STATS™
Player Profiles
1998

STATS, Inc.

Published by STATS Publishing
A Division of Sports Team Analysis & Tracking Systems, Inc.

Cover by Ron Freer

Cover photos by Tony Inzerillo of The Sporting Views

First Edition: November, 1997

Printed in the United States of America

ISBN 1-884064-44-2

Acknowledgments

You'll be hard pressed to find a more comprehensive set of baseball numbers than the one we compile every season in *STATS Player Profiles*. But there are plenty of names behind the numbers, and we wanted to take a minute to give one of the hardest-working staffs in all of sports its due.

John Dewan, STATS President and CEO, continues to lead us into the next millennium. His vision has helped put the STATS name into cyberspace, in book stores, on television, in newspapers and magazines, on video games, on pagers. . . who knows where we'll end up in the next few years! John is assisted by Heather Schwarze, who has the *second*-busiest job in the company.

A book like *Player Profiles* goes nowhere fast without computers, and the machines go nowhere fast without a group of skilled humans at the keyboards. Under the guidance of Sue Dewan, Mike Canter and Art Ashley, the Systems Department adds that human touch. Where do all of these wonderful figures come from, you may ask? From the fingertips of Andrew Bernstein, Dave Carlson, Drew Faust, Kevin Goldstein, Mike Hammer, Stefan Kretschmann, Steve Moyer, Brent Osland, Dean Peterson, Dave Pinto, Pat Quinn, Allan Spear, Jeff Schinski and Kevin Thomas, that's where. Special thanks to Allan, who served as chief programmer for this book.

The Operations Department supplies the raw materials to program. This group, led by Doug Abel, is responsible for overseeing the hunting, gathering, processing and verification of the countless facts and figures you're now holding in your hands. Jeff Chernow, Brian Cousins, Jason Kinsey, Jim Osborne, John Sasman, Matt Senter, Joseph Weindel and Peter Woelflein head up a reporter network that leaves absolutely nothing to the imagination.

Don Zminda and the Publications Department take all the hard work done by the above two groups and turn it into books. Writing, editing, design and layout are the name of the game for Jim Callis, Ethan Cooperson, Kevin Fullam, Jim Henzler, Chuck Miller, Mat Olkin and yours truly. The Fantasy Department, which produces some of the most innovative sports games in existence, consists of Mike Wenz, Jim Musso, Dan Ford and Oscar Palacios.

The Marketing and Sales Departments spread the word and help pay the bills. Steve Byrd heads up Marketing with help from Marc Elman, Ron Freer, Walter Lis and Corey Roberts. Jim Capuano leads the Sales team with the assistance of Kristen Beauregard, Leena Sheth and Lori Smith.

The Departments responsible for Finances and Administration, headed by Bob Meyerhoff, manage the important day-to-day details of our office, from paper clips all the way up to six-figure contracts. Bob's staff consists of Steve Drago, Angela Gabe, Mark Hong, Betty Moy, Carol Savier and Taasha Schroeder. Stephanie Seburn leads our Human Resources Department with help from Tracy Lickton, and Susan Zamechek manages the Administrative staff, which consists of Grant Blair, Ken Gilbert, Sherlinda Johnson, Antoinette Kelly and Kacey Schueler Poulos.

Finally, add your name to the list. As always, thanks for supporting our efforts.

—Tony Nistler

This book is dedicated to my dad, a lifelong Red Sox sufferer, who always wonders how he raised a Yankee fan. You took me to my first game on my eighth birthday, July 22, 1976. I remember it like it was yesterday.
Your son,

Peter Woelflein

Table of Contents

Introduction

In case you missed last year's *STATS Player Profiles,* we'll throw out one little tidbit from that edition: in 1996, Colorado's Larry Walker batted .393 at Coors Field, but only .142 on the road. Since we published that schizophrenic split, Walker's road production has improved to the point where it's on par with his Coors Field hitting—an issue that's become a central point in arguments over the 1997 NL Most Valuable Player Award. "But wait a second," you say to yourself, "What did *Mike Piazza* hit at *Dodger Stadium* last year?" Well, the *roof,* for one thing. We don't keep track of roof shots, but you'll find everything else you can think of in the following pages.

And when we say everything, we mean *everything.* Remember back in August, when Reggie Jefferson, a platoon player, insisted that he be allowed to play full-time, in order to get enough at-bats to win the batting title? Well, was he as capable of hitting southpaws as he claimed to be? If you check his numbers, you'll soon understand exactly why he ended up about 30 points behind Frank Thomas in the batting race. Take a look at Tony Gwynn, too, and ask yourself which is more impressive: his .372 batting average overall, or his .358 batting average *with two strikes.* For any new idea that pops into your head, you can see what the numbers have to say about it. Thirty years ago, when Casey Stengel uttered his now-famous phrase, "You could look it up," he was only half-right. Now, you *can* look it up.

To add some perspective, we include a Leader Boards section in the back of the book. It's one thing to know that Tony Gwynn batted .459 with runners in scoring position (there's that name again!), but it also adds some perspective to know that he led the major leagues in that department. We've presented the leaders in dozens of categories, for last season as well as the last five years combined.

We're always striving to stay on the cutting edge, so you may run into an unfamiliar term now and then. For an explanation or definition, consult the glossary. If it's still not clear, by all means, give us a call. We'd love to hear from you, even if you don't have any questions. Your feedback and ideas help to keep the *Profiles* the most exhaustive and informative statistical compendium around.

—Mat Olkin

Jeff Abbott — White Sox
Age 25 – Bats Right

	Avg	G	AB	R	H	2B	3B	HR	RBI	BB	SO	HBP	GDP	SB	CS	OBP	SLG	IBB	SH	SF	#Pit	#P/PA	GB	FB	G/F
1997 Season	.263	19	38	8	10	1	0	1	2	0	6	0	3	0	0	.263	.368	0	0	0	106	2.79	13	11	1.18

1997 Season

	Avg	AB	H	2B	3B	HR	RBI	BB	SO	OBP	SLG		Avg	AB	H	2B	3B	HR	RBI	BB	SO	OBP	SLG
vs. Left	.333	18	6	1	0	0	0	0	1	.333	.389	Scoring Posn	.000	9	0	0	0	0	0	0	3	.000	.000
vs. Right	.200	20	4	0	0	1	2	0	5	.200	.350	Close & Late	.125	8	1	0	0	0	0	0	3	.125	.250

Kurt Abbott — Marlins
Age 29 – Bats Right

	Avg	G	AB	R	H	2B	3B	HR	RBI	BB	SO	HBP	GDP	SB	CS	OBP	SLG	IBB	SH	SF	#Pit	#P/PA	GB	FB	G/F
1997 Season	.274	94	252	35	69	18	2	6	30	14	68	1	5	3	1	.315	.433	3	6	0	958	3.51	74	68	1.09
Career (1993-1997)	.256	444	1398	184	358	72	19	43	165	91	395	14	26	15	7	.307	.427	9	18	7	5473	3.58	425	371	1.15

1997 Season

	Avg	AB	H	2B	3B	HR	RBI	BB	SO	OBP	SLG		Avg	AB	H	2B	3B	HR	RBI	BB	SO	OBP	SLG
vs. Left	.315	89	28	7	1	2	11	4	19	.344	.483	Scoring Posn	.303	66	20	4	2	2	23	5	21	.361	.515
vs. Right	.252	163	41	11	1	4	19	10	49	.299	.405	Close & Late	.345	55	19	4	0	2	7	2	16	.368	.527
Home	.277	94	26	7	2	1	9	8	25	.333	.426	None on/out	.224	67	15	2	0	0	0	4	17	.268	.254
Away	.272	158	43	11	0	5	21	6	43	.303	.437	Batting #1	.247	77	19	6	0	0	5	3	22	.275	.325
First Pitch	.400	35	14	3	1	1	10	3	0	.447	.629	Batting #3	.310	58	18	3	1	3	8	2	14	.333	.552
Ahead in Count	.408	49	20	6	0	2	9	8	0	.491	.653	Other	.274	117	32	9	1	3	17	9	32	.331	.444
Behind in Count	.172	128	22	7	1	3	9	0	56	.172	.313	Pre-All Star	.285	151	43	10	1	5	21	6	41	.316	.464
Two Strikes	.139	122	17	5	1	2	5	3	68	.160	.246	Post-All Star	.257	101	26	8	1	1	9	8	27	.312	.386

Career (1993-1997)

	Avg	AB	H	2B	3B	HR	RBI	BB	SO	OBP	SLG		Avg	AB	H	2B	3B	HR	RBI	BB	SO	OBP	SLG
vs. Left	.279	408	114	26	5	11	43	23	100	.319	.449	First Pitch	.382	207	79	10	5	9	35	9	0	.417	.609
vs. Right	.246	990	244	46	14	32	122	68	295	.302	.418	Ahead in Count	.360	253	91	19	3	13	51	40	0	.446	.613
Groundball	.258	326	84	14	7	9	48	32	92	.328	.426	Behind in Count	.174	735	128	31	6	16	55	0	352	.181	.298
Flyball	.240	217	52	10	5	6	34	18	74	.297	.415	Two Strikes	.154	695	107	22	6	16	52	42	395	.204	.272
Home	.276	642	177	36	12	23	81	49	177	.332	.477	Batting #7	.245	539	132	23	6	15	57	41	146	.303	.393
Away	.239	756	181	36	7	20	84	42	218	.285	.385	Batting #8	.265	294	78	21	2	7	29	13	90	.304	.422
Day	.254	351	89	15	10	8	33	15	113	.292	.422	Other	.262	565	148	28	11	21	79	37	159	.312	.462
Night	.257	1047	269	57	9	35	132	76	282	.311	.429	March/April	.248	165	41	10	1	5	11	11	62	.311	.412
Grass	.259	1032	267	58	14	31	121	75	289	.315	.432	May	.268	231	62	14	2	7	25	16	56	.317	.437
Turf	.249	366	91	14	5	12	44	16	106	.281	.413	June	.260	254	66	11	3	11	36	12	62	.291	.457
Pre-All Star	.258	752	194	39	7	23	80	44	206	.303	.420	July	.252	290	73	9	6	9	36	14	74	.296	.417
Post-All Star	.254	646	164	33	12	20	85	47	189	.311	.435	August	.248	210	52	17	4	5	25	30	61	.346	.438
Scoring Posn	.261	306	80	12	6	11	119	33	96	.336	.448	Sept/Oct	.258	248	64	11	3	6	32	8	80	.286	.399
Close & Late	.251	243	61	14	1	7	30	20	73	.315	.395	vs. AL	.241	79	19	1	0	3	10	4	27	.277	.367
None on/out	.263	365	96	19	5	10	10	19	92	.303	.425	vs. NL	.257	1319	339	71	19	40	155	87	368	.308	.431

Batter vs. Pitcher (career)

Hits Best Against	Avg	AB	H	2B	3B	HR	RBI	BB	SO	OBP	SLG	Hits Worst Against	Avg	AB	H	2B	3B	HR	RBI	BB	SO	OBP	SLG
Bobby Jones	.545	11	6	2	0	0	0	1	0	.583	.727	Hideo Nomo	.077	13	1	0	0	1	1	0	7	.077	.308
Kevin Ritz	.438	16	7	0	1	1	4	3	3	.526	.750	Pedro Martinez	.091	11	1	0	0	0	0	1	8	.167	.091
Pedro Astacio	.417	12	5	0	2	0	0	1	0	.462	.750	Jon Lieber	.091	11	1	0	0	0	0	1	4	.167	.091
Curt Schilling	.389	18	7	1	0	2	3	1	3	.421	.778	Michael Mimbs	.111	9	1	0	0	1	1	2	3	.273	.111
Paul Wagner	.333	9	3	1	0	1	4	1	2	.455	.778	Allen Watson	.125	16	2	1	0	1	1	0	7	.125	.188

Bob Abreu — Astros
Age 24 – Bats Left

	Avg	G	AB	R	H	2B	3B	HR	RBI	BB	SO	HBP	GDP	SB	CS	OBP	SLG	IBB	SH	SF	#Pit	#P/PA	GB	FB	G/F
1997 Season	.250	59	188	22	47	10	2	3	26	21	48	1	0	7	2	.329	.372	0	0	0	836	3.98	61	45	1.36
Career (1996-1997)	.248	74	210	23	52	11	2	3	27	23	51	1	1	7	2	.325	.362	0	0	0	932	3.98	71	50	1.42

1997 Season

	Avg	AB	H	2B	3B	HR	RBI	BB	SO	OBP	SLG		Avg	AB	H	2B	3B	HR	RBI	BB	SO	OBP	SLG
vs. Left	.182	33	6	3	1	0	6	5	10	.289	.333	Scoring Posn	.349	43	15	3	1	0	19	5	7	.417	.465
vs. Right	.265	155	41	7	1	3	20	16	38	.337	.381	Close & Late	.214	42	9	1	0	1	3	5	10	.298	.310
Home	.277	101	28	5	0	3	15	10	27	.342	.416	None on/out	.208	53	11	2	0	2	2	7	17	.311	.358
Away	.218	87	19	5	2	0	11	11	21	.313	.322	Batting #2	.235	51	12	3	0	2	6	8	9	.339	.412
First Pitch	.444	18	8	1	0	1	1	0	0	.444	.667	Batting #6	.200	50	10	1	0	0	5	4	14	.259	.220
Ahead in Count	.372	43	16	6	1	2	10	12	0	.518	.698	Other	.287	87	25	6	2	1	15	9	25	.361	.437
Behind in Count	.153	85	13	2	1	0	10	0	35	.153	.200	Pre-All Star	.237	152	36	7	2	2	19	19	42	.326	.349
Two Strikes	.188	101	19	3	1	0	13	9	48	.255	.238	Post-All Star	.306	36	11	3	0	1	7	2	6	.342	.472

Juan Acevedo — Mets
Age 28 – Pitches Right (flyball pitcher)

	ERA	W	L	Sv	G	GS	IP	BB	SO	Avg	H	2B	3B	HR	RBI	OBP	SLG	GF	IR	IRS	Hld	SvOp	SB	CS	GB	FB	G/F
1997 Season	3.59	3	1	0	25	2	47.2	22	33	.286	52	13	0	6	26	.366	.456	4	8	4	3	4	5	4	55	51	1.08
Career (1995-1997)	5.24	7	7	0	42	13	113.1	42	73	.304	134	29	0	21	75	.372	.512	4	10	4	4	4	9	7	135	150	0.90

1997 Season

	ERA	W	L	Sv	G	GS	IP	H	HR	BB	SO		Avg	AB	H	2B	3B	HR	RBI	BB	SO	OBP	SLG
Home	2.36	3	0	0	11	2	26.2	22	3	13	19	vs. Left	.330	88	29	7	0	2	14	14	16	.413	.477
Away	5.14	0	1	0	14	0	21.0	30	3	9	14	vs. Right	.245	94	23	6	0	4	12	8	17	.321	.436
Starter	2.25	2	0	0	2	2	12.0	8	1	9	11	Scoring Posn	.222	54	12	2	0	1	17	7	11	.319	.315
Reliever	4.04	1	1	0	23	0	35.2	44	5	13	22	Close & Late	.375	48	18	8	0	2	10	6	6	.464	.667

2

1997 Season

	ERA	W	L	Sv	G	GS	IP	H	HR	BB	SO		Avg	AB	H	2B	3B	HR	RBI	BB	SO	OBP	SLG
0 Days rest (Relief)	6.00	1	0	0	4	0	6.0	8	2	2	2	None on/out	.341	41	14	5	0	1	1	4	10	.413	.537
1 or 2 Days rest	4.11	0	1	0	10	0	15.1	21	1	3	9	First Pitch	.412	34	14	2	0	2	9	2	0	.439	.647
3+ Days rest	3.14	0	0	0	9	0	14.1	15	3	8	11	Ahead in Count	.207	87	18	6	0	3	8	0	26	.213	.379
Pre-All Star	1.88	1	0	0	9	0	14.1	11	2	3	9	Behind in Count	.400	35	14	4	0	0	8	9	0	.511	.514
Post-All Star	4.32	2	1	0	16	2	33.1	41	4	19	24	Two Strikes	.217	83	18	5	0	3	8	11	33	.305	.386

Mark Acre — Athletics   Age 29 – Pitches Right

	ERA	W	L	Sv	G	GS	IP	BB	SO	Avg	H	2B	3B	HR	RBI	OBP	SLG	GF	IR	IRS	Hld	SvOp	SB	CS	GB	FB	G/F
1997 Season	5.74	2	0	0	15	0	15.2	8	12	.318	21	6	0	1	9	.387	.455	5	15	3	0	2	0	1	20	17	1.18
Career (1994-1997)	5.17	9	6	2	114	0	127.0	68	98	.270	135	27	7	16	87	.360	.448	32	81	29	7	10	5	6	166	137	1.21

1997 Season

	ERA	W	L	Sv	G	GS	IP	H	HR	BB	SO		Avg	AB	H	2B	3B	HR	RBI	BB	SO	OBP	SLG
Home	2.00	2	0	0	8	0	9.0	7	0	4	5	vs. Left	.261	23	6	2	0	0	4	2	2	.320	.348
Away	10.80	0	0	0	7	0	6.2	14	1	4	7	vs. Right	.349	43	15	4	0	1	5	6	10	.420	.512

Career (1994-1997)

	ERA	W	L	Sv	G	GS	IP	H	HR	BB	SO		Avg	AB	H	2B	3B	HR	RBI	BB	SO	OBP	SLG
Home	4.85	5	2	1	53	0	59.1	58	7	26	39	vs. Left	.276	217	60	9	2	5	36	38	50	.389	.406
Away	5.45	4	4	1	61	0	67.2	77	9	42	59	vs. Right	.265	283	75	18	5	11	51	30	48	.338	.481
Day	5.47	2	3	2	44	0	51.0	55	7	23	45	Inning 1-6	.270	115	31	6	2	3	18	12	26	.349	.435
Night	4.97	7	3	0	70	0	76.0	80	9	45	53	Inning 7+	.270	385	104	21	5	13	69	56	72	.364	.452
Grass	5.38	7	5	2	98	0	110.1	119	14	53	84	None on	.271	247	67	13	2	10	10	28	48	.357	.462
Turf	3.78	2	1	0	16	0	16.2	16	2	15	14	Runners on	.269	253	68	14	5	6	77	40	50	.364	.435
March/April	2.55	2	0	0	15	0	17.2	17	0	8	12	Scoring Posn	.247	154	38	8	4	3	68	32	30	.368	.409
May	7.42	2	1	0	25	0	30.1	38	3	20	23	Close & Late	.343	143	49	9	3	7	39	32	23	.464	.594
June	4.24	3	1	0	19	0	23.1	15	4	11	18	None on/out	.204	108	22	6	0	4	4	10	24	.289	.370
July	5.40	0	1	0	23	0	26.2	23	4	24	24	vs. 1st Batr (relief)	.260	100	26	6	2	4	18	12	16	.336	.480
August	4.05	1	2	2	14	0	13.1	14	2	10	9	1st Inning Pitched	.266	364	97	23	4	11	63	50	72	.356	.442
Sept/Oct	5.74	0	1	0	18	0	15.2	28	3	5	12	First 15 Pitches	.272	302	82	19	4	10	50	41	53	.361	.460
Starter	0.00	0	0	0	0	0	0.0	0	0	0	0	Pitch 16-30	.267	161	43	8	3	4	26	23	36	.362	.429
Reliever	5.17	9	6	2	114	0	127.0	135	16	68	98	Pitch 31-45	.250	32	8	0	0	2	8	2	8	.306	.438
0 Days rest (Relief)	3.91	3	2	1	18	0	23.0	19	3	13	12	Pitch 46+	.400	5	2	0	0	0	3	2	1	.571	.400
1 or 2 Days rest	5.67	5	1	0	59	0	60.1	69	7	33	50	Ahead in Count	.187	230	43	5	2	5	28	0	89	.192	.291
3+ Days rest	5.15	1	3	1	37	0	43.2	47	6	22	36	Behind in Count	.383	107	41	8	2	6	29	35	0	.535	.664
vs. AL	5.17	9	6	2	114	0	127.0	135	16	68	98	Two Strikes	.200	225	45	8	2	5	35	26	98	.286	.320
vs. NL	0.00	0	0	0	0	0	0.0	0	0	0	0	Pre-All Star	.256	313	80	16	4	8	52	41	59	.347	.409
Pre-All Star	5.27	7	2	0	67	0	80.1	80	8	41	59	Post-All Star	.294	187	55	11	3	8	35	27	39	.382	.513
Post-All Star	5.01	2	4	2	47	0	46.2	55	8	27	39												

Terry Adams — Cubs   Age 25 – Pitches Right (groundball pitcher)

	ERA	W	L	Sv	G	GS	IP	BB	SO	Avg	H	2B	3B	HR	RBI	OBP	SLG	GF	IR	IRS	Hld	SvOp	SB	CS	GB	FB	G/F
1997 Season	4.62	2	9	18	74	0	74.0	40	64	.306	91	15	1	3	39	.388	.394	39	43	7	11	22	8	5	131	42	3.12
Career (1995-1997)	3.92	6	16	23	161	0	193.0	99	157	.268	197	33	6	9	89	.354	.365	68	81	17	22	31	16	7	343	112	3.06

1997 Season

	ERA	W	L	Sv	G	GS	IP	H	HR	BB	SO		Avg	AB	H	2B	3B	HR	RBI	BB	SO	OBP	SLG
Home	5.66	2	5	6	33	0	35.0	49	1	23	28	vs. Left	.297	138	41	10	1	1	15	24	27	.405	.406
Away	3.69	0	4	12	41	0	39.0	42	2	17	36	vs. Right	.314	159	50	5	0	2	24	16	37	.373	.384
Day	6.02	2	5	8	40	0	40.1	53	1	25	34	Inning 1-6	.195	41	8	1	0	0	1	1	16	.214	.220
Night	2.94	0	4	10	34	0	33.2	38	2	15	30	Inning 7+	.324	256	83	14	1	3	38	39	48	.413	.422
Grass	4.85	2	7	11	59	0	59.1	74	3	31	49	None on	.313	134	42	8	1	0	0	18	27	.395	.388
Turf	3.68	0	2	7	15	0	14.2	17	0	9	15	Runners on	.301	163	49	7	0	3	39	22	37	.383	.399
March/April	0.00	0	1	1	10	0	14.0	9	0	2	15	Scoring Posn	.268	97	26	4	0	2	35	17	22	.376	.371
May	1.93	0	0	6	13	0	14.0	12	0	8	11	Close & Late	.321	184	59	13	1	1	26	32	34	.420	.418
June	9.58	1	3	1	11	0	10.1	20	1	8	8	None on/out	.344	61	21	3	1	0	0	8	9	.420	.426
July	6.57	0	1	0	15	0	12.1	19	1	5	9	vs. 1st Batr (relief)	.235	68	16	2	0	1	5	5	12	.297	.309
August	2.35	1	3	5	15	0	15.1	16	0	11	11	1st Inning Pitched	.299	234	70	13	1	3	30	28	49	.374	.402
Sept/Oct	12.38	0	1	5	10	0	8.0	15	1	6	10	First 15 Pitches	.291	189	55	10	1	3	18	20	36	.360	.402
Starter	0.00	0	0	0	0	0	0.0	0	0	0	0	Pitch 16-30	.306	98	30	4	0	0	16	19	24	.415	.347
Reliever	4.62	2	9	18	74	0	74.0	91	3	40	64	Pitch 31-45	.600	10	6	1	0	0	5	1	4	.636	.700
0 Days rest (Relief)	4.50	1	2	6	20	0	18.0	23	1	13	14	Pitch 46+	.000	0	0	0	0	0	0	0	0	.000	.000
1 or 2 Days rest	4.74	1	7	8	41	0	43.2	55	1	20	39	First Pitch	.372	43	16	3	0	1	5	4	0	.426	.512
3+ Days rest	4.38	0	0	4	13	0	12.1	13	1	7	11	Ahead in Count	.236	140	33	5	1	1	10	0	56	.239	.307
vs. AL	5.40	0	0	0	3	0	3.1	4	0	1	3	Behind in Count	.379	66	25	3	0	1	16	17	0	.500	.470
vs. NL	4.58	2	9	18	71	0	70.2	87	3	39	61	Two Strikes	.218	142	31	9	1	1	16	19	64	.313	.317
Pre-All Star	3.60	1	4	8	36	0	40.0	45	1	19	35	Pre-All Star	.296	152	45	8	0	1	19	19	35	.376	.368
Post-All Star	5.82	1	5	10	38	0	34.0	46	2	21	29	Post-All Star	.317	145	46	7	1	2	20	21	29	.401	.421

Career (1995-1997)

	ERA	W	L	Sv	G	GS	IP	H	HR	BB	SO		Avg	AB	H	2B	3B	HR	RBI	BB	SO	OBP	SLG
Home	4.52	5	10	8	82	0	99.2	103	7	58	74	vs. Left	.265	310	82	15	3	4	34	45	55	.359	.371
Away	3.28	1	6	15	79	0	93.1	94	2	41	83	vs. Right	.270	426	115	18	3	5	55	54	102	.351	.362
Day	4.70	6	10	9	95	0	115.0	125	7	66	90	Inning 1-6	.298	104	31	3	1	1	14	5	32	.333	.375
Night	2.77	0	6	14	66	0	78.0	72	2	33	67	Inning 7+	.263	632	166	30	5	8	75	94	125	.357	.364
Grass	4.11	6	12	16	133	0	164.1	170	9	81	127	None on	.266	380	101	16	2	5	5	43	87	.340	.358

Career (1995-1997)																							
	ERA	W	L	Sv	G	GS	IP	H	HR	BB	SO		Avg	AB	H	2B	3B	HR	RBI	BB	SO	OBP	SLG
Turf	2.83	0	4	7	28	0	28.2	27	0	18	30	Runners on	.270	356	96	17	4	4	84	56	70	.368	.374
March/April	1.48	1	1	1	20	0	30.1	23	0	10	25	Scoring Posn	.258	217	56	7	4	2	75	43	44	.378	.355
May	2.67	0	1	6	23	0	30.1	24	1	18	25	Close & Late	.267	375	100	22	2	5	46	61	74	.368	.376
June	3.99	2	4	2	24	0	29.1	32	1	19	22	None on/out	.310	174	54	9	1	4	4	18	32	.375	.443
July	5.40	0	2	2	26	0	30.0	40	4	12	23	vs. 1st Batr (relief)	.247	146	36	9	0	2	10	14	28	.317	.349
August	4.43	1	5	7	38	0	42.2	46	1	23	29	1st Inning Pitched	.257	521	134	26	4	5	63	73	105	.348	.351
Sept/Oct	5.34	2	3	5	30	0	30.1	32	2	17	33	First 15 Pitches	.255	435	111	23	2	5	34	53	81	.337	.352
Starter	0.00	0	0	0	0	0	0.0	0	0	0	0	Pitch 16-30	.263	247	65	9	2	3	44	43	59	.369	.352
Reliever	3.92	6	16	23	161	0	193.0	197	9	99	157	Pitch 31-45	.395	43	17	1	1	1	8	1	14	.409	.535
0 Days rest (Relief)	3.48	3	4	8	37	0	41.1	43	3	26	36	Pitch 46+	.364	11	4	0	1	0	3	2	3	.462	.545
1 or 2 Days rest	3.95	3	12	10	91	0	111.2	110	4	53	85	First Pitch	.315	108	34	6	1	3	12	9	0	.364	.472
3+ Days rest	4.28	0	0	5	33	0	40.0	44	2	20	36	Ahead in Count	.206	339	70	11	3	2	29	0	140	.208	.274
vs. AL	5.40	0	0	0	3	0	3.1	4	0	1	3	Behind in Count	.314	172	54	8	1	3	28	50	0	.464	.424
vs. NL	3.89	6	16	23	158	0	189.2	193	9	98	154	Two Strikes	.182	335	61	13	2	2	30	40	157	.272	.251
Pre-All Star	2.92	3	6	9	72	0	95.2	87	3	51	75	Pre-All Star	.247	352	87	13	2	3	35	51	75	.343	.321
Post-All Star	4.90	3	10	14	89	0	97.1	110	6	48	82	Post-All Star	.286	384	110	20	4	6	54	48	82	.364	.406

Pitcher vs. Batter (career)																				
Pitches Best Vs.	Avg	AB	H	2B	3B	HR	RBI	BB	SO	OBP	SLG	Pitches Worst Vs.	Avg	AB	H	2B	3B	HR	RBI	BB	SO	OBP	SLG
												Craig Biggio	.625	8	5	1	0	0	1	2	1	.636	.750

Willie Adams — Athletics
Age 25 – Pitches Right

	ERA	W	L	Sv	G	GS	IP	BB	SO	Avg	H	2B	3B	HR	RBI	OBP	SLG	CG	ShO	Sup	QS	#P/S	SB	CS	GB	FB	G/F
1997 Season	8.18	3	5	0	13	12	58.1	32	37	.307	73	22	3	9	49	.391	.538	0	0	5.09	1	85	5	2	81	66	1.23
Career (1996-1997)	5.81	6	9	0	25	24	134.2	55	105	.279	149	29	5	20	82	.352	.464	1	1	5.21	8	94	13	2	170	144	1.18

1997 Season																		
	ERA	W	L	Sv	G	GS	IP	H	HR	BB	SO		Avg	AB	H	2B	3B	HR	RBI	BB	SO	OBP	SLG
Home	7.33	0	2	0	5	5	23.1	28	2	12	14	vs. Left	.333	120	40	14	3	4	26	16	18	.407	.600
Away	8.74	3	3	0	8	7	35.0	45	7	20	23	vs. Right	.280	118	33	8	0	5	23	16	19	.374	.475

Joel Adamson — Brewers
Age 26 – Pitches Left

	ERA	W	L	Sv	G	GS	IP	BB	SO	Avg	2B	3B	HR	RBI	OBP	SLG	GF	IR	IRS	Hld	SvOp	SB	CS	GB	FB	G/F
1997 Season	3.54	5	3	0	30	6	76.1	19	56	.265	78	14	0	13	39	.319	.446	3	22	9	1	0	3	3	108	77	1.40
Career (1996-1997)	4.02	5	3	0	39	6	87.1	26	63	.283	96	17	2	14	47	.342	.469	4	27	9	1	0	3	4	124	88	1.41

1997 Season																		
	ERA	W	L	Sv	G	GS	IP	H	HR	BB	SO		Avg	AB	H	2B	3B	HR	RBI	BB	SO	OBP	SLG
Home	4.36	3	1	0	11	3	33.0	38	5	8	26	vs. Left	.238	101	24	5	0	5	11	7	21	.300	.436
Away	2.91	2	2	0	19	3	43.1	40	8	11	30	vs. Right	.280	193	54	9	0	8	28	12	35	.329	.451
Starter	3.06	3	2	0	6	6	32.1	31	5	9	25	Scoring Posn	.242	66	16	4	0	2	25	6	6	.307	.394
Reliever	3.89	2	1	0	24	0	44.0	47	8	10	31	Close & Late	.167	30	5	0	0	1	2	4	7	.278	.267
0 Days rest (Relief)	2.25	0	0	0	3	0	4.0	3	1	1	5	None on/out	.267	75	20	2	0	3	3	2	15	.295	.413
1 or 2 Days rest	4.76	0	1	0	7	0	11.1	12	2	5	6	First Pitch	.390	41	16	3	0	4	13	0	0	.390	.756
3+ Days rest	3.77	2	0	0	14	0	28.2	32	5	4	20	Ahead in Count	.224	125	28	5	0	3	9	0	44	.254	.336
Pre-All Star	5.47	2	1	0	11	1	24.2	30	3	8	14	Behind in Count	.302	63	19	3	0	4	8	8	0	.375	.524
Post-All Star	2.61	3	2	0	19	5	51.2	48	10	11	42	Two Strikes	.203	133	27	4	0	4	11	11	56	.284	.323

Rick Aguilera — Twins
Age 36 – Pitches Right (flyball pitcher)

	ERA	W	L	Sv	G	GS	IP	BB	SO	Avg	H	2B	3B	HR	RBI	OBP	SLG	GF	IR	IRS	Hld	SvOp	SB	CS	GB	FB	G/F
1997 Season	3.82	5	4	26	61	0	68.1	22	68	.257	65	10	2	9	37	.318	.419	57	22	9	0	33	5	4	74	77	0.96
Last Five Years	3.96	21	20	115	241	19	352.0	86	308	.258	352	68	6	51	176	.303	.430	209	77	26	0	138	39	4	402	443	0.91

1997 Season																		
	ERA	W	L	Sv	G	GS	IP	H	HR	BB	SO		Avg	AB	H	2B	3B	HR	RBI	BB	SO	OBP	SLG
Home	2.75	3	2	12	32	0	36.0	26	4	12	33	vs. Left	.235	115	27	4	2	5	17	10	31	.299	.435
Away	5.01	2	2	14	29	0	32.1	39	5	10	35	vs. Right	.275	138	38	6	0	4	20	12	37	.333	.406
Day	4.50	0	1	8	22	0	26.0	26	3	11	16	Inning 1-6	.000	0	0	0	0	0	0	0	0	.000	.000
Night	3.40	5	3	18	39	0	42.1	39	6	11	52	Inning 7+	.257	253	65	10	2	9	37	22	68	.318	.419
Grass	3.86	1	1	13	25	0	28.0	30	5	6	29	None on	.260	146	38	4	2	5	5	7	34	.299	.418
Turf	3.79	4	3	13	36	0	40.1	35	4	16	39	Runners on	.252	107	27	6	0	4	32	15	34	.341	.421
March/April	7.15	1	1	4	11	0	11.1	17	3	8	9	Scoring Posn	.230	61	14	1	0	4	29	11	20	.342	.443
May	3.00	2	0	7	12	0	15.0	11	2	5	15	Close & Late	.269	156	42	6	1	6	24	14	48	.329	.436
June	2.16	0	0	4	8	0	8.1	9	1	0	12	None on/out	.274	62	17	2	0	2	2	2	17	.308	.403
July	3.21	1	2	4	11	0	14.0	12	0	8	16	vs. 1st Batr (relief)	.316	57	18	2	0	3	8	3	12	.361	.509
August	3.38	1	0	3	9	0	10.2	9	1	1	1	1st Inning Pitched	.269	216	58	9	2	9	34	15	58	.319	.454
Sept/Oct	4.00	1	0	4	10	0	9.0	7	2	0	7	First 15 Pitches	.284	162	46	7	2	7	24	10	38	.328	.481
Starter	0.00	0	0	0	0	0	0.0	0	0	0	0	Pitch 16-30	.213	75	16	3	0	2	12	6	26	.277	.333
Reliever	3.82	5	4	26	61	0	68.1	65	9	22	68	Pitch 31-45	.154	13	2	0	0	0	1	4	3	.333	.154
0 Days rest (Relief)	4.63	3	1	6	10	0	11.2	11	3	5	11	Pitch 46+	.333	3	1	0	0	0	2	1	0	.600	.333
1 or 2 Days rest	4.68	2	2	13	30	0	32.2	37	5	8	37	First Pitch	.324	34	11	1	0	3	10	1	0	.351	.618
3+ Days rest	2.25	0	1	7	21	0	24.0	17	1	9	20	Ahead in Count	.177	130	23	3	1	1	6	0	58	.180	.238
vs. AL	3.92	5	4	23	57	0	64.1	62	8	22	63	Behind in Count	.333	36	12	2	0	2	9	14	0	.520	.556
vs. NL	2.25	0	0	3	4	0	4.0	3	1	0	5	Two Strikes	.193	140	27	3	1	2	10	7	68	.230	.271
Pre-All Star	3.86	3	1	16	33	0	37.1	38	6	15	39	Pre-All Star	.270	141	38	6	1	6	19	15	39	.344	.454

1997 Season

	ERA	W	L	Sv	G	GS	IP	H	HR	BB	SO		Avg	AB	H	2B	3B	HR	RBI	BB	SO	OBP	SLG
Post-All Star	3.77	2	3	10	28	0	31.0	27	3	7	29	Post-All Star	.241	112	27	4	1	3	18	7	29	.283	.375

Last Five Years

	ERA	W	L	Sv	G	GS	IP	H	HR	BB	SO		Avg	AB	H	2B	3B	HR	RBI	BB	SO	OBP	SLG
Home	4.00	10	11	54	120	10	177.2	163	25	37	163	vs. Left	.242	715	173	33	5	23	89	42	170	.286	.399
Away	3.92	11	9	61	121	9	174.1	189	26	49	145	vs. Right	.277	647	179	35	1	28	87	44	138	.322	.464
Day	3.46	4	5	36	80	5	117.0	101	19	29	108	Inning 1-6	.273	392	107	30	2	18	58	25	70	.318	.497
Night	4.21	17	15	79	161	14	235.0	251	32	57	200	Inning 7+	.253	970	245	38	4	33	118	61	238	.298	.402
Grass	3.59	12	9	60	116	8	165.1	170	24	37	134	None on	.258	803	207	41	3	29	29	29	179	.288	.425
Turf	4.29	9	11	55	125	11	186.2	182	27	49	174	Runners on	.259	559	145	27	3	22	147	57	129	.324	.436
March/April	5.75	1	2	17	33	1	36.0	47	7	15	32	Scoring Posn	.261	330	86	15	0	15	126	48	77	.347	.442
May	3.14	3	0	24	39	0	43.0	43	5	12	43	Close & Late	.253	600	152	23	2	20	89	45	155	.305	.398
June	2.79	2	4	24	47	4	71.0	60	6	11	65	None on/out	.259	343	89	21	1	13	13	10	68	.282	.440
July	5.11	5	9	21	48	6	79.1	91	12	20	69	vs. 1st Batr (relief)	.234	209	49	7	0	11	27	11	48	.275	.426
August	3.54	4	4	13	38	6	76.1	67	13	16	61	1st Inning Pitched	.262	883	231	36	4	33	119	56	215	.306	.424
Sept/Oct	3.88	6	1	16	36	2	46.1	48	8	12	38	First 15 Pitches	.264	716	189	28	3	28	79	40	167	.304	.429
Starter	5.42	8	6	0	19	19	111.1	124	20	27	83	Pitch 16-30	.236	288	68	12	1	9	49	23	75	.290	.378
Reliever	3.29	13	14	115	222	0	240.2	228	31	59	225	Pitch 31-45	.186	102	19	9	1	2	7	6	18	.229	.353
0 Days rest (Relief)	3.31	4	3	39	51	0	54.1	47	12	13	48	Pitch 46+	.297	256	76	19	1	12	41	17	48	.345	.520
1 or 2 Days rest	3.86	4	5	48	93	0	102.2	106	14	26	104	First Pitch	.323	198	64	13	1	10	37	7	0	.343	.551
3+ Days rest	2.58	1	6	28	78	0	83.2	75	5	20	73	Ahead in Count	.184	679	125	15	2	17	54	0	274	.189	.287
vs. AL	3.98	21	20	112	237	19	348.0	349	50	86	303	Behind in Count	.343	239	82	18	1	11	44	48	0	.448	.565
vs. NL	2.25	0	0	3	4	0	4.0	3	1	0	5	Two Strikes	.173	683	118	22	1	17	58	31	308	.209	.283
Pre-All Star	3.92	7	9	71	134	7	172.0	180	22	45	161	Pre-All Star	.267	674	180	32	3	22	85	45	161	.313	.421
Post-All Star	4.00	14	11	44	107	12	180.0	172	29	41	147	Post-All Star	.250	688	172	36	3	29	91	41	147	.294	.438

Pitcher vs. Batter (career)

Pitches Best Vs.	Avg	AB	H	2B	3B	HR	RBI	BB	SO	OBP	SLG	Pitches Worst Vs.	Avg	AB	H	2B	3B	HR	RBI	BB	SO	OBP	SLG
Gary DiSarcina	.000	12	0	0	0	0	0	1	0	.077	.000	Jim Eisenreich	.583	12	7	1	1	0	0	0	1	.583	.833
Brady Anderson	.083	12	1	0	0	0	0	2	4	.214	.083	Ivan Rodriguez	.500	14	7	1	0	2	5	1	0	.533	1.000
Julio Franco	.100	10	1	0	0	0	1	1	0	.182	.100	Jim Edmonds	.400	10	4	0	0	2	2	1	2	.455	1.000
Bernie Williams	.100	10	1	0	0	0	0	1	3	.182	.100	Mark McGwire	.389	18	7	1	0	3	4	2	4	.476	.944
Travis Fryman	.105	19	2	1	0	0	1	1	5	.150	.158	Dean Palmer	.333	15	5	2	0	2	4	2	4	.412	.867

Jose Alberro — Yankees
Age 29 – Pitches Right (groundball pitcher)

	ERA	W	L	Sv	G	GS	IP	BB	SO	Avg	H	2B	3B	HR	RBI	OBP	SLG	GF	IR	IRS	Hld	SvOp	SB	CS	GB	FB	G/F
1997 Season	7.94	0	3	0	10	4	28.1	17	11	.303	37	10	0	4	27	.390	.484	2	9	2	0	0	1	0	58	25	2.32
Career (1995-1997)	7.41	0	4	0	27	5	58.1	36	23	.312	77	15	2	7	57	.399	.474	10	33	12	1	0	1	1	115	57	2.02

1997 Season

	ERA	W	L	Sv	G	GS	IP	H	HR	BB	SO		Avg	AB	H	2B	3B	HR	RBI	BB	SO	OBP	SLG
Home	10.13	0	2	0	5	2	13.1	18	3	9	5	vs. Left	.349	63	22	5	0	2	14	12	3	.461	.524
Away	6.00	0	1	0	5	2	15.0	19	1	8	6	vs. Right	.254	59	15	5	0	2	13	5	8	.308	.441

Scott Aldred — Twins
Age 30 – Pitches Left (flyball pitcher)

	ERA	W	L	Sv	G	GS	IP	BB	SO	Avg	H	2B	3B	HR	RBI	OBP	SLG	CG	ShO	Sup	QS	#P/S	SB	CS	GB	FB	G/F
1997 Season	7.68	2	10	0	17	15	77.1	28	33	.323	102	24	0	20	63	.382	.589	0	0	5.59	3	81	2	1	108	116	0.93
Last Five Years	6.79	9	19	0	61	40	254.2	106	153	.306	315	73	2	51	190	.374	.530	0	6	6.04	10	89	18	9	302	365	0.83

1997 Season

	ERA	W	L	Sv	G	GS	IP	H	HR	BB	SO		Avg	AB	H	2B	3B	HR	RBI	BB	SO	OBP	SLG
Home	7.88	1	6	0	10	9	45.2	64	11	14	20	vs. Left	.333	72	24	3	0	4	14	2	6	.351	.542
Away	7.39	1	4	0	7	6	31.2	38	9	14	13	vs. Right	.320	244	78	21	0	16	49	26	27	.391	.602
Starter	8.00	2	10	0	15	15	72.0	98	20	28	31	Scoring Posn	.338	71	24	2	0	9	45	8	7	.400	.746
Reliever	3.38	0	0	0	2	0	5.1	4	0	0	2	Close & Late	.375	8	3	0	0	1	3	2	1	.500	.750
0-3 Days Rest (Start)	9.39	1	1	0	2	2	7.2	12	3	4	3	None on/out	.329	82	27	8	0	6	6	9	13	.402	.646
4 Days Rest	7.87	1	8	0	10	10	50.1	66	15	19	23	First Pitch	.372	43	16	6	0	3	9	1	0	.386	.721
5+ Days Rest	7.71	0	1	0	3	3	14.0	20	2	5	7	Ahead in Count	.297	128	38	7	0	8	26	0	26	.305	.539
Pre-All Star	7.68	2	10	0	17	15	77.1	102	20	28	33	Behind in Count	.369	84	31	4	0	4	13	18	0	.485	.560
Post-All Star	0.00	0	0	0	0	0	0.0	0	0	0	0	Two Strikes	.291	134	39	10	0	7	30	9	33	.338	.522

Last Five Years

	ERA	W	L	Sv	G	GS	IP	H	HR	BB	SO		Avg	AB	H	2B	3B	HR	RBI	BB	SO	OBP	SLG
Home	7.86	5	8	0	31	18	121.1	156	30	51	71	vs. Left	.330	230	76	18	1	12	48	18	31	.379	.574
Away	5.81	4	11	0	30	22	133.1	159	21	55	82	vs. Right	.299	798	239	55	1	39	142	88	122	.373	.518
Day	7.70	2	6	0	20	13	69.0	94	13	35	46	Inning 1-6	.305	898	274	64	2	42	162	86	134	.368	.521
Night	6.45	7	13	0	41	27	185.2	221	38	71	107	Inning 7+	.315	130	41	9	0	9	28	20	19	.414	.592
Grass	6.48	4	11	0	32	21	133.1	166	22	64	85	None on	.289	568	164	49	1	21	21	48	90	.352	.489
Turf	7.12	5	8	0	29	19	121.1	149	29	42	68	Runners on	.328	460	151	24	1	30	169	58	63	.401	.580
March/April	7.40	1	4	0	18	10	62.0	75	11	33	44	Scoring Posn	.327	269	88	9	1	19	143	40	41	.406	.580
May	8.22	1	8	0	16	10	61.1	85	14	30	31	Close & Late	.277	47	13	2	0	3	9	4	6	.346	.511
June	7.04	3	3	0	9	7	38.1	54	12	15	19	None on/out	.306	255	78	25	0	13	13	25	44	.377	.557
July	7.50	1	2	0	7	5	36.0	45	8	14	19	vs. 1st Batr (relief)	.350	20	7	4	0	0	3	0	4	.350	.550
August	4.50	1	0	0	5	4	26.0	27	2	8	16	1st Inning Pitched	.322	236	76	23	1	11	49	32	46	.403	.568
Sept/Oct	3.48	1	2	0	6	4	31.0	29	4	6	24	First 75 Pitches	.300	828	248	66	1	37	143	81	132	.365	.516
Starter	7.06	8	19	0	40	40	207.2	264	44	80	119	Pitch 76-90	.259	112	29	2	1	4	21	11	12	.325	.402
Reliever	5.55	1	0	0	21	0	47.0	51	7	26	34	Pitch 91-105	.476	63	30	2	0	6	17	13	6	.566	.794

Last Five Years

	ERA	W	L	Sv	G	GS	IP	H	HR	BB	SO		Avg	AB	H	2B	3B	HR	RBI	BB	SO	OBP	SLG
0-3 Days Rest (Start)	7.71	3	2	0	6	6	30.1	34	8	13	13	Pitch 106+	.320	25	8	3	0	4	9	1	3	.370	.920
4 Days Rest	6.81	4	13	0	26	26	138.2	176	31	47	79	First Pitch	.382	123	47	12	1	9	30	6	0	.417	.715
5+ Days Rest	7.45	1	4	0	8	8	38.2	54	5	20	27	Ahead in Count	.252	425	107	22	1	14	61	0	124	.260	.407
vs. AL	6.56	8	18	0	52	39	238.2	288	47	95	144	Behind in Count	.357	280	100	24	0	16	62	57	0	.466	.614
vs. NL	10.13	1	1	0	9	1	16.0	27	4	11	9	Two Strikes	.230	453	104	23	1	16	60	43	153	.303	.391
Pre-All Star	7.82	6	17	0	45	29	172.2	228	39	85	102	Pre-All Star	.321	710	228	56	2	39	143	85	102	.398	.570
Post-All Star	4.61	3	2	0	16	11	82.0	87	12	21	51	Post-All Star	.274	318	87	17	0	12	47	21	51	.320	.440

Pitcher vs. Batter (career)

Pitches Best Vs.	Avg	AB	H	2B	3B	HR	RBI	BB	SO	OBP	SLG	Pitches Worst Vs.	Avg	AB	H	2B	3B	HR	RBI	BB	SO	OBP	SLG
Eddie Murray	.071	14	1	1	0	0	2	2	1	.188	.143	B.J. Surhoff	.545	11	6	0	0	1	4	2	0	.615	.818
Gary DiSarcina	.083	12	1	0	0	0	1	2	0	.214	.083	Rusty Greer	.500	10	5	2	0	2	6	1	1	.545	1.300
Mike Devereaux	.188	16	3	0	0	0	1	0	3	.176	.188	Edgar Martinez	.462	13	6	1	0	3	6	3	1	.563	1.231
Randy Velarde	.188	16	3	0	0	0	1	2	5	.263	.188	Tim Salmon	.462	13	6	1	0	2	4	2	1	.500	1.000
Mike Bordick	.231	13	3	1	0	0	4	1	0	.286		Mike Stanley	.455	11	5	0	0	3	5	0	2	.500	1.273

Manny Alexander — Cubs   Age 27 – Bats Right

	Avg	G	AB	R	H	2B	3B	HR	RBI	BB	SO	HBP	GDP	SB	CS	OBP	SLG	IBB	SH	SF	#Pit	#P/PA	GB	FB	G/F
1997 Season	.266	87	248	37	66	12	4	3	22	17	54	3	6	13	1	.320	.383	3	3	1	1115	4.10	88	58	1.52
Last Five Years	.233	237	558	79	130	21	5	6	49	40	111	5	10	27	8	.290	.321	3	9	1	2369	3.86	187	161	1.16

1997 Season

	Avg	AB	H	2B	3B	HR	RBI	BB	SO	OBP	SLG		Avg	AB	H	2B	3B	HR	RBI	BB	SO	OBP	SLG
vs. Left	.241	83	20	6	2	0	10	5	19	.292	.361	Scoring Posn	.246	57	14	1	1	0	17	9	16	.362	.298
vs. Right	.279	165	46	6	2	3	12	12	35	.333	.394	Close & Late	.290	31	9	0	1	1	6	3	9	.343	.452
Home	.241	108	26	3	1	0	4	10	21	.311	.287	None on/out	.290	62	18	6	1	3	3	5	9	.343	.565
Away	.286	140	40	9	3	3	18	7	33	.327	.457	Batting #7	.229	48	11	3	0	0	6	2	15	.275	.292
First Pitch	.333	24	8	1	2	0	4	3	0	.429	.542	Batting #8	.311	135	42	5	3	3	13	7	24	.354	.459
Ahead in Count	.296	54	16	3	0	2	7	7	0	.377	.463	Other	.200	65	13	4	1	0	3	8	15	.284	.292
Behind in Count	.208	125	26	6	2	1	4	0	47	.219	.312	Pre-All Star	.235	119	28	6	2	1	9	8	30	.287	.345
Two Strikes	.187	134	25	5	2	1	8	7	54	.236	.276	Post-All Star	.295	129	38	6	2	2	13	9	24	.350	.419

Last Five Years

	Avg	AB	H	2B	3B	HR	RBI	BB	SO	OBP	SLG		Avg	AB	H	2B	3B	HR	RBI	BB	SO	OBP	SLG
vs. Left	.222	194	43	7	3	2	17	13	41	.274	.320	First Pitch	.266	64	17	1	2	1	9	3	0	.319	.391
vs. Right	.239	364	87	14	2	4	32	27	70	.298	.321	Ahead in Count	.311	122	38	7	1	3	16	23	0	.421	.459
Groundball	.193	119	23	4	1	0	7	8	20	.250	.244	Behind in Count	.172	273	47	9	2	2	9	0	97	.181	.242
Flyball	.232	82	19	2	0	1	5	7	20	.292	.293	Two Strikes	.153	274	42	7	2	2	11	14	111	.202	.215
Home	.212	259	55	11	2	2	16	18	51	.269	.270	Batting #2	.223	175	39	7	1	2	23	17	30	.299	.309
Away	.251	299	75	14	4	4	33	22	60	.308	.365	Batting #8	.292	171	50	5	3	4	15	10	28	.339	.427
Day	.242	190	46	7	2	1	13	18	37	.313	.316	Other	.193	212	41	9	1	0	11	13	53	.242	.245
Night	.228	368	84	14	3	5	36	22	74	.277	.323	March/April	.242	66	16	2	0	0	3	4	15	.296	.273
Grass	.234	440	103	19	2	4	38	28	87	.285	.314	May	.237	76	18	3	2	0	5	4	15	.275	.329
Turf	.229	118	27	2	3	2	11	12	24	.308	.347	June	.234	128	30	6	0	2	15	11	22	.293	.328
Pre-All Star	.245	302	74	11	3	3	32	23	57	.302	.331	July	.229	118	27	5	2	3	17	8	29	.289	.381
Post-All Star	.219	256	56	10	2	3	17	17	54	.275	.309	August	.191	89	17	4	0	0	5	7	16	.250	.236
Scoring Posn	.239	134	32	2	1	0	39	14	31	.322	.269	Sept/Oct	.272	81	22	1	1	1	4	6	14	.337	.346
Close & Late	.265	68	18	0	1	1	8	5	12	.311	.338	vs. AL	.207	329	68	9	1	3	28	25	57	.269	.267
None on/out	.246	134	33	7	1	4	4	7	17	.284	.403	vs. NL	.271	229	62	12	4	3	21	15	54	.320	.397

Batter vs. Pitcher (career)

Hits Best Against	Avg	AB	H	2B	3B	HR	RBI	BB	SO	OBP	SLG	Hits Worst Against	Avg	AB	H	2B	3B	HR	RBI	BB	SO	OBP	SLG
												Carlos Perez	.200	10	2	1	1	0	0	2	1	.333	.500

Antonio Alfonseca — Marlins   Age 26 – Pitches Right

	ERA	W	L	Sv	G	GS	IP	BB	SO	Avg	2B	3B	HR	RBI	OBP	SLG	GF	IR	IRS	Hld	SvOp	SB	CS	GB	FB	G/F
1997 Season	4.91	1	3	0	17	0	25.2	10	19	.324	36	9	2	3	17	.385	.523	2	13	4	0	2	0	1	36	33	1.09

1997 Season

	ERA	W	L	Sv	G	GS	IP	H	HR	BB	SO		Avg	AB	H	2B	3B	HR	RBI	BB	SO	OBP	SLG
Home	3.00	0	1	0	9	0	18.0	19	2	6	11	vs. Left	.323	31	10	1	1	1	6	3	4	.382	.516
Away	9.39	1	2	0	8	0	7.2	17	1	4	8	vs. Right	.325	80	26	8	1	2	11	7	15	.386	.525

Edgardo Alfonzo — Mets   Age 24 – Bats Right

	Avg	G	AB	R	H	2B	3B	HR	RBI	BB	SO	HBP	GDP	SB	CS	OBP	SLG	IBB	SH	SF	#Pit	#P/PA	GB	FB	G/F
1997 Season	.315	151	518	84	163	27	2	10	72	63	56	5	4	11	6	.391	.432	0	8	5	2276	3.80	198	161	1.23
Career (1995-1997)	.288	375	1221	146	352	55	9	18	153	100	149	6	19	14	7	.342	.392	3	21	14	5032	3.69	475	369	1.29

1997 Season

	Avg	AB	H	2B	3B	HR	RBI	BB	SO	OBP	SLG		Avg	AB	H	2B	3B	HR	RBI	BB	SO	OBP	SLG
vs. Left	.378	135	51	8	1	4	27	18	11	.448	.541	First Pitch	.358	53	19	3	0	1	4	0	0	.370	.472
vs. Right	.292	383	112	19	1	6	45	45	45	.371	.394	Ahead in Count	.328	116	38	11	0	2	15	41	0	.506	.474
Groundball	.327	98	32	5	1	2	14	18	10	.427	.459	Behind in Count	.288	243	70	8	2	4	32	0	49	.287	.387
Flyball	.261	46	12	1	0	0	4	6	7	.352	.283	Two Strikes	.267	225	60	8	2	5	36	22	56	.333	.387
Home	.327	248	81	16	1	4	42	27	21	.391	.448	Batting #2	.330	406	134	21	2	8	53	43	41	.396	.451
Away	.304	270	82	11	1	6	30	36	35	.390	.419	Batting #5	.219	64	14	2	0	1	9	12	7	.354	.297

1997 Season

	Avg	AB	H	2B	3B	HR	RBI	BB	SO	OBP	SLG		Avg	AB	H	2B	3B	HR	RBI	BB	SO	OBP	SLG
Day	.312	199	62	13	1	2	36	25	23	.389	.417	Other	.313	48	15	4	0	1	10	8	8	.397	.458
Night	.317	319	101	14	1	8	36	38	33	.392	.442	March/April	.268	56	15	4	0	1	9	7	13	.344	.393
Grass	.324	426	138	23	1	9	65	51	39	.398	.446	May	.301	103	31	6	1	2	9	8	8	.351	.437
Turf	.272	92	25	4	1	1	7	12	17	.358	.370	June	.368	76	28	4	0	2	14	8	6	.425	.500
Pre-All Star	.327	260	85	18	1	6	37	25	28	.384	.473	July	.352	88	31	6	0	2	13	12	5	.436	.489
Post-All Star	.302	258	78	9	1	4	35	38	28	.397	.391	August	.350	100	35	5	0	2	21	18	9	.451	.460
Scoring Posn	.417	115	48	10	0	4	60	11	13	.455	.609	Sept/Oct	.242	95	23	2	1	1	6	10	15	.321	.316
Close & Late	.362	94	34	6	1	2	18	17	11	.447	.511	vs. AL	.361	36	13	3	0	0	5	2	6	.410	.444
None on/out	.294	109	32	5	1	2	2	16	14	.389	.413	vs. NL	.311	482	150	24	2	10	67	61	50	.389	.432

1997 By Position

Position	Avg	AB	H	2B	3B	HR	RBI	BB	SO	OBP	SLG	G	GS	Innings	PO	A	E	DP	Fld Pct	Rng Fctr	In Zone	Zone Outs	Zone Rtg	MLB Zone
As 3b	.318	484	154	23	2	10	64	62	48	.399	.436	143	127	1117.0	82	268	12	29	.967	2.82	364	319	.876	.801
As ss	.304	23	7	3	0	0	6	0	4	.292	.435	12	4	49.0	12	15	0	3	1.000	4.96	15	13	.867	.937

Career (1995-1997)

	Avg	AB	H	2B	3B	HR	RBI	BB	SO	OBP	SLG		Avg	AB	H	2B	3B	HR	RBI	BB	SO	OBP	SLG
vs. Left	.317	322	102	16	4	7	55	31	35	.372	.457	First Pitch	.320	128	41	5	1	5	20	3	0	.336	.492
vs. Right	.278	899	250	39	5	11	98	69	114	.330	.369	Ahead in Count	.305	275	84	18	1	4	33	63	0	.434	.422
Groundball	.302	291	88	16	2	3	29	27	34	.359	.402	Behind in Count	.265	577	153	20	3	6	64	0	132	.265	.341
Flyball	.237	152	36	4	0	1	15	13	25	.298	.283	Two Strikes	.243	527	128	19	5	7	71	34	149	.290	.338
Home	.293	597	175	31	4	6	76	52	64	.347	.389	Batting #2	.305	760	232	37	6	14	100	60	84	.354	.425
Away	.284	624	177	24	5	12	77	48	85	.336	.396	Batting #7	.264	220	58	10	1	2	25	15	30	.314	.345
Day	.281	423	119	18	3	4	61	41	55	.343	.366	Other	.257	241	62	8	2	2	28	25	35	.328	.332
Night	.292	798	233	37	6	14	92	59	94	.341	.406	March/April	.245	98	24	6	0	1	12	8	19	.299	.337
Grass	.287	984	282	43	5	13	128	83	112	.341	.380	May	.256	207	53	11	1	3	18	15	23	.308	.362
Turf	.295	237	70	12	4	5	25	17	37	.342	.443	June	.325	203	66	11	2	4	31	11	21	.356	.458
Pre-All Star	.287	585	168	32	4	9	67	37	68	.329	.402	July	.291	278	81	12	2	5	36	21	22	.341	.403
Post-All Star	.289	636	184	23	5	9	86	63	81	.353	.384	August	.298	242	72	8	2	2	38	25	32	.365	.372
Scoring Posn	.332	295	98	20	4	7	132	23	40	.368	.498	Sept/Oct	.290	193	56	7	2	3	18	20	32	.353	.394
Close & Late	.298	228	68	8	2	2	30	29	33	.373	.377	vs. AL	.361	36	13	3	0	0	5	2	6	.410	.444
None on/out	.282	259	73	11	1	3	3	21	29	.338	.367	vs. NL	.286	1185	339	52	9	18	148	98	143	.339	.391

Batter vs. Pitcher (career)

Hits Best Against	Avg	AB	H	2B	3B	HR	RBI	BB	SO	OBP	SLG	Hits Worst Against	Avg	AB	H	2B	3B	HR	RBI	BB	SO	OBP	SLG
Shane Reynolds	.500	18	9	1	0	0	1	1	3	.526	.556	F. Valenzuela	.000	10	0	0	0	0	0	2	3	.167	.000
Carlos Perez	.462	13	6	2	0	1	2	0	2	.462	.846	Kevin Ritz	.100	20	2	0	0	0	1	2	1	.182	.100
Al Leiter	.455	11	5	0	0	1	1	1	0	.500	.727	Pedro Astacio	.143	14	2	0	0	0	0	0	0	.143	.143
Mike Morgan	.364	11	4	1	0	1	3	2	0	.462	.727	Tom Glavine	.154	13	2	0	0	0	0	0	2	.154	.154
Andy Ashby	.333	12	4	1	0	1	1	2	0	.429	.667	Michael Mimbs	.154	13	2	0	0	0	0	0	2	.154	.154

Luis Alicea — Angels

Age 32 – Bats Both

	Avg	G	AB	R	H	2B	3B	HR	RBI	BB	SO	HBP	GDP	SB	CS	OBP	SLG	IBB	SH	SF	#Pit	P/PA	GB	FB	G/F
1997 Season	.253	128	388	59	98	16	7	5	37	69	65	8	4	22	8	.375	.369	3	4	2	1753	3.72	115	143	0.80
Last Five Years	.266	592	1754	259	467	93	21	24	198	261	296	27	29	61	27	.365	.384	19	23	27	7883	3.77	544	568	0.96

1997 Season

	Avg	AB	H	2B	3B	HR	RBI	BB	SO	OBP	SLG		Avg	AB	H	2B	3B	HR	RBI	BB	SO	OBP	SLG
vs. Left	.245	110	27	6	0	0	9	11	11	.317	.300	First Pitch	.403	62	25	3	3	1	7	2	0	.431	.597
vs. Right	.255	278	71	10	7	5	28	58	54	.395	.396	Ahead in Count	.239	88	21	5	3	1	8	36	0	.465	.398
Groundball	.323	65	21	5	2	0	8	13	9	.436	.462	Behind in Count	.198	172	34	3	1	1	12	0	59	.220	.244
Flyball	.151	53	8	0	2	0	2	12	10	.338	.226	Two Strikes	.184	163	30	4	0	2	14	31	65	.323	.245
Home	.235	187	44	12	3	2	23	37	36	.373	.364	Batting #2	.221	86	19	2	2	0	4	15	11	.356	.291
Away	.269	201	54	4	4	3	14	32	29	.377	.373	Batting #8	.286	220	63	12	4	4	27	36	38	.391	.432
Day	.333	99	33	4	3	2	9	20	16	.455	.495	Other	.195	82	16	2	1	1	6	18	16	.352	.280
Night	.225	289	65	12	4	3	28	49	49	.347	.325	March/April	.280	75	21	4	2	0	4	10	11	.372	.387
Grass	.240	341	82	16	6	3	29	58	58	.359	.349	May	.333	78	26	5	2	2	13	13	11	.435	.526
Turf	.340	47	16	0	1	2	8	11	7	.483	.511	June	.232	69	16	3	0	1	6	13	8	.376	.319
Pre-All Star	.288	240	69	12	4	4	25	36	33	.394	.421	July	.232	56	13	1	2	2	8	9	9	.338	.429
Post-All Star	.196	148	29	4	3	1	12	33	32	.346	.284	August	.175	63	11	1	1	0	1	11	14	.297	.222
Scoring Posn	.305	82	25	5	2	2	32	20	14	.438	.488	Sept/Oct	.234	47	11	2	0	0	5	14	12	.415	.277
Close & Late	.268	71	19	3	2	1	5	13	16	.391	.408	vs. AL	.254	354	90	15	7	4	34	65	59	.377	.370
None on/out	.264	106	28	6	4	2	2	21	20	.395	.453	vs. NL	.235	34	8	1	0	1	3	4	6	.350	.353

1997 By Position

Position	Avg	AB	H	2B	3B	HR	RBI	BB	SO	OBP	SLG	G	GS	Innings	PO	A	E	DP	Fld Pct	Rng Fctr	In Zone	Zone Outs	Zone Rtg	MLB Zone
As 2b	.261	345	90	14	7	5	32	60	56	.381	.386	105	100	890.0	219	267	11	61	.978	4.91	290	262	.903	.902
As 3b	.267	30	8	2	0	0	4	9	6	.439	.333	12	8	85.0	5	19	1	1	.960	2.54	28	24	.857	.801

Last Five Years

	Avg	AB	H	2B	3B	HR	RBI	BB	SO	OBP	SLG		Avg	AB	H	2B	3B	HR	RBI	BB	SO	OBP	SLG
vs. Left	.292	391	114	24	0	4	40	49	40	.371	.384	First Pitch	.338	240	81	11	5	1	25	14	0	.377	.438
vs. Right	.259	1363	353	69	21	20	158	212	256	.363	.384	Ahead in Count	.308	448	138	38	5	9	69	115	0	.447	.475
Groundball	.281	462	130	27	6	5	49	53	77	.357	.398	Behind in Count	.199	725	144	22	4	5	54	0	247	.213	.261
Flyball	.240	275	66	12	5	5	30	49	55	.360	.375	Two Strikes	.185	769	142	26	7	9	70	132	296	.308	.272
Home	.251	856	215	44	10	11	98	118	146	.347	.364	Batting #8	.276	536	148	33	7	10	66	86	98	.378	.420
Away	.281	898	252	49	11	13	100	143	150	.382	.403	Batting #9	.275	400	110	17	4	7	47	59	66	.372	.390

7

	Avg	AB	H	2B	3B	HR	RBI	BB	SO	OBP	SLG		Avg	AB	H	2B	3B	HR	RBI	BB	SO	OBP	SLG
Day	.273	523	143	21	9	6	53	75	90	.370	.382	Other	.256	818	209	43	10	7	85	116	132	.353	.358
Night	.263	1231	324	72	12	18	145	186	206	.363	.385	March/April	.234	265	62	12	3	1	17	55	51	.321	.313
Grass	.259	1175	304	57	16	15	113	188	198	.365	.373	May	.289	342	99	20	6	7	49	53	59	.385	.444
Turf	.282	579	163	36	5	9	85	73	98	.365	.408	June	.245	286	70	11	1	5	33	46	45	.359	.343
Pre-All Star	.260	1000	260	46	11	14	107	139	173	.356	.370	July	.286	276	79	15	4	6	36	37	48	.372	.435
Post-All Star	.275	754	207	47	10	10	91	122	123	.377	.403	August	.265	336	89	18	5	4	42	55	52	.367	.384
Scoring Posn	.267	408	109	24	7	9	169	97	74	.396	.426	Sept/Oct	.273	249	68	17	2	1	21	35	41	.370	.369
Close & Late	.282	326	92	21	5	7	46	49	67	.380	.442	vs. AL	.263	773	203	35	10	10	78	128	120	.372	.373
None on/out	.233	468	109	26	6	3	3	66	85	.335	.333	vs. NL	.269	981	264	58	11	14	120	133	176	.359	.393

Batter vs. Pitcher (career)

Hits Best Against	Avg	AB	H	2B	3B	HR	RBI	BB	SO	OBP	SLG	Hits Worst Against	Avg	AB	H	2B	3B	HR	RBI	BB	SO	OBP	SLG
Mike Harkey	.625	8	5	0	0	1	3	2	0	.583	1.000	Bill Swift	.000	12	0	0	0	0	0	0	4	.000	.000
Jack McDowell	.500	8	4	0	0	0	1	0	0	.636	.500	Jaime Navarro	.000	9	0	0	0	0	0	3	1	.250	.000
Darryl Kile	.455	22	10	1	1	0	5	4	3	.536	.591	John Burkett	.077	13	1	0	0	0	0	1	4	.200	.077
Mike Bielecki	.417	12	5	0	1	1	4	1	1	.462	.833	Armando Reynoso	.083	12	1	1	0	0	0	0	1	.083	.167
Mike Mussina	.308	13	4	0	2	0	1	2	4	.400	.615	Mark Portugal	.105	19	2	0	0	0	0	1	4	.150	.105

Jermaine Allensworth — Pirates
Age 26 – Bats Right

	Avg	G	AB	R	H	2B	3B	HR	RBI	BB	SO	HBP	GDP	SB	CS	OBP	SLG	IBB	SH	SF	#Pit	#P/PA	GB	FB	G/F
1997 Season	.255	108	369	55	94	18	2	3	43	44	79	7	5	14	7	.340	.339	1	9	6	1750	4.02	148	94	1.57
Career (1996-1997)	.258	169	598	87	154	27	5	7	74	67	129	11	7	25	13	.339	.355	1	11	8	2793	4.02	232	145	1.60

1997 Season

	Avg	AB	H	2B	3B	HR	RBI	BB	SO	OBP	SLG		Avg	AB	H	2B	3B	HR	RBI	BB	SO	OBP	SLG
vs. Left	.278	97	27	5	1	1	6	18	29	.393	.381	First Pitch	.435	23	10	3	0	0	2	1	0	.481	.565
vs. Right	.246	272	67	13	1	2	37	26	50	.320	.324	Ahead in Count	.395	76	30	4	1	1	21	28	0	.542	.513
Groundball	.246	61	15	3	0	0	5	5	20	.313	.295	Behind in Count	.205	176	36	8	0	1	10	0	62	.211	.267
Flyball	.230	61	14	2	0	0	6	8	16	.319	.262	Two Strikes	.201	194	39	7	1	1	12	15	79	.259	.263
Home	.263	186	49	10	1	1	18	24	34	.356	.344	Batting #1	.364	22	8	2	0	1	3	5	2	.464	.591
Away	.246	183	45	8	1	2	25	20	45	.324	.333	Batting #2	.254	335	85	16	2	2	40	39	72	.339	.331
Day	.234	124	29	3	1	0	13	14	27	.317	.274	Other	.083	12	1	0	0	0	0	0	5	.083	.083
Night	.265	245	65	15	1	3	30	30	52	.352	.371	March/April	.286	91	26	6	0	2	8	14	19	.387	.418
Grass	.252	131	33	5	0	2	18	14	31	.327	.336	May	.184	49	9	2	1	0	7	6	11	.305	.265
Turf	.256	238	61	13	2	1	25	30	48	.348	.340	June	.310	29	9	0	1	0	5	2	6	.355	.379
Pre-All Star	.257	171	44	8	2	2	20	22	36	.354	.363	July	.203	64	13	2	0	0	10	7	20	.280	.234
Post-All Star	.253	198	50	10	0	1	23	22	43	.329	.318	August	.301	93	28	5	0	1	11	10	16	.371	.387
Scoring Posn	.261	88	23	4	1	0	38	16	17	.377	.330	Sept/Oct	.209	43	9	3	0	0	2	5	7	.300	.279
Close & Late	.250	52	13	3	1	0	6	5	13	.316	.346	vs. AL	.143	28	4	1	0	0	0	0	4	.143	.179
None on/out	.203	74	15	3	0	2	2	11	13	.306	.324	vs. NL	.264	341	90	17	2	3	43	44	75	.354	.352

1997 By Position

Position	Avg	AB	H	2B	3B	HR	RBI	BB	SO	OBP	SLG	G	GS	Innings	PO	A	E	DP	Fld Pct	Rng Fctr	In Zone	Zone Outs	Zone Rtg	MLB Zone
As cf	.257	366	94	18	2	3	43	44	77	.343	.342	104	94	837.2	189	5	4	1	.980	2.08	232	184	.793	.815

Carlos Almanzar — Blue Jays
Age 24 – Pitches Right

	ERA	W	L	Sv	G	GS	IP	BB	SO	Avg	H	2B	3B	HR	RBI	OBP	SLG	GF	IR	IRS	Hld	SvOp	SB	CS	GB	FB	G/F
1997 Season	2.70	0	1	0	4	0	3.1	1	4	.091	1	0	0	1	1	.167	.364	2	0	0	0	0	0	0	3	4	0.75

1997 Season

	ERA	W	L	Sv	G	GS	IP	H	HR	BB	SO		Avg	AB	H	2B	3B	HR	RBI	BB	SO	OBP	SLG
Home	0.00	0	0	0	2	0	2.0	0	0	0	4	vs. Left	.143	7	1	0	0	1	1	0	2	.143	.571
Away	6.75	0	1	0	2	0	1.1	1	1	1	0	vs. Right	.000	4	0	0	0	0	0	1	2	.200	.000

Roberto Alomar — Orioles
Age 30 – Bats Both (groundball hitter)

	Avg	G	AB	R	H	2B	3B	HR	RBI	BB	SO	HBP	GDP	SB	CS	OBP	SLG	IBB	SH	SF	#Pit	#P/PA	GB	FB	G/F
1997 Season	.333	112	412	64	137	23	2	14	60	40	43	3	10	9	3	.390	.500	2	7	7	1772	3.78	156	131	1.19
Last Five Years	.319	655	2498	454	797	150	23	74	351	308	261	11	67	130	35	.391	.486	22	32	34	11402	3.95	984	737	1.34

1997 Season

	Avg	AB	H	2B	3B	HR	RBI	BB	SO	OBP	SLG		Avg	AB	H	2B	3B	HR	RBI	BB	SO	OBP	SLG
vs. Left	.248	113	28	5	0	0	8	9	18	.298	.292	First Pitch	.354	48	17	3	0	1	5	2	0	.377	.479
vs. Right	.365	299	109	18	2	14	52	31	25	.423	.579	Ahead in Count	.373	83	31	4	1	3	13	22	0	.491	.554
Groundball	.357	112	40	5	1	3	23	7	12	.390	.500	Behind in Count	.281	192	54	13	0	6	18	0	37	.284	.443
Flyball	.367	49	18	3	0	3	4	8	3	.466	.612	Two Strikes	.269	182	49	11	1	7	24	16	43	.335	.456
Home	.379	211	80	12	0	10	39	22	19	.429	.578	Batting #1	.344	61	21	3	0	2	9	3	3	.369	.492
Away	.284	201	57	11	2	4	21	18	24	.348	.418	Batting #2	.332	337	112	20	2	11	49	36	37	.395	.501
Day	.352	125	44	9	1	8	25	20	16	.433	.632	Other	.286	14	4	0	0	1	2	1	3	.333	.500
Night	.324	287	93	14	1	6	35	20	27	.369	.443	March/April	.258	62	16	1	0	3	11	5	8	.300	.419
Grass	.342	351	120	20	2	13	53	38	36	.403	.521	May	.303	99	30	2	0	3	13	12	10	.375	.414
Turf	.279	61	17	3	0	1	7	2	7	.308	.377	June	.348	89	31	8	1	1	6	10	13	.416	.494
Pre-All Star	.307	274	84	11	2	8	36	30	31	.373	.449	July	.270	89	24	3	1	3	13	8	7	.333	.427
Post-All Star	.384	138	53	12	0	6	24	10	12	.424	.601	August	.333	3	1	0	0	0	0	0	0	.333	.333
Scoring Posn	.286	91	26	4	0	2	39	8	15	.327	.396	Sept/Oct	.500	70	35	9	0	4	17	5	5	.532	.700
Close & Late	.268	56	15	1	0	1	4	4	17	.328	.339	vs. AL	.320	381	122	21	1	13	55	36	41	.378	.483

1997 Season

	Avg	AB	H	2B	3B	HR	RBI	BB	SO	OBP	SLG		Avg	AB	H	2B	3B	HR	RBI	BB	SO	OBP	SLG
None on/out	.363	91	33	4	0	4	4	5	9	.402	.538	vs. NL	.484	31	15	2	1	1	5	4	2	.528	.710

1997 By Position

Position	Avg	AB	H	2B	3B	HR	RBI	BB	SO	OBP	SLG	G	GS	Innings	PO	A	E	DP	Fld Pct	Rng Fctr	In Zone	Outs	Zone Rtg	MLB Zone
As 2b	.333	406	135	22	2	14	60	40	41	.390	.500	109	103	896.2	203	300	6	66	.988	5.05	345	306	.887	.902

Last Five Years

	Avg	AB	H	2B	3B	HR	RBI	BB	SO	OBP	SLG		Avg	AB	H	2B	3B	HR	RBI	BB	SO	OBP	SLG
vs. Left	.262	715	187	35	4	19	92	76	111	.332	.401	First Pitch	.357	249	89	16	1	9	40	16	0	.391	.538
vs. Right	.342	1783	610	115	19	55	259	232	150	.415	.520	Ahead in Count	.354	573	203	41	9	16	83	173	0	.499	.541
Groundball	.309	569	176	24	8	17	89	56	51	.369		Behind in Count	.275	1117	307	60	6	23	120	0	205	.275	.401
Flyball	.341	410	140	23	3	13	52	49	49	.407	.507	Two Strikes	.265	1148	304	59	7	31	145	119	261	.333	.409
Home	.331	1215	402	66	9	43	188	155	123	.402	.506	Batting #2	.317	1341	425	87	13	37	176	169	153	.392	.484
Away	.308	1283	395	84	14	31	163	153	138	.382	.468	Batting #3	.344	616	212	36	7	15	100	80	57	.414	.498
Day	.309	771	238	45	6	28	119	108	82	.391	.492	Other	.296	541	160	27	3	22	75	59	51	.364	.479
Night	.324	1727	559	105	17	46	232	200	179	.391	.484	March/April	.331	366	121	20	5	7	47	43	32	.398	.470
Grass	.333	1520	506	96	14	49	217	183	159	.402	.511	May	.320	478	153	18	3	21	89	65	50	.396	.502
Turf	.298	978	291	54	9	25	134	125	102	.375	.448	June	.333	496	165	33	6	13	54	44	58	.389	.502
Pre-All Star	.320	1479	473	77	15	46	204	174	155	.390	.485	July	.279	438	122	27	5	13	54	62	48	.366	.452
Post-All Star	.318	1019	324	73	8	28	147	134	106	.393	.488	August	.326	399	130	25	1	10	53	46	42	.393	.469
Scoring Posn	.296	564	167	25	7	18	262	166	90	.383	.461	Sept/Oct	.330	321	106	27	3	10	54	48	31	.413	.526
Close & Late	.309	346	107	15	2	11	45	45	52	.387	.460	vs. AL	.317	2467	782	148	22	73	346	304	259	.390	.484
None on/out	.342	576	197	34	4	17	17	51	52	.397	.503	vs. NL	.484	31	15	2	1	1	5	4	2	.528	.710

Batter vs. Pitcher (career)

Hits Best Against	Avg	AB	H	2B	3B	HR	RBI	BB	SO	OBP	SLG	Hits Worst Against	Avg	AB	H	2B	3B	HR	RBI	BB	SO	OBP	SLG
Mike Oquist	.667	9	6	0	0	0	2	2	1	.727	.667	Brian Anderson	.091	11	1	0	0	0	0	0	0	.167	.091
Jeff D'Amico	.625	16	10	3	0	3	5	2	0	.667	1.375	Felipe Lira	.133	15	2	0	0	0	2	1	1	.167	.133
Jack McDowell	.552	29	16	1	0	3	8	7	6	.639	.897	Mike Mussina	.143	28	4	1	0	0	1	1	3	.167	.179
Don Wengert	.500	14	7	0	0	2	6	0	0	.500	.929	Bob Patterson	.154	13	2	0	0	0	0	1	5	.154	.154
Paul Quantrill	.500	8	4	2	0	0	2	3	2	.667	.750	Dan Plesac	.167	18	3	0	0	0	2	1	4	.200	.167

Sandy Alomar Jr. — Indians   Age 32 – Bats Right

	Avg	G	AB	R	H	2B	3B	HR	RBI	BB	SO	HBP	GDP	SB	CS	OBP	SLG	IBB	SH	SF	#Pit	#P/PA	GB	FB	G/F
1997 Season	.324	125	451	63	146	37	0	21	83	19	48	3	16	0	2	.354	.545	2	6	1	1583	3.30	168	139	1.21
Last Five Years	.291	462	1579	216	459	88	2	62	243	81	175	17	54	15	8	.330	.467	4	13	9	5907	3.48	608	486	1.25

1997 Season

	Avg	AB	H	2B	3B	HR	RBI	BB	SO	OBP	SLG		Avg	AB	H	2B	3B	HR	RBI	BB	SO	OBP	SLG
vs. Left	.336	119	40	9	0	5	23	5	11	.363	.538	First Pitch	.373	67	25	9	0	3	15	1	0	.391	.642
vs. Right	.319	332	106	28	0	16	60	14	37	.351	.548	Ahead in Count	.402	117	47	13	0	8	31	9	0	.449	.718
Groundball	.329	85	28	9	0	2	15	4	6	.367	.506	Behind in Count	.270	200	54	8	0	7	26	0	43	.272	.415
Flyball	.329	70	23	4	0	3	13	2	9	.347	.514	Two Strikes	.197	157	31	5	0	4	16	9	48	.244	.306
Home	.294	221	65	19	0	9	44	11	25	.329	.502	Batting #7	.312	157	49	19	0	5	25	5	16	.341	.529
Away	.352	230	81	18	0	12	39	8	23	.379	.587	Batting #8	.330	103	34	6	0	6	17	8	15	.375	.563
Day	.345	113	39	9	0	5	23	7	10	.383	.558	Other	.330	191	63	12	0	10	41	6	17	.354	.550
Night	.317	338	107	28	0	16	60	12	38	.345	.541	March/April	.387	75	29	6	0	8	20	4	11	.425	.787
Grass	.330	385	127	34	0	17	66	18	40	.364	.551	May	.299	67	20	3	0	2	11	5	8	.342	.433
Turf	.288	66	19	3	0	4	17	1	8	.299	.515	June	.420	81	34	13	0	1	10	4	6	.447	.617
Pre-All Star	.375	240	90	23	0	11	44	13	26	.408	.608	July	.239	71	17	4	0	2	9	2	8	.270	.380
Post-All Star	.265	211	56	14	0	10	39	6	22	.292	.474	August	.301	93	28	7	0	3	14	1	10	.316	.473
Scoring Posn	.321	137	44	8	0	6	61	12	14	.377	.511	Sept/Oct	.281	64	18	4	0	5	19	3	5	.313	.578
Close & Late	.397	63	25	8	0	2	10	3	5	.424	.619	vs. AL	.319	405	129	33	0	20	72	19	44	.353	.548
None on/out	.314	102	32	5	0	5	5	2	9	.327	.510	vs. NL	.370	46	17	4	0	1	11	0	4	.370	.522

1997 By Position

Position	Avg	AB	H	2B	3B	HR	RBI	BB	SO	OBP	SLG	G	GS	Innings	PO	A	E	DP	Fld Pct	Rng Fctr	In Zone	Outs	Zone Rtg	MLB Zone
As c	.327	440	144	36	0	21	83	19	46	.359	.552	119	115	1005.0	742	41	12	11	.985	---	---	---	---	---

Last Five Years

	Avg	AB	H	2B	3B	HR	RBI	BB	SO	OBP	SLG		Avg	AB	H	2B	3B	HR	RBI	BB	SO	OBP	SLG
vs. Left	.282	412	116	20	1	14	62	20	47	.315	.437	First Pitch	.315	219	69	17	0	13	45	3	0	.326	.571
vs. Right	.294	1167	343	68	1	48	181	61	128	.336	.477	Ahead in Count	.371	383	142	24	2	16	68	39	0	.433	.569
Groundball	.294	320	94	16	0	8	41	22	44	.347	.419	Behind in Count	.238	682	162	25	0	18	80	0	156	.246	.353
Flyball	.293	283	83	18	0	16	44	13	35	.330	.527	Two Strikes	.213	597	127	19	0	19	69	39	175	.268	.340
Home	.284	749	213	50	1	23	112	43	79	.329	.446	Batting #8	.275	524	144	31	0	18	68	37	65	.326	.437
Away	.296	830	246	38	1	39	131	38	96	.331	.486	Batting #9	.312	471	147	18	1	22	78	22	58	.352	.495
Day	.289	422	122	19	0	18	75	30	45	.340	.462	Other	.288	584	168	39	1	22	97	22	52	.316	.471
Night	.291	1157	337	69	2	44	168	51	130	.327	.468	March/April	.280	246	69	10	0	13	40	19	36	.337	.480
Grass	.295	1350	398	81	2	52	201	73	150	.337	.473	May	.262	206	54	11	0	8	27	14	24	.308	.432
Turf	.266	229	61	7	0	10	42	8	25	.292	.428	June	.345	238	82	19	0	6	30	17	19	.392	.500
Pre-All Star	.301	774	233	46	1	29	110	53	84	.348	.475	July	.290	272	79	11	1	10	42	12	24	.322	.450
Post-All Star	.281	805	226	42	1	33	133	28	91	.313	.458	August	.279	358	100	19	1	12	62	7	41	.303	.439
Scoring Posn	.296	433	128	26	1	15	180	33	55	.349	.464	Sept/Oct	.290	259	75	15	0	13	42	12	31	.330	.498
Close & Late	.335	266	89	14	0	11	40	13	32	.371	.511	vs. AL	.288	1533	442	84	2	61	232	81	171	.329	.465
None on/out	.275	385	106	13	0	16	16	16	39	.309	.434	vs. NL	.370	46	17	4	0	1	11	0	4	.370	.522

Moises Alou — Marlins
Age 31 – Bats Right

	Avg	G	AB	R	H	2B	3B	HR	RBI	BB	SO	HBP	GDP	SB	CS	OBP	SLG	IBB	SH	SF	#Pit	#P/PA	GB	FB	G/F
1997 Season	.292	150	538	88	157	29	5	23	115	70	85	4	13	9	5	.373	.493	9	0	7	2188	3.53	187	185	1.01
Last Five Years	.294	629	2326	374	684	139	18	98	432	228	340	22	52	46	24	.358	.496	41	3	30	8838	3.39	834	744	1.12

1997 Season

	Avg	AB	H	2B	3B	HR	RBI	BB	SO	OBP	SLG		Avg	AB	H	2B	3B	HR	RBI	BB	SO	OBP	SLG
vs. Left	.340	97	33	9	2	5	33	21	15	.454	.629	First Pitch	.380	100	38	10	2	7	25	8	0	.432	.730
vs. Right	.281	441	124	20	3	18	82	49	70	.354	.463	Ahead in Count	.359	131	47	6	2	8	43	36	0	.491	.618
Groundball	.265	83	22	4	1	1	10	11	9	.344	.373	Behind in Count	.220	214	47	8	1	6	28	0	64	.219	.350
Flyball	.239	71	17	3	0	5	15	13	13	.349	.493	Two Strikes	.166	217	36	5	1	5	28	26	85	.255	.267
Home	.276	261	72	12	5	12	62	36	53	.364	.498	Batting #5	.294	293	86	17	5	11	66	36	51	.373	.498
Away	.307	277	85	17	0	11	53	34	32	.382	.487	Batting #6	.322	177	57	7	0	11	37	21	22	.391	.548
Day	.301	156	47	11	1	6	30	25	20	.395	.500	Other	.206	68	14	5	0	1	12	13	12	.329	.324
Night	.288	382	110	18	4	17	85	45	65	.364	.490	March/April	.360	86	31	5	2	8	30	12	13	.430	.744
Grass	.291	437	127	22	5	20	98	59	71	.375	.501	May	.247	97	24	6	1	0	13	15	15	.362	.330
Turf	.297	101	30	7	0	3	17	11	14	.368	.455	June	.293	99	29	6	1	1	21	10	18	.355	.404
Pre-All Star	.293	297	87	18	4	9	65	39	49	.376	.471	July	.268	82	22	6	1	5	14	11	19	.355	.549
Post-All Star	.290	241	70	11	1	14	50	31	36	.370	.519	August	.269	93	25	5	0	4	21	13	11	.355	.452
Scoring Posn	.329	155	51	8	3	7	90	29	20	.419	.555	Sept/Oct	.321	81	26	1	0	5	16	9	9	.389	.519
Close & Late	.253	95	24	3	0	2	14	12	22	.339	.347	vs. AL	.296	54	16	4	0	1	10	4	7	.333	.426
None on/out	.241	116	28	3	0	4	4	16	19	.343	.371	vs. NL	.291	484	141	25	5	22	105	66	78	.377	.500

1997 By Position

Position	Avg	AB	H	2B	3B	HR	RBI	BB	SO	OBP	SLG	G	GS	Innings	PO	A	E	DP	Fld Pct	Rng Fctr	In Zone	In Outs	Zone Rtg	MLB Zone
As lf	.310	310	96	12	1	21	71	35	42	.379	.558	91	85	716.0	123	2	3	0	.977	1.57	159	117	.736	.805
As cf	.278	194	54	16	4	2	42	28	32	.370	.433	54	53	461.2	108	1	0	0	1.000	2.12	135	102	.756	.815
As rf	.194	31	6	1	0	0	1	7	11	.342	.226	18	7	98.2	18	1	0	1	1.000	1.73	26	18	.692	.813

Last Five Years

	Avg	AB	H	2B	3B	HR	RBI	BB	SO	OBP	SLG		Avg	AB	H	2B	3B	HR	RBI	BB	SO	OBP	SLG
vs. Left	.323	561	181	48	4	24	111	61	71	.390	.551	First Pitch	.374	449	168	41	7	28	100	33	0	.424	.684
vs. Right	.285	1765	503	91	14	74	321	167	269	.348	.478	Ahead in Count	.343	557	191	43	5	29	135	112	0	.448	.594
Groundball	.262	606	159	32	6	15	93	46	85	.318	.409	Behind in Count	.237	948	225	30	5	28	129	0	282	.240	.368
Flyball	.260	388	101	27	0	19	74	36	51	.321	.477	Two Strikes	.210	898	189	32	5	22	117	81	340	.277	.331
Home	.294	1092	321	65	11	49	234	121	168	.365	.508	Batting #4	.274	884	242	49	2	31	151	74	134	.333	.439
Away	.294	1234	363	74	7	49	198	107	172	.353	.485	Batting #5	.293	646	189	43	8	15	111	69	101	.363	.454
Day	.282	714	201	49	3	28	116	74	104	.350	.476	Other	.318	796	253	47	8	52	170	85	105	.383	.593
Night	.300	1612	483	90	15	70	316	154	236	.362	.504	March/April	.330	358	118	25	4	20	74	34	49	.386	.589
Grass	.281	1011	284	52	8	40	166	112	153	.354	.467	May	.282	486	137	32	1	8	70	50	71	.357	.401
Turf	.304	1315	400	87	10	58	266	116	187	.362	.518	June	.271	484	131	23	3	21	94	50	71	.336	.461
Pre-All Star	.291	1478	430	91	8	60	267	146	212	.357	.485	July	.300	426	128	28	5	22	81	42	71	.366	.545
Post-All Star	.300	848	254	48	10	38	165	82	128	.362	.514	August	.293	368	108	22	4	17	79	33	56	.348	.514
Scoring Posn	.322	690	222	43	5	28	334	114	99	.406	.520	Sept/Oct	.304	204	62	9	1	10	34	19	22	.369	.505
Close & Late	.273	363	99	16	3	9	59	49	73	.359	.408	vs. AL	.296	54	16	4	0	1	10	4	7	.333	.426
None on/out	.281	519	146	34	7	22	22	39	76	.343	.501	vs. NL	.294	2272	668	135	18	97	422	224	333	.359	.497

Batter vs. Pitcher (career)

Wilson Alvarez — Giants
Age 28 – Pitches Left

	ERA	W	L	Sv	G	GS	IP	BB	SO	Avg	H	2B	3B	HR	RBI	OBP	SLG	CG	ShO	Sup	QS	#P/S	SB	CS	GB	FB	G/F
1997 Season	3.48	13	11	0	33	33	212.0	91	179	.229	180	30	2	18	86	.310	.341	2	1	4.88	21	108	11	9	242	230	1.05
Last Five Years	3.68	63	48	0	152	152	973.2	465	741	.243	882	163	13	90	401	.330	.370	8	3	5.35	90	109	64	50	1133	1076	1.05

1997 Season

	ERA	W	L	Sv	G	GS	IP	H	HR	BB	SO		Avg	AB	H	2B	3B	HR	RBI	BB	SO	OBP	SLG
Home	3.73	5	6	0	17	17	108.2	91	8	46	104	vs. Left	.253	154	39	4	0	5	22	16	29	.328	.377
Away	3.22	8	5	0	16	16	103.1	89	10	45	75	vs. Right	.223	631	141	26	2	13	64	75	150	.306	.333
Day	4.09	4	5	0	13	13	81.1	74	7	38	90	Inning 1-6	.226	687	155	27	1	15	74	80	165	.308	.333
Night	3.10	9	6	0	20	20	130.2	106	11	53	89	Inning 7+	.255	98	25	3	1	3	12	11	14	.327	.398
Grass	3.38	10	10	0	28	28	181.0	152	15	76	153	None on	.233	434	101	15	1	7	7	53	108	.322	.320
Turf	4.06	3	1	0	5	5	31.0	28	3	15	26	Runners on	.225	351	79	15	1	11	79	38	71	.296	.368
March/April	3.16	1	4	0	6	6	37.0	32	4	15	34	Scoring Posn	.268	157	42	7	1	7	69	25	29	.356	.459
May	4.26	2	2	0	5	5	31.2	32	1	12	31	Close & Late	.214	42	9	2	0	2	7	7	8	.327	.405

1997 Season

	ERA	W	L	Sv	G	GS	IP	H	HR	BB	SO
June	0.83	4	0	0	6	6	43.1	31	1	15	24
July	4.54	2	2	0	5	5	33.2	31	3	13	21
August	5.88	3	2	0	6	6	33.2	32	5	20	29
Sept/Oct	3.03	1	1	0	5	5	32.2	22	4	16	40
Starter	3.48	13	11	0	33	33	212.0	180	18	91	179
Reliever	0.00	0	0	0	0	0	0.0	0	0	0	0
0-3 Days Rest (Start)	0.00	0	0	0	0	0	0.0	0	0	0	0
4 Days Rest	3.78	6	7	0	20	20	123.2	103	11	60	104
5+ Days Rest	3.06	7	4	0	13	13	88.1	77	7	31	75
vs. AL	3.65	7	9	0	21	21	133.0	120	10	54	108
vs. NL	3.19	6	2	0	12	12	79.0	60	8	37	71
Pre-All Star	2.57	7	6	0	18	18	119.0	99	6	44	97
Post-All Star	4.65	6	5	0	15	15	93.0	81	12	47	82

	Avg	AB	H	2B	3B	HR	RBI	BB	SO	OBP	SLG
None on/out	.240	196	47	6	0	4	4	23	45	.329	.332
vs. 1st Batr (relief)	.000	0	0	0	0	0	0	0	0	.000	.000
1st Inning Pitched	.248	125	31	5	0	2	13	14	33	.321	.336
First 75 Pitches	.223	524	117	22	1	10	53	53	133	.296	.326
Pitch 76-90	.231	104	24	3	0	2	8	17	19	.341	.317
Pitch 91-105	.217	83	18	0	0	5	17	13	13	.323	.398
Pitch 106+	.284	74	21	5	1	1	8	8	14	.349	.419
First Pitch	.282	85	24	3	0	2	10	4	0	.308	.388
Ahead in Count	.206	407	84	14	0	11	41	0	147	.210	.322
Behind in Count	.291	141	41	9	1	2	17	48	0	.469	.411
Two Strikes	.163	416	68	12	0	9	38	39	179	.236	.257
Post-All Star	.236	343	81	9	0	12	45	47	82	.329	.367

Last Five Years

	ERA	W	L	Sv	G	GS	IP	H	HR	BB	SO
Home	3.74	34	23	0	75	75	476.1	427	39	224	373
Away	3.62	31	25	0	77	77	497.1	455	51	241	368
Day	4.29	14	14	0	45	45	274.2	275	33	137	224
Night	3.44	49	34	0	107	107	699.0	607	57	328	517
Grass	3.69	53	42	0	133	133	854.2	775	81	406	654
Turf	3.63	10	6	0	19	19	119.0	107	9	59	87
March/April	3.14	9	7	0	21	21	132.0	117	15	57	109
May	4.02	14	5	0	27	27	170.1	164	17	93	124
June	3.31	10	10	0	30	30	201.0	184	15	93	141
July	3.50	13	9	0	28	28	185.1	161	15	83	135
August	4.76	9	9	0	24	24	145.2	142	18	65	121
Sept/Oct	3.42	8	8	0	22	22	139.1	114	10	74	111
Starter	3.68	63	48	0	152	152	973.2	882	90	465	741
Reliever	0.00	0	0	0	0	0	0.0	0	0	0	0
0-3 Days Rest (Start)	4.82	2	1	0	3	3	18.2	17	1	10	18
4 Days Rest	3.80	35	29	0	92	92	592.0	530	59	293	444
5+ Days Rest	3.42	26	18	0	57	57	363.0	335	30	162	279
vs. AL	3.72	57	46	0	140	140	894.2	822	82	428	670
vs. NL	3.19	6	2	0	12	12	79.0	60	8	37	71
Pre-All Star	3.59	37	24	0	85	85	546.1	507	50	259	402
Post-All Star	3.79	26	24	0	67	67	427.1	375	40	206	339

	Avg	AB	H	2B	3B	HR	RBI	BB	SO	OBP	SLG
vs. Left	.271	591	160	22	4	10	68	73	111	.355	.372
vs. Right	.238	3035	722	141	9	80	333	392	630	.326	.369
Inning 1-6	.241	3135	754	136	9	81	347	391	673	.326	.367
Inning 7+	.261	491	128	27	4	9	54	74	68	.357	.387
None on/out	.250	2028	506	91	6	44	44	273	426	.342	.365
Runners on	.235	1598	376	72	7	46	357	192	315	.316	.375
Scoring Posn	.249	787	196	47	2	19	282	126	152	.346	.386
Close & Late	.251	251	63	14	2	6	29	48	38	.374	.394
None on/out	.254	925	235	37	2	26	26	110	180	.337	.383
vs. 1st Batr (relief)	.000	0	0	0	0	0	0	0	0	.000	.000
1st Inning Pitched	.240	572	137	27	1	16	66	59	136	.314	.374
First 75 Pitches	.241	2385	575	101	9	57	251	278	523	.322	.363
Pitch 76-90	.241	474	114	16	1	16	60	70	91	.338	.380
Pitch 91-105	.260	396	103	19	0	12	45	66	70	.366	.399
Pitch 106+	.243	371	90	27	3	5	45	51	57	.333	.372
First Pitch	.337	413	139	24	1	21	73	19	0	.364	.552
Ahead in Count	.193	1752	339	54	4	29	148	0	598	.196	.279
Behind in Count	.301	725	218	50	3	21	96	235	0	.469	.465
Two Strikes	.182	1808	329	58	5	30	151	211	741	.269	.269
Post-All Star	.239	1569	375	69	6	40	182	206	339	.329	.369

Pitcher vs. Batter (career)

Pitches Best Vs.	Avg	AB	H	2B	3B	HR	RBI	BB	SO	OBP	SLG
Russ Davis	.000	11	0	0	0	0	0	1	6	.083	.000
Pat Meares	.063	16	1	0	0	0	1	0	4	.063	.063
J.T. Snow	.087	23	2	0	0	0	1	1	6	.125	.087
Gary Gaetti	.115	26	3	0	0	0	1	1	6	.148	.115
Mike Devereaux	.125	32	4	0	0	0	0	0	7	.125	.125

Pitches Worst Vs.	Avg	AB	H	2B	3B	HR	RBI	BB	SO	OBP	SLG
Rex Hudler	.579	19	11	2	0	2	5	1	3	.600	1.000
Derek Jeter	.538	13	7	2	0	0	1	2	0	.600	.692
John Jaha	.444	18	8	3	0	1	8	3	0	.524	.778
Ron Coomer	.400	15	6	4	0	1	5	1	5	.438	.867
Danny Tartabull	.375	16	6	0	0	3	8	5	3	.524	.938

Rich Amaral — Mariners
Age 36 – Bats Right

	Avg	G	AB	R	H	2B	3B	HR	RBI	BB	SO	HBP	GDP	SB	CS	OBP	SLG	IBB	SH	SF	#Pit	#P/PA	GB	FB	G/F
1997 Season	.284	89	190	34	54	5	0	1	21	10	34	3	7	12	8	.327	.326	0	5	2	764	3.64	70	58	1.21
Last Five Years	.283	484	1341	238	380	64	8	9	131	135	204	13	24	82	28	.352	.363	1	24	10	5578	3.66	507	368	1.38

1997 Season

	Avg	AB	H	2B	3B	HR	RBI	BB	SO	OBP	SLG
vs. Left	.279	129	36	4	0	1	15	6	23	.321	.333
vs. Right	.295	61	18	1	0	0	6	4	11	.338	.311
Home	.271	85	23	2	0	0	7	7	17	.294	.370
Away	.295	105	31	3	0	1	14	3	17	.321	.352
First Pitch	.346	26	9	0	0	0	3	0	0	.333	.346
Ahead in Count	.370	46	17	2	0	0	4	0	0	.420	.413
Behind in Count	.212	85	18	3	0	1	10	0	28	.227	.282
Two Strikes	.176	85	15	1	0	1	5	6	34	.239	.224

	Avg	AB	H	2B	3B	HR	RBI	BB	SO	OBP	SLG
Scoring Posn	.204	54	11	4	0	0	20	1	10	.224	.278
Close & Late	.375	32	12	2	0	0	8	0	4	.364	.438
None on/out	.315	54	17	0	0	1	1	4	8	.373	.370
Batting #1	.313	96	30	2	0	1	14	6	15	.356	.365
Batting #9	.219	64	14	1	0	0	3	1	13	.239	.234
Other	.333	30	10	2	0	0	4	3	6	.412	.400
Pre-All Star	.252	111	28	3	0	0	12	7	22	.311	.279
Post-All Star	.329	79	26	2	0	1	9	3	12	.349	.392

Last Five Years

	Avg	AB	H	2B	3B	HR	RBI	BB	SO	OBP	SLG
vs. Left	.305	653	199	38	4	7	72	61	86	.367	.407
vs. Right	.263	688	181	26	4	2	59	74	118	.339	.321
Groundball	.284	257	73	13	0	2	24	35	37	.371	.358
Flyball	.198	227	45	10	1	2	19	21	43	.272	.278
Home	.278	615	171	30	3	4	60	70	90	.357	.356
Away	.288	726	209	34	5	5	71	65	114	.348	.369
Day	.271	388	105	20	4	1	37	38	55	.339	.351
Night	.289	953	275	44	4	8	94	97	149	.358	.368
Grass	.272	593	161	23	3	5	57	55	99	.335	.346
Turf	.293	748	219	41	5	4	74	80	105	.366	.377
Pre-All Star	.280	867	243	46	4	6	81	93	141	.353	.363
Post-All Star	.289	474	137	18	4	3	50	42	63	.350	.363
Scoring Posn	.276	308	85	12	3	2	117	37	46	.347	.354
Close & Late	.277	206	57	9	1	1	28	23	38	.346	.345

	Avg	AB	H	2B	3B	HR	RBI	BB	SO	OBP	SLG
First Pitch	.337	187	63	9	1	3	27	1	0	.340	.444
Ahead in Count	.379	369	140	28	4	3	38	53	0	.455	.501
Behind in Count	.191	530	101	19	0	2	42	0	173	.199	.238
Two Strikes	.197	544	107	17	3	3	35	81	204	.305	.256
Batting #1	.290	713	207	36	4	4	68	73	98	.359	.369
Batting #9	.266	297	79	11	1	1	25	26	56	.332	.320
Other	.284	331	94	17	3	4	38	36	50	.362	.390
March/April	.307	241	74	17	2	2	25	24	36	.375	.419
May	.275	287	79	16	1	4	37	27	52	.340	.380
June	.257	253	65	13	1	0	13	26	37	.331	.316
July	.296	253	75	4	1	1	20	33	33	.379	.332
August	.266	188	50	7	2	1	18	16	28	.332	.340
Sept/Oct	.311	119	37	7	1	1	18	9	18	.354	.412
vs. AL	.284	1336	379	64	8	9	130	134	203	.353	.364

Last Five Years

	Avg	AB	H	2B	3B	HR	RBI	BB	SO	OBP	SLG		Avg	AB	H	2B	3B	HR	RBI	BB	SO	OBP	SLG
None on/out	.281	445	125	24	1	4	4	46	67	.354	.366	vs. NL	.200	5	1	0	0	0	1	1	1	.286	.200

Batter vs. Pitcher (career)

Hits Best Against	Avg	AB	H	2B	3B	HR	RBI	BB	SO	OBP	SLG	Hits Worst Against	Avg	AB	H	2B	3B	HR	RBI	BB	SO	OBP	SLG
Jamie Moyer	.524	21	11	2	0	0	2	1	3	.545	.619	Jose Rosado	.091	11	1	0	0	0	0	0	2	.091	.091
Bobby Witt	.500	10	5	0	0	0	1	1	2	.545	.500	Brian Anderson	.105	19	2	0	0	0	0	1	1	.150	.105
Alex Fernandez	.444	9	4	1	0	0	0	1	1	.545	.556	Mike Mussina	.182	11	2	0	0	0	0	0	4	.182	.182
Jimmy Key	.440	25	11	3	0	0	4	4	6	.500	.560	Arthur Rhodes	.182	11	2	0	0	0	1	0	3	.182	.182
Scott Karl	.412	17	7	2	1	0	2	0	2	.412	.647	Mike Trombley	.182	11	2	0	0	0	0	0	2	.182	.182

Ruben Amaro — Phillies   Age 33 – Bats Both

	Avg	G	AB	R	H	2B	3B	HR	RBI	BB	SO	HBP	GDP	SB	CS	OBP	SLG	IBB	SH	SF	#Pit	#P/PA	GB	FB	G/F
1997 Season	.234	117	175	18	41	6	1	2	21	21	24	2	4	1	1	.320	.314	0	0	2	746	3.73	59	60	0.98
Last Five Years	.262	257	423	49	111	22	3	8	54	42	56	7	9	4	3	.337	.385	1	6	3	1714	3.56	145	139	1.04

1997 Season

	Avg	AB	H	2B	3B	HR	RBI	BB	SO	OBP	SLG		Avg	AB	H	2B	3B	HR	RBI	BB	SO	OBP	SLG
vs. Left	.315	54	17	2	1	0	9	6	8	.383	.389	Scoring Posn	.172	58	10	2	0	0	18	9	5	.286	.207
vs. Right	.198	121	24	4	0	2	12	15	16	.293	.281	Close & Late	.140	43	6	2	0	0	3	3	5	.208	.186
Home	.198	86	17	3	0	1	10	7	10	.274	.267	None on/out	.278	36	10	1	1	0	0	3	2	.333	.361
Away	.270	89	24	3	1	1	11	14	14	.362	.360	Batting #6	.281	32	9	0	0	0	3	3	0	.343	.281
First Pitch	.321	28	9	2	0	1	3	0	0	.321	.500	Batting #9	.193	57	11	3	0	1	9	7	11	.303	.298
Ahead in Count	.319	47	15	2	1	1	11	11	0	.459	.468	Other	.244	86	21	3	1	1	9	11	13	.323	.337
Behind in Count	.155	71	11	2	0	0	4	0	22	.155	.183	Pre-All Star	.250	80	20	4	0	2	11	9	11	.319	.375
Two Strikes	.120	75	9	1	0	0	7	10	24	.221	.133	Post-All Star	.221	95	21	2	1	0	10	12	13	.321	.263

Brady Anderson — Orioles   Age 34 – Bats Left

	Avg	G	AB	R	H	2B	3B	HR	RBI	BB	SO	HBP	GDP	SB	CS	OBP	SLG	IBB	SH	SF	#Pit	#P/PA	GB	FB	G/F
1997 Season	.288	151	590	97	170	39	7	18	73	84	105	19	1	18	12	.393	.469	6	2	1	2581	3.71	180	197	0.91
Last Five Years	.275	696	2736	487	753	170	35	109	361	386	496	71	26	120	40	.377	.482	18	21	15	12711	3.94	847	914	0.93

1997 Season

	Avg	AB	H	2B	3B	HR	RBI	BB	SO	OBP	SLG		Avg	AB	H	2B	3B	HR	RBI	BB	SO	OBP	SLG
vs. Left	.281	192	54	11	3	5	23	24	39	.381	.448	First Pitch	.379	103	39	6	0	4	8	5	0	.423	.553
vs. Right	.291	398	116	28	4	13	50	60	66	.399	.480	Ahead in Count	.415	147	61	13	2	8	28	40	0	.552	.694
Groundball	.310	142	44	11	2	5	22	35	24	.459	.521	Behind in Count	.182	236	43	15	2	4	17	0	88	.209	.314
Flyball	.233	73	17	5	1	1	6	7	13	.309	.370	Two Strikes	.169	254	43	14	3	4	22	39	105	.294	.295
Home	.251	271	68	15	0	8	29	40	47	.366	.395	Batting #1	.293	550	161	36	7	16	67	79	93	.398	.471
Away	.320	319	102	24	7	10	44	44	58	.417	.533	Batting #4	.237	38	9	3	0	2	6	4	10	.326	.474
Day	.289	180	52	14	2	6	25	30	20	.411	.489	Other	.000	2	0	0	0	0	0	1	2	.333	.000
Night	.288	410	118	25	5	12	48	54	85	.385	.461	March/April	.380	79	30	4	2	2	16	18	14	.515	.557
Grass	.285	516	147	36	3	16	64	73	85	.392	.459	May	.291	110	32	7	1	4	16	20	18	.418	.482
Turf	.311	74	23	3	4	2	9	11	20	.400	.541	June	.268	112	30	5	0	1	8	12	23	.349	.339
Pre-All Star	.300	313	94	16	4	7	41	53	56	.421	.444	July	.290	93	27	7	2	3	13	13	11	.385	.505
Post-All Star	.274	277	76	23	3	11	32	31	49	.361	.498	August	.262	107	28	9	1	6	13	12	22	.347	.533
Scoring Posn	.296	115	34	7	4	2	53	25	18	.450	.478	Sept/Oct	.258	89	23	7	1	2	7	9	17	.359	.427
Close & Late	.347	75	26	6	0	2	17	19	15	.495	.507	vs. AL	.299	545	163	38	7	16	66	75	96	.401	.483
None on/out	.263	243	64	19	1	8	8	24	47	.339	.449	vs. NL	.156	45	7	1	0	2	7	9	9	.309	.311

1997 By Position

Position	Avg	AB	H	2B	3B	HR	RBI	BB	SO	OBP	SLG	G	GS	Innings	PO	A	E	DP	Fld Pct	Rng Fctr	In Zone	In Outs	Zone Rtg	MLB Zone
As DH	.366	93	34	5	2	3	18	19	20	.491	.559	25	24	---	---	---	---	---	---	---	---	---	---
As cf	.274	496	136	34	5	15	55	65	84	.374	.454	124	123	1096.0	276	1	3	0	.989	2.27	347	267	.769	.815

Last Five Years

	Avg	AB	H	2B	3B	HR	RBI	BB	SO	OBP	SLG		Avg	AB	H	2B	3B	HR	RBI	BB	SO	OBP	SLG
vs. Left	.251	852	214	48	7	24	106	121	197	.360	.408	First Pitch	.340	326	111	25	1	13	44	14	0	.390	.543
vs. Right	.286	1884	539	122	28	85	255	265	299	.385	.516	Ahead in Count	.371	731	271	65	9	45	132	224	0	.521	.669
Groundball	.317	603	191	40	6	26	91	109	97	.435	.532	Behind in Count	.191	1081	207	46	10	23	92	0	395	.216	.316
Flyball	.223	489	109	24	4	17	50	61	99	.320	.393	Two Strikes	.190	1214	231	50	15	36	126	148	496	.288	.345
Home	.258	1327	343	83	10	46	162	186	246	.363	.440	Batting #1	.275	2371	651	147	30	90	295	332	421	.376	.476
Away	.291	1409	410	87	25	63	199	200	250	.391	.522	Batting #2	.290	303	88	19	5	17	55	46	59	.397	.554
Day	.287	807	232	58	9	37	110	124	131	.391	.519	Other	.226	62	14	4	0	2	11	8	16	.324	.387
Night	.270	1929	521	112	26	72	251	262	365	.371	.467	March/April	.307	381	117	26	6	21	62	60	73	.414	.572
Grass	.274	2360	646	150	26	87	309	340	419	.378	.470	May	.252	507	128	27	3	19	58	74	79	.356	.430
Turf	.285	376	107	20	9	22	52	46	77	.373	.561	June	.257	502	129	29	5	19	57	66	90	.360	.448
Pre-All Star	.272	1513	411	91	18	64	202	222	267	.378	.482	July	.285	460	131	31	8	15	67	60	89	.380	.485
Post-All Star	.280	1223	342	79	17	45	159	164	229	.377	.482	August	.273	458	125	30	7	18	67	70	88	.377	.487
Scoring Posn	.255	581	148	41	6	12	231	121	117	.390	.408	Sept/Oct	.287	428	123	27	6	17	50	56	77	.386	.498
Close & Late	.272	367	100	21	7	9	55	61	84	.384	.441	vs. AL	.277	2691	746	169	35	107	354	377	487	.378	.485
None on/out	.282	1060	299	69	14	51	51	107	194	.360	.518	vs. NL	.156	45	7	1	0	2	7	9	9	.309	.311

Batter vs. Pitcher (career)

Hits Best Against	Avg	AB	H	2B	3B	HR	RBI	BB	SO	OBP	SLG	Hits Worst Against	Avg	AB	H	2B	3B	HR	RBI	BB	SO	OBP	SLG
John Burkett	.900	10	9	0	0	0	1	1	0	.909	.900	Al Leiter	.000	9	0	0	0	0	1	2	0	.167	.000
Heathcliff Slocumb	.571	7	4	1	0	1	4	0	.727	1.143	Rick Aguilera	.083	12	1	0	0	0	0	2	4	.214	.083
Mike Trombley	.545	11	6	2	1	1	1	2	2	.615	1.182	Bob Wickman	.083	12	1	0	0	0	0	2	2	.214	.083

Hits Best Against	Avg	AB	H	2B	3B	HR	RBI	BB	SO	OBP	SLG	Hits Worst Against	Avg	AB	H	2B	3B	HR	RBI	BB	SO	OBP	SLG
James Baldwin	.545	11	6	1	0	2	2	2	1	.615	1.182	Rick Honeycutt	.118	17	2	0	0	0	0	0	6	.167	.118
Kevin Gross	.500	10	5	1	0	4	5	1	2	.583	1.800	Dennis Cook	.143	21	3	0	0	0	2	0	6	.143	.143

Brian Anderson — Indians
Age 26 – Pitches Left (flyball pitcher)

	ERA	W	L	Sv	G	GS	IP	BB	SO	Avg	H	2B	3B	HR	RBI	OBP	SLG	CG	ShO	Sup	QS	#P/S	SB	CS	GB	FB	G/F
1997 Season	4.69	4	2	0	8	8	48.0	11	22	.301	55	3	1	7	28	.332	.443	0	0	6.00	4	93	3	5	61	65	0.94
Career (1993-1997)	5.25	20	16	0	58	53	312.0	84	139	.292	354	72	7	54	174	.337	.497	1	0	6.14	24	89	22	19	366	475	0.77

1997 Season

	ERA	W	L	Sv	G	GS	IP	H	HR	BB	SO		Avg	AB	H	2B	3B	HR	RBI	BB	SO	OBP	SLG
Home	4.32	3	2	0	5	5	33.1	40	5	6	21	vs. Left	.314	35	11	1	0	1	5	1	6	.333	.429
Away	5.52	1	0	0	3	3	14.2	15	2	5	1	vs. Right	.297	148	44	2	1	6	23	10	16	.331	.446

Career (1993-1997)

	ERA	W	L	Sv	G	GS	IP	H	HR	BB	SO		Avg	AB	H	2B	3B	HR	RBI	BB	SO	OBP	SLG
Home	4.75	11	9	0	32	29	180.0	193	28	47	87	vs. Left	.313	243	76	11	1	14	47	7	33	.340	.539
Away	5.93	9	7	0	26	24	132.0	161	26	37	52	vs. Right	.287	969	278	61	6	40	127	77	106	.336	.486
Day	5.28	5	5	0	16	15	92.0	101	14	29	40	Inning 1-6	.289	1060	306	60	7	43	149	77	129	.335	.480
Night	5.24	15	11	0	42	38	220.0	253	40	55	99	Inning 7+	.316	152	48	12	0	11	25	7	10	.354	.612
Grass	5.05	20	15	0	53	49	290.1	324	49	76	127	None on	.291	729	212	44	4	38	38	49	85	.340	.519
Turf	7.89	0	1	0	5	4	21.2	30	5	8	12	Runners on	.294	483	142	28	3	16	136	35	54	.333	.464
March/April	2.95	3	0	0	5	5	36.2	29	2	11	16	Scoring Posn	.307	264	81	18	3	10	120	25	32	.346	.511
May	5.74	0	2	0	6	6	26.2	32	3	6	11	Close & Late	.429	35	15	3	0	3	8	1	1	.459	.771
June	6.27	5	4	0	13	13	70.1	85	14	23	36	None on/out	.262	317	83	24	4	11	11	25	41	.320	.467
July	4.63	7	3	0	11	11	72.0	81	11	19	25	vs. 1st Batr	.800	5	4	1	0	1	2	0	0	.800	1.600
August	6.38	2	5	0	10	10	55.0	70	14	13	30	1st Inning Pitched	.333	228	76	17	0	11	43	17	32	.379	.553
Sept/Oct	4.91	3	2	0	13	8	51.1	57	10	12	21	First 75 Pitches	.295	940	277	53	7	42	135	68	113	.340	.500
Starter	5.36	20	16	0	53	53	300.1	344	53	84	130	Pitch 76-90	.268	157	42	12	0	4	19	7	15	.304	.420
Reliever	2.31	0	0	0	5	0	11.2	10	1	0	9	Pitch 91-105	.233	73	17	2	0	3	8	5	8	.288	.384
0-3 Days Rest (Start)	1.69	2	0	0	2	2	10.2	9	0	2	3	Pitch 106+	.429	42	18	5	0	5	12	4	0	.489	.905
4 Days Rest	5.84	10	12	0	31	31	172.2	205	36	46	87	First Pitch	.304	181	55	13	2	6	17	2	0	.314	.497
5+ Days Rest	5.00	8	4	0	20	20	117.0	130	17	36	40	Ahead in Count	.270	525	142	26	3	15	61	0	110	.274	.417
vs. AL	5.34	19	16	0	57	52	305.0	349	53	84	132	Behind in Count	.325	280	91	19	2	21	61	44	0	.410	.632
vs. NL	1.29	1	0	0	1	1	7.0	5	1	0	7	Two Strikes	.244	512	125	24	2	18	57	38	139	.300	.404
Pre-All Star	5.14	10	8	0	29	29	164.2	181	25	48	70	Pre-All Star	.286	632	181	33	1	25	91	48	70	.335	.460
Post-All Star	5.38	10	8	0	29	24	147.1	173	29	36	69	Post-All Star	.298	580	173	39	6	29	83	36	69	.339	.536

Pitcher vs. Batter (career)

Pitches Best Vs.	Avg	AB	H	2B	3B	HR	RBI	BB	SO	OBP	SLG	Pitches Worst Vs.	Avg	AB	H	2B	3B	HR	RBI	BB	SO	OBP	SLG
Roberto Alomar	.091	11	1	0	0	0	0	0	0	.167	.091	Edgar Martinez	.765	17	13	3	0	3	4	2	0	.789	1.471
Rich Amaral	.105	19	2	0	0	0	1	1	1	.150	.105	Mike Stanley	.500	12	6	1	0	2	3	1	1	.538	1.083
Dan Wilson	.111	9	1	1	0	0	0	2	1	.273	.222	Paul O'Neill	.474	19	9	1	0	4	9	1	4	.500	1.158
Danny Tartabull	.154	13	2	0	0	0	0	0	2	.154	.154	Tino Martinez	.385	13	5	1	0	4	8	0	3	.385	1.385
Dean Palmer	.182	11	2	0	0	0	0	0	0	.182	.182	Travis Fryman	.375	8	3	1	0	2	3	1	1	.455	1.250

Garret Anderson — Angels
Age 26 – Bats Left

	Avg	G	AB	R	H	2B	3B	HR	RBI	BB	SO	HBP	GDP	SB	CS	OBP	SLG	IBB	SH	SF	#Pit	#P/PA	GB	FB	G/F
1997 Season	.303	154	624	76	189	36	3	8	92	30	70	2	20	10	4	.334	.409	6	1	5	2275	3.44	263	156	1.69
Career (1994-1997)	.301	415	1618	205	487	88	6	36	234	76	221	3	49	23	15	.331	.430	15	8	12	5937	3.46	671	415	1.62

1997 Season

	Avg	AB	H	2B	3B	HR	RBI	BB	SO	OBP	SLG		Avg	AB	H	2B	3B	HR	RBI	BB	SO	OBP	SLG
vs. Left	.293	184	54	9	1	0	29	2	28	.296	.353	First Pitch	.300	90	27	6	0	0	10	6	0	.340	.367
vs. Right	.307	440	135	27	2	8	63	28	42	.350	.432	Ahead in Count	.348	132	46	7	0	3	24	18	0	.430	.470
Groundball	.295	105	31	6	0	3	16	6	15	.333	.438	Behind in Count	.251	303	76	13	3	1	28	0	65	.250	.323
Flyball	.309	110	34	8	0	2	27	4	11	.328	.436	Two Strikes	.247	271	67	9	3	3	30	6	70	.265	.336
Home	.327	327	107	20	1	5	45	12	34	.353	.440	Pitch #5	.266	173	46	12	2	4	25	8	19	.302	.428
Away	.276	297	82	16	2	3	47	18	36	.314	.374	Batting #6	.310	319	99	15	1	3	47	17	37	.342	.392
Day	.297	172	51	11	0	1	15	9	17	.328	.378	Other	.333	132	44	9	0	1	20	5	14	.358	.424
Night	.305	452	138	25	3	7	77	21	53	.337	.420	March/April	.337	101	34	1	0	1	12	4	8	.362	.376
Grass	.318	559	178	34	3	8	85	29	62	.352	.433	May	.352	105	37	6	0	1	19	4	11	.378	.438
Turf	.169	65	11	2	0	0	7	1	8	.176	.200	June	.262	103	27	5	2	0	15	3	8	.278	.350
Pre-All Star	.312	327	102	15	2	2	47	12	31	.335	.388	July	.308	104	32	6	1	3	19	9	16	.360	.471
Post-All Star	.293	297	87	21	1	6	45	18	39	.333	.431	August	.227	110	25	9	0	2	12	5	11	.267	.364
Scoring Posn	.303	185	56	10	3	3	80	17	23	.356	.438	Sept/Oct	.337	101	34	9	0	1	15	5	16	.364	.455
Close & Late	.333	111	37	6	0	3	23	5	14	.359	.468	vs. AL	.311	562	175	33	2	8	86	26	65	.341	.420
None on/out	.363	113	41	9	0	1	1	7	9	.400	.469	vs. NL	.226	62	14	3	1	0	6	4	5	.273	.306

1997 By Position

Position	Avg	AB	H	2B	3B	HR	RBI	BB	SO	OBP	SLG	G	GS	Innings	PO	A	E	DP	Fld Pct	Rng Fctr	In Zone Outs	Zone Rtg	MLB Zone
As lf	.316	497	157	28	0	8	78	22	56	.344	.421	130	118	1084.2	260	12	3	1	.989	2.26	310	246	734	.805
As cf	.242	99	24	4	3	0	12	6	8	.290	.343	27	27	214.1	78	2	0	1	1.000	3.36	92	76	826	.815

Career (1994-1997)

	Avg	AB	H	2B	3B	HR	RBI	BB	SO	OBP	SLG		Avg	AB	H	2B	3B	HR	RBI	BB	SO	OBP	SLG
vs. Left	.283	512	145	27	1	8	73	10	95	.293	.387	First Pitch	.313	208	65	15	0	3	26	14	0	.353	.428
vs. Right	.309	1106	342	61	5	28	161	66	126	.348	.449	Ahead in Count	.347	346	120	19	1	15	64	43	0	.419	.538

13

Career (1994-1997)

	Avg	AB	H	2B	3B	HR	RBI	BB	SO	OBP	SLG		Avg	AB	H	2B	3B	HR	RBI	BB	SO	OBP	SLG
Groundball	.296	314	93	23	0	6	50	20	44	.338	.427	Behind in Count	.262	785	206	37	5	10	92	0	201	.262	.361
Flyball	.307	289	89	14	0	9	49	11	38	.328	.448	Two Strikes	.251	705	177	23	4	9	84	19	221	.272	.333
Home	.314	822	258	46	4	19	113	40	118	.346	.449	Batting #5	.262	252	66	16	2	6	45	9	34	.290	.413
Away	.288	796	229	42	2	17	121	36	103	.316	.410	Batting #6	.313	915	286	47	4	25	140	42	128	.341	.455
Day	.287	449	129	25	0	11	54	19	65	.314	.416	Other	.299	451	135	25	0	5	49	25	59	.335	.388
Night	.306	1169	358	63	6	25	180	57	156	.338	.435	March/April	.308	195	60	4	1	3	17	9	20	.337	.385
Grass	.307	1441	443	76	6	32	214	68	199	.338	.435	May	.317	224	71	13	1	5	35	8	28	.342	.451
Turf	.249	177	44	12	0	4	20	8	22	.278	.384	June	.270	270	73	16	3	5	37	15	39	.307	.407
Pre-All Star	.296	764	226	39	5	13	98	37	98	.327	.411	July	.355	318	113	22	1	10	62	19	47	.389	.525
Post-All Star	.306	854	261	49	1	23	136	39	123	.335	.446	August	.266	342	91	22	0	8	44	10	51	.288	.401
Scoring Posn	.280	450	126	24	3	8	184	35	76	.327	.400	Sept/Oct	.294	269	79	11	0	5	39	15	36	.328	.390
Close & Late	.315	251	79	14	2	5	43	11	39	.343	.446	vs. AL	.304	1556	473	85	5	36	228	72	216	.334	.434
None on/out	.336	342	115	16	0	10	10	13	35	.361	.471	vs. NL	.226	62	14	3	1	0	6	4	5	.273	.306

Batter vs. Pitcher (career)

Hits Best Against	Avg	AB	H	2B	3B	HR	RBI	BB	SO	OBP	SLG	Hits Worst Against	Avg	AB	H	2B	3B	HR	RBI	BB	SO	OBP	SLG
Aaron Sele	.600	10	6	4	0	1	6	1	0	.636	1.300	Mike Mussina	.059	17	1	0	0	0	0	1	4	.111	.059
Jamie Moyer	.500	14	7	2	0	1	4	0	0	.500	.857	John Wasdin	.071	14	1	0	0	0	1	1	4	.133	.071
Juan Guzman	.500	12	6	1	0	2	2	0	0	.500	1.083	Rich Robertson	.118	17	2	1	0	0	1	0	2	.118	.176
Kevin Appier	.450	20	9	1	2	0	3	1	2	.476	.700	James Baldwin	.125	16	2	0	0	0	0	0	5	.125	.125
Ariel Prieto	.400	10	4	0	1	1	3	1	0	.455	.900	David Cone	.133	15	2	1	0	0	2	0	4	.133	.200

Shane Andrews — Expos   Age 26 – Bats Right

	Avg	G	AB	R	H	2B	3B	HR	RBI	BB	SO	HBP	GDP	SB	CS	OBP	SLG	IBB	SH	SF	#Pit	#P/PA	GB	FB	G/F
1997 Season	.203	18	64	10	13	3	0	4	9	3	20	0	0	0	0	.232	.438	0	0	2	289	4.19	24	11	2.18
Career (1995-1997)	.220	229	659	80	145	28	3	31	104	55	207	3	6	4	2	.281	.413	10	1	6	2845	3.93	205	166	1.23

1997 Season

	Avg	AB	H	2B	3B	HR	RBI	BB	SO	OBP	SLG		Avg	AB	H	2B	3B	HR	RBI	BB	SO	OBP	SLG
vs. Left	.300	10	3	1	0	2	4	0	1	.300	1.000	Scoring Posn	.118	17	2	1	0	0	4	1	8	.150	.176
vs. Right	.185	54	10	2	0	2	5	3	19	.220	.333	Close & Late	.125	8	1	0	0	0	0	1	3	.222	.125

Career (1995-1997)

	Avg	AB	H	2B	3B	HR	RBI	BB	SO	OBP	SLG		Avg	AB	H	2B	3B	HR	RBI	BB	SO	OBP	SLG
vs. Left	.213	164	35	10	2	5	27	17	49	.288	.390	First Pitch	.396	91	36	7	1	9	30	8	0	.455	.791
vs. Right	.222	495	110	18	1	26	77	38	158	.278	.420	Ahead in Count	.400	100	40	12	0	10	37	29	0	.523	.820
Groundball	.219	178	39	12	1	7	23	17	56	.286	.416	Behind in Count	.148	331	49	5	0	7	24	0	163	.149	.227
Flyball	.271	96	26	4	1	7	18	4	28	.297	.552	Two Strikes	.110	372	41	7	1	8	21	18	207	.152	.199
Home	.217	300	65	14	2	12	52	28	94	.284	.397	Batting #7	.229	201	46	10	2	7	37	16	60	.288	.403
Away	.223	359	80	14	1	19	52	27	113	.278	.426	Batting #8	.225	365	82	16	0	19	55	32	117	.287	.455
Day	.221	204	45	9	1	10	25	20	76	.288	.422	Other	.183	93	17	2	1	5	12	7	30	.240	.387
Night	.220	455	100	19	2	21	79	35	131	.278	.409	March/April	.236	144	34	8	0	10	28	11	49	.289	.500
Grass	.218	220	48	9	1	14	33	16	64	.272	.459	May	.208	96	20	6	1	3	12	12	25	.294	.385
Turf	.221	439	97	19	2	17	71	39	143	.285	.390	June	.278	115	32	4	1	6	20	13	40	.352	.487
Pre-All Star	.241	382	92	19	2	21	64	37	120	.307	.466	July	.185	124	23	4	0	4	13	6	34	.221	.315
Post-All Star	.191	277	53	9	1	10	40	18	87	.244	.339	August	.240	104	25	3	1	4	17	7	33	.295	.404
Scoring Posn	.236	203	48	9	3	11	81	29	69	.329	.473	Sept/Oct	.145	76	11	3	0	4	14	6	26	.214	.342
Close & Late	.173	104	18	4	0	2	11	12	34	.263	.269	vs. AL	.000	0	0	0	0	0	0	0	0	.000	.000
None on/out	.222	171	38	7	0	10	10	8	52	.257	.439	vs. NL	.220	659	145	28	3	31	104	55	207	.281	.413

Batter vs. Pitcher (career)

Hits Best Against	Avg	AB	H	2B	3B	HR	RBI	BB	SO	OBP	SLG	Hits Worst Against	Avg	AB	H	2B	3B	HR	RBI	BB	SO	OBP	SLG
Denny Neagle	.455	11	5	2	0	1	2	0	2	.455	.909	Ramon Martinez	.188	16	3	1	0	0	1	1	4	.278	.250
												Shane Reynolds	.200	10	2	0	0	0	2	1	3	.273	.200

Luis Andujar — Blue Jays   Age 25 – Pitches Right (flyball pitcher)

	ERA	W	L	Sv	G	GS	IP	BB	SO	Avg	H	2B	3B	HR	RBI	OBP	SLG	GF	IR	IRS	Hld	SvOp	SB	CS	GB	FB	G/F
1997 Season	6.48	0	6	0	17	8	50.0	21	28	.352	76	21	1	9	43	.402	.583	5	0	0	1	0	3	2	76	67	1.13
Career (1995-1997)	5.81	3	10	0	30	20	117.2	51	48	.310	148	37	3	21	80	.374	.532	5	2	0	1	0	9	6	156	173	0.90

1997 Season

	ERA	W	L	Sv	G	GS	IP	H	BB	SO		Avg	AB	H	2B	3B	HR	RBI	BB	SO	OBP	SLG
Home	6.35	0	3	0	9	4	22.2	38	5	11	13	vs. Left	.398	103	41	8	0	6	17	11	13	.452	.650
Away	6.59	0	3	0	8	4	27.1	38	4	10	15	vs. Right	.310	113	35	13	1	3	26	10	15	.357	.522

Eric Anthony — Dodgers   Age 30 – Bats Left

	Avg	G	AB	R	H	2B	3B	HR	RBI	BB	SO	HBP	GDP	SB	CS	OBP	SLG	IBB	SH	SF	#Pit	#P/PA	GB	FB	G/F
1997 Season	.243	47	74	8	18	3	2	2	5	12	18	0	0	0	2	.349	.419	1	0	0	347	4.03	22	23	0.96
Last Five Years	.247	397	1141	160	282	50	7	44	146	129	258	2	19	13	10	.323	.419	11	2	7	4924	3.84	420	290	1.45

1997 Season

	Avg	AB	H	2B	3B	HR	RBI	BB	SO	OBP	SLG		Avg	AB	H	2B	3B	HR	RBI	BB	SO	OBP	SLG
vs. Left	.500	2	1	0	0	0	1	0	0	.500	.500	Scoring Posn	.200	15	3	1	0	0	3	6	4	.429	.267
vs. Right	.236	72	17	3	2	2	4	12	18	.345	.417	Close & Late	.136	22	3	1	0	0	0	5	5	.296	.182

Last Five Years

	Avg	AB	H	2B	3B	HR	RBI	BB	SO	OBP	SLG		Avg	AB	H	2B	3B	HR	RBI	BB	SO	OBP	SLG
vs. Left	.242	248	60	10	2	6	34	24	69	.304	.371	First Pitch	.280	143	40	9	2	5	25	8	0	.316	.476
vs. Right	.249	893	222	40	5	38	112	105	189	.328	.432	Ahead in Count	.357	314	112	20	3	19	52	62	0	.460	.621
Groundball	.223	349	78	17	2	10	39	39	82	.300	.370	Behind in Count	.153	451	69	11	1	9	39	0	207	.154	.242
Flyball	.290	200	58	11	2	13	26	23	55	.362	.560	Two Strikes	.152	521	79	13	2	14	46	59	258	.238	.265
Home	.259	526	136	25	4	16	69	60	106	.334	.413	Batting #4	.258	387	100	17	4	14	54	52	76	.348	.432
Away	.237	615	146	25	3	28	77	69	152	.313	.424	Batting #5	.259	259	67	11	0	13	40	21	52	.311	.452
Day	.252	365	92	15	5	16	49	40	70	.325	.452	Other	.232	495	115	22	3	17	52	56	130	.309	.392
Night	.245	776	190	35	2	28	97	89	188	.322	.403	March/April	.273	183	50	9	1	8	30	20	43	.343	.464
Grass	.215	456	98	17	0	22	61	52	108	.294	.397	May	.264	277	73	16	3	9	25	34	60	.343	.440
Turf	.269	685	184	33	7	22	85	77	150	.342	.434	June	.237	207	49	7	1	6	26	20	51	.303	.367
Pre-All Star	.253	743	188	34	5	27	96	80	170	.324	.421	July	.221	181	40	5	0	9	25	20	39	.294	.398
Post-All Star	.236	398	94	16	2	17	50	49	88	.322	.415	August	.297	175	52	7	2	11	26	21	36	.377	.549
Scoring Posn	.229	271	62	9	1	7	94	47	62	.337	.347	Sept/Oct	.153	118	18	6	0	1	14	14	29	.242	.229
Close & Late	.215	186	40	6	0	7	27	26	46	.308	.360	vs. AL	.235	264	62	14	1	10	30	23	67	.295	.409
None on/out	.301	279	84	14	2	19	19	26	55	.363	.570	vs. NL	.251	877	220	36	6	34	116	106	191	.331	.422

Batter vs. Pitcher (career)

Hits Best Against	Avg	AB	H	2B	3B	HR	RBI	BB	SO	OBP	SLG	Hits Worst Against	Avg	AB	H	2B	3B	HR	RBI	BB	SO	OBP	SLG
Rheal Cormier	.417	12	5	1	0	1	4	2	2	.500	.750	Tom Glavine	.000	11	0	0	0	0	0	1	5	.083	.000
Mike Bielecki	.400	10	4	0	0	1	1	1	3	.455	.700	Ken Hill	.100	20	2	0	0	0	0	3	3	.217	.100
Armando Reynoso	.375	16	6	2	0	0	2	1	1	.444	.500	Mel Rojas	.100	10	1	1	0	0	0	1	1	.182	.200
Tom Candiotti	.375	16	6	0	0	1	1	0	4	.375	.563	Dwight Gooden	.120	25	3	1	0	1	6	1	10	.143	.280
John Smoltz	.357	28	10	0	0	1	3	5	7	.455	.464	Pedro Astacio	.182	11	2	0	0	0	0	1	0	.250	.182

Kevin Appier — Royals

Age 30 – Pitches Right

	ERA	W	L	Sv	G	GS	IP	BB	SO	Avg	H	2B	3B	HR	RBI	OBP	SLG	CG	ShO	Sup	QS #P/S	SB	CS	GB	FB	G/F
1997 Season	3.40	9	13	0	34	34	235.2	74	196	.243	215	46	1	24	87	.303	.378	4	1	3.97	19 110	14	9	267	262	1.02
Last Five Years	3.41	63	48	0	154	154	1042.0	373	919	.232	890	178	25	74	368	.302	.349	19	4	4.80	98 110	61	36	1233	1002	1.23

1997 Season

	ERA	W	L	Sv	G	GS	IP	H	HR	BB	SO		Avg	AB	H	2B	3B	HR	RBI	BB	SO	OBP	SLG
Home	3.50	3	7	0	16	16	121.0	106	10	33	98	vs. Left	.257	467	120	27	1	14	48	50	91	.332	.409
Away	3.30	6	6	0	18	18	114.2	109	14	41	98	vs. Right	.227	419	95	19	0	10	39	24	105	.268	.344
Day	3.18	3	3	0	13	13	82.0	77	8	28	72	Inning 1-6	.244	733	179	42	1	18	75	64	166	.307	.374
Night	3.51	6	10	0	21	21	153.2	138	16	46	124	Inning 7+	.235	153	36	4	0	6	12	10	30	.282	.379
Grass	3.32	7	12	0	30	30	214.1	197	21	64	182	None on	.243	540	131	31	1	18	18	40	117	.297	.404
Turf	4.22	2	1	0	4	4	21.1	18	3	10	14	Runners on	.243	346	84	15	0	6	69	34	79	.311	.338
March/April	2.56	3	1	0	6	6	45.2	34	5	12	39	Scoring Posn	.240	192	46	8	0	4	63	20	50	.306	.344
May	2.20	1	3	0	6	6	45.0	30	4	18	44	Close & Late	.223	-112	25	3	0	3	8	8	23	.275	.330
June	3.15	2	1	0	5	5	34.1	30	3	12	21	None on/out	.249	233	58	15	1	8		17	47	.303	.425
July	4.39	0	4	0	6	6	41.0	44	6	12	34	vs. 1st Batr (relief)	.000	0	0	0	0	0	0	0	0	.000	.000
August	3.89	1	2	0	5	5	34.2	34	2	10	26	1st Inning Pitched	.217	120	26	8	0	1	13	13	38	.304	.308
Sept/Oct	4.63	2	2	0	6	6	35.0	43	4	10	32	First 75 Pitches	.240	571	137	30	1	17	55	48	124	.302	.385
Starter	3.40	9	13	0	34	34	235.2	215	24	74	196	Pitch 76-90	.264	129	34	9	0	3	11	8	34	.304	.403
Reliever	0.00	0	0	0	0	0	0.0	0	0	0	0	Pitch 91-105	.241	108	26	6	0	2	12	9	18	.297	.352
0-3 Days Rest (Start)	0.00	0	0	0	0	0	0.0	0	0	0	0	Pitch 106+	.231	78	18	1	0	2	9	9	20	.310	.321
4 Days Rest	3.64	5	11	0	24	24	163.1	156	19	50	136	First Pitch	.259	112	29	6	0	3	10	0	0	.265	.393
5+ Days Rest	2.86	4	2	0	10	10	72.1	59	5	24	60	Ahead in Count	.208	457	95	23	0	9	29	0	169	.213	.317
vs. AL	3.40	7	12	0	31	31	219.2	198	22	71	189	Behind in Count	.260	169	44	8	1	9	24	43	0	.407	.479
vs. NL	3.38	2	1	0	3	3	16.0	17	2	3	7	Two Strikes	.202	456	92	21	0	8	32	31	196	.257	.300
Pre-All Star	2.68	6	6	0	18	18	131.0	103	13	43	109	Pre-All Star	.216	476	103	14	1	13	37	43	109	.286	.332
Post-All Star	4.30	3	7	0	16	16	104.2	112	11	31	87	Post-All Star	.273	410	112	32	0	11	50	31	87	.323	.432

Last Five Years

	ERA	W	L	Sv	G	GS	IP	H	HR	BB	SO		Avg	AB	H	2B	3B	HR	RBI	BB	SO	OBP	SLG
Home	3.50	28	25	0	73	73	520.0	420	40	170	424	vs. Left	.256	2049	525	107	16	44	208	247	435	.338	.388
Away	3.33	35	23	0	81	81	522.0	470	34	194	495	vs. Right	.204	1791	365	71	9	30	160	126	484	.259	.304
Day	2.66	22	10	0	49	49	321.2	264	16	113	300	Inning 1-6	.230	3173	731	150	21	54	306	317	763	.302	.342
Night	3.75	41	38	0	105	105	720.1	626	58	260	619	Inning 7+	.238	667	159	28	4	20	62	56	156	.298	.382
Grass	3.63	42	39	0	112	112	755.1	673	58	267	672	None on	.231	2277	526	110	13	52	52	219	549	.301	.359
Turf	2.83	21	9	0	42	42	286.2	217	16	106	247	Runners on	.233	1563	364	68	12	22	316	154	370	.303	.334
March/April	3.80	11	9	0	25	25	163.1	144	15	56	161	Scoring Posn	.234	873	204	39	9	10	278	90	205	.302	.333
May	3.00	12	11	0	30	30	210.1	185	14	82	193	Close & Late	.248	412	102	16	3	12	43	43	86	.320	.388
June	2.67	15	5	0	26	26	182.1	142	9	59	151	None on/out	.241	1000	241	47	7	23	23	94	223	.310	.371
July	4.26	5	9	0	26	26	167.0	140	16	69	152	vs. 1st Batr (relief)	.000	0	0	0	0	0	0	0	0	.000	.000
August	3.62	9	7	0	24	24	161.2	144	10	50	120	1st Inning Pitched	.230	562	129	27	4	8	65	64	144	.312	.335
Sept/Oct	3.32	11	7	0	23	23	157.1	135	10	57	142	First 75 Pitches	.230	2471	569	112	16	50	227	244	582	.301	.349
Starter	3.41	63	48	0	154	154	1042.0	890	74	373	919	Pitch 76-90	.242	499	121	26	4	7	44	42	114	.309	.353
Reliever	0.00	0	0	0	0	0	0.0	0	0	0	0	Pitch 91-105	.215	452	97	25	1	6	47	41	123	.279	.314
0-3 Days Rest (Start)	3.14	7	3	0	11	11	71.2	62	1	30	78	Pitch 106+	.246	418	103	15	4	11	50	46	100	.321	.380
4 Days Rest	3.42	32	32	0	96	96	668.1	574	49	227	565	First Pitch	.282	447	126	18	5	11	50	10	0	.302	.418
5+ Days Rest	3.46	24	13	0	47	47	302.0	254	24	116	276	Ahead in Count	.193	2019	390	78	11	24	138	0	762	.198	.278
vs. AL	3.41	61	47	0	151	151	1026.0	873	72	370	912	Behind in Count	.317	630	200	46	5	22	84	170	0	.459	.511
vs. NL	3.38	2	1	0	3	3	16.0	17	2	3	7	Two Strikes	.169	2058	348	71	11	26	142	193	919	.244	.252
Pre-All Star	3.30	39	28	0	89	89	600.2	504	41	225	548	Pre-All Star	.228	2212	504	87	18	41	203	225	548	.303	.339
Post-All Star	3.57	24	20	0	65	65	441.1	386	33	148	371	Post-All Star	.237	1628	386	91	7	33	165	148	371	.301	.362

Pitcher vs. Batter (career)

Pitches Best Vs.	Avg	AB	H	2B	3B	HR	RBI	BB	SO	OBP	SLG	Pitches Worst Vs.	Avg	AB	H	2B	3B	HR	RBI	BB	SO	OBP	SLG
Danny Tartabull	.000	18	0	0	0	0	0	1	11	.053	.000	Bob Higginson	.643	14	9	0	0	2	3	2	3	.647	1.071
Rich Becker	.000	12	0	0	0	0	0	2	6	.143	.000	Darryl Hamilton	.538	26	14	1	1	0	2	7	2	.618	.654
Jeff Reboulet	.000	10	0	0	0	0	1	1	3	.091	.000	Garret Anderson	.450	20	9	1	2	0	3	1	1	.476	.700
Gary Gaetti	.077	13	1	0	0	0	0	0	6	.077	.077	Jack Howell	.438	16	7	1	0	1	3	2	5	.500	.688
Benji Gil	.083	12	1	0	0	0	2	1	5	.154	.083	Melvin Nieves	.417	12	5	0	0	2	6	2	5	.500	.917

Alex Arias — Marlins

Age 30 – Bats Right (groundball hitter)

	Avg	G	AB	R	H	2B	3B	HR	RBI	BB	SO	HBP	GDP	SB	CS	OBP	SLG	IBB	SH	SF	#Pit	#P/PA	GB	FB	G/F
1997 Season	.247	74	93	13	23	2	0	1	11	12	12	3	6	0	1	.352	.301	0	4	0	468	4.18	45	21	2.14
Last Five Years	.265	423	895	93	237	32	5	9	98	87	97	12	26	4	3	.335	.342	2	10	8	3867	3.82	401	212	1.89

1997 Season

	Avg	AB	H	2B	3B	HR	RBI	BB	SO	OBP	SLG		Avg	AB	H	2B	3B	HR	RBI	BB	SO	OBP	SLG
vs. Left	.200	20	4	0	0	0	1	5	3	.360	.200	Scoring Posn	.259	27	7	0	0	0	10	4	3	.375	.259
vs. Right	.260	73	19	2	0	1	10	7	9	.349	.329	Close & Late	.200	30	6	0	0	1	3	3	4	.273	.300

Last Five Years

	Avg	AB	H	2B	3B	HR	RBI	BB	SO	OBP	SLG		Avg	AB	H	2B	3B	HR	RBI	BB	SO	OBP	SLG
vs. Left	.254	236	60	9	2	0	21	28	20	.335	.309	First Pitch	.271	70	19	3	0	0	6	1	0	.292	.314
vs. Right	.269	659	177	23	3	9	77	59	77	.336	.354	Ahead in Count	.333	213	71	11	1	3	28	53	0	.459	.437
Groundball	.245	220	54	8	1	2	24	25	27	.327	.318	Behind in Count	.215	405	87	11	1	2	47	0	83	.233	.262
Flyball	.212	165	35	5	1	1	17	9	21	.266	.273	Two Strikes	.208	379	79	9	1	4	38	3	97	.283	.269
Home	.303	386	117	15	1	4	51	37	50	.374	.378	Batting #2	.245	220	54	7	3	2	23	21	23	.314	.332
Away	.236	509	120	17	4	5	47	50	47	.306	.314	Batting #7	.253	292	74	9	1	4	32	30	34	.332	.332
Day	.240	325	78	8	2	5	35	29	29	.307	.323	Other	.285	383	109	16	1	3	43	36	40	.350	.355
Night	.279	570	159	24	3	4	63	58	68	.351	.353	March/April	.244	123	30	8	1	1	19	15	11	.331	.350
Grass	.273	659	180	25	3	9	87	63	71	.344	.361	May	.291	196	57	3	2	3	19	19	20	.367	.372
Turf	.242	236	57	7	2	0	11	24	26	.311	.288	June	.285	137	39	5	0	2	11	12	12	.340	.365
Pre-All Star	.274	519	142	18	4	6	58	52	52	.346	.358	July	.283	145	41	4	1	0	16	12	20	.342	.324
Post-All Star	.253	376	95	14	1	3	40	35	45	.320	.319	August	.176	131	23	5	1	1	16	12	16	.248	.252
Scoring Posn	.258	252	65	10	1	2	88	29	36	.337	.329	Sept/Oct	.288	163	47	7	0	2	17	17	18	.363	.368
Close & Late	.223	193	43	5	1	2	23	24	28	.311	.290	vs. AL	.250	8	2	1	0	0	0	1	1	.400	.375
None on/out	.269	212	57	8	1	2	2	20	25	.338	.344	vs. NL	.265	887	235	31	5	9	98	86	96	.335	.342

Batter vs. Pitcher (career)

Hits Best Against	Avg	AB	H	2B	3B	HR	RBI	BB	SO	OBP	SLG	Hits Worst Against	Avg	AB	H	2B	3B	HR	RBI	BB	SO	OBP	SLG
Kevin Ritz	.333	9	3	1	1	0	1	1	0	.455	.667	Pete Schourek	.000	11	0	0	0	0	0	1	0	.154	.000
												Donovan Osborne	.083	12	1	0	0	0	0	0	1	.083	.083
												Tom Glavine	.133	15	2	0	0	1	1	0	.188	.133
												John Smiley	.143	14	2	0	0	0	0	2	.143	.143
												John Smoltz	.188	16	3	0	0	0	0	0	1	.188	.188

George Arias — Padres

Age 26 – Bats Right

	Avg	G	AB	R	H	2B	3B	HR	RBI	BB	SO	HBP	GDP	SB	CS	OBP	SLG	IBB	SH	SF	#Pit	#P/PA	GB	FB	G/F
1997 Season	.250	9	28	3	7	1	0	0	3	0	1	0	2	0	0	.250	.286	0	0	0	76	2.71	17	7	2.43
Career (1996-1997)	.239	98	280	22	67	9	1	6	31	16	51	0	8	2	0	.280	.343	2	6	0	1100	3.64	92	88	1.05

1997 Season

	Avg	AB	H	2B	3B	HR	RBI	BB	SO	OBP	SLG		Avg	AB	H	2B	3B	HR	RBI	BB	SO	OBP	SLG
vs. Left	.143	7	1	0	0	0	0	0	0	.143	.143	Scoring Posn	.300	10	3	1	0	0	3	0	0	.300	.400
vs. Right	.286	21	6	1	0	0	3	0	1	.286	.333	Close & Late	.000	7	0	0	0	0	0	0	0	.000	.000

Rene Arocha — Giants

Age 32 – Pitches Right (groundball pitcher)

	ERA	W	L	Sv	G	GS	IP	BB	SO	Avg	H	2B	3B	HR	RBI	OBP	SLG	GF	IR	IRS	Hld	SvOp	SB	CS	GB	FB	G/F
1997 Season	11.32	0	0	0	6	0	10.1	5	7	.370	17	3	0	2	12	.434	.565	2	3	1	0	1	5	0	18	12	1.50
Career (1993-1997)	4.11	18	17	11	124	36	331.0	75	190	.282	363	72	13	37	166	.325	.445	40	40	13	20	20	26	19	527	349	1.51

1997 Season

	ERA	W	L	Sv	G	GS	IP	H	HR	BB	SO		Avg	AB	H	2B	3B	HR	RBI	BB	SO	OBP	SLG
Home	11.25	0	0	0	3	0	4.0	8	1	1	3	vs. Left	.286	14	4	2	0	0	3	4	1	.421	.429
Away	11.37	0	0	0	3	0	6.1	9	1	4	4	vs. Right	.406	32	13	1	0	2	9	1	6	.441	.625

Career (1993-1997)

	ERA	W	L	Sv	G	GS	IP	H	HR	BB	SO		Avg	AB	H	2B	3B	HR	RBI	BB	SO	OBP	SLG
Home	3.61	11	8	2	64	19	177.0	189	15	33	111	vs. Left	.297	592	176	33	5	13	76	43	69	.344	.436
Away	4.68	7	9	9	60	17	154.0	174	22	42	79	vs. Right	.269	694	187	39	8	24	90	32	121	.309	.452
Day	4.24	5	7	2	37	11	108.1	111	13	17	67	Inning 1-6	.293	819	240	52	8	22	109	39	117	.328	.457
Night	4.04	13	10	9	87	25	222.2	252	24	58	123	Inning 7+	.263	467	123	20	5	15	57	36	73	.321	.424
Grass	5.14	6	7	5	44	11	105.0	124	17	30	52	None on	.279	750	209	42	10	19	19	32	99	.312	.437
Turf	3.62	12	10	6	80	25	226.0	239	20	45	138	Runners on	.287	536	154	30	3	18	147	43	91	.343	.455
March/April	3.98	5	3	0	11	8	52.0	54	4	7	33	Scoring Posn	.289	342	99	17	3	11	128	37	60	.360	.453
May	5.14	4	3	3	38	5	70.0	85	9	19	42	Close & Late	.255	275	70	12	4	8	37	23	50	.319	.415
June	3.41	4	3	5	30	5	63.1	64	5	18	42	None on/out	.269	327	88	17	5	6	6	13	40	.299	.407
July	3.82	2	3	2	30	5	66.0	72	11	13	45	vs. 1st Batr (relief)	.293	82	24	4	2	5	11	6	16	.341	.573
August	3.86	2	2	1	8	6	44.1	49	3	6	16	1st Inning Pitched	.293	444	130	27	4	11	64	36	65	.348	.446
Sept/Oct	4.33	1	3	0	7	6	35.1	39	5	12	22	First 15 Pitches	.297	387	115	21	5	10	51	33	50	.356	.455

Career (1993-1997)

	ERA	W	L	Sv	G	GS	IP	H	HR	BB	SO
Starter	4.12	12	10	0	36	36	214.1	243	23	35	113
Reliever	4.09	6	7	11	88	0	116.2	120	14	40	77
0 Days rest (Relief)	3.21	3	2	6	26	0	28.0	26	1	13	26
1 or 2 Days rest	3.90	1	4	5	42	0	60.0	65	7	22	34
3+ Days rest	5.34	2	1	0	20	0	28.2	29	6	5	17
vs. AL	0.00	0	0	0	0	0	0.0	0	0	0	0
vs. NL	4.11	18	17	11	124	36	331.0	363	37	75	190
Pre-All Star	4.20	13	11	8	91	20	208.0	230	20	50	121
Post-All Star	3.95	5	6	3	33	16	123.0	133	17	25	69

	Avg	AB	H	2B	3B	HR	RBI	BB	SO	OBP	SLG
Pitch 16-30	.261	268	70	14	2	5	27	12	46	.302	.384
Pitch 31-45	.229	188	43	10	1	4	19	9	36	.274	.356
Pitch 46+	.305	443	135	27	5	18	69	21	58	.333	.510
First Pitch	.311	222	69	11	1	8	35	10	0	.340	.477
Ahead in Count	.219	512	112	22	5	8	42	0	159	.228	.328
Behind in Count	.336	298	100	16	4	16	48	33	0	.398	.577
Two Strikes	.213	544	116	25	6	8	54	32	190	.257	.325
Pre-All Star	.284	810	230	45	10	20	109	50	121	.330	.438
Post-All Star	.279	476	133	27	3	17	57	25	69	.317	.456

Pitcher vs. Batter (career)

Pitches Best Vs.	Avg	AB	H	2B	3B	HR	RBI	BB	SO	OBP	SLG
Jeff Bagwell	.000	13	0	0	0	0	0	1	5	.071	.000
Tony Gwynn	.091	11	1	1	0	0	0	0	0	.091	.182
Delino DeShields	.133	15	2	0	1	0	0	1	1	.188	.267
Darren Lewis	.167	12	2	1	0	0	1	0	0	.167	.250
Larry Walker	.188	16	3	0	0	0	3	0	2	.188	.188

Pitches Worst Vs.	Avg	AB	H	2B	3B	HR	RBI	BB	SO	OBP	SLG
Craig Biggio	.636	11	7	3	0	1	3	1	1	.615	1.182
Rick Wilkins	.600	10	6	0	0	1	1	2	2	.667	.900
Steve Finley	.583	12	7	0	0	1	3	0	0	.583	.833
Phil Plantier	.455	11	5	1	0	2	5	0	2	.455	1.091
Sean Berry	.400	10	4	1	1	1	2	1	2	.455	1.000

Andy Ashby — Padres
Age 30 – Pitches Right (groundball pitcher)

	ERA	W	L	Sv	G	GS	IP	BB	SO	Avg	H	2B	3B	HR	RBI	OBP	SLG	CG	ShO	Sup	QS #P/S	SB	CS	GB	FB	G/F
1997 Season	4.13	9	11	0	30	30	200.2	49	144	.266	207	33	3	17	94	.311	.382	2	0	5.20	17 97	30	10	346	147	2.35
Last Five Years	3.94	39	47	1	141	130	831.1	244	577	.266	847	143	12	86	372	.321	.400	9	2	4.60	68 94	97	33	1405	649	2.16

1997 Season

	ERA	W	L	Sv	G	GS	IP	H	HR	BB	SO
Home	3.29	5	4	0	15	15	109.1	94	12	23	80
Away	5.12	4	7	0	15	15	91.1	113	5	26	64
Day	4.70	2	3	0	10	10	61.1	77	3	14	45
Night	3.88	7	8	0	20	20	139.1	130	14	35	99
Grass	3.81	9	7	0	25	25	174.2	168	15	41	122
Turf	6.23	0	4	0	5	5	26.0	39	2	8	22
March/April	2.11	1	1	0	5	5	38.1	25	3	12	23
May	2.88	1	1	0	4	4	25.0	26	0	4	15
June	5.88	2	2	0	4	4	26.0	37	2	8	15
July	4.93	2	3	0	6	6	38.1	47	4	10	25
August	5.25	1	3	0	6	6	36.0	47	2	8	30
Sept/Oct	3.89	2	1	0	5	5	37.0	25	6	7	36
Starter	4.13	9	11	0	30	30	200.2	207	17	49	144
Reliever	0.00	0	0	0	0	0	0.0	0	0	0	0
0-3 Days Rest (Start)	7.50	0	1	0	1	1	6.0	8	1	3	3
4 Days Rest	3.79	8	6	0	19	19	133.0	136	11	32	99
5+ Days Rest	4.52	1	4	0	10	10	61.2	63	5	16	42
vs. AL	4.05	2	1	0	3	3	20.0	23	1	4	14
vs. NL	4.13	7	10	0	27	27	180.2	184	16	45	130
Pre-All Star	3.54	4	5	0	14	14	96.2	99	5	26	56
Post-All Star	4.67	5	6	0	16	16	104.0	108	12	23	88

	Avg	AB	H	2B	3B	HR	RBI	BB	SO	OBP	SLG
vs. Left	.286	409	117	18	2	14	55	28	66	.332	.443
vs. Right	.244	369	90	15	1	3	39	21	78	.289	.314
Inning 1-6	.262	660	173	26	2	15	79	40	124	.307	.376
Inning 7+	.288	118	34	7	1	2	15	9	20	.339	.415
None on	.266	455	121	19	2	8		26	93	.308	.369
Runners on	.266	323	86	14	1	9	86	23	51	.315	.399
Scoring Posn	.245	192	47	9	1	3	72	17	32	.307	.349
Close & Late	.279	68	19	5	1	1	8	7	14	.347	.426
None on/out	.277	195	54	10	1	3		18	33	.341	.385
vs. 1st Batr (relief)	.000	0	0	0	0	0	0	0	0	.000	.000
1st Inning Pitched	.200	110	22	3	1	1	11	9	21	.262	.273
First 75 Pitches	.255	564	144	21	2	11	63	34	109	.300	.358
Pitch 76-90	.308	104	32	6	0	4	18	10	16	.368	.481
Pitch 91-105	.282	85	24	6	1	1	11	4	13	.315	.412
Pitch 106+	.280	25	7	0	0	1	2	1	6	.308	.400
First Pitch	.339	121	41	6	1	1	22	2	0	.357	.430
Ahead in Count	.187	342	64	11	1	4	25	0	120	.190	.260
Behind in Count	.319	182	58	10	0	5	29	26	0	.405	.456
Two Strikes	.167	317	53	8	1	5	19	21	144	.222	.246
Pre-All Star	.267	371	99	17	2	5	42	26	56	.318	.364
Post-All Star	.265	407	108	16	1	12	52	23	88	.305	.398

Last Five Years

	ERA	W	L	Sv	G	GS	IP	H	HR	BB	SO
Home	3.36	20	17	0	65	60	404.2	378	47	110	296
Away	4.49	19	30	1	76	70	426.2	469	39	134	281
Day	4.12	12	18	0	50	46	284.0	309	25	90	197
Night	3.85	27	29	1	91	84	547.1	538	61	154	380
Grass	3.72	33	30	0	110	101	659.2	662	76	175	447
Turf	4.77	6	17	1	31	29	171.2	185	10	69	130
March/April	3.08	5	6	0	21	21	140.1	121	16	46	83
May	4.05	7	9	1	31	25	160.0	168	12	57	120
June	4.25	8	5	0	25	24	135.2	153	13	34	87
July	4.48	5	10	0	22	22	130.2	132	14	42	88
August	3.54	7	9	0	19	19	124.2	134	11	33	101
Sept/Oct	4.24	7	8	0	23	23	140.0	139	20	32	98
Starter	3.86	39	47	0	130	130	820.0	828	84	236	572
Reliever	9.53	0	0	1	11	0	11.1	19	2	8	5
0-3 Days Rest (Start)	2.37	3	2	0	5	5	30.1	32	2	11	20
4 Days Rest	3.92	24	26	0	73	73	475.1	497	47	130	341
5+ Days Rest	3.92	12	19	0	52	52	314.1	299	35	95	211
vs. AL	4.05	2	1	0	3	3	20.0	23	1	4	14
vs. NL	3.94	37	46	1	138	127	811.1	824	85	240	563
Pre-All Star	3.83	22	23	1	82	71	470.0	474	44	142	314
Post-All Star	4.08	17	24	0	59	59	361.1	373	42	102	263

	Avg	AB	H	2B	3B	HR	RBI	BB	SO	OBP	SLG
vs. Left	.278	1578	439	73	7	40	179	134	242	.336	.409
vs. Right	.254	1605	408	70	5	46	193	110	335	.307	.390
Inning 1-6	.268	2754	739	126	10	75	332	219	505	.325	.403
Inning 7+	.252	429	108	17	2	11	40	25	72	.295	.378
None on	.261	1890	494	83	7	49	49	119	310	.310	.390
Runners on	.273	1293	353	60	5	37	323	125	240	.338	.413
Scoring Posn	.269	767	206	45	5	15	276	97	145	.349	.399
Close & Late	.232	241	56	8	2	4	20	13	48	.275	.332
None on/out	.290	817	237	43	5	21	21	59	116	.342	.432
vs. 1st Batr (relief)	.455	11	5	3	0	1	4	0	1	.455	1.000
1st Inning Pitched	.263	532	140	23	3	12	79	58	92	.339	.385
First 75 Pitches	.265	2408	638	105	10	63	270	184	433	.321	.395
Pitch 76-90	.298	416	124	27	1	14	67	35	66	.353	.469
Pitch 91-105	.257	249	64	11	1	4	27	18	50	.310	.357
Pitch 106+	.191	110	21	0	0	5	8	7	28	.237	.327
First Pitch	.300	490	147	24	1	10	71	19	0	.329	.414
Ahead in Count	.204	1411	288	49	4	24	123	0	487	.212	.296
Behind in Count	.346	706	244	42	4	30	103	120	0	.440	.544
Two Strikes	.184	1366	252	44	4	26	108	105	577	.249	.280
Pre-All Star	.265	1791	474	84	9	44	211	142	314	.322	.395
Post-All Star	.268	1392	373	59	3	42	161	102	263	.321	.405

Pitcher vs. Batter (career)

Pitches Best Vs.	Avg	AB	H	2B	3B	HR	RBI	BB	SO	OBP	SLG
Chipper Jones	.059	17	1	0	0	0	0	0	2	.059	.059
Jay Bell	.077	26	2	0	0	0	0	4	7	.250	.077
Darren Lewis	.083	12	1	0	0	0	0	2	1	.267	.083
Derek Bell	.143	14	2	0	0	0	1	0	4	.133	.143
Royce Clayton	.179	28	5	0	0	0	5	0	3	.172	.179

Pitches Worst Vs.	Avg	AB	H	2B	3B	HR	RBI	BB	SO	OBP	SLG
Jim Eisenreich	.571	14	8	3	0	0	6	1	0	.600	.786
Darrin Fletcher	.471	17	8	2	0	2	5	1	0	.591	.941
Glenallen Hill	.471	17	8	4	0	2	4	1	4	.500	1.059
Andres Galarraga	.467	30	14	4	0	3	10	1	6	.515	.900
Barry Bonds	.441	34	15	3	0	7	10	7	3	.524	1.147

Billy Ashley — Dodgers
Age 27 – Bats Right

	Avg	G	AB	R	H	2B	3B	HR	RBI	BB	SO	HBP	GDP	SB	CS	OBP	SLG	IBB	SH	SF	#Pit	#P/PA	GB	FB	G/F
1997 Season	.244	71	131	12	32	7	0	6	19	8	46	1	2	0	0	.293	.435	0	0	0	554	3.96	38	30	1.27
Last Five Years	.232	239	499	47	116	15	1	23	71	56	191	4	13	0	0	.313	.405	5	0	3	2230	3.97	132	112	1.18

1997 Season

	Avg	AB	H	2B	3B	HR	RBI	BB	SO	OBP	SLG		Avg	AB	H	2B	3B	HR	RBI	BB	SO	OBP	SLG
vs. Left	.289	90	26	7	0	5	17	3	26	.312	.533	Scoring Posn	.211	38	8	2	0	1	12	4	13	.286	.342
vs. Right	.146	41	6	0	0	1	2	5	20	.255	.220	Close & Late	.185	27	5	1	0	1	4	3	12	.267	.333
Home	.224	67	15	3	0	4	16	6	23	.288	.448	None on/out	.217	23	5	1	0	0	0	2	9	.280	.261
Away	.266	64	17	4	0	2	3	2	23	.299	.422	Batting #6	.194	36	7	2	0	1	2	2	14	.237	.333
First Pitch	.462	13	6	1	0	1	2	0	0	.462	.769	Batting #7	.304	56	17	4	0	3	12	3	12	.339	.536
Ahead in Count	.375	32	12	2	0	2	9	4	0	.444	.625	Other	.205	39	8	1	0	2	5	3	20	.279	.385
Behind in Count	.136	59	8	3	0	1	3	0	37	.150	.237	Pre-All Star	.229	96	22	4	0	5	16	7	31	.282	.427
Two Strikes	.141	71	10	3	0	3	5	4	46	.187	.310	Post-All Star	.286	35	10	3	0	1	3	1	15	.324	.457

Last Five Years

	Avg	AB	H	2B	3B	HR	RBI	BB	SO	OBP	SLG		Avg	AB	H	2B	3B	HR	RBI	BB	SO	OBP	SLG
vs. Left	.269	253	68	11	1	15	45	25	90	.336	.498	First Pitch	.369	65	24	2	1	2	11	4	0	.406	.523
vs. Right	.195	246	48	4	0	8	26	31	101	.291	.309	Ahead in Count	.437	87	38	3	0	11	24	22	0	.550	.851
Groundball	.248	113	28	4	0	5	20	21	36	.365	.416	Behind in Count	.136	242	33	6	0	5	20	0	153	.142	.223
Flyball	.235	68	16	1	0	2	9	7	26	.316	.338	Two Strikes	.130	284	37	7	0	7	24	30	191	.215	.229
Home	.264	276	73	9	0	15	50	34	97	.345	.460	Batting #6	.179	95	17	2	1	1	5	9	39	.250	.253
Away	.193	223	43	6	1	8	21	22	94	.273	.336	Batting #7	.191	194	37	6	0	7	22	17	68	.255	.330
Day	.214	112	24	4	0	4	12	19	48	.336	.357	Other	.295	210	62	7	0	15	44	30	84	.390	.543
Night	.238	387	92	11	1	19	59	37	143	.306	.419	March/April	.204	54	11	4	0	4	12	7	18	.290	.500
Grass	.239	414	99	14	0	20	57	48	155	.321	.418	May	.265	147	39	3	1	6	21	10	50	.312	.422
Turf	.200	85	17	1	1	3	14	8	36	.274	.341	June	.192	130	25	2	0	7	18	18	59	.300	.369
Pre-All Star	.228	356	81	11	1	17	53	41	137	.309	.407	July	.224	67	15	5	0	2	8	10	26	.321	.388
Post-All Star	.245	143	35	4	0	6	18	15	54	.323	.399	August	.227	44	10	0	0	2	7	7	18	.340	.364
Scoring Posn	.207	135	28	5	1	7	52	25	53	.329	.415	Sept/Oct	.281	57	16	1	0	2	5	4	20	.339	.404
Close & Late	.197	76	15	2	0	5	13	13	37	.322	.421	vs. AL	.200	10	2	1	0	1	2	3	7	.385	.600
None on/out	.184	114	21	3	0	3	3	7	49	.231	.289	vs. NL	.233	489	114	14	1	22	69	53	184	.311	.401

Batter vs. Pitcher (career)

Hits Best Against	Avg	AB	H	2B	3B	HR	RBI	BB	SO	OBP	SLG	Hits Worst Against	Avg	AB	H	2B	3B	HR	RBI	BB	SO	OBP	SLG
Steve Avery	.400	10	4	2	0	1	4	1	2	.455	.900	Kent Mercker	.000	11	0	0	0	0	0	1	6	.083	.000
Danny Jackson	.385	13	5	1	0	0	2	1	1	.467	.462	Jeff Fassero	.111	9	1	0	0	0	1	3	6	.308	.111
Carlos Perez	.385	13	5	0	0	0	1	0	3	.385	.385	John Smiley	.231	13	3	0	0	1	0	0	6	.231	.231
John Smoltz	.375	8	3	1	0	1	1	3	3	.545	.875												

Paul Assenmacher — Indians
Age 37 – Pitches Left

	ERA	W	L	Sv	G	GS	IP	BB	SO	Avg	H	2B	3B	HR	RBI	OBP	SLG	GF	IR	IRS	Hld	SvOp	SB	CS	GB	FB	G/F
1997 Season	2.94	5	0	4	75	0	49.0	15	53	.231	43	6	0	5	22	.289	.344	20	74	17	20	5	2	2	55	46	1.20
Last Five Years	3.15	20	9	6	301	0	223.0	76	211	.242	201	37	0	16	86	.310	.344	89	244	53	73	17	17	5	271	204	1.33

1997 Season

	ERA	W	L	Sv	G	GS	IP	H	HR	BB	SO		Avg	AB	H	2B	3B	HR	RBI	BB	SO	OBP	SLG
Home	4.15	4	0	2	38	0	26.0	23	3	6	33	vs. Left	.225	89	20	2	0	3	13	6	26	.278	.348
Away	1.57	1	0	2	37	0	23.0	20	2	9	20	vs. Right	.237	97	23	4	0	2	9	9	27	.299	.340
Day	4.50	0	0	2	25	0	16.0	18	2	7	15	Inning 1-6	.429	7	3	1	0	0	1	2	1	.556	.571
Night	2.18	5	0	2	50	0	33.0	25	3	8	38	Inning 7+	.223	179	40	5	0	5	21	13	52	.277	.335
Grass	3.19	5	0	4	66	0	42.1	37	4	13	49	None on	.258	93	24	3	0	3	3	4	24	.296	.387
Turf	1.35	0	0	0	9	0	6.2	6	1	2	4	Runners on	.204	93	19	3	0	2	19	11	29	.283	.301
March/April	9.82	0	0	0	13	0	7.1	11	5	4	6	Scoring Posn	.169	59	10	3	0	0	15	9	17	.271	.220
May	4.91	1	0	0	9	0	3.2	5	0	1	1	Close & Late	.171	82	14	1	0	0	7	7	31	.233	.183
June	3.68	1	0	0	13	0	7.1	9	0	2	9	None on/out	.225	40	9	1	0	1	1	2	12	.262	.325
July	0.00	0	0	1	13	0	9.2	3	0	4	11	vs. 1st Batr (relief)	.258	66	17	2	0	1	11	6	18	.311	.333
August	0.73	2	0	2	15	0	12.1	7	0	1	13	1st Inning Pitched	.234	175	41	6	0	5	22	15	51	.295	.354
Sept/Oct	2.08	1	0	1	12	0	8.2	8	0	3	13	First 15 Pitches	.231	160	37	5	0	4	19	12	48	.286	.338
Starter	0.00	0	0	0	0	0	0.0	0	0	0	0	Pitch 16-30	.231	26	6	1	0	1	3	3	5	.310	.385
Reliever	2.94	5	0	4	75	0	49.0	43	5	15	53	Pitch 31-45	.000	0	0	0	0	0	0	0	0	.000	.000
0 Days rest (Relief)	3.31	3	0	0	24	0	16.1	13	2	5	20	Pitch 46+	.000	0	0	0	0	0	0	0	0	.000	.000
1 or 2 Days rest	2.82	1	0	4	33	0	22.1	22	1	8	24	First Pitch	.208	24	5	1	0	0	4	4	0	.310	.333
3+ Days rest	2.61	1	0	0	18	0	10.1	8	2	2	9	Ahead in Count	.129	93	12	2	0	2	5	0	45	.137	.215
vs. AL	2.95	5	0	3	67	0	42.2	36	5	13	47	Behind in Count	.593	27	16	1	0	3	9	5	0	.656	.963
vs. NL	2.84	0	0	1	8	0	6.1	7	0	2	6	Two Strikes	.115	96	11	3	0	1	4	6	53	.175	.177
Pre-All Star	5.66	2	0	0	38	0	20.2	26	5	8	19	Pre-All Star	.299	87	26	3	0	5	12	8	19	.365	.506
Post-All Star	0.95	3	0	4	37	0	28.1	17	0	7	34	Post-All Star	.172	99	17	3	0	0	10	7	34	.222	.202

Last Five Years

	ERA	W	L	Sv	G	GS	IP	H	HR	BB	SO		Avg	AB	H	2B	3B	HR	RBI	BB	SO	OBP	SLG
Home	3.42	13	5	3	163	0	121.0	114	7	33	123	vs. Left	.224	379	85	9	0	9	45	26	107	.278	.319
Away	2.82	7	4	3	138	0	102.0	87	9	43	88	vs. Right	.257	452	116	28	0	7	41	50	104	.336	.365
Day	3.48	3	3	3	113	0	85.1	80	5	28	70	Inning 1-6	.286	21	6	2	0	0	3	2	2	.348	.381
Night	2.94	17	6	3	188	0	137.2	121	11	48	141	Inning 7+	.241	810	195	35	0	16	83	74	209	.309	.343
Grass	3.26	20	9	6	266	0	199.0	178	12	68	195	None on	.255	416	106	21	0	11	11	30	109	.316	.385
Turf	2.25	0	0	0	35	0	24.0	23	4	8	16	Runners on	.229	415	95	16	0	5	75	46	102	.304	.304
March/April	4.88	1	1	1	44	0	31.1	33	7	14	19	Scoring Posn	.222	261	58	13	0	1	67	40	69	.321	.287
May	4.94	3	3	0	49	0	31.0	32	2	16	27	Close & Late	.230	348	80	11	0	3	39	39	102	.307	.287

Last Five Years

	ERA	W	L	Sv	G	GS	IP	H	HR	BB	SO		Avg	AB	H	2B	3B	HR	RBI	BB	SO	OBP	SLG
June	2.41	3	1	0	58	0	41.0	42	1	14	39	None on/out	.281	196	55	11	0	6	6	10	48	.322	.429
July	0.98	4	1	2	55	0	46.0	33	4	9	54	vs. 1st Batr (relief)	.250	272	68	11	0	6	36	17	71	.296	.357
August	2.23	7	1	2	53	0	40.1	29	1	6	40	1st Inning Pitched	.246	735	181	33	0	15	82	68	187	.314	.352
Sept/Oct	4.86	2	2	1	42	0	33.1	32	1	17	32	First 15 Pitches	.251	689	173	32	0	14	74	60	171	.316	.358
Starter	0.00	0	0	0	0	0	0.0	0	0	0	0	Pitch 16-30	.204	137	28	5	0	2	12	16	38	.290	.285
Reliever	3.15	20	9	6	301	0	223.0	201	16	76	211	Pitch 31-45	.000	5	0	0	0	0	0	0	2	.000	.000
0 Days rest (Relief)	2.62	8	3	1	85	0	65.1	61	5	22	65	Pitch 46+	.000	0	0	0	0	0	0	0	0	.000	.000
1 or 2 Days rest	3.60	9	4	5	124	0	90.0	82	7	32	88	First Pitch	.269	119	32	6	0	2	16	16	0	.353	.370
3+ Days rest	3.06	3	2	0	92	0	67.2	58	4	22	58	Ahead in Count	.181	436	79	12	0	4	27	0	184	.191	.236
vs. AL	3.08	18	8	5	247	0	178.0	150	11	61	171	Behind in Count	.411	146	60	11	0	9	34	31	0	.506	.671
vs. NL	3.40	2	1	1	54	0	45.0	51	5	15	40	Two Strikes	.154	408	63	15	0	2	17	28	211	.217	.206
Pre-All Star	3.60	7	6	2	168	0	120.0	121	12	48	104	Pre-All Star	.264	458	121	22	0	12	52	48	104	.335	.391
Post-All Star	2.62	13	3	4	133	0	103.0	80	4	28	107	Post-All Star	.214	373	80	15	0	4	34	28	107	.278	.287

Pitcher vs. Batter (career)

Pitches Best Vs.	Avg	AB	H	2B	3B	HR	RBI	BB	SO	OBP	SLG	Pitches Worst Vs.	Avg	AB	H	2B	3B	HR	RBI	BB	SO	OBP	SLG
Dave Martinez	.091	22	2	0	0	0	1	1	11	.167	.091	Brett Butler	.692	13	9	1	0	0	4	1	2	.714	.769
Jeff King	.091	11	1	0	0	0	1	0	2	.091	.091	Eric Davis	.625	8	5	0	0	2	4	2	2	.727	1.375
Darryl Strawberry	.107	28	3	1	0	0	4	9	.219	.143	Mo Vaughn	.462	13	6	0	0	1	4	3	3	.588	.692
Larry Walker	.111	18	2	0	0	0	2	2	5	.200	.111	Jay Bell	.455	11	5	1	1	1	2	1	2	.500	1.000
Paul O'Neill	.136	22	3	0	0	2	1	9	.174	.136	Barry Larkin	.400	10	4	1	0	1	2	3	2	.538	.800

Pedro Astacio — Rockies

Age 28 – Pitches Right (groundball pitcher)

	ERA	W	L	Sv	G	GS	IP	BB	SO	Avg	H	2B	3B	HR	RBI	OBP	SLG	CG	ShO	Sup	QS	#P/S	SB	CS	GB	FB	G/F
1997 Season	4.14	12	10	0	33	31	202.1	61	166	.258	200	37	7	24	91	.317	.416	2	1	4.40	19	98	14	6	338	152	2.22
Last Five Years	3.88	48	43	0	170	128	853.1	272	606	.254	817	152	20	86	341	.316	.394	9	5	4.24	77	94	62	35	1317	804	1.64

1997 Season

	ERA	W	L	Sv	G	GS	IP	H	HR	BB	SO		Avg	AB	H	2B	3B	HR	RBI	BB	SO	OBP	SLG
Home	4.63	5	5	0	14	13	83.2	83	13	25	59	vs. Left	.270	337	91	18	4	11	44	35	66	.339	.445
Away	3.79	7	5	0	19	18	118.2	117	11	36	107	vs. Right	.248	439	109	19	3	13	47	26	100	.299	.394
Day	3.46	7	3	0	12	12	80.2	72	8	23	61	Inning 1-6	.255	655	167	28	4	20	81	54	144	.317	.402
Night	4.59	5	7	0	21	19	121.2	128	16	38	105	Inning 7+	.273	121	33	9	3	4	10	7	22	.315	.496
Grass	4.01	11	8	0	26	25	163.2	149	21	51	134	None on	.258	462	119	20	4	15	15	33	106	.314	.416
Turf	4.66	1	2	0	7	6	38.2	51	3	10	32	Runners on	.258	314	81	17	3	9	76	28	60	.320	.417
March/April	2.79	2	0	0	6	4	29.0	22	0	9	17	Scoring Posn	.222	180	40	10	1	3	59	21	39	.303	.339
May	3.14	1	4	0	6	6	43.0	41	6	11	31	Close & Late	.169	59	10	1	1	4	5	12	.246	.271
June	6.55	1	3	0	6	6	34.1	37	4	16	25	None on/out	.257	202	52	10	2	6	6	13	39	.309	.416
July	2.48	3	0	0	5	5	32.2	30	4	8	29	vs. 1st Batr (relief)	.500	2	1	0	0	0	0	0	0	.500	.500
August	6.21	1	2	0	5	5	29.0	38	3	7	30	1st Inning Pitched	.333	141	47	10	1	3	26	13	31	.388	.482
Sept/Oct	3.93	4	1	0	5	5	34.1	32	7	10	34	First 75 Pitches	.251	582	146	28	3	15	66	46	126	.307	.387
Starter	4.22	11	10	0	31	31	198.1	197	24	61	163	Pitch 76-90	.296	98	29	5	2	3	12	7	26	.355	.480
Reliever	0.00	1	0	0	2	0	4.0	3	0	0	3	Pitch 91-105	.222	72	16	3	1	3	8	7	13	.317	.417
0-3 Days Rest (Start)	0.00	1	0	0	1	1	9.0	9	0	3	4	Pitch 106+	.375	24	9	1	1	3	5	1	1	.385	.875
4 Days Rest	4.38	9	6	0	20	20	127.1	122	15	36	105	First Pitch	.288	118	34	7	1	3	13	0	0	.306	.441
5+ Days Rest	4.50	1	4	0	10	10	62.0	66	9	22	54	Ahead in Count	.119	318	38	11	2	3	17	0	142	.124	.195
vs. AL	4.37	2	0	0	3	3	22.2	22	3	5	22	Behind in Count	.407	214	87	13	3	12	38	28	0	.476	.664
vs. NL	4.11	10	10	0	30	28	179.2	178	21	56	144	Two Strikes	.129	326	42	9	3	6	22	33	166	.212	.230
Pre-All Star	4.07	5	7	0	19	17	112.2	107	11	39	80	Pre-All Star	.254	422	107	25	2	11	49	39	80	.319	.400
Post-All Star	4.22	7	3	0	14	14	89.2	93	13	22	86	Post-All Star	.263	354	93	12	5	13	42	22	86	.313	.435

Last Five Years

	ERA	W	L	Sv	G	GS	IP	H	HR	BB	SO		Avg	AB	H	2B	3B	HR	RBI	BB	SO	OBP	SLG
Home	3.42	24	18	0	80	61	421.2	375	39	131	295	vs. Left	.261	1527	399	82	12	46	179	142	253	.324	.421
Away	4.34	24	25	0	90	67	431.2	442	47	141	311	vs. Right	.247	1689	418	70	8	40	162	130	353	.309	.369
Day	3.77	16	11	0	45	38	246.0	222	25	89	163	Inning 1-6	.248	2642	655	113	12	70	285	232	514	.313	.379
Night	3.93	32	32	0	125	90	607.1	595	61	183	443	Inning 7+	.282	574	162	39	8	16	56	40	92	.329	.462
Grass	3.69	37	33	0	131	98	665.2	616	71	209	482	None on	.267	1914	511	93	12	48	48	144	362	.325	.403
Turf	4.56	11	10	0	39	30	187.2	201	15	63	124	Runners on	.235	1302	306	59	8	38	293	128	244	.303	.380
March/April	3.53	6	8	0	21	18	112.1	97	8	47	75	Scoring Posn	.232	691	160	36	4	18	243	89	139	.314	.373
May	3.71	7	10	0	29	29	179.2	181	16	56	123	Close & Late	.233	309	72	12	1	6	28	26	58	.291	.337
June	5.07	7	12	0	30	27	168.2	174	20	54	99	None on/out	.277	851	236	47	8	22	22	61	136	.332	.429
July	4.09	8	8	0	31	20	132.0	125	16	40	92	vs. 1st Batr (relief)	.316	38	12	3	0	1	6	2	4	.341	.474
August	3.91	9	3	0	31	18	129.0	140	13	33	104	1st Inning Pitched	.276	619	171	36	3	17	91	57	102	.338	.426
Sept/Oct	2.67	11	4	0	28	16	131.2	100	13	42	113	First 75 Pitches	.249	2477	617	111	10	62	256	201	470	.309	.377
Starter	3.96	41	41	0	128	128	799.2	773	81	259	562	Pitch 76-90	.284	366	104	18	5	9	39	31	75	.347	.434
Reliever	4.25	7	2	0	42	0	53.2	44	5	13	44	Pitch 91-105	.220	246	54	12	3	7	26	27	44	.299	.378
0-3 Days Rest (Start)	4.50	1	2	0	5	5	30.0	36	5	10	18	Pitch 106+	.331	127	42	11	2	8	20	13	17	.390	.488
4 Days Rest	3.75	23	20	0	64	64	410.2	387	36	121	285	First Pitch	.301	544	164	27	3	18	71	14	0	.323	.461
5+ Days Rest	4.16	17	19	0	59	59	359.0	350	40	128	259	Ahead in Count	.166	1286	214	46	7	20	89	0	508	.172	.260
vs. AL	4.37	2	0	0	3	3	22.2	22	3	5	22	Behind in Count	.338	778	263	43	6	35	115	126	0	.432	.544
vs. NL	3.87	46	43	0	167	125	830.2	795	83	267	584	Two Strikes	.164	1344	221	41	8	19	87	132	606	.242	.249
Pre-All Star	4.12	23	32	0	91	81	509.0	488	50	175	339	Pre-All Star	.255	1912	488	91	10	40	208	175	339	.321	.392
Post-All Star	3.53	25	11	0	79	47	344.1	307	31	92	267	Post-All Star	.252	1304	329	61	10	36	133	97	267	.308	.397

Pitcher vs. Batter (career)

Pitches Best Vs.	Avg	AB	H	2B	3B	HR	RBI	BB	SO	OBP	SLG	Pitches Worst Vs.	Avg	AB	H	2B	3B	HR	RBI	BB	SO	OBP	SLG
Orlando Merced	.000	10	0	0	0	0	0	1	3	.091	.000	Mike Lieberthal	.636	11	7	0	0	1	1	0	1	.636	.909

Pitcher vs. Batter (career)

Pitches Best Vs.	Avg	AB	H	2B	3B	HR	RBI	BB	SO	OBP	SLG	Pitches Worst Vs.	Avg	AB	H	2B	3B	HR	RBI	BB	SO	OBP	SLG
Charles Johnson	.000	9	0	0	0	0	0	1	1	.182	.000	Barry Bonds	.545	11	6	1	1	1	3	3	0	.600	1.091
Henry Rodriguez	.083	12	1	1	0	0	1	0	3	.083	.167	Larry Walker	.500	26	13	3	0	2	7	2	3	.533	.846
Bret Boone	.100	20	2	0	0	0	0	2	2	.182	.100	Nelson Liriano	.500	22	11	5	0	1	4	0	2	.500	.864
Eddie Taubensee	.103	29	3	0	0	0	1	0	8	.100	.103	Ryan Klesko	.368	19	7	1	0	4	7	3	4	.455	1.053

Rich Aurilia — Giants
Age 26 – Bats Right

	Avg	G	AB	R	H	2B	3B	HR	RBI	BB	SO	HBP	GDP	SB	CS	OBP	SLG	IBB	SH	SF	#Pit	#P/PA	GB	FB	G/F
1997 Season	.275	46	102	16	28	8	0	5	19	8	15	0	3	1	1	.321	.500	0	1	2	415	3.67	31	43	0.72
Career (1995-1997)	.257	160	439	47	113	18	1	10	49	34	69	1	5	6	2	.309	.371	2	8	5	1747	3.59	138	168	0.82

1997 Season

	Avg	AB	H	2B	3B	HR	RBI	BB	SO	OBP	SLG		Avg	AB	H	2B	3B	HR	RBI	BB	SO	OBP	SLG
vs. Left	.280	50	14	6	0	3	9	5	6	.345	.580	Scoring Posn	.250	20	5	0	0	2	15	1	5	.261	.550
vs. Right	.269	52	14	2	0	2	10	3	9	.298	.423	Close & Late	.286	14	4	0	0	2	2	0	2	.286	.714

Career (1995-1997)

	Avg	AB	H	2B	3B	HR	RBI	BB	SO	OBP	SLG		Avg	AB	H	2B	3B	HR	RBI	BB	SO	OBP	SLG
vs. Left	.252	119	30	9	0	5	15	11	15	.315	.454	First Pitch	.239	67	16	1	0	1	5	2	0	.268	.299
vs. Right	.259	320	83	9	1	5	34	23	54	.307	.341	Ahead in Count	.340	100	34	6	0	4	13	20	0	.446	.520
Groundball	.256	90	23	0	0	2	8	4	7	.284	.322	Behind in Count	.207	184	38	8	1	4	22	0	59	.203	.326
Flyball	.169	65	11	3	0	0	2	10	14	.280	.215	Two Strikes	.207	188	39	7	1	5	20	12	69	.252	.335
Home	.248	230	57	8	0	2	18	15	39	.296	.309	Batting #7	.308	91	28	3	0	3	9	6	15	.350	.440
Away	.268	209	56	10	1	8	31	19	30	.323	.440	Batting #8	.244	180	44	5	1	4	18	15	24	.303	.357
Day	.272	213	58	9	1	4	30	14	42	.315	.380	Other	.244	168	41	10	0	3	22	13	30	.293	.357
Night	.243	226	55	9	0	6	19	20	27	.304	.363	March/April	.213	47	10	1	1	0	3	3	10	.260	.277
Grass	.269	349	94	14	1	9	40	23	54	.313	.393	May	.230	61	14	2	0	3	7	8	9	.314	.410
Turf	.211	90	19	4	0	1	9	11	15	.294	.289	June	.286	35	10	1	0	3	8	5	7	.390	.571
Pre-All Star	.236	148	35	4	1	7	19	17	27	.317	.419	July	.274	62	17	5	0	2	9	4	10	.318	.452
Post-All Star	.268	291	78	14	0	3	30	17	42	.304	.347	August	.250	120	30	4	0	0	12	8	17	.290	.283
Scoring Posn	.233	103	24	3	0	2	37	13	18	.311	.320	Sept/Oct	.281	114	32	5	0	2	10	6	16	.314	.377
Close & Late	.225	71	16	2	0	2	5	2	11	.247	.338	vs. AL	.222	9	2	0	0	2	5	2	3	.364	.889
None on/out	.306	98	30	5	0	4	4	4	11	.333	.480	vs. NL	.258	430	111	18	1	8	44	32	66	.308	.360

Brad Ausmus — Astros
Age 29 – Bats Right (groundball hitter)

	Avg	G	AB	R	H	2B	3B	HR	RBI	BB	SO	HBP	GDP	SB	CS	OBP	SLG	IBB	SH	SF	#Pit	#P/PA	GB	FB	G/F
1997 Season	.266	130	425	45	113	25	1	4	44	38	78	3	8	14	6	.326	.358	4	6	6	1704	3.56	154	116	1.33
Career (1993-1997)	.257	508	1615	198	415	77	7	26	149	144	297	11	32	41	20	.320	.362	20	22	14	6472	3.58	624	386	1.62

1997 Season

	Avg	AB	H	2B	3B	HR	RBI	BB	SO	OBP	SLG		Avg	AB	H	2B	3B	HR	RBI	BB	SO	OBP	SLG
vs. Left	.240	96	23	6	0	1	11	7	15	.295	.333	First Pitch	.281	89	25	5	0	2	14	4	0	.313	.404
vs. Right	.274	329	90	19	1	3	33	31	63	.335	.365	Ahead in Count	.337	86	29	9	0	0	6	15	0	.431	.442
Groundball	.186	59	11	2	0	0	5	7	12	.269	.220	Behind in Count	.231	182	42	5	1	0	9	0	66	.235	.269
Flyball	.295	61	18	5	0	1	10	6	8	.343	.426	Two Strikes	.206	199	41	9	1	0	10	19	78	.276	.261
Home	.276	196	54	13	0	1	15	21	37	.344	.357	Batting #7	.229	179	41	7	1	1	12	16	39	.291	.296
Away	.258	229	59	12	1	3	29	17	41	.314	.358	Batting #8	.275	160	44	10	0	2	18	19	29	.352	.375
Day	.222	117	26	3	0	0	9	12	23	.298	.248	Other	.326	86	28	8	0	1	14	3	10	.352	.453
Night	.282	308	87	22	1	4	35	26	55	.337	.399	March/April	.344	64	22	6	0	0	6	5	5	.391	.438
Grass	.265	166	44	9	1	2	22	9	26	.308	.367	May	.275	80	22	5	1	1	5	4	12	.310	.400
Turf	.266	259	69	16	0	2	22	29	52	.338	.351	June	.224	67	15	2	0	1	8	6	13	.289	.299
Pre-All Star	.284	229	65	14	1	2	19	16	33	.331	.380	July	.237	76	18	5	0	1	13	5	20	.286	.342
Post-All Star	.245	196	48	11	0	2	25	22	45	.321	.332	August	.280	82	23	4	0	0	4	7	15	.333	.329
Scoring Posn	.259	108	28	5	0	3	41	12	20	.328	.389	Sept/Oct	.232	56	13	3	0	1	8	11	13	.362	.339
Close & Late	.217	83	18	1	1	2	13	9	17	.287	.325	vs. AL	.216	37	8	2	0	1	3	8	.268	.270
None on/out	.272	92	25	5	1	0	0	6	18	.316	.348	vs. NL	.271	388	105	23	1	4	43	35	70	.332	.366

1997 By Position

Position	Avg	AB	H	2B	3B	HR	RBI	BB	SO	OBP	SLG	G	GS	Innings	PO	A	E	DP	Fld Pct	Rng Fctr	In Zone	Zone Outs	Zone Rtg	MLB Zone
As c	.268	421	113	25	1	4	44	38	78	.329	.361	129	113	1032.2	807	74	7	16	.992	---	---	---	---	---

Career (1993-1997)

	Avg	AB	H	2B	3B	HR	RBI	BB	SO	OBP	SLG		Avg	AB	H	2B	3B	HR	RBI	BB	SO	OBP	SLG
vs. Left	.238	386	92	18	2	8	41	36	65	.304	.358	First Pitch	.345	304	105	18	1	9	39	17	0	.380	.500
vs. Right	.263	1229	323	59	5	18	108	108	232	.324	.363	Ahead in Count	.300	323	97	25	1	7	30	66	0	.417	.449
Groundball	.231	433	100	18	4	8	41	35	76	.346	.348	Behind in Count	.203	711	144	20	4	6	41	0	252	.209	.267
Flyball	.223	220	49	11	0	2	19	26	40	.300	.300	Two Strikes	.174	737	128	21	4	5	44	61	297	.239	.233
Home	.265	801	212	38	4	15	75	78	154	.331	.378	Batting #7	.239	456	109	22	1	6	38	40	104	.302	.331
Away	.249	814	203	39	3	11	74	66	143	.308	.345	Batting #8	.267	818	218	38	6	15	72	80	143	.333	.383
Day	.239	427	102	18	0	5	30	39	81	.305	.316	Other	.258	341	88	17	0	5	39	24	50	.311	.352
Night	.263	1188	313	59	7	21	119	105	216	.325	.378	March/April	.262	229	60	14	1	3	23	22	33	.328	.371
Grass	.258	1134	293	51	6	22	110	93	207	.316	.372	May	.258	275	71	17	3	2	18	16	48	.306	.364
Turf	.254	481	122	26	1	4	39	51	90	.327	.337	June	.227	260	59	13	0	4	24	42	.293	.273
Pre-All Star	.249	834	208	37	4	9	63	64	142	.306	.336	July	.258	275	71	14	0	5	30	23	62	.320	.364
Post-All Star	.265	781	207	40	3	17	86	80	155	.334	.389	August	.271	325	88	17	1	8	34	25	64	.320	.403
Scoring Posn	.223	391	87	12	1	9	124	51	90	.309	.327	Sept/Oct	.263	251	66	12	2	5	26	34	48	.351	.386
Close & Late	.222	293	65	11	1	7	34	26	62	.290	.338	vs. AL	.243	263	64	14	0	4	23	29	53	.320	.342

Career (1993-1997)

	Avg	AB	H	2B	3B	HR	RBI	BB	SO	OBP	SLG		Avg	AB	H	2B	3B	HR	RBI	BB	SO	OBP	SLG
None on/out	.271	420	114	25	2	8	8	20	70	.308	.398	vs. NL	.260	1352	351	63	7	22	126	115	244	.319	.365

Batter vs. Pitcher (career)

Hits Best Against	Avg	AB	H	2B	3B	HR	RBI	BB	SO	OBP	SLG	Hits Worst Against	Avg	AB	H	2B	3B	HR	RBI	BB	SO	OBP	SLG
Pete Smith	.545	11	6	2	0	0	0	1	1	.583	.727	Jim Bullinger	.000	11	0	0	0	0	0	0	5	.000	.000
Hideo Nomo	.455	11	5	2	0	0	3	1	2	.500	.636	Ismael Valdes	.000	10	0	0	0	0	0	0	1	.091	.000
Bob Tewksbury	.455	11	5	1	1	0	0	0	0	.455	.727	Tom Glavine	.048	21	1	0	0	0	1	2	1	.130	.048
Terry Mulholland	.400	10	4	1	0	1	5	3	2	.538	.800	Pete Harnisch	.067	15	1	0	0	0	1	0	2	.063	.067
Curt Leskanic	.375	8	3	0	0	1	3	3	3	.545	.750	Curt Schilling	.091	11	1	0	0	0	0	0	3	.091	.091

Bruce Aven — Indians   Age 26 – Bats Right

	Avg	G	AB	R	H	2B	3B	HR	RBI	BB	SO	HBP	GDP	SB	CS	OBP	SLG	IBB	SH	SF	#Pit	P/PA	GB	FB	G/F
1997 Season	.211	13	19	4	4	1	0	0	2	1	5	0	0	0	1	.250	.263	0	0	0	70	3.50	8	2	4.00

1997 Season

	Avg	AB	H	2B	3B	HR	RBI	BB	SO	OBP	SLG		Avg	AB	H	2B	3B	HR	RBI	BB	SO	OBP	SLG
vs. Left	.300	10	3	1	0	0	2	0	3	.300	.400	Scoring Posn	.333	3	1	1	0	0	2	0	1	.333	.667
vs. Right	.111	9	1	0	0	0	0	1	2	.200	.111	Close & Late	.000	2	0	0	0	0	0	1	1	.333	.000

Steve Avery — Red Sox   Age 28 – Pitches Left

	ERA	W	L	Sv	G	GS	IP	BB	SO	Avg	H	2B	3B	HR	RBI	OBP	SLG	CG	ShO	Sup	QS	#P/S	SB	CS	GB	FB	G/F
1997 Season	6.42	6	7	0	22	18	96.2	49	51	.320	127	24	4	15	69	.394	.514	0	0	6.24	1	87	7	4	141	118	1.19
Last Five Years	4.23	46	39	0	134	129	776.0	239	525	.265	781	153	14	76	344	.321	.403	8	2	5.17	67	91	90	38	1077	786	1.37

1997 Season

	ERA	W	L	Sv	G	GS	IP	H	HR	BB	SO		Avg	AB	H	2B	3B	HR	RBI	BB	SO	OBP	SLG
Home	8.59	2	4	0	9	7	36.2	54	5	23	26	vs. Left	.403	62	25	4	2	2	9	16	7	.519	.629
Away	5.10	4	3	0	13	11	60.0	73	10	26	25	vs. Right	.304	335	102	20	2	13	60	33	44	.367	.493
Starter	6.22	6	6	0	18	18	92.2	120	15	47	49	Scoring Posn	.369	103	38	7	2	4	55	14	16	.430	.592
Reliever	11.25	0	1	0	4	0	4.0	7	0	2	2	Close & Late	.333	15	5	2	0	0	3	1	2	.375	.467
0-3 Days Rest (Start)	0.00	0	0	0	0	0	0.0	0	0	0	0	None on/out	.340	97	33	6	1	5	5	13	9	.418	.577
4 Days Rest	7.19	3	3	0	9	9	46.1	61	8	25	21	First Pitch	.371	62	23	2	1	3	16	0	0	.359	.581
5+ Days Rest	5.24	3	3	0	9	9	46.1	59	7	22	28	Ahead in Count	.261	161	42	13	1	5	14	0	41	.268	.447
Pre-All Star	5.55	2	2	0	7	7	35.2	51	8	15	11	Behind in Count	.406	96	39	7	1	4	25	27	0	.532	.625
Post-All Star	6.93	4	5	0	15	11	61.0	76	7	34	40	Two Strikes	.242	161	39	11	2	5	15	22	51	.341	.429

Last Five Years

	ERA	W	L	Sv	G	GS	IP	H	HR	BB	SO		Avg	AB	H	2B	3B	HR	RBI	BB	SO	OBP	SLG
Home	4.10	23	16	0	65	63	384.1	378	37	114	268	vs. Left	.246	468	115	24	2	5	45	53	109	.324	.338
Away	4.37	23	23	0	69	66	391.2	403	39	125	257	vs. Right	.268	2484	666	129	12	71	299	186	416	.320	.415
Day	4.59	9	13	0	37	35	210.0	217	26	67	146	Inning 1-6	.268	2596	696	131	14	71	318	212	464	.324	.411
Night	4.10	37	26	0	97	94	566.0	564	50	172	379	Inning 7+	.239	356	85	22	0	5	26	27	61	.292	.343
Grass	4.07	36	29	0	108	104	626.0	625	61	182	418	None on	.247	1848	456	91	8	46	46	127	347	.298	.379
Turf	4.92	10	10	0	26	25	150.0	156	15	57	107	Runners on	.294	1104	325	62	6	30	298	112	178	.356	.443
March/April	3.61	6	6	0	21	21	129.2	127	14	43	84	Scoring Posn	.294	622	183	33	4	18	260	82	117	.366	.447
May	3.01	13	5	0	26	26	170.2	156	8	47	124	Close & Late	.250	200	50	9	0	2	14	17	31	.309	.325
June	5.75	5	6	0	21	21	119.0	138	13	33	81	None on/out	.243	785	191	43	5	25	25	49	140	.290	.406
July	4.05	9	5	0	24	24	140.0	150	13	43	81	vs. 1st Batr (relief)	.200	5	1	1	0	0	0	0	0	.200	.400
August	5.08	9	9	0	20	20	118.2	115	16	42	81	1st Inning Pitched	.319	533	170	28	1	14	90	44	77	.375	.454
Sept/Oct	4.59	4	8	0	22	17	98.0	95	12	31	74	First 75 Pitches	.267	2300	615	113	10	64	275	172	408	.320	.409
Starter	4.13	46	37	0	129	129	771.1	770	76	235	523	Pitch 76-90	.255	345	88	20	4	8	34	34	69	.317	.406
Reliever	21.21	0	2	0	5	0	4.2	11	0	4	2	Pitch 91-105	.264	227	60	17	0	3	26	25	35	.343	.379
0-3 Days Rest (Start)	6.43	1	2	0	4	4	21.0	23	5	9	14	Pitch 106+	.225	80	18	3	0	1	9	8	13	.292	.300
4 Days Rest	4.03	30	23	0	82	82	498.0	486	52	139	324	First Pitch	.351	445	156	24	3	12	79	13	0	.364	.499
5+ Days Rest	4.14	15	12	0	43	43	252.1	261	19	87	185	Ahead in Count	.196	1336	262	61	5	27	109	0	446	.203	.310
vs. AL	6.17	6	6	0	21	17	93.1	121	13	43	49	Behind in Count	.330	654	216	43	2	30	99	128	0	.438	.540
vs. NL	3.97	40	33	0	113	112	682.2	660	63	196	476	Two Strikes	.179	1344	240	54	7	18	102	98	525	.239	.269
Pre-All Star	4.02	28	19	0	77	77	468.1	475	41	133	314	Pre-All Star	.266	1789	475	104	9	41	200	133	314	.317	.402
Post-All Star	4.56	18	20	0	57	52	307.2	306	35	106	211	Post-All Star	.263	1163	306	49	5	35	144	106	211	.327	.404

Pitcher vs. Batter (career)

Pitches Best Vs.	Avg	AB	H	2B	3B	HR	RBI	BB	SO	OBP	SLG	Pitches Worst Vs.	Avg	AB	H	2B	3B	HR	RBI	BB	SO	OBP	SLG
Luis Gonzalez	.067	15	1	1	0	0	0	2	1	.176	.133	Brian Jordan	.429	21	9	4	1	1	4	1	2	.455	.857
Craig Shipley	.077	13	1	0	0	0	0	1	3	.143	.077	Sammy Sosa	.417	24	10	1	0	3	5	0	6	.417	.833
Darryl Strawberry	.118	17	2	0	0	0	1	1	3	.167	.118	Billy Ashley	.400	10	4	2	0	1	4	1	2	.455	.900
Juan Samuel	.129	31	4	1	0	0	2	0	6	.129	.161	Joe Girardi	.353	17	6	2	0	2	4	3	2	.450	.824
Jose Offerman	.148	27	4	0	0	0	1	1	2	.179	.148	Eric Davis	.350	20	7	3	0	2	7	5	3	.480	.800

Bobby Ayala — Mariners   Age 28 – Pitches Right (groundball pitcher)

	ERA	W	L	Sv	G	GS	IP	BB	SO	Avg	H	2B	3B	HR	RBI	OBP	SLG	GF	IR	IRS	Hld	SvOp	SB	CS	GB	FB	G/F
1997 Season	3.82	10	5	8	71	0	96.2	41	92	.260	91	18	1	14	52	.338	.437	33	55	14	15	12	6	2	132	88	1.50
Last Five Years	4.60	33	26	51	273	9	389.2	167	371	.255	377	69	6	51	239	.335	.414	157	155	49	30	74	26	6	550	351	1.57

1997 Season

	ERA	W	L	Sv	G	GS	IP	H	HR	BB	SO		Avg	AB	H	2B	3B	HR	RBI	BB	SO	OBP	SLG
Home	5.29	6	3	2	38	0	47.2	49	10	23	43	vs. Left	.285	165	47	9	1	7	25	25	42	.380	.479
Away	2.39	4	2	6	33	0	49.0	42	4	18	49	vs. Right	.238	185	44	9	0	7	27	16	50	.298	.400

1997 Season

	ERA	W	L	Sv	G	GS	IP	H	HR	BB	SO
Day	3.56	5	2	3	23	0	30.1	21	4	12	32
Night	3.93	5	3	5	48	0	66.1	70	10	29	60
Grass	2.47	3	2	6	27	0	43.2	39	4	14	41
Turf	4.92	7	3	2	44	0	53.0	52	10	27	51
March/April	5.63	2	1	0	13	0	16.0	22	5	6	11
May	5.28	1	1	0	13	0	15.1	13	4	5	11
June	1.72	2	0	6	12	0	15.2	14	0	5	14
July	8.10	2	2	0	9	0	13.1	18	2	8	13
August	1.56	2	0	1	10	0	17.1	10	2	4	21
Sept/Oct	1.89	1	1	1	14	0	19.0	14	1	13	22
Starter	0.00	0	0	0	0	0	0.0	0	0	0	0
Reliever	3.82	10	5	8	71	0	96.2	91	14	41	92
0 Days rest (Relief)	4.50	3	1	4	18	0	20.0	21	3	10	15
1 or 2 Days rest	3.28	4	4	3	39	0	57.2	51	9	21	63
3+ Days rest	4.74	3	0	1	14	0	19.0	19	2	10	14
vs. AL	3.65	9	5	6	63	0	86.1	80	12	37	83
vs. NL	5.23	1	0	2	8	0	10.1	11	2	4	9
Pre-All Star	4.14	5	2	6	39	0	50.0	51	10	17	38
Post-All Star	3.47	5	3	2	32	0	46.2	40	4	24	54

	Avg	AB	H	2B	3B	HR	RBI	BB	SO	OBP	SLG
Inning 1-6	.167	36	6	0	0	2	3	5	12	.268	.333
Inning 7+	.271	314	85	18	1	12	49	36	80	.345	.449
None on	.275	178	49	7	1	8	8	24	44	.368	.461
Runners on	.244	172	42	11	0	6	44	17	48	.306	.413
Scoring Posn	.230	100	23	6	0	3	36	13	28	.303	.380
Close & Late	.287	178	51	11	1	5	31	17	46	.343	.444
None on/out	.238	80	19	3	1	5	5	10	15	.330	.488
vs. 1st Batr (relief)	.215	65	14	3	0	3	13	4	13	.268	.400
1st Inning Pitched	.218	220	48	9	0	6	31	23	60	.295	.341
First 15 Pitches	.241	191	46	9	0	4	21	16	51	.305	.351
Pitch 16-30	.267	120	32	8	1	7	23	18	32	.355	.525
Pitch 31-45	.353	34	12	1	0	2	6	5	8	.436	.559
Pitch 46+	.200	5	1	0	0	1	2	2	1	.429	.800
First Pitch	.378	45	17	3	0	1	7	2	0	.400	.511
Ahead in Count	.174	172	30	3	1	3	7	0	83	.183	.256
Behind in Count	.329	82	27	5	0	7	28	17	0	.431	.646
Two Strikes	.163	172	28	5	1	5	13	22	92	.264	.291
Pre-All Star	.279	183	51	10	0	10	28	17	38	.341	.497
Post-All Star	.240	167	40	8	1	4	24	24	54	.333	.371

Last Five Years

	ERA	W	L	Sv	G	GS	IP	H	HR	BB	SO
Home	4.82	21	13	23	142	5	203.2	188	28	81	200
Away	4.35	12	13	28	131	4	186.0	189	23	86	171
Day	4.50	12	8	14	76	3	110.0	101	16	41	109
Night	4.63	21	18	37	197	6	279.2	276	35	126	262
Grass	4.59	10	11	23	108	3	153.0	159	17	73	136
Turf	4.60	23	15	28	165	6	236.2	218	34	94	235
March/April	5.32	4	3	3	34	0	45.2	50	9	20	43
May	2.98	3	2	12	40	0	51.1	35	6	19	45
June	3.10	4	3	17	54	0	69.2	59	6	23	66
July	5.55	10	9	9	55	0	73.0	76	9	29	68
August	3.89	6	4	8	46	4	78.2	81	12	34	78
Sept/Oct	6.56	6	5	2	44	5	71.1	76	9	42	71
Starter	8.41	2	6	0	9	9	40.2	60	9	23	29
Reliever	4.15	31	20	51	264	0	349.0	317	42	144	342
0 Days rest (Relief)	4.58	9	6	21	67	0	74.2	71	7	37	63
1 or 2 Days rest	3.91	17	10	20	131	0	191.0	173	25	77	206
3+ Days rest	4.32	5	4	10	66	0	83.1	73	10	30	73
vs. AL	4.22	25	16	46	222	0	281.1	260	33	118	297
vs. NL	5.57	8	10	5	51	9	108.1	117	18	49	74
Pre-All Star	3.69	14	10	35	144	0	190.0	162	25	70	175
Post-All Star	5.45	19	16	16	129	9	199.2	215	26	97	196

	Avg	AB	H	2B	3B	HR	RBI	BB	SO	OBP	SLG
vs. Left	.262	774	203	38	4	26	120	94	206	.344	.422
vs. Right	.248	703	174	31	2	25	119	73	165	.325	.404
Inning 1-6	.283	300	85	14	1	13	54	38	57	.374	.467
Inning 7+	.248	1177	292	55	5	38	185	129	314	.325	.400
None on	.242	784	190	36	4	24	24	77	190	.320	.390
Runners on	.270	693	187	33	2	27	215	90	181	.352	.440
Scoring Posn	.269	431	116	22	1	16	185	67	107	.358	.436
Close & Late	.243	658	160	31	2	18	104	72	184	.320	.378
None on/out	.232	341	79	13	2	11		30	80	.307	.378
vs. 1st Batr (relief)	.217	240	52	7	0	6	32	17	57	.274	.321
1st Inning Pitched	.237	924	219	41	2	24	148	96	254	.313	.364
First 15 Pitches	.227	771	175	32	0	16	81	70	198	.300	.331
Pitch 16-30	.274	463	127	26	5	20	100	64	120	.358	.482
Pitch 31-45	.286	147	42	9	1	6	33	17	31	.364	.483
Pitch 46+	.344	96	33	2	0	9	25	16	22	.452	.646
First Pitch	.340	212	72	11	0	11	46	11	0	.375	.547
Ahead in Count	.195	703	137	23	3	16	74	0	321	.204	.304
Behind in Count	.314	306	96	18	2	15	75	80	0	.452	.533
Two Strikes	.168	713	120	18	3	19	76	76	371	.255	.282
Pre-All Star	.232	698	162	26	3	25	101	70	175	.303	.385
Post-All Star	.276	779	215	43	3	26	138	97	196	.363	.439

Pitcher vs. Batter (career)

Pitches Best Vs.	Avg	AB	H	2B	3B	HR	RBI	BB	SO	OBP	SLG	Pitches Worst Vs.	Avg	AB	H	2B	3B	HR	RBI	BB	SO	OBP	SLG
Travis Fryman	.000	13	0	0	0	0	0	0	5	.000	.000	Paul O'Neill	.400	10	4	2	0	0	7	2	2	.462	.600
Mo Vaughn	.077	13	1	0	0	0	0	1	6	.143	.077	Bobby Bonilla	.375	8	3	0	0	1	2	3	2	.545	.750
Joe Carter	.091	11	1	0	0	0	1	0	2	.091	.091	Wade Boggs	.364	11	4	1	0	0	2	3	1	.500	.455
Tim Raines	.100	10	1	0	0	0	1	1	5	.182	.100	Tim Salmon	.333	12	4	0	0	1	3	2	3	.429	.583
Juan Gonzalez	.111	18	2	1	0	0	0		4	.111	.167	Rusty Greer	.333	12	4	0	0	1	3	1	5	.385	.583

Manny Aybar — Cardinals   Age 23 – Pitches Right (flyball pitcher)

	ERA	W	L	Sv	G	GS	IP	BB	SO	Avg	H	2B	3B	HR	RBI	OBP	SLG	CG	ShO	Sup	QS	#P/S	SB	CS	GB	FB	G/F
1997 Season	4.24	2	4	0	12	12	68.0	29	41	.263	66	11	2	8	32	.344	.418	0	0	3.44	8	88	4	2	80	83	0.96

1997 Season

	ERA	W	L	Sv	G	GS	IP	H	HR	BB	SO
Home	3.07	1	2	0	7	7	44.0	40	4	16	27
Away	6.38	1	2	0	5	5	24.0	26	4	13	14
Starter	4.24	2	4	0	12	12	68.0	66	8	29	41
Reliever	0.00	0	0	0	0	0	0.0	0	0	0	0
0-3 Days Rest (Start)	2.25	1	0	0	2	2	12.0	10	0	3	9
4 Days Rest	4.89	0	3	0	7	7	38.2	40	7	17	21
5+ Days Rest	4.15	1	1	0	3	3	17.1	16	1	9	11
Pre-All Star	0.00	0	0	0	0	0	0.0	0	0	0	0
Post-All Star	4.24	2	4	0	12	12	68.0	66	8	29	41

	Avg	AB	H	2B	3B	HR	RBI	BB	SO	OBP	SLG
vs. Left	.304	135	41	2	2	7	20	17	18	.381	.504
vs. Right	.216	116	25	9	0	1	12	12	23	.301	.319
Scoring Posn	.276	58	16	3	2	1	22	8	9	.343	.448
Close & Late	.500	6	3	1	0	0	1	1	0	.571	.667
None on/out	.250	64	16	3	0	3		7	11	.342	.438
First Pitch	.265	34	9	1	0	2	8	0	0	.250	.471
Ahead in Count	.181	94	17	3	0	3	10	0	35	.196	.309
Behind in Count	.348	69	24	6	0	2	9	20	0	.495	.522
Two Strikes	.115	96	11	0	0	1		9	41	.204	.146

Carlos Baerga — Mets   Age 29 – Bats Both (groundball hitter)

	Avg	G	AB	R	H	2B	3B	HR	RBI	BB	SO	HBP	GDP	SB	CS	OBP	SLG	IBB	SH	SF	#Pit	#P/PA	GB	FB	G/F
1997 Season	.281	133	467	53	131	25	1	9	52	20	54	3	13	2	6	.311	.396	1	3	5	1556	3.12	230	108	2.13
Last Five Years	.298	651	2597	385	774	141	11	76	402	120	225	27	78	37	15	.331	.449	15	11	36	9264	3.32	1181	682	1.73

1997 Season

	Avg	AB	H	2B	3B	HR	RBI	BB	SO	OBP	SLG		Avg	AB	H	2B	3B	HR	RBI	BB	SO	OBP	SLG
vs. Left	.170	94	16	2	0	1	4	3	16	.196	.223	First Pitch	.364	55	20	3	0	1	8	0	0	.375	.473

1997 Season

	Avg	AB	H	2B	3B	HR	RBI	BB	SO	OBP	SLG		Avg	AB	H	2B	3B	HR	RBI	BB	SO	OBP	SLG
vs. Right	.308	373	115	23	1	8	48	17	38	.339	.440	Ahead in Count	.298	121	36	13	1	3	14	16	0	.377	.496
Groundball	.324	102	33	6	0	1	10	3	12	.355	.412	Behind in Count	.225	209	47	6	0	2	17	0	49	.229	.282
Flyball	.375	72	27	8	1	2	13	1	13	.384	.597	Two Strikes	.222	162	36	5	0	3	16	4	54	.244	.309
Home	.319	229	73	15	1	4	28	10	25	.347	.445	Batting #5	.330	91	30	5	1	2	15	8	12	.382	.473
Away	.244	238	58	10	0	5	24	10	29	.277	.349	Batting #6	.307	251	77	15	0	7	32	12	15	.340	.450
Day	.306	173	53	10	0	3	18	6	21	.335	.416	Other	.192	125	24	5	0	0	5	0	27	.192	.232
Night	.265	294	78	15	1	6	34	14	33	.297	.384	March/April	.188	64	12	3	0	0	1	2	9	.212	.234
Grass	.288	403	116	21	1	7	42	17	46	.317	.397	May	.368	95	35	7	0	1	15	3	9	.384	.474
Turf	.234	64	15	4	0	2	10	3	8	.275	.391	June	.256	86	22	2	1	2	9	2	9	.286	.372
Pre-All Star	.290	269	78	13	1	4	28	10	28	.318	.390	July	.273	77	21	3	0	3	8	5	9	.317	.429
Post-All Star	.268	198	53	12	0	5	24	10	26	.302	.404	August	.329	73	24	5	0	2	11	4	6	.363	.479
Scoring Posn	.286	119	34	7	0	3	43	7	18	.323	.420	Sept/Oct	.236	72	17	5	0	1	8	4	12	.273	.347
Close & Late	.321	78	25	5	0	1	12	6	9	.365	.423	vs. AL	.352	54	19	4	0	0	5	1	6	.364	.426
None on/out	.287	115	33	7	1	3	3	7	13	.328	.443	vs. NL	.271	413	112	21	1	9	47	19	48	.305	.392

1997 By Position

Position	Avg	AB	H	2B	3B	HR	RBI	BB	SO	OBP	SLG	G	GS	Innings	PO	A	E	DP	Fld Pct	Rng Fctr	In Zone	Outs	Zone Rtg	MLB Zone
As 2b	.281	459	129	25	1	9	51	20	53	.312	.399	131	122	1048.2	245	371	14	88	.978	5.29	415	361	.870	.902

Last Five Years

	Avg	AB	H	2B	3B	HR	RBI	BB	SO	OBP	SLG		Avg	AB	H	2B	3B	HR	RBI	BB	SO	OBP	SLG
vs. Left	.273	757	207	36	4	19	103	43	87	.317	.407	First Pitch	.359	256	92	11	2	10	51	9	0	.388	.535
vs. Right	.308	1840	567	105	7	57	299	77	138	.337	.466	Ahead in Count	.327	793	259	48	5	34	131	68	0	.378	.528
Groundball	.279	506	141	22	1	12	77	17	45	.304	.397	Behind in Count	.255	1100	281	51	2	18	135	0	199	.263	.355
Flyball	.285	495	141	37	1	7	62	18	55	.317	.406	Two Strikes	.245	917	225	43	1	17	119	42	225	.283	.350
Home	.313	1219	381	66	6	32	211	56	105	.340	.455	Batting #3	.307	1935	595	109	10	62	329	90	165	.340	.470
Away	.285	1378	393	75	5	44	191	64	120	.323	.443	Batting #6	.303	261	79	15	0	8	34	17	15	.346	.452
Day	.317	851	270	50	4	29	147	41	82	.350	.488	Other	.249	401	100	17	1	6	39	13	45	.279	.342
Night	.289	1746	504	91	7	47	255	79	143	.322	.430	March/April	.276	370	102	23	0	9	50	13	37	.302	.411
Grass	.301	2222	669	115	10	63	345	108	188	.334	.447	May	.295	528	156	30	5	15	86	16	50	.320	.456
Turf	.280	375	105	26	1	13	57	12	37	.313	.459	June	.306	552	169	33	3	21	90	23	51	.338	.491
Pre-All Star	.294	1624	478	95	9	51	250	63	152	.324	.458	July	.317	463	147	21	1	14	65	24	36	.357	.462
Post-All Star	.304	973	296	46	2	25	152	57	73	.343	.433	August	.290	431	125	20	2	13	73	29	26	.334	.436
Scoring Posn	.297	715	212	42	3	19	312	62	71	.347	.443	Sept/Oct	.296	253	75	12	0	4	38	15	25	.332	.391
Close & Late	.296	395	117	14	1	7	50	31	30	.351	.390	vs. AL	.307	2101	646	117	10	65	344	96	175	.340	.465
None on/out	.283	513	145	29	4	16	16	23	44	.319	.448	vs. NL	.258	496	128	24	1	11	58	24	50	.296	.377

Batter vs. Pitcher (career)

Hits Best Against	Avg	AB	H	2B	3B	HR	RBI	BB	SO	OBP	SLG	Hits Worst Against	Avg	AB	H	2B	3B	HR	RBI	BB	SO	OBP	SLG
Paul Quantrill	.625	16	10	0	0	1	1	3	0	.684	.813	Hipolito Pichardo	.077	13	1	1	0	0	4	1	1	.125	.154
Mike Magnante	.500	10	5	0	0	1	4	0	0	.455	.800	Tony Castillo	.100	10	1	0	0	0	2	0	2	.083	.100
Jimmy Key	.487	39	19	6	0	1	2	0	3	.487	.718	Sterling Hitchcock	.107	28	3	1	0	0	1	2	7	.188	.143
Tom Candiotti	.462	13	6	1	0	2	3	0	0	.462	1.000	Al Leiter	.143	28	4	0	0	0	2	2	4	.200	.143
Willie Banks	.455	11	5	1	0	1	4	1	0	.500	.818	Rick Honeycutt	.182	11	2	0	0	0	1	0	3	.167	.182

Jeff Bagwell — Astros   Age 30 – Bats Right

	Avg	G	AB	R	H	2B	3B	HR	RBI	BB	SO	HBP	GDP	SB	CS	OBP	SLG	IBB	SH	SF	#Pit	#P/PA	GB	FB	G/F
1997 Season	.286	162	566	109	162	40	2	43	135	127	122	16	10	31	10	.425	.592	27	0	8	2818	3.93	180	180	1.00
Last Five Years	.313	690	2517	488	789	186	10	154	546	468	476	39	67	92	30	.423	.579	79	0	39	11845	3.87	797	834	0.96

1997 Season

	Avg	AB	H	2B	3B	HR	RBI	BB	SO	OBP	SLG		Avg	AB	H	2B	3B	HR	RBI	BB	SO	OBP	SLG
vs. Left	.242	120	29	10	0	5	20	39	21	.432	.450	First Pitch	.516	62	32	11	0	8	29	18	0	.639	1.081
vs. Right	.298	446	133	30	2	38	115	88	101	.423	.630	Ahead in Count	.348	135	47	13	0	13	45	61	0	.547	.733
Groundball	.329	82	27	6	0	6	19	21	18	.457	.622	Behind in Count	.224	245	55	10	2	14	41	0	93	.254	.453
Flyball	.338	77	26	5	0	9	24	22	18	.500	.753	Two Strikes	.185	270	50	9	1	16	39	47	122	.320	.404
Home	.258	264	68	17	1	22	67	66	58	.416	.580	Batting #3	.285	562	160	39	2	43	133	126	122	.424	.591
Away	.311	302	94	23	1	21	68	61	64	.434	.603	Batting #6	1.000	1	1	0	0	0	1		0	1.000	1.000
Day	.304	168	51	11	0	12	40	42	33	.457	.583	Other	.333	3	1	1	0	0	2	0	0	.333	.667
Night	.279	398	111	29	2	31	95	85	89	.412	.595	March/April	.333	99	33	5	1	7	26	12	21	.416	.616
Grass	.318	214	68	15	1	14	46	46	44	.445	.593	May	.320	100	32	12	0	10	26	23	19	.453	.740
Turf	.267	352	94	25	1	29	89	81	78	.413	.591	June	.293	99	29	9	0	5	20	27	24	.438	.535
Pre-All Star	.314	318	100	27	1	24	78	67	67	.437	.632	July	.239	92	22	3	0	6	23	17	20	.383	.467
Post-All Star	.250	248	62	13	1	19	57	60	55	.412	.540	August	.240	96	23	5	1	6	22	18	30		
Scoring Posn	.311	161	50	13	1	9	86	59	38	.494	.571	Sept/Oct	.288	80	23	6	1	6	22	18			
Close & Late	.247	97	24	4	1	5	16	32	24	.435	.464	vs. AL	.236	55	13	3	0	3	9	6			
None on/out	.238	105	25	8	0	11	11	18	21	.365	.629	vs. NL	.292	511	149	37	2	40	126	121			

1997 By Position

Position	Avg	AB	H	2B	3B	HR	RBI	BB	SO	OBP	SLG	G	GS	Innings	PO	A	E	DP	Fld Pct	Rng Fctr	In Zone
As 1b	.286	559	160	38	2	43	133	127	120	.426	.592	159	156	1391.0	1405	136	11	141	.993	---	285

Last Five Years

	Avg	AB	H	2B	3B	HR	RBI	BB	SO	OBP	SLG		Avg	AB	H	2B	3B	HR	RBI	BI
vs. Left	.333	598	199	57	2	38	135	142	91	.461	.625	First Pitch	.393	333	131	25	1	33	97	5
vs. Right	.307	1919	590	129	8	116	411	326	385	.411	.564	Ahead in Count	.422	590	249	64	2	52	179	22
Groundball	.307	639	196	50	1	30	127	109	135	.403	.529	Behind in Count	.233	1049	244	60	5	39	155	

Last Five Years

	Avg	AB	H	2B	3B	HR	RBI	BB	SO	OBP	SLG		Avg	AB	H	2B	3B	HR	RBI	BB	SO	OBP	SLG
Flyball	.287	369	106	23	2	32	86	76	72	.418	.621	Two Strikes	.219	1148	251	56	4	48	177	185	476	.333	.400
Home	.314	1231	386	90	5	80	271	245	237	.432	.590	Batting #3	.310	2228	691	169	8	134	471	428	425	.424	.574
Away	.313	1286	403	96	5	74	275	223	239	.414	.568	Batting #4	.335	269	90	16	2	18	67	37	44	.410	.610
Day	.311	774	241	60	2	49	163	147	143	.426	.584	Other	.400	20	8	1	0	2	8	3	7	.478	.750
Night	.314	1743	548	126	8	105	383	321	333	.422	.577	March/April	.327	388	127	24	4	25	94	64	78	.426	.603
Grass	.314	813	255	57	4	49	171	152	151	.420	.574	May	.318	494	157	35	1	36	115	97	94	.425	.611
Turf	.313	1704	534	129	6	105	375	316	325	.425	.581	June	.310	497	154	46	2	28	95	84	91	.410	.579
Pre-All Star	.313	1535	481	112	7	97	337	277	292	.417	.585	July	.300	493	148	30	1	30	112	94	93	.416	.548
Post-All Star	.314	982	308	74	3	57	209	191	184	.432	.569	August	.328	338	111	28	1	22	67	69	65	.445	.612
Scoring Posn	.305	711	217	50	4	32	366	210	135	.455	.522	Sept/Oct	.300	307	92	23	1	13	63	60	55	.425	.508
Close & Late	.277	393	109	23	2	22	72	103	89	.429	.514	vs. AL	.236	55	13	3	0	3	9	6	10	.338	.455
None on/out	.323	493	159	38	3	43	43	53	89	.395	.673	vs. NL	.315	2462	776	183	10	151	537	462	466	.425	.582

Batter vs. Pitcher (career)

Hits Best Against	Avg	AB	H	2B	3B	HR	RBI	BB	SO	OBP	SLG	Hits Worst Against	Avg	AB	H	2B	3B	HR	RBI	BB	SO	OBP	SLG
Tim Scott	.875	8	7	2	0	1	5	1	0	.818	1.500	Rene Arocha	.000	13	0	0	0	0	0	1	5	.071	.000
Mark Portugal	.647	17	11	5	0	0	3	4	1	.727	.941	Esteban Loaiza	.000	12	0	0	0	0	0	1	1	.077	.000
Jeff Juden	.600	10	6	3	0	2	6	2	3	.615	1.500	Dave Weathers	.083	12	1	0	0	0	0	1	1	.083	.083
Steve Cooke	.583	12	7	1	0	2	5	4	0	.688	1.167	Stan Belinda	.083	12	1	0	0	0	0	3	2	.267	.083
Hideo Nomo	.471	17	8	1	0	4	6	4	2	.571	1.235	Ismael Valdes	.105	19	2	1	0	0	1	1	2	.143	.158

Scott Bailes — Rangers
Age 35 – Pitches Left (groundball pitcher)

	ERA	W	L	Sv	G	GS	IP	BB	SO	Avg	H	2B	3B	HR	RBI	OBP	SLG	GF	IR	IRS	Hld	SvOp	SB	CS	GB	FB	G/F
1997 Season	2.86	1	0	0	24	0	22.0	10	14	.231	18	2	0	2	8	.315	.333	7	13	4	0	0	0	0	33	19	1.74

1997 Season

	ERA	W	L	Sv	G	GS	IP	H	HR	BB	SO		Avg	AB	H	2B	3B	HR	RBI	BB	SO	OBP	SLG
Home	2.89	0	0	0	9	0	9.1	4	1	4	7	vs. Left	.222	36	8	1	0	2	7	5	6	.310	.417
Away	2.84	1	0	0	15	0	12.2	14	1	6	7	vs. Right	.238	42	10	1	0	0	1	5	8	.319	.262

Cory Bailey — Giants
Age 27 – Pitches Right (groundball pitcher)

	ERA	W	L	Sv	G	GS	IP	BB	SO	Avg	H	2B	3B	HR	RBI	OBP	SLG	GF	IR	IRS	Hld	SvOp	SB	CS	GB	FB	G/F
1997 Season	8.38	0	1	0	7	0	9.2	4	5	.375	15	1	1	1	11	.422	.525	4	5	2	0	0	1	0	17	11	1.55
Career (1993-1997)	4.28	5	5	0	77	0	90.1	51	63	.280	96	13	2	4	47	.372	.364	23	47	18	10	2	6	5	150	75	2.00

1997 Season

	ERA	W	L	Sv	G	GS	IP	H	HR	BB	SO		Avg	AB	H	2B	3B	HR	RBI	BB	SO	OBP	SLG
Home	11.12	0	1	0	3	0	5.2	11	1	1	4	vs. Left	.286	14	4	1	0	0	2	2	3	.375	.357
Away	4.50	0	0	0	4	0	4.0	4	0	3	1	vs. Right	.423	26	11	0	1	1	9	2	2	.448	.615

Career (1993-1997)

	ERA	W	L	Sv	G	GS	IP	H	HR	BB	SO		Avg	AB	H	2B	3B	HR	RBI	BB	SO	OBP	SLG
Home	4.29	2	4	0	44	0	50.1	55	3	24	38	vs. Left	.270	122	33	6	1	2	13	27	21	.407	.385
Away	4.28	3	1	0	33	0	40.0	41	1	27	25	vs. Right	.285	221	63	7	1	2	34	24	42	.351	.353
Day	3.00	0	1	0	29	0	36.0	33	1	20	25	Inning 1-6	.362	58	21	1	0	1	11	8	10	.433	.431
Night	5.13	5	4	0	48	0	54.1	63	3	31	38	Inning 7+	.263	285	75	12	2	3	36	43	53	.360	.351
Grass	4.40	3	5	0	65	0	73.2	83	3	43	48	None on	.295	156	46	4	0	1	1	24	30	.389	.340
Turf	3.78	2	0	0	12	0	16.2	13	1	8	15	Runners on	.267	187	50	9	2	3	46	27	33	.358	.385
March/April	4.15	2	0	0	14	0	17.1	16	1	11	19	Scoring Posn	.281	114	32	5	2	2	43	20	19	.384	.412
May	7.71	0	1	0	7	0	7.0	13	0	3	2	Close & Late	.319	135	43	9	0	3	21	20	27	.410	.452
June	1.50	1	0	0	7	0	6.0	7	0	2	5	None on/out	.297	74	22	0	0	1	1	11	15	.388	.338
July	8.53	0	1	0	7	0	6.1	12	2	3	5	vs. 1st Batr (relief)	.250	68	17	1	0	1	6	8	19	.329	.309
August	1.88	0	1	0	12	0	14.1	14	0	8	6	1st Inning Pitched	.288	243	70	10	1	3	39	32	48	.368	.374
Sept/Oct	4.35	2	2	0	30	0	39.1	34	1	24	26	First 15 Pitches	.260	208	54	4	0	1	21	22	41	.329	.293
Starter	0.00	0	0	0	0	0	0.0	0	0	0	0	Pitch 16-30	.323	99	32	7	1	1	16	23	15	.452	.444
Reliever	4.28	5	5	0	77	0	90.1	96	4	51	63	Pitch 31-45	.273	33	9	2	1	2	10	6	6	.375	.576
0 Days rest (Relief)	9.00	1	2	0	15	0	14.0	29	1	11	13	Pitch 46+	.333	3	1	0	0	0	0	0	1	.333	.333
1 or 2 Days rest	2.91	2	1	0	36	0	46.1	35	0	28	28	First Pitch	.333	45	15	1	0	0	2	8	0	.434	.356
3+ Days rest	4.20	2	2	0	26	0	30.0	32	3	12	22	Ahead in Count	.215	158	34	6	2	2	22	0	52	.220	.316
vs. AL	5.40	0	2	0	17	0	21.2	23	2	16	16	Behind in Count	.294	68	20	3	0	1	12	27	0	.490	.382
vs. NL	3.93	5	3	0	60	0	68.2	73	2	35	47	Two Strikes	.241	166	40	4	2	2	20	16	63	.306	.325
Pre-All Star	5.73	3	2	0	31	0	33.0	45	3	18	30	Pre-All Star	.328	137	45	8	0	3	17	18	30	.404	.453
Post-All Star	3.45	2	3	0	46	0	57.1	51	1	33	33	Post-All Star	.248	206	51	5	2	1	30	33	33	.351	.306

Roger Bailey — Rockies
Age 27 – Pitches Right (groundball pitcher)

	ERA	W	L	Sv	G	GS	IP	BB	SO	Avg	H	2B	3B	HR	RBI	OBP	SLG	CG	ShO	Sup	QS	#P/S	SB	CS	GB	FB	G/F
1997 Season	4.29	9	10	0	29	29	191.0	70	84	.283	210	41	7	27	91	.354	.467	5	2	5.89	12	97	16	5	357	166	2.15
Career (1995-1997)	4.90	18	19	1	92	46	356.0	161	162	.284	392	85	14	43	189	.363	.460	5	2	6.17	19	95	30	11	639	341	1.87

1997 Season

	ERA	W	L	Sv	G	GS	IP	H	HR	BB	SO		Avg	AB	H	2B	3B	HR	RBI	BB	SO	OBP	SLG
Home	4.90	5	3	0	14	14	93.2	114	17	31	39	vs. Left	.315	356	112	27	4	11	42	39	44	.383	.506
Away	3.70	4	7	0	15	15	97.1	96	10	39	45	vs. Right	.255	385	98	14	3	16	49	31	40	.327	.431
Day	3.83	6	4	0	15	15	103.1	114	13	29	43	Inning 1-6	.281	630	177	35	6	24	77	63	74	.353	.470
Night	4.83	3	6	0	14	14	87.2	96	14	41	41	Inning 7+	.297	111	33	6	1	3	14	7	10	.358	.450
Grass	4.26	8	5	0	22	22	148.0	167	21	55	62	None on	.299	428	128	24	5	19	19	31	44	.352	.512

24

1997 Season

	ERA	W	L	Sv	G	GS	IP	H	HR	BB	SO		Avg	AB	H	2B	3B	HR	RBI	BB	SO	OBP	SLG
Turf	4.40	1	5	0	7	7	43.0	43	6	15	22	Runners on	.262	313	82	17	2	8	72	39	40	.356	.406
March/April	2.18	3	1	0	4	4	33.0	26	4	4	10	Scoring Posn	.212	184	39	9	1	3	59	24	30	.320	.321
May	3.38	2	3	0	6	6	45.1	45	3	16	18	Close & Late	.316	38	12	2	1	1	5	2	4	.409	.500
June	5.01	3	2	0	5	5	32.1	44	4	15	14	None on/out	.328	192	63	12	0	9	9	15	15	.377	.531
July	5.06	1	2	0	4	4	26.2	28	1	5	13	vs. 1st Batr (relief)	.000	0	0	0	0	0	0	0	0	.000	.000
August	6.91	0	1	0	6	6	28.2	46	9	18	13	1st Inning Pitched	.322	118	38	4	1	4	19	18	18	.413	.475
Sept/Oct	3.96	0	1	0	4	4	25.0	21	6	12	16	First 75 Pitches	.283	538	152	29	5	22	66	53	67	.355	.478
Starter	4.29	9	10	0	29	29	191.0	210	27	70	84	Pitch 76-90	.274	113	31	6	1	3	12	8	11	.322	.425
Reliever	0.00	0	0	0	0	0	0.0	0	0	0	0	Pitch 91-105	.266	64	17	5	1	0	5	7	3	.365	.375
0-3 Days Rest (Start)	0.00	0	0	0	0	0	0.0	0	0	0	0	Pitch 106+	.385	26	10	1	0	2	8	2	3	.433	.654
4 Days Rest	4.51	5	6	0	17	17	107.2	128	12	47	46	First Pitch	.385	130	50	9	3	3	17	1	0	.398	.569
5+ Days Rest	4.00	4	4	0	12	12	83.1	82	15	23	38	Behind in Count	.194	247	48	7	1	4	17	0	70	.207	.279
vs. AL	1.38	1	0	0	2	2	13.0	14	1	7	6	Ahead in Count	.323	235	76	19	1	14	39	37	0	.417	.591
vs. NL	4.50	8	10	0	27	27	178.0	196	26	63	78	Two Strikes	.138	239	33	3	0	5	21	32	84	.247	.213
Pre-All Star	3.50	8	6	0	15	15	110.2	111	11	35	42	Pre-All Star	.271	425	115	28	1	11	45	35	42	.334	.419
Post-All Star	5.38	1	4	0	14	14	80.1	95	16	35	42	Post-All Star	.301	316	95	13	6	16	46	35	42	.380	.532

Career (1995-1997)

	ERA	W	L	Sv	G	GS	IP	H	HR	BB	SO		Avg	AB	H	2B	3B	HR	RBI	BB	SO	OBP	SLG
Home	5.82	12	5	1	46	22	176.1	216	27	72	75	vs. Left	.303	631	191	46	10	16	88	96	81	.394	.483
Away	4.01	6	14	0	46	24	179.2	176	16	89	87	vs. Right	.269	747	201	39	4	27	101	65	81	.336	.440
Day	4.86	8	8	0	37	20	152.0	171	18	62	66	Inning 1-6	.284	1066	303	68	10	34	144	121	129	.361	.462
Night	4.94	10	11	1	55	26	204.0	221	25	99	96	Inning 7+	.285	312	89	17	4	9	45	40	33	.371	.452
Grass	4.99	15	11	1	73	34	274.1	312	36	115	120	None on	.296	766	227	48	7	27	76	84		.363	.483
Turf	4.63	3	8	0	19	12	81.2	80	7	46	42	Runners on	.270	612	165	37	7	16	162	85	78	.364	.431
March/April	3.96	3	1	0	8	4	36.1	32	4	12	14	Scoring Posn	.249	370	92	21	5	8	138	59	60	.357	.397
May	3.00	4	6	0	17	6	63.0	60	3	27	29	Close & Late	.283	99	28	5	3	1	10	16	10	.405	.424
June	4.40	3	2	0	20	5	59.1	68	6	26	30	None on/out	.328	351	115	27	2	15	15	40	25	.396	.544
July	6.60	3	5	0	13	9	58.2	73	6	24	25	vs. 1st Batr (relief)	.244	41	10	2	2	1	4	5	7	.326	.463
August	5.44	4	3	1	18	13	81.0	100	11	42	33	1st Inning Pitched	.288	347	100	19	3	9	60	53	54	.381	.438
Sept/Oct	5.62	1	2	0	16	9	57.2	59	13	30	31	First 75 Pitches	.286	1087	311	71	11	33	152	131	138	.366	.463
Starter	4.76	15	14	0	46	46	289.1	319	37	117	124	Pitch 76-90	.284	162	46	8	1	5	16	15	12	.345	.438
Reliever	5.54	3	5	1	46	0	66.2	73	6	44	38	Pitch 91-105	.253	91	23	5	2	2	12	11	7	.352	.418
0-3 Days Rest (Start)	2.57	0	1	0	1	1	7.0	4	1	2	3	Pitch 106+	.316	38	12	1	0	3	9	4	5	.386	.579
4 Days Rest	5.45	9	8	0	26	26	158.2	200	20	66	62	First Pitch	.357	235	84	18	5	6	32	3	0	.372	.553
5+ Days Rest	4.00	6	5	0	19	19	123.2	115	16	49	59	Ahead in Count	.209	450	94	16	2	7	38	0	132	.215	.300
vs. AL	1.38	1	0	0	2	2	13.0	14	1	7	6	Behind in Count	.323	427	138	34	3	22	80	86	0	.435	.571
vs. NL	5.04	17	19	1	90	44	343.0	378	42	154	156	Two Strikes	.187	445	83	15	1	8	49	72	162	.302	.279
Pre-All Star	4.29	11	11	0	50	16	168.0	175	16	74	75	Pre-All Star	.271	646	175	40	5	16	78	74	75	.351	.423
Post-All Star	5.46	7	8	1	42	30	188.0	217	27	87	87	Post-All Star	.296	732	217	45	9	27	111	87	87	.374	.493

Pitcher vs. Batter (career)

Pitches Best Vs.	Avg	AB	H	2B	3B	HR	RBI	BB	SO	OBP	SLG	Pitches Worst Vs.	Avg	AB	H	2B	3B	HR	RBI	BB	SO	OBP	SLG
Sammy Sosa	.056	18	1	0	0	1	3	0	2	.105	.222	Fred McGriff	.545	11	6	2	0	1	2	2	1	.667	1.000
Gregg Jefferies	.091	11	1	0	0	0	0	1	1	.167	.091	Jeff Bagwell	.545	11	6	2	0	1	6	1	2	.583	1.000
Stan Javier	.100	10	1	0	0	0	0	1	2	.182	.100	Eric Karros	.500	10	5	1	0	2	4	0	0	.455	1.200
Luis Gonzalez	.154	13	2	1	0	0	0	0	0	.154	.231	Jeff Kent	.455	11	5	1	0	2	7	0	1	.455	1.091
Mickey Morandini	.182	11	2	1	0	0	0	0	1	.182	.273	Reggie Sanders	.444	9	4	1	0	2	4	2	1	.583	1.222

Harold Baines — Orioles

Age 39 – Bats Left (groundball hitter)

	Avg	G	AB	R	H	2B	3B	HR	RBI	BB	SO	HBP	GDP	SB	CS	OBP	SLG	IBB	SH	SF	#Pit	#P/PA	GB	FB	G/F
1997 Season	.301	137	452	55	136	23	0	16	67	55	62	0	12	0	1	.375	.458	11	0	3	1784	3.50	184	114	1.61
Last Five Years	.304	619	2074	303	631	105	2	98	357	285	270	2	71	3	4	.386	.499	46	1	16	8459	3.56	853	561	1.52

1997 Season

	Avg	AB	H	2B	3B	HR	RBI	BB	SO	OBP	SLG		Avg	AB	H	2B	3B	HR	RBI	BB	SO	OBP	SLG
vs. Left	.272	92	25	6	0	3	19	4	20	.299	.435	First Pitch	.420	88	37	7	0	7	23	8	0	.459	.739
vs. Right	.308	360	111	17	0	13	48	51	42	.392	.464	Ahead in Count	.267	116	31	4	0	3	11	30	0	.418	.379
Groundball	.321	106	34	4	0	3	18	13	14	.392	.443	Behind in Count	.257	167	43	12	0	5	22	0	43	.257	.419
Flyball	.256	90	23	7	0	5	15	7	17	.306	.500	Two Strikes	.247	174	43	10	0	4	25	17	62	.313	.374
Home	.255	231	59	12	0	6	34	33	35	.346	.385	Batting #5	.305	256	78	15	0	7	35	34	37	.386	.445
Away	.348	221	77	11	0	10	33	22	27	.406	.534	Batting #7	.270	115	31	4	0	3	13	13	15	.341	.383
Day	.310	145	45	7	0	7	24	19	24	.386	.503	Other	.333	81	27	4	0	6	19	8	10	.385	.605
Night	.296	307	91	16	0	9	43	36	38	.369	.436	March/April	.296	71	21	0	0	2	5	16	15	.425	.380
Grass	.294	402	118	22	0	13	54	50	57	.369	.445	May	.329	85	28	12	0	3	19	7	7	.372	.576
Turf	.360	50	18	1	0	3	13	5	5	.418	.560	June	.266	79	21	5	0	4	17	12	12	.363	.481
Pre-All Star	.294	252	74	17	0	9	42	35	35	.377	.468	July	.300	90	27	1	0	3	11	7	14	.351	.411
Post-All Star	.310	200	62	6	0	7	25	20	27	.371	.445	August	.211	71	15	3	0	2	7	8	8	.291	.338
Scoring Posn	.295	129	38	10	0	4	54	25	15	.401	.465	Sept/Oct	.429	56	24	2	0	2	8	5	6	.468	.571
Close & Late	.318	66	21	3	0	2	15	10	12	.408	.455	vs. AL	.299	431	129	23	0	14	63	53	60	.374	.450
None on/out	.298	114	34	6	0	4	4	5	16	.328	.456	vs. NL	.333	21	7	0	0	2	4	2	2	.391	.619

1997 By Position

Position	Avg	AB	H	2B	3B	HR	RBI	BB	SO	OBP	SLG	G	GS	Innings	PO	A	E	DP	Fld Pct	Rng Fctr	In Zone	Zone Outs	Zone Rtg	MLB Zone
As DH	.293	437	128	22	0	15	62	55	62	.370	.446	121	120	---	---	---	---	---	---	---	---	---	---	---
As Pinch Hitter	.533	15	8	1	0	1	5	0	0	.533	.800	16	0	---	---	---	---	---	---	---	---	---	---	---

Last Five Years

	Avg	AB	H	2B	3B	HR	RBI	BB	SO	OBP	SLG
vs. Left	.276	406	112	16	0	15	75	31	71	.325	.426
vs. Right	.311	1668	519	89	2	83	282	254	199	.400	.516
Groundball	.302	490	148	23	1	19	83	62	60	.378	.469
Flyball	.301	418	126	19	1	19	71	59	57	.386	.488
Home	.295	989	292	49	0	45	170	164	141	.393	.481
Away	.312	1085	339	56	2	53	187	121	129	.380	.514
Day	.297	660	196	34	1	31	119	95	83	.382	.492
Night	.308	1414	435	71	1	67	238	190	187	.388	.501
Grass	.306	1812	555	94	2	88	318	256	235	.390	.506
Turf	.290	262	76	11	0	10	39	29	35	.356	.447
Pre-All Star	.303	1139	345	60	2	51	208	154	143	.384	.493
Post-All Star	.306	935	286	45	0	47	149	131	127	.380	.505
Scoring Posn	.280	574	161	31	2	22	254	104	74	.382	.456
Close & Late	.315	311	98	18	1	14	66	40	52	.389	.514
None on/out	.299	531	159	22	0	25		58	64	.348	.482

	Avg	AB	H	2B	3B	HR	RBI	BB	SO	OBP	SLG
First Pitch	.387	395	153	28	2	20	93	37	0	.435	.620
Ahead in Count	.336	554	186	28	0	31	102	141	0	.469	.554
Behind in Count	.217	733	159	28	0	30	92	0	223	.215	.378
Two Strikes	.222	776	172	34	0	28	103	106	270	.313	.374
Batting #4	.305	914	279	48	1	46	167	117	116	.382	.511
Batting #5	.303	712	216	35	0	32	119	102	89	.389	.487
Other	.304	448	136	22	1	20	71	66	65	.389	.491
March/April	.311	270	84	10	1	11	42	39	46	.399	.478
May	.317	344	109	26	0	17	73	45	35	.391	.541
June	.272	401	109	16	1	18	72	53	44	.355	.451
July	.316	393	124	17	0	22	69	48	62	.388	.527
August	.282	362	102	17	0	16	52	54	42	.373	.461
Sept/Oct	.339	304	103	19	0	14	49	46	41	.422	.539
vs. AL	.304	2053	624	105	2	96	353	283	268	.386	.497
vs. NL	.323	21	7	0	0	2	4	2	2	.391	.619

Batter vs. Pitcher (since 1984)

Hits Best Against	Avg	AB	H	2B	3B	HR	RBI	BB	SO	OBP	SLG	Hits Worst Against	Avg	AB	H	2B	3B	HR	RBI	BB	SO	OBP	SLG
Ariel Prieto	.600	10	6	1	0	0	2	2	2	.667	.700	Kenny Rogers	.077	13	1	0	0	0	0	1	3	.143	.077
Pete Harnisch	.500	14	7	1	0	1	3	1	2	.500	.786	Greg Cadaret	.091	11	1	0	0	0	1	4	2	.333	.091
Jose Rosado	.455	11	5	1	0	2	2	2	4	.538	1.091	Mark Langston	.139	36	5	0	0	1	3	0	12	.139	.222
Todd Stottlemyre	.395	38	15	3	0	5	13	5	6	.465	.868	Mariano Rivera	.182	11	2	0	0	0	0	0	2	.182	.182
Shawn Boskie	.375	16	6	1	0	2	2	3	2	.474	.813	Felipe Lira	.188	16	3	1	0	0	0	2	1	.188	.250

James Baldwin — White Sox

Age 26 – Pitches Right (flyball pitcher)

	ERA	W	L	Sv	G	GS	IP	BB	SO	Avg	H	2B	3B	HR	RBI	OBP	SLG	CG	ShO	Sup	QS	#P/S	SB	CS	GB	FB	G/F
1997 Season	5.26	12	15	0	32	32	200.0	83	140	.262	205	53	7	19	110	.334	.421	1	0	5.99	14	103	11	7	239	264	0.91
Career (1995-1997)	5.18	23	22	0	66	64	383.2	149	277	.269	405	86	12	49	207	.336	.439	1	0	5.86	27	98	34	17	427	517	0.83

1997 Season

	ERA	W	L	Sv	G	GS	IP	H	HR	BB	SO
Home	5.17	5	7	0	15	15	94.0	98	7	32	73
Away	5.35	7	8	0	17	17	106.0	107	12	51	67
Day	6.42	4	6	0	14	14	81.1	99	7	39	59
Night	4.47	8	9	0	18	18	118.2	106	12	44	81
Grass	5.56	9	14	0	27	27	168.1	176	17	73	119
Turf	3.69	3	1	0	5	5	31.2	29	2	10	21
March/April	5.08	0	3	0	5	5	33.2	33	2	16	25
May	4.89	2	4	0	6	6	38.2	42	2	17	25
June	3.73	3	1	0	5	5	31.1	24	2	10	23
July	6.15	2	3	0	6	6	33.2	34	3	13	19
August	4.50	4	2	0	6	6	40.0	38	5	22	34
Sept/Oct	8.34	1	2	0	4	4	22.2	34	5	5	14
Starter	5.26	12	15	0	32	32	200.0	205	19	83	140
Reliever	0.00	0	0	0	0	0	0.0	0	0	0	0
0-3 Days Rest (Start)	0.00	0	0	0	0	0	0.0	0	0	0	0
4 Days Rest	4.25	8	7	0	17	17	112.1	104	9	49	76
5+ Days Rest	6.57	4	8	0	15	15	87.2	101	10	34	64
vs. AL	5.41	11	14	0	29	29	183.0	188	19	78	131
vs. NL	3.71	1	1	0	3	3	17.0	17	0	5	9
Pre-All Star	4.70	6	9	0	18	18	115.0	115	6	43	79
Post-All Star	6.04	6	6	0	14	14	85.0	90	13	40	61

	Avg	AB	H	2B	3B	HR	RBI	BB	SO	OBP	SLG
vs. Left	.277	386	107	28	2	8	55	55	62	.365	.422
vs. Right	.247	396	98	25	5	11	55	28	78	.302	.419
Inning 1-6	.250	688	172	46	3	14	91	74	128	.325	.387
Inning 7+	.351	94	33	7	4	5	19	9	12	.404	.670
None on	.244	447	109	26	5	9	9	40	74	.310	.385
Runners on	.287	335	96	27	2	10	101	43	66	.365	.469
Scoring Posn	.285	207	59	18	1	5	87	27	43	.358	.454
Close & Late	.500	46	23	2	3	4	13	6	4	.558	.935
None on/out	.281	196	55	12	2	4	4	19	25	.347	.423
vs. 1st Batr (relief)	.000	0	0	0	0	0	0	0	0	.000	.000
1st Inning Pitched	.229	118	27	6	1	2	11	13	23	.306	.347
First 75 Pitches	.243	534	130	31	3	7	62	58	100	.318	.352
Pitch 76-90	.337	98	33	9	2	3	20	12	18	.420	.561
Pitch 91-105	.298	94	28	9	1	6	20	9	11	.356	.606
Pitch 106+	.250	56	14	4	1	3	8	4	11	.300	.518
First Pitch	.430	100	43	14	2	6	28	3	0	.448	.790
Ahead in Count	.205	375	77	19	3	7	37	0	123	.211	.328
Behind in Count	.293	150	44	9	1	5	28	39	0	.440	.467
Two Strikes	.181	365	66	15	2	5	30	41	140	.265	.274
Pre-All Star	.258	446	115	34	4	6	60	43	79	.323	.392
Post-All Star	.268	336	90	19	3	13	50	40	61	.350	.458

Career (1995-1997)

	ERA	W	L	Sv	G	GS	IP	H	HR	BB	SO
Home	4.71	11	11	0	33	32	200.2	201	25	73	149
Away	5.70	12	11	0	33	32	183.0	204	24	76	128
Day	5.80	11	8	0	30	30	166.0	194	20	67	113
Night	4.71	12	14	0	36	34	217.2	211	29	82	164
Grass	5.36	19	21	0	59	58	345.2	370	47	137	247
Turf	3.55	4	1	0	7	6	38.0	35	2	12	30
March/April	5.13	2	3	0	8	8	47.1	51	3	21	37
May	5.96	4	6	0	16	14	74.0	94	9	33	54
June	3.57	6	1	0	10	10	63.0	55	5	29	44
July	4.59	4	3	0	11	11	68.2	60	7	18	41
August	5.21	5	5	0	12	12	77.2	78	16	33	61
Sept/Oct	6.79	2	4	0	9	9	53.0	67	9	15	40
Starter	5.14	23	22	0	64	64	379.2	400	49	147	274
Reliever	9.00	0	0	0	2	0	4.0	5	0	2	3
0-3 Days Rest (Start)	7.56	1	0	0	2	2	8.1	12	4	2	7
4 Days Rest	4.79	12	13	0	35	35	216.0	212	31	94	159
5+ Days Rest	5.50	10	9	0	27	27	155.1	176	14	51	108
vs. AL	5.25	22	21	0	63	61	366.2	388	49	144	268
vs. NL	3.71	1	1	0	3	3	17.0	17	0	5	9
Pre-All Star	4.95	13	11	0	37	35	201.2	225	17	83	143
Post-All Star	5.44	10	11	0	29	29	182.0	180	32	66	134

	Avg	AB	H	2B	3B	HR	RBI	BB	SO	OBP	SLG
vs. Left	.281	777	218	45	4	21	97	97	136	.359	.430
vs. Right	.256	731	187	41	8	28	110	52	141	.311	.449
Inning 1-6	.265	1343	356	75	8	38	180	136	257	.335	.418
Inning 7+	.297	165	49	11	4	11	27	13	20	.350	.612
None on	.267	879	235	45	7	26	26	73	148	.326	.423
Runners on	.270	629	170	41	5	23	181	76	129	.350	.461
Scoring Posn	.279	362	101	27	3	12	150	46	85	.355	.470
Close & Late	.350	100	35	6	3	10	21	9	11	.409	.770
None on/out	.287	390	112	22	3	14	14	36	55	.349	.467
vs. 1st Batr (relief)	.000	2	0	0	0	0	0	0	0	.000	.000
1st Inning Pitched	.258	252	65	12	2	6	28	33	48	.346	.393
First 75 Pitches	.267	1080	288	54	8	27	132	106	201	.333	.406
Pitch 76-90	.272	191	52	11	2	5	31	18	35	.346	.429
Pitch 91-105	.300	140	42	13	1	11	31	17	23	.373	.643
Pitch 106+	.237	97	23	8	1	6	13	8	18	.295	.526
First Pitch	.394	193	76	18	3	10	46	4	0	.411	.674
Ahead in Count	.197	675	133	27	4	11	61	0	238	.202	.298
Behind in Count	.332	346	115	20	3	22	64	65	0	.438	.598
Two Strikes	.195	687	134	30	4	10	57	80	277	.279	.294
Pre-All Star	.280	804	225	54	6	17	110	83	143	.348	.425
Post-All Star	.256	704	180	32	6	32	97	66	134	.323	.455

Pitcher vs. Batter (career)

Pitches Best Vs.	Avg	AB	H	2B	3B	HR	RBI	BB	SO	OBP	SLG	Pitches Worst Vs.	Avg	AB	H	2B	3B	HR	RBI	BB	SO	OBP	SLG
Tony Pena	.000	12	0	0	0	0	0	0	2	.000	.000	Brady Anderson	.545	11	6	1	0	2	2	2	1	.615	1.182
Otis Nixon	.000	11	0	0	0	0	0	0	2	.000	.000	Tino Martinez	.545	11	6	2	0	2	4	1	2	.583	1.273
Scott Brosius	.000	11	0	0	0	0	0	0	3	.000	.000	Cecil Fielder	.500	14	7	3	0	2	8	2	0	.563	1.143
Terry Steinbach	.000	11	0	0	0	0	0	1	4	.083	.000	Curtis Pride	.500	8	4	1	1	1	3	4	2	.667	1.250
Geronimo Berroa	.000	9	0	0	0	0	0	2	0	.182	.000	Damion Easley	.417	12	5	1	1	2	8	0	2	.417	1.167

Brian Banks — Brewers
Age 27 – Bats Both

	Avg	G	AB	R	H	2B	3B	HR	RBI	BB	SO	HBP	GDP	SB	CS	OBP	SLG	IBB	SH	SF	#Pit	#P/PA	GB	FB	G/F
1997 Season	.206	28	68	9	14	1	0	1	8	6	17	0	1	0	1	.267	.265	0	0	1	273	3.64	18	23	0.78
Career (1996-1997)	.240	32	75	11	18	3	0	2	10	7	19	0	1	0	1	.301	.360	0	0	1	312	3.76	20	24	0.83

1997 Season

	Avg	AB	H	2B	3B	HR	RBI	BB	SO	OBP	SLG		Avg	AB	H	2B	3B	HR	RBI	BB	SO	OBP	SLG
vs. Left	.250	16	4	0	0	0	1	3	5	.350	.250	Scoring Posn	.286	14	4	1	0	1	8	2	2	.353	.571
vs. Right	.192	52	10	1	0	1	7	3	12	.236	.269	Close & Late	.267	15	4	0	0	0	0	0	3	.267	.267

Willie Banks — Yankees
Age 29 – Pitches Right (groundball pitcher)

	ERA	W	L	Sv	G	GS	IP	BB	SO	Avg	H	2B	3B	HR	OBP	SLG	GF	IR	IRS	Hld	SvOp	SB	CS	GB	FB	G/F
1997 Season	1.93	3	0	0	5	1	14.0	6	8	.188	9	2	1	0	3	.291	.291	1	2	0		1	0	0	19	14	1.36
Last Five Years	4.78	24	30	0	84	69	414.1	198	299	.274	440	75	7	47	207	.355	.417	4	6	3	1	2	22	14	628	388	1.62

1997 Season

	ERA	W	L	Sv	G	GS	IP	H	HR	BB	SO		Avg	AB	H	2B	3B	HR	RBI	BB	SO	OBP	SLG
Home	2.08	2	0	0	2	1	8.2	6	0	5	4	vs. Left	.214	28	6	2	0	0	2	1	5	.241	.286
Away	1.69	1	0	0	3	0	5.1	3	0	1	4	vs. Right	.150	20	3	0	1	0	1	5	3	.346	.250

Last Five Years

	ERA	W	L	Sv	G	GS	IP	H	HR	BB	SO		Avg	AB	H	2B	3B	HR	RBI	BB	SO	OBP	SLG
Home	4.26	16	16	0	45	40	239.0	244	24	104	168	vs. Left	.284	839	238	40	4	23	104	87	150	.350	.423
Away	5.49	8	14	0	39	29	175.1	196	23	94	131	vs. Right	.263	768	202	35	3	24	103	111	149	.360	.410
Day	5.14	7	12	0	29	23	140.0	148	14	60	94	Inning 1-6	.267	1423	380	66	6	41	177	175	273	.348	.408
Night	4.59	17	18	0	55	46	274.1	292	33	138	205	Inning 7+	.326	184	60	9	1	6	30	23	26	.405	.484
Grass	5.08	15	15	0	47	37	228.1	247	27	107	164	None on	.271	897	243	39	4	26	26	105	160	.349	.410
Turf	4.40	9	15	0	37	32	186.0	193	20	91	135	Runners on	.277	710	197	36	3	21	181	93	139	.361	.425
March/April	4.21	4	3	0	11	9	57.2	58	6	26	52	Scoring Posn	.274	394	108	16	1	16	164	66	85	.375	.442
May	5.37	6	4	0	18	10	67.0	75	6	32	49	Close & Late	.281	114	32	5	1	3	15	16	19	.379	.421
June	5.80	3	4	0	11	10	59.0	69	10	24	44	None on/out	.274	402	110	17	1	13	13	45	61	.348	.418
July	5.77	2	9	0	16	16	82.2	92	9	40	46	vs. 1st Batr (relief)	.308	13	4	1	0	0	0	2	4	.400	.385
August	3.91	2	6	0	12	12	73.2	75	9	34	57	1st Inning Pitched	.270	311	84	9	1	11	49	40	64	.352	.412
Sept/Oct	3.63	7	4	0	16	12	74.1	71	7	42	51	First 15 Pitches	.285	239	68	9	1	8	28	26	41	.357	.431
Starter	4.44	22	29	0	69	69	393.1	401	41	184	285	Pitch 16-30	.271	273	74	12	1	10	37	37	64	.355	.432
Reliever	11.14	2	1	0	15	0	21.0	39	6	14	14	Pitch 31-45	.244	254	62	8	1	4	28	30	49	.326	.331
0 Days rest (Relief)	0.00	0	0	0	0	0	0.0	0	0	0	0	Pitch 46+	.281	841	236	46	4	25	114	105	145	.362	.434
1 or 2 Days rest	10.00	0	1	0	8	0	9.0	14	2	7	7	First Pitch	.355	234	83	12	1	13	48	8	0	.379	.581
3+ Days rest	12.00	2	0	0	7	0	12.0	25	4	7	7	Ahead in Count	.193	643	124	18	1	12	57	0	250	.199	.280
vs. AL	3.88	14	12	0	36	31	185.1	195	17	84	146	Behind in Count	.359	437	157	33	3	16	69	128	0	.503	.558
vs. NL	5.50	10	18	0	48	38	229.0	245	30	114	153	Two Strikes	.184	705	130	17	2	12	61	62	299	.252	.265
Pre-All Star	5.11	13	16	0	47	36	220.0	237	25	99	167	Pre-All Star	.277	857	237	37	3	25	117	99	167	.353	.414
Post-All Star	4.40	11	14	0	37	33	194.1	203	22	99	132	Post-All Star	.271	750	203	38	4	22	90	99	132	.357	.420

Pitcher vs. Batter (career)

Pitches Best Vs.	Avg	AB	H	2B	3B	HR	RBI	BB	SO	OBP	SLG	Pitches Worst Vs.	Avg	AB	H	2B	3B	HR	RBI	BB	SO	OBP	SLG
Jeff King	.000	12	0	0	0	0	0	4	2	.250	.000	Fred McGriff	.625	8	5	0	0	1	3	3	0	.727	1.000
Scott Livingstone	.091	11	1	0	0	0	0	1	2	.167	.091	Thomas Howard	.500	10	5	1	0	1	1	1	1	.545	.900
Wade Boggs	.100	10	1	0	0	0	0	2	1	.250	.100	Wally Joyner	.467	15	7	3	0	0	4	2	3	.529	.667
Orlando Merced	.143	14	2	1	0	0	0	2	1	.250	.214	Bret Boone	.462	13	6	2	0	1	3	1	3	.467	.846
Derek Bell	.214	14	3	0	0	0	2	0	0	.214	.214	Carlos Baerga	.455	11	5	1	0	1	4	1	0	.500	.818

Manuel Barrios — Astros
Age 23 – Pitches Right

	ERA	W	L	Sv	G	GS	IP	BB	SO	Avg	H	2B	3B	HR	RBI	OBP	SLG	GF	IR	IRS	Hld	SvOp	SB	CS	GB	FB	G/F
1997 Season	12.00	0	0	0	2	0	3.0	3	3	.400	6	2	0	0	4	.500	.533	0	0	0	1	0	0	0	8	2	4.00

1997 Season

	ERA	W	L	Sv	G	GS	IP	H	HR	BB	SO		Avg	AB	H	2B	3B	HR	RBI	BB	SO	OBP	SLG
Home	12.00	0	0	0	2	0	3.0	6	0	3	3	vs. Left	.500	6	3	1	0	0	2	2	0	.625	.667
Away	0.00	0	0	0	0	0	0.0	0	0	0	0	vs. Right	.333	9	3	1	0	0	4	1	3	.400	.444

Tony Barron — Phillies
Age 31 – Bats Right

	Avg	G	AB	R	H	2B	3B	HR	RBI	BB	SO	HBP	GDP	SB	CS	OBP	SLG	IBB	SH	SF	#Pit	#P/PA	GB	FB	G/F
1997 Season	.286	57	189	22	54	12	1	4	24	12	38	2	2	0	1	.330	.423	0	2	3	707	3.38	78	39	2.00

1997 Season

	Avg	AB	H	2B	3B	HR	RBI	BB	SO	OBP	SLG		Avg	AB	H	2B	3B	HR	RBI	BB	SO	OBP	SLG
vs. Left	.339	59	20	7	1	1	7	7	12	.403	.542	Scoring Posn	.256	43	11	1	0	0	16	5	8	.327	.279
vs. Right	.262	130	34	5	0	3	17	5	26	.295	.369	Close & Late	.267	30	8	1	0	0	3	2	6	.313	.300

1997 Season

	Avg	AB	H	2B	3B	HR	RBI	BB	SO	OBP	SLG		Avg	AB	H	2B	3B	HR	RBI	BB	SO	OBP	SLG
Home	.343	108	37	10	1	3	13	9	17	.398	.537	None on/out	.302	53	16	3	0	2	2	1	7	.315	.472
Away	.210	81	17	2	0	1	11	3	21	.239	.272	Batting #6	.192	26	5	0	1	0	4	3	9	.276	.269
First Pitch	.395	38	15	4	0	0	4	0	0	.375	.500	Batting #7	.294	136	40	10	0	3	14	7	26	.333	.434
Ahead in Count	.355	31	11	1	0	2	5	9	0	.488	.581	Other	.333	27	9	2	0	1	6	2	3	.367	.519
Behind in Count	.186	86	16	4	1	1	10	0	31	.205	.291	Pre-All Star	.000	0	0	0	0	0	0	0	0	.000	.000
Two Strikes	.183	82	15	2	1	1	6	3	38	.230	.268	Post-All Star	.286	189	54	12	1	4	24	12	38	.330	.423

Kimera Bartee — Tigers   Age 25 – Bats Both

	Avg	G	AB	R	H	2B	3B	HR	RBI	BB	SO	HBP	GDP	SB	CS	OBP	SLG	IBB	SH	SF	#Pit	#P/PA	GB	FB	G/F
1997 Season	.200	12	5	4	1	0	0	0	0	2	1	0	3	1		.500	.200	0	0	0	31	3.88	1	1	1.00
Career (1996-1997)	.252	122	222	36	56	6	1	1	14	19	79	1	1	23	11	.314	.302	0	13	0	954	3.74	56	41	1.37

1997 Season

	Avg	AB	H	2B	3B	HR	RBI	BB	SO	OBP	SLG		Avg	AB	H	2B	3B	HR	RBI	BB	SO	OBP	SLG
vs. Left	.000	1	0	0	0	0	0	0	1	.500	.000	Scoring Posn	.000	1	0	0	0	0	0	0	0	.000	.000
vs. Right	.250	4	1	0	0	0	0	2	1	.500	.250	Close & Late	.000	0	0	0	0	0	0	0	0	.000	.000

Richard Batchelor — Padres   Age 31 – Pitches Right (groundball pitcher)

	ERA	W	L	Sv	G	GS	IP	BB	SO	Avg	H	2B	3B	HR	RBI	OBP	SLG	GF	IR	IRS	Hld	SvOp	SB	CS	GB	FB	G/F
1997 Season	5.97	3	1	0	23	0	28.2	14	18	.339	40	5	0	2	21	.422	.432	8	13	8	0	2	3	1	49	26	1.88
Career (1993-1997)	5.03	5	1	0	43	0	53.2	18	33	.301	63	9	0	3	29	.362	.388	17	19	10	1	2	5	1	80	51	1.57

1997 Season

	ERA	W	L	Sv	G	GS	IP	H	HR	BB	SO		Avg	AB	H	2B	3B	HR	RBI	BB	SO	OBP	SLG
Home	10.32	2	0	0	11	0	11.1	20	1	10	7	vs. Left	.271	48	13	2	0	1	10	9	9	.386	.375
Away	3.12	1	1	0	12	0	17.1	20	1	4	11	vs. Right	.386	70	27	3	0	1	11	5	9	.449	.471

Jason Bates — Rockies   Age 27 – Bats Both

	Avg	G	AB	R	H	2B	3B	HR	RBI	BB	SO	HBP	GDP	SB	CS	OBP	SLG	IBB	SH	SF	#Pit	#P/PA	GB	FB	G/F
1997 Season	.240	62	121	17	29	10	0	3	11	15	27	3	3	0	1	.338	.397	1	0	0	537	3.86	38	41	0.93
Career (1995-1997)	.245	266	603	78	148	35	5	12	66	80	131	7	14	5	8	.340	.380	5	3	1	2545	3.67	223	162	1.38

1997 Season

	Avg	AB	H	2B	3B	HR	RBI	BB	SO	OBP	SLG		Avg	AB	H	2B	3B	HR	RBI	BB	SO	OBP	SLG
vs. Left	.179	28	5	3	0	0	0	5	8	.361	.286	Scoring Posn	.200	25	5	2	0	0	7	4	9	.333	.280
vs. Right	.258	93	24	7	0	3	11	10	19	.330	.430	Close & Late	.190	21	4	2	0	1	3	2	8	.292	.429
Home	.304	56	17	5	0	1	6	9	8	.409	.446	None on/out	.259	27	7	1	0	2	2	3	5	.355	.519
Away	.185	65	12	5	0	2	5	6	19	.274	.354	Batting #8	.190	63	12	2	0	1	4	5	12	.271	.270
First Pitch	.167	18	3	1	0	0	0	0	0	.211	.222	Batting #9	.308	26	8	7	0	0	2	3	9	.379	.577
Ahead in Count	.250	28	7	2	0	1	3	11	0	.475	.429	Other	.281	32	9	1	0	2	5	7	6	.425	.500
Behind in Count	.238	42	10	4	0	0	5	0	18	.238	.333	Pre-All Star	.238	80	19	6	0	2	8	8	17	.322	.388
Two Strikes	.228	57	13	5	0	1	6	4	27	.279	.368	Post-All Star	.244	41	10	4	0	1	3	7	10	.367	.415

Career (1995-1997)

	Avg	AB	H	2B	3B	HR	RBI	BB	SO	OBP	SLG		Avg	AB	H	2B	3B	HR	RBI	BB	SO	OBP	SLG
vs. Left	.199	141	28	8	1	2	14	22	37	.317	.312	First Pitch	.313	115	36	7	3	3	13	3	0	.347	.504
vs. Right	.260	462	120	27	4	10	52	58	94	.347	.400	Ahead in Count	.288	132	38	12	0	5	17	45	0	.469	.492
Groundball	.262	130	34	7	1	1	16	17	17	.356	.354	Behind in Count	.165	242	40	10	2	1	23	0	109	.169	.236
Flyball	.269	108	29	5	1	6	13	14	24	.352	.500	Two Strikes	.176	273	48	10	2	2	27	32	131	.262	.249
Home	.308	286	88	21	4	6	41	46	56	.409	.472	Batting #2	.233	133	31	8	0	5	18	19	24	.327	.406
Away	.189	317	60	14	1	6	25	34	75	.275	.297	Batting #8	.259	216	56	8	1	3	24	32	49	.365	.347
Day	.246	264	65	19	2	3	27	41	53	.357	.367	Other	.240	254	61	19	4	4	24	29	58	.325	.394
Night	.245	339	83	16	3	9	39	39	78	.326	.389	March/April	.264	91	24	3	1	3	6	9	13	.337	.418
Grass	.246	447	110	29	4	7	52	65	98	.349	.376	May	.256	156	40	5	1	5	17	21	33	.352	.397
Turf	.244	156	38	6	1	5	14	15	33	.314	.391	June	.228	114	26	13	0	1	14	14	24	.323	.368
Pre-All Star	.249	370	92	22	2	9	39	46	71	.339	.392	July	.240	75	18	5	2	1	13	11	10	.333	.400
Post-All Star	.240	233	56	13	3	3	27	34	60	.342	.361	August	.264	87	23	6	0	2	8	13	29	.366	.402
Scoring Posn	.299	137	41	8	2	1	51	29	32	.426	.409	Sept/Oct	.213	80	17	3	1	0	8	12	22	.323	.275
Close & Late	.153	98	15	5	1	2	8	16	32	.284	.286	vs. AL	.143	7	1	0	0	0	1	2	4	.333	.143
None on/out	.256	172	44	11	2	6	6	12	34	.312	.448	vs. NL	.247	596	147	35	5	12	65	78	127	.340	.383

Batter vs. Pitcher (career)

Hits Best Against	Avg	AB	H	2B	3B	HR	RBI	BB	SO	OBP	SLG	Hits Worst Against	Avg	AB	H	2B	3B	HR	RBI	BB	SO	OBP	SLG
												Mark Leiter	.182	11	2	0	0	1	1	2	4	.308	.455

Miguel Batista — Cubs   Age 27 – Pitches Right (groundball pitcher)

	ERA	W	L	Sv	G	GS	IP	BB	SO	Avg	H	2B	3B	HR	RBI	OBP	SLG	CG	ShO	Sup	QS	#P/S	SB	CS	GB	FB	G/F
1997 Season	5.70	0	5	0	11	6	36.1	24	27	.267	36	7	1	4	20	.372	.422	0	0	1.98	3	90	4	2	50	36	1.39
Last Five Years	5.66	0	5	0	20	6	47.2	31	33	.259	45	9	1	4	23	.367	.391	0	0	2.64	3	90	5	2	68	45	1.51

1997 Season

	ERA	W	L	Sv	G	GS	IP	H	HR	BB	SO		Avg	AB	H	2B	3B	HR	RBI	BB	SO	OBP	SLG
Home	6.59	0	2	0	4	3	13.2	15	4	5	10	vs. Left	.258	62	16	4	1	0	5	11	11	.365	.355
Away	5.16	0	3	0	7	3	22.2	21	0	19	17	vs. Right	.274	73	20	3	0	4	15	13	16	.378	.479

Tony Batista — Athletics
Age 24 – Bats Right

	Avg	G	AB	R	H	2B	3B	HR	RBI	BB	SO	HBP	GDP	SB	CS	OBP	SLG	IBB	SH	SF	#Pit	#P/PA	GB	FB	G/F
1997 Season	.202	68	188	22	38	10	1	4	18	14	31	2	8	2	2	.265	.330	0	3	0	764	3.69	78	58	1.34
Career (1996-1997)	.256	142	426	60	109	20	3	10	43	33	80	3	10	9	5	.313	.387	0	3	2	1812	3.88	175	114	1.54

1997 Season

	Avg	AB	H	2B	3B	HR	RBI	BB	SO	OBP	SLG		Avg	AB	H	2B	3B	HR	RBI	BB	SO	OBP	SLG
vs. Left	.150	60	9	3	0	0	2	3	11	.190	.200	Scoring Posn	.256	43	11	5	0	2	16	2	8	.289	.512
vs. Right	.227	128	29	7	1	4	16	11	20	.298	.391	Close & Late	.227	22	5	0	0	0	0	2	5	.292	.227
Home	.206	107	22	5	0	0	5	7	18	.261	.252	None on/out	.217	46	10	2	0	0	0	8	8	.333	.261
Away	.198	81	16	5	1	4	13	7	13	.270	.432	Batting #8	.188	69	13	5	1	1	4	4	8	.233	.333
First Pitch	.176	17	3	1	0	0	3	0	0	.222	.235	Batting #9	.292	48	14	3	0	2	12	5	9	.370	.479
Ahead in Count	.324	34	11	2	0	3	7	10	0	.477	.647	Other	.155	71	11	2	0	1	2	5	14	.221	.225
Behind in Count	.181	94	17	5	1	1	7	0	25	.181	.287	Pre-All Star	.178	101	18	4	1	4	11	7	21	.245	.356
Two Strikes	.191	94	18	5	1	0	3	4	31	.224	.266	Post-All Star	.230	87	20	6	0	0	7	7	10	.287	.299

Danny Bautista — Braves
Age 26 – Bats Right (groundball hitter)

	Avg	G	AB	R	H	2B	3B	HR	RBI	BB	SO	HBP	GDP	SB	CS	OBP	SLG	IBB	SH	SF	#Pit	#P/PA	GB	FB	G/F
1997 Season	.243	64	103	14	25	3	2	3	9	5	24	1	3	2	0	.282	.398	1	2	1	415	3.71	41	22	1.86
Career (1993-1997)	.228	243	618	73	141	21	3	17	69	32	140	2	17	11	6	.268	.354	1	8	2	2346	3.54	248	136	1.82

1997 Season

	Avg	AB	H	2B	3B	HR	RBI	BB	SO	OBP	SLG		Avg	AB	H	2B	3B	HR	RBI	BB	SO	OBP	SLG
vs. Left	.262	61	16	2	0	1	3	3	12	.308	.344	Scoring Posn	.294	17	5	0	0	0	5	2	5	.381	.294
vs. Right	.214	42	9	1	2	2	6	2	12	.244	.476	Close & Late	.407	27	11	2	1	3	5	2	9	.452	.889

Career (1993-1997)

	Avg	AB	H	2B	3B	HR	RBI	BB	SO	OBP	SLG		Avg	AB	H	2B	3B	HR	RBI	BB	SO	OBP	SLG
vs. Left	.229	253	58	7	1	9	28	12	48	.267	.372	First Pitch	.239	88	21	4	1	5	18	1	0	.242	.477
vs. Right	.227	365	83	14	2	8	41	20	92	.268	.342	Ahead in Count	.323	127	41	3	0	7	20	17	0	.403	.512
Groundball	.236	144	34	5	2	5	18	7	34	.270	.403	Behind in Count	.164	292	48	7	0	2	17	0	122	.170	.209
Flyball	.214	103	22	5	0	3	11	4	19	.250	.350	Two Strikes	.146	281	41	6	1	1	13	14	140	.189	.185
Home	.198	288	57	9	3	6	25	17	65	.247	.313	Batting #7	.240	200	48	6	1	8	24	10	46	.276	.400
Away	.255	330	84	12	0	11	44	15	75	.286	.391	Batting #9	.225	151	34	6	1	6	19	8	24	.263	.397
Day	.228	215	49	9	0	7	20	11	59	.265	.367	Other	.221	267	59	9	1	3	26	14	70	.264	.296
Night	.228	403	92	12	3	10	49	21	81	.269	.347	March/April	.321	78	25	2	0	3	14	9	15	.391	.462
Grass	.226	541	122	19	3	14	57	29	120	.267	.349	May	.168	95	16	3	0	2	7	7	33	.225	.263
Turf	.247	77	19	2	0	3	12	3	20	.275	.390	June	.201	134	27	5	1	1	12	5	31	.236	.276
Pre-All Star	.217	341	74	11	1	6	36	23	83	.268	.308	July	.227	119	27	5	2	5	14	6	19	.264	.429
Post-All Star	.242	277	67	10	2	11	33	9	57	.266	.412	August	.177	79	14	1	0	2	8	2	20	.205	.266
Scoring Posn	.221	172	38	6	0	3	47	9	39	.261	.308	Sept/Oct	.283	113	32	5	0	4	14	3	22	.299	.434
Close & Late	.267	90	24	2	1	4	11	6	21	.316	.444	vs. AL	.226	508	115	18	1	14	60	26	114	.264	.348
None on/out	.290	145	42	7	1	9	9	5	27	.313	.538	vs. NL	.236	110	26	3	2	3	9	6	26	.286	.382

Batter vs. Pitcher (career)

Hits Best Against	Avg	AB	H	2B	3B	HR	RBI	BB	SO	OBP	SLG	Hits Worst Against	Avg	AB	H	2B	3B	HR	RBI	BB	SO	OBP	SLG
												Andy Pettitte	.167	12	2	0	0	0	0	0	4	.167	.167
												Mark Langston	.167	12	2	0	0	0	1	1	1	.231	.167
												Chuck Finley	.200	10	2	0	0	0	0	1	3	.273	.200

Jose Bautista — Cardinals
Age 33 – Pitches Right

	ERA	W	L	Sv	G	GS	IP	BB	SO	Avg	H	2B	3B	HR	RBI	OBP	SLG	GF	IR	IRS	Hld	SvOp	SB	CS	GB	FB	G/F
1997 Season	6.66	2	2	0	32	0	52.2	14	23	.318	70	10	0	8	34	.367	.473	7	22	5	2	0	5	1	96	63	1.52
Last Five Years	4.50	22	22	3	237	14	404.0	99	204	.277	436	76	7	63	237	.324	.454	76	149	55	30	7	26	10	614	483	1.27

1997 Season

	ERA	W	L	Sv	G	GS	IP	H	HR	BB	SO		Avg	AB	H	2B	3B	HR	RBI	BB	SO	OBP	SLG
Home	4.91	2	1	0	18	0	36.2	40	6	11	14	vs. Left	.234	94	22	1	0	2	10	7	11	.294	.309
Away	10.69	0	1	0	14	0	16.0	30	2	3	9	vs. Right	.381	126	48	9	0	6	24	7	12	.422	.595
Starter	0.00	0	0	0	0	0	0.0	0	0	0	0	Scoring Posn	.323	65	21	3	0	1	23	5	8	.380	.415
Reliever	6.66	2	2	0	32	0	52.2	70	8	14	23	Close & Late	.357	14	5	1	0	0	2	1	3	.400	.429
0 Days rest (Relief)	0.00	1	0	0	3	0	4.0	3	0	2	2	None on/out	.306	49	15	1	0	0	0	6		.370	.510
1 or 2 Days rest	8.05	0	0	0	14	0	19.0	26	4	5	6	First Pitch	.421	38	16	2	0	4	9	3	0	.476	.789
3+ Days rest	6.67	1	2	0	15	0	29.2	41	4	7	15	Ahead in Count	.231	91	21	5	0	1	8	0	20	.239	.319
Pre-All Star	5.54	2	2	0	18	0	37.1	45	6	10	17	Behind in Count	.362	47	17	3	0	2	11	5	0	.434	.553
Post-All Star	9.39	0	0	0	14	0	15.1	25	2	4	6	Two Strikes	.173	81	14	3	0	0	4	6	23	.239	.210

Last Five Years

	ERA	W	L	Sv	G	GS	IP	H	HR	BB	SO		Avg	AB	H	2B	3B	HR	RBI	BB	SO	OBP	SLG
Home	3.90	14	10	1	128	6	228.1	226	35	56	119	vs. Left	.278	663	184	26	3	25	99	63	80	.342	.439
Away	5.28	8	12	2	109	8	175.2	210	28	43	85	vs. Right	.276	913	252	50	4	38	138	36	124	.310	.464
Day	4.32	9	14	1	122	8	202.0	225	28	54	108	Inning 1-6	.275	687	189	31	1	29	117	39	68	.316	.450
Night	4.68	13	8	2	115	6	202.0	211	35	45	96	Inning 7+	.278	889	247	45	6	34	120	60	136	.330	.457
Grass	4.15	17	15	3	185	11	329.2	348	51	76	168	None on	.271	921	250	51	4	32	32	34	100	.305	.440
Turf	6.05	5	7	0	52	3	74.1	88	12	23	36	Runners on	.284	655	186	25	3	31	205	65	96	.349	.473
March/April	6.37	0	3	0	25	0	41.0	53	8	14	29	Scoring Posn	.298	399	119	16	2	16	167	46	58	.367	.469
May	3.53	3	3	0	45	2	71.1	72	11	14	35	Close & Late	.262	355	93	12	2	10	35	33	53	.327	.392
June	3.64	4	5	1	44	7	99.0	92	13	22	45	None on/out	.264	386	102	18	2	18	18	19	46	.302	.461
July	5.52	8	3	0	52	0	73.1	98	8	21	43	vs. 1st Batr (relief)	.287	209	60	5	3	13	44	7	30	.308	.526

Last Five Years

	ERA	W	L	Sv	G	GS	IP	H	HR	BB	SO		Avg	AB	H	2B	3B	HR	RBI	BB	SO	OBP	SLG
August	3.90	1	6	2	41	1	64.2	59	11	17	27	1st Inning Pitched	.291	829	241	38	6	37	152	46	109	.332	.485
Sept/Oct	5.27	6	2	0	30	4	54.2	62	12	11	25	First 15 Pitches	.292	785	229	35	6	35	127	36	89	.326	.485
Starter	4.63	5	6	0	14	14	83.2	89	13	20	39	Pitch 16-30	.270	411	111	23	1	13	59	43	60	.346	.426
Reliever	4.47	17	16	3	223	0	320.1	347	50	79	165	Pitch 31-45	.288	160	46	6	0	6	27	11	26	.333	.438
0 Days rest (Relief)	2.49	5	6	0	57	0	83.0	71	12	22	49	Pitch 46+	.227	220	50	12	0	9	24	9	29	.264	.405
1 or 2 Days rest	4.02	9	6	3	103	0	138.2	142	18	33	66	First Pitch	.322	276	89	7	3	22	56	16	0	.363	.609
3+ Days rest	6.75	3	4	0	63	0	98.2	134	20	24	50	Ahead in Count	.234	687	161	37	2	11	74	0	176	.242	.342
vs. AL	6.25	2	2	0	21	0	40.1	53	5	12	17	Behind in Count	.361	319	115	19	2	24	75	45	0	.438	.658
vs. NL	4.31	20	20	3	216	14	363.2	383	58	87	187	Two Strikes	.215	627	135	31	2	9	66	38	204	.264	.314
Pre-All Star	4.25	12	12	1	132	9	241.1	258	34	62	127	Pre-All Star	.275	938	258	47	4	34	132	62	127	.326	.442
Post-All Star	4.87	10	10	2	105	5	162.2	178	29	37	77	Post-All Star	.279	638	178	29	3	29	105	37	77	.321	.470

Pitcher vs. Batter (career)

Pitches Best Vs.	Avg	AB	H	2B	3B	HR	RBI	BB	SO	OBP	SLG	Pitches Worst Vs.	Avg	AB	H	2B	3B	HR	RBI	BB	SO	OBP	SLG
Jeff King	.077	13	1	1	0	0	0	0	0	.077	.154	David Segui	.600	10	6	2	0	2	6	2	0	.667	1.400
Brian Jordan	.077	13	1	1	0	0	0	0	0	.143	.154	Rickey Henderson	.556	9	5	2	0	0	0	3	0	.667	.778
Don Slaught	.091	11	1	0	0	0	1	0	3	.091	.091	Mike Piazza	.500	16	8	1	0	2	5	0	1	.471	.938
Carlos Garcia	.100	10	1	0	0	0	0	0	1	.182	.100	Craig Biggio	.500	12	6	1	1	0	3	0	2	.538	.750
Jeff Conine	.111	9	1	0	0	0	1	1	1	.182	.111	Jeff Bagwell	.364	11	4	0	0	2	7	1	2	.385	.909

Trey Beamon — Padres

Age 24 – Bats Left

	Avg	G	AB	R	H	2B	3B	HR	RBI	BB	SO	HBP	GDP	SB	CS	OBP	SLG	IBB	SH	SF	#Pit	#P/PA	GB	FB	G/F
1997 Season	.277	43	65	5	18	3	0	0	7	2	17	1	1	1	2	.309	.323	0	0	0	242	3.56	20	13	1.54
Career (1996-1997)	.250	67	116	12	29	5	0	0	13	6	23	1	1	1	2	.293	.293	0	1	0	448	3.61	42	27	1.56

1997 Season

	Avg	AB	H	2B	3B	HR	RBI	BB	SO	OBP	SLG		Avg	AB	H	2B	3B	HR	RBI	BB	SO	OBP	SLG
vs. Left	.286	7	2	1	0	0	1	0	1	.286	.429	Scoring Posn	.400	15	6	0	0	0	6	0	0	.400	.400
vs. Right	.276	58	16	2	0	0	6	2	16	.311	.310	Close & Late	.154	13	2	0	0	0	1	2	5	.267	.154

Rod Beck — Giants

Age 29 – Pitches Right (flyball pitcher)

	ERA	W	L	Sv	G	GS	IP	BB	SO	Avg	H	2B	3B	HR	RBI	OBP	SLG	GF	IR	IRS	Hld	SvOp	SB	CS	GB	FB	G/F
1997 Season	3.47	7	4	37	73	0	70.0	8	53	.249	67	7	1	7	33	.276	.361	66	15	4	1	45	3	0	86	88	0.98
Last Five Years	3.19	17	24	181	320	0	318.2	65	268	.241	289	35	4	44	149	.282	.386	294	136	37	1	210	14	3	353	414	0.85

1997 Season

	ERA	W	L	Sv	G	GS	IP	H	HR	BB	SO		Avg	AB	H	2B	3B	HR	RBI	BB	SO	OBP	SLG
Home	2.72	4	1	21	40	0	39.2	38	1	6	35	vs. Left	.234	137	32	1	0	2	14	6	27	.271	.285
Away	4.45	3	3	16	33	0	30.1	29	6	2	18	vs. Right	.265	132	35	6	1	5	19	2	26	.281	.439
Day	1.59	5	0	13	32	0	34.0	30	1	3	32	Inning 1-6	.000	0	0	0	0	0	0	0	0	.000	.000
Night	5.25	2	4	24	41	0	36.0	37	6	5	21	Inning 7+	.249	269	67	7	1	7	33	8	53	.276	.361
Grass	3.57	5	3	31	61	0	58.0	57	5	8	45	None on	.228	158	36	2	1	4	4	3	28	.252	.329
Turf	3.00	2	1	6	12	0	12.0	10	2	0	8	Runners on	.279	111	31	5	0	3	29	5	25	.310	.405
March/April	4.66	0	1	11	12	0	9.2	11	2	1	10	Scoring Posn	.321	56	18	4	0	2	27	3	14	.356	.500
May	2.19	3	1	6	14	0	12.1	14	1	2	9	Close & Late	.254	169	43	5	0	4	24	6	34	.284	.355
June	1.42	1	0	9	13	0	12.2	9	1	0	10	None on/out	.246	65	16	1	0	1	1	2	7	.279	.308
July	4.66	0	0	6	11	0	9.2	5	1	2	4	vs. 1st Batr (relief)	.294	68	20	2	0	1	4	3	7	.333	.368
August	5.56	0	1	2	11	0	11.1	14	1	3	7	1st Inning Pitched	.258	256	66	7	1	7	33	8	50	.283	.375
Sept/Oct	3.14	3	1	3	12	0	14.1	14	1	0	13	First 15 Pitches	.243	218	53	4	1	5	17	5	36	.263	.339
Starter	0.00	0	0	0	0	0	0.0	0	0	0	0	Pitch 16-30	.292	48	14	3	0	2	16	3	16	.346	.479
Reliever	3.47	7	4	37	73	0	70.0	67	7	8	53	Pitch 31-45	.000	3	0	0	0	0	0	0	1	.000	.000
0 Days rest (Relief)	3.38	1	0	12	22	0	18.2	19	2	2	23	Pitch 46+	.000	0	0	0	0	0	0	0	0	.000	.000
1 or 2 Days rest	4.14	5	4	19	36	0	37.0	39	4	4	25	First Pitch	.366	41	15	1	0	1	9	2	0	.409	.512
3+ Days rest	1.88	1	0	6	15	0	14.1	9	1	2	5	Ahead in Count	.223	139	31	3	0	3	13	0	46	.229	.309
vs. AL	5.59	1	1	5	10	0	9.2	10	0	2	6	Behind in Count	.256	39	10	0	1	1	5	3	0	.310	.385
vs. NL	3.13	6	3	32	63	0	60.1	57	7	6	47	Two Strikes	.177	130	23	2	0	3	10	3	53	.201	.262
Pre-All Star	2.43	4	2	29	42	0	37.0	34	4	3	30	Pre-All Star	.245	139	34	2	1	4	10	3	30	.261	.360
Post-All Star	4.64	3	2	8	31	0	33.0	33	3	5	23	Post-All Star	.254	130	33	5	0	3	23	5	23	.292	.362

Last Five Years

	ERA	W	L	Sv	G	GS	IP	H	HR	BB	SO		Avg	AB	H	2B	3B	HR	RBI	BB	SO	OBP	SLG
Home	3.05	13	11	91	176	0	177.1	157	23	38	150	vs. Left	.227	600	136	13	3	17	71	43	137	.276	.343
Away	3.38	4	13	90	144	0	141.1	132	21	27	118	vs. Right	.255	601	153	22	1	27	78	22	131	.288	.429
Day	2.48	9	9	88	157	0	163.0	142	25	27	141	Inning 1-6	.000	0	0	0	0	0	0	0	0	.000	.000
Night	3.93	8	15	93	163	0	155.2	147	19	38	127	Inning 7+	.241	1201	289	35	4	44	149	65	268	.282	.386
Grass	3.03	14	19	144	261	0	261.0	230	34	56	218	None on	.243	678	165	21	2	20	20	30	152	.283	.369
Turf	3.90	3	5	37	59	0	57.2	59	10	9	50	Runners on	.237	523	124	14	2	24	129	35	116	.281	.409
March/April	2.08	2	2	26	40	0	39.0	23	3	5	42	Scoring Posn	.231	268	62	7	2	13	104	27	65	.293	.418
May	2.34	7	7	36	65	0	65.1	54	8	11	52	Close & Late	.254	795	202	26	2	31	122	54	179	.304	.409
June	3.21	3	3	29	54	0	53.1	55	9	10	51	None on/out	.220	273	60	7	1	9	9	15	50	.271	.352
July	4.10	5	0	34	62	0	59.1	59	8	16	44	vs. 1st Batr (relief)	.214	295	63	8	1	10	32	16	58	.259	.349
August	4.38	1	3	32	52	0	51.1	56	9	16	40	1st Inning Pitched	.239	1102	263	29	4	38	137	58	241	.278	.376
Sept/Oct	2.86	4	4	24	47	0	50.1	42	7	7	39	First 15 Pitches	.239	948	227	25	4	30	95	38	201	.270	.369
Starter	0.00	0	0	0	0	0	0.0	0	0	0	0	Pitch 16-30	.258	240	62	10	0	14	54	25	64	.330	.475
Reliever	3.19	17	24	181	320	0	318.2	289	44	65	268	Pitch 31-45	.000	13	0	0	0	0	0	0	2	.188	.000
0 Days rest (Relief)	3.56	7	8	64	104	0	101.0	100	15	24	87	Pitch 46+	.000	0	0	0	0	0	0	0	0	.000	.000

Last Five Years

	ERA	W	L	Sv	G	GS	IP	H	HR	BB	SO		Avg	AB	H	2B	3B	HR	RBI	BB	SO	OBP	SLG
1 or 2 Days rest	3.11	9	11	77	135	0	136.0	125	16	27	117	First Pitch	.322	177	57	11	1	3	22	10	0	.366	.446
3+ Days rest	2.87	1	5	40	81	0	81.2	64	13	14	64	Ahead in Count	.200	654	131	14	1	23	69	0	238	.204	.330
vs. AL	5.59	1	1	5	10	0	9.2	10	0	2	6	Behind in Count	.310	184	57	4	1	10	32	21	0	.371	.505
vs. NL	3.12	16	23	176	310	0	309.0	279	44	63	262	Two Strikes	.178	612	109	13	1	22	62	33	268	.223	.310
Pre-All Star	2.68	12	15	103	180	0	177.2	151	25	30	160	Pre-All Star	.230	657	151	18	4	25	69	30	160	.261	.384
Post-All Star	3.83	5	9	78	140	0	141.0	138	19	35	108	Post-All Star	.254	544	138	17	0	19	80	35	108	.306	.390

Pitcher vs. Batter (career)

Pitches Best Vs.	Avg	AB	H	2B	3B	HR	RBI	BB	SO	OBP	SLG	Pitches Worst Vs.	Avg	AB	H	2B	3B	HR	RBI	BB	SO	OBP	SLG
Todd Hundley	.071	14	1	0	0	0	2	0	4	.067	.071	Mike Lansing	.700	10	7	1	0	0	2	0	1	.727	.800
Henry Rodriguez	.077	13	1	0	0	0	0	0	3	.077	.077	Jeff Blauser	.455	11	5	2	0	0	1	3	4	.571	.636
Ryne Sandberg	.091	11	1	0	0	0	2	0	4	.083	.091	Steve Finley	.429	14	6	2	0	3	4	0	1	.429	1.214
Terry Pendleton	.100	20	2	1	0	0	0	1	7	.143	.150	Fred McGriff	.333	12	4	0	0	2	5	0	2	.333	.833
Mickey Morandini	.133	15	2	0	0	0	0	1	2	.188	.133	Derrick May	.308	13	4	0	0	1	1	2	2	.400	.538

Rich Becker — Twins

Age 26 – Bats Left (groundball hitter)

	Avg	G	AB	R	H	2B	3B	HR	RBI	BB	SO	HBP	GDP	SB	CS	OBP	SLG	IBB	SH	SF	#Pit	#P/PA	GB	FB	G/F
1997 Season	.264	132	443	61	117	22	3	10	45	62	130	1	4	17	5	.354	.395	1	2	2	2031	3.98	138	110	1.25
Career (1993-1997)	.267	417	1465	213	391	73	8	25	157	182	372	7	29	51	21	.349	.379	2	14	8	6464	3.85	536	340	1.58

1997 Season

	Avg	AB	H	2B	3B	HR	RBI	BB	SO	OBP	SLG		Avg	AB	H	2B	3B	HR	RBI	BB	SO	OBP	SLG
vs. Left	.156	64	10	2	0	0	3	9	23	.260	.188	First Pitch	.329	70	23	5	1	2	10	0	0	.338	.514
vs. Right	.282	379	107	20	3	10	42	53	107	.370	.430	Ahead in Count	.385	78	30	2	1	2	12	28	0	.547	.513
Groundball	.310	100	31	9	1	1	8	20	29	.425	.450	Behind in Count	.174	195	34	9	1	3	15	0	99	.173	.277
Flyball	.250	72	18	3	0	1	2	6	21	.308	.333	Two Strikes	.188	224	42	10	1	5	18	34	130	.292	.308
Home	.278	223	62	14	1	4	27	34	62	.376	.404	Batting #2	.233	245	57	12	1	4	27	38	68	.333	.339
Away	.250	220	55	8	2	6	18	28	68	.332	.386	Batting #8	.331	124	41	6	2	4	11	11	38	.390	.508
Day	.295	149	44	8	0	5	15	19	40	.375	.450	Other	.257	74	19	4	0	2	7	13	24	.368	.392
Night	.248	294	73	14	3	5	30	43	90	.344	.367	March/April	.216	88	19	0	0	2	9	16	24	.337	.284
Grass	.249	177	44	8	2	4	11	21	55	.328	.384	May	.341	82	28	5	1	1	10	15	23	.439	.463
Turf	.274	266	73	14	1	6	34	41	75	.371	.402	June	.254	63	16	5	0	2	2	6	19	.319	.429
Pre-All Star	.256	250	64	10	1	6	22	38	70	.353	.376	July	.239	71	17	4	1	2	11	5	17	.286	.408
Post-All Star	.275	193	53	12	2	4	23	24	60	.356	.420	August	.278	72	20	6	0	2	7	13	24	.395	.444
Scoring Posn	.243	103	25	4	1	5	36	24	37	.380	.447	Sept/Oct	.254	67	17	2	1	1	6	7	23	.324	.358
Close & Late	.243	70	17	1	1	1	4	3	19	.274	.329	vs. AL	.272	401	109	21	3	7	41	58	121	.362	.392
None on/out	.292	89	26	6	0	1	1	10	19	.364	.393	vs. NL	.190	42	8	1	0	3	4	4	9	.277	.429

1997 By Position

Position	Avg	AB	H	2B	3B	HR	RBI	BB	SO	OBP	SLG	G	GS	Innings	PO	A	E	DP	Fld Pct	Rng Fctr	In Zone	Zone Outs	Zone Rtg	MLB Zone
As Pinch Hitter	.455	11	5	1	0	0	0	0	2	.455	.545	11	0	---	---	---	---	---	---	---	---	---	---	---
As cf	.253	391	99	19	2	10	42	55	115	.345	.389	115	106	932.0	284	5	5	1	.983	2.79	360	280	.778	.815
As rf	.158	19	3	0	0	0	0	5	7	.333	.158	13	5	57.2	18	0	0	0	1.000	2.81	22	18	.818	.813

Career (1993-1997)

	Avg	AB	H	2B	3B	HR	RBI	BB	SO	OBP	SLG		Avg	AB	H	2B	3B	HR	RBI	BB	SO	OBP	SLG
vs. Left	.171	275	47	10	0	0	14	26	100	.254	.207	First Pitch	.362	243	88	20	2	5	30	1	0	.367	.523
vs. Right	.289	1190	344	63	8	25	143	156	272	.370	.418	Ahead in Count	.355	310	110	21	1	5	44	80	0	.486	.477
Groundball	.277	379	105	25	2	3	43	39	87	.344	.377	Behind in Count	.174	632	110	17	4	8	50	0	307	.180	.252
Flyball	.274	219	60	11	1	2	15	36	61	.379	.361	Two Strikes	.175	690	121	16	5	11	55	101	372	.283	.261
Home	.282	721	203	40	2	14	89	88	177	.360	.401	Batting #2	.276	910	251	48	5	16	116	105	210	.349	.392
Away	.253	744	188	33	6	11	68	94	195	.338	.358	Batting #8	.285	228	65	12	2	4	15	24	71	.361	.408
Day	.251	418	105	22	0	10	39	53	110	.339	.376	Other	.229	327	75	13	1	5	26	53	91	.340	.321
Night	.273	1047	286	51	8	15	118	129	262	.353	.380	March/April	.216	199	43	4	0	3	17	38	53	.342	.281
Grass	.250	603	151	26	5	9	51	74	154	.336	.355	May	.312	157	49	10	1	5	18	25	37	.402	.484
Turf	.278	862	240	47	3	16	106	108	218	.358	.396	June	.251	267	67	17	0	4	16	26	70	.316	.360
Pre-All Star	.255	699	178	33	2	13	59	96	183	.343	.363	July	.267	288	77	13	4	6	46	21	70	.316	.403
Post-All Star	.278	766	213	40	6	12	98	86	189	.354	.393	August	.263	293	77	14	0	3	28	39	68	.351	.341
Scoring Posn	.259	374	97	20	3	9	130	57	106	.355	.401	Sept/Oct	.299	261	78	15	3	4	32	33	74	.386	.425
Close & Late	.239	218	52	9	1	4	24	24	61	.318	.344	vs. AL	.269	1423	383	72	8	22	153	178	363	.351	.377
None on/out	.266	308	82	17	2	5	5	37	63	.351	.383	vs. NL	.190	42	8	1	0	3	4	4	9	.277	.429

Batter vs. Pitcher (career)

Hits Best Against	Avg	AB	H	2B	3B	HR	RBI	BB	SO	OBP	SLG	Hits Worst Against	Avg	AB	H	2B	3B	HR	RBI	BB	SO	OBP	SLG
Chad Ogea	.529	17	9	3	0	2	7	2	3	.579	1.059	Kevin Appier	.000	12	0	0	0	0	0	2	6	.143	.000
Aaron Sele	.462	13	6	1	0	0	1	3	2	.563	.538	Todd Stottlemyre	.100	10	1	0	0	0	0	1	6	.182	.100
Scott Sanders	.375	8	3	1	0	1	2	3	2	.545	.875	Scott Erickson	.111	18	2	0	0	0	1	0	2	.111	.111
Tim Belcher	.368	19	7	1	1	1	7	3	3	.455	.684	Juan Guzman	.154	13	2	0	0	0	2	1	2	.214	.154
Roger Pavlik	.318	22	7	2	0	2	6	4	5	.423	.682	Erik Hanson	.188	16	3	0	0	0	1	1	6	.235	.188

Robbie Beckett — Rockies
Age 25 – Pitches Left

	ERA	W	L	Sv	G	GS	IP	BB	SO	Avg	H	2B	3B	HR	RBI	OBP	SLG	GF	IR	IRS	Hld	SvOp	SB	CS	GB	FB	G/F
1997 Season	5.40	0	0	0	2	0	1.2	1	2	.167	1	1	0	0	2	.286	.333	2	1	1	0	0	1	0	3	0	0.00
Career (1996-1997)	11.57	0	0	0	7	0	7.0	10	8	.259	7	1	0	3	12	.447	.630	4	4	4	0	1	1	0	6	12	0.50

1997 Season

	ERA	W	L	Sv	G	GS	IP	H	HR	BB	SO
Home	5.40	0	0	0	2	0	1.2	1	0	1	2
Away	0.00	0	0	0	0	0	0.0	0	0	0	0

	Avg	AB	H	2B	3B	HR	RBI	BB	SO	OBP	SLG
vs. Left	.000	2	0	0	0	0	0	0	2	.000	.000
vs. Right	.250	4	1	1	0	0	2	1	0	.400	.500

Matt Beech — Phillies
Age 26 – Pitches Left (flyball pitcher)

	ERA	W	L	Sv	G	GS	IP	BB	SO	Avg	H	2B	3B	HR	RBI	OBP	SLG	CG	ShO	Sup	QS	#P/S	SB	CS	GB	FB	G/F
1997 Season	5.07	4	9	0	24	24	136.2	57	120	.279	147	26	2	25	72	.351	.478	0	0	4.35	11	100	14	5	137	180	0.76
Career (1996-1997)	5.51	5	13	0	32	32	178.0	68	153	.285	196	35	3	33	102	.351	.489	0	0	4.25	13	97	17	8	173	243	0.71

1997 Season

	ERA	W	L	Sv	G	GS	IP	H	HR	BB	SO
Home	5.26	1	3	0	8	8	49.2	49	12	21	37
Away	4.97	3	6	0	16	16	87.0	98	13	36	83
Day	5.64	0	4	0	8	8	44.2	47	7	19	39
Night	4.79	4	5	0	16	16	92.0	100	18	38	81
Grass	4.43	2	5	0	12	12	67.0	76	8	27	65
Turf	5.68	2	4	0	12	12	69.2	71	17	30	55
March/April	0.00	0	0	0	0	0	0.0	0	0	0	0
May	10.13	0	1	0	2	2	5.1	5	0	9	4
June	5.24	0	2	0	6	6	34.1	38	6	13	31
July	6.44	0	3	0	5	5	29.1	35	8	14	29
August	2.43	3	2	0	6	6	40.2	33	3	17	36
Sept/Oct	6.33	1	1	0	5	5	27.0	36	8	4	20
Starter	5.07	4	9	0	24	24	136.2	147	25	57	120
Reliever	0.00	0	0	0	0	0	0.0	0	0	0	0
0-3 Days Rest (Start)	0.00	0	0	0	0	0	0.0	0	0	0	0
4 Days Rest	4.70	2	3	0	13	13	82.1	86	19	25	71
5+ Days Rest	5.63	2	6	0	11	11	54.1	61	6	32	49
vs. AL	1.80	1	1	0	3	3	20.0	26	3	5	15
vs. NL	5.63	3	8	0	21	21	116.2	121	22	52	105
Pre-All Star	5.72	0	4	0	9	9	45.2	53	8	23	38
Post-All Star	4.75	4	5	0	15	15	91.0	94	17	34	82

	Avg	AB	H	2B	3B	HR	RBI	BB	SO	OBP	SLG
vs. Left	.221	86	19	3	0	3	10	8	16	.292	.360
vs. Right	.290	441	128	23	2	22	62	49	104	.363	.501
Inning 1-6	.279	491	137	26	2	21	68	53	113	.351	.468
Inning 7+	.278	36	10	0	0	4	4	7		.350	.611
None on	.300	300	90	16	2	17	17	26	66	.364	.537
Runners on	.251	227	57	10	0	8	55	31	54	.336	.401
Scoring Posn	.226	124	28	4	0	2	39	21	32	.329	.306
Close & Late	.318	22	7	0	0	2	2	2	5	.375	.591
None on/out	.350	137	48	8	1	10	10	13	25	.418	.642
vs. 1st Batr (relief)	.000	0	0	0	0	0	0	0	0	.000	.000
1st Inning Pitched	.227	88	20	4	0	2	12	19	26	.370	.341
First 75 Pitches	.288	379	109	18	1	16	51	35	91	.353	.467
Pitch 76-90	.250	68	17	3	1	5	9	9	10	.333	.544
Pitch 91-105	.286	56	16	5	0	1	8	8	10	.364	.429
Pitch 106+	.208	24	5	0	0	3	4	5	9	.345	.583
First Pitch	.397	63	25	4	0	3	14	6	0	.452	.603
Ahead in Count	.221	249	55	9	1	7	21	0	102	.230	.349
Behind in Count	.327	110	36	6	0	10	22	28	0	.457	.655
Two Strikes	.190	274	52	12	2	9	24	23	120	.256	.347
Pre-All Star	.308	172	53	9	0	8	30	23	38	.392	.500
Post-All Star	.265	355	94	17	2	17	42	34	82	.330	.468

Tim Belcher — Royals
Age 36 – Pitches Right

	ERA	W	L	Sv	G	GS	IP	BB	SO	Avg	H	2B	3B	HR	RBI	OBP	SLG	CG	ShO	Sup	QS	#P/S	SB	CS	GB	FB	G/F
1997 Season	5.02	13	12	0	32	32	213.1	70	113	.288	242	52	4	31	115	.345	.470	3	1	6.54	18	105	5	6	310	243	1.28
Last Five Years	4.69	57	61	0	154	153	1002.0	378	533	.276	1082	207	35	118	507	.341	.436	16	5	5.38	73	105	46	38	1334	1241	1.07

1997 Season

	ERA	W	L	Sv	G	GS	IP	H	HR	BB	SO
Home	5.87	7	8	0	17	17	112.0	137	15	34	57
Away	4.09	6	4	0	15	15	101.1	105	16	36	56
Day	5.73	4	5	0	13	13	81.2	100	13	26	54
Night	4.58	9	7	0	19	19	131.2	142	18	44	59
Grass	5.51	10	11	0	28	28	184.2	214	29	59	94
Turf	1.88	3	1	0	4	4	28.2	28	2	11	19
March/April	2.63	2	3	0	5	5	37.2	35	4	11	20
May	4.23	3	3	0	6	6	44.2	50	2	16	23
June	3.89	3	1	0	6	6	41.2	46	5	9	28
July	8.79	2	2	0	5	5	28.2	39	7	9	17
August	7.67	2	3	0	5	5	29.1	44	7	8	14
Sept/Oct	4.60	1	0	0	5	5	31.1	28	6	17	11
Starter	5.02	13	12	0	32	32	213.1	242	31	70	113
Reliever	0.00	0	0	0	0	0	0.0	0	0	0	0
0-3 Days Rest (Start)	0.00	0	0	0	0	0	0.0	0	0	0	0
4 Days Rest	4.61	7	7	0	20	20	132.2	145	18	42	73
5+ Days Rest	5.69	6	5	0	12	12	80.2	97	13	28	40
vs. AL	5.05	11	12	0	29	29	192.1	218	30	65	97
vs. NL	4.71	2	0	0	3	3	21.0	24	1	5	16
Pre-All Star	3.92	8	7	0	18	18	131.0	139	13	40	75
Post-All Star	6.78	5	5	0	14	14	82.1	103	18	30	38

	Avg	AB	H	2B	3B	HR	RBI	BB	SO	OBP	SLG
vs. Left	.278	407	113	24	2	17	50	39	58	.344	.472
vs. Right	.297	434	129	28	2	14	65	31	55	.345	.468
Inning 1-6	.277	721	200	44	3	26	97	58	106	.333	.455
Inning 7+	.350	120	42	8	1	5	18	12	7	.410	.558
None on	.275	487	134	26	2	18		38	63	.331	.448
Runners on	.305	354	108	26	2	13	97	32	50	.362	.500
Scoring Posn	.296	196	58	14	2	9	84	20	31	.360	.526
Close & Late	.308	52	16	2	0	3	8	7	6	.390	.519
None on/out	.294	211	62	15	0	8		18	22	.352	.479
vs. 1st Batr (relief)	.000	0	0	0	0	0	0	0	0	.000	.000
1st Inning Pitched	.254	122	31	9	0	2	15	8	19	.298	.377
First 75 Pitches	.258	578	149	30	1	19	64	45	86	.313	.412
Pitch 76-90	.419	124	52	12	3	5	26	12	12	.478	.685
Pitch 91-105	.268	82	22	6	0	3	9	9	10	.341	.451
Pitch 106+	.333	57	19	4	0	4	16	4	5	.371	.614
First Pitch	.288	132	38	6	0	6	15	1	0	.294	.470
Ahead in Count	.231	373	86	23	4	9	38	0	90	.238	.386
Behind in Count	.347	193	67	13	0	10	40	35	0	.445	.570
Two Strikes	.239	351	84	22	2	12	43	34	113	.311	.416
Pre-All Star	.274	507	139	32	2	13	55	40	75	.329	.422
Post-All Star	.308	334	103	20	2	18	60	30	38	.368	.542

Last Five Years

	ERA	W	L	Sv	G	GS	IP	H	HR	BB	SO
Home	4.88	30	29	0	80	80	516.0	581	67	196	277
Away	4.48	27	32	0	74	73	486.0	501	51	182	256
Day	4.92	14	21	0	49	48	307.1	348	41	113	186
Night	4.59	43	40	0	105	105	694.2	734	77	265	347
Grass	4.71	34	45	0	104	103	680.1	754	83	239	333
March/April	4.65	5	11	0	20	20	120.0	139	15	54	53
May	4.39	11	9	0	26	26	174.1	186	21	66	103

	Avg	AB	H	2B	3B	HR	RBI	BB	SO	OBP	SLG
vs. Left	.277	2083	578	99	18	54	256	221	251	.348	.420
vs. Right	.273	1843	504	108	17	64	251	157	282	.334	.455
Inning 1-6	.271	3307	897	179	30	100	440	320	471	.338	.434
Inning 7+	.299	619	185	28	5	18	67	58	62	.360	.447
None on	.260	2239	583	103	19	73	73	210	301	.327	.421
Scoring Posn	.276	934	258	59	7	29	375	114	142	.352	.448
Close & Late	.306	291	89	13	3	9	36	30	29	.369	.464

Last Five Years

	ERA	W	L	Sv	G	GS	IP	H	HR	BB	SO
June	4.09	13	6	0	30	30	202.1	204	24	57	118
July	5.63	13	13	0	29	29	191.2	214	25	83	123
August	4.96	9	13	0	24	24	159.2	183	21	58	66
Sept/Oct	4.38	6	9	0	25	24	154.0	156	12	60	70
Starter	4.69	57	61	0	153	153	1001.0	1082	118	378	532
Reliever	0.00	0	0	0	1	0	1.0	0	0	0	1
0-3 Days Rest (Start)	6.85	3	4	0	8	8	46.0	57	8	26	24
4 Days Rest	4.58	39	39	0	103	103	676.0	742	74	247	345
5+ Days Rest	4.61	15	18	0	42	42	279.0	283	36	105	163
vs. AL	4.72	46	55	0	129	128	844.0	924	106	326	416
vs. NL	4.50	11	6	0	25	25	158.0	158	12	52	117
Pre-All Star	4.41	33	29	0	85	85	558.2	591	67	209	311
Post-All Star	5.03	24	32	0	69	68	443.1	491	51	169	222

	Avg	AB	H	2B	3B	HR	RBI	BB	SO	OBP	SLG
None on/out	.263	996	262	57	6	29	29	86	111	.325	.420
vs. 1st Batr (relief)	.000	1	0	0	0	0	0	0	1	.000	.000
1st Inning Pitched	.243	572	139	27	4	12	57	52	91	.306	.367
First 75 Pitches	.268	2677	717	143	24	74	324	253	392	.334	.422
Pitch 76-90	.308	529	163	31	8	14	78	51	62	.373	.476
Pitch 91-105	.237	389	92	14	0	14	49	44	44	.313	.380
Pitch 106+	.332	331	110	19	3	16	56	30	35	.386	.553
First Pitch	.332	591	196	37	7	21	93	15	0	.349	.525
Ahead in Count	.226	1697	383	72	13	33	164	0	444	.233	.342
Behind in Count	.313	913	286	55	10	40	152	199	0	.434	.527
Two Strikes	.216	1673	361	67	11	37	152	163	533	.291	.335
Pre-All Star	.271	2180	591	116	23	67	272	209	311	.338	.438
Post-All Star	.281	1746	491	91	12	51	235	169	222	.346	.435

Pitcher vs. Batter (career)

Pitches Best Vs.	Avg	AB	H	2B	3B	HR	RBI	BB	SO	OBP	SLG	Pitches Worst Vs.	Avg	AB	H	2B	3B	HR	RBI	BB	SO	OBP	SLG
Dean Palmer	.038	26	1	0	0	0	1	0	8	.038	.038	Jay Buhner	.500	20	10	2	0	4	10	2	1	.545	1.200
Carlos Delgado	.071	14	1	0	0	0	0	1	5	.133	.071	Edgar Martinez	.500	16	8	3	1	0	3	3	0	.600	.813
Jeff King	.083	12	1	0	0	0	1	1	2	.154	.083	Jeromy Burnitz	.455	11	5	2	0	1	3	0	2	.500	.909
Kirt Manwaring	.091	11	1	0	0	0	0	1	2	.091	.091	Dave Clark	.438	16	7	3	0	2	8	0	1	.438	1.000
Wayne Kirby	.118	17	2	0	0	0	1	0	3	.118	.118	Jose Canseco	.412	17	7	2	0	2	2	4	2	.545	.882

Stan Belinda — Reds

Age 31 – Pitches Right (flyball pitcher)

	ERA	W	L	Sv	G	GS	IP	BB	SO	Avg	H	2B	3B	HR	RBI	OBP	SLG	GF	IR	IRS	Hld	SvOp	SB	CS	GB	FB	G/F
1997 Season	3.71	1	5	1	84	0	99.1	33	114	.229	84	22	3	11	48	.304	.395	18	49	18	28	5	18	4	94	113	0.83
Last Five Years	4.10	17	11	33	278	0	316.1	122	281	.235	278	66	7	31	175	.316	.382	112	175	61	65	48	45	8	347	363	0.96

1997 Season

	ERA	W	L	Sv	G	GS	IP	H	HR	BB	SO
Home	4.50	0	4	0	46	0	54.0	49	9	19	62
Away	2.78	1	1	1	38	0	45.1	35	2	14	52
Day	4.50	0	2	1	32	0	40.0	41	6	16	41
Night	3.19	1	3	0	52	0	59.1	43	5	17	73
Grass	3.86	1	1	1	26	0	30.1	27	2	10	34
Turf	3.65	0	4	0	58	0	69.0	57	9	23	80
March/April	5.40	0	0	0	15	0	18.1	22	5	3	14
May	3.14	0	1	0	14	0	14.1	14	2	3	23
June	2.41	0	1	0	16	0	18.2	15	1	5	25
July	0.00	1	0	0	11	0	14.0	5	0	7	15
August	7.31	0	1	1	14	0	16.0	15	1	7	20
Sept/Oct	3.50	0	2	0	13	0	18.0	13	2	8	17
Starter	0.00	0	0	0	0	0	0.0	0	0	0	0
Reliever	3.71	1	5	1	84	0	99.1	84	11	33	114
0 Days rest (Relief)	2.42	0	1	0	27	0	26.0	16	4	7	29
1 or 2 Days rest	4.88	1	5	0	46	0	59.0	61	6	23	70
3+ Days rest	1.26	0	0	0	11	0	14.1	7	1	3	15
vs. AL	1.74	0	0	0	7	0	10.1	8	0	2	14
vs. NL	3.94	1	5	1	77	0	89.0	76	11	31	100
Pre-All Star	3.42	0	2	0	49	0	55.1	52	8	14	65
Post-All Star	4.09	1	3	1	35	0	44.0	32	3	19	49

	Avg	AB	H	2B	3B	HR	RBI	BB	SO	OBP	SLG
vs. Left	.263	160	42	12	2	6	21	16	43	.343	.475
vs. Right	.203	207	42	10	1	5	27	17	71	.275	.333
Inning 1-6	.290	62	18	3	1	1	12	6	18	.357	.419
Inning 7+	.216	305	66	19	2	10	36	27	96	.294	.390
None on	.241	203	49	11	2	7	7	17	67	.303	.419
Runners on	.213	164	35	11	1	4	41	16	47	.306	.366
Scoring Posn	.179	112	20	7	0	4	39	15	35	.302	.348
Close & Late	.215	177	38	13	0	3	22	15	54	.292	.339
None on/out	.244	86	21	5	1	3	3	6	31	.301	.430
vs. 1st Batr (relief)	.233	73	17	5	0	3	12	8	27	.321	.425
1st Inning Pitched	.232	267	62	18	3	8	42	27	80	.316	.412
First 15 Pitches	.253	229	58	16	1	9	35	19	66	.320	.450
Pitch 16-30	.197	117	23	5	2	2	12	11	42	.286	.325
Pitch 31-45	.143	21	3	1	0	0	1	3	6	.240	.190
Pitch 46+	.000	0	0	0	0	0	0	0	0	.000	.000
First Pitch	.262	42	11	2	1	4	13	5	0	.354	.643
Ahead in Count	.167	204	34	8	0	1	12	0	99	.186	.221
Behind in Count	.322	59	19	5	1	3	9	12	0	.421	.593
Two Strikes	.144	201	29	8	0	0	13	16	114	.217	.184
Pre-All Star	.246	211	52	11	3	8	30	14	65	.308	.441
Post-All Star	.205	156	32	11	0	3	18	19	49	.300	.333

Last Five Years

	ERA	W	L	Sv	G	GS	IP	H	HR	BB	SO
Home	4.02	10	5	12	145	0	172.1	147	20	67	146
Away	4.19	7	6	21	133	0	144.0	131	11	55	135
Day	4.93	3	4	10	99	0	118.2	122	12	57	107
Night	3.60	14	7	23	179	0	197.2	156	19	65	174
Grass	4.46	8	5	21	147	0	157.1	138	14	66	131
Turf	3.74	9	6	12	131	0	159.0	140	17	56	150
March/April	5.47	0	2	5	46	0	52.2	54	9	20	37
May	3.95	2	6	6	52	0	54.2	47	6	24	53
June	2.36	5	1	8	49	0	61.0	52	5	16	51
July	4.77	3	2	6	48	0	54.2	45	3	30	51
August	4.07	3	2	8	54	0	55.1	40	4	14	56
Sept/Oct	4.26	4	0	7	29	0	38.0	40	4	18	33
Starter	0.00	0	0	0	0	0	0.0	0	0	0	0
Reliever	4.10	17	11	33	278	0	316.1	278	31	122	281
0 Days rest (Relief)	3.77	2	1	10	75	0	71.2	53	7	28	64
1 or 2 Days rest	4.17	12	8	16	140	0	172.2	168	16	61	152
3+ Days rest	4.25	3	2	7	63	0	72.0	57	8	33	65
vs. AL	4.28	13	5	13	161	0	185.0	167	16	80	151
vs. NL	3.84	4	6	20	117	0	131.1	111	15	42	130
Pre-All Star	4.02	13	6	23	162	0	186.0	170	22	72	158
Post-All Star	4.21	4	5	10	116	0	130.1	108	9	50	123

	Avg	AB	H	2B	3B	HR	RBI	BB	SO	OBP	SLG
vs. Left	.259	509	132	30	5	16	71	66	111	.349	.432
vs. Right	.217	672	146	36	2	15	104	56	170	.291	.344
Inning 1-6	.289	121	35	6	2	2	32	20	23	.397	.421
Inning 7+	.229	1060	243	60	5	29	143	102	258	.306	.377
None on	.223	619	138	29	5	16	16	56	157	.296	.363
Runners on	.249	562	140	37	2	15	159	66	124	.337	.402
Scoring Posn	.241	365	88	25	1	13	151	48	83	.342	.422
Close & Late	.216	612	132	34	2	11	88	55	149	.292	.332
None on/out	.259	263	68	15	2	9	9	23	67	.325	.433
vs. 1st Batr (relief)	.254	240	61	16	2	10	39	32	56	.347	.463
1st Inning Pitched	.243	884	215	56	5	24	151	95	204	.325	.399
First 15 Pitches	.239	762	182	41	5	22	113	75	167	.314	.392
Pitch 16-30	.237	338	80	23	2	7	49	35	97	.324	.379
Pitch 31-45	.149	67	10	2	0	1	7	9	15	.259	.224
Pitch 46+	.429	14	6	0	0	1	6	3	2	.529	.643
First Pitch	.282	149	42	10	2	6	33	15	0	.355	.490
Ahead in Count	.169	574	97	23	2	9	43	0	244	.182	.263
Behind in Count	.346	237	82	17	2	11	57	44	0	.447	.574
Two Strikes	.157	572	90	21	1	5	45	63	281	.248	.224
Pre-All Star	.244	697	170	42	5	22	105	72	158	.325	.413
Post-All Star	.223	484	108	24	2	9	70	50	123	.304	.337

Pitcher vs. Batter (career)

Pitches Best Vs.	Avg	AB	H	2B	3B	HR	RBI	BB	SO	OBP	SLG	Pitches Worst Vs.	Avg	AB	H	2B	3B	HR	RBI	BB	SO	OBP	SLG
Charlie Hayes	.083	12	1	0	0	0	1	0	0	.083	.083	Jeff Blauser	.455	11	5	0	0	0	2	1	3	.500	.455

Pitcher vs. Batter (career)

Pitches Best Vs.	Avg	AB	H	2B	3B	HR	RBI	BB	SO	OBP	SLG	Pitches Worst Vs.	Avg	AB	H	2B	3B	HR	RBI	BB	SO	OBP	SLG
Moises Alou	.083	12	1	1	0	0	0	0	4	.083	.167	Barry Larkin	.444	9	4	0	1	0	3	1	0	.455	.667
Jeff Bagwell	.083	12	1	0	0	0	0	3	2	.267	.083	Paul Molitor	.429	14	6	1	0	0	2	1	0	.438	.500
Ken Caminiti	.125	8	1	0	0	0	2	2	3	.273	.125	Juan Samuel	.429	7	3	2	0	0	4	4	0	.636	.714
Craig Biggio	.133	15	2	0	0	0	1	2	7	.222	.133	Ryne Sandberg	.385	13	5	0	0	1	4	1	2	.400	.615

David Bell — Cardinals   Age 25 – Bats Right

	Avg	G	AB	R	H	2B	3B	HR	RBI	BB	SO	HBP	GDP	SB	CS	OBP	SLG	IBB	SH	SF	#Pit	#P/PA	GB	FB	G/F
1997 Season	.211	66	142	9	30	7	2	1	12	10	28	0	2	1	0	.261	.310	2	2	1	638	4.12	45	55	0.82
Career (1995-1997)	.224	169	433	34	97	20	4	4	40	24	75	3	5	3	3	.268	.316	4	2	3	1740	3.74	140	153	0.92

1997 Season

	Avg	AB	H	2B	3B	HR	RBI	BB	SO	OBP	SLG		Avg	AB	H	2B	3B	HR	RBI	BB	SO	OBP	SLG
vs. Left	.280	50	14	4	0	0	2	3	7	.315	.360	Scoring Posn	.258	31	8	1	0	0	10	4	7	.333	.290
vs. Right	.174	92	16	3	2	1	10	7	21	.232	.283	Close & Late	.226	31	7	1	0	1	6	2	5	.265	.355
Home	.273	77	21	4	1	1	11	4	14	.305	.390	None on/out	.167	42	7	1	1	1	1	2	4	.205	.310
Away	.138	65	9	3	1	0	1	6	14	.211	.215	Batting #7	.242	33	8	2	1	0	4	5	4	.342	.364
First Pitch	.333	21	7	4	0	1	2	2	0	.391	.667	Batting #8	.250	72	18	3	1	1	8	3	12	.276	.361
Ahead in Count	.273	22	6	1	1	0	4	2	0	.333	.409	Other	.108	37	4	2	0	0	0	2	12	.154	.162
Behind in Count	.183	71	13	2	1	0	6	0	24	.181	.239	Pre-All Star	.136	22	3	0	0	0	1	6	.174	.136
Two Strikes	.157	83	13	1	1	0	6	6	28	.211	.193	Post-All Star	.225	120	27	7	2	1	11	9	22	.277	.342

Derek Bell — Astros   Age 29 – Bats Right (groundball hitter)

	Avg	G	AB	R	H	2B	3B	HR	RBI	BB	SO	HBP	GDP	SB	CS	OBP	SLG	IBB	SH	SF	#Pit	#P/PA	GB	FB	G/F
1997 Season	.276	129	493	67	136	29	3	15	71	40	94	12	16	15	7	.344	.438	3	0	2	2015	3.68	200	124	1.61
Last Five Years	.286	657	2548	341	729	129	9	75	396	165	498	41	65	121	32	.336	.432	23	0	27	9894	3.56	1129	547	2.06

1997 Season

	Avg	AB	H	2B	3B	HR	RBI	BB	SO	OBP	SLG		Avg	AB	H	2B	3B	HR	RBI	BB	SO	OBP	SLG
vs. Left	.235	119	28	4	1	1	9	6	23	.270	.311	First Pitch	.278	79	22	6	0	2	5	3	0	.321	.430
vs. Right	.289	374	108	25	2	14	62	34	71	.366	.479	Ahead in Count	.348	112	39	5	1	6	31	18	0	.444	.571
Groundball	.213	75	16	3	2	1	11	2	19	.231	.347	Behind in Count	.219	215	47	12	0	6	17	0	77	.242	.358
Flyball	.283	60	17	7	0	3	9	9	14	.389	.550	Two Strikes	.197	223	44	9	1	3	20	19	94	.274	.287
Home	.295	241	71	18	2	7	40	19	49	.360	.473	Batting #2	.364	154	56	12	3	8	33	9	24	.421	.636
Away	.258	252	65	11	1	8	31	21	45	.329	.405	Batting #5	.242	182	44	12	0	5	23	18	29	.317	.390
Day	.340	141	48	14	0	5	21	13	25	.409	.546	Other	.229	157	36	5	0	2	15	13	41	.299	.299
Night	.250	352	88	15	3	10	50	27	69	.317	.395	March/April	.204	93	19	4	0	0	7	7	19	.282	.247
Grass	.234	192	45	8	1	6	22	16	31	.307	.380	May	.333	42	14	3	1	2	6	5	11	.408	.595
Turf	.302	301	91	21	2	9	49	24	63	.367	.475	June	.266	64	17	3	0	3	11	5	10	.319	.453
Pre-All Star	.247	219	54	10	1	5	26	18	43	.314	.370	July	.256	86	22	5	0	2	12	10	16	.347	.384
Post-All Star	.299	274	82	19	2	10	45	22	51	.367	.493	August	.333	111	37	10	2	5	22	10	13	.398	.595
Scoring Posn	.247	158	39	10	2	3	52	17	31	.346	.392	Sept/Oct	.278	97	27	4	0	3	13	3	25	.324	.412
Close & Late	.261	92	24	4	0	2	9	8	19	.337	.370	vs. AL	.271	59	16	3	0	1	4	4	11	.317	.373
None on/out	.221	95	21	5	0	4	5	19	.267	.400	vs. NL	.276	434	120	26	3	14	67	36	83	.347	.447

1997 By Position

Position	Avg	AB	H	2B	3B	HR	RBI	BB	SO	OBP	SLG	G	GS	Innings	PO	A	E	DP	Fld Pct	Rng Fctr	In Zone	Outs	Zone Rtg	MLB Zone
As cf	.246	134	33	7	1	2	13	12	30	.320	.358	36	34	308.0	65	2	2	1	.971	1.96	81	66	.815	.815
As rf	.285	351	100	22	2	12	57	28	63	.351	.462	89	87	767.2	160	4	6	1	.965	1.92	200	157	.785	.813

Last Five Years

	Avg	AB	H	2B	3B	HR	RBI	BB	SO	OBP	SLG		Avg	AB	H	2B	3B	HR	RBI	BB	SO	OBP	SLG
vs. Left	.301	647	195	28	2	22	103	42	109	.346	.453	First Pitch	.398	430	171	37	2	21	91	19	0	.425	.640
vs. Right	.281	1901	534	101	7	53	293	123	389	.333	.425	Ahead in Count	.346	523	181	31	1	24	123	73	0	.426	.547
Groundball	.245	658	161	29	3	15	88	40	140	.294	.366	Behind in Count	.211	1178	249	37	3	19	114	0	427	.254	.296
Flyball	.290	390	113	25	0	20	72	31	89	.349	.508	Two Strikes	.197	1162	229	40	4	17	119	73	498	.254	.282
Home	.282	1247	352	67	4	38	199	100	241	.345	.434	Batting #4	.292	1375	402	76	5	37	238	95	255	.342	.436
Away	.290	1301	377	62	5	37	197	65	257	.328	.430	Batting #5	.271	558	151	30	0	18	74	41	113	.326	.421
Day	.288	773	223	50	1	19	108	40	136	.334	.429	Other	.286	615	176	23	4	20	84	29	130	.332	.434
Night	.285	1775	506	79	8	56	288	125	362	.337	.433	March/April	.283	385	109	22	2	14	56	27	89	.337	.460
Grass	.284	1278	363	58	4	48	190	78	240	.330	.448	May	.296	473	140	24	2	11	66	29	85	.345	.425
Turf	.288	1270	366	71	5	27	206	87	258	.342	.416	June	.292	486	142	19	1	16	87	36	96	.344	.434
Pre-All Star	.288	1497	431	71	6	43	230	98	300	.338	.430	July	.273	502	137	26	2	11	79	29	100	.319	.398
Post-All Star	.284	1051	298	58	3	32	166	67	198	.333	.436	August	.308	435	134	28	2	17	80	31	73	.359	.499
Scoring Posn	.260	796	207	39	5	18	310	85	170	.337	.389	Sept/Oct	.251	267	67	10	0	6	28	13	55	.300	.356
Close & Late	.259	440	114	21	1	9	67	31	106	.318	.373	vs. AL	.271	59	16	3	0	1	4	4	11	.317	.373
None on/out	.298	571	170	34	2	21	21	27	107	.339	.475	vs. NL	.286	2489	713	126	9	74	392	161	487	.337	.434

Batter vs. Pitcher (career)

Hits Best Against	Avg	AB	H	2B	3B	HR	RBI	BB	SO	OBP	SLG	Hits Worst Against	Avg	AB	H	2B	3B	HR	RBI	BB	SO	OBP	SLG
Terry Mulholland	.625	16	10	0	0	2	9	1	4	.611	1.000	Francisco Cordova	.000	12	0	0	0	0	0	0	6	.000	.000
Jamey Wright	.571	7	4	0	0	2	5	4	2	.750	1.429	Jeff Juden	.000	10	0	0	0	0	1	2	6	.167	.000
Esteban Loaiza	.538	13	7	1	0	2	5	3	2	.625	1.077	Curt Schilling	.048	21	1	0	0	0	1	2	4	.125	.048
Greg Swindell	.467	15	7	0	0	2	4	0	1	.467	.867	Joey Hamilton	.077	13	1	0	0	0	0	1	2	.143	.077
Al Leiter	.417	12	5	2	1	1	5	0	2	.417	1.000	Donovan Osborne	.111	36	4	0	0	0	1	0	9	.111	.111

34

Jay Bell — Royals
Age 32 – Bats Right

	Avg	G	AB	R	H	2B	3B	HR	RBI	BB	SO	HBP	GDP	SB	CS	OBP	SLG	IBB	SH	SF	#Pit	#P/PA	GB	FB	G/F
1997 Season	.291	153	573	89	167	28	3	21	92	71	101	4	13	10	6	.368	.461	2	3	9	2702	4.09	173	196	0.88
Last Five Years	.279	706	2658	403	742	152	23	65	314	306	523	22	67	36	25	.356	.427	15	33	20	12283	4.04	908	756	1.20

1997 Season

	Avg	AB	H	2B	3B	HR	RBI	BB	SO	OBP	SLG		Avg	AB	H	2B	3B	HR	RBI	BB	SO	OBP	SLG
vs. Left	.260	173	45	7	0	4	19	18	31	.330	.370	First Pitch	.373	51	19	4	0	4	10	1	0	.393	.686
vs. Right	.305	400	122	21	3	17	73	53	70	.384	.500	Ahead in Count	.376	125	47	11	0	7	33	41	0	.521	.632
Groundball	.375	96	36	6	0	4	19	17	20	.470	.563	Behind in Count	.247	259	64	9	2	7	35	0	73	.249	.378
Flyball	.277	94	26	7	0	4	12	12	14	.355	.479	Two Strikes	.226	287	65	10	1	5	33	29	101	.298	.321
Home	.287	275	79	16	2	10	45	36	40	.368	.469	Batting #2	.258	97	25	7	0	3	17	20	21	.383	.423
Away	.295	298	88	12	1	11	47	35	61	.368	.453	Batting #3	.303	419	127	18	3	16	67	49	68	.375	.475
Day	.297	182	54	7	1	5	25	19	29	.360	.429	Other	.263	57	15	3	0	2	8	2	12	.283	.421
Night	.289	391	113	21	2	16	67	52	72	.372	.476	March/April	.312	93	29	2	0	6	17	6	12	.350	.527
Grass	.287	485	139	26	2	17	73	60	87	.363	.454	May	.300	100	30	11	0	2	19	18	18	.408	.470
Turf	.318	88	28	2	1	4	19	11	14	.398	.500	June	.218	87	19	2	0	5	19	16	17	.333	.414
Pre-All Star	.279	298	83	16	0	13	56	42	51	.365	.463	July	.292	96	28	3	2	4	15	14	18	.389	.490
Post-All Star	.305	275	84	12	3	8	36	29	50	.372	.458	August	.272	114	31	2	0	3	8	7	19	.311	.368
Scoring Posn	.304	161	49	11	0	5	72	27	25	.392	.466	Sept/Oct	.361	83	30	8	1	1	14	10	17	.426	.518
Close & Late	.260	100	26	2	0	2	11	12	20	.342	.340	vs. AL	.284	524	149	26	3	20	82	58	94	.356	.460
None on/out	.220	100	22	6	1	2	2	9	17	.284	.360	vs. NL	.367	49	18	2	0	1	10	13	7	.484	.469

1997 By Position

Position	Avg	AB	H	2B	3B	HR	RBI	BB	SO	OBP	SLG	G	GS	Innings	PO	A	E	DP	Fld Pct	Rng Fctr	In Zone	Zone Outs	Zone Rtg	MLB Zone
As ss	.290	555	161	24	3	21	91	70	98	.368	.458	149	144	1271.0	226	442	10	103	.985	4.73	476	447	.939	.937

Last Five Years

	Avg	AB	H	2B	3B	HR	RBI	BB	SO	OBP	SLG		Avg	AB	H	2B	3B	HR	RBI	BB	SO	OBP	SLG
vs. Left	.304	716	218	47	5	21	85	98	104	.390	.472	First Pitch	.336	247	83	18	1	11	34	11	0	.367	.551
vs. Right	.270	1942	524	105	18	44	229	208	419	.343	.410	Ahead in Count	.358	587	210	50	5	22	98	167	0	.498	.572
Groundball	.291	767	223	50	5	15	88	81	147	.361	.428	Behind in Count	.238	1253	298	56	13	22	117	0	426	.243	.349
Flyball	.257	412	106	30	1	13	45	52	89	.343	.430	Two Strikes	.214	1348	289	52	10	21	121	128	523	.287	.315
Home	.275	1301	358	84	8	31	151	171	232	.361	.424	Batting #2	.289	1518	438	96	14	31	152	188	300	.371	.431
Away	.283	1357	384	68	15	34	163	135	291	.351	.430	Batting #3	.302	427	129	19	3	16	67	50	70	.374	.473
Day	.296	796	236	53	9	18	83	86	136	.367	.454	Other	.245	713	175	37	6	18	95	68	153	.313	.390
Night	.272	1862	506	99	14	47	231	220	387	.351	.416	March/April	.279	366	102	16	4	13	45	38	71	.345	.451
Grass	.285	1140	325	57	11	35	156	124	230	.355	.446	May	.244	496	121	34	3	9	58	63	107	.331	.379
Turf	.275	1518	417	95	12	30	158	182	293	.357	.412	June	.267	464	124	25	4	10	57	70	98	.363	.403
Pre-All Star	.260	1492	388	87	12	38	179	181	306	.341	.411	July	.268	508	136	26	5	13	57	46	87	.335	.415
Post-All Star	.304	1166	354	65	11	27	135	125	217	.375	.448	August	.306	477	146	28	2	11	49	38	90	.360	.442
Scoring Posn	.270	633	171	35	4	13	235	107	137	.371	.400	Sept/Oct	.326	347	113	23	5	9	48	51	70	.416	.499
Close & Late	.269	443	119	21	4	4	49	58	106	.354	.361	vs. AL	.284	524	149	26	3	20	82	58	94	.356	.460
None on/out	.233	527	123	26	8	10	10	44	94	.294	.370	vs. NL	.278	2134	593	126	20	45	232	248	429	.356	.419

Batter vs. Pitcher (career)

Hits Best Against	Avg	AB	H	2B	3B	HR	RBI	BB	SO	OBP	SLG	Hits Worst Against	Avg	AB	H	2B	3B	HR	RBI	BB	SO	OBP	SLG
Mike Hampton	.615	13	8	3	0	2	4	3	2	.688	1.308	Lee Smith	.000	11	0	0	0	0	0	1	5	.083	.000
Mike Bielecki	.571	21	12	4	2	0	6	3	4	.625	.952	Doug Jones	.000	11	0	0	0	0	0	1	3	.083	.000
Chuck McElroy	.571	14	8	0	1	1	3	2	1	.625	.929	Ismael Valdes	.077	13	1	0	0	0	0	0	6	.077	.077
Kevin Foster	.500	14	7	0	0	1	5	4	2	.632	.714	Ramon Martinez	.091	33	3	0	0	0	4	2	10	.139	.091
Paul Assenmacher	.455	11	5	1	1	2	1	2	.500	1.000	Steve Reed	.111	9	1	0	0	2	0	1	.091	.111

Albert Belle — White Sox
Age 31 – Bats Right

	Avg	G	AB	R	H	2B	3B	HR	RBI	BB	SO	HBP	GDP	SB	CS	OBP	SLG	IBB	SH	SF	#Pit	#P/PA	GB	FB	G/F
1997 Season	.274	161	634	90	174	45	1	30	116	53	105	6	26	4	4	.332	.491	6	0	8	2449	3.49	220	202	1.09
Last Five Years	.306	727	2788	518	853	206	10	202	620	359	439	32	93	52	24	.387	.604	48	2	37	11924	3.70	938	900	1.04

1997 Season

	Avg	AB	H	2B	3B	HR	RBI	BB	SO	OBP	SLG		Avg	AB	H	2B	3B	HR	RBI	BB	SO	OBP	SLG
vs. Left	.295	122	36	7	0	7	21	21	23	.399	.525	First Pitch	.328	116	38	4	1	3	12	5	0	.368	.457
vs. Right	.270	512	138	38	1	23	95	32	82	.315	.482	Ahead in Count	.303	145	44	12	0	12	40	19	0	.389	.634
Groundball	.271	133	36	7	0	6	23	14	27	.349	.459	Behind in Count	.229	253	58	16	0	10	39	0	87	.226	.411
Flyball	.336	113	38	15	0	8	21	10	19	.390	.681	Two Strikes	.163	251	41	13	0	7	29	29	105	.247	.299
Home	.294	313	92	19	1	14	61	19	44	.333	.495	Total	.274	634	174	45	1	30	116	53	105	.332	.491
Away	.255	321	82	26	0	16	55	34	61	.331	.486	Batting #4	.274	634	174	45	1	30	116	53	105	.332	.491
Day	.261	199	52	12	0	8	35	17	33	.320	.442	Other	.000	0	0	0	0	0	0	0	0	.000	.000
Night	.280	435	122	33	1	22	81	36	72	.338	.513	March/April	.206	102	21	6	0	4	14	7	18	.259	.382
Grass	.267	539	144	34	1	25	101	45	88	.325	.473	May	.346	104	36	6	1	7	32	10	21	.403	.625
Turf	.316	95	30	11	0	5	15	8	17	.375	.589	June	.313	112	35	7	0	7	20	10	23	.374	.563
Pre-All Star	.298	339	101	22	1	18	70	30	62	.357	.528	July	.238	105	25	9	0	3	13	9	13	.296	.410
Post-All Star	.247	295	73	23	0	12	46	23	43	.303	.447	August	.259	116	30	9	0	6	21	10	16	.320	.491
Scoring Posn	.253	198	50	10	0	9	86	18	37	.313	.439	Sept/Oct	.284	95	27	8	0	3	16	7	14	.337	.463
Close & Late	.291	86	25	6	1	4	16	15	21	.388	.523	vs. AL	.279	578	161	40	1	28	108	48	94	.336	.460
None on/out	.273	143	39	10	0	8	8	10	24	.320	.524	vs. NL	.232	56	13	5	0	2	8	5	11	.295	.429

1997 By Position

Position	Avg	AB	H	2B	3B	HR	RBI	BB	SO	OBP	SLG	G	GS	Innings	PO	A	E	DP	Fld Pct	Rng Fctr	In Zone	Zone Outs	Zone Rtg	MLB Zone
As lf	.277	610	169	45	1	30	115	48	98	.332	.502	154	154	1333.0	350	1	10	0	.972	2.37	428	342	.799	.805

Last Five Years

	Avg	AB	H	2B	3B	HR	RBI	BB	SO	OBP	SLG		Avg	AB	H	2B	3B	HR	RBI	BB	SO	OBP	SLG
vs. Left	.320	688	220	48	1	51	144	130	107	.425	.615	First Pitch	.362	508	184	37	3	30	107	36	0	.408	.624
vs. Right	.301	2100	633	158	9	151	476	229	332	.373	.601	Ahead in Count	.378	688	260	59	3	76	210	156	0	.492	.804
Groundball	.324	544	176	45	2	39	125	79	92	.414	.629	Behind in Count	.228	1005	229	55	4	54	167	0	334	.233	.452
Flyball	.302	539	163	43	2	45	111	58	87	.371	.640	Two Strikes	.224	1133	254	63	3	63	191	166	439	.327	.452
Home	.319	1330	424	99	8	102	308	173	198	.398	.635	Batting #3	.250	16	4	2	0	0	2	3	4	.368	.375
Away	.294	1458	429	107	2	100	312	186	241	.376	.576	Batting #4	.307	2769	849	204	10	202	618	356	434	.387	.606
Day	.299	916	274	71	3	54	181	109	148	.377	.560	Other	.000	3	0	0	0	0	0	0	1	.000	.000
Night	.309	1872	579	135	7	148	439	250	291	.392	.626	March/April	.298	383	114	25	1	29	80	43	58	.372	.595
Grass	.304	2391	727	171	8	179	536	311	373	.386	.607	May	.331	507	168	41	2	37	122	68	77	.416	.639
Turf	.317	397	126	35	2	23	84	48	66	.394	.589	June	.306	507	155	41	3	32	107	76	101	.393	.588
Pre-All Star	.312	1560	486	121	6	107	343	204	264	.393	.603	July	.298	513	153	31	2	42	123	65	79	.378	.612
Post-All Star	.299	1228	367	85	4	95	277	155	175	.379	.607	August	.300	474	142	33	1	34	103	64	62	.384	.589
Scoring Posn	.297	774	230	52	2	63	429	158	150	.407	.614	Sept/Oct	.300	404	121	35	1	28	85	43	62	.370	.599
Close & Late	.300	410	123	26	2	30	95	72	75	.400	.593	vs. AL	.307	2732	840	201	10	200	612	354	428	.389	.608
None on/out	.324	701	227	62	6	54	54	63	101	.387	.660	vs. NL	.232	56	13	5	0	2	8	5	11	.295	.429

Batter vs. Pitcher (career)

Hits Best Against	Avg	AB	H	2B	3B	HR	RBI	BB	SO	OBP	SLG	Hits Worst Against	Avg	AB	H	2B	3B	HR	RBI	BB	SO	OBP	SLG
Rich Robertson	.875	8	7	1	0	1	4	3	0	.917	1.375	Terry Mulholland	.000	11	0	0	0	0	0	2	3	.154	.000
Brian Bohanon	.600	15	9	3	0	1	6	3	0	.667	1.000	Gregg Olson	.000	10	0	0	0	0	0	1	1	.167	.000
Cal Eldred	.500	28	14	4	1	5	12	3	3	.563	1.250	Dennis Eckersley	.077	13	1	0	1	0	0	0	5	.077	.231
Arthur Rhodes	.400	15	6	3	0	2	7	5	2	.550	1.000	Mike Jackson	.100	10	1	1	0	0	1	1	5	.182	.200
Angel Miranda	.400	10	4	1	0	3	5	4	0	.571	1.400	Ramon Garcia	.167	12	2	0	0	0	0	0	2	.167	.167

Mark Bellhorn — Athletics   Age 23 – Bats Both

	Avg	G	AB	R	H	2B	3B	HR	RBI	BB	SO	HBP	GDP	SB	CS	OBP	SLG	IBB	SH	SF	#Pit	#P/PA	GB	FB	G/F
1997 Season	.228	68	224	33	51	9	1	6	19	32	70	0	1	7	1	.324	.357	0	5	0	1115	4.27	65	52	1.25

1997 Season

	Avg	AB	H	2B	3B	HR	RBI	BB	SO	OBP	SLG		Avg	AB	H	2B	3B	HR	RBI	BB	SO	OBP	SLG
vs. Left	.222	63	14	1	0	2	4	8	26	.310	.333	Scoring Posn	.214	56	12	2	0	0	12	5	21	.279	.250
vs. Right	.230	161	37	8	1	4	15	24	44	.330	.366	Close & Late	.214	42	9	3	0	0	2	6	12	.313	.286
Home	.246	114	28	3	0	3	12	16	32	.338	.351	None on/out	.250	60	15	2	1	2	2	10	18	.357	.417
Away	.209	110	23	6	1	3	7	16	38	.310	.364	Batting #1	.156	96	15	5	0	2	6	9	35	.229	.271
First Pitch	.222	18	4	0	0	1	3	0	0	.222	.389	Batting #9	.275	40	11	0	0	2	5	6	16	.370	.425
Ahead in Count	.391	46	18	2	1	1	5	8	0	.481	.543	Other	.284	88	25	4	1	2	8	17	19	.400	.420
Behind in Count	.156	109	17	3	0	3	7	0	53	.156	.266	Pre-All Star	.321	56	18	0	1	2	6	8	17	.406	.464
Two Strikes	.137	131	18	4	0	2	8	24	70	.271	.214	Post-All Star	.196	168	33	9	0	4	13	24	53	.297	.321

Rafael Belliard — Braves   Age 36 – Bats Right (groundball hitter)

	Avg	G	AB	R	H	2B	3B	HR	RBI	BB	SO	HBP	GDP	SB	CS	OBP	SLG	IBB	SH	SF	#Pit	#P/PA	GB	FB	G/F
1997 Season	.211	72	71	9	15	3	0	1	3	1	17	0	1	0	1	.219	.296	0	4	1	200	2.60	29	11	2.64
Last Five Years	.213	371	592	45	126	24	2	1	28	15	109	7	16	5	6	.240	.265	3	16	3	1863	2.94	274	109	2.51

1997 Season

	Avg	AB	H	2B	3B	HR	RBI	BB	SO	OBP	SLG		Avg	AB	H	2B	3B	HR	RBI	BB	SO	OBP	SLG
vs. Left	.357	14	5	1	0	1	2	0	3	.357	.643	Scoring Posn	.000	13	0	0	0	0	1	0	2	.000	.000
vs. Right	.175	57	10	2	0	0	1	1	14	.186	.211	Close & Late	.333	9	3	1	0	1	2	1	1	.400	.778

Last Five Years

	Avg	AB	H	2B	3B	HR	RBI	BB	SO	OBP	SLG		Avg	AB	H	2B	3B	HR	RBI	BB	SO	OBP	SLG
vs. Left	.238	151	36	6	0	1	9	2	30	.248	.298	First Pitch	.308	143	44	7	1	1	14	3	0	.322	.392
vs. Right	.204	441	90	18	2	0	19	13	79	.237	.254	Ahead in Count	.241	87	21	6	0	0	2	9	0	.320	.310
Groundball	.189	164	31	6	1	0	9	7	31	.225	.238	Behind in Count	.151	304	46	11	1	0	9	0	106	.162	.194
Flyball	.222	90	20	5	0	0	4	2	20	.255	.278	Two Strikes	.109	247	27	4	1	0	4	3	109	.130	.134
Home	.191	267	51	10	0	0	7	6	37	.219	.228	Batting #2	.216	37	8	4	0	1	4	1	7	.250	.405
Away	.231	325	75	14	2	1	21	9	72	.257	.295	Batting #8	.217	498	108	20	2	0	24	13	87	.245	.265
Day	.215	181	39	5	2	0	7	3	28	.231	.265	Other	.175	57	10	0	0	0	0	1	15	.190	.175
Night	.212	411	87	19	0	1	21	12	81	.244	.265	March/April	.245	102	25	5	0	0	3	2	16	.267	.294
Grass	.211	450	95	20	2	1	20	9	75	.232	.271	May	.182	88	16	4	0	0	7	2	16	.215	.227
Turf	.218	142	31	4	0	0	8	6	34	.265	.246	June	.200	60	12	1	0	0	2	2	11	.234	.217
Pre-All Star	.225	302	68	11	0	0	15	6	51	.248	.262	July	.208	125	26	4	0	0	3	1	22	.214	.240
Post-All Star	.200	290	58	13	2	1	13	9	58	.231	.269	August	.190	105	20	4	2	0	6	5	25	.232	.267
Scoring Posn	.176	136	24	3	1	0	23	7	24	.218	.213	Sept/Oct	.241	112	27	6	0	1	7	3	19	.274	.321
Close & Late	.235	68	16	4	0	1	4	3	12	.288	.338	vs. AL	.250	4	1	0	0	0	0	0	1	.250	.250
None on/out	.207	150	31	6	0	0	0	1	30	.217	.247	vs. NL	.213	588	125	24	2	1	28	15	108	.240	.265

Batter vs. Pitcher (since 1984)

Hits Best Against	Avg	AB	H	2B	3B	HR	RBI	BB	SO	OBP	SLG	Hits Worst Against	Avg	AB	H	2B	3B	HR	RBI	BB	SO	OBP	SLG
Mike Morgan	.455	11	5	1	0	0	0	1	2	.500	.545	Ramon Martinez	.071	14	1	0	0	0	0	1	2	.188	.071
Mike Bielecki	.417	12	5	1	0	0	2	1	2	.462	.500	F. Valenzuela	.100	20	2	0	0	0	2	0	1	.100	.100
Shawn Boskie	.364	11	4	1	0	0	1	1	2	.417	.455	Tim Belcher	.105	19	2	1	0	0	1	1	3	.150	.158
John Smiley	.364	11	4	0	0	0	1	0	2	.364	.364	Andy Benes	.111	27	3	0	0	0	1	0	5	.143	.111
Terry Mulholland	.350	20	7	1	1	0	2	1	2	.381	.500	Jeff Brantley	.143	14	2	0	0	0	0	0	2	.143	.143

Rigo Beltran — Cardinals
Age 28 – Pitches Left (flyball pitcher)

	ERA	W	L	Sv	G	GS	IP	BB	SO	Avg	H	2B	3B	HR	RBI	OBP	SLG	GF	IR	IRS	Hld	SvOp	SB	CS	GB	FB	G/F
1997 Season	3.48	1	2	1	35	4	54.1	17	50	.237	47	8	2	3	21	.294	.343	16	11	2	2	1	1	3	51	56	0.91

1997 Season

	ERA	W	L	Sv	G	GS	IP	H	HR	BB	SO		Avg	AB	H	2B	3B	HR	RBI	BB	SO	OBP	SLG
Home	3.33	0	0	1	18	2	27.0	19	0	7	21	vs. Left	.275	40	11	3	1	1	8	7	11	.367	.475
Away	3.62	1	2	0	17	2	27.1	28	3	10	29	vs. Right	.228	158	36	5	1	2	13	10	39	.272	.310
Starter	5.06	0	1	0	4	4	21.1	24	2	7	13	Scoring Posn	.244	45	11	4	0	0	16	5	12	.302	.333
Reliever	2.45	1	1	1	31	0	33.0	23	1	10	37	Close & Late	.182	22	4	0	0	0	3	6	6	.357	.182
0 Days rest (Relief)	0.00	0	0	0	6	0	5.2	2	0	1	7	None on/out	.265	49	13	3	0	0	0	4	15	.321	.327
1 or 2 Days rest	3.52	1	1	1	16	0	15.1	16	0	5	17	First Pitch	.545	22	12	0	1	1	5	0	0	.500	.773
3+ Days rest	2.25	0	0	0	9	0	12.0	5	1	4	13	Ahead in Count	.140	100	14	2	0	2	8	0	44	.140	.220
Pre-All Star	1.93	0	1	0	10	0	9.1	8	0	3	12	Behind in Count	.225	40	9	2	0	0	2	10	0	.373	.275
Post-All Star	3.80	1	1	1	25	4	45.0	39	3	14	38	Two Strikes	.125	96	12	1	0	2	7	7	50	.184	.198

Marvin Benard — Giants
Age 28 – Bats Left

	Avg	G	AB	R	H	2B	3B	HR	RBI	BB	SO	HBP	GDP	SB	CS	OBP	SLG	IBB	SH	SF	#Pit	#P/PA	GB	FB	G/F
1997 Season	.228	84	114	13	26	4	0	1	13	13	29	2	2	3	1	.315	.289	0	0	1	511	3.93	41	28	1.46
Career (1995-1997)	.252	232	636	107	160	23	4	7	44	73	120	6	11	29	12	.333	.333	2	6	2	2727	3.77	268	145	1.85

1997 Season

	Avg	AB	H	2B	3B	HR	RBI	BB	SO	OBP	SLG		Avg	AB	H	2B	3B	HR	RBI	BB	SO	OBP	SLG
vs. Left	.214	14	3	0	0	0	0	2	8	.313	.214	Scoring Posn	.292	24	7	1	0	0	12	5	5	.419	.333
vs. Right	.230	100	23	4	0	1	13	11	21	.316	.300	Close & Late	.188	32	6	1	0	0	4	4	12	.278	.219
Home	.200	55	11	1	0	0	6	5	15	.286	.218	None on/out	.333	39	13	3	0	0	0	3	9	.381	.410
Away	.254	59	15	3	0	1	7	8	14	.343	.356	Batting #1	.200	50	10	1	0	1	3	7	14	.298	.280
First Pitch	.200	15	3	0	0	0	2	0	0	.200	.200	Batting #9	.235	34	8	2	0	0	3	3	7	.297	.294
Ahead in Count	.238	21	5	0	0	0	3	6	0	.393	.238	Other	.267	30	8	1	0	0		7	8	.361	.300
Behind in Count	.200	60	12	3	0	0	6	0	27	.226	.250	Pre-All Star	.250	64	16	1	0	0	6	7	17	.342	.266
Two Strikes	.206	63	13	3	0	1	5	7	29	.296	.302	Post-All Star	.200	50	10	3	0	1	7	6	12	.281	.320

Career (1995-1997)

	Avg	AB	H	2B	3B	HR	RBI	BB	SO	OBP	SLG		Avg	AB	H	2B	3B	HR	RBI	BB	SO	OBP	SLG
vs. Left	.247	89	22	1	0	1	6	9	22	.323	.292	First Pitch	.318	110	35	1	2	2	12	2	0	.342	.418
vs. Right	.252	547	138	22	4	6	38	64	98	.335	.340	Ahead in Count	.312	109	34	8	2	1	14	38	0	.490	.450
Groundball	.253	158	40	3	0	2	7	14	22	.328	.310	Behind in Count	.206	291	60	11	0	3	13	0	105	.214	.275
Flyball	.196	97	19	4	1	2	6	12	26	.284	.320	Two Strikes	.191	304	58	10	0	3	10	33	120	.272	.253
Home	.242	322	78	10	1	2	15	40	59	.332	.298	Batting #1	.249	547	136	20	4	7	32	64	99	.331	.338
Away	.261	314	82	13	3	5	29	33	61	.335	.369	Batting #9	.267	45	12	2	0	0	4	4	10	.327	.311
Day	.233	300	70	10	1	2	15	34	63	.321	.293	Other	.273	44	12	1	0	0	8	5	11	.365	.295
Night	.268	336	90	13	3	5	29	39	57	.345	.369	March/April	.348	92	32	3	0	0	3	10	19	.412	.380
Grass	.244	546	133	19	4	7	37	60	100	.323	.332	May	.231	65	15	2	0	0	4	5	13	.296	.262
Turf	.300	90	27	4	0	0	7	13	20	.394	.344	June	.205	112	23	5	0	0	6	12	23	.286	.250
Pre-All Star	.257	296	76	11	0	0	17	31	59	.330	.294	July	.231	134	31	4	1	3	13	12	24	.295	.343
Post-All Star	.247	340	84	12	4	7	27	42	61	.336	.368	August	.247	93	23	4	1	2	7	16	15	.358	.376
Scoring Posn	.235	115	27	4	1	2	37	14	17	.323	.339	Sept/Oct	.257	140	36	5	2	2	11	18	26	.356	.364
Close & Late	.259	108	28	4	1	4	18	14	27	.344	.426	vs. AL	.222	9	2	1	0	0	1	1	3	.300	.333
None on/out	.298	255	76	10	2	3	3	32	44	.381	.388	vs. NL	.252	627	158	22	4	7	43	72	117	.334	.333

Batter vs. Pitcher (career)

Hits Best Against	Avg	AB	H	2B	3B	HR	RBI	BB	SO	OBP	SLG	Hits Worst Against	Avg	AB	H	2B	3B	HR	RBI	BB	SO	OBP	SLG
Andy Ashby	.364	11	4	1	0	0	0	1	2	.417	.455	Pedro Martinez	.077	13	1	0	0	0	0	0	4	.077	.077
Kevin Brown	.333	12	4	0	0	1	1	0	0	.385	.583	Ramon Martinez	.077	13	1	0	0	1	2	1	5	.143	.308
Frank Castillo	.308	13	4	1	0	0	0	1	2	.357	.385	John Smoltz	.091	11	1	0	0	0	0	1	2	.167	.091
												Andy Benes	.111	9	1	0	0	0	0	2	2	.273	.111
												Shane Reynolds	.200	10	2	0	0	0	0	1	2	.273	.200

Alan Benes — Cardinals
Age 26 – Pitches Right

	ERA	W	L	Sv	G	GS	IP	BB	SO	Avg	H	2B	3B	HR	RBI	OBP	SLG	CG	ShO	Sup	QS	#P/S	SB	CS	GB	FB	G/F
1997 Season	2.89	9	9	0	23	23	161.2	68	160	.219	128	16	4	13	57	.303	.326	2	0	3.56	16	114	10	12	201	140	1.44
Career (1995-1997)	4.17	23	21	0	60	58	368.2	159	311	.250	344	41	17	42	178	.330	.391	5	1	4.52	31	104	19	26	452	393	1.15

1997 Season

	ERA	W	L	Sv	G	GS	IP	H	HR	BB	SO		Avg	AB	H	2B	3B	HR	RBI	BB	SO	OBP	SLG
Home	2.68	3	6	0	12	12	84.0	60	9	34	83	vs. Left	.233	292	68	11	3	8	30	39	73	.325	.373
Away	3.13	6	3	0	11	11	77.2	68	4	34	77	vs. Right	.205	293	60	5	1	5	27	29	87	.279	.280
Day	3.35	3	2	0	6	6	43.0	33	4	22	40	Inning 1-6	.229	490	112	14	2	12	51	54	132	.307	.339
Night	2.73	6	7	0	17	17	118.2	95	9	46	120	Inning 7+	.168	95	16	2	2	1	6	14	28	.282	.263
Grass	2.47	8	7	0	19	19	138.1	95	10	57	140	None on	.209	344	72	9	1	9	9	40	93	.297	.320
Turf	5.40	1	2	0	4	4	23.1	33	3	11	20	Runners on	.232	241	56	7	3	4	48	28	67	.310	.336
March/April	3.62	3	2	0	6	6	37.1	32	3	14	42	Scoring Posn	.216	116	25	2	2	2	40	22	35	.331	.319
May	2.41	1	2	0	5	5	37.1	25	2	13	35	Close & Late	.194	67	13	1	1	1	5	12	19	.316	.284
June	2.03	3	3	0	6	6	44.1	28	5	21	49	None on/out	.191	152	29	5	0	4	4	15	43	.268	.303
July	3.59	2	2	0	6	6	42.2	43	3	20	34	vs. 1st Batr (relief)	.000	0	0	0	0	0	0	0	0	.000	.000
August	0.00	0	0	0	0	0	0.0	0	0	0	0	1st Inning Pitched	.210	81	17	0	0	1	7	10	23	.293	.247
Sept/Oct	0.00	0	0	0	0	0	0.0	0	0	0	0	First 75 Pitches	.227	370	84	9	1	8	35	44	102	.310	.322
Starter	2.89	9	9	0	23	23	161.2	128	13	68	160	Pitch 76-90	.200	80	16	4	0	2	8	6	23	.256	.325
Reliever	0.00	0	0	0	0	0	0.0	0	0	0	0	Pitch 91-105	.213	75	16	1	0	2	7	9	21	.314	.307

37

1997 Season

	ERA	W	L	Sv	G	GS	IP	H	HR	BB	SO		Avg	AB	H	2B	3B	HR	RBI	BB	SO	OBP	SLG
0-3 Days Rest (Start)	0.00	0	0	0	0	0	0.0	0	0	0	0	Pitch 106+	.200	60	12	2	3	1	7	9	14	.304	.383
4 Days Rest	2.57	5	7	0	16	16	112.0	89	10	48	114	First Pitch	.304	69	21	1	2	3	17	2	0	.333	.507
5+ Days Rest	3.62	4	2	0	7	7	49.2	39	3	20	46	Ahead in Count	.173	300	52	7	0	3	16	0	133	.176	.227
vs. AL	1.10	0	1	0	2	2	16.1	9	2	6	21	Behind in Count	.336	107	36	6	1	5	17	31	0	.486	.551
vs. NL	3.10	9	8	0	21	21	145.1	119	11	62	139	Two Strikes	.156	302	47	4	1	3	15	35	160	.241	.205
Pre-All Star	2.55	7	7	0	18	18	127.0	90	11	51	136	Pre-All Star	.200	450	90	12	2	11	40	51	136	.285	.309
Post-All Star	4.15	2	2	0	5	5	34.2	38	2	17	24	Post-All Star	.281	135	38	4	2	2	17	17	24	.359	.385

Career (1995-1997)

	ERA	W	L	Sv	G	GS	IP	H	HR	BB	SO		Avg	AB	H	2B	3B	HR	RBI	BB	SO	OBP	SLG
Home	3.12	11	10	0	27	26	178.2	139	24	74	155	vs. Left	.290	639	185	26	9	20	91	87	124	.376	.452
Away	5.16	12	11	0	33	32	190.0	205	18	85	156	vs. Right	.215	738	159	21	2	22	87	72	187	.288	.339
Day	4.40	7	7	0	17	15	100.1	100	13	47	89	Inning 1-6	.253	1179	298	43	8	34	155	129	267	.329	.389
Night	4.09	16	14	0	43	43	268.1	244	29	112	222	Inning 7+	.232	198	46	4	3	8	23	30	44	.335	.404
Grass	4.03	18	16	0	46	44	283.1	255	35	125	240	None on	.236	787	186	28	4	28	28	97	183	.327	.389
Turf	4.64	5	5	0	14	14	85.1	89	7	34	71	Runners on	.268	590	158	19	7	14	150	62	128	.334	.395
March/April	4.23	6	3	0	12	12	72.1	67	7	28	76	Scoring Posn	.269	305	82	12	3	6	127	48	69	.359	.387
May	4.62	2	4	0	10	10	64.1	53	8	28	57	Close & Late	.267	116	31	2	1	6	18	21	29	.377	.457
June	2.30	6	4	0	11	11	78.1	60	8	30	62	None on/out	.252	353	89	13	3	14	14	43	80	.340	.425
July	4.98	5	4	0	12	12	72.1	78	9	37	55	vs. 1st Batr (relief)	.000	1	0	0	0	0	0	1	0	.500	.000
August	3.69	2	2	0	6	6	39.0	34	7	16	20	1st Inning Pitched	.279	222	62	7	0	2	34	38	52	.387	.338
Sept/Oct	5.95	2	4	0	9	7	42.1	52	3	20	41	First 75 Pitches	.255	941	240	35	7	29	119	110	218	.336	.400
Starter	4.16	22	20	0	58	58	365.2	339	41	157	309	Pitch 76-90	.207	184	38	6	0	5	18	15	40	.266	.321
Reliever	6.00	1	1	0	2	0	3.0	5	1	2	2	Pitch 91-105	.250	136	34	2	0	4	21	19	30	.346	.353
0-3 Days Rest (Start)	4.11	0	1	0	3	3	15.1	19	1	10	10	Pitch 106+	.276	116	32	4	4	4	20	15	23	.359	.483
4 Days Rest	3.91	13	13	0	33	33	212.0	184	22	93	186	First Pitch	.376	181	68	10	2	6	36	5	0	.393	.552
5+ Days Rest	4.55	9	6	0	22	22	138.1	136	18	54	114	Ahead in Count	.185	653	121	16	3	10	55	0	262	.192	.265
vs. AL	1.10	0	1	0	2	2	16.1	9	2	6	21	Behind in Count	.332	295	98	12	4	19	58	81	0	.471	.593
vs. NL	4.32	23	20	0	58	56	352.1	335	40	153	290	Two Strikes	.164	657	108	12	4	7	39	73	311	.249	.227
Pre-All Star	3.71	15	12	0	36	36	233.0	196	25	96	212	Pre-All Star	.229	856	196	32	6	25	106	96	212	.308	.368
Post-All Star	4.98	8	9	0	24	22	135.2	148	17	63	99	Post-All Star	.284	521	148	15	5	17	72	63	99	.365	.430

Pitcher vs. Batter (career)

Pitches Best Vs.	Avg	AB	H	2B	3B	HR	RBI	BB	SO	OBP	SLG	Pitches Worst Vs.	Avg	AB	H	2B	3B	HR	RBI	BB	SO	OBP	SLG
Fred McGriff	.000	13	0	0	0	0	0	0	1	.000	.000	Mark Grace	.778	9	7	0	1	0	1	4	1	.846	1.000
Deion Sanders	.000	11	0	0	0	0	0	1	1	.083	.000	Curtis Goodwin	.700	10	7	1	0	0	1	2	2	.750	.800
Bernard Gilkey	.077	13	1	0	0	0	2	0	2	.071	.077	Jose Vizcaino	.692	13	9	1	2	0	2	0	3	.692	1.077
Chipper Jones	.091	11	1	0	0	0	1	1	2	.167	.091	Barry Bonds	.500	12	6	2	0	2	4	1	1	.538	1.167
Mark Lemke	.167	12	2	0	0	0	1	0	0	.167	.167	Lance Johnson	.455	11	5	1	1	2	4	2	1	.538	1.273

Andy Benes — Cardinals   Age 30 – Pitches Right

	ERA	W	L	Sv	G	GS	IP	BB	SO	Avg	H	2B	3B	HR	RBI	OBP	SLG	CG	ShO	Sup	QS	#P/S	SB	CS	GB	FB	G/F
1997 Season	3.10	10	7	0	26	26	177.0	61	175	.230	149	28	5	9	60	.298	.330	0	0	5.03	20	111	22	9	194	176	1.10
Last Five Years	3.86	60	55	1	152	150	992.0	353	874	.243	912	173	28	98	409	.310	.383	10	6	4.92	94	107	86	40	1109	1109	1.00

1997 Season

	ERA	W	L	Sv	G	GS	IP	H	HR	BB	SO		Avg	AB	H	2B	3B	HR	RBI	BB	SO	OBP	SLG
Home	2.82	7	2	0	13	13	89.1	76	5	27	83	vs. Left	.244	336	82	16	4	6	39	31	80	.306	.369
Away	3.39	3	5	0	13	13	87.2	73	4	34	92	vs. Right	.215	312	67	12	1	3	21	30	95	.290	.288
Day	3.02	3	1	0	9	9	62.2	51	5	16	72	Inning 1-6	.215	549	118	19	5	8	47	50	149	.282	.311
Night	3.15	7	6	0	17	17	114.1	98	4	45	103	Inning 7+	.313	99	31	9	0	1	13	11	26	.387	.434
Grass	3.16	9	6	0	22	22	151.0	125	8	47	147	None on	.215	377	81	16	3	5	5	39	110	.292	.313
Turf	2.77	1	1	0	4	4	26.0	24	1	14	28	Runners on	.251	271	68	12	2	4	55	22	65	.307	.354
March/April	3.60	1	0	0	1	1	5.0	6	0	4	4	Scoring Posn	.199	151	30	6	2	1	46	19	35	.281	.285
May	2.51	2	2	0	6	6	43.0	33	2	12	37	Close & Late	.296	54	16	5	0	0	9	6	15	.367	.389
June	3.69	3	1	0	6	6	39.0	39	1	12	49	None on/out	.253	166	42	10	2	2	2	17	46	.326	.373
July	2.95	1	2	0	5	5	36.2	24	4	12	43	vs. 1st Batr (relief)	.000	0	0	0	0	0	0	0	0	.000	.000
August	3.79	2	2	0	6	6	40.1	36	2	20	32	1st Inning Pitched	.202	94	19	3	2	1	13	11	24	.287	.309
Sept/Oct	1.38	1	0	0	2	2	13.0	11	0	1	10	First 75 Pitches	.219	429	94	14	5	7	37	36	114	.281	.324
Starter	3.10	10	7	0	26	26	177.0	149	9	61	175	Pitch 76-90	.224	85	19	6	0	0	4	6	25	.283	.294
Reliever	0.00	0	0	0	0	0	0.0	0	0	0	0	Pitch 91-105	.233	73	17	4	0	2	10	10	20	.329	.370
0-3 Days Rest (Start)	12.60	0	1	0	1	1	5.0	9	0	2	6	Pitch 106+	.311	61	19	4	0	0	9	9	16	.394	.377
4 Days Rest	3.06	6	5	0	18	18	123.2	100	7	39	118	First Pitch	.367	79	29	6	1	1	4	2	0	.390	.506
5+ Days Rest	2.23	4	1	0	7	7	48.1	40	2	20	51	Ahead in Count	.150	306	46	8	3	0	13	0	137	.160	.196
vs. AL	5.21	1	1	0	3	3	19.0	24	0	3	22	Behind in Count	.371	116	43	8	1	6	22	29	0	.486	.612
vs. NL	2.85	9	6	0	23	23	158.0	125	9	58	153	Two Strikes	.129	348	45	8	2	0	24	30	175	.205	.164
Pre-All Star	3.16	6	3	0	14	14	94.0	83	3	30	100	Pre-All Star	.240	346	83	16	2	3	32	30	100	.302	.324
Post-All Star	3.04	4	4	0	12	12	83.0	66	6	31	75	Post-All Star	.219	302	66	12	3	6	28	31	75	.294	.338

Last Five Years

	ERA	W	L	Sv	G	GS	IP	H	HR	BB	SO		Avg	AB	H	2B	3B	HR	RBI	BB	SO	OBP	SLG
Home	3.84	30	26	1	76	74	498.2	460	54	169	452	vs. Left	.253	1840	466	88	18	39	200	209	354	.330	.384
Away	3.89	30	29	0	76	76	493.1	452	44	184	422	vs. Right	.234	1908	446	85	10	59	209	144	520	.290	.382
Day	3.56	18	12	0	45	44	298.0	258	26	100	276	Inning 1-6	.239	3194	764	139	25	82	351	293	763	.305	.375
Night	3.99	42	43	1	107	106	694.0	654	72	253	598	Inning 7+	.267	554	148	34	3	16	58	60	111	.341	.426
Grass	3.83	45	41	1	116	114	758.1	695	73	249	485	None on	.238	2242	534	99	18	62	62	178	552	.297	.381
Turf	3.97	15	14	0	36	36	233.2	217	25	104	187	Runners on	.251	1506	378	74	10	36	347	175	322	.328	.385
March/April	3.98	7	10	0	19	19	126.2	119	12	40	102	Scoring Posn	.243	836	203	40	7	18	291	132	185	.342	.372

Last Five Years

	ERA	W	L	Sv	G	GS	IP	H	HR	BB	SO
May	3.94	8	16	1	31	30	196.2	188	15	51	178
June	2.98	11	5	0	28	28	196.1	164	17	57	184
July	3.68	11	8	0	27	27	188.1	157	23	65	193
August	4.82	14	9	0	27	27	170.0	171	19	91	144
Sept/Oct	4.03	9	7	0	20	19	114.0	113	12	49	73
Starter	3.85	60	55	0	150	150	991.0	910	98	351	873
Reliever	18.00	0	0	1	2	0	1.0	2	0	2	1
0-3 Days Rest (Start)	5.29	2	2	0	6	6	34.0	36	4	8	26
4 Days Rest	4.01	39	41	0	105	105	685.0	638	71	248	614
5+ Days Rest	3.28	19	12	0	39	39	272.0	236	23	95	233
vs. AL	5.71	8	3	0	15	15	82.0	96	8	36	67
vs. NL	3.70	52	52	1	137	135	910.0	816	90	317	807
Pre-All Star	3.54	30	32	0	86	85	572.1	511	47	167	525
Post-All Star	4.31	30	23	0	66	65	419.2	401	51	186	349

	Avg	AB	H	2B	3B	HR	RBI	BB	SO	OBP	SLG
Close & Late	.237	291	69	15	2	5	29	34	64	.322	.354
None on/out	.268	993	266	49	9	38	38	75	232	.322	.450
1st Batr (relief)	.000	1	0	0	0	0	0	1	0	.500	.000
1st Inning Pitched	.253	577	146	23	3	12	80	78	139	.339	.366
First 75 Pitches	.240	2528	607	114	16	61	256	224	599	.303	.370
Pitch 76-90	.234	500	117	21	6	15	60	50	112	.308	.390
Pitch 91-105	.273	425	116	24	5	16	58	39	89	.339	.466
Pitch 106+	.244	295	72	14	1	6	35	40	74	.333	.359
Ahead in Count	.181	1813	328	63	10	28	140	0	733	.187	.273
Behind in Count	.340	703	239	49	7	32	108	181	0	.471	.566
Two Strikes	.164	1889	310	60	13	27	155	155	874	.231	.253
Pre-All Star	.237	2158	511	108	13	47	211	167	525	.294	.364
Post-All Star	.252	1590	401	65	15	51	198	186	349	.332	.408

Pitcher vs. Batter (career)

Pitches Best Vs.	Avg	AB	H	2B	3B	HR	RBI	BB	SO	OBP	SLG
Ricky Otero	.000	10	0	0	0	0	0	2	3	.167	.000
Kevin Stocker	.042	24	1	0	0	0	0	1	6	.080	.042
Edgar Renteria	.071	14	1	0	0	0	0	0	7	.071	.071
Raul Mondesi	.071	14	1	0	0	0	0	1	4	.133	.071
Damon Berryhill	.083	12	1	0	0	0	0	0	8	.083	.083

Pitches Worst Vs.	Avg	AB	H	2B	3B	HR	RBI	BB	SO	OBP	SLG
Bret Boone	.600	15	9	2	1	1	7	1	4	.625	1.067
Tim Raines	.500	16	8	1	1	2	4	1	3	.529	1.063
Wil Cordero	.500	12	6	1	0	3	6	1	0	.538	1.333
Benito Santiago	.400	15	6	2	0	2	4	2	6	.471	.933
Kevin Mitchell	.367	30	11	4	1	5	10	2	8	.406	1.067

Armando Benitez — Orioles

Age 25 – Pitches Right (flyball pitcher)

	ERA	W	L	Sv	G	GS	IP	BB	SO	Avg	H	2B	3B	HR	RBI	OBP	SLG	GF	IR	IRS	Hld	SvOp	SB	CS	GB	FB	G/F
1997 Season	2.45	4	5	9	71	0	73.1	43	106	.191	49	3	2	7	28	.305	.300	26	57	12	20	10	20	2	46	74	0.62
Career (1994-1997)	3.53	6	10	15	136	0	145.1	90	196	.195	190	11	3	17	66	.318	.327	53	123	31	27	20	27	3	104	160	0.65

1997 Season

	ERA	W	L	Sv	G	GS	IP	H	HR	BB	SO
Home	3.89	2	4	3	34	0	34.2	27	4	25	45
Away	1.16	2	1	6	37	0	38.2	22	3	18	61
Day	1.95	2	2	3	29	0	27.2	16	2	19	37
Night	2.76	2	3	6	42	0	45.2	33	5	24	69
Grass	2.80	4	5	6	63	0	64.1	46	7	40	92
Turf	0.00	0	0	3	8	0	9.0	3	0	3	14
March/April	6.55	0	2	2	9	0	11.0	8	2	11	17
May	0.00	0	0	4	11	0	9.1	3	0	3	11
June	3.29	0	1	0	14	0	13.2	14	3	8	17
July	0.69	1	0	2	13	0	13.0	8	0	7	21
August	1.76	2	1	1	14	0	15.1	9	1	9	25
Sept/Oct	2.45	1	1	0	10	0	11.0	7	1	5	15
Starter	0.00	0	0	0	0	0	0.0	0	0	0	0
Reliever	2.45	4	5	9	71	0	73.1	49	7	43	106
0 Days rest (Relief)	3.06	2	1	2	21	0	17.2	13	2	16	24
1 or 2 Days rest	1.35	1	3	6	34	0	40.0	25	2	15	60
3+ Days rest	4.60	1	1	1	16	0	15.2	11	3	12	22
vs. AL	2.47	4	5	9	62	0	65.2	45	5	39	96
vs. NL	2.35	0	0	0	9	0	7.2	4	2	4	10
Pre-All Star	3.25	0	3	6	36	0	36.0	27	5	23	47
Post-All Star	1.69	4	2	3	35	0	37.1	22	2	20	59

	Avg	AB	H	2B	3B	HR	RBI	BB	SO	OBP	SLG
vs. Left	.204	103	21	2	1	3	12	21	38	.339	.330
vs. Right	.182	154	28	1	1	4	16	22	68	.282	.279
Inning 1-6	.000	0	0	0	0	0	0	0	0	.000	.000
Inning 7+	.191	257	49	3	2	7	28	43	106	.305	.300
None on	.274	113	31	1	1	5	5	19	45	.379	.434
Runners on	.125	144	18	2	1	2	23	24	61	.249	.194
Scoring Posn	.146	89	13	2	1	1	21	17	35	.279	.225
Close & Late	.168	161	27	2	1	2	17	26	70	.281	.230
None on/out	.314	51	16	1	0	3	3	13	13	.453	.510
vs. 1st Batr (relief)	.293	58	17	1	1	1	9	11	18	.408	.397
1st Inning Pitched	.186	215	40	3	2	6	26	36	82	.301	.302
First 15 Pitches	.203	172	35	3	2	4	17	29	61	.320	.314
Pitch 16-30	.177	79	14	0	0	3	10	11	42	.269	.291
Pitch 31-45	.000	6	0	0	0	0	1	3	3	.333	.000
Pitch 46+	.000	0	0	0	0	0	0	0	0	.000	.000
First Pitch	.278	18	5	0	2	0	4	5	0	.417	.500
Ahead in Count	.147	156	23	4	0	4	15	0	87	.151	.237
Behind in Count	.357	42	15	0	0	2	6	19	0	.551	.500
Two Strikes	.130	161	21	2	0	2	13	19	106	.223	.180
Pre-All Star	.214	126	27	1	0	5	16	23	47	.331	.341
Post-All Star	.168	131	22	2	2	2	12	20	59	.278	.260

Career (1994-1997)

	ERA	W	L	Sv	G	GS	IP	H	HR	BB	SO
Home	4.15	3	5	5	66	0	73.2	55	8	47	92
Away	2.89	3	5	10	70	0	71.2	46	9	43	104
Day	2.81	4	3	5	50	0	51.1	31	6	37	73
Night	3.93	2	7	10	86	0	94.0	70	11	53	123
Grass	3.88	5	8	9	115	0	123.0	91	16	83	164
Turf	1.61	1	2	6	21	0	22.1	10	1	7	32
March/April	5.31	1	3	2	17	0	20.1	13	2	18	28
May	2.61	0	2	5	23	0	20.2	10	3	13	23
June	4.57	0	1	0	22	0	21.2	23	4	12	26
July	2.22	2	0	2	20	0	24.1	17	1	13	38
August	3.58	2	3	3	31	0	37.2	24	3	21	54
Sept/Oct	3.05	1	1	3	23	0	20.2	14	4	8	27
Starter	0.00	0	0	0	0	0	0.0	0	0	0	0
Reliever	3.53	6	10	15	136	0	145.1	101	17	90	196
0 Days rest (Relief)	3.27	2	3	3	35	0	33.0	21	3	24	44
1 or 2 Days rest	3.50	2	6	11	66	0	74.2	52	9	42	103
3+ Days rest	3.82	2	1	1	35	0	37.2	28	5	24	49
vs. AL	3.60	6	10	15	127	0	137.2	97	15	86	186
vs. NL	2.35	0	0	0	9	0	7.2	4	2	4	10
Pre-All Star	4.19	2	6	7	68	0	68.2	50	9	52	86
Post-All Star	2.93	4	4	8	68	0	76.2	51	8	38	110

	Avg	AB	H	2B	3B	HR	RBI	BB	SO	OBP	SLG
vs. Left	.218	202	44	7	2	5	19	45	73	.368	.347
vs. Right	.181	315	57	4	1	12	47	45	123	.285	.314
Inning 1-6	.091	11	1	0	0	0	1	4	5	.375	.091
Inning 7+	.198	506	100	11	3	17	65	86	191	.317	.332
None on	.247	231	57	6	2	9	9	40	89	.365	.407
Runners on	.154	286	44	5	1	8	57	50	107	.282	.262
Scoring Posn	.144	180	26	4	1	6	52	37	70	.289	.278
Close & Late	.186	253	47	3	1	8	38	46	101	.312	.300
None on/out	.250	100	25	2	0	3	3	24	38	.405	.360
vs. 1st Batr (relief)	.233	116	27	1	1	5	22	15	44	.324	.388
1st Inning Pitched	.182	391	71	8	3	14	55	65	151	.304	.325
First 15 Pitches	.203	315	64	7	3	12	43	47	117	.316	.359
Pitch 16-30	.167	144	24	2	0	4	16	33	58	.315	.264
Pitch 31-45	.225	40	9	0	0	1	7	5	16	.311	.300
Pitch 46+	.222	18	4	2	0	0	0	5	0	.391	.333
First Pitch	.289	45	13	0	2	3	14	7	0	.400	.556
Ahead in Count	.156	289	45	4	0	6	25	0	153	.165	.232
Behind in Count	.329	85	28	3	0	8	17	39	0	.544	.647
Two Strikes	.139	324	45	4	0	4	22	44	196	.240	.179
Pre-All Star	.207	241	50	3	0	9	37	52	86	.350	.332
Post-All Star	.185	276	51	8	3	8	29	38	110	.288	.322

Pitcher vs. Batter (career)

Pitches Best Vs.	Avg	AB	H	2B	3B	HR	RBI	BB	SO	OBP	SLG	Pitches Worst Vs.	Avg	AB	H	2B	3B	HR	RBI	BB	SO	OBP	SLG
Edgar Martinez	.111	9	1	0	0	1	4	2	4	.273	.444												
Joe Carter	.200	10	2	1	0	0	3	0	3	.182	.300												

Yamil Benitez — Royals   Age 26 – Bats Right

	Avg	G	AB	R	H	2B	3B	HR	RBI	BB	SO	HBP	GDP	SB	CS	OBP	SLG	IBB	SH	SF	#Pit	#P/PA	GB	FB	G/F
1997 Season	.267	53	191	22	51	7	1	8	21	10	49	1	2	2	2	.307	.440	0	2	0	709	3.48	59	49	1.20
Career (1995-1997)	.281	78	242	30	68	9	2	10	30	11	60	1	3	2	4	.315	.459	0	2	0	887	3.46	79	64	1.23

1997 Season

	Avg	AB	H	2B	3B	HR	RBI	BB	SO	OBP	SLG		Avg	AB	H	2B	3B	HR	RBI	BB	SO	OBP	SLG
vs. Left	.241	58	14	2	0	3	8	4	13	.290	.431	Scoring Posn	.200	40	8	1	0	2	13	1	14	.220	.375
vs. Right	.278	133	37	5	1	5	13	6	36	.314	.444	Close & Late	.321	28	9	2	0	1	2	2	6	.387	.500
Home	.314	102	32	0	0	5	12	5	22	.352	.461	None on/out	.318	44	14	2	0	0	0	4	7	.388	.364
Away	.213	89	19	7	1	3	9	5	27	.255	.416	Batting #7	.250	52	13	0	0	1	2	5	15	.328	.308
First Pitch	.483	29	14	1	1	1	4	0	0	.483	.690	Batting #8	.323	62	20	1	0	3	10	1	16	.333	.484
Ahead in Count	.400	20	8	1	0	3	8	6	0	.538	.900	Other	.234	77	18	6	1	4	9	4	18	.272	.494
Behind in Count	.170	106	18	3	0	3	8	0	46	.178	.283	Pre-All Star	.000	0	0	0	0	0	0	0	0	.000	.000
Two Strikes	.122	98	12	3	0	3	7	4	49	.157	.245	Post-All Star	.267	191	51	7	1	8	21	10	49	.307	.440

Mike Benjamin — Red Sox   Age 32 – Bats Right (flyball hitter)

	Avg	G	AB	R	H	2B	3B	HR	RBI	BB	SO	HBP	GDP	SB	CS	OBP	SLG	IBB	SH	SF	#Pit	#P/PA	GB	FB	G/F
1997 Season	.233	49	116	12	27	9	1	0	7	4	27	1	2	2	3	.262	.328	0	1	1	434	3.53	30	32	0.94
Last Five Years	.222	253	613	75	136	32	3	12	57	38	138	11	11	21	5	.279	.343	11	20	1	2394	3.51	183	179	1.02

1997 Season

	Avg	AB	H	2B	3B	HR	RBI	BB	SO	OBP	SLG		Avg	AB	H	2B	3B	HR	RBI	BB	SO	OBP	SLG
vs. Left	.156	32	5	2	0	0	2	3	6	.229	.219	Scoring Posn	.139	36	5	0	1	0	7	2	11	.200	.194
vs. Right	.262	84	22	7	1	0	5	1	21	.276	.369	Close & Late	.231	13	3	1	0	0	1	2	6	.333	.308

Last Five Years

	Avg	AB	H	2B	3B	HR	RBI	BB	SO	OBP	SLG		Avg	AB	H	2B	3B	HR	RBI	BB	SO	OBP	SLG
vs. Left	.261	142	37	14	0	4	19	9	19	.305	.444	First Pitch	.284	102	29	9	1	1	12	7	0	.327	.422
vs. Right	.210	471	99	18	3	8	38	29	119	.271	.312	Ahead in Count	.296	125	37	8	1	7	19	18	0	.401	.544
Groundball	.256	176	45	7	1	2	18	14	39	.328	.341	Behind in Count	.156	302	47	12	1	2	14	0	129	.169	.222
Flyball	.150	107	16	6	1	0	8	4	29	.180	.224	Two Strikes	.136	295	40	9	1	1	11	13	138	.185	.183
Home	.225	276	62	17	0	5	23	16	67	.274	.341	Batting #2	.240	154	37	6	0	4	14	5	38	.267	.357
Away	.220	337	74	15	3	7	34	22	71	.283	.344	Batting #8	.216	342	74	20	1	7	35	29	68	.295	.342
Day	.226	287	65	14	1	7	33	18	65	.284	.355	Other	.214	117	25	6	2	1	8	4	32	.246	.325
Night	.218	326	71	18	2	5	24	20	73	.275	.331	March/April	.294	34	10	2	1	2	6	5	5	.400	.588
Grass	.232	427	99	20	1	10	41	27	96	.286	.354	May	.190	84	16	5	0	1	6	5	20	.253	.286
Turf	.199	186	37	12	2	2	16	11	42	.262	.317	June	.236	220	52	6	1	7	24	15	43	.300	.368
Pre-All Star	.235	392	92	17	2	12	43	29	79	.306	.380	July	.229	96	22	8	0	2	12	5	21	.288	.375
Post-All Star	.199	221	44	15	1	0	14	9	59	.229	.276	August	.267	105	28	9	1	0	6	6	26	.304	.371
Scoring Posn	.232	155	36	7	1	2	38	22	38	.333	.329	Sept/Oct	.108	74	8	2	0	0	3	2	23	.132	.135
Close & Late	.190	100	19	4	0	1	5	8	34	.250	.260	vs. AL	.217	106	23	7	1	0	7	4	25	.250	.302
None on/out	.226	133	30	6	1	3	3	4	25	.254	.353	vs. NL	.223	507	113	25	2	12	50	34	113	.285	.351

Batter vs. Pitcher (career)

Hits Best Against	Avg	AB	H	2B	3B	HR	RBI	BB	SO	OBP	SLG	Hits Worst Against	Avg	AB	H	2B	3B	HR	RBI	BB	SO	OBP	SLG
Jaime Navarro	.389	18	7	0	0	2	4	0	3	.389	.722	Denny Neagle	.091	11	1	0	0	0	0	0	3	.091	.091
												Armando Reynoso	.091	11	1	0	0	0	0	0	1	.091	.091
												Joey Hamilton	.125	8	1	0	0	0	0	3	2	.364	.125
												Steve Avery	.143	14	2	2	0	0	0	2	1	.250	.286
												Willie Blair	.182	11	2	1	0	0	0	0	1	.182	.273

Shayne Bennett — Expos   Age 26 – Pitches Right

	ERA	W	L	Sv	G	GS	IP	BB	SO	Avg	H	2B	3B	HR	RBI	OBP	SLG	GF	IR	IRS	Hld	SvOp	SB	CS	GB	FB	G/F
1997 Season	3.18	0	1	0	16	0	22.2	9	8	.247	21	5	0	2	8	.309	.376	3	3	1	0	0	5	2	34	30	1.13

1997 Season

	ERA	W	L	Sv	G	GS	IP	H	HR	BB	SO		Avg	AB	H	2B	3B	HR	RBI	BB	SO	OBP	SLG
Home	2.00	0	0	0	5	0	9.0	6	1	1	3	vs. Left	.143	28	4	1	0	0	1	4	3	.250	.179
Away	3.95	0	1	0	11	0	13.2	15	1	8	5	vs. Right	.298	57	17	4	0	2	7	5	5	.338	.474

Jeff Berblinger — Cardinals   Age 27 – Bats Right

	Avg	G	AB	R	H	2B	3B	HR	RBI	BB	SO	HBP	GDP	SB	CS	OBP	SLG	IBB	SH	SF	#Pit	#P/PA	GB	FB	G/F
1997 Season	.000	7	5	1	0	0	0	0	0	0	1	0	0	0	0	.000	.000	0	1	0	14	2.33	3	1	3.00

1997 Season

	Avg	AB	H	2B	3B	HR	RBI	BB	SO	OBP	SLG		Avg	AB	H	2B	3B	HR	RBI	BB	SO	OBP	SLG
vs. Left	.000	1	0	0	0	0	0	0	0	.000	.000	Scoring Posn	.000	0	0	0	0	0	0	0	0	.000	.000
vs. Right	.000	4	0	0	0	0	0	0	1	.000	.000	Close & Late	.000	1	0	0	0	0	0	0	0	.000	.000

Jason Bere — White Sox
Age 27 – Pitches Right (flyball pitcher)

	ERA	W	L	Sv	G	GS	IP	BB	SO	Avg	H	2B	3B	HR	RBI	OBP	SLG	CG	ShO	Sup	QS	#P/S	SB	CS	GB	FB	G/F
1997 Season	4.71	4	2	0	6	6	28.2	17	21	.198	20	3	0	4	14	.328	.347	0	0	5.97	2	80	3	0	18	45	0.40
Career (1993-1997)	4.99	36	25	0	86	86	467.1	302	406	.242	425	67	5	57	237	.355	.383	2	0	5.95	37	100	76	21	480	552	0.87

1997 Season

	ERA	W	L	Sv	G	GS	IP	H	HR	BB	SO		Avg	AB	H	2B	3B	HR	RBI	BB	SO	OBP	SLG
Home	4.15	3	1	0	4	4	21.2	12	3	14	12	vs. Left	.280	50	14	2	0	2	8	10	8	.403	.440
Away	6.43	1	1	0	2	2	7.0	8	1	3	9	vs. Right	.118	51	6	1	0	2	6	7	13	.250	.255

Career (1993-1997)

	ERA	W	L	Sv	G	GS	IP	H	HR	BB	SO		Avg	AB	H	2B	3B	HR	RBI	BB	SO	OBP	SLG
Home	4.68	17	11	0	43	43	238.2	204	28	154	195	vs. Left	.256	892	228	37	3	22	112	194	191	.389	.378
Away	5.31	19	14	0	43	43	228.2	221	29	148	211	vs. Right	.228	864	197	30	2	35	125	108	215	.318	.389
Day	4.99	8	7	0	22	22	115.1	108	13	80	91	Inning 1-6	.238	1616	385	57	5	53	221	284	374	.354	.378
Night	4.99	28	18	0	64	64	352.0	317	44	222	315	Inning 7+	.286	140	40	10	0	4	16	18	32	.367	.443
Grass	5.06	33	24	0	79	79	423.1	390	54	276	362	None on	.239	941	225	39	2	30	30	174	220	.362	.380
Turf	4.30	3	1	0	7	7	44.0	35	3	26	44	Runners on	.245	815	200	28	3	27	207	128	186	.347	.387
March/April	6.00	2	3	0	10	10	48.0	45	6	38	49	Scoring Posn	.256	445	114	17	2	14	176	89	104	.373	.398
May	4.39	5	3	0	11	11	69.2	58	8	43	46	Close & Late	.295	88	26	7	0	1	9	12	19	.380	.409
June	4.36	8	5	0	18	18	109.1	95	12	75	107	None on/out	.255	431	110	18	2	17	17	81	85	.378	.425
July	5.74	5	4	0	15	15	78.1	79	9	51	63	vs. 1st Batr (relief)	.000	0	0	0	0	0	0	0	0	.000	.000
August	5.22	7	4	0	16	16	81.0	73	13	47	65	1st Inning Pitched	.265	332	88	16	1	13	71	77	92	.404	.437
Sept/Oct	4.78	9	6	0	16	16	81.0	75	9	48	76	First 75 Pitches	.237	1211	287	43	3	36	163	205	278	.350	.367
Starter	4.99	36	25	0	86	86	467.1	425	57	302	406	Pitch 76-90	.242	223	54	8	1	10	33	40	51	.355	.422
Reliever	0.00	0	0	0	0	0	0.0	0	0	0	0	Pitch 91-105	.270	189	51	10	0	7	25	34	44	.387	.434
0-3 Days Rest (Start)	6.32	2	0	0	3	3	15.2	12	4	8	17	Pitch 106+	.248	133	33	6	1	4	16	23	33	.363	.398
4 Days Rest	5.28	18	14	0	47	47	254.0	229	30	176	215	First Pitch	.284	208	59	10	2	7	33	6	0	.320	.452
5+ Days Rest	4.51	16	11	0	36	36	197.2	174	23	118	174	Ahead in Count	.179	826	148	26	1	14	86	0	336	.184	.264
vs. AL	5.01	35	25	0	85	85	461.1	423	55	300	404	Behind in Count	.331	384	127	18	1	21	66	176	0	.542	.547
vs. NL	3.00	1	0	0	1	1	6.0	2	2	2	2	Two Strikes	.176	894	157	19	2	17	82	120	406	.272	.258
Pre-All Star	5.02	17	13	0	45	45	258.0	234	29	180	226	Pre-All Star	.244	960	234	40	3	29	131	180	226	.363	.382
Post-All Star	4.94	19	12	0	41	41	209.1	191	28	122	180	Post-All Star	.240	796	191	27	2	28	106	122	180	.345	.384

Pitcher vs. Batter (career)

Pitches Best Vs.	Avg	AB	H	2B	3B	HR	RBI	BB	SO	OBP	SLG	Pitches Worst Vs.	Avg	AB	H	2B	3B	HR	RBI	BB	SO	OBP	SLG
Mickey Tettleton	.000	14	0	0	0	0	0	6	9	.300	.000	Gary Gaetti	.471	17	8	1	0	1	6	0	5	.471	.706
B.J. Surhoff	.083	12	1	0	0	0	0	1	5	.154	.083	John Valentin	.444	9	4	1	0	1	3	2	2	.545	.889
Damion Easley	.083	12	1	0	0	0	1	2	5	.200	.083	Mike Macfarlane	.429	14	6	0	0	3	6	5	4	.579	1.071
Joe Carter	.091	11	1	1	0	0	0	1	4	.167	.182	Brady Anderson	.375	8	3	0	0	1	1	8	2	.688	.750
Brian McRae	.111	18	2	0	0	0	0	3	4	.238	.111	Paul Sorrento	.333	15	5	0	0	2	3	5	6	.500	.733

Sean Bergman — Padres
Age 28 – Pitches Right (groundball pitcher)

	ERA	W	L	Sv	G	GS	IP	BB	SO	Avg	H	2B	3B	HR	RBI	OBP	SLG	GF	IR	IRS	Hld	SvOp	SB	CS	GB	FB	G/F
1997 Season	6.09	2	4	0	44	9	99.0	38	74	.316	126	27	7	11	69	.376	.501	13	20	9	1	2	20	3	159	90	1.77
Career (1993-1997)	5.22	18	27	0	125	60	405.0	168	276	.299	483	80	16	52	252	.366	.464	25	39	14	2	2	67	9	670	369	1.82

1997 Season

	ERA	W	L	Sv	G	GS	IP	H	HR	BB	SO		Avg	AB	H	2B	3B	HR	RBI	BB	SO	OBP	SLG
Home	5.40	1	4	0	23	5	46.2	65	6	10	36	vs. Left	.285	165	47	11	2	4	30	25	30	.374	.448
Away	6.71	1	0	0	21	4	52.1	61	5	28	38	vs. Right	.338	234	79	16	5	7	39	13	44	.378	.538
Starter	6.91	1	2	0	9	9	41.2	57	3	19	35	Scoring Posn	.351	114	40	6	2	3	55	20	19	.443	.518
Reliever	5.49	1	2	0	35	0	57.1	69	8	19	39	Close & Late	.421	19	8	1	1	1	7	4	4	.522	.737
0 Days rest (Relief)	0.00	0	0	0	3	0	4.0	2	0	0	3	None on/out	.290	93	27	9	1	0	0	8	16	.347	.409
1 or 2 Days rest	7.17	0	0	0	15	0	21.1	28	4	9	17	First Pitch	.456	68	31	8	3	2	14	2	0	.458	.750
3+ Days rest	5.06	1	2	0	17	0	32.0	39	4	10	19	Ahead in Count	.272	169	46	10	1	5	36	0	63	.277	.432
Pre-All Star	5.01	2	3	0	23	8	64.2	80	4	27	47	Behind in Count	.354	79	28	5	0	3	13	21	0	.490	.532
Post-All Star	8.13	0	1	0	21	1	34.1	46	7	11	27	Two Strikes	.227	185	42	11	2	4	30	15	74	.289	.373

Career (1993-1997)

	ERA	W	L	Sv	G	GS	IP	H	HR	BB	SO		Avg	AB	H	2B	3B	HR	RBI	BB	SO	OBP	SLG
Home	4.97	7	16	0	63	31	201.0	237	24	78	141	vs. Left	.299	783	234	34	10	29	141	103	130	.379	.479
Away	5.47	11	11	0	62	29	204.0	246	28	90	135	vs. Right	.298	835	249	46	6	23	111	65	146	.352	.450
Day	5.11	6	9	0	44	24	149.2	174	14	68	109	Inning 1-6	.305	1317	402	66	13	45	218	145	221	.376	.478
Night	5.29	12	18	0	81	36	255.1	309	38	100	167	Inning 7+	.269	301	81	14	3	7	34	23	55	.319	.405
Grass	5.49	12	25	0	99	51	323.0	398	46	137	222	None on	.305	872	266	47	9	28	28	82	145	.367	.474
Turf	4.17	6	2	0	26	9	82.0	85	6	31	54	Runners on	.291	746	217	33	8	24	224	86	131	.363	.453
March/April	3.50	3	4	0	13	7	46.1	49	3	10	41	Scoring Posn	.317	438	139	21	5	13	193	70	70	.406	.477
May	6.06	1	5	0	20	14	78.2	105	13	35	51	Close & Late	.329	76	25	4	1	2	12	13	17	.427	.487
June	4.60	4	5	0	18	12	78.1	88	11	32	53	None on/out	.311	396	123	24	3	12	12	37	62	.374	.477
July	5.52	3	5	0	27	10	76.2	91	11	38	52	vs. 1st Batr (relief)	.359	64	23	4	0	3	14	1	1	.369	.563
August	5.15	6	6	0	28	11	85.2	95	9	33	53	1st Inning Pitched	.314	474	149	25	5	16	89	49	78	.384	.489
Sept/Oct	6.41	1	2	0	19	6	39.1	55	5	20	26	First 15 Pitches	.325	385	125	19	4	14	54	33	58	.383	.504
Starter	5.55	13	24	0	60	60	303.0	369	40	137	207	Pitch 16-30	.260	354	92	20	2	8	51	34	68	.328	.395
Reliever	4.24	5	3	0	65	0	102.0	114	12	31	69	Pitch 31-45	.317	259	82	16	3	9	35	27	45	.379	.506
0 Days rest (Relief)	2.35	0	0	0	6	0	7.2	4	2	0	5	Pitch 46+	.297	620	184	25	7	21	112	74	105	.370	.461
1 or 2 Days rest	4.75	3	1	0	29	0	41.2	53	4	13	27	First Pitch	.367	226	83	17	3	9	39	10	0	.388	.588
3+ Days rest	4.10	2	2	0	30	0	52.2	57	6	18	37	Ahead in Count	.238	697	166	27	4	18	99	0	244	.245	.366
vs. AL	5.07	10	15	0	44	38	204.0	249	27	105	125	Behind in Count	.371	388	144	25	4	18	79	88	0	.486	.595
vs. NL	5.37	8	12	0	81	22	201.0	234	25	63	151	Two Strikes	.210	686	144	23	6	19	85	70	276	.290	.344

Career (1993-1997)

	ERA	W	L	Sv	G	GS	IP	H	HR	BB	SO		Avg	AB	H	2B	3B	HR	RBI	BB	SO	OBP	SLG
Pre-All Star	4.78	10	15	0	57	35	222.0	264	27	87	157	Pre-All Star	.298	885	264	43	11	27	125	87	157	.359	.463
Post-All Star	5.75	8	12	0	68	25	183.0	219	25	81	119	Post-All Star	.299	733	219	37	5	25	127	81	119	.373	.465

Pitcher vs. Batter (career)

Pitches Best Vs.	Avg	AB	H	2B	3B	HR	RBI	BB	SO	OBP	SLG	Pitches Worst Vs.	Avg	AB	H	2B	3B	HR	RBI	BB	SO	OBP	SLG
John Olerud	.111	9	1	1	0	0	0	4	3	.385	.222	Lance Johnson	.500	20	10	1	1	0	0	0	0	.500	.650
Craig Biggio	.182	11	2	0	0	0	1	0	1	.182	.182	Brian McRae	.500	12	6	0	0	1	1	1	2	.538	.750
Devon White	.182	11	2	1	0	0	1	1	4	.250	.273	Kenny Lofton	.500	10	5	0	1	2	4	3	0	.600	1.300
Paul Molitor	.200	10	2	0	0	1	1	2	1	.333	.500	Chuck Knoblauch	.462	13	6	0	0	0	0	1	2	.500	.462
Carlos Baerga	.231	13	3	0	0	1	5	0	0	.231	.462	Roberto Alomar	.444	9	4	0	0	1	1	2	1	.545	.778

Geronimo Berroa — Orioles
Age 33 – Bats Right

	Avg	G	AB	R	H	2B	3B	HR	RBI	BB	SO	HBP	GDP	SB	CS	OBP	SLG	IBB	SH	SF	#Pit	#P/PA	GB	FB	G/F
1997 Season	.283	156	561	88	159	25	0	26	90	76	120	4	18	4	4	.369	.467	4	0	7	2536	3.91	193	149	1.30
Last Five Years	.285	560	2067	334	589	98	6	97	349	229	409	12	53	18	13	.356	.479	6	0	26	9210	3.95	700	618	1.13

1997 Season

	Avg	AB	H	2B	3B	HR	RBI	BB	SO	OBP	SLG		Avg	AB	H	2B	3B	HR	RBI	BB	SO	OBP	SLG
vs. Left	.358	148	53	8	0	7	29	21	28	.444	.554	First Pitch	.350	60	21	5	0	6	16	2	0	.369	.733
vs. Right	.257	413	106	17	0	19	61	55	92	.342	.436	Ahead in Count	.318	129	41	4	0	5	27	36	0	.461	.465
Groundball	.267	105	28	6	0	4	16	20	20	.386	.438	Behind in Count	.269	264	71	12	0	12	37	0	93	.272	.451
Flyball	.392	74	29	3	0	4	14	8	15	.447	.595	Two Strikes	.220	277	61	10	0	10	32	38	120	.314	.365
Home	.271	273	74	9	0	11	43	27	53	.333	.425	Batting #3	.228	180	41	4	0	8	29	18	48	.302	.383
Away	.295	288	85	16	0	15	47	49	67	.401	.507	Batting #5	.339	186	63	11	0	12	29	26	34	.421	.591
Day	.252	206	52	4	0	14	29	31	54	.356	.476	Other	.282	195	55	10	0	6	32	32	38	.379	.426
Night	.301	355	107	21	0	12	61	45	66	.377	.462	March/April	.350	80	28	4	0	6	13	13	12	.447	.625
Grass	.280	496	139	19	0	23	81	68	104	.367	.458	May	.273	110	30	5	0	5	13	14	28	.352	.455
Turf	.308	65	20	6	0	3	9	8	16	.384	.538	June	.296	81	24	3	0	5	17	9	21	.367	.519
Pre-All Star	.292	298	87	12	0	17	46	42	68	.380	.503	July	.242	99	24	2	0	4	19	13	18	.328	.384
Post-All Star	.274	263	72	13	0	9	44	34	52	.356	.426	August	.281	96	27	5	0	3	18	16	20	.385	.427
Scoring Posn	.265	151	40	5	0	4	66	27	35	.366	.377	Sept/Oct	.274	95	26	6	0	3	10	11	21	.349	.432
Close & Late	.259	81	21	2	0	4	12	18	22	.390	.432	vs. AL	.288	503	145	24	0	26	84	72	109	.377	.491
None on/out	.341	135	46	6	0	12	12	17	23	.414	.652	vs. NL	.241	58	14	1	0	0	6	4	11	.290	.259

1997 By Position

Position	Avg	AB	H	2B	3B	HR	RBI	BB	SO	OBP	SLG	G	GS	Innings	PO	A	E	DP	Fld Pct	Rng Fctr	In Zone	Zone Outs	Zone Rtg	MLB Zone
As DH	.295	258	76	15	0	9	41	34	51	.377	.457	69	65	---	---	---	---	---	---	---	---	---	---
As rf	.270	300	81	10	0	17	48	41	69	.357	.473	83	82	661.1	142	2	4	1	.973	1.96	180	135	.750	.813

Last Five Years

	Avg	AB	H	2B	3B	HR	RBI	BB	SO	OBP	SLG		Avg	AB	H	2B	3B	HR	RBI	BB	SO	OBP	SLG
vs. Left	.314	586	184	32	4	25	108	76	105	.392	.510	First Pitch	.380	279	106	20	0	24	76	3	0	.385	.710
vs. Right	.273	1481	405	66	2	72	241	153	304	.341	.467	Ahead in Count	.348	451	157	30	1	29	104	94	0	.454	.612
Groundball	.284	455	129	23	0	21	75	51	87	.357	.473	Behind in Count	.235	930	219	32	2	30	116	0	327	.238	.371
Flyball	.282	365	103	19	1	14	55	40	83	.350	.455	Two Strikes	.226	1015	229	34	3	30	118	132	409	.315	.354
Home	.284	1015	288	39	3	46	168	111	191	.352	.464	Batting #3	.281	673	189	23	1	29	113	83	135	.359	.447
Away	.286	1052	301	59	3	51	181	118	218	.359	.493	Batting #5	.312	637	199	38	1	40	113	77	132	.385	.564
Day	.288	798	230	38	1	40	141	95	162	.365	.489	Other	.266	757	201	37	4	28	123	69	142	.327	.436
Night	.283	1269	359	60	5	57	208	134	247	.350	.473	March/April	.298	272	81	17	0	15	55	27	49	.361	.526
Grass	.284	1816	516	81	6	84	303	209	365	.357	.473	May	.291	399	116	10	2	24	61	58	83	.380	.506
Turf	.291	251	73	17	0	13	46	20	44	.348	.514	June	.289	408	118	20	1	16	67	40	91	.352	.461
Pre-All Star	.290	1191	345	51	3	58	196	139	245	.364	.484	July	.272	379	103	18	1	20	74	36	67	.334	.483
Post-All Star	.279	876	244	47	3	39	153	90	164	.345	.482	August	.286	315	90	17	2	14	52	41	60	.366	.486
Scoring Posn	.281	544	153	29	3	17	232	74	111	.356	.439	Sept/Oct	.276	294	81	16	0	8	40	27	59	.336	.412
Close & Late	.266	308	82	11	0	12	48	41	71	.354	.419	vs. AL	.289	1975	571	96	6	97	343	223	391	.360	.491
None on/out	.283	453	128	16	2	26	26	45	89	.347	.499	vs. NL	.196	92	18	2	0	0	6	6	18	.245	.217

Batter vs. Pitcher (career)

Hits Best Against	Avg	AB	H	2B	3B	HR	RBI	BB	SO	OBP	SLG	Hits Worst Against	Avg	AB	H	2B	3B	HR	RBI	BB	SO	OBP	SLG
Dennis Martinez	.545	11	6	1	0	1	2	0	3	.545	.909	Dennis Springer	.000	9	0	0	0	0	1	2	4	.167	.000
Andy Pettitte	.500	22	11	0	1	2	5	3	5	.538	.864	James Baldwin	.000	9	0	0	0	0	0	2	0	.182	.000
Bobby Witt	.500	10	5	1	0	2	2	3	1	.615	1.200	Jeff Nelson	.000	9	0	0	0	0	0	3	4	.250	.000
Rich Robertson	.429	14	6	0	0	3	8	1	1	.438	1.071	Jimmy Key	.167	12	2	0	0	1	0	4	.167	.167
Ken Hill	.375	8	3	0	0	1	3	4	3	.538	.750	Hipolito Pichardo	.182	11	2	0	0	0	0	0	2	.182	.182

Sean Berry — Astros
Age 32 – Bats Right

	Avg	G	AB	R	H	2B	3B	HR	RBI	BB	SO	HBP	GDP	SB	CS	OBP	SLG	IBB	SH	SF	#Pit	#P/PA	GB	FB	G/F
1997 Season	.256	96	301	37	77	24	1	8	43	25	53	5	8	1	5	.318	.422	1	1	6	1263	3.73	102	103	0.99
Last Five Years	.279	556	1665	223	465	118	7	64	283	146	284	21	35	42	21	.341	.474	16	10	23	6765	3.63	586	534	1.10

1997 Season

	Avg	AB	H	2B	3B	HR	RBI	BB	SO	OBP	SLG		Avg	AB	H	2B	3B	HR	RBI	BB	SO	OBP	SLG
vs. Left	.240	75	18	5	0	2	12	4	9	.272	.387	First Pitch	.271	48	13	4	1	2	6	1	0	.300	.521
vs. Right	.261	226	59	19	1	6	31	21	44	.332	.434	Ahead in Count	.263	57	15	5	0	2	10	16	0	.416	.456
Groundball	.235	34	8	0	1	4	3	11		.297	.382	Behind in Count	.271	140	38	10	0	4	20	0	46	.278	.429
Flyball	.270	37	10	5	0	0	8	1	5	.293	.405	Two Strikes	.190	142	27	8	0	2	17	8	53	.245	.289
Home	.256	156	40	13	1	4	25	12	26	.322	.429	Batting #5	.246	130	32	11	0	4	14	8	26	.296	.423

1997 Season

	Avg	AB	H	2B	3B	HR	RBI	BB	SO	OBP	SLG		Avg	AB	H	2B	3B	HR	RBI	BB	SO	OBP	SLG
Away	.255	145	37	11	0	4	18	13	27	.313	.414	Batting #6	.252	127	32	8	0	3	15	12	21	.326	.386
Day	.278	97	27	8	1	3	18	7	19	.327	.474	Other	.295	44	13	5	1	1	14	5	6	.353	.523
Night	.245	204	50	16	0	5	25	18	34	.313	.397	March/April	.226	31	7	1	0	1	2	2	6	.294	.355
Grass	.279	104	29	8	0	3	10	9	18	.339	.442	May	.181	94	17	7	0	2	10	6	18	.228	.319
Turf	.244	197	48	16	1	5	33	16	35	.306	.411	June	.293	58	17	2	0	1	4	5	7	.344	.379
Pre-All Star	.227	194	44	12	0	5	19	13	31	.276	.366	July	.319	47	15	5	1	4	14	5	8	.411	.723
Post-All Star	.308	107	33	12	1	3	24	12	22	.386	.523	August	.243	37	9	4	0	0	2	3	9	.300	.351
Scoring Posn	.207	92	19	6	1	1	32	10	14	.275	.326	Sept/Oct	.353	34	12	5	0	0	11	4	5	.405	.500
Close & Late	.159	44	7	2	0	2	6	5	8	.255	.341	vs. AL	.391	23	9	2	0	0	1	2	2	.440	.478
None on/out	.250	68	17	6	0	1	1	1	19	.271	.382	vs. NL	.245	278	68	22	1	8	42	23	51	.308	.417

1997 By Position

Position	Avg	AB	H	2B	3B	HR	RBI	BB	SO	OBP	SLG	G	GS	Innings	PO	A	E	DP	Fld Pct	Rng Fctr	In Zone	In Outs	Zone Rtg	MLB Zone
As Pinch Hitter	.000	9	0	0	0	0	1	2	1	.167	.000	12	0	---	---	---	---	---	---	---	---	---	---	---
As 3b	.254	280	71	23	1	8	41	23	50	.316	.429	85	79	629.1	47	138	16	11	.920	2.65	199	152	.764	.801

Last Five Years

	Avg	AB	H	2B	3B	HR	RBI	BB	SO	OBP	SLG		Avg	AB	H	2B	3B	HR	RBI	BB	SO	OBP	SLG
vs. Left	.265	426	113	27	1	15	68	50	64	.340	.439	First Pitch	.317	221	70	16	2	13	52	14	0	.371	.584
vs. Right	.284	1239	352	91	6	49	215	96	220	.341	.486	Ahead in Count	.360	367	132	39	2	25	89	83	0	.472	.681
Groundball	.270	423	114	20	2	10	55	31	76	.317	.397	Behind in Count	.237	780	185	39	3	20	94	0	254	.243	.372
Flyball	.236	254	60	18	1	12	54	25	51	.314	.457	Two Strikes	.201	751	151	36	3	17	85	49	284	.255	.325
Home	.266	768	204	50	2	22	118	73	142	.333	.422	Batting #5	.287	519	149	43	0	25	99	38	86	.342	.514
Away	.291	897	261	68	5	42	165	73	142	.347	.518	Batting #6	.260	327	85	21	1	12	51	29	42	.329	.440
Day	.270	482	130	45	2	19	90	47	80	.339	.490	Other	.282	819	231	54	6	27	133	79	156	.345	.462
Night	.283	1183	335	73	5	45	193	99	204	.341	.467	March/April	.282	220	62	19	0	3	29	27	32	.370	.409
Grass	.304	589	179	46	4	32	106	49	91	.363	.559	May	.208	313	65	19	0	8	33	20	46	.264	.345
Turf	.266	1076	286	72	3	32	177	97	193	.329	.428	June	.284	289	82	12	0	15	62	20	54	.327	.481
Pre-All Star	.270	934	252	61	1	33	147	75	149	.328	.443	July	.306	340	104	23	3	15	61	31	60	.366	.524
Post-All Star	.291	731	213	57	6	31	136	71	135	.357	.513	August	.295	264	78	26	2	13	54	25	50	.358	.557
Scoring Posn	.268	500	134	34	4	17	217	63	90	.343	.454	Sept/Oct	.310	239	74	19	2	10	44	23	42	.372	.531
Close & Late	.224	277	62	14	1	8	43	19	63	.279	.368	vs. AL	.391	23	9	2	0	0	1	2	2	.440	.478
None on/out	.300	420	126	34	2	14	14	26	71	.348	.491	vs. NL	.278	1642	456	116	7	64	282	144	282	.339	.474

Batter vs. Pitcher (career)

Hits Best Against	Avg	AB	H	2B	3B	HR	RBI	BB	SO	OBP	SLG	Hits Worst Against	Avg	AB	H	2B	3B	HR	RBI	BB	SO	OBP	SLG
Mark Gardner	.563	16	9	3	0	1	4	1	1	.611	.938	Jeff Brantley	.000	12	0	0	0	0	0	0	6	.000	.000
Donovan Osborne	.529	17	9	5	0	1	3	2	2	.579	1.000	Pete Smith	.000	10	0	0	0	0	0	1	1	.091	.000
Frank Castillo	.500	16	8	1	0	2	4	1	4	.556	.938	Greg Swindell	.077	13	1	1	0	0	2	1	4	.143	.154
Kevin Foster	.500	12	6	3	0	1	2	0	2	.500	1.000	Hideo Nomo	.125	16	2	1	0	0	1	0	2	.125	.188
Rene Arocha	.400	10	4	1	1	1	2	1	2	.455	1.000	Tom Glavine	.154	13	2	0	0	0	1	0	2	.154	.154

Damon Berryhill — Giants
Age 34 – Bats Both (flyball hitter)

	Avg	G	AB	R	H	2B	3B	HR	RBI	BB	SO	HBP	GDP	SB	CS	OBP	SLG	IBB	SH	SF	#Pit	#P/PA	GB	FB	G/F
1997 Season	.257	73	167	17	43	8	0	3	23	20	29	0	3	0	0	.335	.359	5	0	1	666	3.54	65	51	1.27
Last Five Years	.247	304	839	77	207	46	4	19	111	70	171	2	19	0	1	.303	.379	8	3	10	3398	3.68	269	263	1.02

1997 Season

	Avg	AB	H	2B	3B	HR	RBI	BB	SO	OBP	SLG		Avg	AB	H	2B	3B	HR	RBI	BB	SO	OBP	SLG
vs. Left	.342	38	13	2	0	0	5	5	6	.419	.395	Scoring Posn	.255	55	14	1	0	1	19	10	5	.364	.327
vs. Right	.233	129	30	6	0	3	18	15	23	.310	.349	Close & Late	.297	37	11	2	0	0	7	2	6	.333	.351
Home	.286	77	22	6	0	2	15	9	14	.356	.442	None on/out	.308	39	12	4	0	0		1	9	.325	.410
Away	.233	90	21	2	0	1	8	11	15	.317	.289	Batting #8	.271	118	32	5	0	3	17	14	20	.346	.390
First Pitch	.353	34	12	2	0	0	4	4	0	.410	.412	Batting #9	.259	27	7	3	0	0	2	5	5	.375	.370
Ahead in Count	.290	31	9	1	0	2	8	9	0	.450	.516	Other	.182	22	4	0	0	0	4	1	4	.217	.182
Behind in Count	.203	79	16	3	0	1	7	0	22	.203	.278	Pre-All Star	.307	88	27	4	0	2	14	13	15	.392	.420
Two Strikes	.205	73	15	3	0	1	9	7	29	.275	.288	Post-All Star	.203	79	16	4	0	1	9	7	14	.267	.291

Last Five Years

	Avg	AB	H	2B	3B	HR	RBI	BB	SO	OBP	SLG		Avg	AB	H	2B	3B	HR	RBI	BB	SO	OBP	SLG
vs. Left	.281	224	63	13	1	4	36	21	36	.333	.402	First Pitch	.325	163	53	11	1	7	28	7	0	.349	.534
vs. Right	.234	615	144	33	3	15	75	49	135	.291	.371	Ahead in Count	.286	154	44	12	1	7	37	27	0	.388	.513
Groundball	.254	232	59	11	1	2	26	17	41	.303	.336	Behind in Count	.187	390	73	14	0	4	26	0	147	.189	.254
Flyball	.248	149	37	11	2	2	18	15	39	.311	.389	Two Strikes	.170	393	67	13	1	4	30	36	171	.241	.239
Home	.272	427	116	29	2	13	65	41	87	.332	.440	Batting #7	.243	375	91	19	2	8	46	25	72	.288	.368
Away	.221	412	91	17	2	6	46	29	84	.272	.316	Batting #8	.252	302	76	16	1	8	45	25	66	.304	.391
Day	.256	289	74	19	0	7	38	21	57	.305	.394	Other	.247	162	40	11	1	3	20	20	33	.333	.383
Night	.242	550	133	27	4	12	73	49	114	.302	.371	March/April	.272	92	25	8	0	2	10	10	16	.340	.424
Grass	.254	646	164	38	3	16	88	51	127	.306	.396	May	.235	136	32	7	0	3	19	8	28	.272	.353
Turf	.223	193	43	8	1	3	23	19	44	.294	.321	June	.239	205	49	12	3	5	28	15	47	.287	.400
Pre-All Star	.252	489	123	30	3	13	68	41	102	.305	.405	July	.256	176	45	8	0	5	25	16	34	.316	.386
Post-All Star	.240	350	84	16	1	6	43	29	69	.300	.343	August	.242	120	29	6	1	2	12	17	19	.341	.358
Scoring Posn	.264	227	60	11	1	5	85	29	39	.335	.388	Sept/Oct	.245	110	27	5	0	2	14	8	27	.274	.345
Close & Late	.247	174	43	10	1	4	25	12	41	.296	.385	vs. AL	.271	277	75	17	2	6	35	22	62	.322	.412
None on/out	.222	176	39	10	1	1	1	9	39	.263	.307	vs. NL	.235	562	132	29	2	13	76	48	109	.294	.363

Batter vs. Pitcher (career)

Hits Best Against	Avg	AB	H	2B	3B	HR	RBI	BB	SO	OBP	SLG	Hits Worst Against	Avg	AB	H	2B	3B	HR	RBI	BB	SO	OBP	SLG
Ken Hill	.333	12	4	3	0	0	1	0	1	.333	.583	Pete Smith	.077	13	1	1	0	0	1	1	3	.143	.154
Pedro Astacio	.333	9	3	1	0	0	0	2	3	.455	.444	Omar Olivares	.077	13	1	0	0	0	2	2	3	.188	.077
Doug Drabek	.325	40	13	4	0	1	7	3	7	.372	.500	Andy Benes	.083	12	1	0	0	0	0	0	8	.083	.083
												Orel Hershiser	.107	28	3	0	0	0	3	1	4	.138	.107
												Mike Morgan	.118	17	2	0	0	0	1	1	1	.167	.118

Mike Bertotti — White Sox
Age 28 – Pitches Left (flyball pitcher)

	ERA	W	L	Sv	G	GS	IP	BB	SO	Avg	H	2B	3B	HR	RBI	OBP	SLG	GF	IR	IRS	Hld	SvOp	SB	CS	GB	FB	G/F
1997 Season	7.36	0	0	0	9	0	3.2	2	4	.450	9	4	0	0	9	.478	.650	2	13	8	0	0	2	0	4	8	0.50
Career (1995-1997)	7.63	3	1	0	28	6	46.0	33	38	.313	60	16	1	11	47	.412	.578	6	22	13	2	1	3	1	48	71	0.68

1997 Season

	ERA	W	L	Sv	G	GS	IP	H	HR	BB	SO		Avg	AB	H	2B	3B	HR	RBI	BB	SO	OBP	SLG
Home	9.00	0	0	0	6	0	2.0	7	0	1	3	vs. Left	.333	9	3	3	0	0	5	1	2	.364	.667
Away	5.40	0	0	0	3	0	1.2	2	0	1	1	vs. Right	.545	11	6	1	0	4	1	2	.583	.636

Brian Bevil — Royals
Age 26 – Pitches Right (flyball pitcher)

	ERA	W	L	Sv	G	GS	IP	BB	SO	Avg	H	2B	3B	HR	RBI	OBP	SLG	GF	IR	IRS	Hld	SvOp	SB	CS	GB	FB	G/F
1997 Season	6.61	1	2	1	18	0	16.1	9	13	.267	16	3	1	1	11	.361	.400	11	9	0	1	5	2	1	19	20	0.95
Career (1996-1997)	6.26	2	2	1	21	0	27.1	14	20	.255	25	5	3	3	18	.345	.459	12	9	0	2	5	2	2	29	33	0.88

1997 Season

	ERA	W	L	Sv	G	GS	IP	H	HR	BB	SO		Avg	AB	H	2B	3B	HR	RBI	BB	SO	OBP	SLG
Home	7.36	1	1	0	8	0	7.1	11	1	3	8	vs. Left	.375	24	9	1	1	0	6	4	2	.448	.500
Away	6.00	0	1	1	10	0	9.0	5	0	6	5	vs. Right	.194	36	7	2	0	1	5	5	11	.302	.333

Dante Bichette — Rockies
Age 34 – Bats Right

	Avg	AB	R	H	2B	3B	HR	RBI	BB	SO	HBP	GDP	SB	CS	OBP	SLG	IBB	SH	SF	#Pit	#P/PA	GB	FB	G/F
1997 Season	.308	151	561	81	173	31	2	26	118	30	90	3	14	6	5	.343	.510	1	0	7	2185	3.63	181	180	1.01
Last Five Years	.316	706	2795	464	882	184	14	145	571	144	460	24	72	85	42	.350	.547	15	0	34	10287	3.43	943	871	1.08

1997 Season

	Avg	AB	H	2B	3B	HR	RBI	BB	SO	OBP	SLG		Avg	AB	H	2B	3B	HR	RBI	BB	SO	OBP	SLG
vs. Left	.263	133	35	7	0	8	28	9	26	.303	.496	First Pitch	.352	91	32	5	0	8	29	0	0	.358	.670
vs. Right	.322	428	138	24	2	18	90	21	64	.355	.514	Ahead in Count	.367	109	40	5	1	9	30	18	0	.454	.679
Groundball	.281	135	38	8	1	5	21	2	23	.291	.467	Behind in Count	.280	261	73	16	1	4	40	0	73	.278	.395
Flyball	.385	91	35	7	0	8	27	6	11	.418	.725	Two Strikes	.252	250	63	15	0	6	36	12	90	.284	.384
Home	.362	301	109	20	1	20	87	18	46	.393	.635	Batting #4	.286	70	20	5	0	4	15	2	14	.311	.529
Away	.246	260	64	11	1	6	31	12	44	.284	.365	Batting #5	.311	418	130	22	1	20	92	20	65	.342	.512
Day	.325	268	87	20	0	12	57	16	48	.359	.534	Other	.315	73	23	4	1	2	11	8	11	.378	.479
Night	.294	293	86	11	2	14	61	14	42	.328	.488	March/April	.322	87	28	4	0	2	22	6	13	.358	.437
Grass	.318	466	148	28	1	22	102	23	73	.346	.524	May	.289	97	28	2	0	5	19	5	17	.324	.464
Turf	.263	95	25	3	1	4	16	7	17	.327	.442	June	.324	111	36	8	1	5	23	5	15	.347	.550
Pre-All Star	.300	317	95	15	1	12	64	16	49	.329	.467	July	.320	100	32	8	1	5	20	5	15	.352	.570
Post-All Star	.320	244	78	16	1	14	54	14	41	.360	.566	August	.299	87	26	6	0	4	17	6	12	.354	.506
Scoring Posn	.322	174	56	15	0	6	87	11	21	.352	.511	Sept/Oct	.291	79	23	3	0	5	17	3	18	.318	.519
Close & Late	.273	66	18	5	1	3	15	1	13	.284	.515	vs. AL	.323	65	21	5	0	1	8	2	9	.343	.446
None on/out	.286	133	38	4	1	5	5	9	23	.336	.444	vs. NL	.306	496	152	26	2	25	110	28	81	.343	.518

1997 By Position

Position	Avg	AB	H	2B	3B	HR	RBI	BB	SO	OBP	SLG	G	GS	Innings	PO	A	E	DP	Fld Pct	Rng Fctr	In Zone	Outs	Zone Rtg	MLB Zone
As lf	.308	497	153	27	2	24	106	22	80	.337	.515	128	128	1000.1	208	3	2	0	.991	1.90	270	198	.733	.805
As rf	.270	37	10	2	0	2	8	7	7	.386	.486	16	9	90.0	17	1	1	1	.947	1.80	25	18	.720	.813

Last Five Years

	Avg	AB	H	2B	3B	HR	RBI	BB	SO	OBP	SLG		Avg	AB	H	2B	3B	HR	RBI	BB	SO	OBP	SLG
vs. Left	.326	645	210	54	3	44	155	41	108	.362	.623	First Pitch	.400	502	201	36	5	38	137	11	0	.411	.719
vs. Right	.313	2150	672	130	11	101	416	103	352	.347	.524	Ahead in Count	.373	498	186	40	4	46	152	69	0	.449	.747
Groundball	.301	797	240	55	4	30	151	27	135	.324	.493	Behind in Count	.253	1362	345	67	3	42	201	0	402	.257	.399
Flyball	.367	466	171	34	2	30	104	28	81	.402	.642	Two Strikes	.223	1209	270	58	3	28	150	64	460	.266	.346
Home	.367	1440	528	106	11	99	375	81	198	.400	.662	Batting #3	.320	1576	505	114	10	82	315	72	266	.352	.562
Away	.261	1355	354	78	3	46	196	63	262	.297	.425	Batting #5	.319	770	246	37	2	44	171	44	119	.357	.544
Day	.315	1075	339	78	2	47	219	52	177	.346	.523	Other	.292	449	131	33	2	19	85	28	75	.334	.501
Night	.316	1720	543	106	12	98	352	92	283	.353	.562	March/April	.329	374	123	23	1	17	87	25	65	.370	.532
Grass	.326	2237	729	149	12	118	462	115	342	.360	.561	May	.305	508	155	26	3	22	92	37	87	.353	.498
Turf	.274	558	153	35	2	27	109	29	118	.311	.489	June	.337	569	192	51	2	27	110	18	84	.355	.572
Pre-All Star	.316	1623	513	110	7	73	321	85	263	.349	.527	July	.297	545	162	38	4	34	121	26	88	.332	.569
Post-All Star	.315	1172	369	74	7	72	250	59	197	.352	.574	August	.308	451	139	25	4	27	81	28	85	.352	.561
Scoring Posn	.328	806	264	46	4	46	417	50	127	.360	.566	Sept/Oct	.319	348	111	21	0	18	80	10	51	.345	.534
Close & Late	.311	386	120	28	1	26	104	16	65	.346	.591	vs. AL	.323	65	21	5	0	1	8	2	9	.343	.446
None on/out	.310	568	176	37	5	26	26	29	91	.348	.530	vs. NL	.315	2730	861	179	14	144	563	142	451	.351	.549

Batter vs. Pitcher (career)

Hits Best Against	Avg	AB	H	2B	3B	HR	RBI	BB	SO	OBP	SLG	Hits Worst Against	Avg	AB	H	2B	3B	HR	RBI	BB	SO	OBP	SLG
Xavier Hernandez	.636	11	7	1	1	0	7	0	3	.636	.909	Jimmy Key	.063	16	1	0	0	0	1	0	2	.059	.063
Donne Wall	.625	16	10	5	0	1	6	0	0	.625	1.125	Todd Stottlemyre	.071	14	1	0	0	0	0	0	4	.071	.071

Batter vs. Pitcher (career)

Hits Best Against	Avg	AB	H	2B	3B	HR	RBI	BB	SO	OBP	SLG	Hits Worst Against	Avg	AB	H	2B	3B	HR	RBI	BB	SO	OBP	SLG
Mark Portugal	.500	20	10	0	1	4	8	1	1	.524	1.200	Mike Jackson	.100	10	1	0	0	0	0	1	4	.182	.100
Terry Mulholland	.462	26	12	4	0	3	10	0	3	.462	.962	Pedro Martinez	.111	18	2	0	0	1	1	0	5	.111	.278
Bill Swift	.417	12	5	2	0	2	3	1	2	.462	1.083	Turk Wendell	.182	11	2	0	0	0	1	0	1	.182	.182

Mike Bielecki — Braves　　　　　　　　　　　　　　　　　Age 38 – Pitches Right

	ERA	W	L	Sv	G	GS	IP	BB	SO	Avg	H	2B	3B	HR	RBI	OBP	SLG	GF	IR	IRS	Hld	SvOp	SB	CS	GB	FB	G/F
1997 Season	4.08	3	7	2	50	0	57.1	21	60	.250	56	8	1	9	31	.316	.415	7	7	3	12	6	4	1	65	58	1.12
Last Five Years	4.59	17	21	4	144	30	303.2	120	232	.267	317	43	4	42	153	.335	.415	24	35	12	15	8	39	8	408	343	1.19

1997 Season

	ERA	W	L	Sv	G	GS	IP	H	HR	BB	SO		Avg	AB	H	2B	3B	HR	RBI	BB	SO	OBP	SLG
Home	4.50	2	5	0	25	0	26.0	26	2	13	26	vs. Left	.267	101	27	4	0	3	13	9	25	.327	.396
Away	3.73	1	2	2	25	0	31.1	30	7	8	34	vs. Right	.236	123	29	4	1	6	18	12	35	.307	.431
Day	2.50	3	1	1	16	0	18.0	13	2	2	23	Inning 1-6	.182	11	2	1	0	0	0	0	5	.182	.273
Night	4.81	0	6	1	34	0	39.1	43	7	19	37	Inning 7+	.254	213	54	7	1	9	31	21	55	.322	.423
Grass	4.30	3	7	2	41	0	44.0	45	4	19	44	None on	.212	137	29	4	0	4	4	10	38	.265	.328
Turf	3.38	0	0	0	9	0	13.1	11	5	2	16	Runners on	.310	87	27	4	1	5	27	11	22	.390	.552
March/April	1.93	1	0	1	13	0	14.0	8	0	2	16	Scoring Posn	.318	44	14	2	0	2	18	8	8	.415	.500
May	2.20	0	3	1	13	0	16.1	14	1	5	15	Close & Late	.282	142	40	5	1	6	20	15	34	.348	.458
June	5.52	2	1	0	11	0	14.2	20	4	4	17	None on/out	.211	57	12	1	0	1	1	6	17	.286	.281
July	8.64	0	2	0	8	0	8.1	10	4	5	8	vs. 1st Batr (relief)	.205	44	9	0	0	2	4	5	11	.280	.341
August	4.50	0	1	0	5	0	4.0	4	0	5	4	1st Inning Pitched	.251	171	43	5	1	5	24	13	44	.306	.380
Sept/Oct	0.00	0	0	0	0	0	0.0	0	0	0	0	First 15 Pitches	.255	137	35	4	1	5	15	7	31	.290	.409
Starter	0.00	0	0	0	0	0	0.0	0	0	0	0	Pitch 16-30	.243	70	17	4	0	1	11	11	24	.354	.343
Reliever	4.08	3	7	2	50	0	57.1	56	9	21	60	Pitch 31-45	.286	14	4	0	0	3	5	3	3	.412	.929
0 Days rest (Relief)	4.26	0	3	1	11	0	12.2	19	1	3	13	Pitch 46+	.000	3	0	0	0	0	0	0	2	.000	.000
1 or 2 Days rest	3.23	2	3	1	25	0	30.2	23	6	8	33	First Pitch	.304	23	7	1	0	1	4	2	0	.360	.478
3+ Days rest	5.79	1	1	0	14	0	14.0	14	2	10	14	Ahead in Count	.179	123	22	1	1	1	8	0	56	.184	.228
vs. AL	7.36	0	1	0	3	0	3.2	9	2	0	7	Behind in Count	.442	43	19	5	0	7	17	11	0	.556	1.047
vs. NL	3.86	3	6	2	47	0	53.2	47	7	21	53	Two Strikes	.156	128	20	2	1	0	7	8	60	.210	.188
Pre-All Star	3.33	3	4	2	38	0	46.0	44	6	11	48	Pre-All Star	.249	177	44	8	0	6	22	11	48	.295	.395
Post-All Star	7.15	0	3	0	12	0	11.1	12	3	10	12	Post-All Star	.255	47	12	0	1	3	9	10	12	.386	.489

Last Five Years

	ERA	W	L	Sv	G	GS	IP	H	HR	BB	SO		Avg	AB	H	2B	3B	HR	RBI	BB	SO	OBP	SLG
Home	4.04	11	10	1	75	14	156.0	156	16	59	111	vs. Left	.257	587	151	20	1	19	67	52	107	.318	.392
Away	5.18	6	11	3	69	16	147.2	161	26	61	121	vs. Right	.276	602	166	23	3	23	86	68	125	.350	.439
Day	4.18	8	4	2	46	9	97.0	91	12	35	88	Inning 1-6	.276	769	212	32	1	26	100	72	134	.337	.421
Night	4.79	9	17	2	98	21	206.2	226	30	85	144	Inning 7+	.250	420	105	11	3	16	53	48	98	.330	.405
Grass	4.67	16	19	3	122	26	262.0	279	33	104	197	None on	.266	692	184	30	1	20	20	54	131	.323	.399
Turf	4.10	1	2	1	22	4	41.2	38	9	16	35	Runners on	.268	497	133	13	3	22	133	66	101	.350	.439
March/April	4.23	3	3	1	30	5	55.1	54	5	16	45	Scoring Posn	.309	259	80	7	1	10	104	47	47	.403	.459
May	4.17	5	6	2	34	8	82.0	84	7	24	51	Close & Late	.251	199	50	6	1	6	24	29	50	.346	.382
June	6.14	3	7	0	30	8	73.1	87	16	32	50	None on/out	.249	305	76	16	0	6	6	24	57	.308	.361
July	4.69	3	3	0	22	3	40.1	41	10	13	38	vs. 1st Batr (relief)	.204	103	21	1	0	4	14	7	27	.246	.330
August	2.53	3	1	0	13	5	32.0	30	2	20	33	1st Inning Pitched	.255	509	130	15	3	12	70	48	115	.320	.367
Sept/Oct	4.79	0	1	1	15	1	20.2	21	2	15	15	First 15 Pitches	.252	413	104	12	3	10	39	28	84	.302	.368
Starter	5.45	9	12	0	30	30	157.0	182	25	64	99	Pitch 16-30	.275	287	79	14	0	6	43	42	60	.369	.387
Reliever	3.68	8	9	4	114	0	146.2	135	17	56	133	Pitch 31-45	.231	160	37	4	0	10	27	8	33	.271	.444
0 Days rest (Relief)	3.26	0	4	2	16	0	19.1	23	1	10	19	Pitch 46+	.295	329	97	13	1	16	44	42	55	.373	.486
1 or 2 Days rest	4.06	4	4	1	49	0	64.1	60	11	18	61	First Pitch	.366	153	56	8	0	4	20	7	0	.389	.497
3+ Days rest	3.43	4	1	1	49	0	63.0	52	5	28	53	Ahead in Count	.176	535	94	14	3	7	38	0	192	.181	.252
vs. AL	5.97	8	12	0	38	24	147.2	179	25	54	90	Behind in Count	.365	277	101	12	0	21	64	65	0	.478	.635
vs. NL	3.29	9	9	4	106	6	156.0	138	17	66	142	Two Strikes	.173	577	100	15	2	10	44	48	232	.240	.258
Pre-All Star	4.76	13	17	3	99	23	227.0	241	31	74	163	Pre-All Star	.270	891	241	39	2	31	156	74	163	.329	.423
Post-All Star	4.11	4	4	1	45	7	76.2	76	11	46	69	Post-All Star	.255	298	76	4	2	11	37	46	69	.351	.393

Pitcher vs. Batter (career)

Pitches Best Vs.	Avg	AB	H	2B	3B	HR	RBI	BB	SO	OBP	SLG	Pitches Worst Vs.	Avg	AB	H	2B	3B	HR	RBI	BB	SO	OBP	SLG
Larry Walker	.083	12	1	0	0	0	0	1	3	.154	.083	Jay Bell	.571	21	12	4	2	0	6	3	4	.625	.952
Stan Javier	.091	11	1	0	0	0	0	0	3	.091	.091	Juan Samuel	.500	20	10	2	0	2	8	2	2	.500	.900
Jeff King	.091	11	1	0	0	0	0	1	3	.167	.091	Steve Finley	.500	18	9	1	2	1	2	1	2	.550	.944
Marquis Grissom	.091	11	1	0	0	0	0	3	0	.286	.091	Mo Vaughn	.500	10	5	1	0	1	3	1	3	.545	.900
Tom Pagnozzi	.176	17	3	0	0	0	2	0	4	.176	.176	Kevin Mitchell	.313	16	5	1	2	2	6	2	2	.389	1.000

Steve Bieser — Mets　　　　　　　　　　　　　　　　　Age 30 – Bats Left

	Avg	G	AB	R	H	2B	3B	HR	RBI	BB	SO	HBP	GDP	SB	CS	OBP	SLG	IBB	SH	SF	#Pit	#P/PA	GB	FB	G/F
1997 Season	.246	47	69	16	17	3	0	0	4	7	20	4	0	2	3	.346	.290	1	0	1	314	3.88	19	14	1.36

1997 Season

	Avg	AB	H	2B	3B	HR	RBI	BB	SO	OBP	SLG		Avg	AB	H	2B	3B	HR	RBI	BB	SO	OBP	SLG
vs. Left	.000	2	0	0	0	0	0	0	1	.000	.000	Scoring Posn	.214	14	3	1	0	0	4	3	5	.368	.286
vs. Right	.254	67	17	3	0	0	4	7	19	.354	.299	Close & Late	.250	12	3	1	0	0	0	1	5	.357	.333

Craig Biggio — Astros
Age 32 – Bats Right

	Avg	G	AB	R	H	2B	3B	HR	RBI	BB	SO	HBP	GDP	SB	CS	OBP	SLG	IBB	SH	SF	#Pit	#P/PA	GB	FB	G/F
1997 Season	.309	162	619	146	191	37	8	22	81	84	107	34	0	47	10	.415	.501	6	0	7	2730	3.67	234	179	1.31
Last Five Years	.300	734	2824	568	846	176	24	86	353	378	415	101	31	159	46	.398	.470	15	25	29	12465	3.71	1061	843	1.26

1997 Season

	Avg	AB	H	2B	3B	HR	RBI	BB	SO	OBP	SLG		Avg	AB	H	2B	3B	HR	RBI	BB	SO	OBP	SLG
vs. Left	.326	138	45	8	2	6	19	26	24	.444	.543	First Pitch	.435	69	30	6	1	4	16	4	0	.535	.725
vs. Right	.304	481	146	29	6	16	62	58	83	.407	.489	Ahead in Count	.400	105	42	8	2	7	17	55	0	.617	.714
Groundball	.347	98	34	5	2	3	12	15	19	.449	.531	Behind in Count	.281	303	85	17	3	8	33	0	81	.304	.436
Flyball	.194	93	18	4	1	3	7	6	20	.283	.355	Two Strikes	.234	290	68	12	1	4	21	25	107	.318	.324
Home	.306	301	92	18	8	7	31	34	51	.406	.488	Batting #1	.311	614	191	37	8	22	80	83	105	.418	.505
Away	.311	318	99	19	0	15	50	50	56	.424	.513	Batting #8	.000	3	0	0	0	0	0	1	1	.250	.000
Day	.261	188	49	7	1	7	21	23	34	.375	.420	Other	.000	2	0	0	0	1	0	1	0	1.000	.000
Night	.329	431	142	30	7	15	60	61	73	.433	.536	March/April	.301	103	31	7	1	3	11	11	18	.387	.476
Grass	.323	229	74	12	0	10	33	35	42	.428	.507	May	.310	113	35	7	1	6	17	9	19	.386	.549
Turf	.300	390	117	25	8	12	48	49	65	.408	.497	June	.318	110	35	8	0	4	15	16	18	.415	.500
Pre-All Star	.305	347	106	24	3	13	44	41	59	.396	.504	July	.354	96	34	6	3	1	14	19	16	.458	.510
Post-All Star	.313	272	85	13	5	9	37	43	48	.439	.496	August	.265	113	30	6	0	6	18	12	19	.385	.478
Scoring Posn	.358	123	44	12	2	4	56	28	25	.485	.585	Sept/Oct	.310	84	26	3	3	2	6	17	17	.473	.488
Close & Late	.275	102	28	3	1	5	18	18	32	.411	.471	vs. AL	.368	57	21	2	1	2	8	6	12	.448	.544
None on/out	.296	270	80	16	4	7	7	29	43	.385	.463	vs. NL	.302	562	170	35	7	20	73	78	95	.412	.496

1997 By Position

Position	Avg	AB	H	2B	3B	HR	RBI	BB	SO	OBP	SLG	G	GS	Innings	PO	A	E	DP	Fld Pct	Rng Fctr	In Zone	Outs	Zone Rtg	MLB Zone
As 2b	.307	612	188	36	8	21	79	84	105	.416	.495	160	155	1384.1	340	503	18	107	.979	5.48	517	481	.930	.902

Last Five Years

	Avg	AB	H	2B	3B	HR	RBI	BB	SO	OBP	SLG		Avg	AB	H	2B	3B	HR	RBI	BB	SO	OBP	SLG
vs. Left	.322	662	213	43	6	26	89	125	73	.438	.523	First Pitch	.387	323	125	30	7	15	61	12	0	.451	.663
vs. Right	.293	2162	633	133	18	60	264	253	342	.385	.454	Ahead in Count	.379	483	183	38	3	23	92	243	0	.590	.613
Groundball	.318	726	231	53	9	20	93	107	102	.416	.499	Behind in Count	.249	1416	353	71	9	28	129	0	349	.270	.371
Flyball	.258	445	115	24	4	16	51	58	76	.364	.438	Two Strikes	.216	1275	275	54	5	21	100	123	415	.301	.315
Home	.293	1370	402	92	13	32	166	194	205	.400	.486	Batting #1	.299	1477	442	99	15	49	177	204	238	.401	.486
Away	.305	1454	444	84	11	54	187	184	210	.395	.490	Batting #2	.303	1019	309	50	6	28	129	127	130	.397	.447
Day	.277	860	238	48	6	31	99	90	136	.366	.455	Other	.290	328	95	27	3	9	47	47	47	.386	.473
Night	.310	1964	608	128	18	55	254	288	279	.411	.477	March/April	.273	385	105	31	2	7	34	60	52	.384	.418
Grass	.291	918	267	45	4	37	112	116	151	.383	.469	May	.313	524	164	39	4	19	69	68	78	.410	.511
Turf	.304	1906	579	131	20	49	241	262	264	.401	.471	June	.275	524	144	32	2	19	69	61	79	.362	.452
Pre-All Star	.295	1611	476	117	12	50	200	212	238	.390	.476	July	.331	520	172	32	7	13	76	72	81	.423	.494
Post-All Star	.305	1213	370	59	12	36	153	166	177	.407	.462	August	.308	477	147	28	4	20	69	61	55	.404	.509
Scoring Posn	.309	641	198	42	4	17	252	109	96	.417	.466	Sept/Oct	.289	394	114	14	5	8	36	56	70	.400	.411
Close & Late	.274	452	124	21	5	13	60	65	88	.386	.429	vs. AL	.368	57	21	2	1	2	8	6	12	.448	.544
None on/out	.287	878	252	53	10	26	26	91	130	.370	.459	vs. NL	.298	2767	825	174	23	84	345	372	403	.397	.469

Batter vs. Pitcher (career)

Hits Best Against	Avg	AB	H	2B	3B	HR	RBI	BB	SO	OBP	SLG	Hits Worst Against	Avg	AB	H	2B	3B	HR	RBI	BB	SO	OBP	SLG
Rene Arocha	.636	11	7	3	0	1	3	1	1	.615	1.182	Hector Carrasco	.000	11	0	0	0	0	0	3	2	.267	.000
Terry Adams	.625	8	5	1	0	0	1	2	1	.636	.750	Dave Mlicki	.056	18	1	0	0	0	0	1	3	.105	.056
Danny Jackson	.500	22	11	1	0	1	6	7	2	.645	.682	Randy Myers	.067	15	1	0	0	0	0	3	3	.222	.067
Roger Bailey	.500	10	5	1	0	1	3	2	1	.615	.900	Kevin Gross	.071	42	3	0	0	0	2	2	8	.114	.071
John Wetteland	.417	12	5	0	0	2	6	3	4	.533	.917	Bret Saberhagen	.071	14	1	0	0	0	0	0	5	.071	.071

Willie Blair — Tigers
Age 32 – Pitches Right

	ERA	W	L	Sv	G	GS	IP	BB	SO	Avg	H	2B	3B	HR	RBI	OBP	SLG	CG	ShO	Sup	QS	#P/S	SB	CS	GB	FB	G/F
1997 Season	4.17	16	8	0	29	27	175.0	46	90	.273	186	38	4	18	75	.319	.420	2	0	6.27	12	97	12	5	240	212	1.13
Last Five Years	4.61	31	34	4	222	58	600.2	201	392	.279	660	108	21	71	333	.338	.433	3	0	4.45	28	96	38	24	851	665	1.28

1997 Season

	ERA	W	L	Sv	G	GS	IP	H	HR	BB	SO		Avg	AB	H	2B	3B	HR	RBI	BB	SO	OBP	SLG
Home	4.65	8	4	0	12	11	69.2	83	7	13	44	vs. Left	.274	347	95	23	1	8	40	25	42	.319	.415
Away	3.84	8	4	0	17	16	105.1	103	11	33	46	vs. Right	.272	334	91	15	3	10	35	21	48	.319	.425
Day	4.13	9	4	0	15	13	80.2	92	10	27	33	Inning 1-6	.277	593	164	35	4	15	68	41	75	.324	.425
Night	4.20	7	4	0	14	14	94.1	94	8	19	57	Inning 7+	.250	88	22	3	0	3	7	5	15	.287	.386
Grass	3.79	16	6	0	27	25	166.1	173	15	42	83	None on	.273	407	111	23	2	9	9	21	51	.310	.405
Turf	11.42	0	2	0	2	2	8.2	13	3	4	7	Runners on	.274	274	75	15	2	9	66	25	39	.332	.442
March/April	6.35	2	2	0	6	5	22.2	31	2	17	7	Scoring Posn	.252	155	39	11	1	5	55	21	29	.333	.432
May	0.00	1	0	0	1	1	5.2	5	0	3	4	Close & Late	.298	47	14	1	0	2	5	3	7	.333	.447
June	3.90	1	2	0	5	5	32.1	33	2	7	16	None on/out	.310	184	57	13	2	6	6	9	17	.342	.440
July	3.96	6	0	0	6	5	36.1	35	6	5	16	vs. 1st Batr (relief)	.500	2	1	0	0	0	0	0	1	.500	.500
August	3.50	4	2	0	6	6	43.2	47	4	10	24	1st Inning Pitched	.223	103	23	7	0	0	8	10	16	.289	.291
Sept/Oct	4.72	2	2	0	5	5	34.1	35	4	4	23	First 75 Pitches	.275	516	142	29	3	13	57	30	67	.315	.409
Starter	4.17	14	8	0	27	27	170.2	182	16	44	87	Pitch 76-90	.294	85	25	4	1	3	9	7	11	.346	.471
Reliever	4.15	2	0	0	2	0	4.1	4	2	2	3	Pitch 91-105	.193	57	11	3	0	1	5	3	6	.242	.298
0-3 Days Rest (Start)	0.00	0	0	0	0	0	0.0	0	0	0	0	Pitch 106+	.348	23	8	2	0	1	4	6	6	.467	.565
4 Days Rest	4.32	9	5	0	15	15	98.0	110	10	22	50	First Pitch	.358	106	38	8	1	4	13	1	0	.370	.566
5+ Days Rest	3.96	5	3	0	12	12	72.2	72	6	22	37	Ahead in Count	.204	285	58	14	2	4	17	0	70	.204	.309
vs. AL	4.08	13	7	0	25	23	150.0	158	18	42	77	Behind in Count	.347	150	52	12	1	5	30	22	0	.425	.540
vs. NL	4.68	3	1	0	4	4	25.0	28	0	4	13	Two Strikes	.191	283	54	9	2	4	16	23	90	.253	.279

1997 Season

	ERA	W	L	Sv	G	GS	IP	H	HR	BB	SO		Avg	AB	H	2B	3B	HR	RBI	BB	SO	OBP	SLG
Pre-All Star	4.66	6	4	0	14	12	67.2	80	6	28	31	Pre-All Star	.300	267	80	19	2	6	32	28	31	.367	.453
Post-All Star	3.86	10	4	0	15	15	107.1	106	12	18	59	Post-All Star	.256	414	106	19	2	12	43	18	59	.287	.399

Last Five Years

	ERA	W	L	Sv	G	GS	IP	H	HR	BB	SO		Avg	AB	H	2B	3B	HR	RBI	BB	SO	OBP	SLG
Home	4.79	13	15	1	111	24	272.1	317	37	88	185	vs. Left	.279	1085	303	60	9	29	152	115	158	.345	.431
Away	4.47	18	19	3	111	34	328.1	343	34	113	207	vs. Right	.280	1277	357	48	12	42	181	86	234	.332	.435
Day	4.49	16	12	2	83	25	234.1	255	29	85	142	Inning 1-6	.276	1599	441	80	17	46	219	132	258	.333	.433
Night	4.69	15	22	2	139	33	366.1	405	42	116	250	Inning 7+	.287	763	219	28	4	25	114	69	134	.350	.434
Grass	4.46	29	28	4	182	49	504.2	558	60	167	322	None on	.274	1340	367	61	7	30	30	91	206	.325	.397
Turf	5.44	2	6	0	40	9	96.0	102	11	34	70	Runners on	.287	1022	293	47	14	41	303	110	186	.355	.480
March/April	5.83	2	5	0	42	5	66.1	77	7	47	41	Scoring Posn	.279	570	159	31	6	24	252	88	120	.369	.481
May	4.29	3	3	1	40	5	79.2	84	4	24	63	Close & Late	.326	298	97	13	2	13	58	31	45	.389	.513
June	4.98	4	10	1	40	11	115.2	134	19	30	65	None on/out	.280	590	165	29	4	14	14	36	84	.323	.414
July	5.17	9	5	1	40	9	109.2	129	16	36	69	vs. 1st Batr (relief)	.217	143	31	3	1	1	18	17	30	.294	.273
August	3.16	9	7	0	33	17	136.2	144	13	33	89	1st Inning Pitched	.244	755	184	32	5	19	131	83	158	.322	.375
Sept/Oct	5.05	4	4	1	27	11	92.2	92	12	31	65	First 75 Pitches	.272	2020	549	89	19	60	288	169	344	.330	.424
Starter	4.42	22	23	0	58	58	356.0	402	39	105	197	Pitch 76-90	.369	176	65	10	2	7	25	16	20	.425	.568
Reliever	4.89	9	11	4	164	0	244.2	258	32	96	195	Pitch 91-105	.297	111	33	4	0	3	15	8	14	.347	.414
0-3 Days Rest (Start)	3.60	1	2	0	4	4	25.0	29	1	6	14	Pitch 106+	.236	55	13	5	0	1	5	8	14	.328	.382
4 Days Rest	5.03	13	15	0	33	33	200.1	234	27	57	120	First Pitch	.353	360	127	24	5	19	77	15	0	.381	.606
5+ Days Rest	3.65	8	6	0	21	21	130.2	139	11	42	63	Ahead in Count	.203	1022	207	33	6	15	79	0	333	.208	.272
vs. AL	4.08	13	7	0	25	23	150.0	158	18	42	77	Behind in Count	.355	516	183	39	7	15	106	93	0	.450	.545
vs. NL	4.79	18	27	4	197	35	450.2	502	53	159	315	Two Strikes	.192	1028	197	20	5	20	79	93	392	.262	.279
Pre-All Star	5.15	11	19	3	134	23	286.2	336	36	109	183	Pre-All Star	.295	1139	336	53	9	36	183	109	183	.359	.452
Post-All Star	4.13	20	15	1	88	35	314.0	324	35	92	209	Post-All Star	.265	1223	324	55	12	35	150	92	209	.319	.415

Pitcher vs. Batter (career)

Pitches Best Vs.	Avg	AB	H	2B	3B	HR	RBI	BB	SO	OBP	SLG	Pitches Worst Vs.	Avg	AB	H	2B	3B	HR	RBI	BB	SO	OBP	SLG
David Justice	.056	18	1	0	0	0	0	2	1	.150	.056	Jody Reed	.571	14	8	1	0	2	5	0	2	.571	1.071
Dave Martinez	.067	15	1	1	0	0	2	1	2	.125	.133	Jose Offerman	.533	15	8	4	0	0	1	2	0	.588	.800
Kevin Stocker	.091	11	1	0	0	0	1	2	2	.231	.091	Sammy Sosa	.476	21	10	1	1	2	10	3	4	.542	.905
Walt Weiss	.143	14	2	0	0	0	1	1	2	.200	.143	Paul Molitor	.455	11	5	1	0	1	5	2	0	.538	.818
Henry Rodriguez	.154	13	2	0	0	0	0	1	3	.214	.154	Andres Galarraga	.364	11	4	1	0	2	5	0	1	.417	1.000

Henry Blanco — Dodgers   Age 26 – Bats Right

	Avg	G	AB	R	H	2B	3B	HR	RBI	BB	SO	HBP	GDP	SB	CS	OBP	SLG	IBB	SH	SF	#Pit	#P/PA	GB	FB	G/F
1997 Season	.400	3	5	1	2	0	0	1	1	0	1	0	1	0	0	0	.400	1.000	0	0	0	14	2.80	2	1	2.00

1997 Season

	Avg	AB	H	2B	3B	HR	RBI	BB	SO	OBP	SLG		Avg	AB	H	2B	3B	HR	RBI	BB	SO	OBP	SLG
vs. Left	.000	1	0	0	0	0	0	0	0	.000	.000	Scoring Posn	.000	0	0	0	0	0	0	0	0	.000	.000
vs. Right	.500	4	2	0	0	1	1	0	1	.500	1.250	Close & Late	.000	0	0	0	0	0	0	0	0	.000	.000

Jeff Blauser — Braves   Age 32 – Bats Right

	Avg	G	AB	R	H	2B	3B	HR	RBI	BB	SO	HBP	GDP	SB	CS	OBP	SLG	IBB	SH	SF	#Pit	#P/PA	GB	FB	G/F
1997 Season	.308	151	519	90	160	31	4	17	70	70	101	20	13	5	1	.405	.482	6	5	9	2331	3.74	180	154	1.17
Last Five Years	.272	606	2192	364	596	111	13	60	254	290	435	59	50	36	15	.368	.417	11	17	25	10042	3.89	744	635	1.17

1997 Season

	Avg	AB	H	2B	3B	HR	RBI	BB	SO	OBP	SLG		Avg	AB	H	2B	3B	HR	RBI	BB	SO	OBP	SLG
vs. Left	.312	125	39	9	1	7	20	23	23	.417	.568	First Pitch	.384	73	28	5	0	3	11	2	0	.408	.575
vs. Right	.307	394	121	22	3	10	50	47	78	.400	.454	Ahead in Count	.368	117	43	8	3	6	27	38	0	.509	.641
Groundball	.269	93	25	6	1	5	14	12	21	.382	.516	Behind in Count	.247	227	56	10	1	3	16	0	81	.291	.339
Flyball	.273	66	18	4	0	2	11	8	12	.351	.424	Two Strikes	.216	231	50	11	1	6	18	30	101	.333	.351
Home	.325	255	83	12	4	9	32	37	48	.425	.510	Batting #1	.301	133	40	9	0	5	21	16	27	.391	.481
Away	.292	264	77	19	0	8	38	33	53	.385	.455	Batting #8	.363	157	57	13	3	5	23	20	21	.449	.580
Day	.340	153	52	8	1	8	21	13	27	.402	.562	Other	.275	229	63	9	1	7	26	34	53	.383	.415
Night	.295	366	108	23	3	9	49	57	74	.405	.448	March/April	.405	79	32	8	1	3	12	7	7	.467	.646
Grass	.301	422	127	21	4	11	46	55	83	.397	.448	May	.337	86	29	6	2	3	15	12	16	.431	.558
Turf	.340	97	33	10	0	6	24	15	18	.434	.629	June	.309	94	29	6	0	5	13	16	19	.431	.532
Pre-All Star	.346	283	98	23	3	12	42	37	48	.439	.576	July	.265	98	26	7	0	2	14	13	21	.353	.398
Post-All Star	.263	236	62	8	1	5	28	33	53	.363	.369	August	.240	96	23	3	0	2	8	8	22	.308	.333
Scoring Posn	.283	113	32	4	1	5	52	27	28	.416	.469	Sept/Oct	.318	66	21	1	1	2	8	14	16	.459	.455
Close & Late	.382	89	34	5	0	3	18	8	22	.437	.539	vs. AL	.259	54	14	3	0	1	4	7	11	.375	.370
None on/out	.281	128	36	9	0	5	14	21	.366	.469	vs. NL	.314	465	146	28	4	16	66	63	90	.408	.495

1997 By Position

Position	Avg	AB	H	2B	3B	HR	RBI	BB	SO	OBP	SLG	G	GS	Innings	PO	A	E	DP	Fld Pct	Rng Fctr	In Zone	Zone Outs	Zone Rtg	MLB Zone
As ss	.308	513	158	31	4	17	67	70	100	.406	.483	149	147	1235.0	204	375	16	80	.973	4.22	431	394	.914	.937

Last Five Years

	Avg	AB	H	2B	3B	HR	RBI	BB	SO	OBP	SLG		Avg	AB	H	2B	3B	HR	RBI	BB	SO	OBP	SLG
vs. Left	.268	537	144	27	4	17	62	90	114	.373	.428	First Pitch	.334	293	98	13	2	10	36	6	0	.359	.495
vs. Right	.273	1655	452	84	9	43	192	200	321	.367	.413	Ahead in Count	.353	510	180	32	7	25	93	150	0	.496	.590
Groundball	.281	620	174	33	7	13	71	77	115	.372	.419	Behind in Count	.193	923	178	33	3	11	56	0	347	.222	.271
Flyball	.245	323	79	15	1	10	37	54	82	.362	.390	Two Strikes	.192	1020	196	40	3	17	78	134	435	.303	.287

Last Five Years

	Avg	AB	H	2B	3B	HR	RBI	BB	SO	OBP	SLG
Home	.263	1079	284	51	9	27	116	158	209	.367	.402
Away	.280	1113	312	60	4	33	138	132	226	.369	.430
Day	.288	614	177	32	5	20	73	74	121	.375	.454
Night	.266	1578	419	79	8	40	181	216	314	.366	.402
Grass	.279	1698	473	82	12	44	182	230	331	.375	.419
Turf	.249	494	123	29	1	16	72	60	104	.345	.409
Pre-All Star	.283	1362	385	75	9	40	159	180	257	.378	.439
Post-All Star	.254	830	211	36	4	20	95	110	178	.353	.380
Scoring Posn	.266	485	129	20	4	11	181	99	117	.388	.392
Close & Late	.296	328	97	15	2	12	59	45	89	.391	.463
None on/out	.264	481	127	29	1	14	14	44	81	.338	.416

	Avg	AB	H	2B	3B	HR	RBI	BB	SO	OBP	SLG
Batting #2	.268	1469	393	68	8	39	166	200	301	.364	.404
Batting #8	.289	298	86	25	3	9	38	42	49	.391	.483
Other	.275	425	117	18	2	12	50	48	85	.367	.412
March/April	.293	328	96	18	2	5	29	41	55	.378	.405
May	.288	416	120	23	4	16	62	58	85	.389	.478
June	.278	478	133	25	3	17	60	63	91	.376	.450
July	.241	428	103	19	1	10	47	60	80	.336	.360
August	.271	284	77	13	2	8	25	34	62	.366	.415
Sept/Oct	.260	258	67	13	1	4	31	34	62	.366	.364
vs. AL	.259	54	14	3	0	1	4	7	11	.375	.370
vs. NL	.272	2138	582	108	13	59	250	283	424	.368	.418

Batter vs. Pitcher (career)

Hits Best Against	Avg	AB	H	2B	3B	HR	RBI	BB	SO	OBP	SLG
Mike Hampton	.588	17	10	2	0	1	3	3	2	.650	.882
Dave Mlicki	.583	12	7	2	0	0	1	2	1	.643	.750
Mike Harkey	.538	13	7	2	0	2	3	1	1	.571	1.154
Bobby Jones	.500	26	13	3	0	2	3	4	2	.567	.846
Mark Leiter	.500	8	4	2	0	1	3	3	1	.667	1.125

Hits Worst Against	Avg	AB	H	2B	3B	HR	RBI	BB	SO	OBP	SLG
Danny Darwin	.053	19	1	0	0	0	0	3	8	.182	.053
David Cone	.077	13	1	0	0	0	0	2	6	.200	.077
Doug Jones	.083	12	1	0	0	0	1	0	5	.083	.083
Andy Benes	.088	57	5	1	0	0	3	4	10	.145	.105
Darryl Kile	.098	41	4	0	0	0	0	4	8	.174	.098

Ron Blazier — Phillies   Age 26 – Pitches Right (flyball pitcher)

	ERA	W	L	Sv	G	GS	IP	BB	SO	Avg	H	2B	3B	HR	RBI	OBP	SLG	GF	IR	IRS	Hld	SvOp	SB	CS	GB	FB	G/F
1997 Season	5.03	1	1	0	36	0	53.2	21	42	.290	62	15	1	8	37	.347	.481	7	27	8	0	0	7	0	57	74	0.77
Career (1996-1997)	5.38	4	2	0	63	0	92.0	31	67	.298	111	24	2	14	61	.347	.487	16	37	11	0	0	11	0	111	121	0.92

1997 Season

	ERA	W	L	Sv	G	GS	IP	H	HR	BB	SO
Home	4.15	1	1	0	20	0	30.1	38	3	16	21
Away	6.17	0	0	0	16	0	23.1	24	5	5	21
Starter	0.00	0	0	0	0	0	0.0	0	0	0	0
Reliever	5.03	1	1	0	36	0	53.2	62	8	21	42
0 Days rest (Relief)	3.46	1	0	0	8	0	13.0	15	0	9	10
1 or 2 Days rest	7.06	0	0	0	15	0	21.2	29	5	5	20
3+ Days rest	3.79	0	1	0	13	0	19.0	18	3	7	12
Pre-All Star	6.63	0	1	0	24	0	38.0	50	8	16	26
Post-All Star	1.15	1	0	0	12	0	15.2	12	0	5	16

	Avg	AB	H	2B	3B	HR	RBI	BB	SO	OBP	SLG
vs. Left	.291	79	23	7	1	2	21	8	14	.341	.481
vs. Right	.289	135	39	8	0	6	16	13	28	.351	.481
Scoring Posn	.284	74	21	4	0	2	30	13	15	.374	.419
Close & Late	.438	16	7	1	0	0	2	1	2	.471	.500
None on/out	.224	49	11	3	0	2	2	1	7	.240	.408
First Pitch	.389	18	7	3	0	0	5	3	0	.455	.556
Ahead in Count	.281	96	27	7	1	5	15	0	33	.273	.531
Behind in Count	.327	49	16	4	0	2	10	10	4	.441	.531
Two Strikes	.243	111	27	5	0	5	15	8	42	.292	.423

Mike Blowers — Mariners   Age 33 – Bats Right (groundball hitter)

	Avg	G	AB	R	H	2B	3B	HR	RBI	BB	SO	HBP	GDP	SB	CS	OBP	SLG	IBB	SH	SF	#Pit	#P/PA	GB	FB	G/F
1997 Season	.293	68	150	22	44	5	0	5	20	21	33	0	4	0	0	.376	.427	1	4	2	667	3.77	56	33	1.70
Last Five Years	.273	506	1555	204	425	84	6	58	260	180	396	4	57	5	8	.348	.447	8	11	12	6996	3.97	559	359	1.56

1997 Season

	Avg	AB	H	2B	3B	HR	RBI	BB	SO	OBP	SLG
vs. Left	.321	109	35	4	0	5	17	19	20	.419	.495
vs. Right	.220	41	9	1	0	0	3	2	13	.250	.244
Home	.280	75	21	2	0	5	13	13	17	.382	.507
Away	.307	75	23	3	0	0	7	8	16	.369	.347
First Pitch	.417	24	10	2	0	1	4	0	0	.417	.625
Ahead in Count	.400	30	12	1	0	1	8	9	0	.525	.533
Behind in Count	.200	65	13	2	0	1	3	0	29	.197	.277
Two Strikes	.183	71	13	1	0	2	4	12	33	.301	.282

	Avg	AB	H	2B	3B	HR	RBI	BB	SO	OBP	SLG
Scoring Posn	.278	36	10	1	0	2	16	5	9	.349	.472
Close & Late	.308	13	4	0	0	1	2	2	5	.400	.538
None on/out	.333	36	12	1	0	1	1	3	7	.385	.444
Batting #6	.232	69	16	3	0	2	8	8	17	.312	.362
Batting #7	.425	40	17	1	0	2	6	7	7	.511	.600
Other	.268	41	11	1	0	1	6	6	9	.347	.366
Pre-All Star	.238	80	19	3	0	3	12	10	17	.319	.388
Post-All Star	.357	70	25	2	0	2	8	11	16	.439	.471

Last Five Years

	Avg	AB	H	2B	3B	HR	RBI	BB	SO	OBP	SLG
vs. Left	.320	591	189	40	3	29	118	70	122	.392	.545
vs. Right	.245	964	236	44	3	29	142	110	274	.321	.387
Groundball	.275	334	92	14	0	12	57	34	81	.341	.425
Flyball	.250	316	79	14	2	15	63	32	62	.319	.449
Home	.275	750	206	42	3	37	134	107	199	.366	.487
Away	.272	805	219	42	3	21	126	73	197	.330	.410
Day	.283	445	126	28	1	13	67	53	117	.356	.438
Night	.269	1110	299	56	5	45	193	127	279	.345	.450
Grass	.272	831	226	44	4	22	120	69	198	.326	.414
Turf	.275	724	199	40	2	36	140	111	198	.371	.485
Pre-All Star	.259	936	242	53	5	28	146	101	224	.330	.416
Post-All Star	.296	619	183	31	1	30	114	79	172	.374	.494
Scoring Posn	.296	426	126	24	3	19	203	65	104	.382	.500
Close & Late	.266	233	62	12	0	12	42	25	62	.336	.472
None on/out	.297	364	108	19	1	10	10	35	89	.358	.437

	Avg	AB	H	2B	3B	HR	RBI	BB	SO	OBP	SLG
First Pitch	.333	201	67	11	0	10	41	5	0	.346	.537
Ahead in Count	.372	317	118	24	2	21	96	70	0	.481	.659
Behind in Count	.190	705	134	26	3	13	66	0	330	.192	.295
Two Strikes	.189	792	150	31	4	15	81	105	396	.285	.295
Batting #6	.284	602	171	37	4	21	102	71	156	.358	.463
Batting #7	.241	515	124	20	1	17	58	65	129	.326	.383
Other	.297	438	130	27	2	20	100	44	111	.359	.500
March/April	.189	227	43	7	1	2	21	28	55	.276	.256
May	.298	299	89	22	2	7	58	29	68	.360	.455
June	.257	296	76	18	2	13	43	33	79	.329	.463
July	.326	267	87	16	0	11	54	29	55	.393	.509
August	.313	233	73	13	0	16	55	31	62	.391	.575
Sept/Oct	.245	233	57	8	1	9	29	30	77	.331	.403
vs. AL	.275	1231	338	64	4	52	221	142	317	.349	.460
vs. NL	.269	324	87	20	2	6	39	38	79	.344	.398

Batter vs. Pitcher (career)

Hits Best Against	Avg	AB	H	2B	3B	HR	RBI	BB	SO	OBP	SLG
Sterling Hitchcock	.500	8	4	0	0	1	3	3	1	.636	.875
Sid Fernandez	.364	11	4	0	0	1	4	1	3	.417	.636
Kenny Rogers	.350	20	7	2	0	1	5	2	3	.409	.600
Chuck Finley	.344	32	11	2	0	2	5	4	9	.417	.594

Hits Worst Against	Avg	AB	H	2B	3B	HR	RBI	BB	SO	OBP	SLG
Todd Stottlemyre	.000	12	0	0	0	0	0	4	3	.250	.000
Alex Fernandez	.071	14	1	0	0	0	2	4	8	.250	.071
Jack McDowell	.077	13	1	0	0	0	0	0	3	.077	.077
Cal Eldred	.083	12	1	0	0	0	0	1	5	.154	.083

Batter vs. Pitcher (career)																				
Hits Best Against	Avg	AB	H	2B	3B	HR	RBI	BB	SO	OBP	SLG	Hits Worst Against	Avg	AB	H	2B	3B	HR	RBI	BB	SO	OBP	SLG
Chris Haney	.333	12	4	2	0	1	6	1	3	.385	.750	Roger Pavlik	.091	11	1	0	0	0	0	2	2	.231	.091

Doug Bochtler — Padres
Age 27 – Pitches Right (flyball pitcher)

	ERA	W	L	Sv	G	GS	IP	BB	SO	Avg	H	2B	3B	HR	RBI	OBP	SLG	GF	IR	IRS	Hld	SvOp	SB	CS	GB	FB	G/F
1997 Season	4.77	3	6	2	54	0	60.1	50	46	.229	51	12	1	3	34	.368	.332	13	38	11	9	3	5	1	61	78	0.78
Career (1995-1997)	3.78	9	14	6	151	0	171.1	108	159	.219	134	26	4	14	82	.335	.343	41	110	31	37	14	21	8	162	198	0.82

1997 Season

	ERA	W	L	Sv	G	GS	IP	H	HR	BB	SO		Avg	AB	H	2B	3B	HR	RBI	BB	SO	OBP	SLG
Home	4.18	1	3	1	27	0	32.1	26	1	20	22	vs. Left	.246	114	28	6	1	3	18	26	27	.383	.395
Away	5.46	2	3	1	27	0	28.0	25	2	30	24	vs. Right	.211	109	23	6	0	0	16	24	19	.353	.266
Day	5.31	1	2	1	19	0	20.1	16	1	15	20	Inning 1-6	.222	9	2	1	0	0	1	1	1	.300	.333
Night	4.50	2	4	1	35	0	40.0	35	2	35	26	Inning 7+	.229	214	49	11	1	3	33	49	45	.371	.332
Grass	5.26	3	6	2	42	0	49.2	40	2	38	40	None on	.178	101	18	6	1	1	1	30	23	.366	.287
Turf	2.53	0	0	0	12	0	10.2	11	1	12	6	Runners on	.270	122	33	6	0	2	33	20	23	.370	.369
March/April	1.69	0	0	0	10	0	10.2	8	0	8	10	Scoring Posn	.250	80	20	4	0	0	29	14	13	.357	.300
May	4.15	0	2	1	12	0	13.0	8	0	13	10	Close & Late	.195	118	23	5	1	2	14	33	25	.364	.305
June	7.90	1	1	1	12	0	13.2	15	0	14	16	None on/out	.109	46	5	3	0	0	0	13	11	.305	.174
July	4.32	1	0	0	7	0	8.1	4	1	4	6	vs. 1st Batr (relief)	.026	39	1	0	0	0	3	13	10	.264	.026
August	3.95	2	2	0	11	0	13.2	14	1	8	4	1st Inning Pitched	.223	166	37	8	1	3	31	39	36	.365	.337
Sept/Oct	18.00	0	0	0	2	0	1.0	2	1	3	0	First 15 Pitches	.215	130	28	9	0	2	23	27	26	.346	.331
Starter	0.00	0	0	0	0	0	0.0	0	0	0	0	Pitch 16-30	.286	77	22	3	1	1	11	21	17	.440	.390
Reliever	4.77	3	6	2	54	0	60.1	51	3	50	46	Pitch 31-45	.000	15	0	0	0	0	0	2	3	.118	.000
0 Days rest (Relief)	2.89	0	1	1	9	0	9.1	1	0	10	9	Pitch 46+	1.000	1	1	0	0	0	0	0	0	1.000	1.000
1 or 2 Days rest	6.50	3	5	1	31	0	36.0	37	2	32	25	First Pitch	.217	23	5	1	0	0	4	4	0	.321	.261
3+ Days rest	1.80	0	0	0	14	0	15.0	13	1	8	12	Ahead in Count	.176	102	18	4	0	0	7	0	36	.176	.216
vs. AL	5.68	1	2	0	6	0	6.1	4	1	7	4	Behind in Count	.400	40	16	4	0	2	12	26	0	.632	.650
vs. NL	4.67	2	4	2	48	0	54.0	47	2	43	42	Two Strikes	.139	115	16	2	0	0	8	20	46	.265	.157
Pre-All Star	5.50	1	4	2	35	0	37.2	32	1	37	37	Pre-All Star	.237	135	32	8	1	2	21	37	37	.398	.333
Post-All Star	3.57	2	2	0	19	0	22.2	19	2	13	9	Post-All Star	.216	88	19	4	0	1	13	13	9	.317	.330

Career (1995-1997)

	ERA	W	L	Sv	G	GS	IP	H	HR	BB	SO		Avg	AB	H	2B	3B	HR	RBI	BB	SO	OBP	SLG
Home	4.30	5	7	2	78	0	92.0	77	9	51	79	vs. Left	.224	281	63	11	4	6	36	59	65	.357	.356
Away	3.18	4	7	4	73	0	79.1	57	5	57	80	vs. Right	.214	332	71	15	0	8	46	49	94	.315	.331
Day	3.14	3	3	2	44	0	51.2	37	2	29	50	Inning 1-6	.188	32	6	2	0	0	4	2	10	.235	.250
Night	4.06	6	11	4	107	0	119.2	97	12	79	109	Inning 7+	.220	581	128	24	4	14	78	106	149	.340	.348
Grass	4.06	9	13	4	124	0	144.0	114	13	86	138	None on	.206	320	66	16	3	6	6	55	90	.324	.331
Turf	2.30	0	1	2	27	0	27.1	20	1	22	21	Runners on	.232	293	68	10	1	8	76	53	69	.346	.355
March/April	1.31	0	1	2	19	0	20.2	14	0	13	20	Scoring Posn	.228	193	44	7	0	2	63	38	41	.349	.295
May	3.08	0	2	2	23	0	26.1	20	0	18	22	Close & Late	.214	360	77	12	3	9	47	77	88	.349	.339
June	8.31	1	2	1	23	0	26.0	33	4	24	29	None on/out	.157	140	22	7	0	1	1	23	40	.276	.229
July	2.17	1	2	0	28	0	37.1	17	3	15	36	vs. 1st Batr (relief)	.121	124	15	6	0	1	15	23	37	.253	.194
August	3.23	4	3	0	36	0	39.0	30	3	25	32	1st Inning Pitched	.214	454	97	19	3	11	71	81	119	.330	.341
Sept/Oct	5.32	3	4	1	22	0	22.0	20	4	13	20	First 15 Pitches	.206	354	73	20	2	8	50	57	88	.315	.342
Starter	0.00	0	0	0	0	0	0.0	0	0	0	0	Pitch 16-30	.257	210	54	6	2	4	27	41	61	.378	.362
Reliever	3.78	9	14	6	151	0	171.1	134	14	108	159	Pitch 31-45	.130	46	6	0	0	2	5	7	10	.245	.261
0 Days rest (Relief)	2.13	2	3	2	26	0	25.1	10	1	25	29	Pitch 46+	.333	3	1	0	0	0	0	3	0	.667	.333
1 or 2 Days rest	5.08	6	9	2	85	0	95.2	89	9	61	77	First Pitch	.263	57	15	2	0	0	7	8	0	.343	.298
3+ Days rest	2.15	1	2	2	40	0	50.1	35	4	22	53	Ahead in Count	.173	307	53	9	1	6	29	0	128	.175	.267
vs. AL	5.68	1	2	0	6	0	6.1	4	1	7	4	Behind in Count	.318	110	35	10	1	5	21	47	0	.522	.564
vs. NL	3.71	8	12	6	145	0	165.0	130	13	101	155	Two Strikes	.156	346	54	7	1	6	31	53	159	.268	.234
Pre-All Star	4.64	1	6	5	70	0	77.2	71	5	57	76	Pre-All Star	.253	281	71	15	2	5	46	57	76	.376	.374
Post-All Star	3.07	8	8	1	81	0	93.2	63	9	51	83	Post-All Star	.190	332	63	11	2	9	36	51	83	.298	.316

Brian Boehringer — Yankees
Age 28 – Pitches Right (flyball pitcher)

	ERA	W	L	Sv	G	GS	IP	BB	SO	Avg	H	2B	3B	HR	RBI	OBP	SLG	GF	IR	IRS	Hld	SvOp	SB	CS	GB	FB	G/F
1997 Season	2.63	3	2	0	34	0	48.0	32	53	.225	39	9	0	4	23	.343	.347	11	30	8	5	3	1	2	35	59	0.59
Career (1995-1997)	5.54	5	9	0	56	6	112.0	75	100	.256	109	3	15	71	.366	.447	12	45	13	9	5	6	2	96	172	0.56

1997 Season

	ERA	W	L	Sv	G	GS	IP	H	HR	BB	SO		Avg	AB	H	2B	3B	HR	RBI	BB	SO	OBP	SLG
Home	3.44	1	1	0	15	0	18.1	15	3	15	18	vs. Left	.152	66	10	2	0	1	4	12	14	.282	.227
Away	2.12	2	1	0	19	0	29.2	24	1	17	35	vs. Right	.271	107	29	7	0	3	19	20	39	.380	.421
Starter	0.00	0	0	0	0	0	0.0	0	0	0	0	Scoring Posn	.275	51	14	3	0	3	21	14	17	.418	.510
Reliever	2.63	3	2	0	34	0	48.0	39	4	32	53	Close & Late	.258	62	16	6	0	1	12	16	19	.400	.403
0 Days rest (Relief)	3.38	0	0	0	7	0	8.0	6	1	2	9	None on/out	.108	37	4	2	0	0	0	8	11	.267	.162
1 or 2 Days rest	3.71	1	1	0	15	0	17.0	18	2	17	19	First Pitch	.526	19	10	4	0	1	5	5	0	.625	.895
3+ Days rest	1.57	2	1	0	12	0	23.0	15	1	13	25	Ahead in Count	.134	82	11	2	0	1	7	0	41	.133	.195
Pre-All Star	3.25	2	2	0	21	0	27.2	29	3	22	31	Behind in Count	.310	29	9	3	0	1	6	13	0	.512	.517
Post-All Star	1.77	1	0	0	13	0	20.1	10	1	10	22	Two Strikes	.146	103	15	2	0	2	8	14	53	.248	.223

Tim Bogar — Astros
Age 31 – Bats Right

	Avg	G	AB	R	H	2B	3B	HR	RBI	BB	SO	HBP	GDP	SB	CS	OBP	SLG	IBB	SH	SF	#Pit	#P/PA	GB	FB	G/F
1997 Season	.249	97	241	30	60	14	4	4	30	24	42	3	4	4	1	.320	.390	1	3	4	943	3.43	87	70	1.24
Career (1993-1997)	.245	394	732	88	179	38	4	10	87	59	127	8	9	7	5	.304	.348	4	11	9	2852	3.48	256	211	1.21

1997 Season

	Avg	AB	H	2B	3B	HR	RBI	BB	SO	OBP	SLG		Avg	AB	H	2B	3B	HR	RBI	BB	SO	OBP	SLG
vs. Left	.279	68	19	4	1	1	12	9	9	.363	.412	Scoring Posn	.277	65	18	5	1	1	26	13	18	.378	.431
vs. Right	.237	173	41	10	3	3	18	15	33	.302	.382	Close & Late	.303	33	10	2	1	0	4	5	7	.395	.424
Home	.220	127	28	8	1	3	14	12	22	.296	.370	None on/out	.271	59	16	3	1	2	2	4	8	.317	.458
Away	.281	114	32	6	3	1	16	12	20	.346	.412	Batting #7	.294	51	15	3	1	2	10	9	8	.393	.510
First Pitch	.318	44	14	5	1	0	3	1	0	.348	.477	Batting #8	.258	159	41	11	2	2	18	12	31	.318	.390
Ahead in Count	.270	37	10	3	1	2	7	10	0	.417	.568	Other	.129	31	4	0	1	0	2	3	3	.200	.194
Behind in Count	.188	128	24	6	1	1	13	0	39	.191	.273	Pre-All Star	.214	98	21	6	1	1	6	9	16	.278	.327
Two Strikes	.170	112	19	5	0	2	9	13	42	.260	.268	Post-All Star	.273	143	39	8	3	3	24	15	26	.348	.434

Career (1993-1997)

	Avg	AB	H	2B	3B	HR	RBI	BB	SO	OBP	SLG		Avg	AB	H	2B	3B	HR	RBI	BB	SO	OBP	SLG
vs. Left	.270	296	80	18	1	5	41	23	45	.322	.389	First Pitch	.291	127	37	8	1	1	14	4	0	.318	.394
vs. Right	.227	436	99	20	3	5	46	36	82	.293	.321	Ahead in Count	.331	142	47	9	1	6	26	24	0	.426	.535
Groundball	.195	164	32	8	0	2	13	9	36	.250	.280	Behind in Count	.178	359	64	15	1	1	25	0	113	.185	.234
Flyball	.216	102	22	3	0	2	15	6	24	.250	.304	Two Strikes	.163	338	55	13	0	2	25	31	127	.239	.219
Home	.218	358	78	18	1	4	30	29	71	.284	.307	Batting #7	.250	128	32	5	1	3	18	10	18	.302	.375
Away	.270	374	101	20	3	6	57	30	56	.324	.388	Batting #8	.242	433	105	24	2	4	46	32	78	.302	.335
Day	.222	212	47	10	0	1	13	22	40	.310	.283	Other	.246	171	42	9	1	3	23	17	31	.313	.363
Night	.254	520	132	28	4	9	74	37	87	.302	.375	March/April	.116	43	5	1	1	0	1	2	9	.156	.186
Grass	.238	446	106	20	1	3	46	37	90	.298	.307	May	.211	71	15	3	0	1	7	6	5	.273	.296
Turf	.255	286	73	18	3	7	41	22	37	.314	.413	June	.272	158	43	10	0	2	20	11	28	.316	.373
Pre-All Star	.237	334	79	16	1	4	33	25	53	.292	.326	July	.214	206	44	7	1	4	18	12	36	.269	.316
Post-All Star	.251	398	100	22	3	6	54	34	74	.314	.367	August	.282	170	48	9	2	3	26	19	29	.352	.412
Scoring Posn	.273	194	53	11	1	4	79	29	39	.364	.402	Sept/Oct	.286	84	24	8	0	0	15	9	20	.365	.381
Close & Late	.244	123	30	5	1	2	18	13	27	.319	.350	vs. AL	.250	28	7	1	0	1	4	3	4	.313	.393
None on/out	.225	182	41	7	4	4	4	9	26	.262	.341	vs. NL	.244	704	172	37	4	9	83	56	123	.304	.347

Batter vs. Pitcher (career)

Hits Best Against	Avg	AB	H	2B	3B	HR	RBI	BB	SO	OBP	SLG	Hits Worst Against	Avg	AB	H	2B	3B	HR	RBI	BB	SO	OBP	SLG
Tom Candiotti	.385	13	5	1	0	0	2	0	2	.429	.462	Michael Mimbs	.083	12	1	1	0	0	0	0	4	.083	.167
Kent Mercker	.333	12	4	0	0	2	5	1	1	.385	.833												

Wade Boggs — Yankees
Age 40 – Bats Left (groundball hitter)

	Avg	G	AB	R	H	2B	3B	HR	RBI	BB	SO	HBP	GDP	SB	CS	OBP	SLG	IBB	SH	SF	#Pit	#P/PA	GB	FB	G/F
1997 Season	.292	103	353	55	103	23	1	4	28	48	38	0	3	0	1	.373	.397	3	2	4	1652	4.06	130	113	1.15
Last Five Years	.313	601	2240	355	702	119	9	24	246	324	198	1	46	4	6	.396	.407	22	6	29	10812	4.16	912	611	1.49

1997 Season

	Avg	AB	H	2B	3B	HR	RBI	BB	SO	OBP	SLG		Avg	AB	H	2B	3B	HR	RBI	BB	SO	OBP	SLG
vs. Left	.361	72	26	3	0	1	4	7	10	.418	.444	First Pitch	.364	22	8	2	0	0	2	2	0	.417	.455
vs. Right	.274	281	77	20	1	3	24	41	28	.362	.384	Ahead in Count	.374	91	34	7	0	3	10	26	0	.513	.549
Groundball	.338	71	24	5	0	1	6	10	5	.420	.451	Behind in Count	.225	151	34	6	1	1	7	0	33	.222	.298
Flyball	.288	59	17	4	0	0	2	3	8	.313	.356	Two Strikes	.195	164	32	9	1	1	8	20	78	.278	.280
Home	.287	157	45	10	0	0	5	20	17	.367	.350	Batting #2	.292	212	62	14	1	2	19	36	17	.390	.396
Away	.296	196	58	13	1	4	23	28	21	.377	.434	Batting #6	.280	75	21	4	0	1	7	8	9	.345	.373
Day	.250	136	34	7	1	1	5	11	16	.306	.338	Other	.303	66	20	5	0	1	2	4	12	.343	.424
Night	.318	217	69	16	0	3	23	37	22	.411	.433	March/April	.311	74	23	2	0	1	6	19	5	.442	.378
Grass	.303	317	96	21	1	4	27	41	30	.378	.413	May	.143	56	8	3	0	0	2	9	6	.262	.196
Turf	.194	36	7	2	0	0	1	7	8	.326	.250	June	.279	61	17	4	0	1	8	6	7	.338	.393
Pre-All Star	.240	204	49	9	0	2	16	34	21	.344	.314	July	.343	67	23	3	0	3	8	12		.413	.433
Post-All Star	.362	149	54	14	1	2	12	14	17	.415	.510	August	.255	47	12	4	0	0	0	1	4	.271	.340
Scoring Posn	.238	84	20	2	1	1	25	18	8	.358	.321	Sept/Oct	.417	48	20	7	1	1	9	5	4	.463	.667
Close & Late	.193	57	11	0	0	1	6	10	6	.266	.193	vs. AL	.293	321	94	22	1	4	26	48	34	.381	.405
None on/out	.373	67	25	6	0	0	4	6	4	.408	.463	vs. NL	.281	32	9	1	0	0	2	0	4	.281	.313

1997 By Position

Position	Avg	AB	H	2B	3B	HR	RBI	BB	SO	OBP	SLG	G	GS	Innings	PO	A	E	DP	Fld Pct	Rng Fctr	In Zone	Zone Outs	Zone Rtg	MLB Zone
As DH	.394	66	26	6	0	1	3	6	12	.444	.530	19	18	---	---	---	---	---	---	---	---	---	---	---
As Pinch Hitter	.000	13	0	0	0	0	0	1	4	.071	.000	14	0	---	---	---	---	---	---	---	---	---	---	---
As 3b	.280	275	77	17	1	3	25	41	23	.369	.382	76	70	611.0	42	141	4	16	.979	2.70	201	165	.821	.801

Last Five Years

	Avg	AB	H	2B	3B	HR	RBI	BB	SO	OBP	SLG		Avg	AB	H	2B	3B	HR	RBI	BB	SO	OBP	SLG
vs. Left	.294	618	182	24	2	4	67	82	61	.371	.359	First Pitch	.339	115	39	7	0	2	7	17	0	.421	.452
vs. Right	.321	1622	520	95	7	20	179	242	137	.405	.425	Ahead in Count	.363	620	225	46	4	12	88	177	0	.499	.508
Groundball	.317	527	167	27	4	6	57	75	60	.402	.417	Behind in Count	.277	962	266	35	4	8	83	0	157	.274	.346
Flyball	.296	416	123	23	0	6	45	63	50	.379	.394	Two Strikes	.266	1067	284	44	5	7	92	129	198	.343	.336
Home	.336	1135	381	63	3	13	114	156	101	.412	.431	Batting #1	.312	766	239	41	5	2	69	115	65	.398	.386
Away	.290	1105	321	56	6	11	132	168	97	.380	.382	Batting #2	.320	1152	369	61	2	19	142	166	94	.401	.426
Day	.313	821	257	49	5	9	98	107	74	.389	.418	Other	.292	322	94	17	2	3	35	43	39	.373	.385
Night	.314	1419	445	70	4	15	148	217	124	.400	.400	March/April	.305	311	95	13	1	1	33	56	29	.405	.363
Grass	.314	1950	613	98	7	21	213	277	175	.395	.404	May	.302	411	124	15	1	8	56	57	31	.380	.401
Turf	.307	290	89	21	2	3	33	47	23	.400	.424	June	.322	438	141	24	3	7	52	64	33	.404	.438

Last Five Years

	Avg	AB	H	2B	3B	HR	RBI	BB	SO	OBP	SLG		Avg	AB	H	2B	3B	HR	RBI	BB	SO	OBP	SLG
Pre-All Star	.301	1277	385	57	5	17	147	194	109	.388	.394	July	.319	401	128	24	0	4	33	57	38	.404	.409
Post-All Star	.329	963	317	62	4	7	99	130	89	.406	.424	August	.318	390	124	22	1	3	33	45	38	.384	.403
Scoring Posn	.299	532	159	21	3	5	213	116	55	.406	.378	Sept/Oct	.311	289	90	21	3	1	39	45	29	.401	.415
Close & Late	.284	299	85	4	3	3	35	53	40	.387	.348	vs. AL	.314	2208	693	118	9	24	244	324	194	.397	.408
None on/out	.304	602	183	27	2	7		72	41	.378	.390	vs. NL	.281	32	9	1	0	2		0	4	.281	.313

Batter vs. Pitcher (since 1984)

Hits Best Against	Avg	AB	H	2B	3B	HR	RBI	BB	SO	OBP	SLG	Hits Worst Against	Avg	AB	H	2B	3B	HR	RBI	BB	SO	OBP	SLG
Eric Plunk	.545	11	6	2	1	0	1	7	0	.722	.909	Scott Karl	.077	13	1	0	0	0	0	1	0	.143	.077
Tim Belcher	.500	28	14	3	0	0	3	4	3	.563	.607	Willie Banks	.100	10	1	0	0	0	0	1	0	.250	.100
Mark Leiter	.462	13	6	1	1	0	2	4	1	.588	.692	Jose Bautista	.111	18	2	0	0	0	1	3	2	.238	.111
Tony Castillo	.417	12	5	1	0	1	3	0	0	.417	.750	Tim Wakefield	.111	9	1	0	0	0	0	2	0	.273	.111
Pete Harnisch	.385	13	5	4	0	0	2	2	1	.467	.692	Randy Johnson	.118	17	2	0	0	0	0	1	8	.167	.118

Brian Bohanon — Mets
Age 29 – Pitches Left (groundball pitcher)

	ERA	W	L	Sv	G	GS	IP	BB	SO	Avg	H	2B	3B	HR	RBI	OBP	SLG	CG	ShO	Sup	QS	#P/S	SB	CS	GB	FB	G/F
1997 Season	3.82	6	4	0	19	14	94.1	34	66	.258	95	19	3	9	40	.328	.399	0	0	4.96	7	96	11	3	146	79	1.85
Last Five Years	5.19	13	12	2	138	37	352.0	148	217	.286	401	89	6	38	212	.358	.440	0	0	5.04	11	85	30	12	554	333	1.66

1997 Season

	ERA	W	L	Sv	G	GS	IP	H	HR	BB	SO		Avg	AB	H	2B	3B	HR	RBI	BB	SO	OBP	SLG
Home	3.38	2	2	0	8	5	40.0	42	5	13	31	vs. Left	.263	76	20	4	0	1	8	5	14	.325	.355
Away	4.14	4	2	0	11	9	54.1	53	4	21	35	vs. Right	.257	292	75	15	3	8	32	29	52	.328	.411
Starter	3.27	6	3	0	14	14	88.0	84	7	29	61	Scoring Posn	.219	96	21	5	1	2	28	14	21	.318	.354
Reliever	11.37	0	1	0	5	0	6.1	11	2	5	5	Close & Late	.429	35	15	3	1	2	5	4	4	.487	.743
0-3 Days Rest (Start)	0.00	0	0	0	0	0	0.0	0	0	0	0	None on/out	.330	94	31	4	1	2	2	6	14	.382	.457
4 Days Rest	2.08	3	1	0	7	7	43.1	39	2	17	27	First Pitch	.317	63	20	2	1	3	8	2	0	.358	.524
5+ Days Rest	4.43	3	2	0	7	7	44.2	45	5	12	34	Ahead in Count	.158	133	21	4	0	1	7	0	56	.170	.211
Pre-All Star	6.75	1	1	0	6	1	13.1	15	2	6	10	Behind in Count	.365	96	35	6	2	3	14	10	0	.425	.563
Post-All Star	3.33	5	3	0	13	13	81.0	80	7	28	56	Two Strikes	.184	136	25	7	0	1	8	22	66	.297	.257

Last Five Years

	ERA	W	L	Sv	G	GS	IP	H	HR	BB	SO		Avg	AB	H	2B	3B	HR	RBI	BB	SO	OBP	SLG
Home	5.57	9	7	0	68	19	171.1	207	24	76	113	vs. Left	.293	358	105	16	0	9	55	35	58	.366	.413
Away	4.83	4	5	2	70	18	180.2	194	14	72	104	vs. Right	.284	1043	296	73	6	29	157	113	159	.355	.449
Day	5.21	3	4	0	59	16	155.1	168	17	69	90	Inning 1-6	.287	1042	299	65	4	25	151	95	167	.350	.429
Night	5.17	10	8	2	79	21	196.2	233	21	79	127	Inning 7+	.284	359	102	24	2	13	61	53	50	.379	.471
Grass	4.77	13	9	0	107	30	284.2	323	27	115	182	None on	.293	728	213	42	1	20	20	69	106	.362	.435
Turf	6.95	0	3	2	31	7	67.1	78	11	33	35	Runners on	.279	673	188	47	5	18	192	79	111	.354	.444
March/April	5.63	1	1	0	24	1	38.1	37	5	24	26	Scoring Posn	.272	408	111	25	4	8	159	56	75	.355	.412
May	5.95	2	1	0	27	3	42.1	51	6	25	26	Close & Late	.344	122	42	9	2	5	22	18	12	.426	.574
June	4.91	1	2	0	11	6	40.1	40	4	18	15	None on/out	.307	329	101	21	1	10	10	29	42	.370	.468
July	6.75	3	2	0	25	9	76.0	96	8	31	52	vs. 1st Batr (relief)	.297	91	27	5	0	4	25	7	12	.356	.484
August	3.54	4	4	0	26	11	94.0	101	10	28	62	1st Inning Pitched	.262	443	116	26	1	14	79	48	79	.337	.420
Sept/Oct	5.16	2	2	1	25	7	61.0	76	5	22	36	First 75 Pitches	.289	1244	359	78	4	33	196	130	194	.359	.437
Starter	4.97	9	9	0	37	37	193.2	212	20	75	122	Pitch 76-90	.287	101	29	6	2	1	7	11	13	.365	.416
Reliever	5.46	4	3	2	101	0	158.1	189	18	73	95	Pitch 91-105	.204	49	10	3	0	3	7	7	10	.304	.449
0-3 Days Rest (Start)	6.68	1	2	0	7	7	33.2	41	3	15	24	Pitch 106+	.429	7	3	2	0	1	2	0	0	.429	1.143
4 Days Rest	4.36	4	3	0	16	16	84.2	88	7	37	49	First Pitch	.379	219	83	17	2	9	43	11	0	.419	.598
5+ Days Rest	4.90	4	4	0	14	14	75.1	83	10	23	49	Ahead in Count	.211	551	116	21	0	10	56	0	184	.219	.303
vs. AL	5.76	8	8	2	120	24	262.2	313	30	115	155	Behind in Count	.356	348	124	28	2	13	71	70	0	.461	.560
vs. NL	3.53	5	4	0	18	13	89.1	88	8	33	62	Two Strikes	.200	546	109	23	2	10	53	67	217	.290	.304
Pre-All Star	5.92	4	4	0	70	14	143.0	159	16	77	84	Pre-All Star	.281	566	159	35	2	16	95	77	84	.367	.435
Post-All Star	4.69	9	8	1	68	23	209.0	242	22	71	133	Post-All Star	.290	835	242	54	4	22	117	71	133	.351	.443

Pitcher vs. Batter (career)

Pitches Best Vs.	Avg	AB	H	2B	3B	HR	RBI	BB	SO	OBP	SLG	Pitches Worst Vs.	Avg	AB	H	2B	3B	HR	RBI	BB	SO	OBP	SLG
Mike Devereaux	.083	12	1	0	0	0	2	0	1	.083	.083	Albert Belle	.600	15	9	3	0	1	6	3	0	.667	1.000
Pat Meares	.091	11	1	0	0	0	0	0	0	.091	.091	Chad Curtis	.556	9	5	2	0	0	1	1	0	.636	.778
Sandy Alomar Jr	.100	10	1	0	0	0	1	0	1	.091	.100	Ken Griffey Jr	.545	11	6	0	0	2	3	1	0	.667	.545
Gary Gaetti	.125	16	2	1	0	0	0	1	3	.176	.188	Brian McRae	.538	13	7	2	1	0	2	0	0	.538	.846
Tony Fernandez	.167	12	2	0	0	0	0	0	1	.167	.167	Tino Martinez	.417	12	5	2	0	2	5	0	3	.385	1.083

Barry Bonds — Giants
Age 33 – Bats Left (flyball hitter)

	Avg	G	AB	R	H	2B	3B	HR	RBI	BB	SO	HBP	GDP	SB	CS	OBP	SLG	IBB	SH	SF	#Pit	#P/PA	GB	FB	G/F
1997 Season	.291	159	532	123	155	26	5	40	101	145	87	8	13	37	8	.446	.585	34	0	5	2519	3.65	162	213	0.76
Last Five Years	.308	732	2485	572	766	139	20	198	538	616	368	22	49	166	46	.446	.619	147	0	25	11615	3.69	733	1000	0.73

1997 Season

	Avg	AB	H	2B	3B	HR	RBI	BB	SO	OBP	SLG		Avg	AB	H	2B	3B	HR	RBI	BB	SO	OBP	SLG
vs. Left	.295	166	49	11	2	11	26	37	24	.427	.584	First Pitch	.360	86	31	4	0	8	19	27	0	.521	.686
vs. Right	.290	366	106	15	3	29	75	108	63	.455	.585	Ahead in Count	.394	155	61	10	2	14	43	76	0	.591	.755
Groundball	.316	114	36	6	2	11	23	25	13	.451	.693	Behind in Count	.200	175	35	9	2	10	23	0	65	.212	.446
Flyball	.228	57	13	3	0	4	11	23	11	.491	.491	Two Strikes	.208	207	43	9	2	13	30	41	87	.343	.459
Home	.326	264	86	15	3	24	61	69	42	.466	.678	Batting #3	.300	310	93	20	2	22	61	94	49	.463	.590
Away	.257	268	69	11	2	16	40	76	45	.428	.493	Batting #4	.281	221	62	6	3	18	40	50	37	.421	.579
Day	.271	240	65	14	2	17	44	64	45	.427	.558	Other	.000	1	0	0	0	0	0	1	1	.500	.000

1997 Season

	Avg	AB	H	2B	3B	HR	RBI	BB	SO	OBP	SLG
Night	.308	292	90	12	3	23	57	81	42	.462	.606
Grass	.299	441	132	21	4	36	89	116	68	.447	.610
Turf	.253	91	23	5	1	4	12	29	19	.444	.462
Pre-All Star	.275	287	79	10	3	20	46	68	46	.418	.540
Post-All Star	.310	245	76	16	2	20	55	77	41	.479	.637
Scoring Posn	.244	135	33	7	1	7	57	63	24	.483	.467
Close & Late	.333	81	27	9	1	3	11	28	12	.509	.580
None on/out	.244	123	30	8	1	9	9	21	22	.363	.545

	Avg	AB	H	2B	3B	HR	RBI	BB	SO	OBP	SLG
March/April	.257	70	18	0	2	3	12	26	8	.465	.443
May	.261	92	24	4	1	5	14	23	20	.402	.489
June	.308	104	32	5	0	11	17	18	14	.415	.673
July	.362	94	34	8	0	8	25	20	22	.483	.702
August	.250	96	24	6	0	4	14	30	20	.433	.438
Sept/Oct	.303	76	23	3	2	9	19	28	3	.491	.750
vs. AL	.310	58	18	4	0	4	5	10	10	.429	.586
vs. NL	.289	474	137	22	5	36	96	135	77	.448	.584

1997 By Position

Position	Avg	AB	H	2B	3B	HR	RBI	BB	SO	OBP	SLG	G	GS	Innings	PO	A	E	DP	Fld Pct	Rng Fctr	In Zone	Outs	Zone Rtg	MLB Zone
As If	.291	532	155	26	5	40	101	145	87	.446	.585	159	158	1372.1	290	10	5	1	.984	1.97	334	267	.799	.805

Last Five Years

	Avg	AB	H	2B	3B	HR	RBI	BB	SO	OBP	SLG
vs. Left	.300	789	237	45	7	54	162	143	117	.410	.580
vs. Right	.312	1696	529	94	13	144	376	473	251	.462	.637
Groundball	.317	697	221	32	5	60	160	148	97	.437	.636
Flyball	.306	356	109	19	2	30	81	98	55	.453	.624
Home	.312	1205	376	68	8	99	268	304	172	.451	.628
Away	.305	1280	390	71	12	99	270	312	196	.441	.611
Day	.309	1191	368	72	7	99	265	297	175	.448	.631
Night	.308	1294	398	67	13	99	273	319	193	.445	.609
Grass	.308	1952	602	102	14	153	423	481	284	.445	.610
Turf	.308	533	164	37	6	45	115	135	84	.450	.653
Pre-All Star	.302	1446	437	75	13	106	292	309	210	.427	.592
Post-All Star	.317	1039	329	64	7	92	246	307	158	.471	.657
Scoring Posn	.317	574	182	39	5	35	306	283	87	.531	.585
Close & Late	.306	382	117	26	1	33	95	109	60	.460	.639
None on/out	.269	602	162	39	6	42	42	82	98	.360	.563

	Avg	AB	H	2B	3B	HR	RBI	BB	SO	OBP	SLG
First Pitch	.348	391	136	17	2	36	94	115	0	.499	.678
Ahead in Count	.386	723	279	48	3	76	205	284	0	.555	.776
Behind in Count	.235	835	196	52	8	45	147	0	269	.242	.478
Two Strikes	.213	949	202	45	9	52	153	215	368	.360	.444
Batting #3	.306	1391	425	78	12	114	309	338	199	.442	.625
Batting #4	.297	538	160	27	4	43	121	151	82	.452	.602
Other	.326	556	181	34	4	41	108	127	87	.450	.622
March/April	.299	321	96	13	5	27	80	91	42	.456	.623
May	.317	489	155	29	6	33	93	98	78	.430	.603
June	.297	488	145	24	2	35	86	94	67	.412	.570
July	.330	469	155	34	1	45	118	111	74	.462	.695
August	.285	372	106	16	2	28	81	114	74	.453	.565
Sept/Oct	.315	346	109	23	4	30	80	108	33	.473	.665
vs. AL	.310	58	18	4	0	4	5	10	10	.429	.586
vs. NL	.308	2427	748	135	20	194	533	606	358	.446	.620

Batter vs. Pitcher (career)

Hits Best Against	Avg	AB	H	2B	3B	HR	RBI	BB	SO	OBP	SLG
Armando Reynoso	.667	15	10	3	1	2	9	8	1	.783	1.400
Pedro Astacio	.545	11	6	1	1	1	3	3	0	.600	1.091
Alan Benes	.500	12	6	2	0	2	4	1	1	.538	1.167
Mark Gardner	.444	9	4	1	0	2	5	3	1	.583	1.222
Mark Leiter	.375	8	3	0	0	2	5	4	1	.583	1.125

Hits Worst Against	Avg	AB	H	2B	3B	HR	RBI	BB	SO	OBP	SLG
Dennis Cook	.000	9	0	0	0	0	0	2	0	.182	.000
Chuck McElroy	.042	24	1	1	0	0	1	1	4	.077	.083
Jon Lieber	.056	18	1	0	0	0	2	3	4	.190	.056
Kevin Brown	.071	14	1	0	0	0	0	4	1	.278	.071
Rick Honeycutt	.083	12	1	1	0	0	1	1	2	.143	.167

Ricky Bones — Royals   Age 29 – Pitches Right

	ERA	W	L	Sv	G	GS	IP	BB	SO	Avg	H	2B	3B	HR	RBI	OBP	SLG	GF	IR	IRS	Hld	SvOp	SB	CS	GB	FB	G/F
1997 Season	6.75	4	8	0	30	13	96.0	36	44	.336	133	18	3	12	72	.394	.487	4	15	6	2	1	9	5	169	109	1.55
Last Five Years	4.98	42	54	0	154	123	822.2	295	304	.285	923	176	27	113	429	.348	.461	7	30	9	5	1	53	25	1204	1062	1.13

1997 Season

	ERA	W	L	Sv	G	GS	IP	H	HR	BB	SO
Home	6.02	2	2	0	13	5	46.1	59	8	8	20
Away	7.43	2	6	0	17	8	49.2	74	4	28	24
Starter	7.62	4	6	0	13	13	65.0	99	7	26	36
Reliever	4.94	0	2	0	17	0	31.0	34	5	10	8
0 Days rest (Relief)	0.00	0	0	0	0	0	0.0	0	0	0	0
1 or 2 Days rest	5.28	0	1	0	9	0	15.1	20	3	1	5
3+ Days rest	4.60	0	1	0	8	0	15.2	14	2	9	3
Pre-All Star	9.00	0	2	0	13	2	23.0	39		12	9
Post-All Star	6.04	4	6	0	17	11	73.0	94		24	35

	Avg	AB	H	2B	3B	HR	RBI	BB	SO	OBP	SLG
vs. Left	.346	188	65	9	1	8	34	15	18	.391	.532
vs. Right	.327	208	68	9	2	4	38	21	26	.396	.447
Scoring Posn	.357	112	40	4	1	2	58	20	15	.433	.464
Close & Late	.292	24	7	1	1	1	5	3	1	.345	.542
None on/out	.327	98	32	6	1	3	3	5	5	.365	.500
First Pitch	.282	71	20	3	1	1	13	2	0	.303	.394
Ahead in Count	.303	155	47	5	1	2	18	0	31	.319	.387
Behind in Count	.422	102	43	6	1	6	31	16	0	.496	.676
Two Strikes	.271	144	39	6	0	0	15	18	44	.359	.313

Last Five Years

	ERA	W	L	Sv	G	GS	IP	H	HR	BB	SO
Home	5.00	19	25	0	68	53	372.1	428	48	117	141
Away	4.96	23	29	0	86	70	450.1	495	65	178	163
Day	4.86	14	15	0	48	38	242.2	281	28	93	102
Night	5.03	28	39	0	106	85	580.0	642	85	202	202
Grass	5.04	32	49	0	129	102	693.0	784	92	247	257
Turf	4.65	10	5	0	25	21	129.2	139	21	48	47
March/April	4.59	5	7	0	24	17	115.2	132	9	49	35
May	5.11	7	10	0	22	21	135.2	138	23	52	48
June	4.20	9	10	0	27	24	158.2	164	26	48	54
July	4.90	8	10	0	30	23	154.1	176	20	50	62
August	5.03	8	10	0	28	22	155.2	177	18	47	62
Sept/Oct	6.49	5	7	0	23	16	102.2	136	17	49	43
Starter	4.94	42	51	0	123	123	772.0	867	105	273	281
Reliever	5.51	0	3	0	31	0	50.2	56	8	22	23
0 Days rest (Relief)	0.00	0	0	0	0	0	0.0	0	0	0	0
1 or 2 Days rest	3.96	0	1	0	15	0	25.0	30	3	6	14
3+ Days rest	7.01	0	2	0	16	0	25.2	26	5	16	9
vs. AL	4.78	42	51	0	142	120	800.0	880	106	278	295
vs. NL	11.91	0	3	0	12	3	22.2	43	7	17	9

	Avg	AB	H	2B	3B	HR	RBI	BB	SO	OBP	SLG
vs. Left	.287	1678	482	87	11	58	203	143	105	.343	.456
vs. Right	.283	1556	441	89	16	55	226	152	199	.352	.467
Inning 1-6	.291	2732	794	155	21	98	391	259	261	.354	.470
Inning 7+	.257	502	129	21	6	15	38	36	43	.310	.412
None on	.279	1919	535	106	14	78	78	146	172	.335	.471
Runners on	.295	1315	388	70	13	35	351	149	132	.364	.448
Scoring Posn	.271	723	196	38	8	22	307	98	85	.350	.437
Close & Late	.244	180	44	5	2	9	16	15	14	.299	.444
None on/out	.286	871	249	49	7	44	44	50	61	.327	.510
vs. 1st Batr (relief)	.222	27	6	1	0	0	5	2	7	.267	.259
1st Inning Pitched	.265	573	152	23	4	19	87	60	59	.342	.419
First 15 Pitches	.268	496	133	24	2	16	51	34	43	.325	.421
Pitch 16-30	.302	477	144	21	6	23	73	56	42	.375	.516
Pitch 31-45	.307	485	149	25	4	14	71	44	44	.369	.462
Pitch 46+	.280	1776	497	106	15	60	234	161	175	.340	.458
First Pitch	.292	535	156	31	6	13	69	9	0	.308	.445
Ahead in Count	.237	1171	278	52	8	32	110	0	247	.248	.377
Behind in Count	.341	858	293	50	9	44	154	160	0	.441	.575
Two Strikes	.237	1208	286	62	5	34	126	126	304	.314	.381

Last Five Years

	ERA	W	L	Sv	G	GS	IP	H	HR	BB	SO		Avg	AB	H	2B	3B	HR	RBI	BB	SO	OBP	SLG
Pre-All Star	4.52	23	31	0	81	69	462.1	485	61	164	153	Pre-All Star	.269	1802	485	97	10	61	225	164	153	.332	.436
Post-All Star	5.57	19	23	0	73	54	360.1	438	52	131	151	Post-All Star	.306	1432	438	79	17	52	204	131	151	.367	.494

Pitcher vs. Batter (career)

Pitches Best Vs.	Avg	AB	H	2B	3B	HR	RBI	BB	SO	OBP	SLG	Pitches Worst Vs.	Avg	AB	H	2B	3B	HR	RBI	BB	SO	OBP	SLG
Craig Paquette	.000	10	0	0	0	0	1	0	2	.000	.000	Rusty Greer	.625	8	5	2	0	0	0	3	1	.727	.875
Darrin Jackson	.000	10	0	0	0	0	0	1	1	.091	.000	Eddie Murray	.545	11	6	1	0	1	2	4	0	.667	.909
Brian McRae	.050	20	1	0	0	0	1	2	2	.130	.050	Scott Stahoviak	.533	15	8	4	0	2	3	0	1	.533	1.200
Dean Palmer	.118	17	2	0	0	0	0	0	9	.118	.118	John Olerud	.478	23	11	3	0	2	7	5	1	.586	.870
Ruben Sierra	.125	32	4	0	0	0	1	0	4	.121	.125	Edgar Martinez	.400	20	8	2	1	3	9	1	3	.409	1.050

Bobby Bonilla — Marlins
Age 35 – Bats Both (flyball hitter)

	Avg	G	AB	R	H	2B	3B	HR	RBI	BB	SO	HBP	GDP	SB	CS	OBP	SLG	IBB	SH	SF	#Pit	#P/PA	GB	FB	G/F
1997 Season	.297	153	562	77	167	39	3	17	96	73	94	5	18	6	6	.378	.468	8	0	8	2438	3.76	191	182	1.05
Last Five Years	.294	700	2616	421	770	148	20	127	465	329	455	12	75	11	20	.371	.512	45	0	39	11371	3.79	854	837	1.02

1997 Season

	Avg	AB	H	2B	3B	HR	RBI	BB	SO	OBP	SLG		Avg	AB	H	2B	3B	HR	RBI	BB	SO	OBP	SLG
vs. Left	.372	113	42	8	0	6	21	9	10	.419	.602	First Pitch	.298	94	28	8	0	4	15	5	0	.330	.511
vs. Right	.278	449	125	31	3	11	75	64	84	.368	.434	Ahead in Count	.392	148	58	15	2	6	34	33	0	.497	.642
Groundball	.299	97	29	8	0	6	19	10	22	.364	.567	Behind in Count	.207	198	41	11	1	4	22	0	69	.214	.333
Flyball	.259	58	15	2	2	0	8	14	11	.421	.362	Two Strikes	.212	231	49	12	0	5	31	35	94	.320	.329
Home	.312	282	88	17	3	8	54	41	52	.401	.479	Batting #4	.270	318	86	16	2	8	48	44	54	.358	.409
Away	.282	280	79	22	0	9	42	32	42	.334	.457	Batting #6	.330	215	71	21	1	7	42	28	37	.410	.535
Day	.267	176	47	8	0	6	22	15	20	.320	.415	Other	.345	29	10	2	0	2	6	1	3	.367	.621
Night	.311	386	120	31	3	11	74	58	74	.403	.492	March/April	.284	88	25	5	1	0	8	8	10	.354	.364
Grass	.291	461	134	29	3	15	82	64	80	.378	.464	May	.382	102	39	16	0	3	23	7	14	.432	.627
Turf	.327	101	33	10	0	2	14	9	14	.378	.485	June	.264	91	24	3	1	4	16	15	17	.361	.451
Pre-All Star	.310	300	93	26	2	7	49	31	46	.378	.480	July	.300	90	27	6	1	4	17	12	19	.381	.522
Post-All Star	.282	262	74	13	1	10	47	42	48	.379	.454	August	.262	107	28	4	0	4	17	16	19	.349	.411
Scoring Posn	.284	169	48	8	2	8	79	30	29	.383	.497	Sept/Oct	.286	84	24	5	0	2	15	15	15	.394	.417
Close & Late	.286	91	26	6	1	3	17	16	19	.394	.473	vs. AL	.231	52	12	2	0	2	6	7	11	.317	.385
None on/out	.307	137	42	10	0	5	5	16	23	.379	.489	vs. NL	.304	510	155	37	3	15	90	66	83	.384	.476

1997 By Position

Position	Avg	AB	H	2B	3B	HR	RBI	BB	SO	OBP	SLG	G	GS	Innings	PO	A	E	DP	Fld Pct	Rng Fctr	In Zone	Zone Outs	Zone Rtg	MLB Zone
As 3b	.299	552	165	38	3	17	96	67	92	.375	.471	149	148	1268.2	104	225	22	29	.937	2.33	343	255	.743	.801

Last Five Years

	Avg	AB	H	2B	3B	HR	RBI	BB	SO	OBP	SLG		Avg	AB	H	2B	3B	HR	RBI	BB	SO	OBP	SLG
vs. Left	.315	746	235	39	6	43	137	71	89	.372	.556	First Pitch	.342	459	157	37	4	26	102	35	0	.387	.610
vs. Right	.286	1870	535	109	14	84	328	258	366	.370	.494	Ahead in Count	.376	643	242	46	6	43	146	127	0	.474	.667
Groundball	.278	686	191	39	5	31	120	84	140	.355	.485	Behind in Count	.215	959	206	41	8	28	107	0	344	.214	.362
Flyball	.265	385	102	16	2	22	57	61	73	.371	.488	Two Strikes	.205	1129	232	46	5	39	133	167	455	.308	.359
Home	.299	1274	381	64	11	57	236	146	205	.368	.501	Batting #4	.288	1925	554	107	15	96	337	236	344	.363	.509
Away	.290	1342	389	84	9	70	229	183	250	.374	.522	Batting #5	.316	367	116	15	4	20	73	51	49	.396	.542
Day	.285	857	244	44	5	42	131	90	136	.347	.495	Other	.309	324	100	26	1	11	55	42	62	.389	.497
Night	.299	1759	526	104	15	85	334	239	319	.382	.520	March/April	.240	346	83	20	1	9	52	47	55	.330	.382
Grass	.294	2114	621	111	16	98	382	271	355	.372	.520	May	.331	481	159	36	3	25	91	53	92	.397	.574
Turf	.297	502	149	37	4	29	83	58	100	.367	.560	June	.291	508	148	21	7	23	78	61	80	.365	.496
Pre-All Star	.290	1487	431	86	11	64	242	178	270	.364	.492	July	.295	492	145	39	2	25	85	61	103	.369	.535
Post-All Star	.300	1129	339	62	9	63	223	151	185	.380	.539	August	.286	475	136	17	4	29	94	64	75	.367	.522
Scoring Posn	.295	681	201	36	6	29	322	132	127	.382	.493	Sept/Oct	.315	314	99	15	3	16	65	43	50	.395	.535
Close & Late	.274	419	115	20	2	24	80	81	88	.386	.504	vs. AL	.296	884	262	41	9	40	168	105	127	.367	.499
None on/out	.289	710	205	31	6	39	39	65	119	.348	.514	vs. NL	.293	1732	508	107	11	87	297	224	328	.373	.518

Batter vs. Pitcher (career)

Hits Best Against	Avg	AB	H	2B	3B	HR	RBI	BB	SO	OBP	SLG	Hits Worst Against	Avg	AB	H	2B	3B	HR	RBI	BB	SO	OBP	SLG
Hideo Nomo	.545	11	6	1	1	1	5	3	1	.625	1.091	Todd Stottlemyre	.000	10	0	0	0	0	0	1	1	.091	.000
Jeff Shaw	.500	12	6	0	0	2	3	0	2	.500	1.000	Tom Gordon	.000	9	0	0	0	0	1	1	4	.091	.000
Pete Smith	.440	25	11	3	0	4	11	5	6	.516	1.040	Danny Darwin	.053	19	1	0	0	0	1	1	2	.100	.053
Jeff Fassero	.400	15	6	0	0	3	6	2	0	.471	1.000	Dennis Cook	.059	17	1	0	0	0	1	1	1	.111	.059
Dave Weathers	.400	10	4	1	1	1	5	3	1	.538	1.000	Bobby Witt	.063	16	1	0	0	1	2	0	3	.059	.250

Aaron Boone — Reds
Age 25 – Bats Right

	Avg	G	AB	R	H	2B	3B	HR	RBI	BB	SO	HBP	GDP	SB	CS	OBP	SLG	IBB	SH	SF	#Pit	#P/PA	GB	FB	G/F
1997 Season	.245	16	49	5	12	1	0	0	5	2	5	0	1	1	0	.275	.265	0	1	0	181	3.48	23	14	1.64

1997 Season

	Avg	AB	H	2B	3B	HR	RBI	BB	SO	OBP	SLG		Avg	AB	H	2B	3B	HR	RBI	BB	SO	OBP	SLG
vs. Left	.364	11	4	0	0	0	0	1	0	.417	.364	Scoring Posn	.154	13	2	1	0	0	5	2	0	.267	.231
vs. Right	.211	38	8	1	0	0	5	1	5	.231	.237	Close & Late	.143	7	1	0	0	0	1	1	0	.250	.143

Bret Boone — Reds
Age 29 – Bats Right (groundball hitter)

	Avg	G	AB	R	H	2B	3B	HR	RBI	BB	SO	HBP	GDP	SB	CS	OBP	SLG	IBB	SH	SF	#Pit	#P/PA	GB	FB	G/F
1997 Season	.223	139	443	40	99	25	1	7	46	45	101	4	12	5	5	.298	.332	4	4	5	2007	4.01	173	102	1.70
Last Five Years	.257	603	2128	249	547	117	10	58	289	158	411	25	51	18	15	.312	.403	6	25	29	8867	3.75	819	587	1.40

1997 Season

	Avg	AB	H	2B	3B	HR	RBI	BB	SO	OBP	SLG		Avg	AB	H	2B	3B	HR	RBI	BB	SO	OBP	SLG
vs. Left	.210	100	21	8	0	0	10	18	30	.328	.290	First Pitch	.436	39	17	3	0	2	9	2	0	.477	.667
vs. Right	.227	343	78	17	1	7	36	27	71	.288	.344	Ahead in Count	.255	98	25	7	0	2	11	28	0	.417	.388
Groundball	.150	80	12	2	0	0	7	7	21	.226	.175	Behind in Count	.163	215	35	9	1	3	17	0	81	.164	.256
Flyball	.151	53	8	4	0	1	6	5	13	.224	.283	Two Strikes	.158	234	37	10	1	3	18	15	101	.210	.248
Home	.247	223	55	12	0	4	26	23	41	.317	.354	Batting #7	.222	176	39	7	0	3	15	19	42	.299	.313
Away	.200	220	44	13	1	3	20	22	60	.278	.309	Batting #8	.234	197	46	9	1	4	20	21	45	.313	.350
Day	.204	152	31	9	1	2	15	18	35	.295	.316	Other	.200	70	14	9	0	0	11	5	14	.250	.329
Night	.234	291	68	16	0	5	31	27	66	.299	.340	March/April	.133	75	10	3	0	0	3	7	13	.224	.173
Grass	.221	145	32	8	1	3	17	18	36	.309	.352	May	.234	77	18	2	0	2	11	12	21	.337	.338
Turf	.225	298	67	17	0	4	29	27	65	.292	.322	June	.240	50	12	5	0	0	6	4	12	.296	.340
Pre-All Star	.190	226	43	12	0	2	24	23	53	.271	.270	July	.276	87	24	8	0	3	14	5	25	.315	.471
Post-All Star	.258	217	56	13	1	5	22	22	48	.326	.396	August	.212	85	18	3	1	1	5	10	19	.299	.306
Scoring Posn	.175	114	20	6	0	3	40	15	30	.261	.307	Sept/Oct	.246	69	17	4	0	1	7	7	11	.312	.348
Close & Late	.160	75	12	4	1	1	6	8	22	.238	.280	vs. AL	.098	41	4	2	0	0	6	2	8	.140	.146
None on/out	.176	108	19	5	0	1	1	6	29	.219	.250	vs. NL	.236	402	95	23	1	7	40	43	93	.313	.351

1997 By Position

Position	Avg	AB	H	2B	3B	HR	RBI	BB	SO	OBP	SLG	G	GS	Innings	PO	A	E	DP	Fld Pct	Rng Fctr	In Zone	Zone Outs	Zone Rtg	MLB Zone
As 2b	.224	438	98	25	1	7	46	45	100	.299	.333	136	127	1115.1	272	333	2	74	.997	4.88	374	341	.912	.902

Last Five Years

	Avg	AB	H	2B	3B	HR	RBI	BB	SO	OBP	SLG		Avg	AB	H	2B	3B	HR	RBI	BB	SO	OBP	SLG
vs. Left	.244	508	124	35	2	16	77	54	100	.313	.415	First Pitch	.339	221	75	15	0	10	38	3	0	.353	.543
vs. Right	.261	1620	423	82	8	42	212	104	311	.311	.399	Ahead in Count	.296	477	141	34	3	17	73	97	0	.411	.486
Groundball	.249	522	130	31	1	5	59	43	100	.312	.341	Behind in Count	.201	1024	206	39	6	16	109	0	351	.211	.298
Flyball	.253	320	81	20	3	17	58	21	73	.298	.494	Two Strikes	.192	1041	200	41	5	20	116	58	411	.238	.299
Home	.257	1039	267	60	6	29	149	89	191	.318	.410	Batting #6	.241	403	97	25	3	12	57	29	67	.291	.407
Away	.257	1089	280	57	4	29	140	69	220	.306	.397	Batting #7	.274	946	259	57	4	24	137	70	187	.330	.419
Day	.249	668	166	33	3	23	95	54	140	.308	.410	Other	.245	779	191	35	3	22	95	59	157	.301	.383
Night	.261	1460	381	84	7	35	194	104	271	.314	.400	March/April	.242	215	52	9	1	3	24	13	44	.289	.335
Grass	.258	728	188	36	3	26	98	50	146	.309	.423	May	.256	359	92	19	0	8	50	30	75	.315	.376
Turf	.256	1400	359	81	7	32	191	108	265	.313	.393	June	.271	361	98	22	1	10	52	31	67	.334	.421
Pre-All Star	.256	1046	268	57	3	22	143	84	207	.315	.380	July	.307	371	114	23	2	18	71	27	80	.357	.526
Post-All Star	.258	1082	279	60	7	36	146	74	204	.309	.426	August	.225	436	98	19	3	11	43	32	78	.283	.358
Scoring Posn	.253	546	138	35	2	12	221	53	138	.316	.390	Sept/Oct	.241	386	93	25	3	8	49	25	67	.290	.383
Close & Late	.251	338	85	16	2	6	38	27	78	.312	.364	vs. AL	.231	312	72	14	2	12	44	19	60	.280	.404
None on/out	.255	513	131	25	2	10	10	26	108	.294	.370	vs. NL	.262	1816	475	103	8	46	245	139	351	.317	.403

Batter vs. Pitcher (career)

Hits Best Against	Avg	AB	H	2B	3B	HR	RBI	BB	SO	OBP	SLG	Hits Worst Against	Avg	AB	H	2B	3B	HR	RBI	BB	SO	OBP	SLG
Greg Swindell	.615	13	8	3	0	2	7	1	0	.600	1.308	Joey Hamilton	.000	14	0	0	0	0	1	1	2	.167	.000
Andy Benes	.600	15	9	2	1	1	7	1	4	.625	1.067	Al Leiter	.063	16	1	0	0	0	2	3	.167	.063
Willie Banks	.462	13	6	2	0	1	3	1	3	.467	.846	John Burkett	.083	12	1	0	0	0	1	0	2	.214	.083
Mark Leiter	.385	13	5	0	0	2	3	3	4	.500	.846	Michael Mimbs	.091	11	1	0	0	0	0	0	1	.091	.091
Pete Harnisch	.364	11	4	2	0	1	3	1	2	.417	.818	Pedro Astacio	.100	20	2	0	0	0	0	0	2	.182	.100

Josh Booty — Marlins
Age 23 – Bats Right

	Avg	G	AB	R	H	2B	3B	HR	RBI	BB	SO	HBP	GDP	SB	CS	OBP	SLG	IBB	SH	SF	#Pit	#P/PA	GB	FB	G/F
1997 Season	.600	4	5	2	3	0	0	0	1	1	1	0	0	0	0	.667	.600	0	0	0	20	3.33	1	0	0.00
Career (1996-1997)	.571	6	7	3	4	0	0	0	1	1	1	0	1	0	0	.625	.571	0	0	0	26	3.25	2	0	0.00

1997 Season

	Avg	AB	H	2B	3B	HR	RBI	BB	SO	OBP	SLG		Avg	AB	H	2B	3B	HR	RBI	BB	SO	OBP	SLG
vs. Left	1.000	1	1	0	0	0	1	0	0	1.000	1.000	Scoring Posn	1.000	1	1	0	0	0	1	1	0	1.000	1.000
vs. Right	.500	4	2	0	0	0	0	1	1	.600	.500	Close & Late	1.000	1	1	0	0	0	0	0	0	1.000	1.000

Pat Borders — Indians
Age 35 – Bats Right

	Avg	G	AB	R	H	2B	3B	HR	RBI	BB	SO	HBP	GDP	SB	CS	OBP	SLG	IBB	SH	SF	#Pit	#P/PA	GB	FB	G/F
1997 Season	.296	55	159	17	47	7	1	4	15	9	27	2	5	0	2	.341	.428	0	0	0	652	3.84	61	32	1.91
Last Five Years	.255	417	1340	109	342	65	3	25	127	62	215	4	37	3	7	.290	.364	4	13	3	5022	3.53	528	338	1.56

1997 Season

	Avg	AB	H	2B	3B	HR	RBI	BB	SO	OBP	SLG		Avg	AB	H	2B	3B	HR	RBI	BB	SO	OBP	SLG
vs. Left	.259	27	7	2	0	0	0	1	6	.286	.333	Scoring Posn	.225	40	9	1	0	0	10	1	5	.279	.250
vs. Right	.303	132	40	5	1	4	15	8	21	.352	.447	Close & Late	.261	23	6	1	0	2	3	1	3	.292	.565
Home	.299	77	23	5	0	0	4	4	15	.341	.364	None on/out	.214	42	9	2	0	1	4	10	.283	.333
Away	.293	82	24	2	1	4	11	5	12	.341	.488	Batting #8	.274	113	31	5	1	2	10	6	22	.322	.389
First Pitch	.360	25	9	1	1	1	4	0	0	.385	.600	Batting #9	.355	31	11	2	0	2	3	1	2	.375	.613
Ahead in Count	.316	38	12	1	0	1	5	3	0	.381	.421	Other	.333	15	5	0	0	0	2	2	3	.412	.333
Behind in Count	.258	62	16	2	0	1	4	0	23	.258	.339	Pre-All Star	.322	59	19	1	0	3	8	5	7	.375	.492
Two Strikes	.250	72	18	2	0	1	4	6	27	.308	.319	Post-All Star	.280	100	28	6	1	1	7	4	20	.321	.390

Last Five Years

	Avg	AB	H	2B	3B	HR	RBI	BB	SO	OBP	SLG		Avg	AB	H	2B	3B	HR	RBI	BB	SO	OBP	SLG
vs. Left	.260	381	99	20	0	8	34	19	59	.294	.375	First Pitch	.301	249	75	12	1	10	32	2	0	.308	.478
vs. Right	.253	959	243	45	3	17	93	43	156	.288	.360	Ahead in Count	.320	278	89	12	2	8	39	37	0	.401	.464
Groundball	.225	253	57	11	1	1	24	14	43	.268	.289	Behind in Count	.203	580	118	24	0	5	39	0	185	.204	.271
Flyball	.258	236	61	13	0	3	18	8	42	.286	.352	Two Strikes	.194	582	113	26	0	4	35	23	215	.226	.259
Home	.260	658	171	26	1	13	70	29	97	.294	.362	Batting #8	.249	846	211	36	2	16	81	39	132	.285	.353
Away	.251	682	171	39	2	12	57	33	118	.286	.367	Batting #9	.289	256	74	20	0	5	28	10	35	.315	.426
Day	.243	457	111	19	1	10	38	16	84	.273	.354	Other	.239	238	57	9	1	4	18	13	48	.279	.336
Night	.262	883	231	46	2	15	89	46	131	.298	.369	March/April	.274	237	65	15	0	2	19	8	38	.297	.363
Grass	.256	758	194	30	2	14	62	38	131	.293	.356	May	.268	224	60	8	0	10	33	6	31	.287	.438
Turf	.254	582	148	35	1	11	65	24	84	.285	.375	June	.228	237	54	12	0	4	18	15	30	.278	.329
Pre-All Star	.254	780	198	41	0	16	76	32	115	.284	.368	July	.257	237	61	12	3	3	25	8	40	.285	.371
Post-All Star	.257	560	144	24	3	9	51	30	100	.290	.359	August	.235	230	54	8	0	2	10	12	47	.275	.296
Scoring Posn	.220	355	78	15	1	2	94	23	67	.271	.285	Sept/Oct	.274	175	48	10	4	4	22	13	29	.324	.400
Close & Late	.271	225	61	16	0	3	23	14	38	.313	.382	vs. AL	.256	1224	313	61	3	25	123	57	194	.290	.372
None on/out	.243	342	83	18	0	7	7	13	51	.270	.357	vs. NL	.250	116	29	4	0		4	5	21	.287	.284

Batter vs. Pitcher (career)

Hits Best Against	Avg	AB	H	2B	3B	HR	RBI	BB	SO	OBP	SLG	Hits Worst Against	Avg	AB	H	2B	3B	HR	RBI	BB	SO	OBP	SLG
Jack McDowell	.467	15	7	2	0	0	2	0	1	.467	.600	Bob Wickman	.000	12	0	0	0	0	1	0	1	.000	.000
Jose Mesa	.462	13	6	2	0	0	2	0	1	.462	.615	Alex Fernandez	.050	20	1	0	0	0	0	0	7	.050	.050
Paul Quantrill	.444	9	4	1	0	1	2	1	1	.545	.556	Dan Plesac	.077	13	1	0	0	0	0	2	1	.200	.077
Kevin Tapani	.333	27	9	1	0	2	3	0	1	.357	.593	Kevin Appier	.100	10	1	0	0	0	0	1	4	.182	.100
Jamie Moyer	.333	21	7	0	1	1	2	1	1	.364	.571	Jaime Navarro	.150	20	3	0	0	0	1	0	1	.150	.150

Mike Bordick — Orioles
Age 32 – Bats Right (groundball hitter)

	Avg	G	AB	R	H	2B	3B	HR	RBI	BB	SO	HBP	GDP	SB	CS	OBP	SLG	IBB	SH	SF	#Pit	#P/PA	GB	FB	G/F
1997 Season	.236	153	509	55	120	19	1	7	46	33	66	2	23	0	2	.283	.318	1	12	4	1957	3.49	213	150	1.42
Last Five Years	.248	707	2399	245	594	89	11	25	229	218	275	22	57	33	23	.313	.325	6	36	23	9959	3.69	986	689	1.43

1997 Season

	Avg	AB	H	2B	3B	HR	RBI	BB	SO	OBP	SLG		Avg	AB	H	2B	3B	HR	RBI	BB	SO	OBP	SLG
vs. Left	.195	154	30	3	0	1	9	8	11	.233	.234	First Pitch	.273	77	21	5	0	0	8	1	0	.272	.338
vs. Right	.254	355	90	16	1	6	37	25	55	.304	.355	Ahead in Count	.358	120	43	7	0	3	13	19	0	.450	.492
Groundball	.326	129	42	6	1	3	13	8	11	.367	.457	Behind in Count	.174	218	38	5	1	2	11	0	57	.177	.234
Flyball	.182	55	10	5	0	1	7	4	7	.237	.327	Two Strikes	.141	206	29	5	1	1	5	13	66	.195	.189
Home	.229	231	53	7	1	5	24	13	35	.274	.333	Batting #8	.348	23	8	0	0	0	2	1	3	.375	.348
Away	.241	278	67	12	0	2	22	20	31	.290	.306	Batting #9	.236	475	112	19	1	7	44	32	62	.285	.324
Day	.228	162	37	6	0	3	15	15	21	.292	.321	Other	.000	11	0	0	0	0	0	0	1	.000	.000
Night	.239	347	83	13	1	4	31	18	45	.278	.317	March/April	.179	78	14	3	0	0	2	8	7	.256	.218
Grass	.227	454	103	16	1	7	42	29	62	.275	.313	May	.247	93	23	3	0	2	13	5	12	.283	.344
Turf	.309	55	17	3	0	0	4	4	4	.350	.364	June	.222	99	22	4	0	1	8	6	12	.267	.293
Pre-All Star	.220	287	63	11	0	3	25	20	32	.269	.289	July	.280	75	21	3	0	0	4	3	7	.300	.320
Post-All Star	.257	222	57	8	1	4	21	13	34	.301	.356	August	.137	73	10	2	1	2	10	6	13	.210	.274
Scoring Posn	.245	110	27	6	0	0	34	15	9	.331	.300	Sept/Oct	.330	91	30	4	0	2	9	5	15	.371	.440
Close & Late	.229	70	16	3	0	2	4	7	20	.270	.271	vs. AL	.228	460	105	17	1	7	41	31	62	.278	.315
None on/out	.270	126	34	6	0	3	3	6	18	.303	.389	vs. NL	.306	49	15	2	0	0	5	2	4	.327	.347

1997 By Position

Position	Avg	AB	H	2B	3B	HR	RBI	BB	SO	OBP	SLG	G	GS	Innings	PO	A	E	DP	Fld Pct	Rng Fctr	In Zone	Outs	Zone Rtg	MLB Zone
As ss	.236	509	120	19	1	7	46	33	66	.283	.318	153	151	1335.1	224	426	13	95	.980	4.38	462	443	.959	.937

Last Five Years

	Avg	AB	H	2B	3B	HR	RBI	BB	SO	OBP	SLG		Avg	AB	H	2B	3B	HR	RBI	BB	SO	OBP	SLG
vs. Left	.235	697	164	24	3	6	57	66	65	.302	.304	First Pitch	.249	313	78	14	1	2	32	3	0	.265	.319
vs. Right	.253	1702	430	65	8	19	172	152	210	.318	.334	Ahead in Count	.309	576	178	33	2	10	73	129	0	.437	.425
Groundball	.258	573	148	23	4	5	56	55	71	.335	.339	Behind in Count	.203	999	203	24	5	6	59	0	232	.209	.255
Flyball	.204	406	83	19	3	4	37	41	51	.280	.296	Two Strikes	.195	981	191	21	5	6	66	86	275	.263	.245
Home	.249	1166	290	44	6	12	104	103	122	.315	.328	Batting #8	.258	682	176	29	4	6	63	57	86	.319	.336
Away	.247	1233	304	45	5	13	125	115	153	.312	.323	Batting #9	.256	1252	321	43	7	16	130	119	140	.324	.340
Day	.240	943	226	31	3	8	96	81	105	.300	.304	Other	.209	465	97	11	1	3	36	42	49	.277	.269
Night	.253	1456	368	58	8	17	133	137	170	.322	.339	March/April	.243	309	75	13	1	2	31	39	38	.334	.311
Grass	.247	2089	515	75	10	25	192	181	233	.310	.328	May	.239	406	97	15	2	3	33	40	49	.308	.308
Turf	.255	310	79	14	1	0	37	37	42	.332	.306	June	.252	461	116	22	2	5	48	41	53	.315	.341
Pre-All Star	.245	1321	324	51	6	11	128	130	152	.315	.318	July	.255	447	114	11	3	2	34	31	43	.300	.306
Post-All Star	.250	1078	270	38	5	14	101	88	123	.311	.334	August	.229	414	95	13	3	9	42	36	43	.301	.341
Scoring Posn	.249	559	139	26	2	3	191	74	69	.331	.318	Sept/Oct	.268	362	97	15	0	4	41	31	49	.329	.343
Close & Late	.240	358	86	8	1	2	32	47	46	.334	.285	vs. AL	.246	2350	579	87	11	25	224	216	271	.313	.325
None on/out	.226	554	125	22	0	9	9	49	52	.297	.314	vs. NL	.306	49	15	2	0	0	5	2	4	.327	.347

Batter vs. Pitcher (career)

Hits Best Against	Avg	AB	H	2B	3B	HR	RBI	BB	SO	OBP	SLG	Hits Worst Against	Avg	AB	H	2B	3B	HR	RBI	BB	SO	OBP	SLG
Paul Quantrill	.500	12	6	1	0	0	0	0	1	.500	.583	Jaime Navarro	.059	17	1	0	1	0	0	1	1	.111	.176
Bobby Witt	.462	13	6	0	0	0	1	3	1	.563	.462	Mark Leiter	.071	14	1	0	1	0	0	0	3	.071	.071
Rich Robertson	.455	11	5	1	1	0	2	0	0	.455	.727	Pat Mahomes	.083	12	1	0	0	0	0	1	1	.154	.083
Orel Hershiser	.385	13	5	0	0	1	1	1	1	.429	.615	Kevin Gross	.091	11	1	0	0	0	0	1	1	.167	.091
Chris Haney	.375	16	6	0	0	1	3	1	0	.412	.563	Jamie Moyer	.125	24	3	1	0	0	0	0	1	.125	.167

Toby Borland — Red Sox
Age 29 – Pitches Right (groundball pitcher)

	ERA	W	L	Sv	G	GS	IP	BB	SO	Avg	H	2B	3B	HR	RBI	OBP	SLG	GF	IR	IRS	Hld	SvOp	SB	CS	GB	FB	G/F
1997 Season	7.56	0	1	1	16	0	16.2	21	8	.262	17	1	0	2	15	.461	.369	5	10	8	1	2	2	0	22	20	1.10
Career (1994-1997)	3.96	9	7	8	159	0	215.2	115	169	.255	212	31	4	15	113	.355	.357	41	87	41	22	14	16	3	348	155	2.25

1997 Season

	ERA	W	L	Sv	G	GS	IP	H	HR	BB	SO		Avg	AB	H	2B	3B	HR	RBI	BB	SO	OBP	SLG
Home	0.00	0	0	1	5	0	7.0	4	0	3	6	vs. Left	.300	30	9	0	0	1	4	8	3	.447	.400
Away	13.03	0	1	0	11	0	9.2	13	0	18	2	vs. Right	.229	35	8	1	0	1	11	13	5	.471	.343

Career (1994-1997)

	ERA	W	L	Sv	G	GS	IP	H	HR	BB	SO		Avg	AB	H	2B	3B	HR	RBI	BB	SO	OBP	SLG
Home	3.40	8	3	5	82	0	113.2	109	6	52	89	vs. Left	.288	344	99	9	1	5	44	39	55	.363	.363
Away	4.59	1	4	3	77	0	102.0	103	9	63	80	vs. Right	.233	486	113	22	3	10	69	76	114	.350	.352
Day	5.66	3	2	2	42	0	49.1	54	1	29	41	Inning 1-6	.224	246	55	10	1	5	45	42	56	.348	.333
Night	3.46	6	5	6	117	0	166.1	158	14	86	128	Inning 7+	.269	584	157	21	3	10	68	73	113	.358	.366
Grass	4.70	1	3	2	58	0	76.2	81	6	47	62	None on	.246	414	102	12	3	9	9	51	98	.338	.355
Turf	3.56	8	4	6	101	0	139.0	131	9	68	107	Runners on	.264	416	110	19	1	6	104	64	71	.372	.358
March/April	6.51	1	1	1	23	0	27.2	26	7	20	21	Scoring Posn	.256	262	67	12	0	3	92	47	50	.377	.336
May	5.06	1	1	1	30	0	42.2	50	3	31	28	Close & Late	.259	232	60	5	2	3	25	28	43	.346	.336
June	3.50	3	1	0	16	0	18.0	15	0	10	15	None on/out	.228	184	42	3	0	6	6	22	44	.330	.342
July	2.47	2	1	3	39	0	54.2	48	2	14	46	vs. 1st Batr (relief)	.205	132	27	3	0	2	20	23	32	.327	.273
August	4.01	1	0	2	29	0	42.2	46	1	26	32	1st Inning Pitched	.249	518	129	19	4	7	83	70	107	.346	.342
Sept/Oct	3.00	1	3	1	22	0	30.0	27	2	14	27	First 15 Pitches	.258	454	117	15	4	10	68	58	83	.351	.374
Starter	0.00	0	0	0	0	0	0.0	0	0	0	0	Pitch 16-30	.244	266	65	10	0	3	30	39	59	.348	.316
Reliever	3.96	9	7	8	159	0	215.2	212	15	115	169	Pitch 31-45	.309	94	29	6	0	1	13	14	20	.414	.404
0 Days rest (Relief)	3.80	3	1	3	41	0	47.1	47	4	19	46	Pitch 46+	.063	16	1	0	0	1	2	4	7	.250	.250
1 or 2 Days rest	3.79	3	6	4	71	0	102.0	107	6	54	77	First Pitch	.306	134	41	5	0	3	21	12	0	.396	.410
3+ Days rest	4.34	3	0	1	47	0	66.1	58	5	42	46	Ahead in Count	.188	361	68	8	1	4	32	0	148	.199	.249
vs. AL	13.50	0	0	0	3	0	3.1	6	1	7	1	Behind in Count	.331	181	60	13	2	5	35	65	0	.508	.508
vs. NL	3.81	9	7	8	156	0	212.1	206	14	108	168	Two Strikes	.191	371	71	9	1	4	36	38	169	.271	.253
Pre-All Star	4.88	6	3	2	78	0	99.2	99	10	65	76	Pre-All Star	.254	389	99	15	2	10	68	65	76	.373	.380
Post-All Star	3.18	3	4	6	81	0	116.0	113	5	50	93	Post-All Star	.256	441	113	16	2	5	45	50	93	.339	.336

Joe Borowski — Yankees
Age 27 – Pitches Right

	ERA	W	L	Sv	G	GS	IP	BB	SO	Avg	H	2B	3B	HR	RBI	OBP	SLG	GF	IR	IRS	Hld	SvOp	SB	CS	GB	FB	G/F
1997 Season	4.15	2	3	0	21	0	26.0	20	8	.284	29	8	0	2	13	.402	.422	9	3	1	2	0	2	0	46	29	1.59
Career (1995-1997)	4.10	4	7	0	49	0	59.1	37	26	.291	67	15	0	6	32	.392	.435	20	23	7	3	0	4	2	98	66	1.48

1997 Season

	ERA	W	L	Sv	G	GS	IP	H	HR	BB	SO		Avg	AB	H	2B	3B	HR	RBI	BB	SO	OBP	SLG
Home	6.17	1	3	0	9	0	11.2	11	1	13	6	vs. Left	.267	45	12	3	0	0	5	14	5	.441	.333
Away	2.51	1	0	0	12	0	14.1	18	1	7	2	vs. Right	.298	57	17	5	0	2	8	6	3	.365	.491

Shawn Boskie — Orioles
Age 31 – Pitches Right (flyball pitcher)

	ERA	W	L	Sv	G	GS	IP	BB	SO	Avg	H	2B	3B	HR	RBI	OBP	SLG	GF	IR	IRS	Hld	SvOp	SB	CS	GB	FB	G/F
1997 Season	6.43	6	6	1	28	9	77.0	26	50	.304	95	24	3	14	53	.354	.535	8	12	3	1	1	9	2	107	99	1.08
Last Five Years	5.27	34	34	1	146	74	534.1	169	334	.283	603	129	9	92	312	.342	.481	20	57	19	8	5	38	9	674	707	0.95

1997 Season

	ERA	W	L	Sv	G	GS	IP	H	HR	BB	SO		Avg	AB	H	2B	3B	HR	RBI	BB	SO	OBP	SLG
Home	6.05	2	2	0	12	4	38.2	50	6	11	24	vs. Left	.322	143	46	7	3	8	28	18	18	.396	.580
Away	6.81	4	4	1	16	5	38.1	45	8	15	26	vs. Right	.290	169	49	17	0	6	25	8	32	.317	.497
Starter	7.01	2	3	0	9	9	43.2	55	9	15	29	Scoring Posn	.300	80	24	6	1	4	42	12	16	.364	.550
Reliever	5.67	4	3	1	19	0	33.1	40	5	11	21	Close & Late	.429	7	3	0	1	1	2	0	0	.375	1.143
0 Days rest (Relief)	0.00	0	0	0	0	0	0.0	0	0	0	0	None on	.350	80	28	9	1	4	4	5	14	.388	.638
1 or 2 Days rest	4.91	3	2	1	10	0	14.2	16	4	4	7	First Pitch	.467	45	21	1	1	4	13	0	0	.447	.800
3+ Days rest	6.27	1	1	0	9	0	18.2	24	1	7	14	Ahead in Count	.199	136	27	10	0	3	13	0	40	.204	.338
Pre-All Star	5.63	4	3	1	18	7	54.1	67	10	18	32	Behind in Count	.375	64	24	6	0	4	12	12	0	.468	.656
Post-All Star	8.34	2	3	0	10	2	22.2	28	4	8	18	Two Strikes	.217	138	30	11	3	4	14	14	50	.291	.362

Last Five Years

	ERA	W	L	Sv	G	GS	IP	H	HR	BB	SO		Avg	AB	H	2B	3B	HR	RBI	BB	SO	OBP	SLG
Home	5.14	17	16	0	72	37	273.0	305	48	89	180	vs. Left	.267	1063	284	52	6	43	141	113	175	.341	.449
Away	5.41	17	18	1	74	37	261.1	298	44	80	154	vs. Right	.298	1069	319	77	3	49	171	56	159	.342	.514
Day	4.05	16	10	0	56	22	184.2	203	28	50	108	Inning 1-6	.287	1739	499	110	7	74	271	135	278	.343	.486
Night	5.92	18	24	1	90	52	349.2	400	64	119	226	Inning 7+	.265	393	104	19	2	18	41	34	56	.334	.461
Grass	5.26	26	26	1	115	55	414.1	467	77	129	262	None on	.289	1203	348	72	5	54	54	92	174	.348	.492
Turf	5.32	8	8	0	31	19	120.0	136	15	40	72	Runners on	.274	929	255	57	4	38	258	77	160	.334	.467
March/April	6.75	2	2	0	18	7	57.1	85	12	20	41	Scoring Posn	.285	502	143	32	3	24	217	57	93	.355	.504
May	3.28	11	3	1	28	13	118.0	101	12	26	68	Close & Late	.288	156	45	9	2	8	19	15	23	.364	.526
June	4.89	10	7	0	25	24	143.2	149	21	45	79	None on/out	.296	540	160	34	4	24	24	37	80	.350	.507
July	5.75	5	6	0	27	12	81.1	90	17	25	56	vs. 1st Batr (relief)	.324	68	22	6	1	1	16	2	9	.347	.485
August	4.26	4	5	0	21	6	61.1	76	10	18	44	1st Inning Pitched	.285	530	151	29	3	23	97	51	87	.353	.481
Sept/Oct	8.42	2	11	0	27	12	72.2	102	20	35	46	First 15 Pitches	.274	423	116	23	1	15	53	25	56	.328	.444
Starter	5.75	23	28	0	74	74	412.0	476	78	132	260	Pitch 16-30	.277	383	106	21	1	14	53	43	73	.353	.446
Reliever	3.68	11	6	1	72	0	122.1	127	14	37	74	Pitch 31-45	.320	322	103	23	3	13	60	24	60	.368	.531
0 Days rest (Relief)	4.67	2	0	0	10	0	17.1	18	3	8	15	Pitch 46+	.277	1004	278	62	3	50	146	77	145	.334	.494
1 or 2 Days rest	2.90	8	4	1	36	0	62.0	56	8	14	31	First Pitch	.337	309	104	20	4	14	60	11	0	.364	.563

Last Five Years

	ERA	W	L	Sv	G	GS	IP	H	HR	BB	SO		Avg	AB	H	2B	3B	HR	RBI	BB	SO	OBP	SLG
3+ Days rest	4.40	1	2	0	26	0	43.0	53	3	15	28	Ahead in Count	.224	994	223	50	1	20	87	0	282	.237	.337
vs. AL	5.52	25	22	1	84	57	375.0	442	69	115	231	Behind in Count	.354	401	142	35	0	33	87	79	0	.458	.688
vs. NL	4.69	9	12	0	62	17	159.1	161	23	54	103	Two Strikes	.222	974	216	47	2	26	99	79	334	.290	.354
Pre-All Star	4.65	24	14	1	81	49	354.1	372	54	102	211	Pre-All Star	.268	1389	372	85	5	54	191	102	211	.322	.453
Post-All Star	6.50	10	20	0	65	25	180.0	231	38	67	123	Post-All Star	.311	743	231	44	4	38	121	67	123	.377	.534

Pitcher vs. Batter (career)

Pitches Best Vs.	Avg	AB	H	2B	3B	HR	RBI	BB	SO	OBP	SLG	Pitches Worst Vs.	Avg	AB	H	2B	3B	HR	RBI	BB	SO	OBP	SLG
Alex Gonzalez	.077	13	1	0	0	0	1	0	7	.077	.077	Mo Vaughn	.556	18	10	4	0	3	10	3	2	.591	1.278
Chris Hoiles	.091	11	1	0	0	0	0	0	4	.091	.091	Alex Rodriguez	.533	15	8	3	0	2	6	0	3	.533	1.133
Ivan Rodriguez	.091	11	1	1	0	0	0	0	2	.091	.182	Orlando Merced	.500	16	8	1	1	2	4	1	3	.529	1.063
Andres Galarraga	.133	15	2	0	0	0	0	0	2	.188	.133	Bernard Gilkey	.500	12	6	1	0	2	3	2	1	.600	1.083
Sandy Alomar Jr	.154	13	2	0	0	0	1	0	0	.143	.154	Barry Bonds	.400	15	6	1	2	2	7	5	2	.550	1.133

Ricky Bottalico — Phillies

Age 28 – Pitches Right

	ERA	W	L	Sv	G	GS	IP	BB	SO	Avg	H	2B	3B	HR	RBI	OBP	SLG	GF	IR	IRS	Hld	SvOp	SB	CS	GB	FB	G/F
1997 Season	3.65	2	5	34	69	0	74.0	42	89	.245	68	15	0	7	38	.347	.375	61	19	8	0	41	7	3	86	59	1.46
Career (1994-1997)	3.02	11	13	69	195	0	232.1	108	253	.203	168	31	4	20	102	.300	.323	140	72	24	20	84	15	7	244	209	1.17

1997 Season

	ERA	W	L	Sv	G	GS	IP	H	HR	BB	SO		Avg	AB	H	2B	3B	HR	RBI	BB	SO	OBP	SLG
Home	3.21	2	3	17	38	0	42.0	33	2	23	46	vs. Left	.257	136	35	8	0	2	17	21	35	.358	.360
Away	4.22	0	2	17	31	0	32.0	35	5	19	43	vs. Right	.234	141	33	7	0	5	21	21	54	.335	.390
Day	5.09	0	1	11	21	0	23.0	22	3	10	31	Inning 1-6	.000	0	0	0	0	0	0	0	0	.000	.000
Night	3.00	2	4	23	48	0	51.0	46	4	32	58	Inning 7+	.245	277	68	15	0	7	38	42	89	.347	.375
Grass	4.88	0	1	12	21	0	24.0	29	5	11	33	None on	.215	144	31	8	0	4	4	23	49	.327	.354
Turf	3.06	2	4	22	48	0	50.0	38	2	31	56	Runners on	.278	133	37	7	0	3	34	19	40	.368	.398
March/April	2.70	0	1	5	9	0	10.0	4	1	5	12	Scoring Posn	.293	75	22	4	0	1	28	14	20	.402	.387
May	2.31	1	0	7	11	0	11.2	13	0	7	13	Close & Late	.247	186	46	9	0	3	30	31	62	.359	.344
June	5.68	0	2	2	12	0	12.2	16	1	12	9	None on/out	.210	62	13	4	0	1	1	7	20	.300	.323
July	4.15	1	0	5	11	0	13.0	14	3	4	17	vs. 1st Batr (relief)	.230	61	14	4	0	1	5	7	17	.309	.344
August	5.28	0	2	7	14	0	15.1	15	2	9	25	1st Inning Pitched	.244	242	59	14	0	3	32	36	77	.339	.339
Sept/Oct	0.79	0	0	8	12	0	11.1	6	0	5	13	First 15 Pitches	.230	183	42	10	0	2	16	26	59	.325	.317
Starter	0.00	0	0	0	0	0	0.0	0	0	0	0	Pitch 16-30	.267	75	20	5	0	3	16	15	22	.391	.453
Reliever	3.65	2	5	34	69	0	74.0	68	7	42	89	Pitch 31-45	.250	16	4	0	0	2	5	1	7	.278	.625
0 Days rest (Relief)	4.67	1	1	10	17	0	17.1	21	1	11	27	Pitch 46+	.667	3	2	0	0	0	0	0	1	.750	.667
1 or 2 Days rest	2.00	1	2	17	32	0	36.0	26	2	18	40	First Pitch	.286	35	10	2	0	0	5	4	0	.375	.343
3+ Days rest	5.66	0	2	7	20	0	20.2	21	4	13	22	Ahead in Count	.158	139	22	3	0	4	14	0	73	.162	.266
vs. AL	8.53	0	1	2	5	0	6.1	10	2	5	7	Behind in Count	.375	48	18	4	0	1	10	21	0	.565	.521
vs. NL	3.19	2	4	32	64	0	67.2	58	5	37	82	Two Strikes	.158	158	25	7	0	4	14	17	89	.243	.278
Pre-All Star	3.82	1	3	15	35	0	37.2	38	3	24	39	Pre-All Star	.268	142	38	9	0	3	21	24	39	.379	.394
Post-All Star	3.47	1	2	19	34	0	36.1	30	4	18	50	Post-All Star	.222	135	30	6	0	4	17	18	50	.312	.356

Career (1994-1997)

	ERA	W	L	Sv	G	GS	IP	H	HR	BB	SO		Avg	AB	H	2B	3B	HR	RBI	BB	SO	OBP	SLG
Home	2.91	8	8	32	103	0	126.2	84	10	56	146	vs. Left	.227	348	79	13	2	8	44	58	90	.340	.345
Away	3.15	3	5	37	92	0	105.2	84	10	52	107	vs. Right	.186	479	89	18	2	12	58	50	163	.269	.307
Day	3.46	3	4	24	65	0	75.1	53	7	29	82	Inning 1-6	.125	24	3	0	0	1	5	8	5	.364	.250
Night	2.81	8	9	45	130	0	157.0	115	13	79	171	Inning 7+	.205	803	165	31	4	19	97	100	248	.297	.325
Grass	2.75	1	3	27	63	0	72.0	57	7	35	76	None on	.180	472	85	15	3	8	8	55	153	.274	.275
Turf	3.14	10	10	42	132	0	160.1	111	13	73	177	Runners on	.234	355	83	16	1	12	94	53	100	.333	.386
March/April	2.55	1	2	13	21	0	24.2	18	1	12	26	Scoring Posn	.261	207	54	10	1	7	82	42	60	.380	.420
May	2.14	4	2	13	34	0	42.0	27	2	26	44	Close & Late	.201	557	112	17	3	13	74	75	173	.300	.312
June	4.54	1	4	5	33	0	35.2	29	4	22	36	None on/out	.155	194	30	7	1	2	2	20	61	.251	.232
July	3.47	1	2	11	35	0	46.2	37	6	13	56	vs. 1st Batr (relief)	.174	172	30	7	0	4	19	18	53	.268	.285
August	3.60	2	3	13	38	0	45.0	37	4	21	56	1st Inning Pitched	.210	656	138	28	2	13	83	91	203	.310	.319
Sept/Oct	1.64	2	0	14	34	0	38.1	20	3	14	43	First 15 Pitches	.197	532	105	22	1	9	50	66	160	.292	.293
Starter	0.00	0	0	0	0	0	0.0	0	0	0	0	Pitch 16-30	.207	237	49	8	3	7	36	37	72	.315	.354
Reliever	3.02	11	13	69	195	0	232.1	168	20	108	253	Pitch 31-45	.218	55	12	1	0	4	15	5	20	.274	.455
0 Days rest (Relief)	2.97	2	2	23	50	0	57.2	41	3	30	68	Pitch 46+	.667	3	2	0	0	0	1	0	1	.750	.667
1 or 2 Days rest	1.87	4	7	32	87	0	110.2	65	7	48	109	First Pitch	.210	105	22	4	0	1	13	8	0	.274	.276
3+ Days rest	5.06	5	4	14	58	0	64.0	62	10	30	76	Ahead in Count	.153	426	65	9	1	8	38	0	213	.155	.235
vs. AL	8.53	0	1	2	5	0	6.1	10	2	5	7	Behind in Count	.301	146	44	7	3	5	26	54	0	.498	.493
vs. NL	2.87	11	12	67	190	0	226.0	158	18	103	246	Two Strikes	.128	445	57	10	1	8	34	46	253	.211	.209
Pre-All Star	3.16	6	8	36	101	0	116.2	89	11	62	120	Pre-All Star	.214	416	89	16	2	11	57	62	120	.324	.341
Post-All Star	2.88	5	5	33	94	0	115.2	79	9	46	133	Post-All Star	.192	411	79	15	2	9	45	46	133	.274	.304

Pitcher vs. Batter (career)

Pitches Best Vs.	Avg	AB	H	2B	3B	HR	RBI	BB	SO	OBP	SLG	Pitches Worst Vs.	Avg	AB	H	2B	3B	HR	RBI	BB	SO	OBP	SLG
Jeff Conine	.200	10	2	0	0	1	3	1	0	.273	.500												

Kent Bottenfield — Cubs
Age 29 – Pitches Right

	ERA	W	L	Sv	G	GS	IP	BB	SO	Avg	H	2B	3B	HR	RBI	OBP	SLG	GF	IR	IRS	Hld	SvOp	SB	CS	GB	FB	G/F
1997 Season	3.86	2	3	2	64	0	84.0	35	74	.259	82	14	1	13	52	.333	.434	20	53	19	8	4	10	6	80	111	0.72
Last Five Years	4.40	13	19	4	165	26	331.2	135	185	.279	353	67	10	42	184	.353	.448	35	86	32	12	8	36	13	444	392	1.13

1997 Season

	ERA	W	L	Sv	G	GS	IP	H	HR	BB	SO
Home	4.93	1	1	1	32	0	38.1	40	11	18	39
Away	2.96	1	2	1	32	0	45.2	42	2	17	35
Day	4.02	1	3	2	38	0	47.0	52	8	18	41
Night	3.65	1	0	0	26	0	37.0	30	5	17	33
Grass	4.43	2	2	1	52	0	65.0	65	13	30	65
Turf	1.89	0	1	1	12	0	19.0	17	0	5	9
March/April	3.94	0	0	0	11	0	16.0	18	1	10	13
May	2.76	1	1	0	10	0	16.1	15	2	6	13
June	1.50	1	0	0	14	0	18.0	12	0	6	18
July	3.78	1	1	1	12	0	16.2	16	2	5	12
August	6.48	0	1	0	9	0	8.1	13	5	5	5
Sept/Oct	8.31	0	0	0	8	0	8.2	8	3	3	13
Starter	0.00	0	0	0	0	0	0.0	0	0	0	0
Reliever	3.86	2	3	2	64	0	84.0	82	13	35	74
0 Days rest (Relief)	1.50	0	1	0	12	0	12.0	9	1	4	8
1 or 2 Days rest	3.75	2	1	2	36	0	48.0	44	8	20	45
3+ Days rest	5.25	0	1	0	16	0	24.0	29	4	11	21
vs. AL	4.15	0	0	0	6	0	4.1	5	0	1	5
vs. NL	3.84	2	3	2	58	0	79.2	77	13	34	69
Pre-All Star	2.44	1	1	2	37	0	55.1	51	3	22	45
Post-All Star	6.59	1	2	0	27	0	28.2	31	10	13	29

	Avg	AB	H	2B	3B	HR	RBI	BB	SO	OBP	SLG
vs. Left	.250	124	31	6	1	1	9	16	26	.340	.339
vs. Right	.266	192	51	8	0	12	43	19	48	.329	.495
Inning 1-6	.265	113	30	3	1	3	23	17	26	.356	.389
Inning 7+	.256	203	52	11	0	10	29	18	48	.320	.458
None on	.261	165	43	6	0	9		16	36	.330	.461
Runners on	.258	151	39	8	1	4	43	19	38	.337	.404
Scoring Posn	.257	105	27	3	1	1	36	13	34	.328	.333
Close & Late	.319	47	15	2	0	5	16	8	13	.418	.681
None on/out	.216	74	16	3	0	4	4	2	16	.247	.419
vs. 1st Batr (relief)	.254	59	15	1	0	4	14	3	9	.281	.475
1st Inning Pitched	.223	202	45	3	0	10	38	23	51	.297	.386
First 15 Pitches	.244	172	42	3	0	10	32	19	37	.320	.436
Pitch 16-30	.278	108	30	8	0	3	15	13	29	.355	.435
Pitch 31-45	.259	27	7	2	1	0	5	3	8	.333	.407
Pitch 46+	.333	9	3	1	0	0	0	0	0	.333	.444
First Pitch	.333	42	14	2	0	2	7	4	0	.404	.524
Ahead in Count	.206	155	32	5	0	5	22	0	64	.206	.335
Behind in Count	.403	62	25	5	1	5	17	13	0	.507	.758
Two Strikes	.160	162	26	5	0	3	17	17	74	.235	.247
Pre-All Star	.249	205	51	10	1	3	23	22	45	.322	.351
Post-All Star	.279	111	31	4	0	10	29	13	29	.354	.586

Last Five Years

	ERA	W	L	Sv	G	GS	IP	H	HR	BB	SO
Home	4.78	6	6	1	82	13	165.2	186	25	67	97
Away	4.01	7	13	3	83	13	166.0	167	17	68	88
Day	4.43	1	9	4	87	10	156.1	171	21	56	97
Night	4.36	12	10	0	78	16	175.1	182	21	79	88
Grass	4.61	11	11	2	116	15	213.0	224	33	86	135
Turf	4.02	2	8	2	49	11	118.2	129	9	49	50
March/April	4.12	1	2	0	15	4	39.1	42	6	18	18
May	4.13	3	2	1	28	1	52.1	52	5	26	33
June	2.80	2	2	1	34	4	64.1	63	3	19	46
July	4.29	4	5	2	32	6	65.0	67	7	27	28
August	5.98	1	6	0	28	5	58.2	73	12	23	25
Sept/Oct	5.19	2	2	0	28	6	52.0	56	9	22	35
Starter	5.53	5	10	0	26	26	138.1	157	21	59	56
Reliever	3.58	8	9	4	139	0	193.1	196	21	76	129
0 Days rest (Relief)	2.63	1	2	1	29	0	37.2	34	2	12	21
1 or 2 Days rest	3.32	6	4	3	77	0	111.0	110	11	44	76
3+ Days rest	5.04	1	3	0	33	0	44.2	52	8	20	32
vs. AL	4.15	0	0	0	6	0	4.1	5	0	1	5
vs. NL	4.40	13	19	4	159	26	327.1	348	42	134	180
Pre-All Star	3.57	6	7	3	86	12	179.0	187	15	68	105
Post-All Star	5.36	7	12	1	79	14	152.2	166	27	67	80

	Avg	AB	H	2B	3B	HR	RBI	BB	SO	OBP	SLG
vs. Left	.303	552	167	34	4	13	54	64	66	.379	.449
vs. Right	.262	711	186	33	6	29	130	71	119	.333	.447
Inning 1-6	.293	793	232	43	8	22	125	95	102	.371	.450
Inning 7+	.257	470	121	24	2	20	59	40	83	.321	.445
None on	.273	677	185	30	4	27		73	94	.348	.449
Runners on	.287	586	168	37	6	15	157	62	91	.358	.447
Scoring Posn	.266	387	103	23	4	7	136	49	72	.347	.401
Close & Late	.288	170	49	10	1	7	27	22	27	.379	.482
None on/out	.307	309	95	15	1	13	13	31	44	.378	.489
vs. 1st Batr (relief)	.256	125	32	6	1	5	22	12	16	.317	.440
1st Inning Pitched	.254	555	141	27	4	17	89	61	92	.327	.409
First 15 Pitches	.267	475	127	25	4	20	72	51	69	.341	.463
Pitch 16-30	.276	337	93	19	0	9	49	40	57	.364	.412
Pitch 31-45	.244	164	40	7	2	1	16	20	33	.324	.329
Pitch 46+	.324	287	93	16	4	12	47	24	26	.377	.533
First Pitch	.291	199	58	9	1	6	27	7	0	.325	.437
Ahead in Count	.238	563	134	30	2	15	68	0	157	.246	.378
Behind in Count	.382	275	105	16	6	15	57	79	0	.521	.647
Two Strikes	.220	563	124	27	2	14	63	48	185	.282	.350
Pre-All Star	.272	687	187	36	7	15	88	68	105	.343	.410
Post-All Star	.288	576	166	31	3	27	96	67	80	.364	.493

Pitcher vs. Batter (career)

Pitches Best Vs.	Avg	AB	H	2B	3B	HR	RBI	BB	SO	OBP	SLG
Eric Davis	.083	12	1	1	0	0	2	1	1	.154	.167
Joe Orsulak	.091	11	1	0	0	0	0	2	1	.231	.091
Brett Butler	.111	9	1	0	0	0	2	3	1	.333	.111
Gregg Jefferies	.167	12	2	0	0	0	0	0	0	.167	.167
Reggie Sanders	.200	10	2	0	0	0	2	1	1	.273	.200

Pitches Worst Vs.	Avg	AB	H	2B	3B	HR	RBI	BB	SO	OBP	SLG
Bernard Gilkey	.636	11	7	2	0	2	3	2	0	.714	1.364
Gary Sheffield	.545	11	6	2	0	1	3	2	0	.643	1.000
Ray Lankford	.500	8	4	0	0	1	3	3	1	.636	.875
Barry Bonds	.444	9	4	0	0	1	1	4	0	.643	.778
Mike Piazza	.364	11	4	0	0	2	9	1	0	.417	.909

Rafael Bournigal — Athletics
Age 32 – Bats Right (groundball hitter)

	Avg	G	AB	R	H	2B	3B	HR	RBI	BB	SO	HBP	GDP	SB	CS	OBP	SLG	IBB	SH	SF	#Pit	#P/PA	GB	FB	G/F
1997 Season	.279	79	222	29	62	9	0	1	20	16	19	4	11	2	1	.339	.333	1	7	0	892	3.58	102	59	1.73
Last Five Years	.260	215	608	64	158	27	3	1	52	41	45	7	20	6	4	.314	.319	2	20	0	2287	3.38	283	167	1.69

1997 Season

	Avg	AB	H	2B	3B	HR	RBI	BB	SO	OBP	SLG
vs. Left	.232	69	16	1	0	0	3	6	5	.293	.246
vs. Right	.301	153	46	8	0	1	17	10	14	.359	.373
Home	.242	120	29	4	0	0	9	11	10	.321	.275
Away	.324	102	33	5	0	1	11	5	9	.361	.402
First Pitch	.280	25	7	3	0	0	7	1	0	.308	.400
Ahead in Count	.267	45	12	2	0	1	6	8	0	.377	.378
Behind in Count	.303	109	33	2	0	0	5	0	18	.315	.321
Two Strikes	.300	90	27	2	0	0	4	7	19	.364	.322

	Avg	AB	H	2B	3B	HR	RBI	BB	SO	OBP	SLG
Scoring Posn	.255	51	13	5	0	0	17	6	4	.345	.353
Close & Late	.300	30	9	0	0	0	3	1	4	.323	.300
None on/out	.261	46	12	0	0	0	0	1	7	.306	.261
Batting #2	.270	122	33	4	0	0	7	9	10	.326	.303
Batting #9	.286	56	16	2	0	1	5	2	5	.333	.375
Other	.295	44	13	3	0	0	8	5	4	.380	.364
Pre-All Star	.307	140	43	7	0	1	16	11	14	.366	.379
Post-All Star	.232	82	19	2	0	0	4	5	5	.292	.256

Last Five Years

	Avg	AB	H	2B	3B	HR	RBI	BB	SO	OBP	SLG
vs. Left	.215	181	39	6	0	0	11	9	10	.253	.249

	Avg	AB	H	2B	3B	HR	RBI	BB	SO	OBP	SLG
First Pitch	.326	95	31	8	2	0	11	1	0	.340	.453

Last Five Years

	Avg	AB	H	2B	3B	HR	RBI	BB	SO	OBP	SLG		Avg	AB	H	2B	3B	HR	RBI	BB	SO	OBP	SLG
vs. Right	.279	427	119	21	3	1	41	32	35	.339	.349	Ahead in Count	.217	115	25	7	1	1	12	24	0	.353	.322
Groundball	.270	148	40	7	0	1	9	12	12	.329	.338	Behind in Count	.263	304	80	9	0	0	22	0	42	.273	.293
Flyball	.292	72	21	2	0	0	6	4	5	.346	.319	Two Strikes	.249	241	60	7	0	0	13	16	45	.307	.278
Home	.239	314	75	12	2	0	23	27	20	.307	.290	Batting #2	.262	279	73	11	2	0	20	22	24	.318	.315
Away	.282	294	83	15	1	1	29	14	25	.322	.350	Batting #8	.251	175	44	6	1	0	18	14	9	.314	.297
Day	.247	251	62	13	2	0	25	16	16	.303	.315	Other	.266	154	41	10	0	1	14	5	12	.307	.351
Night	.269	357	96	14	1	1	27	25	29	.322	.322	March/April	.212	52	11	2	0	0	5	7	3	.317	.250
Grass	.255	510	130	22	3	0	38	35	36	.312	.310	May	.254	59	15	2	0	0	1	0	5	.267	.288
Turf	.286	98	28	5	0	1	14	6	9	.327	.367	June	.365	137	50	11	2	1	18	11	12	.416	.496
Pre-All Star	.300	307	92	18	2	1	29	24	23	.358	.381	July	.223	184	41	7	1	0	18	14	13	.285	.272
Post-All Star	.219	301	66	9	1	0	23	17	22	.268	.256	August	.207	145	30	3	0	0	7	8	10	.258	.228
Scoring Posn	.273	139	38	8	0	0	48	14	13	.353	.331	Sept/Oct	.355	31	11	2	0	0	3	1	2	.375	.419
Close & Late	.293	75	22	4	0	0	9	5	5	.346	.347	vs. AL	.264	458	121	22	2	1	34	30	37	.316	.328
None on/out	.246	134	33	4	2	0	0	6	14	.289	.306	vs. NL	.247	150	37	5	1	0	18	11	8	.307	.293

Batter vs. Pitcher (career)

Hits Best Against	Avg	AB	H	2B	3B	HR	RBI	BB	SO	OBP	SLG	Hits Worst Against	Avg	AB	H	2B	3B	HR	RBI	BB	SO	OBP	SLG
Bob Wolcott	.455	11	5	2	0	0	2	0	1	.455	.636	Ken Hill	.083	12	1	0	0	0	0	0	2	.083	.083
Mike Mussina	.429	14	6	0	0	0	0	0	0	.467	.429	Jeff Fassero	.100	10	1	0	0	0	0	1	0	.182	.100

Mike Bovee — Angels   Age 24 – Pitches Right

	ERA	W	L	Sv	G	GS	IP	BB	SO	Avg	H	2B	3B	HR	RBI	OBP	SLG	GF	IR	IRS	Hld	SvOp	SB	CS	GB	FB	G/F
1997 Season	5.40	0	0	0	3	0	3.1	1	5	.231	3	2	0	1	2	.286	.615	3	1	0	0	0	0	0	1	5	0.20

1997 Season

	ERA	W	L	Sv	G	GS	IP	H	HR	BB	SO		Avg	AB	H	2B	3B	HR	RBI	BB	SO	OBP	SLG
Home	5.40	0	0	0	3	0	3.1	3	1	1	5	vs. Left	.333	6	2	2	0	0	1	0	1	.333	.667
Away	0.00	0	0	0	0	0	0.0	0	0	0	0	vs. Right	.143	7	1	0	0	1	1	1	4	.250	.571

Shane Bowers — Twins   Age 26 – Pitches Right (flyball pitcher)

	ERA	W	L	Sv	G	GS	IP	BB	SO	Avg	H	2B	3B	HR	RBI	OBP	SLG	CG	ShO	Sup	QS	#P/S	SB	CS	GB	FB	G/F
1997 Season	8.05	0	3	0	5	5	19.0	8	7	.329	27	6	3	2	15	.391	.549	0	0	5.21	0	75	1	1	25	30	0.83

1997 Season

	ERA	W	L	Sv	G	GS	IP	H	HR	BB	SO		Avg	AB	H	2B	3B	HR	RBI	BB	SO	OBP	SLG
Home	6.52	0	1	0	2	2	9.2	11	0	3	6	vs. Left	.297	37	11	3	0	1	5	2	4	.341	.459
Away	9.64	0	2	0	3	3	9.1	16	2	5	1	vs. Right	.356	45	16	3	3	1	10	6	3	.431	.622

Darren Bragg — Red Sox   Age 28 – Bats Left

	Avg	G	AB	R	H	2B	3B	HR	RBI	BB	SO	HBP	GDP	SB	CS	OBP	SLG	IBB	SH	SF	#Pit	#P/PA	GB	FB	G/F
1997 Season	.257	153	513	65	132	35	2	9	57	61	102	3	15	10	6	.355	.386	5	5	4	2336	3.99	206	113	1.82
Career (1994-1997)	.254	340	1094	163	278	67	5	22	118	150	218	11	22	33	15	.346	.385	13	8	13	5154	4.04	446	248	1.80

1997 Season

	Avg	AB	H	2B	3B	HR	RBI	BB	SO	OBP	SLG		Avg	AB	H	2B	3B	HR	RBI	BB	SO	OBP	SLG
vs. Left	.242	120	29	7	0	1	16	13	27	.321	.325	First Pitch	.353	68	24	5	0	0	6	3	0	.389	.426
vs. Right	.262	393	103	28	2	8	47	48	75	.342	.405	Ahead in Count	.311	103	32	16	0	3	20	35	0	.482	.553
Groundball	.250	100	25	7	0	2	12	10	16	.315	.380	Behind in Count	.211	228	48	11	1	2	14	0	78	.213	.294
Flyball	.226	84	19	5	1	2	8	9	16	.300	.381	Two Strikes	.185	260	48	14	0	3	19	23	102	.253	.273
Home	.277	260	72	18	1	3	28	37	51	.367	.388	Batting #2	.239	205	49	12	0	3	20	17	44	.296	.341
Away	.237	253	60	17	1	6	29	24	51	.306	.383	Batting #9	.287	167	48	15	1	5	23	14	32	.343	.479
Day	.282	149	42	10	0	0	15	18	32	.355	.349	Other	.248	141	35	8	1	1	14	30	26	.385	.340
Night	.247	364	90	25	2	9	42	43	70	.330	.401	March/April	.306	62	19	5	0	4	12	8	7	.386	.581
Grass	.253	451	114	30	1	4	42	57	93	.337	.350	May	.322	87	28	8	0	1	7	10	18	.392	.448
Turf	.290	62	18	5	1	5	15	4	9	.343	.645	June	.220	123	27	7	0	3	16	7	28	.263	.350
Pre-All Star	.267	296	79	21	0	8	37	29	58	.331	.419	July	.266	94	25	6	1	1	12	23	14	.407	.383
Post-All Star	.244	217	53	14	2	1	20	32	44	.345	.341	August	.212	85	18	3	1	0	5	8	23	.292	.271
Scoring Posn	.248	133	33	8	1	5	48	29	31	.385	.436	Sept/Oct	.242	62	15	6	0	0	5	5	12	.299	.339
Close & Late	.298	94	28	11	0	2	21	11	19	.354	.479	vs. AL	.265	465	123	30	2	9	51	56	93	.347	.396
None on/out	.288	111	32	6	1	2	2	7	22	.331	.414	vs. NL	.188	48	9	5	0	0	6	5	9	.250	.292

1997 By Position

Position	Avg	AB	H	2B	3B	HR	RBI	BB	SO	OBP	SLG	G	GS	Innings	PO	A	E	DP	Fld Pct	Rng Fctr	In Zone	Outs	Zone Rtg	MLB Zone
As Pinch Hitter	.222	9	2	1	0	0	0	2	1	.364	.333	11	0	---	---	---	---	---	---	---	---	---	---	---
As cf	.274	383	105	26	2	9	47	45	79	.352	.423	118	104	945.0	296	9	2	2	.993	2.90	345	274	.794	.815
As rf	.200	120	24	8	0	0	10	14	22	.285	.267	41	30	279.1	69	2	3	1	.959	2.29	77	66	.857	.813

Career (1994-1997)

	Avg	AB	H	2B	3B	HR	RBI	BB	SO	OBP	SLG		Avg	AB	H	2B	3B	HR	RBI	BB	SO	OBP	SLG
vs. Left	.227	220	50	11	0	2	19	33	53	.336	.305	First Pitch	.353	139	49	10	0	2	17	9	0	.400	.468
vs. Right	.261	874	228	56	5	20	99	117	165	.349	.405	Ahead in Count	.309	230	71	23	0	9	37	82	0	.483	.526
Groundball	.259	228	59	16	1	4	29	27	44	.336	.390	Behind in Count	.199	482	96	24	4	4	34	0	170	.207	.290
Flyball	.239	180	43	9	1	7	21	23	31	.333	.417	Two Strikes	.191	545	104	29	3	8	44	59	218	.276	.299
Home	.267	562	150	40	2	11	65	72	113	.365	.404	Batting #1	.262	347	91	18	1	7	30	57	64	.367	.380
Away	.241	532	128	27	3	11	53	78	105	.342	.365	Batting #2	.237	232	55	14	0	4	23	19	50	.297	.349
Day	.273	319	87	22	1	2	32	42	62	.357	.367	Other	.256	515	132	35	4	11	65	74	104	.353	.404

Career (1994-1997)

	Avg	AB	H	2B	3B	HR	RBI	BB	SO	OBP	SLG		Avg	AB	H	2B	3B	HR	RBI	BB	SO	OBP	SLG
Night	.246	775	191	45	4	20	86	108	156	.342	.392	March/April	.252	107	27	6	0	5	16	14	18	.339	.449
Grass	.253	789	200	47	4	11	74	118	160	.352	.365	May	.286	220	63	14	0	5	21	30	45	.375	.418
Turf	.256	305	78	20	1	11	44	32	58	.331	.436	June	.230	222	51	9	1	5	26	28	47	.322	.347
Pre-All Star	.254	610	155	32	2	18	70	80	124	.344	.402	July	.257	179	46	15	2	4	23	29	35	.357	.430
Post-All Star	.254	484	123	35	3	4	48	70	94	.349	.364	August	.236	203	48	11	1	3	18	27	43	.329	.345
Scoring Posn	.239	268	64	18	1	8	95	64	72	.382	.403	Sept/Oct	.264	163	43	12	1	0	14	22	30	.354	.350
Close & Late	.281	167	47	15	1	2	28	28	35	.390	.419	vs. AL	.257	1046	269	62	5	22	112	145	209	.351	.389
None on/out	.247	304	75	12	1	8	8	31	51	.322	.372	vs. NL	.188	48	9	5	0	0	6	5	9	.250	.292

Batter vs. Pitcher (career)

Hits Best Against	Avg	AB	H	2B	3B	HR	RBI	BB	SO	OBP	SLG	Hits Worst Against	Avg	AB	H	2B	3B	HR	RBI	BB	SO	OBP	SLG
James Baldwin	.600	10	6	0	0	0	0	2	0	.667	.600	Roger Clemens	.059	17	1	0	0	0	2	1	5	.150	.059
Omar Olivares	.444	9	4	1	0	0	3	1	3	.455	.556	Scott Erickson	.105	19	2	1	0	0	0	2	3	.190	.158
Bobby Witt	.417	12	5	2	0	1	2	1	4	.462	.833	Ben McDonald	.133	15	2	0	0	0	0	2	5	.235	.133
Brad Radke	.375	16	6	1	0	1	2	4	3	.524	.625	Ramiro Mendoza	.143	14	2	0	0	0	1	0	1	.143	.143
Felipe Lira	.357	14	5	1	1	0	0	0	1	.357	.571	Willie Adams	.182	11	2	0	0	0	2	0	2	.182	.182

Mark Brandenburg — Red Sox
Age 27 – Pitches Right (flyball pitcher)

	ERA	W	L	Sv	G	GS	IP	BB	SO	Avg	H	2B	3B	HR	RBI	OBP	SLG	GF	IR	IRS	Hld	SvOp	SB	CS	GB	FB	G/F
1997 Season	5.49	0	2	0	31	0	41.0	16	34	.299	49	13	1	3	28	.364	.445	5	28	10	3	0	2	1	57	46	1.24
Career (1995-1997)	4.49	5	8	0	97	0	144.1	56	121	.281	161	33	3	16	98	.347	.433	23	80	34	16	2	4	2	165	183	0.90

1997 Season

	ERA	W	L	Sv	G	GS	IP	H	HR	BB	SO		Avg	AB	H	2B	3B	HR	RBI	BB	SO	OBP	SLG
Home	4.66	0	0	0	15	0	19.1	23	2	4	20	vs. Left	.386	70	27	11	0	1	12	9	15	.463	.586
Away	6.23	0	2	0	16	0	21.2	26	1	12	14	vs. Right	.234	94	22	2	1	2	16	7	19	.288	.340
Starter	0.00	0	0	0	0	0	0.0	0	0	0	0	Scoring Posn	.288	59	17	4	1	0	24	11	8	.397	.390
Reliever	5.49	0	2	0	31	0	41.0	49	3	16	34	Close & Late	.333	21	7	1	0	2	5	2	1	.400	.667
0 Days rest (Relief)	4.30	0	0	0	10	0	14.2	19	1	6	11	None on/out	.485	33	16	6	0	0	0	1	7	.500	.667
1 or 2 Days rest	5.51	0	1	0	12	0	16.1	18	2	6	12	First Pitch	.292	24	7	1	0	0	4	3	0	.357	.333
3+ Days rest	7.20	0	1	0	9	0	10.0	12	0	4	11	Ahead in Count	.234	94	22	0	0	1	13	0	30	.247	.351
Pre-All Star	13.94	0	1	0	9	0	10.1	18	1	14	14	Behind in Count	.400	20	8	2	1	1	7	6	0	.538	.750
Post-All Star	2.64	0	1	0	22	0	30.2	31	2	12	20	Two Strikes	.213	89	19	6	0	0	8	7	34	.286	.281

Career (1995-1997)

	ERA	W	L	Sv	G	GS	IP	H	HR	BB	SO		Avg	AB	H	2B	3B	HR	RBI	BB	SO	OBP	SLG
Home	4.64	2	6	0	50	0	73.2	87	10	22	69	vs. Left	.311	257	80	25	2	5	41	28	54	.381	.482
Away	4.33	3	2	0	47	0	70.2	74	6	34	52	vs. Right	.256	316	81	8	1	11	57	28	67	.319	.392
Day	2.89	0	1	0	26	0	46.2	49	4	16	36	Inning 1-6	.264	216	57	10	2	3	43	26	43	.341	.370
Night	5.25	5	7	0	71	0	97.2	112	12	40	85	Inning 7+	.291	357	104	23	1	13	55	30	78	.351	.471
Grass	4.57	4	7	0	86	0	130.0	147	15	45	110	None on	.284	268	76	17	0	10	10	21	63	.342	.459
Turf	3.77	1	1	0	11	0	14.1	14	1	11	11	Runners on	.279	305	85	16	3	6	88	35	58	.351	.410
March/April	1.23	1	0	0	8	0	14.2	16	0	4	13	Scoring Posn	.289	173	50	10	1	2	78	24	32	.369	.393
May	2.89	0	0	0	4	0	9.1	7	0	6	4	Close & Late	.340	103	35	10	0	6	22	9	13	.391	.612
June	8.59	0	1	0	16	0	22.0	32	2	10	23	None on/out	.336	122	41	11	0	5	5	7	29	.382	.549
July	5.66	0	4	0	9	0	20.2	21	4	11	17	vs. 1st Batr (relief)	.236	89	21	7	0	2	19	4	24	.281	.382
August	4.11	3	2	0	34	0	50.1	56	7	11	38	1st Inning Pitched	.268	325	87	21	1	10	68	37	72	.342	.431
Sept/Oct	3.29	1	1	0	26	0	27.1	29	3	14	26	First 15 Pitches	.272	276	75	16	1	10	53	26	54	.335	.446
Starter	0.00	0	0	0	0	0	0.0	0	0	0	0	Pitch 16-30	.280	175	49	10	1	2	21	20	41	.352	.383
Reliever	4.49	5	8	0	97	0	144.1	161	16	56	121	Pitch 31-45	.282	71	20	3	1	2	14	7	17	.358	.437
0 Days rest (Relief)	5.04	2	0	0	19	0	25.0	30	3	10	19	Pitch 46+	.333	51	17	4	0	2	10	3	9	.382	.529
1 or 2 Days rest	4.30	3	6	0	44	0	60.2	59	9	21	52	First Pitch	.387	75	29	3	0	2	22	6	0	.425	.507
3+ Days rest	4.45	0	2	0	34	0	58.2	72	4	25	50	Ahead in Count	.219	311	68	20	2	6	44	0	108	.226	.354
vs. AL	4.39	5	7	0	90	0	135.1	151	13	56	114	Behind in Count	.353	85	30	5	1	4	18	22	0	.486	.576
vs. NL	6.00	0	1	0	7	0	9.0	10	3	0	7	Two Strikes	.195	297	58	15	2	3	32	28	121	.272	.290
Pre-All Star	4.47	1	1	0	30	0	52.1	57	2	23	47	Pre-All Star	.274	208	57	11	2	2	33	23	47	.350	.375
Post-All Star	4.50	4	7	0	67	0	92.0	104	14	33	74	Post-All Star	.285	365	104	22	1	14	65	33	74	.346	.466

Jeff Branson — Indians
Age 31 – Bats Left (groundball hitter)

	Avg	G	AB	R	H	2B	3B	HR	RBI	BB	SO	HBP	GDP	SB	CS	OBP	SLG	IBB	SH	SF	#Pit	#P/PA	GB	FB	G/F
1997 Season	.200	94	170	14	34	7	1	3	12	14	40	1	4	1	2	.262	.306	1	1	2	724	3.85	57	49	1.16
Last Five Years	.245	528	1302	149	319	60	9	33	132	113	265	4	30	9	4	.304	.381	23	19	15	5318	3.66	458	366	1.25

1997 Season

	Avg	AB	H	2B	3B	HR	RBI	BB	SO	OBP	SLG		Avg	AB	H	2B	3B	HR	RBI	BB	SO	OBP	SLG
vs. Left	.389	18	7	1	0	0	0	1	3	.421	.444	Scoring Posn	.097	31	3	1	0	1	9	5	14	.211	.226
vs. Right	.178	152	27	6	1	3	12	13	37	.244	.289	Close & Late	.133	45	6	2	0	1	3	3	12	.188	.244
Home	.229	83	19	4	0	3	9	5	16	.270	.386	None on/out	.222	45	10	1	0	0	0	4	6	.286	.244
Away	.172	87	15	3	1	0	3	9	24	.255	.230	Batting #8	.205	83	17	3	1	3	7		21	.269	.373
First Pitch	.158	19	3	0	0	0	0	0	0	.158	.158	Batting #9	.161	31	5	1	0	0		4	6	.257	.194
Ahead in Count	.375	32	12	1	1	1	3	5	0	.459	.563	Other	.214	56	12	3	0	3			13	.254	.268
Behind in Count	.105	86	9	4	0	0	3	0	35	.114	.151	Pre-All Star	.143	91	13	3	1	1	5	7	20	.204	.231
Two Strikes	.105	86	9	3	0	0	4	9	40	.198	.140	Post-All Star	.266	79	21	4	0	2	7	7	20	.326	.392

Last Five Years

	Avg	AB	H	2B	3B	HR	RBI	BB	SO	OBP	SLG		Avg	AB	H	2B	3B	HR	RBI	BB	SO	OBP	SLG
vs. Left	.234	218	51	12	0	4	20	19	49	.297	.344	First Pitch	.336	226	76	8	3	8	26	18	0	.382	.504

Last Five Years

	Avg	AB	H	2B	3B	HR	RBI	BB	SO	OBP	SLG		Avg	AB	H	2B	3B	HR	RBI	BB	SO	OBP	SLG
vs. Right	.247	1084	268	48	9	29	112	94	216	.305	.388	Ahead in Count	.318	280	89	19	3	12	42	39	0	.396	.536
Groundball	.225	395	89	13	1	10	27	29	74	.276	.339	Behind in Count	.171	556	95	19	1	6	34	0	221	.174	.241
Flyball	.216	222	48	14	2	3	18	17	56	.267	.338	Two Strikes	.156	601	94	22	2	6	35	56	265	.230	.230
Home	.254	594	151	34	2	20	63	42	113	.301	.419	Batting #7	.223	211	47	11	3	8	28	20	41	.292	.417
Away	.237	708	168	26	7	13	69	71	152	.306	.349	Batting #8	.256	675	173	31	5	18	74	62	127	.316	.397
Day	.246	422	104	20	5	13	44	27	97	.292	.410	Other	.238	416	99	18	1	7	30	31	97	.290	.337
Night	.244	880	215	40	4	20	88	86	168	.310	.367	March/April	.270	126	34	3	2	2	12	11	18	.326	.373
Grass	.238	517	123	17	6	13	44	46	113	.298	.369	May	.249	189	47	11	1	3	17	17	42	.311	.365
Turf	.250	785	196	43	3	20	88	67	152	.308	.389	June	.246	228	56	9	2	7	22	16	52	.291	.395
Pre-All Star	.252	642	162	34	7	15	64	50	128	.304	.397	July	.239	268	64	20	3	7	24	21	50	.294	.414
Post-All Star	.238	660	157	26	2	18	68	63	137	.304	.365	August	.259	255	66	9	0	11	40	22	49	.318	.424
Scoring Posn	.202	287	58	11	0	6	92	53	69	.317	.303	Sept/Oct	.220	236	52	8	1	3	17	26	54	.295	.301
Close & Late	.214	234	50	5	0	7	23	18	57	.270	.325	vs. AL	.244	78	19	5	0	2	7	9	18	.322	.385
None on/out	.238	345	82	15	3	10	10	20	66	.281	.386	vs. NL	.245	1224	300	55	9	31	125	104	247	.303	.381

Batter vs. Pitcher (career)

Hits Best Against	Avg	AB	H	2B	3B	HR	RBI	BB	SO	OBP	SLG	Hits Worst Against	Avg	AB	H	2B	3B	HR	RBI	BB	SO	OBP	SLG
Danny Jackson	.500	14	7	1	0	0	1	1	3	.533	.571	Greg Swindell	.083	12	1	0	0	0	0	0	4	.083	.083
Pedro Astacio	.421	19	8	0	1	1	1	0	2	.421	.684	Tom Glavine	.083	12	1	0	0	0	0	0	4	.083	.083
Frank Castillo	.400	10	4	0	2	0	1	1	1	.455	.800	Pat Rapp	.118	17	2	0	0	0	0	1		.118	.118
Jim Bullinger	.364	11	4	1	0	1	1	3	1	.500	.727	Ramon Martinez	.167	12	2	0	0	0	0	1	2	.231	.167
Bobby Jones	.333	21	7	2	0	1	3	1	5	.364	.571	John Burkett	.200	15	3	0	0	0	0	0	5	.200	.200

Jeff Brantley — Reds
Age 34 – Pitches Right (flyball pitcher)

	ERA	W	L	Sv	G	GS	IP	BB	SO	Avg	H	2B	3B	HR	RBI	OBP	SLG	GF	IR	IRS	Hld	SvOp	SB	CS	GB	FB	G/F
1997 Season	3.86	1	1	1	13	0	11.2	7	16	.205	9	1	0	2	6	.340	.364	9	2	1	0	3	0	0	5	18	0.28
Last Five Years	3.20	16	17	88	238	12	332.0	129	293	.226	274	37	4	45	129	.302	.374	163	69	21	11	108	10	9	302	429	0.70

1997 Season

	ERA	W	L	Sv	G	GS	IP	H	HR	BB	SO		Avg	AB	H	2B	3B	HR	RBI	BB	SO	OBP	SLG
Home	1.80	0	0	0	6	0	5.0	2	0	4	6	vs. Left	.056	18	1	0	0	0	1	6	8	.320	.056
Away	5.40	1	1	1	7	0	6.2	7	2	3	10	vs. Right	.308	26	8	1	0	2	5	1	8	.357	.577

Last Five Years

	ERA	W	L	Sv	G	GS	IP	H	HR	BB	SO		Avg	AB	H	2B	3B	HR	RBI	BB	SO	OBP	SLG
Home	3.31	8	8	39	123	5	174.0	130	26	59	146	vs. Left	.245	576	141	26	2	21	53	87	129	.341	.406
Away	3.08	8	9	49	115	7	158.0	144	19	70	147	vs. Right	.209	637	133	11	2	24	76	42	164	.265	.345
Day	2.45	8	3	27	81	6	117.1	94	15	43	101	Inning 1-6	.283	279	79	14	2	12	32	28	37	.355	.477
Night	3.61	8	14	61	157	6	214.2	180	30	86	192	Inning 7+	.209	934	195	23	2	33	97	101	256	.286	.344
Grass	3.24	8	8	33	100	9	161.0	143	23	70	142	None on	.231	723	167	27	1	34	34	69	184	.304	.412
Turf	3.16	8	9	55	138	3	171.0	131	22	59	151	Runners on	.218	490	107	10	3	11	95	60	109	.300	.318
March/April	3.23	2	2	7	30	4	55.2	47	7	22	50	Scoring Posn	.181	254	46	3	0	6	79	46	75	.300	.264
May	4.11	7	5	13	48	6	85.1	77	16	44	71	Close & Late	.207	571	118	15	1	22	70	68	152	.291	.352
June	2.83	5	4	20	41	2	54.0	47	7	15	53	None on/out	.257	315	81	12	1	16	16	23	77	.308	.454
July	1.84	1	2	21	50	0	58.2	43	5	17	61	vs. 1st Batr (relief)	.232	207	48	8	0	11	14	17	59	.289	.430
August	3.59	0	3	16	38	0	42.2	34	6	22	33	1st Inning Pitched	.208	787	164	16	3	25	87	86	220	.286	.332
Sept/Oct	3.28	1	1	11	31	0	35.2	26	4	9	25	First 15 Pitches	.233	657	153	14	3	25	62	54	163	.291	.377
Starter	4.86	3	5	0	12	12	63.0	76	13	25	30	Pitch 16-30	.181	321	58	12	0	9	34	53	96	.301	.302
Reliever	2.81	13	12	88	226	0	269.0	198	32	104	263	Pitch 31-45	.211	95	20	6	0	0	11	13	17	.315	.274
0 Days rest (Relief)	1.79	3	2	34	66	0	70.1	49	7	32	66	Pitch 46+	.307	140	43	5	1	11	22	9	17	.351	.593
1 or 2 Days rest	3.46	7	6	35	95	0	117.0	89	15	42	121	First Pitch	.261	161	42	6	0	6	24	12	0	.306	.410
3+ Days rest	2.76	3	4	19	65	0	81.2	60	10	30	76	Ahead in Count	.191	603	115	12	0	20	44	0	250	.200	.310
vs. AL	0.00	0	0	0	0	0	0.0	0	0	0	0	Behind in Count	.295	207	61	10	4	13	35	64	0	.460	.570
vs. NL	3.20	16	17	88	238	12	332.0	274	45	129	293	Two Strikes	.158	638	101	11	0	17	45	53	293	.228	.255
Pre-All Star	3.46	14	12	48	138	12	213.1	191	32	86	192	Pre-All Star	.241	791	191	30	3	32	96	86	192	.318	.408
Post-All Star	2.73	2	5	40	100	0	118.2	83	13	43	101	Post-All Star	.197	422	83	7	1	13	33	43	101	.273	.310

Pitcher vs. Batter (career)

Pitches Best Vs.	Avg	AB	H	2B	3B	HR	RBI	BB	SO	OBP	SLG	Pitches Worst Vs.	Avg	AB	H	2B	3B	HR	RBI	BB	SO	OBP	SLG
Sean Berry	.000	12	0	0	0	0	0	0	6	.000	.000	Tony Gwynn	.593	27	16	1	0	0	1	5	1	.656	.630
Darren Daulton	.067	15	1	0	0	0	1	1	0	.125	.067	Orlando Merced	.556	9	5	1	0	0	2	7	1	.750	.667
Stan Javier	.091	11	1	1	0	0	2	0	6	.091	.182	Ryne Sandberg	.417	12	5	1	0	1	3	3	3	.563	.750
Henry Rodriguez	.091	11	1	0	0	0	0	0	5	.091	.091	Paul O'Neill	.364	11	4	0	0	2	6	6	1	.588	.909
Barry Larkin	.133	15	2	0	0	0	0	0	1	.133	.133	Moises Alou	.333	9	3	0	0	2	2	2		.455	1.000

Brent Brede — Twins
Age 26 – Bats Left

	Avg	G	AB	R	H	2B	3B	HR	RBI	BB	SO	HBP	GDP	SB	CS	OBP	SLG	IBB	SH	SF	#Pit	#P/PA	GB	FB	G/F
1997 Season	.274	61	190	25	52	11	1	3	21	21	38	1	1	7	2	.347	.389	0	1	1	809	3.78	77	41	1.88
Career (1996-1997)	.276	71	210	27	58	11	2	3	23	22	43	1	2	7	2	.346	.390	0	1	1	880	3.74	83	45	1.84

1997 Season

	Avg	AB	H	2B	3B	HR	RBI	BB	SO	OBP	SLG		Avg	AB	H	2B	3B	HR	RBI	BB	SO	OBP	SLG
vs. Left	.286	14	4	0	0	0	2	0	5	.313	.286	Scoring Posn	.192	52	10	3	1	0	16	7	16	.283	.288
vs. Right	.273	176	48	11	1	3	19	21	33	.350	.398	Close & Late	.480	25	12	1	0	0	4	3	4	.552	.520
Home	.314	70	22	1	0	2	8	8	13	.385	.414	None on/out	.234	47	11	2	0	0	0	2	13	.265	.277
Away	.250	120	30	10	1	1	13	13	25	.326	.375	Batting #2	.247	93	23	6	1	1	8	12	14	.333	.366
First Pitch	.458	24	11	1	1	0	4	0	0	.458	.583	Batting #8	.200	20	4	2	0	0	3	3	9	.292	.300

1997 Season

	Avg	AB	H	2B	3B	HR	RBI	BB	SO	OBP	SLG		Avg	AB	H	2B	3B	HR	RBI	BB	SO	OBP	SLG
Ahead in Count	.265	34	9	3	0	0	4	11	0	.447	.353	Other	.325	77	25	3	0	2	10	6	15	.381	.442
Behind in Count	.208	96	20	3	0	1	6	0	32	.208	.271	Pre-All Star	.279	86	24	5	1	0	7	8	17	.340	.360
Two Strikes	.170	94	16	3	0	0	5	10	38	.250	.202	Post-All Star	.269	104	28	6	0	3	14	13	21	.353	.413

Billy Brewer — Phillies   Age 30 – Pitches Left

	ERA	W	L	Sv	G	GS	IP	BB	SO	Avg	H	2B	3B	HR	RBI	OBP	SLG	GF	IR	IRS	Hld	SvOp	SB	CS	GB	FB	G/F
1997 Season	4.13	1	2	0	28	0	24.0	13	17	.213	19	2	0	0	6	.305	.382	5	13	6	5	2	1	0	37	30	1.23
Career (1993-1997)	4.19	10	9	3	176	0	152.2	77	109	.244	139	19	6	22	98	.335	.415	50	151	40	29	15	12	4	186	172	1.08

1997 Season

	ERA	W	L	Sv	G	GS	IP	H	HR	BB	SO		Avg	AB	H	2B	3B	HR	RBI	BB	SO	OBP	SLG
Home	4.66	1	0	0	12	0	9.2	8	1	2	10	vs. Left	.257	35	9	1	1	2	7	8	5	.395	.514
Away	3.77	0	2	0	16	0	14.1	11	2	11	7	vs. Right	.185	54	10	1	1	0	9	5	12	.242	.296
Starter	0.00	0	0	0	0	0	0.0	0	0	0	0	Scoring Posn	.353	17	6	1	1	1	13	6	4	.462	.706
Reliever	4.13	1	2	0	28	0	24.0	19	3	13	17	Close & Late	.269	26	7	0	2	1	7	5	5	.375	.538
0 Days rest (Relief)	8.22	0	1	0	8	0	7.2	10	1	6	5	None on/out	.217	23	5	1	1	0	0	2	5	.280	.348
1 or 2 Days rest	1.46	1	1	0	14	0	12.1	6	0	5	9	First Pitch	.250	8	2	0	1	0	1	0	0	.222	.500
3+ Days rest	4.50	0	0	0	6	0	4.0	3	2	2	3	Ahead in Count	.216	37	8	2	0	1	5	0	11	.211	.351
Pre-All Star	6.00	0	1	0	9	0	6.0	8	1	5	6	Behind in Count	.190	21	4	0	0	1	3	6	0	.357	.333
Post-All Star	3.50	1	1	0	19	0	18.0	11	2	8	11	Two Strikes	.196	46	9	2	1	1	8	7	17	.296	.348

Career (1993-1997)

	ERA	W	L	Sv	G	GS	IP	H	HR	BB	SO		Avg	AB	H	2B	3B	HR	RBI	BB	SO	OBP	SLG
Home	3.79	6	4	2	90	0	78.1	66	8	33	42	vs. Left	.249	237	59	6	2	14	49	33	46	.343	.468
Away	4.60	4	5	1	86	0	74.1	73	14	44	67	vs. Right	.241	332	80	13	4	8	49	44	63	.330	.377
Day	3.16	3	1	2	57	0	51.1	49	3	22	41	Inning 1-6	.306	72	22	6	1	5	19	12	15	.400	.625
Night	4.71	7	8	1	119	0	101.1	90	19	55	68	Inning 7+	.235	497	117	13	5	17	79	65	94	.326	.384
Grass	4.74	5	7	1	98	0	89.1	94	16	53	64	None on	.249	281	70	7	5	13	13	33	44	.332	.448
Turf	3.41	5	2	2	78	0	63.1	45	6	24	45	Runners on	.240	288	69	12	1	9	85	44	65	.338	.382
March/April	2.33	1	0	1	20	0	19.1	19	2	8	9	Scoring Posn	.243	185	45	9	1	5	77	37	45	.365	.384
May	3.80	2	1	1	29	0	23.2	17	4	9	19	Close & Late	.209	201	42	2	2	7	37	26	38	.303	.343
June	4.76	3	4	0	38	0	28.1	31	3	16	29	None on/out	.326	132	43	3	4	10	10	15	16	.399	.636
July	4.38	3	2	1	46	0	39.0	28	6	22	24	vs. 1st Batr (relief)	.255	145	37	2	3	7	22	25	26	.371	.455
August	4.50	1	1	0	25	0	20.0	20	3	10	15	1st Inning Pitched	.247	450	111	15	6	21	90	54	87	.329	.447
Sept/Oct	4.84	0	1	0	18	0	22.1	24	4	12	13	First 15 Pitches	.249	402	100	11	6	16	63	47	68	.330	.425
Starter	0.00	0	0	0	0	0	0.0	0	0	0	0	Pitch 16-30	.244	135	33	8	0	6	34	25	30	.358	.437
Reliever	4.19	10	9	3	176	0	152.2	139	22	77	109	Pitch 31-45	.188	32	6	0	0	1	5	5	11	.297	.188
0 Days rest (Relief)	4.11	1	2	2	38	0	30.2	31	5	16	24	Pitch 46+	.000	0	0	0	0	0	0	0	0	.000	.000
1 or 2 Days rest	3.66	6	4	0	85	0	66.1	55	9	37	44	First Pitch	.234	64	15	1	2	1	9	5	0	.278	.359
3+ Days rest	4.85	3	3	1	53	0	55.2	53	8	24	41	Ahead in Count	.191	235	45	7	0	7	29	0	84	.197	.311
vs. AL	4.31	9	7	3	153	0	131.2	126	20	67	95	Behind in Count	.320	150	48	9	1	6	32	38	0	.458	.513
vs. NL	3.43	1	2	0	23	0	21.0	13	2	10	14	Two Strikes	.190	263	50	6	2	10	37	34	109	.282	.342
Pre-All Star	3.69	6	5	3	101	0	83.0	76	10	39	61	Pre-All Star	.245	310	76	13	3	10	49	39	61	.336	.403
Post-All Star	4.78	4	4	0	75	0	69.2	63	12	38	48	Post-All Star	.243	259	63	6	3	12	49	38	48	.334	.429

Pitcher vs. Batter (career)

Pitches Best Vs.	Avg	AB	H	2B	3B	HR	RBI	BB	SO	OBP	SLG	Pitches Worst Vs.	Avg	AB	H	2B	3B	HR	RBI	BB	SO	OBP	SLG
Darryl Hamilton	.111	9	1	0	0	0	0	2	2	.273	.111												

Tilson Brito — Athletics   Age 26 – Bats Right

	Avg	G	AB	R	H	2B	3B	HR	RBI	BB	SO	HBP	GDP	SB	CS	OBP	SLG	IBB	SH	SF	#Pit	#P/PA	GB	FB	G/F
1997 Season	.238	66	172	17	41	5	1	2	14	10	38	2	2	1	0	.285	.314	0	2	2	685	3.64	60	49	1.22
Career (1996-1997)	.238	92	252	27	60	12	1	3	21	20	56	5	2	2	1	.305	.329	0	4	2	1035	3.66	85	70	1.21

1997 Season

	Avg	AB	H	2B	3B	HR	RBI	BB	SO	OBP	SLG		Avg	AB	H	2B	3B	HR	RBI	BB	SO	OBP	SLG
vs. Left	.296	54	16	3	0	0	2	2	10	.333	.352	Scoring Posn	.273	44	12	0	0	1	12	3	7	.320	.341
vs. Right	.212	118	25	2	1	2	12	8	28	.264	.297	Close & Late	.318	22	7	0	0	0	1	4	2	.423	.318
Home	.242	66	16	4	0	2	7	7	8	.320	.394	None on/out	.289	38	11	0	0	1	1	4	7	.357	.368
Away	.236	106	25	1	1	0	7	3	30	.261	.264	Batting #8	.162	68	11	0	0	1	5	5	15	.230	.206
First Pitch	.391	23	9	1	1	1	4	0	0	.400	.652	Batting #9	.292	72	21	3	1	1	5	4	15	.333	.403
Ahead in Count	.297	37	11	2	0	1	7	0	0	.409	.351	Other	.281	32	9	2	0	0	4	1	8	.294	.344
Behind in Count	.147	75	11	1	0	1	5	0	32	.156	.200	Pre-All Star	.282	85	24	3	0	0	6	7	17	.340	.318
Two Strikes	.120	83	10	1	0	1	5	3	38	.161	.169	Post-All Star	.195	87	17	2	1	2	8	3	21	.228	.310

Doug Brocail — Tigers   Age 31 – Pitches Right

	ERA	W	L	Sv	G	GS	IP	BB	SO	Avg	H	2B	3B	HR	RBI	OBP	SLG	GF	IR	IRS	Hld	SvOp	SB	CS	GB	FB	G/F
1997 Season	3.23	3	4	2	61	0	78.0	36	60	.256	74	10	1	10	41	.341	.401	20	30	13	16	9	6	4	102	74	1.38
Last Five Years	4.25	14	26	3	156	39	353.2	128	214	.278	383	66	10	44	194	.343	.437	40	68	33	17	11	32	12	513	387	1.33

1997 Season

	ERA	W	L	Sv	G	GS	IP	H	HR	BB	SO		Avg	AB	H	2B	3B	HR	RBI	BB	SO	OBP	SLG
Home	2.45	2	0	0	32	0	40.1	30	4	19	28	vs. Left	.275	131	36	5	0	3	15	18	26	.364	.382
Away	4.06	1	4	2	29	0	37.2	44	6	17	32	vs. Right	.241	158	38	5	1	7	26	18	34	.322	.418
Day	4.36	1	2	1	20	3	33.0	31	5	17	23	Inning 1-6	.302	86	26	4	1	2	12	14	11	.408	.442
Night	2.40	2	2	1	41	1	45.0	43	5	19	37	Inning 7+	.236	203	48	6	0	8	29	22	49	.311	.384

62

1997 Season

	ERA	W	L	Sv	G	GS	IP	H	HR	BB	SO		Avg	AB	H	2B	3B	HR	RBI	BB	SO	OBP	SLG
Grass	3.29	3	4	2	54	3	65.2	62	9	34	50	None on	.202	163	33	3	1	5	5	18	38	.290	.325
Turf	2.92	0	0	0	7	1	12.1	12	1	2	10	Runners on	.325	126	41	7	0	5	36	18	22	.405	.500
March/April	5.64	0	2	0	6	4	22.1	27	2	13	10	Scoring Posn	.310	71	22	5	0	1	28	15	15	.422	.423
May	11.81	0	2	1	7	0	5.1	9	3	5	5	Close & Late	.262	126	33	4	0	6	19	15	33	.336	.437
June	1.86	1	0	1	10	0	9.2	10	2	1	2	None on/out	.243	70	17	1	1	3	3	6	17	.303	.414
July	0.63	1	0	0	13	0	14.1	9	0	6	16	vs. 1st Batr (relief)	.222	54	12	2	0	4	13	2	12	.246	.481
August	0.57	1	0	0	13	0	15.2	10	1	5	13	1st Inning Pitched	.251	183	46	4	0	8	30	19	45	.325	.404
Sept/Oct	2.53	0	0	0	12	0	10.2	9	2	6	14	First 15 Pitches	.252	155	39	4	0	8	26	15	36	.318	.432
Starter	5.48	0	1	0	4	4	21.1	26	2	13	10	Pitch 16-30	.262	61	16	2	0	1	4	10	15	.375	.344
Reliever	2.38	3	3	2	57	0	56.2	48	8	23	50	Pitch 31-45	.087	23	2	0	0	0	2	5	3	.250	.087
0 Days rest (Relief)	1.10	2	0	2	17	0	16.1	14	2	5	13	Pitch 46+	.340	50	17	4	1	1	9	6	6	.414	.520
1 or 2 Days rest	2.08	0	0	0	24	0	26.0	18	3	11	28	First Pitch	.290	31	9	2	0	1	6	2	0	.353	.452
3+ Days rest	4.40	1	3	0	16	0	14.1	16	3	7	9	Ahead in Count	.152	138	21	3	1	3	11	0	50	.150	.254
vs. AL	3.30	3	4	2	55	4	73.2	70	10	36	57	Behind in Count	.410	61	25	3	0	4	17	20	0	.549	.656
vs. NL	2.08	0	0	0	6	0	4.1	4	0	0	3	Two Strikes	.150	147	22	4	1	4	12	14	60	.222	.272
Pre-All Star	5.27	1	4	2	25	4	41.0	48	7	20	21	Pre-All Star	.302	159	48	7	1	7	26	20	21	.386	.491
Post-All Star	0.97	2	0	0	36	0	37.0	26	3	16	39	Post-All Star	.200	130	26	3	0	3	15	16	39	.286	.292

Last Five Years

	ERA	W	L	Sv	G	GS	IP	H	HR	BB	SO		Avg	AB	H	2B	3B	HR	RBI	BB	SO	OBP	SLG
Home	3.84	9	7	0	81	18	180.2	173	17	61	114	vs. Left	.307	613	188	30	5	20	90	74	85	.383	.470
Away	4.68	5	19	3	75	21	173.0	210	27	67	100	vs. Right	.256	763	195	36	5	24	104	54	129	.310	.410
Day	4.71	5	13	1	53	14	122.1	142	16	51	77	Inning 1-6	.290	954	277	47	7	31	141	87	130	.353	.452
Night	4.01	9	13	2	103	25	231.1	241	28	77	137	Inning 7+	.251	422	106	19	3	13	53	41	84	.321	.403
Grass	4.87	6	22	3	99	25	216.1	251	28	89	128	None on	.260	778	202	37	4	28	28	61	126	.319	.425
Turf	3.28	8	4	0	57	14	137.1	132	16	39	86	Runners on	.303	598	181	29	6	16	166	67	88	.372	.452
March/April	4.78	2	4	0	16	6	52.2	54	6	25	35	Scoring Posn	.278	349	97	15	5	9	144	51	55	.369	.427
May	4.95	0	3	1	13	2	20.0	26	6	7	13	Close & Late	.263	224	59	11	1	8	30	27	51	.341	.429
June	3.90	3	3	2	24	7	64.2	70	11	12	37	None on/out	.261	337	88	17	2	11	11	24	53	.310	.421
July	4.06	3	5	0	37	6	68.2	75	5	25	43	vs. 1st Batr (relief)	.206	107	22	4	0	7	24	7	22	.256	.439
August	4.35	3	6	0	35	10	80.2	87	7	31	45	1st Inning Pitched	.269	532	143	21	4	18	89	50	93	.335	.425
Sept/Oct	4.03	3	5	0	31	8	67.0	71	9	28	41	First 15 Pitches	.271	468	127	23	4	18	76	36	75	.326	.453
Starter	4.75	6	19	0	39	39	210.1	230	27	75	112	Pitch 16-30	.291	292	85	15	0	9	28	31	46	.362	.435
Reliever	3.52	8	7	3	117	0	143.1	153	17	53	102	Pitch 31-45	.234	197	46	4	1	2	18	17	32	.295	.294
0 Days rest (Relief)	4.50	3	2	2	29	0	28.0	32	4	7	17	Pitch 46+	.298	419	125	24	5	15	72	44	61	.370	.487
1 or 2 Days rest	2.96	3	2	1	48	0	67.0	59	7	29	54	First Pitch	.356	222	79	9	2	11	47	8	0	.380	.563
3+ Days rest	3.72	2	3	0	40	0	48.1	62	6	17	31	Ahead in Count	.194	582	113	18	2	11	53	0	177	.200	.289
vs. AL	3.30	3	4	2	55	4	73.2	70	10	36	57	Behind in Count	.394	320	126	31	4	17	72	70	0	.501	.675
vs. NL	4.50	11	22	1	101	35	280.0	313	34	92	157	Two Strikes	.172	581	100	14	3	11	50	50	214	.242	.263
Pre-All Star	4.47	6	11	3	66	18	165.0	186	24	53	100	Pre-All Star	.289	644	186	30	5	24	99	53	100	.347	.463
Post-All Star	4.05	8	15	0	90	21	188.2	197	20	75	114	Post-All Star	.269	732	197	36	5	20	95	75	114	.339	.414

Pitcher vs. Batter (career)

Pitches Best Vs.	Avg	AB	H	2B	3B	HR	RBI	BB	SO	OBP	SLG	Pitches Worst Vs.	Avg	AB	H	2B	3B	HR	RBI	BB	SO	OBP	SLG
Marquis Grissom	.154	13	2	0	0	0	1	0	1	.154	.154	Willie McGee	.583	12	7	1	0	0	1	0	1	.583	.667
Moises Alou	.167	12	2	0	0	0	0	0	3	.167	.167	Kevin Stocker	.500	10	5	2	0	0	1	0	1	.545	.700
Charlie Hayes	.200	10	2	2	0	0	0	2	0	.333	.400	Henry Rodriguez	.400	10	4	1	0	2	4	0	2	.364	1.100
Steve Finley	.231	13	3	1	0	0	1	1	0	.286	.308	Will Clark	.375	8	3	1	0	1	6	4	1	.538	.875
Terry Pendleton	.235	17	4	1	0	1	3	1	3	.278	.471	Mike Piazza	.364	11	4	2	0	2	5	2	3	.462	1.091

Chris Brock — Braves
Age 28 – Pitches Right (groundball pitcher)

	ERA	W	L	Sv	G	GS	IP	BB	SO	Avg	H	2B	3B	HR	RBI	OBP	SLG	CG	ShO	Sup	QS	#P/S	SB	CS	GB	FB	G/F
1997 Season	5.58	0	0	0	7	6	30.2	19	16	.288	34	8	2	2	21	.376	.441	0	0	4.99	0	87	3	2	47	30	1.57

1997 Season

	ERA	W	L	Sv	G	GS	IP	H	HR	BB	SO		Avg	AB	H	2B	3B	HR	RBI	BB	SO	OBP	SLG
Home	7.20	0	0	0	3	2	10.0	12	1	8	6	vs. Left	.268	71	19	6	1	1	10	15	8	.391	.423
Away	4.79	0	0	0	4	4	20.2	22	1	11	10	vs. Right	.319	47	15	2	1	1	11	4	8	.352	.468

Rico Brogna — Phillies
Age 28 – Bats Left

	Avg	G	AB	R	H	2B	3B	HR	RBI	BB	SO	HBP	GDP	SB	CS	OBP	SLG	IBB	SH	SF	#Pit	#P/PA	GB	FB	G/F
1997 Season	.252	148	543	68	137	36	1	20	81	33	116	0	13	12	3	.293	.433	4	0	4	2133	3.68	179	154	1.16
Last Five Years	.276	376	1357	174	374	84	6	56	207	97	306	2	29	13	3	.323	.470	12	3	10	5404	3.68	432	379	1.14

1997 Season

	Avg	AB	H	2B	3B	HR	RBI	BB	SO	OBP	SLG		Avg	AB	H	2B	3B	HR	RBI	BB	SO	OBP	SLG
vs. Left	.190	116	22	4	0	1	11	6	30	.228	.250	First Pitch	.333	75	25	9	0	1	16	4	0	.358	.493
vs. Right	.269	427	115	32	1	19	70	27	86	.311	.482	Ahead in Count	.368	117	43	11	0	7	26	18	0	.452	.641
Groundball	.284	81	23	8	0	3	18	8	19	.348	.494	Behind in Count	.196	265	52	10	1	9	28	0	104	.195	.343
Flyball	.283	92	26	9	0	4	12	6	24	.323	.511	Two Strikes	.164	256	42	5	1	11	31	11	116	.198	.320
Home	.254	252	64	14	0	9	38	20	56	.308	.417	Batting #5	.261	249	65	15	1	9	37	14	57	.298	.438
Away	.251	291	73	22	1	11	43	13	60	.280	.447	Batting #6	.247	150	37	11	0	9	27	7	30	.278	.500
Day	.245	163	40	13	0	2	17	8	35	.279	.362	Other	.243	144	35	10	0	2	17	12	29	.299	.354
Night	.255	380	97	23	1	18	64	25	81	.299	.463	March/April	.247	85	21	8	0	1	12	8	16	.305	.376
Grass	.238	202	48	14	1	6	30	11	41	.273	.406	May	.282	103	29	9	0	7	19	4	18	.308	.573
Turf	.261	341	89	22	0	14	51	22	75	.305	.449	June	.231	91	21	7	1	0	8	4	25	.260	.330

	Avg	AB	H	2B	3B	HR	RBI	BB	SO	OBP	SLG		Avg	AB	H	2B	3B	HR	RBI	BB	SO	OBP	SLG
Pre-All Star	.258	298	77	24	1	9	44	18	65	.298	.436	July	.205	88	18	1	0	5	18	6	22	.253	.386
Post-All Star	.245	245	60	12	0	11	37	15	51	.287	.429	August	.256	90	23	5	0	3	15	8	21	.316	.411
Scoring Posn	.278	158	44	11	0	7	63	15	32	.333	.481	Sept/Oct	.291	86	25	6	0	4	9	3	14	.315	.500
Close & Late	.286	77	22	6	0	5	13	3	15	.309	.558	vs. AL	.200	55	11	2	1	0	5	3	14	.237	.273
None on/out	.314	118	37	10	0	7	7	6	25	.347	.576	vs. NL	.258	488	126	34	0	20	76	30	102	.299	.451

1997 By Position

Position	Avg	AB	H	2B	3B	HR	RBI	BB	SO	OBP	SLG	G	GS	Innings	PO	A	E	DP	Fld Pct	Rng Fctr	In Zone	Outs	Zone Rtg	MLB Zone
As 1b	.256	536	137	36	1	20	81	33	114	.297	.438	145	137	1200.0	1054	117	7	102	.994	---	234	202	.863	.874

Last Five Years

	Avg	AB	H	2B	3B	HR	RBI	BB	SO	OBP	SLG		Avg	AB	H	2B	3B	HR	RBI	BB	SO	OBP	SLG
vs. Left	.216	292	63	15	0	3	30	16	87	.257	.298	First Pitch	.375	192	72	20	0	5	36	10	0	.402	.557
vs. Right	.292	1065	311	69	6	53	177	81	219	.340	.517	Ahead in Count	.349	284	99	23	0	17	59	49	0	.444	.609
Groundball	.298	322	96	24	3	13	50	35	67	.365	.512	Behind in Count	.202	635	128	21	4	24	74	0	270	.202	.361
Flyball	.284	211	60	16	0	9	28	14	63	.330	.488	Two Strikes	.185	627	116	19	4	24	68	38	306	.232	.343
Home	.287	635	182	35	4	29	102	52	148	.340	.491	Batting #3	.276	370	102	20	0	10	56	30	83	.328	.411
Away	.266	722	192	49	2	27	105	45	158	.307	.452	Batting #5	.288	507	146	30	4	25	83	40	111	.339	.511
Day	.284	401	114	27	1	13	58	30	90	.331	.454	Other	.263	480	126	34	2	21	68	27	112	.300	.473
Night	.272	956	260	57	5	43	149	67	216	.319	.477	March/April	.285	186	53	19	0	5	30	19	40	.344	.468
Grass	.269	849	228	46	5	37	127	68	193	.321	.465	May	.258	260	67	15	1	15	47	19	60	.306	.496
Turf	.287	508	146	38	1	19	80	29	113	.325	.478	June	.264	242	64	12	2	6	25	12	68	.300	.405
Pre-All Star	.265	766	203	50	3	30	113	56	184	.313	.456	July	.298	265	79	18	1	12	46	18	52	.340	.509
Post-All Star	.289	591	171	34	3	26	94	41	122	.335	.489	August	.267	221	59	9	2	8	29	17	50	.319	.434
Scoring Posn	.278	363	101	23	2	12	146	40	75	.341	.452	Sept/Oct	.284	183	52	11	0	10	30	12	36	.332	.508
Close & Late	.300	237	71	13	1	15	46	21	59	.334	.553	vs. AL	.200	55	11	2	1	0	5	3	14	.237	.273
None on/out	.299	301	90	23	0	17	17	17	65	.339	.545	vs. NL	.279	1302	363	82	5	56	202	94	292	.326	.478

Batter vs. Pitcher (career)

Hits Best Against	Avg	AB	H	2B	3B	HR	RBI	BB	SO	OBP	SLG	Hits Worst Against	Avg	AB	H	2B	3B	HR	RBI	BB	SO	OBP	SLG
John Smoltz	.500	14	7	3	0	0	2	4	2	.611	.714	Armando Reynoso	.000	13	0	0	0	0	0	0	1	.000	.000
Kevin Ritz	.500	10	5	1	0	1	5	4	2	.600	.900	Frank Castillo	.100	20	2	0	0	0	2	0	1	.100	.100
Bobby Witt	.400	10	4	0	1	0	1	3	3	.538	.600	Hideo Nomo	.136	22	3	0	0	0	1	1	6	.174	.136
Darryl Kile	.333	12	4	0	0	2	3	1	2	.385	.833	F. Valenzuela	.143	14	2	0	0	0	1	1	3	.200	.143
Ramon Martinez	.333	9	3	1	0	1	3	2	2	.417	.778	Mark Petkovsek	.231	13	3	0	0	0	2	0	1	.231	.231

Scott Brosius — Athletics

Age 31 – Bats Right (flyball hitter)

	Avg	G	AB	R	H	2B	3B	HR	RBI	BB	SO	HBP	GDP	SB	CS	OBP	SLG	IBB	SH	SF	#Pit	#P/PA	GB	FB	G/F
1997 Season	.203	129	479	59	97	20	1	11	41	34	102	4	9	9	4	.259	.317	1	5	4	2070	3.94	143	163	0.88
Last Five Years	.250	532	1833	258	459	88	5	70	232	172	348	22	38	28	14	.319	.418	5	14	21	7871	3.82	507	666	0.76

1997 Season

	Avg	AB	H	2B	3B	HR	RBI	BB	SO	OBP	SLG		Avg	AB	H	2B	3B	HR	RBI	BB	SO	OBP	SLG
vs. Left	.160	125	20	3	0	2	8	8	32	.215	.232	First Pitch	.412	51	21	5	1	1	8	1	0	.444	.608
vs. Right	.218	354	77	17	1	9	33	26	70	.275	.347	Ahead in Count	.220	91	20	3	0	4	17	17	0	.333	.385
Groundball	.212	113	24	4	1	1	12	8	32	.266	.292	Behind in Count	.156	250	39	11	0	2	9	0	84	.162	.224
Flyball	.200	75	15	2	0	2	4		14	.238	.307	Two Strikes	.145	255	37	8	0	2	9	16	102	.198	.200
Home	.247	219	54	9	1	7	17	18	40	.306	.393	Batting #7	.186	156	29	3	0	6	15	10	28	.238	.321
Away	.165	260	43	11	0	4	24	16	62	.219	.254	Batting #8	.272	125	34	11	0	2	11	6	29	.313	.408
Day	.208	202	42	9	0	6	21	16	42	.269	.342	Other	.172	198	34	6	1	3	15	18	45	.242	.258
Night	.199	277	55	11	1	5	20	18	60	.252	.300	March/April	.181	94	17	1	1	1	7	10	18	.264	.245
Grass	.200	431	86	16	1	10	39	32	91	.259	.311	May	.147	102	15	5	0	1	6	8	21	.207	.225
Turf	.229	48	11	4	0	1	2	2	11	.260	.375	June	.255	98	25	6	0	2	5	4	24	.291	.378
Pre-All Star	.209	320	67	13	1	5	24	22	65	.263	.303	July	.248	101	25	4	0	5	17	7	18	.297	.436
Post-All Star	.189	159	30	7	0	6	17	12	37	.251	.346	August	.182	33	6	2	0	1	1	2	10	.229	.333
Scoring Posn	.121	124	15	3	0	1	28	11	27	.187	.169	Sept/Oct	.176	51	9	2	0	1	5	3	11	.236	.275
Close & Late	.274	73	20	4	0	3	8	9	14	.354	.452	vs. AL	.194	417	81	17	1	10	35	33	88	.258	.312
None on/out	.239	117	28	6	1	5	5	8	22	.288	.436	vs. NL	.258	62	16	3	0	1	6	1	14	.270	.355

1997 By Position

Position	Avg	AB	H	2B	3B	HR	RBI	BB	SO	OBP	SLG	G	GS	Innings	PO	A	E	DP	Fld Pct	Rng Fctr	In Zone	Outs	Zone Rtg	MLB Zone
As 3b	.209	354	74	17	1	7	30	27	75	.269	.322	107	94	825.2	92	205	7	23	.977	3.24	276	243	.880	.801
As ss	.204	54	11	2	0	1	4	3	10	.246	.296	30	12	120.1	25	39	2	8	.970	4.79	45	42	.933	.937
As rf	.229	35	8	1	0	1	3	3	8	.282	.343	11	9	81.1	11	2	0	0	1.000	1.44	15	11	.733	.813

Last Five Years

	Avg	AB	H	2B	3B	HR	RBI	BB	SO	OBP	SLG		Avg	AB	H	2B	3B	HR	RBI	BB	SO	OBP	SLG
vs. Left	.232	538	125	26	2	19	67	57	112	.311	.394	First Pitch	.367	229	84	18	1	11	42	4	0	.388	.598
vs. Right	.258	1295	334	62	3	51	165	115	236	.322	.429	Ahead in Count	.295	370	109	23	2	24	69	87	0	.424	.562
Groundball	.272	448	122	18	1	18	68	30	81	.321	.438	Behind in Count	.198	888	176	32	2	19	78	0	293	.207	.303
Flyball	.245	323	79	15	0	13	39	29	62	.309	.412	Two Strikes	.183	890	163	32	0	22	81	81	348	.254	.293
Home	.265	890	236	39	2	46	118	86	152	.334	.469	Batting #7	.222	571	127	17	2	25	67	60	103	.301	.391
Away	.236	943	223	49	3	24	114	86	196	.305	.371	Batting #8	.282	397	112	23	2	14	63	25	70	.325	.456
Day	.258	755	195	35	1	33	98	74	131	.331	.438	Other	.254	865	220	48	1	31	102	87	175	.328	.420
Night	.245	1078	264	53	4	37	134	98	217	.311	.404	March/April	.253	296	75	8	1	12	44	40	51	.343	.449
Grass	.251	1599	402	73	5	67	204	150	297	.319	.429	May	.218	285	62	19	3	4	23	29	45	.292	.347
Turf	.244	234	57	15	0	3	28	22	51	.315	.346	June	.221	276	61	10	0	11	22	26	63	.294	.377

Last Five Years

	Avg	AB	H	2B	3B	HR	RBI	BB	SO	OBP	SLG		Avg	AB	H	2B	3B	HR	RBI	BB	SO	OBP	SLG
Pre-All Star	.235	962	226	42	4	31	107	103	173	.312	.384	July	.273	363	99	21	0	20	60	32	68	.333	.496
Post-All Star	.268	871	233	46	1	39	125	69	175	.327	.457	August	.284	320	91	15	1	18	51	18	70	.331	.506
Scoring Posn	.240	466	112	19	0	15	164	57	85	.316	.378	Sept/Oct	.242	293	71	15	0	5	32	27	51	.312	.345
Close & Late	.284	264	75	18	1	10	32	35	50	.373	.473	vs. AL	.250	1771	443	85	5	69	226	171	334	.320	.421
None on/out	.261	433	113	21	4	20	20	30	69	.315	.467	vs. NL	.258	62	16	3	0	1	6	1	14	.270	.355

Batter vs. Pitcher (career)

Hits Best Against	Avg	AB	H	2B	3B	HR	RBI	BB	SO	OBP	SLG	Hits Worst Against	Avg	AB	H	2B	3B	HR	RBI	BB	SO	OBP	SLG
Darren Oliver	.444	9	4	0	0	1	3	2	4	.545	.778	James Baldwin	.000	11	0	0	0	0	0	0	3	.000	.000
Roger Pavlik	.412	17	7	0	0	2	2	5	4	.545	.765	Roger Clemens	.071	14	1	0	0	0	0	1	5	.133	.071
Kenny Rogers	.409	22	9	1	0	2	4	0	4	.435	.727	Bob Wolcott	.083	12	1	0	0	0	0	1	4	.154	.083
Chris Haney	.364	11	4	1	2	0	0	1	0	.417	.818	Troy Percival	.091	11	1	0	0	0	0	1	5	.167	.091
Erik Hanson	.360	25	9	2	0	3	4	1	5	.385	.800	Cal Eldred	.125	16	2	0	0	0	0	0	1	.125	.125

Adrian Brown — Pirates   Age 24 – Bats Both

	Avg	G	AB	R	H	2B	3B	HR	RBI	BB	SO	HBP	GDP	SB	CS	OBP	SLG	IBB	SH	SF	#Pit	#P/PA	GB	FB	G/F
1997 Season	.190	48	147	17	28	6	0	1	10	13	18	4	3	8	4	.273	.252	0	2	1	570	3.41	90	17	5.29

1997 Season

	Avg	AB	H	2B	3B	HR	RBI	BB	SO	OBP	SLG		Avg	AB	H	2B	3B	HR	RBI	BB	SO	OBP	SLG
vs. Left	.296	27	8	0	0	1	4	3	4	.367	.407	Scoring Posn	.121	33	4	0	0	1	9	3	4	.231	.212
vs. Right	.167	120	20	6	0	0	6	10	14	.252	.217	Close & Late	.263	19	5	0	0	1	3	1	5	.333	.421
Home	.174	69	12	2	0	0	5	7	10	.284	.203	None on/out	.138	29	4	0	0	0	0	6	5	.286	.138
Away	.205	78	16	4	0	1	5	6	8	.262	.295	Batting #1	.143	14	2	1	0	1	3	3	1	.294	.429
First Pitch	.250	16	4	1	0	0	1	0	0	.294	.313	Batting #2	.200	125	25	5	0	0	7	8	16	.263	.240
Ahead in Count	.294	34	10	2	0	1	6	9	0	.442	.441	Other	.125	8	1	0	0	0	0	2	1	.364	.125
Behind in Count	.145	69	10	2	0	0	2	0	15	.181	.174	Pre-All Star	.195	133	26	6	0	1	10	10	16	.265	.263
Two Strikes	.175	57	10	2	0	0	2	4	18	.254	.211	Post-All Star	.143	14	2	0	0	0	0	3	2	.333	.143

Brant Brown — Cubs   Age 27 – Bats Left

	Avg	G	AB	R	H	2B	3B	HR	RBI	BB	SO	HBP	GDP	SB	CS	OBP	SLG	IBB	SH	SF	#Pit	#P/PA	GB	FB	G/F
1997 Season	.234	46	137	15	32	7	1	5	15	7	28	3	2	2	1	.286	.409	0	1	0	524	3.54	39	46	0.85
Career (1996-1997)	.257	75	206	26	53	8	1	10	24	9	45	4	3	5	4	.300	.451	1	1	1	780	3.53	59	62	0.95

1997 Season

	Avg	AB	H	2B	3B	HR	RBI	BB	SO	OBP	SLG		Avg	AB	H	2B	3B	HR	RBI	BB	SO	OBP	SLG
vs. Left	.118	17	2	0	0	0	1	1	0	.211	.118	Scoring Posn	.250	24	6	3	0	1	10	1	3	.308	.500
vs. Right	.250	120	30	7	1	5	14	6	28	.297	.450	Close & Late	.176	17	3	2	0	0	3	2	4	.300	.294
Home	.241	58	14	4	0	3	5	2	11	.279	.466	None on/out	.292	24	7	1	0	0	1	2	3	.370	.458
Away	.228	79	18	3	1	2	10	5	17	.291	.367	Batting #2	.239	92	22	5	1	4	9	3	17	.278	.446
First Pitch	.318	22	7	0	0	1	2	0	0	.348	.455	Batting #7	.200	20	4	1	0	1	4	1	2	.238	.400
Ahead in Count	.333	27	9	2	0	1	2	6	0	.455	.519	Other	.240	25	6	1	0	0	2	3	9	.345	.280
Behind in Count	.191	68	13	5	1	1	8	0	25	.214	.338	Pre-All Star	.218	119	26	5	1	4	13	6	23	.273	.378
Two Strikes	.164	67	11	3	1	2	7	1	28	.200	.328	Post-All Star	.333	18	6	2	0	1	2	1	5	.368	.611

Emil Brown — Pirates   Age 23 – Bats Right

	Avg	G	AB	R	H	2B	3B	HR	RBI	BB	SO	HBP	GDP	SB	CS	OBP	SLG	IBB	SH	SF	#Pit	#P/PA	GB	FB	G/F
1997 Season	.179	66	95	16	17	2	1	2	6	10	32	7	1	5	1	.304	.284	1	0	0	439	3.92	32	20	1.60

1997 Season

	Avg	AB	H	2B	3B	HR	RBI	BB	SO	OBP	SLG		Avg	AB	H	2B	3B	HR	RBI	BB	SO	OBP	SLG
vs. Left	.184	38	7	1	0	2	4	5	11	.326	.368	Scoring Posn	.045	22	1	0	0	0	2	3	9	.276	.045
vs. Right	.175	57	10	1	1	0	2	5	21	.288	.228	Close & Late	.286	14	4	0	0	0	2	5		.444	.286

Kevin Brown — Marlins   Age 33 – Pitches Right (groundball pitcher)

	ERA	W	L	Sv	G	GS	IP	BB	SO	Avg	H	2B	3B	HR	RBI	OBP	SLG	CG	ShO	Sup	QS	#P/S	SB	CS	GB	FB	G/F
1997 Season	2.69	16	8	0	33	33	237.1	66	205	.240	214	28	6	10	71	.303	.319	6	2	4.36	27	108	19	4	441	121	3.64
Last Five Years	3.21	65	49	0	151	150	1045.2	271	746	.252	1002	143	29	60	356	.308	.348	29	9	4.33	98	106	55	35	1967	668	2.94

1997 Season

	ERA	W	L	Sv	G	GS	IP	H	HR	BB	SO		Avg	AB	H	2B	3B	HR	RBI	BB	SO	OBP	SLG
Home	2.51	8	4	0	17	17	125.1	104	5	38	109	vs. Left	.244	426	104	16	3	4	34	48	76	.328	.324
Away	2.89	8	4	0	16	16	112.0	110	5	28	96	vs. Right	.237	464	110	12	3	6	37	18	129	.278	.315
Day	3.17	7	5	0	16	16	113.2	106	4	32	91	Inning 1-6	.249	738	184	21	4	8	62	57	175	.312	.321
Night	2.26	9	3	0	17	17	123.2	108	6	34	114	Inning 7+	.197	152	30	7	2	2	9	9	30	.256	.309
Grass	2.89	14	7	0	28	28	202.1	185	9	61	165	None on	.231	527	122	19	4	4		35	118	.286	.306
Turf	1.54	2	1	0	5	5	35.0	29	1	5	40	Runners on	.253	363	92	9	2	6	67	31	87	.327	.339
March/April	1.96	3	1	0	6	6	41.1	32	0	15	34	Scoring Posn	.269	201	54	4	2	4	62	17	51	.342	.368
May	3.43	2	2	0	6	6	42.0	45	2	7	47	Close & Late	.136	66	9	3	1	0	2	7	15	.240	.212
June	2.61	2	2	0	5	5	38.0	32	2	7	31	None on/out	.230	226	52	5	2	2		16	44	.284	.296
July	4.96	2	3	0	5	5	32.2	33	3	14	30	vs. 1st Batr (relief)	.000	0	0	0	0	0	0	0	0	.000	.000
August	1.40	3	0	0	6	6	45.0	33	0	13	37	1st Inning Pitched	.205	122	25	2	1	1	9	14	30	.297	.262
Sept/Oct	2.35	4	0	0	5	5	38.1	39	3	10	26	First 75 Pitches	.257	592	152	20	2	6	45	43	142	.316	.328
Starter	2.69	16	8	0	33	33	237.1	214	10	66	205	Pitch 76-90	.195	123	24	1	3	2	13	13	28	.288	.301
Reliever	0.00	0	0	0	0	0	0.0	0	0	0	0	Pitch 91-105	.157	102	16	3	0	0	3	7	24	.225	.186

1997 Season

	ERA	W	L	Sv	G	GS	IP	H	HR	BB	SO		Avg	AB	H	2B	3B	HR	RBI	BB	SO	OBP	SLG
0-3 Days Rest (Start)	0.00	0	0	0	0	0	0.0	0	0	0	0	Pitch 106+	.301	73	22	4	1	2	10	3	11	.329	.466
4 Days Rest	2.31	10	4	0	20	20	148.0	126	5	42	131	First Pitch	.306	134	41	6	0	1	12	7	0	.359	.373
5+ Days Rest	3.32	6	4	0	13	13	89.1	88	5	24	74	Ahead in Count	.202	435	88	14	3	5	31	0	180	.220	.283
vs. AL	2.78	2	0	0	3	3	22.2	22	3	7	15	Behind in Count	.299	164	49	5	1	2	14	27	0	.398	.378
vs. NL	2.68	14	8	0	30	30	214.2	192	7	59	190	Two Strikes	.165	419	69	12	3	6	31	32	205	.232	.251
Pre-All Star	2.67	8	5	0	18	18	128.0	117	5	32	116	Pre-All Star	.241	486	117	17	5	5	38	32	116	.302	.327
Post-All Star	2.72	8	3	0	15	15	109.1	97	5	34	89	Post-All Star	.240	404	97	11	1	5	33	34	89	.303	.309

Last Five Years

	ERA	W	L	Sv	G	GS	IP	H	HR	BB	SO		Avg	AB	H	2B	3B	HR	RBI	BB	SO	OBP	SLG
Home	2.74	40	23	0	81	80	579.0	509	30	134	429	vs. Left	.259	2092	541	79	18	30	189	177	329	.320	.357
Away	3.80	25	26	0	70	70	466.2	493	30	137	317	vs. Right	.244	1887	461	64	11	30	167	94	417	.294	.338
Day	3.45	18	15	0	42	42	289.1	287	19	75	197	Inning 1-6	.255	3213	819	112	23	45	297	220	605	.311	.346
Night	3.12	47	34	0	109	108	756.1	715	41	196	549	Inning 7+	.239	766	183	31	6	15	59	51	141	.294	.354
Grass	3.16	58	41	0	131	130	915.2	862	55	249	641	None on	.245	2403	589	94	19	30	30	139	460	.294	.337
Turf	3.53	7	8	0	20	20	130.0	140	5	22	105	Runners on	.262	1576	413	49	10	30	326	132	286	.329	.363
March/April	3.63	9	9	0	23	23	161.0	178	11	38	108	Scoring Posn	.249	862	215	25	7	17	285	79	174	.326	.354
May	2.99	11	10	0	28	27	198.2	185	14	36	156	Close & Late	.232	380	88	20	3	5	32	29	59	.296	.339
June	3.51	10	11	0	25	25	171.2	171	10	47	118	Behind in Count	.234	1040	243	39	9	13	43	49	199	.274	.326
July	3.99	8	9	0	26	26	167.0	160	10	59	124	vs. 1st Batr (relief)	.000	1	0	0	0	0	0	0	0	.000	.000
August	3.08	11	7	0	26	26	181.0	170	7	50	134	1st Inning Pitched	.254	570	145	16	3	5	53	52	107	.326	.319
Sept/Oct	2.11	16	3	0	23	23	166.1	138	8	41	106	First 75 Pitches	.253	2660	674	91	20	34	231	173	494	.308	.341
Starter	3.19	65	48	0	150	150	1043.2	999	60	270	744	Pitch 76-90	.252	532	134	18	4	13	52	36	100	.307	.374
Reliever	13.50	0	1	0	1	0	2.0	3	0	1	2	Pitch 91-105	.240	445	107	18	2	4	35	30	83	.302	.317
0-3 Days Rest (Start)	3.21	4	3	0	9	9	61.2	62	4	18	45	Pitch 106+	.254	342	87	16	3	9	38	32	69	.319	.398
4 Days Rest	3.10	40	28	0	93	93	659.1	628	34	168	485	First Pitch	.324	580	188	26	5	5	66	14	0	.351	.412
5+ Days Rest	3.38	21	17	0	48	48	322.2	309	22	84	214	Ahead in Count	.193	1837	354	54	9	19	121	0	647	.205	.263
vs. AL	3.91	34	30	0	89	88	598.0	623	45	179	397	Behind in Count	.323	852	275	38	11	19	103	126	0	.413	.460
vs. NL	2.27	31	19	0	62	62	447.2	379	15	92	349	Two Strikes	.165	1784	295	48	9	17	97	131	746	.230	.231
Pre-All Star	3.41	32	32	0	84	83	578.1	583	37	139	421	Pre-All Star	.261	2237	583	83	18	37	219	139	421	.313	.363
Post-All Star	2.97	33	17	0	67	67	467.1	419	23	132	325	Post-All Star	.241	1742	419	60	11	23	137	132	325	.302	.327

Pitcher vs. Batter (career)

Pitches Best Vs.	Avg	AB	H	2B	3B	HR	RBI	BB	SO	OBP	SLG	Pitches Worst Vs.	Avg	AB	H	2B	3B	HR	RBI	BB	SO	OBP	SLG
Kevin Stocker	.000	12	0	0	0	0	0	1	4	.143	.000	Eric Young	.600	10	6	1	1	0	1	1	0	.636	.900
Eric Davis	.000	11	0	0	0	0	0	1	5	.083	.000	Jason Kendall	.500	14	7	2	0	0	3	0	1	.533	.643
Charlie Hayes	.077	13	1	0	0	0	0	0	3	.077	.077	Joe Orsulak	.435	23	10	4	0	1	7	4	1	.519	.739
Tom Lampkin	.077	13	1	0	0	0	0	0	4	.077	.077	Bernard Gilkey	.417	12	5	1	0	2	4	2		.563	1.000
Jeff King	.091	11	1	0	0	0	0	0	4	.091	.091	Mike Stanley	.333	15	5	0	0	3	3	1	7	.375	.933

Kevin L. Brown — Rangers
Age 25 – Bats Right

	Avg	G	AB	R	H	2B	3B	HR	RBI	BB	SO	HBP	GDP	SB	CS	OBP	SLG	IBB	SH	SF	#Pit	#P/PA	GB	FB	G/F
1997 Season	.400	4	5	1	2	0	0	1	1	0	0	0	0	0	0	.400	1.000	0	0	0	14	2.80	0	4	0.00
Career (1996-1997)	.222	7	9	2	2	0	0	1	2	2	2	1	0	0	0	.385	.556	0	0	1	50	3.85	1	5	0.20

1997 Season

	Avg	AB	H	2B	3B	HR	RBI	BB	SO	OBP	SLG		Avg	AB	H	2B	3B	HR	RBI	BB	SO	OBP	SLG
vs. Left	.250	4	1	0	0	0	0	0	0	.250	.250	Scoring Posn	.000	3	0	0	0	0	0	0	0	.000	.000
vs. Right	1.000	1	1	0	0	1	1	0	0	1.000	4.000	Close & Late	.000	1	0	0	0	0	0	0	0	.000	.000

Jacob Brumfield — Blue Jays
Age 33 – Bats Right (flyball hitter)

	Avg	G	AB	R	H	2B	3B	HR	RBI	BB	SO	HBP	GDP	SB	CS	OBP	SLG	IBB	SH	SF	#Pit	#P/PA	GB	FB	G/F
1997 Season	.207	58	174	22	36	5	1	2	20	14	31	1	4	4	4	.268	.282	0	1	1	694	3.63	64	56	1.14
Last Five Years	.261	464	1358	225	355	83	10	30	140	116	242	11	25	67	31	.322	.404	6	7	10	5556	3.70	488	409	1.19

1997 Season

	Avg	AB	H	2B	3B	HR	RBI	BB	SO	OBP	SLG		Avg	AB	H	2B	3B	HR	RBI	BB	SO	OBP	SLG
vs. Left	.245	94	23	4	1	1	9	5	11	.283	.340	Scoring Posn	.250	48	12	3	0	1	18	5	8	.315	.375
vs. Right	.163	80	13	1	0	1	11	9	20	.253	.213	Close & Late	.172	29	5	0	0	0	3	3	12	.250	.172
Home	.200	55	11	2	0	1	8	7	12	.297	.291	None on/out	.136	44	6	0	0	0	0	4	7	.224	.136
Away	.210	119	25	3	1	1	12	7	19	.254	.277	Batting #1	.225	80	18	2	1	1	12	8	12	.295	.313
First Pitch	.303	33	10	1	0	0	4	0	0	.303	.333	Batting #2	.136	22	3	1	0	0	1	4	2	.269	.182
Ahead in Count	.268	41	11	1	1	1	10	3	0	.311	.415	Other	.208	72	15	2	0	1	7	2	17	.237	.278
Behind in Count	.153	72	11	2	0	1	5	0	24	.164	.222	Pre-All Star	.192	104	20	3	0	1	12	8	17	.254	.250
Two Strikes	.096	73	7	2	0	0	5	11	31	.224	.164	Post-All Star	.229	70	16	2	1	1	8	6	14	.289	.329

Last Five Years

	Avg	AB	H	2B	3B	HR	RBI	BB	SO	OBP	SLG		Avg	AB	H	2B	3B	HR	RBI	BB	SO	OBP	SLG
vs. Left	.284	543	154	37	4	12	54	32	73	.325	.433	First Pitch	.301	226	68	17	2	7	37	5	0	.319	.487
vs. Right	.247	815	201	46	6	18	86	84	169	.321	.384	Ahead in Count	.329	328	108	21	2	11	44	51	0	.418	.506
Groundball	.260	334	87	23	2	4	43	32	65	.329	.377	Behind in Count	.197	547	108	29	2	9	44	0	197	.205	.307
Flyball	.230	191	44	13	1	5	14	15	45	.291	.387	Two Strikes	.182	598	109	26	4	9	40	60	242	.259	.284
Home	.267	641	171	43	2	17	69	58	124	.331	.420	Batting #1	.269	806	217	50	6	16	69	70	128	.332	.406
Away	.257	717	184	40	8	13	71	58	118	.315	.389	Batting #2	.216	171	37	8	1	4	18	11	35	.265	.345
Day	.209	449	94	22	1	7	31	41	82	.278	.310	Other	.265	381	101	25	3	10	53	35	79	.327	.425
Night	.287	909	261	61	9	23	109	75	160	.344	.450	March/April	.263	95	25	7	0	3	12	5	19	.307	.432
Grass	.246	513	126	29	6	9	52	44	85	.306	.378	May	.224	196	44	11	2	2	15	18	38	.292	.332

Last Five Years

	Avg	AB	H	2B	3B	HR	RBI	BB	SO	OBP	SLG		Avg	AB	H	2B	3B	HR	RBI	BB	SO	OBP	SLG
Turf	.271	845	229	54	4	21	88	72	157	.332	.419	June	.227	220	50	11	0	6	28	28	36	.319	.359
Pre-All Star	.257	618	159	40	3	16	68	58	109	.325	.409	July	.300	313	94	23	5	8	31	30	58	.363	.482
Post-All Star	.265	740	196	43	7	14	72	58	133	.320	.399	August	.296	280	83	22	2	7	36	21	40	.350	.464
Scoring Posn	.284	296	84	17	3	9	109	42	64	.362	.453	Sept/Oct	.232	254	59	9	1	4	18	14	51	.272	.323
Close & Late	.247	243	60	15	2	6	25	25	67	.320	.399	vs. AL	.240	479	115	24	3	14	72	38	87	.300	.390
None on/out	.276	464	128	30	3	10	10	32	64	.329	.418	vs. NL	.273	879	240	59	7	16	68	78	155	.334	.411

Batter vs. Pitcher (career)

Hits Best Against	Avg	AB	H	2B	3B	HR	RBI	BB	SO	OBP	SLG	Hits Worst Against	Avg	AB	H	2B	3B	HR	RBI	BB	SO	OBP	SLG
Chuck Finley	.455	11	5	1	1	2	4	2	1	.571	1.273	Darren Oliver	.000	9	0	0	0	0	1	2	1	.182	.000
Kevin Foster	.444	9	4	3	0	0	0	1	1	.545	.778	John Burkett	.091	11	1	0	0	0	0	0	2	.091	.091
Mike Morgan	.364	11	4	1	0	0	0	1	1	.417	.455	Jaime Navarro	.100	10	1	0	0	0	0	1	3	.182	.100
Pete Schourek	.364	11	4	1	0	0	0	1	1	.417	.455	Scott Erickson	.100	10	1	0	0	0	0	1	3	.182	.100
Greg Swindell	.333	18	6	2	0	0	2	1	1	.350	.444	Danny Jackson	.125	16	2	0	1	0	3	0	3	.125	.250

Jim Bruske — Dodgers
Age 33 – Pitches Right

	ERA	W	L	Sv	G	GS	IP	BB	SO	Avg	H	2B	3B	HR	RBI	OBP	SLG	GF	IR	IRS	Hld	SvOp	SB	CS	GB	FB	G/F
1997 Season	3.63	4	1	0	28	0	44.2	25	32	.228	37	8	0	4	26	.330	.352	6	31	9	5	1	4	2	56	50	1.12
Career (1995-1997)	4.14	4	1	1	48	0	67.1	32	49	.258	66	12	1	6	43	.344	.383	14	46	16	5	2	5	2	101	68	1.49

1997 Season

	ERA	W	L	Sv	G	GS	IP	H	HR	BB	SO		Avg	AB	H	2B	3B	HR	RBI	BB	SO	OBP	SLG
Home	3.95	2	0	0	9	0	13.2	9	1	8	9	vs. Left	.214	84	18	3	0	2	15	16	13	.343	.321
Away	3.48	2	1	0	19	0	31.0	28	3	17	23	vs. Right	.244	78	19	5	0	2	11	9	19	.315	.385
Starter	0.00	0	0	0	0	0	0.0	0	0	0	0	Scoring Posn	.222	54	12	4	0	0	19	9	11	.318	.296
Reliever	3.63	4	1	0	28	0	44.2	37	4	25	32	Close & Late	.304	23	7	1	0	0	5	4	2	.414	.348
0 Days rest (Relief)	0.00	0	0	0	1	0	1.1	2	0	1	0	None on/out	.263	38	10	2	0	1	1	5	8	.349	.395
1 or 2 Days rest	4.76	3	1	0	19	0	28.1	24	4	19	21	First Pitch	.286	14	4	1	0	0	4	1	0	.294	.357
3+ Days rest	1.80	1	0	0	8	0	15.0	11	0	5	11	Ahead in Count	.134	67	9	1	0	2	7	0	30	.147	.239
Pre-All Star	3.86	1	0	0	5	0	14.0	10	1	6	15	Behind in Count	.270	37	10	1	0	2	7	11	0	.429	.459
Post-All Star	3.52	3	1	0	23	0	30.2	27	3	19	17	Two Strikes	.163	80	13	2	0	2	11	13	32	.287	.263

Damon Buford — Rangers
Age 28 – Bats Right

	Avg	G	AB	R	H	2B	3B	HR	RBI	BB	SO	HBP	GDP	SB	CS	OBP	SLG	IBB	SH	SF	#Pit	#P/PA	GB	FB	G/F
1997 Season	.224	122	366	49	82	18	0	8	39	30	83	3	8	18	7	.287	.339	0	3	2	1632	4.04	117	107	1.09
Career (1993-1997)	.232	337	760	129	176	37	0	20	82	79	172	9	15	38	22	.309	.359	0	8	6	3435	3.98	227	225	1.01

1997 Season

	Avg	AB	H	2B	3B	HR	RBI	BB	SO	OBP	SLG		Avg	AB	H	2B	3B	HR	RBI	BB	SO	OBP	SLG
vs. Left	.252	139	35	5	0	4	14	8	31	.289	.374	First Pitch	.273	22	6	0	0	0	2	0	0	.304	.273
vs. Right	.207	227	47	13	0	4	25	22	52	.286	.317	Ahead in Count	.338	74	25	7	0	2	15	17	0	.457	.514
Groundball	.244	82	20	6	0	3	10	7	15	.319	.427	Behind in Count	.172	192	33	9	0	4	13	0	68	.179	.281
Flyball	.217	46	10	1	0	2	7	2	10	.250	.370	Two Strikes	.155	194	30	4	0	4	15	13	83	.211	.258
Home	.247	178	44	9	0	4	23	17	40	.320	.365	Batting #1	.222	108	24	3	0	3	12	8	17	.274	.333
Away	.202	188	38	9	0	4	16	13	43	.254	.314	Batting #8	.214	154	33	7	0	3	15	15	40	.295	.318
Day	.279	86	24	7	0	5	15	8	16	.340	.535	Other	.240	104	25	8	0	2	12	7	26	.288	.375
Night	.207	280	58	11	0	3	24	22	67	.270	.279	March/April	.232	82	19	5	0	1	9	8	17	.315	.329
Grass	.225	315	71	15	0	7	34	26	69	.289	.340	May	.200	70	14	3	0	3	8	8	20	.282	.371
Turf	.216	51	11	3	0	1	5	4	14	.273	.333	June	.200	90	18	3	0	1	7	6	18	.247	.267
Pre-All Star	.213	263	56	15	0	5	31	24	62	.283	.327	July	.233	73	17	7	0	1	9	5	18	.282	.370
Post-All Star	.252	103	26	3	0	3	8	6	21	.297	.369	August	.286	35	10	0	0	1	3	2	8	.342	.371
Scoring Posn	.233	90	21	7	0	1	29	8	16	.290	.344	Sept/Oct	.250	16	4	0	0	1	3	1	2	.278	.438
Close & Late	.304	46	14	2	0	3	5	6	15	.385	.543	vs. AL	.215	325	70	15	0	7	30	27	75	.280	.326
None on/out	.217	106	23	4	0	4	4	11	27	.291	.358	vs. NL	.293	41	12	3	0	1	9	3	8	.341	.439

1997 By Position

Position	Avg	AB	H	2B	3B	HR	RBI	BB	SO	OBP	SLG	G	GS	Innings	PO	A	E	DP	Fld Pct	Rng Fctr	In Zone	Outs	Zone Rtg	MLB Zone
As cf	.225	360	81	18	0	8	38	30	80	.289	.342	117	102	909.2	282	7	3	5	.990	2.86	318	267	.840	.815

Career (1993-1997)

	Avg	AB	H	2B	3B	HR	RBI	BB	SO	OBP	SLG		Avg	AB	H	2B	3B	HR	RBI	BB	SO	OBP	SLG
vs. Left	.263	308	81	13	0	11	35	28	65	.326	.412	First Pitch	.310	58	18	2	0	2	7	0	0	.344	.448
vs. Right	.210	452	95	24	0	9	47	51	107	.298	.323	Ahead in Count	.321	165	53	10	0	6	23	46	0	.470	.491
Groundball	.251	183	46	10	0	6	20	18	37	.330	.404	Behind in Count	.176	386	68	17	0	5	32	0	147	.182	.259
Flyball	.194	108	21	3	0	3	17	7	28	.261	.306	Two Strikes	.160	393	63	15	0	5	31	33	172	.228	.237
Home	.235	379	89	18	0	9	42	41	86	.315	.354	Batting #1	.211	237	50	6	0	10	30	27	46	.299	.363
Away	.228	381	87	19	0	11	40	38	86	.304	.365	Batting #8	.258	264	68	16	0	6	29	26	61	.333	.386
Day	.263	194	51	13	0	9	34	21	44	.336	.469	Other	.224	259	58	15	0	4	23	26	65	.294	.328
Night	.221	566	125	24	0	11	48	58	128	.300	.322	March/April	.238	101	24	5	0	1	10	21	.316	.317
Grass	.229	632	145	29	0	16	67	63	141	.303	.351	May	.206	194	40	8	0	5	20	24	52	.295	.325
Turf	.242	128	31	8	0	4	15	16	31	.340	.398	June	.217	120	26	5	0	4	14	9	25	.269	.358
Pre-All Star	.219	443	97	22	0	11	53	46	106	.295	.343	July	.256	121	31	12	0	2	14	7	24	.302	.405
Post-All Star	.249	317	79	15	0	9	29	33	66	.320	.382	August	.212	118	25	5	0	2	7	10	27	.290	.305
Scoring Posn	.250	176	44	12	0	4	59	27	39	.343	.386	Sept/Oct	.283	106	30	2	0	6	17	19	23	.392	.472
Close & Late	.248	101	25	7	0	3	11	14	27	.345	.406	vs. AL	.226	583	132	29	0	15	61	57	136	.298	.353
None on/out	.224	219	49	8	0	9	10	24	50	.306	.397	vs. NL	.249	177	44	8	0	5	21	22	36	.345	.379

Batter vs. Pitcher (career)

Hits Best Against	Avg	AB	H	2B	3B	HR	RBI	BB	SO	OBP	SLG	Hits Worst Against	Avg	AB	H	2B	3B	HR	RBI	BB	SO	OBP	SLG
Willie Blair	.545	11	6	0	0	0	0	1	0	.583	.545	David Wells	.167	12	2	0	0	1	3	1	3	.214	.417
												Roger Clemens	.182	11	2	0	0	0	0	1	3	.250	.182
												Andy Pettitte	.235	17	4	0	0	0	0	0	4	.235	.235

Jay Buhner — Mariners   Age 33 – Bats Right (flyball hitter)

	Avg	G	AB	R	H	2B	3B	HR	RBI	BB	SO	HBP	GDP	SB	CS	OBP	SLG	IBB	SH	SF	#Pit	#P/PA	GB	FB	G/F
1997 Season	.243	157	540	104	131	18	2	40	109	119	175	5	23	0	0	.383	.506	3	0	1	2792	4.20	149	155	0.96
Last Five Years	.265	692	2495	462	660	121	9	172	534	429	661	22	68	2	8	.373	.527	29	6	30	11756	3.94	734	789	0.93

1997 Season

	Avg	AB	H	2B	3B	HR	RBI	BB	SO	OBP	SLG		Avg	AB	H	2B	3B	HR	RBI	BB	SO	OBP	SLG
vs. Left	.317	126	40	4	1	11	27	29	32	.449	.627	First Pitch	.411	56	23	4	0	5	12	3	0	.450	.750
vs. Right	.220	414	91	14	1	29	82	90	143	.363	.469	Ahead in Count	.368	114	42	6	1	17	34	62	0	.588	.886
Groundball	.259	116	30	6	2	5	24	31	38	.419	.474	Behind in Count	.154	253	39	3	1	9	36	0	134	.167	.281
Flyball	.209	86	18	1	0	9	20	17	25	.340	.535	Two Strikes	.150	294	44	4	1	11	41	54	175	.288	.282
Home	.235	243	57	13	2	13	45	72	83	.416	.465	Batting #5	.231	402	93	16	2	24	71	79	132	.362	.460
Away	.249	297	74	5	0	27	64	47	92	.354	.539	Batting #6	.264	106	28	2	0	13	30	32	34	.436	.651
Day	.205	171	35	3	0	15	31	39	63	.358	.485	Other	.313	32	10	0	0	3	8	8	9	.463	.594
Night	.260	369	96	15	2	25	78	80	112	.395	.515	March/April	.245	94	23	3	0	4	14	25	30	.403	.404
Grass	.243	259	63	5	0	22	56	40	80	.347	.517	May	.202	89	18	1	0	8	24	22	26	.368	.483
Turf	.242	281	68	13	2	18	53	79	95	.414	.495	June	.268	97	26	5	0	9	23	18	28	.388	.598
Pre-All Star	.239	301	72	9	0	22	64	69	89	.385	.488	July	.255	94	24	4	2	5	15	15	31	.358	.500
Post-All Star	.247	239	59	9	2	18	45	50	86	.381	.527	August	.224	98	22	3	0	6	15	19	35	.361	.490
Scoring Posn	.230	161	37	8	0	9	70	42	50	.393	.447	Sept/Oct	.265	68	18	2	0	8	18	20	25	.432	.647
Close & Late	.215	79	17	2	0	4	18	17	34	.354	.392	vs. AL	.242	488	118	14	2	37	99	102	161	.378	.506
None on/out	.234	128	30	4	0	11	11	27	47	.372	.523	vs. NL	.250	52	13	4	0	3	10	17	14	.435	.500

1997 By Position

Position	Avg	AB	H	2B	3B	HR	RBI	BB	SO	OBP	SLG	G	GS	Innings	PO	A	E	DP	Fld Pct	Rng Fctr	In Zone	Outs	Zone Rtg	MLB Zone
As rf	.243	534	130	18	2	40	107	118	173	.384	.509	154	153	1326.0	294	5	1	4	.997	2.03	349	287	.822	.813

Last Five Years

	Avg	AB	H	2B	3B	HR	RBI	BB	SO	OBP	SLG		Avg	AB	H	2B	3B	HR	RBI	BB	SO	OBP	SLG
vs. Left	.307	651	200	37	2	47	141	123	152	.417	.587	First Pitch	.355	332	118	26	1	30	95	24	0	.401	.711
vs. Right	.249	1844	460	84	7	125	393	306	509	.358	.506	Ahead in Count	.352	534	188	29	2	60	165	204	0	.525	.751
Groundball	.285	586	167	37	3	33	135	91	152	.381	.527	Behind in Count	.197	1134	223	41	4	51	174	0	521	.203	.375
Flyball	.259	451	117	20	1	37	105	82	123	.374	.554	Two Strikes	.171	1241	212	41	4	47	162	200	661	.289	.324
Home	.266	1180	314	70	6	76	251	240	314	.393	.529	Batting #4	.261	1095	286	63	5	57	208	185	262	.369	.484
Away	.263	1315	346	51	3	96	283	189	347	.354	.525	Batting #5	.263	1125	296	50	4	83	243	190	321	.371	.536
Day	.261	719	188	29	1	44	135	127	197	.375	.488	Other	.284	275	78	8	0	32	83	54	78	.399	.662
Night	.266	1776	472	92	8	128	399	304	464	.373	.543	March/April	.295	366	108	19	1	18	69	62	87	.400	.500
Grass	.262	1104	289	43	3	80	230	149	283	.349	.524	May	.271	462	125	23	3	39	112	78	126	.375	.587
Turf	.267	1391	371	78	6	92	304	280	378	.392	.530	June	.267	404	108	24	2	24	77	67	96	.375	.515
Pre-All Star	.273	1363	372	69	6	88	285	222	343	.377	.526	July	.259	456	118	21	2	28	95	79	116	.368	.498
Post-All Star	.254	1132	288	52	3	84	249	207	318	.370	.528	August	.229	420	96	14	1	31	95	84	131	.360	.488
Scoring Posn	.277	747	207	35	1	50	367	167	196	.402	.527	Sept/Oct	.271	387	105	20	0	32	86	59	105	.366	.571
Close & Late	.272	364	99	22	1	18	75	80	99	.403	.486	vs. AL	.265	2443	647	117	9	169	524	412	647	.372	.528
None on/out	.271	609	165	33	3	44	44	90	160	.369	.552	vs. NL	.250	52	13	4	0	3	10	17	14	.435	.500

Batter vs. Pitcher (career)

Hits Best Against	Avg	AB	H	2B	3B	HR	RBI	BB	SO	OBP	SLG	Hits Worst Against	Avg	AB	H	2B	3B	HR	RBI	BB	SO	OBP	SLG
Tim Belcher	.500	20	10	2	0	4	10	2	1	.545	1.200	Mark Leiter	.000	10	0	0	0	0	1	2	5	.154	.000
Albie Lopez	.455	11	5	0	0	2	3	1	0	.500	1.000	Omar Olivares	.071	14	1	0	0	0	0	2	10	.188	.071
Brad Radke	.417	12	5	0	0	3	5	1	4	.462	1.167	Don Wengert	.083	12	1	0	0	0	0	3	4	.267	.083
Ben McDonald	.385	26	10	2	0	3	7	5	2	.484	.808	Tim Wakefield	.105	19	2	0	0	2	1	1	8	.150	.105
Orel Hershiser	.316	19	6	0	0	4	9	1	5	.350	.947	Todd Stottlemyre	.115	26	3	0	0	1	2	0	9	.148	.231

Jim Bullinger — Expos   Age 32 – Pitches Right (groundball pitcher)

	ERA	W	L	Sv	G	GS	IP	BB	SO	Avg	H	2B	3B	HR	RBI	OBP	SLG	CG	ShO	Sup	QS	#P/S	SB	CS	GB	FB	G/F
1997 Season	5.56	7	12	0	36	25	155.1	74	87	.276	165	30	4	17	89	.364	.425	2	2	3.94	12	85	34	6	247	156	1.58
Last Five Years	5.01	32	32	4	145	79	551.1	250	352	.267	566	106	16	53	286	.350	.408	5	4	4.69	34	93	86	21	855	505	1.69

1997 Season

	ERA	W	L	Sv	G	GS	IP	H	HR	BB	SO		Avg	AB	H	2B	3B	HR	RBI	BB	SO	OBP	SLG
Home	4.96	4	4	0	17	12	78.0	85	6	32	35	vs. Left	.265	283	75	15	3	7	44	38	30	.360	.413
Away	6.17	3	8	0	19	13	77.1	80	11	42	52	vs. Right	.287	314	90	15	1	10	45	36	57	.368	.436
Day	7.98	1	5	0	11	8	44.0	48	9	22	19	Inning 1-6	.287	502	144	27	4	12	77	55	75	.365	.420
Night	4.61	6	7	0	25	17	111.1	117	8	52	68	Inning 7+	.221	95	21	3	0	5	12	19	12	.359	.411
Grass	5.40	1	4	0	13	8	55.0	50	8	33	33	None on	.292	322	94	19	2	10	10	31	45	.365	.457
Turf	5.65	6	8	0	23	17	100.1	115	9	41	54	Runners on	.258	275	71	11	2	7	79	43	42	.364	.389
March/April	10.13	1	4	0	6	6	26.2	39	5	18	13	Scoring Posn	.272	169	46	7	1	2	64	34	25	.392	.361
May	4.13	1	0	0	5	5	32.2	22	3	19	24	Close & Late	.203	59	12	2	0	2	6	13	6	.356	.339
June	3.03	3	3	0	6	6	38.2	33	4	14	14	None on/out	.327	150	49	8	2	4	4	16	17	.395	.487
July	6.58	1	3	0	5	5	26.0	35	6	8	15	vs. 1st Batr (relief)	.300	10	3	0	0	0	0	1	1	.364	.300
August	7.17	0	2	0	9	3	21.1	31	3	10	14	1st Inning Pitched	.291	134	39	6	2	4	26	15	15	.368	.455
Sept/Oct	1.80	1	0	0	5	0	10.0	5	0	5	7	First 75 Pitches	.281	491	138	27	3	14	76	54	80	.361	.434

68

1997 Season

	ERA	W	L	Sv	G	GS	IP	H	HR	BB	SO		Avg	AB	H	2B	3B	HR	RBI	BB	SO	OBP	SLG
Starter	5.68	6	12	0	25	25	136.1	150	14	65	73	Pitch 76-90	.276	58	16	1	1	1	8	10	6	.391	.379
Reliever	4.74	1	0	0	11	0	19.0	15	3	9	14	Pitch 91-105	.205	39	8	2	0	0	3	7	1	.326	.256
0-3 Days Rest (Start)	0.00	0	0	0	0	0	0.0	0	0	0	0	Pitch 106+	.333	9	3	0	0	2	2	3	0	.500	1.000
4 Days Rest	4.13	4	5	0	13	13	80.2	73	8	40	47	First Pitch	.300	100	30	9	2	3	14	4	0	.349	.520
5+ Days Rest	7.92	2	7	0	12	12	55.2	77	6	25	26	Ahead in Count	.196	240	47	5	1	6	26	0	76	.219	.300
vs. AL	4.50	0	1	0	2	1	8.0	9	0	5	3	Behind in Count	.389	157	61	10	0	5	33	43	0	.517	.548
vs. NL	5.62	7	11	0	34	24	147.1	156	17	69	84	Two Strikes	.197	233	46	8	2	6	28	27	87	.288	.326
Pre-All Star	5.77	5	8	0	18	18	101.1	100	10	53	52	Pre-All Star	.260	385	100	26	3	10	56	53	52	.351	.421
Post-All Star	5.17	2	4	0	18	7	54.0	65	7	21	35	Post-All Star	.307	212	65	4	1	7	33	21	35	.389	.434

Last Five Years

	ERA	W	L	Sv	G	GS	IP	H	HR	BB	SO		Avg	AB	H	2B	3B	HR	RBI	BB	SO	OBP	SLG
Home	4.97	14	14	2	68	39	270.0	292	24	117	170	vs. Left	.263	968	255	52	10	21	135	134	136	.359	.403
Away	5.05	18	18	2	77	40	281.1	274	29	133	182	vs. Right	.271	1148	311	54	6	32	151	116	216	.343	.412
Day	5.77	13	16	3	67	36	246.1	254	30	114	158	Inning 1-6	.274	1685	461	84	14	43	248	193	285	.353	.417
Night	4.40	19	16	1	78	43	305.0	312	23	136	194	Inning 7+	.244	431	105	22	2	10	38	57	67	.339	.374
Grass	5.07	18	19	3	95	50	356.2	362	39	161	232	None on	.270	1172	316	63	8	25	25	118	181	.343	.401
Turf	4.90	14	13	1	50	29	194.2	204	14	89	120	Runners on	.265	944	250	43	8	28	261	132	171	.358	.416
March/April	8.14	3	6	0	19	13	69.2	93	13	43	43	Scoring Posn	.274	559	153	26	6	12	216	97	104	.383	.406
May	3.56	8	2	1	23	15	108.2	78	9	43	74	Close & Late	.238	172	41	7	1	4	15	24	27	.342	.360
June	4.53	5	8	2	34	11	95.1	89	3	46	56	None on/out	.302	536	162	28	5	13	13	56	72	.372	.446
July	3.97	9	6	0	23	20	131.1	131	11	46	88	vs. Left (relief)	.222	54	12	1	0	0	2	12	10	.364	.241
August	6.39	3	7	0	22	14	87.1	112	12	38	60	1st Inning Pitched	.295	539	159	33	5	14	95	71	68	.376	.453
Sept/Oct	5.03	4	3	1	24	6	59.0	63	5	34	31	First 75 Pitches	.269	1718	463	86	14	43	230	188	291	.346	.411
Starter	5.26	27	31	0	79	79	453.0	477	46	198	282	Pitch 76-90	.271	203	55	10	1	7	32	33	33	.388	.433
Reliever	3.84	5	1	4	66	0	98.1	89	7	52	70	Pitch 91-105	.229	140	32	8	0	0	14	19	22	.321	.286
0-3 Days Rest (Start)	3.25	2	2	0	6	6	36.0	25	1	13	24	Pitch 106+	.291	55	16	2	1	3	10	10	6	.409	.527
4 Days Rest	5.71	12	15	0	39	39	224.0	246	30	112	142	First Pitch	.352	321	113	31	2	14	69	13	0	.381	.592
5+ Days Rest	5.13	13	14	0	34	34	193.0	206	15	73	116	Ahead in Count	.195	841	164	23	5	13	76	0	289	.209	.281
vs. AL	4.50	0	1	0	2	1	8.0	9	0	5	3	Behind in Count	.322	541	174	30	4	17	86	143	0	.464	.486
vs. NL	5.02	32	31	4	143	78	543.1	557	53	245	349	Two Strikes	.176	858	151	23	4	11	77	94	352	.264	.251
Pre-All Star	4.90	18	18	3	83	44	307.0	291	28	145	201	Pre-All Star	.251	1159	291	58	8	28	145	145	201	.337	.387
Post-All Star	5.16	14	14	1	62	35	244.1	275	25	105	151	Post-All Star	.287	957	275	48	8	25	144	105	151	.367	.433

Pitcher vs. Batter (career)

Pitches Best Vs.	Avg	AB	H	2B	3B	HR	RBI	BB	SO	OBP	SLG	Pitches Worst Vs.	Avg	AB	H	2B	3B	HR	RBI	BB	SO	OBP	SLG
Willie Greene	.000	12	0	0	0	0	0	2	5	.143	.000	Ryan Klesko	.615	13	8	1	1	3	9	3	2	.688	1.538
Brad Ausmus	.000	11	0	0	0	0	0	0	5	.000	.000	Javy Lopez	.533	15	8	1	0	2	2	0	2	.533	1.000
Jim Eisenreich	.000	11	0	0	0	0	1	2	2	.143	.000	Brett Butler	.500	16	8	2	0	1	4	0	0	.500	.813
Matt Williams	.133	15	2	0	0	0	1	2	8	.222	.133	Vinny Castilla	.500	10	5	0	0	3	8	5	0	.667	1.400
Carlos Garcia	.167	12	2	0	0	0	1	0	5	.167	.167	Barry Bonds	.364	11	4	1	0	1	3	5	3	.588	.727

Dave Burba — Reds

Age 31 – Pitches Right

	ERA	W	L	Sv	G	GS	IP	H	BB	SO	Avg	H	2B	3B	HR	RBI	OBP	SLG	CG	ShO	Sup	QS	#P/S	SB	CS	GB	FB	G/F
1997 Season	4.72	11	10	0	30	27	160.0	73	131	.255	157	35	3	22	79	.341	.429	2	0	4.28	13	95	12	6	207	175	1.18
Last Five Years	4.21	45	36	0	227	74	631.0	303	547	.245	580	122	10	68	293	.333	.391	3	1	4.92	36	94	57	24	752	701	1.07

1997 Season

	ERA	W	L	Sv	G	GS	IP	H	HR	BB	SO		Avg	AB	H	2B	3B	HR	RBI	BB	SO	OBP	SLG
Home	4.67	7	8	0	18	17	96.1	94	12	46	77	vs. Left	.296	294	87	19	2	10	34	41	51	.389	.476
Away	4.81	4	2	0	12	10	63.2	63	10	27	54	vs. Right	.218	321	70	16	1	12	45	32	80	.296	.386
Day	5.80	4	4	0	11	10	54.1	51	12	27	41	Inning 1-6	.264	568	150	34	3	21	76	66	125	.348	.445
Night	4.17	7	6	0	19	17	105.2	106	10	46	90	Inning 7+	.149	47	7	1	0	1	3	7	6	.259	.234
Grass	6.49	1	2	0	8	6	34.2	42	5	19	26	None on	.237	380	90	25	1	13	13	34	78	.301	.411
Turf	4.24	10	8	0	22	21	125.1	115	17	54	105	Runners on	.285	235	67	10	2	9	66	39	53	.400	.460
March/April	7.57	3	2	0	5	5	27.1	30	7	19	31	Scoring Posn	.296	142	42	5	0	7	59	31	40	.434	.479
May	2.25	1	2	0	7	6	40.0	34	5	11	35	Close & Late	.125	24	3	1	0	0	2	1	3	.160	.167
June	10.23	0	4	0	5	5	22.0	38	3	21	15	None on/out	.210	162	34	10	0	5	5	11	27	.260	.364
July	3.79	2	2	0	6	6	38.0	25	6	15	28	vs. 1st Batr (relief)	.000	3	0	0	0	0	0	0	2	.000	.000
August	3.86	0	0	0	2	0	2.1	2	1	1	2	1st Inning Pitched	.333	126	42	13	1	5	17	11	21	.400	.571
Sept/Oct	2.67	5	0	0	5	5	30.1	28	2	6	20	First 75 Pitches	.251	470	118	29	3	15	55	49	98	.328	.421
Starter	4.80	11	10	0	27	27	155.2	154	21	72	125	Pitch 76-90	.292	72	21	2	0	2	9	12	15	.407	.403
Reliever	2.08	0	0	0	3	0	4.1	3	1	1	6	Pitch 91-105	.286	49	14	4	0	2	8	9	13	.397	.490
0-3 Days Rest (Start)	4.50	0	1	0	1	1	6.0	7	1	3	7	Pitch 106+	.167	24	4	0	0	3	7	3	5	.276	.542
4 Days Rest	4.86	6	4	0	14	14	87.0	81	12	38	73	First Pitch	.337	86	29	4	1	4	16	7	0	.385	.547
5+ Days Rest	4.74	5	5	0	12	12	62.2	66	8	31	45	Ahead in Count	.179	252	45	13	1	3	16	0	98	.197	.274
vs. AL	4.34	2	1	0	3	3	18.2	16	2	11	12	Behind in Count	.367	139	51	8	0	10	27	38	0	.476	.640
vs. NL	4.78	9	9	0	27	24	141.1	141	20	62	119	Two Strikes	.165	261	43	15	2	3	20	37	131	.277	.272
Pre-All Star	5.47	5	8	0	19	18	105.1	110	16	55	88	Pre-All Star	.270	407	110	26	3	16	61	55	88	.364	.467
Post-All Star	3.29	6	2	0	11	9	54.2	47	6	18	43	Post-All Star	.226	208	47	9	0	6	18	18	43	.294	.356

Last Five Years

	ERA	W	L	Sv	G	GS	IP	H	HR	BB	SO		Avg	AB	H	2B	3B	HR	RBI	BB	SO	OBP	SLG
Home	3.75	24	23	0	121	45	367.0	322	30	187	321	vs. Left	.271	1017	276	58	5	30	126	146	180	.365	.427
Away	4.84	21	13	0	106	29	264.0	258	38	116	226	vs. Right	.225	1352	304	62	6	38	167	157	367	.308	.364
Day	5.01	21	20	0	118	32	289.0	278	37	147	258	Inning 1-6	.251	1731	435	92	10	50	229	213	381	.335	.403
Night	3.53	24	16	0	109	42	342.0	302	31	156	289	Inning 7+	.227	638	145	28	1	18	64	90	166	.328	.359
Grass	4.74	19	15	0	142	23	279.0	275	38	131	255	None on	.238	1364	325	67	4	41	41	145	295	.315	.383

Last Five Years

	ERA	W	L	Sv	G	GS	IP	H	HR	BB	SO		Avg	AB	H	2B	3B	HR	RBI	BB	SO	OBP	SLG
Turf	3.78	26	21	0	85	51	352.0	305	30	172	292	Runners on	.254	1005	255	53	7	27	252	158	252	.356	.401
March/April	5.74	5	7	0	28	13	89.1	90	12	50	88	Scoring Posn	.244	598	146	22	3	17	214	111	177	.360	.376
May	3.78	5	10	0	56	12	123.2	106	12	56	111	Close & Late	.202	322	65	15	1	8	34	53	91	.321	.329
June	5.20	4	8	0	45	11	105.2	116	12	61	99	None on/out	.271	616	167	29	2	26	26	46	115	.326	.451
July	3.35	13	3	0	44	13	121.0	95	10	54	90	vs. 1st Batr (relief)	.225	138	31	5	0	8	26	12	35	.285	.435
August	3.51	9	5	0	28	12	97.1	91	10	37	82	1st Inning Pitched	.249	790	197	42	2	25	115	99	192	.337	.403
Sept/Oct	4.02	9	3	0	26	13	94.0	82	12	45	77	First 75 Pitches	.243	1957	476	101	10	53	243	237	458	.328	.386
Starter	4.29	29	26	0	74	74	423.1	408	46	200	328	Pitch 76-90	.265	211	56	9	1	6	22	32	41	.366	.403
Reliever	4.03	16	10	0	153	0	207.2	172	22	103	219	Pitch 91-105	.248	137	34	8	0	4	16	22	34	.350	.394
0-3 Days Rest (Start)	3.76	1	3	0	5	5	26.1	24	2	10	22	Pitch 106+	.219	64	14	2	0	5	12	12	14	.346	.484
4 Days Rest	4.03	19	12	0	40	40	236.2	215	25	114	185	First Pitch	.307	371	114	16	3	16	61	22	0	.346	.496
5+ Days Rest	4.77	9	11	0	29	29	160.1	169	19	76	121	Ahead in Count	.168	1057	178	38	3	12	69	0	434	.175	.244
vs. AL	4.34	2	1	0	3	3	18.2	16	2	11	12	Behind in Count	.340	473	161	36	2	20	86	124	0	.475	.552
vs. NL	4.20	43	35	0	224	71	612.1	564	66	292	535	Two Strikes	.160	1118	179	42	3	13	83	156	547	.266	.238
Pre-All Star	4.53	19	26	0	143	39	355.1	331	39	183	320	Pre-All Star	.248	1333	331	72	8	39	182	183	320	.343	.402
Post-All Star	3.79	26	10	0	84	35	275.2	249	29	120	227	Post-All Star	.240	1036	249	48	3	29	111	120	227	.320	.376

Pitcher vs. Batter (career)

Pitches Best Vs.	Avg	AB	H	2B	3B	HR	RBI	BB	SO	OBP	SLG	Pitches Worst Vs.	Avg	AB	H	2B	3B	HR	RBI	BB	SO	OBP	SLG
Shawon Dunston	.000	12	0	0	0	0	0	0	4	.000	.000	John Mabry	.600	10	6	2	0	0	1	1	2	.636	.800
Greg Vaughn	.000	9	0	0	0	0	0	2	2	.182	.000	Bernard Gilkey	.500	18	9	4	0	1	4	0	1	.474	.889
Benito Santiago	.056	18	1	0	0	0	0	4	5	.227	.056	Larry Walker	.474	19	9	1	1	2	4	4	2	.583	.947
Mark Grudzielanek	.067	15	1	0	0	0	0	0	0	.067	.067	Mike Piazza	.421	19	8	2	0	2	5	2	1	.455	.842
Jody Reed	.125	16	2	0	0	0	1	0	2	.125	.125	Vinny Castilla	.381	21	8	4	0	2	7	1	0	.435	.857

John Burke — Rockies   Age 28 – Pitches Right (flyball pitcher)

	ERA	W	L	Sv	G	GS	IP	BB	SO	Avg	H	2B	3B	HR	RBI	OBP	SLG	CG	ShO	Sup	QS	#P/S	SB	CS	GB	FB	G/F
1997 Season	6.56	2	5	0	17	9	59.0	26	39	.329	83	17	0	13	46	.401	.552	0	0	3.81	2	88	16	1	76	85	0.89
Career (1996-1997)	6.75	4	6	0	28	9	74.2	33	58	.327	104	22	1	16	65	.398	.553	0	0	3.74	2	88	19	1	90	111	0.81

1997 Season

	ERA	W	L	Sv	G	GS	IP	H	HR	BB	SO		Avg	AB	H	2B	3B	HR	RBI	BB	SO	OBP	SLG
Home	9.00	1	3	0	8	4	24.0	38	7	14	22	vs. Left	.364	129	47	10	0	7	23	8	16	.408	.605
Away	4.89	1	2	0	9	5	35.0	45	6	12	17	vs. Right	.293	123	36	7	0	6	23	18	23	.393	.496

John Burkett — Rangers   Age 33 – Pitches Right

	ERA	W	L	Sv	G	GS	IP	BB	SO	Avg	H	2B	3B	HR	RBI	OBP	SLG	CG	ShO	Sup	QS	#P/S	SB	CS	GB	FB	G/F
1997 Season	4.56	9	12	0	30	30	189.1	30	139	.307	240	36	4	20	92	.333	.439	2	0	6.08	12	101	9	8	273	213	1.28
Last Five Years	4.08	62	53	0	153	153	991.1	221	650	.278	1077	190	27	93	437	.321	.414	10	2	5.01	86	99	59	40	1470	1042	1.41

1997 Season

	ERA	W	L	Sv	G	GS	IP	H	HR	BB	SO		Avg	AB	H	2B	3B	HR	RBI	BB	SO	OBP	SLG
Home	5.59	3	5	0	14	14	83.2	114	14	12	62	vs. Left	.298	396	116	18	2	10	48	20	81	.328	.429
Away	3.75	6	7	0	16	16	105.2	126	6	18	77	vs. Right	.315	387	122	18	2	10	44	10	58	.337	.450
Day	4.03	4	4	0	9	9	58.0	63	6	14	50	Inning 1-6	.305	681	208	32	3	19	84	28	129	.333	.445
Night	4.80	5	8	0	21	21	131.1	177	14	16	89	Inning 7+	.314	102	32	4	1	1	8	2	10	.327	.402
Grass	4.79	6	11	0	25	25	156.0	204	19	26	110	None on	.303	446	135	19	3	12	12	17	80	.331	.439
Turf	3.51	3	1	0	5	5	33.1	36	1	4	29	Runners on	.312	337	105	17	1	8	80	13	59	.334	.439
March/April	3.13	1	1	0	5	5	31.2	40	1	4	26	Scoring Posn	.298	171	51	6	0	7	71	9	30	.324	.456
May	6.23	3	2	0	6	6	34.2	51	6	8	22	Close & Late	.357	42	15	3	0	0	3	0	3	.357	.429
June	5.18	1	4	0	6	6	41.2	65	4	6	27	None on/out	.280	193	54	6	1	2		10	39	.315	.352
July	4.66	2	3	0	6	6	36.2	41	5	5	24	vs. 1st Batr (relief)	.000	0	0	0	0	0	0	0	0	.000	.000
August	5.00	1	0	0	2	2	9.0	11	1	1	9	1st Inning Pitched	.309	123	38	7	2	7	19	8	22	.353	.569
Sept/Oct	3.28	2	1	0	5	5	35.2	32	3	6	31	First 75 Pitches	.309	528	163	23	3	15	64	25	104	.342	.449
Starter	4.56	9	12	0	30	30	189.1	240	20	30	139	Pitch 76-90	.320	103	33	6	0	3	18	2	15	.327	.466
Reliever	0.00	0	0	0	0	0	0.0	0	0	0	0	Pitch 91-105	.330	91	30	4	0	1	6	2	13	.344	.407
0-3 Days Rest (Start)	6.00	0	0	0	1	1	6.0	8	2	1	2	Pitch 106+	.230	61	14	3	1	1	4	1	7	.242	.361
4 Days Rest	4.58	7	9	0	20	20	127.2	163	14	18	85	First Pitch	.388	129	50	5	1	2	13	1	0	.397	.488
5+ Days Rest	4.37	2	3	0	9	9	55.2	69	4	11	52	Ahead in Count	.231	334	77	12	0	5	39	0	115	.232	.311
vs. AL	4.62	8	11	0	27	27	169.1	216	19	28	124	Behind in Count	.428	159	68	11	3	8	24	8	0	.453	.686
vs. NL	4.05	1	1	0	3	3	20.0	24	1	2	15	Two Strikes	.199	352	70	12	0	5	32	21	139	.243	.276
Pre-All Star	4.62	6	7	0	18	18	117.0	160	11	19	82	Pre-All Star	.325	492	160	21	3	11	59	19	82	.349	.447
Post-All Star	4.48	3	5	0	12	12	72.1	80	9	11	57	Post-All Star	.275	291	80	15	1	9	33	11	57	.304	.426

Last Five Years

	ERA	W	L	Sv	G	GS	IP	H	HR	BB	SO		Avg	AB	H	2B	3B	HR	RBI	BB	SO	OBP	SLG
Home	4.35	26	27	0	75	75	490.2	536	53	106	334	vs. Left	.277	1948	539	89	17	35	214	129	336	.323	.394
Away	3.81	36	26	0	78	78	500.2	541	40	115	316	vs. Right	.280	1920	538	101	10	58	223	92	314	.319	.434
Day	3.67	21	21	0	55	55	363.0	373	33	79	248	Inning 1-6	.275	3327	914	160	23	77	374	187	575	.317	.406
Night	4.31	41	32	0	98	98	628.1	704	60	142	402	Inning 7+	.301	541	163	30	4	16	63	34	75	.345	.460
Grass	4.26	45	46	0	124	124	800.1	876	79	180	531	None on	.268	2314	619	110	15	50	50	117	398	.308	.393
Turf	3.30	17	7	0	29	29	191.0	201	14	41	119	Runners on	.295	1554	458	80	12	43	387	104	252	.340	.445
March/April	3.15	11	7	0	24	24	157.1	156	13	30	111	Scoring Posn	.283	830	235	35	6	25	324	78	149	.343	.430
May	4.79	10	10	0	28	28	173.0	187	18	53	104	Close & Late	.292	315	92	18	1	6	36	23	44	.343	.413
June	4.04	11	13	0	28	28	194.0	213	20	34	126	None on/out	.256	997	255	40	11	15	15	51	175	.297	.363
July	4.02	10	10	0	28	28	174.2	198	15	39	120	vs. 1st Batr (relief)	.000	0	0	0	0	0	0	0	0	.000	.000

Last Five Years

	ERA	W	L	Sv	G	GS	IP	H	HR	BB	SO		Avg	AB	H	2B	3B	HR	RBI	BB	SO	OBP	SLG
August	4.35	9	6	0	22	22	138.2	160	13	35	84	1st Inning Pitched	.282	593	167	26	8	16	77	38	105	.331	.433
Sept/Oct	4.10	11	7	0	23	23	153.2	163	14	30	105	First 75 Pitches	.272	2797	762	126	21	62	291	152	483	.315	.399
Starter	4.08	62	53	0	153	153	991.1	1077	93	221	650	Pitch 76-90	.300	540	162	33	3	16	75	26	83	.330	.461
Reliever	0.00	0	0	0	0	0	0.0	0	0	0	0	Pitch 91-105	.275	335	92	17	0	11	51	29	55	.339	.424
0-3 Days Rest (Start)	5.25	2	1	0	4	4	24.0	31	4	3	16	Pitch 106+	.311	196	61	14	3	4	20	14	29	.357	.474
4 Days Rest	3.88	45	32	0	103	103	682.2	710	70	159	433	First Pitch	.385	633	244	33	4	14	89	19	0	.413	.517
5+ Days Rest	4.46	15	20	0	46	46	284.2	336	19	59	201	Ahead in Count	.197	1618	318	51	7	21	119	0	553	.204	.276
vs. AL	4.46	13	13	0	37	37	238.0	291	23	44	171	Behind in Count	.344	842	290	63	10	35	137	87	0	.404	.568
vs. NL	3.95	49	40	0	116	116	753.1	786	70	177	479	Two Strikes	.181	1652	299	49	7	17	101	115	650	.237	.250
Pre-All Star	3.98	35	33	0	89	89	583.2	627	56	130	382	Pre-All Star	.277	2262	627	104	13	56	244	130	382	.319	.409
Post-All Star	4.22	27	20	0	64	64	407.2	450	37	91	268	Post-All Star	.280	1606	450	86	14	37	193	91	268	.324	.420

Pitcher vs. Batter (career)

Pitches Best Vs.	Avg	AB	H	2B	3B	HR	RBI	BB	SO	OBP	SLG	Pitches Worst Vs.	Avg	AB	H	2B	3B	HR	RBI	BB	SO	OBP	SLG
Luis Alicea	.077	13	1	0	0	0	0	1	4	.200	.077	Brady Anderson	.900	10	9	0	0	0	1	1	0	.909	.900
Joe Oliver	.083	12	1	0	0	0	0	0	3	.083	.083	Eric Young	.485	33	16	2	3	0	3	1	0	.514	.727
Joe Orsulak	.091	11	1	0	0	0	0	0	1	.091	.091	Wil Cordero	.429	21	9	2	0	3	6	1	2	.455	.952
Jacob Brumfield	.091	11	1	0	0	0	0	0	2	.091	.091	Moises Alou	.421	19	8	3	0	1	4	3	1	.500	.737
Ricky Gutierrez	.091	11	1	0	0	0	2	1	1	.167	.091	Gary Sheffield	.417	12	5	1	0	3	6	1	0	.462	1.250

Ellis Burks — Rockies
Age 33 – Bats Right

	Avg	G	AB	R	H	2B	3B	HR	RBI	BB	SO	HBP	GDP	SB	CS	OBP	SLG	IBB	SH	SF	#Pit	#P/PA	GB	FB	G/F
1997 Season	.290	119	424	91	123	19	2	32	82	47	75	3	17	7	2	.363	.571	0	1	2	1881	3.94	167	118	1.42
Last Five Years	.302	566	1963	382	593	106	23	116	357	223	397	15	57	55	21	.375	.557	7	8	13	8886	4.00	683	570	1.20

1997 Season

	Avg	AB	H	2B	3B	HR	RBI	BB	SO	OBP	SLG		Avg	AB	H	2B	3B	HR	RBI	BB	SO	OBP	SLG
vs. Left	.280	100	28	2	0	5	17	10	15	.345	.450	First Pitch	.311	45	14	2	0	6	9	0	0	.311	.756
vs. Right	.293	324	95	17	2	27	65	37	60	.369	.608	Ahead in Count	.434	106	46	6	1	11	28	23	0	.535	.821
Groundball	.311	90	28	0	0	7	16	16	12	.417	.544	Behind in Count	.227	194	44	6	1	11	28	0	61	.232	.438
Flyball	.370	73	27	5	1	10	20	5	13	.418	.877	Two Strikes	.199	206	41	6	1	10	32	24	75	.283	.383
Home	.337	205	69	11	1	17	45	24	28	.407	.649	Batting #2	.308	331	102	14	2	27	64	39	55	.382	.607
Away	.247	219	54	8	1	15	37	23	47	.322	.498	Batting #5	.270	63	17	5	0	4	13	6	13	.338	.540
Day	.306	180	55	9	1	17	43	25	30	.394	.650	Other	.133	30	4	0	0	1	5	2	7	.212	.233
Night	.279	244	68	10	1	15	39	22	45	.340	.512	March/April	.195	77	15	2	0	6	13	4	16	.241	.455
Grass	.319	335	107	17	2	26	69	39	54	.392	.615	June	.284	88	25	6	0	5	18	12	12	.366	.523
Turf	.180	89	16	2	0	6	13	8	21	.255	.404	July	.143	7	1	0	0	1	2	1	1	.250	.571
Pre-All Star	.253	245	62	11	1	17	49	28	43	.332	.514	August	.309	81	25	4	0	7	12	10	16	.385	.617
Post-All Star	.341	179	61	8	1	15	33	19	32	.407	.648	Sept/Oct	.385	91	35	4	1	7	19	8	15	.440	.681
Scoring Posn	.324	111	36	5	0	8	51	16	17	.412	.586	vs. AL	.354	48	17	1	0	3	9	3	8	.392	.563
Close & Late	.305	59	18	3	1	4	10	7	10	.388	.593	vs. NL	.282	376	106	18	2	29	73	44	67	.360	.572
None on/out	.333	75	25	6	1	6	6	11	17	.419	.680												

1997 By Position

Position	Avg	AB	H	2B	3B	HR	RBI	BB	SO	OBP	SLG	G	GS	Innings	PO	A	E	DP	Fld Pct	Rng Fctr	In Zone	Outs	Zone Rtg	MLB Zone
As lf	.260	96	25	5	0	8	22	5	21	.308	.563	67	17	250.1	53	3	2	0	.966	2.01	63	50	.794	.805
As cf	.305	321	98	14	2	24	59	40	52	.383	.586	89	89	650.0	154	3	2	2	.987	2.17	202	152	.752	.815

Last Five Years

	Avg	AB	H	2B	3B	HR	RBI	BB	SO	OBP	SLG		Avg	AB	H	2B	3B	HR	RBI	BB	SO	OBP	SLG
vs. Left	.333	535	178	28	7	30	95	64	90	.406	.579	First Pitch	.373	209	78	15	2	20	41	5	0	.406	.751
vs. Right	.291	1428	415	78	16	86	262	159	307	.364	.548	Ahead in Count	.409	521	213	36	12	43	136	114	0	.513	.772
Groundball	.309	492	152	24	5	28	85	53	102	.380	.549	Behind in Count	.234	837	196	31	8	34	102	0	324	.241	.412
Flyball	.271	336	91	20	3	25	63	25	72	.325	.571	Two Strikes	.213	945	201	37	7	35	115	104	397	.292	.378
Home	.341	980	334	66	17	62	211	111	193	.411	.633	Batting #2	.320	752	241	41	10	51	146	85	139	.391	.605
Away	.263	983	259	40	6	54	146	112	204	.340	.481	Batting #6	.294	462	136	18	10	25	82	53	97	.367	.539
Day	.316	670	212	41	7	56	148	91	137	.403	.649	Other	.288	749	216	47	3	40	129	85	161	.364	.519
Night	.295	1293	381	65	16	60	209	132	260	.343	.509	March/April	.333	324	108	20	6	21	54	31	62	.398	.627
Grass	.306	1589	486	87	22	95	301	183	319	.379	.568	May	.255	364	93	15	5	21	64	43	86	.337	.487
Turf	.286	374	107	19	1	21	56	40	78	.358	.511	June	.314	338	106	18	2	22	74	42	61	.392	.574
Pre-All Star	.301	1108	333	56	14	68	207	129	224	.377	.560	July	.296	253	75	14	4	14	39	30	55	.370	.549
Post-All Star	.304	855	260	50	9	48	150	94	173	.373	.552	August	.300	360	108	22	3	26	71	31	73	.356	.594
Scoring Posn	.301	534	161	38	6	24	236	72	113	.382	.530	Sept/Oct	.318	324	103	17	3	12	55	46	60	.403	.500
Close & Late	.274	281	77	17	3	10	50	33	70	.351	.463	vs. AL	.282	547	154	25	4	20	83	63	105	.355	.452
None on/out	.324	404	131	22	7	28	28	54	74	.405	.621	vs. NL	.310	1416	439	81	19	96	274	160	292	.383	.597

Batter vs. Pitcher (career)

Hits Best Against	Avg	AB	H	2B	3B	HR	RBI	BB	SO	OBP	SLG	Hits Worst Against	Avg	AB	H	2B	3B	HR	RBI	BB	SO	OBP	SLG
Allen Watson	.700	10	7	1	0	0	1	2	1	.750	.800	Rich DeLucia	.071	14	1	0	0	0	1	0	4	.067	.071
Terry Mulholland	.462	13	6	3	0	1	6	2	4	.563	.923	Darryl Kile	.091	11	1	0	0	0	0	2	4	.231	.091
Jason Isringhausen	.455	11	5	2	1	2	5	3	0	.600	1.364	Jimmy Key	.111	36	4	1	0	0	1	3	7	.179	.139
Bobby Jones	.400	10	4	0	1	3	5	2	2	.500	1.500	Doug Henry	.167	12	2	0	0	0	1	0	3	.167	.167
Chris Hammond	.364	11	4	0	0	3	3	0	1	.417	1.182	Doug Jones	.182	11	2	0	0	0	0	0	1	.182	.182

Jeromy Burnitz — Brewers
Age 29 – Bats Left (flyball hitter)

	Avg	G	AB	R	H	2B	3B	HR	RBI	BB	SO	HBP	GDP	SB	CS	OBP	SLG	IBB	SH	SF	#Pit	#P/PA	GB	FB	G/F
1997 Season	.281	153	494	85	139	37	8	27	85	75	111	5	8	20	13	.382	.553	8	3	0	2331	4.04	157	147	1.07
Career (1993-1997)	.266	387	1107	202	294	66	14	52	178	169	269	11	16	28	21	.367	.491	14	6	4	5221	4.03	325	328	0.99

1997 Season

	Avg	AB	H	2B	3B	HR	RBI	BB	SO	OBP	SLG		Avg	AB	H	2B	3B	HR	RBI	BB	SO	OBP	SLG
vs. Left	.273	121	33	8	1	3	20	10	26	.343	.430	First Pitch	.364	55	20	5	1	5	19	6	0	.435	.764
vs. Right	.284	373	106	29	7	24	65	65	85	.393	.592	Ahead in Count	.406	106	43	13	3	10	28	46	0	.588	.868
Groundball	.337	83	28	7	2	7	20	10	17	.409	.723	Behind in Count	.198	237	47	10	3	8	19	0	91	.202	.367
Flyball	.248	105	26	11	1	3	12	18	27	.368	.457	Two Strikes	.209	263	55	15	4	8	26	23	111	.275	.388
Home	.302	245	74	17	8	18	56	38	55	.402	.657	Batting #2	.279	122	34	11	4	7	21	20	27	.389	.607
Away	.261	249	65	20	0	9	29	37	56	.361	.450	Batting #5	.279	233	65	16	2	13	46	32	54	.368	.532
Day	.280	168	47	11	2	8	25	32	40	.401	.512	Other	.288	139	40	10	2	7	18	23	30	.396	.540
Night	.282	326	92	26	6	19	60	43	71	.371	.574	March/April	.288	59	17	5	1	3	7	12	16	.408	.559
Grass	.287	432	124	30	8	26	79	66	93	.385	.574	May	.313	67	21	6	1	3	11	19	16	.471	.567
Turf	.242	62	15	7	0	1	6	9	18	.356	.403	June	.265	102	27	9	2	5	16	13	21	.359	.539
Pre-All Star	.276	246	68	20	5	12	36	48	57	.401	.545	July	.217	83	18	5	2	5	12	11	23	.309	.506
Post-All Star	.286	248	71	17	3	15	49	27	54	.361	.560	August	.276	98	27	3	1	8	19	9	18	.343	.571
Scoring Posn	.254	130	33	14	2	4	52	19	19	.349	.485	Sept/Oct	.341	85	29	9	1	3	20	11	17	.423	.576
Close & Late	.316	79	25	4	0	6	13	15	16	.432	.595	vs. AL	.283	441	125	33	7	24	76	69	100	.384	.553
None on/out	.248	121	30	7	0	5	5	13	32	.321	.430	vs. NL	.264	53	14	4	1	3	9	6	11	.361	.547

1997 By Position

Position	Avg	AB	H	2B	3B	HR	RBI	BB	SO	OBP	SLG	G	GS	Innings	PO	A	E	DP	Fld Pct	Rng Fctr	In Zone	Outs	Zone Rtg	MLB Zone
As Pinch Hitter	.364	11	4	1	0	2	6	1	0	.417	1.000	14	0	---	---	---	---	---	---	---	---	---	---	---
As cf	.329	73	24	8	2	2	13	15	18	.449	.575	26	19	173.1	50	0	0	0	1.000	2.60	63	49	.778	.815
As rf	.273	400	109	28	6	23	65	57	89	.369	.545	124	111	989.1	202	12	7	3	.968	1.95	242	204	.843	.813

Career (1993-1997)

	Avg	AB	H	2B	3B	HR	RBI	BB	SO	OBP	SLG		Avg	AB	H	2B	3B	HR	RBI	BB	SO	OBP	SLG
vs. Left	.244	217	53	11	3	5	30	23	57	.331	.392	First Pitch	.364	132	48	15	3	14	49	12	0	.433	.841
vs. Right	.271	890	241	55	11	47	148	146	212	.376	.516	Ahead in Count	.441	222	98	22	6	17	61	95	0	.606	.824
Groundball	.286	262	75	18	3	12	50	41	57	.386	.515	Behind in Count	.171	539	92	16	4	14	41	0	220	.175	.293
Flyball	.261	199	52	15	1	11	38	31	55	.370	.513	Two Strikes	.175	594	104	24	4	12	44	62	269	.256	.290
Home	.279	545	152	32	12	31	99	82	128	.379	.552	Batting #5	.270	356	96	21	3	19	69	56	86	.371	.506
Away	.253	562	142	34	2	21	79	87	141	.356	.432	Batting #7	.249	221	55	15	5	9	36	28	58	.339	.484
Day	.276	369	102	23	4	19	55	68	92	.391	.515	Other	.270	530	143	30	6	24	73	85	125	.376	.485
Night	.260	738	192	43	10	33	123	101	177	.355	.480	March/April	.234	128	30	6	1	6	13	23	36	.351	.438
Grass	.268	910	244	54	13	46	145	136	218	.367	.508	May	.292	96	28	7	1	4	15	25	28	.443	.510
Turf	.254	197	50	12	1	6	33	33	51	.369	.416	June	.272	147	40	14	2	8	23	22	34	.378	.558
Pre-All Star	.263	426	112	28	6	22	63	80	110	.385	.512	July	.254	244	62	12	3	12	37	28	61	.337	.475
Post-All Star	.267	681	182	38	8	30	115	89	159	.356	.479	August	.255	251	64	10	4	13	46	36	56	.351	.482
Scoring Posn	.249	301	75	22	4	11	120	38	65	.333	.458	Sept/Oct	.290	241	70	17	3	9	44	35	54	.383	.498
Close & Late	.277	195	54	11	2	11	26	37	47	.396	.523	vs. AL	.281	648	182	48	7	33	116	102	147	.383	.529
None on/out	.241	257	62	15	2	10	10	33	69	.330	.432	vs. NL	.244	459	112	18	7	19	62	67	122	.344	.438

Batter vs. Pitcher (career)

Hits Best Against	Avg	AB	H	2B	3B	HR	RBI	BB	SO	OBP	SLG	Hits Worst Against	Avg	AB	H	2B	3B	HR	RBI	BB	SO	OBP	SLG
Brad Radke	.500	14	7	1	0	2	3	3	3	.588	1.000	Tim Wakefield	.071	14	1	0	0	0	1	4	2	.278	.071
Tim Belcher	.455	11	5	2	0	1	3	0	2	.500	.909	Tom Candiotti	.167	12	2	0	1	0	2	0	2	.167	.333
Brian Moehler	.455	11	5	2	0	1	3	1	1	.500	.909	Kevin Appier	.182	11	2	0	0	1	1	2	1	.308	.455
Scott Erickson	.429	14	6	3	0	1	7	0	3	.429	.857	Greg Maddux	.200	10	2	0	0	0	0	1	3	.273	.200
Mike Mussina	.364	11	4	2	0	1	1	2	4	.462	.818	Pat Hentgen	.200	10	2	0	0	0	0	2	3	.333	.200

Terry Burrows — Padres
Age 29 – Pitches Left

	ERA	W	L	Sv	G	GS	IP	BB	SO	Avg	H	2B	3B	HR	RBI	OBP	SLG	GF	IR	IRS	Hld	SvOp	SB	CS	GB	FB	G/F
1997 Season	10.45	0	2	0	13	0	10.1	8	8	.286	12	4	0	1	6	.412	.452	4	7	0	1	0	1	0	15	10	1.50
Career (1994-1997)	6.42	4	4	1	50	3	68.2	38	35	.306	85	13	1	15	46	.397	.522	14	43	9	7	3	2	3	93	93	1.00

1997 Season

	ERA	W	L	Sv	G	GS	IP	H	R	BB	SO		Avg	AB	H	2B	3B	HR	RBI	BB	SO	OBP	SLG
Home	18.00	0	1	0	9	0	5.0	7	0	6	3	vs. Left	.692	13	9	3	0	1	5	4	1	.765	1.154
Away	3.38	0	1	0	4	0	5.1	5	1	2	5	vs. Right	.103	29	3	1	0	0	4	7		.235	.138

Mike Busby — Cardinals
Age 25 – Pitches Right

	ERA	W	L	Sv	G	GS	IP	BB	SO	Avg	H	2B	3B	HR	RBI	OBP	SLG	CG	ShO	Sup	QS	#P/S	SB	CS	GB	FB	G/F
1997 Season	8.79	0	2	0	3	3	14.1	4	6	.393	24	2	0	2	13	.424	.525	0	0	2.51	1	80	3	2	26	18	1.44
Career (1996-1997)	10.80	0	3	0	4	4	18.1	8	10	.398	33	4	1	6	25	.452	.687	0	0	3.44	1	88	3	2	32	26	1.23

1997 Season

	ERA	W	L	Sv	G	GS	IP	H	HR	BB	SO		Avg	AB	H	2B	3B	HR	RBI	BB	SO	OBP	SLG
Home	5.73	0	1	0	2	2	11.0	17	1	1	5	vs. Left	.375	24	9	0	0	0	3	3	3	.444	.375
Away	18.90	0	1	0	1	1	3.1	7	1	3	1	vs. Right	.405	37	15	2	0	2	10	1	3	.410	.622

Homer Bush — Yankees
Age 25 – Bats Right

	Avg	G	AB	R	H	2B	3B	HR	RBI	BB	SO	HBP	GDP	SB	CS	OBP	SLG	IBB	SH	SF	#Pit	#P/PA	GB	FB	G/F
1997 Season	.364	10	11	2	4	0	0	0	3	0	0	0	0	0	0	.364	.364	0	0	0	23	2.09	4	5	0.80

1997 Season

	Avg	AB	H	2B	3B	HR	RBI	BB	SO	OBP	SLG		Avg	AB	H	2B	3B	HR	RBI	BB	SO	OBP	SLG
vs. Left	.000	0	0	0	0	0	0	0	0	.000	.000	Scoring Posn	.750	4	3	0	0	0	3	0	0	.750	.750
vs. Right	.364	11	4	0	0	0	3	0	0	.364	.364	Close & Late	.000	1	0	0	0	0	0	0	0	.000	.000

Brett Butler — Dodgers
Age 41 – Bats Left (groundball hitter)

	Avg	G	AB	R	H	2B	3B	HR	RBI	BB	SO	HBP	GDP	SB	CS	OBP	SLG	IBB	SH	SF	#Pit	#P/PA	GB	FB	G/F
1997 Season	.283	105	343	52	97	8	3	0	18	42	40	1	1	15	10	.363	.324	0	15	0	1632	4.07	176	48	3.67
Last Five Years	.297	535	2011	311	598	61	32	10	139	272	234	9	14	121	48	.381	.374	3	47	15	9391	3.99	924	354	2.61

1997 Season

	Avg	AB	H	2B	3B	HR	RBI	BB	SO	OBP	SLG		Avg	AB	H	2B	3B	HR	RBI	BB	SO	OBP	SLG
vs. Left	.333	93	31	5	0	0	4	5	10	.367	.387	First Pitch	.214	28	6	0	0	0	0	0	0	.214	.214
vs. Right	.264	250	66	3	3	0	14	37	30	.361	.300	Ahead in Count	.342	76	26	3	1	0	5	21	0	.485	.408
Groundball	.400	55	22	2	1	0	7	8	4	.476	.473	Behind in Count	.232	155	36	2	1	0	7	0	34	.237	.258
Flyball	.231	39	9	0	1	0	2	3	6	.286	.282	Two Strikes	.238	164	39	3	0	0	7	21	40	.328	.256
Home	.288	163	47	4	1	0	3	25	19	.386	.325	Batting #1	.305	292	89	8	3	0	17	36	33	.381	.353
Away	.278	180	50	4	2	0	15	17	21	.340	.322	Batting #2	.107	28	3	0	0	0	1	2	5	.167	.107
Day	.375	80	30	3	1	0	8	10	11	.451	.438	Other	.217	23	5	0	0	0	4	2	.357	.217
Night	.255	263	67	5	2	0	10	32	29	.336	.289	March/April	.360	89	32	4	0	0	2	13	7	.441	.404
Grass	.295	281	83	7	3	0	14	35	31	.375	.342	May	.000	1	0	0	0	0	0	0	0	.000	.000
Turf	.226	62	14	1	0	0	4	7	9	.304	.242	June	.260	77	20	0	1	0	4	16	7	.387	.286
Pre-All Star	.314	185	58	5	1	0	8	29	17	.407	.351	July	.329	85	28	3	1	0	6	7	9	.380	.388
Post-All Star	.247	158	39	3	2	0	10	13	23	.308	.291	August	.197	71	14	1	0	0	4	6	15	.269	.211
Scoring Posn	.205	73	15	2	1	0	17	9	11	.293	.260	Sept/Oct	.150	20	3	0	1	0	2	0	2	.150	.250
Close & Late	.208	53	11	1	1	0	3	6	7	.288	.264	vs. AL	.156	32	5	0	1	0	3	4	3	.270	.219
None on/out	.338	148	50	3	1	0	0	17	17	.406	.372	vs. NL	.296	311	92	8	2	0	15	38	37	.372	.334

1997 By Position

Position	Avg	AB	H	2B	3B	HR	RBI	BB	SO	OBP	SLG	G	GS	Innings	PO	A	E	DP	Fld Pct	Rng Fctr	In Zone	Zone Outs	Zone Rtg	MLB Zone
As Pinch Hitter	.125	8	1	0	0	0	0	1	0	.222	.125	11	0	---	---	---	---	---	---	---	---	---	---	---
As lf	.248	153	38	4	1	0	9	12	25	.307	.288	47	40	322.1	70	2	0	1	1.000	2.01	85	70	.824	.805
As cf	.324	179	58	4	2	0	8	28	14	.415	.369	49	47	408.1	93	2	0	1	1.000	2.09	114	91	.798	.815

Last Five Years

	Avg	AB	H	2B	3B	HR	RBI	BB	SO	OBP	SLG		Avg	AB	H	2B	3B	HR	RBI	BB	SO	OBP	SLG
vs. Left	.307	589	181	19	7	2	43	72	68	.382	.374	First Pitch	.358	257	92	10	7	2	18	2	0	.362	.475
vs. Right	.293	1422	417	42	25	8	96	200	166	.381	.375	Ahead in Count	.368	438	161	31	9	6	49	127	0	.506	.521
Groundball	.326	524	171	17	7	2	39	69	55	.404	.397	Behind in Count	.237	868	206	10	8	1	35	0	195	.242	.271
Flyball	.302	301	91	12	6	1	23	46	43	.390	.392	Two Strikes	.216	944	204	13	8	2	44	143	234	.320	.253
Home	.302	969	293	26	12	2	59	152	114	.396	.360	Batting #1	.301	1796	540	57	29	9	127	238	204	.382	.380
Away	.293	1042	305	35	20	8	80	120	120	.366	.388	Batting #2	.275	189	52	4	3	1	12	29	27	.372	.344
Day	.300	547	164	19	13	4	42	69	71	.378	.404	Other	.231	26	6	0	0	0	0	5	3	.375	.231
Night	.296	1464	434	42	19	6	97	203	163	.363	.363	March/April	.324	386	125	15	5	0	21	61	46	.414	.389
Grass	.303	1551	470	47	20	6	108	226	180	.391	.371	May	.293	321	94	8	7	3	29	36	41	.363	.389
Turf	.278	460	128	14	12	4	31	46	54	.346	.387	June	.276	373	103	8	2	2	34	50	49	.361	.324
Pre-All Star	.293	1221	358	34	16	6	92	157	153	.373	.362	July	.323	399	129	11	10	4	24	45	37	.391	.431
Post-All Star	.304	790	240	27	16	4	47	115	81	.393	.394	August	.273	293	80	13	7	0	12	40	37	.369	.365
Scoring Posn	.276	398	110	11	5	0	123	72	45	.379	.329	Sept/Oct	.280	239	67	6	1	1	19	40	24	.379	.326
Close & Late	.305	341	104	14	6	2	32	56	47	.403	.394	vs. AL	.156	32	5	0	1	0	3	4	3	.270	.219
None on/out	.308	850	262	24	15	7	7	92	103	.376	.396	vs. NL	.300	1979	593	61	31	10	136	268	231	.383	.377

Batter vs. Pitcher (since 1984)

Hits Best Against	Avg	AB	H	2B	3B	HR	RBI	BB	SO	OBP	SLG	Hits Worst Against	Avg	AB	H	2B	3B	HR	RBI	BB	SO	OBP	SLG
Paul Assenmacher	.692	13	9	1	0	0	4	1	2	.714	.769	Esteban Loaiza	.000	11	0	0	0	0	1	4	1	.267	.000
Al Leiter	.556	9	5	0	1	0	3	1	0	.545	.778	Pat Rapp	.000	10	0	0	0	0	0	3	2	.231	.000
Tim Pugh	.522	23	12	2	1	1	5	1	0	.542	.826	Jaime Navarro	.071	14	1	0	0	0	0	0	3	.071	.071
Jim Bullinger	.500	16	8	2	0	1	4	0	0	.500	.813	Mike Stanton	.091	11	1	0	0	0	1	3	1	.286	.091
Pedro Martinez	.364	11	4	1	1	1	2	2	1	.462	.909	Frank Castillo	.125	32	4	0	0	0	0	2	5	.176	.125

Rich Butler — Blue Jays
Age 25 – Bats Left

	Avg	G	AB	R	H	2B	3B	HR	RBI	BB	SO	HBP	GDP	SB	CS	OBP	SLG	IBB	SH	SF	#Pit	#P/PA	GB	FB	G/F
1997 Season	.286	7	14	3	4	1	0	0	2	2	3	0	0	0	1	.375	.357	0	0	0	56	3.50	2	3	0.67

1997 Season

	Avg	AB	H	2B	3B	HR	RBI	BB	SO	OBP	SLG		Avg	AB	H	2B	3B	HR	RBI	BB	SO	OBP	SLG
vs. Left	.000	0	0	0	0	0	0	0	0	.000	.000	Scoring Posn	.500	6	3	1	0	0	2	0	1	.500	.667
vs. Right	.286	14	4	1	0	0	2	2	3	.375	.357	Close & Late	.250	4	1	0	0	0	1	0	1	.400	.250

Rob Butler — Phillies
Age 28 – Bats Left (groundball hitter)

	Avg	G	AB	R	H	2B	3B	HR	RBI	BB	SO	HBP	GDP	SB	CS	OBP	SLG	IBB	SH	SF	#Pit	#P/PA	GB	FB	G/F
1997 Season	.292	43	89	10	26	9	1	0	13	5	8	0	2	1	0	.326	.416	0	0	1	327	3.44	41	20	2.05
Career (1993-1997)	.246	101	211	31	52	13	2	0	20	19	28	2	5	3	3	.311	.327	0	4	3	838	3.51	101	41	2.46

1997 Season

	Avg	AB	H	2B	3B	HR	RBI	BB	SO	OBP	SLG		Avg	AB	H	2B	3B	HR	RBI	BB	SO	OBP	SLG
vs. Left	.167	6	1	0	0	0	2	2	1	.375	.167	Scoring Posn	.333	24	8	1	0	0	11	2	4	.370	.375
vs. Right	.301	83	25	9	1	0	11	3	7	.322	.434	Close & Late	.143	14	2	2	0	0	0	1	2	.200	.286

Paul Byrd — Braves
Age 27 – Pitches Right

	ERA	W	L	Sv	G	GS	IP	BB	SO	Avg	H	2B	3B	HR	RBI	OBP	SLG	GF	IR	IRS	Hld	SvOp	SB	CS	GB	FB	G/F
1997 Season	5.26	4	4	0	31	4	53.0	28	37	.235	47	11	1	6	31	.338	.390	9	9	4	1	0	5	3	68	69	0.99
Career (1995-1997)	4.29	7	6	0	86	4	121.2	56	94	.245	113	26	2	14	68	.330	.400	29	47	18	7	2	13	5	171	132	1.30

1997 Season

	ERA	W	L	Sv	G	GS	IP	H	HR	BB	SO		Avg	AB	H	2B	3B	HR	RBI	BB	SO	OBP	SLG
Home	7.16	2	2	0	18	2	27.2	27	4	19	17	vs. Left	.253	91	23	5	0	1	10	19	14	.382	.341
Away	3.20	2	2	0	13	2	25.1	20	2	9	20	vs. Right	.220	109	24	6	1	5	21	9	23	.298	.431
Starter	4.66	1	3	0	4	4	19.1	19	1	6	14	Scoring Posn	.310	58	18	2	0	3	24	11	13	.408	.500
Reliever	5.61	3	1	0	27	0	33.2	28	5	22	23	Close & Late	.143	21	3	0	0	1	2	4	6	.308	.286
0 Days rest (Relief)	13.50	0	0	0	4	0	3.1	4	0	4	1	None on/out	.255	47	12	4	1	0	0	3	6	.327	.383
1 or 2 Days rest	6.30	2	0	0	9	0	10.0	10	2	3	9	First Pitch	.324	37	12	3	0	2	7	3	0	.395	.568
3+ Days rest	3.98	1	1	0	14	0	20.1	14	3	15	13	Ahead in Count	.170	94	16	4	1	2	9	0	31	.177	.298
Pre-All Star	5.06	3	0	0	22	0	26.2	23	4	17	17	Behind in Count	.350	40	14	3	0	1	9	19	0	.559	.500
Post-All Star	5.47	1	4	0	9	4	26.1	24	2	11	20	Two Strikes	.122	90	11	3	0	1	6		37	.184	.189

Jose Cabrera — Astros
Age 26 – Pitches Right (flyball pitcher)

	ERA	W	L	Sv	G	GS	IP	BB	SO	Avg	H	2B	3B	HR	RBI	OBP	SLG	GF	IR	IRS	Hld	SvOp	SB	CS	GB	FB	G/F
1997 Season	1.17	0	0	0	12	0	15.1	6	18	.125	6	1	0	1	7	.211	.208	6	8	5	2	1	0	0	8	20	0.40

1997 Season

	ERA	W	L	Sv	G	GS	IP	H	HR	BB	SO		Avg	AB	H	2B	3B	HR	RBI	BB	SO	OBP	SLG
Home	2.57	0	0	0	5	0	7.0	3	1	2	9	vs. Left	.095	21	2	0	0	0	3	4	10	.222	.095
Away	0.00	0	0	0	7	0	8.1	3	0	4	9	vs. Right	.148	27	4	1	0	1	4	2	8	.200	.296

Orlando Cabrera — Expos
Age 23 – Bats Right

	Avg	G	AB	R	H	2B	3B	HR	RBI	BB	SO	HBP	GDP	SB	CS	OBP	SLG	IBB	SH	SF	#Pit	#P/PA	GB	FB	G/F
1997 Season	.222	16	18	4	4	0	0	0	2	1	3	0	1	1	2	.263	.222	0	1	0	77	3.85	9	3	3.00

1997 Season

	Avg	AB	H	2B	3B	HR	RBI	BB	SO	OBP	SLG		Avg	AB	H	2B	3B	HR	RBI	BB	SO	OBP	SLG
vs. Left	.143	7	1	0	0	0	1	1	1	.250	.143	Scoring Posn	.333	6	2	0	0	0	2	0	0	.333	.333
vs. Right	.273	11	3	0	0	0	1	0	2	.273	.273	Close & Late	.250	4	1	0	0	0	0	0	2	.250	.250

Greg Cadaret — Angels
Age 36 – Pitches Left (groundball pitcher)

	ERA	W	L	Sv	G	GS	IP	BB	SO	Avg	H	2B	3B	HR	RBI	OBP	SLG	GF	IR	IRS	Hld	SvOp	SB	CS	GB	FB	G/F
1997 Season	3.29	0	0	0	15	0	13.2	8	11	.220	11	2	1	1	4	.350	.360	6	6	1	1	0	1	0	15	20	0.75
Last Five Years	4.34	4	3	3	100	0	101.2	71	65	.270	106	17	1	8	56	.388	.380	41	55	13	10	3	11	5	155	98	1.58

1997 Season

	ERA	W	L	Sv	G	GS	IP	H	HR	BB	SO		Avg	AB	H	2B	3B	HR	RBI	BB	SO	OBP	SLG
Home	5.19	0	0	0	10	0	8.2	9	1	6	6	vs. Left	.174	23	4	1	0	1	1	2	4	.269	.348
Away	0.00	0	0	0	5	0	5.0	2	0	2	5	vs. Right	.259	27	7	1	1	0	3	6	7	.412	.370

Last Five Years

	ERA	W	L	Sv	G	GS	IP	H	HR	BB	SO		Avg	AB	H	2B	3B	HR	RBI	BB	SO	OBP	SLG
Home	3.72	1	2	2	58	0	58.0	61	4	37	35	vs. Left	.291	141	41	5	0	1	15	22	22	.394	.348
Away	5.15	3	1	1	42	0	43.2	45	4	34	30	vs. Right	.259	251	65	12	1	7	41	49	43	.384	.398
Day	5.12	0	1	1	32	0	31.2	29	2	25	20	Inning 1-6	.179	56	10	1	0	0	4	10	11	.303	.196
Night	3.99	4	2	2	68	0	70.0	77	6	46	45	Inning 7+	.286	336	96	16	1	8	52	61	54	.401	.411
Grass	5.29	2	1	1	45	0	49.1	51	3	40	35	None on	.265	189	50	6	1	4	4	30	35	.377	.370
Turf	3.44	2	2	2	55	0	52.1	55	5	31	30	Runners on	.276	203	56	11	0	4	52	41	30	.398	.389
March/April	3.60	0	1	0	18	0	15.0	19	2	7	7	Scoring Posn	.279	129	36	5	0	3	46	31	23	.419	.388
May	4.35	1	0	1	21	0	20.2	20	3	22	14	Close & Late	.314	86	27	1	0	1	14	21	9	.459	.360
June	8.66	1	1	0	15	0	17.2	26	2	14	16	None on/out	.224	85	19	2	0	3	3	13	13	.347	.353
July	3.86	0	0	1	15	0	14.0	13	0	9	8	vs. 1st Batr (relief)	.195	82	16	2	0	2	6	14	13	.333	.293
August	1.46	2	0	1	19	0	24.2	19	0	11	11	1st Inning Pitched	.255	286	73	12	1	2	32	57	48	.386	.325
Sept/Oct	5.59	0	1	0	12	0	9.2	9	1	8	6	First 15 Pitches	.269	249	67	8	1	3	25	43	41	.385	.345
Starter	0.00	0	0	0	0	0	0.0	0	0	0	0	Pitch 16-30	.268	112	30	8	0	3	21	25	18	.401	.420
Reliever	4.34	4	3	3	100	0	101.2	106	8	71	65	Pitch 31-45	.269	26	7	1	0	2	9	2	5	.321	.538
0 Days rest (Relief)	1.54	1	1	2	19	0	23.1	19	1	12	11	Pitch 46+	.400	5	2	0	0	0	1	1	1	.500	.400
1 or 2 Days rest	6.68	0	0	0	38	0	31.0	39	3	30	25	First Pitch	.293	41	12	2	0	0	1	9	0	.431	.341
3+ Days rest	4.18	3	2	1	43	0	47.1	48	4	29	24	Ahead in Count	.188	149	28	2	0	1	9	0	56	.204	.221
vs. AL	4.13	2	2	2	63	0	65.1	63	5	46	40	Behind in Count	.348	115	40	7	0	5	31	36	0	.503	.539
vs. NL	4.71	2	1	1	37	0	36.1	43	3	25	25	Two Strikes	.194	165	32	4	0	3	15	26	65	.314	.273
Pre-All Star	5.37	2	2	1	61	0	62.0	73	7	48	45	Pre-All Star	.293	249	73	11	0	7	45	48	45	.409	.422

	ERA	W	L	Sv	G	GS	IP	H	HR	BB	SO		Avg	AB	H	2B	3B	HR	RBI	BB	SO	OBP	SLG
Post-All Star	2.72	2	1	2	39	0	39.2	33	1	23	20	Post-All Star	.231	143	33	6	1	1	11	23	20	.349	.308

Pitcher vs. Batter (career)

Pitches Best Vs.	Avg	AB	H	2B	3B	HR	RBI	BB	SO	OBP	SLG	Pitches Worst Vs.	Avg	AB	H	2B	3B	HR	RBI	BB	SO	OBP	SLG
Bill Spiers	.000	11	0	0	0	0	0	0	5	.000	.000	Edgar Martinez	.778	9	7	4	0	0	1	2	0	.818	1.222
Mickey Tettleton	.071	14	1	0	0	1	2	0	8	.071	.286	Gary Gaetti	.733	15	11	2	0	1	7	4	1	.750	1.067
Cecil Fielder	.100	10	1	1	0	0	1	1	3	.182	.200	Tony Fernandez	.500	10	5	1	1	1	4	2	1	.538	1.100
Devon White	.115	26	3	0	0	1	3	1	4	.148	.231	Danny Tartabull	.400	10	4	0	0	1	1	3	1	.538	.700
Cal Ripken	.125	16	2	1	0	0	0	1	2	.176	.188	Paul Molitor	.385	13	5	2	0	1	5	5	2	.556	.769

Miguel Cairo — Cubs   Age 24 – Bats Right

	Avg	G	AB	R	H	2B	3B	HR	RBI	BB	SO	HBP	GDP	SB	CS	OBP	SLG	IBB	SH	SF	#Pit	#P/PA	GB	FB	G/F
1997 Season	.241	16	29	7	7	1	0	0	1	2	3	1	0	0	0	.313	.276	0	0	0	102	3.19	11	9	1.22
Career (1996-1997)	.232	25	56	12	13	3	0	0	2	4	12	2	1	0	0	.306	.286	0	0	0	220	3.55	18	14	1.29

1997 Season

	Avg	AB	H	2B	3B	HR	RBI	BB	SO	OBP	SLG		Avg	AB	H	2B	3B	HR	RBI	BB	SO	OBP	SLG
vs. Left	.154	13	2	0	0	0	0	0	2	.154	.154	Scoring Posn	.000	9	0	0	0	0	1	0	1	.000	.000
vs. Right	.313	16	5	1	0	0	1	2	1	.421	.375	Close & Late	.000	7	0	0	0	0	0	0	2	.000	.000

Mike Cameron — White Sox   Age 25 – Bats Right

	Avg	G	AB	R	H	2B	3B	HR	RBI	BB	SO	HBP	GDP	SB	CS	OBP	SLG	IBB	SH	SF	#Pit	#P/PA	GB	FB	G/F
1997 Season	.259	116	379	63	98	18	3	14	55	55	105	5	8	23	2	.356	.433	1	2	5	1776	3.98	100	106	0.94
Career (1995-1997)	.248	155	428	68	106	20	3	15	57	59	123	5	8	23	3	.342	.414	1	5	5	1981	3.95	118	116	1.02

1997 Season

	Avg	AB	H	2B	3B	HR	RBI	BB	SO	OBP	SLG		Avg	AB	H	2B	3B	HR	RBI	BB	SO	OBP	SLG
vs. Left	.228	114	26	7	1	4	15	18	30	.336	.412	First Pitch	.406	32	13	2	0	3	9	0	0	.429	.750
vs. Right	.272	265	72	11	2	10	40	37	75	.365	.442	Ahead in Count	.365	85	31	8	1	4	18	30	0	.526	.624
Groundball	.240	75	18	3	0	2	8	8	26	.313	.360	Behind in Count	.182	187	34	4	2	2	15	0	87	.193	.257
Flyball	.269	52	14	0	2	3	11	9	15	.387	.519	Two Strikes	.155	194	30	4	1	1	15	25	105	.259	.201
Home	.273	176	48	7	1	10	31	28	48	.376	.494	Batting #2	.310	100	31	6	1	6	17	13	31	.391	.570
Away	.246	203	50	11	2	4	24	27	57	.338	.379	Batting #6	.230	174	40	8	1	4	22	29	53	.349	.356
Day	.256	117	30	5	0	3	11	17	31	.351	.376	Other	.257	105	27	4	1	4	16	13	21	.333	.429
Night	.260	262	68	13	3	11	44	38	74	.358	.458	March/April	.000	0	0	0	0	0	0	0	0	.000	.000
Grass	.272	312	85	14	1	12	48	48	81	.373	.439	May	.237	59	14	3	0	1	4	5	17	.297	.339
Turf	.194	67	13	4	2	2	7	7	24	.270	.403	June	.279	61	17	3	0	4	9	9	17	.384	.525
Pre-All Star	.248	137	34	7	0	6	16	16	41	.333	.431	July	.313	80	25	3	2	4	19	10	18	.376	.550
Post-All Star	.264	242	64	11	3	8	39	39	64	.368	.434	August	.208	101	21	4	1	3	17	14	28	.316	.356
Scoring Posn	.312	93	29	7	2	2	41	22	21	.434	.495	Sept/Oct	.269	78	21	5	0	2	6	17	25	.402	.410
Close & Late	.256	43	11	2	0	0	8	12	15	.404	.302	vs. AL	.271	340	92	18	3	14	54	53	93	.368	.465
None on/out	.226	84	19	1	0	2	2	8	24	.301	.310	vs. NL	.154	39	6	0	0	0	1	2	12	.250	.154

1997 By Position

Position	Avg	AB	H	2B	3B	HR	RBI	BB	SO	OBP	SLG	G	GS	Innings	PO	A	E	DP	Fld Pct	Rng Fctr	In Zone	Zone Outs	Zone Rtg	MLB Zone
As cf	.261	341	89	16	3	13	51	51	92	.361	.440	102	99	836.2	297	4	5	1	.984	3.24	331	293	.885	.815
As rf	.243	37	9	2	0	1	4	4	12	.317	.378	37	8	105.0	36	1	0	1	1.000	3.17	34	32	.941	.813

Ken Caminiti — Padres   Age 35 – Bats Both

	Avg	G	AB	R	H	2B	3B	HR	RBI	BB	SO	HBP	GDP	SB	CS	OBP	SLG	IBB	SH	SF	#Pit	#P/PA	GB	FB	G/F
1997 Season	.290	137	486	92	141	28	0	26	90	80	118	3	11	11	2	.389	.508	9	0	7	2259	3.92	150	138	1.09
Last Five Years	.293	680	2507	413	735	157	4	123	464	319	470	10	59	46	20	.371	.506	56	1	29	10420	3.63	830	733	1.13

1997 Season

	Avg	AB	H	2B	3B	HR	RBI	BB	SO	OBP	SLG		Avg	AB	H	2B	3B	HR	RBI	BB	SO	OBP	SLG
vs. Left	.306	144	44	7	0	6	24	24	30	.404	.479	First Pitch	.368	68	25	6	0	6	15	6	0	.434	.721
vs. Right	.284	342	97	21	0	20	66	56	88	.383	.520	Ahead in Count	.370	108	40	6	0	7	28	45	0	.545	.620
Groundball	.306	85	26	8	0	5	18	19	19	.425	.576	Behind in Count	.211	218	46	8	0	9	33	0	98	.212	.372
Flyball	.222	72	16	2	0	5	11	14	24	.348	.458	Two Strikes	.172	238	41	11	0	5	28	2			
Home	.309	230	71	14	0	15	46	39	51	.406	.565	Batting #3	.231	13	3	0	0	0	1				
Away	.273	256	70	14	0	11	44	41	67	.374	.457	Batting #4	.294	470	138	28	0	26	88	7			
Day	.265	151	40	13	0	7	29	20	37	.349	.490	Other	.000	3	0	0	0	0	1				
Night	.301	335	101	15	0	19	61	60	81	.406	.516	March/April	.225	80	18	5	0	2	14				
Grass	.284	394	112	20	0	20	68	64	93	.384	.487	May	.250	52	13	2	0	2	8				
Turf	.315	92	29	8	0	6	22	16	25	.411	.598	June	.271	96	26	5	0	2	13	1			
Pre-All Star	.247	235	58	13	0	6	35	30	62	.337	.379	July	.267	75	20	4	0	5	17	2			
Post-All Star	.331	251	83	15	0	20	55	50	56	.435	.629	August	.376	109	41	9	0	9	20	1			
Scoring Posn	.304	138	42	7	0	8	67	33	32	.421	.529	Sept/Oct	.311	74	23	3	0	6	18	1			
Close & Late	.215	79	17	7	0	0	10	16	25	.351	.304	vs. AL	.346	52	18	6	0	2	8	1			
None on/out	.294	126	37	7	0	10	10	21	30	.395	.587	vs. NL	.283	434	123	22	0	24	82	6			

1997 By Position

Position	Avg	AB	H	2B	3B	HR	RBI	BB	SO	OBP	SLG	G	GS	Innings	PO	A	E	DP	Fld Pct	Rng Fctr	In Zone
As 3b	.292	483	141	28	0	26	89	80	117	.392	.511	133	133	1117.0	90	289	24	23	.940	3.05	410

Last Five Years

	Avg	AB	H	2B	3B	HR	RBI	BB	SO	OBP	SLG		Avg	AB	H	2B	3B	HR	RBI	BB	SO	OBP	SLG
vs. Left	.301	793	239	58	1	41	166	86	104	.368	.532	First Pitch	.346	439	152	37	1	24	92	41	0	.400	.599
vs. Right	.289	1714	496	99	3	82	298	233	366	.373	.494	Ahead in Count	.364	605	220	46	0	32	126	164	0	.497	.598
Groundball	.306	667	204	44	2	29	125	69	112	.369	.508	Behind in Count	.217	995	216	49	0	41	154	0	389	.218	.390
Flyball	.265	392	104	29	1	19	75	53	99	.350	.490	Two Strikes	.201	1054	212	50	2	43	157	114	470	.279	.375
Home	.298	1243	371	77	2	62	247	138	230	.367	.513	Batting #4	.293	1681	492	101	1	89	322	238	337	.379	.513
Away	.288	1264	364	80	2	61	217	181	240	.376	.499	Batting #5	.292	507	148	38	1	17	81	38	76	.340	.471
Day	.281	757	213	53	0	36	139	104	149	.369	.494	Other	.298	319	95	18	2	17	61	43	57	.377	.527
Night	.298	1750	522	104	4	87	325	215	321	.372	.511	March/April	.266	368	98	29	1	9	66	32	73	.327	.424
Grass	.302	1539	465	86	1	91	301	208	301	.384	.537	May	.289	380	110	28	1	21	75	30	54	.341	.534
Turf	.279	968	270	71	3	32	163	111	169	.352	.458	June	.265	501	133	19	0	21	72	51	99	.338	.429
Pre-All Star	.276	1394	385	90	2	55	239	141	254	.344	.462	July	.289	457	132	31	0	18	87	80	87	.391	.475
Post-All Star	.314	1113	350	67	2	68	225	178	216	.404	.562	August	.321	433	139	29	1	28	84	61	83	.398	.587
Scoring Posn	.308	731	225	50	2	38	351	158	141	.418	.538	Sept/Oct	.334	368	123	21	1	26	80	65	74	.430	.609
Close & Late	.245	383	94	24	0	13	52	62	92	.350	.410	vs. AL	.346	52	18	6	0	2	8	13	16	.477	.577
None on/out	.267	633	169	36	0	33	33	48	112	.322	.480	vs. NL	.292	2455	717	151	4	121	456	306	454	.369	.505

Batter vs. Pitcher (career)

Hits Best Against	Avg	AB	H	2B	3B	HR	RBI	BB	SO	OBP	SLG	Hits Worst Against	Avg	AB	H	2B	3B	HR	RBI	BB	SO	OBP	SLG
Chuck McElroy	.727	11	8	1	0	1	3	0	1	.727	1.091	Pete Harnisch	.000	10	0	0	0	0	0	2	5	.167	.000
VanLandingham	.538	13	7	2	0	1	7	1	3	.600	.923	Mel Rojas	.000	9	0	0	0	0	0	4	2	.308	.000
Mark Portugal	.438	16	7	3	0	2	5	1	5	.471	1.000	Norm Charlton	.034	29	1	0	0	1	3	2	8	.097	.138
Mark Clark	.417	12	5	0	0	2	3	2	2	.500	.917	Jaime Navarro	.091	11	1	0	0	0	0	1	4	.167	.091
Ismael Valdes	.400	20	8	0	0	4	8	2	5	.455	1.000	Dwight Gooden	.136	22	3	0	0	0	0	3	5	.160	.136

Casey Candaele — Indians   Age 37 – Bats Both

	Avg	G	AB	R	H	2B	3B	HR	RBI	BB	SO	HBP	GDP	SB	CS	OBP	SLG	IBB	SH	SF	#Pit	#P/PA	GB	FB	G/F
1997 Season	.308	14	26	5	8	1	0	0	4	1	1	0	0	1	0	.333	.346	0	0	0	102	3.78	14	5	2.80
Last Five Years	.251	113	191	31	48	11	0	2	15	12	24	0	0	3	3	.296	.340	0	0	0	783	3.86	78	47	1.66

1997 Season

	Avg	AB	H	2B	3B	HR	RBI	BB	SO	OBP	SLG		Avg	AB	H	2B	3B	HR	RBI	BB	SO	OBP	SLG
vs. Left	.000	2	0	0	0	0	0	0	0	.000	.000	Scoring Posn	.333	12	4	1	0	0	4	1	0	.385	.417
vs. Right	.333	24	8	1	0	0	4	1	1	.360	.375	Close & Late	.200	5	1	0	0	0	1	1	0	.333	.200

Tom Candiotti — Dodgers   Age 40 – Pitches Right

	ERA	W	L	Sv	G	GS	IP	BB	SO	Avg	H	2B	3B	HR	RBI	OBP	SLG	GF	IR	IRS	Hld	SvOp	SB	CS	GB	FB	G/F
1997 Season	3.60	10	7	0	41	18	135.0	40	89	.248	128	24	2	21	52	.314	.424	6	5	1	2	0	16	8	157	173	0.91
Last Five Years	3.71	41	49	0	155	129	844.1	266	566	.257	828	153	14	78	360	.318	.386	6	6	1	2	0	85	35	1129	924	1.22

1997 Season

	ERA	W	L	Sv	G	GS	IP	H	HR	BB	SO		Avg	AB	H	2B	3B	HR	RBI	BB	SO	OBP	SLG
Home	3.16	7	3	0	22	9	74.0	62	14	24	49	vs. Left	.264	246	65	11	1	11	28	20	30	.326	.451
Away	4.13	3	4	0	19	9	61.0	66	7	16	40	vs. Right	.232	271	63	13	1	10	24	20	59	.303	.399
Day	3.39	4	4	0	18	8	61.0	57	9	18	45	Inning 1-6	.245	412	101	20	2	18	42	34	70	.314	.434
Night	3.77	6	3	0	23	10	74.0	71	12	22	44	Inning 7+	.257	105	27	4	0	3	10	6	19	.316	.381
Grass	3.44	9	6	0	32	15	110.0	100	18	36	74	None on	.253	320	81	16	2	14	14	16	51	.299	.447
Turf	4.32	1	1	0	9	3	25.0	28	3	4	15	Runners on	.239	197	47	8	0	7	38	24	38	.336	.386
March/April	2.84	2	1	0	11	0	12.2	8	1	2	9	Scoring Posn	.192	125	24	4	0	4	32	20	27	.313	.320
May	2.25	1	1	0	7	0	8.0	12	0	3	5	Close & Late	.209	43	9	1	0	1	5	1	8	.244	.302
June	2.91	1	0	0	7	2	21.2	14	2	5	15	None on/out	.273	139	38	6	0	9	9	8	19	.331	.511
July	3.35	3	1	0	6	6	37.2	39	7	12	22	vs. 1st Batr (relief)	.100	20	2	2	0	0	1	2	4	.217	.200
August	3.18	2	2	0	6	6	34.0	30	9	9	20	1st Inning Pitched	.245	151	37	7	2	4	18	9	22	.311	.397
Sept/Oct	6.43	1	2	0	4	4	21.0	25	5	9	18	First 15 Pitches	.242	120	29	4	2	6	13	7	19	.298	.458
Starter	3.83	7	5	0	18	18	105.2	103	19	35	68	Pitch 16-30	.290	93	27	7	0	1	8	8	10	.350	.398
Reliever	2.76	3	2	0	23	0	29.1	25	2	5	21	Pitch 31-45	.274	73	20	4	0	1	5	2	15	.312	.370
0 Days rest (Relief)	10.80	0	0	0	2	0	1.2	3	0	0	1	Pitch 46+	.225	231	52	9	0	13	26	23	45	.309	.433
1 or 2 Days rest	0.00	0	0	0	11	0	13.1	3	0	3	10	First Pitch	.284	67	19	5	0	3	9	1	0	.324	.493
3+ Days rest	4.40	0	2	0	10	0	14.1	19	2	2	10	Ahead in Count	.177	231	41	8	0	3	14	0	75	.191	.251
vs. AL	4.02	0	0	0	3	2	15.2	15	5	3	11	Behind in Count	.296	108	32	6	2	7	14	27	0	.447	.583
vs. NL	3.54	10	7	0	38	16	119.1	113	16	37	78	Two Strikes	.156	243	38	8	0	5	16	11	89	.205	.251
Pre-All Star	2.80	5	2	0	27	4	54.2	45	6	13	37	Pre-All Star	.220	205	45	12	1	6	18	13	37	.276	.376
Post-All Star	4.15	5	5	0	14	14	80.1	83	15	27	52	Post-All Star	.266	312	83	12	1	15	34	27	52	.338	.455

Last Five Years

	ERA	W	L	Sv	G	GS	IP	H	HR	BB	SO		Avg	AB	H	2B	3B	HR	RBI	BB	SO	OBP	SLG
Home	3.63	23	24	0	77	62	427.0	414	46	130	292	vs. Left	.254	1550	394	64	8	37	160	154	249	.322	.377
Away	3.80	18	25	0	78	67	417.1	414	32	136	274	vs. Right	.260	1670	434	89	6	41	200	112	317	.314	.394
Day	3.23	14	10	0	45	34	226.0	195	19	72	156	Inning 1-6	.259	2722	705	130	12	66	313	236	483	.322	.388
Night	3.89	27	39	0	110	95	618.1	633	59	194	410	Inning 7+	.247	498	123	23	2	12	47	30	83	.297	.373
Grass	3.64	33	39	0	121	101	669.1	659	65	208	452	None on	.248	1892	470	84	9	48	48	134	340	.305	.378
Turf	3.96	8	10	0	34	28	175.0	169	13	58	114	Runners on	.270	1328	358	69	5	30	312	132	226	.336	.397
March/April	4.36	7	7	0	26	15	97.0	98	11	35	62	Scoring Posn	.236	787	186	34	4	16	268	106	147	.323	.351
May	3.87	8	9	0	31	24	160.1	163	10	50	105	Close & Late	.225	284	64	11	2	7	29	19	47	.282	.352
June	2.81	6	7	0	28	22	160.1	136	8	48	114	None on/out	.257	836	215	40	1	23	23	51	135	.307	.390
July	2.58	10	8	0	26	25	178.0	157	15	60	119	vs. 1st Batr (relief)	.174	23	4	2	0	0	1	2	5	.269	.261
August	4.08	7	7	0	23	23	136.2	141	17	34	94	1st Inning Pitched	.275	607	167	34	7	12	90	59	90	.342	.414

	ERA	W	L	Sv	G	GS	IP	H	HR	BB	SO		Avg	AB	H	2B	3B	HR	RBI	BB	SO	OBP	SLG
Sept/Oct	5.54	3	11	0	21	20	112.0	133	17	39	72	First 15 Pitches	.284	457	130	24	7	11	42	36	60	.339	.440
Starter	3.71	38	47	0	129	129	802.2	788	75	253	537	Pitch 16-30	.260	480	125	30	0	8	64	53	81	.339	.373
Reliever	3.67	3	2	0	26	0	41.2	40	3	13	29	Pitch 31-45	.263	482	127	19	0	10	47	28	94	.309	.365
0 Days rest (Relief)	10.80	0	0	0	2	0	1.2	3	0	0	1	Pitch 46+	.248	1801	446	80	7	49	207	149	331	.309	.381
1 or 2 Days rest	2.08	3	0	0	13	0	21.2	10	1	8	17	First Pitch	.316	450	142	24	2	10	62	5	0	.335	.444
3+ Days rest	4.91	0	2	0	11	0	18.1	27	2	5	11	Ahead in Count	.209	1385	289	50	5	19	125	0	445	.212	.293
vs. AL	4.02	0	0	0	3	2	15.2	15	5	3	11	Behind in Count	.313	674	211	38	5	31	92	140	0	.433	.522
vs. NL	3.70	41	49	0	152	127	828.2	813	73	263	555	Two Strikes	.190	1476	281	50	5	22	129	120	566	.254	.276
Pre-All Star	3.41	24	24	0	95	71	485.2	455	34	146	324	Pre-All Star	.248	1834	455	87	8	34	190	146	324	.308	.360
Post-All Star	4.12	17	25	0	60	58	358.2	373	44	120	242	Post-All Star	.269	1386	373	66	6	44	170	120	242	.331	.421

Pitches Best Vs.	Avg	AB	H	2B	3B	HR	RBI	BB	SO	OBP	SLG	Pitches Worst Vs.	Avg	AB	H	2B	3B	HR	RBI	BB	SO	OBP	SLG
Delino DeShields	.000	8	0	0	0	0	0	3	2	.273	.000	Carlos Baerga	.462	13	6	1	0	2	3	0	0	.462	1.000
Craig Shipley	.083	12	1	0	0	0	1	0	5	.083	.083	Larry Walker	.444	18	8	0	0	4	7	3	0	.500	1.111
Vinny Castilla	.091	11	1	0	0	0	1	1	5	.167	.091	Rafael Palmeiro	.438	16	7	2	0	1	2	1	2	.471	.750
Bill Spiers	.095	21	2	0	0	0	3	1	5	.130	.095	Ryne Sandberg	.417	12	5	3	0	1	3	1	1	.462	.917
Andres Galarraga	.118	17	2	0	0	0	2	0	4	.111	.118	Glenallen Hill	.414	29	12	1	1	4	9	4	3	.485	.931

John Cangelosi — Marlins

Age 35 – Bats Both (groundball hitter)

	Avg	G	AB	R	H	2B	3B	HR	RBI	BB	SO	HBP	GDP	SB	CS	OBP	SLG	IBB	SH	SF	#Pit	#P/PA	GB	FB	G/F
1997 Season	.245	103	192	47	47	8	0	1	12	19	33	3	3	5	1	.321	.302	1	1	1	837	3.88	77	45	1.71
Last Five Years	.272	363	766	137	208	28	6	4	50	130	136	14	11	48	16	.386	.339	4	7	3	3654	3.97	287	174	1.65

1997 Season

	Avg	AB	H	2B	3B	HR	RBI	BB	SO	OBP	SLG		Avg	AB	H	2B	3B	HR	RBI	BB	SO	OBP	SLG
vs. Left	.235	51	12	3	0	0	4	5	12	.310	.294	Scoring Posn	.227	44	10	2	0	0	11	5	5	.300	.273
vs. Right	.248	141	35	5	0	1	8	14	21	.325	.305	Close & Late	.154	39	6	0	0	0	3	6	6	.267	.154
Home	.275	91	25	3	0	1	4	13	18	.371	.341	None on/out	.229	70	16	3	0	1	1	7	11	.299	.314
Away	.218	101	22	5	0	0	8	6	15	.273	.267	Batting #1	.274	106	29	6	0	0	8	11	17	.353	.330
First Pitch	.250	24	6	2	0	0	0	1	0	.308	.333	Batting #9	.205	44	9	2	0	1	1	4	9	.271	.318
Ahead in Count	.385	52	20	4	0	1	5	10	0	.492	.519	Other	.214	42	9	0	0	0	3	4	7	.292	.214
Behind in Count	.159	63	10	0	0	0	3	0	23	.172	.159	Pre-All Star	.243	103	25	4	0	1	8	11	16	.325	.311
Two Strikes	.163	86	14	2	0	4	8	33	0	.240	.186	Post-All Star	.247	89	22	4	0	0	4	8	17	.316	.292

	Avg	AB	H	2B	3B	HR	RBI	BB	SO	OBP	SLG		Avg	AB	H	2B	3B	HR	RBI	BB	SO	OBP	SLG
vs. Left	.232	164	38	10	0	3	14	25	42	.354	.348	First Pitch	.316	98	31	4	1	0	4	3	0	.374	.378
vs. Right	.282	602	170	18	6	1	36	105	94	.399	.337	Ahead in Count	.378	193	73	7	4	2	17	64	0	.535	.487
Groundball	.280	150	42	4	2	1	8	28	22	.403	.353	Behind in Count	.194	288	56	7	1	2	16	0	101	.210	.247
Flyball	.297	118	35	7	0	0	8	18	19	.399	.356	Two Strikes	.193	353	68	8	1	2	22	63	136	.320	.238
Home	.288	406	117	13	5	4	27	72	76	.405	.374	Batting #1	.293	454	133	20	6	2	31	77	77	.401	.377
Away	.253	360	91	15	1	0	23	58	58	.364	.300	Batting #9	.218	119	26	3	0	1	5	22	24	.359	.269
Day	.249	229	57	7	1	2	19	34	34	.358	.314	Other	.254	193	49	5	0	1	14	31	35	.365	.295
Night	.281	537	151	21	5	2	31	96	102	.397	.350	March/April	.254	63	16	2	0	0	1	12	7	.373	.286
Grass	.244	357	87	12	1	1	15	57	67	.355	.291	May	.263	152	40	4	0	0	10	21	23	.365	.289
Turf	.296	409	121	16	5	3	35	73	69	.411	.381	June	.287	136	39	6	2	4	15	34	29	.437	.449
Pre-All Star	.265	407	108	17	3	4	30	72	72	.383	.351	July	.298	151	45	8	1	0	10	17	31	.373	.364
Post-All Star	.279	359	100	11	3	0	20	58	64	.388	.326	August	.291	103	30	3	0	0	5	18	18	.408	.320
Scoring Posn	.244	168	41	4	0	2	48	36	28	.375	.304	Sept/Oct	.236	161	38	5	3	0	9	28	28	.359	.304
Close & Late	.211	185	39	5	0	0	15	39	42	.357	.238	vs. AL	.182	22	4	1	0	1	2	2	3	.250	.364
None on/out	.241	294	71	10	4	2	2	44	50	.350	.323	vs. NL	.274	744	204	27	6	3	48	128	133	.389	.339

Hits Best Against	Avg	AB	H	2B	3B	HR	RBI	BB	SO	OBP	SLG	Hits Worst Against	Avg	AB	H	2B	3B	HR	RBI	BB	SO	OBP	SLG
John Smoltz	.526	19	10	0	0	0	1	5	2	.655	.526	Sid Fernandez	.071	14	1	0	0	0	1	1	.188	.071
Kevin Ritz	.500	10	5	0	1	0	1	2	0	.583	.700	F. Valenzuela	.091	11	1	1	0	0	1	0	3	.167	.182
Hideo Nomo	.417	12	5	2	0	0	1	2	1	.500	.583	Pedro Martinez	.167	18	3	0	0	0	0	1	3	.211	.167
Todd Stottlemyre	.385	13	5	1	0	0	0	4	1	.529	.462	Mark Leiter	.200	10	2	0	0	0	1	1	3	.273	.200
Armando Reynoso	.357	14	5	1	1	0	0	0	2	.400	.571	Greg Maddux	.214	14	3	0	0	0	0	0	3	.313	.214

Jose Canseco — Athletics

Age 33 – Bats Right (flyball hitter)

	Avg	G	AB	R	H	2B	3B	HR	RBI	BB	SO	HBP	GDP	SB	CS	OBP	SLG	IBB	SH	SF	#Pit	#P/PA	GB	FB	G/F
1997 Season	.235	108	388	56	91	19	0	23	74	51	122	3	15	8	2	.325	.461	1	0	4	1861	4.17	94	110	0.85
Last Five Years	.275	477	1804	306	496	99	5	116	373	241	473	24	56	36	17	.365	.528	18	0	17	8823	4.23	502	532	0.94

1997 Season

	Avg	AB	H	2B	3B	HR	RBI	BB	SO	OBP	SLG		Avg	AB	H	2B	3B	HR	RBI	BB	SO	OBP	SLG
vs. Left	.241	79	19	5	0	2	11	9	25	.318	.380	First Pitch	.293	41	12	6	0	1	8	1	0	.311	.512
vs. Right	.233	309	72	14	0	21	63	42	97	.327	.482	Ahead in Count	.346	78	27	7	0	7	25	21	0	.485	.705
Groundball	.239	88	21	4	0	3	14	10	35	.313	.386	Behind in Count	.183	186	34	3	0	9	25	0	100	.189	.344
Flyball	.246	61	15	3	0	8	15	3	16	.288	.689	Two Strikes	.173	220	38	4	0	11	29	29	122	.273	.341
Home	.251	187	47	9	0	10	40	27	54	.350	.460	Batting #3	.263	186	49	8	0	11	37	20	51	.337	.484
Away	.219	201	44	10	0	13	34	24	68	.301	.463	Batting #5	.221	140	31	10	0	8	23	22	52	.329	.464
Day	.214	159	34	4	0	7	25	23	43	.315	.371	Other	.177	62	11	1	0	4	14	9	19	.284	.371
Night	.249	229	57	15	0	16	49	28	79	.332	.524	March/April	.252	107	27	4	0	5	17	9	30	.311	.430
Grass	.228	355	81	15	0	21	68	49	109	.324	.448	May	.225	102	23	4	0	6	21	14	29	.319	.441

1997 Season

	Avg	AB	H	2B	3B	HR	RBI	BB	SO	OBP	SLG		Avg	AB	H	2B	3B	HR	RBI	BB	SO	OBP	SLG
Turf	.303	33	10	4	0	2	6	2	13	.333	.606	June	.241	87	21	7	0	6	16	13	29	.337	.529
Pre-All Star	.241	316	76	16	0	18	57	38	94	.321	.462	July	.218	78	17	4	0	4	13	11	31	.322	.423
Post-All Star	.208	72	15	3	0	5	17	13	28	.341	.458	August	.214	14	3	0	0	2	7	4	3	.400	.643
Scoring Posn	.241	116	28	7	0	8	55	20	35	.343	.509	Sept/Oct	.000	0	0	0	0	0	0	0	0	.000	.000
Close & Late	.217	69	15	5	0	5	14	8	22	.295	.507	vs. AL	.236	360	85	19	0	21	70	43	110	.320	.464
None on/out	.241	83	20	1	0	4	4	11	32	.330	.398	vs. NL	.214	28	6	0	0	2	4	8	12	.389	.429

1997 By Position

Position	Avg	AB	H	2B	3B	HR	RBI	BB	SO	OBP	SLG	G	GS	Innings	PO	A	E	DP	Fld Pct	Rng Fctr	In Zone	Zone Outs	Zone Rtg	MLB Zone
As DH	.248	218	54	13	0	12	40	22	69	.322	.472	60	60	---	---	---	---	---	---	---	---	---	---	---
As lf	.254	63	16	2	0	7	15	13	14	.382	.619	19	17	143.1	25	1	0	0	1.000	1.63	33	24	.727	.805
As rf	.204	103	21	4	0	4	19	16	35	.306	.359	27	27	217.2	49	1	5	0	.909	2.07	55	47	.855	.813

Last Five Years

	Avg	AB	H	2B	3B	HR	RBI	BB	SO	OBP	SLG		Avg	AB	H	2B	3B	HR	RBI	BB	SO	OBP	SLG
vs. Left	.282	397	112	17	2	30	84	73	93	.356	.562	First Pitch	.356	146	52	15	0	10	35	15	0	.424	.664
vs. Right	.273	1407	384	82	3	86	289	168	380	.356	.519	Ahead in Count	.372	436	162	32	2	43	133	102	0	.491	.750
Groundball	.291	422	123	23	0	29	88	49	120	.366	.552	Behind in Count	.205	843	173	31	2	36	115	0	376	.213	.375
Flyball	.295	353	104	18	3	29	76	37	93	.369	.609	Two Strikes	.202	998	202	38	3	47	149	123	473	.293	.388
Home	.289	889	257	44	4	60	195	120	211	.378	.550	Batting #3	.267	798	213	36	2	48	165	102	218	.353	.497
Away	.261	915	239	55	1	56	178	121	262	.352	.507	Batting #4	.289	795	230	48	3	55	165	110	185	.382	.565
Day	.264	561	148	29	1	30	113	73	145	.352	.480	Other	.251	211	53	15	0	13	43	29	70	.344	.507
Night	.280	1243	348	70	4	86	260	168	328	.369	.550	March/April	.259	352	91	17	0	18	72	41	86	.337	.460
Grass	.279	1596	445	80	5	107	341	221	408	.371	.536	May	.265	412	109	23	1	27	85	66	112	.372	.522
Turf	.245	208	51	19	0	9	32	20	65	.312	.466	June	.287	380	109	23	0	31	86	52	102	.376	.592
Pre-All Star	.271	1260	342	70	2	83	262	178	331	.365	.528	July	.283	361	102	16	3	23	71	53	97	.378	.535
Post-All Star	.283	544	154	29	3	33	111	63	142	.363	.529	August	.325	169	55	15	1	13	35	18	41	.395	.657
Scoring Posn	.297	529	157	29	0	34	268	86	118	.390	.544	Sept/Oct	.231	130	30	5	0	4	24	11	35	.306	.362
Close & Late	.286	280	80	16	0	17	66	50	81	.397	.525	vs. AL	.276	1776	490	99	5	114	369	233	461	.364	.530
None on/out	.266	399	106	18	2	26	26	39	117	.339	.516	vs. NL	.214	28	6	0	0	2	4	8	12	.389	.429

Batter vs. Pitcher (career)

Hits Best Against	Avg	AB	H	2B	3B	HR	RBI	BB	SO	OBP	SLG	Hits Worst Against	Avg	AB	H	2B	3B	HR	RBI	BB	SO	OBP	SLG
Arthur Rhodes	.625	8	5	0	0	3	4	4	1	.750	1.750	Erik Hanson	.043	23	1	0	0	0	0	3	11	.154	.043
Tim Belcher	.412	17	7	2	0	2	2	4	2	.545	.882	Chad Ogea	.091	11	1	1	0	0	1	1	4	.167	.182
Terry Mathews	.364	11	4	1	0	2	5	2	1	.462	1.000	Jason Bere	.100	10	1	0	0	0	2	2	3	.250	.100
Tim Wakefield	.333	9	3	1	0	2	6	0	2	.364	1.111	Orel Hershiser	.125	16	2	0	0	0	2	2	8	.211	.125
Todd Stottlemyre	.306	36	11	0	0	8	15	4	12	.390	.972	Rick Aguilera	.167	18	3	0	0	0	1	0	6	.167	.167

Dan Carlson — Giants   Age 28 – Pitches Right (flyball pitcher)

	ERA	W	L	Sv	G	GS	IP	BB	SO	Avg	H	2B	3B	HR	RBI	OBP	SLG	GF	IR	IRS	Hld	SvOp	SB	CS	GB	FB	G/F
1997 Season	7.63	0	0	0	6	0	15.1	8	14	.317	20	5	2	5	13	.389	.698	2	1	1	0	0	0	1	17	29	0.59
Career (1996-1997)	5.68	1	0	0	11	0	25.1	10	18	.314	33	7	2	7	18	.364	.619	5	1	1	0	0	1	1	28	51	0.55

1997 Season

	ERA	W	L	Sv	G	GS	IP	H	HR	BB	SO		Avg	AB	H	2B	3B	HR	RBI	BB	SO	OBP	SLG
Home	7.84	0	0	0	4	0	10.1	14	3	5	9	vs. Left	.250	32	8	2	0	3	5	3	7	.314	.594
Away	7.20	0	0	0	2	0	5.0	6	2	3	5	vs. Right	.387	31	12	3	2	2	8	5	7	.459	.806

Rafael Carmona — Mariners   Age 25 – Pitches Right

	ERA	W	L	Sv	G	GS	IP	BB	SO	Avg	H	2B	3B	HR	RBI	OBP	SLG	GF	IR	IRS	Hld	SvOp	SB	CS	GB	FB	G/F
1997 Season	3.18	0	0	0	4	0	5.2	2	6	.150	3	1	0	1	4	.227	.350	1	3	3	0	0	1	0	4	9	0.44
Career (1995-1997)	4.70	10	7	2	72	4	143.2	91	96	.275	153	33	2	21	88	.378	.455	22	66	26	8	7	7	3	200	179	1.12

1997 Season

	ERA	W	L	Sv	G	GS	IP	H	HR	BB	SO		Avg	AB	H	2B	3B	HR	RBI	BB	SO	OBP	SLG
Home	4.50	0	0	0	2	0	2.0	1	1	0	3	vs. Left	.143	7	1	1	0	0	3	2	2	.333	.286
Away	2.45	0	0	0	2	0	3.2	2	0	2	3	vs. Right	.154	13	2	0	0	1	1	0	4	.154	.385

Career (1995-1997)

	ERA	W	L	Sv	G	GS	IP	H	HR	BB	SO		Avg	AB	H	2B	3B	HR	RBI	BB	SO	OBP	SLG
Home	3.25	5	3	2	36	2	74.2	78	9	47	54	vs. Left	.332	271	90	20	2	12	49	49	47	.433	.554
Away	6.26	5	4	0	36	2	69.0	75	12	44	42	vs. Right	.221	285	63	13	0	9	39	42	49	.322	.361
Day	6.69	2	4	0	20	2	35.0	35	3	31	27	Inning 1-6	.299	278	83	18	1	7	45	51	41	.404	.446
Night	4.06	8	3	2	52	2	108.2	118	18	60	69	Inning 7+	.252	278	70	15	1	14	43	40	55	.351	.464
Grass	6.03	5	4	0	32	2	62.2	68	10	39	36	None on	.278	277	77	14	2	10	10	43	55	.381	.451
Turf	3.67	5	3	2	40	2	81.0	85	11	52	60	Runners on	.272	279	76	19	0	11	78	48	41	.375	.459
March/April	4.50	1	0	0	6	0	6.0	3	0		7	Scoring Posn	.269	175	47	11	0	10	74	31	23	.369	.503
May	4.19	1	1	1	14	1	34.1	31	6	23	25	Close & Late	.230	113	26	4	1	8	18	24	16	.371	.496
June	6.10	3	1	0	16	1	38.1	47	7	29	21	None on/out	.290	124	36	7	1	5	5	24	23	.413	.484
July	5.87	2	3	0	12	1	23.0	28	3	14	15	vs. 1st Batr (relief)	.259	58	15	4	0	2	16	7	7	.343	.431
August	5.21	0	1	0	11	1	19.0	28	3	5	13	1st Inning Pitched	.259	243	63	17	0	5	41	38	37	.358	.391
Sept/Oct	1.57	3	1	1	13	0	23.0	16	2	13	16	First 15 Pitches	.268	190	51	14	0	5	35	32	27	.371	.421
Starter	12.38	0	3	0	4	4	16.0	30	4	10	7	Pitch 16-30	.240	154	37	9	0	6	20	24	31	.344	.416
Reliever	3.74	10	4	2	68	0	127.2	123	17	81	89	Pitch 31-45	.240	104	25	3	1	6	12	17	21	.352	.462
0 Days rest (Relief)	0.00	1	0	0	9	0	12.1	6	0	7	10	Pitch 46+	.370	108	40	7	1	4	21	18	17	.461	.565
1 or 2 Days rest	3.46	4	1	1	27	0	39.0	34	6	29	30	First Pitch	.343	67	23	4	0	4	13	7	0	.405	.582

Career (1995-1997)

	ERA	W	L	Sv	G	GS	IP	H	HR	BB	SO		Avg	AB	H	2B	3B	HR	RBI	BB	SO	OBP	SLG
3+ Days rest	4.48	5	3	1	32	0	76.1	83	11	45	49	Ahead in Count	.183	240	44	8	1	2	22	0	78	.191	.250
vs. AL	4.70	10	7	2	72	4	143.2	153	21	91	96	Behind in Count	.357	143	51	14	0	10	38	47	0	.510	.664
vs. NL	0.00	0	0	0	0	0	0.0	0	0	0	0	Two Strikes	.189	249	47	5	2	5	25	36	96	.296	.285
Pre-All Star	5.08	6	3	1	40	2	83.1	88	15	60	55	Pre-All Star	.278	317	88	23	2	15	57	60	55	.390	.505
Post-All Star	4.18	4	4	1	32	2	60.1	65	6	31	41	Post-All Star	.272	239	65	10	0	6	31	31	41	.361	.389

Chris Carpenter — Blue Jays
Age 23 – Pitches Right (groundball pitcher)

	ERA	W	L	Sv	G	GS	IP	BB	SO	Avg	H	2B	3B	HR	RBI	OBP	SLG	CG	ShO	Sup	QS	#P/S	SB	CS	GB	FB	G/F
1997 Season	5.09	3	7	0	14	13	81.1	37	55	.325	108	18	0	7	43	.394	.443	1	1	3.65	7	98	4	7	136	67	2.03

1997 Season

	ERA	W	L	Sv	G	GS	IP	H	HR	BB	SO		Avg	AB	H	2B	3B	HR	RBI	BB	SO	OBP	SLG
Home	4.22	2	4	0	7	6	42.2	54	5	15	22	vs. Left	.314	172	54	9	0	4	25	16	24	.368	.436
Away	6.05	1	3	0	7	7	38.2	54	2	22	33	vs. Right	.338	160	54	9	0	3	18	21	31	.421	.450
Starter	5.02	3	7	0	13	13	75.1	97	6	34	51	Scoring Posn	.307	88	27	5	0	2	32	11	20	.376	.432
Reliever	6.00	0	0	0	1	0	6.0	11	1	3	4	Close & Late	.259	27	7	1	0	0	3	2	2	.310	.296
0-3 Days Rest (Start)	0.00	0	0	0	0	0	0.0	0	0	0	0	None on/out	.354	79	28	5	0	2	2	9	11	.420	.494
4 Days Rest	2.93	2	2	0	6	6	40.0	36	3	15	31	Ahead in Count	.229	144	33	5	0	3	10	0	48	.240	.326
5+ Days Rest	7.39	1	5	0	7	7	35.1	61	3	19	20	Behind in Count	.397	73	29	7	0	2	20	11	0	.465	.575
Pre-All Star	12.71	0	2	0	3	2	11.1	28	4	8	11	Two Strikes	.241	141	34	4	0	4	10	26	55	.367	.355
Post-All Star	3.86	3	5	0	11	11	70.0	80	3	29	44												

Chuck Carr — Astros
Age 29 – Bats Both (groundball hitter)

	Avg	G	AB	R	H	2B	3B	HR	RBI	BB	SO	HBP	GDP	SB	CS	OBP	SLG	IBB	SH	SF	#Pit	#P/PA	GB	FB	G/F
1997 Season	.248	89	238	37	59	14	2	4	17	17	48	3	0	12	5	.305	.374	2	3	1	887	3.33	84	69	1.22
Last Five Years	.256	469	1636	245	419	78	7	13	119	140	263	12	13	132	50	.318	.336	4	27	10	6312	3.46	629	421	1.49

1997 Season

	Avg	AB	H	2B	3B	HR	RBI	BB	SO	OBP	SLG		Avg	AB	H	2B	3B	HR	RBI	BB	SO	OBP	SLG
vs. Left	.213	47	10	4	0	0	0	3	14	.275	.298	Scoring Posn	.214	56	12	0	0	0	11	6	12	.286	.214
vs. Right	.257	191	49	10	2	4	17	14	34	.313	.393	Close & Late	.233	43	10	4	0	1	3	2	15	.283	.395
Home	.282	131	37	6	2	3	11	5	23	.319	.427	None on/out	.265	68	18	6	0	2	2	4	10	.306	.441
Away	.206	107	22	8	0	1	6	12	25	.308	.308	Batting #2	.278	97	27	4	1	1	8	7	19	.340	.371
First Pitch	.324	37	12	2	0	1	5	2	0	.375	.459	Batting #8	.328	61	20	8	0	3	7	5	11	.373	.607
Ahead in Count	.319	47	15	3	2	1	5	10	0	.431	.532	Other	.150	80	12	2	1	0	2	5	18	.209	.200
Behind in Count	.174	115	20	6	0	1	5	0	42	.181	.252	Pre-All Star	.189	74	14	5	1	0	4	4	17	.241	.284
Two Strikes	.173	98	17	2	0	1	4	5	48	.214	.224	Post-All Star	.274	164	45	9	1	4	13	13	31	.333	.415

Last Five Years

	Avg	AB	H	2B	3B	HR	RBI	BB	SO	OBP	SLG		Avg	AB	H	2B	3B	HR	RBI	BB	SO	OBP	SLG
vs. Left	.248	513	127	34	2	6	45	40	103	.307	.357	First Pitch	.343	312	107	18	0	3	29	3	0	.351	.429
vs. Right	.260	1123	292	44	5	7	74	100	160	.323	.327	Ahead in Count	.340	324	110	23	4	5	32	78	0	.466	.481
Groundball	.248	452	112	21	3	1	27	36	73	.305	.314	Behind in Count	.174	714	124	24	2	2	41	0	231	.178	.221
Flyball	.274	288	79	18	1	5	29	23	43	.328	.396	Two Strikes	.158	677	107	19	2	4	39	59	263	.227	.210
Home	.276	811	224	32	5	8	58	64	125	.332	.358	Batting #1	.267	1068	285	47	4	6	78	82	164	.321	.335
Away	.236	825	195	46	2	5	61	76	138	.304	.315	Batting #2	.236	365	86	16	2	3	24	36	67	.310	.315
Day	.280	375	105	18	2	2	22	31	59	.341	.355	Other	.236	203	48	15	1	4	17	22	32	.313	.379
Night	.249	1261	314	60	5	11	97	109	204	.311	.331	March/April	.243	230	56	14	0	1	14	15	37	.293	.317
Grass	.270	1156	312	54	4	8	85	103	179	.330	.344	May	.285	316	90	15	1	1	34	33	55	.359	.348
Turf	.223	480	107	24	3	5	34	37	84	.286	.317	June	.236	271	64	12	2	2	23	20	38	.283	.317
Pre-All Star	.254	912	232	46	4	4	78	73	144	.311	.327	July	.229	340	78	16	2	1	19	21	62	.285	.297
Post-All Star	.258	724	187	32	3	9	41	67	119	.326	.348	August	.280	289	81	12	1	7	21	26	43	.341	.401
Scoring Posn	.254	346	88	14	0	4	101	48	62	.342	.329	Sept/Oct	.263	190	50	9	1	1	8	25	28	.349	.337
Close & Late	.296	260	77	14	1	2	29	25	57	.360	.381	vs. AL	.227	176	40	9	2	1	14	9	36	.267	.318
None on/out	.278	590	164	25	1	3	3	41	82	.327	.339	vs. NL	.260	1460	379	69	5	12	105	131	227	.323	.338

Batter vs. Pitcher (career)

Hits Best Against	Avg	AB	H	2B	3B	HR	RBI	BB	SO	OBP	SLG	Hits Worst Against	Avg	AB	H	2B	3B	HR	RBI	BB	SO	OBP	SLG
Mike Harkey	.538	13	7	1	0	0	1	0	1	.538	.615	Darryl Kile	.059	17	1	1	0	0	0	0	4	.059	.118
Jeff Fassero	.500	18	9	6	0	0	2	0	3	.500	.833	Bill Swift	.063	16	1	0	0	0	0	0	3	.063	.063
Denny Neagle	.444	9	4	3	0	0	1	3	2	.583	.778	Dennis Martinez	.083	12	1	0	0	0	1	0	1	.083	.083
Frank Castillo	.333	18	6	2	0	0	1	3	1	.429	.444	Dwight Gooden	.083	12	1	0	0	0	0	0	4	.083	.083
Pedro Martinez	.333	18	6	2	0	1	2	1	3	.368	.611	Danny Jackson	.133	15	2	0	0	0	0	0	2	.133	.133

Giovanni Carrara — Reds
Age 30 – Pitches Right (flyball pitcher)

	ERA	W	L	Sv	G	GS	IP	BB	SO	Avg	H	2B	3B	HR	RBI	OBP	SLG	CG	ShO	Sup	QS	#P/S	SB	CS	GB	FB	G/F
1997 Season	7.84	0	1	0	2	2	10.1	6	5	.333	14	0	0	4	9	.417	.619	0	0	4.35	0	87	0	1	16	12	1.33
Career (1995-1997)	7.61	3	6	0	33	14	97.0	56	55	.329	132	20	3	25	86	.413	.581	1	0	5.47	3	89	6	7	120	134	0.90

1997 Season

	ERA	W	L	Sv	G	GS	IP	H	HR	BB	SO		Avg	AB	H	2B	3B	HR	RBI	BB	SO	OBP	SLG
Home	6.75	0	1	0	1	1	5.1	7	1	4	3	vs. Left	.261	23	6	0	0	0	1	4	3	.370	.261
Away	9.00	0	0	0	1	1	5.0	7	3	2	2	vs. Right	.421	19	8	0	0	4	8	2	2	.476	1.053

Hector Carrasco — Royals   Age 28 – Pitches Right

	ERA	W	L	Sv	G	GS	IP	BB	SO	Avg	H	2B	3B	HR	RBI	OBP	SLG	GF	IR	IRS	Hld	SvOp	SB	CS	GB	FB	G/F
1997 Season	4.40	2	8	0	66	0	86.0	41	76	.241	80	14	2	7	46	.336	.358	22	36	13	8	2	7	0	124	85	1.46
Career (1994-1997)	3.76	13	24	11	231	0	304.0	162	240	.234	266	40	8	17	132	.333	.328	89	95	33	37	21	22	2	423	298	1.42

1997 Season

	ERA	W	L	Sv	G	GS	IP	H	HR	BB	SO		Avg	AB	H	2B	3B	HR	RBI	BB	SO	OBP	SLG
Home	3.75	2	3	0	35	0	48.0	38	2	19	34	vs. Left	.265	136	36	6	1	4	29	16	27	.358	.412
Away	5.21	0	5	0	31	0	38.0	42	5	22	42	vs. Right	.224	196	44	8	1	3	17	25	49	.320	.321
Day	7.22	1	4	0	25	0	28.2	38	4	18	24	Inning 1-6	.207	87	18	2	0	1	15	13	22	.321	.264
Night	2.98	1	4	0	41	0	57.1	42	3	23	52	Inning 7+	.253	245	62	12	2	6	31	28	54	.342	.392
Grass	3.97	1	6	0	33	0	45.1	42	3	18	41	None on	.228	167	38	4	1	2	2	20	29	.325	.299
Turf	4.87	1	2	0	33	0	40.2	38	4	23	35	Runners on	.255	165	42	10	1	5	44	21	47	.347	.418
March/April	2.51	1	0	0	12	0	14.1	11	1	8	12	Scoring Posn	.245	98	24	3	1	4	39	15	31	.353	.418
May	1.54	0	1	0	14	0	23.1	21	1	10	20	Close & Late	.292	106	31	5	1	3	17	15	21	.395	.443
June	8.10	0	1	0	11	0	13.1	18	1	6	14	None on/out	.189	74	14	1	1	0	0	9	13	.286	.230
July	6.30	1	1	0	10	0	10.0	9	3	7	10	vs. 1st Batr (relief)	.180	61	11	1	0	1	5	4	14	.242	.246
August	5.02	0	3	0	12	0	14.1	13	1	5	15	1st Inning Pitched	.268	235	63	13	1	7	43	30	57	.361	.421
Sept/Oct	5.91	0	2	0	7	0	10.2	8	0	5	5	First 15 Pitches	.262	206	54	10	1	4	26	19	44	.342	.379
Starter	0.00	0	0	0	0	0	0.0	0	0	0	0	Pitch 16-30	.223	103	23	4	1	3	19	20	26	.352	.369
Reliever	4.40	2	8	0	66	0	86.0	80	7	41	76	Pitch 31-45	.130	23	3	0	0	0	1	2	6	.200	.130
0 Days rest (Relief)	4.15	1	2	0	14	0	17.1	20	3	8	16	Pitch 46+	.000	0	0	0	0	0	0	0	0	.000	.000
1 or 2 Days rest	3.86	1	4	0	39	0	51.1	44	3	23	41	First Pitch	.367	60	22	5	1	3	16	3	0	.441	.633
3+ Days rest	6.23	0	2	0	13	0	17.1	16	1	10	19	Ahead in Count	.158	146	23	3	1	1	11	0	68	.172	.212
vs. AL	6.34	1	5	0	28	0	32.2	32	5	14	30	Behind in Count	.320	75	24	5	0	3	15	22	0	.474	.507
vs. NL	3.21	1	3	0	38	0	53.1	48	2	27	46	Two Strikes	.138	152	21	4	1	0	8	16	76	.233	.178
Pre-All Star	3.53	1	2	0	37	0	51.0	50	3	24	46	Pre-All Star	.248	202	50	7	1	3	25	24	46	.335	.337
Post-All Star	5.66	1	6	0	29	0	35.0	30	4	17	30	Post-All Star	.231	130	30	7	1	4	21	17	30	.338	.392

Career (1994-1997)

	ERA	W	L	Sv	G	GS	IP	H	HR	BB	SO		Avg	AB	H	2B	3B	HR	RBI	BB	SO	OBP	SLG
Home	3.39	6	9	6	119	0	156.2	127	10	70	104	vs. Left	.257	491	126	19	6	10	76	62	85	.346	.381
Away	4.15	7	15	5	112	0	147.1	139	7	92	136	vs. Right	.216	647	140	21	2	7	56	100	155	.323	.287
Day	5.65	4	11	2	76	0	94.0	104	9	60	76	Inning 1-6	.207	164	34	4	1	2	34	29	42	.328	.280
Night	2.91	9	13	9	155	0	210.0	162	8	102	164	Inning 7+	.238	974	232	36	7	15	98	133	198	.333	.336
Grass	4.12	7	14	2	85	0	118.0	109	5	70	104	None on	.220	591	130	19	2	10	10	76	127	.316	.310
Turf	3.53	6	10	9	146	0	186.0	157	12	92	136	Runners on	.249	547	136	21	6	7	122	86	113	.350	.347
March/April	3.31	4	3	2	29	0	35.1	34	3	22	28	Scoring Posn	.246	317	78	8	5	6	113	64	71	.368	.360
May	1.73	2	2	5	31	0	52.0	43	2	24	45	Close & Late	.249	498	124	19	4	6	55	76	97	.354	.339
June	4.13	2	5	2	50	0	65.1	62	4	29	41	None on/out	.213	263	56	7	2	3	3	34	55	.308	.289
July	2.93	3	4	2	48	0	61.1	37	4	33	52	vs. 1st Batr (relief)	.211	199	42	4	1	5	16	30	49	.320	.317
August	4.77	2	6	0	45	0	54.2	52	4	36	49	1st Inning Pitched	.247	788	195	34	7	15	118	123	173	.353	.365
Sept/Oct	6.37	0	4	0	28	0	35.1	38	0	18	25	First 15 Pitches	.252	664	167	30	4	12	76	92	130	.350	.363
Starter	0.00	0	0	0	0	0	0.0	0	0	0	0	Pitch 16-30	.208	365	76	9	4	3	45	55	86	.310	.279
Reliever	3.76	13	24	11	231	0	304.0	266	17	162	240	Pitch 31-45	.198	96	19	1	0	1	10	15	20	.304	.240
0 Days rest (Relief)	3.46	5	5	2	54	0	65.0	60	5	37	50	Pitch 46+	.308	13	4	0	0	1	1	0	4	.308	.538
1 or 2 Days rest	4.03	6	15	8	129	0	167.2	149	9	99	127	First Pitch	.316	196	62	12	3	9	35	11	0	.366	.546
3+ Days rest	3.41	4	4	1	48	0	71.1	57	3	26	63	Ahead in Count	.181	508	92	9	5	2	38	0	208	.192	.230
vs. AL	6.34	1	5	0	28	0	32.2	32	5	14	30	Behind in Count	.304	263	80	16	0	6	48	88	0	.472	.433
vs. NL	3.45	12	19	11	203	0	271.1	234	12	148	210	Two Strikes	.155	522	81	8	4	1	30	63	240	.253	.192
Pre-All Star	3.23	9	13	10	123	0	170.0	152	9	88	130	Pre-All Star	.238	640	152	18	3	9	70	88	130	.329	.317
Post-All Star	4.43	4	11	1	108	0	134.0	114	8	74	110	Post-All Star	.229	498	114	22	5	8	62	74	110	.337	.341

Pitcher vs. Batter (career)

Pitches Best Vs.	Avg	AB	H	2B	3B	HR	RBI	BB	SO	OBP	SLG	Pitches Worst Vs.	Avg	AB	H	2B	3B	HR	RBI	BB	SO	OBP	SLG
Craig Biggio	.000	11	0	0	0	0	0	3	2	.267	.000	Vinny Castilla	.500	12	6	0	0	2	2	0	1	.500	1.000
Jeff Bagwell	.125	16	2	0	1	0	2	2	5	.222	.250	Steve Finley	.400	10	4	1	0	0	3	1	2	.417	.500
Bernard Gilkey	.222	9	2	0	0	0	2	2	1	.364	.222	Sammy Sosa	.364	11	4	1	0	0	2	1	0	.417	.455
Mark Grace	.231	13	3	0	0	0	0	2	1	.231	.231	Jeff Conine	.364	11	4	0	0	0	0	1	0	.417	.364

Joe Carter — Blue Jays   Age 38 – Bats Right (flyball hitter)

	Avg	G	AB	R	H	2B	3B	HR	RBI	BB	SO	HBP	GDP	SB	CS	OBP	SLG	IBB	SH	SF	#Pit	P/PA	GB	FB	G/F
1997 Season	.234	157	612	76	143	30	4	21	102	40	105	7	12	8	2	.284	.399	5	0	9	2349	3.52	154	266	0.58
Last Five Years	.252	719	2833	392	713	146	18	136	509	201	475	28	51	46	12	.303	.460	23	0	43	11312	3.64	688	1211	0.57

1997 Season

	Avg	AB	H	2B	3B	HR	RBI	BB	SO	OBP	SLG		Avg	AB	H	2B	3B	HR	RBI	BB	SO	OBP	SLG
vs. Left	.289	180	52	9	3	6	33	10	27	.328	.472	First Pitch	.376	93	35	9	1	6	23	4	0	.396	.688
vs. Right	.211	432	91	21	1	15	69	30	78	.266	.368	Ahead in Count	.274	113	31	5	2	8	33	24	0	.393	.566
Groundball	.170	106	18	5	0	2	18	8	17	.231	.274	Behind in Count	.170	300	51	11	1	5	29	0	92	.185	.263
Flyball	.184	87	16	4	1	5	18	5	12	.228	.425	Two Strikes	.173	271	47	8	1	5	24	12	105	.219	.266
Home	.217	299	65	11	2	11	59	25	55	.279	.378	Batting #3	.221	263	58	9	0	11	55	20	41	.272	.380
Away	.249	313	78	19	2	10	43	15	50	.290	.419	Batting #4	.244	349	85	21	4	10	47	20	64	.294	.413
Day	.203	222	45	11	2	3	30	15	39	.262	.297	Other	.000	0	0	0	0	0	0	0	0	.000	.000
Night	.251	390	98	18	4	18	72	25	66	.298	.456	March/April	.261	92	24	4	0	2	10	7	18	.324	.370
Grass	.258	260	67	16	2	8	38	11	41	.295	.427	May	.277	101	28	4	1	5	17	5	15	.304	.485
Turf	.216	352	76	14	2	13	64	29	64	.277	.378	June	.182	99	18	5	0	2	20	10	19	.248	.293
Pre-All Star	.235	315	74	13	1	10	51	25	58	.289	.378	July	.257	109	28	5	0	4	22	6	18	.296	.413
Post-All Star	.232	297	69	17	3	11	51	15	47	.279	.421	August	.250	116	29	6	1	7	22	8	20	.315	.500

1997 Season

	Avg	AB	H	2B	3B	HR	RBI	BB	SO	OBP	SLG		Avg	AB	H	2B	3B	HR	RBI	BB	SO	OBP	SLG
Scoring Posn	.265	170	45	7	2	8	85	23	29	.340	.471	Sept/Oct	.168	95	16	6	2	1	11	4	15	.210	.305
Close & Late	.204	98	20	4	0	1	18	14	20	.302	.276	vs. AL	.237	562	133	28	4	19	92	36	92	.287	.402
None on/out	.241	158	38	10	0	8	8	3	25	.264	.456	vs. NL	.200	50	10	2	0	2	10	4	13	.255	.360

1997 By Position

Position	Avg	AB	H	2B	3B	HR	RBI	BB	SO	OBP	SLG	G	GS	Innings	PO	A	E	DP	Fld Pct	Rng Fctr	In Zone	Zone Outs	Zone Rtg	MLB Zone
As DH	.198	253	50	13	1	9	41	15	49	.257	.364	64	64	---	---	---	---	---	---	---	---	---	---	---
As 1b	.261	161	42	8	2	3	23	13	26	.309	.391	42	42	372.0	326	22	1	24	.997	---	55	47	.855	.874
As lf	.258	155	40	6	0	6	29	11	23	.302	.413	41	41	340.2	87	0	3	0	.967	2.30	111	88	.793	.805
As rf	.256	43	11	3	1	3	9	1	7	.289	.581	10	10	90.0	17	1	0	0	1.000	1.80	21	16	.762	.813

Last Five Years

	Avg	AB	H	2B	3B	HR	RBI	BB	SO	OBP	SLG		Avg	AB	H	2B	3B	HR	RBI	BB	SO	OBP	SLG
vs. Left	.284	758	215	40	7	39	142	52	105	.329	.509	First Pitch	.353	411	145	35	2	34	108	17	0	.378	.696
vs. Right	.240	2075	498	106	11	97	367	149	370	.294	.442	Ahead in Count	.301	501	151	26	4	34	113	96	0	.410	.573
Groundball	.260	603	157	28	3	26	104	38	93	.303	.446	Behind in Count	.203	1406	285	56	10	42	183	0	422	.210	.346
Flyball	.233	460	107	26	3	26	84	40	87	.291	.472	Two Strikes	.194	1301	252	49	8	39	155	88	475	.249	.334
Home	.250	1414	353	79	6	77	281	99	262	.300	.477	Batting #3	.231	485	112	20	1	17	85	34	81	.279	.381
Away	.254	1419	360	67	12	59	228	102	213	.307	.443	Batting #4	.256	2345	601	126	17	119	424	166	392	.308	.477
Day	.239	962	230	53	4	45	172	68	167	.292	.443	Other	.000	3	0	0	0	0	0	1	2	.250	.000
Night	.258	1871	483	93	14	91	337	133	308	.309	.469	March/April	.298	392	117	24	2	25	99	32	66	.350	.561
Grass	.261	1161	303	52	11	50	183	85	171	.314	.454	May	.302	506	153	32	7	23	86	31	61	.344	.530
Turf	.245	1672	410	94	7	86	326	116	304	.296	.464	June	.214	495	106	23	3	24	90	39	81	.278	.418
Pre-All Star	.267	1555	415	88	12	81	308	117	236	.321	.495	July	.241	540	130	31	0	24	108	36	103	.291	.431
Post-All Star	.233	1278	298	58	6	55	201	84	239	.282	.417	August	.234	504	118	18	3	25	71	40	99	.292	.431
Scoring Posn	.269	810	218	32	5	45	374	101	154	.341	.488	Sept/Oct	.225	396	89	18	3	15	55	23	65	.268	.399
Close & Late	.231	429	99	19	3	15	64	38	78	.292	.394	vs. AL	.253	2783	703	144	18	134	499	197	462	.304	.462
None on/out	.258	728	188	41	4	43	43	26	102	.290	.503	vs. NL	.200	50	10	2	0	2	10	4	13	.255	.360

Batter vs. Pitcher (since 1984)

Hits Best Against	Avg	AB	H	2B	3B	HR	RBI	BB	SO	OBP	SLG	Hits Worst Against	Avg	AB	H	2B	3B	HR	RBI	BB	SO	OBP	SLG
Scott Karl	.550	20	11	2	1	2	5	2	2	.591	1.050	Rich DeLucia	.000	15	0	0	0	0	0	0	5	.000	.000
Albie Lopez	.429	14	6	1	0	2	4	0	1	.429	.929	Todd Stottlemyre	.000	14	0	0	0	0	0	0	4	.000	.000
Brad Radke	.400	20	8	4	0	2	4	0	4	.381	.900	Roberto Hernandez	.000	11	0	0	0	0	0	0	1	.000	.000
Sid Fernandez	.364	11	4	0	0	2	2	2	4	.462	.909	Al Leiter	.091	11	1	0	0	0	0	0	3	.091	.091
Bob Wolcott	.364	11	4	0	0	2	5	0	0	.417	1.000	Bobby Ayala	.091	11	1	0	0	0	0	1	2	.091	.091

Raul Casanova — Tigers
Age 25 – Bats Both

	Avg	G	AB	R	H	2B	3B	HR	RBI	BB	SO	HBP	GDP	SB	CS	OBP	SLG	IBB	SH	SF	#Pit	#P/PA	GB	FB	G/F
1997 Season	.243	101	304	27	74	10	1	5	24	26	48	3	10	1	1	.308	.332	1	0	1	1231	3.69	142	64	2.22
Career (1996-1997)	.231	126	389	33	90	11	1	9	33	32	66	3	16	1	1	.294	.334	1	0	1	1568	3.69	184	78	2.36

1997 Season

	Avg	AB	H	2B	3B	HR	RBI	BB	SO	OBP	SLG		Avg	AB	H	2B	3B	HR	RBI	BB	SO	OBP	SLG
vs. Left	.237	59	14	1	0	1	5	8	11	.338	.305	First Pitch	.311	45	14	2	0	2	9	1	0	.326	.489
vs. Right	.245	245	60	9	1	4	19	18	37	.301	.339	Ahead in Count	.307	75	23	4	1	2	8	16	0	.430	.467
Groundball	.243	70	17	0	0	0	6	6	12	.321	.243	Behind in Count	.168	125	21	1	0	1	7	0	41	.175	.200
Flyball	.220	50	11	3	0	1	3	5	9	.291	.340	Two Strikes	.159	132	21	3	0	1	6	9	48	.218	.205
Home	.233	150	35	5	1	5	16	13	25	.299	.380	Batting #7	.230	61	14	3	0	2	6	7	12	.314	.377
Away	.253	154	39	5	0	0	8	13	23	.318	.286	Batting #8	.251	203	51	7	1	1	15	18	23	.318	.310
Day	.222	81	18	2	1	0	2	4	16	.267	.272	Other	.225	40	9	0	0	2	3	1	13	.244	.375
Night	.251	223	56	8	0	5	22	22	32	.323	.354	March/April	.214	14	3	0	0	0	0	0	2	.214	.214
Grass	.245	273	67	8	1	5	24	25	45	.312	.337	May	.277	47	13	1	1	0	4	4	5	.358	.340
Turf	.226	31	7	2	0	0	0	1	3	.273	.290	June	.300	70	21	4	0	3	6	5	11	.355	.486
Pre-All Star	.260	146	38	5	1	4	11	10	23	.321	.390	July	.236	55	13	3	0	1	5	6	10	.306	.345
Post-All Star	.228	158	36	5	0	1	13	16	25	.297	.278	August	.200	60	12	0	0	1	5	2	8	.226	.250
Scoring Posn	.192	78	15	1	0	2	20	8	21	.264	.282	Sept/Oct	.207	58	12	2	0	0	4	9	12	.313	.241
Close & Late	.213	47	10	3	0	0	0	4	14	.275	.277	vs. AL	.257	268	69	9	1	4	23	23	40	.322	.343
None on/out	.303	76	23	4	0	0	0	5	8	.354	.355	vs. NL	.139	36	5	1	0	1	1	3	8	.205	.250

1997 By Position

Position	Avg	AB	H	2B	3B	HR	RBI	BB	SO	OBP	SLG	G	GS	Innings	PO	A	E	DP	Fld Pct	Rng Fctr	In Zone	Zone Outs	Zone Rtg	MLB Zone
As Pinch Hitter	.182	11	2	1	0	0	0	2	7	.308	.273	13	0	---	---	---	---	---	---	---	---	---	---	---
As c	.246	293	72	9	1	5	24	24	41	.308	.334	92	83	725.1	543	38	9	7	.985	---	---	---	---	---

Sean Casey — Indians
Age 23 – Bats Left

	Avg	G	AB	R	H	2B	3B	HR	RBI	BB	SO	HBP	GDP	SB	CS	OBP	SLG	IBB	SH	SF	#Pit	#P/PA	GB	FB	G/F
1997 Season	.200	6	10	1	2	0	0	0	1	1	2	0	0	0	0	.333	.200	0	0	0	54	4.50	7	1	7.00

1997 Season

	Avg	AB	H	2B	3B	HR	RBI	BB	SO	OBP	SLG		Avg	AB	H	2B	3B	HR	RBI	BB	SO	OBP	SLG
vs. Left	.000	2	0	0	0	0	0	1	1	.500	.000	Scoring Posn	.000	2	0	0	0	0	1	0	0	.333	.000
vs. Right	.250	8	2	0	0	0	1	0	1	.250	.250	Close & Late	.000	1	0	0	0	0	0	1	0	.500	.000

Larry Casian — Royals   Age 32 – Pitches Left

	ERA	W	L	Sv	G	GS	IP	BB	SO	Avg	H	2B	3B	HR	RBI	OBP	SLG	GF	IR	IRS	Hld	SvOp	SB	CS	GB	FB	G/F
1997 Season	5.70	0	3	0	44	0	36.1	8	23	.318	48	5	0	8	35	.350	.510	7	34	14	5	2	1	0	59	35	1.69
Last Five Years	4.37	8	12	2	215	0	189.1	64	100	.294	217	35	4	24	129	.349	.449	34	191	54	35	10	3	4	283	211	1.34

1997 Season

	ERA	W	L	Sv	G	GS	IP	H	HR	BB	SO		Avg	AB	H	2B	3B	HR	RBI	BB	SO	OBP	SLG
Home	8.64	0	1	0	18	0	16.2	27	7	3	11	vs. Left	.375	64	24	2	0	3	20	1	15	.379	.547
Away	3.20	0	2	0	26	0	19.2	21	1	5	12	vs. Right	.276	87	24	3	0	5	15	7	8	.330	.483
Starter	0.00	0	0	0	0	0	0.0	0	0	0	0	Scoring Posn	.396	48	19	1	0	3	29	5	8	.429	.604
Reliever	5.70	0	3	0	44	0	36.1	48	8	8	23	Close & Late	.211	38	8	0	0	1	6	1	11	.225	.289
0 Days rest (Relief)	3.86	0	0	0	8	0	7.0	7	2	2	3	None on/out	.242	33	8	2	0	0	1		5	.265	.303
1 or 2 Days rest	7.50	0	2	0	20	0	18.0	27	5	5	12	First Pitch	.182	22	4	1	0	0	1	2	0	.240	.227
3+ Days rest	3.97	0	1	0	16	0	11.1	14	1	1	8	Ahead in Count	.259	54	14	1	0	1	7	0	18	.259	.333
Pre-All Star	6.87	0	2	0	26	0	18.1	27	6	4	14	Behind in Count	.359	39	14	1	0	4	15	4	0	.413	.692
Post-All Star	4.50	0	1	0	18	0	18.0	21	2	4	9	Two Strikes	.306	62	19	1	0	4	14	2	23	.328	.532

Last Five Years

	ERA	W	L	Sv	G	GS	IP	H	HR	BB	SO		Avg	AB	H	2B	3B	HR	RBI	BB	SO	OBP	SLG
Home	5.30	2	4	1	101	0	88.1	109	18	26	40	vs. Left	.306	301	92	14	2	9	66	13	52	.332	.455
Away	3.56	6	8	1	114	0	101.0	108	6	38	60	vs. Right	.285	438	125	21	2	15	63	51	48	.360	.445
Day	3.80	2	5	0	88	0	64.0	78	9	22	39	Inning 1-6	.279	197	55	8	0	2	37	17	24	.336	.350
Night	4.67	6	7	2	127	0	125.1	139	15	42	61	Inning 7+	.299	542	162	27	4	22	92	47	76	.354	.485
Grass	4.51	3	10	0	142	0	109.2	137	15	31	60	None on	.272	375	102	16	1	12	12	27	53	.323	.416
Turf	4.18	5	2	2	73	0	79.2	80	9	33	40	Runners on	.316	364	115	19	3	12	117	37	47	.375	.484
March/April	6.26	0	3	0	26	0	27.1	40	8	7	17	Scoring Posn	.322	230	74	14	2	6	101	32	30	.395	.478
May	4.94	1	1	1	26	0	27.1	31	2	9	15	Close & Late	.276	214	59	5	2	5	32	19	30	.335	.388
June	2.73	1	1	0	38	0	29.2	36	4	7	15	None on/out	.245	163	40	11	1	2	2	8	21	.281	.362
July	4.03	1	3	1	36	0	38.0	41	6	9	15	vs. 1st Batr (relief)	.271	188	51	9	2	2	34	17	26	.333	.372
August	3.16	5	2	0	43	0	37.0	31	2	13	35	1st Inning Pitched	.294	541	159	28	4	16	113	55	74	.357	.449
Sept/Oct	5.70	0	2	0	46	0	30.0	38	2	19	14	First 15 Pitches	.299	489	146	27	3	15	91	46	65	.359	.458
Starter	0.00	0	0	0	0	0	0.0	0	0	0	0	Pitch 16-30	.282	163	46	4	1	6	30	12	25	.328	.429
Reliever	4.37	8	12	2	215	0	189.1	217	24	64	100	Pitch 31-45	.310	58	18	2	0	3	7	5	5	.365	.500
0 Days rest (Relief)	4.28	1	3	1	56	0	40.0	43	7	12	21	Pitch 46+	.241	29	7	2	0	0	1	1	5	.267	.310
1 or 2 Days rest	4.70	4	6	1	95	0	84.1	107	13	29	44	First Pitch	.316	95	30	4	0	2	12	10	0	.370	.421
3+ Days rest	4.02	3	3	0	64	0	65.0	67	4	23	35	Ahead in Count	.230	283	65	9	2	5	27	0	81	.232	.329
vs. AL	5.06	6	10	2	124	0	131.2	163	18	36	65	Behind in Count	.397	194	77	13	1	11	55	31	0	.472	.644
vs. NL	2.81	2	2	0	91	0	57.2	54	6	28	35	Two Strikes	.218	293	64	12	1	8	38	22	100	.277	.348
Pre-All Star	4.83	3	6	1	101	0	98.2	126	18	36	54	Pre-All Star	.315	400	126	19	4	18	80	26	54	.356	.518
Post-All Star	3.87	5	6	1	114	0	90.2	91	6	38	46	Post-All Star	.268	339	91	16	0	6	49	38	46	.342	.369

Pitcher vs. Batter (career)

Pitches Best Vs.	Avg	AB	H	2B	3B	HR	RBI	BB	SO	OBP	SLG	Pitches Worst Vs.	Avg	AB	H	2B	3B	HR	RBI	BB	SO	OBP	SLG
												Brian McRae	.636	11	7	2	0	0	0	0	1	.636	.818
												Omar Vizquel	.400	10	4	0	0	0	1	1	1	.455	.400

Vinny Castilla — Rockies   Age 30 – Bats Right

	Avg	G	AB	R	H	2B	3B	HR	RBI	BB	SO	HBP	GDP	SB	CS	OBP	SLG	IBB	SH	SF	#Pit	#P/PA	GB	FB	G/F
1997 Season	.304	159	612	94	186	25	2	40	113	44	108	8	18	2	4	.356	.547	9	0	4	2229	3.34	240	166	1.45
Last Five Years	.299	615	2235	325	669	113	12	124	364	129	351	19	66	15	20	.340	.527	23	5	22	7694	3.19	900	667	1.35

1997 Season

	Avg	AB	H	2B	3B	HR	RBI	BB	SO	OBP	SLG		Avg	AB	H	2B	3B	HR	RBI	BB	SO	OBP	SLG
vs. Left	.380	129	49	6	1	11	31	11	18	.434	.698	First Pitch	.359	117	42	6	1	13	34	6	0	.397	.761
vs. Right	.284	483	137	19	1	29	82	33	90	.335	.507	Ahead in Count	.484	124	60	6	1	18	41	28	0	.578	.984
Groundball	.306	121	37	6	1	7	24	13	18	.384	.545	Behind in Count	.212	278	59	11	0	6	27	0	100	.222	.317
Flyball	.278	97	27	5	0	12	20	12	20	.364	.701	Two Strikes	.161	261	42	8	0	5	20	9	108	.194	.249
Home	.320	316	101	11	1	21	62	18	48	.361	.560	Batting #5	.333	39	13	2	0	3	7	1	11	.350	.615
Away	.287	296	85	14	1	19	51	26	60	.352	.534	Batting #6	.305	544	166	23	2	35	101	43	89	.362	.548
Day	.321	290	93	11	1	20	46	26	48	.385	.572	Other	.241	29	7	0	0	2	5	0	8	.241	.448
Night	.289	322	93	14	1	20	67	18	60	.329	.525	March/April	.360	89	32	2	0	9	25	13	12	.452	.685
Grass	.291	501	146	16	2	31	90	36	83	.346	.517	May	.218	101	22	3	0	4	13	6	16	.259	.366
Turf	.360	111	40	9	0	9	23	8	25	.405	.685	June	.298	114	34	6	2	7	23	5	18	.339	.570
Pre-All Star	.282	326	92	11	2	22	64	24	52	.338	.531	July	.309	110	34	3	0	8	15	2	24	.333	.555
Post-All Star	.329	286	94	14	0	18	49	20	56	.377	.566	August	.360	111	40	10	0	9	20	9	24	.413	.694
Scoring Posn	.310	142	44	5	0	6	65	23	24	.410	.472	Sept/Oct	.276	87	24	1	0	3	17	9	14	.340	.391
Close & Late	.341	91	31	1	1	6	15	4	15	.368	.571	vs. AL	.303	66	20	6	0	3	14	2	13	.324	.530
None on/out	.291	158	46	3	1	10	10	6	25	.317	.513	vs. NL	.304	546	166	19	2	37	99	42	95	.360	.549

1997 By Position

Position	Avg	AB	H	2B	3B	HR	RBI	BB	SO	OBP	SLG	G	GS	Innings	PO	A	E	DP	Fld Pct	Rng Fctr	In Zone	In Outs	Zone Rtg	MLB Zone
As 3b	.303	610	185	25	2	40	113	44	107	.356	.548	157	155	1372.0	111	322	21	42	.954	2.84	465	373	.802	.801

Last Five Years

	Avg	AB	H	2B	3B	HR	RBI	BB	SO	OBP	SLG		Avg	AB	H	2B	3B	HR	RBI	BB	SO	OBP	SLG
vs. Left	.331	523	173	35	3	31	102	36	65	.375	.587	First Pitch	.364	481	175	23	5	43	112	15	0	.384	.701
vs. Right	.290	1712	496	78	9	93	262	93	286	.329	.509	Ahead in Count	.386	498	192	31	3	40	105	75	0	.464	.701
Groundball	.292	558	163	29	2	30	91	31	80	.335	.513	Behind in Count	.221	945	209	40	4	28	106	0	316	.225	.307
Flyball	.295	359	106	20	0	22	66	26	52	.345	.535	Two Strikes	.188	862	162	27	2	24	81	38	351	.223	.307
Home	.341	1146	391	66	10	77	221	68	153	.379	.618	Batting #6	.310	1369	424	77	3	84	239	86	208	.354	.554

Last Five Years

	Avg	AB	H	2B	3B	HR	RBI	BB	SO	OBP	SLG		Avg	AB	H	2B	3B	HR	RBI	BB	SO	OBP	SLG
Away	.255	1089	278	47	2	47	143	61	198	.298	.432	Batting #7	.265	370	98	14	2	13	50	18	64	.300	.419
Day	.310	875	271	50	5	55	152	53	140	.353	.567	Other	.296	496	147	22	7	27	75	25	79	.330	.532
Night	.293	1360	398	63	7	69	212	76	211	.331	.501	March/April	.288	236	68	9	2	14	44	24	35	.360	.521
Grass	.307	1810	556	94	12	101	309	108	274	.348	.540	May	.299	355	106	20	3	12	49	18	40	.333	.473
Turf	.266	425	113	19	0	23	55	21	77	.305	.473	June	.324	487	158	29	6	31	90	20	74	.352	.600
Pre-All Star	.301	1219	367	64	11	64	200	68	177	.339	.529	July	.289	401	116	18	0	25	60	17	78	.322	.521
Post-All Star	.297	1016	302	49	1	60	164	61	174	.340	.525	August	.318	424	135	25	1	32	75	27	71	.361	.608
Scoring Posn	.293	522	153	27	4	22	226	61	87	.363	.487	Sept/Oct	.259	332	86	12	0	10	46	23	53	.309	.386
Close & Late	.299	304	91	15	1	16	48	22	48	.342	.513	vs. AL	.303	66	20	6	0	3	14	2	13	.324	.530
None on/out	.311	540	168	25	3	32	32	20	83	.337	.546	vs. NL	.299	2169	649	107	12	121	350	127	338	.340	.527

Batter vs. Pitcher (career)

Hits Best Against	Avg	AB	H	2B	3B	HR	RBI	BB	SO	OBP	SLG	Hits Worst Against	Avg	AB	H	2B	3B	HR	RBI	BB	SO	OBP	SLG
Terry Mathews	.600	10	6	0	0	1	2	1	1	.636	.900	Pedro Martinez	.000	11	0	0	0	0	0	0	5	.000	.000
Tim Pugh	.583	12	7	1	0	2	5	0	0	.583	1.167	Donne Wall	.000	11	0	0	0	0	1	1	1	.077	.000
Hector Carrasco	.500	12	6	0	0	2	2	0	1	.500	1.000	Mark Portugal	.077	13	1	0	0	0	0	0	3	.077	.077
Jim Bullinger	.500	10	5	0	0	3	8	5	0	.667	1.400	Tom Candiotti	.091	11	1	0	0	0	1	1	5	.167	.091
Kevin Foster	.333	18	6	2	0	4	8	2	3	.400	1.111	Curt Schilling	.105	19	2	1	0	0	0	0	5	.105	.158

Alberto Castillo — Mets
Age 28 – Bats Right

	Avg	G	AB	R	H	2B	3B	HR	RBI	BB	SO	HBP	GDP	SB	CS	OBP	SLG	IBB	SH	SF	#Pit	#P/PA	GB	FB	G/F
1997 Season	.203	35	59	3	12	1	0	0	7	9	16	0	3	0	1	.304	.220	0	2	1	296	4.17	24	8	3.00
Career (1995-1997)	.192	54	99	6	19	1	0	0	7	12	29	1	3	1	1	.283	.202	0	2	1	455	3.96	39	16	2.44

1997 Season

	Avg	AB	H	2B	3B	HR	RBI	BB	SO	OBP	SLG		Avg	AB	H	2B	3B	HR	RBI	BB	SO	OBP	SLG
vs. Left	.192	26	5	0	0	0	1	9	8	.389	.192	Scoring Posn	.217	23	5	1	0	0	7	0	7	.208	.261
vs. Right	.212	33	7	1	0	0	6	0	8	.212	.242	Close & Late	.286	7	2	1	0	0	1	1	2	.375	.429

Carlos Castillo — White Sox
Age 23 – Pitches Right (flyball pitcher)

	ERA	W	L	Sv	G	GS	IP	BB	SO	Avg	H	2B	3B	HR	RBI	OBP	SLG	GF	IR	IRS	Hld	SvOp	SB	CS	GB	FB	G/F
1997 Season	4.48	2	1	1	37	2	66.1	33	43	.265	68	17	2	9	40	.346	.451	14	31	10	3	1	11	1	60	108	0.56

1997 Season

	ERA	W	L	Sv	G	GS	IP	H	HR	BB	SO		Avg	AB	H	2B	3B	HR	RBI	BB	SO	OBP	SLG
Home	4.88	0	0	0	16	2	31.1	31	5	12	21	vs. Left	.297	128	38	7	0	8	26	11	24	.345	.539
Away	4.11	2	1	1	21	0	35.0	37	4	21	22	vs. Right	.233	129	30	10	2	1	14	22	19	.346	.364
Starter	8.64	0	0	0	2	2	8.1	10	2	1	6	Scoring Posn	.269	67	18	4	0	4	32	13	12	.376	.507
Reliever	3.88	2	1	1	35	0	58.0	58	7	32	37	Close & Late	.348	23	8	2	1	1	4	5	3	.452	.652
0 Days rest (Relief)	12.96	1	0	0	7	0	8.1	19	4	6	5	None on/out	.230	61	14	2	1	1	1	5	13	.288	.344
1 or 2 Days rest	3.12	0	1	0	12	0	17.1	14	1	7	10	First Pitch	.333	45	15	2	0	4	10	3	0	.375	.644
3+ Days rest	1.95	1	0	1	16	0	32.1	25	2	19	22	Ahead in Count	.190	116	22	5	1	1	12	0	32	.186	.276
Pre-All Star	4.33	0	1	1	23	1	43.2	46	4	25	28	Behind in Count	.360	50	18	7	0	3	10	14	0	.485	.680
Post-All Star	4.76	2	0	0	14	1	22.2	22	5	8	15	Two Strikes	.186	113	21	4	0	2	15	16	43	.288	.274

Frank Castillo — Rockies
Age 29 – Pitches Right

	ERA	W	L	Sv	G	GS	IP	BB	SO	Avg	H	2B	3B	HR	RBI	OBP	SLG	CG	ShO	Sup	QS	#P/S	SB	CS	GB	FB	G/F
1997 Season	5.42	12	12	0	34	33	184.1	69	126	.300	220	46	5	25	104	.365	.478	0	0	5.81	12	92	13	15	252	223	1.13
Last Five Years	4.66	37	47	0	129	124	719.0	211	503	.281	795	145	16	98	357	.337	.448	6	3	4.93	58	91	50	44	955	779	1.23

1997 Season

	ERA	W	L	Sv	G	GS	IP	H	HR	BB	SO		Avg	AB	H	2B	3B	HR	RBI	BB	SO	OBP	SLG
Home	4.26	7	6	0	19	19	114.0	125	14	39	79	vs. Left	.263	308	81	20	3	4	36	48	59	.361	.386
Away	7.29	5	6	0	15	14	70.1	95	11	30	47	vs. Right	.326	426	139	26	2	21	68	21	67	.368	.545
Day	4.70	7	7	0	18	18	99.2	110	9	37	74	Inning 1-6	.296	675	200	39	5	22	98	65	117	.364	.467
Night	6.27	5	5	0	16	15	84.2	110	16	32	52	Inning 7+	.339	59	20	7	0	3	6	4	9	.375	.610
Grass	5.16	9	9	0	27	26	151.2	179	22	55	100	None on	.291	422	123	28	0	14	14	33	73	.347	.457
Turf	6.61	3	3	0	7	7	32.2	41	3	14	26	Runners on	.311	312	97	18	5	11	90	36	53	.389	.506
March/April	6.29	1	3	0	6	5	24.1	30	2	12	11	Scoring Posn	.300	170	51	12	3	6	74	29	30	.410	.512
May	4.96	1	4	0	6	6	32.2	38	3	15	27	Close & Late	.286	21	6	2	0	0	1	3	3	.360	.381
June	6.75	2	2	0	5	5	21.1	27	1	11	16	None on/out	.314	194	61	14	0	5	5	9	30	.345	.464
July	4.46	4	0	0	6	6	38.1	46	7	11	24	vs. 1st Batr (relief)	1.000	1	1	0	0	0	0	0	0	1.000	1.000
August	4.62	2	2	0	6	6	37.0	44	5	13	28	1st Inning Pitched	.390	146	57	8	1	6	34	13	20	.454	.582
Sept/Oct	6.46	2	1	0	5	5	30.2	35	7	7	20	First 75 Pitches	.302	560	169	32	5	18	80	51	95	.367	.473
Starter	5.29	12	12	0	33	33	183.2	216	24	69	126	Pitch 76-90	.284	95	27	5	0	4	16	11	15	.364	.463
Reliever	40.50	0	0	0	1	0	0.2	4	1	0	0	Pitch 91-105	.328	58	19	7	0	2	7	4	10	.365	.552
0-3 Days Rest (Start)	0.00	0	0	0	0	0	0.0	0	0	0	0	Pitch 106+	.238	21	5	2	0	1	3	3	6	.333	.476
4 Days Rest	5.38	7	7	0	21	21	113.2	135	13	50	77	First Pitch	.370	119	44	14	1	2	14	1	0	.375	.555
5+ Days Rest	5.14	5	5	0	12	12	70.0	81	11	19	49	Ahead in Count	.223	309	69	15	1	9	27	0	113	.233	.366
vs. AL	0.86	2	0	0	3	3	21.0	16	0	7	17	Behind in Count	.391	169	66	9	1	14	46	46	0	.525	.704
vs. NL	6.01	10	12	0	31	30	163.1	204	25	62	109	Two Strikes	.198	323	64	10	2	9	33	22	126	.255	.325
Pre-All Star	5.28	6	9	0	19	18	92.0	106	7	43	65	Pre-All Star	.292	363	106	21	4	7	50	43	65	.370	.430
Post-All Star	5.56	6	3	0	15	15	92.1	114	18	26	61	Post-All Star	.307	371	114	25	1	18	54	26	61	.360	.526

83

Last Five Years

	ERA	W	L	Sv	G	GS	IP	H	HR	BB	SO		Avg	AB	H	2B	3B	HR	RBI	BB	SO	OBP	SLG
Home	4.11	20	24	0	65	65	383.1	406	48	114	278	vs. Left	.268	1222	328	62	8	34	139	133	237	.341	.416
Away	5.28	17	23	0	64	59	335.2	389	50	97	225	vs. Right	.291	1604	467	83	8	64	218	78	266	.333	.473
Day	4.55	20	29	0	69	68	387.2	412	48	123	284	Inning 1-6	.282	2528	712	128	13	89	334	189	453	.337	.448
Night	4.78	17	18	0	60	56	331.1	383	50	88	219	Inning 7+	.279	298	83	17	3	9	23	22	50	.330	.446
Grass	4.26	30	35	0	99	96	578.2	619	76	163	409	None on	.270	1711	462	90	9	59	59	93	314	.314	.437
Turf	6.29	7	12	0	30	28	140.1	176	22	48	94	Runners on	.299	1115	333	55	7	39	298	118	189	.369	.465
March/April	4.80	2	7	0	17	16	86.1	99	12	32	55	Scoring Posn	.293	614	180	31	4	22	250	80	118	.378	.464
May	5.01	5	12	0	23	22	125.2	137	15	37	100	Close & Late	.288	160	46	9	2	4	15	13	25	.341	.444
June	5.56	7	10	0	22	22	115.0	137	16	39	79	None on/out	.298	758	226	48	6	20	20	33	120	.331	.456
July	3.17	12	4	0	22	22	139.0	145	16	35	88	vs. 1st Batr (relief)	.250	4	1	0	0	0	0	0	0	.400	.250
August	4.01	6	9	0	25	25	155.0	164	20	39	110	1st Inning Pitched	.318	519	165	23	3	22	93	48	72	.384	.501
Sept/Oct	6.15	5	5	0	20	17	98.0	113	19	29	71	First 75 Pitches	.283	2191	620	109	12	78	286	159	386	.336	.450
Starter	4.62	37	47	0	124	124	713.1	785	96	210	500	Pitch 76-90	.288	333	96	15	2	13	50	28	55	.352	.462
Reliever	9.53	0	0	0	5	0	5.2	10	2	1	3	Pitch 91-105	.238	206	49	13	1	4	14	13	41	.284	.369
0-3 Days Rest (Start)	4.24	2	2	0	6	6	34.0	32	4	15	27	Pitch 106+	.313	96	30	8	1	3	7	11	21	.394	.510
4 Days Rest	5.21	16	28	0	66	66	359.1	428	52	126	238	First Pitch	.357	442	158	27	4	21	64	5	0	.369	.579
5+ Days Rest	3.99	19	17	0	52	52	320.0	325	40	69	235	Ahead in Count	.209	1271	266	50	2	28	97	0	435	.217	.318
vs. AL	0.86	2	0	0	3	3	21.0	16	0	7	17	Behind in Count	.374	589	220	36	4	42	124	112	0	.478	.662
vs. NL	4.77	35	47	0	126	121	698.0	779	98	204	486	Two Strikes	.182	1280	233	40	5	24	103	94	503	.243	.277
Pre-All Star	4.95	16	31	0	68	66	364.0	408	48	119	261	Pre-All Star	.283	1444	408	69	10	48	192	119	261	.340	.444
Post-All Star	4.36	21	16	0	61	58	355.0	387	50	92	242	Post-All Star	.280	1382	387	76	6	50	165	92	242	.333	.452

Pitcher vs. Batter (career)

Pitches Best Vs.	Avg	AB	H	2B	3B	HR	RBI	BB	SO	OBP	SLG	Pitches Worst Vs.	Avg	AB	H	2B	3B	HR	RBI	BB	SO	OBP	SLG
Willie McGee	.083	12	1	0	0	0	0	1	1	.154	.083	Mike Lieberthal	.636	11	7	1	0	1	1	0	1	.636	1.000
Carl Everett	.091	11	1	0	0	0	1	0	4	.091	.091	Eddie Murray	.588	17	10	2	0	1	8	1	1	.579	.882
Rico Brogna	.100	20	2	0	0	0	2	0	7	.100	.100	Wil Cordero	.529	17	9	4	0	1	3	0	1	.556	.941
Brett Butler	.125	32	4	0	0	0	0	2	5	.176	.125	Sean Berry	.500	16	8	1	0	2	4	1	4	.556	.938
Lenny Harris	.154	13	2	0	0	0	1	0	4	.143	.154	Matt Williams	.429	28	12	3	0	4	11	1	5	.448	.964

Luis Castillo — Marlins
Age 22 – Bats Both

	Avg	G	AB	R	H	2B	3B	HR	RBI	BB	SO	HBP	GDP	SB	CS	OBP	SLG	IBB	SH	SF	#Pit	#P/PA	GB	FB	G/F
1997 Season	.240	75	263	27	63	8	0	0	8	27	53	0	6	16	10	.310	.270	0	1	0	1160	3.99	165	14	11.79
Career (1996-1997)	.248	116	427	53	106	10	1	1	16	41	99	0	6	33	14	.314	.283	0	3	0	1875	3.98	243	31	7.84

1997 Season

	Avg	AB	H	2B	3B	HR	RBI	BB	SO	OBP	SLG		Avg	AB	H	2B	3B	HR	RBI	BB	SO	OBP	SLG
vs. Left	.222	45	10	2	0	0	1	3	9	.271	.267	Scoring Posn	.237	59	14	1	0	0	8	7	12	.318	.254
vs. Right	.243	218	53	6	0	0	7	24	44	.318	.271	Close & Late	.175	40	7	0	0	0	2	6	10	.283	.175
Home	.217	138	30	5	0	0	3	19	26	.312	.254	None on/out	.276	116	32	4	0	0	0	12	24	.344	.310
Away	.264	125	33	3	0	0	5	8	24	.308	.288	Batting #1	.238	210	50	6	0	0	4	20	42	.304	.267
First Pitch	.342	38	13	2	0	0	1	0	0	.342	.395	Batting #8	.321	28	9	2	0	0.	2	2	5	.367	.393
Ahead in Count	.327	52	17	2	0	0	4	12	0	.453	.365	Other	.160	25	4	0	0	0	2	5	6	.300	.160
Behind in Count	.159	107	17	2	0	0	2	0	42	.159	.178	Pre-All Star	.249	225	56	6	0	0	6	22	43	.316	.276
Two Strikes	.154	130	20	1	0	0	1	15	53	.241	.162	Post-All Star	.184	38	7	2	0	0	2	5	10	.279	.237

Tony Castillo — White Sox
Age 35 – Pitches Left

	ERA	W	L	Sv	G	GS	IP	BB	SO	Avg	2B	3B	HR	RBI	OBP	SLG	GF	IR	IRS	Hld	SvOp	SB	CS	GB	FB	G/F
1997 Season	4.91	4	4	4	64	0	62.1	23	42	.296	74	17	0	6	47	.358	.436	20	48	15	15	9	5	5	92	63	1.46
Last Five Years	3.51	18	17	20	266	0	348.2	121	208	.261	343	55	10	34	198	.325	.396	82	219	75	55	41	24	15	469	388	1.21

1997 Season

	ERA	W	L	Sv	G	GS	IP	H	HR	BB	SO		Avg	AB	H	2B	3B	HR	RBI	BB	SO	OBP	SLG
Home	7.50	0	4	2	29	0	30.0	40	5	13	20	vs. Left	.184	87	16	1	0	3	13	3	16	.220	.299
Away	2.51	4	0	2	35	0	32.1	34	1	10	22	vs. Right	.356	163	58	16	0	3	34	20	26	.426	.509
Day	4.91	3	1	0	28	0	29.1	35	1	14	17	Inning 1-6	.235	34	8	1	0	0	3	2	3	.278	.265
Night	4.91	1	3	4	36	0	33.0	39	5	9	25	Inning 7+	.306	216	66	16	0	6	44	21	39	.370	.463
Grass	5.18	2	4	4	59	0	57.1	69	6	21	40	None on	.318	110	35	7	0	5	5	5	18	.348	.518
Turf	1.80	2	0	0	5	0	5.0	5	0	2	2	Runners on	.279	140	39	10	0	1	42	18	24	.365	.371
March/April	7.36	2	2	0	11	0	11.0	13	2	6	9	Scoring Posn	.311	90	28	8	0	1	40	12	15	.398	.433
May	9.82	0	1	0	8	0	7.1	9	1	2	6	Close & Late	.323	93	30	6	0	3	19	6	22	.364	.484
June	3.72	1	0	0	12	0	9.2	15	0	6	3	None on/out	.352	54	19	3	0	2	2	1	7	.364	.519
July	1.98	0	1	0	13	0	13.2	12	1	4	9	vs. 1st Batr (relief)	.328	61	20	3	0	2	12	2	14	.349	.475
August	5.11	0	0	1	11	0	12.1	17	1	5	10	1st Inning Pitched	.281	196	55	13	0	4	37	17	34	.341	.408
Sept/Oct	3.24	1	0	3	9	0	8.1	8	1	0	5	First 15 Pitches	.260	169	44	10	0	5	26	12	27	.313	.408
Starter	0.00	0	0	0	0	0	0.0	0	0	0	0	Pitch 16-30	.400	65	26	4	0	0	18	9	12	.473	.462
Reliever	4.91	4	4	4	64	0	62.1	74	6	23	42	Pitch 31-45	.250	16	4	3	0	1	3	2	3	.333	.625
0 Days rest (Relief)	5.49	2	2	1	21	0	19.2	27	3	8	13	Pitch 46+	.000	0	0	0	0	0	0	0	0	.000	.000
1 or 2 Days rest	5.84	1	1	1	28	0	24.2	31	3	11	17	First Pitch	.235	34	8	3	0	0	4	5	0	.333	.324
3+ Days rest	3.00	1	1	2	15	0	18.0	16	0	4	12	Ahead in Count	.186	118	22	7	0	2	19	0	35	.193	.297
vs. AL	5.43	2	4	4	57	0	56.1	70	6	22	41	Behind in Count	.446	56	25	4	0	4	15	11	0	.537	.732
vs. NL	0.00	2	0	0	7	0	6.0	4	0	1	1	Two Strikes	.211	114	24	7	0	1	16	7	42	.256	.298
Pre-All Star	6.23	3	3	0	33	0	30.1	40	3	14	19	Pre-All Star	.313	128	40	9	0	3	32	14	19	.385	.453
Post-All Star	3.66	1	1	4	31	0	32.0	34	3	9	23	Post-All Star	.279	122	34	8	0	3	15	9	23	.328	.418

Last Five Years

	ERA	W	L	Sv	G	GS	IP	H	HR	BB	SO		Avg	AB	H	2B	3B	HR	RBI	BB	SO	OBP	SLG
Home	4.32	10	13	8	130	0	179.0	179	21	74	105	vs. Left	.247	401	99	15	5	8	66	19	58	.291	.369
Away	2.65	8	4	12	136	0	169.2	164	13	47	103	vs. Right	.268	911	244	40	5	26	132	102	150	.339	.408
Day	4.19	8	5	3	86	0	122.1	135	13	44	78	Inning 1-6	.255	275	70	10	4	4	43	22	44	.313	.364
Night	3.14	10	12	17	180	0	226.1	208	21	77	130	Inning 7+	.263	1037	273	45	6	30	155	99	164	.328	.405
Grass	3.40	5	7	13	156	0	190.1	188	19	56	119	None on	.259	667	173	23	7	22	22	52	103	.317	.414
Turf	3.64	13	10	7	110	0	158.1	155	15	65	89	Runners on	.264	645	170	32	3	12	176	69	105	.333	.378
March/April	5.01	5	3	0	33	0	46.2	45	7	18	31	Scoring Posn	.264	397	105	20	3	7	159	51	65	.343	.383
May	3.15	2	2	0	46	0	60.0	59	3	29	33	Close & Late	.260	561	146	22	3	18	88	51	95	.323	.406
June	3.03	1	2	2	55	0	74.1	75	7	25	40	None on/out	.263	300	79	12	0	10	10	17	42	.307	.403
July	2.27	5	2	7	50	0	75.1	66	7	19	43	vs. 1st Batr (relief)	.293	239	70	10	0	8	53	17	41	.333	.435
August	5.03	1	3	6	47	0	48.1	60	7	19	36	1st Inning Pitched	.254	839	213	33	7	23	147	73	141	.315	.392
Sept/Oct	3.68	4	5	5	35	0	44.0	38	3	11	25	First 15 Pitches	.253	695	176	29	5	20	111	58	107	.313	.396
Starter	0.00	0	0	0	0	0	0.0	0	0	0	0	Pitch 16-30	.265	426	113	16	4	8	54	44	71	.334	.378
Reliever	3.51	18	17	20	266	0	348.2	343	34	121	208	Pitch 31-45	.276	163	45	9	1	6	28	17	26	.343	.454
0 Days rest (Relief)	3.83	4	4	3	49	0	51.2	50	4	17	33	Pitch 46+	.321	28	9	1	0	0	5	2	4	.387	.357
1 or 2 Days rest	3.75	6	7	8	134	0	173.0	177	21	62	109	First Pitch	.277	177	49	11	2	4	29	12	0	.330	.429
3+ Days rest	3.05	8	6	9	83	0	124.0	116	9	42	66	Ahead in Count	.199	593	118	20	4	8	62	0	182	.202	.287
vs. AL	3.57	16	17	20	259	0	342.2	339	34	120	207	Behind in Count	.322	295	95	13	2	13	61	56	0	.429	.512
vs. NL	0.00	2	0	0	7	0	6.0	4	0	1	1	Two Strikes	.207	585	121	23	3	14	73	53	208	.273	.328
Pre-All Star	3.43	10	7	4	146	0	207.1	206	18	78	118	Pre-All Star	.262	787	206	39	4	18	120	78	118	.331	.390
Post-All Star	3.63	8	10	16	120	0	141.1	137	16	43	90	Post-All Star	.254	525	137	16	6	16	78	43	90	.317	.406

Pitcher vs. Batter (career)

Pitches Best Vs.	Avg	AB	H	2B	3B	HR	RBI	BB	SO	OBP	SLG	Pitches Worst Vs.	Avg	AB	H	2B	3B	HR	RBI	BB	SO	OBP	SLG
Mickey Tettleton	.000	10	0	0	0	0	1	2	2	.154	.000	Cal Ripken	.545	11	6	1	0	1	2	0	1	.545	.909
Mike Macfarlane	.071	14	1	0	0	0	1	1	1	.133	.071	Tony Clark	.455	11	5	1	0	1	1	1	3	.500	.818
Eddie Murray	.091	11	1	0	0	0	2	3		.231	.091	Mike Stanley	.455	11	5	0	0	2	3	1	4	.462	1.000
Carlos Baerga	.100	10	1	0	0	0	2	0	2	.083	.100	Wade Boggs	.417	12	5	1	0	1	3	0	0	.417	.750
John Valentin	.182	11	2	0	0	0	0	3		.182	.182	Tino Martinez	.400	10	4	1	0	1	4	1		.500	.800

Juan Castro — Dodgers

Age 26 – Bats Right

	Avg	G	AB	R	H	2B	3B	HR	RBI	BB	SO	HBP	GDP	SB	CS	OBP	SLG	IBB	SH	SF	#Pit	#P/PA	GB	FB	G/F
1997 Season	.147	40	75	3	11	3	1	0	4	7	20	0	2	0	0	.220	.213	1	2	0	286	3.40	28	19	1.47
Career (1995-1997)	.180	121	211	19	38	8	4	0	9	18	48	0	5	1	0	.245	.256	1	6	0	817	3.48	71	61	1.16

1997 Season

	Avg	AB	H	2B	3B	HR	RBI	BB	SO	OBP	SLG		Avg	AB	H	2B	3B	HR	RBI	BB	SO	OBP	SLG
vs. Left	.100	30	3	2	0	0	0	5	9	.229	.167	Scoring Posn	.111	18	2	0	1	0	4	2	8	.200	.222
vs. Right	.178	45	8	1	1	0	4	2	11	.213	.244	Close & Late	.133	15	2	1	0	0	0	0	5	.133	.200

Frank Catalanotto — Tigers

Age 24 – Bats Left

	Avg	G	AB	R	H	2B	3B	HR	RBI	BB	SO	HBP	GDP	SB	CS	OBP	SLG	IBB	SH	SF	#Pit	#P/PA	GB	FB	G/F
1997 Season	.308	13	26	2	8	2	0	0	3	3	7	0	0	0	0	.379	.385	0	0	0	114	3.93	8	4	2.00

1997 Season

	Avg	AB	H	2B	3B	HR	RBI	BB	SO	OBP	SLG		Avg	AB	H	2B	3B	HR	RBI	BB	SO	OBP	SLG
vs. Left	.000	1	0	0	0	0	0	1	1	.500	.000	Scoring Posn	.667	6	4	1	0	0	3	1	1	.714	.833
vs. Right	.320	25	8	2	0	0	3	2	6	.370	.400	Close & Late	.000	2	0	0	0	0	0	0	1	.000	.000

Mike Cather — Braves

Age 27 – Pitches Right (groundball pitcher)

	ERA	W	L	Sv	G	GS	IP	BB	SO	Avg	H	2B	3B	HR	RBI	OBP	SLG	GF	IR	IRS	Hld	SvOp	SB	CS	GB	FB	G/F
1997 Season	2.39	2	4	0	35	0	37.2	19	29	.174	23	7	0	1	12	.288	.250	10	13	4	4	3	0	0	59	25	2.36

1997 Season

	ERA	W	L	Sv	G	GS	IP	H	HR	BB	SO		Avg	AB	H	2B	3B	HR	RBI	BB	SO	OBP	SLG
Home	2.63	1	1	0	22	0	24.0	13	0	12	21	vs. Left	.205	44	9	1	0	1	3	14	9	.397	.295
Away	1.98	1	3	0	13	0	13.2	10	1	7	8	vs. Right	.159	88	14	6	0	0	9	5	20	.221	.227
Starter	0.00	0	0	0	0	0	0.0	0	0	0	0	Scoring Posn	.200	35	7	2	0	0	9	8	7	.378	.257
Reliever	2.39	2	4	0	35	0	37.2	23	1	19	29	Close & Late	.197	71	14	4	0	1	10	12	11	.321	.296
0 Days rest (Relief)	5.23	1	2	0	11	0	10.1	9	0	9	5	None on/out	.100	30	3	1	0	1	1	6	10	.250	.233
1 or 2 Days rest	2.08	0	2	0	18	0	17.1	11	1	8	14	First Pitch	.208	24	5	1	0	0	3	4	0	.321	.250
3+ Days rest	0.00	1	0	0	6	0	10.0	3	0	2	10	Ahead in Count	.123	65	8	1	0	0	3	0	29	.149	.138
Pre-All Star	0.00	0	0	0	0	0	0.0	0	0	0	0	Behind in Count	.304	23	7	3	0	1	5	8	0	.484	.565
Post-All Star	2.39	2	4	0	35	0	37.2	23	1	19	29	Two Strikes	.111	63	7	1	0	0	1	7	29	.222	.127

Domingo Cedeno — Rangers

Age 29 – Bats Both (groundball hitter)

	Avg	G	AB	R	H	2B	3B	HR	RBI	BB	SO	HBP	GDP	SB	CS	OBP	SLG	IBB	SH	SF	#Pit	#P/PA	GB	FB	G/F
1997 Season	.282	113	365	49	103	19	6	4	36	27	77	2	5	3	3	.334	.400	0	2	1	1425	3.59	117	89	1.31
Career (1993-1997)	.258	315	970	132	250	39	12	10	87	63	217	6	18	11	9	.304	.354	0	16	9	3811	3.58	347	227	1.53

1997 Season

	Avg	AB	H	2B	3B	HR	RBI	BB	SO	OBP	SLG		Avg	AB	H	2B	3B	HR	RBI	BB	SO	OBP	SLG
vs. Left	.263	76	20	4	0	0	6	16	27	.317	.316	First Pitch	.382	68	26	3	0	2	9	0	0	.377	.515
vs. Right	.287	289	83	15	6	4	30	21	61	.339	.422	Ahead in Count	.391	64	25	4	2	0	6	12	0	.487	.516
Groundball	.258	97	25	2	1	1	9	4	18	.284	.330	Behind in Count	.199	181	36	10	3	0	13	0	69	.208	.287

1997 Season

	Avg	AB	H	2B	3B	HR	RBI	BB	SO	OBP	SLG		Avg	AB	H	2B	3B	HR	RBI	BB	SO	OBP	SLG
Flyball	.340	50	17	1	2	0	4	8	8	.441	.440	Two Strikes	.197	178	35	9	3	1	14	15	77	.263	.298
Home	.307	163	50	11	4	2	17	13	24	.360	.460	Batting #7	.393	89	35	8	2	0	8	11	14	.460	.528
Away	.262	202	53	8	2	19	14	53		.313	.351	Batting #8	.253	91	23	2	1	0	11	4	16	.292	.297
Day	.228	79	18	5	1	1	7	4	24	.274	.354	Other	.243	185	45	9	3	4	17	12	47	.291	.389
Night	.297	286	85	14	5	3	29	23	53	.350	.413	March/April	.143	7	1	0	0	0	0	1	4	.250	.143
Grass	.283	322	91	18	5	3	29	24	57	.333	.398	May	.267	45	12	3	2	0	5	4	11	.327	.422
Turf	.279	43	12	1	1	1	7	3	20	.340	.419	June	.316	57	18	2	1	2	4	1	11	.328	.491
Pre-All Star	.311	132	41	9	3	2	14	8	28	.350	.470	July	.247	85	21	4	0	0	9	8	19	.319	.294
Post-All Star	.266	233	62	10	3	2	22	19	49	.325	.361	August	.338	74	25	3	2	0	10	6	15	.395	.432
Scoring Posn	.326	86	28	3	2	0	31	6	18	.366	.407	Sept/Oct	.268	97	26	7	1	2	8	7	17	.314	.423
Close & Late	.300	60	18	2	2	0	7	2	18	.333	.400	vs. AL	.274	328	90	18	5	4	29	22	73	.323	.396
None on/out	.272	92	25	6	2	1	1	8	23	.337	.413	vs. NL	.351	37	13	1	1	0	7	5	4	.429	.432

1997 By Position

Position	Avg	AB	H	2B	3B	HR	RBI	BB	SO	OBP	SLG	G	GS	Innings	PO	A	E	DP	Fld Pct	Rng Fctr	In Zone	Zone Outs	Zone Rtg	MLB Zone
As Pinch Hitter	.353	17	6	0	1	1	2	0	6	.389	.647	18	0	---										
As 2b	.279	219	61	13	4	3	24	16	42	.326	.416	65	53	484.1	100	162	11	28	.960	4.87	185	156	.843	.902
As ss	.256	117	30	3	1	0	8	10	28	.320	.299	43	30	279.2	44	89	6	28	.957	4.28	98	96	.980	.937

Career (1993-1997)

	Avg	AB	H	2B	3B	HR	RBI	BB	SO	OBP	SLG		Avg	AB	H	2B	3B	HR	RBI	BB	SO	OBP	SLG
vs. Left	.246	240	59	9	2	2	20	10	53	.275	.325	First Pitch	.349	189	66	12	3	4	25	0	0	.344	.508
vs. Right	.262	730	191	30	10	8	67	53	164	.314	.363	Ahead in Count	.349	166	58	10	4	1	17	28	0	.439	.476
Groundball	.286	259	74	8	3	4	23	9	44	.307	.386	Behind in Count	.180	461	83	15	4	2	29	0	190	.189	.243
Flyball	.229	157	36	4	4	1	14	16	38	.313	.325	Two Strikes	.173	467	81	11	4	2	25	35	217	.236	.227
Home	.266	443	118	21	10	3	39	31	100	.317	.379	Batting #2	.258	434	112	13	4	3	31	27	100	.303	.327
Away	.250	527	132	18	2	7	48	31	129	.294	.332	Batting #9	.216	194	42	8	2	3	23	11	51	.261	.325
Day	.226	287	65	13	4	2	23	23	68	.290	.321	Other	.281	342	96	18	6	4	33	25	66	.331	.404
Night	.271	683	185	26	8	8	64	40	149	.311	.367	March/April	.345	55	19	4	1	1	8	5	12	.381	.509
Grass	.264	606	160	27	5	8	56	39	122	.310	.365	May	.263	224	59	5	5	1	16	13	42	.304	.344
Turf	.247	364	90	12	7	2	31	24	95	.295	.335	June	.245	204	50	9	1	2	11	11	50	.294	.328
Pre-All Star	.270	530	143	22	8	4	41	35	113	.316	.364	July	.237	156	37	7	2	1	16	14	40	.302	.327
Post-All Star	.243	440	107	11	4	6	46	28	104	.290	.341	August	.290	176	51	5	2	3	23	11	43	.333	.392
Scoring Posn	.264	227	60	5	3	3	77	13	48	.299	.352	Sept/Oct	.219	155	34	9	1	2	13	9	30	.260	.329
Close & Late	.244	168	41	4	4	3	20	13	46	.304	.369	vs. AL	.254	933	237	38	11	10	80	58	213	.299	.350
None on/out	.297	219	65	15	4	2	1	8	23	.342	.413	vs. NL	.351	37	13	1	1	0	7	5	4	.429	.432

Batter vs. Pitcher (career)

Hits Best Against	Avg	AB	H	2B	3B	HR	RBI	BB	SO	OBP	SLG	Hits Worst Against	Avg	AB	H	2B	3B	HR	RBI	BB	SO	OBP	SLG
Brad Radke	.500	12	6	1	0	0	0	0	3	.500	.583	Tim Belcher	.111	9	1	0	0	0	0	1	3	.333	.111
Ariel Prieto	.455	11	5	1	0	0	1	0	2	.455	.545	Roger Clemens	.143	14	2	0	0	0	0	1	7	.200	.143
Tim Wakefield	.400	15	6	1	0	0	2	1	2	.412	.467	Bobby Witt	.231	13	3	0	0	0	0		2	.231	.231
Bob Tewksbury	.400	10	4	0	0	1	2	0	1	.364	.700	Mike Mussina	.231	13	3	0	0	0	1	1	7	.286	.231
Charles Nagy	.333	9	3	1	0	0	2	1	2	.364	.444	Kevin Appier	.235	17	4	1	0	1	1	1	3	.278	.471

Roger Cedeno — Dodgers
Age 23 – Bats Both

	Avg	G	AB	H	R	2B	3B	HR	RBI	BB	SO	HBP	GDP	SB	CS	OBP	SLG	IBB	SH	SF	#Pit	#P/PA	GB	FB	G/F
1997 Season	.273	80	194	31	53	10	2	3	17	25	44	3	1	9	1	.362	.392	2	3	2	820	3.61	68	38	1.79
Career (1995-1997)	.257	206	447	61	115	23	3	5	38	52	101	4	2	15	2	.338	.356	2	5	3	1931	3.78	160	99	1.62

1997 Season

	Avg	AB	H	2B	3B	HR	RBI	BB	SO	OBP	SLG		Avg	AB	H	2B	3B	HR	RBI	BB	SO	OBP	SLG
vs. Left	.286	84	24	7	0	2	6	8	22	.358	.440	Scoring Posn	.326	43	14	1	0	2	15	7	8	.415	.488
vs. Right	.264	110	29	3	2	1	11	17	22	.364	.355	Close & Late	.091	33	3	0	0	0	2	2	10	.143	.091
Home	.253	95	24	4	2	3	10	13	18	.345	.432	None on/out	.222	45	10	2	1	1	1	3	13	.255	.378
Away	.293	99	29	6	0	0	7	12	26	.377	.354	Batting #1	.255	47	12	2	1	1	5	3	16	.308	.404
First Pitch	.382	34	13	5	0	2	2	0		.432	.529	Batting #2	.296	98	29	7	0	2	9	13	17	.375	.429
Ahead in Count	.441	34	15	1	0	0	6	14	0	.580	.471	Other	.245	49	12	1	1	0	3	9	11	.383	.306
Behind in Count	.211	90	19	4	2	3	8	0	36	.220	.400	Pre-All Star	.232	95	22	4	1	0	9	12	19	.330	.295
Two Strikes	.135	89	12	1	1		5	9	44	.214	.225	Post-All Star	.313	99	31	6	1	3	8	13	25	.393	.485

Norm Charlton — Mariners
Age 35 – Pitches Left (groundball pitcher)

	ERA	W	L	Sv	G	GS	IP	BB	SO	Avg	H	2B	3B	HR	RBI	OBP	SLG	GF	IR	IRS	Hld	SvOp	SB	CS	GB	FB	G/F
1997 Season	7.27	3	8	14	71	0	69.1	47	55	.312	89	15	2	7	60	.417	.453	38	54	19	9	25	5	5	108	66	1.64
Last Five Years	4.51	12	24	66	230	0	249.1	133	246	.242	225	35	5	22	144	.341	.361	144	144	44	30	89	21	6	330	213	1.55

1997 Season

	ERA	W	L	Sv	G	GS	IP	H	HR	BB	SO		Avg	AB	H	2B	3B	HR	RBI	BB	SO	OBP	SLG
Home	8.17	2	6	7	37	0	36.1	51	5	25	33	vs. Left	.312	93	29	5	0	1	21	13	19	.407	.398
Away	6.27	1	2	7	34	0	33.0	38	2	22	22	vs. Right	.313	192	60	10	2	6	39	34	36	.421	.479
Day	4.55	2	3	6	25	0	27.2	31	2	21	18	Inning 1-6	.231	13	3	0	0	0	2	4	2	.444	.231
Night	9.07	1	5	8	46	0	41.2	58	5	26	37	Inning 7+	.316	272	86	15	2	7	58	43	53	.415	.463
Grass	4.85	1	1	6	28	0	29.2	29	0	17	20	None on	.281	128	36	5	1	2		18	26	.378	.383
Turf	9.08	2	7	8	43	0	39.2	60	7	30	35	Runners on	.338	157	53	10	1	5	58	29	29	.447	.510
March/April	4.50	1	1	7	14	0	14.0	18	2	4	8	Scoring Posn	.314	102	32	9	1	5	58	26	21	.457	.569
May	8.36	1	3	3	12	0	14.0	17	2	12	7	Close & Late	.299	164	49	11	1	4	41	27	34	.404	.451

1997 Season

	ERA	W	L	Sv	G	GS	IP	H	HR	BB	SO		Avg	AB	H	2B	3B	HR	RBI	BB	SO	OBP	SLG
June	9.31	0	1	2	12	0	9.2	13	1	11	9	None on/out	.371	62	23	2	1	2	2	4	9	.409	.532
July	10.61	0	2	2	11	0	9.1	17	1	6	10	vs. 1st Batr (relief)	.344	64	22	4	1	1	12	7	11	.408	.484
August	5.84	1	0	0	12	0	12.1	11	0	9	12	1st Inning Pitched	.313	230	72	12	2	6	52	37	47	.415	.461
Sept/Oct	6.30	0	1	0	10	0	10.0	13	1	5	9	First 15 Pitches	.298	171	51	7	1	3	27	25	37	.391	.404
Starter	0.00	0	0	0	0	0	0.0	0	0	0	0	Pitch 16-30	.366	93	34	8	1	3	27	15	14	.464	.570
Reliever	7.27	3	8	14	71	0	69.1	89	7	47	55	Pitch 31-45	.200	20	4	0	0	1	6	7	4	.429	.350
0 Days rest (Relief)	7.82	1	3	5	17	0	12.2	11	1	10	6	Pitch 46+	.000	1	0	0	0	0	0	0	0	.000	.000
1 or 2 Days rest	4.91	1	4	7	37	0	40.1	51	3	22	35	First Pitch	.364	33	12	3	1	1	8	1	0	.400	.606
3+ Days rest	12.67	1	1	2	17	0	16.1	27	3	15	14	Ahead in Count	.258	120	31	5	0	2	21	0	44	.270	.350
vs. AL	7.20	3	7	14	63	0	60.0	80	7	39	47	Behind in Count	.377	69	26	5	1	2	14	30	0	.566	.565
vs. NL	7.71	0	1	0	8	0	9.1	9	0	8	8	Two Strikes	.222	126	28	3	0	4	25	16	55	.319	.341
Pre-All Star	7.43	2	6	12	40	0	40.0	52	5	28	27	Pre-All Star	.319	163	52	7	2	5	37	28	27	.428	.479
Post-All Star	7.06	1	2	2	31	0	29.1	37	2	19	28	Post-All Star	.303	122	37	8	0	2	23	19	28	.401	.418

Last Five Years

	ERA	W	L	Sv	G	GS	IP	H	HR	BB	SO		Avg	AB	H	2B	3B	HR	RBI	BB	SO	OBP	SLG
Home	4.43	10	10	31	117	0	136.0	112	14	70	140	vs. Left	.226	266	60	8	1	2	38	39	61	.332	.286
Away	4.61	2	14	35	113	0	113.1	113	8	63	106	vs. Right	.248	664	165	27	4	20	106	94	185	.344	.392
Day	3.15	4	6	19	73	0	85.2	71	6	46	85	Inning 1-6	.259	27	7	1	0	0	4	6	6	.412	.296
Night	5.22	8	18	47	157	0	163.2	154	16	87	161	Inning 7+	.241	903	218	34	5	22	140	127	240	.338	.363
Grass	3.86	2	9	28	93	0	100.1	94	5	50	96	None on	.222	460	102	17	2	8	8	52	131	.308	.320
Turf	4.95	10	15	38	137	0	149.0	131	17	83	150	Runners on	.262	470	123	18	3	14	136	81	115	.371	.402
March/April	3.98	2	3	13	32	0	31.2	33	4	10	31	Scoring Posn	.258	302	78	13	2	10	125	62	75	.381	.414
May	5.66	4	5	12	47	0	47.2	41	7	30	39	Close & Late	.230	562	129	21	3	14	101	86	165	.333	.352
June	4.43	1	4	16	41	0	42.2	38	2	28	42	None on/out	.248	202	50	8	2	4	4	15	59	.303	.366
July	7.88	0	7	3	34	0	32.0	46	4	25	36	vs. 1st Batr (relief)	.252	206	52	9	2	2	20	20	54	.320	.345
August	3.08	2	3	5	39	0	49.2	39	2	21	49	1st Inning Pitched	.241	731	176	27	3	17	115	101	195	.337	.356
Sept/Oct	2.96	3	2	17	37	0	45.2	28	3	19	49	First 15 Pitches	.239	594	142	20	2	13	66	74	153	.328	.345
Starter	0.00	0	0	0	0	0	0.0	0	0	0	0	Pitch 16-30	.255	278	71	13	3	6	63	48	79	.367	.388
Reliever	4.51	12	24	66	230	0	249.1	225	22	133	246	Pitch 31-45	.231	52	12	2	0	3	15	11	14	.369	.442
0 Days rest (Relief)	3.56	1	6	20	53	0	48.0	31	1	22	43	Pitch 46+	.000	6	0	0	0	0	0	0	0	.000	.000
1 or 2 Days rest	4.24	6	10	34	112	0	129.1	124	11	72	123	First Pitch	.304	102	31	6	1	6	25	4	0	.339	.559
3+ Days rest	5.63	5	8	12	65	0	72.0	70	10	39	80	Ahead in Count	.184	425	78	9	1	6	46	0	201	.193	.252
vs. AL	4.09	10	18	66	197	0	218.0	193	20	110	226	Behind in Count	.330	215	71	14	2	4	34	77	0	.505	.470
vs. NL	7.47	2	6	0	33	0	31.1	32	2	23	20	Two Strikes	.157	458	72	6	1	8	55	52	246	.250	.227
Pre-All Star	5.37	7	16	42	129	0	130.2	128	15	76	122	Pre-All Star	.261	490	128	17	5	15	87	76	122	.366	.408
Post-All Star	3.56	5	8	24	101	0	118.2	97	7	57	124	Post-All Star	.220	440	97	18	0	7	57	57	124	.312	.309

Pitcher vs. Batter (career)

Pitches Best Vs.	Avg	AB	H	2B	3B	HR	RBI	BB	SO	OBP	SLG	Pitches Worst Vs.	Avg	AB	H	2B	3B	HR	RBI	BB	SO	OBP	SLG
Jeff King	.000	11	0	0	0	0	0	0	1	.000	.000	Terry Pendleton	.500	18	9	1	1	1	6	1	1	.526	.833
Tom Pagnozzi	.000	10	0	0	0	0	0	1	2	.091	.000	Jeff Bagwell	.500	8	4	1	0	1	2	3	1	.636	1.000
Mo Vaughn	.000	8	0	0	0	0	0	2	5	.273	.000	Jay Bell	.444	18	8	0	0	1	2	0	1	.444	.611
Ken Caminiti	.034	29	1	0	0	1	3	2	8	.097	.138	David Justice	.333	15	5	2	0	1	5	2	4	.412	.667
Rafael Palmeiro	.125	16	2	0	0	0	3	0	2	.125	.125	Matt Williams	.308	13	4	1	0	1	3	5	3	.500	.615

Anthony Chavez — Angels

Age 27 – Pitches Right

	ERA	W	L	Sv	G	GS	IP	BB	SO	Avg	H	2B	3B	HR	RBI	OBP	SLG	GF	IR	IRS	Hld	SvOp	SB	CS	GB	FB	G/F
1997 Season	0.93	0	0	0	7	0	9.2	5	10	.206	7	1	0	1	3	.300	.324	2	7	2	0	0	1	0	13	7	1.86

1997 Season

	ERA	W	L	Sv	G	GS	IP	H	HR	BB	SO		Avg	AB	H	2B	3B	HR	RBI	BB	SO	OBP	SLG
Home	1.35	0	0	0	5	0	6.2	6	1	4	6	vs. Left	.133	15	2	1	0	0	0	2	5	.235	.200
Away	0.00	0	0	0	2	0	3.0	1	0	1	4	vs. Right	.263	19	5	0	0	1	3	3	5	.348	.421

Raul Chavez — Expos

Age 25 – Bats Right

	Avg	G	AB	R	H	2B	3B	HR	RBI	BB	SO	HBP	GDP	SB	CS	OBP	SLG	IBB	SH	SF	#Pit	#P/PA	GB	FB	G/F
1997 Season	.269	13	26	0	7	0	0	0	2	0	5	0	0	1	0	.259	.269	0	0	1	89	3.30	8	9	0.89
Career (1996-1997)	.258	16	31	1	8	0	0	0	2	1	6	0	1	2	0	.273	.258	0	0	1	114	3.45	11	10	1.10

1997 Season

	Avg	AB	H	2B	3B	HR	RBI	BB	SO	OBP	SLG		Avg	AB	H	2B	3B	HR	RBI	BB	SO	OBP	SLG
vs. Left	.500	10	5	0	0	0	1	0	1	.500	.500	Scoring Posn	.333	6	2	0	0	0	2	0	1	.286	.333
vs. Right	.125	16	2	0	0	0	1	0	4	.118	.125	Close & Late	.400	5	2	0	0	0	1	0	1	.400	.400

Robinson Checo — Red Sox

Age 26 – Pitches Right (flyball pitcher)

	ERA	W	L	Sv	G	GS	IP	BB	SO	Avg	H	2B	3B	HR	RBI	OBP	SLG	GF	IR	IRS	Hld	SvOp	SB	CS	GB	FB	G/F
1997 Season	3.38	1	1	0	5	2	13.1	3	14	.235	12	5	2	0	4	.278	.412	1	0	0	1	0	0	1	11	19	0.58

1997 Season

	ERA	W	L	Sv	G	GS	IP	H	HR	BB	SO		Avg	AB	H	2B	3B	HR	RBI	BB	SO	OBP	SLG
Home	0.00	0	0	0	1	0	1.0	1	0	0	1	vs. Left	.273	22	6	2	1	0	1	1	6	.304	.455
Away	3.65	1	1	0	4	2	12.1	11	0	3	13	vs. Right	.207	29	6	3	1	0	3	2	8	.258	.379

Jason Christiansen — Pirates
Age 28 – Pitches Left

	ERA	W	L	Sv	G	GS	IP	BB	SO	Avg	H	2B	3B	HR	RBI	OBP	SLG	GF	IR	IRS	Hld	SvOp	SB	CS	GB	FB	G/F
1997 Season	2.94	3	0	0	39	0	33.2	17	37	.274	37	6	0	2	17	.364	.363	9	19	10	8	2	2	3	46	29	1.59
Career (1995-1997)	4.69	7	6	0	135	0	134.1	70	128	.271	142	31	1	14	86	.360	.414	31	83	29	22	8	10	9	164	147	1.12

1997 Season

	ERA	W	L	Sv	G	GS	IP	H	HR	BB	SO		Avg	AB	H	2B	3B	HR	RBI	BB	SO	OBP	SLG
Home	1.08	2	0	0	19	0	16.2	17	0	7	19	vs. Left	.286	42	12	4	0	1	7	7	13	.388	.452
Away	4.76	1	0	0	20	0	17.0	20	2	10	18	vs. Right	.269	93	25	2	0	1	10	10	24	.352	.323
Starter	0.00	0	0	0	0	0	0.0	0	0	0	0	Scoring Posn	.270	37	10	4	0	0	15	6	12	.372	.378
Reliever	2.94	3	0	0	39	0	33.2	37	2	17	37	Close & Late	.324	37	12	1	0	0	5	3	11	.375	.351
0 Days rest (Relief)	8.44	0	0	0	9	0	5.1	5	1	6	5	None on/out	.167	30	5	0	0	1	1	2	12	.219	.267
1 or 2 Days rest	1.52	3	0	0	23	0	23.2	23	1	9	27	First Pitch	.381	21	8	2	0	0	5	1	0	.409	.476
3+ Days rest	3.86	0	0	0	7	0	4.2	9	0	2	5	Ahead in Count	.217	60	13	2	0	1	2	0	26	.230	.300
Pre-All Star	3.60	0	0	0	6	0	5.0	5	0	1	5	Behind in Count	.478	23	11	2	0	1	8	9	0	.636	.696
Post-All Star	2.83	3	0	0	33	0	28.2	32	2	16	32	Two Strikes	.164	67	11	2	0	0	2	6	37	.243	.194

Career (1995-1997)

	ERA	W	L	Sv	G	GS	IP	H	HR	BB	SO		Avg	AB	H	2B	3B	HR	RBI	BB	SO	OBP	SLG
Home	3.95	4	2	0	65	0	66.0	73	3	34	72	vs. Left	.243	177	43	12	1	6	36	26	51	.346	.424
Away	5.40	3	4	0	70	0	68.1	69	11	36	56	vs. Right	.285	347	99	19	0	8	50	44	77	.367	.409
Day	4.30	2	3	0	47	0	46.0	55	7	20	40	Inning 1-6	.281	121	34	9	1	5	33	19	29	.378	.496
Night	4.89	5	3	0	88	0	88.1	87	7	50	88	Inning 7+	.268	403	108	22	0	9	53	51	99	.354	.390
Grass	4.65	2	3	0	43	0	40.2	47	6	19	35	None on	.245	274	67	16	0	5	5	33	66	.332	.358
Turf	4.71	5	3	0	92	0	93.2	95	8	51	93	Runners on	.300	250	75	15	1	9	81	37	62	.389	.476
March/April	10.54	2	2	0	11	0	13.2	22	3	8	17	Scoring Posn	.294	163	48	10	1	4	69	28	52	.392	.442
May	4.18	2	1	0	21	0	23.2	19	4	9	13	Close & Late	.271	144	39	9	0	4	21	25	32	.380	.417
June	3.76	0	0	0	26	0	26.1	30	1	8	20	None on/out	.172	116	20	7	0	2	2	10	32	.244	.284
July	4.74	1	0	0	29	0	24.2	26	1	21	26	vs. 1st Batr (relief)	.215	121	26	6	0	5	22	11	43	.278	.388
August	3.91	1	3	0	24	0	23.0	30	3	18	23	1st Inning Pitched	.275	396	109	25	1	10	75	51	105	.357	.419
Sept/Oct	3.52	1	0	0	24	0	23.0	15	2	6	29	First 15 Pitches	.277	314	87	20	1	7	50	43	78	.359	.414
Starter	0.00	0	0	0	0	0	0.0	0	0	0	0	Pitch 16-30	.269	160	43	8	0	6	28	22	36	.378	.431
Reliever	4.69	7	6	0	135	0	134.1	142	14	70	128	Pitch 31-45	.241	29	7	2	0	1	7	5	9	.343	.414
0 Days rest (Relief)	4.70	1	0	0	26	0	23.0	21	3	14	22	Pitch 46+	.238	21	5	1	0	0	1	0	5	.238	.286
1 or 2 Days rest	4.18	4	5	0	76	0	79.2	85	7	44	79	First Pitch	.426	61	26	7	1	1	16	10	0	.500	.623
3+ Days rest	5.97	2	1	0	33	0	31.2	36	4	12	27	Ahead in Count	.179	246	44	9	0	5	22	0	99	.191	.276
vs. AL	0.00	0	0	0	2	0	1.1	2	0	0	0	Behind in Count	.343	102	35	11	0	5	28	31	0	.493	.598
vs. NL	4.74	7	6	0	133	0	133.0	140	14	70	128	Two Strikes	.167	264	44	6	0	5	27		128	.256	.246
Pre-All Star	5.12	4	3	0	65	0	70.1	78	8	28	57	Pre-All Star	.280	279	78	17	1	8	46	28	57	.346	.434
Post-All Star	4.22	3	3	0	70	0	64.0	64	6	42	71	Post-All Star	.261	245	64	14	0	6	40	42	71	.375	.392

Pitcher vs. Batter (career)

Pitches Best Vs.	Avg	AB	H	2B	3B	HR	RBI	BB	SO	OBP	SLG	Pitches Worst Vs.	Avg	AB	H	2B	3B	HR	RBI	BB	SO	OBP	SLG
Delino DeShields	.000	11	0	0	0	0	0	1	5	.083	.000												

Archi Cianfrocco — Padres
Age 31 – Bats Right

	Avg	G	AB	R	H	2B	3B	HR	RBI	BB	SO	HBP	GDP	SB	CS	OBP	SLG	IBB	SH	SF	#Pit	#P/PA	GB	FB	G/F
1997 Season	.245	89	220	25	54	12	0	4	26	25	80	3	11	7	1	.328	.355	1	1	2	952	3.78	68	35	1.94
Last Five Years	.250	374	972	107	243	51	5	27	150	64	272	14	30	12	3	.303	.396	3	4	11	3974	3.71	308	236	1.31

1997 Season

	Avg	AB	H	2B	3B	HR	RBI	BB	SO	OBP	SLG		Avg	AB	H	2B	3B	HR	RBI	BB	SO	OBP	SLG
vs. Left	.206	68	14	3	0	3	5	8	26	.299	.382	Scoring Posn	.273	55	15	4	0	1	21	10	18	.400	.400
vs. Right	.263	152	40	9	0	1	21	17	54	.341	.342	Close & Late	.219	32	7	2	0	0	4	5	14	.324	.281
Home	.256	121	31	8	0	3	18	15	47	.348	.397	None on/out	.220	50	11	3	0	1	1	5	18	.291	.340
Away	.232	99	23	4	0	1	8	10	33	.303	.303	Batting #5	.286	35	10	2	0	0	6	2	11	.325	.343
First Pitch	.353	34	12	1	0	2	5	1	0	.371	.559	Batting #6	.255	98	25	4	0	2	13	10	37	.336	.357
Ahead in Count	.382	34	13	5	0	1	8	6	0	.463	.618	Other	.218	87	19	6	0	2	7	13	32	.320	.356
Behind in Count	.171	117	20	5	0	1	9	0	70	.190	.239	Pre-All Star	.251	171	43	10	0	3	23	16	63	.319	.363
Two Strikes	.097	113	11	3	0	0	9	18	80	.226	.124	Post-All Star	.224	49	11	2	0	1	3	9	17	.356	.327

Last Five Years

	Avg	AB	H	2B	3B	HR	RBI	BB	SO	OBP	SLG		Avg	AB	H	2B	3B	HR	RBI	BB	SO	OBP	SLG
vs. Left	.263	300	79	19	1	5	37	23	84	.320	.383	First Pitch	.296	135	40	6	0	7	23	2	0	.317	.496
vs. Right	.244	672	164	32	4	22	113	41	188	.295	.402	Ahead in Count	.402	174	70	18	3	8	45	16	0	.447	.678
Groundball	.231	290	67	15	3	8	41	19	84	.291	.386	Behind in Count	.183	508	93	16	2	7	48	0	244	.195	.264
Flyball	.271	144	39	6	0	7	29	9	47	.323	.458	Two Strikes	.136	477	65	10	2	6	49	46	272	.216	.203
Home	.253	513	130	29	4	13	71	35	139	.307	.402	Batting #6	.244	348	85	20	2	7	54	21	97	.293	.374
Away	.246	459	113	22	1	14	79	29	133	.298	.390	Batting #7	.301	209	63	13	1	6	31	18	45	.362	.459
Day	.223	327	73	18	3	9	44	25	88	.287	.379	Other	.229	415	95	18	2	14	65	25	130	.280	.383
Night	.264	645	170	33	2	18	106	39	184	.311	.405	March/April	.247	150	37	12	0	4	21	5	44	.292	.407
Grass	.246	736	181	35	4	22	117	54	203	.303	.394	May	.291	165	48	8	1	3	20	10	52	.330	.406
Turf	.263	236	62	16	1	5	33	10	69	.300	.403	June	.205	156	32	10	0	2	19	7	46	.242	.308
Pre-All Star	.240	524	126	32	1	11	67	27	160	.284	.368	July	.212	151	32	8	1	6	27	13	37	.282	.397
Post-All Star	.261	448	117	19	4	16	83	37	112	.324	.429	August	.312	205	64	10	2	7	37	21	48	.378	.483
Scoring Posn	.304	253	77	14	1	11	126	23	65	.370	.498	Sept/Oct	.207	145	30	3	1	5	26	8	45	.256	.345
Close & Late	.217	180	39	10	1	4	30	12	60	.277	.350	vs. AL	.222	18	4	2	0	1	3	1	6	.263	.500
None on/out	.215	191	41	7	3	4	4	14	50	.272	.346	vs. NL	.251	954	239	49	5	26	147	63	266	.303	.394

Batter vs. Pitcher (career)

Hits Best Against	Avg	AB	H	2B	3B	HR	RBI	BB	SO	OBP	SLG	Hits Worst Against	Avg	AB	H	2B	3B	HR	RBI	BB	SO	OBP	SLG
Terry Mulholland	.600	15	9	3	0	1	5	0	2	.563	1.000	Greg Maddux	.000	11	0	0	0	0	0	1	0	3	.000	.000
Tom Glavine	.471	17	8	0	0	0	4	1	4	.450	.471	Turk Wendell	.000	11	0	0	0	0	0	0	4	.000	.000
Greg Swindell	.455	11	5	1	0	0	2	0	1	.455	.545	Danny Jackson	.067	15	1	0	0	0	0	1	4	.125	.067
Frank Castillo	.375	16	6	1	0	1	3	0	7	.375	.625	Rheal Cormier	.083	12	1	0	0	0	1	1	5	.214	.083
Pat Rapp	.375	8	3	0	1	0	3			.545	.625	Mike Hampton	.143	14	2	0	0	0	2	0	5	.200	.143

Jeff Cirillo — Brewers

Age 28 – Bats Right (flyball hitter)

	Avg	G	AB	R	H	2B	3B	HR	RBI	BB	SO	HBP	GDP	SB	CS	OBP	SLG	IBB	SH	SF	#Pit	#P/PA	GB	FB	G/F
1997 Season	.288	154	580	74	167	46	2	10	82	60	74	14	13	4	3	.367	.426	0	4	3	2457	3.72	216	181	1.19
Career (1994-1997)	.295	476	1600	249	472	120	11	37	216	176	201	27	39	15	15	.372	.453	0	11	13	6870	3.76	623	465	1.34

1997 Season

	Avg	AB	H	2B	3B	HR	RBI	BB	SO	OBP	SLG		Avg	AB	H	2B	3B	HR	RBI	BB	SO	OBP	SLG
vs. Left	.261	165	43	9	0	3	13	18	22	.354	.370	First Pitch	.321	56	18	6	0	1	13	0	0	.367	.482
vs. Right	.299	415	124	37	2	7	69	42	52	.372	.448	Ahead in Count	.348	135	47	11	0	6	28	33	0	.477	.563
Groundball	.313	96	30	12	0	4	16	9	10	.374	.563	Behind in Count	.272	283	77	22	2	2	25	0	61	.285	.385
Flyball	.202	109	22	7	0	0	10	14	13	.298	.266	Two Strikes	.245	257	63	18	1	3	26	27	74	.326	.358
Home	.287	300	86	19	1	6	42	31	37	.363	.417	Batting #2	.291	206	60	18	1	4	34	27	21	.389	.447
Away	.289	280	81	27	1	4	40	29	37	.371	.436	Batting #3	.268	265	71	19	1	4	32	19	39	.325	.392
Day	.301	219	66	16	1	3	28	29	30	.400	.425	Other	.330	109	36	9	0	2	16	14	14	.421	.468
Night	.280	361	101	30	1	7	54	31	44	.346	.427	March/April	.253	83	21	7	0	1	11	16	9	.374	.373
Grass	.289	501	145	35	2	9	76	54	62	.371	.421	May	.309	97	30	9	1	1	21	8	9	.389	.454
Turf	.278	79	22	11	0	1	6	6	12	.337	.456	June	.340	103	35	9	1	4	19	6	14	.384	.563
Pre-All Star	.300	307	92	26	2	6	52	31	35	.377	.456	July	.217	106	23	4	0	1	7	6	15	.278	.283
Post-All Star	.275	273	75	20	0	4	30	29	39	.355	.392	August	.313	99	31	10	0	1	15	13	11	.404	.444
Scoring Posn	.362	149	54	12	0	4	72	17	15	.430	.523	Sept/Oct	.293	92	27	7	0	2	9	11	16	.375	.435
Close & Late	.287	101	29	11	1	2	18	12	13	.374	.475	vs. AL	.279	527	147	39	2	9	74	57	67	.358	.412
None on/out	.325	123	40	15	1	2	10	17		.394	.512	vs. NL	.377	53	20	7	0	1	8	3	7	.450	.566

1997 By Position

Position	Avg	AB	H	2B	3B	HR	RBI	BB	SO	OBP	SLG	G	GS	Innings	PO	A	E	DP	Fld Pct	Rng Fctr	In Zone	Zone Outs	Zone Rtg	MLB Zone
As 3b	.290	568	165	46	2	10	80	59	73	.370	.431	150	148	1294.1	126	318	17	29	.963	3.09	416	369	.887	.801

Career (1994-1997)

	Avg	AB	H	2B	3B	HR	RBI	BB	SO	OBP	SLG		Avg	AB	H	2B	3B	HR	RBI	BB	SO	OBP	SLG
vs. Left	.285	484	138	36	3	11	43	58	64	.370	.440	First Pitch	.376	170	64	16	1	3	36	0	0	.406	.535
vs. Right	.299	1116	334	84	8	26	173	118	137	.372	.459	Ahead in Count	.341	387	132	33	2	16	66	94	0	.469	.561
Groundball	.293	331	97	26	2	7	42	43	47	.376	.447	Behind in Count	.256	734	188	41	6	11	67	0	168	.264	.373
Flyball	.229	275	63	18	0	3	21	33	39	.322	.327	Two Strikes	.228	692	158	38	5	10	64	80	201	.313	.341
Home	.290	799	232	52	5	19	106	94	97	.371	.439	Batting #2	.305	555	169	44	2	14	74	60	58	.380	.467
Away	.300	801	240	68	6	18	110	82	104	.373	.467	Batting #3	.281	363	102	27	1	7	46	31	52	.343	.419
Day	.295	572	169	41	5	12	68	65	80	.377	.448	Other	.295	682	201	49	8	16	96	85	91	.380	.460
Night	.295	1028	303	79	6	25	148	111	121	.369	.456	March/April	.278	169	47	10	1	3	21	23	23	.366	.402
Grass	.300	1391	417	100	10	33	198	157	167	.377	.454	May	.300	237	71	20	1	7	37	27	29	.387	.481
Turf	.263	209	55	20	1	4	18	19	34	.333	.426	June	.348	250	87	20	5	5	36	16	30	.392	.528
Pre-All Star	.306	731	224	52	9	15	100	70	93	.376	.464	July	.281	345	97	18	4	4	35	32	46	.355	.391
Post-All Star	.285	869	248	68	2	22	116	106	108	.368	.444	August	.285	330	94	31	0	10	58	41	35	.363	.470
Scoring Posn	.313	393	123	27	2	12	177	49	44	.385	.483	Sept/Oct	.283	269	76	21	0	8	29	37	38	.375	.450
Close & Late	.306	252	77	20	4	5	38	36	38	.395	.476	vs. AL	.292	1547	452	113	11	36	208	173	194	.369	.449
None on/out	.306	372	114	30	5	7	7	48	53	.400	.470	vs. NL	.377	53	20	7	0	1	8	3	7	.450	.566

Batter vs. Pitcher (career)

Hits Best Against	Avg	AB	H	2B	3B	HR	RBI	BB	SO	OBP	SLG	Hits Worst Against	Avg	AB	H	2B	3B	HR	RBI	BB	SO	OBP	SLG
A.J. Sager	.545	11	6	1	1	0	2	0	1	.545	.818	Justin Thompson	.000	10	0	0	0	0	0	2	2	.167	.000
Andy Pettitte	.450	20	9	1	1	2	3	4	2	.542	.900	Roger Clemens	.067	15	1	1	0	0	0	0	8	.067	.133
Vaughn Eshelman	.417	12	5	0	0	2	3	1	0	.462	.917	Paul Menhart	.111	9	1	0	0	0	0	1	1	.182	.111
Wilson Alvarez	.400	25	10	5	1	0	3	3	4	.464	.680	Bobby Witt	.154	13	2	0	0	0	0	0	3	.154	.154
Juan Guzman	.333	12	4	0	0	2	5	3	2	.467	.833	Jack McDowell	.154	13	2	0	0	0	0	0	1	.154	.154

Dave Clark — Cubs

Age 35 – Bats Left (groundball hitter)

	Avg	G	AB	R	H	2B	3B	HR	RBI	BB	SO	HBP	GDP	SB	CS	OBP	SLG	IBB	SH	SF	#Pit	#P/PA	GB	FB	G/F
1997 Season	.301	102	143	19	43	8	0	5	32	19	34	2	2	1	0	.386	.462	3	0	2	624	3.76	53	24	2.21
Last Five Years	.282	482	1065	157	300	48	5	38	184	137	231	4	32	9	6	.363	.443	12	1	10	4501	3.70	456	224	2.04

1997 Season

	Avg	AB	H	2B	3B	HR	RBI	BB	SO	OBP	SLG		Avg	AB	H	2B	3B	HR	RBI	BB	SO	OBP	SLG
vs. Left	.429	14	6	0	0	0	1	1	3	.467	.429	Scoring Posn	.313	48	15	3	0	1	24	10	12	.417	.438
vs. Right	.287	129	37	8	0	5	31	18	31	.377	.465	Close & Late	.275	40	11	0	0	2	9	5	9	.356	.425
Home	.313	64	20	3	0	1	16	8	17	.400	.406	None on/out	.258	31	8	3	0	0	0	2	6	.303	.355
Away	.291	79	23	5	0	4	16	11	17	.374	.506	Batting #5	.295	78	23	6	0	2	12	13	15	.404	.449
First Pitch	.353	17	6	1	0	0	2	3	0	.450	.412	Batting #9	.292	48	14	1	0	3	13	5	14	.358	.500
Ahead in Count	.395	43	17	4	0	1	13	8	0	.481	.558	Other	.353	17	6	1	0	0	7	1	5	.368	.412
Behind in Count	.228	57	13	1	0	1	6	0	29	.254	.298	Pre-All Star	.301	73	22	6	0	2	14	9	15	.386	.466
Two Strikes	.203	64	13	3	0	2	11	8	34	.288	.344	Post-All Star	.300	70	21	2	0	3	18	10	19	.386	.457

89

Last Five Years

	Avg	AB	H	2B	3B	HR	RBI	BB	SO	OBP	SLG
vs. Left	.278	108	30	4	0	4	19	19	40	.380	.426
vs. Right	.282	957	270	44	5	34	165	118	191	.361	.445
Groundball	.292	349	102	12	0	12	49	49	75	.378	.430
Flyball	.224	170	38	3	2	5	18	17	40	.298	.353
Home	.289	512	148	23	5	24	104	68	117	.372	.494
Away	.275	553	152	25	0	14	80	69	114	.354	.396
Day	.280	350	98	19	1	10	67	52	80	.369	.426
Night	.283	715	202	29	4	28	117	85	151	.359	.452
Grass	.273	440	120	10	0	12	70	57	95	.356	.377
Turf	.288	625	180	38	5	26	114	80	136	.367	.490
Pre-All Star	.301	591	178	33	3	19	110	67	119	.371	.464
Post-All Star	.257	474	122	15	2	19	74	70	112	.352	.418
Scoring Posn	.288	326	94	15	2	10	137	57	85	.384	.439
Close & Late	.278	227	63	6	1	9	44	26	54	.349	.432
None on/out	.268	250	67	15	1	6	6	31	52	.351	.408

	Avg	AB	H	2B	3B	HR	RBI	BB	SO	OBP	SLG
First Pitch	.394	160	63	4	1	6	32	9	0	.421	.544
Ahead in Count	.359	295	106	18	2	14	62	70	0	.481	.576
Behind in Count	.190	420	80	15	2	8	50	0	187	.193	.293
Two Strikes	.156	461	72	13	2	10	57	58	231	.249	.258
Batting #4	.311	302	94	19	0	12	50	40	69	.390	.493
Batting #5	.266	361	96	12	2	13	57	52	71	.362	.418
March/April	.288	104	30	5	3	2	15	13	23	.373	.452
May	.293	198	58	7	0	3	32	23	31	.369	.374
June	.318	220	70	16	0	10	44	26	49	.389	.527
July	.237	211	50	9	0	7	37	26	56	.313	.379
August	.275	200	55	10	0	11	35	29	46	.368	.490
Sept/Oct	.280	132	37	1	2	5	21	20	26	.377	.432
Other	.274	402	110	17	3	13	77	45	91	.343	.428
vs. AL	.350	20	7	0	0	2	9	2	4	.409	.650
vs. NL	.280	1045	293	48	5	36	175	135	227	.362	.439

Batter vs. Pitcher (career)

Hits Best Against	Avg	AB	H	2B	3B	HR	RBI	BB	SO	OBP	SLG
Dave Weathers	.667	15	10	2	0	1	4	0	0	.667	1.000
Tommy Greene	.500	12	6	1	1	2	2	1	1	.538	1.250
Dwight Gooden	.467	15	7	0	0	2	5	4	0	.579	.867
Tim Belcher	.438	16	7	3	0	2	8	0	1	.438	1.000
Kevin Gross	.400	20	8	1	0	2	6	1	3	.429	.750

Hits Worst Against	Avg	AB	H	2B	3B	HR	RBI	BB	SO	OBP	SLG
Bobby Witt	.077	13	1	0	0	0	0	3	1	.250	.077
Shane Reynolds	.091	11	1	0	0	0	0	0	5	.091	.091
Bret Saberhagen	.111	18	2	0	0	0	1	3	7	.227	.111
Ramon Martinez	.133	15	2	1	0	0	3	0	2	.133	.200
Greg Maddux	.143	21	3	0	0	0	0	1	6	.182	.143

Mark Clark — Cubs   Age 30 – Pitches Right

	ERA	W	L	Sv	G	GS	IP	BB	SO	Avg	H	2B	3B	HR	RBI	OBP	SLG	CG	ShO	Sup	QS	#P/S	SB	CS	GB	FB	G/F
1997 Season	3.82	14	8	0	32	31	205.0	59	123	.270	213	43	11	24	85	.322	.443	3	0	5.22	20	96	17	8	302	219	1.38
Last Five Years	4.01	55	34	0	132	119	778.2	214	450	.273	825	160	25	89	345	.322	.431	12	1	5.33	66	95	61	33	1143	857	1.33

1997 Season

	ERA	W	L	Sv	G	GS	IP	H	HR	BB	SO
Home	3.61	6	4	0	16	16	104.2	107	11	31	62
Away	4.04	8	4	0	16	15	100.1	106	13	28	61
Day	4.42	7	4	0	16	15	97.2	101	12	34	62
Night	3.27	7	4	0	16	16	107.1	112	12	25	61
Grass	4.10	10	7	0	26	26	167.0	176	21	48	98
Turf	2.61	4	1	0	6	5	38.0	37	3	11	25
March/April	3.43	3	1	0	6	6	39.1	39	3	18	16
May	4.30	2	2	0	5	5	29.1	37	4	8	17
June	4.33	1	2	0	5	5	35.1	35	6	11	18
July	5.28	1	2	0	5	5	29.0	39	4	9	17
August	3.57	3	0	0	5	5	35.1	32	5	8	30
Sept/Oct	2.45	4	1	0	5	5	36.2	31	2	5	25
Starter	3.74	14	8	0	31	31	202.0	208	24	58	121
Reliever	9.00	0	0	0	1	0	3.0	5	0	1	2
0-3 Days Rest (Start)	2.57	1	0	0	1	1	7.0	7	0	1	4
4 Days Rest	3.71	7	3	0	16	16	102.0	111	8	25	61
5+ Days Rest	3.87	6	5	0	14	14	93.0	90	16	32	56
vs. AL	5.06	2	1	0	3	3	21.1	19	3	8	9
vs. NL	3.68	12	7	0	29	28	183.2	194	21	51	114
Pre-All Star	3.94	7	5	0	18	17	109.2	121	13	39	58
Post-All Star	3.68	7	3	0	14	14	95.1	92	11	20	65

	Avg	AB	H	2B	3B	HR	RBI	BB	SO	OBP	SLG
vs. Left	.298	359	107	16	6	16	45	38	50	.363	.510
vs. Right	.246	431	106	27	5	8	40	21	73	.286	.387
Inning 1-6	.266	688	183	37	10	19	71	52	108	.319	.432
Inning 7+	.294	102	30	6	1	5	14	7	15	.339	.520
None on	.264	478	126	27	7	13		35	77	.317	.431
Runners on	.279	312	87	16	4	11	72	24	46	.330	.462
Scoring Posn	.257	175	45	9	2	6	58	17	31	.323	.434
Close & Late	.296	54	16	2	0	3	7	5	9	.350	.500
None on/out	.220	205	45	9	2	4		12	36	.266	.341
vs. 1st Batr (relief)	1.000	1	1	1	0	0	0	0	0	1.000	2.000
1st Inning Pitched	.302	126	38	9	3	7	20	11	17	.360	.587
First 75 Pitches	.264	621	164	32	10	19	65	42	89	.312	.440
Pitch 76-90	.286	98	28	8	0	2	8	9	24	.352	.429
Pitch 91-105	.291	55	16	1	1	3	11	7	6	.369	.509
Pitch 106+	.313	16	5	2	0	0	1	1	4	.353	.438
First Pitch	.183	126	23	8	1	5	15	1	0	.188	.381
Ahead in Count	.214	327	70	14	3	5	19	0	102	.219	.321
Behind in Count	.356	180	64	12	3	6	26	34	0	.458	.556
Two Strikes	.195	303	59	8	4	6	18	24	123	.256	.307
Pre-All Star	.286	423	121	24	3	13	48	39	58	.346	.449
Post-All Star	.251	367	92	19	8	11	37	20	65	.293	.436

Last Five Years

	ERA	W	L	Sv	G	GS	IP	H	HR	BB	SO
Home	3.65	26	17	0	66	60	400.0	408	49	99	214
Away	4.40	29	17	0	66	59	378.2	417	40	115	236
Day	4.13	22	18	0	60	56	366.1	371	46	102	214
Night	3.91	33	16	0	72	63	412.1	454	43	112	236
Grass	3.96	45	32	0	109	100	657.0	681	79	178	373
Turf	4.29	10	2	0	23	19	121.2	144	10	36	77
March/April	4.92	7	5	0	20	18	115.1	119	20	43	58
May	4.61	10	8	0	32	23	154.1	180	18	46	75
June	3.18	12	5	0	22	21	138.2	135	12	31	83
July	4.69	8	7	0	21	21	121.0	155	18	37	77
August	3.87	8	4	0	17	16	111.2	120	13	30	78
Sept/Oct	2.94	10	5	0	20	20	137.2	116	8	27	79
Starter	3.98	54	34	0	119	119	750.0	790	84	205	436
Reliever	4.71	1	0	0	13	0	28.2	35	5	9	14
0-3 Days Rest (Start)	1.64	3	0	0	3	3	22.0	17	0	3	17
4 Days Rest	4.10	28	15	0	61	61	382.1	421	37	97	227
5+ Days Rest	4.01	23	19	0	55	55	345.2	352	47	105	192
vs. AL	4.49	29	16	0	71	59	382.2	414	48	115	194
vs. NL	3.55	26	18	0	61	60	390.0	411	41	99	256
Pre-All Star	4.22	33	20	0	82	70	451.2	501	53	133	251
Post-All Star	3.72	22	14	0	50	49	327.0	324	36	81	199

	Avg	AB	H	2B	3B	HR	RBI	BB	SO	OBP	SLG
vs. Left	.292	1430	418	75	12	49	188	111	195	.343	.464
vs. Right	.256	1590	407	85	13	40	157	103	255	.303	.401
Inning 1-6	.271	2597	703	141	22	72	300	188	398	.321	.425
Inning 7+	.288	423	122	19	3	17	45	26	52	.330	.468
None on	.274	1809	496	98	17	56	56	107	276	.318	.440
Runners on	.272	1211	329	62	8	33	289	107	174	.328	.418
Scoring Posn	.255	664	169	33	4	17	244	83	108	.333	.393
Close & Late	.232	194	45	5	0	6	17	14	34	.281	.351
None on/out	.255	787	201	30	6	25	25	45	118	.299	.404
vs. 1st Batr (relief)	.500	10	5	2	0	0	5	3	1	.615	.700
1st Inning Pitched	.267	502	134	28	3	15	67	44	80	.326	.424
First 75 Pitches	.269	2295	617	123	21	68	257	154	346	.316	.430
Pitch 76-90	.269	361	97	16	1	12	39	26	60	.319	.418
Pitch 91-105	.325	252	82	12	3	8	40	23	30	.381	.492
Pitch 106+	.259	112	29	9	0	1	9	11	14	.325	.366
First Pitch	.282	479	135	33	5	15	59	8	0	.294	.466
Ahead in Count	.221	1265	280	51	8	23	109	0	368	.227	.329
Behind in Count	.337	659	222	50	4	29	108	111	0	.428	.557
Two Strikes	.208	1250	260	38	8	26	96	95	450	.266	.314
Pre-All Star	.284	1762	501	99	10	53	213	133	251	.336	.442
Post-All Star	.258	1258	324	61	15	36	132	81	199	.303	.416

Pitcher vs. Batter (career)

Pitches Best Vs.	Avg	AB	H	2B	3B	HR	RBI	BB	SO	OBP	SLG	Pitches Worst Vs.	Avg	AB	H	2B	3B	HR	RBI	BB	SO	OBP	SLG
Rondell White	.000	10	0	0	0	0	0	0	3	.091	.000	Chipper Jones	.500	14	7	2	0	1	2	2	1	.563	.857
Joe Oliver	.083	12	1	0	0	0	0	0	2	.083	.083	Damion Easley	.500	10	5	0	1	1	1	1	0	.545	1.000
Lenny Harris	.118	17	2	0	0	0	2	0	0	.118	.118	Darrin Fletcher	.455	11	5	1	0	2	3	0	0	.455	1.091
Terry Steinbach	.154	13	2	0	0	0	1	0	3	.143	.154	Paul O'Neill	.455	11	5	0	0	3	5	0	0	.417	1.273
Brent Gates	.154	13	2	0	0	0	0	0	1	.154	.154	Mickey Tettleton	.444	9	4	1	0	1	3	2	2	.545	.889

Terry Clark — Rangers
Age 37 – Pitches Right (groundball pitcher)

	ERA	W	L	Sv	G	GS	IP	BB	SO	Avg	H	2B	3B	HR	RBI	OBP	SLG	CG	ShO	Sup	QS	#P/S	SB	CS	GB	FB	G/F
1997 Season	6.00	1	7	0	13	9	57.0	23	24	.307	70	15	1	6	33	.373	.461	0	0	2.37	0	93	2	3	102	51	2.00
Last Five Years	5.69	4	15	1	71	9	123.1	52	61	.314	157	36	4	13	79	.381	.480	0	0	3.43	0	93	8	3	225	118	1.91

1997 Season

	ERA	W	L	Sv	G	GS	IP	H	BB	SO		Avg	AB	H	2B	3B	HR	RBI	BB	SO	OBP	SLG
Home	6.40	0	4	0	8	4	32.1	39	5	13	vs. Left	.336	125	42	8	1	5	19	15	12	.413	.536
Away	5.47	1	3	0	5	5	24.2	31	1	10	vs. Right	.272	103	28	7	0	1	14	8	12	.321	.369

Tony Clark — Tigers
Age 26 – Bats Both

	Avg	G	AB	R	H	2B	3B	HR	RBI	BB	SO	HBP	GDP	SB	CS	OBP	SLG	IBB	SH	SF	#Pit	#P/PA	GB	FB	G/F
1997 Season	.276	159	580	105	160	28	3	32	117	93	144	3	11	1	3	.376	.500	13	0	5	2653	3.90	204	137	1.49
Career (1995-1997)	.263	286	1057	171	278	47	4	62	200	130	301	3	20	1	4	.342	.491	14	0	11	4692	3.91	353	240	1.47

1997 Season

	Avg	AB	H	2B	3B	HR	RBI	BB	SO	OBP	SLG		Avg	AB	H	2B	3B	HR	RBI	BB	SO	OBP	SLG
vs. Left	.265	181	48	6	1	10	35	24	44	.350	.475	First Pitch	.443	70	31	6	1	8	23	9	0	.506	.900
vs. Right	.281	399	112	22	2	22	82	69	100	.387	.511	Ahead in Count	.411	107	44	8	0	11	39	44	0	.579	.794
Groundball	.263	114	30	5	0	7	19	22	28	.384	.491	Behind in Count	.201	278	56	11	1	6	31	0	114	.203	.313
Flyball	.291	110	32	6	1	7	20	10	32	.350	.555	Two Strikes	.195	302	59	12	1	8	40	40	144	.291	.321
Home	.267	281	75	12	2	18	57	53	79	.382	.516	Batting #3	.400	15	6	2	0	0	3	2	2	.471	.533
Away	.284	299	85	16	1	14	60	40	65	.370	.485	Batting #4	.273	565	154	26	3	32	114	90	142	.373	.499
Day	.278	230	64	8	2	15	48	42	57	.387	.526	Other	.000	0	0	0	0	0	0	1	0	1.000	.000
Night	.274	350	96	20	1	17	69	51	87	.369	.483	March/April	.288	104	30	3	1	8	27	12	31	.361	.567
Grass	.272	511	139	25	2	30	108	84	127	.375	.505	May	.282	85	24	4	0	9	22	17	22	.408	.647
Turf	.304	69	21	3	1	2	9	9	17	.385	.464	June	.299	87	26	6	0	3	21	23	19	.441	.471
Pre-All Star	.291	299	87	14	2	22	73	60	77	.409	.572	July	.247	93	23	5	1	5	11	18	23	.375	.484
Post-All Star	.260	281	73	14	1	10	44	33	67	.338	.423	August	.261	115	30	6	1	3	17	10	30	.317	.409
Scoring Posn	.315	149	47	13	0	11	86	39	36	.448	.624	Sept/Oct	.281	96	27	4	0	4	19	13	19	.364	.448
Close & Late	.267	86	23	2	0	4	17	16	24	.382	.430	vs. AL	.276	525	145	25	2	30	108	87	128	.379	.503
None on/out	.263	175	46	5	3	8	8	16	46	.325	.463	vs. NL	.273	55	15	3	1	2	9	6	16	.344	.473

1997 By Position

Position	Avg	AB	H	2B	3B	HR	RBI	BB	SO	OBP	SLG		G	GS	Innings	PO	A	E	DP	Fld Pct	Rng Fctr	In Zone	Outs	Zone Rtg	MLB Zone
As 1b	.278	576	160	28	3	32	117	93	142	.378	.503		158	157	1383.2	1424	99	10	131	.993	—	261	243	.931	.874

Career (1995-1997)

	Avg	AB	H	2B	3B	HR	RBI	BB	SO	OBP	SLG		Avg	AB	H	2B	3B	HR	RBI	BB	SO	OBP	SLG
vs. Left	.259	294	76	12	1	16	57	29	77	.323	.469	First Pitch	.402	122	49	8	1	12	31	9	0	.440	.779
vs. Right	.265	763	202	35	3	46	143	101	224	.349	.499	Ahead in Count	.405	200	81	12	0	22	60	65	0	.549	.795
Groundball	.278	216	60	10	0	12	38	32	63	.372	.491	Behind in Count	.172	517	89	17	2	14	65	0	250	.172	.294
Flyball	.262	183	48	10	1	9	32	14	61	.309	.475	Two Strikes	.168	553	93	21	1	14	70	56	301	.245	.286
Home	.257	525	135	23	3	35	110	74	157	.346	.512	Batting #4	.270	603	163	28	3	34	119	91	156	.366	.496
Away	.269	532	143	24	1	27	90	56	144	.338	.470	Batting #5	.225	285	64	8	1	20	55	29	90	.292	.470
Day	.271	413	112	14	3	30	90	54	113	.352	.538	Other	.302	169	51	11	0	8	26	10	55	.339	.509
Night	.258	644	166	33	1	32	110	76	188	.336	.461	March/April	.288	104	30	3	1	8	27	12	31	.361	.567
Grass	.263	924	243	44	3	54	181	115	262	.343	.492	May	.282	85	24	4	0	9	22	17	22	.408	.647
Turf	.263	133	35	3	1	8	19	15	39	.336	.481	June	.289	166	48	12	0	8	38	28	47	.386	.506
Pre-All Star	.281	398	112	20	2	28	91	68	107	.385	.553	July	.228	180	41	6	1	12	23	28	48	.333	.472
Post-All Star	.252	659	166	27	2	34	109	62	194	.315	.454	August	.262	221	58	10	1	9	35	18	61	.317	.439
Scoring Posn	.284	257	73	20	1	19	143	53	71	.394	.591	Sept/Oct	.256	301	77	12	1	16	55	27	92	.313	.462
Close & Late	.232	155	36	5	0	5	22	28	47	.350	.361	vs. AL	.262	1002	263	44	3	60	191	124	285	.342	.492
None on/out	.267	296	79	6	3	20	20	21	80	.315	.510	vs. NL	.273	55	15	3	1	2	9	6	16	.344	.473

Batter vs. Pitcher (career)

Hits Best Against	Avg	AB	H	2B	3B	HR	RBI	BB	SO	OBP	SLG	Hits Worst Against	Avg	AB	H	2B	3B	HR	RBI	BB	SO	OBP	SLG
Orel Hershiser	.500	10	5	0	0	3	5	2	1	.538	1.400	David Cone	.000	11	0	0	0	0	2	0	5	.000	.000
Tony Castillo	.455	11	5	1	0	1	1	1	3	.500	.818	Mike Mussina	.071	14	1	0	0	1	2	0	10	.071	.286
Aaron Sele	.444	9	4	1	0	2	4	3	3	.583	1.222	Ben McDonald	.071	14	1	0	0	0	0	3	4	.235	.071
Brad Radke	.400	10	4	2	1	0	2	1	1	.455	.800	Kenny Rogers	.154	13	2	0	0	1	0	3	.154	.154
Bob Wolcott	.333	12	4	0	0	2	2	1	1	.385	.833	Andy Pettitte	.154	13	2	0	0	0	1	2	.214	.154

91

Will Clark — Rangers
Age 34 – Bats Left (flyball hitter)

	Avg	G	AB	R	H	2B	3B	HR	RBI	BB	SO	HBP	GDP	SB	CS	OBP	SLG	IBB	SH	SF	#Pit	#P/PA	GB	FB	G/F
1997 Season	.326	110	393	56	128	29	1	12	51	49	62	3	4	0	0	.400	.496	11	0	5	1621	3.60	123	120	1.03
Last Five Years	.303	592	2163	365	656	132	9	68	368	315	306	21	36	9	5	.391	.467	39	1	35	9549	3.77	660	737	0.90

1997 Season

	Avg	AB	H	2B	3B	HR	RBI	BB	SO	OBP	SLG		Avg	AB	H	2B	3B	HR	RBI	BB	SO	OBP	SLG
vs. Left	.302	129	39	7	1	3	16	12	20	.366	.442	First Pitch	.462	65	30	8	1	0	10	8	0	.513	.615
vs. Right	.337	264	89	22	0	9	35	37	42	.416	.523	Ahead in Count	.412	85	35	5	0	3	15	23	0	.536	.576
Groundball	.273	99	27	7	0	3	14	14	18	.353	.434	Behind in Count	.210	162	34	9	0	5	16	0	53	.212	.358
Flyball	.340	53	18	4	0	2	7	8	7	.419	.528	Two Strikes	.229	175	40	12	0	8	21	18	62	.301	.434
Home	.351	202	71	16	1	6	26	25	23	.422	.530	Batting #4	.250	32	8	1	0	1	3	3	8	.314	.375
Away	.298	191	57	13	0	6	25	24	39	.377	.461	Batting #5	.331	335	111	25	1	9	43	45	49	.410	.493
Day	.301	73	22	6	0	3	13	10	16	.393	.507	Other	.346	26	9	3	0	2	5	1	5	.370	.692
Night	.331	320	106	23	1	9	38	39	46	.402	.494	March/April	.302	43	13	1	0	1	3	5	9	.388	.395
Grass	.313	342	107	25	1	10	43	46	51	.392	.480	May	.394	99	39	8	0	6	18	20	10	.500	.657
Turf	.412	51	21	4	0	2	8	3	11	.456	.608	June	.288	104	30	8	1	0	5	11	13	.353	.385
Pre-All Star	.331	266	88	18	1	8	30	37	36	.415	.496	July	.365	96	35	10	0	4	17	7	20	.410	.594
Post-All Star	.315	127	40	11	0	4	21	12	26	.368	.494	August	.216	51	11	2	0	1	8	6	10	.283	.314
Scoring Posn	.240	100	24	5	0	4	38	25	21	.382	.410	Sept/Oct	.000	0	0	0	0	0	0	0	0	.000	.000
Close & Late	.222	63	14	4	0	2	8	9	15	.311	.381	vs. AL	.339	363	123	29	1	11	46	41	57	.406	.515
None on/out	.336	113	38	7	1	5	5	2	13	.359	.549	vs. NL	.167	30	5	0	0	1	5	8	5	.333	.267

1997 By Position

Position	Avg	AB	H	2B	3B	HR	RBI	BB	SO	OBP	SLG	G	GS	Innings	PO	A	E	DP	Fld Pct	Rng Fctr	In Zone	Zone Outs	Zone Rtg	MLB Zone
As 1b	.334	365	122	29	1	11	50	46	57	.408	.510	100	98	848.1	879	62	4	86	.996	---	177	150	.847	.874

Last Five Years

	Avg	AB	H	2B	3B	HR	RBI	BB	SO	OBP	SLG		Avg	AB	H	2B	3B	HR	RBI	BB	SO	OBP	SLG
vs. Left	.283	711	201	45	2	13	120	73	98	.354	.406	First Pitch	.399	348	139	35	2	13	76	34	0	.453	.624
vs. Right	.313	1452	455	87	7	55	248	242	208	.409	.497	Ahead in Count	.357	532	190	35	1	22	107	160	0	.501	.551
Groundball	.310	529	164	34	2	16	90	75	76	.394	.473	Behind in Count	.234	855	200	35	2	19	114	0	248	.240	.346
Flyball	.328	412	135	28	1	11	65	51	48	.399	.481	Two Strikes	.214	920	197	39	5	23	116	120	306	.305	.342
Home	.304	1107	337	70	3	39	190	170	150	.396	.479	Batting #3	.294	1303	383	79	6	42	238	180	172	.380	.460
Away	.302	1056	319	62	6	29	178	145	156	.386	.455	Batting #5	.320	507	162	36	1	16	70	75	76	.406	.489
Day	.292	631	184	39	3	17	112	84	96	.374	.444	Other	.314	353	111	17	2	10	60	60	58	.414	.459
Night	.308	1532	472	93	6	51	256	231	210	.398	.477	March/April	.291	309	90	17	1	9	57	50	47	.391	.440
Grass	.303	1824	552	115	9	55	319	274	252	.393	.466	May	.317	480	152	28	1	17	83	83	63	.417	.485
Turf	.307	339	104	17	0	13	49	41	54	.386	.472	June	.307	430	132	33	3	12	75	55	56	.387	.481
Pre-All Star	.311	1315	409	83	5	42	233	202	178	.402	.478	July	.300	360	108	25	0	9	54	43	55	.376	.444
Post-All Star	.291	848	247	49	4	26	135	113	128	.374	.450	August	.289	332	96	19	4	12	63	45	46	.368	.479
Scoring Posn	.288	614	177	34	5	14	282	111	100	.383	.428	Sept/Oct	.310	252	78	10	0	9	36	39	39	.403	.456
Close & Late	.279	308	86	17	1	12	54	52	54	.385	.458	vs. AL	.312	1642	512	105	7	53	290	244	233	.400	.481
None on/out	.344	485	167	30	3	23	23	38	58	.399	.561	vs. NL	.276	521	144	27	2	15	78	71	73	.365	.422

Batter vs. Pitcher (career)

Hits Best Against	Avg	AB	H	2B	3B	HR	RBI	BB	SO	OBP	SLG	Hits Worst Against	Avg	AB	H	2B	3B	HR	RBI	BB	SO	OBP	SLG
Pat Mahomes	.600	15	9	1	0	2	4	2	0	.647	1.067	Mike Harkey	.045	22	1	0	0	0	1	2	4	.125	.045
Todd Worrell	.500	10	5	2	0	1	3	3	2	.615	1.000	Norm Charlton	.083	24	2	0	0	0	0	3	8	.241	.083
Kent Mercker	.471	17	8	2	0	2	7	1	0	.526	.941	Buddy Groom	.100	10	1	0	0	0	0	2	1	.250	.100
Mark Davis	.471	17	8	2	1	1	11	0	3	.471	1.000	Alex Fernandez	.143	14	2	0	0	0	2	1	4	.200	.143
Doug Brocail	.375	8	3	1	0	1	6	4	1	.538	.875	Curt Schilling	.158	19	3	0	0	0	0	2	6	.238	.158

Royce Clayton — Cardinals
Age 28 – Bats Right (groundball hitter)

	Avg	G	AB	R	H	2B	3B	HR	RBI	BB	SO	HBP	GDP	SB	CS	OBP	SLG	IBB	SH	SF	#Pit	#P/PA	GB	FB	G/F
1997 Season	.266	154	576	75	153	39	5	9	61	33	109	3	19	30	10	.306	.398	4	2	5	2145	3.47	236	128	1.84
Last Five Years	.263	682	2510	287	659	123	23	29	254	172	472	15	62	121	47	.311	.365	13	19	21	9809	3.58	1017	587	1.73

1997 Season

	Avg	AB	H	2B	3B	HR	RBI	BB	SO	OBP	SLG		Avg	AB	H	2B	3B	HR	RBI	BB	SO	OBP	SLG
vs. Left	.252	139	35	12	1	2	10	8	33	.295	.396	First Pitch	.336	107	36	13	1	1	16	4	0	.362	.505
vs. Right	.270	437	118	27	4	7	51	25	76	.310	.398	Ahead in Count	.306	111	34	11	1	3	14	17	0	.395	.505
Groundball	.268	112	30	9	0	3	14	9	13	.325	.429	Behind in Count	.209	268	56	9	1	3	16	0	96	.211	.284
Flyball	.188	80	15	2	0	1	6	1	17	.195	.250	Two Strikes	.177	260	46	8	2	4	22	12	109	.215	.269
Home	.298	262	78	19	0	5	32	21	36	.351	.427	Batting #1	.246	175	43	11	0	4	20	10	41	.285	.377
Away	.239	314	75	20	5	4	29	12	73	.267	.373	Batting #8	.280	193	54	15	4	3	27	13	32	.325	.446
Day	.286	203	58	11	1	5	24	15	34	.333	.424	Other	.269	208	56	13	1	2	14	10	36	.306	.370
Night	.255	373	95	28	4	4	37	18	75	.291	.383	March/April	.230	100	23	9	1	2	10	5	14	.264	.400
Grass	.267	468	125	29	4	7	53	26	83	.307	.391	May	.277	101	28	9	0	2	14	8	16	.327	.426
Turf	.259	108	28	10	1	2	8	7	26	.304	.426	June	.268	97	26	5	1	2	11	9	26	.336	.402
Pre-All Star	.264	322	85	23	2	6	36	24	60	.317	.404	July	.224	107	24	6	0	2	7	4	22	.257	.336
Post-All Star	.268	254	68	16	3	3	25	9	49	.292	.390	August	.275	91	25	3	2	0	6	4	19	.313	.352
Scoring Posn	.230	139	32	9	3	0	46	13	31	.291	.338	Sept/Oct	.338	80	27	7	1	1	13	3	12	.353	.488
Close & Late	.246	114	28	5	2	1	11	5	23	.281	.351	vs. AL	.231	52	12	3	0	0	3	0	12	.245	.288
None on/out	.206	165	34	13	0	3	3	10	34	.256	.339	vs. NL	.269	524	141	36	5	9	58	33	97	.312	.408

1997 By Position

Position	Avg	AB	H	2B	3B	HR	RBI	BB	SO	OBP	SLG	G	GS	Innings	PO	A	E	DP	Fld Pct	Rng Fctr	In Zone	Zone Outs	Zone Rtg	MLB Zone
As ss	.266	576	153	39	5	9	61	31	109	.304	.398	153	145	1287.1	229	450	19	95	.973	4.75	495	489	.988	.937

Last Five Years

	Avg	AB	H	2B	3B	HR	RBI	BB	SO	OBP	SLG
vs. Left	.248	633	157	36	4	11	50	38	130	.292	.370
vs. Right	.267	1877	502	87	19	18	204	134	342	.318	.363
Groundball	.260	695	181	33	2	7	67	42	106	.307	.344
Flyball	.222	347	77	9	6	4	41	20	84	.264	.317
Home	.264	1224	323	64	7	19	126	92	221	.316	.374
Away	.261	1286	336	59	16	10	128	80	251	.307	.355
Day	.260	1058	275	45	9	11	116	78	199	.312	.351
Night	.264	1452	384	78	14	18	138	94	273	.311	.375
Grass	.263	1976	520	96	19	26	200	135	362	.311	.370
Turf	.260	534	139	27	4	3	54	37	110	.312	.343
Pre-All Star	.268	1457	390	75	14	17	163	110	278	.319	.341
Post-All Star	.255	1053	269	48	9	12	91	62	194	.300	.352
Scoring Posn	.247	660	163	24	10	6	218	66	145	.309	.341
Close & Late	.224	425	95	14	3	2	33	29	109	.275	.285
None on/out	.263	687	181	45	5	11	11	41	119	.310	.392

	Avg	AB	H	2B	3B	HR	RBI	BB	SO	OBP	SLG
First Pitch	.353	425	150	34	5	6	63	11	0	.369	.499
Ahead in Count	.307	475	146	30	3	12	60	88	0	.413	.459
Behind in Count	.201	1203	242	39	9	8	85	0	420	.203	.268
Two Strikes	.189	1150	217	35	10	8	84	73	472	.239	.257
Batting #6	.263	552	145	24	5	6	72	36	112	.307	.357
Batting #7	.261	767	200	31	9	6	72	64	133	.322	.348
Other	.264	1191	314	68	9	17	110	72	227	.306	.379
March/April	.258	384	99	22	5	5	39	30	72	.308	.380
May	.260	473	123	23	6	6	62	36	78	.313	.372
June	.272	448	122	23	3	4	41	33	96	.325	.364
July	.254	469	119	20	3	5	46	29	91	.301	.341
August	.259	402	104	17	3	5	34	22	79	.301	.353
Sept/Oct	.275	334	92	18	3	4	32	22	56	.320	.383
vs. AL	.231	52	12	3	0	0	3	0	12	.245	.288
vs. NL	.263	2458	647	120	23	29	251	172	460	.313	.366

Batter vs. Pitcher (career)

Hits Best Against	Avg	AB	H	2B	3B	HR	RBI	BB	SO	OBP	SLG
Armando Reynoso	.579	19	11	1	1	1	6	6	0	.630	.895
Pat Rapp	.542	24	13	3	0	0	4	2	4	.577	.667
Steve Cooke	.455	22	10	3	0	1	1	3	3	.520	.727
Kevin Ritz	.429	14	6	1	0	2	5	2	0	.500	.929
Steve Avery	.406	32	13	3	1	2	5	1	8	.412	.750

Hits Worst Against	Avg	AB	H	2B	3B	HR	RBI	BB	SO	OBP	SLG
Jeff Juden	.000	11	0	0	0	0	2	1	4	.077	.000
Jeff Shaw	.056	18	1	0	0	0	0	0	2	.105	.056
Orel Hershiser	.074	27	2	0	0	0	0	1	2	.107	.074
Steve Reed	.083	12	1	0	0	0	1	1	3	.143	.083
Jeff Fassero	.111	18	2	0	0	0	0	0	5	.111	.111

Roger Clemens — Blue Jays

Age 35 – Pitches Right (groundball pitcher)

	ERA	W	L	Sv	G	GS	IP	BB	SO	Avg	H	2B	3B	HR	RBI	OBP	SLG	CG	ShO	Sup	QS	#P/S	SB	CS	GB	FB	G/F
1997 Season	2.05	21	7	0	34	34	264.0	68	292	.213	204	41	3	9	59	.273	.290	9	3	4.98	26	121	10	9	338	193	1.75
Last Five Years	3.32	61	46	0	144	144	1009.0	372	1009	.230	860	160	19	75	359	.306	.343	20	7	4.52	91	117	78	49	1336	780	1.71

1997 Season

	ERA	W	L	Sv	G	GS	IP	H	HR	BB	SO
Home	1.52	10	4	0	18	18	147.2	112	5	33	153
Away	2.71	11	3	0	16	16	116.1	92	4	35	139
Day	1.56	5	3	0	11	11	86.1	61	1	22	92
Night	2.28	16	4	0	23	23	177.2	143	8	46	200
Grass	2.20	10	2	0	14	14	102.1	75	2	33	120
Turf	1.95	11	5	0	20	20	161.2	129	7	35	172
March/April	1.72	4	0	0	5	5	36.2	22	2	11	29
May	1.96	6	0	0	6	6	46.0	35	2	13	51
June	1.64	2	2	0	5	5	38.1	29	1	9	42
July	0.89	4	2	0	6	6	50.1	34	2	9	61
August	2.47	4	0	0	6	6	47.1	43	1	15	54
Sept/Oct	3.57	1	3	0	6	6	45.1	41	1	11	55
Starter	2.05	21	7	0	34	34	264.0	204	9	68	292
Reliever	0.00	0	0	0	0	0	0.0	0	0	0	0
0-3 Days Rest (Start)	0.00	0	0	0	0	0	0.0	0	0	0	0
4 Days Rest	2.39	14	7	0	24	24	188.1	151	7	46	218
5+ Days Rest	1.19	7	0	0	10	10	75.2	53	2	22	74
vs. AL	1.83	21	4	0	31	31	240.2	176	7	64	265
vs. NL	4.24	0	3	0	3	3	23.1	28	2	4	27
Pre-All Star	1.69	13	3	0	18	18	138.1	100	6	36	140
Post-All Star	2.44	8	4	0	16	16	125.2	104	3	32	152

	Avg	AB	H	2B	3B	HR	RBI	BB	SO	OBP	SLG
vs. Left	.205	498	102	21	3	3	32	36	160	.265	.277
vs. Right	.222	459	102	20	0	6	27	32	132	.283	.305
Inning 1-6	.212	736	156	32	2	6	46	55	231	.276	.285
Inning 7+	.217	221	48	9	1	3	13	13	61	.264	.308
None on	.210	587	123	21	1	7	7	43	188	.272	.284
Runners on	.219	370	81	20	2	2	52	25	104	.276	.300
Scoring Posn	.180	194	35	8	2	2	48	17	65	.258	.273
Close & Late	.194	108	21	4	0	3		6	30	.237	.315
vs. 1st Batr (relief)	.000	0	0	0	0	0	0	0	0	.000	.000
1st Inning Pitched	.214	126	27	4	0	0	11	9	46	.281	.246
First 75 Pitches	.223	565	126	26	2	6	37	43	173	.286	.308
Pitch 76-90	.123	114	14	3	0	0		8	48	.187	.149
Pitch 91-105	.198	116	23	3	0	0		3	28	.262	.224
Pitch 106+	.253	162	41	9	1	3	16	8	43	.297	.377
First Pitch	.287	122	35	6	3	0	11	1	0	.313	.410
Ahead in Count	.148	487	72	15	1	2	20	0	241	.156	.195
Behind in Count	.343	175	60	12	2	3	17	26	0	.431	.486
Two Strikes	.123	512	63	13	1	2	18	41	292	.197	.164
Pre-All Star	.204	489	100	16	1	6	25	36	140	.266	.278
Post-All Star	.222	468	104	25	2	3	34	32	152	.281	.303

Last Five Years

	ERA	W	L	Sv	G	GS	IP	H	HR	BB	SO
Home	3.29	32	22	0	71	71	509.1	436	29	171	518
Away	3.35	29	24	0	73	73	499.2	424	46	201	491
Day	3.42	18	17	0	49	49	334.1	306	23	133	325
Night	3.27	43	29	0	95	95	674.2	554	52	239	684
Grass	3.57	46	36	0	109	109	748.2	640	61	292	767
Turf	2.59	15	10	0	35	35	260.1	220	14	80	242
March/April	2.68	10	6	0	22	22	154.1	117	12	54	134
May	2.99	14	5	0	23	23	168.1	129	11	60	192
June	3.75	6	8	0	26	26	175.1	159	16	61	174
July	3.15	11	11	0	26	26	183.0	155	15	69	177
August	3.23	12	7	0	25	25	175.2	163	13	65	166
Sept/Oct	4.14	8	9	0	22	22	152.1	137	8	63	166
Starter	3.32	61	46	0	144	144	1009.0	860	75	372	1009
Reliever	0.00	0	0	0	0	0	0.0	0	0	0	0
0-3 Days Rest (Start)	10.45	0	2	0	2	2	10.1	18	3	4	6
4 Days Rest	3.31	41	35	0	99	99	704.2	608	49	259	723
5+ Days Rest	3.09	20	9	0	43	43	294.0	234	23	109	280
vs. AL	3.30	61	43	0	141	141	985.2	832	73	368	982
vs. NL	4.24	0	3	0	3	3	23.1	28	2	4	27
Pre-All Star	3.12	32	22	0	78	78	548.1	447	43	194	546
Post-All Star	3.56	29	24	0	66	66	460.2	413	32	178	463

	Avg	AB	H	2B	3B	HR	RBI	BB	SO	OBP	SLG
vs. Left	.234	2037	476	90	14	35	190	237	552	.319	.343
vs. Right	.226	1702	384	70	5	40	169	135	457	.289	.343
Inning 1-6	.228	3091	705	134	16	63	308	312	829	.306	.342
Inning 7+	.239	648	155	26	5	12	51	60	180	.305	.350
None on	.225	2223	501	91	10	50	50	216	618	.301	.343
Runners on	.237	1516	359	69	9	25	309	156	391	.311	.344
Scoring Posn	.217	810	176	33	4	10	256	112	225	.314	.305
Close & Late	.208	360	75	12	2	11	34	35	94	.280	.344
None on/out	.228	966	220	28	4	21	21	90	269	.299	.330
vs. 1st Batr (relief)	.000	0	0	0	0	0	0	0	0	.000	.000
1st Inning Pitched	.204	515	105	17	3	2	43	63	145	.298	.260
First 75 Pitches	.239	2296	548	102	13	42	218	224	616	.314	.349
Pitch 76-90	.187	461	86	18	1	10	40	51	127	.271	.295
Pitch 91-105	.200	450	90	14	1	13	47	41	119	.270	.322
Pitch 106+	.256	532	136	26	4	10	54	56	147	.329	.376
First Pitch	.317	483	145	25	1	11	53	5	0	.338	.448
Ahead in Count	.157	1774	279	50	5	24	114	0	831	.167	.232
Behind in Count	.342	739	253	43	9	20	106	158	0	.457	.506
Two Strikes	.145	1958	283	53	6	26	129	208	1009	.231	.218
Pre-All Star	.222	2014	447	94	11	43	198	194	546	.296	.344
Post-All Star	.239	1725	413	66	8	32	177	178	463	.316	.343

Pitcher vs. Batter (career)

Pitches Best Vs.	Avg	AB	H	2B	3B	HR	RBI	BB	SO	OBP	SLG	Pitches Worst Vs.	Avg	AB	H	2B	3B	HR	RBI	BB	SO	OBP	SLG
Ron Karkovice	.000	14	0	0	0	0	0	0	4	.000	.000	Jeff Frye	.667	9	6	1	0	0	0	2	1	.727	.778
Cecil Fielder	.043	46	2	0	0	0	2	4	21	.120	.043	Gary Sheffield	.533	15	8	1	0	0	2	1	1	.563	.600
Jeff Cirillo	.067	15	1	1	0	0	0	0	8	.067	.133	Ken Griffey Jr	.404	57	23	6	0	5	12	10	8	.493	.772
Scott Brosius	.071	14	1	0	0	0	0	1	5	.133	.071	Will Clark	.357	14	5	3	0	1	4	4	4	.500	.786
Pat Listach	.083	24	2	1	0	0	0	0	7	.083	.125	Jim Thome	.333	27	9	2	0	3	8	7	5	.472	.741

Chris Clemons — White Sox
Age 25 – Pitches Right (flyball pitcher)

	ERA	W	L	Sv	G	GS	IP	BB	SO	Avg	H	2B	3B	HR	RBI	OBP	SLG	GF	IR	IRS	Hld	SvOp	SB	CS	GB	FB	G/F
1997 Season	8.53	0	2	0	5	2	12.2	11	8	.345	19	2	0	4	13	.463	.600	3	0	0	0	0	1	1	11	24	0.46

1997 Season

	ERA	W	L	Sv	G	GS	IP	H	HR	BB	SO		Avg	AB	H	2B	3B	HR	RBI	BB	SO	OBP	SLG
Home	7.20	0	0	0	2	0	5.0	6	2	2	1	vs. Left	.344	32	11	1	0	2	6	5	4	.432	.563
Away	9.39	0	2	0	3	2	7.2	13	2	9	7	vs. Right	.348	23	8	1	0	2	7	6	4	.500	.652

Brad Clontz — Braves
Age 27 – Pitches Right (groundball pitcher)

	ERA	W	L	Sv	G	GS	IP	BB	SO	Avg	H	2B	3B	HR	RBI	OBP	SLG	GF	IR	IRS	Hld	SvOp	SB	CS	GB	FB	G/F
1997 Season	3.75	5	1	1	51	0	48.0	18	42	.286	52	12	1	3	34	.350	.412	16	32	15	0	2	5	6	70	35	2.00
Career (1995-1997)	4.51	19	5	6	191	0	197.2	73	146	.267	201	37	3	19	120	.335	.400	41	119	43	23	14	21	9	313	181	1.73

1997 Season

	ERA	W	L	Sv	G	GS	IP	H	HR	BB	SO		Avg	AB	H	2B	3B	HR	RBI	BB	SO	OBP	SLG
Home	4.01	2	0	0	25	0	24.2	24	2	9	21	vs. Left	.284	74	21	8	0	2	17	8	14	.357	.473
Away	3.47	3	1	1	26	0	23.1	28	1	9	21	vs. Right	.287	108	31	4	1	1	17	10	28	.345	.370
Day	6.55	1	1	0	11	0	11.0	17	1	5	9	Inning 1-6	.348	23	8	2	0	1	6	3	5	.407	.565
Night	2.92	4	0	1	40	0	37.0	35	2	13	33	Inning 7+	.277	159	44	10	1	2	28	15	37	.341	.390
Grass	4.30	3	1	0	39	0	37.2	38	3	13	32	None on	.295	78	23	5	0	1	1	10	23	.375	.397
Turf	1.74	2	0	1	12	0	10.1	14	0	5	10	Runners on	.279	104	29	7	1	2	33	8	19	.330	.423
March/April	3.12	2	0	0	10	0	8.2	6	0	3	5	Scoring Posn	.328	61	20	4	1	1	29	8	12	.403	.475
May	3.75	0	0	0	11	0	12.0	14	1	2	10	Close & Late	.170	47	8	2	1	0	7	11	13	.328	.255
June	5.40	1	1	0	10	0	10.0	11	1	7	8	None on/out	.400	35	14	3	0	1	1	7	9	.500	.571
July	3.86	1	0	0	6	0	4.2	6	0	3	5	vs. 1st Batr (relief)	.386	44	17	5	0	2	12	7	9	.471	.636
August	0.00	1	0	0	3	0	3.1	3	0	2	6	1st Inning Pitched	.296	159	47	12	1	2	32	15	37	.356	.421
Sept/Oct	3.86	0	0	1	11	0	9.1	12	1	1	8	First 15 Pitches	.296	135	40	12	0	2	25	14	30	.364	.430
Starter	0.00	0	0	0	0	0	0.0	0	0	0	0	Pitch 16-30	.227	44	10	0	1	1	7	3	11	.271	.341
Reliever	3.75	5	1	1	51	0	48.0	52	3	18	42	Pitch 31-45	.667	3	2	0	0	0	2	1	1	.750	.667
0 Days rest (Relief)	5.17	1	0	0	17	0	15.2	18	1	6	14	Pitch 46+	.000	0	0	0	0	0	0	0	0	.000	.000
1 or 2 Days rest	2.70	3	1	1	18	0	16.2	16	1	6	16	First Pitch	.243	37	9	1	0	1	6	2	0	.282	.351
3+ Days rest	3.45	1	0	0	16	0	15.2	18	1	6	12	Ahead in Count	.205	83	17	5	1	0	4	0	39	.212	.289
vs. AL	0.00	0	0	0	6	0	6.2	2	0	4	10	Behind in Count	.344	32	11	2	0	1	4	10	0	.500	.500
vs. NL	4.35	5	1	1	45	0	41.1	50	3	14	32	Two Strikes	.262	84	22	3	1	1	16	6	42	.315	.357
Pre-All Star	4.01	4	1	0	34	0	33.2	33	2	15	27	Pre-All Star	.266	124	33	8	1	2	23	15	27	.348	.395
Post-All Star	3.14	1	0	1	17	0	14.1	19	1	3	15	Post-All Star	.328	58	19	4	0	1	11	3	15	.355	.448

Career (1995-1997)

	ERA	W	L	Sv	G	GS	IP	H	HR	BB	SO		Avg	AB	H	2B	3B	HR	RBI	BB	SO	OBP	SLG
Home	3.35	10	3	2	96	0	107.1	98	8	37	81	vs. Left	.332	247	82	22	1	9	50	37	38	.417	.538
Away	5.88	9	2	4	95	0	90.1	103	11	36	65	vs. Right	.236	505	119	15	2	10	70	36	108	.291	.333
Day	6.17	5	3	2	64	0	65.2	77	8	25	54	Inning 1-6	.237	169	40	7	1	4	25	15	45	.293	.361
Night	3.68	14	2	4	127	0	132.0	124	11	48	92	Inning 7+	.276	583	161	30	2	15	95	58	101	.347	.412
Grass	4.53	15	5	5	150	0	159.0	155	16	54	121	None on	.268	400	107	21	1	10	10	28	81	.319	.400
Turf	4.42	4	0	1	41	0	38.2	46	3	19	25	Runners on	.267	352	94	16	2	9	110	45	65	.351	.401
March/April	3.13	2	2	2	25	0	23.0	14	2	5	10	Scoring Posn	.282	220	62	9	2	4	96	38	37	.385	.395
May	4.21	2	1	3	34	0	36.1	40	5	10	26	Close & Late	.229	258	59	12	2	8	41	35	40	.326	.384
June	5.45	3	1	0	38	0	38.0	43	3	19	28	None on/out	.272	169	46	9	1	4	4	16	30	.342	.408
July	2.40	7	0	0	27	0	30.0	25	0	12	25	vs. 1st Batr (relief)	.254	173	44	11	0	6	29	14	33	.309	.422
August	6.25	2	0	0	32	0	36.0	37	5	21	31	1st Inning Pitched	.269	617	166	34	1	17	109	56	123	.333	.410
Sept/Oct	4.72	1	1	1	35	0	34.1	42	4	6	26	First 15 Pitches	.276	550	152	31	0	17	85	46	99	.337	.425
Starter	0.00	0	0	0	0	0	0.0	0	0	0	0	Pitch 16-30	.239	184	44	5	2	2	30	24	42	.324	.321
Reliever	4.51	19	5	6	191	0	197.2	201	19	73	146	Pitch 31-45	.294	17	5	1	1	0	5	3	4	.381	.471
0 Days rest (Relief)	4.55	4	2	1	56	0	55.1	62	8	18	48	Pitch 46+	.000	1	0	0	0	0	0	0	1	.000	.000
1 or 2 Days rest	4.40	11	2	5	90	0	92.0	85	6	34	61	First Pitch	.299	137	41	5	1	5	32	11	0	.355	.460
3+ Days rest	4.65	4	1	0	45	0	50.1	54	5	21	37	Ahead in Count	.204	333	68	15	1	5	27	0	128	.212	.300
vs. AL	0.00	0	0	0	6	0	6.2	2	0	4	10	Behind in Count	.372	148	55	11	0	6	23	36	0	.495	.568
vs. NL	4.66	19	5	6	185	0	191.0	199	19	69	136	Two Strikes	.195	333	65	12	1	3	37	26	146	.253	.264
Pre-All Star	4.24	11	4	5	103	0	104.0	102	10	37	71	Pre-All Star	.260	393	102	18	2	10	61	37	71	.327	.392
Post-All Star	4.80	8	1	1	88	0	93.2	99	9	36	75	Post-All Star	.276	359	99	19	1	9	59	36	75	.342	.409

Pitcher vs. Batter (career)

Pitches Best Vs.	Avg	AB	H	2B	3B	HR	RBI	BB	SO	OBP	SLG	Pitches Worst Vs.	Avg	AB	H	2B	3B	HR	RBI	BB	SO	OBP	SLG
Jeff Conine	.200	10	2	0	0	0	2	0	1	.182	.200	Andres Galarraga	.500	10	5	0	0	1	4	0	1	.545	.800

Ken Cloude — Mariners
Age 23 – Pitches Right (flyball pitcher)

	ERA	W	L	Sv	G	GS	IP	BB	SO	Avg	H	2B	3B	HR	RBI	OBP	SLG	CG	ShO	Sup	QS	#P/S	SB	CS	GB	FB	G/F
1997 Season	5.12	4	2	0	10	9	51.0	26	46	.218	41	7	1	8	25	.321	.394	0	0	6.00	5	93	2	3	51	73	0.70

1997 Season

	ERA	W	L	Sv	G	GS	IP	H	HR	BB	SO		Avg	AB	H	2B	3B	HR	RBI	BB	SO	OBP	SLG
Home	5.32	1	2	0	5	4	23.2	20	4	13	26	vs. Left	.210	100	21	4	1	3	12	18	22	.333	.360
Away	4.94	3	0	0	5	5	27.1	21	4	13	20	vs. Right	.227	88	20	3	0	5	13	8	24	.306	.432

Danny Clyburn — Orioles
Age 24 – Bats Right

	Avg	G	AB	R	H	2B	3B	HR	RBI	BB	SO	HBP	GDP	SB	CS	OBP	SLG	IBB	SH	SF	#Pit	#P/PA	GB	FB	G/F
1997 Season	.000	2	3	0	0	0	0	0	0	0	2	0	0	0	0	.000	.000	0	0	0	12	4.00	1	0	0.00

1997 Season

	Avg	AB	H	2B	3B	HR	RBI	BB	SO	OBP	SLG		Avg	AB	H	2B	3B	HR	RBI	BB	SO	OBP	SLG
vs. Left	.000	1	0	0	0	0	0	0	0	.000	.000	Scoring Posn	.000	1	0	0	0	0	0	0	0	.000	.000
vs. Right	.000	2	0	0	0	0	0	0	2	.000	.000	Close & Late	.000	1	0	0	0	0	0	0	0	.000	.000

Greg Colbrunn — Braves
Age 28 – Bats Right

	Avg	G	AB	R	H	2B	3B	HR	RBI	BB	SO	HBP	GDP	SB	CS	OBP	SLG	IBB	SH	SF	#Pit	#P/PA	GB	FB	G/F
1997 Season	.280	98	271	27	76	17	0	7	35	10	49	2	7	1	2	.309	.421	1	1	2	983	3.44	101	84	1.20
Last Five Years	.281	494	1618	189	454	84	3	56	247	72	254	25	48	21	13	.318	.440	7	2	16	6086	3.51	610	511	1.19

1997 Season

	Avg	AB	H	2B	3B	HR	RBI	BB	SO	OBP	SLG		Avg	AB	H	2B	3B	HR	RBI	BB	SO	OBP	SLG
vs. Left	.290	124	36	7	0	4	19	6	25	.321	.444	Scoring Posn	.254	67	17	3	0	2	27	8	12	.333	.388
vs. Right	.272	147	40	10	0	3	16	4	24	.299	.401	Close & Late	.300	40	12	3	0	1	4	2	8	.356	.450
Home	.277	130	36	7	0	3	17	6	30	.304	.400	None on/out	.345	55	19	3	0	2	2	0	14	.345	.509
Away	.284	141	40	10	0	4	18	4	19	.313	.440	Batting #6	.297	91	27	10	0	1	6	1	12	.312	.440
First Pitch	.271	48	13	5	0	1	7	1	0	.275	.438	Batting #7	.353	68	24	2	0	3	13	4	17	.384	.515
Ahead in Count	.480	50	24	7	0	5	4	0	.519	.620	Other	.223	112	25	5	0	3	16	5	20	.261	.348
Behind in Count	.189	127	24	3	0	4	17	0	42	.202	.307	Pre-All Star	.286	175	50	14	0	4	21	8	29	.317	.434
Two Strikes	.200	120	24	4	0	4	18	5	49	.244	.333	Post-All Star	.271	96	26	3	0	3	14	2	20	.293	.396

Last Five Years

	Avg	AB	H	2B	3B	HR	RBI	BB	SO	OBP	SLG		Avg	AB	H	2B	3B	HR	RBI	BB	SO	OBP	SLG
vs. Left	.288	504	145	24	1	19	78	25	85	.318	.452	First Pitch	.309	265	82	14	1	15	64	5	0	.317	.540
vs. Right	.277	1114	309	60	2	37	169	47	169	.318	.434	Ahead in Count	.356	357	127	26	1	18	73	31	0	.407	.585
Groundball	.242	405	98	16	0	13	53	12	67	.280	.378	Behind in Count	.228	746	170	31	0	13	71	0	228	.246	.322
Flyball	.287	272	78	13	0	11	43	17	40	.338	.456	Two Strikes	.222	686	152	26	1	14	65	36	254	.273	.324
Home	.285	783	223	34	3	27	123	38	131	.326	.439	Batting #5	.289	575	166	31	0	25	100	30	82	.328	.473
Away	.277	835	231	50	0	29	124	34	123	.311	.441	Batting #6	.277	506	140	30	2	13	72	19	79	.311	.421
Day	.281	438	123	29	1	16	68	18	64	.322	.461	Other	.276	537	148	23	1	18	75	23	93	.314	.423
Night	.281	1180	331	55	2	40	179	54	190	.317	.432	March/April	.290	224	65	17	0	6	26	9	36	.321	.446
Grass	.293	1064	312	55	3	41	161	47	170	.333	.466	May	.262	317	83	13	0	8	42	16	55	.299	.379
Turf	.256	554	142	29	0	15	86	25	84	.290	.390	June	.309	343	106	20	0	11	58	14	58	.343	.464
Pre-All Star	.284	992	282	58	3	27	141	41	165	.319	.424	July	.278	252	70	16	1	9	43	13	41	.325	.456
Post-All Star	.275	626	172	26	3	29	106	31	89	.318	.465	August	.288	278	80	11	2	16	52	11	32	.327	.514
Scoring Posn	.293	447	131	17	1	18	195	63	38	.345	.456	Sept/Oct	.245	204	50	7	0	6	26	9	32	.284	.368
Close & Late	.271	273	74	15	0	6	35	16	38	.322	.392	vs. AL	.278	230	64	15	0	7	32	9	40	.306	.435
None on/out	.267	371	99	23	1	15	15	11	62	.295	.456	vs. NL	.281	1388	390	69	3	49	215	63	214	.320	.441

Batter vs. Pitcher (career)

Hits Best Against	Avg	AB	H	2B	3B	HR	RBI	BB	SO	OBP	SLG	Hits Worst Against	Avg	AB	H	2B	3B	HR	RBI	BB	SO	OBP	SLG
Donovan Osborne	.643	14	9	1	0	2	4	0	2	.643	1.143	Mark Leiter	.150	20	3	1	0	0	2	0	4	.227	.200
Pedro Astacio	.500	8	4	1	0	2	0	0	.667	.625	Mike Morgan	.154	13	2	0	0	0	1	0	4	.154	.154
Andy Benes	.462	13	6	0	0	1	1	1	3	.500	.692	Greg McMichael	.167	12	2	0	0	0	0	0	4	.167	.167
Pete Harnisch	.417	12	5	1	0	1	2	1	2	.462	.750	Bill Swift	.176	17	3	0	0	0	0	0	7	.176	.176
Rheal Cormier	.400	10	4	0	0	2	2	1	2	.455	1.000	Dave Mlicki	.182	11	2	1	0	0	0	0	3	.182	.273

Michael Coleman — Red Sox
Age 22 – Bats Right

	Avg	G	AB	R	H	2B	3B	HR	RBI	BB	SO	HBP	GDP	SB	CS	OBP	SLG	IBB	SH	SF	#Pit	#P/PA	GB	FB	G/F
1997 Season	.167	8	24	2	4	1	0	0	2	0	11	0	0	1	0	.167	.208	0	1	0	81	3.24	4	7	0.57

1997 Season

	Avg	AB	H	2B	3B	HR	RBI	BB	SO	OBP	SLG		Avg	AB	H	2B	3B	HR	RBI	BB	SO	OBP	SLG
vs. Left	.133	15	2	0	0	0	0	0	9	.133	.133	Scoring Posn	.125	8	1	1	0	0	2	0	5	.125	.250
vs. Right	.222	9	2	1	0	0	0	2	.222	.333	Close & Late	.143	7	1	0	0	0	0	0	5	.143	.143

Vince Coleman — Tigers
Age 36 – Bats Both (groundball hitter)

	Avg	G	AB	R	H	2B	3B	HR	RBI	BB	SO	HBP	GDP	SB	CS	OBP	SLG	IBB	SH	SF	#Pit	#P/PA	GB	FB	G/F
1997 Season	.071	6	14	0	1	0	0	0	0	1	3	0	1	0	0	.133	.071	0	0	0	53	3.53	5	3	1.67
Last Five Years	.260	350	1364	201	354	52	27	10	91	97	244	3	13	142	39	.308	.359	3	13	8	5371	3.62	503	300	1.68

1997 Season

	Avg	AB	H	2B	3B	HR	RBI	BB	SO	OBP	SLG		Avg	AB	H	2B	3B	HR	RBI	BB	SO	OBP	SLG
vs. Left	.000	1	0	0	0	0	0	1	0	.500	.000	Scoring Posn	.000	3	0	0	0	0	0	1	1	.250	.000
vs. Right	.077	13	1	0	0	0	0	0	3	.077	.077	Close & Late	.200	5	1	0	0	0	0	0	0	.200	.200

Last Five Years

	Avg	AB	H	2B	3B	HR	RBI	BB	SO	OBP	SLG		Avg	AB	H	2B	3B	HR	RBI	BB	SO	OBP	SLG
vs. Left	.255	392	100	14	9	6	26	25	62	.300	.383	First Pitch	.350	206	72	7	6	1	13	3	0	.355	.456
vs. Right	.261	972	254	38	18	4	65	72	182	.312	.350	Ahead in Count	.352	256	90	12	9	3	33	51	0	.453	.504
Groundball	.298	359	107	15	5	1	21	18	64	.333	.376	Behind in Count	.209	676	141	19	11	5	34	0	216	.210	.291
Flyball	.229	301	69	12	7	5	22	26	59	.290	.365	Two Strikes	.175	622	109	16	5	3	23	43	244	.231	.232
Home	.286	692	198	25	19	7	56	51	128	.336	.408	Batting #1	.260	1288	335	51	25	10	83	90	230	.308	.362
Away	.232	672	156	27	8	3	35	46	116	.280	.310	Batting #2	.313	48	15	1	1	0	7	3	6	.358	.375
Day	.233	442	103	19	8	5	28	31	72	.283	.346	Other	.143	28	4	0	1	0	1	4	8	.250	.214
Night	.272	922	251	33	19	5	63	66	172	.321	.366	March/April	.207	270	56	7	4	2	15	18	47	.257	.285
Grass	.252	846	213	29	13	6	55	56	143	.297	.338	May	.244	311	76	13	8	2	22	23	52	.294	.357
Turf	.272	518	141	23	14	4	36	41	101	.327	.394	June	.279	298	83	14	6	3	19	26	61	.336	.396
Pre-All Star	.254	996	253	39	20	7	66	73	183	.304	.354	July	.298	248	74	7	5	2	21	11	39	.326	.391
Post-All Star	.274	368	101	13	7	3	25	24	61	.322	.372	August	.265	132	35	3	3	0	6	14	25	.338	.333
Scoring Posn	.259	243	63	9	4	2	80	24	53	.316	.354	Sept/Oct	.286	105	30	8	1	1	8	5	20	.324	.410
Close & Late	.212	208	44	8	2	1	16	17	46	.268	.284	vs. AL	.261	907	237	37	18	7	62	67	155	.312	.365
None on/out	.272	556	151	26	15	5	5	37	102	.399	.348	vs. NL	.256	457	117	15	9	3	29	30	89	.301	.348

Batter vs. Pitcher (career)

Hits Best Against	Avg	AB	H	2B	3B	HR	RBI	BB	SO	OBP	SLG	Hits Worst Against	Avg	AB	H	2B	3B	HR	RBI	BB	SO	OBP	SLG
John Burkett	.583	12	7	0	0	0	0	2	0	.643	.583	Roger Pavlik	.000	11	0	0	0	0	2	2	1	.143	.000
Mark Portugal	.545	11	6	1	1	0	0	1	2	.583	.818	Pete Harnisch	.091	11	1	1	0	0	0	0	3	.091	.182
Tony Castillo	.455	11	5	2	0	0	2	0	1	.455	.636	Mike Morgan	.130	23	3	1	0	0	1	1	3	.167	.174
Rheal Cormier	.417	12	5	2	0	1	2	0	0	.417	.833	Todd Stottlemyre	.133	15	2	0	0	0	0	0	3	.133	.133
Dennis Eckersley	.375	16	6	1	0	2	2	2	2	.444	.563	Chuck Finley	.154	13	2	0	0	0	0	0	4	.154	.154

Darnell Coles — Rockies
Age 36 – Bats Right (flyball hitter)

	Avg	G	AB	R	H	2B	3B	HR	RBI	BB	SO	HBP	GDP	SB	CS	OBP	SLG	IBB	SH	SF	#Pit	#P/PA	GB	FB	G/F
1997 Season	.318	21	22	1	7	1	0	1	2	0	6	1	0	0	0	.348	.500	0	0	0	93	4.04	6	7	0.86
Last Five Years	.235	196	497	55	117	23	2	12	59	42	80	9	6	1	1	.304	.362	2	1	5	2134	3.85	152	182	0.84

1997 Season

	Avg	AB	H	2B	3B	HR	RBI	BB	SO	OBP	SLG		Avg	AB	H	2B	3B	HR	RBI	BB	SO	OBP	SLG
vs. Left	.273	11	3	1	0	1	1	0	3	.273	.636	Scoring Posn	.250	4	1	0	0	0	1	0	1	.250	.250
vs. Right	.364	11	4	0	0	1	0	0	3	.417	.364	Close & Late	.333	6	2	1	0	0	1	0	2	.333	.500

Last Five Years

	Avg	AB	H	2B	3B	HR	RBI	BB	SO	OBP	SLG		Avg	AB	H	2B	3B	HR	RBI	BB	SO	OBP	SLG
vs. Left	.214	201	43	8	1	6	21	15	34	.269	.353	First Pitch	.369	65	24	8	0	2	12	2	0	.394	.585
vs. Right	.250	296	74	15	1	6	38	27	46	.326	.368	Ahead in Count	.298	114	34	8	0	8	21	23	0	.421	.579
Groundball	.216	97	21	6	1	1	7	10	18	.224	.330	Behind in Count	.167	215	36	5	0	1	14	0	67	.174	.205
Flyball	.190	84	16	0	1	3	11	10	17	.292	.321	Two Strikes	.149	228	34	4	0	1	16	17	80	.213	.180
Home	.234	239	56	8	2	7	31	22	38	.312	.372	Batting #6	.262	141	37	8	0	6	17	11	21	.327	.447
Away	.236	258	61	15	0	5	28	20	42	.296	.353	Batting #7	.234	124	29	5	1	4	15	8	19	.281	.387
Day	.268	164	44	12	0	3	19	8	29	.307	.396	Other	.220	232	51	10	1	2	27	23	40	.302	.297
Night	.219	333	73	11	2	9	40	34	51	.302	.345	March/April	.200	50	10	1	1	1	5	8	10	.333	.320
Grass	.229	170	39	8	0	1	17	11	25	.283	.294	May	.252	107	27	3	0	4	18	7	12	.299	.393
Turf	.239	327	78	15	2	11	42	31	55	.314	.398	June	.188	69	13	4	0	0	3	8	12	.273	.246
Pre-All Star	.225	262	59	9	1	8	33	27	42	.304	.359	July	.250	152	38	9	1	4	17	15	24	.327	.401
Post-All Star	.247	235	58	14	1	4	26	15	38	.304	.366	August	.253	87	22	3	0	3	12	3	15	.290	.414
Scoring Posn	.230	135	31	3	0	4	45	15	24	.301	.341	Sept/Oct	.219	32	7	1	0	0	4	1	7	.286	.250
Close & Late	.231	91	21	3	1	1	7	8	20	.314	.319	vs. AL	.234	337	79	15	2	8	41	26	54	.296	.362
None on/out	.252	103	26	7	0	2	2	9	16	.336	.379	vs. NL	.238	160	38	8	0	4	18	16	26	.320	.363

Batter vs. Pitcher (since 1984)

Hits Best Against	Avg	AB	H	2B	3B	HR	RBI	BB	SO	OBP	SLG	Hits Worst Against	Avg	AB	H	2B	3B	HR	RBI	BB	SO	OBP	SLG
Terry Mulholland	.467	15	7	0	0	0	3	1	2	.500	.467	Doug Drabek	.000	11	0	0	0	0	0	1	2	.083	.000
Chris Haney	.400	10	4	1	0	0	0	2	1	.500	.500	David Cone	.000	10	0	0	0	0	0	1	2	.091	.000
Scott Erickson	.364	11	4	0	0	0	0	0	2	.417	.364	Mark Guthrie	.100	10	1	0	0	0	0	1	1	.182	.100
Jamie Moyer	.350	20	7	2	0	3	5	1	2	.381	.900	Jimmy Key	.107	28	3	0	0	0	2	2	2	.167	.107
Bobby Witt	.304	23	7	0	1	1	3	1	7	.333	.522	Kenny Rogers	.182	11	2	0	0	0	2	0	1	.182	.182

Lou Collier — Pirates
Age 24 – Bats Right

	Avg	G	AB	R	H	2B	3B	HR	RBI	BB	SO	HBP	GDP	SB	CS	OBP	SLG	IBB	SH	SF	#Pit	#P/PA	GB	FB	G/F
1997 Season	.135	18	37	3	5	0	0	0	3	1	11	0	1	1	0	.158	.135	0	0	0	135	3.55	12	7	1.71

1997 Season

	Avg	AB	H	2B	3B	HR	RBI	BB	SO	OBP	SLG		Avg	AB	H	2B	3B	HR	RBI	BB	SO	OBP	SLG
vs. Left	.000	4	0	0	0	0	0	0	2	.000	.000	Scoring Posn	.188	16	3	0	0	0	3	1	1	.235	.188
vs. Right	.152	33	5	0	0	0	3	1	9	.176	.152	Close & Late	.143	7	1	0	0	0	1	0	0	.143	.143

Bartolo Colon — Indians
Age 23 – Pitches Right

	ERA	W	L	Sv	G	GS	IP	BB	SO	Avg	H	2B	3B	HR	RBI	OBP	SLG	CG	ShO	Sup	QS	#P/S	SB	CS	GB	FB	G/F
1997 Season	5.65	4	7	0	19	17	94.0	45	66	.286	107	20	2	12	55	.366	.447	1	0	6.70	5	95	10	2	126	103	1.22

1997 Season

	ERA	W	L	Sv	G	GS	IP	H	HR	BB	SO		Avg	AB	H	2B	3B	HR	RBI	BB	SO	OBP	SLG
Home	4.53	2	3	0	8	6	43.2	48	5	11	30	vs. Left	.280	200	56	11	1	5	26	23	35	.353	.420

	ERA	W	L	Sv	G	GS	IP	H	HR	BB	SO		Avg	AB	H	2B	3B	HR	RBI	BB	SO	OBP	SLG
Away	6.62	2	4	0	11	11	50.1	59	7	34	36	vs. Right	.293	174	51	9	1	7	29	22	31	.382	.477
Starter	5.76	3	7	0	17	17	89.0	102	12	44	58	Scoring Posn	.271	107	29	4	2	2	41	13	28	.347	.402
Reliever	3.60	1	0	0	2	0	5.0	5	0	1	8	Close & Late	.400	15	6	0	0	1	2	0	5	.400	.600
0-3 Days Rest (Start)	0.00	0	0	0	0	0	0.0	0	0	0	0	None on/out	.341	91	31	5	0	5	5	12	13	.423	.560
4 Days Rest	6.75	0	5	0	6	6	32.0	40	4	13	16	First Pitch	.415	41	17	3	0	0	5	1	0	.442	.488
5+ Days Rest	5.21	3	2	0	11	11	57.0	62	8	31	42	Ahead in Count	.239	163	39	11	1	2	16	0	55	.238	.356
Pre-All Star	6.75	1	2	0	6	6	26.2	31	5	19	21	Behind in Count	.262	103	27	3	1	4	17	19	0	.387	.427
Post-All Star	5.21	3	5	0	13	11	67.1	76	7	26	45	Two Strikes	.211	171	36	10	0	2	15	25	66	.310	.304

David Cone — Yankees   Age 35 – Pitches Right (flyball pitcher)

	ERA	W	L	Sv	G	GS	IP	BB	SO	Avg	H	2B	3B	HR	RBI	OBP	SLG	CG	ShO	Sup	QS	#P/S	SB	CS	GB	FB	G/F
1997 Season	2.82	12	6	0	29	29	195.0	86	222	.218	155	22	4	17	60	.305	.332	1	0	4.75	21	110	22	8	195	181	1.08
Last Five Years	3.17	64	35	0	127	127	922.0	376	807	.219	735	147	14	79	306	.301	.341	18	6	5.00	84	117	100	36	945	1064	0.89

	ERA	W	L	Sv	G	GS	IP	H	HR	BB	SO		Avg	AB	H	2B	3B	HR	RBI	BB	SO	OBP	SLG
Home	3.20	5	2	0	14	14	90.0	73	7	37	108	vs. Left	.213	371	79	10	2	11	31	54	109	.315	.340
Away	2.49	7	4	0	15	15	105.0	82	10	49	114	vs. Right	.224	339	76	12	2	6	29	32	113	.294	.324
Day	2.55	4	2	0	13	13	84.2	62	6	28	110	Inning 1-6	.206	596	123	16	2	15	50	71	193	.293	.315
Night	3.02	8	4	0	16	16	110.1	93	11	58	112	Inning 7+	.281	114	32	6	2	2	10	15	29	.369	.421
Grass	2.96	10	4	0	25	25	167.0	127	13	78	189	None on	.221	417	92	14	4	11	11	52	128	.309	.353
Turf	1.93	2	2	0	4	4	28.0	28	4	8	33	Runners on	.215	293	63	8	0	6	49	34	94	.301	.304
March/April	2.93	2	2	0	6	6	40.0	33	5	27	49	Scoring Posn	.221	163	36	6	0	4	44	22	63	.321	.331
May	1.65	4	1	0	6	6	43.2	41	1	11	48	Close & Late	.288	73	21	4	1	1	6	12	17	.395	.411
June	3.32	2	0	0	6	6	43.1	30	4	18	56	None on/out	.221	181	40	5	2	5	5	25	49	.316	.354
July	2.21	3	1	0	5	5	36.2	28	3	15	36	vs. 1st Batr (relief)	.000	0	0	0	0	0	0	0	0	.000	.000
August	5.06	1	2	0	4	4	21.1	17	4	10	26	1st Inning Pitched	.198	101	20	3	0	2	8	9	35	.264	.287
Sept/Oct	2.70	0	0	0	2	2	10.0	6	0	5	7	First 75 Pitches	.190	448	85	11	1	12	40	61	146	.289	.299
Starter	2.82	12	6	0	29	29	195.0	155	17	86	222	Pitch 76-90	.255	94	24	4	1	2	5	7	25	.307	.383
Reliever	0.00	0	0	0	0	0	0.0	0	0	0	0	Pitch 91-105	.293	92	27	5	1	1	7	5	29	.333	.402
0-3 Days Rest (Start)	0.00	0	0	0	0	0	0.0	0	0	0	0	Pitch 106+	.250	76	19	2	1	2	8	13	22	.367	.382
4 Days Rest	2.54	9	5	0	21	21	142.0	102	11	68	170	First Pitch	.289	83	24	5	0	4	12	1	0	.314	.494
5+ Days Rest	3.57	3	1	0	8	8	53.0	53	6	18	52	Ahead in Count	.171	386	66	5	1	6	17	0	187	.173	.236
vs. AL	2.93	12	6	0	27	27	178.0	150	17	81	202	Behind in Count	.280	118	33	7	1	2	19	48	0	.485	.407
vs. NL	1.59	0	0	0	2	2	17.0	5	0	5	20	Two Strikes	.133	390	52	4	1	6	12	37	222	.210	.195
Pre-All Star	2.55	8	4	0	19	19	134.1	110	11	60	160	Pre-All Star	.224	491	110	18	1	11	39	60	160	.313	.332
Post-All Star	3.41	4	2	0	10	10	60.2	45	6	26	62	Post-All Star	.205	219	45	4	3	6	21	26	62	.289	.333

	ERA	W	L	Sv	G	GS	IP	H	HR	BB	SO		Avg	AB	H	2B	3B	HR	RBI	BB	SO	OBP	SLG
Home	3.41	30	15	0	61	61	440.2	364	40	181	392	vs. Left	.225	1855	418	72	9	48	176	241	392	.316	.351
Away	2.95	34	20	0	66	66	481.1	371	39	195	415	vs. Right	.210	1506	317	75	5	31	130	135	415	.281	.329
Day	2.87	23	12	0	48	48	345.1	260	24	122	335	Inning 1-6	.211	2687	568	112	9	67	248	303	677	.295	.335
Night	3.36	41	23	0	79	79	576.2	475	55	254	472	Inning 7+	.248	674	167	35	5	12	58	73	130	.325	.368
Grass	3.15	41	20	0	79	79	562.0	436	46	237	515	None on	.219	2049	449	93	9	53	53	206	493	.295	.351
Turf	3.21	23	15	0	48	48	359.1	299	33	139	292	Runners on	.218	1312	286	54	5	26	253	170	314	.309	.326
March/April	3.21	9	8	0	21	21	140.0	120	15	69	129	Scoring Posn	.202	754	152	26	0	15	215	118	196	.308	.296
May	2.16	16	6	0	25	25	195.2	136	11	65	161	Close & Late	.255	377	96	20	3	9	35	51	73	.348	.395
June	3.66	9	6	0	22	22	159.2	132	14	62	144	None on/out	.223	897	200	41	5	32	32	74	201	.287	.387
July	2.84	13	5	0	22	22	167.2	134	15	67	142	vs. 1st Batr (relief)	.000	0	0	0	0	0	0	0	0	.000	.000
August	4.16	9	5	0	18	18	125.1	111	16	52	117	1st Inning Pitched	.229	458	105	26	0	9	55	50	114	.303	.345
Sept/Oct	3.50	8	5	0	19	19	133.2	102	8	61	114	First 75 Pitches	.202	2057	416	84	5	54	179	232	512	.286	.327
Starter	3.17	64	35	0	127	127	922.0	735	79	376	807	Pitch 76-90	.268	425	114	22	2	13	45	44	94	.341	.421
Reliever	0.00	0	0	0	0	0	0.0	0	0	0	0	Pitch 91-105	.236	424	100	23	4	5	35	37	94	.300	.344
0-3 Days Rest (Start)	1.13	1	0	0	1	1	8.0	6	0	3	5	Pitch 106+	.231	455	105	18	3	7	47	63	107	.328	.330
4 Days Rest	3.39	41	25	0	84	84	608.1	500	55	241	559	First Pitch	.285	400	114	31	0	16	65	5	0	.304	.483
5+ Days Rest	2.80	22	10	0	42	42	305.2	229	24	132	243	Ahead in Count	.175	1669	292	51	3	20	90	0	663	.182	.245
vs. AL	3.20	64	35	0	125	125	905.0	730	79	371	787	Behind in Count	.285	652	186	39	5	27	97	194	0	.446	.485
vs. NL	1.59	0	0	0	2	2	17.0	5	0	5	20	Two Strikes	.147	1692	248	41	3	23	82	177	807	.230	.215
Pre-All Star	3.04	37	22	0	75	75	547.2	437	47	214	478	Pre-All Star	.219	1998	437	96	8	47	179	214	478	.298	.345
Post-All Star	3.37	27	13	0	52	52	374.1	298	32	162	329	Post-All Star	.219	1363	298	51	6	32	127	162	329	.305	.335

Pitcher vs. Batter (career)

Pitches Best Vs.	Avg	AB	H	2B	3B	HR	RBI	BB	SO	OBP	SLG	Pitches Worst Vs.	Avg	AB	H	2B	3B	HR	RBI	BB	SO	OBP	SLG
Danny Tartabull	.000	15	0	0	0	0	0	2	4	.118	.000	Fernando Vina	.625	16	10	2	0	0	3	1	1	.667	.750
Tony Batista	.000	12	0	0	0	0	0	0	5	.000	.000	Deion Sanders	.600	10	6	0	0	1	1	1	1	.636	.900
Tony Clark	.000	11	0	0	0	0	2	0	5	.000	.000	Wally Joyner	.556	9	5	0	0	1	3	3	0	.667	.889
Luis Sojo	.000	11	0	0	0	0	1	1	2	.083	.000	Damion Easley	.462	13	6	0	0	1	1	3	4	.563	.692
Darnell Coles	.000	10	0	0	0	0	0	1	2	.091	.000	Shawn Green	.400	10	4	1	0	1	3	1	3	.455	.800

Jeff Conine — Marlins   Age 32 – Bats Right

	Avg	G	AB	R	H	2B	3B	HR	RBI	BB	SO	HBP	GDP	SB	CS	OBP	SLG	IBB	SH	SF	#Pit	#P/PA	GB	FB	G/F
1997 Season	.242	151	405	46	98	13	1	17	61	57	89	2	11	2	0	.337	.405	3	0	2	1829	3.92	121	130	0.93
Last Five Years	.291	718	2531	337	737	122	14	98	422	277	531	13	63	8	8	.360	.467	15	0	31	10908	3.82	749	803	0.93

1997 Season

	Avg	AB	H	2B	3B	HR	RBI	BB	SO	OBP	SLG		Avg	AB	H	2B	3B	HR	RBI	BB	SO	OBP	SLG
vs. Left	.248	105	26	1	1	4	15	12	24	.325	.390	First Pitch	.293	58	17	0	0	2	9	1	0	.305	.397
vs. Right	.240	300	72	12	0	13	46	45	65	.341	.410	Ahead in Count	.290	93	27	3	1	7	22	28	0	.447	.570
Groundball	.192	73	14	1	0	2	10	15	15	.326	.288	Behind in Count	.210	181	38	7	0	7	24	0	72	.214	.365
Flyball	.159	44	7	1	0	0	4	6	11	.260	.182	Two Strikes	.186	194	36	7	0	6	24	28	89	.291	.314
Home	.247	190	47	4	0	7	26	33	37	.360	.379	Batting #6	.222	63	14	0	0	3	10	4	16	.265	.365
Away	.237	215	51	9	1	10	35	24	52	.315	.428	Batting #7	.233	258	60	10	0	7	33	40	59	.337	.353
Day	.241	133	32	3	1	4	16	17	30	.327	.368	Other	.286	84	24	3	1	7	18	13	14	.388	.595
Night	.243	272	66	10	0	13	45	40	59	.342	.423	March/April	.301	73	22	1	1	4	14	13	14	.407	.507
Grass	.234	325	76	7	1	14	47	47	69	.332	.391	May	.163	86	14	2	0	2	7	13	21	.270	.256
Turf	.275	80	22	6	0	3	14	10	20	.356	.463	June	.265	83	22	7	0	1	10	12	19	.365	.386
Pre-All Star	.243	267	65	11	1	8	33	39	57	.341	.382	July	.230	74	17	1	0	2	8	8	15	.305	.324
Post-All Star	.239	138	33	2	0	9	28	18	32	.329	.449	August	.292	48	14	1	0	4	11	6	13	.382	.563
Scoring Posn	.209	110	23	3	0	3	39	30	27	.378	.318	Sept/Oct	.220	41	9	1	0	4	11	5	7	.298	.537
Close & Late	.247	85	21	2	0	5	14	17	22	.373	.447	vs. AL	.132	38	5	1	0	0	3	4	10	.233	.158
None on/out	.292	96	28	3	0	4	4	9	18	.352	.448	vs. NL	.253	367	93	12	1	17	58	53	79	.348	.431

1997 By Position

Position	Avg	AB	H	2B	3B	HR	RBI	BB	SO	OBP	SLG	G	GS	Innings	PO	A	E	DP	Fld Pct	Rng Fctr	In Zone	Outs	Zone Rtg	MLB Zone
As Pinch Hitter	.188	16	3	0	0	1	1	3	5	.316	.375	19	0	---	---	---	---	---	---	---	---	---	---	---
As 1b	.245	387	95	13	1	16	60	54	84	.339	.408	145	102	991.2	896	106	8	100	.992	---	219	203	927	.874

Last Five Years

	Avg	AB	H	2B	3B	HR	RBI	BB	SO	OBP	SLG		Avg	AB	H	2B	3B	HR	RBI	BB	SO	OBP	SLG
vs. Left	.315	650	205	31	5	33	121	80	118	.385	.531	First Pitch	.350	454	159	17	3	19	98	8	0	.358	.526
vs. Right	.283	1881	532	91	9	65	301	197	413	.351	.444	Ahead in Count	.383	507	194	40	5	36	118	123	0	.495	.694
Groundball	.329	677	223	38	4	18	113	68	130	.388	.477	Behind in Count	.211	1099	232	39	3	28	128	0	450	.215	.328
Flyball	.227	414	94	16	3	10	53	46	107	.305	.353	Two Strikes	.193	1163	225	44	5	27	139	146	531	.285	.310
Home	.300	1262	379	52	7	48	216	136	255	.366	.467	Batting #3	.306	683	209	33	3	27	111	78	132	.372	.482
Away	.282	1269	358	70	7	50	206	141	276	.354	.467	Batting #4	.299	995	298	56	8	33	171	94	209	.359	.471
Day	.288	639	184	31	3	30	97	81	140	.367	.487	Other	.270	853	230	33	3	38	140	105	190	.352	.449
Night	.292	1892	553	91	11	68	325	196	391	.358	.460	March/April	.285	355	101	9	2	15	56	41	89	.355	.448
Grass	.291	1994	580	89	11	83	342	213	428	.358	.471	May	.267	445	119	25	2	16	71	75	96	.373	.446
Turf	.292	537	157	33	3	15	80	64	103	.369	.449	June	.323	486	157	30	4	20	83	55	92	.395	.525
Pre-All Star	.292	1461	427	74	8	58	237	184	308	.371	.473	July	.307	475	146	21	1	16	74	38	99	.357	.457
Post-All Star	.290	1070	310	48	6	40	185	93	223	.345	.458	August	.283	417	118	21	4	17	74	36	87	.338	.470
Scoring Posn	.286	706	202	33	1	24	308	117	160	.377	.438	Sept/Oct	.272	353	96	16	1	14	64	32	68	.330	.442
Close & Late	.262	432	113	21	3	14	73	57	96	.346	.421	vs. AL	.132	38	5	1	0	0	3	4	10	.233	.158
None on/out	.268	556	149	25	4	29	29	40	121	.321	.464	vs. NL	.294	2493	732	121	14	98	419	273	521	.362	.471

Batter vs. Pitcher (career)

Hits Best Against	Avg	AB	H	2B	3B	HR	RBI	BB	SO	OBP	SLG	Hits Worst Against	Avg	AB	H	2B	3B	HR	RBI	BB	SO	OBP	SLG
Steve Reed	.500	14	7	2	0	1	2	1	2	.533	.857	Ken Hill	.083	12	1	0	0	0	2	1	5	.154	.083
Salomon Torres	.500	12	6	2	0	2	7	0	3	.500	1.167	Dave Burba	.083	12	1	0	0	0	0	2	4	.214	.083
Shane Reynolds	.476	21	10	2	0	2	9	3	4	.542	.857	Mark Leiter	.087	23	2	0	0	1	2	0	6	.087	.217
Pete Smith	.438	16	7	1	1	1	4	3	2	.526	.813	Hideo Nomo	.105	19	2	0	0	2		3	10	.217	.105
Mike Remlinger	.333	9	3	2	0	1	2	2	2	.455	.889	Jose Bautista	.111	9	1	0	0	0		1	1	.182	.111

Jim Converse — Royals   Age 26 – Pitches Right (groundball pitcher)

	ERA	W	L	Sv	G	GS	IP	BB	SO	Avg	H	2B	3B	HR	RBI	OBP	SLG	GF	IR	IRS	Hld	SvOp	SB	CS	GB	FB	G/F
1997 Season	3.60	0	0	0	3	0	5.0	5	3	.222	4	1	0	2	3	.391	.611	1	1	0	0		2	0	7	5	1.40
Career (1993-1997)	7.21	2	11	1	35	13	97.1	75	66	.325	128	25	6	9	70	.430	.487	6	18	5	1	1	8	6	168	85	1.98

1997 Season

	ERA	W	L	Sv	G	GS	IP	H	HR	BB	SO		Avg	AB	H	2B	3B	HR	RBI	BB	SO	OBP	SLG
Home	3.60	0	0	0	3	0	5.0	4	2	5	3	vs. Left	.333	6	2	1	0	1	1	3	1	.556	1.000
Away	0.00	0	0	0	0	0	0.0	0	0	0	0	vs. Right	.167	12	2	0	0	1	2	2	2	.286	.417

Dennis Cook — Marlins   Age 35 – Pitches Left (flyball pitcher)

	ERA	W	L	Sv	G	GS	IP	BB	SO	Avg	H	2B	3B	HR	RBI	OBP	SLG	GF	IR	IRS	Hld	SvOp	SB	CS	GB	FB	G/F
1997 Season	3.90	1	2	0	59	0	62.1	28	63	.267	64	14	3	4	28	.347	.400	12	24	5	13	2	6	3	55	81	0.68
Last Five Years	4.38	14	12	2	228	7	277.1	119	240	.260	271	59	13	28	163	.340	.422	41	203	52	35	9	14	16	264	364	0.73

1997 Season

	ERA	W	L	Sv	G	GS	IP	H	HR	BB	SO		Avg	AB	H	2B	3B	HR	RBI	BB	SO	OBP	SLG
Home	2.62	1	1	0	32	0	34.1	28	2	13	36	vs. Left	.256	90	23	7	1	1	9	10	26	.330	.389
Away	5.46	0	1	0	27	0	28.0	36	2	15	27	vs. Right	.273	150	41	7	2	3	19	18	37	.357	.407
Day	5.40	0	2	0	17	0	18.1	21	0	11	20	Inning 1-6	.176	17	3	0	0	0	3	5	5	.364	.176
Night	3.27	1	0	0	42	0	44.0	43	4	17	43	Inning 7+	.274	223	61	14	3	4	25	23	58	.345	.417
Grass	3.42	1	2	0	50	0	52.2	50	3	22	55	None on	.273	132	36	9	0	2		12	38	.338	.386
Turf	6.52	0	0	0	9	0	9.2	14	1	6	8	Runners on	.259	108	28	5	3	2	26	16	25	.357	.417
March/April	0.82	0	0	0	8	0	11.0	3	0	3	9	Scoring Posn	.266	64	17	3	1	1	21	13	19	.385	.391

1997 Season

	ERA	W	L	Sv	G	GS	IP	H	HR	BB	SO		Avg	AB	H	2B	3B	HR	RBI	BB	SO	OBP	SLG
May	0.87	0	0	0	10	0	10.1	10	1	4	12	Close & Late	.219	114	25	3	2	1	9	14	37	.305	.307
June	5.40	1	1	0	9	0	6.2	5	0	9	8	None on/out	.232	56	13	4	0	0	0	9	18	.338	.304
July	3.86	0	1	0	12	0	11.2	15	0	6	12	vs. 1st Batr (relief)	.204	49	10	2	1	0	2	10	15	.339	.286
August	8.44	0	0	0	10	0	10.2	18	2	4	10	1st Inning Pitched	.267	180	48	11	3	4	22	25	49	.357	.428
Sept/Oct	4.50	0	0	0	10	0	12.0	13	1	2	12	First 15 Pitches	.262	141	37	7	2	3	11	15	38	.338	.404
Starter	0.00	0	0	0	0	0	0.0	0	0	0	0	Pitch 16-30	.260	73	19	5	1	1	14	11	20	.360	.397
Reliever	3.90	1	2	0	59	0	62.1	64	4	28	63	Pitch 31-45	.217	23	5	2	0	0	0	1	5	.250	.304
0 Days rest (Relief)	3.00	0	0	0	9	0	9.0	8	1	3	10	Pitch 46+	1.000	3	3	0	0	0	3	1	0	1.000	1.000
1 or 2 Days rest	3.33	0	2	0	28	0	27.0	30	0	12	24	Ahead in Count	.226	106	24	5	0	1	11	0	45	.231	.302
3+ Days rest	4.78	1	0	0	22	0	26.1	26	3	13	29	Behind in Count	.383	47	18	6	1	1	8	10	0	.491	.617
vs. AL	16.20	1	1	0	5	0	3.1	5	0	4	2	Two Strikes	.194	129	25	6	1	1	9	14	63	.271	.279
vs. NL	3.20	0	1	0	54	0	59.0	59	4	24	61	Pre-All Star	.214	112	24	7	2	1	11	18	31	.331	.339
Pre-All Star	2.61	1	2	0	30	0	31.0	24	1	18	31	Post-All Star	.313	128	40	7	1	3	17	10	32	.362	.453
Post-All Star	5.17	0	0	0	29	0	31.1	40	3	10	32												

Last Five Years

	ERA	W	L	Sv	G	GS	IP	H	HR	BB	SO		Avg	AB	H	2B	3B	HR	RBI	BB	SO	OBP	SLG
Home	3.65	9	6	1	108	2	138.0	125	14	49	121	vs. Left	.247	389	96	21	4	9	71	37	106	.314	.391
Away	5.10	5	6	1	120	5	139.1	146	14	70	119	vs. Right	.268	653	175	38	9	19	92	82	134	.354	.441
Day	4.82	3	7	0	64	4	89.2	88	11	41	75	Inning 1-6	.270	374	101	30	6	8	73	44	82	.344	.447
Night	4.17	11	5	2	164	3	187.2	183	17	78	165	Inning 7+	.254	668	170	29	7	20	90	75	158	.337	.409
Grass	4.18	14	11	2	200	7	251.2	236	23	102	216	None on	.262	561	147	34	4	15	15	40	128	.318	.417
Turf	6.31	0	1	0	28	0	25.2	35	5	17	24	Runners on	.258	481	124	25	9	13	148	79	112	.362	.428
March/April	4.93	1	0	0	32	0	42.0	34	6	15	35	Scoring Posn	.244	311	76	19	5	7	129	57	82	.354	.405
May	3.30	7	3	0	47	3	71.0	62	6	27	58	Close & Late	.236	276	65	7	4	6	38	36	72	.328	.355
June	4.56	5	4	1	41	3	51.1	46	6	29	44	None on/out	.252	238	60	15	3	2	2	19	57	.318	.366
July	4.24	0	4	0	44	1	51.0	58	4	29	44	vs. 1st Batr (relief)	.208	183	38	9	2	2	34	25	63	.307	.311
August	5.81	0	0	1	32	0	31.0	37	3	9	29	1st Inning Pitched	.243	618	150	37	8	13	110	80	152	.332	.392
Sept/Oct	4.65	1	1	0	32	0	31.0	34	3	10	30	First 15 Pitches	.250	524	131	34	6	13	89	59	122	.328	.412
Starter	8.07	1	4	0	7	7	29.0	35	4	13	17	Pitch 16-30	.236	301	71	9	3	5	40	37	79	.329	.336
Reliever	3.95	13	8	2	221	0	248.1	236	24	106	223	Pitch 31-45	.299	127	38	9	3	7	15	12	25	.357	.583
0 Days rest (Relief)	2.93	2	1	1	38	0	43.0	41	3	22	42	Pitch 46+	.344	90	31	7	1	3	19	11	14	.417	.544
1 or 2 Days rest	4.05	3	7	1	102	0	113.1	111	10	46	93	First Pitch	.352	128	45	10	3	7	23	15	0	.440	.641
3+ Days rest	4.30	8	0	0	81	0	92.0	84	11	38	88	Ahead in Count	.171	484	83	17	5	8	57	0	196	.179	.277
vs. AL	4.70	14	11	2	174	7	218.1	212	24	95	179	Behind in Count	.384	198	76	17	3	9	52	48	0	.500	.636
vs. NL	3.20	0	1	0	54	0	59.0	59	4	24	61	Two Strikes	.167	551	92	21	5	7	55	55	240	.246	.261
Pre-All Star	4.13	13	9	1	136	6	181.0	163	20	88	152	Pre-All Star	.241	677	163	36	10	20	96	80	152	.328	.412
Post-All Star	4.86	1	3	1	92	1	96.1	108	8	39	88	Post-All Star	.296	365	108	23	3	8	67	39	88	.361	.441

Pitcher vs. Batter (career)

Pitches Best Vs.	Avg	AB	H	2B	3B	HR	RBI	BB	SO	OBP	SLG	Pitches Worst Vs.	Avg	AB	H	2B	3B	HR	RBI	BB	SO	OBP	SLG
Mike Devereaux	.000	12	0	0	0	0	0	1	3	.077	.000	Ken Griffey Jr	.545	11	6	0	0	1	7	1	3	.583	.818
Andres Galarraga	.000	10	0	0	0	0	0	1	3	.167	.000	Frank Thomas	.444	9	4	2	0	1	1	3	0	.583	1.000
Barry Bonds	.000	9	0	0	0	0	0	2	0	.182	.000	Darryl Strawberry	.333	9	3	0	0	1	3	4	0	.538	.667
Bobby Bonilla	.059	17	1	0	0	0	0	1	1	.111	.059	Dean Palmer	.333	9	3	2	0	1	2	4	3	.538	.889
Cal Ripken	.077	13	1	0	0	0	0	1	1	.200	.077	John Olerud	.308	13	4	1	0	2	5	2	1	.438	.846

Steve Cooke — Pirates

Age 28 – Pitches Left (groundball pitcher)

	ERA	W	L	Sv	G	GS	IP	BB	SO	Avg	H	2B	3B	HR	RBI	OBP	SLG	CG	ShO	Sup	QS	#P/S	SB	CS	GB	FB	G/F
1997 Season	4.30	9	15	0	32	32	167.1	77	109	.285	184	40	1	15	78	.366	.420	0	0	3.82	16	84	15	12	304	106	2.87
Last Five Years	4.37	23	36	0	92	87	520.2	187	322	.278	559	132	12	59	247	.342	.444	5	1	4.17	49	92	51	24	820	519	1.58

1997 Season

	ERA	W	L	Sv	G	GS	IP	H	HR	BB	SO		Avg	AB	H	2B	3B	HR	RBI	BB	SO	OBP	SLG
Home	4.63	4	9	0	16	16	81.2	95	7	34	50	vs. Left	.283	120	34	4	1	3	13	16	23	.389	.408
Away	3.99	5	6	0	16	16	85.2	89	8	43	59	vs. Right	.285	526	150	36	0	12	65	61	86	.361	.422
Day	5.21	4	8	0	18	18	86.1	111	9	41	59	Inning 1-6	.281	590	166	37	0	15	73	73	100	.366	.420
Night	3.33	5	7	0	14	14	81.0	73	6	36	50	Inning 7+	.321	56	18	3	1	0	5	4	9	.367	.411
Grass	4.67	4	5	0	12	12	61.2	63	8	34	42	None on	.291	347	101	25	1	8	8	35	56	.364	.438
Turf	4.09	5	10	0	20	20	105.2	121	7	43	67	Runners on	.278	299	83	15	0	7	70	42	53	.369	.398
March/April	5.33	1	3	0	5	5	25.1	25	4	13	11	Scoring Posn	.281	178	50	7	0	5	63	31	32	.381	.404
May	2.70	3	3	0	6	6	33.1	35	0	11	19	Close & Late	.282	39	11	1	1	0	3	2	8	.317	.359
June	2.57	1	3	0	5	5	28.0	28	1	13	17	None on/out	.317	164	52	15	0	2	2	14	29	.381	.445
July	3.08	3	1	0	6	6	38.0	42	3	16	29	vs. 1st Batr (relief)	.000	0	0	0	0	0	0	0	0	.000	.000
August	9.00	1	3	0	5	5	18.0	26	4	14	11	1st Inning Pitched	.356	132	47	12	0	8	32	21	20	.436	.629
Sept/Oct	5.84	0	2	0	5	5	24.2	28	3	10	22	First 75 Pitches	.269	510	137	31	0	12	54	57	88	.348	.400
Starter	4.30	9	15	0	32	32	167.1	184	15	77	109	Pitch 76-90	.345	84	29	7	1	2	16	12	11	.423	.524
Reliever	0.00	0	0	0	0	0	0.0	0	0	0	0	Pitch 91-105	.325	40	13	2	0	1	6	6	8	.438	.450
0-3 Days Rest (Start)	0.00	0	0	0	0	0	0.0	0	0	0	0	Pitch 106+	.417	12	5	0	0	0	2	2	2	.500	.417
4 Days Rest	4.02	7	8	0	20	20	105.1	120	9	50	64	First Pitch	.379	95	36	5	0	2	19	7	0	.425	.495
5+ Days Rest	4.79	2	7	0	12	12	62.0	64	6	27	45	Ahead in Count	.212	255	54	11	0	5	10	0	82	.230	.314
vs. AL	3.55	1	2	0	3	3	12.2	14	1	6	10	Behind in Count	.386	158	61	15	0	5	37	41	0	.507	.576
vs. NL	4.36	8	13	0	29	29	154.2	170	14	71	99	Two Strikes	.176	272	48	10	0	6	9	29	109	.266	.279
Pre-All Star	3.10	7	9	0	18	18	101.2	100	9	43	59	Pre-All Star	.265	378	100	24	0	5	34	43	59	.347	.368
Post-All Star	6.17	2	6	0	14	14	65.2	84	10	34	50	Post-All Star	.313	268	84	16	1	10	44	34	50	.394	.493

Last Five Years

	ERA	W	L	Sv	G	GS	IP	H	HR	BB	SO		Avg	AB	H	2B	3B	HR	RBI	BB	SO	OBP	SLG
Home	4.66	12	19	0	45	45	264.1	293	30	84	147	vs. Left	.290	352	102	20	4	9	50	44	66	.377	.446
Away	4.07	11	17	0	47	42	256.1	266	29	103	175	vs. Right	.276	1657	457	112	8	50	197	143	256	.335	.444
Day	4.84	9	16	0	37	35	201.0	241	27	77	121	Inning 1-6	.277	1757	487	115	8	52	226	173	289	.345	.441
Night	4.08	14	20	0	55	52	319.2	318	32	110	201	Inning 7+	.286	252	72	17	4	7	21	14	33	.323	.468
Grass	3.76	8	10	0	31	28	165.0	162	18	74	112	None on	.278	1153	321	88	7	31	31	90	172	.337	.448
Turf	4.66	15	26	0	61	59	355.2	397	41	113	210	Runners on	.278	856	238	44	5	28	216	97	150	.350	.439
March/April	5.00	2	7	0	14	14	81.0	90	13	35	38	Scoring Posn	.285	505	144	27	3	14	181	75	96	.371	.434
May	3.83	6	6	0	19	18	110.1	112	9	36	63	Close & Late	.258	159	41	8	3	4	13	9	25	.298	.421
June	3.03	5	4	0	18	15	110.0	98	7	39	77	None on/out	.297	526	156	46	4	19	19	40	72	.353	.508
July	5.04	4	8	0	17	16	89.1	107	10	33	62	vs. 1st Batr (relief)	.250	4	1	1	0	0	2	1	0	.400	.500
August	5.72	4	7	0	13	13	67.2	89	13	24	38	1st Inning Pitched	.294	354	104	22	1	13	58	45	49	.370	.472
Sept/Oct	4.48	2	4	0	11	11	62.1	63	7	20	44	First 75 Pitches	.272	1506	410	93	7	39	176	147	248	.340	.421
Starter	4.35	22	36	0	87	87	509.0	547	58	179	314	Pitch 76-90	.282	277	78	26	2	8	37	23	39	.344	.477
Reliever	5.40	1	0	0	5	0	11.2	12	1	8	8	Pitch 91-105	.308	156	48	7	2	10	24	12	22	.363	.571
0-3 Days Rest (Start)	63.00	0	1	0	1	1	1.0	5	1	3	0	Pitch 106+	.329	70	23	6	1	2	10	5	13	.373	.529
4 Days Rest	4.60	15	20	0	50	50	289.2	327	32	97	168	First Pitch	.363	273	99	22	1	13	55	15	0	.399	.593
5+ Days Rest	3.75	7	15	0	36	36	218.1	215	25	79	146	Ahead in Count	.200	830	166	40	4	13	49	0	268	.209	.305
vs. AL	3.55	1	2	0	3	3	12.2	14	1	6	10	Behind in Count	.358	514	184	45	5	22	98	95	0	.453	.593
vs. NL	4.39	22	34	0	89	84	508.0	545	58	181	312	Two Strikes	.189	842	159	34	2	16	50	77	322	.263	.291
Pre-All Star	3.82	16	19	0	58	53	342.0	342	31	124	203	Pre-All Star	.266	1287	342	85	5	31	141	124	203	.333	.412
Post-All Star	5.44	7	17	0	34	34	178.2	217	28	63	119	Post-All Star	.301	722	217	47	7	28	106	63	119	.360	.501

Pitcher vs. Batter (career)

Pitches Best Vs.	Avg	AB	H	2B	3B	HR	RBI	BB	SO	OBP	SLG	Pitches Worst Vs.	Avg	AB	H	2B	3B	HR	RBI	BB	SO	OBP	SLG
Gary Sheffield	.000	7	0	0	0	0	1	5	1	.385	.000	Jeff Bagwell	.583	12	7	1	0	2	5	4	0	.688	1.167
Kirt Manwaring	.091	11	1	0	0	0	1	3		.231	.091	Raul Mondesi	.545	11	6	1	1	1	5	0	0	.500	1.091
Sammy Sosa	.111	18	2	0	0	0	2	1	4	.158	.111	Tony Gwynn	.500	20	10	2	0	1	4	1	0	.524	.750
Derek Bell	.133	15	2	1	0	0	1	0	3	.133	.200	Royce Clayton	.455	22	10	3	0	1	1	3	3	.520	.727
Terry Pendleton	.154	13	2	0	0	0	0	1	1	.214	.154	Todd Pratt	.333	12	4	1	0	2	3	0	2	.333	.917

Ron Coomer — Twins

Age 31 – Bats Right

	Avg	G	AB	R	H	2B	3B	HR	RBI	BB	SO	HBP	GDP	SB	CS	OBP	SLG	IBB	SH	SF	#Pit	#P/PA	GB	FB	G/F
1997 Season	.298	140	523	63	156	30	2	13	85	22	91	0	11	4	3	.324	.438	5	0	5	1853	3.37	184	150	1.23
Career (1995-1997)	.293	272	857	112	251	45	4	30	145	48	126	1	30	7	4	.328	.460	6	0	8	3190	3.49	312	271	1.15

1997 Season

	Avg	AB	H	2B	3B	HR	RBI	BB	SO	OBP	SLG		Avg	AB	H	2B	3B	HR	RBI	BB	SO	OBP	SLG
vs. Left	.415	123	51	11	1	3	24	10	13	.459	.593	First Pitch	.355	76	27	3	2	0	16	4	0	.383	.447
vs. Right	.263	400	105	19	1	10	61	12	78	.281	.390	Ahead in Count	.408	130	53	12	0	7	32	10	0	.447	.662
Groundball	.286	119	34	6	0	3	16	5	21	.312	.412	Behind in Count	.229	231	53	9	0	2	19	0	79	.227	.294
Flyball	.309	81	25	6	0	0	15	2	15	.321	.383	Two Strikes	.206	214	44	7	0	0	15	8	91	.232	.238
Home	.310	258	80	20	1	4	40	11	40	.337	.442	Batting #4	.310	129	40	12	1	5	30	5	35	.328	.535
Away	.287	265	76	10	1	9	45	11	51	.311	.434	Batting #5	.289	225	65	9	0	4	24	8	30	.311	.382
Day	.239	163	39	10	1	3	24	7	38	.267	.368	Other	.302	169	51	9	1	4	31	9	26	.337	.438
Night	.325	360	117	20	1	10	61	15	53	.349	.469	March/April	.275	40	11	3	0	2	10	3	10	.326	.500
Grass	.265	226	60	8	1	8	39	11	43	.295	.416	May	.290	69	20	2	0	3	10	4	12	.329	.449
Turf	.323	297	96	22	1	5	46	11	48	.346	.455	June	.350	100	35	6	1	3	20	2	10	.359	.520
Pre-All Star	.305	233	71	11	1	8	41	9	39	.329	.464	July	.317	101	32	4	0	0	10	6	16	.355	.356
Post-All Star	.293	290	85	19	1	5	44	13	52	.319	.417	August	.286	112	32	7	1	1	11	2	23	.298	.393
Scoring Posn	.370	135	50	14	0	4	73	12	23	.408	.563	Sept/Oct	.257	101	26	8	0	4	24	5	20	.282	.455
Close & Late	.261	69	18	1	0	1	5	6	16	.320	.319	vs. AL	.299	469	140	26	2	12	75	22	76	.328	.439
None on/out	.289	128	37	7	0	4		2	30	.286	.426	vs. NL	.296	54	16	4	0	1	10	0	15	.286	.426

1997 By Position

Position	Avg	AB	H	2B	3B	HR	RBI	BB	SO	OBP	SLG	G	GS	Innings	PO	A	E	DP	Fld Pct	Rng Fctr	In Zone	In Outs	Zone Rtg	MLB Zone
As 3b	.308	467	144	27	2	9	72	19	76	.332	.433	119	116	1008.2	66	216	10	20	.966	2.52	301	244	.811	.801

Career (1995-1997)

	Avg	AB	H	2B	3B	HR	RBI	BB	SO	OBP	SLG		Avg	AB	H	2B	3B	HR	RBI	BB	SO	OBP	SLG
vs. Left	.351	316	111	21	2	16	67	28	38	.403	.582	First Pitch	.331	118	39	8	2	1	24	5	0	.352	.458
vs. Right	.259	541	140	24	2	14	78	20	88	.282	.388	Ahead in Count	.367	221	81	13	1	14	52	25	0	.427	.624
Groundball	.285	186	53	9	0	6	27	9	27	.316	.430	Behind in Count	.231	376	87	15	1	10	44	0	110	.232	.356
Flyball	.314	121	38	8	2	2	26	5	19	.336	.463	Two Strikes	.225	351	79	15	1	7	40	18	126	.263	.333
Home	.297	428	127	30	2	11	69	22	61	.330	.453	Batting #5	.287	303	87	14	0	7	41	13	39	.313	.403
Away	.289	429	124	15	2	19	76	26	65	.327	.466	Batting #6	.305	213	65	11	2	7	37	10	26	.338	.474
Day	.273	249	68	13	1	7	41	16	41	.313	.418	Other	.290	341	99	20	2	16	67	25	61	.336	.501
Night	.301	608	183	32	3	23	104	32	85	.334	.477	March/April	.263	80	21	5	0	3	21	5	15	.299	.438
Grass	.272	372	101	12	2	16	64	23	55	.311	.444	May	.320	97	31	3	0	8	17	10	14	.383	.598
Turf	.309	485	150	33	2	14	81	25	71	.342	.472	June	.333	156	52	8	1	4	27	6	14	.354	.474
Pre-All Star	.301	372	112	16	1	16	67	21	52	.335	.478	July	.297	128	38	5	0	1	14	8	22	.338	.359
Post-All Star	.287	485	139	29	3	14	78	27	74	.323	.445	August	.299	204	61	10	2	7	26	7	31	.322	.471
Scoring Posn	.335	233	78	20	1	7	114	22	33	.383	.519	Sept/Oct	.250	192	48	14	1	7	40	12	30	.292	.443
Close & Late	.210	119	25	2	0	2	8	10	23	.271	.277	vs. AL	.293	803	235	41	4	29	135	48	111	.331	.462
None on/out	.286	206	59	10	0	10	10	6	37	.307	.481	vs. NL	.296	54	16	4	0	1	10	0	15	.286	.426

Batter vs. Pitcher (career)

Hits Best Against	Avg	AB	H	2B	3B	HR	RBI	BB	SO	OBP	SLG	Hits Worst Against	Avg	AB	H	2B	3B	HR	RBI	BB	SO	OBP	SLG
David Wells	.615	13	8	0	0	1	2	0	0	.615	.846	Chris Haney	.000	10	0	0	0	0	0	1	1	.091	.000
Jaime Navarro	.500	10	5	0	0	2	3	1	0	.545	1.100	Kenny Rogers	.083	12	1	0	0	0	0	0	2	.083	.083
Darren Oliver	.500	10	5	1	0	1	2	1	0	.545	.900												
Scott Karl	.450	20	9	2	0	4	7	2	1	.500	1.150												
Wilson Alvarez	.400	15	6	4	0	1	5	1	5	.438	.867												

Scott Cooper — Royals
Age 30 – Bats Left

	Avg	G	AB	R	H	2B	3B	HR	RBI	BB	SO	HBP	GDP	SB	CS	OBP	SLG	IBB	SH	SF	#Pit	#P/PA	GB	FB	G/F
1997 Season	.201	75	159	12	32	6	1	3	15	17	32	2	4	1	1	.283	.308	0	2	2	733	4.03	45	54	0.83
Last Five Years	.258	453	1428	157	369	69	10	28	171	154	263	11	27	6	9	.332	.380	20	7	14	6140	3.80	435	442	0.98

1997 Season

	Avg	AB	H	2B	3B	HR	RBI	BB	SO	OBP	SLG		Avg	AB	H	2B	3B	HR	RBI	BB	SO	OBP	SLG
vs. Left	.263	19	5	0	1	1	4	0	5	.300	.526	Scoring Posn	.122	41	5	2	1	0	12	7	7	.240	.220
vs. Right	.193	140	27	6	0	2	11	17	27	.281	.279	Close & Late	.209	43	9	1	0	1	3	5	11	.306	.302
Home	.243	70	17	2	1	3	9	6	12	.321	.429	None on/out	.297	37	11	3	0	2	2	3	6	.366	.541
Away	.169	89	15	4	0	0	6	11	20	.255	.213	Batting #6	.180	50	9	3	0	1	3	4	6	.236	.300
First Pitch	.200	15	3	0	0	0	1	0	0	.235	.200	Batting #8	.289	45	13	2	0	0	6	6	6	.365	.333
Ahead in Count	.286	35	10	2	0	2	5	6	0	.390	.514	Other	.156	64	10	1	1	2	6	7	20	.260	.297
Behind in Count	.149	67	10	3	1	0	8	0	22	.147	.224	Pre-All Star	.209	110	23	5	0	2	10	10	21	.270	.309
Two Strikes	.143	77	11	2	0	0	5	11	32	.242	.169	Post-All Star	.184	49	9	1	1	1	5	7	11	.310	.306

Last Five Years

	Avg	AB	H	2B	3B	HR	RBI	BB	SO	OBP	SLG		Avg	AB	H	2B	3B	HR	RBI	BB	SO	OBP	SLG
vs. Left	.226	368	83	9	4	6	52	32	86	.297	.321	First Pitch	.315	200	63	16	2	7	31	18	0	.372	.520
vs. Right	.270	1060	286	60	6	22	119	122	177	.345	.400	Ahead in Count	.348	325	113	19	3	10	51	58	0	.443	.517
Groundball	.295	295	87	18	2	7	37	18	53	.338	.441	Behind in Count	.187	620	116	24	5	5	54	0	217	.192	.266
Flyball	.264	318	84	17	4	3	38	34	66	.342	.371	Two Strikes	.182	648	118	18	3	4	57	78	263	.271	.238
Home	.283	713	202	38	6	16	85	80	122	.357	.421	Batting #6	.268	447	120	28	2	10	55	45	71	.332	.407
Away	.234	715	167	31	4	12	86	74	141	.307	.338	Batting #7	.268	575	154	25	5	11	61	58	104	.340	.386
Day	.249	482	120	24	3	9	61	64	100	.339	.367	Other	.234	406	95	16	3	7	55	51	88	.323	.340
Night	.263	946	249	45	7	19	110	90	163	.329	.386	March/April	.335	194	65	12	1	10	47	19	42	.392	.562
Grass	.274	1033	283	47	7	24	124	111	178	.345	.403	May	.271	310	84	12	3	4	25	39	53	.359	.368
Turf	.218	395	86	22	3	4	47	43	85	.298	.319	June	.241	315	76	15	1	7	35	33	54	.311	.362
Pre-All Star	.270	926	250	44	7	23	127	100	167	.341	.407	July	.232	271	63	9	2	3	29	28	54	.304	.314
Post-All Star	.237	502	119	25	3	5	44	54	96	.316	.329	August	.212	165	35	10	2	1	17	17	31	.288	.315
Scoring Posn	.257	362	93	25	2	5	140	65	69	.358	.378	Sept/Oct	.266	173	46	11	1	3	18	18	29	.343	.393
Close & Late	.199	246	49	10	2	1	24	36	58	.303	.268	vs. AL	.272	1039	283	51	8	25	131	102	174	.339	.409
None on/out	.262	367	96	23	4	8	61	52	87	.287	.411	vs. NL	.221	389	86	18	2	3	40	52	89	.315	.301

Batter vs. Pitcher (career)

Hits Best Against	Avg	AB	H	2B	3B	HR	RBI	BB	SO	OBP	SLG	Hits Worst Against	Avg	AB	H	2B	3B	HR	RBI	BB	SO	OBP	SLG
Bob Wickman	.545	11	6	2	0	1	4	0	3	.545	1.000	Cal Eldred	.053	19	1	0	0	0	0	5	2	.250	.053
Mark Leiter	.444	9	4	2	1	0	3	7	0	.688	.889	Jose Mesa	.133	15	2	0	0	0	1	2	3	.235	.133
Mike Mussina	.412	17	7	1	0	1	2	2	4	.474	.647	Jaime Navarro	.182	22	4	1	0	1	1	2	2	.250	.364
Ricky Bones	.412	17	7	1	0	1	2	1	0	.421	.647	Bobby Witt	.194	31	6	1	0	0	1	4	7	.286	.226
Scott Erickson	.353	17	6	1	1	1	3	1	0	.389	.706	David Cone	.235	17	4	0	0	0	1	2	1	.316	.235

Rocky Coppinger — Orioles
Age 24 – Pitches Right (flyball pitcher)

	ERA	W	L	Sv	G	GS	IP	BB	SO	Avg	H	2B	3B	HR	RBI	OBP	SLG	CG	ShO	Sup	QS	#P/S	SB	CS	GB	FB	G/F
1997 Season	6.30	1	1	0	5	4	20.0	16	22	.273	21	4	0	2	7	.400	.403	0	0	6.75	1	91	10	2	22	23	0.96
Career (1996-1997)	5.34	11	7	0	28	26	145.0	76	126	.264	147	26	2	27	76	.353	.464	0	0	7.39	10	100	31	5	131	219	0.60

1997 Season

	ERA	W	L	Sv	G	GS	IP	H	HR	BB	SO		Avg	AB	H	2B	3B	HR	RBI	BB	SO	OBP	SLG
Home	8.49	1	1	0	3	3	11.2	15	2	13	16	vs. Left	.219	32	7	0	0	1	3	11	8	.422	.313
Away	3.24	0	0	0	2	1	8.1	6	0	3	6	vs. Right	.311	45	14	4	0	1	4	5	14	.380	.467

Joey Cora — Mariners
Age 33 – Bats Both

	Avg	G	AB	R	H	2B	3B	HR	RBI	BB	SO	HBP	GDP	SB	CS	OBP	SLG	IBB	SH	SF	#Pit	#P/PA	GB	FB	G/F
1997 Season	.300	149	574	105	172	40	4	11	54	53	49	5	6	6	7	.359	.441	2	8	9	2426	3.74	209	190	1.10
Last Five Years	.287	656	2422	409	694	124	29	24	219	230	207	29	45	57	31	.352	.391	3	57	27	10266	3.71	896	739	1.21

1997 Season

	Avg	AB	H	2B	3B	HR	RBI	BB	SO	OBP	SLG		Avg	AB	H	2B	3B	HR	RBI	BB	SO	OBP	SLG
vs. Left	.364	107	39	10	1	5	26	9	10	.403	.617	First Pitch	.359	78	28	5	0	0	8	1	0	.366	.423
vs. Right	.285	467	133	30	3	6	28	44	39	.349	.400	Ahead in Count	.382	136	52	15	1	5	27	37	0	.506	.618
Groundball	.250	128	32	7	0	0	3	13	8	.322	.305	Behind in Count	.235	243	57	11	2	4	9	0	46	.242	.346
Flyball	.384	99	38	8	2	6	15	8	12	.431	.687	Two Strikes	.213	249	53	12	3	5	9	15	49	.264	.345
Home	.300	277	83	20	1	4	25	28	21	.367	.422	Batting #1	.294	551	162	38	4	10	49	47	48	.350	.432
Away	.300	297	89	20	3	7	29	25	28	.352	.458	Batting #9	.474	19	9	1	0	1	5	5	1	.583	.684
Day	.259	185	48	13	3	2	15	18	18	.330	.395	Other	.250	4	1	1	0	0	1	0	0	.400	.500
Night	.319	389	124	27	1	9	39	35	31	.373	.463	March/April	.247	81	20	3	1	1	10	13	4	.347	.346
Grass	.302	252	76	17	1	5	22	22	24	.357	.437	May	.449	107	48	11	1	4	14	10	9	.500	.682
Turf	.298	322	96	23	3	6	32	31	25	.360	.444	June	.271	96	26	11	0	2	7	9	8	.339	.448
Pre-All Star	.330	306	101	26	2	8	33	36	22	.402	.507	July	.312	109	34	7	1	2	12	5	9	.339	.450

1997 Season

	Avg	AB	H	2B	3B	HR	RBI	BB	SO	OBP	SLG
Post-All Star	.265	268	71	14	2	3	21	17	27	.307	.366
Scoring Posn	.311	103	32	9	1	2	43	13	5	.375	.476
Close & Late	.233	73	17	3	0	0	7	15	6	.360	.274
None on/out	.286	241	69	17	0	7		23	24	.353	.444

	Avg	AB	H	2B	3B	HR	RBI	BB	SO	OBP	SLG
August	.231	104	24	5	0	0	6	10	13	.291	.279
Sept/Oct	.260	77	20	3	1	2	5	6	6	.322	.403
vs. AL	.305	511	156	35	4	10	51	46	44	.362	.448
vs. NL	.254	63	16	5	0	1	3	7	5	.333	.381

1997 By Position

Position	Avg	AB	H	2B	3B	HR	RBI	BB	SO	OBP	SLG	G	GS	Innings	PO	A	E	DP	Fld Pct	Rng Fctr	In Zone	Outs	Zone Rtg	MLB Zone
As Pinch Hitter	.143	7	1	1	0	0	0	4	0	.455	.286	11	0	---										
As 2b	.302	567	171	39	4	11	54	49	49	.357	.443	142	138	1192.2	304	310	17	83	.973	4.63	365	299	.819	.902

Last Five Years

	Avg	AB	H	2B	3B	HR	RBI	BB	SO	OBP	SLG
vs. Left	.286	430	123	19	3	5	48	39	49	.346	.379
vs. Right	.287	1992	571	105	26	19	171	191	158	.353	.394
Groundball	.264	587	155	25	6	2	38	56	41	.333	.337
Flyball	.326	476	155	26	8	8	46	44	45	.384	.464
Home	.290	1160	336	61	14	9	99	115	99	.359	.390
Away	.284	1262	358	63	15	15	120	115	108	.345	.393
Day	.279	714	199	40	8	7	56	72	57	.352	.387
Night	.290	1708	495	84	21	17	163	158	150	.352	.393
Grass	.284	1403	398	59	18	12	134	147	125	.354	.377
Turf	.290	1019	296	65	11	12	85	83	82	.349	.411
Pre-All Star	.291	1336	389	75	14	14	125	139	117	.361	.400
Post-All Star	.281	1086	305	49	15	10	94	91	90	.345	.381
Scoring Posn	.300	517	155	25	7	3	186	53	33	.359	.393
Close & Late	.268	343	92	16	4	0	29	38	27	.346	.338
None on/out	.265	762	202	48	8	12	12	83	73	.344	.381

	Avg	AB	H	2B	3B	HR	RBI	BB	SO	OBP	SLG
First Pitch	.340	324	110	16	3	2	35	2	0	.342	.426
Ahead in Count	.314	601	189	45	9	9	93	148	0	.446	.464
Behind in Count	.231	991	229	32	7	10	47	0	180	.245	.308
Two Strikes	.231	999	231	36	10	11	41	80	207	.295	.320
Batting #1	.293	1431	419	85	15	17	122	119	102	.350	.409
Batting #2	.272	831	226	31	11	6	80	92	89	.351	.357
Other	.306	160	49	8	3	1	17	19	16	.379	.413
March/April	.256	336	86	11	6	5	33	38	29	.331	.369
May	.301	432	130	28	5	5	45	43	42	.368	.424
June	.309	453	140	30	3	3	39	44	38	.375	.408
July	.295	464	137	27	5	3	40	33	31	.344	.394
August	.278	396	110	16	5	2	34	37	45	.343	.359
Sept/Oct	.267	341	91	12	5	6	28	35	22	.344	.384
vs. AL	.287	2359	678	119	29	23	216	223	202	.352	.392
vs. NL	.254	63	16	5	0	1	3	7	5	.333	.381

Batter vs. Pitcher (career)

Hits Best Against	Avg	AB	H	2B	3B	HR	RBI	BB	SO	OBP	SLG
Jose Mesa	.556	9	5	1	0	0	1	4	1	.733	.667
Mark Langston	.545	11	6	1	0	1	3	1	1	.615	.909
Woody Williams	.545	11	6	2	0	1	1	0	0	.545	1.000
Rick Aguilera	.500	14	7	1	1	0	2	1	0	.533	.714
Kevin Tapani	.486	35	17	7	0	1	5	0	2	.486	.771

Hits Worst Against	Avg	AB	H	2B	3B	HR	RBI	BB	SO	OBP	SLG
John Smiley	.000	11	0	0	0	0	0	2	1	.214	.000
Aaron Sele	.083	12	1	0	0	0	0	2	0	.214	.083
Sid Fernandez	.100	10	1	0	0	0	0	1	2	.182	.100
Dennis Martinez	.125	16	2	1	0	0	0	0	3	.125	.188
John Burkett	.133	15	2	0	0	0	0	1	2	.188	.133

Wil Cordero — Red Sox

Age 26 – Bats Right

	Avg	G	AB	R	H	2B	3B	HR	RBI	BB	SO	HBP	GDP	SB	CS	OBP	SLG	IBB	SH	SF	#Pit	#P/PA	GB	FB	G/F
1997 Season	.281	140	570	82	160	26	3	18	72	31	122	4	11		3	.320	.432	7	0	4	2164	3.55	212	142	1.49
Last Five Years	.278	578	2172	296	604	137	10	56	279	153	363	28	50	40	15	.332	.428	26	8	13	8534	3.59	855	586	1.46

1997 Season

	Avg	AB	H	2B	3B	HR	RBI	BB	SO	OBP	SLG
vs. Left	.287	174	50	11	1	4	19	11	36	.332	.431
vs. Right	.278	396	110	15	2	14	53	20	86	.315	.432
Groundball	.272	103	28	6	1	4	16	7	25	.330	.466
Flyball	.367	90	33	6	0	3	15	3	19	.394	.533
Home	.267	273	73	12	2	11	35	11	57	.299	.447
Away	.293	297	87	14	1	7	37	20	65	.340	.418
Day	.277	184	51	9	0	5	24	11	43	.318	.408
Night	.282	386	109	17	3	13	48	20	79	.321	.443
Grass	.267	495	132	21	3	15	60	24	106	.302	.412
Turf	.373	75	28	5	0	3	12	7	16	.434	.560
Pre-All Star	.300	280	84	14	0	11	41	16	63	.340	.468
Post-All Star	.262	290	76	12	3	7	31	15	59	.301	.397
Scoring Posn	.264	144	38	10	1	7	56	16	38	.333	.493
Close & Late	.302	96	29	2	0	3	10	9	23	.368	.417
None on/out	.281	128	36	4	1	5	5	2	24	.298	.445

	Avg	AB	H	2B	3B	HR	RBI	BB	SO	OBP	SLG
First Pitch	.357	70	25	5	0	3	11	6	0	.408	.557
Ahead in Count	.331	133	44	11	1	9	24	11	0	.382	.632
Behind in Count	.204	255	52	5	1	4	20	0	102	.208	.278
Two Strikes	.157	242	39	6	0	2	15	14	122	.209	.205
Batting #3	.342	120	41	5	0	5	19	4	32	.365	.508
Batting #5	.272	217	59	9	3	6	21	10	43	.304	.424
Other	.258	233	60	12	0	7	32	17	47	.312	.399
March/April	.300	100	30	5	0	5	17	10	18	.369	.500
May	.327	107	35	6	0	3	12	4	28	.354	.467
June	.260	73	19	3	0	3	12	2	17	.276	.425
July	.232	82	19	3	0	2	9	3	18	.267	.341
August	.270	111	30	5	3	2	13	6	19	.308	.423
Sept/Oct	.278	97	27	4	0	3	9	6	22	.320	.412
vs. AL	.284	553	157	26	3	18	72	30	120	.323	.439
vs. NL	.176	17	3	0	0	0	0	1	2	.222	.176

1997 By Position

Position	Avg	AB	H	2B	3B	HR	RBI	BB	SO	OBP	SLG	G	GS	Innings	PO	A	E	DP	Fld Pct	Rng Fctr	In Zone	Outs	Zone Rtg	MLB Zone
As 1f	.286	560	160	26	3	18	72	31	121	.326	.439	137	137	1199.1	248	8	2		.992	1.92	318	235	.739	.805

Last Five Years

	Avg	AB	H	2B	3B	HR	RBI	BB	SO	OBP	SLG
vs. Left	.287	606	174	48	3	13	78	52	103	.348	.441
vs. Right	.275	1566	430	89	7	43	201	101	260	.325	.423
Groundball	.279	585	163	32	2	7	63	40	96	.332	.376
Flyball	.313	367	115	24	1	13	58	21	58	.358	.490
Home	.270	1014	274	73	6	28	136	74	178	.325	.437
Away	.285	1158	330	64	4	28	143	79	185	.338	.420
Day	.251	696	175	37	2	16	85	39	128	.296	.379
Night	.291	1476	429	100	8	40	194	114	235	.348	.451
Grass	.276	1150	317	59	5	35	155	64	198	.318	.427
Turf	.281	1022	287	78	5	21	124	89	165	.346	.429
Pre-All Star	.286	1309	375	88	5	36	170	100	214	.342	.444
Post-All Star	.265	863	229	49	5	20	109	53	149	.316	.403

	Avg	AB	H	2B	3B	HR	RBI	BB	SO	OBP	SLG
First Pitch	.414	222	92	21	1	12	44	16	0	.461	.680
Ahead in Count	.313	571	179	49	4	22	94	78	0	.398	.529
Behind in Count	.225	993	223	42	4	14	86	0	306	.234	.317
Two Strikes	.204	932	190	39	1	13	86	59	363	.261	.290
Batting #5	.277	382	106	18	3	12	52	26	71	.332	.435
Batting #7	.281	374	105	18	2	8	40	26	52	.334	.404
Other	.278	1416	393	101	5	36	187	101	240	.331	.432
March/April	.265	370	98	22	3	9	55	31	60	.325	.414
May	.290	480	139	36	2	9	52	34	79	.342	.429
June	.291	361	105	25	0	11	47	28	56	.348	.452
July	.284	348	99	21	1	13	53	22	58	.339	.463
August	.260	334	87	18	4	5	34	17	55	.303	.383

	Avg	AB	H	2B	3B	HR	RBI	BB	SO	OBP	SLG		Avg	AB	H	2B	3B	HR	RBI	BB	SO	OBP	SLG
Scoring Posn	.271	553	150	40	2	14	209	74	101	.357	.427	Sept/Oct	.272	279	76	15	0	9	38	21	55	.328	.423
Close & Late	.291	347	101	18	2	11	56	29	64	.352	.450	vs. AL	.285	751	214	40	3	21	109	41	151	.325	.430
None on/out	.277	505	140	28	2	14	14	22	83	.313	.424	vs. NL	.274	1421	390	97	7	35	170	112	212	.335	.426

Batter vs. Pitcher (career)

Hits Best Against	Avg	AB	H	2B	3B	HR	RBI	BB	SO	OBP	SLG	Hits Worst Against	Avg	AB	H	2B	3B	HR	RBI	BB	SO	OBP	SLG
Paul Quantrill	.714	14	10	1	0	0	4	0	1	.714	.786	Chris Hammond	.083	12	1	0	0	0	2	1	0	.143	.083
Frank Castillo	.529	17	9	4	0	1	3	0	1	.556	.941	Bret Saberhagen	.111	18	2	0	1	0	1	1	1	.158	.222
Andy Benes	.500	12	6	1	0	3	6	1	0	.538	1.333	Doug Drabek	.158	19	3	1	0	0	1	0	3	.158	.211
Danny Jackson	.467	15	7	4	0	0	1	4	0	.571	.733	Jason Dickson	.167	12	2	0	0	0	1	0	2	.167	.167
John Burkett	.429	21	9	2	0	3	6	1	2	.455	.952	Rich Robertson	.167	12	2	0	0	0	0	1	4	.231	.167

Francisco Cordova — Pirates Age 26 – Pitches Right (groundball pitcher)

	ERA	W	L	Sv	G	GS	IP	BB	SO	Avg	H	2B	3B	HR	RBI	OBP	SLG	CG	ShO	Sup	QS	#P/S	SB	CS	GB	FB	G/F
1997 Season	3.63	11	8	0	29	29	178.2	49	121	.259	175	40	2	14	69	.314	.386	2	2	5.34	17	88	12	7	292	154	1.90
Career (1996-1997)	3.79	15	15	12	88	35	277.2	69	216	.261	278	60	3	25	119	.310	.393	2	2	5.09	18	85	24	7	438	232	1.89

1997 Season

	ERA	W	L	Sv	G	GS	IP	H	HR	BB	SO		Avg	AB	H	2B	3B	HR	RBI	BB	SO	OBP	SLG
Home	3.59	6	6	0	16	16	97.2	96	10	22	66	vs. Left	.298	346	103	18	2	9	33	28	42	.355	.439
Away	3.67	5	2	0	13	13	81.0	79	4	27	55	vs. Right	.218	330	72	22	0	5	36	21	79	.271	.330
Day	4.78	4	3	0	11	11	64.0	79	8	16	43	Inning 1-6	.250	579	145	35	1	10	57	42	105	.306	.366
Night	2.98	7	5	0	18	18	114.2	96	6	33	78	Inning 7+	.309	97	30	5	1	4	12	7	16	.364	.505
Grass	3.38	3	1	0	9	9	58.2	58	4	21	39	None on	.251	418	105	25	1	8	8	25	67	.303	.373
Turf	3.75	8	7	0	20	20	120.0	117	10	28	82	Runners on	.271	258	70	15	1	6	61	24	54	.332	.407
March/April	1.97	1	2	0	5	5	32.0	28	2	6	14	Scoring Posn	.270	141	38	3	1	5	51	15	31	.337	.411
May	1.50	2	2	0	5	5	36.0	35	1	8	24	Close & Late	.213	47	10	1	0	0	4	2	9	.255	.234
June	4.05	3	1	0	6	6	40.0	38	3	9	25	None on/out	.236	182	43	12	0	1		6	32	.268	.319
July	4.86	1	1	0	5	5	33.1	32	3	8	28	vs. 1st Batr (relief)	.000	0	0	0	0	0	0	0	0	.000	.000
August	5.82	2	1	0	4	4	17.0	21	3	11	11	1st Inning Pitched	.272	114	31	4	0	5	18	12	19	.346	.439
Sept/Oct	5.31	2	1	0	4	4	20.1	21	2	7	19	First 75 Pitches	.258	535	138	33	0	11	54	33	93	.307	.381
Starter	3.63	11	8	0	29	29	178.2	175	14	49	121	Pitch 76-90	.257	74	19	3	1	5		8	16	.325	.365
Reliever	0.00	0	0	0	0	0	0.0	0	0	0	0	Pitch 91-105	.200	45	9	2	1	0	5	8	7	.327	.289
0-3 Days Rest (Start)	0.00	0	0	0	0	0	0.0	0	0	0	0	Pitch 106+	.409	22	9	2	0	2	5	0	5	.435	.773
4 Days Rest	4.48	4	5	0	15	15	86.1	81	8	30	64	First Pitch	.310	113	35	8	0	3	20	3	0	.341	.460
5+ Days Rest	2.83	7	3	0	14	14	92.1	94	6	19	57	Ahead in Count	.180	305	55	14	1	3	16	0	105	.188	.262
vs. AL	7.59	1	1	0	2	2	10.2	13	1	3	7	Behind in Count	.362	141	51	9	0	5	19	26	0	.459	.532
vs. NL	3.38	10	7	0	27	27	168.0	162	13	46	114	Two Strikes	.154	273	42	11	2	1	16	20	121	.211	.220
Pre-All Star	2.82	6	5	0	17	17	115.0	110	7	27	65	Pre-All Star	.255	432	110	24	0	7	36	27	65	.306	.359
Post-All Star	5.09	5	3	0	12	12	63.2	65	7	22	56	Post-All Star	.266	244	65	16	2	7	33	22	56	.330	.434

Marty Cordova — Twins Age 28 – Bats Right

	Avg	G	AB	R	H	2B	3B	HR	RBI	BB	SO	HBP	GDP	SB	CS	OBP	SLG	IBB	SH	SF	#Pit	#P/PA	GB	FB	G/F
1997 Season	.246	103	378	44	93	18	4	15	51	30	92	3	13	5	3	.305	.434	2	0	2	1591	3.85	135	100	1.35
Career (1995-1997)	.282	385	1459	222	411	91	9	55	246	135	299	21	41	36	15	.348	.469	7	0	16	6066	3.72	553	389	1.42

1997 Season

	Avg	AB	H	2B	3B	HR	RBI	BB	SO	OBP	SLG		Avg	AB	H	2B	3B	HR	RBI	BB	SO	OBP	SLG
vs. Left	.212	99	21	5	1	7	20	10	24	.284	.495	First Pitch	.234	64	15	4	1	2	7	2	0	.258	.422
vs. Right	.258	279	72	13	3	8	31	20	68	.313	.412	Ahead in Count	.339	59	20	3	1	5	14	10	0	.443	.678
Groundball	.316	79	25	3	3	5	13	3	22	.357	.620	Behind in Count	.217	175	38	7	1	5	17	0	68	.225	.354
Flyball	.320	50	16	4	0	3	6	5	14	.382	.580	Two Strikes	.208	192	40	7	2	6	25	18	92	.278	.359
Home	.219	183	40	8	2	4	23	17	47	.291	.350	Batting #6	.260	150	39	6	2	8	23	12	36	.315	.487
Away	.272	195	53	10	2	11	28	13	45	.319	.513	Batting #7	.263	114	30	6	1	6	19	8	28	.312	.491
Day	.258	97	25	5	1	0	7	8	27	.315	.330	Other	.211	114	24	6	1	1	9	10	28	.286	.307
Night	.242	281	68	13	3	15	44	22	65	.302	.470	March/April	.280	25	7	3	0	1	4	5	3	.400	.520
Grass	.271	166	45	7	2	9	24	11	39	.318	.500	May	.300	20	6	0	0	2	6	1	6	.333	.600
Turf	.226	212	48	11	2	6	27	19	53	.295	.382	June	.232	82	19	4	0	2	9	7	18	.292	.354
Pre-All Star	.269	145	39	8	0	5	19	15	29	.338	.428	July	.263	76	20	4	0	5	15	5	18	.309	.513
Post-All Star	.232	233	54	10	4	10	32	15	63	.285	.438	August	.202	84	17	4	2	1	7	3	29	.250	.333
Scoring Posn	.214	98	21	6	1	3	30	5	24	.255	.388	Sept/Oct	.264	91	24	3	2	4	10	9	18	.330	.473
Close & Late	.365	52	19	3	1	4	11	4	10	.404	.692	vs. AL	.246	325	80	13	4	14	46	28	80	.310	.440
None on/out	.235	81	19	2	1	3	3	7	15	.295	.395	vs. NL	.245	53	13	5	0	1	5	2	12	.273	.396

1997 By Position

Position	Avg	AB	H	2B	3B	HR	RBI	BB	SO	OBP	SLG	G	GS	Innings	PO	A	E	DP	Fld Pct	Rng Fctr	In Zone	Zone Outs	Zone Rtg	MLB Zone
As lf	.243	367	89	18	3	15	51	29	87	.302	.431	101	99	863.2	214	12	2	2	.991	2.36	245	201	.820	.805

Career (1995-1997)

	Avg	AB	H	2B	3B	HR	RBI	BB	SO	OBP	SLG		Avg	AB	H	2B	3B	HR	RBI	BB	SO	OBP	SLG
vs. Left	.284	352	100	23	4	14	73	39	73	.362	.491	First Pitch	.368	280	103	23	2	16	61	6	0	.377	.636
vs. Right	.281	1107	311	68	5	41	173	96	226	.343	.463	Ahead in Count	.369	241	89	15	2	14	52	52	0	.480	.622
Groundball	.319	370	118	29	6	11	60	25	76	.373	.519	Behind in Count	.218	647	141	33	3	17	83	0	236	.237	.357
Flyball	.228	202	46	11	0	12	33	24	54	.315	.460	Two Strikes	.210	672	141	33	5	16	88	77	299	.304	.345
Home	.282	705	199	43	5	30	133	74	158	.358	.485	Batting #4	.282	524	148	38	2	13	98	52	89	.354	.437
Away	.281	754	212	48	4	25	113	61	141	.338	.455	Batting #5	.303	522	158	32	2	23	87	47	104	.366	.504

Career (1995-1997)

	Avg	AB	H	2B	3B	HR	RBI	BB	SO	OBP	SLG		Avg	AB	H	2B	3B	HR	RBI	BB	SO	OBP	SLG
Day	.265	411	109	33	1	9	59	48	97	.347	.416	Other	.254	413	105	21	5	19	61	36	106	.316	.467
Night	.288	1048	302	58	8	46	187	87	202	.348	.490	March/April	.333	108	36	11	2	3	23	21	23	.446	.556
Grass	.280	636	178	35	4	21	97	50	119	.334	.447	May	.278	223	62	9	0	12	40	15	40	.328	.480
Turf	.283	823	233	56	5	34	149	85	180	.358	.487	June	.283	279	79	23	0	6	41	25	61	.347	.430
Pre-All Star	.289	664	192	45	2	24	112	68	133	.360	.471	July	.292	257	75	16	0	13	50	23	51	.352	.506
Post-All Star	.275	795	219	46	7	31	134	67	166	.337	.468	August	.235	298	70	16	3	10	44	22	73	.298	.409
Scoring Posn	.272	427	116	34	4	12	175	42	101	.337	.454	Sept/Oct	.303	294	89	16	4	11	48	29	51	.369	.497
Close & Late	.269	201	54	8	1	10	32	18	49	.336	.468	vs. AL	.283	1406	398	86	9	54	241	133	287	.350	.472
None on/out	.290	355	103	22	1	12	12	30	65	.351	.459	vs. NL	.245	53	13	5	0	1	5	2	12	.273	.396

Batter vs. Pitcher (career)

Hits Best Against	Avg	AB	H	2B	3B	HR	RBI	BB	SO	OBP	SLG	Hits Worst Against	Avg	AB	H	2B	3B	HR	RBI	BB	SO	OBP	SLG
Ariel Prieto	.455	11	5	2	0	0	2	2	0	.538	.636	Mark Gubicza	.000	15	0	0	0	0	1	1	1	.063	.000
Shawn Boskie	.400	15	6	1	0	1	2	0	0	.400	.667	Darren Oliver	.000	11	0	0	0	0	0	2	3	.154	.000
Bobby Witt	.364	11	4	0	0	1	3	1	1	.417	.636	David Wells	.083	12	1	1	0	0	0	0	2	.083	.167
Tim Belcher	.313	16	5	1	0	3	3	4	3	.450	.938	Kevin Appier	.083	12	1	0	0	0	1	1	5	.154	.083
Alex Fernandez	.308	13	4	1	0	1	4	3	2	.444	.615	David Cone	.111	9	1	0	0	0		2	3	.273	.111

Rheal Cormier — Expos — Age 31 – Pitches Left (groundball pitcher)

	ERA	W	L	Sv	G	GS	IP	BB	SO	Avg	H	2B	3B	HR	RBI	OBP	SLG	CG	ShO	Sup	QS	#P/S	SB	CS	GB	FB	G/F
1997 Season	33.75	0	1	0	1	1	1.1	1	0	.500	4	0	0	1	3	.556	.875	0	0	0.00	0	32	0	0	4	1	1.00
Last Five Years	4.39	24	24	0	127	68	461.0	107	270	.280	503	99	11	53	213	.325	.436	2	1	4.90	29	84	18	16	743	442	1.68

1997 Season

	ERA	W	L	Sv	G	GS	IP	H	HR	BB	SO		Avg	AB	H	2B	3B	HR	RBI	BB	SO	OBP	SLG
Home	33.75	0	1	0	1	1	1.1	4	1	1	0	vs. Left	.500	2	1	0	0	0	0	0	0	.500	.500
Away	0.00	0	0	0	0	0	0.0	0	0	0	0	vs. Right	.500	6	3	0	0	1	3	1	0	.571	1.000

Last Five Years

	ERA	W	L	Sv	G	GS	IP	H	HR	BB	SO		Avg	AB	H	2B	3B	HR	RBI	BB	SO	OBP	SLG
Home	3.97	14	13	0	59	33	233.2	226	23	51	142	vs. Left	.244	389	95	15	2	6	32	20	66	.285	.339
Away	4.83	10	11	0	68	35	227.1	277	30	56	128	vs. Right	.290	1407	408	84	9	47	181	87	204	.335	.463
Day	4.82	7	4	0	38	20	134.1	157	18	22	76	Inning 1-6	.275	1452	400	83	8	45	180	86	223	.320	.437
Night	4.22	17	20	0	89	48	326.2	346	35	85	194	Inning 7+	.299	344	103	16	3	8	33	21	47	.342	.433
Grass	4.07	10	10	0	66	27	203.1	229	22	49	116	None on	.275	1065	293	65	6	27	27	62	178	.320	.423
Turf	4.65	14	14	0	61	41	257.2	274	31	58	154	Runners on	.287	731	210	34	5	26	186	45	92	.330	.454
March/April	5.31	4	5	0	16	16	84.2	88	10	14	60	Scoring Posn	.247	421	104	17	5	10	145	32	53	.303	.382
May	3.56	3	3	0	28	13	93.2	94	7	25	43	Close & Late	.265	166	44	8	1	1	11	9	29	.315	.343
June	4.48	6	4	0	20	9	64.1	77	7	19	35	None on/out	.305	472	144	31	1	16	16	25	75	.347	.477
July	3.90	3	4	0	27	8	80.2	88	10	14	54	vs. 1st Batr (relief)	.283	53	15	4	0	0	1	5	12	.345	.358
August	5.16	5	8	0	17	16	89.0	106	15	23	47	1st Inning Pitched	.286	444	127	24	5	6	59	23	71	.319	.403
Sept/Oct	3.70	3	0	0	19	6	48.2	50	4	12	31	First 75 Pitches	.279	1536	429	83	8	43	176	86	227	.321	.428
Starter	4.58	20	21	0	68	68	379.2	416	49	90	223	Pitch 76-90	.264	163	43	8	0	5	19	11	31	.316	.405
Reliever	3.54	4	3	0	59	0	81.1	87	4	17	47	Pitch 91-105	.342	76	26	5	3	4	16	6	9	.393	.645
0-3 Days Rest (Start)	2.84	1	1	0	4	4	25.1	24	3	1	18	Pitch 106+	.238	21	5	3	0	1	2	4	3	.360	.524
4 Days Rest	3.85	11	9	0	31	31	184.2	204	21	36	100	First Pitch	.359	323	116	28	3	13	60	6	0	.382	.585
5+ Days Rest	5.62	8	11	0	33	33	169.2	188	25	53	105	Ahead in Count	.204	706	144	21	3	9	49	0	230	.214	.280
vs. AL	4.07	7	5	0	48	12	115.0	131	12	31	69	Behind in Count	.333	436	145	32	3	19	66	49	0	.394	.550
vs. NL	4.50	17	19	0	79	56	346.0	372	41	76	201	Two Strikes	.192	717	138	22	5	13	53	52	270	.253	.291
Pre-All Star	4.19	15	13	0	72	42	275.0	287	29	62	161	Pre-All Star	.272	1056	287	51	7	29	122	62	161	.316	.416
Post-All Star	4.69	9	11	0	55	26	186.0	216	24	45	109	Post-All Star	.292	740	216	48	4	24	91	45	109	.336	.465

Pitcher vs. Batter (career)

Pitches Best Vs.	Avg	AB	H	2B	3B	HR	RBI	BB	SO	OBP	SLG	Pitches Worst Vs.	Avg	AB	H	2B	3B	HR	RBI	BB	SO	OBP	SLG
Rey Sanchez	.000	10	0	0	0	0	0	1	0	.091	.000	Joe Oliver	.533	15	8	1	0	1	3	0	0	.533	.800
Mark Lemke	.071	14	1	0	0	0	0	1	0	.133	.071	Barry Larkin	.500	12	6	1	0	1	1	0	0	.538	.833
Darren Daulton	.091	11	1	0	0	0	0	0	4	.091	.091	Benito Santiago	.417	12	5	0	1	3	7	1	2	.462	1.333
Walt Weiss	.091	11	1	0	0	0	0	1	2	.167	.091	Sammy Sosa	.417	12	5	1	0	4	8	1	1	.462	1.500
Hal Morris	.125	16	2	0	0	0	1	0	4	.125	.125	Greg Colbrunn	.400	10	4	0	0	2	2	1	2	.455	1.000

Jim Corsi — Red Sox — Age 36 – Pitches Right (groundball pitcher)

	ERA	W	L	Sv	G	GS	IP	BB	SO	Avg	H	2B	3B	HR	RBI	OBP	SLG	GF	IR	IRS	Hld	SvOp	SB	CS	GB	FB	G/F
1997 Season	3.43	5	3	2	52	0	57.2	21	40	.255	56	10	3	1	31	.327	.341	14	41	14	11	9	1	0	105	37	2.84
Last Five Years	3.71	13	9	7	162	0	196.2	91	116	.259	186	31	5	10	93	.346	.357	46	111	33	35	19	5	4	375	110	3.41

1997 Season

	ERA	W	L	Sv	G	GS	IP	H	HR	BB	SO		Avg	AB	H	2B	3B	HR	RBI	BB	SO	OBP	SLG
Home	2.78	5	1	1	31	0	35.2	34	0	17	22	vs. Left	.221	86	19	5	3	0	15	12	21	.324	.349
Away	4.50	0	2	1	21	0	22.0	22	1	4	18	vs. Right	.276	134	37	5	0	1	16	9	19	.329	.336
Day	5.85	3	2	0	17	0	20.0	26	0	9	14	Inning 1-6	.190	21	4	0	0	0	3	0	4	.190	.190
Night	2.15	2	1	2	35	0	37.2	30	1	12	26	Inning 7+	.261	199	52	10	3	1	28	21	36	.339	.357
Grass	3.14	5	2	1	48	0	51.2	47	1	20	37	None on	.253	99	25	4	1	1		8	21	.327	.343
Turf	6.00	0	1	1	4	0	6.0	9	0	1	3	Runners on	.256	121	31	6	2	0	30	13	19	.326	.339
March/April	8.31	0	1	0	9	0	8.2	11	1	6	6	Scoring Posn	.253	79	20	2	1	0	28	12	14	.347	.304
May	3.77	1	0	0	11	0	14.1	14	0	3	8	Close & Late	.267	131	35	8	1	1	24	15	26	.344	.366
June	0.00	0	0	0	1	0	1.2	3	0	0	0	None on/out	.271	48	13	3	1	1		4	9	.327	.438
July	1.46	1	0	1	12	0	12.1	12	0	4	8	vs. 1st Batr (relief)	.240	50	12	4	1	0	11	1	11	.250	.360

	ERA	W	L	Sv	G	GS	IP	H	HR	BB	SO		Avg	AB	H	2B	3B	HR	RBI	BB	SO	OBP	SLG
August	0.00	1	0	1	8	0	11.0	5	0	3	11	1st Inning Pitched	.244	164	40	9	2	0	26	17	30	.317	.323
Sept/Oct	5.59	2	2	0	11	0	9.2	11	0	5	7	First 15 Pitches	.248	137	34	8	1	0	20	14	25	.321	.321
Starter	0.00	0	0	0	0	0	0.0	0	0	0	0	Pitch 16-30	.264	72	19	2	1	1	8	6	12	.338	.361
Reliever	3.43	5	3	2	52	0	57.2	56	1	21	40	Pitch 31-45	.273	11	3	0	1	0	3	1	3	.333	.455
0 Days rest (Relief)	3.00	1	1	0	12	0	12.0	10	1	5	12	Pitch 46+	.000	0	0	0	0	0	0	0	0	.000	.000
1 or 2 Days rest	3.82	3	1	1	28	0	30.2	31	0	12	17	First Pitch	.323	31	10	2	1	0	9	7	0	.447	.452
3+ Days rest	3.00	1	1	1	12	0	15.0	15	0	4	11	Ahead in Count	.202	89	18	4	0	0	9	0	31	.226	.247
vs. AL	3.83	5	3	1	48	0	51.2	51	1	19	37	Behind in Count	.317	41	13	1	0	0	5	6	0	.388	.341
vs. NL	0.00	0	0	1	4	0	6.0	5	0	2	3	Two Strikes	.214	98	21	6	1	0	11	8	40	.291	.296
Pre-All Star	4.67	1	1	1	22	0	27.0	31	1	9	15	Pre-All Star	.290	107	31	3	1	1	17	9	15	.353	.364
Post-All Star	2.35	4	2	1	30	0	30.2	25	0	12	25	Post-All Star	.221	113	25	7	2	0	14	12	25	.302	.319

	ERA	W	L	Sv	G	GS	IP	H	HR	BB	SO		Avg	AB	H	2B	3B	HR	RBI	BB	SO	OBP	SLG
Home	3.42	10	4	2	81	0	97.1	91	3	48	57	vs. Left	.275	327	90	18	5	3	50	43	48	.364	.388
Away	3.99	3	5	5	81	0	99.1	95	7	43	59	vs. Right	.245	392	96	13	0	7	43	48	68	.331	.332
Day	3.91	8	2	0	58	0	71.1	70	3	36	45	Inning 1-6	.265	102	27	3	1	1	14	8	15	.327	.343
Night	3.59	5	7	7	104	0	125.1	116	7	55	71	Inning 7+	.258	617	159	28	4	9	79	83	101	.349	.360
Grass	3.60	13	6	3	143	0	170.0	160	7	81	101	None on	.255	357	91	13	2	6	6	45	56	.343	.353
Turf	4.39	0	3	4	19	0	26.2	26	3	10	15	Runners on	.262	362	95	18	3	4	87	46	60	.349	.362
March/April	5.06	2	1	1	20	0	26.2	25	4	18	20	Scoring Posn	.238	223	53	8	2	3	80	36	42	.347	.332
May	3.74	2	1	2	33	0	43.1	41	1	18	21	Close & Late	.246	346	85	12	1	8	47	52	56	.347	.355
June	1.69	2	3	1	26	0	37.1	32	1	16	14	None on/out	.251	167	42	6	1	3	3	20	28	.332	.353
July	4.34	3	1	2	25	0	29.0	33	1	12	20	vs. 1st Batr (relief)	.236	148	35	9	1	3	29	9	27	.275	.372
August	3.54	1	0	1	26	0	28.0	24	2	10	21	1st Inning Pitched	.251	501	126	22	4	6	76	65	79	.339	.347
Sept/Oct	4.45	3	3	0	31	0	32.1	31	1	17	20	First 15 Pitches	.260	431	112	18	2	6	58	51	64	.339	.353
Starter	0.00	0	0	0	0	0	0.0	0	0	0	0	Pitch 16-30	.265	234	62	11	2	3	23	29	38	.352	.368
Reliever	3.71	13	9	7	162	0	196.2	186	10	91	116	Pitch 31-45	.208	48	10	1	1	1	11	8	12	.345	.333
0 Days rest (Relief)	3.86	3	1	0	26	0	28.0	25	3	9	19	Pitch 46+	.333	6	2	1	0	0	1	3	2	.556	.500
1 or 2 Days rest	4.19	6	5	6	90	0	105.1	107	6	53	66	First Pitch	.326	89	29	8	1	0	19	14	0	.419	.438
3+ Days rest	2.84	4	3	1	46	0	63.1	54	1	29	31	Ahead in Count	.200	280	56	8	2	1	21	0	87	.212	.254
vs. AL	3.49	13	7	6	143	0	170.1	153	9	79	106	Behind in Count	.354	164	58	7	0	6	27	40	0	.476	.506
vs. NL	5.13	0	2	1	19	0	26.1	33	1	12	10	Two Strikes	.189	307	58	11	3	3	30	37	116	.285	.274
Pre-All Star	3.93	6	6	5	86	0	112.1	109	6	57	57	Pre-All Star	.268	407	109	15	2	6	55	57	59	.362	.359
Post-All Star	3.42	7	3	2	76	0	84.1	77	4	34	57	Post-All Star	.247	312	77	16	3	4	38	34	57	.326	.356

Pitches Best Vs.	Avg	AB	H	2B	3B	HR	RBI	BB	SO	OBP	SLG	Pitches Worst Vs.	Avg	AB	H	2B	3B	HR	RBI	BB	SO	OBP	SLG
Chuck Knoblauch	.091	11	1	0	0	0	1	1	3	.167	.091	Jay Buhner	.400	10	4	0	0	0	1	2	3	.500	.400
Joe Carter	.100	10	1	0	0	0	2	2	1	.250	.100												

Craig Counsell — Marlins
Age 27 – Bats Left

	Avg	G	AB	R	H	2B	3B	HR	RBI	BB	SO	HBP	GDP	SB	CS	OBP	SLG	IBB	SH	SF	#Pit	#P/PA	GB	FB	G/F
1997 Season	.299	52	164	20	49	9	2	1	16	18	17	3	5	1	1	.376	.396	2	3	1	697	3.69	74	37	2.00
Career (1995-1997)	.297	55	165	20	49	9	2	1	16	19	17	3	5	1	1	.378	.394	2	3	1	705	3.69	75	37	2.03

1997 Season

	Avg	AB	H	2B	3B	HR	RBI	BB	SO	OBP	SLG		Avg	AB	H	2B	3B	HR	RBI	BB	SO	OBP	SLG
vs. Left	.308	13	4	2	0	0	1	2	1	.471	.462	Scoring Posn	.349	43	15	2	1	1	16	4	2	.396	.512
vs. Right	.298	151	45	7	2	1	15	16	16	.367	.391	Close & Late	.172	29	5	1	0	0	1	5	3	.314	.207
Home	.293	82	24	1	1	1	10	10	5	.372	.366	None on/out	.233	43	10	2	1	0	0	4	5	.298	.326
Away	.305	82	25	8	1	0	6	8	12	.380	.427	Batting #7	.429	7	3	0	0	0	0	1	0	.500	.429
First Pitch	.333	21	7	1	0	0	5	2	0	.391	.381	Batting #8	.301	153	46	9	2	1	16	17	17	.379	.405
Ahead in Count	.286	35	10	4	0	0	0	12	0	.479	.400	Other	.000	4	0	0	0	0	0	0	0	.000	.000
Behind in Count	.293	82	24	3	2	1	9	0	17	.289	.415	Pre-All Star	.000	0	0	0	0	0	0	0	0	.000	.000
Two Strikes	.295	78	23	4	2	1	11	4	17	.325	.436	Post-All Star	.299	164	49	9	2	1	16	18	17	.376	.396

Tim Crabtree — Blue Jays
Age 28 – Pitches Right (groundball pitcher)

	ERA	W	L	Sv	G	GS	IP	BB	SO	Avg	H	2B	3B	HR	RBI	SLG	GF	IR	IRS	Hld	SvOp	SB	CS	GB	FB	G/F
1997 Season	7.08	2	3	2	37	0	40.2	17	26	.374	65	10	1	7	32	.431 .563	16	12	5	8	5	2	1	68	37	1.84
Career (1995-1997)	3.99	8	8	3	121	0	140.0	52	104	.278	154	28	2	12	79	.345 .401	56	49	21	26	12	9	1	236	102	2.31

1997 Season

	ERA	W	L	Sv	G	GS	IP	H	HR	BB	SO		Avg	AB	H	2B	3B	HR	RBI	BB	SO	OBP	SLG
Home	9.00	2	1	1	14	0	15.0	26	1	6	7	vs. Left	.346	78	27	4	1	4	19	6	10	.384	.577
Away	5.96	1	2	1	23	0	25.2	39	6	11	19	vs. Right	.396	96	38	6	0	3	13	11	16	.468	.552
Starter	0.00	0	0	0	0	0	0.0	0	0	0	0	Scoring Posn	.358	53	19	3	1	1	23	7	9	.429	.509
Reliever	7.08	3	3	2	37	0	40.2	65	7	17	26	Close & Late	.338	65	22	3	0	1	5	8	9	.419	.431
0 Days rest (Relief)	4.82	1	1	0	7	0	9.1	17	1	3	7	None on/out	.410	39	16	3	0	1	1	4	5	.465	.564
1 or 2 Days rest	9.95	1	1	1	17	0	19.0	34	4	8	15	First Pitch	.500	28	14	2	0	2	5	3	0	.548	.786
3+ Days rest	4.38	1	1	1	13	0	12.1	14	2	6	7	Ahead in Count	.319	72	23	5	0	2	8	0	21	.329	.472
Pre-All Star	8.46	2	2	2	21	0	22.1	36	4	9	12	Behind in Count	.405	37	15	0	0	3	12	8	0	.489	.649
Post-All Star	5.40	1	1	0	16	0	18.1	29	3	8	14	Two Strikes	.290	69	20	5	0	1	4	6	26	.347	.406

	ERA	W	L	Sv	G	GS	IP	H	HR	BB	SO		Avg	AB	H	2B	3B	HR	RBI	BB	SO	OBP	SLG
Home	3.60	6	5	2	54	0	65.0	71	4	26	40	vs. Left	.280	268	75	16	1	6	41	22	55	.336	.414

Career (1995-1997)

	ERA	W	L	Sv	G	GS	IP	H	HR	BB	SO		Avg	AB	H	2B	3B	HR	RBI	BB	SO	OBP	SLG
Away	4.32	2	3	1	67	0	75.0	83	8	26	64	vs. Right	.276	286	79	12	1	6	38	30	49	.353	.388
Day	1.99	3	3	0	42	0	49.2	45	2	13	39	Inning 1-6	.346	26	9	2	0	1	7	3	3	.400	.538
Night	5.08	5	5	3	79	0	90.1	109	10	39	65	Inning 7+	.275	528	145	26	2	11	72	49	101	.342	.394
Grass	4.61	2	3	0	59	0	66.1	78	6	25	59	None on	.263	293	77	12	0	7	7	21	66	.316	.375
Turf	3.42	6	5	3	62	0	73.2	76	6	27	45	Runners on	.295	261	77	16	2	5	72	31	38	.374	.429
March/April	2.45	2	2	1	18	0	18.1	15	1	7	10	Scoring Posn	.280	168	47	7	2	1	60	21	24	.360	.363
May	6.18	1	1	1	22	0	27.2	36	4	6	19	Close & Late	.290	241	70	13	1	4	33	30	46	.377	.402
June	3.26	2	1	1	16	0	19.1	20	1	7	17	None on/out	.264	125	33	6	0	4	4	11	25	.328	.408
July	2.93	2	1	0	24	0	27.2	28	2	9	22	vs. 1st Batr (relief)	.324	105	34	5	0	4	14	13	18	.397	.486
August	4.76	1	3	0	25	0	28.1	37	2	18	23	1st Inning Pitched	.257	412	106	21	2	8	56	37	80	.323	.376
Sept/Oct	3.38	0	0	0	16	0	18.2	18	2	5	13	First 15 Pitches	.267	341	91	19	2	7	38	28	67	.326	.396
Starter	0.00	0	0	0	0	0	0.0	0	0	0	0	Pitch 16-30	.274	168	46	6	0	3	26	18	27	.351	.363
Reliever	3.99	8	8	3	121	0	140.0	154	12	52	104	Pitch 31-45	.386	44	17	3	0	2	15	6	10	.462	.591
0 Days rest (Relief)	2.45	2	3	1	21	0	25.2	31	1	10	17	Pitch 46+	.000	1	0	0	0	0	0	0	0	.000	.000
1 or 2 Days rest	5.14	3	3	1	59	0	70.0	84	8	23	53	First Pitch	.321	78	25	7	0	2	11	6	0	.360	.487
3+ Days rest	3.05	3	2	1	41	0	44.1	39	3	19	34	Ahead in Count	.245	265	65	14	0	6	30	0	84	.254	.366
vs. AL	3.91	8	8	3	118	0	135.2	148	12	51	98	Behind in Count	.327	104	34	1	1	4	26	29	0	.471	.471
vs. NL	6.23	0	0	0	3	0	4.1	6	0	1	6	Two Strikes	.210	248	52	12	0	3	21	17	104	.266	.294
Pre-All Star	4.11	5	5	3	62	0	70.0	77	7	21	50	Pre-All Star	.278	277	77	9	1	7	36	21	50	.331	.394
Post-All Star	3.86	3	3	0	59	0	70.0	77	5	31	54	Post-All Star	.278	277	77	19	1	5	43	31	54	.358	.408

Joe Crawford — Mets   Age 28 – Pitches Left

	ERA	W	L	Sv	G	GS	IP	BB	SO	Avg	H	2B	3B	HR	RBI	OBP	SLG	GF	IR	IRS	Hld	SvOp	SB	CS	GB	FB	G/F
1997 Season	3.30	4	3	0	19	2	46.1	13	25	.216	36	5	0	7	21	.272	.371	9	4	3	0	0	3	2	62	50	1.24

1997 Season

	ERA	W	L	Sv	G	GS	IP	H	HR	BB	SO		Avg	AB	H	2B	3B	HR	RBI	BB	SO	OBP	SLG
Home	2.30	4	1	0	11	1	31.1	21	3	7	18	vs. Left	.323	31	10	2	0	2	7	3	3	.382	.581
Away	5.40	0	2	0	8	1	15.0	15	4	6	7	vs. Right	.191	136	26	3	0	5	14	10	22	.247	.324

Doug Creek — Giants   Age 29 – Pitches Left (flyball pitcher)

	ERA	W	L	Sv	G	GS	IP	BB	SO	Avg	H	2B	3B	HR	RBI	OBP	SLG	CG	ShO	Sup	QS	#P/S	SB	CS	GB	FB	G/F
1997 Season	6.75	1	2	0	3	3	13.1	14	14	.240	12	4	1	3	0	.406	.420	0	0	6.75	0	94	1	1	14	15	0.93
Career (1995-1997)	5.93	1	4	0	72	3	68.1	49	62	.230	59	15	3	12	46	.358	.453	0	0	3.82	0	94	6	3	65	99	0.66

1997 Season

	ERA	W	L	Sv	G	GS	IP	H	HR	BB	SO		Avg	AB	H	2B	3B	HR	RBI	BB	SO	OBP	SLG
Home	6.17	1	1	0	2	2	11.2	8	1	12	13	vs. Left	.300	10	3	1	1	0	3	2	3	.417	.600
Away	10.80	0	1	0	1	1	1.2	4	0	2	1	vs. Right	.225	40	9	3	0	1	5	12	11	.404	.375

Career (1995-1997)

	ERA	W	L	Sv	G	GS	IP	H	HR	BB	SO		Avg	AB	H	2B	3B	HR	RBI	BB	SO	OBP	SLG
Home	5.94	1	3	0	30	2	33.1	32	4	28	32	vs. Left	.237	97	23	6	2	4	17	13	24	.333	.464
Away	5.91	0	1	0	42	1	35.0	32	8	21	30	vs. Right	.226	159	36	9	1	8	29	36	38	.372	.447
Day	6.75	0	1	0	35	1	30.2	27	4	28	29	Inning 1-6	.218	87	19	4	2	5	16	19	22	.364	.483
Night	5.26	1	3	0	37	2	37.2	37	8	21	33	Inning 7+	.237	169	40	11	1	7	30	30	40	.355	.438
Grass	6.02	1	4	0	56	3	55.1	51	9	42	47	None on	.198	131	26	5	2	8	8	28	39	.344	.450
Turf	5.54	0	0	0	16	0	13.0	8	3	7	15	Runners on	.264	125	33	10	1	4	38	21	23	.374	.456
March/April	2.53	0	0	0	11	0	10.2	7	0	8	6	Scoring Posn	.306	72	22	6	1	2	32	16	15	.432	.500
May	11.25	0	1	0	12	0	8.0	13	4	7	7	Close & Late	.244	45	11	2	0	2	8	9	10	.370	.422
June	5.40	0	0	0	10	0	6.2	8	1	6	3	None on/out	.150	60	9	2	1	2	2	10	19	.282	.317
July	4.94	1	2	0	15	3	23.2	18	2	18	21	vs. 1st Batr (relief)	.190	58	11	3	0	2	9	9	17	.319	.345
August	11.25	0	0	0	10	0	8.0	9	5	3	10	1st Inning Pitched	.254	193	49	12	3	11	41	32	40	.366	.518
Sept/Oct	3.97	0	0	0	14	0	11.1	4	0	7	15	First 75 Pitches	.231	238	55	15	3	11	45	46	59	.360	.458
Starter	6.75	1	2	0	3	3	13.1	12	1	14	14	Pitch 76-90	.125	8	1	0	0	1	1	0	2	.125	.500
Reliever	5.73	0	2	0	69	0	55.0	47	11	35	48	Pitch 91-105	.200	5	1	0	0	0	0	1	1	.333	.200
0-3 Days Rest (Start)	0.00	0	0	0	0	0	0.0	0	0	0	0	Pitch 106+	.400	5	2	0	0	0	0	2	0	.571	.400
4 Days Rest	0.00	0	0	0	0	0	0.0	0	0	0	0	First Pitch	.357	28	10	3	1	0	4	2	0	.400	.536
5+ Days Rest	6.75	1	2	0	3	3	13.1	12	1	14	14	Ahead in Count	.155	116	18	4	0	3	12	0	50	.162	.267
vs. AL	5.40	1	0	0	1	1	6.2	4	1	5	7	Behind in Count	.356	59	21	7	1	6	22	24	0	.542	.814
vs. NL	5.98	0	4	0	71	2	61.2	55	11	44	55	Two Strikes	.142	134	19	1	0	5	16	23	62	.272	.261
Pre-All Star	5.97	1	1	0	37	1	34.2	35	6	28	26	Pre-All Star	.267	131	35	9	1	6	28	28	26	.400	.489
Post-All Star	5.88	0	3	0	35	2	33.2	24	6	21	36	Post-All Star	.192	125	24	6	2	6	18	21	36	.313	.416

Felipe Crespo — Blue Jays   Age 25 – Bats Both

	Avg	G	AB	R	H	2B	3B	HR	RBI	BB	SO	HBP	GDP	SB	CS	OBP	SLG	IBB	SH	SF	#Pit	#P/PA	GB	FB	G/F
1997 Season	.286	12	28	3	8	0	1	1	5	2	4	0	1	0	0	.333	.464	0	1	0	107	3.45	11	10	1.10
Career (1996-1997)	.221	34	77	9	17	4	1	1	9	14	17	3	1	1	0	.362	.338	0	2	1	334	3.52	24	24	1.00

1997 Season

	Avg	AB	H	2B	3B	HR	RBI	BB	SO	OBP	SLG		Avg	AB	H	2B	3B	HR	RBI	BB	SO	OBP	SLG
vs. Left	.222	9	2	0	1	1	2	0	2	.222	.778	Scoring Posn	.286	7	2	0	0	0	3	0	2	.286	.286
vs. Right	.316	19	6	0	0	0	3	2	2	.381	.316	Close & Late	.222	9	2	0	0	0	2	1	1	.300	.222

Tripp Cromer — Dodgers
Age 30 – Bats Right

	Avg	G	AB	R	H	2B	3B	HR	RBI	BB	SO	HBP	GDP	SB	CS	OBP	SLG	IBB	SH	SF	#Pit	#P/PA	GB	FB	G/F
1997 Season	.291	28	86	8	25	3	0	4	20	6	16	0	2	0	1	.333	.465	3	2	1	307	3.23	25	26	0.96
Career (1993-1997)	.231	145	454	46	105	22	0	9	38	21	88	4	16	0	1	.268	.339	5	3	6	1596	3.27	183	108	1.69

1997 Season

	Avg	AB	H	2B	3B	HR	RBI	BB	SO	OBP	SLG		Avg	AB	H	2B	3B	HR	RBI	BB	SO	OBP	SLG
vs. Left	.321	28	9	1	0	3	8	2	4	.367	.679	Scoring Posn	.583	24	14	3	0	1	17	5	2	.633	.833
vs. Right	.276	58	16	2	0	1	12	4	12	.317	.362	Close & Late	.200	5	1	0	0	0	2	0	1	.167	.200

Career (1993-1997)

	Avg	AB	H	2B	3B	HR	RBI	BB	SO	OBP	SLG		Avg	AB	H	2B	3B	HR	RBI	BB	SO	OBP	SLG
vs. Left	.220	123	27	8	0	5	14	6	21	.258	.407	First Pitch	.317	101	32	7	0	0	7	4	0	.343	.386
vs. Right	.236	331	78	14	0	4	24	15	67	.272	.314	Ahead in Count	.341	88	30	5	0	7	17	5	0	.379	.636
Groundball	.193	119	23	5	0	1	6	5	22	.261	.178	Behind in Count	.132	197	26	6	0	1	7	0	83	.199	.178
Flyball	.227	66	15	3	0	1	3	3	18	.271	.318	Two Strikes	.146	192	28	6	0	2	9	12	88	.198	.208
Home	.244	209	51	12	0	4	16	11	41	.284	.359	Batting #2	.255	149	38	7	0	3	9	5	29	.280	.362
Away	.220	245	54	10	0	5	22	10	47	.255	.322	Batting #8	.230	217	50	13	0	6	22	14	46	.278	.373
Day	.262	164	43	10	0	5	11	12	21	.320	.415	Other	.193	88	17	2	0	0	7	2	13	.223	.216
Night	.214	290	62	12	0	4	27	9	67	.238	.297	March/April	.200	10	2	1	0	0	0	0	1	.200	.300
Grass	.234	214	50	7	0	7	26	11	36	.272	.364	May	.215	65	14	6	0	4	6	6	13	.282	.492
Turf	.229	240	55	15	0	2	12	10	52	.265	.317	June	.268	112	30	4	0	1	8	6	20	.306	.330
Pre-All Star	.257	237	61	12	0	5	20	14	41	.299	.371	July	.235	153	36	5	0	4	21	5	33	.264	.346
Post-All Star	.203	217	44	10	0	4	18	7	47	.234	.304	August	.200	45	9	2	0	0	2	1	8	.217	.244
Scoring Posn	.256	90	23	4	0	1	28	13	19	.330	.333	Sept/Oct	.203	69	14	4	0	0	1	3	13	.243	.261
Close & Late	.241	54	13	2	0	0	5	0	13	.246	.278	vs. AL	.333	9	3	0	0	0	2	0	2	.333	.333
None on/out	.279	104	29	5	0	4	4	2	14	.292	.442	vs. NL	.229	445	102	22	0	9	36	21	86	.267	.339

Batter vs. Pitcher (career)

Hits Best Against	Avg	AB	H	2B	3B	HR	RBI	BB	SO	OBP	SLG	Hits Worst Against	Avg	AB	H	2B	3B	HR	RBI	BB	SO	OBP	SLG
												Mike Hampton	.091	11	1	0	0	0	0	0	1	.091	.091

Jim Crowell — Reds
Age 24 – Pitches Left

	ERA	W	L	Sv	G	GS	IP	BB	SO	Avg	H	2B	3B	HR	RBI	OBP	SLG	CG	ShO	Sup	QS	#P/S	SB	CS	GB	FB	G/F
1997 Season	9.95	0	1	0	2	1	6.1	5	3	.414	12	2	0	2	6	.500	.690	0	0	5.68	0	117	0	0	11	9	1.22

1997 Season

	ERA	W	L	Sv	G	GS	IP	H	HR	BB	SO		Avg	AB	H	2B	3B	HR	RBI	BB	SO	OBP	SLG
Home	0.00	0	0	0	0	0	0.0	0	0	0	0	vs. Left	.143	7	1	1	0	0	1	0	1	.143	.286
Away	9.95	0	1	0	2	1	6.1	12	2	5	3	vs. Right	.500	22	11	1	0	2	5	5	2	.593	.818

Deivi Cruz — Tigers
Age 23 – Bats Right

	Avg	G	AB	R	H	2B	3B	HR	RBI	BB	SO	HBP	GDP	SB	CS	OBP	SLG	IBB	SH	SF	#Pit	#P/PA	GB	FB	G/F
1997 Season	.241	147	436	35	105	26	0	2	40	14	55	0	9	3	6	.263	.314	0	14	3	1561	3.34	194	103	1.88

1997 Season

	Avg	AB	H	2B	3B	HR	RBI	BB	SO	OBP	SLG		Avg	AB	H	2B	3B	HR	RBI	BB	SO	OBP	SLG
vs. Left	.214	112	24	5	0	0	8	7	17	.258	.259	First Pitch	.388	49	19	6	0	0	6	0	0	.388	.510
vs. Right	.250	324	81	21	0	2	32	7	38	.264	.333	Ahead in Count	.223	103	23	7	0	1	12	9	0	.281	.320
Groundball	.233	86	20	7	0	0	10	3	14	.258	.314	Behind in Count	.198	212	42	8	0	0	12	0	53	.197	.236
Flyball	.269	78	21	7	0	1	6	0	10	.269	.397	Two Strikes	.192	182	35	5	0	0	11	5	55	.213	.220
Home	.227	207	47	13	0	0	17	10	29	.260	.290	Batting #8	.250	16	4	1	0	1	5	0	2	.235	.500
Away	.253	229	58	13	0	2	23	4	26	.265	.336	Batting #9	.239	414	99	24	0	1	35	14	53	.263	.304
Day	.194	165	32	11	0	1	15	4	16	.213	.279	Other	.333	6	2	1	0	0	0	0	0	.333	.500
Night	.269	271	73	15	0	1	25	10	39	.292	.336	March/April	.215	79	17	7	0	0	6	2	9	.235	.304
Grass	.236	381	90	24	0	2	37	13	46	.260	.315	May	.206	68	14	4	0	0	6	1	11	.214	.265
Turf	.273	55	15	2	0	0	3	1	9	.281	.309	June	.200	60	12	3	0	1	9	3	9	.231	.300
Pre-All Star	.215	219	47	15	0	1	21	6	33	.232	.297	July	.281	57	16	3	0	0	2	4	6	.333	.333
Post-All Star	.267	217	58	11	0	1	19	8	22	.293	.332	August	.303	89	27	5	0	0	7	1	7	.311	.360
Scoring Posn	.292	96	28	3	0	0	33	3	13	.304	.323	Sept/Oct	.229	83	19	4	0	1	10	3	13	.256	.313
Close & Late	.214	56	12	1	0	0	6	1	7	.224	.232	vs. AL	.232	397	92	25	0	1	34	13	51	.255	.302
None on/out	.229	109	25	9	0	0	0	2	14	.243	.312	vs. NL	.333	39	13	1	0	1	6	1	4	.341	.436

1997 By Position

Position	Avg	AB	H	2B	3B	HR	RBI	BB	SO	OBP	SLG	G	GS	Innings	PO	A	E	DP	Fld Pct	Rng Fctr	In Zone	Zone Outs	Zone Rtg	MLB Zone
As ss	.241	436	105	26	0	2	40	14	55	.263	.314	147	133	1184.0	194	419	13	95	.979	4.66	461	445	.965	.937

Ivan Cruz — Yankees
Age 30 – Bats Left

	Avg	G	AB	R	H	2B	3B	HR	RBI	BB	SO	HBP	GDP	SB	CS	OBP	SLG	IBB	SH	SF	#Pit	#P/PA	GB	FB	G/F
1997 Season	.250	11	20	0	5	1	0	0	3	2	4	0	0	0	0	.318	.300	0	0	0	89	4.05	7	5	1.40

1997 Season

	Avg	AB	H	2B	3B	HR	RBI	BB	SO	OBP	SLG		Avg	AB	H	2B	3B	HR	RBI	BB	SO	OBP	SLG
vs. Left	.000	4	0	0	0	0	0	0	2	.000	.000	Scoring Posn	.222	9	2	0	0	0	3	0	1	.222	.222
vs. Right	.313	16	5	1	0	0	3	2	2	.389	.375	Close & Late	.200	5	1	0	0	0	2	1	0	.333	.200

Jacob Cruz — Giants
Age 25 – Bats Left

	Avg	G	AB	R	H	2B	3B	HR	RBI	BB	SO	HBP	GDP	SB	CS	OBP	SLG	IBB	SH	SF	#Pit	#P/PA	GB	FB	G/F
1997 Season	.160	16	25	3	4	1	0	0	3	4	0	3	0	0	0	.241	.200	0	0	1	118	4.07	13	5	2.60
Career (1996-1997)	.216	49	102	13	22	4	0	3	13	15	28	2	5	0	1	.325	.343	0	1	1	530	4.38	36	22	1.64

1997 Season

	Avg	AB	H	2B	3B	HR	RBI	BB	SO	OBP	SLG		Avg	AB	H	2B	3B	HR	RBI	BB	SO	OBP	SLG
vs. Left	.500	2	1	0	0	0	1	0	1	.500	.500	Scoring Posn	.143	7	1	0	0	0	3	2	1	.300	.143
vs. Right	.130	23	3	1	0	0	2	3	3	.222	.174	Close & Late	.200	10	2	1	0	0	2	1	2	.273	.300

Nelson Cruz — White Sox
Age 25 – Pitches Right (flyball pitcher)

	ERA	W	L	Sv	G	GS	IP	BB	SO	Avg	H	2B	3B	HR	RBI	OBP	SLG	GF	IR	IRS	Hld	SvOp	SB	CS	GB	FB	G/F
1997 Season	6.49	0	2	0	19	0	26.1	9	23	.274	29	7	0	6	15	.330	.509	5	12	2	6	0	2	0	33	35	0.94

1997 Season

	ERA	W	L	Sv	G	GS	IP	H	HR	BB	SO		Avg	AB	H	2B	3B	HR	RBI	BB	SO	OBP	SLG
Home	2.77	0	1	0	10	0	13.0	9	1	4	12	vs. Left	.213	47	10	4	0	2	4	2	9	.245	.426
Away	10.13	0	1	0	9	0	13.1	20	5	5	11	vs. Right	.322	59	19	3	0	4	11	7	14	.394	.576

Jose Cruz Jr. — Blue Jays
Age 24 – Bats Both

	Avg	G	AB	R	H	2B	3B	HR	RBI	BB	SO	HBP	GDP	SB	CS	OBP	SLG	IBB	SH	SF	#Pit	#P/PA	GB	FB	G/F
1997 Season	.248	104	395	59	98	19	1	26	68	41	117	0	5	7	2	.315	.499	2	1	5	1703	3.85	107	119	0.90

1997 Season

	Avg	AB	H	2B	3B	HR	RBI	BB	SO	OBP	SLG		Avg	AB	H	2B	3B	HR	RBI	BB	SO	OBP	SLG
vs. Left	.258	97	25	4	1	5	18	12	23	.333	.474	First Pitch	.473	55	26	3	0	9	23	2	0	.475	1.018
vs. Right	.245	298	73	15	0	21	50	29	94	.309	.507	Ahead in Count	.415	65	27	3	1	7	18	20	0	.547	.815
Groundball	.244	78	19	3	0	8	18	11	25	.333	.590	Behind in Count	.164	195	32	8	0	8	21	0	93	.163	.328
Flyball	.293	58	17	3	0	5	9	6	15	.359	.603	Two Strikes	.146	212	31	8	0	8	18	19	117	.216	.297
Home	.263	175	46	11	0	11	34	20	47	.332	.514	Batting #3	.218	179	39	6	0	11	28	26	62	.311	.436
Away	.236	220	52	8	1	15	34	21	70	.302	.486	Batting #9	.278	79	22	7	1	5	13	5	16	.318	.582
Day	.262	141	37	5	1	11	26	21	44	.356	.546	Other	.270	137	37	6	0	10	27	10	39	.320	.533
Night	.240	254	61	14	0	15	42	20	73	.291	.472	March/April	.000	0	0	0	0	0	0	0	0	.000	.000
Grass	.239	188	45	7	1	13	29	20	57	.311	.495	May	.000	4	0	0	0	0	1	0	0	.000	.000
Turf	.256	207	53	12	0	13	39	21	60	.319	.502	June	.247	93	23	6	0	6	13	8	27	.307	.505
Pre-All Star	.257	113	29	7	0	9	21	10	29	.317	.558	July	.302	86	26	6	1	6	20	5	18	.337	.605
Post-All Star	.245	282	69	12	1	17	47	31	88	.314	.475	August	.256	117	30	2	0	9	22	18	32	.348	.504
Scoring Posn	.189	111	21	1	0	8	39	20	36	.301	.414	Sept/Oct	.200	95	19	5	0	5	12	10	40	.274	.411
Close & Late	.185	65	12	1	1	3	5	5	29	.243	.369	vs. AL	.254	339	86	17	1	20	55	33	94	.316	.487
None on/out	.264	72	19	6	1	1	1	3	19	.293	.417	vs. NL	.214	56	12	2	0	6	13	8	23	.313	.571

1997 By Position

Position	Avg	AB	H	2B	3B	HR	RBI	BB	SO	OBP	SLG	G	GS	Innings	PO	A	E	DP	Fld Pct	Rng Fctr	In Zone	Zone Outs	Zone Rtg	MLB Zone
As lf	.257	382	98	19	1	26	67	38	110	.321	.516	100	98	858.2	176	4	5	1	.973	1.89	224	170	.759	.805

John Cummings — Tigers
Age 29 – Pitches Left

	ERA	W	L	Sv	G	GS	IP	BB	SO	Avg	H	2B	3B	HR	RBI	OBP	SLG	GF	IR	IRS	Hld	SvOp	SB	CS	GB	FB	G/F
1997 Season	5.47	2	0	0	19	0	24.2	14	8	.311	32	3	2	3	15	.393	.466	2	19	5	4	0	5	1	43	26	1.65
Career (1993-1997)	5.33	10	15	0	110	16	216.1	106	114	.292	251	36	2	23	131	.369	.419	23	89	29	11	1	17	7	329	231	1.42

1997 Season

	ERA	W	L	Sv	G	GS	IP	H	HR	BB	SO		Avg	AB	H	2B	3B	HR	RBI	BB	SO	OBP	SLG
Home	8.03	1	0	0	10	0	12.1	19	2	9	5	vs. Left	.310	42	13	1	0	0	1	3	4	.356	.333
Away	2.92	1	0	0	9	0	12.1	13	1	5	3	vs. Right	.311	61	19	2	2	3	14	11	4	.417	.557

Career (1993-1997)

	ERA	W	L	Sv	G	GS	IP	H	HR	BB	SO		Avg	AB	H	2B	3B	HR	RBI	BB	SO	OBP	SLG
Home	7.31	4	8	0	49	6	85.0	109	13	43	46	vs. Left	.312	266	83	13	0	4	39	24	32	.371	.406
Away	4.04	6	7	0	61	10	131.1	142	10	63	68	vs. Right	.283	593	168	23	2	19	92	82	82	.368	.425
Day	5.92	4	6	0	39	5	79.0	95	10	41	44	Inning 1-6	.291	553	161	20	0	12	87	67	67	.366	.392
Night	4.98	6	9	0	71	11	137.1	156	13	65	70	Inning 7+	.294	306	90	16	2	11	44	39	47	.374	.467
Grass	4.59	9	8	0	85	9	151.0	161	13	76	85	None on	.273	447	122	20	1	9	44	56	.342	.383
Turf	7.03	1	7	0	25	7	65.1	90	10	30	29	Runners on	.313	412	129	16	1	14	122	62	58	.396	.459
March/April	5.37	2	5	0	24	5	53.2	69	7	23	26	Scoring Posn	.298	252	75	11	0	9	111	45	37	.391	.448
May	5.93	1	3	0	17	4	41.0	49	4	25	16	Close & Late	.305	118	36	6	1	5	20	16	15	.388	.500
June	8.40	0	1	0	6	1	15.0	21	3	7	10	None on/out	.303	211	64	13	0	7	23	27	.380	.464
July	4.96	1	2	0	13	4	32.2	30	2	15	15	vs. 1st Batr (relief)	.265	83	22	1	0	2	15	9	15	.333	.349
August	3.64	3	1	0	28	2	47.0	44	4	20	32	1st Inning Pitched	.296	361	107	16	1	10	67	45	60	.369	.429
Sept/Oct	6.00	3	3	0	22	0	27.0	38	3	16	15	First 15 Pitches	.322	311	100	15	0	10	49	32	45	.382	.466
Starter	5.46	1	10	0	16	16	84.0	90	10	40	35	Pitch 16-30	.256	227	58	8	1	6	31	28	35	.337	.379
Reliever	5.24	9	5	0	94	0	132.1	161	13	66	79	Pitch 31-45	.240	129	31	5	1	0	17	18	18	.336	.295
0 Days rest (Relief)	5.86	0	0	0	20	0	27.2	39	4	15	21	Pitch 46+	.323	192	62	8	0	7	34	28	16	.407	.474
1 or 2 Days rest	3.04	6	2	0	36	0	53.1	47	4	23	29	First Pitch	.366	142	52	7	1	2	23	10	0	.412	.472
3+ Days rest	7.19	3	3	0	38	0	51.1	75	5	28	29	Ahead in Count	.261	337	88	9	1	6	33	0	96	.264	.347
vs. AL	5.81	7	13	0	71	16	172.0	201	19	94	88	Behind in Count	.313	208	65	17	0	9	42	57	0	.454	.524
vs. NL	3.45	3	2	0	39	0	44.1	50	4	12	26	Two Strikes	.226	337	76	5	0	8	37	39	114	.305	.312
Pre-All Star	5.80	3	10	0	53	11	121.0	148	15	61	57	Pre-All Star	.306	483	148	19	2	15	80	61	57	.380	.447

Career (1993-1997)

	ERA	W	L	Sv	G	GS	IP	H	HR	BB	SO		Avg	AB	H	2B	3B	HR	RBI	BB	SO	OBP	SLG
Post-All Star	4.72	7	5	0	57	5	95.1	103	8	45	57	Post-All Star	.274	376	103	17	0	8	51	45	57	.354	.383

Pitcher vs. Batter (career)

Pitches Best Vs.	Avg	AB	H	2B	3B	HR	RBI	BB	SO	OBP	SLG	Pitches Worst Vs.	Avg	AB	H	2B	3B	HR	RBI	BB	SO	OBP	SLG
Danny Tartabull	.000	7	0	0	0	0	0	6	2	.462	.000	Jim Leyritz	.455	11	5	1	0	2	5	0	1	.455	1.091
Roberto Alomar	.111	9	1	0	0	0	0	2	2	.273	.111												
Bernie Williams	.231	13	3	0	0	0	1	2	2	.333	.231												

Midre Cummings — Phillies
Age 26 – Bats Left

	Avg	G	AB	R	H	2B	3B	HR	RBI	BB	SO	HBP	GDP	SB	CS	OBP	SLG	IBB	SH	SF	#Pit	#P/PA	GB	FB	G/F
1997 Season	.264	115	314	35	83	22	6	4	31	34	56	1	3	2	3	.330	.411	0	2	2	1314	3.75	103	91	1.13
Career (1993-1997)	.244	235	673	75	164	37	8	10	68	52	129	2	5	3	3	.298	.367	3	3	5	2648	3.60	235	199	1.18

1997 Season

	Avg	AB	H	2B	3B	HR	RBI	BB	SO	OBP	SLG		Avg	AB	H	2B	3B	HR	RBI	BB	SO	OBP	SLG
vs. Left	.289	38	11	2	0	0	2	6	7	.386	.342	First Pitch	.295	44	13	4	1	2	6	0	0	.295	.568
vs. Right	.261	276	72	20	6	4	29	25	49	.322	.420	Ahead in Count	.391	69	27	7	2	0	4	15	0	.494	.551
Groundball	.308	52	16	4	1	1	6	5	8	.368	.481	Behind in Count	.188	154	29	9	2	1	15	0	48	.192	.292
Flyball	.180	50	9	2	0	0	2	3	10	.226	.220	Two Strikes	.158	152	24	7	2	1	11	16	56	.238	.250
Home	.291	148	43	13	2	3	18	21	27	.378	.466	Batting #1	.302	192	58	15	4	1	20	23	27	.373	.438
Away	.241	166	40	9	4	1	13	10	29	.284	.361	Batting #3	.239	46	11	4	0	2	5	2	7	.271	.457
Day	.304	125	38	11	5	1	14	8	22	.348	.496	Other	.184	76	14	3	2	1	6	6	22	.253	.316
Night	.238	189	45	11	1	3	17	23	34	.319	.354	March/April	.185	27	5	3	1	0	1	3	8	.267	.370
Grass	.274	113	31	7	3	0	9	6	21	.311	.389	May	.245	49	12	2	1	3	7	4	11	.315	.510
Turf	.259	201	52	15	3	4	22	25	35	.341	.423	June	.100	30	3	1	0	0	0	1	7	.129	.133
Pre-All Star	.189	106	20	6	2	3	8	8	26	.252	.368	July	.333	42	14	3	1	0	5	4	5	.383	.452
Post-All Star	.303	208	63	16	4	1	23	23	30	.369	.433	August	.350	80	28	6	0	1	11	6	9	.391	.463
Scoring Posn	.319	69	22	4	2	0	25	12	12	.417	.435	Sept/Oct	.244	86	21	7	3	0	7	13	16	.343	.395
Close & Late	.289	45	13	2	1	1	8	7	12	.377	.444	vs. AL	.192	26	5	1	0	0	0	2	2	.250	.231
None on/out	.245	110	27	8	2	2	12	12	20	.320	.409	vs. NL	.271	288	78	21	6	4	31	29	54	.338	.427

1997 By Position

Position	Avg	AB	H	2B	3B	HR	RBI	BB	SO	OBP	SLG	G	GS	Innings	PO	A	E	DP	Fld Pct	Rng Fctr	In Zone	Outs	Zone Rtg	MLB Zone
As Pinch Hitter	.189	37	7	2	1	1	6	2	11	.231	.378	39	0	---	---	---	---	---	---	---	---	---	---	---
As lf	.152	46	7	3	0	1	2	2	13	.188	.283	14	11	101.0	19	1	0	0	1.000	1.78	28	19	.679	.805
As cf	.305	197	60	15	4	1	20	22	26	.371	.437	113	50	432.0	113	1	1	1	.991	2.38	147	111	.755	.815
As rf	.265	34	9	2	1	1	3	5	6	.375	.471	13	8	77.2	18	0	0	0	1.000	2.09	25	18	.720	.813

Career (1993-1997)

	Avg	AB	H	2B	3B	HR	RBI	BB	SO	OBP	SLG		Avg	AB	H	2B	3B	HR	RBI	BB	SO	OBP	SLG
vs. Left	.204	108	22	4	0	1	8	6	25	.250	.269	First Pitch	.310	116	36	7	2	5	14	3	0	.328	.534
vs. Right	.251	565	142	33	8	9	60	46	104	.307	.386	Ahead in Count	.305	128	39	9	2	2	12	30	0	.429	.453
Groundball	.265	166	44	8	2	3	15	13	31	.318	.392	Behind in Count	.187	327	61	15	3	2	32	0	116	.188	.269
Flyball	.190	105	20	3	0	1	7	7	23	.239	.248	Two Strikes	.159	320	51	10	3	2	26	19	129	.206	.228
Home	.269	338	91	21	3	7	41	35	65	.337	.411	Batting #1	.284	225	64	16	4	2	24	25	32	.352	.418
Away	.218	335	73	16	5	3	27	17	64	.256	.322	Batting #7	.213	164	35	9	1	0	15	8	41	.253	.280
Day	.264	231	61	14	6	4	27	19	46	.321	.429	Other	.229	284	65	12	3	8	29	19	56	.279	.377
Night	.233	442	103	23	2	6	41	33	83	.285	.335	March/April	.167	36	6	3	1	0	1	5	9	.268	.306
Grass	.250	192	48	10	3	2	16	10	38	.287	.365	May	.246	138	34	6	2	6	14	4	27	.271	.449
Turf	.241	481	116	27	5	8	52	42	91	.302	.368	June	.094	32	3	1	0	0	0	1	7	.121	.125
Pre-All Star	.209	206	43	10	3	6	15	10	43	.248	.374	July	.293	116	34	7	1	1	15	8	19	.333	.397
Post-All Star	.259	467	121	27	5	4	53	42	86	.319	.364	August	.274	179	49	9	0	3	17	12	28	.321	.374
Scoring Posn	.256	160	41	11	3	0	55	23	39	.347	.363	Sept/Oct	.221	172	38	11	4	0	21	22	39	.308	.331
Close & Late	.235	115	27	4	1	1	9	11	25	.299	.313	vs. AL	.192	26	5	1	0	0	0	2	2	.250	.231
None on/out	.252	206	52	12	2	5	5	16	37	.306	.403	vs. NL	.246	647	159	36	8	10	68	50	127	.300	.372

Batter vs. Pitcher (career)

Hits Best Against	Avg	AB	H	2B	3B	HR	RBI	BB	SO	OBP	SLG	Hits Worst Against	Avg	AB	H	2B	3B	HR	RBI	BB	SO	OBP	SLG
												Pedro Martinez	.000	13	0	0	0	0	0	1	3	.071	.000
												Darryl Kile	.083	12	1	0	0	0	0	0	2	.083	.083
												Kevin Foster	.083	12	1	0	0	0	0	0	2	.083	.083

Will Cunnane — Padres
Age 24 – Pitches Right (groundball pitcher)

	ERA	W	L	Sv	G	GS	IP	BB	SO	Avg	H	2B	3B	HR	RBI	OBP	SLG	GF	IR	IRS	Hld	SvOp	SB	CS	GB	FB	G/F
1997 Season	5.81	6	3	0	54	8	91.1	49	79	.305	114	15	2	11	66	.392	.444	16	30	10	4	2	11	6	153	69	2.22

1997 Season

	ERA	W	L	Sv	G	GS	IP	H	HR	BB	SO		Avg	AB	H	2B	3B	HR	RBI	BB	SO	OBP	SLG
Home	3.63	2	1	0	26	2	34.2	40	7	16	31	vs. Left	.287	164	47	8	1	4	26	27	35	.385	.421
Away	7.15	4	2	0	28	6	56.2	74	4	33	48	vs. Right	.319	210	67	7	1	7	40	22	44	.397	.462
Day	3.86	3	0	0	17	1	30.1	32	2	14	23	Inning 1-6	.322	245	79	9	1	10	50	33	50	.409	.490
Night	6.79	3	3	0	37	7	61.0	82	9	35	56	Inning 7+	.271	129	35	6	1	1	16	16	29	.358	.357
Grass	6.28	4	2	0	42	6	67.1	90	11	36	55	None on	.258	198	51	7	0	6	6	19	42	.332	.384
Turf	4.50	2	1	0	12	2	24.0	24	0	13	24	Runners on	.358	176	63	8	2	5	60	30	37	.455	.511
March/April	2.25	0	1	0	6	0	8.0	8	0	4	3	Scoring Posn	.370	100	37	4	2	3	54	24	21	.496	.540
May	5.40	3	0	0	10	1	23.1	30	2	10	19	Close & Late	.280	25	7	0	0	0	3	4	6	.400	.280
June	9.12	1	1	0	7	5	24.2	38	8	14	18	None on/out	.221	86	19	4	0	3	3	8	19	.302	.372

109

1997 Season

	ERA	W	L	Sv	G	GS	IP	H	HR	BB	SO
July	0.64	1	0	0	12	0	14.0	11	0	5	15
August	5.27	1	1	0	11	1	13.2	16	0	9	16
Sept/Oct	10.57	0	0	0	8	1	7.2	11	1	7	8
Starter	8.13	2	2	0	8	8	34.1	47	8	24	25
Reliever	4.42	4	1	0	46	0	57.0	67	3	25	54
0 Days rest (Relief)	6.23	0	0	0	6	0	4.1	9	0	1	4
1 or 2 Days rest	4.05	4	1	0	28	0	40.0	40	2	17	41
3+ Days rest	4.97	0	0	0	12	0	12.2	18	1	7	9
vs. AL	8.78	0	0	0	6	2	13.1	20	3	10	9
vs. NL	5.31	6	3	0	48	6	78.0	94	8	39	70
Pre-All Star	6.29	4	2	0	25	6	58.2	77	10	31	42
Post-All Star	4.96	2	1	0	29	2	32.2	37	1	18	37

	Avg	AB	H	2B	3B	HR	RBI	BB	SO	OBP	SLG
vs. 1st Batr (relief)	.238	42	10	1	0	1	5	4	17	.304	.333
1st Inning Pitched	.333	186	62	8	2	4	45	23	47	.413	.462
First 15 Pitches	.319	138	44	7	0	3	22	14	33	.390	.435
Pitch 16-30	.267	90	24	2	2	2	22	16	21	.380	.400
Pitch 31-45	.232	56	13	2	0	0	5	6	12	.317	.268
Pitch 46+	.367	90	33	4	0	6	17	13	13	.452	.611
First Pitch	.405	37	15	2	0	2	9	1	0	.450	.622
Ahead in Count	.218	165	36	5	1	1	19	0	64	.223	.279
Behind in Count	.423	104	44	5	1	6	28	18	0	.508	.663
Two Strikes	.184	174	32	5	0	2	18	30	79	.311	.247
Pre-All Star	.322	239	77	9	1	10	47	31	42	.407	.494
Post-All Star	.274	135	37	6	1	1	19	18	37	.364	.356

Chad Curtis — Yankees   Age 29 – Bats Right (groundball hitter)

	Avg	G	AB	R	H	2B	3B	HR	RBI	BB	SO	HBP	GDP	SB	CS	OBP	SLG	IBB	SH	SF	#Pit	#P/PA	GB	FB	G/F
1997 Season	.284	115	349	59	99	22	1	15	55	43	59	5	7	12	6	.362	.481	1	2	9	1550	3.80	124	112	1.11
Last Five Years	.269	672	2475	401	665	124	12	65	277	290	398	22	60	130	67	.346	.407	6	22	33	11001	3.87	982	694	1.41

1997 Season

	Avg	AB	H	2B	3B	HR	RBI	BB	SO	OBP	SLG
vs. Left	.314	105	33	8	1	4	18	17	17	.403	.524
vs. Right	.270	244	66	14	0	11	37	26	42	.344	.463
Groundball	.296	71	21	5	0	3	13	8	16	.354	.493
Flyball	.236	55	13	3	1	1	6	5	9	.295	.382
Home	.282	149	42	8	0	4	19	23	28	.372	.416
Away	.285	200	57	14	1	11	36	20	31	.354	.530
Day	.254	126	32	6	0	8	18	16	19	.336	.492
Night	.300	223	67	16	1	7	37	27	40	.376	.475
Grass	.270	293	79	17	1	10	43	41	49	.360	.437
Turf	.357	56	20	5	0	5	12	2	10	.373	.714
Pre-All Star	.240	100	24	6	0	5	14	15	22	.331	.450
Post-All Star	.301	249	75	16	1	10	41	28	37	.375	.494
Scoring Posn	.294	85	25	5	0	3	40	12	19	.355	.459
Close & Late	.289	45	13	2	0	3	6	6	10	.407	.533
None on/out	.333	87	29	9	1	5	10	8	8	.402	.632

	Avg	AB	H	2B	3B	HR	RBI	BB	SO	OBP	SLG
First Pitch	.321	53	17	4	0	3	9	0	0	.309	.566
Ahead in Count	.441	68	30	7	0	4	19	22	0	.559	.721
Behind in Count	.174	161	28	5	1	4	16	0	47	.189	.292
Two Strikes	.163	172	28	4	1	4	16	21	59	.263	.267
Batting #7	.367	139	51	11	1	8	28	18	22	.446	.633
Batting #8	.270	100	27	4	0	3	14	14	14	.347	.400
Other	.191	110	21	7	0	4	13	11	23	.262	.364
March/April	.227	22	5	1	0	3	5	5	8	.370	.682
May	.143	7	1	0	0	0	0	2	2	.333	.143
June	.264	53	14	4	0	2	8	5	9	.317	.453
July	.304	79	24	7	0	2	14	13	8	.392	.468
August	.298	104	31	6	0	6	16	14	20	.395	.529
Sept/Oct	.286	84	24	4	1	2	12	4	12	.315	.429
vs. AL	.289	304	88	18	1	13	51	38	48	.367	.484
vs. NL	.244	45	11	4	0	2	4	5	11	.327	.467

1997 By Position

Position	Avg	AB	H	2B	3B	HR	RBI	BB	SO	OBP	SLG	G	GS	Innings	PO	A	E	DP	Fld Pct	Rng Fctr	In Zone	Zone Outs	Zone Rtg	MLB Zone
As lf	.267	172	46	10	0	7	28	23	26	.360	.448	56	49	421.1	77	4	2	1	.976	1.73	96	76	.792	.805
As cf	.322	149	48	10	1	6	25	16	24	.380	.523	100	55	377.2	55	2	1	1	.990	2.43	115	98	.852	.815

Last Five Years

	Avg	AB	H	2B	3B	HR	RBI	BB	SO	OBP	SLG
vs. Left	.314	663	208	42	7	16	67	87	95	.394	.471
vs. Right	.252	1812	457	82	5	49	210	203	303	.329	.384
Groundball	.277	535	148	32	3	11	50	70	90	.366	.409
Flyball	.258	489	126	21	1	13	56	40	74	.313	.384
Home	.269	1188	320	61	3	29	138	151	190	.353	.399
Away	.268	1287	345	63	9	36	139	139	208	.340	.415
Day	.261	790	206	40	2	18	83	95	122	.342	.385
Night	.272	1685	459	84	10	47	194	195	276	.348	.418
Grass	.264	2087	552	101	9	50	226	246	339	.343	.393
Turf	.291	388	113	23	3	15	51	44	59	.366	.482
Pre-All Star	.269	1368	368	71	7	33	152	163	221	.348	.404
Post-All Star	.268	1107	297	53	5	32	125	127	177	.345	.412
Scoring Posn	.259	555	144	26	2	5	197	69	110	.329	.341
Close & Late	.258	360	93	12	1	8	26	42	64	.343	.364
None on/out	.278	694	193	36	4	21	21	97	92	.371	.425

	Avg	AB	H	2B	3B	HR	RBI	BB	SO	OBP	SLG
First Pitch	.298	322	96	18	0	11	54	3	0	.304	.457
Ahead in Count	.328	525	172	32	5	21	80	181	0	.499	.528
Behind in Count	.224	1143	256	44	5	15	89	0	322	.229	.311
Two Strikes	.198	1186	235	37	6	15	83	106	398	.267	.277
Batting #1	.250	1063	266	51	3	30	113	134	176	.336	.389
Batting #2	.282	956	270	47	7	19	105	144	154	.406	.406
Other	.283	456	129	26	2	16	59	50	78	.355	.454
March/April	.256	313	80	11	1	7	31	41	59	.342	.364
May	.263	426	112	24	4	11	51	62	61	.346	.415
June	.280	468	131	28	2	9	53	53	74	.355	.406
July	.288	483	139	29	0	21	67	59	75	.363	.478
August	.276	453	125	19	2	11	43	49	78	.351	.400
Sept/Oct	.235	332	78	13	3	6	32	36	51	.308	.346
vs. AL	.272	2326	632	115	12	61	264	268	372	.348	.410
vs. NL	.221	149	33	9	0	4	13	22	26	.324	.362

Batter vs. Pitcher (career)

Hits Best Against	Avg	AB	H	2B	3B	HR	RBI	BB	SO	OBP	SLG
Rich Robertson	.700	10	7	1	0	2	7	1	1	.667	1.400
Mark Gubicza	.600	10	6	1	0	0	0	0	0	.636	.700
Brian Bohanon	.556	9	5	2	0	1	1	0	0	.636	.778
Bob Wickman	.500	10	5	1	0	1	2	0	1	.500	.900
Jeff D'Amico	.333	9	3	0	0	2	3	1	2	.364	1.000

Hits Worst Against	Avg	AB	H	2B	3B	HR	RBI	BB	SO	OBP	SLG
Dennis Martinez	.000	10	0	0	0	0	0	1	3	.091	.000
Juan Guzman	.080	25	2	0	0	1	1	0	7	.080	.200
Charles Nagy	.086	35	3	0	0	0	0	4	6	.179	.086
Kevin Appier	.107	28	3	0	0	0	1	1	7	.133	.107
Jaime Navarro	.133	15	2	0	0	0	0	1	4	.188	.133

Jeff D'Amico — Brewers   Age 22 – Pitches Right (flyball pitcher)

	ERA	W	L	Sv	G	GS	IP	BB	SO	Avg	H	2B	3B	HR	RBI	OBP	SLG	CG	ShO	Sup	QS	#P/S	SB	CS	GB	FB	G/F
1997 Season	4.71	9	7	0	23	23	135.2	43	94	.264	139	24	3	25	75	.327	.464	1		4.98	9	96	5	4	159	175	0.91
Career (1996-1997)	4.99	15	13	0	40	40	221.2	74	147	.265	227	45	4	46	123	.327	.488	1		5.40	13	93	10	7	249	309	0.81

1997 Season

	ERA	W	L	Sv	G	GS	IP	H	HR	BB	SO
Home	4.03	4	2	0	11	11	67.0	70	13	21	48
Away	5.37	5	5	0	12	12	68.2	69	12	22	46

	Avg	AB	H	2B	3B	HR	RBI	BB	SO	OBP	SLG
vs. Left	.269	264	71	14	2	15	43	24	39	.333	.508
vs. Right	.260	262	68	10	1	10	32	19	55	.321	.420

1997 Season

	ERA	W	L	Sv	G	GS	IP	H	HR	BB	SO		Avg	AB	H	2B	3B	HR	RBI	BB	SO	OBP	SLG
Day	4.98	3	3	0	8	8	47.0	44	8	18	37	Inning 1-6	.267	490	131	23	3	22	72	43	87	.334	.461
Night	4.57	6	4	0	15	15	88.2	95	17	25	57	Inning 7+	.222	36	8	1	0	3	3	0	7	.222	.500
Grass	4.47	8	5	0	19	19	112.2	119	21	36	76	None on	.262	325	85	15	1	13	13	25	62	.320	.434
Turf	5.87	1	2	0	4	4	23.0	20	4	7	18	Runners on	.269	201	54	9	2	12	62	18	32	.338	.512
March/April	5.65	0	1	0	3	3	14.1	19	2	13	8	Scoring Posn	.301	103	31	4	1	9	53	11	18	.367	.621
May	5.22	2	1	0	5	5	29.1	25	6	14	21	Close & Late	.071	14	1	1	0	0	0	0	4	.071	.143
June	2.68	4	1	0	6	6	43.2	38	2	6	26	None on/out	.324	142	46	9	1	8	8	8	18	.364	.570
July	6.06	2	1	0	3	3	16.1	21	5	4	15	vs. 1st Batr (relief)	.000	0	0	0	0	0	0	0	0	.000	.000
August	0.00	0	0	0	0	0	0.0	0	0	0	0	1st Inning Pitched	.298	94	28	4	0	6	15	16	27	.400	.532
Sept/Oct	5.91	1	0	0	6	6	32.0	36	10	6	24	First 75 Pitches	.280	397	111	21	2	18	56	34	74	.345	.479
Starter	4.71	9	7	0	23	23	135.2	139	25	43	94	Pitch 76-90	.288	73	21	1	1	5	17	4	9	.321	.534
Reliever	0.00	0	0	0	0	0	0.0	0	0	0	0	Pitch 91-105	.156	45	7	2	0	2	2	4	10	.240	.333
0-3 Days Rest (Start)	0.00	0	0	0	0	0	0.0	0	0	0	0	Pitch 106+	.000	11	0	0	0	0	0	1	1	.083	.000
4 Days Rest	4.66	8	6	0	18	18	112.0	115	22	28	79	First Pitch	.297	64	19	5	0	2	9	1	0	.328	.469
5+ Days Rest	4.94	1	1	0	5	5	23.2	24	3	15	15	Ahead in Count	.191	235	45	4	2	7	17	0	79	.212	.315
vs. AL	4.97	7	7	0	20	20	116.0	126	25	38	83	Behind in Count	.370	119	44	9	1	9	27	21	0	.451	.689
vs. NL	3.20	2	0	0	3	3	19.2	13	0	5	11	Two Strikes	.189	243	46	8	2	7	21	21	94	.268	.325
Pre-All Star	4.39	6	4	0	15	15	92.1	91	12	34	61	Pre-All Star	.255	357	91	17	3	12	49	34	61	.327	.420
Post-All Star	5.40	3	3	0	8	8	43.1	48	13	9	33	Post-All Star	.284	169	48	7	0	13	26	9	33	.328	.556

Omar Daal — Blue Jays
Age 26 – Pitches Left (groundball pitcher)

	ERA	W	L	Sv	G	GS	IP	BB	SO	Avg	H	2B	3B	HR	RBI	OBP	SLG	GF	IR	IRS	Hld	SvOp	SB	CS	GB	FB	G/F
1997 Season	7.06	2	3	1	42	3	57.1	21	44	.343	82	17	1	7	43	.399	.510	6	41	13	3	3	2	2	108	43	2.51
Career (1993-1997)	5.27	12	11	1	205	9	213.2	99	165	.283	233	46	2	24	139	.360	.431	32	202	59	26	9	8	5	366	153	2.39

1997 Season

	ERA	W	L	Sv	G	GS	IP	H	HR	BB	SO		Avg	AB	H	2B	3B	HR	RBI	BB	SO	OBP	SLG
Home	7.94	0	2	0	21	1	28.1	42	4	8	21	vs. Left	.370	73	27	7	0	2	23	6	15	.418	.548
Away	6.21	2	1	1	21	2	29.0	40	3	13	23	vs. Right	.331	166	55	10	1	5	20	15	29	.391	.494
Starter	2.50	1	1	0	3	3	18.0	18	2	5	20	Scoring Posn	.282	78	22	7	0	2	35	11	19	.367	.449
Reliever	9.15	1	2	1	39	0	39.1	64	5	16	24	Close & Late	.429	49	21	2	0	1	11	4	6	.472	.531
0 Days rest (Relief)	9.35	1	0	0	10	0	8.2	15	3	2	5	None on/out	.353	51	18	4	0	0	0	4	12	.400	.431
1 or 2 Days rest	12.71	0	1	0	12	0	11.1	19	2	9	5	First Pitch	.372	43	16	5	0	2	6	3	0	.413	.628
3+ Days rest	6.98	0	1	1	17	0	19.1	30	0	5	14	Ahead in Count	.192	104	20	5	0	4	20	0	43	.200	.356
Pre-All Star	9.21	1	1	1	29	0	28.1	41	3	13	16	Behind in Count	.508	63	32	4	1	1	13	7	0	.549	.651
Post-All Star	4.97	1	2	0	13	3	29.0	41	4	8	28	Two Strikes	.221	95	21	0	3	14	11	44	.302	.379

Career (1993-1997)

	ERA	W	L	Sv	G	GS	IP	H	HR	BB	SO		Avg	AB	H	2B	3B	HR	RBI	BB	SO	OBP	SLG
Home	4.71	3	7	0	101	3	109.0	113	12	51	85	vs. Left	.269	316	85	20	0	6	69	33	59	.335	.389
Away	5.85	9	4	1	104	6	104.2	120	12	48	80	vs. Right	.291	508	148	26	2	18	70	66	106	.375	.457
Day	5.21	3	3	1	57	1	57.0	54	6	30	33	Inning 1-6	.298	373	111	24	1	13	66	49	79	.380	.472
Night	5.29	9	8	0	148	8	156.2	179	18	69	132	Inning 7+	.271	451	122	22	1	11	73	50	86	.343	.397
Grass	5.50	9	7	1	104	4	90.0	101	9	50	58	None on	.259	421	109	24	2	11	11	38	88	.323	.404
Turf	5.09	3	4	0	101	5	123.2	132	15	49	107	Runners on	.308	403	124	22	0	13	128	61	77	.396	.459
March/April	4.65	1	2	1	35	0	40.2	32	4	15	26	Scoring Posn	.277	267	74	13	0	6	109	45	59	.374	.393
May	4.82	4	2	0	51	0	37.1	40	3	23	28	Close & Late	.333	168	56	11	0	2	40	27	31	.423	.435
June	6.65	1	0	0	33	0	23.0	31	1	14	17	None on/out	.276	185	51	14	0	4	4	20	36	.344	.416
July	6.75	0	3	0	37	0	29.1	40	3	13	18	vs. 1st Batr (relief)	.269	171	46	6	0	5	36	22	32	.351	.392
August	3.51	2	0	0	25	1	25.2	18	4	11	22	1st Inning Pitched	.284	514	146	27	0	17	111	70	100	.368	.436
Sept/Oct	5.46	4	4	0	24	8	57.2	72	9	23	54	First 15 Pitches	.290	466	135	23	0	15	89	57	88	.366	.436
Starter	4.04	3	4	0	9	9	42.1	44	5	15	47	Pitch 16-30	.277	188	52	16	2	3	30	26	39	.364	.431
Reliever	5.57	9	7	1	196	0	171.1	189	19	84	118	Pitch 31-45	.313	83	26	1	0	4	12	9	15	.387	.470
0 Days rest (Relief)	7.02	2	1	0	59	0	42.1	60	9	15	29	Pitch 46+	.230	87	20	6	0	2	8	7	23	.295	.368
1 or 2 Days rest	5.37	5	4	0	71	0	65.1	64	7	44	41	First Pitch	.349	126	44	9	0	6	21	12	0	.400	.563
3+ Days rest	4.81	2	2	1	66	0	63.2	65	3	25	48	Ahead in Count	.196	372	73	13	0	11	48	0	142	.202	.320
vs. AL	4.00	1	1	0	10	3	27.0	35	3	6	28	Behind in Count	.412	182	75	15	1	5	44	39			
vs. NL	5.45	11	10	1	195	6	186.2	198	21	93	137	Two Strikes	.192	380	73	16	0	8	47	44			
Pre-All Star	5.16	6	4	1	132	0	111.2	115	9	55	79	Pre-All Star	.275	418	115	24	0	9	72	55			
Post-All Star	5.38	6	7	0	73	9	102.0	118	15	44	86	Post-All Star	.291	406	118	22	2	15	67	44			

Pitcher vs. Batter (career)

Pitches Best Vs.	Avg	AB	H	2B	3B	HR	RBI	BB	SO	Pitches Worst Vs.	Avg	AB	H	2B	3B	HR	RBI	BB
Mickey Morandini	.125	16	2	0	0	0	1	2	3	Mark Grace	.545	11	6	3	0	0	2	
Hal Morris	.200	10	2	1	0	0	1	1	2	Fred McGriff	.455	11	5	1	0	0	2	4
Steve Finley	.200	10	2	1	0	0	0	1	1	Jim Eisenreich	.400	10	4	1	0	0	4	1
										Tony Gwynn	.333	15	5	3	0	0	7	1

Johnny Damon — Royals
Age 2

	Avg	G	AB	R	H	2B	3B	HR	RBI	BB	SO	HBP	GDP	SB	CS	OBP	SLG	IBB	SH	SF	#Pit	#P/PA
1997 Season	.275	146	472	70	130	12	8	8	48	42	70	3	3	16	10	.338	.386	2	6	1	1934	3.69
Career (1995-1997)	.274	338	1177	163	323	45	18	17	121	85	156	7	9	48	15	.325	.387	5	18	9	4697	3.62

1997 Season

	Avg	AB	H	2B	3B	HR	RBI	BB	SO	OBP	SLG		Avg	AB	H	2B	3B	HR	RBI	BB
vs. Left	.248	117	29	0	1	2	9	8	13	.307	.316	First Pitch	.349	43	15	0	2	0	5	2

1997 Season

	Avg	AB	H	2B	3B	HR	RBI	BB	SO	OBP	SLG
vs. Right	.285	355	101	12	7	6	39	34	57	.348	.408
Groundball	.291	79	23	1	2	1	6	5	14	.333	.392
Flyball	.226	84	19	2	0	0	7	8	14	.293	.250
Home	.290	231	67	6	6	3	28	20	32	.349	.407
Away	.261	241	63	6	2	5	20	22	38	.327	.365
Day	.185	157	29	5	0	3	14	14	33	.254	.274
Night	.321	315	101	7	8	5	34	28	37	.380	.441
Grass	.281	409	115	11	7	7	43	36	60	.340	.394
Turf	.238	63	15	1	1	1	5	6	10	.324	.333
Pre-All Star	.316	215	68	7	4	4	26	14	30	.359	.442
Post-All Star	.241	257	62	5	4	4	22	28	40	.321	.339
Scoring Posn	.316	114	36	3	6	1	36	12	17	.383	.474
Close & Late	.232	95	22	0	1	1	9	6	14	.277	.284
None on/out	.269	108	29	3	0	2	7	16	33	.319	.352

	Avg	AB	H	2B	3B	HR	RBI	BB	SO	OBP	SLG
Ahead in Count	.289	90	26	3	2	3	17	28	0	.462	.467
Behind in Count	.250	236	59	6	3	3	17	0	65	.249	.339
Two Strikes	.218	225	49	6	2	2	14	12	70	.257	.289
Batting #2	.250	104	26	2	2	1	8	12	18	.328	.337
Batting #9	.362	94	34	3	3	2	14	6	11	.400	.521
Other	.255	274	70	7	3	5	26	24	41	.321	.358
March/April	.295	44	13	2	1	1	7	3	11	.340	.455
May	.356	73	26	2	2	3	10	4	3	.390	.562
June	.300	80	24	3	1	0	7	6	15	.352	.363
July	.250	92	23	0	2	1	12	8	6	.317	.324
August	.216	102	22	2	1	2	7	13	17	.310	.324
Sept/Oct	.272	81	22	2	1	1	5	8	18	.337	.358
vs. AL	.269	413	111	9	7	7	41	37	59	.330	.375
vs. NL	.322	59	19	3	1	1	7	5	11	.394	.458

1997 By Position

Position	Avg	AB	H	2B	3B	HR	RBI	BB	SO	OBP	SLG	G	GS	Innings	PO	A	E	DP	Fld Pct	Rng Fctr	In Zone	Zone Outs	Zone Rtg	MLB Zone
As lf	.277	130	36	3	0	0	11	10	17	.333	.300	48	32	311.1	69	0	1	0	.986	1.99	78	68	.872	.805
As cf	.243	214	52	5	4	4	19	24	36	.322	.360	65	51	480.1	155	1	2	0	.987	2.92	172	152	.884	.815
As rf	.339	121	41	4	4	3	17	8	13	.382	.512	47	35	303.1	99	4	1	3	.990	3.06	116	98	.845	.813

Career (1995-1997)

	Avg	AB	H	2B	3B	HR	RBI	BB	SO	OBP	SLG
vs. Left	.235	289	68	5	3	3	28	23	36	.298	.304
vs. Right	.287	888	255	40	15	14	93	62	120	.334	.413
Groundball	.260	246	64	8	4	5	32	10	33	.284	.386
Flyball	.270	196	53	10	1	3	19	15	30	.322	.378
Home	.276	583	161	24	11	7	60	39	74	.324	.391
Away	.273	594	162	21	7	10	61	46	82	.326	.382
Day	.215	349	75	17	0	5	24	25	58	.268	.307
Night	.300	828	248	28	18	12	97	60	98	.349	.420
Grass	.275	1027	282	38	15	13	105	73	137	.322	.379
Turf	.273	150	41	7	3	4	16	12	19	.343	.440
Pre-All Star	.297	519	154	25	7	8	54	31	66	.338	.418
Post-All Star	.257	658	169	20	11	9	67	54	90	.314	.362
Scoring Posn	.276	268	74	6	10	3	96	26	37	.332	.407
Close & Late	.200	205	41	0	1	2	15	16	30	.260	.239
None on/out	.275	309	85	18	2	5	5	17	38	.319	.395

	Avg	AB	H	2B	3B	HR	RBI	BB	SO	OBP	SLG
First Pitch	.394	132	52	3	5	2	20	4	0	.417	.538
Ahead in Count	.305	233	71	15	3	6	42	55	0	.433	.472
Behind in Count	.231	563	130	15	8	7	43	0	137	.233	.323
Two Strikes	.202	531	107	16	7	6	34	26	156	.241	.292
Batting #1	.270	326	88	19	5	5	32	20	45	.313	.405
Batting #7	.246	191	47	3	1	3	21	20	21	.316	.319
Other	.285	660	188	23	12	9	68	45	90	.333	.397
March/April	.282	142	40	12	1	3	17	10	28	.327	.444
May	.314	159	50	2	4	4	19	10	13	.359	.453
June	.299	174	52	10	1	1	12	10	24	.340	.385
July	.279	190	53	1	5	2	22	15	11	.333	.368
August	.235	272	64	5	5	4	31	27	40	.308	.349
Sept/Oct	.267	240	64	11	2	3	20	13	40	.302	.367
vs. AL	.272	1118	304	42	17	16	114	80	145	.321	.383
vs. NL	.322	59	19	3	1	1	7	5	11	.394	.458

Batter vs. Pitcher (career)

Hits Best Against	Avg	AB	H	2B	3B	HR	RBI	BB	SO	OBP	SLG
Frank Rodriguez	.625	8	5	0	2	1	6	3	0	.727	1.500
Bobby Witt	.571	14	8	1	1	1	4	1	0	.600	1.000
Aaron Sele	.545	11	6	3	0	1	4	0	3	.545	1.091
Wilson Alvarez	.500	14	7	0	1	0	3	1	1	.533	.643
Ricky Bones	.417	12	5	1	1	0	2	2	1	.500	.667

Hits Worst Against	Avg	AB	H	2B	3B	HR	RBI	BB	SO	OBP	SLG
Chad Ogea	.000	12	0	0	0	0	0	0	2	.000	.000
Brad Radke	.133	15	2	0	0	0	0	0	2	.133	.133
Ken Hill	.176	17	3	0	0	0	1	2	4	.250	.176
Alex Fernandez	.214	14	3	1	0	0	0	0	2	.214	.286
Jamie Moyer	.214	14	3	0	0	0	0	1	0	.267	.214

Danny Darwin — Giants

Age 42 – Pitches Right (flyball pitcher)

	ERA	W	L	Sv	G	GS	IP	BB	SO	Avg	H	2B	3B	HR	RBI	OBP	SLG	CG	ShO	Sup	QS	#P/S	SB	CS	GB	FB	G/F
1997 Season	4.35	5	11	0	31	24	157.1	45	92	.286	181	32	1	26	77	.333	.464	1	0	4.12	14	93	10	4	219	208	1.05
Last Five Years	4.50	40	48	0	132	111	726.0	176	430	.272	769	159	14	111	356	.316	.455	4	1	4.72	59	90	44	15	879	990	0.89

1997 Season

	ERA	W	L	Sv	G	GS	IP	H	HR	BB	SO		Avg	AB	H	2B	3B	HR	RBI	BB	SO	OBP	SLG
Home	3.62	1	4	0	14	8	64.2	81	7	18	37	vs. Left	.309	314	97	21	1	17	45	28	39	.361	.545
Away	4.86	4	7	0	17	16	92.2	100	19	27	55	vs. Right	.264	318	84	11	0	9	32	17	53	.304	.384
Day	3.56	2	1	0	8	4	30.1	31	4	10	17	Inning 1-6	.284	587	167	31	1	26	75	40	88	.329	.474
Night	4.54	3	10	0	23	20	127.0	150	22	35	75	Inning 7+	.311	45	14	1	0	0	2	5	4	.380	.333
Grass	4.21	5	8	0	28	21	141.0	158	22	42	82	None on	.317	347	110	17	1	18	18	28	46	.370	.527
Turf	5.51	0	3	0	3	3	16.1	23	4	3	10	Runners on	.249	285	71	15	0	8	59	17	46	.288	.386
March/April	2.33	0	2	0	6	3	27.0	29	4	8	12	Scoring Posn	.219	146	32	6	0	4	46	13	30	.273	.342
May	3.33	1	0	0	5	4	27.0	22	3	13	13	Close & Late	.160	25	4	0	0	0	0	1	3	.192	.160
June	4.32	1	4	0	5	5	33.1	39	7	8	20	None on/out	.319	163	52	7	1	9	9	10	20	.362	.540
July	6.58	2	2	0	5	5	26.0	40	7	2	17	vs. 1st Batr (relief)	.286	7	2	0	0	0	1	0	1	.286	.286
August	5.66	0	1	0	5	3	20.2	27	3	5	16	1st Inning Pitched	.314	121	38	10	1	4	16	4	18	.336	.512
Sept/Oct	4.24	1	2	0	5	4	23.1	24	2	9	14	First 75 Pitches	.280	503	141	30	1	23	62	32	75	.323	.481
Starter	4.33	5	11	0	24	24	143.1	160	23	41	85	Pitch 76-90	.377	77	29	1	0	3	8	6	7	.417	.506
Reliever	4.50	0	0	0	7	0	14.0	21	3	4	7	Pitch 91-105	.205	39	8	1	0	0	4	5	9	.295	.231
0-3 Days Rest (Start)	3.92	0	2	0	3	3	20.2	25	1	7	8	Pitch 106+	.231	13	3	0	0	0	3	2	1	.333	.231
4 Days Rest	4.29	4	4	0	11	11	65.0	74	11	15	39	First Pitch	.306	108	33	7	0	7	20	1	0	.306	.565
5+ Days Rest	4.53	1	5	0	10	10	72.2	61	8	19	46	Ahead in Count	.264	311	82	14	1	8	34	0	82	.263	.392
vs. AL	4.27	4	7	0	21	17	111.2	125	19	35	63	Behind in Count	.330	112	37	8	0	8	15	24	0	.445	.616
vs. NL	4.53	1	4	0	10	7	45.2	56	7	10	29	Two Strikes	.214	285	61	10	1	6	27	20	92	.268	.319
Pre-All Star	3.46	3	6	0	17	13	93.2	98	14	29	49	Pre-All Star	.266	368	98	17	0	14	37	29	49	.318	.427
Post-All Star	5.65	2	5	0	14	11	63.2	83	12	16	43	Post-All Star	.314	264	83	15	1	12	40	16	43	.353	.515

Last Five Years

	ERA	W	L	Sv	G	GS	IP	H	HR	BB	SO
Home	4.54	20	21	0	67	53	359.0	397	49	88	228
Away	4.46	20	27	0	65	58	367.0	372	62	88	202
Day	3.99	17	10	0	38	30	196.1	203	27	55	125
Night	4.69	23	38	0	94	81	529.2	566	84	121	305
Grass	4.25	32	31	0	91	80	521.1	543	76	132	301
Turf	5.14	8	17	0	41	31	204.2	226	35	44	129
March/April	4.13	6	9	0	21	18	113.1	121	21	29	59
May	4.37	10	10	0	27	26	162.2	163	17	43	108
June	4.29	7	14	0	24	24	151.0	169	23	37	71
July	4.85	7	5	0	19	13	91.0	113	13	16	53
August	4.81	6	5	0	20	15	101.0	104	18	23	65
Sept/Oct	4.79	4	5	0	21	15	107.0	99	19	28	74
Starter	4.44	38	48	0	111	111	684.2	714	103	163	405
Reliever	5.44	2	0	0	21	0	41.1	55	8	13	25
0-3 Days Rest (Start)	3.25	1	2	0	5	5	36.0	33	3	10	18
4 Days Rest	4.32	24	20	0	59	59	368.1	370	56	71	228
5+ Days Rest	4.75	13	26	0	47	47	280.1	311	44	82	159
vs. AL	4.73	29	33	0	88	79	515.2	553	88	139	305
vs. NL	3.94	11	15	0	44	32	210.1	216	23	37	125
Pre-All Star	4.26	26	34	0	79	73	464.2	496	62	117	260
Post-All Star	4.92	14	14	0	53	38	261.1	273	49	59	170

	Avg	AB	H	2B	3B	HR	RBI	BB	SO	OBP	SLG
vs. Left	.306	1475	452	95	9	63	195	105	162	.353	.511
vs. Right	.234	1356	317	64	5	48	161	71	268	.275	.395
Inning 1-6	.269	2494	672	144	11	104	324	147	396	.312	.461
Inning 7+	.288	337	97	15	3	7	32	29	34	.341	.412
None on	.280	1702	476	103	8	73	73	91	243	.322	.478
Runners on	.260	1129	293	56	6	38	283	85	187	.308	.421
Scoring Posn	.252	616	155	30	5	22	241	69	108	.318	.424
Close & Late	.262	195	51	10	2	3	19	14	23	.307	.379
None on/out	.317	763	242	58	5	32	32	27	99	.346	.532
vs. 1st Batr (relief)	.263	19	5	1	0	0	2	1	2	.300	.316
1st Inning Pitched	.291	516	150	31	5	23	78	24	82	.327	.504
First 75 Pitches	.269	2268	611	134	12	94	285	129	355	.311	.463
Pitch 76-90	.292	346	101	17	2	12	48	26	45	.343	.457
Pitch 91-105	.254	169	43	6	0	5	16	14	25	.310	.379
Pitch 106+	.292	48	14	2	0	0	7	7	5	.382	.333
First Pitch	.316	490	155	32	5	22	79	16	0	.340	.537
Ahead in Count	.234	1343	314	63	4	41	141	0	374	.236	.378
Behind in Count	.316	538	170	41	2	29	81	84	0	.410	.561
Two Strikes	.206	1221	251	49	4	35	115	76	430	.254	.338
Post-All Star	.271	1008	273	55	7	49	141	59	170	.313	.485

Pitcher vs. Batter (since 1984)

Pitches Best Vs.	Avg	AB	H	2B	3B	HR	RBI	BB	SO	OBP	SLG
Frank Thomas	.000	15	0	0	0	0	0	4	1	.211	.000
Todd Zeile	.000	11	0	0	0	0	0	1	2	.000	.000
Bobby Bonilla	.053	19	1	0	0	0	1	1	2	.100	.053
Pete Incaviglia	.077	13	1	0	0	0	0	0	4	.077	.077
Tino Martinez	.083	12	1	0	0	0	1	1	0	.143	.083

Pitches Worst Vs.	Avg	AB	H	2B	3B	HR	RBI	BB	SO	OBP	SLG
Bip Roberts	.583	12	7	4	0	0	0	1	2	.615	.917
Reggie Jefferson	.563	16	9	1	1	1	5	0	3	.563	.938
Jose Valentin	.545	11	6	1	1	2	4	1	2	.583	1.364
Chad Kreuter	.462	13	6	2	0	2	4	1	3	.500	1.077
Jeff King	.333	12	4	0	0	4	8	1	3	.357	1.333

Jeff Darwin — White Sox
Age 28 – Pitches Right (flyball pitcher)

	ERA	W	L	Sv	G	GS	IP	BB	SO	Avg	H	2B	3B	HR	RBI	OBP	SLG	GF	IR	IRS	Hld	SvOp	SB	CS	GB	FB	G/F
1997 Season	5.27	0	1	0	14	0	13.2	7	9	.298	17	5	1	1	11	.369	.474	6	13	5	2	0	0	0	14	23	0.61
Career (1994-1997)	4.47	0	2	0	38	0	48.1	19	25	.267	50	10	1	7	33	.343	.444	16	36	14	4	1	2	0	59	64	0.92

1997 Season

	ERA	W	L	Sv	G	GS	IP	H	HR	BB	SO		Avg	AB	H	2B	3B	HR	RBI	BB	SO	OBP	SLG
Home	9.00	0	1	0	7	0	7.0	10	1	4	4	vs. Left	.240	25	6	2	0	0	2	4	6	.333	.320
Away	1.35	0	0	0	7	0	6.2	7	0	3	5	vs. Right	.344	32	11	3	1	1	9	3	3	.400	.594

Darren Daulton — Marlins
Age 36 – Bats Left (flyball hitter)

	Avg	G	AB	R	H	2B	3B	HR	RBI	BB	SO	HBP	GDP	SB	CS	OBP	SLG	IBB	SH	SF	#Pit	#P/PA	GB	FB	G/F
1997 Season	.263	136	395	68	104	21	8	14	63	76	74	2	4	6	1	.378	.463	5	0	9	1933	3.99	111	153	0.73
Last Five Years	.263	455	1516	248	399	92	16	62	279	288	285	11	14	18	2	.380	.468	21	0	20	7318	3.98	442	543	0.81

1997 Season

	Avg	AB	H	2B	3B	HR	RBI	BB	SO	OBP	SLG
vs. Left	.262	84	22	4	1	3	10	11	19	.343	.440
vs. Right	.264	311	82	17	7	11	53	65	55	.386	.469
Groundball	.239	71	17	3	3	2	11	8	21	.317	.451
Flyball	.240	50	12	3	2	3	9	17	13	.426	.560
Home	.291	182	53	11	6	6	28	47	32	.426	.516
Away	.239	213	51	10	2	8	35	29	42	.332	.418
Day	.200	90	18	1	1	3	12	17	13	.327	.333
Night	.282	305	86	20	7	11	51	59	61	.392	.502
Grass	.263	190	50	12	1	5	30	34	34	.370	.416
Turf	.263	205	54	9	7	9	33	42	40	.384	.507
Pre-All Star	.267	240	64	10	4	11	36	43	47	.372	.479
Post-All Star	.258	155	40	11	4	3	27	33	27	.385	.439
Scoring Posn	.275	109	30	8	0	3	45	25	26	.383	.431
Close & Late	.255	55	14	5	1	2	10	6	15	.323	.491
None on/out	.236	89	21	3	3	4	16	9		.352	.472

	Avg	AB	H	2B	3B	HR	RBI	BB	SO	OBP	SLG
First Pitch	.440	50	22	6	3	2	11	4	0	.464	.800
Ahead in Count	.336	113	38	9	3	4	32	37	0	.484	.575
Behind in Count	.192	146	28	4	2	5	15	0	50	.200	.349
Two Strikes	.168	173	29	3	1	5	13	35	74	.306	.283
Batting #3	.233	116	27	6	3	5	19	30	27	.383	.466
Batting #4	.299	144	43	7	3	5	22	25	28	.397	.493
Other	.252	135	34	8	2	4	22	21	19	.352	.430
March/April	.294	51	15	3	2	1	6	11	10	.422	.490
May	.287	87	25	4	0	5	15	11	16	.360	.506
June	.269	78	21	3	2	4	13	19	19	.404	.513
July	.232	69	16	4	3	1	10	15	17	.360	.420
August	.261	69	18	6	1	1	11	10	7	.346	.420
Sept/Oct	.220	41	9	1	0	2	8	10	5	.385	.390
vs. AL	.214	42	9	2	0	2	4	3	5	.267	.405
vs. NL	.269	353	95	19	8	12	59	73	69	.389	.470

1997 By Position

Position	Avg	AB	H	2B	3B	HR	RBI	BB	SO	OBP	SLG	G	GS	Innings	PO	A	E	DP	Fld Pct	Rng Fctr	In Zone	Outs	Zone Rtg	MLB Zone
As Pinch Hitter	.154	13	2	0	0	0	2	2	4	.313	.154	16	0	---	---	---	---	---	---	---	---	---	---	---
As 1b	.256	117	30	7	2	4	21	16		.364	.453	42	40	271.0	259	17	4	22	.986	---	47	36	.766	.874
As rf	.286	234	67	13	6	9	42	52	51	.408	.509	73	71	556.2	132	6	3	3	.979	2.23	167	133	.796	.813

Last Five Years

	Avg	AB	H	2B	3B	HR	RBI	BB	SO	OBP	SLG
vs. Left	.243	473	115	27	3	17	80	73	99	.349	.421
vs. Right	.272	1043	284	65	13	45	199	215	186	.394	.489
Groundball	.291	440	128	29	9	21	103	77	82	.392	.541
Flyball	.220	236	52	14	2	9	33	50	54	.359	.411
Home	.272	760	207	44	12	30	137	147	140	.390	.480

	Avg	AB	H	2B	3B	HR	RBI	BB	SO	OBP	SLG
First Pitch	.369	187	69	16	6	11	48	17	0	.417	.695
Ahead in Count	.333	381	127	27	5	21	96	144	0	.511	.596
Behind in Count	.202	608	123	29	3	18	82	0	211	.207	.349
Two Strikes	.187	694	130	34	3	16	86	127	285	.315	.314
Batting #4	.267	453	121	23	6	12	66	72	85	.371	.424

Last Five Years

	Avg	AB	H	2B	3B	HR	RBI	BB	SO	OBP	SLG		Avg	AB	H	2B	3B	HR	RBI	BB	SO	OBP	SLG
Away	.254	756	192	48	4	32	142	141	145	.371	.455	Batting #5	.267	908	242	62	7	43	181	180	161	.386	.492
Day	.251	346	87	22	2	19	75	69	69	.375	.491	Other	.232	155	36	7	3	7	32	36	39	.374	.452
Night	.267	1170	312	70	14	43	204	219	216	.382	.461	March/April	.274	219	60	13	2	12	44	57	42	.427	.516
Grass	.255	525	134	36	2	23	100	107	91	.379	.463	May	.261	368	96	22	2	23	78	59	71	.359	.519
Turf	.267	991	265	56	14	39	179	181	194	.381	.470	June	.276	326	90	18	3	11	60	54	66	.381	.451
Pre-All Star	.258	1009	260	57	8	47	188	182	198	.371	.470	July	.245	245	60	16	6	5	41	51	49	.371	.420
Post-All Star	.274	507	139	35	8	15	91	106	87	.399	.464	August	.263	217	57	15	3	7	35	39	32	.375	.456
Scoring Posn	.265	461	122	32	3	17	207	114	93	.400	.458	Sept/Oct	.255	141	36	8	0	4	21	28	25	.380	.397
Close & Late	.247	239	59	16	1	7	37	56	57	.391	.410	vs. AL	.214	42	9	2	0	2	4	3	5	.267	.405
None on/out	.270	366	99	18	5	19	19	52	52	.366	.503	vs. NL	.265	1474	390	90	16	60	275	285	280	.383	.469

Batter vs. Pitcher (since 1984)

Hits Best Against	Avg	AB	H	2B	3B	HR	RBI	BB	SO	OBP	SLG	Hits Worst Against	Avg	AB	H	2B	3B	HR	RBI	BB	SO	OBP	SLG
Butch Henry	.471	17	8	3	0	1	4	3	0	.550	.824	Bob Patterson	.059	17	1	0	0	0	1	1	3	.105	.059
Donovan Osborne	.455	11	5	1	0	2	7	4	2	.600	1.091	Jeff Brantley	.067	15	1	0	0	0	1	1	0	.125	.067
Jim Bullinger	.400	15	6	1	2	0	4	5	4	.571	.733	John Franco	.071	14	1	1	0	0	0	1	6	.133	.143
Bill Swift	.375	24	9	3	1	2	8	4	2	.464	.833	Rheal Cormier	.091	11	1	0	0	0	0	0	4	.091	.091
Andy Ashby	.357	14	5	1	1	1	5	4	1	.500	.786	Chuck McElroy	.133	15	2	0	0	2	0	0	6	.125	.133

Chili Davis — Royals

Age 38 – Bats Both

	Avg	G	AB	R	H	2B	3B	HR	RBI	BB	SO	HBP	GDP	SB	CS	OBP	SLG	IBB	SH	SF	#Pit	#P/PA	GB	FB	G/F
1997 Season	.279	140	477	71	133	20	0	30	90	85	96	1	15	6	3	.386	.509	16	0	4	2084	3.68	157	135	1.16
Last Five Years	.285	664	2396	371	684	117	1	131	467	400	493	3	75	21	11	.385	.499	62	1	25	10669	3.78	821	657	1.25

1997 Season

	Avg	AB	H	2B	3B	HR	RBI	BB	SO	OBP	SLG		Avg	AB	H	2B	3B	HR	RBI	BB	SO	OBP	SLG
vs. Left	.327	147	48	11	0	9	32	18	25	.395	.585	First Pitch	.275	69	19	2	0	5	12	11	0	.375	.522
vs. Right	.258	330	85	9	0	21	58	67	71	.383	.476	Ahead in Count	.392	102	40	6	0	11	26	41	0	.563	.775
Groundball	.262	84	22	2	0	7	20	21	14	.410	.536	Behind in Count	.210	210	44	6	0	5	26	0	74	.211	.310
Flyball	.317	82	26	5	0	4	10	10	17	.387	.524	Two Strikes	.191	209	40	4	0	6	25	33	96	.300	.297
Home	.265	264	70	9	0	21	53	46	50	.371	.538	Batting #4	.256	250	64	9	0	16	47	41	54	.359	.484
Away	.296	213	63	11	0	9	37	39	46	.406	.474	Batting #5	.316	190	60	9	0	12	35	37	32	.427	.553
Day	.281	153	43	7	0	10	29	20	35	.364	.523	Other	.243	37	9	2	0	2	8	7	10	.356	.459
Night	.278	324	90	13	0	20	61	65	61	.396	.503	March/April	.280	50	14	2	0	2	10	8	9	.390	.440
Grass	.284	426	121	16	0	29	83	73	87	.386	.526	May	.275	91	25	1	0	4	13	24	19	.422	.418
Turf	.235	51	12	4	0	1	7	12	9	.391	.373	June	.311	74	23	4	0	7	25	12	17	.402	.649
Pre-All Star	.298	228	68	7	0	13	48	44	46	.411	.500	July	.286	91	26	6	0	3	14	14	.381	.451
Post-All Star	.261	249	65	13	0	17	42	41	50	.363	.518	August	.327	107	35	6	0	12	26	15	21	.407	.720
Scoring Posn	.314	118	37	5	0	7	60	40	17	.475	.534	Sept/Oct	.156	64	10	1	0	2	8	12	16	.286	.266
Close & Late	.301	83	25	4	0	5	16	14	18	.398	.530	vs. AL	.285	453	129	19	0	29	88	78	90	.388	.519
None on/out	.222	135	30	8	0	8	8	5	28	.250	.459	vs. NL	.167	24	4	1	0	1	2	7	6	.355	.333

1997 By Position

Position	Avg	AB	H	2B	3B	HR	RBI	BB	SO	OBP	SLG	G	GS	Innings	PO	A	E	DP	Fld Pct	Rng Fctr	In Zone Outs	Zone Rtg	MLB Zone
As DH	.280	472	132	20	0	30	90	83	93	.386	.513	133	131	—	—	—	—	—	—	—	—	—	—

Last Five Years

	Avg	AB	H	2B	3B	HR	RBI	BB	SO	OBP	SLG		Avg	AB	H	2B	3B	HR	RBI	BB	SO	OBP	SLG
vs. Left	.308	699	215	38	0	40	155	99	145	.386	.534	First Pitch	.347	378	131	17	0	24	78	49	0	.418	.582
vs. Right	.276	1697	469	79	1	91	312	301	348	.384	.485	Ahead in Count	.392	523	205	40	1	37	145	186	0	.544	.685
Groundball	.287	471	135	23	0	20	76	89	93	.398	.463	Behind in Count	.197	1027	202	34	0	35	132	0	394	.198	.332
Flyball	.272	489	133	29	0	27	89	74	111	.364	.497	Two Strikes	.185	1100	204	26	0	43	139	165	493	.291	.326
Home	.289	1241	359	62	0	74	250	215	250	.391	.518	Batting #4	.281	1915	539	92	1	102	375	313	406	.380	.490
Away	.281	1155	325	55	1	57	217	185	243	.378	.479	Batting #5	.312	420	131	22	0	25	82	73	71	.410	.543
Day	.318	672	214	38	0	43	154	110	145	.411	.567	Other	.230	61	14	3	0	4	10	14	16	.368	.475
Night	.273	1724	470	79	1	88	313	290	348	.375	.473	March/April	.314	287	90	16	0	14	58	40	54	.403	.516
Grass	.288	2108	608	99	1	119	415	351	439	.387	.506	May	.296	470	139	24	1	21	89	106	112	.421	.485
Turf	.264	288	76	18	0	12	52	49	54	.371	.451	June	.281	413	116	19	0	25	92	53	77	.360	.508
Pre-All Star	.303	1285	389	67	1	67	263	222	259	.403	.513	July	.282	433	122	23	0	25	89	80	75	.389	.508
Post-All Star	.266	1111	295	50	0	64	204	178	234	.363	.483	August	.281	455	128	18	0	32	80	79	108	.384	.532
Scoring Posn	.310	636	197	33	0	37	328	167	126	.440	.536	Sept/Oct	.263	338	89	17	0	14	59	44	67	.341	.438
Close & Late	.278	353	98	14	0	16	56	71	74	.399	.453	vs. AL	.287	2372	680	116	1	130	465	393	487	.385	.501
None on/out	.260	643	167	37	0	29	29	62	141	.326	.453	vs. NL	.167	24	4	1	0	1	2	7	6	.355	.333

Batter vs. Pitcher (since 1984)

Hits Best Against	Avg	AB	H	2B	3B	HR	RBI	BB	SO	OBP	SLG	Hits Worst Against	Avg	AB	H	2B	3B	HR	RBI	BB	SO	OBP	SLG
Mike Jackson	.636	11	7	0	0	0	2	7	1	.750	.636	Jeff Montgomery	.050	20	1	0	0	0	0	5	7	.240	.050
Paul Quantrill	.571	14	8	0	0	1	3	1	0	.600	.786	Jesse Orosco	.059	17	1	0	0	0	1	5	8	.273	.059
Scott Radinsky	.556	9	5	2	0	1	8	3	3	.615	1.111	Brad Radke	.154	13	2	0	0	0	0	1	1	.214	.154
Danny Darwin	.400	20	8	1	0	3	4	6	5	.538	.900	Dennis Cook	.167	12	2	0	0	0	0	0	5	.167	.167
Alex Fernandez	.320	25	8	2	0	4	9	4	6	.414	.880	Jose Bautista	.188	16	3	0	0	0	0	0	3	.188	.188

Eric Davis — Orioles
Age 36 – Bats Right

	Avg	G	AB	R	H	2B	3B	HR	RBI	BB	SO	HBP	GDP	SB	CS	OBP	SLG	IBB	SH	SF	#Pit	#P/PA	GB	FB	G/F
1997 Season	.304	42	158	29	48	11	0	8	25	14	47	1	2	6	0	.358	.525	0	0	3	712	4.05	53	38	1.39
Last Five Years	.259	339	1144	200	296	53	1	57	189	157	319	8	26	69	16	.349	.456	10	1	11	5386	4.08	374	308	1.21

1997 Season

	Avg	AB	H	2B	3B	HR	RBI	BB	SO	OBP	SLG		Avg	AB	H	2B	3B	HR	RBI	BB	SO	OBP	SLG
vs. Left	.382	55	21	5	0	3	7	6	15	.443	.636	Scoring Posn	.298	47	14	4	0	1	17	1	13	.294	.447
vs. Right	.262	103	27	6	0	5	18	8	32	.313	.466	Close & Late	.385	26	10	1	0	1	5	4	9	.467	.538
Home	.375	88	33	8	0	7	22	8	19	.418	.705	None on/out	.367	30	11	2	0	2	2	3	9	.424	.633
Away	.214	70	15	3	0	1	3	6	28	.282	.300	Batting #3	.312	109	34	8	0	6	15	9	33	.367	.550
First Pitch	.500	6	3	1	0	1	1	0	0	.500	1.167	Batting #4	.326	43	14	3	0	2	10	5	11	.380	.535
Ahead in Count	.375	32	12	5	0	1	4	8	0	.500	.625	Other	.000	6	0	0	0	0	0	0	3	.000	.000
Behind in Count	.293	82	24	4	0	3	10	0	36	.286	.451	Pre-All Star	.302	129	39	0	0	7	21	13	36	.363	.543
Two Strikes	.221	86	19	4	0	3	10	6	47	.269	.372	Post-All Star	.310	29	9	1	0	1	4	1	11	.333	.448

Last Five Years

	Avg	AB	H	2B	3B	HR	RBI	BB	SO	OBP	SLG		Avg	AB	H	2B	3B	HR	RBI	BB	SO	OBP	SLG
vs. Left	.249	309	77	14	0	11	42	46	84	.348	.401	First Pitch	.275	80	22	7	0	1	8	7	0	.337	.400
vs. Right	.262	835	219	39	1	46	147	111	235	.350	.477	Ahead in Count	.366	265	97	22	0	22	74	78	0	.509	.698
Groundball	.271	291	79	14	0	15	47	51	78	.379	.474	Behind in Count	.205	536	110	15	1	20	69	0	247	.208	.349
Flyball	.268	179	48	9	0	9	31	26	43	.359	.469	Two Strikes	.180	595	107	18	0	24	74	72	319	.271	.331
Home	.277	573	159	28	0	28	105	91	148	.376	.473	Batting #3	.229	375	86	19	0	19	56	44	102	.310	.432
Away	.240	571	137	25	1	29	84	66	171	.321	.440	Batting #5	.299	254	76	11	0	16	52	32	65	.379	.531
Day	.253	384	97	20	1	19	65	56	112	.348	.458	Other	.260	515	134	23	1	22	81	81	152	.362	.437
Night	.262	760	199	33	0	38	124	101	207	.350	.455	March/April	.251	287	72	12	0	12	48	31	77	.322	.418
Grass	.252	769	194	32	1	39	127	102	204	.339	.449	May	.248	234	58	13	0	14	46	42	79	.361	.483
Turf	.272	375	102	21	0	18	62	55	115	.370	.472	June	.254	114	29	6	0	5	22	22	33	.377	.439
Pre-All Star	.258	699	180	34	0	33	122	100	207	.349	.448	July	.279	179	50	11	0	7	22	20	44	.355	.458
Post-All Star	.261	445	116	19	1	24	67	57	112	.349	.470	August	.264	163	43	6	0	10	27	13	39	.324	.485
Scoring Posn	.272	301	82	16	1	13	128	62	92	.388	.462	Sept/Oct	.263	167	44	5	1	9	24	29	47	.376	.467
Close & Late	.223	193	43	4	0	9	28	30	63	.326	.383	vs. AL	.252	353	89	16	1	17	53	46	110	.337	.448
None on/out	.273	245	67	12	0	17	17	28	69	.350	.531	vs. NL	.262	791	207	37	0	40	136	111	209	.354	.460

Batter vs. Pitcher (career)

Hits Best Against	Avg	AB	H	2B	3B	HR	RBI	BB	SO	OBP	SLG	Hits Worst Against	Avg	AB	H	2B	3B	HR	RBI	BB	SO	OBP	SLG
Paul Assenmacher	.625	8	5	0	0	2	4	2	2	.727	1.375	Kevin Brown	.000	11	0	0	0	0	0	1	5	.083	.000
Mike Hampton	.625	8	5	0	0	1	3	2	2	.727	1.000	Ken Hill	.000	9	0	0	0	0	0	2	3	.231	.000
Butch Henry	.500	8	4	2	0	1	4	4	1	.615	1.125	Kent Bottenfield	.083	12	1	1	0	0	2	1	1	.154	.167
John Smoltz	.438	32	14	2	0	5	8	5	5	.514	.969	Darryl Kile	.105	19	2	0	0	1	1	1	9	.150	.263
Xavier Hernandez	.308	13	4	0	0	3	6	2	3	.400	1.000	Donovan Osborne	.125	16	2	0	0	0	0	2	7	.222	.125

Mark Davis — Brewers
Age 37 – Pitches Left (groundball pitcher)

	ERA	W	L	Sv	G	GS	IP	BB	SO	Avg	H	2B	3B	HR	RBI	OBP	SLG	GF	IR	IRS	Hld	SvOp	SB	CS	GB	FB	G/F
1997 Season	5.51	0	0	0	19	0	16.1	5	14	.323	21	1	0	4	13	.380	.523	3	20	5	3	1	1	0	25	12	2.08
Last Five Years	5.19	1	6	4	99	0	102.1	62	99	.293	120	15	3	18	69	.388	.477	19	70	19	12	8	11	2	139	87	1.60

1997 Season

	ERA	W	L	Sv	G	GS	IP	H	HR	BB	SO		Avg	AB	H	2B	3B	HR	RBI	BB	SO	OBP	SLG
Home	7.15	0	0	0	13	0	11.1	18	3	5	9	vs. Left	.286	35	10	0	0	1	5	3	8	.359	.371
Away	1.80	0	0	0	6	0	5.0	3	1	0	5	vs. Right	.367	30	11	1	0	3	8	2	6	.406	.700

Last Five Years

	ERA	W	L	Sv	G	GS	IP	H	HR	BB	SO		Avg	AB	H	2B	3B	HR	RBI	BB	SO	OBP	SLG
Home	5.72	1	3	2	55	0	56.2	64	9	37	53	vs. Left	.257	152	39	4	1	6	23	22	42	.354	.414
Away	4.53	0	3	2	44	0	45.2	56	9	25	46	vs. Right	.315	257	81	11	2	12	46	40	57	.408	.514
Day	4.09	1	1	2	32	0	33.0	39	6	19	33	Inning 1-6	.284	88	25	0	1	8	20	7	18	.337	.580
Night	5.71	0	5	2	67	0	69.1	81	12	43	66	Inning 7+	.296	321	95	15	2	10	49	55	81	.401	.449
Grass	5.21	0	3	2	68	0	67.1	81	11	39	64	None on	.321	184	59	8	1	12	12	32	41	.421	.571
Turf	5.14	1	3	2	31	0	35.0	39	7	23	35	Runners on	.271	225	61	7	2	6	57	30	58	.360	.400
March/April	6.05	0	1	0	20	0	19.1	14	2	19	17	Scoring Posn	.276	145	40	6	1	5	54	20	34	.365	.434
May	8.16	1	2	0	15	0	14.1	23	2	12	15	Close & Late	.293	140	41	3	1	3	22	28	39	.415	.393
June	3.95	0	0	0	9	0	13.2	14	3	4	10	None on/out	.360	89	32	5	0	6	6	19	18	.472	.618
July	4.91	0	0	3	9	0	11.0	14	4	6	17	vs. 1st Batr (relief)	.325	80	26	3	1	6	15	18	16	.455	.613
August	7.20	0	3	0	20	0	15.0	26	1	10	9	1st Inning Pitched	.290	303	88	10	3	13	61	50	71	.393	.472
Sept/Oct	2.79	0	0	1	26	0	29.0	27	6	11	31	First 15 Pitches	.287	261	75	8	2	14	43	37	56	.379	.494
Starter	0.00	0	0	0	0	0	0.0	0	0	0	0	Pitch 16-30	.286	119	34	5	1	4	19	21	34	.393	.445
Reliever	5.19	1	6	4	99	0	102.1	120	18	62	99	Pitch 31-45	.375	24	9	2	0	0	7	4	8	.464	.458
0 Days rest (Relief)	8.28	0	1	1	25	0	25.0	36	7	14	25	Pitch 46+	.400	5	2	0	0	0	0	1	1	.400	.400
1 or 2 Days rest	5.24	0	5	1	47	0	44.2	53	7	31	39	First Pitch	.380	50	19	2	0	1	4	6	0	.446	.480
3+ Days rest	2.76	1	0	2	27	0	32.2	31	4	17	35	Ahead in Count	.192	219	42	4	1	4	28	0	90	.195	.274
vs. AL	5.51	0	0	0	18	0	16.1	20	4	5	14	Behind in Count	.439	82	36	5	1	8	22	27	0	.578	.817
vs. NL	5.13	1	6	4	81	0	86.0	100	14	57	85	Two Strikes	.196	204	40	5	1	9	22	29	99	.299	.319
Pre-All Star	6.26	1	3	0	46	0	50.1	59	9	37	47	Pre-All Star	.286	206	59	10	1	9	34	37	47	.398	.476
Post-All Star	4.15	0	3	4	53	0	52.0	61	9	25	52	Post-All Star	.300	203	61	5	2	9	35	25	52	.378	.478

Pitcher vs. Batter (since 1984)

Pitches Best Vs.	Avg	AB	H	2B	3B	HR	RBI	BB	SO	OBP	SLG	Pitches Worst Vs.	Avg	AB	H	2B	3B	HR	RBI	BB	SO	OBP	SLG
Fred McGriff	.000	9	0	0	0	0	1	4	4	.308	.000	Will Clark	.471	17	8	2	2	1	11	0	3	.471	1.000
Darryl Strawberry	.080	25	2	0	0	1	1	2	12	.148	.200	Mark Grace	.455	11	5	1	0	2	3	0	1	.455	1.091
Mariano Duncan	.105	19	2	1	0	0	0	2	7	.190	.158	Brett Butler	.400	10	4	1	0	0	3	5	3	.600	.500

115

Pitches Best Vs.	Avg	AB	H	2B	3B	HR	RBI	BB	SO	OBP	SLG	Pitches Worst Vs.	Avg	AB	H	2B	3B	HR	RBI	BB	SO	OBP	SLG
Ron Gant	.111	9	1	0	0	0	0	2	3	.273	.111	Barry Bonds	.364	11	4	2	0	0	2	2	4	.462	.545
Roberto Kelly	.125	8	1	0	0	0	2	2	0	.273	.125	Willie McGee	.333	21	7	1	0	2	7	2	7	.391	.667

Russ Davis — Mariners   Age 28 – Bats Right

	Avg	G	AB	R	H	2B	3B	HR	RBI	BB	SO	HBP	GDP	SB	CS	OBP	SLG	IBB	SH	SF	#Pit	#P/PA	GB	FB	G/F
1997 Season	.271	119	420	57	114	29	1	20	63	27	100	2	11	6	2	.317	.488	2	3	2	1626	3.57	114	131	0.87
Career (1994-1997)	.260	214	699	95	182	43	3	27	94	54	180	5	13	8	2	.317	.446	3	7	2	2875	3.74	178	227	0.78

1997 Season

	Avg	AB	H	2B	3B	HR	RBI	BB	SO	OBP	SLG		Avg	AB	H	2B	3B	HR	RBI	BB	SO	OBP	SLG
vs. Left	.248	117	29	7	0	5	19	11	24	.313	.436	First Pitch	.425	87	37	11	1	10	23	1	0	.432	.920
vs. Right	.281	303	85	22	1	15	44	16	76	.319	.508	Ahead in Count	.436	78	34	8	0	7	15	14	0	.522	.808
Groundball	.308	78	24	6	0	3	12	6	16	.365	.500	Behind in Count	.156	179	28	6	0	3	19	0	82	.159	.240
Flyball	.238	63	15	5	1	4	7	3	19	.273	.540	Two Strikes	.136	191	26	7	0	2	17	12	100	.190	.204
Home	.282	213	60	16	0	11	34	13	56	.329	.512	Batting #7	.226	84	19	3	0	5	10	5	23	.267	.440
Away	.261	207	54	13	1	9	29	14	44	.305	.464	Batting #8	.277	321	89	25	1	14	50	20	73	.323	.492
Day	.256	133	34	9	0	7	16	8	32	.298	.481	Other	.400	15	6	1	0	1	3	2	4	.471	.667
Night	.279	287	80	20	1	13	47	19	68	.326	.491	March/April	.337	86	29	9	0	4	15	8	18	.402	.581
Grass	.259	189	49	12	1	7	26	13	39	.304	.444	May	.229	70	16	5	0	2	6	2	13	.250	.386
Turf	.281	231	65	17	0	13	37	14	61	.328	.524	June	.323	96	31	8	0	4	12	4	30	.350	.531
Pre-All Star	.309	272	84	24	0	12	38	16	65	.349	.529	July	.260	96	25	7	1	4	21	6	24	.301	.479
Post-All Star	.203	148	30	5	1	8	25	11	35	.258	.412	August	.183	71	13	0	0	6	9	5	15	.237	.437
Scoring Posn	.287	108	31	11	0	0	38	11	26	.347	.389	Sept/Oct	.000	1	0	0	0	0	0	2	0	.667	.000
Close & Late	.257	74	19	4	0	5	15	5	21	.300	.514	vs. AL	.261	380	99	24	1	15	52	24	88	.306	.447
None on/out	.286	84	24	6	0	7	7	7	18	.348	.607	vs. NL	.375	40	15	5	0	5	11	3	12	.419	.875

1997 By Position

Position	Avg	AB	H	2B	3B	HR	RBI	BB	SO	OBP	SLG	G	GS	Innings	PO	A	E	DP	Fld Pct	Rng Fctr	In Zone	Zone Outs	Zone Rtg	MLB Zone
As 3b	.271	413	112	29	1	19	60	27	98	.318	.484	117	112	992.0	56	216	18	24	.938	2.47	318	248	.780	.801

Tim Davis — Mariners   Age 27 – Pitches Left (groundball pitcher)

	ERA	W	L	Sv	G	GS	IP	BB	SO	Avg	H	2B	3B	HR	RBI	OBP	SLG	GF	IR	IRS	Hld	SvOp	SB	CS	GB	FB	G/F
1997 Season	6.75	0	0	0	2	0	6.2	4	10	.231	6	3	0	1	5	.355	.462	1	1	0	0	0	1	0	8	4	2.00
Career (1994-1997)	4.62	6	5	2	89	6	122.2	64	91	.282	136	27	2	11	75	.367	.414	17	63	23	10	4	7	5	192	118	1.63

1997 Season

	ERA	W	L	Sv	G	GS	IP	H	HR	BB	SO		Avg	AB	H	2B	3B	HR	RBI	BB	SO	OBP	SLG
Home	8.31	0	0	0	1	0	4.1	3	1	4	6	vs. Left	.083	12	1	1	0	0	1	1	6	.214	.167
Away	3.86	0	0	0	1	0	2.1	3	0	0	4	vs. Right	.357	14	5	2	0	1	5	3	4	.471	.714

Career (1994-1997)

	ERA	W	L	Sv	G	GS	IP	H	HR	BB	SO		Avg	AB	H	2B	3B	HR	RBI	BB	SO	OBP	SLG
Home	5.37	4	2	1	45	2	55.1	53	7	31	39	vs. Left	.266	158	42	8	0	3	26	22	30	.357	.373
Away	4.01	2	3	1	44	4	67.1	83	4	33	52	vs. Right	.289	325	94	19	2	8	49	42	61	.372	.434
Day	5.10	1	3	1	25	0	30.0	43	4	15	27	Inning 1-6	.318	258	82	14	2	8	55	34	47	.394	.481
Night	4.47	5	2	1	64	6	92.2	93	7	49	64	Inning 7+	.240	225	54	13	0	3	20	30	44	.336	.338
Grass	3.58	1	2	1	40	2	55.1	64	3	28	45	None on	.266	237	63	17	1	3	3	26	45	.346	.384
Turf	5.48	5	3	1	49	4	67.1	72	8	36	46	Runners on	.297	246	73	10	1	8	72	38	46	.386	.443
March/April	4.24	0	1	1	17	0	23.1	22	2	13	21	Scoring Posn	.284	148	42	6	0	5	64	31	32	.397	.426
May	5.44	2	3	0	31	5	44.2	50	5	30	29	Close & Late	.254	67	17	4	0	2	9	12	17	.375	.403
June	5.40	1	1	1	11	0	10.0	8	0	6	7	None on/out	.257	109	28	8	1	1	1	13	18	.341	.376
July	4.62	1	0	0	18	0	25.1	34	3	13	23	vs. 1st Batr (relief)	.254	71	16	5	0	0	11	10	15	.329	.296
August	2.61	1	0	0	7	1	10.1	13	0	2	6	1st Inning Pitched	.286	262	75	13	1	5	48	36	50	.372	.401
Sept/Oct	3.00	1	0	0	5	0	9.0	9	1	0	5	First 15 Pitches	.292	233	68	14	0	4	37	27	39	.369	.403
Starter	5.90	3	1	0	6	6	29.0	37	2	19	21	Pitch 16-30	.250	104	26	3	1	3	20	16	23	.344	.385
Reliever	4.23	3	4	2	83	0	93.2	99	9	45	70	Pitch 31-45	.288	59	17	7	0	2	8	6	12	.364	.508
0 Days rest (Relief)	3.32	0	0	2	23	0	19.0	13	1	11	14	Pitch 46+	.287	87	25	3	1	2	10	15	17	.392	.414
1 or 2 Days rest	7.90	1	4	0	31	0	27.1	41	4	15	18	First Pitch	.338	68	23	4	0	2	16	5	0	.387	.485
3+ Days rest	2.47	2	0	0	29	0	47.1	45	4	19	38	Ahead in Count	.227	211	48	6	1	4	20	0	79	.233	.322
vs. AL	4.62	6	5	2	89	6	122.2	136	11	64	91	Behind in Count	.319	119	38	8	1	3	21	39	0	.487	.479
vs. NL	0.00	0	0	0	0	0	0.0	0	0	0	0	Two Strikes	.209	211	44	4	1	3	19	20	91	.278	.280
Pre-All Star	4.80	3	5	2	63	5	84.1	85	7	50	61	Pre-All Star	.264	322	85	20	2	7	53	50	61	.367	.404
Post-All Star	4.23	3	0	0	26	1	38.1	51	4	14	30	Post-All Star	.317	161	51	7	0	4	22	14	30	.367	.435

Pitcher vs. Batter (career)

Pitches Best Vs.	Avg	AB	H	2B	3B	HR	RBI	BB	SO	OBP	SLG	Pitches Worst Vs.	Avg	AB	H	2B	3B	HR	RBI	BB	SO	OBP	SLG
												Lance Johnson	.375	8	3	0	0	0	2	2	0	.455	.375

Roland de la Maza — Royals   Age 26 – Pitches Right

	ERA	W	L	Sv	G	GS	IP	BB	SO	Avg	H	2B	3B	HR	RBI	OBP	SLG	GF	IR	IRS	Hld	SvOp	SB	CS	GB	FB	G/F
1997 Season	4.50	0	0	0	1	0	2.0	1	1	.125	1	0	0	1	1	.222	.500	0	0	0	0	0	0	0	4	0	0.00

1997 Season

	ERA	W	L	Sv	G	GS	IP	H	HR	BB	SO		Avg	AB	H	2B	3B	HR	RBI	BB	SO	OBP	SLG
Home	0.00	0	0	0	0	0	0.0	0	0	0	0	vs. Left	.500	2	1	0	0	1	1	1	0	.667	2.000
Away	4.50	0	0	0	1	0	2.0	1	1	1	1	vs. Right	.000	6	0	0	0	0	0	0	0	.000	.000

Rick DeHart — Expos
Age 28 – Pitches Left

	ERA	W	L	Sv	G	GS	IP	BB	SO	Avg	H	2B	3B	HR	RBI	OBP	SLG	GF	IR	IRS	Hld	SvOp	SB	CS	GB	FB	G/F
1997 Season	5.52	2	1	0	23	0	29.1	14	29	.292	33	6	0	7	23	.364	.531	7	20	7	1	1	6	3	35	34	1.03

1997 Season

	ERA	W	L	Sv	G	GS	IP	H	HR	BB	SO		Avg	AB	H	2B	3B	HR	RBI	BB	SO	OBP	SLG
Home	2.16	1	0	0	10	0	16.2	13	2	5	21	vs. Left	.324	37	12	4	0	1	7	2	10	.350	.514
Away	9.95	1	1	0	13	0	12.2	20	5	9	8	vs. Right	.276	76	21	2	0	6	16	12	19	.371	.539

Mike DeJean — Rockies
Age 27 – Pitches Right (groundball pitcher)

	ERA	W	L	Sv	G	GS	IP	BB	SO	Avg	H	2B	3B	HR	RBI	OBP	SLG	GF	IR	IRS	Hld	SvOp	SB	CS	GB	FB	G/F
1997 Season	3.99	5	0	2	56	0	67.2	24	38	.280	74	20	2	4	38	.346	.417	16	27	11	13	4	3	2	120	67	1.79

1997 Season

	ERA	W	L	Sv	G	GS	IP	H	HR	BB	SO		Avg	AB	H	2B	3B	HR	RBI	BB	SO	OBP	SLG
Home	2.58	4	0	0	31	0	38.1	39	2	10	19	vs. Left	.296	142	42	11	1	3	21	12	19	.348	.451
Away	5.83	1	0	2	25	0	29.1	35	2	14	19	vs. Right	.262	122	32	9	1	1	17	12	19	.343	.377
Day	3.90	2	0	1	23	0	27.2	31	0	5	21	Inning 1-6	.292	65	19	7	1	0	13	4	11	.343	.431
Night	4.05	3	0	1	33	0	40.0	43	4	19	17	Inning 7+	.276	199	55	13	1	4	25	20	27	.347	.412
Grass	3.86	4	0	2	51	0	58.1	67	4	20	34	None on	.259	139	36	7	0	3	3	11	20	.313	.374
Turf	4.82	1	0	0	5	0	9.1	7	0	4	4	Runners on	.304	125	38	13	2	1	35	13	18	.380	.464
March/April	0.00	0	0	0	0	0	0.0	0	0	0	0	Scoring Posn	.293	75	22	7	1	0	29	10	10	.379	.413
May	2.75	2	0	1	14	0	19.2	20	0	5	9	Close & Late	.253	79	20	6	1	0	10	14	15	.375	.354
June	4.32	1	0	0	14	0	16.2	18	2	10	10	None on/out	.242	62	15	4	0	0	0	4	11	.288	.306
July	9.72	0	0	0	6	0	8.1	12	2	3	7	vs. 1st Batr (relief)	.275	51	14	5	0	0	5	4	9	.327	.373
August	2.45	1	0	0	10	0	11.0	10	0	2	5	1st Inning Pitched	.313	192	60	17	2	3	33	19	27	.379	.469
Sept/Oct	3.00	1	0	1	12	0	12.0	14	0	4	7	First 15 Pitches	.300	170	51	14	2	2	26	12	24	.351	.441
Starter	0.00	0	0	0	0	0	0.0	0	0	0	0	Pitch 16-30	.267	75	20	5	0	2	10	12	8	.375	.413
Reliever	3.99	5	0	2	56	0	67.2	74	4	24	38	Pitch 31-45	.158	19	3	1	0	0	2	0	6	.158	.211
0 Days rest (Relief)	4.40	2	0	1	16	0	14.1	20	1	11	6	Pitch 46+	.000	0	0	0	0	0	0	0	0	.000	.000
1 or 2 Days rest	4.86	1	0	1	29	0	37.0	43	3	10	23	First Pitch	.368	38	14	5	0	1	8	2	0	.429	.579
3+ Days rest	1.65	2	0	0	11	0	16.1	11	0	3	9	Ahead in Count	.161	118	19	6	0	0	9	0	37	.168	.212
vs. AL	2.00	0	0	0	7	0	9.0	5	0	5	6	Behind in Count	.359	64	23	6	1	1	10	13	0	.468	.531
vs. NL	4.30	5	0	2	49	0	58.2	69	4	19	32	Two Strikes	.171	105	18	5	0	1	10	9	38	.237	.248
Pre-All Star	3.15	3	0	1	30	0	40.0	39	2	16	22	Pre-All Star	.258	151	39	11	0	2	19	16	22	.335	.371
Post-All Star	5.20	2	0	1	26	0	27.2	35	2	8	16	Post-All Star	.310	113	35	9	2	2	19	8	16	.361	.478

Carlos Delgado — Blue Jays
Age 26 – Bats Left

	Avg	G	AB	R	H	2B	3B	HR	RBI	BB	SO	HBP	GDP	SB	CS	OBP	SLG	IBB	SH	SF	#Pit	#P/PA	GB	FB	G/F
1997 Season	.262	153	519	79	136	42	3	30	91	64	133	8	6	0	3	.350	.528	9	0	4	2367	3.98	134	181	0.74
Career (1993-1997)	.253	373	1229	171	311	75	5	67	218	154	344	20	25	1	4	.342	.486	15	0	15	5772	4.07	337	390	0.86

1997 Season

	Avg	AB	H	2B	3B	HR	RBI	BB	SO	OBP	SLG		Avg	AB	H	2B	3B	HR	RBI	BB	SO	OBP	SLG
vs. Left	.254	134	34	14	2	2	16	13	35	.325	.433	First Pitch	.292	48	14	5	0	2	11	8	0	.383	.521
vs. Right	.265	385	102	28	1	28	75	51	98	.358	.561	Ahead in Count	.370	108	40	10	0	14	26	28	0	.500	.852
Groundball	.232	99	23	11	1	4	17	17	20	.350	.485	Behind in Count	.197	259	51	17	1	9	39	0	111	.215	.375
Flyball	.277	65	18	6	0	3	8	11	22	.382	.508	Two Strikes	.195	282	55	18	3	7	31	28	133	.275	.345
Home	.271	258	70	22	2	17	52	37	71	.368	.570	Batting #4	.243	148	36	9	1	9	26	20	46	.333	.500
Away	.253	261	66	20	1	13	39	27	62	.331	.487	Batting #5	.282	248	70	27	2	15	43	30	55	.371	.589
Day	.265	185	49	12	1	6	20	31	48	.383	.438	Other	.244	123	30	6	0	6	22	14	32	.326	.439
Night	.260	334	87	30	2	24	71	33	85	.330	.578	March/April	.345	55	19	1	0	5	15	8	14	.438	.636
Grass	.253	217	55	17	1	10	34	21	51	.327	.479	May	.265	83	22	10	2	3	10	7	17	.337	.542
Turf	.268	302	81	25	2	20	57	43	82	.366	.563	June	.222	90	20	5	0	7	15	12	25	.327	.511
Pre-All Star	.266	248	66	18	2	16	43	32	65	.361	.548	July	.207	92	19	4	1	7	19	13	35	.308	.500
Post-All Star	.258	271	70	24	1	14	48	32	68	.339	.509	August	.255	106	27	9	0	6	23	12	24	.325	.509
Scoring Posn	.266	128	34	7	1	10	64	23	32	.380	.570	Sept/Oct	.312	93	29	13	0	2	9	12	18	.398	.516
Close & Late	.236	89	21	6	0	4	14	15	21	.349	.438	vs. AL	.268	466	125	38	3	25	81	57	118	.355	.524
None on/out	.243	144	35	13	0	6	6	13	34	.314	.458	vs. NL	.208	53	11	4	0	5	10	7	15	.306	.566

1997 By Position

Position	Avg	AB	H	2B	3B	HR	RBI	BB	SO	OBP	SLG	G	GS	Innings	PO	A	E	DP	Fld Pct	Rng Fctr	In Zone	Zone Outs	In Zone Rtg	MLB Zone
As DH	.250	88	22	4	0	5	15	13	20	.353	.466	33	21	---	---	---	---	---	---	---	---	---	---	---
As Pinch Hitter	.267	15	4	1	0	0	0	0	6	.267	.333	15	0	---	---	---	---	---	---	---	---	---	---	---
As 1b	.266	428	114	38	3	25	76	51	111	.351	.544	119	116	1035.2	963	64	12	98	.988	---	212	184	.868	.874

Career (1993-1997)

	Avg	AB	H	2B	3B	HR	RBI	BB	SO	OBP	SLG		Avg	AB	H	2B	3B	HR	RBI	BB	SO	OBP	SLG
vs. Left	.210	271	57	20	3	8	35	22	91	.278	.395	First Pitch	.344	122	42	10	1	5	28	14	0	.415	.566
vs. Right	.265	958	254	55	2	59	183	132	253	.359	.511	Ahead in Count	.372	247	92	19	0	29	69	70	0	.509	.802
Groundball	.251	279	70	18	2	10	45	41	70	.356	.437	Behind in Count	.188	613	115	30	2	20	76	0	280	.202	.341
Flyball	.235	200	47	14	0	8	25	25	64	.325	.425	Two Strikes	.175	693	121	32	4	18	73	70	344	.255	.310
Home	.266	624	166	41	3	36	111	91	187	.364	.514	Batting #3	.267	393	105	28	1	17	71	46	104	.352	.473
Away	.240	605	145	34	2	31	107	63	157	.319	.456	Batting #6	.252	298	75	9	1	20	61	43	100	.348	.490
Day	.271	428	116	21	2	23	70	62	115	.371	.491	Other	.243	538	131	38	3	30	86	65	140	.331	.493
Night	.243	801	195	54	3	44	148	92	229	.336	.483	March/April	.300	223	67	7	0	19	62	34	67	.392	.587
Grass	.237	503	119	30	2	25	87	49	135	.312	.453	May	.243	255	62	18	3	7	24	28	72	.332	.420
Turf	.264	726	192	45	3	42	131	105	209	.362	.508	June	.240	171	41	11	0	11	36	24	53	.351	.497

Career (1993-1997)

	Avg	AB	H	2B	3B	HR	RBI	BB	SO	OBP	SLG		Avg	AB	H	2B	3B	HR	RBI	BB	SO	OBP	SLG
Pre-All Star	.261	689	180	38	3	41	130	94	208	.359	.504	July	.220	168	37	10	1	13	32	26	57	.328	.524
Post-All Star	.243	540	131	37	2	26	88	60	136	.320	.463	August	.271	181	49	13	0	10	38	21	42	.340	.508
Scoring Posn	.262	321	84	12	2	24	160	48	80	.354	.536	Sept/Oct	.238	231	55	16	1	7	26	21	53	.307	.407
Close & Late	.215	200	43	11	0	10	30	24	55	.307	.420	vs. AL	.255	1176	300	71	5	62	208	147	329	.344	.482
None on/out	.228	307	70	23	0	16	16	29	87	.305	.459	vs. NL	.208	53	11	4	0	5	10	7	15	.306	.566

Batter vs. Pitcher (career)

Hits Best Against	Avg	AB	H	2B	3B	HR	RBI	BB	SO	OBP	SLG	Hits Worst Against	Avg	AB	H	2B	3B	HR	RBI	BB	SO	OBP	SLG
Roger Pavlik	.667	12	8	3	0	2	8	1	2	.692	1.417	David Cone	.067	15	1	0	0	0	0	2	7	.176	.067
Dennis Martinez	.600	10	6	1	0	1	5	4	0	.667	1.000	Tim Belcher	.071	14	1	0	0	0	0	1	5	.133	.071
Omar Olivares	.455	11	5	1	0	1	3	0	1	.455	.818	Charles Nagy	.083	12	1	1	0	0	2	1	6	.143	.167
Ariel Prieto	.375	16	6	0	0	3	6	1	4	.444	.938	Felipe Lira	.083	12	1	1	0	0	3	1	4	.154	.167
Jamie Moyer	.375	8	3	1	0	1	1	2	1	.545	.875	Tom Gordon	.091	22	2	0	0	0	1	4	7	.222	.091

Wilson Delgado — Giants
Age 22 – Bats Both

	Avg	G	AB	R	H	2B	3B	HR	RBI	BB	SO	HBP	GDP	SB	CS	OBP	SLG	IBB	SH	SF	#Pit	#P/PA	GB	FB	G/F
1997 Season	.143	8	7	1	1	1	0	0	0	0	2	0	0	0	0	.143	.286	0	1	0	21	2.63	1	3	0.33
Career (1996-1997)	.310	14	29	4	9	1	0	0	2	1	7	2	0	1	0	.375	.345	0	1	0	102	3.09	8	7	1.14

1997 Season

	Avg	AB	H	2B	3B	HR	RBI	BB	SO	OBP	SLG		Avg	AB	H	2B	3B	HR	RBI	BB	SO	OBP	SLG
vs. Left	.000	1	0	0	0	0	0	0	0	.000	.000	Scoring Posn	.000	1	0	0	0	0	0	0	1	.000	.000
vs. Right	.167	6	1	1	0	0	0		2	.167	.333	Close & Late	.000	2	0	0	0	0	0	0	0	.000	.000

David Dellucci — Orioles
Age 24 – Bats Left

	Avg	G	AB	R	H	2B	3B	HR	RBI	BB	SO	HBP	GDP	SB	CS	OBP	SLG	IBB	SH	SF	#Pit	#P/PA	GB	FB	G/F
1997 Season	.222	17	27	3	6	1	0	1	3	4	7	1	2	0	0	.344	.370	1	0	0	124	3.88	12	5	2.40

1997 Season

	Avg	AB	H	2B	3B	HR	RBI	BB	SO	OBP	SLG		Avg	AB	H	2B	3B	HR	RBI	BB	SO	OBP	SLG
vs. Left	.000	2	0	0	0	0	0	0	0	.333	.000	Scoring Posn	.250	8	2	1	0	0	2	1	3	.333	.375
vs. Right	.240	25	6	1	0	1	3	4	7	.345	.400	Close & Late	.200	5	1	0	0	0	0	2	2	.429	.200

Rich DeLucia — Angels
Age 33 – Pitches Right (flyball pitcher)

	ERA	W	L	Sv	G	GS	IP	BB	SO	Avg	H	2B	3B	HR	RBI	OBP	SLG	GF	IR	IRS	Hld	SvOp	SB	CS	GB	FB	G/F
1997 Season	3.89	6	4	3	36	0	44.0	27	44	.227	35	8	3	5	23	.342	.416	13	26	6	8	7	1	6	33	55	0.60
Last Five Years	4.36	20	23	3	186	2	241.1	122	238	.239	215	38	7	31	134	.333	.400	54	115	43	34	14	6	14	229	282	0.81

1997 Season

	ERA	W	L	Sv	G	GS	IP	H	HR	BB	SO		Avg	AB	H	2B	3B	HR	RBI	BB	SO	OBP	SLG
Home	4.84	5	1	0	17	0	22.1	21	4	11	27	vs. Left	.160	50	8	2	0	2	6	17	14	.373	.320
Away	2.91	1	3	3	19	0	21.2	14	1	16	17	vs. Right	.260	104	27	6	3	3	17	10	30	.325	.462
Starter	0.00	0	0	0	0	0	0.0	0	0	0	0	Scoring Posn	.220	41	9	2	1	1	17	17	15	.433	.390
Reliever	3.89	6	4	3	36	0	44.0	35	5	27	44	Close & Late	.221	86	19	4	2	4	16	20	27	.367	.453
0 Days rest (Relief)	6.00	1	1	0	5	0	3.0	6	2	5	1	None on/out	.316	38	12	1	2	2	2	3	6	.381	.605
1 or 2 Days rest	4.24	4	0	1	18	0	23.1	15	2	11	26	First Pitch	.133	15	2	1	0	1	3	2	0	.222	.400
3+ Days rest	3.06	1	3	2	13	0	17.2	14	1	11	17	Ahead in Count	.246	65	16	1	1	1	3	0	29	.258	.338
Pre-All Star	2.62	6	3	2	29	0	34.1	28	3	21	34	Behind in Count	.200	25	5	1	1	0	6	13	0	.462	.320
Post-All Star	8.38	0	1	1	7	0	9.2	7	2	6	10	Two Strikes	.231	91	21	6	2	4	14	12	44	.327	.473

Last Five Years

	ERA	W	L	Sv	G	GS	IP	H	HR	BB	SO		Avg	AB	H	2B	3B	HR	RBI	BB	SO	OBP	SLG
Home	4.77	13	10	0	99	0	126.1	118	17	62	132	vs. Left	.272	335	91	23	2	16	61	70	63	.395	.496
Away	3.91	7	13	3	87	2	115.0	97	14	60	106	vs. Right	.219	565	124	15	5	15	73	52	175	.293	.343
Day	4.68	4	11	2	65	1	82.2	82	7	43	69	Inning 1-6	.259	185	48	9	1	4	30	22	44	.340	.384
Night	4.20	16	12	1	121	1	158.2	133	24	79	169	Inning 7+	.234	715	167	29	6	27	104	100	194	.331	.404
Grass	3.92	10	13	3	110	1	137.2	107	14	68	125	None on	.224	482	108	20	5	15	15	55	117	.309	.380
Turf	4.95	10	10	0	76	1	103.2	108	17	54	113	Runners on	.256	418	107	18	2	16	119	67	121	.359	.423
March/April	1.93	3	0	0	19	0	28.0	19	3	10	29	Scoring Posn	.255	259	66	12	2	10	104	45	71	.361	.432
May	3.92	5	8	1	47	0	62.0	44	3	38	61	Close & Late	.243	407	99	21	4	14	64	73	112	.364	.418
June	5.43	5	5	1	43	2	59.2	63	10	31	61	None on/out	.263	209	55	12	4	6	6	27	44	.353	.445
July	3.04	4	4	1	36	0	47.1	37	7	17	42	vs. 1st Batr (relief)	.264	163	43	9	0	9	28	17	42	.344	.485
August	4.67	1	2	0	14	0	17.1	15	3	12	17	1st Inning Pitched	.247	590	146	29	3	25	106	76	158	.334	.434
Sept/Oct	7.67	2	4	0	27	0	27.0	37	5	14	28	First 15 Pitches	.244	459	112	23	1	21	68	49	116	.319	.436
Starter	10.13	0	2	0	2	2	5.1	11	0	5	3	Pitch 16-30	.237	295	70	9	4	7	47	50	81	.352	.366
Reliever	4.23	20	21	3	184	0	236.0	204	31	117	235	Pitch 31-45	.189	106	20	4	1	3	17	17	33	.310	.330
0 Days rest (Relief)	6.57	4	3	0	35	0	37.0	43	8	23	25	Pitch 46+	.325	40	13	2	1	0	2	6	8	.413	.425
1 or 2 Days rest	4.09	13	11	1	101	0	141.0	116	16	65	149	First Pitch	.292	106	31	5	1	5	22	12	0	.358	.500
3+ Days rest	3.10	3	7	2	48	0	58.0	45	7	29	61	Ahead in Count	.180	417	75	9	3	9	45	0	176	.189	.281
vs. AL	4.28	9	10	3	62	1	82.0	73	10	48	88	Behind in Count	.374	147	55	11	2	9	33	46	0	.518	.660
vs. NL	4.41	11	13	0	124	1	159.1	142	21	74	150	Two Strikes	.173	513	89	16	3	13	60	64	238	.256	.292
Pre-All Star	4.09	14	13	2	119	2	160.2	132	18	86	161	Pre-All Star	.225	587	132	24	4	18	84	86	161	.328	.371
Post-All Star	4.91	6	10	1	67	0	80.2	83	13	36	77	Post-All Star	.265	313	83	14	3	13	50	36	77	.341	.454

Pitcher vs. Batter (career)

Pitches Best Vs.	Avg	AB	H	2B	3B	HR	RBI	BB	SO	OBP	SLG	Pitches Worst Vs.	Avg	AB	H	2B	3B	HR	RBI	BB	SO	OBP	SLG
Joe Carter	.000	15	0	0	0	0	0	0	5	.000	.000	Wally Joyner	.667	6	4	1	0	1	3	5	1	.818	1.333
Ellis Burks	.071	14	1	0	0	0	1	0	4	.067	.071	Jody Reed	.533	15	8	4	0	0	3	2	1	.588	.800
Mark McGwire	.105	19	2	1	0	0	1	1	4	.150	.158	Lance Johnson	.500	20	10	0	2	0	3	1	0	.524	.700
Mike Devereaux	.125	16	2	1	0	0	0	1	3	.176	.188	Cal Ripken	.375	16	6	2	0	2	3	0	1	.375	.875
Devon White	.167	12	2	1	0	0	0	1	3	.231	.250	Cecil Fielder	.308	13	4	0	0	3	11	2	2	.400	1.000

Delino DeShields — Cardinals
Age 29 – Bats Left (groundball hitter)

	Avg	G	AB	R	H	2B	3B	HR	RBI	BB	SO	HBP	GDP	SB	CS	OBP	SLG	IBB	SH	SF	#Pit	#P/PA	GB	FB	G/F
1997 Season	.295	150	572	92	169	26	14	11	58	55	72	3	5	55	14	.357	.448	1	7	6	2340	3.64	244	141	1.73
Last Five Years	.265	643	2379	359	630	84	35	28	198	297	396	8	36	212	56	.346	.365	15	17	15	10780	3.97	987	555	1.78

1997 Season

	Avg	AB	H	2B	3B	HR	RBI	BB	SO	OBP	SLG		Avg	AB	H	2B	3B	HR	RBI	BB	SO	OBP	SLG
vs. Left	.280	118	33	5	3	1	12	13	13	.358	.398	First Pitch	.360	86	31	7	2	1	11	0	0	.364	.523
vs. Right	.300	454	136	21	11	10	46	42	59	.357	.460	Ahead in Count	.398	171	68	11	8	7	22	29	0	.485	.678
Groundball	.299	117	35	7	3	2	8	8	25	.346	.462	Behind in Count	.200	205	41	4	3	1	15	0	56	.205	.263
Flyball	.278	79	22	2	1	5	12	7	6	.333	.519	Two Strikes	.181	221	40	6	3	2	21	26	72	.267	.262
Home	.285	277	79	10	5	6	28	28	33	.353	.422	Batting #1	.287	474	136	21	11	6	48	49	61	.353	.416
Away	.305	295	90	16	9	5	30	27	39	.361	.471	Batting #2	.359	78	28	4	2	3	6	5	8	.398	.577
Day	.363	171	62	12	4	6	27	24	20	.437	.585	Other	.250	20	5	1	1	2	4	1	3	.286	.700
Night	.267	401	107	14	10	5	31	31	52	.321	.389	March/April	.200	75	15	2	2	1	6	6	10	.259	.320
Grass	.304	471	143	25	9	9	48	46	58	.368	.452	May	.330	100	33	7	3	1	9	8	19	.376	.490
Turf	.257	101	26	1	5	2	10	9	14	.307	.426	June	.308	104	32	7	3	3	13	10	11	.368	.519
Pre-All Star	.290	303	88	16	8	5	28	28	44	.349	.446	July	.323	96	31	2	1	4	11	15	7	.414	.490
Post-All Star	.301	269	81	10	6	6	30	27	28	.365	.450	August	.240	104	25	3	3	2	11	5	14	.283	.385
Scoring Posn	.321	109	35	5	4	4	49	13	14	.380	.550	Sept/Oct	.355	93	33	5	2	0	8	11	11	.419	.452
Close & Late	.302	96	29	3	2	3	13	17	14	.400	.469	vs. AL	.217	46	10	0	2	0	2	5	4	.288	.304
None on/out	.289	235	68	9	6	4	4	19	34	.345	.430	vs. NL	.302	526	159	26	12	11	56	50	68	.363	.460

1997 By Position

Position	Avg	AB	H	2B	3B	HR	RBI	BB	SO	OBP	SLG	G	GS	Innings	PO	A	E	DP	Fld Pct	Rng Fctr	In Zone	Outs	Zone Rtg	MLB Zone
As 2b	.295	563	166	26	14	9	55	55	70	.357	.439	147	137	1226.0	270	397	19	93	.972	4.90	424	387	913	.902

Last Five Years

	Avg	AB	H	2B	3B	HR	RBI	BB	SO	OBP	SLG		Avg	AB	H	2B	3B	HR	RBI	BB	SO	OBP	SLG
vs. Left	.258	631	163	25	12	6	60	76	113	.342	.365	First Pitch	.370	273	101	13	6	4	37	12	0	.397	.505
vs. Right	.267	1748	467	59	23	22	138	221	283	.348	.365	Ahead in Count	.314	617	194	29	14	11	65	143	0	.443	.460
Groundball	.254	661	168	27	9	5	58	71	129	.326	.345	Behind in Count	.206	968	199	28	12	4	58	0	324	.208	.272
Flyball	.262	362	95	9	4	11	43	55	58	.358	.401	Two Strikes	.195	1113	217	32	10	8	71	142	396	.285	.263
Home	.267	1128	301	39	13	14	93	155	177	.355	.362	Batting #1	.267	1404	375	49	25	14	107	162	225	.343	.368
Away	.263	1251	329	45	22	14	105	142	219	.338	.368	Batting #2	.279	476	133	17	7	6	44	74	73	.377	.382
Day	.300	673	202	30	12	11	76	97	113	.388	.429	Other	.244	499	122	18	3	8	47	61	98	.325	.341
Night	.251	1706	428	54	23	17	122	200	283	.330	.339	March/April	.228	325	74	13	7	5	30	42	61	.314	.357
Grass	.255	1634	417	62	20	20	140	193	272	.334	.354	May	.273	498	136	16	5	4	29	63	92	.355	.349
Turf	.286	745	213	22	15	8	58	104	124	.374	.388	June	.280	457	128	20	5	6	44	50	62	.353	.385
Pre-All Star	.269	1439	387	54	18	16	108	168	242	.345	.365	July	.271	451	122	10	6	7	37	55	68	.349	.389
Post-All Star	.259	940	243	30	17	12	90	129	154	.348	.365	August	.266	334	89	10	8	5	29	37	60	.343	.389
Scoring Posn	.271	502	136	16	6	8	167	84	84	.371	.375	Sept/Oct	.258	314	81	15	4	1	29	50	53	.358	.341
Close & Late	.277	408	113	9	6	5	48	57	88	.363	.365	vs. AL	.217	46	10	0	2	0	2	5	4	.288	.304
None on/out	.277	813	225	28	15	10	10	79	138	.344	.385	vs. NL	.266	2333	620	84	33	28	196	292	392	.348	.366

Batter vs. Pitcher (career)

Hits Best Against	Avg	AB	H	2B	3B	HR	RBI	BB	SO	OBP	SLG	Hits Worst Against	Avg	AB	H	2B	3B	HR	RBI	BB	SO	OBP	SLG
Donovan Osborne	.545	11	6	1	0	1	2	0	1	.545	.909	John Franco	.000	16	0	0	0	0	0	0	7	.000	.000
Steve Cooke	.455	22	10	2	2	0	2	1	2	.500	.727	Jason Christiansen	.000	11	0	0	0	0	0	1	5	.083	.000
Steve Trachsel	.452	31	14	2	0	2	2	4	2	.485	.710	Mike Stanton	.000	10	0	0	0	0	0	2	3	.167	.000
Al Leiter	.400	10	4	1	3	0	1	1	5	.455	1.100	Tom Candiotti	.000	8	0	0	0	0	0	3	2	.273	.000
Brett Tomko	.375	8	3	1	1	0	0	4	0	.583	.750	Shane Reynolds	.125	24	3	0	0	0	0	0	6	.125	.125

Elmer Dessens — Pirates
Age 26 – Pitches Right (groundball pitcher)

	ERA	W	L	Sv	G	GS	IP	BB	SO	Avg	H	2B	3B	HR	RBI	OBP	SLG	GF	IR	IRS	Hld	SvOp	SB	CS	GB	FB	G/F
1997 Season	0.00	0	0	0	3	0	3.1	0	2	.167	2	1	0	0	1	.231	.250	1	4	1	0	0	0	0	6	4	1.50
Career (1996-1997)	7.31	0	2	0	18	3	28.1	4	15	.362	42	10	0	2	19	.385	.500	2	8	2	3	0	2	1	58	26	2.23

1997 Season

	ERA	W	L	Sv	G	GS	IP	H	HR	BB	SO		Avg	AB	H	2B	3B	HR	RBI	BB	SO	OBP	SLG
Home	0.00	0	0	0	1	0	2.0	2	0	0	2	vs. Left	.000	4	0	0	0	0	0	0	0	.200	.000
Away	0.00	0	0	0	2	0	1.1	0	0	0	0	vs. Right	.250	8	2	1	0	0	1	0	2	.250	.375

Mike Devereaux — Rangers
Age 35 – Bats Right

	Avg	G	AB	R	H	2B	3B	HR	RBI	BB	SO	HBP	GDP	SB	CS	OBP	SLG	IBB	SH	SF	#Pit	#P/PA	GB	FB	G/F
1997 Season	.208	29	72	8	15	3	0	0	7	7	10	0	0	1	0	.275	.250	0	0	1	282	3.53	34	19	1.79
Last Five Years	.247	493	1611	219	398	77	8	42	212	133	296	4	38	21	13	.304	.383	3	6	14	6717	3.80	646	439	1.47

1997 Season

	Avg	AB	H	2B	3B	HR	RBI	BB	SO	OBP	SLG		Avg	AB	H	2B	3B	HR	RBI	BB	SO	OBP	SLG
vs. Left	.227	44	10	2	0	0	1	4	5	.292	.273	Scoring Posn	.333	9	3	1	0	0	7	4	1	.500	.444
vs. Right	.179	28	5	1	0	0	6	3	5	.250	.214	Close & Late	.000	11	0	0	0	0	0	1	4	.083	.000

Last Five Years

	Avg	AB	H	2B	3B	HR	RBI	BB	SO	OBP	SLG		Avg	AB	H	2B	3B	HR	RBI	BB	SO	OBP	SLG
vs. Left	.266	546	145	29	2	17	76	54	86	.331	.419	First Pitch	.273	161	44	9	0	2	22	3	0	.283	.366
vs. Right	.238	1065	253	48	6	25	136	79	210	.290	.364	Ahead in Count	.305	406	124	26	3	12	70	74	0	.406	.473
Groundball	.227	361	82	16	1	5	47	28	75	.282	.319	Behind in Count	.191	743	142	26	2	17	73	0	257	.195	.300
Flyball	.228	281	64	11	1	7	31	21	63	.280	.349	Two Strikes	.176	752	132	22	2	19	73	56	296	.235	.286
Home	.243	733	178	35	4	23	127	74	135	.309	.396	Batting #2	.242	322	78	11	3	7	41	30	63	.309	.360
Away	.251	878	220	42	4	19	85	59	161	.299	.372	Batting #3	.249	289	72	10	1	9	47	28	58	.312	.384
Day	.253	466	118	19	5	12	68	33	79	.304	.393	Other	.248	1000	248	56	4	26	124	75	175	.299	.390
Night	.245	1145	280	58	3	30	144	100	217	.303	.379	March/April	.223	273	61	12	2	8	39	18	54	.270	.370
Grass	.244	1392	339	63	7	40	191	120	252	.303	.385	May	.245	294	72	7	3	4	31	30	52	.318	.330
Turf	.269	219	59	14	1	2	21	13	44	.308	.370	June	.263	319	84	21	1	7	34	25	54	.318	.401
Pre-All Star	.246	1002	246	49	6	21	118	78	179	.301	.369	July	.252	313	79	14	1	10	46	27	55	.309	.399
Post-All Star	.250	609	152	28	2	21	94	55	117	.308	.406	August	.257	272	70	17	1	9	40	25	46	.316	.426
Scoring Posn	.269	442	119	21	3	7	162	42	77	.323	.378	Sept/Oct	.229	140	32	6	0	4	22	8	35	.268	.357
Close & Late	.198	262	52	9	2	4	26	23	59	.260	.294	vs. AL	.247	1556	384	74	8	41	204	131	285	.304	.384
None on/out	.252	349	88	21	1	12	12	28	53	.311	.421	vs. NL	.255	55	14	3	0	1	8	2	11	.281	.364

Batter vs. Pitcher (career)

Hits Best Against	Avg	AB	H	2B	3B	HR	RBI	BB	SO	OBP	SLG	Hits Worst Against	Avg	AB	H	2B	3B	HR	RBI	BB	SO	OBP	SLG
Chris Haney	.400	20	8	3	0	1	3	0	2	.400	.700	Dennis Cook	.000	12	0	0	0	0	0	1	3	.077	.000
Erik Hanson	.391	23	9	1	0	1	5	5	1	.500	.565	Bobby Witt	.053	19	1	0	0	0	1	1	3	.095	.053
Jimmy Key	.364	44	16	4	1	2	7	1	3	.370	.636	Bret Saberhagen	.077	13	1	0	0	0	1	0	3	.077	.077
Jaime Navarro	.359	39	14	3	0	2	6	3	2	.405	.590	Brian Bohanon	.083	12	1	0	0	0	2	0	1	.083	.083
Jeff Nelson	.333	12	4	2	1	0	3	0	3	.333	.667	Wilson Alvarez	.125	32	4	0	0	0	0	0	7	.125	.125

Alex Diaz — Rangers
Age 29 – Bats Both (groundball hitter)

	Avg	G	AB	R	H	2B	3B	HR	RBI	BB	SO	HBP	GDP	SB	CS	OBP	SLG	IBB	SH	SF	#Pit	#P/PA	GB	FB	G/F
1997 Season	.222	28	90	8	20	4	0	2	12	5	13	1	3	1	1	.268	.333	0	0	1	295	3.04	32	32	1.00
Last Five Years	.252	280	695	89	175	27	7	7	62	30	79	5	16	35	20	.285	.341	3	11	7	2250	3.01	311	190	1.64

1997 Season

	Avg	AB	H	2B	3B	HR	RBI	BB	SO	OBP	SLG		Avg	AB	H	2B	3B	HR	RBI	BB	SO	OBP	SLG
vs. Left	.292	24	7	0	0	1	5	1	6	.333	.417	Scoring Posn	.214	28	6	1	0	1	10	1	4	.233	.357
vs. Right	.197	66	13	4	0	1	7	4	7	.243	.303	Close & Late	.211	19	4	1	0	1	3	0	3	.211	.421

Last Five Years

	Avg	AB	H	2B	3B	HR	RBI	BB	SO	OBP	SLG		Avg	AB	H	2B	3B	HR	RBI	BB	SO	OBP	SLG
vs. Left	.291	158	46	8	1	2	18	5	21	.317	.392	First Pitch	.320	175	56	9	3	1	15	2	0	.328	.423
vs. Right	.240	537	129	19	6	5	44	25	58	.275	.326	Ahead in Count	.335	155	52	8	0	3	21	17	0	.397	.445
Groundball	.246	175	43	8	0	1	17	7	18	.280	.309	Behind in Count	.176	278	49	9	3	2	15	0	72	.187	.252
Flyball	.308	130	40	7	1	0	10	3	11	.319	.377	Two Strikes	.148	230	34	8	1	2	15	11	79	.194	.217
Home	.261	360	94	11	4	4	28	16	35	.298	.347	Batting #2	.215	135	29	7	0	0	9	3	12	.238	.267
Away	.242	335	81	16	3	3	34	14	44	.271	.334	Batting #8	.258	186	48	8	2	4	20	10	20	.296	.387
Day	.236	250	59	10	1	1	17	9	33	.265	.296	Other	.262	374	98	12	5	3	33	17	47	.296	.345
Night	.261	445	116	17	6	6	45	21	46	.296	.366	March/April	.238	122	29	3	6	2	14	3	13	.258	.410
Grass	.254	456	116	18	6	3	43	20	54	.285	.340	May	.259	85	22	4	0	0	7	5	8	.300	.306
Turf	.247	239	59	9	1	4	19	10	25	.285	.343	June	.250	148	37	6	1	2	9	10	17	.298	.345
Pre-All Star	.256	398	102	17	7	4	34	18	42	.289	.362	July	.214	117	25	8	0	0	8	2	11	.230	.282
Post-All Star	.246	297	73	10	0	3	28	12	37	.279	.310	August	.261	69	18	3	0	0	10	4	10	.311	.304
Scoring Posn	.224	174	39	7	0	4	55	8	22	.249	.333	Sept/Oct	.286	154	44	3	0	3	14	6	20	.315	.364
Close & Late	.289	135	39	4	1	2	11	9	17	.333	.378	vs. AL	.254	677	172	26	7	7	59	30	76	.288	.344
None on/out	.265	200	53	5	2	2	2	8	27	.340	vs. NL	.167	18	3	1	0	0	3	0	3	.167	.222

Batter vs. Pitcher (career)

Hits Best Against	Avg	AB	H	2B	3B	HR	RBI	BB	SO	OBP	SLG	Hits Worst Against	Avg	AB	H	2B	3B	HR	RBI	BB	SO	OBP	SLG
Jack McDowell	.357	14	5	0	2	0	0	0	0	.357	.643	Tom Gordon	.000	10	0	0	0	0	0	1	2	.091	.000
Randy Johnson	.333	12	4	0	0	0	0	0	6	.333	.333	Pat Hentgen	.133	15	2	0	0	0	0	0	0	.133	.133
Roger Clemens	.333	9	3	1	0	0	1	2	1	.417	.444	Kevin Appier	.200	20	4	0	0	0	1	1	2	.238	.200
												Alex Fernandez	.200	10	2	0	0	0	0	1	2	.273	.200

Eddy Diaz — Brewers
Age 26 – Bats Right

	Avg	G	AB	R	H	2B	3B	HR	RBI	BB	SO	HBP	GDP	SB	CS	OBP	SLG	IBB	SH	SF	#Pit	#P/PA	GB	FB	G/F
1997 Season	.220	16	50	4	11	2	1	0	7	1	5	0	3	0	0	.235	.300	0	0	0	171	3.35	20	15	1.33

1997 Season

	Avg	AB	H	2B	3B	HR	RBI	BB	SO	OBP	SLG		Avg	AB	H	2B	3B	HR	RBI	BB	SO	OBP	SLG
vs. Left	.242	33	8	2	1	0	6	1	2	.265	.364	Scoring Posn	.308	13	4	2	1	0	7	0	2	.308	.615
vs. Right	.176	17	3	0	0	1	0	3	.176	.176	Close & Late	.333	6	2	0	0	0	0	0	1	.333	.333

Einar Diaz — Indians
Age 25 – Bats Right

	Avg	G	AB	R	H	2B	3B	HR	RBI	BB	SO	HBP	GDP	SB	CS	OBP	SLG	IBB	SH	SF	#Pit	#P/PA	GB	FB	G/F
1997 Season	.143	5	7	1	1	1	0	0	1	0	2	0	0	0	0	.143	.286	0	0	0	28	4.00	2	2	1.00

1997 Season

	Avg	AB	H	2B	3B	HR	RBI	BB	SO	OBP	SLG		Avg	AB	H	2B	3B	HR	RBI	BB	SO	OBP	SLG
vs. Left	.000	3	0	0	0	0	0	0	1	.000	.000	Scoring Posn	.000	2	0	0	0	0	0	0	1	.000	.000
vs. Right	.250	4	1	1	0	0	1	0	1	.250	.500	Close & Late	.000	1	0	0	0	0	0	0	1	.000	.000

Jason Dickson — Angels
Age 25 – Pitches Right

	ERA	W	L	Sv	G	GS	IP	BB	SO	Avg	H	2B	3B	HR	RBI	OBP	SLG	CG	ShO	Sup	QS	#P/S	SB	CS	GB	FB	G/F
1997 Season	4.29	13	9	0	33	32	203.2	56	115	.289	236	43	1	32	101	.338	.462	2	1	5.66	20	98	5	7	295	239	1.23
Career (1996-1997)	4.34	14	13	0	40	39	247.0	74	135	.292	288	54	1	38	121	.345	.465	2	1	5.10	24	97	8	12	361	287	1.26

1997 Season

	ERA	W	L	Sv	G	GS	IP	H	HR	BB	SO		Avg	AB	H	2B	3B	HR	RBI	BB	SO	OBP	SLG
Home	4.67	7	5	0	19	18	113.2	137	19	36	64	vs. Left	.308	438	135	22	0	21	59	34	61	.357	.502
Away	3.80	6	4	0	14	14	90.0	99	13	20	51	vs. Right	.267	378	101	21	1	11	42	22	54	.317	.415
Day	4.12	2	3	0	9	9	59.0	62	7	11	39	Inning 1-6	.288	726	209	43	1	28	93	50	107	.338	.466
Night	4.35	11	6	0	24	23	144.2	174	25	45	76	Inning 7+	.300	90	27	0	0	4	8	6	8	.344	.433
Grass	4.42	12	8	0	30	29	183.1	212	28	53	102	None on	.293	492	144	27	0	21	21	26	79	.331	.476
Turf	3.10	1	1	0	3	3	20.1	24	4	3	13	Runners on	.284	324	92	16	1	11	80	30	36	.349	.441
March/April	3.18	4	1	0	6	6	39.2	37	5	7	35	Scoring Posn	.234	188	44	8	0	3	61	20	27	.307	.324
May	4.38	2	1	0	6	6	39.0	39	4	16	17	Close & Late	.319	47	15	0	0	1	3	3	6	.360	.383
June	2.91	2	2	0	5	5	34.0	43	4	4	20	None on/out	.275	211	58	12	0	8	8	11	31	.311	.445
July	4.28	2	0	0	6	6	33.2	47	6	9	24	vs. 1st Batr (relief)	1.000	1	1	0	0	0	1	0	0	1.000	1.000
August	5.10	3	2	0	5	4	30.0	36	5	11	14	1st Inning Pitched	.267	131	35	8	0	5	17	13	31	.347	.443
Sept/Oct	6.59	0	3	0	5	5	27.1	34	8	9	15	First 75 Pitches	.278	609	169	36	1	25	75	41	90	.328	.463
Starter	4.42	12	9	0	32	32	197.1	232	32	52	114	Pitch 76-90	.350	103	36	6	0	4	16	8	13	.393	.524
Reliever	0.00	1	0	0	1	0	6.1	4	0	4	1	Pitch 91-105	.291	86	25	1	0	3	9	5	7	.330	.407
0-3 Days Rest (Start)	1.71	2	0	0	3	3	21.0	23	4	2	12	Pitch 106+	.333	18	6	0	0	1	2	1	5	.400	.333
4 Days Rest	6.41	5	7	0	18	18	99.2	133	21	33	47	First Pitch	.265	117	31	4	0	2	12	3	0	.285	.350
5+ Days Rest	2.58	5	2	0	11	11	76.2	76	7	17	55	Ahead in Count	.273	363	99	15	1	13	43	0	96	.280	.427
vs. AL	4.03	13	6	0	29	28	183.0	200	28	50	98	Behind in Count	.379	177	67	19	0	10	28	29	0	.466	.655
vs. NL	6.53	0	3	0	4	4	20.2	36	4	6	17	Two Strikes	.252	361	91	14	1	12	40	24	115	.304	.396
Pre-All Star	3.41	8	4	0	18	18	118.2	130	13	27	67	Pre-All Star	.280	464	130	21	1	13	50	27	67	.323	.414
Post-All Star	5.51	5	5	0	15	14	85.0	106	19	29	48	Post-All Star	.301	352	106	22	0	19	51	29	48	.358	.526

Mike Difelice — Cardinals
Age 29 – Bats Right

	Avg	G	AB	R	H	2B	3B	HR	RBI	BB	SO	HBP	GDP	SB	CS	OBP	SLG	IBB	SH	SF	#Pit	#P/PA	GB	FB	G/F
1997 Season	.238	93	260	16	62	10	1	4	30	19	61	3	11	1	1	.297	.331	0	6	1	1088	3.76	93	59	1.58
Career (1996-1997)	.240	97	267	16	64	11	1	4	32	19	62	3	11	1	1	.297	.333	0	6	1	1120	3.78	98	60	1.63

1997 Season

	Avg	AB	H	2B	3B	HR	RBI	BB	SO	OBP	SLG		Avg	AB	H	2B	3B	HR	RBI	BB	SO	OBP	SLG
vs. Left	.234	64	15	2	0	2	10	7	17	.315	.359	Scoring Posn	.322	59	19	2	0	0	22	4	12	.369	.356
vs. Right	.240	196	47	8	1	2	20	12	44	.290	.321	Close & Late	.152	33	5	1	0	0	3	2	11	.222	.182
Home	.214	103	22	4	0	1	7	11	25	.287	.282	None on/out	.217	60	13	2	0	1	1	5	12	.277	.300
Away	.255	157	40	6	1	3	23	8	36	.304	.363	Batting #7	.244	246	60	9	1	4	27	19	54	.305	.337
First Pitch	.314	35	11	3	0	2	8	0	0	.324	.571	Batting #8	.182	11	2	1	0	0	3	0	5	.182	.273
Ahead in Count	.304	46	14	2	1	1	8	7	0	.396	.457	Other	.000	3	0	0	0	0	0	0	2	.000	.000
Behind in Count	.181	138	25	3	0	1	8	0	56	.193	.225	Pre-All Star	.213	122	26	6	1	3	13	10	30	.281	.352
Two Strikes	.152	138	21	2	0	1	9	12	61	.230	.188	Post-All Star	.261	138	36	4	0	1	17	9	31	.311	.312

Jerry Dipoto — Rockies
Age 30 – Pitches Right (groundball pitcher)

	ERA	W	L	Sv	G	GS	IP	BB	SO	Avg	H	2B	3B	HR	RBI	OBP	SLG	GF	IR	IRS	Hld	SvOp	SB	CS	GB	FB	G/F
1997 Season	4.70	5	3	16	74	0	95.2	33	74	.288	108	21	0	6	60	.346	.392	33	46	15	10	21	6	3	157	91	1.73
Career (1993-1997)	4.12	20	15	29	242	0	323.2	147	225	.289	359	65	2	14	193	.365	.378	107	150	56	28	49	20	12	576	239	2.41

1997 Season

	ERA	W	L	Sv	G	GS	IP	H	HR	BB	SO		Avg	AB	H	2B	3B	HR	RBI	BB	SO	OBP	SLG
Home	4.08	5	0	8	39	0	53.0	62	3	14	47	vs. Left	.295	190	56	15	0	3	35	15	28	.349	.421
Away	5.48	0	3	8	35	0	42.2	46	3	19	27	vs. Right	.281	185	52	6	0	3	25	18	46	.343	.362
Day	5.56	1	0	9	37	0	45.1	53	2	16	35	Inning 1-6	.345	116	40	6	0	4	28	10	18	.398	.500
Night	3.93	4	3	7	37	0	50.1	55	4	17	39	Inning 7+	.263	259	68	15	0	2	32	23	56	.323	.344
Grass	4.95	5	3	12	61	0	80.0	95	6	25	67	None on	.287	188	54	14	0	2	2	14	39	.340	.394
Turf	3.45	0	0	4	13	0	15.2	13	0	8	7	Runners on	.289	187	54	7	0	4	58	19	35	.352	.390
March/April	5.23	1	0	1	10	0	10.1	12	0	3	7	Scoring Posn	.324	108	35	5	0	4	58	18	20	.412	.481
May	10.22	0	1	0	13	0	12.1	24	2	4	7	Close & Late	.241	145	35	4	0	1	14	16	35	.319	.290
June	2.92	1	0	1	13	0	24.2	22	2	7	22	None on/out	.264	87	23	8	0	1	1	4	22	.297	.391
July	4.58	1	1	0	13	0	19.2	21	0	9	14	vs. 1st Batr (relief)	.229	70	16	6	0	0	7	3	17	.270	.314
August	1.08	2	0	9	14	0	16.2	12	0	4	14	1st Inning Pitched	.282	252	71	14	0	4	48	26	53	.352	.385
Sept/Oct	7.50	0	1	5	11	0	12.0	17	2	6	10	First 15 Pitches	.271	199	54	14	0	2	39	17	38	.329	.372
Starter	0.00	0	0	0	0	0	0.0	0	0	0	0	Pitch 16-30	.290	124	36	4	0	2	21	12	30	.357	.371
Reliever	4.70	5	3	16	74	0	95.2	108	6	33	74	Pitch 31-45	.275	40	11	2	0	1	6	2	5	.302	.400
0 Days rest (Relief)	3.81	3	0	4	20	0	26.0	30	2	10	25	Pitch 46+	.583	12	7	1	0	1	4	2	1	.643	.917
1 or 2 Days rest	4.82	2	3	10	40	0	46.2	55	2	14	36	First Pitch	.340	53	18	4	0	1	13	3	0	.356	.472

1997 Season

	ERA	W	L	Sv	G	GS	IP	H	HR	BB	SO		Avg	AB	H	2B	3B	HR	RBI	BB	SO	OBP	SLG
3+ Days rest	5.48	0	0	2	14	0	23.0	23	2	9	13	Ahead in Count	.259	147	38	7	0	2	18	0	60	.272	.347
vs. AL	1.65	3	0	1	9	0	16.1	15	0	4	14	Behind in Count	.376	85	32	6	0	1	15	16	0	.471	.482
vs. NL	5.33	2	3	15	65	0	79.1	93	6	29	60	Two Strikes	.200	175	35	7	0	3	21	14	74	.269	.291
Pre-All Star	4.97	2	1	2	38	0	50.2	59	4	15	37	Pre-All Star	.289	204	59	9	0	4	34	15	37	.342	.392
Post-All Star	4.40	3	2	14	36	0	45.0	49	2	18	37	Post-All Star	.287	171	49	12	0	2	26	18	37	.351	.392

Career (1993-1997)

	ERA	W	L	Sv	G	GS	IP	H	HR	BB	SO		Avg	AB	H	2B	3B	HR	RBI	BB	SO	OBP	SLG
Home	3.73	11	4	14	123	0	169.0	188	6	71	136	vs. Left	.292	552	161	29	0	5	79	76	77	.378	.371
Away	4.54	9	11	15	119	0	154.2	171	8	76	89	vs. Right	.287	691	198	36	2	9	114	71	148	.354	.384
Day	4.51	4	4	13	86	0	115.2	130	7	51	81	Inning 1-6	.320	266	85	16	0	5	63	27	47	.381	.436
Night	3.89	16	11	16	156	0	208.0	229	7	96	144	Inning 7+	.280	977	274	49	2	9	130	120	178	.360	.362
Grass	4.24	17	13	23	195	0	254.2	291	13	112	187	None on	.301	575	173	37	0	8	8	52	103	.364	.407
Turf	3.65	3	2	6	47	0	69.0	68	1	35	38	Runners on	.278	668	186	28	2	6	185	95	122	.365	.353
March/April	5.33	2	0	1	22	0	27.0	39	0	14	16	Scoring Posn	.294	425	125	18	0	5	176	73	74	.392	.372
May	7.68	0	3	0	31	0	36.1	59	4	13	26	Close & Late	.288	493	142	21	0	4	67	64	91	.371	.355
June	4.94	2	2	1	30	0	47.1	47	4	16	39	None on/out	.310	277	86	18	0	4	4	20	49	.365	.419
July	3.00	8	4	1	54	0	81.0	73	1	37	43	vs. 1st Batr (relief)	.255	216	55	18	0	2	23	18	42	.329	.366
August	3.41	7	1	12	58	0	71.1	72	3	36	54	1st Inning Pitched	.283	828	234	50	1	9	147	103	154	.364	.378
Sept/Oct	3.12	1	5	14	47	0	60.2	69	2	31	47	First 15 Pitches	.285	673	192	45	1	7	89	78	114	.362	.386
Starter	0.00	0	0	0	0	0	0.0	0	0	0	0	Pitch 16-30	.279	401	112	14	1	4	72	49	86	.357	.349
Reliever	4.12	20	15	29	242	0	323.2	359	14	147	225	Pitch 31-45	.298	131	39	4	0	1	19	17	21	.380	.351
0 Days rest (Relief)	3.34	8	2	10	54	0	64.2	67	2	29	53	Pitch 46+	.421	38	16	2	0	2	13	3	4	.452	.632
1 or 2 Days rest	4.15	8	11	17	126	0	169.1	185	4	82	114	First Pitch	.375	192	72	14	1	4	47	24	0	.431	.521
3+ Days rest	4.62	4	2	2	62	0	89.2	107	8	36	58	Ahead in Count	.216	513	111	18	1	3	54	0	185	.227	.273
vs. AL	3.26	7	4	12	62	0	88.1	98	1	44	64	Behind in Count	.315	267	84	10	0	3	42	67	0	.448	.386
vs. NL	4.44	13	11	17	180	0	235.1	261	13	103	161	Two Strikes	.212	556	118	23	1	5	68	56	225	.291	.284
Pre-All Star	5.01	6	5	2	102	0	140.0	166	8	55	94	Pre-All Star	.303	547	166	29	2	8	94	55	94	.367	.408
Post-All Star	3.43	14	10	27	140	0	183.2	193	6	92	131	Post-All Star	.277	696	193	36	0	6	99	92	131	.363	.355

Pitcher vs. Batter (career)

Pitches Best Vs.	Avg	AB	H	2B	3B	HR	RBI	BB	SO	OBP	SLG	Pitches Worst Vs.	Avg	AB	H	2B	3B	HR	RBI	BB	SO	OBP	SLG
Eric Karros	.200	10	2	0	0	0	0	2	3	.333	.200	Brian McRae	.545	11	6	1	0	1	4	1	3	.583	.909
												Ron Gant	.455	11	5	0	0	2	6	0	2	.455	1.000
												Mike Piazza	.375	8	3	1	0	0	2	3	0	.545	.500

Gary DiSarcina — Angels
Age 30 – Bats Right (groundball hitter)

	Avg	G	AB	R	H	2B	3B	HR	RBI	BB	SO	HBP	GDP	SB	CS	OBP	SLG	IBB	SH	SF	#Pit	#P/PA	GB	FB	G/F
1997 Season	.246	154	549	52	135	28	2	4	47	17	29	4	18	7	8	.271	.326	0	8	5	1737	2.98	259	152	1.70
Last Five Years	.259	641	2252	272	583	116	15	20	214	91	156	16	68	24	27	.291	.350	0	46	14	7574	3.13	1054	584	1.80

1997 Season

	Avg	AB	H	2B	3B	HR	RBI	BB	SO	OBP	SLG		Avg	AB	H	2B	3B	HR	RBI	BB	SO	OBP	SLG
vs. Left	.209	158	33	3	0	1	9	6	13	.241	.247	First Pitch	.327	101	33	8	0	0	9	0	0	.333	.406
vs. Right	.261	391	102	25	2	3	38	11	16	.284	.358	Ahead in Count	.227	110	25	6	0	0	8	8	0	.270	.282
Groundball	.283	99	28	5	2	1	10	5	12	.317	.404	Behind in Count	.204	245	50	8	2	2	18	0	26	.213	.278
Flyball	.198	91	18	4	0	0	6	3	1	.237	.242	Two Strikes	.191	157	30	7	1	0	10	9	29	.243	.248
Home	.278	288	80	17	0	2	30	10	16	.298	.358	Batting #8	.100	30	3	1	1	0	2	0	1	.100	.200
Away	.211	261	55	11	2	2	17	7	13	.242	.291	Batting #9	.254	515	131	27	1	4	45	16	27	.280	.334
Day	.250	160	40	9	0	0	9	6	7	.278	.306	Other	.250	4	1	0	0	0	0	1	1	.400	.250
Night	.244	389	95	19	2	4	38	11	22	.268	.334	March/April	.226	84	19	3	0	2	11	1	7	.239	.333
Grass	.250	507	127	27	2	2	42	15	28	.271	.323	May	.289	97	28	9	0	1	12	1	7	.310	.412
Turf	.190	42	8	1	0	2	5	2	1	.271	.357	June	.242	91	22	4	2	0	9	5	2	.286	.330
Pre-All Star	.255	290	74	16	2	3	33	8	18	.282	.355	July	.278	90	25	6	0	0	7	8	6	.333	.344
Post-All Star	.236	259	61	12	0	1	14	9	11	.259	.293	August	.194	98	19	2	0	0	6	2	3	.208	.214
Scoring Posn	.238	143	34	7	1	1	43	7	12	.265	.322	Sept/Oct	.247	89	22	4	0	1	2	0	4	.247	.326
Close & Late	.244	90	22	2	0	2	8	5	10	.293	.333	vs. AL	.253	498	126	26	1	4	43	15	26	.278	.333
None on/out	.248	133	33	8	1	2	2	1	8	.265	.368	vs. NL	.176	51	9	2	1	0	4	2	3	.204	.255

1997 By Position

Position	Avg	AB	H	2B	3B	HR	RBI	BB	SO	OBP	SLG	G	GS	Innings	PO	A	E	DP	Fld Pct	Rng Fctr	In Zone	Zone Outs	Zone Rtg	MLB Zone
As ss	.246	548	135	28	2	4	47	17	29	.272	.327	153	150	1330.1	226	421	15	87	.977	4.38	445	440	989	937

Last Five Years

	Avg	AB	H	2B	3B	HR	RBI	BB	SO	OBP	SLG		Avg	AB	H	2B	3B	HR	RBI	BB	SO	OBP	SLG
vs. Left	.253	655	166	32	4	7	57	21	41	.277	.347	First Pitch	.293	393	115	22	2	2	30	0	0	.299	.374
vs. Right	.261	1597	417	84	11	13	157	70	115	.296	.352	Ahead in Count	.265	520	138	36	3	5	52	55	0	.332	.375
Groundball	.265	456	121	21	3	5	21	21	50	.301	.357	Behind in Count	.243	943	229	35	7	9	83	0	135	.251	.323
Flyball	.230	443	102	20	2	4	38	21	22	.271	.312	Two Strikes	.224	719	161	26	5	5	55	36	156	.267	.295
Home	.262	1179	309	57	7	9	118	44	86	.289	.345	Batting #8	.194	253	49	10	1	1	22	6	19	.214	.253
Away	.255	1073	274	59	8	11	96	47	70	.293	.356	Batting #9	.270	1755	474	91	11	16	176	72	125	.302	.362
Day	.247	612	151	32	4	6	45	27	36	.284	.342	Other	.246	244	60	15	3	3	16	13	12	.286	.369
Night	.263	1640	432	84	11	14	169	64	120	.293	.354	March/April	.242	331	80	14	1	4	35	11	26	.267	.326
Grass	.255	1987	507	101	13	16	181	74	142	.284	.343	May	.284	464	132	30	4	5	57	19	39	.316	.399
Turf	.287	265	76	15	2	4	33	17	14	.338	.404	June	.269	454	122	25	5	4	58	22	34	.304	.372
Pre-All Star	.269	1409	379	76	10	14	163	59	107	.301	.367	July	.270	481	130	24	2	5	39	26	30	.314	.360
Post-All Star	.242	843	204	40	5	6	51	32	49	.273	.323	August	.231	325	75	13	1	1	20	9	16	.255	.286

Last Five Years

	Avg	AB	H	2B	3B	HR	RBI	BB	SO	OBP	SLG		Avg	AB	H	2B	3B	HR	RBI	BB	SO	OBP	SLG
Scoring Posn	.258	569	147	27	4	6	189	33	39	.299	.351	Sept/Oct	.223	197	44	10	2	1	5	4	11	.239	.310
Close & Late	.234	363	85	12	1	3	36	15	37	.275	.298	vs. AL	.261	2201	574	114	14	20	210	89	153	.293	.353
None on/out	.241	543	131	26	5	7	7	15	35	.268	.346	vs. NL	.176	51	9	2	1	0	4	2	3	.204	.255

Batter vs. Pitcher (career)

Hits Best Against	Avg	AB	H	2B	3B	HR	RBI	BB	SO	OBP	SLG	Hits Worst Against	Avg	AB	H	2B	3B	HR	RBI	BB	SO	OBP	SLG
Danny Darwin	.421	19	8	0	0	1	4	0	3	.421	.579	Rick Aguilera	.000	12	0	0	0	0	0	1	0	.077	.000
Brad Radke	.417	12	5	2	0	0	1	0	0	.385	.583	Tim Wakefield	.063	16	1	0	0	0	0	0	0	.063	.063
Brian Bohanon	.400	10	4	1	0	0	3	2	0	.500	.500	John Wasdin	.077	13	1	0	0	0	0	0	1	.077	.077
Jason Bere	.389	18	7	2	0	1	4	1	2	.421	.667	Todd Stottlemyre	.083	24	2	0	0	0	1	0	0	.083	.083
James Baldwin	.364	11	4	3	0	0	4	0	0	.364	.636	Kenny Rogers	.086	35	3	1	0	0	2	0	1	.086	.114

Glenn Dishman — Tigers
Age 27 – Pitches Left

	ERA	W	L	Sv	G	GS	IP	BB	SO	Avg	H	2B	3B	HR	RBI	OBP	SLG	CG	ShO	Sup	QS	#P/S	SB	CS	GB	FB	G/F
1997 Season	5.28	1	2	0	7	4	29.0	8	20	.268	30	7	3	4	19	.323	.491	0	0	4.66	1	91	0	1	32	37	0.86
Career (1995-1997)	5.25	5	10	0	33	21	135.1	45	66	.279	146	33	4	17	73	.339	.454	0	0	5.52	7	90	4	6	189	162	1.17

1997 Season

	ERA	W	L	Sv	G	GS	IP	H	HR	BB	SO		Avg	AB	H	2B	3B	HR	RBI	BB	SO	OBP	SLG
Home	5.93	0	1	0	4	1	13.2	14	3	3	9	vs. Left	.208	24	5	1	1	2	7	2	3	.259	.583
Away	4.70	1	1	0	3	3	15.1	16	1	5	11	vs. Right	.284	88	25	6	2	2	12	6	17	.340	.466

Doug Drabek — White Sox
Age 35 – Pitches Right

	ERA	W	L	Sv	G	GS	IP	BB	SO	Avg	H	2B	3B	HR	RBI	OBP	SLG	CG	ShO	Sup	QS	#P/S	SB	CS	GB	FB	G/F
1997 Season	5.74	12	11	0	31	31	169.1	69	85	.261	170	41	4	30	103	.334	.474	0	0	6.43	12	91	15	7	227	223	1.02
Last Five Years	4.32	50	53	0	149	149	932.0	288	643	.267	957	175	23	101	432	.323	.413	16	5	5.07	81	97	96	36	1396	950	1.47

1997 Season

	ERA	W	L	Sv	G	GS	IP	H	HR	BB	SO		Avg	AB	H	2B	3B	HR	RBI	BB	SO	OBP	SLG
Home	5.66	9	4	0	17	17	95.1	97	18	36	48	vs. Left	.258	310	80	16	2	12	40	46	38	.358	.439
Away	5.84	3	7	0	14	14	74.0	73	12	33	37	vs. Right	.263	342	90	25	2	18	63	23	47	.311	.506
Day	6.00	3	4	0	11	11	57.0	62	9	28	30	Inning 1-6	.258	605	156	39	4	26	96	65	78	.332	.464
Night	5.61	9	7	0	20	20	112.1	108	21	41	55	Inning 7+	.298	47	14	2	0	4	7	4	7	.365	.596
Grass	5.29	11	8	0	26	26	144.2	141	24	60	68	None on	.245	387	95	26	3	11	11	37	53	.318	.413
Turf	8.39	1	3	0	5	5	24.2	29	6	9	17	Runners on	.283	265	75	15	1	19	92	32	32	.358	.562
March/April	7.43	1	3	0	5	5	26.2	29	4	16	9	Scoring Posn	.312	141	44	7	0	10	68	25	19	.411	.574
May	5.27	3	0	0	5	5	27.1	25	5	9	14	Close & Late	.261	23	6	0	0	2	4	3	5	.346	.522
June	7.81	2	2	0	6	6	27.2	44	6	9	12	None on/out	.257	171	44	7	0	8	8	15	23	.328	.439
July	4.03	1	2	0	5	5	29.0	23	3	13	20	vs. 1st Batr (relief)	.000	0	0	0	0	0	0	0	0	.000	.000
August	5.28	3	2	0	5	5	29.0	23	5	11	18	1st Inning Pitched	.274	117	32	6	1	7	20	17	19	.370	.521
Sept/Oct	4.85	2	2	0	5	5	29.2	26	7	11	12	First 75 Pitches	.245	506	124	29	4	18	68	60	64	.326	.425
Starter	5.74	12	11	0	31	31	169.1	170	30	69	85	Pitch 76-90	.359	92	33	7	0	9	26	5	12	.404	.728
Reliever	0.00	0	0	0	0	0	0.0	0	0	0	0	Pitch 91-105	.256	39	10	4	0	3	7	2	7	.293	.590
0-3 Days Rest (Start)	0.00	0	0	0	0	0	0.0	0	0	0	0	Pitch 106+	.200	15	3	1	0	0	2	2	2	.294	.267
4 Days Rest	4.57	4	5	0	14	14	80.2	77	12	29	37	First Pitch	.278	79	22	8	0	1	11	4	0	.321	.418
5+ Days Rest	6.80	8	6	0	17	17	88.2	93	18	40	48	Ahead in Count	.208	265	55	12	3	8	29	0	72	.216	.366
vs. AL	5.95	11	11	0	29	29	157.1	158	30	68	76	Behind in Count	.324	173	56	12	1	15	43	21	0	.397	.665
vs. NL	3.00	1	0	0	2	2	12.0	12	0	1	9	Two Strikes	.185	276	51	9	2	7	27	44	85	.302	.308
Pre-All Star	6.80	6	6	0	17	17	87.1	105	16	34	35	Pre-All Star	.303	346	105	23	3	16	62	34	35	.367	.526
Post-All Star	4.61	6	5	0	14	14	82.0	65	14	35	50	Post-All Star	.212	306	65	18	1	14	41	35	50	.297	.415

Last Five Years

	ERA	W	L	Sv	G	GS	IP	H	HR	BB	SO		Avg	AB	H	2B	3B	HR	RBI	BB	SO	OBP	SLG
Home	3.88	29	27	0	79	79	519.1	513	47	154	385	vs. Left	.269	1769	476	92	11	49	209	172	296	.335	.417
Away	4.86	21	26	0	70	70	412.2	444	54	134	258	vs. Right	.265	1815	481	83	12	52	223	116	347	.312	.410
Day	4.05	18	14	0	49	49	306.2	318	31	88	218	Inning 1-6	.272	3090	839	150	22	89	399	262	546	.328	.421
Night	4.45	32	39	0	100	100	625.1	639	70	200	425	Inning 7+	.239	494	118	25	1	12	33	36	97	.295	.366
Grass	5.04	24	19	0	61	61	353.1	392	49	127	183	None on	.258	2137	551	103	13	52	52	141	386	.308	.391
Turf	3.87	26	34	0	88	88	578.2	565	52	161	460	Runners on	.281	1447	406	72	10	49	380	147	257	.345	.446
March/April	4.17	6	9	0	21	21	131.2	126	16	48	94	Scoring Posn	.268	831	223	37	6	28	313	125	174	.358	.428
May	3.72	13	8	0	29	29	188.2	182	17	63	139	Close & Late	.218	252	55	5	1	8	18	21	57	.284	.341
June	5.00	10	11	0	28	28	171.0	203	18	47	113	None on/out	.267	940	251	37	7	29	29	62	159	.317	.414
July	3.88	6	9	0	27	27	171.2	163	12	52	130	vs. 1st Batr (relief)	.000	0	0	0	0	0	0	0	0	.000	.000
August	4.76	7	9	0	23	23	141.2	143	19	44	97	1st Inning Pitched	.272	578	157	30	5	15	86	69	111	.352	.419
Sept/Oct	4.52	8	7	0	21	21	127.1	140	19	34	70	First 75 Pitches	.272	2634	716	128	20	72	330	224	474	.331	.418
Starter	4.32	50	53	0	149	149	932.0	957	101	288	643	Pitch 76-90	.284	479	136	23	1	21	67	30	75	.330	.468
Reliever	0.00	0	0	0	0	0	0.0	0	0	0	0	Pitch 91-105	.195	313	61	14	2	6	22	18	64	.240	.310
0-3 Days Rest (Start)	4.23	1	2	0	7	7	44.2	44	8	13	39	Pitch 106+	.278	158	44	10	0	2	13	16	30	.345	.380
4 Days Rest	3.84	29	26	0	80	80	527.1	523	49	140	363	First Pitch	.339	566	192	34	6	18	90	21	0	.365	.516
5+ Days Rest	5.03	20	25	0	62	62	360.0	390	44	134	244	Ahead in Count	.197	1566	309	55	11	25	116	0	563	.202	.294
vs. AL	5.95	11	11	0	29	29	157.1	158	30	68	76	Behind in Count	.322	833	268	52	6	35	141	126	0	.410	.525
vs. NL	3.98	39	42	0	120	120	774.2	799	71	220	567	Two Strikes	.183	1561	285	44	8	31	122	141	643	.253	.281
Pre-All Star	4.38	31	31	0	86	86	544.2	569	56	167	389	Pre-All Star	.271	2101	569	104	13	56	258	167	389	.325	.413
Post-All Star	4.23	19	22	0	63	63	387.1	388	45	121	254	Post-All Star	.262	1483	388	71	10	45	174	121	254	.321	.414

Pitcher vs. Batter (career)

Pitches Best Vs.	Avg	AB	H	2B	3B	HR	RBI	BB	SO	OBP	SLG	Pitches Worst Vs.	Avg	AB	H	2B	3B	HR	RBI	BB	SO	OBP	SLG
Cal Ripken	.000	14	0	0	0	0	0	0	0	.000	.000	Fred McGriff	.528	36	19	1	0	4	7	7	8	.591	.889
Cliff Floyd	.000	11	0	0	0	0	0	0	0	.000	.000	Phil Plantier	.462	13	6	3	0	2	6	2	3	.563	1.154
Darnell Coles	.000	11	0	0	0	0	0	1	2	.083	.000	Barry Bonds	.444	27	12	5	1	2	4	7	4	.559	.926
Benito Santiago	.032	31	1	0	1	0	3	2	5	.118	.097	Eric Karros	.409	22	9	3	0	2	7	3	3	.462	.818
Steve Scarsone	.071	14	1	0	0	0	2	0	5	.071	.071	Gary Sheffield	.375	16	6	0	0	2	4	3	2	.500	.750

Darren Dreifort — Dodgers
Age 26 – Pitches Right (groundball pitcher)

	ERA	W	L	Sv	G	GS	IP	BB	SO	Avg	H	2B	3B	HR	RBI	OBP	SLG	GF	IR	IRS	Hld	SvOp	SB	CS	GB	FB	G/F
1997 Season	2.86	5	2	4	48	0	63.0	34	63	.202	45	10	1	3	24	.308	.296	15	28	6	9	7	7	2	86	39	2.21
Career (1994-1997)	4.12	6	11	10	94	0	115.2	61	109	.257	113	20	2	5	53	.352	.346	35	51	17	13	18	11	5	195	63	3.10

1997 Season

	ERA	W	L	Sv	G	GS	IP	H	HR	BB	SO		Avg	AB	H	2B	3B	HR	RBI	BB	SO	OBP	SLG
Home	2.38	4	0	2	23	0	34.0	19	2	13	28	vs. Left	.184	103	19	2	1	0	5	17	24	.306	.223
Away	3.41	1	2	2	25	0	29.0	26	1	21	35	vs. Right	.217	120	26	8	0	3	19	17	39	.309	.358
Starter	0.00	0	0	0	0	0	0.0	0	0	0	0	Scoring Posn	.234	64	15	4	0	0	18	16	17	.378	.297
Reliever	2.86	5	2	4	48	0	63.0	45	3	34	63	Close & Late	.250	96	24	6	1	0	10	18	23	.365	.333
0 Days rest (Relief)	7.00	0	2	1	9	0	9.0	12	0	6	6	None on/out	.151	53	8	4	0	1	1	7	20	.250	.283
1 or 2 Days rest	2.12	2	0	1	24	0	34.0	23	2	18	36	First Pitch	.355	31	11	3	0	2	6	1	0	.375	.645
3+ Days rest	2.25	3	0	2	15	0	20.0	10	1	10	21	Ahead in Count	.106	104	11	1	1	0	5	0	55	.113	.135
Pre-All Star	2.35	3	0	1	20	0	23.0	12	1	14	20	Behind in Count	.304	46	14	4	0	1	8	15	0	.468	.457
Post-All Star	3.15	2	2	3	28	0	40.0	33	2	20	43	Two Strikes	.117	111	13	1	1	0	5	18	63	.246	.144

Rob Ducey — Mariners
Age 33 – Bats Left (flyball hitter)

	Avg	G	AB	R	H	2B	3B	HR	RBI	BB	SO	HBP	GDP	SB	CS	OBP	SLG	IBB	SH	SF	#Pit	#P/PA	GB	FB	G/F
1997 Season	.287	76	143	25	41	15	2	5	10	6	31	0	2	3	3	.311	.524	0	0	2	597	3.95	53	41	1.29
Last Five Years	.272	114	257	41	70	22	5	7	20	18	49	0	4	5	6	.315	.479	2	2	4	1124	4.00	91	78	1.17

1997 Season

	Avg	AB	H	2B	3B	HR	RBI	BB	SO	OBP	SLG		Avg	AB	H	2B	3B	HR	RBI	BB	SO	OBP	SLG
vs. Left	.111	9	1	0	0	0	0	0	3	.111	.111	Scoring Posn	.074	27	2	0	0	0	4	0	7	.069	.074
vs. Right	.299	134	40	15	2	5	10	6	28	.324	.552	Close & Late	.259	27	7	1	0	1	1	1	7	.286	.407
Home	.264	72	19	10	0	0	1	2	19	.280	.403	None on/out	.472	36	17	6	2	3	3	2	6	.500	1.000
Away	.310	71	22	5	2	5	9	4	12	.342	.648	Batting #2	.400	30	12	6	1	2	2	0	4	.400	.867
First Pitch	.313	16	5	2	0	1	1	0	0	.313	.625	Batting #9	.203	59	12	3	1	0	3	5	8	.258	.288
Ahead in Count	.286	28	8	3	0	2	5	3	0	.344	.607	Other	.315	54	17	6	0	3	5	1	19	.327	.593
Behind in Count	.197	71	14	7	1	1	2	0	26	.194	.366	Pre-All Star	.253	75	19	8	0	1	6	5	14	.293	.400
Two Strikes	.221	77	17	8	1	2	4	3	31	.247	.429	Post-All Star	.324	68	22	7	2	4	4	1	17	.333	.662

Mariano Duncan — Blue Jays
Age 35 – Bats Right (groundball hitter)

	Avg	G	AB	R	H	2B	3B	HR	RBI	BB	SO	HBP	GDP	SB	CS	OBP	SLG	IBB	SH	SF	#Pit	#P/PA	GB	FB	G/F
1997 Season	.236	89	339	36	80	14	0	1	25	12	78	3	6	6	3	.268	.286	0	1	0	1196	3.37	139	63	2.21
Last Five Years	.284	491	1847	251	525	110	10	34	238	55	377	13	45	27	16	.307	.410	2	10	16	6577	3.39	768	359	2.14

1997 Season

	Avg	AB	H	2B	3B	HR	RBI	BB	SO	OBP	SLG		Avg	AB	H	2B	3B	HR	RBI	BB	SO	OBP	SLG
vs. Left	.225	102	23	4	0	0	12	3	25	.255	.265	First Pitch	.400	55	22	4	0	0	6	0	0	.400	.473
vs. Right	.241	237	57	10	0	1	13	9	53	.274	.295	Ahead in Count	.235	68	16	2	0	0	1	2	0	.257	.265
Groundball	.139	72	10	1	0	0	2	2	21	.162	.153	Behind in Count	.188	176	33	6	0	1	16	0	70	.192	.239
Flyball	.159	44	7	0	0	0	2	1	13	.178	.159	Two Strikes	.095	147	14	4	0	1	10	10	78	.158	.143
Home	.224	143	32	4	0	1	9	6	33	.265	.273	Batting #2	.217	175	38	6	0	0	12	6	44	.255	.251
Away	.245	196	48	10	0	0	16	6	45	.271	.296	Batting #8	.278	126	35	6	0	1	11	4	21	.300	.349
Day	.162	105	17	3	0	1	5	3	25	.200	.219	Other	.184	38	7	2	0	0	2	2	13	.225	.237
Night	.269	234	63	11	0	0	20	9	53	.299	.316	March/April	.333	66	22	4	0	0	5	4	12	.371	.394
Grass	.250	232	58	9	0	1	18	8	49	.278	.302	May	.214	70	15	3	0	1	6	1	14	.225	.300
Turf	.206	107	22	5	0	0	7	4	29	.248	.252	June	.091	22	2	0	0	0	0	0	6	.091	.091
Pre-All Star	.247	158	39	7	0	1	11	5	32	.270	.310	July	.167	18	3	1	0	0	2	1	8	.211	.222
Post-All Star	.227	181	41	7	0	0	14	7	46	.267	.265	August	.250	108	27	3	0	0	8	5	21	.296	.278
Scoring Posn	.283	99	28	5	0	0	24	3	22	.311	.333	Sept/Oct	.200	55	11	3	0	0	4	1	17	.228	.255
Close & Late	.185	54	10	2	0	0	3	2	13	.214	.222	vs. AL	.239	326	78	13	0	1	25	12	75	.268	.288
None on/out	.178	73	13	1	0	0	5	16	.231	.192	vs. NL	.154	13	2	1	0	0	0	0	3	.267	.231

1997 By Position

Position	Avg	AB	H	2B	3B	HR	RBI	BB	SO	OBP	SLG		G	GS	Innings	PO	A	E	DP	Fld Pct	Rng Fctr	In Zone	Zone Outs	Zone Rtg	MLB Zone
As 2b	.241	311	75	13	0	1	23	11	69	.274	.293		80	78	638.1	139	210	7	44	.980	4.92	232	200	.862	.902

Last Five Years

	Avg	AB	H	2B	3B	HR	RBI	BB	SO	OBP	SLG		Avg	AB	H	2B	3B	HR	RBI	BB	SO	OBP	SLG
vs. Left	.282	648	183	43	3	14	90	24	126	.309	.423	First Pitch	.361	302	109	20	2	9	55	2	0	.363	.530
vs. Right	.285	1199	342	67	7	20	148	31	251	.306	.403	Ahead in Count	.384	344	132	34	4	7	57	25	0	.421	.567
Groundball	.273	527	144	30	0	7	58	13	111	.291	.370	Behind in Count	.212	933	198	44	1	10	85	0	335	.218	.294
Flyball	.302	295	89	20	2	6	54	5	67	.314	.444	Two Strikes	.184	833	153	32	2	10	69	28	377	.216	.263
Home	.294	822	242	42	6	20	114	26	166	.322	.433	Batting #2	.263	1082	285	56	5	19	127	35	220	.293	.377
Away	.276	1025	283	68	4	14	124	29	211	.295	.391	Batting #7	.332	271	90	22	3	5	40	7	51	.346	.491
Day	.271	557	151	31	2	13	80	16	125	.296	.404	Other	.304	494	150	32	2	10	71	13	106	.318	.437

Last Five Years

	Avg	AB	H	2B	3B	HR	RBI	BB	SO	OBP	SLG		Avg	AB	H	2B	3B	HR	RBI	BB	SO	OBP	SLG
Night	.290	1290	374	79	8	21	158	39	252	.312	.412	March/April	.300	277	83	19	1	5	39	13	51	.332	.430
Grass	.299	951	284	56	6	15	122	27	183	.318	.417	May	.256	355	91	20	0	9	49	11	79	.282	.389
Turf	.269	896	241	54	4	19	116	28	194	.296	.402	June	.259	359	93	13	5	4	32	11	69	.286	.357
Pre-All Star	.273	1053	287	58	7	19	126	36	212	.300	.395	July	.335	257	86	19	1	4	39	3	53	.344	.463
Post-All Star	.300	794	238	52	3	15	112	19	165	.317	.429	August	.266	327	87	19	1	7	47	8	69	.285	.394
Scoring Posn	.315	531	167	35	5	10	201	10	106	.324	.456	Sept/Oct	.313	272	85	20	2	5	32	9	56	.336	.456
Close & Late	.274	277	76	19	3	5	42	6	65	.289	.419	vs. AL	.295	726	214	47	3	9	81	21	152	.314	.405
None on/out	.308	360	111	24	3	6	6	19	79	.346	.442	vs. NL	.277	1121	311	63	7	25	157	34	225	.302	.413

Batter vs. Pitcher (career)

Hits Best Against	Avg	AB	H	2B	3B	HR	RBI	BB	SO	OBP	SLG	Hits Worst Against	Avg	AB	H	2B	3B	HR	RBI	BB	SO	OBP	SLG
Frank Rodriguez	.545	11	6	3	0	0	2	0	2	.545	.818	Danny Jackson	.067	15	1	0	0	0	1	1	3	.125	.067
Armando Reynoso	.538	13	7	0	1	2	5	1	0	.571	1.154	Justin Thompson	.083	12	1	0	0	0	0	0	2	.154	.083
Lee Smith	.500	16	8	0	2	1	7	0	1	.500	.938	Bill Swift	.091	22	2	0	0	0	1	0	7	.091	.091
Paul Quantrill	.500	10	5	0	0	1	1	1	1	.545	.800	Butch Henry	.150	20	3	0	0	0	2	0	2	.182	.150
Dennis Springer	.455	11	5	1	0	2	5	0	1	.455	1.091	Bobby Ayala	.154	13	2	0	0	0	0	0	3	.154	.154

Todd Dunn — Brewers
Age 27 – Bats Right

	Avg	G	AB	R	H	2B	3B	HR	RBI	BB	SO	HBP	GDP	SB	CS	OBP	SLG	IBB	SH	SF	#Pit	#P/PA	GB	FB	G/F
1997 Season	.229	44	118	17	27	5	0	3	9	2	39	0	1	3	0	.242	.347	0	0	0	425	3.54	35	30	1.17
Career (1996-1997)	.234	50	128	19	30	6	0	3	10	2	42	0	2	3	0	.246	.352	0	0	0	449	3.45	39	30	1.30

1997 Season

	Avg	AB	H	2B	3B	HR	RBI	BB	SO	OBP	SLG		Avg	AB	H	2B	3B	HR	RBI	BB	SO	OBP	SLG
vs. Left	.241	54	13	3	0	2	6	0	21	.241	.407	Scoring Posn	.296	27	8	2	0	0	6	1	7	.321	.370
vs. Right	.219	64	14	2	0	1	3	2	18	.242	.297	Close & Late	.273	22	6	1	0	1	2	0	7	.273	.455

Shawon Dunston — Pirates
Age 35 – Bats Right (flyball hitter)

	Avg	G	AB	R	H	2B	3B	HR	RBI	BB	SO	HBP	GDP	SB	CS	OBP	SLG	IBB	SH	SF	#Pit	#P/PA	GB	FB	G/F
1997 Season	.300	132	490	71	147	22	5	14	57	8	75	3	9	32	8	.312	.451	0	5	5	1645	3.22	163	141	1.16
Last Five Years	.295	436	1595	197	470	85	13	44	188	47	239	12	29	53	21	.318	.447	6	22	11	5525	3.28	527	496	1.06

1997 Season

	Avg	AB	H	2B	3B	HR	RBI	BB	SO	OBP	SLG		Avg	AB	H	2B	3B	HR	RBI	BB	SO	OBP	SLG
vs. Left	.277	94	26	5	0	3	12	3	13	.293	.426	First Pitch	.463	82	38	5	2	3	19	0	0	.459	.683
vs. Right	.306	396	121	17	5	11	45	5	62	.317	.457	Ahead in Count	.402	102	41	8	1	7	20	5	0	.427	.706
Groundball	.314	102	32	8	3	1	11	3	13	.327	.480	Behind in Count	.199	231	46	8	0	2	10	0	69	.203	.260
Flyball	.272	81	22	3	1	2	7	0	17	.280	.407	Two Strikes	.165	200	33	5	0	2	6	3	75	.177	.220
Home	.319	257	82	13	1	10	33	3	38	.327	.494	Batting #5	.300	210	63	8	0	8	30	4	38	.312	.452
Away	.279	233	65	9	4	4	24	5	37	.296	.403	Batting #6	.329	146	48	7	3	4	20	2	22	.340	.500
Day	.326	242	79	9	1	7	31	4	38	.340	.459	Other	.269	134	36	7	2	2	7	2	15	.283	.396
Night	.274	248	68	13	4	7	26	4	37	.285	.444	March/April	.259	81	21	6	0	1	6	2	8	.291	.370
Grass	.282	372	105	13	4	8	39	7	58	.298	.403	May	.319	91	29	5	2	1	6	3	8	.337	.451
Turf	.356	118	42	9	1	6	18	1	17	.358	.602	June	.265	49	13	4	0	0	6	2	10	.294	.347
Pre-All Star	.295	241	71	15	2	3	22	7	28	.319	.411	July	.314	105	33	2	1	5	16	0	17	.315	.495
Post-All Star	.305	249	76	7	3	11	35	1	47	.306	.490	August	.247	93	23	1	1	2	7	1	21	.255	.344
Scoring Posn	.275	120	33	5	0	4	46	2	21	.276	.417	Sept/Oct	.394	71	28	4	1	5	16	0	11	.389	.690
Close & Late	.308	78	24	3	1	0	3	3	13	.333	.372	vs. AL	.433	30	13	1	0	2	6	0	5	.433	.667
None on/out	.345	110	38	5	2	5	5	1	14	.363	.564	vs. NL	.291	460	134	21	5	12	51	8	70	.305	.437

1997 By Position

Position	Avg	AB	H	2B	3B	HR	RBI	BB	SO	OBP	SLG	G	GS	Innings	PO	A	E	DP	Fld Pct	Rng Fctr	In Zone	Outs	Zone Rtg	MLB Zone
As ss	.302	467	141	20	5	13	55	8	70	.315	.450	126	123	979.2	191	281	15	54	.969	4.34	333	287	862	937

Last Five Years

	Avg	AB	H	2B	3B	HR	RBI	BB	SO	OBP	SLG		Avg	AB	H	2B	3B	HR	RBI	BB	SO	OBP	SLG
vs. Left	.299	384	115	25	3	14	50	14	51	.324	.490	First Pitch	.376	242	91	13	4	11	45	6	0	.398	.599
vs. Right	.293	1211	355	60	10	30	138	33	188	.316	.434	Ahead in Count	.374	281	105	29	3	13	42	26	0	.426	.637
Groundball	.299	441	132	28	5	10	56	10	73	.316	.454	Behind in Count	.231	826	191	31	2	11	67	0	225	.235	.314
Flyball	.282	238	67	15	2	6	18	5	37	.301	.437	Two Strikes	.209	685	143	21	1	7	38	15	239	.227	.273
Home	.303	782	237	41	4	23	94	23	109	.323	.454	Batting #5	.285	365	104	11	2	11	50	9	63	.301	.416
Away	.287	813	233	44	9	21	94	24	130	.313	.440	Batting #6	.321	461	148	26	4	11	56	13	72	.342	.466
Day	.307	789	242	33	5	23	97	28	116	.334	.449	Other	.283	769	218	48	7	22	82	25	104	.311	.450
Night	.283	806	228	52	8	21	91	19	123	.302	.445	March/April	.266	199	53	9	0	4	23	6	26	.292	.372
Grass	.285	1212	346	51	10	32	137	37	188	.310	.423	May	.291	320	93	15	3	6	38	11	35	.313	.413
Turf	.324	383	124	34	3	12	51	10	65	.343	.522	June	.324	315	102	22	4	10	36	11	55	.353	.514
Pre-All Star	.304	942	286	53	7	24	110	32	129	.329	.451	July	.331	359	119	22	3	14	45	12	53	.353	.526
Post-All Star	.282	653	184	32	6	20	78	15	110	.301	.441	August	.214	229	49	9	2	4	17	4	45	.237	.323
Scoring Posn	.297	397	118	15	1	10	143	18	66	.324	.416	Sept/Oct	.312	173	54	8	1	6	29	3	25	.324	.474
Close & Late	.304	260	79	12	3	7	24	11	40	.337	.454	vs. AL	.433	30	13	1	0	2	6	0	5	.433	.667
None on/out	.329	398	131	28	4	15	15	9	51	.350	.533	vs. NL	.292	1565	457	84	13	42	182	47	234	.316	.443

Batter vs. Pitcher (career)

Hits Best Against	Avg	AB	H	2B	3B	HR	RBI	BB	SO	OBP	SLG	Hits Worst Against	Avg	AB	H	2B	3B	HR	RBI	BB	SO	OBP	SLG
Xavier Hernandez	.545	11	6	1	0	0	1	1	0	.583	.636	Dave Burba	.000	12	0	0	0	0	0	0	4	.000	.000
Mike Morgan	.385	26	10	4	0	2	6	2	1	.429	.769	Ismael Valdes	.083	12	1	0	1	0	0	0	3	.083	.250
Bob Tewksbury	.382	34	13	2	3	0	4	1	2	.400	.618	Chan Ho Park	.100	10	1	0	0	0	0	1	5	.182	.100

Todd Dunwoody — Marlins
Age 23 – Bats Left

	Avg	G	AB	R	H	2B	3B	HR	RBI	BB	SO	HBP	GDP	SB	CS	OBP	SLG	IBB	SH	SF	#Pit	#P/PA	GB	FB	G/F
1997 Season	.260	19	50	7	13	2	2	2	7	7	21	1	1	2	0	.362	.500	0	0	0	229	3.95	14	13	1.08

1997 Season

	Avg	AB	H	2B	3B	HR	RBI	BB	SO	OBP	SLG		Avg	AB	H	2B	3B	HR	RBI	BB	SO	OBP	SLG
vs. Left	.222	9	2	0	0	1	2	0	3	.300	.556	Scoring Posn	.364	11	4	1	0	0	3	3	4	.500	.455
vs. Right	.268	41	11	2	2	1	5	7	18	.375	.488	Close & Late	.400	10	4	2	0	1	3	2	3	.500	.900

Roberto Duran — Tigers
Age 25 – Pitches Left (flyball pitcher)

	ERA	W	L	Sv	G	GS	IP	BB	SO	Avg	H	2B	3B	HR	RBI	OBP	SLG	GF	IR	IRS	Hld	SvOp	SB	CS	GB	FB	G/F
1997 Season	7.59	0	0	0	13	0	10.2	15	11	.189	7	2	0	0	8	.446	.243	1	7	5	0	0	0	1	7	15	0.47

1997 Season

	ERA	W	L	Sv	G	GS	IP	H	HR	BB	SO		Avg	AB	H	2B	3B	HR	RBI	BB	SO	OBP	SLG
Home	6.23	0	0	0	5	0	4.1	1	0	3	3	vs. Left	.200	20	4	1	0	0	1	6	4	.448	.250
Away	8.53	0	0	0	8	0	6.1	6	0	12	8	vs. Right	.176	17	3	1	0	0	7	9	7	.444	.235

Ray Durham — White Sox
Age 26 – Bats Both

	Avg	G	AB	R	H	2B	3B	HR	RBI	BB	SO	HBP	GDP	SB	CS	OBP	SLG	IBB	SH	SF	#Pit	#P/PA	GB	FB	G/F
1997 Season	.271	155	634	106	172	27	5	11	53	61	96	6	14	33	16	.337	.382	0	2	8	2807	3.95	264	160	1.65
Career (1995-1997)	.268	436	1662	253	446	87	16	28	169	150	274	22	28	81	25	.334	.390	6	14	19	7199	3.86	613	457	1.34

1997 Season

	Avg	AB	H	2B	3B	HR	RBI	BB	SO	OBP	SLG		Avg	AB	H	2B	3B	HR	RBI	BB	SO	OBP	SLG
vs. Left	.237	177	42	3	0	3	10	12	27	.285	.305	First Pitch	.271	48	13	2	0	0	6	0	0	.265	.313
vs. Right	.284	457	130	24	5	8	43	49	69	.357	.411	Ahead in Count	.365	170	62	6	2	7	23	40	0	.481	.547
Groundball	.268	127	34	5	2	0	3	19	331	.339		Behind in Count	.222	293	65	10	2	1	9	0	83	.237	.280
Flyball	.202	109	22	6	1	1	4	10	25	.275	.303	Two Strikes	.225	320	72	12	3	3	17	21	96	.284	.309
Home	.258	295	76	13	3	3	29	33	40	.328	.353	Batting #1	.268	448	120	20	2	9	28	39	67	.329	.382
Away	.283	339	96	14	2	8	24	28	56	.345	.407	Batting #2	.286	147	42	5	1	2	17	16	22	.353	.374
Day	.295	190	56	9	4	1	17	22	30	.367	.400	Other	.256	39	10	2	0	0	8	6	7	.370	.410
Night	.261	444	116	18	1	10	36	39	66	.324	.374	March/April	.278	97	27	4	2	1	8	15	18	.381	.392
Grass	.274	544	149	22	4	9	50	55	77	.340	.379	May	.260	104	27	4	0	1	12	13	17	.342	.375
Turf	.256	90	23	5	1	2	3	6	19	.316	.400	June	.229	118	27	4	1	3	8	6	19	.266	.356
Pre-All Star	.253	344	87	13	3	5	29	35	59	.323	.352	July	.257	101	26	3	0	2	8	12	17	.333	.347
Post-All Star	.293	290	85	14	2	6	24	26	37	.354	.417	August	.286	112	32	7	1	2	10	9	10	.339	.420
Scoring Posn	.238	130	31	5	1	1	43	19	25	.323	.315	Sept/Oct	.324	102	33	5	1	2	7	6	15	.373	.451
Close & Late	.253	91	23	1	2	0	5	9	17	.324	.308	vs. AL	.272	574	156	26	5	8	48	55	83	.337	.376
None on/out	.293	215	63	9	2	5	5	16	27	.345	.423	vs. NL	.267	60	16	1	0	3	5	6	13	.333	.433

1997 By Position

Position	Avg	AB	H	2B	3B	HR	RBI	BB	SO	OBP	SLG	G	GS	Innings	PO	A	E	DP	Fld Pct	Rng Fctr	In Zone	Zone Outs	Zone Rtg	MLB Zone
As 2b	.273	631	172	27	5	11	53	58	96	.336	.384	153	153	1339.2	270	395	18	77	.974	4.47	472	401	.850	.902

Career (1995-1997)

	Avg	AB	H	2B	3B	HR	RBI	BB	SO	OBP	SLG		Avg	AB	H	2B	3B	HR	RBI	BB	SO	OBP	SLG
vs. Left	.269	494	133	26	6	9	48	38	83	.320	.401	First Pitch	.309	178	55	9	1	2	24	5	0	.337	.404
vs. Right	.268	1168	313	61	10	19	121	112	191	.339	.386	Ahead in Count	.346	370	128	25	5	12	50	95	0	.475	.538
Groundball	.276	388	107	22	3	4	31	39	70	.346	.379	Behind in Count	.221	813	180	38	6	7	59	0	238	.237	.309
Flyball	.252	317	80	18	5	6	33	18	56	.293	.397	Two Strikes	.213	836	178	32	8	10	63	50	274	.270	.306
Home	.251	800	201	40	8	7	80	78	119	.320	.348	Batting #1	.274	526	144	25	4	9	33	46	87	.334	.388
Away	.284	862	245	47	8	21	89	72	155	.347	.430	Batting #7	.273	527	144	29	7	8	74	36	84	.323	.400
Day	.270	486	131	28	6	7	48	58	91	.351	.395	Other	.259	609	158	33	5	11	62	68	103	.341	.384
Night	.268	1176	315	59	10	21	121	92	183	.326	.389	March/April	.267	202	54	11	5	4	23	25	46	.362	.431
Grass	.269	1448	390	77	14	22	147	128	232	.333	.387	May	.300	270	81	12	1	4	38	33	41	.376	.396
Turf	.262	214	56	10	2	6	22	42	.338		.411	June	.248	306	76	13	2	4	23	25	52	.316	.363
Pre-All Star	.260	862	224	45	8	13	87	86	157	.334	.376	July	.257	296	76	15	2	7	26	21	50	.308	.392
Post-All Star	.278	800	222	42	8	15	82	64	117	.333	.406	August	.291	326	95	23	3	5	33	24	44	.338	.426
Scoring Posn	.252	393	99	12	7	5	139	51	75	.331	.356	Sept/Oct	.244	262	64	7	3	4	26	22	41	.308	.340
Close & Late	.241	270	65	11	2	1	21	33	48	.326	.307	vs. AL	.268	1602	430	86	16	25	164	144	261	.334	.389
None on/out	.291	464	135	23	4	8	8	32	69	.343	.409	vs. NL	.267	60	16	1	0	3	5	6	13	.333	.433

Jermaine Dye — Royals
Age 24 – Bats Right

	Avg	G	AB	R	H	2B	3B	HR	RBI	BB	SO	HBP	GDP	SB	CS	OBP	SLG	IBB	SH	SF	#Pit	#P/PA	GB	FB	G/F
1997 Season	.236	75	263	26	62	14	0	7	22	17	51	1	4	2	1	.284	.369	0	1	1	1020	3.60	89	77	1.16
Career (1996-1997)	.259	173	555	58	144	30	0	19	59	25	118	4	15	3	5	.294	.416	0	1	4	2118	3.60	184	158	1.16

1997 Season

	Avg	AB	H	2B	3B	HR	RBI	BB	SO	OBP	SLG		Avg	AB	H	2B	3B	HR	RBI	BB	SO	OBP	SLG
vs. Left	.286	84	24	5	0	4	8	4	13	.315	.488	Scoring Posn	.179	56	10	2	0	1	14	4	8	.242	.268
vs. Right	.212	179	38	9	0	3	14	13	38	.269	.313	Close & Late	.184	49	9	2	0	1	1	5	14	.259	.286
Home	.228	127	29	7	0	3	11	8	24	.274	.354	None on/out	.232	69	16	6	0	1	1	1	13	.243	.362
Away	.243	136	33	7	0	4	11	9	27	.293	.382	Batting #6	.250	80	20	5	0	5	8	5	14	.302	.500
First Pitch	.250	40	10	5	0	1	2	0	0	.268	.450	Batting #7	.202	129	26	5	0	1	6	7	29	.243	.264
Ahead in Count	.370	46	17	5	0	3	10	9	0	.464	.674	Other	.296	54	16	4	0	1	8	5	8	.350	.426
Behind in Count	.180	128	23	3	0	0	5	0	44	.180	.203	Pre-All Star	.214	117	25	7	0	2	9	4	20	.240	.325
Two Strikes	.175	120	21	1	0	1	6	8	51	.227	.208	Post-All Star	.253	146	37	7	0	5	13	13	31	.317	.404

Damion Easley — Tigers
Age 28 – Bats Right (groundball hitter)

	Avg	G	AB	R	H	2B	3B	HR	RBI	BB	SO	HBP	GDP	SB	CS	OBP	SLG	IBB	SH	SF	#Pit	#P/PA	GB	FB	G/F
1997 Season	.264	151	527	97	139	37	3	22	72	68	102	16	18	28	13	.362	.471	3	4	5	2382	3.84	193	150	1.29
Last Five Years	.250	475	1542	220	386	82	8	38	176	167	257	30	42	46	27	.333	.388	6	20	14	6470	3.65	634	411	1.54

1997 Season

	Avg	AB	H	2B	3B	HR	RBI	BB	SO	OBP	SLG		Avg	AB	H	2B	3B	HR	RBI	BB	SO	OBP	SLG
vs. Left	.231	143	33	7	1	7	20	11	29	.299	.441	First Pitch	.414	58	24	4	1	3	9	2	0	.435	.672
vs. Right	.276	384	106	30	2	15	52	57	73	.383	.482	Ahead in Count	.313	112	35	10	1	10	23	28	0	.451	.688
Groundball	.252	103	26	7	0	2	11	16	25	.366	.379	Behind in Count	.213	249	53	15	0	5	24	0	82	.243	.333
Flyball	.261	88	23	10	0	3	9	11	15	.340	.477	Two Strikes	.177	237	42	11	1	4	18	38	102	.312	.283
Home	.250	256	64	14	1	12	31	31	47	.346	.453	Batting #2	.249	257	64	16	2	10	35	38	49	.361	.444
Away	.277	271	75	23	2	10	41	37	55	.377	.487	Batting #6	.279	86	24	6	1	3	15	9	17	.361	.477
Day	.227	198	45	13	0	9	29	28	41	.342	.429	Other	.277	184	51	15	0	9	22	21	36	.364	.505
Night	.286	329	94	24	3	13	43	40	61	.375	.495	March/April	.290	93	27	6	0	3	9	9	17	.358	.452
Grass	.261	463	121	29	3	21	67	62	90	.363	.473	May	.203	79	16	5	1	2	9	16	19	.351	.367
Turf	.281	64	18	8	0	1	5	6	12	.352	.453	June	.292	72	21	4	0	6	13	6	10	.373	.597
Pre-All Star	.272	265	72	18	1	13	34	33	47	.368	.494	July	.267	90	24	6	1	5	11	10	18	.353	.522
Post-All Star	.256	262	67	19	2	9	38	35	55	.356	.447	August	.255	102	26	10	1	3	14	15	21	.367	.461
Scoring Posn	.230	126	29	6	0	6	49	34	25	.404	.421	Sept/Oct	.275	91	25	6	0	3	16	12	17	.370	.440
Close & Late	.347	72	25	4	0	2	11	15	14	.473	.486	vs. AL	.261	479	125	34	3	18	63	62	94	.363	.457
None on/out	.299	107	32	6	1	4	4	10	19	.380	.486	vs. NL	.292	48	14	3	0	4	9	6	8	.357	.604

1997 By Position

Position	Avg	AB	H	2B	3B	HR	RBI	BB	SO	OBP	SLG	G	GS	Innings	PO	A	E	DP	Fld Pct	Rng Fctr	In Zone	In Outs	Zone Rtg	MLB Zone
As 2b	.269	480	129	34	2	21	70	64	88	.368	.479	137	130	1161.2	233	390	12	83	.981	4.83	460	369	.802	.902
As ss	.167	24	4	1	0	0	0	2	9	.286	.208	21	7	68.1	9	16	0	0	1.000	3.29	22	17	.773	.937

Last Five Years

	Avg	AB	H	2B	3B	HR	RBI	BB	SO	OBP	SLG		Avg	AB	H	2B	3B	HR	RBI	BB	SO	OBP	SLG
vs. Left	.255	487	124	27	3	16	56	41	80	.318	.421	First Pitch	.325	212	69	13	2	8	28	4	0	.344	.519
vs. Right	.248	1055	262	55	5	22	120	126	177	.339	.373	Ahead in Count	.296	378	112	26	3	15	55	77	0	.415	.500
Groundball	.210	319	67	16	2	3	27	33	55	.292	.301	Behind in Count	.198	655	130	26	1	8	56	0	216	.220	.278
Flyball	.240	292	70	21	0	9	32	26	47	.309	.404	Two Strikes	.172	640	110	20	2	9	48	86	257	.285	.252
Home	.242	748	181	36	5	18	83	86	116	.328	.376	Batting #2	.237	473	112	26	3	14	55	54	81	.329	.393
Away	.258	794	205	46	3	20	93	81	141	.337	.399	Batting #7	.261	429	112	24	1	7	40	48	80	.340	.371
Day	.222	473	105	22	1	14	51	56	83	.319	.362	Other	.253	640	162	32	4	17	81	65	108	.330	.395
Night	.263	1069	281	60	7	24	125	111	174	.339	.399	March/April	.278	255	71	14	1	8	27	21	43	.342	.435
Grass	.250	1370	342	71	8	34	163	152	233	.334	.388	May	.234	342	80	15	2	5	36	47	51	.336	.333
Turf	.256	172	44	11	0	4	13	15	34	.321	.390	June	.230	239	55	12	1	9	34	19			
Pre-All Star	.247	940	232	50	4	25	110	98	147	.327	.388	July	.241	299	72	16	2	6	27	38			
Post-All Star	.256	602	154	32	4	13	66	69	110	.341	.387	August	.252	262	66	15	2	7	32	24			
Scoring Posn	.230	391	90	16	1	12	136	57	77	.333	.368	Sept/Oct	.290	145	42	10	0	3	20	18			
Close & Late	.294	201	59	8	1	5	31	32	40	.399	.418	vs. AL	.249	1494	372	79	8	34	167	161			
None on/out	.247	365	90	16	3	7	7	36	51	.324	.364	vs. NL	.292	48	14	3	0	4	9	6			

Batter vs. Pitcher (career)

Hits Best Against	Avg	AB	H	2B	3B	HR	RBI	BB	SO	OBP	SLG	Hits Worst Against	Avg	AB	H	2B	3B	HR	RBI	BB	SO
Mark Clark	.500	10	5	0	1	1	1	1	0	.545	1.000	Orel Hershiser	.000	12	0	0	0	0	0	2	
Juan Guzman	.467	15	7	2	0	2	7	4	3	.579	1.000	Rick Helling	.083	12	1	0	0	0	1	0	
David Cone	.462	13	6	0	0	1	1	3	4	.563	.692	Jason Bere	.083	12	1	0	0	0	1	2	
James Baldwin	.417	12	5	1	1	2	8	0	2	.417	1.167	David Wells	.091	11	1	0	0	0	1	0	
Wilson Alvarez	.318	22	7	1	0	2	4	2	5	.375	.636	Randy Johnson	.107	28	3	0	0	0	0	0	

Angel Echevarria — Rockies
Age 27 –

	Avg	G	AB	R	H	2B	3B	HR	RBI	BB	SO	HBP	GDP	SB	CS	OBP	SLG	IBB	SH	SF	#Pit	#P/PA	
1997 Season	.250	15	20	4	5	2	0	0	0	2	5	0	0	0	0	.318	.350	0	0	0	90	4.09	
Career (1996-1997)	.268	41	41	6	11	2	0	0	6	4	10	1	0	0	0	.333	.317	0	0	2	185	3.85	

1997 Season

	Avg	AB	H	2B	3B	HR	RBI	BB	SO	OBP	SLG		Avg	AB	H	2B	3B	HR	RBI	BB	SO	OBP	SLG
vs. Left	.250	8	2	0	0	0	0	0	1	.250	.250	Scoring Posn	.000	2	0	0	0	0	0	0	1	.000	.000

	Avg	AB	H	2B	3B	HR	RBI	BB	SO	OBP	SLG		Avg	AB	H	2B	3B	HR	RBI	BB	SO	OBP	SLG
vs. Right	.250	12	3	2	0	0	0	2	4	.357	.417	Close & Late	.125	8	1	1	0	0	0	1	2	.222	.250

Dennis Eckersley — Cardinals

Age 43 – Pitches Right (flyball pitcher)

	ERA	W	L	Sv	G	GS	IP	H	HR	BB	SO	Avg	H	2B	3B	HR	RBI	OBP	SLG	GF	IR	IRS	Hld	SvOp	SB	CS	GB	FB	G/F
1997 Season	3.91	1	5	36	57	0	53.0	8	45	.238	49	12	0	9	25	.273	.427	47	13	3	0	43	6	2	51	78	0.65
Last Five Years	4.06	12	25	150	281	0	274.2	51	261	.263	283	55	7	34	156	.301	.422	239	106	28	4	186	37	7	271	351	0.77

1997 Season

	ERA	W	L	Sv	G	GS	IP	H	BB	SO		Avg	AB	H	2B	3B	HR	RBI	BB	SO	OBP	SLG
Home	5.02	0	5	20	31	0	28.2	30	5	3	30	vs. Left	.217	106	23	7	0	2	12	4	22	.252	.340
Away	2.59	1	0	16	26	0	24.1	19	4	5	15	vs. Right	.260	100	26	5	0	7	13	4	23	.295	.520
Day	4.87	1	3	12	20	0	20.1	21	5	2	9	Inning 1-6	.000	0	0	0	0	0	0	0	0	.000	.000
Night	3.31	0	2	24	37	0	32.2	28	4	6	36	Inning 7+	.238	206	49	12	0	9	25	8	45	.273	.427
Grass	4.43	1	5	29	47	0	42.2	40	8	8	40	None on	.248	121	30	8	0	6	6	2	31	.266	.463
Turf	1.74	0	0	7	10	0	10.1	9	1	0	5	Runners on	.224	85	19	4	0	3	19	6	14	.283	.376
March/April	2.84	0	1	5	7	0	6.1	4	0	0	7	Scoring Posn	.236	55	13	2	0	2	16	4	9	.300	.382
May	4.00	0	1	6	9	0	9.0	10	2	1	7	Close & Late	.242	161	39	10	0	8	23	8	34	.287	.453
June	4.00	0	0	6	10	0	9.0	9	1	0	7	None on/out	.306	49	15	5	0	2	2	1	8	.333	.531
July	4.91	0	1	9	11	0	11.0	13	2	0	7	vs. 1st Batr (relief)	.259	54	14	4	0	3	5	2	11	.298	.500
August	2.08	0	1	6	11	0	8.2	6	2	5	9	1st Inning Pitched	.236	199	47	11	0	8	23	8	44	.273	.412
Sept/Oct	5.00	1	1	4	10	0	9.0	7	2	2	8	First 15 Pitches	.250	164	41	8	0	8	16	5	37	.276	.445
Starter	0.00	0	0	0	0	0	0.0	0	0	0	0	Pitch 16-30	.195	41	8	4	0	1	9	3	8	.267	.366
Reliever	3.91	1	5	36	57	0	53.0	49	8	8	45	Pitch 31-45	.000	1	0	0	0	0	0	0	0	.000	.000
0 Days rest (Relief)	8.64	0	2	6	10	0	8.1	13	2	2	9	Pitch 46+	.000	0	0	0	0	0	0	0	0	.000	.000
1 or 2 Days rest	2.63	1	1	20	29	0	27.1	19	4	6	21	First Pitch	.269	26	7	2	0	3	6	0	0	.269	.692
3+ Days rest	3.63	0	2	10	18	0	17.1	17	3	0	15	Ahead in Count	.192	130	25	5	0	5	12	0	43	.205	.346
vs. AL	1.50	0	0	6	7	0	6.0	3	1	3	4	Behind in Count	.423	26	11	3	0	1	4	6	0	.531	.654
vs. NL	4.21	1	5	30	50	0	47.0	46	8	5	41	Two Strikes	.140	114	16	4	0	1	4	2	45	.162	.202
Pre-All Star	4.28	0	3	18	28	0	27.1	27	4	1	22	Pre-All Star	.248	109	27	9	0	4	13	1	22	.261	.440
Post-All Star	3.51	1	2	18	29	0	25.2	22	5	7	23	Post-All Star	.227	97	22	3	0	5	12	7	23	.286	.412

Last Five Years

	ERA	W	L	Sv	G	GS	IP	H	HR	BB	SO		Avg	AB	H	2B	3B	HR	RBI	BB	SO	OBP	SLG
Home	3.89	8	15	79	152	0	148.0	150	19	29	157	vs. Left	.303	545	165	37	4	16	87	33	110	.344	.473
Away	4.26	4	10	71	129	0	126.2	133	15	22	104	vs. Right	.223	530	118	18	3	18	69	18	151	.256	.370
Day	3.64	7	13	59	114	0	108.2	105	13	19	92	Inning 1-6	.400	5	2	0	0	0	1	0	0	.400	.400
Night	4.34	5	12	91	167	0	166.0	178	21	32	169	Inning 7+	.263	1070	281	55	7	34	155	51	261	.301	.422
Grass	3.98	10	23	123	235	0	228.2	232	27	48	228	None on	.253	580	147	27	3	19	19	16	152	.281	.409
Turf	4.50	2	2	27	46	0	46.0	51	7	3	33	Runners on	.275	495	136	28	4	15	137	35	109	.323	.438
March/April	2.82	0	7	12	39	0	38.1	42	0	4	40	Scoring Posn	.291	289	84	15	2	9	117	28	64	.352	.450
May	5.63	1	5	28	49	0	48.0	53	7	7	42	Close & Late	.268	765	205	41	4	27	131	41	191	.310	.438
June	3.35	4	1	31	48	0	51.0	52	4	9	46	None on/out	.238	239	57	11	3	6	6	9	56	.272	.385
July	4.47	3	4	32	53	0	52.1	51	10	10	50	vs. 1st Batr (relief)	.226	266	60	9	4	9	24	10	69	.257	.391
August	2.35	2	2	29	50	0	46.0	37	5	16	48	1st Inning Pitched	.261	991	259	49	7	31	144	45	240	.298	.419
Sept/Oct	5.77	2	6	18	42	0	39.0	48	8	5	35	First 15 Pitches	.265	831	220	37	7	30	93	29	202	.294	.434
Starter	0.00	0	0	0	0	0	0.0	0	0	0	0	Pitch 16-30	.270	226	61	18	0	4	61	18	54	.329	.403
Reliever	4.06	12	25	150	281	0	274.2	283	34	51	261	Pitch 31-45	.118	17	2	0	0	0	2	4	5	.286	.118
0 Days rest (Relief)	2.88	3	8	56	79	0	72.0	66	8	16	71	Pitch 46+	.000	1	0	0	0	0	0	0	0	.000	.000
1 or 2 Days rest	2.93	6	7	61	111	0	113.2	102	8	19	102	First Pitch	.338	151	51	11	0	7	31	7	0	.367	.550
3+ Days rest	6.47	3	10	33	91	0	89.0	115	18	16	88	Ahead in Count	.211	612	129	21	4	13	58	0	235	.222	.322
vs. AL	4.29	11	14	90	168	0	167.2	172	18	40	171	Behind in Count	.368	144	53	11	2	8	31	19	0	.442	.639
vs. NL	3.70	1	11	60	113	0	107.0	111	16	11	90	Two Strikes	.185	563	104	17	2	6	48	25	261	.229	.254
Pre-All Star	3.79	6	14	84	154	0	156.2	158	14	22	146	Pre-All Star	.257	614	158	36	4	14	86	22	146	.287	.397
Post-All Star	4.42	6	11	66	127	0	118.0	125	20	29	115	Post-All Star	.271	461	125	19	3	20	70	29	115	.319	.456

Pitcher vs. Batter (since 1984)

Pitches Best Vs.	Avg	AB	H	2B	3B	HR	RBI	BB	SO	OBP	SLG	Pitches Worst Vs.	Avg	AB	H	2B	3B	HR	RBI	BB	SO	OBP	SLG
Albert Belle	.077	13	1	0	1	0	0	0	5	.077	.231	Brian McRae	.500	12	6	1	0	1	3	0	1	.500	.833
Frank Thomas	.077	13	1	0	0	0	0	0	4	.077	.077	Tony Gwynn	.429	14	6	3	0	0	2	0	1	.429	.643
Mike Macfarlane	.083	12	1	0	0	0	1	0	4	.154	.083	Jim Eisenreich	.385	13	5	2	0	1	1	3	.429	.538
Terry Pendleton	.143	14	2	0	0	0	0	3	.143	.143	Vince Coleman	.375	16	6	1	1	0	2	2	2	.444	.563
Joe Carter	.150	20	3	0	0	2	0	5	.150	.150	Paul Molitor	.333	12	4	1	0	2	0	1	.333	.667

Jim Edmonds — Angels

Age 28 – Bats Left (groundball hitter)

	Avg	G	AB	R	H	2B	3B	HR	RBI	BB	SO	HBP	GDP	SB	CS	OBP	SLG	IBB	SH	SF	#Pit	#P/PA	GB	FB	G/F
1997 Season	.291	133	502	82	146	27	0	26	80	60	80	4	7	5	7	.368	.500	5	0	5	2160	3.78	166	170	0.98
Career (1993-1997)	.290	500	1841	315	533	102	9	91	294	189	399	14	29	14	15	.358	.503	15	2	13	8103	3.94	598	515	1.16

1997 Season

	Avg	AB	H	2B	3B	HR	RBI	BB	SO	OBP	SLG		Avg	AB	H	2B	3B	HR	RBI	BB	SO	OBP	SLG
vs. Left	.273	143	39	3	0	6	24	15	20	.342	.420	First Pitch	.365	74	27	6	0	3	12	4	0	.390	.568
vs. Right	.298	359	107	24	0	20	56	45	60	.378	.532	Ahead in Count	.348	115	40	5	0	10	26	29	0	.479	.652
Groundball	.233	90	21	5	0	3	14	10	15	.320	.389	Behind in Count	.248	214	53	10	0	8	24	0	69	.253	.407
Flyball	.244	82	20	4	0	1	9	10	10	.323	.329	Two Strikes	.252	230	58	13	0	11	28	27	80	.329	.452
Home	.295	237	70	10	0	14	42	31	35	.377	.515	Batting #2	.315	127	40	6	0	6	20	19	18	.403	.504
Away	.287	265	76	17	0	12	38	29	45	.359	.487	Batting #4	.300	150	45	10	0	10	26	21	26	.394	.567

1997 Season

	Avg	AB	H	2B	3B	HR	RBI	BB	SO	OBP	SLG		Avg	AB	H	2B	3B	HR	RBI	BB	SO	OBP	SLG
Day	.255	157	40	9	0	6	23	18	27	.331	.427	Other	.271	225	61	11	0	10	34	20	36	.328	.453
Night	.307	345	106	18	0	20	57	42	53	.384	.533	March/April	.315	92	29	6	0	4	17	8	14	.359	.511
Grass	.282	447	126	23	0	23	74	55	70	.362	.488	May	.314	105	33	7	0	6	17	12	14	.387	.552
Turf	.364	55	20	4	0	3	6	5	10	.417	.600	June	.292	89	26	4	0	3	13	5	12	.330	.438
Pre-All Star	.303	297	90	17	0	14	49	27	46	.361	.502	July	.256	82	21	5	0	5	13	15	18	.386	.500
Post-All Star	.273	205	56	10	0	12	31	33	34	.378	.498	August	.220	50	11	4	0	3	8	6	8	.304	.480
Scoring Posn	.271	129	35	8	0	2	48	26	26	.385	.380	Sept/Oct	.310	84	26	1	0	5	12	14	14	.408	.500
Close & Late	.242	91	22	3	0	4	12	15	21	.346	.407	vs. AL	.288	444	128	25	0	22	71	54	68	.366	.493
None on/out	.287	115	33	9	0	8	8	7	20	.333	.574	vs. NL	.310	58	18	2	0	4	9	6	12	.385	.552

1997 By Position

Position	Avg	AB	H	2B	3B	HR	RBI	BB	SO	OBP	SLG	G	GS	Innings	PO	A	E	DP	Fld Pct	Rng Fctr	In Zone	Outs	Zone Rtg	MLB Zone
As 1b	.300	40	12	3	0	1	4	3	6	.349	.450	11	10	84.2	85	7	0	5	1.000	---	18	16	.889	.874
As cf	.295	431	127	23	0	25	74	50	67	.368	.522	115	111	967.0	313	9	5	3	.985	3.00	362	298	.823	.815

Career (1993-1997)

	Avg	AB	H	2B	3B	HR	RBI	BB	SO	OBP	SLG		Avg	AB	H	2B	3B	HR	RBI	BB	SO	OBP	SLG
vs. Left	.261	514	134	22	2	17	71	49	115	.332	.411	First Pitch	.353	238	84	24	2	11	47	13	0	.389	.609
vs. Right	.301	1327	399	80	7	74	223	140	284	.368	.539	Ahead in Count	.385	371	143	23	0	31	82	92	0	.506	.698
Groundball	.272	378	103	15	1	16	66	41	89	.349	.444	Behind in Count	.232	813	189	32	3	29	94	0	317	.240	.386
Flyball	.282	344	97	19	3	19	52	33	80	.344	.520	Two Strikes	.223	923	206	40	5	34	109	84	399	.290	.388
Home	.301	934	281	45	6	50	171	104	202	.371	.522	Batting #2	.308	764	235	44	5	51	152	90	173	.385	.579
Away	.278	907	252	57	3	41	123	85	197	.344	.483	Batting #3	.259	424	110	21	4	13	51	31	98	.307	.420
Day	.283	480	136	25	2	19	70	46	102	.345	.463	Other	.288	653	188	37	0	27	91	68	128	.357	.469
Night	.292	1361	397	77	7	72	224	143	297	.362	.517	March/April	.319	216	69	14	0	12	44	23	43	.385	.551
Grass	.289	1626	470	86	9	82	270	177	353	.361	.504	May	.292	360	105	16	2	18	60	42	75	.369	.497
Turf	.293	215	63	16	0	9	24	12	46	.332	.493	June	.315	292	92	15	0	11	48	17	56	.351	.479
Pre-All Star	.296	947	280	48	2	45	165	92	191	.360	.493	July	.281	331	93	19	1	20	63	44	74	.370	.526
Post-All Star	.283	894	253	54	7	46	129	97	208	.356	.513	August	.277	303	84	23	2	20	48	31	67	.350	.564
Scoring Posn	.276	496	137	24	2	16	191	63	131	.353	.429	Sept/Oct	.265	339	90	15	4	10	31	32	84	.328	.422
Close & Late	.218	266	58	11	0	7	34	31	74	.303	.338	vs. AL	.289	1783	515	100	9	87	285	183	387	.357	.501
None on/out	.295	373	110	28	2	24	24	28	76	.349	.574	vs. NL	.310	58	18	2	0	4	9	6	12	.385	.552

Batter vs. Pitcher (career)

Hits Best Against	Avg	AB	H	2B	3B	HR	RBI	BB	SO	OBP	SLG	Hits Worst Against	Avg	AB	H	2B	3B	HR	RBI	BB	SO	OBP	SLG
Tom Gordon	.516	31	16	3	1	1	2	5	2	.583	.774	Darren Oliver	.000	9	0	0	0	0	0	4	1	.308	.000
Tim Wakefield	.476	21	10	3	0	1	1	1	1	.500	.762	Andy Pettitte	.067	15	1	0	1	0	0	1	3	.125	.200
Felipe Lira	.467	15	7	0	0	3	4	3	2	.556	1.067	David Cone	.176	17	3	0	0	0	1	3	1	.300	.176
Rick Aguilera	.400	10	4	0	0	2	2	1	2	.455	1.000	Woody Williams	.182	11	2	0	0	0	1	0	0	.182	.182
Rich Robertson	.364	11	4	0	0	2	2	2	3	.462	.909	Scott Kamieniecki	.231	13	3	0	0	0	0	2	3	.333	.231

Robert Eenhoorn — Angels   Age 30 – Bats Right

	Avg	G	AB	R	H	2B	3B	HR	RBI	BB	SO	HBP	GDP	SB	CS	OBP	SLG	IBB	SH	SF	#Pit	#P/PA	GB	FB	G/F
1997 Season	.350	11	20	2	7	1	0	1	6	0	2	0	0	0	0	.333	.550	0	0	1	62	2.95	7	5	1.40
Career (1994-1997)	.239	37	67	7	16	3	0	1	10	3	10	0	1	0	0	.260	.328	0	1	3	236	3.19	27	20	1.35

1997 Season

	Avg	AB	H	2B	3B	HR	RBI	BB	SO	OBP	SLG		Avg	AB	H	2B	3B	HR	RBI	BB	SO	OBP	SLG
vs. Left	1.000	1	1	0	0	0	1	0	0	.500	1.000	Scoring Posn	.400	5	2	1	0	0	5	0	1	.333	.600
vs. Right	.316	19	6	1	0	1	5	0	2	.316	.526	Close & Late	.500	4	2	1	0	0	4	0	0	.400	.750

Joey Eischen — Reds   Age 28 – Pitches Left

	ERA	W	L	Sv	G	GS	IP	BB	SO	Avg	H	2B	3B	HR	RBI	OBP	SLG	GF	IR	IRS	Hld	SvOp	SB	CS	GB	FB	G/F
1997 Season	6.75	0	0	0	1	0	1.1	1	2	.333	2	2	0	0	2	.429	.667	0	1	1	0	0	0	0	0	2	0.00
Career (1994-1997)	4.37	1	2	0	71	0	90.2	46	69	.279	100	20	2	8	59	.370	.412	22	48	18	3	2	10	2	135	92	1.47

1997 Season

	ERA	W	L	Sv	G	GS	IP	H	HR	BB	SO		Avg	AB	H	2B	3B	HR	RBI	BB	SO	OBP	SLG
Home	6.75	0	0	0	1	0	1.1	2	0	1	2	vs. Left	1.000	1	1	1	0	0	1	0	0	1.000	2.000
Away	0.00	0	0	0	0	0	0.0	0	0	0	0	vs. Right	.200	5	1	0	0	0	1	1	2	.333	.400

Career (1994-1997)

	ERA	W	L	Sv	G	GS	IP	H	HR	BB	SO		Avg	AB	H	2B	3B	HR	RBI	BB	SO	OBP	SLG
Home	4.09	1	0	0	34	0	50.2	51	3	25	38	vs. Left	.261	115	30	7	1	3	22	13	23	.356	.417
Away	4.72	0	2	0	37	0	40.0	49	5	21	31	vs. Right	.287	244	70	13	1	5	37	33	46	.376	.410
Day	3.20	0	2	0	16	0	19.2	19	3	6	13	Inning 1-6	.314	140	44	9	0	2	35	15	26	.382	.421
Night	4.69	1	0	0	55	0	71.0	81	5	40	56	Inning 7+	.256	219	56	11	2	6	24	31	43	.362	.406
Grass	3.56	1	1	0	55	0	73.1	74	4	36	53	None on	.298	168	50	11	1	3	3	17	30	.376	.429
Turf	7.79	0	1	0	16	0	17.1	26	4	10	16	Runners on	.262	191	50	9	1	5	56	29	39	.364	.398
March/April	2.45	0	0	0	9	0	18.1	13	1	9	18	Scoring Posn	.305	118	36	7	0	3	50	20	27	.408	.441
May	5.79	0	0	0	13	0	14.0	20	2	8	12	Close & Late	.340	47	16	3	1	3	11	9	12	.446	.638
June	7.91	0	0	0	14	0	19.1	28	1	10	16	None on/out	.321	84	27	5	0	3	6	6	16	.387	.488
July	1.93	0	1	0	8	0	9.1	8	1	2	6	vs. 1st Batr (relief)	.419	62	26	7	0	3	15	5	11	.465	.677
August	3.14	1	0	0	10	0	14.1	13	1	7	6	1st Inning Pitched	.307	231	71	16	2	7	46	29	40	.396	.485
Sept/Oct	3.52	0	1	0	17	0	15.1	18	2	10	11	First 15 Pitches	.316	190	60	12	1	6	36	24	35	.400	.484
Starter	0.00	0	0	0	0	0	0.0	0	0	0	0	Pitch 16-30	.231	121	28	8	1	1	15	13	26	.316	.339
Reliever	4.37	1	2	0	71	0	90.2	100	8	46	69	Pitch 31-45	.269	26	7	0	0	0	2	6	4	.406	.269

Career (1994-1997)

	ERA	W	L	Sv	G	GS	IP	H	HR	BB	SO		Avg	AB	H	2B	3B	HR	RBI	BB	SO	OBP	SLG
0 Days rest (Relief)	8.68	0	0	0	11	0	9.1	21	1	7	5	Pitch 46+	.227	22	5	0	0	1	6	3	4	.346	.364
1 or 2 Days rest	3.69	1	1	0	24	0	31.2	26	3	17	23	First Pitch	.344	61	21	6	0	3	16	6	0	.414	.590
3+ Days rest	3.99	0	0	0	36	0	49.2	53	4	22	41	Ahead in Count	.186	156	29	7	0	3	21	0	60	.211	.288
vs. AL	3.24	1	1	0	24	0	25.0	27	3	14	15	Behind in Count	.430	86	37	5	2	2	19	19	0	.528	.605
vs. NL	4.80	1	1	0	47	0	65.2	73	5	32	54	Two Strikes	.147	163	24	7	0	2	18	20	69	.257	.227
Pre-All Star	5.10	0	0	0	38	0	54.2	62	4	28	49	Pre-All Star	.284	218	62	14	1	4	38	28	49	.377	.413
Post-All Star	3.25	1	2	0	33	0	36.0	38	4	18	20	Post-All Star	.270	141	38	6	1	4	21	18	20	.358	.411

Jim Eisenreich — Marlins

Age 39 – Bats Left (groundball hitter)

	Avg	G	AB	R	H	2B	3B	HR	RBI	BB	SO	HBP	GDP	SB	CS	OBP	SLG	IBB	SH	SF	#Pit	#P/PA	GB	FB	G/F
1997 Season	.280	120	293	36	82	19	1	2	34	30	28	1	7	0	0	.345	.372	4	3	4	1145	3.46	125	85	1.47
Last Five Years	.316	619	1660	220	525	97	14	26	227	158	171	5	35	32	3	.374	.439	25	11	16	6616	3.58	702	420	1.67

1997 Season

	Avg	AB	H	2B	3B	HR	RBI	BB	SO	OBP	SLG		Avg	AB	H	2B	3B	HR	RBI	BB	SO	OBP	SLG
vs. Left	.241	29	7	1	0	0	4	6	5	.361	.276	First Pitch	.188	48	9	1	0	0	4	3	0	.235	.208
vs. Right	.284	264	75	18	1	2	30	24	23	.342	.383	Ahead in Count	.351	74	26	4	1	0	12	17	0	.462	.432
Groundball	.314	51	16	5	0	0	7	5	7	.368	.412	Behind in Count	.250	104	26	7	0	1	9	0	26	.255	.346
Flyball	.239	46	11	4	0	0	5	3	3	.288	.326	Two Strikes	.229	109	25	7	0	1	11	10	28	.300	.321
Home	.276	134	37	8	0	2	15	16	16	.353	.381	Batting #3	.209	91	19	4	0	0	9	9	7	.272	.253
Away	.283	159	45	11	1	0	19	14	12	.337	.365	Batting #5	.322	90	29	5	1	2	16	8	8	.378	.467
Day	.286	91	26	5	0	0	8	6	10	.323	.341	Other	.304	112	34	10	0	0	9	13	13	.378	.393
Night	.277	202	56	14	1	2	26	24	18	.354	.386	March/April	.222	36	8	1	0	0	1	4	2	.317	.250
Grass	.289	232	67	14	1	2	27	25	24	.356	.384	May	.316	57	18	3	1	1	8	8	3	.400	.456
Turf	.246	61	15	5	0	0	7	5	4	.299	.328	June	.257	70	18	6	0	0	9	4	5	.286	.343
Pre-All Star	.279	179	50	10	1	1	19	19	11	.347	.363	July	.283	53	15	3	0	1	4	7	8	.367	.396
Post-All Star	.281	114	32	9	0	1	15	11	17	.341	.386	August	.341	44	15	2	0	0	6	4	5	.396	.386
Scoring Posn	.262	84	22	6	1	0	30	15	13	.359	.357	Sept/Oct	.242	33	8	4	0	0	6	3	5	.297	.364
Close & Late	.207	58	12	4	0	0	7	5	8	.273	.276	vs. AL	.306	36	11	4	0	0	9	3	2	.350	.417
None on/out	.234	64	15	3	0	1	1	4	8	.279	.328	vs. NL	.276	257	71	15	1	2	25	27	26	.344	.366

1997 By Position

Position	Avg	AB	H	2B	3B	HR	RBI	BB	SO	OBP	SLG		G	GS	Innings	PO	A	E	DP	Fld Pct	Rng Fctr	In Zone	Outs	Zone Rtg	MLB Zone
As Pinch Hitter	.286	35	10	6	0	0	5	2	6	.333	.457		44	0	---										
As 1b	.296	71	21	7	1	0	11	12	9	.398	.423		29	19	159.0	135	11	1	15	.993	---	21	21	1.000	.874
As lf	.276	127	35	5	0	1	11	12	9	.331	.339		42	32	288.0	58	1	1	0	.983	1.84	68	55	.809	.805
As rf	.308	39	12	0	0	1	5	4	3	.372	.385		13	10	89.2	14	1	0	1	1.000	1.51	16	13	.813	.813

Last Five Years

	Avg	AB	H	2B	3B	HR	RBI	BB	SO	OBP	SLG		Avg	AB	H	2B	3B	HR	RBI	BB	SO	OBP	SLG
vs. Left	.271	255	69	10	1	1	36	26	34	.334	.329	First Pitch	.260	227	59	10	2	7	37	20	0	.317	.414
vs. Right	.325	1405	456	87	13	25	191	132	137	.381	.458	Ahead in Count	.386	427	165	32	5	8	88	93	0	.490	.541
Groundball	.326	466	152	29	2	7	65	47	44	.387	.442	Behind in Count	.281	663	186	37	3	6	59	0	150	.284	.373
Flyball	.298	275	82	19	3	4	36	23	34	.350	.433	Two Strikes	.272	647	176	30	3	6	59	45	171	.323	.355
Home	.334	784	262	51	7	14	105	77	79	.394	.471	Batting #5	.340	497	169	38	5	7	68	47	51	.395	.479
Away	.300	876	263	46	7	12	122	81	92	.356	.410	Batting #6	.331	514	170	21	5	12	79	55	50	.395	.461
Day	.318	471	150	30	3	4	65	31	47	.355	.420	Other	.287	649	186	38	4	7	80	56	70	.342	.390
Night	.315	1189	375	67	11	22	162	127	124	.381	.446	March/April	.258	182	47	5	2	1	21	15	18	.317	.324
Grass	.295	722	213	38	6	9	100	74	76	.357	.402	May	.355	299	106	20	3	2	43	38	27	.426	.462
Turf	.333	938	312	59	8	17	127	84	95	.387	.467	June	.329	347	114	25	4	7	51	25	35	.371	.484
Pre-All Star	.315	951	300	54	9	11	126	93	93	.376	.442	July	.284	356	101	18	1	5	44	37	40	.349	.382
Post-All Star	.317	709	225	43	5	15	101	65	78	.372	.456	August	.356	295	105	21	3	8	42	17	26	.394	.529
Scoring Posn	.316	481	152	22	6	5	186	74	55	.397	.418	Sept/Oct	.287	181	52	8	1	3	26	26	25	.366	.392
Close & Late	.257	338	87	10	1	2	39	31	40	.317	.311	vs. AL	.306	36	11	4	0	0	9	3	2	.350	.417
None on/out	.274	354	97	25	2	8	8	22	45	.318	.394	vs. NL	.317	1624	514	93	14	26	218	155	169	.375	.439

Batter vs. Pitcher (since 1984)

Hits Best Against	Avg	AB	H	2B	3B	HR	RBI	BB	SO	OBP	SLG	Hits Worst Against	Avg	AB	H	2B	3B	HR	RBI	BB	SO	OBP	SLG
Bret Saberhagen	.667	12	8	0	1	0	2	0	2	.667	.833	Jim Bullinger	.000	11	0	0	0	0	1	2	2	.143	.000
Rick Aguilera	.583	12	7	1	1	0	0	0	1	.583	.833	John Smoltz	.080	25	2	0	0	0	1	3	4	.172	.080
Andy Ashby	.571	14	8	3	0	0	6	1	0	.600	.786	David Wells	.091	11	1	0	0	0	0	0	0	.091	.091
Pat Rapp	.421	19	8	1	1	1	7	3	1	.500	.737	Mike Mussina	.091	11	1	1	0	0	0	0	0	.091	.182
Pedro Astacio	.417	24	10	3	1	2	7	2	0	.462	.875	Chuck Finley	.111	9	1	0	0	0	0	2	0	.273	.111

Cal Eldred — Brewers

Age 30 – Pitches Right (flyball pitcher)

	ERA	W	L	Sv	G	GS	IP	BB	SO	Avg	H	2B	3B	HR	RBI	OBP	SLG	CG	ShO	Sup	QS	#P/S	SB	CS	GB	FB	G/F
1997 Season	4.99	13	15	0	34	34	202.0	89	122	.266	207	41	4	31	97	.346	.449	1		5.57	15	101	16	8	236	289	0.82
Last Five Years	4.47	45	47	0	114	114	747.1	312	468	.249	703	146	14	98	343	.327	.415	15		2	4.99	57	109	74	24	882	995	0.89

1997 Season

	ERA	W	L	Sv	G	GS	IP	H	HR	BB	SO		Avg	AB	H	2B	3B	HR	RBI	BB	SO	OBP	SLG
Home	4.42	9	5	0	18	18	114.0	104	17	45	63	vs. Left	.245	412	101	19	3	14	38	49	69	.332	.408
Away	5.73	4	10	0	16	16	88.0	103	14	44	59	vs. Right	.290	365	106	22	1	17	59	40	53	.363	.496
Day	6.97	2	6	0	10	10	50.1	65	9	30	39	Inning 1-6	.267	720	192	39	3	31	97	86	115	.350	.458
Night	4.33	11	9	0	24	24	151.2	142	22	59	83	Inning 7+	.263	57	15	2	1	0	0	3	7	.300	.333
Grass	4.90	13	11	0	29	29	174.1	178	29	73	101	None on	.262	458	120	24	4	18	18	43	56	.332	.450

1997 Season

	ERA	W	L	Sv	G	GS	IP	H	HR	BB	SO		Avg	AB	H	2B	3B	HR	RBI	BB	SO	OBP	SLG
Turf	5.53	0	4	0	5	5	27.2	29	2	16	21	Runners on	.273	319	87	17	0	13	79	46	66	.365	.448
March/April	4.13	3	2	0	5	5	28.1	30	1	18	19	Scoring Posn	.246	179	44	8	0	4	59	34	46	.359	.358
May	5.17	2	3	0	6	6	38.1	43	9	12	26	Close & Late	.275	40	11	2	1	0	0	2	4	.310	.375
June	8.13	2	3	0	6	6	31.0	37	9	20	17	None on/out	.294	201	59	14	3	7	7	20	20	.363	.498
July	3.06	3	2	0	5	5	32.1	22	3	11	20	vs. 1st Batr (relief)	.000	0	0	0	0	0	0	0	0	.000	.000
August	5.22	1	2	0	7	7	39.2	40	4	19	24	1st Inning Pitched	.240	129	31	7	0	6	18	26	27	.367	.434
Sept/Oct	4.18	2	3	0	5	5	32.1	35	5	9	16	First 75 Pitches	.274	559	153	28	2	23	68	63	89	.352	.454
Starter	4.99	13	15	0	34	34	202.0	207	31	89	122	Pitch 76-90	.278	115	32	6	1	5	15	8	16	.336	.478
Reliever	0.00	0	0	0	0	0	0.0	0	0	0	0	Pitch 91-105	.247	73	18	7	1	2	12	12	10	.345	.452
0-3 Days Rest (Start)	0.00	0	0	0	0	0	0.0	0	0	0	0	Pitch 106+	.133	30	4	0	0	1	2	6	7	.278	.233
4 Days Rest	5.34	10	13	0	29	29	170.1	180	30	76	109	First Pitch	.314	86	27	6	2	6	11	0	0	.326	.640
5+ Days Rest	3.13	3	2	0	5	5	31.2	27	1	13	13	Ahead in Count	.207	343	71	12	0	8	25	0	94	.221	.312
vs. AL	5.11	13	14	0	31	31	186.2	194	29	78	110	Behind in Count	.320	181	58	14	1	6	23	50	0	.468	.508
vs. NL	3.52	0	1	0	3	3	15.1	13	2	11	12	Two Strikes	.191	362	69	13	0	11	35	39	122	.280	.318
Pre-All Star	5.50	8	8	0	18	18	104.2	113	19	51	65	Pre-All Star	.278	407	113	22	3	19	60	51	65	.361	.486
Post-All Star	4.44	5	7	0	16	16	97.1	94	12	38	57	Post-All Star	.254	370	94	19	1	12	37	38	57	.330	.408

Last Five Years

	ERA	W	L	Sv	G	GS	IP	H	HR	BB	SO		Avg	AB	H	2B	3B	HR	RBI	BB	SO	OBP	SLG
Home	3.84	26	18	0	57	57	393.2	337	44	143	248	vs. Left	.247	1496	369	73	11	45	157	176	232	.331	.400
Away	5.17	19	29	0	57	57	353.2	366	54	169	220	vs. Right	.252	1328	334	73	3	53	186	136	236	.322	.431
Day	5.37	12	15	0	36	36	223.0	230	29	98	148	Inning 1-6	.249	2417	602	132	10	83	308	283	412	.331	.415
Night	4.09	33	32	0	78	78	524.1	473	69	214	320	Inning 7+	.248	407	101	14	4	15	35	29	56	.299	.413
Grass	4.37	43	39	0	99	99	654.2	609	90	268	412	None on	.251	1694	426	97	11	52	52	159	260	.321	.414
Turf	5.15	2	8	0	15	15	92.2	94	8	44	56	Runners on	.245	1130	277	49	3	46	291	153	208	.335	.416
March/April	3.58	9	6	0	16	16	98.0	86	4	49	72	Scoring Posn	.240	658	158	27	2	24	239	107	135	.340	.397
May	4.98	7	11	0	21	21	141.0	156	25	50	98	Close & Late	.284	222	63	6	3	11	28	14	30	.328	.486
June	4.14	10	7	0	18	18	126.0	102	21	53	62	None on/out	.246	745	200	51	7	22	22	68	106	.335	.444
July	4.99	7	9	0	22	22	140.2	138	21	55	80	vs. 1st Batr (relief)	.000	0	0	0	0	0	0	0	0	.000	.000
August	4.77	8	5	0	21	21	132.0	127	17	63	84	1st Inning Pitched	.245	425	104	22	2	15	68	72	81	.355	.412
Sept/Oct	3.94	4	9	0	16	16	109.2	94	10	42	72	First 75 Pitches	.254	1848	469	99	8	62	223	218	317	.336	.417
Starter	4.47	45	47	0	114	114	747.1	703	98	312	468	Pitch 76-90	.263	419	110	21	1	16	58	36	58	.326	.432
Reliever	0.00	0	0	0	0	0	0.0	0	0	0	0	Pitch 91-105	.251	311	78	21	3	10	43	28	47	.314	.434
0-3 Days Rest (Start)	4.18	1	3	0	4	4	28.0	24	4	8	19	Pitch 106+	.187	246	46	5	2	10	19	30	46	.273	.346
4 Days Rest	4.77	32	38	0	82	82	535.2	527	72	226	347	First Pitch	.313	364	114	22	3	22	55	2	0	.323	.571
5+ Days Rest	3.63	12	6	0	28	28	183.2	152	22	78	110	Ahead in Count	.185	1262	233	45	5	23	92	0	389	.192	.283
vs. AL	4.49	45	46	0	111	111	732.0	690	96	301	456	Behind in Count	.314	634	199	49	4	30	102	168	0	.456	.546
vs. NL	3.52	0	1	0	3	3	15.1	13	2	11	12	Two Strikes	.175	1323	231	43	5	29	115	142	468	.259	.280
Pre-All Star	4.39	28	26	0	61	61	405.2	385	56	169	250	Pre-All Star	.250	1542	385	75	10	56	193	169	250	.325	.420
Post-All Star	4.56	17	21	0	53	53	341.2	318	42	143	218	Post-All Star	.248	1282	318	71	4	42	150	143	218	.329	.408

Pitcher vs. Batter (career)

Pitches Best Vs.	Avg	AB	H	2B	3B	HR	RBI	BB	SO	OBP	SLG	Pitches Worst Vs.	Avg	AB	H	2B	3B	HR	RBI	BB	SO	OBP	SLG
Devon White	.000	18	0	0	0	0	1	2	4	.095	.000	Jeff Frye	.563	16	9	2	0	1	3	0	1	.563	.875
Melvin Nieves	.000	11	0	0	0	0	0	2	5	.214	.000	Chris Gomez	.556	9	5	2	0	1	1	3	1	.667	1.111
Dean Palmer	.053	19	1	0	0	0	1	2	8	.143	.053	Albert Belle	.500	28	14	4	1	5	12	3	3	.563	1.250
Ruben Sierra	.071	14	1	0	0	0	1	2	2	.176	.071	Mark McGwire	.364	11	4	1	0	2	3	0	1	.364	1.000
Mike Blowers	.083	12	1	0	0	0	0	1	5	.154	.083	Juan Gonzalez	.353	17	6	1	0	3	9	1	3	.389	.941

Kevin Elster — Pirates

Age 33 – Bats Right (flyball hitter)

	Avg	G	AB	R	H	2B	3B	HR	RBI	BB	SO	HBP	GDP	SB	CS	OBP	SLG	IBB	SH	SF	#Pit	#P/PA	GB	FB	G/F
1997 Season	.225	39	138	14	31	6	2	7	25	21	39	1	1	0	2	.327	.449	0	2	2	690	4.21	49	39	1.26
Last Five Years	.234	239	743	104	174	43	5	32	133	82	202	4	10	4	3	.308	.435	2	21	15	3470	4.01	196	258	0.76

1997 Season

	Avg	AB	H	2B	3B	HR	RBI	BB	SO	OBP	SLG		Avg	AB	H	2B	3B	HR	RBI	BB	SO	OBP	SLG
vs. Left	.192	26	5	0	1	0	1	5	11	.313	.269	Scoring Posn	.231	39	9	3	0	1	16	6	11	.333	.385
vs. Right	.232	112	26	6	1	7	24	16	28	.331	.491	Close & Late	.320	25	8	3	0	1	7	5	5	.419	.560
Home	.179	56	10	1	1	3	9	11	22	.304	.393	None on/out	.219	32	7	1	1	1	1	5	12	.324	.406
Away	.256	82	21	5	1	4	16	10	17	.344	.488	Total	.225	138	31	6	2	7	25	21	39	.327	.449
First Pitch	.182	11	2	0	0	0	2	0	0	.167	.182	Batting #5	.225	138	31	6	2	7	25	21	39	.327	.449
Ahead in Count	.346	26	9	1	0	3	10	5	0	.438	.731	Other	.000	0	0	0	0	0	0	0	0	.000	.000
Behind in Count	.164	67	11	4	1	2	6	0	29	.164	.343	Pre-All Star	.225	138	31	6	2	7	25	21	39	.327	.449
Two Strikes	.125	72	9	3	1	3	10	16	39	.284	.319	Post-All Star	.000	0	0	0	0	0	0	0	0	.000	.000

Last Five Years

	Avg	AB	H	2B	3B	HR	RBI	BB	SO	OBP	SLG		Avg	AB	H	2B	3B	HR	RBI	BB	SO	OBP	SLG
vs. Left	.247	227	56	16	4	4	36	28	63	.324	.405	First Pitch	.263	80	21	6	1	2	15	2	0	.273	.438
vs. Right	.229	516	118	27	1	28	97	54	139	.301	.448	Ahead in Count	.322	152	49	8	1	11	42	34	0	.439	.605
Groundball	.221	149	33	10	1	4	24	16	38	.290	.383	Behind in Count	.187	374	70	22	1	13	44	0	166	.186	.356
Flyball	.260	127	33	8	1	6	20	13	46	.322	.480	Two Strikes	.152	396	60	17	2	13	57	46	202	.238	.303
Home	.218	344	75	15	3	13	61	42	104	.303	.392	Batting #5	.225	138	31	6	2	7	25	21	39	.327	.449
Away	.248	399	99	28	2	19	72	40	98	.313	.471	Batting #9	.250	504	126	31	2	22	96	51	134	.316	.450
Day	.235	200	47	14	0	10	42	27	52	.323	.455	Other	.168	101	17	6	1	3	12	10	29	.239	.337
Night	.234	543	127	29	5	22	91	55	150	.302	.427	March/April	.251	171	43	13	1	9	37	19	47	.320	.497
Grass	.234	586	137	34	4	25	102	55	154	.299	.433	May	.217	157	34	6	1	9	28	13	46	.273	.439
Turf	.236	157	37	9	1	7	31	25	48	.339	.439	June	.325	77	25	6	1	2	16	19	19	.458	.506
Pre-All Star	.233	447	104	26	3	20	83	54	129	.311	.438	July	.217	120	26	5	0	2	11	11	35	.276	.308

Last Five Years

	Avg	AB	H	2B	3B	HR	RBI	BB	SO	OBP	SLG		Avg	AB	H	2B	3B	HR	RBI	BB	SO	OBP	SLG
Post-All Star	.236	296	70	17	2	12	50	28	73	.304	.429	August	.216	125	27	7	1	9	35	9	26	.277	.504
Scoring Posn	.222	221	49	14	1	5	89	29	58	.297	.362	Sept/Oct	.204	93	19	6	1	1	6	11	29	.290	.323
Close & Late	.194	103	20	7	0	1	19	12	31	.270	.291	vs. AL	.239	552	132	33	2	24	99	54	149	.304	.437
None on/out	.268	183	49	12	1	8	8	15	53	.323	.475	vs. NL	.220	191	42	10	3	8	34	28	53	.320	.429

Batter vs. Pitcher (career)

Hits Best Against	Avg	AB	H	2B	3B	HR	RBI	BB	SO	OBP	SLG	Hits Worst Against	Avg	AB	H	2B	3B	HR	RBI	BB	SO	OBP	SLG
David Wells	.462	13	6	3	0	0	3	1	5	.467	.692	Omar Olivares	.056	18	1	0	0	1	1	1	6	.105	.222
Orel Hershiser	.412	17	7	2	0	1	2	0	2	.444	.706	Mark Portugal	.067	15	1	0	0	0	1	0	1	.063	.067
Steve Avery	.400	15	6	2	1	0	6	0	1	.400	.667	Pete Smith	.091	11	1	1	0	0	0	0	7	.091	.182
Doug Drabek	.370	27	10	1	1	2	7	4	4	.452	.704	Alex Fernandez	.091	11	1	1	0	0	0	0	5	.091	.182
John Wetteland	.333	9	3	0	0	1	4	2	4	.417	.667	Chris Haney	.095	21	2	1	0	0	1	0	3	.095	.143

Alan Embree — Braves
Age 28 – Pitches Left (flyball pitcher)

	ERA	W	L	Sv	G	GS	IP	BB	SO	Avg	H	2B	3B	HR	RBI	OBP	SLG	GF	IR	IRS	Hld	SvOp	SB	CS	GB	FB	G/F
1997 Season	2.54	3	1	0	66	0	46.0	20	45	.221	36	4	0	1	11	.312	.264	15	43	6	16	0	6	1	62	41	1.51
Last Five Years	4.34	7	4	1	113	0	101.2	57	101	.241	89	15	2	13	55	.340	.397	25	87	13	23	1	13	3	111	112	0.99

1997 Season

	ERA	W	L	Sv	G	GS	IP	H	HR	BB	SO		Avg	AB	H	2B	3B	HR	RBI	BB	SO	OBP	SLG
Home	2.96	3	0	0	37	0	27.1	22	1	13	29	vs. Left	.247	73	18	0	0	1	7	9	17	.333	.288
Away	1.93	0	1	0	29	0	18.2	14	0	7	16	vs. Right	.200	90	18	4	0	0	4	11	28	.294	.244
Day	2.57	1	1	0	20	0	14.0	6	1	4	15	Inning 1-6	.095	21	2	0	0	0	1	2	4	.208	.095
Night	2.53	2	0	0	46	0	32.0	30	0	16	30	Inning 7+	.239	142	34	4	0	1	10	18	41	.327	.289
Grass	3.03	3	1	0	55	0	38.2	32	1	17	37	None on	.282	78	22	2	0	1	1	10	18	.371	.346
Turf	0.00	0	0	0	11	0	7.1	4	0	3	8	Runners on	.165	85	14	2	0	0	10	10	27	.258	.188
March/April	4.76	1	1	0	9	0	5.2	5	0	4	2	Scoring Posn	.140	50	7	0	0	0	9	7	15	.241	.140
May	2.61	0	0	0	15	0	10.1	13	0	3	14	Close & Late	.227	66	15	1	0	1	6	11	20	.333	.288
June	1.35	0	0	0	11	0	6.2	3	1	2	3	None on/out	.432	37	16	2	0	1	1	6	8	.523	.568
July	3.12	2	0	0	11	0	8.2	3	0	4	11	vs. 1st Batr (relief)	.291	55	16	1	0	1	4	7	15	.375	.364
August	1.42	0	0	0	10	0	6.1	6	0	3	6	1st Inning Pitched	.219	155	34	4	0	1	11	20	43	.315	.265
Sept/Oct	2.16	0	0	0	10	0	8.1	6	0	4	9	First 15 Pitches	.228	136	31	3	0	1	7	15	38	.312	.272
Starter	0.00	0	0	0	0	0	0.0	0	0	0	0	Pitch 16-30	.185	27	5	1	0	0	4	5	7	.313	.222
Reliever	2.54	3	1	0	66	0	46.0	36	1	20	45	Pitch 31-45	.000	0	0	0	0	0	0	0	0	.000	.000
0 Days rest (Relief)	5.06	1	0	0	18	0	10.2	12	1	7	12	Pitch 46+	.000	0	0	0	0	0	0	0	0	.000	.000
1 or 2 Days rest	1.46	1	1	0	30	0	24.2	19	0	5	25	First Pitch	.400	25	10	2	0	3	2	0		.444	.480
3+ Days rest	2.53	1	0	0	18	0	10.2	5	0	8	8	Ahead in Count	.151	86	13	1	0	1	4	0	39	.170	.198
vs. AL	7.71	0	0	0	5	0	2.1	5	1	2	1	Behind in Count	.321	28	9	1	0	0	1	10	0	.487	.357
vs. NL	2.27	3	1	0	61	0	43.2	31	0	18	44	Two Strikes	.136	81	11	0	0	1	4	8	45	.231	.173
Pre-All Star	2.70	1	1	0	36	0	23.1	21	1	9	19	Pre-All Star	.244	86	21	4	0	1	8	9	19	.320	.326
Post-All Star	2.38	2	0	0	30	0	22.2	15	0	11	26	Post-All Star	.195	77	15	0	0	0	3	11	26	.303	.195

Angelo Encarnacion — Angels
Age 25 – Bats Right

	Avg	G	AB	R	H	2B	3B	HR	RBI	BB	SO	HBP	GDP	SB	CS	OBP	SLG	IBB	SH	SF	#Pit	#P/PA	GB	FB	G/F
1997 Season	.412	11	17	2	7	1	0	1	4	0	1	0	1	2	0	.412	.647	0	0	0	51	3.00	9	4	2.25
Career (1995-1997)	.253	76	198	23	50	10	2	3	15	13	34	0	4	3	1	.299	.369	5	3	0	684	3.20	87	49	1.78

1997 Season

	Avg	AB	H	2B	3B	HR	RBI	BB	SO	OBP	SLG		Avg	AB	H	2B	3B	HR	RBI	BB	SO	OBP	SLG
vs. Left	.667	3	2	0	0	1	4	0	0	.667	1.667	Scoring Posn	.333	6	2	0	0	1	4	0	1	.333	.833
vs. Right	.357	14	5	1	0	0	0	0	1	.357	.429	Close & Late	.000	1	0	0	0	0	0	0	0	.000	.000

Juan Encarnacion — Tigers
Age 22 – Bats Right

	Avg	G	AB	H	2B	3B	HR	RBI	BB	SO	HBP	GDP	SB	CS	OBP	SLG	IBB	SH	SF	#Pit	#P/PA	GB	FB	G/F
1997 Season	.212	11	33	3	7	1	1	1	5	3	12	2	1	3	1	.316	.394	0	0	0	153	4.03	11	8	1.38

1997 Season

	Avg	AB	H	2B	3B	HR	RBI	BB	SO	OBP	SLG		Avg	AB	H	2B	3B	HR	RBI	BB	SO	OBP	SLG
vs. Left	.167	12	2	1	0	1	2	0	5	.231	.500	Scoring Posn	.200	10	2	0	1	0	3	0	3	.200	.400
vs. Right	.238	21	5	0	1	0	3	3	7	.360	.333	Close & Late	.500	2	1	0	0	0	0	1	1	.667	.500

Todd Erdos — Padres
Age 24 – Pitches Right

	ERA	W	L	Sv	G	GS	IP	BB	SO	Avg	H	2B	3B	HR	RBI	OBP	SLG	GF	IR	IRS	Hld	SvOp	SB	CS	GB	FB	G/F
1997 Season	5.27	2	0	0	11	0	13.2	4	13	.293	17	4	1	1	13	.359	.448	2	12	7	0	0	2	0	18	13	1.38

1997 Season

	ERA	W	L	Sv	G	GS	IP	H	HR	BB	SO		Avg	AB	H	2B	3B	HR	RBI	BB	SO	OBP	SLG
Home	4.91	1	0	0	6	0	7.1	10	0	2	8	vs. Left	.357	28	10	3	0	1	8	2	3	.400	.571
Away	5.68	1	0	0	5	0	6.1	7	1	2	5	vs. Right	.233	30	7	1	1	0	5	2	10	.324	.333

John Ericks — Pirates
Age 30 – Pitches Right (flyball pitcher)

	ERA	W	L	Sv	G	GS	IP	BB	SO	Avg	H	2B	3B	HR	RBI	OBP	SLG	GF	IR	IRS	Hld	SvOp	SB	CS	GB	FB	G/F
1997 Season	1.93	1	0	6	10	0	9.1	4	6	.200	7	1	0	1	2	.282	.314	10	0	0	0	7	2	0	12	13	0.92
Career (1995-1997)	4.78	8	14	14	57	22	162.0	73	132	.268	171	29	2	19	88	.343	.410	23	11	5	1	17	26	10	197	204	0.97

1997 Season

	ERA	W	L	Sv	G	GS	IP	H	HR	BB	SO		Avg	AB	H	2B	3B	HR	RBI	BB	SO	OBP	SLG
Home	2.70	1	0	2	4	0	3.1	4	1	1	1	vs. Left	.190	21	4	0	0	0	1	2	3	.261	.190
Away	1.50	0	0	4	6	0	6.0	3	0	3	5	vs. Right	.214	14	3	1	0	1	1	2	3	.313	.500

Scott Erickson — Orioles
Age 30 – Pitches Right (groundball pitcher)

	ERA	W	L	Sv	G	GS	IP	BB	SO	Avg	H	2B	3B	HR	RBI	OBP	SLG	CG	ShO	Sup	QS	#P/S	SB	CS	GB	FB	G/F
1997 Season	3.69	16	7	0	34	33	221.2	61	131	.257	218	35	3	16	84	.309	.362	3	2	4.91	22	96	21	7	440	153	2.88
Last Five Years	4.78	58	59	0	157	155	1003.0	324	557	.287	1132	219	22	87	498	.345	.420	19	5	5.59	75	99	105	28	1953	794	2.46

1997 Season

	ERA	W	L	Sv	G	GS	IP	H	HR	BB	SO		Avg	AB	H	2B	3B	HR	RBI	BB	SO	OBP	SLG
Home	3.29	8	4	0	17	16	109.1	105	5	32	63	vs. Left	.248	452	112	21	2	10	47	35	48	.302	.369
Away	4.09	8	3	0	17	17	112.1	113	11	29	68	vs. Right	.267	397	106	14	1	6	37	26	83	.317	.353
Day	4.32	5	2	0	12	11	73.0	73	7	26	40	Inning 1-6	.257	705	181	27	2	12	73	55	112	.313	.352
Night	3.39	11	5	0	22	22	148.2	145	9	35	91	Inning 7+	.257	144	37	8	1	4	11	6	19	.289	.410
Grass	4.15	12	7	0	29	28	182.0	189	14	59	105	None on	.261	506	132	15	2	8	8	28	87	.305	.346
Turf	1.59	4	0	0	5	5	39.2	29	2	2	26	Runners on	.251	343	86	20	1	8	76	33	44	.315	.385
March/April	2.96	3	1	0	4	4	27.1	21	1	9	11	Scoring Posn	.282	174	49	12	1	7	73	25	24	.368	.483
May	2.93	5	0	0	6	6	43.0	36	3	13	23	Close & Late	.293	82	24	6	1	2	7	6	12	.341	.463
June	4.01	2	2	0	6	5	33.2	35	3	9	17	None on/out	.289	235	68	6	0	5	5	8	36	.313	.379
July	4.86	3	2	0	6	6	37.0	52	4	9	21	vs. 1st Batr (relief)	.000	1	0	0	0	0	0	0	1	.000	.000
August	2.11	2	0	0	6	6	47.0	36	3	8	37	1st Inning Pitched	.296	135	40	3	0	4	23	22	20	.403	.407
Sept/Oct	5.88	1	2	0	6	6	33.2	38	2	13	22	First 75 Pitches	.258	624	161	24	2	11	61	48	101	.314	.356
Starter	3.71	16	7	0	33	33	221.0	218	16	61	130	Pitch 76-90	.276	127	35	6	0	4	16	6	17	.313	.417
Reliever	0.00	0	0	0	1	0	0.2	0	0	0	1	Pitch 91-105	.225	80	18	4	1	0	4	6	10	.279	.300
0-3 Days Rest (Start)	1.17	3	0	0	3	3	23.0	16	1	4	9	Pitch 106+	.222	18	4	1	0	1	3	1	3	.250	.444
4 Days Rest	3.60	9	3	0	22	22	147.2	148	10	43	91	First Pitch	.305	128	39	7	0	4	14	4	0	.333	.453
5+ Days Rest	5.19	4	4	0	8	8	50.1	54	5	14	30	Ahead in Count	.209	364	76	11	1	2	21	0	113	.211	.261
vs. AL	3.73	15	7	0	30	30	202.2	199	14	54	125	Behind in Count	.311	206	64	9	1	6	29	37	0	.418	.451
vs. NL	3.32	1	0	0	4	3	19.0	19	2	7	6	Two Strikes	.188	336	63	12	0	5	27	20	131	.236	.268
Pre-All Star	3.81	11	4	0	18	17	115.2	109	9	37	56	Pre-All Star	.249	438	109	19	2	9	45	37	56	.310	.363
Post-All Star	3.57	5	3	0	16	16	106.0	109	7	24	75	Post-All Star	.265	411	109	16	1	7	39	24	75	.308	.360

Last Five Years

	ERA	W	L	Sv	G	GS	IP	H	HR	BB	SO		Avg	AB	H	2B	3B	HR	RBI	BB	SO	OBP	SLG
Home	4.56	30	28	0	76	75	499.2	538	41	164	301	vs. Left	.305	2187	668	127	18	47	279	192	244	.362	.444
Away	5.01	28	31	0	81	80	503.1	594	46	160	256	vs. Right	.265	1752	464	92	4	40	219	132	313	.325	.390
Day	4.73	19	19	0	49	48	310.1	361	32	97	171	Inning 1-6	.290	3369	976	183	20	74	447	279	484	.347	.422
Night	4.81	39	40	0	108	107	692.2	771	55	227	386	Inning 7+	.274	570	156	36	2	13	51	45	73	.335	.412
Grass	4.67	39	32	0	101	100	641.2	727	56	213	309	None on	.276	2217	613	126	13	49	49	179	336	.335	.411
Turf	4.98	19	27	0	56	55	361.1	405	31	111	248	Runners on	.301	1722	519	93	9	38	449	145	221	.358	.432
March/April	4.85	6	11	0	19	19	115.0	132	13	52	56	Scoring Posn	.308	1004	309	59	6	30	418	106	140	.374	.468
May	4.96	13	8	0	26	26	167.0	164	13	53	96	Close & Late	.299	244	73	20	2	3	25	25	35	.372	.434
June	5.18	9	10	0	30	29	191.0	224	18	58	101	None on/out	.290	1010	293	59	4	26	26	78	137	.334	.434
July	4.91	11	14	0	31	31	196.0	239	20	68	103	vs. 1st Batr (relief)	.000	2	0	0	0	0	0	0	2	.000	.000
August	4.99	10	10	0	28	27	176.2	212	16	51	105	1st Inning Pitched	.301	621	187	24	1	21	101	78	98	.379	.444
Sept/Oct	3.66	9	6	0	23	23	157.1	161	7	42	96	First 75 Pitches	.287	2851	817	143	17	62	357	234	415	.343	.414
Starter	4.78	58	59	0	155	155	1001.1	1130	86	323	555	Pitch 76-90	.316	526	166	38	3	18	84	37	66	.369	.502
Reliever	5.40	0	0	0	2	0	1.2	2	1	1	2	Pitch 91-105	.256	379	97	26	1	5	33	30	52	.317	.369
0-3 Days Rest (Start)	4.58	10	6	0	20	20	131.2	145	15	36	66	Pitch 106+	.284	183	52	12	1	2	24	23	24	.370	.393
4 Days Rest	4.79	33	42	0	104	104	676.1	771	61	224	379	First Pitch	.315	606	191	36	5	12	82	7	0	.347	.450
5+ Days Rest	4.89	15	11	0	31	31	193.1	214	10	63	110	Ahead in Count	.231	1563	361	66	11	20	156	0	464	.236	.326
vs. AL	4.81	57	59	0	153	152	984.0	1113	85	317	551	Behind in Count	.332	1023	340	58	5	39	157	178	0	.431	.513
vs. NL	3.32	1	0	0	4	3	19.0	19	2	7	6	Two Strikes	.203	1466	297	63	7	21	140	138	557	.274	.298
Pre-All Star	4.98	34	32	0	86	85	540.2	601	52	194	284	Pre-All Star	.284	2116	601	120	10	52	282	194	284	.349	.424
Post-All Star	4.56	24	27	0	71	70	462.1	531	35	130	273	Post-All Star	.291	1823	531	99	12	35	216	130	273	.341	.416

Pitcher vs. Batter (career)

Pitches Best Vs.	Avg	AB	H	2B	3B	HR	RBI	BB	SO	OBP	SLG	Pitches Worst Vs.	Avg	AB	H	2B	3B	HR	RBI	BB	SO	OBP	SLG
Billy Ripken	.000	9	0	0	0	0	0	1	3	.182	.000	Chris Hoiles	.471	17	8	3	0	1	1	0	2	.526	.824
Pat Meares	.071	14	1	0	0	0	0	0	7	.071	.071	Alex Rodriguez	.444	18	8	3	0	2	6	2	1	.500	.944
Mark Loretta	.091	11	1	0	0	0	0	1	0	.167	.091	Mark McGwire	.429	28	12	3	0	5	11	3	5	.484	1.071
Jacob Brumfield	.100	10	1	0	0	0	0	1	3	.182	.100	Jim Thome	.400	25	10	2	1	2	9	4	4	.559	.800
Rich Becker	.111	18	2	0	0	0	0	2	7	.111	.111	Matt Lawton	.385	13	5	0	1	2	2	0	2	.385	1.000

Darin Erstad — Angels
Age 24 – Bats Left

	Avg	G	AB	R	H	2B	3B	HR	RBI	BB	SO	HBP	GDP	SB	CS	OBP	SLG	IBB	SH	SF	#Pit	P/PA	GB	FB	G/F
1997 Season	.299	139	539	99	161	34	4	16	77	51	86	4	5	23	8	.360	.466	4	5	6	2344	3.87	180	159	1.13
Career (1996-1997)	.295	196	747	133	220	39	5	20	97	68	115	4	9	23	11	.353	.440	5	6	9	3220	3.86	263	212	1.24

1997 Season

	Avg	AB	H	2B	3B	HR	RBI	BB	SO	OBP	SLG		Avg	AB	H	2B	3B	HR	RBI	BB	SO	OBP	SLG
vs. Left	.302	159	48	7	0	8	31	13	21	.354	.497	First Pitch	.360	25	9	0	0	2	6	4	0	.433	.600

	Avg	AB	H	2B	3B	HR	RBI	BB	SO	OBP	SLG		Avg	AB	H	2B	3B	HR	RBI	BB	SO	OBP	SLG
vs. Right	.297	380	113	27	4	8	46	38	65	.362	.453	Ahead in Count	.349	129	45	8	2	6	24	35	0	.479	.581
Groundball	.284	88	25	7	0	2	11	12	15	.366	.432	Behind in Count	.276	268	74	17	0	6	26	0	76	.284	.407
Flyball	.325	83	27	6	1	3	13	9	9	.404	.530	Two Strikes	.251	263	66	15	0	6	31	12	86	.288	.376
Home	.308	276	85	21	2	8	40	23	42	.361	.486	Batting #1	.261	138	36	7	0	3	20	13	18	.318	.377
Away	.289	263	76	13	2	8	37	28	44	.359	.445	Batting #2	.300	303	91	21	4	8	36	28	47	.366	.475
Day	.278	162	45	14	0	1	15	16	35	.337	.383	Other	.347	98	34	6	0	5	21	10	21	.400	.561
Night	.308	377	116	20	4	15	62	35	51	.370	.501	March/April	.325	77	25	6	0	9	7	7	.381	.442
Grass	.299	489	146	31	4	13	71	43	79	.354	.458	May	.295	105	31	9	0	4	20	6	13	.333	.495
Turf	.300	50	15	3	0	3	6	8	7	.417	.540	June	.280	93	26	3	1	2	10	10	14	.358	.398
Pre-All Star	.304	299	91	19	1	10	43	25	38	.361	.475	July	.298	114	34	4	1	3	11	10	23	.352	.430
Post-All Star	.292	240	70	15	3	6	34	26	48	.359	.454	August	.343	108	37	11	2	3	10	13	18	.415	.565
Scoring Posn	.331	124	41	8	1	5	59	15	26	.399	.532	Sept/Oct	.190	42	8	1	0	3	5	11	.271	.429
Close & Late	.381	84	32	5	1	2	14	8	10	.436	.536	vs. AL	.299	485	145	31	3	13	69	45	78	.359	.456
None on/out	.225	151	34	11	2	3	3	8	19	.269	.384	vs. NL	.296	54	16	3	1	3	8	6	8	.367	.556

1997 By Position

Position	Avg	AB	H	2B	3B	HR	RBI	BB	SO	OBP	SLG	G	GS	Innings	PO	A	E	DP	Fld Pct	Rng Fctr	In Zone	Zone Outs	Zone Rtg	MLB Zone
As 1b	.293	501	147	33	4	16	72	47	80	.355	.471	126	120	1083.0	999	65	11	94	.990	---	195	161	.826	.874

Kelvim Escobar — Blue Jays
Age 22 – Pitches Right (groundball pitcher)

	ERA	W	L	Sv	G	GS	IP	BB	SO	Avg	H	2B	3B	HR	RBI	OBP	SLG	GF	IR	IRS	Hld	SvOp	SB	CS	GB	FB	G/F
1997 Season	2.90	3	2	14	27	0	31.0	19	36	.237	28	6	0	1	11	.343	.314	23	2	1	1	17	2	1	38	21	1.81

1997 Season

	ERA	W	L	Sv	G	GS	IP	H	HR	BB	SO		Avg	AB	H	2B	3B	HR	RBI	BB	SO	OBP	SLG
Home	1.23	1	0	8	13	0	14.2	8	0	7	13	vs. Left	.218	55	12	1	0	0	3	12	18	.358	.236
Away	4.41	2	2	6	14	0	16.1	20	1	12	23	vs. Right	.254	63	16	5	0	1	8	7	18	.329	.381
Starter	0.00	0	0	0	0	0	0.0	0	0	0	0	Scoring Posn	.294	34	10	2	0	0	9	7	11	.415	.353
Reliever	2.90	3	2	14	27	0	31.0	28	1	19	36	Close & Late	.274	73	20	3	0	0	6	11	24	.369	.315
0 Days rest (Relief)	0.00	0	0	5	6	0	4.2	3	0	2	8	None on/out	.115	26	3	1	0	0	6	9	.281	.154
1 or 2 Days rest	3.38	1	1	5	10	0	10.2	11	1	6	12	First Pitch	.333	12	4	1	0	0	1	2	0	.429	.417
3+ Days rest	3.45	2	1	4	11	0	15.2	14	0	11	16	Ahead in Count	.238	63	15	2	0	0	5	0	26	.238	.270
Pre-All Star	1.08	2	0	0	2	0	8.1	3	0	4	8	Behind in Count	.267	15	4	2	0	0	2	8	0	.522	.400
Post-All Star	3.57	1	2	14	25	0	22.2	25	1	15	28	Two Strikes	.205	78	16	3	0	1	8	9	36	.287	.282

Vaughn Eshelman — Red Sox
Age 29 – Pitches Left (groundball pitcher)

	ERA	W	L	Sv	G	GS	IP	BB	SO	Avg	H	2B	3B	HR	RBI	OBP	SLG	GF	IR	IRS	Hld	SvOp	SB	CS	GB	FB	G/F
1997 Season	6.33	3	3	0	21	6	42.2	17	18	.330	58	18	0	3	19	.391	.483	6	15	6	0	1	10	1	82	36	2.28
Career (1995-1997)	6.07	15	9	0	83	30	212.0	111	118	.300	256	56	3	19	131	.380	.440	11	42	14	9	1	13	6	385	179	2.15

1997 Season

	ERA	W	L	Sv	G	GS	IP	H	HR	BB	SO		Avg	AB	H	2B	3B	HR	RBI	BB	SO	OBP	SLG
Home	4.87	2	2	0	9	3	20.1	25	1	11	9	vs. Left	.225	40	9	3	0	1	4	3	7	.295	.375
Away	7.66	1	1	0	12	3	22.1	33	2	6	9	vs. Right	.360	136	49	15	0	2	25	14	11	.418	.515

Career (1995-1997)

	ERA	W	L	Sv	G	GS	IP	H	HR	BB	SO		Avg	AB	H	2B	3B	HR	RBI	BB	SO	OBP	SLG
Home	5.55	8	3	0	40	14	97.1	114	9	55	55	vs. Left	.266	173	46	10	0	4	24	17	36	.337	.393
Away	6.51	7	6	0	43	16	114.2	142	10	56	63	vs. Right	.309	679	210	46	3	15	107	94	82	.391	.452
Day	7.01	3	2	0	26	10	61.2	79	5	36	37	Inning 1-6	.304	680	207	42	2	19	111	85	103	.382	.456
Night	5.69	12	7	0	57	20	150.1	177	14	75	81	Inning 7+	.285	172	49	14	1	0	20	26	15	.376	.378
Grass	5.61	14	9	0	74	27	191.0	223	16	92	105	None on	.282	440	124	25	1	7	7	55	61	.363	.391
Turf	10.29	1	0	0	9	3	21.0	33	3	19	13	Runners on	.320	412	132	31	2	12	124	56	57	.398	.493
March/April	9.95	0	0	0	9	0	6.1	12	0	4	1	Scoring Posn	.315	232	73	16	0	7	108	35	36	.396	.474
May	6.07	3	2	0	9	7	40.0	41	5	24	22	Close & Late	.333	54	18	5	0	0	9	12	5	.456	.426
June	7.34	4	5	0	17	11	65.0	87	7	33	37	None on/out	.284	201	57	11	0	1	1	21	28	.351	.353
July	6.75	3	1	0	14	3	26.2	40	1	14	18	vs. 1st Batr (relief)	.378	45	17	5	0	1	9	4	3	.415	.556
August	2.78	4	0	0	14	5	45.1	46	4	19	24	1st Inning Pitched	.317	278	88	19	0	5	44	42	34	.404	.439
Sept/Oct	6.91	1	1	0	20	4	28.2	30	2	17	16	First 15 Pitches	.335	212	71	16	0	2	21	27	22	.408	.439
Starter	5.68	11	8	0	30	30	149.0	170	12	70	87	Pitch 16-30	.301	166	50	9	0	3	26	26	20	.395	.410
Reliever	7.00	4	1	0	53	0	63.0	86	7	41	31	Pitch 31-45	.238	143	34	5	1	4	20	15	24	.313	.371
0 Days rest (Relief)	6.35	0	0	0	13	0	11.1	12	1	5	4	Pitch 46+	.305	331	101	26	2	10	62	43	52	.384	.486
1 or 2 Days rest	4.71	1	0	0	16	0	21.0	29	1	11	12	First Pitch	.372	137	51	14	0	2	26	6	0	.385	.518
3+ Days rest	8.80	3	1	0	24	0	30.2	45	5	25	15	Ahead in Count	.212	359	76	18	0	5	41	0	98	.216	.304
vs. AL	6.30	13	9	0	81	28	200.0	247	19	109	112	Behind in Count	.395	220	87	17	3	8	37	72	0	.541	.609
vs. NL	2.25	2	0	0	2	2	12.0	9	0	2	6	Two Strikes	.214	364	78	17	0	4	49	33	118	.284	.294
Pre-All Star	6.96	8	7	0	39	20	120.1	154	12	63	64	Pre-All Star	.318	484	154	34	3	12	86	63	64	.397	.475
Post-All Star	4.91	7	2	0	44	10	91.2	101	7	48	54	Post-All Star	.277	368	102	22	0	7	45	48	54	.359	.394

Pitcher vs. Batter (career)

Pitches Best Vs.	Avg	AB	H	2B	3B	HR	RBI	BB	SO	OBP	SLG	Pitches Worst Vs.	Avg	AB	H	2B	3B	HR	RBI	BB	SO	OBP	SLG
Randy Velarde	.100	10	1	0	0	0	0	3	0	.308	.100	Jeff Cirillo	.417	12	5	0	0	2	3	1	0	.462	.917
Jim Leyritz	.182	11	2	0	0	1	3	1	2	.250	.455	Ken Griffey Jr	.400	10	4	1	0	2	8	0	2	.455	1.100
Bernie Williams	.200	10	2	1	0	0	0	3	0	.385	.200	Paul Molitor	.375	8	3	2	0	0	4	2	0	.455	.625

Alvaro Espinoza — Mariners
Age 36 – Bats Right

	Avg	G	AB	R	H	2B	3B	HR	RBI	BB	SO	HBP	GDP	SB	CS	OBP	SLG	IBB	SH	SF	#Pit	#P/PA	GB	FB	G/F
1997 Season	.181	33	72	3	13	1	0	0	7	2	12	1	2	1	1	.213	.194	0	3	0	217	2.78	35	15	2.33
Last Five Years	.254	425	955	110	243	44	4	15	97	28	134	7	28	5	11	.278	.356	0	25	9	3274	3.20	368	266	1.38

1997 Season

	Avg	AB	H	2B	3B	HR	RBI	BB	SO	OBP	SLG		Avg	AB	H	2B	3B	HR	RBI	BB	SO	OBP	SLG
vs. Left	.250	28	7	1	0	0	4	0	5	.250	.286	Scoring Posn	.292	24	7	0	0	0	7	1	5	.346	.292
vs. Right	.136	44	6	0	0	0	3	2	7	.191	.136	Close & Late	.167	6	1	0	0	0	1	0	1	.167	.167

Last Five Years

	Avg	AB	H	2B	3B	HR	RBI	BB	SO	OBP	SLG		Avg	AB	H	2B	3B	HR	RBI	BB	SO	OBP	SLG
vs. Left	.284	363	103	19	2	8	43	9	55	.299	.413	First Pitch	.303	178	54	12	0	1	21	0	0	.308	.388
vs. Right	.236	592	140	25	2	7	54	19	79	.266	.321	Ahead in Count	.277	177	49	7	3	4	19	20	0	.353	.418
Groundball	.249	185	46	10	2	0	14	4	23	.275	.324	Behind in Count	.213	460	98	16	1	3	36	0	123	.217	.272
Flyball	.249	205	51	10	0	4	16	3	33	.258	.356	Two Strikes	.206	379	78	13	1	6	33	8	134	.225	.293
Home	.246	431	106	17	2	7	46	14	59	.272	.343	Batting #2	.278	209	58	14	1	4	25	10	32	.309	.411
Away	.261	524	137	27	2	8	51	14	75	.283	.366	Batting #9	.252	282	71	11	3	5	30	5	36	.271	.365
Day	.246	350	86	18	2	8	33	8	46	.264	.377	Other	.246	464	114	19	0	6	42	13	66	.268	.325
Night	.260	605	157	26	2	7	64	20	88	.286	.344	March/April	.327	55	18	3	0	2	9	1	9	.333	.491
Grass	.259	810	210	36	4	11	80	23	109	.281	.354	May	.257	152	39	7	0	1	15	4	18	.283	.322
Turf	.228	145	33	8	0	4	17	5	25	.263	.366	June	.237	215	51	12	0	3	26	9	34	.276	.335
Pre-All Star	.271	499	135	25	1	6	55	16	72	.298	.361	July	.232	228	53	9	2	2	20	8	36	.261	.316
Post-All Star	.237	456	108	19	3	9	42	12	62	.256	.351	August	.269	197	53	11	1	5	21	5	21	.286	.411
Scoring Posn	.255	247	63	9	1	2	77	8	33	.283	.324	Sept/Oct	.269	108	29	2	1	2	6	1	16	.273	.361
Close & Late	.250	156	39	4	1	3	19	4	26	.268	.346	vs. AL	.246	804	198	37	2	11	79	22	112	.270	.338
None on/out	.273	227	62	12	1	5	5	3	34	.286	.401	vs. NL	.298	151	45	7	2	4	18	6	22	.323	.450

Batter vs. Pitcher (career)

Hits Best Against	Avg	AB	H	2B	3B	HR	RBI	BB	SO	OBP	SLG	Hits Worst Against	Avg	AB	H	2B	3B	HR	RBI	BB	SO	OBP	SLG
Bret Saberhagen	.529	17	9	2	1	0	1	0	0	.529	.765	Tom Gordon	.063	16	1	0	0	0	2	1	5	.118	.063
Kenny Rogers	.471	17	8	0	0	0	1	0	2	.471	.471	Mike Mussina	.091	11	1	1	0	0	1	0	1	.091	.182
Mark Gubicza	.368	19	7	0	1	0	3	0	3	.368	.474	Mark Langston	.154	26	4	0	0	0	0	1	2	.185	.154
Jack McDowell	.333	15	5	0	0	1	2	3	1	.444	.533	Tom Candiotti	.158	19	3	0	0	0	1	0	5	.158	.158
Randy Johnson	.304	23	7	2	0		3	3	8	.385	.522	Todd Stottlemyre	.167	36	6	0	0	0	3	0	7	.162	.167

Bobby Estalella — Phillies
Age 23 – Bats Right

	Avg	G	AB	R	H	2B	3B	HR	RBI	BB	SO	HBP	GDP	SB	CS	OBP	SLG	IBB	SH	SF	#Pit	#P/PA	GB	FB	G/F
1997 Season	.345	13	29	9	10	1	0	4	9	7	7	0	2	0	0	.472	.793	0	0	0	154	4.28	9	9	1.00
Career (1996-1997)	.348	20	46	14	16	1	0	6	13	8	13	0	2	1	0	.444	.761	0	0	0	239	4.43	13	13	1.00

1997 Season

	Avg	AB	H	2B	3B	HR	RBI	BB	SO	OBP	SLG		Avg	AB	H	2B	3B	HR	RBI	BB	SO	OBP	SLG
vs. Left	.125	8	1	0	0	0	0	2	3	.300	.125	Scoring Posn	.300	10	3	0	0	1	4	0	2	.300	.600
vs. Right	.429	21	9	1	0	4	9	5	4	.538	1.048	Close & Late	.250	4	1	0	0	1	1	0	1	.250	1.000

Shawn Estes — Giants
Age 25 – Pitches Left (groundball pitcher)

	ERA	W	L	Sv	G	GS	IP	BB	SO	Avg	H	2B	3B	HR	RBI	OBP	SLG	CG	ShO	Sup	QS	#P/S	SB	CS	GB	FB	G/F
1997 Season	3.18	19	5	0	32	32	201.0	100	181	.223	162	22	3	12	66	.323	.311	3	2	5.96	20	105	8	12	302	149	2.03
Career (1995-1997)	3.50	22	13	0	46	46	288.1	144	255	.228	241	33	6	17	98	.327	.319	3	2	5.31	27	104	13	15	434	223	1.95

1997 Season

	ERA	W	L	Sv	G	GS	IP	H	BB	SO		Avg	AB	H	2B	3B	HR	RBI	BB	SO	OBP	SLG
Home	2.33	11	1	0	15	15	104.1	75	4	45	99	vs. Left	.241	162	39	8	0	1	20	26	28	.363	.309
Away	4.10	8	4	0	17	17	96.2	87	8	55	82	vs. Right	.218	564	123	14	3	11	46	74	153	.311	.312
Day	4.34	8	3	0	15	15	83.0	85	8	44	77	Inning 1-6	.224	633	142	19	3	11	62	84	154	.321	.316
Night	2.36	11	2	0	17	17	118.0	77	4	56	104	Inning 7+	.215	93	20	3	0	1	4	16	27	.336	.280
Grass	3.24	16	4	0	26	26	161.1	135	11	86	147	None on	.211	432	91	9	3	7	7	55	114	.305	.294
Turf	2.95	3	1	0	6	6	39.2	27	1	14	34	Runners on	.241	294	71	13	0	5	59	45	67	.348	.337
March/April	2.28	4	0	0	4	4	27.2	18	2	10	21	Scoring Posn	.228	167	38	4	0	3	50	29	43	.348	.305
May	3.18	3	2	0	6	6	34.0	29	1	22	27	Close & Late	.143	49	7	2	0	0	2	7	16	.263	.184
June	2.63	4	0	0	6	6	41.0	35	3	20	35	None on/out	.228	197	45	6	1	4	4	19	41	.300	.330
July	3.98	3	2	0	5	5	31.2	27	2	13	30	vs. 1st Batr (relief)	.000	0	0	0	0	0	0	0	0	.000	.000
August	3.52	4	0	0	6	6	38.1	32	2	16	37	1st Inning Pitched	.244	119	29	2	2	6	19	17	29	.343	.445
Sept/Oct	3.49	1	1	0	5	5	28.1	21	2	19	31	First 75 Pitches	.205	498	102	11	3	9	42	64	124	.301	.293
Starter	3.18	19	5	0	32	32	201.0	162	12	100	181	Pitch 76-90	.280	100	28	5	0	1	11	12	20	.363	.360
Reliever	0.00	0	0	0	0	0	0.0	0	0	0	0	Pitch 91-105	.282	85	24	4	0	2	9	10	20	.358	.400
0-3 Days Rest (Start)	0.00	0	0	0	0	0	0.0	0	0	0	0	Pitch 106+	.186	43	8	2	0	0	4	14	17	.407	.233
4 Days Rest	3.91	9	1	0	19	19	112.2	100	8	60	99	First Pitch	.388	80	31	1	0	1	7	2	0	.410	.438
5+ Days Rest	2.18	9	1	0	12	12	82.2	58	4	36	78	Ahead in Count	.141	320	45	9	0	2	19	0	143	.146	.188
vs. AL	4.97	1	0	0	2	2	12.2	11	3	9	11	Behind in Count	.291	189	55	6	2	5	24	55	0	.455	.423
vs. NL	3.06	18	5	0	30	30	188.1	151	9	91	170	Two Strikes	.137	357	49	9	1	4	21	43	181	.231	.202
Pre-All Star	2.51	12	2	0	17	17	111.1	83	6	54	94	Pre-All Star	.211	393	83	11	2	6	27	54	94	.314	.295
Post-All Star	4.01	7	3	0	15	15	89.2	79	6	46	87	Post-All Star	.237	333	79	11	1	6	39	46	87	.333	.330

Tony Eusebio — Astros
Age 31 – Bats Right (groundball hitter)

	Avg	G	AB	R	H	2B	3B	HR	RBI	BB	SO	HBP	GDP	SB	CS	OBP	SLG	IBB	SH	SF	#Pit	#P/PA	GB	FB	G/F
1997 Season	.274	60	164	12	45	2	0	1	18	19	27	4	4	0	1	.364	.305	1	0	0	686	3.67	85	29	2.93
Last Five Years	.288	286	843	91	243	39	4	13	125	76	139	7	25	0	5	.348	.390	4	3	12	3508	3.73	417	157	2.66

1997 Season

	Avg	AB	H	2B	3B	HR	RBI	BB	SO	OBP	SLG		Avg	AB	H	2B	3B	HR	RBI	BB	SO	OBP	SLG
vs. Left	.333	48	16	0	0	1	8	4	6	.385	.396	Scoring Posn	.300	50	15	0	0	0	16	9	3	.417	.300
vs. Right	.250	116	29	2	0	0	10	15	21	.356	.267	Close & Late	.263	38	10	1	0	0	4	8	4	.404	.289
Home	.276	87	24	2	0	0	10	10	14	.364	.299	None on/out	.211	38	8	1	0	0	0	4	4	.286	.237
Away	.273	77	21	0	0	1	8	9	13	.364	.312	Batting #6	.200	40	8	0	0	0	2	6	5	.304	.200
First Pitch	.478	23	11	1	0	0	3	0	0	.478	.522	Batting #7	.302	106	32	2	0	1	11	10	18	.373	.349
Ahead in Count	.250	32	8	0	0		4	16	0	.500	.250	Other	.278	18	5	0	0	0	5	3	4	.435	.278
Behind in Count	.232	82	19	0	0	0	6	0	24	.250	.232	Pre-All Star	.277	101	28	1	0	1	10	14	16	.376	.317
Two Strikes	.198	81	16	0	0		4	3	27	.235	.198	Post-All Star	.270	63	17	1	0	0	8	5	11	.343	.286

Last Five Years

	Avg	AB	H	2B	3B	HR	RBI	BB	SO	OBP	SLG		Avg	AB	H	2B	3B	HR	RBI	BB	SO	OBP	SLG
vs. Left	.315	241	76	16	2	6	45	17	38	.359	.473	First Pitch	.367	90	33	5	0	1	16	3	0	.375	.456
vs. Right	.277	602	167	23	2	7	80	59	101	.343	.357	Ahead in Count	.352	196	69	14	2	7	51	49	0	.474	.551
Groundball	.265	200	53	7	1	1	19	18	44	.329	.325	Behind in Count	.231	403	93	12	2	1	31	0	126	.237	.278
Flyball	.340	144	49	10	0	6	31	15	25	.394	.535	Two Strikes	.217	397	86	15	2	2	30	24	139	.264	.280
Home	.272	427	116	20	0	7	61	31	78	.323	.368	Batting #6	.265	230	61	10	3	2	27	23	33	.331	.361
Away	.305	416	127	19	4	6	64	45	61	.372	.413	Batting #7	.311	383	119	19	1	7	60	30	60	.360	.420
Day	.259	255	66	12	3	5	41	23	38	.323	.388	Other	.274	230	63	10	0	4	38	23	46	.345	.370
Night	.301	588	177	27	1	8	84	53	101	.358	.391	March/April	.204	93	19	4	1	2	13	6	14	.253	.333
Grass	.294	245	72	8	2	5	29	28	40	.368	.404	May	.285	130	37	5	0	1	18	8	23	.322	.346
Turf	.286	598	171	31	2	8	96	48	99	.339	.385	June	.327	150	49	7	0	5	24	18	26	.400	.473
Pre-All Star	.284	426	121	20	2	8	64	34	74	.339	.397	July	.331	163	54	10	2	2	27	13	22	.383	.454
Post-All Star	.293	417	122	19	2	5	61	42	65	.356	.384	August	.274	175	48	11	1	2	26	18	34	.337	.383
Scoring Posn	.295	254	75	13	2	6	109	32	37	.368	.433	Sept/Oct	.273	132	36	2	0	1	17	13	20	.347	.311
Close & Late	.299	177	53	9	0	5	32	18	38	.361	.435	vs. AL	.556	9	5	1	0	0	1	2	1	.636	.667
None on/out	.288	198	57	10	1	1		15	30	.338	.364	vs. NL	.285	834	238	38	4	13	124	74	138	.344	.387

Batter vs. Pitcher (career)

Hits Best Against	Avg	AB	H	2B	3B	HR	RBI	BB	SO	OBP	SLG	Hits Worst Against	Avg	AB	H	2B	3B	HR	RBI	BB	SO	OBP	SLG
Denny Neagle	.615	13	8	1	0	0	2	0	2	.615	.692	Joey Hamilton	.200	10	2	0	1	0	1	1	1	.273	.400
Allen Watson	.538	13	7	2	1	0	5	1	1	.571	.846												
F. Valenzuela	.400	10	4	1	0	2	5	2	1	.500	1.100												
John Smiley	.389	18	7	2	0	1	2	0	1	.389	.667												
Pedro Martinez	.313	16	5	1	0	1	3	1	2	.353	.563												

Tom Evans — Blue Jays
Age 23 – Bats Right

	Avg	G	AB	R	H	2B	3B	HR	RBI	BB	SO	HBP	GDP	SB	CS	OBP	SLG	IBB	SH	SF	#Pit	#P/PA	GB	FB	G/F
1997 Season	.289	12	38	7	11	2	0	1	2	2	10	1	0	0	1	.341	.421	0	0	0	137	3.34	8	10	0.80

1997 Season

	Avg	AB	H	2B	3B	HR	RBI	BB	SO	OBP	SLG		Avg	AB	H	2B	3B	HR	RBI	BB	SO	OBP	SLG
vs. Left	.222	9	2	1	0	0	0	2	2	.364	.333	Scoring Posn	.125	8	1	0	0	0	1	2	1	.364	.125
vs. Right	.310	29	9	1	0	1	2	0	8	.333	.448	Close & Late	.222	9	2	1	0	0	0	0	2	.222	.333

Carl Everett — Mets
Age 27 – Bats Both

	Avg	G	AB	R	H	2B	3B	HR	RBI	BB	SO	HBP	GDP	SB	CS	OBP	SLG	IBB	SH	SF	#Pit	#P/PA	GB	FB	G/F
1997 Season	.248	142	443	58	110	28	3	14	57	32	102	7	3	17	9	.308	.420	3	3	2	1798	3.69	139	114	1.22
Career (1993-1997)	.245	349	994	142	244	50	5	29	133	96	246	13	18	30	14	.319	.393	7	5	3	4227	3.80	348	232	1.50

1997 Season

	Avg	AB	H	2B	3B	HR	RBI	BB	SO	OBP	SLG		Avg	AB	H	2B	3B	HR	RBI	BB	SO	OBP	SLG
vs. Left	.208	101	21	6	0	2	9	6	26	.270	.327	First Pitch	.328	67	22	5	0	1	7	2	0	.357	.448
vs. Right	.260	342	89	22	3	12	48	26	76	.319	.447	Ahead in Count	.415	82	34	9	2	6	21	18	0	.510	.793
Groundball	.188	96	18	7	0	0	9	7	27	.250	.260	Behind in Count	.160	219	35	10	1	4	16	0	85	.179	.269
Flyball	.314	70	22	5	0	4	14	3	15	.342	.557	Two Strikes	.160	225	36	9	1	7	26	12	102	.216	.302
Home	.292	219	64	18	3	11	38	21	41	.363	.553	Batting #1	.242	211	51	16	1	5	21	14	54	.294	.398
Away	.205	224	46	10	0	3	19	11	61	.251	.290	Batting #5	.307	75	23	5	0	2	12	5	10	.373	.453
Day	.269	197	53	8	1	9	34	13	44	.326	.457	Other	.229	157	36	7	2	7	24	13	38	.295	.433
Night	.232	246	57	20	2	5	23	19	58	.294	.390	March/April	.170	53	9	0	0	2	7	3	11	.228	.283
Grass	.259	375	97	26	3	13	51	30	85	.319	.448	May	.238	84	20	6	1	2	12	4	19	.270	.405
Turf	.191	68	13	2	0	1	6	2	17	.247	.265	June	.345	87	30	7	1	5	13	7	15	.424	.621
Pre-All Star	.279	247	69	15	3	9	35	16	47	.337	.474	July	.280	82	23	6	1	2	14	6	20	.326	.451
Post-All Star	.209	196	41	13	0	5	22	16	55	.271	.352	August	.197	76	15	7	0	1	4	3	18	.238	.329
Scoring Posn	.280	93	26	5	1	3	42	13	21	.373	.452	Sept/Oct	.213	61	13	2	0	2	7	9	19	.314	.344
Close & Late	.241	83	20	4	0	4	22	11	15	.333	.434	vs. AL	.327	49	16	5	0	2	4	5	10	.389	.551
None on/out	.217	138	30	7	0	4	4	9	28	.280	.355	vs. NL	.239	394	94	23	3	12	53	27	92	.298	.404

1997 By Position

Position	Avg	AB	H	2B	3B	HR	RBI	BB	SO	OBP	SLG	G	GS	Innings	PO	A	E	DP	Fld Pct	Rng Fctr	In Zone	Outs	Zone Rtg	MLB Zone
As Pinch Hitter	.200	25	5	0	0	1	3	3	8	.286	.320	28	0	---	---	---	---	---	---	---	---	---	---	---
As cf	.253	217	55	16	2	4	19	18	54	.324	.401	71	54	486.0	113	4	4	2	.967	2.17	133	109	.820	.815

1997 By Position

Position	Avg	AB	H	2B	3B	HR	RBI	BB	SO	OBP	SLG	G	GS	Innings	PO	A	E	DP	Fld Pct	Rng Fctr	In Zone	Zone Outs	Zone Rtg	MLB Zone
As rf	.255	184	47	11	1	9	35	6	37	.285	.473	65	42	399.2	103	4	3	1	.973	2.41	125	101	.808	.813

Career (1993-1997)

	Avg	AB	H	2B	3B	HR	RBI	BB	SO	OBP	SLG		Avg	AB	H	2B	3B	HR	RBI	BB	SO	OBP	SLG
vs. Left	.207	261	54	15	1	7	31	19	65	.279	.352	First Pitch	.356	135	48	10	1	5	22	4	0	.376	.556
vs. Right	.259	733	190	35	4	22	102	77	181	.333	.408	Ahead in Count	.376	181	68	14	2	11	43	52	0	.513	.657
Groundball	.214	248	53	13	0	1	22	19	73	.275	.278	Behind in Count	.151	483	73	16	1	4	36	0	205	.167	.213
Flyball	.280	157	44	9	0	4	25	17	36	.351	.414	Two Strikes	.153	515	79	15	2	10	47	40	246	.224	.249
Home	.291	468	136	27	4	23	72	57	100	.375	.513	Batting #1	.231	251	58	18	1	7	27	17	72	.288	.394
Away	.205	526	108	23	1	6	61	39	146	.267	.287	Batting #3	.274	270	74	11	2	9	52	39	61	.370	.430
Day	.251	367	92	14	3	13	60	33	88	.319	.411	Other	.237	473	112	21	2	13	54	40	113	.305	.372
Night	.242	627	152	36	2	16	73	63	158	.319	.383	March/April	.221	86	19	1	0	4	13	7	19	.287	.372
Grass	.256	794	203	41	5	25	108	82	190	.330	.414	May	.192	198	38	9	1	5	20	14	57	.248	.323
Turf	.205	200	41	9	0	4	25	14	56	.274	.310	June	.301	113	34	9	2	5	14	10	24	.388	.549
Pre-All Star	.241	436	105	22	4	14	51	34	110	.307	.406	July	.294	163	48	9	1	4	25	9	42	.333	.436
Post-All Star	.249	558	139	28	1	15	82	62	136	.329	.384	August	.221	204	45	13	1	7	26	26	44	.312	.397
Scoring Posn	.260	258	67	13	2	7	105	39	63	.364	.407	Sept/Oct	.261	230	60	9	0	4	35	30	60	.352	.352
Close & Late	.237	207	49	10	1	5	34	23	51	.318	.367	vs. AL	.327	49	16	5	0	2	4	5	10	.389	.551
None on/out	.250	260	65	15	1	6	6	17	61	.306	.385	vs. NL	.241	945	228	45	5	27	129	91	236	.316	.385

Batter vs. Pitcher (career)

Hits Best Against	Avg	AB	H	2B	3B	HR	RBI	BB	SO	OBP	SLG	Hits Worst Against	Avg	AB	H	2B	3B	HR	RBI	BB	SO	OBP	SLG
Denny Neagle	.455	11	5	2	0	0	2	1	3	.500	.636	Ramon Martinez	.000	9	0	0	0	0	1	2	4	.182	.000
Darryl Kile	.429	14	6	2	0	0	2	0	2	.429	.571	Frank Castillo	.091	11	1	0	0	0	1	0	4	.091	.091
Dave Burba	.333	9	3	0	0	1	4	2	2	.455	.667	Tom Candiotti	.091	11	1	1	0	0	0	1	1	.167	.182
John Smoltz	.318	22	7	0	0	1	4	2	4	.375	.455	Mike Hampton	.125	16	2	1	0	0	0	0	4	.125	.188
												Joey Hamilton	.167	18	3	0	0	0	1	1	7	.211	.167

Bryan Eversgerd — Rangers
Age 29 – Pitches Left

	ERA	W	L	Sv	G	GS	IP	BB	SO	Avg	H	2B	3B	HR	RBI	OBP	SLG	GF	IR	IRS	Hld	SvOp	SB	CS	GB	FB	G/F
1997 Season	20.25	0	2	0	3	0	1.1	3	2	.556	5	2	1	0	2	.667	1.000	1	3	0	0	0	0	0	3	3	1.00
Career (1994-1997)	4.90	2	5	0	68	1	90.0	32	57	.296	102	21	2	10	59	.357	.455	14	55	20	3	1	1	3	134	91	1.47

1997 Season

	ERA	W	L	Sv	G	GS	IP	H	HR	BB	SO		Avg	AB	H	2B	3B	HR	RBI	BB	SO	OBP	SLG
Home	9.00	0	0	0	1	0	1.0	2	0	2	2	vs. Left	.500	6	3	2	0	0	1	1	1	.571	.833
Away	54.00	0	2	0	2	0	0.1	3	0	1	0	vs. Right	.667	3	2	0	1	0	1	2	1	.800	1.333

Career (1994-1997)

	ERA	W	L	Sv	G	GS	IP	H	HR	BB	SO		Avg	AB	H	2B	3B	HR	RBI	BB	SO	OBP	SLG
Home	3.66	1	1	0	32	0	51.2	45	5	18	36	vs. Left	.286	105	30	8	0	2	16	10	16	.356	.419
Away	6.57	1	4	0	36	1	38.1	57	5	14	21	vs. Right	.300	240	72	13	2	8	43	22	41	.357	.471
Day	5.90	0	2	0	20	1	29.0	42	2	13	17	Inning 1-6	.293	184	54	10	1	2	29	19	33	.359	.391
Night	4.43	2	3	0	48	1	61.0	60	8	19	40	Inning 7+	.298	161	48	11	1	8	30	13	24	.354	.528
Grass	5.32	1	2	0	22	1	22.0	30	3	10	15	None on	.241	174	42	7	1	6	6	15	33	.305	.397
Turf	4.76	1	3	0	46	0	68.0	72	7	22	42	Runners on	.351	171	60	14	1	4	53	17	24	.407	.515
March/April	0.00	0	0	0	4	0	2.2	2	0	1	1	Scoring Posn	.297	111	33	6	1	1	46	14	18	.374	.396
May	3.81	2	0	0	21	1	28.1	27	5	8	17	Close & Late	.531	32	17	4	1	2	14	3	3	.583	.906
June	4.43	0	0	0	11	0	20.1	21	1	4	20	None on/out	.299	77	23	3	1	3	3	8	13	.365	.481
July	6.53	0	2	0	13	0	20.2	25	3	11	9	vs. 1st Batr (relief)	.364	55	20	2	1	3	12	11	9	.470	.600
August	13.50	0	3	0	4	0	3.1	12	1	2	1	1st Inning Pitched	.353	207	73	14	2	8	51	27	33	.423	.556
Sept/Oct	4.30	0	0	0	15	0	14.2	15	0	6	9	First 15 Pitches	.361	180	65	13	2	7	42	22	27	.432	.572
Starter	0.00	1	0	0	1	1	5.0	4	0	0	4	Pitch 16-30	.255	98	25	5	0	3	12	7	17	.302	.398
Reliever	5.19	1	5	0	67	0	85.0	98	10	32	53	Pitch 31-45	.146	41	6	1	0	0	4	2	11	.200	.171
0 Days rest (Relief)	9.22	1	1	0	14	0	13.2	28	1	6	9	Pitch 46+	.231	26	6	2	0	0	1	1	2	.259	.308
1 or 2 Days rest	3.65	0	2	0	36	0	49.1	41	7	16	24	First Pitch	.333	57	19	4	1	3	12	3	0	.377	.596
3+ Days rest	6.14	0	2	0	17	0	22.0	29	2	10	20	Ahead in Count	.218	133	29	8	0	3	17	0	45	.226	.346
vs. AL	18.00	0	1	0	2	0	1.0	4	0	2	2	Behind in Count	.373	75	28	5	0	3	11	18	0	.495	.560
vs. NL	4.75	2	4	0	66	1	89.0	98	10	30	55	Two Strikes	.185	146	27	5	0	4	20	11	57	.245	.301
Pre-All Star	3.88	2	0	0	39	1	55.2	53	6	15	41	Pre-All Star	.262	202	53	10	0	6	27	15	41	.315	.401
Post-All Star	6.55	0	5	0	29	0	34.1	49	4	17	16	Post-All Star	.343	143	49	11	2	4	32	17	16	.414	.531

Scott Eyre — White Sox
Age 26 – Pitches Left (flyball pitcher)

	ERA	W	L	Sv	G	GS	IP	BB	SO	Avg	H	2B	3B	HR	RBI	OBP	SLG	CG	ShO	Sup	QS	#P/S	SB	CS	GB	FB	G/F
1997 Season	5.04	4	4	0	11	11	60.2	31	36	.267	62	12	1	11	32	.353	.470	0	0	4.01	4	95	7	5	61	95	0.64

1997 Season

	ERA	W	L	Sv	G	GS	IP	H	HR	BB	SO		Avg	AB	H	2B	3B	HR	RBI	BB	SO	OBP	SLG
Home	2.48	4	0	0	5	5	29.0	25	3	10	18	vs. Left	.286	42	12	2	1	4	12	6	4	.375	.667
Away	7.39	0	4	0	6	6	31.2	37	8	21	18	vs. Right	.263	190	50	10	0	7	20	25	32	.349	.426
Starter	5.04	4	4	0	11	11	60.2	62	11	31	36	Scoring Posn	.277	47	13	1	1	3	20	6	10	.357	.532
Reliever	0.00	0	0	0	0	0	0.0	0	0	0	0	Close & Late	.200	5	1	0	0	0	0	1	0	.333	.200
0-3 Days Rest (Start)	0.00	0	0	0	0	0	0.0	0	0	0	0	None on/out	.186	59	11	3	0	2	2	8	8	.284	.339
4 Days Rest	3.38	1	1	0	3	3	16.0	16	3	7	11	First Pitch	.250	28	7	3	0	0	0	0	0	.250	.357
5+ Days Rest	5.64	3	3	0	8	8	44.2	46	8	24	25	Ahead in Count	.223	94	21	2	0	3	9	0	28	.232	.340
Pre-All Star	0.00	0	0	0	0	0	0.0	0	0	0	0	Behind in Count	.359	64	23	6	0	5	16	17	0	.482	.688

	ERA	W	L	Sv	G	GS	IP	H	HR	BB	SO		Avg	AB	H	2B	3B	HR	RBI	BB	SO	OBP	SLG
Post-All Star	5.04	4	4	0	11	11	60.2	62	11	31	36	Two Strikes	.184	98	18	2	1	3	11	14	36	.286	.316

Jorge Fabregas — White Sox   Age 28 – Bats Left

	Avg	G	AB	R	H	2B	3B	HR	RBI	BB	SO	HBP	GDP	SB	CS	OBP	SLG	IBB	SH	SF	#Pit	#P/PA	GB	FB	G/F
1997 Season	.258	121	360	33	93	11	1	7	51	14	46	1	16	1	1	.285	.353	0	6	4	1250	3.25	146	99	1.47
Career (1994-1997)	.267	327	968	87	258	30	1	10	115	55	119	1	37	3	5	.304	.331	4	13	10	3510	3.35	397	253	1.57

1997 Season

	Avg	AB	H	2B	3B	HR	RBI	BB	SO	OBP	SLG		Avg	AB	H	2B	3B	HR	RBI	BB	SO	OBP	SLG
vs. Left	.265	49	13	0	0	1	8	2	9	.288	.327	First Pitch	.333	63	21	1	0	1	11	0	0	.328	.397
vs. Right	.257	311	80	11	1	6	43	12	37	.284	.357	Ahead in Count	.297	111	33	5	1	4	20	8	0	.339	.468
Groundball	.211	71	15	1	1	1	13	3	7	.237	.296	Behind in Count	.155	129	20	2	0	1	11	0	40	.160	.194
Flyball	.306	72	22	2	0	2	9	3	10	.329	.417	Two Strikes	.210	124	26	2	0	2	14	6	46	.252	.274
Home	.238	160	38	7	0	1	19	11	12	.289	.300	Batting #6	.306	85	26	4	0	2	10	2	17	.330	.424
Away	.275	200	55	4	1	6	32	3	34	.282	.395	Batting #7	.275	171	47	4	1	4	25	7	18	.297	.380
Day	.315	92	29	4	1	1	14	5	11	.347	.413	Other	.192	104	20	3	0	1	16	5	11	.229	.250
Night	.239	268	64	7	0	6	37	9	35	.263	.332	March/April	.040	25	1	0	0	0	3	1	1	.077	.040
Grass	.253	297	75	10	1	6	40	12	34	.280	.354	May	.179	39	7	1	0	1	3	2	2	.220	.282
Turf	.286	63	18	1	0	1	11	2	12	.308	.349	June	.325	83	27	2	0	2	18	2	12	.341	.422
Pre-All Star	.231	160	37	4	0	3	26	5	17	.255	.313	July	.289	76	22	3	0	2	7	3	12	.316	.408
Post-All Star	.280	200	56	7	1	4	25	9	29	.308	.385	August	.274	73	20	4	0	2	16	5	11	.313	.411
Scoring Posn	.265	102	27	4	0	3	45	3	13	.275	.392	Sept/Oct	.250	64	16	1	1	0	4	1	8	.265	.250
Close & Late	.245	53	13	0	0	3	9	1	7	.259	.415	vs. AL	.257	315	81	9	1	5	44	11	37	.281	.340
None on/out	.160	75	12	3	0	1	0	0	11	.160	.240	vs. NL	.267	45	12	2	0	2	7	3	9	.313	.444

1997 By Position

Position	Avg	AB	H	2B	3B	HR	RBI	BB	SO	OBP	SLG	G	GS	Innings	PO	A	E	DP	Fld Pct	Rng Fctr	In Zone	Zone Outs	Zone Rtg	MLB Zone
As Pinch Hitter	.083	12	1	0	0	0	4	0	4	.083	.083	12	0	---	---	---	---	---	---	---	---	---	---	---
As c	.262	347	91	11	1	7	47	14	42	.290	.360	113	94	830.2	600	51	8	9	.988	---	---	---	---	---

Career (1994-1997)

	Avg	AB	H	2B	3B	HR	RBI	BB	SO	OBP	SLG		Avg	AB	H	2B	3B	HR	RBI	BB	SO	OBP	SLG
vs. Left	.277	137	38	3	0	2	21	8	24	.311	.343	First Pitch	.396	159	63	7	0	1	26	2	0	.399	.459
vs. Right	.265	831	220	27	1	8	94	47	95	.302	.329	Ahead in Count	.299	281	84	10	1	5	39	27	0	.355	.395
Groundball	.273	220	60	6	1	1	30	7	23	.291	.323	Behind in Count	.193	368	71	7	0	3	33	0	108	.194	.236
Flyball	.326	184	60	6	0	4	23	16	20	.376	.424	Two Strikes	.190	343	65	3	0	3	31	26	119	.249	.224
Home	.249	473	118	15	0	3	46	35	48	.301	.300	Batting #7	.286	224	64	7	1	4	34	9	26	.308	.379
Away	.283	495	140	15	1	7	69	20	71	.307	.360	Batting #8	.262	581	152	17	0	4	63	41	62	.308	.312
Day	.300	223	67	9	1	3	28	7	35	.319	.390	Other	.258	163	42	6	0	2	18	5	31	.281	.331
Night	.256	745	191	21	0	7	87	48	84	.299	.313	March/April	.234	94	22	0	0	1	11	9	7	.298	.266
Grass	.267	832	222	25	1	9	95	48	98	.304	.332	May	.218	174	38	4	0	2	18	9	21	.257	.276
Turf	.265	136	36	5	0	1	20	7	21	.299	.324	June	.318	211	67	8	0	3	29	11	31	.350	.398
Pre-All Star	.260	507	132	13	0	6	61	32	61	.303	.321	July	.255	165	42	5	0	2	15	7	23	.285	.321
Post-All Star	.273	461	126	17	1	4	54	23	58	.304	.341	August	.289	187	54	9	0	2	32	14	19	.329	.369
Scoring Posn	.285	263	75	9	0	3	104	18	34	.320	.354	Sept/Oct	.255	137	35	4	1	0	10	5	18	.283	.299
Close & Late	.267	135	36	1	0	4	17	7	18	.301	.363	vs. AL	.267	923	246	28	1	8	108	52	110	.303	.325
None on/out	.257	214	55	10	0	1	1	10	25	.290	.318	vs. NL	.267	45	12	2	0	2	7	3	9	.313	.444

Batter vs. Pitcher (career)

Hits Best Against	Avg	AB	H	2B	3B	HR	RBI	BB	SO	OBP	SLG	Hits Worst Against	Avg	AB	H	2B	3B	HR	RBI	BB	SO	OBP	SLG
Tim Belcher	.435	23	10	0	0	1	2	3	1	.500	.565	Ben McDonald	.077	13	1	0	0	0	0	0	1	.077	.077
Charles Nagy	.400	15	6	1	0	1	4	0	2	.400	.667	Frank Rodriguez	.083	12	1	0	0	0	0	0	2	.154	.083
Scott Erickson	.389	18	7	1	0	0	2	0	0	.389	.444	Roger Clemens	.143	21	3	0	0	0	0	0	7	.143	.143
Ken Hill	.333	12	4	0	0	0	0	0	1	.333	.333	Chad Ogea	.154	13	2	0	0	0	3	1	2	.214	.154
Tom Gordon	.318	22	7	0	0	1	0	0	4	.304	.318	David Cone	.154	13	2	0	0	0	0	2	1	.267	.154

Steve Falteisek — Expos   Age 26 – Pitches Right

	ERA	W	L	Sv	G	GS	IP	BB	SO	Avg	H	2B	3B	HR	RBI	OBP	SLG	GF	IR	IRS	Hld	SvOp	SB	CS	GB	FB	G/F
1997 Season	3.38	0	0	0	5	0	8.0	3	2	.286	8	1	0	0	5	.353	.321	2	7	2	0		2	0	16	5	3.20

1997 Season

	ERA	W	L	Sv	G	GS	IP	H	HR	BB	SO		Avg	AB	H	2B	3B	HR	RBI	BB	SO	OBP	SLG
Home	6.75	0	0	0	2	0	4.0	6	0	3	2	vs. Left	.200	10	2	0	0	0	1	0	0	.182	.200
Away	0.00	0	0	0	3	0	4.0	2	0	0	0	vs. Right	.333	18	6	1	0	0	4	3	2	.435	.389

Sal Fasano — Royals   Age 26 – Bats Right

	Avg	G	AB	R	H	2B	3B	HR	RBI	BB	SO	HBP	GDP	SB	CS	OBP	SLG	IBB	SH	SF	#Pit	#P/PA	GB	FB	G/F
1997 Season	.211	13	38	4	8	2	0	1	1	1	12	0	1	0	0	.231	.342	0	0	0	149	3.82	10	12	0.83
Career (1996-1997)	.204	64	181	24	37	4	0	7	20	15	37	2	4	1	1	.273	.343	0	0	0	736	3.70	57	60	0.95

1997 Season

	Avg	AB	H	2B	3B	HR	RBI	BB	SO	OBP	SLG		Avg	AB	H	2B	3B	HR	RBI	BB	SO	OBP	SLG
vs. Left	.214	14	3	1	0	0	0	0	3	.214	.286	Scoring Posn	1.000	2	2	0	0	0	0	0	0	1.000	1.000
vs. Right	.208	24	5	1	0	1	1	9	.240	.375	Close & Late	.000	2	0	0	0	0	0	0	1	.000	.000

Jeff Fassero — Mariners
Age 35 – Pitches Left (groundball pitcher)

	ERA	W	L	Sv	G	GS	IP	BB	SO	Avg	H	2B	3B	HR	RBI	OBP	SLG	CG	ShO	Sup	QS	#P/S	SB	CS	GB	FB	G/F
1997 Season	3.61	16	9	0	35	35	234.1	84	189	.249	226	54	3	21	94	.312	.385	2	1	6.30	22	106	15	11	356	235	1.51
Last Five Years	3.38	64	45	1	176	135	943.1	307	834	.247	888	170	16	76	365	.306	.367	10	2	5.26	78	100	76	44	1443	770	1.87

1997 Season

	ERA	W	L	Sv	G	GS	IP	H	HR	BB	SO		Avg	AB	H	2B	3B	HR	RBI	BB	SO	OBP	SLG
Home	3.85	6	5	0	16	16	107.2	97	11	37	86	vs. Left	.263	175	46	8	1	2	13	14	32	.323	.354
Away	3.41	10	4	0	19	19	126.2	129	10	47	103	vs. Right	.246	731	180	46	2	19	81	70	157	.309	.393
Day	2.45	5	2	0	12	12	84.1	70	5	35	58	Inning 1-6	.250	759	190	45	1	17	77	64	157	.307	.379
Night	4.26	11	7	0	23	23	150.0	156	16	49	131	Inning 7+	.245	147	36	9	2	4	17	20	32	.337	.415
Grass	3.87	8	4	0	17	17	109.1	120	10	43	88	None on	.240	538	129	36	1	11	11	41	103	.296	.372
Turf	3.38	8	5	0	18	18	125.0	106	11	41	101	Runners on	.264	368	97	18	2	10	83	43	86	.334	.405
March/April	2.85	4	0	0	6	6	41.0	34	1	17	30	Scoring Posn	.236	220	52	9	2	4	69	29	53	.315	.350
May	5.50	0	2	0	6	6	37.2	46	3	16	29	Close & Late	.205	78	16	5	0	1	8	13	18	.315	.308
June	2.65	4	1	0	5	5	37.1	34	1	14	29	None on/out	.229	236	54	14	0	5	5	16	38	.281	.352
July	5.50	1	3	0	6	6	37.2	44	7	12	36	vs. 1st Batr (relief)	.000	0	0	0	0	0	0	0	0	.000	.000
August	3.40	4	2	0	6	6	39.2	37	6	12	35	1st Inning Pitched	.246	134	33	6	0	1	13	24	307	.313	
Sept/Oct	1.98	3	1	0	6	6	41.0	31	3	13	30	First 75 Pitches	.247	615	152	37	1	11	50	49	126	.301	.364
Starter	3.61	16	9	0	35	35	234.1	226	21	84	189	Pitch 76-90	.205	117	24	6	0	4	18	12	27	.278	.359
Reliever	0.00	0	0	0	0	0	0.0	0	0	0	0	Pitch 91-105	.286	105	30	8	0	3	12	13	22	.370	.448
0-3 Days Rest (Start)	9.00	0	1	0	1	1	3.0	5	2	1	4	Pitch 106+	.290	69	20	3	2	3	14	10	14	.380	.522
4 Days Rest	3.96	11	6	0	23	23	154.2	157	16	53	123	First Pitch	.308	130	40	11	1	2	13	5	0	.333	.454
5+ Days Rest	2.70	5	2	0	11	11	76.2	64	3	30	62	Ahead in Count	.170	436	74	16	0	6	28	0	161	.171	.248
vs. AL	3.49	15	7	0	32	32	214.1	205	17	74	172	Behind in Count	.389	185	72	17	2	10	32	32	0	.475	.665
vs. NL	4.95	1	2	0	3	3	20.0	21	4	10	17	Two Strikes	.159	429	68	12	0	8	34	47	189	.241	.242
Pre-All Star	3.99	8	5	0	19	19	124.0	126	9	51	99	Pre-All Star	.263	479	126	31	2	9	53	51	99	.332	.392
Post-All Star	3.18	8	4	0	16	16	110.1	100	12	33	90	Post-All Star	.234	427	100	23	1	12	41	33	90	.289	.377

Last Five Years

	ERA	W	L	Sv	G	GS	IP	H	HR	BB	SO		Avg	AB	H	2B	3B	HR	RBI	BB	SO	OBP	SLG
Home	3.52	31	24	1	87	67	472.2	418	39	170	407	vs. Left	.218	597	130	23	2	5	50	50	140	.278	.288
Away	3.23	33	21	0	89	68	470.2	470	37	137	427	vs. Right	.253	2998	758	147	14	71	315	257	694	.311	.382
Day	2.98	17	14	0	61	46	329.0	296	22	101	269	Inning 1-6	.248	2956	734	144	13	61	299	249	687	.306	.368
Night	3.59	47	31	1	115	89	614.1	592	54	206	565	Inning 7+	.241	639	154	26	3	15	66	58	147	.304	.362
Grass	3.46	22	17	0	62	52	351.1	364	31	101	328	None on	.240	2149	516	114	9	42	42	156	489	.294	.360
Turf	3.33	42	28	1	114	83	729.0	524	45	206	506	Runners on	.257	1446	372	56	7	34	323	151	345	.323	.376
March/April	3.27	9	4	0	28	18	124.0	114	11	42	95	Scoring Posn	.251	828	208	29	6	16	273	109	196	.330	.359
May	3.41	12	8	0	36	23	169.0	164	10	48	159	Close & Late	.227	335	76	14	0	7	33	34	85	.297	.331
June	3.14	13	7	1	37	22	177.2	143	15	63	148	None on/out	.250	940	235	43	3	18	18	61	192	.298	.366
July	2.98	10	9	0	28	26	172.0	166	12	52	167	vs. 1st Batr (relief)	.286	35	10	1	0	1	5	4	10	.341	.400
August	3.60	13	7	0	23	23	155.0	151	14	52	143	1st Inning Pitched	.243	630	153	23	0	8	69	67	139	.314	.317
Sept/Oct	3.95	7	10	0	24	23	145.2	150	14	50	122	First 75 Pitches	.245	2648	648	121	11	42	233	220	626	.302	.346
Starter	3.45	59	44	0	135	135	888.0	850	73	282	783	Pitch 76-90	.246	455	112	25	1	18	65	38	98	.304	.424
Reliever	2.28	5	1	1	41	0	55.1	38	3	25	51	Pitch 91-105	.233	335	78	15	1	10	38	29	72	.295	.373
0-3 Days Rest (Start)	7.00	0	1	0	2	2	9.0	10	2	5	9	Pitch 106+	.318	157	50	9	3	6	29	20	38	.395	.529
4 Days Rest	3.37	38	26	0	80	80	544.1	503	42	164	482	First Pitch	.348	589	205	35	4	17	86	11	0	.357	.508
5+ Days Rest	3.47	21	17	0	53	53	334.2	337	29	113	292	Ahead in Count	.170	1768	301	58	3	19	117	0	739	.171	.239
vs. AL	3.49	15	7	0	32	32	214.1	205	17	74	172	Behind in Count	.351	676	237	51	7	26	101	147	0	.463	.562
vs. NL	3.35	49	38	1	144	103	729.0	683	59	233	662	Two Strikes	.155	1707	264	42	4	19	100	149	834	.223	.217
Pre-All Star	3.33	36	23	1	111	71	519.0	471	41	167	461	Pre-All Star	.240	1965	471	90	9	41	205	167	461	.299	.357
Post-All Star	3.44	28	22	0	65	64	424.1	417	35	140	373	Post-All Star	.256	1630	417	80	7	35	160	140	273	.314	.378

Pitcher vs. Batter (career)

Pitches Best Vs.	Avg	AB	H	2B	3B	HR	RBI	BB	SO	OBP	SLG	Pitches Worst Vs.	Avg	AB	H	2B	3B	HR	RBI	B
Juan Gonzalez	.000	8	0	0	0	0	1	2	3	.182	.000	Jose Offerman	.632	19	12	2	0	0	1	
Chris Jones	.053	19	1	1	0	0	2	0	6	.053	.105	Chuck Carr	.500	18	9	6	0	0	2	
Al Martin	.063	16	1	0	0	0	1	0	7	.063	.063	Reggie Sanders	.500	12	6	0	0	1	3	
Deivi Cruz	.091	11	1	0	0	0	1	0	1	.091	.091	Bobby Bonilla	.400	15	6	0	0	3	6	
Royce Clayton	.111	18	2	0	0	0	0	0	5	.111	.111	Eric Davis	.333	9	3	2	0	1	1	

Alex Fernandez — Marlins
Age 28 –

	ERA	W	L	Sv	G	GS	IP	BB	SO	Avg	H	2B	3B	HR	RBI	OBP	SLG	CG	ShO	Sup	QS	#P/S	SE
1997 Season	3.59	17	12	0	32	32	220.2	69	183	.238	193	40	9	25	84	.299	.401	5	1	5.18	22	108	7
Last Five Years	3.53	74	46	0	155	155	1100.0	323	833	.247	1025	174	26	130	434	.303	.396	23	8	5.53	96	112	37

1997 Season

	ERA	W	L	Sv	G	GS	IP	H	HR	BB	SO		Avg	AB	H	2B	3B	HR	RBI	BB	SO	OBP	SLG
Home	4.39	7	6	0	14	14	92.1	85	15	31	77	vs. Left	.289	384	111	22	7	12	42				
Away	3.02	10	6	0	18	18	128.1	108	10	38	106	vs. Right	.192	428	82	18	2	13	42				
Day	4.68	5	5	0	10	10	67.1	63	7	19	58	Inning 1-6	.241	692	167	38	8	19	71				
Night	3.11	12	7	0	22	22	153.1	130	18	50	125	Inning 7+	.217	120	26	2	1	6	13				
Grass	4.06	11	12	0	25	25	168.2	159	21	52	136	None on	.229	519	119	23	7	20	20	35	127	.281	.416
Turf	2.08	6	0	0	7	7	52.0	34	4	17	47	Runners on	.253	293	74	17	2	5	64	34	56	.329	.375
March/April	2.73	3	2	0	5	5	33.0	21	1	5	21	Scoring Posn	.218	174	38	6	1	2	53	26	36	.312	.299
May	3.21	2	3	0	6	6	42.0	38	5	14	30	Close & Late	.235	51	12	0	0	4	7	0	13	.235	.471
June	4.54	4	1	0	5	5	33.2	30	4	11	32	None on/out	.252	226	57	14	0	13	13	12	47	.290	.487
July	3.50	3	2	0	5	5	36.0	35	5	15	33	vs. 1st Batr (relief)	.000	0	0	0	0	0	0	0	0	.000	.000
August	2.80	5	1	0	6	6	45.0	39	4	11	44	1st Inning Pitched	.244	123	30	9	1	3	17	15	26	.329	.407

1997 Season

	ERA	W	L	Sv	G	GS	IP	H	HR	BB	SO		Avg	AB	H	2B	3B	HR	RBI	BB	SO	OBP	SLG
Sept/Oct	5.23	0	3	0	5	5	31.0	30	6	13	23	First 75 Pitches	.236	535	126	32	6	11	50	48	125	.300	.379
Starter	3.59	17	12	0	32	32	220.2	193	25	69	183	Pitch 76-90	.294	119	35	4	1	7	15	8	16	.336	.521
Reliever	0.00	0	0	0	0	0	0.0	0	0	0	0	Pitch 91-105	.239	88	21	3	1	4	14	7	25	.302	.432
0-3 Days Rest (Start)	0.00	0	0	0	0	0	0.0	0	0	0	0	Pitch 106+	.157	70	11	1	1	3	5	6	17	.224	.329
4 Days Rest	4.16	10	9	0	21	21	140.2	132	17	46	118	First Pitch	.321	112	36	4	1	5	8	2	0	.339	.509
5+ Days Rest	2.59	7	3	0	11	11	80.0	61	8	23	65	Ahead in Count	.174	403	70	15	4	7	32	0	151	.177	.283
vs. AL	2.93	2	0	0	2	2	15.1	9	2	4	14	Behind in Count	.285	137	39	9	1	8	20	40	0	.444	.540
vs. NL	3.64	15	12	0	30	30	205.1	184	23	65	169	Two Strikes	.200	406	81	18	3	10	45	27	183	.250	.333
Pre-All Star	3.63	9	7	0	17	17	116.2	100	12	31	88	Pre-All Star	.235	426	100	22	7	12	45	31	88	.289	.404
Post-All Star	3.55	8	5	0	15	15	104.0	93	13	38	95	Post-All Star	.241	386	93	18	2	13	39	38	95	.310	.399

Last Five Years

	ERA	W	L	Sv	G	GS	IP	H	HR	BB	SO		Avg	AB	H	2B	3B	HR	RBI	BB	SO	OBP	SLG
Home	3.32	39	21	0	75	75	544.1	474	67	153	420	vs. Left	.265	2098	556	96	19	70	219	176	424	.321	.429
Away	3.74	35	25	0	80	80	555.2	551	63	170	413	vs. Right	.229	2047	469	78	7	60	215	147	409	.284	.362
Day	3.85	18	17	0	47	47	327.2	307	37	95	242	Inning 1-6	.250	3415	853	146	22	107	372	274	684	.306	.399
Night	3.40	56	29	0	108	108	772.1	718	93	228	591	Inning 7+	.236	730	172	28	4	23	62	49	149	.285	.379
Grass	3.64	62	41	0	130	130	920.2	872	115	262	691	None on	.247	2567	633	112	17	86		176	521	.297	.404
Turf	3.01	12	5	0	25	25	179.1	153	15	61	142	Runners on	.248	1578	392	62	9	44	348	147	312	.311	.383
March/April	2.93	12	9	0	22	22	150.2	127	13	46	108	Scoring Posn	.234	808	189	30	5	15	275	99	175	.309	.339
May	3.92	10	12	0	29	29	190.1	187	25	65	146	Close & Late	.241	369	89	15	0	11	35	29	78	.294	.371
June	4.46	12	4	0	26	26	187.2	181	26	68	153	None on/out	.246	1112	274	53	3	39	39	61	208	.287	.405
July	3.80	16	9	0	29	29	208.1	197	25	67	159	vs. 1st Batr (relief)	.000	0	0	0	0	0	0	0	0	.000	.000
August	2.96	15	5	0	26	26	188.2	176	24	37	137	1st Inning Pitched	.233	587	137	26	5	15	57	47	120	.292	.371
Sept/Oct	2.94	9	7	0	23	23	174.1	157	17	40	130	First 75 Pitches	.243	2687	653	110	15	77	253	201	533	.297	.397
Starter	3.53	74	46	0	155	155	1100.0	1025	130	323	833	Pitch 76-90	.252	544	137	21	4	20	67	48	107	.312	.415
Reliever	0.00	0	0	0	0	0	0.0	0	0	0	0	Pitch 91-105	.284	464	132	24	4	19	66	37	101	.337	.476
0-3 Days Rest (Start)	3.21	0	0	0	2	2	14.0	16	4	6	8	Pitch 106+	.229	450	103	19	3	14	48	37	92	.288	.378
4 Days Rest	3.50	52	29	0	106	106	758.1	702	88	220	564	First Pitch	.266	556	148	18	3	19	63	16	0	.288	.412
5+ Days Rest	3.63	22	17	0	47	47	327.2	307	38	97	261	Ahead in Count	.198	1964	389	61	9	35	131	0	689	.202	.292
vs. AL	3.51	59	34	0	125	125	894.2	841	107	258	664	Behind in Count	.340	811	276	54	6	50	135	141	0	.434	.607
vs. NL	3.64	15	12	0	30	30	205.1	184	23	65	169	Two Strikes	.189	1986	375	64	11	37	149	166	833	.254	.288
Pre-All Star	3.87	38	29	0	86	86	593.2	561	71	201	445	Pre-All Star	.251	2237	561	92	15	71	257	201	445	.313	.401
Post-All Star	3.15	36	17	0	69	69	506.1	464	59	122	388	Post-All Star	.243	1908	464	82	11	59	177	122	388	.290	.390

Pitcher vs. Batter (career)

Pitches Best Vs.	Avg	AB	H	2B	3B	HR	RBI	BB	SO	OBP	SLG	Pitches Worst Vs.	Avg	AB	H	2B	3B	HR	RBI	BB	SO	OBP	SLG
Tony Fernandez	.000	15	0	0	0	0	0	3	2	.167	.000	Fred McGriff	.583	12	7	1	0	0	3	2	0	.643	.667
Eric Young	.000	10	0	0	0	0	0	1	0	.091	.000	Marc Newfield	.545	11	6	1	0	2	4	0	0	.545	1.182
Pat Borders	.050	20	1	0	0	0	0	0	7	.050	.050	Geronimo Berroa	.389	18	7	1	0	2	4	2	2	.450	.778
Doug Strange	.050	20	1	0	0	0	0	0	2	.050	.050	Gregg Jefferies	.385	13	5	1	0	2	6	1	2	.429	.923
Derek Jeter	.077	13	1	0	0	0	2	0	3	.067	.077	Chili Davis	.320	25	8	2	0	4	9	4	6	.414	.880

Osvaldo Fernandez — Giants   Age 29 – Pitches Right

	ERA	W	L	Sv	G	GS	IP	BB	SO	Avg	H	2B	3B	HR	RBI	OBP	SLG	CG	ShO	Sup	QS	#P/S	SB	CS	GB	FB	G/F
1997 Season	4.95	3	4	0	11	11	56.1	15	31	.314	74	16	1	9	35	.353	.504	0	0	4.15	5	87	3	7	85	77	1.10
Career (1996-1997)	4.70	10	17	0	41	39	228.0	72	137	.293	267	54	4	29	120	.349	.456	2	0	3.71	19	91	10	12	319	298	1.07

1997 Season

	ERA	W	L	Sv	G	GS	IP	H	HR	BB	SO		Avg	AB	H	2B	3B	HR	RBI	BB	SO	OBP	SLG
Home	6.15	2	3	0	7	7	33.2	47	7	9	18	vs. Left	.259	112	29	4	0	5	23	9	18	.311	.429
Away	3.18	1	1	0	4	4	22.2	27	2	6	13	vs. Right	.363	124	45	12	1	4	12	6	13	.392	.573

Career (1996-1997)

	ERA	W	L	Sv	G	GS	IP	H	HR	BB	SO		Avg	AB	H	2B	3B	HR	RBI	BB	SO	OBP	SLG
Home	4.52	4	9	0	22	21	127.1	146	14	38	80	vs. Left	.283	396	112	19	2	16	67	43	57	.357	.462
Away	4.92	6	8	0	19	18	100.2	121	15	34	57	vs. Right	.300	516	155	35	2	13	53	29	80	.342	.452
Day	4.64	6	9	0	20	20	110.2	135	12	32	63	Inning 1-6	.292	797	233	45	2	27	108	63	118	.349	.455
Night	4.76	4	8	0	21	19	117.1	132	17	40	74	Inning 7+	.296	115	34	9	2	2	12	9	19	.352	.461
Grass	4.62	7	14	0	34	32	187.0	223	24	55	115	None on	.279	502	140	31	2	15	15	38	75	.337	.438
Turf	5.05	3	3	0	7	7	41.0	44	5	17	22	Runners on	.310	410	127	23	2	14	105	34	62	.363	.478
March/April	3.38	6	2	0	10	10	64.0	71	6	18	39	Scoring Posn	.287	247	71	10	1	12	99	24	38	.350	.482
May	6.95	0	5	0	9	9	44.0	66	8	12	34	Close & Late	.300	70	21	5	1	1	7	7	9	.364	.443
June	6.92	1	5	0	8	7	39.0	43	7	16	20	None on/out	.318	233	74	15	0	13	13	19	31	.376	.549
July	4.66	0	3	0	6	5	29.0	35	5	7	16	vs. 1st Batr (relief)	.000	2	0	0	0	0	0	0	2	.000	.000
August	4.08	2	2	0	5	5	28.2	33	3	10	17	1st Inning Pitched	.270	159	43	10	1	4	19	18	24	.350	.421
Sept/Oct	1.16	0	0	0	3	3	23.1	19	0	9	11	First 75 Pitches	.297	694	206	41	2	24	89	51	101	.350	.465
Starter	4.55	10	16	0	39	39	225.1	263	29	71	134	Pitch 76-90	.250	116	29	4	1	2	15	12	19	.320	.353
Reliever	16.88	0	1	0	2	0	2.2	4	0	1	3	Pitch 91-105	.333	72	24	9	0	1	9	7	11	.395	.500
0-3 Days Rest (Start)	10.00	0	2	0	2	2	9.0	13	3	3	5	Pitch 106+	.267	30	8	0	1	2	7	2	6	.313	.533
4 Days Rest	5.03	4	10	0	19	19	110.2	139	14	30	63	First Pitch	.307	153	47	13	2	5	20	6	0	.333	.516
5+ Days Rest	3.66	6	4	0	18	18	110.2	111	12	38	66	Ahead in Count	.235	353	83	16	0	7	36	0	113	.248	.340
vs. AL	0.00	0	0	0	0	0	0.0	0	0	0	0	Behind in Count	.381	223	85	16	1	11	40	47	0	.487	.610
vs. NL	4.70	10	17	0	41	39	228.0	267	29	72	137	Two Strikes	.213	366	78	11	0	5	29	19	137	.260	.284
Pre-All Star	5.38	7	13	0	29	28	157.1	194	24	49	99	Pre-All Star	.302	643	194	40	2	24	93	49	99	.356	.482
Post-All Star	3.18	3	4	0	12	11	70.2	73	5	23	38	Post-All Star	.271	269	73	14	2	5	27	23	38	.332	.394

Pitcher vs. Batter (career)

Pitches Best Vs.	Avg	AB	H	2B	3B	HR	RBI	BB	SO	OBP	SLG	Pitches Worst Vs.	Avg	AB	H	2B	3B	HR	RBI	BB	SO	OBP	SLG
Jeff Conine	.167	12	2	0	0	0	0	0	2	.167	.167	Willie Greene	.455	11	5	1	0	2	5	0	2	.455	1.091
Terry Pendleton	.182	11	2	0	0	0	2	0	1	.250	.182	Gary Sheffield	.444	9	4	0	0	2	3	4	1	.615	1.111
Charles Johnson	.182	11	2	1	0	0	0	1	3	.250	.273	Ray Lankford	.444	9	4	0	1	0	0	2	0	.545	.667
Mark Grudzielanek	.214	14	3	2	0	0	2	0	1	.214	.357	Henry Rodriguez	.417	12	5	1	0	3	7	1	5	.462	1.250
David Segui	.222	9	2	0	0	0	0	2	1	.364	.222												

Sid Fernandez — Astros
Age 35 – Pitches Left (flyball pitcher)

	ERA	W	L	Sv	G	GS	IP	BB	SO	Avg	H	2B	3B	HR	RBI	OBP	SLG	CG	ShO	Sup	QS	#P/S	SB	CS	GB	FB	G/F
1997 Season	3.60	1	0	0	1	1	5.0	2	3	.211	4	1	0	1	2	.286	.421	0	0	7.20	0	76	2	0	9	0	0.22
Last Five Years	4.05	21	23	0	68	67	395.2	148	366	.223	329	65	6	70	172	.296	.418	3	1	4.12	30	96	55	11	271	580	0.47

1997 Season

	ERA	W	L	Sv	G	GS	IP	H	HR	BB	SO		Avg	AB	H	2B	3B	HR	RBI	BB	SO	OBP	SLG
Home	3.60	1	0	0	1	1	5.0	4	1	2	3	vs. Left	.250	4	1	0	0	1	1	0	2	.250	1.000
Away	0.00	0	0	0	0	0	0.0	0	0	0	0	vs. Right	.200	15	3	1	0	0	1	2	1	.294	.267

Last Five Years

	ERA	W	L	Sv	G	GS	IP	H	HR	BB	SO		Avg	AB	H	2B	3B	HR	RBI	BB	SO	OBP	SLG
Home	3.60	11	10	0	33	32	210.0	159	36	66	196	vs. Left	.210	224	47	6	0	6	20	22	56	.285	.317
Away	4.56	10	13	0	35	35	185.2	170	34	82	170	vs. Right	.225	1251	282	59	6	64	152	126	310	.298	.436
Day	4.50	5	8	0	17	17	94.0	80	15	43	82	Inning 1-6	.223	1310	292	59	5	60	154	137	337	.298	.413
Night	3.91	16	15	0	51	50	301.2	249	55	105	284	Inning 7+	.224	165	37	6	1	10	18	11	29	.277	.455
Grass	4.40	13	14	0	41	40	243.1	203	43	97	207	None on	.226	939	212	41	3	44	44	90	215	.296	.416
Turf	3.49	8	9	0	27	27	152.1	126	27	51	159	Runners on	.218	536	117	24	3	26	128	58	151	.296	.420
March/April	3.31	5	2	0	15	15	87.0	68	12	27	78	Scoring Posn	.235	277	65	11	1	11	89	37	86	.320	.401
May	5.69	2	6	0	13	13	68.0	75	12	36	65	Close & Late	.231	104	24	5	0	6	12	6	17	.279	.452
June	4.93	2	6	0	9	9	49.1	44	13	19	50	None on/out	.244	405	99	19	2	18	18	33	91	.303	.435
July	4.67	3	4	0	10	9	54.0	49	13	17	59	vs. 1st Batr (relief)	1.000	1	1	0	0	0	0	0	0	1.000	1.000
August	3.22	7	3	0	13	13	86.2	60	14	31	83	1st Inning Pitched	.214	252	54	11	0	13	30	22	72	.276	.413
Sept/Oct	3.02	2	2	0	8	8	50.2	33	6	18	31	First 75 Pitches	.215	1083	233	46	3	50	114	104	288	.285	.402
Starter	4.06	21	23	0	67	67	394.2	328	70	147	364	Pitch 76-90	.219	178	39	8	1	4	17	24	41	.320	.343
Reliever	0.00	0	0	0	1	0	1.0	1	0	1	2	Pitch 91-105	.271	140	38	7	2	10	28	15	26	.342	.564
0-3 Days Rest (Start)	0.00	0	0	0	0	0	0.0	0	0	0	0	Pitch 106+	.257	74	19	4	0	6	13	5	11	.300	.554
4 Days Rest	3.90	14	11	0	36	36	226.0	186	40	73	191	First Pitch	.287	171	49	7	1	13	27	4	0	.317	.567
5+ Days Rest	4.27	7	12	0	31	31	168.2	142	30	74	173	Ahead in Count	.171	776	133	30	3	22	72	0	322	.173	.303
vs. AL	5.59	6	10	0	27	26	143.1	145	36	63	126	Behind in Count	.319	279	89	16	1	25	45	76	0	.464	.652
vs. NL	3.17	15	13	0	41	41	252.1	184	34	85	240	Two Strikes	.176	774	136	27	4	26	81	68	366	.243	.322
Pre-All Star	4.69	10	14	0	40	39	215.0	202	40	88	203	Pre-All Star	.246	822	202	42	6	40	107	88	203	.320	.457
Post-All Star	3.29	11	9	0	28	28	180.2	127	30	60	163	Post-All Star	.194	653	127	23	0	30	65	60	163	.265	.368

Pitcher vs. Batter (since 1984)

Pitches Best Vs.	Avg	AB	H	2B	3B	HR	RBI	BB	SO	OBP	SLG	Pitches Worst Vs.	Avg	AB	H	2B	3B	HR	RBI	BB	SO	OBP	SLG
Luis Rivera	.000	12	0	0	0	0	0	2	3	.143	.000	Mariano Duncan	.405	42	17	6	2	0	5	3	5	.447	.643
Paul O'Neill	.000	10	0	0	0	0	0	3	5	.231	.000	Larry Walker	.375	16	6	0	0	2	5	1	7	.474	.750
Walt Weiss	.000	9	0	0	0	0	0	2	4	.182	.000	Joe Carter	.364	11	4	0	0	2	2	2	4	.462	.909
John Cangelosi	.071	14	1	0	0	0	0	1	1	.188	.071	Gary Sheffield	.333	12	4	0	0	2	5	0	2	.333	.833
Brian Jordan	.077	13	1	0	0	0	0	1	7	.143	.077	Kevin Mitchell	.320	25	8	2	0	4	5	1	5	.346	.880

Tony Fernandez — Indians
Age 36 – Bats Both (groundball hitter)

	Avg	G	AB	R	H	2B	3B	HR	RBI	BB	SO	HBP	GDP	SB	CS	OBP	SLG	IBB	SH	SF	#Pit	#P/PA	GB	FB	G/F
1997 Season	.286	120	409	55	117	21	1	11	44	22	47	2	11	6	6	.323	.423	0	6	3	1428	3.23	155	107	1.45
Last Five Years	.273	474	1685	227	460	82	20	29	203	164	172	12	47	45	29	.339	.397	15	21	14	6490	3.42	711	437	1.63

1997 Season

	Avg	AB	H	2B	3B	HR	RBI	BB	SO	OBP	SLG		Avg	AB	H	2B	3B	HR	RBI	BB	SO	OBP	SLG
vs. Left	.407	123	50	6	1	5	18	7	7	.435	.593	First Pitch	.414	87	36	6	0	2	8	0	0	.414	.552
vs. Right	.234	286	67	15	0	6	26	15	40	.275	.350	Ahead in Count	.297	101	30	5	1	4	14	11	0	.363	.485
Groundball	.333	66	22	1	1	2	9	4	8	.366	.470	Behind in Count	.167	144	24	6	0	4	15	0	38	.176	.292
Flyball	.286	56	16	3	0	1	4	3	5	.328	.393	Two Strikes	.133	128	17	2	0	3	9	11	47	.213	.219
Home	.297	192	57	9	1	7	24	9	17	.327	.464	Batting #2	.270	204	55	9	1	5	20	10	26	.302	.397
Away	.276	217	60	12	0	4	20	13	30	.320	.387	Batting #8	.310	100	31	6	0	3	15	4	13	.336	.460
Day	.302	129	39	7	0	3	11	8	10	.345	.426	Other	.295	105	31	6	0	3	9	8	8	.351	.438
Night	.279	280	78	14	1	8	33	14	37	.313	.421	March/April	.321	56	18	4	0	1	7	3	11	.356	.446
Grass	.276	351	97	16	1	10	40	18	38	.313	.413	May	.245	94	23	6	0	2	8	5	10	.283	.372
Turf	.345	58	20	5	0	1	4	4	9	.387	.483	June	.167	36	6	1	0	0	1	2	8	.231	.194
Pre-All Star	.274	201	55	14	0	3	19	11	30	.315	.388	July	.375	88	33	6	1	2	15	5	5	.411	.534
Post-All Star	.298	208	62	7	1	8	25	11	17	.332	.457	August	.217	69	15	2	0	2	7	3	11	.243	.333
Scoring Posn	.308	91	28	5	1	0	31	7	13	.353	.385	Sept/Oct	.333	66	22	2	0	4	6	4	2	.371	.545
Close & Late	.354	65	23	6	0	2	12	3	12	.382	.538	vs. AL	.286	381	109	19	1	10	39	20	42	.323	.420
None on/out	.333	90	30	4	0	4	4	4	8	.362	.511	vs. NL	.286	28	8	2	0	1	5	2	5	.323	.464

1997 By Position

Position	Avg	AB	H	2B	3B	HR	RBI	BB	SO	OBP	SLG	G	GS	Innings	PO	A	E	DP	Fld Pct	Rng Fctr	In Zone	Outs	Zone Rtg	MLB Zone
As 2b	.291	371	108	20	1	11	42	20	40	.328	.439	109	94	840.1	208	296	10	62	.981	5.40	327	295	.902	.902
As ss	.250	32	8	1	0	0	2	2	6	.294	.281	10	8	65.2	12	26	1	7	.974	5.21	30	28	.933	.937

Last Five Years

	Avg	AB	H	2B	3B	HR	RBI	BB	SO	OBP	SLG		Avg	AB	H	2B	3B	HR	RBI	BB	SO	OBP	SLG
vs. Left	.281	516	145	21	5	10	61	46	39	.338	.399	First Pitch	.336	330	111	21	5	7	39	12	0	.357	.494
vs. Right	.269	1169	315	61	15	19	142	118	133	.340	.396	Ahead in Count	.295	451	133	26	4	9	64	93	0	.412	.430
Groundball	.275	415	114	13	4	5	39	31	52	.328	.361	Behind in Count	.218	600	131	25	7	8	70	0	134	.230	.323
Flyball	.245	257	63	10	3	3	27	39	26	.344	.342	Two Strikes	.175	589	103	16	4	7	50	59	172	.258	.251
Home	.266	820	218	35	11	14	100	85	74	.337	.387	Batting #2	.255	432	110	15	5	6	44	40	49	.321	.354
Away	.280	865	242	47	9	15	103	79	98	.342	.407	Batting #6	.269	476	128	25	9	9	60	53	49	.343	.416
Day	.251	530	133	23	3	8	61	61	46	.331	.351	Other	.286	777	222	42	6	14	99	71	74	.347	.409
Night	.283	1155	327	59	17	21	142	103	126	.343	.418	March/April	.259	197	51	9	1	6	26	32	28	.366	.406
Grass	.262	1093	286	54	12	20	134	101	109	.324	.388	May	.239	306	73	15	2	3	31	37	32	.322	.330
Turf	.294	592	174	28	8	9	69	63	63	.367	.414	June	.266	312	83	15	6	5	40	31	37	.334	.401
Pre-All Star	.272	940	256	51	10	16	116	112	107	.352	.399	July	.302	371	112	22	4	7	51	27	32	.354	.439
Post-All Star	.274	745	204	31	10	13	87	52	65	.322	.395	August	.252	298	75	11	3	2	32	18	33	.293	.329
Scoring Posn	.314	427	134	20	10	7	173	70	49	.403	.457	Sept/Oct	.328	201	66	10	4	6	23	19	10	.386	.507
Close & Late	.292	277	81	13	0	5	41	29	35	.361	.394	vs. AL	.278	1118	311	57	12	19	134	93	108	.335	.402
None on/out	.274	376	103	15	1	9	9	23	32	.319	.391	vs. NL	.263	567	149	25	8	10	69	71	64	.348	.388

Batter vs. Pitcher (since 1984)

Hits Best Against	Avg	AB	H	2B	3B	HR	RBI	BB	SO	OBP	SLG	Hits Worst Against	Avg	AB	H	2B	3B	HR	RBI	BB	SO	OBP	SLG
Hipolito Pichardo	.500	10	5	0	0	0	0	1	0	.545	.500	Alex Fernandez	.000	15	0	0	0	0	0	3	2	.167	.000
Greg Cadaret	.500	10	5	1	1	1	4	2	1	.538	1.100	Xavier Hernandez	.000	9	0	0	0	0	0	3	1	.250	.000
Jimmy Key	.455	11	5	1	2	0	4	2	0	.538	.909	Chris Haney	.083	12	1	0	0	0	0	0	2	.083	.083
Curt Schilling	.429	14	6	1	0	2		2	3	.500	.714	David Wells	.091	11	1	0	0	0	0	0	1	.091	.091
Jeff Montgomery	.400	10	4	0	1	0	2	1	0	.455	.600	Butch Henry	.100	10	1	0	0	0	0	1	1	.182	.100

Mike Fetters — Brewers   Age 33 – Pitches Right (groundball pitcher)

	ERA	W	L	Sv	G	GS	IP	BB	SO	Avg	H	2B	3B	HR	RBI	OBP	SLG	GF	IR	IRS	Hld	SvOp	SB	CS	GB	FB	G/F
1997 Season	3.45	1	5	6	51	0	70.1	33	62	.244	62	13	2	4	28	.329	.358	20	19	5	11	11	10	3	93	54	1.72
Last Five Years	3.25	8	18	77	239	0	271.2	128	202	.264	267	45	5	15	136	.344	.363	154	110	41	25	96	27	11	423	218	1.94

1997 Season

	ERA	W	L	Sv	G	GS	IP	H	HR	BB	SO		Avg	AB	H	2B	3B	HR	RBI	BB	SO	OBP	SLG
Home	2.29	1	1	4	25	0	35.1	22	2	19	33	vs. Left	.306	111	34	12	0	1	15	11	26	.360	.441
Away	4.63	0	4	2	26	0	35.0	40	2	14	29	vs. Right	.196	143	28	1	2	3	13	22	36	.305	.294
Day	4.66	1	2	2	17	0	19.1	21	1	6	14	Inning 1-6	.059	17	1	0	0	0	1	3	9	.200	.059
Night	3.00	0	3	4	34	0	51.0	41	3	27	48	Inning 7+	.257	237	61	13	2	4	27	30	53	.338	.380
Grass	2.97	1	3	6	44	0	60.2	48	3	30	55	None on	.238	126	30	8	0	3	3	20	29	.347	.373
Turf	6.52	0	2	0	7	0	9.2	14	1	3	7	Runners on	.250	128	32	5	2	1	25	13	33	.310	.344
March/April	0.00	0	0	0	0	0	0.0	0	0	0	0	Scoring Posn	.197	76	15	4	1	1	24	9	21	.270	.316
May	5.40	1	3	0	8	0	10.0	10	0	8	11	Close & Late	.268	164	44	11	2	3	22	26	34	.363	.415
June	3.55	0	1	0	10	0	12.2	11	0	5	11	None on/out	.291	55	16	3	0	2	2	14	10	.443	.455
July	2.16	0	0	5	13	0	16.2	10	1	5	14	vs. 1st Batr (relief)	.256	43	11	2	0	2	5	7	9	.360	.442
August	2.25	0	1	0	10	0	16.0	13	1	7	11	1st Inning Pitched	.230	174	40	7	2	3	20	26	49	.328	.345
Sept/Oct	4.80	0	1	0	10	0	15.0	18	2	8	15	First 15 Pitches	.270	137	37	9	1	3	13	17	33	.350	.416
Starter	0.00	0	0	0	0	0	0.0	0	0	0	0	Pitch 16-30	.207	92	19	3	1	1	13	15	24	.312	.293
Reliever	3.45	1	5	6	51	0	70.1	62	4	33	62	Pitch 31-45	.286	21	6	1	0	0	2	1	3	.318	.333
0 Days rest (Relief)	2.63	0	2	3	10	0	13.2	11	0	6	8	Pitch 46+	.000	4	0	0	0	0	0	0	2	.000	.000
1 or 2 Days rest	2.88	1	1	1	23	0	34.1	29	0	15	34	First Pitch	.294	34	10	4	0	0	2	2	0	.324	.412
3+ Days rest	4.84	0	2	2	18	0	22.1	22	4	12	20	Ahead in Count	.188	112	21	2	0	1	7	0	50	.188	.232
vs. AL	3.21	1	4	6	45	0	61.2	52	3	29	56	Behind in Count	.367	60	22	3	2	1	11	17	0	.506	.583
vs. NL	5.19	0	1	0	6	0	8.2	10	1	4	6	Two Strikes	.148	122	18	4	0	2	11	14	62	.234	.230
Pre-All Star	3.96	1	4	0	21	0	25.0	22	0	13	23	Pre-All Star	.242	91	22	4	0	0	9	13	23	.333	.286
Post-All Star	3.18	0	1	6	30	0	45.1	40	4	20	39	Post-All Star	.245	163	40	7	4	1	19	20	39	.326	.399

Last Five Years

	ERA	W	L	Sv	G	GS	IP	H	HR	BB	SO		Avg	AB	H	2B	3B	HR	RBI	BB	SO	OBP	SLG
Home	3.15	7	8	26	122	0	145.2	127	8	75	112	vs. Left	.278	489	136	26	3	8	72	59	84	.351	.393
Away	3.36	1	10	51	117	0	126.0	140	7	53	90	vs. Right	.250	523	131	19	2	7	64	69	118	.338	.335
Day	3.98	4	7	28	90	0	97.1	104	7	41	72	Inning 1-6	.286	77	22	1	2	2	23	6	14	.333	.429
Night	2.84	4	11	49	149	0	174.1	163	8	87	130	Inning 7+	.262	935	245	44	3	13	113	122	188	.345	.357
Grass	3.05	8	14	61	201	0	230.0	212	14	112	173	None on	.267	472	126	24	0	9	9	64	88	.357	.375
Turf	4.32	0	4	16	38	0	41.2	55	1	16	29	Runners on	.261	540	141	21	5	6	127	64	114	.333	.352
March/April	3.80	1	1	2	22	0	21.1	24	2	11	11	Scoring Posn	.247	316	78	14	3	4	120	46	72	.331	.348
May	2.52	1	5	14	50	0	46.0	42	0	29	35	Close & Late	.268	612	164	30	3	8	85	93	126	.360	.366
June	3.08	3	3	15	49	0	52.2	46	3	25	42	None on/out	.294	218	64	11	0	5	5	28	36	.377	.413
July	3.03	1	4	26	54	0	62.1	60	3	22	49	vs. 1st Batr (relief)	.314	204	64	13	1	5	26	29	33	.401	.461
August	3.00	1	2	16	40	0	51.0	57	4	25	47	1st Inning Pitched	.269	811	218	35	5	11	119	100	167	.346	.365
Sept/Oct	4.98	1	3	7	28	0	34.1	38	3	16	28	First 15 Pitches	.290	665	193	33	4	11	92	76	121	.362	.402
Starter	0.00	0	0	0	0	0	0.0	0	0	0	0	Pitch 16-30	.213	287	61	11	1	3	40	44	71	.311	.289
Reliever	3.25	8	18	77	239	0	271.2	267	15	128	202	Pitch 31-45	.245	53	13	1	0	1	4	8	7	.355	.321
0 Days rest (Relief)	3.12	0	3	25	47	0	49.0	43	2	23	26	Pitch 46+	.000	7	0	0	0	0	0	0	3	.000	.000
1 or 2 Days rest	3.00	4	6	36	94	0	111.0	107	4	46	93	First Pitch	.322	146	47	11	4	4	30	16	0	.379	.479
3+ Days rest	3.55	4	9	16	98	0	111.2	117	9	59	83	Ahead in Count	.173	416	72	14	1	3	36	0	167	.175	.233
vs. AL	3.18	8	17	77	233	0	263.0	257	14	124	196	Behind in Count	.381	257	98	9	3	7	43	68	0	.509	.521
vs. NL	5.19	0	1	0	6	0	8.2	10	1	4	6	Two Strikes	.161	453	73	18	0	4	38	44	202	.235	.227
Pre-All Star	2.85	5	10	35	134	0	142.0	129	5	74	97	Pre-All Star	.254	508	129	20	4	5	69	74	97	.348	.335
Post-All Star	3.68	3	8	42	105	0	129.2	138	10	54	105	Post-All Star	.274	504	138	25	2	10	67	54	105	.340	.391

Pitcher vs. Batter (career)

Pitches Best Vs.	Avg	AB	H	2B	3B	HR	RBI	BB	SO	OBP	SLG	Pitches Worst Vs.	Avg	AB	H	2B	3B	HR	RBI	BB	SO	OBP	SLG
Robin Ventura	.091	11	1	1	0	0	0	4	2	.333	.182	Randy Velarde	.700	10	7	0	0	1	2	2	0	.750	1.000
Paul Sorrento	.100	10	1	0	0	0	1	2	3	.250	.100	Paul Molitor	.556	9	5	1	1	0	1	3	3	.692	.889
Pat Borders	.167	12	2	1	0	0	1	0	3	.167	.250	Rafael Palmeiro	.500	10	5	0	1	1	4	3	0	.643	1.000
Albert Belle	.167	12	2	1	0	0	4	7	.375	.250	Danny Tartabull	.455	11	5	2	0	0	1	2	5	.538	.636
Chuck Knoblauch	.214	14	3	1	0	0	2	1	4	.267	.286	Dean Palmer	.364	11	4	1	0	2	9	0	2	.417	1.000

Cecil Fielder — Yankees   Age 34 – Bats Right (flyball hitter)

	Avg	G	AB	R	H	2B	3B	HR	RBI	BB	SO	HBP	GDP	SB	CS	OBP	SLG	IBB	SH	SF	#Pit	#P/PA	GB	FB	G/F
1997 Season	.260	98	361	40	94	15	0	13	61	51	87	7	14	0	0	.358	.410	3	0	6	1734	4.08	127	92	1.38
Last Five Years	.256	657	2444	342	626	92	3	141	467	353	577	23	88	2	2	.352	.469	42	0	24	11550	4.06	782	692	1.13

1997 Season

	Avg	AB	H	2B	3B	HR	RBI	BB	SO	OBP	SLG		Avg	AB	H	2B	3B	HR	RBI	BB	SO	OBP	SLG
vs. Left	.211	90	19	1	0	1	7	24	29	.379	.256	First Pitch	.333	36	12	3	0	1	13	3	0	.375	.500
vs. Right	.277	271	75	14	0	12	54	27	58	.350	.461	Ahead in Count	.377	69	26	5	0	3	11	25	0	.543	.580
Groundball	.290	93	27	3	0	3	15	11	24	.368	.419	Behind in Count	.199	171	34	5	0	5	21	0	67	.218	.316
Flyball	.254	67	17	3	0	2	4	11	17	.367	.388	Two Strikes	.185	189	35	4	0	6	21	23	87	.284	.302
Home	.277	191	53	8	0	6	28	17	44	.350	.414	Batting #4	.202	89	18	2	0	3	14	17	32	.336	.326
Away	.241	170	41	7	0	7	33	34	43	.365	.406	Batting #5	.266	199	53	8	0	6	33	24	37	.348	.397
Day	.292	130	38	7	0	7	23	18	31	.390	.508	Other	.315	73	23	5	0	4	14	10	18	.412	.548
Night	.242	231	56	8	0	6	38	33	56	.339	.355	March/April	.252	107	27	8	0	1	17	11	18	.336	.355
Grass	.259	336	87	13	0	12	56	44	83	.352	.405	May	.277	94	26	3	0	2	14	12	17	.361	.372
Turf	.280	25	7	2	0	1	5	7	4	.424	.480	June	.262	84	22	2	0	6	18	19	26	.400	.500
Pre-All Star	.259	301	78	13	0	10	50	47	65	.367	.402	July	.176	34	6	1	0	1	2	5	11	.300	.294
Post-All Star	.267	60	16	2	0	3	11	4	22	.308	.450	August	.000	0	0	0	0	0	0	0	0	.000	.000
Scoring Posn	.255	110	28	6	0	4	49	12	25	.323	.418	Sept/Oct	.310	42	13	1	0	3	10	4	15	.362	.548
Close & Late	.240	50	12	2	0	1	5	6	12	.345	.340	vs. AL	.269	335	90	14	0	12	60	45	75	.360	.418
None on/out	.261	92	24	5	0	5	5	13	25	.358	.478	vs. NL	.154	26	4	1	0	1	1	6	12	.333	.308

1997 By Position

Position	Avg	AB	H	2B	3B	HR	RBI	BB	SO	OBP	SLG	G	GS	Innings	PO	A	E	DP	Fld Pct	Rng Fctr	In Zone	Zone Outs	Zone Rtg	MLB Zone
As DH	.263	334	88	14	0	13	58	45	78	.357	.422	89	88	---	---	---	---	---	---	---	---	---	---	---

Last Five Years

	Avg	AB	H	2B	3B	HR	RBI	BB	SO	OBP	SLG		Avg	AB	H	2B	3B	HR	RBI	BB	SO	OBP	SLG
vs. Left	.273	549	150	25	2	32	101	124	127	.405	.501	First Pitch	.326	258	84	14	0	29	83	33	0	.400	.717
vs. Right	.251	1895	476	67	1	109	366	229	450	.336	.460	Ahead in Count	.358	497	178	33	3	42	138	163	0	.516	.690
Groundball	.258	592	153	18	0	20	87	62	127	.334	.390	Behind in Count	.208	1139	237	36	0	41	143	0	433	.215	.348
Flyball	.250	488	122	19	0	37	102	56	120	.327	.516	Two Strikes	.181	1308	237	29	0	47	148	157	577	.271	.311
Home	.266	1198	319	46	1	72	248	170	273	.361	.487	Batting #4	.251	2117	532	77	3	127	409	315	513	.350	.470
Away	.246	1246	307	46	2	69	219	183	304	.344	.453	Batting #5	.255	208	53	8	0	6	33	25	39	.338	.380
Day	.264	886	234	33	3	57	185	123	210	.359	.501	Other	.345	119	41	7	0	8	25	13	25	.418	.605
Night	.252	1558	392	59	0	84	282	230	367	.349	.451	March/April	.249	390	97	18	1	21	77	50	84	.341	.462
Grass	.255	2105	537	70	3	121	398	301	495	.351	.464	May	.255	471	120	16	0	30	84	74	99	.357	.480
Turf	.263	339	89	22	0	20	68	52	82	.361	.504	June	.274	489	134	17	0	29	97	82	116	.379	.487
Pre-All Star	.256	1510	386	55	2	93	300	184	342	.358	.479	July	.245	420	103	17	1	27	90	65	104	.349	.483
Post-All Star	.257	934	240	37	1	48	167	119	235	.342	.453	August	.257	350	90	14	0	19	65	47	96	.345	.460
Scoring Posn	.268	704	189	29	0	38	325	141	150	.386	.472	Sept/Oct	.253	324	82	10	1	15	54	35	78	.329	.429
Close & Late	.215	325	70	11	0	10	38	46	82	.327	.342	vs. AL	.257	2418	622	91	3	140	466	347	565	.353	.471
None on/out	.271	635	172	25	1	39	39	69	140	.347	.498	vs. NL	.154	26	4	1	0	1	1	6	12	.333	.308

Batter vs. Pitcher (career)

Hits Best Against	Avg	AB	H	2B	3B	HR	RBI	BB	SO	OBP	SLG	Hits Worst Against	Avg	AB	H	2B	3B	HR	RBI	BB	SO	OBP	SLG
Bob Wells	.571	7	4	1	0	2	8	4	1	.727	1.571	Mike James	.000	10	0	0	0	0	0	1	1	.091	.043
Frank Rodriguez	.529	17	9	2	0	4	8	1	3	.526	1.353	Roger Clemens	.043	46	2	0	0	0	2	4	21	.120	.043
James Baldwin	.500	14	7	3	0	2	8	2	0	.563	1.143	Woody Williams	.095	21	2	1	0	0	0	0	7	.095	.143
Felipe Lira	.444	9	4	1	0	2	7	2	1	.545	1.222	Mike Jackson	.100	10	1	0	0	0	1	1	4	.182	.100
David Wells	.381	21	8	0	0	4	10	5	4	.500	.952	Steve Karsay	.100	10	1	0	0	0	0	1	2	.182	.100

Mike Figga — Yankees   Age 27 – Bats Right

	Avg	G	AB	R	H	2B	3B	HR	RBI	BB	SO	HBP	GDP	SB	CS	OBP	SLG	IBB	SH	SF	#Pit	#P/PA	GB	FB	G/F
1997 Season	.000	2	4	0	0	0	0	0	0	0	3	0	0	0	0	.000	.000	0	0	0	20	5.00	1	0	0.00

1997 Season

	Avg	AB	H	2B	3B	HR	RBI	BB	SO	OBP	SLG		Avg	AB	H	2B	3B	HR	RBI	BB	SO	OBP	SLG
vs. Left	.000	1	0	0	0	0	0	0	1	.000	.000	Scoring Posn	.000	1	0	0	0	0	0	0	1	.000	.000
vs. Right	.000	3	0	0	0	0	0	0	2	.000	.000	Close & Late	.000	0	0	0	0	0	0	0	0	.000	.000

Chuck Finley — Angels   Age 35 – Pitches Left

	ERA	W	L	Sv	G	GS	IP	BB	SO	Avg	H	2B	3B	HR	RBI	OBP	SLG	CG	ShO	Sup	QS	#P/S	SB	CS	GB	FB	G/F
1997 Season	4.23	13	6	0	25	25	164.0	65	155	.248	152	21	2	20	67	.323	.387	3	1	6.26	13	110	11	6	201	147	1.37
Last Five Years	3.96	69	58	0	152	152	1039.2	405	900	.255	1006	183	9	110	440	.327	.390	29	7	5.06	85	113	97	37	1349	975	1.38

1997 Season

	ERA	W	L	Sv	G	GS	IP	H	HR	BB	SO		Avg	AB	H	2B	3B	HR	RBI	BB	SO	OBP	SLG
Home	3.36	8	1	0	12	12	83.0	66	11	29	81	vs. Left	.164	61	10	2	0	0	3	14	21	.338	.197

1997 Season

	ERA	W	L	Sv	G	GS	IP	H	HR	BB	SO		Avg	AB	H	2B	3B	HR	RBI	BB	SO	OBP	SLG
Away	5.11	5	5	0	13	13	81.0	86	9	36	74	vs. Right	.257	552	142	19	2	20	64	51	134	.321	.408
Day	4.76	4	3	0	8	8	51.0	56	6	25	55	Inning 1-6	.261	525	137	20	1	19	62	56	128	.333	.411
Night	3.98	9	3	0	17	17	113.0	96	14	40	100	Inning 7+	.170	88	15	1	1	1	5	9	27	.263	.239
Grass	3.76	13	5	0	23	23	153.0	135	17	59	143	None on	.245	359	88	12	2	15	15	39	93	.328	.415
Turf	10.64	0	1	0	2	2	11.0	17	3	6	12	Runners on	.252	254	64	9	0	5	52	26	62	.317	.346
March/April	4.86	0	1	0	3	3	16.2	13	4	9	12	Scoring Posn	.273	132	36	3	0	3	45	17	31	.346	.364
May	4.99	3	3	0	6	6	39.2	42	4	10	35	Close & Late	.184	49	9	1	0	1	5	5	14	.273	.265
June	7.12	0	2	0	5	5	30.1	34	9	16	36	None on/out	.269	156	42	5	1	5	5	19	33	.352	.410
July	2.26	7	0	0	7	7	51.2	42	2	19	58	vs. 1st Batr (relief)	.000	0	0	0	0	0	0	0	0	.000	.000
August	3.16	3	0	0	4	4	25.2	21	1	11	14	1st Inning Pitched	.217	92	20	5	0	3	11	15	27	.330	.370
Sept/Oct	0.00	0	0	0	0	0	0.0	0	0	0	0	First 75 Pitches	.278	385	107	16	0	13	50	46	92	.357	.421
Starter	4.23	13	6	0	25	25	164.0	152	20	65	155	Pitch 76-90	.229	83	19	2	1	3	7	6	21	.278	.386
Reliever	0.00	0	0	0	0	0	0.0	0	0	0	0	Pitch 91-105	.217	83	18	3	0	4	8	6	24	.270	.398
0-3 Days Rest (Start)	4.18	4	0	0	5	5	32.1	27	2	12	34	Pitch 106+	.129	62	8	0	1	0	2	7	18	.239	.161
4 Days Rest	4.04	6	5	0	12	12	82.1	75	13	29	84	First Pitch	.377	69	26	6	0	4	12	0	0	.377	.638
5+ Days Rest	4.56	3	1	0	8	8	49.1	50	5	24	37	Ahead in Count	.176	290	51	8	1	1	15	0	124	.181	.221
vs. AL	4.51	12	6	0	23	23	149.2	142	19	59	143	Behind in Count	.330	115	38	3	1	9	21	34	0	.487	.609
vs. NL	1.26	1	0	0	2	2	14.1	10	1	6	12	Two Strikes	.154	324	50	7	0	3	17	31	155	.232	.204
Pre-All Star	4.89	5	6	0	16	16	103.0	98	17	41	102	Pre-All Star	.250	392	98	16	1	17	49	41	102	.326	.426
Post-All Star	3.10	8	0	0	9	9	61.0	54	3	24	53	Post-All Star	.244	221	54	5	1	3	18	24	53	.319	.317

Last Five Years

	ERA	W	L	Sv	G	GS	IP	H	HR	BB	SO		Avg	AB	H	2B	3B	HR	RBI	BB	SO	OBP	SLG
Home	3.47	41	23	0	78	78	557.2	497	63	196	541	vs. Left	.259	537	139	23	0	13	57	69	125	.348	.374
Away	4.54	28	35	0	74	74	482.0	509	47	209	359	vs. Right	.254	3407	861	160	9	97	383	336	775	.324	.392
Day	4.35	20	20	0	44	44	287.2	301	31	129	264	Inning 1-6	.257	3275	843	160	7	96	392	336	751	.329	.398
Night	3.82	49	38	0	108	108	752.0	705	79	276	636	Inning 7+	.244	669	163	23	2	14	48	69	149	.318	.347
Grass	3.91	63	47	0	132	132	903.1	861	97	353	795	None on	.251	2306	579	109	6	73	73	216	528	.320	.399
Turf	4.36	6	11	0	20	20	136.1	145	13	52	105	Runners on	.261	1638	427	74	3	37	367	189	372	.337	.377
March/April	5.62	5	7	0	20	20	123.1	120	22	59	99	Scoring Posn	.266	920	245	37	1	26	332	130	221	.353	.393
May	2.75	16	11	0	30	30	213.0	181	17	76	201	Close & Late	.248	351	87	12	1	6	29	39	73	.327	.339
June	4.48	11	13	0	28	28	197.0	201	23	65	176	None on/out	.268	1033	277	45	2	34	34	82	213	.325	.414
July	4.29	19	8	0	31	31	205.2	210	19	80	190	vs. 1st Batr (relief)	.000	0	0	0	0	0	0	0	0	.000	.000
August	3.67	11	9	0	23	23	161.2	159	13	64	122	1st Inning Pitched	.258	590	152	33	1	18	82	77	140	.345	.408
Sept/Oct	3.50	7	10	0	20	20	139.0	135	16	61	112	First 75 Pitches	.255	2501	637	126	4	65	287	247	581	.324	.386
Starter	3.96	69	58	0	152	152	1039.2	1006	110	405	900	Pitch 76-90	.254	504	128	18	2	16	55	60	101	.337	.393
Reliever	0.00	0	0	0	0	0	0.0	0	0	0	0	Pitch 91-105	.262	481	126	23	2	19	52	38	117	.318	.437
0-3 Days Rest (Start)	2.74	7	0	0	10	10	62.1	50	3	25	67	Pitch 106+	.251	458	115	16	1	10	46	60	101	.342	.356
4 Days Rest	3.95	50	45	0	107	107	751.0	736	85	277	648	First Pitch	.342	529	181	37	1	22	88	4	0	.349	.541
5+ Days Rest	4.33	12	13	0	35	35	226.1	220	22	103	185	Ahead in Count	.175	1749	306	48	3	20	105	0	755	.184	.240
vs. AL	4.00	68	58	0	150	150	1025.1	996	109	399	888	Behind in Count	.348	881	307	66	5	46	143	199	0	.467	.591
vs. NL	1.26	1	0	0	2	2	14.1	10	1	6	12	Two Strikes	.161	1902	307	52	1	21	121	202	900	.247	.223
Pre-All Star	4.06	38	34	0	88	88	600.1	567	68	228	541	Pre-All Star	.250	2270	567	113	4	68	252	228	541	.322	.394
Post-All Star	3.83	31	24	0	64	64	439.1	439	42	177	359	Post-All Star	.262	1674	439	70	4	42	188	177	359	.334	.384

Pitcher vs. Batter (career)

Pitches Best Vs.	Avg	AB	H	2B	3B	HR	RBI	BB	SO	OBP	SLG	Pitches Worst Vs.	Avg	AB	H	2B	3B	HR	RBI	BB	SO	OBP	SLG
Chris Gomez	.059	17	1	0	0	0	0	2	5	.158	.059	Wil Cordero	.500	10	5	1	0	0	1	1	2	.545	.600
Terry Shumpert	.063	16	1	0	0	0	0	1	2	.118	.063	Jacob Brumfield	.455	11	5	1	1	2	4	2	1	.571	1.273
John Flaherty	.077	13	1	0	0	0	0	1	1	.143	.077	Shane Mack	.429	42	18	7	2	2	4	5	7	.500	.833
Jeffrey Hammonds	.133	15	2	0	0	0	0	0	4	.133	.133	Mark Whiten	.429	21	9	3	1	1	4	2	6	.478	.810
Vince Coleman	.154	13	2	0	0	0	0	0	4	.154	.154	Cecil Fielder	.345	55	19	3	1	4	11	14	13	.493	.655

Steve Finley — Padres

Age 33 – Bats Left (groundball hitter)

	Avg	G	AB	R	H	2B	3B	HR	RBI	BB	SO	HBP	GDP	SB	CS	OBP	SLG	IBB	SH	SF	#Pit	#P/PA	GB	FB	G/F
1997 Season	.261	143	560	101	146	26	5	28	92	43	92	3	10	15	3	.313	.475	2	2	7	2220	3.61	180	191	0.94
Last Five Years	.281	679	2695	464	756	125	40	87	308	214	358	15	48	105	36	.335	.453	13	26	18	10594	3.57	1033	782	1.32

1997 Season

	Avg	AB	H	2B	3B	HR	RBI	BB	SO	OBP	SLG		Avg	AB	H	2B	3B	HR	RBI	BB	SO	OBP	SLG
vs. Left	.263	152	40	5	1	5	20	7	24	.309	.408	First Pitch	.304	69	21	4	1	2	11	2	0	.333	.478
vs. Right	.260	408	106	21	4	23	72	36	68	.315	.500	Ahead in Count	.295	112	33	7	0	11	29	26	0	.421	.652
Groundball	.265	102	27	4	2	4	19	10	15	.328	.461	Behind in Count	.205	268	55	8	1	8	36	0	81	.204	.332
Flyball	.281	96	27	6	0	6	15	5	15	.317	.531	Two Strikes	.200	245	49	6	3	5	26	15	92	.246	.310
Home	.216	273	59	12	0	5	30	22	39	.278	.315	Batting #2	.297	195	58	8	1	14	28	14	37	.346	.564
Away	.303	287	87	14	5	23	62	21	53	.347	.627	Batting #3	.247	162	40	11	3	4	32	11	20	.298	.426
Day	.304	191	58	12	3	10	31	15	33	.352	.555	Other	.236	203	48	7	1	10	32	18	35	.295	.429
Night	.238	369	88	14	2	18	61	28	59	.293	.434	March/April	.220	41	9	6	1	0	9	3	7	.283	.415
Grass	.263	438	115	19	2	20	68	37	73	.320	.452	May	.308	104	32	6	0	5	17	8	17	.357	.510
Turf	.254	122	31	7	3	8	24	6	19	.287	.557	June	.283	120	34	5	2	9	24	10	10	.338	.583
Pre-All Star	.279	280	78	17	3	16	55	22	36	.332	.532	July	.234	94	22	1	1	6	19	8	20	.288	.457
Post-All Star	.243	280	68	9	2	12	37	21	56	.294	.418	August	.189	111	21	2	1	3	11	9	20	.246	.306
Scoring Posn	.276	145	40	9	3	7	66	14	27	.325	.524	Sept/Oct	.311	90	28	6	0	5	12	5	18	.354	.544
Close & Late	.275	91	25	4	2	2	15	8	10	.340	.429	vs. AL	.214	56	12	2	0	4	15	4	5	.267	.464
None on/out	.276	123	34	8	0	5	5	15	14	.360	.463	vs. NL	.266	504	134	24	5	24	77	39	87	.318	.476

1997 By Position

Position	Avg	AB	H	2B	3B	HR	RBI	BB	SO	OBP	SLG	G	GS	Innings	PO	A	E	DP	Fld Pct	Rng Fctr	In Zone	Outs	Zone Rtg	MLB Zone
As Pinch Hitter	.500	8	4	0	0	0	2	2	1	.600	.500	10	0	---	---	---	---	---	---	---	---	---	---	---
As cf	.257	552	142	26	5	28	90	41	91	.308	.475	140	131	1179.0	338	10	4	3	.989	2.66	395	329	.833	.815

Last Five Years

	Avg	AB	H	2B	3B	HR	RBI	BB	SO	OBP	SLG		Avg	AB	H	2B	3B	HR	RBI	BB	SO	OBP	SLG
vs. Left	.272	791	215	29	10	15	68	52	111	.324	.391	First Pitch	.346	347	120	16	3	9	47	10	0	.370	.487
vs. Right	.284	1904	541	96	30	72	240	162	247	.339	.480	Ahead in Count	.297	592	176	35	8	24	77	132	0	.423	.505
Groundball	.262	705	185	34	11	12	60	62	100	.325	.393	Behind in Count	.237	1242	294	47	17	29	112	0	314	.239	.372
Flyball	.262	409	107	18	10	23	55	25	55	.305	.523	Two Strikes	.216	1120	242	46	16	30	99	71	358	.264	.366
Home	.270	1277	345	60	17	29	128	103	165	.326	.412	Batting #1	.306	483	148	27	6	12	47	47	60	.370	.462
Away	.290	1418	411	65	23	58	180	111	193	.342	.491	Batting #2	.269	1564	421	60	24	47	149	116	206	.322	.428
Day	.310	888	275	44	15	31	100	69	115	.361	.498	Other	.289	648	187	38	10	28	112	51	92	.339	.508
Night	.266	1807	481	81	25	56	208	145	243	.322	.432	March/April	.249	329	82	16	3	9	38	32	43	.323	.398
Grass	.283	1679	475	81	25	60	205	145	222	.342	.468	May	.281	501	141	22	6	14	51	40	60	.336	.433
Turf	.277	1016	281	44	15	27	103	69	136	.323	.429	June	.257	448	115	22	7	19	55	39	48	.318	.464
Pre-All Star	.272	1444	393	67	21	49	166	126	170	.333	.449	July	.317	537	170	29	10	16	65	40	71	.360	.497
Post-All Star	.290	1251	363	58	19	38	142	88	188	.337	.458	August	.282	476	134	21	9	11	55	35	64	.331	.433
Scoring Posn	.271	613	166	25	11	21	221	66	90	.334	.450	Sept/Oct	.282	404	114	15	5	18	44	28	72	.331	.478
Close & Late	.294	435	128	14	7	17	63	33	48	.347	.476	vs. AL	.214	56	12	2	0	4	15	4	5	.267	.464
None on/out	.308	633	195	31	15	21	21	54	75	.366	.504	vs. NL	.282	2639	744	123	40	83	293	210	353	.336	.453

Batter vs. Pitcher (career)

Hits Best Against	Avg	AB	H	2B	3B	HR	RBI	BB	SO	OBP	SLG	Hits Worst Against	Avg	AB	H	2B	3B	HR	RBI	BB	SO	OBP	SLG
Kevin Ritz	.579	19	11	2	1	3	7	4	1	.652	1.263	Mike Munoz	.063	16	1	0	0	0	0	3	2	.211	.063
Pete Harnisch	.571	14	8	4	2	0	1	1	0	.600	1.143	Matt Ruebel	.091	11	1	0	0	0	0	0	0	.091	.091
Mike Bielecki	.500	18	9	1	2	1	2	1	2	.550	.944	Greg Swindell	.107	28	3	2	0	0	1	6	.138	.179
Omar Olivares	.455	11	5	1	1	1	4	0	1	.455	1.000	Ismael Valdes	.111	27	3	0	0	0	0	2	3	.172	.111
Rod Beck	.429	14	6	2	0	3	4	0	1	.429	1.214	Bruce Ruffin	.133	15	2	1	0	0	0	0	5	.133	.200

John Flaherty — Padres

Age 30 – Bats Right (flyball hitter)

	Avg	G	AB	R	H	2B	3B	HR	RBI	BB	SO	HBP	GDP	SB	CS	OBP	SLG	IBB	SH	SF	#Pit	#P/PA	GB	FB	G/F
1997 Season	.273	129	439	38	120	21	1	9	46	33	62	0	11	4	4	.323	.387	7	2	2	1646	3.46	158	130	1.22
Last Five Years	.261	407	1274	122	333	70	2	33	156	71	187	7	33	7	8	.302	.397	9	17	9	4707	3.42	448	408	1.10

1997 Season

	Avg	AB	H	2B	3B	HR	RBI	BB	SO	OBP	SLG		Avg	AB	H	2B	3B	HR	RBI	BB	SO	OBP	SLG
vs. Left	.265	68	18	5	0	1	5	11	8	.367	.382	First Pitch	.343	67	23	3	0	3	9	6	0	.397	.522
vs. Right	.275	371	102	16	1	8	41	22	54	.314	.388	Ahead in Count	.331	118	39	10	1	4	21	14	0	.398	.534
Groundball	.278	90	25	4	0	0	8	9	8	.343	.322	Behind in Count	.204	167	34	3	0	1	10	0	52	.202	.240
Flyball	.338	68	23	3	0	8	6	1	14	.343	.515	Two Strikes	.200	165	33	3	0	2	8	13	62	.257	.255
Home	.243	214	52	11	1	4	15	15	32	.293	.360	Batting #7	.213	136	29	5	0	3	15	11	15	.272	.316
Away	.302	225	68	10	0	5	31	18	30	.351	.413	Batting #8	.296	267	79	14	1	5	28	16	43	.333	.412
Day	.317	120	38	10	1	3	15	12	9	.373	.492	Other	.333	36	12	2	0	1	3	6	4	.429	.472
Night	.257	319	82	11	0	6	31	21	53	.303	.348	March/April	.205	73	15	2	0	0	5	7	7	.275	.233
Grass	.275	357	98	20	1	9	35	26	48	.323	.412	May	.261	88	23	3	0	3	16	4	10	.290	.398
Turf	.268	82	22	1	0	0	11	7	14	.322	.280	June	.261	88	23	8	0	1	6	2	17	.278	.386
Pre-All Star	.242	264	64	13	0	5	30	13	35	.277	.348	July	.275	69	19	4	0	1	7	5	11	.324	.377
Post-All Star	.320	175	56	8	1	4	16	20	27	.388	.446	August	.307	75	23	4	1	3	10	9	12	.376	.507
Scoring Posn	.265	117	31	4	1	1	37	15	23	.343	.342	Sept/Oct	.370	46	17	0	0	1	2	6	5	.442	.435
Close & Late	.262	65	17	1	0	0	5	7	12	.329	.277	vs. AL	.404	47	19	4	1	2	9	5	3	.462	.660
None on/out	.270	100	27	8	0	3	3	5	12	.305	.440	vs. NL	.258	392	101	17	0	7	37	28	59	.306	.355

1997 By Position

Position	Avg	AB	H	2B	3B	HR	RBI	BB	SO	OBP	SLG	G	GS	Innings	PO	A	E	DP	Fld Pct	Rng Fctr	In Zone	Outs	Zone Rtg	MLB Zone
As c	.273	436	119	21	1	9	46	31	62	.320	.388	124	119	1030.1	753	63	11	14	.987	---	---	---	---	---

Last Five Years

	Avg	AB	H	2B	3B	HR	RBI	BB	SO	OBP	SLG		Avg	AB	H	2B	3B	HR	RBI	BB	SO	OBP	SLG
vs. Left	.249	281	70	19	1	2	34	27	39	.315	.345	First Pitch	.328	186	61	11	1	8	35	8	0	.350	.527
vs. Right	.265	993	263	51	1	31	122	44	148	.298	.412	Ahead in Count	.328	305	100	26	1	15	53	35	0	.398	.567
Groundball	.303	287	87	21	0	6	39	19	27	.350	.439	Behind in Count	.190	541	103	15	0	8	42	0	158	.198	.253
Flyball	.264	227	60	13	0	9	28	5	41	.278	.441	Two Strikes	.180	506	91	13	0	8	35	28	187	.228	.253
Home	.257	611	157	39	2	18	96	36	96	.302	.416	Batting #7	.266	316	84	15	1	9	45	19	35	.309	.405
Away	.265	663	176	31	0	15	82	35	91	.302	.380	Batting #8	.267	480	128	30	1	10	52	27	74	.307	.396
Day	.261	406	106	24	1	13	60	29	66	.307	.421	Other	.253	478	121	25	0	14	59	25	78	.292	.393
Night	.262	868	227	46	1	20	96	42	141	.300	.386	March/April	.211	152	32	7	0	2	15	13	20	.277	.296
Grass	.261	1066	278	65	2	27	127	60	155	.303	.402	May	.269	227	61	14	0	6	33	11	34	.304	.410
Turf	.264	208	55	5	0	6	29	11	32	.299	.375	June	.277	235	65	16	0	12	36	8	36	.298	.498
Pre-All Star	.260	685	178	42	0	22	95	32	102	.294	.418	July	.300	263	79	18	1	6	39	9	44	.327	.445
Post-All Star	.263	589	155	28	2	11	61	39	85	.311	.374	August	.251	223	56	12	1	6	21	19	31	.309	.395
Scoring Posn	.263	323	85	20	2	4	121	24	53	.314	.375	Sept/Oct	.230	174	40	3	0	1	12	11	22	.280	.264
Close & Late	.240	171	41	3	0	4	19	12	29	.292	.327	vs. AL	.246	618	152	41	2	17	78	34	92	.289	.401
None on/out	.278	313	87	17	0	12	12	11	46	.302	.447	vs. NL	.276	656	181	29	0	16	78	37	95	.314	.393

Batter vs. Pitcher (career)

Hits Best Against	Avg	AB	H	2B	3B	HR	RBI	BB	SO	OBP	SLG	Hits Worst Against	Avg	AB	H	2B	3B	HR	RBI	BB	SO	OBP	SLG
Jack McDowell	.500	10	5	1	0	1	3	1	2	.545	.900	Chuck Finley	.077	13	1	0	0	0	0	1	1	.143	.077

Batter vs. Pitcher (career)

Hits Best Against	Avg	AB	H	2B	3B	HR	RBI	BB	SO	OBP	SLG	Hits Worst Against	Avg	AB	H	2B	3B	HR	RBI	BB	SO	OBP	SLG
Mark Leiter	.333	12	4	1	0	1	2	0	4	.333	.667	Tom Candiotti	.154	13	2	1	0	0	0	0	2	.154	.231
Al Leiter	.333	9	3	0	0	0	0	3	0	.500	.333	Kenny Rogers	.154	13	2	1	0	0	3	1	2	.214	.231
												Alex Fernandez	.167	12	2	0	0	0	0	0	0	.167	.167
												Charles Nagy	.200	20	4	2	0	0	0	0	4	.200	.300

Huck Flener — Blue Jays
Age 29 – Pitches Left (flyball pitcher)

	ERA	W	L	Sv	G	GS	IP	BB	SO	Avg	H	2B	3B	HR	RBI	OBP	SLG	GF	IR	IRS	Hld	SvOp	SB	CS	GB	FB	G/F
1997 Season	9.87	0	1	0	8	1	17.1	6	9	.444	40	7	1	3	16	.474	.644	3	2	1	0	0	1	0	26	33	0.79
Career (1993-1997)	5.51	3	3	0	29	12	94.2	43	55	.297	115	27	3	12	54	.365	.475	4	5	1	2	0	4	0	117	130	0.90

1997 Season

	ERA	W	L	Sv	G	GS	IP	H	HR	BB	SO		Avg	AB	H	2B	3B	HR	RBI	BB	SO	OBP	SLG
Home	3.60	0	0	0	2	0	5.0	7	0	3	2	vs. Left	.591	22	13	1	0	0	3	2	2	.600	.636
Away	12.41	0	1	0	6	1	12.1	33	3	3	7	vs. Right	.397	68	27	6	1	3	13	4	7	.431	.647

Darrin Fletcher — Expos
Age 31 – Bats Left (flyball hitter)

	Avg	G	AB	R	H	2B	3B	HR	RBI	BB	SO	HBP	GDP	SB	CS	OBP	SLG	IBB	SH	SF	#Pit	#P/PA	GB	FB	G/F
1997 Season	.277	96	310	39	86	20	1	17	55	17	35	5	6	1	1	.323	.513	3	0	2	1093	3.27	105	113	0.93
Last Five Years	.269	560	1735	183	466	101	4	59	274	135	163	24	47	1	2	.326	.433	14	2	23	6786	3.53	623	618	1.01

1997 Season

	Avg	AB	H	2B	3B	HR	RBI	BB	SO	OBP	SLG		Avg	AB	H	2B	3B	HR	RBI	BB	SO	OBP	SLG
vs. Left	.253	75	19	4	0	4	16	3	11	.291	.467	First Pitch	.188	48	9	3	0	1	3	2	0	.235	.313
vs. Right	.285	235	67	16	1	13	39	14	24	.333	.528	Ahead in Count	.356	87	31	9	1	6	18	8	0	.412	.690
Groundball	.328	58	19	7	0	3	9	4	7	.375	.603	Behind in Count	.256	129	33	4	0	6	23	0	29	.260	.426
Flyball	.256	43	11	2	0	4	8	0	6	.273	.581	Two Strikes	.162	105	17	4	0	1	7	7	35	.219	.229
Home	.307	150	46	9	0	10	27	13	15	.373	.567	Batting #5	.282	131	37	9	1	7	23	10	19	.340	.527
Away	.250	160	40	11	1	7	28	4	20	.274	.463	Batting #6	.217	69	15	3	0	1	9	5	6	.276	.304
Day	.278	97	27	4	1	8	25	5	12	.314	.588	Other	.309	110	34	8	0	9	23	2	10	.333	.627
Night	.277	213	59	16	0	9	30	12	23	.328	.479	March/April	.259	54	14	0	1	3	13	2	6	.281	.463
Grass	.259	116	30	8	0	6	23	4	12	.285	.483	May	.365	63	23	4	0	6	15	5	4	.412	.714
Turf	.289	194	56	12	1	11	32	13	23	.346	.531	June	.200	40	8	3	0	1	7	2	4	.238	.350
Pre-All Star	.288	163	47	7	1	10	35	10	14	.328	.528	July	.268	41	11	3	0	1	1	1	5	.302	.415
Post-All Star	.265	147	39	13	0	7	20	7	21	.319	.497	August	.282	71	20	6	0	6	17	2	8	.311	.620
Scoring Posn	.305	95	29	3	1	5	38	8	12	.370	.516	Sept/Oct	.244	41	10	4	0	0	2	5	8	.360	.341
Close & Late	.345	55	19	3	0	3	9	4	11	.400	.564	vs. AL	.200	25	5	1	0	1	7	2	4	.259	.360
None on/out	.242	66	16	5	0	2	2	3	8	.275	.409	vs. NL	.284	285	81	19	1	16	48	15	31	.329	.526

1997 By Position

Position	Avg	AB	H	2B	3B	HR	RBI	BB	SO	OBP	SLG		G	GS	Innings	PO	A	E	DP	Fld Pct	Rng Fctr	In Zone	Zone Outs	Zone Rtg	MLB Zone
As Pinch Hitter	.214	14	3	1	0	1	1	0	4	.267	.500		15	0	---	---	---	---	---	---	---	---	---	---	---
As c	.280	296	83	19	1	16	54	17	31	.326	.514		83	79	685.2	607	24	4	5	.994	---	---	---	---	---

Last Five Years

	Avg	AB	H	2B	3B	HR	RBI	BB	SO	OBP	SLG		Avg	AB	H	2B	3B	HR	RBI	BB	SO	OBP	SLG
vs. Left	.246	293	72	15	0	10	55	24	39	.311	.399	First Pitch	.248	250	62	13	1	5	32	10	0	.279	.368
vs. Right	.273	1442	394	86	4	49	219	111	124	.329	.440	Ahead in Count	.324	490	159	40	2	19	95	76	0	.413	.531
Groundball	.291	477	139	32	1	15	70	38	45	.348	.457	Behind in Count	.233	678	158	29	1	24	91	0	140	.243	.385
Flyball	.289	287	83	17	2	13	52	23	29	.350	.498	Two Strikes	.224	625	140	29	1	18	78	49	163	.288	.360
Home	.281	818	230	58	1	29	134	69	76	.340	.461	Batting #5	.265	804	213	43	1	30	119	62	66	.324	.433
Away	.257	917	236	43	3	30	140	66	87	.313	.409	Batting #6	.271	388	105	21	0	10	64	36	39	.335	.402
Day	.271	468	127	25	1	19	80	32	46	.320	.451	Other	.273	543	148	37	3	19	91	37	58	.323	.457
Night	.268	1267	339	76	3	40	194	103	117	.328	.427	March/April	.298	248	74	13	1	11	46	18	21	.357	.492
Grass	.261	621	162	25	2	21	98	45	56	.313	.409	May	.252	313	79	13	0	9	50	28	31	.309	.380
Turf	.273	1114	304	76	2	38	176	90	107	.333	.447	June	.280	286	80	22	0	11	57	22	24	.335	.472
Pre-All Star	.276	943	260	52	2	37	174	79	83	.334	.453	July	.290	317	92	19	1	11	52	30	27	.352	.461
Post-All Star	.260	792	206	49	2	22	100	56	80	.317	.410	August	.279	330	92	19	0	15	54	20	36	.328	.473
Scoring Posn	.248	517	128	32	1	17	210	65	57	.330	.412	Sept/Oct	.203	241	49	15	2	2	15	17	24	.269	.307
Close & Late	.294	272	80	18	1	6	41	34	39	.382	.434	vs. AL	.200	25	5	1	0	1	7	2	4	.259	.360
None on/out	.279	376	105	20	2	17	17	21	30	.324	.479	vs. NL	.270	1710	461	100	4	58	267	133	159	.327	.435

Batter vs. Pitcher (career)

Hits Best Against	Avg	AB	H	2B	3B	HR	RBI	BB	SO	OBP	SLG	Hits Worst Against	Avg	AB	H	2B	3B	HR	RBI	BB	SO	OBP	SLG
Orel Hershiser	.600	10	6	1	0	0	1	2	0	.667	.700	Mike Harkey	.000	10	0	0	0	0	0	1	1	.091	.000
Todd Jones	.556	9	5	1	0	0	0	2	1	.636	.667	Tim Pugh	.000	10	0	0	0	0	0	1	0	.167	.000
Jaime Navarro	.500	10	5	0	0	1	1	2	0	.583	.800	Curt Schilling	.031	32	1	0	0	0	4	1	6	.059	.031
Andy Ashby	.471	17	8	2	0	2	5	4	0	.591	.941	Joey Hamilton	.071	14	1	0	0	0	0	1	0	.133	.071
Mark Clark	.455	11	5	1	0	2	3	0	0	.455	1.091	Ismael Valdes	.083	12	1	0	0	0	0	1	0	.154	.083

146

Bryce Florie — Brewers
Age 28 – Pitches Right (groundball pitcher)

	ERA	W	L	Sv	G	GS	IP	BB	SO	Avg	H	2B	3B	HR	RBI	OBP	SLG	GF	IR	IRS	Hld	SvOp	SB	CS	GB	FB	G/F
1997 Season	4.32	4	4	0	32	8	75.0	42	53	.262	74	14	3	4	42	.360	.376	6	32	14	0	1	12	3	138	49	2.82
Career (1994-1997)	3.90	8	9	1	142	8	221.1	123	192	.239	196	31	7	16	112	.344	.353	36	106	40	17	8	34	5	377	138	2.73

1997 Season

	ERA	W	L	Sv	G	GS	IP	H	HR	BB	SO		Avg	AB	H	2B	3B	HR	RBI	BB	SO	OBP	SLG
Home	3.86	0	3	0	16	4	37.1	37	1	20	29	vs. Left	.211	133	28	7	3	1	18	28	29	.354	.331
Away	4.78	4	1	0	16	4	37.2	37	3	22	24	vs. Right	.309	149	46	7	0	3	24	14	24	.365	.416
Starter	3.73	3	3	0	8	8	41.0	33	1	21	31	Scoring Posn	.264	91	24	4	1	2	39	15	15	.355	.396
Reliever	5.03	1	1	0	24	0	34.0	41	3	21	22	Close & Late	.364	33	12	4	0	1	6	6	8	.462	.576
0 Days rest (Relief)	4.91	0	0	0	4	0	3.2	6	0	2	3	None on/out	.323	62	20	6	0	1	9	10	.408	.468
1 or 2 Days rest	6.10	1	0	0	8	0	10.1	15	2	9	6	First Pitch	.263	38	10	2	0	1	6	2	0	.317	.395
3+ Days rest	4.50	1	0	0	12	0	20.0	20	1	10	13	Ahead in Count	.234	111	26	2	2	2	19	0	41	.239	.342
Pre-All Star	5.10	1	1	0	22	0	30.0	36	3	18	21	Behind in Count	.254	63	16	2	0	1	11	21	0	.440	.333
Post-All Star	3.80	3	3	0	10	8	45.0	38	1	24	32	Two Strikes	.211	128	27	5	2	2	22	19	53	.314	.328

Career (1994-1997)

	ERA	W	L	Sv	G	GS	IP	H	HR	BB	SO		Avg	AB	H	2B	3B	HR	RBI	BB	SO	OBP	SLG
Home	3.89	0	6	1	72	4	111.0	106	8	64	107	vs. Left	.222	369	82	15	4	6	46	70	78	.348	.333
Away	3.92	8	3	0	70	4	110.1	90	8	59	85	vs. Right	.253	450	114	16	3	10	66	53	114	.341	.369
Day	3.76	2	1	0	50	1	76.2	63	11	32	68	Inning 1-6	.242	281	68	11	4	5	39	40	60	.336	.363
Night	3.98	6	8	1	92	7	144.2	133	5	91	124	Inning 7+	.238	538	128	20	3	11	73	83	132	.349	.348
Grass	3.62	6	8	1	122	8	191.2	164	14	109	158	None on/out	.249	401	100	15	5	10	10	59	97	.354	.387
Turf	5.76	2	1	0	20	0	29.2	32	2	14	34	Runners on	.230	418	96	16	2	6	102	64	95	.335	.321
March/April	4.61	1	0	0	19	0	27.1	28	2	18	31	Scoring Posn	.226	266	60	8	2	4	94	51	64	.348	.316
May	3.24	1	2	0	24	0	33.1	28	3	19	33	Close & Late	.250	228	57	9	0	6	31	45	63	.375	.368
June	2.17	1	1	0	26	0	37.1	23	2	21	27	None on/out	.256	176	45	7	3	3	30	41	.370	.381
July	3.88	3	2	0	33	3	51.0	51	3	30	44	vs. 1st Batr (relief)	.218	110	24	2	0	2	15	20	29	.351	.291
August	4.50	2	2	1	28	4	54.0	45	3	27	36	1st Inning Pitched	.243	453	110	16	3	8	85	81	102	.365	.344
Sept/Oct	5.89	0	2	0	12	1	18.1	21	3	8	21	First 15 Pitches	.260	369	96	14	2	9	58	63	76	.375	.382
Starter	3.73	3	3	0	8	8	41.0	33	1	21	31	Pitch 16-30	.212	259	55	6	3	3	34	33	69	.306	.293
Reliever	3.94	5	6	1	134	0	180.1	163	15	102	161	Pitch 31-45	.248	101	25	5	1	4	12	11	26	.333	.436
0 Days rest (Relief)	3.48	0	0	0	15	0	20.2	20	2	7	20	Pitch 46+	.222	90	20	6	1	0	8	16	21	.340	.311
1 or 2 Days rest	4.08	4	5	1	69	0	92.2	90	10	54	85	First Pitch	.283	99	28	4	2	3	13	8	0	.372	.455
3+ Days rest	3.90	1	1	0	50	0	67.0	53	3	41	56	Ahead in Count	.192	359	69	9	3	4	38	0	153	.199	.267
vs. AL	4.65	4	5	0	44	8	91.0	91	6	53	64	Behind in Count	.294	180	53	7	0	6	37	69	0	.490	.433
vs. NL	3.38	4	4	1	98	0	130.1	105	10	70	128	Two Strikes	.171	398	68	10	4	3	46	45	192	.259	.239
Pre-All Star	3.58	4	3	0	79	0	110.2	98	8	66	104	Pre-All Star	.240	409	98	17	0	8	57	66	104	.352	.340
Post-All Star	4.23	4	6	1	63	8	110.2	98	8	57	88	Post-All Star	.239	410	98	14	7	8	55	57	88	.337	.366

Cliff Floyd — Marlins
Age 25 – Bats Left (groundball hitter)

	Avg	G	AB	R	H	2B	3B	HR	RBI	BB	SO	HBP	GDP	SB	CS	OBP	SLG	IBB	SH	SF	#Pit	#P/PA	GB	FB	G/F
1997 Season	.234	61	137	23	32	9	1	6	19	24	33	2	4	6	2	.354	.445	0	1	1	661	4.01	42	43	0.98
Career (1993-1997)	.247	317	798	104	197	44	9	18	96	85	179	11	11	26	6	.325	.392	1	4	7	3319	3.67	309	189	1.63

1997 Season

	Avg	AB	H	2B	3B	HR	RBI	BB	SO	OBP	SLG		Avg	AB	H	2B	3B	HR	RBI	BB	SO	OBP	SLG
vs. Left	.250	16	4	2	0	0	0	3	6	.368	.375	Scoring Posn	.176	34	6	0	0	2	11	9	10	.341	.353
vs. Right	.231	121	28	7	1	6	19	21	27	.352	.455	Close & Late	.233	30	7	3	1	1	3	7	6	.378	.500
Home	.239	67	16	7	0	2	8	10	14	.342	.433	None on/out	.250	28	7	2	0	1	1	5	6	.364	.429
Away	.229	70	16	2	1	4	11	14	19	.365	.457	Batting #1	.320	25	8	4	0	0	2	3	5	.393	.480
First Pitch	.222	9	2	1	0	0	0	0	0	.222	.333	Batting #3	.294	51	15	3	0	4	10	4	12	.368	.588
Ahead in Count	.217	46	10	3	0	2	5	10	0	.357	.413	Other	.148	61	9	2	1	2	7	17	16	.329	.311
Behind in Count	.216	51	11	3	1	2	6	0	22	.245	.431	Pre-All Star	.221	86	19	4	1	2	5	16	21	.350	.360
Two Strikes	.169	59	10	3	0	3	11	14	33	.342	.373	Post-All Star	.255	51	13	5	0	4	14	8	12	.361	.588

Career (1993-1997)

	Avg	AB	H	2B	3B	HR	RBI	BB	SO	OBP	SLG		Avg	AB	H	2B	3B	HR	RBI	BB	SO	OBP	SLG
vs. Left	.274	106	29	6	0	0	10	9	27	.325	.330	First Pitch	.310	126	39	9	2	2	16	0	0	.326	.460
vs. Right	.243	692	168	38	9	18	86	76	152	.325	.402	Ahead in Count	.325	203	66	13	2	8	32	39	0	.436	.527
Groundball	.262	221	58	12	1	6	24	18	42	.322	.407	Behind in Count	.176	352	62	18	5	6	33	0	150	.188	.307
Flyball	.187	123	23	5	2	2	15	11	31	.282	.309	Two Strikes	.163	344	56	13	4	6	35	46	179	.270	.276
Home	.243	378	92	23	4	8	49	44	79	.330	.389	Batting #2	.265	181	48	8	3	2	21	15	31	.323	.376
Away	.250	420	105	21	5	10	47	41	100	.320	.395	Batting #3	.229	166	38	9	3	6	18	18	37	.321	.428
Day	.235	230	54	16	1	10	36	29	55	.326	.443	Other	.246	451	111	27	3	10	57	52	111	.327	.386
Night	.252	568	143	28	8	8	60	56	124	.325	.371	March/April	.254	126	32	6	1	2	10	11	28	.312	.365
Grass	.253	372	94	22	3	11	41	41	80	.330	.417	May	.237	173	41	8	2	3	19	22	46	.335	.358
Turf	.242	426	103	22	6	7	55	44	99	.321	.371	June	.262	145	38	8	1	3	23	13	23	.327	.393
Pre-All Star	.256	480	123	26	6	8	58	49	105	.330	.385	July	.299	144	43	11	4	3	17	16	27	.366	.493
Post-All Star	.233	318	74	18	3	10	38	36	74	.318	.403	August	.176	85	15	4	1	1	7	9	26	.278	.282
Scoring Posn	.279	204	57	8	2	6	72	33	49	.374	.426	Sept/Oct	.224	125	28	7	0	6	20	14	29	.308	.424
Close & Late	.280	150	42	8	3	5	20	20	33	.365	.473	vs. AL	.143	21	3	2	0	1	3	3	4	.250	.381
None on/out	.189	169	32	8	1	4	4	10	37	.247	.320	vs. NL	.250	777	194	42	9	17	93	82	175	.327	.393

Batter vs. Pitcher (career)

Hits Best Against	Avg	AB	H	2B	3B	HR	RBI	BB	SO	OBP	SLG	Hits Worst Against	Avg	AB	H	2B	3B	HR	RBI	BB	SO	OBP	SLG
Jon Lieber	.467	15	7	0	1	0	0	1	1	.500	.600	Doug Drabek	.000	11	0	0	0	0	0	0	3	.000	.000
Andy Benes	.364	11	4	0	2	0	3	1	3	.417	.727	Mark Gardner	.154	13	2	0	0	1	3	1	2	.267	.385
Greg Maddux	.313	16	5	1	0	1	4	1	4	.353	.563	Bob Tewksbury	.182	11	2	1	0	0	0	0	2	.182	.273

Batter vs. Pitcher (career)

Hits Best Against	Avg	AB	H	2B	3B	HR	RBI	BB	SO	OBP	SLG	Hits Worst Against	Avg	AB	H	2B	3B	HR	RBI	BB	SO	OBP	SLG
Bobby Jones	.308	13	4	1	0	0	0	2	2	.400	.385	Pedro Astacio	.200	15	3	0	0	0	1	0	1	.200	.200
												Pete Harnisch	.231	13	3	0	0	0	1	0	5	.286	.231

Chad Fonville — White Sox
Age 27 – Bats Both

	Avg	G	AB	R	H	2B	3B	HR	RBI	BB	SO	HBP	GDP	SB	CS	OBP	SLG	IBB	SH	SF	#Pit	#P/PA	GB	FB	G/F
1997 Season	.130	18	23	2	3	0	0	0	2	3	4	0	0	2	1	.231	.130	0	1	0	100	3.70	12	2	6.00
Career (1995-1997)	.244	223	544	79	133	10	2	0	31	43	77	1	4	29	10	.301	.270	2	10	0	2207	3.69	270	74	3.65

1997 Season

	Avg	AB	H	2B	3B	HR	RBI	BB	SO	OBP	SLG		Avg	AB	H	2B	3B	HR	RBI	BB	SO	OBP	SLG
vs. Left	.200	5	1	0	0	0	0	0	0	.200	.200	Scoring Posn	.500	6	3	0	0	0	2	0	1	.500	.500
vs. Right	.111	18	2	0	0	0	2	3	4	.238	.111	Close & Late	.000	5	0	0	0	0	0	2	2	.286	.000

Career (1995-1997)

	Avg	AB	H	2B	3B	HR	RBI	BB	SO	OBP	SLG		Avg	AB	H	2B	3B	HR	RBI	BB	SO	OBP	SLG
vs. Left	.212	151	32	5	0	0	7	7	30	.247	.245	First Pitch	.345	55	19	2	0	0	3	2	0	.368	.382
vs. Right	.257	393	101	5	2	0	24	36	47	.321	.280	Ahead in Count	.243	74	18	1	0	0	4	31	0	.467	.257
Groundball	.259	143	37	3	1	0	10	10	18	.307	.294	Behind in Count	.225	293	66	5	1	0	17	0	73	.228	.249
Flyball	.267	105	28	1	0	0	3	4	17	.300	.276	Two Strikes	.207	266	55	4	1	0	13	10	77	.238	.229
Home	.236	288	68	3	1	0	15	26	46	.299	.253	Batting #1	.236	250	59	6	1	0	16	21	35	.295	.268
Away	.254	256	65	7	1	0	16	17	31	.303	.289	Batting #2	.258	155	40	3	1	0	6	12	13	.311	.290
Day	.233	133	31	3	0	0	3	8	20	.277	.256	Other	.245	139	34	1	0	0	9	10	29	.300	.252
Night	.248	411	102	7	2	0	28	35	57	.309	.275	March/April	.356	45	16	1	0	0	4	7	8	.442	.378
Grass	.254	421	107	7	2	0	24	39	63	.317	.280	May	.143	84	12	2	0	0	1	4	12	.182	.167
Turf	.211	123	26	3	0	0	7	4	14	.242	.236	June	.346	52	18	1	0	0	4	6	6	.414	.365
Pre-All Star	.235	221	52	5	1	0	12	20	35	.299	.267	July	.190	116	22	2	1	0	9	5	23	.223	.224
Post-All Star	.251	323	81	5	1	0	19	23	42	.303	.272	August	.311	119	37	2	0	0	8	13	17	.383	.328
Scoring Posn	.297	118	35	1	2	0	31	11	19	.362	.339	Sept/Oct	.219	128	28	2	1	0	5	8	11	.265	.250
Close & Late	.152	79	12	0	0	0	1	9	19	.239	.152	vs. AL	.111	9	1	0	0	0	1	1	1	.200	.111
None on/out	.253	182	46	4	0	0	10	13	28	.303	.275	vs. NL	.247	535	132	10	2	0	30	42	76	.303	.273

Batter vs. Pitcher (career)

Hits Best Against	Avg	AB	H	2B	3B	HR	RBI	BB	SO	OBP	SLG	Hits Worst Against	Avg	AB	H	2B	3B	HR	RBI	BB	SO	OBP	SLG
Jaime Navarro	.364	11	4	1	0	0	0	2	0	.462	.455	Joey Hamilton	.083	12	1	0	0	0	1	1	3	.154	.083
Mark Leiter	.364	11	4	0	0	0	1	0	1	.364	.364	Kevin Ritz	.154	13	2	0	0	0	1	4	1	.353	.154
Jeff Fassero	.364	11	4	1	0	0	1	0	0	.364	.455												

Tom Fordham — White Sox
Age 24 – Pitches Left (flyball pitcher)

	ERA	W	L	Sv	G	GS	IP	BB	SO	Avg	H	2B	3B	HR	RBI	OBP	SLG	GF	IR	IRS	Hld	SvOp	SB	CS	GB	FB	G/F
1997 Season	6.23	0	1	0	7	1	17.1	10	10	.266	17	3	1	2	15	.364	.438	1	7	5	1	1	1	0	13	32	0.41

1997 Season

	ERA	W	L	Sv	G	GS	IP	H	HR	BB	SO		Avg	AB	H	2B	3B	HR	RBI	BB	SO	OBP	SLG
Home	4.09	0	0	0	5	1	11.0	6	1	5	5	vs. Left	.200	20	4	2	0	0	5	2	3	.261	.300
Away	9.95	0	1	0	2	0	6.1	11	1	5	5	vs. Right	.295	44	13	1	1	2	10	8	7	.407	.500

Brook Fordyce — Reds
Age 28 – Bats Right

	Avg	G	AB	R	H	2B	3B	HR	RBI	BB	SO	HBP	GDP	SB	CS	OBP	SLG	IBB	SH	SF	#Pit	#P/PA	GB	FB	G/F
1997 Season	.208	47	96	7	20	5	0	1	8	8	15	0	0	2	0	.267	.292	1	0	1	390	3.71	36	35	1.03
Career (1995-1997)	.219	55	105	8	23	7	0	1	9	12	16	0	0	2	0	.297	.314	1	0	1	437	3.70	40	38	1.05

1997 Season

	Avg	AB	H	2B	3B	HR	RBI	BB	SO	OBP	SLG		Avg	AB	H	2B	3B	HR	RBI	BB	SO	OBP	SLG
vs. Left	.152	33	5	1	0	0	2	3	2	.216	.212	Scoring Posn	.222	27	6	2	0	0	5	6	9	.353	.296
vs. Right	.238	63	15	4	0	1	6	5	13	.294	.349	Close & Late	.154	13	2	1	0	0	2	2	4	.267	.231

Tony Fossas — Cardinals
Age 40 – Pitches Left

	ERA	W	L	Sv	G	GS	IP	BB	SO	Avg	H	2B	3B	HR	RBI	OBP	SLG	GF	IR	IRS	Hld	SvOp	SB	CS	GB	FB	G/F
1997 Season	3.83	2	7	0	71	0	51.2	26	41	.298	62	8	0	7	25	.377	.438	14	60	6	16	1	10	4	66	57	1.16
Last Five Years	3.57	8	12	3	309	0	209.1	87	187	.253	206	34	2	25	113	.327	.391	78	249	54	72	11	14	5	274	228	1.20

1997 Season

	ERA	W	L	Sv	G	GS	IP	H	HR	BB	SO		Avg	AB	H	2B	3B	HR	RBI	BB	SO	OBP	SLG
Home	3.18	2	4	0	38	0	22.2	30	3	17	22	vs. Left	.266	94	25	4	0	0	6	9	28	.337	.309
Away	4.34	0	3	0	33	0	29.0	32	4	9	19	vs. Right	.325	114	37	4	0	7	19	17	13	.409	.544
Day	6.08	1	2	0	21	0	13.1	18	4	8	13	Inning 1-6	.250	24	6	0	0	1	1	1	4	.280	.375
Night	3.05	1	5	0	50	0	38.1	44	3	18	28	Inning 7+	.304	184	56	8	0	6	24	25	37	.389	.446
Grass	3.60	2	5	0	56	0	40.0	49	6	19	31	None on	.333	96	32	3	0	5	9	15	.491	.521
Turf	4.63	0	2	0	15	0	11.2	13	1	7	10	Runners on	.268	112	30	5	0	2	20	17	26	.362	.366
March/April	2.45	1	0	0	10	0	7.1	3	1	5	9	Scoring Posn	.188	69	13	2	0	1	16	14	19	.321	.261
May	3.00	0	1	0	12	0	6.0	10	0	2	6	Close & Late	.308	104	32	4	0	3	13	17	24	.407	.433
June	0.00	0	0	0	12	0	13.0	9	0	3	10	None on/out	.320	50	16	2	0	2	4	7	.382	.480
July	6.23	0	2	0	13	0	8.2	11	2	7	7	vs. 1st Batr (relief)	.219	64	14	2	0	2	4	17	.296	.250
August	3.38	0	2	0	14	0	8.0	11	2	4	5	1st Inning Pitched	.299	184	55	8	0	5	22	24	37	.381	.424
Sept/Oct	9.35	1	2	0	10	0	8.2	18	2	5	4	First 15 Pitches	.304	161	49	7	0	4	15	21	30	.386	.422

148

1997 Season

	ERA	W	L	Sv	G	GS	IP	H	HR	BB	SO
Starter	0.00	0	0	0	0	0	0.0	0	0	0	0
Reliever	3.83	2	7	0	71	0	51.2	62	7	26	41
0 Days rest (Relief)	5.87	1	5	0	26	0	15.1	19	2	12	18
1 or 2 Days rest	3.92	1	1	0	27	0	20.2	28	3	7	13
3+ Days rest	1.72	0	1	0	18	0	15.2	15	2	7	10
vs. AL	5.06	0	1	0	5	0	5.1	9	3	1	3
vs. NL	3.69	2	6	0	66	0	46.1	53	4	25	38
Pre-All Star	1.88	1	1	0	37	0	28.2	25	3	11	28
Post-All Star	6.26	1	6	0	34	0	23.0	37	4	15	13

	Avg	AB	H	2B	3B	HR	RBI	BB	SO	OBP	SLG
Pitch 16-30	.262	42	11	1	0	2	9	5	11	.340	.429
Pitch 31-45	.400	5	2	0	0	1	1	0	0	.400	1.000
Pitch 46+	.000	0	0	0	0	0	0	0	0	.000	.000
First Pitch	.360	25	9	1	0	2	4	3	0	.429	.640
Ahead in Count	.280	93	26	3	0	3	7	0	29	.287	.409
Behind in Count	.343	35	12	0	0	1	2	14	0	.520	.429
Two Strikes	.220	109	24	3	0	3	11	9	41	.286	.330
Pre-All Star	.229	109	25	4	0	3	12	11	28	.306	.349
Post-All Star	.374	99	37	4	0	4	13	15	13	.452	.535

Last Five Years

	ERA	W	L	Sv	G	GS	IP	H	HR	BB	SO
Home	2.52	6	7	1	155	0	107.0	91	8	51	104
Away	4.66	2	5	2	154	0	102.1	115	17	36	83
Day	3.22	3	4	0	98	0	64.1	64	7	29	58
Night	3.72	5	8	3	211	0	145.0	142	18	58	129
Grass	3.51	6	10	1	227	0	153.2	153	20	68	132
Turf	3.72	2	2	2	82	0	55.2	53	5	19	55
March/April	3.30	2	2	0	43	0	30.0	27	3	15	31
May	2.76	0	2	1	53	0	29.1	23	3	14	28
June	2.74	2	1	1	57	0	42.2	40	7	14	32
July	3.57	2	2	1	56	0	40.1	41	5	17	41
August	4.01	1	2	0	50	0	33.2	34	3	13	26
Sept/Oct	5.13	1	3	0	50	0	33.1	41	4	14	29
Starter	0.00	0	0	0	0	0	0.0	0	0	0	0
Reliever	3.57	8	12	3	309	0	209.1	206	25	87	187
0 Days rest (Relief)	4.00	2	6	1	106	0	63.0	62	6	27	59
1 or 2 Days rest	4.11	4	4	1	118	0	87.2	89	11	37	80
3+ Days rest	2.30	2	2	1	85	0	58.2	55	8	23	48
vs. AL	4.99	3	2	1	120	0	79.1	82	13	31	73
vs. NL	2.70	5	10	2	189	0	130.0	124	12	56	114
Pre-All Star	3.11	4	5	3	167	0	113.0	100	16	45	103
Post-All Star	4.11	4	7	0	142	0	96.1	106	9	42	84

	Avg	AB	H	2B	3B	HR	RBI	BB	SO	OBP	SLG
vs. Left	.204	382	78	15	0	5	45	33	123	.271	.283
vs. Right	.296	433	128	19	2	20	68	54	64	.375	.487
Inning 1-6	.178	101	18	0	1	3	5	10	24	.252	.287
Inning 7+	.263	714	188	34	1	22	108	77	163	.338	.406
None on	.267	397	106	16	1	14	14	35	95	.329	.418
Runners on	.239	418	100	18	1	11	99	52	92	.325	.366
Scoring Posn	.213	263	56	12	0	4	82	40	66	.317	.304
Close & Late	.254	323	82	13	0	10	47	40	79	.338	.387
None on/out	.266	188	50	7	0	7	7	16	43	.330	.415
vs. 1st Batr (relief)	.201	278	56	9	0	6	35	25	79	.275	.299
1st Inning Pitched	.259	718	186	32	1	22	107	79	166	.334	.398
First 15 Pitches	.257	634	163	29	0	16	79	64	143	.328	.379
Pitch 16-30	.242	149	36	4	2	8	32	20	38	.333	.456
Pitch 31-45	.231	26	6	1	0	1	1	3	3	.310	.385
Pitch 46+	.167	6	1	0	0	0	1	0	3	.167	.167
First Pitch	.340	97	33	7	0	5	20	10	0	.404	.567
Ahead in Count	.197	402	79	9	1	13	45	0	148	.198	.321
Behind in Count	.322	146	47	6	1	4	20	43	0	.474	.459
Two Strikes	.189	419	79	8	1	12	50	34	187	.251	.298
Post-All Star	.277	383	106	12	2	9	54	42	84	.351	.389

Pitcher vs. Batter (career)

Pitches Best Vs.	Avg	AB	H	2B	3B	HR	RBI	BB	SO	OBP	SLG
Ryan Klesko	.100	10	1	1	0	0	1	4		.182	.200
Wally Joyner	.118	17	2	0	0	1	6	0	8	.118	.294
Ken Griffey Jr	.130	23	3	0	0	1	3	1	7	.167	.261
Fred McGriff	.200	25	5	1	0	0	2	1	8	.231	.240
Lance Johnson	.214	14	3	0	0	0	1	0	1	.214	.214

Pitches Worst Vs.	Avg	AB	H	2B	3B	HR	RBI	BB	SO	OBP	SLG
Robin Ventura	.500	8	4	0	0	1	2	4	2	.667	.875
John Olerud	.364	11	4	1	0	0	3	2	0	.467	.455
Mickey Tettleton	.333	12	4	1	0	2	5	2	3	.429	.917
Ozzie Guillen	.313	16	5	0	0	0	2	1	6	.353	.313
Jim Eisenreich	.308	13	4	0	0	0	2	0	3	.308	.308

Kevin Foster — Cubs

Age 29 – Pitches Right (flyball pitcher)

	ERA	W	L	Sv	G	GS	IP	BB	SO	Avg	H	2B	3B	HR	RBI	OBP	SLG	CG	ShO	Sup	QS	#P/S	SB	CS	GB	FB	G/F
1997 Season	4.61	10	7	0	26	25	146.1	66	118	.255	141	30	0	27	70	.333	.456	1	0	6.03	17	93	21	6	142	213	0.67
Career (1993-1997)	4.71	32	29	0	88	83	488.2	208	398	.255	471	96	4	85	243	.331	.449	2	0	5.58	41	94	53	24	454	687	0.66

1997 Season

	ERA	W	L	Sv	G	GS	IP	H	HR	BB	SO
Home	3.75	6	2	0	13	13	81.2	73	14	33	62
Away	5.71	4	5	0	13	12	64.2	68	13	33	56
Day	3.77	9	4	0	17	16	100.1	86	18	42	83
Night	6.46	1	3	0	9	9	46.0	55	9	24	35
Grass	4.73	9	6	0	23	22	129.1	128	25	55	100
Turf	3.71	1	1	0	3	3	17.0	13	2	11	18
March/April	4.91	2	2	0	5	5	29.1	30	8	14	18
May	3.25	5	1	0	6	6	36.0	27	4	12	28
June	5.00	2	2	0	5	5	27.0	32	4	17	20
July	5.68	1	1	0	6	6	31.2	36	7	14	39
August	3.54	0	0	0	3	3	20.1	14	3	8	11
Sept/Oct	13.50	1	0	0	1	0	2.0	2	1	1	2
Starter	4.49	10	6	0	25	25	144.1	139	26	65	116
Reliever	13.50	0	1	0	1	0	2.0	2	1	1	2
0-3 Days Rest (Start)	0.00	0	0	0	0	0	0.0	0	0	0	0
4 Days Rest	4.80	8	4	0	17	17	95.2	93	17	45	80
5+ Days Rest	3.88	2	2	0	8	8	48.2	46	9	20	36
vs. AL	2.92	2	0	0	2	2	12.1	14	1	6	7
vs. NL	4.77	8	7	0	24	23	134.0	127	26	60	111
Pre-All Star	4.10	10	5	0	17	17	98.2	96	16	46	70
Post-All Star	5.66	0	2	0	9	8	47.2	45	11	20	48

	Avg	AB	H	2B	3B	HR	RBI	BB	SO	OBP	SLG
vs. Left	.280	261	73	17	0	13	36	33	43	.357	.494
vs. Right	.233	292	68	13	0	14	34	33	75	.311	.421
Inning 1-6	.241	493	119	24	0	24	61	60	109	.323	.436
Inning 7+	.367	60	22	6	0	3	9	6	9	.418	.617
None on	.255	341	87	19	0	17	17	38	67	.332	.460
Runners on	.255	212	54	11	0	10	53	28	51	.335	.448
Scoring Posn	.210	119	25	2	0	4	39	17	33	.299	.328
Close & Late	.406	32	13	5	0	1	6	3	9	.444	.656
None on/out	.287	150	43	9	0	10	10	19	29	.367	.547
vs. 1st Batr (relief)	.000	1	0	0	0	0	0	0	0	.000	.000
1st Inning Pitched	.260	100	26	1	0	5	14	19	22	.383	.420
First 75 Pitches	.239	427	102	20	0	19	53	50	93	.318	.419
Pitch 76-90	.346	78	27	8	0	6	11	9	13	.414	.679
Pitch 91-105	.275	40	11	1	0	2	5	6	10	.370	.450
Pitch 106+	.125	8	1	1	0	0	1	1	2	.200	.250
First Pitch	.305	95	29	4	0	7	15	2	0	.313	.568
Ahead in Count	.191	236	45	9	0	8	25	0	102	.188	.331
Behind in Count	.356	118	42	10	0	9	25	37	0	.506	.669
Two Strikes	.158	240	38	7	0	6	19	27	118	.244	.263
Pre-All Star	.256	375	96	20	0	16	42	46	70	.338	.437
Post-All Star	.253	178	45	10	0	11	28	20	48	.322	.494

Career (1993-1997)

	ERA	W	L	Sv	G	GS	IP	H	HR	BB	SO
Home	3.82	19	9	0	43	39	254.1	226	40	90	196
Away	5.68	13	20	0	45	44	234.1	245	45	118	202
Day	4.19	23	11	0	51	46	288.0	251	49	111	237
Night	5.47	9	18	0	37	37	200.2	220	36	97	161
Grass	4.55	28	21	0	71	67	400.0	379	71	155	310

	Avg	AB	H	2B	3B	HR	RBI	BB	SO	OBP	SLG
vs. Left	.273	880	240	47	1	38	108	101	165	.345	.458
vs. Right	.239	967	231	49	3	47	135	107	233	.319	.442
Inning 1-6	.248	1648	450	79	4	76	216	186	362	.325	.439
Inning 7+	.317	199	63	17	0	9	27	22	36	.381	.538
None on	.257	1145	294	62	2	58	58	116	233	.327	.466

Career (1993-1997)

	ERA	W	L	Sv	G	GS	IP	H	HR	BB	SO		Avg	AB	H	2B	3B	HR	RBI	BB	SO	OBP	SLG
Turf	5.48	4	8	0	17	16	88.2	92	14	53	88	Runners on	.252	702	177	34	2	27	185	92	165	.338	.422
March/April	5.75	6	4	0	12	12	67.1	71	20	29	42	Scoring Posn	.253	399	101	15	1	14	151	60	110	.346	.401
May	5.53	8	3	0	13	13	71.2	67	13	33	57	Close & Late	.316	114	36	11	0	5	20	10	27	.365	.544
June	3.99	5	7	0	17	17	97.0	91	10	51	73	None on/out	.264	493	130	29	1	28	28	56	95	.340	.497
July	4.10	4	4	0	16	16	96.2	93	19	38	104	vs. 1st Batr (relief)	.250	4	1	1	0	0	1	0	0	.200	.500
August	3.40	5	3	0	14	14	87.1	72	9	30	58	1st Inning Pitched	.238	324	77	12	1	12	42	47	71	.342	.392
Sept/Oct	6.42	4	8	0	16	11	68.2	77	14	27	64	First 75 Pitches	.247	1396	345	64	4	61	186	165	310	.327	.430
Starter	4.63	32	28	0	83	83	480.1	460	84	201	389	Pitch 76-90	.293	249	73	20	0	13	30	21	45	.353	.530
Reliever	9.72	0	1	0	5	0	8.1	11	1	7	9	Pitch 91-105	.272	151	41	6	0	10	23	15	31	.337	.510
0-3 Days Rest (Start)	15.00	0	0	0	1	1	3.0	5	2	2	2	Pitch 106+	.235	51	12	6	0	1	4	7	12	.322	.412
4 Days Rest	4.76	21	21	0	51	51	293.0	290	52	128	243	First Pitch	.305	295	90	15	1	16	38	6	0	.317	.525
5+ Days Rest	4.25	11	7	0	31	31	184.1	165	30	71	144	Ahead in Count	.196	830	163	32	1	25	87	0	339	.199	.328
vs. AL	2.92	2	0	0	2	2	12.1	14	1	6	7	Behind in Count	.357	361	129	32	0	27	71	119	0	.516	.670
vs. NL	4.76	30	29	0	86	81	476.1	457	84	202	391	Two Strikes	.182	866	158	30	2	25	91	83	398	.257	.308
Pre-All Star	4.60	21	15	0	47	47	268.0	258	45	128	198	Pre-All Star	.255	1013	258	53	3	45	131	128	198	.338	.446
Post-All Star	4.85	11	14	0	41	36	220.2	213	40	80	200	Post-All Star	.255	834	213	43	1	40	112	80	200	.322	.453

Pitcher vs. Batter (career)

Pitches Best Vs.	Avg	AB	H	2B	3B	HR	RBI	BB	SO	OBP	SLG	Pitches Worst Vs.	Avg	AB	H	2B	3B	HR	RBI	BB	SO	OBP	SLG
Moises Alou	.000	11	0	0	0	0	0	1	0	.083	.000	Eddie Taubensee	.545	11	6	3	0	1	3	0	1	.545	1.091
Reggie Sanders	.083	12	1	0	0	1	1	0	8	.083	.333	Larry Walker	.500	18	9	0	0	4	9	3	4	.545	1.167
Midre Cummings	.083	12	1	0	0	0	0	0	2	.083	.083	Sean Berry	.500	12	6	3	0	1	2	0	2	.500	1.000
Mike Lansing	.091	11	1	1	0	0	0	0	1	.167	.182	Walt Weiss	.444	9	4	2	0	1	3	4	2	.615	1.000
Fred McGriff	.154	13	2	0	0	0	0	1	2	.214	.154	Vinny Castilla	.333	18	6	2	0	4	8	2	3	.400	1.111

Keith Foulke — White Sox Age 25 – Pitches Right

	ERA	W	L	Sv	G	GS	IP	BB	SO	Avg	H	2B	3B	HR	RBI	OBP	SLG	GF	IR	IRS	Hld	SvOp	SB	CS	GB	FB	G/F
1997 Season	6.38	4	5	3	27	8	73.1	23	54	.298	88	13	3	13	40	.356	.495	5	12	2	5	6	8	5	99	89	1.11

1997 Season

	ERA	W	L	Sv	G	GS	IP	H	HR	BB	SO		Avg	AB	H	2B	3B	HR	RBI	BB	SO	OBP	SLG
Home	3.67	3	0	2	15	2	41.2	35	4	9	34	vs. Left	.338	133	45	7	1	5	15	7	25	.369	.519
Away	9.95	1	5	1	12	6	31.2	53	9	14	20	vs. Right	.265	162	43	6	2	8	25	16	29	.346	.475
Starter	6.99	1	4	0	8	8	37.1	50	8	15	28	Scoring Posn	.318	66	21	3	1	3	26	11	12	.418	.530
Reliever	5.75	3	1	3	19	0	36.0	38	5	8	26	Close & Late	.291	55	16	2	0	1	4	2	9	.310	.382
0 Days rest (Relief)	10.80	0	0	0	3	0	1.2	2	0	2	1	None on/out	.286	70	20	5	0	3	3	7	10	.359	.486
1 or 2 Days rest	3.38	2	0	3	9	0	16.0	17	3	2	14	First Pitch	.339	56	19	3	1	2	8	2	0	.362	.536
3+ Days rest	7.36	1	1	0	7	0	18.1	19	2	4	11	Ahead in Count	.205	132	27	3	0	1	7	0	48	.222	.250
Pre-All Star	6.37	1	2	0	8	5	35.1	38	7	12	29	Behind in Count	.400	65	26	4	1	10	20	11	0	.487	.954
Post-All Star	6.39	3	3	3	19	3	38.0	50	6	11	25	Two Strikes	.190	137	26	1	1	1	8	10	54	.258	.241

Andy Fox — Yankees Age 27 – Bats Left

	Avg	G	AB	R	H	2B	3B	HR	RBI	BB	SO	HBP	GDP	SB	CS	OBP	SLG	IBB	SH	SF	#Pit	#P/PA	GB	FB	G/F
1997 Season	.226	22	31	13	7	1	0	0	1	7	9	0	1	2	1	.368	.258	0	2	0	163	4.07	14	5	2.80
Career (1996-1997)	.200	135	220	39	44	5	0	3	14	27	37	1	3	13	4	.290	.264	0	11	0	935	3.61	97	58	1.67

1997 Season

	Avg	AB	H	2B	3B	HR	RBI	BB	SO	OBP	SLG
vs. Left	.333	3	1	0	0	0	0	0	2	.333	.333
vs. Right	.214	28	6	1	0	0	1	7	7	.371	.250
Scoring Posn	.250	8	2	0	0	0	1	4	4	.500	.250
Close & Late	.167	6	1	0	0	0	0	0	3	.167	.167

Chad Fox — Braves Age 27 – Pitches Right (groundball pitcher)

	ERA	W	L	Sv	G	GS	IP	BB	SO	Avg	H	2B	3B	HR	RBI	OBP	SLG	GF	IR	IRS	Hld	SvOp	SB	CS	GB	FB	G/F
1997 Season	3.29	0	1	0	30	0	27.1	16	28	.231	24	2	1	4	11	.333	.385	8	13	1	7	1	4	0	39	22	1.77

1997 Season

	ERA	W	L	Sv	G	GS	IP	H	HR	BB	SO		Avg	AB	H	2B	3B	HR	RBI	BB	SO	OBP	SLG
Home	1.72	0	1	0	16	0	15.2	10	2	5	14	vs. Left	.200	35	7	1	0	1	1	9	11	.364	.314
Away	5.40	0	0	0	14	0	11.2	14	2	11	14	vs. Right	.246	69	17	1	1	3	10	7	17	.316	.420
Starter	0.00	0	0	0	0	0	0.0	0	0	0	0	Scoring Posn	.200	25	5	1	0	0	6	4	10	.310	.240
Reliever	3.29	0	1	0	30	0	27.1	24	4	16	28	Close & Late	.244	41	10	2	0	3	9	8	10	.367	.512
0 Days rest (Relief)	3.86	0	1	0	6	0	4.2	7	0	3	6	None on/out	.125	24	3	0	0	2	2	4	6	.250	.375
1 or 2 Days rest	4.40	0	0	0	17	0	14.1	13	4	9	13	First Pitch	.250	16	4	0	1	1	1	0	0	.250	.563
3+ Days rest	1.08	0	0	0	7	0	8.1	4	0	4	9	Ahead in Count	.111	45	5	1	0	0	0	0	25	.111	.133
Pre-All Star	0.00	0	0	0	0	0	0.0	0	0	0	0	Behind in Count	.480	25	12	1	0	3	9	11	0	.639	.880
Post-All Star	3.29	0	1	0	30	0	27.1	24	4	16	28	Two Strikes	.102	49	5	1	0	0	0	5	28	.185	.122

John Franco — Mets Age 37 – Pitches Left (groundball pitcher)

	ERA	W	L	Sv	G	GS	IP	BB	SO	Avg	H	2B	3B	HR	RBI	OBP	SLG	GF	IR	IRS	Hld	SvOp	SB	CS	GB	FB	G/F
1997 Season	2.55	5	3	36	59	0	60.0	20	53	.226	49	11	0	3	19	.293	.318	53	18	3	0	42	2	0	88	32	2.75
Last Five Years	2.79	19	16	133	240	0	252.0	96	213	.255	244	37	1	17	111	.324	.349	211	82	29	0	167	9	3	394	194	2.03

1997 Season

	ERA	W	L	Sv	G	GS	IP	H	HR	BB	SO		Avg	AB	H	2B	3B	HR	RBI	BB	SO	OBP	SLG
Home	1.95	4	0	17	31	0	32.1	25	1	8	28	vs. Left	.304	46	14	3	0	0	4	5	10	.373	.370

1997 Season

	ERA	W	L	Sv	G	GS	IP	H	HR	BB	SO
Away	3.25	1	3	19	28	0	27.2	24	2	12	25
Day	2.52	2	1	14	24	0	25.0	21	1	9	18
Night	2.57	3	2	22	35	0	35.0	28	2	11	35
Grass	2.82	4	3	29	50	0	51.0	47	3	17	46
Turf	1.00	1	0	7	9	0	9.0	2	0	3	7
March/April	0.66	0	0	6	11	0	13.2	8	0	4	11
May	3.12	0	1	8	10	0	8.2	9	0	3	10
June	6.48	1	0	5	10	0	8.1	10	1	2	6
July	1.98	1	0	9	12	0	13.2	8	1	2	10
August	0.93	2	1	5	11	0	9.2	8	0	6	10
Sept/Oct	4.50	1	1	3	5	0	6.0	6	1	3	6
Starter	0.00	0	0	0	0	0	0.0	0	0	0	0
Reliever	2.55	5	3	36	59	0	60.0	49	3	20	53
0 Days rest (Relief)	3.24	2	0	10	16	0	16.2	15	2	4	12
1 or 2 Days rest	3.42	2	3	16	23	0	23.2	25	1	12	22
3+ Days rest	0.92	1	0	10	20	0	19.2	9	0	4	19
vs. AL	1.93	0	1	4	6	0	4.2	4	0	2	2
vs. NL	2.60	5	2	32	53	0	55.1	45	3	18	51
Pre-All Star	2.86	1	1	20	34	0	34.2	31	1	9	28
Post-All Star	2.13	4	2	16	25	0	25.1	18	2	11	25

	Avg	AB	H	2B	3B	HR	RBI	BB	SO	OBP	SLG
vs. Right	.205	171	35	8	0	3	15	15	43	.271	.304
Inning 1-6	.000	0	0	0	0	0	0	0	0	.000	.000
Inning 7+	.226	217	49	11	0	3	19	20	53	.293	.318
None on	.256	117	30	7	0	1	1	4	27	.281	.342
Runners on	.190	100	19	4	0	2	18	16	26	.305	.290
Scoring Posn	.222	63	14	1	0	2	17	13	14	.359	.333
Close & Late	.227	154	35	7	0	2	17	19	37	.310	.312
None on/out	.364	55	20	5	0	1	1	3	11	.397	.509
vs. 1st Batr (relief)	.327	55	18	5	0	1	3	4	12	.373	.473
1st Inning Pitched	.235	196	46	11	0	3	19	19	46	.304	.337
First 15 Pitches	.258	163	42	10	0	3	14	12	39	.311	.374
Pitch 16-30	.137	51	7	1	0	0	5	7	12	.241	.157
Pitch 31-45	.000	3	0	0	0	0	0	1	2	.250	.000
Pitch 46+	.000	0	0	0	0	0	0	0	0	.000	.000
First Pitch	.294	34	10	2	0	0	2	1	0	.314	.353
Ahead in Count	.154	91	14	2	0	1	9	0	46	.161	.209
Behind in Count	.208	48	10	4	0	2	6	9	0	.333	.417
Two Strikes	.217	106	23	5	0	1	9	10	53	.284	.292
Pre-All Star	.248	125	31	7	0	1	12	9	28	.301	.328
Post-All Star	.196	92	18	4	0	2	7	11	25	.282	.304

Last Five Years

	ERA	W	L	Sv	G	GS	IP	H	HR	BB	SO
Home	2.43	14	4	72	130	0	140.2	129	9	45	117
Away	3.23	5	12	61	110	0	111.1	115	8	51	96
Day	2.47	7	6	42	90	0	94.2	87	6	40	68
Night	2.97	12	10	91	150	0	157.1	157	11	56	145
Grass	2.77	15	14	101	190	0	198.1	192	15	73	166
Turf	2.85	4	2	32	50	0	53.2	52	2	23	47
March/April	2.50	2	1	18	34	0	39.2	33	3	12	39
May	2.44	5	4	25	44	0	44.1	41	3	22	34
June	2.78	1	3	21	45	0	45.1	47	2	23	36
July	2.41	6	1	32	50	0	56.0	55	3	13	45
August	1.77	2	2	23	37	0	35.2	30	1	13	35
Sept/Oct	5.52	3	5	14	30	0	31.0	38	5	13	24
Starter	0.00	0	0	0	0	0	0.0	0	0	0	0
Reliever	2.79	19	16	133	240	0	252.0	244	17	96	213
0 Days rest (Relief)	3.19	4	2	39	53	0	53.2	52	4	16	46
1 or 2 Days rest	3.58	11	9	55	99	0	113.0	120	11	49	99
3+ Days rest	1.48	4	5	39	88	0	85.1	72	2	31	68
vs. AL	1.93	0	1	4	6	0	4.2	4	0	2	2
vs. NL	2.80	19	15	129	234	0	247.1	240	17	94	211
Pre-All Star	2.70	9	8	71	136	0	143.1	135	10	59	116
Post-All Star	2.90	10	8	62	104	0	108.2	109	7	37	97

	Avg	AB	H	2B	3B	HR	RBI	BB	SO	OBP	SLG
vs. Left	.270	215	58	9	0	2	27	19	56	.329	.340
vs. Right	.251	741	186	28	1	15	84	77	157	.322	.352
Inning 1-6	.000	0	0	0	0	0	0	0	0	.000	.000
Inning 7+	.255	956	244	37	1	17	111	96	213	.324	.349
None on	.266	497	132	19	1	11	11	39	114	.319	.374
Runners on	.244	459	112	18	0	6	100	57	99	.329	.322
Scoring Posn	.251	275	69	8	0	4	92	43	51	.352	.324
Close & Late	.258	678	175	27	0	11	90	85	156	.341	.347
None on/out	.280	225	63	10	0	5	5	15	48	.325	.391
vs. 1st Batr (relief)	.274	215	59	8	0	6	19	22	47	.340	.395
1st Inning Pitched	.259	833	216	33	1	15	98	88	176	.331	.355
First 15 Pitches	.272	668	182	30	1	14	66	61	132	.333	.383
Pitch 16-30	.211	247	52	6	0	3	37	29	69	.297	.271
Pitch 31-45	.250	40	10	1	0	0	8	5	12	.333	.275
Pitch 46+	.000	1	0	0	0	0	0	1	0	.500	.000
First Pitch	.294	126	37	6	1	1	12	5	0	.321	.381
Ahead in Count	.192	422	81	10	0	8	40	0	185	.197	.273
Behind in Count	.338	222	75	16	0	7	41	43	0	.445	.505
Two Strikes	.178	439	78	10	0	6	37	48	213	.259	.241
Pre-All Star	.248	544	135	22	1	10	62	59	116	.322	.347
Post-All Star	.265	412	109	15	0	7	49	37	97	.326	.352

Pitcher vs. Batter (career)

Pitches Best Vs.	Avg	AB	H	2B	3B	HR	RBI	BB	SO	OBP	SLG
Delino DeShields	.000	16	0	0	0	0	0	0	7	.000	.000
Tom Pagnozzi	.000	14	0	0	0	0	0	2	6	.125	.000
Darren Daulton	.071	14	1	1	0	0	0	1	6	.133	.143
Sammy Sosa	.100	10	1	0	0	0	1	1	3	.182	.100
Jeff Blauser	.182	11	2	0	0	0	1	0	1	.167	.182

Pitches Worst Vs.	Avg	AB	H	2B	3B	HR	RBI	BB	SO	OBP	SLG
Mariano Duncan	.500	20	10	1	0	0	1	2	5	.545	.550
Todd Zeile	.421	19	8	0	0	1	1	2	4	.476	.579
Ron Gant	.385	13	5	1	0	1	3	2	2	.467	.692
Kevin Mitchell	.357	14	5	0	0	2	2	6	3	.550	.786
Matt Williams	.333	18	6	1	0	1	7	2	4	.400	.556

Julio Franco — Brewers
Age 36 – Bats Right (groundball hitter)

	Avg	G	AB	R	H	2B	3B	HR	RBI	BB	SO	HBP	GDP	SB	CS	OBP	SLG	IBB	SH	SF	#Pit	#P/PA	GB	FB	G/F
1997 Season	.270	120	430	116	116	16	1	7	44	69	116	1	17	15	6	.369	.360	4	1	4	2131	4.22	191	51	3.75
Last Five Years	.299	488	1827	297	547	86	7	55	302	254	368	10	61	40	18	.384	.444	14	6	19	8782	4.15	794	311	2.55

1997 Season

	Avg	AB	H	2B	3B	HR	RBI	BB	SO	OBP	SLG
vs. Left	.252	111	28	3	0	0	9	26	32	.388	.279
vs. Right	.276	319	88	13	1	7	35	43	84	.362	.389
Groundball	.277	65	18	2	0	0	7	7	17	.347	.308
Flyball	.286	77	22	5	0	1	6	13	23	.389	.390
Home	.262	221	58	5	1	5	24	46	61	.385	.362
Away	.278	209	58	11	0	2	20	23	55	.350	.359
Day	.270	111	30	4	0	1	11	30	35	.423	.333
Night	.270	319	86	12	1	6	33	39	81	.348	.370
Grass	.268	377	101	16	1	6	39	62	103	.368	.363
Turf	.283	53	15	0	0	1	5	7	13	.377	.340
Pre-All Star	.288	260	75	13	0	2	21	36	67	.375	.362
Post-All Star	.241	170	41	3	1	5	23	33	49	.361	.359
Scoring Posn	.286	112	32	6	0	3	39	24	36	.400	.420
Close & Late	.298	57	17	0	0	0	3	15	14	.444	.298
None on/out	.295	95	28	3	1	3		16	20	.396	.442

	Avg	AB	H	2B	3B	HR	RBI	BB	SO	OBP	SLG
First Pitch	.423	26	11	4	0	1	3	3	0	.483	.692
Ahead in Count	.372	86	32	2	0	4	11	28	0	.517	.535
Behind in Count	.216	232	50	7	0	1	17	0	97	.217	.259
Two Strikes	.165	237	39	4	1	2	13	38	116	.280	.215
Batting #4	.237	152	36	3	0	5	22	31	44	.362	.355
Batting #7	.305	118	36	3	1	2	11	20	34	.406	.398
Other	.275	160	44	10	0	0	11	18	38	.348	.338
March/April	.333	81	27	3	0	1	10	15	20	.438	.407
May	.330	91	30	7	0	1	7	10	19	.396	.440
June	.220	82	18	3	0	0	4	10	26	.304	.256
July	.200	35	7	0	1	1	4	3	10	.263	.343
August	.288	59	17	3	0	3	11	12	13	.403	.492
Sept/Oct	.207	82	17	0	0	1	8	19	28	.352	.244
vs. AL	.279	390	109	15	1	6	40	61	104	.374	.369
vs. NL	.175	40	7	1	0	1	4	8	12	.327	.275

1997 By Position

Position	Avg	AB	H	2B	3B	HR	RBI	BB	SO	OBP	SLG		G	GS	Innings	PO	A	E	DP	Fld Pct	Rng Fctr	In Zone	Outs	Zone Rtg	MLB Zone
As DH	.295	261	77	12	1	6	30	37	63	.377	.418		70	70	---						---				
As 1b	.130	46	6	0	0	1	3	8	14	.273	.196		14	13	123.1	110	11	1	20	.992	---	28	23	.821	.874
As 2b	.268	123	33	4	0	0	10	22	39	.379	.301		35	34	288.2	69	108	3	23	.983	5.52	131	116	.885	.902

Last Five Years

	Avg	AB	H	2B	3B	HR	RBI	BB	SO	OBP	SLG		Avg	AB	H	2B	3B	HR	RBI	BB	SO	OBP	SLG
vs. Left	.305	440	134	24	2	12	70	76	93	.404	.450	First Pitch	.410	134	55	10	1	5	32	10	0	.447	.612
vs. Right	.298	1387	413	62	5	43	232	178	275	.378	.443	Ahead in Count	.376	399	150	20	2	20	85	119	0	.514	.586
Groundball	.320	384	123	18	2	10	72	49	69	.398	.456	Behind in Count	.247	916	226	39	2	15	109	0	313	.250	.343
Flyball	.294	347	102	21	0	13	70	45	75	.376	.467	Two Strikes	.220	973	214	32	2	19	118	125	368	.310	.316
Home	.328	900	295	47	5	28	163	144	166	.419	.484	Batting #2	.297	593	176	38	0	20	97	82	125	.381	.462
Away	.272	927	252	39	2	27	139	110	202	.350	.406	Batting #4	.296	626	185	24	2	25	129	94	127	.387	.460
Day	.309	489	151	23	1	13	86	79	104	.403	.440	Other	.306	608	186	24	5	10	76	78	116	.385	.411
Night	.296	1338	396	63	6	42	216	175	264	.377	.446	March/April	.297	347	103	15	1	12	59	47	68	.379	.450
Grass	.303	1595	483	80	6	46	269	222	313	.387	.447	May	.305	394	120	29	1	12	74	42	90	.372	.475
Turf	.276	232	64	6	1	9	33	32	55	.365	.427	June	.304	312	95	13	1	6	37	52	64	.406	.410
Pre-All Star	.302	1153	348	61	3	35	193	159	237	.386	.451	July	.281	281	79	9	2	11	48	38	49	.366	.445
Post-All Star	.295	674	199	25	4	20	109	95	131	.381	.433	August	.335	209	70	11	0	8	37	41	35	.447	.502
Scoring Posn	.323	527	170	28	3	15	246	85	114	.407	.472	Sept/Oct	.282	284	80	9	2	6	47	34	62	.354	.391
Close & Late	.272	257	70	4	3	8	37	39	59	.367	.405	vs. AL	.302	1787	540	85	7	54	298	246	356	.386	.448
None on/out	.307	391	120	16	2	12	12	54	71	.394	.450	vs. NL	.175	40	7	1	0	1	4	8	12	.327	.275

Batter vs. Pitcher (since 1984)

Hits Best Against	Avg	AB	H	2B	3B	HR	RBI	BB	SO	OBP	SLG	Hits Worst Against	Avg	AB	H	2B	3B	HR	RBI	BB	SO	OBP	SLG
Andy Pettitte	.545	11	6	1	0	0	0	2	2	.615	.636	Alan Mills	.000	9	0	0	0	0	0	2	4	.182	.000
Erik Hanson	.520	25	13	1	0	1	2	5	1	.600	.680	Rick Aguilera	.100	10	1	0	0	0	1	1	0	.182	.100
Dan Plesac	.500	12	6	0	0	1	1	2	1	.571	.750	Scott Kamieniecki	.143	14	2	0	0	0	2	2	1	.250	.143
Ramon Garcia	.471	17	8	0	0	2	4	2	2	.526	.824	Mike Mussina	.160	25	4	0	0	0	1	1	10	.185	.160
Bob Wickman	.444	9	4	0	1	0	4	2	1	.545	.667	Jose Rosado	.182	11	2	0	0	0	1	0	4	.167	.182

Matt Franco — Mets
Age 28 – Bats Left

	Avg	G	AB	R	H	2B	3B	HR	RBI	BB	SO	HBP	GDP	SB	CS	OBP	SLG	IBB	SH	SF	#Pit	#P/PA	GB	FB	G/F
1997 Season	.276	112	163	21	45	5	0	5	21	13	23	0	4	1	0	.330	.399	4	0	0	574	3.26	68	46	1.48
Career (1995-1997)	.265	142	211	27	56	7	0	6	24	14	32	1	5	1	0	.313	.384	4	0	1	778	3.43	84	62	1.35

1997 Season

	Avg	AB	H	2B	3B	HR	RBI	BB	SO	OBP	SLG		Avg	AB	H	2B	3B	HR	RBI	BB	SO	OBP	SLG
vs. Left	.227	22	5	0	0	0	1	1	3	.261	.227	Scoring Posn	.302	43	13	2	0	1	16	7	5	.400	.419
vs. Right	.284	141	40	5	0	5	20	12	20	.340	.426	Close & Late	.354	48	17	4	0	1	12	3	7	.392	.500
Home	.250	92	23	3	0	3	7	8	12	.310	.380	None on/out	.294	34	10	1	0	3	3	2	2	.333	.588
Away	.310	71	22	2	0	2	14	5	11	.355	.423	Batting #8	.345	29	10	2	0	1	5	4	5	.424	.517
First Pitch	.250	24	6	1	0	1	4	2	0	.308	.417	Batting #9	.234	47	11	1	0	2	4	2	7	.265	.383
Ahead in Count	.293	41	12	1	0	2	5	5	0	.370	.463	Other	.276	87	24	2	0	2	12	7	11	.330	.368
Behind in Count	.279	68	19	2	0	0	20	0		.279	.309	Pre-All Star	.315	92	29	3	0	3	11	7	14	.364	.446
Two Strikes	.281	57	16	0	0	1	5	23		.339	.281	Post-All Star	.225	71	16	2	0	2	10	6	9	.286	.338

Micah Franklin — Cardinals
Age 26 – Bats Both

	Avg	G	AB	R	H	2B	3B	HR	RBI	BB	SO	HBP	GDP	SB	CS	OBP	SLG	IBB	SH	SF	#Pit	#P/PA	GB	FB	G/F
1997 Season	.324	17	34	6	11	0	0	2	2	3	10	0	0	0	0	.378	.500	0	0	0	122	3.30	6	13	0.46

1997 Season

	Avg	AB	H	2B	3B	HR	RBI	BB	SO	OBP	SLG		Avg	AB	H	2B	3B	HR	RBI	BB	SO	OBP	SLG
vs. Left	.111	9	1	0	0	0	0	0	4	.111	.111	Scoring Posn	.000	5	0	0	0	0	0	0	3	.000	.000
vs. Right	.400	25	10	0	0	2	2	3	6	.464	.640	Close & Late	.250	4	1	0	0	0	0	1	3	.400	.250

John Frascatore — Cardinals
Age 28 – Pitches Right (groundball pitcher)

	ERA	W	L	Sv	G	GS	IP	BB	SO	Avg	H	2B	3B	HR	RBI	OBP	SLG	GF	IR	IRS	Hld	SvOp	SB	CS	GB	FB	G/F
1997 Season	2.47	5	2	0	59	0	80.0	33	58	.247	74	9	1	5	33	.329	.334	17	38	15	3	4	15	1	129	60	2.15
Career (1994-1997)	3.41	6	4	0	74	5	116.0	51	81	.269	120	21	2	10	57	.350	.392	20	45	18	3	4	23	5	190	100	1.90

1997 Season

	ERA	W	L	Sv	G	GS	IP	H	HR	SO		Avg	AB	H	2B	3B	HR	RBI	BB	SO	OBP	SLG
Home	2.82	3	0	0	31	0	38.1	37	4	10	31	vs. Left	.214	117	25	4	0	1	11	18	17	.321	.274
Away	2.16	2	2	0	28	0	41.2	37	1	23	27	vs. Right	.269	182	49	5	1	4	22	15	41	.335	.374
Day	3.20	1	1	0	17	0	19.2	23	0	9	17	Inning 1-6	.148	81	12	3	1	1	9	13	17	.283	.247
Night	2.24	4	1	0	42	0	60.1	51	5	24	41	Inning 7+	.284	218	62	6	0	4	24	20	41	.348	.367
Grass	2.73	4	1	0	49	0	62.2	59	5	25	48	None on/out	.279	147	41	4	0	5	5	14	24	.354	.408
Turf	1.56	1	1	0	10	0	17.1	15	0	8	10	Runners on	.217	152	33	5	1	0	28	19	34	.307	.263
March/April	1.32	1	1	0	9	0	13.2	10	0	8	12	Scoring Posn	.186	97	18	5	1	0	28	18	27	.317	.258
May	2.79	1	1	0	6	0	9.2	12	1	2	6	Close & Late	.255	98	25	3	0	1	11	14	15	.348	.316
June	2.87	1	0	0	10	0	15.2	20	0	7	13	None on/out	.292	65	19	2	0	3	3	8	7	.387	.462
July	5.11	1	0	0	11	0	12.1	14	1	5	8	vs. 1st Batr (relief)	.216	51	11	1	0	2	4	5	5	.293	.353
August	0.00	1	0	0	11	0	14.1	7	0	5	9	1st Inning Pitched	.219	183	40	4	0	2	22	19	41	.292	.273
Sept/Oct	3.14	0	0	0	12	0	14.1	11	3	6	10	First 15 Pitches	.245	163	40	4	0	3	18	17	28	.321	.325
Starter	0.00	0	0	0	0	0	0.0	0	0	0	0	Pitch 16-30	.262	107	28	3	1	2	12	12	24	.339	.364

1997 Season

	ERA	W	L	Sv	G	GS	IP	H	HR	BB	SO		Avg	AB	H	2B	3B	HR	RBI	BB	SO	OBP	SLG
Reliever	2.47	5	2	0	59	0	80.0	74	5	33	58	Pitch 31-45	.214	28	6	2	0	0	3	4	5	.353	.286
0 Days rest (Relief)	4.15	1	0	0	8	0	8.2	8	2	3	5	Pitch 46+	.000	1	0	0	0	0	0	0	0	.000	.000
1 or 2 Days rest	1.96	3	1	0	33	0	46.0	43	2	15	33	First Pitch	.333	42	14	0	0	1	2	5	0	.408	.405
3+ Days rest	2.84	1	1	0	18	0	25.1	23	1	15	20	Ahead in Count	.227	141	32	3	1	3	15	0	46	.233	.326
vs. AL	1.80	0	0	0	6	0	5.0	7	0	2	6	Behind in Count	.264	72	19	5	0	0	9	20	0	.432	.333
vs. NL	2.52	5	2	0	53	0	75.0	67	5	31	52	Two Strikes	.150	133	20	2	1	2	10	8	58	.207	.226
Pre-All Star	2.66	3	2	0	27	0	40.2	47	1	18	31	Pre-All Star	.296	159	47	7	1	1	17	18	31	.377	.371
Post-All Star	2.29	2	0	0	32	0	39.1	27	4	15	27	Post-All Star	.193	140	27	2	0	4	16	15	27	.275	.293

Hanley Frias — Rangers   Age 24 – Bats Both

	Avg	G	AB	R	H	2B	3B	HR	RBI	BB	SO	HBP	GDP	SB	CS	OBP	SLG	IBB	SH	SF	#Pit	#P/PA	GB	FB	G/F
1997 Season	.192	14	26	4	5	1	0	0	1	1	4	0	1	0	0	.222	.231	0	0	0	94	3.48	10	6	1.67

1997 Season

	Avg	AB	H	2B	3B	HR	RBI	BB	SO	OBP	SLG		Avg	AB	H	2B	3B	HR	RBI	BB	SO	OBP	SLG
vs. Left	.286	7	2	0	0	0	1	0	3	.286	.286	Scoring Posn	.200	5	1	0	0	0	1	0	2	.200	.200
vs. Right	.158	19	3	1	0	0	1	1		.200	.211	Close & Late	.286	7	2	0	0	0	0	0	1	.286	.286

Jeff Frye — Red Sox   Age 31 – Bats Right

	Avg	G	AB	R	H	2B	3B	HR	RBI	BB	SO	HBP	GDP	SB	CS	OBP	SLG	IBB	SH	SF	#Pit	#P/PA	GB	FB	G/F
1997 Season	.312	127	404	56	126	36	2	3	51	27	44	2	12	19	8	.352	.433	1	2	7	1716	3.88	168	107	1.57
Last Five Years	.298	379	1341	205	400	98	9	11	139	134	169	13	46	46	16	.363	.409	1	20	17	6216	4.08	528	355	1.49

1997 Season

	Avg	AB	H	2B	3B	HR	RBI	BB	SO	OBP	SLG		Avg	AB	H	2B	3B	HR	RBI	BB	SO	OBP	SLG
vs. Left	.322	115	37	14	0	1	17	10	17	.364	.470	First Pitch	.421	19	8	2	0	0	0	1	0	.450	.526
vs. Right	.308	289	89	22	2	2	34	17	27	.347	.419	Ahead in Count	.400	110	44	18	1	1	19	19	0	.481	.609
Groundball	.315	73	23	5	1	0	8	5	3	.363	.411	Behind in Count	.249	185	46	8	1	0	19	0	39	.251	.303
Flyball	.338	71	24	6	0	0	8	3	12	.360	.423	Two Strikes	.235	187	44	8	1	1	23	7	44	.261	.305
Home	.326	181	59	16	0	2	21	12	21	.365	.448	Batting #8	.339	118	40	9	1	1	16	6	9	.365	.458
Away	.300	223	67	20	2	1	30	15	23	.342	.422	Batting #9	.330	115	38	13	0	1	15	7	16	.369	.470
Day	.252	127	32	11	0	1	12	4	15	.273	.362	Other	.281	171	48	14	1	1	20	14	19	.333	.392
Night	.339	277	94	25	2	2	39	23	29	.386	.466	March/April	.414	29	12	1	0	0	4	2	2	.455	.448
Grass	.320	347	111	33	2	3	43	24	35	.362	.452	May	.217	46	10	2	0	0	4	4	6	.269	.261
Turf	.263	57	15	3	0	0	8	3	9	.290	.316	June	.213	47	10	3	0	1	5	3	4	.260	.340
Pre-All Star	.267	135	36	7	1	1	17	9	12	.311	.356	July	.344	93	32	11	1	1	17	7	9	.390	.516
Post-All Star	.335	269	90	29	1	2	34	18	32	.373	.472	August	.280	100	28	10	0	0	10	7	14	.318	.380
Scoring Posn	.314	105	33	10	0	0	43	11	14	.363	.410	Sept/Oct	.382	89	34	9	1	1	11	4	9	.411	.539
Close & Late	.257	70	18	2	2	0	9	6	10	.312	.462	vs. AL	.325	375	122	34	2	3	51	26	37	.366	.451
None on/out	.344	93	32	8	0	1	1	8	7	.402	.462	vs. NL	.138	29	4	2	0	0	0	1	7	.167	.207

1997 By Position

Position	Avg	AB	H	2B	3B	HR	RBI	BB	SO	OBP	SLG	G	GS	Innings	PO	A	E	DP	Fld Pct	Rng Fctr	In Zone	Zone Outs	Zone Rtg	MLB Zone
As DH	.300	10	3	0	0	1	2	1	1	.333	.600	11	1	---	---	---	---	---	---	---	---	---	---	---
As 2b	.334	302	101	31	1	2	40	19	36	.371	.464	80	79	703.0	197	228	4	62	.991	5.44	253	228	.901	.902
As 3b	.255	55	14	3	0	0	5	3	2	.293	.309	18	13	124.1	11	31	6	1	.875	3.04	45	35	.778	.801

Last Five Years

	Avg	AB	H	2B	3B	HR	RBI	BB	SO	OBP	SLG		Avg	AB	H	2B	3B	HR	RBI	BB	SO	OBP	SLG
vs. Left	.294	374	110	32	1	4	45	47	49	.369	.417	First Pitch	.383	47	18	3	0	2	5	1	0	.396	.574
vs. Right	.300	967	290	66	8	7	94	87	120	.361	.406	Ahead in Count	.354	319	113	38	1	3	43	105	0	.509	.508
Groundball	.299	284	85	19	2	0	27	34	27	.383	.380	Behind in Count	.277	686	190	39	4	2	56	0	148	.285	.354
Flyball	.280	261	73	13	5	2	27	13	41	.312	.391	Two Strikes	.248	714	177	35	7	5	69	28	169	.280	.338
Home	.313	638	200	42	4	7	61	72	77	.386	.425	Batting #1	.266	319	85	22	2	0	29	45	41	.358	.348
Away	.284	703	200	56	4	4	78	62	92	.342	.395	Batting #2	.309	612	189	40	4	5	58	54	83	.369	.412
Day	.267	360	96	26	1	5	43	25	44	.315	.386	Other	.307	410	126	36	3	6	52	35	45	.360	.454
Night	.310	981	304	72	8	6	96	109	125	.381	.418	March/April	.373	51	19	4	0	0	4	6	6	.441	.451
Grass	.303	1175	356	90	8	11	123	117	145	.369	.421	May	.311	235	73	12	3	0	23	27	27	.381	.387
Turf	.265	166	44	8	1	0	16	17	24	.328	.325	June	.254	205	52	12	1	1	15	29	22	.349	.337
Pre-All Star	.288	566	163	33	5	1	51	67	60	.365	.369	July	.280	307	86	28	1	2	34	28	44	.343	.397
Post-All Star	.306	775	237	65	4	10	88	67	109	.362	.402	August	.294	306	90	20	1	7	34	29	41	.358	.435
Scoring Posn	.295	305	90	24	1	3	120	35	43	.356	.410	Sept/Oct	.338	237	80	22	3	1	29	15	29	.376	.468
Close & Late	.254	201	51	11	2	1	23	23	32	.332	.343	vs. AL	.302	1312	396	96	9	11	139	133	162	.367	.414
None on/out	.308	321	99	20	2	2	44	31		.402	.402	vs. NL	.138	29	4	2	0	0	0	1	7	.167	.207

Batter vs. Pitcher (career)

Hits Best Against	Avg	AB	H	2B	3B	HR	RBI	BB	SO	OBP	SLG	Hits Worst Against	Avg	AB	H	2B	3B	HR	RBI	BB	SO	OBP	SLG
Roger Clemens	.667	9	6	1	0	0	0	2	1	.727	.778	Jason Dickson	.091	11	1	0	0	0	0	1	0	.167	.091
Scott Karl	.583	12	7	1	0	0	0	2	1	.643	.667	Mike Mussina	.133	15	2	0	0	0	0	0	3	.188	.133
Cal Eldred	.563	16	9	2	0	1	3	0	1	.563	.875	Felipe Lira	.143	14	2	0	0	0	0	1	2	.200	.143
Jaime Navarro	.500	12	6	1	0	0	1	1	1	.538	.583	Woody Williams	.167	12	2	0	0	0	0	0	1	.167	.167
Erik Hanson	.500	12	6	2	0	0	0	0	3	.500	.667	Tom Gordon	.182	11	2	1	0	0	1	0	1	.167	.273

Travis Fryman — Tigers

Age 29 – Bats Right (flyball hitter)

	Avg	G	AB	R	H	2B	3B	HR	RBI	BB	SO	HBP	GDP	SB	CS	OBP	SLG	IBB	SH	SF	#Pit	#P/PA	GB	FB	G/F
1997 Season	.274	154	595	90	163	27	3	22	102	46	113	5	16	16	3	.326	.440	5	0	11	2528	3.85	171	198	0.86
Last Five Years	.277	720	2849	423	788	151	21	99	465	288	587	21	66	35	14	.342	.449	13	3	47	12563	3.92	817	930	0.88

1997 Season

	Avg	AB	H	2B	3B	HR	RBI	BB	SO	OBP	SLG		Avg	AB	H	2B	3B	HR	RBI	BB	SO	OBP	SLG
vs. Left	.298	151	45	9	0	5	21	15	30	.359	.457	First Pitch	.433	67	29	4	0	6	17	2	0	.443	.761
vs. Right	.266	444	118	18	3	17	81	31	83	.314	.435	Ahead in Count	.357	143	51	12	2	6	28	25	0	.451	.594
Groundball	.235	119	28	6	0	3	18	8	23	.277	.361	Behind in Count	.206	272	56	7	1	4	33	0	92	.209	.283
Flyball	.300	100	30	6	0	3	14	13	22	.374	.450	Two Strikes	.191	283	54	7	1	8	38	19	113	.245	.307
Home	.277	282	78	14	1	13	58	26	56	.335	.472	Batting #3	.268	441	118	22	3	18	82	35	88	.321	.454
Away	.272	313	85	13	2	9	44	20	57	.317	.412	Batting #5	.312	138	43	4	0	4	18	9	20	.353	.428
Day	.257	241	62	10	1	8	44	16	49	.303	.407	Other	.125	16	2	1	0	0	2	2	5	.222	.188
Night	.285	354	101	17	2	14	58	30	64	.341	.463	March/April	.308	104	32	4	2	6	21	15	23	.388	.558
Grass	.286	528	151	25	3	22	94	42	97	.339	.470	May	.258	93	24	2	0	2	19	8	15	.318	.344
Turf	.179	67	12	2	0	0	8	4	16	.219	.209	June	.333	75	25	6	1	2	8	4	13	.370	.520
Pre-All Star	.302	301	91	15	3	12	54	29	56	.362	.492	July	.194	108	21	5	0	4	14	10	22	.263	.352
Post-All Star	.245	294	72	12	0	10	48	17	57	.287	.388	August	.273	110	30	2	0	4	26	6	21	.311	.400
Scoring Posn	.275	167	46	4	1	4	79	16	35	.327	.383	Sept/Oct	.295	105	31	8	0	4	14	3	19	.315	.486
Close & Late	.261	88	23	2	0	4	14	5	24	.301	.420	vs. AL	.269	558	150	24	2	21	95	44	107	.322	.432
None on/out	.261	119	31	5	1	7	7	6	23	.296	.496	vs. NL	.351	37	13	3	1	1	7	2	6	.385	.568

1997 By Position

Position	Avg	AB	H	2B	3B	HR	RBI	BB	SO	OBP	SLG	G	GS	Innings	PO	A	E	DP	Fld Pct	Rng Fctr	In Zone	Zone Outs	Zone Rtg	MLB Zone
As 3b	.274	594	163	27	3	22	102	46	112	.326	.441	153	153	1331.2	126	314	10	21	.978	2.97	412	348	845	.801

Last Five Years

	Avg	AB	H	2B	3B	HR	RBI	BB	SO	OBP	SLG		Avg	AB	H	2B	3B	HR	RBI	BB	SO	OBP	SLG
vs. Left	.258	664	171	34	3	25	105	76	141	.332	.431	First Pitch	.358	338	121	22	1	16	71	9	0	.381	.571
vs. Right	.282	2185	617	117	18	74	360	212	446	.345	.454	Ahead in Count	.339	651	221	48	9	33	151	133	0	.443	.593
Groundball	.274	656	180	38	5	18	103	62	135	.336	.430	Behind in Count	.216	1266	273	46	8	24	136	0	477	.218	.321
Flyball	.282	536	151	30	3	16	78	61	113	.352	.438	Two Strikes	.191	1352	258	41	7	31	133	146	587	.270	.300
Home	.284	1351	384	73	8	55	232	161	268	.359	.472	Batting #3	.279	2445	682	130	20	91	413	252	502	.345	.460
Away	.270	1498	404	78	13	44	233	127	319	.327	.427	Batting #5	.281	260	73	15	1	6	31	19	48	.331	.415
Day	.288	1064	306	53	10	34	177	94	201	.344	.452	Other	.229	144	33	6	0	2	21	17	37	.309	.313
Night	.270	1785	482	98	11	65	288	194	386	.341	.446	March/April	.289	398	115	25	5	18	76	42	93	.357	.513
Grass	.279	2462	687	130	18	89	396	254	493	.346	.455	May	.264	512	135	18	3	15	81	51	110	.330	.398
Turf	.261	387	101	21	3	10	69	34	94	.319	.408	June	.287	494	142	31	2	14	74	43	103	.344	.443
Pre-All Star	.281	1586	445	86	10	56	267	153	350	.343	.453	July	.259	540	140	33	5	20	96	62	120	.331	.450
Post-All Star	.272	1263	343	65	11	43	198	135	237	.341	.443	August	.285	491	140	23	3	19	83	48	85	.350	.460
Scoring Posn	.298	783	233	40	7	23	354	104	172	.366	.455	Sept/Oct	.280	414	116	21	3	13	55	42	76	.347	.440
Close & Late	.266	384	102	20	0	14	69	38	93	.327	.427	vs. AL	.276	2812	775	148	20	98	458	286	581	.342	.447
None on/out	.272	541	147	28	6	22	22	44	112	.331	.468	vs. NL	.351	37	13	3	1	1	7	2	6	.385	.568

Batter vs. Pitcher (career)

Hits Best Against	Avg	AB	H	2B	3B	HR	RBI	BB	SO	OBP	SLG	Hits Worst Against	Avg	AB	H	2B	3B	HR	RBI	BB	SO	OBP	SLG
Dennis Martinez	.545	11	6	1	0	0	0	4	2	.667	.636	Bobby Ayala	.000	13	0	0	0	0	0	0	5	.000	.000
Mark Leiter	.462	13	6	2	0	1	3	0	2	.429	.846	John Smiley	.083	12	1	0	0	0	0	1	4	.154	.083
Roberto Hernandez	.375	16	6	0	0	3	7	1	6	.412	.938	Dan Plesac	.091	11	1	0	0	0	0	1	1	.231	.091
Brian Anderson	.375	8	3	1	0	2	3	1	0	.455	1.250	Rick Aguilera	.105	19	2	1	0	0	1	1	5	.150	.158
Tim Wakefield	.353	17	6	1	0	3	5	1	2	.368	.941	Ken Hill	.105	19	2	0	0	0	2	3	4	.217	.105

Brad Fullmer — Expos

Age 23 – Bats Left

	Avg	G	AB	R	H	2B	3B	HR	RBI	BB	SO	HBP	GDP	SB	CS	OBP	SLG	IBB	SH	SF	#Pit	#P/PA	GB	FB	G/F
1997 Season	.300	19	40	4	12	2	0	3	8	2	7	1	0	0	0	.349	.575	1	0	0	144	3.35	14	13	1.08

1997 Season

	Avg	AB	H	2B	3B	HR	RBI	BB	SO	OBP	SLG		Avg	AB	H	2B	3B	HR	RBI	BB	SO	OBP	SLG
vs. Left	.182	11	2	1	0	0	1	1	2	.250	.273	Scoring Posn	.364	11	4	1	0	2	7	1	3	.417	1.000
vs. Right	.345	29	10	1	0	3	7	1	5	.387	.690	Close & Late	.333	6	2	1	0	0	0	1	0	.429	.500

Gary Gaetti — Cardinals

Age 39 – Bats Right

	Avg	G	AB	R	H	2B	3B	HR	RBI	BB	SO	HBP	GDP	SB	CS	OBP	SLG	IBB	SH	SF	#Pit	#P/PA	GB	FB	G/F
1997 Season	.251	148	502	63	126	24	1	17	69	36	88	6	20	7	3	.305	.404	3	4	6	1844	3.33	201	135	1.49
Last Five Years	.263	618	2196	303	578	113	9	101	352	158	426	32	51	13	13	.318	.461	18	14	27	8290	3.42	757	672	1.13

1997 Season

	Avg	AB	H	2B	3B	HR	RBI	BB	SO	OBP	SLG		Avg	AB	H	2B	3B	HR	RBI	BB	SO	OBP	SLG
vs. Left	.277	112	31	6	0	5	18	14	17	.359	.464	First Pitch	.257	109	28	5	0	5	19	1	0	.257	.440
vs. Right	.244	390	95	18	1	12	51	22	71	.289	.387	Ahead in Count	.307	101	31	6	0	3	16	20	0	.423	.455
Groundball	.265	113	30	3	0	2	14	4	17	.288	.345	Behind in Count	.219	215	47	9	1	7	25	0	72	.227	.367
Flyball	.271	70	19	5	0	2	9	5	16	.329	.429	Two Strikes	.177	198	35	5	0	6	16	15	88	.237	.293
Home	.250	256	64	18	0	7	37	17	37	.295	.402	Batting #5	.235	226	53	12	0	7	36	14	39	.279	.381
Away	.252	246	62	6	1	10	32	19	51	.316	.407	Batting #6	.279	179	50	7	1	9	20	12	30	.340	.480
Day	.280	164	46	10	0	5	28	8	26	.316	.433	Other	.237	97	23	5	0	1	13	10	19	.303	.320
Night	.237	338	80	14	1	12	41	28	62	.300	.391	March/April	.218	78	17	3	0	1	7	5	14	.274	.295
Grass	.268	406	109	22	1	14	60	26	58	.316	.431	May	.267	75	20	0	0	4	14	4	12	.321	.507

1997 Season

	Avg	AB	H	2B	3B	HR	RBI	BB	SO	OBP	SLG		Avg	AB	H	2B	3B	HR	RBI	BB	SO	OBP	SLG
Turf	.177	96	17	2	0	3	9	10	30	.262	.292	June	.305	82	25	8	0	1	10	8	18	.363	.439
Pre-All Star	.256	258	66	18	0	6	32	20	46	.316	.395	July	.271	96	26	4	0	6	16	10	16	.343	.500
Post-All Star	.246	244	60	6	1	11	37	16	42	.295	.414	August	.202	94	19	0	1	2	8	7	17	.260	.287
Scoring Posn	.247	146	36	10	0	3	53	8	33	.284	.377	Sept/Oct	.247	77	19	3	0	3	14	2	11	.268	.403
Close & Late	.270	100	27	5	0	4	14	4	26	.299	.440	vs. AL	.340	50	17	3	1	1	6	5	5	.404	.500
None on/out	.258	132	34	7	4	6	6	8	16	.310	.462	vs. NL	.241	452	109	21	0	16	63	31	83	.294	.394

1997 By Position

Position	Avg	AB	H	2B	3B	HR	RBI	BB	SO	OBP	SLG	G	GS	Innings	PO	A	E	DP	Fld Pct	Rng Fctr	In Zone	Outs	Zone Rtg	MLB Zone
As Pinch Hitter	.182	11	2	2	0	0	2	1	1	.250	.364	12	0	---	---	---	---	---	---	---	---	---	---	---
As 1b	.208	24	5	0	0	1	1	3	4	.321	.333	20	4	68.0	61	6	0	8	1.000	---	19	18	.947	.874
As 3b	.255	466	119	22	1	16	66	32	83	.306	.410	132	127	1075.1	72	244	7	27	.978	2.64	321	276	.860	.801

Last Five Years

	Avg	AB	H	2B	3B	HR	RBI	BB	SO	OBP	SLG		Avg	AB	H	2B	3B	HR	RBI	BB	SO	OBP	SLG
vs. Left	.253	541	137	28	3	29	95	60	108	.330	.477	First Pitch	.286	419	120	27	1	18	85	13	0	.305	.484
vs. Right	.266	1655	441	85	6	72	257	98	318	.314	.456	Ahead in Count	.366	459	168	33	1	32	87	76	0	.456	.651
Groundball	.265	475	126	16	3	23	81	31	92	.316	.457	Behind in Count	.203	965	196	34	7	32	114	0	361	.217	.352
Flyball	.268	380	102	20	3	20	62	23	80	.314	.495	Two Strikes	.181	908	164	28	4	24	87	68	426	.248	.300
Home	.279	1079	301	75	7	47	180	76	194	.331	.492	Batting #5	.265	795	211	38	5	26	112	51	154	.316	.424
Away	.248	1117	277	38	2	54	172	82	232	.306	.431	Batting #6	.283	689	195	40	4	36	112	45	136	.332	.509
Day	.275	655	180	34	3	34	121	41	128	.323	.492	Other	.242	712	172	35	0	39	128	62	136	.307	.455
Night	.258	1541	398	79	6	67	231	117	298	.314	.448	March/April	.252	258	65	12	0	9	34	15	46	.299	.403
Grass	.261	1554	405	72	5	75	254	112	279	.316	.458	May	.282	355	100	22	1	17	65	29	60	.347	.493
Turf	.269	642	173	41	4	26	98	46	147	.324	.467	June	.247	397	98	18	1	15	60	27	78	.297	.411
Pre-All Star	.262	1116	292	60	2	48	178	80	206	.316	.437	July	.303	390	118	31	1	18	67	33	82	.363	.526
Post-All Star	.265	1080	286	53	7	57	174	78	220	.320	.485	August	.246	423	104	16	4	21	56	32	86	.302	.452
Scoring Posn	.257	622	160	34	0	27	247	54	134	.319	.442	Sept/Oct	.249	373	93	14	2	21	70	22	74	.297	.466
Close & Late	.290	400	116	15	2	26	72	23	89	.335	.533	vs. AL	.267	1222	326	65	5	62	209	92	246	.324	.480
None on/out	.236	533	126	34	3	24	24	41	85	.316	.436	vs. NL	.259	974	252	48	4	39	143	66	180	.311	.436

Batter vs. Pitcher (since 1984)

Hits Best Against	Avg	AB	H	2B	3B	HR	RBI	BB	SO	OBP	SLG	Hits Worst Against	Avg	AB	H	2B	3B	HR	RBI	BB	SO	OBP	SLG
Greg Cadaret	.733	15	11	2	0	1	7	4	1	.750	1.067	Kevin Appier	.077	13	1	0	0	0	0	0	6	.077	.077
Tim Belcher	.474	19	9	2	0	1	3	1	1	.500	.737	Ramon Martinez	.083	12	1	0	0	0	0	0	0	.083	.083
Jason Bere	.471	17	8	1	0	1	6	0	5	.471	.706	Donn Pall	.083	12	1	0	0	0	0	0	1	.154	.083
Rich DeLucia	.400	10	4	0	0	1	1	1	0	.455	.700	Jose Mesa	.091	11	1	0	0	0	0	0	2	.091	.091
Dennis Cook	.364	11	4	1	0	1	4	2	4	.462	.727	Wilson Alvarez	.115	26	3	0	0	0	0	1	6	.148	.115

Greg Gagne — Dodgers

Age 36 – Bats Right

	Avg	G	AB	R	H	2B	3B	HR	RBI	BB	SO	HBP	GDP	SB	CS	OBP	SLG	IBB	SH	SF	#Pit	P/PA	GB	FB	G/F
1997 Season	.251	144	514	49	129	20	3	9	57	31	120	4	13	2	5	.298	.354	4	3	1	1935	3.50	189	118	1.60
Last Five Years	.261	658	2287	260	596	113	15	42	269	179	445	12	45	29	41	.316	.378	18	20	14	9061	3.61	761	630	1.21

1997 Season

	Avg	AB	H	2B	3B	HR	RBI	BB	SO	OBP	SLG		Avg	AB	H	2B	3B	HR	RBI
vs. Left	.256	133	34	9	0	3	14	9	32	.303	.391	First Pitch	.368	87	32	3	3	2	16
vs. Right	.249	381	95	11	3	6	43	22	88	.297	.341	Ahead in Count	.320	100	32	6	0	5	18
Groundball	.229	96	22	5	1	2	12	5	22	.267	.365	Behind in Count	.169	248	42	7	0	1	11
Flyball	.141	64	9	1	0	1	6	0	11	.154	.203	Two Strikes	.163	239	39	4	0	0	12
Home	.235	260	61	6	1	2	20	14	57	.284	.288	Batting #7	.249	241	60	6	1	6	29
Away	.268	254	68	14	2	7	37	17	63	.313	.421	Batting #8	.247	146	36	5	2	1	14
Day	.256	121	31	9	1	0	12	10	33	.313	.347	Other	.260	127	33	9	0	2	14
Night	.249	393	98	11	2	9	45	21	85	.294	.356	March/April	.356	90	32	3	2	2	13
Grass	.251	419	105	15	2	8	38	24	89	.298	.353	May	.175	97	17	6	0	0	5
Turf	.253	95	24	5	1	1	19	7	31	.301	.358	June	.276	98	27	4	0	3	11
Pre-All Star	.277	310	86	14	3	5	36	15	57	.313	.390	July	.310	71	22	1	1	1	13
Post-All Star	.211	204	43	6	0	4	21	16	63	.277	.299	August	.219	96	21	4	0	2	12
Scoring Posn	.281	128	36	4	3	1	44	13	37	.354	.383	Sept/Oct	.161	62	10	2	0	1	3
Close & Late	.253	91	23	4	1	1	9	8	22	.313	.352	vs. AL	.270	63	17	2	0	0	7
None on/out	.254	118	30	1	0	3	3	7	26	.296	.339	vs. NL	.248	451	112	18	3	9	50

1997 By Position

Position	Avg	AB	H	2B	3B	HR	RBI	BB	SO	OBP	SLG	G	GS	Innings	PO	A	E	DP	Fld Pct	Rng Fctr	Zone
As ss	.251	513	129	20	3	9	57	31	120	.299	.355	143	138	1223.0	174	358	16	55	.971	3.91	38

Last Five Years

	Avg	AB	H	2B	3B	HR	RBI	BB	SO	OBP	SLG		Avg	AB	H	2B	3B	HR	RBI	BB	SO	OBP	SLG
vs. Left	.263	570	150	35	2	10	70	53	113	.324	.384	First Pitch	.351	376	132	27	7	14	73	15	0	.375	.572
vs. Right	.260	1717	446	78	13	32	199	126	332	.313	.376	Ahead in Count	.333	447	149	34	3	10	72	95	0	.448	.490
Groundball	.252	468	118	22	1	7	46	34	75	.308	.348	Behind in Count	.189	1066	202	34	5	9	78	0	399	.194	.256
Flyball	.251	434	109	27	3	12	65	25	96	.291	.410	Two Strikes	.179	1037	186	33	5	10	84	68	445	.233	.250
Home	.267	1105	295	55	6	12	125	90	196	.325	.360	Batting #7	.284	514	146	26	5	11	62	34	105	.333	.418
Away	.255	1182	301	58	9	30	144	89	249	.307	.395	Batting #8	.243	971	236	35	4	18	117	78	217	.302	.343
Day	.261	610	159	35	4	15	82	61	129	.329	.405	Other	.267	802	214	52	6	13	90	67	123	.322	.395
Night	.261	1677	437	78	11	27	187	118	316	.311	.369	March/April	.277	307	85	12	4	7	36	31	46	.345	.410
Grass	.249	1484	369	65	11	28	158	111	283	.303	.364	May	.264	405	107	24	2	6	48	36	86	.325	.378

Last Five Years

	Avg	AB	H	2B	3B	HR	RBI	BB	SO	OBP	SLG		Avg	AB	H	2B	3B	HR	RBI	BB	SO	OBP	SLG
Turf	.283	803	227	48	4	14	111	68	162	.340	.405	June	.256	383	98	18	1	8	41	26	74	.303	.371
Pre-All Star	.272	1207	328	58	9	22	141	101	225	.329	.389	July	.295	403	119	18	4	7	52	28	69	.341	.412
Post-All Star	.248	1080	268	55	6	20	128	78	220	.301	.366	August	.253	446	113	27	4	10	59	30	81	.304	.399
Scoring Posn	.279	570	159	33	8	8	213	66	125	.350	.407	Sept/Oct	.216	343	74	14	0	4	33	28	89	.279	.292
Close & Late	.243	408	99	15	2	6	40	26	96	.289	.333	vs. AL	.266	1408	375	82	10	23	164	100	243	.316	.388
None on/out	.264	515	136	20	3	11	11	40	95	.322	.379	vs. NL	.251	879	221	31	5	19	105	79	202	.316	.363

Batter vs. Pitcher (since 1984)

Hits Best Against	Avg	AB	H	2B	3B	HR	RBI	BB	SO	OBP	SLG	Hits Worst Against	Avg	AB	H	2B	3B	HR	RBI	BB	SO	OBP	SLG
David Cone	.500	12	6	3	0	0	2	0	2	.500	.750	Curt Schilling	.056	18	1	1	0	0	2	0	12	.056	.111
Eddie Guardado	.500	10	5	4	0	0	4	1	1	.545	.900	Ben McDonald	.077	13	1	0	0	0	1	3	.143	.154
Shane Reynolds	.444	9	4	1	0	1	1	3	2	.583	.889	Mike Magnante	.091	11	1	0	0	1	0	2	.091	.182
Scott Bailes	.444	9	4	1	0	0	3	2	0	.545	.556	John Smoltz	.091	11	1	0	0	0	1	8	.167	.091
Tom Candiotti	.400	35	14	8	0	1	3	0	5	.417	.714	Jeff Montgomery	.100	10	1	0	0	0	1	1	.182	.100

Eddie Gaillard — Tigers
Age 27 – Pitches Right (flyball pitcher)

	ERA	W	L	Sv	G	GS	IP	BB	SO	Avg	H	2B	3B	HR	RBI	OBP	SLG	GF	IR	IRS	Hld	SvOp	SB	CS	GB	FB	G/F
1997 Season	5.31	1	0	1	16	0	20.1	10	12	.211	16	2	1	2	9	.295	.342	5	3	0	0	2	3	0	20	29	0.69

1997 Season

	ERA	W	L	Sv	G	GS	IP	H	HR	BB	SO		Avg	AB	H	2B	3B	HR	RBI	BB	SO	OBP	SLG
Home	4.05	0	0	0	6	0	6.2	3	0	3	5	vs. Left	.212	33	7	1	1	1	5	4	3	.289	.394
Away	5.93	1	0	1	10	0	13.2	13	2	7	7	vs. Right	.209	43	9	1	0	1	4	6	9	.300	.302

Andres Galarraga — Rockies
Age 37 – Bats Right (groundball hitter)

	Avg	G	AB	R	H	2B	3B	HR	RBI	BB	SO	HBP	GDP	SB	CS	OBP	SLG	IBB	SH	SF	#Pit	#P/PA	GB	FB	G/F
1997 Season	.318	154	600	120	191	31	3	41	140	54	141	17	16	15	8	.389	.585	2	0	3	2504	3.72	221	147	1.50
Last Five Years	.316	679	2667	476	843	155	13	172	579	169	610	61	55	55	25	.367	.577	31	0	27	10336	3.53	935	705	1.33

1997 Season

	Avg	AB	H	2B	3B	HR	RBI	BB	SO	OBP	SLG		Avg	AB	H	2B	3B	HR	RBI	BB	SO	OBP	SLG
vs. Left	.333	126	42	9	0	10	33	18	24	.426	.643	First Pitch	.457	81	37	4	1	8	34	2	0	.489	.827
vs. Right	.314	474	149	22	3	31	107	36	117	.378	.570	Ahead in Count	.433	141	61	12	0	13	44	24	0	.515	.794
Groundball	.370	119	44	8	0	10	45	15	21	.439	.689	Behind in Count	.219	274	60	8	1	12	37	0	122	.238	.387
Flyball	.223	103	23	4	0	6	21	8	36	.304	.437	Two Strikes	.197	284	56	9	1	12	42	28	141	.281	.363
Home	.342	298	102	17	0	21	89	29	63	.406	.611	Batting #4	.312	539	168	26	3	33	117	48	132	.384	.555
Away	.295	302	89	14	3	20	51	25	78	.372	.560	Batting #5	.397	58	23	5	0	8	23	6	7	.453	.897
Day	.313	281	88	15	1	21	77	25	74	.384	.598	Other	.000	3	0	0	0	0	0	0	2	.000	.000
Night	.323	319	103	16	2	20	63	29	67	.393	.574	March/April	.347	75	26	4	0	5	22	13	16	.462	.600
Grass	.321	492	158	25	2	37	129	43	122	.389	.606	May	.319	116	37	5	1	9	33	9	22	.383	.612
Turf	.306	108	33	6	1	4	11	11	19	.385	.491	June	.342	117	40	5	1	8	29	11	26	.402	.607
Pre-All Star	.323	328	106	15	2	22	84	34	72	.399	.582	July	.267	101	27	5	1	6	17	11	33	.357	.515
Post-All Star	.313	272	85	16	1	19	56	20	69	.375	.588	August	.297	101	30	3	0	8	22	5	21	.349	.564
Scoring Posn	.288	191	55	9	2	9	98	26	56	.379	.497	Sept/Oct	.344	90	31	9	0	5	17	5	23	.394	.611
Close & Late	.238	80	19	2	0	4	17	6	30	.303	.413	vs. AL	.353	68	24	6	0	5	14	3	13	.380	.662
None on/out	.345	142	49	9	4	8	8	12	27	.400	.592	vs. NL	.314	532	167	25	3	36	126	51	128	.390	.575

1997 By Position

Position	Avg	AB	H	2B	3B	HR	RBI	BB	SO	OBP	SLG	G	GS	Innings	PO	A	E	DP	Fld Pct	Rng Fctr	In Zone	Zone Outs	Zone Rtg	MLB Zone
As 1b	.319	599	191	31	3	41	140	54	140	.389	.586	154	150	1325.2	1459	117	15	179	.991	---	334	287	.859	.874

Last Five Years

	Avg	AB	H	2B	3B	HR	RBI	BB	SO	OBP	SLG		Avg	AB	H	2B	3B	HR	RBI	BB	SO	OBP	SLG
vs. Left	.328	609	200	40	3	50	162	51	119	.380	.650	First Pitch	.424	406	172	37	3	34	139	27	0	.473	.781
vs. Right	.312	2058	643	115	10	122	417	118	491	.363	.556	Ahead in Count	.453	618	280	52	4	54	175	69	0	.505	.812
Groundball	.335	723	242	47	4	53	186	48	148	.381	.631	Behind in Count	.218	1210	264	46	4	50	162	0	516	.231	.387
Flyball	.287	436	125	24	1	31	89	38	133	.353	.560	Two Strikes	.189	1200	227	39	4	46	152	72	610	.243	.343
Home	.350	1361	476	84	7	100	355	96	270	.401	.642	Batting #4	.324	1855	601	105	10	114	392	120	433	.375	.576
Away	.281	1306	367	71	6	72	224	73	340	.331	.510	Batting #5	.301	625	188	37	3	51	158	37	136	.350	.614
Day	.319	1033	330	65	6	70	257	77	214	.377	.597	Other	.289	187	54	13	0	7	29	12	41	.341	.471
Night	.314	1634	513	90	7	102	322	92	396	.360	.565	March/April	.317	366	116	22	2	25	97	29	79	.373	.593
Grass	.322	2138	688	117	9	147	502	145	482	.374	.591	May	.311	485	151	26	1	31	113	27	121	.354	.561
Turf	.293	529	155	38	4	25	77	24	128	.336	.522	June	.347	525	182	35	3	33	109	44	123	.406	.613
Pre-All Star	.318	1539	489	92	7	100	352	107	364	.370	.582	July	.291	495	144	22	3	34	94	30	111	.346	.549
Post-All Star	.314	1128	354	63	6	72	227	62	246	.362	.572	August	.309	376	116	17	2	28	80	19	90	.357	.588
Scoring Posn	.335	782	262	58	4	53	417	80	202	.399	.623	Sept/Oct	.319	420	134	33	3	21	86	20	86	.360	.562
Close & Late	.284	352	100	16	3	17	62	31	105	.356	.491	vs. AL	.353	68	24	6	0	5	14	3	13	.380	.662
None on/out	.293	663	194	37	3	32	32	33	148	.331	.502	vs. NL	.315	2599	819	149	13	167	565	166	597	.367	.575

Batter vs. Pitcher (career)

Hits Best Against	Avg	AB	H	2B	3B	HR	RBI	BB	SO	OBP	SLG	Hits Worst Against	Avg	AB	H	2B	3B	HR	RBI	BB	SO	OBP	SLG
Mel Rojas	.750	12	9	3	0	1	5	0	2	.750	1.250	Dennis Cook	.000	10	0	0	0	0	0	1	3	.167	.000
Al Leiter	.625	8	5	2	0	1	6	3	1	.667	1.250	Butch Henry	.083	12	1	1	0	0	1	0	1	.083	.167
Esteban Loaiza	.611	18	11	4	1	0	5	1	1	.632	.944	Tom Candiotti	.118	17	2	0	0	2	0	4	.111	.118
Mike Maddux	.550	20	11	3	0	2	8	1	2	.571	1.000	Hideo Nomo	.125	24	3	0	0	1	2	10	.192	.125
Amaury Telemaco	.364	11	4	0	1	3	7	0	1	.364	1.364	Greg McMichael	.154	13	2	0	0	0	0	7	.154	.154

Mike Gallego — Cardinals   Age 37 – Bats Right

	Avg	G	AB	R	H	2B	3B	HR	RBI	BB	SO	HBP	GDP	SB	CS	OBP	SLG	IBB	SH	SF	#Pit	#P/PA	GB	FB	G/F
1997 Season	.163	27	43	6	7	2	0	0	1	1	6	0	0	0	0	.178	.209	0	1	1	145	3.15	17	14	1.21
Last Five Years	.248	329	1015	131	252	41	2	16	108	110	172	10	23	3	4	.325	.340	2	14	10	4268	3.68	386	274	1.41

1997 Season

	Avg	AB	H	2B	3B	HR	RBI	BB	SO	OBP	SLG		Avg	AB	H	2B	3B	HR	RBI	BB	SO	OBP	SLG
vs. Left	.077	13	1	1	0	0	0	0	3	.077	.154	Scoring Posn	.091	11	1	0	0	0	1	0	1	.083	.091
vs. Right	.200	30	6	1	0	0	1	1	3	.219	.233	Close & Late	.000	6	0	0	0	0	0	0	2	.000	.000

Last Five Years

	Avg	AB	H	2B	3B	HR	RBI	BB	SO	OBP	SLG		Avg	AB	H	2B	3B	HR	RBI	BB	SO	OBP	SLG
vs. Left	.287	328	94	17	0	8	35	37	46	.361	.412	First Pitch	.301	193	58	8	0	3	15	1	0	.304	.389
vs. Right	.230	687	158	24	2	8	73	73	126	.308	.306	Ahead in Count	.306	245	75	14	1	7	45	64	0	.449	.457
Groundball	.261	199	52	9	1	2	23	21	30	.339	.347	Behind in Count	.172	384	66	7	0	1	23	0	146	.177	.198
Flyball	.219	210	46	5	1	3	20	25	33	.301	.295	Two Strikes	.178	428	76	12	1	4	33	45	172	.261	.238
Home	.258	480	124	25	0	7	40	54	86	.340	.354	Batting #8	.241	680	164	27	1	13	72	78	118	.322	.341
Away	.239	535	128	16	2	9	68	56	86	.311	.306	Batting #9	.259	147	38	7	0	0	16	14	24	.325	.306
Day	.247	361	89	12	2	4	33	52	65	.348	.324	Other	.266	188	50	7	1	3	20	18	30	.333	.362
Night	.249	654	163	29	0	12	75	58	107	.312	.349	March/April	.236	106	25	2	0	4	17	12	14	.319	.368
Grass	.253	849	215	35	1	13	89	92	142	.330	.340	May	.229	192	44	8	0	2	19	26	26	.329	.302
Turf	.223	166	37	6	1	3	19	18	30	.299	.325	June	.280	150	42	13	1	2	17	13	22	.333	.420
Pre-All Star	.244	484	118	23	1	8	57	54	67	.324	.345	July	.238	185	44	4	0	2	17	13	36	.294	.292
Post-All Star	.252	531	134	18	1	8	51	56	105	.326	.335	August	.273	220	60	10	1	3	24	22	40	.341	.368
Scoring Posn	.202	277	56	12	0	2	88	36	50	.291	.267	Sept/Oct	.228	162	37	4	0	3	14	24	34	.328	.309
Close & Late	.230	139	32	4	0	3	13	11	21	.301	.324	vs. AL	.258	837	216	37	2	16	103	98	135	.339	.364
None on/out	.259	259	67	13	0	6		26	45	.331	.378	vs. NL	.202	178	36	4	0	5		12	37	.255	.225

Batter vs. Pitcher (career)

Hits Best Against	Avg	AB	H	2B	3B	HR	RBI	BB	SO	OBP	SLG	Hits Worst Against	Avg	AB	H	2B	3B	HR	RBI	BB	SO	OBP	SLG
Mike Timlin	.444	9	4	0	0	0	3	2	1	.545	.444	Juan Guzman	.000	9	0	0	0	0	0	5	3	.357	.000
Kenny Rogers	.400	15	6	1	0	1	2	1	3	.412	.667	Mark Gubicza	.053	19	1	0	0	0	0	3	3	.182	.053
Alex Fernandez	.389	18	7	2	0	1	5	2	3	.429	.667	Ben McDonald	.056	18	1	0	0	0	0	2	5	.150	.056
Al Leiter	.375	8	3	0	0	0	2	3	0	.545	.375	Pat Hentgen	.067	15	1	0	0	0	0	1	2	.125	.067
Jack McDowell	.313	16	5	1	0	1	4	4	2	.450	.563	Greg Swindell	.129	31	4	0	0	0	0	2	9	.182	.129

Ron Gant — Cardinals   Age 33 – Bats Right (flyball hitter)

	Avg	G	AB	R	H	2B	3B	HR	RBI	BB	SO	HBP	GDP	SB	CS	OBP	SLG	IBB	SH	SF	#Pit	#P/PA	GB	FB	G/F
1997 Season	.229	139	502	68	115	21	4	17	62	58	162	1	2	14	6	.310	.388	3	0	1	2343	4.17	139	135	1.03
Last Five Years	.257	537	1937	334	497	81	14	112	349	272	485	9	36	76	27	.348	.486	15	2	17	9034	4.04	553	622	0.89

1997 Season

	Avg	AB	H	2B	3B	HR	RBI	BB	SO	OBP	SLG		Avg	AB	H	2B	3B	HR	RBI	BB	SO	OBP	SLG
vs. Left	.197	122	24	4	2	5	15	17	37	.295	.385	First Pitch	.383	60	23	3	0	4	10	2	0	.403	.633
vs. Right	.239	380	91	17	2	12	47	41	125	.314	.389	Ahead in Count	.349	86	30	8	0	7	19	24	0	.491	.686
Groundball	.238	101	24	5	0	5	15	11	31	.313	.436	Behind in Count	.158	240	38	7	2	2	17	0	117	.158	.229
Flyball	.218	78	17	5	0	1	7	6	26	.274	.321	Two Strikes	.144	291	42	5	2	5	25	32	162	.231	.227
Home	.234	244	57	9	3	11	34	26	75	.307	.430	Batting #2	.251	207	52	10	3	6	26	19	64	.314	.415
Away	.225	258	58	12	1	6	28	32	87	.312	.349	Batting #5	.259	112	29	6	0	4	11	11	38	.325	.420
Day	.248	161	40	6	2	4	19	26	53	.351	.385	Other	.186	183	34	5	1	7	25	28	60	.296	.339
Night	.220	341	75	15	2	13	43	32	109	.289	.390	March/April	.230	87	20	5	1	3	14	11	30	.316	.414
Grass	.230	404	93	14	4	16	50	51	128	.317	.403	May	.198	86	17	2	1	6	14	11	29	.289	.453
Turf	.224	98	22	7	0	1	12	7	34	.276	.327	June	.258	97	25	2	2	3	12	10	31	.333	.412
Pre-All Star	.229	288	66	12	4	12	40	35	97	.315	.424	July	.226	84	19	5	0	2	10	12	23	.320	.357
Post-All Star	.229	214	49	9	0	5	22	23	65	.303	.341	August	.234	94	22	6	0	0	7	10	26	.308	.298
Scoring Posn	.269	130	35	6	2	5	45	23	41	.381	.462	Sept/Oct	.222	54	12	1	0	3	5	4	23	.276	.407
Close & Late	.228	114	26	5	1	4	21	8	36	.279	.395	vs. AL	.150	40	6	3	0	2	5	6	16	.261	.375
None on/out	.145	117	17	2	1	1	1	9	43	.206	.205	vs. NL	.236	462	109	18	4	15	57	52	146	.314	.390

1997 By Position

Position	Avg	AB	H	2B	3B	HR	RBI	BB	SO	OBP	SLG	G	GS	Innings	PO	A	E	DP	Fld Pct	Rng Fctr	In Zone	Zone Outs	Zone Rtg	MLB Zone
As Pinch Hitter	.182	11	2	1	0	0	3	2	5	.308	.273	13	0	---	---	---	---	---	---	---	---	---	---
As lf	.232	487	113	20	4	17	59	56	154	.312	.394	128	125	1084.1	248	4	6	1	.977	2.09	284	240	845	.805

Last Five Years

	Avg	AB	H	2B	3B	HR	RBI	BB	SO	OBP	SLG		Avg	AB	H	2B	3B	HR	RBI	BB	SO	OBP	SLG
vs. Left	.241	449	108	15	3	25	76	81	89	.356	.454	First Pitch	.372	234	87	12	1	23	68	11	0	.400	.726
vs. Right	.261	1488	389	66	11	87	273	191	396	.345	.496	Ahead in Count	.340	397	135	26	4	40	100	137	0	.506	.728
Groundball	.251	542	136	20	5	33	101	72	133	.339	.489	Behind in Count	.191	860	164	27	6	24	99	0	361	.194	.320
Flyball	.236	296	70	14	2	16	52	48	75	.342	.459	Two Strikes	.173	994	172	29	6	27	109	123	485	.267	.296
Home	.254	955	243	37	8	57	173	137	226	.347	.489	Batting #3	.260	959	249	30	6	58	178	142	235	.353	.485
Away	.259	982	254	44	6	55	176	135	259	.350	.484	Batting #4	.253	368	93	14	3	26	81	65	74	.370	.519
Day	.221	566	125	16	4	25	87	91	159	.327	.396	Other	.254	610	155	37	5	28	90	65	176	.326	.469
Night	.271	1371	372	65	10	87	262	181	326	.357	.524	March/April	.222	275	61	12	2	12	44	39	72	.320	.411
Grass	.257	1321	339	50	11	78	240	181	322	.346	.488	May	.272	283	77	13	4	23	72	46	65	.375	.590
Turf	.256	616	158	31	3	34	109	91	163	.353	.482	June	.277	339	94	19	4	22	57	43	87	.361	.552
Pre-All Star	.254	1010	257	51	10	64	190	150	250	.352	.515	July	.246	354	87	15	1	23	58	58	85	.353	.489
Post-All Star	.259	927	240	30	4	48	159	122	235	.344	.455	August	.252	381	96	11	1	19	70	41	93	.322	.436
Scoring Posn	.285	527	150	30	6	33	246	106	143	.397	.552	Sept/Oct	.269	305	82	11	2	13	48	45	83	.361	.446
Close & Late	.275	331	91	15	2	21	67	36	85	.348	.523	vs. AL	.150	40	6	3	0	2	5	6	16	.261	.375

Last Five Years

	Avg	AB	H	2B	3B	HR	RBI	BB	SO	OBP	SLG		Avg	AB	H	2B	3B	HR	RBI	BB	SO	OBP	SLG
None on/out	.231	420	97	13	1	27	27	41	114	.302	.460	vs. NL	.259	1897	491	78	14	110	344	266	469	.350	.489

Batter vs. Pitcher (career)

Hits Best Against	Avg	AB	H	2B	3B	HR	RBI	BB	SO	OBP	SLG	Hits Worst Against	Avg	AB	H	2B	3B	HR	RBI	BB	SO	OBP	SLG
Jaime Navarro	.600	10	6	2	0	2	4	3	1	.692	1.400	Todd Worrell	.000	14	0	0	0	0	0	2	5	.125	.000
Jeff Shaw	.500	10	5	0	0	2	3	3	2	.615	1.100	Pat Rapp	.000	10	0	0	0	0	0	4	6	.286	.000
Bruce Ruffin	.476	21	10	4	1	1	8	3	2	.542	.905	Denny Neagle	.067	15	1	0	0	0	0	3	4	.222	.067
Omar Olivares	.455	22	10	3	1	3	7	4	3	.538	1.091	Sid Fernandez	.080	25	2	0	0	0	2	6	8	.250	.080
Jerry Dipoto	.455	11	5	0	0	2	6	0	2	.455	1.000	Mark Davis	.111	9	1	0	0	0	0	2	3	.273	.111

Rich Garces — Red Sox
Age 27 – Pitches Right (groundball pitcher)

	ERA	W	L	Sv	G	GS	IP	BB	SO	Avg	H	2B	3B	HR	RBI	OBP	SLG	GF	IR	IRS	Hld	SvOp	SB	CS	GB	FB	G/F
1997 Season	4.61	0	1	0	12	0	13.2	9	12	.255	14	1	0	2	15	.364	.382	4	12	8	1	2	4	0	22	13	1.69
Last Five Years	4.50	3	5	0	70	0	86.0	55	92	.254	85	16	3	8	59	.356	.392	21	56	22	6	5	9	2	108	69	1.57

1997 Season

	ERA	W	L	Sv	G	GS	IP	H	HR	BB	SO		Avg	AB	H	2B	3B	HR	RBI	BB	SO	OBP	SLG
Home	7.04	0	1	0	7	0	7.2	9	1	5	8	vs. Left	.370	27	10	1	0	2	12	4	3	.438	.630
Away	1.50	0	0	0	5	0	6.0	5	1	4	4	vs. Right	.143	28	4	0	0	0	3	5	9	.294	.143

Carlos Garcia — Blue Jays
Age 30 – Bats Right (groundball hitter)

	Avg	G	AB	R	H	2B	3B	HR	RBI	BB	SO	HBP	GDP	SB	CS	OBP	SLG	IBB	SH	SF	#Pit	#P/PA	GB	FB	G/F
1997 Season	.220	103	350	29	77	18	2	3	23	16	50	2	7	11	3	.253	.309	0	10	4	1284	3.37	165	75	2.20
Last Five Years	.270	547	2065	262	557	100	15	33	192	110	307	21	29	71	33	.311	.381	12	25	15	7763	3.47	905	502	1.80

1997 Season

	Avg	AB	H	2B	3B	HR	RBI	BB	SO	OBP	SLG		Avg	AB	H	2B	3B	HR	RBI	BB	SO	OBP	SLG
vs. Left	.176	102	18	4	1	1	6	6	17	.227	.265	First Pitch	.159	63	10	1	0	2	4	0	0	.159	.270
vs. Right	.238	248	59	14	1	2	17	9	43	.264	.327	Ahead in Count	.286	70	20	4	0	1	10	11	0	.373	.386
Groundball	.294	51	15	3	1	0	6	0	2	.294	.392	Behind in Count	.201	159	32	8	1	0	3	0	53	.204	.264
Flyball	.189	53	10	4	1	0	1	2	11	.241	.302	Two Strikes	.190	153	29	10	2	0	7	4	60	.213	.281
Home	.228	171	39	8	1	0	6	6	29	.253	.287	Batting #2	.201	134	27	6	2	0	12	5	24	.231	.276
Away	.212	179	38	10	1	3	17	9	31	.254	.330	Batting #9	.266	158	42	9	0	2	9	6	25	.291	.361
Day	.198	131	26	5	0	0	5	6	26	.236	.237	Other	.138	58	8	3	0	0	1	4	11	.206	.241
Night	.233	219	51	13	2	3	18	9	34	.264	.352	March/April	.163	98	16	3	2	0	7	4	16	.196	.235
Grass	.205	146	30	9	1	3	16	6	28	.242	.342	May	.243	74	18	6	0	0	4	13	.278	.324
Turf	.230	204	47	9	1	0	7	9	32	.262	.284	June	.238	63	15	4	0	1	3	9	.273	.349
Pre-All Star	.215	247	53	13	2	1	12	11	40	.247	.296	July	.250	60	15	2	0	2	5	1	.274	.383
Post-All Star	.233	103	24	5	0	2	11	4	20	.268	.340	August	.179	28	5	0	0	0	1	2	7	.226	.179
Scoring Posn	.145	76	11	3	0	0	18	8	19	.225	.184	Sept/Oct	.296	27	8	3	0	0	5	1	6	.323	.407
Close & Late	.242	62	15	3	0	1	8	3	12	.273	.339	vs. AL	.214	309	66	16	2	3	23	12	55	.245	.307
None on/out	.218	78	17	4	1	0		3	12	.247	.295	vs. NL	.268	41	11	2	0	0	0	3	5	.318	.317

1997 By Position

Position	Avg	AB	H	2B	3B	HR	RBI	BB	SO	OBP	SLG	G	GS	Innings	PO	A	E	DP	Fld Pct	Rng Fctr	In Zone	Zone Outs	Zone Rtg	MLB Zone
As 2b	.224	340	76	18	2	3	22	13	56	.253	.315	96	93	821.2	167	252	8	50	.981	4.59	308	263	.854	.902

Last Five Years

	Avg	AB	H	2B	3B	HR	RBI	BB	SO	OBP	SLG		Avg	AB	H	2B	3B	HR	RBI	BB	SO	OBP	SLG
vs. Left	.280	575	161	34	3	10	50	32	79	.318	.402	First Pitch	.279	294	82	13	0	7	23	9	0	.306	.395
vs. Right	.266	1490	396	66	12	23	142	78	228	.309	.372	Ahead in Count	.309	459	142	21	5	13	60	65	0	.394	.462
Groundball	.292	566	165	27	7	8	55	28	65	.332	.406	Behind in Count	.234	930	218	40	6	7	62	0	269	.243	.313
Flyball	.261	326	85	14	3	6	36	19	57	.310	.377	Two Strikes	.224	857	192	40	4	8	58	36	307	.262	.308
Home	.277	1068	296	49	9	18	102	63	167	.320	.390	Batting #1	.276	959	265	38	7	17	77	43	140	.314	.384
Away	.262	997	261	51	6	15	90	47	140	.302	.370	Batting #8	.261	360	94	24	3	5	34	21	48	.306	.386
Day	.294	629	185	29	4	11	51	40	94	.343	.405	Other	.265	746	198	38	5	11	81	46	119	.311	.374
Night	.259	1436	372	71	11	22	141	70	213	.297	.370	March/April	.253	312	79	12	4	5	35	15	49	.291	.365
Grass	.258	644	166	32	5	13	64	36	94	.306	.384	May	.261	360	94	18	3	2	27	29	60	.318	.344
Turf	.275	1421	391	68	10	20	128	74	213	.314	.379	June	.266	444	118	25	3	6	35	19	67	.299	.376
Pre-All Star	.263	1252	329	64	11	14	105	66	199	.303	.365	July	.265	381	101	19	2	9	28	17	57	.301	.396
Post-All Star	.280	813	228	36	4	19	87	44	108	.324	.405	August	.310	255	79	12	1	5	25	16	33	.358	.424
Scoring Posn	.247	437	108	22	3	6	153	50	72	.321	.352	Sept/Oct	.275	313	86	14	2	6	42	14	41	.314	.390
Close & Late	.244	311	76	12	3	3	34	30	59	.316	.331	vs. AL	.214	309	66	16	2	3	23	12	55	.245	.307
None on/out	.268	665	178	31	3	10	10	22	105	.300	.368	vs. NL	.280	1756	491	84	13	30	169	98	252	.323	.394

Batter vs. Pitcher (career)

Hits Best Against	Avg	AB	H	2B	3B	HR	RBI	BB	SO	OBP	SLG	Hits Worst Against	Avg	AB	H	2B	3B	HR	RBI	BB	SO	OBP	SLG
Steve Trachsel	.563	16	9	0	1	1	4	0	0	.563	.875	Shawn Boskie	.067	15	1	0	0	1	2	0	3	.067	.267
Mike Morgan	.467	15	7	0	0	0	1	1	1	.500	.600	Pete Harnisch	.095	21	2	0	0	0	2	0	5	.095	.095
Bob Tewksbury	.435	23	10	2	0	1	6	1	1	.458	.652	Jose Bautista	.100	10	1	0	0	0	0	1	0	.182	.100
Doug Drabek	.429	14	6	2	0	0	1	3	2	.556	.571	Kevin Ritz	.100	10	1	0	0	0	0	1	2	.182	.100
Kevin Brown	.400	10	4	1	1	0	1	1	1	.455	.700	Ramon Martinez	.125	16	2	0	0	0	2	0	2	.125	.188

158

Freddy Garcia — Pirates
Age 25 – Bats Right

	Avg	G	AB	R	H	2B	3B	HR	RBI	BB	SO	HBP	GDP	SB	CS	OBP	SLG	IBB	SH	SF	#Pit	#P/PA	GB	FB	G/F
1997 Season	.150	20	40	4	6	1	0	3	5	2	17	0	0	0	0	.190	.400	0	0	0	171	4.07	9	12	0.75
Career (1995-1997)	.144	62	97	9	14	2	1	3	6	10	34	0	0	0	1	.224	.278	0	1	0	446	4.13	26	28	0.93

1997 Season

	Avg	AB	H	2B	3B	HR	RBI	BB	SO	OBP	SLG		Avg	AB	H	2B	3B	HR	RBI	BB	SO	OBP	SLG
vs. Left	.273	22	6	1	0	3	5	1	7	.304	.727	Scoring Posn	.083	12	1	0	0	1	2	0	2	.083	.333
vs. Right	.000	18	0	0	0	0	0	1	10	.053	.000	Close & Late	.143	7	1	0	0	0	0	1	3	.250	.143

Karim Garcia — Dodgers
Age 22 – Bats Left

	Avg	G	AB	R	H	2B	3B	HR	RBI	BB	SO	HBP	GDP	SB	CS	OBP	SLG	IBB	SH	SF	#Pit	#P/PA	GB	FB	G/F
1997 Season	.128	15	39	5	5	0	0	1	8	6	14	0	0	0	0	.239	.205	1	0	1	157	3.41	10	9	1.11
Career (1995-1997)	.150	29	60	6	9	0	0	1	8	6	19	0	0	0	0	.224	.200	1	0	1	232	3.46	20	14	1.43

1997 Season

	Avg	AB	H	2B	3B	HR	RBI	BB	SO	OBP	SLG		Avg	AB	H	2B	3B	HR	RBI	BB	SO	OBP	SLG
vs. Left	.000	3	0	0	0	0	0	0	2	.000	.000	Scoring Posn	.250	12	3	0	0	1	8	1	4	.286	.500
vs. Right	.139	36	5	0	0	1	8	6	12	.256	.222	Close & Late	.000	7	0	0	0	0	0	1	4	.125	.000

Ramon Garcia — Astros
Age 28 – Pitches Right

	ERA	W	L	Sv	G	GS	IP	BB	SO	Avg	H	2B	3B	HR	RBI	OBP	SLG	GF	IR	IRS	Hld	SvOp	SB	CS	GB	FB	G/F
1997 Season	3.69	9	8	1	42	20	158.2	52	120	.262	155	23	3	20	67	.330	.412	5	9	5	1	1	19	7	217	148	1.47
Last Five Years	4.65	13	12	5	79	22	234.1	73	160	.270	239	38	5	37	126	.334	.450	19	49	16	7	8	24	8	319	243	1.31

1997 Season

	ERA	W	L	Sv	G	GS	IP	H	HR	BB	SO
Home	3.61	4	4	1	18	10	77.1	77	8	22	77
Away	3.76	6	4	0	24	10	81.1	78	12	30	43
Day	3.90	3	2	0	13	8	55.1	54	7	20	40
Night	3.57	6	6	1	29	12	103.1	101	13	32	80
Grass	3.25	4	3	0	16	6	52.2	44	7	19	27
Turf	3.91	5	5	1	26	14	106.0	111	13	33	93
March/April	2.95	2	0	1	7	1	18.1	15	0	7	14
May	6.17	0	3	0	13	1	23.1	31	2	8	12
June	3.60	1	3	0	7	3	25.0	17	3	8	22
July	4.84	1	1	0	4	4	22.1	24	3	5	17
August	3.38	1	1	0	6	6	37.1	40	8	12	32
Sept/Oct	1.95	4	0	0	5	5	32.1	28	4	12	23
Starter	3.46	8	5	0	20	20	117.0	111	17	41	95
Reliever	4.32	1	3	1	22	0	41.2	44	3	11	25
0 Days rest (Relief)	0.93	0	0	1	3	0	9.2	7	0	1	9
1 or 2 Days rest	7.79	0	3	0	13	0	17.1	25	3	7	8
3+ Days rest	2.45	1	0	0	6	0	14.2	12	0	3	8
vs. AL	1.31	2	0	0	3	3	20.2	10	1	10	13
vs. NL	4.04	7	8	1	39	17	138.0	145	19	42	107
Pre-All Star	4.40	3	7	1	28	6	73.2	68	6	25	55
Post-All Star	3.07	6	1	0	14	14	85.0	87	14	27	65

	Avg	AB	H	2B	3B	HR	RBI	BB	SO	OBP	SLG
vs. Left	.250	280	70	13	1	10	25	32	51	.329	.411
vs. Right	.272	312	85	10	2	10	42	20	69	.330	.413
Inning 1-6	.258	469	121	19	1	18	57	43	101	.331	.418
Inning 7+	.276	123	34	4	2	2	10	9	19	.326	.390
None on	.263	365	96	16	3	12	12	24	70	.319	.422
Runners on	.260	227	59	7	0	8	55	28	50	.346	.396
Scoring Posn	.248	125	31	4	0	2	41	21	32	.364	.328
Close & Late	.247	73	18	0	1	1	5	7	15	.313	.315
None on/out	.306	157	48	8	2	5	5	12	25	.366	.478
vs. 1st Batr (relief)	.286	21	6	2	0	1	4	0	2	.318	.524
1st Inning Pitched	.288	156	45	8	0	5	28	14	28	.358	.436
First 15 Pitches	.303	132	40	6	0	4	16	11	21	.367	.439
Pitch 16-30	.250	104	26	4	0	6	22	15	19	.350	.462
Pitch 31-45	.260	100	26	3	0	2	8	4	27	.302	.350
Pitch 46+	.246	256	63	10	3	8	21	22	53	.312	.402
First Pitch	.283	106	30	3	1	5	10	0	0	.290	.472
Behind in Count	.427	124	53	15	0	5	25	34	0	.547	.669
Two Strikes	.155	264	41	3	2	4	16	18	120	.230	.227
Pre-All Star	.249	273	68	9	2	6	38	25	55	.320	.363
Post-All Star	.273	319	87	14	1	14	29	27	65	.338	.455

Nomar Garciaparra — Red Sox
Age 24 – Bats Right

	Avg	G	AB	R	H	2B	3B	HR	RBI	BB	SO	HBP	GDP	SB	CS	OBP	SLG	IBB	SH	SF	#Pit	#P/PA	GB	FB	G/F
1997 Season	.306	153	684	122	209	44	11	30	98	35	92	6	9	22	9	.342	.534	2	2	7	2372	3.23	253	202	1.25
Career (1996-1997)	.298	177	771	133	230	46	14	34	114	39	106	6	9	27	9	.334	.527	2	3	8	2720	3.29	291	227	1.28

1997 Season

	Avg	AB	H	2B	3B	HR	RBI	BB	SO	OBP	SLG		Avg	AB	H	2B	3B	HR	RBI	BB	SO	OBP	SLG
vs. Left	.266	184	49	12	3	9	30	9	30	.303	.511	First Pitch	.385	135	52	11	2	5	20	2	0	.407	.607
vs. Right	.320	500	160	32	8	21	68	26	62	.356	.542	Behind in Count	.291	148	43	7	2	7	20	20	0	.373	.507
Groundball	.339	118	40	6	1	6	16	8	14	.385	.559	Two Strikes	.244	246	60	12	4	11	31	13	92	.281	.459
Flyball	.305	105	32	9	1	4	13	5	14	.345	.524	Batting #1	.306	683	209	44	11	30	98	35	91	.342	.534
Home	.298	356	106	26	5	11	49	17	51	.327	.492	Batting #6	.000	1	0	0	0	0	0	0	1	.000	.000
Away	.314	328	103	18	6	19	49	18	41	.357	.579	Other	.000	0	0	0	0	0	0	0	0	.000	.000
Day	.300	210	63	10	4	7	34	7	29	.320	.486	March/April	.328	116	38	7	1	5	16	7	22	.366	.534
Night	.308	474	146	34	7	23	64	28	63	.351	.555	May	.204	93	19	4	3	1	8	7	11	.257	.344
Grass	.297	599	178	38	11	24	85	31	81	.333	.518	June	.322	121	39	8	1	6	18	8	14	.371	.554
Turf	.365	85	31	6	0	6	13	4	11	.400	.647	July	.317	126	40	9	4	5	18	6	21	.356	.571
Pre-All Star	.291	357	104	20	5	13	44	24	52	.338	.485	August	.372	121	45	6	1	8	22	6	13	.397	.636
Post-All Star	.321	327	105	24	6	17	54	11	40	.346	.587	Sept/Oct	.262	107	28	10	1	5	16	1	11	.273	.514
Scoring Posn	.318	154	49	7	4	5	64	17	31	.371	.513	vs. AL	.311	623	194	42	11	28	92	28	84	.344	.549
Close & Late	.321	106	34	8	3	3	15	8	15	.371	.538	vs. NL	.246	61	15	2	0	2	6	7	8	.319	.377
None on/out	.318	277	88	17	3	12	12	7	31	.339	.531												

1997 By Position

Position	Avg	AB	H	2B	3B	HR	RBI	BB	SO	OBP	SLG	G	GS	Innings	PO	A	E	DP	Fld Pct	Rng Fctr	In Zone	Zone Outs	Zone Rtg	MLB Zone
As ss	.306	684	209	44	11	30	98	35	92	.342	.534	153	152	1344.1	249	450	21	113	.971	4.68	520	491	.944	.937

Mark Gardner — Giants
Age 36 – Pitches Right (flyball pitcher)

	ERA	W	L	Sv	G	GS	IP	BB	SO	Avg	H	2B	3B	HR	RBI	OBP	SLG	CG	ShO	Sup	QS	#P/S	SB	CS	GB	FB	G/F
1997 Season	4.29	12	9	0	30	30	180.1	57	136	.272	188	28	5	28	82	.326	.449	2	1	4.64	16	100	16	16	226	237	0.95
Last Five Years	4.71	37	31	1	136	99	646.0	223	479	.276	686	131	17	101	343	.337	.464	7	3	5.24	42	99	46	51	772	852	0.91

1997 Season

	ERA	W	L	Sv	G	GS	IP	H	HR	BB	SO		Avg	AB	H	2B	3B	HR	RBI	BB	SO	OBP	SLG
Home	4.19	6	4	0	16	16	96.2	106	16	34	75	vs. Left	.305	334	102	13	4	13	38	33	66	.367	.485
Away	4.41	6	5	0	14	14	83.2	82	12	23	61	vs. Right	.242	356	86	15	1	15	44	24	70	.288	.416
Day	4.11	7	4	0	15	15	92.0	94	15	29	73	Inning 1-6	.274	609	167	24	3	23	75	54	115	.331	.437
Night	4.48	5	5	0	15	15	88.1	94	13	28	63	Inning 7+	.259	81	21	4	2	5	7	3	21	.286	.543
Grass	4.44	9	7	0	23	23	135.2	153	23	46	97	None on	.287	435	125	20	2	18	18	31	87	.335	.467
Turf	3.83	3	2	0	7	7	44.2	35	5	11	39	Runners on	.247	255	63	8	3	10	64	26	49	.313	.420
March/April	2.97	2	1	0	6	6	39.1	33	4	7	36	Scoring Posn	.234	141	33	5	1	6	51	21	28	.321	.411
May	3.56	4	0	0	5	5	30.1	33	3	11	19	Close & Late	.314	51	16	3	2	4	6	2	12	.340	.686
June	5.35	2	3	0	6	6	35.1	38	7	17	20	None on/out	.267	187	50	8	1	9	9	12	38	.312	.465
July	2.57	3	0	0	5	5	35.0	35	4	5	35	vs. 1st Batr (relief)	.000	0	0	0	0	0	0	0	0	.000	.000
August	5.35	1	3	0	6	6	35.1	37	7	15	23	1st Inning Pitched	.349	126	44	6	1	8	26	15	25	.410	.603
Sept/Oct	16.20	0	2	0	2	2	5.0	12	3	2	3	First 75 Pitches	.282	489	138	19	1	22	65	40	102	.333	.460
Starter	4.29	12	9	0	30	30	180.1	188	28	57	136	Pitch 76-90	.242	95	23	4	1	4	7	12	294	.432	
Reliever	0.00	0	0	0	0	0	0.0	0	0	0	0	Pitch 91-105	.239	67	16	3	1	1	5	8	16	.320	.358
0-3 Days Rest (Start)	0.00	0	0	0	0	0	0.0	0	0	0	0	Pitch 106+	.282	39	11	2	2	1	5	2	6	.333	.513
4 Days Rest	4.30	6	5	0	16	16	102.2	109	15	35	72	First Pitch	.303	89	27	7	0	5	12	5	0	.337	.551
5+ Days Rest	4.29	6	4	0	14	14	77.2	79	13	22	64	Ahead in Count	.212	335	71	10	2	6	27	0	111	.212	.307
vs. AL	2.38	2	0	0	3	3	22.2	17	2	8	9	Behind in Count	.364	132	48	6	1	13	27	29	0	.478	.720
vs. NL	4.57	10	9	0	27	27	157.2	171	26	49	127	Two Strikes	.224	366	82	11	4	7	34	23	136	.268	.333
Pre-All Star	3.73	9	4	0	18	18	111.0	109	14	36	84	Pre-All Star	.260	419	109	13	4	14	47	36	84	.318	.411
Post-All Star	5.19	3	5	0	12	12	69.1	79	14	21	52	Post-All Star	.292	271	79	15	1	14	35	21	52	.339	.509

Last Five Years

	ERA	W	L	Sv	G	GS	IP	H	HR	BB	SO		Avg	AB	H	2B	3B	HR	RBI	BB	SO	OBP	SLG
Home	4.72	19	14	0	70	52	345.1	374	58	125	250	vs. Left	.297	1160	344	57	12	42	134	117	205	.362	.475
Away	4.70	18	17	1	66	47	300.2	312	43	98	229	vs. Right	.258	1326	342	74	5	59	209	106	274	.315	.455
Day	3.85	17	7	1	49	35	245.1	244	34	71	200	Inning 1-6	.273	2111	577	113	12	83	303	193	401	.336	.456
Night	5.23	20	24	0	87	64	400.2	442	67	152	279	Inning 7+	.291	375	109	18	5	18	40	30	78	.345	.509
Grass	4.58	25	20	0	97	68	452.1	474	77	155	329	None on	.277	1504	416	82	7	63	63	114	294	.330	.466
Turf	5.02	12	11	1	39	31	193.2	212	24	68	150	Runners on	.275	982	270	49	10	38	280	109	185	.348	.461
March/April	4.37	6	3	0	22	14	103.0	93	13	25	84	Scoring Posn	.275	563	155	33	4	21	233	79	115	.359	.460
May	4.42	10	7	0	27	23	134.1	137	19	54	101	Close & Late	.317	145	46	8	3	7	16	15	30	.381	.559
June	5.15	6	8	0	26	20	129.1	138	28	50	83	None on/out	.297	661	196	39	2	30	30	46	128	.344	.498
July	4.03	9	3	0	23	18	118.1	123	14	34	100	vs. 1st Batr (relief)	.212	33	7	0	0	1	4	1	10	.222	.303
August	5.26	4	6	0	24	17	114.2	138	21	41	81	1st Inning Pitched	.291	512	149	25	4	24	90	56	107	.358	.496
Sept/Oct	5.44	2	4	1	14	7	46.1	57	6	19	30	First 75 Pitches	.265	1846	489	96	11	72	251	167	373	.326	.446
Starter	4.69	36	30	0	99	99	589.1	635	91	200	432	Pitch 76-90	.306	307	94	17	1	20	44	22	45	.360	.564
Reliever	4.92	1	1	1	37	0	56.2	51	10	23	47	Pitch 91-105	.309	207	64	12	1	7	30	23	43	.378	.478
0-3 Days Rest (Start)	4.37	3	0	0	4	4	22.2	26	6	11	18	Pitch 106+	.310	126	39	6	4	2	18	11	18	.374	.468
4 Days Rest	4.52	16	12	0	45	45	281.0	318	38	88	213	First Pitch	.318	321	102	22	1	22	59	10	0	.344	.598
5+ Days Rest	4.88	17	18	0	50	50	285.2	291	47	101	201	Ahead in Count	.224	1180	264	53	8	21	120	0	388	.229	.336
vs. AL	5.43	6	6	0	20	19	114.1	109	19	44	63	Behind in Count	.356	505	180	34	4	39	95	101	0	.462	.671
vs. NL	4.55	31	25	1	116	80	531.2	577	82	179	416	Two Strikes	.218	1229	268	50	8	26	130	112	479	.286	.335
Pre-All Star	4.41	26	19	0	82	64	412.0	412	61	141	312	Pre-All Star	.264	1561	412	75	12	61	209	141	312	.327	.445
Post-All Star	5.23	11	12	1	54	35	234.0	274	40	82	167	Post-All Star	.296	925	274	56	5	40	134	82	167	.355	.497

Pitcher vs. Batter (career)

Pitches Best Vs.	Avg	AB	H	2B	3B	HR	RBI	BB	SO	OBP	SLG	Pitches Worst Vs.	Avg	AB	H	2B	3B	HR	RBI	BB	SO	OBP	SLG
Jose Hernandez	.000	9	0	0	0	0	0	2	4	.182	.000	Sean Berry	.563	16	9	3	0	1	4	1	1	.611	.938
Javy Lopez	.083	12	1	0	0	0	0	0	2	.083	.083	Reggie Sanders	.538	13	7	1	0	1	3	4	4	.647	.846
Brad Ausmus	.100	10	1	0	0	0	3	2	3	.214	.100	Brian McRae	.500	12	6	1	1	1	1	0	0	.500	1.000
Brian Jordan	.143	14	2	0	0	0	2	1	7	.188	.143	Barry Bonds	.444	9	4	1	0	2	5	3	1	.583	1.222
Rafael Belliard	.154	13	2	1	0	0	0	1	4	.154	.231	Rickey Henderson	.417	12	5	0	0	3	4	4	3	.563	1.167

Brent Gates — Mariners
Age 28 – Bats Both (groundball hitter)

	Avg	G	AB	R	H	2B	3B	HR	RBI	BB	SO	HBP	GDP	SB	CS	OBP	SLG	IBB	SH	SF	#Pit	#P/PA	GB	FB	G/F
1997 Season	.238	65	151	18	36	8	0	3	20	14	21	0	6	0	0	.298	.351	0	2	3	616	3.62	61	42	1.45
Career (1993-1997)	.269	468	1690	197	455	91	9	19	199	155	247	7	55	14	7	.328	.367	7	20	30	7300	3.84	703	409	1.72

1997 Season

	Avg	AB	H	2B	3B	HR	RBI	BB	SO	OBP	SLG		Avg	AB	H	2B	3B	HR	RBI	BB	SO	OBP	SLG
vs. Left	.148	27	4	4	0	0	5	2	4	.207	.296	Scoring Posn	.250	40	10	4	0	1	.17	5	6	.313	.425
vs. Right	.258	124	32	4	0	3	15	12	17	.317	.363	Close & Late	.240	25	6	1	0	1	2	3	4	.321	.400
Home	.243	74	18	4	0	1	8	8	10	.313	.338	None on/out	.229	35	8	2	0	1	1	3	3	.289	.371
Away	.234	77	18	4	0	2	12	6	11	.282	.364	Batting #8	.276	87	24	5	0	2	10	6	13	.323	.402
First Pitch	.375	16	6	1	0	1	3	0	0	.375	.625	Batting #9	.179	28	5	2	0	0	5	4	4	.273	.250
Ahead in Count	.207	29	6	1	0	1	6	11	0	.415	.345	Other	.194	36	7	1	0	1	5	4	4	.262	.306
Behind in Count	.179	78	14	3	0	1	9	0	19	.177	.256	Pre-All Star	.250	84	21	6	0	2	11	6	13	.293	.393
Two Strikes	.203	74	14	4	0	1	4	3	21	.234	.297	Post-All Star	.224	67	15	2	0	1	9	8	8	.303	.299

Career (1993-1997)

	Avg	AB	H	2B	3B	HR	RBI	BB	SO	OBP	SLG		Avg	AB	H	2B	3B	HR	RBI	BB	SO	OBP	SLG
vs. Left	.257	452	116	30	2	4	50	41	77	.318	.358	First Pitch	.327	153	50	8	0	2	16	5	0	.342	.418

Career (1993-1997)

	Avg	AB	H	2B	3B	HR	RBI	BB	SO	OBP	SLG		Avg	AB	H	2B	3B	HR	RBI	BB	SO	OBP	SLG
vs. Right	.274	1238	339	61	7	15	149	114	170	.331	.371	Ahead in Count	.319	376	120	20	4	7	62	100	0	.451	.449
Groundball	.283	382	108	19	1	3	42	21	44	.316	.361	Behind in Count	.223	802	179	37	4	6	71	0	210	.226	.302
Flyball	.302	348	105	25	2	5	62	32	51	.358	.428	Two Strikes	.220	813	179	39	3	7	76	50	247	.267	.301
Home	.272	806	219	40	3	9	81	77	124	.332	.362	Batting #2	.281	654	184	40	4	8	74	63	83	.343	.391
Away	.267	884	236	51	6	10	118	78	123	.324	.372	Batting #3	.259	293	76	11	1	2	34	24	57	.313	.324
Day	.276	634	175	33	1	5	64	68	100	.342	.355	Other	.262	743	195	40	4	9	91	68	107	.320	.363
Night	.265	1056	280	58	8	14	135	87	147	.319	.375	March/April	.257	140	36	8	0	1	17	18	22	.346	.336
Grass	.261	1365	356	68	7	14	148	121	197	.319	.352	May	.269	379	102	22	2	6	43	42	48	.337	.385
Turf	.305	325	99	23	2	5	51	34	50	.364	.434	June	.275	389	107	22	3	4	51	31	60	.326	.378
Pre-All Star	.267	1028	274	57	5	11	120	99	146	.329	.364	July	.240	267	64	10	0	2	24	19	37	.291	.300
Post-All Star	.273	662	181	34	4	8	79	56	101	.326	.373	August	.293	246	72	13	3	3	30	19	34	.336	.407
Scoring Posn	.252	437	110	26	3	3	169	53	69	.316	.346	Sept/Oct	.275	269	74	16	1	3	34	26	46	.336	.375
Close & Late	.250	268	67	12	1	4	42	24	58	.306	.347	vs. AL	.270	1679	453	90	9	19	197	154	246	.328	.368
None on/out	.300	333	100	26	1	5	5	31	38	.362	.429	vs. NL	.182	11	2	1	0	0	2	1	1	.250	.273

Batter vs. Pitcher (career)

Hits Best Against	Avg	AB	H	2B	3B	HR	RBI	BB	SO	OBP	SLG	Hits Worst Against	Avg	AB	H	2B	3B	HR	RBI	BB	SO	OBP	SLG
Pat Mahomes	.571	14	8	1	0	3	7	1	0	.625	1.286	Brad Radke	.053	19	1	0	1	0	1	2	2	.143	.158
David Wells	.545	11	6	2	0	0	4	0	1	.545	.727	Chris Haney	.071	14	1	0	0	0	1	1	1	.125	.071
Erik Hanson	.522	23	12	4	0	0	0	3	3	.577	.696	Charles Nagy	.071	14	1	0	0	0	1	1	4	.133	.071
Jaime Navarro	.500	10	5	1	0	1	5	1	1	.545	.900	Randy Johnson	.095	21	2	0	0	0	0	2	7	.174	.095
Kevin Tapani	.364	11	4	1	0	1	2	2	0	.462	.727	Jack McDowell	.138	29	4	0	0	0	2	1	3	.167	.138

Jason Giambi — Athletics   Age 27 – Bats Left

	Avg	G	AB	R	H	2B	3B	HR	RBI	BB	SO	HBP	GDP	SB	CS	OBP	SLG	IBB	SH	SF	#Pit	#P/PA	GB	FB	G/F
1997 Season	.293	142	519	66	152	41	2	20	81	55	89	6	11	0	1	.362	.495	3	0	8	2289	3.89	151	191	0.79
Career (1995-1997)	.287	336	1231	177	353	88	3	46	185	134	215	14	30	2	3	.359	.475	6	2	15	5552	3.98	363	415	0.87

1997 Season

	Avg	AB	H	2B	3B	HR	RBI	BB	SO	OBP	SLG		Avg	AB	H	2B	3B	HR	RBI	BB	SO	OBP	SLG
vs. Left	.302	126	38	6	0	6	19	17	28	.397	.492	First Pitch	.333	51	17	4	0	4	9	2	0	.351	.647
vs. Right	.290	393	114	35	2	14	62	38	61	.350	.496	Ahead in Count	.351	134	47	11	0	6	25	30	0	.473	.567
Groundball	.282	117	33	8	0	4	16	18	17	.380	.453	Behind in Count	.248	218	54	15	1	5	26	0	73	.244	.394
Flyball	.308	78	24	5	1	3	13	4	20	.357	.513	Two Strikes	.223	238	53	16	2	5	23	23	89	.292	.370
Home	.314	261	82	20	1	14	41	29	46	.392	.559	Batting #2	.342	149	51	17	0	4	27	13	20	.389	.537
Away	.271	258	70	21	1	6	40	26	43	.332	.430	Batting #5	.275	171	47	13	0	11	34	18	33	.347	.544
Day	.320	225	72	16	1	12	42	26	40	.388	.560	Other	.271	199	54	11	2	5	20	24	36	.355	.422
Night	.272	294	80	25	1	8	39	29	49	.342	.446	March/April	.250	96	24	4	1	3	13	9	15	.312	.406
Grass	.298	457	136	37	2	19	69	53	81	.374	.512	May	.353	85	30	11	0	3	18	10	15	.418	.588
Turf	.258	62	16	4	0	1	12	2	8	.273	.371	June	.364	66	24	7	0	2	11	2	6	.391	.561
Pre-All Star	.302	262	79	22	1	9	44	23	38	.358	.496	July	.195	82	16	4	1	4	8	14	21	.320	.415
Post-All Star	.284	257	73	19	1	11	37	32	51	.366	.494	August	.247	97	24	7	0	4	11	15	14	.360	.443
Scoring Posn	.276	127	35	8	0	8	59	20	32	.363	.528	Sept/Oct	.366	93	34	8	0	4	20	5	18	.386	.581
Close & Late	.338	65	22	0	0	6	17	12	9	.450	.615	vs. AL	.291	484	141	39	2	19	78	51	85	.361	.498
None on/out	.327	110	36	11	0	5	5	10	15	.388	.564	vs. NL	.314	35	11	2	0	1	3	4	4	.385	.457

1997 By Position

Position	Avg	AB	H	2B	3B	HR	RBI	BB	SO	OBP	SLG	G	GS	Innings	PO	A	E	DP	Fld Pct	Rng Fctr	In Zone	Zone Outs	Zone Rtg	MLB Zone
As DH	.286	84	24	8	0	3	16	10	17	.367	.488	25	22	---	---	---	---	---	---	---	---	---	---	---
As 1b	.303	185	56	15	0	8	29	20	30	.368	.514	51	48	433.1	399	40	5	49	.989	---	104	84	.808	.874
As lf	.285	249	71	18	2	9	36	25	42	.351	.482	68	67	541.1	102	5	2	1	.982	1.78	125	94	.752	.805

Career (1995-1997)

	Avg	AB	H	2B	3B	HR	RBI	BB	SO	OBP	SLG		Avg	AB	H	2B	3B	HR	RBI	BB	SO	OBP	SLG
vs. Left	.267	270	72	14	0	9	35	28	64	.353	.419	First Pitch	.307	127	39	7	0	5	19	4	0	.328	.480
vs. Right	.292	961	281	74	3	37	150	106	151	.361	.491	Ahead in Count	.353	289	102	22	0	16	55	86	0	.501	.595
Groundball	.309	298	92	18	0	13	50	31	44	.373	.500	Behind in Count	.230	556	128	30	2	12	61	0	181	.234	.356
Flyball	.271	181	49	12	1	6	22	16	41	.343	.448	Two Strikes	.221	593	131	35	3	16	65	44	215	.281	.371
Home	.299	592	177	49	2	23	88	78	100	.387	.505	Batting #2	.300	257	77	23	1	8	40	22	41	.354	.490
Away	.275	639	176	39	1	23	97	56	115	.333	.448	Batting #3	.288	483	139	33	1	18	71	56	78	.363	.472
Day	.308	530	163	35	2	23	91	61	81	.378	.511	Other	.279	491	137	32	1	20	74	56	96	.359	.470
Night	.271	701	190	53	1	23	94	73	134	.345	.448	March/April	.296	189	56	11	2	6	32	22	35	.367	.471
Grass	.286	1070	306	75	3	44	164	122	189	.363	.485	May	.318	195	62	18	0	8	31	21	32	.386	.533
Turf	.292	161	47	13	0	2	21	12	26	.337	.410	June	.311	167	52	10	0	10	34	9	18	.348	.551
Pre-All Star	.311	605	188	47	2	26	108	57	92	.371	.524	July	.275	255	70	21	1	10	35	34	47	.365	.482
Post-All Star	.264	626	165	41	1	20	77	77	123	.348	.428	August	.268	246	66	16	0	8	28	33	46	.364	.431
Scoring Posn	.293	311	91	24	0	16	139	50	63	.382	.524	Sept/Oct	.263	179	47	12	0	4	25	15	37	.317	.397
Close & Late	.274	175	48	6	0	8	28	28	36	.379	.446	vs. AL	.286	1196	342	86	3	45	182	130	211	.359	.476
None on/out	.301	256	77	17	0	6	6	24	39	.370	.438	vs. NL	.314	35	11	2	0	1	3	4	4	.385	.457

Batter vs. Pitcher (career)

Hits Best Against	Avg	AB	H	2B	3B	HR	RBI	BB	SO	OBP	SLG	Hits Worst Against	Avg	AB	H	2B	3B	HR	RBI	BB	SO	OBP	SLG
Mark Gubicza	.615	13	8	1	0	2	4	1	0	.643	1.154	Roger Pavlik	.077	13	1	0	0	0	0	1	4	.143	.077
Omar Olivares	.600	10	6	1	0	3	9	1	0	.583	1.600	Chris Haney	.118	17	2	1	0	0	1	3	.167	.176
Bobby Witt	.500	12	6	2	0	0	1	2	1	.571	.667	Bob Wolcott	.143	14	2	1	0	0	0	1	.143	.214
Jack McDowell	.462	13	6	2	0	0	2	3	3	.563	.615	Scott Karl	.154	13	2	0	0	0	0	2	2	.267	.154
Juan Guzman	.357	14	5	2	0	1	3	3	1	.471	.714	Kevin Tapani	.214	14	3	1	0	0	1	0	1	.214	.286

Benji Gil — Rangers
Age 25 – Bats Right (flyball hitter)

	Avg	G	AB	R	H	2B	3B	HR	RBI	BB	SO	HBP	GDP	SB	CS	OBP	SLG	IBB	SH	SF	#Pit	#P/PA	GB	FB	G/F
1997 Season	.224	110	317	35	71	13	2	5	31	17	96	1	3	1	2	.263	.325	0	6	4	1358	3.94	97	77	1.26
Career (1993-1997)	.215	267	794	74	171	33	5	14	80	49	266	2	8	4	9	.261	.322	0	21	6	3375	3.87	223	179	1.25

1997 Season

	Avg	AB	H	2B	3B	HR	RBI	BB	SO	OBP	SLG		Avg	AB	H	2B	3B	HR	RBI	BB	SO	OBP	SLG
vs. Left	.243	74	18	5	2	1	5	9	23	.325	.405	First Pitch	.250	36	9	1	0	0	4	0	0	.243	.278
vs. Right	.218	243	53	8	0	4	26	8	73	.242	.300	Ahead in Count	.423	52	22	6	1	2	10	9	0	.484	.692
Groundball	.206	68	14	3	0	0	3	2	21	.236	.250	Behind in Count	.144	167	24	4	0	3	11	0	83	.149	.222
Flyball	.245	53	13	1	1	2	10	2	17	.273	.415	Two Strikes	.134	179	24	5	1	2	9	8	96	.176	.207
Home	.224	165	37	9	1	3	15	9	54	.260	.345	Batting #8	.227	22	5	1	1	0	3	1	4	.261	.364
Away	.224	152	34	4	1	2	16	8	42	.265	.303	Batting #9	.227	291	66	12	1	5	28	16	89	.266	.326
Day	.286	70	20	2	2	0	5	2	19	.315	.371	Other	.000	4	0	0	0	0	0	0	3	.000	.000
Night	.206	247	51	11	0	5	26	15	77	.248	.312	March/April	.226	62	14	2	0	1	7	2	19	.250	.306
Grass	.218	280	61	12	2	5	28	15	83	.254	.329	May	.200	75	15	4	0	1	4	6	20	.256	.293
Turf	.270	37	10	1	0	0	3	2	13	.325	.297	June	.300	40	12	1	0	1	6	5	9	.370	.400
Pre-All Star	.234	188	44	9	0	3	17	13	53	.281	.330	July	.167	18	3	2	0	0	0	0	10	.167	.278
Post-All Star	.209	129	27	4	2	2	14	4	43	.235	.318	August	.225	89	20	2	1	2	13	4	21	.255	.337
Scoring Posn	.212	85	18	1	0	2	26	7	35	.260	.294	Sept/Oct	.212	33	7	2	1	0	1	0	17	.229	.333
Close & Late	.185	27	5	0	0	0	1	1	8	.214	.185	vs. AL	.222	293	65	11	1	5	27	16	91	.262	.317
None on/out	.293	82	24	7	0	1		4	18	.326	.415	vs. NL	.250	24	6	2	1	0	4	1	5	.269	.417

1997 By Position

Position	Avg	AB	H	2B	3B	HR	RBI	BB	SO	OBP	SLG	G	GS	Innings	PO	A	E	DP	Fld Pct	Rng Fctr	In Zone	Zone Outs	Zone Rtg	MLB Zone
As ss	.224	317	71	13	2	5	31	17	96	.263	.325	106	100	860.2	163	327	19	72	.963	5.12	374	359	.960	.937

Career (1993-1997)

	Avg	AB	H	2B	3B	HR	RBI	BB	SO	OBP	SLG		Avg	AB	H	2B	3B	HR	RBI	BB	SO	OBP	SLG
vs. Left	.176	187	33	8	3	1	14	27	70	.278	.267	First Pitch	.323	99	32	4	2	2	15	0	0	.320	.465
vs. Right	.227	607	138	25	2	13	66	22	196	.255	.339	Ahead in Count	.336	125	42	12	1	5	19	25	0	.438	.568
Groundball	.235	179	42	11	1	1	12	11	55	.281	.324	Behind in Count	.158	418	66	13	1	3	25	0	222	.162	.215
Flyball	.174	167	29	3	1	2	15	10	69	.220	.240	Two Strikes	.141	453	64	14	2	2	21	24	266	.186	.194
Home	.228	412	94	23	2	8	40	24	140	.268	.352	Batting #8	.211	38	8	1	1	0	4	4	11	.286	.289
Away	.202	382	77	10	3	6	40	25	126	.253	.291	Batting #9	.217	751	163	32	4	14	76	45	251	.261	.326
Day	.259	170	44	6	3	1	16	13	53	.315	.347	Other	.000	5	0	0	0	0	0	0	4	.000	.000
Night	.204	624	127	27	2	13	64	36	213	.246	.316	March/April	.196	107	21	2	0	1	10	7	36	.246	.243
Grass	.215	699	150	30	5	13	70	47	231	.263	.328	May	.219	196	43	9	0	6	23	16	66	.276	.357
Turf	.221	95	21	3	0	1	10	2	35	.245	.284	June	.267	131	35	7	0	3	15	8	40	.310	.389
Pre-All Star	.224	468	105	21	0	10	48	34	158	.276	.333	July	.159	88	14	5	1	0	3	8	33	.229	.239
Post-All Star	.202	326	66	12	5	4	32	15	108	.238	.307	August	.196	158	31	4	2	4	22	7	43	.229	.323
Scoring Posn	.245	212	52	7	2	4	66	18	80	.297	.354	Sept/Oct	.237	114	27	6	2	0	7	3	48	.261	.325
Close & Late	.125	80	10	1	0	1	5	6	32	.186	.175	vs. AL	.214	770	165	31	4	14	76	48	261	.261	.319
None on/out	.205	190	39	11	0	3	3	9	60	.241	.311	vs. NL	.250	24	6	2	1	0	4	1	5	.269	.417

Batter vs. Pitcher (career)

Hits Best Against	Avg	AB	H	2B	3B	HR	RBI	BB	SO	OBP	SLG	Hits Worst Against	Avg	AB	H	2B	3B	HR	RBI	BB	SO	OBP	SLG
Andy Pettitte	.333	9	3	2	0	0	0	4	2	.538	.556	Roger Clemens	.077	13	1	0	0	0	0	1	5	.200	.077
Mark Langston	.333	9	3	0	0	0	0	2	3	.455	.333	Kevin Appier	.083	12	1	0	0	0	2	1	5	.154	.083
Brad Radke	.313	16	5	2	0	0	0	0	6	.313	.438	David Cone	.200	10	2	0	0	0	0	1	5	.273	.200
												Chuck Finley	.222	9	2	0	0	0	1	2	5	.364	.222

Shawn Gilbert — Mets
Age 30 – Bats Right

	Avg	G	AB	R	H	2B	3B	HR	RBI	BB	SO	HBP	GDP	SB	CS	OBP	SLG	IBB	SH	SF	#Pit	#P/PA	GB	FB	G/F
1997 Season	.136	29	22	3	3	0	0	1	1	1	8	0	0	0	1	0	.174	.273	0	0	0	97	4.22	2	8	0.25

1997 Season

	Avg	AB	H	2B	3B	HR	RBI	BB	SO	OBP	SLG		Avg	AB	H	2B	3B	HR	RBI	BB	SO	OBP	SLG
vs. Left	.143	14	2	0	0	0	0	1	6	.200	.143	Scoring Posn	.000	5	0	0	0	0	0	0	3	.000	.000
vs. Right	.125	8	1	0	0	1	1	0	2	.125	.500	Close & Late	.000	3	0	0	0	0	0	0	1	.000	.000

Brian Giles — Indians
Age 27 – Bats Left

	Avg	G	AB	R	H	2B	3B	HR	RBI	BB	SO	HBP	GDP	SB	CS	OBP	SLG	IBB	SH	SF	#Pit	#P/PA	GB	FB	G/F
1997 Season	.268	130	377	62	101	15	3	17	61	63	50	1	10	13	3	.368	.459	2	3	7	1683	3.73	128	138	0.93
Career (1995-1997)	.294	187	507	94	149	29	4	23	91	82	64	1	15	16	3	.387	.503	6	3	10	2231	3.70	169	187	0.90

1997 Season

	Avg	AB	H	2B	3B	HR	RBI	BB	SO	OBP	SLG		Avg	AB	H	2B	3B	HR	RBI	BB	SO	OBP	SLG
vs. Left	.295	61	18	2	2	1	6	15	11	.429	.443	First Pitch	.384	73	28	3	2	2	14	2	0	.385	.562
vs. Right	.263	316	83	13	1	16	55	48	39	.356	.462	Ahead in Count	.286	105	30	5	1	7	18	28	0	.440	.552
Groundball	.284	88	25	8	0	1	9	10	10	.354	.409	Behind in Count	.205	127	26	3	0	5	17	0	36	.200	.346
Flyball	.268	56	15	0	1	4	13	8	8	.369	.518	Two Strikes	.201	139	28	3	0	4	18	33	50	.351	.309
Home	.239	197	47	8	2	7	28	33	28	.346	.406	Batting #1	.271	85	23	4	1	3	12	9	8	.333	.447
Away	.300	180	54	7	1	10	33	30	22	.393	.512	Batting #7	.254	114	29	6	1	5	22	20	12	.358	.456
Day	.268	138	37	3	0	7	24	24	16	.372	.442	Other	.275	178	49	5	1	9	27	34	30	.391	.466
Night	.268	239	64	12	3	10	37	39	34	.366	.469	March/April	.289	45	13	3	0	4	10	9	7	.400	.622
Grass	.256	324	83	14	2	15	53	55	45	.359	.451	May	.184	38	7	2	0	0	2	11	3	.367	.237
Turf	.340	53	18	1	1	2	8	8	5	.426	.509	June	.277	47	13	2	0	4	9	4	4	.333	.574

1997 Season

	Avg	AB	H	2B	3B	HR	RBI	BB	SO	OBP	SLG		Avg	AB	H	2B	3B	HR	RBI	BB	SO	OBP	SLG
Pre-All Star	.255	149	38	7	1	9	24	26	16	.362	.497	July	.250	68	17	1	1	3	11	17	9	.391	.426
Post-All Star	.276	228	63	8	2	8	37	37	34	.373	.434	August	.288	111	32	5	1	5	17	12	13	.352	.486
Scoring Posn	.299	97	29	5	0	1	39	14	14	.364	.381	Sept/Oct	.279	68	19	2	1	1	12	10	14	.370	.382
Close & Late	.276	58	16	3	0	4	11	10	8	.371	.534	vs. AL	.260	339	88	13	2	15	54	60	47	.366	.442
None on/out	.326	95	31	4	1	9	9	16	11	.429	.674	vs. NL	.342	38	13	2	1	2	7	3	3	.390	.605

1997 By Position

Position	Avg	AB	H	2B	3B	HR	RBI	BB	SO	OBP	SLG	G	GS	Innings	PO	A	E	DP	Fld Pct	Rng Fctr	In Zone	Outs	Zone Rtg	MLB Zone
As Pinch Hitter	.250	12	3	1	0	0	4	3	3	.375	.333	17	0	---	---	---	---	---	---	---	---	---	---	---
As lf	.263	259	68	8	2	13	45	38	36	.352	.459	82	73	647.1	149	5	3	1	.981	2.14	162	144	.889	.805
As cf	.286	49	14	3	1	2	4	7	4	.375	.510	20	13	125.0	28	0	2	0	.933	2.02	33	27	.818	.815
As rf	.308	39	12	2	0	2	8	9	4	.438	.513	25	11	114.0	23	2	1	0	.962	1.97	26	22	.846	.813

Bernard Gilkey — Mets   Age 31 – Bats Right

	Avg	G	AB	R	H	2B	3B	HR	RBI	BB	SO	HBP	GDP	SB	CS	OBP	SLG	IBB	SH	SF	#Pit	#P/PA	GB	FB	G/F
1997 Season	.249	145	518	85	129	31	1	18	78	70	111	6	9	7	11	.338	.417	1	0	12	2326	3.84	156	175	0.89
Last Five Years	.287	661	2506	417	719	170	14	87	379	280	437	29	66	66	44	.361	.470	15	1	30	10692	3.76	858	786	1.09

1997 Season

	Avg	AB	H	2B	3B	HR	RBI	BB	SO	OBP	SLG		Avg	AB	H	2B	3B	HR	RBI	BB	SO	OBP	SLG
vs. Left	.288	139	40	11	0	9	27	23	22	.386	.561	First Pitch	.273	88	24	7	0	2	14	1	0	.283	.420
vs. Right	.235	379	89	20	1	9	51	47	89	.320	.364	Ahead in Count	.346	136	47	8	0	12	34	38	0	.478	.669
Groundball	.257	101	26	4	0	2	20	11	24	.331	.356	Behind in Count	.176	204	36	9	0	2	17	0	90	.182	.250
Flyball	.143	70	10	4	0	1	7	8	15	.248	.243	Two Strikes	.172	233	40	11	0	3	20	31	111	.269	.258
Home	.226	235	53	12	0	7	34	37	48	.333	.366	Batting #3	.282	110	31	5	0	7	27	20	21	.386	.518
Away	.269	283	76	19	1	11	44	33	63	.343	.459	Batting #5	.261	180	47	12	1	6	24	24	38	.354	.439
Day	.250	196	49	11	0	10	39	29	35	.341	.459	Other	.224	228	51	14	0	5	27	26	52	.302	.351
Night	.248	322	80	20	1	8	39	41	76	.337	.391	March/April	.209	91	19	4	0	2	13	11	16	.298	.319
Grass	.251	438	110	26	1	14	67	63	88	.343	.411	May	.213	94	20	5	1	3	13	14	19	.315	.383
Turf	.238	80	19	5	0	4	11	7	23	.311	.450	June	.194	72	14	3	0	2	9	14	17	.318	.319
Pre-All Star	.211	280	59	13	1	8	42	42	56	.311	.350	July	.266	94	25	3	0	4	15	12	19	.339	.426
Post-All Star	.294	238	70	18	0	10	36	28	55	.371	.496	August	.280	82	23	5	0	3	12	10	17	.358	.451
Scoring Posn	.271	133	36	7	0	4	56	17	26	.343	.414	Sept/Oct	.329	85	28	11	0	4	16	9	23	.404	.600
Close & Late	.205	83	17	3	0	3	12	16	21	.340	.349	vs. AL	.327	55	18	4	0	3	13	9	11	.418	.564
None on/out	.259	112	29	8	0	5	5	17	30	.357	.464	vs. NL	.240	463	111	27	1	15	65	61	100	.328	.400

1997 By Position

Position	Avg	AB	H	2B	3B	HR	RBI	BB	SO	OBP	SLG	G	GS	Innings	PO	A	E	DP	Fld Pct	Rng Fctr	In Zone	Outs	Zone Rtg	MLB Zone
As lf	.248	505	125	31	1	16	69	66	109	.334	.408	136	134	1179.2	249	17	3	2	.989	2.03	312	241	.772	.805

Last Five Years

	Avg	AB	H	2B	3B	HR	RBI	BB	SO	OBP	SLG		Avg	AB	H	2B	3B	HR	RBI	BB	SO	OBP	SLG
vs. Left	.315	620	195	43	5	24	94	79	93	.391	.516	First Pitch	.299	394	118	26	1	13	59	10	0	.325	.470
vs. Right	.278	1886	524	127	9	63	285	201	344	.352	.455	Ahead in Count	.367	697	256	52	5	38	149	149	0	.478	.620
Groundball	.290	668	194	45	5	20	116	69	123	.361	.463	Behind in Count	.233	932	217	52	3	19	104	0	355	.240	.356
Flyball	.261	383	100	17	0	15	54	38	67	.333	.423	Two Strikes	.207	1038	215	52	4	19	97	121	437	.293	.320
Home	.277	1197	331	78	9	33	161	133	211	.353	.439	Batting #1	.292	895	261	63	9	25	109	75	124	.351	.466
Away	.296	1309	388	92	5	54	218	147	226	.369	.498	Batting #3	.299	698	209	50	3	38	146	96	147	.383	.543
Day	.296	802	237	54	2	28	123	93	138	.369	.473	Other	.273	913	249	57	2	24	109	166	355	.355	.418
Night	.283	1704	482	116	12	59	256	187	299	.358	.469	March/April	.294	340	100	18	1	10	49	36	52	.363	.441
Grass	.300	1340	402	90	5	60	233	167	251	.377	.509	May	.273	466	127	26	2	17	76	48	80	.347	.446
Turf	.272	1166	317	80	9	27	146	113	186	.343	.425	June	.280	447	125	35	1	12	57	44	75	.345	.443
Pre-All Star	.282	1363	384	85	4	42	198	140	225	.352	.442	July	.288	437	126	21	3	20	70	53	81	.365	.487
Post-All Star	.293	1143	335	85	10	45	181	140	212	.373	.503	August	.282	429	121	37	2	15	69	58	67	.372	.483
Scoring Posn	.322	614	198	44	3	22	285	95	98	.408	.511	Sept/Oct	.310	387	120	33	5	13	58	41	82	.380	.522
Close & Late	.276	413	114	27	2	17	76	57	81	.357	.494	vs. AL	.327	55	18	4	0	3	13	9	11	.418	.564
None on/out	.292	688	201	46	6	27	27	65	120	.357	.494	vs. NL	.286	2451	701	166	14	84	366	271	426	.360	.468

Batter vs. Pitcher (career)

Hits Best Against	Avg	AB	H	2B	3B	HR	RBI	BB	SO	OBP	SLG	Hits Worst Against	Avg	AB	H	2B	3B	HR	RBI	BB	SO	OBP	SLG
Kent Bottenfield	.636	11	7	2	0	2	3	2	0	.714	1.364	Todd Jones	.000	13	0	0	0	0	4	1	1	.125	.000
Shawn Boskie	.500	12	6	1	0	2	3	2	1	.600	1.083	Turk Wendell	.000	8	0	0	0	0	0	3	4	.273	.000
Salomon Torres	.500	10	5	1	0	1	2	2	2	.583	.900	Alan Benes	.077	13	1	0	0	0	2	0	1	.071	.077
Kevin Brown	.417	12	5	1	0	2	4	2	2	.563	1.000	Chan Ho Park	.100	10	1	0	0	0	1	0	5	.091	.100
Scott Sanders	.333	9	3	0	0	2	5	1	2	.364	1.000	Mike Hampton	.118	17	2	0	0	0	1	2	4	.111	.118

Ed Giovanola — Braves   Age 29 – Bats Left

	Avg	G	AB	R	H	2B	3B	HR	RBI	BB	SO	HBP	GDP	SB	CS	OBP	SLG	IBB	SH	SF	#Pit	#P/PA	GB	FB	G/F
1997 Season	.250	14	8	0	2	0	0	0	0	2	1	0	2	0	0	.400	.250	1	0	0	29	2.90	6	1	6.00
Career (1995-1997)	.212	70	104	12	22	2	0	0	7	13	19	1	6	1	0	.303	.231	1	2	1	445	3.68	33	39	0.85

1997 Season

	Avg	AB	H	2B	3B	HR	RBI	BB	SO	OBP	SLG		Avg	AB	H	2B	3B	HR	RBI	BB	SO	OBP	SLG
vs. Left	1.000	1	1	0	0	0	0	0	1	0	1.000	Scoring Posn	.000	1	0	0	0	0	0	0	1	0	.500
vs. Right	.143	7	1	0	0	0	2	1	.333	.143		Close & Late	.500	4	2	0	0	0	0	1	1	.600	.500

Joe Girardi — Yankees

Age 33 – Bats Right (groundball hitter)

	Avg	G	AB	R	H	2B	3B	HR	RBI	BB	SO	HBP	GDP	SB	CS	OBP	SLG	IBB	SH	SF	#Pit	#P/PA	GB	FB	G/F
1997 Season	.264	112	398	38	105	23	1	1	50	26	53	2	15	2	3	.311	.334	1	5	2	1355	3.13	187	78	2.40
Last Five Years	.276	540	1922	238	531	85	15	18	215	130	273	14	60	27	19	.325	.364	3	46	9	6771	3.19	863	423	2.04

1997 Season

	Avg	AB	H	2B	3B	HR	RBI	BB	SO	OBP	SLG		Avg	AB	H	2B	3B	HR	RBI	BB	SO	OBP	SLG
vs. Left	.252	103	26	5	0	0	11	10	10	.319	.301	First Pitch	.255	98	25	7	0	0	16	1	0	.275	.327
vs. Right	.268	295	79	18	1	1	39	16	43	.308	.346	Ahead in Count	.305	95	29	8	0	0	14	14	0	.394	.389
Groundball	.346	81	28	3	0	1	13	6	15	.391	.420	Behind in Count	.221	145	32	4	1	0	12	0	47	.219	.262
Flyball	.262	61	16	3	0	0	4	2	9	.297	.311	Two Strikes	.190	137	26	3	0	1	11	11	53	.248	.234
Home	.283	198	56	9	1	1	24	14	31	.330	.354	Batting #8	.291	148	43	11	1	0	25	11	22	.346	.378
Away	.245	200	49	14	0	0	26	12	22	.292	.315	Batting #9	.244	221	54	10	0	1	24	15	27	.291	.303
Day	.299	147	44	13	1	0	18	13	23	.358	.401	Other	.276	29	8	2	0	0	1	0	4	.276	.345
Night	.243	251	61	10	0	1	32	13	30	.282	.295	March/April	.250	68	17	4	0	1	12	3	11	.278	.353
Grass	.270	337	91	19	1	1	43	26	43	.324	.341	May	.227	66	15	4	0	0	10	1	10	.250	.288
Turf	.230	61	14	4	0	0	7	0	10	.230	.295	June	.288	66	19	2	0	0	6	11	6	.385	.318
Pre-All Star	.269	219	59	12	0	1	29	15	31	.316	.338	July	.266	79	21	4	0	0	9	4	12	.310	.316
Post-All Star	.257	179	46	11	1	0	21	11	22	.304	.330	August	.302	86	26	7	1	0	12	6	11	.348	.407
Scoring Posn	.336	122	41	10	1	0	47	8	15	.371	.434	Sept/Oct	.212	33	7	2	0	0	1	1	3	.235	.273
Close & Late	.268	71	19	4	0	1	9	4	14	.303	.366	vs. AL	.265	362	96	22	1	1	46	20	47	.306	.340
None on/out	.230	74	17	3	0	1	5	5	9	.296	.311	vs. NL	.250	36	9	1	0	0	4	6	6	.349	.278

1997 By Position

Position	Avg	AB	H	2B	3B	HR	RBI	BB	SO	OBP	SLG	G	GS	Innings	PO	A	E	DP	Fld Pct	Rng Fctr	In Zone	Zone Outs	Zone Rtg	MLB Zone
As c	.264	398	105	23	1	1	50	26	53	.311	.334	111	109	979.1	829	54	5	12	.994	—	—	—	—	

Last Five Years

	Avg	AB	H	2B	3B	HR	RBI	BB	SO	OBP	SLG		Avg	AB	H	2B	3B	HR	RBI	BB	SO	OBP	SLG
vs. Left	.270	504	136	23	2	3	42	39	68	.322	.341	First Pitch	.276	434	120	24	1	4	52	1	0	.287	.364
vs. Right	.279	1418	395	62	13	15	173	91	205	.326	.372	Ahead in Count	.307	424	130	29	4	6	56	72	0	.408	.436
Groundball	.282	493	139	15	8	4	62	34	85	.332	.369	Behind in Count	.221	770	170	20	4	5	71	0	250	.225	.277
Flyball	.284	328	93	14	1	4	30	18	44	.327	.369	Two Strikes	.176	681	120	16	2	5	53	57	273	.241	.228
Home	.297	953	283	40	11	11	119	67	129	.346	.397	Batting #2	.292	489	143	23	6	5	47	36	84	.345	.395
Away	.256	969	248	45	4	7	96	63	144	.305	.332	Batting #7	.256	644	165	19	5	7	61	42	90	.303	.334
Day	.295	658	194	42	8	5	73	45	91	.342	.406	Other	.283	789	223	43	4	6	107	52	99	.331	.370
Night	.267	1264	337	43	7	13	142	85	182	.316	.343	March/April	.255	294	75	16	3	1	32	17	49	.298	.340
Grass	.284	1571	446	70	14	17	192	119	215	.338	.379	May	.286	419	120	16	2	2	51	25	63	.327	.348
Turf	.242	351	85	15	1	1	23	11	58	.267	.299	June	.273	297	81	14	2	3	29	29	37	.339	.364
Pre-All Star	.281	1117	314	51	8	7	125	77	159	.329	.360	July	.309	301	93	12	3	3	36	16	41	.345	.399
Post-All Star	.270	805	217	34	7	11	90	53	114	.320	.370	August	.257	338	87	16	3	7	46	22	45	.306	.385
Scoring Posn	.314	503	158	20	6	3	186	51	74	.375	.396	Sept/Oct	.275	273	75	11	2	2	21	21	39	.338	.352
Close & Late	.284	299	85	10	1	2	32	20	47	.330	.344	vs. AL	.281	784	220	44	4	3	91	50	102	.328	.358
None on/out	.285	410	117	19	4	3	3	19	45	.326	.373	vs. NL	.273	1138	311	41	11	15	124	80	171	.324	.368

Batter vs. Pitcher (career)

Hits Best Against	Avg	AB	H	2B	3B	HR	RBI	BB	SO	OBP	SLG	Hits Worst Against	Avg	AB	H	2B	3B	HR	RBI	BB	SO	OBP	SLG
Bruce Ruffin	.500	12	6	2	0	1	4	1	2	.538	.917	Paul Wagner	.000	11	0	0	0	0	0	0	4	.000	.000
Danny Jackson	.455	11	5	0	0	0	1	1	1	.500	.455	Tim Wakefield	.000	10	0	0	0	0	0	1	1	.167	.000
Mark Portugal	.452	31	14	4	0	0	6	0	1	.469	.581	Bob Tewksbury	.056	18	1	0	0	0	0	0	1	.150	.056
Andy Ashby	.385	13	5	0	1	0	0	1	3	.429	.538	Jamie Moyer	.077	13	1	0	0	0	1	0	4	.077	.077
Steve Avery	.353	17	6	2	0	2	4	3	2	.450	.824	Kent Mercker	.083	12	1	0	0	0	0	1	2	.154	.083

Doug Glanville — Cubs

Age 27 – Bats Right

	Avg	G	AB	R	H	2B	3B	HR	RBI	BB	SO	HBP	GDP	SB	CS	OBP	SLG	IBB	SH	SF	#Pit	#P/PA	GB	FB	G/F
1997 Season	.300	146	474	79	142	22	5	4	35	24	46	1	9	19	11	.333	.392	0	9	2	1776	3.48	203	116	1.75
Career (1996-1997)	.291	195	557	89	162	27	6	5	45	27	57	1	11	21	11	.323	.388	0	11	3	2095	3.50	236	145	1.63

1997 Season

	Avg	AB	H	2B	3B	HR	RBI	BB	SO	OBP	SLG		Avg	AB	H	2B	3B	HR	RBI	BB	SO	OBP	SLG
vs. Left	.276	156	43	6	0	3	11	9	8	.317	.372	First Pitch	.333	60	20	4	0	0	9	0	0	.333	.400
vs. Right	.311	318	99	16	5	1	24	15	38	.341	.403	Ahead in Count	.345	87	30	3	1	2	9	20	0	.467	.471
Groundball	.253	79	20	4	1	0	8	4	6	.289	.329	Behind in Count	.291	227	66	10	4	2	11	0	43	.293	.396
Flyball	.265	68	18	3	2	0	3	2	13	.282	.368	Two Strikes	.277	188	52	7	1	1	7	4	46	.295	.340
Home	.327	254	83	11	4	2	25	16	21	.366	.425	Batting #1	.315	248	78	11	3	3	13	11	27	.344	.419
Away	.268	220	59	11	1	2	10	8	25	.294	.355	Batting #2	.285	193	55	9	2	1	15	12	16	.327	.368
Day	.324	278	90	14	3	4	22	19	22	.368	.439	Other	.273	33	9	2	0	0	7	1	3	.294	.333
Night	.265	196	52	8	2	0	13	5	24	.282	.327	March/April	.300	40	12	2	0	0	6	1	2	.326	.350
Grass	.309	375	116	18	4	3	30	19	34	.343	.403	May	.296	71	21	5	3	1	5	6	9	.346	.493
Turf	.263	99	26	4	1	1	5	5	12	.298	.354	June	.299	67	20	2	1	0	3	4	6	.338	.358
Pre-All Star	.305	203	62	10	4	2	15	13	21	.347	.424	July	.313	112	35	7	1	1	8	6	10	.347	.420
Post-All Star	.295	271	80	12	1	2	20	11	25	.323	.369	August	.304	112	34	2	0	2	7	6	10	.339	.375
Scoring Posn	.270	89	24	4	2	0	31	5	6	.302	.360	Sept/Oct	.278	72	20	4	0	0		1	3	.288	.333
Close & Late	.316	76	24	3	2	0	10	1	12	.325	.408	vs. AL	.390	41	16	2	1	0	5	1	3	.405	.634
None on/out	.285	158	45	6	1	1	1	5	14	.307	.354	vs. NL	.291	433	126	20	4	2	30	23	43	.327	.370

1997 By Position

Position	Avg	AB	H	2B	3B	HR	RBI	BB	SO	OBP	SLG	G	GS	Innings	PO	A	E	DP	Fld Pct	Rng Fctr	In Zone	Zone Outs	Zone Rtg	MLB Zone
As Pinch Hitter	.222	9	2	1	0	0	4	0	0	.222	.333	10	0	—	—	—	—	—	—	—	—	—	—	—

Position	Avg	AB	H	2B	3B	HR	RBI	BB	SO	OBP	SLG	G	GS	Innings	PO	A	E	DP	Fld Pct	Rng Fctr	In Zone	Outs	Zone Rtg	MLB Zone
As lf	.294	357	105	17	4	2	25	20	34	.332	.381	120	80	803.0	184	11	3	2	.985	2.19	211	170	.806	.805
As cf	.318	107	34	4	1	2	6	4	12	.342	.430	30	25	218.1	61	1	0	1	1.000	2.56	65	60	.923	.815

Tom Glavine — Braves
Age 32 – Pitches Left

	ERA	W	L	Sv	G	GS	IP	BB	SO	Avg	H	2B	3B	HR	RBI	OBP	SLG	CG	ShO	Sup	QS	#P/S	SB	CS	GB	FB	G/F
1997 Season	2.96	14	7	0	33	33	240.0	79	152	.226	197	29	2	20	74	.292	.333	5	2	4.88	26	111	6	6	348	211	1.65
Last Five Years	3.20	80	39	0	159	159	1078.2	390	720	.249	1010	194	13	69	365	.315	.354	15	5	5.23	108	105	50	24	1542	1032	1.49

1997 Season

	ERA	W	L	Sv	G	GS	IP	H	HR	BB	SO		Avg	AB	H	2B	3B	HR	RBI	BB	SO	OBP	SLG
Home	2.13	5	2	0	13	13	97.1	64	5	36	66	vs. Left	.233	176	41	9	0	4	10	14	28	.292	.352
Away	3.53	9	5	0	20	20	142.2	133	15	43	86	vs. Right	.225	694	156	20	2	16	64	65	124	.292	.329
Day	3.72	1	0	0	7	7	46.0	39	6	17	27	Inning 1-6	.223	691	154	23	2	18	66	70	121	.295	.340
Night	2.78	13	7	0	26	26	194.0	158	14	62	125	Inning 7+	.240	179	43	6	0	2	8	9	31	.279	.307
Grass	2.99	9	6	0	25	25	183.2	149	15	61	119	None on	.239	547	131	22	0	11	11	33	92	.284	.340
Turf	2.88	5	1	0	8	8	56.1	48	5	18	33	Runners on	.204	323	66	7	2	9	63	46	60	.304	.322
March/April	1.64	4	0	0	6	6	44.0	35	1	11	24	Scoring Posn	.183	164	30	3	2	5	54	36	37	.324	.317
May	4.41	1	3	0	5	5	34.2	32	4	13	23	Close & Late	.224	98	22	3	0	1	4	9	18	.296	.286
June	2.09	3	1	0	6	6	47.1	40	1	15	24	None on/out	.242	236	57	9	0	4	4	12	34	.278	.331
July	5.57	2	1	0	5	5	32.1	32	3	11	19	vs. 1st Batr (relief)	.000	0	0	0	0	0	0	0	0	.000	.000
August	2.72	2	1	0	6	6	43.0	30	7	21	30	1st Inning Pitched	.264	125	33	2	0	5	16	12	14	.338	.400
Sept/Oct	2.33	2	1	0	5	5	38.2	28	4	8	32	First 75 Pitches	.220	567	125	21	2	15	49	51	99	.287	.344
Starter	2.96	14	7	0	33	33	240.0	197	20	79	152	Pitch 76-90	.212	113	24	1	0	2	7	12	21	.286	.274
Reliever	0.00	0	0	0	0	0	0.0	0	0	0	0	Pitch 91-105	.242	95	23	2	0	7	10	17		.321	.263
0-3 Days Rest (Start)	0.00	0	0	0	0	0	0.0	0	0	0	0	Pitch 106+	.263	95	25	5	0	3	11	6	15	.301	.411
4 Days Rest	2.59	12	4	0	25	25	181.0	142	15	52	121	First Pitch	.321	106	34	4	1	2	8	3	0	.339	.434
5+ Days Rest	4.12	2	3	0	8	8	59.0	55	5	27	31	Ahead in Count	.160	376	60	8	0	4	12	0	136	.166	.213
vs. AL	1.04	1	0	0	3	3	26.0	19	2	9	13	Behind in Count	.273	205	56	7	1	8	33	49	0	.407	.434
vs. NL	3.20	13	7	0	30	30	214.0	178	18	70	139	Two Strikes	.156	397	62	11	0	7	23	27	152	.213	.237
Pre-All Star	2.62	9	4	0	18	18	134.0	114	6	40	74	Pre-All Star	.235	486	114	17	2	6	37	40	74	.295	.315
Post-All Star	3.40	5	3	0	15	15	106.0	83	14	39	78	Post-All Star	.216	384	83	12	0	14	37	39	78	.289	.357

Last Five Years

	ERA	W	L	Sv	G	GS	IP	H	HR	BB	SO		Avg	AB	H	2B	3B	HR	RBI	BB	SO	OBP	SLG
Home	3.00	37	17	0	75	75	512.2	469	33	195	340	vs. Left	.271	753	204	38	2	9	66	76	151	.339	.363
Away	3.37	43	22	0	84	84	566.0	541	36	195	380	vs. Right	.244	3303	806	156	11	60	299	314	569	.310	.352
Day	3.10	17	7	0	43	43	282.0	259	21	107	192	Inning 1-6	.245	3414	837	163	11	58	313	346	624	.315	.350
Night	3.23	63	32	0	116	116	796.2	751	48	283	528	Inning 7+	.269	642	173	31	2	11	52	44	96	.316	.375
Grass	3.24	57	32	0	122	122	827.1	789	54	305	565	None on	.255	2386	608	116	7	43	43	171	427	.306	.363
Turf	3.04	23	7	0	37	37	251.1	221	15	85	155	Runners on	.241	1670	402	78	6	26	322	219	293	.328	.341
March/April	2.73	11	5	0	23	23	148.1	126	7	65	98	Scoring Posn	.219	892	195	38	6	11	271	165	170	.336	.312
May	3.13	16	8	0	29	29	198.1	164	16	74	144	Close & Late	.246	395	97	17	1	5	27	35	59	.308	.332
June	3.33	12	10	0	28	28	197.1	212	12	68	124	None on/out	.257	1064	273	49	2	21	21	62	178	.299	.366
July	3.39	17	4	0	30	30	209.2	203	10	65	127	vs. 1st Batr (relief)	.000	0	0	0	0	0	0	0	0	.000	.000
August	3.20	11	6	0	25	25	169.0	150	15	72	114	1st Inning Pitched	.269	614	165	34	1	17	84	82	102	.357	.410
Sept/Oct	3.29	13	6	0	24	24	156.0	155	9	46	113	First 75 Pitches	.243	2771	673	133	9	48	236	267	507	.311	.349
Starter	3.20	80	39	0	159	159	1078.2	1010	69	390	720	Pitch 76-90	.254	543	138	28	3	10	50	53	89	.318	.372
Reliever	0.00	0	0	0	0	0	0.0	0	0	0	0	Pitch 91-105	.251	451	113	19	1	4	43	40	79	.313	.324
0-3 Days Rest (Start)	2.76	5	1	0	10	10	65.1	60	3	18	50	Pitch 106+	.296	291	86	14	0	7	36	30	45	.357	.416
4 Days Rest	3.24	48	29	0	103	103	695.1	654	44	259	456	First Pitch	.330	610	201	40	2	17	72	17	0	.347	.485
5+ Days Rest	3.20	27	9	0	46	46	318.0	296	22	113	214	Ahead in Count	.185	1676	310	51	4	20	97	0	616	.189	.256
vs. AL	1.04	1	0	0	3	3	26.0	19	2	9	13	Behind in Count	.297	972	289	58	5	24	125	210	0	.419	.441
vs. NL	3.25	79	39	0	156	156	1052.2	991	67	381	707	Two Strikes	.171	1742	298	59	3	16	105	162	720	.244	.236
Pre-All Star	3.12	46	24	0	89	89	608.2	564	38	219	402	Pre-All Star	.247	2284	564	111	10	38	205	219	402	.313	.354
Post-All Star	3.29	34	15	0	70	70	470.0	446	31	171	318	Post-All Star	.252	1772	446	83	3	31	160	171	318	.318	.354

Pitcher vs. Batter (career)

Pitches Best Vs.	Avg	AB	H	2B	3B	HR	RBI	BB	SO		Avg	AB	H	2B	3B	HR	RBI	BB	SO	OBP	SLG
Al Martin	.000	13	0	0	0	0	0	2	4	.133	.000	Mike Piazza	.393	28	11	2	0	2	4	2	4	.433	.679
Eric Anthony	.000	11	0	0	0	0	0	1	5	.083	.000	Ellis Burks	.385	26	10	5	1	0	4	3	5	.448	.654
Rey Sanchez	.045	22	1	0	0	0	0	0	.045	.045	Carlos Hernandez	.385	13	5	1	0	1	1	1	0	.429	.692
Mark Parent	.050	20	1	0	0	0	0	0	2	.050	.050	Kevin Mitchell	.356	45	16	3	0	5	12	10	7	.473	.756
Jeff Branson	.083	12	1	0	0	0	0	0	2	.083	.083	Ron Gant	.313	16	5	1	0	1	2	7	3	.522	.563

Wayne Gomes — Phillies
Age 25 – Pitches Right (groundball pitcher)

	ERA	W	L	Sv	G	GS	IP	BB	SO	Avg	H	2B	3B	HR	RBI	OBP	SLG	GF	IR	IRS	Hld	SvOp	SB	CS	GB	FB	G/F
1997 Season	5.27	5	1	0	37	0	42.2	24	24	.274	45	9	0	4	24	.370	.402	13	18	5	3	1	2	3	75	42	1.79

1997 Season

	ERA	W	L	Sv	G	GS	IP	H	HR	BB	SO		Avg	AB	H	2B	3B	HR	RBI	BB	SO	OBP	SLG
Home	4.32	3	0	0	18	0	25.0	25	4	9	13	vs. Left	.250	64	16	4	0	1	12	13	9	.377	.359
Away	6.62	2	1	0	19	0	17.2	20	0	15	11	vs. Right	.290	100	29	5	0	3	12	11	15	.366	.430
Starter	0.00	0	0	0	0	0	0.0	0	0	0	0	Scoring Posn	.298	57	17	3	0	2	22	11	7	.412	.456
Reliever	5.27	5	1	0	37	0	42.2	45	4	24	24	Close & Late	.308	52	16	5	0	2	7	6	11	.390	.519
0 Days rest (Relief)	7.00	1	1	0	9	0	9.0	10	0	7	6	None on/out	.324	37	12	4	0	0	0	3	6	.390	.432

1997 Season

	ERA	W	L	Sv	G	GS	IP	H	HR	BB	SO		Avg	AB	H	2B	3B	HR	RBI	BB	SO	OBP	SLG
1 or 2 Days rest	5.95	2	0	0	17	0	19.2	25	1	10	10	First Pitch	.320	25	8	2	0	1	6	0	0	.320	.520
3+ Days rest	3.21	2	0	0	11	0	14.0	10	3	7	8	Ahead in Count	.230	61	14	4	0	0	5	0	18	.230	.295
Pre-All Star	3.68	1	0	0	12	0	14.2	15	0	5	6	Behind in Count	.320	50	16	2	0	3	16	16	0	.493	.540
Post-All Star	6.11	4	1	0	25	0	28.0	30	4	19	18	Two Strikes	.197	61	12	3	0	0	6	8	24	.290	.246

Chris Gomez — Padres
Age 27 – Bats Right

	Avg	G	AB	R	H	2B	3B	HR	RBI	BB	SO	HBP	GDP	SB	CS	OBP	SLG	IBB	SH	SF	#Pit	#P/PA	GB	FB	G/F
1997 Season	.253	150	522	62	132	19	2	5	54	53	114	5	16	5	8	.326	.326	1	3	3	2328	3.95	179	113	1.58
Career (1993-1997)	.247	540	1833	207	453	86	6	28	213	193	375	19	55	19	17	.324	.346	2	18	10	8212	3.96	641	445	1.44

1997 Season

	Avg	AB	H	2B	3B	HR	RBI	BB	SO	OBP	SLG		Avg	AB	H	2B	3B	HR	RBI	BB	SO	OBP	SLG
vs. Left	.294	109	32	3	1	2	15	17	19	.386	.394	First Pitch	.308	65	20	1	1	0	11	1	0	.319	.354
vs. Right	.242	413	100	16	1	3	39	36	95	.309	.308	Ahead in Count	.313	131	41	6	0	2	17	24	0	.417	.405
Groundball	.305	118	36	6	0	1	15	11	20	.364	.381	Behind in Count	.176	227	40	6	1	1	12	0	89	.187	.225
Flyball	.214	84	18	1	0	2	6	14	23	.327	.298	Two Strikes	.183	251	46	10	1	1	19	28	114	.270	.243
Home	.237	266	63	10	0	2	26	23	59	.302	.297	Batting #7	.252	282	71	9	1	3	32	26	64	.325	.323
Away	.270	256	69	9	2	3	28	30	55	.349	.355	Batting #8	.257	148	38	2	1	2	17	18	35	.333	.324
Day	.289	166	48	10	0	3	16	14	32	.348	.404	Other	.250	92	23	8	0	0	5	9	15	.317	.337
Night	.236	356	84	9	2	2	38	39	82	.316	.289	March/April	.275	80	22	2	0	2	8	6	21	.322	.375
Grass	.250	424	106	17	2	5	45	42	94	.321	.335	May	.274	106	29	5	0	1	10	8	21	.330	.349
Turf	.265	98	26	2	0	0	9	11	20	.345	.286	June	.248	113	28	4	1	1	16	9	22	.315	.327
Pre-All Star	.261	318	83	11	1	5	37	27	65	.326	.349	July	.238	80	19	2	1	1	12	14	19	.358	.325
Post-All Star	.240	204	49	8	1	0	17	26	49	.326	.289	August	.240	96	23	4	0	0	7	9	21	.305	.281
Scoring Posn	.234	141	33	5	1	1	44	17	35	.311	.305	Sept/Oct	.234	47	11	2	0	0	1	7	10	.333	.277
Close & Late	.333	78	26	2	2	0	8	14	18	.435	.410	vs. AL	.190	58	11	1	1	1	8	7	9	.284	.293
None on/out	.250	116	29	3	0	2	2	10	21	.315	.328	vs. NL	.261	464	121	18	1	4	46	46	105	.331	.330

1997 By Position

Position	Avg	AB	H	2B	3B	HR	RBI	BB	SO	OBP	SLG	G	GS	Innings	PO	A	E	DP	Fld Pct	Rng Fctr	In Zone	Outs	Zone Rtg	MLB Zone
As ss	.253	522	132	19	2	5	54	53	114	.326	.326	150	146	1279.2	226	432	15	82	.978	4.63	480	439	.915	.937

Career (1993-1997)

	Avg	AB	H	2B	3B	HR	RBI	BB	SO	OBP	SLG		Avg	AB	H	2B	3B	HR	RBI	BB	SO	OBP	SLG
vs. Left	.274	442	121	25	2	6	63	80	145	.367	.380	First Pitch	.285	228	65	8	1	2	34	2	0	.300	.355
vs. Right	.239	1391	332	61	4	22	155	130	295	.309	.336	Ahead in Count	.321	446	143	28	1	13	76	98	0	.445	.475
Groundball	.249	422	105	21	1	2	41	44	94	.326	.318	Behind in Count	.177	803	142	29	1	8	59	0	309	.183	.245
Flyball	.213	324	69	11	1	10	31	41	68	.305	.346	Two Strikes	.181	873	158	35	4	8	72	93	375	.264	.258
Home	.242	885	214	44	3	14	114	97	172	.321	.346	Batting #7	.244	553	135	20	3	7	70	58	120	.324	.329
Away	.252	948	239	42	3	14	99	96	203	.326	.347	Batting #8	.263	419	110	23	2	9	59	48	92	.337	.391
Day	.272	647	176	38	2	13	78	71	125	.350	.397	Other	.242	861	208	43	1	12	84	87	163	.317	.336
Night	.234	1186	277	48	4	15	135	122	250	.309	.319	March/April	.253	150	38	4	0	4	18	19	32	.333	.360
Grass	.249	1513	377	74	6	23	179	162	305	.327	.352	May	.260	292	76	16	0	7	49	30	63	.335	.387
Turf	.238	320	76	12	0	5	34	31	70	.309	.322	June	.258	360	93	13	2	8	49	39	75	.341	.372
Pre-All Star	.261	917	239	39	3	21	134	104	190	.341	.378	July	.262	370	97	21	3	6	40	42	74	.346	.384
Post-All Star	.234	916	214	47	3	7	79	89	185	.305	.314	August	.235	366	86	19	0	1	25	33	72	.299	.285
Scoring Posn	.272	459	125	26	3	4	169	53	101	.350	.368	Sept/Oct	.214	295	63	13	1	2	23	30	59	.286	.285
Close & Late	.215	260	56	4	2	1	17	32	60	.310	.258	vs. AL	.236	1041	246	52	4	21	138	108	206	.312	.354
None on/out	.209	411	86	13	0	10	10	36	83	.281	.314	vs. NL	.261	792	207	34	2	7	75	85	169	.339	.336

Batter vs. Pitcher (career)

Hits Best Against	Avg	AB	H	2B	3B	HR	RBI	BB	SO	OBP	SLG	Hits Worst Against	Avg	AB	H	2B	3B	HR	RBI	BB	SO	OBP	SLG
Cal Eldred	.556	9	5	2	0	1	1	3	1	.667	1.111	Juan Guzman	.000	13	0	0	0	0	0	2	6	.133	.000
Hideo Nomo	.500	10	5	3	0	0	2	2	2	.615	.800	Kevin Gross	.000	10	0	0	0	0	0	1	5	.091	.000
Kevin Ritz	.455	11	5	0	0	1	2	2	1	.538	.727	Chuck Finley	.059	17	1	0	0	0	0	2	5	.158	.059
Mark Clark	.400	20	8	3	0	0	0	0	4	.400	.550	Ismael Valdes	.077	13	1	0	0	0	0	1	4	.143	.077
Andy Pettitte	.333	9	3	0	0	1	1	4	3	.538	.333	Pat Mahomes	.091	11	1	0	0	0	0	1	1	.167	.091

Rene Gonzales — Rockies
Age 36 – Bats Right (groundball hitter)

	Avg	G	AB	R	H	2B	3B	HR	RBI	BB	SO	HBP	GDP	SB	CS	OBP	SLG	IBB	SH	SF	#Pit	#P/PA	GB	FB	G/F
1997 Season	.500	2	2	0	1	0	0	0	1	0	0	0	0	0	0	.500	.500	0	0	0	7	3.50	1	0	0.00
Last Five Years	.253	222	470	60	119	23	1	6	45	64	63	1	16	7	5	.341	.345	2	3	5	2058	3.79	196	122	1.61

1997 Season

	Avg	AB	H	2B	3B	HR	RBI	BB	SO	OBP	SLG		Avg	AB	H	2B	3B	HR	RBI	BB	SO	OBP	SLG
vs. Left	.500	2	1	0	0	0	1	0	0	.500	.500	Scoring Posn	1.000	1	1	0	0	0	1	0	0	1.000	1.000
vs. Right	.000	0	0	0	0	0	0	0	0	.000	.000	Close & Late	.000	0	0	0	0	0	0	0	0	.000	.000

Last Five Years

	Avg	AB	H	2B	3B	HR	RBI	BB	SO	OBP	SLG		Avg	AB	H	2B	3B	HR	RBI	BB	SO	OBP	SLG
vs. Left	.276	185	51	14	0	3	13	26	23	.368	.400	First Pitch	.296	71	21	2	0	3	8	1	0	.306	.451
vs. Right	.239	285	68	9	1	3	32	38	40	.323	.309	Ahead in Count	.296	108	32	12	0	2	18	34	0	.458	.463
Groundball	.227	88	20	2	0	0	5	8	12	.289	.250	Behind in Count	.188	213	40	7	0	1	10	0	56	.187	.239
Flyball	.240	100	24	8	0	1	10	12	14	.319	.350	Two Strikes	.200	205	41	5	1	1	12	29	63	.300	.249
Home	.239	243	58	12	0	2	22	30	31	.322	.313	Batting #6	.230	152	35	7	0	0	8	20	18	.324	.276
Away	.269	227	61	11	1	4	23	34	32	.360	.379	Batting #7	.218	110	24	6	0	1	11	19	16	.331	.300
Day	.285	144	41	7	0	3	19	21	18	.373	.396	Other	.288	208	60	10	1	5	26	25	29	.359	.418

Last Five Years

	Avg	AB	H	2B	3B	HR	RBI	BB	SO	OBP	SLG		Avg	AB	H	2B	3B	HR	RBI	BB	SO	OBP	SLG
Night	.239	326	78	16	1	3	26	43	45	.326	.322	March/April	.241	58	14	3	0	0	6	10	11	.357	.293
Grass	.262	405	106	20	0	6	43	54	53	.346	.356	May	.275	80	22	2	0	1	12	18	9	.404	.338
Turf	.200	65	13	3	1	0	2	10	10	.307	.277	June	.264	87	23	4	1	3	6	10	12	.340	.437
Pre-All Star	.279	265	74	14	1	4	26	39	37	.371	.385	July	.271	96	26	7	0	0	6	10	11	.336	.344
Post-All Star	.220	205	45	9	0	2	19	25	26	.300	.293	August	.273	55	15	4	0	1	7	5	6	.328	.400
Scoring Posn	.271	107	29	2	0	1	37	24	15	.394	.318	Sept/Oct	.202	94	19	3	0	1	8	11	14	.283	.266
Close & Late	.182	66	12	2	0	1	7	13	11	.316	.258	vs. AL	.252	468	118	23	1	6	44	64	63	.340	.344
None on/out	.250	108	27	6	0	1	1	15	17	.341	.333	vs. NL	.500	2	1	0	0	0	1	0	0	.500	.500

Batter vs. Pitcher (career)

Hits Best Against	Avg	AB	H	2B	3B	HR	RBI	BB	SO	OBP	SLG	Hits Worst Against	Avg	AB	H	2B	3B	HR	RBI	BB	SO	OBP	SLG
Randy Johnson	.500	16	8	2	0	1	2	5	2	.667	.813	David Wells	.077	13	1	1	0	0	0	0	1	.077	.154
Jaime Navarro	.500	8	4	1	0	0	1	2	0	.636	.625	Roger Clemens	.136	22	3	1	0	0	0	0	4	.136	.182
Kevin Brown	.444	9	4	0	0	0	0	2	0	.545	.444	Chuck Finley	.154	13	2	1	0	0	0	2	2	.267	.231
Alex Fernandez	.364	11	4	2	0	1	1	1		.417	.545	Kevin Tapani	.188	16	3	0	0	1	1	0	2	.188	.375
Mark Langston	.353	17	6	0	1	0	3	2	3	.421	.471	Jimmy Key	.222	9	2	0	0	0	1	2	2	.333	.222

Alex Gonzalez — Blue Jays
Age 25 – Bats Right (groundball hitter)

	Avg	G	AB	R	H	2B	3B	HR	RBI	BB	SO	HBP	GDP	SB	CS	OBP	SLG	IBB	SH	SF	#Pit	#P/PA	GB	FB	G/F
1997 Season	.239	126	426	46	102	23	2	12	35	34	94	5	9	15	6	.302	.387	1	11	2	1743	3.65	153	111	1.38
Career (1994-1997)	.235	399	1373	168	323	75	12	36	142	127	352	12	30	38	16	.304	.386	2	28	9	5957	3.85	480	335	1.43

1997 Season

	Avg	AB	H	2B	3B	HR	RBI	BB	SO	OBP	SLG		Avg	AB	H	2B	3B	HR	RBI	BB	SO	OBP	SLG
vs. Left	.260	123	32	7	1	3	7	11	18	.326	.407	First Pitch	.286	56	16	5	0	3	8	1	0	.305	.536
vs. Right	.231	303	70	16	1	9	28	23	76	.292	.380	Ahead in Count	.326	92	30	5	0	6	11	21	0	.451	.576
Groundball	.215	65	14	2	0	2	5	3	17	.261	.338	Behind in Count	.223	202	45	10	2	2	12	0	78	.225	.322
Flyball	.259	58	15	6	1	0	4	7	12	.348	.397	Two Strikes	.190	210	40	8	2	2	11	12	94	.233	.276
Home	.234	231	54	8	2	4	15	14	50	.288	.338	Batting #8	.232	125	29	5	0	3	11	9	25	.289	.344
Away	.246	195	48	15	0	8	20	20	44	.318	.446	Batting #9	.265	181	48	13	1	7	14	19	42	.340	.464
Day	.204	152	31	5	0	3	11	6	42	.244	.296	Other	.208	120	25	5	1	2	10	6	27	.256	.317
Night	.259	274	71	18	2	9	24	28	52	.332	.438	March/April	.270	74	20	4	1	2	4	5	19	.333	.432
Grass	.230	152	35	10	0	7	13	18	35	.314	.434	May	.247	97	24	4	0	2	11	7	16	.298	.351
Turf	.245	274	67	13	2	5	22	16	59	.295	.361	June	.231	91	21	4	1	3	8	0	23	.239	.396
Pre-All Star	.241	282	68	13	2	7	24	15	65	.287	.376	July	.160	81	13	5	0	3	5	12	20	.269	.333
Post-All Star	.236	144	34	10	0	5	11	19	29	.329	.410	August	.429	42	18	5	0	2	6	5	7	.490	.690
Scoring Posn	.194	108	21	7	0	1	22	7	26	.246	.287	Sept/Oct	.146	41	6	1	0	0	1	5	9	.250	.171
Close & Late	.230	74	17	1	0	4	6	5	22	.278	.405	vs. AL	.235	391	92	20	2	10	29	34	86	.303	.373
None on/out	.275	102	28	7	1	3	3	4	20	.308	.451	vs. NL	.286	35	10	3	0	2	6	0	8	.286	.543

1997 By Position

Position	Avg	AB	H	2B	3B	HR	RBI	BB	SO	OBP	SLG	G	GS	Innings	PO	A	E	DP	Fld Pct	Rng Fctr	In Zone	Zone Outs	Zone Rtg	MLB Zone
As ss	.239	426	102	23	2	12	35	34	94	.302	.387	125	125	1102.1	209	342	8	77	.986	4.50	366	351	.959	.937

Career (1994-1997)

	Avg	AB	H	2B	3B	HR	RBI	BB	SO	OBP	SLG		Avg	AB	H	2B	3B	HR	RBI	BB	SO	OBP	SLG
vs. Left	.256	414	106	25	6	9	35	44	92	.329	.411	First Pitch	.296	186	55	13	1	8	22	1	0	.307	.505
vs. Right	.226	959	217	50	6	27	107	83	260	.293	.375	Ahead in Count	.344	270	93	22	4	19	51	65	0	.467	.667
Groundball	.214	280	60	11	2	8	31	28	69	.290	.354	Behind in Count	.186	672	125	27	5	5	48	0	299	.191	.263
Flyball	.245	200	49	13	4	1	20	21	58	.327	.365	Two Strikes	.164	718	118	24	5	6	43	61	352	.233	.237
Home	.227	744	169	40	10	15	80	62	200	.293	.368	Batting #8	.210	353	74	15	2	8	34	32	92	.276	.331
Away	.245	629	154	35	2	21	62	65	152	.316	.407	Batting #9	.242	571	138	35	7	15	50	51	146	.311	.406
Day	.222	478	106	24	5	11	47	39	134	.288	.362	Other	.247	449	111	25	3	13	58	44	114	.317	.403
Night	.242	895	217	51	7	25	95	88	218	.312	.399	March/April	.243	235	57	14	2	5	22	15	65	.301	.383
Grass	.250	517	129	27	1	19	51	61	123	.329	.416	May	.233	258	60	15	1	7	35	26	58	.303	.380
Turf	.227	856	194	48	11	17	91	66	229	.288	.368	June	.261	257	67	16	2	6	28	13	64	.299	.409
Pre-All Star	.241	826	199	52	5	18	90	61	209	.297	.381	July	.200	265	53	15	1	7	21	27	73	.276	.343
Post-All Star	.227	547	124	23	7	18	52	66	143	.313	.393	August	.296	186	55	10	3	7	25	28	41	.386	.495
Scoring Posn	.225	342	77	19	2	5	96	34	97	.294	.336	Sept/Oct	.180	172	31	5	3	4	11	18	51	.264	.314
Close & Late	.210	219	46	12	1	7	22	18	63	.275	.370	vs. AL	.234	1338	313	72	12	34	136	127	344	.304	.382
None on/out	.268	340	91	23	4	13	13	24	71	.322	.474	vs. NL	.286	35	10	3	0	2	6	0	8	.286	.543

Batter vs. Pitcher (career)

Hits Best Against	Avg	AB	H	2B	3B	HR	RBI	BB	SO	OBP	SLG	Hits Worst Against	Avg	AB	H	2B	3B	HR	RBI	BB	SO	OBP	SLG
Jimmy Key	.400	15	6	0	0	2	4	0	1	.400	.800	Jose Rosado	.071	14	1	0	0	0	0	1	1	.133	.071
Felipe Lira	.400	10	4	1	0	0	4	1	3	.417	.500	Shawn Boskie	.077	13	1	0	0	0	1	0	7	.071	.077
Tim Wakefield	.375	16	6	0	0	0	1	3	5	.500	.375	Randy Johnson	.083	12	1	0	0	0	0	1	5	.154	.083
Brad Radke	.364	22	8	3	1	1	4	0	4	.364	.727	Kevin Appier	.083	12	1	0	0	0	0	3	4	.267	.083
Scott Karl	.308	13	4	2	1	0	1	0	2	.308	.615	Andy Pettitte	.100	30	3	1	0	0	0	0	10	.100	.233

Jeremi Gonzalez — Cubs
Age 23 – Pitches Right

	ERA	W	L	Sv	G	GS	IP	BB	SO	Avg	H	2B	3B	HR	RBI	OBP	SLG	CG	ShO	Sup	QS	#P/S	SB	CS	GB	FB	G/F
1997 Season	4.25	11	9	0	23	23	144.0	69	93	.236	126	25	4	16	59	.323	.388	1	1	4.69	9	100	17	2	179	156	1.15

1997 Season

	ERA	W	L	Sv	G	GS	IP	H	HR	BB	SO		Avg	AB	H	2B	3B	HR	RBI	BB	SO	OBP	SLG
Home	3.04	6	3	0	11	11	68.0	55	6	32	44	vs. Left	.232	276	64	8	3	10	30	33	52	.310	.391

1997 Season

	ERA	W	L	Sv	G	GS	IP	H	HR	BB	SO		Avg	AB	H	2B	3B	HR	RBI	BB	SO	OBP	SLG
Away	5.33	5	6	0	12	12	76.0	71	10	37	49	vs. Right	.241	257	62	17	1	6	29	36	41	.338	.385
Day	3.35	7	3	0	12	12	75.1	61	8	33	47	Inning 1-6	.231	472	109	22	4	10	47	60	85	.317	.358
Night	5.24	4	6	0	11	11	68.2	65	8	36	46	Inning 7+	.279	61	17	3	0	6	12	9	8	.371	.623
Grass	4.07	9	6	0	18	18	112.2	95	11	53	67	None on	.243	321	78	11	3	9	9	39	52	.327	.380
Turf	4.88	2	3	0	5	5	31.1	31	5	16	26	Runners on	.226	212	48	14	1	7	50	30	41	.319	.401
March/April	0.00	0	0	0	0	0	0.0	0	0	0	0	Scoring Posn	.263	114	30	10	0	5	43	22	27	.369	.482
May	5.06	1	0	0	1	1	5.1	6	1	3	6	Close & Late	.321	28	9	2	0	2	8	5	3	.424	.607
June	2.50	3	2	0	6	6	39.2	29	3	17	27	None on/out	.200	140	28	6	1	2	2	14	21	.277	.300
July	4.86	3	2	0	5	5	33.1	28	6	18	16	vs. 1st Batr (relief)	.000	0	0	0	0	0	0	0	0	.000	.000
August	6.42	3	3	0	6	6	33.2	36	3	18	20	1st Inning Pitched	.264	87	23	1	0	3	5	10	9	.340	.379
Sept/Oct	3.38	1	3	0	5	5	32.0	27	3	13	24	First 75 Pitches	.242	389	94	17	3	9	36	47	61	.322	.370
Starter	4.25	11	9	0	23	23	144.0	126	16	69	93	Pitch 76-90	.229	70	16	5	0	3	10	14	16	.360	.429
Reliever	0.00	0	0	0	0	0	0.0	0	0	0	0	Pitch 91-105	.192	52	10	2	1	2	7	5	12	.263	.385
0-3 Days Rest (Start)	0.00	0	0	0	0	0	0.0	0	0	0	0	Pitch 106+	.273	22	6	1	0	2	6	3	4	.360	.591
4 Days Rest	4.22	6	4	0	13	13	79.0	69	8	44	55	First Pitch	.206	63	13	2	0	4	12	4	0	.257	.429
5+ Days Rest	4.29	5	5	0	10	10	65.0	57	8	25	38	Ahead in Count	.205	249	51	10	3	5	18	0	82	.207	.329
vs. AL	5.60	1	1	0	3	3	17.2	22	3	9	7	Behind in Count	.271	129	35	9	1	5	19	36	0	.428	.473
vs. NL	4.06	10	8	0	20	20	126.1	104	13	60	86	Two Strikes	.188	240	45	11	3	3	19	29	93	.277	.296
Pre-All Star	3.12	5	2	0	8	8	52.0	41	6	24	37	Pre-All Star	.223	184	41	9	2	6	14	24	37	.310	.391
Post-All Star	4.89	6	7	0	15	15	92.0	85	10	45	56	Post-All Star	.244	349	85	16	2	10	45	45	56	.331	.387

Juan Gonzalez — Rangers

Age 28 – Bats Right (flyball hitter)

	Avg	G	AB	R	H	2B	3B	HR	RBI	BB	SO	HBP	GDP	SB	CS	OBP	SLG	IBB	SH	SF	#Pit	#P/PA	GB	FB	G/F
1997 Season	.296	133	533	87	158	24	3	42	131	33	107	3	12	0	0	.335	.589	7	0	10	2075	3.58	142	195	0.73
Last Five Years	.299	604	2384	395	714	128	12	181	560	162	420	26	65	12	5	.348	.591	39	0	23	8975	3.46	698	811	0.86

1997 Season

	Avg	AB	H	2B	3B	HR	RBI	BB	SO	OBP	SLG		Avg	AB	H	2B	3B	HR	RBI	BB	SO	OBP	SLG
vs. Left	.297	148	44	7	0	15	40	14	34	.355	.649	First Pitch	.375	64	24	6	0	9	24	5	0	.414	.891
vs. Right	.296	385	114	17	3	27	91	19	73	.327	.566	Ahead in Count	.387	124	48	2	2	17	47	19	0	.459	.847
Groundball	.242	132	32	5	1	7	26	6	28	.271	.455	Behind in Count	.241	253	61	13	1	8	38	0	91	.242	.395
Flyball	.314	70	22	4	0	5	15	7	17	.363	.586	Two Strikes	.214	248	53	7	1	9	31	9	107	.244	.359
Home	.289	246	71	11	3	18	57	17	45	.336	.577	Batting #3	.250	4	1	0	0	0	0	0	1	.250	.250
Away	.303	287	87	13	0	24	74	16	62	.334	.599	Batting #4	.297	529	157	24	3	42	131	33	106	.336	.592
Day	.266	109	29	4	0	8	32	10	23	.320	.523	Other	.000	0	0	0	0	0	0	0	0	.000	.000
Night	.304	424	129	20	3	34	99	23	84	.339	.606	March/April	.000	0	0	0	0	0	0	0	0	.000	.000
Grass	.292	472	138	18	3	36	114	31	95	.333	.572	May	.274	113	31	6	1	9	31	10	26	.328	.584
Turf	.328	61	20	6	0	6	17	2	12	.349	.721	June	.266	109	29	4	0	8	26	5	22	.305	.523
Pre-All Star	.283	244	69	10	1	20	65	16	50	.325	.578	July	.303	109	33	7	0	5	24	6	19	.333	.505
Post-All Star	.308	289	89	14	2	22	66	17	57	.344	.599	August	.308	107	33	1	1	10	24	4	20	.336	.617
Scoring Posn	.321	165	53	9	1	10	84	18	38	.374	.570	Sept/Oct	.337	95	32	6	1	10	26	6	20	.377	.737
Close & Late	.350	80	28	8	0	6	22	8	19	.400	.675	vs. AL	.291	468	136	21	3	38	115	28	96	.329	.592
None on/out	.311	135	42	8	1	14	14	4	19	.366	.696	vs. NL	.338	65	22	3	0	4	16	5	11	.380	.569

1997 By Position

Position	Avg	AB	H	2B	3B	HR	RBI	BB	SO	OBP	SLG	G	GS	Innings	PO	A	E	DP	Fld Pct	Rng Fctr	In Zone	Zone Outs	Zone Rtg	MLB Zone
As DH	.282	277	78	13	2	23	67	21	65	.327	.592	69	69	---	---	---	---	---	---	---	---	---	---	---
As rf	.313	256	80	11	1	19	64	12	42	.344	.586	64	64	555.2	127	6	4	1	.971	2.15	161	121	.752	.813

Last Five Years

	Avg	AB	H	2B	3B	HR	RBI	BB	SO	OBP	SLG		Avg	AB	H	2B	3B	HR	RBI	BB	SO	OBP	SLG
vs. Left	.328	592	194	37	1	58	157	52	109	.382	.688	First Pitch	.386	345	133	29	0	42	110	30	0	.436	.835
vs. Right	.290	1792	520	91	11	123	403	110	311	.336	.559	Ahead in Count	.368	612	225	32	5	70	198	77	0	.436	.779
Groundball	.290	507	147	33	3	30	123	28	96	.327	.544	Behind in Count	.225	1033	232	43	5	41	162	0	357	.233	.395
Flyball	.274	456	125	23	1	32	89	31	76	.325	.539	Two Strikes	.195	980	191	32	2	37	127	54	420	.243	.345
Home	.308	1145	353	65	11	86	265	92	192	.367	.610	Batting #4	.302	2059	622	114	9	168	493	137	369	.349	.611
Away	.291	1239	361	63	1	95	295	70	228	.329	.574	Batting #5	.284	313	89	14	3	13	64	23	50	.338	.473
Day	.280	539	151	32	2	30	128	34	96	.326	.514	Other	.250	12	3	0	0	0	3	2	1	.357	.250
Night	.305	1845	563	96	10	151	432	128	324	.354	.614	March/April	.286	252	72	11	2	17	58	17	50	.344	.548
Grass	.301	2062	621	106	12	155	497	147	357	.351	.590	May	.290	293	85	19	3	18	69	28	52	.357	.560
Turf	.289	322	93	22	0	26	63	15	63	.325	.599	June	.289	512	148	28	2	38	121	30	84	.332	.574
Pre-All Star	.291	1226	357	65	9	90	295	87	206	.344	.579	July	.322	512	165	27	2	41	125	42	85	.373	.623
Post-All Star	.308	1158	357	63	3	91	265	75	214	.352	.604	August	.296	422	125	16	2	37	98	19	69	.333	.607
Scoring Posn	.306	712	218	45	4	51	367	93	140	.382	.596	Sept/Oct	.303	393	119	27	1	30	89	26	80	.344	.606
Close & Late	.268	343	92	25	1	20	78	29	75	.328	.522	vs. AL	.298	2319	692	125	12	177	544	157	409	.347	.592
None on/out	.324	558	181	35	2	47	47	17	90	.354	.647	vs. NL	.338	65	22	3	0	4	16	5	11	.380	.569

Batter vs. Pitcher (career)

Hits Best Against	Avg	AB	H	2B	3B	HR	RBI	BB	SO	OBP	SLG	Hits Worst Against	Avg	AB	H	2B	3B	HR	RBI	BB	SO	OBP	SLG
Don Wengert	.556	9	5	0	0	4	9	2	0	.583	1.889	Jeff Fassero	.000	8	0	0	0	0	1	2	3	.182	.000
Andy Pettitte	.500	16	8	3	0	1	5	1	3	.529	.875	Brad Radke	.059	17	1	0	1	0	2	0	4	.059	.176
Erik Hanson	.474	19	9	1	0	2	6	2	5	.500	.842	Billy Taylor	.091	11	1	0	0	0	0	0	4	.091	.091
Alan Mills	.462	13	6	2	0	3	9	0	6	.462	1.308	Arthur Rhodes	.105	19	2	1	0	0	0	0	8	.095	.158
Chris Haney	.333	15	5	1	0	3	4	2	1	.412	1.000	Bobby Ayala	.111	18	2	1	0	0	0	1	0	.111	.167

Luis Gonzalez — Astros
Age 30 – Bats Left

	Avg	G	AB	R	H	2B	3B	HR	RBI	BB	SO	HBP	GDP	SB	CS	OBP	SLG	IBB	SH	SF	#Pit	#P/PA	GB	FB	G/F
1997 Season	.258	152	550	78	142	31	2	10	68	71	67	5	12	10	7	.345	.376	7	0	5	2280	3.61	212	185	1.15
Last Five Years	.276	697	2436	356	672	153	21	61	355	285	319	28	59	60	43	.354	.431	36	5	33	9917	3.56	901	782	1.15

1997 Season

	Avg	AB	H	2B	3B	HR	RBI	BB	SO	OBP	SLG		Avg	AB	H	2B	3B	HR	RBI	BB	SO	OBP	SLG
vs. Left	.250	132	33	3	1	3	15	15	21	.338	.356	First Pitch	.355	93	33	9	1	1	16	5	0	.394	.505
vs. Right	.261	418	109	28	1	7	53	56	46	.348	.383	Ahead in Count	.228	158	36	10	1	3	20	36	0	.372	.361
Groundball	.313	80	25	6	0	1	17	13	6	.411	.425	Behind in Count	.252	206	52	7	0	3	19	0	56	.261	.330
Flyball	.293	82	24	7	0	4	14	15	11	.408	.524	Two Strikes	.225	200	45	7	0	3	22	30	67	.329	.305
Home	.261	253	66	15	1	4	30	33	31	.348	.375	Batting #4	.270	419	113	23	1	9	53	53	51	.352	.394
Away	.256	297	76	16	1	6	38	38	36	.343	.377	Batting #5	.226	93	21	5	1	1	9	14	12	.333	.333
Day	.203	177	36	12	0	3	22	20	27	.290	.322	Other	.211	38	8	3	0	0	6	4	4	.302	.289
Night	.284	373	106	19	2	7	46	51	40	.371	.402	March/April	.211	76	16	4	1	0	4	10	12	.318	.289
Grass	.210	210	44	8	0	2	21	26	29	.301	.276	May	.330	94	31	8	0	1	20	17	9	.429	.447
Turf	.288	340	98	23	2	8	47	45	38	.352	.438	June	.295	112	33	6	0	2	11	9	14	.352	.402
Pre-All Star	.280	300	84	19	1	4	37	39	36	.366	.390	July	.278	97	27	6	0	4	17	12	11	.351	.464
Post-All Star	.232	250	58	12	1	6	31	32	31	.321	.360	August	.163	98	16	2	0	0	5	14	10	.272	.184
Scoring Posn	.244	164	40	8	0	1	54	27	18	.348	.311	Sept/Oct	.260	73	19	5	1	3	11	9	11	.345	.479
Close & Late	.219	96	21	5	0	1	8	13	13	.327	.302	vs. AL	.136	44	6	1	0	1	4	6	4	.264	.227
None on/out	.246	142	35	7	2	4	4	15	24	.323	.408	vs. NL	.269	506	136	30	2	9	64	65	63	.353	.389

1997 By Position

Position	Avg	AB	H	2B	3B	HR	RBI	BB	SO	OBP	SLG		G	GS	Innings	PO	A	E	DP	Fld Pct	Rng Fctr	In Zone	Zone Outs	Zone Rtg	MLB Zone
As lf	.260	542	141	31	2	10	67	70	66	.347	.380		146	142	1257.2	263	10	5	1	.982	1.95	317	248	.782	.805

Last Five Years

	Avg	AB	H	2B	3B	HR	RBI	BB	SO	OBP	SLG		Avg	AB	H	2B	3B	HR	RBI	BB	SO	OBP	SLG
vs. Left	.263	597	157	28	5	13	85	55	106	.338	.392	First Pitch	.327	422	138	29	6	14	85	29	0	.377	.524
vs. Right	.280	1839	515	125	16	48	270	230	213	.359	.444	Ahead in Count	.341	657	224	52	4	23	107	145	0	.456	.537
Groundball	.298	662	197	48	6	20	107	71	76	.371	.479	Behind in Count	.214	917	196	42	9	13	98	0	257	.225	.322
Flyball	.282	373	105	25	4	8	62	55	68	.384	.434	Two Strikes	.203	935	190	39	8	12	100	111	319	.295	.301
Home	.285	1181	337	76	10	27	188	137	153	.361	.435	Batting #4	.256	587	150	31	2	13	72	68	70	.331	.382
Away	.267	1255	335	77	11	34	167	148	166	.347	.427	Batting #5	.293	887	260	64	10	20	143	126	117	.383	.455
Day	.275	923	254	71	10	27	138	118	119	.361	.462	Other	.272	962	262	58	9	28	140	91	132	.340	.439
Night	.276	1513	418	82	11	34	217	167	200	.350	.412	March/April	.277	321	89	15	2	7	43	38	42	.368	.402
Grass	.273	1158	316	69	6	31	165	147	151	.357	.429	May	.260	453	118	29	4	13	70	51	53	.335	.428
Turf	.279	1278	356	84	10	31	190	138	168	.351	.433	June	.259	455	118	26	4	8	65	44	71	.325	.387
Pre-All Star	.268	1369	367	82	11	34	203	155	181	.346	.419	July	.293	447	131	32	2	14	69	54	49	.369	.468
Post-All Star	.286	1067	305	71	10	27	152	130	138	.364	.447	August	.283	410	116	28	8	7	57	52	54	.363	.441
Scoring Posn	.286	674	193	47	8	14	282	124	93	.389	.442	Sept/Oct	.286	350	100	23	1	12	51	46	50	.372	.460
Close & Late	.264	383	101	23	2	5	43	47	62	.352	.373	vs. AL	.136	44	6	1	0	1	4	6	4	.264	.227
None on/out	.300	577	173	42	10	16	16	55	77	.368	.490	vs. NL	.278	2392	666	152	21	60	351	279	315	.356	.435

Batter vs. Pitcher (career)

Hits Best Against	Avg	AB	H	2B	3B	HR	RBI	BB	SO	OBP	SLG	Hits Worst Against	Avg	AB	H	2B	3B	HR	RBI	BB	SO	OBP	SLG
Mike Harkey	.615	13	8	1	1	2	6	0	2	.615	1.308	Scott Sanders	.000	11	0	0	0	0	0	1	3	.083	.000
Kevin Ritz	.538	13	7	3	0	0	3	3	2	.667	.769	Chuck McElroy	.000	10	0	0	0	0	0	1	2	.091	.000
Dwight Gooden	.526	19	10	4	0	1	3	1	3	.550	.895	Francisco Cordova	.000	9	0	0	0	0	0	2	0	.182	.000
Paul Quantrill	.500	10	5	4	0	0	2	1	1	.545	.900	Mel Rojas	.083	12	1	0	0	0	0	0	2	.083	.083
Danny Jackson	.438	16	7	1	0	2	4	1	5	.471	.875	Lance Painter	.091	11	1	0	0	0	0	0	1	.091	.091

Dwight Gooden — Yankees
Age 33 – Pitches Right (groundball pitcher)

	ERA	W	L	Sv	G	GS	IP	BB	SO	Avg	H	2B	3B	HR	RBI	OBP	SLG	CG	ShO	Sup	QS	#P/S	SB	CS	GB	FB	G/F
1997 Season	4.91	9	5	0	20	19	106.1	53	66	.283	116	19	1	14	54	.373	.437	0	0	5.76	8	95	8	5	177	98	1.81
Last Five Years	4.47	35	31	0	85	84	527.0	217	381	.259	519	99	9	58	249	.337	.404	8	3	5.04	41	102	71	23	754	491	1.54

1997 Season

	ERA	W	L	Sv	G	GS	IP	H	HR	BB	SO		Avg	AB	H	2B	3B	HR	RBI	BB	SO	OBP	SLG
Home	3.74	4	3	0	9	9	55.1	54	5	26	39	vs. Left	.299	211	63	9	1	8	27	31	34	.393	.464
Away	6.18	5	2	0	11	10	51.0	62	9	27	27	vs. Right	.266	199	53	10	0	6	27	22	32	.351	.407
Starter	4.96	9	5	0	19	19	105.1	114	14	53	66	Scoring Posn	.333	90	30	7	1	3	41	16	21	.431	.533
Reliever	0.00	0	0	0	1	0	1.0	2	0	0	0	Close & Late	.167	12	2	1	0	1	3	2	5	.286	.500
0-3 Days Rest (Start)	0.00	0	0	0	0	0	0.0	0	0	0	0	None on/out	.267	101	27	2	0	4	4	13	13	.357	.406
4 Days Rest	4.80	5	4	0	11	11	60.0	67	8	30	41	First Pitch	.277	47	13	2	0	1	4	0	0	.277	.383
5+ Days Rest	5.16	4	1	0	8	8	45.1	47	6	23	25	Ahead in Count	.191	152	29	4	0	2	14	0	48	.219	.257
Pre-All Star	2.93	3	1	0	5	5	30.2	27	5	10	18	Behind in Count	.361	122	44	8	0	8	18	26	0	.473	.623
Post-All Star	5.71	6	4	0	15	14	75.2	89	9	43	48	Two Strikes	.200	170	34	5	0	1	17	27	66	.325	.247

Last Five Years

	ERA	W	L	Sv	G	GS	IP	H	HR	BB	SO		Avg	AB	H	2B	3B	HR	RBI	BB	SO	OBP	SLG
Home	3.46	21	17	0	48	48	317.2	283	30	112	233	vs. Left	.261	1067	278	51	4	33	123	124	205	.340	.409
Away	6.02	14	14	0	37	36	209.1	236	28	105	148	vs. Right	.257	937	241	48	5	25	126	93	176	.333	.399
Day	3.68	13	9	0	27	26	173.2	164	18	70	120	Inning 1-6	.269	1761	474	91	9	52	232	197	335	.348	.420
Night	4.87	22	22	0	58	58	353.1	355	40	147	261	Inning 7+	.185	243	45	8	0	6	17	20	46	.256	.292
Grass	4.07	34	25	0	76	75	482.1	457	48	193	349	None on	.258	1154	298	53	3	39	39	118	213	.334	.411
Turf	8.87	1	6	0	9	9	44.2	62	10	24	32	Runners on	.260	850	221	46	6	19	210	99	168	.341	.395
March/April	5.24	5	7	0	13	13	79.0	81	10	32	51	Scoring Posn	.249	510	127	27	4	13	186	70	119	.344	.394
May	2.63	6	2	0	11	11	85.2	61	6	34	58	Close & Late	.176	148	26	5	0	4	10	17	29	.269	.291

Last Five Years

	ERA	W	L	Sv	G	GS	IP	H	HR	BB	SO		Avg	AB	H	2B	3B	HR	RBI	BB	SO	OBP	SLG
June	4.04	9	6	0	17	17	111.1	105	12	36	86	None on/out	.258	503	130	26	1	15	15	53	100	.334	.404
July	4.25	7	7	0	16	16	103.2	105	10	49	75	vs. 1st Batr (relief)	1.000	1	1	0	0	0	0	0	0	1.000	2.000
August	4.96	6	7	0	18	18	101.2	105	15	44	81	1st Inning Pitched	.320	344	110	24	1	8	60	42	56	.398	.465
Sept/Oct	7.09	2	2	0	10	9	45.2	62	5	22	30	First 75 Pitches	.271	1426	386	76	5	41	172	139	272	.340	.417
Starter	4.48	35	31	0	84	84	526.0	517	58	217	381	Pitch 76-90	.242	236	57	11	0	10	35	37	47	.355	.415
Reliever	0.00	0	0	0	1	0	1.0	2	0	0	0	Pitch 91-105	.247	198	49	6	2	4	21	21	33	.332	.359
0-3 Days Rest (Start)	1.13	1	0	0	1	1	8.0	4	1	1	9	Pitch 106+	.188	144	27	6	2	3	21	20	25	.287	.319
4 Days Rest	4.38	19	21	0	48	48	316.1	309	33	116	222	First Pitch	.337	273	92	17	3	13	47	3	0	.346	.564
5+ Days Rest	4.78	15	10	0	35	35	201.2	204	24	100	150	Behind in Count	.178	855	152	27	4	11	73	0	293	.195	.257
vs. AL	5.06	20	11	0	45	44	252.1	258	29	129	178	Ahead in Count	.349	484	169	37	1	27	81	109	0	.467	.597
vs. NL	3.93	15	20	0	40	40	274.2	261	29	88	203	Two Strikes	.167	893	149	27	2	12	75	105	381	.266	.242
Pre-All Star	3.95	22	18	0	46	46	312.0	286	31	110	226	Pre-All Star	.244	1171	286	54	4	31	129	110	226	.316	.377
Post-All Star	5.23	13	13	0	39	38	215.0	233	27	107	155	Post-All Star	.280	833	233	45	5	27	120	107	155	.366	.443

Pitcher vs. Batter (career)

Pitches Best Vs.	Avg	AB	H	2B	3B	HR	RBI	BB	SO	OBP	SLG	Pitches Worst Vs.	Avg	AB	H	2B	3B	HR	RBI	BB	SO	OBP	SLG
Rusty Greer	.000	11	0	0	0	0	0	1	2	.083	.000	Roberto Kelly	.636	11	7	3	0	1	2	1	0	.692	1.182
Joe Girardi	.067	15	1	0	0	0	1	2	2	.222	.067	Alex Rodriguez	.600	10	6	2	0	1	1	3	0	.692	1.100
Chuck Carr	.083	12	1	0	0	0	0	0	4	.083	.083	Luis Gonzalez	.526	19	10	4	0	1	3	1	3	.550	.895
Phil Plantier	.083	12	1	0	0	0	1	0	2	.083	.083	Dave Clark	.467	15	7	0	0	2	5	4	0	.579	.867
Tony Fernandez	.118	17	2	0	0	0	1	4	.167	.118	Ken Griffey Jr	.375	8	3	0	0	1	3	5	2	.615	.750

Curtis Goodwin — Reds
Age 25 – Bats Left

	Avg	G	AB	R	H	2B	3B	HR	RBI	BB	SO	HBP	GDP	SB	CS	OBP	SLG	IBB	SH	SF	#Pit	#P/PA	GB	FB	G/F
1997 Season	.253	85	265	27	67	11	0	1	12	24	53	1	6	22	13	.316	.306	0	6	1	1056	3.56	117	43	2.72
Career (1995-1997)	.252	221	690	87	174	25	3	2	41	58	140	3	11	59	23	.311	.306	0	14	4	2932	3.81	312	112	2.79

1997 Season

	Avg	AB	H	2B	3B	HR	RBI	BB	SO	OBP	SLG		Avg	AB	H	2B	3B	HR	RBI	BB	SO	OBP	SLG
vs. Left	.250	56	14	2	0	0	3	9	11	.348	.286	Scoring Posn	.200	50	10	1	0	1	10	7	15	.305	.280
vs. Right	.254	209	53	9	0	1	9	15	42	.307	.311	Close & Late	.298	47	14	1	0	1	6	3	13	.340	.404
Home	.282	149	42	7	0	1	9	12	26	.337	.349	None on/out	.188	64	12	1	0	0	0	8	14	.278	.203
Away	.216	116	25	4	0	0	3	12	27	.289	.250	Batting #1	.114	44	5	1	0	0	2	4	7	.188	.136
First Pitch	.420	50	21	3	0	1	7	0	0	.423	.540	Batting #2	.274	186	51	8	0	1	9	15	38	.330	.333
Ahead in Count	.288	52	15	2	0	0	2	15	0	.448	.327	Other	.314	35	11	2	0	0	1	5	8	.400	.371
Behind in Count	.197	122	24	4	0	0	2	0	46	.197	.230	Pre-All Star	.286	213	61	9	0	1	11	20	36	.349	.343
Two Strikes	.168	119	20	4	0	0	3	9	53	.227	.202	Post-All Star	.115	52	6	2	0	0	1	4	17	.179	.154

Career (1995-1997)

	Avg	AB	H	2B	3B	HR	RBI	BB	SO	OBP	SLG		Avg	AB	H	2B	3B	HR	RBI	BB	SO	OBP	SLG
vs. Left	.251	167	42	5	0	1	11	15	37	.315	.299	First Pitch	.431	102	44	7	0	1	13	0	0	.425	.529
vs. Right	.252	523	132	20	3	1	30	43	103	.310	.308	Ahead in Count	.321	134	43	7	0	0	13	31	0	.448	.373
Groundball	.214	145	31	6	2	2	14	5	28	.250	.324	Behind in Count	.175	326	57	6	1	0	7	0	111	.180	.199
Flyball	.256	121	31	6	0	0	7	12	26	.328	.306	Two Strikes	.152	328	50	7	2	0	10	27	140	.218	.186
Home	.274	372	102	17	1	1	26	31	79	.333	.333	Batting #1	.222	284	63	9	2	1	16	26	54	.286	.278
Away	.226	318	72	8	2	1	15	27	61	.287	.274	Batting #2	.283	198	56	9	0	1	12	15	41	.335	.343
Day	.238	214	51	6	1	1	7	18	44	.300	.290	Other	.264	208	55	7	1	0	13	17	45	.323	.300
Night	.258	476	123	19	2	1	34	40	96	.316	.313	March/April	.333	12	4	1	0	0	1	1	4	.385	.417
Grass	.245	376	92	10	3	0	23	24	73	.291	.287	May	.315	92	29	3	0	1	7	12	13	.400	.380
Turf	.261	314	82	15	0	2	18	34	67	.334	.328	June	.313	230	72	9	0	0	9	15	40	.356	.352
Pre-All Star	.307	388	119	14	0	2	26	34	68	.364	.358	July	.179	151	27	5	1	1	11	12	35	.241	.245
Post-All Star	.182	302	55	11	3	0	15	24	72	.243	.238	August	.215	65	14	2	1	0	5	3	12	.246	.277
Scoring Posn	.218	147	32	2	1	1	35	15	34	.287	.265	Sept/Oct	.200	140	28	5	1	0	8	15	36	.277	.250
Close & Late	.241	112	27	4	0	1	12	6	31	.286	.304	vs. AL	.263	319	84	12	3	1	24	16	56	.300	.329
None on/out	.241	224	54	8	1	0	0	23	44	.315	.286	vs. NL	.243	371	90	13	0	1	17	42	84	.320	.286

Batter vs. Pitcher (career)

Hits Best Against	Avg	AB	H	2B	3B	HR	RBI	BB	SO	OBP	SLG	Hits Worst Against	Avg	AB	H	2B	3B	HR	RBI	BB	SO	OBP	SLG
Alan Benes	.700	10	7	1	0	0	1	2	2	.750	.800	Todd Stottlemyre	.200	10	2	0	0	0	0	1	1	.273	.200

Tom Goodwin — Rangers
Age 29 – Bats Left

	Avg	G	AB	R	H	2B	3B	HR	RBI	BB	SO	HBP	GDP	SB	CS	OBP	SLG	IBB	SH	SF	#Pit	#P/PA	GB	FB	G/F
1997 Season	.260	150	574	90	149	26	6	2	39	44	88	3	7	50	16	.314	.336	1	11	3	2181	3.43	255	119	2.14
Last Five Years	.276	458	1597	248	440	57	13	7	103	122	244	10	18	167	58	.330	.341	1	46	4	6261	3.52	688	309	2.23

1997 Season

	Avg	AB	H	2B	3B	HR	RBI	BB	SO	OBP	SLG		Avg	AB	H	2B	3B	HR	RBI	BB	SO	OBP	SLG
vs. Left	.275	160	44	7	1	0	9	9	28	.318	.331	First Pitch	.299	87	26	2	0	0	7	1	0	.307	.322
vs. Right	.254	414	105	19	5	2	30	35	60	.313	.338	Ahead in Count	.336	122	41	11	1	0	13	30	0	.464	.443
Groundball	.325	114	37	6	1	0	9	4	17	.353	.395	Behind in Count	.222	275	61	9	5	1	16	0	80	.229	.302
Flyball	.168	101	17	5	2	0	0	9	16	.236	.257	Two Strikes	.172	239	41	8	5	0	10	13	88	.220	.247
Home	.281	253	71	9	1	0	16	24	31	.343	.324	Batting #1	.223	233	52	14	2	0	18	26	44	.302	.300
Away	.243	321	78	17	5	2	23	20	57	.291	.346	Batting #2	.269	234	63	8	2	2	16	12	33	.306	.346
Day	.236	165	39	10	1	0	9	11	28	.288	.309	Other	.318	107	34	4	2	0	5	6	11	.360	.393
Night	.269	409	110	16	5	2	30	33	60	.324	.347	March/April	.143	84	12	1	1	0	6	14	.209	.179
Grass	.264	489	129	22	6	1	35	39	72	.320	.339	May	.351	97	34	4	1	0	6	5	10	.388	.412
Turf	.235	85	20	4	0	1	4	5	16	.278	.318	June	.355	107	38	5	2	1	9	3	15	.373	.467

170

1997 Season

	Avg	AB	H	2B	3B	HR	RBI	BB	SO	OBP	SLG		Avg	AB	H	2B	3B	HR	RBI	BB	SO	OBP	SLG
Pre-All Star	.282	308	87	11	4	1	16	14	44	.318	.354	July	.191	94	18	3	1	1	8	9	15	.260	.277
Post-All Star	.233	266	62	15	2	1	23	30	44	.310	.316	August	.240	104	25	7	0	0	11	8	20	.298	.308
Scoring Posn	.261	119	31	6	0	0	35	10	14	.316	.311	Sept/Oct	.250	88	22	6	1	0	5	13	14	.343	.341
Close & Late	.278	97	27	3	2	0	6	8	17	.333	.351	vs. AL	.254	512	130	24	5	2	35	39	77	.309	.332
None on/out	.309	162	50	13	2	0	0	12	23	.356	.414	vs. NL	.306	62	19	2	1	0	4	5	11	.358	.371

1997 By Position

Position	Avg	AB	H	2B	3B	HR	RBI	BB	SO	OBP	SLG	G	GS	Innings	PO	A	E	DP	Fld Pct	Rng Fctr	In Zone	Zone Outs	Zone Rtg	MLB Zone
As cf	.262	569	149	26	6	2	39	41	87	.313	.339	145	141	1228.0	367	6	3	0	.992	2.73	435	351	.807	.815

Last Five Years

	Avg	AB	H	2B	3B	HR	RBI	BB	SO	OBP	SLG		Avg	AB	H	2B	3B	HR	RBI	BB	SO	OBP	SLG
vs. Left	.283	438	124	20	3	0	30	35	75	.339	.342	First Pitch	.329	231	76	9	2	3	21	1	0	.346	.424
vs. Right	.273	1159	316	37	10	7	73	87	169	.327	.340	Ahead in Count	.336	354	119	16	3	2	39	82	0	.459	.415
Groundball	.314	354	111	15	4	0	22	14	56	.345	.379	Behind in Count	.237	742	176	25	6	1	34	0	217	.240	.291
Flyball	.230	270	62	14	3	0	9	24	49	.300	.304	Two Strikes	.197	705	139	20	7	0	24	39	244	.241	.245
Home	.270	760	205	26	5	2	42	56	105	.324	.325	Batting #1	.218	275	60	16	2	0	21	26	50	.286	.291
Away	.281	837	235	31	8	5	61	66	139	.335	.355	Batting #2	.284	1093	310	31	8	7	67	78	160	.335	.346
Day	.277	440	122	14	3	1	22	38	73	.340	.330	Other	.306	229	70	10	3	0	15	18	34	.361	.376
Night	.275	1157	318	43	10	6	81	84	171	.326	.345	March/April	.194	186	36	3	1	0	5	12	27	.250	.220
Grass	.274	1380	378	47	11	5	86	94	201	.324	.335	May	.307	280	86	6	1	1	13	23	41	.363	.346
Turf	.286	217	62	10	2	2	17	28	43	.366	.378	June	.311	296	92	13	3	2	21	21	42	.361	.395
Pre-All Star	.284	849	241	28	7	3	47	61	126	.336	.344	July	.265	309	82	11	3	1	22	21	47	.311	.330
Post-All Star	.266	748	199	29	6	4	56	61	118	.324	.337	August	.266	289	77	14	3	2	27	22	48	.324	.356
Scoring Posn	.264	356	94	16	2	1	95	30	51	.323	.329	Sept/Oct	.283	237	67	10	2	1	15	23	39	.347	.354
Close & Late	.270	237	64	7	3	1	16	20	33	.327	.338	vs. AL	.274	1518	416	54	12	7	98	116	229	.329	.339
None on/out	.288	379	109	20	2	1	1	21	59	.328	.359	vs. NL	.304	79	24	3	1	0	5	6	15	.353	.367

Batter vs. Pitcher (career)

Hits Best Against	Avg	AB	H	2B	3B	HR	RBI	BB	SO	OBP	SLG	Hits Worst Against	Avg	AB	H	2B	3B	HR	RBI	BB	SO	OBP	SLG
Aaron Sele	.583	12	7	1	0	0	2	0	0	.583	.667	Jason Dickson	.000	12	0	0	0	0	0	2	3	.143	.000
Dennis Springer	.545	11	6	1	0	1	3	2	2	.615	.909	Jimmy Key	.083	12	1	1	0	0	1	0	1	.154	.167
Brad Radke	.500	20	10	2	0	1	2	0	2	.500	.750	Juan Guzman	.100	10	1	0	0	0	1	1	0	.182	.100
Mark Clark	.429	14	6	0	0	1	2	1	1	.500	.643	Mike Mussina	.105	19	2	0	0	0	0	2	5	.190	.105
Danny Darwin	.308	13	4	2	1	0	0	2	2	.400	.615	Ben McDonald	.125	16	2	1	0	0	1	0	3	.125	.188

Tom Gordon — Red Sox
Age 30 – Pitches Right (groundball pitcher)

	ERA	W	L	Sv	G	GS	IP	BB	SO	Avg	H	2B	3B	HR	RBI	OBP	SLG	CG	ShO	Sup	QS	#P/S	SB	CS	GB	FB	G/F
1997 Season	3.74	6	10	11	42	25	182.2	78	159	.226	155	30	2	10	77	.306	.319	1	4	4.29	14	106	20	7	271	136	1.99
Last Five Years	4.41	53	44	12	179	128	898.1	436	718	.254	869	161	18	76	418	.337	.377	10	2	5.44	67	107	96	34	1328	755	1.76

1997 Season

	ERA	W	L	Sv	G	GS	IP	H	HR	BB	SO		Avg	AB	H	2B	3B	HR	RBI	BB	SO	OBP	SLG
Home	4.34	2	6	3	22	16	112.0	105	5	46	97	vs. Left	.231	363	84	19	2	3	37	46	85	.320	.320
Away	2.80	4	4	8	20	9	70.2	50	5	32	62	vs. Right	.220	323	71	11	0	7	40	32	74	.290	.319
Day	4.40	3	5	5	17	9	61.1	59	2	33	44	Inning 1-6	.231	524	121	23	2	7	61	56	117	.307	.323
Night	3.41	3	5	6	25	16	121.1	96	8	45	115	Inning 7+	.210	162	34	7	0	3	16	22	42	.304	.309
Grass	3.93	5	9	9	37	24	169.2	150	10	69	143	None on	.219	397	87	18	1	5	5	42	92	.294	.307
Turf	1.38	1	1	2	5	1	13.0	5	0	9	16	Runners on	.235	289	68	12	1	5	72	36	67	.322	.336
March/April	3.23	1	3	0	5	5	30.2	25	3	10	23	Scoring Posn	.256	164	42	9	1	2	66	27	39	.360	.360
May	4.45	2	2	0	5	5	32.1	33	1	14	32	Close & Late	.200	90	18	5	0	2	11	17	20	.327	.322
June	2.49	2	1	0	6	6	43.1	32	1	15	33	None on/out	.218	174	38	9	0	2	2	17	34	.288	.305
July	4.95	0	3	0	6	6	40.0	41	3	21	31	vs. 1st Batr (relief)	.071	14	1	0	0	0	0	3	6	.235	.071
August	2.49	1	0	4	9	3	25.1	17	1	9	23	1st Inning Pitched	.193	145	28	3	0	3	20	23	50	.306	.276
Sept/Oct	6.55	0	1	7	11	0	11.0	7	1	9	17	First 75 Pitches	.225	481	108	21	2	6	59	60	120	.311	.314
Starter	3.59	6	9	0	25	25	165.1	144	9	66	134	Pitch 76-90	.247	89	22	3	0	2	9	5	15	.292	.348
Reliever	5.19	0	1	11	17	0	17.1	11	1	12	25	Pitch 91-105	.209	67	14	3	0	1	6	8	16	.293	.299
0-3 Days Rest (Start)	0.00	0	0	0	0	0	0.0	0	0	0	0	Pitch 106+	.224	49	11	3	0	1	3	5	8	.296	.347
4 Days Rest	4.03	3	7	0	17	17	109.1	101	6	41	84	First Pitch	.357	70	25	4	0	2	9	1	0	.375	.500
5+ Days Rest	2.73	3	2	0	8	8	56.0	43	3	25	50	Ahead in Count	.139	337	47	9	1	2	21	0	140	.141	.190
vs. AL	3.86	6	9	11	38	23	165.1	143	10	69	141	Behind in Count	.301	143	43	7	1	2	25	40	0	.451	.406
vs. NL	2.60	0	1	0	4	2	17.1	12	0	9	18	Two Strikes	.134	337	45	8	1	4	21	37	159	.221	.199
Pre-All Star	3.22	5	7	0	17	17	114.2	95	5	43	94	Pre-All Star	.221	430	95	22	2	5	44	45	94	.294	.316
Post-All Star	4.63	1	3	11	25	8	68.0	60	5	33	65	Post-All Star	.234	256	60	8	0	5	33	33	65	.325	.324

Last Five Years

	ERA	W	L	Sv	G	GS	IP	H	HR	BB	SO		Avg	AB	H	2B	3B	HR	RBI	BB	SO	OBP	SLG
Home	4.16	22	22	4	93	66	485.0	462	37	229	378	vs. Left	.270	1812	490	80	10	35	216	251	361	.359	.384
Away	4.70	31	22	8	86	59	413.1	407	39	207	340	vs. Right	.235	1616	379	81	8	41	202	185	357	.312	.371
Day	5.29	20	14	5	54	37	245.0	266	17	128	178	Inning 1-6	.256	2740	702	132	13	57	337	350	554	.339	.376
Night	4.08	33	30	7	125	91	653.1	603	59	308	540	Inning 7+	.243	688	167	29	5	19	81	86	164	.327	.382
Grass	4.55	34	36	9	123	96	651.1	665	52	311	500	None on	.251	1928	483	98	9	37	37	205	392	.325	.368
Turf	4.05	19	8	3	56	32	249.0	204	24	125	218	Runners on	.257	1500	386	63	9	39	381	231	326	.351	.389
March/April	5.16	4	7	0	24	16	103.0	99	7	66	77	Scoring Posn	.246	877	216	37	5	23	337	165	211	.355	.379
May	4.60	15	5	1	32	21	154.1	149	14	71	133	Close & Late	.243	337	82	18	3	8	46	42	81	.325	.386
June	3.73	9	7	0	33	23	173.2	156	18	75	132	None on/out	.253	865	219	50	3	16	16	85	164	.322	.373
July	4.76	7	10	0	31	26	176.0	177	12	93	145	vs. 1st Batr (relief)	.190	42	8	1	0	1	9	8	12	.314	.286

	ERA	W	L	Sv	G	GS	IP	H	HR	BB	SO		Avg	AB	H	2B	3B	HR	RBI	BB	SO	OBP	SLG
August	3.53	9	8	4	29	23	160.2	135	13	62	128	1st Inning Pitched	.227	640	145	30	1	15	98	116	160	.344	.347
Sept/Oct	5.11	9	7	7	30	19	130.1	143	12	69	103	First 75 Pitches	.253	2349	594	105	11	47	275	332	501	.344	.367
Starter	4.43	49	41	0	128	128	819.0	812	70	387	630	Pitch 76-90	.258	418	108	18	3	9	62	37	72	.321	.380
Reliever	4.20	4	3	12	51	0	79.1	57	6	49	88	Pitch 91-105	.247	369	91	22	1	12	48	35	79	.308	.409
0-3 Days Rest (Start)	5.27	3	4	0	11	11	66.2	80	5	30	46	Pitch 106+	.260	292	76	16	3	8	33	32	66	.334	.418
4 Days Rest	4.41	34	24	0	84	84	538.2	525	41	245	413	First Pitch	.368	408	150	28	4	12	72	14	0	.386	.544
5+ Days Rest	4.21	12	13	0	33	33	213.2	207	24	112	171	Ahead in Count	.176	1586	279	46	8	21	128	0	595	.178	.255
vs. AL	4.44	43	43	12	175	126	881.0	857	76	427	700	Behind in Count	.338	783	265	52	4	30	146	238	0	.490	.530
vs. NL	2.60	0	1	0	4	2	17.1	12	0	9	18	Two Strikes	.156	1605	251	42	6	23	122	184	718	.234	.233
Pre-All Star	4.24	29	22	1	99	67	484.1	454	42	243	387	Pre-All Star	.247	1836	454	84	6	42	216	243	387	.332	.368
Post-All Star	4.61	24	22	11	80	61	414.0	415	34	193	331	Post-All Star	.261	1592	415	77	12	34	202	193	331	.342	.388

Pitcher vs. Batter (career)

Pitches Best Vs.	Avg	AB	H	2B	3B	HR	RBI	BB	SO	OBP	SLG	Pitches Worst Vs.	Avg	AB	H	2B	3B	HR	RBI	BB	SO	OBP	SLG
Alex Diaz	.000	10	0	0	0	0	0	1	2	.091	.000	Jim Edmonds	.516	31	16	3	1	1	2	5	2	.583	.774
Bobby Bonilla	.000	9	0	0	0	0	1	1	4	.091	.000	Mark McGwire	.429	42	18	2	0	5	11	9	6	.519	.833
Alvaro Espinoza	.063	16	1	0	0	0	2	1	5	.118	.063	Jim Thome	.391	23	9	0	1	3	8	8	7	.548	.870
Luis Sojo	.083	12	1	0	0	0	0	0	3	.083	.083	Paul Sorrento	.348	23	8	3	0	2	7	10	3	.545	.739
Roberto Kelly	.091	22	2	0	0	0	1	0	8	.091	.091	Ken Griffey Jr	.341	41	14	1	0	6	13	6	7	.426	.805

Rick Gorecki — Dodgers

Age 24 – Pitches Right

	ERA	W	L	Sv	G	GS	IP	BB	SO	Avg	H	2B	3B	HR	RBI	OBP	SLG	GF	IR	IRS	Hld	SvOp	SB	CS	GB	FB	G/F
1997 Season	15.00	1	0	0	4	1	6.0	6	6	.346	9	1	0	3	8	.469	.731	2	1	0	0	0	1	0	9	9	1.00

1997 Season

	ERA	W	L	Sv	G	GS	IP	H	HR	BB	SO		Avg	AB	H	2B	3B	HR	RBI	BB	SO	OBP	SLG
Home	4.50	0	0	0	2	0	2.0	2	1	1	1	vs. Left	.467	15	7	1	0	2	7	3	1	.556	.933
Away	20.25	1	0	0	2	1	4.0	7	2	5	5	vs. Right	.182	11	2	0	0	1	1	3	5	.357	.455

Mark Grace — Cubs

Age 34 – Bats Left

	Avg	G	AB	R	H	2B	3B	HR	RBI	BB	SO	HBP	GDP	SB	CS	OBP	SLG	IBB	SH	SF	#Pit	#P/PA	GB	FB	G/F
1997 Season	.319	151	555	87	177	32	5	13	78	88	45	2	18	2	4	.409	.465	3	1	8	2430	3.72	216	147	1.47
Last Five Years	.321	697	2651	413	851	184	16	58	387	334	205	6	80	18	14	.394	.468	39	3	33	10489	3.47	1077	705	1.53

1997 Season

	Avg	AB	H	2B	3B	HR	RBI	BB	SO	OBP	SLG		Avg	AB	H	2B	3B	HR	RBI	BB	SO	OBP	SLG
vs. Left	.336	143	48	8	1	3	19	19	9	.412	.469	First Pitch	.281	96	27	3	1	0	10	1	0	.294	.333
vs. Right	.313	412	129	24	4	10	59	69	36	.408	.464	Ahead in Count	.361	155	56	14	2	5	27	54	0	.519	.574
Groundball	.241	112	27	5	1	1	15	19	15	.338	.330	Behind in Count	.257	183	47	6	1	3	23	0	32	.255	.350
Flyball	.310	84	26	3	2	5	14	11	8	.389	.571	Two Strikes	.238	193	46	6	0	2	17	33	45	.346	.301
Home	.355	276	98	19	0	6	43	52	22	.455	.489	Batting #3	.306	490	150	23	5	12	63	74	40	.395	.447
Away	.283	279	79	13	5	7	35	36	23	.361	.441	Batting #4	.419	62	26	9	0	1	14	14	5	.513	.613
Day	.346	301	104	16	3	9	52	54	25	.444	.508	Other	.333	3	1	0	0	0	1	0	0	.333	.333
Night	.287	254	73	16	2	4	26	34	20	.365	.413	March/April	.317	60	19	2	1	3	8	11	3	.423	.533
Grass	.338	452	153	24	5	12	67	76	35	.429	.493	May	.279	104	29	2	0	2	14	21	8	.386	.356
Turf	.233	103	24	8	0	1	11	12	10	.316	.340	June	.360	100	36	9	0	3	13	21	8	.463	.540
Pre-All Star	.324	278	90	13	1	9	42	52	22	.426	.475	July	.355	93	33	9	0	1	18	15	9	.436	.484
Post-All Star	.314	277	87	19	4	4	36	36	23	.391	.455	August	.313	112	35	3	4	1	9	11	8	.379	.438
Scoring Posn	.318	148	47	6	2	0	53	27	15	.404	.385	Sept/Oct	.291	86	25	7	0	3	16	11	8	.367	.477
Close & Late	.301	73	22	3	0	1	9	16	4	.418	.384	vs. AL	.364	55	20	1	2	3	10	13	7	.478	.618
None on/out	.336	119	40	6	1	4	13	7		.406	.504	vs. NL	.314	500	157	31	3	10	68	75	38	.401	.448

1997 By Position

Position	Avg	AB	H	2B	3B	HR	RBI	BB	SO	OBP	SLG	G	GS	Innings	PO	A	E	DP	Fld Pct	Rng Fctr	In Zone	Outs	Zone Rtg	MLB Zone
As 1b	.319	552	176	32	5	13	77	88	45	.409	.466	148	147	1291.0	1202	120	6	94	995	—	278	249	896	874

Last Five Years

	Avg	AB	H	2B	3B	HR	RBI	BB	SO	OBP	SLG		Avg	AB	H	2B	3B	HR	RBI	BB	SO	OBP	SLG
vs. Left	.316	797	252	55	2	14	116	72	77	.372	.443	First Pitch	.323	499	161	29	2	9	69	33	0	.361	.443
vs. Right	.323	1854	599	129	14	44	271	262	128	.403	.479	Ahead in Count	.341	780	266	62	7	20	125	196	0	.469	.515
Groundball	.299	750	224	53	4	13	116	93	69	.372	.432	Behind in Count	.257	905	248	58	4	15	113	0	165	.276	.397
Flyball	.322	398	128	24	4	11	49	48	34	.393	.485	Two Strikes	.257	857	220	49	4	14	104	104	205	.337	.372
Home	.342	1368	468	97	5	24	201	171	103	.412	.473	Batting #3	.317	2205	699	141	14	49	310	270	176	.389	.460
Away	.299	1283	383	87	11	34	186	163	102	.374	.463	Batting #4	.357	384	137	40	1	9	68	59	26	.438	.536
Day	.336	1478	497	92	7	31	217	181	111	.406	.471	Other	.242	62	15	3	1	0	9	5	3	.294	.323
Night	.302	1173	354	92	9	27	170	153	94	.379	.465	March/April	.325	342	111	22	2	8	49	41	20	.392	.471
Grass	.330	2098	692	151	16	49	317	267	158	.402	.482	May	.330	494	163	36	2	10	79	71	39	.409	.472
Turf	.288	553	159	33	1	12	70	67	47	.361	.416	June	.307	459	141	43	2	11	66	56	29	.380	.481
Pre-All Star	.320	1435	459	106	6	34	219	190	97	.395	.473	July	.321	477	153	30	1	9	72	58	40	.390	.444
Post-All Star	.322	1216	392	78	10	24	168	144	108	.392	.463	August	.326	482	157	26	6	10	63	61	42	.405	.467
Scoring Posn	.328	644	211	48	7	7	295	123	54	.418	.457	Sept/Oct	.317	397	126	27	3	10	58	47	35	.384	.476
Close & Late	.344	410	141	23	0	12	58	72	37	.439	.488	vs. AL	.364	55	20	1	2	3	10	13	7	.478	.618
None on/out	.312	516	161	25	3	15	15	52	37	.377	.459	vs. NL	.320	2596	831	183	14	55	377	321	198	.392	.465

Batter vs. Pitcher (career)

Hits Best Against	Avg	AB	H	2B	3B	HR	RBI	BB	SO	OBP	SLG	Hits Worst Against	Avg	AB	H	2B	3B	HR	RBI	BB	SO	OBP	SLG
Alan Benes	.778	9	7	0	1	0	1	4	1	.846	1.000	Mitch Williams	.067	15	1	0	0	0	0	0	3	.067	.067

Batter vs. Pitcher (career)

Hits Best Against	Avg	AB	H	2B	3B	HR	RBI	BB	SO	OBP	SLG	Hits Worst Against	Avg	AB	H	2B	3B	HR	RBI	BB	SO	OBP	SLG
Brian Williams	.583	12	7	2	0	0	4	6	0	.722	.750	Greg McMichael	.083	12	1	0	0	0	0	3	3	.267	.083
Kevin Ritz	.500	24	12	5	0	3	12	4	1	.552	1.083	Robb Nen	.091	11	1	0	0	0	1	1	2	.167	.091
Mark Davis	.455	11	5	1	0	2	3	0	1	.455	1.091	Todd Stottlemyre	.091	11	1	0	0	0	1	2	3	.231	.091
Randy Myers	.429	14	6	0	2	1	6	1	3	.467	.929	Chris Hammond	.148	27	4	0	0	0	4	2	1	.226	.148

Mike Grace — Phillies
Age 28 – Pitches Right (groundball pitcher)

	ERA	W	L	Sv	G	GS	IP	BB	SO	Avg	H	2B	3B	HR	RBI	OBP	SLG	CG	ShO	Sup	QS	#P/S	SB	CS	GB	FB	G/F
1997 Season	3.46	3	2	0	6	6	39.0	10	26	.230	32	6	0	3	16	.285	.338	1	1	4.15	4	89	0	2	55	31	1.77
Career (1995-1997)	3.45	11	5	0	20	20	130.1	30	82	.236	114	22	1	12	50	.283	.360	2	2	5.18	13	89	7	2	206	113	1.82

1997 Season

	ERA	W	L	Sv	G	GS	IP	H	HR	BB	SO		Avg	AB	H	2B	3B	HR	RBI	BB	SO	OBP	SLG
Home	1.41	2	1	0	4	4	32.0	20	1	8	20	vs. Left	.273	77	21	5	0	3	12	7	13	.333	.455
Away	12.86	1	1	0	2	2	7.0	12	2	2	6	vs. Right	.177	62	11	1	0	0	4	3	13	.224	.194

Tony Graffanino — Braves
Age 26 – Bats Right

	Avg	G	AB	R	H	2B	3B	HR	RBI	BB	SO	HBP	GDP	SB	CS	OBP	SLG	IBB	SH	SF	#Pit	#P/PA	GB	FB	G/F
1997 Season	.258	104	186	33	48	9	1	8	20	26	46	1	3	6	4	.344	.446	1	3	5	875	3.96	45	62	0.73
Career (1996-1997)	.241	126	232	40	56	10	2	8	22	30	59	2	3	6	4	.326	.405	1	3	6	1066	3.90	58	79	0.73

1997 Season

	Avg	AB	H	2B	3B	HR	RBI	BB	SO	OBP	SLG		Avg	AB	H	2B	3B	HR	RBI	BB	SO	OBP	SLG
vs. Left	.254	59	15	5	0	3	7	11	12	.361	.492	Scoring Posn	.171	35	6	1	0	0	10	9	11	.306	.200
vs. Right	.260	127	33	4	1	5	13	15	34	.336	.425	Close & Late	.111	36	4	1	1	0	0	5	13	.220	.194
Home	.253	99	25	4	0	5	11	13	22	.330	.444	None on/out	.309	55	17	2	0	6	6	5	12	.367	.673
Away	.264	87	23	5	1	3	9	13	24	.359	.448	Batting #8	.238	126	30	6	0	7	18	17	33	.322	.452
First Pitch	.318	22	7	0	0	1	2	1	0	.333	.455	Batting #9	.407	27	11	2	1	1	1	5	5	.500	.667
Ahead in Count	.439	41	18	6	0	5	9	15	0	.579	.951	Other	.212	33	7	1	0	0	1	4	8	.297	.242
Behind in Count	.140	86	12	1	1	1	5	0	39	.144	.209	Pre-All Star	.286	63	18	3	0	2	7	8	15	.356	.429
Two Strikes	.143	98	14	1	1	2	9	10	46	.216	.235	Post-All Star	.244	123	30	6	1	6	13	18	31	.338	.455

Jeff Granger — Pirates
Age 26 – Pitches Left

	ERA	W	L	Sv	G	GS	IP	BB	SO	Avg	H	2B	3B	HR	RBI	OBP	SLG	GF	IR	IRS	Hld	SvOp	SB	CS	GB	FB	G/F
1997 Season	18.00	0	0	0	9	0	5.0	8	4	.417	10	4	0	3	10	.563	.958	1	5	4	0	0	0	0	6	9	0.67
Career (1993-1997)	9.09	0	1	0	27	2	31.2	26	19	.343	47	12	4	8	34	.449	.664	6	15	6	1	0	2	0	50	40	1.25

1997 Season

	ERA	W	L	Sv	G	GS	IP	H	HR	BB	SO		Avg	AB	H	2B	3B	HR	RBI	BB	SO	OBP	SLG
Home	7.71	0	0	0	4	0	2.1	3	1	4	2	vs. Left	.571	7	4	2	0	1	4	3	0	.700	1.286
Away	27.00	0	0	0	5	0	2.2	7	2	4	2	vs. Right	.353	17	6	2	0	2	6	5	4	.500	.824

Danny Graves — Reds
Age 24 – Pitches Right (groundball pitcher)

	ERA	W	L	Sv	G	GS	IP	BB	SO	Avg	H	2B	3B	HR	RBI	OBP	SLG	GF	IR	IRS	Hld	SvOp	SB	CS	GB	FB	G/F
1997 Season	5.54	0	0	0	15	0	26.0	20	11	.376	41	8	1	2	18	.466	.523	3	10	7	1	0	4	1	49	21	2.33
Career (1996-1997)	5.01	2	0	0	30	0	55.2	30	33	.308	70	16	2	4	37	.385	.449	8	22	15	1	1	8	1	101	38	2.66

1997 Season

	ERA	W	L	Sv	G	GS	IP	H	HR	BB	SO		Avg	AB	H	2B	3B	HR	RBI	BB	SO	OBP	SLG
Home	5.25	0	0	0	6	0	12.0	20	1	12	4	vs. Left	.265	49	13	4	0	0	4	8	4	.368	.347
Away	5.79	0	0	0	9	0	14.0	21	1	8	7	vs. Right	.467	60	28	4	1	2	14	12	7	.541	.667

Craig Grebeck — Angels
Age 33 – Bats Right (flyball hitter)

	Avg	G	AB	R	H	2B	3B	HR	RBI	BB	SO	HBP	GDP	SB	CS	OBP	SLG	IBB	SH	SF	#Pit	#P/PA	GB	FB	G/F
1997 Season	.270	63	126	12	34	9	0	1	6	18	11	0	6	0	1	.359	.365	1	5	1	537	3.58	52	37	1.41
Last Five Years	.252	273	662	81	167	32	0	4	50	81	79	5	22	1	3	.337	.319	2	20	3	2870	3.72	263	190	1.38

1997 Season

	Avg	AB	H	2B	3B	HR	RBI	BB	SO	OBP	SLG		Avg	AB	H	2B	3B	HR	RBI	BB	SO	OBP	SLG
vs. Left	.293	75	22	7	0	0	3	10	8	.372	.387	Scoring Posn	.333	24	8	2	0	0	3	5	2	.433	.417
vs. Right	.235	51	12	2	0	1	3	8	3	.339	.333	Close & Late	.286	21	6	1	0	0	1	3	5	.375	.333
Home	.226	53	12	3	0	1	2	9	4	.339	.340	None on/out	.233	30	7	0	0	0	0	4	5	.324	.233
Away	.301	73	22	6	0	0	4	9	7	.373	.384	Batting #8	.288	66	19	6	0	0	3	4	5	.324	.379
First Pitch	.185	27	5	1	0	0	0	1	0	.214	.222	Batting #9	.308	39	12	3	0	0	2	9	2	.438	.385
Ahead in Count	.440	25	11	5	0	1	5	8	0	.559	.760	Other	.143	21	3	0	0	1	1	5	4	.308	.286
Behind in Count	.226	53	12	2	0	0	0	0	9	.226	.264	Pre-All Star	.304	92	28	9	0	1	6	12	6	.381	.435
Two Strikes	.231	52	12	3	0	0	1	9	11	.344	.288	Post-All Star	.176	34	6	0	0	0	0	6	5	.300	.176

Last Five Years

	Avg	AB	H	2B	3B	HR	RBI	BB	SO	OBP	SLG		Avg	AB	H	2B	3B	HR	RBI	BB	SO	OBP	SLG
vs. Left	.248	339	84	19	0	2	16	36	40	.323	.322	First Pitch	.283	120	34	7	0	2	8	2	0	.301	.392
vs. Right	.257	323	83	13	0	2	34	45	39	.351	.316	Ahead in Count	.324	139	45	15	0	1	19	42	0	.481	.453
Groundball	.259	135	35	5	0	1	5	20	14	.359	.319	Behind in Count	.206	262	54	9	0	0	16	0	63	.211	.240
Flyball	.318	129	41	10	0	1	14	11	12	.366	.419	Two Strikes	.201	278	56	9	0	0	15	37	79	.299	.234
Home	.274	332	91	18	0	1	23	40	36	.358	.337	Batting #2	.204	137	28	5	0	0	6	20	12	.306	.241

Last Five Years

	Avg	AB	H	2B	3B	HR	RBI	BB	SO	OBP	SLG		Avg	AB	H	2B	3B	HR	RBI	BB	SO	OBP	SLG
Away	.230	330	76	14	0	3	27	41	43	.316	.300	Batting #9	.267	258	69	10	0	3	23	39	33	.370	.341
Day	.224	201	45	10	0	3	17	21	25	.302	.318	Other	.262	267	70	17	0	1	21	22	34	.320	.337
Night	.265	461	122	22	0	1	33	60	54	.352	.319	March/April	.198	96	19	3	0	0	4	16	11	.310	.229
Grass	.256	587	150	25	0	3	43	73	67	.342	.313	May	.271	155	42	5	0	4	17	19	15	.350	.381
Turf	.227	75	17	7	0	1	7	8	12	.298	.360	June	.336	110	37	13	0	0	11	10	12	.397	.455
Pre-All Star	.274	430	118	23	0	4	34	53	42	.355	.356	July	.259	139	36	6	0	0	8	18	15	.352	.302
Post-All Star	.211	232	49	9	0	0	16	28	37	.304	.250	August	.229	109	25	4	0	0	8	16	28	.288	.266
Scoring Posn	.277	137	38	6	0	4	43	31	15	.407	.321	Sept/Oct	.151	53	8	1	0	0	2	10	10	.286	.170
Close & Late	.222	90	20	6	0	0	7	10	14	.300	.289	vs. AL	.257	556	143	31	0	3	41	76	63	.350	.329
None on/out	.233	163	38	4	0	2	2	15	22	.309	.294	vs. NL	.226	106	24	1	0	1	9	5	16	.263	.264

Batter vs. Pitcher (career)

Hits Best Against	Avg	AB	H	2B	3B	HR	RBI	BB	SO	OBP	SLG	Hits Worst Against	Avg	AB	H	2B	3B	HR	RBI	BB	SO	OBP	SLG
Mike Mussina	.400	10	4	1	0	0	2	1	3	.455	.500	Randy Johnson	.000	21	0	0	0	0	0	6	5	.250	.000
David Wells	.314	35	11	2	0	2	2	3	2	.368	.543	Mark Langston	.094	32	3	0	0	0	1	3	5	.171	.094
Jamie Moyer	.308	13	4	1	0	0	0	2	0	.400	.385	Erik Hanson	.167	12	2	0	0	0	0	2	2	.286	.167
												Chuck Finley	.192	26	5	1	0	0	2	2	4	.250	.231
												Jaime Navarro	.200	15	3	0	0	0	0	1	2	.250	.200

Scarborough Green — Cardinals

Age 24 – Bats Right

	Avg	G	AB	R	H	2B	3B	HR	RBI	BB	SO	HBP	GDP	SB	CS	OBP	SLG	IBB	SH	SF	#Pit	#P/PA	GB	FB	G/F
1997 Season	.097	20	31	5	3	0	0	0	1	2	5	0	0	0	0	.152	.097	0	0	0	116	3.52	12	8	1.50

1997 Season

	Avg	AB	H	2B	3B	HR	RBI	BB	SO	OBP	SLG		Avg	AB	H	2B	3B	HR	RBI	BB	SO	OBP	SLG
vs. Left	.143	7	1	0	0	0	0	0	1	.143	.143	Scoring Posn	.143	7	1	0	0	0	1	1	0	.250	.143
vs. Right	.083	24	2	0	0	0	1	2	4	.154	.083	Close & Late	.111	9	1	0	0	0	0	0	2	.111	.111

Shawn Green — Blue Jays

Age 25 – Bats Left

	Avg	G	AB	R	H	2B	3B	HR	RBI	BB	SO	HBP	GDP	SB	CS	OBP	SLG	IBB	SH	SF	#Pit	#P/PA	GB	FB	G/F
1997 Season	.287	135	429	57	123	22	4	16	53	36	99	1	4	14	3	.340	.469	4	1	4	1794	3.81	104	103	1.55
Career (1993-1997)	.278	405	1269	162	353	86	11	42	153	90	251	12	16	21	6	.330	.463	10	1	9	5051	3.66	469	319	1.47

1997 Season

	Avg	AB	H	2B	3B	HR	RBI	BB	SO	OBP	SLG		Avg	AB	H	2B	3B	HR	RBI	BB	SO	OBP	SLG
vs. Left	.287	101	29	5	0	0	7	8	27	.339	.337	First Pitch	.258	62	16	4	1	3	7	4	0	.303	.500
vs. Right	.287	328	94	17	4	16	46	28	72	.341	.509	Ahead in Count	.402	87	35	5	1	4	14	11	0	.465	.621
Groundball	.310	84	26	5	1	8	12	7	11	.370	.679	Behind in Count	.231	199	46	7	1	4	13	0	78	.235	.337
Flyball	.261	46	12	2	0	1	7	7	14	.352	.370	Two Strikes	.217	217	47	10	1	4	19	21	99	.288	.327
Home	.276	210	58	9	3	10	33	20	54	.338	.490	Batting #6	.286	140	40	8	1	7	20	9	29	.327	.507
Away	.297	219	65	13	1	6	20	16	45	.343	.447	Batting #7	.294	160	47	7	1	5	18	13	40	.343	.444
Day	.319	160	51	7	4	5	20	13	35	.368	.506	Other	.279	129	36	7	2	4	15	14	30	.352	.457
Night	.268	269	72	15	0	11	33	23	64	.324	.446	March/April	.250	48	12	1	0	4	7	6	11	.345	.521
Grass	.293	191	56	12	1	6	20	14	37	.340	.461	May	.200	45	9	2	0	3	3	11	.245	.244
Turf	.282	238	67	10	3	10	33	22	62	.341	.475	June	.362	47	17	5	1	2	6	3	7	.400	.638
Pre-All Star	.273	161	44	9	1	7	18	14	35	.333	.472	July	.286	91	26	4	0	7	19	6	23	.327	.560
Post-All Star	.295	268	79	13	3	9	35	22	64	.345	.466	August	.318	107	34	7	1	3	8	9	24	.368	.486
Scoring Posn	.284	81	23	6	0	2	32	13	22	.374	.432	Sept/Oct	.275	91	25	3	2	0	10	9	23	.337	.352
Close & Late	.276	87	24	4	1	7	21	8	20	.337	.586	vs. AL	.289	387	112	20	3	13	48	34	89	.345	.457
None on/out	.259	116	30	5	0	6	6	5	28	.289	.457	vs. NL	.262	42	11	2	1	3	5	2	10	.295	.571

1997 By Position

Position	Avg	AB	H	2B	3B	HR	RBI	BB	SO	OBP	SLG	G	GS	Innings	PO	A	E	DP	Fld Pct	Rng Fctr	In Zone	Outs	Zone Rtg	MLB Zone
As DH	.355	124	44	7	0	9	30	10	29	.400	.629	35	33	---	---	---	---	---	---	---	---	---	---	---
As Pinch Hitter	.000	12	0	0	0	0	0	2	7	.143	.000	17	0	---	---	---	---	---	---	---	---	---	---	---
As lf	.273	132	36	8	4	5	12	11	24	.329	.462	45	37	337.2	84	0	1	0	.988	2.24	99	80	.808	.805
As rf	.265	162	43	7	3	2	11	14	40	.322	.383	46	44	393.2	89	6	2	0	.979	2.17	108	84	.778	.813

Career (1993-1997)

	Avg	AB	H	2B	3B	HR	RBI	BB	SO	OBP	SLG		Avg	AB	H	2B	3B	HR	RBI	BB	SO	OBP	SLG
vs. Left	.262	206	54	11	1	1	18	15	47	.317	.340	First Pitch	.356	208	74	19	4	11	35	10	0	.392	.644
vs. Right	.281	1063	299	75	10	41	135	75	204	.332	.486	Ahead in Count	.335	260	87	17	4	13	43	29	0	.399	.581
Groundball	.302	298	90	21	2	15	36	21	51	.355	.537	Behind in Count	.214	579	124	33	2	9	40	0	209	.223	.325
Flyball	.232	198	46	13	1	5	23	19	49	.301	.384	Two Strikes	.193	596	115	33	2	8	47	51	251	.263	.295
Home	.262	607	159	39	5	22	80	48	133	.319	.451	Batting #6	.292	301	88	18	4	12	33	17	58	.331	.498
Away	.293	662	194	47	6	20	73	42	118	.339	.473	Batting #7	.279	670	187	48	4	24	91	47	125	.329	.470
Day	.294	452	133	32	6	14	55	29	76	.344	.485	Other	.262	298	78	20	3	6	29	26	68	.329	.409
Night	.269	817	220	54	5	28	98	61	175	.321	.450	March/April	.255	141	36	7	0	7	18	13	22	.333	.454
Grass	.285	575	164	40	4	18	63	38	98	.335	.463	May	.223	188	42	8	1	5	21	13	45	.276	.356
Turf	.272	694	189	46	7	24	90	52	153	.325	.463	June	.245	196	48	16	4	6	22	15	36	.300	.459
Pre-All Star	.237	579	137	33	5	21	67	45	111	.299	.420	July	.299	231	69	20	0	12	42	12	43	.336	.541
Post-All Star	.313	690	216	53	6	21	86	45	140	.356	.499	August	.336	262	88	20	4	8	26	21	51	.383	.534
Scoring Posn	.256	308	79	21	1	6	99	34	67	.331	.390	Sept/Oct	.279	251	70	15	2	4	24	16	54	.326	.402
Close & Late	.274	215	59	10	1	13	33	15	51	.322	.512	vs. AL	.279	1227	342	84	10	39	148	88	241	.331	.459
None on/out	.282	309	87	22	1	14	14	17	57	.323	.495	vs. NL	.262	42	11	2	1	3	5	2	10	.295	.571

Batter vs. Pitcher (career)

Hits Best Against	Avg	AB	H	2B	3B	HR	RBI	BB	SO	OBP	SLG	Hits Worst Against	Avg	AB	H	2B	3B	HR	RBI	BB	SO	OBP	SLG
Aaron Sele	.667	12	8	2	0	1	4	2	0	.667	1.083	Scott Kamieniecki	.063	16	1	0	0	0	0	0	3	.063	.063
Dennis Martinez	.556	18	10	1	0	3	4	1	0	.600	1.111	Frank Rodriguez	.083	12	1	0	0	0	1	0	5	.077	.083
Ricky Bones	.500	12	6	0	0	1	2	1	0	.538	.750	Mike Oquist	.083	12	1	0	0	0	0	0	0	.083	.083
Jack McDowell	.500	10	5	5	0	0	3	2	1	.583	1.000	Kevin Appier	.095	21	2	1	0	0	2	2	4	.174	.143
Ken Hill	.417	12	5	0	1	1	2	1	3	.462	.833	Tim Belcher	.176	17	3	1	0	0	0	0	5	.176	.235

Tyler Green — Phillies
Age 28 – Pitches Right (groundball pitcher)

	ERA	W	L	Sv	G	GS	IP	BB	SO	Avg	H	2B	3B	HR	RBI	OBP	SLG	CG	ShO	Sup	QS	#P/S	SB	CS	GB	FB	G/F
1997 Season	4.93	4	4	0	14	14	76.2	45	58	.247	72	15	1	8	41	.347	.388	0	0	5.28	6	92	6	6	120	75	1.60
Career (1993-1997)	5.25	12	13	0	43	41	224.2	116	150	.282	245	42	5	24	122	.366	.425	4	2	5.09	19	90	16	14	350	219	1.60

1997 Season

	ERA	W	L	Sv	G	GS	IP	H	HR	BB	SO		Avg	AB	H	2B	3B	HR	RBI	BB	SO	OBP	SLG
Home	6.42	1	3	0	6	6	33.2	38	4	18	28	vs. Left	.286	133	38	8	1	4	16	19	26	.373	.451
Away	3.77	3	1	0	8	8	43.0	34	4	27	30	vs. Right	.215	158	34	7	0	4	25	26	32	.326	.335
Starter	4.93	4	4	0	14	14	76.2	72	8	45	58	Scoring Posn	.247	77	19	6	0	3	33	18	17	.378	.442
Reliever	0.00	0	0	0	0	0	0.0	0	0	0	0	Close & Late	.455	11	5	1	0	0	1	2	1	.538	.545
0-3 Days Rest (Start)	0.00	0	0	0	0	0	0.0	0	0	0	0	None on/out	.333	69	23	5	0	1	1	13	8	.446	.449
4 Days Rest	6.55	2	2	0	7	7	33.0	35	4	20	19	First Pitch	.326	46	15	4	0	3	13	1	0	.354	.609
5+ Days Rest	3.71	2	2	0	7	7	43.2	37	4	25	39	Ahead in Count	.152	105	16	5	0	1	6	0	46	.151	.229
Pre-All Star	0.00	0	0	0	0	0	0.0	0	0	0	0	Behind in Count	.314	86	27	4	0	2	16	25	0	.464	.430
Post-All Star	4.93	4	4	0	14	14	76.2	72	8	45	58	Two Strikes	.168	131	22	6	0	2	9	19	58	.272	.260

Charlie Greene — Orioles
Age 27 – Bats Right

	Avg	G	AB	R	H	2B	3B	HR	RBI	BB	SO	HBP	GDP	SB	CS	OBP	SLG	IBB	SH	SF	#Pit	P/PA	GB	FB	G/F
1997 Season	.000	5	2	0	0	0	0	0	1	0	1	0	0	0	0	.000	.000	0	0	0	6	3.00	1	0	0.00

1997 Season

	Avg	AB	H	2B	3B	HR	RBI	BB	SO	OBP	SLG		Avg	AB	H	2B	3B	HR	RBI	BB	SO	OBP	SLG
vs. Left	.000	1	0	0	0	0	1	0	0	.000	.000	Scoring Posn	.000	1	0	0	0	0	0	1	0	.000	.000
vs. Right	.000	1	0	0	0	0	0	0	1	.000	.000	Close & Late	.000	0	0	0	0	0	0	0	0	.000	.000

Todd Greene — Angels
Age 27 – Bats Right

	Avg	G	AB	R	H	2B	3B	HR	RBI	BB	SO	HBP	GDP	SB	CS	OBP	SLG	IBB	SH	SF	#Pit	P/PA	GB	FB	G/F
1997 Season	.290	34	124	24	36	6	0	9	24	7	25	0	1	2	0	.328	.556	1	0	0	424	3.24	37	37	1.00
Career (1996-1997)	.251	63	203	33	51	7	0	11	33	11	36	1	5	4	0	.293	.448	1	0	0	703	3.27	68	66	1.03

1997 Season

	Avg	AB	H	2B	3B	HR	RBI	BB	SO	OBP	SLG		Avg	AB	H	2B	3B	HR	RBI	BB	SO	OBP	SLG
vs. Left	.318	44	14	4	0	3	8	4	8	.375	.614	Scoring Posn	.262	42	11	3	0	2	16	3	8	.311	.476
vs. Right	.275	80	22	2	0	6	16	3	17	.301	.525	Close & Late	.231	13	3	2	0	0	1	1	2	.286	.385
Home	.319	72	23	5	0	5	13	6	15	.372	.597	None on/out	.360	25	9	1	0	3	3	1	5	.385	.760
Away	.250	52	13	1	0	4	11	1	10	.264	.500	Batting #6	.225	40	9	0	0	3	6	3	8	.279	.450
First Pitch	.367	30	11	1	0	3	6	1	0	.387	.700	Batting #7	.324	34	11	1	0	2	5	1	6	.343	.529
Ahead in Count	.316	19	6	3	0	1	5	2	0	.381	.632	Other	.320	50	16	5	0	4	13	3	11	.358	.660
Behind in Count	.246	57	14	1	0	4	8	0	20	.246	.474	Pre-All Star	.190	21	4	2	0	0	1	2	4	.261	.286
Two Strikes	.196	51	10	1	0	3	6	4	25	.255	.392	Post-All Star	.311	103	32	4	0	9	23	5	21	.343	.612

Tommy Greene — Astros
Age 31 – Pitches Right (flyball pitcher)

	ERA	W	L	Sv	G	GS	IP	BB	SO	Avg	H	2B	3B	HR	RBI	OBP	SLG	CG	ShO	Sup	QS	#P/S	SB	CS	GB	FB	G/F
1997 Season	7.00	0	1	0	2	2	9.0	5	11	.286	14	2	0	2	5	.375	.514	0	0	9.00	0	88	0	1	7	12	0.58
Last Five Years	4.27	18	10	0	51	45	278.1	109	230	.251	267	57	5	25	120	.321	.385	7	2	6.82	21	101	27	11	306	333	0.92

1997 Season

	ERA	W	L	Sv	G	GS	IP	H	HR	BB	SO		Avg	AB	H	2B	3B	HR	RBI	BB	SO	OBP	SLG
Home	5.79	0	1	0	1	1	4.2	4	1	3	4	vs. Left	.267	15	4	1	0	1	4	5	5	.450	.533
Away	8.31	0	0	0	1	1	4.1	6	1	2	7	vs. Right	.300	20	6	1	0	1	1	0	6	.300	.500

Last Five Years

	ERA	W	L	Sv	G	GS	IP	H	HR	BB	SO		Avg	AB	H	2B	3B	HR	RBI	BB	SO	OBP	SLG
Home	3.81	12	4	0	29	24	163.0	143	13	61	137	vs. Left	.260	504	131	27	1	9	57	69	100	.348	.371
Away	4.92	6	6	0	22	21	115.1	124	12	48	93	vs. Right	.243	559	136	30	4	16	63	40	130	.296	.397
Day	5.56	5	2	0	16	12	69.2	63	9	33	58	Inning 1-6	.248	887	220	43	5	22	102	99	198	.324	.382
Night	3.84	13	8	0	35	33	208.2	204	16	76	172	Inning 7+	.267	176	47	14	0	3	18	10	32	.309	.398
Grass	4.10	4	2	0	14	13	74.2	76	8	31	61	None on	.253	612	155	33	3	16	16	60	131	.324	.395
Turf	4.33	14	8	0	37	32	203.2	191	17	78	169	Runners on	.248	451	112	24	2	9	104	49	99	.318	.370
March/April	2.97	2	0	0	7	6	39.1	26	4	15	35	Scoring Posn	.237	274	65	17	2	6	96	37	61	.321	.380
May	2.61	2	0	0	10	10	69.0	57	4	23	56	Close & Late	.296	54	16	7	0	1	10	4	5	.345	.481
June	7.43	2	2	0	8	7	36.1	51	4	15	34	None on/out	.277	278	77	18	1	8	8	21	53	.330	.435
July	4.23	3	2	0	8	6	38.1	37	3	14	28	vs. 1st Batr (relief)	.000	5	0	0	0	0	0	1	2	.167	.000
August	5.98	0	4	0	9	9	46.2	62	7	19	32	1st Inning Pitched	.242	190	46	7 ·	1	4	28	27	42	.336	.353
Sept/Oct	3.70	4	2	0	9	7	48.2	34	3	23	45	First 75 Pitches	.248	758	188	38	3	17	78	81	166	.321	.373
Starter	4.16	18	10	0	45	45	268.1	255	24	107	222	Pitch 76-90	.279	129	36	8	1	6	20	14	24	.354	.496
Reliever	7.20	0	0	0	6	0	10.0	12	1	2	8	Pitch 91-105	.270	89	24	6	1	1	14	7	20	.320	.393
0-3 Days Rest (Start)	1.29	1	0	0	1	1	7.0	2	1	1	8	Pitch 106+	.218	87	19	5	0	1	8	7	20	.274	.310

Last Five Years

	ERA	W	L	Sv	G	GS	IP	H	HR	BB	SO		Avg	AB	H	2B	3B	HR	RBI	BB	SO	OBP	SLG
4 Days Rest	4.62	10	5	0	24	24	142.1	151	12	55	105	First Pitch	.287	115	33	7	2	1	13	2	0	.300	.409
5+ Days Rest	3.78	7	5	0	20	20	119.0	102	11	51	109	Ahead in Count	.213	517	110	25	3	8	39	0	202	.216	.319
vs. AL	0.00	0	0	0	0	0	0.0	0	0	0	0	Behind in Count	.270	222	60	14	0	9	37	58	0	.416	.455
vs. NL	4.27	18	10	0	51	45	278.1	267	25	109	230	Two Strikes	.188	532	100	26	3	8	48	49	230	.259	.293
Pre-All Star	4.14	13	3	0	30	26	165.1	155	14	63	138	Pre-All Star	.248	625	155	29	3	14	65	63	138	.317	.371
Post-All Star	4.46	5	7	0	21	19	113.0	112	11	46	92	Post-All Star	.256	438	112	28	2	11	55	46	92	.327	.404

Pitcher vs. Batter (career)

Pitches Best Vs.	Avg	AB	H	2B	3B	HR	RBI	BB	SO	OBP	SLG	Pitches Worst Vs.	Avg	AB	H	2B	3B	HR	RBI	BB	SO	OBP	SLG
Eric Karros	.059	17	1	0	0	0	0	1	4	.111	.059	Moises Alou	.545	11	6	4	0	0	4	1	1	.583	.909
Todd Hundley	.067	15	1	0	0	0	0	1	4	.125	.067	Dave Clark	.500	12	6	1	1	2	2	1	1	.538	1.250
Otis Nixon	.083	12	1	0	0	0	2	2	1	.214	.083	Barry Bonds	.412	17	7	1	0	3	9	5	4	.522	1.000
Jody Reed	.091	11	1	0	0	0	0	0	3	.091	.091	Mike Piazza	.375	16	6	2	0	2	6	2	4	.444	.875
Eric Young	.100	10	1	0	0	0	0	1	2	.182	.100	Dante Bichette	.375	16	6	2	1	2	4	1	2	.389	1.000

Willie Greene — Reds   Age 26 – Bats Left

	Avg	G	AB	R	H	2B	3B	HR	RBI	BB	SO	HBP	GDP	SB	CS	OBP	SLG	IBB	SH	SF	#Pit	#P/PA	GB	FB	G/F
1997 Season	.253	151	495	62	125	22	1	26	91	78	111	1	10	6	0	.354	.459	5	1	3	2199	3.80	182	145	1.26
Last Five Years	.240	305	888	123	213	30	7	47	162	125	239	1	18	6	1	.332	.448	12	2	6	3935	3.85	307	244	1.26

1997 Season

	Avg	AB	H	2B	3B	HR	RBI	BB	SO	OBP	SLG		Avg	AB	H	2B	3B	HR	RBI	BB	SO	OBP	SLG
vs. Left	.172	99	17	3	0	2	9	18	32	.305	.263	First Pitch	.382	68	26	2	1	8	26	3	0	.403	.794
vs. Right	.273	396	108	19	1	24	82	60	79	.366	.508	Ahead in Count	.350	140	49	10	0	11	38	33	0	.472	.657
Groundball	.286	98	28	5	0	4	15	17	22	.391	.459	Behind in Count	.128	195	25	5	0	3	15	0	96	.128	.200
Flyball	.246	57	14	3	0	4	10	6	10	.313	.509	Two Strikes	.139	216	30	8	0	5	19	42	111	.279	.245
Home	.255	243	62	11	0	13	44	43	49	.369	.461	Batting #4	.268	168	45	6	1	8	25	20	36	.344	.458
Away	.250	252	63	11	1	13	47	35	62	.338	.456	Batting #5	.240	146	35	8	0	5	21	29	40	.367	.397
Day	.247	178	44	9	1	8	30	28	45	.350	.444	Other	.249	181	45	8	0	13	45	29	35	.351	.508
Night	.256	317	81	13	0	18	61	50	66	.356	.467	March/April	.195	82	16	4	1	3	11	13	13	.302	.378
Grass	.239	163	39	9	0	6	24	25	43	.335	.405	May	.239	67	16	5	0	2	14	13	14	.363	.403
Turf	.259	332	86	13	1	20	67	53	68	.363	.485	June	.357	70	25	3	0	6	15	14	14	.464	.657
Pre-All Star	.262	237	62	12	1	13	45	42	45	.371	.485	July	.241	83	20	4	0	4	7	11	22	.330	.434
Post-All Star	.244	258	63	10	0	13	46	36	66	.337	.434	August	.242	95	23	3	0	5	22	13	22	.333	.432
Scoring Posn	.253	158	40	10	1	7	71	34	39	.379	.462	Sept/Oct	.255	98	25	3	0	6	22	14	26	.348	.469
Close & Late	.191	68	13	2	0	1	4	14	17	.329	.265	vs. AL	.275	40	11	1	0	5	9	6	5	.383	.675
None on/out	.261	115	30	4	0	7	7	13	26	.341	.478	vs. NL	.251	455	114	21	1	21	82	72	106	.351	.440

1997 By Position

Position	Avg	AB	H	2B	3B	HR	RBI	BB	SO	OBP	SLG	G	GS	Innings	PO	A	E	DP	Fld Pct	Rng Fctr	In Zone	Zone Outs	Zone Rtg	MLB Zone
As Pinch Hitter	.091	11	1	0	0	0	2	1	1	.167	.091	12	0	—	—	—	—	—	—	—	—	—	—	—
As 3b	.252	349	88	18	1	19	63	53	81	.351	.473	103	100	848.0	54	172	16	7	.934	2.40	259	188	.726	.801
As rf	.292	96	28	3	0	6	17	18	23	.404	.510	33	29	239.2	71	1	1	1	.986	2.70	78	66	.846	.813

Last Five Years

	Avg	AB	H	2B	3B	HR	RBI	BB	SO	OBP	SLG		Avg	AB	H	2B	3B	HR	RBI	BB	SO	OBP	SLG
vs. Left	.156	167	26	4	1	4	18	30	60	.285	.263	First Pitch	.363	124	45	4	2	16	48	6	0	.383	.815
vs. Right	.259	721	187	26	6	43	144	95	179	.344	.491	Ahead in Count	.386	223	86	15	2	18	62	59	0	.512	.713
Groundball	.215	209	45	7	1	5	23	27	62	.304	.330	Behind in Count	.130	378	49	5	2	7	33	0	199	.129	.209
Flyball	.218	124	27	5	1	6	19	11	38	.279	.419	Two Strikes	.130	432	56	9	2	9	35	60	239	.236	.222
Home	.240	445	106	16	2	26	83	65	116	.338	.461	Batting #4	.273	194	53	6	1	15	39	27	47	.343	.546
Away	.239	443	106	14	5	21	79	60	123	.327	.436	Batting #5	.239	188	45	9	0	7	31	33	53	.353	.399
Day	.235	298	70	11	2	14	48	39	84	.322	.426	Other	.227	506	115	15	6	25	92	71	139	.321	.429
Night	.242	590	143	19	5	33	114	86	155	.337	.459	March/April	.201	164	33	6	2	5	22	26	40	.307	.354
Grass	.234	299	70	12	2	13	47	40	87	.322	.418	May	.213	108	23	5	1	3	19	17	32	.320	.361
Turf	.243	589	143	18	5	34	115	85	152	.338	.463	June	.319	141	45	5	2	12	35	19	30	.398	.638
Pre-All Star	.246	431	106	16	5	22	81	64	106	.341	.459	July	.206	126	26	4	0	4	8	19	34	.308	.333
Post-All Star	.234	457	107	14	2	25	81	61	133	.324	.438	August	.239	184	44	5	1	9	36	25	53	.330	.424
Scoring Posn	.233	270	63	11	5	15	119	56	74	.358	.478	Sept/Oct	.255	165	42	5	1	14	42	19	50	.332	.552
Close & Late	.159	126	20	3	0	3	9	26	33	.303	.294	vs. AL	.275	40	11	1	0	5	9	6	5	.383	.675
None on/out	.245	200	49	6	1	13	13	19	54	.314	.480	vs. NL	.238	848	202	29	7	42	153	119	234	.330	.438

Batter vs. Pitcher (career)

Hits Best Against	Avg	AB	H	2B	3B	HR	RBI	BB	SO	OBP	SLG	Hits Worst Against	Avg	AB	H	2B	3B	HR	RBI	BB	SO	OBP	SLG
Pat Rapp	.462	13	6	1	0	0	2	1	2	.500	.538	Jim Bullinger	.000	12	0	0	0	0	0	2	5	.143	.000
Osvald Fernandez	.455	11	5	1	0	2	5	0	2	.455	1.091	John Smoltz	.105	19	2	0	0	0	1	0	5	.105	.105
Alan Benes	.375	8	3	1	0	1	4	3	3	.545	.875	Al Leiter	.111	9	1	0	0	0	0	3	4	.333	.111
Rick Reed	.364	11	4	0	0	1	1	1	2	.417	.636	Pedro Martinez	.150	20	3	1	0	0	2	2	10	.227	.200
												Pedro Astacio	.176	17	3	1	0	0	0	0	1	.176	.235

Rusty Greer — Rangers
Age 29 – Bats Left (flyball hitter)

	Avg	G	AB	R	H	2B	3B	HR	RBI	BB	SO	HBP	GDP	SB	CS	OBP	SLG	IBB	SH	SF	#Pit	#P/PA	GB	FB	G/F
1997 Season	.321	157	601	112	193	42	3	26	87	83	87	3	11	9	5	.405	.531	4	1	2	2739	3.97	202	177	1.14
Career (1994-1997)	.312	507	1837	302	573	120	12	67	294	246	285	9	32	21	6	.392	.500	11	5	19	8334	3.94	599	582	1.03

1997 Season

	Avg	AB	H	2B	3B	HR	RBI	BB	SO	OBP	SLG		Avg	AB	H	2B	3B	HR	RBI	BB	SO	OBP	SLG
vs. Left	.309	178	55	15	0	7	19	28	27	.406	.511	First Pitch	.229	70	16	4	1	2	11	4	0	.276	.400
vs. Right	.326	423	138	27	3	19	68	55	60	.405	.539	Ahead in Count	.348	155	54	11	1	9	30	33	0	.460	.606
Groundball	.301	133	40	7	0	3	19	20	19	.394	.421	Behind in Count	.302	225	68	16	0	8	23	0	67	.305	.480
Flyball	.316	95	30	11	1	3	11	11	16	.387	.547	Two Strikes	.281	263	74	17	0	8	29	46	87	.390	.437
Home	.370	300	111	20	3	18	54	42	39	.446	.637	Batting #3	.321	598	192	42	3	25	84	83	86	.405	.527
Away	.272	301	82	22	0	8	33	41	48	.363	.425	Batting #6	1.000	1	1	0	0	1	3	0	0	1.000	4.000
Day	.361	133	48	10	1	3	15	20	24	.445	.519	Other	.000	2	0	0	0	0	0	0	0	.000	.000
Night	.310	468	145	32	2	23	72	63	63	.393	.534	March/April	.286	84	24	7	0	2	8	17	12	.406	.440
Grass	.330	539	178	36	3	25	76	75	76	.413	.547	May	.324	105	34	5	1	4	15	13	17	.403	.505
Turf	.242	62	15	6	0	1	11	8	11	.338	.387	June	.385	104	40	11	1	5	17	17	12	.475	.654
Pre-All Star	.329	316	104	23	2	13	45	50	43	.423	.538	July	.283	99	28	4	1	5	13	15	14	.374	.495
Post-All Star	.312	285	89	19	1	13	42	33	44	.384	.523	August	.336	116	39	6	0	7	21	13	21	.408	.569
Scoring Posn	.259	170	44	7	1	7	62	33	25	.382	.435	Sept/Oct	.301	93	28	9	0	3	13	8	11	.353	.495
Close & Late	.341	91	31	9	1	5	14	15	18	.434	.626	vs. AL	.315	543	171	36	3	24	77	75	81	.399	.525
None on/out	.358	95	34	11	0	7	7	16	11	.450	.695	vs. NL	.379	58	22	6	0	2	10	8	6	.456	.586

1997 By Position

Position	Avg	AB	H	2B	3B	HR	RBI	BB	SO	OBP	SLG	G	GS	Innings	PO	A	E	DP	Fld Pct	Rng Fctr	In Zone	Zone Outs	Zone Rtg	MLB Zone
As lf	.319	539	172	38	2	22	77	73	74	.402	.519	148	139	1219.1	280	8	11	0	.963	2.13	341	270	.792	.805
As cf	.327	49	16	2	1	3	6	7	9	.411	.592	19	12	102.0	38	1	1	0	.975	3.44	46	37	.804	.815

Career (1994-1997)

	Avg	AB	H	2B	3B	HR	RBI	BB	SO	OBP	SLG		Avg	AB	H	2B	3B	HR	RBI	BB	SO	OBP	SLG
vs. Left	.297	502	149	32	3	18	76	57	80	.370	.480	First Pitch	.308	211	65	12	2	11	49	10	0	.338	.540
vs. Right	.318	1335	424	88	9	49	218	189	205	.400	.507	Ahead in Count	.388	498	193	41	5	26	112	121	0	.502	.647
Groundball	.281	406	114	23	1	10	50	58	62	.370	.416	Behind in Count	.248	715	177	36	3	15	70	0	226	.250	.369
Flyball	.296	358	106	25	2	16	59	45	48	.373	.511	Two Strikes	.223	786	175	36	3	19	79	115	285	.323	.349
Home	.324	904	293	51	7	37	167	135	143	.407	.519	Batting #3	.320	962	308	69	8	38	149	126	146	.399	.527
Away	.300	933	280	69	5	30	127	111	142	.377	.481	Batting #7	.309	369	114	19	2	13	57	44	61	.379	.477
Day	.299	415	124	27	2	10	51	52	76	.381	.446	Other	.298	506	151	32	2	16	88	76	78	.389	.464
Night	.316	1422	449	93	10	57	243	194	209	.396	.515	March/April	.291	199	58	15	1	4	29	32	35	.386	.437
Grass	.312	1626	507	103	10	55	254	225	248	.394	.489	May	.336	307	103	20	3	10	56	35	54	.405	.518
Turf	.313	211	66	17	2	12	40	21	37	.380	.583	June	.303	386	117	27	3	15	61	59	55	.397	.505
Pre-All Star	.307	999	307	63	7	33	164	143	159	.394	.483	July	.288	392	113	17	2	15	57	56	64	.373	.457
Post-All Star	.317	838	266	57	5	34	130	103	126	.390	.519	August	.349	352	123	26	2	16	63	43	48	.422	.571
Scoring Posn	.287	529	152	27	2	21	226	96	88	.389	.465	Sept/Oct	.294	201	59	15	1	7	28	21	29	.354	.483
Close & Late	.300	260	78	15	2	12	51	37	53	.384	.512	vs. AL	.310	1779	551	114	12	65	284	238	279	.390	.497
None on/out	.326	356	116	27	4	15	15	46	49	.403	.551	vs. NL	.379	58	22	6	0	2	10	8	6	.456	.586

Batter vs. Pitcher (career)

Hits Best Against	Avg	AB	H	2B	3B	HR	RBI	BB	SO	OBP	SLG	Hits Worst Against	Avg	AB	H	2B	3B	HR	RBI	BB	SO	OBP	SLG
Juan Guzman	.667	15	10	2	0	1	6	5	1	.750	1.000	Dwight Gooden	.000	11	0	0	0	0	0	1	2	.083	.000
Carlos Reyes	.643	14	9	3	0	1	5	0	0	.643	1.071	David Wells	.071	14	1	0	0	0	1	0	1	.067	.071
Ricky Bones	.625	8	5	2	0	0	0	3	1	.727	.875	Randy Johnson	.083	12	1	0	0	0	1	2	8	.214	.083
Scott Aldred	.500	10	5	2	0	2	6	1	1	.545	1.300	Roger Clemens	.087	23	2	0	0	0	0	4	7	.222	.087
Jaime Navarro	.462	13	6	0	0	2	8	0	1	.462	.923	Omar Olivares	.091	11	1	1	0	0	1	0	1	.091	.182

Tommy Gregg — Braves
Age 34 – Bats Left

	Avg	G	AB	R	H	2B	3B	HR	RBI	BB	SO	HBP	GDP	SB	CS	OBP	SLG	IBB	SH	SF	#Pit	#P/PA	GB	FB	G/F
1997 Season	.263	13	19	1	5	2	0	0	0	1	2	0	0	1	1	.300	.368	0	0	0	74	3.70	5	8	0.63
Last Five Years	.235	95	187	22	44	7	0	6	21	17	35	2	3	4	2	.301	.369	1	0	3	849	4.06	60	64	0.94

1997 Season

	Avg	AB	H	2B	3B	HR	RBI	BB	SO	OBP	SLG		Avg	AB	H	2B	3B	HR	RBI	BB	SO	OBP	SLG
vs. Left	.500	2	1	1	0	0	0	0	0	.500	1.000	Scoring Posn	.000	2	0	0	0	0	0	1	0	.333	.000
vs. Right	.235	17	4	1	0	0	0	1	2	.278	.294	Close & Late	.250	4	1	1	0	0	0	1	1	.400	.500

Ben Grieve — Athletics
Age 22 – Bats Left

	Avg	G	AB	R	H	2B	3B	HR	RBI	BB	SO	HBP	GDP	SB	CS	OBP	SLG	IBB	SH	SF	#Pit	#P/PA	GB	FB	G/F
1997 Season	.312	24	93	12	29	6	0	3	24	13	26	1	1	0	0	.402	.473	1	1	0	434	4.02	29	21	1.38

1997 Season

	Avg	AB	H	2B	3B	HR	RBI	BB	SO	OBP	SLG		Avg	AB	H	2B	3B	HR	RBI	BB	SO	OBP	SLG
vs. Left	.316	38	12	2	0	1	11	5	11	.409	.447	Scoring Posn	.355	31	11	3	0	1	18	5	9	.444	.548
vs. Right	.309	55	17	4	0	2	13	8	14	.397	.491	Close & Late	.286	14	4	0	0	2	4	0	9	.286	.714

Ken Griffey Jr. — Mariners
Age 28 – Bats Left

	Avg	G	AB	R	H	2B	3B	HR	RBI	BB	SO	HBP	GDP	SB	CS	OBP	SLG	IBB	SH	SF	#Pit	#P/PA	GB	FB	G/F
1997 Season	.304	157	608	125	185	34	3	56	147	76	121	8	12	15	4	.382	.646	23	0	12	2550	3.62	164	238	0.69
Last Five Years	.304	636	2428	509	737	129	12	207	528	358	442	23	45	63	19	.394	.622	86	1	30	10428	3.67	672	889	0.76

1997 Season

	Avg	AB	H	2B	3B	HR	RBI	BB	SO	OBP	SLG		Avg	AB	H	2B	3B	HR	RBI	BB	SO	OBP	SLG
vs. Left	.270	196	53	8	1	14	39	14	52	.332	.536	First Pitch	.326	89	29	1	1	5	16	21	0	.465	.528
vs. Right	.320	412	132	26	2	42	108	62	69	.405	.699	Ahead in Count	.386	145	56	12	1	18	43	31	0	.489	.855
Groundball	.317	139	44	9	1	14	34	17	25	.396	.698	Behind in Count	.256	277	71	15	0	22	60	0	99	.254	.549
Flyball	.277	101	28	4	1	10	27	11	20	.348	.634	Two Strikes	.225	276	62	14	0	23	62	23	121	.283	.525
Home	.322	289	93	15	3	27	72	38	51	.396	.675	Batting #1	.000	3	0	0	0	0	0	0	1	.000	.000
Away	.288	319	92	19	0	29	75	38	70	.369	.621	Batting #3	.306	605	185	34	3	56	147	76	120	.384	.650
Day	.271	192	52	7	1	15	42	24	45	.354	.552	Other	.000	0	0	0	0	0	0	0	0	.000	.000
Night	.320	416	133	27	2	41	105	52	76	.395	.690	March/April	.340	103	35	5	1	13	30	12	18	.420	.786
Grass	.298	272	81	17	0	20	59	33	61	.379	.581	May	.291	110	32	4	0	11	32	11	21	.347	.627
Turf	.310	336	104	17	3	36	88	43	60	.385	.699	June	.295	88	26	6	1	5	17	15	19	.400	.557
Pre-All Star	.307	323	99	16	2	30	84	41	64	.384	.647	July	.267	101	27	9	0	3	19	11	22	.328	.446
Post-All Star	.302	285	86	18	1	26	63	35	57	.380	.646	August	.330	115	38	8	1	12	24	14	21	.412	.730
Scoring Posn	.336	146	49	11	1	12	85	27	34	.420	.671	Sept/Oct	.297	91	27	2	0	12	25	13	20	.385	.714
Close & Late	.275	80	22	3	1	7	16	14	22	.385	.600	vs. AL	.304	550	167	28	3	52	132	68	108	.382	.649
None on/out	.279	122	34	9	1	7	7	3	17	.307	.541	vs. NL	.310	58	18	6	0	4	15	8	13	.380	.621

1997 By Position

Position	Avg	AB	H	2B	3B	HR	RBI	BB	SO	OBP	SLG	G	GS	Innings	PO	A	E	DP	Fld Pct	Rng Fctr	In Zone	Outs	Zone Rtg	MLB Zone
As cf	.308	591	182	34	3	54	144	75	115	.386	.650	153	153	1330.2	387	9	6	3	.985	2.68	468	377	.806	.815

Last Five Years

	Avg	AB	H	2B	3B	HR	RBI	BB	SO	OBP	SLG		Avg	AB	H	2B	3B	HR	RBI	BB	SO	OBP	SLG
vs. Left	.294	813	239	36	4	67	184	83	168	.365	.595	First Pitch	.349	367	128	22	2	27	79	77	0	.466	.640
vs. Right	.308	1615	498	93	8	140	344	275	274	.408	.636	Ahead in Count	.386	617	238	43	5	71	166	154	0	.505	.817
Groundball	.319	558	178	29	1	50	115	73	93	.399	.643	Behind in Count	.237	1002	237	41	3	69	177	0	345	.238	.490
Flyball	.288	462	133	25	5	40	104	62	91	.373	.623	Two Strikes	.213	1024	218	38	3	65	173	126	442	.299	.446
Home	.319	1132	361	68	6	105	261	185	200	.416	.668	Batting #2	.291	55	16	3	1	2	5	8	11	.381	.491
Away	.290	1296	376	61	6	102	267	173	242	.374	.583	Batting #3	.305	2361	720	126	11	204	522	349	428	.395	.627
Day	.299	686	205	32	4	58	144	97	128	.386	.611	Other	.083	12	1	0	0	1	1	1	3	.154	.333
Night	.305	1742	532	97	8	149	384	261	314	.397	.627	March/April	.299	384	115	19	6	37	92	55	69	.391	.669
Grass	.294	1067	314	49	5	77	216	145	208	.379	.566	May	.307	499	153	24	1	44	104	73	83	.393	.623
Turf	.311	1361	423	80	7	130	312	213	234	.405	.666	June	.310	364	113	24	1	30	74	49	65	.395	.629
Pre-All Star	.310	1345	417	71	10	115	288	191	233	.396	.634	July	.320	375	120	23	3	28	88	42	68	.387	.621
Post-All Star	.295	1083	320	58	2	92	240	167	209	.391	.608	August	.299	401	120	20	1	35	82	69	82	.405	.616
Scoring Posn	.287	621	178	28	6	51	317	153	139	.415	.597	Sept/Oct	.286	405	116	19	0	33	88	70	75	.391	.578
Close & Late	.288	347	100	15	2	27	70	64	74	.404	.576	vs. AL	.303	2370	719	123	12	203	513	350	429	.394	.622
None on/out	.301	459	138	29	1	43	43	27	74	.345	.649	vs. NL	.310	58	18	6	0	4	15	8	13	.380	.621

Batter vs. Pitcher (career)

Hits Best Against	Avg	AB	H	2B	3B	HR	RBI	BB	SO	OBP	SLG	Hits Worst Against	Avg	AB	H	2B	3B	HR	RBI	BB	SO	OBP	SLG
Bob Tewksbury	.545	11	6	3	0	2	6	0	2	.545	1.364	Eddie Guardado	.000	11	0	0	0	0	0	0	7	.083	.000
Mark Gubicza	.524	21	11	2	0	2	3	8	3	.655	.905	Scott Radinsky	.063	16	1	1	0	0	0	0	7	.118	.125
Albie Lopez	.500	10	5	1	0	2	5	0	2	.455	1.200	Ken Hill	.067	15	1	0	0	0	1	2	2	.167	.067
Vaughn Eshelman	.400	10	4	1	0	2	8	0	2	.455	1.100	Bret Saberhagen	.077	13	1	0	0	0	0	3	4	.250	.077
Aaron Sele	.333	9	3	0	0	2	2	3	3	.500	1.000	Tim Belcher	.091	22	2	0	0	0	2	1	9	.167	.091

Marquis Grissom — Indians
Age 31 – Bats Right

	Avg	G	AB	R	H	2B	3B	HR	RBI	BB	SO	HBP	GDP	SB	CS	OBP	SLG	IBB	SH	SF	#Pit	#P/PA	GB	FB	G/F
1997 Season	.262	144	558	74	146	27	6	12	66	43	89	6	12	22	13	.317	.396	1	6	9	2187	3.52	216	166	1.30
Last Five Years	.284	708	2885	460	820	134	25	77	322	224	365	16	52	162	49	.336	.428	21	11	29	11172	3.53	1219	859	1.42

1997 Season

	Avg	AB	H	2B	3B	HR	RBI	BB	SO	OBP	SLG		Avg	AB	H	2B	3B	HR	RBI	BB	SO	OBP	SLG
vs. Left	.261	138	36	8	1	5	18	11	23	.315	.442	First Pitch	.409	88	36	6	3	4	11	0	0	.418	.682
vs. Right	.262	420	110	19	5	7	48	32	66	.317	.381	Ahead in Count	.277	130	36	4	2	4	24	23	0	.382	.431
Groundball	.212	104	22	8	1	1	8	9	18	.286	.337	Behind in Count	.215	237	51	9	1	2	19	0	73	.215	.287
Flyball	.274	84	23	7	1	0	6	16	.319	.381	Two Strikes	.160	231	37	5	1	3	14	20	89	.234	.229
Home	.255	255	65	13	2	5	31	21	45	.313	.380	Batting #1	.249	354	88	18	4	6	36	31	55	.312	.373
Away	.267	303	81	14	4	7	35	22	44	.319	.409	Batting #9	.258	159	41	7	2	5	24	10	27	.303	.421
Day	.309	181	56	11	0	5	31	18	35	.382	.453	Other	.378	45	17	2	0	1	6	2	7	.404	.489
Night	.239	377	90	16	6	7	35	25	54	.284	.369	March/April	.234	64	15	3	1	1	4	8	5	.329	.359
Grass	.259	471	122	21	5	10	55	36	77	.313	.389	May	.198	96	19	2	0	1	8	6	12	.255	.250
Turf	.276	87	24	6	1	2	11	7	12	.333	.437	June	.333	90	30	5	0	0	16	8	14	.376	.389
Pre-All Star	.260	273	71	11	2	3	32	23	44	.319	.330	July	.257	113	29	8	1	4	16	9	24	.312	.451
Post-All Star	.263	285	75	16	5	10	34	20	55	.314	.460	August	.255	102	26	3	4	4	11	9	21	.327	.480
Scoring Posn	.303	132	40	8	1	4	56	14	16	.361	.470	Sept/Oct	.290	93	27	6	0	2	11	3	13	.306	.419
Close & Late	.271	70	19	3	0	3	12	3	12	.293	.443	vs. AL	.247	502	124	25	6	11	62	39	82	.303	.386
None on/out	.287	174	50	7	3	5	5	17	25	.354	.448	vs. NL	.393	56	22	2	0	1	4	4	7	.443	.482

1997 By Position

Position	Avg	AB	H	2B	3B	HR	RBI	BB	SO	OBP	SLG	G	GS	Innings	PO	A	E	DP	Fld Pct	Rng Fctr	In Zone	Outs	Zone Rtg	MLB Zone
As cf	.262	558	146	27	6	12	66	43	89	.317	.396	144	144	1250.2	357	7	3	3	.992	2.62	409	340	.831	.815

Last Five Years

	Avg	AB	H	2B	3B	HR	RBI	BB	SO	OBP	SLG
vs. Left	.284	742	211	43	7	29	89	59	94	.337	.478
vs. Right	.284	2143	609	91	18	48	233	165	271	.336	.411
Groundball	.282	763	215	33	5	10	63	67	81	.342	.377
Flyball	.283	466	132	24	5	18	62	33	72	.329	.472
Home	.285	1366	389	64	12	34	152	104	177	.336	.424
Away	.284	1519	431	70	13	43	170	120	188	.336	.432
Day	.275	901	248	44	6	26	109	68	126	.328	.424
Night	.288	1984	572	90	19	51	213	156	239	.340	.430
Grass	.271	1780	482	82	19	44	180	143	228	.326	.412
Turf	.306	1105	338	52	6	33	142	81	137	.352	.453
Pre-All Star	.282	1605	453	79	12	39	181	126	208	.334	.419
Post-All Star	.287	1280	367	55	13	38	141	98	157	.338	.439
Scoring Posn	.274	667	183	32	6	19	251	76	81	.340	.426
Close & Late	.311	418	130	18	2	10	66	32	67	.359	.435
None on/out	.287	994	285	51	13	30	30	64	112	.332	.435

	Avg	AB	H	2B	3B	HR	RBI	BB	SO	OBP	SLG
First Pitch	.325	425	138	20	8	14	45	15	0	.352	.508
Ahead in Count	.325	738	240	40	8	22	100	122	0	.417	.491
Behind in Count	.230	1196	275	42	6	23	101	0	308	.231	.333
Two Strikes	.210	1150	241	31	6	17	96	87	365	.267	.291
Batting #1	.283	1983	561	88	20	55	198	154	239	.335	.431
Batting #3	.282	660	186	34	3	15	88	54	88	.336	.411
Other	.302	242	73	12	2	7	36	16	38	.343	.455
March/April	.247	385	95	16	4	9	46	31	56	.307	.379
May	.275	505	139	24	3	12	62	36	59	.324	.406
June	.332	542	180	32	4	14	56	48	69	.384	.483
July	.254	547	139	25	4	19	70	37	70	.313	.419
August	.276	500	138	19	6	11	50	40	69	.333	.404
Sept/Oct	.318	406	129	18	4	12	49	22	42	.349	.470
vs. AL	.247	502	124	25	6	11	62	39	82	.303	.386
vs. NL	.292	2383	696	109	19	66	260	185	283	.343	.437

Batter vs. Pitcher (career)

Hits Best Against	Avg	AB	H	2B	3B	HR	RBI	BB	SO	OBP	SLG
Jon Lieber	.667	9	6	0	0	0	3	2	1	.727	.667
Pedro Martinez	.571	21	12	3	1	1	2	2	2	.609	.952
Greg Swindell	.500	22	11	2	1	5	9	1	3	.522	1.364
Steve Reed	.500	10	5	1	1	0	0	2	1	.583	.800
Todd Stottlemyre	.364	11	4	0	0	3	3	1	2	.417	1.182

Hits Worst Against	Avg	AB	H	2B	3B	HR	RBI	BB	SO	OBP	SLG
Roger Clemens	.000	8	0	0	0	0	0	2	2	.273	.000
Pat Rapp	.071	28	2	0	0	0	0	2	5	.133	.071
F. Valenzuela	.111	27	3	1	0	0	2	1	3	.143	.148
Mike Maddux	.154	13	2	0	0	0	0	0	5	.154	.154
Doug Brocail	.154	13	2	0	0	0	1	0	1	.154	.154

Buddy Groom — Athletics
Age 32 – Pitches Left (groundball pitcher)

	ERA	W	L	Sv	G	GS	IP	BB	SO	Avg	H	2B	3B	HR	RBI	OBP	SLG	GF	IR	IRS	Hld	SvOp	SB	CS	GB	FB	G/F
1997 Season	5.15	2	2	3	78	0	64.2	24	45	.292	75	13	1	9	35	.347	.455	7	72	15	12	5	5	4	100	68	1.47
Last Five Years	5.24	9	10	7	246	8	266.1	116	179	.300	320	51	3	33	169	.370	.447	52	195	54	34	13	24	9	434	256	1.70

1997 Season

	ERA	W	L	Sv	G	GS	IP	H	HR	BB	SO
Home	6.31	0	0	1	41	0	35.2	44	6	17	23
Away	3.72	2	2	2	37	0	29.0	31	3	7	22
Day	6.62	1	1	1	38	0	34.0	41	8	14	21
Night	3.52	1	1	2	40	0	30.2	34	1	10	24
Grass	4.98	2	1	3	71	0	59.2	67	9	21	42
Turf	7.20	0	1	0	7	0	5.0	8	0	3	3
March/April	9.95	1	1	0	13	0	6.1	14	1	4	6
May	1.74	0	0	0	11	0	10.1	12	1	3	4
June	5.40	0	0	2	13	0	10.0	12	0	3	6
July	5.14	0	1	1	14	0	14.0	10	1	4	13
August	3.45	1	0	0	14	0	15.2	13	3	2	11
Sept/Oct	8.64	0	0	0	13	0	8.1	14	3	8	5
Starter	0.00	0	0	0	0	0	0.0	0	0	0	0
Reliever	5.15	2	2	3	78	0	64.2	75	9	24	45
0 Days rest (Relief)	7.79	2	0	1	22	0	17.1	23	2	6	15
1 or 2 Days rest	3.62	0	2	2	41	0	37.1	38	4	17	23
3+ Days rest	6.30	0	0	0	15	0	10.0	14	3	1	7
vs. AL	5.43	2	2	1	70	0	56.1	69	9	20	41
vs. NL	3.24	0	0	2	8	0	8.1	6	0	4	4
Pre-All Star	4.40	1	1	3	40	0	30.2	39	2	11	18
Post-All Star	5.82	1	1	0	38	0	34.0	36	7	13	27

	Avg	AB	H	2B	3B	HR	RBI	BB	SO	OBP	SLG
vs. Left	.231	121	28	5	0	3	14	12	26	.296	.347
vs. Right	.346	136	47	8	1	6	21	12	19	.393	.551
Inning 1-6	.318	88	28	5	0	2	15	7	12	.361	.443
Inning 7+	.278	169	47	8	1	7	20	17	33	.340	.462
None on	.315	127	40	6	1	8	8	13	23	.379	.567
Runners on	.269	130	35	7	0	1	27	11	22	.317	.346
Scoring Posn	.208	77	16	3	0	0	22	7	15	.261	.247
Close & Late	.355	62	22	2	0	4	10	7	11	.414	.581
None on/out	.323	62	21	2	1	4	4	2	10	.359	.597
vs. 1st Batr (relief)	.257	70	18	1	0	1	10	6	14	.308	.314
1st Inning Pitched	.277	188	52	8	1	8	27	16	36	.329	.457
First 15 Pitches	.286	175	50	8	1	8	24	16	34	.340	.480
Pitch 16-30	.338	65	22	5	0	1	7	5	9	.386	.462
Pitch 31-45	.231	13	3	0	0	0	3	1	1	.286	.231
Pitch 46+	.000	4	0	0	0	0	1	2	1	.286	.000
First Pitch	.405	37	15	2	0	3	8	1	0	.410	.703
Ahead in Count	.242	120	29	5	1	2	12	0	37	.238	.350
Behind in Count	.340	50	17	5	0	2	10	6	0	.404	.560
Two Strikes	.240	125	30	4	0	3	13	17	45	.329	.344
Pre-All Star	.315	124	39	8	1	2	18	11	18	.362	.444
Post-All Star	.271	133	36	5	0	7	17	13	27	.333	.466

Last Five Years

	ERA	W	L	Sv	G	GS	IP	H	HR	BB	SO
Home	6.43	1	2	1	125	4	133.0	180	17	68	94
Away	4.05	8	8	6	121	4	133.1	140	16	48	85
Day	6.62	4	4	2	101	3	104.2	147	22	44	79
Night	4.34	5	6	5	145	5	161.2	173	11	72	100
Grass	5.29	8	5	7	216	8	235.0	288	32	99	160
Turf	4.88	1	5	0	30	0	31.1	32	1	17	19
March/April	5.24	2	1	1	30	0	22.1	32	3	12	19
May	4.87	2	2	2	47	6	64.2	81	8	30	43
June	4.01	1	1	2	49	1	51.2	50	5	19	24
July	4.53	2	3	1	45	0	47.2	59	3	14	31
August	6.75	2	3	1	42	1	53.1	66	8	18	42
Sept/Oct	6.75	0	0	0	33	0	26.2	32	6	23	20
Starter	6.69	1	2	0	8	8	35.0	50	3	16	16
Reliever	5.02	8	8	7	238	0	231.1	270	30	100	163
0 Days rest (Relief)	5.85	2	2	2	55	0	47.2	62	5	16	29
1 or 2 Days rest	4.71	3	6	3	117	0	120.1	132	13	60	85
3+ Days rest	4.97	3	0	2	66	0	63.1	76	12	24	49
vs. AL	5.19	8	8	5	224	8	243.0	288	31	106	163
vs. NL	5.79	1	2	2	22	0	23.1	32	2	10	16
Pre-All Star	4.62	5	5	6	140	7	156.0	186	16	66	93
Post-All Star	6.12	4	5	1	106	1	110.1	134	17	50	86

	Avg	AB	H	2B	3B	HR	RBI	BB	SO	OBP	SLG
vs. Left	.273	395	108	17	0	10	60	39	73	.339	.392
vs. Right	.316	670	212	34	3	23	109	77	106	.388	.479
Inning 1-6	.312	417	130	24	1	9	74	52	56	.385	.439
Inning 7+	.293	648	190	27	2	24	95	64	123	.360	.452
None on	.290	534	155	26	3	18	18	46	98	.352	.451
Runners on	.311	531	165	25	0	15	151	70	81	.387	.443
Scoring Posn	.295	312	92	19	0	9	134	53	46	.388	.442
Close & Late	.323	223	72	13	0	9	43	27	46	.391	.502
None on/out	.296	240	71	10	2	7	7	17	41	.350	.442
vs. 1st Batr (relief)	.303	218	66	8	1	5	38	17	43	.353	.417
1st Inning Pitched	.291	678	197	29	3	25	113	75	126	.360	.453
First 15 Pitches	.301	599	180	28	3	20	90	60	111	.364	.457
Pitch 16-30	.286	262	75	11	0	9	36	37	38	.377	.431
Pitch 31-45	.333	99	33	6	0	2	21	9	17	.393	.455
Pitch 46+	.305	105	32	6	0	2	22	10	13	.364	.419
First Pitch	.397	151	60	8	0	4	28	0	0	.434	.530
Ahead in Count	.247	478	118	18	3	13	64	0	147	.252	.379
Behind in Count	.371	232	86	18	0	7	43	51	0	.479	.539
Two Strikes	.232	492	114	17	2	15	73	55	179	.312	.366
Pre-All Star	.300	620	186	31	2	16	87	66	93	.368	.434
Post-All Star	.301	445	134	20	1	17	82	50	86	.373	.465

Pitcher vs. Batter (career)

Pitches Best Vs.	Avg	AB	H	2B	3B	HR	RBI	BB	SO	OBP	SLG	Pitches Worst Vs.	Avg	AB	H	2B	3B	HR	RBI	BB	SO	OBP	SLG
Robin Ventura	.077	13	1	0	0	0	1	0	4	.071	.077	Paul O'Neill	.750	12	9	3	0	1	7	1	0	.769	1.250
Ozzie Guillen	.091	11	1	0	0	0	0	0	1	.091	.091	Frank Thomas	.667	6	4	0	0	1	3	9	0	.867	1.167
Will Clark	.100	10	1	0	0	0	0	2	1	.250	.100	John Valentin	.647	17	11	1	0	1	6	0	0	.647	.882
Troy O'Leary	.125	8	1	0	0	0	1	3	4	.364	.125	Jim Thome	.444	9	4	0	0	2	3	2	2	.545	1.111
Mike Devereaux	.182	11	2	1	0	0	1	0	2	.182	.273	Tim Raines	.400	10	4	1	0	1	1	2	0	.500	.800

Kevin Gross — Angels
Age 37 – Pitches Right

	ERA	W	L	Sv	G	GS	IP	BB	SO	Avg	H	2B	3B	HR	RBI	OBP	SLG	GF	IR	IRS	Hld	SvOp	SB	CS	GB	FB	G/F
1997 Season	6.75	2	1	0	12	3	25.1	20	20	.313	30	3	1	4	17	.429	.490	3	2	2	0	1	2	24	29	0.83
Last Five Years	4.68	44	44	1	129	107	698.0	276	478	.280	767	126	15	76	346	.348	.421	9	16	4	4		65	31	1009	721	1.40

1997 Season

	ERA	W	L	Sv	G	GS	IP	H	HR	BB	SO		Avg	AB	H	2B	3B	HR	RBI	BB	SO	OBP	SLG
Home	2.84	2	0	0	6	1	12.2	8	0	10	15	vs. Left	.268	41	11	1	1	2	7	13	11	.436	.488
Away	10.66	0	1	0	6	2	12.2	22	4	10	5	vs. Right	.345	55	19	2	0	2	10	7	9	.422	.491

Last Five Years

	ERA	W	L	Sv	G	GS	IP	H	HR	SO		Avg	AB	H	2B	3B	HR	RBI	BB	SO	OBP	SLG
Home	4.22	24	17	1	63	50	337.0	344	32	126	242	vs. Left	.280	1399	392	62	9	39	175	169	239	.357	.421
Away	5.11	20	27	0	66	57	361.0	423	44	150	236	vs. Right	.280	1338	375	64	6	37	171	107	239	.338	.420
Day	4.64	9	8	0	27	22	141.2	152	10	56	81	Inning 1-6	.283	2300	652	106	14	70	322	230	423	.350	.433
Night	4.69	35	36	1	102	85	556.1	615	66	220	397	Inning 7+	.263	437	115	20	1	6	24	46	55	.335	.355
Grass	4.67	40	35	1	110	92	599.0	652	64	239	402	None on	.282	1522	429	78	9	52	52	147	261	.349	.447
Turf	4.73	4	9	0	19	15	99.0	115	12	37	76	Runners on	.278	1215	338	48	6	24	294	129	217	.346	.387
March/April	6.49	5	6	0	17	16	86.0	107	13	45	65	Scoring Posn	.287	662	190	27	2	15	269	92	136	.366	.402
May	5.14	9	7	0	21	20	117.1	138	12	48	94	Close & Late	.275	182	50	9	0	0	12	24	27	.361	.324
June	4.14	11	10	0	25	23	156.2	161	14	54	106	None on/out	.282	694	196	38	4	25	25	64	105	.348	.457
July	5.55	5	11	0	29	20	128.0	156	15	63	77	vs. 1st Batr (relief)	.235	17	4	0	0	0	1	4	4	.364	.235
August	3.53	7	7	0	21	16	119.2	116	10	35	85	1st Inning Pitched	.268	481	129	20	3	10	73	72	94	.362	.385
Sept/Oct	3.59	7	3	0	16	12	90.1	89	12	31	51	First 15 Pitches	.267	359	96	15	3	7	30	44	59	.348	.384
Starter	4.84	41	42	0	107	107	656.2	729	75	254	450	Pitch 16-30	.302	424	128	26	1	14	64	55	79	.387	.467
Reliever	2.18	3	2	1	22	0	41.1	38	1	22	28	Pitch 31-45	.263	419	110	10	2	11	54	34	88	.322	.375
0 Days rest (Relief)	0.00	0	0	0	1	0	1.0	0	0	0	0	Pitch 46+	.282	1535	433	75	9	44	198	143	252	.344	.429
1 or 2 Days rest	2.01	1	2	1	13	0	22.1	22	0	14	17	First Pitch	.359	384	138	13	4	11	50	14	0	.382	.500
3+ Days rest	2.50	2	0	0	8	0	18.0	16	1	8	11	Ahead in Count	.222	1202	267	42	5	12	111	0	381	.226	.295
vs. AL	5.34	22	23	0	69	51	334.0	372	48	155	202	Behind in Count	.357	599	214	41	5	32	115	146	0	.481	.603
vs. NL	4.08	22	21	1	60	56	364.0	395	28	121	276	Two Strikes	.197	1209	238	42	3	15	97	116	478	.270	.274
Pre-All Star	5.11	27	27	1	74	66	410.1	464	46	173	300	Pre-All Star	.287	1616	464	83	9	46	219	173	300	.359	.435
Post-All Star	4.07	17	17	0	55	41	287.2	303	30	103	178	Post-All Star	.270	1121	303	43	6	30	127	103	178	.331	.400

Pitcher vs. Batter (since 1984)

Pitches Best Vs.	Avg	AB	H	2B	3B	HR	RBI	BB	SO	OBP	SLG	Pitches Worst Vs.	Avg	AB	H	2B	3B	HR	RBI	BB	SO	OBP	SLG
Scott Servais	.000	11	0	0	0	0	0	0	0	.000	.000	Omar Vizquel	.750	12	9	2	0	0	3	0	0	.750	.917
Chris Gomez	.000	10	0	0	0	0	0	1	5	.091	.000	Edgar Martinez	.545	11	6	2	0	2	3	9	0	.762	1.273
Reggie Sanders	.050	20	1	0	0	0	0	2	6	.136	.050	Pete Incaviglia	.500	12	6	0	0	2	5	0	2	.500	1.000
Craig Biggio	.071	42	3	0	0	0	2	2	8	.114	.071	Brady Anderson	.500	10	5	1	0	4	5	1	2	.583	1.800
Kenny Lofton	.071	14	1	0	0	0	0	0	2	.067	.071	Mark McGwire	.455	11	5	0	0	4	7	2	2	.684	1.545

Mark Grudzielanek — Expos
Age 28 – Bats Right

	Avg	G	AB	R	H	2B	3B	HR	RBI	BB	SO	HBP	GDP	SB	CS	OBP	SLG	IBB	SH	SF	#Pit	#P/PA	GB	FB	G/F
1997 Season	.273	156	649	76	177	54	3	4	51	23	76	10	14	25	9	.307	.384	0	3	3	2263	3.29	282	164	1.72
Career (1995-1997)	.282	387	1575	202	444	100	9	11	120	63	206	26	30	66	19	.319	.378	7	7	6	5582	3.33	686	379	1.81

1997 Season

	Avg	AB	H	2B	3B	HR	RBI	BB	SO	OBP	SLG		Avg	AB	H	2B	3B	HR	RBI	BB	SO	OBP	SLG
vs. Left	.224	147	33	10	0	1	12	5	16	.252	.313	First Pitch	.316	117	37	11	2	1	7	0	0	.333	.470
vs. Right	.287	502	144	44	3	3	39	18	60	.323	.404	Ahead in Count	.313	134	42	14	1	1	9	15	0	.384	.455
Groundball	.283	138	39	11	1	0	10	5	16	.322	.377	Behind in Count	.231	303	70	18	0	1	22	0	69	.243	.300
Flyball	.300	70	21	4	0	0	5	4	9	.338	.357	Two Strikes	.202	253	51	15	0	1	18	8	76	.233	.273
Home	.285	330	94	32	1	1	27	7	44	.308	.397	Batting #1	.258	457	118	32	1	2	33	18	55	.295	.346
Away	.260	319	83	22	2	3	24	16	32	.305	.370	Batting #6	.311	90	28	15	2	0	5	2	10	.326	.522
Day	.295	210	62	15	0	2	18	8	18	.329	.395	Other	.304	102	31	7	0	2	13	3	11	.339	.431
Night	.262	439	115	39	3	2	33	15	58	.296	.378	March/April	.337	98	33	12	0	0	10	2	6	.350	.459
Grass	.277	224	62	12	1	3	14	12	20	.321	.379	May	.270	111	30	7	1	1	10	8	13	.341	.378
Turf	.271	425	115	42	2	1	37	11	56	.299	.386	June	.261	111	29	10	0	1	9	6	14	.322	.378
Pre-All Star	.289	346	100	32	1	2	32	17	37	.337	.405	July	.245	102	25	8	1	0	8	3	11	.267	.343
Post-All Star	.254	303	77	22	2	2	19	6	39	.271	.360	August	.274	113	31	9	1	2	7	3	10	.297	.425
Scoring Posn	.237	139	33	10	0	1	46	8	13	.283	.331	Sept/Oct	.254	114	29	8	0	0	7	1	22	.263	.325
Close & Late	.296	98	29	10	0	2	14	7	13	.346	.459	vs. AL	.290	62	18	5	0	1	6	2	8	.323	.419
None on/out	.271	240	65	18	3	1		4	34	.271	.379	vs. NL	.271	587	159	49	3	3	45	21	68	.305	.380

1997 By Position

Position	Avg	AB	H	2B	3B	HR	RBI	BB	SO	OBP	SLG	G	GS	Innings	PO	A	E	DP	Fld Pct	Rng Fctr	In Zone	Zone Outs	Zone Rtg	MLB Zone
As ss	.273	649	177	54	3	4	51	23	76	.307	.384	156	156	1368.1	237	446	32	99	.955	4.49	512	474	.926	.937

180

Career (1995-1997)

	Avg	AB	H	2B	3B	HR	RBI	BB	SO	OBP	SLG		Avg	AB	H	2B	3B	HR	RBI	BB	SO	OBP	SLG
vs. Left	.280	350	98	22	1	2	26	12	49	.309	.366	First Pitch	.320	269	86	22	4	6	23	5	0	.341	.498
vs. Right	.282	1225	346	78	8	9	94	51	157	.322	.381	Ahead in Count	.352	315	111	30	1	3	27	40	0	.426	.483
Groundball	.249	345	86	16	3	3	27	13	53	.290	.339	Behind in Count	.228	738	168	28	1	1	43	0	185	.244	.272
Flyball	.329	225	74	16	2	0	10	9	37	.355	.418	Two Strikes	.208	638	133	21	2	1	43	18	206	.244	.252
Home	.308	746	230	60	5	7	64	28	89	.343	.430	Batting #1	.281	1112	312	65	5	8	77	38	141	.313	.370
Away	.258	829	214	40	4	4	56	35	117	.298	.331	Batting #8	.294	136	40	4	1	1	19	11	23	.356	.360
Day	.297	498	148	36	1	2	35	21	60	.334	.386	Other	.281	327	92	31	3	2	24	14	42	.324	.413
Night	.275	1077	296	64	8	9	85	42	146	.312	.374	March/April	.345	226	78	19	0	3	26	6	21	.369	.469
Grass	.259	580	150	24	3	3	38	27	78	.299	.326	May	.292	288	84	16	4	4	23	16	38	.348	.417
Turf	.295	995	294	76	6	8	82	36	128	.331	.408	June	.259	282	73	16	2	1	19	14	33	.307	.340
Pre-All Star	.298	856	255	56	6	8	73	37	101	.340	.405	July	.271	214	58	15	2	0	14	7	28	.294	.360
Post-All Star	.263	719	189	44	3	4	47	26	105	.295	.345	August	.254	236	60	15	1	2	12	11	30	.296	.352
Scoring Posn	.251	347	87	15	0	1	104	28	51	.314	.303	Sept/Oct	.277	329	91	19	0	1	26	9	56	.302	.343
Close & Late	.297	239	71	13	1	3	22	16	41	.350	.397	vs. AL	.290	62	18	5	0	1	6	2	8	.323	.419
None on/out	.295	600	177	37	6	4	43	13	83	.319	.397	vs. NL	.282	1513	426	95	9	10	114	61	198	.319	.376

Batter vs. Pitcher (career)

Hits Best Against	Avg	AB	H	2B	3B	HR	RBI	BB	SO	OBP	SLG	Hits Worst Against	Avg	AB	H	2B	3B	HR	RBI	BB	SO	OBP	SLG
Mike Williams	.556	9	5	0	0	0	0	3	1	.667	.556	Armando Reynoso	.000	10	0	0	0	0	0	0	1	.167	.000
Pedro Astacio	.500	20	10	2	1	0	0	0	1	.500	.500	Dave Burba	.067	15	1	0	0	0	0	0	0	.067	.067
Dave Mlicki	.500	12	6	1	0	0	1	1	1	.538	.583	Jamey Wright	.067	15	1	0	0	0	2	0	0	.067	.067
Bobby Jones	.450	20	9	2	0	0	1	1	2	.476	.550	Tom Glavine	.133	30	4	1	0	0	2	0	4	.129	.167
Terry Mulholland	.346	26	9	3	1	1	4	0	1	.346	.654	Tom Candiotti	.154	13	2	0	0	0	0	0	1	.154	.154

Ken Grundt — Red Sox
Age 28 – Pitches Left

	ERA	W	L	Sv	G	GS	IP	BB	SO	Avg	H	2B	3B	HR	RBI	OBP	SLG	GF	IR	IRS	Hld	SvOp	SB	CS	GB	FB	G/F
1997 Season	9.00	0	0	0	2	0	3.0	0	0	.357	5	2	1	0	3	.357	.643	0	0	0	0	0	0	0	3	4	0.75
Career (1996-1997)	10.80	0	0	0	3	0	3.1	0	0	.375	6	3	1	0	3	.375	.688	0	0	0	0	0	0	0	4	4	1.00

1997 Season

	ERA	W	L	Sv	G	GS	IP	H	HR	BB	SO		Avg	AB	H	2B	3B	HR	RBI	BB	SO	OBP	SLG
Home	0.00	0	0	0	0	0	0.0	0	0	0	0	vs. Left	.500	6	3	1	1	0	1	0	0	.500	1.000
Away	9.00	0	0	0	2	0	3.0	5	0	0	0	vs. Right	.250	8	2	1	0	0	2	0	0	.250	.375

Eddie Guardado — Twins
Age 27 – Pitches Left (flyball pitcher)

	ERA	W	L	Sv	G	GS	IP	BB	SO	Avg	H	2B	3B	HR	RBI	OBP	SLG	GF	IR	IRS	Hld	SvOp	SB	CS	GB	FB	G/F
1997 Season	3.91	0	4	1	69	0	46.0	17	54	.251	45	7	1	7	30	.322	.419	20	57	17	13	1	6	1	34	57	0.60
Career (1993-1997)	5.47	13	28	7	226	25	322.2	135	253	.281	354	75	11	48	208	.350	.473	49	160	52	36	13	27	12	287	505	0.57

1997 Season

	ERA	W	L	Sv	G	GS	IP	H	HR	BB	SO		Avg	AB	H	2B	3B	HR	RBI	BB	SO	OBP	SLG
Home	3.00	0	1	0	35	0	24.0	22	3	8	30	vs. Left	.253	75	19	4	1	4	16	6	26	.309	.493
Away	4.91	0	3	1	34	0	22.0	23	4	9	24	vs. Right	.250	104	26	3	0	3	14	11	28	.331	.365
Day	3.57	0	2	0	22	0	17.2	12	3	5	19	Inning 1-6	.133	15	2	1	0	0	1	1	2	.188	.200
Night	4.13	0	2	1	47	0	28.1	33	4	12	35	Inning 7+	.262	164	43	6	1	7	29	16	52	.333	.439
Grass	4.74	0	2	0	28	0	19.0	19	4	7	20	None on	.244	86	21	5	0	5	5	10	29	.330	.477
Turf	3.33	0	2	1	41	0	27.0	26	3	10	34	Runners on	.258	93	24	2	1	2	25	7	25	.314	.366
March/April	6.43	0	0	0	13	0	7.0	7	2	3	8	Scoring Posn	.288	59	17	2	1	2	25	4	15	.314	.458
May	2.25	0	1	0	14	0	8.0	6	1	2	11	Close & Late	.277	47	13	4	1	2	9	3	20	.314	.532
June	4.15	0	1	0	9	0	4.1	4	2	2	8	None on/out	.229	35	8	3	0	0	0	5	13	.325	.314
July	2.70	0	1	1	12	0	13.1	13	1	3	16	vs. 1st Batr (relief)	.242	62	15	2	1	1	10	5	20	.294	.355
August	2.08	0	1	0	12	0	8.2	6	0	3	6	1st Inning Pitched	.259	162	42	6	1	6	28	16	49	.331	.420
Sept/Oct	9.64	0	0	0	9	0	4.2	9	1	4	5	First 15 Pitches	.255	137	35	6	1	7	24	12	40	.322	.467
Starter	0.00	0	0	0	0	0	0.0	0	0	0	0	Pitch 16-30	.216	37	8	0	0	0	5	4	13	.293	.216
Reliever	3.91	0	4	1	69	0	46.0	45	7	17	54	Pitch 31-45	.500	4	2	1	0	0	1	0	0	.500	.750
0 Days rest (Relief)	3.29	0	2	1	23	0	13.2	12	2	4	17	Pitch 46+	.000	1	0	0	0	0	0	1	1	.500	.000
1 or 2 Days rest	6.19	0	1	0	27	0	16.0	22	3	4	20	First Pitch	.500	26	13	1	0	4	12	1	0	.552	1.000
3+ Days rest	2.20	0	1	0	19	0	16.1	11	2	9	17	Ahead in Count	.181	105	19	3	0	1	9	0	49	.181	.238
vs. AL	4.01	0	2	1	63	0	42.2	42	6	16	53	Behind in Count	.375	24	9	2	1	1	6	8	0	.531	.667
vs. NL	2.70	0	2	0	6	0	3.1	3	1	1	1	Two Strikes	.126	103	13	1	0	1	7	8	54	.189	.165
Pre-All Star	4.22	0	3	0	39	0	21.1	20	6	7	27	Pre-All Star	.247	81	20	2	0	6	18	7	27	.319	.494
Post-All Star	3.65	0	1	1	30	0	24.2	25	1	10	27	Post-All Star	.255	98	25	5	1	1	12	10	27	.324	.357

Career (1993-1997)

	ERA	W	L	Sv	G	GS	IP	H	HR	BB	SO		Avg	AB	H	2B	3B	HR	RBI	BB	SO	OBP	SLG
Home	5.08	7	12	4	113	9	150.2	161	23	62	117	vs. Left	.245	400	98	15	5	10	60	23	100	.286	.383
Away	5.81	6	16	3	113	16	172.0	193	25	73	136	vs. Right	.298	859	256	60	6	38	148	112	153	.378	.515
Day	5.32	8	8	2	75	9	110.0	125	20	43	80	Inning 1-6	.303	646	196	50	8	24	114	64	88	.363	.517
Night	5.54	5	20	5	151	16	212.2	229	28	92	173	Inning 7+	.258	613	158	25	3	24	94	71	165	.336	.426
Grass	5.86	4	13	2	96	14	165.0	165	24	63	112	None on	.264	697	184	43	4	30	30	72	144	.335	.466
Turf	5.13	9	15	5	130	11	175.1	189	24	72	141	Runners on	.302	562	170	32	7	18	178	63	109	.368	.480
March/April	5.19	0	2	0	31	0	26.0	23	4	10	23	Scoring Posn	.329	331	109	22	6	12	162	38	63	.386	.541
May	4.01	2	5	0	35	3	51.2	52	6	21	47	Close & Late	.254	272	69	16	2	12	45	33	80	.332	.460
June	7.26	1	6	2	33	6	48.1	61	9	27	33	None on/out	.252	301	76	16	0	10	10	31	63	.322	.406
July	6.28	4	7	1	45	6	76.0	92	12	30	54	vs. 1st Batr (relief)	.212	179	38	4	1	6	27	15	49	.278	.346
August	4.52	4	5	1	43	6	69.2	73	10	21	49	1st Inning Pitched	.256	634	162	31	4	22	115	66	163	.328	.421

Career (1993-1997)

	ERA	W	L	Sv	G	GS	IP	H	HR	BB	SO		Avg	AB	H	2B	3B	HR	RBI	BB	SO	OBP	SLG
Sept/Oct	5.47	2	3	3	39	2	51.0	53	7	26	47	First 15 Pitches	.253	541	137	25	3	24	86	53	132	.322	.444
Starter	6.95	3	15	0	25	25	125.2	169	19	50	60	Pitch 16-30	.248	266	66	14	3	9	47	37	56	.339	.425
Reliever	4.52	10	13	7	201	0	197.0	185	29	85	193	Pitch 31-45	.245	159	39	8	0	5	17	14	26	.305	.390
0 Days rest (Relief)	3.93	4	5	3	65	0	55.0	43	8	28	55	Pitch 46+	.382	293	112	28	5	10	58	31	39	.435	.614
1 or 2 Days rest	4.85	6	6	4	86	0	89.0	85	14	32	88	First Pitch	.445	155	69	12	0	13	48	6	0	.462	.774
3+ Days rest	4.58	0	2	0	50	0	53.0	57	7	25	50	Ahead in Count	.222	632	140	30	3	14	80	0	211	.223	.345
vs. AL	5.50	13	26	7	220	25	319.1	351	47	134	252	Behind in Count	.344	250	86	18	6	15	53	66	0	.475	.644
vs. NL	2.70	0	2	0	6	0	3.1	3	1	1	1	Two Strikes	.207	638	132	32	2	14	71	63	253	.280	.329
Pre-All Star	5.47	5	16	2	114	13	156.1	171	24	64	116	Pre-All Star	.282	607	171	37	6	24	104	64	116	.349	.481
Post-All Star	5.46	8	12	5	112	12	166.1	183	24	71	137	Post-All Star	.281	652	183	38	5	24	104	71	137	.351	.465

Pitcher vs. Batter (career)

Pitches Best Vs.	Avg	AB	H	2B	3B	HR	RBI	BB	SO	OBP	SLG	Pitches Worst Vs.	Avg	AB	H	2B	3B	HR	RBI	BB	SO	OBP	SLG
Ken Griffey Jr	.000	11	0	0	0	0	0	0	7	.083	.000	Dean Palmer	.600	5	3	1	0	0	0	6	0	.818	.800
Brady Anderson	.143	14	2	1	0	0	0	2	3	.250	.214	Greg Gagne	.500	10	5	4	0	0	4	1	1	.545	.900
Rafael Palmeiro	.167	12	2	1	0	0	1	0	3	.167	.250	Bernie Williams	.429	14	6	2	0	2	5	2	2	.500	1.000
Omar Vizquel	.182	11	2	0	0	0	2	0	0	.182	.182	Jim Edmonds	.400	10	4	1	0	1	5	0	4	.364	.800
Will Clark	.214	14	3	0	0	0	1	3		.267	.214	Chili Davis	.333	12	4	0	0	2	5			.400	.833

Mark Gubicza — Angels
Age 35 – Pitches Right (groundball pitcher)

	ERA	W	L	Sv	G	GS	IP	BB	SO	Avg	H	2B	3B	HR	RBI	OBP	SLG	CG	ShO	Sup	QS	#P/S	SB	CS	GB	FB	G/F
1997 Season	25.07	0	1	0	2	2	4.2	3	5	.481	13	2	0	2	10	.533	.815	0	0	17.36	0	56	1	0	5	11	0.45
Last Five Years	4.55	28	44	2	125	82	571.2	168	280	.290	653	120	11	58	293	.341	.431	5	3	4.06	40	95	32	14	1020	488	2.09

1997 Season

	ERA	W	L	Sv	G	GS	IP	H	HR	BB	SO		Avg	AB	H	2B	3B	HR	RBI	BB	SO	OBP	SLG
Home	17.18	0	0	0	1	1	3.2	6	1		3	vs. Left	.417	12	5	1	0	1	5	2	3	.500	.750
Away	54.00	0	1	0	1	1	1.0	7	1	0	2	vs. Right	.533	15	8	2	0	1	5	1	2	.563	.867

Last Five Years

	ERA	W	L	Sv	G	GS	IP	H	HR	BB	SO		Avg	AB	H	2B	3B	HR	RBI	BB	SO	OBP	SLG
Home	4.40	17	23	2	72	45	335.2	366	33	106	172	vs. Left	.291	1183	344	62	8	24	154	93	115	.344	.418
Away	4.77	11	21	0	53	37	236.0	287	25	62	108	vs. Right	.290	1065	309	58	3	34	139	75	165	.338	.446
Day	4.35	9	14	1	40	26	184.1	225	22	43	81	Inning 1-6	.291	1803	524	100	10	49	241	119	210	.336	.439
Night	4.65	19	30	1	85	56	387.1	428	36	125	199	Inning 7+	.290	445	129	20	1	9	52	49	70	.358	.400
Grass	4.56	15	34	0	72	59	391.0	441	48	118	181	None on	.272	1307	355	66	5	32	32	90	159	.322	.403
Turf	4.53	13	10	2	53	23	180.2	212	10	50	99	Runners on	.317	941	298	54	6	26	261	78	121	.365	.470
March/April	6.86	2	10	0	16	16	78.2	113	11	26	32	Scoring Posn	.317	533	169	35	4	16	228	53	74	.367	.488
May	4.77	7	11	0	26	20	139.2	152	17	44	63	Close & Late	.298	228	68	10	1	2	27	34	34	.385	.377
June	3.58	5	11	0	29	19	146.0	143	15	36	80	None on/out	.275	582	160	34	2	15	15	25	67	.312	.418
July	4.32	6	3	1	22	12	85.1	94	7	26	52	vs. 1st Batr (relief)	.342	38	13	2	2	0	9	4	4	.405	.500
August	2.99	5	4	1	19	9	78.1	83	1	19	36	1st Inning Pitched	.276	474	131	27	2	5	64	28	68	.319	.373
Sept/Oct	6.18	3	5	0	13	6	43.2	68	7	17	17	First 75 Pitches	.293	1775	520	98	10	45	229	125	223	.342	.435
Starter	4.69	23	40	0	82	82	499.1	572	57	137	219	Pitch 76-90	.301	239	72	15	1	4	36	22	23	.356	.423
Reliever	3.61	5	4	2	43	0	72.1	81	1	31	61	Pitch 91-105	.271	166	45	5	0	7	22	15	22	.324	.428
0-3 Days Rest (Start)	4.70	6	7	0	14	14	88.0	94	8	26	43	Pitch 106+	.235	68	16	2	0	2	6	6	12	.307	.353
4 Days Rest	4.44	10	23	0	46	46	290.0	336	36	71	126	First Pitch	.318	337	107	18	0	4	45	14	0	.343	.407
5+ Days Rest	5.27	7	10	0	22	22	121.1	142	13	40	50	Ahead in Count	.224	765	171	31	4	12	70	0	205	.231	.322
vs. AL	4.55	28	44	2	125	82	571.2	653	58	168	280	Behind in Count	.360	619	223	45	1	28	115	76	0	.427	.572
vs. NL	0.00	0	0	0	0	0	0.0	0	0	0	0	Two Strikes	.219	866	190	37	6	12	78	78	280	.286	.318
Pre-All Star	4.70	17	34	0	80	60	398.2	441	44	115	196	Pre-All Star	.282	1564	441	77	9	44	210	115	196	.332	.427
Post-All Star	4.21	11	10	2	45	22	173.0	212	14	53	84	Post-All Star	.310	684	212	43	2	14	83	53	84	.360	.440

Pitcher vs. Batter (career)

Pitches Best Vs.	Avg	AB	H	2B	3B	HR	RBI	BB	SO	OBP	SLG	Pitches Worst Vs.	Avg	AB	H	2B	3B	HR	RBI	BB	SO	OBP	SLG
Stan Javier	.000	19	0	0	0	0	0	0	2	.000	.000	Jason Giambi	.615	13	8	1	0	2	4	1	0	.643	1.154
Marty Cordova	.000	15	0	0	0	0	1	1	1	.063	.000	Ken Griffey Jr	.524	21	11	2	0	2	8		3	.655	.905
Mike Gallego	.053	19	1	0	0	0	0	3	3	.182	.053	Fred McGriff	.500	20	10	3	0	4	4	3	3	.583	1.250
Matt Walbeck	.100	10	1	0	0	0	1		0	.182	.100	Rusty Greer	.500	14	7	2	1	0	2	2	0	.563	.786
Mark McLemore	.115	26	3	0	0	0	1		2	.148	.115	Albert Belle	.429	14	6	0	0	2	5	2	2	.500	.857

Vladimir Guerrero — Expos
Age 22 – Bats Right

	Avg	G	AB	R	H	2B	3B	HR	RBI	BB	SO	HBP	GDP	SB	CS	OBP	SLG	IBB	SH	SF	#Pit	#P/PA	GB	FB	G/F
1997 Season	.302	90	325	44	98	22	2	11	40	19	39	7	11	3	4	.350	.483	2	0	3	1082	3.06	143	81	1.77
Career (1996-1997)	.293	99	352	46	103	22	2	12	41	19	42	7	12	3	4	.339	.469	2	0	3	1160	3.04	156	87	1.79

1997 Season

	Avg	AB	H	2B	3B	HR	RBI	BB	SO	OBP	SLG		Avg	AB	H	2B	3B	HR	RBI	BB	SO	OBP	SLG
vs. Left	.301	93	28	5	1	4	12	6	10	.350	.505	First Pitch	.361	61	22	5	1	2	9	2	0	.385	.574
vs. Right	.302	232	70	17	1	7	28	13	29	.350	.474	Ahead in Count	.400	60	24	6	0	6	13	12	0	.500	.800
Groundball	.292	72	21	4	0	2	9	3	8	.342	.431	Behind in Count	.245	155	38	9	1	2	12	0	36	.263	.355
Flyball	.371	35	13	3	0	4	6	3	2	.421	.800	Two Strikes	.212	113	24	5	1	1	5	5	39	.256	.301
Home	.265	166	44	9	2	5	21	11	24	.315	.434	Batting #3	.284	116	33	9	2	5	16	3	16	.317	.526
Away	.340	159	54	13	0	6	19	8	15	.387	.535	Batting #6	.383	81	31	7	0	3	15	8	5	.452	.580
Day	.328	137	45	11	0	5	17	4	13	.357	.518	Other	.266	128	34	6	0	3	9	8	18	.312	.383
Night	.282	188	53	11	2	6	23	15	26	.346	.457	March/April	.000	0	0	0	0	0	0	0	0	.000	.000
Grass	.354	127	45	11	0	4	15	6	12	.399	.535	May	.282	85	24	6	0	1	12	8	14	.357	.388

1997 Season

	Avg	AB	H	2B	3B	HR	RBI	BB	SO	OBP	SLG		Avg	AB	H	2B	3B	HR	RBI	BB	SO	OBP	SLG
Turf	.268	198	53	11	2	7	25	13	27	.319	.449	June	.367	60	22	3	1	3	6	2	6	.387	.600
Pre-All Star	.323	167	54	10	2	6	26	13	20	.376	.515	July	.390	41	16	2	1	2	8	3	1	.435	.634
Post-All Star	.278	158	44	12	0	5	14	6	19	.321	.449	August	.275	102	28	10	0	2	8	5	12	.321	.431
Scoring Posn	.263	76	20	3	1	2	26	7	13	.337	.408	Sept/Oct	.216	37	8	1	0	3	6	1	6	.256	.486
Close & Late	.298	57	17	4	0	1	5	4	6	.365	.421	vs. AL	.303	33	10	3	0	3	7	1	3	.343	.667
None on/out	.328	64	21	4	1	0	0	2	6	.358	.422	vs. NL	.301	292	88	19	2	8	33	18	36	.351	.462

1997 By Position

Position	Avg	AB	H	2B	3B	HR	RBI	BB	SO	OBP	SLG	G	GS	Innings	PO	A	E	DP	Fld Pct	Rng Fctr	In Zone	Zone Outs	Zone Rtg	MLB Zone
As rf	.306	320	98	22	2	11	40	19	39	.355	.491	84	84	721.0	146	10	12	3	.929	1.95	164	141	.860	.813

Wilton Guerrero — Dodgers
Age 23 – Bats Both

	Avg	G	AB	R	H	2B	3B	HR	RBI	BB	SO	HBP	GDP	SB	CS	OBP	SLG	IBB	SH	SF	#Pit	#P/PA	GB	FB	G/F
1997 Season	.291	111	357	39	104	10	9	4	32	8	52	0	7	6	5	.305	.403	1	13	2	1251	3.29	154	70	2.20
Career (1996-1997)	.290	116	359	40	104	10	9	4	32	8	54	0	7	6	5	.304	.401	1	13	2	1258	3.29	154	70	2.20

1997 Season

	Avg	AB	H	2B	3B	HR	RBI	BB	SO	OBP	SLG		Avg	AB	H	2B	3B	HR	RBI	BB	SO	OBP	SLG
vs. Left	.220	91	20	1	1	3	8	2	12	.234	.352	First Pitch	.373	51	19	1	1	1	8	1	0	.377	.490
vs. Right	.316	266	84	9	8	1	24	6	40	.330	.421	Ahead in Count	.322	59	19	3	1	1	5	6	0	.385	.458
Groundball	.308	52	16	2	1	1	5	0	7	.302	.442	Behind in Count	.247	182	45	5	5	1	12	0	51	.247	.346
Flyball	.222	45	10	2	0	0	3	3	13	.271	.267	Two Strikes	.209	158	33	3	5	1	12	1	52	.213	.310
Home	.273	176	48	5	6	2	13	6	23	.297	.403	Batting #2	.297	118	35	1	3	3	15	2	18	.303	.432
Away	.309	181	56	5	3	2	19	2	29	.314	.403	Batting #8	.323	96	31	6	1	1	7	4	12	.350	.438
Day	.313	115	36	1	3	2	15	4	18	.333	.426	Other	.266	143	38	3	5	0	10	2	22	.276	.357
Night	.281	242	68	9	6	2	17	4	34	.291	.393	March/April	.275	80	22	3	1	7	3	11	.298	.425
Grass	.275	298	82	7	7	4	24	8	44	.293	.386	May	.307	88	27	3	3	0	6	0	14	.307	.409
Turf	.373	59	22	3	2	0	8	0	8	.367	.492	June	.299	77	23	3	2	1	10	3	9	.321	.429
Pre-All Star	.289	249	72	9	8	2	23	6	36	.304	.414	July	.286	56	16	1	1	1	7	0	6	.286	.393
Post-All Star	.296	108	32	1	1	2	9	2	16	.309	.380	August	.283	46	13	0	0	1	2	2	10	.313	.348
Scoring Posn	.321	81	26	2	4	0	26	1	9	.321	.444	Sept/Oct	.300	10	3	0	0	0	0	0	2	.300	.300
Close & Late	.250	60	15	2	2	0	4	2	15	.270	.350	vs. AL	.241	29	7	1	0	1	2	1	6	.258	.379
None on/out	.330	97	32	3	3	1	1	3	18	.350	.454	vs. NL	.296	328	97	9	9	3	30	7	46	.310	.405

1997 By Position

Position	Avg	AB	H	2B	3B	HR	RBI	BB	SO	OBP	SLG	G	GS	Innings	PO	A	E	DP	Fld Pct	Rng Fctr	In Zone	Zone Outs	Zone Rtg	MLB Zone
As Pinch Hitter	.250	12	3	0	1	0	0	1	4	.308	.417	13	0	---	---	---	---	---	---	---	---	---	---	---
As 2b	.291	330	96	10	8	4	31	7	48	.304	.406	91	84	739.2	141	221	4	24	.989	4.40	256	229	.895	.902

Giomar Guevara — Mariners
Age 25 – Bats Right

	Avg	G	AB	R	H	2B	3B	HR	RBI	BB	SO	HBP	GDP	SB	CS	OBP	SLG	IBB	SH	SF	#Pit	#P/PA	GB	FB	G/F
1997 Season	.000	5	4	0	0	0	0	0	0	0	2	0	0	0	0	.000	.000	0	0	0	17	4.25	1	1	1.00

1997 Season

	Avg	AB	H	2B	3B	HR	RBI	BB	SO	OBP	SLG		Avg	AB	H	2B	3B	HR	RBI	BB	SO	OBP	SLG
vs. Left	.000	1	0	0	0	0	0	0	1	.000	.000	Scoring Posn	.000	0	0	0	0	0	0	0	0	.000	.000
vs. Right	.000	3	0	0	0	0	0	0	1	.000	.000	Close & Late	.000	0	0	0	0	0	0	0	0	.000	.000

Jose Guillen — Pirates
Age 22 – Bats Right

	Avg	G	AB	R	H	2B	3B	HR	RBI	BB	SO	HBP	GDP	SB	CS	OBP	SLG	IBB	SH	SF	#Pit	#P/PA	GB	FB	G/F
1997 Season	.267	143	498	58	133	20	5	14	70	17	88	8	16	1	2	.300	.412	0	0	3	1645	3.13	222	121	1.83

1997 Season

	Avg	AB	H	2B	3B	HR	RBI	BB	SO	OBP	SLG		Avg	AB	H	2B	3B	HR	RBI	BB	SO	OBP	SLG
vs. Left	.263	99	26	4	0	3	13	6	16	.302	.394	First Pitch	.278	97	27	6	1	2	9	0	0	.290	.423
vs. Right	.268	399	107	16	5	11	57	11	72	.300	.416	Ahead in Count	.389	90	35	8	1	6	28	9	0	.446	.700
Groundball	.211	76	16	7	0	2	7	0	7	.211	.382	Behind in Count	.220	245	54	6	3	3	22	0	80	.232	.306
Flyball	.274	95	26	3	2	1	8	4	29	.317	.379	Two Strikes	.168	197	33	1	2	1	15	8	88	.208	.208
Home	.269	242	65	9	3	5	32	10	40	.304	.393	Batting #7	.273	461	126	19	5	13	67	16	78	.305	.421
Away	.266	256	68	11	2	9	38	7	48	.297	.430	Batting #8	.050	20	1	0	0	0	0	0	4	.050	.050
Day	.310	145	45	8	1	8	27	7	34	.353	.545	Other	.353	17	6	1	0	1	3	1	6	.450	.588
Night	.249	353	88	12	4	6	43	10	54	.278	.357	March/April	.282	78	22	2	0	2	5	4	14	.329	.385
Grass	.267	172	46	9	0	7	28	3	27	.291	.442	May	.191	89	17	5	1	2	9	3	14	.223	.337
Turf	.267	326	87	11	5	7	42	14	61	.305	.396	June	.295	95	28	6	2	2	15	3	15	.323	.463
Pre-All Star	.261	283	74	13	4	7	35	10	45	.294	.410	July	.286	84	24	4	1	3	11	2	15	.302	.464
Post-All Star	.274	215	59	7	1	7	35	7	43	.308	.414	August	.272	81	22	2	0	3	15	2	12	.298	.407
Scoring Posn	.240	154	37	1	1	5	55	5	32	.268	.357	Sept/Oct	.282	71	20	1	1	2	15	3	18	.333	.408
Close & Late	.247	93	23	4	2	1	10	1	15	.258	.366	vs. AL	.325	40	13	1	2	0	5	1	5	.341	.450
None on/out	.270	111	30	5	1	3	3	4	21	.302	.414	vs. NL	.262	458	120	19	3	14	65	16	83	.297	.408

1997 By Position

Position	Avg	AB	H	2B	3B	HR	RBI	BB	SO	OBP	SLG	G	GS	Innings	PO	A	E	DP	Fld Pct	Rng Fctr	In Zone	Zone Outs	Zone Rtg	MLB Zone
As rf	.269	480	129	20	5	14	70	16	84	.302	.419	134	130	1108.2	224	9	9	4	.963	1.89	293	216	.737	.813

Ozzie Guillen — White Sox
Age 34 – Bats Left (groundball hitter)

	Avg	G	AB	R	H	2B	3B	HR	RBI	BB	SO	HBP	GDP	SB	CS	OBP	SLG	IBB	SH	SF	#Pit	#P/PA	GB	FB	G/F
1997 Season	.245	142	490	59	120	21	6	4	52	22	24	0	7	5	3	.275	.337	1	11	4	1465	2.78	219	167	1.31
Last Five Years	.264	648	2226	261	587	97	26	14	227	69	152	0	39	27	23	.283	.350	4	47	22	6765	2.86	997	601	1.66

1997 Season

	Avg	AB	H	2B	3B	HR	RBI	BB	SO	OBP	SLG		Avg	AB	H	2B	3B	HR	RBI	BB	SO	OBP	SLG
vs. Left	.278	108	30	4	2	1	9	7	8	.322	.380	First Pitch	.257	140	36	4	4	0	12	0	0	.254	.343
vs. Right	.236	382	90	17	4	3	43	15	16	.262	.325	Ahead in Count	.316	98	31	6	2	3	20	20	0	.432	.510
Groundball	.235	98	23	7	0	1	11	3	5	.252	.337	Behind in Count	.222	189	42	10	0	0	12	0	21	.221	.275
Flyball	.212	99	21	3	3	1	12	3	5	.235	.333	Two Strikes	.220	141	31	7	0	0	9	2	24	.229	.270
Home	.263	236	62	14	4	1	24	15	12	.307	.369	Batting #2	.242	33	8	1	0	0	2	1	2	.257	.273
Away	.228	254	58	7	2	3	28	7	12	.245	.307	Batting #9	.244	447	109	20	6	4	49	21	20	.276	.342
Day	.235	166	39	7	3	2	19	12	9	.283	.349	Other	.300	10	3	0	0	0	1	0	2	.300	.300
Night	.250	324	81	14	3	2	33	10	15	.271	.330	March/April	.234	77	18	3	1	1	7	6	3	.289	.338
Grass	.254	409	104	17	5	4	46	20	19	.286	.350	May	.278	79	22	2	0	3	8	1	3	.345	.304
Turf	.198	81	16	4	1	0	6	2	5	.217	.272	June	.305	95	29	5	3	0	8	3	4	.327	.421
Pre-All Star	.273	271	74	11	4	1	18	17	11	.316	.354	July	.250	88	22	4	0	1	10	2	6	.264	.330
Post-All Star	.210	219	46	10	2	3	34	5	13	.224	.315	August	.174	92	16	3	1	1	13	2	5	.191	.261
Scoring Posn	.284	102	29	6	2	2	45	6	3	.313	.441	Sept/Oct	.220	59	13	4	1	1	11	1	5	.222	.373
Close & Late	.256	86	22	3	0	1	11	9	3	.323	.326	vs. AL	.248	443	110	19	6	4	49	21	20	.281	.345
None on/out	.185	135	25	5	3	0	0	10	7	.241	.267	vs. NL	.213	47	10	2	0	0	3	1	4	.224	.255

1997 By Position

Position	Avg	AB	H	2B	3B	HR	RBI	BB	SO	OBP	SLG	G	GS	Innings	PO	A	E	DP	Fld Pct	Rng Fctr	In Zone	Zone Outs	Zone Rtg	MLB Zone
As ss	.245	485	119	21	6	4	52	22	23	.276	.338	139	134	1191.1	207	348	15	77	.974	4.19	422	386	915	937

Last Five Years

	Avg	AB	H	2B	3B	HR	RBI	BB	SO	OBP	SLG		Avg	AB	H	2B	3B	HR	RBI	BB	SO	OBP	SLG
vs. Left	.242	571	138	19	5	3	43	17	48	.263	.308	First Pitch	.290	573	166	23	12	4	74	2	0	.288	.393
vs. Right	.271	1655	449	78	21	11	184	52	104	.290	.364	Ahead in Count	.321	417	134	30	7	7	58	59	0	.404	.477
Groundball	.271	560	152	23	6	3	61	14	38	.285	.350	Behind in Count	.233	931	217	35	5	1	70	0	138	.231	.285
Flyball	.258	481	124	18	9	2	41	10	46	.272	.345	Two Strikes	.218	697	152	24	4	1	44	8	152	.226	.268
Home	.270	1067	288	47	16	5	112	41	73	.294	.358	Batting #2	.186	59	11	2	0	0	3	2	3	.210	.220
Away	.258	1159	299	50	10	9	115	28	79	.273	.342	Batting #9	.266	2136	568	93	26	14	220	67	147	.286	.353
Day	.238	647	154	27	6	5	70	27	40	.265	.321	Other	.258	31	8	2	0	0	4	0	2	.250	.323
Night	.274	1579	433	70	20	9	157	42	112	.291	.361	March/April	.236	318	75	11	4	1	32	15	21	.266	.318
Grass	.263	1908	502	80	23	11	190	60	122	.283	.346	May	.298	369	110	11	2	2	37	14	14	.321	.355
Turf	.267	318	85	17	3	3	37	9	30	.285	.368	June	.287	450	129	23	8	2	48	18	29	.312	.387
Pre-All Star	.276	1273	351	57	16	7	129	50	80	.300	.362	July	.259	424	110	20	2	4	37	13	42	.278	.344
Post-All Star	.248	953	236	40	10	7	98	19	72	.260	.333	August	.231	385	89	14	6	3	42	7	30	.243	.322
Scoring Posn	.276	548	151	24	5	7	199	21	41	.291	.376	Sept/Oct	.264	280	74	14	4	2	31	2	16	.267	.364
Close & Late	.251	411	103	19	3	2	40	20	35	.282	.326	vs. AL	.265	2179	577	95	26	14	224	68	148	.284	.352
None on/out	.242	559	135	25	8	0	0	24	34	.273	.315	vs. NL	.213	47	10	2	0	0	3	1	4	.224	.255

Batter vs. Pitcher (career)

Hits Best Against	Avg	AB	H	2B	3B	HR	RBI	BB	SO	OBP	SLG	Hits Worst Against	Avg	AB	H	2B	3B	HR	RBI	BB	SO	OBP	SLG
Bob Tewksbury	.571	14	8	2	0	0	3	0	1	.533	.714	Jesse Orosco	.000	14	0	0	0	0	0	0	4	.000	.000
Mark Leiter	.545	11	6	0	1	0	2	0	1	.545	.727	Dennis Martinez	.038	26	1	0	0	0	0	1	1	.074	.038
Brian Bohanon	.455	11	5	0	1	0	2	0	1	.455	.636	Kenny Rogers	.067	15	1	0	0	0	2	0	0	.067	.067
Felipe Lira	.455	11	5	2	1	0	3	0	0	.455	.818	Buddy Groom	.091	11	1	0	0	0	0	0	1	.091	.091
Mike Magnante	.400	10	4	2	1	0	2	1	0	.455	.800	Scott Bailes	.118	17	2	0	0	0	0	0	2	.118	.118

Mike Gulan — Cardinals
Age 27 – Bats Right

	Avg	G	AB	R	H	2B	3B	HR	RBI	BB	SO	HBP	GDP	SB	CS	OBP	SLG	IBB	SH	SF	#Pit	#P/PA	GB	FB	G/F
1997 Season	.000	5	9	2	0	0	0	0	1	1	5	0	0	0	0	.100	.000	0	0	0	49	4.90	2	1	2.00

1997 Season

	Avg	AB	H	2B	3B	HR	RBI	BB	SO	OBP	SLG		Avg	AB	H	2B	3B	HR	RBI	BB	SO	OBP	SLG
vs. Left	.000	2	0	0	0	0	0	1	2	.333	.000	Scoring Posn	.000	3	0	0	0	0	1	1	1	.250	.000
vs. Right	.000	7	0	0	0	0	1	0	3	.000	.000	Close & Late	.000	1	0	0	0	0	0	1	1	.500	.000

Eric Gunderson — Rangers
Age 32 – Pitches Left

	ERA	W	L	Sv	G	GS	IP	BB	SO	Avg	H	2B	3B	HR	RBI	OBP	SLG	GF	IR	IRS	Hld	SvOp	SB	CS	GB	FB	G/F
1997 Season	3.26	2	1	1	60	0	49.2	15	31	.241	45	8	0	5	28	.300	.364	11	54	14	12	4	0	0	65	59	1.10
Last Five Years	4.07	5	4	1	151	0	112.2	44	70	.259	109	31	1	12	67	.334	.423	24	144	40	23	7	1	2	149	123	1.21

1997 Season

	ERA	W	L	Sv	G	GS	IP	H	HR	BB	SO		Avg	AB	H	2B	3B	HR	RBI	BB	SO	OBP	SLG
Home	2.93	1	1	0	30	0	27.2	25	1	6	18	vs. Left	.253	91	23	3	0	3	18	8	17	.317	.385
Away	3.68	1	0	1	30	0	22.0	20	4	9	13	vs. Right	.229	96	22	5	0	2	10	7	14	.283	.344
Day	3.00	1	0	0	14	0	12.0	8	2	1	8	Inning 1-6	.235	34	8	2	0	1	7	2	7	.270	.382
Night	3.35	1	1	1	46	0	37.2	37	3	14	23	Inning 7+	.242	153	37	6	0	4	21	13	24	.306	.359
Grass	3.27	2	1	0	54	0	44.0	40	4	13	27	None on	.228	92	21	4	0	2	2	7	14	.297	.337
Turf	3.18	0	0	1	6	0	5.2	5	1	2	4	Runners on	.253	95	24	4	0	3	26	8	17	.302	.389
March/April	1.17	0	0	1	9	0	7.2	2	1	1	5	Scoring Posn	.226	53	12	1	0	2	23	4	12	.267	.358
May	3.38	0	0	0	12	0	10.2	9	1	5	9	Close & Late	.250	56	14	2	0	2	8	5	7	.317	.393
June	0.84	1	0	0	11	0	10.2	4	0	0	6	None on/out	.237	38	9	3	0	1	1	6	4	.341	.395

	ERA	W	L	Sv	G	GS	IP	H	HR	BB	SO		Avg	AB	H	2B	3B	HR	RBI	BB	SO	OBP	SLG
July	1.35	1	0	0	14	0	13.1	11	1	2	6	vs. 1st Batr (relief)	.241	54	13	4	0	2	13	4	10	.288	.426
August	12.71	0	1	0	9	0	5.2	11	2	4	3	1st Inning Pitched	.260	150	39	6	0	5	27	14	26	.325	.400
Sept/Oct	10.80	0	0	0	5	0	1.2	8	0	3	2	First 15 Pitches	.246	138	34	6	0	5	20	13	22	.316	.399
Starter	0.00	0	0	0	0	0	0.0	0	0	0	0	Pitch 16-30	.275	40	11	2	0	0	8	1	6	.286	.325
Reliever	3.26	2	1	1	60	0	49.2	45	5	15	31	Pitch 31-45	.000	9	0	0	0	0	0	1	3	.100	.000
0 Days rest (Relief)	1.59	0	0	0	12	0	11.1	4	1	0	6	Pitch 46+	.000	0	0	0	0	0	0	0	0	.000	.000
1 or 2 Days rest	4.85	1	1	0	33	0	26.0	33	2	9	19	First Pitch	.458	24	11	2	0	1	5	2	0	.500	.667
3+ Days rest	1.46	1	0	1	15	0	12.1	8	2	6	6	Ahead in Count	.130	77	10	1	0	1	7	0	27	.141	.182
vs. AL	3.45	2	1	1	57	0	47.0	43	5	15	29	Behind in Count	.391	46	18	3	0	3	12	6	0	.446	.652
vs. NL	0.00	0	0	0	3	0	2.2	2	0	0	2	Two Strikes	.148	81	12	2	0	1	8	7	31	.216	.210
Pre-All Star	1.78	1	0	1	35	0	30.1	16	2	6	20	Pre-All Star	.152	105	16	4	0	2	11	6	20	.202	.248
Post-All Star	5.59	1	1	0	25	0	19.1	29	3	9	11	Post-All Star	.354	82	29	4	0	3	17	9	11	.419	.512

Last Five Years

	ERA	W	L	Sv	G	GS	IP	H	HR	BB	SO		Avg	AB	H	2B	3B	HR	RBI	BB	SO	OBP	SLG
Home	3.90	2	3	0	79	0	57.2	55	4	21	38	vs. Left	.245	200	49	12	0	8	37	17	41	.309	.425
Away	4.25	3	1	1	72	0	55.0	54	8	23	32	vs. Right	.271	221	60	19	1	4	30	27	29	.355	.421
Day	6.35	2	0	0	44	0	28.1	37	8	10	19	Inning 1-6	.192	78	15	6	0	1	15	7	22	.261	.308
Night	3.31	3	4	1	107	0	84.1	72	4	34	51	Inning 7+	.274	343	94	25	1	11	52	37	48	.350	.449
Grass	4.03	4	4	0	130	0	91.2	87	9	38	57	None on	.268	205	55	16	1	7	7	14	31	.324	.459
Turf	4.29	1	0	1	21	0	21.0	22	3	6	13	Runners on	.250	216	54	15	0	5	60	30	39	.342	.389
March/April	0.82	0	0	1	13	0	11.0	3	1	2	7	Scoring Posn	.235	132	31	9	0	3	54	21	27	.333	.371
May	4.22	1	0	0	26	0	21.1	21	3	7	14	Close & Late	.291	141	41	10	0	4	24	15	17	.366	.447
June	2.96	1	2	0	30	0	24.1	18	0	6	13	None on/out	.253	87	22	9	0	3	3	10	9	.330	.460
July	1.88	1	0	0	37	0	28.2	26	4	9	16	vs. 1st Batr (relief)	.262	130	34	13	0	4	30	14	24	.338	.454
August	5.66	2	1	0	27	0	20.2	24	3	9	13	1st Inning Pitched	.276	344	95	25	1	11	63	40	61	.355	.451
Sept/Oct	17.55	0	1	0	18	0	6.2	17	1	11	7	First 15 Pitches	.267	318	85	23	1	10	51	36	56	.346	.440
Starter	0.00	0	0	0	0	0	0.0	0	0	0	0	Pitch 16-30	.247	85	21	7	0	1	13	7	11	.305	.365
Reliever	4.07	5	4	1	151	0	112.2	109	12	44	70	Pitch 31-45	.167	18	3	1	0	1	3	1	3	.250	.389
0 Days rest (Relief)	3.42	2	1	0	42	0	26.1	19	3	8	17	Pitch 46+	.000	0	0	0	0	0	0	0	0	.000	.000
1 or 2 Days rest	4.35	1	1	0	64	0	51.2	56	5	21	38	First Pitch	.448	58	26	8	1	2	11	8	0	.515	.724
3+ Days rest	4.15	2	2	1	45	0	34.2	34	4	15	15	Ahead in Count	.171	175	30	8	0	3	18	0	63	.193	.269
vs. AL	4.81	4	3	1	104	0	76.2	77	10	32	45	Behind in Count	.368	106	39	9	0	6	27	19	0	.458	.623
vs. NL	2.50	1	1	0	47	0	36.0	32	2	12	25	Two Strikes	.156	186	29	8	0	4	18	17	70	.236	.263
Pre-All Star	3.21	2	2	1	76	0	61.2	46	7	15	38	Pre-All Star	.204	225	46	14	0	7	32	15	38	.262	.360
Post-All Star	5.12	3	2	0	75	0	51.0	63	5	29	32	Post-All Star	.321	196	63	17	1	5	35	29	32	.411	.495

Mark Guthrie — Dodgers   Age 32 – Pitches Left

	ERA	W	L	Sv	G	GS	IP	BB	SO	Avg	H	2B	3B	HR	RBI	OBP	SLG	GF	IR	IRS	Hld	SvOp	SB	CS	GB	FB	G/F
1997 Season	5.32	1	4	1	62	0	69.1	30	42	.272	71	11	1	12	45	.344	.460	18	32	9	13	4	8	5	90	87	1.03
Last Five Years	4.36	14	15	3	260	2	276.2	111	218	.272	287	56	6	31	166	.340	.425	63	176	56	60	13	30	12	360	300	1.20

1997 Season

	ERA	W	L	Sv	G	GS	IP	H	HR	BB	SO		Avg	AB	H	2B	3B	HR	RBI	BB	SO	OBP	SLG
Home	3.94	1	3	0	29	0	29.2	24	3	9	19	vs. Left	.282	85	24	3	0	3	15	9	18	.351	.424
Away	6.35	0	1	1	33	0	39.2	47	9	21	23	vs. Right	.267	176	47	8	1	9	30	21	24	.340	.477
Day	4.50	0	1	0	17	0	20.0	22	4	10	10	Inning 1-6	.364	44	16	5	1	3	11	8	6	.462	.727
Night	5.66	1	3	1	45	0	49.1	49	8	20	32	Inning 7+	.253	217	55	6	0	9	34	22	36	.318	.406
Grass	5.40	1	4	0	54	0	56.2	61	10	20	31	None on	.263	156	41	6	0	7	7	13	26	.320	.436
Turf	4.97	0	0	1	8	0	12.2	10	2	10	11	Runners on	.286	105	30	5	1	5	38	17	16	.376	.495
March/April	2.35	1	0	0	12	0	15.1	6	1	6	8	Scoring Posn	.268	71	19	4	1	4	35	14	13	.375	.521
May	3.24	0	1	0	11	0	8.1	10	1	4	9	Close & Late	.261	92	24	3	0	6	26	12	18	.340	.489
June	5.14	0	1	0	13	0	14.0	20	3	6	9	None on/out	.294	68	20	4	0	2	2	8	10	.368	.441
July	8.18	0	1	0	10	0	11.0	17	1	1	5	vs. 1st Batr (relief)	.302	53	16	2	0	1	8	7	10	.377	.396
August	2.25	0	0	1	8	0	16.0	9	2	7	10	1st Inning Pitched	.289	194	56	9	1	9	40	27	30	.371	.485
Sept/Oct	23.14	0	1	0	8	0	4.2	9	4	6	1	First 15 Pitches	.286	161	46	6	0	8	30	18	26	.354	.472
Starter	0.00	0	0	0	0	0	0.0	0	0	0	0	Pitch 16-30	.253	79	20	4	1	3	12	10	11	.333	.443
Reliever	5.32	1	4	1	62	0	69.1	71	12	30	42	Pitch 31-45	.278	18	5	1	0	1	3	2	4	.350	.500
0 Days rest (Relief)	8.53	0	1	0	13	0	12.2	16	4	7	6	Pitch 46+	.000	3	0	0	0	0	0	0	0	.000	.000
1 or 2 Days rest	3.50	1	2	0	33	0	36.0	32	4	10	25	First Pitch	.405	37	15	3	0	4	9	4	0	.463	.811
3+ Days rest	6.53	0	1	1	16	0	20.2	23	4	13	11	Ahead in Count	.229	109	25	2	0	4	17	0	36	.229	.358
vs. AL	7.36	0	0	0	9	0	7.1	12	2	3	5	Behind in Count	.328	67	22	3	0	4	15	17	0	.453	.552
vs. NL	5.08	1	4	1	56	0	62.0	59	10	27	37	Two Strikes	.177	113	20	2	0	4	17	9	42	.236	.301
Pre-All Star	3.73	1	2	0	38	0	41.0	40	5	16	27	Pre-All Star	.258	155	40	3	0	5	23	16	27	.324	.374
Post-All Star	7.62	0	2	1	24	0	28.1	31	7	14	15	Post-All Star	.292	106	31	8	1	7	22	14	15	.372	.585

Last Five Years

	ERA	W	L	Sv	G	GS	IP	H	HR	BB	SO		Avg	AB	H	2B	3B	HR	RBI	BB	SO	OBP	SLG
Home	3.53	8	8	2	127	0	127.1	117	9	51	110	vs. Left	.256	359	92	13	1	7	50	35	79	.321	.357
Away	5.06	6	7	1	133	2	149.1	170	22	60	108	vs. Right	.281	695	195	43	5	24	116	76	139	.350	.460
Day	4.70	2	6	0	78	0	82.1	96	13	33	68	Inning 1-6	.327	171	56	12	3	5	37	21	33	.403	.520
Night	4.21	12	9	3	182	2	194.1	191	18	78	150	Inning 7+	.262	883	231	44	3	26	129	90	185	.328	.407
Grass	4.01	6	11	1	168	1	181.2	187	21	58	138	None on	.273	565	154	28	2	18	18	44	119	.328	.425
Turf	5.02	8	4	2	92	1	95.0	100	10	53	80	Runners on	.272	489	133	28	4	13	148	67	99	.353	.425
March/April	5.21	4	2	0	48	0	57.0	57	8	29	39	Scoring Posn	.295	308	91	20	3	9	134	49	66	.378	.468
May	4.09	5	3	0	53	0	55.0	63	7	20	57	Close & Late	.266	432	115	26	0	15	74	43	100	.329	.431
June	3.51	2	2	1	49	0	51.1	51	6	18	45	None on/out	.284	250	71	15	1	7	7	16	49	.332	.436

Last Five Years

	ERA	W	L	Sv	G	GS	IP	H	HR	BB	SO
July	4.15	3	3	0	46	0	47.2	45	2	16	31
August	4.05	0	2	2	34	0	40.0	39	3	15	31
Sept/Oct	5.61	0	3	0	30	0	25.2	32	5	13	15
Starter	21.60	0	1	0	2	2	5.0	16	2	1	1
Reliever	4.04	14	14	3	258	0	271.2	271	29	110	217
0 Days rest (Relief)	3.54	5	4	1	72	0	68.2	69	9	18	53
1 or 2 Days rest	3.86	4	8	1	117	0	128.1	122	10	56	98
3+ Days rest	4.82	5	2	1	69	0	74.2	80	10	36	66
vs. AL	5.39	11	6	1	114	2	122.0	144	17	53	106
vs. NL	3.55	3	9	2	146	0	154.2	143	14	58	112
Pre-All Star	4.28	12	7	1	164	2	181.0	189	22	73	153
Post-All Star	4.52	2	8	2	96	2	95.2	98	9	38	65

	Avg	AB	H	2B	3B	HR	RBI	BB	SO	OBP	SLG
vs. 1st Batr (relief)	.296	230	68	12	0	8	40	22	43	.357	.452
1st Inning Pitched	.277	773	214	42	2	23	128	91	155	.350	.426
First 15 Pitches	.279	659	184	34	2	20	102	72	130	.348	.428
Pitch 16-30	.258	287	74	18	2	8	44	28	62	.325	.418
Pitch 31-45	.266	79	21	3	1	2	17	9	18	.341	.405
Pitch 46+	.276	29	8	1	1	1	3	2	8	.313	.483
First Pitch	.397	136	54	9	0	6	31	13	0	.444	.596
Ahead in Count	.228	469	107	21	2	14	62	0	180	.233	.371
Behind in Count	.289	253	73	13	2	9	49	58	0	.411	.462
Two Strikes	.186	489	91	20	2	10	53	40	218	.248	.309
Pre-All Star	.274	690	189	35	4	22	113	73	153	.341	.432
Post-All Star	.269	364	98	21	2	9	53	38	65	.337	.412

Pitcher vs. Batter (career)

Pitches Best Vs.	Avg	AB	H	2B	3B	HR	RBI	BB	SO	OBP	SLG
Greg Vaughn	.071	14	1	0	0	0	0	1	4	.133	.071
John Olerud	.100	10	1	0	0	0	1	1	7	.167	.100
Darnell Coles	.100	10	1	0	0	0	0	1	1	.182	.100
Paul Molitor	.133	15	2	0	0	0	1	0	4	.133	.133
Darryl Hamilton	.182	11	2	0	0	0	0	0	3	.182	.182

Pitches Worst Vs.	Avg	AB	H	2B	3B	HR	RBI	BB	SO	OBP	SLG
Mark McGwire	.556	9	5	0	0	2	4	2	4	.692	.556
Terry Steinbach	.545	11	6	0	0	3	13	1	1	.583	1.364
Jody Reed	.500	10	5	1	0	0	0	4	3	.643	.600
Glenallen Hill	.438	16	7	2	0	1	4	0	3	.438	.750
Danny Tartabull	.429	14	6	0	0	1	5	6	4	.600	.857

Ricky Gutierrez — Astros

Age 28 – Bats Right (groundball hitter)

	Avg	G	AB	R	H	2B	3B	HR	RBI	BB	SO	HBP	GDP	SB	CS	OBP	SLG	IBB	SH	SF	#Pit	#P/PA	GB	FB	G/F
1997 Season	.261	102	303	33	79	14	4	3	34	21	50	3	17	5	2	.315	.363	2	0	0	1191	3.64	147	58	2.53
Career (1993-1997)	.259	466	1390	186	360	49	12	10	115	136	276	14	39	22	12	.330	.333	11	8	6	5959	3.83	616	240	2.57

1997 Season

	Avg	AB	H	2B	3B	HR	RBI	BB	SO	OBP	SLG
vs. Left	.256	78	20	4	0	1	9	5	12	.301	.346
vs. Right	.262	225	59	10	4	2	25	16	38	.320	.369
Groundball	.370	46	17	3	1	1	13	1	6	.383	.543
Flyball	.271	48	13	2	0	0	5	5	5	.352	.313
Home	.202	129	26	4	2	0	12	9	22	.264	.264
Away	.305	174	53	10	2	3	22	12	28	.353	.437
Day	.269	104	28	8	1	0	13	8	18	.321	.365
Night	.256	199	51	6	3	3	21	13	32	.312	.362
Grass	.294	119	35	4	2	3	16	6	20	.328	.437
Turf	.239	184	44	10	2	0	18	15	30	.307	.315
Pre-All Star	.256	117	30	4	0	1	13	9	19	.320	.316
Post-All Star	.263	186	49	10	4	2	21	12	31	.312	.392
Scoring Posn	.236	89	21	3	2	0	27	10	15	.313	.315
Close & Late	.191	68	13	2	0	0	5	4	11	.247	.221
None on/out	.209	67	14	2	0	2	2	3	10	.243	.328

	Avg	AB	H	2B	3B	HR	RBI	BB	SO	OBP	SLG
First Pitch	.327	49	16	7	1	1	8	2	0	.353	.571
Ahead in Count	.329	70	23	1	2	1	11	8	0	.397	.443
Behind in Count	.197	127	25	4	1	1	12	0	38	.215	.268
Two Strikes	.168	137	23	4	1	1	12	11	50	.235	.226
Batting #7	.286	98	28	4	3	1	14	7	17	.340	.418
Batting #8	.267	60	16	2	0	0	3	5	7	.343	.300
Other	.241	145	35	8	1	2	17	9	26	.286	.352
March/April	.000	0	0	0	0	0	0	0	0	.000	.000
May	.328	58	19	4	0	1	9	3	8	.381	.448
June	.182	55	10	0	0	0	6	4	10	.262	.182
July	.300	40	12	2	1	0	0	3	3	.349	.400
August	.263	57	15	5	0	1	5	3	10	.300	.404
Sept/Oct	.247	93	23	3	3	1	12	6	19	.300	.376
vs. AL	.174	23	4	1	0	0	1	2	1	.240	.217
vs. NL	.268	280	75	13	4	3	33	19	49	.321	.375

1997 By Position

Position	Avg	AB	H	2B	3B	HR	RBI	BB	SO	OBP	SLG	G	GS	Innings	PO	A	E	DP	Fld Pct	Rng Fctr	In Zone	Zone Outs	Zone Rtg	MLB Zone
As Pinch Hitter	.231	13	3	0	0	0	4	1	0	.333	.231	16	0	---	---	---	---	---	---	---	---	---	---	---
As 3b	.288	66	19	3	0	2	8	4	16	.329	.424	22	17	155.0	10	36	0	3	1.000	2.67	45	40	.889	.801
As ss	.261	211	55	9	4	1	22	15	33	.316	.355	64	52	469.1	85	152	8	36	.967	4.54	173	157	.908	.937

Career (1993-1997)

	Avg	AB	H	2B	3B	HR	RBI	BB	SO	OBP	SLG
vs. Left	.274	438	120	16	4	5	35	42	84	.339	.363
vs. Right	.252	952	240	33	8	5	80	94	192	.326	.319
Groundball	.273	363	99	16	3	2	26	30	71	.332	.350
Flyball	.229	223	51	6	2	1	17	23	40	.311	.287
Home	.260	670	174	16	4	7	53	67	142	.335	.327
Away	.258	720	186	33	8	3	62	69	134	.325	.339
Day	.280	447	125	24	3	3	39	52	86	.358	.367
Night	.249	943	235	25	9	7	76	84	190	.316	.317
Grass	.264	788	208	24	5	9	65	89	162	.343	.341
Turf	.252	602	152	25	7	1	50	47	114	.313	.322
Pre-All Star	.269	692	186	24	6	3	57	71	136	.340	.334
Post-All Star	.249	698	174	25	6	7	58	65	140	.320	.332
Scoring Posn	.234	364	85	8	3	0	95	51	76	.326	.272
Close & Late	.262	256	67	8	2	1	18	30	59	.343	.320
None on/out	.266	346	92	10	3	5	5	29	69	.328	.355

	Avg	AB	H	2B	3B	HR	RBI	BB	SO	OBP	SLG
First Pitch	.304	171	52	13	2	2	16	7	0	.331	.439
Ahead in Count	.330	270	89	7	7	5	35	69	0	.468	.463
Behind in Count	.208	677	141	17	3	3	45	0	236	.220	.256
Two Strikes	.193	698	135	18	2	2	51	60	276	.260	.234
Batting #7	.262	408	107	15	5	1	35	36	75	.326	.331
Batting #8	.286	381	109	10	2	2	34	39	73	.358	.339
Other	.240	601	144	24	5	7	46	61	128	.314	.331
March/April	.260	131	34	6	1	0	10	8	31	.303	.321
May	.248	210	52	8	1	2	18	24	37	.331	.324
June	.299	268	80	7	2	1	24	29	49	.369	.351
July	.248	242	60	7	5	2	20	32	48	.341	.343
August	.242	265	64	13	0	2	14	23	48	.311	.313
Sept/Oct	.255	274	70	8	3	3	29	20	63	.312	.339
vs. AL	.174	23	4	1	0	0	1	2	1	.240	.217
vs. NL	.260	1367	356	48	12	10	114	134	275	.331	.335

Batter vs. Pitcher (career)

Hits Best Against	Avg	AB	H	2B	3B	HR	RBI	BB	SO	OBP	SLG
Jaime Navarro	.462	13	6	1	0	0	5	3	2	.563	.538
Mark Portugal	.462	13	6	1	0	0	2	0	2	.462	.538
Frank Castillo	.417	12	5	0	1	0	2	2	1	.500	.583
Steve Trachsel	.333	12	4	1	0	1	1	2	2	.429	.667
Steve Avery	.333	12	4	0	1	1	1	0	1	.333	.583

Hits Worst Against	Avg	AB	H	2B	3B	HR	RBI	BB	SO	OBP	SLG
Kirk Rueter	.000	14	0	0	0	0	0	0	3	.000	.000
Pete Schourek	.000	12	0	0	0	0	0	2	3	.143	.000
John Burkett	.091	11	1	0	0	0	0	2	1	.167	.091
Pete Harnisch	.100	10	1	0	0	0	0	1	4	.182	.100
Bobby Jones	.100	10	1	0	0	0	0	0	1	.182	.100

Juan Guzman — Blue Jays

	ERA	W	L	Sv	G	GS	IP	BB	SO	Avg	H	2B	3B	HR	RBI	OBP	SLG	CG	ShO	Sup	QS	#P/S	SB	CS	GB	FB	G/F
1997 Season	4.95	3	6	0	13	13	60.0	31	52	.213	48	7	0	14	37	.312	.431	0	0	4.35	3	78	12	1	81	63	1.29
Last Five Years	4.55	44	42	0	122	122	751.1	343	629	.255	733	127	9	84	360	.336	.393	11	2	5.35	57	105	93	30	915	821	1.11

1997 Season

	ERA	W	L	Sv	G	GS	IP	H	HR	BB	SO
Home	3.77	1	3	0	6	6	31.0	20	4	16	34
Away	6.21	2	3	0	7	7	29.0	28	10	15	18
Starter	4.95	3	6	0	13	13	60.0	48	14	31	52
Reliever	0.00	0	0	0	0	0	0.0	0	0	0	0
0-3 Days Rest (Start)	0.00	0	0	0	0	0	0.0	0	0	0	0
4 Days Rest	7.39	1	5	0	7	7	31.2	30	10	14	27
5+ Days Rest	2.22	2	1	0	6	6	28.1	18	4	17	25
Pre-All Star	4.13	3	5	0	11	11	52.1	38	8	29	44
Post-All Star	10.57	0	1	0	2	2	7.2	10	6	2	8

	Avg	AB	H	2B	3B	HR	RBI	BB	SO	OBP	SLG
vs. Left	.216	116	25	3	0	4	13	17	25	.319	.345
vs. Right	.211	109	23	4	0	10	24	14	27	.304	.523
Scoring Posn	.255	51	13	0	0	4	24	6	16	.333	.490
Close & Late	.167	12	2	1	0	0	0	1	2	.231	.250
None on/out	.254	63	16	3	0	5	5	5	14	.309	.540
First Pitch	.259	27	7	1	0	1	1	0	0	.259	.407
Ahead in Count	.126	103	13	2	0	3	10	0	37	.143	.233
Behind in Count	.370	46	17	2	0	8	14	17	0	.540	.935
Two Strikes	.138	109	15	4	0	2	10	14	52	.240	.229

Last Five Years

	ERA	W	L	Sv	G	GS	IP	H	HR	BB	SO
Home	4.29	21	18	0	61	61	387.2	395	39	145	336
Away	4.83	23	24	0	61	61	363.2	338	45	198	293
Day	4.96	16	13	0	42	42	261.1	274	29	120	207
Night	4.33	28	29	0	80	80	490.0	459	55	223	422
Grass	5.15	15	24	0	50	50	286.2	277	37	151	225
Turf	4.18	29	18	0	72	72	464.2	456	47	192	404
March/April	4.27	11	5	0	21	21	145.1	136	18	62	119
May	6.02	5	9	0	24	24	128.2	147	18	70	97
June	4.58	8	10	0	22	22	133.2	123	17	64	119
July	4.45	9	9	0	27	27	153.2	157	17	70	138
August	3.82	6	5	0	15	15	96.2	90	4	41	92
Sept/Oct	3.86	5	4	0	13	13	93.1	80	10	36	64
Starter	4.55	44	42	0	122	122	751.1	733	84	343	629
Reliever	0.00	0	0	0	0	0	0.0	0	0	0	0
0-3 Days Rest (Start)	5.63	0	1	0	1	1	8.0	9	0	2	3
4 Days Rest	4.76	28	29	0	78	78	480.1	480	56	214	418
5+ Days Rest	4.14	16	12	0	43	43	263.0	244	28	127	208
vs. AL	4.55	44	42	0	122	122	751.1	733	84	343	629
vs. NL	0.00	0	0	0	0	0	0.0	0	0	0	0
Pre-All Star	4.93	27	27	0	75	75	456.2	461	55	223	377
Post-All Star	3.97	17	15	0	47	47	294.2	272	29	120	252

	Avg	AB	H	2B	3B	HR	RBI	BB	SO	OBP	SLG
vs. Left	.272	1506	409	64	6	33	178	199	266	.356	.388
vs. Right	.236	1370	324	63	3	51	182	144	363	.313	.399
Inning 1-6	.248	2435	603	106	8	70	300	300	560	.331	.384
Inning 7+	.295	441	130	21	1	14	60	43	69	.361	.442
None on	.245	1650	404	65	3	47	47	188	363	.325	.373
Runners on	.268	1226	329	62	6	37	313	155	266	.350	.419
Scoring Posn	.253	699	177	31	3	20	264	103	170	.347	.392
Close & Late	.308	208	64	8	0	8	30	24	25	.380	.452
None on/out	.243	723	176	22	2	26	26	85	150	.325	.387
vs. 1st Batr (relief)	.000	0	0	0	0	0	0	0	0	.000	.000
1st Inning Pitched	.233	443	103	23	2	13	55	75	108	.342	.381
First 75 Pitches	.244	1868	456	82	7	55	222	236	439	.330	.384
Pitch 76-90	.291	375	109	14	1	14	52	41	68	.365	.445
Pitch 91-105	.249	329	82	15	0	5	38	35	68	.322	.340
Pitch 106+	.283	304	86	16	1	10	48	31	54	.354	.441
First Pitch	.284	377	107	15	1	11	46	11	0	.307	.416
Ahead in Count	.197	1277	252	39	2	20	105	0	506	.203	.278
Behind in Count	.357	613	219	41	5	32	120	162	0	.489	.597
Two Strikes	.171	1378	235	45	2	19	114	170	629	.263	.247
Pre-All Star	.263	1754	461	83	7	55	244	223	377	.347	.412
Post-All Star	.242	1122	272	44	2	29	116	120	252	.319	.363

Pitcher vs. Batter (career)

Pitches Best Vs.	Avg	AB	H	2B	3B	HR	RBI	BB	SO	OBP	SLG
Chris Gomez	.000	13	0	0	0	0	0	2	6	.133	.000
Mark McGwire	.000	11	0	0	0	0	0	2	5	.214	.000
Chad Curtis	.080	25	2	0	0	1	1	0	7	.080	.200
Scott Livingstone	.091	11	1	0	0	0	0	0	1	.091	.091
Pat Meares	.133	15	2	0	0	0	1	0	6	.133	.133

Pitches Worst Vs.	Avg	AB	H	2B	3B	HR	RBI	BB	SO	OBP	SLG
Rusty Greer	.667	15	10	2	0	1	6	5	1	.750	1.000
Garret Anderson	.500	12	6	1	0	2	2	0	0	.500	1.083
Wally Joyner	.471	17	8	1	1	1	3	2	1	.526	.824
Damion Easley	.467	15	7	2	0	2	7	4	3	.579	1.000
Jody Reed	.462	13	6	1	0	0	3	2	1	.533	.769

Tony Gwynn — Padres

	Avg	G	AB	R	H	2B	3B	HR	RBI	BB	SO	HBP	GDP	SB	CS	OBP	SLG	IBB	SH	SF	#Pit	#P/PA	GB	FB	G/F
1997 Season	.372	149	592	97	220	49	2	17	119	43	28	3	12	12	5	.409	.547	12	1	12	2138	3.28	261	156	1.67
Last Five Years	.368	632	2486	395	916	185	9	48	382	201	98	8	85	59	15	.412	.508	61	4	36	8780	3.21	1195	560	2.13

1997 Season

	Avg	AB	H	2B	3B	HR	RBI	BB	SO	OBP	SLG
vs. Left	.356	163	58	17	1	6	48	11	10	.391	.583
vs. Right	.378	429	162	32	1	11	71	32	18	.416	.534
Groundball	.378	119	45	10	0	5	30	6	5	.398	.588
Flyball	.427	96	41	0	1	17	4	6		.441	.542
Home	.378	296	112	25	2	8	63	18	17	.408	.557
Away	.365	296	108	24	0	9	56	25	11	.411	.537
Day	.365	192	70	14	0	2	40	11	9	.389	.469
Night	.375	400	150	35	2	15	79	32	19	.419	.585
Grass	.366	484	177	39	2	14	101	33	21	.403	.541
Turf	.398	108	43	10	0	3	18	10	7	.434	.574
Pre-All Star	.394	330	130	23	1	13	71	26	12	.431	.588
Post-All Star	.344	262	90	26	1	4	48	17	16	.381	.496
Scoring Posn	.459	146	67	13	2	9	99	18	9	.489	.760
Close & Late	.395	86	34	9	1	4	30	13	6	.461	.663
None on/out	.369	103	38	5	0	2	2	8	4	.414	.476

	Avg	AB	H	2B	3B	HR	RBI	BB	SO	OBP	SLG
First Pitch	.423	97	41	11	0	5	33	10	0	.468	.691
Ahead in Count	.374	179	67	17	1	5	30	22	0	.441	.564
Two Strikes	.355	220	78	16	1	6	37	10	28	.387	.568
Batting #2	.411	124	51	10	0	3	15	7	8	.447	.565
Batting #3	.359	465	167	39	2	14	101	36	19	.398	.542
Other	.667	3	2	0	0	0	3	0	1	.667	.667
March/April	.367	98	36	2	1	5	21	5	4	.390	.561
May	.447	103	46	9	0	4	20	9	3	.478	.650
June	.362	105	38	11	0	4	26	10	4	.419	.581
July	.387	106	41	9	1	3	28	8	6	.422	.575
August	.323	99	32	12	0	0	10	7	7	.355	.444
Sept/Oct	.333	81	27	6	0	1	14	4	4	.379	.444
vs. AL	.313	67	21	5	0	1	9	4	5	.356	.433
vs. NL	.379	525	199	44	2	16	110	39	23	.416	.562

1997 By Position

Position	Avg	AB	H	2B	3B	HR	RBI	BB	SO	OBP	SLG	G	GS	Innings	PO	A	E	DP	Fld Pct	Rng Fctr	In Zone	Zone Outs	Zone Rtg	MLB Zone
As rf	.376	575	216	48	2	17	114	43	26	.414	.555	143	143	1203.1	218	8	4	4	.983	1.69	253	203	.802	.813

Last Five Years

	Avg	AB	H	2B	3B	HR	RBI	BB	SO	OBP	SLG
vs. Left	.353	818	289	57	3	14	132	55	33	.392	.482
vs. Right	.376	1668	627	128	6	34	250	146	65	.421	.521

	Avg	AB	H	2B	3B	HR	RBI	BB	SO	OBP	SLG
First Pitch	.401	399	160	44	0	13	100	47	0	.451	.609
Ahead in Count	.389	691	269	61	3	19	102	112	0	.472	.569

Last Five Years

	Avg	AB	H	2B	3B	HR	RBI	BB	SO	OBP	SLG		Avg	AB	H	2B	3B	HR	RBI	BB	SO	OBP	SLG
Groundball	.347	660	229	46	2	15	101	50	23	.389	.491	Behind in Count	.326	936	305	53	2	12	124	0	89	.324	.425
Flyball	.392	395	155	30	1	7	58	23	12	.421	.527	Two Strikes	.337	735	248	47	2	12	100	41	98	.372	.456
Home	.379	1242	471	93	6	23	191	104	61	.423	.519	Batting #2	.389	560	218	40	2	9	56	33	20	.424	.516
Away	.358	1244	445	92	3	25	191	97	37	.401	.497	Batting #3	.366	1723	630	127	6	38	304	144	62	.409	.512
Day	.380	789	300	57	2	14	129	57	34	.419	.511	Other	.335	203	68	18	1	1	22	24	16	.402	.448
Night	.363	1697	616	128	7	34	253	144	64	.409	.507	March/April	.372	360	134	21	2	9	48	24	13	.409	.517
Grass	.375	1915	719	147	6	37	302	166	77	.421	.516	May	.354	509	180	32	2	8	73	50	18	.408	.472
Turf	.345	571	197	38	3	11	80	35	21	.380	.480	June	.349	467	163	39	2	15	88	41	20	.398	.537
Pre-All Star	.363	1475	536	101	7	34	235	129	57	.411	.511	July	.386	425	164	34	2	10	86	35	17	.427	.546
Post-All Star	.376	1011	380	84	2	14	147	72	41	.413	.504	August	.383	412	158	37	0	4	46	27	16	.415	.502
Scoring Posn	.387	558	216	50	4	16	321	93	26	.454	.577	Sept/Oct	.374	313	117	22	1	2	41	24	14	.419	.470
Close & Late	.409	416	170	33	2	11	88	49	20	.466	.577	vs. AL	.313	67	21	5	0	1	9	4	5	.356	.433
None on/out	.382	474	181	34	4	10	10	38	21	.429	.534	vs. NL	.370	2419	895	180	9	47	373	197	93	.413	.510

Batter vs. Pitcher (since 1984)

Hits Best Against	Avg	AB	H	2B	3B	HR	RBI	BB	SO	OBP	SLG	Hits Worst Against	Avg	AB	H	2B	3B	HR	RBI	BB	SO	OBP	SLG
Jeff Brantley	.593	27	16	1	0	0	1	5	1	.656	.630	Omar Olivares	.050	20	1	0	0	1	2	1	1	.095	.200
Steve Cooke	.500	20	10	2	0	1	4	1	0	.524	.750	Allen Watson	.067	15	1	0	0	0	0	2	0	.176	.067
Ismael Valdes	.480	25	12	5	0	1	3	1	1	.500	.800	Jaime Navarro	.083	12	1	1	0	0	0	0	0	.083	.167
Hideo Nomo	.471	17	8	1	1	1	4	2	0	.526	.824	Rene Arocha	.091	11	1	1	0	0	0	0	0	.091	.182
Paul Wagner	.438	16	7	2	0	2	6	2	1	.500	.938	Mel Rojas	.118	17	2	1	0	2	0	0	0	.105	.176

Chip Hale — Dodgers   Age 33 – Bats Left

	Avg	G	AB	R	H	2B	3B	HR	RBI	BB	SO	HBP	GDP	SB	CS	OBP	SLG	IBB	SH	SF	#Pit	#P/PA	GB	FB	G/F
1997 Season	.083	14	12	0	1	0	0	0	0	2	4	0	0	0	0	.214	.083	0	0	0	64	4.57	5	3	1.67
Last Five Years	.287	304	506	56	145	24	1	7	72	57	61	7	14	2	3	.364	.379	4	3	4	2133	3.70	200	139	1.44

1997 Season

	Avg	AB	H	2B	3B	HR	RBI	BB	SO	OBP	SLG		Avg	AB	H	2B	3B	HR	RBI	BB	SO	OBP	SLG
vs. Left	.000	0	0	0	0	0	0	0	0	.000	.000	Scoring Posn	.000	2	0	0	0	0	0	0	2	.000	.000
vs. Right	.083	12	1	0	0	0	0	2	4	.214	.083	Close & Late	.000	5	0	0	0	0	0	0	2	.000	.000

Last Five Years

	Avg	AB	H	2B	3B	HR	RBI	BB	SO	OBP	SLG		Avg	AB	H	2B	3B	HR	RBI	BB	SO	OBP	SLG
vs. Left	.286	21	6	2	0	1	3	2	5	.375	.524	First Pitch	.382	76	29	3	1	1	18	4	0	.413	.487
vs. Right	.287	485	139	22	1	6	69	55	56	.364	.373	Ahead in Count	.342	117	40	7	0	2	22	34	0	.494	.453
Groundball	.328	137	45	7	0	3	25	17	14	.399	.445	Behind in Count	.230	222	51	7	0	3	19	0	49	.242	.302
Flyball	.331	127	42	9	1	1	20	13	15	.411	.441	Two Strikes	.216	231	50	10	0	2	21	19	61	.282	.286
Home	.289	256	74	13	1	1	30	33	34	.375	.359	Batting #2	.313	112	35	6	1	1	16	11	11	.366	.411
Away	.284	250	71	11	0	6	42	24	27	.352	.400	Batting #6	.228	101	23	3	0	4	12	10	11	.310	.376
Day	.307	163	50	5	1	4	25	20	22	.390	.423	March/April	.278	54	15	1	0	1	6	10	8	.391	.352
Night	.277	343	95	19	0	3	47	37	39	.351	.359	May	.193	57	11	6	0	0	3	11	11	.324	.298
Grass	.264	216	57	7	0	4	38	21	24	.336	.352	June	.357	115	41	6	1	3	22	8	10	.405	.504
Turf	.303	290	88	17	1	3	34	36	37	.385	.400	July	.258	97	25	5	0	0	9	11	13	.348	.309
Pre-All Star	.291	275	80	16	1	4	37	33	33	.373	.400	August	.234	111	26	4	0	2	15	9	11	.298	.324
Post-All Star	.281	231	65	8	0	3	35	24	28	.354	.355	Sept/Oct	.375	72	27	2	0	1	17	8	8	.438	.444
Scoring Posn	.301	136	41	7	0	2	63	22	23	.400	.397	vs. AL	.291	494	144	24	1	7	72	55	57	.368	.387
Close & Late	.282	149	42	6	0	1	31	17	23	.360	.342	vs. NL	.083	12	1	0	0	0	0	2	4	.214	.083
None on/out	.267	105	28	6	0	1	1	8	7	.330	.352												

Batter vs. Pitcher (career)

Hits Best Against	Avg	AB	H	2B	3B	HR	RBI	BB	SO	OBP	SLG	Hits Worst Against	Avg	AB	H	2B	3B	HR	RBI	BB	SO	OBP	SLG
Roger Clemens	.500	12	6	0	0	0	1	2	1	.600	.500	Juan Guzman	.111	9	1	0	0	0	0	3	0	.333	.111
Bobby Witt	.385	13	5	0	0	0	3	1	1	.400	.385	Jack McDowell	.182	11	2	1	0	0	0	0	3	.182	.273
Bob Wickman	.364	11	4	0	0	0	1	1	1	.417	.364												
David Cone	.313	16	5	1	0	1	1	2	2	.389	.563												

Darren Hall — Dodgers   Age 33 – Pitches Right (groundball pitcher)

	ERA	W	L	Sv	G	GS	IP	BB	SO	Avg	H	2B	3B	HR	RBI	OBP	SLG	GF	IR	IRS	Hld	SvOp	SB	CS	GB	FB	G/F
1997 Season	2.30	3	2	2	63	0	54.2	26	39	.283	58	11	1	3	24	.362	.390	20	46	12	15	5	9	2	108	27	4.00
Career (1994-1997)	3.30	5	9	22	119	0	114.2	54	90	.271	118	19	2	10	53	.352	.392	62	71	16	20	30	17	2	204	79	2.58

1997 Season

	ERA	W	L	Sv	G	GS	IP	H	HR	BB	SO		Avg	AB	H	2B	3B	HR	RBI	BB	SO	OBP	SLG
Home	0.33	2	0	2	30	0	27.2	19	0	12	21	vs. Left	.325	83	27	4	0	1	5	10	9	.398	.410
Away	4.33	1	2	0	33	0	27.0	39	3	14	18	vs. Right	.254	122	31	7	1	2	19	16	30	.338	.377
Day	2.70	1	0	0	20	0	20.0	21	3	9	13	Inning 1-6	.333	12	4	1	0	0	4	3	2	.467	.417
Night	2.08	2	2	2	43	0	34.2	37	0	17	26	Inning 7+	.280	193	54	10	1	3	20	23	37	.355	.389
Grass	2.20	3	2	2	51	0	45.0	49	3	22	31	None on	.299	97	29	6	0	3		9	15	.358	.454
Turf	2.79	0	0	0	12	0	9.2	9	0	4	8	Runners on	.269	108	29	5	1	0	21	17	24	.365	.333
March/April	2.08	0	1	0	11	0	8.2	9	0	8	7	Scoring Posn	.279	68	19	3	1	0	21	14	14	.398	.353
May	2.70	0	1	0	13	0	10.0	9	1	4	6	Close & Late	.273	99	27	5	0	1	10	17	20	.379	.354
June	0.87	2	0	2	11	0	10.1	10	0	4	13	None on/out	.244	45	11	1	0	2	2	3	8	.292	.400
July	4.50	0	0	0	9	0	10.0	16	1	6	2	vs. 1st Batr (relief)	.212	52	11	1	1	1	9	9	17	.323	.327
August	1.00	0	0	0	11	0	9.0	6	1	2	6	1st Inning Pitched	.276	170	47	11	1	2	20	24	32	.364	.388
Sept/Oct	2.70	1	0	0	8	0	6.2	8	0	2	5	First 15 Pitches	.293	157	46	10	1	2	18	22	29	.378	.408
Starter	0.00	0	0	0	0	0	0.0	0	0	0	0	Pitch 16-30	.256	39	10	1	0	1	4	4	8	.326	.359

1997 Season

	ERA	W	L	Sv	G	GS	IP	H	HR	BB	SO		Avg	AB	H	2B	3B	HR	RBI	BB	SO	OBP	SLG
Reliever	2.30	3	2	2	63	0	54.2	58	3	26	39	Pitch 31-45	.250	8	2	0	0	0	2	0	2	.250	.250
0 Days rest (Relief)	3.18	0	2	0	10	0	5.2	7	0	6	1	Pitch 46+	.000	1	0	0	0	0	0	0	0	.000	.000
1 or 2 Days rest	1.97	2	0	2	34	0	32.0	34	1	14	24	First Pitch	.324	34	11	1	0	2	5	5	0	.410	.529
3+ Days rest	2.65	1	0	0	19	0	17.0	17	2	6	14	Ahead in Count	.169	89	15	3	1	1	10	0	33	.167	.258
vs. AL	0.00	2	0	0	6	0	5.1	5	0	1	3	Behind in Count	.417	48	20	4	0	6	12	0	.533	.507
vs. NL	2.55	1	2	2	57	0	49.1	53	3	25	36	Two Strikes	.113	80	9	2	1	0	6	9	39	.200	.163
Pre-All Star	2.27	2	2	2	37	0	31.2	35	2	17	27	Pre-All Star	.287	122	35	7	0	2	11	17	27	.371	.393
Post-All Star	2.35	1	0	0	26	0	23.0	23	1	9	12	Post-All Star	.277	83	23	4	1	1	13	9	12	.348	.386

Joe Hall — Tigers
Age 32 – Bats Right

	Avg	G	AB	R	H	2B	3B	HR	RBI	BB	SO	HBP	GDP	SB	CS	OBP	SLG	IBB	SH	SF	#Pit	#P/PA	GB	FB	G/F
1997 Season	.500	2	4	1	2	1	0	0	3	0	0	0	0	0	0	.500	.750	0	0	0	13	3.25	1	0	0.00
Career (1994-1997)	.319	26	47	9	15	4	0	1	8	4	7	1	3	0	0	.385	.468	0	0	0	218	4.19	19	9	2.11

1997 Season

	Avg	AB	H	2B	3B	HR	RBI	BB	SO	OBP	SLG		Avg	AB	H	2B	3B	HR	RBI	BB	SO	OBP	SLG
vs. Left	1.000	2	2	1	0	0	3	0	0	1.000	1.500	Scoring Posn	1.000	1	1	0	0	0	2	0	0	1.000	1.000
vs. Right	.000	2	0	0	0	0	0	0	0	.000	.000	Close & Late	.000	0	0	0	0	0	0	0	0	.000	.000

Shane Halter — Royals
Age 28 – Bats Right

	Avg	G	AB	R	H	2B	3B	HR	RBI	BB	SO	HBP	GDP	SB	CS	OBP	SLG	IBB	SH	SF	#Pit	#P/PA	GB	FB	G/F
1997 Season	.276	74	123	16	34	5	1	2	10	10	28	2	1	4	3	.341	.382	0	4	0	521	3.75	38	28	1.36

1997 Season

	Avg	AB	H	2B	3B	HR	RBI	BB	SO	OBP	SLG		Avg	AB	H	2B	3B	HR	RBI	BB	SO	OBP	SLG
vs. Left	.286	63	18	1	0	2	4	3	21	.328	.397	Scoring Posn	.129	31	4	2	0	0	7	0	9	.156	.194
vs. Right	.267	60	16	4	1	0	6	7	7	.353	.367	Close & Late	.167	18	3	1	0	0	3	3	5	.318	.222
Home	.265	49	13	2	0	1	5	7	5	.379	.367	None on/out	.200	30	6	0	0	1	1	2	7	.250	.300
Away	.284	74	21	3	1	1	5	3	23	.312	.392	Batting #2	.255	55	14	3	0	2	6	3	13	.305	.418
First Pitch	.500	14	7	1	0	2	3	0	0	.500	1.000	Batting #8	.192	26	5	1	0	0	1	2	9	.250	.231
Ahead in Count	.227	22	5	2	1	0	3	9	0	.469	.409	Other	.357	42	15	1	1	0	3	5	6	.438	.429
Behind in Count	.239	67	16	1	0	3	0	25	.250	.254	Pre-All Star	.281	32	9	0	0	1	6	7	.410	.281
Two Strikes	.185	65	12	0	0	1	1	28	.209	.185	Post-All Star	.275	91	25	5	1	2	9	4	21	.313	.418

Bob Hamelin — Tigers
Age 30 – Bats Left (flyball hitter)

	Avg	G	AB	R	H	2B	3B	HR	RBI	BB	SO	HBP	GDP	SB	CS	OBP	SLG	IBB	SH	SF	#Pit	#P/PA	GB	FB	G/F
1997 Season	.270	110	318	47	86	15	0	18	52	48	72	1	8	2	1	.366	.487	3	0	2	1447	3.91	90	96	0.94
Career (1993-1997)	.250	388	1126	164	281	64	3	60	187	190	263	10	27	11	7	.359	.472	9	0	12	5376	4.01	317	356	0.89

1997 Season

	Avg	AB	H	2B	3B	HR	RBI	BB	SO	OBP	SLG		Avg	AB	H	2B	3B	HR	RBI	BB	SO	OBP	SLG
vs. Left	.209	43	9	1	0	2	4	8	11	.346	.372	First Pitch	.292	48	14	5	0	4	10				
vs. Right	.280	275	77	14	0	16	48	40	61	.369	.505	Ahead in Count	.369	65	24	3	0	5	15	3			
Groundball	.242	62	15	1	0	0	2	12	19	.365	.258	Behind in Count	.174	132	23	4	0	2	13				
Flyball	.267	60	16	1	0	5	11	12	14	.384	.533	Two Strikes	.186	161	30	6	0	5	18	1			
Home	.251	167	42	5	0	10	26	32	35	.373	.461	Batting #5	.279	172	48	12	0	11	29	3			
Away	.291	151	44	10	0	8	26	16	37	.357	.517	Batting #6	.241	79	19	3	0	4	12	1			
Day	.292	106	31	4	0	9	17	18	14	.397	.585	Other	.284	67	19	0	0	3	11				
Night	.259	212	55	11	0	9	35	30	58	.350	.439	March/April	.000	0	0	0	0	0	0				
Grass	.257	288	74	12	0	17	45	45	68	.358	.476	May	.311	45	14	1	0	3	10				
Turf	.400	30	12	3	0	1	7	3	4	.441	.600	June	.338	68	23	5	0	3	8	1			
Pre-All Star	.303	132	40	6	0	9	25	20	21	.399	.553	July	.219	64	14	4	0	5	15	1			
Post-All Star	.247	186	46	9	0	9	27	28	51	.343	.441	August	.303	89	27	4	0	5	14				
Scoring Posn	.274	84	23	4	0	4	32	14	15	.376	.464	Sept/Oct	.154	52	8	1	0	2	5	1			
Close & Late	.297	37	11	1	0	2	6	8	12	.422	.486	vs. AL	.275	287	79	15	0	17	48	4			
None on/out	.205	73	15	3	0	5	5	5	19	.256	.452	vs. NL	.226	31	7	0	0	1	4				

1997 By Position

Position	Avg	AB	H	2B	3B	HR	RBI	BB	SO	OBP	SLG	G	GS	Innings	PO	A	E	DP	Fld Pct	Rng Fctr	In Zone
As DH	.275	298	82	15	0	18	51	46	66	.372	.507	95	87	---	---	---	---	---	---	---	---
As Pinch Hitter	.214	14	3	0	0	0	1	1	4	.267	.214	16	0	---	---	---	---	---	---	---	---

Career (1993-1997)

	Avg	AB	H	2B	3B	HR	RBI	BB	SO	OBP	SLG		Avg	AB	H	2B	3B	HR	RBI	BB	SO	OBP	SLG
vs. Left	.235	170	40	7	1	6	24	30	48	.362	.394	First Pitch	.310	171	53	14	0	12	34	7	0	.344	.602
vs. Right	.252	956	241	57	2	54	163	160	215	.359	.485	Ahead in Count	.355	228	81	16	1	20	67	108	0	.557	.697
Groundball	.212	255	54	11	2	8	32	48	71	.337	.365	Behind in Count	.169	478	81	18	2	14	46	0	205	.174	.303
Flyball	.246	244	60	10	0	17	43	49	54	.368	.496	Two Strikes	.176	575	101	27	1	21	62	75	263	.271	.336
Home	.244	561	137	33	2	29	91	99	115	.360	.465	Batting #4	.254	355	90	28	0	18	58	56	91	.356	.485
Away	.255	565	144	31	1	31	96	91	148	.359	.478	Batting #5	.237	452	107	27	1	22	70	86	101	.359	.447
Day	.244	340	83	23	0	16	53	70	73	.374	.453	Other	.263	319	84	9	2	20	59	48	71	.363	.492
Night	.252	786	198	41	3	44	134	120	190	.353	.480	March/April	.269	134	36	5	0	8	28	36	31	.417	.485
Grass	.233	825	192	42	2	36	123	138	202	.345	.419	May	.202	218	44	9	1	11	42	41	56	.335	.404
Turf	.296	301	89	22	1	24	64	52	61	.398	.615	June	.289	180	52	19	1	6	22	24	28	.382	.526
Pre-All Star	.250	609	152	36	2	33	110	111	126	.368	.478	July	.242	244	59	13	0	18	47	41	66	.351	.516

Career (1993-1997)

	Avg	AB	H	2B	3B	HR	RBI	BB	SO	OBP	SLG		Avg	AB	H	2B	3B	HR	RBI	BB	SO	OBP	SLG
Post-All Star	.250	517	129	28	1	27	77	79	137	.349	.464	August	.319	182	58	12	0	10	28	20	40	.385	.549
Scoring Posn	.212	307	65	14	1	14	120	70	68	.350	.401	Sept/Oct	.190	168	32	6	1	7	20	28	42	.305	.363
Close & Late	.279	154	43	8	1	13	33	36	41	.415	.597	vs. AL	.250	1095	274	64	3	59	183	186	258	.361	.476
None on/out	.248	262	65	15	1	14	14	27	62	.328	.473	vs. NL	.226	31	7	0	0	1	4	5	.314	.323

Batter vs. Pitcher (career)

Hits Best Against	Avg	AB	H	2B	3B	HR	RBI	BB	SO	OBP	SLG	Hits Worst Against	Avg	AB	H	2B	3B	HR	RBI	BB	SO	OBP	SLG
Ricky Bones	.471	17	8	1	0	2	3	3	3	.550	.882	Mike Mussina	.000	21	0	0	0	0	1	1	4	.045	.000
Shawn Boskie	.444	9	4	2	0	1	2	1	0	.545	1.000	Juan Guzman	.091	11	1	1	0	0	0	1	3	.167	.182
Bob Wolcott	.429	14	6	3	0	1	5	2	0	.500	.857	Kevin Tapani	.100	10	1	1	0	0	0	1	4	.182	.200
Tim Belcher	.412	17	7	1	0	2	5	3	1	.500	.824	Charles Nagy	.111	18	2	0	0	0	1	1	9	.158	.111
Bobby Witt	.391	23	9	4	0	2	8	0	4	.375	.826	Roger Clemens	.154	13	2	0	0	1	1	1	5	.267	.154

Darryl Hamilton — Giants

Age 33 – Bats Left (groundball hitter)

	Avg	G	AB	R	H	2B	3B	HR	RBI	BB	SO	HBP	GDP	SB	CS	OBP	SLG	IBB	SH	SF	#Pit	#P/PA	GB	FB	G/F
1997 Season	.270	125	460	78	124	23	3	5	43	61	61	0	6	15	10	.354	.365	1	6	2	2125	4.02	190	123	1.54
Last Five Years	.286	556	2146	323	614	103	15	26	199	222	241	8	39	65	29	.353	.384	14	27	13	9540	3.95	876	564	1.55

1997 Season

	Avg	AB	H	2B	3B	HR	RBI	BB	SO	OBP	SLG		Avg	AB	H	2B	3B	HR	RBI	BB	SO	OBP	SLG
vs. Left	.250	104	26	3	1	1	12	11	20	.316	.327	First Pitch	.346	52	18	4	1	2	9	1	0	.358	.577
vs. Right	.275	356	98	20	2	4	31	50	41	.365	.376	Ahead in Count	.312	93	29	6	0	2	12	31	0	.484	.441
Groundball	.323	93	30	3	1	1	12	6	10	.360	.409	Behind in Count	.235	204	48	9	1	0	12	0	48	.234	.289
Flyball	.217	46	10	1	1	0	3	9	9	.345	.283	Two Strikes	.238	214	51	8	2	1	18	29	61	.327	.308
Home	.251	203	51	9	2	1	14	31	28	.349	.330	Batting #1	.269	446	120	21	3	5	40	57	59	.350	.363
Away	.284	257	73	14	1	4	29	30	33	.358	.393	Batting #2	.000	5	0	0	0	0	0	1	1	.286	.000
Day	.287	178	51	14	2	1	16	32	24	.392	.404	Other	.444	9	4	2	0	0	3	2	1	.545	.667
Night	.259	282	73	9	1	4	27	29	37	.328	.340	March/April	.244	45	11	0	0	1	7	6	.346	.244
Grass	.274	361	99	18	3	5	36	54	48	.367	.382	May	.317	41	13	2	0	0	6	7	7	.417	.366
Turf	.253	99	25	5	0	0	7	7	13	.302	.303	June	.278	108	30	8	2	2	10	6	13	.313	.444
Pre-All Star	.276	214	59	11	2	2	18	23	27	.345	.374	July	.346	81	28	6	1	1	4	18	9	.465	.481
Post-All Star	.264	246	65	12	1	3	25	38	34	.361	.358	August	.208	120	25	4	0	1	9	17	.262	.267
Scoring Posn	.320	100	32	4	1	2	37	10	11	.375	.440	Sept/Oct	.262	65	17	3	0	1	13	14	9	.392	.354
Close & Late	.294	68	20	5	0	1	10	6	12	.351	.412	vs. AL	.228	57	13	5	0	1	3	8	5	.323	.368
None on/out	.238	193	46	9	1	0	0	29	28	.338	.295	vs. NL	.275	403	111	18	3	4	40	53	56	.358	.365

1997 By Position

Position	Avg	AB	H	2B	3B	HR	RBI	BB	SO	OBP	SLG	G	GS	Innings	PO	A	E	DP	Fld Pct	Rng Fctr	In Zone	Outs	Zone Rtg	MLB Zone
As cf	.272	453	123	23	3	5	43	60	59	.355	.369	119	112	961.2	245	1	5	0	.980	2.30	297	232	.781	.815

Last Five Years

	Avg	AB	H	2B	3B	HR	RBI	BB	SO	OBP	SLG		Avg	AB	H	2B	3B	HR	RBI	BB	SO	OBP	SLG
vs. Left	.256	613	157	15	7	3	49	61	84	.326	.318	First Pitch	.376	178	67	12	3	3	27	12	0	.417	.528
vs. Right	.298	1533	457	88	8	23	150	161	157	.364	.411	Ahead in Count	.328	460	151	22	3	11	62	110	0	.456	.461
Groundball	.279	480	134	25	7	3	46	38	53	.333	.379	Behind in Count	.257	986	253	45	7	6	68	0	205	.259	.335
Flyball	.288	368	106	16	2	6	37	44	49	.368	.391	Two Strikes	.247	962	238	44	6	9	78	100	241	.319	.334
Home	.297	1052	312	49	7	11	106	131	105	.375	.388	Batting #1	.290	1613	468	77	11	18	142	164	186	.355	.385
Away	.276	1094	302	54	8	15	93	91	136	.332	.381	Batting #2	.262	374	98	17	4	6	40	43	38	.343	.377
Day	.287	729	209	36	5	7	60	69	88	.347	.379	Other	.302	159	48	9	0	2	17	15	17	.362	.396
Night	.286	1417	405	67	10	19	139	153	153	.356	.387	March/April	.278	317	88	10	2	0	18	40	42	.358	.322
Grass	.293	1787	524	87	14	23	170	197	203	.363	.396	May	.317	325	103	18	1	3	30	38	34	.389	.406
Turf	.251	359	90	16	1	3	29	25	38	.301	.326	June	.292	425	124	25	4	6	49	29	47	.333	.407
Pre-All Star	.293	1177	345	60	8	9	102	116	135	.355	.381	July	.310	358	111	19	4	4	29	43	42	.385	.419
Post-All Star	.278	969	269	43	7	17	97	106	106	.351	.389	August	.274	420	115	18	4	9	44	37	44	.335	.400
Scoring Posn	.285	463	132	21	5	3	160	69	52	.372	.371	Sept/Oct	.243	301	73	13	1	4	29	35	32	.324	.332
Close & Late	.268	306	82	18	1	3	33	34	36	.342	.363	vs. AL	.289	1743	503	85	12	22	159	169	185	.352	.389
None on/out	.299	780	233	39	5	9	9	71	90	.359	.396	vs. NL	.275	403	111	18	3	4	40	53	56	.358	.365

Batter vs. Pitcher (career)

Hits Best Against	Avg	AB	H	2B	3B	HR	RBI	BB	SO	OBP	SLG	Hits Worst Against	Avg	AB	H	2B	3B	HR	RBI	BB	SO	OBP	SLG
Kevin Appier	.538	26	14	1	1	0	2	1	2	.618	.654	Sterling Hitchcock	.083	12	1	0	0	0	2	0	1	.214	.083
Andy Ashby	.500	12	6	1	0	1	1	1	2	.538	.750	Jeff Montgomery	.118	17	2	0	0	1	1	1	.167	.118
Jason Bere	.455	11	5	1	0	0	4	2	.600	.545	Mark Langston	.125	16	2	0	0	0	0	3	.176	.125
Kevin Tapani	.438	32	14	3	1	1	7	3	3	.486	.688	Jamie Moyer	.167	18	3	0	0	0	0	1	1	.211	.167
Bret Saberhagen	.364	11	4	1	0	1	4	5	.417	.727	Mark Guthrie	.182	11	2	0	0	0	0	3	.182	.182

Joey Hamilton — Padres

Age 27 – Pitches Right (groundball pitcher)

	ERA	W	L	Sv	G	GS	IP	BB	SO	Avg	H	2B	3B	HR	RBI	OBP	SLG	CG	ShO	Sup	QS	#P/S	SB	CS	GB	FB	G/F
1997 Season	4.25	12	7	0	31	29	192.2	69	124	.271	199	36	3	22	90	.340	.418	1	0	4.67	16	101	13	12	305	162	1.88
Career (1994-1997)	3.70	42	31	0	112	108	717.1	237	492	.255	692	100	17	65	290	.322	.376	7	4	4.55	67	102	38	28	1210	557	2.17

1997 Season

	ERA	W	L	Sv	G	GS	IP	H	HR	BB	SO		Avg	AB	H	2B	3B	HR	RBI	BB	SO	OBP	SLG
Home	4.56	3	6	0	17	16	102.2	108	16	42	80	vs. Left	.306	360	110	23	3	14	52	35	43	.372	.503
Away	3.90	9	1	0	14	13	90.0	91	6	27	44	vs. Right	.238	374	89	13	0	8	38	34	81	.310	.337
Day	3.86	6	2	0	14	12	84.0	79	7	32	68	Inning 1-6	.274	631	173	31	3	19	80	63	108	.347	.423
Night	4.56	6	5	0	17	17	108.2	120	9	37	56	Inning 7+	.252	103	26	5	0	3	10	6	16	.297	.388

190

1997 Season

	ERA	W	L	Sv	G	GS	IP	H	HR	BB	SO		Avg	AB	H	2B	3B	HR	RBI	BB	SO	OBP	SLG
Grass	4.28	8	6	0	24	22	147.1	154	19	52	99	None on	.270	437	118	21	3	14	14	32	76	.327	.428
Turf	4.17	4	1	0	7	7	45.1	45	3	17	25	Runners on	.273	297	81	15	0	8	76	37	48	.358	.404
March/April	4.56	1	1	0	4	4	23.2	28	4	11	21	Scoring Posn	.257	175	45	7	0	4	67	27	28	.355	.366
May	3.50	2	1	0	3	3	18.0	14	3	5	11	Close & Late	.273	55	15	2	0	1	5	4	6	.322	.364
June	4.75	2	1	0	6	6	36.0	37	3	21	24	None on/out	.289	194	56	10	3	8	8	13	25	.340	.495
July	3.55	3	0	0	6	5	38.0	40	3	14	25	vs. 1st Batr (relief)	.000	2	0	0	0	0	0	0	1	.000	.000
August	4.91	2	1	0	6	6	44.0	48	4	8	23	1st Inning Pitched	.254	114	29	7	0	2	13	18	14	.368	.368
Sept/Oct	3.82	2	3	0	6	5	33.0	32	5	10	20	First 75 Pitches	.264	519	137	27	3	14	58	54	80	.341	.408
Starter	4.32	11	7	0	29	29	187.2	197	22	69	121	Pitch 76-90	.287	108	31	3	0	4	16	4	17	.319	.426
Reliever	1.80	1	0	0	2	0	5.0	2	0	0	3	Pitch 91-105	.292	72	21	3	0	1	8	10	16	.381	.375
0-3 Days Rest (Start)	0.00	0	0	0	0	0	0.0	0	0	0	0	Pitch 106+	.286	35	10	3	0	3	8	1	11	.306	.629
4 Days Rest	4.09	8	6	0	20	20	134.1	137	17	46	80	First Pitch	.352	125	44	8	0	3	20	2	0	.373	.488
5+ Days Rest	4.89	3	1	0	9	9	53.1	60	5	23	41	Ahead in Count	.213	320	68	10	1	5	19	0	106	.229	.297
vs. AL	6.46	1	1	0	3	3	15.1	21	5	9	8	Behind in Count	.366	142	52	10	2	7	24	42	0	.505	.613
vs. NL	4.06	11	6	0	28	26	177.1	178	17	60	116	Two Strikes	.173	306	53	7	0	6	25	25	124	.255	.255
Pre-All Star	4.21	6	3	0	15	14	87.2	89	12	40	61	Pre-All Star	.271	329	89	14	1	12	40	40	61	.355	.429
Post-All Star	4.29	6	4	0	16	15	105.0	110	10	29	63	Post-All Star	.272	405	110	22	2	10	50	29	63	.327	.410

Career (1994-1997)

	ERA	W	L	Sv	G	GS	IP	H	HR	BB	SO		Avg	AB	H	2B	3B	HR	RBI	BB	SO	OBP	SLG
Home	3.43	22	18	0	59	57	375.2	351	37	127	281	vs. Left	.268	1285	344	53	9	34	143	119	203	.334	.402
Away	4.00	20	13	0	53	51	341.2	341	28	110	211	vs. Right	.244	1427	348	47	8	31	147	118	289	.311	.353
Day	4.36	17	8	0	36	33	214.2	218	25	81	179	Inning 1-6	.253	2342	593	87	15	58	259	201	440	.319	.377
Night	3.42	25	23	0	76	75	502.2	474	40	156	313	Inning 7+	.268	370	99	13	2	7	31	36	52	.338	.370
Grass	3.69	33	24	0	90	87	575.1	558	57	188	408	None on	.252	1600	403	61	14	41	41	128	285	.314	.384
Turf	3.74	9	7	0	22	21	142.0	134	8	49	84	Runners on	.260	1112	289	39	3	24	249	109	207	.332	.365
March/April	3.63	6	2	0	11	11	69.1	67	4	24	54	Scoring Posn	.256	614	157	23	3	11	217	73	121	.335	.357
May	4.06	7	5	0	16	16	99.2	98	13	24	71	Close & Late	.272	235	64	7	0	4	21	29	29	.357	.353
June	3.51	8	5	0	24	24	164.0	142	13	66	96	None on/out	.261	709	185	27	9	22	22	47	107	.314	.417
July	3.76	8	7	0	23	20	139.1	143	11	50	106	vs. 1st Batr (relief)	.000	4	0	0	0	0	0	0	2	.000	.000
August	3.48	9	4	0	21	21	144.2	139	10	37	100	1st Inning Pitched	.252	416	105	18	3	10	54	61	65	.357	.382
Sept/Oct	3.93	4	8	0	17	16	100.2	103	10	36	65	First 75 Pitches	.242	1895	460	72	13	38	185	174	339	.314	.354
Starter	3.73	41	31	0	108	108	709.2	689	65	236	486	Pitch 76-90	.296	402	119	13	2	15	55	21	71	.332	.450
Reliever	1.17	1	0	0	4	0	7.2	1	0	1	6	Pitch 91-105	.242	273	66	7	1	7	26	22	55	.302	.352
0-3 Days Rest (Start)	4.15	1	1	0	2	2	13.0	15	1	5	8	Pitch 106+	.345	142	49	8	1	5	24	20	27	.429	.521
4 Days Rest	3.22	27	25	0	72	72	492.1	457	45	152	329	First Pitch	.343	399	137	21	0	12	60	8	0	.372	.486
5+ Days Rest	4.93	13	5	0	34	34	204.1	217	19	79	149	Ahead in Count	.204	1255	256	29	9	18	82	0	418	.215	.284
vs. AL	6.46	1	1	0	3	3	15.1	21	5	9	8	Behind in Count	.305	534	163	30	6	20	79	128	0	.438	.496
vs. NL	3.64	41	30	0	109	105	702.0	671	60	228	484	Two Strikes	.183	1243	227	36	8	17	86	101	492	.251	.265
Pre-All Star	3.73	24	13	0	59	56	371.1	345	39	126	244	Pre-All Star	.250	1380	345	44	9	39	154	126	244	.322	.380
Post-All Star	3.67	18	18	0	53	52	346.0	347	26	111	248	Post-All Star	.261	1332	347	56	8	26	136	111	248	.322	.373

Pitcher vs. Batter (career)

Pitches Best Vs.	Avg	AB	H	2B	3B	HR	RBI	BB	SO	OBP	SLG	Pitches Worst Vs.	Avg	AB	H	2B	3B	HR	RBI	BB	SO	OBP	SLG
Bret Boone	.000	14	0	0	0	0	1	1	2	.167	.000	Ellis Burks	.462	13	6	3	0	1	4	2	1	.533	.923
Darrin Fletcher	.071	14	1	0	0	0	0	1	0	.133	.071	Dante Bichette	.450	20	9	2	0	2	4	1	5	.476	.850
Derek Bell	.077	13	1	0	0	0	0	1	2	.143	.077	Ryan Klesko	.375	16	6	0	0	2	3	2	3	.444	.750
Chad Fonville	.083	12	1	0	0	0	1	1	3	.154	.083	Barry Bonds	.353	17	6	0	1	3	6	2	2	.421	1.000
Mike Lansing	.105	19	2	0	0	0	1	0	4	.150	.105	Chipper Jones	.350	20	7	2	0	2	4	2	1	.409	.750

Chris Hammond — Red Sox

Age 32 – Pitches Left (groundball pitcher)

	ERA	W	L	Sv	G	GS	IP	BB	SO	Avg	H	2B	3B	HR	RBI	OBP	SLG	GF	IR	IRS	Hld	SvOp	SB	CS	GB	FB	G/F
1997 Season	5.92	3	4	1	29	8	65.1	27	48	.310	81	15	0	5	40	.375	.425	6	17	7	4	2	4	2	116	45	2.58
Last Five Years	4.63	32	34	1	137	86	571.2	190	372	.281	628	116	15	59	293	.340	.426	11	36	19	9	2	12	19	888	591	1.50

1997 Season

	ERA	W	L	Sv	G	GS	IP	H	HR	BB	SO		Avg	AB	H	2B	3B	HR	RBI	BB	SO	OBP	SLG
Home	3.57	3	2	1	18	4	40.1	39	1	16	29	vs. Left	.297	74	22	6	0	1	17	2	19	.312	.419
Away	9.72	0	2	0	11	4	25.0	42	4	11	19	vs. Right	.316	187	59	9	0	4	23	25	29	.398	.428
Starter	6.48	2	3	0	8	8	41.2	55	3	13	28	Scoring Posn	.389	72	28	5	0	2	34	9	11	.447	.542
Reliever	4.94	1	1	1	21	0	23.2	26	2	14	20	Close & Late	.324	37	12	4	0	2	8	4	10	.381	.595
0 Days rest (Relief)	6.75	0	0	0	6	0	4.0	3	0	0	6	None on/out	.333	63	21	5	0	1	1	5	12	.382	.460
1 or 2 Days rest	6.28	0	1	0	10	0	14.1	21	2	11	10	First Pitch	.525	40	21	5	0	1	11	0	0	.578	.725
3+ Days rest	0.00	1	0	0	5	0	5.1	2	0	3	4	Ahead in Count	.221	122	27	7	0	1	18	0	44	.220	.303
Pre-All Star	5.92	3	4	1	29	8	65.1	81	5	27	48	Behind in Count	.362	58	21	3	0	1	6	19	0	.513	.466
Post-All Star	0.00	0	0	0	0	0	0.0	0	0	0	0	Two Strikes	.208	120	25	6	0	2	1	4	48	.232	.308

Last Five Years

	ERA	W	L	Sv	G	GS	IP	H	HR	BB	SO		Avg	AB	H	2B	3B	HR	RBI	BB	SO	OBP	SLG
Home	3.79	17	14	1	67	39	271.0	273	18	80	186	vs. Left	.270	470	127	24	3	10	64	38	87	.328	.398
Away	5.39	15	20	0	70	47	300.2	355	41	110	186	vs. Right	.284	1762	501	92	12	49	229	152	285	.343	.434
Day	5.95	6	10	0	36	21	130.0	161	15	48	79	Inning 1-6	.280	1830	512	92	14	46	237	158	304	.339	.421
Night	4.24	26	24	1	101	65	441.2	467	44	142	293	Inning 7+	.289	402	116	24	1	13	56	32	68	.345	.450
Grass	4.08	29	24	1	109	67	452.0	452	41	149	296	None on	.257	1282	330	59	8	30	30	99	227	.314	.386
Turf	6.69	3	10	0	28	19	119.2	154	18	49	76	Runners on	.314	950	298	57	7	29	263	91	145	.374	.480
March/April	5.17	3	10	0	25	17	101.0	112	13	43	55	Scoring Posn	.298	560	167	30	5	13	209	59	95	.363	.439
May	3.71	10	5	0	28	19	123.2	105	15	46	79	Close & Late	.288	184	53	13	1	6	28	14	35	.340	.467
June	3.72	10	4	1	28	15	116.0	141	8	31	69	None on/out	.284	573	163	27	2	17	17	45	87	.340	.428

Last Five Years

	ERA	W	L	Sv	G	GS	IP	H	HR	BB	SO
July	4.66	4	4	0	13	13	77.1	81	8	21	48
August	7.39	2	6	0	21	10	70.2	102	7	18	51
Sept/Oct	4.23	3	5	0	22	12	83.0	87	8	31	70
Starter	4.74	28	31	0	86	86	501.1	552	52	162	319
Reliever	3.84	4	3	1	51	0	70.1	76	7	28	53
0 Days rest (Relief)	5.40	1	0	0	7	0	5.0	3	0	0	6
1 or 2 Days rest	5.23	1	2	1	28	0	41.1	59	6	22	27
3+ Days rest	1.13	2	1	0	16	0	24.0	14	1	6	20
vs. AL	6.38	3	4	0	26	8	60.2	78	5	25	44
vs. NL	4.42	29	30	1	111	78	511.0	550	54	165	328
Pre-All Star	4.16	24	19	1	84	54	361.0	381	37	123	215
Post-All Star	5.43	8	15	0	53	32	210.2	247	22	67	157

	Avg	AB	H	2B	3B	HR	RBI	BB	SO	OBP	SLG
vs. 1st Batr (relief)	.326	46	15	3	0	1	14	4	11	.380	.457
1st Inning Pitched	.286	497	142	22	4	14	78	47	100	.348	.431
First 15 Pitches	.295	438	129	22	4	12	51	35	73	.351	.445
Pitch 16-30	.249	409	102	19	2	16	55	29	95	.300	.423
Pitch 31-45	.287	349	100	19	6	4	44	32	55	.345	.410
Pitch 46+	.287	1036	297	56	3	27	143	94	149	.349	.425
First Pitch	.364	324	118	26	5	9	54	6	0	.378	.559
Ahead in Count	.216	982	212	41	4	14	102	0	323	.223	.309
Behind in Count	.322	538	173	32	5	16	73	121	0	.449	.489
Two Strikes	.202	968	196	35	4	14	98	63	372	.255	.290
Pre-All Star	.274	1392	381	61	7	37	167	123	215	.334	.407
Post-All Star	.294	840	247	55	8	22	126	67	157	.350	.457

Pitcher vs. Batter (career)

Pitches Best Vs.	Avg	AB	H	2B	3B	HR	RBI	BB	SO	OBP	SLG
Jeff Kent	.067	15	1	1	0	0	1	0	3	.067	.133
Mark Whiten	.077	13	1	0	0	0	0	0	6	.077	.077
Wil Cordero	.083	12	1	0	0	0	2	1	0	.143	.083
Kirt Manwaring	.111	18	2	1	0	0	1	1	3	.158	.167
Moises Alou	.133	15	2	0	0	0	0	1	4	.188	.133

Pitches Worst Vs.	Avg	AB	H	2B	3B	HR	RBI	BB	SO	OBP	SLG
Larry Walker	.600	15	9	0	0	2	3	1	2	.647	1.000
Bernard Gilkey	.560	25	14	2	0	0	5	5	1	.633	.640
Kevin Mitchell	.500	10	5	1	0	1	3	1	0	.545	.900
Reggie Sanders	.438	16	7	1	3	1	6	2	1	.500	1.063
Ellis Burks	.364	11	4	0	0	3	3	0	1	.417	1.182

Jeffrey Hammonds — Orioles

Age 27 – Bats Right (flyball hitter)

	Avg	G	AB	R	H	2B	3B	HR	RBI	BB	SO	HBP	GDP	SB	CS	OBP	SLG	IBB	SH	SF	#Pit	#P/PA	GB	FB	G/F
1997 Season	.264	118	397	71	105	19	3	21	55	32	73	3	6	15	1	.323	.486	1	0	2	1605	3.70	120	157	0.76
Career (1993-1997)	.263	347	1178	182	310	64	7	45	155	83	211	10	21	31	6	.314	.444	4	8	12	4659	3.61	365	442	0.83

1997 Season

	Avg	AB	H	2B	3B	HR	RBI	BB	SO	OBP	SLG
vs. Left	.277	148	41	5	3	8	18	13	25	.333	.514
vs. Right	.257	249	64	14	0	13	37	19	48	.316	.470
Groundball	.299	87	26	3	1	2	8	16		.361	.425
Flyball	.265	34	9	2	0	4	10	2	5	.297	.676
Home	.258	194	50	6	1	9	21	16	40	.316	.438
Away	.271	203	55	13	2	12	34	16	33	.329	.532
Day	.313	147	46	7	1	13	25	12	30	.365	.639
Night	.236	250	59	12	2	8	30	20	43	.298	.396
Grass	.277	354	98	18	3	19	52	29	60	.335	.506
Turf	.163	43	7	1	0	2	3	3	13	.217	.326
Pre-All Star	.287	230	66	13	1	14	37	12	42	.327	.535
Post-All Star	.234	167	39	6	2	7	18	20	31	.317	.419
Scoring Posn	.209	91	19	5	0	1	24	13	19	.308	.297
Close & Late	.234	64	15	1	1	4	14	9	11	.333	.469
None on/out	.222	90	20	2	2	4	4	4	15	.263	.422

	Avg	AB	H	2B	3B	HR	RBI	BB	SO	OBP	SLG
First Pitch	.333	57	19	3	0	4	8	1	0	.350	.596
Ahead in Count	.354	96	34	4	0	12	25	16	0	.446	.771
Behind in Count	.208	159	33	4	3	3	11	0	57	.211	.327
Two Strikes	.163	166	27	2	1	4	12	15	73	.236	.259
Batting #6	.270	126	34	6	0	9	21	4	19	.301	.532
Batting #7	.240	125	30	4	0	8	19	14	29	.321	.464
Other	.281	146	41	9	3	4	15	14	25	.342	.466
March/April	.263	76	20	2	0	2	8	5	8	.309	.368
May	.235	34	8	2	0	3	7	3	12	.316	.559
June	.301	93	28	6	0	5	13	4	17	.333	.527
July	.296	98	29	7	2	6	14	4	18	.330	.592
August	.209	43	9	0	1	2	4	3	8	.261	.395
Sept/Oct	.208	53	11	2	0	3	9	10	13	.358	.415
vs. AL	.277	347	96	19	3	20	49	28	59	.334	.522
vs. NL	.180	50	9	0	0	1	6	4	14	.241	.240

1997 By Position

Position	Avg	AB	H	2B	3B	HR	RBI	BB	SO	OBP	SLG	G	GS	Innings	PO	A	E	DP	Fld Pct	Rng Fctr	In Zone	Outs	Zone Rtg	MLB Zone
As lf	.247	89	22	3	1	8	14	2	14	.277	.573	31	23	207.2	55	2	2	0	.966	2.47	59	50	.847	.805
As cf	.293	140	41	6	2	8	20	14	26	.357	.536	40	36	319.0	94	1	1	0	.990	2.68	109	93	.853	.815
As rf	.242	157	38	9	0	5	21	14	31	.306	.395	54	40	375.0	91	1	2	0	.979	2.21	115	90	.783	.813

Career (1993-1997)

	Avg	AB	H	2B	3B	HR	RBI	BB	SO	OBP	SLG
vs. Left	.255	388	99	18	4	14	45	32	65	.309	.430
vs. Right	.267	790	211	46	3	31	110	51	146	.317	.451
Groundball	.275	255	70	14	1	8	32	22	46	.339	.431
Flyball	.240	175	42	10	1	5	26	8	32	.270	.394
Home	.270	577	156	26	3	22	70	41	105	.320	.440
Away	.256	601	154	38	4	23	85	42	106	.308	.448
Day	.265	374	99	19	2	18	52	30	70	.317	.471
Night	.262	804	211	45	5	27	103	55	141	.313	.432
Grass	.267	1043	279	57	7	41	138	75	175	.320	.453
Turf	.230	135	31	7	0	4	17	8	36	.269	.370
Pre-All Star	.267	795	212	42	5	34	115	49	136	.312	.460
Post-All Star	.256	383	98	22	2	11	40	34	75	.318	.410
Scoring Posn	.252	282	71	16	2	9	104	34	54	.324	.418
Close & Late	.238	189	45	6	1	7	27	15	33	.297	.392
None on/out	.243	272	66	12	2	11	11	18	37	.295	.423

	Avg	AB	H	2B	3B	HR	RBI	BB	SO	OBP	SLG
First Pitch	.313	160	50	13	0	7	25	3	0	.321	.525
Ahead in Count	.306	271	83	14	1	20	52	49	0	.414	.587
Behind in Count	.242	504	122	25	5	11	48	0	168	.249	.377
Two Strikes	.185	503	93	16	2	11	39	31	211	.237	.290
Batting #2	.278	266	74	14	3	3	30	8	39	.305	.387
Batting #9	.259	301	78	18	1	13	42	23	57	.315	.455
Other	.259	611	158	32	3	29	83	52	115	.318	.463
March/April	.277	249	69	14	2	9	32	11	34	.313	.458
May	.248	149	37	6	1	8	23	15	30	.329	.423
June	.276	286	79	13	1	9	33	16	55	.315	.423
July	.290	290	84	22	2	11	41	17	51	.328	.493
August	.201	139	28	6	1	5	17	10	29	.257	.367
Sept/Oct	.200	65	13	3	0	3	9	14	12	.338	.385
vs. AL	.267	1128	301	64	7	44	149	79	197	.317	.453
vs. NL	.180	50	9	0	0	1	6	4	14	.241	.240

Batter vs. Pitcher (career)

Hits Best Against	Avg	AB	H	2B	3B	HR	RBI	BB	SO	OBP	SLG
Charles Nagy	.385	13	5	1	0	0	1	1	5	.429	.462
Kenny Rogers	.364	11	4	0	0	1	3	2	1	.462	.636
Kevin Appier	.364	11	4	1	0	0	0	1	2	.462	.455
James Baldwin	.364	11	4	1	0	2	3	2	3	.462	1.000
Tom Gordon	.333	12	4	2	0	0	2	0	3	.333	.500

Hits Worst Against	Avg	AB	H	2B	3B	HR	RBI	BB	SO	OBP	SLG
Pat Hentgen	.077	13	1	0	0	0	1	0	3	.077	.077
Kevin Tapani	.083	12	1	0	0	0	0	0	2	.083	.083
Chuck Finley	.133	15	2	0	0	0	0	0	4	.133	.133
Dennis Martinez	.167	12	2	0	0	0	0	0	2	.167	.167
Rich Robertson	.167	12	2	1	0	0	1	2	3	.286	.250

Mike Hampton — Astros

	ERA	W	L	Sv	G	GS	IP	BB	SO	Avg	H	2B	3B	HR	RBI	OBP	SLG	CG	ShO	Sup	QS	#P/S	SB	CS	GB	FB	G/F
1997 Season	3.83	15	10	0	34	34	223.0	77	139	.257	217	41	4	16	88	.318	.372	7	2	6.17	20	98	4	7	394	174	2.26
Career (1993-1997)	3.80	37	32	1	142	88	592.1	208	387	.266	607	115	10	48	259	.328	.389	9	3	5.64	48	93	39	22	1034	463	2.23

1997 Season

	ERA	W	L	Sv	G	GS	IP	H	HR	BB	SO		Avg	AB	H	2B	3B	HR	RBI	BB	SO	OBP	SLG
Home	3.09	10	2	0	16	16	113.2	99	5	34	81	vs. Left	.303	155	47	8	1	3	24	12	21	.353	.426
Away	4.61	5	8	0	18	18	109.1	118	11	43	58	vs. Right	.247	689	170	33	3	13	64	65	118	.311	.360
Day	3.01	6	2	0	12	12	86.2	67	6	32	63	Inning 1-6	.258	705	182	34	3	14	79	68	120	.322	.374
Night	4.36	9	8	0	22	22	136.1	150	10	45	76	Inning 7+	.252	139	35	7	1	2	9	9	19	.297	.360
Grass	5.27	3	7	0	14	14	80.1	97	8	33	42	None on	.251	487	122	21	3	8	8	35	74	.301	.355
Turf	3.03	12	3	0	20	20	142.2	120	8	44	97	Runners on	.266	357	95	20	1	8	80	42	65	.341	.395
March/April	5.52	1	3	0	6	6	31.0	40	2	10	19	Scoring Posn	.278	187	52	8	0	5	70	29	34	.366	.401
May	5.81	1	1	0	5	5	26.1	28	4	14	18	Close & Late	.271	48	13	2	1	1	5	2	8	.300	.417
June	4.74	1	3	0	6	6	38.0	38	3	15	25	None on/out	.300	223	67	16	0	4	4	16	25	.347	.426
July	2.25	5	0	0	6	6	48.0	41	1	5	30	vs. 1st Batr (relief)	.000	0	0	0	0	0	0	0	0	.000	.000
August	3.27	3	2	0	6	6	44.0	37	4	22	25	1st Inning Pitched	.268	127	34	5	2	2	20	21	25	.371	.386
Sept/Oct	2.78	4	1	0	5	5	35.2	33	2	11	22	First 75 Pitches	.248	612	152	29	3	8	59	60	107	.315	.345
Starter	3.83	15	10	0	34	34	223.0	217	16	77	139	Pitch 76-90	.308	120	37	4	1	7	21	9	13	.354	.533
Reliever	0.00	0	0	0	0	0	0.0	0	0	0	0	Pitch 91-105	.225	71	16	4	0	0	4	6	9	.282	.282
0-3 Days Rest (Start)	9.00	0	0	0	1	1	5.0	9	1	1	7	Pitch 106+	.293	41	12	4	0	1	4	2	10	.326	.463
4 Days Rest	3.71	11	6	0	24	24	160.0	148	11	53	100	First Pitch	.287	129	37	15	0	2	18	2	0	.301	.450
5+ Days Rest	3.72	4	4	0	9	9	58.0	60	4	23	32	Ahead in Count	.224	357	80	8	2	8	39	0	117	.222	.325
vs. AL	4.87	1	2	0	3	3	20.1	30	1	4	7	Behind in Count	.300	207	62	12	1	3	18	47	0	.426	.411
vs. NL	3.73	14	8	0	31	31	202.2	187	15	73	132	Two Strikes	.211	351	74	8	2	9	36	28	139	.268	.322
Pre-All Star	5.19	4	7	0	19	19	109.1	125	10	41	72	Pre-All Star	.290	431	125	25	3	10	60	41	72	.349	.432
Post-All Star	2.53	11	3	0	15	15	113.2	92	6	36	67	Post-All Star	.223	413	92	16	1	6	28	36	67	.286	.310

Career (1993-1997)

	ERA	W	L	Sv	G	GS	IP	H	HR	BB	SO		Avg	AB	H	2B	3B	HR	RBI	BB	SO	OBP	SLG
Home	3.40	23	13	0	68	43	310.0	300	20	92	233	vs. Left	.294	496	146	25	4	12	67	37	80	.348	.433
Away	4.24	14	19	1	74	45	282.1	307	28	116	154	vs. Right	.258	1784	461	90	6	36	192	171	307	.323	.376
Day	3.19	11	11	0	47	32	217.1	208	16	73	142	Inning 1-6	.263	1856	489	97	8	38	216	168	327	.325	.386
Night	4.15	26	21	1	95	56	375.0	399	32	135	245	Inning 7+	.278	424	118	18	2	10	43	40	60	.343	.401
Grass	4.72	7	14	1	45	28	173.2	205	18	75	86	None on	.264	1267	334	60	7	23	23	103	224	.321	.376
Turf	3.42	30	18	0	97	60	418.2	402	30	133	301	Runners on	.269	1013	273	55	3	25	236	105	163	.337	.404
March/April	4.03	5	7	0	25	13	82.2	87	6	30	59	Scoring Posn	.260	573	149	28	1	16	203	76		.342	.396
May	4.56	3	5	0	24	12	73.0	77	5	32	56	Close & Late	.254	189	48	6	1	3	20	15	27	.312	.344
June	3.58	4	5	0	26	15	103.0	103	9	37	64	None on/out	.299	571	171	36	3	9	9	50	88	.357	.420
July	3.60	12	4	1	35	18	137.2	139	8	34	91	vs. 1st Batr (relief)	.308	52	16	5	0	2	9	2	9	.333	.519
August	4.23	8	7	0	20	18	117.0	127	13	51	70	1st Inning Pitched	.264	497	131	24	5	9	67	55	78	.333	.386
Sept/Oct	2.85	5	4	0	12	12	79.0	74	7	24	47	First 75 Pitches	.260	1778	463	92	9	33	187	165	306	.324	.378
Starter	3.79	34	31	0	88	88	541.0	547	44	183	358	Pitch 76-90	.315	270	85	12	1	11	42	24	37	.370	.489
Reliever	3.86	3	1	1	54	0	51.1	60	4	25	29	Pitch 91-105	.244	164	40	7	0	3	23	13	29	.296	.341
0-3 Days Rest (Start)	5.40	1	1	0	4	4	20.0	29	4	2	18	Pitch 106+	.279	68	19	4	0	1	7	6	15	.347	.382
4 Days Rest	3.62	18	17	0	49	49	318.0	302	20	110	198	First Pitch	.324	358	116	28	5	7	48	9	0	.345	.489
5+ Days Rest	3.90	15	13	0	35	35	203.0	216	20	71	142	Ahead in Count	.210	995	209	36	2	13	92	0	331	.212	.289
vs. AL	6.99	2	5	1	16	6	37.1	58	4	21	15	Behind in Count	.334	542	181	33	2	19	75	111	0	.446	.517
vs. NL	3.58	35	27	0	126	82	555.0	549	44	187	372	Two Strikes	.199	967	192	29	2	14	76	88	387	.266	.276
Pre-All Star	4.06	16	19	0	87	47	310.0	330	26	111	211	Pre-All Star	.274	1205	330	62	5	26	150	111	211	.335	.398
Post-All Star	3.51	21	13	1	55	41	282.1	277	22	97	176	Post-All Star	.258	1075	277	53	5	22	109	97	176	.321	.378

Pitcher vs. Batter (career)

Pitches Best Vs.	Avg	AB	H	2B	3B	HR	RBI	BB	SO	OBP	SLG	Pitches Worst Vs.	Avg	AB	H	2B	3B	HR	RBI	BB	SO	OBP	SLG
Sammy Sosa	.000	23	0	0	0	0	0	1	7	.042	.000	Eric Davis	.625	8	5	0	0	1	3	2	2	.727	1.000
Mickey Morandini	.000	12	0	0	0	0	0	2	1	.143	.000	Jay Bell	.615	13	8	3	0	2	4	3	2	.688	1.308
Ryan Klesko	.063	16	1	0	0	0	0		6	.063	.063	Jeff Blauser	.588	17	10	2	0	1	3	3	2	.650	.882
Danny Sheaffer	.083	12	1	0	0	0	0		3	.083	.083	Eric Young	.563	16	9	2	0	0	4	1	1	.611	.688
Tripp Cromer	.091	11	1	0	0	0	0		1	.091	.091	Mike Piazza	.455	11	5	1	0	1	3	1		.500	.818

Chris Haney — Royals

	ERA	W	L	Sv	G	GS	IP	BB	SO	Avg	H	2B	3B	HR	RBI	OBP	SLG	GF	IR	IRS	Hld	SvOp	SB	CS	GB	FB	G/F
1997 Season	4.38	1	2	0	8	3	24.2	5	16	.290	29	6	0	1	13	.333	.380	1	0	1	0		2	1	34	28	1.21
Last Five Years	5.00	25	31	0	88	80	486.1	153	245	.287	551	109	9	52	265	.341	.435	1	2	2	3	0	21	19	711	547	1.30

1997 Season

	ERA	W	L	Sv	G	GS	IP	H	HR	BB	SO		Avg	AB	H	2B	3B	HR	RBI	BB	SO	OBP	SLG
Home	3.29	1	1	0	3	2	13.2	14	1	2	10	vs. Left	.250	28	7	0	0	0	3	0	8	.276	.250
Away	5.73	0	1	0	5	1	11.0	15	0	3	6	vs. Right	.306	72	22	6	0	1	10	5	8	.354	.431

Last Five Years

	ERA	W	L	Sv	G	GS	IP	H	HR	BB	SO		Avg	AB	H	2B	3B	HR	RBI	BB	SO	OBP	SLG
Home	5.40	11	19	0	43	41	250.0	299	29	58	121	vs. Left	.267	359	96	14	1	6	43	27	42	.327	.362
Away	4.57	14	12	0	45	39	236.1	252	23	95	124	vs. Right	.292	1558	455	95	8	46	222	126	203	.344	.452
Day	3.77	4	4	0	23	20	126.2	122	10	50	60	Inning 1-6	.287	1658	476	94	8	47	238	140	215	.343	.438
Night	5.43	21	27	0	65	60	359.2	429	42	103	185	Inning 7+	.290	259	75	15	1	5	27	13	30	.330	.413
Grass	4.41	17	20	0	60	54	348.2	381	40	106	176	None on	.277	1087	301	66	9	27	27	77	130	.328	.423
Turf	6.47	8	11	0	28	26	137.2	170	12	47	69	Runners on	.301	830	250	43	3	25	238	76	115	.357	.451
March/April	7.67	1	6	0	11	10	54.0	78	8	22	28	Scoring Posn	.301	465	140	22	3	11	203	52	78	.362	.432

Last Five Years

	ERA	W	L	Sv	G	GS	IP	H	HR	BB	SO
May	3.46	7	3	0	16	14	93.2	82	5	29	46
June	4.35	6	4	0	21	19	113.2	121	12	28	58
July	5.73	7	8	0	17	17	99.0	123	16	30	46
August	3.63	3	5	0	10	10	69.1	72	3	20	34
Sept/Oct	6.67	3	10	0	13	10	56.2	75	8	24	33
Starter	5.15	25	31	0	80	80	470.0	536	52	151	237
Reliever	0.55	0	0	0	8	0	16.1	15	0	2	8
0 Days rest (Relief)	0.00	0	0	0	1	0	1.0	1	0	0	1
1 or 2 Days rest	0.00	0	0	0	0	0	0.0	0	0	0	0
3+ Days rest	0.59	0	0	0	7	0	15.1	14	0	2	7
vs. AL	5.03	25	30	0	86	79	479.2	545	52	151	241
vs. NL	2.70	0	1	0	2	1	6.2	6	0	2	4
Pre-All Star	4.84	17	15	0	54	49	295.2	321	32	89	144
Post-All Star	5.24	8	16	0	34	31	190.2	230	20	64	101

	Avg	AB	H	2B	3B	HR	RBI	BB	SO	OBP	SLG
Close & Late	.252	147	37	4	0	3	15	6	20	.288	.340
None on/out	.275	494	136	32	3	14	14	31	59	.322	.437
vs. 1st Batr (relief)	.286	7	2	0	0	0	0	1	0	.375	.286
1st Inning Pitched	.308	347	107	17	1	6	52	41	46	.384	.415
First 15 Pitches	.313	265	83	15	1	5	18	25	28	.378	.434
Pitch 16-30	.236	276	65	14	0	6	43	36	49	.322	.351
Pitch 31-45	.301	306	92	15	3	5	39	18	39	.340	.418
Pitch 46+	.291	1070	311	65	5	36	165	74	129	.337	.462
First Pitch	.378	288	109	24	1	12	57	5	0	.384	.594
Ahead in Count	.235	813	191	34	4	11	85	0	218	.242	.327
Behind in Count	.331	465	154	34	3	14	65	81	0	.428	.508
Two Strikes	.217	808	175	34	3	14	83	67	245	.280	.318
Pre-All Star	.280	1147	321	65	7	32	153	89	144	.332	.432
Post-All Star	.299	770	230	44	2	20	112	64	101	.354	.439

Pitcher vs. Batter (career)

Pitches Best Vs.	Avg	AB	H	2B	3B	HR	RBI	BB	SO	OBP	SLG
Rex Hudler	.000	13	0	0	0	0	0	0	2	.000	.000
Ron Coomer	.000	10	0	0	0	0	0	1	1	.091	.000
Rickey Henderson	.000	10	0	0	0	0	0	3	0	.231	.000
Brent Gates	.071	14	1	0	0	0	1	1	1	.125	.071
Tony Fernandez	.083	12	1	0	0	0	0	0	2	.083	.083

Pitches Worst Vs.	Avg	AB	H	2B	3B	HR	RBI	BB	SO	OBP	SLG
Frank Thomas	.556	9	5	0	0	1	2	2	0	.583	.889
B.J. Surhoff	.500	16	8	3	0	1	4	0	0	.500	.875
Jim Leyritz	.462	13	6	2	0	2	5	4	4	.588	1.077
Cal Ripken	.400	15	6	0	0	3	7	1	1	.412	1.000
Juan Gonzalez	.333	15	5	1	0	3	4	2	1	.412	1.000

Greg Hansell — Brewers

Age 27 – Pitches Right

	ERA	W	L	Sv	G	GS	IP	BB	SO	Avg	H	2B	3B	HR	RBI	OBP	SLG	GF	IR	IRS	Hld	SvOp	SB	CS	GB	FB	G/F
1997 Season	9.64	0	0	0	3	0	4.2	1	5	.263	5	1	0	1	5	.333	.474	1	0	0	0	0	0	0	8	4	2.00
Career (1995-1997)	6.22	3	1	3	73	0	98.1	38	64	.298	117	20	2	20	85	.364	.511	31	50	30	4	5	3	3	128	122	1.05

1997 Season

	ERA	W	L	Sv	G	GS	IP	H	HR	BB	SO
Home	9.64	0	0	0	3	0	4.2	5	1	1	5
Away	0.00	0	0	0	0	0	0.0	0	0	0	0

	Avg	AB	H	2B	3B	HR	RBI	BB	SO	OBP	SLG
vs. Left	.375	8	3	1	0	0	2	1	3	.444	.500
vs. Right	.182	11	2	0	0	1	3	0	2	.250	.455

Career (1995-1997)

	ERA	W	L	Sv	G	GS	IP	H	HR	BB	SO
Home	5.91	2	0	2	44	0	64.0	76	9	22	42
Away	6.82	1	1	1	29	0	34.1	41	11	16	22
Day	6.03	1	1	2	23	0	31.1	29	6	13	23
Night	6.31	2	0	1	50	0	67.0	88	14	25	41
Grass	7.48	1	1	1	35	0	43.1	55	13	16	30
Turf	5.24	2	0	2	38	0	55.0	62	7	22	34
March/April	5.00	2	0	1	10	0	18.0	19	3	10	13
May	4.88	1	1	0	19	0	24.0	26	5	7	14
June	5.76	0	0	2	17	0	25.0	30	5	6	16
July	8.44	0	0	0	13	0	16.0	27	5	4	9
August	7.94	0	0	0	10	0	11.1	12	2	7	11
Sept/Oct	9.00	0	0	0	4	0	4.0	3	0	4	1
Starter	0.00	0	0	0	0	0	0.0	0	0	0	0
Reliever	6.22	3	1	3	73	0	98.1	117	20	38	64
0 Days rest (Relief)	8.22	0	1	0	18	0	23.0	30	7	5	21
1 or 2 Days rest	5.52	1	0	1	21	0	29.1	36	2	14	18
3+ Days rest	5.67	2	0	2	34	0	46.0	51	11	19	25
vs. AL	5.92	3	0	3	53	0	79.0	88	15	32	51
vs. NL	7.45	0	1	0	20	0	19.1	29	5	6	13
Pre-All Star	5.76	3	1	3	49	0	70.1	83	17	24	46
Post-All Star	7.39	0	0	0	24	0	28.0	34	3	14	18

	Avg	AB	H	2B	3B	HR	RBI	BB	SO	OBP	SLG
vs. Left	.268	168	45	9	0	11	32	19	33	.356	.518
vs. Right	.320	225	72	11	2	9	53	19	31	.371	.507
Inning 1-6	.307	137	42	10	0	8	39	11	31	.359	.555
Inning 7+	.293	256	75	10	2	12	46	27	33	.367	.488
None on	.263	217	57	9	0	8	8	19	37	.328	.415
Runners on	.341	176	60	11	2	12	77	19	27	.408	.631
Scoring Posn	.355	107	38	9	2	7	66	12	22	.419	.673
Close & Late	.315	54	17	1	1	2	14	8	7	.413	.481
None on/out	.274	95	26	1	0	3	3	6	17	.317	.379
vs. 1st Batr (relief)	.304	69	21	1	1	4	24	3	15	.329	.522
1st Inning Pitched	.315	260	82	12	2	14	69	26	46	.377	.538
First 15 Pitches	.325	203	66	11	1	12	56	16	36	.374	.567
Pitch 16-30	.289	121	35	6	1	4	22	16	20	.379	.455
Pitch 31-45	.234	47	11	1	0	2	5	5	4	.333	.383
Pitch 46+	.227	22	5	2	0	2	2	1	4	.261	.591
First Pitch	.196	51	10	1	0	0	6	2	0	.226	.216
Ahead in Count	.222	180	40	6	0	6	22	0	56	.238	.356
Behind in Count	.494	89	44	7	1	13	40	20	0	.582	1.034
Two Strikes	.220	186	41	7	0	6	26	16	64	.291	.355
Pre-All Star	.302	275	83	12	1	17	57	24	46	.363	.538
Post-All Star	.288	118	34	8	1	3	28	14	18	.368	.449

Dave Hansen — Cubs

Age 29 – Bats Left

	Avg	G	AB	R	H	2B	3B	HR	RBI	BB	SO	HBP	GDP	SB	CS	OBP	SLG	IBB	SH	SF	#Pit	#P/PA	GB	FB	G/F
1997 Season	.311	90	151	19	47	8	2	3	21	31	32	1	0	1	2	.429	.450	1	2	1	766	4.12	63	25	2.52
Last Five Years	.299	394	585	61	175	25	2	8	76	96	100	2	9	1	3	.397	.390	9	2	4	2725	3.96	234	135	1.73

1997 Season

	Avg	AB	H	2B	3B	HR	RBI	BB	SO	OBP	SLG
vs. Left	.286	7	2	0	0	0	0	0	2	.375	.286
vs. Right	.313	144	45	8	2	3	21	31	30	.432	.458
Home	.308	52	16	1	1	1	4	11	9	.429	.423
Away	.313	99	31	7	1	2	17	20	23	.430	.465
First Pitch	.333	18	6	1	0	1	5	1	0	.368	.556
Ahead in Count	.343	35	12	5	1	1	9	22	0	.596	.629
Behind in Count	.274	73	20	1	1	1	5	0	28	.280	.356
Two Strikes	.256	78	20	1	0	1	4	8	32	.333	.308

	Avg	AB	H	2B	3B	HR	RBI	BB	SO	OBP	SLG
Scoring Posn	.310	29	9	1	0	1	17	14	5	.523	.448
Close & Late	.355	31	11	2	1	1	3	8	6	.487	.581
None on/out	.355	31	11	2	1	0	0	6	8	.459	.484
Batting #5	.286	56	16	1	2	1	6	7	15	.365	.429
Batting #9	.308	26	8	2	0	1	1	6	4	.438	.500
Other	.333	69	23	5	0	1	14	18	13	.472	.449
Pre-All Star	.276	98	27	7	0	1	14	21	22	.405	.378
Post-All Star	.377	53	20	1	2	2	7	10	10	.476	.585

Last Five Years

	Avg	AB	H	2B	3B	HR	RBI	BB	SO	OBP	SLG
vs. Left	.222	27	6	2	0	0	2	2	5	.290	.296
vs. Right	.303	558	169	23	2	8	74	94	95	.402	.394

	Avg	AB	H	2B	3B	HR	RBI	BB	SO	OBP	SLG
First Pitch	.315	92	29	5	0	2	15	7	0	.360	.435
Ahead in Count	.260	146	38	9	1	2	25	55	0	.463	.377

Last Five Years

	Avg	AB	H	2B	3B	HR	RBI	BB	SO	OBP	SLG		Avg	AB	H	2B	3B	HR	RBI	BB	SO	OBP	SLG
Groundball	.288	146	42	6	0	0	17	31	24	.412	.329	Behind in Count	.283	237	67	3	1	1	21	0	81	.285	.316
Flyball	.330	115	38	5	0	4	23	7	31	.365	.478	Two Strikes	.295	275	81	8	0	2	23	34	100	.375	.345
Home	.295	258	76	3	1	3	26	41	41	.390	.349	Batting #7	.279	129	36	6	0	1	7	20	15	.380	.349
Away	.303	327	99	22	1	5	50	55	59	.403	.422	Batting #9	.315	149	47	7	0	2	21	22	30	.404	.403
Day	.258	194	50	9	2	3	22	38	32	.380	.371	Other	.300	307	92	12	2	5	48	54	55	.402	.401
Night	.320	391	125	16	0	5	54	58	68	.399	.406	March/April	.240	75	18	3	0	0	3	12	8	.348	.280
Grass	.301	459	138	15	2	5	48	80	75	.405	.375	May	.228	101	23	1	0	0	7	21	20	.361	.238
Turf	.294	126	37	10	0	3	28	16	25	.370	.444	June	.316	76	24	5	0	3	15	14	14	.429	.500
Pre-All Star	.264	296	78	14	0	3	33	50	53	.370	.341	July	.340	103	35	7	0	0	18	19	18	.435	.408
Post-All Star	.336	289	97	11	2	5	43	46	47	.426	.439	August	.292	130	38	4	1	2	10	13	27	.354	.385
Scoring Posn	.306	170	52	7	0	2	64	39	33	.427	.382	Sept/Oct	.370	100	37	5	1	3	23	17	13	.462	.530
Close & Late	.311	148	46	7	1	4	30	27	33	.417	.382	vs. AL	.125	8	1	1	0	0	0	0	3	.125	.250
None on/out	.345	113	39	3	1	1	1	14	17	.417	.416	vs. NL	.302	577	174	24	2	8	76	96	97	.401	.392

Batter vs. Pitcher (career)

Hits Best Against	Avg	AB	H	2B	3B	HR	RBI	BB	SO	OBP	SLG	Hits Worst Against	Avg	AB	H	2B	3B	HR	RBI	BB	SO	OBP	SLG
Mike Morgan	.462	13	6	1	0	0	2	3	1	.563	.538	Darryl Kile	.063	16	1	1	0	0	0	1	0	.118	.125
John Burkett	.400	15	6	1	0	1	6	0	3	.375	.667	Greg Maddux	.143	14	2	0	0	0	0	2	3	.250	.143
Bret Saberhagen	.400	10	4	1	0	0	1	2	0	.500	.500	Mark Portugal	.154	13	2	0	0	1	2	0	3	.154	.385
Curt Schilling	.385	13	5	1	0	1	1	0	5	.385	.692	Mark Gardner	.167	18	3	1	0	1	2	0	4	.167	.389
Mark Leiter	.385	13	5	0	0	1	4	0	2	.385	.615	Pete Harnisch	.214	14	3	0	0	1	2	0	5	.214	.429

Jed Hansen — Royals
Age 25 – Bats Right

	Avg	G	AB	R	H	2B	3B	HR	RBI	BB	SO	HBP	GDP	SB	CS	OBP	SLG	IBB	SH	SF	#Pit	#P/PA	GB	FB	G/F
1997 Season	.309	34	94	11	29	6	1	1	14	13	29	1	2	3	2	.394	.426	0	2	1	456	4.11	23	26	0.88

1997 Season

	Avg	AB	H	2B	3B	HR	RBI	BB	SO	OBP	SLG		Avg	AB	H	2B	3B	HR	RBI	BB	SO	OBP	SLG
vs. Left	.357	42	15	4	0	0	3	4	11	.413	.452	Scoring Posn	.353	17	6	1	1	0	11	4	4	.455	.529
vs. Right	.269	52	14	2	1	1	11	9	18	.381	.404	Close & Late	.227	22	5	1	0	0	3	5	8	.370	.273

Erik Hanson — Blue Jays
Age 33 – Pitches Right (groundball pitcher)

	ERA	W	L	Sv	G	GS	IP	BB	SO	Avg	H	2B	3B	HR	RBI	OBP	SLG	CG	ShO	Sup	QS	#P/S	SB	CS	GB	FB	G/F
1997 Season	7.80	0	0	0	3	2	15.0	6	18	.254	15	3	0	3	12	.323	.458	0	0	4.80	0	108	3	0	17	14	1.21
Last Five Years	4.40	44	39	0	120	117	754.0	250	577	.272	797	160	16	73	353	.329	.412	12	2	5.31	64	104	43	38	1120	691	1.62

1997 Season

	ERA	W	L	Sv	G	GS	IP	H	HR	BB	SO		Avg	AB	H	2B	3B	HR	RBI	BB	SO	OBP	SLG
Home	7.20	0	0	0	1	1	5.0	4	1	3	8	vs. Left	.241	29	7	1	0	1	7	4	9	.333	.379
Away	8.10	0	0	0	2	1	10.0	11	2	3	10	vs. Right	.267	30	8	2	0	2	5	2	9	.313	.533

Last Five Years

	ERA	W	L	Sv	G	GS	IP	H	HR	BB	SO		Avg	AB	H	2B	3B	HR	RBI	BB	SO	OBP	SLG
Home	4.03	17	16	0	57	56	364.0	371	37	104	277	vs. Left	.243	1513	368	64	9	31	173	133	327	.304	.359
Away	4.75	27	23	0	63	61	390.0	426	36	146	300	vs. Right	.303	1417	429	96	7	42	180	117	250	.357	.469
Day	4.24	13	13	0	38	38	233.1	258	30	72	192	Inning 1-6	.278	2560	711	141	14	62	324	219	492	.334	.416
Night	4.48	31	26	0	82	79	520.2	539	43	178	385	Inning 7+	.232	370	86	19	2	11	29	31	85	.295	.384
Grass	4.79	24	23	0	64	62	394.2	437	39	142	292	None on	.256	1696	435	99	11	39	39	145	351	.317	.397
Turf	3.98	20	16	0	56	55	359.1	360	34	108	285	Runners on	.293	1234	362	61	5	34	314	105	226	.346	.434
March/April	4.82	7	5	0	18	18	106.1	114	13	45	83	Scoring Posn	.274	718	197	32	4	21	277	71	137	.335	.418
May	3.63	12	8	0	24	24	153.2	170	10	37	142	Close & Late	.260	204	53	11	2	8	20	20	43	.326	.451
June	4.95	5	8	0	22	20	136.1	149	17	46	94	None on/out	.272	756	206	56	5	18	18	53	132	.320	.431
July	4.62	6	8	0	22	22	132.1	144	12	44	94	vs. 1st Batr (relief)	.000	2	0	0	0	0	0	1	0	.333	.000
August	4.49	9	6	0	18	18	120.1	115	13	44	86	1st Inning Pitched	.268	444	119	24	3	10	53	52	81	.341	.403
Sept/Oct	4.03	5	4	0	16	15	105.0	105	8	34	78	First 75 Pitches	.284	2013	571	120	12	51	250	170	393	.339	.431
Starter	4.35	44	38	0	117	117	744.2	784	72	247	570	Pitch 76-90	.258	372	96	19	2	11	59	36	69	.323	.409
Reliever	8.68	0	1	0	3	0	9.1	13	1	3	7	Pitch 91-105	.243	329	80	12	1	7	27	24	64	.299	.350
0-3 Days Rest (Start)	2.25	1	0	0	2	2	12.0	8	1	2	10	Pitch 106+	.231	216	50	9	1	4	17	20	51	.301	.338
4 Days Rest	4.30	31	24	0	78	78	506.1	543	49	161	387	First Pitch	.377	393	148	28	2	8	66	7	0	.384	.519
5+ Days Rest	4.57	12	14	0	37	37	226.1	233	22	84	173	Ahead in Count	.176	1213	214	35	1	15	96	0	472	.182	.244
vs. AL	4.46	39	34	0	98	96	631.0	660	63	227	476	Behind in Count	.378	724	274	62	9	39	139	112	0	.457	.651
vs. NL	4.11	5	5	0	22	21	122.2	137	10	23	101	Two Strikes	.174	1359	237	47	3	13	94	131	577	.249	.242
Pre-All Star	4.37	27	23	0	72	70	449.0	488	44	141	358	Pre-All Star	.276	1766	488	91	10	44	209	141	358	.332	.414
Post-All Star	4.46	17	16	0	48	47	305.0	309	29	109	219	Post-All Star	.265	1164	309	69	6	29	144	109	219	.326	.410

Pitcher vs. Batter (career)

Pitches Best Vs.	Avg	AB	H	2B	3B	HR	RBI	BB	SO	OBP	SLG	Pitches Worst Vs.	Avg	AB	H	2B	3B	HR	RBI	BB	SO	OBP	SLG
Reggie Jefferson	.000	11	0	0	0	0	0	1	3	.083	.000	Bob Higginson	.600	10	6	2	0	3	5	1	1	.636	1.700
Jose Canseco	.043	23	1	0	0	0	0	3	11	.154	.043	Juan Gonzalez	.474	19	9	1	0	2	6	2	5	.500	.842
Pat Kelly	.071	14	1	0	0	0	0	0	5	.071	.071	Edgar Martinez	.455	11	5	0	0	4	5	4	0	.600	1.545
Bill Spiers	.100	20	2	0	0	0	0	0	5	.100	.100	Fred McGriff	.375	8	3	0	0	2	3	5	1	.615	1.125
Scott Livingstone	.105	19	2	0	0	0	1	0	4	.100	.105												

Jason Hardtke — Mets
Age 26 – Bats Both

	Avg	G	AB	R	H	2B	3B	HR	RBI	BB	SO	HBP	GDP	SB	CS	OBP	SLG	IBB	SH	SF	#Pit	#P/PA	GB	FB	G/F
1997 Season	.268	30	56	9	15	2	0	2	8	4	6	1	3	1	1	.323	.411	1	0	1	226	3.65	22	19	1.16
Career (1996-1997)	.230	49	113	12	26	7	0	2	14	6	18	2	4	1	1	.279	.345	1			456	3.74	39	38	1.03

1997 Season

	Avg	AB	H	2B	3B	HR	RBI	BB	SO	OBP	SLG		Avg	AB	H	2B	3B	HR	RBI	BB	SO	OBP	SLG
vs. Left	.286	21	6	0	0	1	5	3	4	.375	.429	Scoring Posn	.250	16	4	0	0	0	6	2	3	.316	.250
vs. Right	.257	35	9	2	0	1	3	1	2	.289	.400	Close & Late	.364	11	4	0	0	1	2	2	0	.500	.636

Mike Harkey — Dodgers
Age 31 – Pitches Right

	ERA	W	L	Sv	G	GS	IP	BB	SO	Avg	H	2B	3B	HR	RBI	OBP	SLG	GF	IR	IRS	Hld	SvOp	SB	CS	GB	FB	G/F
1997 Season	4.30	1	0	0	10	0	14.2	5	6	.211	12	3	1	3	8	.274	.456	5	8	0	0	0	0	0	16	26	0.62
Last Five Years	5.41	20	25	0	88	61	391.0	130	168	.308	479	86	13	54	218	.361	.484	9	13	0	0	0	32	18	573	469	1.22

1997 Season

	ERA	W	L	Sv	G	GS	IP	H	HR	BB	SO		Avg	AB	H	2B	3B	HR	RBI	BB	SO	OBP	SLG
Home	2.45	0	0	0	6	0	11.0	6	1	4	6	vs. Left	.185	27	5	1	0	2	4	2	2	.241	.444
Away	9.82	1	0	0	4	0	3.2	6	2	1	0	vs. Right	.233	30	7	2	1	1	4	3	4	.303	.467

Last Five Years

	ERA	W	L	Sv	G	GS	IP	H	HR	BB	SO		Avg	AB	H	2B	3B	HR	RBI	BB	SO	OBP	SLG
Home	5.06	11	15	0	50	34	226.0	268	35	82	102	vs. Left	.306	790	242	45	5	32	120	84	83	.372	.497
Away	5.89	9	10	0	38	27	165.0	211	19	48	66	vs. Right	.309	767	237	41	8	22	98	46	85	.349	.469
Day	5.87	8	15	0	38	32	188.2	234	29	66	83	Inning 1-6	.310	1361	422	75	12	47	198	110	149	.362	.486
Night	4.98	12	10	0	50	29	202.1	245	25	64	85	Inning 7+	.291	196	57	11	1	7	20	20	19	.356	.464
Grass	5.09	18	21	0	76	53	343.1	415	48	116	147	None on	.302	915	276	44	8	34	67	96	96	.352	.479
Turf	7.74	2	4	0	12	8	47.2	64	6	14	21	Runners on	.316	642	203	42	5	20	184	63	72	.373	.491
March/April	4.69	3	2	0	9	9	55.2	66	3	22	27	Scoring Posn	.315	356	112	25	3	11	155	47	44	.383	.494
May	6.66	4	7	0	17	14	73.0	106	13	23	33	Close & Late	.352	54	19	3	0	3	9	9	7	.438	.574
June	5.29	3	1	0	17	9	63.0	67	8	33	26	None on/out	.279	405	113	16	3	14	14	27	41	.329	.437
July	5.22	3	7	0	13	11	69.0	81	9	20	26	vs. 1st Batr (relief)	.160	25	4	1	1	0	0	2	4	.222	.280
August	5.13	3	5	0	17	12	80.2	106	15	19	33	1st Inning Pitched	.334	356	119	23	3	12	68	30	37	.382	.517
Sept/Oct	5.26	4	3	0	15	6	49.2	53	6	13	23	First 15 Pitches	.353	292	103	20	5	11	42	22	28	.396	.568
Starter	5.57	17	24	0	61	61	339.1	420	44	116	144	Pitch 16-30	.292	291	85	10	0	12	50	30	37	.360	.450
Reliever	4.35	3	1	0	27	0	51.2	59	10	14	24	Pitch 31-45	.301	282	85	15	4	8	35	12	23	.329	.468
0 Days rest (Relief)	20.25	0	0	0	1	0	1.1	2	1	1	1	Pitch 46+	.298	692	206	41	4	23	91	66	80	.359	.468
1 or 2 Days rest	6.00	1	0	0	10	0	15.0	22	3	3	6	First Pitch	.376	242	91	16	3	9	34	8	0	.399	.579
3+ Days rest	3.06	2	1	0	16	0	35.1	35	6	10	17	Ahead in Count	.245	637	156	21	5	16	73	0	137	.247	.369
vs. AL	5.40	8	9	0	27	20	128.1	156	24	48	56	Behind in Count	.361	393	142	27	4	18	64	66	0	.451	.588
vs. NL	5.41	12	16	0	61	41	262.2	323	30	82	112	Two Strikes	.226	602	136	19	4	22	75	56	168	.293	.380
Pre-All Star	5.45	11	14	0	50	37	229.2	280	29	88	96	Pre-All Star	.308	909	280	57	8	29	131	88	96	.370	.484
Post-All Star	5.36	9	11	0	38	24	161.1	199	20	42	72	Post-All Star	.307	648	199	29	5	25	87	42	72	.348	.483

Pitcher vs. Batter (career)

Pitches Best Vs.	Avg	AB	H	2B	3B	HR	RBI	BB	SO	OBP	SLG	Pitches Worst Vs.	Avg	AB	H	2B	3B	HR	RBI	BB	SO	OBP	SLG
Darrin Fletcher	.000	10	0	0	0	0	0	1	1	.091	.000	Luis Alicea	.625	8	5	0	0	1	3	2	0	.583	1.000
Will Clark	.045	22	1	0	0	1	2	4		.125	.045	Luis Gonzalez	.615	13	8	1	1	2	6	0	2	.615	1.308
Jeff Conine	.118	17	2	1	0	0	1	1	2	.167	.176	Jeff Blauser	.538	13	7	2	0	2	3	1	1	.571	1.154
Jay Bell	.167	12	2	0	0	0	0	0	1	.167	.167	Paul O'Neill	.500	16	8	1	0	3	6	3	1	.579	1.125
Juan Samuel	.188	16	3	0	0	0	0	0	0	.188	.188	Bobby Bonilla	.467	15	7	0	0	2	4	3	1	.556	.867

Pete Harnisch — Brewers
Age 31 – Pitches Right (flyball pitcher)

	ERA	W	L	Sv	G	GS	IP	BB	SO	Avg	H	2B	3B	HR	RBI	OBP	SLG	CG	ShO	Sup	QS	#P/S	SB	CS	GB	FB	G/F
1997 Season	7.03	1	2	0	10	8	39.2	23	22	.300	48	17	0	6	23	.387	.519	0	0	4.54	1	86	1	2	48	51	0.94
Last Five Years	4.05	35	36	0	109	107	657.0	226	465	.250	625	125	15	82	295	.314	.410	8	5	5.12	65	96	60	18	782	852	0.92

1997 Season

	ERA	W	L	Sv	G	GS	IP	H	HR	BB	SO		Avg	AB	H	2B	3B	HR	RBI	BB	SO	OBP	SLG
Home	7.48	1	1	0	6	4	21.2	27	2	16	12	vs. Left	.386	70	27	9	0	2	11	14	5	.488	.600
Away	6.50	0	1	0	4	4	18.0	21	4	7	10	vs. Right	.233	90	21	8	0	4	12	9	17	.300	.456

Last Five Years

	ERA	W	L	Sv	G	GS	IP	H	HR	BB	SO		Avg	AB	H	2B	3B	HR	RBI	BB	SO	OBP	SLG
Home	3.66	21	19	0	62	60	388.0	345	48	131	283	vs. Left	.273	1218	332	60	14	36	139	137	191	.348	.433
Away	4.62	14	17	0	47	47	269.0	280	34	95	182	vs. Right	.228	1286	293	65	1	46	156	89	274	.281	.387
Day	4.12	7	7	0	31	31	181.1	167	18	66	131	Inning 1-6	.255	2255	574	116	13	77	281	203	410	.319	.420
Night	4.03	28	29	0	78	76	475.2	458	64	160	334	Inning 7+	.205	249	51	9	2	5	14	23	55	.274	.317
Grass	4.25	16	20	0	62	60	360.1	361	47	123	242	None on	.248	1511	374	67	13	53	53	116	283	.306	.414
Turf	3.82	16	16	0	47	47	296.2	264	35	103	223	Runners on	.253	993	251	58	2	29	242	110	182	.326	.403
March/April	4.70	6	4	0	17	17	95.2	84	13	41	60	Scoring Posn	.253	570	144	39	1	15	205	78	112	.335	.404
May	4.35	5	7	0	19	19	113.2	113	16	28	83	Close & Late	.224	134	30	6	1	4	13	12	33	.291	.373
June	4.98	3	7	0	17	17	97.2	113	12	34	76	None on/out	.248	664	165	23	7	31	31	41	113	.294	.444
July	3.08	11	7	0	22	22	146.1	136	22	36	111	vs. 1st Batr (relief)	.000	2	0	0	0	0	0	0	0	.000	.000
August	4.75	5	7	0	20	19	119.1	113	16	49	81	1st Inning Pitched	.289	425	123	21	4	14	66	44	79	.354	.456
Sept/Oct	2.56	5	4	0	14	13	84.1	66	3	38	54	First 75 Pitches	.256	1862	476	98	12	58	221	159	350	.316	.415
Starter	4.04	35	36	0	107	107	655.0	624	82	222	463	Pitch 76-90	.253	336	85	16	2	14	47	32	53	.321	.438
Reliever	9.00	0	0	0	2	0	2.0	1	0	4	2	Pitch 91-105	.202	208	42	6	1	9	22	22	40	.280	.370
0-3 Days Rest (Start)	2.00	2	1	0	4	4	27.0	18	3	10	17	Pitch 106+	.224	98	22	5	0	1	5	13	22	.321	.306

Last Five Years

	ERA	W	L	Sv	G	GS	IP	H	HR	BB	SO		Avg	AB	H	2B	3B	HR	RBI	BB	SO	OBP	SLG
4 Days Rest	4.02	22	22	0	58	58	351.1	346	42	113	260	First Pitch	.286	402	115	21	2	14	58	12	0	.313	.453
5+ Days Rest	4.26	11	13	0	45	45	276.2	260	37	99	186	Ahead in Count	.196	1152	226	48	7	23	97	0	386	.201	.310
vs. AL	5.14	1	1	0	4	3	14.0	13	1	12	10	Behind in Count	.316	512	162	34	2	32	87	87	0	.412	.578
vs. NL	4.03	34	35	0	105	104	643.0	612	81	214	455	Two Strikes	.170	1138	193	35	7	25	89	127	465	.255	.279
Pre-All Star	4.44	18	23	0	62	62	366.2	363	51	124	264	Pre-All Star	.256	1417	363	70	10	51	193	124	264	.317	.428
Post-All Star	3.56	17	13	0	47	45	290.1	262	31	102	201	Post-All Star	.241	1087	262	55	5	31	102	102	201	.310	.386

Pitcher vs. Batter (career)

Pitches Best Vs.	Avg	AB	H	2B	3B	HR	RBI	BB	SO	OBP	SLG	Pitches Worst Vs.	Avg	AB	H	2B	3B	HR	RBI	BB	SO	OBP	SLG
Devon White	.000	13	0	0	0	0	0	0	3	.071	.000	Steve Finley	.571	14	8	4	2	0	1	1	0	.600	1.143
Ken Caminiti	.000	10	0	0	0	0	0	2	5	.167	.000	Harold Baines	.500	14	7	1	0	1	3	1	2	.500	.786
Brad Ausmus	.067	15	1	0	0	0	1	0	3	.063	.067	Thomas Howard	.429	14	6	1	0	2	2	0	5	.429	.929
Ruben Sierra	.067	15	1	0	0	0	1	1	3	.118	.067	Don Slaught	.368	19	7	2	0	2	9	2	1	.478	.789
Carlos Garcia	.095	21	2	0	0	0	2	0	5	.095	.095	Bret Boone	.364	11	4	2	0	1	3	1	2	.417	.818

Lenny Harris — Reds
Age 33 – Bats Left (groundball hitter)

	Avg	G	AB	R	H	2B	3B	HR	RBI	BB	SO	HBP	GDP	SB	CS	OBP	SLG	IBB	SH	SF	#Pit	#P/PA	GB	FB	G/F
1997 Season	.273	120	238	32	65	13	1	3	28	18	18	2	10	4	3	.327	.374	1	3	2	831	3.16	111	70	1.59
Last Five Years	.262	519	997	130	261	47	8	12	101	73	97	3	23	38	13	.312	.361	6	13	7	3587	3.28	483	248	1.95

1997 Season

	Avg	AB	H	2B	3B	HR	RBI	BB	SO	OBP	SLG		Avg	AB	H	2B	3B	HR	RBI	BB	SO	OBP	SLG
vs. Left	.250	24	6	1	0	0	2	0	2	.250	.292	Scoring Posn	.237	59	14	4	0	0	22	5	6	.309	.305
vs. Right	.276	214	59	12	1	3	26	18	16	.335	.383	Close & Late	.191	47	9	1	0	0	5	2	3	.240	.213
Home	.293	123	36	6	1	2	13	7	8	.328	.407	None on/out	.265	49	13	4	0	1	1	3	4	.308	.408
Away	.252	115	29	7	0	1	15	11	10	.326	.339	Batting #2	.219	73	16	4	1	1	8	2	7	.240	.342
First Pitch	.352	54	19	6	0	1	10	1	0	.364	.519	Batting #3	.245	49	12	4	0	0	1	4	2	.302	.327
Ahead in Count	.299	67	20	4	0	1	12	15	0	.422	.403	Other	.319	116	37	5	0	2	19	12	9	.386	.414
Behind in Count	.219	73	16	2	1	1	6	0	15	.237	.315	Pre-All Star	.258	155	40	9	1	3	20	6	11	.288	.387
Two Strikes	.224	76	17	3	0	1	6	2	18	.259	.303	Post-All Star	.301	83	25	4	0	0	8	12	7	.392	.349

Last Five Years

	Avg	AB	H	2B	3B	HR	RBI	BB	SO	OBP	SLG		Avg	AB	H	2B	3B	HR	RBI	BB	SO	OBP	SLG
vs. Left	.313	112	35	6	0	2	15	6	15	.353	.420	First Pitch	.290	200	58	12	3	3	30	5	0	.307	.425
vs. Right	.255	885	226	41	8	10	86	67	82	.307	.354	Ahead in Count	.335	260	87	23	1	2	25	49	0	.436	.454
Groundball	.257	269	69	14	0	6	27	12	23	.287	.312	Behind in Count	.206	373	77	7	3	5	34	0	85	.211	.282
Flyball	.261	157	41	5	0	1	11	16	18	.329	.312	Two Strikes	.189	349	66	6	0	4	24	19	97	.233	.241
Home	.261	467	122	22	2	4	40	34	44	.308	.343	Batting #2	.257	296	76	16	2	5	30	7	27	.275	.375
Away	.262	530	139	25	6	8	61	39	53	.315	.377	Batting #9	.218	197	43	8	2	2	21	16	27	.278	.310
Day	.246	341	84	14	4	6	36	26	24	.300	.364	Other	.282	504	142	23	4	5	50	50	43	.346	.373
Night	.270	656	177	33	4	6	65	47	73	.318	.360	March/April	.232	99	23	5	2	1	16	5	14	.274	.354
Grass	.275	400	110	19	5	6	46	24	44	.317	.393	May	.303	175	53	9	3	3	24	11	21	.340	.440
Turf	.253	597	151	28	3	6	55	49	53	.309	.340	June	.252	222	56	15	1	1	19	12	23	.291	.342
Pre-All Star	.258	577	149	33	6	5	64	39	70	.304	.362	July	.254	213	54	9	2	1	14	16	16	.303	.329
Post-All Star	.267	420	112	14	2	7	37	34	27	.322	.360	August	.220	168	37	5	0	3	11	12	26	.284	.304
Scoring Posn	.306	232	71	10	5	1	80	21	25	.364	.405	Sept/Oct	.317	120	38	4	0	3	11	13	11	.390	.425
Close & Late	.237	219	52	6	0	1	22	16	25	.292	.279	vs. AL	.294	17	5	2	0	0	3	1	2	.333	.412
None on/out	.254	248	63	15	0	5	5	25	23	.322	.375	vs. NL	.261	980	256	45	8	12	98	72	95	.312	.360

Batter vs. Pitcher (career)

Hits Best Against	Avg	AB	H	2B	3B	HR	RBI	BB	SO	OBP	SLG	Hits Worst Against	Avg	AB	H	2B	3B	HR	RBI	BB	SO	OBP	SLG
Bob Tewksbury	.500	16	8	3	0	0	2	0	0	.500	.688	Ramon Martinez	.000	9	0	0	0	0	1	2	2	.167	.000
Omar Olivares	.462	13	6	2	0	0	1	2	1	.533	.615	Mel Rojas	.100	10	1	0	0	0	1	1	1	.167	.100
Mark Portugal	.406	32	13	0	0	1	5	4	4	.472	.500	Mark Clark	.118	17	2	0	0	0	2	0	4	.118	.118
Bill Swift	.389	18	7	0	0	1	2	0	1	.389	.556	Rick Reed	.133	15	2	0	0	0	0	1	0	.188	.133
Shane Reynolds	.333	12	4	1	0	1	1	1	1	.385	.667	Frank Castillo	.154	13	2	0	0	0	1	0	4	.143	.154

Pep Harris — Angels
Age 25 – Pitches Right

	ERA	W	L	Sv	G	GS	IP	BB	SO	Avg	H	2B	3B	HR	RBI	OBP	SLG	GF	IR	IRS	Hld	SvOp	SB	CS	GB	FB	G/F
1997 Season	3.62	5	4	0	61	0	79.2	38	56	.274	82	10	3	7	40	.356	.398	17	54	13	10	3	1	5	118	77	1.53
Career (1996-1997)	3.70	7	4	0	72	3	112.0	55	76	.268	113	20	4	11	55	.354	.413	17	67	15	12	3	2	5	163	117	1.39

1997 Season

	ERA	W	L	Sv	G	GS	IP	H	HR	BB	SO		Avg	AB	H	2B	3B	HR	RBI	BB	SO	OBP	SLG
Home	2.68	3	1	0	33	0	43.2	46	1	20	33	vs. Left	.270	111	30	2	1	5	16	19	18	.377	.441
Away	4.75	2	3	0	28	0	36.0	36	6	18	23	vs. Right	.277	188	52	8	2	2	24	19	38	.343	.372
Day	2.81	2	1	0	19	0	25.2	24	3	15	19	Inning 1-6	.311	61	19	2	1	2	12	10	9	.397	.475
Night	4.00	3	3	0	42	0	54.0	58	4	23	37	Inning 7+	.265	238	63	8	2	5	28	28	47	.344	.378
Grass	3.36	5	3	0	56	0	72.1	73	6	37	52	None on	.256	160	41	5	3	4	4	18	35	.331	.400
Turf	6.14	0	1	0	5	0	7.1	9	1	1	4	Runners on	.295	139	41	5	0	3	36	20	21	.382	.396
March/April	1.83	0	0	0	12	0	19.2	20	2	8	10	Scoring Posn	.281	89	25	2	0	2	34	16	16	.380	.371
May	6.92	0	1	0	10	0	13.0	15	2	8	9	Close & Late	.254	130	33	5	0	4	17	17	21	.347	.385
June	4.38	1	1	0	9	0	12.1	13	1	8	10	None on/out	.270	63	17	3	0	2	2	6	14	.333	.413
July	4.66	1	0	0	10	0	9.2	10	0	6	7	vs. 1st Batr (relief)	.315	54	17	2	0	3	9	5	9	.361	.519
August	4.70	0	1	0	9	0	7.2	9	2	3	11	1st Inning Pitched	.283	191	54	5	2	2	34	25	38	.362	.440
Sept/Oct	1.56	3	1	0	11	0	17.1	15	0	5	17	First 15 Pitches	.252	155	39	4	2	5	22	21	30	.339	.400
Starter	0.00	0	0	0	0	0	0.0	0	0	0	0	Pitch 16-30	.314	118	37	5	1	2	16	13	20	.383	.424

1997 Season

	ERA	W	L	Sv	G	GS	IP	H	HR	BB	SO		Avg	AB	H	2B	3B	HR	RBI	BB	SO	OBP	SLG
Reliever	3.62	5	4	0	61	0	79.2	82	7	38	56	Pitch 31-45	.250	20	5	0	0	0	3	3	4	.348	.250
0 Days rest (Relief)	5.79	0	1	0	6	0	4.2	2	0	7	4	Pitch 46+	.167	6	1	1	0	0	0	1	2	.286	.333
1 or 2 Days rest	4.07	4	2	0	38	0	55.1	62	7	25	41	First Pitch	.286	35	10	2	0	2	5	5	0	.375	.514
3+ Days rest	1.83	1	1	0	17	0	19.2	18	0	6	11	Ahead in Count	.229	131	30	3	2	2	12	0	46	.235	.328
vs. AL	3.41	5	4	0	55	0	71.1	71	6	35	51	Behind in Count	.351	77	27	4	1	2	20	20	0	.470	.506
vs. NL	5.40	0	0	0	9	0	8.1	11	1	3	5	Two Strikes	.193	135	26	2	2	2	7	13	56	.268	.281
Pre-All Star	4.24	1	2	0	33	0	46.2	54	5	24	29	Pre-All Star	.297	182	54	6	3	5	26	24	29	.380	.445
Post-All Star	2.73	4	2	0	28	0	33.0	28	2	14	27	Post-All Star	.239	117	28	4	0	2	14	14	27	.319	.325

Reggie Harris — Phillies
Age 29 – Pitches Right (flyball pitcher)

	ERA	W	L	Sv	G	GS	IP	BB	SO	Avg	H	2B	3B	HR	RBI	OBP	SLG	GF	IR	IRS	Hld	SvOp	SB	CS	GB	FB	G/F
1997 Season	5.30	1	3	0	50	0	54.1	43	45	.263	55	10	2	1	33	.395	.344	13	34	11	1	0	9	2	60	67	0.90
Last Five Years	5.83	1	3	0	54	0	58.2	48	49	.273	62	12	2	3	40	.407	.383	14	36	13	1	1	9	2	66	70	0.94

1997 Season

	ERA	W	L	Sv	G	GS	IP	H	HR	BB	SO		Avg	AB	H	2B	3B	HR	RBI	BB	SO	OBP	SLG
Home	3.38	1	2	0	23	0	26.2	20	0	17	23	vs. Left	.315	89	28	6	2	0	17	24	14	.453	.427
Away	7.16	0	1	0	27	0	27.2	35	1	26	22	vs. Right	.225	120	27	4	0	1	16	19	31	.347	.283
Day	4.67	0	1	0	16	0	17.1	19	0	13	22	Inning 1-6	.269	78	21	4	0	1	15	16	18	.404	.359
Night	5.59	1	2	0	34	0	37.0	36	1	30	23	Inning 7+	.260	131	34	6	2	0	18	27	27	.389	.336
Grass	5.82	0	1	0	19	0	21.2	27	1	19	22	None on	.241	83	20	3	2	0	0	13	9	.370	.325
Turf	4.96	1	2	0	31	0	32.2	28	0	24	23	Runners on	.278	126	35	7	0	1	33	30	36	.410	.357
March/April	7.45	0	1	0	11	0	9.2	7	0	17	9	Scoring Posn	.269	93	25	6	0	1	32	22	28	.400	.366
May	3.98	0	1	0	14	0	20.1	15	0	8	12	Close & Late	.211	19	4	0	0	0	0	8	4	.444	.211
June	5.79	0	1	0	10	0	9.1	13	0	9	11	None on/out	.250	40	10	1	1	0	0	1	8	.388	.325
July	4.15	1	0	0	8	0	8.2	7	1	6	8	vs. 1st Batr (relief)	.300	40	12	3	1	1	7	9	4	.440	.500
August	10.13	0	0	0	4	0	2.2	9	0	2	8	1st Inning Pitched	.291	151	44	7	1	1	29	32	25	.419	.371
Sept/Oct	4.91	0	0	0	3	0	3.2	4	0	1	4	First 15 Pitches	.281	114	32	4	1	1	14	21	16	.403	.360
Starter	0.00	0	0	0	0	0	0.0	0	0	0	0	Pitch 16-30	.222	72	16	5	1	0	16	16	19	.366	.319
Reliever	5.30	1	3	0	50	0	54.1	55	1	43	45	Pitch 31-45	.278	18	5	1	0	0	3	6	8	.458	.333
0 Days rest (Relief)	4.70	1	1	0	10	0	7.2	4	0	6	4	Pitch 46+	.400	5	2	0	0	0	0	0	2	.400	.400
1 or 2 Days rest	6.94	0	2	0	19	0	23.1	26	1	18	18	First Pitch	.269	26	7	1	0	0	2	1	0	.321	.308
3+ Days rest	3.86	0	0	0	21	0	23.1	25	0	19	23	Ahead in Count	.211	90	19	3	2	0	8	10	0	.226	.289
vs. AL	10.80	0	0	0	3	0	3.1	7	0	7	5	Behind in Count	.321	56	18	5	0	1	16	28	0	.534	.464
vs. NL	4.94	1	3	0	47	0	51.0	48	1	36	40	Two Strikes	.191	94	18	1	1	0	10	14	45	.309	.245
Pre-All Star	5.02	1	3	0	38	0	43.0	38	0	35	34	Pre-All Star	.239	159	38	8	1	0	20	35	34	.383	.302
Post-All Star	6.35	0	0	0	12	0	11.1	17	1	8	11	Post-All Star	.340	50	17	2	1	1	13	8	11	.433	.480

Shigetoshi Hasegawa — Angels
Age 29 – Pitches Right

	ERA	W	L	Sv	G	GS	IP	BB	SO	Avg	H	2B	3B	HR	RBI	OBP	SLG	GF	IR	IRS	Hld	SvOp	SB	CS	GB	FB	G/F
1997 Season	3.93	3	7	0	50	7	116.2	46	83	.269	118	28	2	14	56	.339	.438	17	37	15	3	1	3	4	145	127	1.14

1997 Season

	ERA	W	L	Sv	G	GS	IP	H	HR	BB	SO		Avg	AB	H	2B	3B	HR	RBI	BB	SO	OBP	SLG
Home	4.23	0	4	0	26	4	66.0	70	11	23	45	vs. Left	.278	176	49	13	0	5	16	19	32	.350	.438
Away	3.55	3	3	0	24	3	50.2	48	3	23	38	vs. Right	.263	262	69	15	2	9	40	27	51	.332	.439
Day	3.78	2	3	0	16	2	33.1	38	3	18	29	Inning 1-6	.280	264	74	17	1	9	38	27	49	.347	.455
Night	4.00	1	4	0	34	5	83.1	80	11	28	54	Inning 7+	.253	174	44	11	1	5	18	19	34	.328	.414
Grass	4.17	3	7	0	48	7	110.0	116	14	43	79	None on	.265	245	65	18	1	7	7	26	46	.341	.441
Turf	0.00	0	0	0	2	0	6.2	2	0	3	4	Runners on	.275	193	53	10	1	7	49	20	37	.338	.446
March/April	7.63	1	1	0	8	1	15.1	19	4	6	10	Scoring Posn	.227	110	25	6	1	3	39	16	21	.313	.382
May	4.13	0	1	0	8	3	24.0	28	3	4	12	Close & Late	.290	69	20	7	0	2	9	11	17	.378	.478
June	2.45	0	2	0	11	0	22.0	17	2	14	18	None on/out	.254	114	29	10	1	2	2	6	25	.298	.412
July	2.20	1	1	0	9	0	16.1	12	2	4	7	vs. 1st Batr (relief)	.162	37	6	0	0	2	3	3	11	.220	.162
August	3.86	0	1	0	8	0	14.0	16	2	10	10	1st Inning Pitched	.223	157	35	7	1	5	22	22	37	.317	.376
Sept/Oct	3.96	1	1	0	6	3	25.0	26	1	8	26	First 15 Pitches	.216	125	27	4	1	4	17	16	27	.299	.360
Starter	6.62	0	3	0	7	7	34.0	49	5	10	24	Pitch 16-30	.200	120	24	4	1	4	10	13	23	.287	.350
Reliever	2.83	3	4	0	43	0	82.2	69	9	36	59	Pitch 31-45	.338	71	24	7	0	2	6	9	13	.420	.521
0 Days rest (Relief)	3.55	0	0	0	5	0	12.2	8	2	6	8	Pitch 46+	.352	122	43	13	0	4	23	8	20	.389	.557
1 or 2 Days rest	4.02	2	1	0	19	0	31.1	35	5	10	18	First Pitch	.326	46	15	5	0	3	10	6	0	.396	.630
3+ Days rest	1.63	1	3	0	19	0	38.2	26	2	20	33	Ahead in Count	.195	190	37	7	0	3	10	0	65	.206	.279
vs. AL	3.98	3	6	0	43	7	104.0	108	13	39	71	Behind in Count	.406	96	39	10	1	6	23	24	0	.512	.719
vs. NL	3.55	0	1	0	7	0	12.2	10	1	7	12	Two Strikes	.194	227	44	10	1	4	18	16	83	.255	.300
Pre-All Star	4.21	1	4	0	29	4	66.1	66	10	26	42	Pre-All Star	.268	246	66	13	1	10	32	26	42	.338	.451
Post-All Star	3.58	2	3	0	21	3	50.1	52	4	20	41	Post-All Star	.271	192	52	15	1	4	24	20	41	.341	.422

Bill Haselman — Red Sox
Age 32 – Bats Right (groundball hitter)

	Avg	G	AB	R	H	2B	3B	HR	RBI	BB	SO	HBP	GDP	SB	CS	OBP	SLG	IBB	SH	SF	#Pit	#P/PA	GB	FB	G/F
1997 Season	.236	67	212	22	50	15	0	6	26	15	44	2	8	0	2	.290	.392	2	1	2	798	3.44	78	53	1.47
Last Five Years	.247	304	821	109	203	49	3	25	107	66	156	7	32	7	7	.306	.406	5	4	7	3379	3.73	338	206	1.64

1997 Season

	Avg	AB	H	2B	3B	HR	RBI	BB	SO	OBP	SLG		Avg	AB	H	2B	3B	HR	RBI	BB	SO	OBP	SLG
vs. Left	.265	102	27	9	0	4	10	8	19	.319	.471	Scoring Posn	.264	53	14	4	0	1	17	4	10	.305	.396
vs. Right	.209	110	23	6	0	2	16	7	25	.263	.318	Close & Late	.171	35	6	4	0	0	2	3	10	.237	.286

1997 Season

	Avg	AB	H	2B	3B	HR	RBI	BB	SO	OBP	SLG		Avg	AB	H	2B	3B	HR	RBI	BB	SO	OBP	SLG
Home	.250	96	24	5	0	3	13	6	23	.291	.396	None on/out	.259	54	14	3	0	2	2	2	12	.298	.426
Away	.224	116	26	10	0	3	13	9	21	.289	.388	Batting #7	.200	35	7	2	0	1	6	0	5	.216	.343
First Pitch	.313	32	10	2	0	1	3	2	0	.353	.469	Batting #8	.267	135	36	12	0	5	19	11	27	.327	.467
Ahead in Count	.241	54	13	4	0	3	10	9	0	.349	.481	Other	.167	42	7	1	0	0	1	4	12	.234	.190
Behind in Count	.198	96	19	6	0	1	7	0	38	.214	.292	Pre-All Star	.242	149	36	12	0	3	18	11	35	.298	.383
Two Strikes	.179	95	17	4	0	1	7	4	44	.225	.253	Post-All Star	.222	63	14	3	0	3	8	4	9	.271	.413

Last Five Years

	Avg	AB	H	2B	3B	HR	RBI	BB	SO	OBP	SLG		Avg	AB	H	2B	3B	HR	RBI	BB	SO	OBP	SLG
vs. Left	.277	310	86	29	2	8	43	28	42	.337	.461	First Pitch	.272	103	28	6	1	3	10	5	0	.318	.437
vs. Right	.229	511	117	20	1	17	64	38	114	.287	.372	Ahead in Count	.337	187	63	19	0	12	37	28	0	.423	.631
Groundball	.260	150	39	9	1	3	23	11	32	.324	.393	Behind in Count	.175	378	66	13	1	5	30	0	131	.254	.254
Flyball	.233	150	35	11	1	7	17	9	32	.281	.460	Two Strikes	.168	394	66	14	1	6	35	33	156	.238	.254
Home	.261	380	99	18	2	15	54	36	75	.325	.437	Batting #7	.253	170	43	9	1	6	21	13	32	.310	.424
Away	.236	441	104	31	1	10	53	30	81	.290	.379	Batting #8	.264	435	115	32	1	16	62	35	75	.324	.453
Day	.265	306	81	23	1	11	44	29	53	.331	.454	Other	.208	216	45	8	1	3	24	18	49	.267	.296
Night	.237	515	122	26	2	14	63	37	103	.291	.377	March/April	.275	142	39	14	0	3	18	15	31	.346	.437
Grass	.254	610	155	32	2	20	85	49	124	.312	.411	May	.253	178	45	10	2	4	19	13	40	.310	.399
Turf	.227	211	48	17	1	5	22	17	32	.291	.389	June	.200	130	26	5	0	5	16	6	21	.239	.354
Pre-All Star	.246	479	118	31	2	12	55	36	94	.303	.395	July	.273	77	21	5	0	2	10	5	10	.317	.416
Post-All Star	.249	342	85	18	1	13	52	30	62	.311	.421	August	.248	117	29	5	0	3	14	9	21	.297	.368
Scoring Posn	.267	217	58	14	1	5	79	28	49	.349	.410	Sept/Oct	.243	177	43	10	1	8	30	18	33	.320	.446
Close & Late	.211	142	30	8	0	5	16	12	37	.276	.373	vs. AL	.250	808	202	49	3	25	107	66	154	.310	.411
None on/out	.240	192	46	12	0	7	7	10	30	.281	.411	vs. NL	.077	13	1	0	0	0	0	0	2	.077	.077

Batter vs. Pitcher (career)

Hits Best Against	Avg	AB	H	2B	3B	HR	RBI	BB	SO	OBP	SLG	Hits Worst Against	Avg	AB	H	2B	3B	HR	RBI	BB	SO	OBP	SLG
Jimmy Key	.364	11	4	2	0	0	1	4	0	.533	.545	Kenny Rogers	.100	10	1	1	0	0	3	1	2	.182	.200
Rich Robertson	.333	9	3	2	0	0	3	1	2	.364	.556	Alex Fernandez	.133	15	2	0	0	2	3	0	2	.133	.533
Mike Mussina	.308	13	4	2	0	1	3	0	2	.357	.692	Andy Pettitte	.200	15	3	2	0	0	0	0	2	.200	.333
												David Wells	.211	19	4	0	0	1	2	0	5	.211	.368
												Chuck Finley	.217	23	5	2	0	0	3	0	4	.217	.304

Scott Hatteberg — Red Sox   Age 28 – Bats Left

	Avg	G	AB	R	H	2B	3B	HR	RBI	BB	SO	HBP	GDP	SB	CS	OBP	SLG	IBB	SH	SF	#Pit	#P/PA	GB	FB	G/F
1997 Season	.277	114	350	46	97	23	1	10	44	40	70	2	11	0	1	.354	.434	2	2	1	1617	4.09	111	97	1.14
Career (1995-1997)	.275	126	363	50	100	24	1	10	44	43	72	2	14	0	1	.355	.430	2	2	1	1699	4.13	117	99	1.18

1997 Season

	Avg	AB	H	2B	3B	HR	RBI	BB	SO	OBP	SLG		Avg	AB	H	2B	3B	HR	RBI	BB	SO	OBP	SLG
vs. Left	.225	80	18	8	1	0	12	11	21	.333	.350	First Pitch	.276	29	8	4	0	0	1	1	0	.300	.414
vs. Right	.293	270	79	15	0	10	32	29	49	.360	.459	Ahead in Count	.360	86	31	7	0	7	22	22	0	.491	.686
Groundball	.214	56	12	3	0	1	6	9	12	.333	.321	Behind in Count	.176	159	28	3	0	0	4	0	60	.181	.195
Flyball	.237	59	14	2	0	2	4	7	14	.318	.373	Two Strikes	.215	181	39	7	0	2	15	17	70	.283	.287
Home	.279	179	50	11	1	5	24	23	41	.368	.436	Batting #7	.268	194	52	15	1	3	22	17	41	.329	.402
Away	.275	171	47	12	0	5	20	17	29	.339	.433	Batting #9	.259	58	15	3	0	3	7	7	8	.338	.466
Day	.230	87	20	4	0	0	5	9	20	.302	.276	Other	.306	98	30	5	0	4	15	16	21	.409	.480
Night	.293	263	77	19	1	10	39	31	50	.370	.487	March/April	.353	17	6	3	0	0	0	3	5	.450	.529
Grass	.289	308	89	22	1	9	38	36	58	.367	.455	May	.238	42	10	1	0	3	8	5	7	.319	.476
Turf	.190	42	8	1	0	1	6	4	12	.255	.286	June	.321	78	25	3	1	2	8	12	12	.418	.462
Pre-All Star	.286	161	46	9	1	5	19	21	26	.375	.447	July	.220	82	18	4	0	2	9	10	19	.342	.341
Post-All Star	.270	189	51	14	0	5	25	19	44	.355	.423	August	.289	76	22	7	0	1	11	5	13	.329	.421
Scoring Posn	.233	90	21	5	0	2	32	18	23	.364	.356	Sept/Oct	.291	55	16	5	0	2	8	5	14	.350	.491
Close & Late	.207	58	12	4	0	1	6	8	15	.313	.328	vs. AL	.277	311	86	22	0	9	42	33	60	.345	.434
None on/out	.396	91	36	9	1	5	5	7	13	.440	.436	vs. NL	.282	39	11	1	1	2		7	10	.417	.436

1997 By Position

Position	Avg	AB	H	2B	3B	HR	RBI	BB	SO	OBP	SLG	G	GS	Innings	PO	A	E	DP	Fld Pct	Rng Fctr	In Zone Outs	Zone Rtg	MLB Zone
As Pinch Hitter	.222	9	2	0	0	1	2	2	2	.364	.556	14	0	—	—	—	—	—	—	—	—	—	—
As c	.280	339	95	23	1	9	42	38	68	.355	.434	106	93	839.1	574	45	11	13	.983	—	—	—	—

Gary Haught — Athletics   Age 27 – Pitches Right

	ERA	W	L	Sv	G	GS	IP	BB	SO	Avg	H	2B	3B	HR	RBI	OBP	SLG	GF	IR	IRS	Hld	SvOp	SB	CS	GB	FB	G/F
1997 Season	7.15	0	0	0	6	0	11.1	6	11	.279	12	3	1	3	8	.385	.605	2	0	0	1	0	0	1	12	12	1.00

1997 Season

	ERA	W	L	Sv	G	GS	IP	H	HR	BB	SO		Avg	AB	H	2B	3B	HR	RBI	BB	SO	OBP	SLG
Home	6.35	0	0	0	3	0	5.2	5	0	4	5	vs. Left	.200	20	4	0	1	1	3	1	5	.227	.450
Away	7.94	0	0	0	3	0	5.2	7	3	2	6	vs. Right	.348	23	8	3	0	2	5	5	6	.500	.739

LaTroy Hawkins — Twins
Age 25 – Pitches Right

	ERA	W	L	Sv	G	GS	IP	BB	SO	Avg	H	2B	3B	HR	RBI	OBP	SLG	CG	ShO	Sup	QS	#P/S	SB	CS	GB	FB	G/F
1997 Season	5.84	6	12	0	20	20	103.1	47	58	.317	134	29	4	19	67	.389	.539	0	0	5.31	9	83	6	2	165	107	1.54
Career (1995-1997)	6.72	9	16	0	33	32	156.2	68	91	.330	215	47	6	30	116	.395	.559	1	0	5.86	9	83	2	1	236	179	1.32

1997 Season

	ERA	W	L	Sv	G	GS	IP	H	HR	BB	SO
Home	4.62	4	5	0	9	9	48.2	54	4	19	28
Away	6.91	2	7	0	11	11	54.2	80	15	28	30
Starter	5.84	6	12	0	20	20	103.1	134	19	47	58
Reliever	0.00	0	0	0	0	0	0.0	0	0	0	0
0-3 Days Rest (Start)	6.00	0	1	0	1	1	6.0	6	0	2	4
4 Days Rest	5.71	3	9	0	13	13	64.2	95	13	29	34
5+ Days Rest	6.06	3	2	0	6	6	32.2	33	6	16	20
Pre-All Star	4.78	1	4	0	5	5	26.1	30	2	14	11
Post-All Star	6.19	5	8	0	15	15	77.0	104	17	33	47

	Avg	AB	H	2B	3B	HR	RBI	BB	SO	OBP	SLG
vs. Left	.368	209	77	18	3	12	39	33	27	.453	.656
vs. Right	.266	214	57	11	1	7	28	14	31	.320	.425
Scoring Posn	.260	131	34	7	1	5	44	7	21	.298	.443
Close & Late	.125	8	1	0	0	0	0	0	0	.125	.125
None on/out	.320	100	32	6	1	4		15	12	.414	.520
Ahead in Count	.274	190	52	7	1	3	17	0	54	.281	.368
Behind in Count	.349	86	30	6	1	8	26	29	0	.509	.721
Two Strikes	.271	188	51	9	1	5	18	18	58	.338	.410

Charlie Hayes — Yankees
Age 33 – Bats Right

	Avg	G	AB	R	H	2B	3B	HR	RBI	BB	SO	HBP	GDP	SB	CS	OBP	SLG	IBB	SH	SF	#Pit	#P/PA	GB	FB	G/F
1997 Season	.258	100	353	39	91	16	0	11	53	40	66	1	13	3	2	.332	.397				1484	3.73	105	106	0.99
Last Five Years	.277	659	2404	290	667	138	11	69	361	206	397	13	89	28	15	.335	.430	18	4	22	9601	3.62	836	700	1.19

1997 Season

	Avg	AB	H	2B	3B	HR	RBI	BB	SO	OBP	SLG
vs. Left	.311	135	42	7	0	8	29	18	16	.394	.541
vs. Right	.225	218	49	9	0	3	24	22	50	.292	.307
Groundball	.275	69	19	1	0	2	6	4	12	.311	.377
Flyball	.261	46	12	3	0	1	7	3	9	.314	.391
Home	.269	182	49	13	0	5	26	22	31	.348	.423
Away	.246	171	42	3	0	6	27	18	35	.314	.368
Day	.315	127	40	11	0	5	25	21	27	.409	.520
Night	.226	226	51	5	0	6	28	19	39	.285	.327
Grass	.262	302	79	14	0	10	46	34	49	.333	.407
Turf	.235	51	12	2	0	1	7	6	17	.322	.333
Pre-All Star	.277	141	39	8	0	6	21	23	31	.380	.461
Post-All Star	.245	212	52	8	0	5	32	17	35	.297	.354
Scoring Posn	.206	107	22	5	0	2	38	17	24	.305	.308
Close & Late	.309	55	17	2	0	5	16	13	16	.441	.618
None on/out	.293	75	22	3	0	1	1	8	12	.361	.373

	Avg	AB	H	2B	3B	HR	RBI	BB	SO	OBP	SLG
First Pitch	.283	60	17	4	0	0	3	2	0	.308	.350
Ahead in Count	.333	81	27	3	0	4	16	21	0	.471	.519
Behind in Count	.237	156	37	5	0	7	24	0	49	.236	.404
Two Strikes	.190	163	31	5	0	6	25	17	66	.264	.331
Batting #6	.277	159	44	13	0	5	23	11	34	.322	.453
Batting #7	.242	95	23	2	0	2	13	15	19	.345	.326
Other	.242	99	24	1	0	4	17	14	13	.333	.374
March/April	.242	33	8	2	0	0	2	5	6	.342	.303
May	.269	52	14	1	0	3	6	11	13	.400	.462
June	.356	45	16	4	0	3	13	6	9	.431	.644
July	.237	76	18	4	0	2	15	6	9	.289	.368
August	.240	96	23	4	0	3	9	8	21	.295	.375
Sept/Oct	.235	51	12	1	0	0	0	4	8	.286	.255
vs. AL	.254	323	82	14	0	11	50	37	63	.329	.399
vs. NL	.300	30	9	2	0	0	3	3	3	.364	.367

1997 By Position

Position	Avg	AB	H	2B	3B	HR	RBI	BB	SO	OBP	SLG	G	GS	Innings	PO	A	E	DP	Fld Pct	Rng Fctr	In Zone	Zone Outs	Zone Rtg	MLB Zone
As 3b	.256	347	89	16	0	10	49	37	66	.326	.389	98	89	806.0	65	168	13	19	.947	2.60	250	205	.820	.801

Last Five Years

	Avg	AB	H	2B	3B	HR	RBI	BB	SO	OBP	SLG
vs. Left	.306	625	191	44	2	24	100	56	87	.364	.498
vs. Right	.268	1779	476	94	9	45	261	150	310	.325	.406
Groundball	.265	703	186	34	5	11	86	46	120	.310	.374
Flyball	.255	381	97	22	2	8	54	28	75	.309	.386
Home	.298	1177	351	87	8	37	198	110	177	.359	.480
Away	.258	1227	316	51	3	32	163	96	220	.312	.382
Day	.284	803	228	43	4	25	125	69	148	.340	.441
Night	.274	1601	439	95	7	44	236	137	249	.332	.425
Grass	.280	1451	406	78	6	48	214	120	230	.335	.441
Turf	.274	953	261	60	5	21	147	86	167	.335	.413
Pre-All Star	.284	1315	374	75	6	42	210	134	215	.351	.446
Post-All Star	.269	1089	293	63	5	27	151	72	182	.315	.410
Scoring Posn	.286	668	191	43	4	18	291	96	215	.359	.443
Close & Late	.278	360	100	24	1	10	65	41	68	.350	.433
None on/out	.263	563	148	40	2	19	19	37	88	.311	.442

	Avg	AB	H	2B	3B	HR	RBI	BB	SO	OBP	SLG
First Pitch	.316	411	130	31	3	14	62	15	0	.347	.509
Ahead in Count	.334	527	176	36	1	19	86	99	0	.440	.514
Behind in Count	.250	1066	267	54	7	29	143	0	334	.250	.396
Two Strikes	.213	1074	229	46	6	28	143	92	397	.275	.345
Batting #5	.280	1069	299	66	7	29	158	92	165	.338	.436
Batting #6	.267	671	179	46	1	22	105	47	124	.314	.437
Other	.285	664	189	26	3	18	98	67	108	.350	.414
March/April	.261	307	80	14	1	9	35	27	47	.323	.401
May	.279	455	127	23	3	18	68	53	84	.355	.462
June	.303	409	124	28	1	13	86	42	62	.367	.472
July	.264	478	126	24	4	10	66	36	80	.315	.393
August	.270	433	117	27	1	11	52	24	69	.308	.413
Sept/Oct	.289	322	93	22	1	8	54	24	55	.341	.438
vs. AL	.259	390	101	17	0	13	63	38	75	.323	.403
vs. NL	.281	2014	566	121	11	56	298	168	322	.337	.435

Batter vs. Pitcher (career)

Hits Best Against	Avg	AB	H	2B	3B	HR	RBI	BB	SO	OBP	SLG	Hits Worst Against	Avg	AB	H	2B	3B	HR	RBI	BB	SO	OBP	SLG
Dave Mlicki	.583	12	7	0	0	0	4	3	0	.667	.583	VanLandingham	.000	15	0	0	0	0	0	2	4	.118	.000
Greg Swindell	.563	16	9	4	0	2	3	0	1	.563	1.188	Randy Johnson	.000	9	0	0	0	0	2	0	0	.091	.000
Rick Reed	.556	18	10	1	0	2	6	0	3	.556	.944	David Cone	.053	19	1	1	0	0	1	0	7	.053	.105
Kevin Gross	.526	19	10	1	0	2	4	2	0	.571	.895	Kevin Brown	.077	13	1	0	0	0	0	0	3	.077	.077
Denny Neagle	.444	9	4	3	0	0	1	3	1	.583	.778	Kevin Ritz	.077	13	1	0	0	0	0	0	2	.077	.077

Jimmy Haynes — Athletics
Age 25 – Pitches Right

	ERA	W	L	Sv	G	GS	IP	BB	SO	Avg	H	2B	3B	HR	RBI	OBP	SLG	CG	ShO	Sup	QS	#P/S	SB	CS	GB	FB	G/F
1997 Season	4.42	3	6	0	13	13	73.1	40	65	.262	74	13	0	7	33	.354	.383	0	0	4.17	5	99	3	2	101	76	1.33
Career (1995-1997)	5.99	8	13	1	43	27	186.1	110	152	.284	207	33	4	23	116	.377	.435	0	0	5.22	9	99	6	6	236	227	1.04

1997 Season

	ERA	W	L	Sv	G	GS	IP	H	HR	BB	SO		Avg	AB	H	2B	3B	HR	RBI	BB	SO	OBP	SLG
Home	4.91	1	5	0	8	8	44.0	49	4	23	37	vs. Left	.248	141	35	6	0	4	13	21	29	.339	.376

1997 Season

	ERA	W	L	Sv	G	GS	IP	H	HR	BB	SO		Avg	AB	H	2B	3B	HR	RBI	BB	SO	OBP	SLG
Away	3.68	2	1	0	5	5	29.1	25	3	17	28	vs. Right	.277	141	39	7	0	3	20	19	36	.368	.390
Starter	4.42	3	6	0	13	13	73.1	74	7	40	65	Scoring Posn	.197	76	15	2	0	1	25	13	19	.309	.263
Reliever	0.00	0	0	0	0	0	0.0	0	0	0	0	Close & Late	.000	0	0	0	0	0	0	0	0	.000	.000
0-3 Days Rest (Start)	3.52	1	1	0	3	3	15.1	14	1	7	9	None on/out	.236	72	17	4	0	3	3	8	13	.313	.417
4 Days Rest	4.85	2	4	0	7	7	42.2	43	5	19	47	First Pitch	.308	39	12	2	0	2	13	1	0	.317	.513
5+ Days Rest	4.11	0	1	0	3	3	15.1	17	1	14	9	Behind in Count	.181	116	21	6	0	0	6	0	55	.179	.233
Pre-All Star	0.00	0	0	0	0	0	0.0	0	0	0	0	Ahead in Count	.384	73	28	5	0	4	10	25	0	.535	.616
Post-All Star	4.42	3	6	0	13	13	73.1	74	7	40	65	Two Strikes	.156	128	20	5	0	0	3	14	65	.248	.195

Rick Helling — Rangers
Age 27 – Pitches Right (flyball pitcher)

	ERA	W	L	Sv	G	GS	IP	BB	SO	Avg	H	2B	3B	HR	RBI	OBP	SLG	GF	IR	IRS	Hld	SvOp	SB	CS	GB	FB	G/F
1997 Season	4.47	5	9	0	41	16	131.0	69	99	.233	108	21	4	17	63	.335	.406	9	20	6	6	1	8	13	104	178	0.58
Career (1994-1997)	4.85	11	16	0	64	34	243.1	111	171	.248	224	40	10	42	128	.332	.454	11	24	9	7	1	19	14	217	364	0.60

1997 Season

	ERA	W	L	Sv	G	GS	IP	H	HR	BB	SO		Avg	AB	H	2B	3B	HR	RBI	BB	SO	OBP	SLG
Home	3.84	2	4	0	18	7	58.2	48	4	30	34	vs. Left	.220	223	49	11	2	9	30	40	58	.340	.408
Away	4.98	3	5	0	23	9	72.1	60	13	39	65	vs. Right	.246	240	59	10	2	8	33	29	41	.330	.404
Day	5.74	1	4	0	12	4	31.1	35	7	18	21	Inning 1-6	.242	330	80	19	3	11	42	50	65	.344	.418
Night	4.06	4	5	0	29	12	99.2	73	10	51	78	Inning 7+	.211	133	28	2	1	6	21	14	34	.310	.376
Grass	4.33	4	7	0	36	14	114.1	92	14	62	77	None on	.222	284	63	11	2	11	11	33	61	.309	.391
Turf	5.40	1	2	0	5	2	16.2	16	3	7	22	Runners on	.251	179	45	10	2	6	52	36	38	.370	.430
March/April	1.59	0	1	0	10	0	17.0	9	2	6	7	Scoring Posn	.229	105	24	7	2	1	41	28	23	.371	.362
May	3.26	1	2	0	4	3	19.1	13	2	7	14	Close & Late	.271	48	13	1	1	3	11	8	10	.407	.521
June	7.61	1	2	0	6	5	23.2	27	6	24	18	None on/out	.240	121	29	8	1	3	3	13	29	.319	.397
July	4.38	0	1	0	9	0	12.1	9	2	7	12	vs. 1st Batr (relief)	.190	21	4	0	0	3	2	3		.240	.190
August	1.88	1	1	0	7	3	28.2	14	2	12	20	1st Inning Pitched	.235	132	31	7	1	6	21	6	21	.348	.439
Sept/Oct	6.90	2	2	0	5	5	30.0	36	3	13	28	First 15 Pitches	.260	100	26	6	1	5	15	13	13	.342	.490
Starter	5.48	5	7	0	16	16	90.1	85	13	50	70	Pitch 16-30	.229	96	22	3	0	3	10	15	30	.327	.354
Reliever	2.21	0	2	0	25	0	40.2	23	4	19	29	Pitch 31-45	.254	63	16	4	2	2	15	15	18	.407	.476
0 Days rest (Relief)	4.50	0	0	0	1	0	2.0	3	1	0	3	Pitch 46+	.216	204	44	8	1	7	23	26	58	.309	.368
1 or 2 Days rest	0.00	0	0	0	11	0	18.1	4	0	5	12	First Pitch	.300	60	18	3	2	4	10	2	0	.338	.617
3+ Days rest	3.98	0	2	0	13	0	20.1	16	3	14	14	Ahead in Count	.208	197	41	6	1	5	20	0	81	.222	.325
vs. AL	4.74	3	3	0	11	8	57.0	51	4	27	51	Behind in Count	.279	111	31	5	1	5	19	25	0	.397	.477
vs. NL	4.26	2	6	0	30	8	74.0	57	13	42	48	Two Strikes	.172	221	38	8	1	3	24	42	99	.305	.258
Pre-All Star	4.74	2	5	0	22	8	62.2	52	10	41	41	Pre-All Star	.236	220	52	14	3	10	36	41	41	.358	.464
Post-All Star	4.21	3	4	0	19	8	68.1	56	7	28	58	Post-All Star	.230	243	56	7	1	7	27	28	58	.312	.354

Todd Helton — Rockies
Age 24 – Bats Left

	Avg	G	AB	R	H	2B	3B	HR	RBI	BB	SO	HBP	GDP	SB	CS	OBP	SLG	IBB	SH	SF	#Pit	P/PA	GB	FB	G/F
1997 Season	.280	35	93	13	26	2	1	5	11	8	11	0	1	0	1	.337	.484	0	0	0	402	3.98	32	34	0.94

1997 Season

	Avg	AB	H	2B	3B	HR	RBI	BB	SO	OBP	SLG		Avg	AB	H	2B	3B	HR	RBI	BB	SO	OBP	SLG
vs. Left	.200	10	2	0	0	0	0	0	0	.200	.200	Scoring Posn	.214	28	6	0	0	2	8	2	5	.267	.429
vs. Right	.289	83	24	2	1	5	11	8	11	.352	.518	Close & Late	.368	19	7	0	1	0	2	1	0	.400	.474

Rickey Henderson — Angels
Age 39 – Bats Right

	Avg	G	AB	R	H	2B	3B	HR	RBI	BB	SO	HBP	GDP	SB	CS	OBP	SLG	IBB	SH	SF	#Pit	#P/PA	GB	FB	G/F
1997 Season	.248	120	403	84	100	14	0	8	34	97	85	6	10	45	8	.400	.342	2	1	2	2316	4.55	137	107	1.28
Last Five Years	.268	601	2052	441	550	97	5	53	196	486	351	29	32	189	48	.413	.398	14	4	13	11496	4.45	692	609	1.14

1997 Season

	Avg	AB	H	2B	3B	HR	RBI	BB	SO	OBP	SLG		Avg	AB	H	2B	3B	HR	RBI	BB	SO	OBP	SLG
vs. Left	.273	77	21	3	0	4	9	28	17	.481	.468	First Pitch	.417	24	10	0	0	1	4	0	0	.440	.542
vs. Right	.242	326	79	11	0	4	25	69	68	.378	.313	Ahead in Count	.300	80	24	6	0	2	7	50	0	.569	.450
Groundball	.230	87	20	2	0	2	13	11	21	.323	.322	Behind in Count	.196	179	35	1	0	0	6	0	62	.216	.201
Flyball	.241	58	14	2	0	2	8	16	13	.403	.379	Two Strikes	.213	244	52	5	0	5	20	47	85	.349	.295
Home	.230	209	48	8	0	6	18	49	46	.379	.354	Batting #1	.255	388	99	14	0	7	32	89	78	.399	.345
Away	.268	194	52	6	0	2	16	48	39	.421	.330	Batting #9	.125	8	1	0	0	1	2	5	4	.500	.500
Day	.268	138	37	5	0	4	16	35	24	.420	.391	Other	.000	7	0	0	0	0	0	3	3	.300	.000
Night	.238	265	63	9	0	4	18	62	61	.389	.317	March/April	.173	52	9	2	0	1	5	17	13	.394	.269
Grass	.252	369	93	13	0	8	32	92	77	.406	.352	May	.111	9	1	0	0	0	0	3	3	.333	.111
Turf	.206	34	7	1	0	0	2	5	8	.325	.235	June	.370	92	34	3	0	2	9	24	10	.500	.467
Pre-All Star	.289	180	52	7	0	5	20	46	38	.439	.411	July	.242	99	24	5	0	2	9	18	29	.364	.354
Post-All Star	.215	223	48	7	0	3	14	51	47	.367	.287	August	.263	95	25	4	0	3	10	24	20	.413	.400
Scoring Posn	.279	61	17	4	0	1	26	21	15	.459	.393	Sept/Oct	.125	56	7	0	0	0	1	11	10	.279	.125
Close & Late	.254	59	15	1	0	1	3	21	14	.444	.322	vs. AL	.212	146	31	5	0	4	14	29	35	.354	.329
None on/out	.193	171	33	3	0	6	6	35	43	.316	.316	vs. NL	.268	257	69	9	0	4	20	68	50	.424	.350

1997 By Position

Position	Avg	AB	H	2B	3B	HR	RBI	BB	SO	OBP	SLG	G	GS	Innings	PO	A	E	DP	Fld Pct	Rng Fctr	In Zone	Zone Outs	Zone Rtg	MLB Zone
As DH	.185	81	15	2	0	2	6	17	22	.340	.284	21	21	—	—	—	—	—	—	—	—	—	—	—
As Pinch Hitter	.143	7	1	0	0	1	1	3	3	.400	.571	10	0	—	—	—	—	—	—	—	—	—	—	—

1997 By Position

Position	Avg	AB	H	2B	3B	HR	RBI	BB	SO	OBP	SLG	G	GS	Innings	PO	A	E	DP	Fld Pct	Rng Fctr	In Zone	Zone Outs	Zone Rtg	MLB Zone
As lf	.291	234	68	9	0	4	20	48	43	.414	.380	66	61	526.1	128	3	4	0	.970	2.24	143	118	.825	.805
As cf	.175	57	10	3	0	0	3	18	15	.382	.228	19	17	139.1	47	1	1	1	.980	3.10	52	44	.846	.815

Last Five Years

	Avg	AB	H	2B	3B	HR	RBI	BB	SO	OBP	SLG
vs. Left	.267	546	146	20	0	25	58	152	100	.430	.441
vs. Right	.268	1506	404	77	5	28	138	334	251	.406	.406
Groundball	.259	441	114	22	1	11	51	107	72	.408	.388
Flyball	.293	358	105	20	2	14	43	95	67	.449	.478
Home	.269	1033	278	45	2	29	93	244	177	.412	.401
Away	.267	1019	272	52	3	24	103	242	174	.413	.395
Day	.270	737	199	36	1	17	64	193	124	.427	.391
Night	.267	1315	351	61	4	36	132	293	227	.405	.402
Grass	.270	1681	454	78	4	45	156	406	285	.416	.399
Turf	.259	371	96	19	3	8	40	80	66	.397	.391
Pre-All Star	.273	1131	309	51	4	33	124	289	198	.427	.413
Post-All Star	.262	921	241	46	1	20	72	197	153	.395	.379
Scoring Posn	.263	377	99	20	2	8	143	125	78	.443	.390
Close & Late	.255	310	79	14	3	5	23	84	55	.415	.368
None on/out	.266	865	230	42	0	32	32	176	164	.399	.425

	Avg	AB	H	2B	3B	HR	RBI	BB	SO	OBP	SLG
First Pitch	.304	102	31	3	0	4	13	9	0	.379	.451
Ahead in Count	.335	504	169	36	0	26	70	271		.566	.562
Behind in Count	.215	912	196	23	1	10	52	0	276	.229	.275
Two Strikes	.230	1149	264	38	4	18	83	206	351	.352	.317
Batting #1	.272	1989	541	96	5	51	189	459	330	.413	.402
Batting #9	.136	22	3	0	0	1	3	9	9	.394	.273
Other	.146	41	6	1	0	1	4	18	12	.417	.244
March/April	.228	259	59	12	2	5	27	80	47	.417	.347
May	.251	283	71	12	1	9	34	68	67	.401	.396
June	.300	443	133	20	0	12	40	110	56	.444	.427
July	.292	448	131	32	1	14	45	93	87	.421	.462
August	.282	354	100	11	1	7	26	83	57	.420	.379
Sept/Oct	.211	265	56	10	0	6	24	52	37	.343	.317
vs. AL	.277	1330	369	71	3	40	147	293	211	.411	.426
vs. NL	.251	722	181	26	2	13	49	193	140	.415	.346

Batter vs. Pitcher (since 1984)

Hits Best Against	Avg	AB	H	2B	3B	HR	RBI	BB	SO	OBP	SLG
Jose Bautista	.556	9	5	2	0	0	0	3	0	.667	.778
Mike Morgan	.500	12	6	0	0	3	3	2	2	.571	1.250
Scott Bailes	.500	10	5	1	1	0	1	7	2	.706	.800
Donn Pall	.462	13	6	1	0	1	7	2	0	.533	.769
Mark Gardner	.417	12	5	0	0	3	4	4	3	.563	1.167

Hits Worst Against	Avg	AB	H	2B	3B	HR	RBI	BB	SO	OBP	SLG
Chris Haney	.000	10	0	0	0	0	0	3	0	.231	.000
John Smiley	.063	16	1	0	0	0	0	2	2	.167	.063
Brad Radke	.091	11	1	0	0	0	0	2	1	.231	.091
Andy Benes	.100	10	1	0	0	0	1	1	2	.167	.100
Pedro Astacio	.150	20	3	0	0	0	0	0	3	.150	.150

Oscar Henriquez — Astros
Age 24 – Pitches Right

	ERA	W	L	Sv	G	GS	IP	BB	SO	Avg	H	2B	3B	HR	RBI	OBP	SLG	GF	IR	IRS	Hld	SvOp	SB	CS	GB	FB	G/F
1997 Season	4.50	0	1	0	4	0	4.0	3	3	.167	2	0	0	0	2	.375	.167	1	0	0	1	0	2	0	6	3	2.00

1997 Season

	ERA	W	L	Sv	G	GS	IP	H	HR	BB	SO		Avg	AB	H	2B	3B	HR	RBI	BB	SO	OBP	SLG
Home	6.00	0	1	0	3	0	3.0	2	0	3	3	vs. Left	.167	6	1	0	0	0	1	2	1	.375	.167
Away	0.00	0	0	0	1	0	1.0	0	0	0	0	vs. Right	.167	6	1	0	0	0	1	1	2	.375	.167

Butch Henry — Red Sox
Age 29 – Pitches Left

	ERA	W	L	Sv	G	GS	IP	BB	SO	Avg	H	2B	3B	HR	RBI	OBP	SLG	GF	IR	IRS	Hld	SvOp	SB	CS	GB	FB	G/F
1997 Season	3.52	7	3	6	36	5	84.1	19	51	.277	89	12	2	6	33	.315	.383	13	19	3	4	8	6	4	112	102	1.10
Last Five Years	3.67	25	24	7	111	57	421.1	95	228	.274	454	39	8	42	173	.317	.413	18	31	8	6	9	30	20	628	470	1.34

1997 Season

	ERA	W	L	Sv	G	GS	IP	H	HR	BB	SO		Avg	AB	H	2B	3B	HR	RBI	BB	SO	OBP	SLG
Home	2.37	3	1	0	16	2	38.0	41	1	10	19	vs. Left	.308	65	20	3	0	1	5	4	10	.343	.400
Away	4.47	4	2	6	20	3	46.1	48	5	9	32	vs. Right	.270	256	69	9	2	5	28	15	41	.308	.379
Starter	1.48	2	1	0	5	5	30.1	25	1	7	14	Scoring Posn	.232	82	19	2	0	3	28	5	13	.283	.366
Reliever	4.67	5	2	6	31	0	54.0	64	5	12	37	Close & Late	.283	106	30	4	1	3	11	7	16	.327	.425
0 Days rest (Relief)	0.00	0	0	0	0	0	0.0	0	0	0	0	None on/out	.316	79	25	3	1	2		4	15	.349	.456
1 or 2 Days rest	4.00	3	2	4	20	0	36.0	38	5	6	25	First Pitch	.320	50	16	3	0	0	4		5	.349	.456
3+ Days rest	6.00	2	0	2	11	0	18.0	26	0	0	12	Ahead in Count	.255	149	38	2	0	4	15	0	46	.255	.349
Pre-All Star	2.96	2	2	4	15	0	27.1	30	0	6	20	Behind in Count	.343	67	23	5	2	1	9		5	.378	.522
Post-All Star	3.79	5	1	2	21	5	57.0	59	6	13	31	Two Strikes	.204	137	28	2	0	2	10	12	51	.268	.263

Last Five Years

	ERA	W	L	Sv	G	GS	IP	H	HR	BB	SO		Avg	AB	H	2B	3B	HR	RBI	BB	SO	OBP	SLG
Home	3.81	9	11	1	53	25	189.0	229	21	43	103	vs. Left	.291	350	102	23	2	7	34	22	43	.333	.429
Away	3.56	16	13	6	58	32	232.1	225	21	52	125	vs. Right	.274	1284	352	56	6	35	139	73	185	.312	.409
Day	4.79	5	7	1	34	12	97.2	128	10	24	55	Inning 1-6	.276	1270	351	62	4	36	136	68	171	.313	.417
Night	3.34	20	17	6	77	45	323.2	326	32	71	173	Inning 7+	.283	364	103	17	4	6	37	27	57	.329	.401
Grass	4.38	16	11	4	64	27	220.0	256	21	51	110	None on	.275	962	265	51	5	24	24	47	139	.309	.414
Turf	2.91	9	13	3	47	30	201.1	198	21	44	118	Runners on	.281	672	189	28	3	18	149	48	89	.327	.412
March/April	3.35	2	4	4	18	5	53.2	57	6	11	30	Scoring Posn	.260	373	97	17	2	11	129	34	56	.317	.405
May	4.76	4	7	0	22	16	92.2	98	12	23	47	Close & Late	.292	168	49	5	2	5	17	13	27	.342	.435
June	3.42	5	4	1	19	11	81.2	89	7	23	42	None on/out	.294	428	126	30	2	11	11	21	51	.327	.451
July	3.55	9	5	0	23	13	99.0	112	10	20	58	vs. 1st Batr (relief)	.294	51	15	3	1	1	6	3	7	.333	.451
August	3.76	3	2	2	16	7	52.2	60	6	8	31	1st Inning Pitched	.262	401	105	18	3	10	55	29	54	.309	.397
Sept/Oct	2.38	2	2	0	13	5	41.2	38	1	10	20	First 15 Pitches	.279	362	101	16	3	10	35	16	42	.308	.420
Starter	3.53	20	21	0	57	57	329.1	350	36	74	166	Pitch 16-30	.283	357	101	23	1	12	47	23	67	.324	.454
Reliever	4.21	5	3	7	54	0	92.0	104	6	21	62	Pitch 31-45	.276	283	78	13	2	5	23	15	33	.311	.389
0 Days rest (Relief)	6.75	0	0	0	2	0	1.1	2	0	0	1	Pitch 46+	.275	632	174	28	2	15	68	41	86	.320	.397
1 or 2 Days rest	4.70	3	3	5	31	0	51.2	60	6	10	35	First Pitch	.316	291	92	21	2	6	39	8	0	.333	.464
3+ Days rest	3.46	2	0	2	21	0	39.0	42	0	11	26	Ahead in Count	.233	737	172	24	2	13	60	0	203	.236	.324
vs. AL	3.63	7	3	6	35	4	79.1	87	5	17	47	Behind in Count	.323	331	107	19	4	12	39	34	0	.382	.514
vs. NL	3.68	18	21	1	76	53	342.0	367	37	78	181	Two Strikes	.214	674	144	26	1	15	50	53	228	.272	.322

Last Five Years

	ERA	W	L	Sv	G	GS	IP	H	HR	BB	SO		Avg	AB	H	2B	3B	HR	RBI	BB	SO	OBP	SLG
Pre-All Star	4.13	13	18	5	67	38	263.2	290	29	64	141	Pre-All Star	.283	1026	290	52	3	29	119	64	141	.325	.424
Post-All Star	2.91	12	6	2	44	19	157.2	164	13	31	87	Post-All Star	.270	608	164	27	5	13	54	31	87	.302	.395

Pitcher vs. Batter (career)

Pitches Best Vs.	Avg	AB	H	2B	3B	HR	RBI	BB	SO	OBP	SLG	Pitches Worst Vs.	Avg	AB	H	2B	3B	HR	RBI	BB	SO	OBP	SLG
Andres Galarraga	.083	12	1	1	0	0	1	0	1	.083	.167	Dave Hollins	.652	23	15	3	0	6	11	2	5	.667	1.565
Darrin Jackson	.091	11	1	0	0	0	0	0	2	.091	.091	Eric Davis	.500	8	4	2	0	1	4	4	1	.615	1.125
Tony Fernandez	.100	10	1	0	0	0	0	1	1	.182	.100	Reggie Sanders	.471	17	8	3	0	1	4	3	0	.550	.824
Eric Karros	.150	20	3	0	0	0	0		4	.150	.150	Darren Daulton	.455	11	5	1	0	3	4	1	1	.500	1.364
Mariano Duncan	.150	20	3	0	0	0		2		.182	.150	Barry Larkin	.417	12	5	1	0	1	4	2	1	.500	.750

Doug Henry — Giants

	ERA	W	L	Sv	G	GS	IP	BB	SO	Avg	H	2B	3B	HR	RBI	OBP	SLG	GF	IR	IRS	Hld	SvOp	SB	CS	GB	FB	G/F
1997 Season	4.71	4	5	3	75	0	70.2	41	69	.261	70	13	0	5	36	.358	.366	25	39	11	21	6	7	3	74	85	0.87
Last Five Years	4.45	15	26	33	263	0	299.0	150	247	.260	299	50	6	33	165	.345	.400	126	127	46	39	51	30	6	366	339	1.08

1997 Season

	ERA	W	L	Sv	G	GS	IP	H	HR	BB	SO		Avg	AB	H	2B	3B	HR	RBI	BB	SO	OBP	SLG
Home	3.30	4	2	1	44	0	43.2	37	3	24	42	vs. Left	.240	104	25	5	0	2	15	19	30	.360	.346
Away	7.00	0	3	2	31	0	27.0	33	2	17	27	vs. Right	.274	164	45	8	0	3	21	22	39	.356	.378
Day	5.45	3	2	2	39	0	36.1	37	3	20	31	Inning 1-6	.143	14	2	1	0	0	4	1	2	.188	.214
Night	3.93	1	3	1	36	0	34.1	33	2	21	38	Inning 7+	.268	254	68	12	0	5	32	40	67	.367	.374
Grass	4.76	4	4	1	65	0	58.2	60	5	35	55	None on	.228	136	31	4	0	2	2	17	36	.314	.301
Turf	4.50	0	1	2	10	0	12.0	10	0	6	14	Runners on	.295	132	39	9	0	3	34	24	33	.400	.432
March/April	1.42	2	0	0	13	0	12.2	6	0	5	13	Scoring Posn	.292	72	21	5	0	2	31	18	19	.419	.444
May	1.13	0	1	1	13	0	16.0	16	1	7	15	Close & Late	.298	124	37	10	0	2	20	20	35	.390	.427
June	9.53	0	2	1	16	0	11.1	18	2	6	12	None on/out	.258	62	16	2	0	1	1	8	13	.343	.339
July	5.79	1	1	0	11	0	9.1	4	2	11	7	vs. 1st Batr (relief)	.290	69	20	3	0	1	8	5	15	.333	.377
August	6.14	1	1	1	13	0	14.2	16	0	8	13	1st Inning Pitched	.267	225	60	12	0	5	33	37	62	.368	.387
Sept/Oct	6.75	0	0	0	9	0	6.2	10	0	4	9	First 15 Pitches	.260	181	47	10	0	2	17	28	45	.358	.348
Starter	0.00	0	0	0	0	0	0.0	0	0	0	0	Pitch 16-30	.244	78	19	3	0	3	16	12	24	.341	.397
Reliever	4.71	4	5	3	75	0	70.2	70	5	41	69	Pitch 31-45	.500	8	4	0	0	0	3	1	0	.556	.500
0 Days rest (Relief)	11.37	1	2	1	18	0	12.2	17	1	13	12	Pitch 46+	.000	1	0	0	0	0	0	0	0	.000	.000
1 or 2 Days rest	3.19	3	2	1	42	0	42.1	39	3	20	44	First Pitch	.406	32	13	1	0	0	4	5	0	.474	.438
3+ Days rest	3.45	0	1	1	15	0	15.2	14	1	8	13	Ahead in Count	.213	127	27	8	0	1	15	0	60	.217	.299
vs. AL	3.38	0	0	1	7	0	5.1	4	0	2	7	Behind in Count	.246	57	14	2	0	3	14	16	0	.405	.404
vs. NL	4.82	4	5	2	68	0	65.1	66	5	39	62	Two Strikes	.194	124	24	6	0	1	8	20	69	.308	.266
Pre-All Star	3.43	2	3	2	44	0	42.0	40	3	19	42	Pre-All Star	.255	157	40	5	0	3	17	19	42	.335	.344
Post-All Star	6.59	2	2	1	31	0	28.2	30	2	22	27	Post-All Star	.270	111	30	8	0	2	19	22	27	.388	.396

Last Five Years

	ERA	W	L	Sv	G	GS	IP	H	HR	BB	SO		Avg	AB	H	2B	3B	HR	RBI	BB	SO	OBP	SLG
Home	4.38	12	9	12	143	0	162.1	161	23	79	131	vs. Left	.254	497	126	18	2	16	70	78	109	.354	.394
Away	4.54	3	17	21	120	0	136.2	138	10	71	116	vs. Right	.265	654	173	32	4	17	95	72	138	.338	.404
Day	5.05	7	7	10	103	0	108.2	109	13	57	87	Inning 1-6	.226	106	24	6	0	3	16	13	19	.323	.368
Night	4.11	8	19	23	160	0	190.1	190	20	93	160	Inning 7+	.263	1045	275	44	6	30	149	137	228	.348	.403
Grass	4.57	14	22	26	221	0	248.1	257	30	128	205	None on	.249	607	151	26	3	17	17	62	124	.322	.386
Turf	3.91	1	4	7	42	0	50.2	42	3	22	42	Runners on	.272	544	148	24	3	16	148	88	123	.369	.415
March/April	4.14	3	0	6	38	0	41.1	42	3	20	33	Scoring Posn	.262	324	85	14	2	9	130	66	79	.380	.401
May	2.89	3	6	8	52	0	65.1	62	7	29	50	Close & Late	.284	559	159	26	5	18	101	75	130	.368	.445
June	5.29	1	7	9	51	0	51.0	57	8	19	48	None on/out	.223	264	59	13	1	6	6	30	50	.307	.348
July	5.51	3	6	5	43	0	50.2	42	8	31	35	vs. 1st Batr (relief)	.270	230	62	16	0	5	27	30	50	.354	.404
August	3.86	5	3	4	49	0	60.2	56	5	32	56	1st Inning Pitched	.265	848	225	44	4	24	137	112	188	.352	.412
Sept/Oct	6.30	0	4	1	30	0	30.0	40	2	19	25	First 15 Pitches	.278	684	190	39	4	21	103	88	139	.360	.439
Starter	0.00	0	0	0	0	0	0.0	0	0	0	0	Pitch 16-30	.223	363	81	10	2	7	45	46	83	.312	.320
Reliever	4.45	15	26	33	263	0	299.0	299	33	150	247	Pitch 31-45	.278	90	25	1	0	4	16	16	21	.383	.422
0 Days rest (Relief)	6.82	2	5	4	43	0	33.0	42	2	24	25	Pitch 46+	.214	14	3	0	0	1	1	0	4	.214	.429
1 or 2 Days rest	4.15	6	14	17	135	0	158.1	164	18	82	143	First Pitch	.363	146	53	5	2	8	38	23	0	.442	.589
3+ Days rest	4.18	7	7	12	85	0	107.2	93	13	44	79	Ahead in Count	.178	512	91	21	2	6	46	0	209	.186	.262
vs. AL	5.11	6	7	18	86	0	91.2	103	14	50	65	Behind in Count	.372	242	90	14	0	14	56	61	0	.495	.603
vs. NL	4.17	9	19	15	177	0	207.1	196	19	100	182	Two Strikes	.163	575	94	18	2	6	44	66	247	.251	.233
Pre-All Star	3.99	9	13	26	157	0	178.0	174	22	73	146	Pre-All Star	.256	680	174	29	2	22	96	73	146	.328	.401
Post-All Star	5.13	6	13	7	106	0	121.0	125	11	77	101	Post-All Star	.265	471	125	21	4	11	69	77	101	.370	.397

Pitcher vs. Batter (career)

Pitches Best Vs.	Avg	AB	H	2B	3B	HR	RBI	BB	SO	OBP	SLG	Pitches Worst Vs.	Avg	AB	H	2B	3B	HR	RBI	BB	SO	OBP	SLG
Greg Gagne	.167	12	2	0	0	0	0	0	3	.167	.167												
Ellis Burks	.167	12	2	0	0	0	1	0	3	.167	.167												
Vinny Castilla	.182	11	2	0	0	0	0	0	3	.182	.182												
Thomas Howard	.182	11	2	0	0	0	1	1	3	.250	.182												

Pat Hentgen — Blue Jays
Age 29 – Pitches Right

	ERA	W	L	Sv	G	GS	IP	BB	SO	Avg	H	2B	3B	HR	RBI	OBP	SLG	CG	ShO	Sup	QS	#P/S	SB	CS	GB	FB	G/F
1997 Season	3.68	15	10	0	35	35	264.0	71	160	.254	253	42	7	31	107	.308	.404	2	3	4.94	20	112	12	15	355	303	1.17
Last Five Years	3.82	77	51	0	158	156	1121.1	388	741	.256	1100	196	22	123	480	.321	.398	30	9	5.36	86	112	55	47	1387	1362	1.02

1997 Season

	ERA	W	L	Sv	G	GS	IP	H	HR	BB	SO		Avg	AB	H	2B	3B	HR	RBI	BB	SO	OBP	SLG
Home	3.33	8	5	0	17	17	135.0	125	19	33	73	vs. Left	.241	511	123	21	4	14	58	44	79	.308	.380
Away	4.05	7	5	0	18	18	129.0	128	12	38	87	vs. Right	.269	484	130	21	3	17	49	27	81	.307	.430
Day	3.32	4	4	0	15	15	111.0	96	11	36	76	Inning 1-6	.240	775	186	31	5	21	78	55	129	.293	.374
Night	3.94	11	6	0	20	20	153.0	157	20	35	84	Inning 7+	.305	220	67	11	2	10	29	16	31	.360	.509
Grass	4.66	5	5	0	16	16	112.0	116	12	35	76	None on	.256	610	156	27	1	19	19	36	94	.302	.397
Turf	2.96	10	5	0	19	19	152.0	137	19	36	84	Runners on	.252	385	97	15	6	12	88	35	66	.317	.416
March/April	4.43	1	1	0	6	6	44.2	51	4	11	26	Scoring Posn	.293	188	55	8	4	10	79	24	28	.367	.537
May	1.50	4	1	0	6	6	48.0	32	0	14	40	Close & Late	.331	130	43	8	1	8	20	9	23	.378	.592
June	3.46	3	3	0	6	6	52.0	49	10	10	27	None on/out	.272	265	72	8	1	9	9	15	33	.316	.411
July	4.21	2	2	0	5	5	36.1	38	6	14	19	vs. 1st Batr (relief)	.000	0	0	0	0	0	0	0	0	.000	.000
August	4.00	4	1	0	6	6	45.0	44	5	11	22	1st Inning Pitched	.256	133	34	3	0	3	11	11	17	.315	.346
Sept/Oct	4.97	1	2	0	6	6	38.0	39	6	11	26	First 75 Pitches	.239	639	153	24	3	15	52	45	105	.291	.357
Starter	3.68	15	10	0	35	35	264.0	253	31	71	160	Pitch 76-90	.266	143	38	10	2	5	20	8	21	.314	.469
Reliever	0.00	0	0	0	0	0	0.0	0	0	0	0	Pitch 91-105	.276	127	35	6	0	6	19	8	21	.321	.465
0-3 Days Rest (Start)	0.00	0	0	0	0	0	0.0	0	0	0	0	Pitch 106+	.314	86	27	2	2	5	16	10	13	.394	.558
4 Days Rest	4.00	11	9	0	26	26	191.1	197	24	49	118	First Pitch	.282	177	50	6	2	8	21	2	0	.298	.475
5+ Days Rest	2.85	4	1	0	9	9	72.2	62	7	22	42	Ahead in Count	.219	429	94	16	2	9	41	0	128	.225	.329
vs. AL	3.86	14	9	0	32	32	240.0	236	28	67	146	Behind in Count	.338	207	70	11	3	8	26	36	0	.434	.534
vs. NL	1.88	1	2	0	3	3	24.0	17	3	4	14	Two Strikes	.190	441	84	13	1	8	35	33	160	.252	.279
Pre-All Star	3.27	8	6	0	19	19	151.1	142	15	39	96	Pre-All Star	.249	570	142	18	5	15	55	39	96	.302	.377
Post-All Star	4.23	7	4	0	16	16	112.2	111	16	32	64	Post-All Star	.261	425	111	24	2	16	52	32	64	.315	.440

Last Five Years

	ERA	W	L	Sv	G	GS	IP	H	HR	BB	SO		Avg	AB	H	2B	3B	HR	RBI	BB	SO	OBP	SLG
Home	3.80	35	30	0	84	82	603.1	586	75	202	396	vs. Left	.266	2245	598	104	13	61	260	206	352	.332	.406
Away	3.84	42	21	0	74	74	518.0	514	48	186	345	vs. Right	.246	2044	502	92	9	62	220	182	389	.309	.390
Day	3.40	28	12	0	52	51	371.0	327	34	132	250	Inning 1-6	.257	3486	897	158	19	96	401	323	605	.323	.396
Night	4.03	49	39	0	106	105	750.1	773	89	256	491	Inning 7+	.253	803	203	38	3	27	79	65	136	.313	.408
Grass	4.12	35	19	0	65	65	448.0	460	45	159	298	None on	.256	2460	630	120	12	73	73	213	433	.320	.404
Turf	3.62	42	32	0	93	91	673.1	640	78	229	443	Runners on	.257	1829	470	76	10	50	407	175	308	.322	.391
March/April	4.04	11	6	0	23	21	156.0	148	11	54	101	Scoring Posn	.252	974	245	40	6	27	343	107	181	.322	.388
May	3.32	15	9	0	30	30	211.1	189	19	78	150	Close & Late	.247	430	106	21	1	14	39	32	92	.303	.398
June	3.80	13	8	0	27	27	189.1	184	25	68	115	None on/out	.261	1089	284	49	10	30	30	91	178	.322	.391
July	4.21	15	10	0	27	27	192.1	192	25	79	123	vs. 1st Batr (relief)	.000	1	0	0	0	0	0	0	0	.000	.000
August	3.92	15	8	0	27	27	204.1	202	26	62	117	1st Inning Pitched	.276	615	170	30	2	15	85	61	104	.343	.405
Sept/Oct	3.70	8	10	0	24	24	168.0	176	17	47	135	First 75 Pitches	.257	2736	703	117	12	73	289	241	477	.320	.405
Starter	3.82	77	50	0	156	156	1113.2	1093	123	381	736	Pitch 76-90	.267	562	150	40	4	19	77	57	87	.337	.454
Reliever	3.52	0	1	0	2	0	7.2	7	0	7	5	Pitch 91-105	.236	542	128	24	1	14	52	45	99	.294	.362
0-3 Days Rest (Start)	0.89	3	0	0	3	3	20.1	15	1	4	17	Pitch 106+	.265	449	119	15	5	17	62	45	78	.337	.434
4 Days Rest	4.06	51	33	0	102	102	716.1	726	80	256	474	First Pitch	.305	643	196	32	10	31	97	8	0	.321	.530
5+ Days Rest	3.53	23	17	0	51	51	377.0	352	42	121	245	Ahead in Count	.212	1891	400	64	5	30	156	0	608	.216	.298
vs. AL	3.86	76	49	0	155	153	1097.1	1083	120	384	727	Behind in Count	.323	968	313	58	4	44	150	204	0	.440	.528
vs. NL	1.88	1	2	0	3	3	24.0	17	3	4	14	Two Strikes	.193	1931	372	62	7	28	143	176	741	.263	.276
Pre-All Star	3.80	44	27	0	89	87	618.0	596	64	221	406	Pre-All Star	.252	2362	596	104	13	64	256	221	406	.319	.389
Post-All Star	3.84	33	24	0	69	69	503.1	504	59	167	335	Post-All Star	.262	1927	504	92	9	59	224	167	335	.323	.410

Pitcher vs. Batter (career)

Pitches Best Vs.	Avg	AB	H	2B	3B	HR	RBI	BB	SO	OBP	SLG	Pitches Worst Vs.	Avg	AB	H	2B	3B	HR	RBI	BB	SO	OBP	SLG
Tony Pena	.000	12	0	0	0	0	0	1	4	.077	.000	Nomar Garciaparra	.467	15	7	2	0	2	2	0	0	.500	1.000
Pat Meares	.059	17	1	0	0	0	0	0	6	.059	.059	Omar Vizquel	.400	25	10	2	1	2	3	2	2	.444	.800
Mike Gallego	.067	15	1	0	0	0	0	1	2	.125	.067	Michael Tucker	.400	10	4	1	0	1	4	4	3	.571	.800
Jeffrey Hammonds	.077	13	1	0	0	0	1	0	3	.077	.077	Cecil Fielder	.375	48	18	2	0	8	16	5	8	.434	.917
Brian L. Hunter	.091	11	1	0	0	0	0	0	0	.091	.091	Tony Phillips	.367	30	11	2	0	4	11	6	3	.472	.833

Felix Heredia — Marlins
Age 22 – Pitches Left (flyball pitcher)

	ERA	W	L	Sv	G	GS	IP	BB	SO	Avg	H	2B	3B	HR	RBI	OBP	SLG	GF	IR	IRS	Hld	SvOp	SB	CS	GB	FB	G/F
1997 Season	4.29	5	3	0	56	0	56.2	30	54	.243	53	14	1	3	30	.345	.358	10	37	13	7	1	3	1	64	70	0.91
Career (1996-1997)	4.30	6	4	0	77	0	73.1	40	64	.260	74	18	2	4	41	.357	.379	15	51	19	9	1	5	2	83	90	0.92

1997 Season

	ERA	W	L	Sv	G	GS	IP	H	HR	BB	SO		Avg	AB	H	2B	3B	HR	RBI	BB	SO	OBP	SLG
Home	3.06	2	0	0	31	0	32.1	24	0	17	29	vs. Left	.188	69	13	2	1	0	6	11	24	.325	.246
Away	5.92	3	3	0	25	0	24.1	29	3	13	25	vs. Right	.268	149	40	12	0	3	24	19	30	.355	.409
Day	1.37	3	1	0	17	0	19.2	12	1	6	13	Inning 1-6	.167	54	9	3	0	0	9	12	22	.292	.222
Night	5.84	2	2	0	39	0	37.0	41	2	24	41	Inning 7+	.268	164	44	11	1	3	21	21	42	.363	.402
Grass	3.38	3	1	0	47	0	48.0	34	0	24	42	None on	.220	109	24	6	1	2	2	14	25	.325	.349
Turf	9.35	2	2	0	9	0	8.2	19	3	6	12	Runners on	.266	109	29	8	0	1	28	16	29	.364	.367
March/April	4.91	1	0	0	6	0	7.1	6	0	3	2	Scoring Posn	.250	68	17	3	0	0	24	12	19	.361	.294
May	2.25	1	0	0	9	0	8.0	11	0	3	10	Close & Late	.225	80	18	5	0	3	10	8	20	.311	.400
June	0.54	2	0	0	11	0	16.2	7	0	5	8	None on/out	.200	50	10	1	1	2	2	9	9	.333	.420
July	12.38	0	1	0	9	0	8.0	15	2	1	10	vs. 1st Batr (relief)	.208	48	10	2	0	2	2	5	4	.304	.375
August	4.50	0	1	0	10	0	8.0	7	0	10	12	1st Inning Pitched	.265	170	45	11	1	3	29	22	42	.359	.394

1997 Season

	ERA	W	L	Sv	G	GS	IP	H	HR	BB	SO		Avg	AB	H	2B	3B	HR	RBI	BB	SO	OBP	SLG
Sept/Oct	5.19	1	1	0	11	0	8.2	7	1	8	12	First 15 Pitches	.285	144	41	11	1	3	23	17	30	.370	.438
Starter	0.00	0	0	0	0	0	0.0	0	0	0	0	Pitch 16-30	.169	65	11	3	0	0	7	9	21	.286	.215
Reliever	4.29	5	3	0	56	0	56.2	53	3	30	54	Pitch 31-45	.000	7	0	0	0	0	0	4	2	.364	.000
0 Days rest (Relief)	3.52	0	0	0	7	0	7.2	5	0	3	5	Pitch 46+	.500	2	1	0	0	0	0	0	1	.500	.500
1 or 2 Days rest	3.86	3	2	0	28	0	28.0	24	2	16	27	First Pitch	.333	21	7	2	0	1	3	1	0	.423	.571
3+ Days rest	5.14	2	1	0	21	0	21.0	24	1	11	22	Ahead in Count	.164	116	19	6	0	0	8	0	48	.169	.216
vs. AL	0.93	1	0	0	9	0	9.2	2	0	7	9	Behind in Count	.385	39	15	3	0	0	10	16	0	.571	.462
vs. NL	4.98	4	3	0	47	0	47.0	51	3	23	45	Two Strikes	.122	115	14	5	0	0	12	13	54	.215	.165
Pre-All Star	1.85	4	0	0	28	0	34.0	24	0	11	23	Pre-All Star	.195	123	24	7	1	0	7	11	23	.275	.268
Post-All Star	7.94	1	3	0	28	0	22.2	29	3	19	31	Post-All Star	.305	95	29	7	0	3	23	19	31	.427	.474

Wilson Heredia — Rangers
Age 26 – Pitches Right (flyball pitcher)

	ERA	W	L	Sv	G	GS	IP	BB	SO	Avg	H	2B	3B	HR	RBI	OBP	SLG	GF	IR	IRS	Hld	SvOp	SB	CS	GB	FB	G/F
1997 Season	3.20	1	0	0	10	0	19.2	16	8	.197	14	3	0	2	10	.337	.324	3	9	2	0	0	1	1	30	26	1.15
Career (1995-1997)	3.41	1	1	0	16	0	31.2	31	14	.207	23	5	0	4	16	.372	.360	3	17	6	0	0	2	1	36	46	0.78

1997 Season

	ERA	W	L	Sv	G	GS	IP	H	HR	BB	SO		Avg	AB	H	2B	3B	HR	RBI	BB	SO	OBP	SLG
Home	2.61	1	0	0	5	0	10.1	7	1	12	3	vs. Left	.235	34	8	2	0	1	4	9	4	.395	.382
Away	3.86	0	0	0	5	0	9.1	7	1	4	5	vs. Right	.162	37	6	1	0	1	6	7	4	.283	.270

Dustin Hermanson — Expos
Age 25 – Pitches Right (flyball pitcher)

	ERA	W	L	Sv	G	GS	IP	BB	SO	Avg	H	2B	3B	HR	RBI	OBP	SLG	CG	ShO	Sup	QS	#P/S	SB	CS	GB	FB	G/F
1997 Season	3.69	8	8	0	32	28	158.1	66	136	.234	134	26	4	15	63	.312	.372	1	1	5.06	13	83	11	7	162	175	0.93
Career (1995-1997)	4.51	12	9	0	66	28	203.2	92	166	.249	187	36	4	26	106	.329	.412	1	1	5.52	13	83	14	7	222	230	0.97

1997 Season

	ERA	W	L	Sv	G	GS	IP	H	HR	BB	SO		Avg	AB	H	2B	3B	HR	RBI	BB	SO	OBP	SLG
Home	4.12	3	4	0	14	12	67.2	61	7	30	61	vs. Left	.232	276	64	12	1	8	33	36	56	.323	.370
Away	3.38	5	4	0	18	16	90.2	73	8	36	75	vs. Right	.236	296	70	14	3	7	30	30	80	.301	.375
Day	3.49	1	3	0	11	9	56.2	38	4	25	46	Inning 1-6	.232	518	120	25	3	13	58	64	120	.314	.367
Night	3.81	7	5	0	21	19	101.2	96	11	41	90	Inning 7+	.259	54	14	1	1	2	5	2	16	.286	.426
Grass	2.35	4	3	0	13	12	69.0	44	5	28	62	None on	.235	353	83	18	3	9	9	36	89	.306	.380
Turf	4.74	4	5	0	19	16	89.1	90	10	38	74	Runners on	.233	219	51	8	1	6	54	30	47	.320	.361
March/April	4.40	1	1	0	6	2	14.1	14	1	10	19	Scoring Posn	.236	123	29	3	0	3	44	19	23	.324	.333
May	2.94	1	2	0	6	5	33.2	28	3	13	26	Close & Late	.154	13	2	1	0	0	0	2	15	.214	.231
June	3.38	1	1	0	5	5	24.0	19	4	12	20	None on/out	.223	157	35	10	0	5	5	13	35	.282	.382
July	5.74	2	1	0	5	5	26.2	29	3	2	24	vs. 1st Batr (relief)	.333	3	1	0	0	0	0	1	1	.500	.333
August	2.08	3	0	0	5	5	30.1	16	3	14	29	1st Inning Pitched	.172	99	17	2	1	2	9	24	25	.331	.273
Sept/Oct	4.30	0	3	0	5	5	29.1	28	1	15	18	First 75 Pitches	.226	461	104	22	4	8	45	57	116	.309	.343
Starter	3.73	8	8	0	28	28	149.2	126	15	61	121	Pitch 76-90	.271	70	19	3	0	6	11	5	10	.320	.571
Reliever	3.12	0	0	0	4	0	8.2	8	0	5	15	Pitch 91-105	.172	29	5	0	0	1	5	3	9	.250	.276
0-3 Days Rest (Start)	0.00	0	0	0	0	0	0.0	0	0	0	0	Pitch 106+	.500	12	6	1	0	0	2	1	1	.538	.583
4 Days Rest	4.86	3	7	0	15	15	74.0	71	10	32	54	First Pitch	.288	73	21	3	0	4	7	2	0	.316	.493
5+ Days Rest	2.62	5	1	0	13	13	75.2	55	5	29	67	Ahead in Count	.174	288	50	13	3	3	20	0	116	.172	.271
vs. AL	6.97	1	0	0	2	2	10.1	12	4	4	10	Behind in Count	.354	96	34	7	0	5	22	30	0	.500	.583
vs. NL	3.47	7	8	0	30	26	148.0	122	11	62	126	Two Strikes	.150	287	43	12	2	2	21	34	136	.239	.226
Pre-All Star	3.77	3	4	0	18	14	76.1	67	10	37	68	Pre-All Star	.239	280	67	10	4	10	31	37	68	.327	.411
Post-All Star	3.62	5	4	0	14	14	82.0	67	5	29	68	Post-All Star	.229	292	67	16	0	5	32	29	68	.296	.336

Carlos Hernandez — Padres
Age 31 – Bats Right (groundball hitter)

	Avg	G	AB	R	H	2B	3B	HR	RBI	BB	SO	HBP	GDP	SB	CS	OBP	SLG	IBB	SH	SF	#Pit	#P/PA	GB	FB	G/F
1997 Season	.313	50	134	15	42	7	1	3	14	3	27	0	5	0	2	.328	.448	0	1	0	453	3.28	53	25	2.12
Last Five Years	.244	190	405	31	99	15	1	9	35	15	79	1	10	0	2	.273	.353	0	3	0	1401	3.30	165	86	1.92

1997 Season

	Avg	AB	H	2B	3B	HR	RBI	BB	SO	OBP	SLG		Avg	AB	H	2B	3B	HR	RBI	BB	SO	OBP	SLG
vs. Left	.324	37	12	2	0	1	1	2	6	.359	.459	Scoring Posn	.300	30	9	2	1	0	9	0	10	.300	.433
vs. Right	.309	97	30	5	1	2	13	1	21	.316	.443	Close & Late	.273	22	6	1	0	0	0	0	3	.273	.318
Home	.277	65	18	2	1	2	7	2	15	.299	.431	None on/out	.308	39	12	1	0	0	0	0	6	.308	.333
Away	.348	69	24	5	0	1	7	1	12	.357	.464	Batting #7	.280	25	7	0	0	0	2	0	7	.280	.280
First Pitch	.333	21	7	2	0	2	0	0	0	.333	.429	Batting #8	.337	83	28	6	1	2	10	3	13	.360	.506
Ahead in Count	.346	26	9	1	0	3	1	0	0	.370	.385	Other	.269	26	7	1	0	1	2	0	7	.269	.423
Behind in Count	.254	71	18	1	0	2	6	0	25	.254	.352	Pre-All Star	.292	72	21	4	0	1	5	2	15	.311	.389
Two Strikes	.224	58	13	1	0	2	6	2	27	.250	.397	Post-All Star	.339	62	21	3	1	2	9	1	12	.349	.516

Fernando Hernandez — Tigers
Age 27 – Pitches Right

	ERA	W	L	Sv	G	GS	IP	BB	SO	Avg	H	2B	3B	HR	RBI	OBP	SLG	GF	IR	IRS	Hld	SvOp	SB	CS	GB	FB	G/F
1997 Season	40.50	0	0	0	2	0	1.1	3	2	.556	5	2	1	0	7	.692	1.000	0	1	1	0	0	0	0	1	2	0.50

1997 Season

	ERA	W	L	Sv	G	GS	IP	H	HR	BB	SO		Avg	AB	H	2B	3B	HR	RBI	BB	SO	OBP	SLG
Home	0.00	0	0	0	0	0	0.0	0	0	0	0	vs. Left	.500	4	2	0	1	0	2	2	2	.667	1.000
Away	40.50	0	0	0	2	0	1.1	5	0	3	2	vs. Right	.600	5	3	2	0	0	5	1	0	.714	1.000

Jose Hernandez — Cubs
Age 28 – Bats Right (groundball hitter)

	Avg	G	AB	R	H	2B	3B	HR	RBI	BB	SO	HBP	GDP	SB	CS	OBP	SLG	IBB	SH	SF	#Pit	#P/PA	GB	FB	G/F
1997 Season	.273	121	183	33	50	8	5	7	26	14	42	0	5	2	5	.323	.486	2	1	1	725	3.64	69	44	1.57
Last Five Years	.249	401	891	140	222	35	13	31	116	59	237	2	27	9	7	.296	.422	9	19	5	3573	3.66	336	191	1.76

1997 Season

	Avg	AB	H	2B	3B	HR	RBI	BB	SO	OBP	SLG		Avg	AB	H	2B	3B	HR	RBI	BB	SO	OBP	SLG
vs. Left	.250	84	21	2	3	3	11	9	19	.319	.452	Scoring Posn	.217	46	10	0	1	2	15	7	15	.315	.391
vs. Right	.293	99	29	6	2	4	15	5	23	.327	.515	Close & Late	.283	46	13	1	2	1	4	3	15	.327	.457
Home	.274	84	23	4	3	4	14	8	18	.337	.536	None on/out	.289	38	11	1	1	2	2	3	5	.341	.526
Away	.273	99	27	4	2	3	12	6	24	.311	.444	Batting #7	.250	64	16	3	3	2	8	4	14	.294	.484
First Pitch	.200	15	3	0	0	0	1	0		.250	.200	Batting #9	.216	37	8	1	0	1	3	4	8	.286	.324
Ahead in Count	.429	49	21	2	3	4	11	8	0	.509	.837	Other	.317	82	26	4	2	4	15	6	20	.364	.561
Behind in Count	.216	88	19	4	1	2	10	0	35	.213	.352	Pre-All Star	.281	96	27	3	2	3	10	7	20	.327	.448
Two Strikes	.205	83	17	3	1	1	8	5	42	.247	.301	Post-All Star	.264	87	23	5	3	4	16	7	22	.319	.529

Last Five Years

	Avg	AB	H	2B	3B	HR	RBI	BB	SO	OBP	SLG		Avg	AB	H	2B	3B	HR	RBI	BB	SO	OBP	SLG
vs. Left	.235	268	63	9	5	9	31	17	65	.279	.407	First Pitch	.333	102	34	5	2	4	20	7	0	.376	.539
vs. Right	.255	623	159	26	8	22	85	42	172	.303	.429	Ahead in Count	.346	182	63	9	5	14	33	27	0	.425	.681
Groundball	.251	231	58	6	2	11	28	9	60	.278	.437	Behind in Count	.181	448	81	12	4	10	38	0	206	.182	.292
Flyball	.182	132	24	2	1	4	8	11	41	.245	.303	Two Strikes	.167	456	76	11	4	7	38	25	237	.211	.254
Home	.238	433	103	13	6	14	56	35	122	.293	.393	Batting #7	.252	226	57	10	4	9	36	19	63	.309	.451
Away	.260	458	119	22	7	17	60	24	115	.298	.450	Batting #8	.237	354	84	14	3	13	44	23	86	.286	.404
Day	.224	518	116	15	7	17	67	39	142	.277	.378	Other	.260	311	81	11	6	9	36	17	77	.297	.421
Night	.284	373	106	20	6	14	49	20	95	.322	.483	March/April	.243	74	18	1	1	0	9	10	23	.333	.284
Grass	.251	686	172	22	11	27	95	44	178	.295	.433	May	.295	112	33	5	1	5	12	5	24	.325	.491
Turf	.244	205	50	13	2	4	21	15	59	.299	.385	June	.224	183	41	6	2	5	19	8	52	.255	.361
Pre-All Star	.252	449	113	14	6	11	49	29	117	.298	.383	July	.249	209	52	10	3	7	23	12	47	.291	.426
Post-All Star	.247	442	109	21	7	20	67	30	120	.294	.462	August	.253	170	43	6	0	10	31	13	44	.308	.465
Scoring Posn	.237	219	52	3	4	3	72	22	70	.301	.329	Sept/Oct	.245	143	35	7	6	4	22	11	47	.295	.462
Close & Late	.238	185	44	8	4	5	17	14	57	.299	.405	vs. AL	.176	17	3	1	0	0	1	2	6	.263	.235
None on/out	.264	208	55	12	3	11	11	13	47	.311	.510	vs. NL	.251	874	219	34	13	31	115	57	231	.296	.426

Batter vs. Pitcher (career)

Hits Best Against	Avg	AB	H	2B	3B	HR	RBI	BB	SO	OBP	SLG	Hits Worst Against	Avg	AB	H	2B	3B	HR	RBI	BB	SO	OBP	SLG
Andy Ashby	.600	10	6	0	0	0	1	1	2	.636	.600	Mark Gardner	.000	9	0	0	0	0	0	2	4	.182	.000
Willie Blair	.417	12	5	2	0	0	1	1	4	.462	.583	Bobby Jones	.063	16	1	0	0	0	0	0	5	.063	.063
Mike Hampton	.385	13	5	1	2	0	1	0	2	.385	.769	Denny Neagle	.150	20	3	0	0	0	0	0	6	.150	.150
Kevin Ritz	.333	15	5	1	0	1	0	0	4	.333	.467	Ismael Valdes	.182	11	2	0	0	0	0	1	4	.250	.182
Tom Glavine	.333	12	4	2	0	0	3	1	2	.385	.500	Darryl Kile	.231	13	3	0	0	0	3	3	5	.412	.231

Livan Hernandez — Marlins
Age 23 – Pitches Right (flyball pitcher)

	ERA	W	L	Sv	G	GS	IP	BB	SO	Avg	H	2B	3B	HR	RBI	OBP	SLG	CG	ShO	Sup	QS	#P/S	SB	CS	GB	FB	G/F
1997 Season	3.18	9	3	0	17	17	96.1	38	72	.229	81	17	4	5	32	.304	.343	0	0	6.35	8	96	4	3	111	112	0.99
Career (1996-1997)	3.08	9	3	0	18	17	99.1	40	74	.231	84	17	4	5	32	.307	.341	0	0	6.25	8	96	4	3	114	116	0.98

1997 Season

	ERA	W	L	Sv	G	GS	IP	H	HR	BB	SO		Avg	AB	H	2B	3B	HR	RBI	BB	SO	OBP	SLG
Home	3.45	5	3	0	10	10	57.1	47	3	24	41	vs. Left	.248	157	39	8	3	3	11	23	22	.344	.395
Away	2.77	4	0	0	7	7	39.0	34	2	14	31	vs. Right	.214	196	42	9	1	2	21	15	50	.271	.301
Starter	3.18	9	3	0	17	17	96.1	81	5	38	72	Scoring Posn	.152	79	12	3	1	1	26	8	18	.229	.253
Reliever	0.00	0	0	0	0	0	0.0	0	0	0	0	Close & Late	.200	10	2	0	0	0	0	1	2	.273	.200
0-3 Days Rest (Start)	0.00	0	0	0	0	0	0.0	0	0	0	0	None on/out	.237	93	22	6	1	2	10	19	.311	.387
4 Days Rest	3.31	5	2	0	9	9	51.2	48	3	17	36	First Pitch	.195	41	8	2	0	1	7	0	0	.178	.317
5+ Days Rest	3.02	4	1	0	8	8	44.2	33	2	21	36	Ahead in Count	.193	150	29	6	2	0	11	0	51	.197	.260
Pre-All Star	4.11	2	0	0	3	3	15.1	15	0	7	15	Behind in Count	.325	80	26	8	1	1	6	24	0	.481	.488
Post-All Star	3.00	7	3	0	14	14	81.0	66	5	31	57	Two Strikes	.182	181	33	5	2	2	14	14	72	.240	.265

Roberto Hernandez — Giants
Age 33 – Pitches Right

	ERA	W	L	Sv	G	GS	IP	BB	SO	Avg	H	2B	3B	HR	RBI	OBP	SLG	GF	IR	IRS	Hld	SvOp	SB	CS	GB	FB	G/F
1997 Season	2.45	10	3	31	74	0	80.2	38	82	.225	67	4	1	7	33	.314	.315	50	46	14	9	39	10	3	119	66	1.80
Last Five Years	2.87	26	23	153	321	0	351.1	143	372	.231	305	31	9	29	171	.307	.330	278	165	60	9	191	26	11	408	320	1.28

1997 Season

	ERA	W	L	Sv	G	GS	IP	H	HR	BB	SO		Avg	AB	H	2B	3B	HR	RBI	BB	SO	OBP	SLG
Home	2.06	4	0	17	35	0	39.1	28	2	15	44	vs. Left	.194	160	31	1	0	2	13	21	50	.287	.238
Away	2.83	6	3	14	39	0	41.1	39	5	23	38	vs. Right	.261	138	36	3	1	5	20	17	32	.344	.406
Day	2.34	4	1	13	31	0	34.2	28	2	13	39	Inning 1-6	.000	1	0	0	0	0	0	0	1	.000	.000
Night	2.54	6	2	18	43	0	46.0	39	5	25	43	Inning 7+	.226	297	67	4	1	7	33	38	81	.315	.316
Grass	2.39	8	2	27	62	0	67.2	56	6	34	72	None on	.279	140	39	4	0	4	4	18	35	.365	.393
Turf	2.77	2	1	4	12	0	13.0	11	1	4	10	Runners on	.177	158	28	0	1	3	29	20	47	.268	.247
March/April	5.19	1	1	3	8	0	8.2	11	2	2	9	Scoring Posn	.180	100	18	0	2	26	15	35	.284	.240
May	2.08	2	0	7	11	0	13.0	7	2	7	14	Close & Late	.220	218	48	1	1	5	28	26	61	.302	.303
June	0.66	1	0	9	15	0	13.2	9	0	10	11	None on/out	.277	65	18	2	0	2	7	12	.347	.400
July	2.84	1	0	8	12	0	12.2	11	1	5	13	vs. 1st Batr (relief)	.217	69	15	2	0	2	5	18	.270	.333
August	2.12	1	1	1	14	0	17.0	15	1	6	18	1st Inning Pitched	.237	253	60	4	1	7	32	35	68	.331	.344
Sept/Oct	2.87	4	1	3	14	0	15.2	14	1	8	17	First 15 Pitches	.261	188	49	4	1	7	25	23	46	.344	.404
Starter	0.00	0	0	0	0	0	0.0	0	0	0	0	Pitch 16-30	.167	102	17	0	0	7	14	32	.265	.167

1997 Season

	ERA	W	L	Sv	G	GS	IP	H	HR	BB	SO		Avg	AB	H	2B	3B	HR	RBI	BB	SO	OBP	SLG
Reliever	2.45	10	3	31	74	0	80.2	67	7	38	82	Pitch 31-45	.125	8	1	0	0	0	1	1	4	.222	.125
0 Days rest (Relief)	1.82	2	1	13	26	0	24.2	22	1	15	25	Pitch 46+	.000	0	0	0	0	0	0	0	0	.000	.000
1 or 2 Days rest	2.16	3	2	11	28	0	33.1	23	2	11	32	First Pitch	.235	34	8	1	0	0	3	4	0	.316	.265
3+ Days rest	3.57	5	0	7	20	0	22.2	22	4	12	25	Ahead in Count	.170	159	27	1	1	0	12	0	69	.175	.189
vs. AL	2.17	5	1	25	47	0	49.2	41	5	25	51	Behind in Count	.318	44	14	1	0	3	7	20	0	.531	.545
vs. NL	2.90	5	2	6	27	0	31.0	26	2	13	31	Two Strikes	.150	173	26	1	1	2	13	14	82	.217	.202
Pre-All Star	3.05	5	1	20	37	0	38.1	34	5	20	38	Pre-All Star	.239	142	34	2	1	5	19	20	38	.331	.373
Post-All Star	1.91	5	2	11	37	0	42.1	33	2	18	44	Post-All Star	.212	156	33	2	0	2	14	18	44	.297	.263

Last Five Years

	ERA	W	L	Sv	G	GS	IP	H	HR	BB	SO		Avg	AB	H	2B	3B	HR	RBI	BB	SO	OBP	SLG
Home	2.60	12	8	83	161	0	173.1	152	12	56	179	vs. Left	.217	658	143	10	2	12	76	84	217	.306	.293
Away	3.13	14	15	70	160	0	178.0	153	17	87	193	vs. Right	.244	665	162	21	5	17	95	59	155	.308	.367
Day	2.65	9	6	50	111	0	122.1	107	6	46	132	Inning 1-6	.000	1	0	0	0	0	0	1	0	.000	.000
Night	2.99	17	17	103	210	0	229.0	198	23	97	240	Inning 7+	.231	1322	305	31	7	29	171	143	371	.307	.331
Grass	2.67	22	17	134	275	0	300.1	259	24	122	326	None on	.228	637	145	17	3	12	12	72	180	.309	.320
Turf	4.06	4	6	19	46	0	51.0	46	5	21	46	Runners on	.233	686	160	14	4	17	159	71	192	.305	.340
March/April	2.01	2	2	17	38	0	44.2	33	3	23	57	Scoring Posn	.227	401	91	7	2	12	141	58	118	.323	.344
May	3.20	4	3	28	52	0	56.1	49	6	22	58	Close & Late	.233	922	215	17	6	23	134	102	257	.310	.339
June	4.25	4	5	31	64	0	65.2	61	7	35	53	None on/out	.216	282	61	8	0	6	25	81	280	.309
July	2.11	2	4	33	61	0	64.0	49	6	22	67	vs. 1st Batr (relief)	.224	294	66	11	1	6	34	25	79	.288	.330
August	1.81	6	4	21	57	0	64.2	49	4	18	70	1st Inning Pitched	.228	1111	253	26	7	28	156	121	308	.305	.339
Sept/Oct	3.70	8	5	23	49	0	56.0	64	3	23	67	First 15 Pitches	.225	861	194	25	6	21	100	87	229	.298	.341
Starter	0.00	0	0	0	0	0	0.0	0	0	0	0	Pitch 16-30	.248	391	97	5	0	8	61	49	116	.331	.322
Reliever	2.87	26	23	153	321	0	351.1	305	29	143	372	Pitch 31-45	.203	64	13	1	1	0	10	7	25	.284	.250
0 Days rest (Relief)	3.07	6	6	45	88	0	88.0	81	10	40	91	Pitch 46+	.143	7	1	0	0	0	0	0	2	.143	.143
1 or 2 Days rest	2.77	7	13	84	148	0	162.2	138	11	60	171	First Pitch	.273	154	42	5	1	3	18	12	0	.325	.377
3+ Days rest	2.86	13	4	24	85	0	100.2	86	8	43	110	Ahead in Count	.172	723	124	10	4	7	69	0	324	.174	.225
vs. AL	2.87	21	21	147	294	0	320.1	279	27	130	341	Behind in Count	.323	201	65	8	0	9	33	61	0	.479	.498
vs. NL	2.90	5	2	6	27	0	31.0	26	2	13	31	Two Strikes	.161	752	121	8	3	12	74	70	372	.235	.227
Pre-All Star	3.16	12	10	84	175	0	188.0	162	17	86	192	Pre-All Star	.231	701	162	17	4	17	99	86	192	.317	.340
Post-All Star	2.53	14	13	69	146	0	163.1	143	12	57	180	Post-All Star	.230	622	143	14	3	12	72	57	180	.295	.320

Pitcher vs. Batter (career)

Pitches Best Vs.	Avg	AB	H	2B	3B	HR	RBI	BB	SO	OBP	SLG	Pitches Worst Vs.	Avg	AB	H	2B	3B	HR	RBI	BB	SO	OBP	SLG
Joe Carter	.000	11	0	0	0	0	0	0	1	.000	.000	Ruben Sierra	.417	12	5	1	0	2	7	2	1	.500	1.000
Cal Ripken	.000	10	0	0	0	0	0	1	1	.091	.000	Travis Fryman	.375	16	6	0	0	3	7	1	6	.412	.938
Mo Vaughn	.071	14	1	0	0	1	1	0	8	.071	.286	Ivan Rodriguez	.375	8	3	0	0	0	1	3	3	.545	.375
John Jaha	.100	10	1	0	0	0	0	2	3	.250	.100	Roberto Alomar	.364	11	4	1	0	1	2	2	3	.462	.727
Paul Sorrento	.125	16	2	0	0	2	0	5	.125	.125	Jay Buhner	.364	11	4	1	1	0	1	1	3	.417	.636

Xavier Hernandez — Rangers
Age 32 – Pitches Right

	ERA	W	L	Sv	G	GS	IP	BB	SO	Avg	H	2B	3B	HR	RBI	OBP	SLG	GF	IR	IRS	Hld	SvOp	SB	CS	GB	FB	G/F
1997 Season	4.56	0	4	0	44	0	49.1	22	36	.262	51	12	0	7	31	.341	.431	20	37	13	13	1	3	0	72	54	1.33
Last Five Years	4.19	20	20	24	267	0	354.0	130	339	.255	346	80	7	41	190	.323	.415	109	151	56	49	40	27	3	436	365	1.19

1997 Season

	ERA	W	L	Sv	G	GS	IP	H	HR	BB	SO		Avg	AB	H	2B	3B	HR	RBI	BB	SO	OBP	SLG
Home	4.26	0	2	0	20	0	25.1	28	3	12	15	vs. Left	.250	72	18	2	0	3	11	11	14	.349	.403
Away	4.88	0	2	0	24	0	24.0	23	4	10	21	vs. Right	.268	123	33	10	0	4	20	11	22	.336	.447
Starter	0.00	0	0	0	0	0	0.0	0	0	0	0	Scoring Posn	.286	63	18	2	0	2	24	9	12	.370	.413
Reliever	4.56	0	4	0	44	0	49.1	51	7	22	36	Close & Late	.298	94	28	7	0	2	16	12	18	.383	.436
0 Days rest (Relief)	6.75	0	0	0	5	0	8.0	11	3	3	7	None on/out	.154	39	6	2	0	1	1	4	8	.233	.282
1 or 2 Days rest	3.68	0	2	0	29	0	29.1	28	2	13	21	First Pitch	.321	28	9	1	0	2	9	3	0	.387	.571
3+ Days rest	5.25	0	2	0	10	0	12.0	12	2	6	8	Ahead in Count	.215	65	14	1	0	3	13	0	31	.227	.369
Pre-All Star	3.77	0	2	0	35	0	43.0	36	5	19	33	Behind in Count	.339	56	19	4	0	2	8	8	0	.424	.518
Post-All Star	9.95	0	2	0	9	0	6.1	15	2	3	3	Two Strikes	.179	78	14	3	0	2	11	11	36	.281	.295

Last Five Years

	ERA	W	L	Sv	G	GS	IP	H	HR	BB	SO		Avg	AB	H	2B	3B	HR	RBI	BB	SO	OBP	SLG
Home	4.48	10	10	15	133	0	170.2	168	15	63	165	vs. Left	.268	529	142	32	4	21	86	69	134	.352	.463
Away	3.93	10	10	9	134	0	183.1	178	26	67	174	vs. Right	.247	827	204	48	3	20	104	61	205	.303	.385
Day	3.73	8	4	5	81	0	113.1	106	14	44	101	Inning 1-6	.293	229	67	14	1	6	35	15	49	.336	.441
Night	4.41	12	16	19	186	0	240.2	240	27	86	238	Inning 7+	.248	1127	279	66	6	35	155	115	290	.320	.410
Grass	4.65	6	12	12	126	0	164.2	172	26	63	143	None on	.256	719	184	40	4	24	24	62	184	.319	.423
Turf	3.80	14	8	12	141	0	189.1	174	15	67	196	Runners on	.254	637	162	40	3	17	166	68	155	.327	.407
March/April	4.72	2	0	5	37	0	47.2	45	6	25	45	Scoring Posn	.267	393	105	26	3	6	138	51	99	.347	.394
May	3.88	6	4	4	55	0	69.2	64	8	25	62	Close & Late	.247	603	149	34	1	17	86	58	167	.317	.391
June	5.27	2	7	3	57	0	70.0	74	8	29	65	None on/out	.234	316	74	16	2	9	9	23	75	.288	.383
July	3.45	5	4	3	51	0	73.0	76	9	22	70	vs. 1st Batr (relief)	.266	246	63	16	2	4	29	18	60	.303	.386
August	3.00	2	6	3	36	0	54.0	49	8	8	55	1st Inning Pitched	.262	897	235	56	6	29	143	83	204	.325	.435
Sept/Oct	5.22	2	3	3	31	0	39.2	38	2	21	42	First 15 Pitches	.266	807	215	49	4	27	111	66	179	.323	.437
Starter	0.00	0	0	0	0	0	0.0	0	0	0	0	Pitch 16-30	.239	426	102	27	3	10	62	53	127	.328	.387
Reliever	4.19	20	20	24	267	0	354.0	346	41	130	339	Pitch 31-45	.243	111	27	4	0	4	16	10	31	.315	.387
0 Days rest (Relief)	3.99	3	3	5	46	0	58.2	58	9	16	59	Pitch 46+	.167	12	2	0	0	0	1	1	2	.214	.167
1 or 2 Days rest	3.82	9	9	16	148	0	197.2	185	18	72	183	First Pitch	.358	218	78	10	3	9	55	12	0	.399	.555
3+ Days rest	5.07	8	8	3	73	0	97.2	103	14	42	97	Ahead in Count	.149	571	85	19	0	8	42	0	301	.153	.224
vs. AL	5.31	4	8	6	71	0	84.2	95	14	42	68	Behind in Count	.358	330	118	28	1	17	61	57	0	.449	.603

207

Last Five Years

	ERA	W	L	Sv	G	GS	IP	H	HR	BB	SO		Avg	AB	H	2B	3B	HR	RBI	BB	SO	OBP	SLG
vs. NL	3.84	16	12	18	196	0	269.1	251	27	88	271	Two Strikes	.141	597	84	19	1	9	45	61	339	.221	.221
Pre-All Star	4.41	10	13	14	165	0	208.0	203	23	85	201	Pre-All Star	.255	795	203	51	4	23	115	85	201	.331	.416
Post-All Star	3.88	10	7	10	102	0	146.0	143	18	45	138	Post-All Star	.255	561	143	29	3	18	75	45	138	.312	.414

Pitcher vs. Batter (career)

Pitches Best Vs.	Avg	AB	H	2B	3B	HR	RBI	BB	SO	OBP	SLG	Pitches Worst Vs.	Avg	AB	H	2B	3B	HR	RBI	BB	SO	OBP	SLG
Tony Fernandez	.000	9	0	0	0	0	0	3	1	.250	.000	Dante Bichette	.636	11	7	1	1	0	7	0	3	.636	.909
Eric Karros	.067	15	1	0	0	0	1	1	8	.125	.067	Orlando Merced	.600	10	6	1	0	1	2	2	2	.667	1.000
Otis Nixon	.091	11	1	0	0	0	1	0	1	.083	.091	Shawon Dunston	.545	11	6	1	0	0	1	1	0	.583	.636
Brian Jordan	.091	11	1	0	0	0	1	0	3	.091	.091	Matt Williams	.438	16	7	3	0	2	9	0	2	.438	1.000
Jay Bell	.125	24	3	0	0	0	1	0	9	.125	.125	Eric Davis	.308	13	4	0	0	3	6	2	3	.400	1.000

Orel Hershiser — Indians   Age 39 – Pitches Right (groundball pitcher)

	ERA	W	L	Sv	G	GS	IP	BB	SO	Avg	H	2B	3B	HR	RBI	OBP	SLG	CG	ShO	Sup	QS	#P/S	SB	CS	GB	FB	G/F
1997 Season	4.47	14	6	0	32	32	195.1	69	107	.272	199	33	7	26	97	.340	.443	1	0	6.04	16	91	4	8	343	154	2.23
Last Five Years	4.00	63	41	0	145	145	919.2	292	556	.266	935	191	21	100	420	.326	.417	9	2	5.58	88	92	34	28	1629	732	2.23

1997 Season

	ERA	W	L	Sv	G	GS	IP	H	HR	BB	SO		Avg	AB	H	2B	3B	HR	RBI	BB	SO	OBP	SLG
Home	3.87	6	1	0	16	16	100.0	92	12	34	48	vs. Left	.282	340	96	21	3	12	49	44	41	.367	.468
Away	5.10	8	5	0	16	16	95.1	107	14	35	59	vs. Right	.263	392	103	12	4	14	48	25	66	.316	.421
Day	6.65	4	2	0	9	9	47.1	60	10	22	26	Inning 1-6	.271	663	180	30	6	24	91	63	97	.340	.443
Night	3.77	10	4	0	23	23	148.0	139	16	47	81	Inning 7+	.275	69	19	3	1	2	6	6	10	.342	.435
Grass	4.14	11	4	0	26	26	161.0	156	23	58	83	None on	.243	432	105	19	3	16	16	41	59	.322	.412
Turf	6.03	3	2	0	6	6	34.1	43	3	11	24	Runners on	.313	300	94	14	4	10	81	28	48	.367	.487
March/April	6.06	2	0	0	6	6	35.2	44	8	13	24	Scoring Posn	.293	164	48	8	2	7	69	17	32	.351	.494
May	4.12	3	2	0	6	6	39.1	43	8	11	14	Close & Late	.429	35	15	1	0	2	5	2	3	.459	.629
June	2.68	2	2	0	5	5	37.0	30	2	10	19	None on/out	.261	184	48	11	1	6	6	22	22	.349	.429
July	7.58	2	1	0	6	6	29.2	33	4	13	19	vs. 1st Batr (relief)	.000	0	0	0	0	0	0	0	0	.000	.000
August	2.55	3	0	0	4	4	24.2	21	2	9	13	1st Inning Pitched	.269	119	32	9	1	3	15	14	21	.341	.437
Sept/Oct	3.72	2	1	0	5	5	29.0	28	2	13	18	First 75 Pitches	.262	577	151	27	4	20	76	55	89	.330	.426
Starter	4.47	14	6	0	32	32	195.1	199	26	69	107	Pitch 76-90	.330	106	35	2	3	4	15	6	12	.379	.519
Reliever	0.00	0	0	0	0	0	0.0	0	0	0	0	Pitch 91-105	.295	44	13	4	0	2	6	7	6	.404	.523
0-3 Days Rest (Start)	17.18	0	0	0	1	1	3.2	8	0	1	2	Pitch 106+	.000	5	0	0	0	0	0	1	0	.167	.000
4 Days Rest	4.76	10	5	0	21	21	128.2	125	22	42	76	First Pitch	.359	103	37	5	0	3	13	0	0	.374	.495
5+ Days Rest	3.14	4	1	0	10	10	63.0	66	4	26	29	Ahead in Count	.189	318	60	7	2	4	23	0	97	.207	.277
vs. AL	4.50	13	4	0	28	28	170.0	171	26	62	89	Behind in Count	.359	181	65	11	4	11	34	43	0	.476	.646
vs. NL	4.26	1	2	0	4	4	25.1	28	0	7	18	Two Strikes	.171	293	50	9	2	4	20	26	107	.257	.256
Pre-All Star	4.95	7	5	0	19	19	120.0	132	18	37	64	Pre-All Star	.286	461	132	21	5	18	70	37	64	.344	.471
Post-All Star	3.70	7	1	0	13	13	75.1	67	8	32	43	Post-All Star	.247	271	67	12	2	8	27	32	43	.334	.395

Last Five Years

	ERA	W	L	Sv	G	GS	IP	H	HR	BB	SO		Avg	AB	H	2B	3B	HR	RBI	BB	SO	OBP	SLG
Home	3.48	28	17	0	69	69	445.1	423	40	139	269	vs. Left	.282	1855	524	116	15	45	215	191	233	.352	.434
Away	4.50	35	24	0	76	76	474.1	512	60	153	287	vs. Right	.247	1666	411	75	6	55	205	101	323	.297	.398
Day	4.98	20	15	0	46	46	274.2	304	34	112	162	Inning 1-6	.264	3068	809	165	19	84	375	246	488	.323	.412
Night	3.59	43	26	0	99	99	645.0	631	66	180	394	Inning 7+	.278	453	126	26	2	16	45	46	68	.348	.450
Grass	3.92	52	35	0	122	122	775.2	771	83	250	452	None on	.254	2081	529	117	7	65	65	144	326	.311	.411
Turf	4.44	11	6	0	23	23	144.0	164	17	42	104	Runners on	.282	1440	406	74	14	35	355	148	230	.348	.426
March/April	4.43	8	4	0	22	22	138.0	150	16	44	85	Scoring Posn	.276	842	232	48	10	22	312	106	157	.354	.435
May	4.20	13	9	0	29	29	178.0	189	24	45	110	Close & Late	.283	205	58	13	1	6	23	28	30	.372	.444
June	3.67	10	9	0	26	26	174.1	172	20	54	94	None on/out	.274	919	252	55	3	32	32	63	125	.327	.445
July	4.35	9	9	0	24	24	144.2	152	13	52	81	vs. 1st Batr (relief)	.000	0	0	0	0	0	0	0	0	.000	.000
August	3.71	14	4	0	23	23	150.1	145	14	50	94	1st Inning Pitched	.245	543	133	30	4	6	63	47	94	.311	.348
Sept/Oct	3.68	9	6	0	21	21	134.1	127	13	47	92	First 75 Pitches	.260	2739	713	139	17	74	310	208	440	.317	.405
Starter	4.00	63	41	0	145	145	919.2	935	100	292	556	Pitch 76-90	.286	454	130	32	4	13	59	38	62	.345	.460
Reliever	0.00	0	0	0	0	0	0.0	0	0	0	0	Pitch 91-105	.273	249	68	13	0	9	39	31	46	.361	.434
0-3 Days Rest (Start)	6.39	1	0	0	2	2	12.2	17	0	1	7	Pitch 106+	.304	79	24	7	0	4	12	15	8	.411	.544
4 Days Rest	4.10	34	21	0	73	73	454.2	464	50	128	277	First Pitch	.337	596	201	45	3	16	95	19	0	.367	.503
5+ Days Rest	3.84	28	20	0	70	70	452.1	454	50	163	272	Ahead in Count	.201	1474	297	49	6	28	119	0	491	.213	.300
vs. AL	4.21	44	19	0	87	87	543.1	560	68	171	325	Behind in Count	.348	853	297	64	11	39	138	167	0	.453	.586
vs. NL	3.71	19	22	0	58	58	376.1	375	32	121	231	Two Strikes	.177	1382	244	52	5	20	94	106	556	.245	.265
Pre-All Star	4.12	33	26	0	85	85	538.0	573	61	159	314	Pre-All Star	.275	2085	573	110	11	61	253	159	314	.329	.426
Post-All Star	3.84	30	15	0	60	60	381.2	362	39	133	242	Post-All Star	.252	1436	362	81	10	39	167	133	242	.322	.404

Pitcher vs. Batter (since 1984)

Pitches Best Vs.	Avg	AB	H	2B	3B	HR	RBI	BB	SO	OBP	SLG	Pitches Worst Vs.	Avg	AB	H	2B	3B	HR	RBI	BB	SO	OBP	SLG
Cal Ripken	.000	16	0	0	0	0	2	4	2	.182	.000	Mark McGwire	.583	12	7	1	0	3	7	0	3	.583	1.417
Damion Easley	.000	12	0	0	0	0	0	2	2	.143	.000	Sammy Sosa	.529	17	9	1	0	3	6	2	2	.579	1.118
Darren Lewis	.069	29	2	0	0	0	2	1	5	.100	.069	Frank Thomas	.529	17	9	2	0	2	5	1	1	.526	1.000
Royce Clayton	.074	27	2	0	0	0	2	1	2	.107	.074	Tony Clark	.500	10	5	0	0	3	5	2	1	.538	1.400
Tim Salmon	.083	12	1	0	0	0	1	1	4	.154	.083	Edgar Martinez	.385	13	5	2	0	2	5	4	2	.529	1.000

Richard Hidalgo — Astros
Age 22 – Bats Right

	Avg	G	AB	R	H	2B	3B	HR	RBI	BB	SO	HBP	GDP	SB	CS	OBP	SLG	IBB	SH	SF	#Pit	#P/PA	GB	FB	G/F
1997 Season	.306	19	62	8	19	5	0	2	6	4	18	1	0	1	0	.358	.484	0	0	0	271	4.04	14	21	0.67

1997 Season

	Avg	AB	H	2B	3B	HR	RBI	BB	SO	OBP	SLG		Avg	AB	H	2B	3B	HR	RBI	BB	SO	OBP	SLG
vs. Left	.455	22	10	2	0	1	2	1	6	.478	.682	Scoring Posn	.231	13	3	0	0	0	3	2	3	.333	.231
vs. Right	.225	40	9	3	0	1	4	3	12	.295	.375	Close & Late	.182	11	2	1	0	0	0	1	5	.250	.273

Bob Higginson — Tigers
Age 27 – Bats Left

	Avg	G	AB	R	H	2B	3B	HR	RBI	BB	SO	HBP	GDP	SB	CS	OBP	SLG	IBB	SH	SF	#Pit	#P/PA	GB	FB	G/F
1997 Season	.299	146	546	94	163	30	5	27	101	70	85	3	10	12	7	.379	.520	2	0	4	2489	4.00	178	174	1.02
Career (1995-1997)	.284	407	1396	230	396	82	10	67	225	197	258	9	22	24	14	.372	.501	12	5	17	6607	4.07	418	464	0.90

1997 Season

	Avg	AB	H	2B	3B	HR	RBI	BB	SO	OBP	SLG		Avg	AB	H	2B	3B	HR	RBI	BB	SO	OBP	SLG
vs. Left	.301	156	47	8	3	7	35	17	27	.375	.526	First Pitch	.318	44	14	1	0	2	9	2	0	.340	.477
vs. Right	.297	390	116	22	2	20	66	53	58	.380	.518	Ahead in Count	.383	154	59	16	3	12	44	35	0	.495	.760
Groundball	.292	106	31	11	1	3	19	18	16	.392	.500	Behind in Count	.226	230	52	9	1	7	31	0	70	.233	.365
Flyball	.287	101	29	4	3	5	16	10	13	.348	.535	Two Strikes	.221	244	54	9	2	8	31	33	85	.315	.373
Home	.322	236	76	13	2	16	56	41	41	.423	.597	Batting #2	.316	253	80	16	4	13	45	34	36	.398	.565
Away	.281	310	87	17	3	11	45	29	44	.342	.461	Batting #3	.288	146	42	8	0	8	30	20	24	.367	.507
Day	.294	214	63	13	1	11	48	34	32	.394	.519	Other	.279	147	41	6	1	6	26	16	25	.358	.456
Night	.301	332	100	17	4	16	53	36	53	.368	.521	March/April	.261	92	24	4	0	3	13	13	16	.358	.402
Grass	.303	478	145	25	2	24	96	67	75	.389	.515	May	.272	92	25	6	0	4	17	12	17	.358	.467
Turf	.265	68	18	5	3	3	5	3	10	.296	.559	June	.260	50	13	1	1	5	12	7	7	.351	.620
Pre-All Star	.267	258	69	12	1	14	49	35	45	.357	.484	July	.315	89	28	8	0	6	21	14	19	.404	.607
Post-All Star	.326	288	94	18	4	13	52	35	40	.399	.552	August	.347	121	42	6	4	5	15	14	11	.416	.587
Scoring Posn	.338	151	51	11	2	10	79	22	30	.416	.636	Sept/Oct	.304	102	31	5	0	4	23	10	15	.363	.471
Close & Late	.263	76	20	6	2	1	6	10	13	.349	.434	vs. AL	.301	512	154	29	5	23	88	65	79	.381	.512
None on/out	.267	105	28	4	1	4	4	12	14	.347	.438	vs. NL	.265	34	9	1	0	4	13	5	6	.350	.647

1997 By Position

Position	Avg	AB	H	2B	3B	HR	RBI	BB	SO	OBP	SLG	G	GS	Innings	PO	A	E	DP	Fld Pct	Rng Fctr	In Zone	Zone Outs	Zone Rtg	MLB Zone
As lf	.274	351	96	19	2	18	67	43	57	.353	.493	105	90	809.2	195	17	6	6	.972	2.36	231	189	.818	.805
As rf	.344	189	65	11	3	9	33	27	27	.427	.577	57	51	435.1	91	3	3	0	.969	1.94	108	87	.806	.813

Career (1995-1997)

	Avg	AB	H	2B	3B	HR	RBI	BB	SO	OBP	SLG		Avg	AB	H	2B	3B	HR	RBI	BB	SO	OBP	SLG
vs. Left	.265	283	75	11	3	10	52	40	55	.355	.431	First Pitch	.323	133	43	7	1	6	24	11	0	.367	.526
vs. Right	.288	1113	321	71	7	57	173	157	203	.376	.518	Ahead in Count	.366	344	126	33	3	30	85	97	0	.499	.741
Groundball	.268	314	84	23	1	14	47	40	46	.350	.481	Behind in Count	.223	609	136	26	2	16	65	0	204	.233	.351
Flyball	.262	256	67	12	4	10	35	34	50	.348	.457	Two Strikes	.208	693	144	28	5	18	71	89	258	.301	.341
Home	.294	674	198	37	6	41	119	101	139	.385	.549	Batting #2	.301	355	107	20	5	19	61	54	52	.394	.546
Away	.274	722	198	44	4	26	106	96	119	.359	.456	Batting #6	.252	218	55	11	2	9	30	28	54	.335	.445
Day	.296	527	156	36	4	25	97	83	88	.394	.522	Other	.284	823	234	51	3	39	134	115	152	.372	.496
Night	.276	869	240	46	6	42	128	114	170	.377	.488	March/April	.251	183	46	10	0	6	28	27	31	.351	.404
Grass	.289	1215	351	67	7	63	208	173	223	.377	.511	May	.257	210	54	10	0	10	35	27	46	.346	.448
Turf	.249	181	45	15	3	4	17	24	35	.338	.431	June	.315	197	62	15	2	16	40	32	40	.406	.655
Pre-All Star	.273	660	180	37	3	38	119	97	130	.365	.511	July	.284	243	69	18	1	13	47	41	53	.380	.527
Post-All Star	.293	736	216	45	7	29	106	100	128	.378	.492	August	.301	286	86	15	5	13	36	36	41	.382	.524
Scoring Posn	.304	329	100	28	2	15	159	68	66	.410	.538	Sept/Oct	.285	277	79	14	2	9	39	34	47	.362	.448
Close & Late	.251	203	51	10	4	7	18	31	42	.350	.443	vs. AL	.284	1362	387	81	10	63	212	192	252	.372	.497
None on/out	.250	336	84	17	3	16	16	31	66	.341	.461	vs. NL	.265	34	9	1	0	4	13	5	6	.350	.647

Batter vs. Pitcher (career)

Hits Best Against	Avg	AB	H	2B	3B	HR	RBI	BB	SO	OBP	SLG	Hits Worst Against	Avg	AB	H	2B	3B	HR	RBI	BB	SO	OBP	SLG
Kevin Appier	.643	14	9	0	0	2	3	2	3	.647	1.071	Roger Pavlik	.100	20	2	0	0	1	1	1	6	.143	.250
Erik Hanson	.600	10	6	2	0	3	5	1	1	.636	1.700	Chuck Finley	.100	10	1	1	0	0	1	1	3	.182	.200
Ricky Bones	.455	11	5	0	1	1	2	0	1	.417	.909	Jeff Fassero	.167	12	2	0	1	0	2	0	3	.167	.333
Bob Wickman	.375	8	3	0	0	1	2	3	1	.545	.750	Pat Hentgen	.182	33	6	1	0	0	2	4	7	.270	.212
Frank Rodriguez	.368	19	7	2	0	3	9	2	1	.429	.947	Ken Hill	.182	22	4	1	0	0	3	0	3	.174	.227

Glenallen Hill — Giants
Age 33 – Bats Right

	Avg	G	AB	R	H	2B	3B	HR	RBI	BB	SO	HBP	GDP	SB	CS	OBP	SLG	IBB	SH	SF	#Pit	#P/PA	GB	FB	G/F
1997 Season	.261	128	398	47	104	28	4	11	64	19	87	4	8	7	4	.297	.435	0	0	7	1505	3.52	135	128	1.05
Last Five Years	.272	544	1804	255	490	109	11	79	302	137	408	12	34	65	21	.324	.476	8	1	17	6955	3.53	614	535	1.15

1997 Season

	Avg	AB	H	2B	3B	HR	RBI	BB	SO	OBP	SLG		Avg	AB	H	2B	3B	HR	RBI	BB	SO	OBP	SLG
vs. Left	.270	111	30	8	0	4	17	7	21	.311	.450	First Pitch	.333	75	25	6	2	5	17	0	0	.316	.667
vs. Right	.258	287	74	20	4	7	47	12	66	.291	.429	Ahead in Count	.275	80	22	6	2	2	16	7	0	.330	.475
Groundball	.307	101	31	9	1	4	18	2	18	.308	.535	Behind in Count	.199	171	34	10	0	3	20	0	71	.215	.310
Flyball	.200	45	9	2	0	2	11	4	20	.260	.378	Two Strikes	.214	182	39	13	0	1	19	12	87	.275	.302
Home	.228	193	44	11	1	3	24	11	47	.276	.342	Batting #3	.248	157	39	12	3	3	26	6	32	.278	.420
Away	.293	205	60	17	3	8	40	8	40	.317	.522	Batting #6	.234	145	34	10	1	6	21	5	31	.266	.441
Day	.263	167	44	13	2	3	30	8	35	.298	.419	Other	.323	96	31	6	0	2	17	8	24	.371	.527
Night	.260	231	60	15	2	8	34	11	52	.296	.446	March/April	.286	91	26	9	2	3	18	3	23	.309	.527

1997 Season

	Avg	AB	H	2B	3B	HR	RBI	BB	SO	OBP	SLG		Avg	AB	H	2B	3B	HR	RBI	BB	SO	OBP	SLG
Grass	.241	323	78	22	2	7	44	15	75	.277	.387	May	.200	100	20	4	0	3	16	6	24	.248	.330
Turf	.347	75	26	6	2	4	20	4	12	.378	.640	June	.260	77	20	5	2	2	13	1	17	.263	.455
Pre-All Star	.248	282	70	18	4	8	48	10	64	.273	.426	July	.261	46	12	3	0	0	2	1	6	.292	.326
Post-All Star	.293	116	34	10	0	3	16	9	23	.352	.457	August	.311	45	14	4	0	2	9	5	8	.380	.533
Scoring Posn	.317	104	33	8	1	0	45	9	18	.366	.413	Sept/Oct	.308	39	12	3	0	1	6	3	9	.364	.462
Close & Late	.355	62	22	7	1	2	22	5	15	.391	.597	vs. AL	.244	41	10	2	0	0	4	3	6	.289	.293
None on/out	.239	88	21	7	1	1	1	3	19	.264	.375	vs. NL	.263	357	94	26	4	11	60	16	81	.298	.451

1997 By Position

Position	Avg	AB	H	2B	3B	HR	RBI	BB	SO	OBP	SLG	G	GS	Innings	PO	A	E	DP	Fld Pct	Rng Fctr	In Zone	Zone Outs	Zone Rtg	MLB Zone
As Pinch Hitter	.360	25	9	4	0	0	5	2	8	.393	.520	28	0	---	---	---	---	---	---	---	---	---	---	---
As rf	.255	349	89	23	4	11	55	15	76	.290	.438	97	92	744.2	158	2	9	0	.947	1.93	198	150	.758	.813

Last Five Years

	Avg	AB	H	2B	3B	HR	RBI	BB	SO	OBP	SLG		Avg	AB	H	2B	3B	HR	RBI	BB	SO	OBP	SLG
vs. Left	.293	540	158	25	2	34	100	42	106	.341	.535	First Pitch	.336	372	125	25	4	24	80	6	0	.345	.618
vs. Right	.263	1264	332	84	9	45	202	95	302	.317	.450	Ahead in Count	.346	298	103	21	4	22	70	63	0	.454	.664
Groundball	.322	456	147	35	4	22	80	29	99	.358	.561	Behind in Count	.203	832	169	40	2	25	108	0	355	.210	.346
Flyball	.233	275	64	13	1	14	46	24	84	.291	.440	Two Strikes	.196	831	163	39	2	21	103	68	408	.261	.324
Home	.255	858	219	51	4	33	142	66	193	.312	.439	Batting #5	.275	506	139	30	2	22	93	48	114	.339	.472
Away	.286	946	271	58	7	46	160	71	215	.336	.508	Batting #6	.247	466	115	23	3	26	77	29	111	.294	.476
Day	.270	848	229	56	4	35	154	68	188	.326	.469	Other	.284	832	236	56	6	31	132	60	183	.333	.477
Night	.273	956	261	53	7	44	148	69	220	.323	.481	March/April	.266	286	76	21	3	9	51	15	80	.302	.455
Grass	.267	1385	370	85	8	58	235	110	320	.322	.466	May	.253	367	93	17	1	17	54	30	80	.310	.449
Turf	.286	419	120	24	3	21	67	27	88	.332	.508	June	.258	256	66	14	3	9	47	18	49	.302	.441
Pre-All Star	.259	1008	261	57	4	38	161	73	226	.308	.442	July	.289	284	82	16	2	11	47	27	61	.352	.475
Post-All Star	.288	796	229	52	4	41	141	64	182	.345	.518	August	.286	322	92	25	1	12	44	28	80	.347	.481
Scoring Posn	.284	517	147	30	4	13	203	65	113	.360	.433	Sept/Oct	.280	289	81	16	1	21	59	19	58	.330	.561
Close & Late	.256	312	80	23	2	8	62	22	77	.304	.420	vs. AL	.228	215	49	9	2	5	20	14	56	.272	.358
None on/out	.276	402	111	28	2	18	18	19	93	.310	.490	vs. NL	.278	1589	441	100	9	74	273	123	352	.331	.492

Batter vs. Pitcher (career)

Hits Best Against	Avg	AB	H	2B	3B	HR	RBI	BB	SO	OBP	SLG	Hits Worst Against	Avg	AB	H	2B	3B	HR	RBI	BB	SO	OBP	SLG
Kevin Ritz	.500	22	11	2	1	2	5	2	2	.542	.955	Kevin Tapani	.000	12	0	0	0	0	1	0	2	.000	.000
Darryl Kile	.500	10	5	2	1	1	8	6	2	.684	1.200	Dave Veres	.000	11	0	0	0	0	1	0	5	.000	.000
Andy Ashby	.471	17	8	4	0	2	4	1	4	.500	1.059	Pat Rapp	.000	11	0	0	0	0	0	1	0	.083	.000
Terry Mulholland	.462	13	6	1	0	2	3	0	0	.462	1.000	John Smoltz	.077	13	1	1	0	0	0	0	7	.077	.154
Shane Reynolds	.400	15	6	0	2	2	4	0	5	.375	1.067	Pedro Martinez	.105	19	2	0	0	0	0	0	8	.100	.105

Ken Hill — Angels

Age 32 – Pitches Right (groundball pitcher)

	ERA	W	L	Sv	G	GS	IP	BB	SO	Avg	H	2B	3B	HR	RBI	OBP	SLG	CG	ShO	Sup	QS	#P/S	SB	CS	GB	FB	G/F
1997 Season	4.55	9	12	0	31	31	190.0	95	106	.268	194	41	5	19	91	.352	.417	1	0	5.26	16	98	19	8	287	208	1.38
Last Five Years	3.87	60	42	0	147	146	964.0	385	549	.260	954	194	25	78	399	.332	.391	13	4	5.60	86	103	96	41	1490	967	1.54

1997 Season

	ERA	W	L	Sv	G	GS	IP	H	HR	BB	SO		Avg	AB	H	2B	3B	HR	RBI	BB	SO	OBP	SLG
Home	5.11	2	6	0	14	14	86.1	108	13	37	51	vs. Left	.264	387	102	21	1	12	43	58	47	.359	.416
Away	4.08	7	6	0	17	17	103.2	86	6	58	55	vs. Right	.272	338	92	20	4	7	48	37	59	.343	.417
Day	5.35	1	4	0	6	6	37.0	43	3	18	28	Inning 1-6	.272	640	174	37	4	17	86	80	95	.352	.422
Night	4.35	8	8	0	25	25	153.0	151	16	77	78	Inning 7+	.235	85	20	4	1	2	5	15	11	.350	.376
Grass	4.69	6	10	0	26	26	157.1	167	17	77	80	None on	.258	414	107	24	3	15	15	54	54	.347	.440
Turf	3.86	3	2	0	5	5	32.2	27	2	18	26	Runners on	.280	311	87	17	2	4	76	41	52	.358	.386
March/April	3.75	2	2	0	6	6	36.0	32	4	18	29	Scoring Posn	.275	189	52	10	1	4	73	30	32	.366	.402
May	2.08	2	0	0	2	2	13.0	10	0	7	4	Close & Late	.313	32	10	2	0	1	4	11	6	.488	.469
June	5.14	0	3	0	6	6	35.0	50	6	13	20	None on/out	.318	195	62	13	2	7	7	13	20	.361	.513
July	7.56	2	3	0	6	6	33.1	42	2	25	19	vs. 1st Batr (relief)	.000	0	0	0	0	0	0	0	0	.000	.000
August	6.17	1	3	0	6	6	35.0	44	6	15	14	1st Inning Pitched	.254	118	30	6	1	2	14	14	18	.338	.373
Sept/Oct	1.43	2	1	0	5	5	37.2	16	1	17	20	First 75 Pitches	.279	520	145	29	4	15	69	63	70	.357	.437
Starter	4.55	9	12	0	31	31	190.0	194	19	95	106	Pitch 76-90	.283	92	26	7	0	2	13	13	17	.367	.424
Reliever	0.00	0	0	0	0	0	0.0	0	0	0	0	Pitch 91-105	.198	86	17	3	1	2	6	6	14	.250	.326
0-3 Days Rest (Start)	7.64	0	2	0	3	3	17.2	25	2	6	15	Pitch 106+	.222	27	6	2	0	0	3	13	5	.475	.296
4 Days Rest	4.05	5	7	0	17	17	102.1	104	11	41	52	First Pitch	.325	117	38	10	1	1	16	2	0	.333	.453
5+ Days Rest	4.50	4	3	0	11	11	70.0	65	6	48	39	Ahead in Count	.222	315	70	12	3	7	32	0	87	.226	.346
vs. AL	4.68	8	12	0	29	29	175.0	178	17	90	99	Behind in Count	.306	157	48	11	0	6	20	55	0	.479	.490
vs. NL	3.00	1	0	0	2	2	15.0	16	2	5	7	Two Strikes	.211	303	64	9	3	7	33	38	106	.301	.330
Pre-All Star	4.17	5	5	0	15	15	90.2	100	11	41	58	Pre-All Star	.284	352	100	20	4	11	44	41	58	.358	.457
Post-All Star	4.89	4	7	0	16	16	99.1	94	8	54	48	Post-All Star	.252	373	94	21	1	8	47	54	48	.347	.378

Last Five Years

	ERA	W	L	Sv	G	GS	IP	H	HR	BB	SO		Avg	AB	H	2B	3B	HR	RBI	BB	SO	OBP	SLG
Home	4.06	27	25	0	73	72	476.2	504	39	184	246	vs. Left	.262	1931	505	107	14	37	197	237	227	.342	.389
Away	3.69	33	17	0	74	74	487.1	450	39	201	303	vs. Right	.259	1736	449	87	11	41	202	148	322	.319	.392
Day	4.28	16	16	0	41	40	267.0	275	28	107	159	Inning 1-6	.257	3118	801	157	20	64	346	339	488	.331	.382
Night	3.72	44	26	0	106	106	697.0	679	50	278	390	Inning 7+	.279	549	153	37	5	14	53	46	61	.336	.441
Grass	3.96	33	25	0	88	87	574.2	584	53	222	343	None on	.261	2073	542	112	11	52	52	216	272	.335	.401
Turf	3.74	27	17	0	59	59	389.1	370	25	163	206	Runners on	.258	1594	412	82	14	26	347	169	277	.328	.376
March/April	3.13	13	5	0	23	23	158.0	133	11	63	105	Scoring Posn	.247	941	232	53	7	16	307	122	167	.328	.369

Last Five Years

	ERA	W	L	Sv	G	GS	IP	H	HR	BB	SO		Avg	AB	H	2B	3B	HR	RBI	BB	SO	OBP	SLG
May	2.90	16	3	0	26	26	174.0	148	13	55	93	Close & Late	.303	231	70	16	2	6	28	27	32	.375	.468
June	5.01	5	11	0	26	26	163.1	194	18	75	81	None on/out	.284	951	270	55	7	25	25	81	107	.343	.435
July	4.34	10	8	0	25	25	163.2	169	12	74	104	vs. 1st Batr (relief)	1.000	1	1	0	0	0	0	0	0	1.000	1.000
August	4.25	8	8	0	26	26	171.2	192	17	56	86	1st Inning Pitched	.254	562	143	28	6	9	77	76	91	.347	.374
Sept/Oct	3.58	8	7	0	21	20	133.1	118	7	62	80	First 75 Pitches	.255	2551	651	126	15	51	268	273	393	.329	.376
Starter	3.87	60	42	0	146	146	962.0	952	78	385	547	Pitch 76-90	.294	489	144	29	6	10	61	53	67	.361	.440
Reliever	4.50	0	0	0	1	0	2.0	2	0	0	2	Pitch 91-105	.247	405	100	24	3	9	39	28	60	.296	.388
0-3 Days Rest (Start)	5.61	1	2	0	4	4	25.2	29	3	7	18	Pitch 106+	.266	222	59	15	1	8	31	31	29	.355	.450
4 Days Rest	3.75	38	26	0	84	84	563.2	558	54	214	325	First Pitch	.297	595	177	43	4	10	82	16	0	.311	.434
5+ Days Rest	3.94	21	14	0	58	58	372.2	365	21	164	204	Ahead in Count	.214	1615	346	48	16	29	133	0	453	.220	.318
vs. AL	4.05	28	23	0	76	75	500.0	505	41	217	317	Behind in Count	.327	791	259	57	3	23	107	204	0	.463	.494
vs. NL	3.69	32	19	0	71	71	463.2	449	37	168	232	Two Strikes	.188	1547	291	42	12	27	125	165	549	.270	.283
Pre-All Star	3.72	38	21	0	82	82	543.2	529	46	214	317	Pre-All Star	.255	2075	529	100	17	46	219	214	317	.326	.386
Post-All Star	4.07	22	21	0	65	64	420.1	425	32	171	232	Post-All Star	.267	1592	425	94	8	32	180	171	232	.339	.396

Pitcher vs. Batter (career)

Pitches Best Vs.	Avg	AB	H	2B	3B	HR	RBI	BB	SO	OBP	SLG	Pitches Worst Vs.	Avg	AB	H	2B	3B	HR	RBI	BB	SO	OBP	SLG
Ruben Amaro	.000	10	0	0	0	0	0	0	1	.091	.000	Mo Vaughn	.563	16	9	3	0	1	3	1	1	.611	.938
Luis Gonzalez	.059	34	2	0	1	0	3	1	5	.086	.118	Tim Raines	.550	20	11	3	1	0	5	7	2	.667	.800
Scott Stahoviak	.067	15	1	0	0	0	0	1	3	.125	.067	Sammy Sosa	.500	12	6	1	0	2	3	1	1	.600	1.083
Rafael Bournigal	.083	12	1	0	0	0	0	0	2	.083	.083	Brady Anderson	.500	8	4	1	0	1	1	5	1	.692	1.000
Darren Lewis	.105	19	2	0	0	0	1	0	0	.105	.105	Rafael Palmeiro	.417	12	5	0	0	2	5	4	1	.563	.917

Sterling Hitchcock — Padres
Age 27 – Pitches Left

	ERA	W	L	Sv	G	GS	IP	BB	SO	Avg	H	2B	3B	HR	RBI	OBP	SLG	CG	ShO	Sup	QS	#P/S	SB	CS	GB	FB	G/F
1997 Season	5.20	10	11	0	32	28	161.0	55	106	.276	172	40	6	24	88	.337	.475	1	0	5.37	12	89	26	9	217	182	1.19
Last Five Years	5.00	39	33	2	123	101	606.1	239	422	.278	652	130	11	80	317	.345	.445	6	1	5.61	45	97	66	34	774	716	1.08

1997 Season

	ERA	W	L	Sv	G	GS	IP	H	HR	BB	SO		Avg	AB	H	2B	3B	HR	RBI	BB	SO	OBP	SLG
Home	4.04	6	4	0	15	12	75.2	66	11	22	50	vs. Left	.316	117	37	8	2	4	12	6	18	.370	.521
Away	6.22	4	7	0	17	16	85.1	106	13	33	56	vs. Right	.267	506	135	32	4	20	76	49	88	.329	.464
Day	5.45	3	6	0	12	12	66.0	79	10	27	48	Inning 1-6	.281	563	158	38	5	23	82	53	96	.343	.488
Night	5.02	7	5	0	20	16	95.0	93	14	28	58	Inning 7+	.233	60	14	2	1	1	6	2	10	.270	.350
Grass	4.22	7	7	0	24	21	128.0	125	17	42	87	None on	.294	360	106	22	2	16	16	30	60	.352	.500
Turf	9.00	3	4	0	8	7	33.0	47	7	13	19	Runners on	.251	263	66	18	4	8	72	25	46	.316	.441
March/April	2.92	2	2	0	7	5	37.0	31	2	9	25	Scoring Posn	.257	152	39	12	1	5	62	19	31	.335	.447
May	5.12	3	3	0	6	6	38.2	37	7	13	25	Close & Late	.241	29	7	1	0	0	3	1	4	.290	.276
June	9.00	0	0	0	1	1	5.0	9	2	2	4	None on/out	.346	162	56	13	1	7	7	14	18	.404	.568
July	4.85	2	1	0	6	6	29.2	33	5	16	20	vs. 1st Batr (relief)	.250	4	1	0	0	0	0	1	.250	.250
August	5.14	3	2	0	6	6	35.0	37	5	5	18	1st Inning Pitched	.314	121	38	10	1	6	27	18	20	.411	.562
Sept/Oct	10.34	0	3	0	6	4	15.2	25	3	10	14	First 75 Pitches	.277	484	134	35	6	21	72	43	87	.338	.504
Starter	5.26	10	11	0	28	28	159.0	171	24	55	105	Pitch 76-90	.265	83	22	3	0	2	9	10	12	.351	.373
Reliever	0.00	0	0	0	4	0	2.0	1	0	0	1	Pitch 91-105	.275	40	11	0	0	1	5	1	5	.279	.350
0-3 Days Rest (Start)	2.66	1	2	0	3	3	20.1	15	4	6	16	Pitch 106+	.313	16	5	2	0	0	2	1	2	.353	.438
4 Days Rest	4.78	5	6	0	15	15	90.1	96	12	24	58	First Pitch	.303	76	23	9	2	1	11	0	0	.304	.513
5+ Days Rest	7.26	4	3	0	10	10	48.1	60	8	25	31	Ahead in Count	.199	272	54	11	2	2	23	0	89	.201	.276
vs. AL	7.27	1	0	0	2	2	8.2	11	2	3	4	Behind in Count	.363	157	57	10	0	14	32	33	0	.474	.694
vs. NL	5.08	9	11	0	30	26	152.1	161	22	52	102	Two Strikes	.163	270	44	7	2	3	18	22	106	.229	.237
Pre-All Star	4.64	5	5	0	15	13	83.1	81	12	36	52	Pre-All Star	.258	314	81	17	2	12	36	26	54	.317	.439
Post-All Star	5.79	5	6	0	17	15	77.2	91	12	29	52	Post-All Star	.294	309	91	23	4	12	52	29	52	.357	.511

Last Five Years

	ERA	W	L	Sv	G	GS	IP	H	HR	BB	SO		Avg	AB	H	2B	3B	HR	RBI	BB	SO	OBP	SLG
Home	4.59	19	16	1	57	47	296.0	299	32	100	200	vs. Left	.269	461	124	31	3	13	61	40	86	.334	.434
Away	5.39	20	17	1	66	54	310.1	353	48	139	222	vs. Right	.280	1887	528	99	8	67	256	199	336	.347	.447
Day	4.96	12	10	1	36	30	183.1	198	21	71	141	Inning 1-6	.280	2050	574	119	9	71	284	213	367	.348	.451
Night	5.02	27	23	1	87	71	423.0	454	59	168	281	Inning 7+	.262	298	78	11	2	9	33	26	55	.322	.403
Grass	4.40	28	23	2	89	70	438.0	442	53	173	312	None on	.276	1352	373	78	4	45	45	131	241	.344	.439
Turf	6.58	11	10	0	34	31	168.1	210	27	66	110	Runners on	.280	996	279	52	7	35	272	108	181	.346	.452
March/April	4.00	5	3	0	16	11	74.1	71	5	25	51	Scoring Posn	.292	538	157	32	3	19	228	72	101	.363	.468
May	5.30	6	8	2	25	18	120.2	121	18	48	89	Close & Late	.262	149	39	6	1	1	18	14	26	.327	.336
June	5.24	5	2	0	20	12	77.1	91	11	33	58	None on/out	.284	603	171	37	2	18	18	59	99	.351	.441
July	4.33	9	4	0	20	20	116.1	127	15	48	82	vs. 1st Batr (relief)	.263	19	5	2	0	0	1	3	6	.364	.368
August	5.23	9	9	0	21	21	127.1	139	18	45	74	1st Inning Pitched	.255	432	110	22	2	13	62	53	95	.335	.405
Sept/Oct	5.78	5	7	0	21	19	90.1	103	13	40	68	First 75 Pitches	.278	1727	480	101	11	56	227	169	322	.341	.446
Starter	4.98	38	32	0	101	101	585.2	631	79	227	403	Pitch 76-90	.294	289	85	16	0	12	43	38	46	.380	.474
Reliever	5.66	1	1	2	22	0	20.2	21	1	12	19	Pitch 91-105	.255	196	50	6	0	7	26	22	32	.330	.393
0-3 Days Rest (Start)	4.95	1	3	0	6	6	36.1	37	9	8	26	Pitch 106+	.272	136	37	7	0	5	21	10	22	.331	.434
4 Days Rest	5.09	24	19	0	62	62	364.1	390	47	142	263	First Pitch	.350	260	91	25	2	12	46	4	0	.354	.600
5+ Days Rest	4.77	13	10	0	33	33	185.0	204	23	77	114	Ahead in Count	.197	1023	202	31	3	16	94	0	351	.203	.281
vs. AL	4.98	30	22	2	93	75	454.0	491	58	187	320	Behind in Count	.367	577	212	42	3	37	108	119	0	.473	.643
vs. NL	5.08	9	11	0	30	26	152.1	161	22	52	102	Two Strikes	.185	1073	198	30	3	16	92	116	422	.266	.263
Pre-All Star	4.91	17	14	2	65	45	296.2	304	40	116	216	Pre-All Star	.267	1137	304	61	5	40	146	116	216	.335	.435
Post-All Star	5.09	22	19	0	58	56	309.2	348	40	123	206	Post-All Star	.287	1211	348	69	6	40	171	123	206	.354	.453

211

Pitcher vs. Batter (career)

Pitches Best Vs.	Avg	AB	H	2B	3B	HR	RBI	BB	SO	OBP	SLG	Pitches Worst Vs.	Avg	AB	H	2B	3B	HR	RBI	BB	SO	OBP	SLG
Danny Tartabull	.000	10	0	0	0	0	0	3	6	.231	.000	Frank Thomas	.571	14	8	3	0	2	4	2	1	.625	1.214
Jose Valentin	.077	13	1	0	0	0	0	0	6	.077	.077	Roberto Alomar	.500	16	8	3	1	0	1	0	2	.500	.813
Mike Devereaux	.083	12	1	1	0	0	1	0	2	.083	.167	Mike Blowers	.500	8	4	0	0	1	3	3	1	.636	.875
Joe Oliver	.083	12	1	0	0	0	0	1	4	.154	.083	Rafael Palmeiro	.440	25	11	5	0	2	7	4	2	.517	.880
Darryl Hamilton	.083	12	1	0	0	0	2	0	1	.214	.083	Terry Steinbach	.400	10	4	0	0	2	4	1	3	.417	1.000

Denny Hocking — Twins
Age 28 – Bats Both (groundball hitter)

	Avg	G	AB	R	H	2B	3B	HR	RBI	BB	SO	HBP	GDP	SB	CS	OBP	SLG	IBB	SH	SF	#Pit	P/PA	GB	FB	G/F
1997 Season	.257	115	253	28	65	12	4	2	25	18	51	1	6	3	5	.308	.360	0	5	1	1096	3.94	94	62	1.52
Career (1993-1997)	.233	199	472	58	110	22	6	3	40	34	89	1	12	10	8	.285	.324	1	7	2	1955	3.79	181	123	1.47

1997 Season

	Avg	AB	H	2B	3B	HR	RBI	BB	SO	OBP	SLG		Avg	AB	H	2B	3B	HR	RBI	BB	SO	OBP	SLG
vs. Left	.310	84	26	7	1	1	9	6	14	.363	.452	Scoring Posn	.319	72	23	4	1	1	23	6	17	.367	.444
vs. Right	.231	169	39	5	3	1	16	12	37	.280	.314	Close & Late	.244	45	11	2	1	0	2	2	10	.277	.333
Home	.284	95	27	3	2	0	9	5	21	.327	.358	None on/out	.214	56	12	2	1	0	0	5	7	.290	.286
Away	.241	158	38	9	2	2	16	13	30	.297	.361	Batting #2	.219	73	16	4	2	0	5	4	18	.256	.329
First Pitch	.360	25	9	1	0	0	1	0	0	.360	.400	Batting #9	.305	131	40	8	1	2	18	11	21	.359	.427
Ahead in Count	.362	58	21	5	3	0	8	9	0	.441	.552	Other	.184	49	9	0	1	0	2	3	12	.245	.224
Behind in Count	.227	128	29	5	1	2	13	0	45	.233	.328	Pre-All Star	.277	112	31	5	1	1	13	5	24	.314	.366
Two Strikes	.205	132	27	4	1	1	14	9	51	.255	.273	Post-All Star	.241	141	34	7	3	1	12	13	27	.303	.355

Trevor Hoffman — Padres
Age 30 – Pitches Right (flyball pitcher)

	ERA	W	L	Sv	G	GS	IP	BB	SO	Avg	H	2B	3B	HR	RBI	OBP	SLG	GF	IR	IRS	Hld	SvOp	SB	CS	GB	FB	G/F
1997 Season	2.66	6	4	37	70	0	81.1	24	111	.200	59	9	3	9	36	.259	.342	59	44	14	0	44	4	5	75	75	1.00
Career (1993-1997)	3.03	30	23	135	309	0	368.2	128	421	.204	276	53	12	39	152	.272	.347	239	172	41	16	162	18	8	332	412	0.81

1997 Season

	ERA	W	L	Sv	G	GS	IP	H	HR	BB	SO		Avg	AB	H	2B	3B	HR	RBI	BB	SO	OBP	SLG
Home	2.85	6	0	16	37	0	41.0	32	6	7	63	vs. Left	.185	157	29	5	2	3	17	9	63	.229	.299
Away	2.45	0	4	21	33	0	40.1	27	3	17	48	vs. Right	.217	138	30	4	1	6	19	15	48	.292	.391
Day	1.75	2	1	13	21	0	25.2	16	2	9	35	Inning 1-6	.000	0	0	0	0	0	0	0	0	.000	.000
Night	3.07	4	3	24	49	0	55.2	43	7	15	76	Inning 7+	.200	295	59	9	3	9	36	24	111	.259	.342
Grass	3.09	6	3	30	57	0	64.0	49	9	17	87	None on	.186	167	31	7	0	3	3	10	67	.232	.281
Turf	1.04	0	1	7	13	0	17.1	10	0	7	24	Runners on	.219	128	28	2	3	6	33	14	44	.294	.422
March/April	6.48	0	2	3	10	0	8.1	12	2	3	11	Scoring Posn	.221	77	17	1	2	4	27	9	21	.299	.442
May	1.54	2	1	4	10	0	11.2	7	0	3	18	Close & Late	.185	216	40	7	2	5	29	19	77	.250	.306
June	4.30	1	0	8	12	0	14.2	14	3	5	18	None on/out	.159	69	11	3	0	2	2	2	31	.183	.290
July	2.35	1	1	10	16	0	15.1	8	2	5	20	vs. 1st Batr (relief)	.147	68	10	2	1	2	6	1	31	.159	.294
August	1.47	2	0	7	13	0	18.1	9	1	2	28	1st Inning Pitched	.212	236	50	8	3	8	33	13	90	.252	.373
Sept/Oct	1.38	0	0	5	9	0	13.0	9	1	6	16	First 15 Pitches	.201	204	41	7	3	6	26	8	74	.230	.353
Starter	0.00	0	0	0	0	0	0.0	0	0	0	0	Pitch 16-30	.206	68	14	2	0	3	9	11	29	.316	.368
Reliever	2.66	6	4	37	70	0	81.1	59	9	24	111	Pitch 31-45	.200	20	4	0	0	0	1	5	6	.360	.200
0 Days rest (Relief)	1.69	1	0	16	20	0	21.1	14	2	4	28	Pitch 46+	.000	3	0	0	0	0	0	0	2	.000	.000
1 or 2 Days rest	3.69	4	3	16	33	0	39.0	34	5	9	54	First Pitch	.276	29	8	1	0	0	2	3	0	.344	.310
3+ Days rest	1.71	1	1	5	17	0	21.0	11	2	11	29	Ahead in Count	.144	180	26	4	1	3	13	0	99	.144	.228
vs. AL	3.00	0	0	4	7	0	9.0	8	2	4	11	Behind in Count	.308	39	12	2	1	2	9	7	0	.413	.564
vs. NL	2.61	6	4	33	63	0	72.1	51	7	20	100	Two Strikes	.151	186	28	3	1	6	17	14	111	.209	.274
Pre-All Star	4.06	3	3	16	35	0	37.2	36	6	12	53	Pre-All Star	.254	142	36	7	2	6	22	12	53	.310	.458
Post-All Star	1.44	3	1	21	35	0	43.2	23	3	12	58	Post-All Star	.150	153	23	2	1	3	14	12	58	.212	.235

Career (1993-1997)

	ERA	W	L	Sv	G	GS	IP	H	HR	BB	SO		Avg	AB	H	2B	3B	HR	RBI	BB	SO	OBP	SLG
Home	2.65	22	7	62	155	0	180.1	135	17	51	205	vs. Left	.194	653	127	19	7	14	66	78	209	.280	.309
Away	3.39	8	16	73	154	0	188.1	141	22	77	216	vs. Right	.213	701	149	34	5	25	86	50	212	.265	.382
Day	2.67	5	8	48	106	0	131.1	88	17	56	157	Inning 1-6	.222	18	4	2	1	1	4	0	3	.200	.611
Night	3.22	25	15	87	203	0	237.1	188	22	72	264	Inning 7+	.204	1336	272	51	11	38	148	128	418	.273	.344
Grass	2.99	25	18	110	245	0	286.1	217	32	96	324	None on	.193	766	148	30	6	21	21	55	233	.249	.330
Turf	3.17	5	5	25	64	0	82.1	59	7	32	97	Runners on	.218	588	128	23	6	18	131	73	188	.301	.369
March/April	3.00	4	3	12	41	0	48.0	33	5	23	60	Scoring Posn	.185	362	67	10	3	13	110	61	118	.297	.337
May	2.50	8	4	19	52	0	57.2	47	5	27	45	Close & Late	.199	950	189	38	8	20	111	94	294	.271	.319
June	3.66	5	5	25	56	0	66.1	61	7	15	67	None on/out	.212	326	69	15	4	11	11	16	95	.253	.383
July	4.19	4	6	27	60	0	68.2	50	10	30	83	vs. 1st Batr (relief)	.197	289	57	13	5	11	27	16	97	.240	.391
August	2.12	4	3	31	55	0	68.0	46	3	15	70	1st Inning Pitched	.210	1043	219	43	8	33	129	94	319	.274	.361
Sept/Oct	2.55	5	2	21	45	0	60.0	39	7	18	76	First 15 Pitches	.205	882	181	40	7	29	99	63	255	.257	.365
Starter	0.00	0	0	0	0	0	0.0	0	0	0	0	Pitch 16-30	.197	365	72	8	4	7	38	50	129	.294	.299
Reliever	3.03	30	23	135	309	0	368.2	276	39	128	421	Pitch 31-45	.229	96	22	5	1	3	14	14	30	.330	.396
0 Days rest (Relief)	2.34	5	0	48	67	0	69.1	46	8	20	75	Pitch 46+	.091	11	1	0	0	0	1	1	7	.167	.091
1 or 2 Days rest	3.09	20	16	67	164	0	206.2	167	19	66	245	First Pitch	.273	132	36	6	1	6	18	25	0	.390	.470
3+ Days rest	3.40	5	7	20	78	0	92.2	63	12	42	101	Ahead in Count	.154	774	119	20	5	16	61	0	370	.155	.255
vs. AL	3.00	0	0	4	7	0	9.0	8	2	4	11	Behind in Count	.288	198	57	15	2	6	32	52	0	.433	.475
vs. NL	3.03	30	23	131	302	0	359.2	268	37	124	410	Two Strikes	.153	798	122	17	5	18	64	51	421	.204	.254
Pre-All Star	3.36	17	13	61	166	0	192.2	162	20	74	221	Pre-All Star	.223	725	162	37	6	20	92	74	221	.294	.374
Post-All Star	2.66	13	10	74	143	0	176.0	114	19	54	200	Post-All Star	.181	629	114	16	6	19	60	54	200	.247	.316

Pitcher vs. Batter (career)

Pitches Best Vs.	Avg	AB	H	2B	3B	HR	RBI	BB	SO	OBP	SLG	Pitches Worst Vs.	Avg	AB	H	2B	3B	HR	RBI	BB	SO	OBP	SLG
Mickey Morandini	.000	11	0	0	0	0	0	1	4	.083	.000	Barry Bonds	.444	9	4	0	0	1	3	4	0	.615	.778
Rick Wilkins	.000	8	0	0	0	0	0	3	5	.273	.000	Charlie Hayes	.333	12	4	2	0	1	3	1	1	.385	.750
Mike Lansing	.083	12	1	0	0	0	0	1	1	.154	.083	Dante Bichette	.333	12	4	1	0	2	5	0	4	.333	.917
Craig Biggio	.091	11	1	1	0	0	1	1	3	.167	.182	Jay Bell	.333	9	3	2	0	0	3	1	1	.364	.556
Vinny Castilla	.154	13	2	0	0	0	3	0	1	.143	.154												

Chris Hoiles — Orioles

Age 33 – Bats Right (flyball hitter)

	Avg	G	AB	R	H	2B	3B	HR	RBI	BB	SO	HBP	GDP	SB	CS	OBP	SLG	IBB	SH	SF	#Pit	#P/PA	GB	FB	G/F
1997 Season	.259	99	320	45	83	15	0	12	49	51	86	10	7	1	0	.375	.419	3	0	3	1563	4.07	72	105	0.69
Last Five Years	.267	565	1830	287	488	81	1	104	315	307	430	37	41	5	2	.379	.483	13	5	20	9113	4.14	433	691	0.63

1997 Season

	Avg	AB	H	2B	3B	HR	RBI	BB	SO	OBP	SLG		Avg	AB	H	2B	3B	HR	RBI	BB	SO	OBP	SLG
vs. Left	.245	94	23	5	0	5	18	20	24	.385	.457	First Pitch	.333	21	7	1	0	2	5	3	0	.440	.667
vs. Right	.265	226	60	10	0	7	31	31	62	.371	.403	Ahead in Count	.402	87	35	7	0	4	17	24	0	.535	.621
Groundball	.314	70	22	5	0	4	10	19	18	.479	.557	Behind in Count	.190	153	29	5	0	2	17	0	68	.209	.261
Flyball	.200	30	6	0	0	0	1	4	7	.368	.200	Two Strikes	.169	166	28	6	0	2	21	24	86	.292	.241
Home	.345	145	50	6	0	9	22	23	33	.454	.572	Batting #7	.259	54	14	3	0	2	5	6	17	.375	.426
Away	.189	175	33	9	0	3	27	28	53	.310	.291	Batting #8	.271	225	61	10	0	7	32	32	56	.374	.409
Day	.277	112	31	5	0	7	18	22	36	.404	.509	Other	.195	41	8	2	0	3	12	13	13	.382	.463
Night	.250	208	52	10	0	5	31	29	50	.359	.370	March/April	.309	68	21	3	0	3	8	9	15	.413	.485
Grass	.253	293	74	12	0	11	43	43	77	.363	.406	May	.269	67	18	2	0	4	15	13	13	.417	.478
Turf	.333	27	9	3	0	1	6	8	9	.486	.556	June	.268	41	11	1	0	1	7	5	20	.362	.366
Pre-All Star	.284	176	50	6	0	8	30	27	48	.403	.455	July	.152	33	5	1	0	1	5	5	10	.263	.273
Post-All Star	.229	144	33	9	0	4	19	24	38	.341	.375	August	.290	62	18	4	0	2	10	10	13	.390	.452
Scoring Posn	.333	75	25	8	0	2	37	19	16	.475	.520	Sept/Oct	.204	49	10	4	0	1	4	9	15	.328	.347
Close & Late	.255	55	14	4	0	1	8	9	19	.369	.382	vs. AL	.256	297	76	13	0	10	45	50	75	.376	.401
None on/out	.237	76	18	3	0	4	4	10	25	.341	.434	vs. NL	.304	23	7	2	0	2	4	1	11	.360	.652

1997 By Position

Position	Avg	AB	H	2B	3B	HR	RBI	BB	SO	OBP	SLG	G	GS	Innings	PO	A	E	DP	Fld Pct	Rng Fctr	In Zone	Zone Outs	Zone Rtg	MLB Zone
As c	.263	285	75	12	0	9	38	39	75	.369	.400	87	85	729.2	602	28	0	4	1.000	—	—	—	—	—

Last Five Years

	Avg	AB	H	2B	3B	HR	RBI	BB	SO	OBP	SLG		Avg	AB	H	2B	3B	HR	RBI	BB	SO	OBP	SLG
vs. Left	.293	505	148	23	1	42	109	95	102	.403	.592	First Pitch	.284	141	40	5	0	12	35	9	0	.348	.574
vs. Right	.257	1325	340	58	0	62	206	212	328	.370	.441	Ahead in Count	.385	468	180	34	0	51	123	155	0	.538	.784
Groundball	.317	404	128	23	1	27	73	68	92	.430	.579	Behind in Count	.189	797	151	25	0	21	92	0	336	.201	.300
Flyball	.208	283	59	7	0	15	40	60	67	.356	.392	Two Strikes	.185	905	167	29	1	25	111	142	430	.303	.302
Home	.280	897	251	31	0	58	161	162	201	.398	.508	Batting #7	.288	521	150	32	1	34	89	82	112	.393	.549
Away	.254	933	237	50	1	46	154	145	229	.361	.458	Batting #8	.269	516	139	19	0	24	83	79	122	.375	.446
Day	.258	480	124	21	0	28	74	100	139	.392	.477	Other	.251	793	199	30	0	46	143	146	196	.373	.463
Night	.270	1350	364	60	1	76	241	207	291	.375	.484	March/April	.252	282	71	12	0	17	38	43	74	.364	.475
Grass	.273	1602	437	66	0	93	280	271	373	.385	.488	May	.243	366	89	16	0	16	57	67	91	.371	.418
Turf	.224	228	51	15	1	11	35	36	57	.338	.443	June	.240	321	77	7	0	21	54	44	81	.341	.458
Pre-All Star	.254	1072	272	42	0	65	178	174	258	.369	.475	July	.268	287	77	13	0	18	60	47	52	.381	.502
Post-All Star	.285	758	216	39	1	39	137	133	172	.394	.493	August	.301	292	88	14	1	18	58	47	72	.395	.541
Scoring Posn	.280	436	122	21	1	21	195	102	109	.412	.477	Sept/Oct	.305	282	86	19	0	14	48	59	60	.428	.521
Close & Late	.235	285	67	12	0	13	46	49	88	.364	.414	vs. AL	.266	1807	481	79	1	102	311	306	419	.379	.480
None on/out	.274	419	115	19	0	24	24	52	102	.367	.492	vs. NL	.304	23	7	2	0	2	4	1	11	.360	.652

Batter vs. Pitcher (career)

Hits Best Against	Avg	AB	H	2B	3B	HR	RBI	BB	SO	OBP	SLG	Hits Worst Against	Avg	AB	H	2B	3B	HR	RBI	BB	SO	OBP	SLG
Bob Wickman	.500	12	6	0	0	2	3	3	3	.588	1.000	Eric Plunk	.000	7	0	0	0	0	1	3	2	.273	.000
Scott Erickson	.471	17	8	3	0	1	1	0	2	.526	.824	Pat Hentgen	.067	15	1	0	0	0	0	4	2	.263	.067
Brian Anderson	.455	11	5	0	0	2	2	2	2	.538	1.000	Jose Mesa	.077	13	1	0	0	0	2	3	7	.235	.077
Ken Hill	.385	13	5	1	0	2	2	1	4	.467	.923	David Wells	.083	12	1	0	0	0	0	1	3	.154	.083
David Cone	.333	12	4	1	0	1	2	5	4	.556	.667	Shawn Boskie	.091	11	1	0	0	0	0	0	4	.091	.091

Todd Hollandsworth — Dodgers

Age 25 – Bats Left

	Avg	G	AB	R	H	2B	3B	HR	RBI	BB	SO	HBP	GDP	SB	CS	OBP	SLG	IBB	SH	SF	#Pit	#P/PA	GB	FB	G/F
1997 Season	.247	106	296	39	73	20	2	4	31	17	60	0	8	5	5	.286	.368	2	2	2	1136	3.58	116	69	1.68
Career (1995-1997)	.269	296	877	119	236	48	6	21	103	68	182	3	11	28	12	.322	.409	5	5	5	3540	3.70	324	221	1.47

1997 Season

	Avg	AB	H	2B	3B	HR	RBI	BB	SO	OBP	SLG		Avg	AB	H	2B	3B	HR	RBI	BB	SO	OBP	SLG
vs. Left	.348	46	16	2	0	1	7	1	9	.362	.457	First Pitch	.211	38	8	3	1	0	2	1	0	.231	.342
vs. Right	.228	250	57	18	2	3	24	16	51	.272	.352	Ahead in Count	.319	47	15	6	0	2	13	11	0	.441	.574
Groundball	.400	35	14	3	1	0	6	3	6	.436	.543	Behind in Count	.232	164	38	7	0	2	9	0	51	.230	.311
Flyball	.308	39	12	3	0	1	4	3	5	.357	.462	Two Strikes	.184	147	27	4	0	0	2	5	60	.241	.211
Home	.288	153	44	13	0	1	14	7	26	.315	.392	Batting #1	.259	58	15	5	1	1	7	2	6	.283	.431
Away	.203	143	29	7	2	3	17	10	34	.255	.343	Batting #6	.219	96	21	4	0	1	6	6	14	.265	.292
Day	.239	92	22	5	1	3	16	6	17	.286	.413	Other	.261	142	37	11	1	2	18	9	40	.301	.394
Night	.250	204	51	15	1	1	15	11	43	.286	.348	March/April	.250	88	22	4	0	1	7	6	18	.295	.330
Grass	.254	248	63	18	1	3	24	12	53	.286	.371	May	.205	83	17	6	1	1	8	3	15	.233	.337
Turf	.208	48	10	2	1	1	7	5	7	.283	.354	June	.225	40	9	1	0	0	3	5	7	.311	.250

1997 Season

	Avg	AB	H	2B	3B	HR	RBI	BB	SO	OBP	SLG			Avg	AB	H	2B	3B	HR	RBI	BB	SO	OBP	SLG
Pre-All Star	.229	223	51	14	1	2	18	16	42	.279	.327		July	.321	56	18	5	1	1	6	3	13	.350	.500
Post-All Star	.301	73	22	6	1	2	13	1	18	.307	.493		August	.600	5	3	2	0	0	3	0	0	.600	1.000
Scoring Posn	.264	72	19	6	0	2	26	5	15	.304	.431		Sept/Oct	.167	24	4	2	0	1	4	0	7	.167	.375
Close & Late	.164	61	10	1	0	0	4	3	9	.200	.180		vs. AL	.167	18	3	3	0	0	0	2	4	.250	.333
None on/out	.227	75	17	6	0	0		3	14	.256	.307		vs. NL	.252	278	70	17	2	4	31	15	56	.288	.371

1997 By Position

Position	Avg	AB	H	2B	3B	HR	RBI	BB	SO	OBP	SLG	G	GS	Innings	PO	A	E	DP	Fld Pct	Rng Fctr	In Zone	Zone Outs	Zone Rtg	MLB Zone
As Pinch Hitter	.429	14	6	2	0	0	3	1	3	.467	.571	15	0	---	---	---	---	---	---	---	---	---	---	---
As lf	.240	175	42	10	1	2	12	13	38	.293	.343	80	39	439.1	132	1	2	0	.985	2.72	137	129	.942	.805
As cf	.235	98	23	7	1	1	13	3	18	.252	.357	30	25	202.2	51	1	1	0	.981	2.31	60	50	.833	.815

Career (1995-1997)

	Avg	AB	H	2B	3B	HR	RBI	BB	SO	OBP	SLG			Avg	AB	H	2B	3B	HR	RBI	BB	SO	OBP	SLG
vs. Left	.302	106	32	4	2	2	9	7	27	.345	.434		First Pitch	.295	112	33	9	2	2	13	4	0	.316	.464
vs. Right	.265	771	204	44	4	19	94	61	155	.319	.406		Ahead in Count	.347	150	52	11	0	7	30	36	0	.473	.560
Groundball	.293	184	54	7	3	3	28	17	34	.350	.413		Behind in Count	.229	455	104	19	1	10	42	0	155	.231	.341
Flyball	.268	153	41	8	1	5	16	14	26	.329	.431		Two Strikes	.190	436	83	13	2	6	32	28	182	.241	.271
Home	.285	414	118	21	1	6	39	27	80	.329	.384		Batting #1	.291	206	60	13	4	7	28	13	34	.336	.495
Away	.255	463	118	27	5	15	64	41	102	.316	.432		Batting #7	.298	178	53	12	1	7	33	24	45	.380	.494
Day	.253	265	67	13	3	9	41	23	57	.313	.426		Other	.249	493	123	23	1	7	42	31	103	.294	.343
Night	.276	612	169	35	3	12	62	45	125	.326	.402		March/April	.237	139	33	6	0	1	13	16	30	.314	.302
Grass	.275	730	201	39	5	17	84	52	154	.324	.412		May	.257	152	39	11	1	4	17	12	32	.311	.421
Turf	.238	147	35	9	1	4	19	16	28	.313	.395		June	.246	126	31	2	0	1	13	10	24	.299	.286
Pre-All Star	.254	453	115	22	2	7	47	41	97	.316	.358		July	.303	201	61	13	2	7	30	14	49	.350	.493
Post-All Star	.285	424	121	26	4	14	56	27	85	.329	.465		August	.290	124	36	8	0	4	18	9	23	.343	.452
Scoring Posn	.294	204	60	13	2	4	76	14	40	.335	.436		Sept/Oct	.267	135	36	8	3	4	12	7	24	.303	.459
Close & Late	.254	142	36	5	0	3	12	16	30	.325	.352		vs. AL	.167	18	3	3	0	0	0	2	4	.250	.333
None on/out	.218	225	49	11	0	4	4	20	52	.287	.320		vs. NL	.271	859	233	45	6	21	103	66	178	.324	.411

Batter vs. Pitcher (career)

Hits Best Against	Avg	AB	H	2B	3B	HR	RBI	BB	SO	OBP	SLG		Hits Worst Against	Avg	AB	H	2B	3B	HR	RBI	BB	SO	OBP	SLG
Shane Reynolds	.500	12	6	2	0	2	5	1	3	.538	1.167		Steve Trachsel	.091	11	1	0	0	0	0	1	1	.167	.091
Mark Leiter	.429	21	9	2	0	0	4	3	2	.500	.524		Doug Drabek	.100	10	1	0	0	0	0	1	1	.182	.100
Todd Stottlemyre	.417	12	5	0	0	1	2	2	3	.500	.667		Curt Schilling	.150	20	3	1	0	0	2	2	10	.227	.200
Mike Williams	.417	12	5	0	0	1	2	1	2	.462	.667		Andy Ashby	.182	11	2	0	0	0	0	0	0	.182	.182
John Smoltz	.400	10	4	0	0	0	2	1	3	.500	.400		Pat Rapp	.231	13	3	0	0	0	0	0	4	.231	.231

Dave Hollins — Angels   Age 32 – Bats Both

	Avg	G	AB	R	H	2B	3B	HR	RBI	BB	SO	HBP	GDP	SB	CS	OBP	SLG	IBB	SH	SF	#Pit	#P/PA	GB	FB	G/F
1997 Season	.288	149	572	101	165	29	2	16	85	62	124	8	12	16	6	.363	.430	2	1	5	2411	3.72	213	135	1.58
Last Five Years	.265	555	2011	369	533	107	9	61	308	311	427	35	48	26	16	.370	.418	18	2	21	9275	3.90	722	530	1.36

1997 Season

	Avg	AB	H	2B	3B	HR	RBI	BB	SO	OBP	SLG			Avg	AB	H	2B	3B	HR	RBI	BB	SO	OBP	SLG
vs. Left	.326	175	57	11	0	8	29	17	50	.382	.526		First Pitch	.352	105	37	6	1	2	23	1	0	.370	.524
vs. Right	.272	397	108	18	2	8	56	45	74	.351	.388		Ahead in Count	.385	96	37	5	0	4	12	30	0	.528	.563
Groundball	.250	104	26	2	1	2	16	7	23	.307	.346		Behind in Count	.231	273	63	12	1	5	29	0	106	.245	.337
Flyball	.352	88	31	9	0	5	14	5	19	.394	.625		Two Strikes	.193	270	52	8	1	6	30	31	124	.284	.296
Home	.317	290	92	15	1	15	60	28	55	.382	.531		Batting #3	.277	408	113	20	2	12	62	46	93	.356	.427
Away	.259	282	73	14	1	1	25	34	69	.345	.326		Batting #5	.352	71	25	2	0	2	11	10	12	.439	.465
Day	.221	136	30	5	0	2	7	13	25	.301	.301		Other	.290	93	27	0	0	2	12	6	19	.333	.430
Night	.310	436	135	24	2	14	78	49	99	.383	.470		March/April	.326	89	29	4	0	1	11	9	17	.400	.404
Grass	.297	519	154	27	2	16	80	52	108	.368	.449		May	.287	94	27	3	1	6	20	13	15	.373	.532
Turf	.208	53	11	2	0	0	5	10	16	.318	.245		June	.267	101	27	5	0	3	12	10	30	.342	.406
Pre-All Star	.292	301	88	12	1	11	48	36	65	.374	.449		July	.280	93	26	4	0	1	13	15	18	.391	.355
Post-All Star	.284	271	77	17	1	5	37	26	59	.349	.410		August	.272	103	28	10	1	2	18	6	29	.318	.447
Scoring Posn	.255	161	41	10	1	5	70	30	30	.369	.422		Sept/Oct	.304	92	28	3	0	3	11	9	15	.359	.435
Close & Late	.293	99	29	9	1	2	15	13	18	.377	.465		vs. AL	.291	516	150	27	2	15	81	55	111	.364	.438
None on/out	.280	100	28	0	0	1		1	25	.327	.310		vs. NL	.268	56	15	2	0	1	4	7	13	.359	.357

1997 By Position

Position	Avg	AB	H	2B	3B	HR	RBI	BB	SO	OBP	SLG	G	GS	Innings	PO	A	E	DP	Fld Pct	Rng Fctr	In Zone	Zone Outs	Zone Rtg	MLB Zone
As 1b	.357	56	20	1	0	3	8	5	5	.410	.536	14	14	122.0	107	8	0	10	1.000	---	24	21	.875	.874
As 3b	.282	514	145	28	2	13	77	57	118	.360	.420	135	131	1148.1	100	241	29	19	.922	2.67	374	277	.741	.801

Last Five Years

	Avg	AB	H	2B	3B	HR	RBI	BB	SO	OBP	SLG			Avg	AB	H	2B	3B	HR	RBI	BB	SO	OBP	SLG
vs. Left	.305	629	192	40	5	25	96	76	132	.390	.504		First Pitch	.392	296	116	22	2	9	72	16	0	.428	.571
vs. Right	.247	1382	341	67	4	36	212	235	295	.361	.379		Ahead in Count	.336	438	147	25	2	25	92	158	0	.509	.573
Groundball	.247	511	126	25	3	14	79	64	116	.307	.389		Behind in Count	.188	874	164	30	4	14	80	0	340	.209	.279
Flyball	.276	315	87	22	4	12	47	44	68	.370	.473		Two Strikes	.171	939	161	31	3	16	135	137	427	.241	.256
Home	.272	998	271	54	2	37	160	150	202	.373	.441		Batting #3	.271	446	121	21	2	13	67	48	100	.349	.415
Away	.259	1013	262	53	7	24	148	161	225	.367	.396		Batting #4	.256	895	229	46	6	27	142	156	186	.369	.411
Day	.264	557	147	36	1	16	84	89	110	.372	.418		Other	.273	670	183	40	1	21	99	107	141	.358	.430
Night	.265	1454	386	71	8	45	224	222	317	.369	.418		March/April	.289	356	103	20	1	14	71	55	73	.392	.469
Grass	.282	1047	295	55	4	32	175	138	213	.372	.434		May	.249	454	113	24	3	16	68	85	87	.371	.421

Last Five Years

	Avg	AB	H	2B	3B	HR	RBI	BB	SO	OBP	SLG		Avg	AB	H	2B	3B	HR	RBI	BB	SO	OBP	SLG
Turf	.247	964	238	52	5	29	133	173	214	.367	.401	June	.236	263	62	10	0	7	32	45	67	.354	.354
Pre-All Star	.257	1194	307	60	4	39	185	203	253	.372	.412	July	.242	356	86	16	3	7	42	51	75	.348	.362
Post-All Star	.277	817	226	47	5	22	123	108	174	.366	.427	August	.278	295	82	27	1	8	42	36	75	.366	.458
Scoring Posn	.252	600	151	37	2	16	232	119	139	.376	.400	Sept/Oct	.303	287	87	10	1	9	53	39	50	.385	.439
Close & Late	.252	322	81	15	2	11	56	45	74	.345	.413	vs. AL	.275	1045	287	56	2	31	160	143	235	.370	.421
None on/out	.249	453	113	12	1	7	7	67	105	.356	.327	vs. NL	.255	966	246	51	7	30	148	168	192	.369	.415

Batter vs. Pitcher (career)

Hits Best Against	Avg	AB	H	2B	3B	HR	RBI	BB	SO	OBP	SLG	Hits Worst Against	Avg	AB	H	2B	3B	HR	RBI	BB	SO	OBP	SLG
Butch Henry	.652	23	15	3	0	6	11	2	5	.667	1.565	Randy Johnson	.083	12	1	0	0	0	1	1	3	.154	.083
Danny Jackson	.500	10	5	3	0	1	4	3	1	.600	1.100	Kevin Gross	.091	11	1	0	0	0	3	1	3	.167	.091
Kenny Rogers	.455	11	5	0	0	2	3	4	1	.600	1.000	Mel Rojas	.091	11	1	0	0	0	1	1	3	.167	.091
Mike Stanton	.357	14	5	3	0	1	1	2	2	.438	.786	Bobby Witt	.100	10	1	0	0	0	0	1	1	.182	.100
Kent Mercker	.333	6	2	2	0	0	3	5	1	.636	.667	Mike Maddux	.100	10	1	0	0	0	0	1	6	.182	.100

Darren Holmes — Rockies
Age 32 – Pitches Right (groundball pitcher)

	ERA	W	L	Sv	G	GS	IP	BB	SO	Avg	H	2B	3B	HR	RBI	OBP	SLG	GF	IR	IRS	Hld	SvOp	SB	CS	GB	FB	G/F
1997 Season	5.34	9	2	3	42	6	89.1	36	70	.314	113	25	2	12	56	.373	.494	10	11	6	5	4	5	3	136	82	1.66
Last Five Years	4.42	23	13	46	263	6	328.0	136	297	.268	341	66	11	34	187	.339	.417	129	105	42	30	67	25	14	483	308	1.57

1997 Season

	ERA	W	L	Sv	G	GS	IP	H	HR	BB	SO		Avg	AB	H	2B	3B	HR	RBI	BB	SO	OBP	SLG
Home	5.03	5	1	2	21	3	48.1	59	10	13	32	vs. Left	.339	180	61	15	2	3	27	20	36	.403	.494
Away	5.71	4	1	1	21	3	41.0	54	2	23	38	vs. Right	.289	180	52	10	0	9	29	16	34	.342	.494
Starter	6.25	2	0	0	6	6	31.2	39	5	11	30	Scoring Posn	.264	106	28	9	1	2	41	17	25	.354	.425
Reliever	4.84	7	2	3	36	0	57.2	74	7	25	40	Close & Late	.372	78	29	4	1	3	18	7	8	.419	.564
0 Days rest (Relief)	8.44	0	1	0	4	0	5.1	9	1	3	4	None on/out	.360	89	32	4	0	4	4	7	14	.406	.539
1 or 2 Days rest	7.25	3	1	0	15	0	22.1	33	6	8	18	First Pitch	.346	52	18	6	1	4	15	3	0	.382	.731
3+ Days rest	2.40	4	0	3	17	0	30.0	32	0	14	18	Ahead in Count	.278	180	50	8	0	5	23	0	61	.272	.406
Pre-All Star	4.08	3	1	1	21	5	57.1	65	5	21	46	Behind in Count	.388	67	26	7	0	1	7	17	0	.512	.537
Post-All Star	7.59	6	1	2	21	1	32.0	48	7	15	24	Two Strikes	.215	149	32	6	0	2	13	16	70	.287	.295

Last Five Years

	ERA	W	L	Sv	G	GS	IP	H	HR	BB	SO		Avg	AB	H	2B	3B	HR	RBI	BB	SO	OBP	SLG
Home	4.74	16	7	24	139	3	178.2	200	22	59	164	vs. Left	.268	590	158	31	8	11	85	72	114	.350	.403
Away	4.04	7	6	22	124	3	149.1	141	12	77	133	vs. Right	.268	683	183	35	3	23	102	64	183	.328	.429
Day	4.60	5	5	19	99	2	123.1	138	15	53	107	Inning 1-6	.304	270	82	22	2	10	51	25	61	.365	.511
Night	4.31	18	8	27	164	4	204.2	203	19	83	190	Inning 7+	.258	1003	259	44	9	24	136	111	236	.332	.392
Grass	4.46	21	10	35	212	5	266.2	278	28	103	234	None on	.262	676	177	30	5	18	54	58	158	.320	.401
Turf	4.26	2	3	11	51	1	61.1	63	6	33	63	Runners on	.275	597	164	36	6	16	169	82	139	.358	.436
March/April	6.00	1	4	5	37	1	48.0	57	3	34	47	Scoring Posn	.268	373	100	26	4	8	148	63	96	.366	.424
May	4.37	5	2	5	44	0	47.1	52	6	18	40	Close & Late	.279	524	146	24	4	14	87	66	113	.358	.424
June	5.29	4	4	3	44	3	63.0	73	9	21	58	None on/out	.295	295	87	11	3	7	7	27	65	.358	.424
July	4.30	2	1	17	50	2	67.0	70	9	25	60	vs. 1st Batr (relief)	.311	228	71	12	3	4	17	25	42	.387	.443
August	2.72	3	1	10	42	0	49.2	47	2	23	46	1st Inning Pitched	.274	915	251	46	10	27	155	105	206	.350	.435
Sept/Oct	3.74	8	1	6	46	0	53.0	42	5	15	46	First 15 Pitches	.286	751	215	36	7	23	105	71	150	.349	.445
Starter	6.25	2	0	0	6	6	31.2	39	5	11	30	Pitch 16-30	.234	351	82	17	4	7	61	46	104	.323	.365
Reliever	4.22	21	13	46	257	0	296.1	302	29	125	267	Pitch 31-45	.236	89	21	6	0	1	8	7	24	.286	.337
0 Days rest (Relief)	5.02	1	2	13	52	0	52.0	66	3	23	68	Pitch 46+	.280	82	23	7	0	3	13	12	19	.372	.476
1 or 2 Days rest	4.29	13	7	20	136	0	159.1	147	21	62	158	First Pitch	.326	144	47	10	2	6	26	12	0	.380	.549
3+ Days rest	3.60	7	4	13	69	0	85.0	89	5	40	61	Ahead in Count	.225	662	149	25	4	10	73	0	249	.226	.320
vs. AL	9.00	1	0	0	5	2	13.0	22	2	6	6	Behind in Count	.333	240	80	18	1	10	48	58	0	.463	.542
vs. NL	4.23	22	13	46	258	4	315.0	319	32	130	291	Two Strikes	.197	630	124	22	3	6	61	66	297	.272	.270
Pre-All Star	4.88	10	10	19	143	5	182.2	200	20	85	167	Pre-All Star	.279	718	200	41	8	20	118	85	167	.354	.442
Post-All Star	3.84	13	3	27	120	1	145.1	141	14	69	51	Post-All Star	.254	555	141	25	3	14	69	130	.318	.386

Pitcher vs. Batter (career)

Pitches Best Vs.	Avg	AB	H	2B	3B	HR	RBI	BB	SO	OBP	SLG	Pitches Worst Vs.	Avg	AB	H	2B	3B	HR	RBI	BB	SO	OBP	SLG
Eric Karros	.000	8	0	0	0	0	0	3	5	.273	.000	Mike Lansing	.545	11	6	1	0	1	4	2	1	.615	.909
Greg Gagne	.083	12	1	0	0	1	1	0	7	.083	.333	Ray Lankford	.455	11	5	1	0	1	2	2	1	.538	.818
Glenallen Hill	.100	10	1	0	0	0	1	1	4	.167	.100	Sammy Sosa	.417	12	5	1	0	2	6	0	3	.417	1.000
Jim Eisenreich	.182	11	2	0	0	0	2	1	3	.250	.182	Gary Sheffield	.400	10	4	3	0	0	0	4	3	.571	.700
Gregg Jefferies	.231	13	3	0	0	0	1	0	.231	.231	Mike Piazza	.385	13	5	1	0	2	7	0	3	.385	.923

Chris Holt — Astros
Age 26 – Pitches Right (groundball pitcher)

	ERA	W	L	Sv	G	GS	IP	BB	SO	Avg	H	2B	3B	HR	RBI	OBP	SLG	CG	ShO	Sup	QS	#P/S	SB	CS	GB	FB	G/F
1997 Season	3.52	8	12	0	33	32	209.2	61	95	.263	211	40	3	17	82	.320	.384	0	0	4.25	22	96	13	12	391	186	2.10
Career (1996-1997)	3.57	8	13	0	37	32	214.1	64	95	.263	216	41	3	17	86	.321	.382	0	0	4.37	22	96	13	13	406	188	2.16

1997 Season

	ERA	W	L	Sv	G	GS	IP	H	HR	BB	SO		Avg	AB	H	2B	3B	HR	RBI	BB	SO	OBP	SLG
Home	3.52	3	8	0	17	16	107.1	103	6	28	63	vs. Left	.302	391	118	27	2	12	55	38	32	.366	.473
Away	3.52	5	4	0	16	16	102.1	108	11	33	32	vs. Right	.226	411	93	13	1	5	27	23	63	.273	.299
Day	3.47	2	3	0	10	9	59.2	59	4	25	30	Inning 1-6	.256	706	181	34	3	15	75	52	89	.312	.377
Night	3.54	6	9	0	23	23	150.0	152	13	36	65	Inning 7+	.313	96	30	6	0	2	7	9	6	.377	.438
Grass	3.62	3	2	0	11	11	69.2	71	8	25	19	None on	.242	472	114	19	1	12	12	39	51	.302	.362
Turf	3.47	5	10	0	22	21	140.0	140	9	36	76	Runners on	.294	330	97	21	2	5	70	22	44	.344	.415

1997 Season

	ERA	W	L	Sv	G	GS	IP	H	HR	BB	SO		Avg	AB	H	2B	3B	HR	RBI	BB	SO	OBP	SLG
March/April	3.63	2	2	0	5	5	34.2	35	3	5	18	Scoring Posn	.303	185	56	14	1	2	60	18	28	.359	.422
May	4.66	3	2	0	7	7	38.2	53	2	16	18	Close & Late	.333	57	19	3	0	1	5	7	3	.415	.439
June	3.82	2	1	0	5	5	33.0	32	4	13	15	None on/out	.241	203	49	5	0	5	5	22	15	.319	.340
July	3.03	0	2	0	5	5	32.2	34	0	10	15	vs. 1st Batr (relief)	.000	1	0	0	0	0	0	0	1	.000	.000
August	2.31	1	2	0	5	5	35.0	24	5	6	10	1st Inning Pitched	.304	125	38	5	0	3	15	9	22	.356	.416
Sept/Oct	3.53	0	3	0	6	5	35.2	33	3	11	19	First 75 Pitches	.258	620	160	28	3	14	64	48	76	.317	.381
Starter	3.54	8	12	0	32	32	208.2	211	17	61	92	Pitch 76-90	.268	112	30	9	0	1	12	5	13	.297	.375
Reliever	0.00	0	0	0	1	0	1.0	0	0	0	0	Pitch 91-105	.241	54	13	1	0	2	5	5	5	.317	.370
0-3 Days Rest (Start)	3.00	1	0	0	2	2	12.0	13	0	2	7	Pitch 106+	.500	16	8	2	0	0	1	3	1	.579	.625
4 Days Rest	4.43	3	9	0	17	17	107.2	121	11	33	49	First Pitch	.336	140	47	8	2	2	16	1	0	.352	.464
5+ Days Rest	2.53	4	3	0	13	13	89.0	77	6	26	36	Ahead in Count	.190	336	64	13	0	6	25	0	84	.202	.283
vs. AL	4.79	0	1	0	3	3	20.2	25	1	10	10	Behind in Count	.310	187	58	13	0	8	29	36	0	.416	.508
vs. NL	3.38	8	11	0	30	29	189.0	186	16	51	85	Two Strikes	.185	324	60	11	1	6	28	24	95	.250	.281
Pre-All Star	4.30	7	5	0	18	18	113.0	131	9	36	56	Pre-All Star	.290	451	131	29	2	9	52	36	56	.349	.424
Post-All Star	2.61	1	7	0	15	14	96.2	80	8	25	39	Post-All Star	.228	351	80	11	1	8	30	25	39	.282	.333

Mike Holtz — Angels   Age 25 – Pitches Left (groundball pitcher)

	ERA	W	L	Sv	G	GS	IP	BB	SO	Avg	H	2B	3B	HR	RBI	OBP	SLG	GF	IR	IRS	Hld	SvOp	SB	CS	GB	FB	G/F
1997 Season	3.32	3	4	2	66	0	43.1	15	40	.228	38	10	0	7	26	.296	.413	11	56	12	14	8	6	2	67	34	1.97
Career (1996-1997)	2.97	6	7	2	96	0	72.2	34	71	.219	59	15	0	8	36	.314	.363	19	85	18	19	8	8	3	97	60	1.62

1997 Season

	ERA	W	L	Sv	G	GS	IP	H	HR	BB	SO		Avg	AB	H	2B	3B	HR	RBI	BB	SO	OBP	SLG
Home	3.32	1	2	1	32	0	21.2	20	3	9	19	vs. Left	.198	91	18	5	0	2	10	7	26	.260	.319
Away	3.32	2	2	1	34	0	21.2	18	4	6	21	vs. Right	.263	76	20	5	0	5	16	8	14	.337	.526
Day	0.90	0	1	0	17	0	10.0	6	1	1	8	Inning 1-6	.000	0	0	0	0	0	0	0	0	.000	.000
Night	4.05	3	3	2	49	0	33.1	32	6	14	32	Inning 7+	.228	167	38	10	0	7	26	15	40	.296	.413
Grass	3.32	3	4	2	59	0	40.2	34	7	15	37	None on	.230	87	20	3	0	4	4	5	17	.280	.402
Turf	3.38	0	0	0	7	0	2.2	4	0	0	3	Runners on	.225	80	18	7	0	3	22	10	23	.312	.425
March/April	0.96	2	0	0	11	0	9.1	4	0	4	11	Scoring Posn	.209	43	9	3	0	2	18	9	12	.345	.419
May	1.80	0	1	0	11	0	5.0	4	1	2	2	Close & Late	.223	103	23	6	0	4	19	9	26	.283	.398
June	1.29	0	2	0	12	0	7.0	6	1	2	5	None on/out	.205	44	9	0	0	3	3	2	8	.255	.409
July	3.38	1	1	0	10	0	8.0	8	2	1	7	vs. 1st Batr (relief)	.250	60	15	3	0	2	10	4	12	.303	.400
August	0.96	0	1	0	12	0	9.1	5	1	3	10	1st Inning Pitched	.229	144	33	8	0	6	24	14	32	.302	.410
Sept/Oct	17.36	0	1	0	4	0	4.2	11	2	3	5	First 15 Pitches	.237	131	31	7	0	5	19	12	26	.308	.405
Starter	0.00	0	0	0	0	0	0.0	0	0	0	0	Pitch 16-30	.206	34	7	3	0	2	7	2	13	.243	.471
Reliever	3.32	3	4	2	66	0	43.1	38	7	15	40	Pitch 31-45	.000	2	0	0	0	0	0	1	1	.333	.000
0 Days rest (Relief)	4.35	0	1	1	20	0	10.1	14	5	2	11	Pitch 46+	.000	0	0	0	0	0	0	0	0	.000	.000
1 or 2 Days rest	3.26	2	3	1	28	0	19.1	16	1	11	16	First Pitch	.333	18	6	1	0	1	2	3	0	.455	.556
3+ Days rest	2.63	1	0	0	18	0	13.2	8	1	2	13	Ahead in Count	.194	67	13	3	0	3	10	0	30	.194	.373
vs. AL	3.58	3	3	2	59	0	37.2	35	6	15	36	Behind in Count	.270	37	10	3	0	3	10	12	0	.440	.595
vs. NL	1.59	0	1	0	7	0	5.2	3	1	0	4	Two Strikes	.171	82	14	5	0	2	9	9	40	.171	.305
Pre-All Star	1.23	2	2	1	35	0	22.0	14	2	8	18	Pre-All Star	.179	78	14	4	0	2	6	8	18	.264	.308
Post-All Star	5.48	1	2	1	31	0	21.1	24	5	7	22	Post-All Star	.270	89	24	6	0	5	20	7	22	.323	.506

Mark Holzemer — Mariners   Age 28 – Pitches Left (groundball pitcher)

	ERA	W	L	Sv	G	GS	IP	BB	SO	Avg	H	2B	3B	HR	RBI	OBP	SLG	GF	IR	IRS	Hld	SvOp	SB	CS	GB	FB	G/F
1997 Season	6.00	0	0	1	14	0	9.0	8	7	.250	2	0	0	4	.386	.306	2	15	3	1	1	0	0	16	6	2.67	
Career (1993-1997)	7.99	1	4	1	56	4	65.1	36	42	.319	89	17	1	10	62	.409	.495	11	51	14	2	1	4	2	105	62	1.69

1997 Season

	ERA	W	L	Sv	G	GS	IP	H	HR	BB	SO		Avg	AB	H	2B	3B	HR	RBI	BB	SO	OBP	SLG
Home	3.38	0	0	0	4	0	2.2	2	0	1	2	vs. Left	.217	23	5	1	0	0	3	4	4	.333	.261
Away	7.11	0	0	1	10	0	6.1	7	0	7	5	vs. Right	.308	13	4	1	0	0	1	4	3	.471	.385

Rick Honeycutt — Cardinals   Age 44 – Pitches Left (groundball pitcher)

	ERA	W	L	Sv	G	GS	IP	BB	SO	Avg	H	2B	3B	HR	RBI	OBP	SLG	GF	IR	IRS	Hld	SvOp	SB	CS	GB	FB	G/F
1997 Season	13.50	0	0	0	2	0	2.0	1	2	.500	5	0	0	0	2	.545	.500	2	0	0	0	0	0	0	5	0	0.00
Last Five Years	3.67	9	8	8	209	0	161.2	47	92	.256	153	22	1	15	85	.311	.371	37	156	46	62	17	8	5	252	165	1.53

1997 Season

	ERA	W	L	Sv	G	GS	IP	H	HR	BB	SO		Avg	AB	H	2B	3B	HR	RBI	BB	SO	OBP	SLG
Home	9.00	0	0	0	1	0	1.0	3	0	0	0	vs. Left	.000	1	0	0	0	0	0	0	0	.000	.000
Away	18.00	0	0	0	1	0	1.0	2	0	1	2	vs. Right	.556	9	5	0	0	0	2	1	2	.600	.556

Last Five Years

	ERA	W	L	Sv	G	GS	IP	H	HR	BB	SO		Avg	AB	H	2B	3B	HR	RBI	BB	SO	OBP	SLG
Home	3.38	7	4	4	103	0	80.0	73	8	18	49	vs. Left	.256	258	66	12	1	5	37	14	41	.292	.368
Away	3.97	2	4	4	106	0	81.2	80	7	29	43	vs. Right	.256	340	87	10	0	10	48	33	51	.324	.374
Day	3.80	4	3	2	79	0	68.2	64	8	18	34	Inning 1-6	.410	61	25	3	0	2	21	5	9	.448	.557
Night	3.58	5	5	6	130	0	93.0	89	7	29	58	Inning 7+	.238	537	128	19	1	13	64	42	83	.295	.350
Grass	3.60	8	7	8	181	0	142.1	132	12	38	83	None on	.229	319	73	12	1	6	6	19	46	.281	.329
Turf	4.19	1	1	0	28	0	19.1	21	3	9	9	Runners on	.287	279	80	10	0	9	79	28	46	.343	.419
March/April	5.26	0	2	2	32	0	25.2	22	3	7	15	Scoring Posn	.331	163	54	6	0	6	72	20	25	.387	.479
May	4.86	1	2	2	45	0	37.0	42	1	15	21	Close & Late	.236	301	71	8	1	5	38	32	49	.311	.319

Last Five Years

	ERA	W	L	Sv	G	GS	IP	H	HR	BB	SO		Avg	AB	H	2B	3B	HR	RBI	BB	SO	OBP	SLG
June	2.59	4	1	1	34	0	24.1	24	2	5	20	None on/out	.219	137	30	4	1	2	2	4	20	.246	.307
July	3.22	2	0	1	29	0	22.1	24	5	7	13	vs. 1st Batr (relief)	.264	193	51	5	1	8	33	7	32	.289	.425
August	2.96	1	3	1	39	0	27.1	25	1	8	15	1st Inning Pitched	.259	522	135	17	1	13	80	40	82	.309	.370
Sept/Oct	2.52	1	0	1	30	0	25.0	16	3	5	8	First 15 Pitches	.261	479	125	17	1	13	71	35	72	.311	.382
Starter	0.00	0	0	0	0	0	0.0	0	0	0	0	Pitch 16-30	.243	111	27	5	0	2	13	12	19	.320	.342
Reliever	3.67	9	8	8	209	0	161.2	153	15	47	92	Pitch 31-45	.125	8	1	0	0	0	1	0	1	.125	.125
0 Days rest (Relief)	4.21	1	3	3	52	0	36.1	35	2	13	18	Pitch 46+	.000	0	0	0	0	0	0	0	0	.000	.000
1 or 2 Days rest	2.71	5	3	4	95	0	76.1	67	9	16	49	First Pitch	.214	70	15	3	0	0	11	8	0	.291	.257
3+ Days rest	4.78	3	2	1	62	0	49.0	51	4	18	25	Ahead in Count	.225	302	68	6	1	4	28	0	82	.231	.291
vs. AL	3.85	7	7	4	146	0	112.1	106	12	39	60	Behind in Count	.330	115	38	7	0	6	24	18	0	.418	.548
vs. NL	3.28	2	1	4	63	0	49.1	47	3	8	32	Two Strikes	.214	295	63	8	0	6	25	19	92	.266	.302
Pre-All Star	4.24	7	5	5	116	0	91.1	91	7	27	58	Pre-All Star	.264	345	91	16	0	7	52	27	58	.321	.371
Post-All Star	2.94	2	3	3	93	0	70.1	62	8	20	34	Post-All Star	.245	253	62	6	1	8	33	20	34	.296	.372

Pitcher vs. Batter (since 1984)

Pitches Best Vs.	Avg	AB	H	2B	3B	HR	RBI	BB	SO	OBP	SLG	Pitches Worst Vs.	Avg	AB	H	2B	3B	HR	RBI	BB	SO	OBP	SLG
Bip Roberts	.000	11	0	0	0	0	0	1	2	.083	.000	Kevin Mitchell	.538	13	7	2	0	2	3	0	0	.538	1.154
Barry Bonds	.083	12	1	1	0	0	1	1	2	.143	.167	Wade Boggs	.500	14	7	0	0	0	3	2	1	.529	.500
Brady Anderson	.118	17	2	0	0	0	0	6	6	.167	.118	Chili Davis	.367	30	11	1	0	4	8	1	1	.387	.800
Tony Fernandez	.154	13	2	0	0	0	0	0	5	.154	.154	Tony Pena	.364	11	4	1	0	0	3	1	0	.417	.455
Carlos Baerga	.182	11	2	0	0	0	1	0	3	.167	.182	Ryne Sandberg	.333	30	10	2	0	1	2	2	3	.375	.500

Tyler Houston — Cubs

Age 27 – Bats Left

	Avg	G	AB	R	H	2B	3B	HR	RBI	BB	SO	HBP	GDP	SB	CS	OBP	SLG	IBB	SH	SF	#Pit	#P/PA	GB	FB	G/F
1997 Season	.260	72	196	15	51	10	0	2	28	9	35	0	4	1	0	.290	.342	1	0	2	692	3.34	80	41	1.95
Career (1996-1997)	.284	151	338	36	96	19	1	5	55	18	62	0	9	4	0	.318	.391	2	0	3	1166	3.26	132	72	1.83

1997 Season

	Avg	AB	H	2B	3B	HR	RBI	BB	SO	OBP	SLG		Avg	AB	H	2B	3B	HR	RBI	BB	SO	OBP	SLG
vs. Left	.154	13	2	1	0	0	2	0	4	.154	.231	Scoring Posn	.362	47	17	6	0	0	25	3	9	.385	.489
vs. Right	.268	183	49	9	0	2	26	9	31	.299	.350	Close & Late	.194	36	7	2	0	1	5	1	7	.216	.333
Home	.250	96	24	6	0	0	15	5	20	.282	.313	None on/out	.261	46	12	2	0	1	1	1	10	.277	.370
Away	.270	100	27	4	0	2	13	4	15	.298	.370	Batting #5	.212	52	11	3	0	0	8	2	10	.236	.269
First Pitch	.298	47	14	4	0	2	7	1	0	.313	.511	Batting #7	.362	47	17	1	0	2	9	1	8	.367	.511
Ahead in Count	.385	39	15	2	0	0	11	2	0	.415	.436	Other	.237	97	23	6	0	0	11	6	17	.282	.299
Behind in Count	.169	83	14	1	0	0	8	0	30	.165	.181	Pre-All Star	.222	90	20	6	0	1	16	2	14	.234	.322
Two Strikes	.188	85	16	2	0	0	7	6	35	.239	.212	Post-All Star	.292	106	31	4	0	1	12	7	21	.336	.358

David Howard — Royals

Age 31 – Bats Both

	Avg	G	AB	R	H	2B	3B	HR	RBI	BB	SO	HBP	GDP	SB	CS	OBP	SLG	IBB	SH	SF	#Pit	#P/PA	GB	FB	G/F
1997 Season	.241	80	162	24	39	8	1	1	13	10	31	1	1	2	2	.287	.321	1	3	1	636	3.59	42	47	0.89
Last Five Years	.233	379	944	112	220	39	11	6	95	87	174	6	16	17	11	.299	.317	2	31	10	3811	3.54	282	275	1.03

1997 Season

	Avg	AB	H	2B	3B	HR	RBI	BB	SO	OBP	SLG		Avg	AB	H	2B	3B	HR	RBI	BB	SO	OBP	SLG
vs. Left	.235	51	12	2	1	0	3	3	8	.278	.314	Scoring Posn	.237	38	9	1	0	1	13	3	7	.286	.342
vs. Right	.243	111	27	6	0	1	10	7	23	.292	.324	Close & Late	.273	33	9	1	0	0	1	2	9	.314	.303
Home	.196	92	18	1	0	0	6	6	19	.250	.207	None on/out	.295	44	13	2	1	0	2	2	8	.326	.386
Away	.300	70	21	7	1	1	7	4	12	.338	.471	Batting #8	.292	48	14	3	0	1	8	3	10	.333	.417
First Pitch	.259	27	7	1	0	0	2	1	0	.286	.296	Batting #9	.173	75	13	2	0	0	4	6	14	.241	.200
Ahead in Count	.308	39	12	2	0	1	4	3	0	.349	.436	Other	.308	39	12	3	1	0	1	1	7	.325	.436
Behind in Count	.183	71	13	2	1	0	4	0	28	.194	.239	Pre-All Star	.279	104	29	6	1	1	12	6	20	.321	.385
Two Strikes	.188	69	13	4	0	0	6	6	31	.263	.246	Post-All Star	.172	58	10	2	0	0	1	4	11	.226	.207

Last Five Years

	Avg	AB	H	2B	3B	HR	RBI	BB	SO	OBP	SLG		Avg	AB	H	2B	3B	HR	RBI	BB	SO	OBP	SLG
vs. Left	.223	323	72	13	3	3	31	30	55	.288	.310	First Pitch	.224	183	41	8	3	1	18	2	0	.231	.317
vs. Right	.238	621	148	26	8	3	64	57	119	.305	.320	Ahead in Count	.323	195	63	12	4	4	32	46	0	.448	.487
Groundball	.239	201	48	11	1	1	16	17	35	.306	.318	Behind in Count	.189	408	77	9	4	1	27	0	149	.195	.238
Flyball	.199	161	32	6	0	1	14	15	38	.264	.255	Two Strikes	.170	407	69	10	3	1	30	39	174	.245	.216
Home	.250	503	126	19	8	3	54	49	87	.317	.338	Batting #8	.224	255	57	14	2	1	21	21	47	.281	.306
Away	.213	441	94	20	3	3	41	38	87	.277	.293	Batting #9	.231	527	122	17	6	4	58	48	103	.296	.309
Day	.224	263	59	9	1	1	18	29	51	.306	.278	Other	.253	162	41	8	3	1	16	18	24	.335	.358
Night	.236	681	161	30	10	5	77	58	123	.296	.332	March/April	.275	138	38	6	3	3	19	15	26	.348	.428
Grass	.234	743	174	27	10	4	67	63	129	.297	.314	May	.194	165	32	5	1	0	13	10	36	.239	.236
Turf	.229	201	46	12	1	2	28	24	45	.304	.328	June	.245	147	36	5	2	0	12	10	23	.294	.306
Pre-All Star	.239	539	129	20	6	4	53	45	99	.298	.321	July	.250	248	62	13	2	2	21	21	37	.309	.343
Post-All Star	.225	405	91	19	5	2	42	42	75	.300	.311	August	.237	152	36	7	3	1	23	15	29	.308	.342
Scoring Posn	.224	245	55	11	3	3	87	32	53	.306	.331	Sept/Oct	.170	94	16	3	0	0	7	16	23	.296	.202
Close & Late	.229	170	39	6	1	0	12	17	47	.305	.276	vs. AL	.230	916	211	36	11	6	94	85	169	.297	.313
None on/out	.214	248	53	10	3	0	0	18	43	.270	.278	vs. NL	.321	28	9	3	0	0	1	2	5	.367	.429

Batter vs. Pitcher (career)

Hits Best Against	Avg	AB	H	2B	3B	HR	RBI	BB	SO	OBP	SLG	Hits Worst Against	Avg	AB	H	2B	3B	HR	RBI	BB	SO	OBP	SLG
Brad Radke	.364	11	4	2	0	0	0	1	0	.417	.545	Jose Mesa	.000	9	0	0	0	0	0	3	4	.250	.000
Jack McDowell	.357	14	5	0	1	0	1	3	2	.471	.500	Randy Johnson	.077	26	2	1	0	0	1	1	8	.111	.115
												Wilson Alvarez	.150	20	3	1	0	0	1	1	4	.190	.200

Batter vs. Pitcher (career)																						
Hits Best Against	Avg	AB	H	2B	3B	HR	RBI	BB	SO	OBP	SLG	Hits Worst Against	Avg	AB	H	2B	3B	HR	RBI	BB	SO	OBP	SLG
												David Wells	.167	12	2	1	0	0	0	0	0	.167	.250
												Chuck Finley	.167	12	2	0	0	0	1	6	.231	.167

Thomas Howard — Astros
Age 33 – Bats Left (groundball hitter)

	Avg	G	AB	R	H	2B	3B	HR	RBI	BB	SO	HBP	GDP	SB	CS	OBP	SLG	IBB	SH	SF	#Pit	#P/PA	GB	FB	G/F
1997 Season	.247	107	255	24	63	16	1	3	22	26	48	3	3	1	2	.323	.353	1	1	1	1030	3.60	112	61	1.84
Last Five Years	.268	536	1393	188	374	76	16	24	150	97	229	7	22	38	24	.317	.398	5	7	12	5354	3.53	559	369	1.51

1997 Season

	Avg	AB	H	2B	3B	HR	RBI	BB	SO	OBP	SLG		Avg	AB	H	2B	3B	HR	RBI	BB	SO	OBP	SLG
vs. Left	.333	18	6	0	1	0	1	1	4	.400	.444	Scoring Posn	.156	64	10	2	0	0	13	13	16	.295	.188
vs. Right	.241	237	57	16	0	3	21	25	44	.317	.346	Close & Late	.298	57	17	5	0	0	4	8	13	.397	.386
Home	.192	120	23	8	0	0	7	11	25	.274	.258	None on/out	.237	59	14	4	0	0	1	1	12	.274	.305
Away	.296	135	40	8	1	3	15	15	23	.367	.437	Batting #2	.269	104	28	6	1	2	12	8	20	.321	.404
First Pitch	.273	33	9	3	0	0	3	1	0	.286	.364	Batting #6	.232	56	13	2	0	0	3	7	6	.323	.268
Ahead in Count	.328	64	21	7	0	1	7	13	0	.449	.484	Other	.232	95	22	8	0	1	7	11	22	.324	.347
Behind in Count	.165	109	18	4	0	0	5	0	42	.180	.202	Pre-All Star	.247	158	39	11	0	2	16	16	30	.318	.354
Two Strikes	.142	106	15	4	0	1	6	12	48	.235	.208	Post-All Star	.247	97	24	5	1	1	6	10	18	.330	.351

Last Five Years

	Avg	AB	H	2B	3B	HR	RBI	BB	SO	OBP	SLG		Avg	AB	H	2B	3B	HR	RBI	BB	SO	OBP	SLG
vs. Left	.195	241	47	7	1	1	20	19	66	.256	.245	First Pitch	.286	217	62	14	2	4	23	4	0	.291	.424
vs. Right	.284	1152	327	69	15	23	130	78	163	.330	.430	Ahead in Count	.333	285	95	22	4	7	41	49	0	.432	.512
Groundball	.292	343	100	24	3	6	41	21	42	.333	.431	Behind in Count	.244	657	160	31	7	11	66	0	199	.247	.362
Flyball	.287	223	64	15	5	5	27	11	45	.313	.466	Two Strikes	.196	606	119	21	5	10	52	43	229	.252	.297
Home	.263	666	175	38	8	11	68	51	103	.317	.393	Batting #1	.291	505	147	30	10	8	48	32	67	.335	.438
Away	.274	727	199	38	8	13	82	46	126	.316	.402	Batting #2	.237	337	80	11	2	5	34	18	72	.274	.326
Day	.269	443	119	31	5	6	48	29	70	.314	.402	Other	.267	551	147	35	4	11	68	47	90	.326	.405
Night	.268	950	255	45	11	18	102	68	159	.318	.396	March/April	.309	139	43	7	0	4	24	12	26	.359	.446
Grass	.260	569	148	22	6	13	59	41	93	.307	.388	May	.209	230	48	6	0	2	16	15	46	.257	.261
Turf	.274	824	226	54	10	11	91	56	136	.323	.404	June	.259	251	65	19	2	3	29	20	38	.311	.386
Pre-All Star	.261	706	184	36	2	13	83	51	125	.309	.373	July	.286	245	70	11	3	6	34	14	37	.327	.429
Post-All Star	.277	687	190	40	14	11	67	46	104	.325	.424	August	.327	245	80	15	5	7	31	18	38	.373	.514
Scoring Posn	.262	324	85	14	6	6	119	37	59	.329	.398	Sept/Oct	.240	283	68	18	6	2	16	18	44	.290	.367
Close & Late	.304	270	82	17	1	3	47	25	56	.361	.407	vs. AL	.240	196	47	8	0	3	24	13	45	.285	.327
None on/out	.289	409	118	32	4	9	9	23	56	.333	.452	vs. NL	.273	1197	327	68	16	21	126	84	184	.322	.409

Batter vs. Pitcher (career)																						
Hits Best Against	Avg	AB	H	2B	3B	HR	RBI	BB	SO	OBP	SLG	Hits Worst Against	Avg	AB	H	2B	3B	HR	RBI	BB	SO	OBP	SLG
VanLandingham	.800	10	8	1	0	0	3	0	0	.727	.900	Ken Hill	.100	10	1	0	0	0	1	1	1	.182	.200
Willie Banks	.500	10	5	1	0	1	1	1	1	.545	.900	Pedro Martinez	.118	17	2	2	0	0	1	0	5	.111	.235
Pete Harnisch	.429	14	6	1	0	2	2	0	5	.429	.929	Tom Glavine	.154	13	2	1	0	0	0	0	4	.154	.154
John Smiley	.417	12	5	1	0	1	3	0	4	.417	.750	Mike Williams	.154	13	2	1	0	0	0	0	0	.154	.231
Ramon Martinez	.406	32	13	2	1	3	4	3	2	.457	.813	Tom Candiotti	.176	17	3	1	0	0	1	0	3	.176	.235

Jack Howell — Angels
Age 36 – Bats Left

	Avg	G	AB	R	H	2B	3B	HR	RBI	BB	SO	HBP	GDP	SB	CS	OBP	SLG	IBB	SH	SF	#Pit	#P/PA	GB	FB	G/F
1997 Season	.259	77	174	25	45	7	0	14	34	13	36	0	4	1	0	.305	.540	2	1	3	679	3.55	55	56	0.98
Last Five Years	.263	143	300	45	79	11	1	22	55	23	66	0	7	1	1	.313	.527	2	1	3	1194	3.65	94	99	0.95

1997 Season

	Avg	AB	H	2B	3B	HR	RBI	BB	SO	OBP	SLG		Avg	AB	H	2B	3B	HR	RBI	BB	SO	OBP	SLG
vs. Left	.261	23	6	2	0	0	4	1	2	.292	.348	Scoring Posn	.207	58	12	3	0	3	19	3	17	.234	.414
vs. Right	.258	151	39	5	0	14	30	12	34	.307	.570	Close & Late	.296	27	8	3	0	2	6	2	9	.333	.630
Home	.272	81	22	5	0	5	16	9	19	.333	.519	None on/out	.188	32	6	0	0	5	5	3	6	.257	.656
Away	.247	93	23	2	0	9	18	4	17	.278	.559	Batting #6	.180	61	11	2	0	4	10	5	12	.239	.410
First Pitch	.333	27	9	5	0	3	8	1	0	.357	.852	Batting #7	.313	80	25	1	0	9	19	5	15	.349	.663
Ahead in Count	.488	41	20	1	0	7	15	6	0	.542	1.024	Other	.273	33	9	4	0	1	5	3	9	.324	.485
Behind in Count	.127	71	9	0	0	2	6	0	30	.123	.211	Pre-All Star	.278	72	20	4	0	3	9	6	14	.325	.458
Two Strikes	.117	77	9	1	0	3	8	6	36	.179	.247	Post-All Star	.245	102	25	3	0	11	25	7	22	.291	.598

Mike Hubbard — Cubs
Age 27 – Bats Right

	Avg	G	AB	R	H	2B	3B	HR	RBI	BB	SO	HBP	GDP	SB	CS	OBP	SLG	IBB	SH	SF	#Pit	#P/PA	GB	FB	G/F
1997 Season	.203	29	64	4	13	0	0	1	2	2	21	0	1	0	0	.227	.250	1	0	0	228	3.45	19	11	1.73
Career (1995-1997)	.168	65	125	7	21	0	0	2	7	4	38	0	3	0	0	.192	.216	1	0	1	472	3.63	37	31	1.19

1997 Season

	Avg	AB	H	2B	3B	HR	RBI	BB	SO	OBP	SLG		Avg	AB	H	2B	3B	HR	RBI	BB	SO	OBP	SLG
vs. Left	.250	36	9	0	0	0	1	0	14	.250	.250	Scoring Posn	.071	14	1	0	0	0	1	2	6	.188	.071
vs. Right	.143	28	4	0	0	1	1	2	7	.200	.250	Close & Late	.182	11	2	0	0	0	1	0	2	.182	.182

Trent Hubbard — Indians

	Avg	G	AB	R	H	2B	3B	HR	RBI	BB	SO	HBP	GDP	SB	CS	OBP	SLG	IBB	SH	SF	#Pit	#P/PA	GB	FB	G/F
1997 Season	.250	7	12	3	3	1	0	0	0	1	3	0	0	2	0	.308	.333	0	0	0	53	4.08	4	3	1.33
Career (1994-1997)	.255	104	184	34	47	11	3	6	26	23	40	1	6	6	1	.341	.446	0	1	0	828	3.96	64	45	1.42

1997 Season

	Avg	AB	H	2B	3B	HR	RBI	BB	SO	OBP	SLG		Avg	AB	H	2B	3B	HR	RBI	BB	SO	OBP	SLG
vs. Left	.125	8	1	0	0	0	0	1	3	.222	.125	Scoring Posn	.000	2	0	0	0	0	0	0	1	.000	.000
vs. Right	.500	4	2	1	0	0	0	0	0	.500	.750	Close & Late	.000	1	0	0	0	0	0	0	1	.000	.000

John Hudek — Astros

	ERA	W	L	Sv	G	GS	IP	BB	SO	Avg	H	2B	3B	HR	RBI	OBP	SLG	GF	IR	IRS	Hld	SvOp	SB	CS	GB	FB	G/F
1997 Season	5.98	1	3	4	40	0	40.2	33	36	.252	38	5	2	8	27	.396	.470	20	14	5	2	8	2	5	40	52	0.77
Career (1994-1997)	4.42	5	7	29	116	0	116.0	61	118	.219	93	12	5	18	63	.322	.399	75	55	15	4	37	6	5	106	137	0.77

1997 Season

	ERA	W	L	Sv	G	GS	IP	H	HR	BB	SO		Avg	AB	H	2B	3B	HR	RBI	BB	SO	OBP	SLG
Home	3.38	0	1	1	21	0	21.1	12	2	14	19	vs. Left	.255	51	13	1	2	2	9	19	11	.465	.471
Away	8.84	1	2	3	21	0	19.1	26	6	19	17	vs. Right	.250	100	25	4	0	6	18	14	25	.353	.470
Starter	0.00	0	0	0	0	0	0.0	0	0	0	0	Scoring Posn	.262	42	11	0	1	4	20	9	7	.415	.595
Reliever	5.98	1	3	4	40	0	40.2	38	8	33	36	Close & Late	.289	83	24	4	1	6	19	20	13	.438	.578
0 Days rest (Relief)	0.00	1	0	1	4	0	5.1	2	0	5	4	None on/out	.270	37	10	2	0	1	1	6	9	.372	.405
1 or 2 Days rest	9.37	0	2	1	19	0	16.1	24	3	14	14	First Pitch	.421	19	8	1	0	2	7	0	0	.450	.789
3+ Days rest	4.74	0	1	2	17	0	19.0	12	5	14	18	Ahead in Count	.203	69	14	3	0	1	7	0	25	.225	.290
Pre-All Star	6.23	0	0	4	26	0	26.0	27	6	20	22	Behind in Count	.333	30	10	0	2	4	10	19	0	.592	.867
Post-All Star	5.52	1	3	0	14	0	14.2	11	2	13	14	Two Strikes	.158	76	12	2	0	0	5	14	36	.304	.184

Career (1994-1997)

	ERA	W	L	Sv	G	GS	IP	H	HR	BB	SO		Avg	AB	H	2B	3B	HR	RBI	BB	SO	OBP	SLG
Home	3.18	4	2	11	58	0	62.1	36	6	30	67	vs. Left	.247	166	41	4	5	10	34	34	43	.379	.512
Away	5.87	1	5	18	58	0	53.2	57	12	31	51	vs. Right	.202	258	52	8	0	8	29	27	75	.281	.326
Day	3.00	1	2	13	37	0	39.0	24	5	20	42	Inning 1-6	.231	26	6	2	1	1	5	3	9	.333	.500
Night	5.14	4	5	16	79	0	77.0	69	13	41	76	Inning 7+	.219	398	87	10	4	17	58	58	109	.321	.392
Grass	5.86	1	3	10	37	0	35.1	41	7	18	28	None on	.221	231	51	5	0	8	8	27	71	.308	.346
Turf	3.79	4	4	19	79	0	80.2	52	11	43	90	Runners on	.218	193	42	7	5	10	55	34	47	.338	.461
March/April	1.26	0	0	5	13	0	14.1	5	1	6	16	Scoring Posn	.202	119	24	2	2	8	45	22	27	.331	.454
May	3.62	2	0	10	34	0	32.1	28	4	16	43	Close & Late	.222	248	55	8	3	12	44	38	64	.330	.423
June	7.46	0	2	8	25	0	25.1	25	6	15	22	None on/out	.235	102	24	4	0	3	3	11	27	.310	.363
July	7.07	0	3	4	15	0	14.0	15	4	7	9	vs. 1st Batr (relief)	.204	103	21	5	0	2	5	12	28	.293	.311
August	4.85	1	2	1	14	0	13.0	10	2	9	10	1st Inning Pitched	.224	371	83	10	5	16	59	53	104	.326	.407
Sept/Oct	1.59	2	0	1	15	0	17.0	10	1	8	18	First 15 Pitches	.223	291	65	10	2	10	35	37	81	.317	.375
Starter	0.00	0	0	0	0	0	0.0	0	0	0	0	Pitch 16-30	.217	120	26	2	3	7	26	24	33	.347	.458
Reliever	4.42	5	7	29	116	0	116.0	93	18	61	118	Pitch 31-45	.154	13	2	0	1	0	2	0	4	.154	.385
0 Days rest (Relief)	3.29	3	0	5	12	0	13.2	5	2	10	12	Pitch 46+	.000	0	0	0	0	0	0	0	0	.000	.000
1 or 2 Days rest	5.84	1	6	16	62	0	57.0	63	10	30	55	First Pitch	.339	56	19	3	0	4	12	3	0	.383	.607
3+ Days rest	2.98	1	1	8	42	0	45.1	25	6	21	51	Ahead in Count	.141	205	29	5	1	3	16	0	93	.149	.220
vs. AL	16.20	0	1	0	3	0	1.2	4	0	2	2	Behind in Count	.356	73	26	1	4	8	25	27	0	.530	.808
vs. NL	4.25	5	6	29	113	0	114.1	89	18	59	116	Two Strikes	.128	235	30	6	1	4	20	31	118	.233	.213
Pre-All Star	4.27	2	3	26	78	0	78.0	64	12	37	85	Pre-All Star	.222	288	64	8	3	12	37	37	85	.311	.396
Post-All Star	4.74	3	4	3	38	0	38.0	29	6	24	33	Post-All Star	.213	136	29	4	2	6	28	24	33	.344	.404

Rex Hudler — Phillies

	Avg	G	AB	R	H	2B	3B	HR	RBI	BB	SO	HBP	GDP	SB	CS	OBP	SLG	IBB	SH	SF	#Pit	#P/PA	GB	FB	G/F
1997 Season	.221	50	122	17	27	4	0	5	10	6	28	1	2	1	0	.264	.377	1	1	0	493	3.79	31	43	0.72
Last Five Years	.281	282	771	124	217	48	3	35	97	18	130	7	15	30	7	.315	.488	2	9	4	3128	3.80	238	236	1.01

1997 Season

	Avg	AB	H	2B	3B	HR	RBI	BB	SO	OBP	SLG		Avg	AB	H	2B	3B	HR	RBI	BB	SO	OBP	SLG
vs. Left	.253	91	23	4	0	5	10	4	20	.284	.462	Scoring Posn	.167	24	4	1	0	0	3	3	8	.259	.208
vs. Right	.129	31	4	0	0	0	0	2	8	.206	.129	Close & Late	.400	15	6	0	0	2	4	3	4	.526	.800
Home	.289	76	22	2	0	5	10	3	15	.325	.513	None on/out	.262	42	11	2	0	3	3	1	5	.279	.524
Away	.109	46	5	2	0	0	0	3	13	.163	.152	Batting #1	.306	62	19	4	0	3	7	2	14	.328	.516
First Pitch	.333	3	1	0	0	0	0	1	0	.500	.333	Batting #5	.143	21	3	0	0	1	2	1	6	.217	.286
Ahead in Count	.250	24	6	2	0	1	3	4	0	.357	.458	Other	.128	39	5	0	0	1	1	3	8	.190	.205
Behind in Count	.189	74	14	1	0	2	4	0	26	.189	.284	Pre-All Star	.145	55	8	0	0	1	1	3	14	.203	.200
Two Strikes	.209	67	14	1	0	3	5	1	28	.221	.358	Post-All Star	.284	67	19	4	0	4	9	3	14	.314	.522

Last Five Years

	Avg	AB	H	2B	3B	HR	RBI	BB	SO	OBP	SLG		Avg	AB	H	2B	3B	HR	RBI	BB	SO	OBP	SLG
vs. Left	.300	397	119	30	2	21	56	20	79	.334	.544	First Pitch	.413	46	19	1	0	1	3	2	0	.471	.500
vs. Right	.262	374	98	18	1	14	41	11	79	.295	.428	Ahead in Count	.333	138	46	9	0	8	28	21	0	.420	.572
Groundball	.258	151	39	7	0	9	24	9	30	.301	.483	Behind in Count	.232	453	105	24	3	15	44	0	148	.232	.397
Flyball	.257	140	36	8	0	3	18	6	27	.305	.379	Two Strikes	.239	418	100	25	1	16	39	8	158	.254	.419
Home	.285	376	107	26	1	19	47	18	74	.323	.511	Batting #1	.300	273	82	20	1	17	36	9	50	.339	.568
Away	.278	395	110	22	2	16	50	13	84	.308	.466	Batting #2	.258	132	34	8	0	4	16	5	27	.290	.409
Day	.292	233	68	18	1	10	30	10	46	.332	.506	Other	.276	366	101	20	2	14	45	17	81	.315	.456
Night	.277	538	149	30	2	25	67	21	112	.308	.480	March/April	.281	64	18	4	0	3	5	6	12	.338	.484
Grass	.273	597	163	40	3	28	76	25	119	.307	.491	May	.327	165	54	15	0	11	26	5	30	.353	.618
Turf	.310	174	54	8	0	7	21	6	39	.344	.477	June	.240	150	36	9	0	5	23	6	28	.274	.400

Last Five Years

	Avg	AB	H	2B	3B	HR	RBI	BB	SO	OBP	SLG		Avg	AB	H	2B	3B	HR	RBI	BB	SO	OBP	SLG
Pre-All Star	.284	437	124	31	0	22	60	19	85	.317	.506	July	.289	149	43	6	0	7	17	7	35	.321	.470
Post-All Star	.278	334	93	17	3	13	37	12	73	.314	.464	August	.233	120	28	6	3	2	7	3	23	.264	.383
Scoring Posn	.281	153	43	17	0	6	59	10	37	.325	.510	Sept/Oct	.309	123	38	8	0	7	19	4	30	.346	.545
Close & Late	.241	112	27	3	0	5	14	5	26	.286	.402	vs. AL	.294	657	193	45	3	30	88	26	131	.327	.508
None on/out	.288	226	65	13	1	12	12	8	50	.321	.513	vs. NL	.211	114	24	3	0	5	9	5	27	.250	.368

Batter vs. Pitcher (career)

Hits Best Against	Avg	AB	H	2B	3B	HR	RBI	BB	SO	OBP	SLG	Hits Worst Against	Avg	AB	H	2B	3B	HR	RBI	BB	SO	OBP	SLG
Wilson Alvarez	.579	19	11	2	0	2	5	1	3	.600	1.000	Chris Haney	.000	13	0	0	0	0	0	0	2	.000	.000
David Wells	.400	15	6	1	0	2	6	1	1	.438	.867	Mitch Williams	.091	11	1	0	0	0	0	0	3	.091	.091
Randy Johnson	.389	18	7	3	0	1	5	0	7	.389	.722	Norm Charlton	.100	10	1	0	0	0	0	1	3	.182	.100
Jamie Moyer	.375	16	6	2	0	3	5	1	1	.412	1.063	Terry Mulholland	.179	28	5	1	0	0	0	0	3	.179	.214
Tom Gordon	.308	13	4	0	1	1	3	1	1	.357	.692	Randy Myers	.235	17	4	0	0	0	0	0	2	.235	.235

Joe Hudson — Red Sox
Age 27 – Pitches Right (groundball pitcher)

	ERA	W	L	Sv	G	GS	IP	BB	SO	Avg	H	2B	3B	HR	RBI	OBP	SLG	GF	IR	IRS	Hld	SvOp	SB	CS	GB	FB	G/F
1997 Season	3.53	3	1	0	26	0	35.2	14	14	.289	39	8	0	1	21	.373	.370	9	24	8	0	0	4	1	69	31	2.23
Career (1995-1997)	4.41	6	7	2	101	0	126.2	69	62	.304	149	26	0	7	87	.394	.400	36	85	32	11	9	9	2	230	103	2.23

1997 Season

	ERA	W	L	Sv	G	GS	IP	H	HR	BB	SO		Avg	AB	H	2B	3B	HR	RBI	BB	SO	OBP	SLG
Home	2.50	1	0	0	13	0	18.0	22	0	5	8	vs. Left	.370	54	20	4	0	0	4	9	6	.477	.444
Away	4.58	2	1	0	13	0	17.2	17	1	9	6	vs. Right	.235	81	19	4	0	1	17	5	8	.295	.321
Starter	0.00	0	0	0	0	0	0.0	0	0	0	0	Scoring Posn	.333	48	16	3	0	0	18	5	2	.418	.396
Reliever	3.53	3	1	0	26	0	35.2	39	1	14	14	Close & Late	.267	15	4	1	0	1	4	1	4	.313	.533
0 Days rest (Relief)	6.00	0	0	0	5	0	6.0	7	0	6	2	None on/out	.222	27	6	2	0	0	0	4	5	.323	.296
1 or 2 Days rest	3.46	1	1	0	10	0	13.0	15	1	3	5	First Pitch	.381	21	8	2	0	0	3	1	0	.409	.476
3+ Days rest	2.70	2	0	0	11	0	16.2	17	0	5	7	Ahead in Count	.205	39	8	0	0	0	6	0	10	.225	.205
Pre-All Star	2.65	1	0	0	11	0	17.0	16	0	7	7	Behind in Count	.333	42	14	4	0	0	9	5	0	.429	.429
Post-All Star	4.34	2	1	0	15	0	18.2	23	1	7	7	Two Strikes	.220	50	11	0	0	0	6	7	14	.328	.220

Career (1995-1997)

	ERA	W	L	Sv	G	GS	IP	H	HR	BB	SO		Avg	AB	H	2B	3B	HR	RBI	BB	SO	OBP	SLG
Home	2.50	2	2	2	50	0	72.0	73	2	30	38	vs. Left	.341	211	72	12	0	3	33	34	23	.436	.441
Away	6.91	4	5	0	51	0	54.2	76	5	39	24	vs. Right	.276	279	77	14	0	4	54	35	39	.362	.369
Day	7.27	3	3	1	28	0	34.2	46	4	23	11	Inning 1-6	.345	116	40	6	0	0	28	16	8	.433	.397
Night	3.33	3	4	1	73	0	92.0	103	3	46	51	Inning 7+	.291	374	109	20	0	7	59	53	54	.382	.401
Grass	3.74	5	5	2	85	0	108.1	121	5	57	50	None on	.277	235	65	12	0	1	1	28	36	.358	.340
Turf	8.35	1	2	0	16	0	18.1	28	2	12	12	Runners on	.329	255	84	14	0	6	86	41	26	.426	.455
March/April	12.27	0	1	0	3	0	3.2	6	1	4	1	Scoring Posn	.329	170	56	9	0	3	77	31	13	.432	.435
May	0.00	0	0	0	0	0	0.0	0	0	0	0	Close & Late	.319	119	38	7	0	4	20	20	18	.417	.479
June	2.40	3	1	0	28	0	41.1	35	0	22	23	None on/out	.259	108	28	7	0	1	1	8	18	.316	.352
July	5.81	1	1	1	22	0	26.1	30	2	16	9	vs. 1st Batr (relief)	.358	81	29	5	0	1	17	16	12	.470	.457
August	3.72	2	0	1	29	0	38.2	49	2	19	24	1st Inning Pitched	.307	322	99	18	0	7	75	47	44	.396	.429
Sept/Oct	7.02	0	4	0	19	0	16.2	29	2	8	5	First 15 Pitches	.325	271	88	16	0	5	56	42	31	.415	.439
Starter	0.00	0	0	0	0	0	0.0	0	0	0	0	Pitch 16-30	.283	152	43	6	0	2	25	18	23	.366	.362
Reliever	4.41	6	7	2	101	0	126.2	149	7	69	62	Pitch 31-45	.264	53	14	3	0	0	6	8	6	.381	.321
0 Days rest (Relief)	3.63	2	0	0	23	0	22.1	24	0	20	10	Pitch 46+	.286	14	4	1	0	0	0	1	2	.333	.357
1 or 2 Days rest	4.07	1	5	1	42	0	55.1	60	3	29	30	First Pitch	.373	59	22	4	0	1	12	4	0	.413	.492
3+ Days rest	5.14	3	2	1	36	0	49.0	65	4	20	22	Ahead in Count	.226	186	42	8	0	1	20	0	50	.238	.285
vs. AL	4.13	6	6	2	93	0	120.0	137	6	65	60	Behind in Count	.388	147	57	10	0	2	39	47	0	.535	.497
vs. NL	9.45	0	1	0	8	0	6.2	12	1	4	2	Two Strikes	.217	189	41	5	0	2	24	17	62	.284	.275
Pre-All Star	4.10	4	3	0	37	0	48.1	49	2	31	26	Pre-All Star	.268	183	49	9	0	2	32	31	26	.376	.350
Post-All Star	4.60	2	4	2	64	0	78.1	100	5	38	36	Post-All Star	.326	307	100	17	0	5	55	38	36	.406	.430

Todd Hundley — Mets
Age 29 – Bats Both

	Avg	G	AB	R	H	2B	3B	HR	RBI	BB	SO	HBP	GDP	SB	CS	OBP	SLG	IBB	SH	SF	#Pit	#P/PA	GB	FB	G/F
1997 Season	.273	132	417	78	114	21	2	30	86	83	116	3	10	2	3	.394	.549	16	0	5	2186	4.30	97	149	0.65
Last Five Years	.255	596	1940	287	495	91	6	113	344	252	461	16	36	7	8	.343	.483	47	6	15	8900	3.99	586	620	0.95

1997 Season

	Avg	AB	H	2B	3B	HR	RBI	BB	SO	OBP	SLG		Avg	AB	H	2B	3B	HR	RBI	BB	SO	OBP	SLG
vs. Left	.219	96	21	6	0	3	14	27	33	.391	.375	First Pitch	.318	22	7	0	0	4	10	11	0	.545	.864
vs. Right	.290	321	93	15	2	27	72	56	83	.395	.601	Ahead in Count	.381	105	40	10	0	9	25	40	0	.551	.733
Groundball	.407	86	35	5	0	9	32	17	15	.505	.779	Behind in Count	.241	187	45	5	2	10	33	0	80	.244	.449
Flyball	.222	72	16	1	1	4	9	8	24	.300	.431	Two Strikes	.185	233	43	7	2	12	34	32	116	.285	.386
Home	.281	196	55	9	1	14	39	31	54	.377	.551	Batting #4	.275	374	103	19	2	30	82	76	98	.397	.578
Away	.267	221	59	12	1	16	47	52	62	.407	.548	Batting #5	.267	30	8	2	0	0	4	6	13	.395	.333
Day	.324	145	47	6	0	14	33	34	38	.456	.655	Other	.231	13	3	0	0	0	0	1	5	.286	.231
Night	.246	272	67	15	2	16	53	49	78	.359	.493	March/April	.244	82	20	4	0	6	20	14	22	.350	.512
Grass	.266	353	94	19	1	25	76	66	95	.381	.538	May	.347	75	26	6	1	6	20	22	18	.485	.693
Turf	.313	64	20	2	1	5	10	17	21	.458	.609	June	.278	79	22	5	0	7	10	23	27	.441	.608
Pre-All Star	.300	243	73	16	1	19	51	62	68	.437	.609	July	.274	62	17	4	0	3	14	12	19	.400	.484
Post-All Star	.236	174	41	5	1	11	35	21	48	.325	.466	August	.195	87	17	2	1	6	16	10	20	.286	.448
Scoring Posn	.280	125	35	10	0	9	57	35	32	.431	.576	Sept/Oct	.375	32	12	0	0	2	6	2	10	.412	.563
Close & Late	.253	75	19	1	0	5	15	17	18	.387	.467	vs. AL	.271	48	13	2	0	1	5	9	16	.397	.375

1997 Season

	Avg	AB	H	2B	3B	HR	RBI	BB	SO	OBP	SLG		Avg	AB	H	2B	3B	HR	RBI	BB	SO	OBP	SLG
None on/out	.330	103	34	3	1	10	10	18	33	.430	.670	vs. NL	.274	369	101	19	2	29	81	74	100	.393	.572

1997 By Position

Position	Avg	AB	H	2B	3B	HR	RBI	BB	SO	OBP	SLG	G	GS	Innings	PO	A	E	DP	Fld Pct	Rng Fctr	In Zone Outs	Zone Rtg	MLB Zone
As Pinch Hitter	.273	11	3	0	0	0	0	1	3	.333	.273	12	0	--	--	--	--	--	--	--	--	--	--
As c	.272	401	109	21	2	30	86	79	111	.390	.559	122	116	1006.1	677	55	10	6	.987	--	--	--	--

Last Five Years

	Avg	AB	H	2B	3B	HR	RBI	BB	SO	OBP	SLG		Avg	AB	H	2B	3B	HR	RBI	BB	SO	OBP	SLG
vs. Left	.226	412	93	22	0	14	57	67	136	.339	.381	First Pitch	.280	193	54	5	1	19	57	34	0	.392	.611
vs. Right	.263	1528	402	69	6	99	287	185	325	.344	.510	Ahead in Count	.348	480	167	34	0	39	109	126	0	.484	.663
Groundball	.295	535	158	32	1	26	98	72	119	.381	.505	Behind in Count	.207	875	181	29	5	34	114	0	369	.214	.368
Flyball	.201	304	61	11	1	15	47	32	82	.288	.391	Two Strikes	.177	1002	177	34	5	36	115	92	461	.249	.328
Home	.253	924	234	41	2	53	156	119	204	.342	.474	Batting #4	.269	707	190	39	2	51	146	127	191	.380	.546
Away	.257	1016	261	50	4	60	188	133	257	.345	.491	Batting #7	.212	264	56	7	1	8	36	26	45	.290	.337
Day	.263	632	166	31	0	50	119	80	143	.349	.549	Other	.257	969	249	45	3	54	162	99	225	.330	.477
Night	.252	1308	329	60	6	63	225	172	318	.340	.451	March/April	.279	287	80	18	1	24	71	36	72	.361	.599
Grass	.257	1538	396	72	3	92	283	202	351	.347	.488	May	.252	357	90	18	2	18	64	43	81	.340	.465
Turf	.246	402	99	19	3	21	61	50	110	.329	.465	June	.245	384	94	14	1	23	66	61	96	.352	.466
Pre-All Star	.258	1154	298	55	4	75	221	159	274	.352	.508	July	.251	371	93	15	1	24	64	55	85	.347	.491
Post-All Star	.251	786	197	36	2	38	123	93	187	.330	.447	August	.236	276	65	11	1	15	43	31	67	.314	.446
Scoring Posn	.269	525	141	25	3	33	234	108	125	.392	.516	Sept/Oct	.275	265	73	15	0	9	36	26	60	.339	.434
Close & Late	.217	374	81	13	1	17	61	58	93	.323	.393	vs. AL	.271	48	13	2	0	1	5	9	16	.397	.375
None on/out	.270	429	116	16	1	33	33	51	104	.351	.543	vs. NL	.255	1892	482	89	6	112	339	243	445	.342	.486

Batter vs. Pitcher (career)

Hits Best Against	Avg	AB	H	2B	3B	HR	RBI	BB	SO	OBP	SLG	Hits Worst Against	Avg	AB	H	2B	3B	HR	RBI	BB	SO	OBP	SLG
Mark Thompson	.556	9	5	0	0	1	4	2	0	.636	.889	Shawn Estes	.000	12	0	0	0	0	1	2	7	.143	.000
Jason Schmidt	.533	15	8	2	0	3	9	2	3	.556	1.267	Dan Plesac	.000	11	0	0	0	0	0	1	7	.083	.000
Kevin Ritz	.467	15	7	3	0	1	6	3	2	.556	.867	Todd Worrell	.000	10	0	0	0	0	0	0	5	.091	.000
Steve Trachsel	.462	13	6	0	0	3	4	0	2	.462	1.154	Tommy Greene	.067	15	1	0	0	0	0	1	4	.125	.067
Esteban Loaiza	.375	8	3	0	0	2	2	3	1	.545	1.125	Rod Beck	.071	14	1	0	0	0	2	0	4	.067	.071

Brian L. Hunter — Tigers

Age 27 – Bats Right

	Avg	G	AB	R	H	2B	3B	HR	RBI	BB	SO	HBP	GDP	SB	CS	OBP	SLG	IBB	SH	SF	#Pit	#P/PA	GB	FB	G/F
1997 Season	.269	162	658	112	177	29	7	4	45	66	121	1	13	74	18	.334	.353	1	8	5	2820	3.82	287	140	2.05
Career (1994-1997)	.278	378	1529	240	425	71	14	11	108	105	271	5	21	135	35	.323	.364	1	12	15	6071	3.64	660	347	1.90

1997 Season

	Avg	AB	H	2B	3B	HR	RBI	BB	SO	OBP	SLG		Avg	AB	H	2B	3B	HR	RBI	BB	SO	OBP	SLG
vs. Left	.264	159	42	8	3	1	9	18	23	.337	.371	First Pitch	.395	76	30	4	2	2	7	0	0	.385	.579
vs. Right	.271	499	135	21	4	3	36	48	98	.333	.347	Ahead in Count	.313	112	35	10	1	0	9	32	0	.459	.420
Groundball	.294	136	40	7	0	0	5	10	25	.364	.346	Behind in Count	.229	345	79	11	3	0	22	0	107	.231	.278
Flyball	.259	116	30	3	1	1	9	10	25	.315	.328	Two Strikes	.227	344	78	8	2	1	23	34	121	.296	.270
Home	.272	313	85	14	5	2	24	41	57	.355	.367	Batting #1	.268	641	172	26	7	4	44	63	116	.332	.349
Away	.267	345	92	15	2	2	21	25	64	.315	.339	Batting #2	.273	11	3	1	0	0	1	2	3	.385	.455
Day	.310	255	79	14	3	2	15	26	49	.370	.412	Other	.333	6	2	1	0	0	0	1	2	.429	.500
Night	.243	403	98	15	4	2	30	40	72	.312	.315	March/April	.246	114	28	5	0	2	7	9	17	.301	.342
Grass	.281	577	162	26	7	4	43	63	102	.350	.371	May	.250	100	25	3	2	1	10	14	16	.342	.350
Turf	.185	81	15	3	0	0	2	3	19	.214	.222	June	.217	106	23	4	2	0	7	9	22	.282	.292
Pre-All Star	.256	347	89	13	4	4	32	33	60	.320	.352	July	.336	107	36	3	1	1	12	10	18	.383	.411
Post-All Star	.283	311	88	16	3	0	13	33	61	.350	.354	August	.273	121	33	9	0	0	5	15	19	.353	.347
Scoring Posn	.300	130	39	6	1	1	41	14	24	.356	.385	Sept/Oct	.291	110	32	5	2	0	4	9	29	.342	.373
Close & Late	.220	100	22	5	0	0	7	6	24	.278	.270	vs. AL	.262	600	157	24	6	4	41	60	106	.328	.342
None on/out	.247	279	69	9	4	1	1	27	61	.316	.319	vs. NL	.345	58	20	5	1	0	4	6	15	.400	.466

1997 By Position

Position	Avg	AB	H	2B	3B	HR	RBI	BB	SO	OBP	SLG	G	GS	Innings	PO	A	E	DP	Fld Pct	Rng Fctr	In Zone Outs	Zone Rtg	MLB Zone
As cf	.269	658	177	29	7	4	45	66	121	.334	.353	162	162	1422.2	408	8	4	0	.990	2.63	474	403	.850	.815

Career (1994-1997)

	Avg	AB	H	2B	3B	HR	RBI	BB	SO	OBP	SLG		Avg	AB	H	2B	3B	HR	RBI	BB	SO	OBP	SLG
vs. Left	.268	373	100	18	7	1	25	28	55	.315	.362	First Pitch	.380	229	87	13	3	2	20	0	0	.376	.489
vs. Right	.281	1156	325	53	7	10	83	77	216	.326	.365	Ahead in Count	.321	262	84	19	3	6	22	46	0	.417	.485
Groundball	.323	334	108	17	3	2	25	23	62	.367	.410	Behind in Count	.232	760	176	24	5	0	45	0	231	.234	.276
Flyball	.250	260	65	8	1	3	22	17	53	.292	.323	Two Strikes	.218	731	159	16	5	1	38	59	271	.277	.257
Home	.282	742	209	36	7	3	44	59	130	.334	.361	Batting #1	.281	1380	388	64	13	11	93	99	240	.328	.370
Away	.274	787	216	35	7	8	64	46	141	.313	.367	Batting #6	.236	72	17	3	0	0	10	2	15	.253	.278
Day	.282	517	146	26	3	3	27	41	92	.333	.362	Other	.260	77	20	4	1	0	5	4	16	.301	.338
Night	.276	1012	279	45	11	8	81	64	179	.319	.366	March/April	.285	235	67	10	0	2	15	13	41	.323	.353
Grass	.280	838	235	40	8	8	70	78	148	.331	.376	May	.257	206	53	8	3	3	16	16	36	.310	.369
Turf	.275	691	190	31	6	3	38	27	123	.302	.350	June	.259	290	75	11	5	1	25	21	59	.311	.341
Pre-All Star	.277	784	217	34	8	7	66	51	144	.322	.367	July	.332	184	61	8	2	1	16	11	28	.367	.413
Post-All Star	.279	745	208	37	6	4	42	54	127	.325	.361	August	.281	334	94	22	1	3	19	27	49	.333	.380
Scoring Posn	.253	332	84	12	4	1	96	28	62	.301	.322	Sept/Oct	.268	280	75	12	3	1	17	17	58	.307	.342
Close & Late	.284	243	69	11	2	2	21	11	49	.311	.370	vs. AL	.262	600	157	24	6	4	41	60	106	.328	.342
None on/out	.284	613	174	28	5	7	7	44	111	.334	.380	vs. NL	.288	929	268	47	8	7	67	45	165	.321	.379

Batter vs. Pitcher (career)

Hits Best Against	Avg	AB	H	2B	3B	HR	RBI	BB	SO	OBP	SLG	Hits Worst Against	Avg	AB	H	2B	3B	HR	RBI	BB	SO	OBP	SLG
Kevin Ritz	.429	14	6	1	1	0	1	0	2	.429	.643	Jeff Juden	.077	13	1	1	0	0	1	1	2	.133	.154
Bobby Witt	.429	7	3	1	0	0	3	1	5	.545	.571	Pat Hentgen	.091	11	1	0	0	0	0	0	0	.091	.091
Chuck Finley	.400	10	4	0	1	0	0	1	4	.455	.600	John Smiley	.136	22	3	0	0	0	1	1	4	.174	.136
Jeff Fassero	.379	29	11	3	1	0	3	3	3	.438	.552	VanLandingham	.143	14	2	0	0	0	2	0	4	.133	.143
Allen Watson	.375	16	6	0	1	1	2	0	0	.353	.688	Danny Darwin	.154	13	2	0	0	0	0	0	4	.154	.154

Jimmy Hurst — Tigers   Age 26 – Bats Right

	Avg	G	AB	R	H	2B	3B	HR	RBI	BB	SO	HBP	GDP	SB	CS	OBP	SLG	IBB	SH	SF	#Pit	#P/PA	GB	FB	G/F
1997 Season	.176	13	17	1	3	1	0	1	1	2	6	0	0	0	0	.263	.412	0	0	0	69	3.63	5	5	1.00

1997 Season

	Avg	AB	H	2B	3B	HR	RBI	BB	SO	OBP	SLG		Avg	AB	H	2B	3B	HR	RBI	BB	SO	OBP	SLG
vs. Left	.500	6	3	1	0	1	1	2	1	.625	1.167	Scoring Posn	.000	5	0	0	0	0	0	1	2	.167	.000
vs. Right	.000	11	0	0	0	0	0	0	5	.000	.000	Close & Late	.500	2	1	0	0	0	1	1	1	.500	2.000

Edwin Hurtado — Mariners   Age 28 – Pitches Right

	ERA	W	L	Sv	G	GS	IP	BB	SO	Avg	H	2B	3B	HR	RBI	OBP	SLG	GF	IR	IRS	Hld	SvOp	SB	CS	GB	FB	G/F
1997 Season	9.00	1	2	0	14	1	19.0	15	10	.329	31	3	1	5	19	.447	.592	2	4	2	1	0	0	1	21	31	0.68
Career (1995-1997)	6.67	8	9	2	43	15	144.1	85	79	.299	167	30	3	26	108	.392	.503	8	15	7	2	3	14	6	214	173	1.24

1997 Season

	ERA	W	L	Sv	G	GS	IP	H	HR	BB	SO		Avg	AB	H	2B	3B	HR	RBI	BB	SO	OBP	SLG
Home	11.37	1	1	0	7	1	12.2	19	4	12	7	vs. Left	.250	28	7	0	0	4	10	6	3	.389	.679
Away	4.26	0	1	0	6	0	6.1	6	1	3	3	vs. Right	.375	48	18	3	1	1	9	9	7	.483	.542

Butch Huskey — Mets   Age 26 – Bats Right

	Avg	G	AB	R	H	2B	3B	HR	RBI	BB	SO	HBP	GDP	SB	CS	OBP	SLG	IBB	SH	SF	#Pit	#P/PA	GB	FB	G/F
1997 Season	.287	142	471	61	135	26	2	24	81	25	84	1	21	8	5	.319	.503	5	0	8	1723	3.41	170	143	1.19
Career (1993-1997)	.269	301	1016	114	273	44	4	42	155	63	190	1	34	10	7	.308	.444	9	1	15	3864	3.53	361	305	1.18

1997 Season

	Avg	AB	H	2B	3B	HR	RBI	BB	SO	OBP	SLG		Avg	AB	H	2B	3B	HR	RBI	BB	SO	OBP	SLG
vs. Left	.338	139	47	8	0	7	26	9	18	.373	.547	First Pitch	.537	54	29	4	0	7	17	3	0	.550	1.000
vs. Right	.265	332	88	18	2	17	55	16	66	.296	.485	Ahead in Count	.319	119	38	11	0	10	25	12	0	.379	.664
Groundball	.326	89	29	8	1	0	13	7	15	.371	.438	Behind in Count	.197	203	40	6	0	3	21	0	70	.193	.271
Flyball	.281	57	16	2	0	5	12	2	16	.290	.579	Two Strikes	.126	191	24	2	0	3	20	10	84	.167	.183
Home	.306	235	72	18	0	7	36	10	43	.328	.472	Batting #4	.362	105	38	6	0	5	19	6	12	.389	.562
Away	.267	236	63	8	2	17	45	15	41	.310	.534	Batting #7	.289	142	41	6	2	8	25	9	24	.321	.528
Day	.268	183	49	6	1	8	27	10	34	.299	.443	Other	.250	224	56	14	0	11	37	10	48	.284	.460
Night	.299	288	86	20	1	16	54	15	50	.331	.542	March/April	.213	61	13	5	0	2	11	0	12	.206	.393
Grass	.284	391	111	22	2	17	65	20	67	.315	.481	May	.338	80	27	5	0	7	19	7	13	.386	.663
Turf	.300	80	24	4	0	7	16	5	17	.337	.613	June	.304	69	21	3	0	1	9	5	11	.333	.391
Pre-All Star	.272	228	62	14	0	10	39	12	39	.300	.465	July	.243	74	18	4	1	4	13	5	13	.291	.486
Post-All Star	.300	243	73	12	2	14	42	13	45	.337	.539	August	.293	92	27	6	1	3	14	4	15	.320	.478
Scoring Posn	.270	122	33	3	0	1	48	12	26	.317	.344	Sept/Oct	.305	95	29	3	0	7	15	4	20	.340	.558
Close & Late	.250	88	22	0	0	5	13	6	18	.298	.420	vs. AL	.240	50	12	2	0	2	5	1	9	.255	.400
None on/out	.339	112	38	7	1	9	9	5	15	.373	.661	vs. NL	.292	421	123	24	2	22	76	24	75	.326	.515

1997 By Position

Position	Avg	AB	H	2B	3B	HR	RBI	BB	SO	OBP	SLG	G	GS	Innings	PO	A	E	DP	Fld Pct	Rng Fctr	In Zone	Outs	Zone Rtg	MLB Zone
As Pinch Hitter	.313	16	5	1	0	2	4	1	3	.353	.750	18	0	—	—	—	—	—	—	—	—	—	—	—
As 1b	.419	74	31	6	0	4	17	5	8	.450	.662	22	18	156.2	182	10	2	19	.990	—	45	40	.889	.874
As 3b	.163	49	8	2	0	1	8	0	9	.157	.265	15	12	108.0	17	22	7	3	.848	3.25	43	33	.767	.801
As lf	.299	77	23	2	0	3	5	3	12	.321	.442	30	18	180.0	47	4	3	0	.944	2.55	58	46	.793	.805
As rf	.276	239	66	15	2	14	46	16	49	.319	.531	131	2	537.1	72	68	3	1	.978	2.23	145	122	.841	.813

Career (1993-1997)

	Avg	AB	H	2B	3B	HR	RBI	BB	SO	OBP	SLG		Avg	AB	H	2B	3B	HR	RBI	BB	SO	OBP	SLG
vs. Left	.289	287	83	12	0	13	40	22	49	.337	.467	First Pitch	.429	133	57	7	0	11	29	7	0	.455	.729
vs. Right	.261	729	190	32	4	29	115	41	141	.296	.435	Ahead in Count	.301	226	68	14	2	21	48	25	0	.366	.659
Groundball	.309	223	69	14	3	3	33	15	39	.347	.439	Behind in Count	.199	468	93	14	0	4	41	0	164	.196	.254
Flyball	.254	142	36	3	0	6	21	10	35	.295	.401	Two Strikes	.149	449	67	9	0	4	42	31	190	.202	.196
Home	.289	530	153	27	1	18	75	25	100	.315	.445	Batting #4	.304	217	66	8	0	10	32	10	33	.330	.479
Away	.247	486	120	17	3	24	80	38	90	.300	.444	Batting #7	.273	406	111	17	4	19	69	28	82	.314	.475
Day	.270	352	95	13	1	16	54	19	69	.302	.449	Other	.244	393	96	19	0	13	54	25	75	.289	.392
Night	.268	664	178	31	3	26	101	44	121	.311	.441	March/April	.209	139	29	7	0	3	16	2	29	.217	.324
Grass	.274	826	226	35	3	32	124	44	148	.307	.439	May	.313	150	47	5	0	9	26	12	24	.362	.527
Turf	.247	190	47	9	1	10	31	19	42	.311	.463	June	.284	141	40	10	0	3	25	10	28	.321	.418
Pre-All Star	.263	472	124	24	1	16	71	28	89	.299	.419	July	.301	183	55	6	3	11	33	14	34	.345	.546
Post-All Star	.274	544	149	20	3	26	84	35	101	.316	.465	August	.281	153	43	7	1	5	23	9	23	.317	.438
Scoring Posn	.253	261	66	12	0	4	100	22	48	.295	.345	Sept/Oct	.236	250	59	9	0	11	32	16	52	.283	.404
Close & Late	.273	176	48	4	1	8	23	8	38	.303	.443	vs. AL	.240	50	12	2	0	2	5	1	9	.255	.400
None on/out	.300	243	73	10	1	17	17	14	37	.341	.560	vs. NL	.270	966	261	42	4	40	150	62	181	.310	.446

Batter vs. Pitcher (career)

Hits Best Against	Avg	AB	H	2B	3B	HR	RBI	BB	SO	OBP	SLG	Hits Worst Against	Avg	AB	H	2B	3B	HR	RBI	BB	SO	OBP	SLG
Kevin Ritz	.600	15	9	2	0	1	4	1	0	.625	.933	Ramon Martinez	.000	10	0	0	0	0	0	1	2	.091	.000
Mike Morgan	.500	10	5	2	0	0	3	1	1	.545	.700	Todd Stottlemyre	.083	12	1	0	0	1	0	0	4	.083	.333
Calvin Maduro	.500	10	5	3	0	2	6	1	0	.545	1.400	Ismael Valdes	.100	10	1	0	0	0	0	1	2	.182	.100
Terry Mulholland	.471	17	8	2	0	1	3	1	2	.500	.765	Andy Benes	.182	11	2	0	0	0	1	1	3	.250	.182
F. Valenzuela	.462	13	6	1	0	1	2	0	1	.462	.769	Carlos Perez	.214	14	3	0	0	0	2	0	2	.214	.214

Jeff Huson — Brewers
Age 33 – Bats Left

	Avg	G	AB	R	H	2B	3B	HR	RBI	BB	SO	HBP	GDP	SB	CS	OBP	SLG	IBB	SH	SF	#Pit	#P/PA	GB	FB	G/F
1997 Season	.203	84	143	12	29	3	0	0	11	5	15	2	7	3	0	.238	.224	0	2	1	519	3.37	61	39	1.56
Last Five Years	.223	190	377	44	84	9	3	1	34	21	48	3	11	8	4	.267	.271	1	5	3	1458	3.56	146	119	1.23

1997 Season

	Avg	AB	H	2B	3B	HR	RBI	BB	SO	OBP	SLG		Avg	AB	H	2B	3B	HR	RBI	BB	SO	OBP	SLG
vs. Left	.286	7	2	0	0	0	2	0	0	.375	.286	Scoring Posn	.300	30	9	1	0	0	11	2	4	.333	.333
vs. Right	.199	136	27	3	0	0	9	5	15	.231	.221	Close & Late	.188	48	9	1	0	0	6	3	5	.250	.208
Home	.212	66	14	0	0	0	4	3	6	.254	.212	None on/out	.192	52	10	2	0	0	3	5	.250	.231
Away	.195	77	15	3	0	0	7	2	9	.225	.234	Batting #7	.139	36	5	1	0	0	4	1	5	.162	.167
First Pitch	.188	32	6	1	0	0	3	0	0	.182	.219	Batting #8	.122	41	5	0	0	0	2	2	5	.159	.122
Ahead in Count	.269	26	7	0	0	0	2	1	0	.296	.269	Other	.288	66	19	2	0	0	5	2	5	.329	.318
Behind in Count	.167	60	10	1	0	0	1	0	13	.194	.183	Pre-All Star	.266	79	21	1	0	0	7	5	11	.322	.278
Two Strikes	.211	57	12	2	0	0	5	4	15	.286	.246	Post-All Star	.125	64	8	2	0	0	4	0	4	.125	.156

Mark Hutton — Rockies
Age 28 – Pitches Right

	ERA	W	L	Sv	G	GS	IP	BB	SO	Avg	H	2B	3B	HR	RBI	OBP	SLG	GF	IR	IRS	Hld	SvOp	SB	CS	GB	FB	G/F
1997 Season	4.48	3	2	0	40	1	60.1	26	39	.314	72	8	4	10	38	.392	.515	9	24	9	4	3	6	1	83	69	1.20
Career (1993-1997)	4.48	9	6	0	74	16	172.2	79	108	.272	179	24	6	21	88	.355	.422	17	32	13	5	3	21	4	248	194	1.28

1997 Season

	ERA	W	L	Sv	G	GS	IP	H	HR	BB	SO		Avg	AB	H	2B	3B	HR	RBI	BB	SO	OBP	SLG
Home	6.31	3	2	0	25	1	35.2	52	8	18	24	vs. Left	.256	90	23	1	3	2	12	13	15	.352	.400
Away	1.82	0	0	0	15	0	24.2	20	2	8	15	vs. Right	.353	139	49	7	1	8	26	13	24	.420	.590
Starter	8.44	0	1	0	1	1	5.1	11	1	1	3	Scoring Posn	.281	64	18	2	0	4	30	10	12	.390	.500
Reliever	4.09	3	1	0	39	0	55.0	61	9	25	36	Close & Late	.339	56	19	1	1	5	13	11	12	.471	.661
0 Days rest (Relief)	3.38	1	0	0	4	0	5.1	5	2	1	2	None on/out	.375	56	21	2	4	4	4	5	9	.435	.768
1 or 2 Days rest	4.79	0	1	0	15	0	20.2	21	3	10	11	First Pitch	.528	36	19	0	0	3	11	3	0	.564	.778
3+ Days rest	3.72	2	0	0	20	0	29.0	35	4	14	23	Ahead in Count	.250	92	23	5	2	3	18	0	33	.260	.446
Pre-All Star	3.70	3	1	0	26	0	41.1	40	6	16	26	Behind in Count	.296	54	16	3	1	4	8	16	0	.467	.611
Post-All Star	6.16	0	1	0	14	1	19.0	32	4	10	13	Two Strikes	.212	99	21	5	3	3	18	7	39	.266	.414

Raul Ibanez — Mariners
Age 2

	Avg	G	AB	R	H	2B	3B	HR	RBI	BB	SO	HBP	GDP	SB	CS	OBP	SLG	IBB	SH	SF	#Pit	#P/PA
1997 Season	.154	11	26	3	4	0	1	1	4	0	6	0	0	0	0	.154	.346	0	0	0	109	4.19
Career (1996-1997)	.129	15	31	3	4	0	1	1	4	0	7	1	0	0	0	.156	.290	0	0	0	127	3.97

1997 Season

	Avg	AB	H	2B	3B	HR	RBI	BB	SO	OBP	SLG		Avg	AB	H	2B	3B	HR	RBI	BB
vs. Left	.250	4	1	0	0	0	0	0	1	.250	.250	Scoring Posn	.300	10	3	0	0	1	3	0
vs. Right	.136	22	3	0	1	1	4	0	5	.136	.364	Close & Late	.250	4	1	0	0	0	0	0

Pete Incaviglia — Yankees
Age 34

	Avg	G	AB	R	H	2B	3B	HR	RBI	BB	SO	HBP	GDP	SB	CS	OBP	SLG	IBB	SH	SF	#Pit	#P/PA
1997 Season	.247	53	154	19	38	4	0	5	12	11	46	3	1	0	0	.308	.370	2	0	1	591	3.50
Last Five Years	.251	360	1068	144	268	39	6	60	183	78	288	14	19	4	1	.307	.467	8	0	11	4288	3.66

1997 Season

	Avg	AB	H	2B	3B	HR	RBI	BB	SO	OBP	SLG		Avg	AB	H	2B	3B	HR	RBI	BB	SO	OBP	SLG
vs. Left	.306	72	22	3	0	3	9	8	17	.383	.472	Scoring Posn	.176	34	6	0	0	0	7	3			
vs. Right	.195	82	16	1	0	2	3	3	29	.239	.280	Close & Late	.190	21	4	1	0	0	1	2			
Home	.243	74	18	3	0	2	2	3	23	.300	.365	None on/out	.190	42	8	0	0	1	1	1	12	.209	.262
Away	.250	80	20	1	0	3	10	8	23	.315	.375	Batting #6	.267	60	16	1	0	2	5	6	17	.348	.383
First Pitch	.400	35	14	2	0	2	3	1	0	.432	.629	Batting #7	.200	50	10	2	0	1	1	3	11	.259	.300
Ahead in Count	.273	22	6	0	0	1	1	4	0	.407	.409	Other	.273	44	12	1	0	2	6	2	18	.304	.432
Behind in Count	.155	71	11	0	0	0	2	0	40	.167	.155	Pre-All Star	.248	137	34	4	0	5	12	11	42	.316	.387
Two Strikes	.107	75	8	1	0	3	6	6	46	.171	.120	Post-All Star	.235	17	4	0	0	0	0	0	4	.235	.235

Last Five Years

	Avg	AB	H	2B	3B	HR	RBI	BB	SO	OBP	SLG		Avg	AB	H	2B	3B	HR	RBI	BB	SO	OBP	SLG
vs. Left	.290	411	119	19	2	28	76	35	87	.348	.550	First Pitch	.316	193	61	14	2	12	28	4	0	.333	.596
vs. Right	.227	657	149	20	4	32	107	43	201	.282	.416	Ahead in Count	.346	208	72	9	0	24	68	39	0	.451	.736
Groundball	.234	278	65	11	1	16	38	22	83	.299	.453	Behind in Count	.157	465	73	6	3	10	40	0	233	.170	.247
Flyball	.224	152	34	3	2	5	27	21	36	.322	.368	Two Strikes	.145	517	75	9	3	14	49	35	288	.204	.255
Home	.252	516	130	19	4	29	82	37	133	.310	.473	Batting #4	.250	252	63	6	0	14	36	18	77	.308	.440
Away	.250	552	138	20	2	31	101	41	155	.305	.462	Batting #6	.271	336	91	15	5	22	73	26	76	.327	.542
Day	.241	324	78	9	1	19	51	21	87	.289	.451	Other	.238	480	114	18	1	24	74	34	135	.293	.429
Night	.255	744	190	30	5	41	132	57	201	.315	.474	March/April	.237	173	41	4	0	8	27	9	55	.281	.399

Last Five Years

	Avg	AB	H	2B	3B	HR	RBI	BB	SO	OBP	SLG
Grass	.246	447	110	18	2	21	68	28	131	.296	.436
Turf	.254	621	158	21	4	39	115	50	157	.315	.490
Pre-All Star	.250	757	189	26	4	43	127	54	211	.308	.465
Post-All Star	.254	311	79	13	2	17	56	24	77	.306	.473
Scoring Posn	.233	317	74	5	1	19	133	33	102	.304	.435
Close & Late	.176	187	33	7	0	3	21	13	60	.225	.262
None on/out	.246	252	62	14	0	12	12	14	54	.294	.444

	Avg	AB	H	2B	3B	HR	RBI	BB	SO	OBP	SLG
May	.297	259	77	11	2	24	61	17	67	.349	.633
June	.231	247	57	6	0	11	34	20	69	.296	.389
July	.193	181	35	9	3	6	20	15	50	.263	.376
August	.302	126	38	5	0	10	29	15	31	.373	.579
Sept/Oct	.244	82	20	4	1	1	12	2	16	.261	.354
vs. AL	.257	179	46	5	0	7	20	9	51	.304	.402
vs. NL	.250	889	222	34	6	53	163	69	237	.308	.480

Batter vs. Pitcher (career)

Hits Best Against	Avg	AB	H	2B	3B	HR	RBI	BB	SO	OBP	SLG
Scott Bailes	.643	14	9	2	0	4	8	1	0	.667	1.643
Kevin Gross	.500	12	6	0	0	2	5	0	2	.500	1.000
Armando Reynoso	.438	16	7	2	0	1	4	3	3	.526	.750
Denny Neagle	.400	10	4	1	0	0	0	3	3	.538	.500
Greg Cadaret	.364	11	4	2	0	1	6	1	3	.417	.818

Hits Worst Against	Avg	AB	H	2B	3B	HR	RBI	BB	SO	OBP	SLG
Dan Plesac	.045	22	1	0	0	0	2	1	5	.087	.045
Doug Drabek	.071	14	1	0	0	0	0	1	5	.188	.071
Danny Darwin	.077	13	1	0	0	0	0	0	4	.077	.077
Jeff Montgomery	.083	12	1	0	0	0	1	2	5	.214	.083
Donovan Osborne	.167	12	2	0	0	0	0	0	2	.167	.167

Garey Ingram — Dodgers   Age 27 – Bats Right

	Avg	G	AB	R	H	2B	3B	HR	RBI	BB	SO	HBP	GDP	SB	CS	OBP	SLG	IBB	SH	SF	#Pit	#P/PA	GB	FB	G/F
1997 Season	.444	12	9	2	4	0	0	0	1	1	3	0		1	0	.500	.444	0	0	0	41	4.10	3	0	0.00
Career (1994-1997)	.261	82	142	17	37	3	0	3	12	17	33	0	2	4	0	.340	.345	3	3	0	595	3.67	40	39	1.03

1997 Season

	Avg	AB	H	2B	3B	HR	RBI	BB	SO	OBP	SLG
vs. Left	.500	6	3	0	0	0	1	1	2	.571	.500
vs. Right	.333	3	1	0	0	0	0	0	1	.333	.333

	Avg	AB	H	2B	3B	HR	RBI	BB	SO	OBP	SLG
Scoring Posn	.500	2	1	0	0	0	1	0	0	.500	.500
Close & Late	.000	0	0	0	0	0	0	0	2	.000	.000

Hideki Irabu — Yankees   Age 29 – Pitches Right

	ERA	W	L	Sv	G	GS	IP	BB	SO	Avg	H	2B	3B	HR	RBI	OBP	SLG	CG	ShO	Sup	QS	#P/S	SB	CS	GB	FB	G/F
1997 Season	7.09	5	4	0	13	9	53.1	20	56	.311	69	13	2	15	41	.367	.590	0	0	7.09	2	78	9	2	62	62	1.00

1997 Season

	ERA	W	L	Sv	G	GS	IP	H	HR	BB	SO
Home	6.91	3	2	0	7	4	27.1	34	7	12	29
Away	7.27	2	2	0	6	5	26.0	35	8	8	27

	Avg	AB	H	2B	3B	HR	RBI	BB	SO	OBP	SLG
vs. Left	.328	119	39	8	0	9	21	11	25	.379	.622
vs. Right	.291	103	30	5	2	6	20	9	31	.354	.553

Jason Isringhausen — Mets   Age 25 – Pitches Right (groundball pitcher)

	ERA	W	L	Sv	G	GS	IP	BB	SO	Avg	H	2B	3B	HR	RBI	OBP	SLG	CG	ShO	Sup	QS	#P/S	SB	CS	GB	FB	G/F
1997 Season	7.58	2	2	0	6	6	29.2	22	25	.336	40	7	1	3	24	.438	.471	0	0	6.37	1	98	3	1	42	31	1.35
Career (1995-1997)	4.43	17	18	0	47	47	294.1	126	194	.280	318	32	7	22	134	.354	.379	3	1	4.13	25	101	44	8	459	286	1.60

1997 Season

	ERA	W	L	Sv	G	GS	IP	H	HR	BB	SO
Home	6.08	2	1	0	5	5	26.2	30	1	22	22
Away	21.00	0	1	0	1	1	3.0	10	2	0	3

	Avg	AB	H	2B	3B	HR	RBI	BB	SO	OBP	SLG
vs. Left	.362	69	25	1	1	2	13	11	13	.451	.493
vs. Right	.300	50	15	4	0	1	11	11	12	.419	.440

Career (1995-1997)

	ERA	W	L	Sv	G	GS	IP	H	HR	BB	SO
Home	3.49	12	9	0	27	27	180.1	175	9	75	124
Away	5.92	5	9	0	20	20	114.0	143	13	51	70
Day	2.95	7	3	0	15	15	100.2	92	5	38	73
Night	5.20	10	15	0	32	32	193.2	226	17	88	121
Grass	4.06	14	14	0	39	39	246.1	255	17	102	164
Turf	6.38	3	4	0	8	8	48.0	63	5	24	30
March/April	4.85	1	2	0	5	5	29.2	30	4	17	21
May	3.14	1	5	0	6	6	43.0	39	0	20	26
June	6.06	2	3	0	6	6	35.2	45	3	12	30
July	4.55	2	1	0	8	8	55.1	64	5	24	34
August	4.96	4	4	0	8	8	49.0	55	4	19	29
Sept/Oct	3.86	7	3	0	14	14	81.2	85	6	34	54
Starter	4.43	17	18	0	47	47	294.1	318	22	126	194
Reliever	0.00	0	0	0	0	0	0.0	0	0	0	0
0-3 Days Rest (Start)	0.00	0	0	0	0	0	0.0	0	0	0	0
4 Days Rest	4.66	11	9	0	27	27	164.0	187	16	68	113
5+ Days Rest	4.14	6	9	0	20	20	130.1	131	6	58	81
vs. AL	0.00	1	0	0	1	1	6.0	2	0	6	6
vs. NL	4.53	16	18	0	46	46	288.1	316	22	120	188
Pre-All Star	4.78	4	10	0	18	18	113.0	123	7	55	80
Post-All Star	4.22	13	8	0	29	29	181.1	195	15	71	114

	Avg	AB	H	2B	3B	HR	RBI	BB	SO	OBP	SLG
vs. Left	.316	528	167	15	3	8	67	58	74	.385	.402
vs. Right	.249	606	151	17	4	14	67	68	120	.327	.360
Inning 1-6	.284	989	281	31	7	21	128	113	175	.359	.393
Inning 7+	.255	145	37	1	0	1	6	13	19	.323	.283
None on	.257	650	167	20	3	12	12	54	120	.320	.352
Runners on	.312	484	151	12	4	10	122	72	74	.397	.415
Scoring Posn	.278	295	82	7	2	2	102	55	50	.380	.336
Close & Late	.241	83	20	0	0	1	5	8	11	.319	.277
None on/out	.262	290	76	5	1	5	5	19	44	.312	.338
vs. 1st Batr (relief)	.000	0	0	0	0	0	0	0	0	.000	.000
1st Inning Pitched	.326	193	63	2	2	9	37	20	32	.387	.497
First 75 Pitches	.283	809	229	25	7	16	92	84	134	.352	.391
Pitch 76-90	.312	138	43	3	0	4	27	23	26	.410	.420
Pitch 91-105	.239	109	26	3	0	1	8	7	22	.282	.294
Pitch 106+	.256	78	20	1	0	1	7	12	12	.366	.308
First Pitch	.331	175	58	5	3	3	25	4	0	.357	.446
Ahead in Count	.212	462	98	11	1	6	40	0	169	.221	.279
Behind in Count	.340	297	101	15	3	8	45	73	0	.464	.492
Two Strikes	.197	473	93	9	1	5	40	49	194	.276	.252
Pre-All Star	.283	434	123	12	3	7	54	55	80	.370	.373
Post-All Star	.279	700	195	20	4	15	80	71	114	.344	.383

Pitcher vs. Batter (career)

Pitches Best Vs.	Avg	AB	H	2B	3B	HR	RBI	BB	SO	OBP	SLG
Jody Reed	.100	10	1	0	0	0	0	2	1	.250	.100
F.P. Santangelo	.111	9	1	0	0	0	1	1	0	.250	.111
Fred McGriff	.143	7	1	0	0	0	2	3	2	.364	.143
Tony Gwynn	.167	12	2	0	0	0	1	1	2	.231	.167
Moises Alou	.182	11	2	0	0	1	3	3	0	.357	.455

Pitches Worst Vs.	Avg	AB	H	2B	3B	HR	RBI	BB	SO	OBP	SLG
Ellis Burks	.455	11	5	2	1	2	5	3	0	.600	1.364
Ryan Klesko	.455	11	5	1	0	1	1	1	0	.500	.818
Darrin Fletcher	.429	14	6	2	0	0	2	1	0	.500	.571
Orlando Merced	.429	14	6	1	0	2	4	1	1	.467	.929
Vinny Castilla	.429	14	6	0	0	2	3	0	2	.429	.857

Damian Jackson — Reds
Age 24 – Bats Right

	Avg	G	AB	R	H	2B	3B	HR	RBI	BB	SO	HBP	GDP	SB	CS	OBP	SLG	IBB	SH	SF	#Pit	#P/PA	GB	FB	G/F
1997 Season	.194	20	36	8	7	2	1	1	2	4	8	1	0	2	1	.293	.389	1	1	0	146	3.48	7	15	0.47
Career (1996-1997)	.217	25	46	10	10	4	1	1	3	5	12	1	0	2	1	.308	.413	1	1	0	195	3.68	8	16	0.50

1997 Season

	Avg	AB	H	2B	3B	HR	RBI	BB	SO	OBP	SLG		Avg	AB	H	2B	3B	HR	RBI	BB	SO	OBP	SLG
vs. Left	.400	5	2	1	0	1	1	1	0	.500	1.200	Scoring Posn	.182	11	2	0	1	0	1	2	3	.308	.364
vs. Right	.161	31	5	1	1	0	1	3	8	.257	.258	Close & Late	.000	4	0	0	0	0	0	0	1	.000	.000

Danny Jackson — Padres
Age 36 – Pitches Left (groundball pitcher)

	ERA	W	L	Sv	G	GS	IP	BB	SO	Avg	H	2B	3B	HR	RBI	OBP	SLG	CG	ShO	Sup	QS	#P/S	SB	CS	GB	FB	G/F
1997 Season	7.58	2	9	0	17	13	67.2	28	32	.351	98	27	1	11	61	.413	.573	0	0	5.05	3	81	8	3	113	83	1.36
Last Five Years	4.45	31	39	0	106	93	594.1	218	360	.280	648	139	13	49	305	.343	.415	8	3	5.38	50	97	48	16	928	589	1.58

1997 Season

	ERA	W	L	Sv	G	GS	IP	H	HR	BB	SO		Avg	AB	H	2B	3B	HR	RBI	BB	SO	OBP	SLG
Home	5.30	2	3	0	8	6	35.2	42	2	15	18	vs. Left	.286	35	10	3	0	1	3	9	8	.457	.457
Away	10.13	0	6	0	9	7	32.0	56	9	13	14	vs. Right	.361	244	88	24	1	10	58	19	24	.406	.590
Starter	7.75	2	9	0	13	13	65.0	95	11	27	32	Scoring Posn	.386	83	32	9	0	6	53	12	9	.446	.711
Reliever	3.38	0	0	0	4	0	2.2	3	0	1	0	Close & Late	.500	2	1	1	0	0	0	1	0	.667	1.000
0-3 Days Rest (Start)	9.00	0	1	0	1	1	4.0	6	2	1	2	None on/out	.419	62	26	6	0	1	1	10	10	.500	.565
4 Days Rest	7.90	0	6	0	7	7	35.1	60	5	11	16	First Pitch	.367	60	22	5	1	3	11	3	0	.391	.633
5+ Days Rest	7.36	2	2	0	5	5	25.2	29	4	15	14	Behind in Count	.276	105	29	5	0	1	15	0	28	.296	.352
Pre-All Star	7.63	1	7	0	9	9	46.0	68	8	20	25	Ahead in Count	.375	72	27	10	0	4	23	12	0	.466	.681
Post-All Star	7.48	1	2	0	8	4	21.2	30	3	8	7	Two Strikes	.284	102	29	9	0	3	19	13	32	.368	.461

Last Five Years

	ERA	W	L	Sv	G	GS	IP	H	HR	BB	SO		Avg	AB	H	2B	3B	HR	RBI	BB	SO	OBP	SLG
Home	4.05	20	17	0	56	47	322.0	345	23	97	207	vs. Left	.279	365	102	15	1	7	47	37	78	.355	.384
Away	4.92	11	22	0	50	46	272.1	303	26	121	153	vs. Right	.281	1946	546	124	12	42	258	181	282	.341	.421
Day	4.61	8	13	0	36	33	201.0	216	14	81	144	Inning 1-6	.280	2012	564	122	9	46	272	196	318	.344	.418
Night	4.37	23	26	0	70	60	393.1	432	35	137	216	Inning 7+	.281	299	84	17	4	3	33	22	42	.339	.395
Grass	4.77	11	19	0	49	38	234.0	273	22	96	133	None on	.273	1242	339	76	7	23	23	117	192	.341	.401
Turf	4.25	20	20	0	57	55	360.1	375	27	122	227	Runners on	.289	1069	309	63	6	26	282	101	168	.348	.432
March/April	3.53	4	1	0	11	11	74.0	70	6	28	51	Scoring Posn	.276	608	168	32	3	18	248	68	115	.339	.428
May	4.76	7	8	0	19	19	119.0	136	9	42	76	Close & Late	.310	100	31	8	1	2	18	8	13	.364	.470
June	5.04	7	11	0	21	21	130.1	139	16	51	67	None on/out	.274	570	156	39	2	12	12	53	89	.340	.412
July	4.40	8	11	0	24	22	141.0	167	9	51	80	vs. 1st Batr (relief)	.273	11	3	0	0	0	0				
August	3.18	3	5	0	18	10	70.2	74	6	19	45	1st Inning Pitched	.283	403	114	24	3	9	67				
Sept/Oct	5.31	2	3	0	13	10	59.1	62	3	27	41	First 75 Pitches	.283	1717	486	111	8	32	220	1			
Starter	4.45	31	39	0	93	93	578.0	626	47	211	351	Pitch 76-90	.258	295	76	18	2	10	41				
Reliever	4.41	0	0	0	13	0	16.1	22	2	7	9	Pitch 91-105	.295	200	59	4	2	5	28				
0-3 Days Rest (Start)	4.24	1	1	0	3	3	17.0	14	3	6	10	Pitch 106+	.273	99	27	6	1	2	16				
4 Days Rest	4.25	21	25	0	60	60	378.2	425	27	121	233	First Pitch	.332	385	128	25	4	13	67				
5+ Days Rest	4.89	9	13	0	30	30	182.1	187	17	84	108	Ahead in Count	.223	1025	229	37	2	11	95				
vs. AL	12.60	0	1	0	1	0	5.0	7	2	5	1	Behind in Count	.325	538	175	46	3	13	83	1			
vs. NL	4.38	31	38	0	105	92	589.1	641	47	213	359	Two Strikes	.218	957	209	41	3	14	94				
Pre-All Star	4.69	20	25	0	58	58	366.2	413	35	133	218	Pre-All Star	.288	1436	413	92	10	35	201	1			
Post-All Star	4.07	11	14	0	48	35	227.2	235	14	85	142	Post-All Star	.269	875	235	47	3	14	104				

Pitcher vs. Batter (since 1984)

Pitches Best Vs.	Avg	AB	H	2B	3B	HR	RBI	BB	SO	OBP	SLG	Pitches Worst Vs.	Avg	AB	H	2B	3B	HR	RBI
Mariano Duncan	.067	15	1	0	0	0	1	1	3	.125	.067	Steve Scarsone	.600	10	6	1	0	0	3
Archi Cianfrocco	.067	15	1	0	0	0	0	1	4	.125	.067	Ellis Burks	.500	18	9	3	1	0	0
Dave Magadan	.077	13	1	0	0	0	2	0	2	.077	.077	Reggie Sanders	.500	18	9	1	0	2	9
Derek Bell	.107	28	3	1	0	0	2	0	5	.107	.143	Dave Hollins	.500	10	5	3	0	1	4
Chuck Carr	.133	15	2	0	0	0	0	0	2	.133	.133	Luis Gonzalez	.438	16	7	1	0	2	4

Darrin Jackson — Brewers
Age 34 – Bats Right

	Avg	G	AB	R	H	2B	3B	HR	RBI	BB	SO	HBP	GDP	SB	CS	OBP	SLG	IBB	SH	SF	#Pit	#P/PA	GB	FB	G/F
1997 Season	.261	75	211	26	55	9	1	5	36	6	31	0	5	4	1	.279	.384	0	5	2	746	3.33	83	64	1.30
Last Five Years	.267	256	843	88	225	35	4	21	113	43	162	3	19	11	4	.303	.393	3	13	5	3098	3.42	290	227	1.28

1997 Season

	Avg	AB	H	2B	3B	HR	RBI	BB	SO	OBP	SLG		Avg	AB	H	2B	3B	HR	RBI	BB	SO	OBP	SLG
vs. Left	.268	97	26	6	0	2	16	3	12	.287	.392	Scoring Posn	.317	60	19	5	0	3	33	3	13	.338	.550
vs. Right	.254	114	29	3	1	3	20	3	19	.271	.377	Close & Late	.229	35	8	1	0	1	4	0	8	.229	.343
Home	.254	122	31	4	0	4	24	5	17	.279	.385	None on/out	.255	47	12	1	0	0	0	0	7	.255	.277
Away	.270	89	24	5	1	1	12	1	14	.278	.382	Batting #7	.222	45	10	2	0	1	4	1	5	.239	.333
First Pitch	.342	38	13	1	0	2	10	0	0	.342	.526	Batting #8	.253	75	19	1	1	1	8	3	13	.282	.333
Ahead in Count	.293	41	12	4	0	1	11	3	0	.326	.463	Other	.286	91	26	6	0	3	24	2	13	.295	.451
Behind in Count	.232	95	22	3	1	0	7	0	29	.232	.284	Pre-All Star	.244	78	19	2	0	3	18	2	14	.256	.385
Two Strikes	.181	83	15	1	0	2	8	3	31	.209	.265	Post-All Star	.271	133	36	7	1	2	18	4	17	.292	.383

Last Five Years

	Avg	AB	H	2B	3B	HR	RBI	BB	SO	OBP	SLG		Avg	AB	H	2B	3B	HR	RBI	BB	SO	OBP	SLG
vs. Left	.283	304	86	13	1	9	38	16	48	.317	.421	First Pitch	.338	136	46	6	0	5	33	3	0	.348	.493
vs. Right	.258	539	139	22	3	12	75	27	114	.295	.377	Ahead in Count	.331	160	53	13	1	7	25	15	0	.388	.556

Last Five Years

	Avg	AB	H	2B	3B	HR	RBI	BB	SO	OBP	SLG
Groundball	.254	193	49	7	1	3	23	10	39	.291	.347
Flyball	.231	173	40	11	2	4	23	9	31	.272	.387
Home	.282	419	118	21	1	12	62	21	71	.316	.422
Away	.252	424	107	14	3	9	51	22	91	.290	.363
Day	.245	237	58	6	1	7	31	15	53	.290	.367
Night	.276	606	167	29	3	14	82	28	109	.308	.403
Grass	.289	571	165	27	3	12	78	28	94	.324	.410
Turf	.221	272	60	8	1	9	35	15	68	.260	.357
Pre-All Star	.262	583	153	25	1	18	88	31	121	.302	.401
Post-All Star	.277	260	72	10	3	3	25	12	41	.307	.373
Scoring Posn	.262	237	62	10	0	9	97	18	49	.313	.418
Close & Late	.262	130	34	8	0	2	12	4	29	.284	.369
None on/out	.263	194	51	7	1	4	4	3	39	.278	.371

	Avg	AB	H	2B	3B	HR	RBI	BB	SO	OBP	SLG
Behind in Count	.207	420	87	12	2	3	32	0	148	.211	.267
Two Strikes	.176	369	65	7	2	6	28	25	162	.228	.255
Batting #6	.300	487	146	26	3	11	69	32	92	.345	.433
Batting #7	.220	123	27	5	0	4	10	4	26	.242	.358
March/April	.311	148	46	10	1	6	21	13	38	.366	.514
May	.245	204	50	10	0	8	37	8	41	.276	.412
June	.255	184	47	4	0	3	22	9	35	.290	.326
July	.270	137	37	2	3	2	12	8	23	.315	.372
August	.250	56	14	1	0	0	4	2	8	.271	.268
Sept/Oct	.272	114	31	8	0	2	17	3	17	.288	.395
vs. AL	.276	751	207	34	4	20	105	41	140	.314	.411
vs. NL	.196	92	18	2	1	0	1	8	22	.211	.239

Batter vs. Pitcher (career)

Hits Best Against	Avg	AB	H	2B	3B	HR	RBI	BB	SO	OBP	SLG
Jimmy Key	.500	12	6	1	0	1	1	0	1	.500	.833
Donovan Osborne	.467	15	7	0	0	1	2	1	2	.500	.667
Danny Jackson	.417	24	10	1	0	2	5	3	4	.464	.708
Doug Drabek	.417	12	5	0	0	1	3	1	1	.462	.667
John Smoltz	.400	20	8	3	0	4	0	4		.400	.700

Hits Worst Against	Avg	AB	H	2B	3B	HR	RBI	BB	SO	OBP	SLG
Ricky Bones	.000	10	0	0	0	0	0	1	1	.091	.000
Ramon Martinez	.059	17	1	0	0	0	0	0	2	.059	.059
Butch Henry	.091	11	1	0	0	0	0	0	2	.091	.091
Randy Myers	.100	10	1	0	0	0	1	2	0	.250	.100
Charles Nagy	.125	16	2	0	0	0	1	4		.176	.125

Mike Jackson — Indians   Age 33 – Pitches Right (flyball pitcher)

	ERA	W	L	Sv	G	GS	IP	BB	SO	Avg	H	2B	3B	HR	RBI	OBP	SLG	GF	IR	IRS	Hld	SvOp	SB	CS	GB	FB	G/F
1997 Season	3.24	2	5	15	71	0	75.0	29	74	.215	59	12	0	3	24	.297	.292	38	29	5	14	17	4	0	82	70	1.17
Last Five Years	2.91	18	15	28	301	0	315.2	107	306	.208	239	40	4	30	150	.283	.329	100	208	62	81	41	12	6	337	342	0.99

1997 Season

	ERA	W	L	Sv	G	GS	IP	H	HR	BB	SO
Home	4.33	1	3	8	34	0	35.1	29	2	16	37
Away	2.27	1	2	7	37	0	39.2	30	1	13	37
Day	3.09	1	1	2	21	0	23.1	20	1	13	23
Night	3.31	1	4	13	50	0	51.2	39	2	16	51
Grass	3.73	2	5	11	61	0	62.2	54	3	27	62
Turf	0.73	0	0	4	10	0	12.1	5	0	2	12
March/April	4.02	0	1	2	12	0	15.2	10	0	9	12
May	1.54	0	0	4	10	0	11.2	10	0	4	14
June	1.38	0	0	3	13	0	13.0	10	0	2	11
July	1.50	2	1	5	11	0	12.0	5	1	4	14
August	8.18	0	2	0	12	0	11.0	14	0	5	12
Sept/Oct	3.09	0	1	1	13	0	11.2	10	2	5	13
Starter	0.00	0	0	0	0	0	0.0	0	0	0	0
Reliever	3.24	2	5	15	71	0	75.0	59	3	29	74
0 Days rest (Relief)	2.28	0	1	6	21	0	23.2	16	1	9	27
1 or 2 Days rest	3.06	2	2	7	33	0	35.1	27	2	14	32
3+ Days rest	5.06	0	2	2	17	0	16.0	16	0	6	15
vs. AL	3.41	2	5	13	64	0	68.2	54	3	27	65
vs. NL	1.42	0	0	2	7	0	6.1	5	0	2	9
Pre-All Star	2.27	1	1	11	38	0	43.2	31	0	16	39
Post-All Star	4.60	1	4	4	33	0	31.1	28	3	13	35

	Avg	AB	H	2B	3B	HR	RBI	BB	SO	OBP	SLG
vs. Left	.299	117	35	9	0	0	18	18	18	.391	.376
vs. Right	.153	157	24	3	0	3	6	11	56	.221	.229
Inning 1-6	.200	10	2	0	0	0	1	3	1	.385	.200
Inning 7+	.216	264	57	12	0	3	23	26	73	.293	.295
None on	.235	153	36	6	0	3	3	14	38	.308	.333
Runners on	.190	121	23	6	0	0	21	15	36	.284	.240
Scoring Posn	.258	62	16	5	0	0	20	8	18	.338	.339
Close & Late	.192	151	29	7	0	1	11	18	49	.285	.258
None on/out	.238	63	15	0	0	2	2	8	14	.333	.333
vs. 1st Batr (relief)	.206	68	14	0	0	1	2	3	17	.239	.250
1st Inning Pitched	.230	222	51	12	0	3	21	20	58	.298	.324
First 15 Pitches	.236	191	45	8	0	3	13	17	43	.303	.325
Pitch 16-30	.178	73	13	4	0	0	9		26	.279	.233
Pitch 31-45	.100	10	1	0	0	0	2	3	5	.308	.100
Pitch 46+	.000	0	0	0	0	0	0	0	0	.000	.000
First Pitch	.308	39	12	1	0	2	4	5	0	.378	.487
Ahead in Count	.178	146	26	6	0	0	10	0	67	.199	.219
Behind in Count	.316	38	12	3	0	0	6	11	0	.460	.395
Two Strikes	.151	152	23	4	0	1	10	13	74	.231	.197
Pre-All Star	.199	156	31	8	0	0	14	16	39	.274	.250
Post-All Star	.237	118	28	4	0	3	10	13	35	.326	.347

Last Five Years

	ERA	W	L	Sv	G	GS	IP	H	HR	BB	SO
Home	3.05	11	8	17	151	0	156.1	126	16	53	162
Away	2.77	7	7	11	150	0	159.1	113	14	54	144
Day	2.44	9	4	11	122	0	132.2	97	10	44	128
Night	3.25	9	11	17	179	0	183.0	142	20	63	178
Grass	3.55	12	13	18	200	0	202.2	164	21	78	198
Turf	1.75	6	2	10	101	0	113.0	75	9	29	108
March/April	2.63	3	2	8	50	0	51.1	37	2	19	51
May	2.44	4	2	4	54	0	62.2	44	8	15	62
June	4.03	2	2	5	52	0	51.1	39	7	16	48
July	2.32	6	2	7	48	0	50.1	40	6	20	45
August	4.40	1	5	2	42	0	45.0	38	2	16	42
Sept/Oct	1.96	2	2	2	55	0	55.0	41	5	21	58
Starter	0.00	0	0	0	0	0	0.0	0	0	0	0
Reliever	2.91	18	15	28	301	0	315.2	239	30	107	306
0 Days rest (Relief)	2.51	7	4	11	90	0	89.2	64	8	22	91
1 or 2 Days rest	2.93	9	8	14	148	0	163.0	123	17	63	155
3+ Days rest	3.43	2	3	3	63	0	63.0	52	5	22	60
vs. AL	3.52	3	6	19	137	0	140.2	115	14	51	135
vs. NL	2.42	15	9	9	164	0	175.0	124	16	56	171
Pre-All Star	2.88	11	6	20	173	0	184.2	137	18	58	178
Post-All Star	2.95	7	9	8	128	0	131.0	102	12	49	128

	Avg	AB	H	2B	3B	HR	RBI	BB	SO	OBP	SLG
vs. Left	.249	473	118	16	3	11	72	57	78	.333	.366
vs. Right	.180	674	121	24	1	19	78	50	228	.247	.303
Inning 1-6	.245	53	13	3	0	1	14	5	12	.317	.358
Inning 7+	.207	1094	226	37	4	29	136	102	294	.282	.327
None on	.214	612	131	23	2	12	12	52	162	.286	.317
Runners on	.202	535	108	17	2	18	138	55	144	.280	.342
Scoring Posn	.214	308	66	13	2	10	119	37	78	.302	.342
Close & Late	.196	626	123	20	2	17	80	58	171	.267	.316
None on/out	.241	253	61	8	0	5	5	22	58	.312	.332
vs. 1st Batr (relief)	.222	279	62	9	0	6	38	18	74	.270	.319
1st Inning Pitched	.212	915	194	33	3	24	130	74	245	.278	.333
First 15 Pitches	.223	817	182	29	3	21	108	60	200	.284	.343
Pitch 16-30	.181	299	54	11	0	9	36	40	97	.284	.308
Pitch 31-45	.100	30	3	0	1	0	6	7	9	.270	.167
Pitch 46+	.000	1	0	0	0	0	0	0	0	.000	.000
First Pitch	.313	144	45	4	2	8	32	13	0	.370	.535
Ahead in Count	.158	584	92	18	2	8	50	0	252	.169	.236
Behind in Count	.317	199	63	10	0	10	36	45	0	.444	.518
Two Strikes	.126	618	78	15	2	7	48	49	306	.199	.191
Pre-All Star	.207	661	137	20	2	18	102	58	178	.281	.325
Post-All Star	.210	486	102	20	2	12	48	49	128	.287	.333

Pitcher vs. Batter (career)

Pitches Best Vs.	Avg	AB	H	2B	3B	HR	RBI	BB	SO	OBP	SLG
Paul Molitor	.056	18	1	1	0	0	1	1	4	.105	.111

Pitches Worst Vs.	Avg	AB	H	2B	3B	HR	RBI	BB	SO	OBP	SLG
Chili Davis	.636	11	7	0	0	0	2	7	1	.750	.636

Pitcher vs. Batter (career)

Pitches Best Vs.	Avg	AB	H	2B	3B	HR	RBI	BB	SO	OBP	SLG	Pitches Worst Vs.	Avg	AB	H	2B	3B	HR	RBI	BB	SO	OBP	SLG
Roberto Kelly	.077	13	1	0	0	0	0	1	7	.200	.077	Rafael Palmeiro	.636	11	7	1	0	2	3	2	1	.714	1.273
Casey Candaele	.100	10	1	0	0	0	1	0	1	.091	.100	Dave Martinez	.444	9	4	0	0	0	1	3	2	.538	.444
Cecil Fielder	.100	10	1	0	0	0	0	1	4	.182	.100	Jeff Bagwell	.364	11	4	0	0	1	4	1	3	.417	.636
Dante Bichette	.100	10	1	0	0	0	0	1	4	.182	.100	Cal Ripken	.333	18	6	1	0	3	10	1	4	.368	.889

Jason Jacome — Indians

Age 27 – Pitches Left

	ERA	W	L	Sv	G	GS	IP	BB	SO	Avg	H	2B	3B	HR	RBI	OBP	SLG	GF	IR	IRS	Hld	SvOp	SB	CS	GB	FB	G/F
1997 Season	5.84	2	0	0	28	4	49.1	20	27	.296	58	12	0	10	38	.362	.510	1	22	7	1	1	0	1	78	52	1.50
Career (1994-1997)	5.17	10	17	1	105	33	256.0	95	139	.305	313	62	9	36	159	.365	.489	22	59	17	7	5	11	7	400	271	1.48

1997 Season

	ERA	W	L	Sv	G	GS	IP	H	HR	BB	SO		Avg	AB	H	2B	3B	HR	RBI	BB	SO	OBP	SLG
Home	3.67	1	0	0	14	2	27.0	27	4	11	17	vs. Left	.296	54	16	3	0	7	16	8	9	.381	.741
Away	8.46	1	0	0	14	2	22.1	31	8	9	10	vs. Right	.296	142	42	9	0	3	22	12	18	.355	.423
Starter	4.82	2	0	0	4	4	18.2	19	2	5	8	Scoring Posn	.400	45	18	2	0	3	28	11	6	.509	.644
Reliever	6.46	0	0	0	24	0	30.2	39	8	15	19	Close & Late	.500	18	9	2	0	5	8	3	3	.571	1.444
0 Days rest (Relief)	10.38	0	0	0	3	0	4.1	9	3	2	2	None on/out	.277	47	13	3	0	1	1	2	9	.306	.404
1 or 2 Days rest	6.75	0	0	0	6	0	5.1	5	1	1	4	First Pitch	.346	26	9	3	0	1	6	4	0	.419	.577
3+ Days rest	5.57	0	0	0	15	0	21.0	25	4	12	13	Behind in Count	.190	84	16	3	0	3	7	0	20	.200	.333
Pre-All Star	10.97	0	0	0	10	1	10.2	20	4	8	6	Behind in Count	.415	41	17	3	0	4	11	8	0	.510	.780
Post-All Star	4.42	2	0	0	18	3	38.2	38	6	12	21	Two Strikes	.200	85	17	5	0	1	9	8	27	.277	.294

Career (1994-1997)

	ERA	W	L	Sv	G	GS	IP	H	HR	BB	SO		Avg	AB	H	2B	3B	HR	RBI	BB	SO	OBP	SLG
Home	4.70	7	7	0	49	16	122.2	140	12	47	55	vs. Left	.281	231	65	10	1	12	39	25	45	.355	.489
Away	5.60	3	10	1	56	17	133.1	173	24	48	84	vs. Right	.312	794	248	52	8	24	120	70	94	.368	.489
Day	5.85	2	5	1	32	9	67.2	81	14	32	40	Inning 1-6	.306	728	223	43	9	26	125	70	93	.366	.497
Night	4.92	8	12	0	73	24	188.1	232	22	63	99	Inning 7+	.303	297	90	19	0	10	34	25	46	.362	.468
Grass	4.97	8	12	1	87	24	201.0	234	28	74	105	None on	.320	562	180	36	3	18	18	32	75	.361	.491
Turf	5.89	2	5	0	18	9	55.0	79	8	21	34	Runners on	.287	463	133	26	6	18	141	63	64	.370	.486
March/April	7.76	0	1	0	16	3	26.2	40	5	13	14	Scoring Posn	.323	260	84	19	5	9	122	46	39	.417	.538
May	9.12	0	4	0	13	4	24.2	39	4	17	17	Close & Late	.341	82	28	2	0	7	13	10	10	.419	.622
June	4.72	0	1	0	14	1	13.1	18	2	8	9	None on/out	.288	250	72	14	1	5	5	16	31	.336	.412
July	3.47	6	3	0	20	9	70.0	76	6	21	36	vs. 1st Batr (relief)	.250	64	16	4	0	2	12	8	13	.333	.406
August	3.48	4	3	0	23	10	77.2	75	10	21	43	1st Inning Pitched	.294	330	97	18	2	8	52	39	53	.370	.433
Sept/Oct	7.21	0	5	1	19	6	43.2	65	9	15	20	First 15 Pitches	.293	280	82	14	0	8	30	26	44	.355	.429
Starter	5.63	10	14	0	33	33	180.2	219	25	62	88	Pitch 16-30	.341	217	74	13	3	8	43	25	28	.410	.539
Reliever	4.06	0	3	1	72	0	75.1	94	11	33	51	Pitch 31-45	.266	158	42	10	2	5	15	8	23	.306	.449
0 Days rest (Relief)	3.21	0	1	0	15	0	14.0	21	3	6	11	Pitch 46+	.311	370	115	25	4	15	71	36	44	.371	.522
1 or 2 Days rest	4.42	0	2	0	21	0	18.1	23	2	7	14	First Pitch	.374	147	55	9	0	5	25	9	0	.403	.537
3+ Days rest	4.19	0	1	0	36	0	43.0	50	6	20	26	Ahead in Count	.233	433	101	16	4	12	49	0	110	.238	.372
vs. AL	5.30	6	10	1	91	20	180.0	224	30	63	98	Behind in Count	.361	238	86	20	1	12	39	57	0	.485	.605
vs. NL	4.86	4	7	0	14	13	76.0	89	6	32	41	Two Strikes	.228	421	96	21	4	9	54	29	139	.284	.361
Pre-All Star	6.11	1	7	0	48	10	84.0	117	11	41	52	Pre-All Star	.333	351	117	25	4	11	62	41	52	.408	.521
Post-All Star	4.71	9	10	1	57	23	172.0	196	25	54	87	Post-All Star	.291	674	196	37	5	25	97	54	87	.342	.472

Pitcher vs. Batter (career)

Pitches Best Vs.	Avg	AB	H	2B	3B	HR	RBI	BB	SO	OBP	SLG	Pitches Worst Vs.	Avg	AB	H	2B	3B	HR	RBI	BB	SO	OBP	SLG
B.J. Surhoff	.077	13	1	0	0	0	0	0	1	.077	.077												
Chuck Knoblauch	.182	11	2	0	1	0	3	1	1	.250	.364												

John Jaha — Brewers

Age 32 – Bats Right

	Avg	G	AB	R	H	2B	3B	HR	RBI	BB	SO	HBP	GDP	SB	CS	OBP	SLG	IBB	SH	SF	#Pit	#P/PA	GB	FB	G/F
1997 Season	.247	46	162	25	40	7	0	11	26	25	40	3	6	1	0	.354	.494	1	0	2	804	4.19	55	45	1.22
Last Five Years	.278	519	1827	315	508	90	3	96	318	229	408	30	44	22	14	.365	.488	9	5	14	8462	4.02	685	467	1.47

1997 Season

	Avg	AB	H	2B	3B	HR	RBI	BB	SO	OBP	SLG		Avg	AB	H	2B	3B	HR	RBI	BB	SO	OBP	SLG
vs. Left	.333	42	14	2	0	6	11	4	7	.391	.810	Scoring Posn	.184	49	9	0	0	2	15	13	18	.344	.306
vs. Right	.217	120	26	5	0	5	15	21	33	.342	.383	Close & Late	.320	25	8	1	0	3	6	9	6	.500	.720
Home	.197	76	15	4	0	1	7	14	21	.319	.289	None on/out	.243	37	9	3	0	3	3	6	5	.349	.568
Away	.291	86	25	3	0	10	19	11	19	.386	.674	Batting #4	.253	150	38	7	0	10	25	23	38	.360	.500
First Pitch	.364	11	4	1	0	0	1	0	0	.417	.455	Batting #5	.167	12	2	0	0	1	1	2	2	.286	.417
Ahead in Count	.353	34	12	2	0	2	6	11	0	.500	.588	Other	.000	0	0	0	0	0	0	0	0	.000	.000
Behind in Count	.167	84	14	3	0	4	9	0	34	.186	.345	Pre-All Star	.247	162	40	7	0	11	26	25	40	.354	.494
Two Strikes	.174	92	16	2	0	7	15	13	40	.290	.424	Post-All Star	.000	0	0	0	0	0	0	0	0	.000	.000

Last Five Years

	Avg	AB	H	2B	3B	HR	RBI	BB	SO	OBP	SLG		Avg	AB	H	2B	3B	HR	RBI	BB	SO	OBP	SLG
vs. Left	.299	469	140	25	0	26	85	67	95	.385	.518	First Pitch	.401	217	87	20	0	13	51	8	0	.441	.673
vs. Right	.271	1358	368	65	3	70	233	162	313	.358	.478	Ahead in Count	.360	383	138	22	1	32	91	103	0	.498	.674
Groundball	.310	419	130	29	2	17	75	49	91	.392	.511	Behind in Count	.210	844	177	30	1	32	105	0	332	.220	.361
Flyball	.299	328	98	16	1	23	60	37	81	.376	.564	Two Strikes	.196	936	183	26	1	33	114	118	408	.290	.331
Home	.272	853	232	38	1	36	140	113	204	.363	.445	Batting #4	.279	505	141	30	1	29	92	85	118	.386	.515
Away	.283	974	276	52	2	60	178	116	204	.367	.526	Batting #5	.306	428	131	21	0	26	90	57	96	.391	.537
Day	.271	643	174	32	2	28	110	91	143	.369	.457	Other	.264	894	236	39	2	41	136	87	194	.340	.450
Night	.282	1184	334	58	1	68	208	138	265	.363	.505	March/April	.257	303	78	11	0	15	50	32	71	.344	.442

Last Five Years

	Avg	AB	H	2B	3B	HR	RBI	BB	SO	OBP	SLG		Avg	AB	H	2B	3B	HR	RBI	BB	SO	OBP	SLG
Grass	.279	1557	435	76	3	77	261	195	348	.366	.480	May	.249	357	89	19	1	14	55	49	91	.348	.426
Turf	.270	270	73	14	0	19	57	34	60	.361	.533	June	.275	327	90	14	1	18	53	45	68	.373	.489
Pre-All Star	.263	1076	283	51	2	47	166	131	248	.353	.445	July	.270	222	60	10	0	9	31	18	49	.329	.437
Post-All Star	.300	751	225	39	1	49	152	98	160	.383	.550	August	.302	338	102	19	0	22	71	43	78	.381	.553
Scoring Posn	.278	496	138	25	1	27	222	84	111	.379	.496	Sept/Oct	.318	280	89	17	1	18	51	42	51	.409	.579
Close & Late	.287	279	80	10	1	15	52	39	61	.385	.491	vs. AL	.278	1827	508	90	3	96	318	229	408	.365	.488
None on/out	.300	443	133	28	0	30	30	58	86	.390	.567	vs. NL	.000	0	0	0	0	0	0	0	0	.000	.000

Batter vs. Pitcher (career)

Hits Best Against	Avg	AB	H	2B	3B	HR	RBI	BB	SO	OBP	SLG	Hits Worst Against	Avg	AB	H	2B	3B	HR	RBI	BB	SO	OBP	SLG
Mike Trombley	.538	13	7	2	0	3	9	1	2	.571	1.385	Randy Johnson	.083	24	2	0	0	0	0	3	10	.185	.083
Wilson Alvarez	.444	18	8	3	0	1	8	3	4	.524	.778	Dennis Cook	.100	10	1	0	0	0	0	1	4	.182	.100
Mike Mussina	.368	19	7	1	1	3	7	2	7	.429	1.000	Roberto Hernandez	.100	10	1	0	0	0	0	2	3	.250	.100
Chris Haney	.364	11	4	0	0	2	3	1	1	.417	.909	Jack McDowell	.136	22	3	0	0	0	1	1	5	.174	.136
Ken Hill	.333	21	7	2	1	3	7	3	5	.417	.952	Jason Bere	.200	10	2	0	0	0	1	0	2	.182	.200

Mike James — Angels
Age 30 – Pitches Right

	ERA	W	L	Sv	G	GS	IP	BB	SO	Avg	H	2B	3B	HR	RBI	OBP	SLG	GF	IR	IRS	Hld	SvOp	SB	CS	GB	FB	G/F
1997 Season	4.31	5	5	7	58	0	62.2	28	57	.283	69	13	2	3	33	.367	.389	22	36	12	12	13	4	3	90	55	1.64
Career (1995-1997)	3.52	13	10	9	173	0	199.1	96	158	.243	180	29	5	16	99	.342	.361	56	125	44	33	21	5	7	265	200	1.33

1997 Season

	ERA	W	L	Sv	G	GS	IP	H	HR	BB	SO		Avg	AB	H	2B	3B	HR	RBI	BB	SO	OBP	SLG
Home	2.94	5	2	3	31	0	33.2	31	1	10	26	vs. Left	.315	92	29	10	1	0	9	20	22	.434	.446
Away	5.90	0	3	4	27	0	29.0	38	2	18	31	vs. Right	.263	152	40	3	1	3	24	8	35	.321	.355
Day	4.03	2	2	1	20	0	22.1	22	1	12	20	Inning 1-6	.429	7	3	0	0	0	2	0	0	.429	.429
Night	4.46	3	3	6	38	0	40.1	47	2	16	37	Inning 7+	.278	237	66	13	2	3	31	28	55	.365	.388
Grass	4.19	5	3	7	53	0	58.0	64	3	25	52	None on	.268	127	34	8	1	2	2	12	33	.345	.394
Turf	5.79	0	2	0	5	0	4.2	5	0	3	5	Runners on	.299	117	35	5	1	1	31	16	24	.390	.385
March/April	2.57	2	2	2	12	0	14.0	14	0	6	11	Scoring Posn	.294	68	20	2	0	0	27	13	15	.410	.324
May	6.17	0	0	4	11	0	11.2	11	0	11	12	Close & Late	.276	170	47	6	1	2	22	16	37	.353	.359
June	6.00	2	0	0	12	0	12.0	18	1	4	9	None on/out	.304	56	17	4	0	2	2	3	19	.339	.482
July	7.36	0	1	1	3	0	3.2	5	0	2	2	vs. 1st Batr (relief)	.204	54	11	2	0	2	7	2	14	.241	.352
August	3.09	0	1	0	11	0	11.2	13	2	1	9	1st Inning Pitched	.298	188	56	10	2	2	31	20	46	.379	.404
Sept/Oct	2.79	1	1	0	9	0	9.2	8	0	4	14	First 15 Pitches	.258	163	42	9	2	3	21	17	41	.341	.393
Starter	0.00	0	0	0	0	0	0.0	0	0	0	0	Pitch 16-30	.388	67	26	4	0	0	12	11	14	.481	.448
Reliever	4.31	5	5	7	58	0	62.2	69	3	28	57	Pitch 31-45	.071	14	1	0	0	0	0	0	2	.071	.071
0 Days rest (Relief)	6.17	2	2	1	11	0	11.2	15	0	4	5	Pitch 46+	.000	0	0	0	0	0	0	0	0	.000	.000
1 or 2 Days rest	3.21	1	1	6	32	0	33.2	34	2	15	36	First Pitch	.226	31	7	2	0	0	1	4	0	.314	.290
3+ Days rest	5.19	1	2	0	15	0	17.1	20	1	9	16	Ahead in Count	.194	124	24	4	1	0	11	0	52	.219	.242
vs. AL	3.42	4	5	7	50	0	55.1	50	1	25	51	Behind in Count	.438	48	21	4	1	3	10	14	0	.565	.750
vs. NL	11.05	1	0	0	8	0	7.1	19	2	3	6	Two Strikes	.197	127	25	4	1	0	12	10	57	.266	.244
Pre-All Star	4.85	4	2	6	36	0	39.0	45	1	22	32	Pre-All Star	.292	154	45	9	2	1	20	22	32	.388	.396
Post-All Star	3.42	1	3	1	22	0	23.2	24	2	6	25	Post-All Star	.267	90	24	4	0	2	13	6	25	.330	.378

Career (1995-1997)

	ERA	W	L	Sv	G	GS	IP	H	HR	BB	SO		Avg	AB	H	2B	3B	HR	RBI	BB	SO	OBP	SLG
Home	2.20	10	3	4	94	0	102.1	80	7	38	73	vs. Left	.267	307	82	18	4	8	38	54	69	.381	.430
Away	4.92	3	7	5	79	0	97.0	100	9	58	85	vs. Right	.226	433	98	11	1	8	61	42	89	.312	.312
Day	4.89	3	6	1	49	0	57.0	55	6	40	50	Inning 1-6	.267	60	16	3	0	2	12	6	15	.343	.417
Night	2.97	10	4	8	124	0	142.1	125	10	56	108	Inning 7+	.241	680	164	26	5	14	87	90	143	.342	.356
Grass	3.12	12	8	9	154	0	178.2	157	14	83	141	None on	.227	387	88	13	3	9	9	49	87	.330	.346
Turf	6.97	1	2	0	19	0	20.2	23	2	13	17	Runners on	.261	353	92	16	2	7	90	47	71	.355	.377
March/April	2.48	6	4	2	25	0	32.2	23	1	17	26	Scoring Posn	.244	193	47	6	0	4	78	35	42	.359	.337
May	3.16	0	4	4	27	0	31.1	26	2	17	31	Close & Late	.251	383	96	14	2	7	56	51	81	.347	.352
June	5.21	2	1	2	36	0	38.0	48	4	13	23	None on/out	.207	164	34	6	0	5	5	20	41	.309	.335
July	3.69	2	3	1	22	0	31.2	22	3	18	22	vs. 1st Batr (relief)	.212	151	32	6	0	6	31	14	34	.292	.371
August	2.09	2	1	0	33	0	38.2	38	3	12	30	1st Inning Pitched	.253	529	134	24	3	14	89	62	115	.344	.389
Sept/Oct	4.67	1	1	0	30	0	27.0	23	1	19	26	First 15 Pitches	.242	472	114	21	2	15	54	50	102	.331	.390
Starter	0.00	0	0	0	0	0	0.0	0	0	0	0	Pitch 16-30	.257	218	56	8	2	0	21	35	43	.366	.312
Reliever	3.52	13	10	9	173	0	199.1	180	16	96	158	Pitch 31-45	.196	46	9	0	1	1	4	8	11	.309	.304
0 Days rest (Relief)	4.50	3	2	1	37	0	38.0	37	3	14	24	Pitch 46+	.250	4	1	0	0	0	0	3	2	.571	.250
1 or 2 Days rest	3.33	7	5	8	91	0	105.1	98	9	53	88	First Pitch	.265	102	27	7	0	2	13	12	0	.345	.392
3+ Days rest	3.21	3	3	0	45	0	56.0	45	4	29	46	Ahead in Count	.164	360	59	5	2	2	27	0	143	.191	.206
vs. AL	3.23	12	10	9	165	0	192.0	161	14	93	152	Behind in Count	.333	165	55	13	1	10	35	52	0	.491	.606
vs. NL	11.05	1	0	0	8	0	7.1	19	2	3	6	Two Strikes	.159	346	55	5	2	1	28	32	158	.247	.194
Pre-All Star	3.65	9	6	8	95	0	113.1	103	10	56	86	Pre-All Star	.243	423	103	20	3	10	58	56	86	.342	.376
Post-All Star	3.35	4	4	1	78	0	86.0	77	6	40	72	Post-All Star	.243	317	77	9	2	6	41	40	72	.342	.341

Pitcher vs. Batter (career)

Pitches Best Vs.	Avg	AB	H	2B	3B	HR	RBI	BB	SO	OBP	SLG	Pitches Worst Vs.	Avg	AB	H	2B	3B	HR	RBI	BB	SO	OBP	SLG
Cecil Fielder	.000	10	0	0	0	0	0	1	1	.091	.000	John Valentin	.462	13	6	1	0	1	6	0	1	.462	.769
												Frank Thomas	.375	8	3	1	0	1	2	3	1	.583	.875

Marty Janzen — Blue Jays
Age 25 – Pitches Right

	ERA	W	L	Sv	G	GS	IP	BB	SO	Avg	H	2B	3B	HR	RBI	OBP	SLG	GF	IR	IRS	Hld	SvOp	SB	CS	GB	FB	G/F
1997 Season	3.60	2	1	0	12	0	25.0	13	17	.250	23	3	0	4	11	.343	.413	6	4	0	0	0	1	1	41	20	2.05
Career (1996-1997)	6.39	6	7	0	27	11	98.2	51	64	.302	118	20	2	20	68	.383	.517	9	6	0	0	0	5	2	146	102	1.43

1997 Season

	ERA	W	L	Sv	G	GS	IP	H	HR	BB	SO		Avg	AB	H	2B	3B	HR	RBI	BB	SO	OBP	SLG
Home	4.63	1	0	0	5	0	11.2	13	3	5	6	vs. Left	.217	46	10	2	0	1	1	4	4	.280	.326
Away	2.70	1	1	0	7	0	13.1	10	1	8	11	vs. Right	.283	46	13	1	0	3	10	9	13	.400	.500

Kevin Jarvis — Tigers
Age 28 – Pitches Right (groundball pitcher)

	ERA	W	L	Sv	G	GS	IP	BB	SO	Avg	H	2B	3B	HR	RBI	OBP	SLG	GF	IR	IRS	Hld	SvOp	SB	CS	GB	FB	G/F
1997 Season	7.68	0	4	1	32	5	68.0	29	48	.334	99	20	1	17	61	.394	.581	13	15	5	0	1	13	3	92	93	0.99
Career (1994-1997)	6.38	12	18	1	81	39	285.0	109	154	.309	364	68	6	51	197	.368	.506	17	25	9	0	1	43	8	485	323	1.50

1997 Season

	ERA	W	L	Sv	G	GS	IP	H	HR	BB	SO		Avg	AB	H	2B	3B	HR	RBI	BB	SO	OBP	SLG
Home	6.96	0	1	1	16	2	32.1	50	7	16	24	vs. Left	.369	130	48	11	0	10	32	10	19	.418	.685
Away	8.33	0	3	0	16	3	35.2	49	10	13	24	vs. Right	.307	166	51	9	1	7	29	19	29	.376	.500
Starter	9.45	0	3	0	5	5	20.0	34	5	10	13	Scoring Posn	.357	98	35	5	1	4	43	14	18	.434	.551
Reliever	6.94	0	1	1	27	0	48.0	65	12	19	35	Close & Late	.167	12	2	0	0	0	1	1	2	.286	.167
0 Days rest (Relief)	0.00	0	1	0	2	0	1.1	1	0	1	0	None on/out	.362	69	25	4	0	7	7	6	12	.421	.725
1 or 2 Days rest	15.43	0	0	0	12	0	14.0	28	6	3	11	Ahead in Count	.444	45	20	4	0	3	8	0	0	.457	.733
3+ Days rest	3.58	0	0	1	13	0	32.2	36	6	10	24	Behind in Count	.238	126	30	6	1	4	19	0	40	.236	.397
Pre-All Star	10.67	0	1	1	18	2	28.2	49	8	15	22	Behind in Count	.403	72	29	7	0	6	20	19	0	.527	.750
Post-All Star	5.49	0	3	0	14	3	39.1	50	9	14	26	Two Strikes	.217	120	26	6	1	5	20	10	48	.275	.408

Career (1994-1997)

	ERA	W	L	Sv	G	GS	IP	H	HR	BB	SO		Avg	AB	H	2B	3B	HR	RBI	BB	SO	OBP	SLG
Home	6.03	7	6	1	39	19	140.1	176	22	47	78	vs. Left	.317	501	159	28	3	29	91	50	54	.380	.559
Away	6.72	5	12	0	42	20	144.2	188	29	62	76	vs. Right	.302	678	205	40	3	22	106	59	100	.359	.468
Day	6.75	2	5	1	22	10	72.0	89	12	24	41	Inning 1-6	.314	1003	315	64	6	45	179	95	125	.372	.524
Night	6.25	10	13	0	59	29	213.0	275	39	85	113	Inning 7+	.278	176	49	4	0	6	18	14	29	.345	.403
Grass	5.83	3	9	0	42	14	125.0	153	22	51	64	None on	.304	645	196	37	4	34	34	55	83	.362	.532
Turf	6.81	9	9	1	39	25	160.0	211	29	58	90	Runners on	.315	534	168	31	2	17	163	54	71	.375	.476
March/April	7.67	0	1	1	13	3	27.0	40	6	10	20	Scoring Posn	.298	342	102	15	2	11	140	41	48	.366	.450
May	4.30	2	2	0	10	6	44.0	39	8	21	18	Close & Late	.167	30	5	0	0	2	3	3	5	.286	.367
June	7.41	3	4	0	18	12	64.1	98	14	24	29	None on/out	.288	285	82	11	2	19	19	30	36	.360	.540
July	5.33	2	3	0	10	6	54.0	59	4	15	25	vs. 1st Batr (relief)	.324	37	12	2	0	3	7	4	7	.405	.622
August	7.08	4	6	0	15	9	61.0	89	13	23	38	1st Inning Pitched	.317	334	106	18	3	12	67	34	47	.379	.497
Sept/Oct	6.49	1	2	0	15	3	34.2	39	6	16	24	First 15 Pitches	.329	252	83	15	3	13	42	26	23	.394	.567
Starter	6.19	12	15	0	39	39	206.1	259	32	75	104	Pitch 16-30	.295	264	78	16	0	7	44	22	44	.347	.436
Reliever	6.86	0	3	1	42	0	78.2	105	19	34	50	Pitch 31-45	.279	215	60	15	1	6	30	16	33	.328	.442
0 Days rest (Relief)	0.00	0	1	0	3	0	3.1	3	0	1	2	Pitch 46+	.319	448	143	22	2	25	81	45	54	.384	.545
1 or 2 Days rest	14.10	0	2	0	17	0	22.1	43	10	13	16	First Pitch	.389	203	79	16	0	11	38	3	0	.399	.631
3+ Days rest	4.25	0	0	1	22	0	53.0	59	9	20	32	Ahead in Count	.226	473	107	20	4	9	54	0	129	.229	.342
vs. AL	7.32	0	3	0	22	5	51.2	75	12	21	33	Behind in Count	.379	301	114	22	1	22	65	72	0	.496	.678
vs. NL	6.17	12	15	1	59	34	233.1	289	39	64	121	Two Strikes	.215	432	93	16	3	10	55	34	154	.275	.336
Pre-All Star	6.38	5	7	1	45	22	151.0	194	29	63	73	Pre-All Star	.311	624	194	35	3	29	107	63	73	.374	.516
Post-All Star	6.38	7	11	0	36	17	134.0	170	22	46	81	Post-All Star	.306	555	170	33	3	22	90	46	81	.361	.495

Pitcher vs. Batter (career)

Pitches Best Vs.	Avg	AB	H	2B	3B	HR	RBI	BB	SO	OBP	SLG	Pitches Worst Vs.	Avg	AB	H	2B	3B	HR	RBI	BB	SO	OBP	SLG
Gregg Jefferies	.091	11	1	0	0	0	0	0	0	.091	.091	Eric Young	.556	9	5	0	0	0	0	2	0	.636	.556
Jay Bell	.154	13	2	0	0	0	0	1	4	.214	.154	Greg Colbrunn	.400	10	4	2	0	0	1	1	0	.455	.600
Walt Weiss	.167	12	2	0	0	1	1	4	0	.412	.417	Andres Galarraga	.385	13	5	0	0	3	4	0	2	.385	1.077
Vinny Castilla	.200	15	3	0	0	2	2	1	4	.250	.600	Todd Zeile	.364	11	4	0	0	1	2	2	0	.429	.636
												Gary Sheffield	.364	11	4	1	0	1	4	1	0	.417	.727

Stan Javier — Giants
Age 34 – Bats Both (groundball hitter)

	Avg	G	AB	R	H	2B	3B	HR	RBI	BB	SO	HBP	GDP	SB	CS	OBP	SLG	IBB	SH	SF	#Pit	#P/PA	GB	FB	G/F
1997 Season	.286	142	440	69	126	16	4	8	50	56	70	5	5	25	3	.368	.395	1	2	7	1941	3.81	174	118	1.47
Last Five Years	.279	544	1812	302	506	94	10	31	200	206	293	14	31	114	19	.354	.393	6	20	17	7938	3.84	702	446	1.57

1997 Season

	Avg	AB	H	2B	3B	HR	RBI	BB	SO	OBP	SLG		Avg	AB	H	2B	3B	HR	RBI	BB	SO	OBP	SLG
vs. Left	.252	135	34	6	2	10	16	23		.314	.341	First Pitch	.317	63	20	3	0	2	17	0	0	.314	.460
vs. Right	.302	305	92	10	4	6	40	40	47	.382	.420	Ahead in Count	.407	91	37	5	1	5	20	34	0	.559	.648
Groundball	.287	87	25	5	0	2	7	10	13	.364	.414	Behind in Count	.209	191	40	4	2	0	6	0	57	.218	.251
Flyball	.238	42	10	1	1	8	4	12		.340	.381	Two Strikes	.193	197	38	7	1	1	10	22	70	.281	.254
Home	.305	220	67	7	1	6	27	30	34	.391	.427	Batting #1	.242	132	32	3	2	0	7	19	23	.350	.295
Away	.268	220	59	9	3	2	23	26	36	.345	.364	Batting #6	.328	116	38	1	0	2	22	18	13	.410	.388
Day	.272	228	62	10	2	4	25	20	40	.335	.386	Other	.292	192	56	12	2	6	21	19	34	.354	.469
Night	.302	212	64	6	2	4	25	36	30	.402	.406	March/April	.237	38	9	1	1	0	0	4	7	.256	.316
Grass	.305	367	112	13	3	8	44	51	56	.393	.422	May	.254	63	16	2	1	0	6	11	13	.390	.286
Turf	.192	73	14	3	1	0	6	5	14	.238	.260	June	.367	90	33	6	2	5	14	12	15	.437	.644
Pre-All Star	.311	209	65	11	3	5	22	25	34	.392	.464	July	.299	97	29	4	0	1	12	11	14	.366	.371
Post-All Star	.264	231	61	5	1	3	28	31	36	.347	.333	August	.210	81	17	2	0	1	10	17	11	.340	.272
Scoring Posn	.275	102	28	1	2	2	41	19	14	.372	.382	Sept/Oct	.310	71	22	1	1	1	8	5	13	.351	.394

229

1997 Season

	Avg	AB	H	2B	3B	HR	RBI	BB	SO	OBP	SLG		Avg	AB	H	2B	3B	HR	RBI	BB	SO	OBP	SLG
Close & Late	.299	77	23	2	1	1	15	12	16	.385	.390	vs. AL	.259	54	14	2	0	3	8	5	6	.311	.463
None on/out	.254	122	31	4	1	2	2	19	26	.355	.352	vs. NL	.290	386	112	14	4	5	42	51	64	.376	.386

1997 By Position

Position	Avg	AB	H	2B	3B	HR	RBI	BB	SO	OBP	SLG	G	GS	Innings	PO	A	E	DP	Fld Pct	Rng Fctr	In Zone	Zone Outs	Zone Rtg	MLB Zone
As Pinch Hitter	.133	15	2	1	0	1	2	3	6	.278	.400	18	0	---	---	---	---	---	---	---	---	---	---	---
As cf	.282	156	44	5	1	0	10	20	22	.374	.327	46	40	353.2	99	1	3	1	.971	2.54	120	99	.825	.815
As rf	.300	247	74	7	2	7	38	31	38	.373	.429	95	60	580.0	154	1	3	1	.981	2.41	169	148	.876	.813

Last Five Years

	Avg	AB	H	2B	3B	HR	RBI	BB	SO	OBP	SLG		Avg	AB	H	2B	3B	HR	RBI	BB	SO	OBP	SLG
vs. Left	.287	571	164	39	2	10	60	61	81	.359	.415	First Pitch	.374	235	88	16	2	7	46	5	0	.384	.549
vs. Right	.276	1241	342	55	8	21	140	145	212	.352	.384	Ahead in Count	.351	365	128	21	1	10	59	103	0	.487	.496
Groundball	.297	408	121	23	1	7	40	42	58	.366	.409	Behind in Count	.209	803	168	32	5	3	44	0	245	.217	.273
Flyball	.268	332	89	16	2	9	40	36	63	.339	.410	Two Strikes	.208	835	174	42	4	9	62	98	293	.295	.301
Home	.279	816	228	42	4	11	87	105	135	.364	.381	Batting #1	.242	495	120	23	3	3	36	66	90	.335	.319
Away	.279	996	278	52	6	20	113	101	158	.364	.404	Batting #2	.297	583	173	38	1	11	63	54	90	.357	.422
Day	.286	745	213	48	5	13	89	71	124	.348	.416	Other	.290	734	213	33	6	17	101	86	113	.366	.402
Night	.275	1067	293	46	5	18	111	135	169	.359	.378	March/April	.320	172	55	8	1	4	19	12	32	.367	.448
Grass	.277	1495	414	74	8	24	159	178	241	.356	.385	May	.244	406	99	20	1	4	28	52	73	.335	.328
Turf	.290	317	92	16	2	7	41	28	52	.347	.432	June	.283	403	114	23	3	12	46	41	67	.348	.444
Pre-All Star	.277	1106	306	64	6	21	107	120	196	.349	.402	July	.269	353	95	23	1	4	40	37	53	.338	.374
Post-All Star	.283	706	200	30	4	10	93	86	97	.362	.380	August	.280	264	74	12	0	2	36	36	31	.368	.348
Scoring Posn	.254	460	117	15	5	6	158	58	84	.330	.348	Sept/Oct	.322	214	69	8	4	5	31	28	37	.402	.467
Close & Late	.258	291	75	5	3	4	45	42	72	.347	.337	vs. AL	.278	1152	320	55	6	24	136	130	178	.351	.398
None on/out	.267	490	131	29	1	6	6	61	80	.350	.367	vs. NL	.282	660	186	39	4	7	64	76	115	.360	.385

Batter vs. Pitcher (career)

Hits Best Against	Avg	AB	H	2B	3B	HR	RBI	BB	SO	OBP	SLG	Hits Worst Against	Avg	AB	H	2B	3B	HR	RBI	BB	SO	OBP	SLG
John Burkett	.600	10	6	0	0	0	0	1	1	.636	.600	Mark Gubicza	.000	19	0	0	0	0	0	0	2	.000	.000
Scott Erickson	.538	13	7	1	0	0	3	0	0	.538	.615	Greg Maddux	.071	14	1	0	0	0	1	0	4	.133	.071
Kevin Gross	.462	13	6	1	0	0	1	1	1	.588	.538	Tom Glavine	.074	27	2	0	0	0	0	3	4	.167	.074
Curt Schilling	.444	9	4	2	0	0	1	1	1	.455	.667	Mike Bielecki	.091	11	1	0	0	0	0	0	2	.091	.091
Erik Hanson	.400	25	10	1	1	1	5	2	4	.444	.640	Mark Langston	.111	18	2	0	0	0	0	0	5	.111	.111

Gregg Jefferies — Phillies Age 30 – Bats Both

	Avg	G	AB	R	H	2B	3B	HR	RBI	BB	SO	HBP	GDP	SB	CS	OBP	SLG	IBB	SH	SF	#Pit	#P/PA	GB	FB	G/F
1997 Season	.256	130	476	68	122	25	3	11	48	53	27	2	8	12	6	.333	.391	7	0	0	1899	3.58	207	146	1.42
Last Five Years	.305	593	2301	337	702	124	12	57	293	231	132	6	55	99	12	.367	.444	37	0	19	9022	3.53	975	713	1.37

1997 Season

	Avg	AB	H	2B	3B	HR	RBI	BB	SO	OBP	SLG		Avg	AB	H	2B	3B	HR	RBI	BB	SO	OBP	SLG
vs. Left	.333	111	37	5	1	5	21	12	6	.398	.532	First Pitch	.204	49	10	2	0	2	6	6	0	.291	.367
vs. Right	.233	365	85	20	2	6	27	41	21	.314	.348	Ahead in Count	.317	145	46	11	2	6	20	32	0	.441	.545
Groundball	.361	72	26	3	2	1	5	11	4	.446	.500	Behind in Count	.221	190	42	7	1	3	16	0	24	.229	.316
Flyball	.181	72	13	5	0	1	5	11	6	.306	.292	Two Strikes	.198	162	32	5	1	3	11	15	27	.270	.296
Home	.292	202	59	14	2	5	24	23	10	.364	.411	Batting #1	.247	166	41	7	1	4	16	15	8	.313	.373
Away	.230	274	63	11	1	9	24	30	17	.310	.376	Batting #3	.259	185	48	10	1	4	16	18	10	.328	.389
Day	.237	139	33	6	0	3	13	16	11	.316	.345	Other	.264	125	33	8	1	3	16	20	9	.366	.416
Night	.264	337	89	19	3	8	35	37	16	.340	.409	March/April	.214	84	18	7	0	0	6	4	3	.298	.298
Grass	.244	193	47	9	1	7	17	21	9	.318	.409	May	.250	112	28	3	1	4	11	10	5	.311	.402
Turf	.265	283	75	16	2	4	31	32	18	.344	.378	June	.298	84	25	5	1	0	12	5	5	.385	.381
Pre-All Star	.251	303	76	16	2	5	28	32	14	.324	.366	July	.208	96	20	3	0	5	10	11	5	.290	.396
Post-All Star	.266	173	46	9	1	6	20	21	13	.349	.434	August	.333	57	19	4	0	2	9	7	4	.406	.509
Scoring Posn	.239	109	26	6	1	0	31	21	10	.366	.312	Sept/Oct	.279	43	12	3	1	0	2	4	4	.354	.395
Close & Late	.353	68	24	5	1	2	13	9	4	.429	.544	vs. AL	.455	44	20	2	0	0	5	2	2	.478	.500
None on/out	.278	144	40	6	1	4	4	12	4	.333	.417	vs. NL	.236	432	102	23	3	11	43	51	25	.320	.380

1997 By Position

Position	Avg	AB	H	2B	3B	HR	RBI	BB	SO	OBP	SLG	G	GS	Innings	PO	A	E	DP	Fld Pct	Rng Fctr	In Zone	Zone Outs	Zone Rtg	MLB Zone
As lf	.255	471	120	25	3	11	47	51	26	.330	.391	124	122	1021.0	211	5	3	3	.986	1.90	279	206	.738	.805

Last Five Years

	Avg	AB	H	2B	3B	HR	RBI	BB	SO	OBP	SLG		Avg	AB	H	2B	3B	HR	RBI	BB	SO	OBP	SLG
vs. Left	.329	620	204	37	2	20	88	49	27	.376	.492	First Pitch	.329	231	76	12	3	3	30	26	0	.392	.446
vs. Right	.296	1681	498	87	10	37	205	182	105	.364	.426	Ahead in Count	.331	683	226	43	3	22	103	152	0	.450	.499
Groundball	.339	611	207	39	3	10	80	70	38	.403	.462	Behind in Count	.277	893	247	42	6	21	105	0	118	.279	.408
Flyball	.261	372	97	20	0	9	38	41	20	.337	.387	Two Strikes	.277	779	216	39	2	21	96	53	132	.324	.413
Home	.321	1080	347	64	9	27	160	117	69	.387	.472	Batting #1	.241	170	41	7	1	4	16	15	8	.306	.365
Away	.291	1221	355	60	3	30	133	114	63	.350	.419	Batting #3	.314	1855	582	102	10	48	240	181	107	.373	.457
Day	.306	657	201	44	1	18	83	68	45	.368	.458	Other	.286	276	79	15	1	5	37	35	17	.368	.402
Night	.305	1644	501	80	11	39	210	163	87	.367	.438	March/April	.273	267	73	11	2	7	36	29	17	.346	.408
Grass	.289	757	219	42	3	17	76	73	34	.350	.420	May	.266	406	108	20	1	10	46	44	22	.338	.394
Turf	.313	1544	483	82	9	40	217	158	98	.376	.455	June	.328	408	134	31	4	10	48	38	25	.383	.498
Pre-All Star	.293	1244	364	67	7	33	152	123	74	.355	.451	July	.308	509	157	21	1	15	68	43	26	.361	.442
Post-All Star	.320	1057	338	57	5	24	141	108	58	.381	.451	August	.315	416	131	23	3	11	48	44	25	.377	.464
Scoring Posn	.309	556	172	23	4	11	220	97	43	.403	.424	Sept/Oct	.336	295	99	18	1	4	47	33	17	.402	.444

Last Five Years

	Avg	AB	H	2B	3B	HR	RBI	BB	SO	OBP	SLG		Avg	AB	H	2B	3B	HR	RBI	BB	SO	OBP	SLG
Close & Late	.312	349	109	19	2	8	52	50	19	.397	.447	vs. AL	.455	44	20	2	0	0	5	2	2	.478	.500
None on/out	.289	456	132	26	3	16	16	35	17	.341	.465	vs. NL	.302	2257	682	122	12	57	288	229	130	.365	.443

Batter vs. Pitcher (career)

Hits Best Against	Avg	AB	H	2B	3B	HR	RBI	BB	SO	OBP	SLG	Hits Worst Against	Avg	AB	H	2B	3B	HR	RBI	BB	SO	OBP	SLG
Jose Mesa	.615	13	8	2	0	1	1	0	0	.615	1.000	Lance Painter	.000	12	0	0	0	0	0	1	1	.077	.000
Brian Williams	.571	14	8	1	1	1	4	3	1	.647	1.000	Kevin Jarvis	.091	11	1	0	0	0	0	1	0	.091	.091
Pedro Martinez	.542	24	13	2	1	1	3	2	1	.607	.833	Jack McDowell	.091	11	1	0	0	0	0	1	0	.167	.091
Bill Swift	.417	12	5	0	0	2	7	2	0	.500	.917	Roger Bailey	.091	11	1	0	0	0	0	1	1	.167	.091
Kirk Rueter	.400	15	6	2	0	2	2	1	0	.438	.933	Pete Schourek	.133	15	2	0	0	0	0	0	1	.133	.133

Reggie Jefferson — Red Sox — Age 29 – Bats Left (groundball hitter)

	Avg	G	AB	R	H	2B	3B	HR	RBI	BB	SO	HBP	GDP	SB	CS	OBP	SLG	IBB	SH	SF	#Pit	#P/PA	GB	FB	G/F
1997 Season	.319	136	489	74	156	33	1	13	67	24	93	7	17	1	2	.358	.470	5	1	3	1827	3.49	208	95	2.19
Last Five Years	.308	480	1524	221	469	93	7	55	233	103	316	16	44	2	5	.356	.486	23	4	11	5888	3.55	629	296	2.13

1997 Season

	Avg	AB	H	2B	3B	HR	RBI	BB	SO	OBP	SLG		Avg	AB	H	2B	3B	HR	RBI	BB	SO	OBP	SLG
vs. Left	.198	106	21	3	0	0	6	5	28	.267	.226	First Pitch	.314	86	27	7	0	0	7	5	0	.372	.395
vs. Right	.352	383	135	30	1	13	61	19	65	.383	.538	Ahead in Count	.404	104	42	9	0	4	24	11	0	.449	.606
Groundball	.289	83	24	3	0	1	0	6	15	.333	.361	Behind in Count	.276	214	59	10	0	6	25	0	77	.286	.407
Flyball	.357	84	30	6	1	2	12	4	11	.389	.524	Two Strikes	.251	219	55	11	0	3	20	8	93	.287	.342
Home	.337	246	83	21	0	6	34	7	41	.363	.496	Batting #4	.346	344	119	26	0	10	47	16	64	.383	.509
Away	.300	243	73	12	1	7	33	17	52	.354	.444	Batting #5	.250	136	34	6	1	3	18	7	25	.295	.375
Day	.336	152	51	16	0	3	22	4	27	.354	.500	Other	.333	9	3	1	0	0	2	1	4	.364	.444
Night	.312	337	105	17	1	10	45	20	66	.359	.457	March/April	.364	44	16	2	0	3	12	0	12	.356	.614
Grass	.329	438	144	31	1	12	62	21	83	.367	.486	May	.279	68	19	1	0	4	14	5	15	.320	.471
Turf	.235	51	12	2	0	1	5	3	10	.278	.333	June	.379	95	36	10	1	1	8	1	14	.398	.537
Pre-All Star	.341	229	78	14	1	8	36	10	46	.371	.515	July	.406	96	39	8	0	1	11	6	14	.447	.521
Post-All Star	.300	260	78	19	0	5	31	14	47	.345	.431	August	.270	100	27	7	0	4	16	7	18	.342	.460
Scoring Posn	.289	128	37	7	0	3	50	8	21	.329	.414	Sept/Oct	.221	86	19	5	0	0	6	3	20	.264	.279
Close & Late	.208	72	15	1	0	2	8	6	19	.269	.306	vs. AL	.321	452	145	32	1	12	65	20	87	.356	.476
None on/out	.299	137	41	7	1	2	2	6	27	.347	.409	vs. NL	.297	37	11	1	0	1	2	4	6	.381	.405

1997 By Position

Position	Avg	AB	H	2B	3B	HR	RBI	BB	SO	OBP	SLG	G	GS	Innings	PO	A	E	DP	Fld Pct	Rng Fctr	In Zone	Zone Outs	Zone Rtg	MLB Zone
As DH	.325	452	147	29	1	13	62	21	86	.362	.480	119	115	---	---	---	---	---	---	---	---	---	---	---
As Pinch Hitter	.300	10	3	1	0	0	2	1	4	.333	.400	12	0	---	---	---	---	---	---	---	---	---	---	---
As 1b	.226	31	7	3	0	0	3	2	5	.294	.323	12	8	80.0	74	5	2	9	.975	---	15	11	.733	.874

Last Five Years

	Avg	AB	H	2B	3B	HR	RBI	BB	SO	OBP	SLG		Avg	AB	H	2B	3B	HR	RBI	BB	SO	OBP	SLG
vs. Left	.215	279	60	10	0	2	24	21	74	.294	.272	First Pitch	.375	267	100	21	2	11	48	18	0	.419	.592
vs. Right	.329	1245	409	83	7	53	209	82	242	.370	.534	Ahead in Count	.363	325	118	20	2	15	65	38	0	.423	.575
Groundball	.315	292	92	20	0	6	50	23	62	.367	.445	Behind in Count	.234	661	155	27	2	18	74	0	272	.243	.363
Flyball	.298	295	88	12	3	13	43	23	60	.355	.492	Two Strikes	.234	697	163	34	2	15	66	47	316	.287	.353
Home	.325	742	241	51	5	27	122	48	152	.368	.516	Batting #4	.349	505	176	40	1	18	80	26	100	.387	.539
Away	.292	782	228	42	2	28	111	55	164	.343	.458	Batting #6	.279	402	112	17	2	18	54	26	89	.327	.465
Day	.306	477	146	32	2	14	73	27	100	.342	.470	Other	.293	617	181	36	4	19	99	51	127	.348	.457
Night	.309	1047	323	61	5	41	160	76	216	.362	.494	March/April	.355	197	70	15	2	10	34	16	49	.402	.604
Grass	.317	1282	407	80	7	47	193	85	254	.364	.501	May	.277	256	71	12	0	10	42	15	53	.313	.441
Turf	.256	242	62	13	0	8	40	18	62	.308	.409	June	.333	324	108	19	3	14	48	18	54	.376	.540
Pre-All Star	.313	850	266	48	5	36	134	56	179	.358	.508	July	.288	260	75	13	0	7	33	18	53	.342	.419
Post-All Star	.301	674	203	45	2	19	99	47	137	.352	.458	August	.298	302	90	22	2	11	51	21	61	.351	.493
Scoring Posn	.308	389	120	24	1	15	173	46	76	.375	.491	Sept/Oct	.297	185	55	12	0	3	25	15	42	.356	.411
Close & Late	.245	237	58	9	0	7	29	22	54	.312	.371	vs. AL	.308	1487	458	92	7	54	231	99	310	.355	.488
None on/out	.271	410	111	23	1	10	10	20	86	.316	.405	vs. NL	.297	37	11	1	0	1	2	4	6	.381	.405

Batter vs. Pitcher (career)

Hits Best Against	Avg	AB	H	2B	3B	HR	RBI	BB	SO	OBP	SLG	Hits Worst Against	Avg	AB	H	2B	3B	HR	RBI	BB	SO	OBP	SLG
Paul Quantrill	.667	12	8	3	0	0	3	2	2	.714	.917	Erik Hanson	.000	11	0	0	0	0	0	1	3	.083	.000
Danny Darwin	.563	16	9	1	1	1	5	0	3	.563	.938	Kevin Appier	.143	14	2	1	0	0	0	0	5	.143	.214
Ramiro Mendoza	.545	11	6	2	0	0	2	0	1	.545	.727	Randy Johnson	.143	14	2	0	0	0	1	0	7	.200	.143
Scott Kamieniecki	.474	19	9	4	0	1	3	1	3	.500	.842	Jimmy Key	.182	11	2	1	0	0	2	0	4	.182	.273
Kevin Tapani	.400	10	4	1	0	1	1	1	3	.455	.800	Jaime Navarro	.200	15	3	1	0	0	2	1	3	.250	.267

Robin Jennings — Cubs — Age 26 – Bats Left

	Avg	G	AB	R	H	2B	3B	HR	RBI	BB	SO	HBP	GDP	SB	CS	OBP	SLG	IBB	SH	SF	#Pit	#P/PA	GB	FB	G/F
1997 Season	.167	9	18	1	3	1	0	0	2	0	2	0	0	0	0	.158	.222	0	0	1	74	3.89	1	12	0.08
Career (1996-1997)	.211	40	76	8	16	6	0	0	6	3	11	1	1	1	1	.247	.289	0	0	1	297	3.67	23	28	0.82

1997 Season

	Avg	AB	H	2B	3B	HR	RBI	BB	SO	OBP	SLG		Avg	AB	H	2B	3B	HR	RBI	BB	SO	OBP	SLG
vs. Left	.000	0	0	0	0	0	0	0	0	.000	.000	Scoring Posn	.750	4	3	1	0	0	2	0	0	.600	1.000
vs. Right	.167	18	3	1	0	0	2	0	2	.158	.222	Close & Late	.000	4	0	0	0	0	0	0	0	.000	.000

Marcus Jensen — Tigers
Age 25 – Bats Both

	Avg	G	AB	R	H	2B	3B	HR	RBI	BB	SO	HBP	GDP	SB	CS	OBP	SLG	IBB	SH	SF	#Pit	#P/PA	GB	FB	G/F
1997 Season	.153	38	85	6	13	2	0	1	4	8	28	0	2	0	0	.226	212	1	0	0	355	3.82	32	17	1.88
Career (1996-1997)	.163	47	104	10	17	3	0	1	8	16	35	0	3	0	0	.275	221	1	0	0	493	4.11	36	21	1.71

1997 Season

	Avg	AB	H	2B	3B	HR	RBI	BB	SO	OBP	SLG		Avg	AB	H	2B	3B	HR	RBI	BB	SO	OBP	SLG
vs. Left	.129	31	4	0	0	0	1	3	9	.206	.129	Scoring Posn	.211	19	4	0	0	1	4	3	4	.318	.368
vs. Right	.167	54	9	2	0	1	3	5	19	.237	.259	Close & Late	.063	16	1	0	0	0	0	1	7	.118	.063

Derek Jeter — Yankees
Age 24 – Bats Right

	Avg	G	AB	R	H	2B	3B	HR	RBI	BB	SO	HBP	GDP	SB	CS	OBP	SLG	IBB	SH	SF	#Pit	#P/PA	GB	FB	G/F
1997 Season	.291	159	654	116	190	31	7	10	70	74	125	10	14	23	12	.370	.405	0	8	2	2923	3.91	308	101	3.05
Career (1995-1997)	.300	331	1284	225	385	60	14	20	155	125	238	19	27	37	19	.368	.415	1	14	11	5550	3.82	580	227	2.56

1997 Season

	Avg	AB	H	2B	3B	HR	RBI	BB	SO	OBP	SLG		Avg	AB	H	2B	3B	HR	RBI	BB	SO	OBP	SLG
vs. Left	.290	169	49	7	0	5	21	19	28	.366	.420	First Pitch	.413	92	38	8	1	3	14	0	0	.419	.620
vs. Right	.291	485	141	24	7	5	49	55	97	.372	.400	Ahead in Count	.376	125	47	8	3	1	19	33	0	.506	.512
Groundball	.232	138	32	6	1	1	10	19	27	.342	.312	Behind in Count	.237	291	69	11	3	3	14	0	93	.253	.326
Flyball	.373	102	38	5	1	5	16	9	17	.420	.588	Two Strikes	.215	321	69	10	3	4	24	41	125	.313	.302
Home	.284	313	89	12	3	5	39	38	53	.367	.390	Batting #1	.321	427	137	21	6	6	44	47	85	.394	.440
Away	.296	341	101	19	4	5	31	36	72	.373	.419	Batting #7	.254	126	32	5	1	2	12	14	20	.347	.357
Day	.271	247	67	12	1	2	26	26	48	.347	.352	Other	.208	101	21	5	0	2	14	13	20	.298	.317
Night	.302	407	123	19	6	8	44	48	77	.384	.437	March/April	.309	110	34	4	3	1	12	18	22	.415	.427
Grass	.296	565	167	26	7	9	64	67	106	.378	.414	May	.227	110	25	4	0	3	13	7	19	.280	.345
Turf	.258	89	23	5	0	1	6	7	19	.320	.348	June	.324	102	33	4	3	0	11	12	25	.403	.422
Pre-All Star	.285	347	99	13	6	4	37	39	73	.365	.392	July	.318	107	34	6	0	0	3	9	16	.381	.374
Post-All Star	.296	307	91	18	1	6	33	35	52	.376	.420	August	.289	121	35	6	1	4	20	15	21	.372	.455
Scoring Posn	.228	149	34	6	0	2	57	32	32	.368	.309	Sept/Oct	.279	104	29	7	0	2	11	13	22	.364	.404
Close & Late	.273	99	27	2	1	3	14	14	26	.374	.404	vs. AL	.293	591	173	29	7	10	63	69	107	.375	.416
None on/out	.338	225	76	14	2	4	4	15	42	.384	.471	vs. NL	.270	63	17	2	0	0	7	5	18	.329	.302

1997 By Position

Position	Avg	AB	H	2B	3B	HR	RBI	BB	SO	OBP	SLG	G	GS	Innings	PO	A	E	DP	Fld Pct	Rng Fctr	In Zone	Zone Outs	Zone Rtg	MLB Zone
As ss	.291	654	190	31	7	10	70	74	125	.370	.405	159	159	1417.0	245	455	18	88	.975	4.45	525	480	.914	.937

Career (1995-1997)

	Avg	AB	H	2B	3B	HR	RBI	BB	SO	OBP	SLG		Avg	AB	H	2B	3B	HR	RBI	BB	SO	OBP	SLG
vs. Left	.316	345	109	15	1	7	37	35	55	.386	.426	First Pitch	.435	200	87	15	3	5	34	0	0	.434	.615
vs. Right	.294	939	276	45	13	13	118	90	183	.361	.411	Ahead in Count	.395	261	103	16	5	4	44	62	0	.511	.540
Groundball	.254	279	71	11	3	2	22	29	53	.337	.337	Behind in Count	.219	567	124	18	4	6	36	0	187	.233	.296
Flyball	.365	208	76	12	4	9	36	19	44	.415	.591	Two Strikes	.215	615	132	22	4	7	50	63	238	.295	.298
Home	.289	634	183	26	7	8	84	69	104	.362	.390	Batting #1	.323	601	194	30	8	6	62	61	107	.390	.439
Away	.311	650	202	34	7	12	71	56	134	.373	.440	Batting #9	.326	307	100	10	3	6	44	23	69	.374	.436
Day	.291	481	140	27	1	8	58	46	94	.356	.401	Other	.242	376	91	20	3	6	49	41	62	.327	.359
Night	.305	803	245	33	13	12	97	79	144	.374	.423	March/April	.295	183	54	4	4	2	22	31	40	.408	.393
Grass	.303	1116	338	51	14	17	139	113	201	.373	.419	May	.239	209	50	7	2	4	25	21	43	.316	.349
Turf	.280	168	40	7	0	3	16	12	37	.328	.387	June	.292	240	70	14	4	1	29	19	49	.346	.396
Pre-All Star	.278	679	189	26	10	8	81	74	141	.355	.381	July	.346	205	71	13	0	2	13	13	28	.391	.494
Post-All Star	.324	605	196	34	4	12	74	51	97	.382	.453	August	.307	241	74	10	2	7	36	23	34	.373	.452
Scoring Posn	.248	314	78	14	0	4	128	51	74	.352	.331	Sept/Oct	.320	206	66	12	2	4	30	18	44	.379	.456
Close & Late	.269	186	50	4	1	6	27	26	42	.364	.398	vs. AL	.301	1221	368	58	14	20	148	120	220	.370	.420
None on/out	.345	403	139	24	4	10	10	28	67	.394	.499	vs. NL	.270	63	17	2	0	0	7	5	18	.329	.302

Batter vs. Pitcher (career)

Hits Best Against	Avg	AB	H	2B	3B	HR	RBI	BB	SO	OBP	SLG	Hits Worst Against	Avg	AB	H	2B	3B	HR	RBI	BB	SO	OBP	SLG
Jason Dickson	.545	11	6	1	1	1	5	2	3	.615	1.091	Jeff Fassero	.071	14	1	0	0	1	2	1	1	.133	.286
Wilson Alvarez	.538	13	7	2	0	0	1	2	0	.600	.692	Alex Fernandez	.077	13	1	0	0	0	2	0	3	.067	.077
Dave Telgheder	.455	11	5	0	0	1	1	1	1	.500	.727	Roger Clemens	.105	19	2	1	0	0	1	1	5	.150	.158
Woody Williams	.357	14	5	1	0	2	2	0	4	.357	.857	Chuck Finley	.118	17	2	0	0	0	1	3	4	.286	.118
Bobby Witt	.333	9	3	0	0	1	1	3	3	.500	.667	Jamie Moyer	.200	15	3	0	0	0	0	0	0	.200	.200

Brian Johnson — Giants
Age 30 – Bats Right (groundball hitter)

	Avg	G	AB	R	H	2B	3B	HR	RBI	BB	SO	HBP	GDP	SB	CS	OBP	SLG	IBB	SH	SF	#Pit	#P/PA	GB	FB	G/F
1997 Season	.261	101	318	32	83	13	3	13	45	19	45	2	11	1	1	.303	.443	8	5	4	1174	3.37	127	100	1.27
Career (1994-1997)	.260	287	861	77	224	39	5	27	125	39	141	7	25	1	1	.293	.411	12	10	13	3145	3.38	327	248	1.32

1997 Season

	Avg	AB	H	2B	3B	HR	RBI	BB	SO	OBP	SLG		Avg	AB	H	2B	3B	HR	RBI	BB	SO	OBP	SLG
vs. Left	.226	93	21	3	1	1	10	6	10	.267	.312	First Pitch	.216	51	11	1	0	4	12	7	0	.311	.471
vs. Right	.276	225	62	10	2	12	35	13	35	.318	.498	Ahead in Count	.375	64	24	5	1	2	9	8	0	.438	.578
Groundball	.250	48	12	1	0	2	7	1	3	.260	.396	Behind in Count	.219	155	34	4	1	6	17	0	40	.223	.374
Flyball	.136	44	6	0	0	0	3	2	10	.170	.136	Two Strikes	.210	143	30	5	2	4	17	4	45	.235	.357
Home	.266	158	42	5	2	8	23	7	21	.302	.475	Batting #7	.313	48	15	3	1	0	4	1	4	.327	.417
Away	.256	160	41	8	1	5	22	12	24	.305	.413	Batting #8	.257	257	66	10	2	13	40	15	40	.299	.463
Day	.281	153	43	7	0	6	23	12	17	.333	.444	Other	.154	13	2	0	0	0	1	3	1	.313	.154
Night	.242	165	40	6	3	7	22	7	28	.274	.442	March/April	.250	56	14	3	0	1	11	1	7	.263	.357

	Avg	AB	H	2B	3B	HR	RBI	BB	SO	OBP	SLG		Avg	AB	H	2B	3B	HR	RBI	BB	SO	OBP	SLG
Grass	.261	257	67	11	2	11	36	14	38	.300	.447	May	.116	43	5	0	1	0	1	1	4	.136	.163
Turf	.262	61	16	2	1	2	9	5	7	.318	.426	June	.379	29	11	3	0	0	2	2	6	.406	.483
Pre-All Star	.237	139	33	6	1	2	18	5	19	.262	.338	July	.317	41	13	2	0	5	10	5	3	.391	.732
Post-All Star	.279	179	50	7	2	11	27	14	26	.333	.525	August	.274	84	23	3	1	4	11	7	14	.330	.476
Scoring Posn	.161	87	14	2	0	1	28	11	11	.252	.218	Sept/Oct	.262	65	17	2	1	3	10	3	11	.301	.462
Close & Late	.317	60	19	3	0	4	9	2	12	.339	.567	vs. AL	.242	149	36	5	1	3	21	6	22	.269	.349
None on/out	.349	63	22	3	0	8	8	4	10	.388	.778	vs. NL	.278	169	47	8	2	10	24	13	23	.332	.527

1997 By Position

Position	Avg	AB	H	2B	3B	HR	RBI	BB	SO	OBP	SLG	G	GS	Innings	PO	A	E	DP	Fld Pct	Rng Fctr	In Zone	Zone Outs	Zone Rtg	MLB Zone
As c	.260	315	82	13	3	13	44	18	44	.301	.444	98	86	773.2	561	33	5	8	.992	---	---	---	---	---

Career (1994-1997)

	Avg	AB	H	2B	3B	HR	RBI	BB	SO	OBP	SLG		Avg	AB	H	2B	3B	HR	RBI	BB	SO	OBP	SLG
vs. Left	.272	250	68	15	1	4	33	14	32	.307	.388	First Pitch	.264	148	39	6	0	5	23	10	0	.311	.405
vs. Right	.255	611	156	24	4	23	92	25	109	.283	.421	Ahead in Count	.330	185	61	10	2	11	37	18	0	.380	.584
Groundball	.247	178	44	7	0	5	20	8	22	.282	.371	Behind in Count	.206	393	81	14	2	8	44	0	124	.211	.313
Flyball	.225	120	27	5	0	2	17	4	25	.254	.317	Two Strikes	.189	366	69	14	3	4	34	11	141	.217	.276
Home	.268	406	109	12	4	15	56	13	65	.295	.429	Batting #7	.239	272	65	12	2	3	29	11	39	.270	.331
Away	.253	455	115	27	1	12	69	26	76	.292	.396	Batting #8	.265	378	100	16	2	17	59	21	66	.303	.452
Day	.245	376	92	16	0	10	57	19	61	.284	.367	Other	.280	211	59	11	1	7	37	7	36	.307	.441
Night	.272	485	132	23	5	17	68	20	80	.301	.445	March/April	.230	100	23	5	0	2	20	2	20	.245	.340
Grass	.262	664	174	25	4	21	90	28	110	.294	.407	May	.253	150	38	5	2	5	25	3	23	.272	.413
Turf	.254	197	50	14	1	6	35	11	31	.290	.426	June	.311	132	41	9	0	4	14	10	15	.359	.470
Pre-All Star	.259	448	116	20	2	13	75	17	76	.286	.400	July	.247	162	40	8	1	7	33	10	26	.288	.438
Post-All Star	.262	413	108	19	3	14	50	22	65	.302	.424	August	.265	162	43	8	1	5	17	9	38	.302	.420
Scoring Posn	.218	243	53	12	1	6	94	20	41	.275	.350	Sept/Oct	.252	155	39	4	1	4	16	5	19	.283	.368
Close & Late	.292	161	47	10	0	9	32	3	31	.305	.522	vs. AL	.242	149	36	5	1	3	21	6	22	.269	.349
None on/out	.284	201	57	9	0	12	12	5	37	.301	.424	vs. NL	.264	712	188	34	4	24	104	33	119	.298	.424

Batter vs. Pitcher (career)

Hits Best Against	Avg	AB	H	2B	3B	HR	RBI	BB	SO	OBP	SLG	Hits Worst Against	Avg	AB	H	2B	3B	HR	RBI	BB	SO	OBP	SLG
Michael Mimbs	.500	10	5	1	0	1	1	1	0	.583	.900	Darryl Kile	.182	11	2	0	0	0	2	0	4	.250	.182
Mark Portugal	.500	10	5	2	0	1	4	0	0	.455	1.000												
Bobby Jones	.429	14	6	0	0	1	2	0	2	.429	.643												
Jason Isringhausen	.364	11	4	0	0	0	2	2	3	.467	.364												
Shane Reynolds	.308	13	4	0	0	2	3	1	1	.357	.769												

Charles Johnson — Marlins

Age 26 – Bats Right

	Avg	G	AB	R	H	2B	3B	HR	RBI	BB	SO	HBP	GDP	SB	CS	OBP	SLG	IBB	SH	SF	#Pit	#P/PA	GB	FB	G/F
1997 Season	.250	124	416	43	104	26	1	19	63	60	109	3	13	0	2	.347	.454	6	3	2	1894	3.91	123	129	0.95
Career (1994-1997)	.241	345	1128	122	272	55	3	44	143	147	275	9	45	1	4	.331	.412	14	9	9	5008	3.84	370	327	1.13

1997 Season

	Avg	AB	H	2B	3B	HR	RBI	BB	SO	OBP	SLG		Avg	AB	H	2B	3B	HR	RBI	BB	SO	OBP	SLG
vs. Left	.300	90	27	7	0	5	15	10	21	.376	.544	First Pitch	.291	55	16	5	0	2	9	5	0	.350	.491
vs. Right	.236	326	77	19	1	14	48	50	88	.339	.429	Ahead in Count	.312	93	29	7	1	5	15	18	0	.420	.570
Groundball	.207	58	12	2	0	2	5	4	13	.258	.345	Behind in Count	.210	186	39	10	0	6	28	0	89	.217	.360
Flyball	.283	53	15	2	1	2	7	6	21	.356	.472	Two Strikes	.160	200	32	10	0	6	20	37	109	.299	.300
Home	.243	206	50	11	0	7	22	36	54	.359	.398	Batting #7	.278	194	54	12	0	12	35	30	51	.376	.526
Away	.257	210	54	15	1	12	41	24	55	.335	.510	Batting #8	.226	221	50	14	1	7	28	30	58	.335	.394
Day	.236	110	26	6	0	6	15	18	22	.349	.455	Other	.000	1	0	0	0	0	0	0	0	.000	.000
Night	.255	306	78	20	1	13	48	42	87	.347	.454	March/April	.237	59	14	5	0	2	9	11	14	.361	.424
Grass	.236	348	82	19	0	14	45	49	91	.332	.411	May	.215	65	14	3	0	1	4	9	20	.300	.308
Turf	.324	68	22	7	1	5	18	11	18	.425	.676	June	.230	74	17	4	1	3	11	8	18	.305	.432
Pre-All Star	.226	212	48	14	1	6	25	30	56	.327	.387	July	.348	69	24	7	0	6	14	9	17	.423	.710
Post-All Star	.275	204	56	12	0	13	38	30	53	.369	.525	August	.309	81	25	5	0	6	19	14	20	.412	.593
Scoring Posn	.225	111	25	8	0	5	41	28	36	.380	.432	Sept/Oct	.147	68	10	2	0	1	6	9	20	.247	.221
Close & Late	.247	73	18	4	1	3	14	8	20	.317	.452	vs. AL	.316	38	12	3	0	1	5	6	13	.409	.474
None on/out	.352	88	31	5	0	5	5	8	15	.406	.580	vs. NL	.243	378	92	23	1	18	58	54	96	.341	.452

1997 By Position

Position	Avg	AB	H	2B	3B	HR	RBI	BB	SO	OBP	SLG	G	GS	Innings	PO	A	E	DP	Fld Pct	Rng Fctr	In Zone	Zone Outs	Zone Rtg	MLB Zone
As c	.251	415	104	26	1	19	63	60	109	.348	.455	123	123	1076.2	902	68	0	16	1.000	---	---	---	---	---

Career (1994-1997)

	Avg	AB	H	2B	3B	HR	RBI	BB	SO	OBP	SLG		Avg	AB	H	2B	3B	HR	RBI	BB	SO	OBP	SLG
vs. Left	.267	262	70	18	0	9	33	38	57	.360	.439	First Pitch	.292	154	45	12	0	8	23	9	0	.343	.526
vs. Right	.233	866	202	37	3	35	110	109	218	.322	.404	Ahead in Count	.307	241	74	16	2	17	42	61	0	.443	.602
Groundball	.222	234	52	7	1	7	19	19	51	.312	.349	Behind in Count	.194	505	98	21	0	12	51	0	226	.200	.307
Flyball	.285	186	53	10	2	7	29	19	51	.349	.473	Two Strikes	.171	545	93	18	1	11	42	77	275	.275	.268
Home	.235	582	137	21	2	20	60	75	134	.326	.381	Batting #7	.233	546	127	24	1	22	67	69	128	.319	.401
Away	.247	546	135	34	1	24	83	72	141	.336	.445	Batting #8	.248	556	138	30	2	21	72	74	140	.341	.423
Day	.220	255	56	10	0	12	32	35	60	.316	.400	Other	.269	26	7	1	0	1	4	4	7	.355	.423
Night	.247	873	216	45	3	32	111	112	215	.335	.416	March/April	.218	156	34	10	0	4	15	21	43	.313	.359
Grass	.230	900	207	35	2	34	102	113	217	.318	.387	May	.216	241	52	5	0	10	29	34	61	.312	.361
Turf	.285	228	65	20	1	10	41	34	58	.380	.513	June	.209	234	49	12	2	7	28	19	55	.273	.368

Career (1994-1997)

	Avg	AB	H	2B	3B	HR	RBI	BB	SO	OBP	SLG		Avg	AB	H	2B	3B	HR	RBI	BB	SO	OBP	SLG
Pre-All Star	.217	686	149	31	3	22	77	80	173	.301	.367	July	.290	207	60	10	1	12	30	25	45	.368	.522
Post-All Star	.278	442	123	24	4	22	66	67	102	.376	.482	August	.327	101	33	9	0	6	22	17	24	.430	.594
Scoring Posn	.213	291	62	17	1	9	92	54	73	.333	.371	Sept/Oct	.233	189	44	9	0	5	19	31	47	.344	.360
Close & Late	.263	179	47	7	1	7	29	25	46	.348	.430	vs. AL	.316	38	12	3	0	1	5	6	13	.409	.474
None on/out	.287	251	72	10	0	12	12	28	54	.363	.470	vs. NL	.239	1090	260	52	3	43	138	141	262	.328	.410

Batter vs. Pitcher (career)

Hits Best Against	Avg	AB	H	2B	3B	HR	RBI	BB	SO	OBP	SLG	Hits Worst Against	Avg	AB	H	2B	3B	HR	RBI	BB	SO	OBP	SLG
Danny Darwin	.375	8	3	1	0	0	2	2	1	.455	.500	Pedro Astacio	.000	9	0	0	0	0	0	1	1	.182	.000
Jon Lieber	.364	11	4	0	0	0	0	0	3	.364	.364	Jaime Navarro	.077	13	1	0	0	0	0	0	1	.077	.077
Curt Schilling	.353	17	6	2	0	1	4	2	9	.421	.647	Andy Benes	.100	10	1	0	0	0	0	1	4	.182	.100
John Smiley	.318	22	7	2	0	0	1	2	3	.375	.409	Hideo Nomo	.118	17	2	1	0	0	0	2	13	.211	.176
												Greg Maddux	.154	13	2	0	0	0	0	0	0	.154	.154

Dane Johnson — Athletics Age 35 – Pitches Right

	ERA	W	L	Sv	G	GS	IP	BB	SO	Avg	H	2B	3B	HR	RBI	OBP	SLG	GF	IR	IRS	Hld	SvOp	SB	CS	GB	FB	G/F
1997 Season	4.53	4	1	2	38	0	45.2	31	43	.272	49	8	1	4	38	.378	.394	12	35	19	2	4	7	1	63	47	1.34
Career (1994-1997)	4.70	6	2	2	63	0	67.0	47	57	.269	70	8	1	6	55	.379	.377	18	51	28	6	4	11	1	95	72	1.32

1997 Season

	ERA	W	L	Sv	G	GS	IP	H	HR	BB	SO		Avg	AB	H	2B	3B	HR	RBI	BB	SO	OBP	SLG
Home	6.65	1	1	1	20	0	23.0	26	2	20	21	vs. Left	.301	83	25	4	1	1	16	15	16	.404	.410
Away	2.38	3	0	1	18	0	22.2	23	2	11	22	vs. Right	.247	97	24	4	0	3	22	16	27	.356	.381
Starter	0.00	0	0	0	0	0	0.0	0	0	0	0	Scoring Posn	.329	70	23	3	1	3	37	16	17	.440	.529
Reliever	4.53	4	1	2	38	0	45.2	49	4	31	43	Close & Late	.207	29	6	2	0	0	8	9	7	.425	.276
0 Days rest (Relief)	0.00	0	0	1	4	0	2.0	6	0	0	1	None on/out	.256	39	10	2	0	1	1	6	7	.356	.385
1 or 2 Days rest	3.79	4	1	0	27	0	35.2	32	1	23	33	First Pitch	.353	17	6	1	1	0	5	4	0	.476	.529
3+ Days rest	9.00	0	0	1	7	0	8.0	11	3	8	9	Ahead in Count	.213	80	17	4	0	2	10	0	36	.217	.338
Pre-All Star	4.12	3	0	2	18	0	19.2	24	3	12	24	Behind in Count	.357	56	20	1	0	2	15	13	0	.465	.482
Post-All Star	4.85	1	1	0	20	0	26.0	25	1	19	19	Two Strikes	.205	83	17	5	0	1	13	14	43	.323	.301

Jason Johnson — Pirates Age 24 – Pitches Right

	ERA	W	L	Sv	G	GS	IP	BB	SO	Avg	H	2B	3B	HR	RBI	OBP	SLG	GF	IR	IRS	Hld	SvOp	SB	CS	GB	FB	G/F
1997 Season	6.00	0	0	0	3	0	6.0	1	3	.400	10	0	1	2	6	.407	.720	0	2	2	0	0	0	2	7	6	1.17

1997 Season

	ERA	W	L	Sv	G	GS	IP	H	HR	BB	SO		Avg	AB	H	2B	3B	HR	RBI	BB	SO	OBP	SLG
Home	4.50	0	0	0	2	0	4.0	7	2	0	3	vs. Left	.429	7	3	0	1	0	1	1	1	.500	.714
Away	9.00	0	0	0	1	0	2.0	3	1	0	0	vs. Right	.389	18	7	0	0	2	5	0	2	.368	.722

Lance Johnson — Cubs Age 34 – Bats Left (groundball hitter)

	Avg	G	AB	R	H	2B	3B	HR	RBI	BB	SO	HBP	GDP	SB	CS	OBP	SLG	IBB	SH	SF	#Pit	P/PA	GB	FB	G/F
1997 Season	.307	111	410	60	126	16	8	5	39	42	31	0	8	20	12	.370	.422	3	0	2	1514	3.33	196	93	2.11
Last Five Years	.310	666	2651	406	821	94	69	27	266	169	158	4	40	171	43	.350	.428	19	8	13	8600	3.02	1263	625	2.02

1997 Season

	Avg	AB	H	2B	3B	HR	RBI	BB	SO	OBP	SLG		Avg	AB	H	2B	3B	HR	RBI	BB	SO	OBP	SLG
vs. Left	.298	131	39	6	2	1	14	11	8	.350	.397	First Pitch	.312	93	29	2	0	0	6	2	0	.326	.333
vs. Right	.312	279	87	10	6	4	25	31	23	.379	.434	Ahead in Count	.398	98	39	7	2	1	16	27	0	.528	.541
Groundball	.325	83	27	2	0	0	8	11	6	.404	.349	Behind in Count	.264	144	38	5	3	0	8	0	26	.260	.340
Flyball	.255	55	14	1	0	1	7	7	6	.333	.327	Two Strikes	.254	142	36	5	2	1	10	13	31	.312	.338
Home	.346	179	62	8	5	4	24	20	14	.410	.514	Batting #1	.306	396	121	15	8	5	36	41	29	.369	.422
Away	.277	231	64	8	3	1	15	22	17	.339	.351	Batting #9	.444	9	4	1	0	0	3	0	0	.444	.556
Day	.299	174	52	6	2	4	23	17	14	.358	.425	Other	.200	5	1	0	0	0	0	1	2	.333	.200
Night	.314	236	74	10	6	1	16	25	17	.379	.419	March/April	.299	97	29	4	1	0	13	19	6	.410	.361
Grass	.289	336	97	10	6	5	34	33	24	.351	.399	May	.000	1	0	0	0	0	0	0	0	.000	.000
Turf	.392	74	29	6	2	0	5	9	7	.452	.527	June	.275	51	14	3	1	1	2	2	5	.302	.431
Pre-All Star	.297	172	51	8	2	1	17	24	13	.381	.384	July	.311	90	28	2	2	0	6	11	8	.386	.378
Post-All Star	.315	238	75	8	6	4	22	18	18	.362	.450	August	.293	92	27	1	2	0	9	3	7	.316	.413
Scoring Posn	.337	89	30	5	2	0	32	12	7	.408	.438	Sept/Oct	.354	79	28	6	2	2	9	7	5	.402	.557
Close & Late	.296	71	21	4	1	0	9	11	9	.381	.380	vs. AL	.260	50	13	0	0	0	5	2	4	.288	.260
None on/out	.304	171	52	10	3	2	14	13	.433	.459		vs. NL	.314	360	113	16	8	5	34	40	27	.381	.444

1997 By Position

Position	Avg	AB	H	2B	3B	HR	RBI	BB	SO	OBP	SLG	G	GS	Innings	PO	A	E	DP	Fld Pct	Rng Fctr	In Zone	Zone Outs	Zone Rtg	MLB Zone
As Pinch Hitter	.300	10	3	0	0	0	2	0	2	.273	.300	11	0	---	---	---	---	---	---	---	---	---	---	---
As cf	.306	395	121	16	8	5	35	42	29	.372	.425	105	94	836.1	231	4	7	2	.971	2.53	266	229	.861	.815

Last Five Years

	Avg	AB	H	2B	3B	HR	RBI	BB	SO	OBP	SLG		Avg	AB	H	2B	3B	HR	RBI	BB	SO	OBP	SLG
vs. Left	.298	762	227	26	14	3	76	45	65	.336	.381	First Pitch	.354	692	245	27	17	8	60	15	0	.367	.477
vs. Right	.314	1889	594	68	55	24	190	124	93	.356	.447	Ahead in Count	.328	646	212	21	16	6	88	113	0	.428	.438
Groundball	.310	681	211	15	12	6	76	38	43	.346	.394	Behind in Count	.268	870	233	34	19	3	74	0	147	.267	.361
Flyball	.279	517	144	11	9	7	45	26	24	.358	.402	Two Strikes	.259	752	195	28	17	4	62	41	158	.295	.358
Home	.300	1285	385	38	36	8	123	80	77	.340	.404	Batting #1	.318	1647	524	61	39	24	163	104	102	.357	.446
Away	.319	1366	436	56	33	19	143	89	81	.360	.450	Batting #7	.295	779	230	25	25	3	82	55	41	.342	.403

Last Five Years

	Avg	AB	H	2B	3B	HR	RBI	BB	SO	OBP	SLG		Avg	AB	H	2B	3B	HR	RBI	BB	SO	OBP	SLG
Day	.305	840	256	29	21	11	98	56	61	.347	.429	Other	.298	225	67	8	5	0	21	10	15	.326	.378
Night	.312	1811	565	65	48	16	168	113	97	.352	.427	March/April	.288	399	115	13	10	1	50	32	24	.339	.378
Grass	.301	2220	669	67	52	22	203	139	128	.342	.408	May	.294	412	121	10	9	1	29	21	23	.327	.369
Turf	.353	431	152	27	17	5	63	30	30	.394	.529	June	.280	460	129	15	14	4	44	36	29	.333	.400
Pre-All Star	.295	1452	428	46	41	8	144	97	86	.338	.399	July	.322	525	169	18	14	6	55	36	35	.366	.444
Post-All Star	.328	1199	393	48	28	19	122	72	72	.365	.462	August	.322	460	148	16	8	10	48	23	29	.353	.457
Scoring Posn	.321	582	187	20	23	7	233	53	40	.370	.471	Sept/Oct	.352	395	139	22	14	5	40	21	18	.384	.516
Close & Late	.306	422	129	14	11	4	51	36	39	.359	.419	vs. AL	.299	1609	481	47	40	13	163	96	91	.338	.402
None on/out	.321	896	288	41	20	12	12	45	47	.355	.452	vs. NL	.326	1042	340	47	29	14	103	73	67	.369	.467

Batter vs. Pitcher (career)

Hits Best Against	Avg	AB	H	2B	3B	HR	RBI	BB	SO	OBP	SLG	Hits Worst Against	Avg	AB	H	2B	3B	HR	RBI	BB	SO	OBP	SLG
Jim Poole	.571	14	8	1	2	0	6	0	0	.571	.929	Chris Haney	.083	12	1	1	0	0	0	1	2	.154	.167
Darryl Kile	.563	16	9	3	0	0	0	0	0	.563	.750	Dennis Martinez	.100	20	2	0	0	0	1	1	1	.143	.100
Pat Mahomes	.529	17	9	1	1	0	3	0	0	.529	.706	Roger Pavlik	.120	25	3	0	0	0	1	1	3	.154	.120
Curt Schilling	.500	12	6	0	1	1	3	0	0	.462	.917	Roger Clemens	.125	40	5	0	0	0	0	0	7	.125	.125
Alan Benes	.455	11	5	1	1	2	4	2	1	.538	1.273	Jamie Moyer	.133	15	2	0	0	0	0	0	2	.133	.133

Mark Johnson — Reds
Age 30 – Bats Left

	Avg	G	AB	R	H	2B	3B	HR	RBI	BB	SO	HBP	GDP	SB	CS	OBP	SLG	IBB	SH	SF	#Pit	#P/PA	GB	FB	G/F
1997 Season	.215	78	219	30	47	10	0	4	29	43	78	2	1	1	1	.345	.315	1	0	3	1128	4.22	50	64	0.78
Career (1995-1997)	.239	284	783	117	187	40	1	30	104	124	208	9	8	12	7	.346	.407	6	0	8	3685	3.99	209	273	0.77

1997 Season

	Avg	AB	H	2B	3B	HR	RBI	BB	SO	OBP	SLG		Avg	AB	H	2B	3B	HR	RBI	BB	SO	OBP	SLG
vs. Left	.314	35	11	1	0	0	5	5	11	.390	.343	Scoring Posn	.219	64	14	3	0	1	22	19	20	.398	.313
vs. Right	.196	184	36	9	0	4	24	38	67	.336	.310	Close & Late	.293	41	12	3	0	0	8	8	17	.400	.366
Home	.223	94	21	4	0	2	14	17	36	.345	.330	None on/out	.259	54	14	2	0	1	1	7	14	.344	.352
Away	.208	125	26	6	0	2	15	26	42	.344	.304	Batting #4	.238	160	38	8	0	3	19	31	56	.366	.344
First Pitch	.462	26	12	4	0	2	11	0	0	.444	.846	Batting #6	.167	30	5	0	0	1	6	8	11	.325	.267
Ahead in Count	.302	43	13	3	0	0	7	23	0	.552	.372	Other	.138	29	4	2	0	0	0	4	11	.242	.207
Behind in Count	.141	99	14	2	0	1	5	0	57	.149	.192	Pre-All Star	.214	187	40	8	0	4	26	39	64	.348	.321
Two Strikes	.129	116	15	3	0	2	10	20	78	.261	.207	Post-All Star	.219	32	7	2	0	0	3	4	14	.324	.281

Career (1995-1997)

	Avg	AB	H	2B	3B	HR	RBI	BB	SO	OBP	SLG		Avg	AB	H	2B	3B	HR	RBI	BB	SO	OBP	SLG
vs. Left	.253	87	22	3	0	3	13	9	24	.327	.391	First Pitch	.376	101	38	9	0	8	28	4	0	.389	.703
vs. Right	.237	696	165	37	1	27	91	115	184	.349	.409	Ahead in Count	.317	164	52	12	0	9	36	64	0	.511	.555
Groundball	.262	202	53	10	0	3	18	37	57	.377	.356	Behind in Count	.179	352	63	14	0	6	21	0	157	.189	.270
Flyball	.206	136	28	7	0	4	17	14	40	.279	.346	Two Strikes	.159	384	61	14	1	9	25	56	208	.271	.271
Home	.251	351	88	19	1	19	52	61	98	.370	.473	Batting #4	.243	358	87	16	0	12	49	59	100	.353	.388
Away	.229	432	99	21	0	11	52	63	110	.327	.354	Batting #5	.235	187	44	12	0	6	19	25	43	.333	.396
Day	.239	255	61	15	1	10	36	36	71	.334	.424	Other	.235	238	56	12	1	12	36	40	65	.346	.445
Night	.239	528	126	25	0	20	68	88	137	.352	.400	March/April	.232	112	26	6	0	4	17	15	33	.331	.393
Grass	.244	324	79	16	0	5	34	40	79	.326	.340	May	.236	165	39	10	1	6	23	32	50	.360	.418
Turf	.235	459	108	24	1	25	70	84	129	.360	.455	June	.265	151	40	6	0	8	25	26	35	.365	.464
Pre-All Star	.253	455	115	25	1	20	68	79	128	.362	.444	July	.267	131	35	4	0	8	20	19	37	.372	.481
Post-All Star	.220	328	72	15	0	10	36	45	80	.324	.357	August	.188	133	25	9	0	3	13	19	37	.294	.323
Scoring Posn	.206	218	45	9	0	5	62	41	54	.332	.317	Sept/Oct	.242	91	22	5	0	1	6	13	16	.346	.330
Close & Late	.263	137	36	7	0	4	20	23	43	.372	.401	vs. AL	.083	12	1	1	0	0	0	2	3	.250	.167
None on/out	.230	183	42	8	0	5	5	27	42	.332	.355	vs. NL	.241	771	186	39	1	30	102	121	204	.348	.411

Batter vs. Pitcher (career)

Hits Best Against	Avg	AB	H	2B	3B	HR	RBI	BB	SO	OBP	SLG	Hits Worst Against	Avg	AB	H	2B	3B	HR	RBI	BB	SO	OBP	SLG
Jamey Wright	.500	8	4	2	0	0	5	3	1	.636	.750	Curt Schilling	.118	17	2	1	0	1	2	0	8	.118	.353
Ismael Valdes	.444	9	4	0	0	0	0	6	1	.667	.444	Dave Burba	.125	8	1	0	0	0	1	3	6	.385	.125
Kevin Ritz	.444	9	4	1	0	0	1	3	1	.583	.556	Greg Maddux	.133	15	2	0	0	0	1	0	8	.133	.133
Frank Castillo	.308	13	4	1	1	1	1	1	5	.357	.769	Steve Trachsel	.154	13	2	1	0	0	0	1	3	.214	.231
Andy Benes	.308	13	4	1	0	1	3	1	5	.333	.615	Pedro Martinez	.154	13	2	0	0	0	1	2	5	.267	.154

Mike Johnson — Expos
Age 22 – Pitches Right (flyball pitcher)

	ERA	W	L	Sv	G	GS	IP	BB	SO	Avg	H	2B	3B	HR	RBI	OBP	SLG	CG	ShO	Sup	QS	#P/S	SB	CS	GB	FB	G/F
1997 Season	6.83	2	6	2	25	16	89.2	37	57	.295	106	17	1	20	64	.359	.515	0	0	5.22	3	70	14	3	111	129	0.86

1997 Season

	ERA	W	L	Sv	G	GS	IP	H	HR	BB	SO		Avg	AB	H	2B	3B	HR	RBI	BB	SO	OBP	SLG
Home	4.62	1	2	1	14	6	48.2	48	8	18	25	vs. Left	.330	194	64	6	1	10	38	21	32	.390	.526
Away	9.44	0	5	1	11	10	41.0	58	12	19	32	vs. Right	.255	165	42	11	0	10	26	16	25	.322	.503
Starter	8.13	2	6	0	16	16	65.1	80	16	33	40	Scoring Posn	.290	93	27	4	1	4	42	17	21	.391	.484
Reliever	3.33	0	0	2	9	0	24.1	26	4	4	17	Close & Late	.500	2	1	0	0	0	1	1	0	.500	2.000
0-3 Days Rest (Start)	0.00	0	0	0	0	0	0.0	0	0	0	0	None on/out	.301	93	28	2	0	4	4	6	15	.343	.452
4 Days Rest	6.97	1	4	0	9	9	40.0	45	9	17	20	First Pitch	.415	53	22	2	0	3	7	4	0	.441	.623
5+ Days Rest	9.95	1	2	0	7	7	25.1	35	7	16	20	Ahead in Count	.208	144	30	4	1	3	16	0	47	.212	.313
Pre-All Star	8.23	0	1	2	12	5	35.0	43	11	15	26	Behind in Count	.376	93	35	10	0	6	21	19	0	.478	.677
Post-All Star	5.93	2	5	0	13	11	54.2	63	9	22	31	Two Strikes	.209	158	33	5	0	8	29	14	57	.276	.392

Randy Johnson — Mariners
Age 34 – Pitches Left

	ERA	W	L	Sv	G	GS	IP	BB	SO	Avg	H	2B	3B	HR	RBI	OBP	SLG	CG	ShO	Sup	QS	#P/S	SB	CS	GB	FB	G/F
1997 Season	2.28	20	4	0	30	29	213.0	77	291	.194	147	32	1	20	56	.277	.318	5	2	4.86	23	120	13	16	198	187	1.06
Last Five Years	2.86	75	20	2	132	124	916.0	338	1182	.203	671	144	11	76	284	.284	.322	30	12	5.30	90	121	90	53	950	767	1.24

1997 Season

	ERA	W	L	Sv	G	GS	IP	H	HR	BB	SO		Avg	AB	H	2B	3B	HR	RBI	BB	SO	OBP	SLG
Home	1.89	9	1	0	16	15	114.0	71	10	40	173	vs. Left	.260	77	20	4	0	4	7	5	28	.329	.468
Away	2.73	11	3	0	14	14	99.0	76	10	37	118	vs. Right	.186	681	127	28	1	16	49	72	263	.271	.301
Day	2.18	6	1	0	10	9	66.0	39	5	34	85	Inning 1-6	.194	623	121	29	1	17	48	58	236	.271	.326
Night	2.33	14	3	0	20	20	147.0	108	15	43	206	Inning 7+	.193	135	26	3	0	3	8	19	55	.299	.281
Grass	2.87	10	3	0	13	13	91.0	70	10	36	109	None on	.201	477	96	16	1	13	13	53	195	.287	.321
Turf	1.84	10	1	0	17	16	122.0	77	10	41	182	Runners on	.181	281	51	16	0	7	43	24	96	.260	.313
March/April	2.73	3	0	0	5	5	33.0	23	4	13	39	Scoring Posn	.154	143	22	9	0	4	34	11	54	.233	.301
May	2.31	4	1	0	6	6	42.0	29	4	17	57	Close & Late	.217	83	18	3	0	1	5	10	32	.316	.289
June	0.92	4	1	0	6	6	49.0	25	3	14	68	None on/out	.155	194	30	7	0	2	2	20	81	.241	.222
July	3.16	3	1	0	5	5	37.0	34	4	17	54	vs. 1st Batr (relief)	.000	1	0	0	0	0	0	0	1	.000	.000
August	1.86	3	1	0	4	4	29.0	15	2	12	46	1st Inning Pitched	.178	107	19	5	0	2	7	10	45	.254	.280
Sept/Oct	1.96	3	0	0	4	3	23.0	21	3	4	27	First 75 Pitches	.179	463	83	18	1	9	26	42	174	.258	.281
Starter	2.30	19	4	0	29	29	211.0	145	20	77	288	Pitch 76-90	.216	88	19	6	0	5	10	7	36	.274	.455
Reliever	0.00	1	0	0	2	0	2.0	2	0	0	3	Pitch 91-105	.233	90	21	5	0	2	9	11	32	.330	.356
0-3 Days Rest (Start)	0.00	0	0	0	0	0	0.0	0	0	0	0	Pitch 106+	.205	117	24	3	0	4	11	17	49	.309	.333
4 Days Rest	2.41	14	2	0	19	19	142.0	102	14	56	187	First Pitch	.351	77	27	6	1	5	15	1	0	.375	.649
5+ Days Rest	2.09	5	2	0	10	10	69.0	43	6	21	101	Ahead in Count	.121	406	49	10	0	5	14	0	234	.131	.182
vs. AL	2.33	19	4	0	29	28	205.0	145	19	75	279	Behind in Count	.333	132	44	12	0	8	18	37	0	.482	.606
vs. NL	1.13	1	0	0	1	1	8.0	0	0	2	12	Two Strikes	.095	451	43	11	0	5	16	39	291	.174	.153
Pre-All Star	2.20	12	2	0	18	18	131.0	83	13	48	168	Pre-All Star	.182	455	83	15	1	13	32	48	168	.269	.305
Post-All Star	2.41	8	2	0	12	11	82.0	64	7	29	123	Post-All Star	.211	303	64	17	0	7	24	29	123	.288	.337

Last Five Years

	ERA	W	L	Sv	G	GS	IP	H	HR	BB	SO		Avg	AB	H	2B	3B	HR	RBI	BB	SO	OBP	SLG
Home	2.61	40	8	2	70	65	497.0	347	42	179	681	vs. Left	.198	323	64	16	1	5	27	19	131	.264	.300
Away	3.16	35	12	0	62	59	419.0	324	34	159	501	vs. Right	.204	2980	607	128	10	71	257	319	1051	.286	.325
Day	2.85	20	4	0	36	33	246.2	172	17	110	304	Inning 1-6	.207	2620	542	118	10	58	224	259	914	.285	.326
Night	2.86	55	16	2	96	91	669.1	499	59	228	878	Inning 7+	.189	683	129	26	1	18	60	79	268	.282	.309
Grass	3.20	29	10	0	53	50	351.2	274	27	144	428	None on	.205	2058	422	92	9	46	46	196	729	.281	.326
Turf	2.65	46	10	2	79	74	564.1	397	49	194	754	Runners on	.200	1245	249	52	2	30	238	142	453	.289	.317
March/April	3.43	13	3	0	23	23	157.1	117	19	71	181	Scoring Posn	.195	707	138	35	1	15	202	83	283	.283	.311
May	3.01	16	4	0	26	26	170.1	134	12	66	206	Close & Late	.201	348	70	14	0	9	40	32	140	.281	.319
June	2.30	14	4	0	23	23	183.2	115	13	63	252	None on/out	.196	863	169	36	4	16	16	84	303	.276	.302
July	3.97	8	6	0	20	20	140.2	125	13	57	192	vs. 1st Batr (relief)	.625	8	5	2	0	0	2	0	2	.625	.875
August	2.59	11	3	2	24	17	142.1	102	11	47	192	1st Inning Pitched	.194	463	90	17	2	9	39	52	173	.283	.298
Sept/Oct	1.78	13	0	0	16	15	121.2	78	8	34	159	First 75 Pitches	.203	1978	402	81	10	38	153	191	711	.281	.312
Starter	2.86	74	20	0	124	124	896.0	654	74	333	1148	Pitch 76-90	.226	380	86	20	0	18	40	38	125	.300	.421
Reliever	2.70	1	0	2	8	0	20.0	17	2	5	34	Pitch 91-105	.206	383	79	15	1	9	39	41	124	.294	.321
0-3 Days Rest (Start)	2.48	5	0	0	7	7	54.1	35	5	13	70	Pitch 106+	.185	562	104	28	0	11	52	68	222	.279	.294
4 Days Rest	2.67	47	13	0	79	79	577.0	411	47	215	735	First Pitch	.322	311	100	16	3	20	56	4	0	.343	.585
5+ Days Rest	3.37	22	7	0	38	38	264.2	208	22	105	343	Ahead in Count	.138	1854	255	55	6	20	92	0	1013	.147	.206
vs. AL	2.87	74	20	2	131	123	908.0	669	75	336	1170	Behind in Count	.324	555	180	46	2	19	73	164	0	.482	.517
vs. NL	1.13	1	0	0	1	1	8.0	0	2	1	12	Two Strikes	.121	2005	242	44	4	26	102	170	1182	.194	.186
Pre-All Star	2.95	46	12	0	79	79	563.2	414	49	218	699	Pre-All Star	.206	2014	414	84	7	49	174	218	699	.290	.327
Post-All Star	2.71	29	8	2	53	45	352.1	257	27	110	483	Post-All Star	.199	1289	257	60	4	27	110	120	483	.275	.315

Pitcher vs. Batter (career)

Pitches Best Vs.	Avg	AB	H	2B	3B	HR	RBI	BB	SO	OBP	SLG	Pitches Worst Vs.	Avg	AB	H	2B	3B	HR	RBI	BB	SO	OBP	SLG
Jose Valentin	.000	13	0	0	0	0	0	2	6	.133	.000	Rene Gonzales	.500	16	8	2	0	1	2	5	2	.667	.813
Charlie Hayes	.000	9	0	0	0	0	2	0	2	.091	.000	Jack Voigt	.417	12	5	1	0	1	2	1	4	.462	.750
Mark Loretta	.000	9	0	0	0	0	0	2	5	.182	.000	Mo Vaughn	.389	18	7	2	0	2	4	0	7	.450	.833
Rafael Palmeiro	.048	21	1	0	0	0	0	0	5	.048	.048	Ellis Burks	.333	18	6	1	0	2	6	2	6	.400	.722
David Howard	.077	26	2	0	0	0	1	1	8	.111	.115	Jim Edmonds	.313	16	5	2	0	2	3	1	4	.389	.813

Russ Johnson — Astros
Age 25 – Bats Right

	Avg	G	AB	R	H	2B	3B	HR	RBI	BB	SO	HBP	GDP	SB	CS	OBP	SLG	IBB	SH	SF	#Pit	#P/PA	GB	FB	G/F
1997 Season	.300	21	60	7	18	1	0	2	9	6	14	0	2	1	1	.364	.417	0	1	0	273	4.07	19	12	1.58

1997 Season

	Avg	AB	H	2B	3B	HR	RBI	BB	SO	OBP	SLG		Avg	AB	H	2B	3B	HR	RBI	BB	SO	OBP	SLG
vs. Left	.238	21	5	1	0	0	4	2	3	.304	.286	Scoring Posn	.412	17	7	1	0	0	7	3	5	.500	.471
vs. Right	.333	39	13	0	0	2	5	4	11	.395	.487	Close & Late	.222	18	4	0	0	1	2	1	8	.263	.389

John Johnstone — Giants
Age 29 – Pitches Right (flyball pitcher)

	ERA	W	L	Sv	G	GS	IP	BB	SO	Avg	H	2B	3B	HR	RBI	OBP	SLG	GF	IR	IRS	Hld	SvOp	SB	CS	GB	FB	G/F
1997 Season	3.24	0	0	0	18	0	25.0	14	19	.250	22	7	0	1	17	.364	.364	3	17	9	1	0	7	1	23	35	0.66
Career (1993-1997)	4.82	2	4	0	55	0	74.2	44	55	.287	85	21	5	9	57	.382	.483	19	33	15	4	0	10	3	92	104	0.88

1997 Season

	ERA	W	L	Sv	G	GS	IP	H	HR	BB	SO		Avg	AB	H	2B	3B	HR	RBI	BB	SO	OBP	SLG
Home	4.32	0	0	0	7	0	8.1	7	0	8	5	vs. Left	.270	37	10	3	0	0	3	6	5	.372	.351
Away	2.70	0	0	0	11	0	16.2	15	1	6	14	vs. Right	.235	51	12	4	0	1	14	8	14	.358	.373

Andruw Jones — Braves

	Avg	G	AB	R	H	2B	3B	HR	RBI	BB	SO	HBP	GDP	SB	CS	OBP	SLG	IBB	SH	SF	#Pit	#P/PA	GB	FB	G/F
1997 Season	.231	153	399	60	92	18	1	18	70	56	107	4	11	20	11	.329	.416	2	5	3	1776	3.80	134	108	1.24
Career (1996-1997)	.228	184	505	71	115	25	2	23	83	63	136	4	12	23	11	.317	.422	2	5	3	2179	3.76	168	140	1.20

1997 Season

	Avg	AB	H	2B	3B	HR	RBI	BB	SO	OBP	SLG			Avg	AB	H	2B	3B	HR	RBI	BB	SO	OBP	SLG
vs. Left	.281	139	39	7	1	7	28	23	31	.383	.496		First Pitch	.373	59	22	8	1	5	19	1	0	.397	.797
vs. Right	.204	260	53	11	0	11	42	33	76	.300	.373		Ahead in Count	.325	83	27	7	0	7	25	28	0	.496	.663
Groundball	.231	65	15	2	0	2	9	7	19	.315	.354		Behind in Count	.144	188	27	2	0	4	17	0	89	.143	.218
Flyball	.239	46	11	3	0	3	10	8	15	.368	.500		Two Strikes	.112	197	22	2	0	3	18	27	107	.218	.168
Home	.203	187	38	9	1	5	30	37	51	.336	.342		Batting #5	.252	159	40	8	1	7	22	20	47	.339	.447
Away	.255	212	54	9	0	13	40	19	56	.322	.481		Batting #6	.191	152	29	10	0	3	24	22	41	.302	.316
Day	.185	119	22	3	0	6	16	14	33	.274	.361		Other	.261	88	23	0	0	8	24	14	19	.359	.534
Night	.250	280	70	15	1	12	54	42	74	.352	.439		March/April	.254	59	15	4	0	2	7	7	13	.333	.424
Grass	.212	307	65	14	1	12	50	48	88	.319	.381		May	.281	32	9	2	0	0	4	7	6	.410	.344
Turf	.293	92	27	4	0	6	20	8	19	.363	.533		June	.282	78	22	2	1	4	15	13	24	.389	.487
Pre-All Star	.272	195	53	11	1	7	31	27	52	.363	.446		July	.234	107	25	8	0	6	20	10	28	.299	.477
Post-All Star	.191	204	39	7	0	11	39	29	55	.297	.387		August	.218	55	12	1	0	3	14	14	16	.380	.400
Scoring Posn	.234	124	29	5	0	4	48	11	25	.295	.371		Sept/Oct	.132	68	9	1	0	3	10	5	20	.203	.279
Close & Late	.205	73	15	2	0	3	9	14	23	.341	.356		vs. AL	.282	39	11	2	1	1	6	6	17	.370	.462
None on/out	.194	93	18	1	0	4	4	15	24	.312	.355		vs. NL	.225	360	81	16	0	17	64	50	90	.325	.411

1997 By Position

Position	Avg	AB	H	2B	3B	HR	RBI	BB	SO	OBP	SLG	G	GS	Innings	PO	A	E	DP	Fld Pct	Rng Fctr	In Zone	Zone Outs	Zone Rtg	MLB Zone
As Pinch Hitter	.045	22	1	0	0	0	2	6	5	.250	.045	29	0	---	---	---	---	---	---	---	---	---	---	---
As cf	.258	163	42	10	1	10	33	25	45	.359	.515	57	41	415.1	139	8	2	1	.987	3.19	150	130	.867	.815
As rf	.225	213	48	8	0	7	34	25	57	.311	.362	95	55	553.2	148	7	5	1	.969	2.52	166	140	.843	.813

Bobby Jones — Mets

	ERA	W	L	Sv	G	GS	IP	BB	SO	Avg	H	2B	3B	HR	RBI	OBP	SLG	CG	ShO	Sup	QS	#P/S	SB	CS	GB	FB	G/F
1997 Season	3.63	15	9	0	30	30	193.1	63	125	.242	177	35	2	24	83	.303	.395	2	1	4.75	20	98	11	6	278	199	1.40
Career (1993-1997)	3.86	51	38	0	124	124	806.1	240	483	.266	823	158	13	86	355	.320	.409	9	4	4.53	74	98	59	22	1171	857	1.37

1997 Season

	ERA	W	L	Sv	G	GS	IP	H	HR	BB	SO			Avg	AB	H	2B	3B	HR	RBI	BB	SO	OBP	SLG
Home	3.59	5	4	0	14	14	90.1	82	13	28	64		vs. Left	.237	355	84	18	1	13	49	37	67	.311	.403
Away	3.67	10	5	0	16	16	103.0	95	11	35	61		vs. Right	.248	375	93	17	1	11	34	26	58	.295	.387
Day	3.57	5	3	0	10	10	68.0	65	11	21	35		Inning 1-6	.250	615	154	29	2	21	75	54	113	.311	.407
Night	3.66	10	6	0	20	20	125.1	112	13	42	90		Inning 7+	.200	115	23	6	0	3	8	9	12	.258	.330
Grass	3.65	12	7	0	25	25	160.1	145	20	58	104		None on	.243	456	111	19	0	15	15	36	81	.302	.384
Turf	3.55	3	2	0	5	5	33.0	32	4	5	21		Runners on	.241	274	66	16	2	9	68	27	44	.305	.412
March/April	3.40	4	2	0	6	6	42.1	35	6	10	28		Scoring Posn	.268	142	38	9	2	6	59	19	27	.345	.486
May	1.15	5	0	0	5	5	39.0	27	2	13	21		Close & Late	.197	66	13	5	0	2	6	5	6	.254	.364
June	3.51	3	2	0	5	5	33.1	34	4	11	25		None on/out	.189	190	36	5	0	5	5	13	35	.241	.295
July	6.00	0	2	0	6	6	33.0	37	7	10	26		vs. 1st Batr (relief)	.000	0	0	0	0	0	0	0	0	.000	.000
August	5.32	1	2	0	4	4	23.2	29	4	7	9		1st Inning Pitched	.286	119	34	9	0	5	23	17	24	.380	.487
Sept/Oct	3.27	2	1	0	4	4	22.0	15	1	12	16		First 75 Pitches	.268	507	136	25	1	18	62	48	95	.332	.428
Starter	3.63	15	9	0	30	30	193.1	177	24	63	125		Pitch 76-90	.185	92	17	5	1	2	13	5	15	.224	.326
Reliever	0.00	0	0	0	0	0	0.0	0	0	0	0		Pitch 91-105	.193	83	16	4	0	4	6	8	10	.264	.386
0-3 Days Rest (Start)	3.86	0	0	0	1	1	7.0	6	2	2	5		Pitch 106+	.167	48	8	1	0	0	2	2	5	.200	.188
4 Days Rest	3.59	8	5	0	16	16	97.2	86	11	39	65		First Pitch	.267	101	27	4	2	3	14	3	0	.292	.436
5+ Days Rest	3.65	7	4	0	13	13	88.2	85	11	22	55		Ahead in Count	.199	346	69	11	0	8	22	0	108	.199	.301
vs. AL	12.38	0	2	0	2	2	8.0	15	5	2	9		Behind in Count	.319	163	52	13	0	10	27	26	0	.408	.583
vs. NL	3.25	15	7	0	28	28	185.1	162	19	61	116		Two Strikes	.165	339	56	7	0	7	22	34	125	.243	.248
Pre-All Star	3.08	12	5	0	18	18	125.2	110	16	36	81		Pre-All Star	.235	469	110	18	2	16	46	36	81	.291	.384
Post-All Star	4.66	3	4	0	12	12	67.2	67	8	27	44		Post-All Star	.257	261	67	17	0	8	37	27	44	.323	.414

Career (1993-1997)

	ERA	W	L	Sv	G	GS	IP	H	HR	BB	SO			Avg	AB	H	2B	3B	HR	RBI	BB	SO	OBP	SLG
Home	3.73	19	20	0	60	60	397.2	414	41	122	252		vs. Left	.257	1500	385	84	7	38	164	138	242	.319	.398
Away	3.99	32	18	0	64	64	408.2	409	45	118	231		vs. Right	.275	1595	438	74	6	48	191	102	241	.321	.419
Day	4.33	17	9	0	38	38	247.1	269	37	62	149		Inning 1-6	.266	2593	689	133	13	78	315	201	426	.320	.417
Night	3.65	34	29	0	86	86	559.0	554	49	178	334		Inning 7+	.267	502	134	25	0	8	40	39	57	.322	.365
Grass	4.09	36	32	0	98	98	634.1	656	76	192	394		None on	.264	1832	483	98	4	46		136	290	.318	.397
Turf	3.03	15	6	0	26	26	172.0	167	10	48	89		Runners on	.269	1263	340	60	9	40	309	104	193	.323	.426
March/April	4.23	8	5	0	17	17	106.1	96	13	34	68		Scoring Posn	.256	661	169	33	6	16	247	85	117	.335	.396
May	2.33	15	5	0	23	23	166.1	150	8	45	85		Close & Late	.221	249	55	11	0	4	20	20	30	.279	.313
June	3.86	7	10	0	20	20	137.2	154	20	35	87		None on/out	.247	801	198	38	2	18	18	56	124	.300	.367
July	4.73	8	6	0	24	24	142.2	167	14	45	92		vs. 1st Batr (relief)	.000	0	0	0	0	0	0	0	0	.000	.000
August	4.87	6	6	0	19	19	116.1	128	16	33	65		1st Inning Pitched	.277	477	132	32	0	13	50	46	85	.342	.426
Sept/Oct	3.68	7	6	0	19	19	137.0	128	11	48	86		First 75 Pitches	.268	2211	593	108	11	68	256	173	368	.322	.419
Starter	3.86	51	38	0	124	124	806.1	823	86	240	483		Pitch 76-90	.254	390	99	24	1	8	55	29	46	.308	.382
Reliever	0.00	0	0	0	0	0	0.0	0	0	0	0		Pitch 91-105	.286	315	90	22	1	8	27	28	46	.348	.438
0-3 Days Rest (Start)	2.96	1	0	0	4	4	27.1	28	4	7	12		Pitch 106+	.229	179	41	4	0	2	17	10	23	.274	.285
4 Days Rest	3.80	29	21	0	71	71	459.0	464	50	151	279		First Pitch	.327	508	166	26	6	22	80	13	0	.343	.531
5+ Days Rest	4.02	21	16	0	49	49	320.0	331	32	82	192		Ahead in Count	.214	1355	290	47	2	26	107	0	429	.218	.309
vs. AL	12.38	0	2	0	2	2	8.0	15	5	2	9		Behind in Count	.308	737	227	55	4	26	95	122	0	.404	.499

Career (1993-1997)

	ERA	W	L	Sv	G	GS	IP	H	HR	BB	SO		Avg	AB	H	2B	3B	HR	RBI	BB	SO	OBP	SLG
vs. NL	3.78	51	36	0	122	122	798.1	808	81	238	474	Two Strikes	.197	1318	259	45	1	23	98	105	483	.260	.285
Pre-All Star	3.48	33	23	0	68	68	455.2	456	46	128	272	Pre-All Star	.263	1737	456	74	7	46	191	128	272	.316	.393
Post-All Star	4.36	18	15	0	56	56	350.2	367	40	112	211	Post-All Star	.270	1358	367	84	6	40	164	112	211	.326	.429

Pitcher vs. Batter (career)

Pitches Best Vs.	Avg	AB	H	2B	3B	HR	RBI	BB	SO	OBP	SLG	Pitches Worst Vs.	Avg	AB	H	2B	3B	HR	RBI	BB	SO	OBP	SLG
David Segui	.000	15	0	0	0	0	0	1	5	.063	.000	Bill Mueller	.600	10	6	3	0	0	1	3	2	.692	.900
Henry Rodriguez	.045	22	1	0	0	0	1	1	5	.087	.045	Jeff Blauser	.500	26	13	0	2	3	4	2	5	.567	.846
Scott Servais	.056	18	1	0	0	0	0	1	1	.150	.056	Ryan Klesko	.500	26	13	1	1	3	12	4	3	.567	.962
Jose Hernandez	.063	16	1	0	0	0	0	0	5	.063	.063	Moises Alou	.467	15	7	2	0	2	7	2	2	.529	1.000
Rey Sanchez	.091	11	1	0	0	0	1	0	0	.091	.091	Ellis Burks	.400	10	4	0	1	3	5	2	2	.500	1.500

Bobby M. Jones — Rockies
Age 26 – Pitches Left (flyball pitcher)

	ERA	W	L	Sv	G	GS	IP	BB	SO	Avg	H	2B	3B	HR	RBI	OBP	SLG	CG	ShO	Sup	QS	#P/S	SB	CS	GB	FB	G/F
1997 Season	8.38	1	1	0	4	4	19.1	12	5	.380	30	8	2	2	16	.447	.608	0	0	6.05	0	84	4	1	31	34	0.91

1997 Season

	ERA	W	L	Sv	G	GS	IP	H	HR	BB	SO		Avg	AB	H	2B	3B	HR	RBI	BB	SO	OBP	SLG
Home	8.10	1	0	0	1	1	6.2	11	0	2	0	vs. Left	.250	8	2	0	1	0	3	0	0	.222	.500
Away	8.53	0	1	0	3	3	12.2	19	2	10	5	vs. Right	.394	71	28	8	1	2	13	12	5	.471	.620

Chipper Jones — Braves
Age 26 – Bats Both

	Avg	G	AB	R	H	2B	3B	HR	RBI	BB	SO	HBP	GDP	SB	CS	OBP	SLG	IBB	SH	SF	#Pit	#P/PA	GB	FB	G/F
1997 Season	.295	157	597	100	176	41	3	21	111	76	88	0	20	20	5	.371	.479	8	0	6	2437	3.59	247	156	1.58
Career (1993-1997)	.292	462	1722	303	502	96	11	74	307	237	276	0	44	42	10	.374	.489	9	2	17	7285	3.68	701	469	1.49

1997 Season

	Avg	AB	H	2B	3B	HR	RBI	BB	SO	OBP	SLG		Avg	AB	H	2B	3B	HR	RBI	BB	SO	OBP	SLG
vs. Left	.250	196	49	15	0	1	21	22	37	.324	.342	First Pitch	.328	116	38	8	0	5	26	7	0	.357	.526
vs. Right	.317	401	127	26	3	20	90	54	51	.393	.546	Ahead in Count	.353	153	54	14	1	9	45	38	0	.474	.634
Groundball	.270	115	31	7	0	4	21	9	17	.317	.435	Behind in Count	.229	210	48	14	1	3	20	0	72	.229	.348
Flyball	.278	72	20	3	1	3	19	8	10	.346	.472	Two Strikes	.219	228	50	16	0	1	15	31	88	.313	.303
Home	.316	304	96	24	1	7	56	45	42	.402	.470	Batting #3	.298	567	169	39	3	19	106	73	85	.375	.478
Away	.273	293	80	17	2	14	55	31	46	.338	.488	Batting #4	.150	20	3	0	0	2	5	2	3	.227	.450
Day	.314	175	55	13	2	7	37	22	23	.385	.531	Other	.400	10	4	2	0	0	1	0	.455	.600
Night	.287	422	121	28	1	14	74	54	65	.365	.457	March/April	.322	90	29	7	0	2	20	13	14	.400	.467
Grass	.293	478	140	29	3	14	87	65	71	.373	.454	May	.237	97	23	5	0	3	13	12	16	.321	.381
Turf	.303	119	36	12	0	7	24	11	17	.362	.580	June	.345	110	38	9	0	8	29	15	16	.417	.645
Pre-All Star	.307	319	98	22	0	14	69	43	48	.385	.508	July	.325	114	37	8	1	4	24	8	15	.366	.518
Post-All Star	.281	278	78	19	3	7	42	33	40	.355	.446	August	.283	99	28	5	2	1	17	16	14	.379	.404
Scoring Posn	.314	172	54	15	0	6	90	25	23	.389	.506	Sept/Oct	.241	87	21	7	0	3	8	12	13	.333	.425
Close & Late	.256	90	23	4	0	0	15	13	14	.350	.300	vs. AL	.288	59	17	4	1	2	8	4	11	.333	.492
None on/out	.299	107	32	10	0	6	6	17	10	.395	.561	vs. NL	.296	538	159	37	2	19	103	72	77	.375	.478

1997 By Position

Position	Avg	AB	H	2B	3B	HR	RBI	BB	SO	OBP	SLG	G	GS	Innings	PO	A	E	DP	Fld Pct	Rng Fctr	In Zone	Zone Outs	Zone Rtg	MLB Zone
As 3b	.299	581	174	41	3	21	111	74	87	.375	.489	152	151	1300.2	77	240	15	18	.955	2.19	326	268	822	801

Career (1993-1997)

	Avg	AB	H	2B	3B	HR	RBI	BB	SO	OBP	SLG		Avg	AB	H	2B	3B	HR	RBI	BB	SO	OBP	SLG
vs. Left	.276	497	137	27	2	10	63	66	89	.359	.398	First Pitch	.360	328	118	22	4	17	72	8	0	.367	.607
vs. Right	.298	1225	365	69	9	64	244	171	187	.380	.526	Ahead in Count	.356	436	155	32	2	26	104	128	0	.496	.617
Groundball	.266	425	113	22	2	17	67	44	69	.331	.447	Behind in Count	.225	630	142	28	2	17	74	0	222	.225	.357
Flyball	.289	242	70	12	1	9	48	34	36	.373	.459	Two Strikes	.213	686	146	23	3	20	76	101	276	.313	.343
Home	.311	866	269	56	5	40	171	121	130	.392	.525	Batting #2	.350	20	7	2	1	0	2	4	1	.458	.550
Away	.272	856	233	40	6	34	136	116	146	.356	.452	Batting #3	.294	1658	487	92	10	72	298	229	269	.376	.492
Day	.293	508	149	26	5	21	96	79	80	.383	.488	Other	.182	44	8	2	0	2	7	4	6	.250	.364
Night	.291	1214	353	70	6	53	211	158	196	.370	.489	March/April	.289	201	58	11	1	5	42	25	33	.362	.428
Grass	.291	1361	396	76	9	57	245	187	215	.373	.486	May	.281	302	85	19	1	15	54	46	52	.376	.500
Turf	.294	361	106	20	2	17	62	50	61	.380	.501	June	.294	326	96	20	1	19	70	36	50	.359	.537
Pre-All Star	.288	904	260	51	3	44	182	125	145	.371	.497	July	.314	296	93	15	1	14	53	45	38	.402	.514
Post-All Star	.296	818	242	45	8	30	125	112	131	.377	.480	August	.313	320	100	14	5	13	57	47	50	.397	.509
Scoring Posn	.311	453	141	26	2	16	222	70	76	.391	.483	Sept/Oct	.253	277	70	17	2	8	31	38	53	.340	.415
Close & Late	.280	268	75	13	2	12	53	42	47	.375	.478	vs. AL	.288	59	17	4	1	2	8	4	11	.333	.492
None on/out	.288	320	92	20	1	21	21	42	40	.370	.553	vs. NL	.292	1663	485	92	10	72	299	233	265	.375	.489

Batter vs. Pitcher (career)

Hits Best Against	Avg	AB	H	2B	3B	HR	RBI	BB	SO	OBP	SLG	Hits Worst Against	Avg	AB	H	2B	3B	HR	RBI	BB	SO	OBP	SLG
Michael Mimbs	.600	10	6	1	1	0	1	6	2	.750	.900	Hideo Nomo	.000	15	0	0	0	0	0	3	6	.167	.000
Armando Reynoso	.545	11	6	1	1	2	4	2	0	.615	1.364	Andy Ashby	.059	17	1	0	0	0	0	2	1	.059	.059
Todd Stottlemyre	.500	14	7	1	0	3	7	4	1	.611	1.214	John Smiley	.063	16	1	0	0	0	1	3	4	.211	.063
Allen Watson	.500	12	6	1	0	2	6	0	2	.500	1.083	Pat Rapp	.071	14	1	0	0	0	1	1	2	.133	.071
Dave Mlicki	.467	15	7	2	0	2	9	2	1	.529	1.000	Alan Benes	.091	11	1	0	0	0	0	1	2	.167	.091

238

Chris Jones — Padres
Age 32 – Bats Right (groundball hitter)

	Avg	G	AB	R	H	2B	3B	HR	RBI	BB	SO	HBP	GDP	SB	CS	OBP	SLG	IBB	SH	SF	#Pit	#P/PA	GB	FB	G/F
1997 Season	.243	92	152	24	37	9	0	7	25	16	45	2	4	7	2	.322	.441	0	1	1	692	4.02	53	32	1.66
Last Five Years	.264	367	732	114	193	35	7	25	107	53	194	5	16	19	8	.316	.433	4	8	5	3064	3.82	281	148	1.90

1997 Season

	Avg	AB	H	2B	3B	HR	RBI	BB	SO	OBP	SLG		Avg	AB	H	2B	3B	HR	RBI	BB	SO	OBP	SLG
vs. Left	.228	57	13	2	0	2	9	6	19	.308	.368	Scoring Posn	.250	44	11	3	0	2	18	7	10	.346	.455
vs. Right	.253	95	24	7	0	5	16	10	26	.330	.484	Close & Late	.160	25	4	1	0	0	1	1	10	.192	.200
Home	.231	78	18	3	0	4	13	8	27	.299	.423	None on/out	.314	35	11	1	0	1	1	1	9	.333	.429
Away	.257	74	19	6	0	3	12	8	18	.345	.459	Batting #5	.256	43	11	3	0	4	9	3	13	.304	.605
First Pitch	.214	14	3	2	0	0	5	0	0	.200	.357	Batting #6	.292	24	7	0	0	1	3	2	5	.346	.417
Ahead in Count	.444	18	8	0	0	3	8	6	0	.600	.944	Other	.224	85	19	6	0	2	13	11	27	.323	.365
Behind in Count	.167	90	15	5	0	1	6	0	40	.176	.256	Pre-All Star	.236	89	21	7	0	5	17	9	23	.320	.483
Two Strikes	.179	84	15	6	0	0	2	10	45	.274	.250	Post-All Star	.254	63	16	2	0	2	8	7	22	.324	.381

Last Five Years

	Avg	AB	H	2B	3B	HR	RBI	BB	SO	OBP	SLG		Avg	AB	H	2B	3B	HR	RBI	BB	SO	OBP	SLG
vs. Left	.263	319	84	18	2	8	36	19	87	.306	.408	First Pitch	.308	91	28	6	0	4	30	4	0	.330	.505
vs. Right	.264	413	109	17	5	17	71	34	107	.323	.453	Ahead in Count	.398	103	41	9	1	8	23	18	0	.492	.738
Groundball	.288	191	55	11	2	10	36	13	49	.332	.524	Behind in Count	.205	395	81	16	3	7	38	0	167	.209	.314
Flyball	.190	121	23	5	0	3	16	4	32	.227	.306	Two Strikes	.175	394	69	12	4	4	26	32	194	.241	.256
Home	.243	358	87	13	4	12	44	26	96	.296	.402	Batting #5	.278	151	42	6	3	9	30	10	38	.325	.536
Away	.283	374	106	22	3	13	63	27	98	.334	.463	Batting #6	.252	143	36	5	0	4	17	6	36	.282	.371
Day	.247	247	61	15	5	7	34	18	64	.301	.433	Other	.263	438	115	24	4	12	60	37	120	.323	.418
Night	.272	485	132	20	2	18	73	35	130	.323	.433	March/April	.273	33	9	1	0	2	7	3	7	.351	.485
Grass	.265	544	144	27	6	17	78	48	143	.326	.430	May	.220	123	27	2	0	7	12	9	40	.278	.407
Turf	.261	188	49	8	1	8	29	5	51	.284	.441	June	.320	175	56	12	2	7	28	16	43	.377	.531
Pre-All Star	.288	416	120	21	4	17	64	29	109	.339	.481	July	.312	170	53	10	3	5	35	9	35	.346	.494
Post-All Star	.231	316	73	14	3	8	43	24	85	.286	.370	August	.172	134	23	5	0	1	16	7	40	.221	.231
Scoring Posn	.278	194	54	12	0	8	79	20	45	.338	.464	Sept/Oct	.258	97	25	5	2	3	9	9	29	.318	.443
Close & Late	.250	160	40	6	2	6	29	15	43	.320	.425	vs. AL	.250	28	7	3	0	1	8	2	5	.323	.464
None on/out	.321	159	51	7	3	3	3	5	34	.345	.459	vs. NL	.264	704	186	32	7	24	99	51	189	.315	.432

Batter vs. Pitcher (career)

Hits Best Against	Avg	AB	H	2B	3B	HR	RBI	BB	SO	OBP	SLG	Hits Worst Against	Avg	AB	H	2B	3B	HR	RBI	BB	SO	OBP	SLG
Chris Hammond	.417	12	5	1	0	0	1	0	2	.417	.500	Jeff Fassero	.053	19	1	1	0	0	2	0	6	.053	.105
Terry Mulholland	.375	24	9	1	0	1	4	1	4	.385	.542	Steve Avery	.174	23	4	1	0	1	2	3	6	.269	.348
												Al Leiter	.182	11	2	0	0	1	2	1	7	.250	.455
												Tom Glavine	.188	16	3	1	0	0	0	0	7	.188	.250
												Denny Neagle	.188	16	3	0	0	0	1	0	3	.188	.188

Doug Jones — Brewers
Age 41 – Pitches Right

	ERA	W	L	Sv	G	GS	IP	BB	SO	Avg	H	2B	3B	HR	RBI	OBP	SLG	GF	IR	IRS	Hld	SvOp	SB	CS	GB	FB	G/F
1997 Season	2.02	6	6	36	75	0	80.1	9	82	.215	62	11	1	4	20	.242	.301	73	18	4	0	38	2	6	88	91	0.97
Last Five Years	3.54	19	26	114	297	0	330.1	72	288	.267	346	53	2	26	170	.310	.373	243	116	46	3	137	6	5	456	330	1.38

1997 Season

	ERA	W	L	Sv	G	GS	IP	H	HR	BB	SO		Avg	AB	H	2B	3B	HR	RBI	BB	SO	OBP	SLG
Home	1.55	6	2	19	40	0	46.1	34	2	6	49	vs. Left	.228	149	34	5	1	3	12	5	42	.258	.336
Away	2.65	0	4	17	35	0	34.0	28	2	3	33	vs. Right	.200	140	28	6	0	1	8	4	40	.224	.264
Day	2.59	3	2	13	29	0	31.1	25	3	2	32	Inning 1-6	.000	0	0	0	0	0	0	0	0	.000	.000
Night	1.65	3	4	23	46	0	49.0	37	1	7	50	Inning 7+	.215	289	62	11	1	4	20	9	82	.242	.301
Grass	2.02	6	6	30	66	0	71.1	57	4	7	72	None on	.210	181	38	8	1	3	3	6	52	.243	.315
Turf	2.00	0	0	6	9	0	9.0	5	0	2	10	Runners on	.222	108	24	3	0	1	17	3	30	.239	.278
March/April	1.80	2	0	5	10	0	10.0	7	1	1	12	Scoring Posn	.213	61	13	2	0	1	17	3	19	.232	.295
May	2.93	1	1	7	16	0	15.1	18	0	3	15	Close & Late	.224	183	41	8	0	2	14	6	53	.256	.301
June	3.00	0	2	7	14	0	15.0	14	1	0	18	None on/out	.224	76	17	6	0	1	1	1	23	.234	.342
July	2.57	0	1	4	8	0	7.0	6	1	0	5	vs. 1st Batr (relief)	.194	72	14	5	0	1	3	1	22	.200	.306
August	0.47	3	1	6	16	0	19.1	7	1	3	15	1st Inning Pitched	.214	257	55	9	1	4	17	9	76	.245	.304
Sept/Oct	1.98	0	1	7	11	0	13.2	6	1	3	15	First 15 Pitches	.224	219	49	9	1	3	14	7	61	.252	.315
Starter	0.00	0	0	0	0	0	0.0	0	0	0	0	Pitch 16-30	.186	59	11	1	0	1	5	2	19	.213	.254
Reliever	2.02	6	6	36	75	0	80.1	62	4	9	82	Pitch 31-45	.200	10	2	1	0	0	0	0	2	.200	.300
0 Days rest (Relief)	1.72	4	3	17	32	0	36.2	30	1	4	37	Pitch 46+	.000	1	0	0	0	0	0	0	1	.000	.000
1 or 2 Days rest	2.33	2	3	14	27	0	27.0	25	1	4	28	First Pitch	.359	39	14	4	0	0	3	0	0	.359	.462
3+ Days rest	2.16	0	0	5	16	0	16.2	7	2	1	17	Ahead in Count	.196	184	36	4	1	2	12	0	76	.199	.261
vs. AL	2.23	5	6	31	68	0	72.2	60	4	7	76	Behind in Count	.211	38	8	2	0	1	1	6	0	.318	.342
vs. NL	0.00	1	0	5	7	0	7.2	2	0	2	6	Two Strikes	.133	165	22	2	1	1	6	3	82	.152	.176
Pre-All Star	2.70	3	3	20	43	0	43.1	41	3	4	47	Pre-All Star	.256	160	41	7	1	3	15	4	47	.271	.341
Post-All Star	1.22	3	3	16	32	0	37.0	21	1	5	35	Post-All Star	.163	129	21	4	0	1	5	5	35	.206	.217

Last Five Years

	ERA	W	L	Sv	G	GS	IP	H	HR	BB	SO		Avg	AB	H	2B	3B	HR	RBI	BB	SO	OBP	SLG
Home	3.41	15	12	56	148	0	171.1	177	14	35	148	vs. Left	.264	640	169	25	2	13	86	40	140	.313	.370
Away	3.68	4	14	58	149	0	159.0	169	12	37	140	vs. Right	.270	655	177	28	1	13	84	32	148	.307	.376
Day	2.76	9	10	40	112	0	130.1	127	10	23	107	Inning 1-6	.240	50	12	1	0	2	8	3	13	.309	.380
Night	4.05	10	16	74	185	0	200.0	219	16	49	181	Inning 7+	.268	1245	334	52	3	24	162	69	275	.310	.373
Grass	3.88	13	19	71	199	0	218.0	234	19	45	197	None on	.254	696	177	28	2	13	33	33	151	.294	.356
Turf	2.88	6	7	43	98	0	112.1	112	7	27	91	Runners on	.282	599	169	25	1	13	157	39	137	.328	.392
March/April	2.55	5	2	15	46	0	53.0	51	6	6	46	Scoring Posn	.279	351	98	17	0	8	143	33	84	.342	.396

Last Five Years

	ERA	W	L	Sv	G	GS	IP	H	HR	BB	SO
May	4.24	3	8	27	66	0	70.0	79	6	14	58
June	4.47	2	5	23	52	0	58.1	74	1	10	49
July	2.93	0	5	24	44	0	43.0	44	5	12	31
August	3.28	7	5	13	56	0	68.2	60	5	21	58
Sept/Oct	3.38	2	1	12	33	0	37.1	38	3	9	46
Starter	0.00	0	0	0	0	0	0.0	0	0	0	0
Reliever	3.54	19	26	114	297	0	330.1	346	26	72	288
0 Days rest (Relief)	3.00	8	11	50	96	0	105.0	107	8	21	89
1 or 2 Days rest	3.50	10	9	44	121	0	139.0	151	7	30	126
3+ Days rest	4.27	1	6	20	80	0	86.1	88	11	21	73
vs. AL	3.34	10	10	54	144	0	151.0	146	13	36	152
vs. NL	3.71	9	16	60	153	0	179.1	200	13	36	136
Pre-All Star	3.84	10	16	70	179	0	196.2	220	16	33	162
Post-All Star	3.10	9	10	44	118	0	133.2	126	10	39	126

	Avg	AB	H	2B	3B	HR	RBI	BB	SO	OBP	SLG
Close & Late	.277	734	203	30	1	14	115	46	164	.322	.377
None on/out	.257	307	79	12	1	7	7	7	63	.276	.371
vs. 1st Batr (relief)	.281	281	79	13	0	7	29	10	54	.307	.402
1st Inning Pitched	.262	1065	279	43	1	24	143	57	247	.305	.372
First 15 Pitches	.276	903	249	37	1	22	111	44	190	.315	.392
Pitch 16-30	.248	339	84	15	1	3	50	24	84	.298	.324
Pitch 31-45	.250	52	13	1	1	1	9	4	14	.304	.365
Pitch 46+	.000	1	0	0	0	0	0	0	0	.000	.000
First Pitch	.380	171	65	13	0	4	30	14	0	.431	.526
Ahead in Count	.214	742	159	19	3	9	73	0	260	.219	.284
Behind in Count	.345	200	69	13	0	6	39	43	0	.462	.500
Two Strikes	.176	663	117	15	2	9	57	15	288	.197	.246
Pre-All Star	.282	781	220	30	2	16	105	33	162	.313	.387
Post-All Star	.245	514	126	23	1	10	65	39	126	.305	.352

Pitcher vs. Batter (since 1984)

Pitches Best Vs.	Avg	AB	H	2B	3B	HR	RBI	BB	SO	OBP	SLG
Jay Bell	.000	11	0	0	0	0	0	1	3	.083	.000
Fred McGriff	.059	17	1	0	0	0	1	2	5	.158	.059
Kevin Seitzer	.077	13	1	0	0	0	1	0	1	.077	.077
Jeff Blauser	.083	12	1	0	0	0	1	0	5	.083	.083
Jose Offerman	.083	12	1	0	0	0	1	0	2	.083	.083

Pitches Worst Vs.	Avg	AB	H	2B	3B	HR	RBI	BB	SO	OBP	SLG
Terry Steinbach	.600	10	6	1	0	0	4	0	1	.545	.700
Greg Vaughn	.500	14	7	4	0	1	3	0	2	.500	1.000
Travis Fryman	.500	12	6	3	0	0	3	0	3	.500	.750
Cal Ripken	.455	22	10	3	0	1	6	2	4	.500	.727
Edgar Martinez	.333	9	3	2	0	1	4	2	3	.500	.889

Todd Jones — Tigers   Age 30 – Pitches Right (groundball pitcher)

	ERA	W	L	Sv	G	GS	IP	BB	SO	Avg	H	2B	3B	HR	RBI	OBP	SLG	GF	IR	IRS	Hld	SvOp	SB	CS	GB	FB	G/F
1997 Season	3.09	5	4	31	68	0	70.0	35	70	.231	60	8	0	3	26	.320	.296	51	35	10	5	36	6	1	96	51	1.88
Career (1993-1997)	3.23	23	16	70	262	0	337.0	160	298	.233	290	52	4	23	143	.324	.336	156	158	45	28	91	29	7	513	262	1.96

1997 Season

	ERA	W	L	Sv	G	GS	IP	H	HR	BB	SO
Home	3.66	1	2	16	33	0	32.0	27	1	16	28
Away	2.61	4	2	15	35	0	38.0	33	2	19	42
Day	3.14	1	0	13	29	0	28.2	28	0	15	27
Night	3.05	4	4	18	39	0	41.1	32	3	20	43
Grass	3.23	5	2	27	59	0	61.1	51	3	30	58
Turf	2.08	0	2	4	9	0	8.2	9	0	5	12
March/April	4.26	1	1	3	14	0	12.2	13	0	12	10
May	2.61	0	1	2	9	0	10.1	6	0	6	8
June	3.86	0	1	4	10	0	9.1	8	2	8	12
July	1.29	1	0	10	13	0	14.0	12	0	4	15
August	4.09	0	0	6	11	0	11.0	11	1	1	12
Sept/Oct	2.84	3	1	6	11	0	12.2	10	0	4	13
Starter	0.00	0	0	0	0	0	0.0	0	0	0	0
Reliever	3.09	5	4	31	68	0	70.0	60	3	35	70
0 Days rest (Relief)	1.71	1	1	13	19	0	21.0	14	0	8	25
1 or 2 Days rest	3.79	4	1	13	33	0	35.2	34	3	20	31
3+ Days rest	3.38	0	2	5	16	0	13.1	12	0	7	14
vs. AL	2.98	5	3	27	61	0	63.1	50	2	33	62
vs. NL	4.05	0	1	4	7	0	6.2	10	1	2	8
Pre-All Star	3.50	1	3	13	37	0	36.0	31	2	28	33
Post-All Star	2.65	4	1	18	31	0	34.0	29	1	7	37

	Avg	AB	H	2B	3B	HR	RBI	BB	SO	OBP	SLG
vs. Left	.246	134	33	6	0	3	15	16	35	.322	.358
vs. Right	.214	126	27	2	0	0	11	19	35	.318	.230
Inning 1-6	.000	0	0	0	0	0	0	0	0	.000	.000
Inning 7+	.231	260	60	8	0	3	26	35	70	.320	.296
None on	.293	123	36	3	0	1		17	32	.383	.341
Runners on	.175	137	24	5	0	2	25	18	38	.264	.255
Scoring Posn	.149	74	11	3	0	1	22	13	22	.264	.230
Close & Late	.210	181	38	5	0	2	19	25	51	.303	.271
None on/out	.300	60	18	2	0	1		5	16	.364	.383
vs. 1st Batr (relief)	.230	61	14	2	0	0	4	6	18	.294	.262
1st Inning Pitched	.236	233	55	8	0	3	26	30	63	.318	.309
First 15 Pitches	.253	178	45	7	0	1	13	22	46	.332	.309
Pitch 16-30	.203	74	15	1	0	2	13	12	22	.307	.297
Pitch 31-45	.000	8	0	0	0	0	0	0	2	.111	.000
Pitch 46+	.000	0	0	0	0	0	0	1	0	1.000	.000
First Pitch	.185	27	5	3	0	0	1	2	0	.241	.185
Ahead in Count	.198	131	26	2	0	1	10	0	60	.201	.237
Behind in Count	.333	60	20	3	0	1	9	19	0	.494	.467
Two Strikes	.167	144	24	1	0	1	10	14	70	.241	.201
Pre-All Star	.235	132	31	6	0	2	18	28	33	.366	.326
Post-All Star	.227	128	29	2	0	1	8	7	37	.265	.266

Career (1993-1997)

	ERA	W	L	Sv	G	GS	IP	H	HR	BB	SO
Home	2.78	12	10	33	125	0	165.0	133	7	68	150
Away	3.66	11	6	37	137	0	172.0	157	16	92	148
Day	4.28	5	6	24	87	0	101.0	109	8	58	102
Night	2.78	18	10	46	175	0	236.0	181	15	102	196
Grass	3.79	7	6	39	119	0	140.0	126	11	72	125
Turf	2.83	16	10	31	143	0	197.0	164	12	88	173
March/April	4.60	4	4	7	40	0	43.0	43	3	25	39
May	1.71	4	1	11	46	0	63.1	35	3	29	51
June	2.72	5	2	12	41	0	56.1	53	5	28	54
July	2.61	5	2	18	50	0	72.1	63	4	31	76
August	4.42	3	3	13	46	0	55.0	49	5	24	40
Sept/Oct	4.21	4	4	9	39	0	47.0	47	3	23	38
Starter	0.00	0	0	0	0	0	0.0	0	0	0	0
Reliever	3.23	23	16	70	262	0	337.0	290	23	160	298
0 Days rest (Relief)	2.90	7	3	26	61	0	71.1	59	5	42	68
1 or 2 Days rest	3.57	11	9	32	134	0	179.0	158	15	79	154
3+ Days rest	2.80	5	4	12	67	0	86.2	73	3	39	76
vs. AL	2.98	5	3	27	61	0	63.1	50	2	33	62
vs. NL	3.29	18	13	43	201	0	273.2	240	21	127	236
Pre-All Star	2.76	15	7	37	144	0	185.2	151	13	91	167
Post-All Star	3.81	8	9	33	118	0	151.1	139	10	69	131

	Avg	AB	H	2B	3B	HR	RBI	BB	SO	OBP	SLG
vs. Left	.261	570	149	29	3	10	60	83	135	.352	.375
vs. Right	.209	676	141	23	1	13	81	77	163	.300	.303
Inning 1-6	.215	107	23	7	0	2	16	18	19	.333	.336
Inning 7+	.234	1139	267	45	4	21	127	142	279	.323	.336
None on	.247	628	155	30	2	11		70	149	.326	.354
Runners on	.218	618	135	22	2	12	132	90	149	.322	.319
Scoring Posn	.207	376	78	14	2	6	116	79	94	.347	.303
Close & Late	.234	723	169	27	2	14	94	102	191	.331	.335
None on/out	.253	288	73	16	1	5	5	23	70	.311	.368
vs. 1st Batr (relief)	.219	237	52	13	0	3	22	21	58	.284	.312
1st Inning Pitched	.245	884	217	41	3	16	118	120	204	.338	.353
First 15 Pitches	.261	701	183	37	4	11	76	88	147	.349	.372
Pitch 16-30	.211	445	94	15	0	9	56	55	119	.298	.306
Pitch 31-45	.134	97	13	0	0	3	11	15	30	.267	.227
Pitch 46+	.000	3	0	0	0	0	0	0	2	.000	.000
First Pitch	.299	137	41	6	1	2	23	24	0	.413	.401
Ahead in Count	.175	605	106	17	2	7	44	0	263	.179	.245
Behind in Count	.294	293	86	23	1	9	44	79	0	.447	.477
Two Strikes	.169	635	107	19	0	7	49	56	298	.239	.231
Pre-All Star	.223	676	151	30	1	13	78	91	167	.316	.328
Post-All Star	.244	570	139	22	3	10	65	69	131	.334	.346

Pitcher vs. Batter (career)

Pitches Best Vs.	Avg	AB	H	2B	3B	HR	RBI	BB	SO	OBP	SLG	Pitches Worst Vs.	Avg	AB	H	2B	3B	HR	RBI	BB	SO	OBP	SLG
Bernard Gilkey	.000	13	0	0	0	0	4	1	1	.125	.000	Darrin Fletcher	.556	9	5	1	0	0	0	2	1	.636	.667
Mike Lansing	.000	10	0	0	0	1	2	0	0	.167	.000	Andres Galarraga	.455	11	5	1	0	1	7	0	2	.455	.818
Reggie Sanders	.077	13	1	0	0	1	1	6	.143	.077	Todd Zeile	.364	11	4	0	0	0	2	1	3	.417	.364
Moises Alou	.091	11	1	0	0	1	2	0	1	.091	.364												
Orlando Merced	.111	9	1	0	0	0	0	2	3	.273	.111												

Brian Jordan — Cardinals
Age 31 – Bats Right (groundball hitter)

	Avg	G	AB	R	H	2B	3B	HR	RBI	BB	SO	HBP	GDP	SB	CS	OBP	SLG	IBB	SH	SF	#Pit	#P/PA	GB	FB	G/F
1997 Season	.234	47	145	17	34	5	0	0	10	10	21	6	4	6	1	.311	.269	1	0	0	531	3.30	55	44	1.25
Last Five Years	.292	438	1549	229	453	79	13	54	254	89	259	29	27	62	24	.339	.465	9	2	16	5797	3.44	601	447	1.34

1997 Season

	Avg	AB	H	2B	3B	HR	RBI	BB	SO	OBP	SLG		Avg	AB	H	2B	3B	HR	RBI	BB	SO	OBP	SLG
vs. Left	.286	35	10	3	0	0	3	4	4	.359	.371	Scoring Posn	.244	41	10	1	0	0	9	7	6	.380	.268
vs. Right	.218	110	24	2	0	0	7	6	17	.295	.236	Close & Late	.207	29	6	1	0	0	2	4	5	.303	.241
Home	.250	72	18	2	0	0	8	6	7	.316	.278	None on/out	.270	37	10	2	0	0	1	9	.308	.324
Away	.219	73	16	3	0	0	2	4	14	.305	.260	Batting #2	.159	44	7	1	0	0	1	4	.196	.182
First Pitch	.385	26	10	1	0	0	0	1	0	.429	.423	Batting #4	.280	93	26	3	0	0	9	16	.374	.312
Ahead in Count	.360	25	9	3	0	0	3	5	0	.467	.480	Other	.125	8	1	0	0	1	0	1	.125	.250
Behind in Count	.154	65	10	1	0	0	4	0	20	.214	.169	Pre-All Star	.254	114	29	4	0	0	9	9	18	.341	.289
Two Strikes	.169	59	10	1	0	0	5	4	21	.279	.186	Post-All Star	.161	31	5	1	0	0	1	3	.188	.194

Last Five Years

	Avg	AB	H	2B	3B	HR	RBI	BB	SO	OBP	SLG		Avg	AB	H	2B	3B	HR	RBI	BB	SO	OBP	SLG
vs. Left	.307	388	119	23	5	17	65	31	65	.361	.523	First Pitch	.374	281	105	16	4	15	53	8	0	.404	.619
vs. Right	.288	1161	334	56	8	37	189	58	194	.332	.445	Ahead in Count	.373	316	118	24	5	17	73	39	0	.437	.642
Groundball	.271	446	121	18	2	15	61	25	78	.317	.422	Behind in Count	.222	686	152	26	4	11	75	0	230	.235	.319
Flyball	.300	243	73	16	1	9	40	15	53	.345	.486	Two Strikes	.192	655	126	18	2	9	58	42	259	.254	.267
Home	.309	839	259	50	10	25	141	48	132	.352	.482	Batting #4	.316	534	169	32	2	18	101	35	77	.371	.485
Away	.273	710	194	29	3	29	113	41	127	.324	.445	Batting #5	.283	329	93	16	4	15	51	17	65	.324	.492
Day	.309	457	141	25	5	17	85	26	67	.355	.497	Other	.278	686	191	31	7	21	102	37	117	.322	.436
Night	.286	1092	312	54	8	37	169	63	192	.333	.451	March/April	.258	244	63	14	1	5	26	16	58	.314	.385
Grass	.288	767	221	42	3	21	118	45	126	.335	.433	May	.241	224	54	4	1	6	30	18	39	.305	.348
Turf	.297	782	232	37	10	33	136	44	133	.344	.496	June	.302	325	98	19	6	9	50	15	50	.339	.480
Pre-All Star	.282	909	256	44	9	27	135	56	175	.331	.439	July	.319	288	92	18	1	16	69	15	50	.358	.556
Post-All Star	.308	640	197	35	4	27	119	33	84	.351	.502	August	.310	310	96	17	4	9	47	17	35	.353	.477
Scoring Posn	.320	431	138	23	3	18	196	45	72	.387	.513	Sept/Oct	.316	158	50	7	0	9	32	8	27	.366	.532
Close & Late	.276	257	71	13	2	7	33	20	62	.333	.424	vs. AL	.143	21	3	1	0	0	0	0	3	.182	.190
None on/out	.246	370	91	15	3	9	9	13	68	.281	.376	vs. NL	.295	1528	450	78	13	54	254	89	256	.341	.469

Batter vs. Pitcher (career)

Hits Best Against	Avg	AB	H	2B	3B	HR	RBI	BB	SO	OBP	SLG	Hits Worst Against	Avg	AB	H	2B	3B	HR	RBI	BB	SO	OBP	SLG
Bret Saberhagen	.455	11	5	0	0	1	2	0	2	.455	.727	Sid Fernandez	.077	13	1	0	0	0	0	1	7	.143	.077
Steve Avery	.429	21	9	4	1	1	4	1	2	.455	.857	Jose Bautista	.077	13	1	1	0	0	0	0	0	.143	.154
Andy Ashby	.421	19	8	2	1	0	0	0	2	.450	.632	Xavier Hernandez	.091	11	1	0	0	0	1	0	3	.091	.091
VanLandingham	.400	10	4	3	0	0	2	1	1	.455	.700	Mark Gardner	.143	14	2	0	0	0	2	1	1	.188	.143
Greg Swindell	.333	21	7	2	0	2	5	2	4	.391	.714	Scott Sanders	.182	11	2	0	0	0	0	0	5	.182	.182

Kevin Jordan — Phillies
Age 28 – Bats Right

	Avg	G	AB	R	H	2B	3B	HR	RBI	BB	SO	HBP	GDP	SB	CS	OBP	SLG	IBB	SH	SF	#Pit	#P/PA	GB	FB	G/F
1997 Season	.266	84	177	19	47	8	0	6	30	3	26	0	5	0	1	.273	.412	0	0	3	665	3.63	63	57	1.11
Career (1995-1997)	.260	151	362	40	94	19	0	11	48	10	55	2	8	2	2	.280	.403	3	5	1392	3.64	132	108	1.22

1997 Season

	Avg	AB	H	2B	3B	HR	RBI	BB	SO	OBP	SLG		Avg	AB	H	2B	3B	HR	RBI	BB	SO	OBP	SLG
vs. Left	.240	75	18	4	0	4	18	3	10	.259	.453	Scoring Posn	.273	66	18	4	0	0	22	1	11	.271	.333
vs. Right	.284	102	29	4	0	2	12	0	16	.284	.382	Close & Late	.324	37	12	1	0	2	7	1	7	.342	.514
Home	.246	118	29	4	0	4	19	3	16	.258	.381	None on/out	.361	36	13	2	0	2	2	0	3	.361	.583
Away	.305	59	18	4	0	2	11	0	10	.305	.475	Batting #3	.233	43	10	2	0	2	7	1	4	.250	.419
First Pitch	.500	10	5	1	0	2	3	0	0	.500	1.200	Batting #5	.283	53	15	2	0	0	4	0	9	.273	.321
Ahead in Count	.447	38	17	3	0	1	11	1	0	.462	.605	Other	.272	81	22	4	0	4	19	2	13	.286	.469
Behind in Count	.200	95	19	3	0	2	12	0	21	.194	.295	Pre-All Star	.222	63	14	2	0	3	9	1	11	.224	.397
Two Strikes	.159	82	13	4	0	1	8	2	26	.174	.244	Post-All Star	.289	114	33	6	0	3	21	2	15	.302	.421

Ricardo Jordan — Mets
Age 28 – Pitches Left

	ERA	W	L	Sv	G	GS	IP	BB	SO	Avg	H	2B	3B	HR	RBI	OBP	SLG	GF	IR	IRS	Hld	SvOp	SB	CS	GB	FB	G/F
1997 Season	5.33	1	2	0	22	0	27.0	15	19	.304	31	5	1	1	13	.397	.402	4	7	1	1	0	4	0	38	21	1.81
Career (1995-1997)	4.30	4	4	1	63	0	67.0	40	46	.268	67	10	3	4	44	.371	.380	9	48	21	6	1	6	0	88	64	1.38

1997 Season

	ERA	W	L	Sv	G	GS	IP	H	HR	BB	SO		Avg	AB	H	2B	3B	HR	RBI	BB	SO	OBP	SLG
Home	5.79	0	0	0	11	0	14.0	18	0	6	13	vs. Left	.366	41	15	2	1	0	6	1	7	.400	.463
Away	4.85	1	2	0	11	0	13.0	13	1	9	6	vs. Right	.262	61	16	3	0	1	7	14	12	.395	.361

241

Wally Joyner — Padres
Age 36 – Bats Left

	Avg	G	AB	R	H	2B	3B	HR	RBI	BB	SO	HBP	GDP	SB	CS	OBP	SLG	IBB	SH	SF	#Pit	#P/PA	GB	FB	G/F
1997 Season	.327	135	455	59	149	29	2	13	83	51	51	2	14	3	5	.390	.486	5	0	10	1821	3.52	172	137	1.26
Last Five Years	.303	625	2213	322	671	142	9	56	353	302	297	10	46	19	21	.384	.451	39	10	33	9396	3.66	724	710	1.02

1997 Season

	Avg	AB	H	2B	3B	HR	RBI	BB	SO	OBP	SLG		Avg	AB	H	2B	3B	HR	RBI	BB	SO	OBP	SLG
vs. Left	.263	80	21	4	0	3	15	6	13	.307	.425	First Pitch	.453	86	39	7	0	4	21	3	0	.473	.674
vs. Right	.341	375	128	25	2	10	68	45	38	.407	.499	Ahead in Count	.402	122	49	9	0	3	25	26	0	.487	.549
Groundball	.385	91	35	12	1	1	23	11	8	.448	.571	Behind in Count	.235	162	38	7	2	6	24	0	41	.233	.414
Flyball	.242	66	16	3	0	1	9	8	10	.320	.333	Two Strikes	.216	167	36	8	2	4	22	22	51	.305	.359
Home	.324	216	70	12	1	6	34	20	24	.377	.472	Batting #5	.333	255	85	19	2	8	52	27	28	.392	.518
Away	.331	239	79	17	1	7	49	31	27	.401	.498	Batting #6	.328	131	43	7	0	2	17	14	15	.383	.427
Day	.349	166	58	13	2	2	26	14	18	.395	.488	Other	.304	69	21	3	0	3	14	10	8	.395	.478
Night	.315	289	91	16	0	11	57	37	33	.387	.484	March/April	.324	71	23	3	0	1	7	3	4	.342	.408
Grass	.340	365	124	24	2	11	66	40	37	.400	.507	May	.255	55	14	3	0	3	14	11	8	.373	.473
Turf	.278	90	25	5	0	2	17	11	14	.350	.400	June	.392	102	40	9	0	4	26	16	11	.467	.598
Pre-All Star	.337	246	83	18	0	8	49	31	26	.403	.508	July	.347	75	26	7	1	0	11	10	9	.411	.467
Post-All Star	.316	209	66	11	2	5	34	20	25	.374	.459	August	.319	91	29	6	1	2	15	3	9	.344	.473
Scoring Posn	.353	133	47	8	1	3	65	17	14	.404	.496	Sept/Oct	.279	61	17	1	0	3	10	8	10	.362	.443
Close & Late	.347	75	26	6	1	0	13	5	11	.383	.453	vs. AL	.442	52	23	4	0	2	13	6	3	.500	.635
None on/out	.280	107	30	8	1	3	9	9	15	.336	.458	vs. NL	.313	403	126	25	2	11	70	45	48	.376	.467

1997 By Position

Position	Avg	AB	H	2B	3B	HR	RBI	BB	SO	OBP	SLG	G	GS	Innings	PO	A	E	DP	Fld Pct	Rng Fctr	In Zone	Zone Outs	Zone Rtg	MLB Zone
As Pinch Hitter	.455	11	5	1	0	0	5	0	2	.455	.545	11	0	—	—	—	—	—	—	—	—	—	—	—
As 1b	.324	444	144	28	2	13	78	51	49	.389	.484	131	122	1045.2	1027	88	4	85	.996	—	192	172	.896	.874

Last Five Years

	Avg	AB	H	2B	3B	HR	RBI	BB	SO	OBP	SLG		Avg	AB	H	2B	3B	HR	RBI	BB	SO	OBP	SLG
vs. Left	.264	633	167	31	0	8	81	61	99	.329	.351	First Pitch	.340	373	127	24	2	15	73	25	0	.376	.536
vs. Right	.319	1580	504	111	9	48	272	241	198	.405	.492	Ahead in Count	.353	546	193	52	0	10	103	152	0	.488	.504
Groundball	.345	447	154	38	2	4	69	55	43	.416	.465	Behind in Count	.244	861	210	40	7	14	91	0	242	.245	.355
Flyball	.297	407	121	25	2	12	78	62	65	.387	.457	Two Strikes	.241	897	216	36	5	18	102	125	297	.334	.352
Home	.317	1078	342	72	6	23	172	136	135	.390	.459	Batting #3	.321	651	209	45	3	21	123	100	86	.406	.496
Away	.290	1135	329	70	3	33	181	166	162	.379	.444	Batting #5	.298	708	211	47	3	16	109	91	103	.378	.441
Day	.292	682	199	46	5	14	99	92	99	.373	.435	Other	.294	854	251	50	3	19	121	111	108	.373	.426
Night	.308	1531	472	96	4	42	254	210	198	.389	.459	March/April	.327	330	108	28	2	4	39	52	32	.420	.461
Grass	.298	1431	427	81	3	40	223	194	198	.380	.443	May	.291	440	128	27	1	19	87	74	70	.390	.486
Turf	.312	782	244	61	6	16	130	108	99	.393	.467	June	.311	351	109	24	0	7	61	52	46	.397	.439
Pre-All Star	.309	1201	371	86	4	33	202	185	157	.398	.470	July	.337	418	141	23	4	11	76	48	58	.400	.490
Post-All Star	.296	1012	300	56	5	23	151	117	140	.367	.430	August	.276	427	118	24	2	7	54	42	51	.340	.391
Scoring Posn	.317	597	189	37	2	14	284	122	91	.416	.456	Sept/Oct	.271	247	67	16	0	8	36	34	40	.357	.433
Close & Late	.319	351	112	27	1	7	55	54	58	.409	.462	vs. AL	.309	1377	425	88	6	37	218	188	178	.389	.462
None on/out	.265	498	132	31	5	18	18	40	60	.322	.456	vs. NL	.294	836	246	54	3	19	135	114	119	.377	.434

Batter vs. Pitcher (career)

Hits Best Against	Avg	AB	H	2B	3B	HR	RBI	BB	SO	OBP	SLG	Hits Worst Against	Avg	AB	H	2B	3B	HR	RBI	BB	SO	OBP	SLG
Rich DeLucia	.667	6	4	1	0	1	3	5	1	.818	1.333	Andy Benes	.091	11	1	0	0	0	0	2	4	.231	.091
Kevin Ritz	.643	14	9	1	0	0	2	4	0	.737	.714	Mark Langston	.103	39	4	0	0	1	2	1	6	.125	.179
Eric Plunk	.625	16	10	2	0	3	8	3	1	.684	1.313	Danny Jackson	.143	14	2	0	0	0	0	0	4	.143	.143
David Cone	.556	9	5	0	0	1	3	3	0	.667	.889	Terry Mulholland	.167	12	2	0	0	0	2	0	2	.154	.167
Juan Guzman	.471	17	8	1	1	1	3	2	1	.526	.824	Gregg Olson	.167	12	2	0	0	0	2	0	3	.154	.167

Mike Judd — Dodgers
Age 23 – Pitches Right

	ERA	W	L	Sv	G	GS	IP	BB	SO	Avg	H	2B	3B	HR	RBI	OBP	SLG	GF	IR	IRS	Hld	SvOp	SB	CS	GB	FB	G/F
1997 Season	0.00	0	0	0	1	0	2.2	0	4	.364	4	0	0	0	2	.364	.364	0	2	2	0	1	1	1	3	2	1.50

1997 Season

	ERA	W	L	Sv	G	GS	IP	H	HR	BB	SO		Avg	AB	H	2B	3B	HR	RBI	BB	SO	OBP	SLG
Home	0.00	0	0	0	0	0	0.0	0	0	0	0	vs. Left	.429	7	3	0	0	0	2	0	3	.429	.429
Away	0.00	0	0	0	1	0	2.2	4	0	0	4	vs. Right	.250	4	1	0	0	0	0	0	1	.250	.250

Jeff Juden — Indians
Age 27 – Pitches Right

	ERA	W	L	Sv	G	GS	IP	BB	SO	Avg	H	2B	3B	HR	RBI	OBP	SLG	CG	ShO	Sup	QS	#P/S	SB	CS	GB	FB	G/F
1997 Season	4.46	11	6	0	30	27	161.1	72	136	.257	157	27	2	23	79	.342	.421	3	0	5.86	13	91	50	6	193	184	1.05
Last Five Years	4.27	19	15	0	109	42	331.0	153	273	.247	304	55	4	42	161	.336	.400	4	0	5.11	21	92	82	11	450	330	1.36

1997 Season

	ERA	W	L	Sv	G	GS	IP	H	HR	BB	SO		Avg	AB	H	2B	3B	HR	RBI	BB	SO	OBP	SLG
Home	4.17	7	3	0	15	14	90.2	87	13	34	78	vs. Left	.299	281	84	12	1	10	35	49	53	.403	.456
Away	4.84	4	3	0	15	13	70.2	70	10	38	58	vs. Right	.221	330	73	15	1	13	44	23	83	.286	.391
Day	4.52	7	2	0	15	14	81.2	84	12	40	69	Inning 1-6	.264	534	141	25	2	16	69	68	119	.354	.408
Night	4.41	4	4	0	15	13	79.2	70	11	32	67	Inning 7+	.208	77	16	2	0	7	10	4	17	.247	.506
Grass	5.29	2	2	0	15	12	68.0	76	11	34	52	None on	.275	360	99	18	2	12	12	32	81	.344	.436
Turf	3.86	9	4	0	15	15	93.1	81	12	38	84	Runners on	.231	251	58	9	0	11	67	40	55	.339	.398
March/April	4.09	2	0	0	5	5	22.0	18	0	14	12	Scoring Posn	.204	157	32	3	0	4	51	35	38	.348	.299
May	5.13	3	1	0	6	6	33.1	41	5	16	25	Close & Late	.250	36	9	0	0	4	5	1	10	.270	.583

1997 Season

	ERA	W	L	Sv	G	GS	IP	H	HR	BB	SO		Avg	AB	H	2B	3B	HR	RBI	BB	SO	OBP	SLG
June	3.19	4	1	0	5	5	36.2	29	4	12	30	None on/out	.289	159	46	9	0	4	4	14	35	.354	.421
July	4.50	2	3	0	6	6	38.0	37	8	15	40	vs. 1st Batr (relief)	.000	2	0	0	0	0	0	1	0	.333	.000
August	7.16	0	1	0	5	3	16.1	21	5	12	14	1st Inning Pitched	.301	113	34	6	1	5	26	25	22	.433	.504
Sept/Oct	3.60	0	0	0	3	2	15.0	11	1	3	15	First 75 Pitches	.255	459	117	22	2	15	58	60	104	.347	.410
Starter	4.40	11	6	0	27	27	157.2	153	21	69	133	Pitch 76-90	.309	81	25	3	0	3	13	9	16	.383	.457
Reliever	7.36	0	0	0	3	0	3.2	4	2	3	3	Pitch 91-105	.236	55	13	2	0	4	7	2	12	.263	.491
0-3 Days Rest (Start)	2.57	0	0	0	1	1	7.0	4	1	0	7	Pitch 106+	.125	16	2	0	0	1	1	1	4	.222	.313
4 Days Rest	4.02	7	4	0	12	12	78.1	75	14	29	71	First Pitch	.295	88	26	4	1	4	11	2	0	.340	.500
5+ Days Rest	4.98	4	2	0	14	14	72.1	74	6	40	55	Ahead in Count	.138	282	39	9	0	3	17	0	123	.144	.202
vs. AL	3.75	2	1	0	9	7	48.0	38	7	17	51	Behind in Count	.407	135	55	10	0	9	31	47	0	.551	.681
vs. NL	4.76	9	5	0	21	20	113.1	119	16	55	85	Two Strikes	.149	275	41	10	1	2	14	23	136	.220	.215
Pre-All Star	3.70	11	2	0	18	18	109.1	96	11	45	92	Pre-All Star	.238	403	96	17	1	11	44	45	92	.321	.367
Post-All Star	6.06	0	4	0	12	9	52.0	61	12	27	44	Post-All Star	.293	208	61	10	1	12	35	27	44	.382	.524

Last Five Years

	ERA	W	L	Sv	G	GS	IP	H	HR	BB	SO		Avg	AB	H	2B	3B	HR	RBI	BB	SO	OBP	SLG
Home	4.06	12	5	0	52	22	177.1	158	23	75	153	vs. Left	.289	533	154	24	1	21	71	91	107	.392	.456
Away	4.51	7	10	0	57	20	153.2	146	19	78	120	vs. Right	.214	700	150	31	4	21	90	62	166	.291	.357
Day	4.96	10	7	0	43	20	139.2	141	19	64	119	Inning 1-6	.248	935	232	44	2	28	125	121	207	.341	.389
Night	3.76	9	8	0	66	22	191.1	163	23	89	154	Inning 7+	.242	298	72	11	2	14	36	32	66	.319	.433
Grass	4.85	5	6	0	63	16	144.2	145	23	66	117	None on	.257	709	182	32	3	26	26	78	157	.338	.420
Turf	3.82	14	9	0	46	26	186.1	159	19	87	156	Runners on	.233	524	122	23	1	16	135	75	116	.333	.372
March/April	4.17	5	2	0	21	8	58.1	49	3	28	37	Scoring Posn	.206	320	66	12	1	7	111	64	84	.338	.316
May	5.81	3	3	0	19	8	52.2	64	12	28	43	Close & Late	.244	123	30	4	1	4	10	11	29	.309	.390
June	3.45	5	1	0	15	5	47.0	40	5	16	39	None on/out	.286	318	91	18	1	12	12	35	62	.366	.462
July	4.03	3	3	0	14	7	51.1	47	8	23	50	vs. 1st Batr (relief)	.286	56	16	3	1	5	11	10	12	.403	.643
August	4.43	2	3	0	21	9	67.0	60	10	39	52	1st Inning Pitched	.266	380	101	22	3	17	73	64	86	.374	.474
Sept/Oct	3.62	1	3	0	19	5	54.2	44	4	19	52	First 75 Pitches	.246	1001	246	46	4	34	130	131	227	.340	.402
Starter	4.49	14	14	0	42	42	240.2	227	29	111	195	Pitch 76-90	.279	122	34	6	0	3	21	12	25	.345	.402
Reliever	3.69	5	1	0	67	0	90.1	77	13	42	78	Pitch 91-105	.241	79	19	3	0	4	9	7	17	.302	.430
0-3 Days Rest (Start)	2.57	0	0	0	1	1	7.0	4	1	0	7	Pitch 106+	.161	31	5	0	0	1	1	3	4	.257	.258
4 Days Rest	4.01	10	7	0	19	19	119.0	105	18	52	102	First Pitch	.351	154	54	10	1	8	33	5	0	.391	.584
5+ Days Rest	5.10	4	7	0	22	22	114.2	118	10	59	86	Ahead in Count	.153	583	89	20	1	7	40	0	241	.161	.226
vs. AL	3.75	2	1	0	9	7	48.0	38	7	17	51	Behind in Count	.362	268	97	14	0	17	54	91	0	.516	.604
vs. NL	4.36	17	14	0	100	35	283.0	266	35	136	222	Two Strikes	.142	583	83	18	2	6	34	57	273	.224	.211
Pre-All Star	4.18	16	6	0	60	23	178.2	164	22	77	149	Pre-All Star	.247	664	164	30	2	22	87	77	149	.329	.398
Post-All Star	4.37	3	9	0	49	19	152.1	140	20	76	124	Post-All Star	.246	569	140	25	2	20	74	76	124	.344	.402

Pitcher vs. Batter (career)

Pitches Best Vs.	Avg	AB	H	2B	3B	HR	RBI	BB	SO	OBP	SLG	Pitches Worst Vs.	Avg	AB	H	2B	3B	HR	RBI	BB	SO	OBP	SLG
Royce Clayton	.000	11	0	0	0	0	2	1	4	.077	.000	Jeff Bagwell	.600	10	6	3	0	2	6	2	3	.615	1.500
Derek Bell	.000	10	0	0	0	0	1	2	6	.167	.000	Hal Morris	.500	16	8	2	0	2	4	1	4	.500	1.000
Brian L. Hunter	.077	13	1	1	0	0	1	1	2	.133	.154	Craig Biggio	.417	12	5	1	0	0	0	1	1	.462	.500
Raul Mondesi	.091	11	1	0	0	0	0	1	1	.167	.091	Barry Larkin	.364	11	4	1	1	0	2	2	1	.462	.636
Edgar Renteria	.214	14	3	0	0	0	0		4	.214	.214	Mark Lemke	.357	14	5	2	0	1	3	2	3	.438	.714

David Justice — Indians

Age 32 – Bats Left (flyball hitter)

	Avg	G	AB	R	H	2B	3B	HR	RBI	BB	SO	HBP	GDP	SB	CS	OBP	SLG	IBB	SH	SF	#Pit	#P/PA	GB	FB	G/F
1997 Season	.329	139	495	84	163	31	1	33	101	80	79	0	12	3	5	.418	.596	11	0	7	2329	4.00	157	148	1.06
Last Five Years	.292	560	1983	331	580	88	9	122	383	321	304	8	39	13	17	.390	.531	34	0	19	9334	4.00	627	671	0.93

1997 Season

	Avg	AB	H	2B	3B	HR	RBI	BB	SO	OBP	SLG		Avg	AB	H	2B	3B	HR	RBI	BB	SO	OBP	SLG
vs. Left	.322	146	47	10	0	11	32	15	22	.380	.616	First Pitch	.308	39	12	2	0	6	14	9	0	.429	.821
vs. Right	.332	349	116	21	1	22	69	65	57	.432	.587	Ahead in Count	.420	138	58	12	0	10	35	42	0	.549	.725
Groundball	.326	95	31	8	0	8	20	14	17	.409	.663	Behind in Count	.255	220	56	14	1	8	27	0	65	.253	.436
Flyball	.344	61	21	4	0	5	12	10	9	.431	.656	Two Strikes	.245	229	56	11	1	9	31	29	79	.328	.419
Home	.353	238	84	15	0	17	55	41	32	.440	.630	Batting #5	.335	478	160	31	1	32	99	75	77	.420	.605
Away	.307	257	79	16	1	16	46	39	47	.396	.564	Batting #7	.286	7	2	0	0	0	0	3	0	.500	.286
Day	.355	166	59	10	0	8	31	28	26	.444	.560	Other	.100	10	1	0	0	1	2	2	2	.250	.400
Night	.316	329	104	21	1	25	70	52	53	.404	.614	March/April	.386	83	32	7	1	7	18	22	7	.509	.747
Grass	.328	430	141	24	1	31	91	68	64	.414	.605	May	.381	84	32	5	0	9	26	14	9	.455	.762
Turf	.338	65	22	7	0	2	10	12	15	.442	.538	June	.176	51	9	2	0	1	3	4	10	.232	.275
Pre-All Star	.335	218	73	14	1	17	47	40	26	.430	.642	July	.286	70	20	3	0	2	11	13	19	.393	.414
Post-All Star	.325	277	90	17	0	16	54	40	53	.408	.563	August	.385	104	40	7	0	11	28	18	13	.475	.769
Scoring Posn	.354	127	45	7	0	11	74	35	20	.473	.669	Sept/Oct	.291	103	30	7	0	3	15	9	21	.345	.447
Close & Late	.338	65	22	4	0	5	18	7	11	.382	.631	vs. AL	.336	464	156	29	1	32	97	76	71	.424	.610
None on/out	.333	126	42	6	1	9	9	15	20	.404	.611	vs. NL	.226	31	7	2	0	1	4	4	8	.314	.387

1997 By Position

Position	Avg	AB	H	2B	3B	HR	RBI	BB	SO	OBP	SLG	G	GS	Innings	PO	A	E	DP	Fld Pct	Rng Fctr	In Zone	Zone Outs	Zone Rtg	MLB Zone
As DH	.333	231	77	10	0	14	41	26	41	.399	.558	61	59	—	—	—	—	—	—	—	—	—	—	—
As lf	.332	250	83	20	1	18	57	52	37	.438	.636	115	74	622.1		2	2	0	.983	1.69	147	112	.762	.805

Last Five Years

	Avg	AB	H	2B	3B	HR	RBI	BB	SO	OBP	SLG		Avg	AB	H	2B	3B	HR	RBI	BB	SO	OBP	SLG
vs. Left	.290	639	185	28	3	36	119	97	91	.382	.512	First Pitch	.321	224	72	8	1	19	59	26	0	.391	.621

Last Five Years

	Avg	AB	H	2B	3B	HR	RBI	BB	SO	OBP	SLG		Avg	AB	H	2B	3B	HR	RBI	BB	SO	OBP	SLG
vs. Right	.294	1344	395	60	6	86	264	224	213	.394	.539	Ahead in Count	.380	479	182	30	2	48	134	154	0	.524	.752
Groundball	.282	553	156	27	1	32	99	90	90	.380	.508	Behind in Count	.236	850	201	36	3	29	99	0	236	.237	.388
Flyball	.285	309	88	12	1	18	60	63	50	.408	.505	Two Strikes	.227	935	212	31	5	33	118	141	304	.328	.376
Home	.315	969	305	47	3	64	196	142	133	.401	.568	Batting #4	.237	211	50	7	2	14	43	28	32	.332	.488
Away	.271	1014	275	41	6	58	187	179	171	.379	.495	Batting #5	.293	1575	461	71	6	95	303	261	253	.391	.526
Day	.304	572	174	26	2	35	112	96	79	.402	.540	Other	.350	197	69	10	1	13	37	32	19	.442	.609
Night	.288	1411	406	62	7	87	271	225	225	.385	.527	March/April	.280	343	96	18	1	17	53	56	55	.382	.487
Grass	.294	1589	467	67	9	101	309	232	235	.383	.538	May	.321	390	125	19	2	28	83	61	52	.411	.595
Turf	.287	394	113	21	0	21	74	89	69	.418	.500	June	.268	261	70	13	2	13	47	51	45	.386	.483
Pre-All Star	.300	1095	328	57	6	66	212	187	160	.402	.543	July	.292	346	101	14	1	19	70	69	48	.408	.503
Post-All Star	.284	888	252	31	3	56	171	134	144	.375	.515	August	.315	340	107	11	1	34	79	49	47	.401	.653
Scoring Posn	.317	521	165	20	2	34	265	133	88	.445	.559	Sept/Oct	.267	303	81	13	2	11	51	35	56	.340	.432
Close & Late	.290	290	84	7	2	21	59	44	47	.377	.545	vs. AL	.336	464	156	29	1	32	97	76	71	.424	.610
None on/out	.273	501	137	21	1	30	30	65	67	.358	.499	vs. NL	.279	1519	424	59	8	90	286	245	233	.379	.506

Batter vs. Pitcher (career)

Hits Best Against	Avg	AB	H	2B	3B	HR	RBI	BB	SO	OBP	SLG	Hits Worst Against	Avg	AB	H	2B	3B	HR	RBI	BB	SO	OBP	SLG
Kevin Gross	.400	20	8	0	0	2	5	4	5	.462	.700	Mike Maddux	.000	9	0	0	0	0	1	4	2	.286	.000
Paul Wagner	.368	19	7	0	0	3	6	1	3	.400	.842	Willie Blair	.056	18	1	0	0	0	0	2	1	.150	.056
Curt Schilling	.360	25	9	2	0	3	11	6	5	.484	.800	Cal Eldred	.111	9	1	0	0	0	1	2	2	.250	.111
Greg Swindell	.350	20	7	0	0	3	3	2	3	.409	.800	Bret Saberhagen	.143	14	2	1	0	0	2	0	1	.143	.214
Doug Brocail	.308	13	4	1	0	2	4	0	1	.333	.846	Mitch Williams	.154	13	2	0	0	0	0	1	4	.214	.154

Scott Kamieniecki — Orioles
Age 34 – Pitches Right

	ERA	W	L	Sv	G	GS	IP	BB	SO	Avg	H	2B	3B	HR	RBI	OBP	SLG	CG	ShO	Sup	QS	#P/S	SB	CS	GB	FB	G/F
1997 Season	4.01	10	6	0	30	30	179.1	67	109	.261	179	38	3	20	81	.328	.413	0	0	4.27	17	98	25	4	287	200	1.43
Last Five Years	4.27	36	27	1	106	87	563.1	253	310	.268	576	115	12	64	265	.347	.421	4	0	5.40	43	98	47	23	867	593	1.46

1997 Season

	ERA	W	L	Sv	G	GS	IP	H	HR	BB	SO		Avg	AB	H	2B	3B	HR	RBI	BB	SO	OBP	SLG
Home	3.41	6	3	0	17	17	105.2	98	10	37	67	vs. Left	.257	350	90	21	3	8	34	39	51	.330	.403
Away	4.89	4	3	0	13	13	73.2	81	10	30	42	vs. Right	.265	336	89	17	0	12	47	28	58	.325	.423
Day	2.26	4	0	0	8	8	51.2	46	4	15	41	Inning 1-6	.264	639	169	36	3	18	77	63	104	.331	.415
Night	4.72	6	6	0	22	22	127.2	133	16	52	68	Inning 7+	.213	47	10	2	0	2	4		5	.288	.383
Grass	3.89	7	5	0	26	26	155.0	154	14	58	93	None on	.251	407	102	27	2	10	10	35	64	.315	.400
Turf	4.81	3	1	0	4	4	24.1	25	6	9	16	Runners on	.276	279	77	11	1	10	71	32	45	.346	.430
March/April	3.41	2	0	0	5	5	29.0	21	3	15	19	Scoring Posn	.258	182	47	6	1	5	60	21	30	.325	.385
May	3.58	2	2	0	5	5	32.2	32	3	12	18	Close & Late	.158	19	3	0	0	1	2	2	2	.273	.316
June	4.34	2	2	0	5	5	29.0	30	3	11	12	None on/out	.250	172	44	13	1	3	3	16	27	.317	.390
July	5.14	1	1	0	5	5	28.0	35	8	10	23	vs. 1st Batr (relief)	.000	0	0	0	0	0	0	1	0	1.000	.000
August	3.73	2	0	0	5	5	31.1	28	1	7	22	1st Inning Pitched	.281	114	32	5	0	2	17	21	13	.390	.377
Sept/Oct	3.99	1	1	0	5	5	29.1	33	2	12	15	First 75 Pitches	.270	514	139	29	3	14	62	53	81	.339	.420
Starter	4.01	10	6	0	30	30	179.1	179	20	67	109	Pitch 76-90	.222	81	18	5	0	3	10	9	15	.297	.395
Reliever	0.00	0	0	0	0	0	0	0	0	0	0	Pitch 91-105	.225	71	16	3	0	2	6	5	9	.286	.352
0-3 Days Rest (Start)	18.90	0	0	0	1	1	3.1	8	0	2	0	Pitch 106+	.300	20	6	1	0	1	3	0	4	.300	.500
4 Days Rest	4.00	6	4	0	17	17	105.2	112	11	37	60	First Pitch	.282	85	24	6	1	2	6	1	0	.291	.447
5+ Days Rest	3.33	4	2	0	12	12	70.1	59	9	28	49	Ahead in Count	.190	289	55	11	1	6	22	0	86	.195	.298
vs. AL	3.91	9	6	0	26	26	156.2	148	15	62	99	Behind in Count	.358	159	57	13	1	8	35	31	0	.462	.604
vs. NL	4.76	1	0	0	4	4	22.2	31	5	5	10	Two Strikes	.208	303	63	13	0	6	23	35	109	.293	.310
Pre-All Star	3.92	6	4	0	16	16	96.1	92	12	39	52	Pre-All Star	.250	368	92	20	1	12	45	39	52	.320	.408
Post-All Star	4.12	4	2	0	14	14	83.0	87	8	28	57	Post-All Star	.274	318	87	18	2	8	36	28	57	.337	.418

Last Five Years

	ERA	W	L	Sv	G	GS	IP	H	HR	BB	SO		Avg	AB	H	2B	3B	HR	RBI	BB	SO	OBP	SLG
Home	4.16	19	12	0	56	46	305.1	315	33	117	177	vs. Left	.269	1068	287	62	7	29	115	134	144	.352	.421
Away	4.40	17	15	1	50	41	258.0	261	31	136	133	vs. Right	.267	1084	289	53	5	35	150	119	166	.341	.422
Day	3.46	14	9	1	38	30	213.0	196	18	92	128	Inning 1-6	.271	1869	507	105	12	57	234	223	278	.351	.432
Night	4.75	22	18	0	68	57	350.1	380	46	161	182	Inning 7+	.244	283	69	10	0	7	31	30	32	.319	.353
Grass	4.26	27	23	1	92	73	479.1	492	52	217	262	None on	.263	1253	330	70	7	33	33	124	182	.334	.409
Turf	4.29	9	4	0	14	14	84.0	84	12	36	48	Runners on	.274	899	246	45	5	31	232	129	128	.364	.438
March/April	3.94	5	1	1	18	10	77.2	76	8	43	47	Scoring Posn	.270	515	139	24	2	16	191	87	80	.369	.417
May	5.10	4	5	0	22	13	84.2	93	12	46	47	Close & Late	.225	102	23	3	0	3	11	17	15	.339	.343
June	4.84	5	6	0	15	14	87.1	88	9	34	36	None on/out	.258	554	143	27	3	13	13	50	79	.322	.388
July	4.22	9	6	0	19	19	117.1	127	19	44	78	vs. 1st Batr (relief)	.467	15	7	1	0	1	1	4	2	.550	.733
August	3.74	8	4	0	16	16	101.0	90	7	48	50	1st Inning Pitched	.316	418	132	24	1	16	78	59	52	.399	.493
Sept/Oct	3.87	5	5	0	16	15	95.1	102	9	38	52	First 75 Pitches	.279	1602	447	90	11	47	200	191	230	.358	.437
Starter	4.26	35	26	0	87	87	515.0	523	57	233	279	Pitch 76-90	.263	236	62	14	1	10	37	31	44	.349	.458
Reliever	4.28	1	1	1	19	0	48.1	53	7	20	31	Pitch 91-105	.207	203	42	8	0	4	18	14	21	.264	.305
0-3 Days Rest (Start)	18.90	0	0	0	1	1	3.1	8	0	2	0	Pitch 106+	.225	111	25	3	0	3	10	17	15	.331	.333
4 Days Rest	4.39	20	15	0	49	49	287.1	298	27	131	152	First Pitch	.312	276	86	20	3	13	41	9	0	.336	.547
5+ Days Rest	3.89	15	11	0	37	37	224.1	217	30	100	127	Ahead in Count	.209	900	188	31	5	15	75	0	248	.217	.304
vs. AL	4.24	35	27	1	102	83	540.2	545	59	248	300	Behind in Count	.338	539	182	39	3	26	102	132	0	.465	.566
vs. NL	4.76	1	0	0	4	4	22.2	31	5	5	10	Two Strikes	.210	949	199	35	2	14	74	112	310	.297	.295
Pre-All Star	4.70	15	15	1	60	42	279.2	297	35	134	145	Pre-All Star	.274	1084	297	61	5	35	148	134	145	.355	.436
Post-All Star	3.84	21	12	0	46	45	283.2	279	29	119	165	Post-All Star	.261	1068	279	54	7	29	117	119	165	.339	.406

Pitcher vs. Batter (career)

Pitches Best Vs.	Avg	AB	H	2B	3B	HR	RBI	BB	SO	OBP	SLG	Pitches Worst Vs.	Avg	AB	H	2B	3B	HR	RBI	BB	SO	OBP	SLG
Greg Myers	.000	10	0	0	0	0	0	1	5	.091	.000	Tim Salmon	.647	17	11	2	0	2	8	2	5	.667	1.118
Shawn Green	.063	16	1	0	0	0	0	0	3	.063	.063	Tim Naehring	.583	12	7	2	0	1	8	7	0	.737	1.000
Tony Pena	.100	10	1	0	0	0	1	0	1	.182	.100	Devon White	.500	16	8	0	1	2	5	1	3	.529	1.000
Tim Raines	.125	16	2	0	0	0	0	2	2	.222	.125	Mark McGwire	.444	18	8	2	0	4	8	2	3	.500	1.222
Julio Franco	.143	14	2	0	0	0	0	2	1	.250	.143	Frank Thomas	.412	17	7	1	0	2	5	6	1	.565	.824

Matt Karchner — White Sox

Age 31 – Pitches Right

	ERA	W	L	Sv	G	GS	IP	BB	SO	Avg	H	2B	3B	HR	RBI	OBP	SLG	GF	IR	IRS	Hld	SvOp	SB	CS	GB	FB	G/F
1997 Season	2.91	3	1	15	52	0	52.2	26	30	.258	50	7	1	4	22	.344	.366	25	37	10	12	16	7	2	71	61	1.16
Career (1995-1997)	3.81	14	7	16	133	0	144.0	79	100	.266	144	21	2	16	81	.357	.400	48	101	33	38	25	12	5	183	158	1.16

1997 Season

	ERA	W	L	Sv	G	GS	IP	H	HR	BB	SO		Avg	AB	H	2B	3B	HR	RBI	BB	SO	OBP	SLG
Home	3.38	3	1	8	26	0	26.2	26	3	10	16	vs. Left	.250	72	18	4	1	1	8	13	11	.360	.375
Away	2.42	0	0	7	26	0	26.0	24	1	16	14	vs. Right	.262	122	32	3	0	3	14	13	19	.333	.361
Day	3.32	1	0	7	22	0	21.2	29	1	13	14	Inning 1-6	.250	4	1	1	0	0	0	0	0	.250	.500
Night	2.61	2	1	8	30	0	31.0	21	3	13	16	Inning 7+	.258	190	49	6	1	4	22	26	30	.346	.363
Grass	3.35	3	1	12	45	0	43.0	42	4	17	25	None on	.283	99	28	5	1	3	3	8	13	.336	.444
Turf	0.93	0	0	3	7	0	9.2	8	0	9	5	Runners on	.232	95	22	2	0	1	19	18	17	.351	.284
March/April	0.00	0	0	0	0	0	0.0	0	0	0	0	Scoring Posn	.231	65	15	2	0	0	17	12	13	.346	.262
May	5.00	0	0	0	7	0	9.0	8	1	6	1	Close & Late	.211	114	24	2	0	3	11	15	20	.302	.307
June	0.00	2	0	0	12	0	13.2	9	0	3	7	None on/out	.326	43	14	1	1	2	2	3	6	.370	.535
July	4.50	1	0	1	14	0	12.0	14	3	5	8	vs. 1st Batr (relief)	.311	45	14	1	0	1	6	6	7	.385	.400
August	0.00	0	0	11	13	0	13.0	8	0	10	9	1st Inning Pitched	.272	158	43	6	1	3	20	20	25	.352	.380
Sept/Oct	10.80	0	1	3	6	0	5.0	11	0	2	5	First 15 Pitches	.277	130	36	3	1	3	13	17	17	.358	.385
Starter	0.00	0	0	0	0	0	0.0	0	0	0	0	Pitch 16-30	.236	55	13	4	0	1	9	5	12	.300	.364
Reliever	2.91	3	1	15	52	0	52.2	50	4	26	30	Pitch 31-45	.125	8	1	0	0	0	0	4	1	.417	.125
0 Days rest (Relief)	2.87	1	1	5	15	0	15.2	13	0	7	9	Pitch 46+	.000	1	0	0	0	0	0	0	0	.000	.000
1 or 2 Days rest	3.33	1	0	8	26	0	24.1	27	3	12	15	First Pitch	.333	18	6	0	0	1	5	3	0	.409	.500
3+ Days rest	2.13	1	0	2	11	0	12.2	10	1	7	6	Ahead in Count	.189	95	18	3	1	1	8	0	25	.189	.274
vs. AL	3.09	3	1	12	46	0	46.2	45	4	21	25	Behind in Count	.364	33	12	2	0	0	4	12	0	.533	.424
vs. NL	1.50	0	0	3	6	0	6.0	5	0	5	5	Two Strikes	.176	91	16	4	1	2	11				
Pre-All Star	2.16	2	0	0	22	0	25.0	20	1	11	10	Pre-All Star	.222	90	20	2	1	1	7				
Post-All Star	3.58	1	1	15	30	0	27.2	30	3	15	20	Post-All Star	.288	104	30	5	0	3	15				

Career (1995-1997)

	ERA	W	L	Sv	G	GS	IP	H	HR	BB	SO		Avg	AB	H	2B	3B	HR	RBI
Home	5.37	6	6	8	64	0	70.1	80	11	36	48	vs. Left	.272	224	61	8	2	5	30
Away	2.32	8	1	8	69	0	73.2	64	5	43	52	vs. Right	.261	318	83	13	0	11	51
Day	3.80	7	2	7	43	0	45.0	48	5	30	34	Inning 1-6	.227	22	5	2	1	0	5
Night	3.82	7	5	9	90	0	99.0	96	11	49	66	Inning 7+	.267	520	139	19	1	16	76
Grass	4.39	14	7	13	116	0	123.0	132	16	63	81	None on	.297	256	76	13	1	11	11
Turf	0.43	0	0	3	17	0	21.0	12	0	16	19	Runners on	.238	286	68	8	1	5	70
March/April	1.69	3	0	1	12	0	16.0	10	2	11	16	Scoring Posn	.244	176	43	7	1	2	64
May	4.21	1	0	0	19	0	25.2	22	4	12	12	Close & Late	.251	327	82	10	0	12	47
June	4.50	3	2	0	23	0	26.0	22	3	17	13	None on/out	.331	118	39	7	1	6	6
July	4.11	4	2	1	32	0	30.2	37	5	13	23	vs. 1st Batr (relief)	.284	116	33	8	0	3	16
August	3.52	1	1	11	30	0	30.2	33	1	18	26	1st Inning Pitched	.270	407	110	17	2	11	69
Sept/Oct	4.20	2	2	3	17	0	15.0	20	1	8	10	First 15 Pitches	.276	340	94	13	2	11	51
Starter	0.00	0	0	0	0	0	0.0	0	0	0	0	Pitch 16-30	.229	166	38	8	0	2	21
Reliever	3.81	14	7	16	133	0	144.0	144	16	79	100	Pitch 31-45	.364	33	12	0	0	3	9
0 Days rest (Relief)	1.91	4	2	5	29	0	33.0	25	2	13	21	Pitch 46+	.000	3	0	0	0	0	0
1 or 2 Days rest	4.50	6	4	9	74	0	78.0	91	10	45	59	First Pitch	.297	64	19	2	1	1	15
3+ Days rest	4.09	4	1	2	30	0	33.0	28	4	21	20	Ahead in Count	.204	255	52	9	1	3	27
vs. AL	3.91	14	7	13	127	0	138.0	139	16	74	95	Behind in Count	.381	105	40	6	0	8	27
vs. NL	1.50	0	0	3	6	0	6.0	5	0	5	5	Two Strikes	.186	258	48	11	1	5	28
Pre-All Star	3.77	9	2	1	61	0	74.0	61	9	43	47	Pre-All Star	.228	268	61	10	2	9	38
Post-All Star	3.86	5	5	15	72	0	70.0	83	7	36	53	Post-All Star	.303	274	83	11	0	7	43

(partial right-hand column values: First Pitch .382 .406; Ahead in Count 9 0 .207 .282; Behind in Count 39 0 .537 .667; Two Strikes 43 100 .273 .295; Pre-All Star 43 47 .333 .381; Post-All Star 36 53 .381 .420)

Ron Karkovice — White Sox

Age 34 – Bats Right (flyball hitter)

	Avg	G	AB	R	H	2B	3B	HR	RBI	BB	SO	HBP	GDP	SB	CS	OBP	SLG	IBB	SH	SF	#Pit	#P/PA	GB	FB	G/F
1997 Season	.181	51	138	10	25	3	0	6	18	11	32	3	3	0	0	.248	.333	0	4	5	560	3.48	48	43	1.12
Last Five Years	.217	480	1426	191	309	65	3	60	190	139	403	15	27	4	8	.289	.393	5	33	20	6062	3.71	364	454	0.80

1997 Season

	Avg	AB	H	2B	3B	HR	RBI	BB	SO	OBP	SLG		Avg	AB	H	2B	3B	HR	RBI	BB	SO	OBP	SLG
vs. Left	.214	56	12	1	0	2	4	5	11	.270	.339	Scoring Posn	.114	35	4	0	0	1	11	4	10	.200	.200
vs. Right	.159	82	13	2	0	4	14	6	21	.234	.329	Close & Late	.308	13	4	1	0	1	2	2	0	.375	.615
Home	.191	68	13	2	0	4	11	7	18	.269	.397	None on/out	.125	32	4	0	0	3	3	2	8	.176	.406
Away	.171	70	12	1	0	2	7	4	14	.228	.271	Batting #7	.455	11	5	0	0	1	1	0	2	.500	.727
First Pitch	.214	28	6	0	0	2	5	0	0	.200	.429	Batting #8	.173	110	19	3	0	4	15	10	25	.246	.309
Ahead in Count	.194	31	6	2	0	3	5	5	0	.350	.548	Other	.059	17	1	0	0	1	2	1	5	.105	.235
Behind in Count	.098	61	6	0	0	1	0	28	.097	.098	Pre-All Star	.173	98	17	3	0	3	12	9	23	.250	.296
Two Strikes	.143	63	9	0	0	1	7	6	32	.211	.190	Post-All Star	.200	40	8	0	0	3	6	2	9	.244	.425

245

Last Five Years

	Avg	AB	H	2B	3B	HR	RBI	BB	SO	OBP	SLG		Avg	AB	H	2B	3B	HR	RBI	BB	SO	OBP	SLG
vs. Left	.229	445	102	20	1	19	58	55	117	.314	.407	First Pitch	.289	201	58	5	0	8	30	4	0	.305	.433
vs. Right	.211	981	207	45	2	41	132	84	286	.278	.386	Ahead in Count	.270	293	79	24	0	14	50	74	0	.418	.495
Groundball	.229	341	78	19	0	15	50	32	97	.298	.416	Behind in Count	.167	688	115	25	2	25	66	0	347	.173	.318
Flyball	.191	267	51	9	0	13	36	23	85	.270	.371	Two Strikes	.141	711	100	18	1	25	63	61	403	.213	.274
Home	.216	689	149	35	1	26	93	59	181	.281	.383	Batting #7	.230	261	60	12	0	9	28	20	60	.287	.379
Away	.217	737	160	30	2	34	97	80	222	.297	.402	Batting #8	.216	1126	243	52	3	50	157	115	334	.292	.401
Day	.226	402	91	22	1	18	55	38	121	.296	.420	Other	.154	39	6	1	0	1	5	4	9	.227	.256
Night	.213	1024	218	43	2	42	135	101	282	.287	.382	March/April	.224	245	55	15	0	11	37	43	66	.342	.420
Grass	.222	1250	277	60	2	54	174	115	345	.291	.402	May	.220	300	66	15	0	11	41	28	77	.285	.380
Turf	.182	176	32	5	1	6	16	24	58	.277	.324	June	.234	261	61	10	2	12	34	21	71	.294	.425
Pre-All Star	.217	889	193	41	2	39	121	99	248	.297	.399	July	.192	239	46	4	1	12	31	18	67	.256	.368
Post-All Star	.216	537	116	24	1	21	69	40	155	.277	.382	August	.231	242	56	14	0	14	34	18	74	.287	.413
Scoring Posn	.176	374	66	17	0	14	124	62	105	.289	.334	Sept/Oct	.180	139	25	7	0	4	13	11	48	.252	.317
Close & Late	.182	198	36	7	1	11	23	7	51	.216	.394	vs. AL	.217	1418	308	65	3	60	190	139	400	.290	.394
None on/out	.244	353	86	18	1	21	21	21	99	.290	.479	vs. NL	.125	8	1	0	0	0	0	0	3	.125	.125

Batter vs. Pitcher (career)

Hits Best Against	Avg	AB	H	2B	3B	HR	RBI	BB	SO	OBP	SLG	Hits Worst Against	Avg	AB	H	2B	3B	HR	RBI	BB	SO	OBP	SLG
Chris Haney	.429	14	6	1	0	0	1	2	3	.500	.500	Roger Clemens	.000	14	0	0	0	0	0	0	4	.000	.000
Cal Eldred	.385	13	5	2	0	0	2	3	4	.529	.538	Jaime Navarro	.000	14	0	0	0	0	0	1	7	.125	.000
Felipe Lira	.364	11	4	0	0	2	4	2	4	.462	.909	Hipolito Pichardo	.067	15	1	0	0	0	0	0	4	.067	.067
Roger Pavlik	.333	18	6	3	0	1	3	3	5	.455	.667	Ben McDonald	.071	14	1	1	0	0	1	0	3	.067	.143
David Wells	.318	22	7	0	0	3	6	1	5	.333	.727	Greg Swindell	.071	14	1	0	0	0	0	1	1	.133	.071

Scott Karl — Brewers
Age 26 – Pitches Left

	ERA	W	L	Sv	G	GS	IP	BB	SO	Avg	H	2B	3B	HR	RBI	OBP	SLG	CG	ShO	Sup	QS	#P/S	SB	CS	GB	FB	G/F
1997 Season	4.47	10	13	0	32	32	193.1	67	119	.279	212	47	3	23	91	.340	.439	1	0	4.33	19	100	7	6	289	210	1.38
Career (1995-1997)	4.55	29	29	0	89	82	524.2	189	299	.278	573	127	12	62	262	.342	.441	5	1	5.35	48	101	21	16	787	570	1.38

1997 Season

	ERA	W	L	Sv	G	GS	IP	H	HR	BB	SO		Avg	AB	H	2B	3B	HR	RBI	BB	SO	OBP	SLG
Home	4.32	5	6	0	15	15	93.2	112	13	30	54	vs. Left	.241	116	28	7	0	1	4	10	15	.313	.328
Away	4.61	5	7	0	17	17	99.2	100	10	37	65	vs. Right	.286	644	184	40	3	22	87	57	104	.345	.460
Day	5.45	0	6	0	12	12	66.0	81	7	33	40	Inning 1-6	.275	694	191	41	3	21	84	63	111	.338	.434
Night	3.96	10	7	0	20	20	127.1	131	16	34	79	Inning 7+	.318	66	21	6	0	2	7	4	8	.357	.500
Grass	4.49	10	10	0	29	29	174.1	196	20	60	111	None on	.279	448	125	29	3	15	15	33	72	.333	.458
Turf	4.26	0	3	0	3	3	19.0	16	3	7	8	Runners on	.279	312	87	18	0	8	76	34	47	.350	.413
March/April	5.73	0	5	0	6	6	33.0	33	6	23	17	Scoring Posn	.266	184	49	13	0	3	64	22	33	.344	.386
May	4.15	2	1	0	5	5	30.1	32	3	12	21	Close & Late	.333	36	12	5	0	2	6	2	2	.368	.639
June	5.40	0	3	0	5	5	30.0	37	2	11	20	None on/out	.266	207	55	14	2	12	12	12	36	.309	.527
July	3.41	4	1	0	5	5	34.1	39	3	5	17	vs. 1st Batr (relief)	.000	0	0	0	0	0	0	0	0	.000	.000
August	2.78	4	0	0	5	5	32.1	34	3	4	22	1st Inning Pitched	.220	118	26	7	0	2	11	11	18	.292	.331
Sept/Oct	5.40	0	3	0	6	6	33.1	37	6	12	22	First 75 Pitches	.273	557	152	36	2	17	64	50	86	.336	.436
Starter	4.47	10	13	0	32	32	193.1	212	23	67	119	Pitch 76-90	.287	101	29	6	1	1	12	10	17	.351	.396
Reliever	0.00	0	0	0	0	0	0.0	0	0	0	0	Pitch 91-105	.311	74	23	3	0	5	15	4	12	.346	.554
0-3 Days Rest (Start)	2.57	1	0	0	1	1	7.0	6	1	3	5	Pitch 106+	.286	28	8	2	0	0	0	3	4	.355	.357
4 Days Rest	4.79	4	9	0	21	21	124.0	144	16	51	78	First Pitch	.357	98	35	4	0	6	19	1	0	.376	.582
5+ Days Rest	4.04	5	4	0	10	10	62.1	62	6	16	38	Ahead in Count	.232	327	76	17	1	6	34	0	96	.234	.346
vs. AL	4.43	9	11	0	29	29	174.2	189	22	62	109	Behind in Count	.316	174	55	17	0	10	26	34	0	.426	.586
vs. NL	4.82	1	2	0	3	3	18.2	23	1	5	10	Two Strikes	.217	355	77	13	1	6	32	32	119	.283	.310
Pre-All Star	5.44	2	10	0	17	17	97.2	113	13	48	59	Pre-All Star	.294	385	113	25	2	13	57	48	59	.372	.470
Post-All Star	3.48	8	3	0	15	15	95.2	99	10	19	60	Post-All Star	.264	375	99	22	1	10	34	19	60	.304	.408

Career (1995-1997)

	ERA	W	L	Sv	G	GS	IP	H	HR	BB	SO		Avg	AB	H	2B	3B	HR	RBI	BB	SO	OBP	SLG
Home	4.64	15	15	0	44	41	262.0	309	33	87	143	vs. Left	.234	364	85	15	0	10	36	30	43	.310	.357
Away	4.45	14	14	0	45	41	262.2	264	29	102	156	vs. Right	.287	1698	488	112	12	52	226	159	256	.349	.459
Day	5.18	3	13	0	33	29	175.1	205	21	79	93	Inning 1-6	.277	1811	501	108	10	57	235	172	269	.342	.442
Night	4.23	26	16	0	56	53	349.1	368	41	110	206	Inning 7+	.287	251	72	19	2	5	27	17	30	.338	.438
Grass	4.47	25	23	0	78	71	452.2	499	50	162	264	None on	.272	1196	325	74	6	40	40	98	178	.333	.444
Turf	5.00	4	6	0	11	11	72.0	74	12	27	35	Runners on	.286	866	248	53	6	22	222	91	121	.355	.438
March/April	4.84	2	6	0	11	11	67.0	63	8	36	40	Scoring Posn	.270	497	134	34	2	11	189	64	81	.351	.412
May	4.50	5	2	0	15	10	72.0	72	9	27	37	Close & Late	.325	80	26	9	1	2	11	8	6	.386	.538
June	4.72	3	4	0	12	11	68.2	87	5	24	41	None on/out	.252	539	136	32	3	21	21	38	82	.309	.440
July	5.03	7	5	0	17	16	98.1	123	14	37	52	vs. 1st Batr (relief)	.500	4	2	0	0	0	0	3	1	.714	1.000
August	3.97	8	3	0	17	17	113.1	111	11	32	69	1st Inning Pitched	.243	338	82	19	1	5	39	33	58	.316	.349
Sept/Oct	4.44	4	9	0	17	17	105.1	117	15	33	60	First 75 Pitches	.278	1493	415	93	6	43	186	139	218	.343	.435
Starter	4.56	29	29	0	82	82	513.0	557	61	183	293	Pitch 76-90	.265	279	74	19	1	7	33	28	40	.334	.416
Reliever	3.86	0	0	0	7	0	11.2	16	1	6	6	Pitch 91-105	.303	208	63	10	4	10	38	12	25	.345	.534
0-3 Days Rest (Start)	4.74	1	1	0	3	3	19.0	22	2	5	12	Pitch 106+	.256	82	21	5	1	2	5	10	16	.344	.415
4 Days Rest	4.81	17	18	0	52	52	323.2	369	40	122	187	Ahead in Count	.228	846	193	43	4	17	90	0	241	.234	.349
5+ Days Rest	4.07	11	10	0	27	27	170.1	166	19	56	94	Behind in Count	.308	513	158	38	5	21	72	87	0	.408	.524
vs. AL	4.54	28	27	0	86	79	506.0	550	61	184	289	Two Strikes	.216	889	192	32	5	20	93	95	299	.296	.331
vs. NL	4.82	1	2	0	3	3	18.2	23	1	5	10	Pre-All Star	.276	906	250	55	5	27	122	98	129	.350	.437
Pre-All Star	4.69	11	14	0	42	36	232.0	250	27	98	123	Post-All Star	.279	1156	323	72	7	35	140	91	170	.336	.445
Post-All Star	4.43	18	15	0	47	46	292.2	323	35	91	170												

Pitcher vs. Batter (career)

Pitches Best Vs.	Avg	AB	H	2B	3B	HR	RBI	BB	SO	OBP	SLG	Pitches Worst Vs.	Avg	AB	H	2B	3B	HR	RBI	BB	SO	OBP	SLG
Tino Martinez	.000	17	0	0	0	0	1	1	2	.053	.000	Tim Salmon	.615	13	8	1	0	1	5	2	3	.667	.923
Bernie Williams	.059	17	1	0	0	0	0	1	4	.111	.059	Frank Thomas	.583	12	7	1	0	4	8	4	1	.688	1.667
Wade Boggs	.077	13	1	0	0	0	0	1	0	.143	.077	Joe Carter	.550	20	11	2	1	2	5	2	2	.591	1.000
B.J. Surhoff	.083	12	1	0	0	0	0	0	0	.154	.083	Sandy Alomar Jr	.500	18	9	5	0	2	6	2	3	.524	1.111
Craig Paquette	.091	11	1	0	0	0	0		5	.091	.091	Ron Coomer	.450	20	9	2	0	4	7	2	1	.500	1.150

Ryan Karp — Phillies
Age 28 – Pitches Left (flyball pitcher)

	ERA	W	L	Sv	G	GS	IP	BB	SO	Avg	H	2B	3B	HR	RBI	OBP	SLG	GF	IR	IRS	Hld	SvOp	SB	CS	GB	FB	G/F
1997 Season	5.40	1	1	0	15	1	15.0	9	18	.218	12	1	0	2	11	.348	.345	1	10	2	5	1	0	1	15	15	1.00
Career (1995-1997)	5.29	1	1	0	16	1	17.0	12	20	.210	13	1	0	2	12	.355	.323	1	10	2	5	1	0	1	15	18	0.83

1997 Season

	ERA	W	L	Sv	G	GS	IP	H	HR	BB	SO		Avg	AB	H	2B	3B	HR	RBI	BB	SO	OBP	SLG
Home	5.23	0	1	0	9	1	10.1	8	1	5	14	vs. Left	.067	15	1	0	0	1	3	4	3	.300	.267
Away	5.79	1	0	0	6	0	4.2	4	1	4	4	vs. Right	.275	40	11	1	0	1	8	5	15	.370	.375

Eric Karros — Dodgers
Age 30 – Bats Right

	Avg	G	AB	R	H	2B	3B	HR	RBI	BB	SO	HBP	GDP	SB	CS	OBP	SLG	IBB	SH	SF	#Pit	#P/PA	GB	FB	G/F
1997 Season	.266	162	628	86	167	28	0	31	104	61	116	2	10	15	7	.329	.459	2	0	9	2683	3.83	190	216	0.88
Last Five Years	.267	728	2812	378	750	134	7	134	446	238	487	11	82	29	12	.323	.462	10	0	35	11774	3.80	928	909	1.02

1997 Season

	Avg	AB	H	2B	3B	HR	RBI	BB	SO	OBP	SLG		Avg	AB	H	2B	3B	HR	RBI	BB	SO	OBP	SLG
vs. Left	.229	153	35	5	0	6	26	18	22	.306	.379	First Pitch	.315	92	29	7	0	3	17	2	0	.316	.489
vs. Right	.278	475	132	23	0	25	78	43	94	.336	.484	Ahead in Count	.364	118	43	6	0	13	35	28	0	.483	.746
Groundball	.311	103	32	4	0	4	23	10	20	.371	.466	Behind in Count	.211	280	59	11	0	7	32	0	92	.215	.325
Flyball	.203	74	15	2	0	4	9	12	14	.322	.392	Two Strikes	.178	298	53	12	0	9	29	31	116	.258	.309
Home	.267	296	79	14	0	13	48	36	57	.343	.446	Batting #4	.275	512	141	27	0	23	84	49	95	.335	.463
Away	.265	332	88	14	0	18	56	25	59	.315	.470	Batting #5	.225	102	23	1	0	6	17	12	19	.307	.412
Day	.318	179	57	10	0	12	35	22	35	.388	.575	Other	.214	14	3	0	0	2	3	0	2	.250	.643
Night	.245	449	110	18	0	19	69	39	81	.304	.412	March/April	.228	92	21	4	0	2	12	10	13	.301	.337
Grass	.265	505	134	20	0	27	86	56	96	.335	.465	May	.245	102	25	2	0	5	10	13	20	.336	.412
Turf	.268	123	33	8	0	4	18	5	20	.300	.431	June	.318	110	35	8	0	9	25	14	13	.392	.636
Pre-All Star	.270	330	89	15	0	20	56	38	52	.344	.497	July	.262	103	27	4	0	8	27	9	24	.316	.534
Post-All Star	.262	298	78	13	0	11	48	23	64	.311	.416	August	.276	123	34	4	0	4	17	7	27	.308	.407
Scoring Posn	.251	167	42	10	0	7	71	16	36	.302	.437	Sept/Oct	.255	98	25	6	0	3	13	8	19	.311	.408
Close & Late	.255	98	25	3	0	9	18	17	21	.365	.561	vs. AL	.303	66	20	1	0	10	16	3	9	.329	.773
None on/out	.285	151	43	6	0	6	6	15	29	.349	.444	vs. NL	.262	562	147	27	0	21	88	58	107	.329	.422

1997 By Position

Position	Avg	AB	H	2B	3B	HR	RBI	BB	SO	OBP	SLG	G	GS	Innings	PO	A	E	DP	Fld Pct	Rng Fctr	In Zone	Outs	Zone Rtg	MLB Zone
As 1b	.266	628	167	28	0	31	104	61	116	.329	.459	162	162	1447.2	1318	120	11	89	.992	—	292	258	.884	.874

Last Five Years

	Avg	AB	H	2B	3B	HR	RBI	BB	SO	OBP	SLG		Avg	AB	H	2B	3B	HR	RBI	BB	SO	OBP	SLG
vs. Left	.288	650	187	34	3	25	108	68	87	.352	.465	First Pitch	.325	416	135	31	0	25	88	9	0	.339	.579
vs. Right	.260	2162	563	100	4	109	338	170	400	.314	.462	Ahead in Count	.336	602	202	32	2	54	138	97	0	.425	.664
Groundball	.262	728	191	25	0	25	104	59	114	.318	.400	Behind in Count	.203	1247	253	40	3	29	121	0	411	.204	.310
Flyball	.275	436	120	20	0	23	77	44	83	.341	.479	Two Strikes	.187	1304	244	45	3	34	128	132	487	.263	.304
Home	.266	1340	356	54	2	66	221	124	217	.325	.457	Batting #4	.262	1822	478	89	3	90	305	174	346	.325	.463
Away	.268	1472	394	80	5	68	225	114	270	.320	.467	Batting #5	.269	528	142	24	2	25	91	37	75	.318	.464
Day	.278	776	216	49	4	39	120	78	153	.344	.503	Other	.281	462	130	21	2	19	50	27	66	.319	.459
Night	.262	2036	534	85	3	95	326	160	334	.315	.447	March/April	.259	359	93	15	0	9	53	36	58	.327	.376
Grass	.266	2206	587	101	4	117	366	193	379	.324	.475	May	.271	521	141	22	1	25	62	49	83	.334	.461
Turf	.269	606	163	33	3	17	80	45	108	.319	.417	June	.292	514	150	30	0	30	84	40	80	.339	.525
Pre-All Star	.273	1552	424	73	2	71	223	135	245	.330	.460	July	.260	497	129	24	3	22	83	36	82	.309	.453
Post-All Star	.259	1260	326	61	5	63	223	103	242	.313	.465	August	.247	494	122	23	2	28	93	40	100	.302	.472
Scoring Posn	.271	746	202	40	2	32	310	92	146	.339	.458	Sept/Oct	.269	427	115	20	1	20	71	37	84	.325	.461
Close & Late	.228	461	105	17	0	24	64	55	91	.310	.421	vs. AL	.303	66	20	1	0	10	16	3	9	.329	.773
None on/out	.274	715	196	33	2	35	35	53	122	.324	.473	vs. NL	.266	2746	730	133	7	124	430	235	478	.323	.455

Batter vs. Pitcher (career)

Hits Best Against	Avg	AB	H	2B	3B	HR	RBI	BB	SO	OBP	SLG	Hits Worst Against	Avg	AB	H	2B	3B	HR	RBI	BB	SO	OBP	SLG
F. Valenzuela	.571	14	8	0	0	2	5	0	1	.571	1.000	Darren Holmes	.000	8	0	0	0	0	0	3	5	.273	.000
Allen Watson	.500	14	7	2	0	1	2	1	4	.533	.857	Tommy Greene	.059	17	1	0	0	0	0	1	4	.111	.059
Roger Bailey	.500	10	5	1	0	2	4	0	0	.455	1.200	Xavier Hernandez	.067	15	1	0	0	0	1	1	8	.125	.067
Paul Quantrill	.417	12	5	3	0	1	3	0	1	.417	.917	Greg Maddux	.083	24	2	1	0	0	2	1	4	.120	.125
Pedro Martinez	.333	12	4	1	0	2	2	2	5	.467	.917	Todd Stottlemyre	.083	12	1	0	0	0	1	1	4	.143	.083

Steve Karsay — Athletics
Age 26 – Pitches Right

	ERA	W	L	Sv	G	GS	IP	BB	SO	Avg	H	2B	3B	HR	RBI	OBP	SLG	CG	ShO	Sup	QS	#P/S	SB	CS	GB	FB	G/F
1997 Season	5.77	3	12	0	24	24	132.2	47	92	.304	166	39	6	20	79	.366	.507	0	0	3.80	10	95	17	1	209	160	1.31
Career (1993-1997)	4.94	7	16	0	36	36	209.2	71	140	.287	241	49	9	25	107	.348	.456	1	0	4.55	17	96	22	4	301	253	1.19

1997 Season

	ERA	W	L	Sv	G	GS	IP	H	HR	BB	SO		Avg	AB	H	2B	3B	HR	RBI	BB	SO	OBP	SLG
Home	6.52	1	5	0	12	12	67.2	86	9	24	50	vs. Left	.296	287	85	24	4	16	48	32	54	.369	.575
Away	4.98	2	7	0	12	12	65.0	80	11	23	42	vs. Right	.313	259	81	15	2	4	31	15	38	.362	.432
Day	4.77	1	6	0	10	10	54.2	66	8	17	45	Inning 1-6	.301	522	157	39	5	19	75	45	90	.360	.504
Night	6.46	2	6	0	14	14	78.0	100	12	30	47	Inning 7+	.375	24	9	0	1	1	4	2	2	.467	.583
Grass	6.29	1	11	0	21	21	113.0	152	18	41	75	None on	.313	313	98	26	3	12	12	18	54	.354	.530
Turf	2.75	2	1	0	3	3	19.2	14	2	6	17	Runners on	.292	233	68	13	3	8	67	29	38	.380	.476
March/April	3.30	0	2	0	5	5	30.0	37	3	9	29	Scoring Posn	.277	137	38	7	1	5	56	25	21	.399	.453
May	6.75	1	3	0	6	6	36.0	41	6	10	25	Close & Late	.417	12	5	0	1	1	3	1	1	.500	.833
June	4.93	2	0	0	6	6	34.2	38	6	17	20	None on/out	.314	140	44	12	3	5	5	6	25	.351	.550
July	9.36	1	4	0	6	6	25.0	43	4	10	15	vs. 1st Batr (relief)	.000	0	0	0	0	0	0	0	0	.000	.000
August	2.57	0	1	0	1	1	7.0	7	1	1	3	1st Inning Pitched	.321	106	34	2	2	17	11	17	.381	.434
Sept/Oct	0.00	0	0	0	0	0	0.0	0	0	0	0	First 75 Pitches	.316	415	131	33	5	13	61	31	70	.365	.513
Starter	5.77	3	12	0	24	24	132.2	166	20	47	92	Pitch 76-90	.295	78	23	3	1	5	11	9	.364	.551
Reliever	0.00	0	0	0	0	0	0.0	0	0	0	0	Pitch 91-105	.220	41	9	3	0	0	4	5	9	.353	.293
0-3 Days Rest (Start)	8.59	0	2	0	2	2	7.1	16	2	3	5	Pitch 106+	.250	12	3	0	0	2	3	3	4	.438	.750
4 Days Rest	6.92	1	6	0	12	12	65.0	80	13	22	46	First Pitch	.400	75	30	10	1	4	10	2	0	.430	.720
5+ Days Rest	4.18	2	4	0	10	10	60.1	70	5	22	41	Ahead in Count	.245	237	58	11	1	6	29	0	77	.253	.376
vs. AL	5.82	3	12	0	23	23	125.1	157	19	44	89	Behind in Count	.357	143	51	13	3	4	27	17	0	.428	.573
vs. NL	4.91	0	0	0	1	1	7.1	9	1	3	3	Two Strikes	.220	241	53	14	1	7	28	28	92	.301	.373
Pre-All Star	5.49	2	8	0	18	18	105.0	125	17	37	77	Pre-All Star	.293	426	125	29	3	17	61	37	77	.359	.495
Post-All Star	6.83	1	4	0	6	6	27.2	41	3	10	15	Post-All Star	.342	120	41	10	3	3	18	10	15	.389	.550

Takashi Kashiwada — Mets
Age 27 – Pitches Left

	ERA	W	L	Sv	G	GS	IP	BB	SO	Avg	H	2B	3B	HR	RBI	OBP	SLG	GF	IR	IRS	Hld	SvOp	SB	CS	GB	FB	G/F
1997 Season	4.31	3	1	0	35	0	31.1	18	19	.289	35	9	0	4	16	.389	.463	11	17	5	3	2	4	1	50	39	1.28

1997 Season

	ERA	W	L	Sv	G	GS	IP	H	HR	BB	SO		Avg	AB	H	2B	3B	HR	RBI	BB	SO	OBP	SLG
Home	2.19	2	0	0	12	0	12.1	11	1	8	9	vs. Left	.289	45	13	2	0	1	5	9	7	.411	.400
Away	5.68	1	1	0	23	0	19.0	24	3	10	10	vs. Right	.289	76	22	7	0	3	11	9	12	.375	.500
Starter	0.00	0	0	0	0	0	0.0	0	0	0	0	Scoring Posn	.290	31	9	1	0	1	10	7	6	.400	.419
Reliever	4.31	3	1	0	35	0	31.1	35	4	18	19	Close & Late	.355	31	11	1	0	2	7	5	5	.447	.581
0 Days rest (Relief)	3.38	0	0	0	7	0	8.0	8	1	3	5	None on/out	.281	32	9	3	0	1	1	1	4	.324	.469
1 or 2 Days rest	3.38	0	1	0	15	0	13.1	17	1	5	8	First Pitch	.455	22	10	5	0	0	1	0	0	.478	.682
3+ Days rest	6.30	3	0	0	13	0	10.0	10	2	10	6	Ahead in Count	.145	55	8	1	0	2	8	0	17	.143	.273
Pre-All Star	4.64	2	0	0	23	0	21.1	22	3	11	13	Behind in Count	.579	19	11	3	0	2	5	12	0	.758	1.053
Post-All Star	3.60	1	1	0	12	0	10.0	13	1	7	6	Two Strikes	.174	46	8	1	0	2	7	6	19	.264	.326

Greg Keagle — Tigers
Age 27 – Pitches Right (flyball pitcher)

	ERA	W	L	Sv	G	GS	IP	BB	SO	Avg	H	2B	3B	HR	RBI	OBP	SLG	CG	ShO	Sup	QS	#P/S	SB	CS	GB	FB	G/F
1997 Season	6.55	3	5	0	11	10	45.1	18	33	.309	58	10	1	9	29	.382	.516	0	0	6.55	2	83	5	1	46	65	0.71
Career (1996-1997)	7.11	6	11	0	37	16	133.0	86	103	.302	162	38	6	22	105	.406	.518	0	0	4.74	2	84	12	2	152	161	0.94

1997 Season

	ERA	W	L	Sv	G	GS	IP	H	HR	BB	SO		Avg	AB	H	2B	3B	HR	RBI	BB	SO	OBP	SLG
Home	5.63	2	2	0	5	5	24.0	27	4	10	19	vs. Left	.321	109	35	7	1	8	20	11	19	.400	.624
Away	7.59	1	3	0	6	5	21.1	31	5	8	14	vs. Right	.291	79	23	3	0	1	9	7	14	.356	.367

Mike Kelly — Reds
Age 28 – Bats Right (flyball hitter)

	Avg	G	AB	R	H	2B	3B	HR	RBI	BB	SO	HBP	GDP	SB	CS	OBP	SLG	IBB	SH	SF	#Pit	#P/PA	GB	FB	G/F
1997 Season	.293	73	140	27	41	13	2	6	19	10	30	0	3	6	1	.338	.543	0	0	1	615	4.07	42	42	1.00
Career (1994-1997)	.241	219	403	72	97	33	4	12	52	32	107	5	8	17	5	.303	.432	0	2	2	1793	4.04	125	107	1.17

1997 Season

	Avg	AB	H	2B	3B	HR	RBI	BB	SO	OBP	SLG		Avg	AB	H	2B	3B	HR	RBI	BB	SO	OBP	SLG
vs. Left	.297	64	19	9	1	3	11	5	16	.343	.609	Scoring Posn	.186	43	8	2	2	1	12	4	10	.250	.395
vs. Right	.289	76	22	4	1	3	8	5	14	.333	.487	Close & Late	.258	31	8	2	1	2	7	2	9	.294	.581
Home	.333	90	30	9	0	3	13	7	14	.378	.533	None on/out	.258	31	8	2	0	1	1	2	9	.303	.419
Away	.220	50	11	4	2	3	6	3	16	.264	.560	Batting #2	.429	28	12	4	1	0	3	3	3	.484	.643
First Pitch	.500	10	5	1	1	2	3	0	0	.500	1.400	Batting #6	.233	43	10	1	1	1	6	2	13	.267	.372
Ahead in Count	.485	33	16	7	0	1	6	5	0	.538	.788	Other	.275	69	19	8	0	5	10	5	14	.320	.609
Behind in Count	.173	75	13	3	1	2	7	0	26	.173	.320	Pre-All Star	.254	63	16	5	1	2	10	5	13	.309	.460
Two Strikes	.175	80	14	5	1	2	8	5	30	.224	.338	Post-All Star	.325	77	25	8	1	4	9	5	17	.361	.610

Pat Kelly — Yankees

	Avg	G	AB	R	H	2B	3B	HR	RBI	BB	SO	HBP	GDP	SB	CS	OBP	SLG	IBB	SH	SF	#Pit	#P/PA	GB	FB	G/F
1997 Season	.242	67	120	25	29	6	1	2	10	14	37	1	4	8	1	.324	.358	1	2	1	526	3.81	26	32	0.81
Last Five Years	.260	389	1103	145	287	63	5	16	133	82	230	16	29	36	21	.317	.370	2	36	14	4519	3.61	308	320	0.96

1997 Season

	Avg	AB	H	2B	3B	HR	RBI	BB	SO	OBP	SLG		Avg	AB	H	2B	3B	HR	RBI	BB	SO	OBP	SLG
vs. Left	.211	38	8	1	0	0	1	2	12	.250	.237	Scoring Posn	.125	40	5	1	0	1	7	7	17	.265	.225
vs. Right	.256	82	21	5	1	2	9	12	25	.354	.415	Close & Late	.250	12	3	0	1	0	1	4	1	.438	.417
Home	.200	65	13	1	0	1	4	4	20	.246	.262	None on/out	.316	19	6	1	0	1		2	4	.381	.526
Away	.291	55	16	5	1	1	6	10	17	.403	.473	Batting #2	.303	66	20	4	1	2	9	5	18	.361	.485
First Pitch	.471	17	8	0	0	0	1	0	0	.474	.471	Batting #9	.111	36	4	0	0	0	1	4	17	.195	.111
Ahead in Count	.364	22	8	4	1	1	6	8	0	.533	.773	Other	.278	18	5	2	0	0		5	2	.435	.389
Behind in Count	.121	58	7	2	0	1	3	0	26	.121	.207	Pre-All Star	.221	68	15	4	1	0	4	12	23	.333	.309
Two Strikes	.129	70	9	2	0	2		6	37	.197	.157	Post-All Star	.269	52	14	2	0	2	6	2	14	.309	.423

Last Five Years

	Avg	AB	H	2B	3B	HR	RBI	BB	SO	OBP	SLG		Avg	AB	H	2B	3B	HR	RBI	BB	SO	OBP	SLG
vs. Left	.279	377	105	20	2	7	44	24	63	.327	.398	First Pitch	.314	194	61	8	1	3	26	1	0	.322	.412
vs. Right	.251	726	182	43	3	9	89	58	167	.312	.355	Ahead in Count	.356	205	73	21	2	4	34	35	0	.453	.537
Groundball	.229	249	57	13	1	0	28	13	49	.271	.289	Behind in Count	.198	500	99	25	2	7	48	0	187	.207	.298
Flyball	.277	224	62	16	1	6	38	16	42	.331	.438	Two Strikes	.183	514	94	22	2	6	55	46	230	.258	.268
Home	.247	546	135	29	1	7	53	43	109	.308	.342	Batting #2	.290	69	20	4	1	2	9	5	19	.347	.464
Away	.273	557	152	34	4	9	80	39	121	.325	.397	Batting #9	.256	990	253	56	3	13	119	71	200	.311	.358
Day	.253	411	104	22	1	4	52	31	83	.312	.341	Other	.318	44	14	3	1	1	5	6	11	.400	.500
Night	.264	692	183	41	4	12	81	51	147	.320	.387	March/April	.252	159	40	12	0	2	18	17	29	.328	.365
Grass	.257	946	243	50	4	12	102	71	197	.316	.356	June	.284	162	46	13	1	2	25	18	31	.358	.414
Turf	.280	157	44	13	1	4	31	11	33	.320	.452	July	.260	258	67	8	2	5	34	14	52	.308	.364
Pre-All Star	.274	594	163	34	1	10	69	56	121	.340	.386	August	.228	224	51	16	1	1	24	12	53	.270	.321
Post-All Star	.244	509	124	29	4	6	64	26	109	.288	.352	Sept/Oct	.253	91	23	5	1	1	10	3	20	.289	.363
Scoring Posn	.223	305	68	19	0	2	107	26	82	.291	.305	vs. AL	.260	1091	284	63	4	16	132	77	228	.315	.369
Close & Late	.255	137	35	8	1	2	19	14	32	.322	.372	vs. NL	.250	12	3	0	1	0	1	5	2	.471	.417
None on/out	.245	257	63	13	2	5	5	18	40	.297	.370												

Batter vs. Pitcher (career)

Hits Best Against	Avg	AB	H	2B	3B	HR	RBI	BB	SO	OBP	SLG	Hits Worst Against	Avg	AB	H	2B	3B	HR	RBI	BB	SO	OBP	SLG
Kenny Rogers	.429	14	6	1	0	1	2	1	2	.467	.714	Erik Hanson	.071	14	1	0	0	0	0	0	5	.071	.071
Mike Mussina	.429	14	6	2	0	1	5	0	2	.429	.786	Kevin Brown	.077	13	1	0	0	0	0	0	2	.143	.077
Woody Williams	.400	10	4	1	0	0	1	1	3	.417	.500	Todd Stottlemyre	.091	33	3	0	1	0	2	1	7	.118	.152
Cal Eldred	.333	9	3	1	0	0	1	2	2	.455	.444	Roger Clemens	.091	11	1	0	0	0	0	1	4	.167	.091
Matt Whiteside	.333	9	3	1	0	0	2	2	3	.455	.444	Wilson Alvarez	.111	18	2	0	0	0	0	2	6	.200	.111

Roberto Kelly — Mariners

	Avg	G	AB	R	H	2B	3B	HR	RBI	BB	SO	HBP	GDP	SB	CS	OBP	SLG	IBB	SH	SF	#Pit	#P/PA	GB	FB	G/F
1997 Season	.291	105	368	58	107	26	2	12	59	22	67	3	6	9	5	.333	.470	0	2	3	1348	3.39	128	113	1.13
Last Five Years	.298	527	1948	274	580	106	14	43	243	119	313	21	55	78	33	.341	.433	7	2	21	7580	3.58	767	500	1.53

1997 Season

	Avg	AB	H	2B	3B	HR	RBI	BB	SO	OBP	SLG		Avg	AB	H	2B	3B	HR	RBI	BB	SO	OBP	SLG
vs. Left	.298	124	37	10	0	5	24	11	24	.355	.500	First Pitch	.268	56	15	3	0	1	12	0	0	.268	.375
vs. Right	.287	244	70	16	2	7	35	11	43	.322	.455	Ahead in Count	.278	72	20	3	0	6	14	14	0	.395	.569
Groundball	.274	73	20	5	0	3	16	8	17	.345	.466	Behind in Count	.289	180	52	14	2	3	22	0	58	.297	.439
Flyball	.232	56	13	5	0	0	7	2	13	.254	.321	Two Strikes	.199	156	31	11	1	1	11	8	67	.243	.301
Home	.266	188	50	12	1	8	30	7	38	.299	.468	Batting #2	.307	179	55	13	0	8	31	9	27	.342	.514
Away	.317	180	57	14	1	4	29	15	29	.367	.472	Batting #7	.235	68	16	4	1	3	11	6	14	.316	.456
Day	.327	104	34	10	0	2	20	2	14	.336	.481	Other	.298	121	36	9	1	1	17	7	26	.331	.413
Night	.277	264	73	16	2	10	39	20	53	.332	.466	March/April	.283	46	13	5	0	1	11	2	8	.314	.457
Grass	.307	140	43	12	0	4	20	11	21	.353	.479	May	.265	68	18	3	1	0	4	6	15	.333	.338
Turf	.281	228	64	14	2	8	39	11	46	.321	.465	June	.273	44	12	5	1	0	3	8	6	.385	.432
Pre-All Star	.292	171	50	14	2	1	20	16	30	.356	.415	July	.356	59	21	3	0	3	12	1	11	.367	.559
Post-All Star	.289	197	57	12	0	11	39	6	37	.312	.518	August	.267	75	20	5	0	4	13	1	17	.276	.493
Scoring Posn	.315	89	28	11	0	3	43	4	18	.333	.539	Sept/Oct	.303	76	23	5	0	4	16	4	10	.341	.526
Close & Late	.236	55	13	3	0	1	8	3	10	.271	.345	vs. AL	.294	327	96	25	1	11	55	17	60	.331	.475
None on/out	.232	82	19	2	2	5	5	5	15	.276	.341	vs. NL	.268	41	11	1	1	1	4	5	7	.348	.415

1997 By Position

Position	Avg	AB	H	2B	3B	HR	RBI	BB	SO	OBP	SLG		G	GS	Innings	PO	A	E	DP	Fld Pct	Rng Fctr	In Zone	Zone Outs	Zone Rtg	MLB Zone
As DH	.250	44	11	3	0	1	10	2	9	.286	.386		13	10	---	---	---	---	---	---	---	---	---	---	---
As Pinch Hitter	.286	14	4	1	0	0	4	1	4	.313	.357		17	0	---	---	---	---	---	---	---	---	---	---	---
As lf	.306	121	37	7	0	7	23	5	17	.339	.537		29	28	246.0	55	1	0	0	1.000	2.05	68	54	.794	.805
As rf	.288	191	55	15	2	4	30	14	39	.340	.450		57	50	433.1	99	1	0	0	1.000	2.08	117	95	.812	.813

Last Five Years

	Avg	AB	H	2B	3B	HR	RBI	BB	SO	OBP	SLG		Avg	AB	H	2B	3B	HR	RBI	BB	SO	OBP	SLG
vs. Left	.314	573	180	39	3	16	79	42	94	.364	.476	First Pitch	.299	244	73	10	3	1	39	6	0	.319	.377
vs. Right	.291	1375	400	67	11	27	164	77	219	.332	.415	Ahead in Count	.339	428	145	24	5	16	62	59	0	.417	.530
Groundball	.312	587	183	37	3	11	65	38	95	.356	.441	Behind in Count	.255	934	238	50	2	17	85	0	268	.263	.367
Flyball	.300	323	97	19	3	9	51	13	55	.329	.461	Two Strikes	.235	852	200	42	3	12	74	54	313	.284	.333
Home	.282	939	265	43	8	21	116	58	150	.329	.412	Batting #2	.314	404	127	24	3	13	54	21	63	.353	.485
Away	.312	1009	315	63	6	22	127	61	163	.353	.452	Batting #5	.276	391	108	18	4	9	50	21	77	.316	.412

Last Five Years

	Avg	AB	H	2B	3B	HR	RBI	BB	SO	OBP	SLG		Avg	AB	H	2B	3B	HR	RBI	BB	SO	OBP	SLG
Day	.316	535	169	35	4	12	78	20	86	.340	.464	Other	.299	1153	345	64	7	21	139	77	173	.346	.422
Night	.291	1413	411	71	10	31	165	99	227	.342	.421	March/April	.285	295	84	15	3	5	39	17	57	.327	.407
Grass	.299	933	279	56	6	22	100	59	137	.340	.443	May	.301	465	140	24	2	7	44	33	70	.354	.406
Turf	.297	1015	301	50	8	21	143	60	176	.342	.424	June	.312	420	131	29	5	6	44	30	63	.362	.448
Pre-All Star	.305	1267	386	75	11	19	134	85	200	.353	.424	July	.272	316	86	13	1	8	45	14	58	.301	.396
Post-All Star	.285	681	194	31	3	24	109	34	113	.320	.445	August	.298	245	73	10	1	9	36	8	37	.319	.457
Scoring Posn	.315	479	151	26	4	10	193	43	69	.367	.449	Sept/Oct	.319	207	66	15	2	8	35	17	28	.377	.527
Close & Late	.307	277	85	17	3	6	43	14	40	.339	.455	vs. AL	.308	649	200	42	5	17	102	40	113	.354	.467
None on/out	.289	488	141	29	5	11	11	23	70	.326	.436	vs. NL	.293	1299	380	64	9	26	141	79	200	.335	.416

Batter vs. Pitcher (career)

Hits Best Against	Avg	AB	H	2B	3B	HR	RBI	BB	SO	OBP	SLG	Hits Worst Against	Avg	AB	H	2B	3B	HR	RBI	BB	SO	OBP	SLG
Darren Oliver	.667	9	6	1	0	2	4	2	2	.727	1.444	John Smoltz	.000	13	0	0	0	0	0	1	2	.071	.000
Dwight Gooden	.636	11	7	3	0	1	2	1	0	.692	1.182	Andy Pettitte	.000	12	0	0	0	0	0	0	5	.000	.000
Jimmy Haynes	.636	11	7	1	0	0	3	0	1	.583	.727	Jack McDowell	.000	9	0	0	0	0	0	2	5	.182	.000
Scott Aldred	.500	12	6	1	0	1	4	0	4	.500	.833	Allen Watson	.077	13	1	0	0	0	1	0	6	.077	.077
Bruce Ruffin	.500	8	4	1	0	0	4	3	3	.636	.625	Tom Gordon	.091	22	2	0	0	0	1	0	8	.091	.091

Jason Kendall — Pirates

Age 24 – Bats Right

	Avg	G	AB	R	H	2B	3B	HR	RBI	BB	SO	HBP	GDP	SB	CS	OBP	SLG	IBB	SH	SF	#Pit	#P/PA	GB	FB	G/F
1997 Season	.294	144	486	71	143	36	4	8	49	49	53	31	11	18	6	.391	.434	2	1	5	2177	3.81	213	141	1.51
Career (1996-1997)	.297	274	900	125	267	59	9	11	91	84	83	46	18	23	8	.382	.419	13	4	9	3931	3.77	404	257	1.57

1997 Season

	Avg	AB	H	2B	3B	HR	RBI	BB	SO	OBP	SLG		Avg	AB	H	2B	3B	HR	RBI	BB	SO	OBP	SLG
vs. Left	.297	101	30	8	0	3	10	8	9	.374	.465	First Pitch	.342	38	13	4	0	1	2	2	0	.444	.526
vs. Right	.294	385	113	28	4	5	39	41	44	.395	.426	Ahead in Count	.330	112	37	7	1	4	15	31	0	.483	.518
Groundball	.265	83	22	6	0	0	7	6	13	.326	.337	Behind in Count	.233	232	54	15	1	3	21	0	47	.287	.345
Flyball	.293	92	27	9	0	3	10	6	12	.363	.489	Two Strikes	.242	211	51	15	3	2	14	16	53	.336	.370
Home	.308	234	72	16	2	5	24	29	21	.409	.457	Batting #6	.309	337	104	26	3	5	38	28	36	.393	.448
Away	.282	252	71	20	2	3	25	20	32	.373	.413	Batting #8	.306	62	19	6	0	2	6	9	7	.419	.500
Day	.309	149	46	12	1	2	22	13	18	.399	.443	Other	.230	87	20	4	1	1	5	12	10	.362	.333
Night	.288	337	97	24	3	6	27	36	35	.387	.430	March/April	.247	77	19	7	0	0	6	4	9	.318	.338
Grass	.248	165	41	9	1	2	16	16	21	.345	.352	May	.326	89	29	6	3	2	13	10	11	.417	.528
Turf	.318	321	102	27	3	6	33	33	32	.414	.477	June	.244	78	19	5	1	0	6	12	7	.402	.333
Pre-All Star	.268	261	70	19	4	2	27	27	29	.377	.395	July	.321	84	27	6	0	2	9	8	9	.406	.464
Post-All Star	.324	225	73	17	0	6	22	22	24	.407	.480	August	.318	85	27	5	0	2	9	5	11	.379	.447
Scoring Posn	.256	121	31	8	1	0	38	10	14	.321	.339	Sept/Oct	.301	73	22	7	0	2	6	10	6	.414	.479
Close & Late	.373	75	28	9	0	0	12	9	13	.479	.493	vs. AL	.200	45	9	3	0	0	3	3	3	.321	.267
None on/out	.377	106	40	12	1	5	5	16	8	.496	.651	vs. NL	.304	441	134	33	4	8	49	46	50	.398	.451

1997 By Position

Position	Avg	AB	H	2B	3B	HR	RBI	BB	SO	OBP	SLG	G	GS	Innings	PO	A	E	DP	Fld Pct	Rng Fctr	In Zone	Zone Outs	Zone Rtg	MLB Zone
As c	.293	484	142	36	4	8	49	49	52	.390	.434	142	139	1218.0	953	101	11	20	.990	---	---	---	---	

Career (1996-1997)

	Avg	AB	H	2B	3B	HR	RBI	BB	SO	OBP	SLG		Avg	AB	H	2B	3B	HR	RBI	BB	SO	OBP	SLG
vs. Left	.296	179	53	11	3	3	15	17	11	.373	.441	First Pitch	.348	66	23	7	3	1	6	7	0	.463	.591
vs. Right	.297	721	214	48	6	8	76	67	72	.384	.413	Ahead in Count	.336	214	72	12	2	5	26	53	0	.475	.481
Groundball	.270	189	51	10	1	1	17	19	24	.349	.349	Behind in Count	.251	439	110	26	2	3	38	0	72	.293	.339
Flyball	.308	156	48	11	2	4	19	9	18	.374	.481	Two Strikes	.248	399	99	21	4	3	38	24	83	.325	.343
Home	.307	450	138	28	5	7	50	38	36	.382	.438	Batting #6	.311	338	105	26	3	5	39	28	36	.394	.450
Away	.287	450	129	31	4	4	41	46	47	.382	.400	Batting #8	.303	445	135	28	5	4	45	40	36	.381	.416
Day	.304	260	79	19	3	4	36	20	28	.378	.446	Other	.231	117	27	5	1	2	7	16	11	.353	.342
Night	.294	640	188	40	6	7	55	64	55	.384	.408	March/April	.267	150	40	12	1	0	15	6	15	.319	.360
Grass	.252	301	76	14	3	3	28	36	31	.356	.349	May	.323	161	52	9	4	3	24	13	17	.389	.484
Turf	.319	599	191	45	6	8	63	48	52	.396	.454	June	.264	144	38	6	2	0	12	21	14	.394	.333
Pre-All Star	.280	489	137	29	7	3	53	42	50	.363	.387	July	.281	153	43	10	0	2	13	12	13	.349	.386
Post-All Star	.316	411	130	30	2	8	38	42	33	.404	.457	August	.363	160	58	13	0	3	18	11	14	.425	.500
Scoring Posn	.276	221	61	13	2	0	73	28	32	.372	.353	Sept/Oct	.273	132	36	9	2	3	9	21	11	.411	.439
Close & Late	.359	142	51	14	2	2	26	14	20	.454	.528	vs. AL	.200	45	9	3	0	0	3	3	3	.321	.267
None on/out	.320	203	65	17	2	6	6	23	17	.418	.512	vs. NL	.302	855	258	56	9	11	91	81	80	.385	.427

Batter vs. Pitcher (career)

Hits Best Against	Avg	AB	H	2B	3B	HR	RBI	BB	SO	OBP	SLG	Hits Worst Against	Avg	AB	H	2B	3B	HR	RBI	BB	SO	OBP	SLG
Kevin Brown	.500	14	7	2	0	0	3	0	1	.533	.643	Shane Reynolds	.111	9	1	0	0	0	0	2	0	.333	.111
Terry Mulholland	.500	10	5	1	0	0	2	1	0	.583	.600	Kirk Rueter	.111	9	1	0	0	0	0	3	0	.333	.111
Pedro Astacio	.417	12	5	2	0	0	1	1	2	.500	.583	Mark Clark	.182	11	2	0	0	0	1	0	0	.182	.182
John Smoltz	.364	22	8	1	1	0	2	1	1	.391	.500	Darryl Kile	.200	15	3	2	0	0	1	0	1	.294	.333
Andy Ashby	.308	13	4	1	0	0	0	0	2	.308	.385	Curt Schilling	.231	13	3	0	0	0	1	1	2	.286	.231

Jeff Kent — Giants

Age 30 – Bats Right (flyball hitter)

	Avg	G	AB	R	H	2B	3B	HR	RBI	BB	SO	HBP	GDP	SB	CS	OBP	SLG	IBB	SH	SF	#Pit	#P/PA	GB	FB	G/F
1997 Season	.250	155	580	90	145	38	2	29	121	48	133	13	14	11	3	.316	.472	6	0	10	2343	3.60	154	210	0.73
Last Five Years	.273	655	2400	334	655	135	11	96	389	161	472	41	49	25	18	.326	.458	15	9	27	9176	3.48	738	768	0.96

1997 Season

	Avg	AB	H	2B	3B	HR	RBI	BB	SO	OBP	SLG		Avg	AB	H	2B	3B	HR	RBI	BB	SO	OBP	SLG
vs. Left	.230	148	34	7	1	6	21	17	24	.307	.412	First Pitch	.181	83	15	6	0	3	11	6	0	.266	.361
vs. Right	.257	432	111	31	1	23	100	31	109	.320	.493	Ahead in Count	.333	138	46	18	1	9	36	25	0	.440	.674
Groundball	.191	115	22	6	0	4	18	12	30	.280	.348	Behind in Count	.213	272	58	8	1	9	43	0	118	.217	.349
Flyball	.349	63	22	6	0	2	11	7	13	.425	.540	Two Strikes	.190	268	51	7	0	12	50	17	133	.245	.351
Home	.246	281	69	19	0	13	58	27	69	.321	.452	Batting #4	.249	341	85	21	2	15	67	28	72	.318	.455
Away	.254	299	76	19	2	16	63	21	64	.312	.492	Batting #5	.230	187	43	12	0	11	47	17	44	.302	.471
Day	.232	263	61	20	0	5	39	22	61	.303	.365	Other	.327	52	17	5	0	3	7	3	17	.364	.596
Night	.265	317	84	18	2	24	82	26	72	.328	.562	March/April	.286	77	22	10	0	5	26	8	18	.341	.610
Grass	.239	477	114	29	1	22	97	39	112	.306	.442	May	.235	98	23	3	0	6	20	7	22	.313	.449
Turf	.301	103	31	9	1	7	24	9	21	.365	.612	June	.248	101	25	7	0	5	15	6	30	.309	.465
Pre-All Star	.252	298	75	20	0	18	64	24	74	.320	.500	July	.221	104	23	3	1	6	21	9	20	.287	.442
Post-All Star	.248	282	70	18	2	11	57	24	59	.313	.443	August	.301	103	31	10	1	4	22	13	17	.383	.534
Scoring Posn	.271	199	54	11	2	8	91	25	49	.365	.467	Sept/Oct	.216	97	21	5	0	3	17	5	26	.262	.361
Close & Late	.236	89	21	2	0	4	21	10	19	.317	.393	vs. AL	.294	68	20	5	0	5	11	5	20	.342	.588
None on/out	.224	116	26	5	0	11	11	5	27	.268	.552	vs. NL	.244	512	125	33	2	24	110	43	113	.313	.457

1997 By Position

Position	Avg	AB	H	2B	3B	HR	RBI	BB	SO	OBP	SLG	G	GS	Innings	PO	A	E	DP	Fld Pct	Rng Fctr	In Zone	Zone Outs	Zone Rtg	MLB Zone
As 1b	.154	39	6	0	0	1	3	3	7	.214	.231	13	8	81.2	80	4	0	6	1.000	—	15	15	1.000	.874
As 2b	.258	539	139	38	2	28	118	45	126	.325	.492	148	143	1274.1	323	425	16	104	.979	5.49	450	420	.933	.902

Last Five Years

	Avg	AB	H	2B	3B	HR	RBI	BB	SO	OBP	SLG		Avg	AB	H	2B	3B	HR	RBI	BB	SO	OBP	SLG
vs. Left	.275	662	182	43	3	13	69	64	97	.338	.408	First Pitch	.264	416	110	27	3	15	64	13	0	.302	.452
vs. Right	.272	1738	473	92	8	83	320	97	375	.321	.478	Ahead in Count	.355	493	175	47	1	26	117	83	0	.450	.613
Groundball	.285	663	189	36	2	30	117	44	133	.336	.481	Behind in Count	.223	1087	242	36	5	28	127	0	412	.229	.342
Flyball	.240	341	82	16	0	10	41	20	74	.289	.375	Two Strikes	.196	1037	203	31	4	31	127	65	472	.247	.323
Home	.277	1167	323	68	8	47	200	80	230	.329	.470	Batting #5	.271	852	231	48	4	33	138	58	177	.326	.453
Away	.269	1233	332	67	3	49	189	81	242	.323	.448	Batting #6	.294	643	189	30	4	28	108	40	116	.339	.484
Day	.273	847	231	50	1	36	128	60	171	.329	.462	Other	.260	905	235	57	3	35	143	63	179	.317	.445
Night	.273	1553	424	85	10	60	261	101	301	.324	.457	March/April	.291	333	97	26	0	17	71	23	76	.344	.523
Grass	.267	1899	507	102	9	78	316	129	375	.320	.453	May	.249	450	112	17	4	18	62	33	95	.315	.424
Turf	.295	501	148	33	2	18	73	32	97	.348	.477	June	.275	473	130	26	3	17	59	22	87	.317	.450
Pre-All Star	.272	1394	379	75	7	56	209	85	291	.324	.456	July	.274	398	109	18	2	17	69	26	77	.319	.457
Post-All Star	.274	1006	276	60	4	40	180	76	181	.329	.461	August	.286	405	116	24	2	13	62	35	69	.348	.452
Scoring Posn	.276	678	187	35	6	24	285	72	147	.348	.451	Sept/Oct	.267	341	91	24	0	14	66	22	68	.316	.460
Close & Late	.257	428	110	16	0	20	60	28	99	.309	.435	vs. AL	.276	170	47	12	0	8	27	15	42	.333	.488
None on/out	.272	558	152	36	1	24	24	24	93	.308	.470	vs. NL	.273	2230	608	123	11	88	362	146	430	.325	.456

Batter vs. Pitcher (career)

Hits Best Against	Avg	AB	H	2B	3B	HR	RBI	BB	SO	OBP	SLG	Hits Worst Against	Avg	AB	H	2B	3B	HR	RBI	BB	SO	OBP	SLG
Dave Weathers	.600	15	9	3	1	0	8	3	2	.684	.933	Chris Hammond	.067	15	1	1	0	0	1	0	3	.067	.133
Carlos Perez	.462	13	6	1	1	2	4	0	2	.462	1.154	Scott Sanders	.077	13	1	0	0	0	0	0	5	.077	.077
Roger Bailey	.455	11	5	1	0	2	7	0	1	.455	1.091	Orel Hershiser	.167	12	2	0	0	0	1	0	4	.154	.167
Pat Rapp	.400	25	10	1	0	4	10	3	4	.464	.920	Alan Benes	.167	12	2	0	0	0	1	0	2	.167	.167
Greg McMichael	.333	12	4	1	0	2	3	3	4	.467	.917	Steve Reed	.182	11	2	0	0	0	1	0	2	.167	.182

Jimmy Key — Orioles

Age 37 – Pitches Left

	ERA	W	L	Sv	G	GS	IP	BB	SO	Avg	H	2B	3B	HR	RBI	OBP	SLG	CG	ShO	Sup	QS	#P/S	SB	CS	GB	FB	G/F
1997 Season	3.43	16	10	0	34	34	212.1	82	141	.261	210	30	4	24	77	.331	.398	1	1	5.34	19	105	11	13	282	236	1.19
Last Five Years	3.61	64	33	0	128	128	816.2	241	541	.263	817	136	18	84	319	.316	.399	6	3	6.03	77	103	37	29	1175	843	1.39

1997 Season

	ERA	W	L	Sv	G	GS	IP	H	HR	BB	SO		Avg	AB	H	2B	3B	HR	RBI	BB	SO	OBP	SLG
Home	3.93	6	8	0	16	16	100.2	95	15	40	68	vs. Left	.263	137	36	6	0	5	17	18	24	.356	.416
Away	2.98	10	2	0	18	18	111.2	115	9	42	73	vs. Right	.261	667	174	24	4	19	60	64	117	.326	.394
Day	3.59	5	3	0	10	10	62.2	63	8	28	45	Inning 1-6	.258	730	188	29	3	23	75	74	129	.328	.400
Night	3.37	11	7	0	24	24	149.2	147	16	54	96	Inning 7+	.297	74	22	1	1	1	2	8	12	.366	.378
Grass	3.51	15	10	0	31	31	194.2	193	21	74	128	None on	.283	495	140	23	3	13	13	31	85	.328	.420
Turf	2.55	1	0	0	3	3	17.2	17	3	8	13	Runners on	.227	309	70	7	1	11	64	51	56	.336	.362
March/April	2.48	4	0	0	5	5	32.2	32	3	14	20	Scoring Posn	.179	156	28	5	0	7	54	35	27	.330	.346
May	2.15	5	1	0	6	6	37.2	38	1	11	11	Close & Late	.304	23	7	0	0	0	0	4	6	.407	.304
June	3.32	2	3	0	6	6	38.0	34	5	12	34	None on/out	.250	212	53	8	1	3	3	8	31	.281	.340
July	1.99	2	2	0	6	6	40.2	37	4	12	28	vs. 1st Batr (relief)	.000	0	0	0	0	0	0	0	0	.000	.000
August	5.05	1	2	0	6	6	35.2	35	9	20	29	1st Inning Pitched	.308	143	44	9	0	8	25	11	24	.361	.538
Sept/Oct	6.51	2	2	0	5	5	27.2	34	2	13	19	First 75 Pitches	.266	556	148	21	2	17	54	55	84	.332	.403
Starter	3.43	16	10	0	34	34	212.1	210	24	82	141	Pitch 76-90	.223	103	23	7	1	5	15	10	31	.298	.456
Reliever	0.00	0	0	0	0	0	0.0	0	0	0	0	Pitch 91-105	.243	103	25	1	0	2	6	8	18	.304	.311
0-3 Days Rest (Start)	0.00	0	0	0	0	0	0.0	0	0	0	0	Pitch 106+	.333	42	14	1	1	0	2	9	8	.451	.405
4 Days Rest	3.01	11	7	0	23	23	143.1	137	17	56	90	First Pitch	.377	106	40	3	2	6	16	1	0	.385	.613
5+ Days Rest	4.30	5	3	0	11	11	69.0	73	7	26	51	Ahead in Count	.212	326	69	8	1	7	19	0	111	.213	.307
vs. AL	3.51	15	8	0	31	31	192.1	196	21	72	128	Behind in Count	.283	184	52	9	1	6	25	45	0	.423	.440

1997 Season

	ERA	W	L	Sv	G	GS	IP	H	HR	BB	SO		Avg	AB	H	2B	3B	HR	RBI	BB	SO	OBP	SLG
vs. NL	2.70	1	2	0	3	3	20.0	14	3	10	13	Two Strikes	.190	379	72	12	1	9	24	36	141	.260	.298
Pre-All Star	2.55	12	4	0	18	18	116.1	109	10	39	68	Pre-All Star	.249	438	109	13	3	10	33	39	68	.311	.361
Post-All Star	4.50	4	6	0	16	16	96.0	101	14	43	73	Post-All Star	.276	366	101	17	1	14	44	43	73	.354	.443

Last Five Years

	ERA	W	L	Sv	G	GS	IP	H	HR	BB	SO		Avg	AB	H	2B	3B	HR	RBI	BB	SO	OBP	SLG
Home	3.90	26	21	0	62	62	397.1	396	42	113	263	vs. Left	.241	507	122	22	1	13	54	36	91	.299	.365
Away	3.35	38	12	0	66	66	419.1	421	42	128	278	vs. Right	.267	2602	695	114	17	71	265	205	450	.319	.406
Day	4.30	16	11	0	37	37	234.1	254	25	63	156	Inning 1-6	.264	2755	726	120	17	74	289	222	485	.319	.400
Night	3.34	48	22	0	91	91	582.1	563	59	178	385	Inning 7+	.257	354	91	16	1	10	30	19	56	.293	.393
Grass	3.73	55	32	0	111	111	712.2	716	75	210	469	None on	.272	1878	511	91	13	48	48	117	317	.317	.411
Turf	2.86	9	1	0	17	17	104.0	101	9	31	72	Runners on	.249	1231	306	45	5	36	271	124	224	.314	.381
March/April	3.18	13	4	0	22	22	141.2	127	12	37	90	Scoring Posn	.238	625	149	24	2	20	227	87	114	.325	.379
May	3.48	11	7	0	25	25	165.2	170	15	33	95	Close & Late	.263	137	36	5	0	3	14	7	19	.295	.365
June	3.38	13	4	0	21	21	133.0	135	12	44	97	None on/out	.258	811	209	38	6	19	19	44	119	.299	.390
July	3.14	13	8	0	25	25	166.0	160	19	52	110	vs. 1st Batr (relief)	.000	0	0	0	0	0	0	0	0	.000	.000
August	4.73	7	6	0	19	19	112.1	121	20	39	78	1st Inning Pitched	.276	489	135	23	5	12	61	36	97	.330	.417
Sept/Oct	4.32	7	4	0	16	16	98.0	104	6	36	71	First 75 Pitches	.260	2164	563	90	15	56	206	175	369	.315	.393
Starter	3.61	64	33	0	128	128	816.2	817	84	241	541	Pitch 76-90	.280	443	124	28	1	12	58	28	82	.324	.429
Reliever	0.00	0	0	0	0	0	0.0	0	0	0	0	Pitch 91-105	.275	338	93	14	1	12	41	23	58	.322	.429
0-3 Days Rest (Start)	0.00	0	0	0	0	0	0.0	0	0	0	0	Pitch 106+	.226	164	37	4	1	4	14	15	32	.291	.335
4 Days Rest	3.63	47	25	0	90	90	574.2	585	60	170	394	First Pitch	.304	424	129	23	2	13	55	4	0	.311	.460
5+ Days Rest	3.57	17	8	0	38	38	242.0	232	24	71	147	Ahead in Count	.198	1277	253	42	4	23	87	0	446	.200	.291
vs. AL	3.64	63	31	0	125	125	796.2	803	81	231	528	Behind in Count	.325	738	240	39	3	29	101	124	0	.420	.504
vs. NL	2.70	1	2	0	3	3	20.0	14	3	10	13	Two Strikes	.195	1436	280	47	7	29	104	113	541	.253	.298
Pre-All Star	3.27	42	16	0	75	75	487.1	474	42	128	311	Pre-All Star	.257	1845	474	79	10	42	170	128	311	.304	.379
Post-All Star	4.13	22	17	0	53	53	329.1	343	42	113	230	Post-All Star	.271	1264	343	57	8	42	149	113	230	.332	.429

Pitcher vs. Batter (career)

Pitches Best Vs.	Avg	AB	H	2B	3B	HR	RBI	BB	SO	OBP	SLG	Pitches Worst Vs.	Avg	AB	H	2B	3B	HR	RBI	BB	SO	OBP	SLG
Dante Bichette	.063	16	1	0	0	0	1	0	2	.059	.063	Darrin Jackson	.500	12	6	1	0	1	1	0	1	.500	.833
Eddie Williams	.071	14	1	1	0	0	0	0	3	.071	.143	Tony Fernandez	.455	11	5	1	2	0	4	2	0	.538	.909
Lee Tinsley	.071	14	1	0	0	0	0	0	5	.133	.071	Rickey Henderson	.412	85	35	4	1	9	14	13	8	.485	.800
J.T. Snow	.071	14	1	0	0	0	1	5	.133	.071	Joe Vitiello	.400	10	4	2	0	1	4	0	5	.364	.900
Juan Samuel	.077	13	1	0	0	0	1	0	3	.077	.077	Cecil Fielder	.333	45	15	1	0	7	15	4	8	.388	.822

Brooks Kieschnick — Cubs
Age 26 – Bats Left

	Avg	G	AB	R	H	2B	3B	HR	RBI	BB	SO	HBP	GDP	SB	CS	OBP	SLG	IBB	SH	SF	#Pit	#P/PA	GB	FB	G/F
1997 Season	.200	39	90	9	18	2	0	4	12	12	21	0	2	1	0	.294	.356	0	0	0	411	4.03	29	29	1.00
Career (1996-1997)	.235	64	119	15	28	4	0	5	18	15	29	0	2	1	0	.321	.395	0	0	0	523	3.90	35	40	0.88

1997 Season

	Avg	AB	H	2B	3B	HR	RBI	BB	SO	OBP	SLG		Avg	AB	H	2B	3B	HR	RBI	BB	SO	OBP	SLG
vs. Left	.286	7	2	0	0	0	1	0	2	.286	.286	Scoring Posn	.333	21	7	0	0	3	11	4	6	.440	.762
vs. Right	.193	83	16	2	0	4	11	12	19	.295	.361	Close & Late	.000	7	0	0	0	0	0	2	2	.222	.000

Darryl Kile — Astros
Age 29 – Pitches Right

	ERA	W	L	Sv	G	GS	IP	BB	SO	Avg	H	2B	3B	HR	RBI	OBP	SLG	CG	ShO	Sup	QS	#P/S	SB	CS	GB	FB	G/F
1997 Season	2.57	19	7	0	34	34	255.2	94	205	.225	208	38	4	19	76	.301	.337	6	4	5.46	26	113	20	4	365	231	1.58
Last Five Years	3.78	59	44	0	150	138	921.0	415	783	.250	860	148	22	65	365	.339	.363	14	6	5.36	85	105	69	25	1234	882	1.40

1997 Season

	ERA	W	L	Sv	G	GS	IP	H	HR	BB	SO		Avg	AB	H	2B	3B	HR	RBI	BB	SO	OBP	SLG
Home	2.59	10	3	0	17	17	132.0	104	11	38	124	vs. Left	.233	486	113	20	1	11	39	53	108	.306	.346
Away	2.55	9	4	0	17	17	123.2	104	8	56	81	vs. Right	.217	438	95	18	3	8	37	41	97	.294	.326
Day	2.14	6	1	0	10	10	75.2	62	3	28	55	Inning 1-6	.231	719	166	26	3	14	59	76	161	.308	.334
Night	2.75	13	6	0	24	24	180.0	146	16	66	150	Inning 7+	.205	205	42	12	1	5	17	18	44	.275	.346
Grass	2.40	6	2	0	12	12	90.0	73	6	42	56	None on	.243	536	130	27	3	12	12	55	115	.318	.371
Turf	2.66	13	5	0	22	22	165.2	135	13	52	149	Runners on	.201	388	78	11	1	7	64	39	90	.278	.289
March/April	3.12	1	2	0	6	6	43.1	36	3	18	28	Scoring Posn	.171	210	36	5	0	4	56	31	61	.270	.252
May	1.20	5	0	0	6	6	45.0	31	1	19	35	Close & Late	.232	125	29	8	1	4	13	10	23	.298	.408
June	2.40	3	1	0	6	6	45.0	39	4	15	34	None on/out	.277	242	67	9	3	7	7	27	47	.354	.426
July	1.59	5	0	0	6	6	51.0	36	2	11	46	vs. 1st Batr (relief)	.000	0	0	0	0	0	0	0	0	.000	.000
August	3.68	2	1	0	5	5	36.2	41	6	11	30	1st Inning Pitched	.210	119	25	6	0	1	8	18	35	.319	.286
Sept/Oct	4.15	2	3	0	5	5	34.2	25	3	20	32	First 75 Pitches	.242	612	148	23	3	13	53	57	129	.307	.353
Starter	2.57	19	7	0	34	34	255.2	208	19	94	205	Pitch 76-90	.165	115	19	4	0	1	7	13	35	.254	.226
Reliever	0.00	0	0	0	0	0	0.0	0	0	0	0	Pitch 91-105	.204	108	22	8	0	4	8	17	21	.323	.389
0-3 Days Rest (Start)	0.00	1	0	0	1	1	9.0	4	0	3	6	Pitch 106+	.213	89	19	3	1	1	8	7	20	.287	.303
4 Days Rest	2.57	14	5	0	23	23	171.1	139	10	65	138	First Pitch	.324	148	48	12	2	3	13	0	0	.331	.493
5+ Days Rest	2.87	3	3	0	10	10	75.1	65	9	26	61	Ahead in Count	.167	414	69	12	2	4	20	0	173	.172	.234
vs. AL	3.63	0	2	0	3	3	22.1	17	4	4	20	Behind in Count	.275	218	60	10	0	9	28	51	0	.412	.445
vs. NL	2.47	19	5	0	31	31	233.1	191	15	90	185	Two Strikes	.139	417	58	8	0	4	22	43	205	.222	.187
Pre-All Star	2.17	10	3	0	19	19	141.1	108	9	56	109	Pre-All Star	.215	503	108	16	2	9	37	56	109	.298	.308
Post-All Star	3.07	9	4	0	15	15	114.1	100	7	38	96	Post-All Star	.238	421	100	22	2	10	39	38	96	.304	.371

Last Five Years

	ERA	W	L	Sv	G	GS	IP	H	HR	BB	SO		Avg	AB	H	2B	3B	HR	RBI	BB	SO	OBP	SLG
Home	3.54	28	24	0	75	70	476.0	427	38	193	425	vs. Left	.261	1720	449	75	7	38	190	239	348	.352	.379
Away	4.04	31	20	0	75	68	445.0	433	27	222	358	vs. Right	.240	1716	411	73	15	27	175	176	435	.326	.347
Day	3.46	22	11	0	49	45	314.1	299	21	133	278	Inning 1-6	.250	2872	718	121	19	50	316	362	659	.341	.358
Night	3.95	37	33	0	101	93	606.2	561	44	282	505	Inning 7+	.252	564	142	27	3	15	49	53	124	.326	.390
Grass	3.97	19	14	0	52	47	310.2	303	22	158	254	None on	.253	1876	475	88	16	38	38	230	433	.344	.378
Turf	3.69	40	30	0	98	91	610.1	557	43	257	529	Runners on	.247	1560	385	60	6	27	327	185	350	.333	.345
March/April	3.80	7	6	0	22	19	120.2	116	16	59	103	Scoring Posn	.235	872	205	33	2	13	280	134	223	.337	.322
May	3.25	12	6	0	30	27	180.0	139	5	103	136	Close & Late	.245	306	75	13	2	9	27	23	67	.313	.389
June	3.74	13	7	0	28	27	180.2	176	12	70	160	None on/out	.271	876	237	42	11	23	23	103	181	.354	.422
July	3.48	14	9	0	29	29	196.1	183	12	85	161	vs. 1st Batr (relief)	.625	8	5	0	0	1	1	4	1	.750	1.000
August	4.60	8	7	0	20	19	125.1	136	11	45	104	1st Inning Pitched	.269	565	152	25	2	9	78	89	135	.376	.368
Sept/Oct	4.27	5	9	0	21	17	118.0	110	9	53	119	First 75 Pitches	.257	2391	614	101	16	43	257	268	547	.339	.366
Starter	3.79	58	44	0	138	138	906.1	845	63	405	773	Pitch 76-90	.225	409	92	18	3	6	41	67	91	.344	.328
Reliever	3.07	1	0	0	12	0	14.2	15	2	10	10	Pitch 91-105	.246	378	93	20	1	12	42	51	87	.339	.399
0-3 Days Rest (Start)	3.68	4	4	0	9	9	58.2	51	5	29	54	Pitch 106+	.236	258	61	9	2	4	25	29	58	.331	.333
4 Days Rest	3.60	38	24	0	78	78	535.0	499	33	227	474	First Pitch	.344	509	175	34	5	10	61	10	0	.377	.489
5+ Days Rest	4.14	16	16	0	51	51	312.2	295	25	149	245	Ahead in Count	.164	1499	246	43	5	12	101	0	669	.176	.223
vs. AL	3.63	0	2	0	3	3	22.1	17	4	4	20	Behind in Count	.331	876	290	46	8	30	140	235	0	.471	.505
vs. NL	3.79	59	42	0	147	135	898.2	843	61	411	763	Two Strikes	.153	1570	240	39	6	16	106	170	783	.243	.216
Pre-All Star	3.48	37	21	0	88	81	540.1	480	37	256	448	Pre-All Star	.241	1992	480	79	16	37	199	256	448	.338	.352
Post-All Star	4.21	22	23	0	62	57	380.2	380	28	156	335	Post-All Star	.263	1444	380	69	6	28	166	159	335	.341	.377

Pitcher vs. Batter (career)

Pitches Best Vs.	Avg	AB	H	2B	3B	HR	RBI	BB	SO	OBP	SLG	Pitches Worst Vs.	Avg	AB	H	2B	3B	HR	RBI	BB	SO	OBP	SLG
John Vander Wal	.000	12	0	0	0	0	0	3	3	.200	.000	Lance Johnson	.563	16	9	3	0	0	0	0	0	.563	.750
Chuck Carr	.059	17	1	1	0	0	0	0	4	.059	.118	Mark Whiten	.526	19	10	1	1	1	4	2	1	.571	.842
Dave Hansen	.063	16	1	1	0	0	0	1	0	.118	.125	Glenallen Hill	.500	10	5	2	1	1	8	6	2	.684	1.200
Darren Lewis	.067	15	1	0	0	0	0	2	4	.176	.067	Kevin Mitchell	.500	10	5	1	0	2	5	3	0	.571	1.200
Midre Cummings	.083	12	1	0	0	0	0	0	2	.083	.083	Ryne Sandberg	.400	20	8	3	0	1	5	6	4	.567	.700

Curtis King — Cardinals
Age 27 – Pitches Right (groundball pitcher)

	ERA	W	L	Sv	G	GS	IP	BB	SO	Avg	H	2B	3B	HR	RBI	OBP	SLG	GF	IR	IRS	Hld	SvOp	SB	CS	GB	FB	G/F
1997 Season	2.76	4	2	0	30	0	29.1	11	13	.325	38	4	0	0	16	.379	.359	8	21	4	10	3	2	0	65	17	3.82

1997 Season

	ERA	W	L	Sv	G	GS	IP	H	HR	BB	SO		Avg	AB	H	2B	3B	HR	RBI	BB	SO	OBP	SLG
Home	2.20	2	1	0	16	0	16.1	17	0	6	7	vs. Left	.231	39	9	1	0	0	4	5	5	.311	.256
Away	3.46	2	1	0	14	0	13.0	21	0	5	6	vs. Right	.372	78	29	3	0	0	12	6	8	.414	.410
Starter	0.00	0	0	0	0	0	0.0	0	0	0	0	Scoring Posn	.350	40	14	0	0	0	16	4	3	.383	.350
Reliever	2.76	4	2	0	30	0	29.1	38	0	11	13	Close & Late	.337	83	28	2	0	0	14	8	9	.394	.361
0 Days rest (Relief)	1.00	0	1	0	10	0	9.0	6	0	3	1	None on/out	.261	23	6	1	0	0	0	2	4	.320	.304
1 or 2 Days rest	3.38	4	0	0	18	0	18.2	27	0	6	12	First Pitch	.438	16	7	1	0	0	2	0	0	.412	.500
3+ Days rest	5.40	0	1	0	2	0	1.2	5	0	2	0	Ahead in Count	.209	43	9	0	0	0	3	0	13	.222	.209
Pre-All Star	0.00	0	0	0	0	0	0.0	0	0	0	0	Behind in Count	.394	33	13	3	0	0	7	6	0	.475	.485
Post-All Star	2.76	4	2	0	30	0	29.1	38	0	11	13	Two Strikes	.225	40	9	0	0	0	5	5	13	.326	.225

Jeff King — Royals
Age 33 – Bats Right (flyball hitter)

	Avg	G	AB	R	H	2B	3B	HR	RBI	BB	SO	HBP	GDP	SB	CS	OBP	SLG	IBB	SH	SF	#Pit	#P/PA	GB	FB	G/F
1997 Season	.238	155	543	84	129	30	1	28	112	89	96	2	9	16	5	.341	.451	4	1	12	2590	4.00	139	225	0.62
Last Five Years	.267	684	2529	354	676	151	10	90	450	303	346	9	60	49	18	.343	.442	17	5	43	11107	3.84	845	948	0.89

1997 Season

	Avg	AB	H	2B	3B	HR	RBI	BB	SO	OBP	SLG		Avg	AB	H	2B	3B	HR	RBI	BB	SO	OBP	SLG
vs. Left	.268	149	40	11	0	9	28	32	25	.391	.523	First Pitch	.344	61	21	5	0	3	16	3	0	.364	.574
vs. Right	.226	394	89	19	1	19	84	57	71	.320	.424	Ahead in Count	.288	118	34	4	1	14	47	42	0	.467	.695
Groundball	.263	99	26	5	0	6	21	16	18	.368	.495	Behind in Count	.180	250	45	16	0	6	26	0	71	.181	.316
Flyball	.242	91	22	6	0	4	17	14	20	.330	.440	Two Strikes	.178	258	46	16	0	9	33	44	96	.295	.345
Home	.250	272	68	17	1	11	52	42	46	.347	.441	Batting #4	.256	289	74	17	1	14	66	47	55	.357	.467
Away	.225	271	61	13	0	17	60	47	50	.334	.461	Batting #5	.219	105	23	4	0	5	18	14	15	.306	.400
Day	.244	164	40	10	0	7	28	30	27	.352	.433	Other	.215	149	32	9	0	9	28	28	26	.333	.456
Night	.235	379	89	20	1	21	84	59	69	.336	.459	March/April	.314	70	22	6	0	4	18	25	13	.485	.571
Grass	.242	466	113	27	1	22	97	75	84	.343	.446	May	.170	100	17	5	0	1	10	16	19	.288	.250
Turf	.208	77	16	3	0	6	15	14	12	.326	.481	June	.355	93	33	7	1	10	29	14	14	.435	.774
Pre-All Star	.258	279	72	18	1	15	57	59	48	.386	.491	July	.146	103	15	4	0	1	9	8	15	.205	.214
Post-All Star	.216	264	57	12	0	13	55	30	48	.289	.409	August	.215	93	20	4	0	4	16	11	16	.292	.387
Scoring Posn	.277	148	41	10	1	7	76	30	25	.377	.500	Sept/Oct	.262	84	22	4	0	8	30	15	19	.359	.595
Close & Late	.200	95	19	5	0	5	23	12	16	.279	.411	vs. AL	.227	494	112	28	1	21	93	81	89	.332	.415
None on/out	.181	127	23	7	0	3	3	26	22	.320	.307	vs. NL	.347	49	17	2	0	7	19	8	7	.431	.816

1997 By Position

Position	Avg	AB	H	2B	3B	HR	RBI	BB	SO	OBP	SLG	G	GS	Innings	PO	A	E	DP	Fld Pct	Rng Fctr	In Zone	Zone Outs	Zone Rtg	MLB Zone
As 1b	.240	529	127	30	1	27	106	87	89	.343	.454	150	147	1291.0	1217	146	5	136	.996	—	309	298	.964	.874

Last Five Years

	Avg	AB	H	2B	3B	HR	RBI	BB	SO	OBP	SLG		Avg	AB	H	2B	3B	HR	RBI	BB	SO	OBP	SLG
vs. Left	.280	672	188	46	5	29	112	104	73	.372	.493	First Pitch	.325	311	101	22	1	12	67	11	0	.339	.518

Last Five Years

	Avg	AB	H	2B	3B	HR	RBI	BB	SO	OBP	SLG
vs. Right	.263	1857	488	105	5	61	338	199	273	.331	.423
Groundball	.279	724	202	46	3	18	123	84	85	.354	.425
Flyball	.244	409	100	26	0	19	70	50	59	.321	.447
Home	.270	1273	344	84	7	38	230	149	184	.342	.437
Away	.264	1256	332	67	3	52	220	154	162	.343	.447
Day	.281	691	194	45	3	28	129	79	85	.349	.476
Night	.262	1838	482	106	7	62	321	224	261	.340	.429
Grass	.249	1076	268	60	3	41	192	144	161	.336	.425
Turf	.281	1453	408	91	7	49	258	159	185	.344	.454
Pre-All Star	.272	1383	376	83	3	52	245	164	193	.348	.449
Post-All Star	.262	1146	300	68	7	38	205	139	153	.336	.433
Scoring Posn	.281	711	200	51	5	18	329	117	96	.348	.443
Close & Late	.231	411	95	18	2	10	73	50	75	.311	.358
None on/out	.270	611	165	39	1	19	19	65	68	.341	.430

	Avg	AB	H	2B	3B	HR	RBI	BB	SO	OBP	SLG
Ahead in Count	.285	561	160	35	2	35	138	163	0	.440	.542
Behind in Count	.233	1108	258	61	5	27	160	0	274	.233	.370
Two Strikes	.226	1114	252	60	4	29	157	128	346	.305	.365
Batting #3	.274	594	163	35	4	32	113	77	95	.356	.508
Batting #4	.269	1225	330	79	3	38	223	153	161	.348	.432
Other	.258	710	183	37	3	20	114	73	90	.323	.403
March/April	.272	345	94	24	0	13	61	48	49	.358	.455
May	.239	460	110	31	0	11	81	52	73	.320	.378
June	.315	422	133	25	2	23	82	52	53	.387	.547
July	.235	502	118	22	2	12	64	40	60	.291	.359
August	.289	450	130	27	6	16	91	49	56	.350	.482
Sept/Oct	.260	350	91	22	0	15	71	62	55	.364	.451
vs. AL	.227	494	112	28	1	21	93	81	89	.332	.415
vs. NL	.277	2035	564	123	9	69	357	222	257	.345	.448

Batter vs. Pitcher (career)

Hits Best Against	Avg	AB	H	2B	3B	HR	RBI	BB	SO	OBP	SLG
Jaime Navarro	.478	23	11	2	0	2	11	0	2	.478	.826
F. Valenzuela	.400	15	6	4	0	0	0	4	1	.526	.667
Tim Scott	.400	10	4	1	0	1	4	2	0	.500	.800
Andy Benes	.379	29	11	1	0	3	7	7	0	.500	.724
Danny Darwin	.333	12	4	0	0	4	8	1	3	.357	1.333

Hits Worst Against	Avg	AB	H	2B	3B	HR	RBI	BB	SO	OBP	SLG
Norm Charlton	.000	11	0	0	0	0	0	0	1	.000	.000
David Wells	.000	10	0	0	0	0	0	2	2	.167	.000
John Wetteland	.050	20	1	0	0	0	1	1	8	.091	.050
Paul Assenmacher	.091	11	1	0	0	0	0	0	1	.091	.091
Kevin Brown	.091	11	1	0	0	0	0	0	4	.091	.091

Wayne Kirby — Dodgers
Age 34 – Bats Left (groundball hitter)

	Avg	G	AB	R	H	2B	3B	HR	RBI	BB	SO	HBP	GDP	SB	CS	OBP	SLG	IBB	SH	SF	#Pit	#P/PA	GB	FB	G/F
1997 Season	.169	46	65	6	11	2	0	0	4	10	12	0	1	0	0	.280	.200	0	0	0	270	3.60	25	18	1.39
Last Five Years	.257	448	1106	165	284	48	8	13	113	92	151	6	18	42	15	.315	.350	3	11	9	4479	3.66	433	296	1.46

1997 Season

	Avg	AB	H	2B	3B	HR	RBI	BB	SO	OBP	SLG
vs. Left	.286	7	2	1	0	0	0	0		.286	.429
vs. Right	.155	58	9	1	0	0	4	10	12	.279	.172

	Avg	AB	H	2B	3B	HR	RBI	BB	SO	OBP	SLG
Scoring Posn	.056	18	1	1	0	0	4	5	4	.261	.111
Close & Late	.053	19	1	0	0	0	2	5	5	.250	.053

Last Five Years

	Avg	AB	H	2B	3B	HR	RBI	BB	SO	OBP	SLG
vs. Left	.244	193	47	11	1	0	16	16	38	.307	.311
vs. Right	.260	913	237	37	7	13	97	76	113	.317	.358
Groundball	.305	233	71	14	3	1	27	25	34	.373	.403
Flyball	.196	214	42	8	0	6	19	16	32	.252	.318
Home	.260	507	132	19	5	7	53	50	67	.328	.359
Away	.254	599	152	29	3	6	60	42	84	.304	.342
Day	.283	361	102	13	4	5	40	31	48	.341	.382
Night	.244	745	182	35	4	8	73	61	103	.302	.334
Grass	.255	898	229	37	7	10	92	83	118	.320	.345
Turf	.264	208	55	11	1	3	21	9	33	.294	.370
Pre-All Star	.258	484	125	19	3	7	57	38	60	.312	.353
Post-All Star	.256	622	159	29	5	6	56	54	91	.317	.347
Scoring Posn	.260	288	75	8	3	5	96	27	39	.317	.361
Close & Late	.253	198	50	6	1	2	25	23	42	.330	.323
None on/out	.244	254	62	10	2	2		31	39	.329	.323

	Avg	AB	H	2B	3B	HR	RBI	BB	SO	OBP	SLG
First Pitch	.298	141	42	2	0	2	15	2	0	.306	.355
Ahead in Count	.301	209	63	15	3	3	27	58	0	.451	.445
Behind in Count	.206	548	113	20	5	5	46	0	136	.209	.288
Two Strikes	.200	511	102	16	4	4	40	32	151	.247	.270
Batting #1	.221	249	55	13	2	2	10	19	38	.282	.313
Batting #2	.283	587	166	28	4	9	71	45	65	.333	.390
Other	.233	270	63	7	2	2	22	28	48	.305	.296
March/April	.298	57	17	2	0	0	9	5	7	.355	.333
May	.256	180	46	5	1	2	21	12	22	.304	.328
June	.246	171	42	9	1	4	19	16	24	.307	.380
July	.245	265	65	12	2	5	23	22	37	.303	.362
August	.272	235	64	8	4	2	28	16	38	.323	.348
Sept/Oct	.253	198	50	12	0	0	13	21	23	.326	.313
vs. AL	.260	854	222	36	7	12	98	65	122	.313	.361
vs. NL	.246	252	62	12	1	1	15	27	29	.320	.313

Batter vs. Pitcher (career)

Hits Best Against	Avg	AB	H	2B	3B	HR	RBI	BB	SO	OBP	SLG
Scott Erickson	.500	18	9	1	0	0	4	4	2	.565	.556
Mark Leiter	.500	14	7	3	0	0	2	1	0	.533	.714
Kevin Appier	.462	13	6	1	0	0	3	1	2	.500	.538
Ricky Bones	.385	13	5	0	0	1	3	0	0	.385	.615
Mark Gardner	.364	11	4	2	0	1	2	0	0	.333	.818

Hits Worst Against	Avg	AB	H	2B	3B	HR	RBI	BB	SO	OBP	SLG
Roger Clemens	.000	10	0	0	0	0	0	2	1	.231	.000
Tim Belcher	.118	17	2	0	0	0	0	0	3	.118	.118
Jason Bere	.154	13	2	1	0	0	0	2	0	.267	.231
Aaron Sele	.182	11	2	0	0	0	0	1	1	.250	.182
Jack McDowell	.214	14	3	1	0	0	2	0	4	.214	.286

Ryan Klesko — Braves
Age 27 – Bats Left (flyball hitter)

	Avg	G	AB	R	H	2B	3B	HR	RBI	BB	SO	HBP	GDP	SB	CS	OBP	SLG	IBB	SH	SF	#Pit	#P/PA	GB	FB	G/F
1997 Season	.261	143	467	67	122	23	6	24	84	48	130	4	11	4	4	.334	.490	5	1	2	2000	3.81	150	110	1.36
Last Five Years	.282	517	1586	250	447	83	15	100	299	192	383	9	36	16	11	.360	.542	29	1	13	6837	3.78	493	465	1.06

1997 Season

	Avg	AB	H	2B	3B	HR	RBI	BB	SO	OBP	SLG
vs. Left	.198	106	21	2	2	3	14	12	36	.283	.340
vs. Right	.280	361	101	21	4	21	70	36	94	.349	.535
Groundball	.275	91	25	6	1	4	12	8	18	.340	.495
Flyball	.170	53	9	3	0	1	4	5	21	.241	.283
Home	.270	230	62	10	3	10	44	26	58	.346	.470
Away	.253	237	60	13	3	14	40	22	72	.322	.511
Day	.266	143	38	8	1	7	27	17	43	.352	.483
Night	.259	324	84	15	5	17	57	31	87	.326	.494
Grass	.270	385	104	17	6	21	74	38	108	.339	.509
Turf	.220	82	18	6	0	3	10	10	22	.312	.402
Pre-All Star	.260	262	68	14	4	14	48	28	74	.336	.504

	Avg	AB	H	2B	3B	HR	RBI	BB	SO	OBP	SLG
First Pitch	.309	68	21	5	3	5	20	5	0	.360	.691
Ahead in Count	.379	95	36	4	1	7	23	23	0	.504	.663
Behind in Count	.202	198	40	10	2	5	17	0	99	.210	.348
Two Strikes	.151	239	36	10	2	3	14	20	130	.215	.247
Batting #5	.283	382	108	22	3	22	76	37	103	.350	.529
Batting #7	.189	37	7	0	2	1	4	8	16	.340	.378
Other	.146	48	7	1	1	1	4	3	11	.196	.271
March/April	.243	70	17	4	2	4		6	15	.299	.443
May	.262	84	22	4	1	7	12	12	30	.361	.583
June	.227	97	22	5	1	3	16	9	29	.296	.392
July	.316	79	25	6	0	6	20	8	19	.386	.620

1997 Season

	Avg	AB	H	2B	3B	HR	RBI	BB	SO	OBP	SLG
Post-All Star	.263	205	54	9	2	10	36	20	56	.332	.473
Scoring Posn	.286	119	34	5	1	7	55	17	39	.374	.521
Close & Late	.103	58	6	0	0	1	3	12	22	.257	.155
None on/out	.252	131	33	5	2	7	7	14	34	.324	.481

	Avg	AB	H	2B	3B	HR	RBI	BB	SO	OBP	SLG
August	.219	73	16	3	2	2	9	9	18	.313	.397
Sept/Oct	.313	64	20	1	0	4	13	4	19	.353	.516
vs. AL	.327	49	16	4	0	4	14	3	17	.377	.653
vs. NL	.254	418	106	19	6	20	70	45	113	.329	.471

1997 By Position

Position	Avg	AB	H	2B	3B	HR	RBI	BB	SO	OBP	SLG	G	GS	Innings	PO	A	E	DP	Fld Pct	Rng Fctr	In Zone	Zone Outs	Zone Rtg	MLB Zone
As 1b	.214	28	6	2	0	2	9	3	7	.290	.500	22	6	78.0	63	3	0	7	1.000	---	13	12	.923	.874
As lf	.269	432	116	21	6	22	75	44	120	.340	.498	182	130	992.1	126	3	6	0	.969	1.68	238	180	.756	.805

Last Five Years

	Avg	AB	H	2B	3B	HR	RBI	BB	SO	OBP	SLG
vs. Left	.223	346	77	10	5	9	40	36	102	.303	.358
vs. Right	.298	1240	370	73	10	91	259	156	281	.376	.594
Groundball	.304	415	126	26	4	26	80	45	81	.372	.573
Flyball	.258	217	56	8	3	15	39	33	66	.357	.530
Home	.294	795	234	34	6	54	157	85	179	.364	.556
Away	.269	791	213	49	9	46	142	107	204	.356	.528
Day	.280	472	132	30	3	27	93	66	130	.369	.528
Night	.283	1114	315	53	12	73	206	126	253	.356	.548
Grass	.288	1275	367	60	12	84	247	147	305	.363	.551
Turf	.257	311	80	23	3	16	52	45	78	.350	.505
Pre-All Star	.292	896	262	49	10	61	166	101	219	.363	.574
Post-All Star	.268	690	185	34	5	39	133	91	164	.357	.501
Scoring Posn	.282	394	111	20	2	26	189	70	106	.383	.541
Close & Late	.213	230	49	8	2	6	24	37	70	.323	.343
None on/out	.304	375	114	19	3	30	92	35	92	.367	.611

	Avg	AB	H	2B	3B	HR	RBI	BB	SO	OBP	SLG
First Pitch	.385	244	94	19	4	20	67	25	0	.445	.742
Ahead in Count	.380	366	139	21	7	33	98	89	0	.499	.746
Behind in Count	.198	666	132	23	4	23	68	0	292	.201	.348
Two Strikes	.175	760	133	27	4	24	74	77	383	.250	.316
Batting #5	.284	809	230	41	6	51	164	92	197	.359	.539
Batting #6	.301	386	116	27	2	27	75	51	82	.381	.591
Other	.258	391	101	15	7	22	60	49	104	.342	.501
March/April	.300	227	68	9	4	19	50	30	54	.378	.626
May	.242	273	66	12	2	14	31	32	81	.322	.454
June	.324	324	105	23	4	24	72	32	69	.382	.642
July	.268	287	77	17	0	19	57	35	64	.352	.526
August	.250	260	65	12	5	8	40	37	60	.348	.427
Sept/Oct	.307	215	66	10	0	16	49	26	55	.381	.577
vs. AL	.327	49	16	4	0	4	14	3	17	.377	.653
vs. NL	.280	1537	431	79	15	96	285	189	366	.359	.539

Batter vs. Pitcher (career)

Hits Best Against	Avg	AB	H	2B	3B	HR	RBI	BB	SO	OBP	SLG
Jim Bullinger	.615	13	8	1	1	3	9	3	2	.688	1.538
Jon Lieber	.545	11	6	2	0	1	4	2	1	.615	1.000
Bobby Jones	.500	26	13	1	1	3	12	4	3	.567	.962
Kirk Rueter	.500	12	6	0	0	2	5	1	2	.538	1.000
Kevin Ritz	.417	12	5	2	0	2	5	1	3	.462	1.083

Hits Worst Against	Avg	AB	H	2B	3B	HR	RBI	BB	SO	OBP	SLG
Curt Schilling	.000	13	0	0	0	0	0	2	7	.133	.000
Matt Beech	.000	10	0	0	0	0	1	0	4	.083	.000
Mike Hampton	.063	16	1	0	0	0	0	0	6	.063	.063
Armando Reynoso	.091	11	1	1	0	0	0	2	0	.231	.182
Tony Fossas	.100	10	1	1	0	0	1	1	4	.182	.200

Steve Kline — Expos
Age 25 – Pitches Left (groundball pitcher)

	ERA	W	L	Sv	G	GS	IP	BB	SO	Avg	H	2B	3B	HR	RBI	OBP	SLG	GF	IR	IRS	Hld	SvOp	SB	CS	GB	FB	G/F
1997 Season	5.98	4	4	0	46	1	52.2	23	37	.338	73	9	2	10	41	.403	.537	7	29	14	5	3	8	3	91	45	2.02

1997 Season

	ERA	W	L	Sv	G	GS	IP	H	HR	BB	SO
Home	3.22	1	2	0	18	1	22.1	23	1	12	18
Away	8.01	3	2	0	28	0	30.1	50	9	11	19
Starter	10.80	0	1	0	1	1	1.2	3	1	4	2
Reliever	5.82	4	3	0	45	0	51.0	70	9	19	35
0 Days rest (Relief)	4.05	2	1	0	13	0	13.1	12	1	7	11
1 or 2 Days rest	9.14	1	2	0	23	0	21.2	40	8	7	17
3+ Days rest	2.81	1	0	0	9	0	16.0	18	0	5	7
Pre-All Star	5.81	3	1	0	20	1	26.1	42	6	13	17
Post-All Star	6.15	1	3	0	26	0	26.1	31	4	10	20

	Avg	AB	H	2B	3B	HR	RBI	BB	SO	OBP	SLG
vs. Left	.354	82	29	2	2	4	23	9	18	.382	.573
vs. Right	.328	134	44	7	0	6	18	20	19	.416	.515
Scoring Posn	.313	64	20	2	2	4	33	10	14	.395	.594
Close & Late	.284	67	19	2	1	2	9	5	14	.333	.433
None on/out	.286	49	14	2	0	1	1	4	8	.364	.388
First Pitch	.412	34	14	0	0	4	8	4	0	.474	.765
Ahead in Count	.174	92	16	2	0	2	9	0	33	.170	.261
Behind in Count	.577	52	30	5	1	3	21	13	0	.672	.885
Two Strikes	.232	95	22	3	1	3	11	6	37	.272	.379

Chuck Knoblauch — Twins
Age 29 – Bats Right (groundball hitter)

	Avg	G	AB	R	H	2B	3B	HR	RBI	BB	SO	HBP	GDP	SB	CS	OBP	SLG	IBB	SH	SF	#Pit	#P/PA	GB	FB	G/F
1997 Season	.291	156	611	117	178	26	10	9	58	84	84	17	11	62	10	.390	.411	6	0	4	2896	4.04	239	189	1.26
Last Five Years	.310	707	2774	531	860	167	39	40	285	366	353	65	59	217	59	.400	.442	18	4	21	12483	3.86	1105	781	1.41

1997 Season

	Avg	AB	H	2B	3B	HR	RBI	BB	SO	OBP	SLG
vs. Left	.295	132	39	0	2	3	17	22	12	.404	.394
vs. Right	.290	479	139	26	8	6	41	62	72	.386	.415
Groundball	.263	137	36	4	2	2	15	20	14	.370	.365
Flyball	.343	99	34	3	1	2	6	11	13	.420	.455
Home	.289	305	88	16	3	2	23	37	44	.384	.380
Away	.294	306	90	10	7	7	35	47	40	.395	.441
Day	.318	179	57	12	2	2	16	28	23	.415	.441
Night	.280	432	121	14	8	7	42	56	61	.379	.398
Grass	.269	253	68	8	4	5	25	37	34	.369	.391
Turf	.307	358	110	18	6	4	33	47	50	.404	.425
Pre-All Star	.289	325	94	15	5	5	36	58	46	.405	.412
Post-All Star	.294	286	84	11	5	4	22	26	38	.372	.409
Scoring Posn	.313	131	41	4	5	0	45	28	24	.437	.420
Close & Late	.178	73	13	2	0	1	7	15	14	.326	.247
None on/out	.292	243	71	9	3	4	4	27	34	.370	.403

	Avg	AB	H	2B	3B	HR	RBI	BB	SO	OBP	SLG
First Pitch	.319	47	15	1	0	2	7	5	0	.404	.468
Ahead in Count	.347	121	42	4	3	2	16	37	0	.503	.479
Behind in Count	.255	298	76	16	5	2	22	0	66	.284	.362
Two Strikes	.245	294	72	13	5	2	22	42	84	.359	.344
Batting #1	.293	608	178	26	10	9	58	84	84	.390	.413
Batting #2	.000	3	0	0	0	0	0	0	0	.250	.000
Other	.000	0	0	0	0	0	0	0	0	.000	.000
March/April	.244	90	22	4	2	2	11	27	12	.421	.400
May	.290	107	31	2	1	1	13	18	13	.402	.355
June	.337	101	34	6	1	1	11	12	15	.419	.446
July	.271	96	26	7	3	2	8	12	12	.375	.469
August	.322	121	39	5	2	3	10	4	22	.346	.471
Sept/Oct	.271	96	26	2	1	0	5	12	10	.375	.313
vs. AL	.288	548	158	24	9	9	51	79	71	.391	.414
vs. NL	.317	63	20	2	1	0	7	5	13	.377	.381

1997 By Position

Position	Avg	AB	H	2B	3B	HR	RBI	BB	SO	OBP	SLG	G	GS	Innings	PO	A	E	DP	Fld Pct	Rng Fctr	In Zone	Zone Outs	Zone Rtg	MLB Zone
As 2b	.289	602	174	26	10	9	57	83	84	.388	.410	154	154	1316.2	283	425	11	101	.985	4.84	462	422	.913	.902

Last Five Years

	Avg	AB	H	2B	3B	HR	RBI	BB	SO	OBP	SLG		Avg	AB	H	2B	3B	HR	RBI	BB	SO	OBP	SLG
vs. Left	.320	681	218	39	8	13	86	78	89	.393	.458	First Pitch	.347	326	113	25	3	4	35	15	0	.389	.479
vs. Right	.307	2093	642	128	31	27	199	288	264	.402	.436	Ahead in Count	.331	598	198	40	10	13	66	188	0	.491	.497
Groundball	.317	659	209	39	7	10	75	91	86	.411	.443	Behind in Count	.285	1266	361	70	15	15	109	0	289	.307	.400
Flyball	.316	488	154	28	8	8	53	49	75	.386	.455	Two Strikes	.268	1220	327	54	16	15	122	163	353	.369	.375
Home	.320	1426	456	90	17	16	147	183	179	.406	.440	Batting #1	.313	2397	750	145	37	38	249	329	321	.406	.452
Away	.300	1348	404	77	22	24	138	183	174	.394	.443	Batting #2	.293	365	107	21	2	2	35	35	32	.362	.378
Day	.309	807	249	54	7	12	77	99	100	.395	.437	Other	.250	12	3	1	0	0	1	2	0	.357	.333
Night	.311	1967	611	113	32	28	208	267	253	.402	.443	March/April	.276	373	103	24	5	5	44	67	51	.397	.408
Grass	.299	1103	330	59	18	19	111	151	139	.393	.437	May	.327	465	152	32	6	2	48	51	58	.403	.434
Turf	.317	1671	530	108	21	21	174	215	214	.405	.445	June	.317	527	167	30	6	7	57	65	65	.394	.436
Pre-All Star	.314	1530	480	99	22	19	174	197	197	.399	.444	July	.325	507	165	38	10	10	49	65	61	.417	.499
Post-All Star	.305	1244	380	68	17	21	111	169	156	.401	.438	August	.314	493	155	26	7	10	49	57	77	.392	.456
Scoring Posn	.329	574	189	37	11	3	226	98	79	.428	.448	Sept/Oct	.289	409	118	17	5	6	38	61	41	.397	.399
Close & Late	.245	367	90	17	4	4	43	59	53	.358	.346	vs. AL	.310	2711	840	165	38	40	278	361	340	.401	.443
None on/out	.311	1041	324	54	15	20	20	127	139	.398	.381	vs. NL	.317	63	20	2	1	0	7	5	13	.377	.381

Batter vs. Pitcher (career)

Hits Best Against	Avg	AB	H	2B	3B	HR	RBI	BB	SO	OBP	SLG	Hits Worst Against	Avg	AB	H	2B	3B	HR	RBI	BB	SO	OBP	SLG
Woody Williams	.545	11	6	2	0	1	2	0	1	.545	1.000	Bob Wolcott	.000	14	0	0	0	0	0	0	2	.000	.000
Roger Pavlik	.484	31	15	2	1	2	4	6	0	.579	.806	Jose Mesa	.050	20	1	0	0	0	1	2	3	.167	.050
Jeff Suppan	.444	9	4	0	1	0	2	2	0	.545	.667	Steve Karsay	.071	14	1	0	0	0	0	0	0	.071	.071
Ariel Prieto	.417	12	5	1	0	1	2	5	1	.611	.750	Jim Corsi	.091	11	1	0	0	0	1	1	3	.167	.091
Jimmy Haynes	.364	11	4	2	1	0	2	2	0	.462	.727	Randy Johnson	.146	41	6	2	0	0	0	2	10	.205	.195

Randy Knorr — Astros   Age 29 – Bats Right

	Avg	G	AB	R	H	2B	3B	HR	RBI	BB	SO	HBP	GDP	SB	CS	OBP	SLG	IBB	SH	SF	#Pit	#P/PA	GB	FB	G/F
1997 Season	.375	4	8	1	3	0	0	1	1	0	2	0	0	0	0	.375	.750	0	0	0	22	2.75	2	4	0.50
Last Five Years	.228	165	452	57	103	18	2	16	63	35	112	2	15	0	1	.285	.383	2	3	2	1799	3.64	143	129	1.11

1997 Season

	Avg	AB	H	2B	3B	HR	RBI	BB	SO	OBP	SLG		Avg	AB	H	2B	3B	HR	RBI	BB	SO	OBP	SLG
vs. Left	1.000	1	1	0	0	0	0	0	0	1.000	1.000	Scoring Posn	.000	1	0	0	0	0	0	0	1	.000	.000
vs. Right	.286	7	2	0	0	1	1	0	2	.286	.714	Close & Late	1.000	2	2	0	0	1	1	0	0	1.000	2.500

Last Five Years

	Avg	AB	H	2B	3B	HR	RBI	BB	SO	OBP	SLG		Avg	AB	H	2B	3B	HR	RBI	BB	SO	OBP	SLG
vs. Left	.259	162	42	8	1	8	29	13	37	.314	.469	First Pitch	.317	63	20	5	1	2	17	1	0	.333	.524
vs. Right	.210	290	61	10	1	8	34	22	75	.269	.334	Ahead in Count	.330	109	36	7	1	4	18	18	0	.425	.523
Groundball	.206	102	21	5	0	2	7	7	24	.255	.314	Behind in Count	.141	206	29	3	0	6	17	0	102	.144	.243
Flyball	.228	79	18	1	1	3	10	7	22	.291	.380	Two Strikes	.150	207	31	4	0	7	19	16	112	.213	.271
Home	.236	220	52	8	1	10	33	18	54	.295	.418	Batting #8	.188	234	44	6	1	8	29	19	60	.251	.325
Away	.220	232	51	10	1	6	30	17	58	.276	.349	Batting #9	.271	203	55	10	0	8	32	15	46	.323	.438
Day	.242	190	46	8	1	10	33	13	49	.298	.453	Other	.267	15	4	2	1	0	2	1	6	.313	.533
Night	.218	262	57	10	1	6	30	22	63	.276	.332	March/April	.139	36	5	2	0	0	4	3	11	.205	.194
Grass	.218	188	41	10	1	5	26	16	49	.283	.362	May	.209	115	24	5	0	4	15	7	31	.254	.357
Turf	.235	264	62	8	1	11	37	19	63	.287	.398	June	.189	74	14	0	0	5	10	8	19	.268	.392
Pre-All Star	.196	260	51	8	0	10	31	21	66	.256	.342	July	.238	105	25	3	1	4	13	6	27	.283	.400
Post-All Star	.271	192	52	10	2	6	32	14	46	.324	.438	August	.373	59	22	5	0	1	11	4	11	.415	.508
Scoring Posn	.235	119	28	8	0	3	43	13	31	.311	.378	Sept/Oct	.206	63	13	3	1	2	10	7	13	.286	.381
Close & Late	.306	49	15	1	1	2	5	1	4	.320	.490	vs. AL	.232	357	83	13	2	14	55	30	92	.293	.398
None on/out	.224	98	22	2	0	4	4	9	21	.290	.367	vs. NL	.211	95	20	5	0	2	8	5	20	.255	.326

Paul Konerko — Dodgers   Age 22 – Bats Right

	Avg	G	AB	R	H	2B	3B	HR	RBI	BB	SO	HBP	GDP	SB	CS	OBP	SLG	IBB	SH	SF	#Pit	#P/PA	GB	FB	G/F
1997 Season	.143	6	7	0	1	0	0	0	0	1	2	0	1	0	0	.250	.143	0	0	0	29	3.63	2	2	1.00

1997 Season

	Avg	AB	H	2B	3B	HR	RBI	BB	SO	OBP	SLG		Avg	AB	H	2B	3B	HR	RBI	BB	SO	OBP	SLG
vs. Left	.250	4	1	0	0	0	0	0	1	.250	.250	Scoring Posn	.000	2	0	0	0	0	0	0	1	.000	.000
vs. Right	.000	3	0	0	0	0	0	1	1	.250	.000	Close & Late	1.000	1	1	0	0	0	0	0	1	1.000	1.000

Mark Kotsay — Marlins   Age 22 – Bats Left

	Avg	G	AB	R	H	2B	3B	HR	RBI	BB	SO	HBP	GDP	SB	CS	OBP	SLG	IBB	SH	SF	#Pit	#P/PA	GB	FB	G/F
1997 Season	.192	14	52	5	10	1	1	0	4	4	7	0	1	3	0	.250	.250	0	1	0	220	3.86	20	17	1.18

1997 Season

	Avg	AB	H	2B	3B	HR	RBI	BB	SO	OBP	SLG		Avg	AB	H	2B	3B	HR	RBI	BB	SO	OBP	SLG
vs. Left	.000	1	0	0	0	0	0	0	0	.000	.000	Scoring Posn	.167	12	2	0	1	0	4	1	4	.231	.333
vs. Right	.196	51	10	1	1	0	4	4	7	.255	.255	Close & Late	.000	4	0	0	0	0	1	0	2	.000	.000

Chad Kreuter — Angels

	Avg	G	AB	R	H	2B	3B	HR	RBI	BB	SO	HBP	GDP	SB	CS	OBP	SLG	IBB	SH	SF	#Pit	#P/PA	GB	FB	G/F
1997 Season	.231	89	255	25	59	9	2	5	21	29	66	0	7	0	3	.310	.341	0	1	0	1068	3.75	84	52	1.62
Last Five Years	.249	345	988	127	246	53	5	25	117	124	245	7	17	2	5	.335	.389	4	8	8	4556	4.01	307	243	1.26

1997 Season

	Avg	AB	H	2B	3B	HR	RBI	BB	SO	OBP	SLG		Avg	AB	H	2B	3B	HR	RBI	BB	SO	OBP	SLG
vs. Left	.247	77	19	2	0	3	10	9	26	.326	.390	Scoring Posn	.172	64	11	1	0	0	12	8	19	.264	.188
vs. Right	.225	178	40	7	2	2	11	20	40	.303	.320	Close & Late	.158	38	6	1	0	0	2	4	13	.238	.184
Home	.207	121	25	4	1	3	13	22	33	.329	.331	None on/out	.273	66	18	4	1	1	7	13	.342	.409
Away	.254	134	34	5	1	2	8	7	33	.291	.351	Batting #7	.250	92	23	4	0	1	8	6	19	.296	.326
First Pitch	.293	41	12	1	0	0	3	0	0	.293	.317	Batting #8	.221	154	34	4	1	4	12	19	45	.306	.338
Ahead in Count	.373	59	22	4	0	1	8	13	0	.486	.492	Other	.222	9	2	1	0	1	.4	2	.462	.556
Behind in Count	.153	111	17	1	1	2	5	0	61	.153	.234	Pre-All Star	.230	122	28	4	2	2	10	13	31	.304	.344
Two Strikes	.133	113	15	4	2	3	7	16	66	.240	.283	Post-All Star	.233	133	31	5	0	3	11	16	35	.315	.338

Last Five Years

	Avg	AB	H	2B	3B	HR	RBI	BB	SO	OBP	SLG		Avg	AB	H	2B	3B	HR	RBI	BB	SO	OBP	SLG
vs. Left	.224	277	62	13	0	10	41	33	76	.304	.379	First Pitch	.353	133	47	8	0	2	20	4	0	.367	.459
vs. Right	.259	711	184	40	5	15	76	91	169	.346	.392	Ahead in Count	.382	217	83	19	3	9	32	57	0	.507	.622
Groundball	.229	218	50	12	0	2	20	24	51	.315	.312	Behind in Count	.160	426	68	13	1	7	36	0	206	.168	.244
Flyball	.282	174	49	11	0	9	30	22	49	.367	.500	Two Strikes	.153	497	76	21	2	9	42	63	245	.251	.258
Home	.247	485	120	25	2	15	69	70	130	.341	.400	Batting #7	.248	363	90	24	2	7	41	41	92	.324	.383
Away	.250	503	126	28	3	10	48	54	115	.328	.378	Batting #8	.242	401	97	19	1	14	49	53	109	.336	.399
Day	.277	401	111	23	2	11	59	47	83	.354	.426	Other	.263	224	59	10	2	4	27	30	44	.349	.379
Night	.230	587	135	30	3	14	58	77	162	.321	.363	March/April	.325	114	37	9	1	4	16	14	18	.397	.526
Grass	.257	806	207	45	4	22	97	102	200	.343	.404	May	.230	230	53	10	1	4	25	38	64	.340	.335
Turf	.214	182	39	8	1	3	20	22	45	.298	.319	June	.258	260	67	17	3	4	25	22	58	.323	.392
Pre-All Star	.253	675	171	39	5	14	72	80	159	.335	.388	July	.197	152	30	10	0	4	18	19	37	.282	.342
Post-All Star	.240	313	75	14	0	11	45	44	86	.333	.390	August	.233	116	27	4	0	3	17	18	31	.341	.345
Scoring Posn	.208	259	54	13	1	4	85	44	65	.322	.313	Sept/Oct	.276	116	32	3	0	6	16	13	37	.351	.457
Close & Late	.199	171	34	9	0	2	18	24	51	.301	.287	vs. AL	.248	957	237	51	5	25	113	122	241	.335	.390
None on/out	.259	251	65	12	3	8	25	51	.331	.426	vs. NL	.290	31	9	2	0	0	4	2	4	.333	.355

Batter vs. Pitcher (career)

Hits Best Against	Avg	AB	H	2B	3B	HR	RBI	BB	SO	OBP	SLG	Hits Worst Against	Avg	AB	H	2B	3B	HR	RBI	BB	SO	OBP	SLG
Jose Mesa	.500	12	6	2	0	1	4	1	4	.571	.917	Charles Nagy	.091	11	1	1	0	0	0	1	4	.167	.182
Danny Darwin	.462	13	6	2	0	2	4	1	3	.500	1.077	Kevin Brown	.167	18	3	1	0	0	2	1	6	.211	.222
Kevin Tapani	.364	11	4	1	0	0	1	0	1	.364	.455	Juan Guzman	.182	11	2	0	0	0	1	0	4	.182	.182
Chuck Finley	.316	19	6	2	0	2	3	2	4	.381	.737	Ricky Bones	.182	11	2	0	0	0	1	0	16	.182	.182
												Bobby Witt	.200	10	2	1	0	0	1	0	3	.182	.300

Rick Krivda — Orioles

	ERA	W	L	Sv	G	GS	IP	BB	SO	Avg	H	2B	3B	HR	RBI	OBP	SLG	CG	ShO	Sup	QS	#P/S	SB	CS	GB	FB	G/F
1997 Season	6.30	4	2	0	10	10	50.0	18	29	.328	67	17	3	7	33	.379	.544	0	0	7.02	3	87	6	3	84	57	1.47
Career (1995-1997)	5.13	9	14	0	45	34	207.0	82	136	.288	232	54	6	30	109	.354	.482	1	0	4.96	12	92	17	12	261	252	1.04

1997 Season

	ERA	W	L	Sv	G	GS	IP	H	HR	BB	SO		Avg	AB	H	2B	3B	HR	RBI	BB	SO	OBP	SLG
Home	8.49	1	1	0	5	5	23.1	37	5	8	13	vs. Left	.385	39	15	4	1	4	10	4	6	.442	.846
Away	4.39	3	1	0	5	5	26.2	30	2	10	16	vs. Right	.315	165	52	13	2	3	23	14	23	.365	.473

Marc Kroon — Padres

	ERA	W	L	Sv	G	GS	IP	BB	SO	Avg	H	2B	3B	HR	RBI	OBP	SLG	GF	IR	IRS	Hld	SvOp	SB	CS	GB	FB	G/F
1997 Season	7.15	0	1	0	12	0	11.1	5	12	.280	14	4	0	2	10	.357	.480	2	3	3	1	0	0	0	17	13	1.31
Career (1995-1997)	7.62	0	2	0	14	0	13.0	7	14	.273	15	4	0	2	10	.365	.455	3	4	3	1	0	0	1	20	13	1.54

1997 Season

	ERA	W	L	Sv	G	GS	IP	H	HR	BB	SO		Avg	AB	H	2B	3B	HR	RBI	BB	SO	OBP	SLG
Home	5.68	0	0	0	6	0	6.1	9	2	2	5	vs. Left	.130	23	3	1	0	0	2	2	7	.231	.174
Away	9.00	0	1	0	6	0	5.0	5	0	3	7	vs. Right	.407	27	11	3	0	2	8	3	5	.467	.741

Tim Kubinski — Athletics

	ERA	W	L	Sv	G	GS	IP	BB	SO	Avg	H	2B	3B	HR	RBI	OBP	SLG	GF	IR	IRS	Hld	SvOp	SB	CS	GB	FB	G/F
1997 Season	5.68	0	0	0	11	0	12.2	6	10	.255	12	1	0	2	12	.339	.404	3	11	3	1	0	2	0	20	17	1.18

1997 Season

	ERA	W	L	Sv	G	GS	IP	H	HR	BB	SO		Avg	AB	H	2B	3B	HR	RBI	BB	SO	OBP	SLG
Home	11.57	0	0	0	5	0	2.1	4	1	2	2	vs. Left	.190	21	4	0	0	0	4	5	2	.357	.190
Away	4.35	0	0	0	6	0	10.1	8	1	4	8	vs. Right	.308	26	8	1	0	2	8	1	8	.321	.577

Kerry Lacy — Red Sox
Age 25 – Pitches Right (groundball pitcher)

	ERA	W	L	Sv	G	GS	IP	BB	SO	Avg	H	2B	3B	HR	RBI	OBP	SLG	GF	IR	IRS	Hld	SvOp	SB	CS	GB	FB	G/F
1997 Season	6.11	1	1	3	33	0	45.2	22	18	.314	60	14	1	7	38	.381	.508	12	23	11	5	3	2	0	91	47	1.94
Career (1996-1997)	5.59	3	1	3	44	0	56.1	30	27	.318	75	16	2	9	46	.394	.517	15	32	16	6	5	2	0	109	54	2.02

1997 Season

	ERA	W	L	Sv	G	GS	IP	H	HR	BB	SO			Avg	AB	H	2B	3B	HR	RBI	BB	SO	OBP	SLG
Home	5.16	1	1	1	18	0	29.2	38	3	9	10	vs. Left		.293	92	27	6	1	4	19	12	8	.375	.511
Away	7.88	0	0	2	15	0	16.0	22	4	13	8	vs. Right		.333	99	33	8	0	3	19	10	10	.387	.505
Starter	0.00	0	0	0	0	0	0.0	0	0	0	0	Scoring Posn		.298	57	17	1	0	2	29	9	7	.382	.421
Reliever	6.11	1	1	3	33	0	45.2	60	7	22	18	Close & Late		.250	40	10	4	1	5	5	5	5	.333	.475
0 Days rest (Relief)	1.13	0	0	1	8	0	8.0	8	0	6	2	None on/out		.375	40	15	4	1	0	0	5	2	.444	.525
1 or 2 Days rest	7.40	1	1	1	17	0	24.1	36	3	9	10	First Pitch		.300	40	12	3	0	3	11	3	0	.349	.600
3+ Days rest	6.75	0	0	1	8	0	13.1	16	4	7	6	Ahead in Count		.219	73	16	5	0	2	9	0	13	.216	.370
Pre-All Star	6.12	0	1	3	23	0	32.1	40	4	14	10	Behind in Count		.432	44	19	3	1	0	9	13	0	.561	.545
Post-All Star	6.08	1	0	0	10	0	13.1	20	3	8	8	Two Strikes		.205	73	15	6	0	2	6	6	18	.266	.370

Tim Laker — Orioles
Age 28 – Bats Right (groundball hitter)

	Avg	G	AB	R	H	2B	3B	HR	RBI	BB	SO	HBP	GDP	SB	CS	OBP	SLG	IBB	SH	SF	#Pit	#P/PA	GB	FB	G/F
1997 Season	.000	7	14	0	0	0	0	0	1	2	9	0	0	0	0	.118	.000	0	1	1	75	4.17	1	4	0.25
Last Five Years	.207	114	241	20	50	10	2	3	28	18	63	2	7	2	1	.265	.303	4	5	3	1010	3.75	90	58	1.55

1997 Season

	Avg	AB	H	2B	3B	HR	RBI	BB	SO	OBP	SLG			Avg	AB	H	2B	3B	HR	RBI	BB	SO	OBP	SLG
vs. Left	.000	3	0	0	0	0	1	0	3	.000	.000	Scoring Posn		.000	3	0	0	0	0	1	0	2	.000	.000
vs. Right	.000	11	0	0	0	0	0	2	6	.154	.000	Close & Late		.000	2	0	0	0	0	0	0	2	.000	.000

Tom Lampkin — Cardinals
Age 34 – Bats Left (groundball hitter)

	Avg	G	AB	R	H	2B	3B	HR	RBI	BB	SO	HBP	GDP	SB	CS	OBP	SLG	IBB	SH	SF	#Pit	#P/PA	GB	FB	G/F
1997 Season	.245	108	229	28	56	8	1	7	22	28	30	4	8	2	1	.335	.380	5	4	2	960	3.60	97	57	1.70
Last Five Years	.233	312	644	84	150	26	1	18	85	77	86	10	13	12	9	.321	.360	11	6	8	2644	3.55	258	201	1.28

1997 Season

	Avg	AB	H	2B	3B	HR	RBI	BB	SO	OBP	SLG			Avg	AB	H	2B	3B	HR	RBI	BB	SO	OBP	SLG
vs. Left	.250	36	9	1	0	0	4	4	9	.341	.278	Scoring Posn		.209	43	9	1	0	0	12	10	6	.368	.233
vs. Right	.244	193	47	7	1	7	18	24	21	.333	.399	Close & Late		.196	56	11	1	0	1	4	5	11	.274	.268
Home	.193	119	23	5	0	2	9	18	21	.302	.286	None on/out		.183	60	11	1	0	3	3	7	4	.279	.350
Away	.300	110	33	3	1	5	13	10	9	.371	.482	Batting #7		.281	121	34	2	0	4	10	14	15	.360	.397
First Pitch	.229	35	8	0	1	0	2	2	0	.282	.286	Batting #8		.240	75	18	5	1	2	8	12	11	.352	.413
Ahead in Count	.219	64	14	2	0	3	8	17	0	.383	.391	Other		.121	33	4	1	0	1	4	2	4	.194	.242
Behind in Count	.275	91	25	6	0	3	10	0	25	.290	.440	Pre-All Star		.226	159	36	6	1	5	15	17	19	.311	.371
Two Strikes	.239	92	22	4	0	3	7	8	30	.307	.380	Post-All Star		.286	70	20	2	0	2	7	11	11	.386	.400

Last Five Years

	Avg	AB	H	2B	3B	HR	RBI	BB	SO	OBP	SLG			Avg	AB	H	2B	3B	HR	RBI	BB	SO	OBP	SLG
vs. Left	.183	104	19	5	0	2	15	10	20	.267	.288	First Pitch		.268	97	26	4	1	1	10	6	0	.314	.361
vs. Right	.243	540	131	21	1	16	70	67	66	.331	.374	Ahead in Count		.272	173	47	5	0	8	37	54	0	.440	.439
Groundball	.221	149	33	5	0	2	12	15	20	.291	.295	Behind in Count		.187	268	50	11	0	5	21	0	76	.203	.284
Flyball	.280	107	30	6	0	3	16	10	9	.336	.421	Two Strikes		.181	259	47	10	0	6	24	16	86	.234	.290
Home	.201	328	66	12	0	9	42	46	50	.302	.320	Batting #7		.237	224	53	4	0	6	24	24	32	.312	.335
Away	.266	316	84	14	1	9	43	31	36	.341	.402	Batting #8		.234	171	40	8	1	3	16	25	28	.343	.345
Day	.239	255	61	11	0	6	32	34	37	.331	.353	Other		.229	249	57	14	0	9	45	28	26	.312	.394
Night	.229	389	89	15	1	12	53	43	49	.314	.365	March/April		.200	70	14	1	1	2	8	5	10	.263	.329
Grass	.226	521	118	20	1	16	67	62	72	.316	.361	May		.246	130	32	5	0	2	12	12	15	.313	.331
Turf	.260	123	32	6	0	2	18	15	14	.343	.358	June		.239	138	33	9	0	5	22	24	19	.355	.413
Pre-All Star	.228	364	83	16	1	10	44	42	48	.312	.360	July		.248	125	31	7	0	4	16	18	18	.356	.400
Post-All Star	.239	280	67	10	0	8	41	35	38	.331	.361	August		.233	120	28	3	0	4	20	12	14	.304	.358
Scoring Posn	.247	146	36	9	0	5	64	33	20	.379	.411	Sept/Oct		.197	61	12	1	0	1	7	6	10	.275	.262
Close & Late	.212	156	33	5	0	2	17	18	26	.299	.282	vs. AL		.219	178	39	9	0	6	28	23	31	.302	.371
None on/out	.185	162	30	3	0	4	4	14	15	.263	.278	vs. NL		.238	466	111	17	1	12	57	54	55	.328	.356

Batter vs. Pitcher (career)

Hits Best Against	Avg	AB	H	2B	3B	HR	RBI	BB	SO	OBP	SLG	Hits Worst Against	Avg	AB	H	2B	3B	HR	RBI	BB	SO	OBP	SLG
Hideo Nomo	.375	8	3	1	0	1	3	2	0	.545	.875	Kevin Brown	.077	13	1	0	0	0	0	0	4	.077	.077
Mark Clark	.308	13	4	0	0	0	2	0	1	.308	.308	Curt Schilling	.200	10	2	0	0	1	1	1	3	.273	.500
												Pedro Martinez	.222	9	2	0	0	0	0	2	1	.364	.222

Mark Langston — Angels
Age 37 – Pitches Left

	ERA	W	L	Sv	G	GS	IP	BB	SO	Avg	H	2B	3B	HR	RBI	OBP	SLG	CG	ShO	Sup	QS	#P/S	SB	CS	GB	FB	G/F
1997 Season	5.85	2	4	0	9	9	47.2	29	30	.316	61	11	0	8	32	.402	.497	0	0	5.66	4	95	1	2	70	50	1.40
Last Five Years	4.25	46	35	0	111	111	747.0	277	560	.258	730	134	9	88	341	.323	.404	13	2	5.43	59	104	36	39	1010	761	1.33

1997 Season

	ERA	W	L	Sv	G	GS	IP	H	HR	BB	SO			Avg	AB	H	2B	3B	HR	RBI	BB	SO	OBP	SLG
Home	5.97	1	3	0	6	6	31.2	37	7	16	21	vs. Left		.185	27	5	0	0	1	1	3	6	.267	.296
Away	5.63	1	1	0	3	3	16.0	24	1	13	9	vs. Right		.337	166	56	11	0	7	31	26	24	.423	.530

Last Five Years

	ERA	W	L	Sv	G	GS	IP	H	HR	BB	SO
Home	4.18	25	17	0	56	56	383.2	354	57	139	308
Away	4.33	21	18	0	55	55	363.1	376	31	138	252
Day	4.75	11	12	0	31	31	199.0	219	20	72	156
Night	4.07	35	23	0	80	80	548.0	511	68	205	404
Grass	4.15	42	28	0	96	96	648.1	621	79	237	490
Turf	4.93	4	7	0	15	15	98.2	109	9	40	70
March/April	3.52	7	3	0	19	19	128.0	122	10	54	103
May	3.91	8	5	0	19	19	122.0	117	15	51	86
June	4.82	11	5	0	22	22	145.2	146	18	45	103
July	3.93	7	7	0	21	21	151.1	143	18	58	117
August	4.24	9	6	0	16	16	108.1	102	14	37	78
Sept/Oct	5.40	4	9	0	14	14	91.2	100	13	32	73
Starter	4.25	46	35	0	111	111	747.0	730	88	277	560
Reliever	0.00	0	0	0	0	0	0.0	0	0	0	0
0-3 Days Rest (Start)	2.76	3	1	0	5	5	32.2	34	2	11	21
4 Days Rest	4.59	27	21	0	66	66	454.2	453	45	164	334
5+ Days Rest	3.85	16	13	0	40	40	259.2	243	41	102	205
vs. AL	4.25	46	35	0	111	111	747.0	730	88	277	560
vs. NL	0.00	0	0	0	0	0	0.0	0	0	0	0
Pre-All Star	4.06	29	16	0	68	68	457.0	441	51	172	340
Post-All Star	4.56	17	19	0	43	43	290.0	289	37	105	220

	Avg	AB	H	2B	3B	HR	RBI	BB	SO	OBP	SLG
vs. Left	.221	408	90	10	0	9	37	30	83	.274	.311
vs. Right	.264	2426	640	124	9	79	304	247	477	.331	.420
Inning 1-6	.259	2401	622	116	9	74	299	237	496	.324	.407
Inning 7+	.249	433	108	18	0	14	42	40	64	.314	.388
None on	.238	1673	399	71	3	55	55	174	343	.312	.383
Runners on	.285	1161	331	63	6	33	286	103	217	.338	.435
Scoring Posn	.292	617	180	38	4	13	234	57	117	.341	.429
Close & Late	.248	286	71	10	0	8	26	30	44	.322	.367
None on/out	.266	747	199	40	3	29	29	63	150	.324	.444
vs. 1st Batr (relief)	.000	0	0	0	0	0	0	0	0	.000	.000
1st Inning Pitched	.269	417	112	19	0	17	55	43	84	.335	.436
First 75 Pitches	.262	1964	514	96	9	59	226	182	403	.324	.410
Pitch 76-90	.230	374	86	16	0	11	55	42	71	.303	.361
Pitch 91-105	.274	314	86	14	0	11	34	22	55	.322	.424
Pitch 106+	.242	182	44	8	0	7	26	31	31	.349	.401
First Pitch	.343	470	161	28	5	18	73	4	0	.347	.538
Ahead in Count	.191	1259	240	51	2	21	112	0	480	.192	.284
Behind in Count	.324	632	205	36	2	35	96	149	0	.450	.554
Two Strikes	.168	1252	210	46	2	15	96	124	560	.243	.244
Pre-All Star	.254	1734	441	84	6	51	201	172	340	.321	.398
Post-All Star	.263	1100	289	50	3	37	140	105	220	.325	.415

Pitcher vs. Batter (career)

Pitches Best Vs.	Avg	AB	H	2B	3B	HR	RBI	BB	SO	OBP	SLG
Jack Voigt	.000	12	0	0	0	0	0	0	3	.000	.000
Ryne Sandberg	.000	8	0	0	0	0	0	3	3	.273	.000
Craig Grebeck	.094	32	3	0	0	0	1	3	5	.171	.094
Walt Weiss	.100	10	1	0	0	0	0	1	2	.182	.100
Stan Javier	.111	18	2	0	0	0	0	0	5	.111	.111

Pitches Worst Vs.	Avg	AB	H	2B	3B	HR	RBI	BB	SO	OBP	SLG
Joey Cora	.545	11	6	1	0	1	3	1	1	.615	.909
Kevin Mitchell	.471	17	8	2	0	1	4	0	3	.471	.765
Paul Molitor	.429	63	27	6	0	4	15	11	9	.507	.714
Frank Thomas	.429	49	21	2	0	6	13	17	8	.567	.837
David Segui	.353	17	6	1	0	1	3	3	2	.450	.588

Ray Lankford — Cardinals

Age

	Avg	G	AB	R	H	2B	3B	HR	RBI	BB	SO	HBP	GDP	SB	CS	OBP	SLG	IBB	SH	SF	#Pit	#P/
1997 Season	.295	133	465	94	137	36	3	31	98	95	125	0	9	21	11	.411	.585	10	0	5	2408	4.
Last Five Years	.272	650	2316	428	629	149	21	103	368	376	592	12	36	105	50	.373	.487	36	2	24	11327	4.

1997 Season

	Avg	AB	H	2B	3B	HR	RBI	BB	SO	OBP	SLG
vs. Left	.301	136	41	11	1	12	38	15	39	.368	.662
vs. Right	.292	329	96	25	2	19	60	80	86	.426	.553
Groundball	.305	82	25	6	0	4	16	18	17	.422	.524
Flyball	.263	57	15	5	0	2	7	15	24	.417	.456
Home	.290	259	75	26	2	10	45	45	64	.392	.521
Away	.301	206	62	10	1	21	53	50	61	.432	.665
Day	.263	152	40	13	0	9	37	30	44	.376	.526
Night	.310	313	97	23	3	22	61	65	81	.427	.613
Grass	.287	397	114	33	3	22	76	78	100	.400	.552
Turf	.338	68	23	3	0	9	22	17	25	.471	.779
Pre-All Star	.333	240	80	22	1	17	61	43	53	.427	.646
Post-All Star	.253	225	57	14	2	14	37	52	72	.394	.520
Scoring Posn	.272	114	31	9	0	11	70	42	33	.423	.640
Close & Late	.247	93	23	8	1	3	12	14	19	.346	.452
None on/out	.370	100	37	12	1	3	3	15	26	.452	.600

	Avg	AB	H	2B	3B	HR	RBI	BB	SO	OBP	SLG
First Pitch	.515	33	17	6	0	4	10				
Ahead in Count	.396	91	36	5	1	10	26				
Behind in Count	.223	229	51	16	1	8	34				
Two Strikes	.204	275	56	16	1	8	40				
Batting #3	.318	258	82	20	1	16	55				
Batting #4	.266	199	53	16	2	14	42				
Other	.250	8	2	0	0	1	1				
March/April	.462	26	12	2	0	3	6				
May	.330	97	32	9	0	6	27				
June	.289	97	28	8	1	7	20				
July	.302	96	29	8	2	6	21				
August	.271	70	19	4	0	3	11			.393	.457
Sept/Oct	.215	79	17	5	0	6	13	27	26	.415	.506
vs. AL	.205	44	9	3	1	0	2	10	11	.352	.318
vs. NL	.304	421	128	33	2	31	96	85	114	.417	.613

1997 By Position

Position	Avg	AB	H	2B	3B	HR	RBI	BB	SO	OBP	SLG	G	GS	Innings	PO	A	E	DP	Fld Pct	Rng Fctr	In Zone	Outs	Zone Rtg	MLB Zone
As cf	.296	463	137	36	3	31	98	95	124	.412	.587	132	130	1141.1	292	4	9	2	.970	2.33	356	281	.789	.815

Last Five Years

	Avg	AB	H	2B	3B	HR	RBI	BB	SO	OBP	SLG
vs. Left	.248	621	154	36	7	18	105	84	180	.337	.415
vs. Right	.280	1695	475	113	14	85	263	292	412	.386	.514
Groundball	.281	595	167	31	2	19	81	93	138	.379	.435
Flyball	.263	373	98	32	5	15	50	58	112	.359	.496
Home	.294	1145	337	93	11	48	197	182	272	.388	.521
Away	.249	1171	292	56	10	55	171	194	320	.348	.455
Day	.249	696	173	52	6	20	106	113	204	.351	.427
Night	.281	1620	456	97	15	83	262	263	388	.382	.514
Grass	.265	1237	328	84	13	50	185	215	312	.372	.475
Turf	.279	1079	301	65	8	53	183	161	280	.373	.501
Pre-All Star	.285	1342	382	91	11	61	218	210	328	.379	.505
Post-All Star	.254	974	247	58	10	42	150	166	264	.364	.463
Scoring Posn	.278	597	166	40	6	29	268	148	169	.411	.511
Close & Late	.237	393	93	25	5	14	55	55	96	.330	.433
None on/out	.294	589	173	42	8	27	27	65	140	.367	.530

	Avg	AB	H	2B	3B	HR	RBI	BB	SO	OBP	SLG
First Pitch	.370	184	68	16	2	12	40	23	0	.437	.674
Ahead in Count	.373	485	181	40	7	35	120	168	0	.528	.701
Behind in Count	.200	1156	231	54	9	30	123	0	477	.204	.340
Two Strikes	.183	1275	233	47	6	30	124	185	592	.288	.300
Batting #3	.298	795	237	60	7	45	146	119	178	.384	.561
Batting #4	.260	723	188	40	6	33	125	131	193	.375	.469
Other	.256	798	204	49	8	25	97	126	221	.359	.431
March/April	.308	305	94	17	3	17	52	45	69	.397	.551
May	.297	499	148	32	4	19	81	79	135	.388	.491
June	.252	436	110	32	2	20	65	74	101	.360	.472
July	.267	415	111	28	6	18	76	56	104	.358	.494
August	.249	354	88	21	2	12	47	52	92	.349	.421
Sept/Oct	.254	307	78	19	4	17	47	70	91	.389	.508
vs. AL	.205	44	9	3	1	0	2	10	11	.352	.318
vs. NL	.273	2272	620	146	20	103	366	366	581	.373	.491

Batter vs. Pitcher (career)

Hits Best Against	Avg	AB	H	2B	3B	HR	RBI	BB	SO	OBP	SLG	Hits Worst Against	Avg	AB	H	2B	3B	HR	RBI	BB	SO	OBP	SLG
Mitch Williams	.500	10	5	1	1	0	2	4	3	.643	.800	Hideo Nomo	.056	18	1	0	0	0	1	0	5	.056	.056
Kent Bottenfield	.500	8	4	0	0	1	3	3	1	.636	.875	Bob Patterson	.067	15	1	0	1	0	1	0	5	.067	.200
Mike Williams	.462	13	6	2	0	2	3	1	4	.500	1.077	Bruce Ruffin	.100	20	2	0	0	0	0	4	5	.250	.100
VanLandingham	.455	11	5	1	0	2	6	2	0	.538	1.091	Pedro Martinez	.105	19	2	1	0	0	1	3	10	.227	.158
Chan Ho Park	.429	7	3	0	0	2	2	6	4	.692	1.286	Randy Myers	.118	17	2	0	0	0	0	1	2	.167	.118

Mike Lansing — Expos
Age 30 – Bats Right (groundball hitter)

	Avg	G	AB	R	H	2B	3B	HR	RBI	BB	SO	HBP	GDP	SB	CS	OBP	SLG	IBB	SH	SF	#Pit	#P/PA	GB	FB	G/F
1997 Season	.281	144	572	86	161	45	2	20	70	45	92	5	9	11	5	.338	.472	2	6	3	2233	3.54	194	175	1.11
Career (1993-1997)	.276	677	2565	340	709	165	9	49	265	193	335	30	68	96	30	.333	.405	10	28	12	9856	3.49	1041	704	1.48

1997 Season

	Avg	AB	H	2B	3B	HR	RBI	BB	SO	OBP	SLG		Avg	AB	H	2B	3B	HR	RBI	BB	SO	OBP	SLG
vs. Left	.299	117	35	10	0	4	16	12	18	.364	.487	First Pitch	.389	95	37	13	0	2	11	0	0	.396	.589
vs. Right	.277	455	126	35	2	16	54	33	74	.331	.468	Ahead in Count	.402	132	53	13	0	8	23	26	0	.497	.682
Groundball	.320	128	41	15	2	5	18	6	22	.355	.586	Behind in Count	.163	246	40	10	1	6	20	0	80	.171	.285
Flyball	.266	64	17	6	0	1	7	10	9	.373	.406	Two Strikes	.181	237	43	13	1	6	21	19	92	.249	.321
Home	.297	259	77	24	0	11	32	23	38	.361	.517	Total	.281	572	161	45	2	20	70	45	92	.338	.472
Away	.268	313	84	21	2	9	38	22	54	.318	.435	Batting #2	.281	572	161	45	2	20	70	45	92	.338	.472
Day	.286	189	54	16	2	10	31	18	32	.352	.550	Other	.000	0	0	0	0	0	0	0	0	.000	.000
Night	.279	383	107	29	0	10	39	27	60	.330	.433	March/April	.215	79	17	6	0	2	7	8	11	.281	.367
Grass	.281	228	64	14	0	7	27	19	37	.339	.434	May	.307	114	35	8	0	6	15	9	20	.365	.535
Turf	.282	344	97	31	2	13	43	26	55	.337	.497	June	.286	112	32	9	0	4	16	10	16	.350	.473
Pre-All Star	.278	327	91	28	0	12	40	29	50	.340	.474	July	.347	101	35	11	2	2	11	10	9	.405	.554
Post-All Star	.286	245	70	17	2	8	30	16	42	.335	.469	August	.313	83	26	5	0	2	11	3	15	.352	.446
Scoring Posn	.297	128	38	13	1	3	46	14	26	.367	.484	Sept/Oct	.193	83	16	6	0	4	10	5	21	.239	.410
Close & Late	.237	93	22	5	0	2	13	16	311	.355	vs. AL	.246	65	16	6	0	2	6	3	10	.279	.431
None on/out	.299	97	29	9	1	3	3	9	13	.364	.505	vs. NL	.286	507	145	39	2	18	64	42	82	.345	.477

1997 By Position

Position	Avg	AB	H	2B	3B	HR	RBI	BB	SO	OBP	SLG	G	GS	Innings	PO	A	E	DP	Fld Pct	Rng Fctr	In Zone	Zone Outs	Zone Rtg	MLB Zone
As 2b	.281	572	161	45	2	20	70	45	92	.338	.472	144	143	1234.0	280	395	9	97	.987	4.92	425	402	946	902

Career (1993-1997)

	Avg	AB	H	2B	3B	HR	RBI	BB	SO	OBP	SLG		Avg	AB	H	2B	3B	HR	RBI	BB	SO	OBP	SLG
vs. Left	.282	600	169	32	1	13	59	53	74	.339	.403	First Pitch	.330	421	139	37	0	8	40	6	0	.351	.475
vs. Right	.275	1965	540	133	8	36	206	140	261	.331	.406	Ahead in Count	.347	669	232	51	3	22	100	103	0	.434	.531
Groundball	.295	675	199	38	3	13	84	46	88	.343	.418	Behind in Count	.191	1047	200	45	4	11	73	0	288	.201	.273
Flyball	.272	386	105	27	2	3	27	25	53	.325	.376	Two Strikes	.204	985	201	45	4	11	78	84	335	.274	.291
Home	.275	1252	344	87	3	22	126	102	161	.336	.402	Batting #2	.281	1482	416	101	6	32	147	117	203	.339	.422
Away	.278	1313	365	78	6	27	139	91	174	.330	.408	Batting #6	.260	404	105	21	2	7	48	21	51	.300	.374
Day	.277	779	216	52	2	20	80	65	126	.342	.426	Other	.277	679	188	43	1	10	70	55	81	.337	.387
Night	.276	1786	493	113	7	29	185	128	209	.329	.396	March/April	.290	362	105	28	1	6	35	34	49	.354	.423
Grass	.288	845	243	43	2	23	100	56	113	.337	.425	May	.280	514	144	28	3	14	57	41	73	.342	.428
Turf	.271	1720	466	122	7	26	165	137	222	.331	.395	June	.251	427	107	30	0	7	46	31	46	.310	.370
Pre-All Star	.272	1446	393	97	4	29	150	118	184	.334	.405	July	.302	463	140	34	3	8	42	42	58	.366	.441
Post-All Star	.282	1119	316	68	5	20	115	75	151	.332	.406	August	.288	424	122	24	1	7	48	20	52	.322	.399
Scoring Posn	.293	608	178	46	2	17	215	78	90	.375	.459	Sept/Oct	.243	375	91	21	1	7	37	25	57	.295	.360
Close & Late	.266	395	105	24	0	5	47	36	56	.333	.365	vs. AL	.246	65	16	6	0	2	6	3	10	.279	.431
None on/out	.265	567	150	41	3	5	5	31	64	.308	.374	vs. NL	.277	2500	693	159	9	47	259	190	325	.334	.404

Batter vs. Pitcher (career)

Hits Best Against	Avg	AB	H	2B	3B	HR	RBI	BB	SO	OBP	SLG	Hits Worst Against	Avg	AB	H	2B	3B	HR	RBI	BB	SO	OBP	SLG
Rod Beck	.700	10	7	1	0	0	2	0	1	.727	.800	Todd Jones	.000	10	0	0	0	0	1	2	0	.167	.000
Mike Morgan	.556	18	10	2	2	0	1	2	2	.619	.889	Scott Sanders	.071	14	1	0	0	0	0	0	3	.133	.071
Darren Holmes	.545	11	6	1	0	1	4	2	1	.615	.909	Trevor Hoffman	.083	12	1	0	0	0	0	1	1	.154	.083
Willie Blair	.500	14	7	1	1	0	1	0	3	.500	.714	Joey Hamilton	.105	19	2	0	0	0	1	0	3	.150	.105
Steve Reed	.385	13	5	1	0	1	4	1	0	.429	.692	Pete Harnisch	.143	21	3	0	0	0	1	0	3	.143	.143

Barry Larkin — Reds
Age 34 – Bats Right (groundball hitter)

	Avg	G	AB	R	H	2B	3B	HR	RBI	BB	SO	HBP	GDP	SB	CS	OBP	SLG	IBB	SH	SF	#Pit	#P/PA	GB	FB	G/F
1997 Season	.317	73	224	34	71	17	3	4	20	47	24	3	3	14	3	.440	.473	6	1	1	1070	3.88	92	57	1.61
Last Five Years	.304	566	2048	384	623	121	21	69	278	319	216	14	48	141	21	.398	.485	20	10	20	9735	4.04	837	597	1.40

1997 Season

	Avg	AB	H	2B	3B	HR	RBI	BB	SO	OBP	SLG		Avg	AB	H	2B	3B	HR	RBI	BB	SO	OBP	SLG
vs. Left	.447	47	21	4	2	1	1	4	1	.559	.745	Scoring Posn	.219	64	14	3	1	1	16	29	8	.463	.344
vs. Right	.282	177	50	13	1	2	9	36	22	.407	.401	Close & Late	.273	33	9	2	1	0	1	8	6	.415	.394
Home	.391	110	43	13	2	0	12	29	11	.518	.545	None on/out	.318	44	14	5	2	1	1	6	4	.400	.591
Away	.246	114	28	4	1	4	8	18	13	.358	.404	Batting #3	.275	153	42	9	1	1	12	34	18	.407	.366
First Pitch	.286	21	6	2	0	0	2	5	0	.444	.381	Batting #4	.455	55	25	8	2	3	8	11	5	.559	.836
Ahead in Count	.295	61	18	4	1	2	7	29	0	.527	.492	Other	.250	16	4	0	0	0	0	2	1	.333	.250
Behind in Count	.306	98	30	5	1	1	5	0	21	.303	.408	Pre-All Star	.317	186	59	14	3	4	18	41	22	.446	.489
Two Strikes	.266	94	25	4	1	0	6	13	24	.358	.330	Post-All Star	.316	38	12	3	0	0	2	6	2	.409	.395

Last Five Years

	Avg	AB	H	2B	3B	HR	RBI	BB	SO	OBP	SLG		Avg	AB	H	2B	3B	HR	RBI	BB	SO	OBP	SLG
vs. Left	.319	476	152	32	5	26	89	91	42	.425	.571	First Pitch	.308	143	44	5	0	4	23	16	0	.380	.427
vs. Right	.300	1572	471	89	16	43	189	228	174	.390	.459	Ahead in Count	.343	545	187	37	7	26	94	206	0	.520	.580
Groundball	.292	624	182	32	3	18	83	113	66	.399	.439	Behind in Count	.256	884	226	49	9	18	82	0	170	.259	.393
Flyball	.267	315	84	17	3	11	50	43	37	.354	.444	Two Strikes	.260	942	245	55	11	22	95	97	216	.333	.412
Home	.306	1046	320	65	9	29	138	196	107	.414	.468	Batting #2	.302	625	189	35	9	21	75	75	71	.375	.488
Away	.302	1002	303	56	12	40	140	123	109	.380	.502	Batting #3	.296	1105	327	63	9	37	164	188	109	.398	.470
Day	.309	624	193	41	4	29	85	124	57	.425	.527	Other	.336	318	107	23	3	11	39	56	36	.440	.531
Night	.302	1424	430	80	17	40	193	195	159	.386	.466	March/April	.274	343	94	15	3	9	34	73	34	.400	.414
Grass	.307	615	189	36	9	30	94	87	71	.394	.541	May	.317	467	148	27	6	12	75	74	50	.412	.478
Turf	.303	1433	434	85	12	39	184	232	145	.400	.461	June	.298	383	114	19	5	8	44	53	43	.386	.436
Pre-All Star	.299	1344	402	72	14	36	168	214	143	.396	.454	July	.319	395	126	25	4	17	57	41	44	.379	.532
Post-All Star	.314	704	221	49	7	33	110	105	73	.403	.544	August	.325	305	99	26	2	13	47	50	26	.418	.551
Scoring Posn	.311	501	156	25	5	16	203	132	59	.443	.477	Sept/Oct	.271	155	42	9	1	10	21	28	19	.389	.535
Close & Late	.292	301	88	10	4	10	37	61	42	.412	.452	vs. AL	.316	19	6	4	0	0	1	1	0	.350	.526
None on/out	.334	434	145	32	4	18	18	47	33	.400	.551	vs. NL	.304	2029	617	117	21	69	277	318	216	.399	.484

Batter vs. Pitcher (career)

Hits Best Against	Avg	AB	H	2B	3B	HR	RBI	BB	SO	OBP	SLG	Hits Worst Against	Avg	AB	H	2B	3B	HR	RBI	BB	SO	OBP	SLG
Paul Wagner	.524	21	11	3	1	1	4	4	0	.600	.571	Steve Reed	.000	10	0	0	0	0	0	2	2	.167	.000
Michael Mimbs	.500	10	5	0	0	2	6	2	0	.583	1.100	John Wetteland	.077	13	1	1	0	0	3	0	0	.071	.154
Mark Thompson	.429	14	6	1	0	2	4	1	1	.467	.929	Kirk Rueter	.091	11	1	0	0	0	1	1	1	.154	.091
Al Leiter	.400	5	2	0	0	1	1	6	1	.727	1.000	Bret Saberhagen	.100	10	1	0	0	0	0	1	3	.182	.100
Greg McMichael	.375	8	3	1	0	1	4	3	1	.545	.875	Jeff Brantley	.133	15	2	0	0	0	0	0	1	.133	.133

Chris Latham — Twins
Age 25 – Bats Both

	Avg	G	AB	R	H	2B	3B	HR	RBI	BB	SO	HBP	GDP	SB	CS	OBP	SLG	IBB	SH	SF	#Pit	#P/PA	GB	FB	G/F
1997 Season	.182	15	22	4	4	1	0	0	1	0	8	0	0	0	0	.182	.227	0	0	0	79	3.59	5	8	0.63

1997 Season

	Avg	AB	H	2B	3B	HR	RBI	BB	SO	OBP	SLG		Avg	AB	H	2B	3B	HR	RBI	BB	SO	OBP	SLG
vs. Left	.167	12	2	1	0	0	1	0	5	.167	.250	Scoring Posn	.125	8	1	1	0	0	1	0	3	.125	.250
vs. Right	.200	10	2	0	0	0	0	0	3	.200	.200	Close & Late	.000	4	0	0	0	0	0	0	2	.000	.000

Matt Lawton — Twins
Age 26 – Bats Left

	Avg	G	AB	R	H	2B	3B	HR	RBI	BB	SO	HBP	GDP	SB	CS	OBP	SLG	IBB	SH	SF	#Pit	#P/PA	GB	FB	G/F
1997 Season	.248	142	460	74	114	29	3	14	60	76	81	10	7	7	4	.366	.415	3	1	1	2140	3.91	150	155	0.97
Career (1995-1997)	.256	242	772	119	198	40	5	21	114	111	120	17	14	12	9	.361	.403	4	1	3	3466	3.83	280	240	1.17

1997 Season

	Avg	AB	H	2B	3B	HR	RBI	BB	SO	OBP	SLG		Avg	AB	H	2B	3B	HR	RBI	BB	SO	OBP	SLG
vs. Left	.274	84	23	4	0	1	12	13	13	.386	.357	First Pitch	.341	82	28	7	0	7	17	3	0	.372	.683
vs. Right	.242	376	91	25	3	13	48	63	68	.361	.428	Ahead in Count	.286	112	32	12	1	5	25	42	0	.481	.545
Groundball	.278	115	32	10	1	3	18	18	21	.385	.461	Behind in Count	.139	166	23	4	1	1	11	0	63	.178	.193
Flyball	.246	65	16	9	1	0	5	10	11	.380	.415	Two Strikes	.139	202	28	5	1	1	10	31	81	.275	.188
Home	.248	218	54	16	1	8	26	44	43	.389	.440	Batting #2	.328	119	39	9	0	6	27	20	16	.430	.555
Away	.248	242	60	13	2	6	34	32	38	.343	.393	Batting #5	.225	89	20	6	0	1	6	18	16	.361	.326
Day	.229	140	32	9	1	2	21	29	23	.372	.350	Other	.218	252	55	14	3	7	27	38	49	.337	.381
Night	.256	320	82	20	2	12	39	47	58	.363	.444	March/April	.305	95	29	10	1	2	10	17	16	.421	.495
Grass	.244	205	50	11	2	4	28	21	33	.320	.376	May	.224	85	19	5	2	1	10	11	19	.327	.365
Turf	.251	255	64	18	1	10	32	55	48	.398	.447	June	.262	65	17	1	0	3	7	7	11	.338	.415
Pre-All Star	.257	261	67	16	3	6	29	35	48	.354	.410	July	.179	67	12	3	0	0	5	4	12	.225	.224
Post-All Star	.236	199	47	13	0	8	31	41	33	.380	.422	August	.237	76	18	4	0	3	12	20	13	.414	.408
Scoring Posn	.279	104	29	6	0	4	42	24	16	.433	.452	Sept/Oct	.264	72	19	6	0	5	16	17	10	.418	.556
Close & Late	.308	65	20	5	0	2	10	13	11	.430	.477	vs. AL	.249	425	106	28	3	12	55	70	76	.366	.414
None on/out	.271	96	26	4	1	4	4	19	15	.402	.458	vs. NL	.229	35	8	1	0	2	5	6	5	.357	.429

1997 By Position

Position	Avg	AB	H	2B	3B	HR	RBI	BB	SO	OBP	SLG	G	GS	Innings	PO	A	E	DP	Fld Pct	Rng Fctr	In Zone	Zone Outs	Zone Rtg	MLB Zone
As Pinch Hitter	.250	8	2	1	0	0	0	4	1	.500	.375	13	0	---	---	---	---	---	---	---	---	---	---	---
As lf	.249	197	49	15	2	3	20	22	37	.338	.391	58	51	460.1	108	5	2	2	.983	2.21	135	104	.770	.805
As cf	.246	57	14	4	0	3	8	14	6	.394	.474	23	16	141.1	43	0	3	0	.935	2.74	53	44	.830	.815
As rf	.247	198	49	9	1	8	32	36	37	.377	.424	67	59	522.1	129	4	2	1	.985	2.29	150	119	.793	.813

Career (1995-1997)

	Avg	AB	H	2B	3B	HR	RBI	BB	SO	OBP	SLG		Avg	AB	H	2B	3B	HR	RBI	BB	SO	OBP	SLG
vs. Left	.253	150	38	5	0	1	18	22	22	.354	.307	First Pitch	.356	135	48	12	0	8	28	4	0	.387	.622
vs. Right	.257	622	160	35	5	20	93	93	98	.363	.426	Ahead in Count	.270	178	48	14	2	7	37	66	0	.466	.489
Groundball	.260	192	50	10	3	7	40	29	29	.377	.453	Behind in Count	.175	291	51	5	2	2	28	0	95	.205	.227
Flyball	.220	109	24	10	1	0	9	12	18	.325	.330	Two Strikes	.156	334	52	6	1	4	25	41	120	.266	.216
Home	.251	351	88	23	3	10	51	61	61	.376	.419	Batting #2	.313	227	71	14	2	9	52	33	32	.410	.511
Away	.261	421	110	17	2	11	63	50	59	.347	.390	Batting #8	.248	129	32	4	0	3	15	13	17	.329	.349
Day	.247	267	66	11	1	5	37	40	44	.354	.352	Other	.228	416	95	22	3	9	47	65	71	.344	.361
Night	.261	505	132	29	4	16	77	71	76	.365	.430	March/April	.260	173	45	11	2	2	20	29	29	.376	.382
Grass	.257	369	95	14	2	9	57	36	52	.331	.379	May	.224	85	19	5	2	1	10	11	19	.327	.365
Turf	.256	403	103	26	3	12	57	75	68	.386	.424	June	.286	98	28	1	0	5	14	10	14	.355	.449
Pre-All Star	.248	400	99	18	4	8	50	51	65	.341	.373	July	.182	99	18	4	0	0	9	5	14	.221	.222

Career (1995-1997)

	Avg	AB	H	2B	3B	HR	RBI	BB	SO	OBP	SLG		Avg	AB	H	2B	3B	HR	RBI	BB	SO	OBP	SLG
Post-All Star	.266	372	99	22	1	13	64	60	55	.382	.435	August	.299	147	44	7	0	7	29	29	18	.425	.490
Scoring Posn	.313	195	61	10	2	8	91	33	23	.429	.508	Sept/Oct	.259	170	44	12	1	6	32	27	26	.380	.447
Close & Late	.272	114	31	6	0	3	19	16	15	.371	.404	vs. AL	.258	737	190	39	5	19	109	105	115	.361	.402
None on/out	.217	166	36	5	1	6	6	26	25	.333	.367	vs. NL	.229	35	8	1	0	2	5	6	5	.357	.429

Batter vs. Pitcher (career)

Hits Best Against	Avg	AB	H	2B	3B	HR	RBI	BB	SO	OBP	SLG	Hits Worst Against	Avg	AB	H	2B	3B	HR	RBI	BB	SO	OBP	SLG
Jeff D'Amico	.500	10	5	1	1	0	3	0	0	.545	.800	Scott Kamieniecki	.182	11	2	1	0	0	0	1	1	.250	.273
Ken Hill	.455	11	5	2	1	0	2	1	0	.538	.818	Roger Clemens	.200	10	2	0	0	0	1	1	2	.273	.200
Scott Erickson	.385	13	5	0	1	2	2	0	2	.385	1.000	Pat Hentgen	.222	9	2	0	0	0	1	1	1	.364	.222
												Charles Nagy	.222	9	2	2	0	0	4	3	3	.417	.444
												Tom Gordon	.231	13	3	0	0	1	2	1	3	.286	.462

Aaron Ledesma — Orioles   Age 27 – Bats Right

	Avg	G	AB	R	H	2B	3B	HR	RBI	BB	SO	HBP	GDP	SB	CS	OBP	SLG	IBB	SH	SF	#Pit	#P/PA	GB	FB	G/F
1997 Season	.352	43	88	24	31	5	1	2	11	13	9	1	1	1	0	.437	.500	0	1	1	363	3.49	37	26	1.42
Career (1995-1997)	.322	64	121	28	39	5	1	2	14	19	16	1	3	1	0	.415	.430	1	1	1	496	3.47	53	30	1.77

1997 Season

	Avg	AB	H	2B	3B	HR	RBI	BB	SO	OBP	SLG		Avg	AB	H	2B	3B	HR	RBI	BB	SO	OBP	SLG
vs. Left	.375	40	15	2	0	1	5	4	3	.422	.500	Scoring Posn	.238	21	5	2	0	0	9	5	1	.393	.333
vs. Right	.333	48	16	3	1	1	6	9	6	.448	.500	Close & Late	.154	13	2	0	0	0	1	4	1	.353	.154

Derrek Lee — Padres   Age 22 – Bats Right

	Avg	G	AB	R	H	2B	3B	HR	RBI	BB	SO	HBP	GDP	SB	CS	OBP	SLG	IBB	SH	SF	#Pit	#P/PA	GB	FB	G/F
1997 Season	.259	22	54	9	14	3	0	1	4	9	24	0	1	0	0	.365	.370	0	0	0	269	4.27	15	6	2.50

1997 Season

	Avg	AB	H	2B	3B	HR	RBI	BB	SO	OBP	SLG		Avg	AB	H	2B	3B	HR	RBI	BB	SO	OBP	SLG
vs. Left	.250	16	4	2	0	0	0	4	7	.400	.375	Scoring Posn	.200	15	3	0	0	1	4	2	8	.294	.400
vs. Right	.263	38	10	1	0	1	4	5	17	.349	.368	Close & Late	.357	14	5	0	0	1	3	2	4	.438	.571

Al Leiter — Marlins   Age 32 – Pitches Left

	ERA	W	L	Sv	G	GS	IP	BB	SO	Avg	H	2B	3B	HR	RBI	OBP	SLG	CG	ShO	Sup	QS	#P/S	SB	CS	GB	FB	G/F
1997 Season	4.34	11	9	0	27	27	151.1	91	132	.241	133	22	9	13	72	.359	.384	0	0	4.70	13	102	12	16	163	178	0.92
Last Five Years	3.85	53	45	2	142	120	766.1	439	651	.237	666	128	18	56	307	.344	.355	6	3	4.80	63	107	39	43	909	806	1.13

1997 Season

	ERA	W	L	Sv	G	GS	IP	H	HR	BB	SO		Avg	AB	H	2B	3B	HR	RBI	BB	SO	OBP	SLG
Home	2.28	6	2	0	12	12	75.0	48	5	39	64	vs. Left	.204	98	20	2	5	0	5	14	28	.310	.327
Away	6.37	5	7	0	15	15	76.1	85	8	52	68	vs. Right	.249	454	113	20	4	13	67	77	104	.369	.396
Day	6.49	2	4	0	7	7	34.2	42	2	19	24	Inning 1-6	.250	528	132	22	8	13	71	87	126	.366	.396
Night	3.70	9	5	0	20	20	116.2	93	11	72	108	Inning 7+	.042	24	1	0	1	0	1	4	6	.207	.125
Grass	4.24	8	6	0	20	20	114.2	101	11	66	102	None on	.228	294	67	11	6	7	7	50	66	.351	.378
Turf	4.66	3	3	0	7	7	36.2	32	2	25	30	Runners on	.256	258	66	11	3	6	65	41	66	.367	.391
March/April	5.12	3	2	0	6	6	31.2	29	3	22	25	Scoring Posn	.281	139	39	8	2	2	55	27	34	.405	.410
May	5.40	1	1	0	2	2	10.0	9	2	6	11	Close & Late	.000	12	0	0	0	0	0	3	5	.200	.000
June	4.15	3	2	0	6	6	34.2	33	0	21	30	None on/out	.237	131	31	4	4	4	4	27	31	.383	.420
July	3.00	1	1	0	4	4	24.0	16	4	17	25	vs. 1st Batr (relief)	.000	0	0	0	0	0	0	0	0	.000	.000
August	4.30	1	3	0	4	4	23.0	20	1	14	18	1st Inning Pitched	.245	98	24	3	0	1	10	16	25	.368	.306
Sept/Oct	4.50	2	0	0	5	5	28.0	26	3	11	23	First 75 Pitches	.245	388	95	15	5	6	45	63	90	.359	.356
Starter	4.34	11	9	0	27	27	151.1	133	13	91	132	Pitch 76-90	.301	73	22	4	2	4	18	9	20	.393	.575
Reliever	0.00	0	0	0	0	0	0.0	0	0	0	0	Pitch 91-105	.245	53	13	3	1	3	8	12	10	.403	.509
0-3 Days Rest (Start)	0.00	0	0	0	0	0	0.0	0	0	0	0	Pitch 106+	.079	38	3	0	1	0	1	7	12	.222	.132
4 Days Rest	5.29	3	7	0	15	15	80.0	77	6	48	65	First Pitch	.439	57	25	5	1	0	1	0		.435	.561
5+ Days Rest	3.28	8	2	0	12	12	71.1	56	7	43	67	Ahead in Count	.173	237	41	7	5	3	21	0	102	.200	.283
vs. AL	4.71	1	1	0	4	4	21.0	21	1	15	16	Behind in Count	.313	128	40	7	3	5	25	45	0	.497	.531
vs. NL	4.28	10	8	0	23	23	130.1	112	12	76	116	Two Strikes	.154	280	43	6	5	6	27	45	132	.280	.275
Pre-All Star	5.02	7	6	0	15	15	80.2	77	7	54	67	Pre-All Star	.256	301	77	12	5	7	43	54	67	.379	.399
Post-All Star	3.57	4	3	0	12	12	70.2	56	6	37	65	Post-All Star	.223	251	56	10	4	6	29	37	65	.333	.367

Last Five Years

	ERA	W	L	Sv	G	GS	IP	H	HR	BB	SO		Avg	AB	H	2B	3B	HR	RBI	BB	SO	OBP	SLG
Home	2.99	33	13	0	72	58	403.1	317	28	204	356	vs. Left	.240	516	124	18	10	9	54	54	122	.313	.366
Away	4.81	20	32	2	70	62	363.0	349	28	235	295	vs. Right	.236	2299	542	110	8	47	253	385	529	.351	.352
Day	4.32	15	22	0	48	43	262.1	230	19	154	231	Inning 1-6	.238	2503	595	117	16	51	282	376	588	.343	.358
Night	3.61	38	23	2	94	77	504.0	436	37	285	420	Inning 7+	.228	312	71	11	2	5	25	63	63	.359	.324
Grass	3.81	30	31	2	83	75	468.0	389	37	263	404	None on	.235	1563	368	76	14	32	32	230	352	.339	.363
Turf	3.92	23	14	0	59	45	298.1	277	19	176	247	Runners on	.238	1252	298	52	4	24	275	209	299	.351	.343
March/April	4.00	11	6	0	21	21	123.2	106	9	81	100	Scoring Posn	.238	677	161	32	3	9	235	129	176	.361	.334
May	4.22	6	11	0	22	20	121.2	108	6	65	107	Close & Late	.250	144	36	7	0	3	12	34	32	.392	.361
June	3.12	11	6	1	27	24	144.1	126	7	81	118	None on/out	.234	692	162	32	7	17	17	112	144	.346	.374
July	4.21	10	8	0	26	20	130.1	109	10	88	117	vs. 1st Batr (relief)	.118	17	2	0	0	1	5	3	1	.238	.294
August	4.33	7	9	1	25	17	124.2	116	13	73	105	1st Inning Pitched	.216	501	108	18	1	10	48	71	122	.315	.315
Sept/Oct	3.33	8	5	0	21	18	121.2	101	11	51	104	First 75 Pitches	.240	1964	472	88	11	33	196	283	437	.341	.347
Starter	3.87	50	44	0	120	120	725.1	622	53	421	624	Pitch 76-90	.253	356	90	20	3	11	45	51	86	.356	.419

262

Last Five Years

	ERA	W	L	Sv	G	GS	IP	H	HR	BB	SO		Avg	AB	H	2B	3B	HR	RBI	BB	SO	OBP	SLG
Reliever	3.51	3	1	2	22	0	41.0	44	3	18	27	Pitch 91-105	.198	278	55	12	2	7	40	57	75	.341	.331
0-3 Days Rest (Start)	5.73	0	1	0	2	2	11.0	9	1	8	11	Pitch 106+	.226	217	49	8	2	5	26	48	53	.361	.350
4 Days Rest	4.16	23	29	0	67	67	405.0	345	32	249	346	First Pitch	.351	342	120	29	2	9	52	7	0	.367	.526
5+ Days Rest	3.43	27	14	0	51	51	309.1	268	20	164	267	Ahead in Count	.171	1184	202	31	8	11	85	0	509	.182	.238
vs. AL	4.19	27	25	2	86	64	420.2	401	30	244	335	Behind in Count	.319	661	211	49	7	19	94	241	0	.503	.501
vs. NL	3.44	26	20	0	56	56	345.2	265	26	195	316	Two Strikes	.149	1363	203	33	8	19	100	191	651	.258	.227
Pre-All Star	4.09	28	27	1	78	71	422.2	379	27	261	345	Pre-All Star	.243	1562	379	70	11	27	182	261	345	.356	.353
Post-All Star	3.56	25	18	1	64	49	343.2	287	20	178	306	Post-All Star	.229	1253	287	58	7	29	125	178	306	.329	.356

Pitcher vs. Batter (career)

Pitches Best Vs.	Avg	AB	H	2B	3B	HR	RBI	BB	SO	OBP	SLG	Pitches Worst Vs.	Avg	AB	H	2B	3B	HR	RBI	BB	SO	OBP	SLG
Brady Anderson	.000	9	0	0	0	0	1	2	0	.167	.000	Andres Galarraga	.625	8	5	2	0	1	6	3	1	.667	1.250
Bret Boone	.063	16	1	0	0	0	0	2	3	.063	.063	Mark McLemore	.500	18	9	3	0	1	3	1	1	.571	.833
Joe Carter	.091	11	1	0	0	0	0	0	3	.091	.091	Derek Bell	.417	12	5	2	1	1	5	0	2	.417	1.000
Hal Morris	.091	11	1	0	0	0	1	0	0	.091	.091	Delino DeShields	.400	10	4	1	3	0	1	1	5	.455	1.100
Mark Lemke	.100	10	1	0	0	0	2	1	1	.154	.100	Barry Larkin	.400	5	2	0	0	1	6	1	.727	1.000

Mark Leiter — Phillies

Age 35 – Pitches Right

	ERA	W	L	Sv	G	GS	IP	BB	SO	Avg	H	2B	3B	HR	RBI	OBP	SLG	CG	ShO	Sup	QS	#P/S	SB	CS	GB	FB	G/F
1997 Season	5.67	10	17	0	31	31	182.2	64	148	.292	216	58	7	25	121	.352	.491	3	0	5.37	13	96	19	6	258	197	1.31
Last Five Years	4.77	38	54	2	163	114	785.1	267	582	.271	830	177	17	111	424	.338	.449	13	1	4.92	54	98	68	27	979	960	1.02

1997 Season

	ERA	W	L	Sv	G	GS	IP	H	HR	BB	SO		Avg	AB	H	2B	3B	HR	RBI	BB	SO	OBP	SLG
Home	5.46	5	7	0	15	15	90.2	104	11	25	72	vs. Left	.316	374	118	29	5	13	66	46	57	.389	.524
Away	5.87	5	10	0	16	16	92.0	112	14	39	76	vs. Right	.268	366	98	29	2	12	55	18	91	.311	.456
Day	6.06	2	4	0	7	7	35.2	49	4	15	31	Inning 1-6	.294	659	194	52	5	23	113	60	132	.357	.493
Night	5.57	8	13	0	24	24	147.0	167	21	49	117	Inning 7+	.272	81	22	6	2	2	8	4	16	.307	.469
Grass	5.17	4	7	0	11	11	62.2	69	8	31	54	None on	.300	410	123	31	3	13	13	30	88	.351	.485
Turf	5.93	6	10	0	20	20	120.0	147	17	33	94	Runners on	.282	330	93	27	4	12	108	34	60	.354	.497
March/April	3.23	3	2	0	6	6	39.0	37	3	15	23	Scoring Posn	.303	198	60	16	3	8	96	28	33	.387	.535
May	7.96	1	4	0	6	6	31.2	39	7	13	21	Close & Late	.200	20	4	0	0	1	2	3	4	.292	.350
June	5.75	0	2	0	4	4	20.1	30	2	5	8	None on/out	.261	180	47	11	0	8	8	18	38	.328	.456
July	10.71	2	3	0	5	5	21.0	30	6	13	26	vs. 1st Batr (relief)	.000	0	0	0	0	0	0	0	0	.000	.000
August	3.83	3	3	0	6	6	42.1	48	4	12	40	1st Inning Pitched	.313	131	41	11	0	6	28	12	20	.378	.534
Sept/Oct	5.40	1	3	0	4	4	28.1	32	3	6	30	First 75 Pitches	.298	544	162	47	3	17	87	46	102	.360	.489
Starter	5.67	10	17	0	31	31	182.2	216	25	64	148	Pitch 76-90	.237	93	22	3	2	4	16	10	27	.305	.441
Reliever	0.00	0	0	0	0	0	0.0	0	0	0	0	Pitch 91-105	.317	63	20	4	0	4	12	6	12	.371	.571
0-3 Days Rest (Start)	1.13	1	0	0	1	1	8.0	3	0	1	5	Pitch 106+	.300	40	12	4	2	0	6	2	7	.326	.500
4 Days Rest	5.42	4	9	0	17	17	98.0	118	14	37	75	First Pitch	.350	137	48	17	1	2	26	3	0	.369	.533
5+ Days Rest	6.46	5	8	0	13	13	76.2	95	11	26	68	Ahead in Count	.185	324	60	8	3	5	21	0	130	.195	.275
vs. AL	5.00	0	2	0	2	2	9.0	13	0	4	10	Behind in Count	.417	132	55	18	2	9	35	31	0	.524	.788
vs. NL	5.70	10	15	0	29	29	173.2	203	25	60	138	Two Strikes	.196	336	66	11	3	8	30	148	262	.318
Pre-All Star	5.89	4	9	0	17	17	94.2	115	13	33	58	Pre-All Star	.297	387	115	37	1	13	67	33	58	.356	.499
Post-All Star	5.42	6	8	0	14	14	88.0	101	12	31	90	Post-All Star	.286	353	101	21	6	12	54	31	90	.348	.482

Last Five Years

	ERA	W	L	Sv	G	GS	IP	H	HR	BB	SO		Avg	AB	H	2B	3B	HR	RBI	BB	SO	OBP	SLG
Home	4.92	18	27	0	86	56	404.1	426	59	126	306	vs. Left	.285	1400	399	74	12	56	201	169	229	.364	.475
Away	4.61	20	27	2	77	58	381.0	404	52	141	276	vs. Right	.260	1659	431	103	5	55	223	98	353	.314	.427
Day	4.58	12	15	1	51	34	238.0	252	34	86	198	Inning 1-6	.278	2521	701	155	11	93	370	221	469	.344	.459
Night	4.85	26	39	1	112	80	547.1	578	77	181	384	Inning 7+	.240	538	129	22	6	18	54	46	113	.309	.403
Grass	4.66	25	39	2	116	71	521.1	531	70	201	398	None on	.265	1780	471	97	9	75	75	136	354	.324	.456
Turf	4.98	13	15	0	47	43	264.0	299	41	66	184	Runners on	.281	1279	359	80	8	36	349	131	228	.355	.440
March/April	3.68	9	8	0	24	19	129.2	127	14	47	85	Scoring Posn	.284	754	214	47	5	22	308	105	142	.375	.447
May	5.02	8	9	0	30	23	159.2	172	26	57	106	Close & Late	.234	248	58	7	1	10	26	27	45	.319	.391
June	4.89	6	11	0	32	22	147.1	160	20	51	103	None on/out	.258	786	203	37	2	40	40	56	163	.313	.463
July	5.92	4	10	2	35	16	111.0	125	19	44	105	vs. 1st Batr (relief)	.233	43	10	2	0	2	4	3	11	.292	.419
August	3.85	10	8	0	24	18	133.1	126	18	38	98	1st Inning Pitched	.287	613	176	34	4	22	102	65	121	.370	.463
Sept/Oct	5.52	3	9	0	18	16	104.1	120	14	30	85	First 75 Pitches	.281	2333	655	144	12	85	322	197	439	.346	.462
Starter	4.70	35	47	0	114	114	699.1	742	98	231	508	Pitch 76-90	.240	342	82	16	3	14	45	26	71	.298	.427
Reliever	5.34	3	7	2	49	0	86.0	88	13	36	74	Pitch 91-105	.258	248	64	9	0	10	42	28	41	.337	.415
0-3 Days Rest (Start)	5.47	1	2	0	5	5	24.2	30	1	5	18	Pitch 106+	.213	136	29	8	2	2	15	16	31	.299	.346
4 Days Rest	4.43	19	28	0	68	68	426.2	438	59	133	295	First Pitch	.339	516	175	39	1	19	87	20	0	.373	.529
5+ Days Rest	5.08	15	17	0	41	41	248.0	274	38	93	195	Ahead in Count	.196	1340	263	48	6	26	109	0	493	.214	.299
vs. AL	4.73	10	15	2	69	22	211.0	223	30	83	151	Behind in Count	.336	619	208	48	5	42	128	126	0	.448	.633
vs. NL	4.78	28	39	0	94	92	574.1	607	81	184	431	Two Strikes	.180	1358	245	47	7	33	122	120	582	.256	.298
Pre-All Star	4.75	21	31	1	98	69	468.0	501	65	169	320	Pre-All Star	.274	1831	501	102	8	65	251	169	320	.341	.445
Post-All Star	4.79	17	23	1	65	45	317.1	329	46	98	262	Post-All Star	.268	1228	329	75	9	46	173	98	262	.333	.456

Pitcher vs. Batter (career)

Pitches Best Vs.	Avg	AB	H	2B	3B	HR	RBI	BB	SO	OBP	SLG	Pitches Worst Vs.	Avg	AB	H	2B	3B	HR	RBI	BB	SO	OBP	SLG
Tony Phillips	.000	10	0	0	0	0	1	0	2	.000	.000	John Olerud	.727	11	8	2	1	0	4	4	1	.800	1.091
Jay Buhner	.000	10	0	0	0	0	0	2	5	.154	.000	Rafael Palmeiro	.632	19	12	2	0	3	7	5	1	.708	1.211
Mike Bordick	.071	14	1	0	0	0	1	0	3	.071	.071	Paul O'Neill	.600	10	6	0	0	2	4	2	0	.667	1.200
Terry Shumpert	.091	11	1	0	0	0	0	0	2	.091	.091	Jeff Blauser	.500	8	4	2	0	1	3	3	1	.667	1.125
Gregg Jefferies	.143	14	2	0	0	0	0	0	0	.143	.143	Barry Bonds	.375	8	3	0	0	2	5	4	1	.583	1.125

Mark Lemke — Braves
Age 32 – Bats Both (groundball hitter)

	Avg	G	AB	R	H	2B	3B	HR	RBI	BB	SO	HBP	GDP	SB	CS	OBP	SLG	IBB	SH	SF	#Pit	#P/PA	GB	FB	G/F
1997 Season	.245	109	351	33	86	17	1	2	26	33	51	0	10	2	0	.306	.316	2	8	5	1319	3.32	159	74	2.15
Last Five Years	.259	615	2091	231	541	84	8	22	181	233	226	0	67	10	9	.330	.338	32	31	20	7910	3.33	963	509	1.89

1997 Season

	Avg	AB	H	2B	3B	HR	RBI	BB	SO	OBP	SLG		Avg	AB	H	2B	3B	HR	RBI	BB	SO	OBP	SLG
vs. Left	.261	69	18	4	0	1	6	8	10	.329	.362	First Pitch	.244	90	22	5	1	0	6	1	0	.250	.322
vs. Right	.241	282	68	13	1	1	20	25	41	.300	.305	Ahead in Count	.364	66	24	4	0	1	12	22	0	.505	.470
Groundball	.194	62	12	3	0	0	3	10	11	.301	.242	Behind in Count	.159	132	21	4	0	0	4	0	43	.158	.189
Flyball	.297	37	11	2	0	1	5	4	7	.349	.432	Two Strikes	.181	138	25	7	0	0	4	10	51	.235	.232
Home	.258	178	46	7	0	2	11	12	28	.302	.331	Batting #7	.207	121	25	3	0	1	6	9	17	.258	.256
Away	.231	173	40	10	1	0	15	21	23	.310	.301	Batting #8	.297	148	44	11	1	0	14	17	19	.367	.385
Day	.269	104	28	9	0	0	6	7	13	.315	.356	Other	.207	82	17	3	0	1	6	7	15	.264	.280
Night	.235	247	58	8	1	2	20	26	38	.302	.300	March/April	.276	76	21	3	0	1	4	7	9	.329	.368
Grass	.245	277	68	13	0	2	18	24	39	.301	.314	May	.200	80	16	3	0	1	8	7	12	.258	.275
Turf	.243	74	18	4	1	0	8	9	12	.325	.324	June	.214	70	15	3	0	0	5	3	13	.247	.257
Pre-All Star	.224	245	55	10	1	2	19	20	37	.279	.298	July	.280	82	23	5	1	0	6	9	9	.352	.366
Post-All Star	.292	106	31	7	0	0	7	13	14	.367	.358	August	.256	43	11	2	0	0	3	7	8	.353	.302
Scoring Posn	.253	79	20	3	1	0	23	8	14	.304	.316	Sept/Oct	.000	0	0	0	0	0	0	0	0	.000	.000
Close & Late	.241	58	14	3	1	0	3	6	9	.313	.328	vs. AL	.200	30	6	2	0	0	1	0	7	.200	.267
None on/out	.253	95	24	5	0	1	1	6	13	.297	.337	vs. NL	.249	321	80	15	1	2	25	33	44	.315	.321

1997 By Position

Position	Avg	AB	H	2B	3B	HR	RBI	BB	SO	OBP	SLG	G	GS	Innings	PO	A	E	DP	Fld Pct	Rng Fctr	In Zone	Outs	Zone Rtg	MLB Zone
As 2b	.246	350	86	17	1	2	24	32	50	.306	.317	104	101	849.2	191	308	10	65	.980	5.29	342	315	.921	.902

Last Five Years

	Avg	AB	H	2B	3B	HR	RBI	BB	SO	OBP	SLG		Avg	AB	H	2B	3B	HR	RBI	BB	SO	OBP	SLG
vs. Left	.275	531	146	24	3	14	52	67	53	.353	.411	First Pitch	.238	499	119	20	2	0	39	22	0	.267	.287
vs. Right	.253	1560	395	60	5	8	129	166	173	.322	.313	Ahead in Count	.345	466	161	19	4	12	70	152	0	.500	.481
Groundball	.262	604	158	23	3	6	56	75	72	.340	.339	Behind in Count	.209	743	155	25	2	3	37	0	190	.207	.260
Flyball	.276	315	87	20	0	4	24	32	32	.340	.378	Two Strikes	.219	725	159	31	1	7	44	59	226	.277	.294
Home	.276	1061	293	39	4	13	96	105	115	.339	.357	Batting #2	.281	537	151	24	1	6	38	49	53	.340	.363
Away	.241	1030	248	45	4	9	85	128	111	.321	.318	Batting #8	.254	1212	308	49	6	12	111	147	127	.332	.334
Day	.279	613	171	29	3	7	51	64	65	.346	.370	Other	.240	342	82	11	1	4	32	37	46	.311	.313
Night	.250	1478	370	55	5	15	130	169	161	.324	.325	March/April	.249	317	79	11	0	8	25	42	30	.333	.360
Grass	.258	1629	420	60	6	18	136	181	166	.329	.335	May	.291	413	120	22	3	5	41	46	48	.360	.395
Turf	.262	462	121	24	2	4	45	52	60	.335	.348	June	.256	379	97	13	2	4	40	43	44	.332	.332
Pre-All Star	.261	1219	318	49	6	18	114	145	132	.338	.355	July	.249	409	102	17	1	1	27	41	44	.315	.303
Post-All Star	.256	872	223	35	2	4	67	88	94	.320	.314	August	.240	337	81	11	2	1	32	45	40	.322	.294
Scoring Posn	.259	474	123	20	5	3	151	90	50	.365	.342	Sept/Oct	.263	236	62	10	0	3	16	16	20	.308	.343
Close & Late	.251	343	86	10	3	7	35	37	40	.321	.359	vs. AL	.200	30	6	2	0	0	1	0	7	.200	.267
None on/out	.251	505	127	21	1	6	6	39	53	.305	.333	vs. NL	.260	2061	535	82	8	22	180	233	219	.332	.339

Batter vs. Pitcher (career)

Hits Best Against	Avg	AB	H	2B	3B	HR	RBI	BB	SO	OBP	SLG	Hits Worst Against	Avg	AB	H	2B	3B	HR	RBI	BB	SO	OBP	SLG
Steve Trachsel	.500	10	5	1	1	0	3	3	1	.615	.800	Mike Morgan	.045	22	1	0	0	0	0	3	4	.160	.045
Curt Schilling	.484	31	15	1	0	2	5	3	4	.529	.710	Rheal Cormier	.071	14	1	0	0	0	0	1	0	.133	.071
Dave Burba	.455	11	5	1	0	1	3	1	1	.462	.818	Todd Stottlemyre	.091	11	1	0	0	0	1	2	1	.214	.091
Michael Mimbs	.417	12	5	1	0	1	2	1	1	.462	.750	Al Leiter	.100	10	1	0	0	0	2	1	1	.154	.100
F. Valenzuela	.400	20	8	1	0	2	4	2	4	.455	.750	Steve Reed	.100	10	1	0	0	0	0	1	0	.182	.100

Patrick Lennon — Athletics
Age 30 – Bats Right

	Avg	G	AB	R	H	2B	3B	HR	RBI	BB	SO	HBP	GDP	SB	CS	OBP	SLG	IBB	SH	SF	#Pit	#P/PA	GB	FB	G/F
1997 Season	.293	56	116	14	34	6	1	1	14	15	35	0	3	0	1	.374	.388	0	0	0	522	3.98	38	21	1.81
Last Five Years	.281	70	146	19	41	9	1	1	15	22	45	0	3	0	1	.375	.377	0	0	0	701	4.17	49	25	1.96

1997 Season

	Avg	AB	H	2B	3B	HR	RBI	BB	SO	OBP	SLG		Avg	AB	H	2B	3B	HR	RBI	BB	SO	OBP	SLG
vs. Left	.337	83	28	6	1	0	13	15	25	.439	.434	Scoring Posn	.348	23	8	3	0	0	13	6	9	.483	.478
vs. Right	.182	33	6	0	0	1	1	0	10	.182	.273	Close & Late	.158	19	3	1	0	0	4	4	8	.304	.211
Home	.338	68	23	5	1	1	11	6	19	.392	.485	None on/out	.240	25	6	1	1	0	0	2	8	.296	.360
Away	.229	48	11	1	0	0	3	9	16	.351	.250	Batting #2	.227	44	10	3	0	0	8	8	16	.346	.295
First Pitch	.529	17	9	2	1	1	3	0	0	.529	.941	Batting #3	.370	27	10	2	0	0	6	4	6	.452	.444
Ahead in Count	.412	17	7	0	0	0	4	6	0	.565	.412	Other	.311	45	14	1	1	1	5	3	13	.354	.444
Behind in Count	.219	64	14	4	0	0	6	0	31	.219	.281	Pre-All Star	.352	54	19	3	0	0	11	9	16	.444	.407
Two Strikes	.162	68	11	2	0	0	4	9	35	.260	.191	Post-All Star	.242	62	15	3	1	1	3	6	19	.309	.371

John LeRoy — Braves
Age 23 – Pitches Right

	ERA	W	L	Sv	G	GS	IP	BB	SO	Avg	H	2B	3B	HR	RBI	OBP	SLG	GF	IR	IRS	Hld	SvOp	SB	CS	GB	FB	G/F
1997 Season	0.00	1	0	0	1	0	2.0	3	3	.143	1	0	0	0	0	.400	.143	0	0	0	0	0	0	0	2	2	1.00

1997 Season

	ERA	W	L	Sv	G	GS	IP	H	HR	BB	SO		Avg	AB	H	2B	3B	HR	RBI	BB	SO	OBP	SLG
Home	0.00	0	0	0	0	0	0.0	0	0	0	0	vs. Left	.000	4	0	0	0	0	0	0	2	2	.333	.000
Away	0.00	1	0	0	1	0	2.0	1	0	3	3	vs. Right	.333	3	1	0	0	0	0	1	1	.500	.333

Brian Lesher — Athletics
Age 27 – Bats Right

	Avg	G	AB	R	H	2B	3B	HR	RBI	BB	SO	HBP	GDP	SB	CS	OBP	SLG	IBB	SH	SF	#Pit	#P/PA	GB	FB	G/F
1997 Season	.229	46	131	17	30	4	1	4	16	9	30	0	4	4	1	.275	.366	0	0	2	543	3.82	37	48	0.77
Career (1996-1997)	.230	72	213	28	49	7	1	9	32	14	47	1	6	4	1	.277	.399	0	1	3	922	3.97	64	74	0.86

1997 Season

	Avg	AB	H	2B	3B	HR	RBI	BB	SO	OBP	SLG		Avg	AB	H	2B	3B	HR	RBI	BB	SO	OBP	SLG
vs. Left	.345	58	20	2	1	3	10	5	6	.391	.569	Scoring Posn	.241	29	7	1	0	0	9	4	6	.314	.276
vs. Right	.137	73	10	2	0	1	6	4	24	.179	.205	Close & Late	.111	18	2	0	0	0	1	0	5	.111	.111
Home	.200	80	16	1	1	2	8	5	20	.244	.313	None on/out	.147	34	5	0	0	0	0	2	8	.194	.147
Away	.275	51	14	3	0	2	8	4	10	.321	.451	Batting #4	.270	37	10	1	0	0	5	2	5	.293	.297
First Pitch	.150	20	3	1	0	2	4	0	0	.150	.500	Batting #7	.200	40	8	2	0	1	3	1	14	.220	.325
Ahead in Count	.393	28	11	1	1	0	3	5	0	.485	.500	Other	.222	54	12	1	1	3	8	6	11	.300	.444
Behind in Count	.169	59	10	1	0	1	1	0	28	.169	.237	Pre-All Star	.000	0	0	0	0	0	0	0	0	.000	.000
Two Strikes	.148	61	9	1	0	1	4	4	30	.197	.213	Post-All Star	.229	131	30	4	1	4	16	9	30	.275	.366

Curt Leskanic — Rockies
Age 30 – Pitches Right (groundball pitcher)

	ERA	W	L	Sv	G	GS	IP	BB	SO	Avg	H	2B	3B	HR	RBI	OBP	SLG	GF	IR	IRS	Hld	SvOp	SB	CS	GB	FB	G/F
1997 Season	5.55	4	0	2	55	0	58.1	24	53	.271	59	11	3	8	42	.337	.459	23	25	11	6	4	2	3	81	61	1.33
Career (1993-1997)	5.00	19	14	18	227	11	309.1	132	283	.262	310	55	10	36	180	.335	.417	85	104	33	34	30	16	13	443	291	1.52

1997 Season

	ERA	W	L	Sv	G	GS	IP	H	HR	BB	SO		Avg	AB	H	2B	3B	HR	RBI	BB	SO	OBP	SLG
Home	5.70	3	0	2	31	0	30.0	33	4	17	26	vs. Left	.312	93	29	7	1	4	20	14	21	.394	.538
Away	5.40	1	0	0	24	0	28.1	26	4	7	27	vs. Right	.240	125	30	4	2	4	22	10	32	.292	.400
Day	5.61	4	0	0	26	0	25.2	27	3	9	22	Inning 1-6	.184	38	7	1	0	2	9	4	10	.256	.368
Night	5.51	0	0	2	29	0	32.2	32	5	15	31	Inning 7+	.289	180	52	10	3	6	33	20	43	.355	.478
Grass	4.96	4	0	2	49	0	49.0	49	4	23	43	None on	.207	116	24	3	1	2	2	13	36	.287	.302
Turf	8.68	0	0	0	6	0	9.1	10	4	1	10	Runners on	.343	102	35	8	2	6	40	11	17	.393	.637
March/April	13.50	0	0	0	2	0	2.2	6	1		2	Scoring Posn	.333	63	21	4	0	3	30	6	12	.370	.540
May	0.00	0	0	0	3	0	2.2	2	0	0	1	Close & Late	.234	64	15	3	1	3	13	8	16	.319	.453
June	3.38	1	0	1	13	0	13.1	13	2	6	11	None on/out	.184	49	9	1	1	1	1	3	16	.231	.306
July	8.53	1	0	0	12	0	12.2	13	2	8	12	vs. 1st Batr (relief)	.280	50	14	2	2	1	6	5	15	.345	.460
August	8.10	1	0	0	12	0	16.2	20	3	3	13	1st Inning Pitched	.275	182	50	8	3	8	38	23	48	.351	.484
Sept/Oct	0.00	1	0	1	13	0	10.1	7	0	4	12	First 15 Pitches	.282	149	42	5	3	5	24	16	37	.347	.456
Starter	0.00	0	0	0	0	0	0.0	0	0	0	0	Pitch 16-30	.268	56	15	5	0	3	17	8	14	.348	.518
Reliever	5.55	4	0	2	55	0	58.1	59	8	24	53	Pitch 31-45	.000	9	0	0	0	0	0	0	1	.000	.000
0 Days rest (Relief)	7.59	3	0	0	14	0	10.2	13	2	4	11	Pitch 46+	.500	4	2	1	0	0	0	0	1	.500	.750
1 or 2 Days rest	4.75	1	0	2	30	0	36.0	31	5	16	33	First Pitch	.300	30	9	1	0	2	10	0	0	.290	.533
3+ Days rest	6.17	0	0	0	11	0	11.2	15	1	4	9	Ahead in Count	.216	88	19	5	1	1	10	0	41	.209	.330
vs. AL	8.44	1	0	0	6	0	5.1	6	0	4	3	Behind in Count	.436	55	24	3	0	3	14	12	0	.537	.655
vs. NL	5.26	3	0	2	49	0	53.0	53	8	20	50	Two Strikes	.144	97	14	4	1	3	13	12	53	.234	.299
Pre-All Star	5.95	1	0	1	19	0	19.2	22	3	11	16	Pre-All Star	.301	73	22	5	1	3	14	11	16	.384	.521
Post-All Star	5.35	3	0	1	36	0	38.2	37	5	13	37	Post-All Star	.255	145	37	6	2	5	28	13	37	.313	.428

Career (1993-1997)

	ERA	W	L	Sv	G	GS	IP	H	HR	BB	SO		Avg	AB	H	2B	3B	HR	RBI	BB	SO	OBP	SLG
Home	4.83	12	3	11	116	5	156.2	165	17	61	129	vs. Left	.266	530	141	28	5	20	91	72	123	.351	.451
Away	5.19	7	11	7	111	6	152.2	145	19	71	154	vs. Right	.259	652	169	27	5	16	89	60	160	.321	.390
Day	5.37	9	4	8	93	4	114.0	112	14	56	101	Inning 1-6	.230	383	88	12	2	9	54	42	78	.306	.342
Night	4.79	10	10	10	134	7	195.1	198	22	76	182	Inning 7+	.278	799	222	43	8	27	126	90	205	.349	.453
Grass	4.99	18	10	16	188	9	252.1	263	29	108	216	None on	.243	642	156	25	4	14	14	60	170	.311	.360
Turf	5.05	1	4	2	39	2	57.0	47	7	24	67	Runners on	.285	540	154	30	6	22	166	72	113	.363	.485
March/April	5.19	3	1	6	20	0	26.0	30	3	11	24	Scoring Posn	.271	325	88	17	2	11	131	43	67	.344	.437
May	6.25	2	3	0	28	0	31.2	39	3	20	38	Close & Late	.243	391	95	21	3	12	62	47	107	.321	.404
June	3.72	2	1	4	30	2	48.1	43	7	14	43	None on/out	.250	280	70	10	2	7	7	23	81	.309	.375
July	5.63	7	3	1	55	6	86.1	83	11	41	79	vs. 1st Batr (relief)	.256	195	50	7	2	3	12	21	50	.329	.359
August	5.98	3	3	2	50	1	64.2	64	9	24	64	1st Inning Pitched	.250	748	187	33	7	21	122	89	195	.327	.397
Sept/Oct	3.10	2	3	5	44	2	52.1	51	3	22	45	First 15 Pitches	.252	622	157	27	3	15	76	63	153	.320	.378
Starter	4.87	2	5	0	11	11	61.0	61	6	25	35	Pitch 16-30	.260	319	83	17	5	11	63	46	90	.350	.448
Reliever	5.04	17	9	18	216	0	248.1	249	30	107	248	Pitch 31-45	.324	102	33	6	2	6	25	10	20	.381	.588
0 Days rest (Relief)	6.07	7	2	5	52	0	43.0	48	5	20	56	Pitch 46+	.266	139	37	5	0	4	16	13	20	.333	.388
1 or 2 Days rest	4.35	8	4	12	128	0	161.1	143	17	66	155	First Pitch	.333	159	53	13	1	8	35	2	0	.348	.579
3+ Days rest	6.55	2	3	1	36	0	44.0	58	8	18	37	Ahead in Count	.217	543	118	23	4	10	66	0	220	.214	.330
vs. AL	8.44	1	0	0	6	0	5.1	6	0	4	3	Behind in Count	.363	234	85	12	2	12	51	72	0	.510	.585
vs. NL	4.94	18	14	18	221	11	304.0	304	36	128	280	Two Strikes	.176	580	102	19	3	11	64	58	283	.249	.276
Pre-All Star	4.57	10	5	11	91	5	136.0	139	15	57	125	Pre-All Star	.270	514	139	26	3	15	80	57	125	.341	.420
Post-All Star	5.35	9	9	7	136	6	173.1	165	21	100	158	Post-All Star	.256	668	171	29	7	21	100	75	158	.331	.415

Pitcher vs. Batter (career)

Pitches Best Vs.	Avg	AB	H	2B	3B	HR	RBI	BB	SO	OBP	SLG	Pitches Worst Vs.	Avg	AB	H	2B	3B	HR	RBI	BB	SO	OBP	SLG
Rick Wilkins	.000	11	0	0	0	0	0	0	7	.000	.000	Fred McGriff	.545	11	6	0	0	1	2	3	2	.643	.818
Terry Pendleton	.000	11	0	0	0	0	0	1	2	4	.154	.000	Steve Finley	.375	16	6	0	2	0	2	0	3	.375	.625
Brian McRae	.091	11	1	0	0	0	0	0		.091	.091	Brad Ausmus	.375	8	3	0	0	1	3	3	3	.545	.750
Ryne Sandberg	.182	11	2	0	0	0	0	2	2	.308	.182	Jeff Conine	.357	14	5	1	0	0	2	2	4	.438	.429
Rey Sanchez	.231	13	3	0	0	0	0	0	2	.231	.231	Raul Mondesi	.353	17	6	1	1	0	1	1	4	.389	.529

Al Levine — White Sox
Age 30 – Pitches Right (groundball pitcher)

	ERA	W	L	Sv	G	GS	IP	BB	SO	Avg	H	2B	3B	HR	RBI	OBP	SLG	GF	IR	IRS	Hld	SvOp	SB	CS	GB	FB	G/F
1997 Season	6.91	2	2	0	25	0	27.1	16	22	.313	35	7	0	4	15	.402	.482	6	11	2	3	1	3	0	42	23	1.83
Career (1996-1997)	6.31	2	3	0	41	0	45.2	23	34	.303	57	11	0	5	24	.382	.441	11	20	3	3	2	6	0	80	37	2.16

1997 Season

	ERA	W	L	Sv	G	GS	IP	H	HR	BB	SO		Avg	AB	H	2B	3B	HR	RBI	BB	SO	OBP	SLG
Home	5.54	2	1	0	12	0	13.0	18	2	6	18	vs. Left	.348	46	16	5	0	2	9	8	9	.439	.587
Away	8.16	0	1	0	13	0	14.1	17	2	10	4	vs. Right	.288	66	19	2	0	2	6	8	13	.373	.409
Starter	0.00	0	0	0	0	0	0.0	0	0	0	0	Scoring Posn	.257	35	9	1	0	1	10	5	9	.349	.371
Reliever	6.91	2	2	0	25	0	27.1	35	4	16	22	Close & Late	.260	50	13	2	0	0	3	8	11	.356	.300
0 Days rest (Relief)	1.59	2	0	0	4	0	5.2	5	0	4	4	None on/out	.286	28	8	1	0	1	1	5	6	.412	.429
1 or 2 Days rest	12.54	0	2	0	12	0	9.1	18	4	7	7	First Pitch	.600	10	6	1	0	1	3	1	0	.636	1.000
3+ Days rest	5.11	0	0	0	9	0	12.1	12	0	5	11	Ahead in Count	.256	43	11	2	0	2	0		17	.273	.302
Pre-All Star	6.87	2	2	0	18	0	18.1	22	2	11	16	Behind in Count	.375	32	12	4	0	2	7	11	0	.523	.688
Post-All Star	7.00	0	0	0	7	0	9.0	13	2	5	6	Two Strikes	.260	50	13	0	0	1	4		22	.327	.340

Jesse Levis — Brewers
Age 30 – Bats Left (groundball hitter)

	Avg	G	AB	R	H	2B	3B	HR	RBI	BB	SO	HBP	GDP	SB	CS	OBP	SLG	IBB	SH	SF	#Pit	#P/PA	GB	FB	G/F
1997 Season	.285	99	200	19	57	7	0	1	19	24	17	1	4	1	0	.361	.335	0	5	2	827	3.56	96	49	1.96
Last Five Years	.252	247	515	54	130	17	1	2	47	65	42	3	12	1	0	.337	.301	0	8	5	2205	3.70	252	124	2.03

1997 Season

	Avg	AB	H	2B	3B	HR	RBI	BB	SO	OBP	SLG		Avg	AB	H	2B	3B	HR	RBI	BB	SO	OBP	SLG
vs. Left	.222	18	4	1	0	0	1	3	3	.333	.278	Scoring Posn	.349	43	15	3	0	0	17	6	3	.412	.419
vs. Right	.291	182	53	6	0	1	18	21	14	.364	.341	Close & Late	.206	63	13	2	0	0	4	8	9	.296	.238
Home	.313	80	25	3	0	1	7	12	5	.409	.388	None on/out	.300	50	15	2	0	0	0	7	3	.386	.340
Away	.267	120	32	4	0	0	12	12	12	.328	.300	Batting #8	.273	44	12	1	0	0	5	3	3	.313	.295
First Pitch	.273	22	6	0	0	0	1	0	0	.273	.273	Batting #9	.285	144	41	6	0	1	14	18	13	.366	.347
Ahead in Count	.281	57	16	3	0	0	7	15	0	.425	.333	Other	.333	12	4	0	0	0	0	3	1	.467	.333
Behind in Count	.314	86	27	3	0	1	9	0	16	.322	.384	Pre-All Star	.263	95	25	1	0	1	10	11	11	.336	.305
Two Strikes	.292	72	21	2	0	0	5	9	17	.378	.319	Post-All Star	.305	105	32	6	0	0	9	13	6	.383	.362

Last Five Years

	Avg	AB	H	2B	3B	HR	RBI	BB	SO	OBP	SLG		Avg	AB	H	2B	3B	HR	RBI	BB	SO	OBP	SLG
vs. Left	.246	69	17	1	0	0	9	9	9	.333	.261	First Pitch	.274	62	17	2	0	1	7	0	0	.270	.355
vs. Right	.253	446	113	16	1	2	38	56	33	.337	.307	Ahead in Count	.279	136	38	6	1	0	16	44	0	.454	.338
Groundball	.255	110	28	1	0	0	7	18	10	.357	.264	Behind in Count	.229	218	50	6	0	1	15	0	38	.235	.271
Flyball	.220	82	18	3	0	1	10	9	8	.299	.293	Two Strikes	.217	207	45	5	0	0	13	21	42	.291	.242
Home	.258	260	67	8	1	1	23	32	19	.341	.308	Batting #8	.259	54	14	2	0	0	5	4	5	.305	.296
Away	.247	255	63	9	0	1	24	33	23	.332	.294	Batting #9	.242	426	103	14	1	2	37	54	36	.328	.293
Day	.262	210	55	11	0	0	20	28	15	.347	.314	Other	.371	35	13	1	0	0	5	7	1	.477	.400
Night	.246	305	75	6	1	2	27	37	27	.329	.292	March/April	.298	47	14	0	0	1	9	6	3	.382	.362
Grass	.254	452	115	16	1	2	47	59	37	.341	.308	May	.186	70	13	1	0	0	5	4	9	.227	.200
Turf	.238	63	15	1	0	0	0	6	5	.304	.254	June	.216	97	21	2	1	0	8	7	9	.267	.258
Pre-All Star	.228	237	54	3	1	1	23	19	24	.285	.262	July	.287	101	29	4	0	0	12	15	7	.379	.327
Post-All Star	.273	278	76	14	0	1	24	46	18	.378	.335	August	.265	113	30	5	0	0	5	16	8	.357	.310
Scoring Posn	.254	138	35	4	1	0	43	19	10	.333	.297	Sept/Oct	.264	87	23	5	0	1	8	17	6	.389	.356
Close & Late	.229	140	32	4	0	1	12	14	19	.297	.279	vs. AL	.256	496	127	16	1	2	46	64	40	.342	.304
None on/out	.283	113	32	6	0	1	1	17	9	.386	.363	vs. NL	.158	19	3	1	0	0	1	1	2	.200	.211

Batter vs. Pitcher (career)

Hits Best Against	Avg	AB	H	2B	3B	HR	RBI	BB	SO	OBP	SLG	Hits Worst Against	Avg	AB	H	2B	3B	HR	RBI	BB	SO	OBP	SLG
Scott Erickson	.308	13	4	1	0	0	0	0	1	.308	.385	Jack McDowell	.091	11	1	0	0	0	0	1	1	.167	.091
												Roger Clemens	.235	17	4	0	0	0	1	2	2	.300	.235

Darren Lewis — Dodgers
Age 30 – Bats Right (groundball hitter)

	Avg	G	AB	R	H	2B	3B	HR	RBI	BB	SO	HBP	GDP	SB	CS	OBP	SLG	IBB	SH	SF	#Pit	#P/PA	GB	FB	G/F
1997 Season	.266	107	154	22	41	4	1	1	15	17	31	0	3	14	6	.339	.325	0	7	0	663	3.72	69	23	3.00
Last Five Years	.250	630	1936	297	484	61	22	12	169	179	218	22	31	143	57	.319	.323	1	50	8	7783	3.55	901	423	2.13

1997 Season

	Avg	AB	H	2B	3B	HR	RBI	BB	SO	OBP	SLG		Avg	AB	H	2B	3B	HR	RBI	BB	SO	OBP	SLG
vs. Left	.266	64	17	1	1	0	4	5	9	.319	.313	Scoring Posn	.303	33	10	2	0	1	14	5	5	.395	.455
vs. Right	.267	90	24	3	0	1	11	12	22	.353	.333	Close & Late	.222	27	6	1	1	0	2	0	8	.222	.333
Home	.263	80	21	3	1	0	7	11	16	.352	.325	None on/out	.243	37	9	0	0	0	3	10		.300	.243
Away	.270	74	20	1	0	1	8	6	15	.325	.324	Batting #7	.264	53	14	2	0	1	6	6	10	.339	.358
First Pitch	.273	22	6	0	0	1	3	0	0	.273	.409	Batting #8	.278	36	10	1	1	0	3	4	7	.350	.361
Ahead in Count	.313	32	10	0	1	0	3	6	0	.421	.375	Other	.262	65	17	1	0	0	6	7	14	.333	.277
Behind in Count	.211	71	15	2	0	0	6	0	26	.211	.239	Pre-All Star	.196	56	11	1	0	0	4	9	13	.308	.214
Two Strikes	.162	68	11	2	0	0	3	11	31	.211	.191	Post-All Star	.306	98	30	3	1	1	11	8	18	.358	.388

Last Five Years

	Avg	AB	H	2B	3B	HR	RBI	BB	SO	OBP	SLG		Avg	AB	H	2B	3B	HR	RBI	BB	SO	OBP	SLG
vs. Left	.235	567	133	18	6	2	46	49	52	.296	.298	First Pitch	.289	305	88	11	2	1	36	1	0	.292	.348
vs. Right	.256	1369	351	43	16	10	123	130	166	.329	.333	Ahead in Count	.277	408	113	17	6	3	38	91	0	.416	.370
Groundball	.255	548	140	11	8	6	56	44	64	.318	.338	Behind in Count	.223	835	186	19	10	6	62	0	183	.233	.291
Flyball	.246	301	74	11	4	0	30	31	33	.314	.309	Two Strikes	.206	767	158	17	9	6	58	87	218	.296	.275
Home	.244	950	232	34	6	7	87	91	104	.315	.315	Batting #1	.254	1242	316	36	17	6	84	103	118	.319	.325

Last Five Years

	Avg	AB	H	2B	3B	HR	RBI	BB	SO	OBP	SLG
Away	.256	986	252	27	16	5	82	88	114	.324	.331
Day	.246	856	211	27	10	9	80	89	94	.325	.333
Night	.253	1080	273	34	12	3	89	90	124	.315	.315
Grass	.251	1455	365	52	16	11	140	127	162	.317	.331
Turf	.247	481	119	9	6	1	29	52	56	.326	.297
Pre-All Star	.256	1200	307	39	15	8	102	123	138	.331	.333
Post-All Star	.240	736	177	22	7	4	67	56	80	.300	.306
Scoring Posn	.288	416	120	14	4	6	155	39	50	.355	.385
Close & Late	.246	289	71	6	3	1	27	26	41	.323	.298
None on/out	.240	647	155	18	9	4	4	65	80	.315	.314

	Avg	AB	H	2B	3B	HR	RBI	BB	SO	OBP	SLG
Batting #2	.262	317	83	13	3	4	43	34	46	.339	.360
Other	.225	377	85	12	2	2	42	42	54	.304	.284
March/April	.241	241	58	9	4	1	13	37	31	.345	.324
May	.245	441	108	15	7	4	45	38	49	.314	.338
June	.265	388	103	13	3	0	28	41	44	.339	.314
July	.244	397	97	13	4	5	33	27	35	.300	.335
August	.284	215	61	4	2	1	23	15	28	.339	.335
Sept/Oct	.224	254	57	7	2	1	27	21	31	.285	.280
vs. AL	.230	434	100	14	2	4	60	56	59	.319	.300
vs. NL	.256	1502	384	47	20	8	109	123	159	.319	.330

Batter vs. Pitcher (career)

Hits Best Against	Avg	AB	H	2B	3B	HR	RBI	BB	SO	OBP	SLG
Pat Rapp	.538	13	7	0	1	0	1	3	2	.625	.692
Shawn Boskie	.500	12	6	0	0	1	3	0	1	.500	.750
Tim Wakefield	.500	10	5	2	0	0	1	1	1	.545	.700
Bret Saberhagen	.400	15	6	1	0	1	1	0	2	.400	.667
Greg Swindell	.370	27	10	3	1	1	8	2	0	.414	.667

Hits Worst Against	Avg	AB	H	2B	3B	HR	RBI	BB	SO	OBP	SLG
Donovan Osborne	.067	15	1	0	1	0	0	1	2	.125	.200
Darryl Kile	.067	15	1	0	0	0	0	2	4	.176	.067
Orel Hershiser	.069	29	2	0	0	0	2	1	5	.100	.069
Ken Hill	.105	19	2	0	0	0	1	0	0	.105	.105
Rheal Cormier	.111	18	2	0	0	0	0	1	0	.158	.111

Mark Lewis — Giants

Age 28 – Bats Right (flyball hitter)

	Avg	G	AB	R	H	2B	3B	HR	RBI	BB	SO	HBP	GDP	SB	CS	OBP	SLG	IBB	SH	SF	#Pit	#P/PA	GB	FB	G/F
1997 Season	.267	118	341	50	91	14	6	10	42	23	62	4	8	3	2	.318	.431	2	1	3	1344	3.61	109	110	0.99
Last Five Years	.274	378	1182	156	324	64	10	26	140	88	224	9	24	13	6	.327	.411	4	7	8	4909	3.79	390	338	1.15

1997 Season

	Avg	AB	H	2B	3B	HR	RBI	BB	SO	OBP	SLG
vs. Left	.290	124	36	7	4	1	15	9	22	.343	.435
vs. Right	.253	217	55	7	2	9	27	14	40	.304	.429
Groundball	.324	74	24	0	2	15	5	9		.370	.459
Flyball	.513	39	20	3	2	3	9	3	3	.545	.923
Home	.237	152	36	4	4	4	21	13	26	.308	.395
Away	.291	189	55	10	2	6	21	10	36	.327	.460
Day	.279	136	38	7	0	4	14	14	27	.359	.419
Night	.259	205	53	7	6	6	28	9	35	.289	.439
Grass	.283	279	79	11	5	8	35	20	47	.339	.444
Turf	.194	62	12	3	1	2	7	3	15	.224	.371
Pre-All Star	.284	190	54	8	3	6	23	15	34	.341	.453
Post-All Star	.245	151	37	6	3	4	19	8	28	.288	.404
Scoring Posn	.273	88	24	4	1	2	32	8	14	.343	.409
Close & Late	.370	54	20	5	1	2	11	5	11	.426	.611
None on/out	.263	76	20	4	1	4	4	3	12	.291	.500

	Avg	AB	H	2B	3B	HR	RBI	BB	SO	OBP	SLG
First Pitch	.411	56	23	1	2	3	6	2	0	.431	.661
Ahead in Count	.321	81	26	5	2	3	15	9	0	.394	.543
Behind in Count	.176	148	26	6	0	2	13	0	56	.174	.257
Two Strikes	.209	158	33	6	0	3	16	12	62	.269	.304
Batting #6	.303	89	27	4	2	5	20	10	16	.374	.562
Batting #7	.231	134	31	3	2	2	9	7	24	.278	.328
Other	.280	118	33	7	2	3	13	6	22	.320	.449
March/April	.270	37	10	1	1	2	5	2	5	.308	.514
May	.274	73	20	3	0	2	7	6	15	.346	.397
June	.295	61	18	4	0	2	10	4	8	.333	.459
July	.256	78	20	3	2	2	8	5	13	.310	.423
August	.196	56	11	1	2	2	7	2	16	.220	.393
Sept/Oct	.333	36	12	2	1	0	5	4	5	.405	.444
vs. AL	.235	34	8	0	1	1	6	4	7	.308	.382
vs. NL	.270	307	83	14	5	9	36	19	55	.319	.436

1997 By Position

Position	Avg	AB	H	2B	3B	HR	RBI	BB	SO	OBP	SLG	G	GS	Innings	PO	A	E	DP	Fld Pct	Rng Fctr	In Zone	Outs	Zone Rtg	MLB Zone
As Pinch Hitter	.286	21	6	2	0	0	2	3	2	.375	.381	24	0	---	---	---	---	---	---	---	---	---	---	---
As 2b	.314	86	27	3	1	6	15	3	18	.337	.581	29	19	192.2	40	54	6	14	.940	4.39	65	58	.892	.902
As 3b	.245	229	56	9	4	4	24	17	41	.304	.371	69	64	530.0	33	103	8	10	.944	2.31	145	116	.800	.801

Last Five Years

	Avg	AB	H	2B	3B	HR	RBI	BB	SO	OBP	SLG
vs. Left	.315	425	134	26	7	7	55	35	71	.366	.459
vs. Right	.251	757	190	38	3	19	85	53	153	.305	.384
Groundball	.280	254	71	15	0	6	36	32	43	.366	.409
Flyball	.320	175	56	10	4	5	20	14	36	.372	.509
Home	.258	598	154	30	5	15	77	40	109	.311	.400
Away	.291	584	170	34	5	11	63	48	115	.344	.423
Day	.280	432	121	28	0	12	62	36	88	.340	.428
Night	.271	750	203	36	10	14	78	52	136	.320	.401
Grass	.268	889	238	45	8	21	105	64	155	.321	.407
Turf	.294	293	86	19	2	5	35	24	69	.347	.423
Pre-All Star	.297	671	199	35	7	17	78	44	117	.341	.446
Post-All Star	.245	511	125	29	3	9	62	44	107	.309	.366
Scoring Posn	.294	289	85	18	2	5	110	35	52	.367	.422
Close & Late	.284	183	52	12	2	4	22	15	43	.337	.437
None on/out	.290	241	70	15	2	6	6	16	41	.342	.444

	Avg	AB	H	2B	3B	HR	RBI	BB	SO	OBP	SLG
First Pitch	.381	147	56	7	4	6	23	4	0	.405	.605
Ahead in Count	.350	286	100	21	4	9	45	42	0	.430	.545
Behind in Count	.202	506	102	25	0	8	42	0	182	.202	.298
Two Strikes	.193	549	106	22	0	6	46	42	224	.253	.266
Batting #2	.249	346	86	20	3	4	37	24	65	.317	.358
Batting #7	.270	396	107	18	2	9	42	23	75	.317	.394
Other	.298	440	131	26	5	13	61	41	84	.358	.468
March/April	.305	200	61	11	2	8	28	8	35	.333	.500
May	.259	220	57	9	2	6	20	13	45	.306	.400
June	.332	202	67	12	1	3	26	15	28	.374	.446
July	.243	185	45	9	2	4	17	22	40	.333	.378
August	.227	176	40	13	2	3	26	19	41	.303	.375
Sept/Oct	.271	199	54	10	1	2	23	11	35	.312	.362
vs. AL	.260	704	183	37	4	14	74	48	136	.310	.384
vs. NL	.295	478	141	27	6	12	66	40	88	.352	.452

Batter vs. Pitcher (career)

Hits Best Against	Avg	AB	H	2B	3B	HR	RBI	BB	SO	OBP	SLG
Sterling Hitchcock	.500	12	6	1	0	0	1	1	2	.538	.583
Jeff Fassero	.500	10	5	0	0	0	3	2	0	.583	.500
Roger Pavlik	.417	12	5	1	1	1	3	2	2	.467	.917
Terry Mulholland	.364	11	4	1	0	1		0	2	.364	.455
Scott Erickson	.318	22	7	4	0	0	2	2	1	.375	.500

Hits Worst Against	Avg	AB	H	2B	3B	HR	RBI	BB	SO	OBP	SLG
Jack McDowell	.083	12	1	0	0	0	1	0	2	.083	.083
Jaime Navarro	.150	20	3	1	0	0	0		1	.150	.200
Roger Clemens	.154	13	2	0	0	0	0		6	.154	.154
Wilson Alvarez	.158	19	3	0	0	0	1	1	2	.200	.158
Jimmy Key	.188	16	3	0	0	0	0		2	.188	.188

Richie Lewis — Reds

Age 32 – Pitches Right

	ERA	W	L	Sv	G	GS	IP	BB	SO	Avg	H	2B	3B	HR	RBI	OBP	SLG	GF	IR	IRS	Hld	SvOp	SB	CS	GB	FB	G/F
1997 Season	8.88	2	0	0	18	0	24.1	18	16	.292	28	3	1	10	28	.405	.656	5	18	9	0	0	2	2	35	32	1.09
Last Five Years	4.56	13	14	2	213	1	282.0	179	236	.251	266	47	14	42	194	.358	.440	53	209	80	13	8	29	11	341	319	1.07

1997 Season

	ERA	W	L	Sv	G	GS	IP	H	HR	BB	SO		Avg	AB	H	2B	3B	HR	RBI	BB	SO	OBP	SLG
Home	8.31	2	0	0	10	0	13.0	14	3	9	8	vs. Left	.359	39	14	0	1	5	18	4	4	.419	.795
Away	9.53	0	0	0	8	0	11.1	14	7	9	8	vs. Right	.246	57	14	3	0	5	10	14	12	.397	.561

Last Five Years

	ERA	W	L	Sv	G	GS	IP	H	HR	BB	SO		Avg	AB	H	2B	3B	HR	RBI	BB	SO	OBP	SLG
Home	4.86	10	7	1	115	1	159.1	144	22	104	129	vs. Left	.264	459	121	20	6	17	91	86	88	.379	.444
Away	4.18	3	7	1	98	0	122.2	122	20	75	107	vs. Right	.241	602	145	27	8	25	103	93	148	.342	.437
Day	4.23	4	5	2	60	0	72.1	70	9	48	63	Inning 1-6	.244	406	99	18	4	12	75	67	77	.345	.394
Night	4.68	9	9	0	153	1	209.2	196	33	131	173	Inning 7+	.255	655	167	29	10	30	119	114	159	.367	.467
Grass	5.00	12	12	1	171	1	223.0	216	37	143	179	None on	.247	530	131	21	7	23	23	72	118	.342	.443
Turf	2.90	1	2	1	42	0	59.0	50	5	36	57	Runners on	.254	531	135	26	7	19	171	107	118	.374	.437
March/April	4.80	3	2	1	45	0	54.1	47	9	34	43	Scoring Posn	.216	371	80	14	6	12	151	89	93	.358	.383
May	4.60	4	6	0	39	0	58.2	51	10	39	57	Close & Late	.247	287	71	13	4	9	52	65	66	.388	.415
June	3.16	2	1	1	30	0	42.2	39	2	28	40	None on/out	.239	230	55	7	3	11	11	29	43	.332	.439
July	6.64	0	2	0	35	0	42.0	47	9	32	30	vs. 1st Batr (relief)	.237	177	42	6	3	7	35	30	40	.344	.424
August	4.73	4	1	0	29	1	45.2	48	9	23	33	1st Inning Pitched	.240	658	158	26	9	23	148	106	140	.345	.412
Sept/Oct	3.26	0	2	0	35	0	38.2	34	3	23	33	First 15 Pitches	.255	553	141	24	9	21	119	79	107	.346	.445
Starter	2.70	0	0	0	1	1	6.2	6	1	2	5	Pitch 16-30	.250	340	85	15	3	13	50	73	92	.384	.426
Reliever	4.61	13	14	2	212	0	275.1	260	41	177	231	Pitch 31-45	.248	121	30	5	1	6	22	21	27	.359	.455
0 Days rest (Relief)	4.93	4	1	1	42	0	45.2	37	5	42	33	Pitch 46+	.213	47	10	3	1	2	3	6	10	.302	.447
1 or 2 Days rest	4.32	4	11	1	107	0	141.2	134	22	83	125	First Pitch	.307	127	39	4	0	9	30	18	0	.379	.551
3+ Days rest	4.91	5	2	0	63	0	88.0	89	14	52	73	Ahead in Count	.200	470	94	23	7	11	59	0	198	.208	.349
vs. AL	5.12	6	6	2	86	0	109.0	102	16	80	90	Behind in Count	.324	281	91	12	5	15	65	90	0	.485	.562
vs. NL	4.21	7	8	0	127	1	173.0	164	26	99	146	Two Strikes	.165	510	84	19	4	11	51	70	236	.272	.282
Pre-All Star	4.47	9	9	2	121	0	163.0	146	22	106	144	Pre-All Star	.241	605	146	21	5	22	105	106	144	.354	.402
Post-All Star	4.69	4	5	0	92	1	119.0	120	20	73	92	Post-All Star	.263	456	120	26	9	20	89	73	92	.364	.491

Pitcher vs. Batter (career)

Pitches Best Vs.	Avg	AB	H	2B	3B	HR	RBI	BB	SO	OBP	SLG	Pitches Worst Vs.	Avg	AB	H	2B	3B	HR	RBI	BB	SO	OBP	SLG
Todd Zeile	.100	10	1	0	0	0	0	1	4	.182	.100	Wil Cordero	.333	9	3	0	0	0	0	2	1	.455	.333
Roberto Kelly	.200	10	2	1	0	0	4	1	2	.250	.300												

Jim Leyritz — Rangers

Age 34 – Bats Right

	Avg	G	AB	R	H	2B	3B	HR	RBI	BB	SO	HBP	GDP	SB	CS	OBP	SLG	IBB	SH	SF	#Pit	#P/PA	GB	FB	G/F
1997 Season	.277	121	379	58	105	11	0	11	64	60	78	6	13	2	1	.379	.393	2	4	6	1763	3.87	161	86	1.87
Last Five Years	.277	456	1416	208	392	59	0	56	252	199	339	37	49	5	2	.377	.437	11	6	14	6656	3.98	505	335	1.51

1997 Season

	Avg	AB	H	2B	3B	HR	RBI	BB	SO	OBP	SLG		Avg	AB	H	2B	3B	HR	RBI	BB	SO	OBP	SLG
vs. Left	.297	118	35	1	0	5	23	23	21	.411	.432	First Pitch	.365	52	19	2	0	3	11	2	0	.379	.577
vs. Right	.268	261	70	10	0	6	41	37	57	.364	.375	Ahead in Count	.338	80	27	2	0	4	16	24	0	.495	.513
Groundball	.313	80	25	2	0	3	12	9	20	.385	.450	Behind in Count	.201	169	34	5	0	2	18	0	65	.217	.266
Flyball	.276	58	16	1	0	1	8	11	10	.386	.345	Two Strikes	.173	173	30	2	0	3	23	34	78	.319	.237
Home	.278	180	50	3	0	3	23	26	36	.379	.344	Batting #4	.244	119	29	4	0	3	21	17	28	.350	.353
Away	.276	199	55	8	0	8	41	34	42	.379	.437	Batting #6	.322	87	28	4	0	3	19	18	13	.430	.471
Day	.205	88	18	2	0	1	11	14	19	.314	.261	Other	.277	173	48	3	0	5	24	25	37	.373	.382
Night	.299	291	87	9	0	10	53	46	59	.399	.433	March/April	.348	69	24	4	0	4	19	7	15	.410	.580
Grass	.288	340	98	9	0	9	57	56	73	.393	.394	May	.289	83	24	3	0	3	10	7	18	.341	.398
Turf	.179	39	7	2	0	2	7	4	5	.250	.385	June	.247	73	18	3	0	3	13	13	9	.360	.411
Pre-All Star	.281	242	68	7	0	10	42	28	47	.357	.434	July	.217	69	15	0	0	1	8	10	14	.321	.261
Post-All Star	.270	137	37	4	0	1	22	32	31	.414	.321	August	.292	65	19	4	0	0	11	22	15	.484	.354
Scoring Posn	.304	112	34	2	0	3	54	16	21	.396	.402	Sept/Oct	.250	20	5	0	0	0	3	1	7	.286	.250
Close & Late	.348	66	23	5	0	0	10	7	11	.429	.424	vs. AL	.284	345	98	10	0	11	63	51	69	.378	.409
None on/out	.310	84	26	5	0	3	3	14	16	.414	.476	vs. NL	.206	34	7	1	0	0	1	9	9	.386	.235

1997 By Position

Position	Avg	AB	H	2B	3B	HR	RBI	BB	SO	OBP	SLG	G	GS	Innings	PO	A	E	DP	Fld Pct	Rng Fctr	In Zone Outs	Zone Rtg	MLB Zone
As DH	.159	69	11	0	0	1	9	15	20	.318	.203	22	20	---	---	---	---	---	---	---	---	---	---
As Pinch Hitter	.444	9	4	0	0	0	2	2	3	.538	.444	13	0	---	---	---	---	---	---	---	---	---	---
As c	.324	241	78	9	0	9	45	34	45	.407	.473	69	65	576.2	417	44	1	6	.998	---	---	---	---
As 1b	.200	60	12	2	0	1	9	10	10	.319	.283	24	17	151.0	138	7	2	21	.986	---	37	29	.784	.874

Last Five Years

	Avg	AB	H	2B	3B	HR	RBI	BB	SO	OBP	SLG		Avg	AB	H	2B	3B	HR	RBI	BB	SO	OBP	SLG
vs. Left	.281	587	165	22	0	22	87	106	139	.397	.431	First Pitch	.395	147	58	8	0	8	41	9	0	.424	.612
vs. Right	.274	829	227	37	0	34	165	93	200	.362	.441	Ahead in Count	.400	315	126	24	0	20	79	101	0	.548	.667
Groundball	.258	295	76	10	0	9	50	35	79	.346	.383	Behind in Count	.182	649	118	15	0	13	71	0	272	.208	.265
Flyball	.268	250	67	10	0	7	36	34	65	.369	.392	Two Strikes	.174	713	124	15	0	16	83	89	339	.279	.262
Home	.289	678	196	26	0	19	108	90	154	.384	.412	Batting #4	.291	265	77	13	0	11	59	36	66	.397	.464
Away	.266	738	196	33	0	37	144	109	185	.370	.461	Batting #6	.263	312	82	13	0	12	53	49	72	.368	.420
Day	.289	485	140	23	0	21	88	63	109	.385	.466	Other	.278	839	233	33	0	33	140	111	201	.374	.435
Night	.271	931	252	36	0	35	164	136	230	.373	.422	March/April	.359	195	70	10	0	17	52	22	42	.425	.672
Grass	.277	1229	340	50	0	45	216	176	293	.379	.427	May	.279	362	101	16	0	13	66	40	88	.368	.431

Last Five Years

	Avg	AB	H	2B	3B	HR	RBI	BB	SO	OBP	SLG		Avg	AB	H	2B	3B	HR	RBI	BB	SO	OBP	SLG
Turf	.278	187	52	9	0	11	36	23	46	.363	.503	June	.252	294	74	12	0	10	42	56	72	.381	.395
Pre-All Star	.279	925	258	41	0	40	165	122	225	.375	.453	July	.250	240	60	8	0	6	36	25	58	.332	.358
Post-All Star	.273	491	134	18	0	16	87	77	114	.381	.407	August	.280	193	54	9	0	5	29	41	45	.417	.404
Scoring Posn	.291	416	121	23	0	16	196	65	105	.395	.462	Sept/Oct	.250	132	33	4	0	5	27	15	34	.338	.394
Close & Late	.284	194	55	10	0	5	30	21	53	.380	.412	vs. AL	.279	1382	385	58	0	56	251	190	330	.377	.442
None on/out	.298	302	90	15	0	9	9	37	58	.386	.437	vs. NL	.206	34	7	1	0	0	1	9	9	.386	.235

Batter vs. Pitcher (career)

Hits Best Against	Avg	AB	H	2B	3B	HR	RBI	BB	SO	OBP	SLG	Hits Worst Against	Avg	AB	H	2B	3B	HR	RBI	BB	SO	OBP	SLG
Sterling Hitchcock	.500	12	6	1	0	0	1	0	1	.500	.583	Jaime Navarro	.077	13	1	1	0	0	0	4	0	.294	.154
Chris Haney	.462	13	6	2	0	2	5	4	4	.588	1.077	Mark Langston	.125	32	4	0	0	0	0	2	12	.176	.125
John Cummings	.455	11	5	1	0	2	5	0	1	.455	1.091	Kevin Tapani	.125	16	2	0	0	0	0	1	3	.222	.125
Roger Clemens	.385	13	5	1	0	1	4	0	4	.385	.692	Felipe Lira	.125	8	1	0	0	0	1	2	2	.273	.125
Tom Gordon	.308	13	4	0	0	1	1	2	3	.438	.538	Paul Quantrill	.143	14	2	1	0	0	0	1	4	.250	.214

Cory Lidle — Mets
Age 26 – Pitches Right (groundball pitcher)

	ERA	W	L	Sv	G	GS	IP	BB	SO	Avg	H	2B	3B	HR	RBI	OBP	SLG	GF	IR	IRS	Hld	SvOp	SB	CS	GB	FB	G/F
1997 Season	3.53	7	2	2	54	2	81.2	20	54	.274	86	14	2	7	42	.320	.398	20	29	11	9	3	3	2	152	56	2.71

1997 Season

	ERA	W	L	Sv	G	GS	IP	H	HR	BB	SO		Avg	AB	H	2B	3B	HR	RBI	BB	SO	OBP	SLG
Home	4.15	2	1	1	25	1	39.0	41	1	9	25	vs. Left	.321	137	44	8	2	5	20	10	18	.362	.518
Away	2.95	5	1	1	29	1	42.2	45	6	11	29	vs. Right	.237	177	42	6	0	2	22	10	36	.286	.305
Day	-4.01	2	1	2	19	2	33.2	40	1	4	25	Inning 1-6	.302	116	35	8	0	1	20	3	21	.328	.397
Night	3.19	5	1	0	35	0	48.0	46	6	16	29	Inning 7+	.258	198	51	6	2	6	22	17	33	.315	.399
Grass	3.76	5	1	2	43	1	64.2	65	6	16	45	None on	.235	170	40	5	2	4	4	8	31	.274	.359
Turf	2.65	2	1	0	11	1	17.0	21	1	4	9	Runners on	.319	144	46	9	0	3	38	12	23	.370	.444
March/April	0.00	0	0	0	0	0	0.0	0	0	0	0	Scoring Posn	.319	91	29	5	0	1	32	11	14	.389	.407
May	1.64	3	0	0	8	0	11.0	12	1	2	6	Close & Late	.239	88	21	3	1	2	8	11	13	.323	.364
June	5.64	0	1	1	12	2	22.1	32	2	1	18	None on/out	.229	70	16	1	0	2	2	7	11	.299	.329
July	1.84	1	0	0	13	0	14.2	13	1	6	8	vs. 1st Batr (relief)	.289	45	13	2	0	2	5	6	13	.365	.467
August	3.68	2	0	1	12	0	22.0	20	2	5	17	1st Inning Pitched	.270	185	50	8	1	5	26	15	32	.324	.405
Sept/Oct	3.09	1	1	0	9	0	11.2	9	1	6	5	First 15 Pitches	.259	174	45	7	1	4	19	14	30	.318	.379
Starter	7.71	0	1	0	2	2	7.0	12	0	0	4	Pitch 16-30	.244	86	21	4	1	2	11	4	14	.275	.384
Reliever	3.13	7	1	2	52	0	74.2	74	7	20	50	Pitch 31-45	.400	25	10	1	0	0	5	2	3	.464	.440
0 Days rest (Relief)	0.00	3	0	0	10	0	8.2	4	0	2	6	Pitch 46+	.345	29	10	2	0	1	7	0	7	.333	.517
1 or 2 Days rest	4.23	4	1	2	35	0	55.1	58	7	14	40	First Pitch	.328	61	20	3	0	2	13	4	0	.364	.475
3+ Days rest	0.00	0	0	0	7	0	10.2	12	0	4	4	Ahead in Count	.195	128	25	4	1	1	8	0	47	.206	.266
vs. AL	2.92	0	0	1	5	0	12.1	10	3	2	12	Behind in Count	.389	72	28	4	0	4	16	11	0	.464	.611
vs. NL	3.63	7	2	1	49	2	69.1	76	4	18	42	Two Strikes	.153	124	19	4	1	0	7	5	54	.197	.202
Pre-All Star	4.06	3	1	1	24	2	37.2	47	4	3	27	Pre-All Star	.307	153	47	6	1	4	20	3	27	.325	.438
Post-All Star	3.07	4	1	1	30	0	44.0	39	3	17	27	Post-All Star	.242	161	39	8	1	3	22	17	27	.315	.360

Jon Lieber — Pirates
Age 28 – Pitches Right (groundball pitcher)

	ERA	W	L	Sv	G	GS	IP	BB	SO	Avg	H	2B	3B	HR	RBI	OBP	SLG	CG	ShO	Sup	QS	#P/S	SB	CS	GB	FB	G/F
1997 Season	4.49	11	14	0	33	32	188.1	51	160	.263	193	39	7	23	85	.309	.429	1	0	4.35	18	86	16	4	293	162	1.81
Career (1994-1997)	4.45	30	33	1	122	76	511.2	118	370	.263	568	104	18	61	257	.321	.441	2	0	4.75	38	87	48	21	831	490	1.70

1997 Season

	ERA	W	L	Sv	G	GS	IP	H	HR	BB	SO		Avg	AB	H	2B	3B	HR	RBI	BB	SO	OBP	SLG
Home	4.25	6	5	0	15	15	95.1	91	12	24	91	vs. Left	.304	378	115	22	6	15	48	34	65	.360	.513
Away	4.74	5	9	0	18	17	93.0	102	11	27	69	vs. Right	.219	356	78	17	1	8	37	17	95	.253	.340
Day	3.40	3	1	0	9	8	50.1	51	4	12	39	Inning 1-6	.267	673	180	36	7	22	83	46	149	.312	.440
Night	4.89	8	13	0	24	24	138.0	142	19	39	121	Inning 7+	.213	61	13	3	0	1	2	5	11	.273	.311
Grass	4.45	9	6	0	12	12	64.2	75	4	17	45	None on	.271	442	120	22	5	16	16	26	95	.313	.452
Turf	4.51	8	8	0	21	20	123.2	118	19	34	115	Runners on	.250	292	73	17	2	7	69	25	65	.302	.394
March/April	3.28	1	2	0	6	6	35.2	40	3	9	27	Scoring Posn	.267	161	43	13	1	5	63	18	38	.328	.453
May	6.28	1	4	0	5	5	28.2	32	6	9	25	Close & Late	.211	38	8	3	0	0	1	3	8	.268	.289
June	3.28	3	2	0	6	6	35.2	30	2	11	29	None on/out	.296	196	58	9	4	8	8	10	34	.330	.505
July	7.13	1	3	0	5	5	24.0	29	2	9	21	vs. 1st Batr (relief)	.000	1	0	0	0	0	0	0	0	.000	.000
August	3.49	3	1	0	6	6	38.2	40	3	10	35	1st Inning Pitched	.279	129	36	7	5	1	17	5	27	.297	.434
Sept/Oct	4.91	2	2	0	5	4	25.2	22	7	3	23	First 75 Pitches	.264	588	155	32	5	19	69	37	137	.305	.432
Starter	4.54	11	14	0	32	32	186.1	193	23	51	159	Pitch 76-90	.292	89	26	5	1	4	10	7	12	.347	.506
Reliever	0.00	0	0	0	1	0	2.0	0	0	0	1	Pitch 91-105	.213	47	10	2	1	0	5	5	9	.283	.298
0-3 Days Rest (Start)	0.00	0	0	0	0	0	0.0	0	0	0	0	Pitch 106+	.200	10	2	0	0	0	1	2	2	.333	.200
4 Days Rest	5.81	6	10	0	18	18	96.0	117	12	30	76	First Pitch	.333	126	42	8	2	4	22	0	0	.361	.524
5+ Days Rest	3.19	5	4	0	14	14	90.1	76	11	21	83	Ahead in Count	.187	337	63	12	4	7	26	0	141	.188	.309
vs. AL	2.53	2	1	0	3	3	21.1	16	1	5	22	Behind in Count	.341	138	47	11	1	7	26	22	0	.423	.587
vs. NL	4.74	9	13	0	30	29	167.0	177	22	46	138	Two Strikes	.169	325	55	10	2	6	21	23	160	.224	.268
Pre-All Star	4.08	6	8	0	18	18	106.0	108	11	31	85	Pre-All Star	.263	411	108	24	4	11	49	31	85	.312	.421
Post-All Star	5.03	5	6	0	15	14	82.1	85	12	20	75	Post-All Star	.263	323	85	15	3	12	36	20	75	.305	.440

Career (1994-1997)

	ERA	W	L	Sv	G	GS	IP	H	HR	BB	SO		Avg	AB	H	2B	3B	HR	RBI	BB	SO	OBP	SLG
Home	4.54	17	15	0	58	41	279.1	306	33	67	211	vs. Left	.312	1008	314	62	13	34	140	74	152	.357	.500
Away	4.34	13	18	1	64	35	232.1	262	28	51	159	vs. Right	.251	1011	254	42	5	27	117	44	218	.285	.383

Career (1994-1997)

	ERA	W	L	Sv	G	GS	IP	H	HR	BB	SO		Avg	AB	H	2B	3B	HR	RBI	BB	SO	OBP	SLG
Day	3.13	10	7	0	39	20	149.1	153	12	35	90	Inning 1-6	.279	1686	470	86	17	47	219	100	311	.319	.434
Night	4.99	20	26	1	83	56	362.1	415	49	83	280	Inning 7+	.294	333	98	18	1	14	38	18	59	.330	.480
Grass	4.06	8	9	1	41	22	146.1	170	14	27	95	None on	.286	1176	336	52	11	42	42	61	224	.324	.456
Turf	4.61	22	24	0	81	54	365.1	398	47	91	275	Runners on	.275	843	232	52	7	19	215	57	146	.317	.421
March/April	4.28	1	3	1	20	7	54.2	66	8	12	42	Scoring Posn	.296	467	138	29	6	13	194	42	80	.345	.467
May	4.63	3	10	0	23	14	95.1	99	13	23	68	Close & Late	.286	161	46	14	1	6	19	12	30	.335	.497
June	4.70	8	6	0	25	16	103.1	123	10	23	69	None on/out	.305	525	160	24	7	21	21	25	79	.340	.497
July	5.84	5	9	0	19	15	89.1	105	14	27	64	vs. 1st Batr (relief)	.311	45	14	3	0	3	7	1	3	.326	.578
August	3.42	6	3	0	14	14	92.0	93	8	18	71	1st Inning Pitched	.275	444	122	17	8	7	56	20	78	.304	.396
Sept/Oct	3.62	7	2	0	21	10	77.0	82	8	15	56	First 75 Pitches	.274	1666	457	81	14	51	203	95	314	.313	.432
Starter	4.58	27	30	0	76	76	447.2	504	51	104	324	Pitch 76-90	.335	206	69	16	1	7	29	14	31	.383	.524
Reliever	3.52	3	3	1	46	0	64.0	64	10	14	46	Pitch 91-105	.288	111	32	5	3	3	22	7	15	.328	.468
0-3 Days Rest (Start)	8.01	2	3	0	6	6	30.1	46	3	4	21	Pitch 106+	.278	36	10	2	0	0	3	2	10	.316	.333
4 Days Rest	5.04	15	17	0	40	40	226.2	276	24	57	162	First Pitch	.335	352	118	22	5	13	56	10	0	.354	.537
5+ Days Rest	3.49	10	10	0	30	30	190.2	182	24	43	141	Ahead in Count	.208	929	193	30	9	23	92	0	332	.211	.334
vs. AL	2.53	2	1	0	3	3	21.1	16	1	5	22	Behind in Count	.378	392	148	28	2	17	70	56	0	.451	.589
vs. NL	4.53	28	32	1	119	73	490.1	552	60	113	348	Two Strikes	.189	861	163	25	6	17	74	52	370	.238	.292
Pre-All Star	4.68	14	21	1	74	40	276.2	314	34	64	197	Pre-All Star	.288	1091	314	61	11	34	147	64	197	.327	.457
Post-All Star	4.17	16	12	0	48	36	235.0	254	27	54	173	Post-All Star	.274	928	254	43	7	27	110	54	173	.315	.422

Pitcher vs. Batter (career)

Pitches Best Vs.	Avg	AB	H	2B	3B	HR	RBI	BB	SO	OBP	SLG	Pitches Worst Vs.	Avg	AB	H	2B	3B	HR	RBI	BB	SO	OBP	SLG
Greg Vaughn	.000	12	0	0	0	0	0	0	3	.000	.000	Bill Mueller	.714	14	10	1	0	0	2	0	1	.714	.786
Brian McRae	.000	11	0	0	0	0	0	2	1	.154	.000	Marquis Grissom	.667	9	6	0	0	0	3	2	1	.727	.667
Barry Bonds	.056	18	1	0	0	0	2	3	4	.190	.056	Ryan Klesko	.545	11	6	2	0	1	4	2	1	.615	1.000
Terry Pendleton	.071	14	1	0	0	1	0	1	1	.071	.071	Ken Caminiti	.440	25	11	3	1	2	6	1	5	.462	.880
Kurt Abbott	.091	11	1	0	0	0	0	1	4	.167	.091	Eric Karros	.364	11	4	0	0	2	0	0	2	.417	.909

Mike Lieberthal — Phillies

Age 26 – Bats Right (groundball hitter)

	Avg	G	AB	R	H	2B	3B	HR	RBI	BB	SO	HBP	GDP	SB	CS	OBP	SLG	IBB	SH	SF	#Pit	#P/PA	GB	FB	G/F
1997 Season	.246	134	455	59	112	27	1	20	77	44	76	4	10	3	4	.314	.442	1	0	7	1865	3.66	158	157	1.01
Career (1994-1997)	.250	224	747	87	187	40	2	28	109	62	116	7	19	3	4	.310	.422	1	3	11	2964	3.57	263	254	1.04

1997 Season

	Avg	AB	H	2B	3B	HR	RBI	BB	SO	OBP	SLG		Avg	AB	H	2B	3B	HR	RBI	BB	SO	OBP	SLG
vs. Left	.245	106	26	8	0	5	25	12	13	.319	.462	First Pitch	.263	76	20	2	0	5	19	0	0	.269	.487
vs. Right	.246	349	86	19	1	15	52	32	63	.312	.436	Ahead in Count	.294	102	30	8	0	9	26	24	0	.429	.637
Groundball	.274	62	17	3	0	1	7	9	15	.366	.371	Behind in Count	.183	202	37	11	0	3	18	0	63	.190	.282
Flyball	.299	67	20	6	0	6	15	5	16	.347	.657	Two Strikes	.206	204	42	13	1	4	20	19	76	.276	.338
Home	.228	219	50	13	0	11	35	28	42	.319	.438	Batting #5	.167	168	28	6	0	5	24	17	26	.249	.292
Away	.263	236	62	14	1	9	42	16	34	.309	.445	Batting #6	.292	120	35	5	1	5	21	12	15	.350	.475
Day	.252	115	29	5	0	4	17	11	17	.323	.400	Other	.293	167	49	16	0	10	32	15	35	.353	.569
Night	.244	340	83	22	1	16	60	33	59	.311	.456	March/April	.219	73	16	3	0	7	15	2	11	.250	.548
Grass	.280	168	47	12	0	7	30	14	27	.335	.476	May	.127	71	9	3	0	0	2	6	9	.205	.169
Turf	.226	287	65	15	1	13	47	30	49	.301	.422	June	.261	69	18	7	0	3	10	7	13	.329	.493
Pre-All Star	.227	229	52	18	0	12	31	16	36	.283	.463	July	.400	80	32	10	0	4	17	10	14	.468	.675
Post-All Star	.265	226	60	9	1	8	46	28	40	.342	.420	August	.261	88	23	1	0	5	23	4	15	.287	.443
Scoring Posn	.248	129	32	5	1	9	61	11	20	.297	.512	Sept/Oct	.189	74	14	3	1	1	10	15	14	.315	.297
Close & Late	.230	74	17	2	0	2	9	9	16	.310	.338	vs. AL	.279	43	12	5	0	1	6	8	10	.392	.465
None on/out	.276	105	29	10	0	3	8	24		.439		vs. NL	.243	412	100	22	1	19	71	36	66	.305	.439

1997 By Position

Position	Avg	AB	H	2B	3B	HR	RBI	BB	SO	OBP	SLG	G	GS	Innings	PO	A	E	DP	Fld Pct	Rng Fctr	In Zone	Zone Outs	MLB Rtg	Zone
As c	.249	442	110	27	1	20	77	44	71	.318	.450	129	119	1059.0	933	73	12	9	.988	---	---	---	---

Kerry Ligtenberg — Braves

Age 27 – Pitches Right (flyball pitcher)

	ERA	W	L	Sv	G	GS	IP	BB	SO	Avg	H	2B	3B	HR	RBI	OBP	SLG	GF	IR	IRS	Hld	SvOp	SB	CS	GB	FB	G/F
1997 Season	3.00	1	0	1	15	0	15.0	4	19	.211	12	1	0	4	9	.262	.439	9	10	4	0	1	4	0	10	17	0.59

1997 Season

	ERA	W	L	Sv	G	GS	IP	H	HR	BB	SO		Avg	AB	H	2B	3B	HR	RBI	BB	SO	OBP	SLG
Home	2.79	1	0	0	9	0	9.2	8	1	4	11	vs. Left	.214	28	6	0	0	2	6	1	9	.241	.429
Away	3.38	0	0	1	6	0	5.1	4	2	0	8	vs. Right	.207	29	6	1	0	2	3	3	10	.281	.448

Jose Lima — Astros

Age 25 – Pitches Right

	ERA	W	L	Sv	G	GS	IP	BB	SO	Avg	H	2B	3B	HR	RBI	OBP	SLG	GF	IR	IRS	Hld	SvOp	SB	CS	GB	FB	G/F
1997 Season	5.28	1	6	2	52	1	75.0	16	63	.271	79	17	2	9	46	.317	.436	15	36	15	3	2	3	4	77	100	0.77
Career (1994-1997)	5.92	9	22	5	109	21	228.0	59	166	.288	262	53	7	34	141	.338	.473	31	63	24	9	11	5	290	275	1.05

1997 Season

	ERA	W	L	Sv	G	GS	IP	H	HR	BB	SO		Avg	AB	H	2B	3B	HR	RBI	BB	SO	OBP	SLG
Home	3.89	0	3	1	22	1	34.2	26	1	9	27	vs. Left	.230	122	28	6	1	3	17	8	26	.275	.369
Away	6.47	1	3	1	30	0	40.1	53	8	7	36	vs. Right	.302	169	51	11	1	6	29	8	37	.348	.485
Day	4.40	0	1	0	14	1	14.1	12	2	2	16	Inning 1-6	.240	125	30	7	0	3	19	5	28	.278	.368
Night	5.49	1	5	2	38	0	60.2	67	7	14	47	Inning 7+	.295	166	49	10	2	6	27	11	35	.346	.488

1997 Season

	ERA	W	L	Sv	G	GS	IP	H	HR	BB	SO		Avg	AB	H	2B	3B	HR	RBI	BB	SO	OBP	SLG
Grass	6.60	1	3	1	22	0	30.0	40	6	6	29	None on	.244	168	41	7	0	5	5	8	39	.291	.375
Turf	4.40	0	3	1	30	1	45.0	39	3	10	34	Runners on	.309	123	38	10	2	4	41	8	24	.353	.520
March/April	7.71	0	1	0	7	0	7.0	7	1	4	4	Scoring Posn	.310	71	22	4	1	2	33	6	16	.358	.479
May	2.05	0	2	0	14	0	22.0	17	1	3	18	Close & Late	.318	66	21	3	1	1	9	7	15	.392	.439
June	6.23	1	0	1	13	0	21.2	29	4	3	19	None on/out	.227	66	15	4	0	1	1	4	14	.292	.333
July	4.82	0	1	0	6	0	9.1	13	0	0	7	vs. 1st Batr (relief)	.289	45	13	2	1	2	14	2	12	.320	.511
August	7.36	0	2	1	8	0	11.0	8	3	4	11	1st Inning Pitched	.247	162	40	8	2	4	32	11	35	.294	.395
Sept/Oct	9.00	0	0	0	4	1	4.0	5	0	2	4	First 15 Pitches	.278	158	44	10	2	4	29	8	32	.312	.443
Starter	0.00	0	0	0	1	1	2.0	0	0	0	1	Pitch 16-30	.286	84	24	4	0	4	13	8	18	.368	.476
Reliever	5.42	1	6	2	51	0	73.0	79	9	15	63	Pitch 31-45	.211	38	8	2	0	1	4	0	10	.231	.342
0 Days rest (Relief)	3.86	0	1	2	9	0	11.2	11	2	0	8	Pitch 46+	.273	11	3	1	0	0	0	0	3	.273	.364
1 or 2 Days rest	5.75	1	3	0	26	0	40.2	45	6	10	37	First Pitch	.308	52	16	5	1	1	4	2	0	.327	.500
3+ Days rest	5.66	0	2	0	16	0	20.2	23	1	5	18	Ahead in Count	.245	163	40	6	0	4	21	0	59	.266	.356
vs. AL	7.45	0	1	0	5	0	9.2	10	4	1	11	Behind in Count	.350	40	14	3	1	3	12	7	0	.438	.700
vs. NL	4.96	1	5	2	47	1	65.1	69	5	15	52	Two Strikes	.243	148	36	6	0	3	22	7	63	.294	.345
Pre-All Star	4.61	1	4	1	36	0	52.2	57	6	10	44	Pre-All Star	.274	208	57	10	2	6	33	10	44	.309	.428
Post-All Star	6.85	0	2	1	16	1	22.1	22	3	6	19	Post-All Star	.265	83	22	7	0	3	13	6	19	.337	.458

Felipe Lira — Mariners   Age 26 – Pitches Right

	ERA	W	L	Sv	G	GS	IP	BB	SO	Avg	H	2B	3B	HR	RBI	OBP	SLG	CG	ShO	Sup	QS	#P/S	SB	CS	GB	FB	G/F
1997 Season	6.34	5	11	0	28	18	110.2	55	73	.295	132	29	3	18	70	.376	.493	1	1	3.98	7	95	22	3	153	132	1.16
Career (1995-1997)	5.20	20	38	1	97	72	451.2	177	275	.276	487	93	11	65	238	.346	.452	4	3	4.18	32	96	45	14	609	536	1.14

1997 Season

	ERA	W	L	Sv	G	GS	IP	H	HR	BB	SO		Avg	AB	H	2B	3B	HR	RBI	BB	SO	OBP	SLG
Home	5.40	3	5	0	12	10	63.1	65	11	35	44	vs. Left	.288	226	65	16	1	10	41	25	32	.363	.500
Away	7.61	2	6	0	16	8	47.1	67	7	20	29	vs. Right	.302	222	67	13	2	8	29	30	41	.389	.486
Starter	5.98	5	9	0	18	18	96.1	112	16	46	67	Scoring Posn	.283	127	36	9	1	4	49	22	22	.391	.465
Reliever	8.79	0	2	0	10	0	14.1	20	2	9	6	Close & Late	.308	26	8	0	0	1	3	7	3	.457	.423
0-3 Days Rest (Start)	7.00	0	1	0	2	2	9.0	15	2	6	5	None on/out	.321	112	36	5	2	5	5	9	16	.377	.536
4 Days Rest	7.33	2	2	0	5	5	27.0	36	5	9	17	First Pitch	.339	59	20	4	0	1	9	2	0	.369	.458
5+ Days Rest	5.22	3	6	0	11	11	60.1	61	9	31	45	Ahead in Count	.247	186	46	8	1	4	23	0	59	.255	.366
Pre-All Star	5.60	5	5	0	18	13	82.0	83	14	39	56	Behind in Count	.416	113	47	12	1	12	32	33	0	.544	.858
Post-All Star	8.48	0	6	0	10	5	28.2	49	4	16	17	Two Strikes	.223	197	44	7	2	4	21	20	73	.305	.340

Career (1995-1997)

	ERA	W	L	Sv	G	GS	IP	H	HR	BB	SO		Avg	AB	H	2B	3B	HR	RBI	BB	SO	OBP	SLG
Home	4.18	12	19	0	47	39	254.1	238	38	94	154	vs. Left	.276	967	267	47	8	36	133	99	148	.348	.453
Away	6.52	8	19	1	50	33	197.1	249	27	83	121	vs. Right	.276	796	220	46	3	29	105	78	127	.344	.451
Day	5.18	7	13	0	37	25	161.2	181	25	60	88	Inning 1-6	.272	1528	415	82	10	57	210	151	243	.342	.450
Night	5.21	13	25	1	60	47	290.0	306	40	117	187	Inning 7+	.306	235	72	11	1	8	28	26	32	.372	.464
Grass	4.98	17	33	1	83	62	393.2	414	57	154	226	None on	.267	1012	270	50	4	35	35	86	159	.335	.428
Turf	6.67	3	5	0	14	10	58.0	73	8	23	49	Runners on	.289	751	217	43	7	30	203	91	116	.361	.485
March/April	6.53	1	5	0	14	8	51.0	62	9	21	33	Scoring Posn	.256	403	103	17	2	14	161	69	73	.352	.412
May	4.87	7	4	0	20	12	81.1	81	15	24	61	Close & Late	.315	143	45	7	0	6	18	18	21	.390	.490
June	4.70	6	6	0	16	15	92.0	90	10	45	52	None on/out	.269	453	122	18	2	15	15	34	67	.337	.417
July	5.26	4	6	0	19	16	99.1	124	15	32	61	vs. 1st Batr (relief)	.263	19	5	0	1	1	3	5	4	.440	.526
August	4.89	1	8	1	16	10	70.0	72	8	29	34	1st Inning Pitched	.230	348	80	14	2	16	55	37	58	.312	.420
Sept/Oct	5.59	1	9	0	12	11	58.0	58	8	26	34	First 75 Pitches	.277	1312	364	71	10	43	181	137	197	.352	.445
Starter	5.13	18	33	0	72	72	412.1	443	59	159	249	Pitch 76-90	.268	198	53	9	1	13	31	19	35	.327	.520
Reliever	5.95	2	5	1	25	0	39.1	44	6	18	26	Pitch 91-105	.305	164	50	9	0	8	19	13	30	.352	.506
0-3 Days Rest (Start)	5.46	2	1	0	6	6	31.1	39	5	14	21	Pitch 106+	.225	89	20	4	0	1	7	8	13	.286	.303
4 Days Rest	4.24	11	16	0	39	39	239.2	238	26	80	139	First Pitch	.366	246	90	11	1	9	36	7	0	.389	.528
5+ Days Rest	6.56	5	16	0	27	27	141.1	166	28	65	89	Ahead in Count	.213	736	157	30	5	15	70	0	221	.224	.329
vs. AL	5.26	20	38	1	96	71	444.2	485	65	173	269	Behind in Count	.343	432	148	35	3	27	80	104	0	.466	.625
vs. NL	1.29	0	0	0	1	1	7.0	2	0	4	6	Two Strikes	.205	772	158	31	4	20	71	66	275	.275	.333
Pre-All Star	5.03	17	16	0	56	41	264.2	276	37	101	166	Pre-All Star	.268	1030	276	52	5	37	128	101	166	.337	.436
Post-All Star	5.44	3	22	1	41	31	187.0	211	28	76	109	Post-All Star	.288	733	211	41	6	28	110	76	109	.358	.475

Pitcher vs. Batter (career)

Pitches Best Vs.	Avg	AB	H	2B	3B	HR	RBI	BB	SO	OBP	Pitches Worst Vs.	Avg	AB	H	2B	3B	HR	RBI	BB	SO	OBP	SLG
Tim Raines	.000	9	0	0	0	0		4	2	.308	Rafael Palmeiro	.526	19	10	0	0	2	5	0	0	.550	.842
Carlos Delgado	.083	12	1	1	0	0	3	1	4	.154	Jim Edmonds	.467	15	7	0	0	3	4	3	2	.556	1.067
Mickey Tettleton	.091	11	1	0	0	0	1	0	5	.083	Jim Thome	.455	11	5	1	0	1	1	4	2	.625	.818
Roberto Alomar	.133	15	2	0	0	0	2	1	1	.167	Cecil Fielder	.444	9	4	1	0	2	7	2	1	.545	1.222
Jeff Frye	.143	14	2	0	0	0	0	1	2	.200	Tino Martinez	.409	22	9	2	0	4	7	1	1	.435	1.045

Nelson Liriano — Dodgers   Age 34 – Bats Both (groundball hitter)

	Avg	G	AB	R	H	2B	3B	HR	RBI	BB	SO	HBP	GDP	SB	CS	OBP	SLG	IBB	SH	SF	#Pit	#P/PA	GB	FB	G/F
1997 Season	.227	76	88	10	20	6	0	1	11	6	12	0	1	0	0	.274	.330	1	2	1	346	3.57	43	22	1.95
Last Five Years	.271	430	970	129	263	55	11	14	125	104	134	2	14	10	8	.339	.394	13	11	11	3931	3.58	408	252	1.62

1997 Season

	Avg	AB	H	2B	3B	HR	RBI	BB	SO	OBP	SLG		Avg	AB	H	2B	3B	HR	RBI	BB	SO	OBP	SLG
vs. Left	.167	12	2	1	0	0	0	1	4	.231	.250	Scoring Posn	.241	29	7	2	0	1	11	2	5	.281	.414
vs. Right	.237	76	18	5	0	1	11	5	8	.280	.342	Close & Late	.212	33	7	4	0	1	5	4	8	.297	.424

Last Five Years

	Avg	AB	H	2B	3B	HR	RBI	BB	SO	OBP	SLG		Avg	AB	H	2B	3B	HR	RBI	BB	SO	OBP	SLG
vs. Left	.226	168	38	6	1	4	26	20	35	.309	.345	First Pitch	.316	171	54	14	3	2	29	9	0	.346	.468
vs. Right	.281	802	225	49	10	10	99	84	99	.346	.404	Ahead in Count	.309	243	75	16	1	3	41	44	0	.408	.420
Groundball	.263	259	68	12	1	0	25	33	39	.344	.317	Behind in Count	.222	370	82	12	4	6	25	0	116	.223	.324
Flyball	.254	169	43	10	2	4	26	22	29	.337	.408	Two Strikes	.227	405	92	19	5	5	32	51	134	.313	.336
Home	.264	455	120	29	8	4	60	50	61	.337	.389	Batting #1	.286	192	55	10	4	3	18	14	28	.333	.427
Away	.278	515	143	26	3	10	65	54	73	.342	.398	Batting #8	.245	273	67	13	4	4	35	43	41	.343	.366
Day	.299	338	101	17	7	8	55	32	51	.357	.462	Other	.279	505	141	32	3	7	72	47	65	.340	.396
Night	.256	632	162	38	4	6	70	72	83	.331	.358	March/April	.247	85	21	5	0	1	4	9	15	.319	.341
Grass	.284	580	165	37	10	8	84	67	77	.354	.424	May	.241	170	41	8	1	4	18	25	28	.338	.371
Turf	.251	390	98	18	1	6	41	37	57	.318	.344	June	.254	189	48	13	2	0	24	21	21	.329	.344
Pre-All Star	.253	501	127	27	4	6	50	62	73	.336	.359	July	.276	185	51	7	3	4	26	18	29	.332	.411
Post-All Star	.290	469	136	28	7	8	75	42	61	.344	.431	August	.273	172	47	11	1	3	23	14	18	.328	.401
Scoring Posn	.290	241	70	17	5	4	108	36	35	.368	.452	Sept/Oct	.325	169	55	11	4	2	30	17	23	.383	.473
Close & Late	.253	217	55	14	1	3	31	27	45	.337	.369	vs. AL	.125	8	1	0	0	0	0	0	2	.125	.125
None on/out	.235	302	71	15	2	3	3	19	46	.283	.328	vs. NL	.272	962	262	55	11	14	125	104	132	.341	.396

Batter vs. Pitcher (career)

Hits Best Against	Avg	AB	H	2B	3B	HR	RBI	BB	SO	OBP	SLG	Hits Worst Against	Avg	AB	H	2B	3B	HR	RBI	BB	SO	OBP	SLG
Kevin Foster	.636	11	7	2	0	0	1	1	1	.667	.818	Greg Maddux	.067	15	1	0	0	0	0	0	5	.067	.067
Greg Swindell	.615	13	8	1	0	1	3	0	3	.615	.923	Doug Drabek	.067	15	1	0	0	0	0	3	3	.222	.067
Pedro Astacio	.500	22	11	5	0	1	4	0	2	.500	.864	Pat Rapp	.083	12	1	0	0	0	0	1	3	.154	.083
Darryl Kile	.455	11	5	2	0	0	2	3	2	.571	.636	Erik Hanson	.154	13	2	0	0	0	0	0	6	.154	.154
Doug Jones	.400	10	4	0	0	1	2	3	0	.500	.700	Kevin Brown	.167	12	2	0	0	0	0	0	1	.167	.167

Pat Listach — Astros
Age 30 – Bats Both (groundball hitter)

	Avg	G	AB	R	H	2B	3B	HR	RBI	BB	SO	HBP	GDP	SB	CS	OBP	SLG	IBB	SH	SF	#Pit	#P/PA	GB	FB	G/F
1997 Season	.182	52	132	13	24	2	2	0	6	11	24	1	7	4	2	.247	.227	2	5	2	577	3.82	62	27	2.30
Last Five Years	.231	354	1193	157	276	44	7	4	96	112	214	7	23	62	20	.299	.290	2	23	7	5148	3.84	486	253	1.92

1997 Season

	Avg	AB	H	2B	3B	HR	RBI	BB	SO	OBP	SLG		Avg	AB	H	2B	3B	HR	RBI	BB	SO	OBP	SLG
vs. Left	.146	41	6	1	0	0	0	1	8	.167	.171	Scoring Posn	.067	30	2	0	1	0	6	4	8	.167	.133
vs. Right	.198	91	18	1	2	0	6	10	16	.279	.253	Close & Late	.000	22	0	0	0	0	0	2	6	.083	.000
Home	.185	65	12	1	1	0	4	4	11	.239	.231	None on/out	.310	29	9	1	0	0	0	4	6	.394	.345
Away	.179	67	12	1	1	0	2	7	13	.253	.224	Batting #2	.280	50	14	1	1	0	3	2	7	.315	.340
First Pitch	.318	22	7	0	0	0	1	2	0	.375	.318	Batting #8	.129	62	8	1	0	0	2	6	13	.206	.145
Ahead in Count	.138	29	4	1	0	0	1	3	0	.219	.172	Other	.100	20	2	0	1	0	1	3	4	.208	.200
Behind in Count	.130	54	7	0	1	0	2	0	23	.143	.167	Pre-All Star	.182	132	24	2	2	0	6	11	24	.247	.227
Two Strikes	.175	63	11	1	2	0	4	6	24	.250	.254	Post-All Star	.000	0	0	0	0	0	0	0	0	.000	.000

Last Five Years

	Avg	AB	H	2B	3B	HR	RBI	BB	SO	OBP	SLG		Avg	AB	H	2B	3B	HR	RBI	BB	SO	OBP	SLG
vs. Left	.263	453	119	24	3	3	29	39	71	.324	.349	First Pitch	.286	182	52	10	0	0	17	2	0	.298	.341
vs. Right	.212	740	157	20	4	1	67	73	143	.285	.254	Ahead in Count	.294	238	70	12	0	2	26	50	0	.419	.370
Groundball	.229	266	61	10	2	1	29	26	51	.297	.293	Behind in Count	.192	530	102	15	1	2	38	0	179	.197	.236
Flyball	.217	207	45	5	0	0	9	20	46	.293	.242	Two Strikes	.172	574	99	14	5	2	42	60	214	.254	.225
Home	.244	603	147	23	2	1	56	62	107	.316	.294	Batting #1	.236	643	152	26	5	2	48	60	120	.302	.302
Away	.219	590	129	21	5	3	40	50	107	.283	.283	Batting #8	.216	292	63	9	0	0	22	26	48	.279	.247
Day	.243	452	110	20	3	3	32	49	74	.323	.321	Other	.236	258	61	9	2	2	26	26	46	.315	.310
Night	.224	741	166	24	4	1	64	63	140	.285	.271	March/April	.253	269	68	12	0	1	21	23	41	.316	.309
Grass	.235	960	226	37	4	2	78	95	164	.306	.289	May	.196	260	51	7	1	1	13	20	54	.254	.242
Turf	.215	233	50	7	3	2	18	17	50	.270	.296	June	.257	171	44	5	3	0	15	18	26	.328	.322
Pre-All Star	.230	713	164	24	4	2	49	63	124	.295	.283	July	.215	181	39	9	1	0	16	26	38	.313	.276
Post-All Star	.233	480	112	20	3	2	47	49	90	.307	.300	August	.230	200	46	9	0	1	21	21	33	.307	.290
Scoring Posn	.247	279	69	12	1	1	90	25	63	.307	.308	Sept/Oct	.250	112	28	2	2	1	10	4	22	.282	.330
Close & Late	.215	191	41	5	1	0	22	16	46	.275	.251	vs. AL	.237	1074	255	43	6	4	90	102	193	.306	.300
None on/out	.230	392	90	16	2	3	3	36	61	.298	.304	vs. NL	.176	119	21	1	1	0	6	10	21	.242	.202

Batter vs. Pitcher (career)

Hits Best Against	Avg	AB	H	2B	3B	HR	RBI	BB	SO	OBP	SLG	Hits Worst Against	Avg	AB	H	2B	3B	HR	RBI	BB	SO	OBP	SLG
Todd Stottlemyre	.467	15	7	1	0	1	4	1	1	.529	.733	Roger Clemens	.083	24	2	1	0	0	0	0	7	.083	.125
F. Valenzuela	.385	13	5	1	0	0	0	1	2	.429	.462	Wilson Alvarez	.133	15	2	0	0	0	0	0	1	.133	.133
Jimmy Key	.379	29	11	1	2	0	1	2	4	.419	.552	Erik Hanson	.150	20	3	1	0	0	4	1	6	.190	.200
Al Leiter	.333	9	3	0	1	0	0	2	0	.455	.556	Scott Kamieniecki	.167	12	2	0	0	0	0	1	2	.231	.167
Kevin Appier	.313	16	5	0	1	0	3	4	3	.476	.438	Danny Darwin	.200	20	4	0	0	0	0	0	5	.200	.200

Scott Livingstone — Cardinals
Age 32 – Bats Left

	Avg	G	AB	R	H	2B	3B	HR	RBI	BB	SO	HBP	GDP	SB	CS	OBP	SLG	IBB	SH	SF	#Pit	#P/PA	GB	FB	G/F
1997 Season	.164	65	67	4	11	2	0	0	6	3	11	0	1	1	0	.194	.194	0	0	2	264	3.67	22	24	0.92
Last Five Years	.288	436	942	100	271	44	4	11	108	53	113	0	19	6	7	.322	.378	2	1	11	3361	3.34	372	238	1.56

1997 Season

	Avg	AB	H	2B	3B	HR	RBI	BB	SO	OBP	SLG		Avg	AB	H	2B	3B	HR	RBI	BB	SO	OBP	SLG
vs. Left	.000	4	0	0	0	0	0	0	0	.000	.000	Scoring Posn	.250	12	3	1	0	0	6	0	1	.214	.333
vs. Right	.175	63	11	2	0	0	6	3	11	.206	.206	Close & Late	.167	24	4	0	0	0	3	2	4	.222	.167

Last Five Years

	Avg	AB	H	2B	3B	HR	RBI	BB	SO	OBP	SLG		Avg	AB	H	2B	3B	HR	RBI	BB	SO	OBP	SLG
vs. Left	.274	73	20	1	0	2	8	3	9	.303	.370	First Pitch	.342	184	63	5	1	2	15	2	0	.346	.413
vs. Right	.289	869	251	43	4	9	100	50	104	.324	.379	Ahead in Count	.282	216	61	14	1	3	24	28	0	.360	.398
Groundball	.258	229	59	13	0	4	15	11	36	.289	.367	Behind in Count	.257	385	99	14	1	4	42	0	99	.254	.330
Flyball	.298	191	57	8	0	3	29	8	26	.317	.387	Two Strikes	.221	353	78	12	0	3	37	23	113	.266	.280
Home	.275	462	127	19	4	3	46	27	55	.314	.353	Batting #5	.326	221	72	19	1	3	31	16	21	.368	.462
Away	.300	480	144	25	0	8	62	26	58	.329	.402	Batting #8	.266	229	61	9	1	1	28	15	28	.306	.328
Day	.279	337	94	15	1	2	31	18	50	.312	.347	Other	.280	492	138	16	2	7	49	22	64	.308	.364
Night	.293	605	177	29	3	9	77	35	63	.328	.395	March/April	.295	105	31	4	0	2	17	7	9	.336	.390
Grass	.285	766	218	34	4	7	79	47	93	.324	.367	May	.269	186	50	9	1	1	17	10	23	.305	.344
Turf	.301	176	53	10	0	4	29	6	20	.316	.426	June	.228	180	41	8	1	0	12	6	22	.247	.283
Pre-All Star	.260	558	145	24	2	4	48	25	69	.289	.332	July	.255	196	50	6	0	2	14	8	27	.284	.316
Post-All Star	.328	384	126	20	2	7	60	28	44	.369	.445	August	.374	155	58	9	1	5	30	16	19	.423	.542
Scoring Posn	.289	239	69	10	1	2	98	18	32	.325	.364	Sept/Oct	.342	120	41	8	1	1	18	6	13	.370	.450
Close & Late	.309	178	55	7	0	4	28	11	20	.344	.416	vs. AL	.286	332	95	11	2	2	40	20	36	.321	.349
None on/out	.300	200	60	15	1	3	3	12	24	.340	.393	vs. NL	.289	610	176	33	2	9	68	33	77	.323	.393

Batter vs. Pitcher (career)

Hits Best Against	Avg	AB	H	2B	3B	HR	RBI	BB	SO	OBP	SLG	Hits Worst Against	Avg	AB	H	2B	3B	HR	RBI	BB	SO	OBP	SLG
Kevin Foster	.636	11	7	1	0	0	1	0	1	.636	.727	Juan Guzman	.091	11	1	0	0	0	0	0	1	.091	.091
Jose Mesa	.533	15	8	1	0	0	4	2	0	.533	.600	Willie Banks	.091	11	1	0	0	0	0	1	2	.167	.091
Tom Candiotti	.333	18	6	2	1	0	3	0	3	.316	.556	Erik Hanson	.105	19	2	0	0	0	1	0	4	.100	.105
Scott Erickson	.333	12	4	1	0	0	3	1	0	.385	.417	Cal Eldred	.176	17	3	0	0	0	0	0	0	.176	.176
												Danny Darwin	.176	17	3	0	0	0	2	1	4	.211	.176

Graeme Lloyd — Yankees
Age 31 – Pitches Left (groundball pitcher)

	ERA	W	L	Sv	G	GS	IP	BB	SO	Avg	H	2B	3B	HR	RBI	OBP	SLG	GF	IR	IRS	Hld	SvOp	SB	CS	GB	FB	G/F
1997 Season	3.31	1	1	1	46	0	49.0	20	26	.293	55	12	0	6	30	.355	.452	17	39	10	2	1	5	0	81	43	1.88
Career (1993-1997)	3.91	8	19	8	242	0	248.1	78	131	.269	257	36	5	23	150	.325	.390	79	232	77	37	22	17	3	400	249	1.61

1997 Season

	ERA	W	L	Sv	G	GS	IP	H	HR	BB	SO		Avg	AB	H	2B	3B	HR	RBI	BB	SO	OBP	SLG
Home	2.45	0	0	1	20	0	22.0	24	3	9	10	vs. Left	.279	68	19	5	0	3	9	3	13	.306	.485
Away	4.00	1	1	0	26	0	27.0	31	3	11	16	vs. Right	.300	120	36	7	0	3	21	17	13	.380	.433
Starter	0.00	0	0	0	0	0	0.0	0	0	0	0	Scoring Posn	.169	59	10	4	0	1	23	15	7	.316	.288
Reliever	3.31	1	1	1	46	0	49.0	55	6	20	26	Close & Late	.200	20	4	1	0	0	3	5	2	.346	.250
0 Days rest (Relief)	1.59	0	1	0	10	0	11.1	9	1	8	5	None on/out	.357	42	15	0	0	1	1	2	8	.400	.429
1 or 2 Days rest	2.08	1	0	0	16	0	17.1	15	1	7	10	Ahead in Count	.440	25	11	2	0	2	4	6	0	.548	.760
3+ Days rest	5.31	0	0	1	20	0	20.1	31	4	5	11	Behind in Count	.231	78	18	4	0	3	13	0	20	.235	.397
Pre-All Star	3.86	1	1	1	24	0	21.0	28	3	10	9	Two Strikes	.236	72	17	3	0	1	13	9	26	.321	.319
Post-All Star	2.89	0	0	0	22	0	28.0	27	3	10	17												

Career (1993-1997)

	ERA	W	L	Sv	G	GS	IP	H	HR	BB	SO		Avg	AB	H	2B	3B	HR	RBI	BB	SO	OBP	SLG
Home	4.09	4	7	4	120	0	121.0	144	10	33	59	vs. Left	.233	344	80	11	1	7	49	22	56	.280	.331
Away	3.75	4	12	4	122	0	127.1	113	13	45	72	vs. Right	.290	611	177	25	4	16	101	56	75	.349	.422
Day	3.96	4	6	4	86	0	84.0	94	9	25	44	Inning 1-6	.198	111	22	5	0	3	26	7	21	.252	.324
Night	3.89	4	13	4	156	0	164.1	163	14	53	87	Inning 7+	.278	844	235	31	5	20	124	71	110	.334	.398
Grass	3.85	8	17	7	210	0	217.1	227	19	66	114	None on	.272	464	126	15	2	10	10	27	67	.316	.377
Turf	4.35	0	2	1	32	0	31.0	30	4	12	17	Runners on	.267	491	131	21	3	13	140	51	64	.332	.401
March/April	2.79	2	3	4	40	0	42.0	42	3	13	25	Scoring Posn	.272	290	79	14	2	8	128	43	43	.355	.417
May	3.81	2	4	3	52	0	54.1	57	5	18	31	Close & Late	.298	342	102	10	3	5	49	38	44	.362	.389
June	3.66	3	4	1	49	0	59.0	61	6	14	24	None on/out	.256	199	51	4	2	4	13	13	36	.305	.357
July	3.18	1	3	0	49	0	45.1	43	4	10	24	vs. 1st Batr (relief)	.266	218	58	5	2	6	45	16	31	.306	.390
August	6.97	0	5	0	30	0	31.0	34	4	17	16	1st Inning Pitched	.260	695	181	23	4	18	127	53	92	.312	.383
Sept/Oct	4.32	0	0	0	22	0	16.2	22	1	6	11	First 15 Pitches	.273	664	181	23	4	14	114	50	83	.323	.401
Starter	0.00	0	0	0	0	0	0.0	0	0	0	0	Pitch 16-30	.268	250	67	10	1	5	31	24	38	.335	.376
Reliever	3.91	8	19	8	242	0	248.1	257	23	78	131	Pitch 31-45	.250	36	9	3	0	0	5	4	9	.317	.333
0 Days rest (Relief)	4.18	7	4	1	57	0	56.0	52	7	27	28	Pitch 46+	.000	5	0	0	0	0	0	0	1	.000	.000
1 or 2 Days rest	3.68	7	5	3	110	0	115.0	108	6	34	67	First Pitch	.351	131	46	6	0	6	27	17	0	.432	.534
3+ Days rest	4.07	0	7	1	75	0	77.1	87	10	17	36	Ahead in Count	.232	380	88	12	2	9	49	0	105	.232	.345
vs. AL	4.00	8	19	8	235	0	240.2	252	23	77	126	Behind in Count	.297	273	81	14	2	4	49	31	0	.365	.407
vs. NL	1.17	0	0	0	7	0	7.2	5	0	1	5	Two Strikes	.220	386	85	11	2	5	48	29	131	.274	.298
Pre-All Star	3.49	7	12	8	157	0	170.0	171	15	48	90	Pre-All Star	.263	649	171	23	4	15	89	48	90	.315	.381
Post-All Star	4.83	1	7	0	85	0	78.1	86	8	30	41	Post-All Star	.281	306	86	13	1	8	61	30	41	.343	.408

Pitcher vs. Batter (career)

Pitches Best Vs.	Avg	AB	H	2B	3B	HR	RBI	BB	SO	OBP	SLG	Pitches Worst Vs.	Avg	AB	H	2B	3B	HR	RBI	BB	SO	OBP	SLG
Kenny Lofton	.154	13	2	1	0	0	0	0	1	.154	.231	Lance Johnson	.385	13	5	0	0	0	1	0	0	.385	.385
Rafael Palmeiro	.167	18	3	0	0	0	0	1	3	.211	.167												
Paul O'Neill	.182	11	2	0	0	0	1	1	1	.250	.182												
Mo Vaughn	.231	13	3	0	0	2	3	3	4	.375	.692												

Esteban Loaiza — Pirates
Age 26 – Pitches Right (groundball pitcher)

	ERA	W	L	Sv	G	GS	IP	BB	SO	Avg	H	2B	3B	HR	RBI	OBP	SLG	CG	ShO	Sup	QS	#P/S	SB	CS	GB	FB	G/F
1997 Season	4.13	11	11	0	33	32	196.1	56	122	.279	214	38	6	17	92	.335	.411	1	0	4.95	21	92	20	10	318	178	1.79
Career (1995-1997)	4.65	21	23	0	75	73	421.2	130	239	.292	484	93	10	49	224	.347	.448	3	1	4.99	40	86	43	21	696	421	1.65

1997 Season

	ERA	W	L	Sv	G	GS	IP	H	HR	BB	SO		Avg	AB	H	2B	3B	HR	RBI	BB	SO	OBP	SLG
Home	4.69	4	6	0	15	14	86.1	95	10	23	52	vs. Left	.289	405	117	19	1	7	39	32	54	.348	.393
Away	3.68	7	5	0	18	18	110.0	119	7	33	70	vs. Right	.269	361	97	19	5	10	53	24	68	.322	.432
Day	4.91	4	0	0	7	6	36.2	46	4	12	25	Inning 1-6	.277	696	193	31	6	16	86	50	112	.333	.408
Night	3.95	7	11	0	26	26	159.2	168	13	44	97	Inning 7+	.300	70	21	7	0	1	6	6	10	.359	.443
Grass	3.46	6	2	0	11	11	67.2	71	5	19	45	None on	.277	430	119	19	3	13	13	27	67	.324	.426
Turf	4.48	5	9	0	22	21	128.2	143	12	37	77	Runners on	.283	336	95	19	3	4	79	29	55	.349	.393
March/April	1.83	2	0	0	5	5	34.1	31	0	10	21	Scoring Posn	.265	189	50	8	1	1	66	23	32	.351	.333
May	4.89	2	2	0	6	6	38.2	40	5	13	20	Close & Late	.395	38	15	5	0	1	5	5	4	.455	.605
June	5.79	1	3	0	5	5	28.0	37	1	7	20	None on/out	.310	197	61	8	0	7	7	13	26	.352	.457
July	5.20	3	2	0	5	5	27.2	36	3	7	20	vs. 1st Batr (relief)	.000	1	0	0	0	0	0	0	0	.000	.000
August	4.59	2	2	0	7	6	33.1	42	4	12	18	1st Inning Pitched	.271	129	35	4	2	4	17	10	25	.326	.426
Sept/Oct	2.88	1	2	0	5	5	34.1	28	4	7	23	First 75 Pitches	.273	594	162	26	6	13	68	41	99	.329	.402
Starter	4.19	11	11	0	32	32	193.1	213	17	54	120	Pitch 76-90	.333	102	34	6	0	4	18	9	13	.389	.510
Reliever	0.00	0	0	0	1	0	3.0	1	0	2	2	Pitch 91-105	.277	47	13	5	0	0	5	6	8	.352	.383
0-3 Days Rest (Start)	0.00	0	0	0	0	0	0.0	0	0	0	0	Pitch 106+	.217	23	5	1	0	0	1	0	2	.217	.261
4 Days Rest	4.42	9	3	0	16	16	93.2	111	11	21	64	First Pitch	.382	131	50	9	0	5	25	7	0	.404	.565
5+ Days Rest	3.97	2	8	0	16	16	99.2	102	6	33	56	Ahead in Count	.228	347	79	17	3	6	30	0	98	.237	.346
vs. AL	8.66	0	3	0	3	3	17.2	22	3	5	13	Behind in Count	.333	159	53	6	1	5	25	28	0	.438	.478
vs. NL	3.68	11	8	0	30	29	178.2	192	14	51	109	Two Strikes	.194	324	63	11	4	4	27	21	122	.253	.290
Pre-All Star	4.04	6	5	0	17	17	107.0	115	6	31	66	Pre-All Star	.282	408	115	20	4	6	46	31	66	.340	.395
Post-All Star	4.23	5	6	0	16	15	89.1	99	11	25	56	Post-All Star	.277	358	99	18	2	11	46	25	56	.330	.430

Career (1995-1997)

	ERA	W	L	Sv	G	GS	IP	H	HR	BB	SO		Avg	AB	H	2B	3B	HR	RBI	BB	SO	OBP	SLG
Home	5.35	7	15	0	36	34	193.1	231	29	59	115	vs. Left	.284	804	228	46	1	16	97	79	112	.352	.403
Away	4.06	14	8	0	39	39	228.1	253	20	71	124	vs. Right	.299	856	256	47	9	33	127	51	127	.342	.491
Day	4.86	8	3	0	20	18	107.1	129	15	30	61	Inning 1-6	.291	1507	439	82	10	44	211	117	218	.346	.447
Night	4.58	13	20	0	55	55	314.1	355	34	100	178	Inning 7+	.294	153	45	11	0	5	13	13	21	.355	.464
Grass	4.15	10	3	0	24	24	141.0	157	14	43	81	None on	.286	944	270	50	6	36	36	64	135	.335	.466
Turf	4.91	11	20	0	51	49	280.2	327	35	87	158	Runners on	.299	716	214	43	4	13	188	66	104	.361	.425
March/April	1.60	3	0	0	6	6	39.1	36	0	10	23	Scoring Posn	.297	424	126	24	1	5	160	49	65	.369	.394
May	6.50	2	4	0	12	11	62.1	77	9	19	35	Close & Late	.328	67	22	5	0	3	7	9	6	.410	.537
June	5.88	5	4	0	14	14	75.0	96	9	21	43	None on/out	.282	422	119	20	1	16	16	30	65	.333	.448
July	4.76	4	4	0	11	11	62.1	70	7	21	37	vs. 1st Batr (relief)	.000	2	0	0	0	0	0	0	0	.000	.000
August	5.05	4	4	0	15	14	76.2	107	11	25	36	1st Inning Pitched	.273	286	78	11	2	7	39	22	50	.326	.399
Sept/Oct	3.48	3	7	0	17	17	106.0	98	13	34	65	First 75 Pitches	.290	1328	385	70	9	41	174	102	194	.345	.449
Starter	4.72	21	23	0	73	73	415.2	480	49	128	236	Pitch 76-90	.327	205	67	13	1	7	36	13	26	.372	.502
Reliever	0.00	0	0	0	2	0	6.0	4	0	2	3	Pitch 91-105	.276	87	24	9	0	1	11	12	13	.360	.414
0-3 Days Rest (Start)	4.74	5	1	0	8	8	49.1	54	7	11	27	Pitch 106+	.200	40	8	1	0	0	3	3	6	.256	.225
4 Days Rest	4.29	13	11	0	37	37	218.1	247	25	60	130	First Pitch	.380	300	114	22	1	14	63	9	0	.394	.600
5+ Days Rest	5.35	3	11	0	28	28	148.0	179	17	57	79	Ahead in Count	.233	748	174	40	4	11	71	0	200	.238	.341
vs. AL	8.66	0	3	0	3	3	17.2	22	3	5	13	Behind in Count	.366	331	121	16	2	18	60	73	0	.481	.589
vs. NL	4.48	21	20	0	72	70	404.0	462	46	125	226	Two Strikes	.203	666	135	24	5	8	56	48	239	.260	.290
Pre-All Star	4.76	12	8	0	35	34	198.1	226	19	56	112	Pre-All Star	.293	772	226	47	6	19	105	56	112	.346	.443
Post-All Star	4.55	9	15	0	40	39	223.1	258	30	74	127	Post-All Star	.291	888	258	46	4	30	119	74	127	.348	.453

Pitcher vs. Batter (career)

Pitches Best Vs.	Avg	AB	H	2B	3B	HR	RBI	BB	SO	OBP	SLG	Pitches Worst Vs.	Avg	AB	H	2B	3B	HR	RBI	BB	SO	OBP	SLG
Jeff Bagwell	.000	12	0	0	0	0	0	1	1	.077	.000	Andres Galarraga	.611	18	11	4	1	0	5	1	1	.632	.944
Brett Butler	.000	11	0	0	0	0	1	4	1	.267	.000	Mike Piazza	.600	10	6	0	0	1	2	1	1	.636	.900
Delino DeShields	.143	14	2	0	0	0	1	0	1	.200	.143	Derek Bell	.538	13	7	1	0	2	5	3	2	.625	1.077
Chuck Carr	.182	11	2	0	0	0	0	0	0	.182	.182	Walt Weiss	.462	13	6	3	0	1	4	2	1	.533	.923
Quilvio Veras	.182	11	2	0	0	0	1	1	.250	.182	Todd Hundley	.375	8	3	0	0	2	3	1	.545	1.125

Keith Lockhart — Braves
Age 33 – Bats Left (flyball hitter)

	Avg	G	AB	R	H	2B	3B	HR	RBI	BB	SO	HBP	GDP	SB	CS	OBP	SLG	IBB	SH	SF	#Pit	#P/PA	GB	FB	G/F
1997 Season	.279	96	147	25	41	5	3	6	32	14	17	1	4	0	7	.337	.476	0	3	4	605	3.58	63	45	1.40
Career (1994-1997)	.285	355	897	119	256	57	9	21	126	62	88	8	14	20	7	.331	.439	6	6	17	3267	3.30	308	325	0.95

1997 Season

	Avg	AB	H	2B	3B	HR	RBI	BB	SO	OBP	SLG		Avg	AB	H	2B	3B	HR	RBI	BB	SO	OBP	SLG
vs. Left	.667	9	6	0	2	1	5	1	1	.700	1.444	Scoring Posn	.289	38	11	2	1	2	25	6	3	.367	.553
vs. Right	.254	138	35	5	1	5	27	13	16	.314	.413	Close & Late	.265	34	9	1	0	1	6	4	4	.350	.382
Home	.309	55	17	2	1	3	14	7	8	.381	.545	None on/out	.324	34	11	2	1	2	2	0	4	.324	.618
Away	.261	92	24	3	2	3	18	7	9	.311	.435	Batting #2	.324	37	12	0	1	2	6	3	7	.375	.541
First Pitch	.294	17	5	0	0	0	0	0	0	.294	.294	Batting #9	.265	49	13	3	0	2	16	7	3	.351	.449
Ahead in Count	.364	33	12	1	1	3	13	12	0	.522	.727	Other	.262	61	16	2	2	2	10	4	7	.304	.459
Behind in Count	.203	74	15	2	1	1	12	0	15	.205	.297	Pre-All Star	.229	83	19	3	1	3	20	7	5	.277	.398
Two Strikes	.238	63	15	2	2	14	2	17	.265	.429	Post-All Star	.344	64	22	2	2	3	12	7	12	.417	.578

Career (1994-1997)

	Avg	AB	H	2B	3B	HR	RBI	BB	SO	OBP	SLG		Avg	AB	H	2B	3B	HR	RBI	BB	SO	OBP	SLG
vs. Left	.244	90	22	4	4	1	10	3	15	.277	.411	First Pitch	.309	149	46	4	4	2	18	6	0	.335	.430

Career (1994-1997)

	Avg	AB	H	2B	3B	HR	RBI	BB	SO	OBP	SLG		Avg	AB	H	2B	3B	HR	RBI	BB	SO	OBP	SLG
vs. Right	.290	807	234	53	5	20	116	59	73	.337	.442	Ahead in Count	.314	223	70	16	1	13	44	40	0	.412	.570
Groundball	.271	221	60	10	2	4	27	20	18	.331	.389	Behind in Count	.264	390	103	25	3	2	44	0	77	.268	.359
Flyball	.272	147	40	7	2	1	18	15	17	.347	.367	Two Strikes	.220	322	71	18	3	5	35	16	88	.266	.342
Home	.300	407	122	23	2	12	63	35	34	.353	.455	Batting #3	.290	393	114	30	4	8	60	19	23	.323	.448
Away	.273	490	134	34	7	9	63	27	54	.313	.427	Batting #5	.319	119	38	7	2	2	14	8	13	.370	.462
Day	.297	246	73	18	3	8	42	21	24	.351	.492	Other	.270	385	104	20	3	11	52	35	52	.327	.423
Night	.281	651	183	39	6	13	84	41	64	.323	.419	March/April	.282	110	31	5	0	3	21	12	14	.352	.409
Grass	.286	748	214	46	5	18	102	52	72	.331	.433	May	.262	107	28	7	1	3	15	11	12	.325	.430
Turf	.282	149	42	11	4	3	24	10	16	.333	.470	June	.333	168	56	11	4	3	27	13	12	.383	.500
Pre-All Star	.299	442	132	29	5	9	70	36	41	.351	.448	July	.231	173	40	12	0	2	15	3	10	.249	.335
Post-All Star	.273	455	124	28	4	12	56	26	47	.312	.431	August	.296	179	53	11	2	4	28	14	15	.345	.447
Scoring Posn	.260	235	61	17	2	6	99	27	24	.320	.426	Sept/Oct	.300	160	48	11	2	6	20	9	25	.333	.506
Close & Late	.241	145	35	3	3	3	16	17	21	.323	.366	vs. AL	.294	748	220	53	7	15	95	47	66	.336	.444
None on/out	.304	194	59	12	3	8	8	7	19	.332	.521	vs. NL	.242	149	36	4	2	6	31	15	22	.310	.416

Batter vs. Pitcher (career)

Hits Best Against	Avg	AB	H	2B	3B	HR	RBI	BB	SO	OBP	SLG	Hits Worst Against	Avg	AB	H	2B	3B	HR	RBI	BB	SO	OBP	SLG
Alex Fernandez	.368	19	7	3	0	1	2	0	1	.368	.684	Chad Ogea	.182	11	2	0	0	0	0	0	1	.182	.182
Brad Radke	.357	14	5	3	0	1	6	0	1	.357	.786	Orel Hershiser	.182	11	2	1	1	0	0	1	2	.250	.455
Roger Pavlik	.333	12	4	0	0	1	2	0	1	.333	.583	Pat Hentgen	.200	15	3	0	0	0	0	0	1	.200	.200
Aaron Sele	.333	9	3	0	0	1	3	2	1	.417	.667												
Scott Erickson	.308	13	4	0	0	1	4	1	0	.357	.538												

Kenny Lofton — Braves

Age 31 – Bats Left (groundball hitter)

	Avg	G	AB	R	H	2B	3B	HR	RBI	BB	SO	HBP	GDP	SB	CS	OBP	SLG	IBB	SH	SF	#Pit	#P/PA	GB	FB	G/F
1997 Season	.333	122	493	90	164	20	6	5	48	64	83	2	10	27	20	.409	.428	5	2	3	2234	3.96	190	87	2.18
Last Five Years	.326	654	2664	536	868	137	40	39	267	298	353	6	36	286	78	.392	.451	25	19	22	11290	3.75	1062	572	1.86

1997 Season

	Avg	AB	H	2B	3B	HR	RBI	BB	SO	OBP	SLG		Avg	AB	H	2B	3B	HR	RBI	BB	SO	OBP	SLG
vs. Left	.336	152	51	6	3	2	22	10	24	.382	.454	First Pitch	.364	44	16	2	1	1	9	4	0	.429	.523
vs. Right	.331	341	113	14	3	3	26	54	59	.421	.416	Ahead in Count	.389	126	49	6	3	1	14	33	0	.513	.508
Groundball	.353	102	36	4	3	3	18	12	21	.414	.539	Behind in Count	.275	207	57	3	1	1	12	0	69	.274	.343
Flyball	.314	70	22	1	0	0	5	10	13	.402	.329	Two Strikes	.267	243	65	9	1	3	18	27	83	.338	.350
Home	.322	258	83	7	3	3	23	32	40	.399	.407	Batting #1	.331	492	163	20	6	5	47	64	83	.409	.427
Away	.345	235	81	13	3	2	25	32	43	.420	.451	Batting #9	1.000	1	1	0	0	0	1	0	0	.500	1.000
Day	.301	136	41	9	2	3	10	11	21	.354	.463	Other	.000	0	0	0	0	0	0	0	0	.000	.000
Night	.345	357	123	11	4	2	38	53	62	.429	.415	March/April	.395	114	45	4	1	2	13	8	15	.434	.500
Grass	.335	415	139	18	6	5	45	54	67	.411	.443	May	.296	115	34	5	1	1	13	12	20	.359	.383
Turf	.321	78	25	2	0	0	3	10	16	.398	.346	June	.339	56	19	2	1	0	7	8	10	.415	.411
Pre-All Star	.344	288	99	11	3	3	33	30	45	.403	.434	July	.385	13	5	0	1	0	1	4	3	.529	.538
Post-All Star	.317	205	65	9	3	2	15	34	38	.417	.420	August	.363	113	41	6	2	2	9	15	22	.442	.504
Scoring Posn	.351	111	39	1	2	1	40	16	20	.427	.423	Sept/Oct	.244	82	20	3	0	0	5	17	13	.376	.280
Close & Late	.338	74	25	3	1	0	7	6	14	.388	.405	vs. AL	.289	38	11	2	0	0	1	3	7	.341	.342
None on/out	.354	198	70	13	4	3	3	30	29	.436	.465	vs. NL	.336	455	153	18	6	5	47	61	76	.415	.435

1997 By Position

Position	Avg	AB	H	2B	3B	HR	RBI	BB	SO	OBP	SLG	G	GS	Innings	PO	A	E	DP	Fld Pct	Rng Fctr	In Zone	Outs	Zone Rtg	MLB Zone
As cf	.333	493	164	20	6	5	48	64	83	.409	.428	122	121	1047.1	289	5	5	1	.983	2.53	337	282	837	815

Last Five Years

	Avg	AB	H	2B	3B	HR	RBI	BB	SO	OBP	SLG		Avg	AB	H	2B	3B	HR	RBI	BB	SO	OBP	SLG
vs. Left	.307	897	275	46	11	7	84	98	152	.376	.406	First Pitch	.379	327	124	13	4	3	44	21	0	.411	.471
vs. Right	.336	1767	593	91	29	32	183	200	201	.400	.474	Ahead in Count	.412	763	314	58	17	16	90	154	0	.507	.595
Groundball	.326	500	163	21	12	9	59	55	65	.389	.470	Behind in Count	.244	1048	256	40	10	6	66	0	299	.245	.319
Flyball	.316	490	155	23	6	10	47	53	68	.382	.449	Two Strikes	.235	1118	263	38	11	12	73	123	353	.311	.321
Home	.331	1330	440	62	23	26	133	160	168	.401	.471	Batting #1	.326	2658	866	137	40	39	266	297	353	.392	.451
Away	.321	1334	428	75	17	13	134	138	185	.383	.432	Batting #9	.333	3	1	0	0	0	1	1	0	.400	.333
Day	.321	845	271	50	15	10	87	94	114	.385	.451	Other	.333	3	1	0	0	0	0	0	0	.333	.333
Night	.328	1819	597	87	25	29	180	204	239	.395	.451	March/April	.345	397	137	14	7	7	45	47	51	.411	.469
Grass	.329	2299	757	124	38	37	236	262	304	.396	.465	May	.333	532	177	26	7	8	49	54	69	.394	.453
Turf	.304	365	111	13	2	2	31	36	49	.366	.367	June	.327	495	162	32	10	7	60	54	68	.390	.475
Pre-All Star	.335	1568	525	83	26	25	170	168	210	.397	.469	July	.310	374	116	25	4	5	37	38	47	.393	.439
Post-All Star	.313	1096	343	54	14	14	97	130	143	.385	.426	August	.331	501	166	25	11	9	53	47	74	.390	.479
Scoring Posn	.330	533	176	18	10	8	216	85	75	.410	.447	Sept/Oct	.301	365	110	15	1	3	23	58	44	.397	.373
Close & Late	.284	394	112	16	4	2	34	48	55	.360	.360	vs. AL	.324	2209	715	119	34	34	220	237	277	.387	.455
None on/out	.329	1071	352	59	13	21	21	114	138	.394	.467	vs. NL	.336	455	153	18	6	5	47	61	76	.415	.435

Batter vs. Pitcher (career)

Hits Best Against	Avg	AB	H	2B	3B	HR	RBI	BB	SO	OBP	SLG	Hits Worst Against	Avg	AB	H	2B	3B	HR	RBI	BB	SO	OBP	SLG
John Smiley	.545	11	6	1	0	1	1	0	0	.545	.909	Mike Mohler	.000	9	0	0	0	0	0	4	2	.308	.000
Sean Bergman	.500	10	5	0	1	2	4	3	0	.600	1.300	Kevin Gross	.071	14	1	0	0	0	1	0	0	.067	.071
Kevin Ritz	.500	8	4	1	1	0	1	3	0	.636	.875	Jesse Orosco	.083	12	1	0	0	0	0	0	3	.154	.083
Frank Rodriguez	.455	11	5	1	0	1	1	0	0	.455	.818	Jimmy Key	.118	17	2	0	0	0	1	0	4	.118	.118
Cal Eldred	.353	17	6	1	0	2	2	4	2	.476	.765	Graeme Lloyd	.154	13	2	1	0	0	0	0	1	.154	.231

Rich Loiselle — Pirates
Age 26 – Pitches Right (groundball pitcher)

	ERA	W	L	Sv	G	GS	IP	BB	SO	Avg	H	2B	3B	HR	RBI	OBP	SLG	GF	IR	IRS	Hld	SvOp	SB	CS	GB	FB	G/F
1997 Season	3.10	1	5	29	72	0	72.2	24	66	.269	76	10	3	7	39	.326	.399	58	26	16	5	34	3	2	122	54	2.26
Career (1996-1997)	3.09	2	5	29	77	3	93.1	32	75	.268	98	14	3	10	44	.328	.405	58	26	16	5	34	4	3	162	72	2.25

1997 Season

	ERA	W	L	Sv	G	GS	IP	H	HR	BB	SO		Avg	AB	H	2B	3B	HR	RBI	BB	SO	OBP	SLG
Home	3.44	0	2	14	35	0	34.0	33	3	13	41	vs. Left	.309	123	38	7	2	2	18	16	26	.386	.447
Away	2.79	1	3	15	37	0	38.2	43	4	11	25	vs. Right	.238	160	38	3	1	5	21	8	40	.276	.363
Day	3.45	0	1	9	30	0	31.1	32	5	10	27	Inning 1-6	.250	8	2	0	0	0	1	0	3	.222	.250
Night	2.83	1	4	20	42	0	41.1	44	2	14	39	Inning 7+	.269	275	74	10	3	7	38	24	63	.329	.404
Grass	2.83	1	2	11	27	0	28.2	29	3	10	21	None on	.267	135	36	5	1	5		15	33	.344	.430
Turf	3.27	0	3	18	45	0	44.0	47	4	14	45	Runners on	.270	148	40	5	2	2	34	9	33	.308	.372
March/April	3.68	1	0	0	11	0	14.2	15	2	5	12	Scoring Posn	.351	74	26	5	1	0	29	6	16	.390	.446
May	3.86	0	1	4	10	0	9.1	10	1	3	7	Close & Late	.268	198	53	7	2	5	27	17	48	.324	.399
June	2.00	0	0	3	9	0	9.0	11	1	4	7	None on/out	.290	62	18	1	0	4	4	8	17	.371	.500
July	2.76	0	1	9	16	0	16.1	15	2	3	17	vs. 1st Batr (relief)	.227	66	15	2	1	3	9	5	18	.278	.424
August	2.13	0	1	8	15	0	12.2	10	0	6	16	1st Inning Pitched	.273	253	69	9	2	6	36	22	61	.332	.395
Sept/Oct	4.22	0	2	5	11	0	10.2	15	2	2	7	First 15 Pitches	.280	207	58	8	2	5	27	16	46	.333	.411
Starter	0.00	0	0	0	0	0	0.0	0	0	0	0	Pitch 16-30	.254	71	18	2	1	2	12	7	17	.316	.394
Reliever	3.10	1	5	29	72	0	72.2	76	7	24	66	Pitch 31-45	.000	5	0	0	0	0	0	1	3	.167	.000
0 Days rest (Relief)	2.51	0	2	8	16	0	14.1	14	2	6	14	Pitch 46+	.000	0	0	0	0	0	0	0	0	.000	.000
1 or 2 Days rest	3.38	0	3	16	40	0	40.0	43	3	15	34	Ahead in Count	.211	142	30	5	1	3		0	57	.214	.324
3+ Days rest	2.95	1	0	5	16	0	18.1	19	2	3	18	Behind in Count	.350	40	14	0	2	2	7	10	0	.480	.600
vs. AL	1.80	0	0	5	5	0	5.0	4	0	0	2	Two Strikes	.191	141	27	5	0	3	17	13	66	.261	.291
vs. NL	3.19	1	5	24	67	0	67.2	72	7	24	64												
Pre-All Star	3.13	1	1	10	34	0	37.1	40	4	12	28	Pre-All Star	.274	146	40	5	2	4	19	12	28	.331	.418
Post-All Star	3.06	0	4	19	38	0	35.1	36	3	12	38	Post-All Star	.263	137	36	5	1	3	20	12	38	.320	.380

Joey Long — Padres
Age 27 – Pitches Left (groundball pitcher)

	ERA	W	L	Sv	G	GS	IP	BB	SO	Avg	H	2B	3B	HR	RBI	OBP	SLG	GF	IR	IRS	Hld	SvOp	SB	CS	GB	FB	G/F
1997 Season	8.18	0	0	0	10	0	11.0	8	8	.340	17	5	0	1	9	.441	.500	4	4	2	0	0	4	1	18	10	1.80

1997 Season

	ERA	W	L	Sv	G	GS	IP	H	HR	BB	SO		Avg	AB	H	2B	3B	HR	RBI	BB	SO	OBP	SLG
Home	7.20	0	0	0	4	0	5.0	8	1	0	6	vs. Left	.231	13	3	0	0	0	2	1	4	.286	.231
Away	9.00	0	0	0	6	0	6.0	9	0	8	2	vs. Right	.378	37	14	5	0	1	7	7	4	.489	.595

Ryan Long — Royals
Age 25 – Bats Right

	Avg	G	AB	R	H	2B	3B	HR	RBI	BB	SO	HBP	GDP	SB	CS	OBP	SLG	IBB	SH	SF	#Pit	#P/PA	GB	FB	G/F
1997 Season	.222	6	9	2	2	0	0	0	2	0	3	1	0	0	0	.300	.222	0	0	0	31	3.10	2	4	0.50

1997 Season

	Avg	AB	H	2B	3B	HR	RBI	BB	SO	OBP	SLG		Avg	AB	H	2B	3B	HR	RBI	BB	SO	OBP	SLG
vs. Left	.250	4	1	0	0	0	1	0	2	.250	.250	Scoring Posn	.400	5	2	0	0	0	2	0	1	.400	.400
vs. Right	.200	5	1	0	0	0	1	0	1	.333	.200	Close & Late	.000	2	0	0	0	0	0	0	2	.000	.000

Albie Lopez — Indians
Age 26 – Pitches Right (groundball pitcher)

	ERA	W	L	Sv	G	GS	IP	BB	SO	Avg	H	2B	3B	HR	RBI	OBP	SLG	GF	IR	IRS	Hld	SvOp	SB	CS	GB	FB	G/F
1997 Season	6.93	3	7	0	37	6	76.2	40	63	.322	101	16	2	11	61	.403	.490	10	15	9	4	1	11	6	131	71	1.85
Career (1993-1997)	5.99	12	14	0	69	31	228.1	107	173	.293	267	40	2	39	146	.371	.470	10	21	10	4	1	20	15	348	226	1.54

1997 Season

	ERA	W	L	Sv	G	GS	IP	H	HR	BB	SO		Avg	AB	H	2B	3B	HR	RBI	BB	SO	OBP	SLG
Home	6.06	1	2	0	19	3	35.2	43	5	16	30	vs. Left	.333	153	51	7	1	7	34	17	29	.401	.529
Away	7.68	2	5	0	18	3	41.0	58	6	24	33	vs. Right	.311	161	50	9	1	4	27	23	34	.404	.453
Starter	6.59	2	2	0	6	6	28.2	36	1	18	19	Scoring Posn	.356	90	32	7	1	3	47	23	14	.478	.556
Reliever	7.13	1	5	0	31	0	48.0	65	10	22	44	Close & Late	.339	56	19	4	1	6	16	7	13	.424	.768
0 Days rest (Relief)	7.20	0	0	0	4	0	5.0	7	1	1	4	None on/out	.266	79	21	2	0	4	4		11	.318	.443
1 or 2 Days rest	11.02	0	3	0	13	0	16.1	25	7	8	16	First Pitch	.333	33	11	1	0	1	7	5	0	.436	.455
3+ Days rest	4.72	1	2	0	14	0	26.2	33	2	13	24	Ahead in Count	.301	143	43	6	0	2	15	0	52	.306	.385
Pre-All Star	6.57	3	4	0	21	6	50.2	68	4	32	39	Behind in Count	.387	75	29	5	2	7	26	21	0	.521	.787
Post-All Star	7.62	0	3	0	16	0	26.0	33	7	8	24	Two Strikes	.256	160	41	6	0	3	18	14	63	.322	.350

Javy Lopez — Braves
Age 27 – Bats Right (groundball hitter)

	Avg	G	AB	R	H	2B	3B	HR	RBI	BB	SO	HBP	GDP	SB	CS	OBP	SLG	IBB	SH	SF	#Pit	#P/PA	GB	FB	G/F
1997 Season	.295	123	414	52	122	28	1	23	68	40	82	5	9	1	1	.361	.534	10	1	4	1531	3.30	160	104	1.54
Last Five Years	.287	449	1529	173	439	68	7	74	225	99	286	16	51	2	10	.334	.486	15	4	14	5479	3.30	635	372	1.71

1997 Season

	Avg	AB	H	2B	3B	HR	RBI	BB	SO	OBP	SLG		Avg	AB	H	2B	3B	HR	RBI	BB	SO	OBP	SLG
vs. Left	.330	97	32	4	0	4	14	14	14	.414	.495	First Pitch	.456	90	41	11	0	9	25	8	0	.515	.878
vs. Right	.284	317	90	24	1	19	54	26	68	.344	.546	Ahead in Count	.301	73	22	3	0	6	12	16	0	.427	.589
Groundball	.329	79	26	10	0	6	15	5	15	.384	.684	Behind in Count	.222	194	43	8	0	7	21	0	72	.225	.371
Flyball	.300	40	12	2	0	5	12	3	10	.356	.725	Two Strikes	.183	186	34	7	1	5	12	16	82	.252	.312
Home	.306	183	56	9	0	11	34	23	41	.387	.536	Batting #6	.303	284	86	20	1	17	46	32	58	.377	.560

1997 Season

	Avg	AB	H	2B	3B	HR	RBI	BB	SO	OBP	SLG		Avg	AB	H	2B	3B	HR	RBI	BB	SO	OBP	SLG
Away	.286	231	66	19	1	12	34	17	41	.339	.532	Batting #7	.292	96	28	7	0	5	19	3	15	.320	.521
Day	.279	111	31	10	1	7	17	7	25	.331	.577	Other	.235	34	8	1	0	1	3	5	9	.333	.353
Night	.300	303	91	18	0	16	51	33	57	.371	.518	March/April	.342	76	26	6	0	6	17	9	15	.412	.658
Grass	.287	335	96	23	1	14	51	32	67	.351	.487	May	.234	77	18	5	0	3	11	11	16	.326	.416
Turf	.329	79	26	5	0	9	17	8	15	.400	.734	June	.333	69	23	8	0	4	10	3	12	.373	.623
Pre-All Star	.311	238	74	20	0	14	42	24	46	.376	.571	July	.283	46	13	1	0	3	8	1	6	.300	.500
Post-All Star	.273	176	48	8	1	9	26	16	36	.340	.483	August	.256	82	21	4	0	5	14	6	21	.322	.488
Scoring Posn	.271	107	29	10	0	5	44	21	21	.383	.505	Sept/Oct	.328	64	21	4	1	2	8	10	12	.419	.516
Close & Late	.288	73	21	3	0	4	8	13	20	.404	.493	vs. AL	.279	43	12	5	0	2	5	3	5	.340	.535
None on/out	.353	102	36	8	0	7	7	3	19	.377	.637	vs. NL	.296	371	110	23	1	21	63	37	77	.363	.534

1997 By Position

Position	Avg	AB	H	2B	3B	HR	RBI	BB	SO	OBP	SLG	G	GS	Innings	PO	A	E	DP	Fld Pct	Rng Fctr	In Zone Outs	Zone Rtg	MLB Zone
As Pinch Hitter	.167	12	2	0	0	0	1	2	4	.286	.167	15	0	---	---	---	---	---	---	---	---	---	---
As c	.299	402	120	28	1	23	67	38	78	.363	.545	117	107	951.0	791	57	6	9	.993	---	---	---	---

Last Five Years

	Avg	AB	H	2B	3B	HR	RBI	BB	SO	OBP	SLG		Avg	AB	H	2B	3B	HR	RBI	BB	SO	OBP	SLG
vs. Left	.285	393	112	16	0	15	49	32	71	.339	.440	First Pitch	.387	326	126	19	1	22	69	13	0	.413	.653
vs. Right	.288	1136	327	52	7	59	176	67	215	.333	.502	Ahead in Count	.394	277	109	12	1	22	52	46	0	.485	.682
Groundball	.311	412	128	20	1	20	62	22	77	.351	.510	Behind in Count	.210	714	150	28	3	21	71	0	247	.213	.346
Flyball	.259	212	55	5	0	10	27	10	49	.292	.425	Two Strikes	.182	644	117	20	3	17	51	40	286	.232	.301
Home	.286	731	209	25	3	33	105	48	131	.333	.464	Batting #6	.287	654	188	35	2	28	88	58	135	.350	.476
Away	.288	798	230	43	4	41	120	51	155	.335	.506	Batting #7	.302	702	212	29	4	37	116	28	110	.333	.513
Day	.255	475	121	24	2	22	67	21	93	.292	.453	Other	.225	173	39	4	1	9	21	13	41	.280	.416
Night	.302	1054	318	44	5	52	158	78	193	.353	.501	March/April	.296	260	77	11	0	18	55	21	55	.346	.546
Grass	.290	1227	356	57	6	57	186	76	215	.335	.486	May	.281	295	83	14	2	13	43	22	57	.336	.475
Turf	.275	302	83	11	1	17	39	23	71	.332	.487	June	.260	285	74	12	1	11	28	12	49	.300	.425
Pre-All Star	.278	902	251	39	4	43	132	58	171	.326	.471	July	.309	230	71	10	0	12	37	9	35	.335	.509
Post-All Star	.300	627	188	29	4	31	93	41	115	.346	.507	August	.255	259	66	11	2	11	37	18	50	.307	.440
Scoring Posn	.272	378	103	18	2	12	142	49	78	.351	.426	Sept/Oct	.340	200	68	10	2	9	25	17	40	.395	.545
Close & Late	.286	287	82	13	1	12	48	28	59	.351	.463	vs. AL	.279	43	12	5	0	2	5	3	5	.340	.535
None on/out	.320	378	121	16	3	25	25	10	65	.346	.577	vs. NL	.287	1486	427	63	7	72	220	96	281	.334	.485

Batter vs. Pitcher (career)

Hits Best Against	Avg	AB	H	2B	3B	HR	RBI	BB	SO	OBP	SLG	Hits Worst Against	Avg	AB	H	2B	3B	HR	RBI	BB	SO	OBP	SLG
Jim Bullinger	.533	15	8	1	0	2	2	0	2	.533	1.000	John Smiley	.000	18	0	0	0	0	0	0	2	.000	.000
Terry Mulholland	.500	12	6	2	0	0	2	0	1	.500	.667	Francisco Cordova	.000	10	0	0	0	0	0	1	2	.091	.000
Shawn Estes	.500	10	5	0	0	0	0	2	1	.583	.500	Mark Gardner	.083	12	1	0	0	0	0	0	2	.083	.083
Kevin Ritz	.417	12	5	3	0	0	2	0	1	.417	.667	Tony Saunders	.091	11	1	0	0	0	0	1	2	.167	.091
Shane Reynolds	.400	15	6	1	0	1	1	0	1	.400	.667	Bob Tewksbury	.125	16	2	0	0	0	1	0	2	.125	.125

Luis Lopez — Mets

Age 27 – Bats Both

	Avg	G	AB	R	H	2B	3B	HR	RBI	BB	SO	HBP	GDP	SB	CS	OBP	SLG	IBB	SH	SF	#Pit	#P/PA	GB	FB	G/F
1997 Season	.270	78	178	19	48	12	1	1	19	12	42	4	2	2	4	.330	.365	2	2	0	673	3.43	63	37	1.70
Career (1993-1997)	.240	235	595	59	143	32	2	5	51	34	124	8	16	5	6	.291	.326	5	5	4	2242	3.46	229	128	1.79

1997 Season

	Avg	AB	H	2B	3B	HR	RBI	BB	SO	OBP	SLG		Avg	AB	H	2B	3B	HR	RBI	BB	SO	OBP	SLG
vs. Left	.235	51	12	3	0	1	4	5	7	.339	.353	Scoring Posn	.275	51	14	6	1	0	17	4	12	.339	.431
vs. Right	.283	127	36	9	1	0	15	7	35	.326	.370	Close & Late	.143	42	6	3	0	0	3	5	15	.250	.214
Home	.208	96	20	3	0	1	7	11	27	.303	.271	None on/out	.209	43	9	2	0	0	0	3	10	.277	.256
Away	.341	82	28	9	1	0	12	1	15	.365	.476	Batting #7	.235	34	8	3	0	1	4	5	5	.333	.412
First Pitch	.395	38	15	4	0	1	7	1	0	.425	.579	Batting #8	.300	80	24	5	1	0	10	3	20	.349	.388
Ahead in Count	.405	37	15	5	0	0	6	9	0	.532	.541	Other	.250	64	16	4	0	0	5	4	17	.304	.313
Behind in Count	.151	73	11	2	0	0	3	0	37	.162	.178	Pre-All Star	.270	74	20	4	1	0	5	6	16	.349	.351
Two Strikes	.118	76	9	2	0	0	2	2	42	.145	.145	Post-All Star	.269	104	28	8	0	1	14	6	26	.315	.375

Career (1993-1997)

	Avg	AB	H	2B	3B	HR	RBI	BB	SO	OBP	SLG		Avg	AB	H	2B	3B	HR	RBI	BB	SO	OBP	SLG
vs. Left	.248	113	28	5	0	1	10	10	17	.333	.319	First Pitch	.291	103	30	6	0	2	13	4	0	.324	.408
vs. Right	.239	482	115	27	2	4	41	26	107	.280	.328	Ahead in Count	.361	122	44	13	0	2	17	19	0	.456	.516
Groundball	.228	171	39	6	1	1	10	5	38	.251	.292	Behind in Count	.185	270	50	9	1	0	13	0	108	.190	.226
Flyball	.189	74	14	2	0	1	8	7	15	.268	.257	Two Strikes	.163	264	43	8	0	0	12	13	124	.206	.193
Home	.218	293	64	15	0	4	27	25	67	.283	.311	Batting #7	.199	196	39	11	0	3	16	14	36	.254	.301
Away	.262	302	79	17	2	1	24	11	57	.299	.341	Batting #8	.283	173	49	11	1	1	15	10	39	.337	.376
Day	.265	230	61	13	0	2	26	12	49	.304	.348	Other	.243	226	55	10	1	1	20	12	49	.288	.310
Night	.225	365	82	19	2	3	25	24	75	.283	.312	March/April	.289	38	11	4	0	1	3	3	10	.341	.474
Grass	.243	470	114	29	1	4	39	31	96	.294	.334	May	.274	106	29	7	0	2	16	10	17	.339	.434
Turf	.232	125	29	3	1	1	12	5	28	.278	.296	June	.224	143	32	8	2	0	10	8	32	.288	.308
Pre-All Star	.250	336	84	20	2	4	32	26	66	.314	.357	July	.247	146	36	4	0	1	8	9	25	.293	.295
Post-All Star	.228	259	59	12	0	1	19	10	58	.259	.286	August	.280	82	23	7	0	0	9	1	19	.286	.366
Scoring Posn	.230	148	34	9	1	1	44	14	30	.298	.324	Sept/Oct	.150	80	12	2	0	1	5	5	21	.207	.213
Close & Late	.185	130	24	7	0	2	11	10	37	.246	.285	vs. AL	.250	28	7	3	0	0	4	2	3	.344	.357
None on/out	.247	146	36	8	1	0	0	8	31	.295	.315	vs. NL	.240	567	136	29	2	5	47	34	121	.288	.325

Batter vs. Pitcher (career)

Hits Best Against	Avg	AB	H	2B	3B	HR	RBI	BB	SO	OBP	SLG	Hits Worst Against	Avg	AB	H	2B	3B	HR	RBI	BB	SO	OBP	SLG
												Kevin Gross	.100	10	1	0	0	0	0	1	3	.182	.100
												Darryl Kile	.182	11	2	1	0	0	1	0	1	.182	.273

Mark Loretta — Brewers
Age 26 – Bats Right

	Avg	G	AB	R	H	2B	3B	HR	RBI	BB	SO	HBP	GDP	SB	CS	OBP	SLG	IBB	SH	SF	#Pit	#P/PA	GB	FB	G/F
1997 Season	.287	132	418	56	120	17	5	5	47	47	60	2	16	5	5	.354	.388	2	5	10	1951	4.05	164	106	1.55
Career (1995-1997)	.283	224	622	89	176	23	5	7	63	65	82	3	23	8	7	.349	.370	2	8	10	2798	3.95	240	161	1.49

1997 Season

	Avg	AB	H	2B	3B	HR	RBI	BB	SO	OBP	SLG		Avg	AB	H	2B	3B	HR	RBI	BB	SO	OBP	SLG
vs. Left	.255	137	35	4	1	1	14	20	22	.348	.321	First Pitch	.469	32	15	4	1	2	9	1	0	.471	.844
vs. Right	.302	281	85	13	4	4	33	27	38	.358	.420	Ahead in Count	.221	68	15	2	2	2	9	34	0	.467	.397
Groundball	.320	75	24	4	1	0	7	4	4	.363	.400	Behind in Count	.250	220	55	6	2	0	17	0	51	.253	.295
Flyball	.262	65	17	3	0	0	4	7	17	.324	.308	Two Strikes	.277	231	64	8	1	1	19	12	60	.317	.333
Home	.329	207	68	11	3	2	24	26	35	.398	.440	Batting #1	.260	131	34	9	1	1	12	10	26	.317	.366
Away	.246	211	52	6	2	3	23	21	25	.311	.336	Batting #7	.304	102	31	2	2	3	14	10	13	.366	.451
Day	.302	159	48	5	0	2	15	14	22	.356	.371	Other	.297	185	55	6	2	1	21	27	21	.372	.368
Night	.278	259	72	12	5	3	32	33	38	.353	.398	March/April	.238	63	15	1	1	0	5	8	11	.324	.286
Grass	.308	373	115	17	5	3	42	41	53	.370	.368	May	.250	68	17	2	0	2	10	6	12	.308	.368
Turf	.111	45	5	0	0	2	5	6	7	.226	.244	June	.421	95	40	7	2	2	14	13	12	.482	.600
Pre-All Star	.297	246	73	10	3	4	29	27	38	.362	.411	July	.193	57	11	5	0	0	2	4	11	.246	.281
Post-All Star	.273	172	47	7	2	1	18	20	22	.343	.355	August	.257	74	19	1	2	1	10	5	5	.301	.365
Scoring Posn	.290	93	27	3	3	1	40	15	16	.367	.419	Sept/Oct	.295	61	18	1	0	0	6	11	9	.392	.311
Close & Late	.250	76	19	1	1	1	6	7	14	.313	.329	vs. AL	.290	372	108	15	5	4	44	42	54	.357	.390
None on/out	.279	111	31	6	1	2	2	16	22	.370	.405	vs. NL	.261	46	12	2	0	1	3	5	6	.333	.370

1997 By Position

Position	Avg	AB	H	2B	3B	HR	RBI	BB	SO	OBP	SLG	G	GS	Innings	PO	A	E	DP	Fld Pct	Rng Fctr	In Zone	Zone Outs	Zone Rtg	MLB Zone
As 1b	.267	60	16	1	1	1	10	5	5	.309	.367	19	16	147.0	151	7	2	10	.988	---	36	29	.806	.874
As 2b	.337	202	68	14	2	4	25	21	32	.397	.485	63	56	497.0	126	170	6	52	.980	5.36	182	169	.929	.902
As 3b	.216	37	8	0	1	0	5	4	3	.273	.270	15	10	92.0	9	16	1	3	.962	2.45	22	20	.909	.801
As ss	.246	114	28	2	1	0	7	16	18	.338	.281	44	29	276.0	51	83	6	23	.957	4.37	102	90	.882	.937

Andrew Lorraine — Athletics
Age 25 – Pitches Left (flyball pitcher)

	ERA	W	L	Sv	G	GS	IP	BB	SO	Avg	H	2B	3B	HR	RBI	OBP	SLG	CG	ShO	Sup	QS	#P/S	SB	CS	GB	FB	G/F
1997 Season	6.37	3	1	0	12	6	29.2	15	18	.354	45	12	2	2	20	.418	.528	0	0	11.83	1	73	2	1	42	43	0.98
Career (1994-1997)	7.35	3	3	0	21	9	56.1	28	33	.331	78	16	3	9	41	.400	.538	0	0	7.99	1	80	4	1	74	82	0.90

1997 Season

	ERA	W	L	Sv	G	GS	IP	H	HR	BB	SO		Avg	AB	H	2B	3B	HR	RBI	BB	SO	OBP	SLG
Home	9.37	1	1	0	8	4	16.1	30	1	6	11	vs. Left	.371	35	13	4	0	1	5	2	8	.410	.571
Away	2.70	2	0	0	4	2	13.1	15	1	9	7	vs. Right	.348	92	32	8	2	1	15	13	10	.421	.511

Derek Lowe — Red Sox
Age 25 – Pitches Right (groundball pitcher)

	ERA	W	L	Sv	G	GS	IP	BB	SO	Avg	H	2B	3B	HR	RBI	OBP	SLG	GF	IR	IRS	Hld	SvOp	SB	CS	GB	FB	G/F
1997 Season	6.13	2	6	0	20	9	69.0	23	52	.279	74	16	0	11	40	.344	.464	1	5	2	1	2	4	2	107	61	1.75

1997 Season

	ERA	W	L	Sv	G	GS	IP	H	HR	BB	SO		Avg	AB	H	2B	3B	HR	RBI	BB	SO	OBP	SLG
Home	7.20	1	4	0	9	5	35.0	39	7	14	27	vs. Left	.348	135	47	12	0	8	24	16	22	.419	.615
Away	5.03	1	2	0	11	4	34.0	35	4	9	25	vs. Right	.208	130	27	4	0	3	16	7	30	.259	.308
Starter	7.89	2	3	0	9	9	43.1	49	9	18	34	Scoring Posn	.313	64	20	8	0	3	30	7	12	.370	.578
Reliever	3.16	0	3	0	11	0	25.2	25	2	5	18	Close & Late	.292	24	7	1	0	0	1	2	5	.370	.333
0 Days rest (Relief)	0.00	0	0	0	0	0	0.0	0	0	0	0	None on/out	.277	65	18	6	0	3	3	9	14	.365	.508
1 or 2 Days rest	0.00	0	0	0	3	0	6.1	4	0	0	5	First Pitch	.226	31	7	2	0	1	5	1	0	.250	.387
3+ Days rest	4.19	0	3	0	8	0	19.1	21	2	5	13	Ahead in Count	.192	120	23	5	0	3	10	0	47	.203	.308
Pre-All Star	6.46	2	3	0	11	8	47.1	51	11	17	31	Behind in Count	.394	71	28	8	0	6	20	13	0	.488	.761
Post-All Star	5.40	0	3	0	9	1	21.2	23	0	6	21	Two Strikes	.186	118	22	5	0	3	11	9	52	.248	.305

Sean Lowe — Cardinals
Age 27 – Pitches Right (groundball pitcher)

	ERA	W	L	Sv	G	GS	IP	BB	SO	Avg	H	2B	3B	HR	RBI	OBP	SLG	CG	ShO	Sup	QS	#P/S	SB	CS	GB	FB	G/F
1997 Season	9.35	0	2	0	6	4	17.1	10	8	.365	27	5	0	2	17	.437	.514	0	0	2.60	0	69	2	0	37	13	2.85

1997 Season

	ERA	W	L	Sv	G	GS	IP	H	HR	BB	SO		Avg	AB	H	2B	3B	HR	RBI	BB	SO	OBP	SLG
Home	11.25	0	1	0	2	1	4.0	6	0	1	2	vs. Left	.419	31	13	3	0	1	9	5	3	.486	.613
Away	8.78	0	1	0	4	3	13.1	21	2	9	6	vs. Right	.326	43	14	2	0	1	8	5	5	.400	.442

Terrell Lowery — Cubs
Age 27 – Bats Right

	Avg	G	AB	R	H	2B	3B	HR	RBI	BB	SO	HBP	GDP	SB	CS	OBP	SLG	IBB	SH	SF	#Pit	#P/PA	GB	FB	G/F
1997 Season	.286	9	14	2	4	0	0	0	0	3	3	0	0	1	0	.412	.286	0	0	0	69	4.06	6	4	1.50

1997 Season

	Avg	AB	H	2B	3B	HR	RBI	BB	SO	OBP	SLG		Avg	AB	H	2B	3B	HR	RBI	BB	SO	OBP	SLG
vs. Left	.250	12	3	0	0	0	0	3	3	.400	.250	Scoring Posn	.333	3	1	0	0	0	0	2	1	.600	.333
vs. Right	.500	2	1	0	0	0	0	0	0	.500	.500	Close & Late	.000	1	0	0	0	0	0	1	1	.500	.000

Eric Ludwick — Athletics
Age 26 – Pitches Right

	ERA	W	L	Sv	G	GS	IP	BB	SO	Avg	H	2B	3B	HR	RBI	OBP	SLG	GF	IR	IRS	Hld	SvOp	SB	CS	GB	FB	G/F
1997 Season	8.51	1	5	0	11	5	30.2	22	21	.346	44	4	0	8	25	.447	.567	3	3	0	0	0	12'	1	36	34	1.06
Career (1996-1997)	8.63	1	6	0	17	6	40.2	25	33	.329	55	4	0	12	34	.421	.569	5	3	0	0	0	15	2	46	44	1.05

1997 Season

	ERA	W	L	Sv	G	GS	IP	H	HR	BB	SO		Avg	AB	H	2B	3B	HR	RBI	BB	SO	OBP	SLG
Home	8.27	0	2	0	5	2	16.1	22	5	9	12	vs. Left	.396	53	21	3	0	6	14	5	8	.458	.792
Away	8.79	1	3	0	6	3	14.1	22	3	13	9	vs. Right	.311	74	23	1	0	2	11	17	13	.440	.405

John Mabry — Cardinals
Age 27 – Bats Left

	Avg	G	AB	R	H	2B	3B	HR	RBI	BB	SO	HBP	GDP	SB	CS	OBP	SLG	IBB	SH	SF	#Pit	#P/PA	GB	FB	G/F
1997 Season	.284	116	388	40	110	19	0	5	36	39	77	3	11	0	1	.352	.371	9	2	2	1448	3.34	154	78	1.97
Career (1994-1997)	.296	402	1342	140	397	73	3	23	154	102	210	8	38	3	6	.347	.406	25	5	11	4745	3.23	591	305	1.94

1997 Season

	Avg	AB	H	2B	3B	HR	RBI	BB	SO	OBP	SLG		Avg	AB	H	2B	3B	HR	RBI	BB	SO	OBP	SLG
vs. Left	.266	94	25	6	0	0	10	5	23	.307	.330	First Pitch	.316	79	25	6	0	0	4				
vs. Right	.289	294	85	13	0	5	26	34	54	.366	.384	Ahead in Count	.419	74	31	4	0	1	10	1			
Groundball	.309	81	25	2	0	1	7	11	14	.391	.370	Behind in Count	.193	176	34	8	0	1	14				
Flyball	.237	59	14	5	0	1	4	4	19	.297	.373	Two Strikes	.194	165	32	5	0	1	15	1			
Home	.292	192	56	12	0	5	20	21	39	.367	.432	Batting #5	.261	138	36	2	0	3	16	2			
Away	.276	196	54	7	0	0	16	18	38	.336	.311	Batting #6	.295	176	52	12	0	2	17	1			
Day	.312	138	43	3	0	3	14	10	26	.360	.399	Other	.297	74	22	5	0	0	3				
Night	.268	250	67	16	0	2	22	29	51	.348	.356	March/April	.239	71	17	4	0	1	6	1			
Grass	.278	324	90	15	0	5	33	35	69	.353	.370	May	.320	97	31	3	0	1	11				
Turf	.313	64	20	4	0	0	3	4	8	.348	.375	June	.340	94	32	8	0	3	17	1			
Pre-All Star	.295	285	84	15	0	5	35	35	56	.372	.400	July	.231	91	21	2	0	0	1				
Post-All Star	.252	103	26	4	0	0	1	4	21	.294	.291	August	.257	35	9	2	0	0	1				
Scoring Posn	.280	82	23	6	0	2	31	26	18	.460	.427	Sept/Oct	.000	0	0	0	0	0	0				
Close & Late	.313	67	21	5	0	0	6	10	13	.425	.388	vs. AL	.345	29	10	3	0	2	6				
None on/out	.294	102	30	2	0	2	2	4	16	.321	.373	vs. NL	.279	359	100	16	0	3	30				

1997 By Position

Position	Avg	AB	H	2B	3B	HR	RBI	BB	SO	OBP	SLG	G	GS	Innings	PO	A	E	DP	Fld Pct	Rng Fctr	In Zone
As 1b	.297	138	41	6	0	3	11	12	28	.355	.406	49	38	331.2	346	22	1	34	.997	---	60
As rf	.284	225	64	10	0	1	21	22	45	.349	.342	71	61	527.1	96	8	0	1	1.000	1.77	115

Career (1994-1997)

	Avg	AB	H	2B	3B	HR	RBI	BB	SO	OBP	SLG		Avg	AB	H	2B	3B	HR	RBI	BB	SO	OBP	SLG
vs. Left	.314	293	92	16	1	5	43	14	53	.350	.427	First Pitch	.396	280	111	24	1	4	37	20	0	.438	.532
vs. Right	.291	1049	305	57	2	18	111	88	157	.345	.400	Ahead in Count	.377	305	115	16	2	8	54	52	0	.467	.521
Groundball	.313	307	96	14	1	4	29	28	40	.369	.404	Behind in Count	.205	565	116	23	0	5	37	0	186	.207	.273
Flyball	.252	202	51	11	0	6	14	15	46	.306	.396	Two Strikes	.176	500	88	19	0	7	36	30	210	.221	.256
Home	.287	668	192	46	1	10	75	55	107	.344	.404	Batting #5	.289	464	134	24	0	10	58	38	63	.341	.405
Away	.304	674	205	27	2	13	79	47	103	.349	.408	Batting #6	.299	575	172	33	2	9	76	48	97	.353	.410
Day	.326	438	143	26	0	8	53	32	63	.372	.441	Other	.300	303	91	16	1	4	20	16	50	.344	.399
Night	.281	904	254	47	3	15	101	70	147	.334	.389	March/April	.267	180	48	10	0	2	18	19	37	.338	.356
Grass	.282	877	247	49	2	13	99	72	161	.339	.387	May	.332	259	86	14	1	4	31	15	42	.369	.440
Turf	.323	465	150	24	1	10	55	30	49	.362	.443	June	.332	241	80	21	0	6	36	23	40	.391	.494
Pre-All Star	.312	764	238	45	1	13	93	65	130	.367	.424	July	.244	270	66	3	2	5	24	22	40	.303	.326
Post-All Star	.275	578	159	28	2	10	61	37	80	.319	.382	August	.282	220	62	13	0	4	22	9	40	.313	.395
Scoring Posn	.296	318	94	18	0	5	124	59	56	.404	.399	Sept/Oct	.320	172	55	12	0	2	23	14	11	.368	.424
Close & Late	.309	230	71	16	1	1	25	25	43	.383	.400	vs. AL	.345	29	10	3	0	2	6	7	2	.472	.655
None on/out	.269	335	90	16	2	7	7	10	45	.292	.391	vs. NL	.295	1313	387	70	3	21	148	95	208	.343	.401

Batter vs. Pitcher (career)

Hits Best Against	Avg	AB	H	2B	3B	HR	RBI	BB	SO	OBP	SLG	Hits Worst Against	Avg	AB	H	2B	3B	HR	RBI	BB	SO	OBP	SLG
Dave Burba	.600	10	6	2	0	0	1	1	2	.636	.800	Dave Mlicki	.000	10	0	0	0	0	0	1	2	.091	.000
Mark Portugal	.400	10	4	1	0	1	4	1	2	.455	.800	Bobby Jones	.125	16	2	0	0	1	2	1	1	.167	.313
Armando Reynoso	.389	18	7	3	0	1	3	1	0	.421	.722	Kevin Ritz	.133	15	2	0	0	0	0	1	2	.188	.133
Doug Drabek	.333	12	4	0	0	1	2	1	2	.385	.583	Pete Harnisch	.167	12	2	2	0	0	0	0	2	.167	.333
VanLandingham	.333	9	3	0	0	1	1	3	0	.500	.667	Esteban Loaiza	.211	19	4	1	0	0	4	1	4	.238	.263

Mike Macfarlane — Royals
Age 34 – Bats Right (flyball hitter)

	Avg	G	AB	R	H	2B	3B	HR	RBI	BB	SO	HBP	GDP	SB	CS	OBP	SLG	IBB	SH	SF	#Pit	#P/PA	GB	FB	G/F
1997 Season	.237	82	257	34	61	14	2	8	35	24	47	6	4	0	2	.316	.401	3	3	1	1029	3.54	83	86	0.97
Last Five Years	.254	518	1702	245	433	100	8	76	254	168	336	61	34	8	11	.340	.457	11	4	16	6948	3.56	530	589	0.90

1997 Season

	Avg	AB	H	2B	3B	HR	RBI	BB	SO	OBP	SLG		Avg	AB	H	2B	3B	HR	RBI	BB	SO	OBP	SLG
vs. Left	.200	80	16	4	0	2	12	3	16	.229	.325	Scoring Posn	.286	63	18	5	0	2	26	9	15	.387	.460
vs. Right	.254	177	45	10	2	6	23	21	31	.351	.435	Close & Late	.273	44	12	0	1	1	5	4	6	.340	.386
Home	.284	134	38	10	2	5	21	11	24	.360	.500	None on/out	.154	65	10	4	1	2	2	7	11	.247	.338
Away	.187	123	23	4	0	3	14	13	23	.268	.293	Batting #8	.295	122	36	9	1	5	23	11	19	.365	.508
First Pitch	.352	54	19	4	0	1	8	3	0	.397	.481	Batting #9	.214	70	15	3	1	3	7	8	16	.313	.414
Ahead in Count	.300	50	15	4	0	4	12	13	0	.444	.620	Other	.154	65	10	2	0	0	5	5	12	.225	.185
Behind in Count	.163	104	17	5	2	1	9	0	41	.185	.279	Pre-All Star	.182	148	27	3	0	3	17	14	25	.262	.264
Two Strikes	.128	109	14	2	2	2	9	8	47	.207	.239	Post-All Star	.312	109	34	11	2	5	18	10	22	.387	.587

Last Five Years

	Avg	AB	H	2B	3B	HR	RBI	BB	SO	OBP	SLG		Avg	AB	H	2B	3B	HR	RBI	BB	SO	OBP	SLG
vs. Left	.246	540	133	33	3	25	83	59	112	.326	.457	First Pitch	.333	309	103	22	2	17	61	8	0	.377	.583
vs. Right	.258	1162	300	67	5	51	171	109	224	.346	.456	Ahead in Count	.334	353	118	31	2	19	60	89	0	.469	.595
Groundball	.284	320	91	16	1	15	57	38	57	.380	.481	Behind in Count	.179	745	133	25	3	26	81	0	297	.209	.325
Flyball	.219	320	70	14	3	16	47	28	69	.298	.431	Two Strikes	.172	748	129	30	3	28	82	71	336	.266	.333
Home	.277	862	239	69	6	37	139	81	154	.358	.500	Batting #4	.246	586	144	28	1	26	74	66	128	.344	.430
Away	.231	840	194	31	2	39	115	87	182	.321	.412	Batting #8	.279	412	115	38	3	10	57	39	62	.361	.459
Day	.281	501	141	29	1	27	87	50	97	.361	.505	Other	.247	704	174	34	4	40	123	63	146	.324	.477
Night	.243	1201	292	71	7	49	167	118	239	.331	.436	March/April	.214	206	44	7	2	7	29	22	40	.299	.398
Grass	.257	1139	293	60	6	55	164	110	217	.342	.465	May	.263	289	76	19	0	17	54	33	55	.362	.505
Turf	.249	563	140	40	2	21	90	58	119	.337	.439	June	.239	348	83	15	2	14	46	32	69	.328	.414
Pre-All Star	.245	957	234	48	4	45	152	97	190	.335	.444	July	.243	317	77	20	0	16	44	31	65	.342	.457
Post-All Star	.267	745	199	52	4	31	102	71	146	.346	.472	August	.267	315	84	24	4	14	46	28	69	.342	.502
Scoring Posn	.239	464	111	25	2	22	183	62	99	.346	.444	Sept/Oct	.304	227	69	15	0	8	35	22	38	.362	.476
Close & Late	.238	290	69	13	1	13	40	29	59	.319	.424	vs. AL	.254	1674	426	97	8	76	246	161	331	.339	.458
None on/out	.253	438	111	31	2	20	20	40	82	.330	.470	vs. NL	.250	28	7	3	0	1	8	7	5	.405	.357

Batter vs. Pitcher (career)

Hits Best Against	Avg	AB	H	2B	3B	HR	RBI	BB	SO	OBP	SLG	Hits Worst Against	Avg	AB	H	2B	3B	HR	RBI	BB	SO	OBP	SLG
Alan Mills	.500	10	5	1	1	2	4	2	3	.583	1.400	Tony Castillo	.071	14	1	0	0	0	0	1	1	.133	.071
Aaron Sele	.500	10	5	1	0	1	2	2	2	.583	.900	Dennis Eckersley	.083	12	1	0	0	0	1	0	4	.154	.083
Charles Nagy	.474	19	9	0	0	3	6	0	5	.474	.947	Angel Miranda	.083	12	1	0	0	0	0	1	5	.154	.083
Jason Bere	.429	14	6	0	0	3	6	5	4	.579	1.071	Wilson Alvarez	.100	10	1	0	0	0	2	3	3	.286	.100
Mike Mussina	.357	28	10	2	0	4	5	2	5	.387	.857	Greg Swindell	.130	23	3	0	0	1	0	6	.130	.130

Robert Machado — White Sox
Age 25 – Bats Right

	Avg	G	AB	R	H	2B	3B	HR	RBI	BB	SO	HBP	GDP	SB	CS	OBP	SLG	IBB	SH	SF	#Pit	#P/PA	GB	FB	G/F
1997 Season	.200	10	15	3	3	0	1	0	2	1	6	0	0	0	0	.250	.333	0	1	0	60	3.53	3	4	0.75
Career (1996-1997)	.333	14	21	2	7	1	2	0	4	1	6	0	1	0	0	.364	.476	0	1	0	74	3.22	6	5	1.20

1997 Season

	Avg	AB	H	2B	3B	HR	RBI	BB	SO	OBP	SLG		Avg	AB	H	2B	3B	HR	RBI	BB	SO	OBP	SLG
vs. Left	.000	5	0	0	0	0	0	0	3	.000	.000	Scoring Posn	.333	3	1	0	1	0	2	1	2	.500	1.000
vs. Right	.300	10	3	0	1	0	2	1	3	.364	.500	Close & Late	.500	2	1	0	0	0	0	0	0	.500	.500

Shane Mack — Red Sox
Age 34 – Bats Right (groundball hitter)

	Avg	G	AB	R	H	2B	3B	HR	RBI	BB	SO	HBP	GDP	SB	CS	OBP	SLG	IBB	SH	SF	#Pit	#P/PA	GB	FB	G/F
1997 Season	.315	60	130	13	41	7	0	3	17	9	24	3	3	2	1	.368	.438	1	2	2	480	3.29	55	32	1.72
Last Five Years	.300	269	936	134	281	58	6	28	139	82	151	13	27	21	7	.362	.465	3	6	9	3738	3.57	434	218	1.99

1997 Season

	Avg	AB	H	2B	3B	HR	RBI	BB	SO	OBP	SLG		Avg	AB	H	2B	3B	HR	RBI	BB	SO	OBP	SLG
vs. Left	.305	59	18	3	0	1	5	5	8	.373	.407	Scoring Posn	.244	41	10	3	0	0	13	5	5	.340	.317
vs. Right	.324	71	23	4	0	2	12	4	16	.364	.465	Close & Late	.261	23	6	1	0	0	3	2	5	.320	.304
Home	.275	69	19	3	0	2	8	6	13	.338	.406	None on/out	.321	28	9	0	0	1	1	2	6	.387	.429
Away	.361	61	22	4	0	1	9	3	11	.403	.475	Batting #8	.273	22	6	1	0	0	2	3	3	.333	.318
First Pitch	.433	30	13	4	0	1	3	1	0	.469	.667	Batting #9	.329	76	25	5	0	2	11	4	17	.373	.474
Ahead in Count	.389	18	7	1	0	2	5	5	0	.500	.778	Other	.313	32	10	1	0	1	4	3	4	.378	.438
Behind in Count	.241	58	14	2	0	0	8	0	19	.262	.276	Pre-All Star	.316	95	30	5	0	3	12	6	17	.359	.463
Two Strikes	.232	56	13	0	0	0	3	1	24	.279	.232	Post-All Star	.314	35	11	2	0	0	5	3	7	.390	.371

Last Five Years

	Avg	AB	H	2B	3B	HR	RBI	BB	SO	OBP	SLG		Avg	AB	H	2B	3B	HR	RBI	BB	SO	OBP	SLG
vs. Left	.332	256	85	19	2	8	36	18	28	.379	.516	First Pitch	.368	136	50	13	2	6	22	3	0	.390	.625
vs. Right	.288	680	196	39	4	20	103	64	123	.355	.446	Ahead in Count	.374	195	73	15	1	6	43	45	0	.484	.554
Groundball	.311	167	52	8	1	5	29	21	31	.395	.461	Behind in Count	.226	438	99	25	1	11	51	0	131	.237	.363
Flyball	.305	190	58	12	3	9	36	14	33	.361	.542	Two Strikes	.215	414	89	17	0	8	43	34	151	.280	.314
Home	.302	453	137	31	4	13	70	42	75	.366	.475	Batting #1	.278	259	72	16	1	4	28	16	35	.324	.394
Away	.298	483	144	27	2	15	69	40	76	.357	.455	Batting #5	.293	157	46	11	0	4	21	15	25	.358	.439
Day	.253	269	68	14	3	4	41	21	49	.315	.372	Other	.313	520	163	31	5	20	90	51	91	.381	.508
Night	.319	667	213	44	3	24	98	61	102	.380	.502	March/April	.233	103	24	6	0	0	11	5	17	.275	.291
Grass	.300	437	131	26	1	14	63	42	72	.367	.460	May	.283	145	41	11	1	6	29	9	18	.331	.497

Last Five Years

	Avg	AB	H	2B	3B	HR	RBI	BB	SO	OBP	SLG		Avg	AB	H	2B	3B	HR	RBI	BB	SO	OBP	SLG
Turf	.301	499	150	32	5	14	76	40	79	.356	.469	June	.286	234	67	12	4	11	41	30	42	.374	.513
Pre-All Star	.291	560	163	36	5	19	93	55	90	.359	.475	July	.345	232	80	19	0	7	33	20	38	.397	.517
Post-All Star	.314	376	118	22	1	9	46	27	61	.366	.449	August	.319	166	53	5	1	3	22	14	26	.380	.416
Scoring Posn	.320	225	72	15	2	11	115	29	31	.398	.551	Sept/Oct	.286	56	16	5	0	1	3	4	10	.333	.429
Close & Late	.250	144	36	10	1	5	26	13	25	.319	.438	vs. AL	.298	910	271	57	6	27	132	80	147	.360	.463
None on/out	.271	266	72	12	0	8	8	12	41	.310	.406	vs. NL	.385	26	10	1	0	1	7	2	4	.414	.538

Batter vs. Pitcher (career)

Hits Best Against	Avg	AB	H	2B	3B	HR	RBI	BB	SO	OBP	SLG	Hits Worst Against	Avg	AB	H	2B	3B	HR	RBI	BB	SO	OBP	SLG
Cal Eldred	.500	12	6	2	0	0	0	1	3	.538	.667	Bob Wickman	.083	12	1	0	0	0	0	2	4	.214	.083
Jimmy Key	.464	28	13	1	0	1	6	3	2	.516	.607	Alex Fernandez	.103	29	3	0	0	0	2	1	9	.129	.103
Ben McDonald	.450	20	9	2	0	3	5	2	4	.500	1.000	Mike Magnante	.125	16	2	0	0	0	0	0	0	.125	.125
Chuck Finley	.429	42	18	7	2	2	4	5	7	.500	.833	Greg Swindell	.167	12	2	0	0	0	1	1	2	.231	.167
Kenny Rogers	.333	18	6	3	0	1	2	2	2	.400	.667	Jeff Montgomery	.200	15	3	0	0	0	1	0	2	.200	.200

Greg Maddux — Braves

Age 32 – Pitches Right (groundball pitcher)

	ERA	W	L	Sv	G	GS	IP	BB	SO	Avg	H	2B	3B	HR	RBI	OBP	SLG	CG	ShO	Sup	QS	#P/S	SB	CS	GB	FB	G/F
1997 Season	2.20	19	4	0	33	33	232.2	20	177	.236	200	31	3	9	56	.256	.311	5	2	5.34	27	86	20	8	379	164	2.31
Last Five Years	2.13	89	33	0	157	157	1156.1	154	883	.254	950	158	13	46	282	.254	.300	38	10	4.45	126	94	116	31	1993	736	2.71

1997 Season

	ERA	W	L	Sv	G	GS	IP	H	HR	BB	SO		Avg	AB	H	2B	3B	HR	RBI	BB	SO	OBP	SLG
Home	2.18	8	3	0	18	18	132.0	118	4	13	97	vs. Left	.213	394	84	16	1	6	31	13	97	.239	.305
Away	2.24	11	1	0	15	15	100.2	82	5	7	80	vs. Right	.255	455	116	15	2	3	25	7	80	.271	.316
Day	1.94	10	0	0	11	11	79.0	50	3	6	60	Inning 1-6	.244	717	175	24	3	7	48	15	149	.262	.315
Night	2.34	9	4	0	22	22	153.2	150	6	14	117	Inning 7+	.189	132	25	7	0	2	8	5	28	.223	.288
Grass	1.89	15	3	0	28	28	204.2	166	7	18	154	None on	.245	543	133	21	2	4	4	10	117	.265	.313
Turf	4.50	4	1	0	5	5	28.0	34	2	2	23	Runners on	.219	306	67	10	1	5	52	10	60	.241	.307
March/April	1.13	3	1	0	5	5	32.0	22	0	3	29	Scoring Posn	.208	159	33	2	1	4	47	9	39	.244	.308
May	1.90	3	0	0	6	6	42.2	41	1	6	33	Close & Late	.186	97	18	4	0	1	6	5	22	.223	.258
June	4.29	4	2	0	6	6	42.0	38	3	4	29	None on/out	.268	228	61	9	2	1	1	5	51	.289	.338
July	1.66	5	0	0	5	5	38.0	25	2	4	30	vs. 1st Batr (relief)	.000	0	0	0	0	0	0	0	0	.000	.000
August	2.36	2	0	0	6	6	42.0	43	2	2	30	1st Inning Pitched	.220	118	26	3	0	2	9	3	28	.242	.297
Sept/Oct	1.50	2	1	0	5	5	36.0	31	1	1	26	First 75 Pitches	.234	718	168	21	3	8	46	12	149	.250	.305
Starter	2.20	19	4	0	33	33	232.2	200	9	20	177	Pitch 76-90	.253	87	22	7	0	1	8	5	17	.301	.368
Reliever	0.00	0	0	0	0	0	0.0	0	0	0	0	Pitch 91-105	.294	34	10	3	0	0	2	3	9	.342	.382
0-3 Days Rest (Start)	1.23	2	0	0	3	3	22.0	17	1	2	19	Pitch 106+	.000	10	0	0	0	0	0	0	2	.000	.000
4 Days Rest	2.04	13	1	0	21	21	149.2	118	8	8	102	First Pitch	.288	153	44	7	0	3	12	5	0	.308	.392
5+ Days Rest	2.95	4	3	0	9	9	61.0	65	0	10	56	Ahead in Count	.178	433	77	14	2	1	17	0	164	.188	.224
vs. AL	3.10	2	2	0	4	4	29.0	25	1	0	25	Behind in Count	.319	138	44	7	0	3	17	7	0	.345	.435
vs. NL	2.08	17	2	0	29	29	203.2	175	8	20	152	Two Strikes	.152	361	55	7	2	1	16	8	177	.176	.191
Pre-All Star	2.36	11	3	0	18	18	125.2	104	4	13	99	Pre-All Star	.228	456	104	20	1	4	33	13	99	.252	.303
Post-All Star	2.02	8	1	0	15	15	107.0	96	5	7	78	Post-All Star	.244	393	96	11	2	5	23	7	78	.262	.321

Last Five Years

	ERA	W	L	Sv	G	GS	IP	H	HR	BB	SO		Avg	AB	H	2B	3B	HR	RBI	BB	SO	OBP	SLG
Home	2.18	40	16	0	78	78	589.1	480	26	74	444	vs. Left	.215	2066	445	66	7	20	130	91	473	.250	.283
Away	2.08	49	17	0	79	79	567.0	470	20	80	439	vs. Right	.232	2177	505	92	6	26	152	63	410	.258	.316
Day	1.86	33	6	0	46	46	333.1	262	10	42	242	Inning 1-6	.225	3367	759	125	11	31	221	116	704	.254	.297
Night	2.24	56	27	0	111	111	823.0	688	36	112	641	Inning 7+	.219	874	191	33	2	15	61	38	179	.254	.312
Grass	2.17	67	22	0	119	119	882.2	717	39	122	658	None on	.227	2712	616	105	11	28	28	74	574	.251	.305
Turf	2.01	22	11	0	38	38	273.2	233	7	32	225	Runners on	.218	1529	334	53	2	18	254	80	309	.259	.291
March/April	1.91	14	6	0	24	24	174.2	136	8	25	137	Scoring Posn	.204	866	177	28	2	14	232	69	188	.263	.290
May	2.48	14	5	0	29	29	214.0	173	9	32	181	Close & Late	.227	559	127	19	1	12	50	30	128	.270	.329
June	2.71	14	8	0	28	28	206.0	189	8	30	138	None on/out	.254	1148	292	46	4	12	12	32	242	.278	.333
July	2.04	19	8	0	29	29	220.2	176	8	25	178	vs. 1st Batr (relief)	.000	0	0	0	0	0	0	0	0	.000	.000
August	1.83	16	3	0	26	26	201.2	160	10	24	142	1st Inning Pitched	.235	595	140	28	0	6	51	25	113	.269	.313
Sept/Oct	1.61	12	3	0	21	21	139.1	107	3	18	107	First 75 Pitches	.219	3277	718	115	10	31	199	100	674	.245	.289
Starter	2.13	89	33	0	157	157	1156.1	950	46	154	883	Pitch 76-90	.254	531	135	28	2	7	45	21	115	.286	.354
Reliever	0.00	0	0	0	0	0	0.0	0	0	0	0	Pitch 91-105	.228	312	71	10	1	6	28	23	71	.279	.324
0-3 Days Rest (Start)	1.64	6	0	0	10	10	77.0	56	4	9	62	Pitch 106+	.215	121	26	5	0	2	10	10	23	.278	.306
4 Days Rest	2.16	54	24	0	101	101	729.2	601	29	103	557	First Pitch	.264	770	203	28	2	6	60	22	0	.286	.329
5+ Days Rest	2.19	29	9	0	46	46	349.2	293	13	42	264	Ahead in Count	.165	2057	339	60	4	18	95	0	764	.172	.224
vs. AL	3.10	2	2	0	4	4	29.0	25	1	0	25	Behind in Count	.318	702	223	35	3	10	69	66	0	.373	.419
vs. NL	2.11	87	31	0	153	153	1127.1	925	45	154	858	Two Strikes	.134	1807	243	42	4	14	76	66	883	.169	.185
Pre-All Star	2.34	47	23	0	91	91	669.2	560	26	95	526	Pre-All Star	.227	2463	560	99	7	26	178	95	526	.258	.305
Post-All Star	1.85	42	10	0	66	66	486.2	390	20	59	357	Post-All Star	.219	1778	390	59	6	20	104	59	357	.248	.293

Pitcher vs. Batter (career)

Pitches Best Vs.	Avg	AB	H	2B	3B	HR	RBI	BB	SO	OBP	SLG	Pitches Worst Vs.	Avg	AB	H	2B	3B	HR	RBI	BB	SO	OBP	SLG
Archi Cianfrocco	.000	11	0	0	0	0	1	0	3	.000	.000	Raul Mondesi	.500	12	6	2	0	0	1	1	0	.538	.667
Phil Plantier	.053	19	1	0	0	0	0	0	6	.053	.053	Bip Roberts	.471	34	16	4	0	0	3	7	4	.561	.588
Nelson Liriano	.067	15	1	0	0	0	0	0	5	.067	.067	Ricky Otero	.467	15	7	2	0	0	0	0	0	.467	.600
Rey Sanchez	.071	14	1	0	0	0	0	0	1	.071	.071	Tony Gwynn	.459	74	34	6	1	0	8	10	0	.524	.568
Don Slaught	.091	11	1	0	0	0	0	0	3	.091	.091	Marquis Grissom	.405	42	17	4	0	1	3	0	3	.409	.571

Mike Maddux — Mariners
Age 36 – Pitches Right (groundball pitcher)

	ERA	W	L	Sv	G	GS	IP	BB	SO	Avg	H	2B	3B	HR	RBI	OBP	SLG	GF	IR	IRS	Hld	SvOp	SB	CS	GB	FB	G/F
1997 Season	10.13	1	0	0	6	0	10.2	8	7	.400	20	6	0	1	9	.492	.580	1	4	2	0	0	0	0	22	13	1.69
Last Five Years	4.43	14	12	8	158	11	292.2	93	197	.270	308	68	8	28	161	.328	.417	53	93	39	12	16	32	7	476	251	1.90

1997 Season

	ERA	W	L	Sv	G	GS	IP	H	HR	BB	SO		Avg	AB	H	2B	3B	HR	RBI	BB	SO	OBP	SLG
Home	15.43	0	0	0	1	0	2.1	7	0	1	0	vs. Left	.294	17	5	1	0	0	2	4	3	.429	.353
Away	8.64	1	0	0	5	0	8.1	13	1	7	7	vs. Right	.455	33	15	5	0	1	7	4	4	.526	.697

Last Five Years

	ERA	W	L	Sv	G	GS	IP	H	HR	BB	SO		Avg	AB	H	2B	3B	HR	RBI	BB	SO	OBP	SLG
Home	4.08	9	5	2	77	5	143.1	158	16	33	85	vs. Left	.284	525	149	36	3	16	81	53	90	.350	.455
Away	4.76	5	7	6	81	6	149.1	150	12	60	112	vs. Right	.258	617	159	32	5	12	80	40	107	.309	.384
Day	3.64	5	2	3	59	4	106.1	103	11	27	70	Inning 1-6	.270	549	148	33	2	14	77	34	87	.316	.413
Night	4.88	9	10	5	99	7	186.1	205	17	66	127	Inning 7+	.270	593	160	35	6	14	84	59	110	.339	.420
Grass	4.32	11	10	5	122	10	225.0	240	23	72	153	None on	.250	616	154	30	7	13	13	42	106	.304	.385
Turf	4.79	3	2	3	36	1	67.2	68	5	21	44	Runners on	.293	526	154	38	1	15	148	51	91	.355	.454
March/April	4.17	0	2	4	31	0	45.1	45	5	20	20	Scoring Posn	.263	338	89	26	1	7	127	43	61	.343	.408
May	6.27	2	3	0	27	0	37.1	43	6	15	32	Close & Late	.313	233	73	16	4	5	43	29	38	.389	.481
June	5.87	2	1	0	31	0	53.2	74	2	14	40	None on/out	.267	270	72	17	3	2	2	20	34	.320	.374
July	1.54	2	2	1	22	1	41.0	29	2	13	21	vs. 1st Batr (relief)	.326	135	44	14	2	3	23	9	15	.370	.526
August	4.36	6	1	1	24	5	64.0	69	6	15	41	1st Inning Pitched	.274	552	151	34	3	11	89	50	96	.335	.406
Sept/Oct	4.21	2	2	1	23	5	51.1	48	7	16	43	First 15 Pitches	.290	496	144	32	4	7	65	39	77	.344	.413
Starter	3.77	5	1	0	11	11	62.0	62	8	14	35	Pitch 16-30	.207	304	63	13	1	10	43	29	68	.279	.355
Reliever	4.60	9	11	8	147	0	230.2	246	20	79	162	Pitch 31-45	.259	174	45	12	2	3	24	17	34	.332	.402
0 Days rest (Relief)	2.95	1	1	0	15	0	21.1	17	3	7	12	Pitch 46+	.333	168	56	11	1	8	29	8	18	.372	.554
1 or 2 Days rest	5.16	5	5	8	76	0	122.0	145	8	36	86	First Pitch	.314	172	54	13	0	3	31	15	0	.365	.442
3+ Days rest	4.23	3	5	0	56	0	87.1	84	9	36	64	Ahead in Count	.221	520	115	17	2	14	58	0	170	.229	.342
vs. AL	4.21	8	3	1	64	11	162.1	175	18	49	104	Behind in Count	.346	237	82	19	2	8	47	37	0	.429	.544
vs. NL	4.70	6	9	7	94	0	130.1	133	10	44	93	Two Strikes	.206	499	103	20	2	9	51	40	197	.270	.309
Pre-All Star	5.00	4	8	6	95	0	151.1	175	13	52	102	Pre-All Star	.290	603	175	40	4	13	93	52	102	.348	.434
Post-All Star	3.82	10	4	2	63	11	141.1	133	15	41	95	Post-All Star	.247	539	133	28	4	15	68	41	95	.306	.397

Pitcher vs. Batter (career)

Pitches Best Vs.	Avg	AB	H	2B	3B	HR	RBI	BB	SO	Pitches Worst Vs.	Avg	AB	H	2B	3B	HR	RBI	BB	SO	OBP	SLG
David Justice	.000	9	0	0	0	0	1	4	2	Dave Martinez	.583	12	7	0	0	0	3	1	.688	.583
Larry Walker	.100	10	1	0	0	0	2	0	2	Jose Offerman	.556	9	5	0	0	0	2	1	.636	.556
Dave Hollins	.100	10	1	0	0	0	0	1	6	Andres Galarraga	.550	20	11	3	0	2	8	1	2	.571	1.000
Marquis Grissom	.154	13	2	0	0	0	0	5	Mark Grace	.409	22	9	1	0	1	6	3	2	.462	.591
Damon Berryhill	.167	12	2	0	0	0	2	0	2	.167	.167	Shawon Dunston	.333	18	6	3	0	1	2	2	6	.400	.667

Calvin Maduro — Phillies
Age 23 – Pitches Right (flyball pitcher)

	ERA	W	L	Sv	G	GS	IP	BB	SO	Avg	H	2B	3B	HR	RBI	OBP	SLG	CG	ShO	Sup	QS	#P/S	SB	CS	GB	FB	G/F
1997 Season	7.23	3	7	0	15	13	71.0	41	31	.294	83	22	3	12	51	.385	.521	0	0	4.06	4	92	4	3	88	107	0.82
Career (1996-1997)	6.57	3	8	0	19	15	86.1	44	42	.284	96	25	3	13	55	.371	.491	0	0	3.96	5	93	5	4	104	122	0.85

1997 Season

	ERA	W	L	Sv	G	GS	IP	H	HR	BB	SO		Avg	AB	H	2B	3B	HR	RBI	BB	SO	OBP	SLG
Home	6.80	3	3	0	8	8	43.2	53	10	18	20	vs. Left	.303	109	33	8	1	1	14	24	9	.437	.422
Away	7.90	0	4	0	7	5	27.1	30	2	23	11	vs. Right	.289	173	50	14	2	11	37	17	22	.349	.584
Starter	7.38	3	7	0	13	13	68.1	81	12	37	31	Scoring Posn	.316	76	24	5	2	3	38	17	8	.429	.553
Reliever	3.38	0	0	0	2	0	2.2	2	0	4	0	Close & Late	.167	6	1	1	0	0	1	0	.143	.333
0-3 Days Rest (Start)	0.00	0	0	0	0	0	0.0	0	0	0	0	None on/out	.301	73	22	4	0	4	4	6	6	.363	.521
4 Days Rest	8.14	1	6	0	9	9	45.1	50	9	29	20	First Pitch	.267	30	8	4	1	1	4	3	0	.324	.567
5+ Days Rest	5.87	2	1	0	4	4	23.0	31	3	8	11	Ahead in Count	.250	108	27	7	1	4	13	0	24	.250	.444
Pre-All Star	7.23	3	7	0	15	13	71.0	83	12	41	31	Behind in Count	.372	86	32	8	0	4	25	23	0	.504	.605
Post-All Star	0.00	0	0	0	0	0	0.0	0	0	0	0	Two Strikes	.196	112	22	5	1	2	12	15	31	.289	.313

Dave Magadan — Athletics
Age 35 – Bats Left

	Avg	G	AB	R	H	2B	3B	HR	RBI	BB	SO	HBP	GDP	SB	CS	OBP	SLG	IBB	SH	SF	#Pit	#P/PA	GB	FB	G/F
1997 Season	.303	128	271	38	82	10	1	4	30	50	40	2	7	1	0	.414	.391	1	4	1	1451	4.42	105	60	1.75
Last Five Years	.286	544	1454	184	416	74	1	15	165	269	207	4	39	5	4	.396	.369	20	8	14	7255	4.15	550	358	1.54

1997 Season

	Avg	AB	H	2B	3B	HR	RBI	BB	SO	OBP	SLG		Avg	AB	H	2B	3B	HR	RBI	BB	SO	OBP	SLG
vs. Left	.220	41	9	0	0	0	7	6	6	.313	.220	First Pitch	.294	17	5	1	0	0	3	1	0	.368	.353
vs. Right	.317	230	73	10	1	4	23	44	34	.431	.422	Ahead in Count	.277	47	13	2	0	1	5	24	0	.514	.383
Groundball	.273	55	15	0	0	0	0	16	7	.437	.273	Behind in Count	.288	125	36	5	0	1	10	0	30	.294	.352
Flyball	.264	53	14	3	0	0	5	7	1	.361	.321	Two Strikes	.268	153	41	5	1	1	11	25	40	.374	.333
Home	.302	129	39	3	0	2	15	23	15	.409	.372	Batting #2	.242	95	23	3	0	0	8	19	11	.374	.274
Away	.303	142	43	7	1	2	15	27	25	.418	.408	Batting #6	.365	52	19	4	1	3	12	8	.492	.500
Day	.319	119	38	3	0	2	14	18	17	.410	.395	Other	.323	124	40	3	1	3	19	19	21	.410	.435
Night	.289	152	44	7	1	2	16	32	23	.416	.388	March/April	.292	24	7	0	0	1	6	3	.433	.417
Grass	.308	247	76	10	1	4	28	46	34	.419	.405	May	.268	41	11	0	0	1	4	9	5	.348	.341
Turf	.250	24	6	0	0	0	2	4	6	.357	.250	June	.233	43	10	2	0	0	5	8	7	.365	.279
Pre-All Star	.272	114	31	2	0	3	9	22	19	.394	.368	July	.326	43	14	3	0	0	9	4	.444	.465
Post-All Star	.325	157	51	8	1	1	21	28	21	.428	.408	August	.426	61	26	2	1	1	8	9	8	.500	.541
Scoring Posn	.258	62	16	2	0	0	23	18	10	.427	.290	Sept/Oct	.237	59	14	3	0	0	9	13	9	.375	.288

282

	Avg	AB	H	2B	3B	HR	RBI	BB	SO	OBP	SLG		Avg	AB	H	2B	3B	HR	RBI	BB	SO	OBP	SLG
Close & Late	.297	64	19	1	0	0	7	7	9	.366	.313	vs. AL	.304	250	76	10	1	3	28	44	38	.409	.388
None on/out	.258	62	16	1	1	1	4	4	10	.303	.355	vs. NL	.286	21	6	0	0	1	2	6	2	.464	.429

1997 By Position

Position	Avg	AB	H	2B	3B	HR	RBI	BB	SO	OBP	SLG	G	GS	Innings	PO	A	E	DP	Fld Pct	Rng Fctr	In Zone	Outs	Zone Rtg	MLB Zone
As DH	.310	87	27	5	1	1	12	19	10	.439	.425	25	24	---	---	---	---	---	---	---	---	---	---	---
As Pinch Hitter	.289	45	13	0	0	0	8	6	10	.365	.289	53	0	---	---	---	---	---	---	---	---	---	---	---
As 1b	.250	52	13	2	0	0	3	7	8	.339	.288	30	10	126.0	123	11	0	15	1.000		28	25	.893	.874
As 3b	.330	88	29	3	0	3	7	18	13	.449	.466	49	25	233.1	25	54	5	7	.940	3.05	81	64	.790	.801

Last Five Years

	Avg	AB	H	2B	3B	HR	RBI	BB	SO	OBP	SLG		Avg	AB	H	2B	3B	HR	RBI	BB	SO	OBP	SLG
vs. Left	.238	269	64	12	0	0	33	36	47	.322	.283	First Pitch	.329	140	46	8	0	2	18	14	0	.389	.429
vs. Right	.297	1185	352	62	1	15	132	233	160	.412	.389	Ahead in Count	.328	357	117	20	0	4	48	145	0	.516	.417
Groundball	.302	358	108	10	0	5	33	66	40	.407	.372	Behind in Count	.231	620	143	27	0	3	42	0	172	.233	.289
Flyball	.230	274	63	12	0	2	24	51	44	.352	.296	Two Strikes	.245	713	175	33	1	6	64	110	207	.347	.320
Home	.302	685	207	38	0	8	85	139	79	.417	.393	Batting #2	.243	341	83	12	0	2	26	56	46	.350	.296
Away	.272	769	209	36	1	7	80	130	128	.376	.349	Batting #5	.257	432	111	28	0	2	42	83	56	.374	.336
Day	.268	488	131	20	0	5	44	84	66	.375	.340	Other	.326	681	222	34	1	11	97	130	105	.432	.427
Night	.295	966	285	54	1	10	121	185	141	.406	.384	March/April	.315	165	52	5	0	3	20	39	22	.449	.400
Grass	.286	914	261	41	1	15	102	169	137	.395	.382	May	.238	256	61	12	0	3	29	55	35	.366	.320
Turf	.287	540	155	33	0	0	63	100	70	.396	.348	June	.269	234	63	9	0	2	18	41	41	.379	.333
Pre-All Star	.273	741	202	33	0	9	83	156	108	.397	.354	July	.316	263	83	17	0	2	32	48	37	.420	.403
Post-All Star	.300	713	214	41	1	6	82	113	99	.394	.386	August	.301	259	78	11	1	3	28	39	32	.390	.386
Scoring Posn	.255	385	98	22	0	2	144	97	63	.394	.327	Sept/Oct	.285	277	79	20	0	2	38	47	40	.388	.379
Close & Late	.254	279	71	6	0	2	38	48	43	.364	.297	vs. AL	.282	478	135	21	1	4	49	80	71	.384	.356
None on/out	.238	315	75	17	1	2	2	45	46	.335	.317	vs. NL	.288	976	281	53	0	11	116	189	136	.402	.376

Batter vs. Pitcher (career)

Hits Best Against	Avg	AB	H	2B	3B	HR	RBI	BB	SO	OBP	SLG	Hits Worst Against	Avg	AB	H	2B	3B	HR	RBI	BB	SO	OBP	SLG
Bill Swift	.500	14	7	1	0	0	3	3	0	.588	.571	Danny Jackson	.077	13	1	0	0	0	2	0	2	.077	.077
Andy Ashby	.500	12	6	0	0	1	1	2	0	.571	.750	Scott Erickson	.167	12	2	0	0	0	0	2	4	.286	.167
Jim Bullinger	.500	10	5	2	0	0	4	1	0	.545	.700	Pedro Martinez	.167	12	2	0	0	0	0	2	4	.286	.167
Armando Reynoso	.444	9	4	1	0	0	0	1	0	.545	.556	Joey Hamilton	.182	11	2	0	0	0	1	1	2	.250	.182
Pete Harnisch	.364	22	8	3	0	1	3	6	1	.500	.636	Bret Saberhagen	.182	11	2	0	0	0	1	2	3	.308	.182

Wendell Magee — Phillies
Age 25 – Bats Right

	Avg	G	AB	R	H	2B	3B	HR	RBI	BB	SO	HBP	GDP	SB	CS	OBP	SLG	IBB	SH	SF	#Pit	#P/PA	GB	FB	G/F
1997 Season	.200	38	115	7	23	4	0	1	9	9	20	0	8	1	4	.254	.261	1	0	2	424	3.37	45	30	1.50
Career (1996-1997)	.202	76	257	16	52	11	0	3	23	18	53	0	10	1	4	.253	.280	1	0	2	979	3.53	103	66	1.56

1997 Season

	Avg	AB	H	2B	3B	HR	RBI	BB	SO	OBP	SLG		Avg	AB	H	2B	3B	HR	RBI	BB	SO	OBP	SLG
vs. Left	.100	20	2	1	0	0	3	0	4	.091	.150	Scoring Posn	.310	29	9	0	0	0	8	4	4	.371	.310
vs. Right	.221	95	21	3	0	1	6	9	16	.288	.284	Close & Late	.200	15	3	1	0	1	1	1	3	.250	.467
Home	.232	56	13	4	0	0	5	2	10	.254	.304	None on/out	.200	35	7	3	0	0	0	2	7	.243	.286
Away	.169	59	10	0	0	1	4	7	10	.254	.220	Batting #7	.217	83	18	3	0	0	8	6	15	.264	.253
First Pitch	.294	17	5	0	0	0	1	0	0	.294	.294	Batting #8	.167	30	5	1	0	1	1	3	5	.242	.300
Ahead in Count	.308	26	8	2	0	1	3	8	0	.471	.500	Other	.000	2	0	0	0	0	0	0	0	.000	.000
Behind in Count	.151	53	8	1	0	0	4	0	19	.148	.170	Pre-All Star	.200	115	23	4	0	1	9	9	20	.254	.261
Two Strikes	.173	52	9	2	0	0	3	1	20	.189	.212	Post-All Star	.000	0	0	0	0	0	0	0	0	.000	.000

Mike Magnante — Astros
Age 33 – Pitches Left

	ERA	W	L	Sv	G	GS	IP	BB	SO	Avg	H	2B	3B	HR	RBI	OBP	SLG	GF	IR	IRS	Hld	SvOp	SB	CS	FB	GB	G/F
1997 Season	2.27	3	1	1	40	0	47.2	11	43	.223	39	5	0	2	19	.266	.286	14	39	9	3	5	4	3	71	36	1.97
Last Five Years	4.21	9	9	1	149	7	228.2	78	140	.269	234	34	8	21	131	.330	.399	40	130	40	19	7	20	12	319	244	1.31

1997 Season

	ERA	W	L	Sv	G	GS	IP	H	HR	BB	SO		Avg	AB	H	2B	3B	HR	RBI	BB	SO	OBP	SLG
Home	0.35	1	0	0	18	0	26.0	14	0	5	25	vs. Left	.154	39	6	0	0	0	1	4	6	.233	.154
Away	4.57	2	1	1	22	0	21.2	25	2	6	18	vs. Right	.243	136	33	5	0	2	18	7	37	.276	.324
Starter	0.00	0	0	0	0	0	0.0	0	0	0	0	Scoring Posn	.189	53	10	1	0	1	17	6	10	.262	.264
Reliever	2.27	3	1	1	40	0	47.2	39	2	11	43	Close & Late	.290	69	20	2	0	1	10	6	10	.347	.362
0 Days rest (Relief)	4.32	0	0	0	8	0	8.1	9	1	2	8	None on/out	.184	38	7	0	0	0	0	2	11	.225	.184
1 or 2 Days rest	0.68	2	0	0	20	0	26.1	17	0	7	24	First Pitch	.182	22	4	0	0	0	1	1	0	.208	.182
3+ Days rest	4.15	1	1	1	12	0	13.0	13	1	2	11	Ahead in Count	.167	90	15	3	0	1	8	0	34	.165	.233
Pre-All Star	3.24	2	0	0	13	0	16.2	14	1	4	15	Behind in Count	.367	30	11	1	0	1	8	6	0	.472	.500
Post-All Star	1.74	1	1	1	27	0	31.0	25	1	7	28	Two Strikes	.136	88	12	4	0	0	6	4	43	.172	.182

Last Five Years

	ERA	W	L	Sv	G	GS	IP	H	HR	BB	SO		Avg	AB	H	2B	3B	HR	RBI	BB	SO	OBP	SLG
Home	1.83	6	2	0	70	3	118.1	89	5	37	76	vs. Left	.251	271	68	9	1	5	33	30	41	.337	.347
Away	6.77	3	7	1	79	4	110.1	145	16	41	64	vs. Right	.277	599	166	25	7	16	98	48	99	.327	.422
Day	5.72	2	4	1	47	4	74.0	79	2	23	46	Inning 1-6	.286	405	116	16	3	11	66	40	56	.347	.422
Night	3.49	7	5	0	102	3	154.2	156	12	55	94	Inning 7+	.254	465	118	18	5	10	63	38	84	.315	.378
Grass	4.39	6	5	1	90	2	131.1	135	15	46	82	None on	.267	460	123	18	4	9	9	39	77	.329	.383
Turf	3.98	3	4	0	59	5	97.1	99	6	32	58	Runners on	.271	410	111	16	4	12	122	39	63	.331	.417

Last Five Years

	ERA	W	L	Sv	G	GS	IP	H	HR	BB	SO
March/April	5.90	1	2	0	20	0	29.0	33	1	15	8
May	3.32	0	0	0	15	0	19.0	16	3	6	12
June	5.09	4	2	0	25	1	35.1	38	5	8	27
July	2.36	2	1	1	25	0	49.2	40	4	15	30
August	3.79	1	2	0	36	3	54.2	60	3	18	35
Sept/Oct	5.49	1	2	0	28	3	41.0	47	5	16	28
Starter	6.50	1	3	0	7	7	36.0	46	5	11	17
Reliever	3.78	8	6	1	142	0	192.2	188	16	67	123
0 Days rest (Relief)	4.26	0	0	1	21	0	19.0	26	2	6	12
1 or 2 Days rest	3.84	4	4	0	66	0	96.0	93	5	35	66
3+ Days rest	3.59	4	2	0	55	0	77.2	69	9	26	45
vs. AL	4.65	6	8	0	113	7	185.2	199	19	67	100
vs. NL	2.30	3	1	1	36	0	43.0	35	2	11	40
Pre-All Star	4.85	5	5	0	68	1	94.2	101	11	32	52
Post-All Star	3.76	4	4	1	81	6	134.0	133	10	46	88

	Avg	AB	H	2B	3B	HR	RBI	BB	SO	OBP	SLG
Scoring Posn	.285	235	67	8	4	10	113	31	38	.359	.481
Close & Late	.278	205	57	7	2	3	36	19	31	.345	.376
None on/out	.266	199	53	8	2	3	16	34		.324	.372
vs. 1st Batr (relief)	.234	124	29	4	0	3	20	15	26	.317	.339
1st Inning Pitched	.263	445	117	20	1	9	85	51	79	.339	.373
First 15 Pitches	.262	393	103	14	0	8	59	46	64	.342	.359
Pitch 16-30	.271	262	71	13	4	9	47	16	50	.310	.454
Pitch 31-45	.241	112	27	5	2	0	9	8	13	.290	.321
Pitch 46+	.320	103	33	2	2	4	16	8	13	.377	.495
First Pitch	.265	132	35	8	1	1	16	4	0	.293	.364
Ahead in Count	.227	397	90	12	4	7	49	0	117	.229	.330
Behind in Count	.347	176	61	7	1	9	44	45	0	.480	.551
Two Strikes	.215	395	85	11	4	8	46	29	140	.267	.324
Pre-All Star	.272	372	101	16	5	11	65	32	52	.328	.430
Post-All Star	.267	498	133	18	3	10	66	46	88	.331	.376

Pitcher vs. Batter (career)

Pitches Best Vs.	Avg	AB	H	2B	3B	HR	RBI	BB	SO	OBP	SLG
Greg Gagne	.091	11	1	1	0	0	1	0	2	.091	.182
Shane Mack	.125	16	2	0	0	0	0	0	0	.125	.125
John Olerud	.167	12	2	0	0	0	0	1	2	.231	.167
Chili Davis	.200	10	2	0	0	0	0	1	3	.273	.200
Mike Devereaux	.200	10	2	0	0	0	1	1	3	.273	.200

Pitches Worst Vs.	Avg	AB	H	2B	3B	HR	RBI	BB	SO	OBP	SLG
Carlos Baerga	.500	10	5	0	0	1	4	0	0	.455	.800
Cal Ripken	.455	11	5	2	0	0	2	0	0	.455	.636
Roberto Alomar	.429	14	6	0	1	0	1	2	1	.500	.571
Robin Ventura	.400	15	6	0	0	1	1	2	1	.471	.600
Ozzie Guillen	.400	10	4	2	1	0	2	1	0	.455	.800

Ron Mahay — Red Sox
Age 27 – Pitches Left (flyball pitcher)

	ERA	W	L	Sv	G	GS	IP	BB	SO	Avg	H	2B	3B	HR	RBI	OBP	SLG	GF	IR	IRS	Hld	SvOp	SB	CS	GB	FB	G/F
1997 Season	2.52	3	0	0	28	0	25.0	11	22	.204	19	1	0	3	6	.288	.312	7	11	0	5	1	3	0	24	32	0.75

1997 Season

	ERA	W	L	Sv	G	GS	IP	H	HR	BB	SO
Home	2.81	2	0	0	13	0	16.0	13	2	5	14
Away	2.00	1	0	0	15	0	9.0	6	1	6	8
Starter	0.00	0	0	0	0	0	0.0	0	0	0	0
Reliever	2.52	3	0	0	28	0	25.0	19	3	11	22
0 Days rest (Relief)	3.00	1	0	0	5	0	3.0	2	1	1	4
1 or 2 Days rest	2.00	2	0	0	17	0	18.0	11	1	9	15
3+ Days rest	6.75	0	0	0	6	0	2.2	6	1	1	3
Pre-All Star	0.00	0	0	0	0	0	0.0	0	0	0	0
Post-All Star	2.52	3	0	0	28	0	25.0	19	3	11	22

	Avg	AB	H	2B	3B	HR	RBI	BB	SO	OBP	SLG
vs. Left	.231	39	9	0	0	1	2	7	12	.348	.308
vs. Right	.185	54	10	1	0	2	4	4	10	.241	.315
Scoring Posn	.222	18	4	0	0	0	3	2	4	.300	.222
Close & Late	.231	26	6	0	0	1	3	4	5	.333	.346
None on/out	.200	25	5	0	0	2	2	3	4	.286	.440
First Pitch	.222	9	2	0	0	0	1	0	0	.222	.222
Ahead in Count	.176	51	9	1	0	3		0	18	.176	.373
Behind in Count	.214	14	3	0	0	1		6	0	.450	.214
Two Strikes	.148	54	8	0	0	3		5	22	.220	.315

Pat Mahomes — Red Sox
Age 27 – Pitches Right (flyball pitcher)

	ERA	W	L	Sv	G	GS	IP	BB	SO	Avg	H	2B	3B	HR	RBI	OBP	SLG	GF	IR	IRS	Hld	SvOp	SB	CS	GB	FB	G/F
1997 Season	8.10	1	0	0	10	0	10.0	10	5	.366	15	2	0	2	11	.500	.561	2	10	4	1	0	2	0	13	16	0.81
Last Five Years	6.06	18	24	5	121	38	319.1	168	184	.285	355	73	8	67	225	.370	.518	32	64	25	14	9	33	15	378	483	0.78

1997 Season

	ERA	W	L	Sv	G	GS	IP	H	HR	BB	SO
Home	2.25	0	0	0	4	0	4.0	3	0	3	2
Away	12.00	1	0	0	6	0	6.0	12	2	7	3

	Avg	AB	H	2B	3B	HR	RBI	BB	SO	OBP	SLG
vs. Left	.313	16	5	1	0	1	3	2	2	.421	.563
vs. Right	.400	25	10	1	0	1	8	8	3	.543	.560

Last Five Years

	ERA	W	L	Sv	G	GS	IP	H	HR	BB	SO
Home	6.60	8	13	1	65	21	166.1	186	33	95	97
Away	5.47	10	11	4	56	17	153.0	169	34	73	87
Day	6.49	7	5	1	43	11	105.1	125	27	61	56
Night	5.85	11	19	4	78	27	214.0	230	40	107	128
Grass	5.48	8	10	5	53	15	133.0	146	28	67	67
Turf	6.47	10	14	0	68	23	186.1	209	39	101	117
March/April	8.96	3	6	0	32	9	68.1	97	19	40	34
May	5.71	3	6	0	22	13	88.1	91	18	44	49
June	5.94	4	4	0	15	11	66.2	85	16	40	46
July	2.70	1	1	0	12	3	30.0	19	2	13	20
August	4.25	4	2	1	16	2	36.0	32	3	19	19
Sept/Oct	6.30	3	5	4	24	0	30.0	31	9	12	16
Starter	6.66	9	17	0	38	38	196.0	232	46	106	101
Reliever	5.11	9	7	5	83	0	123.1	123	21	62	83
0 Days rest (Relief)	11.49	3	1	2	16	0	15.2	21	5	13	7
1 or 2 Days rest	4.55	4	5	3	36	0	55.1	54	9	25	41
3+ Days rest	3.78	2	1	0	31	0	52.1	48	7	24	35
vs. AL	6.06	18	24	5	121	38	319.1	355	67	168	184
vs. NL	0.00	0	0	0	0	0	0.0	0	0	0	0
Pre-All Star	6.70	10	17	0	72	34	233.2	282	55	127	138
Post-All Star	4.31	8	7	5	49	4	85.2	73	12	41	46

	Avg	AB	H	2B	3B	HR	RBI	BB	SO	OBP	SLG
vs. Left	.306	643	197	41	3	36	106	91	82	.394	.547
vs. Right	.262	602	158	32	5	31	119	77	102	.344	.487
Inning 1-6	.293	846	248	48	6	49	155	115	114	.377	.538
Inning 7+	.268	399	107	25	2	18	70	53	70	.354	.476
None on	.284	676	192	40	2	37	37	98	96	.377	.513
Runners on	.286	569	163	33	6	30	188	70	88	.361	.524
Scoring Posn	.293	314	92	16	4	15	150	47	48	.376	.513
Close & Late	.281	167	47	7	0	8	24	23	36	.368	.467
None on/out	.284	292	83	17	0	14	14	44	34	.380	.486
vs. 1st Batr (relief)	.284	67	19	6	0	2	15	14	6	.410	.463
1st Inning Pitched	.278	403	112	23	1	20	82	55	61	.366	.489
First 15 Pitches	.294	313	92	21	1	17	59	40	37	.376	.530
Pitch 16-30	.283	272	77	12	1	18	50	41	54	.379	.533
Pitch 31-45	.291	179	52	9	2	5	28	30	30	.390	.447
Pitch 46+	.279	481	134	31	4	27	88	57	63	.352	.528
First Pitch	.344	131	45	5	2	10	31	2	0	.365	.641
Ahead in Count	.215	522	112	21	3	14	61	0	153	.217	.347
Behind in Count	.367	335	123	27	1	30	77	95	0	.502	.722
Two Strikes	.219	567	124	24	3	17	81	71	184	.306	.362
Pre-All Star	.301	936	282	53	8	55	175	127	138	.385	.551
Post-All Star	.236	309	73	20	0	12	50	41	46	.324	.417

Pitcher vs. Batter (career)

Pitches Best Vs.	Avg	AB	H	2B	3B	HR	RBI	BB	SO	OBP	SLG
Ivan Rodriguez	.000	11	0	0	0	0	1	0	0	.000	.000

Pitches Worst Vs.	Avg	AB	H	2B	3B	HR	RBI	BB	SO	OBP	SLG
Will Clark	.600	15	9	1	0	2	4	2	0	.647	1.067

Pitcher vs. Batter (career)

Pitches Best Vs.	Avg	AB	H	2B	3B	HR	RBI	BB	SO	OBP	SLG	Pitches Worst Vs.	Avg	AB	H	2B	3B	HR	RBI	BB	SO	OBP	SLG
Cecil Fielder	.083	12	1	0	0	1	2	1	5	.154	.333	Brent Gates	.571	14	8	1	0	3	7	1	0	.625	1.286
Mike Bordick	.083	12	1	0	0	2	1	1	4	.154	.083	Mickey Tettleton	.500	6	3	1	0	2	3	5	2	.727	1.667
Chris Gomez	.091	11	1	0	0	0	0	1	1	.167	.091	Mark McLemore	.429	14	6	2	0	1	3	5	3	.579	.786
Jose Canseco	.158	19	3	0	0	1	2	1	10	.200	.316	Eddie Murray	.385	13	5	2	0	2	6	0	2	.385	1.000

Jose Malave — Red Sox
Age 27 – Bats Right

	Avg	G	AB	R	H	2B	3B	HR	RBI	BB	SO	HBP	GDP	SB	CS	OBP	SLG	IBB	SH	SF	#Pit	#P/PA	GB	FB	G/F
1997 Season	.000	4	4	0	0	0	0	0	0	0	2	0	1	0	0	.000	.000	0	0	0	13	3.25	1	1	1.00
Career (1996-1997)	.226	45	106	12	24	3	0	4	17	2	27	1	1	0	0	.248	.368	0	0	0	404	3.71	31	28	1.11

1997 Season

	Avg	AB	H	2B	3B	HR	RBI	BB	SO	OBP	SLG		Avg	AB	H	2B	3B	HR	RBI	BB	SO	OBP	SLG
vs. Left	.000	1	0	0	0	0	0	0	1	.000	.000	Scoring Posn	.000	1	0	0	0	0	0	0	1	.000	.000
vs. Right	.000	3	0	0	0	0	0	0	1	.000	.000	Close & Late	.000	0	0	0	0	0	0	0	0	.000	.000

Sean Maloney — Brewers
Age 27 – Pitches Right

	ERA	W	L	Sv	G	GS	IP	BB	SO	Avg	H	2B	3B	HR	RBI	OBP	SLG	GF	IR	IRS	Hld	SvOp	SB	CS	GB	FB	G/F
1997 Season	5.14	0	0	0	3	0	7.0	2	5	.304	7	1	0	1	7	.379	.478	2	4	3	0	0	0	0	6	8	0.75

1997 Season

	ERA	W	L	Sv	G	GS	IP	H	HR	BB	SO		Avg	AB	H	2B	3B	HR	RBI	BB	SO	OBP	SLG
Home	0.00	0	0	0	1	0	1.0	0	0	1	2	vs. Left	.500	12	6	0	0	1	5	1	2	.500	.750
Away	6.00	0	0	0	2	0	6.0	7	1	1	3	vs. Right	.091	11	1	1	0	2	1	1	3	.267	.182

Jeff Manto — Indians
Age 33 – Bats Right (flyball hitter)

	Avg	G	AB	R	H	2B	3B	HR	RBI	BB	SO	HBP	GDP	SB	CS	OBP	SLG	IBB	SH	SF	#Pit	#P/PA	GB	FB	G/F
1997 Season	.267	16	30	3	8	3	0	2	7	1	10	0	2	0	0	.290	.567	0	0	0	128	4.13	8	8	1.00
Last Five Years	.233	156	404	49	94	18	1	22	55	42	106	4	10	0	4	.311	.446	0	0	0	1799	4.00	118	134	0.88

1997 Season

	Avg	AB	H	2B	3B	HR	RBI	BB	SO	OBP	SLG		Avg	AB	H	2B	3B	HR	RBI	BB	SO	OBP	SLG
vs. Left	.267	15	4	1	0	1	3	1	5	.313	.533	Scoring Posn	.500	6	3	2	0	1	5	0	2	.500	1.333
vs. Right	.267	15	4	2	0	1	4	0	5	.267	.600	Close & Late	.400	5	2	0	0	2	0	1	.400	1.000

Last Five Years

	Avg	AB	H	2B	3B	HR	RBI	BB	SO	OBP	SLG		Avg	AB	H	2B	3B	HR	RBI	BB	SO	OBP	SLG
vs. Left	.292	154	45	10	0	11	28	20	43	.381	.571	First Pitch	.286	42	12	0	0	4	6	0	0	.286	.571
vs. Right	.196	250	49	8	1	11	27	22	63	.266	.368	Ahead in Count	.344	93	32	5	0	9	26	22	0	.479	.688
Groundball	.240	96	23	6	0	3	12	8	19	.305	.396	Behind in Count	.169	189	32	8	0	4	10	0	91	.174	.275
Flyball	.256	86	22	3	0	8	17	8	23	.326	.570	Two Strikes	.153	203	31	6	0	3	12	20	106	.232	.227
Home	.252	214	54	10	1	17	40	20	52	.316	.547	Batting #7	.274	146	40	8	0	8	20	15	33	.342	.493
Away	.211	190	40	8	0	5	15	22	54	.306	.332	Batting #8	.155	142	22	4	1	5	10	16	43	.245	.303
Day	.299	87	26	5	0	4	13	8	19	.358	.494	Other	.276	116	32	9	0	9	25	11	30	.354	.560
Night	.215	317	68	13	1	18	42	34	87	.299	.432	March/April	.000	0	0	0	0	0	0	0	0	.000	.000
Grass	.246	338	83	15	1	20	48	35	90	.320	.473	May	.263	76	20	6	1	3	10	4	20	.309	.487
Turf	.167	66	11	3	0	2	7	7	16	.267	.303	June	.255	98	25	2	0	9	20	5	19	.291	.551
Pre-All Star	.254	177	45	8	1	12	30	9	41	.294	.514	July	.164	61	10	3	0	3	6	5	19	.227	.361
Post-All Star	.216	227	49	10	0	10	25	33	65	.323	.392	August	.232	112	26	5	0	4	8	19	32	.353	.384
Scoring Posn	.202	99	20	3	0	5	30	12	28	.295	.384	Sept/Oct	.228	57	13	2	0	3	11	9	16	.343	.421
Close & Late	.175	63	11	0	0	4	9	5	18	.246	.365	vs. AL	.242	385	93	18	1	22	55	42	103	.321	.465
None on/out	.290	100	29	6	0	5	5	10	24	.355	.500	vs. NL	.053	19	1	0	0	0	0	0	3	.100	.053

Batter vs. Pitcher (career)

Hits Best Against	Avg	AB	H	2B	3B	HR	RBI	BB	SO	OBP	SLG	Hits Worst Against	Avg	AB	H	2B	3B	HR	RBI	BB	SO	OBP	SLG
Bobby Witt	.375	8	3	2	0	0	3	2	1	.545	.625	Chuck Finley	.100	10	1	0	0	0	0	1	2	.250	.100
David Wells	.353	17	6	0	0	2	5	0	5	.353	.706	Jimmy Key	.133	15	2	0	0	0	1	2	4	.235	.133

Barry Manuel — Mets
Age 32 – Pitches Right (flyball pitcher)

	ERA	W	L	Sv	G	GS	IP	BB	SO	Avg	H	2B	3B	HR	RBI	OBP	SLG	GF	IR	IRS	Hld	SvOp	SB	CS	GB	FB	G/F
1997 Season	5.26	1	0	1	9	0	25.2	13	21	.324	35	6	0	6	23	.402	.546	6	8	6	1	0	1	1	23	32	0.72
Last Five Years	3.71	4	2	0	72	0	111.2	39	83	.246	105	23	2	16	64	.320	.423	13	57	23	3	0	20	2	128	140	0.91

1997 Season

	ERA	W	L	Sv	G	GS	IP	H	HR	BB	SO		Avg	AB	H	2B	3B	HR	RBI	BB	SO	OBP	SLG
Home	4.72	0	0	0	9	0	13.1	16	3	9	10	vs. Left	.276	58	16	3	0	3	12	5	14	.333	.483
Away	5.84	1	0	1	10	0	12.1	19	3	4	11	vs. Right	.380	50	19	3	0	3	11	8	7	.475	.620

Kirt Manwaring — Rockies
Age 32 – Bats Right (groundball hitter)

	Avg	G	AB	R	H	2B	3B	HR	RBI	BB	SO	HBP	GDP	SB	CS	OBP	SLG	IBB	SH	SF	#Pit	#P/PA	GB	FB	G/F
1997 Season	.226	104	337	22	76	6	4	1	27	30	78	2	10	1	5	.291	.276	0	4	2	1425	3.80	102	105	0.97
Last Five Years	.249	535	1691	135	421	62	8	12	159	142	316	26	46	4	10	.315	.316	23	19	13	6682	3.53	604	493	1.23

1997 Season

	Avg	AB	H	2B	3B	HR	RBI	BB	SO	OBP	SLG		Avg	AB	H	2B	3B	HR	RBI	BB	SO	OBP	SLG
vs. Left	.231	117	27	1	1	0	7	7	25	.270	.256	First Pitch	.316	38	12	1	1	0	6	0	0	.308	.395

1997 Season

	Avg	AB	H	2B	3B	HR	RBI	BB	SO	OBP	SLG		Avg	AB	H	2B	3B	HR	RBI	BB	SO	OBP	SLG
vs. Right	.223	220	49	5	3	1	20	23	53	.302	.286	Ahead in Count	.303	76	23	4	1	0	10	13	0	.400	.382
Groundball	.311	61	19	1	2	1	8	3	9	.338	.443	Behind in Count	.146	151	22	1	1	1	8	0	64	.151	.185
Flyball	.250	52	13	1	0	3	6	-16		.328	.308	Two Strikes	.160	163	26	1	1	0	8	17	78	.239	.178
Home	.251	175	44	6	2	1	14	12	31	.303	.326	Batting #7	.233	301	70	6	4	1	23	22	64	.285	.289
Away	.198	162	32	0	2	0	13	18	47	.279	.222	Batting #8	.133	30	4	0	0	0	2	6	12	.297	.133
Day	.241	158	38	1	0	8	14	40		.306	.278	Other	.333	6	2	0	0	0	2	2		.500	.333
Night	.212	179	38	2	3	1	19	16	38	.278	.274	March/April	.304	56	17	3	1	0	9	7	12	.375	.393
Grass	.231	277	64	6	3	1	19	28	64	.306	.285	May	.203	59	12	1	0	1	2	6	15	.288	.271
Turf	.200	60	12	0	1	0	8	2	14	.219	.233	June	.260	77	20	1	2	0	4	6	20	.321	.325
Pre-All Star	.246	203	50	5	3	1	15	21	52	.322	.315	July	.143	49	7	0	1	0	5	7	14	.246	.184
Post-All Star	.194	134	26	1	1	0	12	9	26	.243	.216	August	.237	59	14	1	0	0	4	3	10	.274	.254
Scoring Posn	.291	79	23	2	1	0	25	6	10	.333	.342	Sept/Oct	.162	37	6	0	0	0	3	1	7	.184	.162
Close & Late	.211	38	8	1	0	0	0	4	10	.286	.237	vs. AL	.139	36	5	0	0	0	0	3	16	.225	.139
None on/out	.162	74	12	1	0	1	1	6	12	.235	.216	vs. NL	.236	301	71	6	4	1	27	27	62	.299	.292

1997 By Position

Position	Avg	AB	H	2B	3B	HR	RBI	BB	SO	OBP	SLG	G	GS	Innings	PO	A	E	DP	Fld Pct	Rng Fctr	In Zone	Zone Outs	Zone Rtg	MLB Zone
As c	.227	335	76	6	4	1	27	29	78	.291	.278	100	95	829.2	488	39	3	8	.994	—	—	—	—	—

Last Five Years

	Avg	AB	H	2B	3B	HR	RBI	BB	SO	OBP	SLG		Avg	AB	H	2B	3B	HR	RBI	BB	SO	OBP	SLG
vs. Left	.250	488	122	17	2	7	38	47	103	.319	.336	First Pitch	.305	282	86	12	2	2	30	18	0	.356	.383
vs. Right	.249	1203	299	45	6	5	121	95	213	.313	.308	Ahead in Count	.327	333	109	22	1	2	38	66	0	.442	.417
Groundball	.283	467	132	23	2	4	42	27	67	.328	.366	Behind in Count	.193	788	152	21	3	5	64	0	272	.202	.246
Flyball	.238	231	55	8	1	2	29	22	53	.309	.307	Two Strikes	.170	748	127	14	3	4	45	58	316	.232	.213
Home	.266	827	220	34	4	9	79	62	148	.324	.349	Batting #7	.260	530	138	17	4	5	48	39	95	.313	.336
Away	.233	864	201	28	4	3	80	80	168	.305	.285	Batting #8	.244	1146	280	45	4	7	109	101	216	.316	.309
Day	.246	778	191	36	4	5	66	70	151	.314	.321	Other	.200	15	3	0	0	0	2	5		.294	.200
Night	.252	913	230	26	4	7	93	72	165	.315	.312	March/April	.247	215	53	11	2	2	28	19	36	.315	.344
Grass	.247	1277	316	48	5	11	122	110	242	.314	.319	May	.274	288	79	10	1	2	26	22	52	.339	.337
Turf	.254	414	105	14	3	1	37	32	74	.317	.309	June	.266	354	94	12	3	1	29	29	66	.326	.325
Pre-All Star	.256	967	248	35	4	5	91	80	176	.321	.321	July	.235	315	74	10	1	5	33	35	61	.316	.321
Post-All Star	.239	724	173	27	2	7	68	62	140	.306	.311	August	.217	290	63	10	0	2	23	21	58	.278	.272
Scoring Posn	.257	432	111	22	1	0	138	50	76	.337	.313	Sept/Oct	.253	229	58	9	1	0	16	16	43	.310	.301
Close & Late	.206	257	53	12	0	0	17	17	58	.265	.253	vs. AL	.139	36	5	0	0	0	0	3	16	.225	.139
None on/out	.273	418	114	16	4	3	3	28	73	.352	.349	vs. NL	.251	1655	416	62	8	12	159	139	300	.317	.320

Batter vs. Pitcher (career)

Hits Best Against	Avg	AB	H	2B	3B	HR	RBI	BB	SO	OBP	SLG	Hits Worst Against	Avg	AB	H	2B	3B	HR	RBI	BB	SO	OBP	SLG
Shane Reynolds	.545	11	6	2	0	0	0	0	1	.545	.727	Pedro Martinez	.000	9	0	0	0	0	1	1	5	.250	.000
Butch Henry	.438	16	7	1	1	0	1	0	2	.438	.625	Dennis Martinez	.083	12	1	0	0	0	1	0	1	.083	.083
Mike Hampton	.375	16	6	1	1	3	1	1		.389	.750	Tim Belcher	.091	11	1	0	0	0	0	0	2	.091	.091
Frank Castillo	.353	17	6	1	0	1	2	0	3	.333	.588	Mike Morgan	.103	29	3	0	0	0	1	2	5	.156	.103
Joey Hamilton	.333	9	3	1	0	1		2	0	.500	.444	Bobby Jones	.150	20	3	0	0	0	0	0	5	.150	.150

Josias Manzanillo — Mariners   Age 30 – Pitches Right

	ERA	W	L	Sv	G	GS	IP	BB	SO	Avg	H	2B	3B	HR	RBI	OBP	SLG	GF	IR	IRS	Hld	SvOp	SB	CS	GB	FB	G/F
1997 Season	5.40	0	1	0	16	0	18.1	17	18	.275	19	2	0	3	23	.409	.435	4	18	12	1	1	1	2	16	24	0.67
Last Five Years	4.57	5	6	3	92	1	128.0	64	112	.247	120	27	1	13	90	.339	.387	32	73	37	12	8	5	5	165	132	1.25

1997 Season

	ERA	W	L	Sv	G	GS	IP	H	HR	BB	SO		Avg	AB	H	2B	3B	HR	RBI	BB	SO	OBP	SLG
Home	2.89	0	0	0	8	0	9.1	7	1	9	10	vs. Left	.296	27	8	1	0	1	10	11	6	.500	.444
Away	8.00	0	1	0	8	0	9.0	12	2	8	8	vs. Right	.262	42	11	1	0	2	13	6	12	.340	.429

Last Five Years

	ERA	W	L	Sv	G	GS	IP	H	HR	BB	SO		Avg	AB	H	2B	3B	HR	RBI	BB	SO	OBP	SLG
Home	4.73	3	5	0	47	1	64.2	56	9	30	52	vs. Left	.280	211	59	10	1	5	40	34	50	.382	.408
Away	4.41	2	1	3	45	0	63.1	64	4	34	60	vs. Right	.222	275	61	17	0	8	50	30	62	.306	.371
Day	6.36	2	4	2	30	1	46.2	50	6	26	44	Inning 1-6	.285	137	39	11	0	3	37	23	30	.384	.431
Night	3.54	3	2	1	62	0	81.1	70	7	38	68	Inning 7+	.232	349	81	16	1	10	53	41	82	.321	.370
Grass	5.29	5	6	2	70	1	97.0	96	11	43	76	None on	.220	254	56	11	1	7	7	17	60	.283	.354
Turf	2.32	0	0	1	22	0	31.0	24	2	21	36	Runners on	.276	232	64	16	0	6	83	47	52	.394	.422
March/April	9.97	1	2	0	15	1	21.2	33	4	11	15	Scoring Posn	.278	158	44	11	0	3	76	40	32	.415	.405
May	4.53	1	3	2	32	0	45.2	40	5	25	39	Close & Late	.220	150	33	11	1	3	22	17	47	.308	.367
June	1.23	1	0	1	23	0	29.1	25	1	13	26	None on/out	.208	106	22	3	1	2	2	10	22	.288	.311
July	4.66	2	1	0	16	0	19.1	14	2	6	21	vs. 1st Batr (relief)	.256	78	20	5	1	1	17	9	18	.326	.385
August	4.50	0	0	0	3	0	6.0	2	0	5	4	1st Inning Pitched	.259	317	82	19	1	7	73	48	74	.355	.391
Sept/Oct	1.50	0	0	0	3	0	6.0	6	1	4	7	First 15 Pitches	.257	269	69	14	1	8	48	31	56	.338	.405
Starter	7.20	0	1	0	1	1	5.0	5	1	1	0	Pitch 16-30	.214	145	31	9	0	2	28	20	42	.315	.317
Reliever	4.46	5	5	3	91	0	123.0	115	12	63	112	Pitch 31-45	.241	58	14	2	0	2	10	8	13	.333	.379
0 Days rest (Relief)	2.78	1	0	0	16	0	22.2	19	1	11	27	Pitch 46+	.429	14	6	2	0	1	4	5	1	.571	.786
1 or 2 Days rest	3.75	2	4	2	45	0	57.2	47	8	32	46	First Pitch	.310	71	22	5	0	5	19	9	0	.383	.592
3+ Days rest	6.33	2	1	1	30	0	42.2	49	3	20	39	Ahead in Count	.195	241	47	12	1	2	27	0	93	.211	.270
vs. AL	6.02	1	2	1	35	1	49.1	59	5	35	35	Behind in Count	.359	103	37	6	0	5	34	26	0	.485	.563
vs. NL	3.66	4	4	2	57	0	78.2	61	8	29	77	Two Strikes	.154	240	37	10	1	2	22	28	112	.254	.229
Pre-All Star	4.64	4	5	3	77	1	106.2	105	11	52	90	Pre-All Star	.257	408	105	24	0	11	74	52	90	.346	.397

286

	ERA	W	L	Sv	G	GS	IP	H	HR	BB	SO		Avg	AB	H	2B	3B	HR	RBI	BB	SO	OBP	SLG
Post-All Star	4.22	1	1	0	15	0	21.1	15	2	12	22	Post-All Star	.192	78	15	3	1	2	16	12	22	.304	.333

Eli Marrero — Cardinals   Age 24 – Bats Right

	Avg	G	AB	R	H	2B	3B	HR	RBI	BB	SO	HBP	GDP	SB	CS	OBP	SLG	IBB	SH	SF	#Pit	#P/PA	GB	FB	G/F
1997 Season	.244	17	45	4	11	2	0	2	7	2	13	0	1	4	0	.271	.422	1	0	1	179	3.73	13	16	0.81

1997 Season

	Avg	AB	H	2B	3B	HR	RBI	BB	SO	OBP	SLG		Avg	AB	H	2B	3B	HR	RBI	BB	SO	OBP	SLG
vs. Left	.100	10	1	1	0	0	0	0	4	.100	.200	Scoring Posn	.273	11	3	0	0	1	6	2	2	.357	.545
vs. Right	.286	35	10	1	0	2	7	2	9	.316	.486	Close & Late	.143	7	1	0	0	1	2	0	1	.125	.571

Al Martin — Pirates   Age 30 – Bats Left

	Avg	G	AB	R	H	2B	3B	HR	RBI	BB	SO	HBP	GDP	SB	CS	OBP	SLG	IBB	SH	SF	#Pit	#P/PA	GB	FB	G/F
1997 Season	.291	113	423	64	123	24	7	13	59	45	83	3	8	23	7	.359	.473	7	1	5	1637	3.43	156	116	1.34
Last Five Years	.289	617	2248	368	650	127	23	71	269	219	469	10	29	112	45	.353	.461	23	5	16	9032	3.62	819	600	1.37

1997 Season

	Avg	AB	H	2B	3B	HR	RBI	BB	SO	OBP	SLG		Avg	AB	H	2B	3B	HR	RBI	BB	SO	OBP	SLG
vs. Left	.326	92	30	4	2	1	16	14	17	.417	.446	First Pitch	.380	92	35	9	1	3	14	4	0	.398	.598
vs. Right	.281	331	93	20	5	12	43	31	66	.342	.473	Ahead in Count	.297	91	27	1	3	3	13	20	0	.412	.473
Groundball	.273	77	21	3	0	3	11	9	15	.349	.429	Behind in Count	.254	173	44	12	1	4	17	0	66	.263	.405
Flyball	.304	79	24	3	2	1	8	3	15	.333	.430	Two Strikes	.211	171	36	5	2	5	19	21	83	.304	.351
Home	.302	202	61	13	6	8	32	19	38	.361	.545	Batting #3	.294	419	123	24	7	13	59	44	82	.361	.477
Away	.281	221	62	11	1	5	27	26	45	.357	.407	Batting #7	.000	2	0	0	0	0	0	0	1	.000	.000
Day	.282	149	42	9	1	3	18	15	34	.349	.416	Other	.000	2	0	0	0	0	0	1	0	.333	.000
Night	.296	274	81	15	6	10	41	30	49	.365	.504	March/April	.300	70	21	3	1	0	7	8	18	.372	.371
Grass	.273	165	45	7	1	3	20	24	34	.366	.382	May	.317	60	19	1	0	5	13	13	14	.438	.583
Turf	.302	258	78	17	6	10	39	21	49	.354	.531	June	.360	25	9	2	2	2	5	2	4	.407	.840
Pre-All Star	.295	176	52	7	4	7	26	28	40	.390	.500	July	.238	101	24	9	1	1	9	14	23	.333	.376
Post-All Star	.287	247	71	17	3	6	33	17	43	.336	.453	August	.293	99	29	4	3	2	11	5	13	.330	.455
Scoring Posn	.280	125	35	8	2	5	48	23	21	.387	.496	Sept/Oct	.309	68	21	5	0	3	14	3	11	.333	.515
Close & Late	.230	61	14	3	0	0	5	11	14	.356	.279	vs. AL	.361	36	13	3	1	0	3	1	5	.395	.500
None on/out	.338	74	25	4	3	3	9	16	410	.410	.595	vs. NL	.284	387	110	21	6	13	56	44	78	.356	.470

1997 By Position

Position	Avg	AB	H	2B	3B	HR	RBI	BB	SO	OBP	SLG	G	GS	Innings	PO	A	E	DP	Fld Pct	Rng Fctr	In Zone	Zone Outs	Zone Rtg	MLB Zone
As lf	.292	421	123	24	7	13	59	44	82	.359	.475	110	107	929.2	125	8	6	1	.957	1.29	177	127	.718	.805

Last Five Years

	Avg	AB	H	2B	3B	HR	RBI	BB	SO	OBP	SLG		Avg	AB	H	2B	3B	HR	RBI	BB	SO	OBP	SLG
vs. Left	.225	436	98	18	3	8	56	48	111	.301	.335	First Pitch	.423	397	168	29	7	17	76	14	0	.436	.660
vs. Right	.305	1812	552	109	20	63	213	171	358	.365	.491	Ahead in Count	.335	502	168	31	9	21	76	95	0	.436	.558
Groundball	.275	652	179	36	5	11	64	59	146	.334	.396	Behind in Count	.206	956	197	44	2	22	75	0	384	.211	.325
Flyball	.279	344	96	20	4	10	32	38	69	.351	.448	Two Strikes	.173	978	169	31	4	19	66	110	469	.259	.271
Home	.298	1129	336	66	16	45	158	106	246	.357	.504	Batting #2	.296	744	220	48	1	20	85	64	133	.351	.444
Away	.281	1119	314	61	7	26	111	114	223	.348	.417	Batting #3	.280	625	175	32	7	17	76	70	138	.355	.435
Day	.266	685	182	43	2	18	70	57	149	.324	.413	Other	.290	879	255	47	15	34	108	85	198	.353	.494
Night	.299	1563	468	84	21	53	199	162	320	.365	.482	March/April	.283	336	95	17	6	9	41	27	66	.334	.449
Grass	.289	766	221	41	5	18	80	87	151	.362	.426	May	.264	413	109	21	2	11	36	49	101	.343	.404
Turf	.289	1482	429	86	18	53	189	132	318	.347	.479	June	.270	397	107	15	4	18	48	41	85	.342	.463
Pre-All Star	.274	1269	348	58	14	40	136	128	279	.342	.437	July	.310	378	117	27	3	7	39	39	96	.374	.452
Post-All Star	.308	979	302	69	9	31	133	91	190	.367	.492	August	.314	392	123	22	5	9	40	30	59	.362	.464
Scoring Posn	.259	541	140	25	5	15	184	90	125	.360	.407	Sept/Oct	.298	332	99	25	3	17	65	33	62	.360	.545
Close & Late	.271	343	93	15	1	8	31	53	91	.367	.391	vs. AL	.361	36	13	3	1	0	3	1	5	.395	.500
None on/out	.291	547	159	30	12	15	15	48	107	.348	.472	vs. NL	.288	2212	637	124	22	71	266	218	464	.352	.460

Batter vs. Pitcher (career)

Hits Best Against	Avg	AB	H	2B	3B	HR	RBI	BB	SO	OBP	SLG	Hits Worst Against	Avg	AB	H	2B	3B	HR	RBI	BB	SO	OBP	SLG
Jamey Wright	.583	12	7	1	0	1	1	4	0	.688	.917	Tom Glavine	.000	13	0	0	0	0	0	2	4	.133	.000
John Smoltz	.513	39	20	5	1	1	7	6	5	.578	.769	F. Valenzuela	.000	8	0	0	0	0	0	3	0	.273	.000
Alan Benes	.429	14	6	2	0	1	4	2	5	.579	.786	Jeff Fassero	.063	16	1	0	0	0	1	0	7	.063	.063
Roger Bailey	.400	15	6	2	1	2	5	1	.550	.867	Orel Hershiser	.091	11	1	0	0	0	1	1	0	.167	.091
Dave Mlicki	.333	12	4	0	1	2	4	1	3	.385	1.000	Curt Schilling	.100	20	2	0	0	0	0	1	7	.100	.250

Norberto Martin — White Sox   Age 31 – Bats Right (groundball hitter)

	Avg	G	AB	R	H	2B	3B	HR	RBI	BB	SO	HBP	GDP	SB	CS	OBP	SLG	IBB	SH	SF	#Pit	#P/PA	GB	FB	G/F
1997 Season	.300	71	213	24	64	7	1	2	27	6	31	0	2	1	4	.320	.371	0	0	0	702	3.21	116	31	3.74
Career (1993-1997)	.299	266	658	93	197	28	6	6	76	25	90	1	13	20	8	.323	.388	0	9	6	2314	3.31	343	103	3.33

1997 Season

	Avg	AB	H	2B	3B	HR	RBI	BB	SO	OBP	SLG		Avg	AB	H	2B	3B	HR	RBI	BB	SO	OBP	SLG
vs. Left	.346	81	28	1	0	1	13	3	6	.369	.395	Scoring Posn	.386	57	22	0	0	1	26	2	11	.407	.439
vs. Right	.273	132	36	6	1	1	14	3	25	.289	.356	Close & Late	.357	42	15	1	0	1	5	2	5	.386	.452
Home	.295	105	31	4	1	1	11	3	19	.315	.381	None on/out	.211	57	12	2	0	1	1	3	8	.250	.298
Away	.306	108	33	3	0	1	16	3	12	.324	.361	Batting #2	.289	45	13	1	0	0	5	2	6	.319	.311
First Pitch	.375	40	15	0	0	2	13	0	0	.375	.525	Batting #7	.354	48	17	3	0	1	9	2	5	.380	.479

287

1997 Season

	Avg	AB	H	2B	3B	HR	RBI	BB	SO	OBP	SLG		Avg	AB	H	2B	3B	HR	RBI	BB	SO	OBP	SLG
Ahead in Count	.390	41	16	1	1	0	3	4	0	.444	.463	Other	.283	120	34	3	1	1	13	2	20	.295	.350
Behind in Count	.223	103	23	4	0	0	6	0	29	.223	.262	Pre-All Star	.281	114	32	4	0	2	15	5	15	.311	.368
Two Strikes	.200	90	18	2	0	0	7	2	31	.217	.222	Post-All Star	.323	99	32	3	1	0	12	1	16	.330	.374

Career (1993-1997)

	Avg	AB	H	2B	3B	HR	RBI	BB	SO	OBP	SLG		Avg	AB	H	2B	3B	HR	RBI	BB	SO	OBP	SLG
vs. Left	.304	313	95	15	0	4	36	13	39	.331	.390	First Pitch	.407	123	50	6	2	4	27	0	0	.403	.585
vs. Right	.296	345	102	13	6	2	40	12	51	.316	.386	Ahead in Count	.343	108	37	5	2	1	15	9	0	.387	.454
Groundball	.275	171	47	6	1	2	21	6	26	.296	.357	Behind in Count	.240	325	78	12	1	1	22	0	80	.241	.292
Flyball	.381	105	40	9	3	1	15	1	10	.387	.552	Two Strikes	.226	274	62	8	0	0	17	16	90	.271	.255
Home	.315	314	99	14	4	2	36	9	47	.331	.404	Batting #1	.286	168	48	9	0	1	17	7	27	.311	.357
Away	.285	344	98	14	2	4	40	16	43	.316	.372	Batting #7	.324	145	47	5	2	2	25	4	14	.340	.428
Day	.303	208	63	11	2	1	24	11	31	.335	.389	Other	.296	345	102	14	4	3	34	14	49	.322	.386
Night	.298	450	134	17	4	5	52	14	59	.318	.387	March/April	.267	30	8	1	0	1	4	2	5	.313	.400
Grass	.303	591	179	25	5	5	71	22	82	.326	.387	May	.275	102	28	3	1	1	11	4	11	.299	.353
Turf	.269	67	18	3	1	1	5	3	8	.296	.388	June	.265	136	36	6	0	1	10	6	24	.301	.331
Pre-All Star	.284	306	87	15	1	3	30	18	42	.315	.369	July	.345	142	49	8	1	0	11	4	14	.356	.415
Post-All Star	.313	352	110	13	5	3	46	12	48	.331	.403	August	.351	134	47	7	3	3	19	6	20	.373	.515
Scoring Posn	.336	152	51	5	2	2	71	8	18	.355	.434	Sept/Oct	.254	114	29	3	1	0	11	3	16	.274	.298
Close & Late	.330	112	37	3	2	2	17	7	20	.367	.446	vs. AL	.301	647	195	28	6	6	76	25	89	.325	.391
None on/out	.254	181	46	10	1	2	2	10	26	.293	.354	vs. NL	.182	11	2	0	0	0	0	0	1	.182	.182

Batter vs. Pitcher (career)

Hits Best Against	Avg	AB	H	2B	3B	HR	RBI	BB	SO	OBP	SLG	Hits Worst Against	Avg	AB	H	2B	3B	HR	RBI	BB	SO	OBP	SLG
Chuck Finley	.429	14	6	0	0	0	0	0	0	.429	.429	Scott Karl	.167	12	2	0	0	0	1	2	2	.286	.167
Mike Mussina	.375	16	6	2	1	0	1	0	2	.375	.625	Roger Clemens	.182	11	2	0	0	0	1	0	0	.182	.182
Andy Pettitte	.333	12	4	0	0	0	0	0	1	.333	.333	Darren Oliver	.214	14	3	0	0	1	4	0	4	.200	.429
Kenny Rogers	.318	22	7	1	0	0	1		2	.348	.364	Mark Langston	.217	23	5	2	0	0	1		2	.280	.304

Tom Martin — Astros
Age 28 – Pitches Left (groundball pitcher)

	ERA	W	L	Sv	G	GS	IP	BB	SO	Avg	H	2B	3B	HR	RBI	OBP	SLG	GF	IR	IRS	Hld	SvOp	SB	CS	GB	FB	G/F
1997 Season	2.09	5	3	2	55	0	56.0	23	36	.254	52	7	0	2	30	.330	.317	18	39	19	7	3	5	1	84	48	1.75

1997 Season

	ERA	W	L	Sv	G	GS	IP	H	HR	BB	SO		Avg	AB	H	2B	3B	HR	RBI	BB	SO	OBP	SLG
Home	3.00	5	2	1	29	0	30.0	33	2	12	23	vs. Left	.262	61	16	1	0	0	9	10	14	.361	.279
Away	1.04	0	1	1	26	0	26.0	19	0	11	13	vs. Right	.250	144	36	6	0	2	21	13	22	.316	.333
Day	2.14	3	1	1	19	0	21.0	18	0	8	14	Inning 1-6	.333	6	2	0	0	0	3	0	1	.333	.333
Night	2.06	2	2	1	36	0	35.0	34	2	15	22	Inning 7+	.251	199	50	7	0	2	27	23	35	.330	.317
Grass	0.00	0	0	1	19	0	19.0	10	0	7	10	None on	.263	95	25	5	0	0		13	18	.352	.316
Turf	3.16	5	3	1	36	0	37.0	42	2	16	26	Runners on	.245	110	27	2	0	2	30	10	18	.311	.318
March/April	0.00	1	0	0		0	7.2	7	0	3	4	Scoring Posn	.258	66	17	2	0	1	28	6	12	.324	.333
May	2.92	1	1	0	11	0	12.1	11	1	7	5	Close & Late	.277	119	33	4	0	2	18	10	18	.333	.361
June	3.86	0	1	0	5	0	4.2	9	1	1	2	None on/out	.283	46	13	3	0	0		5	7	.353	.348
July	1.42	1	0	1	10	0	12.2	9	0	5	10	vs. 1st Batr (relief)	.348	46	16	2	0	0	13	7		.434	.391
August	3.86	2	1	1	12	0	11.2	12	0	5	7	1st Inning Pitched	.260	169	44	5	0	2	29	23	32	.351	.325
Sept/Oct	0.00	0	0	0	8	0	7.0	4	0	2	8	First 15 Pitches	.266	143	38	5	0	1	22	19	25	.350	.322
Starter	0.00	0	0	0	0	0	0.0	0	0	0	0	Pitch 16-30	.217	60	13	2	0	1	7	4	10	.277	.300
Reliever	2.09	5	3	2	55	0	56.0	52	2	23	36	Pitch 31-45	.500	2	1	0	0	0	0	0	1	.500	.500
0 Days rest (Relief)	2.61	1	1	0	9	0	10.1	8	1	4	4	Pitch 46+	.000	0	0	0	0	0	0	0	1	.000	.000
1 or 2 Days rest	2.13	0	1	2	26	0	25.1	18	1	12	20	First Pitch	.464	28	13	1	0	1	7	1	0	.483	.607
3+ Days rest	1.77	4	1	0	20	0	20.1	26	0	7	12	Ahead in Count	.206	102	21	3	0	1	8	0	32	.214	.265
vs. AL	4.50	0	1	0	4	0	4.0	5	1	3	2	Behind in Count	.167	36	6	2	0	0		10	14	.392	.222
vs. NL	1.90	5	2	2	51	0	52.0	47	1	20	34	Two Strikes	.180	100	18	3	0	0	5	8	36	.248	.240
Pre-All Star	2.00	2	2	0	28	0	27.0	29	2	12	13	Pre-All Star	.284	102	29	2	0	2	15	12	13	.362	.363
Post-All Star	2.17	3	1	2	27	0	29.0	23	0	11	23	Post-All Star	.223	103	23	2	0	0	15	11	23	.298	.272

Dave Martinez — White Sox
Age 33 – Bats Left

	Avg	G	AB	R	H	2B	3B	HR	RBI	BB	SO	HBP	GDP	SB	CS	OBP	SLG	IBB	SH	SF	#Pit	#P/PA	GB	FB	G/F
1997 Season	.286	145	504	78	144	16	6	12	55	55	69	3	4	12	6	.356	.413	7	5	6	2291	4.00	172	164	1.05
Last Five Years	.286	597	1723	263	493	73	22	36	199	187	223	9	25	44	22	.357	.417	14	18	11	7637	3.92	616	525	1.17

1997 Season

	Avg	AB	H	2B	3B	HR	RBI	BB	SO	OBP	SLG		Avg	AB	H	2B	3B	HR	RBI	BB	SO	OBP	SLG
vs. Left	.259	85	22	1	1	3	8	9	17	.333	.400	First Pitch	.257	35	9	0	1	1	1	4	0	.333	.400
vs. Right	.291	419	122	15	5	9	47	46	52	.360	.415	Ahead in Count	.322	149	48	7	0	5	22	28	0	.422	.474
Groundball	.340	106	36	6	3	1	10	11	9	.397	.481	Behind in Count	.262	210	55	5	0	3	19	0	52	.269	.329
Flyball	.225	102	23	2	0	4	13	9	17	.288	.363	Two Strikes	.252	234	59	7	2	4	16	23	69	.323	.350
Home	.307	241	74	9	3	5	28	26	32	.375	.432	Batting #2	.296	284	84	9	2	6	20	28	44	.359	.405
Away	.266	263	70	7	3	7	27	29	37	.338	.395	Batting #7	.303	109	33	2	3	4	22	11	8	.360	.486
Day	.300	160	48	5	3	2	17	19	24	.376	.406	Other	.243	111	27	5	1	2	13	16	17	.344	.360
Night	.279	344	96	11	3	10	38	36	45	.346	.416	March/April	.250	88	22	2	2	1	11	5	9	.290	.352
Grass	.288	437	126	14	6	10	51	45	56	.353	.416	May	.292	65	19	1	1	2	12	9	10	.367	.431
Turf	.269	67	18	2	0	2	4	10	13	.372	.388	June	.315	92	29	4	0	7	15	18	15	.425	.587
Pre-All Star	.281	256	72	8	3	10	38	33	38	.362	.453	July	.203	79	16	3	0	0	0	8	17	.284	.241
Post-All Star	.290	248	72	8	3	2	17	22	31	.348	.371	August	.340	103	35	5	2	1	6	6	10	.376	.456

1997 Season

	Avg	AB	H	2B	3B	HR	RBI	BB	SO	OBP	SLG		Avg	AB	H	2B	3B	HR	RBI	BB	SO	OBP	SLG
Scoring Posn	.265	117	31	3	1	2	40	22	17	.374	.359	Sept/Oct	.299	77	23	1	1	1	11	9	8	.372	.377
Close & Late	.338	77	26	2	0	1	11	13	15	.435	.403	vs. AL	.281	462	130	14	6	9	50	45	62	.344	.396
None on/out	.281	121	34	3	2	5	5	5	14	.310	.463	vs. NL	.333	42	14	2	0	3	5	10	7	.472	.595

1997 By Position

Position	Avg	AB	H	2B	3B	HR	RBI	BB	SO	OBP	SLG	G	GS	Innings	PO	A	E	DP	Fld Pct	Rng Fctr	In Zone	Zone Outs	Zone Rtg	MLB Zone
As Pinch Hitter	.200	10	2	0	1	0	1	2	3	.333	.400	13	0	---	---								.864	.874
As 1b	.250	108	27	2	0	2	12	14	9	.339	.324	52	29	284.0	256	24	6	23	.979				.864	.874
As cf	.309	162	50	5	2	4	22	12	22	.356	.438	45	42	332.0	104	3	0	0	1.000	2.90	127	-104	.819	.815
As rf	.291	223	65	9	3	6	20	27	35	.366	.439	75	58	507.1	125	3	1	2	.992	2.27	146	119	.815	.813

Last Five Years

	Avg	AB	H	2B	3B	HR	RBI	BB	SO	OBP	SLG		Avg	AB	H	2B	3B	HR	RBI	BB	SO	OBP	SLG
vs. Left	.267	247	66	9	5	4	20	31	45	.353	.393	First Pitch	.355	152	54	10	4	4	25	11	0	.398	.553
vs. Right	.289	1476	427	64	17	32	179	156	178	.358	.421	Ahead in Count	.340	488	166	30	6	16	68	97	0	.448	.525
Groundball	.297	511	152	23	10	7	48	46	58	.356	.423	Behind in Count	.236	728	172	19	4	10	64	0	170	.241	.315
Flyball	.261	326	85	17	6	8	37	33	43	.329	.423	Two Strikes	.228	775	177	23	4	13	66	79	223	.302	.319
Home	.264	825	218	28	14	12	83	90	112	.339	.376	Batting #2	.286	706	202	32	7	16	68	80	89	.360	.419
Away	.306	898	275	45	8	24	116	97	111	.373	.454	Batting #6	.314	306	96	12	7	7	39	24	42	.366	.467
Day	.284	617	175	33	7	7	71	70	93	.356	.394	Other	.274	711	195	29	8	13	92	83	92	.351	.392
Night	.288	1106	318	40	15	29	128	117	130	.356	.429	March/April	.213	207	44	7	4	2	22	17	26	.272	.314
Grass	.279	1447	404	57	20	26	163	150	184	.348	.400	May	.305	200	61	10	2	5	34	21	31	.370	.450
Turf	.322	276	89	16	2	10	36	37	39	.404	.504	June	.302	328	99	13	3	16	48	47	45	.389	.506
Pre-All Star	.270	827	223	34	9	24	111	90	121	.346	.420	July	.268	328	88	11	3	4	25	28	49	.335	.357
Post-All Star	.301	896	270	39	13	12	88	92	103	.367	.414	August	.299	384	115	20	6	6	36	35	47	.358	.430
Scoring Posn	.293	399	117	17	3	8	156	73	53	.397	.411	Sept/Oct	.312	276	86	12	4	3	34	39	25	.393	.417
Close & Late	.314	280	88	14	4	5	32	43	44	.408	.446	vs. AL	.301	1205	363	50	18	24	140	129	155	.369	.432
None on/out	.284	394	112	18	7	11	11	22	45	.324	.449	vs. NL	.251	518	130	23	4	12	59	58	65	.330	.380

Batter vs. Pitcher (career)

Hits Best Against	Avg	AB	H	2B	3B	HR	RBI	BB	SO	OBP	SLG	Hits Worst Against	Avg	AB	H	2B	3B	HR	RBI	BB	SO	OBP	SLG
Mike Maddux	.583	12	7	0	0	0		3	1	.688	.583	Willie Blair	.067	15	1	1	0	0	2	1	2	.125	.133
Brian Williams	.500	10	5	1	0	0	1	1	0	.545	.600	Paul Assenmacher	.091	22	2	0	0	0	1	1	11	.167	.091
Tom Gordon	.455	11	5	1	0	0	1	2	0	.538	.545	Rich Rodriguez	.100	10	1	0	0	0	0	1	5	.182	.100
Kevin Appier	.385	13	5	0	0	1	1	3	0	.500	.615	Jeff Brantley	.100	10	1	0	0	0	1	2	0	.250	.100
Jack McDowell	.333	18	6	0	0	2	4	1	3	.368	.143	Chuck McElroy	.143	14	2	0	0	0	0	0	8	.143	.143

Dennis Martinez — Mariners

Age 43 – Pitches Right (groundball pitcher)

	ERA	W	L	Sv	G	GS	IP	BB	SO	Avg	H	2B	3B	HR	RBI	OBP	SLG	CG	ShO	Sup	QS	#P/S	SB	CS	GB	FB	G/F
1997 Season	7.71	1	5	0	9	9	49.0	29	17	.327	65	7	2	8	37	.424	.503	0	0	4.96	3	98	11	5	88	61	1.44
Last Five Years	3.93	48	31	1	116	115	749.1	220	394	.257	738	132	21	78	312	.317	.399	13	6	5.51	69	99	87	23	1257	682	1.84

1997 Season

	ERA	W	L	Sv	G	GS	IP	H	HR	BB	SO		Avg	AB	H	2B	3B	HR	RBI	BB	SO	OBP	SLG
Home	7.50	0	2	0	3	3	18.0	26	1	8	8	vs. Left	.333	93	31	3	2	5	22	20	9	.447	.570
Away	7.84	1	3	0	6	6	31.0	39	7	21	9	vs. Right	.321	106	34	4	0	3	15	9	8	.403	.443

Last Five Years

	ERA	W	L	Sv	G	GS	IP	H	HR	BB	SO		Avg	AB	H	2B	3B	HR	RBI	BB	SO	OBP	SLG
Home	3.86	20	14	1	56	55	364.0	375	35	88	179	vs. Left	.258	1531	395	57	12	42	166	132	195	.316	.393
Away	3.99	28	17	0	60	60	385.1	363	43	132	215	vs. Right	.256	1339	343	75	9	36	146	88	199	.317	.406
Day	4.30	15	14	1	41	40	251.1	262	32	79	141	Inning 1-6	.254	2432	618	113	19	68	279	194	335	.316	.400
Night	3.74	33	18	0	75	75	498.0	476	46	141	253	Inning 7+	.274	438	120	19	2	10	36	26	59	.320	.395
Grass	4.02	31	25	0	78	78	504.1	503	51	140	255	None on	.271	1722	466	89	13	51	51	100	226	.316	.426
Turf	3.75	17	6	1	38	37	245.0	235	27	80	139	Runners on	.237	1148	272	43	8	27	261	120	168	.317	.359
March/April	4.62	7	11	0	24	24	146.0	148	16	50	67	Scoring Posn	.217	673	146	23	6	17	227	94	111	.322	.345
May	4.22	12	5	0	26	26	168.2	185	19	50	84	Close & Late	.276	225	62	10	1	2	20	14	29	.320	.356
June	3.55	11	3	0	23	23	154.2	161	14	41	79	None on/out	.281	759	213	39	6	26	26	40	92	.321	.451
July	3.13	9	6	1	19	18	126.1	107	12	29	72	vs. 1st Batr (relief)	.000	1	0	0	0	0	0	0	1	.000	.000
August	4.68	3	4	0	13	13	82.2	78	13	31	44	1st Inning Pitched	.277	444	123	15	5	15	76	52	73	.359	.435
Sept/Oct	3.17	6	2	0	11	11	71.0	59	4	19	48	First 75 Pitches	.255	1994	509	89	17	52	224	169	274	.321	.395
Starter	3.93	48	31	0	115	115	749.0	738	78	220	393	Pitch 76-90	.260	419	109	20	1	15	38	17	49	.290	.420
Reliever	0.00	0	0	1	1	0	0.1	0	0	0	1	Pitch 91-105	.258	295	76	15	3	10	38	23	49	.321	.431
0-3 Days Rest (Start)	5.73	0	2	0	2	2	11.0	12	0	3	9	Pitch 106+	.272	162	44	8	0	1	12	11	22	.324	.340
4 Days Rest	3.77	32	18	0	67	67	446.0	442	41	114	234	First Pitch	.279	420	117	24	1	11	53	0	0	.296	.419
5+ Days Rest	4.10	16	11	0	46	46	292.0	284	37	103	156	Ahead in Count	.230	1267	291	44	11	30	114	0	324	.239	.353
vs. AL	3.96	33	22	0	81	81	524.2	527	51	156	256	Behind in Count	.313	623	195	34	5	26	94	117	0	.425	.509
vs. NL	3.85	15	9	1	35	34	224.2	211	27	64	138	Two Strikes	.197	1213	239	37	4	21	94	95	394	.259	.294
Pre-All Star	3.99	35	19	1	79	78	504.2	518	51	144	251	Pre-All Star	.265	1958	518	95	15	51	211	144	251	.321	.407
Post-All Star	3.79	13	12	0	37	37	244.2	220	27	76	143	Post-All Star	.241	912	220	37	6	27	101	76	143	.307	.384

Pitcher vs. Batter (since 1984)

Pitches Best Vs.	Avg	AB	H	2B	3B	HR	RBI	BB	SO	OBP	SLG	Pitches Worst Vs.	Avg	AB	H	2B	3B	HR	RBI	BB	SO	OBP	SLG
Chad Curtis	.000	10	0	0	0	0	0	1	3	.091	.000	Carlos Delgado	.600	10	6	1	0	1	5	4	0	.667	1.000
Ozzie Guillen	.038	26	1	0	0	0	0	1	1	.074	.038	Shawn Green	.556	18	10	1	0	3	4	1	0	.600	1.111
Mickey Morandini	.045	22	1	0	0	0	0	1	3	.087	.045	Geronimo Berroa	.545	11	6	1	0	1	3	0	1	.545	.909
Kirt Manwaring	.083	12	1	0	0	0	1	0	1	.083	.083	Troy O'Leary	.462	13	6	1	1	2	3	0	1	.462	1.154
Chuck Carr	.083	12	1	0	0	0	0	0	1	.083	.083	Frank Thomas	.381	21	8	1	0	3	8	6	2	.519	.857

Edgar Martinez — Mariners
Age 35 – Bats Right

	Avg	G	AB	R	H	2B	3B	HR	RBI	BB	SO	HBP	GDP	SB	CS	OBP	SLG	IBB	SH	SF	#Pit	#P/PA	GB	FB	G/F
1997 Season	.330	155	542	104	179	35	1	28	108	119	86	11	21	2	4	.456	.554	11	0	6	2799	4.13	196	.163	1.20
Last Five Years	.322	570	2013	413	649	169	4	100	388	439	318	30	53	15	12	.447	.559	46	3	18	10348	4.13	707	613	1.15

1997 Season

	Avg	AB	H	2B	3B	HR	RBI	BB	SO	OBP	SLG		Avg	AB	H	2B	3B	HR	RBI	BB	SO	OBP	SLG
vs. Left	.282	131	37	6	0	4	15	28	21	.413	.420	First Pitch	.390	41	16	3	0	3	13	4	0	.468	.683
vs. Right	.345	411	142	29	1	24	93	91	65	.469	.596	Ahead in Count	.453	161	73	10	1	16	45	68	0	.614	.826
Groundball	.298	121	36	6	0	5	22	25	20	.428	.471	Behind in Count	.242	219	53	11	0	5	36	0	61	.248	.361
Flyball	.354	82	29	5	0	3	17	16	13	.455	.524	Two Strikes	.253	249	63	15	0	6	38	46	86	.374	.386
Home	.321	268	86	21	1	12	50	61	48	.450	.541	Batting #3	.000	8	0	0	0	0	0	1	2	.111	.000
Away	.339	274	93	14	0	16	58	58	38	.462	.566	Batting #4	.335	531	178	35	1	27	107	117	84	.460	.557
Day	.301	163	49	13	1	9	31	38	29	.432	.558	Other	.333	3	1	0	0	1	1	1	0	.500	1.333
Night	.343	379	130	22	0	19	77	81	57	.466	.551	March/April	.300	100	30	8	0	4	16	16	14	.393	.500
Grass	.329	237	78	14	0	13	48	55	33	.463	.553	May	.376	101	38	7	0	3	24	21	9	.496	.535
Turf	.331	305	101	21	1	15	60	64	53	.450	.554	June	.351	94	33	5	0	6	21	17	16	.447	.596
Pre-All Star	.342	310	106	20	0	16	66	62	41	.455	.561	July	.292	89	26	3	0	4	17	24	18	.452	.461
Post-All Star	.315	232	73	15	1	12	42	57	45	.457	.543	August	.307	88	27	8	1	7	18	29	18	.492	.659
Scoring Posn	.307	150	46	9	0	6	74	46	23	.458	.487	Sept/Oct	.357	70	25	4	0	4	12	12	11	.451	.586
Close & Late	.328	67	22	8	0	1	9	23	12	.516	.493	vs. AL	.319	502	160	32	1	21	94	107	79	.444	.512
None on/out	.376	125	47	8	0	8	29	24		.503	.632	vs. NL	.475	40	19	3	0	7	14	12	7	.593	1.075

1997 By Position

Position	Avg	AB	H	2B	3B	HR	RBI	BB	SO	OBP	SLG	G	GS	Innings	PO	A	E	DP	Fld Pct	Rng Fctr	In Zone	Zone Outs	Zone Rtg	MLB Zone
As DH	.326	513	167	33	1	23	100	115	82	.455	.528	144	144	—	—	—	—	—	—	—	—	—	—	—

Last Five Years

	Avg	AB	H	2B	3B	HR	RBI	BB	SO	OBP	SLG		Avg	AB	H	2B	3B	HR	RBI	BB	SO	OBP	SLG
vs. Left	.330	491	162	36	0	24	87	128	64	.468	.550	First Pitch	.375	168	63	18	0	12	50	28	0	.473	.696
vs. Right	.320	1522	487	133	4	76	301	311	254	.440	.562	Ahead in Count	.423	555	235	56	2	47	155	229	1	.591	.786
Groundball	.319	489	156	39	0	22	88	101	83	.441	.534	Behind in Count	.256	841	215	61	1	23	109	0	234	.261	.413
Flyball	.365	351	128	33	2	26	76	69	47	.471	.692	Two Strikes	.251	950	238	67	1	29	135	180	318	.373	.415
Home	.336	934	314	95	1	47	193	218	158	.464	.591	Batting #3	.330	400	132	40	0	25	93	120	59	.490	.618
Away	.310	1079	335	74	3	53	195	221	160	.432	.532	Batting #4	.327	1184	387	94	3	56	222	251	202	.448	.553
Day	.302	589	178	50	4	28	102	112	92	.415	.543	Other	.303	429	130	35	1	19	73	68	57	.400	.522
Night	.331	1424	471	119	0	72	286	327	226	.460	.566	March/April	.316	215	68	23	2	10	39	41	35	.424	.581
Grass	.305	905	276	62	2	43	159	192	137	.432	.520	May	.335	427	143	44	1	18	86	70	63	.435	.569
Turf	.337	1108	373	107	2	57	229	247	181	.460	.591	June	.335	406	136	30	0	25	95	92	53	.454	.594
Pre-All Star	.332	1154	383	104	3	63	240	240	165	.448	.591	July	.304	372	113	29	0	15	60	94	62	.449	.503
Post-All Star	.310	859	266	65	1	37	148	199	153	.446	.517	August	.325	329	107	26	1	21	74	92	62	.483	.602
Scoring Posn	.321	552	177	47	1	22	273	184	95	.484	.529	Sept/Oct	.311	264	82	17	0	11	34	50	52	.423	.500
Close & Late	.343	268	92	28	2	7	56	95	45	.521	.541	vs. AL	.319	1973	630	166	4	93	374	427	311	.444	.549
None on/out	.340	465	158	41	1	24	24	88	74	.453	.587	vs. NL	.475	40	19	3	0	7	14	12	7	.593	1.075

Batter vs. Pitcher (career)

Hits Best Against	Avg	AB	H	2B	3B	HR	RBI	BB	SO	OBP	SLG	Hits Worst Against	Avg	AB	H	2B	3B	HR	RBI	BB	SO	OBP	SLG
Greg Cadaret	.778	9	7	4	0	0	1	2	0	.818	1.222	Omar Olivares	.091	11	1	0	0	0	1	2	2	.231	.091
Brian Anderson	.765	17	13	3	0	3	4	2	0	.789	1.471	Billy Taylor	.111	9	1	0	0	0	1	2	1	.273	.111
Kevin Gross	.545	11	6	2	0	2	3	9	0	.762	1.273	Alex Fernandez	.139	36	5	2	0	0	0	7	2	.279	.194
Scott Aldred	.462	13	6	1	0	3	6	3	1	.563	1.231	Jeff Montgomery	.143	14	2	0	0	0	0	2	6	.250	.143
Erik Hanson	.455	11	5	0	0	4	5	4	0	.600	1.545	Tom Candiotti	.154	13	2	1	0	0	0	1	5	.214	.231

Felix Martinez — Royals
Age 24 – Bats Both

	Avg	G	AB	R	H	2B	3B	HR	RBI	BB	SO	HBP	GDP	SB	CS	OBP	SLG	IBB	SH	SF	#Pit	#P/PA	GB	FB	G/F
1997 Season	.226	16	31	3	7	1	1	0	3	6	8	0	1	0	0	.351	.323	0	1	0	136	3.58	11	5	2.20

1997 Season

	Avg	AB	H	2B	3B	HR	RBI	BB	SO	OBP	SLG		Avg	AB	H	2B	3B	HR	RBI	BB	SO	OBP	SLG
vs. Left	.091	11	1	0	0	0	0	2	2	.231	.091	Scoring Posn	.300	10	3	1	1	0	3	4	1	.500	.600
vs. Right	.300	20	6	1	1	0	3	4	6	.417	.450	Close & Late	.500	8	4	1	0	0	1	1	1	.556	.625

Pedro Martinez — Expos
Age 26 – Pitches Right

	ERA	W	L	Sv	G	GS	IP	BB	SO	Avg	H	2B	3B	HR	RBI	OBP	SLG	CG	ShO	Sup	QS	#P/S	SB	CS	GB	FB	G/F
1997 Season	1.90	17	8	0	31	31	241.1	67	305	.184	158	24	4	16	62	.250	.277	13	4	3.54	25	117	20	5	260	184	1.41
Last Five Years	3.01	65	38	3	183	119	904.1	305	962	.213	696	127	25	72	297	.286	.333	20	8	4.40	74	105	75	28	947	869	1.09

1997 Season

	ERA	W	L	Sv	G	GS	IP	H	HR	BB	SO		Avg	AB	H	2B	3B	HR	RBI	BB	SO	OBP	SLG
Home	1.99	9	5	0	18	18	140.1	96	9	46	177	vs. Left	.183	469	86	14	2	8	29	42	149	.252	.273
Away	1.78	8	3	0	13	13	101.0	62	7	21	128	vs. Right	.184	391	72	10	2	8	33	25	156	.247	.281
Day	1.35	7	1	0	10	10	80.0	43	4	23	99	Inning 1-6	.176	653	115	13	2	12	44	58	244	.252	.257
Night	2.18	10	7	0	21	21	161.1	115	12	44	206	Inning 7+	.208	207	43	11	2	4	18	9	61	.243	.338
Grass	1.43	4	3	0	7	7	56.2	34	3	12	82	None on	.182	549	100	14	3	13	13	34	190	.238	.290
Turf	2.05	13	5	0	24	24	184.2	124	13	55	223	Runners on	.186	311	58	10	1	3	49	33	115	.270	.254
March/April	0.44	3	0	0	3	3	20.1	12	1	7	23	Scoring Posn	.205	161	33	5	0	2	45	25	63	.317	.273
May	1.76	5	1	0	6	6	46.0	34	3	7	50	Close & Late	.203	128	26	8	1	2	13	7	39	.248	.328
June	1.78	2	2	0	6	6	50.2	29	3	15	72	None on/out	.203	231	47	5	2	6	6	15	69	.261	.320

1997 Season

	ERA	W	L	Sv	G	GS	IP	H	HR	BB	SO		Avg	AB	H	2B	3B	HR	RBI	BB	SO	OBP	SLG
July	2.61	2	2	0	5	5	38.0	24	3	12	44	vs. 1st Batr (relief)	.000	0	0	0	0	0	0	0	0	.000	.000
August	1.09	4	1	0	6	6	49.1	24	2	18	66	1st Inning Pitched	.118	102	12	2	0	0	0	7	42	.182	.137
Sept/Oct	3.41	1	2	0	5	5	37.0	35	4	8	50	First 75 Pitches	.176	522	92	12	2	10	33	47	206	.255	.264
Starter	1.90	17	8	0	31	31	241.1	158	16	67	305	Pitch 76-90	.195	113	22	2	0	1	7	6	33	.235	.239
Reliever	0.00	0	0	0	0	0	0.0	0	0	0	0	Pitch 91-105	.198	96	19	3	1	2	11	8	25	.260	.313
0-3 Days Rest (Start)	0.00	0	0	0	0	0	0.0	0	0	0	0	Pitch 106+	.194	129	25	7	1	3	11	6	41	.234	.333
4 Days Rest	2.08	10	6	0	20	20	155.2	105	11	44	203	First Pitch	.351	111	39	10	0	3	11	5	0	.385	.523
5+ Days Rest	1.58	7	2	0	11	11	85.2	53	5	23	102	Ahead in Count	.112	492	55	6	0	3	18	0	271	.119	.142
vs. AL	1.00	3	0	0	3	3	27.0	11	1	4	34	Behind in Count	.342	111	38	7	2	5	19	26	0	.471	.577
vs. NL	2.02	14	8	0	28	28	214.1	147	15	63	271	Two Strikes	.092	501	46	1	1	3	15	36	305	.157	.116
Pre-All Star	1.74	10	4	0	16	16	124.0	81	8	35	154	Pre-All Star	.184	441	81	12	3	8	31	35	154	.250	.279
Post-All Star	2.07	7	4	0	15	15	117.1	77	8	32	151	Post-All Star	.184	419	77	12	1	8	31	32	151	.249	.274

Last Five Years

	ERA	W	L	Sv	G	GS	IP	H	HR	BB	SO		Avg	AB	H	2B	3B	HR	RBI	BB	SO	OBP	SLG
Home	2.79	34	21	2	89	58	451.0	344	29	155	497	vs. Left	.224	1740	389	74	15	34	152	164	441	.294	.342
Away	3.22	31	17	1	94	61	453.1	352	43	150	465	vs. Right	.201	1531	307	53	10	38	145	141	521	.277	.323
Day	2.83	21	16	1	59	41	308.2	226	28	109	316	Inning 1-6	.215	2479	533	99	20	60	244	232	733	.289	.344
Night	3.10	44	22	2	124	78	595.2	470	44	196	646	Inning 7+	.206	792	163	28	5	12	53	73	229	.278	.299
Grass	3.23	25	15	2	86	39	326.1	253	33	113	371	None on	.208	2033	423	77	17	47	47	172	588	.279	.332
Turf	2.88	40	23	1	97	80	578.0	443	39	192	591	Runners on	.221	1238	273	50	8	25	250	133	374	.298	.334
March/April	2.70	7	4	0	21	14	103.1	71	8	35	112	Scoring Posn	.211	668	141	24	2	14	210	91	231	.307	.316
May	2.41	14	4	1	34	23	175.2	129	13	52	168	Close & Late	.198	491	97	17	3	8	36	47	157	.274	.293
June	3.08	12	8	1	35	23	178.0	143	11	56	204	None on/out	.223	862	192	36	8	22	22	77	225	.295	.360
July	4.11	13	8	1	35	22	164.1	130	19	59	169	vs. 1st Batr (relief)	.193	57	11	2	0	1	2	6	15	.281	.281
August	2.58	13	7	0	32	20	160.2	115	14	62	167	1st Inning Pitched	.209	627	131	28	4	16	56	62	195	.286	.343
Sept/Oct	3.09	6	7	0	26	17	122.1	108	7	41	142	First 75 Pitches	.210	2282	480	87	17	51	207	232	710	.290	.330
Starter	3.10	55	35	0	119	119	804.0	631	67	252	848	Pitch 76-90	.232	401	93	10	5	12	43	26	87	.284	.372
Reliever	2.24	10	3	3	64	0	100.1	65	5	53	114	Pitch 91-105	.193	306	59	10	2	6	29	26	88	.257	.297
0-3 Days Rest (Start)	1.80	1	1	0	2	2	15.0	12	0	4	13	Pitch 106+	.227	282	64	20	1	3	18	21	77	.287	.337
4 Days Rest	2.90	34	15	0	67	67	463.0	358	38	152	503	First Pitch	.317	463	147	33	8	10	45	14	0	.346	.488
5+ Days Rest	3.45	20	19	0	50	50	326.0	261	29	96	332	Ahead in Count	.152	1693	258	49	6	15	102	0	802	.162	.215
vs. AL	1.00	3	0	0	3	3	27.0	11	1	4	34	Behind in Count	.312	519	162	29	4	28	85	136	0	.456	.545
vs. NL	3.07	62	38	3	180	116	877.1	685	71	301	928	Two Strikes	.136	1785	242	41	7	18	101	155	962	.210	.197
Pre-All Star	2.87	35	18	2	102	66	502.0	378	37	166	527	Pre-All Star	.208	1813	378	79	12	37	157	166	527	.281	.327
Post-All Star	3.18	30	20	1	81	53	402.1	318	35	139	435	Post-All Star	.218	1458	318	48	13	35	140	139	435	.292	.341

Pitcher vs. Batter (career)

Pitches Best Vs.	Avg	AB	H	2B	3B	HR	RBI	BB	SO	OBP	SLG	Pitches Worst Vs.	Avg	AB	H	2B	3B	HR	RBI	BB	SO	OBP	SLG
Midre Cummings	.000	13	0	0	0	0	0	1	3	.071	.000	Marquis Grissom	.571	21	12	3	1	1	2	2	2	.609	.952
Vinny Castilla	.000	11	0	0	0	0	0	1	5	.000	.000	Gregg Jefferies	.542	24	13	2	1	1	3	2	1	.607	.833
David Segui	.000	10	0	0	0	0	0	1	5	.091	.000	Bip Roberts	.438	16	7	2	1	1	2	3	1	.526	.875
Don Slaught	.000	10	0	0	0	0	0	2	3	.167	.000	Mike Piazza	.412	17	7	1	0	3	5	0	3	.412	1.000
Marvin Benard	.077	13	1	0	0	0	0	0	4	.077	.077	Eric Karros	.333	12	4	1	0	2	2	1	5	.467	.917

Pedro A. Martinez — Reds

Age 29 – Pitches Left

	ERA	W	L	Sv	G	GS	IP	BB	SO	Avg	H	2B	3B	HR	RBI	OBP	SLG	GF	IR	IRS	Hld	SvOp	SB	CS	GB	FB	G/F
1997 Season	9.45	1	1	0	8	0	6.2	7	4	.286	8	0	1	1	12	.432	.464	1	13	5	3	0	1	0	12	9	1.33
Career (1993-1997)	3.97	7	4	3	122	1	142.2	93	114	.232	125	25	3	14	88	.348	.367	31	96	32	13	6	15	10	180	151	1.19

1997 Season

	ERA	W	L	Sv	G	GS	IP	H	HR	BB	SO		Avg	AB	H	2B	3B	HR	RBI	BB	SO	OBP	SLG
Home	11.57	0	0	0	3	0	2.1	3	1	2	0	vs. Left	.182	11	2	0	0	0	4	0	2	.231	.182
Away	8.31	1	1	0	5	0	4.1	5	0	5	4	vs. Right	.353	17	6	0	1	1	8	7	2	.542	.647

Career (1993-1997)

	ERA	W	L	Sv	G	GS	IP	H	HR	BB	SO		Avg	AB	H	2B	3B	HR	RBI	BB	SO	OBP	SLG
Home	2.84	4	2	1	57	0	69.2	42	8	41	57	vs. Left	.260	192	50	8	1	6	34	23	37	.347	.406
Away	5.05	3	2	2	65	1	73.0	83	6	52	57	vs. Right	.216	347	75	17	2	8	54	70	77	.348	.346
Day	4.12	3	2	1	37	0	39.1	39	8	32	25	Inning 1-6	.209	177	37	8	1	2	26	35	42	.349	.299
Night	3.92	4	2	2	85	1	103.1	86	6	61	89	Inning 7+	.243	362	88	17	2	12	62	58	72	.348	.401
Grass	3.05	5	4	3	76	0	97.1	73	8	58	79	None on	.236	242	57	10	1	4	4	38	50	.342	.335
Turf	5.96	2	0	0	46	1	45.1	52	6	35	35	Runners on	.229	297	68	15	2	10	84	55	64	.353	.394
March/April	1.00	0	0	1	12	0	18.0	10	0	6	13	Scoring Posn	.226	186	42	7	1	6	70	40	39	.365	.371
May	5.20	1	1	0	20	1	27.2	28	1	21	24	Close & Late	.191	141	27	7	0	4	20	29	34	.331	.326
June	5.57	1	2	0	32	0	32.1	36	8	20	27	None on/out	.272	114	31	6	0	1	1	14	26	.357	.351
July	2.01	2	1	0	20	0	22.1	17	0	14	12	vs. 1st Batr (relief)	.330	103	34	6	0	5	23	12	19	.412	.534
August	3.97	3	1	0	19	0	22.2	17	2	15	22	1st Inning Pitched	.251	371	93	19	2	12	75	64	73	.366	.410
Sept/Oct	4.58	0	1	0	19	0	19.2	17	3	7	16	First 75 Pitches	.267	311	83	18	1	10	61	47	55	.368	.428
Starter	11.57	0	0	0	1	1	2.1	4	0	4	1	Pitch 16-30	.189	159	30	5	2	4	20	32	45	.326	.321
Reliever	3.85	7	4	3	121	0	140.1	121	14	89	113	Pitch 31-45	.180	50	9	2	0	0	7	11	11	.323	.220
0 Days rest (Relief)	4.61	2	2	2	24	0	27.1	25	3	18	20	Pitch 46+	.158	19	3	0	0	0	0	3	3	.273	.158
1 or 2 Days rest	3.58	1	2	0	51	0	60.1	54	7	37	54	First Pitch	.317	63	20	2	0	4	18	13	0	.449	.540
3+ Days rest	3.76	4	0	1	46	0	52.2	42	4	34	39	Ahead in Count	.158	234	37	9	1	4	28	0	93	.161	.256
vs. AL	0.00	0	0	0	2	0	0.2	0	0	0	0	Behind in Count	.264	125	33	5	1	3	21	41	0	.440	.392
vs. NL	3.99	7	4	3	120	1	142.0	125	14	93	114	Two Strikes	.173	255	44	12	1	2	26	39	114	.283	.251
Pre-All Star	4.27	2	1	3	72	1	86.1	80	9	59	70	Pre-All Star	.245	327	80	19	1	9	55	59	70	.362	.391
Post-All Star	3.51	5	3	0	50	0	56.1	45	5	34	44	Post-All Star	.212	212	45	6	2	5	33	34	44	.325	.330

	ERA	W	L	Sv	G	GS	IP	BB	SO	Avg	H	2B	3B	HR	RBI	OBP	SLG	CG	ShO	Sup	QS	#P/S	SB	CS	GB	FB	G/F
1997 Season	3.64	10	5	0	22	22	133.2	68	120	.243	123	35	0	14	52	.337	.394	1	0	5.52	12	104	13	7	164	139	1.18
Last Five Years	3.62	64	37	0	136	135	890.1	395	637	.245	814	140	17	78	333	.328	.367	15	10	5.08	81	107	68	40	1161	946	1.23

1997 Season

	ERA	W	L	Sv	G	GS	IP	H	HR	BB	SO
Home	3.70	7	3	0	13	13	80.1	74	9	39	80
Away	3.54	3	2	0	9	9	53.1	49	5	29	40
Day	3.40	2	2	0	7	7	39.2	35	4	23	33
Night	3.73	8	3	0	15	15	94.0	88	10	45	87
Grass	3.71	8	4	0	18	18	111.2	102	12	57	102
Turf	3.27	2	1	0	4	4	22.0	21	2	11	18
March/April	3.82	2	2	0	6	6	35.1	38	3	22	32
May	2.83	2	1	0	6	6	41.1	31	3	18	32
June	4.00	2	0	0	3	3	18.0	20	3	8	23
July	0.00	0	0	0	0	0	0.0	0	0	0	0
August	1.64	2	0	0	2	2	11.0	8	1	3	12
Sept/Oct	5.14	2	2	0	5	5	28.0	26	4	17	21
Starter	3.64	10	5	0	22	22	133.2	123	14	68	120
Reliever	0.00	0	0	0	0	0	0.0	0	0	0	0
0-3 Days Rest (Start)	8.44	0	0	0	1	1	5.1	9	0	3	4
4 Days Rest	4.02	6	4	0	13	13	80.2	74	10	37	79
5+ Days Rest	2.45	4	1	0	8	8	47.2	40	4	28	37
vs. AL	5.40	1	0	0	2	2	10.0	9	3	7	12
vs. NL	3.49	9	5	0	20	20	123.2	114	11	61	108
Pre-All Star	3.42	6	3	0	15	15	94.2	89	9	48	87
Post-All Star	4.15	4	2	0	7	7	39.0	34	5	20	33

	Avg	AB	H	2B	3B	HR	RBI	BB	SO	OBP	SLG
vs. Left	.269	245	66	18	0	7	30	48	47	.384	.429
vs. Right	.218	262	57	17	0	7	22	20	73	.288	.363
Inning 1-6	.254	464	118	33	0	14	52	67	112	.353	.416
Inning 7+	.116	43	5	2	0	0	0	1	8	.136	.163
None on	.285	281	80	22	0	12	12	31	74	.360	.491
Runners on	.190	226	43	13	0	2	40	37	46	.310	.274
Scoring Posn	.190	142	27	9	0	1	37	27	34	.316	.275
Close & Late	.103	29	3	1	0	0	0	1	4	.133	.138
None on/out	.282	131	37	11	0	3	3	9	32	.329	.435
vs. 1st Batr (relief)	.000	0	0	0	0	0	0	0	0	.000	.000
1st Inning Pitched	.184	76	14	2	0	2	7	10	19	.292	.289
First 75 Pitches	.236	348	82	24	0	11	32	45	86	.327	.399
Pitch 76-90	.355	76	27	8	0	2	11	12	13	.440	.549
Pitch 91-105	.146	48	7	0	0	1	6	9	12	.300	.208
Pitch 106+	.200	35	7	3	0	0	3	2	9	.243	.286
First Pitch	.282	78	22	0	0	1	8	0	0	.296	.397
Ahead in Count	.127	220	28	5	0	0	8	0	99	.135	.150
Behind in Count	.378	111	42	13	0	8	21	36	0	.530	.712
Two Strikes	.142	246	35	9	0	2	10	32	120	.246	.203
Pre-All Star	.247	360	89	27	0	9	35	48	87	.337	.399
Post-All Star	.231	147	34	8	0	5	17	20	33	.335	.388

Last Five Years

	ERA	W	L	Sv	G	GS	IP	H	HR	BB	SO
Home	3.64	33	22	0	72	71	479.1	442	37	192	344
Away	3.59	31	15	0	64	64	411.0	372	41	203	293
Day	3.55	13	13	0	38	37	228.1	210	31	101	168
Night	3.64	51	24	0	98	98	662.0	604	47	294	469
Grass	3.73	47	30	0	108	107	700.1	653	63	300	514
Turf	3.22	17	7	0	28	28	190.0	161	15	95	123
March/April	4.00	6	8	0	20	20	117.0	107	13	67	95
May	3.23	14	3	0	26	26	181.1	156	10	82	115
June	4.23	12	7	0	23	23	151.0	160	16	55	114
July	3.42	11	8	0	24	24	166.0	152	18	69	105
August	2.79	10	6	0	21	20	145.0	116	9	59	107
Sept/Oct	4.29	11	5	0	22	22	130.0	123	12	63	101
Starter	3.61	64	36	0	135	135	886.1	810	78	391	632
Reliever	4.50	0	1	0	1	0	4.0	4	0	4	5
0-3 Days Rest (Start)	4.81	1	2	0	4	4	24.1	30	2	7	20
4 Days Rest	3.79	31	19	0	72	72	475.1	436	43	201	348
5+ Days Rest	3.33	32	15	0	59	59	386.2	344	33	183	264
vs. AL	5.40	1	0	0	2	2	10.0	9	3	7	12
vs. NL	3.60	63	37	0	134	133	880.1	805	75	388	625
Pre-All Star	3.87	35	21	0	76	76	495.0	465	44	232	357
Post-All Star	3.30	29	16	0	60	59	395.1	349	34	163	280

	Avg	AB	H	2B	3B	HR	RBI	BB	SO	OBP	SLG
vs. Left	.249	1551	386	69	7	40	163	265	273	.357	.380
vs. Right	.241	1777	428	71	10	38	170	130	364	.300	.356
Inning 1-6	.246	2825	694	126	14	67	299	337	547	.329	.371
Inning 7+	.239	503	120	14	3	11	34	58	90	.320	.344
None on	.249	1929	481	89	12	53	53	208	387	.327	.390
Runners on	.238	1399	333	51	5	25	280	187	250	.320	.335
Scoring Posn	.215	769	165	27	5	11	244	127	146	.322	.306
Close & Late	.230	244	56	4	1	6	21	25	43	.309	.328
None on/out	.257	871	224	46	8	24	24	74	150	.320	.411
vs. 1st Batr (relief)	.000	1	0	0	0	0	0	0	1	.000	.000
1st Inning Pitched	.228	500	114	19	1	13	47	46	89	.299	.348
First 75 Pitches	.247	2215	547	103	10	52	229	249	422	.325	.373
Pitch 76-90	.260	465	121	21	2	13	49	64	79	.355	.398
Pitch 91-105	.235	341	80	8	3	11	44	39	73	.320	.372
Pitch 106+	.215	307	66	8	2	2	22	42	63	.311	.274
First Pitch	.290	466	135	21	3	13	62	17	0	.318	.431
Ahead in Count	.183	1370	251	39	6	12	86	0	518	.189	.247
Behind in Count	.315	790	249	40	4	32	111	194	0	.450	.504
Two Strikes	.165	1481	245	42	7	20	89	183	687	.261	.244
Pre-All Star	.251	1854	465	89	8	44	192	232	357	.336	.379
Post-All Star	.237	1474	349	51	9	34	141	163	280	.316	.353

Pitcher vs. Batter (career)

Pitches Best Vs.	Avg	AB	H	2B	3B	HR	RBI	BB	SO	OBP	SLG
Steve Scarsone	.000	12	0	0	0	0	0	0	5	.000	.000
Butch Huskey	.000	10	0	0	0	0	0	1	2	.091	.000
Darrin Jackson	.059	17	1	0	0	0	0	0	2	.059	.059
Darryl Strawberry	.067	15	1	0	0	0	1	0	4	.067	.067
Orlando Miller	.077	13	1	0	0	0	0	0	4	.077	.077

Pitches Worst Vs.	Avg	AB	H	2B	3B	HR	RBI	BB	SO	OBP	SLG
Will Clark	.415	41	17	4	0	3	8	4	4	.478	.732
Thomas Howard	.406	32	13	2	1	3	4	3	2	.457	.813
Eddie Murray	.364	11	4	0	0	2	3	3	2	.500	.909
Bobby Bonilla	.343	35	12	0	1	6	12	4	9	.410	.914
Rico Brogna	.333	9	3	1	0	1	3	2	1	.417	.778

Sandy Martinez — Blue Jays   Age 25 – Bats Left

	Avg	G	AB	R	H	2B	3B	HR	RBI	BB	SO	HBP	GDP	SB	CS	OBP	SLG	IBB	SH	SF	#Pit	#P/PA	GB	FB	G/F
1997 Season	.000	3	2	1	0	0	0	0	0	0	1	0	0	0	0	.333	.000	0	0	0	12	4.00	0	1	0.00
Career (1995-1997)	.232	141	422	30	98	21	3	5	43	24	104	5	5	0	0	.280	.332	0	1	2	1636	3.60	149	105	1.42

1997 Season

	Avg	AB	H	2B	3B	HR	RBI	BB	SO	OBP	SLG
vs. Left	.000	0	0	0	0	0	0	0	0	.000	.000
vs. Right	.000	2	0	0	0	0	0	1	1	.333	.000

	Avg	AB	H	2B	3B	HR	RBI	BB	SO	OBP	SLG
Scoring Posn	.000	0	0	0	0	0	0	0	0	.000	.000
Close & Late	.000	0	0	0	0	0	0	1	0	1.000	.000

Career (1995-1997)

	Avg	AB	H	2B	3B	HR	RBI	BB	SO	OBP	SLG
vs. Left	.203	59	12	4	0	1	5	4	20	.254	.322
vs. Right	.237	363	86	17	3	4	38	20	84	.285	.333
Groundball	.276	105	29	7	0	1	18	5	23	.316	.371
Flyball	.222	81	18	5	0	0	5	7	22	.300	.284
Home	.228	197	45	13	1	3	19	11	49	.285	.350
Away	.236	225	53	8	2	2	24	13	55	.282	.316
Day	.220	150	33	5	2	2	10	6	43	.253	.320

	Avg	AB	H	2B	3B	HR	RBI	BB	SO	OBP	SLG
First Pitch	.260	73	19	3	0	1	7	0	0	.260	.342
Ahead in Count	.274	95	26	5	1	3	14	8	0	.333	.442
Behind in Count	.168	190	32	10	0	0	13	0	91	.172	.221
Two Strikes	.116	189	22	4	1	0	9	16	104	.184	.148
Batting #8	.225	284	64	17	3	3	30	19	69	.286	.338
Batting #9	.222	117	26	3	0	1	11	3	29	.238	.274
Other	.381	21	8	1	0	1	2	2	6	.435	.571

Career (1995-1997)

	Avg	AB	H	2B	3B	HR	RBI	BB	SO	OBP	SLG		Avg	AB	H	2B	3B	HR	RBI	BB	SO	OBP	SLG
Night	.239	272	65	16	1	3	33	18	61	.295	.338	March/April	.250	40	10	2	1	1	5	3	7	.302	.425
Grass	.241	191	46	7	1	2	23	12	43	.291	.319	May	.169	59	10	2	0	0	7	4	18	.234	.203
Turf	.225	231	52	14	2	3	20	12	61	.271	.342	June	.320	50	16	3	2	1	4	5	11	.382	.520
Pre-All Star	.242	178	43	7	3	3	17	14	48	.304	.365	July	.217	106	23	5	0	1	5	4	30	.265	.292
Post-All Star	.225	244	55	14	0	2	26	10	56	.263	.307	August	.237	93	22	4	0	1	17	5	16	.270	.312
Scoring Posn	.243	107	26	6	1	2	39	7	28	.291	.374	Sept/Oct	.230	74	17	5	0	1	5	3	22	.269	.338
Close & Late	.217	60	13	2	0	1	8	4	17	.266	.300	vs. AL	.232	422	98	21	3	5	43	24	104	.280	.332
None on/out	.226	106	24	5	0	2	2	4	23	.268	.330	vs. NL	.000	0	0	0	0	0	0	0	0	.000	.000

Batter vs. Pitcher (career)

Hits Best Against	Avg	AB	H	2B	3B	HR	RBI	BB	SO	OBP	SLG	Hits Worst Against	Avg	AB	H	2B	3B	HR	RBI	BB	SO	OBP	SLG
Mike Mussina	.333	12	4	2	0	0	2	0	2	.333	.500												

Tino Martinez — Yankees
Age 30 – Bats Left

	Avg	G	AB	R	H	2B	3B	HR	RBI	BB	SO	HBP	GDP	SB	CS	OBP	SLG	IBB	SH	SF	#Pit	#P/PA	GB	FB	G/F
1997 Season	.296	158	594	96	176	31	2	44	141	75	75	3	15	3	1	.371	.577	14	0	13	2560	3.74	195	227	0.86
Last Five Years	.285	660	2445	360	696	140	6	137	490	279	359	15	57	6	7	.358	.515	44	10	30	10594	3.81	804	856	0.94

1997 Season

	Avg	AB	H	2B	3B	HR	RBI	BB	SO	OBP	SLG		Avg	AB	H	2B	3B	HR	RBI	BB	SO	OBP	SLG
vs. Left	.268	231	62	10	2	12	55	22	27	.330	.485	First Pitch	.393	56	22	6	0	6	15	10	0	.493	.821
vs. Right	.314	363	114	21	0	32	86	53	48	.396	.636	Ahead in Count	.385	130	50	9	0	16	44	40	0	.514	.823
Groundball	.350	123	43	6	0	10	32	14	18	.417	.642	Behind in Count	.225	280	63	9	2	12	54	0	60	.222	.400
Flyball	.226	93	21	6	0	4	12	10	15	.290	.419	Two Strikes	.221	258	57	13	1	13	47	25	75	.285	.430
Home	.282	280	79	12	2	18	63	38	23	.361	.532	Batting #4	.298	463	138	24	2	31	107	59	58	.374	.559
Away	.309	314	97	19	0	26	78	37	52	.380	.618	Batting #5	.294	126	37	7	0	12	33	15	14	.361	.635
Day	.273	238	65	17	1	16	53	26	37	.340	.555	Other	.200	5	1	0	0	1	1	1	3	.333	.800
Night	.312	356	111	14	1	28	88	49	38	.391	.593	March/April	.327	113	37	7	0	9	34	12	10	.377	.628
Grass	.294	513	151	27	2	36	116	68	54	.371	.565	May	.282	103	29	1	1	11	22	15	17	.373	.631
Turf	.309	81	25	4	0	8	25	7	21	.371	.654	June	.312	93	29	8	0	8	20	11	7	.381	.656
Pre-All Star	.302	331	100	19	1	28	78	39	41	.370	.619	July	.266	94	25	5	1	8	23	12	12	.358	.596
Post-All Star	.289	263	76	12	1	16	63	36	34	.372	.525	August	.327	110	36	8	0	5	26	16	17	.408	.536
Scoring Posn	.317	186	59	10	1	15	105	38	33	.409	.624	Sept/Oct	.247	81	20	2	0	3	16	9	12	.312	.383
Close & Late	.378	90	34	6	1	8	22	10	8	.436	.733	vs. AL	.311	540	168	29	2	44	139	74	64	.390	.617
None on/out	.254	134	34	5	0	6	6	10	14	.315	.425	vs. NL	.148	54	8	2	0	0	2	1	11	.161	.185

1997 By Position

Position	Avg	AB	H	2B	3B	HR	RBI	BB	SO	OBP	SLG	G	GS	Innings	PO	A	E	DP	Fld Pct	Rng Fctr	In Zone	Zone Outs	Zone Rtg	MLB Zone
As 1b	.298	570	170	30	2	43	136	74	72	.375	.584	150	147	1309.1	1304	104	8	127	.994	---	260	224	.862	.874

Last Five Years

	Avg	AB	H	2B	3B	HR	RBI	BB	SO	OBP	SLG		Avg	AB	H	2B	3B	HR	RBI	BB	SO	OBP	SLG
vs. Left	.279	811	226	48	4	37	173	78	142	.347	.485	First Pitch	.367	215	79	19	0	13	53	32	0	.453	.637
vs. Right	.288	1634	470	92	2	100	317	201	217	.365	.530	Ahead in Count	.344	544	187	39	1	46	144	140	0	.473	.673
Groundball	.293	542	159	27	1	26	103	56	75	.362	.491	Behind in Count	.234	1143	268	54	3	47	191	0	299	.237	.410
Flyball	.273	466	127	33	0	24	80	45	76	.333	.498	Two Strikes	.222	1106	246	51	3	47	180	106	359	.291	.401
Home	.271	1136	308	59	3	58	240	150	151	.356	.482	Batting #4	.296	864	256	46	4	56	201	106	124	.372	.553
Away	.296	1309	388	81	3	79	250	129	208	.359	.544	Batting #5	.267	891	238	47	0	45	167	88	121	.332	.471
Day	.287	830	238	48	1	52	179	94	121	.358	.535	Other	.293	690	202	47	2	36	122	85	114	.371	.523
Night	.284	1615	458	92	5	85	311	185	238	.358	.505	March/April	.259	359	93	19	0	17	70	48	45	.344	.454
Grass	.292	1612	471	90	4	91	320	172	223	.359	.522	May	.276	468	129	16	2	33	92	62	77	.361	.530
Turf	.270	833	225	50	2	46	170	107	136	.355	.501	June	.284	493	140	40	2	26	94	46	63	.344	.531
Pre-All Star	.276	1458	402	89	4	84	284	163	210	.348	.515	July	.303	459	139	30	1	29	100	49	65	.374	.562
Post-All Star	.298	987	294	51	2	53	206	116	149	.371	.515	August	.314	389	122	20	1	22	81	43	63	.381	.540
Scoring Posn	.305	691	211	47	2	45	373	127	110	.401	.524	Sept/Oct	.264	277	73	15	0	10	53	31	46	.335	.426
Close & Late	.312	397	124	29	1	26	93	55	67	.393	.587	vs. AL	.288	2391	688	138	6	137	488	278	348	.362	.522
None on/out	.259	595	154	23	0	29	29	52	76	.320	.444	vs. NL	.148	54	8	2	0	0	2	1	11	.161	.185

Batter vs. Pitcher (career)

Hits Best Against	Avg	AB	H	2B	3B	HR	RBI	BB	SO	OBP	SLG	Hits Worst Against	Avg	AB	H	2B	3B	HR	RBI	BB	SO	OBP	SLG
James Baldwin	.545	11	6	2	0	2	4	1	2	.583	1.273	Scott Karl	.000	17	0	0	0	0	1	1	2	.053	.000
Mike Myers	.455	11	5	2	1	1	2	1	2	.500	1.091	Danny Darwin	.083	12	1	0	0	1	1	0	.143	.083
Felipe Lira	.409	22	9	2	0	4	7	1	1	.435	1.045	Jesse Orosco	.105	19	2	1	0	0	2	2	6	.182	.158
Brian Anderson	.385	13	5	1	0	4	8	0	3	.385	1.385	Kevin Brown	.118	34	4	0	0	0	0	1	6	.143	.118
Mike Mohler	.364	11	4	0	2	7	1	2		.385	1.091	Rick Krivda	.182	11	2	0	0	0	0	0	4	.182	.182

John Marzano — Mariners
Age 35 – Bats Right (groundball hitter)

	Avg	G	AB	R	H	2B	3B	HR	RBI	BB	SO	HBP	GDP	SB	CS	OBP	SLG	IBB	SH	SF	#Pit	#P/PA	GB	FB	G/F
1997 Season	.287	39	87	7	25	3	0	1	10	7	15	0	2	0	0	.340	.356	0	2	0	355	3.70	28	26	1.08
Last Five Years	.266	82	199	16	53	9	0	1	16	14	30	4	4	4	0	.327	.327	0	5	0	789	3.55	75	59	1.27

1997 Season

	Avg	AB	H	2B	3B	HR	RBI	BB	SO	OBP	SLG		Avg	AB	H	2B	3B	HR	RBI	BB	SO	OBP	SLG
vs. Left	.391	23	9	2	0	0	4	3	3	.462	.478	Scoring Posn	.286	21	6	0	0	1	9	3	6	.375	.429
vs. Right	.250	64	16	1	0	1	6	4	12	.294	.313	Close & Late	.000	6	0	0	0	0	0	1	3	.143	.000

Damon Mashore — Athletics
Age 28 – Bats Right

	Avg	G	AB	R	H	2B	3B	HR	RBI	BB	SO	HBP	GDP	SB	CS	OBP	SLG	IBB	SH	SF	#Pit	#P/PA	GB	FB	G/F
1997 Season	.247	92	279	55	69	10	2	3	18	50	82	5	5	5	4	.370	.330	1	7	1	1387	4.06	105	45	2.33
Career (1996-1997)	.253	142	384	75	97	17	3	6	30	66	113	6	7	9	4	.369	.359	1	8	2	1892	4.06	140	72	1.94

1997 Season

	Avg	AB	H	2B	3B	HR	RBI	BB	SO	OBP	SLG		Avg	AB	H	2B	3B	HR	RBI	BB	SO	OBP	SLG
vs. Left	.297	74	22	4	1	2	7	14	22	.416	.459	First Pitch	.286	35	10	3	1	1	3	0	0	.278	.514
vs. Right	.229	205	47	6	1	1	11	36	60	.354	.283	Ahead in Count	.451	51	23	5	1	1	6	29	0	.659	.647
Groundball	.294	51	15	1	1	0	2	12	10	.438	.353	Behind in Count	.173	139	24	2	0	1	5	0	67	.184	.209
Flyball	.195	41	8	4	0	1	4	7	13	.313	.366	Two Strikes	.167	150	25	2	0	1	7	21	82	.277	.200
Home	.227	110	25	5	0	1	5	24	33	.380	.300	Batting #1	.253	261	66	9	2	3	15	45	74	.370	.337
Away	.260	169	44	5	2	2	13	26	49	.364	.349	Batting #2	.167	6	1	0	0	0	0	3	4	.444	.167
Day	.287	115	33	4	2	2	9	21	33	.406	.409	Other	.167	12	2	1	0	0	3	2	4	.333	.250
Night	.220	164	36	6	0	1	9	29	49	.345	.274	March/April	.347	75	26	3	1	1	5	11	12	.437	.453
Grass	.241	253	61	8	2	3	17	45	72	.365	.324	May	.220	118	26	5	1	0	7	21	37	.340	.280
Turf	.308	26	8	2	0	1	5	10		.419	.385	June	.180	50	9	2	0	1	4	11	19	.349	.280
Pre-All Star	.243	251	61	10	2	2	16	45	71	.365	.323	July	.222	36	8	0	0	1	2	7	14	.364	.306
Post-All Star	.286	28	8	0	0	1	2	5	11	.412	.393	August	.000	0	0	0	0	0	0	0	0	.000	.000
Scoring Posn	.255	51	13	1	1	0	14	14	15	.409	.314	Sept/Oct	.000	0	0	0	0	0	0	0	0	.000	.000
Close & Late	.314	35	11	2	0	1	1	12	15	.500	.371	vs. AL	.262	260	68	10	2	3	18	45	72	.379	.350
None on/out	.281	114	32	5	1	2	2	12	35	.359	.395	vs. NL	.053	19	1	0	0	0	0	5	10	.250	.053

1997 By Position

Position	Avg	AB	H	2B	3B	HR	RBI	BB	SO	OBP	SLG	G	GS	Innings	PO	A	E	DP	Fld Pct	Rng Fctr	In Zone	Zone Outs	Zone Rtg	MLB Zone
As lf	.273	22	6	1	0	0	1	7	6	.448	.318	28	3	79.0	24	1	0	0	1.000	2.85	28	22	.786	.805
As cf	.249	253	63	9	2	3	16	41	74	.363	.336	71	68	557.0	175	9	2	3	.989	2.97	213	167	.784	.815

Mike Matheny — Brewers
Age 27 – Bats Right (groundball hitter)

	Avg	G	AB	R	H	2B	3B	HR	RBI	BB	SO	HBP	GDP	SB	CS	OBP	SLG	IBB	SH	SF	#Pit	#P/PA	GB	FB	G/F
1997 Season	.244	123	320	29	78	16	1	4	32	17	68	7	9	0	1	.294	.338	0	9	3	1229	3.45	103	82	1.26
Career (1994-1997)	.229	337	852	76	195	43	4	13	101	46	189	14	22	5	5	.277	.335	0	18	7	3339	3.56	291	214	1.36

1997 Season

	Avg	AB	H	2B	3B	HR	RBI	BB	SO	OBP	SLG		Avg	AB	H	2B	3B	HR	RBI	BB	SO	OBP	SLG
vs. Left	.264	110	29	7	1	1	8	5	19	.308	.373	First Pitch	.333	51	17	5	1	1	7	0	0	.352	.529
vs. Right	.233	210	49	9	0	3	24	12	49	.287	.319	Ahead in Count	.382	55	21	4	0	0	9	10	0	.485	.455
Groundball	.293	58	17	1	1	2	10	1	16	.317	.448	Behind in Count	.153	163	25	4	0	2	13	0	61	.172	.215
Flyball	.327	49	16	3	0	1	5	1	11	.389	.449	Two Strikes	.158	152	24	3	0	2	12	7	68	.213	.217
Home	.237	152	36	6	1	2	21	9	32	.289	.329	Batting #8	.214	14	3	0	0	0	2	3	2	.333	.214
Away	.250	168	42	10	0	2	11	8	36	.298	.345	Batting #9	.250	292	73	16	1	4	29	12	64	.294	.353
Day	.271	107	29	4	0	4	17	3	16	.307	.421	Other	.143	14	2	0	0	0	1	2	2	.250	.143
Night	.230	213	49	12	1	0	15	14	52	.288	.296	March/April	.259	54	14	2	0	1	7	3	11	.310	.352
Grass	.249	281	70	12	1	3	25	13	58	.297	.331	May	.233	60	14	6	0	1	6	3	15	.281	.383
Turf	.205	39	8	4	0	1	7	4	10	.273	.385	June	.207	58	12	3	0	0	2	2	13	.242	.259
Pre-All Star	.233	180	42	11	0	3	17	8	41	.275	.344	July	.268	56	15	3	0	1	6	1	13	.288	.375
Post-All Star	.257	140	36	5	1	1	15	9	27	.318	.329	August	.254	63	16	1	1	1	9	4	10	.304	.349
Scoring Posn	.253	79	20	4	0	3	30	4	23	.311	.418	Sept/Oct	.241	29	7	1	0	0	2	4	6	.371	.276
Close & Late	.265	34	9	1	1	0	1	5		.286	.353	vs. AL	.253	289	73	15	1	4	29	15	61	.304	.353
None on/out	.247	81	20	4	1	2	2	7	14	.315	.358	vs. NL	.161	31	5	1	0	0	3	2	7	.206	.194

1997 By Position

Position	Avg	AB	H	2B	3B	HR	RBI	BB	SO	OBP	SLG	G	GS	Innings	PO	A	E	DP	Fld Pct	Rng Fctr	In Zone	Zone Outs	Zone Rtg	MLB Zone
As c	.239	318	76	16	0	4	32	17	68	.290	.327	121	112	929.2	697	57	5	8	.993	—	—	—	—	—

Career (1994-1997)

	Avg	AB	H	2B	3B	HR	RBI	BB	SO	OBP	SLG		Avg	AB	H	2B	3B	HR	RBI	BB	SO	OBP	SLG
vs. Left	.245	298	73	18	1	2	29	15	54	.287	.332	First Pitch	.295	129	38	9	2	3	24	0	0	.313	.465
vs. Right	.220	554	122	25	3	11	72	31	135	.272	.336	Ahead in Count	.346	162	56	13	0	3	27	20	0	.418	.481
Groundball	.230	187	43	7	2	5	29	10	47	.291	.369	Behind in Count	.148	427	63	12	2	5	39	0	170	.162	.220
Flyball	.242	149	36	6	1	2	12	11	29	.302	.336	Two Strikes	.122	403	49	5	0	5	28	26	189	.187	.171
Home	.251	431	108	23	2	8	61	27	86	.301	.369	Batting #8	.241	158	38	8	0	0	20	15	27	.315	.291
Away	.207	421	87	20	2	5	40	19	103	.253	.299	Batting #9	.228	619	141	31	4	11	71	24	146	.266	.344
Day	.242	306	74	10	1	7	49	12	59	.278	.350	Other	.213	75	16	4	0	2	10	7	16	.289	.347
Night	.222	546	121	33	3	6	52	34	130	.277	.326	March/April	.244	135	33	5	0	4	23	8	29	.301	.370
Grass	.234	731	171	37	3	11	86	38	156	.282	.338	May	.234	167	39	14	2	1	22	7	41	.268	.359
Turf	.198	121	24	6	1	2	15	8	33	.250	.314	June	.174	132	23	5	0	1	9	6	31	.213	.235
Pre-All Star	.212	472	100	25	2	7	56	21	111	.251	.318	July	.249	193	48	12	1	3	17	9	44	.288	.368
Post-All Star	.250	380	95	18	2	6	45	25	78	.309	.355	August	.267	120	32	3	1	2	20	7	19	.310	.358
Scoring Posn	.276	221	61	13	1	4	89	12	55	.316	.398	Sept/Oct	.190	105	20	4	0	2	10	9	25	.286	.286
Close & Late	.239	92	22	2	1	1	4	3	16	.278	.315	vs. AL	.231	821	190	42	4	13	98	44	182	.280	.340
None on/out	.218	197	43	12	1	1	1	17	43	.290	.365	vs. NL	.161	31	5	1	0	0	3	2	7	.206	.194

Batter vs. Pitcher (career)

Hits Best Against	Avg	AB	H	2B	3B	HR	RBI	BB	SO	OBP	SLG	Hits Worst Against	Avg	AB	H	2B	3B	HR	RBI	BB	SO	OBP	SLG
Bob Wells	.364	11	4	1	1	1	2	0	4	.364	.909	Jamie Moyer	.091	11	1	0	0	0	0	0	4	.091	.091
Orel Hershiser	.333	12	4	0	0	1	3	1	2	.467	.583	Jimmy Key	.091	11	1	0	0	0	0	1	5	.167	.091
Pat Hentgen	.313	16	5	1	0	0	3	1	2	.353	.375	Tim Wakefield	.095	21	2	0	0	1	2	1	6	.174	.238
												Charles Nagy	.167	12	2	1	0	0	0	0	8	.167	.250

Batter vs. Pitcher (career)

Hits Best Against	Avg	AB	H	2B	3B	HR	RBI	BB	SO	OBP	SLG	Hits Worst Against	Avg	AB	H	2B	3B	HR	RBI	BB	SO	OBP	SLG
												Andy Pettitte	.182	11	2	1	0	0	1	0	2	.182	.273

T.J. Mathews — Athletics
Age 28 – Pitches Right

	ERA	W	L	Sv	G	GS	IP	BB	SO	Avg	H	2B	3B	HR	RBI	OBP	SLG	GF	IR	IRS	Hld	SvOp	SB	CS	GB	FB	G/F
1997 Season	3.01	10	6	3	64	0	74.2	30	70	.260	75	11	2	9	33	.333	.406	26	25	8	12	9	13	0	100	79	1.27
Career (1995-1997)	2.78	13	13	11	154	0	188.0	73	178	.226	158	11	3	18	73	.302	.348	61	67	16	28	22	21	3	215	212	1.01

1997 Season

	ERA	W	L	Sv	G	GS	IP	H	HR	BB	SO		Avg	AB	H	2B	3B	HR	RBI	BB	SO	OBP	SLG
Home	2.56	9	3	2	40	0	45.2	46	7	19	38	vs. Left	.323	124	40	8	1	5	21	16	20	.397	.524
Away	3.72	1	3	1	24	0	29.0	29	2	11	32	vs. Right	.213	164	35	3	1	4	12	14	50	.283	.317
Day	3.26	2	2	2	24	0	30.1	35	5	12	29	Inning 1-6	.118	17	2	0	0	0	1	1	5	.167	.118
Night	2.84	8	4	1	40	0	44.1	40	4	18	41	Inning 7+	.269	271	73	11	2	9	32	29	65	.343	.424
Grass	2.86	10	5	2	57	0	66.0	68	8	27	58	None on	.291	148	43	7	0	7	11	33	.344	.480
Turf	4.15	0	1	1	7	0	8.2	7	1	3	12	Runners on	.229	140	32	4	2	2	26	19	37	.323	.329
March/April	1.86	0	0	0	8	0	9.2	7	0	5	10	Scoring Posn	.204	93	19	2	1	1	21	14	25	.306	.280
May	2.70	2	2	0	11	0	10.0	12	0	2	9	Close & Late	.287	150	43	6	1	3	20	20	37	.378	.400
June	1.35	1	1	0	10	0	13.1	11	1	5	13	None on/out	.238	63	15	2	0	1	1	3	16	.284	.317
July	2.77	1	1	0	11	0	13.0	11	3	6	14	vs. 1st Batr (relief)	.259	58	15	0	2	0	5	5	13	.317	.328
August	4.40	4	2	1	12	0	14.1	18	3	5	13	1st Inning Pitched	.242	215	52	8	2	7	26	21	53	.314	.395
Sept/Oct	4.40	2	0	2	12	0	14.1	16	2	7	11	Pitch 16-30	.290	93	27	6	0	3	12	11	22	.365	.452
Starter	0.00	0	0	0	0	0	0.0	0	0	0	0	Pitch 31-45	.313	16	5	0	0	0	4	5	2	.476	.313
Reliever	3.01	10	6	3	64	0	74.2	75	9	30	70	Pitch 46+	.000	1	0	0	0	0	0	1	0	.000	.000
0 Days rest (Relief)	0.84	3	1	1	9	0	10.2	7	0	5	9	First Pitch	.333	39	13	0	0	4	7	4	0	.395	.641
1 or 2 Days rest	3.48	6	3	2	44	0	51.2	53	8	17	50	Ahead in Count	.252	155	39	7	0	3	17	0	59	.256	.355
3+ Days rest	2.92	1	2	0	11	0	12.1	15	1	8	11	Behind in Count	.194	31	6	2	0	0	1	12	0	.419	.258
vs. AL	3.77	6	2	3	26	0	31.0	35	4	10	24	Two Strikes	.251	167	42	8	1	4	19	14	70	.313	.383
vs. NL	2.47	4	4	0	38	0	43.2	40	5	20	46	Pre-All Star	.241	133	32	4	2	1	9	13	35	.313	.323
Pre-All Star	1.73	3	3	0	32	0	36.1	32	1	13	35	Post-All Star	.277	155	43	7	0	8	24	17	35	.351	.477
Post-All Star	4.23	7	3	3	32	0	38.1	43	8	17	35												

Career (1995-1997)

	ERA	W	L	Sv	G	GS	IP	H	HR	BB	SO		Avg	AB	H	2B	3B	HR	RBI	BB	SO	OBP	SLG
Home	2.16	12	5	5	84	0	104.0	81	11	36	91	vs. Left	.269	253	68	11	1	8	38	40	45	.367	.415
Away	3.54	1	8	6	70	0	84.0	77	7	37	87	vs. Right	.202	446	90	14	2	10	35	33	133	.263	.309
Day	3.17	4	3	3	44	0	54.0	51	5	22	51	Inning 1-6	.137	51	7	2	0	2	6	4	15	.214	.294
Night	2.62	9	10	8	110	0	134.0	107	13	51	127	Inning 7+	.233	648	151	23	3	16	67	69	163	.309	.352
Grass	2.94	12	9	7	116	0	140.2	119	14	59	130	None on	.235	375	88	13	0	11	11	32	95	.298	.357
Turf	2.28	1	4	4	38	0	47.1	39	4	14	48	Runners on	.216	324	70	12	3	7	62	41	83	.307	.336
March/April	1.00	1	1	1	20	0	27.0	14	2	13	28	Scoring Posn	.189	201	38	5	2	3	49	30	51	.293	.279
May	3.96	2	3	2	23	0	25.0	23	2	9	17	Close & Late	.246	350	86	11	2	6	40	44	90	.333	.340
June	2.05	1	1	0	17	0	22.0	19	1	9	23	None on/out	.214	159	34	5	0	4	4	10	42	.265	.321
July	3.54	1	3	1	24	0	28.0	26	4	11	26	vs. 1st Batr (relief)	.237	139	33	4	2	2	10	14	34	.307	.338
August	2.79	6	4	2	36	0	48.1	41	6	13	53	1st Inning Pitched	.224	505	113	18	3	13	56	56	124	.306	.349
Sept/Oct	3.11	2	1	5	34	0	37.2	35	3	18	31	First 15 Pitches	.218	418	91	12	2	9	31	43	101	.296	.321
Starter	0.00	0	0	0	0	0	0.0	0	0	0	0	Pitch 16-30	.247	235	58	13	1	9	36	23	62	.314	.426
Reliever	2.78	13	13	11	154	0	188.0	158	18	73	178	Pitch 31-45	.200	45	9	0	0	0	6	7	14	.308	.200
0 Days rest (Relief)	1.89	3	3	4	27	0	33.1	22	3	12	39	Pitch 46+	.000	1	0	0	0	0	0	1	0	.000	.000
1 or 2 Days rest	2.89	8	7	5	89	0	106.0	92	12	34	100	First Pitch	.346	78	27	4	0	6	13	9	0	.414	.628
3+ Days rest	3.14	2	3	2	38	0	48.2	44	3	27	39	Ahead in Count	.191	393	75	8	1	6	30	0	151	.193	.262
vs. AL	3.77	6	2	3	26	0	31.0	35	4	10	24	Behind in Count	.240	104	25	7	0	1	5	40	0	.459	.337
vs. NL	2.58	7	11	8	128	0	157.0	123	14	63	154	Two Strikes	.185	401	74	9	2	9	40	24	178	.232	.284
Pre-All Star	2.04	4	5	3	67	0	84.0	62	5	32	78	Pre-All Star	.207	300	62	11	2	5	25	32	78	.287	.307
Post-All Star	3.38	9	8	8	87	0	104.0	96	13	41	100	Post-All Star	.241	399	96	14	1	13	48	41	100	.314	.378

Pitcher vs. Batter (career)

Pitches Best Vs.	Avg	AB	H	2B	3B	HR	RBI	BB	SO	OBP	SLG	Pitches Worst Vs.	Avg	AB	H	2B	3B	HR	RBI	BB	SO	OBP	SLG
Eric Karros	.182	11	2	1	0	1	1	0	3	.182	.545												

Terry Mathews — Orioles
Age 33 – Pitches Right (flyball pitcher)

	ERA	W	L	Sv	G	GS	IP	BB	SO	Avg	H	2B	3B	HR	RBI	OBP	SLG	GF	IR	IRS	Hld	SvOp	SB	CS	GB	FB	G/F
1997 Season	4.41	4	4	1	57	0	63.1	36	39	.267	63	13	0	8	32	.359	.424	19	42	12	8	2	6	1	69	85	0.81
Last Five Years	3.94	14	15	8	209	2	262.2	106	194	.260	257	53	3	31	140	.332	.414	62	135	47	37	16	17	14	283	342	0.83

1997 Season

	ERA	W	L	Sv	G	GS	IP	H	HR	BB	SO		Avg	AB	H	2B	3B	HR	RBI	BB	SO	OBP	SLG
Home	6.41	1	2	0	26	0	26.2	34	7	13	15	vs. Left	.256	82	21	8	0	3	14	16	7	.370	.463
Away	2.95	3	2	1	31	0	36.2	29	1	23	24	vs. Right	.273	154	42	5	0	5	18	20	32	.352	.403
Day	5.17	1	1	1	14	0	15.2	18	2	13	7	Inning 1-6	.241	29	7	1	0	1	7	7	5	.389	.379
Night	4.15	3	3	0	43	0	47.2	45	6	23	32	Inning 7+	.271	207	56	12	0	7	25	29	34	.354	.430
Grass	4.94	4	3	1	52	0	54.2	57	7	35	31	None on	.270	126	34	6	0	2	2	16	22	.352	.365
Turf	1.04	0	1	0	5	0	8.2	6	1	1	8	Runners on	.264	110	29	7	0	6	30	20	17	.366	.491
March/April	2.25	0	1	0	8	0	12.0	8	1	2	11	Scoring Posn	.190	63	12	2	0	3	23	15	11	.329	.365
May	6.75	0	0	0	7	0	8.0	6	1	11	6	Close & Late	.258	89	23	6	0	4	12	17	17	.374	.461
June	3.24	1	0	0	10	0	8.1	7	0	5	5	None on/out	.286	56	16	3	0	1	1	8	12	.375	.393
July	2.03	1	0	0	13	0	13.1	16	0	1	8	vs. 1st Batr (relief)	.360	50	18	2	0	1	6	5	9	.411	.460

1997 Season

	ERA	W	L	Sv	G	GS	IP	H	HR	BB	SO
August	7.15	1	2	0	7	0	11.1	12	4	4	5
Sept/Oct	6.10	1	1	1	12	0	10.1	14	2	8	4
Starter	0.00	0	0	0	0	0	0.0	0	0	0	0
Reliever	4.41	4	4	1	57	0	63.1	63	8	36	39
0 Days rest (Relief)	5.91	2	2	1	12	0	10.2	12	1	6	7
1 or 2 Days rest	4.39	1	1	0	25	0	26.2	28	3	17	12
3+ Days rest	3.81	1	1	0	20	0	26.0	23	4	13	20
vs. AL	4.31	3	2	1	50	0	54.1	53	8	31	37
vs. NL	5.00	1	2	0	7	0	9.0	10	0	5	2
Pre-All Star	3.34	1	1	0	29	0	32.1	22	2	20	28
Post-All Star	5.52	3	3	1	28	0	31.0	41	6	16	11

	Avg	AB	H	2B	3B	HR	RBI	BB	SO	OBP	SLG
1st Inning Pitched	.256	168	43	9	0	7	29	27	26	.354	.435
First 15 Pitches	.284	141	40	8	0	5	21	20	20	.366	.447
Pitch 16-30	.224	76	17	3	0	3	10	16	16	.359	.382
Pitch 31-45	.308	13	4	2	0	0	1	0	3	.286	.462
Pitch 46+	.333	6	2	0	0	0	0	0	0	.333	.333
First Pitch	.400	35	14	2	0	4	10	2	0	.421	.800
Ahead in Count	.229	109	25	6	0	2	10	0	32	.225	.339
Behind in Count	.306	49	15	2	0	2	9	17	0	.478	.469
Two Strikes	.210	105	22	5	0	2	13	17	39	.315	.314
Pre-All Star	.191	115	22	4	0	2	10	20	28	.309	.261
Post-All Star	.339	121	41	11	0	6	22	16	11	.407	.579

Last Five Years

	ERA	W	L	Sv	G	GS	IP	H	HR	BB	SO
Home	4.22	4	9	3	102	1	130.0	125	15	48	104
Away	3.66	10	6	5	107	1	132.2	132	16	58	90
Day	4.90	3	4	2	50	1	60.2	67	7	30	44
Night	3.65	11	11	6	159	1	202.0	190	24	76	150
Grass	4.29	11	13	5	169	1	203.1	200	24	88	161
Turf	2.73	3	2	3	40	1	59.1	57	7	18	33
March/April	2.89	0	1	1	16	0	18.2	18	1	9	19
May	4.23	1	0	3	33	0	38.1	39	4	21	32
June	2.98	4	2	1	37	1	60.1	53	7	19	36
July	3.82	4	5	1	53	1	66.0	61	8	27	52
August	5.62	1	3	1	33	0	41.2	46	6	14	27
Sept/Oct	4.06	4	4	1	37	0	37.2	40	5	16	28
Starter	4.09	1	1	0	2	2	11.0	15	1	1	6
Reliever	3.93	13	14	8	207	0	251.2	242	30	105	188
0 Days rest (Relief)	4.34	6	7	5	52	0	56.0	51	9	22	42
1 or 2 Days rest	3.79	5	4	3	102	0	130.2	125	15	53	91
3+ Days rest	3.88	2	3	0	53	0	65.0	66	6	30	55
vs. AL	4.07	5	4	1	64	0	73.0	73	11	38	50
vs. NL	3.89	9	11	7	145	2	189.2	184	20	68	144
Pre-All Star	3.41	6	6	5	103	2	142.2	131	14	58	112
Post-All Star	4.57	8	9	3	106	0	120.0	126	16	48	82

	Avg	AB	H	2B	3B	HR	RBI	BB	SO	OBP	SLG
vs. Left	.289	387	112	31	2	15	56	50	48	.370	.496
vs. Right	.241	602	145	22	1	16	84	56	146	.306	.360
Inning 1-6	.263	236	62	17	2	6	36	22	36	.324	.428
Inning 7+	.259	753	195	36	1	25	104	84	158	.334	.409
None on	.259	556	144	34	1	16	16	51	121	.321	.410
Runners on	.261	433	113	19	2	15	124	55	73	.344	.418
Scoring Posn	.282	255	72	11	2	10	112	44	43	.386	.459
Close & Late	.282	333	94	15	1	15	61	48	69	.371	.468
None on/out	.270	237	64	13	1	6	6	20	48	.327	.409
vs. 1st Batr (relief)	.263	186	49	6	2	5	30	17	42	.322	.398
1st Inning Pitched	.248	644	160	29	2	20	113	73	128	.326	.393
First 15 Pitches	.261	559	146	27	2	16	84	59	107	.331	.403
Pitch 16-30	.250	280	70	14	0	9	41	38	60	.342	.396
Pitch 31-45	.264	91	24	7	1	2	7	1	19	.269	.429
Pitch 46+	.288	59	17	5	0	4	8	8	8	.373	.576
First Pitch	.318	132	42	5	1	4	21	9	0	.364	.462
Ahead in Count	.201	497	100	24	1	12	43	0	174	.204	.326
Behind in Count	.356	191	68	13	1	10	44	48	0	.483	.592
Two Strikes	.198	486	96	23	1	10	59	49	194	.270	.348
Pre-All Star	.247	531	131	31	2	14	60	58	112	.320	.392
Post-All Star	.275	458	126	21	1	17	80	48	82	.344	.439

Pitcher vs. Batter (career)

Pitches Best Vs.	Avg	AB	H	2B	3B	HR	RBI	BB	SO	OBP	SLG
Dante Bichette	.167	12	2	0	0	1	3	0	4	.167	.417
Andres Galarraga	.200	10	2	1	0	0	1	0	8	.273	.300
Jay Buhner	.200	10	2	1	0	0	1		3	.273	.300
Jeff King	.222	9	2	1	0	1	4	1	0	.273	.667

Pitches Worst Vs.	Avg	AB	H	2B	3B	HR	RBI	BB	SO	OBP	SLG
Vinny Castilla	.600	10	6	0	0	1	2	1	1	.636	.900
Jose Canseco	.364	11	4	1	0	2	5	2	1	.462	1.000
Roberto Kelly	.364	11	4	0	0	1	2	1	1	.417	.636
Mark Whiten	.333	9	3	0	0	1	4	2	0	.455	.667

Darrell May — Angels
Age 26 – Pitches Left (flyball pitcher)

	ERA	W	L	Sv	G	GS	IP	BB	SO	Avg	H	2B	3B	HR	RBI	OBP	SLG	GF	IR	IRS	Hld	SvOp	SB	CS	GB	FB	G/F
1997 Season	5.23	2	1	0	29	2	51.2	25	42	.277	56	15	2	6	34	.351	.460	7	22	8	2	1	2	0	48	77	0.62
Career (1995-1997)	6.31	2	2	0	41	4	67.0	31	49	.308	84	17	2	12	58	.372	.516	10	36	16	3	1	6	0	70	105	0.67

1997 Season

	ERA	W	L	Sv	G	GS	IP	H	HR	BB	SO
Home	3.27	1	0	0	16	0	22.0	20	4	10	17
Away	6.67	1	1	0	13	2	29.2	36	2	15	25
Starter	9.00	1	0	0	2	2	8.0	11	1	5	7
Reliever	4.53	1	1	0	27	0	43.2	45	5	20	35
0 Days rest (Relief)	5.40	0	0	0	2	0	1.2	3	1	0	1
1 or 2 Days rest	3.20	1	0	0	11	0	19.2	13	2	7	13
3+ Days rest	5.64	0	1	0	14	0	22.1	29	2	13	21
Pre-All Star	4.85	0	0	0	7	0	13.0	13	1	6	8
Post-All Star	5.35	2	1	0	22	2	38.2	43	5	19	34

	Avg	AB	H	2B	3B	HR	RBI	BB	SO	OBP	SLG
vs. Left	.262	84	22	5	0	2	13	9	13	.330	.393
vs. Right	.288	118	34	10	2	4	21	16	29	.365	.508
Scoring Posn	.327	55	18	7	1	4	28	9	11	.397	.545
Close & Late	.200	20	4	0	0	1	2	2	3	.273	.350
None on/out	.240	50	12	5	1	1		3	12	.283	.440
First Pitch	.368	19	7	2	1	0	3	2	0	.409	.579
Ahead in Count	.245	110	27	7	0	2	17	0	35	.241	.364
Behind in Count	.324	34	11	0	0	3	11	13	0	.500	.676
Two Strikes	.226	106	24	6	1	2	13	10	42	.288	.358

Derrick May — Phillies
Age 29 – Bats Left (groundball hitter)

	Avg	G	AB	R	H	2B	3B	HR	RBI	BB	SO	HBP	GDP	SB	CS	OBP	SLG	IBB	SH	SF	#Pit	#P/PA	GB	FB	G/F
1997 Season	.228	83	149	8	34	5	1	1	13	8	26	0	4	4	1	.266	.295	3	0	1	581	3.65	64	41	1.56
Last Five Years	.276	530	1537	181	424	79	10	33	224	123	176	5	38	24	9	.329	.405	21	1	15	5637	3.35	647	415	1.56

1997 Season

	Avg	AB	H	2B	3B	HR	RBI	BB	SO	OBP	SLG
vs. Left	.200	5	1	0	0	0	2	1	0	.333	.200
vs. Right	.229	144	33	5	1	1	11	7	26	.263	.299
Home	.210	62	13	2	0	0	4	2	9	.231	.242
Away	.241	87	21	3	1	1	9	6	17	.290	.333
First Pitch	.308	26	8	2	0	0	2	1	0	.333	.385
Ahead in Count	.273	33	9	2	0	1	3	3	0	.324	.424
Behind in Count	.179	56	10	0	0	0	5	0	18	.179	.179
Two Strikes	.219	64	14	1	0	0	6	4	26	.265	.266

	Avg	AB	H	2B	3B	HR	RBI	BB	SO	OBP	SLG
Scoring Posn	.263	38	10	1	0	0	11	3	8	.310	.289
Close & Late	.241	29	7	1	1	0	1	0	4	.241	.345
None on/out	.156	32	5	1	0	0	0	2	5	.206	.188
Batting #4	.313	48	15	3	0	1	5	0	6	.306	.438
Batting #7	.204	54	11	0	1	0	6	3	9	.246	.241
Other	.170	47	8	2	0	0	2	3	9	.250	.213
Pre-All Star	.245	110	27	5	0	1	11	5	17	.276	.318
Post-All Star	.179	39	7	0	1	0	2	3	9	.238	.231

Last Five Years

	Avg	AB	H	2B	3B	HR	RBI	BB	SO	OBP	SLG
vs. Left	.263	213	56	9	1	6	44	6	27	.286	.399
vs. Right	.278	1324	368	70	9	27	180	117	149	.335	.406
Groundball	.285	471	134	24	2	8	64	32	53	.330	.395
Flyball	.254	280	71	10	3	4	32	14	29	.287	.354
Home	.275	755	208	40	4	14	108	66	89	.335	.395
Away	.276	782	216	39	6	19	116	57	87	.323	.414
Day	.288	732	211	39	4	20	112	53	83	.335	.434
Night	.265	805	213	40	6	13	112	70	93	.323	.378
Grass	.286	1001	286	49	8	22	141	70	111	.332	.417
Turf	.257	536	138	30	2	11	83	53	65	.323	.382
Pre-All Star	.277	918	254	43	4	18	129	69	103	.326	.391
Post-All Star	.275	619	170	36	6	15	95	54	73	.332	.425
Scoring Posn	.286	455	130	26	2	12	187	61	59	.361	.431
Close & Late	.274	266	73	14	1	7	44	21	40	.325	.414
None on/out	.264	368	97	17	2	11	11	19	39	.305	.410

	Avg	AB	H	2B	3B	HR	RBI	BB	SO	OBP	SLG
First Pitch	.311	299	93	25	3	5	46	12	0	.334	.465
Ahead in Count	.321	393	126	25	4	15	77	54	0	.401	.519
Behind in Count	.214	562	120	19	1	4	55	0	146	.216	.272
Two Strikes	.213	544	116	15	2	5	54	56	176	.286	.276
Batting #4	.289	577	167	32	3	13	91	46	56	.339	.423
Batting #5	.267	490	131	27	4	9	67	35	52	.318	.394
Other	.268	470	126	20	3	11	66	42	68	.328	.394
March/April	.296	226	67	11	0	7	43	18	29	.347	.438
May	.297	293	87	13	0	7	43	16	31	.333	.413
June	.230	296	68	16	4	3	31	24	33	.288	.341
July	.298	349	104	14	3	7	49	37	36	.363	.415
August	.256	234	60	14	1	4	33	16	26	.302	.376
Sept/Oct	.273	139	38	11	2	5	25	12	21	.331	.489
vs. AL	.233	133	31	3	1	1	11	6	18	.271	.293
vs. NL	.280	1404	393	76	9	32	213	117	158	.334	.415

Batter vs. Pitcher (career)

Hits Best Against	Avg	AB	H	2B	3B	HR	RBI	BB	SO	OBP	SLG
Omar Olivares	.600	10	6	2	0	0	3	1	1	.636	.800
Paul Wagner	.571	14	8	0	0	0	4	2	0	.588	.571
Pedro Astacio	.545	11	6	1	0	0	3	0	0	.545	.636
Dennis Martinez	.400	20	8	2	0	2	8	2	1	.455	.800
Frank Castillo	.364	11	4	2	0	1	2	1	4	.417	.818

Hits Worst Against	Avg	AB	H	2B	3B	HR	RBI	BB	SO	OBP	SLG
Armando Reynoso	.000	9	0	0	0	0	0	2	2	.250	.000
Joey Hamilton	.095	21	2	0	0	1	1	1	3	.136	.238
Greg Maddux	.158	19	3	0	0	0	1	0	3	.158	.158
Jeff Shaw	.182	11	2	0	0	0	1	1	0	.231	.182
Tim Belcher	.214	14	3	0	0	0	1	0	0	.214	.214

Brent Mayne — Athletics
Age 30 – Bats Left (groundball hitter)

	Avg	G	AB	R	H	2B	3B	HR	RBI	BB	SO	HBP	GDP	SB	CS	OBP	SLG	IBB	SH	SF	#Pit	#P/PA	GB	FB	G/F
1997 Season	.289	85	256	29	74	12	0	6	22	18	33	4	7	1	0	.343	.406	1	2	2	1111	3.94	112	63	1.78
Last Five Years	.263	382	1011	102	266	50	3	12	97	87	154	8	36	5	4	.326	.354	11	18	3	4170	3.70	409	224	1.83

1997 Season

	Avg	AB	H	2B	3B	HR	RBI	BB	SO	OBP	SLG
vs. Left	.279	43	12	2	0	0	2	3	9	.326	.326
vs. Right	.291	213	62	10	0	6	20	15	24	.346	.423
Home	.315	130	41	6	0	4	15	13	16	.381	.454
Away	.262	126	33	6	0	2	7	5	17	.301	.357
First Pitch	.300	30	9	0	0	2	4	0	0	.290	.500
Ahead in Count	.392	51	20	6	0	1	6	15	0	.522	.569
Behind in Count	.252	111	28	3	0	3	9	0	30	.272	.360
Two Strikes	.252	123	31	5	0	2	10	3	33	.287	.341

	Avg	AB	H	2B	3B	HR	RBI	BB	SO	OBP	SLG
Scoring Posn	.214	56	12	2	0	0	12	7	7	.303	.250
Close & Late	.316	38	12	2	0	0	2	1	7	.350	.368
None on/out	.329	73	24	4	0	1	1	5	9	.372	.425
Batting #7	.279	68	19	2	0	1	3	3	9	.315	.353
Batting #9	.256	78	20	4	0	1	6	5	6	.314	.346
Other	.318	110	35	6	0	4	13	10	18	.380	.482
Pre-All Star	.195	87	17	2	0	2	7	7	8	.260	.287
Post-All Star	.337	169	57	10	0	4	15	11	25	.386	.467

Last Five Years

	Avg	AB	H	2B	3B	HR	RBI	BB	SO	OBP	SLG
vs. Left	.233	133	31	5	0	0	7	7	31	.271	.271
vs. Right	.268	878	235	45	3	12	90	80	123	.333	.367
Groundball	.274	234	64	16	1	1	21	21	26	.333	.363
Flyball	.267	232	62	13	2	5	23	16	42	.320	.405
Home	.296	497	147	24	3	6	53	50	74	.363	.392
Away	.232	514	119	26	0	6	44	37	80	.288	.317
Day	.263	372	98	22	0	4	39	37	59	.337	.355
Night	.263	639	168	28	3	8	58	50	95	.319	.354
Grass	.260	712	185	38	1	10	63	59	99	.321	.358
Turf	.271	299	81	12	2	2	34	28	55	.337	.344
Pre-All Star	.228	531	121	21	1	7	48	41	81	.285	.311
Post-All Star	.302	480	145	29	2	5	49	46	73	.369	.402
Scoring Posn	.275	233	64	12	1	2	78	28	37	.353	.361
Close & Late	.270	174	47	7	0	2	15	13	36	.324	.345
None on/out	.288	250	72	16	0	2	2	16	33	.333	.376

	Avg	AB	H	2B	3B	HR	RBI	BB	SO	OBP	SLG
First Pitch	.246	134	33	7	0	5	16	9	0	.292	.410
Ahead in Count	.311	251	78	16	1	1	24	55	0	.432	.394
Behind in Count	.215	451	97	17	2	5	39	0	141	.227	.295
Two Strikes	.209	446	93	15	2	3	34	23	154	.254	.271
Batting #7	.274	248	68	11	2	4	29	23	37	.339	.383
Batting #9	.239	297	71	16	1	1	22	24	38	.302	.310
Other	.273	466	127	23	0	7	46	40	79	.333	.367
March/April	.254	114	29	5	0	3	15	9	22	.320	.377
May	.263	175	46	9	1	2	18	16	25	.325	.360
June	.196	179	35	6	0	1	8	11	27	.242	.246
July	.241	199	48	9	1	1	22	12	26	.288	.312
August	.275	178	49	8	1	3	14	23	27	.365	.382
Sept/Oct	.355	166	59	13	0	2	20	16	27	.416	.470
vs. AL	.261	886	231	42	3	9	84	70	129	.320	.345
vs. NL	.280	125	35	8	0	3	13	17	25	.364	.416

Batter vs. Pitcher (career)

Hits Best Against	Avg	AB	H	2B	3B	HR	RBI	BB	SO	OBP	SLG
Alex Fernandez	.429	14	6	1	0	1	3	0	2	.429	.714
Cal Eldred	.417	12	5	0	0	1	2	3	1	.563	.667
Roger Clemens	.414	29	12	1	0	0	2	3	6	.500	.448
Kevin Brown	.375	16	6	2	0	0	2	2	3	.444	.500
Mike Mussina	.348	23	8	1	1	2	4	0	2	.348	.739

Hits Worst Against	Avg	AB	H	2B	3B	HR	RBI	BB	SO	OBP	SLG
Roger Pavlik	.077	13	1	0	0	0	2	3	3	.250	.077
Jack McDowell	.167	18	3	0	0	0	2	1	2	.250	.167
Kevin Tapani	.182	22	4	1	0	0	2	1	5	.217	.227
Dennis Eckersley	.182	11	2	0	0	0	2	0	2	.182	.182
Scott Erickson	.185	27	5	3	0	0	3	2	2	.241	.296

Jamie McAndrew — Brewers
Age 30 – Pitches Right (groundball pitcher)

	ERA	W	L	Sv	G	GS	IP	BB	SO	Avg	H	2B	3B	HR	RBI	OBP	SLG	CG	ShO	Sup	QS	#P/S	SB	CS	GB	FB	G/F
1997 Season	8.38	1	1	0	5	4	19.1	23	8	.304	24	5	0	1	16	.471	.405	0	0	4.66	0	84	0	2	35	17	2.06
Career (1995-1997)	5.98	3	4	0	15	8	55.2	35	27	.280	61	12	0	3	30	.387	.376	0	0	5.98	2	79	5	3	95	49	1.94

1997 Season

	ERA	W	L	Sv	G	GS	IP	H	HR	BB	SO		Avg	AB	H	2B	3B	HR	RBI	BB	SO	OBP	SLG
Home	8.64	0	0	0	2	2	8.1	11	1	10	4	vs. Left	.244	41	10	1	0	0	8	13	3	.436	.268
Away	8.18	1	1	0	3	2	11.0	13	0	13	4	vs. Right	.368	38	14	1	0	1	8	10	5	.510	.553

Greg McCarthy — Mariners

Age 29 – Pitches Left

	ERA	W	L	Sv	G	GS	IP	BB	SO	Avg	H	2B	3B	HR	RBI	OBP	SLG	GF	IR	IRS	Hld	SvOp	SB	CS	GB	FB	G/F
1997 Season	5.46	1	1	0	37	0	29.2	16	34	.230	26	6	0	4	13	.331	.389	4	24	4	8	0	4	1	39	26	1.50
Career (1996-1997)	4.58	1	1	0	47	0	39.1	20	41	.230	4	4	0	4	16	.339	.365	5	34	6	9	0	4	1	49	37	1.32

1997 Season

	ERA	W	L	Sv	G	GS	IP	H	HR	BB	SO		Avg	AB	H	2B	3B	HR	RBI	BB	SO	OBP	SLG
Home	5.51	0	0	0	18	0	16.1	13	2	11	17	vs. Left	.212	52	11	2	0	2	3	6	10	.305	.365
Away	5.40	1	1	0	19	0	13.1	13	2	5	17	vs. Right	.246	61	15	4	0	2	10	10	24	.352	.410
Starter	0.00	0	0	0	0	0	0.0	0	0	0	0	Scoring Posn	.182	33	6	1	0	1	9	4	7	.289	.303
Reliever	5.46	1	1	0	37	0	29.2	26	4	16	34	Close & Late	.308	26	8	2	0	1	3	5	13	.419	.500
0 Days rest (Relief)	4.50	1	0	0	8	0	6.0	4	1	2	5	None on/out	.217	23	5	1	0	1	1	6	8	.379	.391
1 or 2 Days rest	4.85	0	1	0	18	0	13.0	12	2	4	19	First Pitch	.118	17	2	0	0	1	3	0	0	.118	.294
3+ Days rest	6.75	0	0	0	11	0	10.2	10	1	10	10	Ahead in Count	.236	55	13	2	0	2	6	0	24	.236	.382
Pre-All Star	4.50	1	1	0	35	0	28.0	22	3	14	34	Behind in Count	.500	16	8	0	0	1	3	7	0	.652	.938
Post-All Star	21.60	0	0	0	2	0	1.2	4	1	2	0	Two Strikes	.161	56	9	1	0	1	1	8	34	.277	.232

Quinton McCracken — Rockies

Age 28 – Bats Both

	Avg	G	AB	R	H	2B	3B	HR	RBI	BB	SO	HBP	GDP	SB	CS	OBP	SLG	IBB	SH	SF	#Pit	#P/PA	GB	FB	G/F
1997 Season	.292	147	325	69	95	11	1	3	36	42	62	1	6	28	11	.374	.360	0	6	1	1506	4.02	138	66	2.09
Career (1995-1997)	.291	274	609	119	177	24	7	6	76	74	125	2	11	45	17	.368	.383	4	18	2	2812	3.99	240	122	1.97

1997 Season

	Avg	AB	H	2B	3B	HR	RBI	BB	SO	OBP	SLG		Avg	AB	H	2B	3B	HR	RBI	BB	SO	OBP	SLG
vs. Left	.233	86	20	0	0	1	6	9	14	.305	.267	First Pitch	.441	34	15	2	0	0	7	0	0	.441	.500
vs. Right	.314	239	75	11	1	2	30	33	48	.398	.393	Ahead in Count	.338	71	24	2	0	1	8	22	0	.489	.408
Groundball	.347	49	17	1	0	0	8	6	3	.418	.367	Behind in Count	.221	154	34	4	1	2	12	0	54	.226	.299
Flyball	.226	62	14	1	0	3	6	5	16	.279	.387	Two Strikes	.213	169	36	4	1	1	16	20	62	.300	.266
Home	.325	157	51	6	1	1	21	19	25	.398	.395	Batting #2	.275	160	44	2	0	3	15	24	28	.368	.344
Away	.262	168	44	5	0	2	15	23	37	.352	.327	Batting #8	.306	72	22	3	1	0	5	8	13	.375	.375
Day	.343	178	61	6	1	3	22	29	31	.435	.438	Other	.312	93	29	6	0	0	16	10	21	.385	.376
Night	.231	147	34	5	0	0	14	13	31	.296	.265	March/April	.358	53	19	2	0	1	6	4	7	.404	.453
Grass	.285	263	75	9	1	3	30	36	46	.373	.361	May	.271	48	13	2	0	1	7	8	9	.368	.375
Turf	.323	62	20	2	0	0	6	6	16	.377	.355	June	.234	64	15	2	0	1	7	8	13	.319	.313
Pre-All Star	.258	186	48	6	0	3	21	21	34	.332	.339	July	.228	92	21	2	1	0	5	11	18	.311	.272
Post-All Star	.338	139	47	5	1	0	15	21	28	.424	.388	August	.386	44	17	3	0	0	6	9	11	.491	.455
Scoring Posn	.318	85	27	6	0	0	32	7	19	.366	.388	Sept/Oct	.417	24	10	0	0	0	5	2	4	.481	.417
Close & Late	.222	54	12	2	0	0	3	7	12	.317	.259	vs. AL	.158	38	6	2	0	0	8	4	9	.238	.211
None on/out	.244	90	22	1	0	2	2	13	14	.346	.322	vs. NL	.310	287	89	9	1	3	28	38	53	.391	.380

1997 By Position

Position	Avg	AB	H	2B	3B	HR	RBI	BB	SO	OBP	SLG		G	GS	Innings	PO	A	E	DP	Fld Pct	Rng Fctr	In Zone	In Outs	Zone Rtg	MLB Zone
As Pinch Hitter	.333	12	4	0	0	0	1	2	3	.429	.333		16	0	---	---	---	---	---	---	---	---	---	---	---
As cf	.291	313	91	11	1	3	35	40	59	.372	.361		133	71	756.0	194	5	4	3	.980	2.37	271	192	.708	.815

Career (1995-1997)

	Avg	AB	H	2B	3B	HR	RBI	BB	SO	OBP	SLG		Avg	AB	H	2B	3B	HR	RBI	BB	SO	OBP	SLG
vs. Left	.253	154	39	4	0	1	12	15	27	.320	.299	First Pitch	.324	71	23	3	0	0	9	2	0	.342	.366
vs. Right	.303	455	138	20	7	5	64	59	98	.384	.411	Ahead in Count	.394	127	50	5	2	2	24	36	0	.521	.512
Groundball	.310	126	39	3	2	0	13	13	23	.374	.365	Behind in Count	.214	285	61	9	4	2	22	0	103	.220	.295
Flyball	.229	105	24	4	1	3	10	11	25	.305	.371	Two Strikes	.214	323	69	9	2	2	29	36	125	.296	.272
Home	.327	297	97	16	4	3	49	39	52	.404	.438	Batting #2	.263	293	77	6	6	5	32	41	62	.354	.375
Away	.256	312	80	8	3	3	27	35	73	.334	.330	Batting #8	.356	160	57	9	1	1	22	19	29	.425	.444
Day	.338	314	106	12	4	4	46	41	67	.413	.439	Other	.276	156	43	9	0	0	22	14	34	.337	.333
Night	.241	295	71	12	3	2	30	33	58	.320	.322	March/April	.308	78	24	3	1	1	8	6	13	.360	.410
Grass	.303	505	153	22	6	6	68	63	96	.382	.406	May	.250	64	16	3	1	0	9	11	10	.355	.344
Turf	.231	104	24	2	1	0	8	11	29	.302	.269	June	.257	105	27	5	0	1	12	14	24	.345	.333
Pre-All Star	.257	280	72	11	1	3	31	33	56	.335	.336	July	.285	172	49	6	1	1	20	21	34	.363	.349
Post-All Star	.319	329	105	13	6	3	45	41	69	.396	.422	August	.330	91	30	4	2	1	14	14	23	.419	.451
Scoring Posn	.329	173	57	12	2	2	69	20	35	.398	.457	Sept/Oct	.313	99	31	3	3	1	13	8	21	.370	.434
Close & Late	.252	107	27	5	2	0	11	10	26	.336	.336	vs. AL	.158	38	6	2	0	0	8	4	9	.238	.211
None on/out	.261	142	37	2	1	2	2	17	25	.344	.331	vs. NL	.299	571	171	22	7	6	68	70	116	.377	.394

Batter vs. Pitcher (career)

Hits Best Against	Avg	AB	H	2B	3B	HR	RBI	BB	SO	OBP	SLG	Hits Worst Against	Avg	AB	H	2B	3B	HR	RBI	BB	SO	OBP	SLG
John Smoltz	.385	13	5	0	0	0	0	0	3	.385	.385	Tom Glavine	.125	16	2	0	0	0	0	1	2	.176	.125
Jim Bullinger	.357	14	5	1	0	0	2	0	0	.357	.429	Hideo Nomo	.143	14	2	0	0	0	0	1	1	.200	.143
												Frank Castillo	.222	9	2	0	0	0	2	3	4	.417	.222

Jeff McCurry — Rockies

Age 28 – Pitches Right (groundball pitcher)

	ERA	W	L	Sv	G	GS	IP	BB	SO	Avg	H	2B	3B	HR	RBI	OBP	SLG	GF	IR	IRS	Hld	SvOp	SB	CS	GB	FB	G/F
1997 Season	4.43	1	4	0	33	0	40.2	20	19	.277	43	7	1	7	23	.358	.471	13	19	9	4	2	5	1	76	40	1.90
Career (1995-1997)	5.40	2	8	1	90	0	105.0	52	46	.321	134	27	4	19	75	.402	.542	24	61	22	9	5	9	5	184	112	1.64

1997 Season

	ERA	W	L	Sv	G	GS	IP	H	HR	BB	SO		Avg	AB	H	2B	3B	HR	RBI	BB	SO	OBP	SLG
Home	5.21	0	2	0	14	0	19.0	23	4	7	10	vs. Left	.238	80	19	4	1	3	13	10	6	.319	.425
Away	3.74	1	2	0	19	0	21.2	20	3	13	9	vs. Right	.320	75	24	3	0	4	10	10	13	.400	.520

1997 Season

	ERA	W	L	Sv	G	GS	IP	H	HR	BB	SO		Avg	AB	H	2B	3B	HR	RBI	BB	SO	OBP	SLG
Starter	0.00	0	0	0	0	0	0.0	0	0	0	0	Scoring Posn	.255	51	13	1	1	2	18	9	7	.361	.431
Reliever	4.43	1	4	0	33	0	40.2	43	7	20	19	Close & Late	.353	34	12	3	1	2	9	6	3	.439	.676
0 Days rest (Relief)	7.88	1	3	0	8	0	8.0	11	2	5	7	None on/out	.306	36	11	2	0	3	3	4	2	.375	.611
1 or 2 Days rest	5.56	0	0	0	8	0	11.1	14	2	8	3	First Pitch	.318	22	7	0	0	2	6	0	0	.318	.591
3+ Days rest	2.53	0	1	0	17	0	21.1	18	3	7	9	Ahead in Count	.214	56	12	1	1	1	7	0	17	.214	.321
Pre-All Star	3.67	1	1	0	22	0	27.0	26	3	14	12	Behind in Count	.308	52	16	2	0	3	4	12	0	.438	.519
Post-All Star	5.93	0	3	0	11	0	13.2	17	4	6	7	Two Strikes	.184	49	9	1	1	1	7	8	19	.298	.306

Allen McDill — Royals   Age 26 – Pitches Left

	ERA	W	L	Sv	G	GS	IP	BB	SO	Avg	H	2B	3B	HR	RBI	OBP	SLG	GF	IR	IRS	Hld	SvOp	SB	CS	GB	FB	G/F
1997 Season	13.50	0	0	0	3	0	4.0	8	2	.214	3	0	0	1	4	.522	.429	1	0	0	0	0	0	0	5	4	1.25

1997 Season

	ERA	W	L	Sv	G	GS	IP	H	HR	BB	SO		Avg	AB	H	2B	3B	HR	RBI	BB	SO	OBP	SLG
Home	18.00	0	0	0	2	0	3.0	3	1	7	2	vs. Left	.000	4	0	0	0	0	0	2	1	.333	.000
Away	0.00	0	0	0	1	0	1.0	0	0	1	0	vs. Right	.300	10	3	0	0	1	4	6	1	.588	.600

Ben McDonald — Brewers   Age 30 – Pitches Right (groundball pitcher)

	ERA	W	L	Sv	G	GS	IP	BB	SO	Avg	H	2B	3B	HR	RBI	OBP	SLG	CG	ShO	Sup	QS	#P/S	SB	CS	GB	FB	G/F
1997 Season	4.06	8	7	0	21	21	133.0	36	110	.237	120	27	4	13	58	.294	.383	1	0	5.14	12	97	20	4	186	130	1.43
Last Five Years	3.85	50	44	0	128	127	812.0	281	583	.244	751	135	16	79	323	.311	.376	16	2	5.31	74	102	80	35	1188	777	1.53

1997 Season

	ERA	W	L	Sv	G	GS	IP	H	HR	BB	SO		Avg	AB	H	2B	3B	HR	RBI	BB	SO	OBP	SLG
Home	2.97	5	2	0	11	11	72.2	65	5	17	64	vs. Left	.259	255	66	11	2	9	33	27	51	.337	.424
Away	5.37	3	5	0	10	10	60.1	55	8	19	46	vs. Right	.215	251	54	16	2	4	25	9	59	.247	.343
Day	4.40	5	4	0	12	12	75.2	72	7	22	62	Inning 1-6	.240	455	109	26	2	11	54	33	96	.297	.378
Night	3.61	3	3	0	9	9	57.1	48	6	14	48	Inning 7+	.216	51	11	1	2	2	4	3	14	.268	.431
Grass	3.95	7	6	0	19	19	123.0	109	12	33	100	None on	.215	316	68	13	3	4		20	68	.266	.313
Turf	5.40	1	1	0	2	2	10.0	11	1	3	10	Runners on	.274	190	52	14	1	9	54	16	42	.338	.500
March/April	4.74	3	2	0	6	6	38.0	35	3	15	24	Scoring Posn	.269	104	28	5	1	4	41	14	26	.364	.452
May	3.46	3	1	0	6	6	39.0	42	5	9	38	Close & Late	.237	38	9	1	2	1	3	3	12	.286	.447
June	4.24	0	2	0	5	5	34.0	28	4	9	33	None on/out	.224	134	30	6	1	2	2		8	.278	.328
July	3.68	2	2	0	4	4	22.0	15	1	3	15	1st Inning Pitched	.260	77	20	5	0	1	11	10	18	.352	.364
August	0.00	0	0	0	0	0	0.0	0	0	0	0	First 75 Pitches	.218	363	79	20	2	8	37	27	80	.279	.354
Sept/Oct	0.00	0	0	0	0	0	0.0	0	0	0	0	Pitch 76-90	.297	74	22	6	0	1	8	3	13	.321	.419
Starter	4.06	8	7	0	21	21	133.0	120	13	36	110	Pitch 91-105	.273	55	15	1	2	3	11	6	13	.344	.527
Reliever	0.00	0	0	0	0	0	0.0	0	0	0	0	Pitch 106+	.286	14	4	0	0	1	2	0	4	.333	.500
0-3 Days Rest (Start)	3.00	1	0	0	1	1	6.0	3	0	0	4	First Pitch	.259	58	15	6	0	3	6	0	0	.271	.517
4 Days Rest	4.15	7	6	0	15	15	93.1	87	9	26	83	Ahead in Count	.186	210	39	8	1	5	21	0	92	.190	.305
5+ Days Rest	4.01	0	1	0	5	5	33.2	30	4	10	23	Behind in Count	.289	128	37	7	2	3	21	18	0	.378	.445
vs. AL	4.17	8	6	0	19	19	121.0	110	13	34	95	Two Strikes	.159	227	36	11	1	4	19	18	110	.220	.271
vs. NL	3.00	0	1	0	2	2	12.0	10	0	2	15	Pre-All Star	.245	466	114	24	4	12	55	34	102	.301	.391
Pre-All Star	4.24	7	6	0	19	19	121.0	114	12	34	102	Post-All Star	.150	40	6	3	0	1	3	2	8	.209	.300
Post-All Star	2.25	1	1	0	2	2	12.0	6	1	2	8												

Last Five Years

	ERA	W	L	Sv	G	GS	IP	H	HR	BB	SO		Avg	AB	H	2B	3B	HR	RBI	BB	SO	OBP	SLG
Home	3.56	28	19	0	65	65	422.2	389	39	135	311	vs. Left	.243	1647	401	68	12	44	169	160	310	.313	.379
Away	4.16	22	25	0	63	62	389.1	362	40	146	272	vs. Right	.246	1425	350	67	4	35	154	121	273	.308	.372
Day	4.08	15	17	0	44	43	282.2	274	24	95	203	Inning 1-6	.244	2638	644	116	13	72	294	254	498	.314	.380
Night	3.72	35	27	0	84	84	529.1	477	55	186	380	Inning 7+	.247	434	107	19	3	7	29	27	85	.292	.353
Grass	3.58	49	35	0	115	114	748.1	669	66	249	529	None on	.235	1909	449	85	10	49	49	145	359	.293	.367
Turf	6.93	1	9	0	13	13	63.2	82	13	32	54	Runners on	.260	1163	302	50	6	30	274	136	224	.339	.390
March/April	3.88	13	5	0	23	23	141.1	140	13	48	86	Scoring Posn	.237	670	159	25	4	13	228	101	142	.338	.345
May	4.70	8	11	0	29	29	172.1	182	26	65	135	Close & Late	.254	197	50	7	3	2	14	16	44	.307	.350
June	4.04	9	8	0	24	24	156.0	147	16	52	113	None on/out	.239	821	196	40	7	21	21	59	148	.292	.381
July	3.03	10	9	0	24	24	157.2	123	12	49	109	vs. 1st Batr (relief)	.000	1	0	0	0	0	0	0	0	.000	.000
August	4.57	3	7	0	13	13	84.2	91	7	31	51	1st Inning Pitched	.230	465	107	18	1	9	43	50	91	.308	.331
Sept/Oct	2.70	7	4	0	15	14	100.0	68	5	36	89	First 75 Pitches	.243	2144	521	95	12	50	225	199	412	.302	.368
Starter	3.85	50	44	0	127	127	808.0	748	79	280	581	Pitch 76-90	.245	408	100	20	2	16	42	31	66	.302	.422
Reliever	2.25	0	0	0	1	0	4.0	3	0	1	2	Pitch 91-105	.269	334	90	14	2	10	44	34	64	.337	.413
0-3 Days Rest (Start)	3.00	1	0	0	1	1	6.0	3	0	0	4	Pitch 106+	.215	186	40	6	0	3	12	17	41	.296	.296
4 Days Rest	4.08	35	35	0	87	87	554.1	533	56	180	398	First Pitch	.318	346	110	26	2	15	42	3	0	.330	.535
5+ Days Rest	3.38	14	9	0	39	39	247.2	212	23	100	179	Ahead in Count	.176	1262	222	42	3	19	86	0	503	.181	.259
vs. AL	3.86	50	43	0	126	125	800.0	741	79	279	568	Behind in Count	.308	799	246	42	4	32	121	151	0	.416	.491
vs. NL	3.00	0	1	0	2	2	12.0	10	0	2	15	Two Strikes	.175	1396	244	49	4	26	101	127	583	.247	.271
Pre-All Star	4.09	33	27	0	84	84	521.1	511	57	182	361	Pre-All Star	.255	2001	511	87	12	57	226	182	361	.321	.396
Post-All Star	3.41	17	17	0	44	43	290.2	240	22	99	222	Post-All Star	.224	1071	240	48	4	22	97	99	222	.292	.338

Pitcher vs. Batter (career)

Pitches Best Vs.	Avg	AB	H	2B	3B	HR	RBI	BB	SO	OBP	SLG	Pitches Worst Vs.	Avg	AB	H	2B	3B	HR	RBI	BB	SO	OBP	SLG
Ruben Sierra	.033	30	1	0	0	0	0	1	1	.065	.033	Shane Mack	.450	20	9	2	0	3	5	2	4	.500	1.000
Mike Gallego	.056	18	1	0	0	0	0	2	5	.150	.056	Dave Nilsson	.429	14	6	1	0	1	2	4	1	.556	.714
Ron Karkovice	.071	14	1	1	0	0	1	0	3	.067	.143	Jay Buhner	.385	26	10	2	0	3	7	5	2	.484	.808
Jorge Fabregas	.077	13	1	0	0	0	0	0	1	.077	.077	Tino Martinez	.385	26	10	3	0	3	5	3	5	.448	.846

Pitcher vs. Batter (career)

Pitches Best Vs.	Avg	AB	H	2B	3B	HR	RBI	BB	SO	OBP	SLG	Pitches Worst Vs.	Avg	AB	H	2B	3B	HR	RBI	BB	SO	OBP	SLG
Greg Gagne	.077	13	1	1	0	0	1	1	3	.143	.154	John Olerud	.333	36	12	1	1	5	8	5	5	.415	.833

Jason McDonald — Athletics
Age 26 – Bats Both

	Avg	G	AB	R	H	2B	3B	HR	RBI	BB	SO	HBP	GDP	SB	CS	OBP	SLG	IBB	SH	SF	#Pit	#P/PA	GB	FB	G/F
1997 Season	.263	78	236	47	62	11	4	4	14	36	49	1	0	13	8	.361	.394	0	2	1	1117	4.05	68	68	1.00

1997 Season

	Avg	AB	H	2B	3B	HR	RBI	BB	SO	OBP	SLG		Avg	AB	H	2B	3B	HR	RBI	BB	SO	OBP	SLG
vs. Left	.250	52	13	2	0	0	3	12	15	.391	.288	Scoring Posn	.238	42	10	1	0	1	10	11	11	.389	.333
vs. Right	.266	184	49	9	4	4	11	24	34	.352	.424	Close & Late	.343	35	12	2	0	1	6	6	11	.439	.486
Home	.262	126	33	5	1	1	5	19	23	.359	.341	None on/out	.216	97	21	4	2	2	2	12	18	.309	.361
Away	.264	110	29	6	3	3	9	17	26	.364	.455	Batting #1	.261	226	59	10	4	4	12	32	47	.351	.394
First Pitch	.344	32	11	2	1	1	2	0	0	.344	.563	Batting #3	.500	2	1	1	0	0	2	2	0	.750	1.000
Ahead in Count	.288	59	17	4	1	1	2	11	0	.400	.441	Other	.250	8	2	0	0	0	0	2	2	.455	.250
Behind in Count	.204	93	19	2	2	1	4	0	39	.213	.301	Pre-All Star	.224	85	19	4	1	2	4	12	19	.320	.365
Two Strikes	.193	109	21	2	1	0	5	25	49	.346	.248	Post-All Star	.285	151	43	7	3	2	10	24	30	.384	.411

Jack McDowell — Indians
Age 32 – Pitches Right

	ERA	W	L	Sv	G	GS	IP	BB	SO	Avg	H	2B	3B	HR	RBI	OBP	SLG	CG	ShO	Sup	QS	#P/S	SB	CS	GB	FB	G/F
1997 Season	5.09	3	3	0	8	6	40.2	18	38	.282	44	10	0	6	22	.356	.462	0	0	7.52	3	103	4	1	51	39	1.31
Last Five Years	4.03	63	41	0	127	125	888.0	274	621	.267	916	168	22	85	383	.323	.404	29	9	5.24	73	110	79	37	1167	946	1.23

1997 Season

	ERA	W	L	Sv	G	GS	IP	H	HR	BB	SO		Avg	AB	H	2B	3B	HR	RBI	BB	SO	OBP	SLG
Home	4.55	3	2	0	5	4	27.2	28	2	15	27	vs. Left	.342	79	27	4	0	5	17	10	15	.411	.582
Away	6.23	0	1	0	3	2	13.0	16	4	3	11	vs. Right	.221	77	17	6	0	1	5	8	23	.299	.338

Last Five Years

	ERA	W	L	Sv	G	GS	IP	H	HR	BB	SO		Avg	AB	H	2B	3B	HR	RBI	BB	SO	OBP	SLG
Home	4.48	31	24	0	66	65	453.2	491	46	147	315	vs. Left	.268	1814	487	82	14	46	208	158	304	.327	.405
Away	3.56	32	17	0	61	60	434.1	425	39	127	306	vs. Right	.266	1613	429	86	8	39	175	116	317	.318	.402
Day	4.34	15	15	0	33	32	222.0	237	20	75	156	Inning 1-6	.270	2768	748	134	19	68	326	229	513	.327	.406
Night	3.93	48	26	0	94	93	666.0	679	65	199	465	Inning 7+	.255	659	168	34	3	17	57	45	108	.305	.393
Grass	4.09	57	37	0	114	112	794.2	819	78	243	550	None on	.275	1968	541	98	13	54	54	145	338	.328	.420
Turf	3.57	6	4	0	13	13	93.1	97	7	31	71	Runners on	.257	1459	375	70	9	31	329	129	283	.315	.381
March/April	4.76	10	6	0	21	19	128.2	150	13	55	80	Scoring Posn	.250	831	208	37	7	14	280	82	172	.312	.362
May	4.53	8	13	0	27	27	188.2	195	23	55	131	Close & Late	.248	404	100	17	3	10	41	22	66	.289	.379
June	4.26	11	6	0	22	22	154.1	151	21	48	96	None on/out	.280	879	246	43	5	20	20	57	132	.327	.408
July	3.57	16	5	0	23	23	171.1	179	13	44	136	vs. 1st Batr (relief)	.000	2	0	0	0	0	0	0	2	.000	.000
August	3.47	9	8	0	19	19	140.0	147	8	41	98	1st Inning Pitched	.272	482	131	17	6	17	70	42	101	.333	.438
Sept/Oct	3.43	9	3	0	15	15	105.0	94	7	31	80	First 75 Pitches	.273	2232	609	109	17	59	252	176	405	.327	.416
Starter	4.06	62	41	0	125	125	882.0	912	85	271	615	Pitch 76-90	.261	433	113	22	2	8	51	41	75	.324	.376
Reliever	0.00	1	0	0	2	0	6.0	4	0	3	6	Pitch 91-105	.265	400	106	20	0	8	44	30	69	.319	.375
0-3 Days Rest (Start)	2.25	3	0	0	3	3	24.0	19	1	5	30	Pitch 106+	.243	362	88	17	3	10	36	27	72	.298	.390
4 Days Rest	3.86	39	30	0	81	81	594.2	599	59	177	404	First Pitch	.347	501	174	25	5	19	80	0	0	.363	.531
5+ Days Rest	4.68	20	11	0	41	41	263.1	294	25	89	181	Ahead in Count	.209	1610	336	50	13	24	133	0	513	.213	.301
vs. AL	4.03	63	41	0	127	125	888.0	916	85	274	621	Behind in Count	.344	652	224	55	4	27	103	134	0	.455	.564
vs. NL	0.00	0	0	0	0	0	0.0	0	0	0	0	Two Strikes	.195	1592	311	58	9	21	119	129	621	.258	.283
Pre-All Star	4.35	35	27	0	79	77	540.1	560	62	176	356	Pre-All Star	.269	2080	560	107	12	62	248	176	356	.328	.422
Post-All Star	3.55	28	14	0	48	48	347.2	356	23	98	265	Post-All Star	.264	1347	356	61	10	23	135	98	265	.314	.376

Pitcher vs. Batter (career)

Pitches Best Vs.	Avg	AB	H	2B	3B	HR	RBI	BB	SO	OBP	SLG	Pitches Worst Vs.	Avg	AB	H	2B	3B	HR	RBI	BB	SO	OBP	SLG
Roberto Kelly	.000	9	0	0	0	0	0	2	5	.182	.000	Roberto Alomar	.552	29	16	1	0	3	8	7	6	.639	.897
Walt Weiss	.048	21	1	0	0	0	1	0	4	.048	.048	Shawn Green	.500	10	5	5	0	0	3	2	1	.583	1.000
Billy Ripken	.077	13	1	0	0	0	0	2	0	.077	.077	John Flaherty	.500	10	5	1	0	1	3	1	2	.545	.900
Mike Blowers	.077	13	1	0	0	0	0	0	3	.077	.077	Don Slaught	.455	11	5	2	0	1	1	0	0	.500	.909
Mark Lewis	.083	12	1	0	0	0	1	0	2	.083	.083	Fred McGriff	.400	10	4	1	1	1	1	1	3	.455	1.000

Chuck McElroy — White Sox
Age 30 – Pitches Left

	ERA	W	L	Sv	G	GS	IP	BB	SO	Avg	H	2B	3B	HR	RBI	OBP	SLG	GF	IR	IRS	Hld	SvOp	SB	CS	GB	FB	G/F
1997 Season	3.84	1	3	1	61	0	75.0	22	62	.252	73	12	0	5	33	.306	.345	16	42	10	15	6	4	0	93	89	1.04
Last Five Years	3.98	14	12	6	258	0	269.1	100	203	.260	267	49	3	21	145	.327	.375	63	187	62	39	22	15	11	347	301	1.15

1997 Season

	ERA	W	L	Sv	G	GS	IP	H	HR	BB	SO		Avg	AB	H	2B	3B	HR	RBI	BB	SO	OBP	SLG
Home	2.18	0	1	1	31	0	41.1	33	5	7	30	vs. Left	.229	105	24	5	0	2	14	7	18	.272	.333
Away	5.88	1	2	0	30	0	33.2	40	0	15	32	vs. Right	.265	185	49	7	0	3	19	15	44	.325	.351
Day	3.38	0	1	0	16	0	13.1	13	1	6	10	Inning 1-6	.236	89	21	3	0	1	10	7	18	.289	.303
Night	3.94	1	2	1	45	0	61.2	60	4	16	52	Inning 7+	.259	201	52	9	0	4	23	15	44	.314	.363
Grass	3.59	1	2	1	51	0	62.2	61	5	18	52	None on	.226	155	35	7	0	4	10	3	23	.281	.348
Turf	5.11	0	1	0	10	0	12.1	12	0	4	10	Runners on	.281	135	38	5	0	1	29	12	29	.333	.341
March/April	3.55	0	0	0	8	0	12.2	12	2	2	13	Scoring Posn	.289	76	22	4	0	0	26	8	17	.345	.342
May	3.38	0	0	0	11	0	8.0	10	1	4	7	Close & Late	.286	91	26	3	0	3	14	12	22	.371	.418
June	7.62	0	1	0	11	0	13.0	18	0	5	7	None on/out	.224	67	15	3	0	2	5	5	12	.297	.358
July	1.15	0	0	0	8	0	15.2	10	1	2	11	vs. 1st Batr (relief)	.255	51	13	2	0	1	9	7	13	.333	.353

1997 Season

	ERA	W	L	Sv	G	GS	IP	H	HR	BB	SO		Avg	AB	H	2B	3B	HR	RBI	BB	SO	OBP	SLG
August	4.86	0	2	0	13	0	16.2	14	1	7	14	1st Inning Pitched	.295	183	54	10	0	3	26	16	40	.350	.399
Sept/Oct	2.00	1	0	1	10	0	9.0	9	0	2	10	First 15 Pitches	.289	152	44	9	0	3	21	13	29	.343	.408
Starter	0.00	0	0	0	0	0	0.0	0	0	0	0	Pitch 16-30	.247	85	21	2	0	1	9	6	20	.304	.306
Reliever	3.84	1	3	1	61	0	75.0	73	5	22	62	Pitch 31-45	.108	37	4	0	0	1	3	1	8	.132	.189
0 Days rest (Relief)	3.86	0	0	0	10	0	7.0	7	0	3	3	Pitch 46+	.250	16	4	1	0	0	0	2	5	.333	.313
1 or 2 Days rest	6.03	1	2	1	30	0	37.1	43	5	11	33	First Pitch	.344	32	11	1	0	2	12	1	0	.353	.563
3+ Days rest	1.17	0	1	0	21	0	30.2	23	0	8	26	Ahead in Count	.224	156	35	5	0	0	8	0	59	.229	.256
vs. AL	3.68	1	3	1	57	0	71.0	69	5	21	59	Behind in Count	.188	48	9	2	0	1	4	11	0	.344	.292
vs. NL	6.75	0	0	0	4	0	4.0	4	0	1	3	Two Strikes	.248	157	39	7	0	2	13	10	62	.298	.331
Pre-All Star	4.35	0	1	0	32	0	39.1	42	3	12	29	Pre-All Star	.269	156	42	7	0	3	20	12	29	.318	.372
Post-All Star	3.28	1	2	1	29	0	35.2	31	2	10	33	Post-All Star	.231	134	31	5	0	2	13	10	33	.293	.313

Last Five Years

	ERA	W	L	Sv	G	GS	IP	H	HR	BB	SO		Avg	AB	H	2B	3B	HR	RBI	BB	SO	OBP	SLG
Home	3.53	7	4	5	134	0	150.1	134	11	48	96	vs. Left	.253	372	94	18	1	8	60	39	68	.321	.371
Away	4.54	7	8	1	124	0	119.0	133	10	52	107	vs. Right	.265	654	173	31	2	13	85	61	135	.331	.378
Day	4.26	4	4	4	95	0	88.2	95	11	44	60	Inning 1-6	.266	259	69	15	0	3	40	27	54	.334	.359
Night	3.84	10	8	2	163	0	180.2	172	10	56	143	Inning 7+	.258	767	198	34	3	18	105	73	149	.325	.381
Grass	4.00	9	6	2	154	0	164.1	169	15	70	125	None on	.230	534	123	21	3	10	10	45	112	.295	.337
Turf	3.94	5	6	4	104	0	105.0	98	6	30	78	Runners on	.293	492	144	28	0	11	135	55	91	.361	.417
March/April	2.25	1	2	1	29	0	36.0	24	3	15	33	Scoring Posn	.302	285	86	16	0	7	119	43	48	.388	.432
May	3.42	3	1	1	50	0	52.2	47	4	22	39	Close & Late	.266	335	89	15	2	7	43	37	62	.341	.385
June	5.40	6	4	2	55	0	61.2	73	7	16	44	None on/out	.253	229	58	12	0	5	5	22	43	.329	.371
July	2.00	1	1	0	46	0	45.0	39	2	18	33	vs. 1st Batr (relief)	.285	221	63	12	0	3	35	29	47	.370	.380
August	5.93	1	3	1	44	0	44.0	52	2	20	34	1st Inning Pitched	.290	739	214	39	3	17	127	83	144	.361	.419
Sept/Oct	4.20	2	1	1	34	0	30.0	32	3	9	20	First 15 Pitches	.296	655	194	38	2	14	105	70	118	.364	.424
Starter	0.00	0	0	0	0	0	0.0	0	0	0	0	Pitch 16-30	.222	270	60	9	1	6	35	23	64	.286	.330
Reliever	3.98	14	12	6	258	0	269.1	267	21	100	203	Pitch 31-45	.118	76	9	1	0	1	5	5	15	.183	.171
0 Days rest (Relief)	5.37	3	4	3	69	0	60.1	68	8	18	44	Pitch 46+	.160	25	4	1	0	0	2	2	6	.222	.200
1 or 2 Days rest	4.14	6	5	3	109	0	115.1	119	11	46	88	First Pitch	.363	124	45	8	0	4	26	11	0	.416	.524
3+ Days rest	2.88	5	3	0	80	0	93.2	80	2	36	71	Ahead in Count	.194	494	96	14	2	2	42	0	179	.198	.243
vs. AL	3.43	6	4	1	97	0	107.2	101	7	34	91	Behind in Count	.299	221	66	15	1	6	36	51	0	.426	.457
vs. NL	4.34	8	8	5	161	0	161.2	166	14	66	112	Two Strikes	.199	498	99	17	2	5	49	38	203	.261	.271
Pre-All Star	3.83	10	7	4	149	0	164.1	157	15	57	126	Pre-All Star	.253	620	157	33	2	15	84	57	126	.316	.385
Post-All Star	4.20	4	5	2	109	0	105.0	110	6	43	77	Post-All Star	.271	406	110	16	1	6	61	43	77	.344	.360

Pitcher vs. Batter (career)

Pitches Best Vs.	Avg	AB	H	2B	3B	HR	RBI	BB	SO	OBP	SLG	Pitches Worst Vs.	Avg	AB	H	2B	3B	HR	RBI	BB	SO	OBP	SLG
Luis Gonzalez	.000	10	0	0	0	0	0	1	2	.091	.000	Ken Caminiti	.727	11	8	1	0	1	3	0	1	.727	1.091
Barry Bonds	.042	24	1	1	0	0	1	1	4	.077	.083	Jay Bell	.571	14	8	0	1	1	3	2	1	.625	.929
Todd Zeile	.071	14	1	0	0	0	0	2	1	.188	.071	Bobby Bonilla	.500	14	7	1	1	0	0	2	4	.563	.714
Todd Hundley	.091	11	1	0	0	0	0	1	5	.167	.091	Brett Butler	.364	11	4	2	0	0	2	6	5	.588	.545
Darren Daulton	.133	15	2	0	0	0		2	6	.125	.133	Fred McGriff	.333	21	7	3	0	2	6	2	5	.391	.762

Willie McGee — Cardinals

Age 39 – Bats Both (groundball hitter)

	Avg	G	AB	R	H	2B	3B	HR	RBI	BB	SO	HBP	GDP	SB	CS	OBP	SLG	IBB	SH	SF	#Pit	#P/PA	GB	FB	G/F
1997 Season	.300	122	300	29	90	19	4	3	38	22	59	6	8	2		.347	.420	2	0	1	1107	3.43	133	55	2.42
Last Five Years	.298	487	1440	185	429	76	10	19	163	102	251	3	39	31	15	.343	.404	13	10	11	5427	3.47	733	219	3.35

1997 Season

	Avg	AB	H	2B	3B	HR	RBI	BB	SO	OBP	SLG		Avg	AB	H	2B	3B	HR	RBI	BB	SO	OBP	SLG
vs. Left	.274	95	26	6	1	1	12	7	21	.324	.389	First Pitch	.452	62	28	7	0	3	11	2	0	.469	.710
vs. Right	.312	205	64	13	3	2	26	15	38	.357	.434	Ahead in Count	.479	48	23	6	0	0	6	10	0	.569	.604
Groundball	.352	71	25	3	2	0	11	7	17	.410	.451	Behind in Count	.199	141	28	4	3	0	17	0	52	.199	.270
Flyball	.371	35	13	3	1	1	6	3	7	.421	.600	Two Strikes	.165	127	21	3	2	0	11	10	59	.226	.220
Home	.336	128	43	10	1	2	18	9	21	.380	.477	Batting #2	.255	98	25	4	0	1	9	4	18	.284	.327
Away	.273	172	47	9	3	1	20	13	38	.323	.378	Batting #3	.273	66	18	5	1	0	8	7	11	.342	.379
Day	.319	113	36	5	2	1	20	8	16	.361	.425	Other	.346	136	47	10	3	2	21	11	30	.392	.507
Night	.289	187	54	14	2	2	18	14	43	.338	.417	March/April	.268	41	11	3	2	1	3	6	10	.362	.512
Grass	.300	243	73	15	4	3	30	15	48	.340	.432	May	.245	49	12	2	0	1	5	4	16	.302	.347
Turf	.298	57	17	4	0	0	8	7	11	.375	.368	June	.380	50	19	0	1	0	11	5	7	.436	.420
Pre-All Star	.303	155	47	6	3	3	21	16	35	.368	.439	July	.240	25	6	1	0	1	2	5	6	.296	.400
Post-All Star	.297	145	43	13	1	0	17	6	24	.322	.400	August	.333	69	23	8	1	0	6	4	11	.370	.478
Scoring Posn	.310	84	26	4	3	1	34	12	15	.392	.464	Sept/Oct	.288	66	19	5	0	0	11	1	10	.294	.364
Close & Late	.262	84	22	5	2	2	11	8	23	.323	.440	vs. AL	.314	35	11	2	1	1	5	1	2	.333	.514
None on/out	.375	56	21	3	0	0	0	5	4	.426	.429	vs. NL	.298	265	79	17	3	2	33	21	57	.348	.408

1997 By Position

Position	Avg	AB	H	2B	3B	HR	RBI	BB	SO	OBP	SLG	G	GS	Innings	PO	A	E	DP	Fld Pct	Rng Fctr	In Zone	Zone Outs	Zone Rtg	MLB Zone
As Pinch Hitter	.314	51	16	5	2	1	6	5	9	.375	.549	56	0	---	---	---	---	---	---	---	---	---	---	---
As lf	.341	44	15	2	0	2	9	3	8	.383	.523	18	9	92.0	15	1	0	1	1.000	1.57	19	14	.737	.805
As cf	.259	54	14	3	1	0	8	5	6	.322	.352	18	11	122.1	26	1	1		.964	1.99	37	27	.730	.815
As rf	.312	138	43	9	0	0	12	9	36	.351	.377	53	29	297.2	58	4	1		.984	1.87	71	56	.789	.813

Last Five Years

	Avg	AB	H	2B	3B	HR	RBI	BB	SO	OBP	SLG		Avg	AB	H	2B	3B	HR	RBI	BB	SO	OBP	SLG
vs. Left	.305	455	139	27	4	9	54	22	85	.335	.442	First Pitch	.383	282	108	22	4	6	39	12	0	.405	.553

Last Five Years

	Avg	AB	H	2B	3B	HR	RBI	BB	SO	OBP	SLG
vs. Right	.294	985	290	49	6	10	109	80	166	.347	.387
Groundball	.309	385	119	19	3	5	39	29	71	.356	.413
Flyball	.345	200	69	15	3	5	28	12	32	.380	.525
Home	.322	698	225	38	5	7	76	50	110	.367	.421
Away	.275	742	204	38	5	12	87	52	141	.321	.388
Day	.292	592	173	25	4	8	74	43	91	.337	.389
Night	.302	848	256	51	6	11	89	59	160	.348	.415
Grass	.300	1188	356	63	6	14	128	75	197	.340	.405
Turf	.290	252	73	13	0	5	35	27	54	.357	.401
Pre-All Star	.313	782	245	39	5	13	98	66	130	.364	.426
Post-All Star	.280	658	184	37	5	6	65	36	121	.318	.378
Scoring Posn	.288	378	109	19	5	5	142	46	71	.359	.405
Close & Late	.317	290	92	14	3	4	38	26	60	.371	.428
None on/out	.298	349	104	16	0	4	4	26	58	.347	.378

	Avg	AB	H	2B	3B	HR	RBI	BB	SO	OBP	SLG
Ahead in Count	.406	249	101	21	0	5	37	53	0	.503	.550
Behind in Count	.220	660	145	22	3	4	54	0	216	.220	.280
Two Strikes	.205	623	128	20	3	4	51	37	251	.249	.266
Batting #1	.286	357	102	17	2	4	27	21	69	.324	.378
Batting #3	.249	281	70	13	1	3	29	26	51	.311	.335
Other	.320	802	257	46	7	12	107	55	131	.363	.440
March/April	.282	266	75	13	2	4	29	19	48	.328	.391
May	.313	281	88	15	1	6	32	26	48	.368	.438
June	.344	180	62	8	1	1	27	16	27	.396	.417
July	.315	165	52	8		4	19	8	32	.349	.461
August	.266	301	80	16	3	4	33	15	53	.301	.379
Sept/Oct	.291	247	72	16	1	0	23	18	43	.340	.364
vs. AL	.289	235	68	13	4	3	20	10	43	.315	.417
vs. NL	.300	1205	361	63	6	16	143	92	208	.349	.402

Batter vs. Pitcher (since 1984)

Hits Best Against	Avg	AB	H	2B	3B	HR	RBI	BB	SO	OBP	SLG
Doug Brocail	.583	12	7	1	0	0	1	0	1	.583	.667
Jim Bullinger	.538	13	7	1	0	0	2	0	1	.538	.615
Paul Assenmacher	.529	17	9	1	0	0	3	1	3	.556	.588
Darryl Kile	.457	35	16	4	0	0	5	4	6	.513	.571
Pete Harnisch	.452	31	14	1	2	1	4	2	0	.485	.710

Hits Worst Against	Avg	AB	H	2B	3B	HR	RBI	BB	SO	OBP	SLG
Frank Castillo	.083	12	1	0	0	0	0	1	1	.154	.083
Tim Wakefield	.133	15	2	0	0	0	1	0	4	.133	.133
Curt Schilling	.133	15	2	0	0	0	1	1	3	.188	.133
Norm Charlton	.143	14	2	0	0	0	0	0	6	.143	.143
Steve Avery	.176	34	6	0	0	0	0	2	8	.222	.176

Tom McGraw — Cardinals   Age 30 – Pitches Left

	ERA	W	L	Sv	G	GS	IP	BB	SO	Avg	H	2B	3B	HR	RBI	OBP	SLG	GF	IR	IRS	Hld	SvOp	SB	CS	GB	FB	G/F
1997 Season	0.00	0	0	0	2	0	1.2	1	0	.333	2	1	0	0	3	.375	.500	2	3	3	0	0	0	0	3	4	0.75

1997 Season

	ERA	W	L	Sv	G	GS	IP	H	HR	BB	SO
Home	0.00	0	0	0	2	0	1.2	2	0	1	0
Away	0.00	0	0	0	0	0	0.0	0	0	0	0

	Avg	AB	H	2B	3B	HR	RBI	BB	SO	OBP	SLG
vs. Left	.000	1	0	0	0	0	1	1	0	.500	.000
vs. Right	.400	5	2	1	0	0	2	0	0	.333	.600

Fred McGriff — Braves   Age 34 – Bats Left

	Avg	G	AB	R	H	2B	3B	HR	RBI	BB	SO	HBP	GDP	SB	CS	OBP	SLG	IBB	SH	SF	#Pit	#P/PA	GB	FB	G/F
1997 Season	.277	152	564	77	156	25	1	22	97	68	112	4	22	5	0	.356	.441	4	0	5	2336	3.64	229	139	1.65
Last Five Years	.291	719	2690	435	783	143	6	148	492	327	509	14	84	27	15	.368	.514	36	0	23	11346	3.72	959	748	1.28

1997 Season

	Avg	AB	H	2B	3B	HR	RBI	BB	SO	OBP	SLG
vs. Left	.268	183	49	5	1	6	28	25	42	.362	.404
vs. Right	.281	381	107	20	0	16	69	43	70	.353	.437
Groundball	.211	109	23	3	0	5	13	14	24	.306	.376
Flyball	.297	64	19	1	0	4	11	7	19	.366	.500
Home	.265	294	78	14	1	8	52	33	60	.338	.401
Away	.289	270	78	11	0	14	45	35	52	.375	.485
Day	.258	155	40	6	1	6	24	17	33	.331	.426
Night	.284	409	116	19	0	16	73	51	79	.365	.447
Grass	.271	472	128	19	1	16	83	57	94	.351	.417
Turf	.304	92	28	6	0	6	14	11	18	.379	.565
Pre-All Star	.281	313	88	11	1	10	50	41	53	.362	.419
Post-All Star	.271	251	68	14	0	12	47	27	59	.347	.470
Scoring Posn	.259	174	45	6	1	2	67	31	39	.365	.339
Close & Late	.222	81	18	2	1	5	12	10	23	.315	.457
None on/out	.301	133	40	7	0	9	9	13	25	.363	.496

	Avg	AB	H	2B	3B	HR	RBI	BB	SO	OBP	SLG
First Pitch	.307	101	31	4	0	5	15	2	0	.320	.495
Ahead in Count	.359	142	51	8	0	10	34	39	0	.492	.627
Behind in Count	.206	218	45	8	0	4	25	0	92	.219	.298
Two Strikes	.215	237	51	9	1	2	30	26	112	.298	.287
Batting #4	.280	550	154	25	1	21	95	67	105	.359	.444
Batting #5	.250	8	2	0	0	1	2	0	3	.250	.625
Other	.000	6	0	0	0	0	0	1	4	.143	.000
March/April	.299	97	29	3	0	4	19	13	16	.382	.454
May	.252	107	27	0	0	3	14	8	17	.299	.336
June	.293	92	27	6	1	3	15	15	15	.409	.478
July	.319	91	29	9	0	5	15		16	.411	.582
August	.216	102	22	2	0	5	16	7	32	.279	.382
Sept/Oct	.293	75	22	5	0	2	18	7	16	.360	.440
vs. AL	.279	43	12	0	0	3	9	6	10	.373	.488
vs. NL	.276	521	144	25	1	19	88	62	102	.354	.438

1997 By Position

Position	Avg	AB	H	2B	3B	HR	RBI	BB	SO	OBP	SLG	G	GS	Innings	PO	A	E	DP	Fld Pct	Rng Fctr	In Zone	Zone Outs	Rtg	MLB Zone
As 1b	.278	562	156	25	1	22	97	67	111	.356	.443	149	149	1263.2	1190	97	13	112	990	---	234	193	825	874

Last Five Years

	Avg	AB	H	2B	3B	HR	RBI	BB	SO	OBP	SLG
vs. Left	.283	929	263	40	4	41	162	99	116	.354	.467
vs. Right	.295	1761	520	103	2	107	330	228	331	.354	.538
Groundball	.281	740	208	36	1	46	129	88	154	.360	.519
Flyball	.291	419	122	25	2	22	80	51	87	.366	.518
Home	.280	1323	371	66	3	68	250	165	237	.359	.489
Away	.301	1367	412	77	3	80	242	162	272	.376	.538
Day	.309	794	245	53	3	41	134	98	152	.383	.538
Night	.284	1896	538	90	3	107	358	229	357	.365	.504
Grass	.289	2111	610	105	4	111	389	249	394	.364	.500
Turf	.299	579	173	38	2	37	103	78	115	.383	.563
Pre-All Star	.289	1531	443	78	5	82	272	195	278	.362	.508
Post-All Star	.293	1159	340	65	1	66	220	132	231	.369	.522
Scoring Posn	.277	733	203	34	3	36	325	141	147	.388	.479
Close & Late	.282	390	110	20	3	20	61	70	91	.394	.503
None on/out	.280	718	201	43	2	36	36	51	129	.329	.496

	Avg	AB	H	2B	3B	HR	RBI	BB	SO	OBP	SLG
First Pitch	.356	494	176	31	0	37	107	27	0	.387	.644
Ahead in Count	.384	657	252	52	1	58	175	138	0	.488	.731
Behind in Count	.204	1029	210	35	4	31	122	0	403	.211	.336
Two Strikes	.199	1162	231	39	5	34	143	161	509	.299	.329
Batting #3	.185	27	5	0	0	1	2	5	4	.313	.296
Batting #4	.293	2645	775	142	6	146	488	321	497	.370	.517
Other	.167	18	3	1	0	1	2	1	8	.211	.389
March/April	.292	380	111	18	0	20	75	55	80	.380	.497
May	.288	514	148	17	3	30	86	58	97	.359	.508
June	.275	484	133	31	2	24	78	72	69	.367	.496
July	.305	475	145	30	1	29	94	45	94	.362	.556
August	.286	476	136	21	0	28	86	42	98	.348	.506
Sept/Oct	.305	361	110	26	0	17	73	55	71	.401	.518
vs. AL	.279	43	12	0	0	3	9	6	10	.373	.488
vs. NL	.291	2647	771	143	6	145	483	321	499	.368	.514

Batter vs. Pitcher (career)

Hits Best Against	Avg	AB	H	2B	3B	HR	RBI	BB	SO	OBP	SLG	Hits Worst Against	Avg	AB	H	2B	3B	HR	RBI	BB	SO	OBP	SLG
Willie Banks	.625	8	5	0	0	1	3	3	0	.727	1.000	Alan Benes	.000	13	0	0	0	0	0	0	1	.000	.000
Roger Bailey	.545	11	6	2	0	1	2	2	1	.667	1.000	Mark Davis	.000	9	0	0	0	0	1	4	4	.308	.000
Tim Pugh	.538	13	7	0	1	2	5	4	1	.647	1.154	Doug Jones	.059	17	1	0	0	0	1	2	5	.158	.059
Mark Gubicza	.500	20	10	3	0	4	4	3	3	.583	1.250	Matt Beech	.091	11	1	0	0	0	2	1	1	.167	.091
Erik Hanson	.375	8	3	0	0	2	3	5	1	.615	1.125	Donovan Osborne	.136	22	3	0	0	0	1	1	4	.174	.136

Ryan McGuire — Expos
Age 26 – Bats Left

	Avg	G	AB	R	H	2B	3B	HR	RBI	BB	SO	HBP	GDP	SB	CS	OBP	SLG	IBB	SH	SF	#Pit	#P/PA	GB	FB	G/F
1997 Season	.256	84	199	22	51	15	2	3	17	19	34	0	3	1	4	.320	.397	1	3	1	836	3.77	78	51	1.53

1997 Season

	Avg	AB	H	2B	3B	HR	RBI	BB	SO	OBP	SLG		Avg	AB	H	2B	3B	HR	RBI	BB	SO	OBP	SLG
vs. Left	.200	65	13	2	1	1	2	5	11	.257	.308	Scoring Posn	.216	37	8	4	1	0	12	6	6	.318	.378
vs. Right	.284	134	38	13	1	2	15	14	23	.349	.440	Close & Late	.225	40	9	2	0	0	2	6	7	.326	.275
Home	.295	88	26	7	1	2	8	12	8	.380	.466	None on/out	.273	55	15	5	0	1	1	3	10	.310	.418
Away	.225	111	25	8	1	1	9	7	26	.269	.342	Batting #7	.127	63	8	0	1	0	5	6	14	.203	.159
First Pitch	.400	30	12	2	1	3	5	1	0	.419	.833	Batting #8	.385	78	30	11	1	3	9	8	9	.437	.667
Ahead in Count	.278	54	15	7	0	0	5	9	0	.381	.407	Other	.224	58	13	4	0	0	3	5	11	.286	.293
Behind in Count	.186	86	16	3	1	0	7	0	30	.184	.244	Pre-All Star	.329	76	25	7	0	3	9	8	10	.393	.539
Two Strikes	.156	90	14	3	1	0	6	9	34	.230	.211	Post-All Star	.211	123	26	8	2	0	8	11	24	.274	.309

Mark McGwire — Cardinals
Age 34 – Bats Right (flyball hitter)

	Avg	G	AB	R	H	2B	3B	HR	RBI	BB	SO	HBP	GDP	SB	CS	OBP	SLG	IBB	SH	SF	#Pit	#P/PA	GB	FB	G/F
1997 Season	.274	156	540	86	148	27	0	58	123	101	159	9	9	3	0	.393	.646	16	0	7	2419	3.68	105	200	0.53
Last Five Years	.286	464	1499	307	429	70	0	167	375	363	407	29	35	4	2	.431	.667	45	0	15	7306	3.83	282	602	0.47

1997 Season

	Avg	AB	H	2B	3B	HR	RBI	BB	SO	OBP	SLG		Avg	AB	H	2B	3B	HR	RBI	BB	SO	OBP	SLG
vs. Left	.282	117	33	8	0	12	27	32	40	.436	.658	First Pitch	.356	90	32	6	0	8	24	14	0	.443	.689
vs. Right	.272	423	115	19	0	46	96	69	119	.380	.643	Ahead in Count	.439	114	50	9	0	25	50	44	0	.590	1.175
Groundball	.272	103	28	7	0	10	26	22	31	.406	.631	Behind in Count	.165	230	38	6	0	16	27	0	125	.179	.400
Flyball	.216	88	19	3	0	7	13	17	19	.355	.489	Two Strikes	.140	250	35	5	0	14	27	43	159	.269	.328
Home	.315	248	78	18	0	30	60	52	64	.438	.750	Batting #3	.281	128	36	3	0	20	34	36	46	.447	.773
Away	.240	292	70	9	0	28	63	49	95	.354	.558	Batting #4	.265	407	108	24	0	37	87	64	112	.368	.597
Day	.280	193	54	11	0	20	39	41	50	.415	.648	Other	.800	5	4	0	0	1	2	1	1	.833	1.400
Night	.271	347	94	16	0	38	84	60	109	.380	.646	March/April	.322	87	28	8	0	11	25	23	16	.464	.793
Grass	.281	467	131	23	0	51	108	94	136	.405	.657	May	.253	99	25	3	0	8	19	12	20	.325	.525
Turf	.233	73	17	4	0	7	15	7	23	.314	.575	June	.266	94	25	6	0	10	19	11	31	.352	.649
Pre-All Star	.288	299	86	19	0	31	71	50	73	.389	.662	July	.302	86	26	7	0	5	18	12	31	.394	.558
Post-All Star	.257	241	62	8	0	27	52	51	86	.397	.627	August	.211	76	16	2	0	9	18	23	25	.408	.592
Scoring Posn	.232	142	33	12	0	11	63	37	43	.399	.549	Sept/Oct	.286	98	28	1	0	15	24	20	36	.413	.755
Close & Late	.264	87	23	2	0	8	19	26	29	.431	.563	vs. AL	.276	344	95	20	0	33	75	59	95	.383	.622
None on/out	.326	141	46	7	0	21	21	22	38	.417	.823	vs. NL	.270	196	53	7	0	25	48	42	64	.409	.689

1997 By Position

Position	Avg	AB	H	2B	3B	HR	RBI	BB	SO	OBP	SLG	G	GS	Innings	PO	A	E	DP	Fld Pct	Rng Fctr	In Zone	Zone Outs	Zone Rtg	MLB Zone
As 1b	.269	535	144	27	0	57	121	100	159	.389	.639	152	150	1287.1	1326	94	7	130	.995	—	273	223	.817	.874

Last Five Years

	Avg	AB	H	2B	3B	HR	RBI	BB	SO	OBP	SLG		Avg	AB	H	2B	3B	HR	RBI	BB	SO	OBP	SLG
vs. Left	.301	382	115	20	0	45	106	116	100	.467	.707	First Pitch	.370	254	94	18	0	36	88	33	0	.452	.866
vs. Right	.281	1117	314	50	0	122	269	247	307	.418	.654	Ahead in Count	.428	283	121	19	0	57	119	169	0	.642	1.099
Groundball	.325	335	109	17	0	40	85	87	86	.472	.734	Behind in Count	.192	650	125	19	0	41	89	0	309	.204	.411
Flyball	.229	280	64	9	0	29	65	66	77	.388	.571	Two Strikes	.152	710	108	15	0	39	87	161	407	.313	.338
Home	.292	709	207	37	0	80	184	179	187	.442	.683	Batting #3	.277	130	36	3	0	20	34	37	47	.445	.762
Away	.281	790	222	33	0	87	191	184	220	.420	.653	Batting #4	.289	1252	362	65	0	137	319	297	334	.431	.669
Day	.293	584	171	32	0	67	141	147	148	.444	.692	Other	.265	117	31	2	0	10	22	29	26	.412	.538
Night	.282	915	258	38	0	100	234	216	259	.422	.651	March/April	.288	222	64	14	0	21	55	65	58	.451	.635
Grass	.289	1328	384	64	0	146	330	328	361	.435	.667	May	.315	314	99	19	0	33	82	62	63	.431	.691
Turf	.263	171	45	6	0	21	45	35	46	.394	.667	June	.285	281	80	14	0	36	71	72	79	.436	.719
Pre-All Star	.300	911	273	51	0	99	233	222	224	.440	.683	July	.273	253	69	11	0	24	54	50	70	.399	.601
Post-All Star	.265	588	156	19	0	68	142	141	183	.416	.645	August	.270	185	50	4	0	20	46	49	59	.427	.616
Scoring Posn	.282	383	108	25	0	39	201	142	107	.475	.653	Sept/Oct	.275	244	67	8	0	33	67	68	78	.439	.713
Close & Late	.266	218	58	5	0	19	48	76	69	.461	.550	vs. AL	.289	1303	376	63	0	142	327	321	343	.434	.664
None on/out	.284	387	110	16	0	51	51	74	109	.407	.721	vs. NL	.270	196	53	7	0	25	48	42	64	.409	.689

Batter vs. Pitcher (career)

Hits Best Against	Avg	AB	H	2B	3B	HR	RBI	BB	SO	OBP	SLG	Hits Worst Against	Avg	AB	H	2B	3B	HR	RBI	BB	SO	OBP	SLG
Rich Robertson	.600	10	6	1	0	3	7	3	1	.692	1.600	Juan Guzman	.000	11	0	0	0	0	0	2	5	.214	.000
Orel Hershiser	.583	12	7	1	0	3	7	0	3	.583	1.417	Roger Clemens	.085	47	4	1	0	2	6	6	14	.189	.234
John Smiley	.500	10	5	2	0	2	2	3	2	.615	1.300	Rich DeLucia	.105	19	2	1	0	0	1	1	4	.150	.158
Kevin Gross	.455	11	5	0	0	4	7	7	2	.684	1.545	Eric Plunk	.154	13	2	0	0	0	3	2	7	.267	.154
Scott Kamieniecki	.444	18	8	2	0	4	8	2	3	.500	1.222	Matt Whiteside	.154	13	2	0	0	0	0	2	4	.267	.154

Walt McKeel — Red Sox   Age 26 – Bats Right

	Avg	G	AB	R	H	2B	3B	HR	RBI	BB	SO	HBP	GDP	SB	CS	OBP	SLG	IBB	SH	SF	#Pit	#P/PA	GB	FB	G/F
1997 Season	.000	5	3	0	0	0	0	0	0	0	1	0	0	0	0	.000	.000	0	0	0	12	4.00	0	2	0.00

1997 Season

	Avg	AB	H	2B	3B	HR	RBI	BB	SO	OBP	SLG		Avg	AB	H	2B	3B	HR	RBI	BB	SO	OBP	SLG
vs. Left	.000	2	0	0	0	0	0	0	1	.000	.000	Scoring Posn	.000	2	0	0	0	0	0	0	1	.000	.000
vs. Right	.000	1	0	0	0	0	0	0	0	.000	.000	Close & Late	.000	0	0	0	0	0	0	0	0	.000	.000

Mark McLemore — Rangers   Age 33 – Bats Both (groundball hitter)

	Avg	G	AB	R	H	2B	3B	HR	RBI	BB	SO	HBP	GDP	SB	CS	OBP	SLG	IBB	SH	SF	#Pit	#P/PA	GB	FB	G/F
1997 Season	.261	89	349	47	91	17	2	1	25	40	54	2	5	7	5	.338	.330	1	6	2	1499	3.76	145	70	2.07
Last Five Years	.273	617	2257	329	616	98	17	18	213	301	336	7	58	96	46	.358	.355	19	33	17	9792	3.74	936	520	1.80

1997 Season

	Avg	AB	H	2B	3B	HR	RBI	BB	SO	OBP	SLG		Avg	AB	H	2B	3B	HR	RBI	BB	SO	OBP	SLG
vs. Left	.267	90	24	6	0	0	3	9	15	.330	.333	First Pitch	.357	42	15	2	0	1	5	1	0	.364	.476
vs. Right	.259	259	67	11	2	1	22	31	39	.341	.328	Ahead in Count	.318	88	28	5	0	0	9	26	0	.470	.375
Groundball	.303	89	27	6	1	0	6	8	14	.364	.393	Behind in Count	.209	139	29	7	1	0	4	0	44	.214	.273
Flyball	.316	57	18	4	1	1	9	3	12	.350	.474	Two Strikes	.205	151	31	7	2	0	6	13	54	.273	.278
Home	.234	188	44	10	1	0	16	22	32	.313	.298	Batting #1	.265	268	71	14	1	0	14	36	32	.355	.325
Away	.292	161	47	7	1	1	9	18	22	.368	.366	Batting #2	.262	65	17	2	0	1	8	2	18	.279	.338
Day	.229	83	19	7	1	0	6	8	14	.293	.337	Other	.188	16	3	1	1	0	3	2	4	.278	.375
Night	.271	266	72	10	1	1	19	32	40	.352	.327	March/April	.167	84	14	3	0	0	3	14	8	.290	.202
Grass	.261	322	84	15	1	1	24	34	49	.331	.323	May	.194	31	6	2	0	0	0	5		.194	.258
Turf	.259	27	7	2	1	0	1	6	5	.412	.407	June	.329	73	24	3	1	0	7	11	6	.424	.397
Pre-All Star	.250	212	53	8	1	0	14	31	22	.350	.297	July	.313	112	35	8	1	1	7	13	23	.384	.429
Post-All Star	.277	137	38	9	1	1	11	9	32	.320	.380	August	.245	49	12	1	0	0	6	2	12	.269	.265
Scoring Posn	.214	70	15	1	0	0	23	9	20	.305	.229	Sept/Oct	.000	0	0	0	0	0	0	0	0	.000	.000
Close & Late	.283	60	17	7	1	0	5	5	9	.338	.400	vs. AL	.238	307	73	15	1	1	19	36	52	.320	.303
None on/out	.267	116	31	8	1	1		16	14	.356	.379	vs. NL	.429	42	18	2	1	0	6	4	2	.478	.524

1997 By Position

Position	Avg	AB	H	2B	3B	HR	RBI	BB	SO	OBP	SLG	G	GS	Innings	PO	A	E	DP	Fld Pct	Rng Fctr	In Zone	Outs	Zone Rtg	MLB Zone
As 2b	.261	348	91	17	2	1	25	39	54	.338	.330	89	86	742.1	149	254	8	60	.981	4.89	263	244	928	902

Last Five Years

	Avg	AB	H	2B	3B	HR	RBI	BB	SO	OBP	SLG		Avg	AB	H	2B	3B	HR	RBI	BB	SO	OBP	SLG
vs. Left	.240	597	143	22	2	2	34	76	92	.326	.293	First Pitch	.338	311	105	14	2	6	25	13	0	.363	.453
vs. Right	.285	1660	473	76	15	16	179	225	244	.369	.378	Ahead in Count	.347	603	209	36	5	3	68	172	0	.488	.438
Groundball	.277	498	138	28	4	1	41	67	74	.364	.355	Behind in Count	.196	849	166	33	4	7	74	0	271	.198	.269
Flyball	.297	434	129	27	3	4	47	56	69	.374	.401	Two Strikes	.186	929	173	35	7	7	77	115	336	.276	.262
Home	.285	1135	324	49	10	10	116	155	174	.370	.373	Batting #2	.262	883	231	37	9	10	92	104	138	.339	.358
Away	.260	1122	292	49	7	8	97	146	162	.346	.338	Batting #8	.288	572	165	24	1	3	55	88	86	.381	.350
Day	.273	594	162	31	6	5	57	69	95	.349	.370	Other	.274	802	220	37	7	5	66	109	112	.362	.357
Night	.273	1663	454	67	11	13	156	232	241	.361	.350	March/April	.257	307	79	10	1	2	33	45	48	.348	.316
Grass	.270	1963	530	88	13	15	185	260	301	.354	.351	May	.269	401	108	17	3	3	35	58	61	.364	.349
Turf	.293	294	86	10	4	3	28	41	35	.383	.384	June	.323	424	137	19	3	4	51	61	54	.409	.410
Pre-All Star	.284	1290	367	54	9	10	136	184	184	.374	.364	July	.261	494	129	31	6	4	38	62	75	.343	.372
Post-All Star	.257	967	249	44	8	8	77	117	152	.336	.344	August	.272	367	100	15	3	2	33	40	52	.341	.346
Scoring Posn	.268	533	143	23	2	6	193	105	96	.382	.353	Sept/Oct	.239	264	63	6	1	3	23	35	46	.326	.303
Close & Late	.274	339	93	16	4	2	31	48	53	.362	.363	vs. AL	.270	2215	598	96	16	18	207	297	334	.356	.352
None on/out	.263	559	147	21	3	6	6	65	83	.340	.343	vs. NL	.429	42	18	2	1	0	6	4	2	.478	.524

Batter vs. Pitcher (career)

Hits Best Against	Avg	AB	H	2B	3B	HR	RBI	BB	SO	OBP	SLG	Hits Worst Against	Avg	AB	H	2B	3B	HR	RBI	BB	SO	OBP	SLG
Al Leiter	.500	18	9	3	0	1	3	3	1	.571	.833	Aaron Sele	.000	12	0	0	0	0	0	1	3	.077	.000
Danny Darwin	.458	24	11	1	0	1	5	1	1	.480	.625	Kenny Rogers	.071	14	1	0	0	0	0	1	2	.133	.071
Mike Trombley	.455	11	5	0	1	0	2	2	2	.538	.636	Jamie Moyer	.077	13	1	0	0	0	1	2	5	.200	.077
Bobby Witt	.438	16	7	1	1	0	4	3	1	.500	.625	Mark Gubicza	.115	26	3	0	0	0	1	1	2	.148	.115
Pat Mahomes	.429	14	6	2	0	1	3	5	3	.579	.786	Charles Nagy	.143	28	4	1	0	0	2	2	5	.194	.179

Greg McMichael — Mets   Age 31 – Pitches Right (groundball pitcher)

	ERA	W	L	Sv	G	GS	IP	BB	SO	Avg	H	2B	3B	HR	RBI	OBP	SLG	GF	IR	IRS	Hld	SvOp	SB	CS	GB	FB	G/F
1997 Season	2.98	7	10	7	73	0	87.2	27	81	.233	73	14	2	8	38	.295	.367	23	52	15	19	18	10	1	125	60	2.08
Career (1993-1997)	2.91	25	24	51	338	0	405.1	134	369	.235	355	66	6	24	146	.297	.334	134	131	41	70	82	32	9	579	324	1.79

1997 Season

	ERA	W	L	Sv	G	GS	IP	H	HR	BB	SO		Avg	AB	H	2B	3B	HR	RBI	BB	SO	OBP	SLG
Home	1.41	4	4	4	34	0	44.2	31	3	13	46	vs. Left	.259	139	36	5	2	3	15	16	39	.338	.388
Away	4.60	3	6	3	39	0	43.0	42	5	14	35	vs. Right	.213	174	37	9	0	5	23	11	42	.259	.351
Day	3.03	2	4	3	29	0	35.2	36	3	13	26	Inning 1-6	.667	3	2	0	0	0	2	0	0	.667	.667
Night	2.94	5	6	4	44	0	52.0	37	5	14	55	Inning 7+	.229	310	71	14	2	8	36	27	81	.292	.365
Grass	2.72	6	8	7	62	0	76.0	59	6	21	66	None on	.235	162	38	9	1	3	3	11	42	.287	.358
Turf	4.63	1	2	0	11	0	11.2	14	2	6	15	Runners on	.232	151	35	5	1	5	35	16	39	.302	.377
March/April	2.30	1	2	1	12	0	15.2	17	2	4	13	Scoring Posn	.180	100	18	1	1	2	28	16	26	.289	.270
May	2.77	2	2	1	12	0	13.0	13	1	4	11	Close & Late	.239	226	54	12	2	6	30	24	61	.312	.389
June	1.80	1	2	1	11	0	10.0	7	0	4	9	None on/out	.229	70	16	6	1	0	0	3	16	.270	.343

1997 Season

	ERA	W	L	Sv	G	GS	IP	H	HR	BB	SO		Avg	AB	H	2B	3B	HR	RBI	BB	SO	OBP	SLG
July	4.24	3	2	3	14	0	17.0	12	3	6	11	vs. 1st Batr (relief)	.231	65	15	5	0	0	9	5	15	.288	.308
August	3.24	0	2	0	13	0	16.2	14	2	5	14	1st Inning Pitched	.236	233	55	11	1	6	33	20	60	.295	.369
Sept/Oct	2.93	0	0	1	11	0	15.1	10	0	4	23	First 15 Pitches	.259	197	51	9	1	5	24	17	45	.317	.391
Starter	0.00	0	0	0	0	0	0.0	0	0	0	0	Pitch 16-30	.196	107	21	4	1	3	14	9	33	.263	.336
Reliever	2.98	7	10	7	73	0	87.2	73	8	27	81	Pitch 31-45	.111	9	1	1	0	0	0	1	3	.200	.222
0 Days rest (Relief)	3.78	1	5	1	14	0	16.2	16	1	5	18	Pitch 46+	.000	0	0	0	0	0	0	0	0	.000	.000
1 or 2 Days rest	3.34	4	5	6	46	0	56.2	48	6	18	48	First Pitch	.333	42	14	5	1	1	4	1	0	.349	.571
3+ Days rest	0.63	2	0	0	13	0	14.1	9	1	4	15	Behind in Count	.182	165	30	4	0	3	15	0	69	.189	.261
vs. AL	4.91	0	1	0	7	0	7.1	5	2	2	4	Behind in Count	.319	47	15	4	1	1	7	17	0	.492	.511
vs. NL	2.80	7	9	7	66	0	80.1	68	6	25	77	Two Strikes	.150	167	25	2	0	4	15	8	81	.197	.234
Pre-All Star	2.47	4	6	4	38	0	43.2	40	4	15	35	Pre-All Star	.255	157	40	8	1	4	18	15	35	.314	.395
Post-All Star	3.48	3	4	3	35	0	44.0	33	4	12	46	Post-All Star	.212	156	33	6	1	4	20	12	46	.275	.340

Career (1993-1997)

	ERA	W	L	Sv	G	GS	IP	H	HR	BB	SO		Avg	AB	H	2B	3B	HR	RBI	BB	SO	OBP	SLG
Home	2.96	13	11	22	168	0	203.2	187	14	57	186	vs. Left	.247	718	177	31	5	11	72	58	173	.303	.350
Away	2.86	12	13	29	170	0	201.2	168	10	77	183	vs. Right	.224	793	178	35	1	13	74	76	196	.291	.300
Day	3.28	6	8	17	119	0	145.1	141	9	51	118	Inning 1-6	.252	115	29	4	0	3	20	4	29	.273	.365
Night	2.70	19	16	34	219	0	260.0	214	15	83	251	Inning 7+	.234	1396	326	62	6	21	126	130	340	.299	.332
Grass	2.83	24	17	43	273	0	333.2	288	21	98	302	None on	.233	847	197	45	1	14	14	58	215	.283	.338
Turf	3.27	1	7	8	65	0	71.2	67	3	36	67	Runners on	.238	664	158	21	5	10	132	76	154	.313	.330
March/April	3.21	4	4	7	47	0	61.2	56	5	19	51	Scoring Posn	.210	415	87	11	4	3	114	64	108	.310	.277
May	2.59	7	5	7	58	0	73.0	76	6	25	69	Close & Late	.253	877	222	45	5	16	98	96	213	.326	.371
June	2.85	4	7	63	0	72.2	59	0	23	58		None on/out	.215	367	79	19	1	6	6	26	100	.269	.322
July	4.46	6	5	10	63	0	70.2	60	6	23	67	vs. 1st Batr (relief)	.220	309	68	14	0	2	23	23	86	.273	.285
August	1.52	2	3	10	60	0	71.0	49	3	19	66	1st Inning Pitched	.245	1159	284	55	5	15	126	102	292	.305	.340
Sept/Oct	2.88	2	2	10	47	0	56.1	55	4	25	58	First 15 Pitches	.256	992	254	52	1	13	80	77	239	.309	.350
Starter	0.00	0	0	0	0	0	0.0	0	0	0	0	Pitch 16-30	.201	462	93	12	5	10	63	53	117	.283	.314
Reliever	2.91	25	24	51	338	0	405.1	355	24	134	369	Pitch 31-45	.140	57	8	2	0	1	3	4	13	.194	.228
0 Days rest (Relief)	2.63	5	10	15	85	0	96.0	90	5	31	93	Pitch 46+	.000	0	0	0	0	0	0	0	0	.000	.000
1 or 2 Days rest	2.65	16	11	32	189	0	234.1	193	13	75	208	First Pitch	.315	184	58	11	2	3	16	20	0	.382	.446
3+ Days rest	4.08	4	3	4	64	0	75.0	72	6	28	68	Ahead in Count	.188	804	151	22	2	11	64	0	316	.188	.261
vs. AL	4.91	0	1	0	7	0	7.1	5	2	2	4	Behind in Count	.288	240	69	17	1	5	29	71	0	.446	.429
vs. NL	2.87	25	23	51	331	0	398.0	350	22	132	365	Two Strikes	.167	791	132	18	3	10	61	42	369	.210	.235
Pre-All Star	2.88	16	14	24	188	0	231.0	203	13	75	205	Pre-All Star	.235	863	203	37	2	13	79	75	205	.295	.328
Post-All Star	2.94	9	10	27	150	0	174.1	152	11	59	164	Post-All Star	.235	648	152	29	4	11	67	59	164	.300	.343

Pitcher vs. Batter (career)

Pitches Best Vs.	Avg	AB	H	2B	3B	HR	RBI	BB	SO	OBP	SLG	Pitches Worst Vs.	Avg	AB	H	2B	3B	HR	RBI	BB	SO	OBP	SLG
Moises Alou	.000	8	0	0	0	0	0	3	0	.273	.000	David Segui	.545	11	6	1	0	1	3	0	2	.545	.909
Mark Grace	.083	12	1	0	0	0	0	3	3	.267	.083	Larry Walker	.500	12	6	0	1	2	3	1	0	.538	1.167
Andres Galarraga	.154	13	2	0	0	0	2	0	1	.154	.154	Sammy Sosa	.444	9	4	2	0	0	1	3	2	.583	.667
Greg Colbrunn	.167	12	2	0	0	0	0	0	4	.167	.167	Barry Larkin	.375	8	3	1	0	1	4	3	1	.545	.875
Rick Wilkins	.182	11	2	0	0	0	0	1	6	.250	.182	Jeff Kent	.333	12	4	1	0	2	3	3	4	.467	.917

Billy McMillon — Phillies
Age 26 – Bats Left

	Avg	G	AB	R	H	2B	3B	HR	RBI	BB	SO	HBP	GDP	SB	CS	OBP	SLG	IBB	SH	SF	#Pit	#P/PA	GB	FB	G/F
1997 Season	.256	37	90	10	23	5	1	2	14	6	24	0	1	2	1	.293	.400	0	0	3	371	3.75	23	25	0.92
Career (1996-1997)	.241	65	141	14	34	5	1	2	18	11	38	0	2	2	1	.290	.333	1	0	3	612	3.95	46	33	1.39

1997 Season

	Avg	AB	H	2B	3B	HR	RBI	BB	SO	OBP	SLG		Avg	AB	H	2B	3B	HR	RBI	BB	SO	OBP	SLG
vs. Left	.333	15	5	1	0	1	2	3	2	.421	.600	Scoring Posn	.233	30	7	2	1	1	13	1	9	.235	.467
vs. Right	.240	75	18	4	1	1	12	3	22	.263	.360	Close & Late	.133	15	2	1	1	0	3	1	4	.176	.333

Brian McRae — Mets
Age 30 – Bats Both (groundball hitter)

	Avg	G	AB	R	H	2B	3B	HR	RBI	BB	SO	HBP	GDP	SB	CS	OBP	SLG	IBB	SH	SF	#Pit	#P/PA	GB	FB	G/F
1997 Season	.242	153	562	86	136	32	7	11	43	65	84	6	13	17	10	.326	.383	2	4	2	2454	3.84	235	143	1.64
Last Five Years	.273	714	2829	438	771	152	34	56	266	276	432	35	47	132	49	.343	.410	13	29	14	12106	3.80	1198	647	1.85

1997 Season

	Avg	AB	H	2B	3B	HR	RBI	BB	SO	OBP	SLG		Avg	AB	H	2B	3B	HR	RBI	BB	SO	OBP	SLG
vs. Left	.278	144	40	8	2	4	9	10	20	.333	.444	First Pitch	.261	92	24	5	0	3	5	1	0	.277	.413
vs. Right	.230	418	96	24	5	7	34	55	64	.324	.361	Ahead in Count	.277	130	36	5	2	3	10	24	0	.391	.415
Groundball	.280	107	30	5	2	3	8	15	18	.374	.449	Behind in Count	.185	222	41	9	4	2	14	0	67	.199	.288
Flyball	.176	85	15	4	2	1	2	8	15	.247	.306	Two Strikes	.185	254	47	12	3	3	21	40	84	.303	.291
Home	.276	297	82	18	5	6	23	31	46	.348	.431	Batting #1	.237	397	94	21	5	7	22	34	58	.304	.388
Away	.204	265	54	14	2	5	20	34	38	.301	.328	Batting #2	.254	122	31	9	1	2	9	24	17	.381	.393
Day	.240	283	68	16	4	6	27	29	40	.315	.389	Other	.256	43	11	2	1	2	12	7	9	.353	.488
Night	.244	279	68	16	3	5	16	36	44	.336	.376	March/April	.167	96	16	5	2	1	3	8	16	.236	.292
Grass	.248	492	122	27	6	9	37	52	74	.326	.382	May	.364	110	40	11	2	3	12	6	14	.397	.582
Turf	.200	70	14	5	1	2	6	13	10	.325	.386	June	.147	102	15	2	0	0	4	12	17	.250	.167
Pre-All Star	.233	330	77	22	5	4	21	31	48	.304	.367	July	.267	90	24	9	1	0	7	22	7	.416	.389
Post-All Star	.254	232	59	10	2	7	22	34	36	.356	.405	August	.255	98	25	4	2	3	8	12	16	.333	.429
Scoring Posn	.262	103	27	6	1	1	31	22	17	.391	.369	Sept/Oct	.242	66	16	1	0	4	9	5	14	.315	.439
Close & Late	.275	80	22	5	1	3	7	13	11	.383	.475	vs. AL	.273	55	15	6	0	0	5	5	7	.333	.382

1997 Season

	Avg	AB	H	2B	3B	HR	RBI	BB	SO	OBP	SLG		Avg	AB	H	2B	3B	HR	RBI	BB	SO	OBP	SLG
None on/out	.217	198	43	13	2	3	3	17	28	.292	.348	vs. NL	.239	507	121	26	7	11	38	60	77	.325	.383

1997 By Position

Position	Avg	AB	H	2B	3B	HR	RBI	BB	SO	OBP	SLG	G	GS	Innings	PO	A	E	DP	Fld Pct	Rng Fctr	In Zone	Outs	Zone Rtg	MLB Zone
As cf	.239	556	133	32	7	10	39	64	82	.323	.376	148	138	1222.0	308	4	4	2	.987	2.30	358	299	835	815

Last Five Years

	Avg	AB	H	2B	3B	HR	RBI	BB	SO	OBP	SLG		Avg	AB	H	2B	3B	HR	RBI	BB	SO	OBP	SLG
vs. Left	.305	775	236	42	10	14	77	41	100	.345	.439	First Pitch	.353	436	154	18	4	9	44	9	0	.375	.475
vs. Right	.260	2054	535	110	24	42	189	235	332	.342	.399	Ahead in Count	.304	598	182	36	13	17	78	118	0	.422	.493
Groundball	.282	606	171	33	6	10	56	60	95	.356	.406	Behind in Count	.225	1192	268	50	11	20	75	0	359	.236	.336
Flyball	.256	492	126	22	4	13	35	44	79	.327	.396	Two Strikes	.208	1271	264	61	12	19	90	149	432	.298	.319
Home	.285	1426	406	76	19	28	152	141	208	.355	.424	Batting #1	.273	1865	509	106	20	39	154	175	286	.342	.414
Away	.260	1403	365	76	15	28	114	135	224	.331	.396	Batting #2	.274	771	211	36	11	12	85	76	119	.344	.396
Day	.274	1259	345	69	18	25	122	128	183	.348	.417	Other	.264	193	51	10	3	5	27	25	27	.348	.425
Night	.271	1570	426	83	16	31	144	148	249	.339	.404	March/April	.271	406	110	24	7	5	35	36	53	.333	.401
Grass	.275	1847	508	96	22	40	163	180	280	.347	.416	May	.301	529	159	38	9	4	39	50	79	.363	.429
Turf	.268	982	263	56	12	16	103	96	152	.336	.398	June	.251	546	137	22	5	9	54	56	79	.328	.359
Pre-All Star	.277	1642	455	95	23	22	142	155	238	.344	.403	July	.283	519	147	31	7	11	50	53	83	.357	.434
Post-All Star	.266	1187	316	57	11	34	124	121	194	.341	.419	August	.297	454	135	22	4	14	51	53	69	.378	.456
Scoring Posn	.266	582	155	28	7	9	207	91	100	.368	.385	Sept/Oct	.221	375	83	15	2	13	37	28	69	.282	.376
Close & Late	.268	456	122	26	6	10	51	56	70	.353	.417	vs. AL	.278	1118	311	56	15	16	114	96	179	.339	.398
None on/out	.279	965	269	62	12	16	16	80	140	.340	.418	vs. NL	.269	1711	460	96	19	40	152	180	253	.346	.417

Batter vs. Pitcher (career)

Hits Best Against	Avg	AB	H	2B	3B	HR	RBI	BB	SO	OBP	SLG	Hits Worst Against	Avg	AB	H	2B	3B	HR	RBI	BB	SO	OBP	SLG
Larry Casian	.636	11	7	2	0	0	0	0	1	.636	.818	Kirk Rueter	.000	11	0	0	0	0	0	0	1	.000	.000
Jerry Dipoto	.545	11	6	1	0	1	4	1	3	.583	.909	Jon Lieber	.000	11	0	0	0	0	0	2	1	.154	.000
Brian Bohanon	.538	13	7	2	1	0	2	0	0	.538	.846	Danny Darwin	.040	25	1	0	0	1	1	1	5	.077	.160
Mark Gardner	.500	12	6	1	1	1	1	0	0	.500	1.000	Ricky Bones	.050	20	1	0	0	1	2	2	1	.130	.050
Allen Watson	.455	11	5	3	0	1	8	1	1	.500	1.000	Curt Leskanic	.091	11	1	0	0	0	0	0	0	.091	.091

Pat Meares — Twins
Age 29 – Bats Right (groundball hitter)

	Avg	G	AB	R	H	2B	3B	HR	RBI	BB	SO	HBP	GDP	SB	CS	OBP	SLG	IBB	SH	SF	#Pit	#P/PA	GB	FB	G/F
1997 Season	.276	134	439	63	121	23	3	10	60	18	86	16	9	7	7	.323	.410	0	3	7	1690	3.50	155	128	1.21
Career (1993-1997)	.267	593	1921	248	512	94	18	32	233	71	346	39	58	35	21	.303	.384	1	21	25	7092	3.41	709	557	1.27

1997 Season

	Avg	AB	H	2B	3B	HR	RBI	BB	SO	OBP	SLG		Avg	AB	H	2B	3B	HR	RBI	BB	SO	OBP	SLG
vs. Left	.182	99	18	5	0	1	12	2	19	.243	.263	First Pitch	.298	47	14	0	0	2	3	0	0	.340	.298
vs. Right	.303	340	103	18	3	9	48	16	67	.347	.453	Ahead in Count	.364	88	32	6	1	4	20	7	0	.418	.591
Groundball	.234	94	22	7	0	1	8	4	21	.294	.340	Behind in Count	.223	220	49	12	1	5	26	0	74	.254	.355
Flyball	.293	58	17	1	0	3	11	1	2	.328	.466	Two Strikes	.221	204	45	13	1	5	25	11	86	.289	.368
Home	.244	246	60	12	2	5	33	10	47	.288	.370	Batting #8	.322	118	38	9	1	3	19	4	20	.362	.492
Away	.316	193	61	11	1	5	27	8	39	.366	.461	Batting #9	.261	280	73	13	2	7	36	13	54	.315	.396
Day	.280	132	37	7	1	3	20	3	21	.322	.417	Other	.244	41	10	1	0	0	5	1	12	.267	.268
Night	.274	307	84	16	2	7	40	15	65	.323	.407	March/April	.272	81	22	5	1	3	11	3	15	.322	.469
Grass	.343	166	57	10	1	5	26	7	28	.388	.506	May	.304	79	24	7	0	2	14	4	14	.345	.468
Turf	.234	273	64	13	2	5	34	11	58	.283	.352	June	.284	81	23	5	1	2	10	4	17	.344	.444
Pre-All Star	.276	261	72	18	2	8	38	13	50	.328	.452	July	.256	86	22	4	0	1	9	3	18	.309	.337
Post-All Star	.275	178	49	5	1	2	22	5	36	.316	.348	August	.234	47	11	1	1	0	6	1	8	.265	.298
Scoring Posn	.307	114	35	8	1	4	51	6	27	.338	.500	Sept/Oct	.292	65	19	1	0	2	10	3	14	.329	.400
Close & Late	.328	58	19	1	1	2	9	2	16	.365	.483	vs. AL	.270	389	105	20	2	9	50	15	76	.315	.401
None on/out	.255	98	25	5	1	1	1	5	14	.324	.357	vs. NL	.320	50	16	3	1	1	10	3	10	.382	.480

1997 By Position

Position	Avg	AB	H	2B	3B	HR	RBI	BB	SO	OBP	SLG	G	GS	Innings	PO	A	E	DP	Fld Pct	Rng Fctr	In Zone	Outs	Zone Rtg	MLB Zone
As ss	.277	437	121	23	3	10	59	18	85	.324	.412	134	129	1131.1	212	415	20	93	.969	4.99	463	426	920	937

Career (1993-1997)

	Avg	AB	H	2B	3B	HR	RBI	BB	SO	OBP	SLG		Avg	AB	H	2B	3B	HR	RBI	BB	SO	OBP	SLG
vs. Left	.243	515	125	23	3	10	60	18	99	.281	.357	First Pitch	.313	294	92	16	1	5	29	1	0	.336	.425
vs. Right	.275	1406	387	71	15	22	173	53	247	.311	.394	Ahead in Count	.347	380	132	28	9	8	71	33	0	.400	.532
Groundball	.271	447	121	23	2	5	55	20	78	.315	.365	Behind in Count	.207	935	194	35	5	12	87	0	309	.226	.294
Flyball	.254	299	76	17	1	7	34	9	57	.290	.388	Two Strikes	.186	861	160	29	3	12	74	37	346	.237	.268
Home	.260	977	254	46	11	11	114	31	169	.291	.363	Batting #8	.294	354	104	20	4	8	50	14	60	.329	.441
Away	.273	944	258	48	7	21	119	40	177	.315	.406	Batting #9	.253	1239	314	55	12	17	140	51	221	.293	.358
Day	.260	549	143	25	6	10	62	14	108	.288	.383	Other	.287	328	94	19	2	7	43	6	65	.311	.421
Night	.269	1372	369	69	12	22	171	57	238	.308	.385	March/April	.284	236	67	11	4	6	39	16	50	.340	.441
Grass	.280	768	215	42	7	17	96	33	123	.320	.419	May	.282	344	97	23	2	6	41	12	68	.311	.413
Turf	.258	1153	297	52	11	15	137	38	223	.290	.361	June	.293	372	109	23	3	9	44	11	69	.320	.444
Pre-All Star	.277	1044	289	62	9	22	134	45	207	.313	.417	July	.239	380	91	19	3	2	32	13	76	.276	.321
Post-All Star	.254	877	223	32	9	10	99	26	139	.290	.345	August	.244	299	73	8	4	3	34	9	40	.283	.328
Scoring Posn	.272	486	132	25	6	12	198	30	103	.308	.422	Sept/Oct	.259	290	75	10	2	6	43	10	43	.294	.369
Close & Late	.319	238	76	17	2	4	36	9	52	.352	.458	vs. AL	.265	1871	496	91	17	31	223	68	336	.300	.382
None on/out	.266	455	121	21	2	8	8	17	70	.306	.374	vs. NL	.320	50	16	3	1	1	10	3	10	.382	.480

Batter vs. Pitcher (career)

Hits Best Against	Avg	AB	H	2B	3B	HR	RBI	BB	SO	OBP	SLG	Hits Worst Against	Avg	AB	H	2B	3B	HR	RBI	BB	SO	OBP	SLG
Bob Wickman	.500	16	8	2	0	0	5	3	0	.600	.625	Pat Hentgen	.059	17	1	0	0	0	0	0	6	.059	.059
Ken Hill	.435	23	10	1	0	2	3	1	3	.458	.739	Wilson Alvarez	.063	16	1	0	0	0	1	0	4	.063	.063
Bob Wolcott	.417	12	5	1	0	1	4	0	1	.385	.750	Scott Erickson	.071	14	1	0	0	0	0	0	7	.071	.071
Todd Stottlemyre	.357	14	5	1	0	1	3	0	4	.357	.643	Alex Fernandez	.083	12	1	0	0	0	0	0	1	.083	.083
Scott Karl	.316	19	6	2	1	1	5	0	1	.300	.684	Angel Miranda	.091	11	1	0	0	0	3	0	3	.083	.091

Jim Mecir — Yankees
Age 28 – Pitches Right

	ERA	W	L	Sv	G	GS	IP	BB	SO	Avg	H	2B	3B	HR	RBI	OBP	SLG	GF	IR	IRS	Hld	SvOp	SB	CS	GB	FB	G/F
1997 Season	5.88	0	4	0	25	0	33.2	10	25	.279	36	7	0	5	26	.338	.450	11	35	9	1	1	3	3	54	27	2.00
Career (1995-1997)	5.15	1	5	0	53	0	78.2	35	66	.276	83	15	2	11	66	.350	.449	22	65	25	1	1	8	3	105	73	1.44

1997 Season

	ERA	W	L	Sv	G	GS	IP	H	HR	BB	SO		Avg	AB	H	2B	3B	HR	RBI	BB	SO	OBP	SLG
Home	7.36	0	2	0	12	0	14.2	16	2	7	10	vs. Left	.175	40	7	1	0	2	7	3	11	.233	.350
Away	4.74	0	2	0	13	0	19.0	20	3	3	15	vs. Right	.326	89	29	6	0	3	19	7	14	.384	.494
Starter	0.00	0	0	0	0	0	0.0	0	0	0	0	Scoring Posn	.385	39	15	3	0	2	21	6	6	.468	.615
Reliever	5.88	0	4	0	25	0	33.2	36	5	10	25	Close & Late	.440	25	11	2	0	1	6	4	6	.533	.640
0 Days rest (Relief)	15.19	0	2	0	6	0	5.1	10	1	5	2	None on/out	.185	27	5	1	0	1	2	7	.241	.333
1 or 2 Days rest	3.06	0	1	0	10	0	17.2	15	2	3	12	First Pitch	.385	13	5	1	0	2	0	0	.385	.462
3+ Days rest	5.91	0	1	0	9	0	10.2	11	2	2	11	Ahead in Count	.176	51	9	1	0	2	10	0	17	.204	.314
Pre-All Star	6.43	0	4	0	20	0	28.0	34	5	7	20	Behind in Count	.375	32	12	3	0	2	7	4	0	.444	.656
Post-All Star	3.18	0	0	0	5	0	5.2	2	0	3	5	Two Strikes	.213	61	13	3	0	2	14	5	25	.290	.361

Roberto Mejia — Cardinals
Age 26 – Bats Right

	Avg	G	AB	R	H	2B	3B	HR	RBI	BB	SO	HBP	GDP	SB	CS	OBP	SLG	IBB	SH	SF	#Pit	#P/PA	GB	FB	G/F
1997 Season	.071	7	14	0	1	1	0	0	2	0	5	0	0	0	0	.067	.143	0	1	1	63	3.94	5	5	1.00
Career (1993-1997)	.219	133	411	47	90	24	6	10	40	28	118	2	4	7	3	.270	.380	3	5	4	1677	3.73	118	116	1.02

1997 Season

	Avg	AB	H	2B	3B	HR	RBI	BB	SO	OBP	SLG		Avg	AB	H	2B	3B	HR	RBI	BB	SO	OBP	SLG
vs. Left	.167	6	1	1	0	0	1	0	2	.167	.333	Scoring Posn	.500	2	1	1	0	0	2	0	0	.333	1.000
vs. Right	.000	8	0	0	0	0	1	0	3	.000	.000	Close & Late	.000	6	0	0	0	0	0	0	3	.000	.000

Career (1993-1997)

	Avg	AB	H	2B	3B	HR	RBI	BB	SO	OBP	SLG		Avg	AB	H	2B	3B	HR	RBI	BB	SO	OBP	SLG
vs. Left	.223	103	23	5	3	3	14	8	28	.277	.417	First Pitch	.391	46	18	7	0	2	4	2	0	.420	.674
vs. Right	.218	308	67	19	3	7	26	20	90	.267	.367	Ahead in Count	.328	64	21	2	2	5	11	15	0	.444	.656
Groundball	.199	151	30	4	3	1	11	10	45	.248	.285	Behind in Count	.145	221	32	9	3	1	11	0	99	.148	.226
Flyball	.173	81	14	6	0	1	5	6	23	.230	.284	Two Strikes	.123	227	28	10	2	0	12	11	118	.163	.185
Home	.246	203	50	12	5	5	28	16	52	.302	.429	Batting #2	.233	116	27	7	3	1	9	9	36	.291	.371
Away	.192	208	40	12	1	5	12	12	66	.236	.332	Batting #8	.225	267	60	17	3	9	30	16	69	.268	.412
Day	.216	162	35	11	1	7	20	17	41	.291	.426	Other	.107	28	3	0	0	0	1	3	13	.194	.107
Night	.221	249	55	13	5	3	20	11	77	.255	.349	March/April	.188	85	16	5	1	2	13	4	22	.228	.341
Grass	.234	304	71	18	6	9	36	21	88	.284	.421	May	.230	87	20	5	0	3	7	11	28	.313	.391
Turf	.178	107	19	6	0	1	4	7	30	.228	.262	June	.100	10	1	0	0	0	0	0	5	.100	.100
Pre-All Star	.203	182	37	10	1	5	20	15	55	.264	.352	July	.258	62	16	5	3	1	8	5	16	.319	.484
Post-All Star	.231	229	53	14	5	5	20	13	63	.275	.402	August	.193	88	17	2	0	1	5	4	30	.228	.250
Scoring Posn	.153	98	15	8	1	0	25	10	32	.237	.255	Sept/Oct	.253	79	20	7	2	3	7	4	17	.289	.506
Close & Late	.270	63	17	8	2	1	6	4	19	.313	.508	vs. AL	.000	0	0	0	0	0	0	0	0	.000	.000
None on/out	.250	104	26	8	3	2	2	1	20	.257	.442	vs. NL	.219	411	90	24	6	10	40	28	118	.270	.380

Batter vs. Pitcher (career)

Hits Best Against	Avg	AB	H	2B	3B	HR	RBI	BB	SO	OBP	SLG	Hits Worst Against	Avg	AB	H	2B	3B	HR	RBI	BB	SO	OBP	SLG
												Danny Jackson	.182	11	2	0	0	0	1	2	2	.308	.182

Carlos Mendoza — Mets
Age 23 – Bats Left

	Avg	G	AB	R	H	2B	3B	HR	RBI	BB	SO	HBP	GDP	SB	CS	OBP	SLG	IBB	SH	SF	#Pit	#P/PA	GB	FB	G/F
1997 Season	.250	15	12	6	3	0	0	0	1	4	2	2	0	0	0	.500	.250	0	0	0	65	3.61	6	2	3.00

1997 Season

	Avg	AB	H	2B	3B	HR	RBI	BB	SO	OBP	SLG		Avg	AB	H	2B	3B	HR	RBI	BB	SO	OBP	SLG
vs. Left	.250	4	1	0	0	0	1	0	1	.500	.250	Scoring Posn	.000	1	0	0	0	0	1	1	0	.667	.000
vs. Right	.250	8	2	0	0	0	0	4	1	.500	.250	Close & Late	.000	3	0	0	0	0	0	2	1	.400	.000

Ramiro Mendoza — Yankees
Age 26 – Pitches Right (groundball pitcher)

	ERA	W	L	Sv	G	GS	IP	BB	SO	Avg	H	2B	3B	HR	RBI	OBP	SLG	GF	IR	IRS	Hld	SvOp	SB	CS	GB	FB	G/F
1997 Season	4.24	8	6	2	39	15	133.2	28	82	.292	157	34	2	15	64	.330	.447	9	8	3	4	4	8	2	251	104	2.41
Career (1996-1997)	4.97	12	11	2	51	26	186.2	38	116	.308	237	60	2	20	101	.345	.469	9	8	3	4	4	15	2	368	143	2.57

1997 Season

	ERA	W	L	Sv	G	GS	IP	H	HR	BB	SO		Avg	AB	H	2B	3B	HR	RBI	BB	SO	OBP	SLG
Home	3.67	3	4	1	20	8	76.0	78	7	14	44	vs. Left	.300	250	75	13	1	7	25	17	33	.344	.444
Away	4.99	5	2	1	19	7	57.2	79	8	14	38	vs. Right	.286	287	82	21	1	8	39	11	49	.318	.449
Day	4.83	3	4	2	18	5	63.1	70	7	17	33	Inning 1-6	.285	417	119	25	2	14	54	24	64	.325	.456
Night	3.71	5	2	0	21	10	70.1	87	8	11	49	Inning 7+	.317	120	38	9	0	1	10	4	18	.349	.417

1997 Season

	ERA	W	L	Sv	G	GS	IP	H	HR	BB	SO		Avg	AB	H	2B	3B	HR	RBI	BB	SO	OBP	SLG
Grass	3.97	7	5	2	34	13	115.2	133	12	22	71	None on	.281	295	83	21	1	9	9	17	53	.327	.451
Turf	6.00	1	1	0	5	2	18.0	24	3	6	11	Runners on	.306	242	74	13	1	6	55	11	29	.335	.442
March/April	6.89	1	1	0	3	3	15.2	22	0	7	13	Scoring Posn	.274	135	37	9	0	3	46	7	15	.309	.407
May	4.71	2	1	0	6	5	28.2	39	4	3	18	Close & Late	.362	47	17	4	0	0	5	1	8	.388	.447
June	4.05	0	0	0	6	1	13.1	12	2	3	8	vs. 1st Batr (relief)	.273	22	6	0	0	1	4	1	4	.292	.409
July	2.67	0	2	1	7	2	27.0	26	3	7	14	1st Inning Pitched	.259	143	37	7	1	1	15	4	17	.285	.343
August	5.76	2	1	0	9	1	25.0	35	4	3	13	First 15 Pitches	.261	134	35	6	1	2	12	4	20	.284	.366
Sept/Oct	2.25	3	1	0	8	3	24.0	23	2	5	16	Pitch 16-30	.228	114	26	7	0	1	10	2	21	.248	.316
Starter	4.93	5	5	0	15	15	87.2	110	11	23	59	Pitch 31-45	.354	79	28	7	1	4	10	6	14	.402	.620
Reliever	2.93	3	1	2	24	0	46.0	47	4	5	23	Pitch 46+	.324	210	68	14	0	8	32	16	27	.374	.505
0 Days rest (Relief)	1.32	2	0	0	4	0	13.2	8	1	1	4	First Pitch	.329	85	28	6	0	4	16	1	0	.348	.541
1 or 2 Days rest	4.42	1	1	2	10	0	18.1	29	2	3	9	Ahead in Count	.229	258	59	13	1	4	23	0	71	.232	.333
3+ Days rest	2.57	0	0	0	10	0	14.0	10	1	1	10	Behind in Count	.356	104	37	7	1	5	18	17	0	.447	.587
vs. AL	4.51	8	5	2	35	14	121.2	147	14	28	73	None on/out	.242	231	56	17	1	5	21	10	62	.275	.390
vs. NL	1.50	0	1	0	4	1	12.0	10	1	0	9												
Pre-All Star	4.60	3	4	0	17	11	72.1	87	7	17	48	Pre-All Star	.298	292	87	17	1	7	36	17	48	.339	.435
Post-All Star	3.82	5	2	2	22	4	61.1	70	8	11	34	Post-All Star	.286	245	70	17	1	8	28	11	34	.320	.461

Paul Menhart — Padres

Age 29 – Pitches Right (groundball pitcher)

	ERA	W	L	Sv	G	GS	IP	BB	SO	Avg	H	2B	3B	HR	RBI	OBP	SLG	CG	ShO	Sup	QS	#P/S	SB	CS	GB	FB	G/F
1997 Season	4.70	2	3	0	9	8	44.0	13	22	.256	42	10	1	6	21	.309	.439	0	0	4.70	3	79	3	3	68	45	1.51
Career (1995-1997)	5.47	5	9	0	41	23	164.2	85	90	.272	169	35	7	24	98	.364	.466	1	0	4.37	8	89	9	6	254	153	1.66

1997 Season

	ERA	W	L	Sv	G	GS	IP	H	HR	BB	SO		Avg	AB	H	2B	3B	HR	RBI	BB	SO	OBP	SLG
Home	4.55	2	1	0	5	5	27.2	25	2	9	14	vs. Left	.250	72	18	4	1	1	8	8	7	.321	.375
Away	4.96	0	2	0	4	3	16.1	17	4	4	8	vs. Right	.261	92	24	6	0	5	13	5	15	.299	.489

Orlando Merced — Blue Jays

Age 31 – Bats Left (groundball hitter)

	Avg	G	AB	R	H	2B	3B	HR	RBI	BB	SO	HBP	GDP	SB	CS	OBP	SLG	IBB	SH	SF	#Pit	#P/PA	GB	FB	G/F
1997 Season	.266	98	368	45	98	23	2	9	40	47	62	3	6	7	3	.352	.413	1	0	2	1597	3.80	132	97	1.36
Last Five Years	.289	595	2141	305	619	123	14	58	324	269	332		6	50	29	13	.368	.441	30	0	14	9019	3.71	845	607	1.39

1997 Season

	Avg	AB	H	2B	3B	HR	RBI	BB	SO	OBP	SLG		Avg	AB	H	2B	3B	HR	RBI	BB	SO	OBP	SLG
vs. Left	.223	121	27	5	0	4	18	14	26	.312	.364	First Pitch	.229	35	8	2	1	0	3	1	0	.256	.343
vs. Right	.287	247	71	18	2	5	22	33	36	.372	.437	Ahead in Count	.304	102	31	9	0	3	21	28	0	.454	.480
Groundball	.274	62	17	3	0	0	6	8	10	.366	.323	Behind in Count	.200	155	31	8	1	1	8	0	51	.205	.284
Flyball	.242	62	15	5	0	2	7	5	12	.299	.419	Two Strikes	.196	153	30	6	1	5	12	18	62	.281	.346
Home	.307	192	59	15	2	3	22	31	26	.409	.453	Batting #2	.279	215	60	11	1	6	24	30	32	.371	.423
Away	.222	176	39	8	0	6	18	16	36	.287	.369	Batting #3	.252	151	38	12	1	3	16	16	30	.321	.404
Day	.277	130	36	9	2	1	9	13	27	.340	.400	Other	.000	2	0	0	0	0	0	1	0	.500	.000
Night	.261	238	62	14	0	8	31	34	35	.359	.420	March/April	.258	89	23	8	1	3	13	10	17	.330	.472
Grass	.233	146	34	6	0	6	17	12	28	.292	.397	May	.243	107	26	6	0	3	11	8	21	.296	.383
Turf	.288	222	64	17	2	3	23	35	34	.390	.423	June	.352	88	31	7	1	1	11	14	8	.442	.489
Pre-All Star	.282	309	87	21	2	8	36	34	49	.353	.440	July	.214	84	18	2	0	2	5	15	16	.347	.310
Post-All Star	.186	59	11	2	0	1	4	13	13	.351	.271	August	.000	0	0	0	0	0	0	0	0	.000	.000
Scoring Posn	.205	88	18	3	1	0	25	20	14	.351	.261	Sept/Oct	.000	0	0	0	0	0	0	1	0	.000	.000
Close & Late	.211	57	12	2	0	4	14	14	11	.366	.246	vs. AL	.266	334	89	21	2	9	39	40	57	.348	.422
None on/out	.294	68	20	3	0	2	5	12		.351	.324	vs. NL	.265	34	9	2	0	0	1	7	5	.390	.324

1997 By Position

Position	Avg	AB	H	2B	3B	HR	RBI	BB	SO	OBP	SLG	G	GS	Innings	PO	A	E	DP	Fld Pct	Rng Fctr	In Zone	Zone Outs	Zone Rtg	MLB Zone
As rf	.269	360	97	23	2	9	40	46	61	.355	.419	96		827.0	190	10	3	4	.985	2.18	220	187	.850	.813

Last Five Years

	Avg	AB	H	2B	3B	HR	RBI	BB	SO	OBP	SLG		Avg	AB	H	2B	3B	HR	RBI	BB	SO	OBP	SLG
vs. Left	.256	562	144	28	6	14	85	70	109	.339	.402	First Pitch	.316	269	85	14	2	7	46	27	0	.373	.461
vs. Right	.301	1579	475	95	8	44	239	199	223	.378	.455	Ahead in Count	.344	573	197	44	6	23	126	128	0	.461	.542
Groundball	.264	622	164	21	1	11	76	57	102	.325	.354	Behind in Count	.230	895	206	42	5	12	92	0	272	.233	.328
Flyball	.267	337	90	19	1	13	55	46	60	.353	.445	Two Strikes	.207	893	185	37	5	20	101	114	332	.297	.327
Home	.297	1045	310	70	6	27	147	144	153	.383	.453	Batting #3	.259	800	207	42	4	18	103	97	129	.337	.389
Away	.282	1096	309	53	8	31	177	125	179	.354	.430	Batting #4	.316	554	175	31	2	21	107	73	75	.395	.493
Day	.279	620	173	39	4	9	74	80	115	.360	.398	Other	.301	787	237	50	8	19	114	99	128	.381	.457
Night	.293	1521	446	84	10	49	250	189	217	.371	.458	March/April	.272	327	89	20	2	9	46	46	64	.363	.428
Grass	.276	729	201	30	5	23	131	84	119	.349	.425	May	.305	384	117	22	1	9	51	45	66	.376	.438
Turf	.296	1412	418	93	9	35	193	185	213	.378	.449	June	.305	466	142	26	4	14	72	55	60	.380	.468
Pre-All Star	.303	1335	404	79	8	38	195	162	215	.378	.459	July	.289	461	133	29	3	17	64	50	70	.359	.475
Post-All Star	.267	806	215	44	6	20	129	107	117	.351	.411	August	.278	263	73	20	0	7	44	38	35	.366	.433
Scoring Posn	.301	595	179	35	5	18	258	110	85	.403	.467	Sept/Oct	.271	240	65	6	4	2	44	35	37	.358	.354
Close & Late	.282	347	98	19	0	11	59	59	65	.384	.432	vs. AL	.266	334	89	21	2	9	39	40	57	.348	.422
None on/out	.297	427	127	26	1	12	12	44	77	.342	.444	vs. NL	.293	1807	530	102	12	49	285	229	275	.372	.444

Batter vs. Pitcher (career)

Hits Best Against	Avg	AB	H	2B	3B	HR	RBI	BB	SO	OBP	SLG	Hits Worst Against	Avg	AB	H	2B	3B	HR	RBI	BB	SO	OBP	SLG
Paul Quantrill	.615	13	8	2	1	1	3	1	1	.643	1.154	Steve Trachsel	.000	15	0	0	0	0	0	0	2	.000	.000

Batter vs. Pitcher (career)

Hits Best Against	Avg	AB	H	2B	3B	HR	RBI	BB	SO	OBP	SLG	Hits Worst Against	Avg	AB	H	2B	3B	HR	RBI	BB	SO	OBP	SLG
Xavier Hernandez	.600	10	6	1	0	1	2	2	2	.667	1.000	Pedro Astacio	.000	10	0	0	0	0	0	1	3	.091	.000
Armando Reynoso	.563	16	9	2	0	2	8	1	2	.588	1.063	Pete Schourek	.083	12	1	1	0	0	1	0	1	.083	.167
Jeff Brantley	.556	9	5	1	0	0	2	7	1	.750	.667	Jeff Fassero	.091	22	2	1	0	0	0	2	7	.167	.136
Shawn Boskie	.500	16	8	1	1	2	4	1	3	.529	1.063	Bill Swift	.125	16	2	1	0	0	0	0	1	.125	.188

Henry Mercedes — Rangers
Age 28 – Bats Right (groundball hitter)

	Avg	G	AB	R	H	2B	3B	HR	RBI	BB	SO	HBP	GDP	SB	CS	OBP	SLG	IBB	SH	SF	#Pit	#P/PA	GB	FB	G/F
1997 Season	.213	23	47	4	10	4	0	0	4	6	25	0	0	0	0	.302	.298	0	3	0	206	3.68	8	9	0.89
Last Five Years	.227	70	141	17	32	8	0	0	16	16	54	2	0	1	1	.311	.284	0	4	2	625	3.79	43	26	1.65

1997 Season

	Avg	AB	H	2B	3B	HR	RBI	BB	SO	OBP	SLG		Avg	AB	H	2B	3B	HR	RBI	BB	SO	OBP	SLG
vs. Left	.400	15	6	1	0	0	2	2	5	.471	.467	Scoring Posn	.188	16	3	1	0	0	4	2	9	.278	.250
vs. Right	.125	32	4	3	0	0	2	4	20	.222	.219	Close & Late	.000	5	0	0	0	0	0	1	2	.167	.000

Jose Mercedes — Brewers
Age 27 – Pitches Right

	ERA	W	L	Sv	G	GS	IP	BB	SO	Avg	H	2B	3B	HR	RBI	OBP	SLG	CG	ShO	Sup	QS	#P/S	SB	CS	GB	FB	G/F
1997 Season	3.79	7	10	0	29	23	159.0	53	80	.248	146	26	2	24	70	.314	.422	2	1	4.42	9	95	9	7	213	186	1.15
Career (1994-1997)	4.21	9	13	0	64	23	214.0	82	103	.253	200	34	3	35	107	.326	.437	2	1	4.88	9	95	11	8	291	254	1.15

1997 Season

	ERA	W	L	Sv	G	GS	IP	H	HR	BB	SO		Avg	AB	H	2B	3B	HR	RBI	BB	SO	OBP	SLG
Home	2.74	4	4	0	15	10	75.2	67	10	20	39	vs. Left	.278	313	87	21	1	12	35	34	36	.348	.466
Away	4.75	3	6	0	14	13	83.1	79	14	33	41	vs. Right	.215	275	59	5	1	12	35	19	44	.275	.371
Day	2.45	3	3	0	12	8	62.1	45	10	18	31	Inning 1-6	.256	493	126	22	2	20	62	47	69	.323	.430
Night	4.66	4	7	0	17	15	96.2	101	14	35	49	Inning 7+	.211	95	20	4	0	4	8	6	11	.265	.379
Grass	3.57	6	8	0	25	19	133.2	120	21	45	69	None on	.241	365	88	17	1	15	15	34	46	.309	.416
Turf	4.97	1	2	0	4	4	25.1	26	3	8	11	Runners on	.260	223	58	9	1	9	55	19	34	.321	.430
March/April	5.25	1	0	0	5	0	12.0	12	5	7	10	Scoring Posn	.221	122	27	4	0	4	41	8	23	.277	.352
May	4.74	0	1	0	5	4	24.2	24	3	8	12	Close & Late	.243	37	9	2	0	1	3	1	8	.263	.378
June	4.35	2	2	0	5	5	31.0	32	5	11	12	None on/out	.281	160	45	10	0	7	7	11	19	.331	.475
July	4.06	1	3	0	5	5	31.0	28	3	8	13	vs. 1st Batr (relief)	.500	6	3	1	0	1	2	0	1	.500	1.167
August	2.52	2	2	0	6	6	39.1	34	4	14	23	1st Inning Pitched	.286	112	32	8	0	6	18	14	19	.362	.518
Sept/Oct	3.00	1	2	0	3	3	21.0	16	4	5	10	First 75 Pitches	.256	464	119	24	2	18	57	43	66	.322	.433
Starter	3.69	6	10	0	23	23	146.1	134	19	45	69	Pitch 76-90	.212	66	14	1	0	3	6	7	10	.289	.364
Reliever	4.97	1	0	0	6	0	12.2	12	5	8	11	Pitch 91-105	.213	47	10	0	0	2	5	3	2	.275	.340
0-3 Days Rest (Start)	0.00	0	0	0	1	1	7.0	2	0	2	6	Pitch 106+	.273	11	3	1	0	1	2	0	2	.273	.636
4 Days Rest	3.83	5	7	0	15	15	91.2	89	14	30	42	First Pitch	.323	93	30	7	0	3	14	1	0	.354	.495
5+ Days Rest	3.97	1	3	0	7	7	47.2	43	5	13	21	Ahead in Count	.160	256	41	8	0	6	18	0	70	.160	.262
vs. AL	3.81	7	8	0	26	20	139.1	124	22	48	70	Behind in Count	.301	113	34	8	2	9	19	28	0	.437	.646
vs. NL	3.66	0	2	0	3	3	19.2	22	2	5	10	Two Strikes	.176	250	44	7	0	5	16	24	80	.248	.264
Pre-All Star	4.72	3	4	0	16	10	74.1	72	14	28	37	Pre-All Star	.261	276	72	14	2	14	38	28	37	.330	.478
Post-All Star	2.98	4	6	0	13	13	84.2	74	10	25	43	Post-All Star	.237	312	74	12	0	10	32	25	43	.299	.372

Kent Mercker — Reds
Age 30 – Pitches Left (flyball pitcher)

	ERA	W	L	Sv	G	GS	IP	BB	SO	Avg	H	2B	3B	HR	RBI	OBP	SLG	CG	ShO	Sup	QS	#P/S	SB	CS	GB	FB	G/F
1997 Season	3.92	8	11	0	28	25	144.2	62	75	.250	135	25	4	16	53	.328	.401	0	3	3.86	13	86	14	5	176	192	0.92
Last Five Years	4.15	31	30	0	144	86	535.2	242	376	.248	500	94	13	63	231	.329	.402	2	1	4.57	38	89	46	17	628	650	0.97

1997 Season

	ERA	W	L	Sv	G	GS	IP	H	HR	BB	SO		Avg	AB	H	2B	3B	HR	RBI	BB	SO	OBP	SLG
Home	3.58	4	5	0	13	12	70.1	68	10	24	36	vs. Left	.269	134	36	6	1	3	14	11	13	.327	.396
Away	4.24	4	6	0	15	13	74.1	67	6	38	39	vs. Right	.244	405	99	19	3	13	39	51	62	.328	.402
Day	4.91	0	3	0	9	7	40.1	43	5	22	21	Inning 1-6	.253	509	129	23	3	16	50	57	72	.329	.405
Night	3.54	8	8	0	19	18	104.1	92	11	40	54	Inning 7+	.200	30	6	2	1	0	3	5	3	.314	.333
Grass	4.89	3	4	0	11	9	49.2	51	4	25	25	None on	.255	314	80	15	1	12	12	36	43	.335	.424
Turf	3.41	5	7	0	17	16	95.0	84	12	37	50	Runners on	.244	225	55	10	3	4	41	26	32	.318	.369
March/April	5.75	1	3	0	6	3	20.1	25	1	12	12	Scoring Posn	.186	118	22	5	2	1	34	18	18	.286	.288
May	3.29	1	2	0	5	5	27.1	22	2	13	10	Close & Late	.111	9	1	1	0	0	0	4	0	.385	.222
June	1.96	4	0	0	6	6	41.1	29	4	16	20	None on/out	.252	139	35	8	0	6	6	16	13	.329	.439
July	5.40	1	2	0	4	4	21.2	26	5	9	14	vs. 1st Batr (relief)	.333	3	1	0	0	0	1	0	1	.333	.333
August	5.21	1	2	0	4	4	19.0	17	2	9	10	1st Inning Pitched	.255	102	26	8	0	1	12	16	14	.352	.363
Sept/Oct	4.20	0	2	0	3	3	15.0	16	2	3	9	First 75 Pitches	.252	441	111	21	3	14	47	47	65	.324	.408
Starter	4.03	7	11	0	25	25	140.2	132	16	58	73	Pitch 76-90	.254	67	17	2	1	2	5	9	6	.342	.403
Reliever	0.00	1	0	0	3	0	4.0	3	0	4	2	Pitch 91-105	.233	30	7	2	0	0	1	5	4	.343	.300
0-3 Days Rest (Start)	0.00	0	0	0	0	0	0.0	0	0	0	0	Pitch 106+	.000	1	0	0	0	0	0	1	0	.500	.000
4 Days Rest	2.73	4	3	0	10	10	59.1	45	5	20	25	First Pitch	.351	77	27	5	1	1	10	3	0	.351	.481
5+ Days Rest	4.98	3	8	0	15	15	81.1	87	11	38	48	Ahead in Count	.220	259	57	13	0	4	19	0	68	.222	.317
vs. AL	1.80	2	0	0	2	2	15.0	11	2	2	3	Behind in Count	.248	121	30	4	3	8	17	38	0	.425	.529
vs. NL	4.16	6	11	0	26	23	129.2	124	14	60	72	Two Strikes	.190	248	47	9	0	5	17	21	75	.252	.286
Pre-All Star	3.19	6	6	0	18	15	96.0	80	7	44	45	Pre-All Star	.232	345	80	17	2	7	28	44	45	.320	.354
Post-All Star	5.36	2	5	0	10	10	48.2	55	9	18	30	Post-All Star	.284	194	55	8	2	9	25	18	30	.343	.485

	ERA	W	L	Sv	G	GS	IP	H	HR	BB	SO
Home	4.39	14	14	0	73	43	268.1	261	37	117	192
Away	3.91	17	16	0	71	43	267.1	239	26	125	184
Day	3.60	8	6	0	43	23	147.2	144	14	68	98
Night	4.36	23	24	0	101	63	388.0	356	49	174	278
Grass	4.42	21	17	0	104	59	362.2	351	45	166	269
Turf	3.59	10	13	0	40	27	173.0	149	18	76	107
March/April	5.86	5	4	0	25	12	73.2	80	7	43	56
May	3.66	7	6	0	29	16	98.1	87	7	57	66
June	4.33	10	7	0	26	20	129.0	119	19	52	89
July	3.54	3	6	0	22	15	96.2	80	15	43	79
August	4.56	4	5	0	21	14	81.0	86	10	32	46
Sept/Oct	2.84	2	2	0	21	9	57.0	48	5	15	40
Starter	4.31	27	29	0	86	86	474.1	450	60	201	325
Reliever	2.93	4	1	0	58	0	61.1	50	3	41	51
0-3 Days Rest (Start)	10.00	0	1	0	2	2	9.0	11	3	5	8
4 Days Rest	3.69	12	11	0	34	34	188.0	161	24	73	125
5+ Days Rest	4.54	15	17	0	50	50	277.1	278	33	123	192
vs. AL	6.06	0	6	0	26	14	84.2	94	15	40	32
vs. NL	3.79	25	24	0	118	72	451.0	406	48	202	344
Pre-All Star	4.20	22	18	0	86	52	332.0	304	35	164	239
Post-All Star	4.07	9	12	0	58	34	203.2	196	28	78	137

	Avg	AB	H	2B	3B	HR	RBI	BB	SO	OBP	SLG
vs. Left	.239	398	95	18	2	7	34	50	73	.324	.347
vs. Right	.251	1615	405	76	11	56	197	192	303	.330	.415
Inning 1-6	.252	1765	445	84	10	58	212	209	324	.331	.410
Inning 7+	.222	248	55	10	3	5	19	33	52	.318	.347
None on	.252	1167	294	55	6	40	40	134	225	.332	.412
Runners on	.243	846	206	39	7	23	191	108	151	.325	.388
Scoring Posn	.217	470	102	18	5	13	163	68	97	.307	.360
Close & Late	.243	107	26	7	0	3	11	19	19	.367	.393
None on/out	.244	524	128	28	3	17	17	52	92	.313	.406
vs. 1st Batr (relief)	.184	49	9	0	1	0	4	7	16	.293	.224
1st Inning Pitched	.236	492	116	24	4	9	68	71	103	.331	.356
First 75 Pitches	.246	1624	399	77	10	48	181	194	314	.326	.394
Pitch 76-90	.279	240	67	11	3	11	34	28	34	.354	.488
Pitch 91-105	.212	113	24	3	0	2	8	16	20	.310	.292
Pitch 106+	.278	36	10	3	0	2	8	4	8	.366	.528
First Pitch	.307	274	84	16	2	10	36	12	0	.331	.489
Ahead in Count	.175	921	161	33	1	13	67	0	321	.180	.255
Behind in Count	.336	446	150	29	8	27	92	134	0	.486	.619
Two Strikes	.159	954	152	28	2	18	62	96	376	.239	.249
Pre-All Star	.246	1235	304	60	8	35	141	164	239	.335	.393
Post-All Star	.252	778	196	34	5	28	90	78	137	.319	.416

Pitcher vs. Batter (career)

Pitches Best Vs.	Avg	AB	H	2B	3B	HR	RBI	BB	SO	OBP	SLG
Billy Ashley	.000	11	0	0	0	0	0	1	6	.083	.000
Joe Girardi	.083	12	1	0	0	0	0	1	2	.154	.083
Juan Samuel	.100	10	1	0	0	0	0	2	3	.231	.100
Delino DeShields	.107	28	3	0	0	0	1	3	7	.194	.107
Don Slaught	.182	11	2	0	0	0	0	0	5	.182	.182

Pitches Worst Vs.	Avg	AB	H	2B	3B	HR	RBI	BB	SO	OBP	SLG
Will Clark	.471	17	8	2	0	2	7	1	0	.526	.941
Andres Galarraga	.389	18	7	0	0	2	6	2	6	.450	.722
Sammy Sosa	.333	15	5	0	0	2	3	4	5	.474	.733
Tim Bogar	.333	12	4	0	0	2	5	1	1	.385	.833
Dave Hollins	.333	6	2	2	0	0	3	5	1	.636	.667

Jose Mesa — Indians   Age 32 – Pitches Right

	ERA	W	L	Sv	G	GS	IP	BB	SO	Avg	H	2B	3B	HR	RBI	OBP	SLG	GF	IR	IRS	Hld	SvOp	SB	CS	GB	FB	G/F
1997 Season	2.40	4	4	16	66	0	82.1	28	69	.259	83	12	1	7	30	.322	.368	38	36	8	9	21	2	3	103	93	1.11
Last Five Years	3.69	26	28	103	282	33	500.1	161	372	.264	504	69	4	40	205	.324	.368	177	102	28	17	119	25	21	680	505	1.35

1997 Season

	ERA	W	L	Sv	G	GS	IP	H	HR	BB	SO
Home	2.09	2	1	7	36	0	47.1	43	3	10	42
Away	2.83	2	3	9	30	0	35.0	40	4	18	27
Day	3.38	0	2	5	23	0	29.1	29	3	12	29
Night	1.87	4	2	11	43	0	53.0	54	4	16	40
Grass	2.76	3	4	13	57	0	71.2	75	7	25	59
Turf	0.00	1	0	3	9	0	10.2	8	0	3	10
March/April	6.43	0	2	3	8	0	7.0	13	2	3	2
May	6.17	0	1	0	10	0	11.2	19	3	7	17
June	3.38	1	1	0	6	0	10.2	12	1	3	8
July	1.13	0	0	0	15	0	24.0	21	0	5	22
August	0.56	2	0	6	14	0	16.0	11	1	5	12
Sept/Oct	0.69	1	0	7	13	0	13.0	7	0	0	8
Starter	0.00	0	0	0	0	0	0.0	0	0	0	0
Reliever	2.40	4	4	16	66	0	82.1	83	7	28	69
0 Days rest (Relief)	0.00	1	0	9	19	0	26.0	17	0	6	23
1 or 2 Days rest	2.68	2	1	7	31	0	37.0	43	2	16	31
3+ Days rest	5.12	1	3	0	16	0	19.1	23	5	6	15
vs. AL	2.64	2	4	15	60	0	75.0	76	7	26	65
vs. NL	0.00	2	0	1	6	0	7.1	7	0	2	4
Pre-All Star	4.25	1	4	3	27	0	36.0	46	6	14	32
Post-All Star	0.97	3	0	13	39	0	46.1	37	1	14	37

	Avg	AB	H	2B	3B	HR	RBI	BB	SO	OBP	SLG
vs. Left	.309	149	46	6	0	1	13	12	25	.364	.369
vs. Right	.215	172	37	6	1	6	17	16	44	.286	.366
Inning 1-6	.295	61	18	3	0	1	7	4	15	.333	.393
Inning 7+	.250	260	65	9	1	6	23	24	54	.319	.362
None on	.305	154	47	7	0	6	6	18	33	.378	.468
Runners on	.216	167	36	5	1	1	24	10	36	.269	.275
Scoring Posn	.193	88	17	3	1	0	22	7	20	.263	.250
Close & Late	.239	138	33	4	0	4	14	15	28	.312	.355
None on/out	.321	78	25	3	0	5	5	5	16	.361	.551
vs. 1st Batr (relief)	.254	59	15	2	0	3	6	7	10	.333	.441
1st Inning Pitched	.251	231	58	10	1	5	24	22	49	.323	.368
First 15 Pitches	.237	186	44	6	1	4	14	19	36	.314	.344
Pitch 16-30	.277	101	28	5	0	2	12	8	22	.333	.386
Pitch 31-45	.333	24	8	0	0	1	4	1	5	.346	.458
Pitch 46+	.300	10	3	1	0	0	0	0	6	.300	.400
First Pitch	.390	59	23	4	0	1	5	2	0	.429	.508
Ahead in Count	.160	131	21	4	0	1	7	0	54	.167	.214
Behind in Count	.354	65	23	3	1	3	13	15	0	.463	.569
Two Strikes	.149	141	21	4	0	3	8	11	69	.216	.241
Pre-All Star	.311	148	46	7	0	6	19	14	32	.380	.480
Post-All Star	.214	173	37	5	1	1	11	14	37	.271	.272

Last Five Years

	ERA	W	L	Sv	G	GS	IP	H	HR	BB	SO
Home	3.14	15	15	48	143	16	263.1	241	17	82	198
Away	4.29	11	13	55	139	17	237.0	263	23	79	174
Day	4.40	5	14	33	97	10	157.1	174	14	69	135
Night	3.36	21	14	70	185	23	343.0	330	26	92	237
Grass	3.70	23	25	85	242	28	435.2	432	35	142	318
Turf	3.62	3	3	18	40	5	64.2	72	5	19	54
March/April	3.73	5	3	14	38	4	62.2	63	10	17	44
May	3.03	5	5	22	55	6	95.0	89	8	31	83
June	4.57	6	7	13	47	6	86.2	91	7	36	53
July	3.39	4	4	10	51	6	98.1	101	4	30	83
August	3.21	3	4	21	50	6	92.2	88	6	24	62
Sept/Oct	4.57	3	5	23	41	5	65.0	72	5	23	47
Starter	4.94	10	12	0	33	33	202.2	232	21	62	118
Reliever	2.80	16	16	103	249	0	292.2	272	19	99	254
0 Days rest (Relief)	1.67	6	2	41	74	0	86.1	64	6	23	80
1 or 2 Days rest	3.10	7	7	46	119	0	142.1	134	6	55	123

	Avg	AB	H	2B	3B	HR	RBI	BB	SO	OBP	SLG
vs. Left	.277	905	251	29	0	11	86	89	158	.344	.346
vs. Right	.253	1001	253	40	4	29	119	72	214	.306	.388
Inning 1-6	.278	787	219	33	3	19	102	60	124	.330	.400
Inning 7+	.255	1119	285	36	1	21	103	101	248	.320	.345
None on	.263	1049	276	45	1	25	25	90	208	.324	.379
Runners on	.266	857	228	24	3	15	180	71	164	.324	.354
Scoring Posn	.256	473	121	17	2	7	162	55	95	.330	.345
Close & Late	.253	731	185	23	0	12	72	72	157	.320	.334
None on/out	.256	473	121	20	0	15	15	31	94	.303	.393
vs. 1st Batr (relief)	.210	229	48	6	0	7	21	18	54	.266	.328
1st Inning Pitched	.244	979	239	29	2	19	104	89	223	.310	.336
First 15 Pitches	.244	787	192	22	2	17	66	66	161	.304	.342
Pitch 16-30	.279	430	120	15	0	8	60	45	105	.352	.370
Pitch 31-45	.238	202	48	7	1	4	21	16	36	.296	.342
Pitch 46+	.296	487	144	25	1	11	58	34	70	.343	.419
First Pitch	.408	262	107	15	1	6	35	16	0	.442	.542

Last Five Years

	ERA	W	L	Sv	G	GS	IP	H	HR	BB	SO		Avg	AB	H	2B	3B	HR	RBI	BB	SO	OBP	SLG
3+ Days rest	3.66	3	7	16	56	0	64.0	74	9	21	51	Ahead in Count	.214	919	197	25	2	13	81	0	316	.222	.288
vs. AL	3.74	24	28	102	276	33	493.0	497	40	159	368	Behind in Count	.286	384	110	18	1	9	45	72	0	.396	.409
vs. NL	0.00	2	0	1	6	0	7.1	7	0	2	4	Two Strikes	.203	913	185	22	2	15	67	73	372	.268	.280
Pre-All Star	3.68	17	17	50	151	18	268.2	267	25	94	197	Pre-All Star	.262	1021	267	38	2	25	110	94	197	.327	.376
Post-All Star	3.69	9	11	53	131	15	231.2	237	15	67	175	Post-All Star	.268	885	237	31	2	15	95	67	175	.321	.358

Pitcher vs. Batter (career)

Pitches Best Vs.	Avg	AB	H	2B	3B	HR	RBI	BB	SO	OBP	SLG	Pitches Worst Vs.	Avg	AB	H	2B	3B	HR	RBI	BB	SO	OBP	SLG
David Howard	.000	9	0	0	0	0	0	3	4	.250	.000	Gregg Jefferies	.615	13	8	2	0	1	1	0	0	.615	1.000
Chuck Knoblauch	.050	20	1	0	0	0	1	2	3	.167	.050	Joey Cora	.556	9	5	1	0	0	1	4	1	.733	.667
Tim Raines	.077	13	1	0	0	0	0	0	0	.077	.077	Danny Tartabull	.545	11	6	3	0	0	2	0	1	.545	.818
Gary Gaetti	.091	11	1	0	0	0	0	0	2	.091	.091	Ken Griffey Jr	.500	24	12	2	0	1	3	2	1	.538	.708
Luis Soio	.091	11	1	0	0	0	0	0	3	.091	.091	Chad Kreuter	.500	12	6	2	0	1	4	1	1	.571	.917

Hensley Meulens — Expos
Age 31 – Bats Right (groundball hitter)

	Avg	G	AB	R	H	2B	3B	HR	RBI	BB	SO	HBP	GDP	SB	CS	OBP	SLG	IBB	SH	SF	#Pit	#P/PA	GB	FB	G/F
1997 Season	.292	16	24	6	7	1	0	2	6	4	10	0	0	0	1	.379	.583	0	0	1	120	4.14	1	10	0.10
Last Five Years	.208	46	77	14	16	2	1	4	11	12	29	0	2	0	2	.311	.416	0	0	1	353	3.92	15	23	0.65

1997 Season

	Avg	AB	H	2B	3B	HR	RBI	BB	SO	OBP	SLG		Avg	AB	H	2B	3B	HR	RBI	BB	SO	OBP	SLG
vs. Left	.353	17	6	1	0	2	6	3	5	.429	.765	Scoring Posn	.500	2	1	0	0	0	3	1	0	.500	.500
vs. Right	.143	7	1	0	0	0	0	1	5	.250	.143	Close & Late	.000	4	0	0	0	0	1	0	4	.000	.000

Dan Miceli — Tigers
Age 27 – Pitches Right (flyball pitcher)

	ERA	W	L	Sv	G	GS	IP	BB	SO	Avg	H	2B	3B	HR	RBI	OBP	SLG	GF	IR	IRS	Hld	SvOp	SB	CS	GB	FB	G/F
1997 Season	5.01	3	2	3	71	0	82.2	38	79	.248	77	17	3	13	59	.330	.448	24	62	29	11	8	5	2	87	100	0.87
Career (1993-1997)	5.28	11	17	27	210	9	259.0	125	232	.270	271	55	8	40	187	.352	.461	102	131	51	21	39	40	10	285	334	0.85

1997 Season

	ERA	W	L	Sv	G	GS	IP	H	HR	BB	SO		Avg	AB	H	2B	3B	HR	RBI	BB	SO	OBP	SLG
Home	2.70	1	1	0			40.0	28	6	15	44	vs. Left	.260	127	33	9	2	5	26	20	26	.365	.480
Away	7.17	2	1	3	38	0	42.2	49	7	23	35	vs. Right	.240	183	44	8	1	8	33	18	53	.304	.426
Day	6.11	0	0	0	26	0	28.0	32	6	17	26	Inning 1-6	.263	38	10	2	1	1	10	7	9	.370	.447
Night	4.45	3	2	3	45	0	54.2	45	7	21	53	Inning 7+	.246	272	67	15	2	12	49	31	70	.324	.449
Grass	4.38	3	1	3	60	0	74.0	64	11	27	69	None on	.190	174	33	8	0	7	7	20	54	.277	.356
Turf	10.38	0	1	0	11	0	8.2	13	2	11	10	Runners on	.324	136	44	9	3	6	52	18	25	.395	.566
March/April	8.80	0	1	1	14	0	15.1	17	3	12	13	Scoring Posn	.337	86	29	8	3	2	43	14	15	.417	.570
May	1.54	0	0	0	9	0	11.2	7	0	5	12	Close & Late	.340	94	32	9	1	3	25	8	23	.394	.553
June	3.65	1	0	0	12	0	12.1	10	3	5	12	None on/out	.214	70	15	1	0	4	4	9	24	.304	.400
July	9.82	1	0	0	12	0	11.0	20	1	4	11	vs. 1st Batr (relief)	.286	63	18	4	1	2	16	7	2	.357	.476
August	3.72	1	1	0	12	0	19.1	15	3	7	20	1st Inning Pitched	.245	216	53	11	2	10	47	28	59	.332	.454
Sept/Oct	2.77	0	0	2	12	0	13.0	8	3	5	11	First 15 Pitches	.249	181	45	8	1	8	37	25	49	.341	.436
Starter	0.00	0	0	0	0	0	0.0	0	0	0	0	Pitch 16-30	.248	105	26	8	2	5	19	10	24	.308	.505
Reliever	5.01	3	2	3	71	0	82.2	77	13	38	79	Pitch 31-45	.250	24	6	1	0	0	0	3	6	.333	.292
0 Days rest (Relief)	6.43	2	0	1	17	0	14.0	13	5	8	13	Pitch 46+	.000	0	0	0	0	0	0	0	0	.000	.000
1 or 2 Days rest	3.32	0	1	1	36	0	43.1	35	5	21	40	First Pitch	.220	41	9	3	0	1	8	3	0	.267	.366
3+ Days rest	7.11	1	1	1	18	0	25.1	29	3	9	26	Ahead in Count	.185	146	27	3	0	5	14	0	70	.184	.308
vs. AL	4.85	3	2	3	66	0	78.0	72	12	36	75	Behind in Count	.412	68	28	7	3	6	30	17	0	.523	.868
vs. NL	7.71	0	0	0	5	0	4.2	5	1	2	4	Two Strikes	.167	144	24	6	0	4	12	18	79	.259	.292
Pre-All Star	5.53	2	1	1	39	0	42.1	39	7	23	39	Pre-All Star	.241	162	39	10	0	7	38	23	39	.332	.432
Post-All Star	4.46	1	1	2	32	0	40.1	38	6	15	40	Post-All Star	.257	148	38	7	3	6	21	15	40	.327	.466

Career (1993-1997)

	ERA	W	L	Sv	G	GS	IP	H	HR	BB	SO		Avg	AB	H	2B	3B	HR	RBI	BB	SO	OBP	SLG
Home	4.21	7	8	13	109	4	132.2	113	20	62	132	vs. Left	.297	394	117	28	6	17	79	62	72	.390	.528
Away	6.41	4	9	14	101	5	126.1	158	20	63	100	vs. Right	.253	609	154	27	2	23	108	63	160	.326	.417
Day	4.54	1	5	7	66	3	83.1	75	10	43	74	Inning 1-6	.307	244	75	13	4	12	51	31	49	.379	.541
Night	5.64	10	12	20	144	6	175.2	196	30	82	158	Inning 7+	.258	759	196	42	4	28	136	94	183	.343	.435
Grass	5.03	4	9	10	99	3	125.1	132	23	49	110	None on	.242	528	128	23	2	22	22	60	132	.325	.419
Turf	5.52	7	11	17	111	6	133.2	139	17	76	122	Runners on	.301	475	143	32	6	18	165	65	100	.380	.507
March/April	8.70	0	2	2	28	0	30.0	35	10	17	27	Scoring Posn	.298	305	91	22	4	11	142	51	69	.388	.505
May	3.96	1	2	6	36	0	36.1	27	4	23	40	Close & Late	.271	336	91	20	1	10	71	46	87	.358	.426
June	3.48	2	3	4	39	0	44.0	45	5	13	39	None on/out	.266	229	61	10	1	14	14	25	54	.346	.502
July	4.42	4	3	5	38	5	59.0	62	8	18	50	vs. 1st Batr (relief)	.266	177	47	9	1	11	35	20	49	.345	.514
August	6.55	3	5	5	34	4	56.1	68	6	38	48	1st Inning Pitched	.253	681	172	34	6	27	132	92	165	.346	.439
Sept/Oct	5.40	1	5	5	35	0	33.1	34	7	16	28	First 15 Pitches	.258	542	140	25	4	23	95	72	126	.351	.446
Starter	6.86	1	5	0	9	9	42.0	52	8	21	34	Pitch 16-30	.273	289	79	20	4	9	59	36	69	.349	.464
Reliever	4.98	10	12	27	201	0	217.0	219	32	104	198	Pitch 31-45	.283	92	26	4	0	2	18	10	18	.346	.391
0 Days rest (Relief)	3.96	5	1	9	40	0	36.1	33	8	15	33	Pitch 46+	.325	80	26	6	0	6	15	7	19	.375	.625
1 or 2 Days rest	3.86	4	6	11	94	0	107.1	97	14	51	95	First Pitch	.339	127	43	12	2	3	32	13	0	.405	.535
3+ Days rest	7.12	1	5	7	67	0	73.1	89	10	38	70	Ahead in Count	.209	497	104	14	1	14	60	0	203	.211	.326
vs. AL	4.85	3	2	3	66	0	78.0	72	12	36	75	Behind in Count	.337	199	67	18	3	14	63	66	0	.493	.668
vs. NL	5.47	8	15	24	144	9	181.0	199	28	89	157	Two Strikes	.194	494	96	19	1	13	51	45	232	.264	.316
Pre-All Star	5.21	4	8	12	113	1	122.2	120	22	56	115	Pre-All Star	.255	470	120	23	2	22	100	56	115	.337	.453
Post-All Star	5.35	7	9	15	97	8	136.1	151	18	69	117	Post-All Star	.283	533	151	32	6	18	87	69	117	.365	.467

Matt Mieske — Brewers
Age 30 – Bats Right

	Avg	G	AB	R	H	2B	3B	HR	RBI	BB	SO	HBP	GDP	SB	CS	OBP	SLG	IBB	SH	SF	#Pit	#P/PA	GB	FB	G/F
1997 Season	.249	84	253	39	63	15	3	5	21	19	50	0	12	1	0	.300	.391	2	0	1	1038	3.80	92	66	1.39
Career (1993-1997)	.260	435	1211	175	315	65	8	44	178	97	247	9	37	7	16	.317	.436	4	4	13	5252	3.94	409	361	1.13

1997 Season

	Avg	AB	H	2B	3B	HR	RBI	BB	SO	OBP	SLG		Avg	AB	H	2B	3B	HR	RBI	BB	SO	OBP	SLG
vs. Left	.255	106	27	9	2	3	11	8	14	.304	.462	Scoring Posn	.200	65	13	4	0	0	12	9	14	.293	.262
vs. Right	.245	147	36	6	1	2	10	11	36	.297	.340	Close & Late	.214	42	9	1	1	1	2	5	8	.298	.357
Home	.284	116	33	9	0	1	10	4		.328	.388	None on/out	.261	46	12	3	1	2	3	9		.306	.500
Away	.219	137	30	6	3	4	11	11	26	.277	.394	Batting #5	.235	68	16	5	0	2	5	3	15	.268	.397
First Pitch	.222	27	6	1	1	0	1	0		.250	.333	Batting #6	.278	97	27	8	1	1	9	9	24	.340	.412
Ahead in Count	.328	61	20	4	0	2	3	13	0	.446	.492	Other	.227	88	20	2	2	2	7	11		.281	.364
Behind in Count	.188	112	21	5	2	2	10	0	42	.188	.321	Pre-All Star	.264	182	48	12	3	2	14	16	35	.322	.396
Two Strikes	.202	119	24	7	2	3	13	5	50	.234	.370	Post-All Star	.211	71	15	3	0	3	7	3	15	.243	.380

Career (1993-1997)

	Avg	AB	H	2B	3B	HR	RBI	BB	SO	OBP	SLG		Avg	AB	H	2B	3B	HR	RBI	BB	SO	OBP	SLG
vs. Left	.305	462	141	32	6	28	96	42	64	.362	.582	First Pitch	.356	132	47	7	1	9	27	1	0	.368	.629
vs. Right	.232	749	174	33	2	16	82	55	183	.288	.346	Ahead in Count	.367	305	112	22	2	21	76	68	0	.479	.659
Groundball	.250	244	61	9	0	7	26	17	59	.302	.373	Behind in Count	.184	528	97	20	3	9	44	0	215	.186	.284
Flyball	.252	238	60	7	2	10	38	19	52	.304	.433	Two Strikes	.190	600	114	24	4	11	55	28	247	.229	.298
Home	.254	595	151	27	2	21	79	50	112	.314	.412	Batting #6	.263	400	105	29	3	12	58	36	89	.323	.440
Away	.266	616	164	38	6	23	99	47	135	.319	.459	Batting #7	.268	369	99	19	3	10	52	20	67	.306	.417
Day	.280	450	126	24	5	14	75	47	79	.346	.449	Other	.251	442	111	17	2	22	68	41	91	.320	.448
Night	.248	761	189	41	3	30	103	50	168	.298	.428	March/April	.302	139	42	9	0	4	20	13	19	.369	.453
Grass	.262	1066	279	55	7	35	149	87	215	.319	.425	May	.279	280	78	18	3	10	39	27	56	.340	.471
Turf	.248	145	36	10	1	9	29	10	32	.297	.517	June	.252	242	61	8	4	9	33	20	51	.316	.430
Pre-All Star	.274	712	195	38	7	26	103	65	142	.338	.456	July	.251	235	59	11	0	12	35	15	50	.296	.451
Post-All Star	.240	499	120	27	1	18	75	32	105	.286	.407	August	.211	166	35	13	1	3	23	10	25	.256	.355
Scoring Posn	.256	347	89	18	3	12	133	33	71	.314	.429	Sept/Oct	.268	149	40	6	0	6	28	12	41	.321	.430
Close & Late	.237	190	45	4	1	8	30	13	41	.288	.395	vs. AL	.260	1206	314	65	8	44	178	97	247	.317	.437
None on/out	.271	266	72	14	3	10	10	21	54	.324	.459	vs. NL	.200	5	1	0	0	0	0	0	0	.200	.200

Batter vs. Pitcher (career)

Hits Best Against	Avg	AB	H	2B	3B	HR	RBI	BB	SO	OBP	SLG	Hits Worst Against	Avg	AB	H	2B	3B	HR	RBI	BB	SO	OBP	SLG
Rich Robertson	.455	11	5	2	0	1	4	2	2	.467	.909	Dennis Martinez	.083	12	1	1	0	0	0	0	4	.154	.167
Jimmy Key	.375	16	6	2	1	1	1	0	1	.375	.813	Roger Clemens	.133	15	2	0	0	0	0	0	5	.133	.133
Mark Langston	.368	19	7	3	0	0	1	0	3	.400	.526	Jamie Moyer	.143	21	3	0	0	0	1	2	4	.217	.143
Chuck Finley	.316	19	6	0	0	1	7	2	4	.364	.474	Charles Nagy	.182	11	2	0	0	0	1		5	.250	.182
Tom Gordon	.313	16	5	0	0	1	4	1	4	.353	.500	Tim Wakefield	.188	16	3	1	0	1	1		6	.222	.250

Damian Miller — Twins
Age 28 – Bats Right

	Avg	G	AB	R	H	2B	3B	HR	RBI	BB	SO	HBP	GDP	SB	CS	OBP	SLG	IBB	SH	SF	#Pit	#P/PA	GB	FB	G/F
1997 Season	.273	25	66	5	18	1	0	2	13	2	12	0	2	0	0	.282	.379	0	0	3	224	3.15	19	26	0.73

1997 Season

	Avg	AB	H	2B	3B	HR	RBI	BB	SO	OBP	SLG		Avg	AB	H	2B	3B	HR	RBI	BB	SO	OBP	SLG
vs. Left	.182	22	4	0	0	0	1	0	4	.182	.182	Scoring Posn	.278	18	5	0	0	1	11	0	4	.238	.444
vs. Right	.318	44	14	1	0	2	12	2	8	.327	.477	Close & Late	.000	4	0	0	0	0	0	0	0	.000	.000

Kurt Miller — Marlins
Age 25 – Pitches Right

	ERA	W	L	Sv	G	GS	IP	BB	SO	Avg	H	2B	3B	HR	RBI	OBP	SLG	GF	IR	IRS	Hld	SvOp	SB	CS	GB	FB	G/F
1997 Season	9.82	0	1	0	7	0	7.1	7	7	.364	12	2	0	2	7	.488	.606	1	0	0	0	0	0	0	9	10	0.90
Career (1994-1997)	7.45	2	7	0	37	9	73.2	47	48	.320	95	16	2	10	61	.419	.488	7	19	5	0	2	2	2	101	86	1.17

1997 Season

	ERA	W	L	Sv	G	GS	IP	H	HR	BB	SO		Avg	AB	H	2B	3B	HR	RBI	BB	SO	OBP	SLG
Home	0.00	0	0	0	5	0	5.0	3	0	4	5	vs. Left	.167	12	2	1	0	0	2	1	4	.286	.250
Away	30.86	0	1	0	2	0	2.1	9	2	3	2	vs. Right	.476	21	10	1	0	2	5	6	3	.593	.810

Orlando Miller — Tigers
Age 29 – Bats Right

	Avg	G	AB	R	H	2B	3B	HR	RBI	BB	SO	HBP	GDP	SB	CS	OBP	SLG	IBB	SH	SF	#Pit	#P/PA	GB	FB	G/F
1997 Season	.234	50	111	13	26	7	1	2	10	5	24	4	1	1	0	.289	.369	0	1	1	447	3.66	42	32	1.31
Career (1994-1997)	.259	297	943	95	244	53	5	24	113	43	223	21	22	8	11	.305	.402	14	6	4	3690	3.63	352	224	1.57

1997 Season

	Avg	AB	H	2B	3B	HR	RBI	BB	SO	OBP	SLG		Avg	AB	H	2B	3B	HR	RBI	BB	SO	OBP	SLG
vs. Left	.250	32	8	2	1	1	4	2	9	.314	.469	Scoring Posn	.160	25	4	3	0	0	7	4	5	.290	.280
vs. Right	.228	79	18	5	0	1	6	3	15	.279	.329	Close & Late	.100	20	2	1	0	0	2	0	6	.143	.150

Career (1994-1997)

	Avg	AB	H	2B	3B	HR	RBI	BB	SO	OBP	SLG		Avg	AB	H	2B	3B	HR	RBI	BB	SO	OBP	SLG
vs. Left	.220	205	45	15	3	3	19	13	45	.276	.366	First Pitch	.364	110	40	10	1	4	21	10	0	.426	.582
vs. Right	.270	738	199	38	2	21	94	30	178	.313	.412	Ahead in Count	.372	199	74	17	1	11	32	14	0	.424	.633
Groundball	.252	226	57	11	1	3	26	8	51	.288	.350	Behind in Count	.186	488	91	18	2	6	41	0	198	.202	.268
Flyball	.263	160	42	13	1	3			6	44	.304	.413	Two Strikes	.184	467	86	16	0	5	39	19	223	.228	.251
Home	.231	468	108	24	2	10	56	18	112	.267	.355	Batting #7	.188	191	36	9	2	5	17	7	52	.224	.335
Away	.286	475	136	29	3	14	57	25	111	.340	.448	Batting #8	.279	530	148	31	2	15	69	27	123	.330	.430

Career (1994-1997)

	Avg	AB	H	2B	3B	HR	RBI	BB	SO	OBP	SLG		Avg	AB	H	2B	3B	HR	RBI	BB	SO	OBP	SLG
Day	.253	304	77	14	1	8	46	13	72	.294	.385	Other	.270	222	60	13	1	4	27	9	48	.311	.392
Night	.261	639	167	39	4	16	67	30	151	.310	.410	March/April	.308	91	28	6	0	4	16	6	21	.354	.505
Grass	.246	378	93	19	1	11	33	20	89	.299	.389	May	.280	150	42	10	1	1	10	7	37	.333	.380
Turf	.267	565	151	34	4	13	80	23	134	.308	.411	June	.254	213	54	15	1	7	35	11	39	.289	.432
Pre-All Star	.271	535	145	33	2	14	72	27	116	.316	.419	July	.244	246	60	7	2	7	29	14	67	.302	.374
Post-All Star	.243	408	99	20	3	10	41	16	107	.290	.380	August	.262	149	39	10	1	3	16	4	38	.302	.403
Scoring Posn	.247	247	61	12	1	4	86	26	69	.331	.352	Sept/Oct	.223	94	21	5	0	2	7	1	21	.255	.340
Close & Late	.273	165	45	9	0	5	18	7	41	.310	.418	vs. AL	.213	94	20	5	1	0	7	2	21	.250	.287
None on/out	.258	225	58	14	1	8	8	6	44	.292	.436	vs. NL	.264	849	224	48	4	24	106	41	202	.311	.415

Batter vs. Pitcher (career)

Hits Best Against	Avg	AB	H	2B	3B	HR	RBI	BB	SO	OBP	SLG	Hits Worst Against	Avg	AB	H	2B	3B	HR	RBI	BB	SO	OBP	SLG
VanLandingham	.364	11	4	0	0	0	2	1	2	.417	.364	Ramon Martinez	.077	13	1	0	0	0	1	0	4	.077	.077
Greg Maddux	.333	12	4	1	0	0	0	0	3	.333	.417	John Smiley	.091	11	1	0	0	0	0	0	3	.091	.091
Steve Trachsel	.333	12	4	2	0	0	1	0	3	.333	.500	Kevin Ritz	.118	17	2	0	0	1	0	0	3	.118	.118
John Smoltz	.313	16	5	1	0	1	1	4	.353	.438	Pedro Martinez	.167	12	2	0	0	0	0	0	5	.167	.167
Curt Schilling	.313	16	5	1	0	0	2	0	3	.313	.375	Bobby Jones	.167	12	2	0	0	0	0	0	0	.167	.167

Travis Miller — Twins
Age 25 – Pitches Left

	ERA	W	L	Sv	G	GS	IP	BB	SO	Avg	H	2B	3B	HR	RBI	OBP	SLG	CG	ShO	Sup	QS	#P/S	SB	CS	GB	FB	G/F
1997 Season	7.63	1	5	0	13	7	48.1	23	26	.320	64	14	0	8	42	.389	.510	0	0	4.66	1	81	4	3	67	66	1.02
Career (1996-1997)	8.20	2	7	0	20	14	74.2	32	41	.345	109	20	0	15	67	.405	.551	0	0	5.91	3	74	8	6	113	93	1.22

1997 Season

	ERA	W	L	Sv	G	GS	IP	H	HR	BB	SO		Avg	AB	H	2B	3B	HR	RBI	BB	SO	OBP	SLG
Home	7.20	1	3	0	5	4	20.0	28	2	11	10	vs. Left	.260	50	13	2	0	1	7	5	6	.327	.360
Away	7.94	0	2	0	8	3	28.1	36	6	12	16	vs. Right	.340	150	51	12	0	7	35	18	20	.409	.560

Ralph Milliard — Marlins
Age 24 – Bats Right

	Avg	G	AB	R	H	2B	3B	HR	RBI	BB	SO	HBP	GDP	SB	CS	OBP	SLG	IBB	SH	SF	#Pit	#P/PA	GB	FB	G/F
1997 Season	.200	8	30	2	6	0	0	0	2	3	3	2	2	1	1	.314	.200	0	1	0	132	3.67	16	6	2.67
Career (1996-1997)	.174	32	92	9	16	2	0	0	3	17	19	2	3	3	1	.313	.196	1	1	1	466	4.12	40	24	1.67

1997 Season

	Avg	AB	H	2B	3B	HR	RBI	BB	SO	OBP	SLG		Avg	AB	H	2B	3B	HR	RBI	BB	SO	OBP	SLG
vs. Left	.125	8	1	0	0	0	1	1	0	.222	.125	Scoring Posn	.182	11	2	0	0	0	2	1	1	.250	.182
vs. Right	.227	22	5	0	0	0	1	2	3	.346	.227	Close & Late	.500	2	1	0	0	0	0	0	1	.500	.500

Alan Mills — Orioles
Age 31 – Pitches Right (flyball pitcher)

	ERA	W	L	Sv	G	GS	IP	BB	SO	Avg	H	2B	3B	HR	RBI	OBP	SLG	GF	IR	IRS	Hld	SvOp	SB	CS	GB	FB	G/F
1997 Season	4.89	2	3	0	39	0	38.2	33	32	.270	41	10	2	5	23	.401	.461	11	17	3	7	0	8	1	46	53	0.87
Last Five Years	4.40	16	12	9	201	0	262.0	161	210	.242	234	43	5	40	159	.352	.420	69	182	58	35	20	29	6	273	344	0.79

1997 Season

	ERA	W	L	Sv	G	GS	IP	H	HR	BB	SO		Avg	AB	H	2B	3B	HR	RBI	BB	SO	OBP	SLG
Home	5.29	1	1	0	21	0	17.0	17	2	14	14	vs. Left	.333	48	16	5	1	2	10	15	7	.492	.604
Away	4.57	1	2	0	18	0	21.2	24	3	19	18	vs. Right	.240	104	25	5	1	3	13	18	25	.355	.394
Starter	0.00	0	0	0	0	0	0.0	0	0	0	0	Scoring Posn	.196	46	9	1	0	2	17	18	12	.424	.348
Reliever	4.89	2	3	0	39	0	38.2	41	5	33	32	Close & Late	.270	63	17	5	1	8	14	14	.403	.460
0 Days rest (Relief)	7.88	0	0	0	7	0	8.0	12	2	6	5	None on/out	.211	38	8	1	0	1	1	9	.231	.316
1 or 2 Days rest	3.00	2	2	0	20	0	21.0	17	2	10	20	First Pitch	.250	20	5	0	1	1	4	1	0	.286	.500
3+ Days rest	6.52	0	1	0	12	0	9.2	12	1	17	7	Ahead in Count	.177	62	11	2	1	1	7	0	24	.190	.290
Pre-All Star	4.85	1	1	0	10	0	13.0	13	2	11	12	Behind in Count	.303	33	10	4	0	2	7	16	0	.520	.606
Post-All Star	4.91	1	2	0	29	0	25.2	28	3	22	20	Two Strikes	.159	69	11	3	1	1	6	16	32	.326	.275

Last Five Years

	ERA	W	L	Sv	G	GS	IP	H	HR	BB	SO		Avg	AB	H	2B	3B	HR	RBI	BB	SO	OBP	SLG
Home	4.04	10	5	3	101	0	129.1	111	23	71	101	vs. Left	.291	350	102	18	2	10	52	63	53	.401	.440
Away	4.75	6	7	6	100	0	132.2	123	17	90	109	vs. Right	.214	618	132	25	3	30	107	98	157	.324	.409
Day	4.50	2	3	2	58	0	74.0	63	10	49	74	Inning 1-6	.212	250	53	5	0	12	42	38	53	.323	.376
Night	4.36	14	9	7	143	0	188.0	171	30	112	136	Inning 7+	.252	718	181	38	5	28	117	123	157	.362	.436
Grass	4.37	14	11	8	178	0	232.2	202	38	145	187	None on	.251	505	127	28	2	21	21	70	102	.347	.440
Turf	4.60	2	1	1	23	0	29.1	32	2	16	23	Runners on	.231	463	107	15	3	19	138	91	108	.357	.400
March/April	8.59	1	2	0	27	0	29.1	31	9	18	22	Scoring Posn	.217	299	65	11	0	12	118	69	83	.362	.375
May	3.64	4	3	1	38	0	54.1	46	5	36	41	Close & Late	.262	347	91	19	4	14	69	65	84	.379	.461
June	3.60	3	1	2	37	0	50.0	44	6	25	45	None on/out	.262	229	60	7	1	12	12	22	45	.329	.459
July	4.43	1	1	0	31	0	42.2	39	9	30	24	vs. 1st Batr (relief)	.243	173	42	7	1	10	35	22	43	.332	.468
August	4.11	3	1	2	38	0	50.1	44	7	38	46	1st Inning Pitched	.240	570	137	27	1	21	114	96	132	.351	.402
Sept/Oct	3.57	4	4	4	30	0	35.1	30	4	14	26	First 15 Pitches	.246	491	121	25	1	21	92	76	107	.351	.430
Starter	0.00	0	0	0	0	0	0.0	0	0	0	0	Pitch 16-30	.245	277	68	11	1	14	48	47	63	.356	.444
Reliever	4.40	16	12	9	201	0	262.0	234	40	161	210	Pitch 31-45	.242	132	32	4	2	4	11	20	30	.346	.394
0 Days rest (Relief)	5.32	1	2	3	38	0	44.0	42	9	26	37	Pitch 46+	.191	68	13	3	1	1	8	18	10	.356	.309
1 or 2 Days rest	4.10	11	5	5	92	0	109.2	92	13	63	90	First Pitch	.275	131	36	6	1	6	30	10	0	.326	.473
3+ Days rest	4.32	4	5	1	71	0	108.1	100	18	72	83	Ahead in Count	.160	399	64	8	1	8	35	0	160	.176	.246
vs. AL	4.27	16	12	9	197	0	257.0	225	39	156	206	Behind in Count	.305	203	62	12	1	15	43	77	0	.495	.596
vs. NL	10.80	0	0	0	4	0	5.0	9	1	5	4	Two Strikes	.156	463	72	13	3	10	51	74	210	.277	.261

313

	ERA	W	L	Sv	G	GS	IP	H	HR	BB	SO		Avg	AB	H	2B	3B	HR	RBI	BB	SO	OBP	SLG
												Last Five Years											
Pre-All Star	5.05	9	7	3	111	0	149.2	140	27	93	123	Pre-All Star	.248	564	140	26	2	27	101	93	123	.358	.445
Post-All Star	3.53	7	5	6	90	0	112.1	94	13	68	87	Post-All Star	.233	404	94	17	3	13	58	68	87	.344	.386

Pitcher vs. Batter (career)

Pitches Best Vs.	Avg	AB	H	2B	3B	HR	RBI	BB	SO	OBP	SLG	Pitches Worst Vs.	Avg	AB	H	2B	3B	HR	RBI	BB	SO	OBP	SLG
Julio Franco	.000	9	0	0	0	0	0	2	4	.182	.000	Mike Macfarlane	.500	10	5	1	1	2	4	2	3	.583	1.400
Dean Palmer	.083	12	1	0	0	0	0	1	6	.154	.083	Lance Johnson	.500	10	5	0	0	0	2	1	0	.545	.500
Danny Tartabull	.100	10	1	0	0	0	2	1	6	.167	.100	Juan Gonzalez	.462	13	6	2	0	3	9	0	6	.462	1.308
Terry Steinbach	.100	10	1	0	0	0	0	1	2	.182	.100	Edgar Martinez	.364	11	4	2	0	0	1	4	2	.533	.545
Kevin Seitzer	.143	14	2	1	0	0	1	1	1	.200	.214	Chili Davis	.308	13	4	1	0	2	4	1	.471	.615

Kevin Millwood — Braves
Age 23 – Pitches Right

	ERA	W	L	Sv	G	GS	IP	BB	SO	Avg	H	2B	3B	HR	RBI	OBP	SLG	CG	ShO	Sup	QS	#P/S	SB	CS	GB	FB	G/F
1997 Season	4.03	5	3	0	12	8	51.1	21	42	.282	55	11	0	1	25	.350	.354	0	0	8.42	5	92	11	3	57	47	1.21

1997 Season

	ERA	W	L	Sv	G	GS	IP	H	HR	BB	SO		Avg	AB	H	2B	3B	HR	RBI	BB	SO	OBP	SLG
Home	2.53	3	1	0	6	3	21.1	22	0	8	18	vs. Left	.306	108	33	6	0	1	16	14	14	.384	.389
Away	5.10	2	2	0	6	5	30.0	33	1	13	24	vs. Right	.253	87	22	5	0	0	9	7	28	.306	.310

Michael Mimbs — Phillies
Age 29 – Pitches Left

	ERA	W	L	Sv	G	GS	IP	BB	SO	Avg	H	2B	3B	HR	RBI	OBP	SLG	GF	IR	IRS	Hld	SvOp	SB	CS	GB	FB	G/F
1997 Season	7.53	0	3	0	17	1	28.2	27	29	.272	31	8	2	6	26	.424	.535	2	13	4	0	0	1	0	31	40	0.78
Career (1995-1997)	5.03	12	19	1	73	37	264.2	143	178	.270	274	59	4	29	144	.362	.421	8	28	10	0	1	7	12	366	263	1.39

1997 Season

	ERA	W	L	Sv	G	GS	IP	H	HR	BB	SO		Avg	AB	H	2B	3B	HR	RBI	BB	SO	OBP	SLG
Home	8.56	0	1	0	9	0	13.2	14	4	13	15	vs. Left	.244	41	10	2	2	1	6	9	12	.380	.463
Away	6.60	0	2	0	8	1	15.0	17	2	14	14	vs. Right	.288	73	21	6	0	5	20	18	17	.447	.575

Career (1995-1997)

	ERA	W	L	Sv	G	GS	IP	H	HR	BB	SO		Avg	AB	H	2B	3B	HR	RBI	BB	SO	OBP	SLG
Home	5.29	7	13	1	42	21	153.0	152	20	82	105	vs. Left	.274	219	60	16	2	3	27	31	38	.363	.406
Away	4.67	5	6	0	31	16	111.2	122	9	61	73	vs. Right	.269	797	214	43	2	26	117	112	140	.362	.425
Day	5.35	4	4	0	24	9	69.0	73	7	35	51	Inning 1-6	.277	846	234	48	3	23	124	117	147	.367	.422
Night	4.92	8	15	1	49	28	195.2	201	22	108	127	Inning 7+	.235	170	40	11	1	6	20	26	31	.338	.418
Grass	4.50	4	5	0	25	14	94.0	97	7	54	56	None on	.274	548	150	26	3	12	12	65	109	.355	.398
Turf	5.33	8	14	1	48	23	170.2	177	22	89	122	Runners on	.265	468	124	33	1	17	132	78	69	.371	.449
March/April	4.67	0	2	0	11	1	17.1	17	2	18	15	Scoring Posn	.271	251	68	15	1	11	112	46	35	.382	.470
May	6.54	3	4	0	18	10	63.1	71	9	39	47	Close & Late	.190	63	12	4	0	0	6	8	11	.282	.254
June	3.98	3	3	0	8	8	54.1	54	4	19	33	None on/out	.283	251	71	13	1	3	25	47	.353	.378
July	5.24	2	5	0	12	9	56.2	60	5	36	37	vs. 1st Batr (relief)	.242	33	8	4	0	0	9	3	6	.306	.364
August	4.50	1	1	0	13	1	24.0	25	2	13	18	1st Inning Pitched	.275	269	74	17	2	10	50	48	48	.384	.465
Sept/Oct	4.41	3	4	0	11	8	49.0	47	7	18	28	First 15 Pitches	.291	196	57	16	1	6	29	34	30	.394	.474
Starter	4.56	10	17	0	37	37	211.0	217	19	105	129	Pitch 16-30	.291	206	60	13	2	6	43	26	37	.371	.461
Reliever	6.88	2	2	1	36	0	53.2	57	10	38	49	Pitch 31-45	.207	164	34	6	0	6	18	21	37	.309	.354
0 Days rest (Relief)	7.07	0	1	1	6	0	14.0	17	3	6	14	Pitch 46+	.273	450	123	24	1	11	54	62	74	.364	.404
1 or 2 Days rest	7.27	0	1	0	15	0	17.1	20	3	18	16	First Pitch	.264	140	37	9	0	4	20	4	0	.289	.414
3+ Days rest	6.45	2	0	0	15	0	22.1	20	4	14	19	Ahead in Count	.199	407	81	12	1	8	47	0	147	.203	.292
vs. AL	0.00	0	0	0	0	0	0.0	0	0	0	0	Behind in Count	.365	260	95	24	2	13	50	86	0	.524	.623
vs. NL	5.03	12	19	1	73	37	264.2	274	29	143	178	Two Strikes	.158	425	67	12	2	6	35	53	178	.254	.238
Pre-All Star	5.10	6	11	0	40	22	153.2	163	15	90	102	Pre-All Star	.275	592	163	36	2	15	86	90	102	.376	.419
Post-All Star	4.95	6	8	1	33	15	111.0	111	14	53	76	Post-All Star	.262	424	111	23	2	14	58	53	76	.342	.425

Pitcher vs. Batter (career)

Pitches Best Vs.	Avg	AB	H	2B	3B	HR	RBI	BB	SO	OBP	SLG	Pitches Worst Vs.	Avg	AB	H	2B	3B	HR	RBI	BB	SO	OBP	SLG
Tony Gwynn	.071	14	1	0	0	0	1	4	1	.263	.071	Chipper Jones	.600	10	6	1	1	0	1	6	2	.750	.900
Tim Bogar	.083	12	1	1	0	0	0	0	4	.083	.167	Barry Larkin	.500	10	5	0	0	2	6	2	0	.583	1.100
Bret Boone	.091	11	1	0	0	0	0	0	1	.091	.091	Brian Johnson	.500	10	5	1	0	1	1	1	0	.583	.900
Kurt Abbott	.111	9	1	0	0	0	1	2	3	.273	.111	Quilvio Veras	.462	13	6	1	0	0	2	6	2	.650	.538
Edgardo Alfonzo	.154	13	2	0	0	0	1	0	2	.154	.154	Mark Lemke	.417	12	5	1	0	1	2	1	1	.462	.750

Nate Minchey — Rockies
Age 28 – Pitches Right

	ERA	W	L	Sv	G	GS	IP	BB	SO	Avg	H	2B	3B	HR	RBI	OBP	SLG	GF	IR	IRS	Hld	SvOp	SB	CS	GB	FB	G/F
1997 Season	13.50	0	0	0	2	0	2.0	1	1	.556	5	0	0	0	3	.600	.556	0	0	0	0	0	1	0	3	2	1.50
Career (1993-1997)	6.75	3	7	0	15	12	64.0	28	38	.365	100	21	2	7	46	.418	.533	0	0	0	0	0	4	2	101	68	1.49

1997 Season

	ERA	W	L	Sv	G	GS	IP	H	HR	BB	SO		Avg	AB	H	2B	3B	HR	RBI	BB	SO	OBP	SLG
Home	13.50	0	0	0	2	0	2.0	5	0	1	1	vs. Left	.000	2	0	0	0	0	1	1	0	.333	.000
Away	0.00	0	0	0	0	0	0.0	0	0	0	0	vs. Right	.714	7	5	0	0	0	2	0	1	.714	.714

314

Blas Minor — Astros — Age 32 – Pitches Right

	ERA	W	L	Sv	G	GS	IP	BB	SO	Avg	H	2B	3B	HR	RBI	OBP	SLG	GF	IR	IRS	Hld	SvOp	SB	CS	GB	FB	G/F
1997 Season	4.50	1	0	1	11	0	12.0	5	6	.277	13	2	0	1	5	.352	.383	5	10	3	2	3	0	0	19	12	1.58
Last Five Years	4.40	13	10	5	156	0	223.0	70	184	.268	228	40	5	29	117	.326	.429	45	93	38	14	9	9	8	299	217	1.38

1997 Season

	ERA	W	L	Sv	G	GS	IP	H	HR	BB	SO		Avg	AB	H	2B	3B	HR	RBI	BB	SO	OBP	SLG
Home	5.40	0	0	0	5	0	6.2	6	1	3	3	vs. Left	.133	15	2	0	0	0	2	2	2	.222	.133
Away	3.38	1	0	1	6	0	5.1	7	0	2	3	vs. Right	.344	32	11	2	0	1	3	3	4	.417	.500

Last Five Years

	ERA	W	L	Sv	G	GS	IP	H	HR	BB	SO		Avg	AB	H	2B	3B	HR	RBI	BB	SO	OBP	SLG
Home	4.60	4	4	2	85	0	119.1	127	14	35	96	vs. Left	.281	335	94	15	3	12	53	33	58	.343	.451
Away	4.17	4	6	3	71	0	103.2	101	15	35	88	vs. Right	.260	516	134	25	2	17	64	37	126	.315	.415
Day	3.32	5	3	1	42	0	62.1	52	5	15	39	Inning 1-6	.266	289	77	11	0	10	48	21	64	.320	.408
Night	4.82	8	7	4	114	0	160.2	176	24	55	145	Inning 7+	.269	562	151	29	5	19	69	49	122	.330	.440
Grass	3.14	7	6	3	72	0	106.0	95	11	26	93	None on	.264	485	128	21	4	15	15	32	110	.316	.416
Turf	5.54	6	4	2	84	0	117.0	133	18	44	91	Runners on	.273	366	100	19	1	14	102	38	74	.339	.445
March/April	4.10	4	0	0	29	0	37.1	34	5	9	32	Scoring Posn	.284	211	60	10	0	10	90	32	45	.371	.474
May	4.46	1	3	0	28	0	38.1	38	7	13	44	Close & Late	.250	240	60	10	1	9	25	22	54	.316	.413
June	4.82	3	2	3	41	0	56.0	64	6	18	45	None on/out	.284	204	58	12	4	6	6	12	43	.333	.471
July	4.36	2	3	1	31	0	53.2	56	8	20	35	vs. 1st Batr (relief)	.315	143	45	7	2	6	30	8	30	.348	.517
August	6.19	1	1	1	12	0	16.0	19	2	6	18	1st Inning Pitched	.279	512	143	25	3	19	88	41	103	.337	.451
Sept/Oct	2.49	2	1	0	15	0	21.2	17	1	4	20	First 15 Pitches	.290	473	137	25	4	17	73	32	89	.338	.467
Starter	0.00	0	0	0	0	0	0.0	0	0	0	0	Pitch 16-30	.253	257	65	11	1	4	28	22	64	.312	.350
Reliever	4.40	13	10	5	156	0	223.0	228	29	70	184	Pitch 31-45	.190	79	15	3	0	5	9	12	20	.304	.418
0 Days rest (Relief)	4.55	3	4	0	24	0	29.2	27	1	6	17	Pitch 46+	.262	42	11	1	0	3	7	4	11	.326	.500
1 or 2 Days rest	4.01	6	2	4	67	0	94.1	90	11	31	83	First Pitch	.356	132	47	9	1	10	21	5	0	.386	.667
3+ Days rest	4.73	4	4	1	65	0	99.0	111	17	33	84	Ahead in Count	.166	379	63	9	3	4	25	0	154	.172	.237
vs. AL	4.50	0	1	0	15	0	32.0	31	7	14	18	Behind in Count	.365	189	69	13	0	9	46	42	0	.475	.577
vs. NL	4.38	13	9	5	141	0	191.0	197	22	56	166	Two Strikes	.163	381	62	12	2	5	25	23	184	.216	.244
Pre-All Star	4.50	9	6	4	112	0	152.0	154	21	48	129	Pre-All Star	.266	578	154	30	4	21	87	48	129	.326	.441
Post-All Star	4.18	4	4	1	44	0	71.0	74	8	22	55	Post-All Star	.271	273	74	10	1	8	30	22	55	.327	.403

Pitcher vs. Batter (career)

Pitches Best Vs.	Avg	AB	H	2B	3B	HR	RBI	BB	SO	OBP	SLG	Pitches Worst Vs.	Avg	AB	H	2B	3B	HR	RBI	BB	SO	OBP	SLG
Jeff Blauser	.200	10	2	0	0	0	0	1	1	.273	.200												

Doug Mirabelli — Giants — Age 27 – Bats Right

	Avg	G	AB	R	H	2B	3B	HR	RBI	BB	SO	HBP	GDP	SB	CS	OBP	SLG	IBB	SH	SF	#Pit	#P/PA	GB	FB	G/F
1997 Season	.143	6	7	0	1	0	0	0	0	1	3	0	0	0	0	.250	.143	0	0	0	40	5.00	3	1	3.00
Career (1996-1997)	.200	15	25	2	5	1	0	0	1	4	7	0	0	0	0	.310	.240	0	0	0	115	3.97	10	7	1.43

1997 Season

	Avg	AB	H	2B	3B	HR	RBI	BB	SO	OBP	SLG		Avg	AB	H	2B	3B	HR	RBI	BB	SO	OBP	SLG
vs. Left	.000	2	0	0	0	0	0	0	1	.000	.000	Scoring Posn	.000	1	0	0	0	0	0	0	0	.000	.000
vs. Right	.200	5	1	0	0	0	0	1	2	.333	.200	Close & Late	.000	2	0	0	0	0	0	0	1	.333	.000

Angel Miranda — Rangers — Age 28 – Pitches Left

	ERA	W	L	Sv	G	GS	IP	BB	SO	Avg	H	2B	3B	HR	RBI	OBP	SLG	GF	IR	IRS	Hld	SvOp	SB	CS	GB	FB	G/F
1997 Season	3.86	0	0	0	10	0	14.0	9	8	.309	17	2	0	1	8	.433	.400	1	8	4	2	0	1	1	18	16	1.13
Career (1993-1997)	4.46	17	21	2	116	47	363.1	206	243	.260	355	84	11	41	182	.356	.427	11	58	20	11	5	22	13	445	434	1.03

1997 Season

	ERA	W	L	Sv	G	GS	IP	H	HR	BB	SO		Avg	AB	H	2B	3B	HR	RBI	BB	SO	OBP	SLG
Home	3.00	0	0	0	5	0	6.0	7	1	5	4	vs. Left	.346	26	9	2	0	0	4	3	3	.433	.423
Away	4.50	0	0	0	5	0	8.0	10	0	4	4	vs. Right	.276	29	8	0	0	1	4	6	5	.432	.379

Career (1993-1997)

	ERA	W	L	Sv	G	GS	IP	H	HR	BB	SO		Avg	AB	H	2B	3B	HR	RBI	BB	SO	OBP	SLG
Home	4.16	8	11	2	59	26	192.2	176	18	111	124	vs. Left	.280	304	85	22	2	4	38	52	41	.386	.405
Away	4.80	9	10	0	57	21	170.2	179	23	95	119	vs. Right	.254	1064	270	62	9	37	144	154	202	.347	.433
Day	2.70	8	7	1	43	18	146.2	107	12	79	101	Inning 1-6	.262	1051	275	69	10	31	150	158	179	.357	.435
Night	5.65	9	14	1	73	29	216.2	248	29	127	142	Inning 7+	.252	317	80	15	1	10	32	48	64	.351	.401
Grass	4.46	14	19	2	101	42	315.0	308	36	183	208	None on	.253	772	195	49	7	22	22	95	135	.336	.420
Turf	4.47	3	2	0	15	5	48.1	47	5	23	35	Runners on	.268	596	160	35	4	19	160	111	108	.379	.436
March/April	2.36	2	0	1	15	3	34.1	23	2	13	30	Scoring Posn	.242	347	84	25	2	4	126	77	70	.369	.360
May	6.67	2	5	0	15	10	55.1	69	7	38	30	Close & Late	.253	166	42	11	0	7	19	30	31	.369	.446
June	4.76	3	4	0	19	11	64.1	69	8	52	40	None on/out	.254	350	89	21	3	14	14	38	58	.329	.451
July	4.88	2	5	0	22	10	75.2	65	12	42	50	vs. 1st Batr (relief)	.309	55	17	3	1	0	8	10	12	.424	.400
August	3.59	7	6	1	28	8	90.1	83	9	38	59	1st Inning Pitched	.268	384	103	25	4	6	68	74	83	.382	.401
Sept/Oct	3.95	1	1	0	17	5	43.1	46	3	23	34	First 15 Pitches	.261	295	77	18	3	5	34	50	58	.370	.393
Starter	4.50	11	18	0	47	47	264.0	251	32	144	171	Pitch 16-30	.241	266	64	12	2	7	44	43	59	.342	.380
Reliever	4.35	6	3	2	69	0	99.1	104	9	62	72	Pitch 31-45	.293	225	66	18	1	7	37	32	42	.381	.476
0 Days rest (Relief)	6.14	0	0	1	8	0	7.1	12	3	1	7	Pitch 46+	.254	582	148	36	5	22	67	81	84	.345	.447
1 or 2 Days rest	5.28	3	3	1	27	0	29.0	32	2	25	23	First Pitch	.328	180	59	17	2	4	28	10	0	.365	.511
3+ Days rest	3.71	3	0	0	34	0	63.0	60	4	36	42	Ahead in Count	.167	544	91	17	3	9	49	0	194	.171	.259
vs. AL	4.46	17	21	2	116	47	363.1	355	41	206	243	Behind in Count	.361	371	134	35	4	21	58	107	0	.499	.647
vs. NL	0.00	0	0	0	0	0	0.0	0	0	0	0	Two Strikes	.164	604	99	19	4	7	56	89	243	.273	.243

Career (1993-1997)

	ERA	W	L	Sv	G	GS	IP	H	HR	BB	SO		Avg	AB	H	2B	3B	HR	RBI	BB	SO	OBP	SLG
Pre-All Star	4.94	8	10	1	55	28	176.2	182	20	119	110	Pre-All Star	.270	673	182	51	7	20	97	119	110	.381	.456
Post-All Star	4.00	9	11	1	61	19	186.2	173	21	87	133	Post-All Star	.249	695	173	33	4	21	85	87	133	.330	.399

Pitcher vs. Batter (career)

Pitches Best Vs.	Avg	AB	H	2B	3B	HR	RBI	BB	SO	OBP	SLG	Pitches Worst Vs.	Avg	AB	H	2B	3B	HR	RBI	BB	SO	OBP	SLG
Mike Macfarlane	.083	12	1	0	0	0	0	1	5	.154	.083	Mickey Tettleton	.571	14	8	1	0	3	5	0	3	.571	1.286
Pat Meares	.091	11	1	0	0	0	3	0	0	.083	.091	John Valentin	.500	12	6	1	1	0	1	3	0	.625	.750
Cecil Fielder	.100	10	1	0	0	0	0	2	3	.250	.100	Rafael Palmeiro	.417	12	5	1	0	2	6	1	0	.462	1.000
Mike Devereaux	.100	10	1	0	0	0	1	2	2	.250	.100	Mo Vaughn	.400	15	6	2	0	1	4	4	2	.526	.733
Ruben Sierra	.167	12	2	0	0	0	1	4	.231	.167	Albert Belle	.400	10	4	1	0	3	5	4	0	.571	1.400

Mike Misuraca — Brewers
Age 29 – Pitches Right (flyball pitcher)

	ERA	W	L	Sv	G	GS	IP	BB	SO	Avg	H	2B	3B	HR	RBI	OBP	SLG	GF	IR	IRS	Hld	SvOp	SB	CS	GB	FB	G/F
1997 Season	11.32	0	0	0	5	0	10.1	7	10	.333	15	5	0	5	13	.423	.778	2	0	0	2	0	0	0	12	18	0.67

1997 Season

	ERA	W	L	Sv	G	GS	IP	H	HR	BB	SO		Avg	AB	H	2B	3B	HR	RBI	BB	SO	OBP	SLG
Home	7.88	0	0	0	3	0	8.0	9	3	5	8	vs. Left	.533	15	8	1	0	3	7	3	1	.611	1.200
Away	23.14	0	0	0	2	0	2.1	6	2	2	2	vs. Right	.233	30	7	4	0	2	6	4	9	.324	.567

Kevin Mitchell — Indians
Age 36 – Bats Right (flyball hitter)

	Avg	G	AB	R	H	2B	3B	HR	RBI	BB	SO	HBP	GDP	SB	CS	OBP	SLG	IBB	SH	SF	#Pit	#P/PA	GB	FB	G/F
1997 Season	.153	20	59	7	9	1	0	4	11	9	11	1	2	1	0	.275	.373	2	0	0	247	3.58	20	22	0.91
Last Five Years	.317	272	898	147	285	55	4	61	191	130	151	6	36	4	0	.402	.591	23	0	13	3768	3.60	287	311	0.92

1997 Season

	Avg	AB	H	2B	3B	HR	RBI	BB	SO	OBP	SLG		Avg	AB	H	2B	3B	HR	RBI	BB	SO	OBP	SLG
vs. Left	.111	18	2	0	0	1	2	2	2	.200	.278	Scoring Posn	.150	20	3	0	0	2	9	6	3	.346	.450
vs. Right	.171	41	7	1	0	3	9	7	9	.306	.415	Close & Late	.000	9	0	0	0	0	0	1	0	.100	.000

Last Five Years

	Avg	AB	H	2B	3B	HR	RBI	BB	SO	OBP	SLG		Avg	AB	H	2B	3B	HR	RBI	BB	SO	OBP	SLG
vs. Left	.358	240	86	14	2	21	50	31	27	.430	.696	First Pitch	.347	147	51	9	1	12	42	15	0	.399	.667
vs. Right	.302	658	199	41	2	40	141	99	124	.392	.553	Ahead in Count	.401	237	95	18	1	21	65	62	0	.515	.751
Groundball	.356	284	101	19	2	20	67	35	43	.425	.648	Behind in Count	.251	359	90	22	2	15	51	0	119	.260	.448
Flyball	.306	147	45	10	1	10	27	17	31	.382	.592	Two Strikes	.232	353	82	18	1	17	50	51	151	.336	.433
Home	.341	490	167	34	2	35	115	79	72	.429	.633	Batting #4	.333	739	246	50	4	52	164	103	127	.411	.622
Away	.289	408	118	21	2	26	76	51	79	.369	.542	Batting #8	.209	43	9	1	0	4	11	8	9	.333	.512
Day	.326	301	98	18	0	24	70	43	59	.413	.625	Other	.259	116	30	4	0	5	16	19	15	.372	.422
Night	.313	597	187	37	4	37	121	87	92	.397	.592	March/April	.263	194	51	9	0	11	37	19	31	.332	.479
Grass	.303	347	105	18	1	26	76	47	59	.388	.585	May	.342	196	67	7	1	15	40	19	33	.398	.617
Turf	.327	551	180	37	3	35	115	83	92	.411	.595	June	.368	144	53	12	2	9	30	22	21	.447	.667
Pre-All Star	.316	591	187	33	4	41	120	66	97	.385	.591	July	.321	156	50	12	0	13	41	34	28	.440	.647
Post-All Star	.319	307	98	22	1	20	71	64	54	.434	.593	August	.295	190	56	13	1	11	37	28	35	.382	.547
Scoring Posn	.310	268	83	19	1	14	131	71	53	.439	.545	Sept/Oct	.444	18	8	2	0	2	6	8	3	.615	.889
Close & Late	.237	139	33	7	0	7	25	30	24	.370	.439	vs. AL	.245	151	37	5	0	6	24	20	25	.341	.397
None on/out	.276	221	61	10	1	16	16	21	39	.342	.548	vs. NL	.332	747	248	50	4	55	167	110	126	.414	.631

Batter vs. Pitcher (career)

Hits Best Against	Avg	AB	H	2B	3B	HR	RBI	BB	SO	OBP	SLG	Hits Worst Against	Avg	AB	H	2B	3B	HR	RBI	BB	SO	OBP	SLG
Rick Honeycutt	.538	13	7	2	0	2	3	0	0	.538	1.154	Paul Assenmacher	.100	10	1	0	0	0	3	3	.308	.100
Greg Swindell	.500	12	6	1	0	2	5	0	0	.500	1.083	Curt Schilling	.111	9	1	1	0	0	1	2	1	.273	.222
Darryl Kile	.500	10	5	1	0	2	5	3	0	.571	1.200	Kevin Gross	.128	39	5	1	1	0	6	3	12	.222	.205
Chris Hammond	.500	10	5	1	0	1	3	1	0	.545	.900	Pete Smith	.143	21	3	1	1	0	2	2	6	.217	.286
Andy Benes	.367	30	11	4	1	5	10	2	8	.406	1.067	Shawn Boskie	.200	15	3	0	0	0	2	.200	.200

Dave Mlicki — Mets
Age 30 – Pitches Right

	ERA	W	L	Sv	G	GS	IP	BB	SO	Avg	H	2B	3B	HR	RBI	OBP	SLG	CG	ShO	Sup	QS	#P/S	SB	CS	GB	FB	G/F
1997 Season	4.00	8	12	0	32	32	193.2	76	157	.259	194	40	6	21	79	.329	.413	1	1	3.76	20	94	26	5	272	184	1.48
Last Five Years	3.93	23	26	1	115	62	457.2	169	370	.260	460	85	10	55	204	.329	.413	1	1	4.62	32	99	47	12	613	476	1.29

1997 Season

	ERA	W	L	Sv	G	GS	IP	H	HR	BB	SO		Avg	AB	H	2B	3B	HR	RBI	BB	SO	OBP	SLG
Home	2.53	6	5	0	14	14	89.0	80	9	26	74	vs. Left	.246	362	89	22	5	7	34	40	64	.320	.392
Away	5.25	2	7	0	18	18	104.2	114	12	50	83	vs. Right	.272	386	105	18	1	14	45	36	93	.338	.433
Day	4.88	3	5	0	11	11	62.2	68	7	24	53	Inning 1-6	.254	669	170	35	6	18	74	72	146	.328	.405
Night	3.57	5	7	0	21	21	131.0	126	14	52	104	Inning 7+	.304	79	24	5	0	3	5	4	11	.337	.481
Grass	3.74	8	9	0	27	27	166.0	164	19	66	135	None on	.267	431	115	17	5	14	14	35	87	.329	.427
Turf	5.53	0	3	0	5	5	27.2	30	2	10	22	Runners on	.249	317	79	23	1	7	65	41	70	.330	.394
March/April	3.99	0	2	0	5	5	29.1	24	1	16	22	Scoring Posn	.224	174	39	16	1	2	54	29	42	.325	.362
May	5.01	1	2	0	6	6	32.1	35	6	15	27	Close & Late	.293	58	17	4	0	2	4	3	8	.328	.466
June	4.24	3	2	0	5	5	34.0	42	2	10	29	None on/out	.230	191	44	6	3	7	7	15	41	.297	.403
July	4.91	1	1	0	5	5	29.1	30	2	15	20	vs. 1st Batr (relief)	.000	0	0	0	0	0	0	0	0	.000	.000
August	4.38	1	3	0	6	6	37.0	43	7	12	27	1st Inning Pitched	.231	121	28	4	2	1	7	6	31	.266	.322
Sept/Oct	1.42	2	2	0	5	5	31.2	20	3	8	32	First 75 Pitches	.256	567	145	30	5	14	59	60	126	.328	.400
Starter	4.00	8	12	0	32	32	193.2	194	21	76	157	Pitch 76-90	.240	100	24	5	0	4	11	8	18	.306	.410
Reliever	0.00	0	0	0	0	0	0.0	0	0	0	0	Pitch 91-105	.300	60	18	4	1	3	8	6	7	.364	.550

1997 Season

	ERA	W	L	Sv	G	GS	IP	H	HR	BB	SO		Avg	AB	H	2B	3B	HR	RBI	BB	SO	OBP	SLG
0-3 Days Rest (Start)	0.00	0	0	0	0	0	0.0	0	0	0	0	Pitch 106+	.333	21	7	1	0	0	1	2	6	.375	.381
4 Days Rest	3.81	4	7	0	18	18	108.2	100	11	46	88	First Pitch	.310	126	39	13	0	6	19	4	0	.336	.556
5+ Days Rest	4.24	4	5	0	14	14	85.0	94	10	30	69	Ahead in Count	.206	339	70	15	1	3	20	0	132	.211	.283
vs. AL	2.73	2	1	0	4	4	26.1	25	3	10	25	Behind in Count	.335	161	54	7	3	10	27	38	0	.461	.602
vs. NL	4.20	6	11	0	28	28	167.1	169	18	66	132	Two Strikes	.198	323	64	11	3	3	17	34	157	.274	.279
Pre-All Star	4.65	4	7	0	17	17	100.2	108	10	45	81	Pre-All Star	.272	397	108	27	3	10	46	45	81	.347	.431
Post-All Star	3.29	4	5	0	15	15	93.0	86	11	31	76	Post-All Star	.245	351	86	13	3	11	33	31	76	.309	.393

Last Five Years

	ERA	W	L	Sv	G	GS	IP	H	HR	BB	SO		Avg	AB	H	2B	3B	HR	RBI	BB	SO	OBP	SLG
Home	3.14	13	12	1	53	30	229.1	207	29	72	184	vs. Left	.272	827	225	44	8	26	97	88	136	.346	.439
Away	4.73	10	14	0	62	32	228.1	253	26	97	186	vs. Right	.250	939	235	41	2	29	107	81	234	.313	.391
Day	4.28	8	9	0	41	19	141.0	148	17	51	121	Inning 1-6	.256	1391	356	71	9	42	158	133	297	.324	.410
Night	3.78	15	17	1	74	43	316.2	312	38	118	249	Inning 7+	.277	375	104	14	1	13	46	36	73	.346	.424
Grass	3.72	19	20	1	92	51	380.0	383	45	143	314	None on	.272	1017	277	43	7	34	34	72	207	.328	.429
Turf	4.98	4	6	0	23	11	77.2	77	10	26	56	Runners on	.244	749	183	42	3	21	170	97	163	.329	.393
March/April	3.65	2	4	0	11	7	49.1	46	5	21	38	Scoring Posn	.233	421	98	26	3	11	146	69	106	.337	.387
May	3.86	2	3	0	20	11	77.0	75	12	24	59	Close & Late	.293	232	68	11	1	6	29	26	41	.370	.427
June	4.45	8	6	1	21	11	87.0	99	10	29	73	None on/out	.280	457	128	17	4	14	14	25	95	.326	.427
July	5.69	2	3	0	17	8	61.2	64	10	29	51	vs. 1st Batr (relief)	.275	51	14	2	0	0	3	0	22	.269	.314
August	3.53	4	6	0	23	11	86.2	91	10	32	69	1st Inning Pitched	.249	429	107	17	3	8	40	29	96	.300	.359
Sept/Oct	2.91	5	4	0	23	14	96.0	85	8	34	80	First 75 Pitches	.261	1383	361	68	9	39	149	127	300	.327	.408
Starter	4.16	16	21	0	62	62	374.2	381	49	137	291	Pitch 76-90	.229	179	41	8	0	6	22	20	36	.314	.374
Reliever	2.93	7	5	1	53	0	83.0	79	6	32	79	Pitch 91-105	.267	131	35	7	1	5	20	12	19	.329	.450
0-3 Days Rest (Start)	3.00	1	0	0	2	2	12.0	10	2	1	16	Pitch 106+	.315	73	23	2	0	5	13	10	15	.393	.548
4 Days Rest	4.18	8	12	0	33	33	204.1	203	27	81	155	First Pitch	.309	246	76	20	0	11	36	11	0	.344	.524
5+ Days Rest	4.21	7	9	0	27	27	158.1	168	20	55	120	Ahead in Count	.195	790	154	28	3	12	64	0	307	.205	.284
vs. AL	2.95	2	1	0	7	7	39.2	36	5	16	32	Behind in Count	.333	406	135	22	5	19	61	82	0	.440	.552
vs. NL	4.03	21	25	1	108	55	418.0	424	50	153	338	Two Strikes	.194	825	160	26	5	16	67	76	370	.267	.296
Pre-All Star	4.13	12	14	1	56	31	229.0	237	31	82	184	Pre-All Star	.265	893	237	48	7	31	105	82	184	.331	.439
Post-All Star	3.74	11	12	0	59	31	228.2	223	24	87	186	Post-All Star	.255	873	223	37	3	24	99	87	186	.326	.387

Pitcher vs. Batter (career)

Pitches Best Vs.	Avg	AB	H	2B	3B	HR	RBI	BB	SO	OBP	SLG	Pitches Worst Vs.	Avg	AB	H	2B	3B	HR	RBI	BB	SO	OBP	SLG
John Mabry	.000	10	0	0	0	0	0	1	2	.091	.000	Jeff Blauser	.583	12	7	2	0	0	1	2	1	.643	.750
Raul Mondesi	.053	19	1	0	0	1	1	0	8	.053	.211	Barry Bonds	.500	14	7	2	0	2	3	2	0	.563	1.071
Craig Biggio	.056	18	1	0	0	0	0	1	3	.105	.056	Chipper Jones	.467	15	7	2	0	2	9	2	1	.529	1.000
Mickey Morandini	.077	13	1	0	0	0	0	0	4	.077	.077	Ken Caminiti	.417	12	5	2	0	1	2	5	2	.579	.833
Kirt Manwaring	.154	13	2	0	0	0	0	0	4	.154	.154	Ryan Klesko	.417	12	5	2	0	1	2	4	3	.563	.833

Brian Moehler — Tigers

Age 26 – Pitches Right (groundball pitcher)

	ERA	W	L	Sv	G	GS	IP	BB	SO	Avg	H	2B	3B	HR	RBI	OBP	SLG	CG	ShO	Sup	QS	#P/S	SB	CS	GB	FB	G/F
1997 Season	4.67	11	12	0	31	31	175.1	61	97	.285	198	37	4	22	80	.343	.445	2	1	5.39	12	93	21	5	286	186	1.54
Career (1996-1997)	4.65	11	13	0	33	33	185.2	69	99	.284	209	43	5	23	89	.346	.449	2	1	5.24	12	92	21	5	309	197	1.57

1997 Season

	ERA	W	L	Sv	G	GS	IP	H	HR	BB	SO		Avg	AB	H	2B	3B	HR	RBI	BB	SO	OBP	SLG
Home	4.90	5	6	0	15	15	82.2	101	11	30	48	vs. Left	.321	374	120	25	4	12	48	32	45	.374	.505
Away	4.47	6	6	0	16	16	92.2	97	11	31	49	vs. Right	.243	321	78	12	0	10	32	29	52	.308	.374
Day	5.16	2	6	0	12	12	68.0	80	8	28	36	Inning 1-6	.291	625	182	35	3	22	79	57	89	.351	.462
Night	4.36	9	6	0	19	19	107.1	118	14	33	61	Inning 7+	.229	70	16	2	1	0	1	4	8	.270	.286
Grass	4.73	10	10	0	28	28	158.0	181	21	60	88	None on	.270	422	114	22	2	18	18	34	65	.329	.460
Turf	4.15	1	2	0	3	3	17.1	17	1	1	9	Runners on	.308	273	84	15	2	4	62	27	32	.365	.421
March/April	2.45	2	1	0	5	5	33.0	28	3	12	16	Scoring Posn	.310	145	45	11	1	1	54	20	16	.383	.421
May	5.97	1	3	0	5	5	28.2	34	6	10	20	Close & Late	.188	32	6	0	1	0	0	1	5	.212	.250
June	5.19	2	2	0	5	5	26.0	32	5	5	15	None on/out	.258	182	47	11	1	9	9	14	30	.315	.478
July	5.14	2	3	0	6	6	35.0	40	4	18	17	vs. 1st Batr (relief)	.000	0	0	0	0	0	0	0	0	.000	.000
August	5.21	1	1	0	4	4	19.0	25	2	6	18	1st Inning Pitched	.267	120	32	8	2	2	18	19	14	.366	.417
Sept/Oct	4.54	3	2	0	6	6	33.2	39	2	10	11	First 75 Pitches	.292	514	150	30	3	17	61	45	75	.350	.461
Starter	4.67	11	12	0	31	31	175.1	198	22	61	97	Pitch 76-90	.281	96	27	4	0	4	12	8	14	.336	.448
Reliever	0.00	0	0	0	0	0	0.0	0	0	0	0	Pitch 91-105	.269	67	18	3	1	1	7	5	4	.319	.388
0-3 Days Rest (Start)	0.00	0	0	0	0	0	0.0	0	0	0	0	Pitch 106+	.167	18	3	0	0	0	0	3	4	.286	.167
4 Days Rest	5.66	6	8	0	19	19	103.1	126	16	37	50	First Pitch	.368	95	35	4	1	8	19	1	0	.374	.684
5+ Days Rest	3.25	5	4	0	12	12	72.0	72	6	24	47	Ahead in Count	.214	290	62	12	2	6	19	0	74	.223	.331
vs. AL	4.78	9	11	0	28	28	158.0	178	21	58	91	Behind in Count	.337	172	58	14	1	2	23	33	0	.438	.465
vs. NL	3.63	2	1	0	3	3	17.1	20	1	3	6	Two Strikes	.213	300	64	14	2	9	24	27	97	.282	.363
Pre-All Star	4.22	6	6	0	17	17	98.0	106	14	30	54	Pre-All Star	.275	385	106	18	2	14	39	30	54	.331	.442
Post-All Star	5.24	5	6	0	14	14	77.1	92	8	31	43	Post-All Star	.297	310	92	19	2	8	41	31	43	.358	.448

Mike Mohler — Athletics
Age 29 – Pitches Left (flyball pitcher)

	ERA	W	L	Sv	G	GS	IP	BB	SO	Avg	H	2B	3B	HR	RBI	OBP	SLG	GF	IR	IRS	Hld	SvOp	SB	CS	GB	FB	G/F
1997 Season	5.13	1	10	1	62	10	101.2	54	66	.301	116	20	1	11	74	.391	.444	16	55	17	11	4	9	5	131	118	1.11
Career (1993-1997)	4.65	9	21	9	205	20	273.0	159	191	.266	270	49	6	31	178	.367	.418	56	168	52	29	20	19	11	325	326	1.00

1997 Season

	ERA	W	L	Sv	G	GS	IP	H	HR	BB	SO		Avg	AB	H	2B	3B	HR	RBI	BB	SO	OBP	SLG
Home	5.43	1	6	0	35	5	54.2	60	6	37	32	vs. Left	.339	115	39	7	0	2	31	11	15	.406	.452
Away	4.79	0	4	1	27	5	47.0	56	5	17	34	vs. Right	.285	270	77	13	1	9	43	43	51	.384	.441
Day	4.22	1	5	0	29	7	59.2	59	4	31	33	Inning 1-6	.311	257	80	15	1	6	51	33	42	.388	.447
Night	6.43	0	5	1	33	3	42.0	57	7	23	33	Inning 7+	.281	128	36	5	0	5	23	21	24	.396	.438
Grass	5.21	1	9	1	54	8	84.2	95	11	49	57	None on	.296	186	55	10	1	6	6	25	33	.391	.457
Turf	4.76	0	1	0	8	2	17.0	21	0	5	9	Runners on	.307	199	61	10	0	5	68	29	33	.391	.432
March/April	4.80	0	3	0	5	5	30.0	31	2	12	24	Scoring Posn	.311	122	38	6	0	2	60	18	22	.389	.410
May	9.88	0	5	0	9	5	27.1	44	7	19	12	Close & Late	.327	52	17	3	0	1	17	11	7	.455	.442
June	4.15	0	0	0	14	0	8.2	9	1	5	8	None on/out	.315	89	28	5	0	3	3	12	18	.413	.472
July	1.59	1	0	0	9	0	11.1	10	0	7	6	vs. 1st Batr (relief)	.302	43	13	1	0	0	9	5	11	.373	.326
August	2.70	0	2	1	16	0	13.1	11	1	10	4	1st Inning Pitched	.271	166	45	4	1	5	35	24	32	.362	.398
Sept/Oct	1.64	0	0	0	9	0	11.0	11	0	1	12	First 15 Pitches	.282	142	40	3	1	4	29	18	23	.361	.401
Starter	6.83	0	7	0	10	10	54.0	67	7	27	34	Pitch 16-30	.226	84	19	2	0	2	8	14	16	.356	.321
Reliever	3.21	1	3	1	52	0	47.2	49	4	27	32	Pitch 31-45	.286	42	12	4	0	0	4	5	8	.354	.381
0 Days rest (Relief)	4.22	0	2	0	13	0	10.2	15	1	12	7	Pitch 46+	.385	117	45	11	0	5	33	17	19	.464	.607
1 or 2 Days rest	3.33	1	1	1	30	0	27.0	24	3	14	16	First Pitch	.392	51	20	3	0	2	11	4	0	.439	.569
3+ Days rest	1.80	0	0	0	9	0	10.0	10	0	1	9	Ahead in Count	.205	156	32	8	0	3	20	0	57	.211	.314
vs. AL	4.99	1	9	1	56	10	97.1	106	11	51	61	Behind in Count	.398	88	35	4	0	1	23	29	0	.545	.477
vs. NL	8.31	0	1	0	6	0	4.1	10	0	3	5	Two Strikes	.211	175	37	9	1	5	24	21	66	.300	.360
Pre-All Star	6.68	0	8	0	30	10	68.2	89	10	38	46	Pre-All Star	.330	270	89	18	1	10	61	38	46	.413	.515
Post-All Star	1.91	1	2	1	32	0	33.0	27	1	16	20	Post-All Star	.235	115	27	2	0	1	13	16	20	.338	.278

Career (1993-1997)

	ERA	W	L	Sv	G	GS	IP	H	HR	BB	SO		Avg	AB	H	2B	3B	HR	RBI	BB	SO	OBP	SLG
Home	4.74	2	11	3	103	10	133.0	130	15	76	96	vs. Left	.273	330	90	17	2	7	71	43	68	.361	.400
Away	4.56	7	10	6	102	10	140.0	140	16	83	95	vs. Right	.263	685	180	32	4	24	107	116	123	.369	.426
Day	4.55	3	9	3	95	13	144.1	135	16	82	92	Inning 1-6	.285	481	137	26	1	16	91	72	80	.377	.443
Night	4.76	6	12	6	110	7	128.2	135	15	77	99	Inning 7+	.249	534	133	23	5	15	87	87	111	.358	.395
Grass	4.63	5	19	9	180	18	235.1	232	29	143	167	None on	.259	498	129	23	2	13	13	71	91	.358	.392
Turf	4.78	4	2	0	25	2	37.2	38	2	16	24	Runners on	.273	517	141	26	4	18	165	88	100	.375	.443
March/April	4.13	2	3	2	23	5	56.2	51	5	27	54	Scoring Posn	.263	308	81	15	1	12	144	60	62	.373	.435
May	6.66	1	6	2	33	5	48.2	64	7	37	26	Close & Late	.281	274	77	17	1	6	56	41	47	.377	.416
June	4.97	0	2	0	35	0	25.1	27	2	20	20	None on/out	.263	236	62	9	0	6	6	24	48	.341	.377
July	2.79	3	2	1	35	5	51.2	42	2	30	43	vs. 1st Batr (relief)	.277	155	43	2	2	2	34	19	33	.354	.355
August	5.24	2	7	2	42	4	55.0	51	10	31	20	1st Inning Pitched	.239	564	135	18	5	12	102	92	116	.345	.353
Sept/Oct	4.29	1	3	0	37	1	35.2	35	5	14	28	First 15 Pitches	.249	474	118	15	3	10	82	72	81	.348	.357
Starter	6.87	0	13	0	20	20	90.1	105	14	47	59	Pitch 16-30	.226	252	57	11	3	7	29	43	60	.344	.377
Reliever	3.55	9	8	9	185	0	182.2	165	16	112	132	Pitch 31-45	.288	111	32	7	0	3	15	20	26	.394	.432
0 Days rest (Relief)	2.97	2	4	3	38	0	36.1	37	2	29	27	Pitch 46+	.354	178	63	16	0	11	52	24	24	.433	.629
1 or 2 Days rest	3.48	4	2	6	101	0	95.2	79	10	55	69	First Pitch	.306	134	41	7	0	5	22	15	0	.377	.470
3+ Days rest	4.09	3	2	0	46	0	50.2	49	4	28	36	Ahead in Count	.193	409	79	18	4	6	48	0	155	.198	.301
vs. AL	4.59	9	20	9	199	20	268.2	260	31	156	186	Behind in Count	.349	241	84	12	1	12	70	76	0	.503	.556
vs. NL	8.31	0	1	0	6	0	4.1	10	0	3	5	Two Strikes	.188	462	87	18	5	7	68	61	191	.294	.294
Pre-All Star	4.97	4	9	6	99	12	145.0	158	14	90	112	Pre-All Star	.291	543	158	32	2	14	100	90	112	.393	.435
Post-All Star	4.29	5	12	3	106	8	128.0	112	17	69	79	Post-All Star	.237	472	112	17	4	17	78	69	79	.336	.398

Pitcher vs. Batter (career)

Pitches Best Vs.	Avg	AB	H	2B	3B	HR	RBI	BB	SO	OBP	SLG	Pitches Worst Vs.	Avg	AB	H	2B	3B	HR	RBI	BB	SO	OBP	SLG
Kenny Lofton	.000	9	0	0	0	0	0	4	2	.308	.000	Frank Thomas	.429	7	3	0	0	1	1	4	1	.636	.857
Brady Anderson	.091	11	1	0	0	0	0	4	3	.375	.091	Paul O'Neill	.400	15	6	1	0	1	6	2	1	.444	.667
Chili Davis	.111	9	1	0	0	0	0	3	1	.333	.111	Tony Phillips	.400	10	4	1	0	0	1	6	3	.625	.500
Joe Carter	.200	10	2	1	0	1	1	1	2	.273	.600	Rafael Palmeiro	.375	16	6	2	0	1	7	3	2	.474	.688
Harold Baines	.200	10	2	1	0	0	3	2	1	.308	.300	Tino Martinez	.364	11	4	2	0	2	7	1	2	.385	1.091

Izzy Molina — Athletics
Age 27 – Bats Right

	Avg	G	AB	R	H	2B	3B	HR	RBI	BB	SO	HBP	GDP	SB	CS	OBP	SLG	IBB	SH	SF	#Pit	#P/PA	GB	FB	G/F
1997 Season	.198	48	111	6	22	3	1	3	7	3	17	0	1	0	0	.219	.324	0	1	0	419	3.64	44	32	1.38
Career (1996-1997)	.199	62	136	6	27	5	1	3	8	4	20	0	1	0	0	.221	.316	0	1	0	510	3.62	53	41	1.29

1997 Season

	Avg	AB	H	2B	3B	HR	RBI	BB	SO	OBP	SLG		Avg	AB	H	2B	3B	HR	RBI	BB	SO	OBP	SLG
vs. Left	.185	54	10	1	1	1	2	1	6	.200	.296	Scoring Posn	.263	19	5	1	0	0	4	2	5	.333	.316
vs. Right	.211	57	12	2	0	2	5	2	11	.237	.351	Close & Late	.313	16	5	1	0	1	2	1	3	.353	.563

Paul Molitor — Twins
Age 41 – Bats Right

	Avg	G	AB	R	H	2B	3B	HR	RBI	BB	SO	HBP	GDP	SB	CS	OBP	SLG	IBB	SH	SF	#Pit	#P/PA	GB	FB	G/F
1997 Season	.305	135	538	63	164	32	4	10	89	45	73	0	8	11	4	.351	.435	8	2	12	2064	3.46	216	152	1.42
Last Five Years	.319	701	2813	432	897	171	23	70	448	294	321	12	65	83	14	.381	.471	26	6	38	11323	3.58	1133	780	1.45

1997 Season

	Avg	AB	H	2B	3B	HR	RBI	BB	SO	OBP	SLG		Avg	AB	H	2B	3B	HR	RBI	BB	SO	OBP	SLG
vs. Left	.336	113	38	8	0	0	16	13	9	.395	.407	First Pitch	.430	79	34	7	0	2	20	6	0	.465	.595

1997 Season

	Avg	AB	H	2B	3B	HR	RBI	BB	SO	OBP	SLG		Avg	AB	H	2B	3B	HR	RBI	BB	SO	OBP	SLG
vs. Right	.296	425	126	24	4	10	73	32	64	.339	.442	Ahead in Count	.394	142	56	13	3	2	33	21	0	.456	.570
Groundball	.254	126	32	7	1	1	17	10	22	.302	.349	Behind in Count	.197	229	45	5	1	4	23	0	70	.193	.279
Flyball	.316	98	31	4	0	2	10	3	12	.330	.418	Two Strikes	.207	203	42	8	1	2	20	18	73	.269	.286
Home	.322	289	93	16	3	5	51	23	33	.365	.450	Batting #3	.306	532	163	32	4	10	89	45	70	.353	.438
Away	.285	249	71	16	1	5	38	22	40	.336	.418	Batting #4	.200	5	1	0	0	0	0	0	2	.200	.200
Day	.331	157	52	10	1	3	33	18	21	.385	.465	Other	.000	1	0	0	0	0	0	0	1	.000	.000
Night	.294	381	112	22	3	7	56	27	52	.337	.423	March/April	.326	43	14	1	0	1	11	2	4	.333	.419
Grass	.301	219	66	16	1	4	34	21	33	.354	.438	May	.310	100	31	6	0	0	12	14	15	.388	.370
Turf	.307	319	98	16	3	6	55	24	40	.350	.433	June	.337	101	34	10	2	2	20	7	10	.376	.535
Pre-All Star	.318	264	84	18	2	4	47	24	36	.366	.447	July	.286	98	28	5	0	3	20	6	16	.321	.429
Post-All Star	.292	274	80	14	2	6	42	21	37	.337	.423	August	.257	113	29	5	0	2	12	7	18	.293	.354
Scoring Posn	.325	169	55	7	2	3	75	24	28	.385	.444	Sept/Oct	.337	83	28	5	2	2	14	9	10	.398	.518
Close & Late	.302	63	19	3	1	2	14	8	12	.375	.476	vs. AL	.299	489	146	30	3	8	79	43	67	.348	.421
None on/out	.229	96	22	6	0	0	0	3	11	.292	.292	vs. NL	.367	49	18	2	1	2	10	2	6	.385	.571

1997 By Position

Position	Avg	AB	H	2B	3B	HR	RBI	BB	SO	OBP	SLG	G	GS	Innings	PO	A	E	DP	Fld Pct	Rng Fctr	In Zone	Zone Outs	Zone Rtg	MLB Zone
As DH	.303	489	148	30	4	8	80	41	69	.349	.429	122	121	—	—	—	—	—	—	—	—	—	—	—
As 1b	.333	48	16	2	0	2	9	4	3	.385	.500	12	12	97.1	99	7	1	6	.991	—	23	20	.870	.874

Last Five Years

	Avg	AB	H	2B	3B	HR	RBI	BB	SO	OBP	SLG		Avg	AB	H	2B	3B	HR	RBI	BB	SO	OBP	SLG
vs. Left	.345	653	225	43	7	18	108	98	69	.426	.515	First Pitch	.360	425	153	28	3	14	89	21	0	.387	.539
vs. Right	.311	2160	672	128	16	52	340	196	252	.367	.457	Ahead in Count	.387	754	292	55	7	24	154	169	0	.493	.574
Groundball	.293	627	184	33	2	13	92	63	83	.358	.415	Behind in Count	.247	1134	280	47	10	18	121	0	287	.251	.354
Flyball	.322	488	157	39	3	15	73	4	54	.381	.506	Two Strikes	.239	1064	254	49	9	19	118	104	321	.310	.355
Home	.340	1421	483	93	12	38	246	139	152	.397	.502	Batting #2	.290	403	117	26	2	14	51	47	43	.365	.469
Away	.297	1392	414	78	11	32	202	155	169	.365	.438	Batting #3	.322	2298	741	136	20	52	375	240	262	.384	.467
Day	.326	896	292	50	9	27	145	115	104	.399	.492	Other	.348	112	39	9	1	4	22	7	16	.379	.554
Night	.316	1917	605	121	14	43	303	179	217	.373	.461	March/April	.332	355	118	19	4	7	66	39	40	.394	.468
Grass	.301	1150	346	60	9	26	173	129	140	.368	.437	May	.308	506	156	23	1	9	65	54	47	.376	.411
Turf	.331	1663	551	111	14	44	275	165	181	.390	.494	June	.297	508	151	35	2	14	86	59	57	.369	.457
Pre-All Star	.310	1538	477	88	7	36	242	170	166	.377	.447	July	.328	527	173	27	4	19	98	55	64	.389	.503
Post-All Star	.329	1275	420	83	16	34	206	124	155	.385	.500	August	.331	511	169	37	5	12	77	51	66	.387	.493
Scoring Posn	.351	795	279	44	7	15	355	128	94	.427	.481	Sept/Oct	.320	406	130	30	7	9	56	36	47	.373	.495
Close & Late	.311	392	122	17	4	10	70	51	50	.389	.452	vs. AL	.318	2764	879	169	22	68	438	292	315	.381	.469
None on/out	.319	492	157	34	1	15	15	42	51	.375	.484	vs. NL	.367	49	18	2	1	2	10	2	6	.385	.571

Batter vs. Pitcher (since 1984)

Hits Best Against	Avg	AB	H	2B	3B	HR	RBI	BB	SO	OBP	SLG	Hits Worst Against	Avg	AB	H	2B	3B	HR	RBI	BB	SO	OBP	SLG
Mike Fetters	.556	9	5	1	1	0	1	3	3	.692	.889	Mike Jackson	.056	18	1	1	0	0	1	1	4	.105	.111
Eric Plunk	.464	28	13	1	1	2	7	6	5	.559	.786	Darren Oliver	.077	13	1	1	0	0	0	0	2	.077	.154
Willie Blair	.455	11	5	1	0	1	5	2	0	.538	.818	Albie Lopez	.091	11	1	0	0	0	0	0	1	.091	.091
Greg Cadaret	.385	13	5	2	0	1	5	5	2	.556	.769	Mark Guthrie	.133	15	2	0	0	0	1	1	4	.133	.133
Scott Aldred	.385	13	5	1	0	2	4	4	1	.500	.923	Tim Wakefield	.143	14	2	0	0	0	1	0	4	.200	.143

Raul Mondesi — Dodgers

Age 27 – Bats Right

	Avg	G	AB	R	H	2B	3B	HR	RBI	BB	SO	HBP	GDP	SB	CS	OBP	SLG	IBB	SH	SF	#Pit	#P/PA	GB	FB	G/F
1997 Season	.310	159	616	95	191	42	5	30	87	44	105	6	11	32	15	.360	.541	7	1	3	2255	3.37	202	194	1.04
Career (1993-1997)	.299	609	2306	360	690	135	27	100	329	129	417	17	34	88	35	.339	.511	25	2	14	8388	3.40	824	702	1.17

1997 Season

	Avg	AB	H	2B	3B	HR	RBI	BB	SO	OBP	SLG		Avg	AB	H	2B	3B	HR	RBI	BB	SO	OBP	SLG
vs. Left	.284	148	42	9	1	7	23	17	19	.355	.500	First Pitch	.333	120	40	9	0	6	15	3	0	.362	.558
vs. Right	.318	468	149	33	4	23	64	27	86	.362	.553	Ahead in Count	.356	146	52	13	1	13	35	22	0	.441	.726
Groundball	.282	103	29	9	2	3	10	2	4	.306	.495	Behind in Count	.254	228	58	11	3	7	23	0	89	.257	.421
Flyball	.296	81	24	3	1	4	9	4	20	.329	.506	Two Strikes	.233	240	56	12	2	4	21	19	105	.288	.350
Home	.316	304	96	25	0	16	40	18	50	.360	.556	Batting #3	.261	161	42	4	1	9	21	11	32	.322	.466
Away	.304	312	95	17	5	14	47	26	55	.360	.526	Batting #5	.332	425	141	36	4	21	65	31	68	.377	.584
Day	.248	165	41	11	1	5	20	16	35	.319	.418	Other	.267	30	8	2	0	0	1	2	5	.333	.333
Night	.333	451	150	31	4	25	67	28	70	.376	.585	March/April	.283	92	26	2	1	6	15	10	14	.362	.522
Grass	.325	507	165	38	2	28	72	33	81	.373	.574	May	.257	109	28	9	0	5	16	5	15	.287	.477
Turf	.239	109	26	4	3	2	15	11	24	.303	.385	June	.327	98	32	8	1	5	16	6	12	.377	.582
Pre-All Star	.295	325	96	21	2	17	48	21	44	.346	.529	July	.345	110	38	9	0	7	13	3	19	.368	.618
Post-All Star	.326	291	95	21	3	13	39	23	61	.377	.553	August	.328	116	38	6	2	3	16	12	22	.388	.491
Scoring Posn	.258	151	39	10	3	4	54	21	30	.343	.444	Sept/Oct	.319	91	29	8	1	4	11	8	23	.380	.560
Close & Late	.327	110	36	7	0	7	17	6	17	.359	.582	vs. AL	.359	64	23	7	0	3	11	4	7	.397	.609
None on/out	.372	156	58	11	1	10	10	4	21	.399	.647	vs. NL	.304	552	168	35	5	27	76	40	98	.356	.533

1997 By Position

Position	Avg	AB	H	2B	3B	HR	RBI	BB	SO	OBP	SLG	G	GS	Innings	PO	A	E	DP	Fld Pct	Rng Fctr	In Zone	Zone Outs	Zone Rtg	MLB Zone
As rf	.309	615	190	41	5	30	87	44	105	.359	.538	159	157	1390.0	338	10	4	1	.989	2.25	387	323	.835	.813

Career (1993-1997)

	Avg	AB	H	2B	3B	HR	RBI	BB	SO	OBP	SLG		Avg	AB	H	2B	3B	HR	RBI	BB	SO	OBP	SLG
vs. Left	.273	549	150	30	6	22	76	39	95	.322	.470	First Pitch	.352	454	160	33	2	27	78	20	0	.383	.612
vs. Right	.307	1757	540	105	21	78	253	90	322	.344	.524	Ahead in Count	.349	479	167	33	8	37	90	53	0	.416	.683

Career (1993-1997)

	Avg	AB	H	2B	3B	HR	RBI	BB	SO	OBP	SLG		Avg	AB	H	2B	3B	HR	RBI	BB	SO	OBP	SLG
Groundball	.304	575	175	37	8	14	66	23	104	.333	.470	Behind in Count	.236	966	228	48	11	20	101	0	344	.240	.371
Flyball	.281	391	110	19	4	27	58	19	90	.318	.558	Two Strikes	.221	956	211	40	10	15	86	56	417	.266	.331
Home	.300	1112	334	68	6	52	154	58	194	.337	.513	Batting #3	.293	539	158	24	5	26	86	34	95	.340	.501
Away	.298	1194	356	67	21	48	175	71	223	.341	.510	Batting #5	.301	1099	331	72	11	51	158	61	207	.340	.526
Day	.291	639	186	37	10	23	84	45	132	.340	.488	Other	.301	668	201	39	11	23	85	34	115	.337	.496
Night	.302	1667	504	98	17	77	245	84	285	.339	.520	March/April	.273	308	84	13	3	15	51	17	49	.314	.481
Grass	.310	1832	568	114	17	86	266	105	323	.346	.532	May	.282	450	127	31	5	24	70	23	83	.319	.533
Turf	.257	474	122	21	10	14	63	24	94	.296	.432	June	.329	395	130	19	7	19	52	18	64	.362	.557
Pre-All Star	.298	1275	380	71	15	61	187	61	217	.334	.521	July	.301	429	129	28	1	13	42	20	75	.335	.462
Post-All Star	.301	1031	310	64	12	39	142	68	200	.346	.500	August	.284	380	108	20	7	14	59	30	83	.334	.484
Scoring Posn	.289	546	158	32	9	26	228	59	115	.354	.524	Sept/Oct	.326	344	112	24	4	15	55	21	63	.371	.549
Close & Late	.302	391	118	18	5	15	55	20	73	.337	.488	vs. AL	.359	64	23	7	0	3	11	4	7	.397	.609
None on/out	.329	535	176	31	9	26	26	21	82	.360	.566	vs. NL	.298	2242	667	128	27	97	318	125	410	.337	.508

Batter vs. Pitcher (career)

Hits Best Against	Avg	AB	H	2B	3B	HR	RBI	BB	SO	OBP	SLG	Hits Worst Against	Avg	AB	H	2B	3B	HR	RBI	BB	SO	OBP	SLG
Steve Cooke	.545	11	6	1	1	1	5	0	0	.500	1.091	Dave Mlicki	.053	19	1	0	0	1	1	0	8	.053	.211
Mark Gardner	.462	13	6	2	0	1	1	1	2	.500	.846	Andy Benes	.071	14	1	0	0	0	0	1	4	.133	.071
Donovan Osborne	.455	11	5	0	0	1	4	3	1	.600	.727	Jeff Juden	.091	11	1	0	0	0	0	1	1	.167	.091
Mark Thompson	.357	14	5	1	0	3	6	0	1	.357	1.071	John Smiley	.105	19	2	1	0	0	0	2	2	.190	.158
Frank Castillo	.333	15	5	1	0		5	0	1	.333	1.000	Doug Drabek	.154	13	2	1	0	0	0	0	2	.154	.231

Jeff Montgomery — Royals   Age 36 – Pitches Right (groundball pitcher)

	ERA	W	L	Sv	G	GS	IP	BB	SO	Avg	H	2B	3B	HR	RBI	OBP	SLG	GF	IR	IRS	Hld	SvOp	SB	CS	GB	FB	G/F
1997 Season	3.49	1	4	14	55	0	59.1	18	48	.240	53	7	0	9	32	.295	.394	37	24	10	3	17	3	2	88	49	1.80
Last Five Years	3.37	16	21	141	268	0	320.1	100	258	.241	285	49	5	38	154	.302	.387	225	108	38	3	172	20	5	435	286	1.52

1997 Season

	ERA	W	L	Sv	G	GS	IP	H	HR	BB	SO		Avg	AB	H	2B	3B	HR	RBI	BB	SO	OBP	SLG
Home	4.13	0	1	5	30	0	32.2	30	5	8	23	vs. Left	.267	101	27	3	0	6	16	9	18	.327	.475
Away	2.70	1	3	9	25	0	26.2	23	4	10	25	vs. Right	.217	120	26	4	0	3	16	9	30	.267	.325
Day	5.79	0	2	3	17	0	18.2	21	3	10	18	Inning 1-6	.000	1	0	0	0	0	0	0	0	.000	.000
Night	2.43	1	2	11	38	0	40.2	32	6	8	30	Inning 7+	.241	220	53	7	0	9	32	18	48	.296	.395
Grass	3.76	0	4	12	48	0	52.2	48	8	17	42	None on	.259	135	35	5	0	7	7	5	27	.286	.452
Turf	1.35	1	0	2	7	0	6.2	5	1	1	6	Runners on	.209	86	18	2	0	2	25	13	21	.307	.302
March/April	16.62	0	1	0	5	0	4.1	10	3	3	5	Scoring Posn	.268	56	15	2	0	0	21	10	12	.368	.304
May	6.17	0	0	0	11	0	11.2	16	3	6	10	Close & Late	.240	121	29	4	0	4	16	12	29	.306	.372
June	3.86	0	2	3	9	0	9.1	9	1	1	5	None on/out	.356	59	21	3	0	4	0	0	11	.356	.610
July	1.64	1	0	2	10	0	11.0	5	2	1	10	vs. 1st Batr (relief)	.302	53	16	3	0	4	10	0	8	.291	.585
August	0.00	0	0	6	11	0	12.0	5	0	1	8	1st Inning Pitched	.242	186	45	6	0	9	28	9	40	.274	.419
Sept/Oct	0.82	0	1	3	9	0	11.0	6	0	6	10	First 15 Pitches	.252	163	41	6	0	7	22	6	30	.275	.417
Starter	0.00	0	0	0	0	0	0.0	0	0	0	0	Pitch 16-30	.220	50	11	1	0	2	9	9	14	.339	.360
Reliever	3.49	1	4	14	55	0	59.1	53	9	18	48	Pitch 31-45	.125	8	1	0	0	0	1	3	4	.364	.125
0 Days rest (Relief)	0.00	0	0	4	7	0	6.0	5	0	2	4	Pitch 46+	.000	0	0	0	0	0	0	0	0	.000	.000
1 or 2 Days rest	2.55	1	2	7	30	0	35.1	29	5	9	28	First Pitch	.414	29	12	1	0	2	10	2	0	.438	.655
3+ Days rest	6.50	0	2	3	18	0	18.0	19	4	7	14	Ahead in Count	.145	117	17	4	0	1	6	0	44	.144	.205
vs. AL	3.70	1	4	13	51	0	56.0	51	9	17	46	Behind in Count	.429	35	15	1	0	4	11	10	0	.556	.800
vs. NL	0.00	0	0	1	4	0	3.1	2	0	1	2	Two Strikes	.104	106	11	2	0	2	5	5	48	.144	.179
Pre-All Star	7.01	0	3	3	26	0	25.2	37	7	10	20	Pre-All Star	.339	109	37	5	0	7	28	10	20	.392	.578
Post-All Star	0.80	1	1	11	29	0	33.2	16	2	8	28	Post-All Star	.143	112	16	2	0	2	4	8	28	.198	.214

Last Five Years

	ERA	W	L	Sv	G	GS	IP	H	HR	BB	SO		Avg	AB	H	2B	3B	HR	RBI	BB	SO	OBP	SLG
Home	3.40	12	8	51	132	0	164.1	140	19	41	120	vs. Left	.261	625	163	28	4	19	89	58	110	.325	.410
Away	3.35	4	13	90	136	0	156.0	145	19	59	138	vs. Right	.218	559	122	21	1	19	65	42	148	.275	.361
Day	3.88	2	9	38	85	0	102.0	96	17	37	96	Inning 1-6	.000	1	0	0	0	0	0	0	0	.000	.000
Night	3.13	14	12	103	183	0	218.1	189	21	63	162	Inning 7+	.241	1183	285	49	5	38	154	100	258	.302	.387
Grass	3.33	8	11	88	177	0	213.1	190	30	73	173	None on	.241	659	159	29	2	24	24	42	145	.291	.401
Turf	3.45	8	10	53	91	0	107.0	95	8	27	85	Runners on	.240	525	126	20	3	14	130	58	113	.315	.370
March/April	4.17	1	3	13	33	0	41.0	38	5	16	32	Scoring Posn	.240	321	77	15	3	3	105	39	70	.321	.333
May	4.06	2	4	28	56	0	68.2	75	8	25	58	Close & Late	.247	843	208	35	2	24	116	81	188	.314	.378
June	4.37	1	7	27	49	0	56.2	53	10	13	41	None on/out	.277	282	78	14	1	12	12	13	52	.311	.461
July	1.67	5	1	30	50	0	59.1	39	4	11	51	vs. 1st Batr (relief)	.274	248	68	16	0	12	30	15	53	.318	.484
August	2.70	3	4	30	49	0	56.2	44	6	19	45	1st Inning Pitched	.245	946	232	41	3	32	127	73	206	.300	.386
Sept/Oct	3.46	4	2	13	31	0	39.0	36	5	16	31	First 15 Pitches	.240	797	191	35	1	26	89	54	167	.289	.384
Starter	0.00	0	0	0	0	0	0.0	0	0	0	0	Pitch 16-30	.260	338	88	14	4	12	63	39	76	.341	.432
Reliever	3.37	16	21	141	268	0	320.1	285	38	100	258	Pitch 31-45	.125	48	6	0	0	0	2	7	14	.236	.125
0 Days rest (Relief)	2.57	2	2	47	64	0	73.2	61	8	19	62	Pitch 46+	.000	1	0	0	0	0	0	0	1	.000	.000
1 or 2 Days rest	3.33	6	11	67	115	0	135.1	123	14	45	112	First Pitch	.310	142	44	11	0	7	32	0	1	.366	.535
3+ Days rest	3.96	8	8	27	89	0	111.1	101	16	36	84	Ahead in Count	.184	631	116	22	2	9	47	0	227	.189	.268
vs. AL	3.41	16	21	140	264	0	317.0	283	38	99	256	Behind in Count	.352	213	75	11	1	10	42	54	0	.481	.532
vs. NL	0.00	0	0	1	4	0	3.1	2	0	1	2	Two Strikes	.162	591	96	19	4	10	47	32	258	.210	.259
Pre-All Star	4.07	6	15	74	151	0	179.0	176	24	56	146	Pre-All Star	.261	675	176	33	3	24	105	56	146	.322	.425
Post-All Star	2.48	10	6	67	117	0	141.1	109	14	44	112	Post-All Star	.214	509	109	16	2	14	49	44	112	.275	.336

Pitcher vs. Batter (career)

Pitches Best Vs.	Avg	AB	H	2B	3B	HR	RBI	BB	SO	OBP	SLG	Pitches Worst Vs.	Avg	AB	H	2B	3B	HR	RBI	BB	SO	OBP	SLG
Randy Velarde	.000	11	0	0	0	0	0	1	7	.083	.000	Joe Orsulak	.462	13	6	2	0	0	2	1	0	.500	.615

Pitcher vs. Batter (career)

Pitches Best Vs.	Avg	AB	H	2B	3B	HR	RBI	BB	SO	OBP	SLG	Pitches Worst Vs.	Avg	AB	H	2B	3B	HR	RBI	BB	SO	OBP	SLG
Chili Davis	.050	20	1	0	0	0	0	5	7	.240	.050	Cal Ripken	.421	19	8	4	0	0	1	6	2	.560	.632
Pete Incaviglia	.083	12	1	0	0	0	1	2	5	.214	.083	Jose Canseco	.417	12	5	2	0	1	4	1	3	.462	.833
Greg Gagne	.100	10	1	0	0	0	0	1	1	.182	.100	John Olerud	.368	19	7	3	0	1	1	1	3	.400	.684
Darryl Hamilton	.118	17	2	0	0	0	1	1	1	.167	.118	Rusty Greer	.364	11	4	2	0	1	3	0	2	.364	.818

Ray Montgomery — Astros
Age 28 – Bats Right

	Avg	G	AB	R	H	2B	3B	HR	RBI	BB	SO	HBP	GDP	SB	CS	OBP	SLG	IBB	SH	SF	#Pit	#P/PA	GB	FB	G/F
1997 Season	.235	29	68	8	16	4	1	0	4	5	18	0	2	0	0	.276	.324	0	0	3	295	3.88	23	19	1.21
Career (1996-1997)	.232	41	82	12	19	5	1	0	8	6	23	0	2	0	0	.275	.354	0	0	3	349	3.84	24	26	0.92

1997 Season

	Avg	AB	H	2B	3B	HR	RBI	BB	SO	OBP	SLG		Avg	AB	H	2B	3B	HR	RBI	BB	SO	OBP	SLG
vs. Left	.111	27	3	1	0	0	2	1	5	.133	.148	Scoring Posn	.200	15	3	1	0	0	4	4	3	.318	.267
vs. Right	.317	41	13	3	1	0	2	4	13	.370	.439	Close & Late	.111	18	2	0	0	0	0	0	6	.111	.111

Steve Montgomery — Athletics
Age 27 – Pitches Right (flyball pitcher)

	ERA	W	L	Sv	G	GS	IP	BB	SO	Avg	H	2B	3B	HR	RBI	OBP	SLG	GF	IR	IRS	Hld	SvOp	SB	CS	GB	FB	G/F
1997 Season	9.95	0	1	0	4	0	6.1	8	1	.385	10	2	0	2	5	.514	.692	0	1	0	1	0	2	1	9	10	0.90
Career (1996-1997)	9.45	1	1	0	12	0	20.0	21	9	.333	28	5	0	7	19	.462	.643	0	7	3	1	0	4	1	27	29	0.93

1997 Season

	ERA	W	L	Sv	G	GS	IP	H	HR	BB	SO		Avg	AB	H	2B	3B	HR	RBI	BB	SO	OBP	SLG
Home	7.20	0	0	0	2	0	5.0	7	2	4	1	vs. Left	.286	14	4	1	0	1	2	6	0	.500	.571
Away	20.25	0	1	0	2	0	1.1	3	0	4	0	vs. Right	.500	12	6	1	0	1	3	2	1	.533	.833

Eric Moody — Rangers
Age 27 – Pitches Right (flyball pitcher)

	ERA	W	L	Sv	G	GS	IP	BB	SO	Avg	H	2B	3B	HR	RBI	OBP	SLG	GF	IR	IRS	Hld	SvOp	SB	CS	GB	FB	G/F
1997 Season	4.26	0	1	0	10	1	19.0	2	12	.329	26	2	0	4	13	.341	.506	3	9	5	0	1	3	1	24	26	0.92

1997 Season

	ERA	W	L	Sv	G	GS	IP	H	HR	BB	SO		Avg	AB	H	2B	3B	HR	RBI	BB	SO	OBP	SLG
Home	3.72	0	0	0	5	0	9.2	12	1	2	7	vs. Left	.355	31	11	1	0	3	4	1	4	.375	.677
Away	4.82	0	1	0	5	1	9.1	14	3	0	5	vs. Right	.313	48	15	1	0	1	9	1	8	.320	.396

Mickey Morandini — Phillies
Age 32 – Bats Left (groundball hitter)

	Avg	G	AB	R	H	2B	3B	HR	RBI	BB	SO	HBP	GDP	SB	CS	OBP	SLG	IBB	SH	SF	#Pit	#P/PA	GB	FB	G/F
1997 Season	.295	150	553	83	163	40	2	1	39	62	91	8	16	13	9	.371	.380	0	12	5	2431	3.80	202	135	1.50
Last Five Years	.273	624	2285	309	623	133	29	15	179	221	364	35	44	74	31	.344	.376	10	29	12	9576	3.71	858	558	1.54

1997 Season

	Avg	AB	H	2B	3B	HR	RBI	BB	SO	OBP	SLG		Avg	AB	H	2B	3B	HR	RBI	BB	SO	OBP	SLG
vs. Left	.304	125	38	8	0	0	17	22	14	.417	.368	First Pitch	.464	84	39	10	1	1	12	0	0	.477	.643
vs. Right	.292	428	125	32	2	1	22	40	77	.356	.383	Ahead in Count	.363	91	33	9	0	0	14	37	0	.538	.462
Groundball	.250	92	23	5	0	1	5	9	16	.320	.337	Behind in Count	.205	263	54	12	0	0	8	0	80	.216	.251
Flyball	.362	94	34	10	0	0	5	5	17	.400	.468	Two Strikes	.212	259	55	13	1	0	6	25	91	.287	.270
Home	.288	267	77	18	1	1	22	33	48	.371	.375	Batting #1	.189	37	7	0	0	0	0	3	6	.250	.189
Away	.301	286	86	22	1	0	17	29	43	.371	.385	Batting #2	.304	510	155	39	2	1	39	58	82	.379	.394
Day	.327	153	50	11	0	1	16	26	24	.423	.418	Other	.167	6	1	1	0	0	0	1	3	.375	.333
Night	.283	400	113	29	2	0	23	36	67	.350	.365	March/April	.242	91	22	3	0	0	4	14	16	.349	.275
Grass	.284	208	59	11	1	0	13	18	36	.346	.346	May	.367	98	36	13	1	0	5	10	13	.432	.520
Turf	.301	345	104	29	1	1	26	44	55	.385	.400	June	.316	98	31	10	0	1	4	9	15	.380	.449
Pre-All Star	.308	305	94	28	1	1	15	38	44	.390	.416	July	.240	96	23	6	1	0	9	12	10	.327	.323
Post-All Star	.278	248	69	12	1	0	24	24	47	.348	.335	August	.322	90	29	5	0	0	8	11	20	.398	.378
Scoring Posn	.257	113	29	6	0	1	37	12	26	.321	.336	Sept/Oct	.275	80	22	3	0	0	9	6	17	.333	.313
Close & Late	.323	62	20	4	0	0	12	13	9	.427	.387	vs. AL	.204	49	10	3	0	0	1	7	9	.298	.265
None on/out	.294	102	30	8	1	0	15	7	15	.395	.392	vs. NL	.304	504	153	37	2	1	38	55	82	.378	.391

1997 By Position

Position	Avg	AB	H	2B	3B	HR	RBI	BB	SO	OBP	SLG		G	GS	Innings	PO	A	E	DP	Fld Pct	Rng Fctr	In Zone	Zone Outs	Zone Rtg	MLB Zone
As 2b	.292	548	160	39	2	1	38	62	90	.368	.376		146	143	1220.2	256	350	6	88	.990	4.47	364	335	.920	.902

Last Five Years

	Avg	AB	H	2B	3B	HR	RBI	BB	SO	OBP	SLG		Avg	AB	H	2B	3B	HR	RBI	BB	SO	OBP	SLG
vs. Left	.248	484	120	24	6	2	48	56	74	.338	.335	First Pitch	.363	372	135	20	7	4	39	8	0	.384	.487
vs. Right	.279	1801	503	109	23	13	131	165	290	.346	.387	Ahead in Count	.311	492	153	34	9	2	60	121	0	.449	.429
Groundball	.250	641	160	34	12	5	40	59	91	.320	.363	Behind in Count	.191	985	188	43	7	6	48	0	314	.203	.267
Flyball	.284	366	104	28	3	3	24	22	57	.337	.402	Two Strikes	.189	984	186	39	8	7	47	92	364	.264	.266
Home	.272	1138	309	66	12	9	96	114	181	.344	.374	Batting #1	.246	366	90	18	5	3	24	37	62	.328	.347
Away	.274	1147	314	67	17	6	83	107	183	.345	.378	Batting #2	.283	1499	424	90	16	8	121	144	235	.351	.380
Day	.294	660	194	40	9	5	56	70	108	.368	.405	Other	.260	420	109	25	8	4	34	40	67	.335	.386
Night	.264	1625	429	93	20	10	123	151	256	.335	.364	March/April	.238	303	72	14	4	2	18	41	46	.329	.330
Grass	.255	788	201	38	10	4	54	61	127	.318	.344	May	.283	467	132	33	4	2	30	40	67	.346	.383
Turf	.282	1497	422	95	19	11	125	160	237	.358	.393	June	.299	385	115	30	8	4	30	34	64	.369	.449
Pre-All Star	.277	1318	365	83	16	11	98	136	194	.351	.389	July	.270	471	127	22	5	5	49	45	60	.337	.369

	Avg	AB	H	2B	3B	HR	RBI	BB	SO	OBP	SLG		Avg	AB	H	2B	3B	HR	RBI	BB	SO	OBP	SLG
Post-All Star	.267	967	258	50	13	4	81	85	170	.336	.358	August	.275	346	95	14	4	1	27	34	70	.348	.347
Scoring Posn	.284	493	140	28	6	4	156	73	86	.384	.389	Sept/Oct	.262	313	82	20	4	1	25	27	57	.332	.361
Close & Late	.236	352	83	16	3	4	40	42	62	.323	.332	vs. AL	.204	49	10	3	0	0	1	7	9	.298	.265
None on/out	.267	532	142	30	9	4	4	51	72	.338	.380	vs. NL	.274	2236	613	130	29	15	178	214	355	.345	.378

							Batter vs. Pitcher (career)														

Hits Best Against	Avg	AB	H	2B	3B	HR	RBI	BB	SO	OBP	SLG	Hits Worst Against	Avg	AB	H	2B	3B	HR	RBI	BB	SO	OBP	SLG
Armando Reynoso	.545	11	6	2	2	0	0	1	2	.583	1.091	Mike Hampton	.000	12	0	0	0	0	0	2	1	.143	.000
Esteban Loaiza	.500	12	6	2	0	0	0	2	1	.571	.667	Trevor Hoffman	.000	11	0	0	0	0	0	1	4	.083	.000
John Ericks	.500	8	4	0	0	0	0	1	1	.636	.500	Dennis Martinez	.045	22	1	0	0	0	0	1	3	.087	.045
Kevin Gross	.467	15	7	2	0	0	4	4	2	.579	.600	Omar Olivares	.059	17	1	0	0	0	0	1	1	.111	.059
Steve Trachsel	.412	17	7	2	0	1	2	3	1	.500	.706	Dave Mlicki	.077	13	1	0	0	0	0	0	4	.077	.077

Mike Mordecai — Braves   Age 30 – Bats Right

	Avg	G	AB	R	H	2B	3B	HR	RBI	BB	SO	HBP	GDP	SB	CS	OBP	SLG	IBB	SH	SF	#Pit	#P/PA	GB	FB	G/F
1997 Season	.173	61	81	8	14	2	1	0	3	6	16	0	4	0	1	.227	.222	0	1	1	319	3.58	28	31	0.90
Career (1994-1997)	.231	200	268	31	62	13	1	6	25	25	56	0	5	1	1	.294	.354	1	7	3	1131	3.73	80	92	0.87

								1997 Season													

	Avg	AB	H	2B	3B	HR	RBI	BB	SO	OBP	SLG		Avg	AB	H	2B	3B	HR	RBI	BB	SO	OBP	SLG
vs. Left	.176	34	6	1	0	0	1	2	8	.216	.206	Scoring Posn	.050	20	1	0	0	0	2	3	7	.167	.050
vs. Right	.170	47	8	1	1	0	2	4	8	.235	.234	Close & Late	.103	29	3	0	0	0	0	2	7	.161	.103

Ramon Morel — Cubs   Age 23 – Pitches Right (groundball pitcher)

	ERA	W	L	Sv	G	GS	IP	BB	SO	Avg	H	2B	3B	HR	RBI	OBP	SLG	GF	IR	IRS	Hld	SvOp	SB	CS	GB	FB	G/F
1997 Season	4.76	0	0	0	8	0	11.1	7	7	.304	14	1	1	3	9	.396	.565	5	5	3	0		1	0	20	13	1.54
Career (1995-1997)	4.98	2	2	0	42	0	59.2	28	32	.318	77	8	3	7	39	.390	.463	9	23	8	2	1	2	1	110	62	1.77

								1997 Season													

	ERA	W	L	Sv	G	GS	IP	H	HR	BB	SO		Avg	AB	H	2B	3B	HR	RBI	BB	SO	OBP	SLG
Home	5.14	0	0	0	4	0	7.0	10	2	2	3	vs. Left	.368	19	7	0	0	1	3	1	2	.400	.526
Away	4.15	0	0	0	4	0	4.1	4	1	5	4	vs. Right	.259	27	7	1	1	2	6	6	5	.394	.593

Kevin Morgan — Mets   Age 28 – Bats Right

	Avg	G	AB	R	H	2B	3B	HR	RBI	BB	SO	HBP	GDP	SB	CS	OBP	SLG	IBB	SH	SF	#Pit	#P/PA	GB	FB	G/F
1997 Season	.000	1	1	0	0	0	0	0	0	0	0	0	0	0	0	.000	.000	0	0	0	1	1.00	0	1	0.00

								1997 Season													

	Avg	AB	H	2B	3B	HR	RBI	BB	SO	OBP	SLG		Avg	AB	H	2B	3B	HR	RBI	BB	SO	OBP	SLG
vs. Left	.000	1	0	0	0	0	0	0	0	.000	.000	Scoring Posn	.000	0	0	0	0	0	0	0	0	.000	.000
vs. Right	.000	0	0	0	0	0	0	0	0	.000	.000	Close & Late	.000	0	0	0	0	0	0	0	0	.000	.000

Mike Morgan — Reds   Age 38 – Pitches Right (groundball pitcher)

	ERA	W	L	Sv	G	GS	IP	BB	SO	Avg	H	2B	3B	HR	RBI	OBP	SLG	CG	ShO	Sup	QS	#P/S	SB	CS	GB	FB	G/F
1997 Season	4.78	9	12	0	31	30	162.0	49	103	.266	165	45	8	13	82	.327	.427	1	0	4.28	12	78	15	6	292	132	2.21
Last Five Years	4.53	34	55	0	122	121	712.0	239	406	.279	761	147	19	68	345	.340	.421	4	1	4.11	56	87	71	34	1277	558	2.29

								1997 Season													

	ERA	W	L	Sv	G	GS	IP	H	HR	BB	SO		Avg	AB	H	2B	3B	HR	RBI	BB	SO	OBP	SLG
Home	4.76	5	5	0	14	14	75.2	81	4	23	47	vs. Left	.271	291	79	19	4	7	40	25	50	.330	.436
Away	4.80	4	7	0	17	16	86.1	84	9	26	56	vs. Right	.261	329	86	26	4	6	42	24	53	.324	.419
Day	4.94	0	4	0	10	10	51.0	53	3	20	29	Inning 1-6	.269	579	156	42	7	13	81	46	98	.331	.434
Night	4.70	9	8	0	21	20	111.0	112	10	29	74	Inning 7+	.220	41	9	3	1	0	1	3	5	.273	.341
Grass	5.33	2	5	0	11	10	50.2	55	5	17	30	None on	.234	372	87	25	3	4	4	26	66	.288	.349
Turf	4.53	7	7	0	20	20	111.1	110	8	32	73	Runners on	.315	248	78	20	5	9	78	23	37	.384	.544
March/April	5.87	3	0	0	5	5	23.0	26	1	16	20	Scoring Posn	.303	152	46	10	2	6	64	19	30	.386	.513
May	5.45	2	2	0	7	6	33.0	37	1	6	17	Close & Late	.286	14	4	2	1	0	1	3	1	.412	.571
June	6.55	0	0	0	3	3	11.0	17	2	4	8	None on/out	.259	162	42	10	3	2	2	11	25	.310	.395
July	4.44	1	4	0	5	5	26.1	25	3	9	13	vs. 1st Batr (relief)	.000	1	0	0	0	0	0	0	0	.000	.000
August	4.58	2	2	0	6	6	35.1	31	4	8	25	1st Inning Pitched	.241	112	27	4	0	4	11	6	19	.286	.384
Sept/Oct	3.24	4	1	0	5	5	33.1	29	2	6	20	First 75 Pitches	.266	541	144	38	6	10	70	46	92	.332	.414
Starter	4.79	9	12	0	30	30	161.2	164	13	47	103	Pitch 76-90	.281	57	16	7	1	2	9	1	9	.288	.544
Reliever	0.00	0	0	0	1	0	0.1	1	0	2	0	Pitch 91-105	.227	22	5	0	1	1	3	2	2	.292	.455
0-3 Days Rest (Start)	30.86	0	1	0	1	1	2.1	8	0	1	2	Pitch 106+	.000	0	0	0	0	0	0	0	0	.000	.000
4 Days Rest	3.86	6	5	0	16	16	93.1	83	5	24	56	First Pitch	.361	97	35	9	1	4	19	5	0	.404	.598
5+ Days Rest	5.18	3	6	0	13	13	66.0	73	8	22	45	Ahead in Count	.230	270	62	16	4	6	29	0	92	.240	.385
vs. AL	6.00	0	1	0	1	1	6.0	5	2	1	5	Behind in Count	.298	151	45	15	0	1	23	23	0	.389	.417
vs. NL	4.73	9	11	0	30	29	156.0	160	11	48	98	Two Strikes	.211	251	53	13	3	7	25	21	103	.276	.371
Pre-All Star	5.63	3	5	0	16	15	72.0	85	4	29	47	Pre-All Star	.300	283	85	24	3	4	40	29	47	.373	.449
Post-All Star	4.10	6	7	0	15	15	90.0	80	9	20	56	Post-All Star	.237	337	80	21	5	9	42	20	56	.287	.409

								Last Five Years													

	ERA	W	L	Sv	G	GS	IP	H	HR	BB	SO		Avg	AB	H	2B	3B	HR	RBI	BB	SO	OBP	SLG
Home	3.96	15	25	0	57	57	345.2	359	27	103	205	vs. Left	.277	1290	357	74	9	29	150	146	190	.351	.416
Away	5.06	19	30	0	65	64	366.1	402	41	136	201	vs. Right	.280	1441	404	73	10	39	195	93	216	.329	.426

Last Five Years

	ERA	W	L	Sv	G	GS	IP	H	HR	BB	SO		Avg	AB	H	2B	3B	HR	RBI	BB	SO	OBP	SLG
Day	4.49	9	28	0	53	53	313.0	345	25	107	176	Inning 1-6	.280	2486	696	134	17	62	325	222	378	.342	.422
Night	4.56	25	27	0	69	68	399.0	416	43	132	230	Inning 7+	.265	245	65	13	2	6	20	17	28	.312	.408
Grass	4.54	17	33	0	72	71	412.2	436	45	153	233	None on	.274	1589	435	92	11	33	33	111	242	.326	.408
Turf	4.51	17	22	0	50	50	299.1	325	23	86	173	Runners on	.285	1142	326	55	8	35	312	128	164	.358	.440
March/April	5.35	1	10	0	14	14	74.0	81	6	39	51	Scoring Posn	.278	697	194	29	5	22	271	95	119	.362	.429
May	4.76	8	8	0	20	19	109.2	113	6	40	55	Close & Late	.279	122	34	6	1	3	9	11	14	.338	.418
June	4.50	8	8	0	20	20	122.0	132	13	46	64	None on/out	.307	711	218	47	6	16	16	48	101	.357	.457
July	3.87	6	10	0	24	24	146.2	151	15	40	81	vs. 1st Batr (relief)	.000	1	0	0	0	0	0	0	0	.000	.000
August	5.47	6	13	0	23	23	130.0	164	15	38	78	1st Inning Pitched	.274	464	127	21	3	14	73	42	76	.336	.422
Sept/Oct	3.68	9	6	0	21	21	129.2	120	13	36	77	First 75 Pitches	.282	2216	625	121	16	51	290	193	346	.344	.420
Starter	4.53	34	55	0	121	121	711.2	760	68	237	406	Pitch 76-90	.252	310	78	15	1	11	34	28	35	.310	.413
Reliever	0.00	0	0	0	1	0	0.1	1	0	2	0	Pitch 91-105	.268	168	45	9	2	4	11	14	19	.324	.417
0-3 Days Rest (Start)	30.86	0	1	0	1	1	2.1	8	0	1	2	Pitch 106+	.351	37	13	2	0	2	10	4	6	.415	.568
4 Days Rest	4.44	18	33	0	70	70	427.1	461	33	145	232	First Pitch	.333	469	156	32	3	14	70	13	0	.359	.503
5+ Days Rest	4.44	16	21	0	50	50	282.0	291	35	91	172	Ahead in Count	.229	1129	258	43	8	20	109	0	352	.234	.334
vs. AL	6.00	0	1	0	1	1	6.0	5	2	1	5	Behind in Count	.323	662	214	47	5	24	109	132	0	.435	.518
vs. NL	4.51	34	54	0	121	120	706.0	756	66	238	401	Two Strikes	.219	1070	234	39	6	20	98	94	406	.282	.322
Pre-All Star	4.87	16	29	0	62	61	353.1	385	30	138	198	Pre-All Star	.283	1360	385	81	10	30	173	138	198	.352	.424
Post-All Star	4.19	18	26	0	60	60	358.2	376	38	101	208	Post-All Star	.274	1371	376	66	9	38	172	101	208	.327	.419

Pitcher vs. Batter (since 1984)

Pitches Best Vs.	Avg	AB	H	2B	3B	HR	RBI	BB	SO	OBP	SLG	Pitches Worst Vs.	Avg	AB	H	2B	3B	HR	RBI	BB	SO	OBP	SLG
Mark Lemke	.045	22	1	0	0	0	0	3	4	.160	.045	Danny Tartabull	.727	11	8	0	0	1	4	1	0	.750	1.000
Rondell White	.071	14	1	1	0	0	0	1	1	.133	.143	Mike Lansing	.556	18	10	2	2	0	1	2	2	.619	.889
Cal Ripken	.091	22	2	0	0	0	0	4	4	.091	.091	Don Slaught	.533	15	8	1	0	2	4	3	0	.632	1.000
Kirt Manwaring	.103	29	3	0	0	1	2	5	.156	.103	Rickey Henderson	.500	12	6	0	0	3	3	2	2	.571	1.250
Eddie Taubensee	.105	19	2	0	0	2	0	5	.100	.105	Ellis Burks	.385	13	5	1	0	2	4	3	3	.529	.923

Alvin Morman — Indians
Age 29 – Pitches Left

	ERA	W	L	Sv	G	GS	IP	BB	SO	Avg	H	2B	3B	HR	RBI	OBP	SLG	GF	IR	IRS	Hld	SvOp	SB	CS	GB	FB	G/F
1997 Season	5.89	0	0	2	34	0	18.1	14	13	.268	19	2	2	2	13	.395	.437	7	26	3	5	2	7	1	22	19	1.16
Career (1996-1997)	5.22	4	1	2	87	0	60.1	38	44	.263	62	10	2	10	48	.366	.449	16	77	21	12	4	9	2	92	63	1.46

1997 Season

	ERA	W	L	Sv	G	GS	IP	H	HR	BB	SO		Avg	AB	H	2B	3B	HR	RBI	BB	SO	OBP	SLG
Home	5.00	0	0	1	17	0	9.0	9	1	7	8	vs. Left	.268	41	11	1	1	0	7	4	9	.348	.341
Away	6.75	0	0	1	17	0	9.1	10	1	7	5	vs. Right	.267	30	8	1	1	2	6	10	4	.450	.567
Starter	0.00	0	0	0	0	0	0.0	0	0	0	0	Scoring Posn	.182	33	6	1	1	0	11	7	10	.325	.273
Reliever	5.89	0	0	2	34	0	18.1	19	2	14	13	Close & Late	.222	18	4	0	0	0	3	3	2	.364	.222
0 Days rest (Relief)	8.44	0	0	0	9	0	5.1	6	0	4	4	None on/out	.500	12	6	1	1	1	1	4	1	.647	1.000
1 or 2 Days rest	5.40	0	0	0	12	0	6.2	9	2	6	3	First Pitch	.556	9	5	0	1	0	2	2	0	.636	.778
3+ Days rest	4.26	0	0	2	13	0	6.1	4	0	4	6	Ahead in Count	.156	32	5	0	1	1	5	0	12	.156	.313
Pre-All Star	1.17	0	0	2	16	0	7.2	3	1	5	4	Behind in Count	.250	16	4	1	0	1	4	4	0	.429	.313
Post-All Star	9.28	0	0	0	18	0	10.2	16	1	9	9	Two Strikes	.147	34	5	1	0	1	5	8	13	.310	.265

Russ Morman — Marlins
Age 36 – Bats Right (flyball hitter)

	Avg	G	AB	R	H	2B	3B	HR	RBI	BB	SO	HBP	GDP	SB	CS	OBP	SLG	IBB	SH	SF	#Pit	#P/PA	GB	FB	G/F
1997 Season	.286	4	7	3	2	1	0	1	2	0	2	0	0	0	1	0	.286	.857	0	0	0	28	4.00	2	3	0.67
Last Five Years	.254	57	118	14	30	4	2	5	11	6	25	2	7	1	0	.302	.449	0	0	0	462	3.67	44	29	1.52

1997 Season

	Avg	AB	H	2B	3B	HR	RBI	BB	SO	OBP	SLG		Avg	AB	H	2B	3B	HR	RBI	BB	SO	OBP	SLG
vs. Left	1.000	1	1	0	0	1	2	0	0	1.000	4.000	Scoring Posn	1.000	1	1	0	0	1	2	0	0	1.000	4.000
vs. Right	.167	6	1	1	0	0	0	0	2	.167	.333	Close & Late	.000	2	0	0	0	0	0	0	1	.000	.000

Hal Morris — Reds
Age 33 – Bats Left (groundball hitter)

	Avg	G	AB	R	H	2B	3B	HR	RBI	BB	SO	HBP	GDP	SB	CS	OBP	SLG	IBB	SH	SF	#Pit	#P/PA	GB	FB	G/F
1997 Season	.276	96	333	42	92	20	1	1	33	23	43	3	10	3	1	.328	.351	2	4	1	1268	3.48	169	55	3.07
Last Five Years	.306	552	2035	285	623	125	11	45	291	170	290	16	53	19	11	.361	.445	26	4	12	8050	3.57	895	429	2.09

1997 Season

	Avg	AB	H	2B	3B	HR	RBI	BB	SO	OBP	SLG		Avg	AB	H	2B	3B	HR	RBI	BB	SO	OBP	SLG
vs. Left	.250	72	18	3	0	0	12	3	13	.286	.292	First Pitch	.317	60	19	2	0	0	8	2	0	.349	.350
vs. Right	.284	261	74	17	1	1	21	20	30	.339	.368	Ahead in Count	.222	81	18	4	1	1	4	9	0	.300	.333
Groundball	.246	65	16	2	0	0	8	4	9	.290	.277	Behind in Count	.259	135	35	10	0	0	13	0	41	.263	.333
Flyball	.275	51	14	5	0	0	2	0	8	.275	.373	Two Strikes	.220	127	28	4	0	0	11	12	43	.291	.252
Home	.299	167	50	13	0	1	19	11	15	.343	.395	Batting #3	.232	69	16	5	0	0	3	4	4	.284	.304
Away	.253	166	42	7	1	0	14	12	28	.313	.307	Batting #5	.313	144	45	9	1	0	20	9	18	.353	.389
Day	.269	134	36	6	0	1	14	6	18	.298	.336	Other	.258	120	31	6	0	1	10	10	21	.323	.333
Night	.281	199	56	14	1	0	19	17	25	.347	.362	March/April	.244	90	22	5	0	1	9	7	13	.306	.333
Grass	.184	114	21	2	0	0	4	9	16	.248	.202	May	.258	89	23	7	0	0	5	4	8	.287	.337
Turf	.324	219	71	18	1	1	29	14	27	.370	.429	June	.266	79	21	4	0	0	8	5	8	.326	.316
Pre-All Star	.268	276	74	16	0	1	25	18	34	.319	.337	July	.347	75	26	4	1	0	11	7	14	.402	.427
Post-All Star	.316	57	18	4	1	0	8	5	9	.371	.421	August	.000	0	0	0	0	0	0	0	0	.000	.000
Scoring Posn	.197	76	15	3	0	0	26	9	10	.287	.237	Sept/Oct	.000	0	0	0	0	0	0	0	0	.000	.000

323

1997 Season

	Avg	AB	H	2B	3B	HR	RBI	BB	SO	OBP	SLG		Avg	AB	H	2B	3B	HR	RBI	BB	SO	OBP	SLG
Close & Late	.246	57	14	2	0	0	3	3	10	.283	.281	vs. AL	.370	27	10	2	0	0	4	3	4	.452	.444
None on/out	.210	81	17	3	0	0	0	7	8	.273	.247	vs. NL	.268	306	82	18	1	1	29	20	39	.316	.343

1997 By Position

Position	Avg	AB	H	2B	3B	HR	RBI	BB	SO	OBP	SLG	G	GS	Innings	PO	A	E	DP	Fld Pct	Rng Fctr	In Zone	Zone Outs	Zone Rtg	MLB Zone
As Pinch Hitter	.091	11	1	0	0	0	0	0	1	.091	.091	11	0	—	—	—	—	—	—	—	—	—	—	—
As 1b	.283	322	91	20	1	1	33	23	42	.335	.360	89	84	749.0	672	51	7	67	.990	—	130	107	.823	.874

Last Five Years

	Avg	AB	H	2B	3B	HR	RBI	BB	SO	OBP	SLG		Avg	AB	H	2B	3B	HR	RBI	BB	SO	OBP	SLG
vs. Left	.252	468	118	26	0	1	61	34	91	.309	.314	First Pitch	.367	376	138	24	2	9	59	18	0	.399	.513
vs. Right	.322	1567	505	99	11	44	230	136	199	.377	.484	Ahead in Count	.371	491	182	36	6	24	98	80	0	.455	.615
Groundball	.299	618	185	39	2	11	83	44	92	.346	.422	Behind in Count	.234	822	192	42	3	5	72	0	251	.240	.310
Flyball	.278	313	87	17	0	5	37	25	48	.329	.380	Two Strikes	.211	825	174	40	2	4	71	72	290	.278	.279
Home	.326	994	324	84	6	21	153	80	125	.377	.486	Batting #2	.292	524	153	35	3	8	64	42	74	.342	.416
Away	.287	1041	299	41	5	24	138	90	165	.346	.405	Batting #3	.307	651	200	35	4	17	98	45	89	.352	.452
Day	.311	627	195	35	7	13	87	54	87	.365	.451	Other	.314	860	270	55	4	20	129	83	127	.379	.457
Night	.304	1408	428	90	4	32	204	116	203	.359	.442	March/April	.279	294	82	17	0	7	38	26	47	.340	.408
Grass	.270	677	183	22	3	16	83	59	109	.327	.383	May	.283	346	98	23	4	4	43	24	40	.325	.408
Turf	.324	1358	440	103	8	29	208	111	181	.378	.476	June	.304	378	115	18	2	5	48	23	53	.349	.402
Pre-All Star	.296	1108	328	63	6	19	150	87	154	.348	.415	July	.313	367	115	24	1	8	62	32	60	.370	.450
Post-All Star	.318	927	295	62	5	26	141	83	136	.376	.480	August	.326	359	117	22	3	12	56	34	46	.387	.504
Scoring Posn	.273	535	146	29	2	6	216	79	90	.357	.368	Sept/Oct	.330	291	96	21	1	9	44	31	44	.396	.502
Close & Late	.292	325	95	19	0	9	47	30	61	.350	.434	vs. AL	.370	27	10	2	0	0	4	3	4	.452	.444
None on/out	.292	448	131	26	1	14	14	28	54	.340	.449	vs. NL	.305	2008	613	123	11	45	287	167	286	.360	.445

Batter vs. Pitcher (career)

Hits Best Against	Avg	AB	H	2B	3B	HR	RBI	BB	SO	OBP	SLG	Hits Worst Against	Avg	AB	H	2B	3B	HR	RBI	BB	SO	OBP	SLG
Rick Reed	.615	13	8	2	0	0	1	0	1	.615	.769	Darryl Kile	.053	19	1	1	0	0	0	1	4	.143	.105
Mel Rojas	.588	17	10	2	0	1	3	0	1	.556	.882	Pedro Martinez	.083	24	2	0	0	0	0	0	4	.083	.083
Andy Ashby	.500	16	8	1	0	1	2	3	3	.579	.750	Pete Smith	.083	12	1	1	0	0	2	0	1	.083	.167
Jeff Juden	.500	16	8	2	0	2	4	1	4	.500	1.000	Al Leiter	.091	11	1	0	0	0	1	0	0	.091	.091
Tim Worrell	.417	12	5	1	0	1	5	2	1	.500	.750	Rheal Cormier	.125	16	2	0	0	0	1	0	4	.125	.125

Matt Morris — Cardinals
Age 23 – Pitches Right (groundball pitcher)

	ERA	W	L	Sv	G	GS	IP	BB	SO	Avg	H	2B	3B	HR	RBI	OBP	SLG	CG	ShO	Sup	QS	#P/S	SB	CS	GB	FB	G/F
1997 Season	3.19	12	9	0	33	33	217.0	69	149	.258	208	32	4	12	81	.319	.352	3	0	4.60	22	100	11	7	345	177	1.95

1997 Season

	ERA	W	L	Sv	G	GS	IP	H	BB	SO		Avg	AB	H	2B	3B	HR	RBI	BB	SO	OBP	SLG
Home	2.73	9	5	0	21	21	141.2	132	7	43	108	vs. Left	.259	405	105	18	3	8	55	46	80	.333	.378
Away	4.06	3	4	0	12	12	75.1	76	5	26	41	vs. Right	.257	401	103	14	1	4	26	23	69	.306	.327
Day	4.35	6	5	0	16	16	99.1	96	8	33	74	Inning 1-6	.255	689	176	29	1	10	70	60	128	.316	.344
Night	2.22	6	4	0	17	17	117.2	112	4	36	75	Inning 7+	.274	117	32	3	3	2	11	9	21	.338	.402
Grass	3.29	12	8	0	30	30	197.0	188	12	62	144	None on	.249	473	118	18	3	5	5	40	90	.313	.332
Turf	2.25	0	1	0	3	3	20.0	20	0	7	5	Runners on	.270	333	90	14	1	7	76	29	59	.328	.381
March/April	2.65	0	1	0	4	4	17.0	20	1	4	12	Scoring Posn	.286	189	54	9	0	3	63	23	36	.352	.381
May	2.63	2	2	0	6	6	41.0	35	2	11	29	Close & Late	.291	79	23	2	2	2	8	5	11	.349	.443
June	2.88	4	1	0	6	6	40.2	42	4	11	26	None on/out	.258	209	54	8	0	2	2	19	33	.320	.325
July	2.18	2	2	0	6	6	41.1	32	1	19	33	vs. 1st Batr (relief)	.000	0	0	0	0	0	0	0	0	.000	.000
August	5.17	1	2	0	5	5	31.1	38	1	11	23	1st Inning Pitched	.287	122	35	6	0	2	15	15	27	.364	.385
Sept/Oct	3.74	3	1	0	6	6	45.2	41	3	13	26	First 75 Pitches	.261	567	148	24	1	9	60	52	103	.323	.354
Starter	3.19	12	9	0	33	33	217.0	208	12	69	149	Pitch 76-90	.217	120	26	4	0	1	8	6	25	.260	.275
Reliever	0.00	0	0	0	0	0	0.0	0	0	0	0	Pitch 91-105	.278	79	22	3	2	2	7	8	11	.352	.443
0-3 Days Rest (Start)	0.00	0	0	0	0	0	0.0	0	0	0	0	Pitch 106+	.300	40	12	1	1	0	6	3	10	.370	.375
4 Days Rest	3.21	8	3	0	21	21	140.0	124	6	47	90	First Pitch	.254	114	29	4	0	1	13	2	0	.263	.316
5+ Days Rest	3.16	4	6	0	12	12	77.0	84	6	22	59	Ahead in Count	.215	377	81	13	3	2	23	0	136	.222	.287
vs. AL	1.19	2	0	0	3	3	22.2	16	2	4	12	Behind in Count	.331	172	57	9	1	6	28	32	0	.432	.500
vs. NL	3.43	10	9	0	30	30	194.1	192	10	65	137	Two Strikes	.190	369	70	11	1	1	19	35	149	.268	.233
Pre-All Star	2.82	6	5	0	17	17	105.1	103	7	30	76	Pre-All Star	.263	391	103	13	0	7	35	30	76	.319	.350
Post-All Star	3.55	6	4	0	16	16	111.2	105	5	39	73	Post-All Star	.253	415	105	19	4	5	46	39	73	.320	.354

Julio Mosquera — Blue Jays
Age 26 – Bats Right

	Avg	G	AB	R	H	2B	3B	HR	RBI	BB	SO	HBP	GDP	SB	CS	OBP	SLG	IBB	SH	SF	#Pit	#P/PA	GB	FB	G/F
1997 Season	.250	3	8	0	2	1	0	0	0	0	2	0	0	0	0	.250	.375	0	0	0	25	3.13	3	1	3.00
Career (1996-1997)	.233	11	30	2	7	3	0	0	2	1	7	0	0	0	1	.258	.333	0	0	0	90	2.90	16	4	4.00

1997 Season

	Avg	AB	H	2B	3B	HR	RBI	BB	SO	OBP	SLG		Avg	AB	H	2B	3B	HR	RBI	BB	SO	OBP	SLG
vs. Left	.000	0	0	0	0	0	0	0	0	.000	.000	Scoring Posn	.000	4	0	0	0	0	0	0	1	.000	.000
vs. Right	.250	8	2	1	0	0	0	0	2	.250	.375	Close & Late	.000	1	0	0	0	0	0	0	0	.000	.000

James Mouton — Astros

	Avg	G	AB	R	H	2B	3B	HR	RBI	BB	SO	HBP	GDP	SB	CS	OBP	SLG	IBB	SH	SF	#Pit	#P/PA	GB	FB	G/F
1997 Season	.211	86	180	24	38	9	1	3	23	18	30	2	3	9	7	.287	.322	0	2	2	784	3.84	57	64	0.89
Career (1994-1997)	.249	411	1088	149	271	53	4	12	100	108	213	11	23	79	29	.321	.338	3	9	7	4718	3.86	387	307	1.26

1997 Season

	Avg	AB	H	2B	3B	HR	RBI	BB	SO	OBP	SLG		Avg	AB	H	2B	3B	HR	RBI	BB	SO	OBP	SLG
vs. Left	.263	99	26	6	1	3	15	11	16	.336	.434	Scoring Posn	.196	56	11	4	0	0	20	2	8	.230	.268
vs. Right	.148	81	12	3	0	0	8	7	14	.225	.185	Close & Late	.139	36	5	2	0	0	2	4	10	.225	.194
Home	.269	78	21	4	1	1	13	9	16	.348	.385	None on/out	.303	33	10	3	0	0	0	2	5	.361	.394
Away	.167	102	17	5	0	2	10	9	14	.239	.275	Batting #2	.241	79	19	6	0	2	12	10	8	.330	.392
First Pitch	.310	29	9	3	1	1	5	0	0	.333	.586	Batting #8	.214	28	6	1	1	2	2	8	.290	.429
Ahead in Count	.290	31	9	2	0	2	5	9	0	.450	.548	Other	.178	73	13	2	0	0	6	14	.228	.205
Behind in Count	.200	80	16	4	0	0	10	0	24	.205	.250	Pre-All Star	.220	123	27	8	1	2	15	12	19	.290	.350
Two Strikes	.169	89	15	4	0	0	11	9	30	.248	.213	Post-All Star	.193	57	11	1	0	1	8	6	11	.281	.263

Career (1994-1997)

	Avg	AB	H	2B	3B	HR	RBI	BB	SO	OBP	SLG		Avg	AB	H	2B	3B	HR	RBI	BB	SO	OBP	SLG
vs. Left	.313	438	137	21	3	8	46	46	76	.378	.429	First Pitch	.323	158	51	9	2	4	24	1	0	.341	.481
vs. Right	.206	650	134	32	1	4	54	62	137	.283	.277	Ahead in Count	.310	168	52	12	1	3	17	57	0	.487	.446
Groundball	.273	245	67	17	1	2	24	17	46	.330	.376	Behind in Count	.208	542	113	21	0	1	38	0	176	.212	.253
Flyball	.216	176	38	7	1	2	14	13	40	.270	.301	Two Strikes	.198	570	113	22	1	3	39	49	213	.264	.256
Home	.267	521	139	26	3	6	48	48	102	.332	.363	Batting #1	.260	430	112	18	1	3	23	39	97	.332	.328
Away	.233	567	132	27	1	6	52	60	111	.312	.316	Batting #7	.240	229	55	12	1	2	28	24	42	.311	.328
Day	.276	315	87	17	1	3	28	42	63	.366	.365	Other	.242	429	104	23	2	7	49	45	74	.316	.354
Night	.238	773	184	36	3	9	72	66	150	.302	.327	March/April	.208	154	32	9	0	2	17	13	36	.269	.305
Grass	.210	338	71	14	0	4	30	36	67	.288	.287	May	.259	278	72	14	3	3	23	25	68	.331	.363
Turf	.267	750	200	39	4	8	70	72	146	.336	.361	June	.245	184	45	7	0	1	21	18	30	.314	.299
Pre-All Star	.246	688	169	34	3	8	67	65	146	.315	.339	July	.266	188	50	9	0	3	11	20	39	.341	.362
Post-All Star	.255	400	102	19	1	4	33	43	67	.331	.338	August	.242	182	44	11	1	2	19	21	23	.325	.346
Scoring Posn	.222	293	65	14	0	3	84	32	55	.305	.300	Sept/Oct	.275	102	28	3	0	1	9	11	17	.342	.333
Close & Late	.199	186	37	9	1	2	15	23	44	.291	.290	vs. AL	.125	16	2	0	0	0	0	2	3	.222	.125
None on/out	.266	316	84	18	1	2	2	25	66	.328	.348	vs. NL	.251	1072	269	53	4	12	100	106	210	.323	.341

Batter vs. Pitcher (career)

Hits Best Against	Avg	AB	H	2B	3B	HR	RBI	BB	SO	OBP	SLG	Hits Worst Against	Avg	AB	H	2B	3B	HR	RBI	BB	SO	OBP	SLG
F. Valenzuela	.462	13	6	0	0	2	4	2	0	.500	.923	Steve Trachsel	.100	10	1	0	0	1	2	1	4	.182	.400
Jeff Fassero	.375	16	6	2	0	0	0	0	3	.375	.500	John Smoltz	.182	11	2	0	0	0	0	0	4	.182	.182
Al Leiter	.364	11	4	1	0	0	2	2	0	.462	.455	Steve Avery	.182	11	2	0	0	0	0	0	3	.182	.182
Chris Hammond	.364	11	4	1	0	0	0	1	3	.417	.455	Ramon Martinez	.214	14	3	0	0	0	0	0	5	.214	.214
Frank Castillo	.364	11	4	2	0	0	2	0	2	.364	.545	Denny Neagle	.214	14	3	0	0	0	0	2	5	.313	.214

Lyle Mouton — White Sox

	Avg	G	AB	R	H	2B	3B	HR	RBI	BB	SO	HBP	GDP	SB	CS	OBP	SLG	IBB	SH	SF	#Pit	#P/PA	GB	FB	G/F
1997 Season	.269	88	242	26	65	9	0	5	23	14	66	1	8	4	4	.308	.368	1	0	3	947	3.64	88	53	1.66
Career (1995-1997)	.287	233	635	74	182	33	1	17	89	55	162	5	18	8	4	.345	.422	5	0	7	2619	3.73	221	139	1.59

1997 Season

	Avg	AB	H	2B	3B	HR	RBI	BB	SO	OBP	SLG		Avg	AB	H	2B	3B	HR	RBI	BB	SO	OBP	SLG
vs. Left	.280	100	28	4	0	2	11	3	22	.298	.380	Scoring Posn	.259	54	14	4	0	0	17	8	19	.338	.333
vs. Right	.261	142	37	5	0	3	12	11	44	.314	.359	Close & Late	.323	31	10	0	0	0	3	5	10	.405	.323
Home	.267	120	32	6	0	4	12	2	31	.282	.417	None on/out	.262	61	16	0	0	1	1	2	14	.286	.311
Away	.270	122	33	3	0	1	11	12	35	.331	.320	Batting #5	.241	112	27	5	0	2	12	4	27	.265	.339
First Pitch	.385	39	15	2	0	1	7	1	0	.390	.513	Batting #6	.315	92	29	3	0	3	8	9	23	.375	.446
Ahead in Count	.359	39	14	2	0	2	6	6	0	.444	.564	Other	.237	38	9	1	0	0	3	1	16	.256	.263
Behind in Count	.184	125	23	2	0	1	5	0	60	.189	.224	Pre-All Star	.286	161	46	6	0	4	20	8	41	.318	.398
Two Strikes	.167	126	21	3	0	2	9	7	66	.213	.238	Post-All Star	.235	81	19	3	0	1	3	6	25	.287	.309

Career (1995-1997)

	Avg	AB	H	2B	3B	HR	RBI	BB	SO	OBP	SLG		Avg	AB	H	2B	3B	HR	RBI	BB	SO	OBP	SLG
vs. Left	.290	303	88	16	0	7	44	24	73	.340	.413	First Pitch	.287	101	29	4	0	2	13	4	0	.311	.386
vs. Right	.283	332	94	17	1	10	45	31	89	.349	.431	Ahead in Count	.395	114	45	5	1	5	23	25	0	.507	.588
Groundball	.308	143	44	10	1	5	26	14	36	.377	.497	Behind in Count	.212	312	66	14	0	6	25	0	142	.218	.314
Flyball	.355	93	33	8	0	4	15	9	28	.413	.570	Two Strikes	.195	323	63	16	0	6	33	26	162	.258	.300
Home	.299	308	92	17	1	12	45	25	74	.349	.477	Batting #5	.228	171	39	7	0	5	24	10	42	.269	.357
Away	.275	327	90	16	0	5	44	30	88	.341	.370	Batting #6	.304	263	80	16	1	9	35	30	66	.379	.475
Day	.297	185	55	11	1	9	27	17	46	.363	.514	Other	.313	201	63	10	0	3	30	15	54	.360	.408
Night	.282	450	127	22	0	8	62	38	116	.337	.384	March/April	.284	67	19	3	0	2	10	9	19	.359	.418
Grass	.311	541	168	28	1	16	78	50	127	.369	.455	May	.320	75	24	3	1	2	8	3	15	.363	.467
Turf	.149	94	14	5	0	1	11	5	35	.198	.234	June	.271	129	35	5	0	5	20	14	39	.336	.426
Pre-All Star	.284	285	81	11	1	9	40	26	79	.343	.425	July	.295	95	28	5	0	2	12	3	21	.316	.411
Post-All Star	.289	350	101	22	0	8	49	29	83	.346	.420	August	.306	144	44	7	0	2	19	16	40	.380	.396
Scoring Posn	.283	173	49	12	1	3	71	31	53	.382	.416	Sept/Oct	.256	125	32	10	0	4	20	10	28	.314	.420
Close & Late	.352	88	31	4	1	5	17	11	27	.420	.591	vs. AL	.290	606	176	31	1	16	84	54	155	.350	.424
None on/out	.294	143	42	6	0	4	4	6	21	.322	.420	vs. NL	.207	29	6	2	0	1	5	1	7	.233	.379

Batter vs. Pitcher (career)

Hits Best Against	Avg	AB	H	2B	3B	HR	RBI	BB	SO	OBP	SLG	Hits Worst Against	Avg	AB	H	2B	3B	HR	RBI	BB	SO	OBP	SLG
Mike Mussina	.462	13	6	0	0	1	1	0	3	.462	.692	Rich Robertson	.000	13	0	0	0	0	3	1	2	.063	.000
Kenny Rogers	.409	22	9	2	0	0	4	1	1	.435	.500	Mark Langston	.231	13	3	0	0	0	1	1	6	.267	.231
Ben McDonald	.385	13	5	1	0	1	1	2	2	.467	.692	Chuck Finley	.231	13	3	1	0	0	0	6	5	.474	.308

Hits Best Against	Avg	AB	H	2B	3B	HR	RBI	BB	SO	OBP	SLG	Hits Worst Against	Avg	AB	H	2B	3B	HR	RBI	BB	SO	OBP	SLG
Darren Oliver	.385	13	5	1	0	0	0	1	3	.429	.462												
Andy Pettitte	.313	16	5	1	0	0	1	0	5	.313	.375												

Jamie Moyer — Mariners

Age 35 – Pitches Left

	ERA	W	L	Sv	G	GS	IP	BB	SO	Avg	H	2B	3B	HR	RBI	OBP	SLG	CG	ShO	Sup	QS	#P/S	SB	CS	GB	FB	G/F
1997 Season	3.86	17	5	0	30	30	188.2	43	113	.256	187	29	0	21	70	.303	.382	2	0	7.73	19	98	14	6	271	220	1.23
Last Five Years	4.18	55	30	0	139	117	766.0	195	434	.266	793	140	7	96	336	.314	.414	5	1	6.13	63	95	53	21	1116	899	1.24

1997 Season

	ERA	W	L	Sv	G	GS	IP	H	HR	BB	SO		Avg	AB	H	2B	3B	HR	RBI	BB	SO	OBP	SLG
Home	3.63	12	2	0	16	16	101.2	98	12	27	61	vs. Left	.322	183	59	8	0	6	20	12	25	.380	.464
Away	4.14	5	3	0	14	14	87.0	89	9	16	52	vs. Right	.234	547	128	21	0	15	50	31	88	.277	.355
Day	3.38	5	1	0	9	9	56.0	53	8	14	26	Inning 1-6	.250	656	164	27	0	20	65	38	103	.297	.383
Night	4.07	12	4	0	21	21	132.2	134	13	29	87	Inning 7+	.311	74	23	2	0	1	5	5	10	.363	.378
Grass	4.10	4	3	0	12	12	74.2	78	9	13	44	None on	.252	433	109	17	0	12	12	23	64	.297	.374
Turf	3.71	13	2	0	18	18	114.0	109	12	30	69	Runners on	.263	297	78	12	0	9	58	20	49	.313	.394
March/April	3.18	0	0	0	1	1	5.2	5	1	0	1	Scoring Posn	.253	154	39	8	0	4	48	13	28	.314	.383
May	5.02	4	2	0	6	6	37.2	44	7	11	18	Close & Late	.321	28	9	1	0	1	4	2	1	.387	.464
June	4.40	3	0	0	5	5	28.2	26	3	6	10	None on/out	.259	193	50	5	0	6	6	11	25	.302	.378
July	3.91	4	2	0	7	7	48.1	47	6	11	36	vs. 1st Batr (relief)	.000	0	0	0	0	0	0	0	0	.000	.000
August	2.58	3	0	0	6	6	38.1	32	1	10	28	1st Inning Pitched	.309	123	38	4	0	6	16	9	20	.361	.488
Sept/Oct	3.60	3	1	0	5	5	30.0	33	3	5	20	First 75 Pitches	.264	535	141	20	0	18	56	29	84	.307	.402
Starter	3.86	17	5	0	30	30	188.2	187	21	43	113	Pitch 76-90	.225	102	23	5	0	1	6	9	13	.301	.304
Reliever	0.00	0	0	0	0	0	0.0	0	0	0	0	Pitch 91-105	.235	68	16	4	0	1	3	4	10	.278	.338
0-3 Days Rest (Start)	2.57	0	0	0	2	2	14.0	10	2	3	5	Pitch 106+	.280	25	7	0	0	1	5	1	6	.308	.400
4 Days Rest	3.68	17	3	0	22	22	141.2	141	16	34	88	First Pitch	.365	104	38	5	0	4	14	1	0	.377	.529
5+ Days Rest	5.18	0	2	0	6	6	33.0	36	3	6	20	Ahead in Count	.206	311	64	12	0	8	22	0	93	.215	.322
vs. AL	4.09	15	5	0	27	27	169.1	176	19	37	104	Behind in Count	.298	161	48	3	0	7	19	17	0	.365	.447
vs. NL	1.86	2	0	0	3	3	19.1	11	2	6	9	Two Strikes	.191	330	63	13	0	7	20	25	113	.251	.294
Pre-All Star	4.34	8	2	0	14	14	85.0	85	12	23	36	Pre-All Star	.258	330	85	14	0	12	30	23	36	.311	.400
Post-All Star	3.47	9	3	0	16	16	103.2	102	9	20	77	Post-All Star	.255	400	102	15	0	9	40	20	77	.297	.360

Last Five Years

	ERA	W	L	Sv	G	GS	IP	H	HR	BB	SO		Avg	AB	H	2B	3B	HR	RBI	BB	SO	OBP	SLG
Home	4.45	27	17	0	71	60	386.1	401	52	110	228	vs. Left	.310	625	194	30	0	23	80	49	79	.370	.469
Away	3.91	28	13	0	68	57	379.2	392	44	85	206	vs. Right	.254	2355	599	110	7	73	256	146	355	.299	.400
Day	4.32	20	10	0	47	42	270.2	282	43	60	137	Inning 1-6	.260	2568	667	126	7	77	296	176	374	.310	.404
Night	4.11	35	20	0	92	75	495.1	511	53	135	297	Inning 7+	.306	412	126	14	0	19	40	19	60	.341	.478
Grass	4.46	35	26	0	104	84	551.1	588	72	143	305	None on	.255	1837	469	77	6	57	57	100	273	.298	.397
Turf	3.48	20	4	0	35	33	214.2	205	24	52	129	Runners on	.283	1143	324	63	1	39	279	95	161	.339	.443
March/April	5.84	3	3	0	14	11	74.0	85	14	18	36	Scoring Posn	.276	594	164	36	0	19	226	61	94	.339	.433
May	4.98	7	7	0	27	16	112.0	133	16	38	59	Close & Late	.294	163	48	4	0	8	17	12	23	.350	.466
June	4.48	8	5	0	27	20	132.2	141	15	43	71	None on/out	.255	801	204	28	2	25	25	41	121	.295	.388
July	3.51	17	6	0	28	28	182.0	173	18	36	109	vs. 1st Batr (relief)	.238	21	5	0	0	1	6	0	2	.227	.381
August	3.96	13	3	0	27	27	168.0	158	17	40	107	1st Inning Pitched	.294	538	158	24	3	20	85	45	92	.347	.461
Sept/Oct	3.24	7	6	0	16	15	97.1	103	12	20	52	First 75 Pitches	.265	2244	595	107	6	68	254	148	337	.314	.409
Starter	4.18	53	29	0	117	117	719.1	742	91	173	401	Pitch 76-90	.270	371	100	21	1	13	41	26	45	.323	.437
Reliever	4.24	2	1	0	22	0	46.2	51	5	22	33	Pitch 91-105	.236	259	61	10	0	7	22	12	35	.272	.355
0-3 Days Rest (Start)	4.10	2	0	0	7	7	37.1	33	6	13	22	Pitch 106+	.349	106	37	2	0	8	19	9	17	.400	.594
4 Days Rest	4.13	40	19	0	77	77	483.2	503	62	113	272	First Pitch	.338	450	152	20	2	21	60	5	0	.351	.531
5+ Days Rest	4.31	11	10	0	33	33	198.1	206	23	47	107	Ahead in Count	.217	1289	280	51	2	33	114	0	356	.223	.337
vs. AL	4.24	53	30	0	136	114	746.2	782	94	189	425	Behind in Count	.306	648	198	35	2	28	90	83	0	.383	.495
vs. NL	1.86	2	0	0	3	3	19.1	11	2	6	9	Two Strikes	.212	1283	272	48	3	30	112	107	434	.275	.324
Pre-All Star	4.57	24	16	0	78	57	386.1	414	55	114	205	Pre-All Star	.274	1510	414	69	3	55	175	114	205	.327	.433
Post-All Star	3.79	31	14	0	61	60	379.2	379	41	81	229	Post-All Star	.258	1470	379	71	4	41	161	81	229	.301	.395

Pitcher vs. Batter (career)

Pitches Best Vs.	Avg	AB	H	2B	3B	HR	RBI	BB	SO	OBP	SLG	Pitches Worst Vs.	Avg	AB	H	2B	3B	HR	RBI	BB	SO	OBP	SLG
Otis Nixon	.059	17	1	0	0	0	0	0	1	.059	.059	Bernie Williams	.514	37	19	6	0	5	10	2	3	.538	1.081
Joe Girardi	.077	13	1	0	0	0	1	0	4	.077	.077	Frank Thomas	.471	17	8	1	0	2	6	4	1	.545	.882
Mike Matheny	.091	11	1	0	0	0	0	0	1	.091	.091	Brady Anderson	.462	13	6	0	0	3	4	1	2	.500	1.154
Luis Rivera	.130	23	3	0	0	0	0	0	3	.130	.130	Mo Vaughn	.444	9	4	0	0	2	3	1	2	.583	1.111
Lance Johnson	.133	15	2	0	0	0	1	0	2	.133	.133	Rex Hudler	.375	16	6	2	0	2	3	1	2	.412	1.063

Bill Mueller — Giants

Age 27 – Bats Both

	Avg	G	AB	R	H	2B	3B	HR	RBI	BB	SO	HBP	GDP	SB	CS	OBP	SLG	IBB	SH	SF	#Pit	#P/PA	GB	FB	G/F
1997 Season	.292	128	390	51	114	26	3	7	44	48	71	3	10	4	3	.369	.428	1	6	6	1705	3.76	158	107	1.48
Career (1996-1997)	.305	183	590	82	180	41	4	7	63	72	97	4	11	4	3	.380	.424	1	7	8	2540	3.73	239	163	1.47

1997 Season

	Avg	AB	H	2B	3B	HR	RBI	BB	SO	OBP	SLG		Avg	AB	H	2B	3B	HR	RBI	BB	SO	OBP	SLG
vs. Left	.282	85	24	7	0	2	10	11	14	.365	.435	First Pitch	.328	67	22	3	1	1	5	0	0	.328	.448
vs. Right	.295	305	90	19	3	5	34	37	57	.370	.426	Ahead in Count	.384	86	33	8	0	2	10	33	0	.557	.547
Groundball	.274	84	23	5	1	0	7	6	12	.315	.357	Behind in Count	.229	153	35	13	0	2	13	0	60	.231	.353
Flyball	.205	44	9	2	1	2	9	8	11	.352	.432	Two Strikes	.197	178	35	9	0	4	14	15	71	.259	.315
Home	.291	189	55	8	1	5	24	28	32	.385	.423	Batting #2	.309	136	42	8	1	2	12	17	28	.394	.426

1997 Season

	Avg	AB	H	2B	3B	HR	RBI	BB	SO	OBP	SLG		Avg	AB	H	2B	3B	HR	RBI	BB	SO	OBP	SLG
Away	.294	201	59	18	2	2	20	20	39	.354	.433	Batting #7	.271	177	48	13	1	4	22	23	31	.351	.424
Day	.295	190	56	11	0	5	21	19	31	.362	.432	Other	.312	77	24	5	1	1	10	8	12	.368	.442
Night	.290	200	58	15	3	2	23	29	40	.376	.425	March/April	.271	59	16	5	0	0	4	7	10	.343	.356
Grass	.302	321	97	20	2	7	37	40	54	.379	.442	May	.286	56	16	2	1	0	6	7	8	.373	.357
Turf	.246	69	17	6	1	0	7	8	17	.325	.362	June	.257	70	18	4	0	2	8	7	12	.316	.400
Pre-All Star	.270	185	50	11	1	2	18	21	30	.343	.373	July	.306	36	11	0	0	2	6	3	10	.375	.472
Post-All Star	.312	205	64	15	2	5	26	27	41	.393	.478	August	.349	83	29	10	2	3	15	15	12	.444	.627
Scoring Posn	.260	96	25	5	2	1	36	18	17	.364	.385	Sept/Oct	.279	86	24	5	0	0	5	9	19	.347	.337
Close & Late	.328	67	22	5	1	1	13	10	17	.418	.478	vs. AL	.361	36	13	6	0	1	4	3	3	.410	.611
None on/out	.256	90	23	7	1	0	0	6	17	.309	.356	vs. NL	.285	354	101	20	3	6	40	45	68	.365	.410

1997 By Position

Position	Avg	AB	H	2B	3B	HR	RBI	BB	SO	OBP	SLG	G	GS	Innings	PO	A	E	DP	Fld Pct	Rng Fctr	In Zone	Zone Outs	Zone Rtg	MLB Zone
As 3b	.298	383	114	26	3	7	43	47	70	.374	.436	122	98	916.0	85	217	14	18	.956	2.97	306	252	.824	.801

Terry Mulholland — Giants
Age 35 – Pitches Left (groundball pitcher)

	ERA	W	L	Sv	G	GS	IP	BB	SO	Avg	H	2B	3B	HR	RBI	OBP	SLG	CG	ShO	Sup	QS	#P/S	SB	CS	GB	FB	G/F
1997 Season	4.24	6	13	0	40	27	186.2	51	99	.267	190	45	2	24	92	.324	.437	1	0	2.84	14	90	1	4	303	179	1.69
Last Five Years	4.71	42	53	0	155	131	850.0	215	438	.281	939	197	18	115	450	.327	.454	15	2	4.57	65	90	5	18	1376	893	1.54

1997 Season

	ERA	W	L	Sv	G	GS	IP	H	HR	BB	SO		Avg	AB	H	2B	3B	HR	RBI	BB	SO	OBP	SLG
Home	3.43	2	5	0	18	13	94.1	87	13	26	59	vs. Left	.271	140	38	10	0	2	11	10	13	.327	.386
Away	5.07	4	8	0	22	14	92.1	103	11	25	40	vs. Right	.266	571	152	35	2	22	81	41	86	.324	.450
Day	4.09	2	5	0	21	14	92.1	99	14	28	49	Inning 1-6	.260	597	155	40	2	16	79	48	85	.323	.414
Night	4.39	4	8	0	19	13	94.1	91	10	23	50	Inning 7+	.307	114	35	5	0	8	13	3	14	.333	.561
Grass	4.09	4	10	0	33	22	154.0	153	19	44	84	None on	.282	422	119	25	0	18	18	28	69	.334	.469
Turf	4.96	2	3	0	7	5	32.2	37	5	7	15	Runners on	.246	289	71	20	2	6	74	23	30	.311	.391
March/April	3.22	1	3	0	6	6	36.1	41	2	13	14	Scoring Posn	.273	161	44	17	2	1	61	15	18	.339	.422
May	1.94	3	1	0	6	6	41.2	37	4	5	24	Close & Late	.383	60	23	4	0	5	8	2	4	.406	.700
June	6.06	1	5	0	6	6	35.2	37	5	8	24	None on/out	.324	188	61	8	0	9	9	13	24	.383	.511
July	4.50	1	2	0	6	6	38.0	40	8	13	20	vs. 1st Batr (relief)	.167	12	2	0	0	0	1	0	3	.154	.167
August	5.50	0	1	0	8	1	18.0	14	2	8	11	1st Inning Pitched	.257	144	37	7	1	4	21	12	20	.314	.403
Sept/Oct	6.35	0	1	0	8	2	17.0	21	3	4	17	First 75 Pitches	.253	581	147	34	1	13	65	42	83	.311	.382
Starter	4.05	6	13	0	27	27	169.0	175	23	47	88	Pitch 76-90	.367	90	33	10	1	10	26	6	10	.414	.833
Reliever	6.11	0	0	0	13	0	17.2	15	1	4	11	Pitch 91-105	.237	38	9	1	0	1	1	2	6	.293	.342
0-3 Days Rest (Start)	6.32	0	2	0	3	3	15.2	25	2	4	10	Pitch 106+	.500	2	1	0	0	0	0	0	0	.667	.500
4 Days Rest	3.33	6	6	0	16	16	108.0	99	15	19	48	First Pitch	.348	115	40	8	0	5	20	3	0	.367	.548
5+ Days Rest	4.96	0	5	0	8	8	45.1	51	6	24	30	Ahead in Count	.231	320	74	19	0	7	32	0	88	.244	.356
vs. AL	3.86	0	2	0	6	2	21.0	16	2	6	14	Behind in Count	.296	169	50	12	1	9	28	28	0	.403	.538
vs. NL	4.29	6	11	0	34	25	165.2	174	22	45	85	Two Strikes	.183	284	52	13	0	6	27	20	99	.251	.292
Pre-All Star	3.72	6	9	0	19	19	118.2	120	13	28	55	Pre-All Star	.264	454	120	34	1	13	53	28	55	.315	.430
Post-All Star	5.16	0	4	0	21	8	68.0	70	11	23	44	Post-All Star	.272	257	70	11	1	11	39	23	44	.340	.451

Last Five Years

	ERA	W	L	Sv	G	GS	IP	H	HR	BB	SO		Avg	AB	H	2B	3B	HR	RBI	BB	SO	OBP	SLG
Home	4.70	20	23	0	71	60	390.1	417	63	94	225	vs. Left	.262	596	156	31	4	14	76	42	68	.311	.398
Away	4.72	22	30	0	84	71	459.2	522	52	121	213	vs. Right	.285	2749	783	166	14	101	374	173	370	.330	.466
Day	4.79	14	23	0	65	55	351.2	373	55	101	167	Inning 1-6	.281	2818	793	167	18	92	381	191	375	.330	.451
Night	4.66	28	30	0	90	76	498.1	566	60	114	271	Inning 7+	.277	527	146	30	0	23	69	24	63	.310	.465
Grass	4.69	23	32	0	97	78	516.2	573	77	141	266	None on	.272	1975	538	113	7	71	71	107	288	.315	.445
Turf	4.75	19	21	0	58	53	333.1	366	38	74	172	Runners on	.293	1370	401	84	11	44	379	108	150	.343	.466
March/April	4.67	7	11	0	22	22	135.0	153	11	43	59	Scoring Posn	.304	734	223	56	8	16	308	68	78	.357	.467
May	4.38	15	10	0	30	30	193.1	209	26	39	76	Close & Late	.309	262	81	22	0	11	39	11	26	.338	.519
June	4.88	6	11	0	23	23	145.2	167	24	34	95	None on/out	.290	868	252	42	4	37	37	51	122	.338	.476
July	5.17	4	11	0	27	24	151.1	180	26	39	82	vs. 1st Batr (relief)	.217	23	5	0	0	2	6	0	5	.208	.478
August	4.92	5	3	0	29	15	120.2	123	19	30	71	1st Inning Pitched	.293	601	176	31	9	23	103	50	77	.350	.489
Sept/Oct	4.24	5	7	0	24	17	104.0	107	9	30	55	First 75 Pitches	.276	2626	726	146	16	84	335	167	355	.322	.440
Starter	4.69	42	53	0	131	131	815.2	910	110	208	416	Pitch 76-90	.313	390	122	31	2	20	72	26	41	.358	.556
Reliever	5.24	0	0	0	24	0	34.1	29	5	7	22	Pitch 91-105	.249	233	58	8	0	8	25	12	31	.286	.386
0-3 Days Rest (Start)	4.50	2	3	0	7	7	38.0	47	6	12	20	Pitch 106+	.344	96	33	12	0	3	18	10	11	.406	.563
4 Days Rest	4.96	23	34	0	79	79	484.0	547	71	120	234	First Pitch	.316	554	175	35	2	23	79	10	0	.331	.511
5+ Days Rest	4.26	17	16	0	45	45	293.2	316	33	76	162	Ahead in Count	.219	1455	319	62	6	30	136	0	388	.227	.372
vs. AL	5.63	11	13	0	42	33	211.0	241	31	71	120	Behind in Count	.359	788	283	63	4	46	157	119	0	.440	.624
vs. NL	4.41	31	40	0	113	98	639.0	698	84	144	318	Two Strikes	.192	1295	248	59	5	25	117	86	438	.249	.303
Pre-All Star	4.77	29	35	0	83	83	515.1	589	69	125	255	Pre-All Star	.288	2042	589	130	8	69	277	125	255	.332	.461
Post-All Star	4.63	13	18	0	72	48	334.2	350	41	90	183	Post-All Star	.269	1303	350	67	10	46	173	90	183	.319	.441

Pitcher vs. Batter (career)

Pitches Best Vs.	Avg	AB	H	2B	3B	HR	RBI	BB	SO	OBP	SLG	Pitches Worst Vs.	Avg	AB	H	2B	3B	HR	RBI	BB	SO	OBP	SLG
Albert Belle	.000	11	0	0	0	0	0	2	3	.154	.000	Derek Bell	.625	16	10	0	0	2	9	1	4	.611	1.000
Devon White	.000	10	0	0	0	0	0	2	2	.167	.000	Archi Cianfrocco	.600	15	9	3	0	1	5	0	2	.563	1.000
Darrin Jackson	.120	25	3	0	1	0	3	1	5	.154	.200	Dante Bichette	.462	26	12	4	0	3	10	0	3	.462	.962
Wally Joyner	.167	12	2	0	0	0	2	0	2	.154	.167	Ellis Burks	.462	13	6	3	0	1	6	2	4	.563	.923
Rey Sanchez	.176	17	3	0	0	0	1	0	0	.176	.176	Glenallen Hill	.462	13	6	1	0	2	3	0	0	.462	1.000

327

Bobby Munoz — Phillies   Age 30 – Pitches Right (groundball pitcher)

	ERA	W	L	Sv	G	GS	IP	BB	SO	Avg	H	2B	3B	HR	RBI	OBP	SLG	CG	ShO	Sup	QS	#P/S	SB	CS	GB	FB	G/F
1997 Season	8.91	1	5	0	8	7	33.1	15	20	.338	47	13	2	4	34	.403	.547	0	0	4.32	1	84	9	2	58	34	1.71
Career (1993-1997)	4.93	11	18	1	76	30	224.1	92	126	.286	253	52	6	20	127	.352	.426	1	0	4.21	13	89	37	4	398	206	1.93

1997 Season

	ERA	W	L	Sv	G	GS	IP	H	HR	BB	SO		Avg	AB	H	2B	3B	HR	RBI	BB	SO	OBP	SLG
Home	10.80	0	3	0	4	3	15.0	28	1	4	8	vs. Left	.313	64	20	4	1	1	10	10	9	.408	.453
Away	7.36	1	2	0	4	4	18.1	19	3	11	12	vs. Right	.360	75	27	9	1	3	24	5	11	.398	.627

Career (1993-1997)

	ERA	W	L	Sv	G	GS	IP	H	HR	BB	SO		Avg	AB	H	2B	3B	HR	RBI	BB	SO	OBP	SLG
Home	5.30	7	7	0	36	13	105.1	128	4	38	53	vs. Left	.260	392	102	17	2	6	41	49	60	.338	.360
Away	4.61	4	11	1	40	17	119.0	125	16	54	73	vs. Right	.306	494	151	35	4	14	86	43	66	.364	.478
Day	4.32	1	6	1	26	7	66.2	72	6	26	38	Inning 1-6	.289	636	184	35	5	17	96	56	86	.347	.440
Night	5.19	10	12	0	50	23	157.2	181	14	66	88	Inning 7+	.276	250	69	17	1	3	31	36	40	.364	.388
Grass	4.64	6	10	1	47	14	116.1	112	15	54	76	None on	.268	500	134	20	2	11	11	32	75	.315	.392
Turf	5.25	5	8	0	29	16	108.0	141	5	38	50	Runners on	.308	386	119	27	4	9	116	60	51	.396	.469
March/April	8.13	0	4	1	10	4	27.2	39	2	14	13	Scoring Posn	.259	247	64	16	2	3	97	45	41	.362	.377
May	5.25	1	2	0	8	4	24.0	29	3	11	19	Close & Late	.298	124	37	10	0	2	20	23	24	.403	.427
June	2.83	6	3	0	20	8	63.2	55	4	31	41	None on/out	.243	218	53	12	1	5	5	14	30	.289	.376
July	4.62	3	3	0	18	9	64.1	71	7	21	27	vs. 1st Batr (relief)	.167	36	6	2	0	0	3	9	12	.326	.222
August	6.97	0	6	0	10	5	31.0	45	3	11	19	1st Inning Pitched	.295	264	78	17	1	5	52	41	41	.385	.424
Sept/Oct	4.61	0	0	0	10	0	13.2	14	1	4	7	First 75 Pitches	.288	753	217	44	5	16	101	75	108	.353	.424
Starter	4.81	8	15	0	30	30	166.2	188	19	56	88	Pitch 76-90	.256	78	20	3	1	3	16	12	10	.355	.436
Reliever	5.31	3	3	1	46	0	57.2	65	1	36	38	Pitch 91-105	.333	45	15	5	0	1	10	3	6	.360	.511
0-3 Days Rest (Start)	4.50	1	0	0	1	1	6.0	3	1	3	2	Pitch 106+	.100	10	1	0	0	0	0	2	2	.250	.100
4 Days Rest	4.07	4	9	0	17	17	95.0	103	11	32	58	First Pitch	.295	122	36	14	2	3	21	6	0	.323	.516
5+ Days Rest	5.89	3	6	0	12	12	65.2	82	7	21	28	Ahead in Count	.262	359	94	17	1	8	46	0	102	.269	.382
vs. AL	5.32	3	3	0	38	0	45.2	48	1	26	33	Behind in Count	.342	237	81	14	3	4	41	54	0	.463	.477
vs. NL	4.84	8	15	1	38	30	178.2	205	19	66	93	Two Strikes	.206	359	74	12	1	5	27	32	126	.275	.287
Pre-All Star	4.55	7	11	1	43	18	132.2	143	12	61	85	Pre-All Star	.272	525	143	30	4	12	72	61	85	.348	.413
Post-All Star	5.50	4	7	0	33	12	91.2	110	8	31	41	Post-All Star	.305	361	110	22	2	8	55	31	41	.359	.443

Pitcher vs. Batter (career)

Pitches Best Vs.	Avg	AB	H	2B	3B	HR	RBI	BB	SO	OBP	SLG	Pitches Worst Vs.	Avg	AB	H	2B	3B	HR	RBI	BB	SO	OBP	SLG
Andres Galarraga	.200	10	2	0	0	0	3	0	1	.273	.200	Tony Gwynn	.429	7	3	0	0	0	2	2	0	.455	.429
Dante Bichette	.200	10	2	0	0	0	4	1	1	.273	.400												

Mike Munoz — Rockies   Age 32 – Pitches Left (groundball pitcher)

	ERA	W	L	Sv	G	GS	IP	BB	SO	Avg	H	2B	3B	HR	RBI	OBP	SLG	GF	IR	IRS	Hld	SvOp	SB	CS	GB	FB	G/F
1997 Season	4.53	3	3	2	64	0	45.2	13	26	.294	52	7	0	4	24	.339	.401	16	52	11	19	2	2	0	82	42	1.95
Last Five Years	5.47	13	13	5	268	0	200.2	102	157	.285	223	41	7	22	131	.366	.440	60	187	50	58	13	9	3	326	160	2.04

1997 Season

	ERA	W	L	Sv	G	GS	IP	H	HR	BB	SO		Avg	AB	H	2B	3B	HR	RBI	BB	SO	OBP	SLG
Home	4.03	1	0	1	34	0	29.0	32	4	7	19	vs. Left	.337	83	28	3	0	3	13	7	11	.380	.482
Away	5.40	2	3	1	30	0	16.2	20	0	6	7	vs. Right	.255	94	24	4	0	1	11	6	15	.300	.330
Day	6.00	1	1	1	28	0	18.0	24	0	7	11	Inning 1-6	.429	21	9	0	0	1	7	0	3	.429	.571
Night	3.58	2	2	1	36	0	27.2	28	4	6	15	Inning 7+	.276	156	43	7	0	3	17	13	23	.327	.378
Grass	4.35	3	2	2	55	0	41.1	46	4	12	23	None on	.267	86	23	3	0	4	4	6	12	.315	.442
Turf	6.23	0	1	0	9	0	4.1	6	0	1	3	Runners on	.319	91	29	4	0	0	20	7	14	.360	.363
March/April	7.71	0	0	0	9	0	7.0	9	1	1	1	Scoring Posn	.292	65	19	2	0	0	20	5	13	.333	.323
May	4.15	1	0	1	13	0	8.2	7	1	3	5	Close & Late	.265	68	18	3	0	0	5	3	12	.292	.309
June	5.23	0	2	0	15	0	10.1	14	1	2	5	None on/out	.308	39	12	3	0	2	2	2	4	.341	.538
July	3.00	0	1	0	9	0	6.0	5	1	1	5	vs. 1st Batr (relief)	.310	58	18	4	0	1	8	5	7	.359	.431
August	3.68	1	0	0	9	0	7.1	4	0	4	4	1st Inning Pitched	.304	161	49	7	0	3	23	12	23	.349	.404
Sept/Oct	2.84	1	0	1	9	0	6.1	8	0	2	3	First 15 Pitches	.303	142	43	7	0	3	17	10	20	.344	.415
Starter	0.00	0	0	0	0	0	0.0	0	0	0	0	Pitch 16-30	.280	25	7	0	0	0	3	3	5	.357	.280
Reliever	4.53	3	3	2	64	0	45.2	52	4	13	26	Pitch 31-45	.143	7	1	0	0	0	1	0	1	.143	.571
0 Days rest (Relief)	4.82	0	3	1	16	0	9.1	9	1	3	2	Pitch 46+	.333	3	1	0	0	0	0	0	0	.333	.333
1 or 2 Days rest	1.74	1	0	0	27	0	20.2	14	1	6	14	First Pitch	.316	19	6	0	0	0	8	0	0	.300	.316
3+ Days rest	8.04	1	0	0	21	0	15.2	29	2	4	10	Ahead in Count	.278	79	22	5	0	1	8	0	21	.275	.380
vs. AL	3.00	0	1	1	5	0	3.0	2	0	0	2	Behind in Count	.302	43	13	1	0	2	6	10	0	.434	.465
vs. NL	4.64	3	2	1	59	0	42.2	50	4	13	24	Two Strikes	.263	76	20	6	0	1	7	3	26	.288	.382
Pre-All Star	5.74	1	3	1	39	0	26.2	33	3	6	14	Pre-All Star	.308	107	33	4	0	3	17	6	14	.342	.430
Post-All Star	2.84	2	0	1	25	0	19.0	19	1	7	12	Post-All Star	.271	70	19	3	0	1	7	7	12	.333	.357

Last Five Years

	ERA	W	L	Sv	G	GS	IP	H	HR	BB	SO		Avg	AB	H	2B	3B	HR	RBI	BB	SO	OBP	SLG
Home	5.63	10	1	2	142	0	115.0	135	17	54	96	vs. Left	.274	336	92	15	1	13	48	35	70	.342	.440
Away	5.25	3	12	3	126	0	85.2	88	5	48	61	vs. Right	.294	446	131	26	6	9	83	67	87	.383	.439
Day	4.91	6	6	2	106	0	80.2	85	8	37	63	Inning 1-6	.269	119	32	5	1	5	35	18	25	.362	.454
Night	5.85	7	7	3	162	0	120.0	138	14	65	94	Inning 7+	.288	663	191	36	6	17	96	84	132	.367	.437
Grass	5.36	12	6	5	216	0	163.0	181	20	79	125	None on	.278	388	108	19	1	15	15	38	76	.344	.448
Turf	5.97	1	7	0	52	0	37.2	42	2	23	32	Runners on	.292	394	115	22	6	7	116	64	81	.385	.431
March/April	7.03	1	3	0	45	0	32.0	34	5	21	17	Scoring Posn	.290	255	74	15	3	5	107	49	59	.394	.431
May	5.35	2	1	1	48	0	33.2	32	4	20	32	Close & Late	.302	278	84	15	5	5	35	36	55	.379	.446
June	2.68	2	4	3	50	0	40.1	34	1	22	24	None on/out	.256	180	46	11	0	5	5	15	36	.316	.400
July	6.82	2	3	0	48	0	31.2	39	2	13	28	vs. 1st Batr (relief)	.250	240	60	14	3	6	27	25	41	.317	.408

Last Five Years

	ERA	W	L	Sv	G	GS	IP	H	HR	BB	SO		Avg	AB	H	2B	3B	HR	RBI	BB	SO	OBP	SLG
August	7.12	4	1	0	33	0	30.1	46	5	14	21	1st Inning Pitched	.288	697	201	39	7	16	117	93	136	.370	.433
Sept/Oct	4.68	2	1	1	44	0	32.2	38	5	12	35	First 15 Pitches	.299	588	176	35	7	17	89	71	104	.371	.469
Starter	0.00	0	0	0	0	0	0.0	0	0	0	0	Pitch 16-30	.242	161	39	5	0	3	35	30	43	.364	.329
Reliever	5.47	13	13	5	268	0	200.2	223	22	102	157	Pitch 31-45	.233	30	7	1	0	2	7	1	10	.258	.467
0 Days rest (Relief)	5.09	4	5	2	94	0	70.2	73	6	40	51	Pitch 46+	.333	3	1	0	0	0	0	0	0	.333	.333
1 or 2 Days rest	5.05	8	4	3	110	0	87.1	89	11	40	72	First Pitch	.314	102	32	2	0	3	21	9	0	.366	.422
3+ Days rest	6.96	1	4	0	64	0	42.2	61	5	22	34	Ahead in Count	.247	332	82	19	2	5	36	0	132	.246	.361
vs. AL	4.50	0	2	1	13	0	6.0	6	1	6	3	Behind in Count	.302	199	60	11	4	7	38	52	0	.443	.503
vs. NL	5.50	13	11	4	255	0	194.2	217	21	96	154	Two Strikes	.214	355	76	20	3	9	47	41	157	.295	.363
Pre-All Star	5.02	6	9	4	158	0	114.2	110	10	66	82	Pre-All Star	.255	432	110	15	5	10	73	66	82	.352	.382
Post-All Star	6.07	7	4	1	110	0	86.0	113	12	36	75	Post-All Star	.323	350	113	26	2	12	58	36	75	.384	.511

Pitcher vs. Batter (career)

Pitches Best Vs.	Avg	AB	H	2B	3B	HR	RBI	BB	SO	OBP	SLG	Pitches Worst Vs.	Avg	AB	H	2B	3B	HR	RBI	BB	SO	OBP	SLG
Steve Finley	.063	16	1	0	0	0	0	3	2	.211	.063	Darrin Fletcher	.400	10	4	0	0	0	2	0	0	.455	.400
Mark Grace	.154	13	2	1	0	0	1	1	2	.200	.231	Al Martin	.364	11	4	0	0	1	1	2	4	.462	.636
Fred McGriff	.200	20	4	1	0	1	6	3	4	.304	.400	Wally Joyner	.333	9	3	0	0	0	0	2	0	.455	.333
Orlando Merced	.200	10	2	0	0	0	0	1	3	.273	.200												
Delino DeShields	.200	10	2	1	0	0	2	2	4	.333	.300												

Eddie Murray — Dodgers
Age 42 – Bats Both

	Avg	G	AB	R	H	2B	3B	HR	RBI	BB	SO	HBP	GDP	SB	CS	OBP	SLG	IBB	SH	SF	#Pit	#P/PA	GB	FB	G/F
1997 Season	.222	55	167	13	37	7	0	3	18	15	26	0	10	1	0	.281	.317	0	0	3	647	3.50	72	46	1.57
Last Five Years	.275	582	2212	284	609	98	3	90	355	186	292	0	72	20	7	.327	.444	21	0	30	8663	3.57	817	699	1.17

1997 Season

	Avg	AB	H	2B	3B	HR	RBI	BB	SO	OBP	SLG		Avg	AB	H	2B	3B	HR	RBI	BB	SO	OBP	SLG
vs. Left	.281	64	18	2	0	0	7	3	8	.309	.313	Scoring Posn	.217	46	10	1	0	1	15	7	10	.304	.304
vs. Right	.184	103	19	5	0	3	11	12	18	.265	.320	Close & Late	.189	37	7	2	0	0	5	5	8	.279	.243
Home	.233	86	20	5	0	2	12	8	13	.289	.360	None on/out	.200	30	6	0	0	1	1	3	6	.273	.300
Away	.210	81	17	2	0	1	6	7	13	.273	.272	Batting #6	.200	20	4	0	0	1	1	1	3	.238	.300
First Pitch	.303	33	10	3	0	1	3	0	0	.303	.485	Batting #7	.221	140	31	7	0	3	14	13	20	.282	.336
Ahead in Count	.229	35	8	0	0	1	9	10	0	.383	.314	Other	.286	7	2	0	0	0	3	1	3	.375	.286
Behind in Count	.178	73	13	3	0	1	5	0	25	.176	.260	Pre-All Star	.219	146	32	6	0	3	14	11	20	.270	.322
Two Strikes	.183	71	13	2	0	1	6	5	26	.234	.254	Post-All Star	.238	21	5	1	0	0	4	4	6	.346	.286

Last Five Years

	Avg	AB	H	2B	3B	HR	RBI	BB	SO	OBP	SLG		Avg	AB	H	2B	3B	HR	RBI	BB	SO	OBP	SLG
vs. Left	.270	660	178	28	0	22	95	50	79	.317	.412	First Pitch	.364	401	146	28	1	23	82	17	0	.383	.611
vs. Right	.278	1552	431	70	3	68	260	136	213	.332	.458	Ahead in Count	.335	553	185	30	0	36	127	93	0	.423	.584
Groundball	.270	548	148	32	2	17	80	33	77	.309	.429	Behind in Count	.199	874	174	22	2	20	83	0	241	.198	.297
Flyball	.248	432	107	17	1	26	73	40	58	.310	.472	Two Strikes	.191	889	170	22	2	19	88	76	292	.253	.285
Home	.277	1071	297	44	3	48	178	89	134	.328	.458	Batting #3	.285	592	169	28	1	24	96	39	59	.325	.458
Away	.273	1141	312	54	0	42	177	97	158	.327	.431	Batting #5	.284	1027	292	44	2	43	176	88	147	.338	.457
Day	.281	704	198	25	1	32	126	59	98	.332	.456	Other	.250	593	148	26	0	23	83	59	86	.312	.410
Night	.273	1508	411	73	2	58	229	127	194	.325	.439	March/April	.268	354	95	12	0	11	53	28	49	.320	.395
Grass	.278	1893	526	86	3	76	311	161	250	.330	.447	May	.260	435	113	14	2	15	54	36	61	.312	.405
Turf	.260	319	83	12	0	14	44	25	42	.314	.429	June	.284	429	122	25	0	19	86	36	62	.333	.476
Pre-All Star	.270	1331	360	55	2	50	214	108	181	.321	.427	July	.276	297	82	13	0	16	56	32	50	.322	.481
Post-All Star	.283	881	249	43	1	40	141	78	111	.338	.470	August	.256	391	100	19	1	15	51	30	50	.304	.425
Scoring Posn	.297	565	168	29	1	23	257	77	94	.365	.474	Sept/Oct	.317	306	97	15	0	14	55	34	34	.383	.503
Close & Late	.246	357	88	13	1	18	48	39	66	.318	.440	vs. AL	.271	1595	433	70	2	63	252	144	229	.328	.436
None on/out	.246	501	123	19	1	25	25	35	67	.295	.437	vs. NL	.285	617	176	28	1	27	103	42	63	.326	.465

Batter vs. Pitcher (since 1984)

Hits Best Against	Avg	AB	H	2B	3B	HR	RBI	BB	SO	OBP	SLG	Hits Worst Against	Avg	AB	H	2B	3B	HR	RBI	BB	SO	OBP	SLG
Frank Castillo	.588	17	10	2	0	1	8	1	1	.579	.882	Mike Stanton	.067	15	1	0	0	0	0	0	1	.067	.067
Ricky Bones	.545	11	6	1	0	1	2	4	0	.667	.909	Curt Schilling	.077	26	2	0	0	0	0	2	6	.143	.077
Kevin Gross	.406	32	13	1	1	4	7	7	2	.513	.875	Wilson Alvarez	.115	26	3	0	0	0	0	2	1	.179	.115
Pat Mahomes	.385	13	5	2	0	2	6	0	2	.385	1.000	Pat Hentgen	.118	17	2	0	0	0	0	1	3	.167	.118
Ramon Martinez	.364	11	4	0	0	2	3	3	2	.500	.909	Bob Patterson	.143	14	2	0	0	0	1	0	3	.133	.143

Heath Murray — Padres
Age 25 – Pitches Left (groundball pitcher)

	ERA	W	L	Sv	G	GS	IP	BB	SO	Avg	H	2B	3B	HR	RBI	OBP	SLG	GF	IR	IRS	Hld	SvOp	SB	CS	GB	FB	G/F
1997 Season	6.75	1	2	0	17	3	33.1	21	16	.376	50	6	0	3	25	.472	.489	1	20	8	1	0	2	1	61	29	2.10

1997 Season

	ERA	W	L	Sv	G	GS	IP	H	HR	BB	SO		Avg	AB	H	2B	3B	HR	RBI	BB	SO	OBP	SLG
Home	6.87	0	1	0	10	1	18.1	26	1	15	8	vs. Left	.364	44	16	1	0	1	10	9	7	.472	.455
Away	6.60	1	1	0	7	2	15.0	24	2	6	8	vs. Right	.382	89	34	5	0	2	15	12	9	.472	.506

Mike Mussina — Orioles
Age 29 – Pitches Right

	ERA	W	L	Sv	G	GS	IP	BB	SO	Avg	H	2B	3B	HR	RBI	OBP	SLG	CG	ShO	Sup	QS	#P/S	SB	CS	GB	FB	G/F
1997 Season	3.20	15	8	0	33	33	224.2	54	218	.234	197	41	4	27	78	.282	.388	4	1	5.53	25	105	9	6	287	207	1.39
Last Five Years	3.78	83	39	0	150	150	1033.2	259	796	.248	974	214	16	121	417	.295	.404	21	8	5.78	94	107	29	32	1293	1187	1.09

1997 Season

	ERA	W	L	Sv	G	GS	IP	H	HR	BB	SO		Avg	AB	H	2B	3B	HR	RBI	BB	SO	OBP	SLG
Home	2.68	8	4	0	17	17	117.2	96	13	25	120	vs. Left	.221	429	95	25	1	14	41	32	110	.276	.382
Away	3.79	7	4	0	16	16	107.0	101	14	29	98	vs. Right	.246	414	102	16	3	13	37	22	108	.288	.394
Day	4.63	5	4	0	13	13	81.2	83	13	17	79	Inning 1-6	.235	711	167	37	3	22	69	45	185	.283	.388
Night	2.39	10	4	0	20	20	143.0	114	14	37	139	Inning 7+	.227	132	30	4	1	5	9	9	33	.275	.386
Grass	3.01	15	6	0	30	30	206.0	171	22	45	203	None on	.239	536	128	25	4	14	14	39	143	.290	.379
Turf	5.30	0	2	0	3	3	18.2	26	5	9	15	Runners on	.225	307	69	16	0	13	64	15	75	.266	.404
March/April	4.22	3	1	0	5	5	32.0	30	2	6	25	Scoring Posn	.193	161	31	8	0	4	41	10	43	.246	.317
May	3.35	4	0	0	6	6	40.1	33	6	7	41	Close & Late	.239	46	11	2	0	2	3	6	15	.327	.413
June	2.20	3	1	0	6	6	45.0	34	3	12	42	None on/out	.280	232	65	14	2	8		11	59	.313	.461
July	3.72	1	2	0	5	5	36.1	32	6	11	35	vs. 1st Batr (relief)	.000	0	0	0	0	0	0	0	0	.000	.000
August	2.77	2	2	0	6	6	39.0	36	4	11	45	1st Inning Pitched	.248	125	31	8	0	5	20	13	40	.319	.432
Sept/Oct	3.38	2	2	0	5	5	32.0	32	6	7	30	First 75 Pitches	.216	556	120	27	3	17	51	37	157	.267	.367
Starter	3.20	15	8	0	33	33	224.2	197	27	54	218	Pitch 76-90	.289	121	35	6	0	4	11	7	25	.328	.438
Reliever	0.00	0	0	0	0	0	0.0	0	0	0	0	Pitch 91-105	.246	114	28	5	1	5	13	5	24	.283	.439
0-3 Days Rest (Start)	0.00	0	0	0	0	0	0.0	0	0	0	0	Pitch 106+	.269	52	14	3	0	1	3	5	12	.328	.385
4 Days Rest	3.27	10	4	0	23	23	154.0	139	22	37	151	First Pitch	.381	105	40	5	1	6	21	2	0	.389	.619
5+ Days Rest	3.06	5	4	0	10	10	70.2	58	5	17	67	Ahead in Count	.169	438	74	20	1	7	21	0	190	.170	.267
vs. AL	3.27	14	8	0	30	30	203.2	178	25	52	192	Behind in Count	.285	144	41	9	1	8	20	25	0	.398	.528
vs. NL	2.57	1	0	0	3	3	21.0	19	2	2	26	Two Strikes	.158	456	72	16	1	9	22	27	218	.207	.257
Pre-All Star	3.26	10	2	0	18	18	124.1	103	12	28	122	Pre-All Star	.224	459	103	25	3	12	41	28	122	.269	.370
Post-All Star	3.14	5	6	0	15	15	100.1	94	15	26	96	Post-All Star	.245	384	94	16	1	15	37	26	96	.296	.409

Last Five Years

	ERA	W	L	Sv	G	GS	IP	H	HR	BB	SO		Avg	AB	H	2B	3B	HR	RBI	BB	SO	OBP	SLG
Home	4.01	41	21	0	79	79	533.2	528	76	125	422	vs. Left	.234	2053	480	102	9	42	181	154	434	.287	.354
Away	3.53	42	18	0	71	71	500.0	446	45	134	374	vs. Right	.264	1869	494	112	7	79	236	105	362	.305	.459
Day	3.68	30	13	0	55	55	374.1	337	43	94	298	Inning 1-6	.251	3221	810	179	12	100	354	214	666	.298	.408
Night	3.84	53	26	0	95	95	659.1	637	78	165	498	Inning 7+	.234	701	164	35	4	21	63	45	130	.282	.385
Grass	3.98	72	37	0	134	134	912.1	869	111	234	711	None on	.242	2468	598	132	14	73	73	159	515	.290	.396
Turf	2.30	11	2	0	16	16	121.1	105	10	25	85	Runners on	.259	1454	376	82	2	48	344	100	281	.305	.417
March/April	3.42	14	5	0	23	23	165.2	140	17	34	103	Scoring Posn	.257	782	201	47	1	25	287	63	158	.307	.416
May	3.64	17	5	0	29	29	203.0	191	33	42	162	Close & Late	.215	316	68	16	1	9	28	29	64	.282	.358
June	4.33	16	9	0	28	28	185.0	192	18	55	140	None on/out	.259	1059	274	64	4	38	38	52	211	.295	.434
July	4.93	13	7	0	26	26	171.2	187	25	49	126	vs. 1st Batr (relief)	.000	0	0	0	0	0	0	0	0	.000	.000
August	2.43	14	6	0	23	23	166.2	136	11	41	136	1st Inning Pitched	.237	557	132	32	0	18	71	55	141	.306	.391
Sept/Oct	3.88	9	7	0	21	21	141.2	128	17	38	129	First 75 Pitches	.246	2602	640	140	9	88	284	179	557	.294	.408
Starter	3.78	83	39	0	150	150	1033.2	974	121	259	796	Pitch 76-90	.262	519	136	27	3	17	55	29	90	.303	.424
Reliever	0.00	0	0	0	0	0	0.0	0	0	0	0	Pitch 91-105	.243	481	117	25	2	11	44	20	83	.276	.372
0-3 Days Rest (Start)	5.46	2	1	0	4	4	28.0	30	3	8	21	Pitch 106+	.253	320	81	22	2	5	34	31	66	.318	.381
4 Days Rest	3.76	58	27	0	106	106	727.1	700	87	181	572	First Pitch	.294	571	168	35	2	29	89	7	0	.300	.515
5+ Days Rest	3.65	23	11	0	40	40	278.1	244	31	70	203	Ahead in Count	.204	1936	394	81	5	34	145	0	672	.205	.303
vs. AL	3.80	82	39	0	147	147	1012.2	955	119	257	770	Behind in Count	.318	704	224	61	5	33	105	122	0	.420	.560
vs. NL	2.57	1	0	0	3	3	21.0	19	2	2	26	Two Strikes	.181	1916	347	69	4	30	122	130	796	.235	.268
Pre-All Star	3.88	53	20	0	88	88	606.0	577	78	144	456	Pre-All Star	.250	2309	577	116	9	78	250	144	456	.294	.409
Post-All Star	3.64	30	19	0	62	62	427.2	397	43	115	340	Post-All Star	.246	1613	397	98	7	43	167	115	340	.297	.396

Pitcher vs. Batter (career)

Pitches Best Vs.	Avg	AB	H	2B	3B	HR	RBI	BB	SO	OBP	SLG	Pitches Worst Vs.	Avg	AB	H	2B	3B	HR	RBI	BB	SO	OBP	SLG
Bob Hamelin	.000	21	0	0	0	0	1	1	4	.045	.045	Frank Thomas	.457	46	21	5	0	6	11	7	8	.528	.957
Garret Anderson	.059	17	1	0	0	0	0	1	4	.111	.059	Danny Tartabull	.429	14	6	0	0	3	4	1	4	.467	1.071
Dave Nilsson	.077	26	2	0	0	1	4	0	9	.074	.192	Edgar Martinez	.419	31	13	2	2	3	8	3	1	.471	.903
Rafael Palmeiro	.091	22	2	1	0	0	1	1	3	.125	.136	Albert Belle	.395	38	15	4	0	5	9	3	6	.439	.895
Roberto Kelly	.133	15	2	0	0	0	1	0	2	.125	.133	John Jaha	.368	19	7	1	1	3	7	2	7	.429	1.000

Greg Myers — Braves
Age 32 – Bats Left

	Avg	G	AB	R	H	2B	3B	HR	RBI	BB	SO	HBP	GDP	SB	CS	OBP	SLG	IBB	SH	SF	#Pit	#P/PA	GB	FB	G/F
1997 Season	.259	71	174	24	45	11	1	5	29	17	32	0	4	0	0	.321	.420	2	0	2	671	3.48	56	56	1.00
Last Five Years	.264	406	1192	133	315	61	6	29	162	80	207	3	30	3	6	.309	.398	13	9	13	4435	3.42	456	322	1.42

1997 Season

	Avg	AB	H	2B	3B	HR	RBI	BB	SO	OBP	SLG		Avg	AB	H	2B	3B	HR	RBI	BB	SO	OBP	SLG
vs. Left	.533	15	8	3	0	1	4	2	1	.556	.933	Scoring Posn	.224	58	13	6	1	1	23	6	12	.288	.414
vs. Right	.233	159	37	8	1	4	25	15	31	.297	.371	Close & Late	.207	29	6	1	0	0	4	5	6	.324	.241
Home	.314	86	27	7	1	3	18	8	16	.368	.523	None on/out	.263	38	10	1	0	1	1	1	7	.282	.368
Away	.205	88	18	4	0	2	11	9	16	.276	.318	Batting #4	.272	92	25	8	1	3	19	6	18	.313	.478
First Pitch	.259	27	7	2	0	1	4	2	0	.310	.444	Batting #5	.280	25	7	2	0	1	4	3	4	.345	.480
Ahead in Count	.340	50	17	5	0	2	13	7	0	.421	.560	Other	.228	57	13	1	0	1	6	8	10	.323	.298
Behind in Count	.211	71	15	3	0	1	7	0	27	.208	.296	Pre-All Star	.275	120	33	9	1	3	21	13	22	.341	.442
Two Strikes	.154	65	10	3	0	0	6	8	32	.240	.200	Post-All Star	.222	54	12	2	0	2	8	4	10	.276	.370

Last Five Years

	Avg	AB	H	2B	3B	HR	RBI	BB	SO	OBP	SLG		Avg	AB	H	2B	3B	HR	RBI	BB	SO	OBP	SLG
vs. Left	.307	166	51	12	1	1	21	10	43	.348	.410	First Pitch	.283	226	64	12	2	8	34	7	0	.301	.460

Last Five Years

	Avg	AB	H	2B	3B	HR	RBI	BB	SO	OBP	SLG
vs. Right	.257	1026	264	49	5	28	141	70	164	.303	.397
Groundball	.285	270	77	13	1	9	37	14	44	.319	.441
Flyball	.254	209	53	12	3	5	29	11	40	.288	.411
Home	.280	611	171	36	4	17	89	39	116	.321	.435
Away	.248	581	144	25	2	12	73	41	91	.296	.360
Day	.292	380	111	21	3	10	54	28	80	.339	.442
Night	.251	812	204	40	3	19	108	52	127	.295	.378
Grass	.241	772	186	33	1	20	92	52	144	.287	.364
Turf	.307	420	129	28	5	9	70	28	63	.349	.462
Pre-All Star	.274	687	188	44	4	18	108	61	114	.329	.428
Post-All Star	.251	505	127	17	2	11	54	19	93	.280	.358
Scoring Posn	.258	337	87	18	2	3	125	32	70	.315	.350
Close & Late	.265	189	50	11	0	5	27	11	33	.308	.402
None on/out	.244	258	63	13	2	8	8	13	44	.280	.403

	Avg	AB	H	2B	3B	HR	RBI	BB	SO	OBP	SLG
Ahead in Count	.366	290	106	21	0	14	56	43	0	.448	.583
Behind in Count	.184	477	88	16	1	5	43	0	173	.184	.254
Two Strikes	.180	462	83	16	0	4	45	30	207	.228	.240
Batting #5	.284	236	67	15	2	7	35	11	39	.317	.453
Batting #6	.241	291	70	13	1	7	27	25	50	.303	.364
Other	.268	665	178	33	3	15	100	44	118	.309	.394
March/April	.254	181	46	13	0	1	16	12	34	.297	.343
May	.281	242	68	16	4	9	39	20	39	.332	.492
June	.301	183	55	11	0	6	39	20	27	.362	.459
July	.216	222	48	7	0	3	22	13	41	.262	.288
August	.307	205	63	12	0	7	30	12	36	.347	.468
Sept/Oct	.220	159	35	2	2	3	16	3	30	.236	.314
vs. AL	.263	1162	306	58	6	27	155	78	202	.308	.393
vs. NL	.300	30	9	3	0	2	7	2	5	.344	.600

Batter vs. Pitcher (career)

Hits Best Against	Avg	AB	H	2B	3B	HR	RBI	BB	SO	OBP	SLG
Bob Wells	.455	11	5	1	0	2	4	1	1	.500	1.091
Juan Guzman	.375	8	3	1	0	0	1	3	0	.545	.500
Kevin Tapani	.357	28	10	2	0	0	0	2	2	.400	.429
Bobby Witt	.313	16	5	1	0	0	2	3	4	.421	.500
Tim Belcher	.313	16	5	1	1	0	3	1	0	.353	.500

Hits Worst Against	Avg	AB	H	2B	3B	HR	RBI	BB	SO	OBP	SLG
Scott Kamieniecki	.000	10	0	0	0	0	0	1	5	.091	.000
Tom Gordon	.091	22	2	0	0	0	1	1	4	.130	.091
Roger Pavlik	.143	14	2	0	0	0	1	0	3	.133	.143
Cal Eldred	.167	12	2	0	0	0	1	0	1	.167	.167
Ricky Bones	.182	11	2	0	0	0	2	0	1	.182	.182

Mike Myers — Tigers
Age 29 – Pitches Left

	ERA	W	L	Sv	G	GS	IP	BB	SO	Avg	H	2B	3B	HR	RBI	OBP	SLG	GF	IR	IRS	Hld	SvOp	SB	CS	GB	FB	G/F
1997 Season	5.70	0	4	2	88	0	53.2	25	50	.274	58	9	1	12	52	.351	.495	23	81	27	18	5	5	1	71	60	1.18
Career (1995-1997)	5.47	2	9	8	184	0	126.2	66	123	.277	139	11	9	19	99	.367	.451	53	164	48	36	14	12	3	163	135	1.21

1997 Season

	ERA	W	L	Sv	G	GS	IP	H	HR	BB	SO		Avg	AB	H	2B	3B	HR	RBI	BB	SO	OBP	SLG
Home	5.54	0	2	1	39	0	26.0	28	7	6	28	vs. Left	.252	107	27	1	1	5	24	13	35	.336	.421
Away	5.86	0	2	1	49	0	27.2	30	5	19	22	vs. Right	.295	105	31	8	0	7	28	12	15	.367	.571
Day	5.82	0	3	1	33	0	21.2	25	6	12	19	Inning 1-6	.286	7	2	0	0	0	2	1	2	.375	.286
Night	5.63	0	1	1	55	0	32.0	33	6	13	31	Inning 7+	.273	205	56	9	1	12	50	24	48	.350	.502
Grass	5.59	0	4	2	74	0	46.2	51	10	18	44	None on	.260	104	27	5	1	6	6	7	25	.313	.500
Turf	6.43	0	0	0	14	0	7.0	7	2	7	6	Runners on	.287	108	31	4	0	6	46	18	25	.385	.491
March/April	6.75	0	2	0	15	0	6.2	11	1	8	7	Scoring Posn	.329	73	24	4	0	3	40	15	15	.435	.507
May	1.93	0	0	2	14	0	9.1	4	1	2	9	Close & Late	.284	74	21	0	1	7	25	13	19	.386	.595
June	9.45	0	2	0	14	0	6.2	7	3	3	6	None on/out	.239	46	11	2	0	3	3	1	12	.271	.478
July	6.57	0	0	0	18	0	12.1	16	3	5	12	vs. 1st Batr (relief)	.307	75	23	2	1	4	17	9	15	.391	.520
August	8.00	0	0	0	15	0	9.0	13	3	4	5	1st Inning Pitched	.277	195	54	8	1	11	50	25	45	.360	.497
Sept/Oct	2.79	0	0	0	12	0	9.2	7	1	3	11	First 15 Pitches	.266	169	45	7	1	10	39	19	37	.342	.497
Starter	0.00	0	0	0	0	0	0.0	0	0	0	0	Pitch 16-30	.250	40	10	1	0	2	10	5	13	.333	.425
Reliever	5.70	0	4	2	88	0	53.2	58	12	25	50	Pitch 31-45	1.000	2	2	1	0	0	2	1	0	1.000	1.500
0 Days rest (Relief)	6.55	0	1	1	43	0	22.0	28	4	15	20	Pitch 46+	1.000	1	1	0	0	0	1	0	0	1.000	1.000
1 or 2 Days rest	7.32	0	3	0	31	0	19.2	21	7	7	20	First Pitch	.421	19	8	1	0	2	9	2	0	.476	.789
3+ Days rest	1.50	0	0	1	14	0	12.0	9	1	3	10	Ahead in Count	.167	96	16	3	1	3	13	0	38	.173	.313
vs. AL	6.04	0	4	2	79	0	47.2	53	12	22	47	Behind in Count	.347	49	17	3	0	3	12	11	0	.468	.592
vs. NL	3.00	0	0	0	9	0	6.0	5	0	3	3	Two Strikes	.185	108	20	4	1	4	19	12	50	.262	.352
Pre-All Star	6.00	0	4	2	48	0	27.0	28	6	16	25	Pre-All Star	.275	102	28	4	0	6	25	16	25	.372	.490
Post-All Star	5.40	0	0	0	40	0	26.2	30	6	9	25	Post-All Star	.273	110	30	5	1	6	27	9	25	.331	.500

Career (1995-1997)

	ERA	W	L	Sv	G	GS	IP	H	HR	BB	SO		Avg	AB	H	2B	3B	HR	RBI	BB	SO	OBP	SLG
Home	5.60	1	4	3	86	0	64.1	71	10	29	68	vs. Left	.238	240	57	9	1	6	36	28	80	.320	.358
Away	5.34	1	5	5	98	0	62.1	68	9	37	55	vs. Right	.314	261	82	19	0	13	63	38	43	.409	.536
Day	4.87	2	4	3	72	0	57.1	60	8	30	61	Inning 1-6	.267	30	8	2	0	0	8	7	6	.395	.333
Night	5.97	0	5	5	112	0	69.1	79	11	36	62	Inning 7+	.278	471	131	26	1	19	91	59	117	.365	.459
Grass	5.06	2	9	8	158	0	110.1	122	14	53	110	None on	.259	232	60	13	1	10	10	21	59	.333	.453
Turf	8.27	0	0	0	26	0	16.1	17	5	13	13	Runners on	.294	269	79	15	0	9	89	45	64	.394	.450
March/April	6.33	0	3	0	31	0	21.1	28	4	16	23	Scoring Posn	.303	175	53	12	0	5	79	37	44	.423	.457
May	3.33	0	1	4	31	0	24.1	21	2	11	17	Close & Late	.277	191	53	6	1	8	42	27	45	.369	.445
June	9.00	0	4	0	29	0	16.0	20	3	13	19	None on/out	.220	109	24	4	0	5	5	4	26	.261	.394
July	4.21	0	0	1	33	0	25.2	28	4	10	25	vs. 1st Batr (relief)	.226	159	36	6	1	5	28	18	42	.311	.371
August	5.87	0	0	3	26	0	15.1	18	4	5	13	1st Inning Pitched	.279	445	124	26	1	17	92	58	100	.367	.456
Sept/Oct	5.63	2	1	0	34	0	24.0	24	2	11	26	First 15 Pitches	.267	374	100	21	1	15	71	49	91	.359	.449
Starter	0.00	0	0	0	0	0	0.0	0	0	0	0	Pitch 16-30	.282	110	31	5	0	3	23	14	29	.368	.409
Reliever	5.47	2	9	8	184	0	126.2	139	19	66	123	Pitch 31-45	.429	14	6	2	0	1	4	3	2	.529	.786
0 Days rest (Relief)	5.47	2	5	1	76	0	49.1	60	7	31	48	Pitch 46+	.667	3	2	0	0	0	1	0	1	.667	.667
1 or 2 Days rest	6.15	0	4	4	77	0	52.2	59	10	24	52	First Pitch	.320	50	16	2	0	3	13	10	0	.443	.540
3+ Days rest	4.01	0	0	3	31	0	24.2	20	2	11	23	Ahead in Count	.188	234	44	11	1	4	29	0	99	.203	.295
vs. AL	5.69	2	9	8	173	0	118.2	133	19	60	120	Behind in Count	.374	107	40	8	0	5	29	24	0	.489	.589
vs. NL	2.25	0	0	0	11	0	8.0	6	0	6	3	Two Strikes	.185	259	48	9	1	7	33	32	123	.279	.309
Pre-All Star	5.77	0	8	5	99	0	68.2	76	10	43	67	Pre-All Star	.284	268	76	15	0	10	54	43	67	.387	.451
Post-All Star	5.12	2	1	3	85	0	58.0	63	9	23	56	Post-All Star	.270	233	63	13	1	9	45	23	56	.344	.451

Pitches Best Vs.	Avg	AB	H	2B	3B	HR	RBI	BB	SO	OBP	SLG	Pitches Worst Vs.	Avg	AB	H	2B	3B	HR	RBI	BB	SO	OBP	SLG
												Tino Martinez	.455	11	5	2	1	1	2	1	2	.500	1.091

Randy Myers — Orioles
Age 35 – Pitches Left (flyball pitcher)

	ERA	W	L	Sv	G	GS	IP	BB	SO	Avg	H	2B	3B	HR	RBI	OBP	SLG	GF	IR	IRS	Hld	SvOp	SB	CS	GB	FB	G/F
1997 Season	1.51	2	3	45	61	0	59.2	22	56	.217	47	7	1	2	18	.289	.286	57	20	6	2	46	0	1	55	79	0.70
Last Five Years	3.11	10	18	188	291	0	289.2	121	307	.240	261	46	4	26	134	.315	.362	257	121	38	4	213	5	5	303	320	0.95

1997 Season

	ERA	W	L	Sv	G	GS	IP	H	HR	BB	SO		Avg	AB	H	2B	3B	HR	RBI	BB	SO	OBP	SLG
Home	2.40	1	2	22	30	0	30.0	26	2	10	31	vs. Left	.188	48	9	1	1	1	5	9	12	.316	.313
Away	0.61	1	1	23	31	0	29.2	21	0	12	25	vs. Right	.225	169	38	6	0	1	13	13	44	.280	.278
Day	3.06	0	3	13	18	0	17.2	14	2	8	21	Inning 1-6	.000	0	0	0	0	0	0	0	0	.000	.000
Night	0.86	2	0	32	43	0	42.0	33	0	14	35	Inning 7+	.217	217	47	7	1	2	18	22	56	.289	.286
Grass	1.78	2	3	39	51	0	50.2	38	2	21	48	None on	.223	103	23	3	1	0	0	16	30	.328	.272
Turf	0.00	0	0	6	10	0	9.0	9	0	1	8	Runners on	.211	114	24	4	0	2	18	6	26	.250	.298
March/April	0.00	0	0	10	11	0	10.1	9	0	4	14	Scoring Posn	.220	59	13	2	0	2	17	5	5	.281	.356
May	2.25	0	2	7	12	0	12.0	13	1	3	14	Close & Late	.207	179	37	3	1	2	12	21	51	.290	.268
June	2.00	1	1	8	10	0	9.0	7	0	6	6	None on/out	.186	43	8	2	0	0	0	9	15	.327	.233
July	1.80	1	0	5	9	0	10.0	9	0	4	9	vs. 1st Batr (relief)	.154	52	8	1	0	0	1	9	17	.279	.173
August	1.69	0	0	10	11	0	10.2	6	1	5	5	1st Inning Pitched	.210	210	44	6	1	2	17	20	56	.278	.276
Sept/Oct	1.17	0	0	5	8	0	7.2	2	0	0	7	First 15 Pitches	.209	153	32	6	1	2	12	15	40	.280	.301
Starter	0.00	0	0	0	0	0	0.0	0	0	0	0	Pitch 16-30	.220	59	13	1	0	0	5	7	15	.303	.237
Reliever	1.51	2	3	45	61	0	59.2	47	2	22	56	Pitch 31-45	.400	5	2	0	0	0	1	0	1	.400	.400
0 Days rest (Relief)	0.50	0	0	13	20	0	18.0	16	0	4	14	Pitch 46+	.000	0	0	0	0	0	0	0	0	.000	.000
1 or 2 Days rest	2.49	1	3	18	22	0	21.2	16	1	13	17	First Pitch	.227	22	5	0	0	0	2	0	0	.292	.227
3+ Days rest	1.35	1	0	14	19	0	20.0	15	1	5	25	Ahead in Count	.164	116	19	3	1	1	7	0	48	.164	.233
vs. AL	1.51	2	3	40	55	0	53.2	44	2	17	49	Behind in Count	.303	33	10	1	0	1	7	6	0	.410	.424
vs. NL	1.50	0	0	5	6	0	6.0	3	0	5	7	Two Strikes	.185	119	22	2	1	0	4	14	56	.271	.218
Pre-All Star	1.35	1	3	27	35	0	33.1	29	1	15	39	Pre-All Star	.225	129	29	2	1	1	11	15	39	.306	.279
Post-All Star	1.71	1	0	18	26	0	26.1	18	1	7	17	Post-All Star	.205	88	18	5	0	1	7	7	17	.263	.295

Last Five Years

	ERA	W	L	Sv	G	GS	IP	H	HR	BB	SO		Avg	AB	H	2B	3B	HR	RBI	BB	SO	OBP	SLG
Home	3.14	3	8	91	143	0	143.1	129	13	66	155	vs. Left	.171	216	37	5	2	5	27	35	69	.287	.282
Away	3.08	7	10	97	148	0	146.1	132	13	55	152	vs. Right	.257	871	224	41	2	21	107	86	238	.322	.381
Day	3.63	3	8	85	136	0	136.1	116	16	64	144	Inning 1-6	.000	0	0	0	0	0	0	0	0	.000	.000
Night	2.64	7	10	103	155	0	153.1	145	10	57	163	Inning 7+	.240	1087	261	46	4	26	134	121	307	.315	.362
Grass	3.07	9	13	149	231	0	226.0	203	18	97	246	None on	.237	548	130	24	4	13	13	63	155	.317	.367
Turf	3.25	1	5	39	60	0	63.2	58	8	24	61	Runners on	.243	539	131	22	0	13	121	58	152	.313	.356
March/April	1.11	0	1	28	43	0	40.2	26	1	22	46	Scoring Posn	.254	299	76	14	0	10	111	48	81	.350	.401
May	3.10	0	8	38	53	0	52.1	55	4	26	61	Close & Late	.245	829	203	36	2	20	109	98	232	.323	.366
June	1.64	3	2	30	47	0	49.1	38	2	13	55	None on/out	.229	236	54	8	2	5	5	24	62	.300	.343
July	5.96	2	4	29	50	0	54.1	65	7	25	51	vs. 1st Batr (relief)	.209	258	54	8	2	3	12	28	72	.287	.291
August	4.18	4	5	29	50	0	47.1	46	8	22	38	1st Inning Pitched	.237	987	234	40	4	23	123	104	279	.309	.356
Sept/Oct	1.97	1	0	34	48	0	45.2	31	4	13	56	First 15 Pitches	.240	739	177	36	3	18	78	79	199	.312	.369
Starter	0.00	0	0	0	0	0	0.0	0	0	0	0	Pitch 16-30	.233	318	74	8	1	7	48	37	102	.311	.330
Reliever	3.11	10	18	188	291	0	289.2	261	26	121	307	Pitch 31-45	.333	30	10	2	0	1	8	5	6	.429	.500
0 Days rest (Relief)	3.66	0	7	57	87	0	78.2	82	8	31	73	Pitch 46+	.000	0	0	0	0	0	0	0	0	.000	.000
1 or 2 Days rest	3.21	7	6	79	116	0	117.2	103	10	53	130	First Pitch	.372	113	42	4	2	2	14	5	0	.398	.496
3+ Days rest	2.51	3	5	52	88	0	93.1	76	8	37	104	Ahead in Count	.167	575	96	15	1	7	39	0	263	.168	.233
vs. AL	2.56	6	7	71	117	0	112.1	104	9	46	123	Behind in Count	.353	184	65	16	1	9	46	57	0	.500	.598
vs. NL	3.45	4	11	117	174	0	177.1	157	17	75	184	Two Strikes	.152	611	93	13	1	7	40	59	307	.226	.211
Pre-All Star	2.55	3	12	110	162	0	162.2	141	9	70	190	Pre-All Star	.230	613	141	25	3	9	70	70	190	.307	.325
Post-All Star	3.83	7	6	78	129	0	127.0	120	17	51	117	Post-All Star	.253	474	120	21	1	17	64	51	117	.325	.409

Pitcher vs. Batter (career)

Pitches Best Vs.	Avg	AB	H	2B	3B	HR	RBI	BB	SO	OBP	SLG	Pitches Worst Vs.	Avg	AB	H	2B	3B	HR	RBI	BB	SO	OBP	SLG
Craig Biggio	.067	15	1	0	0	0	0	3	3	.222	.067	Mark Grace	.429	14	6	0	2	1	6	1	3	.467	.929
Larry Walker	.071	14	1	1	0	0	2	4	4	.176	.143	Bobby Bonilla	.417	24	10	1	0	1	7	6	4	.500	.583
Darrin Jackson	.100	10	1	0	0	0	1	2	0	.250	.100	Jeff Bagwell	.417	12	5	3	0	2	5	1	4	.462	1.167
Ray Lankford	.118	17	2	0	0	0	0	1	2	.167	.118	Luis Gonzalez	.385	13	5	3	0	0	5	1	5	.429	.615
Jose Offerman	.125	16	2	0	0	0	0	1	8	.176	.125	Andres Galarraga	.350	20	7	0	0	3	11	5	7	.480	.800

Rod Myers — Royals
Age 25 – Bats Left

	Avg	G	AB	R	H	2B	3B	HR	RBI	BB	SO	HBP	GDP	SB	CS	OBP	SLG	IBB	SH	SF	#Pit	#P/PA	GB	FB	G/F
1997 Season	.257	31	101	14	26	7	0	2	9	17	22	1	2	4	0	.370	.386	0	2	0	479	3.96	27	29	0.93
Career (1996-1997)	.268	53	164	23	44	14	0	3	20	24	38	1	3	7	2	.365	.409	0	2	0	778	4.07	41	47	0.87

1997 Season

	Avg	AB	H	2B	3B	HR	RBI	BB	SO	OBP	SLG		Avg	AB	H	2B	3B	HR	RBI	BB	SO	OBP	SLG
vs. Left	.211	19	4	1	0	0	3	3	5	.318	.263	Scoring Posn	.160	25	4	0	0	0	5	6	6	.323	.160
vs. Right	.268	82	22	6	0	2	6	14	17	.381	.415	Close & Late	.346	26	9	4	0	0	3	6	7	.469	.500

Rodney Myers — Cubs
Age 29 – Pitches Right

	ERA	W	L	Sv	G	GS	IP	BB	SO	Avg	H	2B	3B	HR	RBI	OBP	SLG	GF	IR	IRS	Hld	SvOp	SB	CS	GB	FB	G/F
1997 Season	6.00	0	0	0	5	1	9.0	7	6	.333	12	0	1	1	7	.455	.472	2	3	1	0	0	2	0	10	10	1.00
Career (1996-1997)	4.83	2	1	0	50	1	76.1	45	56	.254	73	12	3	7	54	.358	.390	10	31	14	1	0	13	2	106	74	1.43

1997 Season

	ERA	W	L	Sv	G	GS	IP	H	HR	BB	SO		Avg	AB	H	2B	3B	HR	RBI	BB	SO	OBP	SLG
Home	4.91	0	0	0	2	0	3.2	3	1	1	3	vs. Left	.333	18	6	0	1	0	5	1	3	.368	.444
Away	6.75	0	0	0	3	1	5.1	9	0	6	3	vs. Right	.333	18	6	0	0	1	2	6	3	.520	.500

Tim Naehring — Red Sox
Age 31 – Bats Right

	Avg	G	AB	R	H	2B	3B	HR	RBI	BB	SO	HBP	GDP	SB	CS	OBP	SLG	IBB	SH	SF	#Pit	#P/PA	GB	FB	G/F
1997 Season	.286	70	259	38	74	18	1	9	40	38	40	1	10	1	1	.375	.467	0	0	3	1213	4.03	99	75	1.32
Last Five Years	.294	431	1546	231	455	89	4	44	221	204	251	13	54	5	7	.379	.442	10	16	11	7084	3.96	537	448	1.20

1997 Season

	Avg	AB	H	2B	3B	HR	RBI	BB	SO	OBP	SLG		Avg	AB	H	2B	3B	HR	RBI	BB	SO	OBP	SLG
vs. Left	.292	72	21	5	1	2	5	16	12	.416	.472	First Pitch	.484	31	15	2	0	1	5	0	0	.469	.645
vs. Right	.283	187	53	13	0	7	35	22	28	.358	.465	Ahead in Count	.274	62	17	5	0	3	7	20	0	.451	.500
Groundball	.250	40	10	3	0	1	9	4	6	.311	.400	Behind in Count	.242	99	24	7	0	4	13	0	35	.245	.434
Flyball	.359	39	14	2	0	2	4	10	6	.490	.564	Two Strikes	.205	117	24	7	0	3	19	18	40	.312	.342
Home	.282	117	33	8	1	4	23	24	19	.406	.470	Batting #5	.279	147	41	10	0	7	29	27	25	.386	.490
Away	.289	142	41	10	0	5	17	14	21	.348	.465	Batting #6	.315	92	29	6	1	2	8	7	11	.370	.467
Day	.238	84	20	5	0	3	12	15	9	.354	.405	Other	.200	20	4	2	0	0	3	4	4	.320	.300
Night	.309	175	54	13	1	6	28	23	31	.386	.497	March/April	.310	87	27	8	0	6	20	17	15	.415	.609
Grass	.283	230	65	15	1	7	33	35	39	.377	.448	May	.290	93	27	5	1	2	9	11			
Turf	.310	29	9	3	0	2	7	3	1	.364	.621	June	.253	79	20	5	0	1	11	10			
Pre-All Star	.286	259	74	18	1	9	40	38	40	.375	.467	July	.000	0	0	0	0	0	0	0			
Post-All Star	.000	0	0	0	0	0	0	0	0	.000	.000	August	.000	0	0	0	0	0	0	0			
Scoring Posn	.258	66	17	6	0	3	34	15	10	.381	.485	Sept/Oct	.000	0	0	0	0	0	0	0			
Close & Late	.167	42	7	4	0	0	5	5	9	.250	.262	vs. AL	.288	236	68	15	1	9	35	34			
None on/out	.302	53	16	6	0	2	2	3	8	.339	.528	vs. NL	.261	23	6	3	0	0	5	4			

1997 By Position

Position	Avg	AB	H	2B	3B	HR	RBI	BB	SO	OBP	SLG	G	GS	Innings	PO	A	E	DP	Fld Pct	Rng Fctr	In Zone
As 3b	.288	257	74	18	1	9	40	38	39	.378	.471	68	68	602.1	40	110	3	10	.980	2.24	156

Last Five Years

	Avg	AB	H	2B	3B	HR	RBI	BB	SO	OBP	SLG		Avg	AB	H	2B	3B	HR	RBI	BB			
vs. Left	.280	418	117	23	2	11	49	73	69	.387	.423	First Pitch	.398	176	70	14	1	5	30				
vs. Right	.300	1128	338	66	2	33	172	131	182	.376	.449	Ahead in Count	.364	407	148	33	0	16	73	11			
Groundball	.298	272	81	20	0	5	44	36	35	.382	.426	Behind in Count	.228	632	144	27	2	13	71				
Flyball	.242	293	71	18	0	6	27	39	57	.335	.365	Two Strikes	.217	706	153	28	1	15	78	8			
Home	.312	763	238	52	2	22	134	111	133	.402	.472	Batting #5	.283	456	129	23	0	23	83	6			
Away	.277	783	217	37	2	22	87	93	118	.355	.414	Batting #6	.283	441	125	28	3	8	50	6			
Day	.335	495	166	27	0	15	78	63	73	.413	.481	Other	.310	649	201	38	1	13	88	76	111	.385	.431
Night	.275	1051	289	62	4	29	143	141	178	.363	.424	March/April	.321	209	67	12	1	12	46	33	30	.415	.560
Grass	.296	1380	409	80	3	38	202	170	230	.376	.441	May	.322	360	116	23	1	9	49	47	61	.404	.467
Turf	.277	166	46	9	1	6	19	34	21	.401	.452	June	.301	266	80	18	0	10	48	31	31	.371	.481
Pre-All Star	.308	903	278	54	3	32	151	118	134	.389	.481	July	.264	265	70	11	1	6	29	35	41	.351	.381
Post-All Star	.275	643	177	35	1	12	70	86	117	.364	.389	August	.234	248	58	8	0	4	22	34	49	.334	.315
Scoring Posn	.297	414	123	27	2	12	182	78	70	.406	.459	Sept/Oct	.323	198	64	17	1	3	27	24	39	.396	.465
Close & Late	.252	234	59	11	1	7	31	29	52	.336	.397	vs. AL	.295	1523	449	86	4	44	216	200	245	.379	.443
None on/out	.316	342	108	25	0	10	10	29	45	.371	.477	vs. NL	.261	23	6	3	0	0	5	4	6	.357	.391

Batter vs. Pitcher (career)

Hits Best Against	Avg	AB	H	2B	3B	HR	RBI	BB	SO	OBP	SLG	Hits Worst Against	Avg	AB	H	2B	3B	HR	RBI	BB	SO	OBP	SLG
Scott Kamieniecki	.583	12	7	2	0	1	8	7	0	.737	1.000	Tom Gordon	.063	16	1	0	0	0	0	2	5	.167	.063
Shawn Boskie	.583	12	7	2	1	0	2	0	2	.583	.917	Ben McDonald	.077	13	1	0	0	0	0	4	4	.294	.077
Bob Wolcott	.500	12	6	1	0	1	3	3	1	.625	.833	Charles Nagy	.143	14	2	0	0	0	0		1	.143	.143
Ricky Bones	.389	18	7	0	0	2	5	2	3	.450	.722	Kevin Appier	.167	24	4	0	0	0	2	1	6	.200	.167
Mike Mussina	.368	19	7	2	0	2	5	2	1	.429	.789	Orel Hershiser	.200	15	3	1	0	0	0	3		.200	.267

Charles Nagy — Indians
Age 31 – Pitches Right (groundball pitcher)

	ERA	W	L	Sv	G	GS	IP	BB	SO	Avg	H	2B	3B	HR	RBI	OBP	SLG	CG	ShO	Sup	QS	#P/S	SB	CS	GB	FB	G/F
1997 Season	4.28	15	11	0	34	34	227.0	77	149	.283	253	48	3	27	108	.342	.434	1	1	5.59	18	106	24	10	413	178	2.32
Last Five Years	4.06	60	36	0	127	127	845.0	260	593	.274	905	169	9	89	374	.329	.411	12	2	6.39	70	105	80	23	1468	674	2.18

1997 Season

	ERA	W	L	Sv	G	GS	IP	H	HR	BB	SO		Avg	AB	H	2B	3B	HR	RBI	BB	SO	OBP	SLG
Home	4.37	9	6	0	19	19	129.2	141	19	43	78	vs. Left	.279	419	117	23	1	13	49	44	71	.348	.432
Away	4.16	6	5	0	15	15	97.1	112	8	34	71	vs. Right	.286	476	136	25	2	14	59	33	78	.337	.435
Day	4.32	7	4	0	11	11	73.0	75	8	22	41	Inning 1-6	.276	756	209	43	2	22	96	60	122	.331	.426
Night	4.27	8	7	0	23	23	154.0	178	19	55	108	Inning 7+	.317	139	44	5	1	5	12	17	27	.400	.475
Grass	4.40	14	9	0	30	30	200.1	220	26	70	127	None on	.288	520	150	31	3	20	20	35	79	.336	.475
Turf	3.38	1	2	0	4	4	26.2	33	1	7	22	Runners on	.275	375	103	17	0	7	88	42	70	.350	.376
March/April	4.99	4	1	0	6	6	39.2	47	6	12	30	Scoring Posn	.265	223	59	11	0	5	80	31	39	.356	.381
May	2.40	2	2	0	6	6	45.0	46	5	20	32	Close & Late	.316	57	18	4	1	4	8	9	11	.409	.632

1997 Season

	ERA	W	L	Sv	G	GS	IP	H	HR	BB	SO
June	4.50	2	1	0	5	5	30.0	35	4	11	15
July	6.08	2	3	0	6	6	37.0	44	5	11	24
August	3.19	3	2	0	6	6	42.1	44	5	10	30
Sept/Oct	5.18	2	2	0	5	5	33.0	37	2	13	18
Starter	4.28	15	11	0	34	34	227.0	253	27	77	149
Reliever	0.00	0	0	0	0	0	0.0	0	0	0	0
0-3 Days Rest (Start)	0.00	0	0	0	0	0	0.0	0	0	0	0
4 Days Rest	3.67	15	8	0	25	25	169.0	176	17	53	112
5+ Days Rest	6.05	0	3	0	9	9	58.0	77	10	24	37
vs. AL	4.54	13	11	0	31	31	206.0	235	27	70	138
vs. NL	1.71	2	0	0	3	3	21.0	18	0	7	11
Pre-All Star	3.92	9	4	0	18	18	121.2	134	16	45	81
Post-All Star	4.70	6	7	0	16	16	105.1	119	11	32	68

	Avg	AB	H	2B	3B	HR	RBI	BB	SO	OBP	SLG
None on/out	.258	233	60	12	2	7	7	10	36	.291	.416
	.000	0	0	0	0	0	0	0	0	.000	.000
1st Inning Pitched	.246	130	32	7	0	4	16	14	23	.319	.392
First 75 Pitches	.266	601	160	31	1	19	70	50	97	.322	.416
Pitch 76-90	.353	119	42	10	1	3	15	9	19	.408	.529
Pitch 91-105	.284	102	29	5	1	3	14	9	18	.348	.441
Pitch 106+	.301	73	22	2	0	2	9	9	15	.393	.411
Ahead in Count	.241	394	95	21	0	7	34	0	118	.247	.348
Behind in Count	.351	191	67	14	2	11	33	44	0	.473	.618
Two Strikes	.216	394	85	17	0	8	33	29	149	.268	.320
Pre-All Star	.282	476	134	22	2	16	56	45	81	.343	.437
Post-All Star	.284	419	119	26	1	11	52	32	68	.341	.430

Last Five Years

	ERA	W	L	Sv	G	GS	IP	H	HR	BB	SO
Home	3.70	34	16	0	66	66	459.1	455	48	139	333
Away	4.48	26	20	0	61	61	385.2	450	41	121	260
Day	4.23	24	10	0	41	41	265.2	283	32	80	195
Night	3.98	36	26	0	86	86	579.1	622	57	180	398
Grass	3.98	55	29	0	110	110	740.1	770	84	225	513
Turf	4.64	5	7	0	17	17	104.2	135	5	35	80
March/April	5.15	10	6	0	22	22	136.1	158	17	35	89
May	3.02	14	7	0	25	25	169.2	173	15	58	126
June	3.83	8	5	0	21	21	141.0	153	16	40	89
July	4.45	9	9	0	24	24	164.0	166	18	60	108
August	4.20	8	4	0	18	18	120.0	138	15	32	92
Sept/Oct	3.87	11	5	0	17	17	114.0	117	8	35	89
Starter	4.06	60	36	0	127	127	845.0	905	89	260	593
Reliever	0.00	0	0	0	0	0	0.0	0	0	0	0
0-3 Days Rest (Start)	0.00	0	0	0	0	0	0.0	0	0	0	0
4 Days Rest	3.89	38	23	0	77	77	523.0	529	55	145	346
5+ Days Rest	4.33	22	13	0	50	50	322.0	376	34	115	247
vs. AL	4.12	58	36	0	124	124	824.0	887	89	253	582
vs. NL	1.71	2	0	0	3	3	21.0	18	0	7	11
Pre-All Star	3.85	36	20	0	75	75	502.0	527	56	147	342
Post-All Star	4.36	24	16	0	52	52	343.0	378	33	113	251

	Avg	AB	H	2B	3B	HR	RBI	BB	SO	OBP	SLG
vs. Left	.272	1664	452	87	5	36	170	148	268	.332	.395
vs. Right	.276	1644	453	82	4	53	204	112	325	.326	.427
Inning 1-6	.275	2788	766	147	8	73	331	213	503	.329	.412
Inning 7+	.267	520	139	22	1	16	43	47	90	.333	.406
None on	.291	1899	552	109	8	53	53	122	312	.336	.440
Runners on	.251	1409	353	60	1	36	321	138	281	.320	.371
Scoring Posn	.261	802	209	36	1	22	284	93	164	.337	.390
Close & Late	.265	226	60	8	1	11	25	23	42	.335	.456
None on/out	.288	848	244	50	5	19	19	38	125	.322	.422
vs. 1st Batr (relief)	.000	0	0	0	0	0	0	0	0	.000	.000
1st Inning Pitched	.285	506	144	28	0	13	75	52	83	.355	.417
First 75 Pitches	.274	2264	621	124	6	60	258	179	404	.329	.414
Pitch 76-90	.274	441	121	16	1	15	54	28	82	.324	.417
Pitch 91-105	.277	365	101	22	2	9	34	21	60	.321	.422
Pitch 106+	.261	238	62	7	0	5	28	32	47	.354	.450
First Pitch	.324	476	154	22	2	19	62	7	0	.336	.498
Ahead in Count	.217	1459	317	59	2	24	115	0	492	.224	.310
Behind in Count	.342	725	248	55	4	29	113	143	0	.449	.549
Two Strikes	.201	1478	297	51	3	24	110	110	593	.259	.288
Pre-All Star	.269	1956	527	90	6	56	215	147	342	.322	.407
Post-All Star	.280	1352	378	79	3	33	159	113	251	.339	.416

Pitcher vs. Batter (career)

Pitches Best Vs.	Avg	AB	H	2B	3B	HR	RBI	BB	SO	OBP	SLG
Billy Ripken	.000	14	0	0	0	0	1	1	4	.067	.000
Lenny Webster	.000	10	0	0	0	0	0	2	3	.167	.000
Warren Newson	.056	18	1	0	0	0	0	2	2	.150	.056
Brent Gates	.071	14	1	0	0	0	1	1	4	.133	.071
Chad Curtis	.086	35	3	0	0	0	0	4	6	.179	.086

Pitches Worst Vs.	Avg	AB	H	2B	3B	HR	RBI	BB	SO	OBP	SLG
Mike Macfarlane	.474	19	9	0	0	3	6	0	5	.474	.947
John Jaha	.444	18	8	0	0	2	4	1	2	.500	.778
Mike Stanley	.435	23	10	1	0	3	9	4	2	.519	.870
Dean Palmer	.394	33	13	3	0	4	13	0	6	.394	.848
Mickey Tettleton	.382	34	13	1	0	5	9	8	12	.488	.853

Bob Natal — Marlins
Age 32 – Bats Right

	Avg	G	AB	R	H	2B	3B	HR	RBI	BB	SO	HBP	GDP	SB	CS	OBP	SLG	IBB	SH	SF	#Pit	#P/PA	GB	FB	G/F
1997 Season	.500	4	4	2	2	1	0	1	3	2	0	0	0	0	0	.571	1.500	0	0	1	19	2.71	1	3	0.33
Last Five Years	.201	115	283	13	57	10	3	4	19	29	67	4	9	2	1	.282	.300	5	4	3	1222	3.78	105	75	1.40

1997 Season

	Avg	AB	H	2B	3B	HR	RBI	BB	SO	OBP	SLG		Avg	AB	H	2B	3B	HR	RBI	BB	SO	OBP	SLG
vs. Left	1.000	2	2	1	0	1	2	0	0	1.000	3.000	Scoring Posn	.000	0	0	0	0	0	0	1	1	.500	.000
vs. Right	.000	2	0	0	0	1	2	0		.400	.000	Close & Late	.000	0	0	0	0	0	0	1	1	.500	.000

Dan Naulty — Twins
Age 28 – Pitches Right (flyball pitcher)

	ERA	W	L	Sv	G	GS	IP	BB	SO	Avg	H	2B	3B	HR	RBI	OBP	SLG	GF	IR	IRS	Hld	SvOp	SB	CS	GB	FB	G/F
1997 Season	5.87	1	1	1	29	0	30.2	10	23	.254	29	7	0	8	23	.305	.526	8	30	7	8	3	1	1	31	49	0.63
Career (1996-1997)	4.52	4	3	5	78	0	87.2	45	79	.224	72	16	2	13	51	.315	.407	23	63	20	12	12	6	2	91	111	0.82

1997 Season

	ERA	W	L	Sv	G	GS	IP	H	HR	BB	SO
Home	5.25	1	1	1	15	0	12.0	7	2	5	7
Away	6.27	0	0	0	14	0	18.2	22	6	5	16
Starter	0.00	0	0	0	0	0	0.0	0	0	0	0
Reliever	5.87	1	1	1	29	0	30.2	29	8	10	23
0 Days rest (Relief)	0.00	0	0	1	5	0	2.1	0	0	0	1
1 or 2 Days rest	5.51	0	1	0	15	0	16.1	10	3	7	12
3+ Days rest	7.50	1	0	0	9	0	12.0	19	5	3	10
Pre-All Star	4.87	1	1	1	22	0	20.1	15	3	6	16
Post-All Star	7.84	0	0	0	7	0	10.1	14	5	4	7

	Avg	AB	H	2B	3B	HR	RBI	BB	SO	OBP	SLG
vs. Left	.268	41	11	3	0	4	10	6	7	.347	.634
vs. Right	.247	73	18	4	0	4	13	4	16	.278	.466
Scoring Posn	.163	43	7	1	0	2	15	4	7	.216	.326
Close & Late	.241	29	7	2	0	2	9	1	8	.242	.517
None on/out	.250	20	5	1	0	2	2	3	3	.348	.600
First Pitch	.368	19	7	3	0	3	3	0	0	.368	.842
Ahead in Count	.171	41	7	3	0	1	10	0	15	.163	.317
Behind in Count	.269	26	7	1	0	1	4	5	0	.375	.423
Two Strikes	.135	52	7	1	0	2	9	5	23	.207	.288

Jaime Navarro — White Sox
Age 30 – Pitches Right (groundball pitcher)

	ERA	W	L	Sv	G	GS	IP	BB	SO	Avg	H	2B	3B	HR	RBI	OBP	SLG	CG	ShO	Sup	QS	#P/S	SB	CS	GB	FB	G/F
1997 Season	5.79	9	14	0	33	33	209.2	73	142	.309	267	51	5	22	140	.359	.455	2	0	5.37	16	107	23	7	331	226	1.46
Last Five Years	4.77	53	53	0	161	141	950.2	309	607	.286	1074	186	26	97	500	.341	.427	12	3	4.95	71	103	107	36	1469	962	1.53

1997 Season

	ERA	W	L	Sv	G	GS	IP	H	HR	BB	SO		Avg	AB	H	2B	3B	HR	RBI	BB	SO	OBP	SLG
Home	4.57	6	6	0	15	15	102.1	116	6	33	80	vs. Left	.321	396	127	26	4	9	61	49	66	.392	.475
Away	6.96	3	8	0	18	18	107.1	151	16	40	62	vs. Right	.299	469	140	25	1	13	79	24	76	.329	.439
Day	3.86	4	3	0	11	11	81.2	85	5	26	67	Inning 1-6	.302	731	221	42	5	17	119	60	120	.353	.443
Night	7.03	5	11	0	22	22	128.0	182	17	47	75	Inning 7+	.343	134	46	9	0	5	21	13	22	.399	.522
Grass	5.81	8	11	0	27	27	172.0	216	15	60	118	None on	.291	468	136	29	4	10	10	32	82	.340	.434
Turf	5.73	1	3	0	6	6	37.2	51	7	13	24	Runners on	.330	397	131	22	1	12	130	41	60	.381	.481
March/April	4.50	2	1	0	6	6	40.0	41	3	16	34	Scoring Posn	.327	248	81	13	0	8	117	28	45	.376	.476
May	4.66	2	3	0	6	6	38.2	46	2	16	28	Close & Late	.370	73	27	8	0	1	13	6	12	.418	.521
June	5.66	2	2	0	5	5	35.0	41	3	12	21	None on/out	.303	211	64	11	1	5	5	13	38	.347	.436
July	7.58	2	3	0	6	6	38.0	57	5	10	20	vs. 1st Batr (relief)	.000	0	0	0	0	0	0	0	0	.000	.000
August	6.21	1	3	0	5	5	33.1	45	4	10	22	1st Inning Pitched	.311	135	42	7	1	4	21	8	21	.345	.467
Sept/Oct	6.57	0	2	0	5	5	24.2	37	5	9	17	First 75 Pitches	.304	585	178	36	4	13	92	46	92	.354	.446
Starter	5.79	9	14	0	33	33	209.2	267	22	73	142	Pitch 76-90	.354	99	35	8	1	4	19	13	18	.421	.576
Reliever	0.00	0	0	0	0	0	0.0	0	0	0	0	Pitch 91-105	.260	96	25	4	0	0	12	4	17	.282	.302
0-3 Days Rest (Start)	0.00	0	0	0	0	0	0.0	0	0	0	0	Pitch 106+	.341	85	29	3	0	5	17	10	15	.406	.553
4 Days Rest	6.37	4	10	0	17	17	101.2	138	16	40	66	First Pitch	.292	120	35	9	1	4	25	4	0	.310	.483
5+ Days Rest	5.25	5	4	0	16	16	108.0	129	6	33	76	Ahead in Count	.268	366	98	23	3	4	39	0	113	.268	.380
vs. AL	5.63	9	11	0	30	30	193.1	243	19	68	129	Behind in Count	.427	211	90	14	1	8	41	26	0	.483	.616
vs. NL	7.71	0	3	0	3	3	16.1	24	3	5	13	Two Strikes	.220	369	81	13	3	2	35	43	142	.300	.287
Pre-All Star	4.77	6	7	0	18	18	120.2	134	9	45	87	Pre-All Star	.277	483	134	25	4	9	71	45	87	.333	.402
Post-All Star	7.18	3	7	0	15	15	89.0	133	13	28	55	Post-All Star	.348	382	133	26	1	13	69	28	55	.393	.524

Last Five Years

	ERA	W	L	Sv	G	GS	IP	H	HR	BB	SO		Avg	AB	H	2B	3B	HR	RBI	BB	SO	OBP	SLG
Home	4.61	22	27	0	76	66	455.0	496	33	151	317	vs. Left	.297	1739	517	89	22	44	233	165	291	.357	.450
Away	4.92	31	26	0	85	75	495.2	578	64	158	290	vs. Right	.276	2019	557	97	4	53	267	144	316	.328	.407
Day	4.15	25	20	0	72	64	445.0	476	36	129	312	Inning 1-6	.290	3200	928	160	26	77	444	262	505	.345	.428
Night	5.32	28	33	0	89	77	505.2	598	61	180	295	Inning 7+	.262	558	146	26	0	20	56	47	102	.321	.416
Grass	4.79	42	41	0	130	112	760.2	843	75	251	509	None on	.272	2158	586	98	17	52	52	155	357	.325	.405
Turf	4.69	11	12	0	31	29	190.0	231	22	58	98	Runners on	.305	1600	488	88	9	44	448	154	250	.362	.456
March/April	5.03	5	8	0	22	22	141.1	145	13	53	102	Scoring Posn	.286	935	267	55	2	23	384	113	168	.353	.422
May	4.33	11	10	0	29	27	178.2	212	13	54	109	Close & Late	.285	291	83	21	0	8	33	22	43	.339	.440
June	4.28	9	7	0	30	23	168.1	162	17	58	103	None on/out	.272	951	259	44	7	22	22	63	146	.322	.403
July	5.48	9	12	0	30	22	157.2	198	20	47	79	vs. 1st Batr (relief)	.250	16	4	0	0	0	2	3	3	.400	.250
August	4.67	12	7	0	27	24	165.2	193	16	46	112	1st Inning Pitched	.311	636	198	37	7	18	116	60	113	.366	.476
Sept/Oct	4.99	7	9	0	23	23	139.0	164	18	51	102	First 75 Pitches	.288	2665	767	137	22	58	364	215	421	.343	.421
Starter	4.76	51	50	0	141	141	911.0	1035	94	291	580	Pitch 76-90	.295	498	147	26	2	19	69	41	71	.349	.470
Reliever	4.99	2	3	0	20	0	39.2	39	3	18	27	Pitch 91-105	.263	358	94	16	1	11	36	28	66	.318	.405
0-3 Days Rest (Start)	4.09	1	2	0	5	5	33.0	24	2	11	21	Pitch 106+	.278	237	66	7	1	9	31	25	49	.345	.430
4 Days Rest	4.78	27	28	0	80	80	512.0	589	65	172	311	First Pitch	.346	552	191	37	5	17	90	18	0	.374	.524
5+ Days Rest	4.80	23	20	0	56	56	366.0	422	27	108	248	Ahead in Count	.226	1614	364	70	9	21	150	0	514	.230	.319
vs. AL	5.68	24	32	0	94	74	497.1	612	50	176	308	Behind in Count	.370	860	318	54	8	39	166	132	0	.449	.587
vs. NL	3.77	29	21	0	67	67	453.1	462	47	133	299	Two Strikes	.202	1611	326	59	10	18	140	159	607	.275	.285
Pre-All Star	4.45	27	29	0	91	79	540.1	572	47	176	341	Pre-All Star	.271	2114	572	101	17	47	270	176	341	.327	.401
Post-All Star	5.20	26	24	0	70	62	410.1	502	50	133	266	Post-All Star	.305	1644	502	85	9	50	230	133	266	.360	.459

Pitcher vs. Batter (career)

Pitches Best Vs.	Avg	AB	H	2B	3B	HR	RBI	BB	SO	OBP	SLG	Pitches Worst Vs.	Avg	AB	H	2B	3B	HR	RBI	BB	SO	OBP	SLG
Ron Karkovice	.000	14	0	0	0	0	0	1	7	.125	.000	Ron Gant	.600	10	6	2	0	2	4	3	1	.692	1.400
Mickey Morandini	.000	13	0	0	0	0	0	3	2	.188	.000	Ron Coomer	.500	10	5	0	0	2	3	1	0	.545	1.100
Brett Butler	.071	14	1	0	0	0	0	0	3	.071	.071	Danny Tartabull	.480	25	12	1	0	3	8	4	8	.567	.880
Charles Johnson	.077	13	1	0	0	0	0	0	1	.077	.077	Gary Sheffield	.455	11	5	0	0	2	5	4	0	.625	1.000
Tony Gwynn	.083	12	1	1	0	0	0	0	0	.083	.167	Tony Tarasco	.364	11	4	1	0	2	4	2	1	.462	1.000

Denny Neagle — Braves
Age 29 – Pitches Left

	ERA	W	L	Sv	G	GS	IP	BB	SO	Avg	H	2B	3B	HR	RBI	OBP	SLG	CG	ShO	Sup	QS	#P/S	SB	CS	GB	FB	G/F
1997 Season	2.97	20	5	0	34	34	233.1	49	172	.233	204	46	6	18	80	.277	.362	4	4	5.67	27	106	14	8	253	293	0.86
Last Five Years	3.76	61	37	1	172	129	882.2	228	666	.258	868	166	26	92	365	.306	.404	13	5	5.00	84	100	76	41	1069	1037	1.03

1997 Season

	ERA	W	L	Sv	G	GS	IP	H	HR	BB	SO		Avg	AB	H	2B	3B	HR	RBI	BB	SO	OBP	SLG
Home	3.06	10	1	0	18	18	120.2	102	14	22	85	vs. Left	.236	174	41	11	1	5	14	8	33	.272	.397
Away	2.88	10	4	0	16	16	112.2	102	4	27	87	vs. Right	.233	700	163	35	5	13	66	41	139	.278	.353
Day	3.65	4	4	0	9	9	61.2	58	7	17	47	Inning 1-6	.232	740	172	36	6	16	71	43	151	.277	.362
Night	2.73	16	1	0	25	25	171.2	146	11	32	125	Inning 7+	.239	134	32	10	0	2	9	6	21	.277	.358
Grass	2.95	16	4	0	28	28	192.0	160	16	42	138	None on	.213	569	121	27	4	10	10	28	113	.253	.327
Turf	3.05	4	1	0	6	6	41.1	44	2	7	34	Runners on	.272	305	83	19	2	8	70	21	59	.319	.426
March/April	4.15	4	1	0	6	6	39.0	40	1	9	22	Scoring Posn	.244	172	42	9	2	3	54	13	39	.295	.372
May	2.75	3	1	0	6	6	39.1	36	3	9	28	Close & Late	.281	64	18	8	0	0	7	5	10	.343	.406
June	2.89	4	0	0	5	5	37.1	33	3	6	25	None on/out	.197	234	46	9	3	4	4	11	45	.236	.312
July	2.83	3	1	0	6	6	41.1	37	1	7	30	vs. 1st Batr (relief)	.000	0	0	0	0	0	0	0	0	.000	.000
August	1.65	4	1	0	6	6	43.2	32	2	11	38	1st Inning Pitched	.194	124	24	5	1	0	10	9	22	.257	.250

	ERA	W	L	Sv	G	GS	IP	H	HR	BB	SO
Sept/Oct	3.86	2	2	0	5	5	32.2	26	5	7	29
Starter	2.97	20	5	0	34	34	233.1	204	18	49	172
Reliever	0.00	0	0	0	0	0	0.0	0	0	0	0
0-3 Days Rest (Start)	3.55	0	0	0	2	2	12.2	16	1	4	4
4 Days Rest	2.60	16	2	0	21	21	148.2	127	7	31	117
5+ Days Rest	3.63	4	3	0	11	11	72.0	61	10	16	51
vs. AL	0.35	3	0	0	3	3	25.2	16	0	3	15
vs. NL	3.29	17	5	0	31	31	207.2	189	18	46	157
Pre-All Star	3.20	12	2	0	19	19	129.1	123	8	27	85
Post-All Star	2.68	8	3	0	15	15	104.0	81	10	22	87

	Avg	AB	H	2B	3B	HR	RBI	BB	SO	OBP	SLG
First 75 Pitches	.219	575	126	30	4	8	44	30	125	.261	.327
Pitch 76-90	.304	125	38	6	0	4	17	10	21	.355	.448
Pitch 91-105	.245	106	26	5	2	4	13	4	14	.273	.443
Pitch 106+	.206	68	14	5	0	2	6	5	12	.270	.368
First Pitch	.254	122	31	6	1	6	13			.276	.467
Ahead in Count	.213	445	95	21	4	5	32	0	144	.220	.312
Behind in Count	.256	125	32	9	1	4	13	19	0	.354	.440
Two Strikes	.183	460	84	21	3	5	32	26	172	.231	.274
Pre-All Star	.248	495	123	27	5	8	49	27	85	.291	.372
Post-All Star	.214	379	81	19	1	10	31	22	87	.259	.348

Last Five Years

	ERA	W	L	Sv	G	GS	IP	H	HR	BB	SO
Home	3.60	31	8	0	82	60	414.2	403	49	101	317
Away	3.90	30	29	1	96	69	468.0	465	43	127	349
Day	3.83	11	12	0	40	27	192.2	188	20	57	139
Night	3.74	50	25	0	132	102	690.0	680	72	171	527
Grass	3.36	33	17	1	77	63	439.1	400	42	98	319
Turf	4.16	28	20	0	95	66	443.1	468	50	130	347
March/April	3.90	9	6	0	27	18	127.0	122	9	35	106
May	3.53	14	4	0	32	23	158.0	164	17	36	130
June	3.56	14	9	0	28	28	179.2	171	20	47	124
July	3.74	10	3	0	30	25	168.2	164	19	40	122
August	3.81	9	8	1	29	20	144.0	139	15	41	105
Sept/Oct	4.27	6	6	0	26	15	105.1	108	12	29	79
Starter	3.72	60	35	0	129	129	834.0	821	88	212	622
Reliever	4.44	1	2	1	43	0	48.2	47	4	16	44
0-3 Days Rest (Start)	3.04	4	4	0	12	12	77.0	81	7	10	51
4 Days Rest	3.62	37	16	0	74	74	490.0	483	50	127	357
5+ Days Rest	4.11	19	15	0	43	43	267.0	257	31	75	214
vs. AL	0.35	3	0	0	3	3	25.2	15	0	3	15
vs. NL	3.86	58	37	1	169	126	857.0	853	92	225	651
Pre-All Star	3.79	40	22	0	97	77	515.2	521	50	133	397
Post-All Star	3.73	21	15	1	75	52	367.0	347	42	95	269

	Avg	AB	H	2B	3B	HR	RBI	BB	SO	OBP	SLG
vs. Left	.255	599	153	30	8	17	63	45	144	.310	.417
vs. Right	.258	2769	715	136	18	75	302	183	522	.305	.402
Inning 1-6	.255	2770	705	131	20	79	301	189	557	.303	.402
Inning 7+	.273	598	163	35	6	13	64	39	109	.321	.416
None on	.251	2079	522	96	16	58	58	119	412	.295	.396
Runners on	.268	1289	346	70	10	34	307	109	254	.324	.417
Scoring Posn	.267	707	189	37	8	14	252	80	157	.337	.402
Close & Late	.268	291	78	21	3	8	38	23	56	.327	.443
None on/out	.250	884	221	35	9	24	24	51	167	.295	.391
vs. 1st Batr (relief)	.162	37	6	0	0	0	6	6	9	.279	.162
1st Inning Pitched	.265	630	167	32	7	10	85	54	123	.326	.386
First 75 Pitches	.250	2423	606	120	19	63	259	158	505	.298	.393
Pitch 76-90	.290	442	128	26	1	15	50	33	78	.337	.455
Pitch 91-105	.270	318	86	10	3	9	35	23	45	.320	.406
Pitch 106+	.259	185	48	10	3	5	21	14	38	.315	.427
First Pitch	.361	468	169	37	4	21	71	12	0	.379	.592
Ahead in Count	.208	1690	351	63	13	20	116	0	566	.211	.296
Behind in Count	.327	597	195	40	7	38	101	108	0	.429	.608
Two Strikes	.179	1654	296	56	11	20	124	107	666	.230	.262
Pre-All Star	.263	1982	521	102	18	50	215	133	397	.310	.408
Post-All Star	.250	1386	347	64	8	42	150	95	269	.300	.399

Pitcher vs. Batter (career)

Pitches Best Vs.	Avg	AB	H	2B	3B	HR	RBI	BB	SO	OBP	SLG	Pitches Worst Vs.	Avg	AB	H	2B	3B	HR	RBI	BB	SO	OBP	SLG
Rey Ordonez	.000	11	0	0	0	0	0	0	2	.000	.000	Shane Andrews	.455	11	5	2	0	1	2	0	2	.455	.909
Ron Gant	.067	15	1	0	0	0	0	3	4	.222	.067	Charlie Hayes	.444	9	4	3	0	0	1	3	1	.583	.778
Mike Benjamin	.091	11	1	0	0	0	0	0	1	.091	.091	Chuck Carr	.444	9	4	3	0	0	1	3	2	.583	.778
Mike Kelly	.091	11	1	0	0	0	0	1	6	.167	.091	Reggie Sanders	.423	26	11	3	0	3	8	2	8	.483	.885
Rey Sanchez	.100	20	2	0	0	0	0	1	2	.143	.100	Benito Santiago	.421	19	8	1	0	3	4	2	3	.476	.947

Jeff Nelson — Yankees
Age 31 – Pitches Right (groundball pitcher)

	ERA	W	L	Sv	G	GS	IP	BB	SO	Avg	H	2B	3B	HR	RBI	OBP	SLG	GF	IR	IRS	Hld	SvOp	SB	CS	GB	FB	G/F
1997 Season	2.86	3	7	0	77	0	78.2	37	81	.191	53	14	1	7	34	.294	.325	22	53	11	22	8	13	2	94	61	1.54
Last Five Years	3.29	19	17	7	311	0	334.0	154	373	.229	278	55	4	25	169	.326	.342	93	271	85	65	27	47	11	417	252	1.65

1997 Season

	ERA	W	L	Sv	G	GS	IP	H	HR	BB	SO
Home	2.88	2	2	0	36	0	40.2	23	4	18	43
Away	2.84	1	5	2	41	0	38.0	30	3	25	38
Day	2.62	2	2	1	32	0	34.1	20	2	14	36
Night	3.05	1	5	1	45	0	44.1	33	5	23	45
Grass	3.03	3	7	1	67	0	71.1	51	7	31	71
Turf	1.23	0	0	1	10	0	7.1	2	0	6	10
March/April	3.52	1	3	0	16	0	15.1	14	1	7	12
May	2.70	0	1	1	12	0	13.1	8	1	6	18
June	3.21	1	1	0	11	0	14.0	15	1	7	12
July	0.68	1	1	0	14	0	13.1	2	1	6	16
August	4.15	0	1	1	14	0	13.0	11	3	6	13
Sept/Oct	2.79	0	1	0	10	0	9.2	3	0	9	10
Starter	0.00	0	0	0	0	0	0.0	0	0	0	0
Reliever	2.86	3	7	0	77	0	78.2	53	7	37	81
0 Days rest (Relief)	1.08	2	0	1	24	0	25.0	9	1	6	25
1 or 2 Days rest	3.52	1	5	1	38	0	38.1	30	3	25	44
3+ Days rest	4.11	0	2	0	15	0	15.1	14	3	6	12
vs. AL	2.79	3	7	2	69	0	71.0	47	7	30	68
vs. NL	3.52	0	0	0	8	0	7.2	6	0	7	13
Pre-All Star	3.02	1	5	1	42	0	44.2	37	3	20	45
Post-All Star	2.65	2	2	1	35	0	34.0	16	4	17	36

	Avg	AB	H	2B	3B	HR	RBI	BB	SO	OBP	SLG
vs. Left	.235	98	23	9	1	3	12	17	23	.364	.439
vs. Right	.168	179	30	5	0	4	22	20	58	.252	.263
Inning 1-6	.143	7	1	0	0	0	0	0	1	.143	.143
Inning 7+	.193	270	52	14	1	7	34	37	80	.297	.330
None on	.182	154	28	10	1	3	13		42	.254	.318
Runners on	.203	123	25	4	0	4	31	24	39	.338	.333
Scoring Posn	.232	95	22	4	0	4	31	21	34	.375	.400
Close & Late	.245	139	34	9	1	4	24	18	41	.338	.410
None on/out	.186	59	11	6	0	1	1	8	17	.294	.339
vs. 1st Batr (relief)	.143	63	9	3	0	2	6	12	26	.280	.286
1st Inning Pitched	.193	212	41	12	1	6	28	31	66	.300	.344
First 15 Pitches	.174	190	33	9	0	5	19	22	54	.262	.300
Pitch 16-30	.233	73	17	5	1	2	13	15	24	.374	.411
Pitch 31-45	.214	14	3	0	0	0	0	2	0	.267	.214
Pitch 46+	.000	0	0	0	0	0	0	0	0	.000	.000
First Pitch	.435	23	10	2	0	0	3	11	0	.618	.522
Ahead in Count	.168	161	27	8	0	4	18	0	65	.177	.292
Behind in Count	.289	38	11	3	0	2	9	11	0	.451	.526
Two Strikes	.142	162	23	1	1	5	17	15	81	.219	.302
Pre-All Star	.223	166	37	9	1	3	19	20	45	.312	.343
Post-All Star	.144	111	16	5	0	4	15	17	36	.267	.297

Last Five Years

	ERA	W	L	Sv	G	GS	IP	H	HR	BB	SO
Home	3.16	11	7	3	148	0	171.0	131	14	68	198
Away	3.42	8	10	4	163	0	163.0	147	11	86	175
Day	3.16	7	7	1	103	0	116.2	79	7	52	144
Night	3.35	12	10	6	208	0	217.1	199	18	102	229

	Avg	AB	H	2B	3B	HR	RBI	BB	SO	OBP	SLG
vs. Left	.274	441	121	28	3	14	68	63	110	.384	.447
vs. Right	.203	775	157	27	1	11	101	91	263	.292	.283
Inning 1-6	.244	176	43	9	2	3	33	21	53	.338	.369
Inning 7+	.226	1040	235	46	2	22	136	133	320	.324	.338

Last Five Years

	ERA	W	L	Sv	G	GS	IP	H	HR	BB	SO		Avg	AB	H	2B	3B	HR	RBI	BB	SO	OBP	SLG
Grass	3.64	11	15	3	198	0	203.0	174	18	106	214	None on	.217	621	135	29	1	11	11	56	191	.296	.320
Turf	2.75	8	2	4	113	0	131.0	104	7	48	159	Runners on	.240	595	143	26	3	14	158	98	182	.356	.365
March/April	2.98	2	3	1	40	0	42.1	40	1	25	38	Scoring Posn	.230	408	94	16	2	11	145	80	134	.365	.360
May	3.39	3	3	3	59	0	66.1	54	3	38	68	Close & Late	.255	440	112	17	1	10	76	67	126	.358	.366
June	2.83	4	3	0	51	0	57.1	53	5	24	60	None on/out	.242	273	66	15	0	4	4	21	83	.312	.341
July	1.87	4	1	1	57	0	67.1	41	7	16	75	vs. 1st Batr (relief)	.245	265	65	10	1	10	53	34	83	.332	.404
August	6.23	4	5	2	53	0	56.1	60	8	29	79	1st Inning Pitched	.235	892	210	40	4	21	148	106	268	.325	.360
Sept/Oct	2.44	2	2	0	51	0	44.1	30	1	22	53	First 15 Pitches	.232	746	173	33	2	18	116	83	220	.317	.354
Starter	0.00	0	0	0	0	0	0.0	0	0	0	0	Pitch 16-30	.239	339	81	17	2	5	42	52	109	.354	.345
Reliever	3.29	19	17	7	311	0	334.0	278	25	154	373	Pitch 31-45	.194	108	21	4	0	2	9	14	36	.293	.287
0 Days rest (Relief)	2.35	5	2	2	92	0	95.2	58	4	43	106	Pitch 46+	.130	23	3	1	0	0	2	5	8	.355	.174
1 or 2 Days rest	4.44	10	12	3	150	0	154.0	151	15	82	181	First Pitch	.358	95	34	8	0	2	23	28	0	.500	.505
3+ Days rest	2.24	4	3	2	69	0	84.1	69	6	29	86	Ahead in Count	.178	659	117	21	2	9	68	0	307	.196	.256
vs. AL	3.28	19	17	7	303	0	326.1	272	25	147	360	Behind in Count	.332	223	74	18	0	10	47	58	0	.478	.547
vs. NL	3.52	0	0	0	8	0	7.2	6	0	7	13	Two Strikes	.162	716	116	23	3	10	66	68	373	.249	.244
Pre-All Star	3.05	10	9	4	163	0	177.0	154	11	89	179	Pre-All Star	.237	650	154	25	2	11	81	89	179	.338	.332
Post-All Star	3.55	9	8	3	148	0	157.0	124	14	65	194	Post-All Star	.219	566	124	30	2	14	88	65	194	.313	.353

Pitcher vs. Batter (career)

Pitches Best Vs.	Avg	AB	H	2B	3B	HR	RBI	BB	SO	OBP	SLG	Pitches Worst Vs.	Avg	AB	H	2B	3B	HR	RBI	BB	SO	OBP	SLG
Geronimo Berroa	.000	9	0	0	0	0	0	3	4	.250	.000	Chad Curtis	.400	10	4	0	0	0	1	1	2	.500	.400
Joe Carter	.063	16	1	0	0	0	0	2	4	.167	.063	Sandy Alomar Jr	.364	11	4	0	0	0	1	1	0	.417	.364
Randy Velarde	.077	13	1	0	1	0	0	0	5	.143	.231	Mike Devereaux	.333	12	4	2	1	0	3	0	3	.333	.667
John Valentin	.091	11	1	0	0	0	0	1	2	.167	.091	Mike Bordick	.333	9	3	0	0	0	2	2	2	.500	.333
Dean Palmer	.118	17	2	1	0	0	3	2	8	.211	.176	Jose Canseco	.316	19	6	2	0	1	5	2	4	.381	.579

Robb Nen — Marlins   Age 28 – Pitches Right

	ERA	W	L	Sv	G	GS	IP	BB	SO	Avg	H	2B	3B	HR	RBI	OBP	SLG	GF	IR	IRS	Hld	SvOp	SB	CS	GB	FB	G/F
1997 Season	3.89	9	3	35	73	0	74.0	40	81	.250	72	10	2	7	44	.338	.372	65	20	10	0	42	9	0	108	65	1.66
Career (1993-1997)	3.61	21	17	108	278	4	336.2	147	340	.244	310	71	9	27	157	.322	.378	218	106	28	1	128	32	5	425	319	1.33

1997 Season

	ERA	W	L	Sv	G	GS	IP	H	HR	BB	SO		Avg	AB	H	2B	3B	HR	RBI	BB	SO	OBP	SLG
Home	3.89	7	1	16	39	0	39.1	42	4	22	39	vs. Left	.222	144	32	4	0	4	21	20	40	.313	.333
Away	3.89	2	2	19	34	0	34.2	30	3	18	42	vs. Right	.278	144	40	6	2	3	23	20	41	.364	.410
Day	2.55	2	0	11	24	0	24.2	17	1	16	24	Inning 1-6	.000	0	0	0	0	0	0	0	0	.000	.000
Night	4.56	7	3	24	49	0	49.1	55	6	24	57	Inning 7+	.250	288	72	10	2	7	44	40	81	.338	.372
Grass	3.98	8	2	28	60	0	61.0	64	5	35	66	None on	.230	126	29	5	1	4	4	20	44	.336	.381
Turf	3.46	1	1	7	13	0	13.0	8	2	5	15	Runners on	.265	162	43	5	1	3	40	20	37	.341	.364
March/April	7.36	1	1	7	12	0	11.0	18	0	6	17	Scoring Posn	.234	111	26	4	0	2	37	17	26	.328	.324
May	3.86	3	1	6	13	0	14.0	16	1	11	15	Close & Late	.245	208	51	7	2	5	37	27	57	.328	.370
June	2.03	1	0	10	14	0	13.1	8	0	4	17	None on/out	.241	54	13	3	1	2	2	15	17	.406	.444
July	4.38	2	0	4	9	0	12.1	10	2	12	7	vs. 1st Batr (relief)	.283	60	17	3	1	3	6	13	21	.411	.517
August	2.63	2	0	5	14	0	13.2	10	2	1	17	1st Inning Pitched	.257	272	70	10	2	7	44	33	78	.334	.386
Sept/Oct	3.72	0	1	3	11	0	9.2	10	2	6	8	First 15 Pitches	.270	204	55	7	1	6	24	24	57	.343	.402
Starter	0.00	0	0	0	0	0	0.0	0	0	0	0	Pitch 16-30	.194	72	14	2	1	1	17	14	23	.322	.292
Reliever	3.89	9	3	35	73	0	74.0	72	7	40	81	Pitch 31-45	.250	12	3	1	0	0	3	2	1	.357	.333
0 Days rest (Relief)	2.30	2	0	5	17	0	15.2	11	1	4	21	Pitch 46+	.000	0	0	0	0	0	0	0	0	.000	.000
1 or 2 Days rest	3.38	4	3	24	39	0	37.1	36	5	16	47	First Pitch	.379	29	11	1	0	1	6	5	0	.444	.517
3+ Days rest	6.00	3	0	6	17	0	21.0	25	1	20	13	Ahead in Count	.215	172	37	7	0	4	24	0	76	.214	.326
vs. AL	3.38	1	0	3	9	0	8.0	3	0	3	9	Behind in Count	.265	49	13	2	2	1	9	19	0	.471	.449
vs. NL	3.95	8	3	32	64	0	66.0	69	7	37	72	Two Strikes	.168	161	27	6	0	2	19	16	81	.242	.242
Pre-All Star	3.92	5	2	24	41	0	41.1	42	1	25	50	Pre-All Star	.256	164	42	6	2	1	26	25	50	.351	.335
Post-All Star	3.86	4	1	11	32	0	32.2	30	6	15	31	Post-All Star	.242	124	30	4	0	6	18	15	31	.321	.419

Career (1993-1997)

	ERA	W	L	Sv	G	GS	IP	H	HR	BB	SO		Avg	AB	H	2B	3B	HR	RBI	BB	SO	OBP	SLG
Home	3.52	15	8	52	153	2	192.0	181	15	78	192	vs. Left	.227	596	135	29	5	8	63	73	147	.310	.332
Away	3.73	6	9	56	125	2	144.2	129	12	69	148	vs. Right	.260	674	175	42	4	19	94	74	193	.342	.418
Day	3.13	8	2	25	75	2	95.0	81	9	58	93	Inning 1-6	.280	200	56	15	2	6	39	37	38	.389	.465
Night	3.80	13	15	83	203	2	241.2	229	18	89	247	Inning 7+	.237	1070	254	56	7	21	118	110	302	.308	.362
Grass	3.62	19	11	84	222	3	271.1	259	23	117	275	None on	.249	622	155	40	6	15	15	75	190	.331	.405
Turf	3.58	2	6	24	56	1	65.1	51	4	30	65	Runners on	.239	648	155	31	3	12	142	72	150	.313	.352
March/April	5.23	3	3	11	36	1	43.0	51	2	25	45	Scoring Posn	.230	408	94	21	1	6	123	52	100	.313	.331
May	3.51	6	6	17	52	2	74.1	67	6	38	73	Close & Late	.228	685	156	32	4	14	90	66	206	.295	.347
June	3.11	2	4	22	51	0	55.0	52	4	18	58	None on/out	.264	277	73	20	3	10	10	39	81	.356	.466
July	2.75	5	1	18	46	1	55.2	41	5	28	57	vs. 1st Batr (relief)	.273	249	68	17	3	9	19	23	75	.339	.474
August	2.49	5	0	26	53	0	61.1	42	7	15	63	1st Inning Pitched	.237	971	230	54	6	19	114	101	273	.308	.382
Sept/Oct	5.32	0	3	14	44	0	47.1	57	3	23	44	First 15 Pitches	.250	807	202	46	4	16	76	74	225	.313	.377
Starter	4.50	2	1	0	4	4	18.0	14	1	16	14	Pitch 16-30	.218	326	71	17	4	8	54	45	90	.310	.368
Reliever	3.56	19	16	108	274	0	318.2	296	26	131	326	Pitch 31-45	.247	81	20	3	1	1	13	17	18	.378	.346
0 Days rest (Relief)	3.43	5	4	41	70	0	76.0	66	8	21	89	Pitch 46+	.304	56	17	5	0	2	14	11	7	.412	.500
1 or 2 Days rest	3.75	10	12	53	132	0	151.0	149	13	65	157	First Pitch	.326	144	47	11	0	1	22	16	0	.389	.424
3+ Days rest	3.34	4	0	14	72	0	91.2	81	5	45	80	Ahead in Count	.188	704	132	27	3	13	74	0	310	.187	.290
vs. AL	5.58	2	1	3	18	3	30.2	31	1	29	21	Behind in Count	.348	227	79	21	5	8	40	81	0	.516	.590
vs. NL	3.41	19	16	105	260	1	306.0	279	26	118	319	Two Strikes	.168	680	114	23	2	7	53	50	340	.224	.238
Pre-All Star	3.68	12	13	55	153	3	186.0	181	13	88	185	Pre-All Star	.257	703	181	45	6	13	94	88	185	.339	.394

Career (1993-1997)

	ERA	W	L	Sv	G	GS	IP	H	HR	BB	SO		Avg	AB	H	2B	3B	HR	RBI	BB	SO	OBP	SLG
Post-All Star	3.52	9	4	53	125	1	150.2	129	14	59	155	Post-All Star	.228	567	129	26	3	14	63	59	155	.300	.358

Pitcher vs. Batter (career)

Pitches Best Vs.	Avg	AB	H	2B	3B	HR	RBI	BB	SO	OBP	SLG	Pitches Worst Vs.	Avg	AB	H	2B	3B	HR	RBI	BB	SO	OBP	SLG
Charlie Hayes	.083	12	1	0	0	0	2	1	4	.154	.083	Jose Vizcaino	.545	11	6	3	1	0	1	0	2	.545	1.000
Mark Grace	.091	11	1	0	0	0	0	1	2	.167	.091	Jeff Bagwell	.500	8	4	2	0	0	3	0		.636	.750
Todd Zeile	.125	8	1	0	0	1	2	4	2	.417	.500	Sammy Sosa	.364	11	4	0	1	3	5	0	3	.364	1.364
Andres Galarraga	.182	11	2	0	0	1	4	0	3	.182	.455												
Mickey Morandini	.182	11	2	1	0	0	0	3		.182	.273												

Phil Nevin — Tigers
Age 27 – Bats Right

	Avg	G	AB	R	H	2B	3B	HR	RBI	BB	SO	HBP	GDP	SB	CS	OBP	SLG	IBB	SH	SF	#Pit	#P/PA	GB	FB	G/F
1997 Season	.235	93	251	32	59	16	1	9	35	25	68	1	5	0	1	.306	.414	1	0	1	1116	4.01	78	69	1.13
Career (1995-1997)	.231	178	527	60	122	25	2	19	67	51	147	6	11	2	1	.305	.395	2	1	2	2331	3.97	164	143	1.15

1997 Season

	Avg	AB	H	2B	3B	HR	RBI	BB	SO	OBP	SLG		Avg	AB	H	2B	3B	HR	RBI	BB	SO	OBP	SLG
vs. Left	.307	114	35	10	1	6	21	11	27	.368	.570	Scoring Posn	.273	66	18	7	0	1	21	14	15	.395	.424
vs. Right	.175	137	24	6	0	3	14	14	41	.255	.285	Close & Late	.310	42	13	1	0	3	8	4	14	.370	.548
Home	.214	112	24	5	1	4	15	16	29	.315	.384	None on/out	.196	56	11	2	0	0	0	4	15	.250	.232
Away	.252	139	35	11	0	5	20	9	39	.297	.439	Batting #5	.284	102	29	11	1	4	19	12	26	.357	.529
First Pitch	.444	27	12	4	0	2	9	1	0	.464	.815	Batting #7	.185	92	17	2	0	2	7	10	26	.272	.272
Ahead in Count	.343	35	12	2	1	3	7	6	0	.429	.714	Other	.228	57	13	3	0	3	9	3	16	.267	.439
Behind in Count	.169	130	22	6	0	2	9	0	52	.176	.262	Pre-All Star	.277	101	28	10	0	4	20	15	21	.373	.495
Two Strikes	.146	137	20	5	0	4	10	18	68	.250	.270	Post-All Star	.207	150	31	6	1	5	15	10	47	.256	.360

Marc Newfield — Brewers
Age 25 – Bats Right (groundball hitter)

	Avg	G	AB	R	H	2B	3B	HR	RBI	BB	SO	HBP	GDP	SB	CS	OBP	SLG	IBB	SH	SF	#Pit	#P/PA	GB	FB	G/F
1997 Season	.229	50	157	14	36	8	0	1	18	14	27	2	4	0	0	.295	.299	0	0	3	689	3.91	68	39	1.74
Career (1993-1997)	.252	262	771	83	194	46	1	19	107	50	133	10	21	1	3	.302	.388	3	0	11	3174	3.77	320	189	1.69

1997 Season

	Avg	AB	H	2B	3B	HR	RBI	BB	SO	OBP	SLG		Avg	AB	H	2B	3B	HR	RBI	BB	SO	OBP	SLG
vs. Left	.241	54	13	2	0	0	7	3	6	.288	.278	Scoring Posn	.200	55	11	4	0	0	15	6	5	.266	.273
vs. Right	.223	103	23	6	0	1	11	11	21	.299	.311	Close & Late	.455	22	10	3	0	0	6	3	2	.500	.591
Home	.210	81	17	5	0	0	11	8	16	.275	.272	None on/out	.147	34	5	2	0	0	0	1	11	.194	.206
Away	.250	76	19	3	0	1	7	6	11	.318	.329	Batting #5	.233	60	14	5	0	0	4	7	10	.319	.317
First Pitch	.231	13	3	0	0	0	1	0	0	.286	.231	Batting #6	.260	50	13	2	0	1	10	4	5	.315	.360
Ahead in Count	.310	29	9	1	0	1	4	7	0	.444	.448	Other	.191	47	9	1	0	0	4	3	12	.245	.213
Behind in Count	.160	75	12	2	0	0	9	0	26	.165	.187	Pre-All Star	.236	123	29	7	0	1	17	12	19	.302	.317
Two Strikes	.183	82	15	5	0	0	10	7	27	.242	.244	Post-All Star	.206	34	7	1	0	0	1	2	8	.270	.235

Career (1993-1997)

	Avg	AB	H	2B	3B	HR	RBI	BB	SO	OBP	SLG		Avg	AB	H	2B	3B	HR	RBI	BB	SO	OBP	SLG
vs. Left	.266	244	65	17	0	5	32	14	45	.304	.398	First Pitch	.267	101	27	4	0	6	22	1	0	.296	.485
vs. Right	.245	527	129	29	1	14	75	36	88	.301	.383	Ahead in Count	.353	156	55	13	1	6	30	24	0	.440	.564
Groundball	.178	169	30	8	0	2	19	13	22	.241	.260	Behind in Count	.190	368	70	18	0	5	35	0	117	.194	.280
Flyball	.234	141	33	7	0	3	11	13	27	.299	.348	Two Strikes	.184	376	69	17	0	5	36	25	133	.234	.269
Home	.225	378	85	18	0	7	51	25	64	.271	.328	Batting #5	.260	192	50	11	0	5	30	17	28	.322	.396
Away	.277	393	109	28	1	12	56	25	69	.332	.445	Batting #6	.259	282	73	21	1	5	40	14	44	.301	.394
Day	.263	278	73	16	0	9	47	15	40	.302	.417	Other	.239	297	71	14	0	9	37	19	61	.288	.377
Night	.245	493	121	30	1	10	60	35	93	.301	.371	March/April	.322	115	37	10	0	3	21	14	20	.397	.487
Grass	.258	590	152	36	0	15	81	37	94	.308	.395	May	.202	114	23	3	0	1	12	9	20	.256	.254
Turf	.232	181	42	10	1	4	26	13	39	.281	.365	June	.222	117	26	5	0	4	16	8	24	.278	.368
Pre-All Star	.239	414	99	20	0	10	61	34	72	.298	.360	July	.184	163	30	5	0	3	18	6	31	.226	.270
Post-All Star	.266	357	95	26	1	9	46	16	61	.306	.420	August	.291	117	34	9	0	6	21	8	17	.346	.521
Scoring Posn	.230	230	53	14	0	5	81	23	43	.293	.357	Sept/Oct	.303	145	44	14	1	2	19	5	21	.327	.455
Close & Late	.281	121	34	8	0	2	18	13	20	.353	.397	vs. AL	.246	525	129	30	0	13	74	32	81	.295	.377
None on/out	.230	174	40	13	0	4	4	2	33	.251	.374	vs. NL	.264	246	65	16	1	6	33	18	52	.316	.411

Batter vs. Pitcher (career)

Hits Best Against	Avg	AB	H	2B	3B	HR	RBI	BB	SO	OBP	SLG	Hits Worst Against	Avg	AB	H	2B	3B	HR	RBI	BB	SO	OBP	SLG
Alex Fernandez	.545	11	6	1	0	2	4	0	0	.545	1.182	Orel Hershiser	.091	11	1	0	0	1	0	0	3	.154	.182
Mike Mussina	.364	11	4	0	0	1	2	1	0	.417	.636	Wilson Alvarez	.231	13	3	2	0	0	2	0	1	.231	.385
Jack McDowell	.333	9	3	0	0	0	1	1	2	.455	.333												

Warren Newson — Rangers
Age 33 – Bats Left (groundball hitter)

	Avg	G	AB	R	H	2B	3B	HR	RBI	BB	SO	HBP	GDP	SB	CS	OBP	SLG	IBB	SH	SF	#Pit	#P/PA	GB	FB	G/F
1997 Season	.213	81	169	23	36	10	1	10	23	31	53	0	4	3	0	.333	.462	2	0	1	838	4.17	51	43	1.19
Last Five Years	.249	345	703	116	175	31	4	29	82	130	215	1	14	9	1	.366	.428	5	2	2	3636	4.34	253	129	1.96

1997 Season

	Avg	AB	H	2B	3B	HR	RBI	BB	SO	OBP	SLG		Avg	AB	H	2B	3B	HR	RBI	BB	SO	OBP	SLG
vs. Left	.077	13	1	0	0	0	0	1	8	.143	.077	Scoring Posn	.156	32	5	3	0	1	10	10	13	.349	.344
vs. Right	.224	156	35	10	1	10	23	30	45	.348	.494	Close & Late	.222	27	6	3	0	2	4	8	13	.400	.556
Home	.183	93	17	7	1	2	8	22	32	.339	.344	None on/out	.170	47	8	1	0	2	2	11	12	.328	.319

338

1997 Season

	Avg	AB	H	2B	3B	HR	RBI	BB	SO	OBP	SLG		Avg	AB	H	2B	3B	HR	RBI	BB	SO	OBP	SLG
Away	.250	76	19	3	0	8	15	9	21	.326	.605	Batting #1	.274	62	17	5	1	3	7	8	17	.357	.532
First Pitch	.235	17	4	0	0	2	4	1	0	.278	.588	Batting #7	.197	71	14	3	0	5	11	16	17	.341	.451
Ahead in Count	.556	27	15	6	1	4	9	17	0	.727	1.296	Other	.139	36	5	2	0	2	5	7	19	.279	.361
Behind in Count	.074	94	7	1	0	0	2	0	50	.074	.085	Pre-All Star	.243	115	28	9	1	4	14	22	33	.362	.443
Two Strikes	.071	99	7	1	0	2	3	13	53	.179	.141	Post-All Star	.148	54	8	1	0	6	9	9	20	.270	.500

Last Five Years

	Avg	AB	H	2B	3B	HR	RBI	BB	SO	OBP	SLG		Avg	AB	H	2B	3B	HR	RBI	BB	SO	OBP	SLG
vs. Left	.200	50	10	1	0	0	3	15	27	.394	.220	First Pitch	.339	59	20	2	1	5	11	3	0	.371	.661
vs. Right	.253	653	165	30	4	29	79	115	188	.364	.444	Ahead in Count	.382	144	55	14	1	10	28	51	0	.544	.701
Groundball	.227	194	44	9	0	4	15	32	53	.336	.335	Behind in Count	.168	339	57	8	1	9	22	0	170	.170	.277
Flyball	.258	128	33	4	1	12	25	17	47	.349	.586	Two Strikes	.159	395	63	9	1	9	24	76	215	.294	.256
Home	.239	360	86	15	3	15	49	68	111	.360	.422	Batting #6	.293	184	54	6	2	7	17	26	46	.381	.462
Away	.259	343	89	16	1	14	33	62	104	.372	.434	Batting #7	.252	214	54	12	1	12	30	38	65	.362	.486
Day	.230	204	47	7	0	9	21	45	64	.369	.397	Other	.220	305	67	13	1	10	35	66	104	.360	.367
Night	.257	499	128	24	4	20	61	85	151	.365	.441	March/April	.214	56	12	2	0	2	7	14	17	.366	.357
Grass	.245	600	147	28	4	25	71	107	187	.360	.430	May	.299	194	58	15	1	8	27	36	55	.411	.510
Turf	.272	103	28	3	0	4	11	23	28	.402	.417	June	.213	141	30	6	2	5	14	23	43	.323	.390
Pre-All Star	.249	421	105	24	3	17	53	76	127	.364	.442	July	.242	149	36	4	1	7	17	24	50	.345	.423
Post-All Star	.248	282	70	7	1	12	29	54	88	.369	.408	August	.216	111	24	3	0	5	11	21	33	.341	.378
Scoring Posn	.202	168	34	5	1	1	45	44	59	.367	.262	Sept/Oct	.288	52	15	1	0	2	6	12	17	.422	.423
Close & Late	.299	137	41	7	0	3	16	22	55	.400	.416	vs. AL	.250	695	174	31	4	29	82	130	213	.368	.432
None on/out	.256	168	43	8	1	9	9	26	45	.356	.476	vs. NL	.125	8	1	0	0	0	0	0	2	.125	.125

Batter vs. Pitcher (career)

Hits Best Against	Avg	AB	H	2B	3B	HR	RBI	BB	SO	OBP	SLG	Hits Worst Against	Avg	AB	H	2B	3B	HR	RBI	BB	SO	OBP	SLG
Tom Gordon	.500	12	6	0	0	0	0	4	3	.625	.500	Juan Guzman	.000	9	0	0	0	0	0	4	3	.308	.000
Jeff Montgomery	.400	10	4	1	0	0	1	2	4	.455	.500	Charles Nagy	.056	18	1	0	0	0	0	2	2	.150	.056
Mark Gubicza	.370	27	10	3	0	1	3	2	6	.414	.593	Bobby Witt	.100	10	1	0	0	0	0	1	4	.182	.100
Rick Aguilera	.333	9	3	0	0	0	1	4	3	.538	.333	Scott Erickson	.111	9	1	0	0	0	2	4	3	.385	.111
David Cone	.313	16	5	1	0	1	2	4	4	.450	.563	Erik Hanson	.143	14	2	0	0	0	0	0	5	.143	.143

Melvin Nieves — Tigers

Age 26 – Bats Both (groundball hitter)

	Avg	G	AB	R	H	2B	3B	HR	RBI	BB	SO	HBP	GDP	SB	CS	OBP	SLG	IBB	SH	SF	#Pit	#P/PA	GB	FB	G/F
1997 Season	.228	116	359	46	82	18	1	20	64	39	157	5	3	1	7	.311	.451	6	0	2	1591	3.93	96	64	1.50
Last Five Years	.229	363	1090	155	250	48	6	61	169	108	434	17	22	4	12	.307	.452	8	1	8	4814	3.93	321	209	1.54

1997 Season

	Avg	AB	H	2B	3B	HR	RBI	BB	SO	OBP	SLG		Avg	AB	H	2B	3B	HR	RBI	BB	SO	OBP	SLG
vs. Left	.241	112	27	9	0	4	25	15	48	.331	.429	First Pitch	.400	50	20	5	0	5	14	4	0	.455	.800
vs. Right	.223	247	55	9	1	16	39	24	109	.302	.462	Ahead in Count	.386	44	17	3	1	5	16	15	0	.533	.841
Groundball	.239	71	17	3	1	5	13	8	26	.316	.521	Behind in Count	.137	190	26	7	0	5	22	0	122	.150	.253
Flyball	.182	66	12	1	0	3	12	9	38	.282	.333	Two Strikes	.113	221	25	6	0	5	16	20	157	.189	.208
Home	.235	162	38	10	0	7	23	22	70	.332	.426	Batting #6	.253	277	70	15	1	16	52	31	115	.334	.487
Away	.223	197	44	8	1	13	41	17	87	.294	.472	Batting #7	.036	28	1	0	0	1	4	3	16	.152	.143
Day	.266	128	34	10	0	6	22	18	54	.362	.484	Other	.204	54	11	3	0	3	8	5	26	.279	.426
Night	.208	231	48	8	1	14	42	21	103	.281	.433	March/April	.271	70	19	6	0	3	16	8	31	.346	.486
Grass	.232	314	73	17	0	18	57	37	136	.321	.459	May	.278	72	20	4	1	3	8	13	29	.402	.486
Turf	.200	45	9	1	1	2	7	2	21	.234	.400	June	.241	83	20	5	0	4	17	9	36	.312	.446
Pre-All Star	.262	237	62	15	1	11	43	33	100	.355	.473	July	.211	71	15	2	0	5	13	4	32	.273	.451
Post-All Star	.164	122	20	3	0	9	21	6	57	.220	.410	August	.154	39	6	1	0	4	8	2	14	.209	.487
Scoring Posn	.270	89	24	7	1	8	46	14	40	.374	.640	Sept/Oct	.083	24	2	0	0	1	2	3	15	.185	.208
Close & Late	.246	65	16	2	0	3	13	7	24	.319	.415	vs. AL	.238	328	78	18	1	19	60	35	139	.320	.473
None on/out	.250	72	18	4	0	4	4	10	28	.349	.472	vs. NL	.129	31	4	0	0	1	4	4	18	.222	.226

1997 By Position

Position	Avg	AB	H	2B	3B	HR	RBI	BB	SO	OBP	SLG	G	GS	Innings	PO	A	E	DP	Fld Pct	Rng Fctr	In Zone Outs	Zone Rtg	MLB Zone
As DH	.310	29	9	1	0	1	7	5	16	.412	.448	11	7	---	---	---	---	---	---	---	---	---	---
As Pinch Hitter	.063	16	1	0	0	1	3	2	11	.167	.250	19	0	---	---	---	---	---	---	---	---	---	---
As rf	.225	315	71	17	1	17	53	33	131	.307	.448	101	84	752.1	189	4	4	1	.980	2.31	227 188	.828	.813

Last Five Years

	Avg	AB	H	2B	3B	HR	RBI	BB	SO	OBP	SLG		Avg	AB	H	2B	3B	HR	RBI	BB	SO	OBP	SLG
vs. Left	.223	287	64	14	2	15	55	26	105	.291	.443	First Pitch	.438	146	64	11	1	14	41	6	0	.468	.815
vs. Right	.232	803	186	34	4	46	114	82	329	.312	.456	Ahead in Count	.361	169	61	10	3	17	43	41	0	.481	.757
Groundball	.237	257	61	7	2	17	36	26	93	.311	.479	Behind in Count	.125	546	68	16	1	14	42	0	346	.143	.234
Flyball	.145	166	24	2	1	5	21	18	84	.240	.259	Two Strikes	.110	626	69	17	1	13	36	61	434	.196	.203
Home	.213	526	112	18	2	24	66	49	214	.287	.392	Batting #5	.218	248	54	16	1	11	26	32	92	.315	.423
Away	.245	564	138	30	4	37	103	59	220	.325	.509	Batting #6	.254	602	153	27	4	35	101	58	233	.326	.487
Day	.253	384	97	25	2	20	53	45	151	.337	.484	Other	.179	240	43	5	1	15	42	18	109	.248	.396
Night	.217	706	153	23	4	41	116	63	283	.290	.435	March/April	.287	157	45	15	1	6	32	17	61	.356	.510
Grass	.229	957	219	42	3	55	150	95	378	.307	.451	May	.238	227	54	7	1	13	28	30	85	.337	.449
Turf	.233	133	31	6	3	6	19	13	56	.307	.459	June	.228	167	38	10	1	5	24	17	62	.305	.389
Pre-All Star	.241	619	149	33	4	26	90	74	241	.323	.433	July	.214	210	45	5	2	15	34	21	93	.297	.471
Post-All Star	.214	471	101	15	2	35	79	34	193	.276	.478	August	.231	117	27	3	1	11	31	8	44	.292	.556
Scoring Posn	.232	263	61	12	1	15	108	30	111	.311	.456	Sept/Oct	.193	212	41	8	0	11	20	15	89	.253	.387
Close & Late	.254	189	48	4	0	11	31	16	68	.316	.450	vs. AL	.242	759	184	41	5	43	120	79	297	.321	.480

Last Five Years

	Avg	AB	H	2B	3B	HR	RBI	BB	SO	OBP	SLG		Avg	AB	H	2B	3B	HR	RBI	BB	SO	OBP	SLG
None on/out	.216	259	56	14	2	14	14	24	107	.293	.448	vs. NL	.199	331	66	7	1	18	49	29	137	.273	.390

Batter vs. Pitcher (career)

Hits Best Against	Avg	AB	H	2B	3B	HR	RBI	BB	SO	OBP	SLG	Hits Worst Against	Avg	AB	H	2B	3B	HR	RBI	BB	SO	OBP	SLG
Kevin Appier	.417	12	5	0	0	2	6	2	5	.500	.917	Cal Eldred	.000	11	0	0	0	0	0	2	5	.214	.000
Tony Castillo	.400	10	4	3	0	0	3	1	1	.455	.700	Tom Gordon	.077	13	1	0	0	0	0	2	5	.250	.077
Charles Nagy	.308	13	4	0	0	1	1	3	4	.438	.538	James Baldwin	.111	18	2	0	0	0	1	1	7	.158	.111
												Pat Hentgen	.154	13	2	0	0	0	0	0	6	.154	.154
												Jose Rosado	.182	11	2	0	0	0	0	0	2	.182	.182

Dave Nilsson — Brewers

Age 28 – Bats Left

	Avg	G	AB	R	H	2B	3B	HR	RBI	BB	SO	HBP	GDP	SB	CS	OBP	SLG	IBB	SH	SF	#Pit	#P/PA	GB	FB	G/F
1997 Season	.278	156	554	71	154	33	0	20	81	65	88	2	7	2	3	.352	.446	8	1	7	2415	3.84	168	199	0.84
Last Five Years	.286	569	1963	279	562	116	8	68	327	217	294	7	36	10	12	.355	.457	32	6	26	8408	3.79	669	618	1.08

1997 Season

	Avg	AB	H	2B	3B	HR	RBI	BB	SO	OBP	SLG		Avg	AB	H	2B	3B	HR	RBI	BB	SO	OBP	SLG
vs. Left	.236	199	47	5	0	4	21	12	47	.282	.322	First Pitch	.286	49	14	2	0	2	6	7	0	.375	.449
vs. Right	.301	355	107	28	0	16	60	53	41	.388	.515	Ahead in Count	.306	124	38	10	0	4	12	39	0	.470	.484
Groundball	.207	92	19	1	0	4	9	11	15	.286	.348	Behind in Count	.250	264	66	13	0	9	44	0	72	.248	.402
Flyball	.276	105	29	7	0	4	15	16	15	.371	.457	Two Strikes	.234	261	61	14	0	10	40	19	88	.285	.402
Home	.300	257	77	20	0	5	38	38	32	.389	.436	Batting #3	.281	292	82	18	0	5	34	39	37	.364	.394
Away	.259	297	77	13	0	15	43	27	56	.318	.455	Batting #4	.284	229	65	14	0	14	44	20	41	.336	.528
Day	.295	207	61	16	0	4	31	29	45	.377	.430	Other	.212	33	7	0	0	1	3	6	10	.350	.333
Night	.268	347	93	17	0	16	50	36	43	.337	.455	March/April	.299	87	26	4	0	4	14	12	17	.380	.483
Grass	.288	479	138	30	0	18	75	57	76	.361	.463	May	.286	98	28	7	0	1	13	14	8	.372	.388
Turf	.213	75	16	3	0	2	6	8	12	.289	.333	June	.232	99	23	5	0	2	13	9	23	.288	.343
Pre-All Star	.279	301	84	19	0	7	43	39	51	.357	.412	July	.333	99	33	5	0	10	24	8	16	.380	.687
Post-All Star	.277	253	70	14	0	13	38	26	37	.346	.486	August	.275	109	30	8	0	3	15	10	13	.339	.431
Scoring Posn	.237	152	36	10	0	1	52	21	24	.317	.322	Sept/Oct	.226	62	14	4	0	0	2	12	11	.360	.290
Close & Late	.267	86	23	3	0	2	9	13	16	.360	.372	vs. AL	.275	502	138	27	0	20	79	56	79	.346	.448
None on/out	.311	122	38	8	0	7	7	13	19	.382	.549	vs. NL	.308	52	16	6	0	0	2	9	9	.410	.423

1997 By Position

Position	Avg	AB	H	2B	3B	HR	RBI	BB	SO	OBP	SLG	G	GS	Innings	PO	A	E	DP	Fld Pct	Rng Fctr	In Zone	Zone Outs	Zone Rtg	MLB Zone
As DH	.274	215	59	13	0	3	28	19	42	.329	.377	59	59	—										
As 1b	.268	272	73	11	0	17	48	34	38	.351	.496	74	72	589.2	609	36	6	72	.991	—	125	107	.856	.874
As lf	.333	63	21	8	0	0	5	11	5	.427	.460	31	1	141.0	22		0	0	1.000	2.04	47	29	.617	.805

Last Five Years

	Avg	AB	H	2B	3B	HR	RBI	BB	SO	OBP	SLG		Avg	AB	H	2B	3B	HR	RBI	BB	SO	OBP	SLG
vs. Left	.244	532	130	19	3	11	75	36	119	.293	.353	First Pitch	.295	210	62	13	1	6	31	26	0	.376	.452
vs. Right	.302	1431	432	97	5	57	252	181	175	.377	.496	Ahead in Count	.331	493	163	34	5	26	91	104	0	.443	.578
Groundball	.297	404	120	23	1	10	68	51	58	.370	.433	Behind in Count	.249	866	216	44	2	22	134	0	236	.248	.381
Flyball	.267	363	97	22	1	13	59	38	64	.334	.441	Two Strikes	.223	866	193	40	2	22	122	87	294	.293	.350
Home	.302	983	297	69	5	24	170	112	141	.370	.456	Batting #3	.282	489	138	27	1	9	57	60	69	.362	.397
Away	.270	980	265	47	3	44	157	105	153	.341	.456	Batting #4	.302	605	183	39	2	29	125	65	99	.367	.517
Day	.291	625	182	40	4	14	95	77	112	.365	.435	Other	.277	869	241	50	5	30	145	92	126	.343	.450
Night	.284	1338	380	76	4	54	232	140	182	.351	.468	March/April	.277	195	54	9	0	9	29	16	27	.329	.462
Grass	.290	1719	499	105	8	50	278	195	259	.360	.448	May	.293	290	85	21	1	8	41	30	37	.357	.455
Turf	.258	244	63	11	0	18	49	22	35	.323	.525	June	.270	319	86	22	2	11	65	35	68	.335	.455
Pre-All Star	.283	930	263	59	4	30	158	95	148	.344	.452	July	.318	424	135	25	2	20	88	48	57	.384	.528
Post-All Star	.289	1033	299	57	4	38	169	122	146	.365	.463	August	.290	442	128	24	2	14	70	48	57	.359	.448
Scoring Posn	.273	561	153	34	3	15	245	92	67	.362	.424	Sept/Oct	.253	293	74	15	1	6	34	40	48	.345	.372
Close & Late	.281	295	83	14	1	10	46	31	48	.345	.437	vs. AL	.286	1911	546	110	8	68	325	208	285	.354	.458
None on/out	.297	435	129	28	0	19		19	39	.356	.492	vs. NL	.308	52	16	6	0	0	2	9	9	.410	.423

Batter vs. Pitcher (career)

Hits Best Against	Avg	AB	H	2B	3B	HR	RBI	BB	SO	OBP	SLG	Hits Worst Against	Avg	AB	H	2B	3B	HR	RBI	BB	SO	OBP	SLG
Tim Wakefield	.640	25	16	5	0	1	4	7	1	.719	.960	Jimmy Key	.071	14	1	0	0	0	0	3	5	.235	.071
James Baldwin	.636	11	7	0	0	1	3	1	0	.667	.909	Mike Mussina	.077	26	2	0	0	1	4	0	9	.074	.192
Kevin Gross	.500	10	5	3	0	0	3	1	2	.545	.800	David Wells	.077	13	1	0	0	0	0	1		.077	.077
Ben McDonald	.429	14	6	1	0	1	2	4	1	.556	.714	Jeff Suppan	.100	10	1	0	0	0	2	1	1	.182	.100
Tom Gordon	.375	24	9	4	1	1	7	4	3	.464	.750	Paul Assenmacher	.200	10	2	0	0	0	3	0	3	.167	.200

Otis Nixon — Dodgers

Age 39 – Bats Both (groundball hitter)

	Avg	G	AB	R	H	2B	3B	HR	RBI	BB	SO	HBP	GDP	SB	CS	OBP	SLG	IBB	SH	SF	#Pit	#P/PA	GB	FB	G/F
1997 Season	.266	145	576	84	153	18	3	2	44	65	78	0	12	59	12	.337	.318	0	8	6	2423	3.70	259	97	2.67
Last Five Years	.279	646	2520	395	702	81	10	4	167	310	359	1	35	252	69	.356	.323	5	32	16	10731	3.73	1162	388	2.99

1997 Season

	Avg	AB	H	2B	3B	HR	RBI	BB	SO	OBP	SLG		Avg	AB	H	2B	3B	HR	RBI	BB	SO	OBP	SLG
vs. Left	.214	168	36	6	2	1	12	14	18	.273	.292	First Pitch	.367	90	33	2	0	0	11	0	0	.363	.389
vs. Right	.287	408	117	12	1	1	32	51	60	.362	.328	Ahead in Count	.270	122	33	4	0	0	10	35	0	.425	.303
Groundball	.344	90	31	6	0	0	7	6	10	.385	.411	Behind in Count	.222	252	56	6	2	1	13	0	70	.222	.274
Flyball	.276	58	16	2	1	0	5	9	14	.368	.345	Two Strikes	.195	256	50	10	2	1	10	30	78	.279	.262
Home	.262	298	78	8	1	0	22	29	45	.326	.295	Batting #1	.254	473	120	15	1	1	31	57	64	.330	.296

	Avg	AB	H	2B	3B	HR	RBI	BB	SO	OBP	SLG		Avg	AB	H	2B	3B	HR	RBI	BB	SO	OBP	SLG
Away	.270	278	75	10	2	2	22	36	33	.348	.342	Batting #2	.372	78	29	2	2	1	11	3	8	.395	.487
Day	.325	169	55	7	1	1	20	22	21	.397	.396	Other	.160	25	4	1	0	0	2	5	6	.300	.200
Night	.241	407	98	11	2	1	24	43	57	.311	.285	March/April	.212	85	18	1	0	0	6	14	10	.323	.224
Grass	.259	290	75	10	2	2	27	26	33	.316	.328	May	.295	95	28	4	1	0	5	11	13	.361	.358
Turf	.273	286	78	8	1	0	17	39	45	.358	.308	June	.310	87	27	2	0	0	7	16	14	.410	.333
Pre-All Star	.266	289	77	7	1	0	18	44	44	.359	.298	July	.202	94	19	2	0	0	3	8	14	.262	.223
Post-All Star	.265	287	76	11	2	2	26	21	34	.313	.338	August	.267	116	31	5	0	1	13	10	16	.325	.336
Scoring Posn	.270	115	31	3	1	0	39	19	13	.357	.313	Sept/Oct	.303	99	30	4	2	1	10	6	11	.340	.414
Close & Late	.309	94	29	3	0	0	9	10	15	.368	.340	vs. AL	.275	393	108	14	2	1	30	49	45	.352	.328
None on/out	.221	226	50	8	0	0	0	24	38	.296	.257	vs. NL	.246	183	45	4	1	1	14	16	33	.303	.295

1997 By Position

Position	Avg	AB	H	2B	3B	HR	RBI	BB	SO	OBP	SLG	G	GS	Innings	PO	A	E	DP	Fld Pct	Rng Fctr	In Zone	Zone Outs	Zone Rtg	MLB Zone
As cf	.264	571	151	18	3	2	44	65	78	.336	.317	144	143	1263.2	351	2	2	0	.994	2.51	410	341	.832	.815

Last Five Years

	Avg	AB	H	2B	3B	HR	RBI	BB	SO	OBP	SLG		Avg	AB	H	2B	3B	HR	RBI	BB	SO	OBP	SLG
vs. Left	.271	756	205	20	7	2	47	72	89	.334	.324	First Pitch	.330	409	135	13	1	0	32	3	0	.333	.367
vs. Right	.282	1764	497	61	3	2	120	238	270	.365	.323	Ahead in Count	.314	566	178	23	1	0	42	166	0	.465	.359
Groundball	.272	599	163	21	3	0	31	65	92	.341	.317	Behind in Count	.241	1067	257	27	4	3	49	0	306	.241	.282
Flyball	.285	432	123	22	1	0	44	58	72	.368	.340	Two Strikes	.210	1098	231	29	6	3	53	140	359	.299	.256
Home	.276	1287	355	41	5	2	97	166	175	.358	.320	Batting #1	.278	2401	667	77	8	3	152	300	337	.356	.320
Away	.281	1233	347	40	5	2	70	144	184	.354	.327	Batting #2	.380	79	30	2	2	1	11	3	8	.402	.494
Day	.292	734	214	24	1	2	49	99	95	.375	.335	Other	.125	40	5	2	0	0	4	7	14	.255	.175
Night	.273	1786	488	57	9	2	118	211	264	.348	.319	March/April	.244	389	95	11	1	1	30	59	56	.341	.285
Grass	.282	1696	478	57	7	3	124	196	228	.354	.329	May	.287	481	138	15	2	0	33	59	64	.363	.326
Turf	.272	824	224	24	3	1	43	114	131	.360	.312	June	.284	356	101	12	1	0	19	48	50	.367	.323
Pre-All Star	.270	1336	361	43	4	1	86	185	184	.357	.311	July	.255	439	112	14	1	1	24	48	64	.327	.298
Post-All Star	.288	1184	341	38	6	3	81	125	175	.354	.338	August	.274	464	127	14	1	1	33	47	78	.341	.315
Scoring Posn	.266	537	143	20	1	0	157	75	78	.347	.307	Sept/Oct	.330	391	129	15	4	1	28	49	47	.402	.396
Close & Late	.275	363	100	10	1	0	32	51	63	.361	.309	vs. AL	.284	1876	533	65	6	2	129	233	263	.362	.328
None on/out	.278	994	276	29	4	2	2	130	147	.362	.321	vs. NL	.262	644	169	16	4	2	38	77	96	.338	.309

Batter vs. Pitcher (since 1984)

Hits Best Against	Avg	AB	H	2B	3B	HR	RBI	BB	SO	OBP	SLG	Hits Worst Against	Avg	AB	H	2B	3B	HR	RBI	BB	SO	OBP	SLG
Mike Bielecki	.529	17	9	1	1	0	4	1	4	.556	.706	James Baldwin	.000	11	0	0	0	0	0	0	2	.000	.000
Ken Hill	.500	24	12	2	0	0	0	5	2	.586	.583	Jamie Moyer	.059	17	1	0	0	0	0	0	1	.059	.059
Mike Oquist	.500	10	5	1	0	0	3	1	0	.545	.600	Tommy Greene	.083	12	1	0	0	0	2	2	1	.214	.083
Sterling Hitchcock	.455	11	5	1	0	0	1	2	2	.538	.545	Xavier Hernandez	.091	11	1	0	0	0	0	1	0	.083	.091
Bobby Witt	.438	16	7	1	1	0	1	2	1	.500	.625	Kevin Brown	.133	15	2	0	0	0	2	0	3	.133	.133

Hideo Nomo — Dodgers

Age 29 – Pitches Right (flyball pitcher)

	ERA	W	L	Sv	G	GS	IP	BB	SO	Avg	H	2B	3B	HR	RBI	OBP	SLG	CG	ShO	Sup	QS	#P/S	SB	CS	GB	FB	G/F
1997 Season	4.25	14	12	0	33	33	207.1	92	233	.243	193	34	11	23	91	.328	.400	1	0	5.73	18	101	15	10	216	233	0.93
Career (1995-1997)	3.34	43	29	0	94	94	627.0	255	703	.216	497	88	16	60	227	.297	.346	8	5	5.00	60	104	96	26	617	651	0.95

1997 Season

	ERA	W	L	Sv	G	GS	IP	H	HR	BB	SO		Avg	AB	H	2B	3B	HR	RBI	BB	SO	OBP	SLG
Home	3.60	6	7	0	17	17	110.0	95	13	40	121	vs. Left	.252	413	104	17	6	9	42	45	107	.330	.387
Away	4.99	8	5	0	16	16	97.1	98	10	52	112	vs. Right	.233	382	89	17	5	14	49	47	126	.325	.414
Day	5.61	2	2	0	7	7	43.1	51	7	16	54	Inning 1-6	.233	700	163	28	10	19	75	79	214	.317	.383
Night	3.90	12	10	0	26	26	164.0	142	16	76	179	Inning 7+	.316	95	30	6	1	4	16	13	19	.404	.526
Grass	4.28	9	11	0	26	26	164.0	151	18	70	177	None on	.241	460	111	21	4	14	14	52	123	.324	.396
Turf	4.15	5	1	0	7	7	43.1	42	5	22	56	Runners on	.245	335	82	13	7	9	77	40	110	.333	.406
March/April	3.50	3	2	0	6	6	36.0	26	4	16	42	Scoring Posn	.215	191	41	7	5	3	60	28	68	.326	.351
May	3.67	2	2	0	5	5	34.1	34	1	10	38	Close & Late	.278	36	10	2	0	2	7	6	4	.381	.500
June	4.81	2	3	0	6	6	39.1	32	5	21	45	None on/out	.234	201	47	12	3	4	4	18	49	.300	.383
July	2.76	2	1	0	5	5	29.1	30	1	16	28	vs. 1st Batr (relief)	.000	0	0	0	0	0	0	0	0	.000	.000
August	4.97	4	2	0	6	6	38.0	45	6	19	48	1st Inning Pitched	.301	136	41	5	4	4	25	18	43	.389	.485
Sept/Oct	5.64	1	2	0	5	5	30.1	26	6	10	32	First 75 Pitches	.230	570	131	16	9	16	54	62	169	.310	.374
Starter	4.25	14	12	0	33	33	207.1	193	23	92	233	Pitch 76-90	.333	108	36	12	1	4	20	9	30	.400	.574
Reliever	0.00	0	0	0	0	0	0.0	0	0	0	0	Pitch 91-105	.188	69	13	3	0	1	5	14	24	.333	.275
0-3 Days Rest (Start)	0.00	0	0	0	0	0	0.0	0	0	0	0	Pitch 106+	.271	48	13	3	1	2	12	7	10	.364	.500
4 Days Rest	4.47	6	8	0	18	18	112.2	104	11	48	117	First Pitch	.376	109	41	8	0	6	19	2	0	.395	.615
5+ Days Rest	3.99	8	4	0	15	15	94.2	89	12	44	116	Ahead in Count	.139	353	49	7	2	3	20	0	190	.146	.195
vs. AL	4.15	2	1	0	5	5	30.1	22	2	20	35	Behind in Count	.344	189	65	11	7	7	26	54	0	.496	.587
vs. NL	4.27	12	11	0	28	28	177.0	171	21	72	198	Two Strikes	.105	371	39	7	1	4	20	36	233	.190	.162
Pre-All Star	3.81	8	7	0	18	18	115.2	95	10	52	131	Pre-All Star	.221	430	95	19	5	10	45	52	131	.316	.358
Post-All Star	4.81	6	5	0	15	15	91.2	98	13	40	102	Post-All Star	.268	365	98	15	6	13	46	40	102	.342	.449

Career (1995-1997)

	ERA	W	L	Sv	G	GS	IP	H	HR	BB	SO		Avg	AB	H	2B	3B	HR	RBI	BB	SO	OBP	SLG
Home	2.73	23	15	0	49	49	343.0	252	29	122	376	vs. Left	.225	1086	244	38	10	25	109	309	.302	.347
Away	4.09	20	14	0	45	45	284.0	245	31	133	327	vs. Right	.208	1217	253	50	6	35	125	141	394	.293	.345
Day	4.64	9	6	0	23	23	141.2	147	20	66	159	Inning 1-6	.214	1943	415	74	14	51	190	215	613	.295	.345
Night	2.97	34	23	0	71	71	485.1	350	40	189	544	Inning 7+	.228	360	82	14	2	9	37	40	90	.309	.353
Grass	3.18	33	24	0	76	76	517.1	399	50	195	576	None on	.211	1420	299	52	7	37	37	134	395	.283	.335

Career (1995-1997)

	ERA	W	L	Sv	G	GS	IP	H	HR	BB	SO		Avg	AB	H	2B	3B	HR	RBI	BB	SO	OBP	SLG
Turf	4.10	10	5	0	18	18	109.2	98	10	60	127	Runners on	.224	883	198	36	9	23	190	121	308	.319	.364
March/April	3.38	7	4	0	12	12	77.1	57	10	35	83	Scoring Posn	.209	536	112	24	7	10	156	92	216	.325	.336
May	3.94	4	5	0	16	16	98.1	93	6	44	122	Close & Late	.178	157	28	3	1	5	16	24	38	.291	.306
June	2.91	10	6	0	18	18	130.0	93	11	47	153	None on/out	.225	608	137	24	4	13	13	51	160	.289	.342
July	2.55	6	4	0	15	15	102.1	72	8	37	106	vs. 1st Batr (relief)	.000	0	0	0	0	0	0	0	0	.000	.000
August	4.05	9	6	0	17	17	113.1	106	15	50	137	1st Inning Pitched	.244	352	86	14	5	10	48	53	119	.345	.398
Sept/Oct	3.32	7	4	0	16	16	105.2	76	10	42	102	First 75 Pitches	.207	1604	332	50	13	39	134	177	509	.289	.327
Starter	3.34	43	29	0	94	94	627.0	497	60	255	703	Pitch 76-90	.269	308	83	20	1	11	47	30	83	.338	.448
Reliever	0.00	0	0	0	0	0	0.0	0	0	0	0	Pitch 91-105	.224	237	53	13	0	4	22	29	70	.310	.329
0-3 Days Rest (Start)	0.00	0	0	0	0	0	0.0	0	0	0	0	Pitch 106+	.188	154	29	5	2	6	24	19	41	.280	.364
4 Days Rest	3.30	25	17	0	54	54	365.2	277	37	145	401	First Pitch	.315	346	109	18	1	14	45	9	0	.337	.494
5+ Days Rest	3.41	18	12	0	40	40	261.1	220	23	110	302	Ahead in Count	.120	1065	128	17	3	14	59	0	595	.125	.181
vs. AL	4.15	2	1	0	5	5	30.1	22	2	20	35	Behind in Count	.320	503	161	33	8	18	72	129	0	.458	.525
vs. NL	3.30	41	28	0	89	89	596.2	475	58	235	668	Two Strikes	.102	1132	116	17	2	14	58	117	703	.189	.158
Pre-All Star	3.20	23	15	0	49	49	326.2	253	27	137	383	Pre-All Star	.211	1201	253	46	7	27	113	137	383	.297	.328
Post-All Star	3.51	20	14	0	45	45	300.1	244	33	118	320	Post-All Star	.221	1102	244	42	9	33	114	118	320	.297	.366

Pitcher vs. Batter (career)

Pitches Best Vs.	Avg	AB	H	2B	3B	HR	RBI	BB	SO	OBP	SLG	Pitches Worst Vs.	Avg	AB	H	2B	3B	HR	RBI	BB	SO	OBP	SLG
Chipper Jones	.000	15	0	0	0	0	0	3	6	.167	.000	Gary Sheffield	.571	14	8	0	0	3	5	2	2	.625	1.214
Ray Lankford	.056	18	1	0	0	0	1	0	5	.056	.056	Bobby Bonilla	.545	11	6	1	1	1	5	3	1	.625	1.091
Jay Bell	.083	12	1	0	0	0	0	1	7	.154	.083	Jeff Bagwell	.471	17	8	1	0	4	6	4	2	.571	1.235
Benito Santiago	.100	10	1	0	0	0	0	1	1	.182	.100	Moises Alou	.417	12	5	1	1	1	7	2	1	.500	.917
Rico Brogna	.136	22	3	0	0	1	1	1	6	.174	.136	Tom Lampkin	.375	8	3	1	0	1	3	2	0	.545	.875

Greg Norton — White Sox
Age 25 – Bats Both

	Avg	G	AB	R	H	2B	3B	HR	RBI	BB	SO	HBP	GDP	SB	CS	OBP	SLG	IBB	SH	SF	#Pit	#P/PA	GB	FB	G/F
1997 Season	.265	18	34	5	9	2	2	0	1	2	8	0	0	0	0	.306	.441	0	1	0	141	3.81	9	10	0.90
Career (1996-1997)	.246	29	57	9	14	2	2	2	4	6	14	0	0	0	1	.317	.456	0	1	0	262	4.09	15	18	0.83

1997 Season

	Avg	AB	H	2B	3B	HR	RBI	BB	SO	OBP	SLG		Avg	AB	H	2B	3B	HR	RBI	BB	SO	OBP	SLG
vs. Left	.000	1	0	0	0	0	0	0	0	.000	.000	Scoring Posn	.125	8	1	1	0	0	1	1	4	.222	.250
vs. Right	.273	33	9	2	2	0	1	2	8	.314	.455	Close & Late	.000	5	0	0	0	0	0	0	2	.000	.000

Abraham Nunez — Pirates
Age 22 – Bats Both

	Avg	G	AB	R	H	2B	3B	HR	RBI	BB	SO	HBP	GDP	SB	CS	OBP	SLG	IBB	SH	SF	#Pit	#P/PA	GB	FB	G/F
1997 Season	.225	19	40	3	9	2	2	0	6	3	10	1	1	1	0	.289	.375	0	0	1	155	3.44	19	6	3.17

1997 Season

	Avg	AB	H	2B	3B	HR	RBI	BB	SO	OBP	SLG		Avg	AB	H	2B	3B	HR	RBI	BB	SO	OBP	SLG
vs. Left	.375	8	3	0	2	0	3	1	3	.444	.875	Scoring Posn	.273	11	3	1	1	0	5	0	2	.250	.545
vs. Right	.188	32	6	2	0	0	3	2	7	.250	.250	Close & Late	.500	6	3	0	0	0	1	0	0	.500	.500

Jon Nunnally — Reds
Age 26 – Bats Left

	Avg	G	AB	R	H	2B	3B	HR	RBI	BB	SO	HBP	GDP	SB	CS	OBP	SLG	IBB	SH	SF	#Pit	#P/PA	GB	FB	G/F
1997 Season	.309	78	230	46	71	12	4	14	39	31	58	2	2	7	3	.394	.578	0	1	1	1056	3.97	67	64	1.05
Career (1995-1997)	.263	232	623	113	164	32	11	33	98	95	169	4	6	13	7	.363	.509	7	5	2	2950	4.04	172	174	0.99

1997 Season

	Avg	AB	H	2B	3B	HR	RBI	BB	SO	OBP	SLG		Avg	AB	H	2B	3B	HR	RBI	BB	SO	OBP	SLG
vs. Left	.258	31	8	3	0	1	8	3	9	.343	.452	Scoring Posn	.360	50	18	2	1	1	24	8	16	.441	.500
vs. Right	.317	199	63	9	4	13	31	28	49	.402	.598	Close & Late	.206	34	7	1	2	1	7	2	12	.250	.441
Home	.277	94	26	4	1	7	18	19	23	.398	.564	None on/out	.278	54	15	4	2	2	2	5	10	.339	.537
Away	.331	136	45	8	3	7	21	12	35	.391	.588	Batting #2	.319	141	45	10	2	8	26	21	33	.407	.589
First Pitch	.342	38	13	3	1	2	5	0	0	.342	.632	Batting #7	.414	29	12	1	2	3	6	2	7	.469	.897
Ahead in Count	.541	37	20	4	1	4	12	15	0	.679	1.027	Other	.233	60	14	1	0	3	7	8	18	.329	.400
Behind in Count	.237	114	27	3	1	8	19	0	52	.241	.491	Pre-All Star	.273	22	6	0	1	0	2	2	6	.333	.364
Two Strikes	.216	125	27	4	1	5	17	16	58	.308	.384	Post-All Star	.313	208	65	12	3	14	37	29	52	.400	.601

Career (1995-1997)

	Avg	AB	H	2B	3B	HR	RBI	BB	SO	OBP	SLG		Avg	AB	H	2B	3B	HR	RBI	BB	SO	OBP	SLG
vs. Left	.200	75	15	4	1	2	12	10	24	.302	.360	First Pitch	.292	89	26	5	1	3	9	6	0	.351	.472
vs. Right	.272	548	149	28	10	31	86	85	145	.371	.529	Ahead in Count	.500	98	49	10	3	11	36	45	0	.660	1.000
Groundball	.244	123	30	5	0	7	18	16	32	.340	.455	Behind in Count	.188	309	58	10	5	14	37	0	141	.190	.388
Flyball	.216	111	24	4	3	6	16	15	33	.310	.468	Two Strikes	.169	349	59	11	4	13	41	44	169	.263	.335
Home	.232	280	65	10	5	15	41	52	76	.353	.464	Batting #2	.316	152	48	10	2	9	27	22	37	.402	.586
Away	.289	343	99	22	6	18	57	43	93	.372	.545	Batting #7	.247	158	39	7	4	6	24	26	48	.364	.456
Day	.242	194	47	11	2	11	32	25	54	.335	.490	Other	.246	313	77	15	5	18	47	47	84	.344	.498
Night	.273	429	117	21	9	22	66	70	115	.376	.517	March/April	.455	11	5	0	0	1	3	1	3	.500	.727
Grass	.252	448	113	20	7	20	57	61	122	.345	.462	May	.205	39	8	0	1	2	5	6	13	.311	.410
Turf	.291	175	51	12	4	13	41	34	46	.408	.629	June	.260	104	27	6	2	7	18	17	27	.366	.558
Pre-All Star	.268	179	48	6	4	12	30	26	49	.362	.547	July	.254	122	31	7	2	7	19	18	30	.352	.516
Post-All Star	.261	444	116	26	7	21	68	69	120	.364	.493	August	.228	158	36	5	4	6	20	17	47	.311	.424
Scoring Posn	.288	146	42	10	1	6	64	36	42	.430	.493	Sept/Oct	.302	189	57	14	2	10	33	36	49	.413	.556
Close & Late	.196	102	20	4	2	6	20	11	32	.272	.451	vs. AL	.238	437	104	21	8	20	65	70	120	.345	.460

Career (1995-1997)

	Avg	AB	H	2B	3B	HR	RBI	BB	SO	OBP	SLG		Avg	AB	H	2B	3B	HR	RBI	BB	SO	OBP	SLG
None on/out	.252	159	40	8	3	9	9	12	33	.304	.509	vs. NL	.323	186	60	11	3	13	33	25	49	.407	.624

Batter vs. Pitcher (career)

Hits Best Against	Avg	AB	H	2B	3B	HR	RBI	BB	SO	OBP	SLG	Hits Worst Against	Avg	AB	H	2B	3B	HR	RBI	BB	SO	OBP	SLG
Alex Fernandez	.375	8	3	2	0	0	0	3	2	.545	.625	Kevin Tapani	.000	11	0	0	0	0	0	1	5	.083	.000
Charles Nagy	.333	9	3	2	0	2	3	1	.500	.556												
Ricky Bones	.333	9	3	1	0	1	1	2	1	.455	.778												

Ryan Nye — Phillies
Age 25 – Pitches Right

	ERA	W	L	Sv	G	GS	IP	BB	SO	Avg	H	2B	3B	HR	RBI	OBP	SLG	CG	ShO	Sup	QS	#P/S	SB	CS	GB	FB	G/F
1997 Season	8.25	0	2	0	4	2	12.0	9	7	.392	20	5	0	2	12	.484	.608	0	0	3.00	1	89	0	0	18	17	1.06

1997 Season

	ERA	W	L	Sv	G	GS	IP	H	HR	BB	SO		Avg	AB	H	2B	3B	HR	RBI	BB	SO	OBP	SLG
Home	8.59	0	1	0	2	1	7.1	12	1	5	5	vs. Left	.391	23	9	1	0	1	6	2	5	.429	.565
Away	7.71	0	1	0	2	1	4.2	8	0	4	2	vs. Right	.393	28	11	4	0	1	6	7	2	.528	.643

Charlie O'Brien — Blue Jays
Age 37 – Bats Right (flyball hitter)

	Avg	G	AB	R	H	2B	3B	HR	RBI	BB	SO	HBP	GDP	SB	CS	OBP	SLG	IBB	SH	SF	#Pit	#P/PA	GB	FB	G/F
1997 Season	.218	69	225	22	49	15	1	4	27	22	45	11	6	0	2	.311	.347	1	3	6	1013	3.			
Last Five Years	.236	363	1087	112	256	61	1	38	145	109	191	39	31	1	5	.324	.398	7	10	10	4755	3.			

1997 Season

	Avg	AB	H	2B	3B	HR	RBI	BB	SO	OBP	SLG		Avg	AB	H	2B	3B	HR	RBI
vs. Left	.267	75	20	10	1	2	10	7	9	.341	.507	Scoring Posn	.235	51	12	1	0	2	22
vs. Right	.193	150	29	5	0	2	17	15	36	.296	.267	Close & Late	.196	46	9	2	0	3	11
Home	.237	97	23	10	1	2	9	13	20	.370	.423	None on/out	.167	54	9	5	0	0	0
Away	.203	128	26	5	0	2	18	9	25	.262	.289	Batting #7	.198	116	23	5	1	2	14
First Pitch	.132	38	5	3	1	1	7	1	0	.227	.342	Batting #8	.240	96	23	9	0	2	11
Ahead in Count	.324	34	11	5	0	0	4	11	0	.500	.471	Other	.231	13	3	1	0	0	2
Behind in Count	.198	116	23	5	0	1	9	0	35	.213	.267	Pre-All Star	.243	111	27	9	1	3	21
Two Strikes	.181	116	21	3	0	1	8	10	45	.260	.233	Post-All Star	.193	114	22	6	0	1	6

Last Five Years

	Avg	AB	H	2B	3B	HR	RBI	BB	SO	OBP	SLG		Avg	AB	H	2B	3B	HR	RBI	BB	SO	OBP	SLG
vs. Left	.253	387	98	30	1	10	47	40	44	.333	.413	First Pitch	.286	189	54	13	1	8	30				
vs. Right	.226	700	158	31	0	28	98	69	147	.320	.390	Ahead in Count	.299	221	66	16	0	17	41				
Groundball	.224	277	62	15	0	11	37	25	50	.304	.397	Behind in Count	.169	510	86	22	0	7	44				
Flyball	.240	154	37	13	0	5	22	18	33	.344	.422	Two Strikes	.172	517	89	19	0	8	48				
Home	.238	516	123	30	1	21	67	48	94	.328	.422	Batting #7	.223	641	143	33	1	21	76				
Away	.233	571	133	31	0	17	78	61	97	.321	.377	Batting #8	.255	275	70	19	0	14	50	27	45	.337	.476
Day	.236	385	91	26	1	13	54	32	63	.303	.410	Other	.251	171	43	9	0	3	19	16	24	.321	.357
Night	.235	702	165	35	0	25	91	77	128	.336	.392	March/April	.236	127	30	9	1	4	26	16	20	.359	.417
Grass	.227	635	144	23	0	24	80	66	108	.312	.376	May	.288	163	47	9	0	8	30	7	24	.331	.491
Turf	.248	452	112	38	1	14	65	43	83	.342	.429	June	.253	174	44	12	0	7	23	22	34	.354	.443
Pre-All Star	.256	535	137	40	1	19	86	48	91	.341	.441	July	.235	230	54	13	0	12	36	22	45	.326	.448
Post-All Star	.216	552	119	21	0	19	59	61	100	.308	.357	August	.209	230	48	10	0	4	18	39	18	.284	.304
Scoring Posn	.239	280	67	16	0	10	102	38	50	.346	.404	Sept/Oct	.202	163	33	8	0	3	12	24	29	.311	.307
Close & Late	.231	195	45	12	0	10	36	16	49	.298	.446	vs. AL	.233	532	124	31	1	17	69	50	111	.327	.391
None on/out	.248	238	59	17	0	9	9	26	49	.337	.433	vs. NL	.238	555	132	30	0	21	76	59	80	.322	.405

Batter vs. Pitcher (career)

Hits Best Against	Avg	AB	H	2B	3B	HR	RBI	BB	SO	OBP	SLG	Hits Worst Against	Avg	AB	H	2B	3B	HR	RBI	BB	SO	OBP	SLG
Pat Rapp	.545	11	6	0	0	1	1	2	1	.643	.818	Chris Hammond	.100	10	1	0	0	0	1	1	1	.250	.100
Andy Pettitte	.417	12	5	2	0	0	3	3	.563	.583	Omar Olivares	.125	16	2	1	0	0	2	3	2	.263	.188
Tom Glavine	.389	18	7	4	0	2	1	1	.421	.611	Terry Mulholland	.167	18	3	0	0	0	1	1	2	.211	.167
Butch Henry	.357	14	5	1	0	1	2	0	3	.357	.643	Tom Candiotti	.167	12	2	0	0	0	1	0	2	.231	.167
Rheal Cormier	.353	17	6	2	0	0	0	1	1	.389	.471	Steve Avery	.214	14	3	0	0	0	1	3	.267	.214

Troy O'Leary — Red Sox
Age 28 – Bats Left (groundball hitter)

	Avg	G	AB	R	H	2B	3B	HR	RBI	BB	SO	HBP	GDP	SB	CS	OBP	SLG	IBB	SH	SF	#Pit	#P/PA	GB	FB	G/F
1997 Season	.309	146	499	65	154	32	4	15	80	39	70	2	12	0	5	.358	.479	7	1	4	1947	3.57	216	120	1.80
Career (1993-1997)	.290	453	1502	205	436	95	16	42	220	125	235	8	34	9	11	.346	.459	14	8	10	5969	3.61	604	371	1.63

1997 Season

	Avg	AB	H	2B	3B	HR	RBI	BB	SO	OBP	SLG		Avg	AB	H	2B	3B	HR	RBI	BB	SO	OBP	SLG
vs. Left	.277	101	28	9	0	2	18	8	23	.327	.426	First Pitch	.281	57	16	4	2	0	8	5	0	.349	.421
vs. Right	.317	398	126	23	4	13	62	31	47	.366	.492	Ahead in Count	.397	146	58	13	1	8	38	17	0	.457	.664
Groundball	.281	89	25	9	1	1	16	9	16	.340	.438	Behind in Count	.239	209	50	8	1	3	23	0	61	.239	.330
Flyball	.281	89	25	4	0	3	18	5	8	.313	.427	Two Strikes	.223	197	44	8	1	2	20	17	70	.281	.305
Home	.317	246	78	21	3	5	40	22	32	.375	.488	Batting #6	.314	287	90	18	1	9	52	22	33	.361	.477
Away	.300	253	76	11	1	10	40	17	38	.342	.470	Batting #7	.303	152	46	8	2	5	19	11	21	.348	.480
Day	.268	142	38	8	0	3	23	13	18	.321	.387	Other	.300	60	18	6	1	1	9	6	16	.373	.483
Night	.325	357	116	24	4	12	57	26	52	.374	.515	March/April	.338	74	25	7	1	3	14	7	11	.390	.581
Grass	.307	443	136	30	4	11	70	34	63	.356	.467	May	.180	61	11	0	0	2	2	4	10	.231	.279
Turf	.321	56	18	2	0	4	10	5	7	.377	.571	June	.315	92	29	8	0	3	16	10	11	.385	.500

343

1997 Season

	Avg	AB	H	2B	3B	HR	RBI	BB	SO	OBP	SLG		Avg	AB	H	2B	3B	HR	RBI	BB	SO	OBP	SLG
Pre-All Star	.298	248	74	17	1	8	38	22	35	.354	.472	July	.402	87	35	8	2	1	13	2	13	.418	.575
Post-All Star	.319	251	80	15	3	7	42	17	35	.363	.486	August	.330	100	33	7	1	4	26	7	14	.370	.540
Scoring Posn	.341	132	45	16	2	3	62	24	16	.438	.561	Sept/Oct	.247	85	21	2	0	2	9	9	11	.319	.341
Close & Late	.310	84	26	6	1	0	15	10	19	.389	.405	vs. AL	.313	451	141	26	4	13	67	34	61	.359	.475
None on/out	.299	117	35	5	1	6	6	4	17	.322	.513	vs. NL	.271	48	13	6	0	2	13	5	9	.352	.521

1997 By Position

Position	Avg	AB	H	2B	3B	HR	RBI	BB	SO	OBP	SLG	G	GS	Innings	PO	A	E	DP	Fld Pct	Rng Fctr	In Zone	Zone Outs	Zone Rtg	MLB Zone
As Pinch Hitter	.364	11	4	1	0	0	5	2	3	.462	.455	13	0	---	---	---	---	---	---	---	---	---	---	---
As lf	.346	78	27	7	0	3	18	6	8	.398	.551	24	20	186.1	37	3	2	0	.952	1.93	51	34	.667	.805
As rf	.300	410	123	24	4	12	57	31	59	.348	.466	119	108	967.2	229	5	4	1	.983	2.18	252	210	.833	.813

Career (1993-1997)

	Avg	AB	H	2B	3B	HR	RBI	BB	SO	OBP	SLG		Avg	AB	H	2B	3B	HR	RBI	BB	SO	OBP	SLG
vs. Left	.230	269	62	13	2	2	38	28	60	.304	.316	First Pitch	.354	192	68	17	4	4	33	9	0	.385	.547
vs. Right	.303	1233	374	82	14	40	182	97	175	.355	.490	Ahead in Count	.361	399	144	40	4	18	92	51	0	.430	.617
Groundball	.265	325	86	16	2	7	47	29	53	.324	.391	Behind in Count	.215	636	137	22	7	8	53	0	196	.218	.310
Flyball	.259	278	72	13	4	6	45	28	38	.322	.399	Two Strikes	.199	609	121	22	6	7	55	65	235	.276	.289
Home	.317	761	241	61	12	20	124	68	101	.375	.507	Batting #6	.300	456	137	27	3	15	70	36	61	.351	.471
Away	.263	741	195	34	4	22	96	57	134	.315	.409	Batting #7	.293	410	120	20	6	12	49	40	62	.359	.459
Day	.275	466	128	29	5	12	79	38	67	.327	.436	Other	.281	636	179	48	7	15	101	49	112	.333	.450
Night	.297	1036	308	66	11	30	141	87	168	.354	.469	March/April	.322	174	56	9	3	7	26	12	24	.364	.529
Grass	.294	1328	391	88	15	33	195	105	207	.348	.458	May	.256	238	61	14	2	7	38	17	40	.310	.420
Turf	.259	174	45	7	1	9	25	20	28	.330	.466	June	.309	269	83	17	2	7	38	29	40	.380	.465
Pre-All Star	.292	753	220	44	9	24	117	67	115	.351	.470	July	.297	266	79	23	5	5	37	21	46	.347	.477
Post-All Star	.288	749	216	51	7	18	103	58	120	.340	.447	August	.326	316	103	20	4	14	61	24	45	.374	.547
Scoring Posn	.314	382	120	31	8	12	179	66	61	.411	.531	Sept/Oct	.226	239	54	12	0	2	20	22	40	.291	.301
Close & Late	.267	240	64	13	4	4	36	33	54	.360	.404	vs. AL	.291	1454	423	89	16	40	207	120	226	.346	.457
None on/out	.266	365	97	20	3	14	14	18	55	.302	.452	vs. NL	.271	48	13	6	0	2	13	5	9	.352	.521

Batter vs. Pitcher (career)

Hits Best Against	Avg	AB	H	2B	3B	HR	RBI	BB	SO	OBP	SLG	Hits Worst Against	Avg	AB	H	2B	3B	HR	RBI	BB	SO	OBP	SLG
Dennis Martinez	.462	13	6	1	1	2	3	0	1	.462	1.154	Ken Hill	.077	13	1	1	0	0	2	1	4	.133	.154
Chad Ogea	.417	12	5	2	0	0	1	2	0	.500	.583	Mark Gubicza	.143	14	2	0	0	0	0	0	1	.143	.143
Bob Wells	.364	11	4	2	0	0	2	1	.462	.545	Juan Guzman	.150	20	3	0	0	0	0	1	6	.227	.150
Mark Clark	.353	17	6	3	0	0	0	1	3	.421	.529	Bobby Witt	.154	13	2	0	0	0	0	0	3	.154	.154
Brad Radke	.333	21	7	1	0	3	4	0	1	.333	.810	Cal Eldred	.167	12	2	0	0	0	1	0	2	.167	.167

Paul O'Neill — Yankees   Age 35 – Bats Left

	Avg	G	AB	R	H	2B	3B	HR	RBI	BB	SO	HBP	GDP	SB	CS	OBP	SLG	IBB	SH	SF	#Pit	#P/PA	GB	FB	G/F
1997 Season	.324	149	553	89	179	42	0	21	117	75	92	0	16	10	7	.399	.514	8	0	9	2427	3.81	216	134	1.61
Last Five Years	.317	670	2425	399	769	166	7	103	462	364	369	7	87	18	18	.403	.519	42	0	34	10664	3.77	889	655	1.36

1997 Season

	Avg	AB	H	2B	3B	HR	RBI	BB	SO	OBP	SLG		Avg	AB	H	2B	3B	HR	RBI	BB	SO	OBP	SLG
vs. Left	.280	189	53	15	0	4	33	20	41	.343	.423	First Pitch	.378	90	34	13	0	4	18	5	0	.406	.656
vs. Right	.346	364	126	27	0	17	84	55	51	.427	.560	Ahead in Count	.391	115	45	7	0	8	38	39	0	.528	.661
Groundball	.287	108	31	8	0	2	26	17	22	.381	.417	Behind in Count	.289	235	68	16	0	5	41	0	72	.287	.421
Flyball	.354	99	35	8	0	9	25	7	17	.393	.707	Two Strikes	.273	256	70	15	0	7	46	31	92	.348	.414
Home	.308	263	81	19	0	10	53	40	44	.393	.494	Batting #3	.368	190	70	12	0	9	46	31	30	.453	.574
Away	.338	290	98	23	0	11	64	35	48	.404	.531	Batting #5	.267	180	48	10	0	5	35	24	34	.346	.406
Day	.316	206	65	15	0	12	57	27	36	.390	.563	Other	.333	183	61	20	0	7	36	20	28	.393	.557
Night	.329	347	114	27	0	9	60	48	56	.404	.484	March/April	.352	91	32	12	0	4	22	11	12	.413	.615
Grass	.328	481	158	38	0	20	106	64	72	.401	.532	May	.278	90	25	5	0	6	36	14	19	.375	.533
Turf	.292	72	21	4	0	1	11	11	20	.386	.389	June	.349	86	30	9	0	1	16	19	10	.462	.488
Pre-All Star	.313	288	90	27	0	11	56	45	47	.402	.521	July	.354	99	35	7	0	4	27	10	13	.405	.545
Post-All Star	.336	265	89	15	0	10	61	30	45	.395	.506	August	.286	105	30	4	0	3	24	9	19	.333	.410
Scoring Posn	.428	159	68	15	0	9	101	34	22	.505	.692	Sept/Oct	.329	82	27	5	0	3	12	12	19	.411	.500
Close & Late	.337	83	28	7	0	2	19	9	14	.394	.494	vs. AL	.332	503	167	40	0	21	114	67	83	.405	.537
None on/out	.310	116	36	13	0	3	3	9	25	.360	.500	vs. NL	.240	50	12	2	0	0	3	8	9	.339	.280

1997 By Position

Position	Avg	AB	H	2B	3B	HR	RBI	BB	SO	OBP	SLG	G	GS	Innings	PO	A	E	DP	Fld Pct	Rng Fctr	In Zone	Zone Outs	Zone Rtg	MLB Zone
As rf	.325	547	178	42	0	21	117	75	90	.401	.517	146	145	1263.0	293	7	5	0	.984	2.14	343	279	.813	.813

Last Five Years

	Avg	AB	H	2B	3B	HR	RBI	BB	SO	OBP	SLG		Avg	AB	H	2B	3B	HR	RBI	BB	SO	OBP	SLG
vs. Left	.260	796	207	46	2	29	151	105	160	.344	.432	First Pitch	.389	383	149	37	0	19	79	34	0	.438	.634
vs. Right	.345	1629	562	120	5	74	311	259	209	.431	.561	Ahead in Count	.399	544	217	37	2	38	150	187	0	.544	.684
Groundball	.315	562	177	39	1	15	103	83	94	.399	.468	Behind in Count	.262	978	256	63	2	27	147	0	284	.260	.413
Flyball	.333	469	156	33	2	29	104	65	64	.410	.597	Two Strikes	.249	1032	257	62	5	30	158	143	369	.338	.406
Home	.333	1166	388	76	6	47	232	185	175	.420	.529	Batting #3	.311	1169	364	76	2	48	218	198	166	.408	.503
Away	.303	1259	381	90	1	56	230	179	194	.387	.509	Batting #5	.329	761	250	52	2	33	182	95	110	.400	.532
Day	.323	879	284	62	3	39	183	125	134	.405	.534	Other	.313	495	155	38	3	22	108	71	93	.395	.535
Night	.314	1546	485	104	4	64	279	239	235	.402	.510	March/April	.373	311	116	28	2	14	73	48	46	.451	.611
Grass	.321	2091	671	140	7	92	404	318	317	.406	.527	May	.332	407	135	31	1	19	63	73	57	.434	.553
Turf	.293	334	98	26	0	11	58	46	52	.381	.470	June	.314	488	153	33	1	18	89	69	69	.396	.496

Last Five Years

	Avg	AB	H	2B	3B	HR	RBI	BB	SO	OBP	SLG
Pre-All Star	.337	1337	450	97	5	57	249	211	195	.425	.545
Post-All Star	.293	1088	319	69	2	46	213	153	174	.375	.487
Scoring Posn	.338	683	231	55	2	23	346	143	111	.436	.526
Close & Late	.339	316	107	26	1	12	67	60	58	.437	.541
None on/out	.326	503	164	31	2	25	25	57	89	.397	.545

	Avg	AB	H	2B	3B	HR	RBI	BB	SO	OBP	SLG
July	.312	459	143	29	2	20	97	70	70	.399	.514
August	.290	427	124	24	0	18	81	57	58	.371	.473
Sept/Oct	.294	333	98	21	1	14	59	47	69	.375	.489
vs. AL	.319	2375	757	164	7	103	459	356	360	.404	.524
vs. NL	.240	50	12	2	0	0	3	8	9	.339	.280

Batter vs. Pitcher (career)

Hits Best Against	Avg	AB	H	2B	3B	HR	RBI	BB	SO	OBP	SLG
Buddy Groom	.750	12	9	3	0	1	7	1	0	.769	1.250
Mark Leiter	.600	10	6	0	0	2	4	2	0	.667	1.200
Mike Harkey	.500	16	8	1	0	3	6	3	1	.579	1.125
Dennis Springer	.462	13	6	4	0	2	4	1	0	.467	1.231
Mark Clark	.455	11	5	0	0	3	5	0	0	.417	1.273

Hits Worst Against	Avg	AB	H	2B	3B	HR	RBI	BB	SO	OBP	SLG
Jesse Orosco	.000	14	0	0	0	0	0	5	4	.263	.000
Sid Fernandez	.000	10	0	0	0	0	0	3	5	.231	.000
David Wells	.071	14	1	0	0	0	0	0	1	.071	.071
Curt Schilling	.083	12	1	0	0	0	0	1	6	.154	.083
Norm Charlton	.100	10	1	0	0	0	0	1	2	.182	.100

Sherman Obando — Expos
Age 28 – Bats Right

	Avg	G	AB	R	H	2B	3B	HR	RBI	BB	SO	HBP	GDP	SB	CS	OBP	SLG	IBB	SH	SF	#Pit	#P/PA	GB	FB	G/F
1997 Season	.128	41	47	3	6	1	0	2	9	6	14	1	0	0	0	.241	.277	0	0	0	220	4.07	15	15	1.00
Career (1993-1997)	.239	177	355	41	85	13	0	13	49	34	100	3	3	3	0	.310	.386	1	0	2	1575	4.00	111	89	1.25

1997 Season

	Avg	AB	H	2B	3B	HR	RBI	BB	SO	OBP	SLG
vs. Left	.133	30	4	1	0	1	7	5	8	.278	.267
vs. Right	.118	17	2	0	0	1	2	1	6	.147	.294

	Avg	AB	H	2B	3B	HR	RBI	BB	SO	OBP	SLG
Scoring Posn	.133	15	2	0	0	1	8	3	4	.278	.333
Close & Late	.000	12	0	0	0	0	2	3	6	.200	.000

Career (1993-1997)

	Avg	AB	H	2B	3B	HR	RBI	BB	SO	OBP	SLG
vs. Left	.222	162	36	8	0	5	29	16	41	.293	.364
vs. Right	.254	193	49	5	0	8	20	18	59	.324	.404
Groundball	.173	81	14	2	0	0	7	8	21	.244	.198
Flyball	.183	71	13	2	0	2	8	5	26	.237	.296
Home	.241	187	45	7	0	8	31	17	44	.311	.406
Away	.238	168	40	6	0	5	18	17	56	.308	.363
Day	.230	126	29	2	0	7	18	11	40	.290	.413
Night	.245	229	56	11	0	6	31	23	60	.320	.371
Grass	.243	169	41	5	0	5	21	13	50	.299	.361
Turf	.237	186	44	8	0	8	28	21	50	.319	.409
Pre-All Star	.240	283	68	10	0	8	36	22	80	.298	.360
Post-All Star	.236	72	17	3	0	5	13	12	20	.353	.486
Scoring Posn	.230	100	23	0	0	2	34	18	30	.347	.310
Close & Late	.163	80	13	1	0	2	7	8	24	.239	.250
None on/out	.289	83	24	5	0	4	4	2	24	.322	.494

	Avg	AB	H	2B	3B	HR	RBI	BB	SO	OBP	SLG
First Pitch	.386	44	17	2	0	1	6	0	0	.378	.500
Ahead in Count	.342	76	26	6	0	7	22	13	0	.438	.697
Behind in Count	.166	169	28	4	0	4	10	0	85	.180	.260
Two Strikes	.143	189	27	3	0	2	13	20	100	.229	.190
Batting #6	.218	110	24	7	0	3	15	10	26	.279	.364
Batting #9	.172	64	11	1	0	2	9	4	27	.221	.281
Other	.276	181	50	5	0	8	25	20	47	.358	.436
March/April	.193	88	17	3	0	4	14	4	25	.234	.364
May	.307	140	43	5	0	2	17	13	40	.364	.386
June	.157	51	8	2	0	2	5	4	15	.232	.314
July	.242	33	8	1	0	2	5	9	6	.419	.455
August	.194	31	6	1	0	3	7	2	11	.242	.516
Sept/Oct	.250	12	3	1	0	0	1	2	3	.357	.333
vs. AL	.269	134	36	3	0	4	19	6	39	.303	.381
vs. NL	.222	221	49	10	0	9	30	28	61	.313	.389

Batter vs. Pitcher (career)

Hits Best Against	Avg	AB	H	2B	3B	HR	RBI	BB	SO	OBP	SLG

Hits Worst Against	Avg	AB	H	2B	3B	HR	RBI	BB	SO	OBP	SLG
Terry Mulholland	.188	16	3	1	0	0	2	2	4	.278	.250

Alex Ochoa — Mets
Age 26 – Bats Right

	Avg	G	AB	R	H	2B	3B	HR	RBI	BB	SO	HBP	GDP	SB	CS	OBP	SLG	IBB	SH	SF	#Pit	#P/PA	GB	FB	G/F
1997 Season	.244	113	238	31	58	14	1	3	22	37	72	2	7	3	4	.300	.349	0	2	2	972	3.71	116	51	2.27
Career (1995-1997)	.273	206	557	75	152	34	4	7	55	55	72	4	10	8	7	.320	.386	0	2	5	2195	3.63	269	114	2.36

1997 Season

	Avg	AB	H	2B	3B	HR	RBI	BB	SO	OBP	SLG
vs. Left	.224	107	24	4	0	1	10	3	14	.250	.290
vs. Right	.260	131	34	10	1	2	12	15	58	.338	.397
Home	.261	119	31	8	1	1	13	11	11	.323	.370
Away	.227	119	27	6	0	2	9	7	21	.276	.328
First Pitch	.273	33	9	3	0	1	8	0	0	.265	.455
Ahead in Count	.436	39	17	4	0	2	6	13	0	.577	.692
Behind in Count	.168	113	19	2	1	0	4	0	24	.181	.204
Two Strikes	.150	100	15	3	1	0	5	5	32	.206	.200

	Avg	AB	H	2B	3B	HR	RBI	BB	SO	OBP	SLG
Scoring Posn	.191	68	13	2	0	0	17	8	8	.278	.221
Close & Late	.263	57	15	3	0	1	6	3	7	.300	.368
None on/out	.284	67	19	2	1	1	1	2	10	.304	.388
Batting #6	.219	73	16	4	0	1	8	4	15	.253	.315
Batting #7	.272	81	22	6	0	1	6	6	14	.322	.383
Other	.238	84	20	4	1	1	8	8	7	.319	.345
Pre-All Star	.220	150	33	8	1	1		10	19	.270	.307
Post-All Star	.284	88	25	6	0	2	11	18	13	.351	.420

Career (1995-1997)

	Avg	AB	H	2B	3B	HR	RBI	BB	SO	OBP	SLG
vs. Left	.278	216	60	12	3	3	22	11	23	.313	.403
vs. Right	.270	341	92	22	1	4	33	26	49	.324	.375
Groundball	.297	118	35	7	0	3	16	8	16	.344	.432
Flyball	.338	74	25	8	1	1	9	3	5	.372	.514
Home	.267	288	77	17	1	2	27	22	30	.354	.354
Away	.279	269	75	17	3	5	28	15	42	.321	.420
Day	.231	208	48	11	0	1	19	8	32	.262	.298
Night	.298	349	104	23	4	6	36	29	40	.353	.438
Grass	.267	430	115	24	3	4	38	33	53	.321	.365
Turf	.291	127	37	10	1	3	17	4	19	.316	.457
Pre-All Star	.250	208	52	14	2	4	26	12	26	.293	.394
Post-All Star	.287	349	100	20	2	3	29	25	46	.336	.381
Scoring Posn	.250	144	36	5	2	1	46	12	16	.302	.333
Close & Late	.246	114	28	5	0	3	12	5	15	.275	.368

	Avg	AB	H	2B	3B	HR	RBI	BB	SO	OBP	SLG
First Pitch	.316	79	25	4	0	1	10	0	0	.329	.405
Ahead in Count	.397	116	46	14	0	3	14	20	0	.482	.595
Behind in Count	.201	244	49	8	2	2	16	0	59	.206	.275
Two Strikes	.202	228	46	8	3	1	20	17	72	.261	.276
Batting #6	.267	247	66	17	2	4	33	17	36	.315	.401
Batting #7	.274	106	29	9	0	1	6	6	14	.313	.387
Other	.279	204	57	8	2	2	16	14	22	.360	.368
March/April	.212	66	14	2	0	0	7	3	8	.243	.242
May	.189	37	7	2	0	0	2	5	4	.279	.243
June	.297	74	22	8	1	1	8	4	10	.338	.473
July	.285	123	35	7	1	4	17	4	14	.321	.455
August	.286	112	32	9	1	0	9	12	14	.355	.384
Sept/Oct	.290	145	42	6	1	2	12	9	22	.329	.386
vs. AL	.350	20	7	3	0	1	2	0	2	.350	.650

Career (1995-1997)

	Avg	AB	H	2B	3B	HR	RBI	BB	SO	OBP	SLG		Avg	AB	H	2B	3B	HR	RBI	BB	SO	OBP	SLG
None on/out	.284	162	46	9	1	2	2	9	20	.322	.389	vs. NL	.270	537	145	31	4	6	53	37	70	.319	.376

Batter vs. Pitcher (career)

Hits Best Against	Avg	AB	H	2B	3B	HR	RBI	BB	SO	OBP	SLG	Hits Worst Against	Avg	AB	H	2B	3B	HR	RBI	BB	SO	OBP	SLG
Terry Mulholland	.364	11	4	1	1	0	1	0	0	.364	.636	Carlos Perez	.000	12	0	0	0	0	1	0	1	.000	.000
Denny Neagle	.364	11	4	1	1	0	2	0	0	.364	.636	Shawn Estes	.222	9	2	0	1	0	0	4	1	.462	.444
John Smiley	.357	14	5	1	0	0	1	0	0	.357	.429												

Jose Offerman — Royals
Age 29 – Bats Both (groundball hitter)

	Avg	G	AB	R	H	2B	3B	HR	RBI	BB	SO	HBP	GDP	SB	CS	OBP	SLG	IBB	SH	SF	#Pit	#P/PA	GB	FB	G/F
1997 Season	.297	106	424	59	126	23	6	2	39	41	64	0	5	9	10	.359	.394	3	6	0	1876	3.98	181	90	2.01
Last Five Years	.280	606	2247	317	629	99	30	13	206	293	342	6	37	67	41	.363	.368	17	54	12	10053	3.85	879	522	1.68

1997 Season

	Avg	AB	H	2B	3B	HR	RBI	BB	SO	OBP	SLG		Avg	AB	H	2B	3B	HR	RBI	BB	SO	OBP	SLG
vs. Left	.380	129	49	12	3	0	11	12	22	.433	.519	First Pitch	.378	45	17	5	1	0	10	1	0	.391	.533
vs. Right	.261	295	77	11	3	2	28	29	42	.337	.339	Ahead in Count	.338	74	25	7	1	1	10	15	0	.449	.500
Groundball	.291	79	23	3	2	0	7	11	12	.378	.380	Behind in Count	.250	204	51	6	3	1	14	0	54	.250	.324
Flyball	.221	68	15	2	2	1	9	7	12	.293	.353	Two Strikes	.249	217	54	6	0	0	13	25	64	.326	.295
Home	.301	206	62	9	4	2	22	26	30	.379	.413	Batting #1	.309	350	108	20	6	2	36	32	49	.366	.417
Away	.294	218	64	14	2	0	17	15	34	.339	.376	Batting #2	.250	52	13	3	0	0	2	6	10	.328	.308
Day	.336	128	43	6	4	1	14	12	22	.393	.469	Other ·	.227	22	5	0	0	0	1	3	5	.320	.227
Night	.280	296	83	17	2	1	25	29	42	.345	.361	March/April	.292	24	7	1	1	1	3	2	5	.346	.542
Grass	.288	382	110	18	5	2	36	36	57	.349	.377	May	.286	112	32	5	2	1	13	18	14	.385	.393
Turf	.381	42	16	5	1	0	3	5	7	.447	.548	June	.342	114	39	7	2	0	11	6	17	.375	.439
Pre-All Star	.312	260	81	14	5	2	28	26	38	.374	.427	July	.255	51	13	0	0	2	5	8	.321	.314
Post-All Star	.274	164	45	9	1	0	11	15	26	.335	.341	August	.327	49	16	2	1	0	3	3	12	.365	.408
Scoring Posn	.265	98	26	9	4	1	38	11	18	.339	.469	Sept/Oct	.257	74	19	5	0	0	7	7	8	.321	.324
Close & Late	.250	76	19	3	2	0	3	5	18	.296	.342	vs. AL	.292	394	115	20	6	2	36	37	57	.353	.388
None on/out	.338	160	54	8	0	0	15	19	.394	.388	vs. NL	.367	30	11	3	0	0	3	4	7	.441	.467

1997 By Position

Position	Avg	AB	H	2B	3B	HR	RBI	BB	SO	OBP	SLG		G	GS	Innings	PO	A	E	DP	Fld Pct	Rng Fctr	In Zone	Zone Outs	Zone Rtg	MLB Zone
As 2b	.300	416	125	22	6	2	38	39	62	.360	.397		101	100	870.0	202	254	9	64	.981	4.72	274	256	.934	.902

Last Five Years

	Avg	AB	H	2B	3B	HR	RBI	BB	SO	OBP	SLG		Avg	AB	H	2B	3B	HR	RBI	BB	SO	OBP	SLG
vs. Left	.274	697	191	38	8	6	56	82	106	.350	.377	First Pitch	.351	276	97	17	4	1	36	13	0	.379	.453
vs. Right	.283	1550	438	61	22	7	150	211	236	.368	.364	Ahead in Count	.326	500	163	34	7	5	54	120	0	.454	.452
Groundball	.294	551	162	19	7	2	59	75	83	.374	.365	Behind in Count	.229	987	226	27	11	4	73	0	299	.232	.291
Flyball	.258	365	94	15	6	2	42	48	57	.345	.348	Two Strikes	.222	1049	233	31	12	3	81	160	342	.327	.283
Home	.293	1090	319	49	12	6	100	149	154	.377	.376	Batting #1	.297	778	231	44	14	6	71	76	127	.361	.413
Away	.268	1157	310	50	18	7	106	144	188	.349	.360	Batting #2	.271	949	257	36	10	5	85	133	136	.360	.346
Day	.281	583	164	21	8	5	56	81	103	.368	.370	Other	.271	520	141	19	6	2	50	84	79	.371	.342
Night	.279	1664	465	78	22	8	150	212	239	.361	.367	March/April	.237	266	63	10	3	1	23	32	49	.321	.308
Grass	.278	1851	514	75	19	12	164	247	283	.362	.358	May	.299	489	146	21	8	3	53	84	70	.400	.393
Turf	.290	396	115	24	11	1	42	46	59	.364	.414	June	.279	476	133	22	6	1	34	57	72	.355	.357
Pre-All Star	.280	1350	378	62	19	5	122	182	211	.365	.365	July	.277	358	99	15	6	3	34	34	60	.338	.377
Post-All Star	.280	897	251	37	11	8	84	111	131	.359	.372	August	.280	379	106	16	5	2	35	48	59	.361	.364
Scoring Posn	.281	523	147	19	14	1	184	87	88	.376	.377	Sept/Oct	.294	279	82	15	2	3	27	38	32	.379	.394
Close & Late	.255	364	93	9	4	0	32	62	69	.360	.302	vs. AL	.298	955	285	53	14	7	83	111	155	.371	.405
None on/out	.283	598	169	25	7	6	6	65	54			vs. NL	.266	1292	344	46	16	6	123	182	187	.357	.341

Batter vs. Pitcher (career)

Hits Best Against	Avg	AB	H	2B	3B	HR	RBI	BB	SO	OBP	SLG	Hits Worst Against	Avg	AB	H	2B	3B	HR	RBI	BB	SO	OBP	SLG
Jeff Fassero	.632	19	12	2	0	0	1	2	4	.667	.737	Doug Jones	.083	12	1	0	0	0	1	0	2	.083	.083
Rich Robertson	.556	9	5	2	0	0	2	2	0	.636	.778	Curt Schilling	.083	12	1	0	0	0	0	1	5	.154	.083
Dave Weathers	.545	11	6	1	0	0	2	1	0	.583	.636	David Cone	.087	23	2	0	0	0	0	1	7	.125	.087
Willie Blair	.533	15	8	4	0	0	1	2	0	.588	.800	Pete Smith	.125	16	2	0	0	0	0	0	0	.125	.125
Allen Watson	.462	13	6	1	0	2	0	2		.462	.769	Randy Myers	.125	16	2	0	0	0	0	0	8	.176	.125

Chad Ogea — Indians
Age 27 – Pitches Right (flyball pitcher)

	ERA	W	L	Sv	G	GS	IP	BB	SO	Avg	H	2B	3B	HR	RBI	OBP	SLG	CG	ShO	Sup	QS	#P/S	SB	CS	GB	FB	G/F
1997 Season	4.99	8	9	0	21	21	126.1	47	80	.283	139	32	1	13	67	.348	.431	0	0	5.91	11	94	9	8	151	154	0.98
Career (1994-1997)	4.44	26	19	0	74	57	395.2	128	249	.265	406	93	3	48	192	.324	.423	3	1	6.21	30	96	33	19	495	498	0.99

1997 Season

	ERA	W	L	Sv	G	GS	IP	H	HR	BB	SO		Avg	AB	H	2B	3B	HR	RBI	BB	SO	OBP	SLG
Home	5.20	3	6	0	10	10	62.1	68	7	17	36	vs. Left	.306	245	75	17	1	8	39	28	39	.378	.482
Away	4.78	5	3	0	11	11	64.0	71	6	30	44	vs. Right	.259	247	64	15	0	5	28	19	41	.317	.381
Day	5.27	3	1	0	7	7	42.2	39	3	18	29	Inning 1-6	.283	452	128	29	1	13	62	41	74	.346	.438
Night	4.84	5	8	0	14	14	83.2	100	10	29	51	Inning 7+	.275	40	11	3	0	0	5	6	6	.370	.350
Grass	4.85	6	9	0	19	19	115.0	127	11	43	73	None on	.278	284	79	18	0	9	9	25	45	.341	.437
Turf	6.35	2	0	0	2	2	11.1	12	2	4	7	Runners on	.288	208	60	14	1	4	58	22	35	.357	.423
March/April	6.98	2	2	0	5	5	29.2	41	4	10	21	Scoring Posn	.268	127	34	9	0	3	54	16	23	.351	.409
May	3.19	3	1	0	6	6	42.1	31	4	18	30	Close & Late	.333	15	5	2	0	0	3	1	1	.444	.467
June	7.52	0	5	0	5	5	26.1	37	4	10	13	None on/out	.258	124	32	9	0	2	2	11	20	.319	.379

1997 Season

	ERA	W	L	Sv	G	GS	IP	H	HR	BB	SO		Avg	AB	H	2B	3B	HR	RBI	BB	SO	OBP	SLG
July	0.00	0	0	0	0	0	0.0	0	0	0	0	vs. 1st Batr (relief)	.000	0	0	0	0	0	0	0	0	.000	.000
August	0.00	0	0	0	0	0	0.0	0	0	0	0	1st Inning Pitched	.293	82	24	6	1	6	14	9	16	.355	.610
Sept/Oct	3.21	3	1	0	5	5	28.0	30	1	9	16	First 75 Pitches	.302	367	111	24	1	10	50	36	60	.365	.455
Starter	4.99	8	9	0	21	21	126.1	139	13	47	80	Pitch 76-90	.212	66	14	3	0	3	9	4	11	.270	.394
Reliever	0.00	0	0	0	0	0	0.0	0	0	0	0	Pitch 91-105	.273	44	12	5	0	0	8	6	5	.373	.386
0-3 Days Rest (Start)	4.05	0	1	0	1	1	6.2	6	1	3	1	Pitch 106+	.133	15	2	0	0	0	0	1	4	.188	.133
4 Days Rest	4.55	4	4	0	10	10	61.1	69	4	21	41	First Pitch	.338	80	27	10	1	2	17	3	0	.365	.563
5+ Days Rest	5.55	4	4	0	10	10	58.1	64	8	23	38	Ahead in Count	.186	204	38	6	0	3	13	0	60	.196	.260
vs. AL	4.95	7	7	0	18	18	109.0	121	11	39	72	Behind in Count	.430	100	43	11	0	6	22	24	0	.536	.720
vs. NL	5.19	1	2	0	3	3	17.1	18	2	8	8	Two Strikes	.204	206	42	8	0	2	17	20	80	.281	.272
Pre-All Star	5.49	5	8	0	16	16	98.1	109	12	38	64	Pre-All Star	.283	385	109	27	1	12	58	38	64	.353	.452
Post-All Star	3.21	3	1	0	5	5	28.0	30	1	9	16	Post-All Star	.280	107	30	5	0	1	9	9	16	.331	.355

Career (1994-1997)

	ERA	W	L	Sv	G	GS	IP	H	HR	BB	SO		Avg	AB	H	2B	3B	HR	RBI	BB	SO	OBP	SLG
Home	3.99	15	8	0	39	29	207.2	203	19	54	128	vs. Left	.270	818	221	46	2	25	103	75	129	.329	.423
Away	4.93	11	11	0	35	28	188.0	203	29	74	121	vs. Right	.258	716	185	47	1	23	89	53	120	.318	.423
Day	4.40	8	4	0	28	19	139.0	134	14	48	103	Inning 1-6	.266	1363	363	80	3	47	179	108	226	.323	.433
Night	4.45	18	15	0	46	38	256.2	272	34	80	146	Inning 7+	.251	171	43	13	0	1	13	20	23	.330	.345
Grass	4.11	22	16	0	66	50	354.1	362	36	111	222	None on	.263	909	239	54	1	30	30	71	148	.321	.424
Turf	7.19	4	3	0	8	7	41.1	44	12	17	27	Runners on	.267	625	167	39	2	18	162	57	101	.327	.422
March/April	7.95	4	2	0	10	6	43.0	64	8	14	29	Scoring Posn	.237	371	88	20	1	10	138	37	69	.304	.377
May	3.54	3	1	0	9	6	53.1	42	5	23	36	Close & Late	.254	63	16	6	0	1	5	9	10	.347	.397
June	4.62	5	6	0	18	11	85.2	92	7	25	49	None on/out	.246	398	98	24	1	12	12	27	65	.297	.402
July	4.82	3	4	0	11	11	65.1	61	11	23	39	vs. 1st Batr (relief)	.059	17	1	0	0	0	1	0	3	.059	.059
August	4.09	4	4	0	11	10	66.0	72	11	24	46	1st Inning Pitched	.253	277	70	15	1	14	36	26	51	.315	.466
Sept/Oct	2.95	7	2	0	15	13	82.1	75	6	19	50	First 75 Pitches	.272	1163	316	64	1	40	157	87	204	.324	.432
Starter	4.33	23	19	0	57	57	347.0	357	40	113	217	Pitch 76-90	.252	202	51	14	0	6	16	18	24	.319	.411
Reliever	5.18	3	0	0	17	0	48.2	49	8	15	32	Pitch 91-105	.230	122	28	11	1	2	19	19	12	.338	.385
0-3 Days Rest (Start)	5.51	0	2	0	3	3	16.1	20	1	8	7	Pitch 106+	.234	47	11	4	1	0	0	4	9	.294	.362
4 Days Rest	3.94	13	9	0	30	30	187.1	178	23	52	116	First Pitch	.295	234	69	22	1	8	38	7	0	.314	.500
5+ Days Rest	4.71	10	8	0	24	24	143.1	159	16	53	94	Ahead in Count	.208	691	144	26	1	12	49	0	200	.218	.301
vs. AL	4.40	25	17	0	71	54	378.1	388	46	120	241	Behind in Count	.358	302	108	33	0	18	64	58	0	.457	.646
vs. NL	5.19	1	2	0	3	3	17.1	18	2	8	8	Two Strikes	.192	691	133	24	2	10	54	63	249	.266	.276
Pre-All Star	4.80	14	10	0	41	27	208.1	215	24	70	128	Pre-All Star	.266	808	215	47	1	24	108	70	128	.330	.416
Post-All Star	4.04	12	9	0	33	30	187.1	191	24	58	121	Post-All Star	.263	726	191	46	2	24	84	58	121	.317	.431

Pitcher vs. Batter (career)

Pitches Best Vs.	Avg	AB	H	2B	3B	HR	RBI	BB	SO	OBP	SLG	Pitches Worst Vs.	Avg	AB	H	2B	3B	HR	RBI	BB	SO	OBP	SLG
Johnny Damon	.000	12	0	0	0	0	0	0	2	.000	.000	Rich Becker	.529	17	9	3	0	2	7	2	3	.579	1.059
Jose Canseco	.091	11	1	1	0	0	1	1	4	.167	.182	Craig Paquette	.429	14	6	3	0	1	1	0	1	.429	.857
Gary DiSarcina	.091	11	1	1	0	0	0	1	0	.167	.182	Troy O'Leary	.417	12	5	2	0	0	1	2	0	.500	.583
Cal Ripken	.107	28	3	1	0	0	0	2	4	.167	.143	Scott Stahoviak	.400	15	6	1	0	1	4	3	3	.500	.667
Joey Cora	.182	11	2	0	0	0	0	0	0	.182	.182	Shawn Green	.385	13	5	2	0	1	4	2	1	.438	.769

Kirt Ojala — Marlins
Age 29 – Pitches Left

	ERA	W	L	Sv	G	GS	IP	BB	SO	Avg	H	2B	3B	HR	RBI	OBP	SLG	CG	ShO	Sup	QS	#P/S	SB	CS	GB	FB	G/F
1997 Season	3.14	1	2	0	7	5	28.2	18	19	.252	28	2	0	4	9	.354	.378	0	0	4.71	3	93	1	2	39	38	1.03

1997 Season

	ERA	W	L	Sv	G	GS	IP	H	HR	BB	SO		Avg	AB	H	2B	3B	HR	RBI	BB	SO	OBP	SLG
Home	3.66	1	1	0	4	4	19.2	20	4	9	13	vs. Left	.556	9	5	0	0	0	1	5	1	.714	.556
Away	2.00	0	1	0	3	1	9.0	8	0	8	6	vs. Right	.225	102	23	2	0	4	8	13	18	.310	.363

John Olerud — Mets
Age 29 – Bats Left

	Avg	G	AB	R	H	2B	3B	HR	RBI	BB	SO	HBP	GDP	SB	CS	OBP	SLG	IBB	SH	SF	#Pit	#P/PA	GB	FB	G/F
1997 Season	.294	154	524	90	154	34	1	22	102	85	67	13	19	0	0	.400	.489	5	0	8	2387	3.79	192	157	1.22
Last Five Years	.307	680	2349	377	720	174	5	84	391	404	276	37	69	2	4	.413	.492	66	0	22	10284	3.66	832	716	1.16

1997 Season

	Avg	AB	H	2B	3B	HR	RBI	BB	SO	OBP	SLG		Avg	AB	H	2B	3B	HR	RBI	BB	SO	OBP	SLG
vs. Left	.276	145	40	9	1	6	38	28	18	.414	.476	First Pitch	.283	60	17	4	0	4	14	1	0	.318	.550
vs. Right	.301	379	114	25	0	16	64	57	49	.394	.493	Ahead in Count	.380	158	60	19	1	9	46	44	0	.510	.684
Groundball	.321	112	36	5	0	2	18	17	14	.405	.420	Behind in Count	.255	200	51	7	0	6	26	0	51	.275	.380
Flyball	.295	78	23	7	0	7	14	13	19	.402	.654	Two Strikes	.197	198	39	7	0	3	20	40	67	.343	.278
Home	.304	247	75	18	1	13	57	44	30	.417	.543	Batting #2	.302	43	13	4	0	1	5	8	9	.404	.465
Away	.285	277	79	16	0	9	45	41	37	.385	.440	Batting #3	.297	471	140	29	1	21	95	74	55	.398	.497
Day	.325	194	63	17	0	12	45	31	29	.421	.598	Other	.100	10	1	1	0	0	2	3	3	.471	.200
Night	.276	330	91	17	1	10	57	54	38	.387	.424	March/April	.356	101	36	11	0	3	19	12	15	.426	.554
Grass	.311	438	136	30	1	19	86	68	57	.412	.514	May	.308	91	28	3	0	6	21	18	6	.435	.538
Turf	.209	86	18	4	0	3	16	17	10	.340	.360	June	.297	91	27	9	0	4	18	10	10	.375	.527
Pre-All Star	.305	308	94	23	0	13	61	44	32	.398	.506	July	.198	81	16	1	0	1	8	14	12	.327	.247
Post-All Star	.278	216	60	11	1	9	41	41	35	.402	.463	August	.275	91	25	5	0	2	12	13	13	.380	.396
Scoring Posn	.385	130	50	11	1	7	75	31	11	.497	.646	Sept/Oct	.319	69	22	5	1	6	24	18	11	.456	.681
Close & Late	.287	94	27	4	1	5	21	19	16	.414	.511	vs. AL	.163	49	8	3	0	1	6	7	6	.293	.286
None on/out	.256	86	22	4	0	4	4	11	8	.354	.442	vs. NL	.307	475	146	31	1	21	96	78	61	.411	.509

1997 By Position

Position	Avg	AB	H	2B	3B	HR	RBI	BB	SO	OBP	SLG	G	GS	Innings	PO	A	E	DP	Fld Pct	Rng Fctr	In Zone	Outs	Zone Rtg	MLB Zone
As Pinch Hitter	.000	6	0	0	0	0	1	2	2	.400	.000	10	0											
As 1b	.297	518	154	34	1	22	101	83	65	.400	.494	146	141	1236.1	1292	119	7	126	.995	—	271	242	.893	.874

Last Five Years

	Avg	AB	H	2B	3B	HR	RBI	BB	SO	OBP	SLG		Avg	AB	H	2B	3B	HR	RBI	BB	SO	OBP	SLG
vs. Left	.268	645	173	36	1	15	117	97	95	.375	.397	First Pitch	.374	342	128	33	1	11	60	51	0	.464	.573
vs. Right	.321	1704	547	138	4	69	274	307	181	.427	.528	Ahead in Count	.381	683	260	73	1	37	143	188	0	.512	.653
Groundball	.312	523	163	39	2	10	79	89	55	.416	.451	Behind in Count	.247	860	212	41	1	23	120	0	210	.259	.377
Flyball	.297	421	125	24	1	25	70	69	64	.398	.537	Two Strikes	.214	883	189	42	2	15	106	165	276	.343	.317
Home	.307	1144	351	90	3	38	184	200	130	.417	.490	Batting #3	.292	479	140	29	1	21	95	74	56	.392	.489
Away	.306	1205	369	84	2	46	207	204	146	.409	.494	Batting #5	.323	1260	407	101	4	39	203	233	144	.430	.502
Day	.309	809	250	65	2	41	142	136	100	.412	.546	Other	.284	610	173	44	0	24	93	97	76	.394	.474
Night	.305	1540	470	109	3	43	249	268	176	.413	.464	March/April	.343	373	128	31	0	15	71	55	45	.431	.547
Grass	.317	1215	385	85	3	50	215	206	145	.421	.515	May	.306	458	140	26	1	19	72	78	47	.409	.491
Turf	.295	1134	335	89	2	34	176	198	131	.404	.467	June	.275	414	114	43	0	13	76	70	41	.385	.473
Pre-All Star	.303	1394	422	113	1	53	238	228	151	.404	.499	July	.306	399	122	27	1	18	59	76	54	.420	.514
Post-All Star	.312	955	298	61	4	31	153	176	125	.425	.482	August	.330	403	133	27	2	10	63	62	46	.424	.481
Scoring Posn	.322	612	197	54	2	18	296	180	68	.472	.505	Sept/Oct	.275	302	83	20	1	9	50	63	43	.411	.437
Close & Late	.288	368	106	18	2	12	56	71	55	.403	.446	vs. AL	.306	1874	574	143	4	63	295	326	215	.413	.488
None on/out	.311	570	177	46	2	32	32	65	66	.387	.567	vs. NL	.307	475	146	31	1	21	96	78	61	.411	.509

Batter vs. Pitcher (career)

Hits Best Against	Avg	AB	H	2B	3B	HR	RBI	BB	SO	OBP	SLG	Hits Worst Against	Avg	AB	H	2B	3B	HR	RBI	BB	SO	OBP	SLG
Mark Leiter	.727	11	8	2	1	0	4	4	1	.800	1.091	Frank Rodriguez	.000	8	0	0	0	0	1	3	0	.273	.000
Bob Wickman	.556	9	5	2	1	0	0	2	0	.636	1.000	Mark Guthrie	.100	10	1	0	0	0	1	1	7	.167	.100
Ricky Bones	.478	23	11	3	0	2	7	5	1	.586	.870	Carlos Perez	.111	9	1	0	0	0	0	2	0	.273	.111
F. Valenzuela	.455	11	5	1	0	1	1	4	1	.600	.818	Scott Radinsky	.118	17	2	1	0	0	2	3	1	.211	.176
Tim Belcher	.412	17	7	0	0	2	2	5	0	.545	.765	Tom Candiotti	.133	15	2	0	0	0	0	1	4	.188	.133

Omar Olivares — Mariners   Age 30 – Pitches Right (groundball pitcher)

	ERA	W	L	Sv	G	GS	IP	BB	SO	Avg	H	2B	3B	HR	RBI	OBP	SLG	CG	ShO	Sup	QS	#P/S	SB	CS	GB	FB	G/F
1997 Season	4.97	6	10	0	32	31	177.1	81	103	.276	191	42	3	18	98	.360	.424	3	2	5.43	12	95	3	4	297	168	1.77
Last Five Years	5.03	22	32	2	145	83	571.1	270	295	.285	633	135	13	59	311	.369	.437	8	2	5.21	29	96	30	14	979	543	1.80

1997 Season

	ERA	W	L	Sv	G	GS	IP	H	HR	BB	SO		Avg	AB	H	2B	3B	HR	RBI	BB	SO	OBP	SLG
Home	4.20	4	3	0	16	15	90.0	84	6	46	50	vs. Left	.305	370	113	24	2	14	60	53	50	.398	.495
Away	5.77	2	7	0	16	16	87.1	107	12	35	53	vs. Right	.243	321	78	18	1	4	38	28	53	.314	.343
Day	4.13	4	1	0	11	11	65.1	57	5	33	33	Inning 1-6	.283	630	178	41	3	18	97	72	96	.364	.443
Night	5.46	2	9	0	21	20	112.0	134	13	48	70	Inning 7+	.213	61	13	1	0	0	1	9	7	.314	.230
Grass	5.17	5	7	0	22	22	125.1	129	14	65	68	None on	.269	361	97	22	2	5	5	52	52	.373	.382
Turf	4.50	1	3	0	10	9	52.0	62	4	16	35	Runners on	.285	330	94	20	1	13	93	29	51	.345	.470
March/April	3.64	1	1	0	5	5	29.2	21	3	18	19	Scoring Posn	.310	155	48	10	0	8	79	17	25	.374	.529
May	2.57	1	2	0	6	6	42.0	32	0	15	27	Close & Late	.281	32	9	0	0	0	1	4	6	.361	.281
June	6.40	1	2	0	5	5	32.1	36	4	11	22	None on/out	.287	167	48	11	1	2	2	21	19	.380	.401
July	7.15	1	1	0	6	5	22.2	36	1	17	11	vs. 1st Batr (relief)	.000	0	0	0	0	0	0	1	0	1.000	.000
August	5.08	0	3	0	5	5	28.1	38	2	13	13	1st Inning Pitched	.237	114	27	5	2	1	18	17	18	.348	.342
Sept/Oct	6.85	0	1	0	5	5	22.1	28	8	7	11	First 75 Pitches	.286	521	149	33	2	14	78	60	78	.367	.438
Starter	4.87	6	10	0	31	31	177.1	191	18	79	103	Pitch 76-90	.257	74	19	6	1	3	13	13	12	.380	.486
Reliever	0	0	0	0	1	0	0.0	0	0	0	0	Pitch 91-105	.258	62	16	2	0	1	6	6	10	.324	.339
0-3 Days Rest (Start)	0.71	1	0	0	2	2	12.2	10	0	4	7	Pitch 106+	.206	34	7	1	0	0	1	2	3	.250	.235
4 Days Rest	5.50	3	4	0	12	12	68.2	70	6	34	40	First Pitch	.385	96	37	9	1	2	12	2	0	.423	.563
5+ Days Rest	4.97	2	6	0	17	17	96.0	111	12	41	56	Ahead in Count	.216	278	60	13	0	5	28	0	81	.227	.317
vs. AL	4.99	5	8	0	28	27	149.2	160	11	76	88	Behind in Count	.331	163	54	10	1	7	39	47	0	.474	.534
vs. NL	4.88	1	2	0	4	4	27.2	31	7	5	15	Two Strikes	.200	300	60	6	1	6	31	32	103	.282	.287
Pre-All Star	4.56	5	5	0	17	17	106.2	95	7	48	71	Pre-All Star	.239	397	95	23	1	7	52	48	71	.331	.355
Post-All Star	5.60	1	5	0	15	14	70.2	96	11	32	32	Post-All Star	.327	294	96	19	2	11	46	33	32	.399	.517

Last Five Years

	ERA	W	L	Sv	G	GS	IP	H	HR	BB	SO		Avg	AB	H	2B	3B	HR	RBI	BB	SO	OBP	SLG
Home	4.92	11	15	2	70	39	276.1	290	22	135	148	vs. Left	.299	1112	333	84	9	34	172	166	145	.392	.483
Away	5.13	11	17	0	75	44	295.0	343	37	135	147	vs. Right	.270	1211	300	51	4	25	139	104	150	.344	.391
Day	4.41	11	4	0	34	23	155.0	142	17	68	77	Inning 1-6	.289	1804	522	107	10	45	256	228	241	.375	.435
Night	5.25	11	28	2	111	60	416.1	491	42	202	218	Inning 7+	.265	419	111	28	3	14	55	42	54	.341	.446
Grass	4.93	14	22	0	76	53	339.2	365	41	171	172	None on	.285	1138	324	78	9	31	31	157	148	.381	.451
Turf	5.17	8	10	2	69	30	231.2	268	18	99	123	Runners on	.285	1085	309	57	4	28	280	113	147	.355	.422
March/April	3.39	4	2	1	17	11	82.1	60	7	37	54	Scoring Posn	.277	600	166	28	3	19	250	79	84	.358	.428
May	4.81	3	7	0	18	16	91.2	100	5	47	49	Close & Late	.274	179	49	15	0	5	22	21	27	.360	.441
June	5.05	6	3	1	25	15	112.1	137	15	46	55	None on/out	.303	532	161	36	3	12	12	66	62	.388	.449
July	6.67	4	11	0	39	17	118.2	146	14	67	54	vs. 1st Batr (relief)	.382	55	21	4	0	1	9	7	3	.452	.509
August	4.38	3	5	0	27	13	102.2	117	7	41	51	1st Inning Pitched	.297	519	154	34	3	12	85	58	61	.379	.443
Sept/Oct	5.37	2	4	0	19	11	63.2	73	11	32	32	First 75 Pitches	.287	1708	491	105	10	43	230	210	223	.371	.436
Starter	5.06	19	30	0	83	83	483.2	529	49	233	253	Pitch 76-90	.270	230	62	11	2	10	48	28	30	.357	.465
Reliever	4.83	3	2	2	62	0	87.2	104	10	37	42	Pitch 91-105	.333	153	51	8	1	5	22	21	22	.417	.497
0-3 Days Rest (Start)	3.58	1	0	0	6	6	37.2	41	3	11	18	Pitch 106+	.220	132	29	11	0	1	11	11	20	.295	.326
4 Days Rest	4.92	10	13	0	39	39	234.1	241	21	125	127	First Pitch	.370	330	122	29	3	11	59	12	0	.409	.576
5+ Days Rest	5.49	7	16	0	38	38	211.2	247	25	97	108	Ahead in Count	.218	857	187	42	2	8	73	0	233	.231	.300

Last Five Years

	ERA	W	L	Sv	G	GS	IP	H	HR	BB	SO		Avg	AB	H	2B	3B	HR	RBI	BB	SO	OBP	SLG
vs. AL	4.94	12	19	0	53	52	309.2	329	27	151	169	Behind in Count	.332	575	191	34	3	29	118	148	0	.465	.553
vs. NL	5.12	10	13	2	92	31	261.2	304	32	119	126	Two Strikes	.218	886	193	40	3	10	82	110	295	.311	.304
Pre-All Star	4.89	13	16	2	72	47	322.0	344	35	147	174	Pre-All Star	.278	1239	344	75	6	35	170	147	174	.361	.433
Post-All Star	5.20	9	16	0	73	36	249.1	289	24	123	121	Post-All Star	.294	984	289	60	7	24	141	123	121	.378	.442

Pitcher vs. Batter (career)

Pitches Best Vs.	Avg	AB	H	2B	3B	HR	RBI	BB	SO	OBP	SLG	Pitches Worst Vs.	Avg	AB	H	2B	3B	HR	RBI	BB	SO	OBP	SLG
Kevin Seitzer	.000	11	0	0	0	0	0	2	1	.154	.000	Derrick May	.600	10	6	2	0	0	3	1	1	.636	.800
Mickey Morandini	.059	17	1	0	0	0	0	1	1	.111	.059	Jason Giambi	.600	10	6	1	0	3	9	1	0	.583	1.600
Jay Buhner	.071	14	1	0	0	0	0	2	10	.188	.071	Roberto Alomar	.471	17	8	1	1	1	5	2	2	.526	.824
Damon Berryhill	.077	13	1	0	0	0	2	2	3	.188	.077	Ron Gant	.455	22	10	3	1	3	7	4	3	.538	1.091
Jose Vizcaino	.105	19	2	0	0	0	1	1	1	.150	.105	Steve Finley	.455	11	5	1	1	1	4	0	1	.455	1.000

Darren Oliver — Rangers

Age 27 – Pitches Left

	ERA	W	L	Sv	G	GS	IP	BB	SO	Avg	H	2B	3B	HR	RBI	OBP	SLG	CG	ShO	Sup	QS	#P/S	SB	CS	GB	FB	G/F
1997 Season	4.20	13	12	0	32	32	201.1	82	104	.271	213	43	6	29	98	.346	.451	3	1	5.68	15	100	14	10	277	246	1.13
Career (1993-1997)	4.28	35	20	2	124	69	477.1	226	309	.267	492	88	11	57	230	.353	.419	4	2	6.15	30	96	36	20	668	514	1.30

1997 Season

	ERA	W	L	Sv	G	GS	IP	H	HR	BB	SO		Avg	AB	H	2B	3B	HR	RBI	BB	SO	OBP	SLG
Home	4.34	7	6	0	17	17	110.0	119	18	43	49	vs. Left	.246	118	29	6	0	4	15	16	13	.357	.398
Away	4.04	6	6	0	15	15	91.1	94	11	39	55	vs. Right	.275	669	184	37	6	25	83	66	91	.344	.460
Day	4.04	3	3	0	8	8	42.1	47	5	21	23	Inning 1-6	.272	677	184	36	4	26	83	70	87	.347	.452
Night	4.25	10	9	0	24	24	159.0	166	24	61	81	Inning 7+	.264	110	29	7	2	3	15	12	17	.336	.445
Grass	4.03	13	10	0	29	29	183.0	193	26	71	90	None on	.278	453	126	24	3	16	16	44	59	.351	.450
Turf	5.89	0	2	0	3	3	18.1	20	3	11	14	Runners on	.260	334	87	19	3	13	82	38	45	.339	.452
March/April	3.48	1	2	0	4	4	20.2	18	0	8	10	Scoring Posn	.259	185	48	12	0	8	67	20	32	.333	.454
May	5.61	1	4	0	6	6	33.2	41	5	20	17	Close & Late	.321	28	9	2	1	0	5	6	4	.444	.464
June	3.23	2	3	0	6	6	39.0	41	5	13	25	None on/out	.287	202	58	8	1	8	8	22	24	.371	.455
July	3.82	3	1	0	5	5	35.1	32	5	11	19	vs. 1st Batr (relief)	.000	0	0	0	0	0	0	0	0	.000	.000
August	4.02	4	0	0	6	6	40.1	43	10	17	19	1st Inning Pitched	.343	137	47	18	0	6	27	13	14	.399	.606
Sept/Oct	5.01	2	2	0	5	5	32.1	38	4	13	14	First 75 Pitches	.280	558	156	31	2	20	73	54	71	.350	.450
Starter	4.20	13	12	0	32	32	201.1	213	29	82	104	Pitch 76-90	.230	113	26	6	2	5	11	17	304	.304	.372
Reliever	0.00	0	0	0	0	0	0.0	0	0	0	0	Pitch 91-105	.289	76	22	3	1	5	13	12	11	.382	.553
0-3 Days Rest (Start)	0.00	0	0	0	0	0	0.0	0	0	0	0	Pitch 106+	.225	40	9	3	1	2	7	5	5	.326	.500
4 Days Rest	3.79	9	11	0	22	22	135.1	138	16	64	74	First Pitch	.385	122	47	8	1	8	25	2	0	.405	.664
5+ Days Rest	5.05	4	1	0	10	10	66.0	75	13	18	30	Ahead in Count	.217	313	68	20	3	7	31	0	92	.228	.367
vs. AL	4.11	12	11	0	28	28	175.0	182	25	79	94	Behind in Count	.342	196	67	10	2	11	31	53	0	.482	.582
vs. NL	4.78	1	1	0	4	4	26.1	31	4	3	10	Two Strikes	.203	311	63	18	2	5	26	27	104	.275	.322
Pre-All Star	4.07	5	9	0	17	17	101.2	104	11	43	56	Pre-All Star	.268	388	104	19	1	11	48	43	56	.347	.407
Post-All Star	4.33	8	3	0	15	15	99.2	109	18	39	48	Post-All Star	.273	399	109	24	5	18	50	39	48	.345	.494

Career (1993-1997)

	ERA	W	L	Sv	G	GS	IP	H	HR	BB	SO		Avg	AB	H	2B	3B	HR	RBI	BB	SO	OBP	SLG
Home	4.18	21	9	2	67	39	269.0	276	35	110	176	vs. Left	.228	329	75	14	2	8	36	48	77	.336	.356
Away	4.41	14	11	0	57	30	208.1	216	22	116	133	vs. Right	.275	1515	417	74	9	49	194	178	232	.357	.433
Day	4.31	10	6	0	32	19	121.0	124	13	71	82	Inning 1-6	.273	1462	399	76	7	48	183	168	228	.354	.433
Night	4.27	25	14	2	92	50	356.1	368	44	155	227	Inning 7+	.243	382	93	12	4	9	47	58	81	.350	.366
Grass	4.18	32	17	2	112	62	430.2	439	51	197	274	None on	.274	1036	284	52	6	36	36	106	163	.347	.440
Turf	5.21	3	3	0	12	7	46.2	53	6	29	35	Runners on	.257	808	208	36	5	21	194	120	146	.361	.392
March/April	3.56	2	2	0	13	7	43.0	35	3	25	26	Scoring Posn	.246	476	117	20	0	14	171	75	96	.359	.376
May	5.28	5	7	0	33	14	102.1	121	13	62	52	Close & Late	.218	142	31	4	2	1	15	25	33	.345	.296
June	3.13	8	4	1	29	17	115.0	104	11	53	90	None on/out	.283	466	132	24	4	19	19	46	75	.358	.474
July	4.21	8	3	1	22	11	83.1	77	9	31	64	vs. 1st Batr (relief)	.208	48	10	1	0	0	6	6	12	.296	.229
August	5.38	7	2	0	16	11	72.0	86	14	30	41	1st Inning Pitched	.253	423	107	27	1	8	60	60	85	.354	.378
Sept/Oct	4.09	5	2	0	11	9	61.2	69	7	25	36	First 75 Pitches	.271	1385	376	67	5	41	183	178	240	.362	.416
Starter	4.28	30	20	0	69	69	410.0	432	52	176	247	Pitch 76-90	.234	248	58	10	2	5	17	19	39	.293	.351
Reliever	4.28	5	0	2	55	0	67.1	60	5	50	62	Pitch 91-105	.272	147	40	7	3	8	20	22	22	.359	.524
0-3 Days Rest (Start)	0.00	0	0	0	0	0	0.0	0	0	0	0	Pitch 106+	.281	64	18	4	1	3	10	9	8	.378	.516
4 Days Rest	4.15	17	18	0	45	45	264.1	281	29	126	161	First Pitch	.396	275	109	21	3	11	43	7	0	.421	.615
5+ Days Rest	4.51	13	2	0	24	24	145.2	151	23	50	86	Ahead in Count	.191	782	149	29	5	15	67	0	275	.206	.292
vs. AL	4.25	34	19	2	120	65	451.0	461	53	223	299	Behind in Count	.345	444	153	26	3	21	73	131	0	.494	.559
vs. NL	4.78	1	1	0	4	4	26.1	31	4	3	10	Two Strikes	.183	786	144	30	3	14	66	88	309	.275	.282
Pre-All Star	3.96	18	13	1	81	40	279.1	273	28	148	184	Pre-All Star	.257	1062	273	46	3	28	131	148	184	.354	.385
Post-All Star	4.73	17	7	1	43	29	198.0	219	30	78	125	Post-All Star	.280	782	219	42	8	29	99	78	125	.353	.465

Pitcher vs. Batter (career)

Pitches Best Vs.	Avg	AB	H	2B	3B	HR	RBI	BB	SO	OBP	SLG	Pitches Worst Vs.	Avg	AB	H	2B	3B	HR	RBI	BB	SO	OBP	SLG
Tomas Perez	.000	12	0	0	0	0	0	1	1	.077	.000	Roberto Kelly	.667	9	6	1	0	2	4	2	2	.727	1.444
Marty Cordova	.000	11	0	0	0	0	0	2	3	.154	.000	Ron Coomer	.500	10	5	1	0	1	2	1	0	.545	.900
Jacob Brumfield	.000	9	0	0	0	0	1	2	1	.182	.000	Scott Brosius	.444	9	4	0	0	1	3	2	4	.545	.778
Paul Molitor	.077	13	1	1	0	0	0	0	2	.077	.154	Bernie Williams	.429	14	6	2	0	1	4	3	0	.529	.786
Darin Erstad	.091	11	1	0	0	0	0	2	1	.091	.091	John Valentin	.417	12	5	0	1	1	3	1	0	.462	.833

Joe Oliver — Reds
Age 32 – Bats Right

	Avg	G	AB	R	H	2B	3B	HR	RBI	BB	SO	HBP	GDP	SB	CS	OBP	SLG	IBB	SH	SF	#Pit	#P/PA	GB	FB	G/F
1997 Season	.258	111	349	28	90	13	0	14	43	25	58	5	7	1	3	.313	.415	1	2	5	1341	3.47	125	113	1.11
Last Five Years	.251	459	1476	143	371	73	1	52	220	109	272	11	39	5	7	.304	.408	11	9	17	5769	3.56	497	471	1.06

1997 Season

	Avg	AB	H	2B	3B	HR	RBI	BB	SO	OBP	SLG		Avg	AB	H	2B	3B	HR	RBI	BB	SO	OBP	SLG
vs. Left	.279	86	24	3	0	2	8	9	15	.354	.384	First Pitch	.292	72	21	1	0	3	12	1	0	.303	.431
vs. Right	.251	263	66	10	0	12	35	16	43	.299	.426	Ahead in Count	.309	55	17	5	0	2	8	11	0	.426	.509
Groundball	.288	59	17	3	0	2	8	2	11	.317	.441	Behind in Count	.200	155	31	4	0	4	9	0	49	.208	.303
Flyball	.182	55	10	0	0	4	9	4	13	.237	.400	Two Strikes	.190	153	29	3	0	6	13	13	58	.251	.327
Home	.243	169	41	7	0	7	23	15	23	.318	.408	Batting #6	.284	109	31	3	0	4	16	5	19	.319	.422
Away	.272	180	49	6	0	7	20	10	35	.307	.422	Batting #7	.258	155	40	5	0	8	19	10	26	.314	.445
Day	.248	109	27	5	0	3	10	8	16	.299	.376	Other	.224	85	19	5	0	2	8	10	13	.302	.353
Night	.263	240	63	8	0	11	33	17	42	.318	.433	March/April	.000	0	0	0	0	0	0	0	0	.000	.000
Grass	.261	111	29	2	0	6	11	7	22	.303	.441	May	.311	61	19	4	0	2	6	4	10	.354	.475
Turf	.256	238	61	11	0	8	32	18	36	.317	.403	June	.257	74	19	1	0	3	12	6	13	.313	.392
Pre-All Star	.299	157	47	6	0	7	24	12	26	.349	.471	July	.273	77	21	3	0	4	15	6	7	.329	.468
Post-All Star	.224	192	43	7	0	7	19	13	32	.283	.370	August	.268	71	19	3	0	4	7	3	14	.321	.479
Scoring Posn	.259	85	22	1	0	3	30	6	18	.306	.424	Sept/Oct	.182	66	12	2	0	1	3	6	14	.247	.258
Close & Late	.262	65	17	2	0	4	9	5	17	.319	.477	vs. AL	.364	44	16	3	0	2	5	4	6	.417	.568
None on/out	.314	86	27	4	0	2	2	5	13	.359	.430	vs. NL	.243	305	74	10	0	12	38	21	52	.298	.393

1997 By Position

Position	Avg	AB	H	2B	3B	HR	RBI	BB	SO	OBP	SLG	G	GS	Innings	PO	A	E	DP	Fld Pct	Rng Fctr	In Zone	Zone Outs	Zone Rtg	MLB Zone
As c	.263	335	88	13	0	14	42	25	56	.319	.427	106	93	837.0	667	52	7	10	.990	---	---	---	---	---

Last Five Years

	Avg	AB	H	2B	3B	HR	RBI	BB	SO	OBP	SLG		Avg	AB	H	2B	3B	HR	RBI	BB	SO	OBP	SLG
vs. Left	.269	412	111	25	0	14	58	37	63	.333	.432	First Pitch	.300	243	73	12	0	11	51	7	0	.318	.486
vs. Right	.244	1064	260	48	1	38	162	72	209	.293	.398	Ahead in Count	.348	256	89	22	0	14	51	43	0	.438	.598
Groundball	.251	423	106	22	0	14	65	24	71	.292	.402	Behind in Count	.195	698	136	24	1	17	77	0	230	.200	.305
Flyball	.238	244	58	13	1	12	42	16	52	.290	.447	Two Strikes	.180	661	119	23	1	13	72	59	272	.248	.277
Home	.249	704	175	38	0	25	111	56	113	.309	.409	Batting #7	.260	507	132	19	0	24	89	26	92	.300	.440
Away	.254	772	196	35	1	27	109	53	159	.300	.407	Batting #8	.256	485	124	34	1	15	73	44	91	.317	.423
Day	.231	420	97	20	0	12	66	35	67	.291	.364	Other	.238	484	115	20	0	13	58	39	89	.296	.360
Night	.259	1056	274	53	1	40	154	74	205	.310	.425	March/April	.242	153	37	8	0	5	28	12	24	.297	.392
Grass	.255	652	166	35	1	22	92	44	124	.304	.413	May	.275	284	78	23	1	7	38	18	47	.319	.437
Turf	.249	824	205	38	0	30	128	65	148	.305	.404	June	.245	273	67	14	0	10	41	20	58	.291	.407
Pre-All Star	.267	810	216	48	1	29	125	58	145	.314	.436	July	.294	252	74	8	0	14	41	21	40	.355	.492
Post-All Star	.233	666	155	25	0	23	95	51	127	.292	.374	August	.211	261	55	15	0	9	45	18	52	.268	.372
Scoring Posn	.279	409	114	22	0	14	167	44	78	.340	.435	Sept/Oct	.237	253	60	5	0	7	27	20	51	.294	.340
Close & Late	.226	235	53	8	1	7	30	15	50	.272	.357	vs. AL	.283	381	108	23	0	14	56	31	72	.342	.454
None on/out	.258	333	86	13	0	9	9	34	93	.310	.378	vs. NL	.240	1095	263	50	1	38	164	78	200	.291	.392

Batter vs. Pitcher (career)

Hits Best Against	Avg	AB	H	2B	3B	HR	RBI	BB	SO	OBP	SLG	Hits Worst Against	Avg	AB	H	2B	3B	HR	RBI	BB	SO	OBP	SLG
Pete Smith	.636	11	7	0	0	1	6	0	0	.636	.909	Bill Swift	.063	16	1	0	0	0	0	0	1	.063	.063
Pete Schourek	.545	11	6	3	0	1	4	0	2	.545	1.091	John Burkett	.083	12	1	0	0	0	0	0	3	.083	.083
Rheal Cormier	.533	15	8	1	0	1	3	0	0	.533	.800	Mark Clark	.083	12	1	0	0	0	0	0	2	.083	.083
Danny Darwin	.417	12	5	0	0	2	2	1	1	.462	.917	Pedro Martinez	.083	12	1	0	0	0	1	0	4	.083	.083
Allen Watson	.400	10	4	0	0	2	4	1	4	.455	1.000	Armando Reynoso	.083	12	1	0	0	0	0	1	4	.154	.083

Gregg Olson — Royals
Age 31 – Pitches Right (groundball pitcher)

	ERA	W	L	Sv	G	GS	IP	BB	SO	Avg	H	2B	3B	HR	RBI	OBP	SLG	GF	IR	IRS	Hld	SvOp	SB	CS	GB	FB	G/F
1997 Season	5.58	4	3	1	45	0	50.0	28	34	.299	58	8	1	3	36	.388	.397	18	30	12	5	4	9	4	89	38	2.34
Last Five Years	4.52	11	10	42	186	0	195.0	113	146	.265	197	36	3	16	138	.361	.386	111	115	53	9	55	29	10	302	178	1.70

1997 Season

	ERA	W	L	Sv	G	GS	IP	H	HR	BB	SO		Avg	AB	H	2B	3B	HR	RBI	BB	SO	OBP	SLG
Home	6.08	2	1	0	21	0	23.2	32	1	8	15	vs. Left	.253	75	19	5	1	2	19	6	18	.305	.427
Away	5.13	2	2	1	24	0	26.1	26	2	20	19	vs. Right	.328	119	39	3	0	1	17	22	16	.437	.378
Starter	0.00	0	0	0	0	0	0.0	0	0	0	0	Scoring Posn	.350	60	21	4	1	0	31	17	9	.494	.450
Reliever	5.58	4	3	1	45	0	50.0	58	3	28	34	Close & Late	.344	64	22	2	1	2	15	13	14	.455	.500
0 Days rest (Relief)	2.70	1	0	0	7	0	6.2	4	0	3	6	None on/out	.289	45	13	2	0	2	4	7	.347	.467
1 or 2 Days rest	4.40	2	3	1	25	0	30.2	37	2	16	22	First Pitch	.344	32	11	1	0	1	4	3	0	.417	.469
3+ Days rest	9.95	1	0	0	13	0	12.2	17	1	9	6	Ahead in Count	.284	95	27	5	1	0	16	0	31	.281	.358
Pre-All Star	16.20	0	0	0	13	0	10.0	21	1	12	6	Behind in Count	.333	33	11	1	0	0	8	10	0	.488	.364
Post-All Star	2.93	4	3	1	32	0	40.0	37	2	16	28	Two Strikes	.245	94	23	2	0	1	12	15	34	.349	.298

Last Five Years

	ERA	W	L	Sv	G	GS	IP	H	HR	BB	SO		Avg	AB	H	2B	3B	HR	RBI	BB	SO	OBP	SLG
Home	4.36	6	4	20	90	0	95.0	95	10	44	77	vs. Left	.237	342	81	19	1	9	64	39	75	.315	.377
Away	4.68	5	6	22	96	0	100.0	102	6	69	69	vs. Right	.289	402	116	17	2	7	74	74	71	.398	.393
Day	4.79	5	4	8	54	0	56.1	61	5	41	41	Inning 1-6	.254	67	17	2	1	0	15	11	14	.354	.313
Night	4.41	6	6	34	132	0	138.2	136	11	72	105	Inning 7+	.266	677	180	34	2	16	123	102	132	.362	.393
Grass	4.46	8	7	36	141	0	147.1	148	16	81	107	None on	.238	366	87	16	0	8	8	44	67	.320	.347
Turf	4.72	3	3	6	45	0	47.2	49	0	32	39	Runners on	.291	378	110	20	3	8	130	69	79	.398	.423
March/April	7.94	0	1	5	23	0	22.2	33	1	14	16	Scoring Posn	.312	250	78	15	3	7	126	58	53	.435	.480
May	4.37	0	0	5	25	0	22.2	21	3	22	21	Close & Late	.244	311	76	15	1	5	63	56	71	.356	.347

Last Five Years

	ERA	W	L	Sv	G	GS	IP	H	HR	BB	SO		Avg	AB	H	2B	3B	HR	RBI	BB	SO	OBP	SLG
June	4.89	1	0	14	35	0	35.0	31	3	18	24	None on/out	.231	156	36	3	0	4	20	31		.318	.327
July	2.43	2	3	9	38	0	40.2	37	1	19	28	vs. 1st Batr (relief)	.279	154	43	5	0	5	31	28	30	.391	.409
August	4.97	3	3	7	37	0	38.0	38	5	22	26	1st Inning Pitched	.271	624	169	29	3	15	123	91	125	.363	.399
Sept/Oct	4.00	5	3	2	28	0	36.0	37	3	18	31	First 15 Pitches	.268	481	129	23	3	10	83	70	90	.361	.391
Starter	0.00	0	0	0	0	0	0.0	0	0	0	0	Pitch 16-30	.246	224	55	9	0	5	40	37	51	.351	.353
Reliever	4.52	11	10	42	186	0	195.0	197	16	113	146	Pitch 31-45	.297	37	11	4	0	0	11	6	5	.395	.405
0 Days rest (Relief)	5.33	2	0	9	27	0	25.1	30	3	12	22	Pitch 46+	1.000	2	2	0	0	1	4	0	0	1.000	2.500
1 or 2 Days rest	3.85	6	7	24	98	0	107.2	106	6	62	86	First Pitch	.357	98	35	9	0	4	25	11	0	.416	.571
3+ Days rest	5.37	3	3	9	61	0	62.0	61	7	39	38	Ahead in Count	.199	322	64	13	1	0	33	0	125	.198	.245
vs. AL	4.05	10	7	41	158	0	169.0	162	14	91	125	Behind in Count	.330	182	60	8	2	8	50	46	0	.463	.527
vs. NL	7.62	1	3	1	28	0	26.0	35	2	22	21	Two Strikes	.181	353	64	9	0	3	48	56	146	.293	.232
Pre-All Star	5.24	1	2	27	93	0	89.1	92	8	59	63	Pre-All Star	.267	344	92	19	0	8	71	59	63	.372	.392
Post-All Star	3.92	10	8	15	93	0	105.2	105	8	54	83	Post-All Star	.263	400	105	17	3	8	67	54	83	.351	.380

Pitcher vs. Batter (career)

Pitches Best Vs.	Avg	AB	H	2B	3B	HR	RBI	BB	SO	OBP	SLG	Pitches Worst Vs.	Avg	AB	H	2B	3B	HR	RBI	BB	SO	OBP	SLG
Ruben Sierra	.000	12	0	0	0	0	0	1	3	.077	.000	Sandy Alomar Jr	.444	9	4	0	0	0	3	2	2	.545	.444
Albert Belle	.000	10	0	0	0	0	0	1	1	.167	.000	Danny Tartabull	.400	15	6	0	0	1	7	3	4	.500	.600
Travis Fryman	.111	9	1	0	0	0	2	2	4	.250	.111	Mark McGwire	.400	10	4	0	0	1	4	5	3	.600	.700
Rafael Palmeiro	.143	14	2	0	0	0	3	1	2	.200	.143	Robin Ventura	.400	10	4	0	0	0	2	2	0	.500	.400
Wally Joyner	.167	12	2	0	0	0	2	0	3	.154	.167	Tony Phillips	.357	14	5	1	0	0	2	2	1	.438	.429

Mike Oquist — Athletics
Age 30 – Pitches Right

	ERA	W	L	Sv	G	GS	IP	BB	SO	Avg	H	2B	3B	HR	RBI	OBP	SLG	CG	ShO	Sup	QS	#P/S	SB	CS	GB	FB	G/F
1997 Season	5.02	4	6	0	19	17	107.2	43	72	.266	111	21	2	15	54	.340	.433	1	0	5.68	5	100	3	4	136	137	0.99
Career (1993-1997)	4.96	9	10	0	74	26	239.1	122	150	.274	255	52	4	28	128	.362	.428	1	0	5.26	7	94	9	7	312	310	1.01

1997 Season

	ERA	W	L	Sv	G	GS	IP	H	HR	BB	SO		Avg	AB	H	2B	3B	HR	RBI	BB	SO	OBP	SLG
Home	4.96	2	3	0	9	8	49.0	53	4	19	31	vs. Left	.260	219	57	11	2	8	29	27	39	.345	.438
Away	5.06	2	3	0	10	9	58.2	58	11	24	41	vs. Right	.271	199	54	10	0	7	25	16	33	.335	.427
Starter	4.81	4	5	0	17	17	101.0	101	13	40	71	Scoring Posn	.312	77	24	3	0	5	38	15	12	.417	.545
Reliever	8.10	0	1	0	2	0	6.2	10	2	3	1	Close & Late	.333	15	5	1	0	0	1	2	1	.444	.400
0-3 Days Rest (Start)	0.00	0	0	0	0	0	0.0	0	0	0	0	None on/out	.219	105	23	6	1	4	4	10	14	.305	.410
4 Days Rest	4.40	3	3	0	12	12	75.2	73	10	27	53	First Pitch	.288	52	15	4	1	1	3	1	0	.302	.462
5+ Days Rest	6.04	1	2	0	5	5	25.1	28	3	13	18	Ahead in Count	.213	183	39	4	1	4	18	0	58	.236	.311
Pre-All Star	4.03	2	2	0	10	8	58.0	60	7	20	32	Behind in Count	.298	104	31	7	0	4	16	24	0	.430	.481
Post-All Star	6.16	2	4	0	9	9	49.2	51	8	23	40	Two Strikes	.188	191	36	6	1	7	20	18	72	.269	.340

Luis Ordaz — Cardinals
Age 22 – Bats Right

	Avg	G	AB	R	H	2B	3B	HR	RBI	BB	SO	HBP	GDP	SB	CS	OBP	SLG	IBB	SH	SF	#Pit	#P/PA	GB	FB	G/F
1997 Season	.273	12	22	3	6	1	0	0	1	1	2	0	0	3	0	.304	.318	0	0	0	71	3.09	9	8	1.13

1997 Season

	Avg	AB	H	2B	3B	HR	RBI	BB	SO	OBP	SLG		Avg	AB	H	2B	3B	HR	RBI	BB	SO	OBP	SLG
vs. Left	.000	2	0	0	0	0	0	0	0	.000	.000	Scoring Posn	.000	3	0	0	0	0	1	0	0	.000	.000
vs. Right	.300	20	6	1	0	0	1	1	2	.333	.350	Close & Late	.000	2	0	0	0	0	0	0	0	.000	.000

Magglio Ordonez — White Sox
Age 24 – Bats Right

	Avg	G	AB	R	H	2B	3B	HR	RBI	BB	SO	HBP	GDP	SB	CS	OBP	SLG	IBB	SH	SF	#Pit	#P/PA	GB	FB	G/F
1997 Season	.319	21	69	12	22	6	0	4	11	2	8	0	1	0	1	2	.338	.580	0	1	0	221	3.03	30	19	1.58

1997 Season

	Avg	AB	H	2B	3B	HR	RBI	BB	SO	OBP	SLG		Avg	AB	H	2B	3B	HR	RBI	BB	SO	OBP	SLG
vs. Left	.294	17	5	2	0	1	1	0	0	.294	.588	Scoring Posn	.267	15	4	1	0	1	6	1	1	.313	.533
vs. Right	.327	52	17	4	0	3	10	2	8	.352	.577	Close & Late	.364	11	4	0	0	1	1	0	0	.364	.636

Rey Ordonez — Mets
Age 25 – Bats Right

	Avg	G	AB	R	H	2B	3B	HR	RBI	BB	SO	HBP	GDP	SB	CS	OBP	SLG	IBB	SH	SF	#Pit	#P/PA	GB	FB	G/F
1997 Season	.216	120	356	35	77	5	3	1	33	18	36	1	10	11	5	.255	.256	3	14	2	1202	3.07	165	83	1.99
Career (1996-1997)	.240	271	858	86	206	17	7	2	63	40	89	2	22	12	8	.275	.283	15	18	3	2798	3.04	428	173	2.47

1997 Season

	Avg	AB	H	2B	3B	HR	RBI	BB	SO	OBP	SLG		Avg	AB	H	2B	3B	HR	RBI	BB	SO	OBP	SLG
vs. Left	.270	100	27	3	0	0	11	5	7	.308	.300	First Pitch	.250	56	14	1	1	0	11	1	0	.259	.304
vs. Right	.195	256	50	2	3	1	22	13	29	.233	.238	Ahead in Count	.300	70	21	1	0	0	5	14	0	.412	.314
Groundball	.257	70	18	0	0	0	6	6	9	.316	.257	Behind in Count	.154	169	26	2	0	2	9	0	35	.159	.189
Flyball	.205	44	9	1	0	0	3	1	5	.222	.227	Two Strikes	.152	125	19	1	2	1	7	3	36	.172	.216
Home	.238	164	39	3	2	1	17	12	14	.288	.299	Batting #2	.286	14	4	0	0	0	2	0	1	.286	.286
Away	.198	192	38	2	1	0	16	6	22	.225	.219	Batting #8	.216	328	71	5	3	1	30	17	35	.256	.259
Day	.239	138	33	1	1	0	14	9	10	.284	.261	Other	.143	14	2	0	0	0	1	1	0	.200	.143
Night	.202	218	44	4	2	1	19	9	26	.236	.252	March/April	.253	79	20	1	1	0	5	3	6	.280	.291
Grass	.221	298	66	4	2	1	25	17	28	.262	.258	May	.239	67	16	0	1	0	7	3	8	.271	.269
Turf	.190	58	11	1	1	0	8	1	8	.217	.241	June	.500	4	2	0	1	0	3	0	1	.500	1.000
Pre-All Star	.253	150	38	1	3	0	15	6	15	.282	.300	July	.208	53	11	2	0	0	5	5	6	.271	.245

1997 Season

	Avg	AB	H	2B	3B	HR	RBI	BB	SO	OBP	SLG		Avg	AB	H	2B	3B	HR	RBI	BB	SO	OBP	SLG
Post-All Star	.189	206	39	4	0	1	18	12	21	.235	.223	August	.209	86	18	1	0	0	7	3	9	.236	.221
Scoring Posn	.279	86	24	2	0	2	31	8	10	.333	.349	Sept/Oct	.149	67	10	1	0	1	6	4	6	.205	.209
Close & Late	.220	50	11	1	0	0	7	4	5	.278	.240	vs. AL	.273	22	6	1	0	1	5	1	0	.304	.455
None on/out	.144	97	14	0	0	0	5	10	.194	.144		vs. NL	.213	334	71	4	3	0	28	17	36	.251	.243

1997 By Position

Position	Avg	AB	H	2B	3B	HR	RBI	BB	SO	OBP	SLG	G	GS	Innings	PO	A	E	DP	Fld Pct	Rng Fctr	In Zone	Zone Outs	Zone Rtg	MLB Zone
As ss	.215	354	76	5	3	1	31	18	36	.253	.254	118	112	956.1	170	355	9	72	.983	4.94	366	358	.978	.937

Career (1996-1997)

	Avg	AB	H	2B	3B	HR	RBI	BB	SO	OBP	SLG		Avg	AB	H	2B	3B	HR	RBI	BB	SO	OBP	SLG
vs. Left	.264	220	58	5	1	0	21	8	15	.291	.295	First Pitch	.272	151	41	6	1	1	19	11	0	.319	.344
vs. Right	.232	638	148	12	6	2	42	32	74	.269	.279	Ahead in Count	.316	158	50	2	2	0	11	22	0	.398	.354
Groundball	.264	197	52	3	1	0	14	14	22	.311	.289	Behind in Count	.197	406	80	7	3	0	18	0	88	.200	.229
Flyball	.235	119	28	4	2	0	11	4	12	.260	.303	Two Strikes	.174	298	52	2	2	1	14	6	89	.190	.205
Home	.232	410	95	9	2	1	28	27	35	.280	.271	Batting #2	.182	22	4	0	0	0	2	0	3	.182	.182
Away	.248	448	111	8	5	1	35	13	54	.269	.295	Batting #8	.243	815	198	17	7	2	60	39	86	.278	.288
Day	.270	304	82	7	2	0	25	15	30	.304	.306	Other	.190	21	4	0	0	0	1	1	0	.227	.190
Night	.224	554	124	10	5	2	38	25	59	.258	.271	March/April	.304	161	49	5	3	0	10	5	15	.325	.373
Grass	.242	716	173	14	5	1	48	37	71	.279	.279	May	.258	155	40	4	1	0	12	8	17	.294	.297
Turf	.232	142	33	3	2	1	15	3	18	.253	.303	June	.170	88	15	1	1	0	4	5	10	.223	.205
Pre-All Star	.258	422	109	10	5	0	28	18	42	.290	.306	July	.241	137	33	2	1	0	8	8	15	.281	.270
Post-All Star	.222	436	97	7	2	2	35	22	47	.260	.261	August	.250	176	44	3	1	0	13	6	16	.275	.278
Scoring Posn	.259	201	52	4	3	0	58	23	19	.333	.308	Sept/Oct	.177	141	25	2	0	2	16	8	16	.224	.234
Close & Late	.248	133	33	2	1	0	15	7	13	.291	.278	vs. AL	.273	22	6	1	0	1	5	1	0	.304	.455
None on/out	.218	234	51	2	0	0	7	25	.244	.256		vs. NL	.239	836	200	16	7	1	58	39	89	.274	.279

Batter vs. Pitcher (career)

Hits Best Against	Avg	AB	H	2B	3B	HR	RBI	BB	SO	OBP	SLG	Hits Worst Against	Avg	AB	H	2B	3B	HR	RBI	BB	SO	OBP	SLG
Joey Hamilton	.438	16	7	0	0	0	1	1	1	.471	.438	Denny Neagle	.000	11	0	0	0	0	0	0	2	.000	.000
F. Valenzuela	.333	12	4	0	0	0	1	0	0	.333	.333	Shawn Estes	.077	13	1	0	0	0	0	0	1	.077	.077
John Smiley	.333	12	4	1	0	0	1	0	0	.333	.417	Todd Stottlemyre	.118	17	2	0	0	0	0	0	5	.118	.118
Jeff Fassero	.333	12	4	1	0	0	0	0	2	.333	.417	Darryl Kile	.167	12	2	0	0	0	2	0	2	.167	.167
Andy Ashby	.308	13	4	1	0	1	0	2	.308	.385		Shane Reynolds	.200	15	3	0	0	0	0	2	.200	.200

Kevin Orie — Cubs
Age 25 – Bats Right

	Avg	G	AB	R	H	2B	3B	HR	RBI	BB	SO	HBP	GDP	SB	CS	OBP	SLG	IBB	SH	SF	#Pit	#P/PA	GB	FB	G/F
1997 Season	.275	114	364	40	100	23	5	8	44	39	57	5	13	2	2	.350	.431	3	3	4	1527	3.65	142	97	1.46

1997 Season

	Avg	AB	H	2B	3B	HR	RBI	BB	SO	OBP	SLG		Avg	AB	H	2B	3B	HR	RBI	BB	SO	OBP	SLG
vs. Left	.207	87	18	4	0	2	10	8	10	.281	.322	First Pitch	.258	62	16	5	0	2	9	2	0	.288	.435
vs. Right	.296	277	82	19	5	6	34	31	47	.370	.466	Ahead in Count	.288	73	21	7	2	0	9	19	0	.426	.438
Groundball	.261	69	18	4	2	1	10	8	13	.350	.420	Behind in Count	.229	153	35	4	2	3	17	0	49	.237	.340
Flyball	.262	42	11	3	0	2	4	2	5	.295	.476	Two Strikes	.176	148	26	2	2	3	12	18	57	.268	.277
Home	.284	204	58	8	2	6	27	24	33	.365	.431	Batting #6	.291	179	52	8	3	6	22	17	22	.355	.469
Away	.263	160	42	15	3	2	17	15	24	.330	.431	Batting #7	.208	130	27	8	1	1	12	16	26	.300	.308
Day	.294	214	63	12	3	7	30	25	32	.369	.477	Other	.382	55	21	7	1	1	10	6	9	.452	.600
Night	.247	150	37	11	2	1	14	14	25	.322	.367	March/April	.239	67	16	8	0	0	4	11	10	.354	.358
Grass	.262	301	79	15	3	7	36	32	51	.340	.402	May	.400	5	2	1	0	0	2	1	1	.500	.600
Turf	.333	63	21	8	2	1	8	7	6	.392	.571	June	.313	64	20	3	1	3	11	10	6	.408	.531
Pre-All Star	.272	147	40	12	1	3	19	23	18	.371	.429	July	.250	76	19	4	1	1	7	5	17	.298	.368
Post-All Star	.276	217	60	11	4	5	25	16	39	.333	.433	August	.256	90	23	1	1	4	15	5	18	.299	.422
Scoring Posn	.303	89	27	8	1	1	36	19	11	.421	.449	Sept/Oct	.323	62	20	6	2	0	5	7	5	.400	.484
Close & Late	.279	68	19	2	1	1	9	4	18	.319	.382	vs. AL	.318	44	14	1	1	1	5	6	5	.400	.455
None on/out	.235	81	19	3	1	1	1	7	17	.303	.333	vs. NL	.269	320	86	22	4	7	39	33	52	.343	.428

1997 By Position

Position	Avg	AB	H	2B	3B	HR	RBI	BB	SO	OBP	SLG	G	GS	Innings	PO	A	E	DP	Fld Pct	Rng Fctr	In Zone	Zone Outs	Zone Rtg	MLB Zone
As 3b	.271	358	97	23	5	6	42	39	56	.347	.413	112	106	901.0	91	212	9	15	.971	3.03	301	248	.824	.801

Jesse Orosco — Orioles
Age 41 – Pitches Left (flyball pitcher)

	ERA	W	L	Sv	G	GS	IP	BB	SO	Avg	H	2B	3B	HR	RBI	OBP	SLG	GF	IR	IRS	Hld	SvOp	SB	CS	GB	FB	G/F
1997 Season	2.32	6	3	0	71	0	50.1	30	46	.169	29	5	0	6	26	.289	.302	12	68	16	21	4	5	2	49	64	0.77
Last Five Years	3.37	17	14	11	299	0	251.1	128	259	.199	178	33	2	21	119	.301	.311	77	254	61	74	30	28	10	253	263	0.96

1997 Season

	ERA	W	L	Sv	G	GS	IP	H	HR	BB	SO		Avg	AB	H	2B	3B	HR	RBI	BB	SO	OBP	SLG
Home	2.66	2	1	0	36	0	23.2	17	3	13	19	vs. Left	.101	79	8	3	0	1	7	12	26	.215	.177
Away	2.03	4	2	0	35	0	26.2	12	3	17	27	vs. Right	.226	93	21	2	0	5	19	18	20	.351	.409
Day	1.37	2	0	0	24	0	19.2	10	1	12	19	Inning 1-6	.111	9	1	0	0	1	5	2	4	.273	.444
Night	2.93	4	3	0	47	0	30.2	19	5	18	27	Inning 7+	.172	163	28	5	0	5	21	28	42	.290	.294
Grass	2.64	3	3	0	63	0	44.1	28	6	28	39	None on	.155	84	13	5	0	0	0	15	16	.283	.214
Turf	0.00	3	0	0	8	0	6.0	1	0	2	7	Runners on	.182	88	16	0	0	6	26	15	30	.295	.386
March/April	0.00	0	0	0	6	0	3.0	1	0	5	2	Scoring Posn	.155	58	9	0	0	4	22	9	22	.261	.362
May	0.82	1	0	0	13	0	11.0	4	0	8	5	Close & Late	.190	100	19	2	0	4	15	14	26	.287	.330

1997 Season

	ERA	W	L	Sv	G	GS	IP	H	HR	BB	SO
June	2.89	1	0	0	13	0	9.1	8	1	6	11
July	3.48	1	2	0	13	0	10.1	7	2	5	9
August	1.42	2	1	0	12	0	6.1	3	0	4	9
Sept/Oct	3.48	1	0	0	14	0	10.1	6	3	2	10
Starter	0.00	0	0	0	0	0	0.0	0	0	0	0
Reliever	2.32	6	3	0	71	0	50.1	29	6	30	46
0 Days rest (Relief)	3.29	2	1	0	22	0	13.2	10	4	8	16
1 or 2 Days rest	0.98	4	1	0	34	0	27.2	11	0	14	22
3+ Days rest	5.00	0	1	0	15	0	9.0	8	2	8	8
vs. AL	2.27	6	3	0	62	0	43.2	26	5	27	38
vs. NL	2.70	0	0	0	9	0	6.2	3	1	3	8
Pre-All Star	2.13	2	1	0	35	0	25.1	15	2	20	20
Post-All Star	2.52	4	2	0	36	0	25.0	14	4	10	26

	Avg	AB	H	2B	3B	HR	RBI	BB	SO	OBP	SLG
None on/out	.135	37	5	0	0	0	0	6	4	.256	.135
vs. 1st Batr (relief)	.070	57	4	0	0	3	11	12	21	.232	.228
1st Inning Pitched	.155	155	24	4	0	6	26	28	42	.281	.297
First 15 Pitches	.178	135	24	4	0	5	20	23	34	.296	.319
Pitch 16-30	.139	36	5	1	0	1	6	7	12	.273	.250
Pitch 31-45	.000	1	0	0	0	0	0	0	0	.000	.000
Pitch 46+	.000	0	0	0	0	0	0	0	0	.000	.000
Ahead in Count	.095	74	7	0	0	1	5	0	31	.093	.135
Behind in Count	.207	29	6	0	0	2	8	11	0	.425	.414
Two Strikes	.128	94	12	2	0	2	11	19	46	.272	.213
Pre-All Star	.174	86	15	3	0	2	10	20	20	.327	.279
Post-All Star	.163	86	14	2	0	4	16	10	26	.247	.326

Last Five Years

	ERA	W	L	Sv	G	GS	IP	H	HR	BB	SO
Home	3.49	5	9	8	162	0	136.2	105	14	69	140
Away	3.22	12	5	3	137	0	114.2	73	7	59	119
Day	3.31	4	5	4	97	0	84.1	61	8	38	84
Night	3.40	13	9	7	202	0	167.0	117	13	90	175
Grass	3.38	12	14	10	266	0	226.1	164	21	119	229
Turf	3.24	5	0	1	33	0	25.0	14	0	9	30
March/April	9.86	2	1	1	32	0	21.0	30	3	20	21
May	2.55	3	1	0	54	0	53.0	26	2	26	42
June	3.72	1	3	0	56	0	46.0	38	4	25	52
July	1.98	4	3	1	51	0	41.0	31	3	18	42
August	2.59	4	3	3	58	0	48.2	26	2	20	56
Sept/Oct	3.02	3	3	6	48	0	41.2	27	7	19	46
Starter	0.00	0	0	0	0	0	0.0	0	0	0	0
Reliever	3.37	17	14	11	299	0	251.1	178	21	128	259
0 Days rest (Relief)	4.98	3	5	3	85	0	65.0	56	13	35	79
1 or 2 Days rest	2.11	8	3	5	131	0	115.1	63	4	52	114
3+ Days rest	3.93	6	6	3	83	0	71.0	59	4	41	66
vs. AL	3.38	17	14	11	290	0	244.2	175	20	125	251
vs. NL	2.70	0	0	0	9	0	6.2	3	1	3	8
Pre-All Star	4.41	6	6	1	155	0	128.2	106	11	75	124
Post-All Star	2.27	11	8	10	144	0	122.2	72	10	53	135

	Avg	AB	H	2B	3B	HR	RBI	BB	SO	OBP	SLG
vs. Left	.199	351	70	15	1	6	40	41	102	.283	.299
vs. Right	.199	544	108	18	1	15	79	87	157	.313	.318
Inning 1-6	.185	54	10	2	0	4	13	8	13	.313	.444
Inning 7+	.200	841	168	31	2	17	106	120	246	.301	.302
None on	.191	445	85	17	0	9	9	55	131	.286	.290
Runners on	.207	450	93	16	2	12	110	73	128	.316	.331
Scoring Posn	.191	282	54	10	0	9	98	55	80	.317	.323
Close & Late	.186	469	87	18	2	11	60	59	149	.282	.303
None on/out	.195	190	37	9	0	5	5	25	44	.288	.321
vs. 1st Batr (relief)	.182	258	47	13	1	6	35	32	70	.278	.310
1st Inning Pitched	.198	734	145	30	2	18	115	105	201	.299	.317
First 15 Pitches	.210	662	139	30	2	18	99	88	177	.305	.343
Pitch 16-30	.167	198	33	2	0	3	18	32	69	.285	.222
Pitch 31-45	.171	35	6	1	0	0	1	7	13	.310	.200
Pitch 46+	.000	0	0	0	0	0	0	1	1	1.000	.000
First Pitch	.315	108	34	8	0	3	19	13	0	.387	.472
Ahead in Count	.154	436	67	10	2	7	43	0	205	.161	.234
Behind in Count	.241	162	39	5	0	8	29	51	0	.419	.420
Two Strikes	.134	478	64	15	1	4	41	64	259	.188	.195
Pre-All Star	.226	470	106	23	1	11	70	75	124	.332	.349
Post-All Star	.169	425	72	10	1	10	49	53	135	.266	.268

Pitcher vs. Batter (since 1984)

Pitches Best Vs.	Avg	AB	H	2B	3B	HR	RBI	BB	SO	OBP	SLG
Ozzie Guillen	.000	14	0	0	0	0	0	0	4	.000	.000
Paul O'Neill	.000	14	0	0	0	0	0	5	4	.263	.000
Terry Pendleton	.063	16	1	0	0	0	0	4	4	.250	.063
Kenny Lofton	.083	12	1	0	0	0	0	1	3	.154	.083
Cal Ripken	.133	15	2	0	0	0	2	0	4	.188	.133

Pitches Worst Vs.	Avg	AB	H	2B	3B	HR	RBI	BB	SO	OBP	SLG
Robin Ventura	.500	12	6	1	1	2	4	3	3	.600	1.250
Tony Gwynn	.375	16	6	0	0	1	4	2	0	.444	.563
Mike Stanley	.357	14	5	1	0	2	5	0	2	.357	.857
Ruben Sierra	.333	18	6	3	0	1	7	2	0	.333	.667
Juan Gonzalez	.333	9	3	2	0	0	2	2	0	.455	.556

Joe Orsulak — Expos
Age 36 – Bats Left

	Avg	G	AB	R	H	2B	3B	HR	RBI	BB	SO	HBP	GDP	SB	CS	OBP	SLG	IBB	SH	SF	#Pit	#P/PA	GB	FB	G/F
1997 Season	.227	106	150	13	34	12	1	1	7	18	17	0	2	0	1	.310	.340	0	2	0	601	3.54	64	47	1.36
Last Five Years	.262	564	1358	175	356	55	8	20	140	97	136	6	26	11	11	.311	.359	6	3	16	5040	3.41	555	412	1.35

1997 Season

	Avg	AB	H	2B	3B	HR	RBI	BB	SO	OBP	SLG
vs. Left	.000	14	0	0	0	0	1	1	2	.067	.000
vs. Right	.250	136	34	12	1	1	6	17	15	.333	.375
Home	.198	81	16	5	1	0	4	11	6	.293	.284
Away	.261	69	18	7	0	1	3	7	11	.329	.406
First Pitch	.292	24	7	2	0	0	2	0	0	.292	.375
Ahead in Count	.176	34	6	4	0	0	1	11	0	.378	.294
Behind in Count	.200	70	14	4	1	0	0	0	16	.200	.286
Two Strikes	.138	58	8	2	1	1	3	7	17	.231	.259

	Avg	AB	H	2B	3B	HR	RBI	BB	SO	OBP	SLG
Scoring Posn	.063	32	2	1	0	1	7	7	4	.231	.188
Close & Late	.250	32	8	2	1	0	0	4	2	.333	.375
None on/out	.135	37	5	3	0	0	0	3	6	.200	.216
Batting #7	.211	38	8	2	1	0	0	5	6	.302	.316
Batting #9	.200	35	7	2	0	0	0	6	3	.317	.257
Other	.247	77	19	8	0	1	7	7	8	.310	.390
Pre-All Star	.233	103	24	7	1	1	7	14	11	.325	.350
Post-All Star	.213	47	10	5	0	0	0	4	6	.275	.319

Last Five Years

	Avg	AB	H	2B	3B	HR	RBI	BB	SO	OBP	SLG
vs. Left	.234	145	34	4	1	0	20	4	17	.265	.276
vs. Right	.265	1213	322	51	7	20	120	93	119	.316	.369
Groundball	.225	386	87	8	2	5	39	23	33	.266	.295
Flyball	.292	185	54	7	3	4	25	17	25	.359	.427
Home	.281	633	178	23	4	12	81	54	43	.334	.387
Away	.246	725	178	32	4	8	59	43	93	.290	.334
Day	.240	421	101	14	4	4	37	41	54	.301	.321
Night	.272	937	255	41	4	16	103	56	82	.311	.376
Grass	.269	979	263	34	5	17	112	67	93	.313	.366
Turf	.245	379	93	21	3	3	28	30	43	.304	.340
Pre-All Star	.266	787	209	31	2	14	85	55	71	.314	.363
Post-All Star	.257	571	147	24	6	6	55	42	65	.306	.352
Scoring Posn	.267	311	83	11	1	6	120	39	40	.335	.367
Close & Late	.269	301	81	11	3	5	45	20	33	.317	.375

	Avg	AB	H	2B	3B	HR	RBI	BB	SO	OBP	SLG
First Pitch	.271	225	61	9	2	1	17	6	0	.285	.342
Ahead in Count	.271	321	87	17	2	9	41	63	0	.384	.421
Behind in Count	.235	561	132	17	3	4	51	0	113	.240	.298
Two Strikes	.220	487	107	15	3	6	52	28	136	.264	.300
Batting #5	.302	295	89	18	2	3	33	21	22	.347	.407
Batting #6	.245	200	49	7	1	3	17	7	28	.267	.335
Other	.253	863	218	30	5	14	90	69	86	.308	.348
March/April	.234	158	37	8	0	2	14	10	17	.287	.323
May	.293	283	83	7	1	6	36	21	26	.343	.389
June	.256	242	62	11	1	5	28	17	19	.302	.372
July	.264	277	73	15	0	3	28	19	24	.306	.350
August	.273	220	60	10	2	4	23	15	26	.316	.391
Sept/Oct	.230	178	41	4	4	0	11	15	24	.294	.298
vs. AL	.000	7	0	0	0	0	0	0	0	.000	.000

Last Five Years

	Avg	AB	H	2B	3B	HR	RBI	BB	SO	OBP	SLG		Avg	AB	H	2B	3B	HR	RBI	BB	SO	OBP	SLG
None on/out	.251	343	86	20	2	6	6	19	37	.294	.373	vs. NL	.264	1351	356	55	8	20	140	97	136	.312	.360

Batter vs. Pitcher (since 1984)

Hits Best Against	Avg	AB	H	2B	3B	HR	RBI	BB	SO	OBP	SLG	Hits Worst Against	Avg	AB	H	2B	3B	HR	RBI	BB	SO	OBP	SLG
Jeff Montgomery	.462	13	6	2	0	0	2	1	0	.500	.615	Mel Rojas	.000	10	0	0	0	0	0	0	2	.091	.000
Jack McDowell	.458	24	11	2	0	2	5	1	1	.480	.792	Greg Swindell	.091	11	1	0	0	0	0	0	1	.091	.091
Frank Castillo	.438	16	7	3	0	0	2	0	1	.438	.625	John Burkett	.091	11	1	0	0	0	0	0	1	.091	.091
Kevin Brown	.435	23	10	4	0	1	7	4	1	.519	.739	Kent Bottenfield	.091	11	1	0	0	0	0	2	1	.231	.091
Tim Pugh	.429	14	6	1	1	0	2	0	0	.429	.643	Doug Jones	.182	11	2	0	0	0	2	0	1	.182	.182

David Ortiz — Twins
Age 22 – Bats Left

	Avg	G	AB	R	H	2B	3B	HR	RBI	BB	SO	HBP	GDP	SB	CS	OBP	SLG	IBB	SH	SF	#Pit	#P/PA	GB	FB	G/F
1997 Season	.327	15	49	10	16	3	0	1	6	2	19	0	1	0	0	.353	.449	0	0	0	182	3.57	10	10	1.00

1997 Season

	Avg	AB	H	2B	3B	HR	RBI	BB	SO	OBP	SLG		Avg	AB	H	2B	3B	HR	RBI	BB	SO	OBP	SLG
vs. Left	.222	9	2	1	0	0	1	0	3	.222	.333	Scoring Posn	.400	15	6	0	0	1	6	2	6	.471	.600
vs. Right	.350	40	14	2	0	1	5	2	16	.381	.475	Close & Late	.000	4	0	0	0	0	0	0	1	.000	.000

Donovan Osborne — Cardinals
Age 29 – Pitches Left

	ERA	W	L	Sv	G	GS	IP	BB	SO	Avg	H	2B	3B	HR	RBI	OBP	SLG	CG	ShO	Sup	QS	#P/S	SB	CS	GB	FB	G/F
1997 Season	4.93	3	7	0	14	14	80.1	23	51	.274	84	17	1	10	43	.323	.433	0	0	4.48	8		3	5	102	86	1.19
Last Five Years	3.86	30	29	0	89	89	548.0	161	350	.259	540	107	11	67	231	.314	.417	3	1	4.17	58		96	21	28	704	634	1.11

1997 Season

	ERA	W	L	Sv	G	GS	IP	H	HR	BB	SO		Avg	AB	H	2B	3B	HR	RBI	BB	SO	OBP	SLG
Home	3.18	2	1	0	5	5	34.0	27	1	7	22	vs. Left	.343	35	12	2	0	0	2	9	.378	.400
Away	6.22	1	6	0	9	9	46.1	57	9	16	29	vs. Right	.265	272	72	15	1	10	41	21	42	.316	.438
Starter	4.93	3	7	0	14	14	80.1	84	10	23	51	Scoring Posn	.266	79	21	4	0	2	31	7	17	.315	.392
Reliever	0.00	0	0	0	0	0	0.0	0	0	0	0	Close & Late	.000	5	0	0	0	0	1	2	.167	.000
0-3 Days Rest (Start)	0.00	0	0	0	0	0	0.0	0	0	0	0	None on/out	.364	77	28	8	1	2	2	8	14	.430	.571
4 Days Rest	5.23	3	3	0	8	8	43.0	44	7	13	27	First Pitch	.378	45	17	4	1	1	7	1	0	.391	.578
5+ Days Rest	4.58	0	4	0	6	6	37.1	40	3	10	24	Ahead in Count	.257	62	16	5	0	5	19	0	43	.259	.404
Pre-All Star	3.60	1	2	0	6	6	35.0	39	3	11	26	Behind in Count	.339	62	21	6	0	2	12	8	0	.408	.532
Post-All Star	5.96	2	5	0	8	8	45.1	45	7	12	25	Two Strikes	.236	140	33	5	0	6	17	14	51	.308	.400

Last Five Years

	ERA	W	L	Sv	G	GS	IP	H	HR	BB	SO		Avg	AB	H	2B	3B	HR	RBI	BB	SO	OBP	SLG
Home	3.13	20	9	0	44	44	290.2	267	26	71	183	vs. Left	.241	332	80	19	2	9	28	27	67	.298	.392
Away	4.69	10	20	0	45	45	257.1	273	41	90	167	vs. Right	.262	1753	460	88	9	58	203	134	283	.317	.422
Day	4.14	8	9	0	31	31	193.2	183	28	56	132	Inning 1-6	.254	1857	472	88	9	61	208	152	327	.313	.410
Night	3.71	22	20	0	58	58	354.1	357	39	105	218	Inning 7+	.298	228	68	19	2	6	23	9	23	.324	.478
Grass	4.10	15	13	0	46	46	281.0	278	35	80	188	None on	.249	1299	324	69	10	40	40	94	229	.302	.410
Turf	3.61	15	16	0	43	43	267.0	262	32	81	162	Runners on	.275	786	216	38	1	27	191	67	121	.333	.429
March/April	3.66	3	4	0	14	14	86.0	83	9	24	55	Scoring Posn	.279	430	120	21	0	11	152	46	72	.346	.405
May	3.81	4	4	0	15	15	89.2	98	16	27	48	Close & Late	.273	128	35	12	2	4	17	7	16	.309	.492
June	3.09	7	2	0	11	11	75.2	74	6	13	44	None on/out	.255	550	140	29	7	12	12	39	89	.306	.398
July	4.10	5	6	0	14	14	85.2	79	13	28	63	vs. 1st Batr (relief)	.000	0	0	0	0	0	0	0	0	.000	.000
August	4.17	5	11	0	23	23	136.0	133	15	45	87	1st Inning Pitched	.257	338	87	16	3	10	47	28	69	.314	.411
Sept/Oct	4.08	6	2	0	12	12	75.0	73	8	24	53	First 75 Pitches	.256	1540	394	68	8	49	166	121	270	.311	.406
Starter	3.86	30	29	0	89	89	548.0	540	67	161	350	Pitch 76-90	.255	267	68	20	1	10	29	23	36	.312	.449
Reliever	0.00	0	0	0	0	0	0.0	0	0	0	0	Pitch 91-105	.262	187	49	12	2	5	24	10	36	.307	.428
0-3 Days Rest (Start)	11.25	0	1	0	1	1	4.0	6	2	2	6	Pitch 106+	.319	91	29	7	0	3	12	7	8	.374	.495
4 Days Rest	4.15	21	16	0	56	56	338.1	342	41	96	216	Ahead in Count	.204	931	190	28	3	20	85	0	295	.209	.305
5+ Days Rest	3.24	9	13	0	32	32	205.2	192	24	63	128	Behind in Count	.333	463	154	35	3	27	73	75	0	.424	.596
vs. AL	4.50	1	0	0	1	1	6.0	5	2	1	4	Two Strikes	.187	961	180	31	3	21	71	76	350	.251	.291
vs. NL	3.85	29	29	0	88	88	542.0	535	65	160	346	Pre-All Star	.257	1042	268	59	7	33	108	68	159	.305	.422
Pre-All Star	3.45	17	10	0	43	43	274.0	268	33	68	159	Post-All Star	.261	1043	272	48	4	34	123	93	191	.323	.412
Post-All Star	4.27	13	19	0	46	46	274.0	272	34	93	191												

Pitcher vs. Batter (career)

Pitches Best Vs.	Avg	AB	H	2B	3B	HR	RBI	BB	SO	OBP	SLG	Pitches Worst Vs.	Avg	AB	H	2B	3B	HR	RBI	BB	SO	OBP	SLG
Jeff King	.077	26	2	0	0	0	0	1	1	.111	.077	Greg Colbrunn	.643	14	9	1	0	2	4	0	2	.643	1.143
Alex Arias	.083	12	1	0	0	0	0	0	1	.083	.083	Delino DeShields	.545	11	6	1	0	1	2	0	0	.545	.909
Mickey Morandini	.091	11	1	0	0	0	0	0	1	.091	.091	Ryne Sandberg	.538	13	7	1	0	2	6	4	2	.647	1.154
Kevin Young	.091	11	1	0	0	0	0	0	7	.091	.091	Sean Berry	.529	17	9	5	0	1	3	2	2	.579	1.000
Derek Bell	.111	36	4	0	0	0	1	0	9	.111	.111	Darren Daulton	.455	11	5	1	0	2	7	4	2	.600	1.091

Keith Osik — Pirates
Age 29 – Bats Right

	Avg	G	AB	R	H	2B	3B	HR	RBI	BB	SO	HBP	GDP	SB	CS	OBP	SLG	IBB	SH	SF	#Pit	#P/PA	GB	FB	G/F
1997 Season	.257	49	105	10	27	9	1	0	7	9	21	1	1	0	1	.322	.362	1	2	0	427	3.65	38	28	1.36
Career (1996-1997)	.278	97	245	28	68	23	2	1	21	22	43	2	4	1	1	.344	.400	2	3	0	983	3.60	89	68	1.31

1997 Season

	Avg	AB	H	2B	3B	HR	RBI	BB	SO	OBP	SLG		Avg	AB	H	2B	3B	HR	RBI	BB	SO	OBP	SLG
vs. Left	.375	16	6	1	0	0	0	3	2	.474	.438	Scoring Posn	.304	23	7	2	1	0	6	3	4	.385	.478
vs. Right	.236	89	21	8	1	0	7	6	19	.292	.348	Close & Late	.200	20	4	2	0	0	1	3	4	.304	.300

Antonio Osuna — Dodgers

	ERA	W	L	Sv	G	GS	IP	BB	SO	Avg	H	2B	3B	HR	RBI	OBP	SLG	GF	IR	IRS	Hld	SvOp	SB	CS	GB	FB	G/F
1997 Season	2.19	3	4	0	48	0	61.2	19	68	.209	46	11	0	6	17	.274	.341	18	24	3	10	0	2	2	60	56	1.07
Career (1995-1997)	3.07	14	14	4	160	0	190.1	71	199	.221	150	27	4	17	68	.296	.348	47	83	19	37	11	13	5	184	189	0.97

1997 Season

	ERA	W	L	Sv	G	GS	IP	H	HR	BB	SO		Avg	AB	H	2B	3B	HR	RBI	BB	SO	OBP	SLG
Home	2.51	1	2	0	21	0	28.2	23	2	9	30	vs. Left	.192	104	20	6	0	2	6	11	30	.276	.308
Away	1.91	2	2	0	27	0	33.0	23	4	10	38	vs. Right	.224	116	26	5	0	4	11	8	38	.272	.371
Starter	0.00	0	0	0	0	0	0.0	0	0	0	0	Scoring Posn	.091	66	6	2	0	1	11	8	21	.197	.167
Reliever	2.19	3	4	0	48	0	61.2	46	6	19	68	Close & Late	.220	100	22	5	0	1	7	9	33	.284	.300
0 Days rest (Relief)	0.00	0	0	0	9	0	9.1	4	0	2	16	None on/out	.216	51	11	3	0	1		3	17	.259	.333
1 or 2 Days rest	3.07	0	4	0	22	0	29.1	22	4	12	31	First Pitch	.375	24	9	4	0	0	6	2	0	.429	.542
3+ Days rest	1.96	3	0	0	17	0	23.0	20	2	5	21	Ahead in Count	.144	118	17	2	0	2	4	0	57	.144	.212
Pre-All Star	3.00	1	3	0	21	0	24.0	20	3	9	29	Behind in Count	.294	34	10	3	0	2	3	10	0	.455	.559
Post-All Star	1.67	2	1	0	27	0	37.2	26	3	10	39	Two Strikes	.153	131	20	4	0	3	5	7	68	.196	.252

Career (1995-1997)

	ERA	W	L	Sv	G	GS	IP	H	HR	BB	SO		Avg	AB	H	2B	3B	HR	RBI	BB	SO	OBP	SLG
Home	2.78	4	7	3	76	0	90.2	60	4	30	95	vs. Left	.229	271	62	13	2	6	23	45	72	.339	.358
Away	3.34	10	7	1	84	0	99.2	90	13	41	104	vs. Right	.216	407	88	14	2	11	45	26	127	.265	.342
Day	2.53	7	4	0	43	0	57.0	38	8	17	64	Inning 1-6	.109	46	5	1	0	0	1	6	17	.222	.130
Night	3.31	7	10	4	117	0	133.1	112	9	54	135	Inning 7+	.229	632	145	26	4	17	67	65	182	.302	.364
Grass	3.34	10	12	3	131	0	153.2	119	15	61	159	Runners on	.231	281	65	15	0	8	59	42	79	.330	.370
Turf	1.96	4	2	1	29	0	36.2	31	2	10	40	Scoring Posn	.189	185	35	9	0	5	50	33	54	.308	.319
March/April	4.58	2	3	0	15	0	19.2	12	1	12	16	Close & Late	.223	386	86	17	3	6	43	41	115	.297	.329
May	2.21	3	3	1	28	0	36.2	34	4	15	37	None on/out	.227	163	37	5	3	2	2	9	48	.272	.331
June	3.90	0	2	1	26	0	27.2	23	4	11	27	vs. 1st Batr (relief)	.236	148	35	8	1	1	6	7	42	.277	.324
July	2.45	4	1	0	20	0	25.2	16	3	11	33	1st Inning Pitched	.224	491	110	22	1	14	55	49	145	.294	.358
August	2.23	4	1	1	35	0	44.1	35	3	8	49	First 15 Pitches	.225	423	95	17	2	11	39	30	121	.276	.352
Sept/Oct	3.96	1	4	1	36	0	36.1	30	2	14	37	Pitch 16-30	.237	190	45	9	1	6	22	31	62	.348	.389
Starter	0.00	0	0	0	0	0	0.0	0	0	0	0	Pitch 31-45	.118	51	6	1	0	0	5	5	13	.193	.137
Reliever	3.07	14	14	4	160	0	190.1	150	17	71	199	Pitch 46+	.286	14	4	0	1	0	2	5	3	.474	.429
0 Days rest (Relief)	2.10	6	2	2	47	0	51.1	34	4	13	60	First Pitch	.295	88	26	4	0	3	15	12	0	.379	.443
1 or 2 Days rest	3.70	5	9	1	74	0	87.2	77	9	32	91	Ahead in Count	.152	348	53	9	3	5	19	0	168	.157	.239
3+ Days rest	2.98	3	3	1	39	0	51.1	39	4	26	48	Behind in Count	.342	111	38	9	0	7	25	30	0	.483	.613
vs. AL	3.68	1	1	0	8	0	7.1	11	2	3	7	Two Strikes	.174	380	66	12	2	6	21	26	199	.228	.263
vs. NL	3.05	13	13	4	152	0	183.0	139	15	68	192	Pre-All Star	.225	316	71	10	2	10	29	40	86	.311	.364
Pre-All Star	3.24	6	8	2	72	0	89.0	71	10	40	86	Post-All Star	.218	362	79	17	2	7	39	31	113	.283	.334
Post-All Star	2.93	8	6	2	88	0	101.1	79	7	31	113												

Pitcher vs. Batter (career)

Pitches Best Vs.	Avg	AB	H	2B	3B	HR	RBI	BB	SO	OBP	SLG	Pitches Worst Vs.	Avg	AB	H	2B	3B	HR	RBI	BB	SO	OBP	SLG
Dante Bichette	.111	9	1	0	0	1	2	2	5	.273	.444												

Ricky Otero — Phillies

	Avg	G	AB	R	H	2B	3B	HR	RBI	BB	SO	HBP	GDP	SB	CS	OBP	SLG	IBB	SH	SF	#Pit	#P/PA	GB	FB	G/F
1997 Season	.252	50	151	20	38	6	2	0	3	19	15	1	2	0	3	.339	.318	0	3	0	674	3.87	54	43	1.26
Career (1995-1997)	.256	189	613	79	157	19	9	2	36	56	55	3	6	18	14	.320	.326	0	4	2	2500	3.69	249	170	1.46

1997 Season

	Avg	AB	H	2B	3B	HR	RBI	BB	SO	OBP	SLG		Avg	AB	H	2B	3B	HR	RBI	BB	SO	OBP	SLG
vs. Left	.313	32	10	2	0	0	2	4	3	.405	.375	Scoring Posn	.103	29	3	1	0	0	3	1	4	.161	.138
vs. Right	.235	119	28	4	2	0	1	15	12	.321	.303	Close & Late	.158	19	3	1	0	0	1	4	3	.304	.211
Home	.253	79	20	3	0	0	1	10	9	.337	.291	None on/out	.246	69	17	3	1	0	0	9	8	.333	.319
Away	.250	72	18	3	2	0	2	9	6	.341	.347	Batting #1	.246	134	33	4	2	0	3	18	13	.336	.306
First Pitch	.000	9	0	0	0	0	1	0	0	.100	.000	Batting #9	.400	10	4	1	0	0		1	1	.455	.500
Ahead in Count	.308	26	8	1	0	0	0	11	0	.514	.346	Other	.143	7	1	1	0	0	0	0	1	.250	.286
Behind in Count	.253	79	20	5	2	0	2	0	13	.253	.367	Pre-All Star	.232	99	23	3	2	0	1	11	11	.309	.303
Two Strikes	.188	64	12	3	0	0	2		7	.234	.234	Post-All Star	.288	52	15	3	0	0	2	8	4	.393	.346

Career (1995-1997)

	Avg	AB	H	2B	3B	HR	RBI	BB	SO	OBP	SLG		Avg	AB	H	2B	3B	HR	RBI	BB	SO	OBP	SLG
vs. Left	.252	131	33	6	0	0	5	13	14	.324	.298	First Pitch	.306	49	15	2	1	0	11	0	0	.320	.388
vs. Right	.257	482	124	13	9	2	31	43	41	.319	.334	Ahead in Count	.283	127	36	4	3	0	8	40	0	.453	.362
Groundball	.254	185	47	3	3	0	12	12	18	.299	.303	Behind in Count	.232	315	73	13	5	1	12	0	51	.234	.314
Flyball	.237	93	22	5	0	4	8	10		.304	.290	Two Strikes	.214	266	57	9	2	2	13	16	55	.259	.286
Home	.250	336	84	10	7	0	15	32	34	.316	.321	Batting #1	.264	557	147	16	9	2	36	52	45	.328	.336
Away	.264	277	73	9	2	2	21	24	21	.326	.332	Batting #9	.250	28	7	2	0	0	0	2	3	.300	.321
Day	.302	182	55	10	2	0	12	18	13	.365	.379	Other	.107	28	3	1	0	0	0	2	7	.194	.143
Night	.237	431	102	9	7	2	24	38	42	.302	.304	March/April	.250	4	1	0	0	0	0	0	0	.250	.250
Grass	.278	194	54	6	0	2	18	19	15	.344	.340	May	.197	61	12	2	0	0	1	8	10	.290	.230
Turf	.246	419	103	13	9	0	18	37	40	.309	.320	June	.228	180	41	5	2	2	13	18	22	.300	.311
Pre-All Star	.234	299	70	9	3	2	17	28	35	.301	.304	July	.322	174	56	5	4	0	13	12	8	.367	.397
Post-All Star	.277	314	87	10	6	0	19	28	20	.339	.347	August	.216	102	22	4	0	0	1	8	7	.279	.255
Scoring Posn	.215	121	26	2	0	0	30	4	9	.242	.231	Sept/Oct	.272	92	25	3	3	0	6	9	6	.343	.370
Close & Late	.215	93	20	1	0	1	5	12	13	.305	.258	vs. AL	.048	21	1	0	0	0	0	1	1	.091	.048
None on/out	.259	274	71	8	4	0	0	27	25	.328	.318	vs. NL	.264	592	156	19	9	2	36	55	54	.328	.326

Batter vs. Pitcher (career)

Hits Best Against	Avg	AB	H	2B	3B	HR	RBI	BB	SO	OBP	SLG	Hits Worst Against	Avg	AB	H	2B	3B	HR	RBI	BB	SO	OBP	SLG
Steve Trachsel	.538	13	7	0	1	1	2	0	1	.500	.923	Andy Benes	.000	10	0	0	0	0	0	2	3	.167	.000
Greg Maddux	.467	15	7	2	0	0	0	0	0	.467	.600	Frank Castillo	.200	10	2	0	1	0	0	1	1	.273	.400
Mark Clark	.364	11	4	0	0	0	0	0	0	.364	.364	Jeff Fassero	.214	14	3	0	0	0	0	1	3	.267	.214

Eric Owens — Reds
Age 27 – Bats Right

	Avg	G	AB	R	H	2B	3B	HR	RBI	BB	SO	HBP	GDP	SB	CS	OBP	SLG	IBB	SH	SF	#Pit	#P/PA	GB	FB	G/F
1997 Season	.263	27	57	8	15	0	0	0	3	4	11	0	2	3	2	.311	.263	0	0	0	232	3.80	25	12	2.08
Career (1995-1997)	.220	117	264	34	58	6	0	0	13	27	49	1	4	19	4	.293	.242	1	2	2	1099	3.71	103	68	1.51

1997 Season

	Avg	AB	H	2B	3B	HR	RBI	BB	SO	OBP	SLG		Avg	AB	H	2B	3B	HR	RBI	BB	SO	OBP	SLG
vs. Left	.217	23	5	0	0	0	0	2	3	.280	.217	Scoring Posn	.214	14	3	0	0	0	3	1	5	.267	.214
vs. Right	.294	34	10	0	0	0	3	2	8	.333	.294	Close & Late	.375	8	3	0	0	0	0	1	2	.444	.375

Tom Pagnozzi — Cardinals
Age 35 – Bats Right

	Avg	G	AB	R	H	2B	3B	HR	RBI	BB	SO	HBP	GDP	SB	CS	OBP	SLG	IBB	SH	SF	#Pit	#P/PA	GB	FB	G/F
1997 Season	.220	25	50	4	11	3	0	1	8	1	7	0	2	0	0	.235	.340	0	0	0	173	3.39	18	14	1.29
Last Five Years	.255	368	1249	121	319	67	3	30	159	76	185	4	30	5	2	.298	.386	13	3	12	4615	3.43	408	454	0.90

1997 Season

	Avg	AB	H	2B	3B	HR	RBI	BB	SO	OBP	SLG		Avg	AB	H	2B	3B	HR	RBI	BB	SO	OBP	SLG
vs. Left	.357	14	5	2	0	0	2	0	1	.357	.500	Scoring Posn	.211	19	4	2	0	0	6	0	5	.211	.316
vs. Right	.167	36	6	1	0	1	6	1	6	.189	.278	Close & Late	.143	7	1	1	0	0	2	1	1	.250	.286

Last Five Years

	Avg	AB	H	2B	3B	HR	RBI	BB	SO	OBP	SLG		Avg	AB	H	2B	3B	HR	RBI	BB	SO	OBP	SLG
vs. Left	.298	255	76	17	0	6	32	20	26	.345	.435	First Pitch	.321	221	71	21	1	6	31	9	0	.349	.507
vs. Right	.244	994	243	50	3	24	127	56	159	.285	.373	Ahead in Count	.287	279	80	16	1	9	44	44	0	.382	.448
Groundball	.276	355	98	21	0	7	48	19	53	.312	.394	Behind in Count	.214	542	116	19	1	10	57	0	164	.215	.308
Flyball	.199	201	40	7	2	3	21	14	28	.249	.299	Two Strikes	.204	496	101	22	1	9	53	22	185	.239	.306
Home	.269	603	162	32	2	14	78	41	84	.313	.398	Batting #7	.247	675	167	34	0	15	78	36	110	.285	.364
Away	.243	646	157	35	1	16	81	35	101	.282	.375	Batting #8	.260	473	123	26	3	11	66	36	56	.311	.397
Day	.288	351	101	24	1	10	49	24	49	.334	.447	Other	.287	101	29	7	0	4	15	4	19	.318	.475
Night	.243	898	218	43	2	20	110	52	136	.283	.362	March/April	.196	97	19	4	0	1	7	6	9	.236	.268
Grass	.292	636	186	35	1	21	95	36	100	.330	.450	May	.297	259	77	22	1	7	44	18	36	.342	.471
Turf	.217	613	133	32	2	9	64	40	85	.264	.320	June	.241	232	56	8	1	4	23	10	38	.272	.336
Pre-All Star	.260	689	179	41	2	15	86	39	104	.297	.390	July	.260	265	69	13	0	6	32	17	49	.302	.377
Post-All Star	.250	560	140	26	1	15	73	37	81	.298	.380	August	.230	248	57	11	1	10	33	14	29	.274	.403
Scoring Posn	.237	346	82	11	1	5	118	37	63	.301	.318	Sept/Oct	.277	148	41	9	0	2	20	11	24	.331	.378
Close & Late	.200	220	44	6	0	6	25	18	42	.259	.309	vs. AL	.125	8	1	0	0	0	2	1	0	.222	.250
None on/out	.260	288	75	19	0	6	12	29	.292	.389		vs. NL	.256	1241	318	66	3	30	157	75	185	.298	.387

Batter vs. Pitcher (career)

Hits Best Against	Avg	AB	H	2B	3B	HR	RBI	BB	SO	OBP	SLG	Hits Worst Against	Avg	AB	H	2B	3B	HR	RBI	BB	SO	OBP	SLG
Chris Hammond	.533	15	8	1	0	0	4	3	1	.611	.600	John Franco	.000	14	0	0	0	0	0	2	6	.125	.000
Tim Scott	.500	12	6	3	0	0	1	0	2	.500	.750	Norm Charlton	.000	10	0	0	0	0	0	1	2	.091	.000
Armando Reynoso	.455	11	5	1	1	0	2	1	1	.500	.727	Andy Benes	.059	17	1	0	0	0	2	0	2	.059	.235
Steve Trachsel	.438	16	7	4	1	1	3	2	3	.500	1.000	Mark Portugal	.059	17	1	0	0	0	1	2	1	.150	.059
Pete Schourek	.438	16	7	3	0	2	6	0	1	.471	1.000	Mel Rojas	.071	14	1	0	0	0	0	0	3	.071	.071

Lance Painter — Cardinals
Age 30 – Pitches Left

	ERA	W	L	Sv	G	GS	IP	BB	SO	Avg	H	2B	3B	HR	RBI	OBP	SLG	GF	IR	IRS	Hld	SvOp	SB	CS	GB	FB	G/F
1997 Season	4.76	1	1	0	14	0	17.0	8	11	.213	13	2	1	1	6	.304	.328	4	4	0	3	0	0	2	23	19	1.21
Career (1993-1997)	5.58	14	11	1	106	22	225.2	78	152	.295	267	52	10	36	144	.352	.494	18	55	17	11	2	16	10	329	262	1.26

1997 Season

	ERA	W	L	Sv	G	GS	IP	H	HR	BB	SO		Avg	AB	H	2B	3B	HR	RBI	BB	SO	OBP	SLG
Home	0.00	1	0	0	4	0	7.1	1	0	3	9	vs. Left	.250	24	6	0	1	1	4	2	6	.308	.458
Away	8.38	0	1	0	10	0	9.2	12	1	5	2	vs. Right	.189	37	7	2	0	0	2	6	5	.302	.243

Career (1993-1997)

	ERA	W	L	Sv	G	GS	IP	H	HR	BB	SO		Avg	AB	H	2B	3B	HR	RBI	BB	SO	OBP	SLG
Home	5.96	10	4	0	54	10	116.1	143	21	41	77	vs. Left	.261	207	54	7	4	4	28	26	43	.349	.391
Away	5.19	4	7	1	52	12	109.1	124	15	37	75	vs. Right	.306	697	213	45	6	32	116	52	109	.353	.525
Day	6.13	6	6	1	37	9	79.1	94	13	30	54	Inning 1-6	.311	676	210	38	7	31	124	56	107	.363	.525
Night	5.29	8	5	0	69	13	146.1	173	23	48	98	Inning 7+	.250	228	57	14	3	5	20	22	45	.322	.404
Grass	5.71	13	9	0	83	15	176.2	218	29	56	122	None on	.292	497	145	32	4	18	36	84	.342	.481
Turf	5.14	1	2	1	23	7	49.0	49	7	22	30	Runners on	.300	407	122	20	6	18	126	42	68	.364	.511
March/April	5.87	1	1	0	12	1	23.0	23	5	10	19	Scoring Posn	.307	238	73	11	5	10	103	36	44	.389	.521
May	10.43	1	4	0	16	5	33.2	52	7	15	21	Close & Late	.233	90	21	5	0	0	3	18	24	.364	.289
June	7.91	4	0	0	18	5	38.2	56	9	22	23	None on/out	.290	224	65	11	2	7	7	18	37	.348	.451
July	3.32	1	4	0	22	5	59.2	57	8	17	53	vs. 1st Batr (relief)	.151	73	11	2	1	1	8	10	12	.262	.247
August	4.13	3	1	0	16	3	32.2	35	2	1	14	1st Inning Pitched	.282	351	99	16	4	13	61	34	64	.349	.462
Sept/Oct	3.55	4	1	0	22	3	38.0	44	5	13	22	First 15 Pitches	.276	275	76	13	3	7	33	26	49	.346	.422
Starter	6.11	7	9	0	22	22	116.1	148	17	38	61	Pitch 16-30	.281	199	56	14	2	11	38	16	30	.333	.538
Reliever	5.02	7	2	1	84	0	109.1	119	19	40	91	Pitch 31-45	.294	143	42	10	1	3	25	17	28	.364	.441

Career (1993-1997)

	ERA	W	L	Sv	G	GS	IP	H	BB	SO		Avg	AB	H	2B	3B	HR	RBI	BB	SO	OBP	SLG
0 Days rest (Relief)	4.43	0	1	0	15	0	20.1	20	3	8	19	Pitch 46+	.324	287	93	15	4	15	48	19	45	.366	.561
1 or 2 Days rest	4.41	5	1	0	36	0	51.0	53	8	17	40	First Pitch	.361	122	44	11	1	6	25	5	0	.380	.615
3+ Days rest	6.16	2	0	1	33	0	38.0	46	8	15	32	Ahead in Count	.255	381	97	13	5	13	55	0	122	.263	.417
vs. AL	0.00	0	0	0	0	0	0.0	0	0	0	0	Behind in Count	.347	219	76	16	2	13	40	43	0	.454	.616
vs. NL	5.58	14	11	1	106	22	225.2	267	36	78	152	Two Strikes	.222	396	88	14	6	11	54	30	152	.282	.371
Pre-All Star	7.46	6	7	0	50	13	114.2	149	25	55	79	Pre-All Star	.318	469	149	23	4	25	94	55	79	.386	.544
Post-All Star	3.65	8	4	1	56	9	111.0	118	11	23	73	Post-All Star	.271	435	118	29	6	11	50	23	73	.314	.441

Pitcher vs. Batter (career)

Pitches Best Vs.	Avg	AB	H	2B	3B	HR	RBI	BB	SO	OBP	SLG	Pitches Worst Vs.	Avg	AB	H	2B	3B	HR	RBI	BB	SO	OBP	SLG
Gregg Jefferies	.000	12	0	0	0	0	0	1	1	.077	.000	Ken Caminiti	.500	14	7	2	0	0	5	2	1	.563	.643
Luis Gonzalez	.091	11	1	0	0	0	0	0	1	.091	.091	Jeff Bagwell	.500	10	5	1	0	1	2	1	1	.545	.900
Craig Biggio	.222	9	2	1	0	1	1	3	0	.417	.667												

Donn Pall — Marlins
Age 36 – Pitches Right

	ERA	W	L	Sv	G	GS	IP	H	HR	BB	SO	Avg	H	2B	3B	HR	RBI	OBP	SLG	GF	IR	IRS	Hld	SvOp	SB
1997 Season	3.86	0	0	0	2	0	2.1	1	0	.300	3	0	0	1	.364	.600	0	0	0	1	0				
Last Five Years	3.63	5	6	1	89	0	136.1	34	72	273	147	22	2	14	72	.318	.399	20	53	24	13	3	6		

1997 Season

	ERA	W	L	Sv	G	GS	IP	H	HR	BB	SO		Avg	AB	H	2B	3B	HR	RBI
Home	0.00	0	0	0	0	0	0.0	0	0	0	0	vs. Left	.333	3	1	0	0	0	0
Away	3.86	0	0	0	2	0	2.1	3	1	1	0	vs. Right	.286	7	2	0	0	1	1

Last Five Years

	ERA	W	L	Sv	G	GS	IP	H	HR	BB	SO		Avg	AB	H	2B	3B	HR	RBI						
Home	4.21	3	3	1	45	0	66.1	78	6	20	38	vs. Left	.285	239	68	14	0	7	36						
Away	3.09	2	3	0	44	0	70.0	69	8	14	34	vs. Right	.263	300	79	8	2	7	36						
Day	5.12	1	3	0	26	0	38.2	58	6	12	19	Inning 1-6	.268	183	49	9	1	5	32						
Night	3.04	4	3	1	63	0	97.2	89	8	22	53	Inning 7+	.275	356	98	13	1	9	40						
Grass	3.66	4	5	1	69	0	103.1	111	12	26	52	None on	.243	313	76	12	1	7	7						
Turf	3.55	1	1	0	20	0	33.0	36	2	8	20	Runners on	.314	226	71	10	1	7	65						
March/April	2.01	1	2	0	13	0	22.1	20	2	2	12	Scoring Posn	.284	148	42	3	1	3	54						
May	4.84	1	1	0	13	0	22.1	27	2	7	12	Close & Late	.304	135	41	5	1	2	16						
June	1.98	1	1	1	18	0	27.1	22	2	4	15	None on/out	.246	134	33	6	0	4	4						
July	4.76	1	1	0	24	0	34.0	40	4	13	16	vs. 1st Batr (relief)	.301	83	25	3	0	4	15						
August	6.39	0	1	0	13	0	12.2	23	3	5	6	1st Inning Pitched	.266	305	81	8	2	11	56	26	40	.325	.413		
Sept/Oct	2.55	1	0	0	8	0	17.2	15	1	3	11	First 15 Pitches	.278	295	82	10	2	11	44	15	31	.318	.437		
Starter	0.00	0	0	0	0	0	0.0	0	0	0	0	Pitch 16-30	.252	163	41	7	0	2	17	14	30	.307	.331		
Reliever	3.63	5	6	1	89	0	136.1	147	14	34	72	Pitch 31-45	.297	64	19	4	0	1	10	5	8	.348	.406		
0 Days rest (Relief)	3.60	3	0	0	9	0	15.0	14	1	4	12	Pitch 46+	.294	17	5	1	0	0	1	0	3	.294	.353		
1 or 2 Days rest	5.25	0	3	0	36	0	48.0	56	8	14	24	First Pitch	.311	74	23	3	0	2	13	4	0	.338	.432		
3+ Days rest	2.58	2	3	1	44	0	73.1	77	5	16	36	Ahead in Count	.221	240	53	6	1	6	26	0	60	.226	.329		
vs. AL	3.36	3	5	1	65	0	93.2	105	8	20	50	Behind in Count	.358	106	38	7	1	4	19	16	0	.443	.557		
vs. NL	4.22	2	1	0	24	0	42.2	42	6	14	22	Two Strikes	.221	226	50	7	1	5	31	14	72	.269	.327		
Pre-All Star	2.84	3	4	1	52	0	85.2	84	6	18	46	Pre-All Star	.253	332	84	14	2	6	38	18	46	.293	.361		
Post-All Star	4.97	2	2	0	37	0	50.2	63	8	16	26	Post-All Star	.304	207	63	8	0	8	34	16	26	.357	.459		

Pitcher vs. Batter (career)

Pitches Best Vs.	Avg	AB	H	2B	3B	HR	RBI	BB	SO	OBP	SLG	Pitches Worst Vs.	Avg	AB	H	2B	3B	HR	RBI	BB	SO	OBP	SLG
Gary Gaetti	.083	12	1	0	0	0	0	0	1	.154	.083	Rickey Henderson	.462	13	6	1	0	1	7	2	0	.533	.769
Joe Carter	.083	12	1	0	0	0	0	1	1	.154	.083	Mark McGwire	.385	13	5	1	0	1	2	3	2	.500	.692
Tony Phillips	.143	21	3	0	0	0	0	2	2	.217	.143	Rafael Palmeiro	.364	11	4	2	0	1	2	3	0	.500	.818
Travis Fryman	.167	12	2	0	0	0	2	0	0	.167	.167	Julio Franco	.364	11	4	1	0	1	1	2	1	.462	.727
Dean Palmer	.182	11	2	0	0	0	2	0	1	.167	.182	Mickey Tettleton	.364	11	4	0	0	1	3	1	3	.417	.636

Orlando Palmeiro — Angels
Age 29 – Bats Left

	Avg	G	AB	R	H	2B	3B	HR	RBI	BB	SO	HBP	GDP	SB	CS	OBP	SLG	IBB	SH	SF	#Pit	#P/PA	GB	FB	G/F
1997 Season	.216	74	134	19	29	2	2	0	8	17	11	1	4	2	2	.307	.261	1	3	1	675	4.33	64	35	1.83
Career (1995-1997)	.253	139	241	28	61	8	3	0	15	26	25	3	5	2	3	.332	.311	2	4	1	1138	4.14	104	59	1.76

1997 Season

	Avg	AB	H	2B	3B	HR	RBI	BB	SO	OBP	SLG		Avg	AB	H	2B	3B	HR	RBI	BB	SO	OBP	SLG
vs. Left	.351	37	13	1	0	0	2	2	1	.385	.378	Scoring Posn	.167	30	5	1	1	0	8	8	1	.333	.267
vs. Right	.165	97	16	1	2	0	6	15	10	.281	.216	Close & Late	.379	29	11	0	1	0	2	6	2	.486	.448
Home	.215	65	14	2	1	0	6	13	4	.354	.277	None on/out	.260	50	13	0	1	0	0	2	5	.288	.300
Away	.217	69	15	0	1	0	2	4	7	.257	.246	Batting #1	.211	71	15	1	1	0	6	8	3	.296	.254
First Pitch	.091	11	1	0	0	0	1	1	0	.167	.091	Batting #2	.174	23	4	0	1	0	1	1	4	.208	.261
Ahead in Count	.235	17	4	1	0	0	1	8	0	.480	.294	Other	.250	40	10	1	0	0	1	8	4	.375	.275
Behind in Count	.230	74	17	1	1	0	3	0	8	.237	.270	Pre-All Star	.250	72	18	2	0	0	5	12	4	.353	.278
Two Strikes	.192	78	15	1	0	0	6	8	11	.273	.231	Post-All Star	.177	62	11	0	2	0	3	5	7	.250	.242

357

Rafael Palmeiro — Orioles

Age 33 – Bats Left (flyball hitter)

	Avg	G	AB	R	H	2B	3B	HR	RBI	BB	SO	HBP	GDP	SB	CS	OBP	SLG	IBB	SH	SF	#Pit	#P/PA	GB	FB	G/F
1997 Season	.254	158	614	95	156	24	2	38	110	67	109	5	13	5	2	.329	.485	7	0	6	2518	3.64	162	236	0.69
Last Five Years	.291	734	2827	500	824	166	8	176	537	351	418	18	52	45	9	.369	.543	47	2	34	11916	3.69	795	1097	0.72

1997 Season

	Avg	AB	H	2B	3B	HR	RBI	BB	SO	OBP	SLG		Avg	AB	H	2B	3B	HR	RBI	BB	SO	OBP	SLG
vs. Left	.213	225	48	6	0	15	39	17	45	.275	.440	First Pitch	.352	125	44	4	2	10	31	6	0	.385	.656
vs. Right	.278	389	108	18	2	23	71	50	64	.360	.512	Ahead in Count	.299	137	41	6	0	8	27	25	0	.406	.518
Groundball	.275	149	41	4	0	7	36	23	22	.373	.443	Behind in Count	.170	229	39	9	0	9	30	0	86	.177	.328
Flyball	.260	73	19	4	1	3	7	7	9	.333	.466	Two Strikes	.160	262	42	11	0	11	29	36	109	.261	.328
Home	.247	299	74	8	0	20	50	33	57	.326	.475	Batting #3	.241	261	63	10	1	15	47	28	61	.311	.460
Away	.260	315	82	16	2	18	60	34	52	.332	.495	Batting #4	.248	242	60	8	1	11	29	26	35	.331	.426
Day	.260	208	54	6	1	11	36	24	39	.340	.457	Other	.297	111	33	6	0	12	34	13	13	.370	.676
Night	.251	406	102	18	1	27	74	43	70	.324	.500	March/April	.289	97	28	4	0	5	20	9	17	.343	.485
Grass	.253	542	137	19	2	36	96	65	95	.336	.494	May	.269	108	29	6	0	5	17	13	21	.347	.463
Turf	.264	72	19	5	0	2	14	2	14	.276	.417	June	.206	107	22	3	1	3	13	12	17	.292	.336
Pre-All Star	.260	342	89	13	2	16	55	37	61	.334	.450	July	.302	106	32	2	1	10	21	11	22	.375	.623
Post-All Star	.246	272	67	11	0	22	55	30	48	.324	.529	August	.236	106	25	4	0	8	20	9	16	.299	.500
Scoring Posn	.237	156	37	6	0	10	69	34	29	.369	.468	Sept/Oct	.222	90	20	5	0	7	19	13	16	.321	.511
Close & Late	.234	94	22	4	0	8	18	13	25	.327	.532	vs. AL	.262	553	145	24	2	34	104	59	101	.335	.497
None on/out	.197	142	28	4	1	10	10	12	27	.265	.451	vs. NL	.180	61	11	0	0	4	6	8	8	.275	.377

1997 By Position

Position	Avg	AB	H	2B	3B	HR	RBI	BB	SO	OBP	SLG	G	GS	Innings	PO	A	E	DP	Fld Pct	Rng Fctr	In Zone	Zone Outs	Zone Rtg	MLB Zone
As 1b	.253	600	152	23	2	38	108	65	107	.329	.488	155	151	1356.0	1303	113	10	126	.993	---	252	227	.901	.874

Last Five Years

	Avg	AB	H	2B	3B	HR	RBI	BB	SO	OBP	SLG		Avg	AB	H	2B	3B	HR	RBI	BB	SO	OBP	SLG
vs. Left	.280	965	270	53	0	55	180	93	144	.344	.506	First Pitch	.350	477	167	31	2	35	107	37	0	.397	.644
vs. Right	.298	1862	554	113	8	121	357	258	274	.382	.562	Ahead in Count	.362	726	263	59	1	59	177	151	0	.470	.690
Groundball	.295	631	186	39	1	31	115	77	87	.372	.507	Behind in Count	.223	1053	235	48	2	42	157	0	330	.225	.392
Flyball	.293	474	139	31	3	37	95	78	67	.391	.605	Two Strikes	.201	1125	226	44	2	48	147	163	418	.302	.372
Home	.294	1366	402	74	1	95	268	190	217	.378	.559	Batting #3	.298	1778	529	113	3	106	328	235	274	.378	.543
Away	.289	1461	422	92	7	81	269	161	201	.361	.528	Batting #4	.277	685	190	35	4	43	131	79	101	.355	.528
Day	.300	818	245	51	2	46	163	120	124	.389	.538	Other	.288	364	105	18	1	27	78	37	43	.350	.566
Night	.288	2009	579	115	5	130	374	231	294	.361	.545	March/April	.277	386	107	20	1	20	71	48	55	.351	.490
Grass	.290	2457	713	140	6	161	477	327	359	.373	.549	May	.301	495	149	26	3	27	86	73	69	.390	.529
Turf	.300	370	111	26	2	15	60	24	59	.343	.497	June	.297	532	158	37	1	25	88	52	79	.363	.511
Pre-All Star	.295	1592	469	90	6	84	283	193	230	.370	.517	July	.313	514	161	31	1	46	125	66	84	.389	.646
Post-All Star	.287	1235	355	76	2	92	254	158	188	.369	.576	August	.277	491	136	30	2	31	92	56	63	.359	.536
Scoring Posn	.285	705	201	44	3	41	343	172	108	.413	.530	Sept/Oct	.276	409	113	22	0	27	75	56	66	.358	.528
Close & Late	.288	372	107	22	0	26	76	58	73	.380	.556	vs. AL	.294	2766	813	166	8	172	531	343	410	.371	.546
None on/out	.300	607	182	38	1	40	40	45	79	.352	.563	vs. NL	.180	61	11	0	0	4	6	8	8	.275	.377

Batter vs. Pitcher (career)

Hits Best Against	Avg	AB	H	2B	3B	HR	RBI	BB	SO	OBP	SLG	Hits Worst Against	Avg	AB	H	2B	3B	HR	RBI	BB	SO	OBP	SLG
Mike Jackson	.636	11	7	1	0	2	3	2	1	.714	1.273	Dennis Springer	.000	15	0	0	0	0	0	0	3	.000	.000
Mark Leiter	.632	19	12	2	0	3	7	5	1	.708	1.211	Jim Poole	.000	11	0	0	0	0	1	1	1	.083	.000
Mike Fetters	.500	10	5	0	1	1	4	3	0	.643	1.000	Randy Johnson	.048	21	1	0	0	0	0	0	5	.048	.048
Hipolito Pichardo	.467	15	7	2	0	2	3	1	1	.529	1.000	John Smiley	.050	20	1	0	0	0	0	4	2	.208	.050
Justin Thompson	.462	13	6	1	2	2	7	0	2	.462	1.077	Norm Charlton	.125	16	2	0	0	0	3	0	2	.125	.125

Dean Palmer — Royals

Age 29 – Bats Right (flyball hitter)

	Avg	G	AB	R	H	2B	3B	HR	RBI	BB	SO	HBP	GDP	SB	CS	OBP	SLG	IBB	SH	SF	#Pit	#P/PA	GB	FB	G/F
1997 Season	.256	143	542	70	139	31	1	23	86	41	134	3	7	2	2	.310	.445	2	1	5	2308	3.90	158	165	0.96
Last Five Years	.263	574	2104	336	553	108	7	122	372	200	543	22	36	19	17	.331	.495	11	1	18	9178	3.91	521	687	0.76

1997 Season

	Avg	AB	H	2B	3B	HR	RBI	BB	SO	OBP	SLG		Avg	AB	H	2B	3B	HR	RBI	BB	SO	OBP	SLG
vs. Left	.240	146	35	5	0	8	17	9	32	.285	.438	First Pitch	.422	64	27	6	0	5	8	2	0	.448	.750
vs. Right	.263	396	104	26	1	15	69	32	102	.319	.447	Ahead in Count	.271	96	26	6	0	5	18	17	0	.374	.490
Groundball	.289	114	33	8	0	4	19	9	23	.339	.465	Behind in Count	.204	270	55	17	0	6	39	0	105	.205	.333
Flyball	.241	87	21	5	1	2	10	5	26	.283	.391	Two Strikes	.180	283	51	14	1	4	28	22	134	.239	.279
Home	.239	272	65	12	0	10	40	22	69	.298	.393	Batting #5	.266	173	46	7	0	9	31	12	44	.310	.462
Away	.274	270	74	19	1	13	46	19	65	.322	.496	Batting #6	.242	265	64	19	0	10	40	13	61	.278	.426
Day	.256	133	34	5	1	6	27	12	34	.320	.444	Other	.279	104	29	5	1	4	15	16	29	.382	.462
Night	.257	409	105	26	0	17	59	29	100	.306	.445	March/April	.294	85	25	4	0	4	15	11	20	.378	.482
Grass	.242	472	114	22	1	22	76	35	116	.295	.432	May	.187	91	17	6	0	1	12	6	21	.232	.286
Turf	.357	70	25	9	0	1	10	6	18	.408	.529	June	.234	111	26	8	0	2	12	4	27	.261	.360
Pre-All Star	.239	297	71	19	0	8	42	23	69	.293	.384	July	.290	93	27	5	0	7	19	8	26	.359	.570
Post-All Star	.278	245	68	12	1	15	44	18	65	.330	.518	August	.286	91	26	3	0	5	18	4	22	.316	.484
Scoring Posn	.255	145	37	10	0	5	63	14	34	.315	.428	Sept/Oct	.254	71	18	5	1	4	10	7	18	.321	.521
Close & Late	.289	83	24	1	1	5	16	7	20	.344	.506	vs. AL	.255	482	123	26	1	19	71	37	121	.309	.432
None on/out	.256	129	33	4	1	10	10	7	29	.294	.535	vs. NL	.267	60	16	5	0	4	15	4	13	.313	.550

1997 By Position

Position	Avg	AB	H	2B	3B	HR	RBI	BB	SO	OBP	SLG	G	GS	Innings	PO	A	E	DP	Fld Pct	Rng Fctr	In Zone	Zone Outs	Zone Rtg	MLB Zone
As 3b	.256	540	138	31	1	23	85	40	134	.308	.444	141	140	1227.0	99	246	19	18	.948	2.53	362	276	.762	.801

Last Five Years

	Avg	AB	H	2B	3B	HR	RBI	BB	SO	OBP	SLG		Avg	AB	H	2B	3B	HR	RBI	BB	SO	OBP	SLG
vs. Left	.281	512	144	21	1	33	88	54	132	.355	.520	First Pitch	.342	219	75	15	1	18	50	9	0	.379	.667
vs. Right	.257	1592	409	87	6	89	284	146	411	.323	.487	Ahead in Count	.370	405	150	24	2	30	93	94	0	.489	.662
Groundball	.252	436	110	22	1	21	91	47	104	.330	.452	Behind in Count	.203	1038	211	46	2	43	140	0	449	.210	.376
Flyball	.241	423	102	25	2	26	59	41	119	.314	.494	Two Strikes	.176	1079	190	37	2	41	124	97	543	.246	.328
Home	.254	1057	269	47	1	57	181	106	284	.325	.463	Batting #5	.250	521	130	24	0	28	83	55	140	.323	.457
Away	.271	1047	284	61	6	65	191	94	259	.336	.527	Batting #6	.268	1166	312	61	4	71	221	95	296	.325	.509
Day	.286	539	154	33	3	33	115	51	132	.353	.542	Other	.266	417	111	23	3	23	68	50	107	.356	.501
Night	.255	1565	399	75	4	89	257	149	411	.330	.479	March/April	.289	325	94	19	2	21	64	37	75	.371	.554
Grass	.262	1824	477	86	6	107	323	175	459	.331	.491	May	.241	440	106	23	0	24	78	49	124	.317	.457
Turf	.271	280	76	22	1	15	49	25	84	.331	.518	June	.264	375	99	27	2	18	62	36	94	.330	.491
Pre-All Star	.266	1256	334	74	5	75	246	69	222	.318	.469	July	.267	382	102	15	1	25	76	33	106	.333	.508
Post-All Star	.258	848	219	34	2	47	126	131	321	.339	.512	August	.255	322	82	11	0	20	58	25	81	.313	.475
Scoring Posn	.227	573	130	27	1	25	229	67	170	.306	.408	Sept/Oct	.269	260	70	13	2	14	34	20	63	.321	.496
Close & Late	.250	300	75	9	1	20	47	32	90	.325	.487	vs. AL	.263	2044	537	103	7	118	357	196	530	.331	.493
None on/out	.285	470	134	21	4	29	29	40	107	.348	.532	vs. NL	.267	60	16	5	0	4	15	4	13	.313	.550

Batter vs. Pitcher (career)

Hits Best Against	Avg	AB	H	2B	3B	HR	RBI	BB	SO	OBP	SLG	Hits Worst Against	Avg	AB	H	2B	3B	HR	RBI	BB	SO	OBP	SLG
Eddie Guardado	.600	5	3	1	0	0	0	6	0	.818	.800	Tim Belcher	.038	26	1	0	0	0	1	0	8	.038	.038
Tim Wakefield	.500	12	6	1	0	1	1	2	2	.571	.833	Cal Eldred	.053	19	1	0	0	0	1	2	8	.143	.053
Bobby Witt	.417	12	5	1	0	3	6	2	3	.500	1.250	Alan Mills	.083	12	1	0	0	0	0	1	6	.154	.083
Mike Fetters	.364	11	4	1	0	2	9	0	2	.417	1.000	John Smiley	.091	11	1	0	0	0	0	0	3	.091	.091
Dennis Cook	.333	9	3	2	0	1	2	4	3	.538	.889	Ricky Bones	.118	17	2	0	0	0	0	0	9	.118	.118

Jose Paniagua — Expos

Age 24 – Pitches Right (groundball pitcher)

	ERA	W	L	Sv	G	GS	IP	BB	SO	Avg	H	2B	3B	HR	RBI	OBP	SLG	GF	IR	IRS	Hld	SvOp	SB	CS	GB	FB	G/F
1997 Season	12.00	1	2	0	9	3	18.0	16	8	.372	29	7	1	2	23	.495	.564	0	4	1	0	0	5	0	35	17	2.06
Career (1996-1997)	5.74	3	6	0	22	14	69.0	39	35	.308	84	17	1	9	43	.405	.476	0	4	1	0	0	12	2	127	66	1.92

1997 Season

	ERA	W	L	Sv	G	GS	IP	H	HR	BB	SO		Avg	AB	H	2B	3B	HR	RBI	BB	SO	OBP	SLG
Home	9.00	0	0	0	4	0	6.0	6	0	7	2	vs. Left	.400	30	12	3	0	1	10	8	2	.537	.600
Away	13.50	1	2	0	5	3	12.0	23	2	9	6	vs. Right	.354	48	17	4	1	1	13	8	6	.466	.542

Craig Paquette — Royals

Age 29 – Bats Right

	Avg	G	AB	R	H	2B	3B	HR	RBI	BB	SO	HBP	GDP	SB	CS	OBP	SLG	IBB	SH	SF	#Pit	#P/PA	GB	FB	G/F
1997 Season	.230	77	252	26	58	15	1	8	33	10	57	2	13	2	2	.263	.393	0	1	2	869	3.25	104	55	1.89
Career (1993-1997)	.232	419	1406	164	326	65	7	55	195	59	368	5	36	17	9	.263	.405	4	9	13	5296	3.55	472	357	1.32

1997 Season

	Avg	AB	H	2B	3B	HR	RBI	BB	SO	OBP	SLG		Avg	AB	H	2B	3B	HR	RBI	BB	SO	OBP	SLG
vs. Left	.228	101	23	5	0	5	21	2	22	.238	.426	Scoring Posn	.191	68	13	4	0	3	25	2	13	.219	.382
vs. Right	.232	151	35	10	1	3	12	8	35	.280	.371	Close & Late	.289	38	11	2	0	1	7	0	7	.308	.421
Home	.266	124	33	5	0	7	18	8	26	.313	.476	None on/out	.259	58	15	4	1	1	1	2	10	.283	.414
Away	.195	128	25	10	1	1	15	2	31	.212	.313	Batting #6	.218	119	26	10	0	4	18	8	28	.269	.403
First Pitch	.449	49	22	7	0	3	15	0	0	.440	.776	Batting #7	.279	68	19	3	0	2	7	1	14	.300	.412
Ahead in Count	.294	51	15	5	1	2	7	7	0	.379	.549	Other	.200	65	13	2	1	2	8	1	15	.212	.354
Behind in Count	.124	113	14	2	0	1	3	0	51	.139	.168	Pre-All Star	.221	231	51	14	1	8	28	10	53	.257	.394
Two Strikes	.095	105	10	1	0	0	2	3	57	.127	.105	Post-All Star	.333	21	7	1	0	0	5	0	4	.333	.381

Career (1993-1997)

	Avg	AB	H	2B	3B	HR	RBI	BB	SO	OBP	SLG		Avg	AB	H	2B	3B	HR	RBI	BB	SO	OBP	SLG
vs. Left	.244	504	123	19	2	23	73	34	141	.290	.427	First Pitch	.298	208	62	20	2	6	45	3	0	.304	.500
vs. Right	.225	902	203	46	5	32	122	25	227	.248	.394	Ahead in Count	.330	282	93	13	2	23	56	30	0	.395	.635
Groundball	.230	278	64	12	1	5	29	10	81	.256	.335	Behind in Count	.153	691	106	19	1	16	59	3	320	.157	.253
Flyball	.240	233	56	0	3	11	35	6	67	.256	.421	Two Strikes	.133	676	90	14	0	10	40	26	368	.165	.198
Home	.248	660	164	25	3	35	90	30	171	.281	.455	Batting #6	.258	318	82	22	2	12	49	17	82	.298	.453
Away	.217	746	162	40	4	20	105	29	197	.247	.362	Batting #7	.234	338	79	17	2	12	34	9	92	.255	.402
Day	.210	461	97	21	3	12	46	15	131	.237	.347	Other	.220	750	165	26	3	31	112	33	194	.251	.387
Night	.242	945	229	44	4	43	149	44	237	.276	.434	March/April	.266	109	29	9	2	3	12	6	19	.304	.468
Grass	.237	1173	278	52	4	46	152	47	301	.267	.406	May	.171	164	28	5	0	6	22	9	49	.219	.311
Turf	.206	233	48	13	3	9	43	12	67	.241	.403	June	.268	351	94	18	1	18	58	8	87	.283	.479
Pre-All Star	.232	708	164	34	3	31	103	26	179	.258	.419	July	.213	254	54	13	0	8	36	14	64	.251	.358
Post-All Star	.232	698	162	31	4	24	92	33	189	.268	.391	August	.276	294	81	15	3	14	48	17	80	.315	.490
Scoring Posn	.229	384	88	21	3	17	147	17	104	.257	.432	Sept/Oct	.171	234	40	5	1	6	19	5	69	.190	.278
Close & Late	.248	210	52	10	0	7	35	4	64	.266	.395	vs. AL	.232	1387	322	62	7	55	195	59	364	.264	.406
None on/out	.218	331	72	12	3	9	43	14	83	.249	.353	vs. NL	.211	19	4	3	0	0	0	0	4	.211	.368

Batter vs. Pitcher (career)

Hits Best Against	Avg	AB	H	2B	3B	HR	RBI	BB	SO	OBP	SLG	Hits Worst Against	Avg	AB	H	2B	3B	HR	RBI	BB	SO	OBP	SLG
Ben McDonald	.462	13	6	1	0	1	4	0	3	.462	.769	Ricky Bones	.000	10	0	0	0	0	0	1	2	.000	.000
Chad Ogea	.429	14	6	3	0	1	1	0	1	.429	.857	Juan Guzman	.083	12	1	1	0	0	1	1	3	.154	.167
Jamie Moyer	.370	27	10	1	0	2	7	3	4	.433	.630	Scott Karl	.091	11	1	0	0	0	0	0	5	.091	.091
Brad Radke	.368	19	7	0	1	3	4	1	4	.400	.947	Alex Fernandez	.143	14	2	0	0	0	2	0	4	.143	.143
Jimmy Key	.333	15	5	2	0	1	2	1	4	.375	.667	Justin Thompson	.167	12	2	0	0	0	1	0	3	.167	.167

Mark Parent — Phillies

Age 36 – Bats Right

	Avg	G	AB	R	H	2B	3B	HR	RBI	BB	SO	HBP	GDP	SB	CS	OBP	SLG	IBB	SH	SF	#Pit	#P/PA	GB	FB	G/F
1997 Season	.150	39	113	4	17	3	0	0	8	7	39	0	3	0	1	.198	.177	0	0	1	482	3.98	36	27	1.33
Last Five Years	.225	242	668	66	150	27	0	34	97	54	183	1	18	0	2	.282	.418	3	6	5	2795	3.81	214	185	1.16

1997 Season

	Avg	AB	H	2B	3B	HR	RBI	BB	SO	OBP	SLG		Avg	AB	H	2B	3B	HR	RBI	BB	SO	OBP	SLG
vs. Left	.120	25	3	0	0	0	2	3	10	.214	.120	Scoring Posn	.240	25	6	1	0	0	7	2	8	.286	.280
vs. Right	.159	88	14	3	0	0	6	4	29	.194	.193	Close & Late	.091	11	1	0	0	0	0	0	3	.091	.091

Last Five Years

	Avg	AB	H	2B	3B	HR	RBI	BB	SO	OBP	SLG		Avg	AB	H	2B	3B	HR	RBI	BB	SO	OBP	SLG
vs. Left	.235	213	50	5	0	15	34	25	43	.314	.469	First Pitch	.333	93	31	2	0	5	23	1	0	.340	.516
vs. Right	.220	455	100	22	0	19	63	29	140	.266	.393	Ahead in Count	.383	128	49	12	0	15	29	24	0	.480	.828
Groundball	.228	180	41	8	0	6	21	12	48	.273	.372	Behind in Count	.124	306	38	10	0	5	21	0	151	.123	.206
Flyball	.194	108	21	4	0	12	26	14	36	.285	.565	Two Strikes	.118	338	40	8	0	7	23	29	183	.186	.204
Home	.224	339	76	18	0	12	45	30	94	.285	.383	Batting #7	.210	291	61	10	0	14	38	22	71	.263	.388
Away	.225	329	74	9	0	22	52	24	89	.278	.453	Batting #8	.257	202	52	9	0	10	25	20	57	.324	.450
Day	.218	293	64	9	0	17	41	18	81	.262	.423	Other	.211	175	37	8	0	10	34	12	55	.262	.429
Night	.229	375	86	18	0	17	56	36	102	.296	.413	March/April	.188	69	13	5	0	3	9	9	26	.282	.391
Grass	.239	393	94	17	0	22	64	26	101	.285	.450	May	.256	129	33	5	0	7	22	13	34	.324	.457
Turf	.204	275	56	10	0	12	33	28	82	.276	.371	June	.286	119	34	5	0	5	17	5	31	.317	.454
Pre-All Star	.251	358	90	17	0	17	54	31	100	.311	.441	July	.218	119	26	5	0	7	17	12	33	.286	.437
Post-All Star	.194	310	60	10	0	17	43	23	83	.247	.390	August	.171	164	28	4	0	7	20	11	40	.220	.323
Scoring Posn	.199	166	33	6	0	6	56	21	54	.281	.343	Sept/Oct	.235	68	16	3	0	5	12	4	19	.278	.500
Close & Late	.211	109	23	4	0	6	21	5	38	.243	.413	vs. AL	.227	203	46	9	0	13	35	8	56	.254	.463
None on/out	.274	175	48	10	0	10	10	12	41	.324	.503	vs. NL	.224	465	104	18	0	21	62	46	127	.293	.398

Batter vs. Pitcher (career)

Hits Best Against	Avg	AB	H	2B	3B	HR	RBI	BB	SO	OBP	SLG	Hits Worst Against	Avg	AB	H	2B	3B	HR	RBI	BB	SO	OBP	SLG
F. Valenzuela	.583	12	7	1	0	2	4	0	1	.583	1.167	Tom Glavine	.050	20	1	0	0	0	0	0	2	.050	.050
Doug Drabek	.385	13	5	0	0	1	4	1	2	.400	.615	Ismael Valdes	.091	11	1	0	0	0	0	0	1	.091	.091
Greg Swindell	.364	11	4	2	0	2	4	2	1	.462	1.091	Jeff Fassero	.100	10	1	0	0	0	0	2	4	.250	.100
Kevin Gross	.364	11	4	1	0	0	2	0	2	.333	.455	Greg Maddux	.154	13	2	0	0	0	0	1	0	.214	.154
												Danny Jackson	.231	13	3	0	0	0	0	2	1	.333	.231

Chan Ho Park — Dodgers

Age 25 – Pitches Right

	ERA	W	L	Sv	G	GS	IP	BB	SO	Avg	H	2B	3B	HR	RBI	OBP	SLG	CG	ShO	Sup	QS	#P/S	SB	CS	GB	FB	G/F
1997 Season	3.38	14	8	0	32	29	192.0	70	166	.213	149	21	3	24	71	.290	.354	2	0	4.55	21	106	6	10	206	205	1.00
Career (1994-1997)	3.59	19	13	0	84	40	308.2	148	298	.212	238	37	3	33	118	.309	.338	2	0	4.08	24	101	10	15	345	302	1.14

1997 Season

	ERA	W	L	Sv	G	GS	IP	H	HR	BB	SO		Avg	AB	H	2B	3B	HR	RBI	BB	SO	OBP	SLG
Home	2.92	8	3	0	16	15	104.2	79	16	32	79	vs. Left	.237	363	86	11	2	13	37	49	73	.330	.386
Away	3.92	6	5	0	16	14	87.1	70	8	38	87	vs. Right	.187	337	63	10	1	11	34	21	93	.245	.320
Day	4.20	4	0	0	5	5	30.0	35	4	10	26	Inning 1-6	.212	612	130	18	3	21	64	61	149	.289	.355
Night	3.22	10	8	0	27	24	162.0	114	20	60	140	Inning 7+	.216	88	19	3	0	3	7	9	17	.296	.352
Grass	2.95	14	5	0	28	25	170.2	125	22	59	141	None on	.212	434	92	10	2	15	15	50	105	.298	.348
Turf	6.75	0	3	0	4	4	21.1	24	2	11	25	Runners on	.214	266	57	11	1	9	56	20	61	.277	.365
March/April	2.42	1	1	0	6	3	22.1	13	4	4	16	Scoring Posn	.239	109	26	6	1	2	40	13	28	.328	.367
May	3.48	2	1	0	5	5	31.0	23	4	15	26	Close & Late	.204	54	11	0	0	3	6	6	10	.295	.370
June	3.89	2	3	0	6	6	39.1	36	6	17	34	None on/out	.231	182	42	8	1	4	4	22	40	.317	.352
July	1.96	5	0	0	6	6	41.1	27	1	14	34	vs. 1st Batr (relief)	.000	3	0	0	0	0	0	0	0	.000	.000
August	3.78	3	1	0	5	5	33.1	28	4	9	24	1st Inning Pitched	.260	123	32	4	1	6	16	11	19	.336	.455
Sept/Oct	5.11	1	2	0	4	4	24.2	22	5	11	24	First 75 Pitches	.207	497	103	13	3	16	44	47	120	.282	.342
Starter	3.40	14	8	0	29	29	187.2	147	23	70	162	Pitch 76-90	.270	89	24	2	0	5	13	10	21	.347	.461
Reliever	2.08	0	0	0	3	0	4.1	2	1	0	4	Pitch 91-105	.181	72	13	4	0	2	11	8	14	.259	.319
0-3 Days Rest (Start)	1.50	1	0	0	2	2	12.0	4	2	4	9	Pitch 106+	.214	42	9	2	0	1	3	5	11	.313	.333
4 Days Rest	3.39	9	4	0	16	16	106.1	76	15	44	101	First Pitch	.230	87	20	1	0	4	7	1	0	.253	.379
5+ Days Rest	3.76	4	4	0	11	11	69.1	67	6	22	52	Ahead in Count	.140	314	44	5	2	6	22	0	138	.150	.226
vs. AL	2.13	0	0	0	2	2	12.2	10	1	5	9	Behind in Count	.377	159	60	11	1	10	28	30	0	.469	.648
vs. NL	3.46	14	8	0	30	27	179.1	139	23	65	157	Two Strikes	.121	339	41	5	2	5	22	39	166	.219	.192
Pre-All Star	3.29	5	5	0	18	15	98.1	76	15	40	80	Pre-All Star	.217	351	76	9	1	15	36	40	80	.300	.376
Post-All Star	3.46	9	3	0	14	14	93.2	73	9	30	86	Post-All Star	.209	349	73	12	2	9	35	30	86	.280	.332

Bob Patterson — Cubs

Age 39 – Pitches Left (flyball pitcher)

	ERA	W	L	Sv	G	GS	IP	BB	SO	Avg	H	2B	3B	HR	RBI	OBP	SLG	GF	IR	IRS	Hld	SvOp	SB	CS	GB	FB	G/F
1997 Season	3.34	1	6	0	76	0	59.1	10	58	.222	47	10	1	9	32	.252	.406	12	68	17	22	3	6	1	45	74	0.61
Last Five Years	3.64	13	18	10	316	0	262.0	71	228	.242	235	46	5	35	142	.294	.408	99	285	71	65	17	15	10	222	345	0.64

1997 Season

	ERA	W	L	Sv	G	GS	IP	H	HR	BB	SO		Avg	AB	H	2B	3B	HR	RBI	BB	SO	OBP	SLG
Home	3.34	1	3	0	42	0	35.0	21	7	4	35	vs. Left	.167	96	16	3	1	2	16	4	26	.196	.281
Away	3.33	0	3	0	34	0	24.1	26	2	6	23	vs. Right	.267	116	31	7	0	7	16	6	32	.298	.509
Day	3.47	1	2	0	45	0	36.1	30	8	5	32	Inning 1-6	.182	11	2	1	0	0	4	0	5	.182	.273
Night	3.13	0	4	0	31	0	23.0	17	1	5	26	Inning 7+	.224	201	45	9	1	9	28	10	53	.256	.413
Grass	3.20	1	5	0	64	0	50.2	39	9	7	53	None on	.210	105	22	4	0	5	5	4	27	.239	.390
Turf	4.15	0	1	0	12	0	8.2	8	0	3	5	Runners on	.234	107	25	6	1	4	27	6	31	.265	.421
March/April	3.75	1	1	0	13	0	12.0	13	1	1	11	Scoring Posn	.169	77	13	2	1	2	21	5	25	.209	.299

1997 Season

	ERA	W	L	Sv	G	GS	IP	H	HR	BB	SO		Avg	AB	H	2B	3B	HR	RBI	BB	SO	OBP	SLG
May	2.89	0	1	0	13	0	9.1	7	2	1	12	Close & Late	.240	121	29	5	0	4	17	5	35	.264	.380
June	5.23	0	1	0	14	0	10.1	7	2	4	6	None on/out	.213	47	10	0	0	2	2	1	10	.229	.340
July	0.93	0	1	0	13	0	9.2	7	0	1	11	vs. 1st Batr (relief)	.186	70	13	2	0	2	8	2	19	.205	.300
August	3.65	0	2	0	15	0	12.1	9	3	3	13	1st Inning Pitched	.212	184	39	8	1	6	27	9	50	.244	.364
Sept/Oct	3.18	0	0	0	8	0	5.2	4	1	0	5	First 15 Pitches	.243	169	41	8	1	6	28	8	40	.271	.408
Starter	0.00	0	0	0	0	0	0.0	0	0	0	0	Pitch 16-30	.146	41	6	2	0	3	4	2	17	.186	.415
Reliever	3.34	1	6	0	76	0	59.1	47	9	10	58	Pitch 31-45	.000	2	0	0	0	0	0	0	1	.000	.000
0 Days rest (Relief)	2.41	0	2	0	25	0	18.2	15	4	4	20	Pitch 46+	.000	0	0	0	0	0	0	0	0	.000	.000
1 or 2 Days rest	3.64	1	2	0	36	0	29.2	23	4	5	29	Ahead in Count	.159	113	18	4	0	4	15	0	52	.157	.301
3+ Days rest	4.09	0	2	0	15	0	11.0	9	1	1	9	Behind in Count	.395	43	17	5	1	3	10	3	0	.426	.767
vs. AL	0.00	0	0	0	8	0	5.0	4	0	1	2	Two Strikes	.111	117	13	3	0	3	11	6	58	.152	.214
vs. NL	3.64	1	6	0	68	0	54.1	43	9	9	56	Pre-All Star	.250	128	32	8	1	5	22	7	33	.281	.445
Pre-All Star	3.89	1	4	0	44	0	34.2	32	5	7	33	Post-All Star	.179	84	15	2	0	4	10	3	25	.207	.345
Post-All Star	2.55	0	2	0	32	0	24.2	15	4	3	25												

Last Five Years

	ERA	W	L	Sv	G	GS	IP	H	HR	BB	SO		Avg	AB	H	2B	3B	HR	RBI	BB	SO	OBP	SLG
Home	3.50	9	9	3	160	0	138.2	124	23	36	116	vs. Left	.204	402	82	20	2	7	53	25	97	.250	.316
Away	3.79	4	9	7	156	0	123.1	111	12	35	112	vs. Right	.269	568	153	26	3	28	89	46	131	.325	.474
Day	3.90	2	3	5	131	0	99.1	92	17	30	87	Inning 1-6	.268	71	19	6	0	3	18	9	20	.350	.479
Night	3.49	15	15	5	185	0	162.2	143	18	41	141	Inning 7+	.240	899	216	40	5	32	124	62	208	.290	.403
Grass	3.62	13	16	8	268	0	223.2	197	31	61	192	None on	.239	494	118	22	1	20	20	28	107	.285	.409
Turf	3.76	0	2	2	48	0	38.1	38	4	10	36	Runners on	.246	476	117	24	4	15	122	43	121	.303	.408
March/April	3.50	3	4	0	50	0	43.2	43	5	14	44	Scoring Posn	.249	297	74	13	3	10	107	34	75	.318	.414
May	3.50	4	5	1	52	0	46.1	44	7	14	37	Close & Late	.227	427	97	16	3	9	55	38	110	.289	.342
June	3.59	3	3	1	61	0	47.2	38	8	16	46	None on/out	.233	202	47	9	1	6	6	15	41	.292	.376
July	3.40	3	2	3	56	0	47.1	40	3	12	45	vs. 1st Batr (relief)	.217	286	62	13	1	7	44	19	83	.265	.343
August	3.86	0	2	4	57	0	49.0	42	10	8	31	1st Inning Pitched	.239	813	194	36	5	28	128	58	190	.289	.399
Sept/Oct	4.82	0	2	1	40	0	28.0	28	2	7	25	First 15 Pitches	.241	733	177	35	5	24	115	51	166	.290	.401
Starter	0.00	0	0	0	0	0	0.0	0	0	0	0	Pitch 16-30	.240	200	48	9	0	9	22	15	51	.300	.420
Reliever	3.64	13	18	10	316	0	262.0	235	35	71	228	Pitch 31-45	.242	33	8	1	0	2	5	5	10	.333	.455
0 Days rest (Relief)	3.05	3	6	6	93	0	76.2	62	8	24	82	Pitch 46+	.500	4	2	1	0	0	0	0	1	.500	.750
1 or 2 Days rest	3.59	6	8	3	140	0	117.2	108	17	26	91	First Pitch	.292	96	28	4	1	5	19	10	0	.357	.510
3+ Days rest	4.39	4	4	1	83	0	67.2	65	10	21	55	Ahead in Count	.199	522	104	20	2	14	59	0	192	.203	.326
vs. AL	3.82	9	9	2	169	0	153.0	146	20	40	119	Behind in Count	.316	177	56	12	1	10	30	29	0	.409	.565
vs. NL	3.39	4	9	8	147	0	109.0	89	15	31	109	Two Strikes	.170	505	86	15	1	15	62	32	228	.223	.293
Pre-All Star	3.49	12	14	3	181	0	154.2	143	22	49	144	Pre-All Star	.250	573	143	30	2	22	86	49	144	.306	.424
Post-All Star	3.86	1	4	7	135	0	107.1	92	13	22	84	Post-All Star	.232	397	92	16	3	13	56	22	84	.276	.385

Pitcher vs. Batter (career)

Pitches Best Vs.	Avg	AB	H	2B	3B	HR	RBI	BB	SO	OBP	SLG	Pitches Worst Vs.	Avg	AB	H	2B	3B	HR	RBI	BB	SO	OBP	SLG
Larry Walker	.000	9	0	0	0	0	1	1	3	.091	.000	Casey Candaele	.583	12	7	2	0	0	1	0	0	.583	.750
Darren Daulton	.059	17	1	0	0	0	1	1	3	.105	.059	Todd Hundley	.444	9	4	0	0	0	1	2	2	.545	.444
Ray Lankford	.067	15	1	0	1	0	1	0	5	.067	.200	Ryne Sandberg	.417	12	5	1	0	0	0	0	0	.417	.500
Eddie Murray	.143	14	2	0	0	0	1	0	3	.133	.143	Ken Caminiti	.385	13	5	1	1	1	5	1	6	.429	.846
Roberto Alomar	.154	13	2	0	0	0	0		5	.154	.154	Todd Zeile	.333	12	4	2	0	0	1	4	0	.333	.750

Danny Patterson — Rangers

Age 27 – Pitches Right (groundball pitcher)

	ERA	W	L	Sv	G	GS	IP	BB	SO	Avg	H	2B	3B	HR	RBI	OBP	SLG	GF	IR	IRS	Hld	SvOp	SB	CS	GB	FB	G/F
1997 Season	3.42	10	6	1	54	0	71.0	23	69	.263	70	12	2	3	38	.318	.357	17	50	19	9	8	3	4	119	41	2.90
Career (1996-1997)	3.05	10	6	1	61	0	79.2	26	74	.266	80	12	2	3	43	.321	.349	22	55	20	9	8	3	5	139	48	2.90

1997 Season

	ERA	W	L	Sv	G	GS	IP	H	HR	BB	SO		Avg	AB	H	2B	3B	HR	RBI	BB	SO	OBP	SLG
Home	4.58	5	5	1	28	0	37.1	38	0	15	37	vs. Left	.236	110	26	2	2	0	12	14	28	.323	.291
Away	2.14	5	1	0	26	0	33.2	32	3	8	32	vs. Right	.282	156	44	10	0	3	26	9	41	.315	.404
Day	1.53	2	1	0	13	0	17.2	12	1	4	25	Inning 1-6	.143	21	3	3	0	0	3	0	7	.143	.286
Night	4.05	6	6	1	41	0	53.1	58	2	19	44	Inning 7+	.273	245	67	9	2	3	35	23	62	.332	.363
Grass	3.65	8	6	1	50	0	66.2	67	3	23	62	None on	.258	132	34	4	0	3	3	10	35	.310	.356
Turf	0.00	2	0	0	4	0	4.1	3	0	0	7	Runners on	.269	134	36	8	2	0	35	13	34	.327	.358
March/April	1.93	2	2	0	10	0	9.1	9	0	2	14	Scoring Posn	.256	86	22	6	2	0	35	11	23	.330	.372
May	1.29	2	1	0	8	0	14.0	6	0	5	13	Close & Late	.283	159	45	7	1	3	29	16	40	.343	.396
June	4.50	1	0	0	7	0	10.0	8	0	6	8	None on/out	.268	56	15	1	0	1	1	5	14	.328	.339
July	3.52	2	1	0	10	0	15.1	15	2	4	11	vs. 1st Batr (relief)	.320	50	16	2	0	1	12	2	14	.333	.420
August	6.39	1	1	0	10	0	12.2	20	1	4	11	1st Inning Pitched	.291	179	52	8	1	2	33	15	47	.340	.380
Sept/Oct	2.79	2	1	0	9	0	9.2	12	0	2	12	First 15 Pitches	.301	166	50	8	1	3	29	12	40	.344	.416
Starter	0.00	0	0	0	0	0	0.0	0	0	0	0	Pitch 16-30	.183	82	15	4	0	0	7	9	24	.261	.232
Reliever	3.42	10	6	1	54	0	71.0	70	3	23	69	Pitch 31-45	.278	18	5	0	1	0	2	2	5	.350	.389
0 Days rest (Relief)	10.13	0	1	0	5	0	5.1	8	1	2	4	Pitch 46+	.000	0	0	0	0	0	0	0	0	.000	.000
1 or 2 Days rest	3.05	8	3	1	32	0	44.1	36	3	14	40	First Pitch	.340	47	16	4	1	0	15	3	0	.373	.468
3+ Days rest	2.53	2	2	0	17	0	21.1	26	0	7	25	Ahead in Count	.171	129	22	5	1	0	9	0	62	.169	.225
vs. AL	3.58	8	6	1	50	0	65.1	63	3	20	64	Behind in Count	.353	51	18	1	0	3	11	9	0	.443	.549
vs. NL	1.59	2	0	0	4	0	5.2	7	0	3	5	Two Strikes	.127	118	15	4	0	0	5	11	69	.202	.161
Pre-All Star	2.78	5	3	1	27	0	35.2	26	0	13	38	Pre-All Star	.208	125	26	5	0	0	15	13	38	.277	.248
Post-All Star	4.08	5	3	0	27	0	35.1	44	3	10	31	Post-All Star	.312	141	44	7	2	3	23	10	31	.358	.454

Roger Pavlik — Rangers
Age 30 – Pitches Right

	ERA	W	L	Sv	G	GS	IP	BB	SO	Avg	H	2B	3B	HR	RBI	OBP	SLG	CG	ShO	Sup	QS	#P/S	SB	CS	GB	FB	G/F
1997 Season	4.37	3	5	0	11	11	57.2	31	35	.267	59	15	0	7	25	.358	.430	0	0	4.68	7	89	2	2	83	61	1.36
Last Five Years	4.63	42	34	0	113	113	667.0	312	473	.260	661	122	17	80	304	.343	.416	11	1	5.09	62	97	35	25	877	733	1.20

1997 Season

	ERA	W	L	Sv	G	GS	IP	H	HR	BB	SO		Avg	AB	H	2B	3B	HR	RBI	BB	SO	OBP	SLG
Home	3.13	3	2	0	6	6	31.2	28	2	14	20	vs. Left	.221	113	25	5	0	1	6	20	20	.336	.292
Away	5.88	0	3	0	5	5	26.0	31	5	17	15	vs. Right	.315	108	34	10	0	6	19	11	15	.383	.574

Last Five Years

	ERA	W	L	Sv	G	GS	IP	H	HR	BB	SO		Avg	AB	H	2B	3B	HR	RBI	BB	SO	OBP	SLG
Home	4.63	26	16	0	59	59	352.0	332	37	147	248	vs. Left	.252	1373	346	57	11	36	151	176	259	.337	.388
Away	4.63	16	18	0	54	54	315.0	329	43	165	225	vs. Right	.270	1168	315	65	6	44	153	136	214	.351	.449
Day	4.35	13	8	0	26	26	147.0	146	17	72	111	Inning 1-6	.260	2189	570	108	15	68	273	278	409	.346	.417
Night	4.71	29	26	0	87	87	520.0	515	63	240	362	Inning 7+	.259	352	91	14	2	12	31	34	64	.323	.412
Grass	4.40	38	25	0	95	95	571.0	543	65	262	401	None on	.254	1524	387	76	13	49	49	157	295	.326	.417
Turf	6.00	4	9	0	18	18	96.0	118	15	50	72	Runners on	.269	1017	274	46	4	31	255	155	178	.367	.414
March/April	6.94	5	2	0	12	12	58.1	64	10	39	38	Scoring Posn	.262	603	158	30	2	20	224	93	105	.359	.418
May	4.30	9	6	0	18	18	115.0	128	12	36	79	Close & Late	.266	199	53	7	2	7	21	22	41	.338	.427
June	6.69	6	7	0	20	20	106.1	118	14	58	68	None on/out	.266	676	180	33	5	25	25	67	121	.336	.441
July	4.05	7	8	0	19	19	113.1	120	12	55	84	vs. 1st Batr (relief)	.000	0	0	0	0	0	0	0	0	.000	.000
August	4.21	7	7	0	20	20	132.2	120	20	56	101	1st Inning Pitched	.318	444	141	30	4	14	93	69	74	.409	.498
Sept/Oct	3.25	8	4	0	24	24	141.1	111	12	68	103	First 75 Pitches	.268	1794	480	88	15	55	233	236	324	.355	.425
Starter	4.63	42	34	0	113	113	667.0	661	80	312	473	Pitch 76-90	.233	339	79	17	1	11	31	34	76	.308	.386
Reliever	0.00	0	0	0	0	0	0.0	0	0	0	0	Pitch 91-105	.239	259	62	7	1	10	23	23	44	.304	.390
0-3 Days Rest (Start)	1.98	4	2	0	10	10	68.1	43	6	27	48	Pitch 106+	.268	149	40	10	0	4	17	19	29	.351	.416
4 Days Rest	4.73	20	20	0	62	62	369.1	374	40	171	247	First Pitch	.331	369	122	27	2	15	56	11	0	.353	.537
5+ Days Rest	5.26	18	12	0	41	41	229.1	244	34	114	178	Ahead in Count	.189	1124	212	39	2	28	113	0	401	.194	.302
vs. AL	4.63	42	34	0	113	113	667.0	661	80	312	473	Behind in Count	.317	574	182	32	8	25	82	176	0	.474	.531
vs. NL	0.00	0	0	0	0	0	0.0	0	0	0	0	Two Strikes	.188	1134	213	42	3	25	100	125	473	.274	.296
Pre-All Star	5.43	24	17	0	56	56	316.1	352	38	147	213	Pre-All Star	.284	1241	352	63	9	38	167	147	213	.361	.441
Post-All Star	3.90	18	17	0	57	57	350.2	309	42	165	260	Post-All Star	.238	1300	309	59	8	42	137	165	260	.327	.392

Pitcher vs. Batter (career)

Pitches Best Vs.	Avg	AB	H	2B	3B	HR	RBI	BB	SO	OBP	SLG	Pitches Worst Vs.	Avg	AB	H	2B	3B	HR	RBI	BB	SO	OBP	SLG
Manny Ramirez	.000	13	0	0	0	0	1	2	3	.133	.000	Carlos Delgado	.667	12	8	3	0	2	8	1	2	.692	1.417
Vince Coleman	.000	11	0	0	0	0	2	2	1	.143	.000	Rafael Palmeiro	.533	15	8	0	1	3	2	2	2	.579	.733
Jason Giambi	.077	13	1	0	0	0	1	4		.143	.077	Chuck Knoblauch	.484	31	15	2	1	2	4	6	0	.579	.806
Lance Johnson	.120	25	3	0	0	0	1	3		.154	.120	Mark Lewis	.417	12	5	1	1	1	3	2	2	.467	.917
Greg Myers	.143	14	2	0	0	0	1	0	3	.133	.143	Scott Brosius	.412	17	7	0	0	2	2	5	4	.545	.765

Rudy Pemberton — Red Sox
Age 28 – Bats Right

	Avg	G	AB	R	H	2B	3B	HR	RBI	BB	SO	HBP	GDP	SB	CS	OBP	SLG	IBB	SH	SF	#Pit	#P/PA	GB	FB	G/F
1997 Season	.238	27	63	8	15	2	0	2	10	4	13	3	0	0	0	.314	.365	0	0	0	231	3.30	20	18	1.11
Career (1995-1997)	.336	52	134	22	45	13	1	3	23	7	22	6	3	3	1	.395	.515	0	0	0	472	3.21	44	37	1.19

1997 Season

	Avg	AB	H	2B	3B	HR	RBI	BB	SO	OBP	SLG		Avg	AB	H	2B	3B	HR	RBI	BB	SO	OBP	SLG
vs. Left	.218	55	12	2	0	2	9	3	12	.283	.364	Scoring Posn	.250	16	4	0	0	2	10	2	4	.368	.625
vs. Right	.375	8	3	0	0	1	1	1	1	.500	.375	Close & Late	.125	8	1	1	0	0	1	1	2	.300	.250

Tony Pena — Astros
Age 41 – Bats Right (groundball hitter)

	Avg	G	AB	R	H	2B	3B	HR	RBI	BB	SO	HBP	GDP	SB	CS	OBP	SLG	IBB	SH	SF	#Pit	#P/PA	GB	FB	G/F
1997 Season	.174	40	86	6	15	4	0	0	10	10	16	0	3	0	0	.255	.221	0	0	2	398	4.06	33	23	1.43
Last Five Years	.219	364	939	83	206	42	1	12	94	73	142	3	37	2	5	.275	.305	1	20	10	3909	3.74	397	228	1.74

1997 Season

	Avg	AB	H	2B	3B	HR	RBI	BB	SO	OBP	SLG		Avg	AB	H	2B	3B	HR	RBI	BB	SO	OBP	SLG
vs. Left	.268	41	11	3	0	0	6	5	3	.348	.341	Scoring Posn	.227	22	5	1	0	0	9	4	6	.321	.273
vs. Right	.089	45	4	1	0	0	4	5	13	.173	.111	Close & Late	.200	10	2	1	0	0	1	1	3	.273	.300

Last Five Years

	Avg	AB	H	2B	3B	HR	RBI	BB	SO	OBP	SLG		Avg	AB	H	2B	3B	HR	RBI	BB	SO	OBP	SLG
vs. Left	.278	324	90	16	1	6	33	16	29	.311	.389	First Pitch	.293	164	48	6	0	2	15	1	0	.292	.366
vs. Right	.189	615	116	26	0	6	61	57	113	.257	.260	Ahead in Count	.260	200	52	8	0	5	27	43	0	.392	.375
Groundball	.230	148	34	9	0	1	20	12	26	.288	.311	Behind in Count	.172	395	68	19	1	3	32	0	117	.175	.248
Flyball	.204	181	37	8	0	5	14	14	37	.266	.331	Two Strikes	.164	427	70	18	1	3	37	29	142	.218	.232
Home	.191	445	85	24	0	4	42	42	75	.260	.272	Batting #8	.198	388	77	11	0	3	38	31	55	.254	.250
Away	.245	494	121	18	1	8	52	31	67	.289	.334	Batting #9	.238	530	126	31	1	8	53	40	85	.293	.345
Day	.231	342	79	15	1	3	33	34	42	.296	.307	Other	.143	21	3	0	0	1	3	2	2	.217	.286
Night	.213	597	127	27	0	9	61	39	100	.263	.303	March/April	.202	119	24	3	0	0	10	8	14	.246	.227
Grass	.208	788	164	33	0	10	75	66	127	.270	.288	May	.260	204	53	10	1	3	21	18	36	.318	.363
Turf	.278	151	42	9	1	2	19	7	15	.304	.391	June	.213	174	37	9	0	3	10	19	32	.290	.391
Pre-All Star	.229	558	128	27	1	6	47	50	86	.291	.314	July	.198	182	36	8	0	3	17	13	23	.254	.291
Post-All Star	.205	381	78	15	0	6	47	23	56	.252	.291	August	.158	139	22	5	0	1	16	7	21	.201	.216
Scoring Posn	.231	255	59	13	1	3	81	22	51	.285	.325	Sept/Oct	.281	121	34	7	0	2	20	8	16	.323	.388
Close & Late	.202	99	20	6	0	1	4	8	20	.269	.293	vs. AL	.220	920	202	39	1	12	92	71	140	.275	.303
None on/out	.237	207	49	0	0	3	3	16	23	.291	.319	vs. NL	.211	19	4	3	0	0	2	2	2	.273	.368

Batter vs. Pitcher (since 1984)

Hits Best Against	Avg	AB	H	2B	3B	HR	RBI	BB	SO	OBP	SLG	Hits Worst Against	Avg	AB	H	2B	3B	HR	RBI	BB	SO	OBP	SLG
Kenny Rogers	.500	12	6	2	0	0	1	1	0	.538	.667	James Baldwin	.000	12	0	0	0	0	0	0	2	.000	.000
Terry Mulholland	.455	11	5	1	0	0	0	1	0	.500	.545	Pat Hentgen	.000	12	0	0	0	0	0	0	4	.077	.000
Chris Haney	.455	11	5	0	0	1	1	0	0	.455	.727	Scott Erickson	.100	20	2	0	0	0	1	3	5	.217	.100
Jimmy Key	.444	36	16	2	0	2	6	0	1	.444	.667	Scott Kamieniecki	.100	10	1	0	0	0	1	0	1	.182	.100
Ben McDonald	.381	21	8	2	0	0	3	6	4	.519	.476	Kevin Tapani	.111	18	2	1	0	0	1	2	.158	.167

Terry Pendleton — Reds
Age 37 – Bats Both

	Avg	G	AB	R	H	2B	3B	HR	RBI	BB	SO	HBP	GDP	SB	CS	OBP	SLG	IBB	SH	SF	#Pit	#P/PA	GB	FB	G/F
1997 Season	.248	50	113	11	28	9	0	1	17	12	14	0	1	2	1	.320	.354	1	0	0	470	3.76	45	38	1.18
Last Five Years	.263	574	2136	238	562	118	6	50	284	139	363	8	52	12	7	.308	.394	22	7	16	8538	3.70	800	613	1.31

1997 Season

	Avg	AB	H	2B	3B	HR	RBI	BB	SO	OBP	SLG		Avg	AB	H	2B	3B	HR	RBI	BB	SO	OBP	SLG
vs. Left	.316	38	12	4	0	0	6	6	3	.409	.421	Scoring Posn	.297	37	11	3	0	1	16	4	3	.366	.459
vs. Right	.213	75	16	5	0	1	11	6	11	.272	.320	Close & Late	.158	19	3	3	0	0	2	4	4	.304	.316
Home	.274	73	20	6	0	1	14	6	8	.329	.397	None on/out	.238	21	5	2	0	0	0	2	4	.304	.333
Away	.200	40	8	3	0	0	3	6	6	.304	.275	Batting #3	.250	44	11	5	0	1	9	6	5	.340	.432
First Pitch	.235	17	4	3	0	0	2	1	0	.278	.412	Batting #6	.190	21	4	1	0	0	3	2	2	.261	.238
Ahead in Count	.313	32	10	3	0	0	4	9	0	.463	.406	Other	.271	48	13	3	0	0	5	1	4	.327	.333
Behind in Count	.184	38	7	2	0	1	7	0	13	.184	.316	Pre-All Star	.248	113	28	9	0	1	17	12>14		.320	.354
Two Strikes	.170	47	8	2	0	1	8	2	14	.204	.277	Post-All Star	.000	0	0	0	0	0	0	0	0	.000	.000

Last Five Years

	Avg	AB	H	2B	3B	HR	RBI	BB	SO	OBP	SLG		Avg	AB	H	2B	3B	HR	RBI	BB	SO	OBP	SLG
vs. Left	.282	571	161	28	2	9	78	30	56	.318	.385	First Pitch	.297	300	89	19	2	9	63	17	0	.329	.463
vs. Right	.256	1565	401	90	4	41	206	109	307	.305	.397	Ahead in Count	.290	420	122	28	1	14	65	73	0	.392	.462
Groundball	.242	586	142	31	1	14	69	41	103	.292	.370	Behind in Count	.227	1018	231	44	2	13	91	0	314	.230	.312
Flyball	.274	369	101	18	4	9	51	23	60	.318	.417	Two Strikes	.193	1005	194	39	3	11	81	49	363	.231	.271
Home	.274	1081	296	61	4	27	156	67	191	.314	.413	Batting #5	.261	437	114	26	1	9	59	29	73	.306	.387
Away	.252	1055	266	57	2	23	128	72	172	.303	.375	Batting #6	.273	667	182	40	5	19	102	43	121	.319	.433
Day	.271	580	157	27	1	11	69	39	107	.316	.378	Other	.258	1032	266	52	0	22	123	67	169	.302	.372
Night	.260	1556	405	91	5	39	215	100	256	.305	.400	March/April	.243	317	77	10	1	8	33	23	50	.294	.356
Grass	.270	1647	444	90	5	41	218	101	279	.312	.405	May	.231	459	106	20	2	6	57	20	81	.264	.322
Turf	.241	489	118	28	1	9	66	38	84	.298	.358	June	.295	373	110	31	0	5	46	19	60	.331	.418
Pre-All Star	.259	1255	325	70	3	22	155	75	204	.302	.372	July	.280	322	90	19	1	9	47	23	53	.328	.429
Post-All Star	.269	881	237	48	3	28	129	64	159	.318	.426	August	.301	356	107	21	1	9	54	28	57	.351	.441
Scoring Posn	.280	574	161	35	1	12	219	62	87	.344	.408	Sept/Oct	.233	309	72	17	1	13	47	26	62	.292	.421
Close & Late	.259	328	85	16	1	6	33	37	67	.334	.369	vs. AL	.348	23	8	1	0	1	6	4	1	.444	.522
None on/out	.265	479	127	23	1	14	14	19	98	.295	.405	vs. NL	.262	2113	554	117	6	49	278	135	362	.307	.393

Batter vs. Pitcher (career)

Hits Best Against	Avg	AB	H	2B	3B	HR	RBI	BB	SO	OBP	SLG	Hits Worst Against	Avg	AB	H	2B	3B	HR	RBI	BB	SO	OBP	SLG
Shane Reynolds	.600	10	6	2	0	0	3	0	0	.545	.800	Curt Leskanic	.000	11	0	0	0	0	1	2	4	.154	.000
Brian Williams	.571	14	8	1	0	1	7	0	3	.571	.857	Jon Lieber	.071	14	1	0	0	0	1	0	1	.071	.071
Norm Charlton	.500	18	9	1	1	1	6	1	1	.526	.833	Rod Beck	.100	20	2	1	0	0	1	7	.143	.150
Mike Williams	.500	12	6	4	0	0	3	1	0	.538	.833	Todd Worrell	.100	10	1	0	0	0	2	1	3	.182	.100
Shawn Boskie	.471	17	8	4	0	1	1	1	1	.500	.882	Dennis Eckersley	.143	14	2	0	0	0	0	3	.143	.143

Troy Percival — Angels
Age 28 – Pitches Right (flyball pitcher)

	ERA	W	L	Sv	G	GS	IP	BB	SO	Avg	H	2B	3B	HR	RBI	OBP	SLG	GF	IR	IRS	Hld	SvOp	SB	CS	GB	FB	G/F
1997 Season	3.46	5	5	27	55	0	52.0	22	72	.205	40	9	0	6	21	.296	.344	46	27	5	0	31	4	1	33	66	0.50
Career (1995-1997)	2.47	8	9	66	179	0	200.0	79	266	.164	115	21	0	20	66	.254	.279	114	108	18	31	76	26	3	119	238	0.50

1997 Season

	ERA	W	L	Sv	G	GS	IP	H	HR	BB	SO		Avg	AB	H	2B	3B	HR	RBI	BB	SO	OBP	SLG
Home	3.03	4	3	14	32	0	29.2	20	4	12	36	vs. Left	.235	102	24	6	0	2	10	13	42	.331	.353
Away	4.03	1	2	13	23	0	22.1	20	2	10	36	vs. Right	.172	93	16	3	0	4	11	9	30	.257	.333
Day	1.69	0	0	10	15	0	16.0	11	0	8	26	Inning 1-6	.000	0	0	0	0	0	0	0	0	.000	.000
Night	4.25	5	5	17	40	0	36.0	29	6	14	46	Inning 7+	.205	195	40	9	0	6	21	22	72	.296	.344
Grass	3.78	5	5	24	50	0	47.2	40	6	22	65	None on	.216	97	21	6	0	4	9	35	.296	.402
Turf	0.00	0	0	3	5	0	4.1	0	0	0	7	Runners on	.194	98	19	3	0	2	17	13	37	.296	.286
March/April	20.25	0	2	0	3	0	2.2	6	2	4	4	Scoring Posn	.179	67	12	2	0	1	15	11	26	.296	.254
May	0.00	2	0	3	5	0	5.2	3	0	0	6	Close & Late	.204	137	28	4	0	6	19	15	52	.299	.365
June	1.38	0	1	6	13	0	13.0	5	1	5	11	None on/out	.128	39	5	2	0	0	5	16	.227	.179
July	6.55	2	2	5	13	0	11.0	10	3	7	18	vs. 1st Batr (relief)	.106	47	5	2	0	1	3	8	20	.236	.213
August	1.80	0	0	9	11	0	10.0	7	0	1	16	1st Inning Pitched	.203	182	37	9	0	5	20	21	68	.297	.335
Sept/Oct	1.86	1	0	4	10	0	9.2	9	0	5	17	First 15 Pitches	.180	133	24	6	0	4	12	11	50	.255	.316
Starter	0.00	0	0	0	0	0	0.0	0	0	0	0	Pitch 16-30	.276	58	16	3	0	2	8	21	.364	.431
Reliever	3.46	5	5	27	55	0	52.0	40	6	22	72	Pitch 31-45	.000	4	0	0	0	0	3	3	1	.500	.000
0 Days rest (Relief)	3.46	0	2	10	16	0	13.0	13	3	3	19	Pitch 46+	.000	0	0	0	0	0	0	0	.000	.000
1 or 2 Days rest	2.96	2	2	13	25	0	24.1	15	3	12	30	First Pitch	.375	16	6	3	0	1	1	0	.412	.563
3+ Days rest	4.30	3	1	4	14	0	14.2	12	0	7	23	Ahead in Count	.182	121	22	3	0	3	9	0	61	.200	.281
vs. AL	3.50	5	3	24	47	0	43.2	34	4	20	64	Behind in Count	.208	24	5	1	0	3	10	0	.441	.417
vs. NL	3.24	0	2	3	8	0	8.1	6	2	2	8	Two Strikes	.161	124	20	3	0	3	10	11	72	.245	.258
Pre-All Star	3.24	3	4	10	24	0	25.0	16	4	10	23	Pre-All Star	.178	90	16	3	0	4	8	10	23	.279	.344
Post-All Star	3.67	2	1	17	31	0	27.0	24	2	12	49	Post-All Star	.229	105	24	6	0	2	13	12	49	.311	.343

Career (1995-1997)

	ERA	W	L	Sv	G	GS	IP	H	HR	BB	SO		Avg	AB	H	2B	3B	HR	RBI	BB	SO	OBP	SLG
Home	2.32	5	5	32	97	0	104.2	57	13	43	146	vs. Left	.174	351	61	14	0	6	26	45	133	.272	.265
Away	2.64	3	4	34	82	0	95.1	58	7	36	120	vs. Right	.154	351	54	7	0	14	40	34	133	.235	.293
Day	1.85	0	0	16	51	0	63.1	33	3	25	94	Inning 1-6	.000	4	0	0	0	0	0	0	1	.000	.000
Night	2.77	8	9	50	128	0	136.2	82	17	54	172	Inning 7+	.165	698	115	21	0	20	66	79	265	.255	.281
Grass	2.58	8	9	60	160	0	177.2	106	20	74	235	None on	.166	379	63	14	0	12	12	38	145	.251	.298
Turf	1.61	0	0	6	19	0	22.1	9	0	5	31	Runners on	.161	323	52	7	0	8	54	41	121	.257	.257
March/April	4.80	0	2	8	15	0	15.0	15	2	5	19	Scoring Posn	.175	194	34	6	0	4	46	28	73	.278	.268
May	2.59	3	1	8	28	0	31.1	18	6	8	43	Close & Late	.168	477	80	7	0	17	53	49	171	.251	.289
June	1.54	0	1	15	38	0	41.0	18	3	22	44	None on/out	.136	147	20	6	0	1	1	19	59	.244	.197
July	2.50	3	2	11	35	0	39.2	25	4	16	49	vs. 1st Batr (relief)	.131	160	21	5	0	3	14	15	68	.213	.219
August	1.69	0	0	17	33	0	37.1	17	2	8	53	1st Inning Pitched	.160	575	92	19	0	16	56	55	219	.240	.277
Sept/Oct	3.28	2	3	7	30	0	35.2	22	3	20	58	First 15 Pitches	.159	441	70	16	0	13	41	35	166	.227	.283
Starter	0.00	0	0	0	0	0	0.0	0	0	0	0	Pitch 16-30	.180	222	40	5	0	6	17	30	84	.281	.284
Reliever	2.47	8	9	66	179	0	200.0	115	20	79	266	Pitch 31-45	.143	35	5	0	0	1	8	13	14	.388	.229
0 Days rest (Relief)	2.93	2	4	24	49	0	46.0	30	10	10	60	Pitch 46+	.000	4	0	0	0	0	0	1	2	.200	.000
1 or 2 Days rest	2.09	2	3	31	80	0	94.2	50	6	39	123	First Pitch	.246	65	16	5	0	2	6	7	0	.319	.415
3+ Days rest	2.73	4	2	11	50	0	59.1	35	4	30	83	Ahead in Count	.132	425	56	9	0	10	30	0	220	.140	.224
vs. AL	2.44	8	7	63	171	0	191.2	109	18	71	258	Behind in Count	.198	81	16	4	0	3	11	31	0	.416	.358
vs. NL	3.24	2	3	8	0	8.1		6	2	2	8	Two Strikes	.127	458	58	9	0	13	35	41	266	.206	.231
Pre-All Star	2.36	4	5	32	89	0	99.0	55	12	39	120	Pre-All Star	.159	345	55	10	0	12	33	39	120	.253	.293
Post-All Star	2.58	4	4	34	90	0	101.0	60	8	40	146	Post-All Star	.168	357	60	11	0	8	33	40	146	.255	.266

Pitcher vs. Batter (career)

Pitches Best Vs.	Avg	AB	H	2B	3B	HR	RBI	BB	SO	OBP	SLG	Pitches Worst Vs.	Avg	AB	H	2B	3B	HR	RBI	BB	SO	OBP	SLG
Scott Brosius	.091	11	1	0	0	0	0	1	5	.167	.091	Geronimo Berroa	.333	9	3	0	0	1	4	4	3	.538	.667
Mark McGwire	.091	11	1	0	0	0	0	4	5	.333	.091												

Carlos Perez — Expos

Age 27 – Pitches Left

	ERA	W	L	Sv	G	GS	IP	BB	SO	Avg	H	2B	3B	HR	RBI	OBP	SLG	CG	ShO	Sup	QS	#P/S	SB	CS	GB	FB	G/F
1997 Season	3.88	12	13	0	33	32	206.2	48	110	.260	206	51	9	21	101	.303	.426	8	5	4.31	15	89	11	4	291	241	1.21
Career (1995-1997)	3.80	22	21	0	61	55	348.0	76	216	.259	348	79	12	39	157	.301	.422	10	6	4.45	27	88	25	11	513	375	1.37

1997 Season

	ERA	W	L	Sv	G	GS	IP	H	HR	BB	SO		Avg	AB	H	2B	3B	HR	RBI	BB	SO	OBP	SLG
Home	4.26	7	5	0	18	17	107.2	118	8	24	59	vs. Left	.194	139	27	4	0	2	14	11	20	.257	.266
Away	3.45	5	8	0	15	15	99.0	88	13	24	51	vs. Right	.274	654	179	47	9	19	87	37	90	.313	.460
Day	4.42	2	3	0	7	6	36.2	38	5	8	14	Inning 1-6	.264	658	174	45	9	19	92	45	91	.312	.447
Night	3.76	10	10	0	26	26	170.0	168	16	40	96	Inning 7+	.237	135	32	6	0	2	9	3	19	.257	.326
Grass	3.26	4	6	0	12	12	77.1	67	10	17	35	None on	.235	485	114	29	4	11	11	35	82	.289	.379
Turf	4.24	8	7	0	21	20	129.1	139	11	31	75	Runners on	.299	308	92	22	5	10	90	13	28	.324	.500
March/April	3.51	4	1	0	6	5	33.1	36	2	8	16	Scoring Posn	.303	175	53	12	5	6	78	9	16	.332	.531
May	6.18	0	3	0	5	5	27.2	29	6	13	9	Close & Late	.257	70	18	2	0	2	7	1	8	.274	.371
June	1.96	4	1	0	6	6	46.0	39	1	8	21	None on/out	.249	205	51	11	2	6	6	15	30	.303	.410
July	5.13	2	1	0	5	5	33.1	36	7	7	19	vs. 1st Batr (relief)	1.000	1	1	0	0	0	0	0	0	1.000	1.000
August	6.00	1	4	0	6	6	36.0	42	4	6	26	1st Inning Pitched	.248	125	31	8	2	3	19	17	17	.336	.416
Sept/Oct	1.19	1	3	0	5	5	30.1	24	2	6	19	First 75 Pitches	.260	603	157	39	7	17	78	41	85	.308	.433
Starter	3.85	12	13	0	32	32	205.2	203	21	48	109	Pitch 76-90	.250	108	27	8	2	2	13	3	16	.274	.417
Reliever	9.00	0	0	0	1	0	1.0	3	0	0	1	Pitch 91-105	.262	61	16	4	0	2	10	4	6	.308	.426
0-3 Days Rest (Start)	0.00	0	0	0	0	0	0.0	0	0	0	0	Pitch 106+	.286	21	6	0	0	0	0	0	3	.286	.286
4 Days Rest	3.69	6	8	0	18	18	114.2	106	12	29	66	First Pitch	.347	124	43	10	3	6	21	1	0	.357	.621
5+ Days Rest	4.05	6	5	0	14	14	91.0	97	9	19	43	Ahead in Count	.209	369	77	19	2	4	25	0	103	.212	.304
vs. AL	1.39	3	0	0	4	4	32.1	23	0	2	16	Behind in Count	.323	158	51	15	3	7	33	28	0	.416	.589
vs. NL	4.34	9	13	0	29	28	174.1	183	21	46	94	Two Strikes	.180	305	55	12	2	6	27	19	110	.232	.292
Pre-All Star	3.52	8	5	0	18	17	115.0	112	9	30	50	Pre-All Star	.256	438	112	31	6	9	54	30	50	.305	.416
Post-All Star	4.32	4	8	0	15	15	91.2	94	12	18	60	Post-All Star	.265	355	94	20	3	12	47	18	60	.301	.439

Eddie Perez — Braves

Age 30 – Bats Right

	Avg	G	AB	R	H	2B	3B	HR	RBI	BB	SO	HBP	GDP	SB	CS	OBP	SLG	IBB	SH	SF	#Pit	#P/PA	GB	FB	G/F
1997 Season	.215	73	191	20	41	5	0	6	18	10	35	2	8	0	1	.259	.335	0	1	2	752	3.65	69	63	1.10
Career (1995-1997)	.236	148	360	40	85	15	1	9	39	18	56	3	14	0	1	.275	.375	0	1	4	1329	3.44	132	120	1.10

1997 Season

	Avg	AB	H	2B	3B	HR	RBI	BB	SO	OBP	SLG		Avg	AB	H	2B	3B	HR	RBI	BB	SO	OBP	SLG
vs. Left	.170	53	9	2	0	2	6	1	8	.185	.321	Scoring Posn	.128	47	6	0	0	1	13	2	6	.173	.191
vs. Right	.232	138	32	3	0	4	12	9	27	.285	.341	Close & Late	.192	26	5	0	0	2	2	4	5	.300	.423
Home	.260	100	26	2	0	4	11	3	18	.295	.400	None on/out	.209	43	9	2	0	1	1	3	9	.261	.326
Away	.165	91	15	3	0	2	7	7	17	.220	.264	Batting #7	.216	139	30	4	0	5	13	7	24	.262	.353
First Pitch	.233	30	7	0	0	0	4	0	0	.250	.233	Batting #8	.207	29	6	0	0	0	3	3	8	.273	.207
Ahead in Count	.235	34	8	1	0	0	4	8	0	.372	.265	Other	.217	23	5	1	0	1	2	0	3	.217	.391
Behind in Count	.176	102	18	1	0	4	7	0	31	.184	.304	Pre-All Star	.250	96	24	3	0	3	8	7	16	.298	.375
Two Strikes	.153	98	15	3	0	5	8	2	35	.178	.337	Post-All Star	.179	95	17	2	0	3	10	3	19	.218	.295

Eduardo Perez — Reds

	Avg	G	AB	R	H	2B	3B	HR	RBI	BB	SO	HBP	GDP	SB	CS	OBP	SLG	IBB	SH	SF	#Pit	#P/PA	GB	FB	G/F
1997 Season	.253	106	297	44	75	18	0	16	52	29	76	2	6	5	1	.321	.475	1	0	2	1342	4.07	100	80	1.25
Career (1993-1997)	.234	243	713	87	167	35	3	29	110	67	162	6	20	13	7	.303	.414	3	1	5	3035	3.83	245	209	1.17

1997 Season

	Avg	AB	H	2B	3B	HR	RBI	BB	SO	OBP	SLG		Avg	AB	H	2B	3B	HR	RBI	BB	SO	OBP	SLG
vs. Left	.275	102	28	6	0	8	24	13	19	.362	.569	First Pitch	.296	27	8	1	0	1	5	0	0	.286	.444
vs. Right	.241	195	47	12	0	8	28	16	57	.299	.426	Ahead in Count	.368	57	21	6	0	6	17	16	0	.507	.789
Groundball	.250	56	14	4	0	1	6	9	18	.364	.375	Behind in Count	.219	151	33	8	0	6	20	0	65	.229	.391
Flyball	.231	39	9	0	0	3	8	2	13	.268	.462	Two Strikes	.172	163	28	5	0	7	22	12	76	.236	.331
Home	.235	153	36	9	0	7	26	20	46	.324	.431	Batting #4	.261	211	55	17	0	12	38	21	57	.331	.512
Away	.271	144	39	9	0	9	26	9	30	.318	.521	Batting #5	.237	38	9	0	0	2	8	3	8	.293	.395
Day	.233	120	28	7	0	4	18	10	35	.290	.392	Other	.229	48	11	1	0	2	6	5	11	.302	.375
Night	.266	177	47	11	0	12	34	19	41	.342	.531	March/April	.324	34	11	1	0	0	6	3	8	.378	.353
Grass	.275	102	28	6	0	7	19	5	20	.309	.539	May	.219	32	7	1	0	2	4	5	8	.324	.438
Turf	.241	195	47	12	0	9	33	24	56	.327	.441	June	.256	39	10	3	0	2	5	3	8	.310	.487
Pre-All Star	.259	112	29	5	0	4	16	11	26	.325	.411	July	.241	29	7	1	0	3	8	5	9	.371	.586
Post-All Star	.249	185	46	13	0	12	36	18	50	.319	.514	August	.305	105	32	9	0	7	24	8	24	.353	.590
Scoring Posn	.250	92	23	5	0	5	39	19	27	.377	.467	Sept/Oct	.138	58	8	3	0	2	5	5	19	.206	.293
Close & Late	.372	43	16	4	0	3	7	6	8	.449	.674	vs. AL	.227	22	5	2	0	1	3	3	4	.346	.455
None on/out	.197	76	15	2	0	3	3	7	17	.274	.342	vs. NL	.255	275	70	16	0	15	49	26	72	.319	.476

1997 By Position

Position	Avg	AB	H	2B	3B	HR	RBI	BB	SO	OBP	SLG	G	GS	Innings	PO	A	E	DP	Fld Pct	Rng Fctr	In Zone	Outs	Zone Rtg	MLB Zone
As Pinch Hitter	.238	21	5	1	0	1	2	3	3	.333	.429	27	0	—	—	—	—	—	—	—	—	—	—	—
As 1b	.241	220	53	14	0	13	37	20	59	.307	.482	67	58	525.0	489	33	2	37	.996	—	87	75	.862	.874
As lf	.323	31	10	2	0	1	8	0	6	.323	.484	11	9	65.1	12	0	0	0	1.000	1.65	18	12	.667	.805

Career (1993-1997)

	Avg	AB	H	2B	3B	HR	RBI	BB	SO	OBP	SLG		Avg	AB	H	2B	3B	HR	RBI	BB	SO	OBP	SLG
vs. Left	.251	239	60	13	1	13	50	29	42	.337	.477	First Pitch	.271	85	23	5	0	2	11	2	0	.292	.400
vs. Right	.226	474	107	22	2	16	60	38	120	.286	.382	Ahead in Count	.333	129	43	11	1	11	34	32	0	.466	.690
Groundball	.211	147	31	6	0	3	16	21	36	.312	.313	Behind in Count	.191	367	70	15	1	11	41	0	143	.200	.327
Flyball	.233	146	34	4	1	8	27	8	33	.276	.438	Two Strikes	.158	366	58	12	1	11	43	32	162	.230	.287
Home	.213	357	76	15	3	15	53	44	86	.300	.398	Batting #4	.255	216	55	17	0	12	38	21	58	.324	.500
Away	.256	356	91	20	0	14	57	23	76	.307	.430	Batting #6	.229	214	49	12	2	11	41	23	50	.305	.458
Day	.244	242	59	14	0	7	30	22	67	.307	.388	Other	.223	283	63	6	1	6	31	23	54	.286	.314
Night	.229	471	108	21	3	22	80	45	95	.302	.427	March/April	.231	130	30	6	1	5	22	15	27	.313	.408
Grass	.209	412	86	17	3	16	61	32	84	.268	.381	May	.205	127	26	7	0	2	9	17	26	.301	.307
Turf	.269	301	81	18	0	13	49	35	78	.351	.458	June	.222	45	10	3	0	2	5	3	10	.271	.422
Pre-All Star	.215	312	67	16	1	9	37	35	67	.296	.359	July	.271	59	16	2	0	7	15	7	12	.358	.661
Post-All Star	.249	401	100	19	2	20	73	32	95	.309	.456	August	.275	211	58	12	1	9	40	14	48	.323	.469
Scoring Posn	.248	202	50	11	3	10	87	33	55	.354	.480	Sept/Oct	.191	141	27	5	1	4	19	11	39	.253	.326
Close & Late	.304	112	34	7	1	5	19	10	22	.368	.518	vs. AL	.221	402	89	19	3	11	56	36	81	.291	.366
None on/out	.204	167	34	9	0	4	4	16	40	.277	.329	vs. NL	.251	311	78	16	0	18	54	31	81	.319	.476

Batter vs. Pitcher (career)

Hits Best Against	Avg	AB	H	2B	3B	HR	RBI	BB	SO	OBP	SLG	Hits Worst Against	Avg	AB	H	2B	3B	HR	RBI	BB	SO	OBP	SLG
Denny Neagle	.417	12	5	0	0	0	4	0	1	.417	.417	Randy Johnson	.182	11	2	0	0	0	1	0	3	.182	.182
Todd Stottlemyre	.385	13	5	2	1	0	5	0	1	.357	.692	Wilson Alvarez	.182	11	2	0	0	2	1	2	.308	.182
Al Leiter	.333	12	4	3	0	1	4	3	.529	.583	Ricky Bones	.200	15	3	2	0	2	1	2	.250	.333

Mike Perez — Royals

	ERA	W	L	Sv	G	GS	IP	BB	SO	Avg	H	2B	3B	HR	RBI	OBP	SLG	GF	IR	IRS	Hld	SvOp	SB	CS	GB	FB	G/F
1997 Season	3.54	2	0	0	16	0	20.1	8	17	.214	15	2	1	2	13	.304	.357	4	16	9	1	0	1	0	3	26	12 2.17
Last Five Years	4.09	14	11	21	209	0	222.1	78	166	.275	233	34	5	21	124	.340	.401	69	115	40	37	27	26	10	280	233	1.20

1997 Season

	ERA	W	L	Sv	G	GS	IP	H	HR	BB	SO		Avg	AB	H	2B	3B	HR	RBI	BB	SO	OBP	SLG
Home	0.82	1	0	0	8	0	11.0	5	1	3	6	vs. Left	.200	20	4	0	0	0	3	2	4	.273	.200
Away	6.75	1	0	0	8	0	9.1	10	1	5	11	vs. Right	.220	50	11	2	1	2	10	6	13	.316	.420

Last Five Years

	ERA	W	L	Sv	G	GS	IP	H	HR	BB	SO		Avg	AB	H	2B	3B	HR	RBI	BB	SO	OBP	SLG
Home	4.08	12	7	7	108	0	117.0	123	10	45	77	vs. Left	.301	332	100	13	1	7	43	33	50	.373	.410
Away	4.10	2	4	14	101	0	105.1	110	11	33	89	vs. Right	.258	516	133	21	4	14	81	45	116	.318	.395
Day	3.79	6	7	9	92	0	97.1	92	10	40	77	Inning 1-6	.239	88	21	4	1	2	19	12	24	.330	.375
Night	4.32	8	4	12	117	0	125.0	141	11	38	89	Inning 7+	.279	760	212	30	4	19	105	66	142	.341	.404
Grass	3.95	5	8	8	124	0	132.0	130	15	53	107	None on	.284	436	124	18	4	10	10	33	79	.343	.413
Turf	4.28	9	3	13	85	0	90.1	103	6	25	59	Runners on	.265	412	109	16	1	11	114	45	87	.336	.388
March/April	2.54	3	1	7	33	0	39.0	36	3	11	37	Scoring Posn	.272	250	68	10	0	8	104	37	54	.354	.408
May	4.98	3	4	6	48	0	47.0	54	4	15	32	Close & Late	.277	404	112	16	3	11	60	31	81	.332	.413
June	4.30	1	3	4	43	0	44.0	48	5	21	31	None on/out	.299	197	59	9	3	8	8	19	33	.364	.497
July	5.81	2	2	0	29	0	31.0	35	4	14	22	vs. 1st Batr (relief)	.296	189	56	8	1	7	30	16	39	.344	.460
August	2.56	2	0	0	29	0	31.2	31	2	8	25	1st Inning Pitched	.271	682	185	27	2	17	107	69	132	.341	.391
Sept/Oct	4.25	3	1	4	27	0	29.2	29	3	9	19	First 15 Pitches	.272	581	158	25	2	15	75	48	107	.329	.399
Starter	0.00	0	0	0	0	0	0.0	0	0	0	0	Pitch 16-30	.289	225	65	7	3	5	44	27	43	.374	.413
Reliever	4.09	14	11	21	209	0	222.1	233	21	78	166	Pitch 31-45	.250	40	10	2	0	1	5	3	16	.302	.375
0 Days rest (Relief)	3.13	5	4	8	62	0	69.0	71	1	15	51	Pitch 46+	.000	2	0	0	0	0	0	0	0	.000	.000

Last Five Years

	ERA	W	L	Sv	G	GS	IP	H	HR	BB	SO		Avg	AB	H	2B	3B	HR	RBI	BB	SO	OBP	SLG
1 or 2 Days rest	4.54	6	3	7	104	0	111.0	116	12	45	86	First Pitch	.331	124	41	5	1	8	33	6	0	.363	.581
3+ Days rest	4.46	3	4	6	43	0	42.1	46	8	18	29	Ahead in Count	.207	391	81	9	3	3	28	0	139	.216	.269
vs. AL	3.54	2	0	0	16	0	20.1	15	2	8	17	Behind in Count	.371	167	62	13	1	4	31	37	0	.481	.533
vs. NL	4.14	12	11	21	193	0	202.0	218	19	70	149	Two Strikes	.204	397	81	8	3	5	37	34	166	.275	.277
Pre-All Star	4.24	8	8	17	136	0	140.0	156	13	49	103	Pre-All Star	.286	545	156	25	3	13	78	49	103	.350	.415
Post-All Star	3.83	6	3	4	73	0	82.1	77	8	29	63	Post-All Star	.254	303	77	9	2	8	46	29	63	.321	.376

Pitcher vs. Batter (career)

Pitches Best Vs.	Avg	AB	H	2B	3B	HR	RBI	BB	SO	OBP	SLG	Pitches Worst Vs.	Avg	AB	H	2B	3B	HR	RBI	BB	SO	OBP	SLG
Matt Williams	.111	9	1	0	0	0	0	2	1	.273	.111	Orlando Merced	.600	10	6	0	0	0	1	1	0	.636	.600
Eric Karros	.125	8	1	0	0	0	0	3	3	.364	.125	Ron Gant	.500	10	5	0	0	0	0	2	4	.583	.500
												Andres Galarraga	.364	11	4	1	0	1	4	1	2	.417	.727
												Barry Larkin	.364	11	4	0	0	1	1	1	4	.417	.636
												Marquis Grissom	.353	17	6	1	0	1	4	1	3	.389	.588

Neifi Perez — Rockies

Age 23 – Bats Both

	Avg	G	AB	R	H	2B	3B	HR	RBI	BB	SO	HBP	GDP	SB	CS	OBP	SLG	IBB	SH	SF	#Pit	#P/PA	GB	FB	G/F
1997 Season	.291	83	313	46	91	13	10	5	31	21	43	1	3	4	3	.333	.444	4	5	4	1118	3.25	111	103	1.08
Career (1996-1997)	.274	100	358	50	98	15	10	5	34	21	51	1	5	6	5	.313	.413	4	6	4	1282	3.29	127	117	1.09

1997 Season

	Avg	AB	H	2B	3B	HR	RBI	BB	SO	OBP	SLG		Avg	AB	H	2B	3B	HR	RBI	BB	SO	OBP	SLG
vs. Left	.312	77	24	4	3	2	10	3	9	.333	.519	First Pitch	.311	61	19	2	3	0	9	2	0	.328	.443
vs. Right	.284	236	67	9	7	3	21	18	34	.333	.419	Ahead in Count	.456	57	26	5	3	1	10	14	0	.548	.702
Groundball	.224	67	15	3	1	2	5	4	5	.268	.388	Behind in Count	.207	145	30	6	1	2	7	0	40	.212	.303
Flyball	.364	44	16	3	3	0	4	4	6	.400	.568	Two Strikes	.175	126	22	4	2	1	4	5	43	.206	.262
Home	.343	169	58	7	6	3	19	9	18	.378	.509	Batting #2	.309	110	34	5	0	4	11	8	16	.361	.464
Away	.229	144	33	6	4	2	12	12	25	.283	.368	Batting #8	.303	142	43	6	7	1	17	10	18	.342	.465
Day	.287	122	35	8	1	3	12	6	15	.320	.443	Other	.230	61	14	2	3	0	3	3	9	.262	.361
Night	.293	191	56	5	9	2	19	15	28	.341	.445	March/April	.000	0	0	0	0	0	0	0	0	.000	.000
Grass	.302	258	78	10	9	4	25	16	32	.343	.457	May	.000	0	0	0	0	0	0	0	0	.000	.000
Turf	.236	55	13	3	1	1	6	5	11	.290	.382	June	.250	24	6	1	1	2	5	0	3	.250	.625
Pre-All Star	.250	36	9	3	1	2	5	0	6	.250	.556	July	.322	87	28	6	0	1	5	7	12	.379	.425
Post-All Star	.296	277	82	10	9	3	26	21	37	.343	.430	August	.280	107	30	3	5	2	10	10	15	.336	.458
Scoring Posn	.264	72	19	2	2	0	23	9	8	.329	.347	Sept/Oct	.284	95	27	3	4	0	11	4	13	.307	.400
Close & Late	.231	52	12	3	1	0	7	3	5	.268	.327	vs. AL	.323	31	10	2	2	0	1	2	3	.364	.516
None on/out	.343	67	23	4	2	0	4	9	.389	.463		vs. NL	.287	282	81	11	8	5	30	19	40	.330	.436

1997 By Position

Position	Avg	AB	H	2B	3B	HR	RBI	BB	SO	OBP	SLG	G	GS	Innings	PO	A	E	DP	Fld Pct	Rng Fctr	In Zone	Zone Outs	Zone Rtg	MLB Zone
As 2b	.304	148	45	4	6	0	11	6	22	.325	.412	41	39	333.2	105	131	2	40	.992	6.37	131	118	.901	.902
As ss	.295	156	46	9	4	5	20	15	18	.358	.500	45	38	359.0	77	155	6	35	.975	5.82	158	145	.918	.937

Robert Perez — Blue Jays

Age 29 – Bats Right

	Avg	G	AB	R	H	2B	3B	HR	RBI	BB	SO	HBP	GDP	SB	CS	OBP	SLG	IBB	SH	SF	#Pit	#P/PA	GB	FB	G/F
1997 Season	.192	37	78	4	15	4	1	2	6	0	16	0	2	0	0	.192	.346	0	0	0	267	3.42	24	26	0.92
Career (1994-1997)	.271	144	336	36	91	16	5	5	30	8	39	1	10	3	0	.289	.369	0	4	1	1082	3.09	144	80	1.80

1997 Season

	Avg	AB	H	2B	3B	HR	RBI	BB	SO	OBP	SLG		Avg	AB	H	2B	3B	HR	RBI	BB	SO	OBP	SLG
vs. Left	.188	64	12	4	1	0	4	0	13	.188	.281	Scoring Posn	.267	15	4	2	0	0	4	0	2	.267	.400
vs. Right	.214	14	3	0	0	2	2	0	3	.214	.643	Close & Late	.375	8	3	1	0	1	2	0	2	.375	.875

Tomas Perez — Blue Jays

Age 24 – Bats Both

	Avg	G	AB	R	H	2B	3B	HR	RBI	BB	SO	HBP	GDP	SB	CS	OBP	SLG	IBB	SH	SF	#Pit	#P/PA	GB	FB	G/F
1997 Season	.195	40	123	9	24	3	2	0	9	11	28	1	2	1	1	.267	.252	0	3	0	538	3.90	43	31	1.39
Career (1995-1997)	.236	172	516	45	122	19	7	2	36	43	75	2	18	2	4	.297	.312	0	9	2	2153	3.76	230	107	2.15

1997 Season

	Avg	AB	H	2B	3B	HR	RBI	BB	SO	OBP	SLG		Avg	AB	H	2B	3B	HR	RBI	BB	SO	OBP	SLG
vs. Left	.111	27	3	0	0	0	1	1	5	.143	.111	Scoring Posn	.175	40	7	0	1	0	9	3	7	.233	.225
vs. Right	.219	96	21	3	2	0	8	10	23	.299	.292	Close & Late	.188	16	3	0	1	0	2	1	4	.235	.188
Home	.182	66	12	1	1	0	3	5	15	.239	.227	None on/out	.077	26	2	0	1	0	0	3	6	.172	.154
Away	.211	57	12	2	1	0	6	6	13	.297	.281	Batting #8	.222	9	2	0	0	0	1	2	.300	.222
First Pitch	.167	12	2	0	0	0	1	0	0	.167	.167	Batting #9	.193	114	22	3	2	0	9	10	26	.264	.254
Ahead in Count	.273	22	6	0	2	0	5	7	0	.467	.455	Other	.000	0	0	0	0	0	0	0	0	.000	.000
Behind in Count	.157	70	11	3	0	0	2	0	27	.157	.200	Pre-All Star	.167	6	1	0	0	0	1	2	1	.375	.167
Two Strikes	.185	65	12	3	0	0	3	4	28	.232	.231	Post-All Star	.197	117	23	3	2	0	9	27	.260	.256

Career (1995-1997)

	Avg	AB	H	2B	3B	HR	RBI	BB	SO	OBP	SLG		Avg	AB	H	2B	3B	HR	RBI	BB	SO	OBP	SLG
vs. Left	.218	142	31	6	2	2	16	10	22	.270	.331	First Pitch	.301	83	25	4	0	1	5	0	0	.298	.386
vs. Right	.243	374	91	13	5	0	20	33	53	.307	.305	Ahead in Count	.258	89	23	4	3	0	13	23	0	.412	.371
Groundball	.171	117	20	3	0	0	2	8	17	.224	.197	Behind in Count	.194	258	50	7	3	0	12	0	69	.197	.244
Flyball	.184	76	14	2	0	1	8	6	8	.244	.250	Two Strikes	.191	256	49	9	3	0	12	20	75	.250	.250
Home	.199	276	55	8	5	2	21	22	44	.258	.286	Batting #2	.258	89	23	5	3	0	6	11	13	.340	.382

366

Career (1995-1997)

	Avg	AB	H	2B	3B	HR	RBI	BB	SO	OBP	SLG		Avg	AB	H	2B	3B	HR	RBI	BB	SO	OBP	SLG
Away	.279	240	67	11	2	0	15	21	31	.341	.342	Batting #9	.236	390	92	14	4	2	29	31	57	.294	.308
Day	.274	175	48	7	1	1	13	20	27	.347	.343	Other	.189	37	7	0	0	0	1	1	5	.211	.189
Night	.217	341	74	12	6	1	23	23	48	.270	.296	March/April	.000	0	0	0	0	0	0	0	0	.000	.000
Grass	.274	219	60	10	2	0	13	20	29	.339	.338	May	.250	12	3	1	0	0	1	0	2	.250	.333
Turf	.209	297	62	9	5	2	23	23	46	.265	.293	June	.268	82	22	5	0	1	10	7	6	.326	.366
Pre-All Star	.262	122	32	6	0	1	11	8	10	.313	.336	July	.240	104	25	3	2	1	8	11	14	.319	.337
Post-All Star	.228	394	90	13	7	1	25	35	65	.292	.305	August	.242	157	38	8	3	0	10	10	24	.288	.331
Scoring Posn	.196	148	29	1	3	2	34	14	22	.262	.284	Sept/Oct	.211	161	34	2	2	0	7	15	29	.278	.248
Close & Late	.215	79	17	2	0	0	6	5	14	.271	.241	vs. AL	.239	497	119	18	7	2	36	42	68	.300	.316
None on/out	.220	118	26	5	1	0	0	9	17	.276	.280	vs. NL	.158	19	3	1	0	0	0	1	7	.200	.211

Batter vs. Pitcher (career)

Hits Best Against	Avg	AB	H	2B	3B	HR	RBI	BB	SO	OBP	SLG	Hits Worst Against	Avg	AB	H	2B	3B	HR	RBI	BB	SO	OBP	SLG
												Darren Oliver	.000	12	0	0	0	0	0	1	1	.077	.000
												Tim Wakefield	.100	10	1	0	0	0	0	1	1	.182	.100
												Alex Fernandez	.200	10	2	0	0	0	0	1	4	.273	.200

Yorkis Perez — Mets
Age 30 – Pitches Left (flyball pitcher)

	ERA	W	L	Sv	G	GS	IP	BB	SO	Avg	H	2B	3B	HR	RBI	OBP	SLG	GF	IR	IRS	Hld	SvOp	SB	CS	GB	FB	G/F
1997 Season	8.31	0	1	0	9	0	8.2	4	7	.375	15	0	0	2	9	.422	.525	1	7	4	1	1	2	0	11	16	0.69
Last Five Years	4.95	8	11	1	186	0	143.2	77	142	.245	134	24	4	14	85	.340	.380	38	147	38	42	9	13	3	156	167	0.93

1997 Season

	ERA	W	L	Sv	G	GS	IP	H	HR	BB	SO		Avg	AB	H	2B	3B	HR	RBI	BB	SO	OBP	SLG
Home	13.50	0	0	0	5	0	3.1	7	1	1	3	vs. Left	.400	15	6	0	0	0	2	0	3	.375	.400
Away	5.06	0	1	0	4	0	5.1	8	1	3	4	vs. Right	.360	25	9	0	0	2	7	4	4	.448	.600

Last Five Years

	ERA	W	L	Sv	G	GS	IP	H	HR	BB	SO		Avg	AB	H	2B	3B	HR	RBI	BB	SO	OBP	SLG
Home	3.09	6	3	1	97	0	84.1	63	6	35	90	vs. Left	.229	253	58	8	3	6	38	28	70	.309	.356
Away	7.58	2	8	0	89	0	59.1	71	8	42	52	vs. Right	.258	295	76	16	1	8	47	49	72	.365	.400
Day	6.82	0	4	0	51	0	33.0	37	1	21	40	Inning 1-6	.382	55	21	4	1	1	20	6	8	.435	.545
Night	4.39	8	7	1	135	0	110.2	97	13	56	102	Inning 7+	.229	493	113	20	3	13	65	71	134	.329	.361
Grass	4.56	6	8	1	148	0	120.1	107	10	64	124	None on	.238	290	69	16	4	5	5	36	68	.326	.372
Turf	6.94	2	3	0	38	0	23.1	27	4	13	18	Runners on	.252	258	65	8	0	9	80	41	74	.354	.388
March/April	5.27	1	0	0	21	0	13.2	12	0	9	18	Scoring Posn	.255	161	41	5	0	3	65	31	52	.374	.342
May	4.95	1	2	0	44	0	40.0	37	5	19	36	Close & Late	.248	246	61	9	1	8	32	50	56	.378	.390
June	4.12	3	2	1	29	0	19.2	15	1	14	19	None on/out	.191	131	25	3	2	2	2	14	31	.279	.290
July	4.18	2	2	0	39	0	28.0	28	2	16	30	vs. 1st Batr (relief)	.199	161	32	5	1	1	18	22	51	.299	.261
August	7.27	1	2	0	32	0	26.0	29	4	11	29	1st Inning Pitched	.239	457	109	22	2	12	80	61	118	.331	.374
Sept/Oct	3.31	1	2	0	21	0	16.1	13	2	8	10	First 15 Pitches	.235	388	91	19	2	9	59	54	92	.333	.363
Starter	0.00	0	0	0	0	0	0.0	0	0	0	0	Pitch 16-30	.266	128	34	5	2	5	26	21	40	.364	.453
Reliever	4.95	8	11	1	186	0	143.2	134	14	77	142	Pitch 31-45	.259	27	7	0	0	0	2	2	10	.310	.259
0 Days rest (Relief)	5.11	3	4	1	68	0	44.0	38	7	30	48	Pitch 46+	.400	5	2	0	0	0	0	0	0	.400	.400
1 or 2 Days rest	4.94	4	5	0	72	0	62.0	60	5	29	60	First Pitch	.219	73	16	4	0	3	7	7	0	.313	.397
3+ Days rest	4.78	1	2	0	46	0	37.2	36	2	18	34	Ahead in Count	.177	260	46	6	1	5	35	0	125	.177	.265
vs. AL	0.00	0	0	0	0	0	0.0	0	0	0	0	Behind in Count	.381	105	40	8	2	5	24	35	0	.535	.638
vs. NL	4.95	8	11	1	186	0	143.2	134	14	77	142	Two Strikes	.179	285	51	6	2	4	38	34	142	.265	.256
Pre-All Star	4.52	4	6	1	110	0	87.2	77	6	47	87	Pre-All Star	.235	328	77	15	2	6	41	47	87	.332	.348
Post-All Star	5.63	4	5	0	76	0	56.0	57	8	30	55	Post-All Star	.259	220	57	9	2	8	44	30	55	.350	.427

Pitcher vs. Batter (career)

Pitches Best Vs.	Avg	AB	H	2B	3B	HR	RBI	BB	SO	OBP	SLG	Pitches Worst Vs.	Avg	AB	H	2B	3B	HR	RBI	BB	SO	OBP	SLG
Mickey Morandini	.200	10	2	0	0	0	0	0	1	.273	.200	Ken Caminiti	.444	9	4	0	0	0	3	2	1	.545	.444
Ryan Klesko	.200	10	2	0	0	0	0	1	2	.333	.200	Fred McGriff	.389	18	7	1	0	1	5	2	1	.450	.611
Jim Eisenreich	.214	14	3	0	0	0	2	0	3	.214	.214												

Matt Perisho — Angels
Age 23 – Pitches Left (groundball pitcher)

	ERA	W	L	Sv	G	GS	IP	BB	SO	Avg	H	2B	3B	HR	RBI	OBP	SLG	CG	ShO	Sup	QS	#P/S	SB	CS	GB	FB	G/F
1997 Season	6.00	0	2	0	11	8	45.0	28	35	.324	59	6	1	6	29	.419	.467	0	0	3.80	2	94	8	1	62	41	1.51

1997 Season

	ERA	W	L	Sv	G	GS	IP	H	HR	BB	SO		Avg	AB	H	2B	3B	HR	RBI	BB	SO	OBP	SLG
Home	4.63	0	0	0	6	4	23.1	27	5	13	16	vs. Left	.316	19	6	0	0	1	6	6	5	.481	.474
Away	7.48	0	2	0	5	4	21.2	32	1	15	19	vs. Right	.325	163	53	6	1	5	23	22	30	.410	.466

Robert Person — Blue Jays
Age 28 – Pitches Right (flyball pitcher)

	ERA	W	L	Sv	G	GS	IP	BB	SO	Avg	H	2B	3B	HR	RBI	OBP	SLG	CG	ShO	Sup	QS	#P/S	SB	CS	GB	FB	G/F
1997 Season	5.61	5	10	0	23	22	128.1	60	99	.255	125	33	3	19	73	.338	.450	0	0	3.79	8	98	3	4	115	197	0.58
Career (1995-1997)	4.93	10	15	0	53	36	230.0	97	185	.245	216	49	4	36	117	.322	.432	0	0	3.72	15	95	11	5	218	328	0.66

1997 Season

	ERA	W	L	Sv	G	GS	IP	H	HR	BB	SO		Avg	AB	H	2B	3B	HR	RBI	BB	SO	OBP	SLG
Home	4.54	2	5	0	12	11	69.1	63	6	30	53	vs. Left	.243	251	61	14	1	11	35	35	55	.334	.438
Away	6.86	3	5	0	11	11	59.0	62	13	30	46	vs. Right	.267	240	64	19	2	8	38	25	44	.342	.463
Day	4.43	2	4	0	7	6	40.2	36	4	17	34	Inning 1-6	.236	440	104	28	3	19	65	52	96	.318	.443
Night	6.16	3	6	0	16	16	87.2	89	15	43	65	Inning 7+	.412	51	21	5	0	0	8	8	3	.500	.510

1997 Season

	ERA	W	L	Sv	G	GS	IP	H	HR	BB	SO
Grass	8.14	1	5	0	9	9	45.1	50	12	22	37
Turf	4.23	4	5	0	14	13	83.0	75	7	38	62
March/April	2.77	0	1	0	3	2	13.0	13	1	5	9
May	6.92	0	2	0	3	3	13.0	11	2	5	12
June	4.13	3	2	0	5	5	32.2	31	4	11	24
July	6.39	1	2	0	5	5	31.0	31	6	12	28
August	6.91	1	3	0	5	5	28.2	28	4	20	22
Sept/Oct	6.30	0	0	0	2	2	10.0	11	2	7	4
Starter	5.58	5	10	0	22	22	127.1	123	19	58	99
Reliever	9.00	0	0	0	1	0	1.0	2	0	2	0
0-3 Days Rest (Start)	0.00	0	0	0	0	0	0.0	0	0	0	0
4 Days Rest	6.45	2	4	0	12	12	67.0	60	14	34	52
5+ Days Rest	4.62	3	6	0	10	10	60.1	63	5	24	47
vs. AL	5.75	4	9	0	19	18	103.1	98	15	47	81
vs. NL	5.04	1	1	0	4	4	25.0	27	4	13	18
Pre-All Star	4.80	3	5	0	12	11	65.2	62	9	23	53
Post-All Star	6.46	2	5	0	11	11	62.2	63	10	37	46

	Avg	AB	H	2B	3B	HR	RBI	BB	SO	OBP	SLG
None on	.227	304	69	13	1	13	13	27	61	.294	.405
Runners on	.299	187	56	20	2	6	60	33	38	.402	.524
Scoring Posn	.308	107	33	14	2	4	52	20	24	.412	.589
Close & Late	.400	45	18	4	0	0	6	7	3	.491	.489
None on/out	.269	130	35	7	0	6	6	11	23	.336	.462
vs. 1st Batr (relief)	.000	1	0	0	0	0	0	0	0	.000	.000
1st Inning Pitched	.320	97	31	9	0	5	20	14	22	.404	.567
First 75 Pitches	.238	349	83	20	3	17	49	43	82	.322	.458
Pitch 76-90	.242	62	15	5	0	0	7	10	9	.356	.323
Pitch 91-105	.311	61	19	6	0	2	15	3	5	.353	.508
Pitch 106+	.421	19	8	2	0	0	2	4	3	.522	.526
First Pitch	.328	64	21	7	1	3	12	2	0	.343	.609
Ahead in Count	.202	213	43	11	0	4	19	0	81	.210	.310
Behind in Count	.279	104	29	6	0	7	22	30	0	.434	.538
Two Strikes	.223	238	53	13	2	3	24	28	99	.306	.332
Pre-All Star	.245	253	62	17	2	9	34	23	53	.311	.435
Post-All Star	.265	238	63	16	1	10	39	37	46	.365	.466

Roberto Petagine — Mets
Age 27 – Bats Left

	Avg	G	AB	R	H	2B	3B	HR	RBI	BB	SO	HBP	GDP	SB	CS	OBP	SLG	IBB	SH	SF	#Pit	#P/PA	GB	FB	G/F
1997 Season	.067	12	15	2	1	0	0	0	2	3	6	0	0	0	0	.222	.067	0	0	0	73	4.06	3	3	1.00
Career (1994-1997)	.216	159	245	27	53	11	0	7	36	39	77	3	6	0	0	.330	.347	3	3	1	1147	3.94	66	58	1.14

1997 Season

	Avg	AB	H	2B	3B	HR	RBI	BB	SO	OBP	SLG
vs. Left	.000	2	0	0	0	0	0	0	1	.000	.000
vs. Right	.077	13	1	0	0	0	2	3	5	.250	.077

	Avg	AB	H	2B	3B	HR	RBI	BB	SO	OBP	SLG
Scoring Posn	.200	5	1	0	0	0	2	0	1	.200	.200
Close & Late	.000	7	0	0	0	0	0	1	3	.125	.000

Chris Peters — Pirates
Age 26 – Pitches Left (groundball pitcher)

	ERA	W	L	Sv	G	GS	IP	BB	SO	Avg	H	2B	3B	HR	RBI	OBP	SLG	GF	IR	IRS	Hld	SvOp	SB	CS	GB	FB	G/F
1997 Season	4.58	2	2	0	31	1	37.1	21	17	.277	38	7	1	6	25	.383	.474	5	25	8	2	1	2	3	65	29	2.24
Career (1996-1997)	5.24	4	6	0	47	11	101.1	46	45	.284	110	22	5	15	66	.362	.482	5	33	12	4	1	11	3	189	90	2.10

1997 Season

	ERA	W	L	Sv	G	GS	IP	H	HR	BB	SO
Home	3.97	1	1	0	15	1	22.2	24	3	10	10
Away	5.52	1	1	0	16	0	14.2	14	3	11	7
Starter	0.00	0	0	0	1	1	7.0	6	0	1	2
Reliever	5.64	2	2	0	30	0	30.1	32	6	20	15
0 Days rest (Relief)	3.86	0	0	0	4	0	4.2	4	0	2	5
1 or 2 Days rest	4.15	1	1	0	16	0	17.1	17	2	12	7
3+ Days rest	9.72	1	1	0	10	0	8.1	11	4	6	3
Pre-All Star	5.96	2	2	0	21	1	22.2	23	4	13	11
Post-All Star	2.45	0	0	0	10	1	14.2	15	2	8	6

	Avg	AB	H	2B	3B	HR	RBI	BB	SO	OBP	SLG
vs. Left	.271	48	13	1	1	3	11	5	5	.352	.521
vs. Right	.281	89	25	6	0	3	14	16	12	.398	.449
Scoring Posn	.200	50	10	1	0	2	19	11	6	.359	.340
Close & Late	.294	17	5	1	0	3	7	3	1	.429	.882
None on/out	.382	34	13	1	3	3	3	2	2	.432	.794
First Pitch	.346	26	9	3	1	2	3	3	0	.414	.769
Ahead in Count	.234	47	11	1	0	2	10	0	13	.245	.383
Behind in Count	.222	36	8	2	0	2	10	12	0	.417	.444
Two Strikes	.229	48	11	1	0	2	7	6	17	.309	.375

Mark Petkovsek — Cardinals
Age 32 – Pitches Right (groundball pitcher)

	ERA	W	L	Sv	G	GS	IP	BB	SO	Avg	H	2B	3B	HR	RBI	OBP	SLG	GF	IR	IRS	Hld	SvOp	SB	CS	GB	FB	G/F
1997 Season	5.06	4	7	2	55	2	96.0	31	51	.292	109	15	6	14	61	.354	.477	19	19	8	5	2	7	4	164	85	1.93
Last Five Years	4.44	24	15	2	155	29	354.1	110	181	.274	371	60	15	41	192	.334	.431	35	71	26	15	5	31	12	667	273	2.44

1997 Season

	ERA	W	L	Sv	G	GS	IP	H	HR	BB	SO
Home	3.77	2	1	0	28	1	45.1	48	4	13	19
Away	6.22	2	6	2	27	1	50.2	61	10	18	32
Day	5.73	2	3	1	21	0	37.2	41	7	10	18
Night	4.63	2	4	1	34	2	58.1	68	7	21	33
Grass	5.05	3	6	2	44	1	73.0	81	12	24	34
Turf	5.09	1	1	0	11	1	23.0	28	2	7	17
March/April	1.96	2	3	0	8	1	23.0	18	2	5	13
May	2.70	0	1	0	9	0	13.1	16	2	6	3
June	5.40	1	0	1	10	0	15.0	20	2	6	11
July	7.71	1	0	0	10	1	16.1	22	2	6	4
August	8.36	0	1	0	9	0	14.0	18	5	3	10
Sept/Oct	5.65	0	2	1	9	0	14.1	15	1	5	10
Starter	7.71	0	1	0	2	2	9.1	14	1	3	
Reliever	4.78	4	6	2	53	0	86.2	95	13	28	47
0 Days rest (Relief)	4.61	0	1	1	8	0	13.2	17	1	6	7
1 or 2 Days rest	5.01	2	4	0	24	0	41.1	42	8	12	22
3+ Days rest	4.55	2	1	1	21	0	31.2	36	4	10	18
vs. AL	19.06	1	0	0	4	0	5.2	13	4	4	3
vs. NL	4.18	3	7	2	51	2	90.1	96	10	27	48
Pre-All Star	3.40	4	4	1	30	1	55.2	60	7	18	27
Post-All Star	7.36	0	3	1	25	1	40.1	49	7	13	24

	Avg	AB	H	2B	3B	HR	RBI	BB	SO	OBP	SLG
vs. Left	.262	168	44	7	1	3	18	10	22	.317	.369
vs. Right	.317	205	65	8	5	11	43	21	29	.384	.566
Inning 1-6	.294	170	50	8	4	6	37	13	22	.348	.494
Inning 7+	.291	203	59	7	2	8	24	18	29	.360	.463
None on	.246	224	55	8	2	8	8	15	37	.307	.406
Runners on	.362	149	54	7	4	6	53	16	14	.423	.584
Scoring Posn	.379	87	33	4	3	4	45	13	9	.451	.598
Close & Late	.318	85	27	3	1	4	15	11	3	.402	.518
None on/out	.221	95	21	3	1	3	3	4	14	.267	.368
vs. 1st Batr (relief)	.240	50	12	2	0	2	6	1	7	.283	.400
1st Inning Pitched	.322	199	64	9	3	5	36	20	29	.395	.472
First 15 Pitches	.314	169	53	10	3	4	23	14	24	.380	.479
Pitch 16-30	.268	112	30	3	0	3	22	11	12	.333	.375
Pitch 31-45	.300	50	15	2	1	3	5	2	9	.327	.560
Pitch 46+	.262	42	11	0	2	4	11	4	6	.340	.643
First Pitch	.383	60	23	1	1	3	12	4	0	.433	.583
Ahead in Count	.229	131	30	6	1	0	15	0	39	.244	.290
Behind in Count	.315	92	29	4	2	5	17	15	0	.411	.565
Two Strikes	.206	131	27	5	0	0	12	12	51	.281	.244
Pre-All Star	.278	216	60	7	3	7	26	18	27	.342	.435
Post-All Star	.312	157	49	8	3	7	35	13	24	.371	.535

Last Five Years

	ERA	W	L	Sv	G	GS	IP	H	HR	BB	SO		Avg	AB	H	2B	3B	HR	RBI	BB	SO	OBP	SLG
Home	3.38	16	4	0	81	16	189.1	186	17	53	83	vs. Left	.280	589	165	29	7	13	74	43	64	.332	.419
Away	5.67	8	11	2	74	13	165.0	185	24	57	98	vs. Right	.269	766	206	31	8	28	118	67	117	.336	.440
Day	5.81	8	5	1	48	5	91.1	108	15	31	48	Inning 1-6	.277	889	246	40	9	29	138	67	117	.332	.440
Night	3.97	16	10	1	107	24	263.0	263	26	79	133	Inning 7+	.268	466	125	20	6	12	54	43	64	.338	.414
Grass	4.87	18	11	2	102	14	207.0	220	28	69	109	None on	.253	774	196	30	10	23	23	51	111	.310	.407
Turf	3.85	6	4	0	53	15	147.1	151	13	41	72	Runners on	.301	581	175	30	5	18	169	59	70	.365	.463
March/April	2.45	3	3	0	11	3	33.0	28	4	8	19	Scoring Posn	.309	353	109	19	4	11	150	44	43	.382	.479
May	4.38	2	2	0	20	4	49.1	60	7	21	15	Close & Late	.266	214	57	7	3	5	27	26	32	.352	.397
June	3.96	7	1	1	28	5	61.1	69	5	15	26	None on/out	.252	329	83	11	7	9	9	23	48	.315	.410
July	4.96	5	3	0	31	5	65.1	65	6	26	29	vs. 1st Batter (relief)	.252	111	28	4	2	3	12	9	17	.325	.405
August	4.65	3	2	0	38	5	79.1	78	15	19	52	1st Inning Pitched	.293	552	162	25	8	16	101	55	73	.367	.455
Sept/Oct	5.18	4	4	1	27	7	66.0	71	4	21	40	First 15 Pitches	.287	487	140	25	9	12	69	35	55	.344	.450
Starter	4.04	8	7	0	29	29	164.2	166	16	46	86	Pitch 16-30	.232	315	73	9	1	8	45	32	45	.311	.343
Reliever	4.79	16	8	2	126	0	189.2	205	25	64	95	Pitch 31-45	.283	198	56	7	1	5	17	9	34	.314	.404
0 Days rest (Relief)	7.40	0	1	1	15	0	20.2	31	2	12	9	Pitch 46+	.287	355	102	19	4	16	61	34	47	.353	.499
1 or 2 Days rest	3.90	10	5	0	64	0	99.1	92	16	26	45	First Pitch	.338	216	73	11	4	11	40	10	0	.379	.579
3+ Days rest	5.30	6	1	0	47	0	69.2	82	7	26	41	Ahead in Count	.227	520	118	18	4	8	62	0	154	.237	.323
vs. AL	19.06	1	0	0	4	0	5.2	13	4	4	3	Behind in Count	.292	359	105	19	5	11	55	53	0	.383	.465
vs. NL	4.21	23	15	2	151	29	348.2	358	37	106	178	Two Strikes	.208	518	108	16	3	7	52	47	181	.277	.292
Pre-All Star	4.04	13	8	1	66	14	162.2	176	19	52	69	Pre-All Star	.281	627	176	28	7	19	80	52	69	.342	.439
Post-All Star	4.79	11	9	1	89	15	191.2	195	22	58	112	Post-All Star	.268	728	195	32	8	22	112	58	112	.328	.424

Pitcher vs. Batter (career)

Pitches Best Vs.	Avg	AB	H	2B	3B	HR	RBI	BB	SO	OBP	SLG	Pitches Worst Vs.	Avg	AB	H	2B	3B	HR	RBI	BB	SO	OBP	SLG
Scott Servais	.100	10	1	0	0	0	0	1	2	.182	.100	Jose Vizcaino	.500	12	6	2	0	0	0	0	0	.500	.667
Walt Weiss	.143	21	3	0	0	0	0	1	2	.182	.143	Sammy Sosa	.455	11	5	1	0	3	8	1	0	.500	1.364
Luis Gonzalez	.182	11	2	0	0	0	2	0	0	.182	.182	Andres Galarraga	.423	26	11	2	1	2	7	2	5	.483	.808
Vinny Castilla	.200	25	5	0	0	1	2	1	3	.231	.320	Brett Butler	.400	10	4	0	2	0	0	1	1	.455	.800
Rico Brogna	.231	13	3	0	0	0	2	0	2	.231	.231	Ellis Burks	.333	12	4	1	0	1	2	5	1	.529	.667

Andy Pettitte — Yankees

Age 26 – Pitches Left (groundball pitcher)

	ERA	W	L	Sv	G	GS	IP	BB	SO	Avg	H	2B	3B	HR	RBI	OBP	SLG	CG	ShO	Sup	QS	#P/S	SB	CS	GB	FB	G/F
1997 Season	2.88	18	7	0	35	35	240.1	65	166	.256	233	43	4	7	72	.307	.335	4	1	6.52	24	104	16	7	384	182	2.11
Career (1995-1997)	3.58	51	24	0	101	95	636.1	200	442	.266	645	114	14	45	234	.322	.380	9	1	6.12	56	104	35	26	962	571	1.68

1997 Season

	ERA	W	L	Sv	G	GS	IP	H	HR	BB	SO		Avg	AB	H	2B	3B	HR	RBI	BB	SO	OBP	SLG
Home	2.65	9	4	0	17	17	118.2	110	6	23	86	vs. Left	.318	192	61	10	2	1	24	7	32	.343	.406
Away	3.11	9	3	0	18	18	121.2	123	1	42	80	vs. Right	.240	718	172	33	2	6	48	58	134	.298	.316
Day	3.25	6	3	0	14	14	97.0	99	2	28	74	Inning 1-6	.230	738	170	33	2	6	51	57	143	.288	.305
Night	2.64	12	4	0	21	21	143.1	134	5	37	92	Inning 7+	.366	172	63	10	2	1	21	8	23	.394	.465
Grass	3.02	15	7	0	31	31	211.1	206	7	54	137	None on	.242	542	131	22	2	6	6	32	94	.286	.323
Turf	1.86	3	0	0	4	4	29.0	27	0	11	29	Runners on	.277	368	102	21	2	1	66	33	72	.337	.353
March/April	2.32	5	0	0	6	6	42.2	38	3	13	27	Scoring Posn	.277	202	56	14	1	0	63	22	48	.348	.356
May	3.80	2	3	0	6	6	42.2	44	1	13	32	Close & Late	.380	71	27	6	2	0	14	4	10	.413	.521
June	3.89	1	2	0	6	6	39.1	41	1	11	26	None on/out	.221	240	53	6	1	1	1	11	41	.255	.267
July	2.70	4	1	0	5	5	36.2	39	0	4	20	vs. 1st Batr (relief)	.000	0	0	0	0	0	0	0	0	.000	.000
August	2.25	4	1	0	7	7	52.0	52	2	15	35	1st Inning Pitched	.257	136	35	8	1	2	9	10	25	.308	.375
Sept/Oct	2.33	2	0	0	5	5	27.0	19	0	9	26	First 75 Pitches	.233	615	143	26	1	5	40	52	113	.293	.302
Starter	2.88	18	7	0	35	35	240.1	233	7	65	166	Pitch 76-90	.286	126	36	7	1	1	10	2	27	.302	.381
Reliever	0.00	0	0	0	0	0	0.0	0	0	0	0	Pitch 91-105	.333	114	38	10	1	0	16	7	17	.377	.439
0-3 Days Rest (Start)	3.66	0	0	0	3	3	19.2	22	1	7	12	Pitch 106+	.291	55	16	0	1	1	6	4	9	.339	.382
4 Days Rest	2.79	13	2	0	21	21	142.0	135	5	36	107	First Pitch	.343	134	46	7	0	1	10	0	0	.341	.418
5+ Days Rest	2.86	5	5	0	11	11	78.2	76	1	22	47	Ahead in Count	.199	412	82	11	2	1	19	0	133	.201	.243
vs. AL	2.89	17	6	0	32	32	221.0	216	7	61	152	Behind in Count	.300	190	57	12	1	3	26	34	0	.410	.421
vs. NL	2.79	1	1	0	3	3	19.1	17	0	4	14	Two Strikes	.193	420	81	17	2	0	19	31	166	.248	.243
Pre-All Star	3.10	9	5	0	19	19	133.2	129	5	39	91	Pre-All Star	.257	501	129	26	1	5	43	39	91	.313	.343
Post-All Star	2.62	9	2	0	16	16	106.2	104	2	26	75	Post-All Star	.254	409	104	17	3	2	29	26	75	.300	.325

Career (1995-1997)

	ERA	W	L	Sv	G	GS	IP	H	HR	BB	SO		Avg	AB	H	2B	3B	HR	RBI	BB	SO	OBP	SLG
Home	2.84	27	10	0	48	47	339.0	307	25	91	233	vs. Left	.306	461	141	18	5	3	46	25	84	.342	.386
Away	4.42	24	14	0	53	48	297.1	338	20	109	209	vs. Right	.256	1965	504	96	9	42	188	175	358	.319	.379
Day	3.27	22	8	0	43	39	267.1	270	16	81	204	Inning 1-6	.255	2001	510	95	11	41	194	178	390	.317	.375
Night	3.80	29	16	0	58	56	369.0	375	29	119	238	Inning 7+	.318	425	135	19	3	4	40	22	52	.350	.405
Grass	3.62	45	22	0	90	85	569.2	582	43	174	389	None on	.255	1427	364	66	9	30	30	114	269	.312	.377
Turf	3.24	6	2	0	11	10	66.2	63	2	26	53	Runners on	.281	999	281	48	5	15	204	86	173	.337	.384
March/April	3.70	8	1	0	14	12	80.1	88	6	24	49	Scoring Posn	.277	545	151	30	2	8	185	56	109	.341	.383
May	3.70	6	6	0	16	12	87.2	88	8	33	63	Close & Late	.318	176	56	9	2	2	22	9	23	.351	.443
June	3.47	9	6	0	18	18	116.2	118	8	38	72	None on/out	.255	640	163	26	6	12	12	37	118	.296	.370
July	4.17	10	5	0	16	16	105.2	124	4	31	62	vs. 1st Batr (relief)	.333	6	2	0	0	0	0	0	0	.333	.333
August	3.78	9	4	0	20	20	131.0	134	12	45	105	1st Inning Pitched	.294	398	117	23	5	10	55	34	80	.349	.452
Sept/Oct	2.74	9	2	0	17	17	115.0	119	2	29	91	First 75 Pitches	.258	1631	421	79	10	31	156	153	308	.322	.376
Starter	3.58	50	24	0	95	95	626.1	633	45	199	435	Pitch 76-90	.274	318	87	13	2	4	25	17	62	.311	.365
Reliever	3.60	1	0	0	6	0	10.0	12	0	1	7	Pitch 91-105	.316	285	90	18	1	5	36	18	44	.357	.439
0-3 Days Rest (Start)	4.35	2	2	0	7	7	41.1	41	4	22	28	Pitch 106+	.245	192	47	4	1	5	17	12	28	.289	.354
4 Days Rest	3.46	39	12	0	66	66	437.1	437	35	129	320	First Pitch	.356	343	122	18	2	11	44	1	0	.357	.516

Career (1995-1997)

	ERA	W	L	Sv	G	GS	IP	H	HR	BB	SO		Avg	AB	H	2B	3B	HR	RBI	BB	SO	OBP	SLG
5+ Days Rest	3.72	9	10	0	22	22	147.2	155	6	48	87	Ahead in Count	.194	1055	205	33	5	9	51	0	371	.197	.261
vs. AL	3.60	50	23	0	98	98	617.0	628	45	196	428	Behind in Count	.320	553	177	35	3	16	85	99	0	.421	.481
vs. NL	2.79	1	1	0	3	3	19.1	17	0	1	14	Two Strikes	.198	1109	220	45	4	10	62	99	442	.266	.273
Pre-All Star	3.70	25	15	0	52	46	309.1	324	23	104	197	Pre-All Star	.276	1175	324	60	4	23	120	104	197	.335	.392
Post-All Star	3.47	26	9	0	49	49	327.0	321	22	96	245	Post-All Star	.257	1251	321	54	10	22	114	96	245	.311	.369

Pitcher vs. Batter (career)

Pitches Best Vs.	Avg	AB	H	2B	3B	HR	RBI	BB	SO	OBP	SLG	Pitches Worst Vs.	Avg	AB	H	2B	3B	HR	RBI	BB	SO	OBP	SLG
Roberto Kelly	.000	12	0	0	0	0	0	0	5	.000	.000	Manny Ramirez	.500	18	9	2	0	2	7	0	3	.500	.944
Billy Ripken	.000	11	0	0	0	0	0	0	1	.000	.000	Juan Gonzalez	.500	16	8	3	0	1	5	1	3	.529	.875
John Valentin	.067	15	1	1	0	0	1	1	2	.125	.133	Frank Thomas	.500	14	7	2	0	2	6	5	0	.632	1.071
Jim Edmonds	.067	15	1	0	1	0	1	1	3	.125	.200	Greg Vaughn	.500	10	5	1	0	1	5		0	.615	.900
Mike Devereaux	.100	10	1	0	0	0	1	1	2	.182	.100	Jeff Cirillo	.450	20	9	1	1	2	3	4	2	.542	.900

J.R. Phillips — Astros   Age 28 – Bats Left (flyball hitter)

	Avg	G	AB	R	H	2B	3B	HR	RBI	BB	SO	HBP	GDP	SB	CS	OBP	SLG	IBB	SH	SF	#Pit	#P/PA	GB	FB	G/F
1997 Season	.133	13	15	2	2	0	0	1	4	0	7	0	0	0	0	.125	.333	0	0	1	53	3.31	3	6	0.50
Career (1993-1997)	.183	181	404	43	74	15	1	19	54	31	145	1	5	1	2	.242	.366	3	2	2	1698	3.86	105	116	0.91

1997 Season

	Avg	AB	H	2B	3B	HR	RBI	BB	SO	OBP	SLG		Avg	AB	H	2B	3B	HR	RBI	BB	SO	OBP	SLG
vs. Left	.000	2	0	0	0	0	0	0	2	.000	.000	Scoring Posn	.143	7	1	0	0	1	4	0	3	.125	.571
vs. Right	.154	13	2	0	0	1	4	0	5	.143	.385	Close & Late	.143	7	1	0	0	1	3	0	3	.143	.571

Career (1993-1997)

	Avg	AB	H	2B	3B	HR	RBI	BB	SO	OBP	SLG		Avg	AB	H	2B	3B	HR	RBI	BB	SO	OBP	SLG
vs. Left	.152	46	7	0	0	1	7	2	20	.200	.217	First Pitch	.291	55	16	2	0	5	13	1	0	.304	.600
vs. Right	.187	358	67	15	1	18	47	29	125	.247	.385	Ahead in Count	.284	67	19	4	1	6	15	16	0	.422	.642
Groundball	.159	113	18	3	0	3	12	9	37	.221	.265	Behind in Count	.124	217	27	8	0	6	19	0	124	.127	.244
Flyball	.155	71	11	5	0	1	7	5	25	.211	.268	Two Strikes	.101	227	23	6	0	5	15	14	145	.157	.194
Home	.190	210	40	6	0	10	29	12	74	.233	.362	Batting #6	.184	98	18	3	1	6	11	9	33	.250	.418
Away	.175	194	34	9	1	9	25	19	71	.251	.371	Batting #7	.181	182	33	8	0	7	17	13	65	.236	.341
Day	.168	214	36	7	0	12	32	16	71	.225	.369	Other	.185	124	23	4	0	6	26	9	47	.244	.363
Night	.200	190	38	8	1	7	22	15	74	.261	.363	March/April	.150	40	6	0	0	3	8	3		.227	.375
Grass	.181	277	50	8	0	12	33	20	95	.238	.339	May	.104	115	12	3	0	4	8	10	33	.183	.235
Turf	.189	127	24	7	1	7	21	11	50	.250	.425	June	.185	108	20	2	0	5	15	6	41	.226	.343
Pre-All Star	.158	284	45	9	0	12	31	24	103	.226	.317	July	.230	61	14	5	0	2	8	7	22	.304	.410
Post-All Star	.242	120	29	6	1	7	23	7	42	.281	.483	August	.243	37	9	0	0	3	10	2	14	.282	.486
Scoring Posn	.186	113	21	5	0	7	38	12	41	.260	.416	Sept/Oct	.302	43	13	5	1	7	21	2	14	.333	.605
Close & Late	.175	80	14	3	0	5	26	7	26	.224	.288	vs. AL	.000	0	0	0	0	0	0	0	0	.000	.000
None on/out	.202	94	19	3	0	6	6	5	32	.250	.426	vs. NL	.183	404	74	15	1	19	54	31	145	.242	.366

Batter vs. Pitcher (career)

Hits Best Against	Avg	AB	H	2B	3B	HR	RBI	BB	SO	OBP	SLG	Hits Worst Against	Avg	AB	H	2B	3B	HR	RBI	BB	SO	OBP	SLG
Andy Benes	.333	12	4	2	0	1	4	1	4	.385	.750	Greg Maddux	.083	12	1	0	0	1	1	0	4	.083	.333

Tony Phillips — Angels   Age 39 – Bats Both (groundball hitter)

	Avg	G	AB	R	H	2B	3B	HR	RBI	BB	SO	HBP	GDP	SB	CS	OBP	SLG	IBB	SH	SF	#Pit	#P/PA	GB	FB	G/F
1997 Season	.275	141	534	96	147	34	2	8	57	102	118	3	11	13	10	.392	.391	5	5	4	2687	4.15	171	142	1.20
Last Five Years	.282	698	2644	538	745	130	9	73	299	567	592	16	41	68	44	.409	.421	28	8	20	13787	4.24	949	603	1.57

1997 Season

	Avg	AB	H	2B	3B	HR	RBI	BB	SO	OBP	SLG		Avg	AB	H	2B	3B	HR	RBI	BB	SO	OBP	SLG
vs. Left	.245	139	34	8	1	1	12	34	26	.397	.338	First Pitch	.264	53	14	5	1	0	5	0	0	.259	.396
vs. Right	.286	395	113	26	1	7	45	68	92	.390	.410	Ahead in Count	.357	115	41	12	1	1	12	51	0	.557	.504
Groundball	.323	96	31	7	0	2	13	21	27	.445	.458	Behind in Count	.225	253	57	11	0	5	24	0	95	.230	.328
Flyball	.274	84	23	7	1	2	6	20	18	.419	.452	Two Strikes	.220	287	63	15	0	4	31	51	118	.335	.314
Home	.246	272	67	12	0	5	35	50	66	.365	.346	Batting #1	.279	448	125	26	2	8	48	81	93	.389	.400
Away	.305	262	80	22	2	3	22	52	52	.420	.439	Batting #2	.262	84	22	8	0	0	9	20	24	.410	.357
Day	.265	166	44	12	1	2	16	38	42	.403	.386	Other	.000	2	0	0	0	0	0	1	1	.333	.000
Night	.280	368	103	22	1	6	41	64	76	.387	.394	March/April	.292	89	26	3	0	1	5	20	23	.427	.360
Grass	.266	466	124	32	1	7	53	90	109	.385	.384	May	.270	89	24	4	0	1	6	23	15	.425	.348
Turf	.338	68	23	2	1	1	4	12	9	.438	.441	June	.321	106	34	7	1	1	10	17	16	.415	.434
Pre-All Star	.290	307	89	16	1	4	25	65	58	.417	.388	July	.245	110	27	9	1	3	22	11	28	.304	.427
Post-All Star	.256	227	58	18	1	4	32	37	60	.357	.396	August	.281	64	18	7	0	1	13	11	11	.410	.438
Scoring Posn	.325	117	38	6	0	2	49	29	19	.447	.427	Sept/Oct	.237	76	18	4	0	1	3	18	25	.383	.329
Close & Late	.230	74	17	5	0	0	6	20	24	.400	.297	vs. AL	.274	468	128	28	2	6	49	92	106	.393	.380
None on/out	.254	197	50	11	2	5	5	29	48	.352	.406	vs. NL	.288	66	19	6	0	2	8	10	12	.382	.470

1997 By Position

Position	Avg	AB	H	2B	3B	HR	RBI	BB	SO	OBP	SLG	G	GS	Innings	PO	A	E	DP	Fld Pct	Rng Fctr	In Zone	Outs	Zone Rtg	MLB Zone
As DH	.245	110	27	6	0	1	14	13	19	.320	.327	26	26	---	---	---	---	---	---	---	---	---	---	---
As 2b	.286	168	48	14	1	2	22	28	45	.389	.417	43	42	367.2	78	100	6	21	.967	4.36	101	90	.891	.902
As 3b	.244	41	10	2	0	2	7	10	10	.354	.293	10	10	83.2	7	13	1	1	.952	2.15	22	16	.727	.801
As lf	.250	104	26	7	1	3	10	22	20	.383	.423	31	29	240.0	48	1	2	0	.961	1.84	57	48	.842	.805
As rf	.330	100	33	6	0	2	7	29	21	.485	.430	31	28	245.2	73	3	2	1	.974	2.78	89	75	.843	.813

Last Five Years

	Avg	AB	H	2B	3B	HR	RBI	BB	SO	OBP	SLG		Avg	AB	H	2B	3B	HR	RBI	BB	SO	OBP	SLG
vs. Left	.285	699	199	35	4	16	71	182	127	.434	.415	First Pitch	.342	266	91	18	1	7	36	18	0	.389	.496
vs. Right	.281	1945	546	95	5	57	228	385	465	.399	.423	Ahead in Count	.389	558	217	47	4	32	100	260	0	.580	.659
Groundball	.319	568	181	25	4	14	64	130	132	.447	.451	Behind in Count	.216	1207	261	36	2	16	93	0	460	.220	.289
Flyball	.289	532	154	29	1	24	79	108	117	.410	.483	Two Strikes	.204	1414	289	39	3	17	106	289	592	.340	.272
Home	.271	1297	352	56	3	39	155	288	301	.404	.409	Batting #1	.282	2539	717	122	9	72	288	541	562	.409	.423
Away	.292	1347	393	74	6	34	144	279	291	.414	.431	Batting #2	.258	89	23	8	0	0	9	21	27	.405	.348
Day	.278	877	244	40	1	29	114	201	208	.410	.425	Other	.313	16	5	0	0	1	2	5	3	.476	.500
Night	.284	1767	501	90	8	44	185	366	384	.408	.418	March/April	.289	377	109	12	0	10	51	81	75	.413	.401
Grass	.280	2282	640	116	7	57	253	483	518	.406	.412	May	.290	496	144	25	1	12	59	118	106	.428	.417
Turf	.290	362	105	14	2	16	46	84	74	.426	.472	June	.294	496	146	30	3	13	61	110	102	.419	.446
Pre-All Star	.291	1546	450	77	4	43	196	346	320	.420	.429	July	.289	532	154	32	3	17	67	99	124	.400	.457
Post-All Star	.269	1098	295	53	5	30	103	221	272	.394	.408	August	.255	384	98	17	1	12	40	86	99	.397	.398
Scoring Posn	.282	574	162	22	3	17	230	146	124	.419	.420	Sept/Oct	.262	359	94	14	1	9	21	73	86	.389	.382
Close & Late	.269	353	95	17	0	9	46	92	102	.421	.394	vs. AL	.282	2578	726	124	9	71	291	557	580	.410	.419
None on/out	.285	1080	308	53	3	32	32	188	238	.382	.470	vs. NL	.288	66	19	6	0	2	8	10	12	.382	.470

Batter vs. Pitcher (since 1984)

Hits Best Against	Avg	AB	H	2B	3B	HR	RBI	BB	SO	OBP	SLG	Hits Worst Against	Avg	AB	H	2B	3B	HR	RBI	BB	SO	OBP	SLG
Ken Hill	.500	14	7	3	0	0	3	2	2	.563	.714	Mark Leiter	.000	10	0	0	0	0	0	1	0	2	.000
Felipe Lira	.467	15	7	3	0	1	4	1	3	.500	.867	Ariel Prieto	.111	18	2	0	0	0	1	2	8	.200	.111
Rich Robertson	.444	9	4	0	1	0	0	3		.583	.667	Dennis Martinez	.118	17	2	0	0	0	1	3	6	.250	.118
Pat Hentgen	.367	30	11	2	0	4	11	6	3	.472	.833	Mike Mussina	.130	54	7	2	0	0	1	4	18	.190	.167
Scott Erickson	.354	48	17	4	0	5	9	15	7	.508	.750	Donn Pall	.143	21	3	0	0	0	0	2	2	.217	.143

Mike Piazza — Dodgers

Age 29 – Bats Right

	Avg	G	AB	R	H	2B	3B	HR	RBI	BB	SO	HBP	GDP	SB	CS	OBP	SLG	IBB	SH	SF	#Pit	#P/PA	GB	FB	G/F
1997 Season	.362	152	556	104	201	32	1	40	124	69	77	3	18	5	1	.431	.638	11	0	5	2208	3.49	218	151	1.44
Last Five Years	.337	668	2489	418	838	107	3	167	526	268	401	9	70	10	11	.401	.583	58	0	16	9880	3.55	956	673	1.42

1997 Season

	Avg	AB	H	2B	3B	HR	RBI	BB	SO	OBP	SLG		Avg	AB	H	2B	3B	HR	RBI	BB	SO	OBP	SLG
vs. Left	.363	124	45	9	1	7	27	20	20	.450	.621	First Pitch	.360	89	32	2	0	9	27	7	0	.420	.685
vs. Right	.361	432	156	23	0	33	97	49	57	.426	.644	Ahead in Count	.459	122	56	7	0	12	36	48	0	.612	.811
Groundball	.270	89	24	5	1	3	17	8	9	.323	.449	Behind in Count	.309	246	76	13	1	12	38	0	65	.309	.516
Flyball	.397	73	29	5	0	4	12	8	14	.457	.630	Two Strikes	.311	238	74	13	1	15	41	14	77	.346	.563
Home	.355	279	99	12	0	22	61	39	40	.432	.634	Batting #3	.361	468	169	29	1	37	112	52	64	.423	.665
Away	.368	277	102	20	1	18	63	30	35	.431	.643	Batting #4	.381	84	32	3	0	3	12	16	12	.485	.524
Day	.377	159	60	10	0	10	34	16	20	.435	.629	Other	.000	4	0	0	0	0	0	0	1	.200	.000
Night	.355	397	141	22	1	30	90	53	57	.430	.642	March/April	.319	72	23	3	0	4	12	12	12	.424	.528
Grass	.353	465	164	24	1	31	95	53	64	.417	.609	May	.323	93	30	6	0	3	10	12	11	.396	.484
Turf	.407	91	37	8	0	9	29	16	13	.500	.791	June	.431	109	47	8	0	9	25	11	14	.475	.752
Pre-All Star	.357	300	107	19	0	16	51	37	40	.424	.580	July	.349	83	29	6	0	6	23	8	12	.404	.639
Post-All Star	.367	256	94	13	1	24	73	32	37	.440	.707	August	.320	103	33	5	0	10	27	19	20	.431	.660
Scoring Posn	.361	147	53	8	0	11	81	30	17	.456	.639	Sept/Oct	.406	96	39	4	1	8	27	7	8	.447	.719
Close & Late	.310	84	26	5	0	3	19	15	14	.414	.476	vs. AL	.435	62	27	6	1	3	12	6	8	.478	.710
None on/out	.333	114	38	3	0	9	9	15	17	.415	.596	vs. NL	.352	494	174	26	0	37	112	63	69	.426	.630

1997 By Position

Position	Avg	AB	H	2B	3B	HR	RBI	BB	SO	OBP	SLG	G	GS	Innings	PO	A	E	DP	Fld Pct	Rng Fctr	In Zone	Zone Outs	Zone Rtg	MLB Zone
As c	.358	520	186	29	0	40	118	68	73	.432	.644	140	139	1199.1	1044	74	16	11	.986	---	---	---	---	---

Last Five Years

	Avg	AB	H	2B	3B	HR	RBI	BB	SO	OBP	SLG		Avg	AB	H	2B	3B	HR	RBI	BB	SO	OBP	SLG
vs. Left	.352	542	191	27	1	41	120	61	90	.416	.633	First Pitch	.438	368	161	15	0	46	140	43	0	.495	.853
vs. Right	.332	1947	647	80	2	126	406	207	311	.396	.570	Ahead in Count	.405	513	208	30	1	41	121	145	0	.537	.708
Groundball	.298	634	189	24	1	22	109	58	59	.356	.443	Behind in Count	.277	1148	318	36	2	58	171	0	333	.277	.463
Flyball	.372	382	142	19	1	35	104	46	76	.440	.702	Two Strikes	.243	1101	267	34	2	46	140	80	401	.294	.402
Home	.316	1236	391	41	0	79	245	127	217	.380	.543	Batting #3	.337	1800	607	78	1	130	408	208	292	.406	.598
Away	.357	1253	447	66	2	88	281	141	184	.421	.623	Batting #4	.364	321	117	15	0	16	54	34	46	.423	.561
Day	.363	656	238	31	0	51	152	81	92	.431	.643	Other	.310	368	114	14	2	21	64	26	63	.356	.530
Night	.327	1833	600	76	3	116	374	187	309	.390	.562	March/April	.330	355	117	15	0	17	67	31	64	.382	.515
Grass	.326	1992	650	79	2	124	407	214	330	.391	.555	May	.371	404	150	20	0	26	84	36	60	.423	.614
Turf	.378	497	188	28	1	43	119	54	71	.439	.698	June	.346	480	166	19	1	42	113	50	66	.406	.652
Pre-All Star	.344	1388	478	57	1	92	285	127	218	.399	.586	July	.308	435	134	15	1	23	79	45	71	.374	.506
Post-All Star	.327	1101	360	50	2	75	241	141	183	.404	.580	August	.337	430	145	24	0	33	92	58	77	.415	.623
Scoring Posn	.351	667	234	28	0	45	351	113	105	.437	.595	Sept/Oct	.327	385	126	14	1	26	91	48	63	.401	.571
Close & Late	.294	408	120	17	1	23	75	57	83	.381	.510	vs. AL	.435	62	27	6	1	3	12	6	8	.478	.710
None on/out	.346	482	167	18	0	36	36	40	71	.400	.608	vs. NL	.334	2427	811	101	2	164	514	262	393	.399	.580

Batter vs. Pitcher (career)

Hits Best Against	Avg	AB	H	2B	3B	HR	RBI	BB	SO	OBP	SLG	Hits Worst Against	Avg	AB	H	2B	3B	HR	RBI	BB	SO	OBP	SLG
Tim Worrell	.615	13	8	1	0	3	6	2	0	.667	1.385	Mel Rojas	.077	13	1	0	0	0	1	1	7	.143	.077
Esteban Loaiza	.600	10	6	0	0	1	2	1	1	.636	.900	Tim Scott	.091	11	1	1	0	0	1	0	4	.091	.182
Steve Reed	.583	12	7	1	0	4	9	1	1	.667	1.667	Jeff Juden	.125	8	1	0	0	0	0	3	1	.364	.125
Mike Remlinger	.375	8	3	2	0	1	2	3	3	.545	1.000	Chris Hammond	.154	13	2	0	0	0	1	2	1	.250	.154
Doug Brocail	.364	11	4	2	0	2	5	2	3	.462	1.091	Mark Clark	.154	13	2	0	0	0	1	3	2	.313	.154

Hipolito Pichardo — Royals

Age 28 – Pitches Right (groundball pitcher)

	ERA	W	L	Sv	G	GS	IP	BB	SO	Avg	H	2B	3B	HR	RBI	OBP	SLG	GF	IR	IRS	Hld	SvOp	SB	CS	GB	FB	G/F
1997 Season	4.22	3	5	11	47	0	49.0	24	34	.273	51	5	2	7	19	.358	.433	26	24	5	4	13	0	2	80	38	2.11
Last Five Years	4.48	26	25	18	223	25	413.2	157	226	.283	456	84	6	30	202	.351	.398	91	113	36	33	25	17	12	756	307	2.46

1997 Season

	ERA	W	L	Sv	G	GS	IP	H	HR	BB	SO		Avg	AB	H	2B	3B	HR	RBI	BB	SO	OBP	SLG
Home	5.06	1	3	2	20	0	21.1	25	5	11	11	vs. Left	.301	83	25	2	1	5	10	14	17	.408	.530
Away	3.58	2	2	9	27	0	27.2	26	2	13	23	vs. Right	.250	104	26	3	1	2	9	10	17	.316	.356
Starter	0.00	0	0	0	0	0	0.0	0	0	0	0	Scoring Posn	.146	48	7	1	0	1	11	14	9	.339	.229
Reliever	4.22	3	5	11	47	0	49.0	51	7	24	34	Close & Late	.292	120	35	3	0	5	14	14	18	.366	.442
0 Days rest (Relief)	3.60	0	1	5	9	0	10.0	12	1	4	4	None on/out	.273	44	12	1	0	2	2	2	10	.319	.432
1 or 2 Days rest	5.33	2	4	4	26	0	27.0	26	5	16	23	First Pitch	.345	29	10	0	0	4	11	8	0	.486	.759
3+ Days rest	2.25	1	0	2	12	0	12.0	13	1	4	7	Ahead in Count	.209	91	19	2	1	3	0	0	32	.217	.286
Pre-All Star	5.61	2	4	9	32	0	33.2	39	5	17	19	Behind in Count	.410	39	16	2	1	1	7	0	0	.500	.590
Post-All Star	1.17	1	1	2	15	0	15.1	12	2	7	15	Two Strikes	.238	84	20	3	1	2	6	9	34	.319	.369

Last Five Years

	ERA	W	L	Sv	G	GS	IP	H	HR	BB	SO		Avg	AB	H	2B	3B	HR	RBI	BB	SO	OBP	SLG
Home	4.62	15	13	5	106	14	208.2	241	17	75	100	vs. Left	.301	788	237	41	3	16	97	78	87	.364	.421
Away	4.35	11	12	13	117	11	205.0	215	13	82	126	vs. Right	.266	824	219	43	3	14	105	79	139	.339	.376
Day	4.77	10	8	3	76	8	128.1	145	10	50	68	Inning 1-6	.297	691	205	48	2	12	96	57	74	.351	.424
Night	4.35	16	17	15	147	17	285.1	311	20	107	158	Inning 7+	.273	921	251	36	4	18	106	100	152	.351	.379
Grass	4.22	17	16	12	157	7	232.2	228	14	101	141	None on	.291	843	245	46	6	17	17	65	127	.346	.420
Turf	4.82	9	9	6	66	18	181.0	228	16	56	85	Runners on	.274	769	211	38	0	13	185	92	99	.356	.375
March/April	5.05	3	5	5	40	4	71.1	76	1	29	47	Scoring Posn	.285	452	129	26	0	6	167	72	69	.382	.383
May	3.71	4	4	6	46	5	85.0	96	7	28	43	Close & Late	.285	498	142	19	2	9	61	61	80	.368	.386
June	5.29	8	5	2	43	5	80.0	84	5	35	40	None on/out	.277	379	105	17	3	9	9	24	60	.327	.409
July	4.57	6	6	2	37	5	82.2	91	7	25	42	vs. 1st Batr (relief)	.254	181	46	5	2	4	19	12	27	.313	.370
August	4.99	2	2	0	24	3	39.2	50	4	21	24	1st Inning Pitched	.292	758	221	31	3	16	110	75	125	.359	.404
Sept/Oct	3.27	3	3	3	33	3	55.0	59	6	19	30	First 15 Pitches	.278	661	184	24	3	13	73	54	101	.335	.383
Starter	4.00	7	7	0	25	25	155.1	170	10	52	64	Pitch 16-30	.289	394	114	18	3	4	49	56	68	.384	.381
Reliever	4.77	19	18	18	198	0	258.1	286	20	105	162	Pitch 31-45	.298	191	57	14	0	6	31	16	20	.369	.466
0 Days rest (Relief)	6.14	5	4	5	29	0	36.2	55	4	15	22	Pitch 46+	.276	366	101	28	0	7	49	31	37	.333	.410
1 or 2 Days rest	4.20	10	9	8	106	0	145.2	134	9	62	96	First Pitch	.274	241	66	13	2	6	35	22	0	.341	.419
3+ Days rest	5.21	4	5	5	63	0	76.0	97	7	28	44	Ahead in Count	.248	661	164	29	1	8	55	0	187	.260	.331
vs. AL	4.47	26	25	17	219	25	409.0	453	30	156	222	Behind in Count	.356	376	134	21	3	12	71	63	0	.448	.524
vs. NL	5.79	0	0	1	4	0	4.2	3	0	1	4	Two Strikes	.243	686	167	22	1	10	59	71	226	.319	.322
Pre-All Star	4.61	17	17	13	142	16	263.1	285	16	98	143	Pre-All Star	.280	1018	285	57	5	16	131	98	143	.347	.393
Post-All Star	4.25	9	8	5	81	9	150.1	171	14	59	83	Post-All Star	.288	594	171	27	1	14	71	59	83	.359	.407

Pitcher vs. Batter (career)

Pitches Best Vs.	Avg	AB	H	2B	3B	HR	RBI	BB	SO	OBP	SLG	Pitches Worst Vs.	Avg	AB	H	2B	3B	HR	RBI	BB	SO	OBP	SLG
Mo Vaughn	.000	11	0	0	0	0	0	1	3	.083	.000	John Olerud	.500	12	6	2	0	0	2	3	2	.600	.667
Ron Karkovice	.067	15	1	0	0	0	0	0	4	.067	.067	Mike Stanley	.500	8	4	1	0	0	1	2	2	.636	.625
Carlos Baerga	.077	13	1	1	0	0	4	1	1	.125	.154	Rafael Palmeiro	.467	15	7	2	0	2	3	1	1	.529	1.000
Joe Carter	.125	16	2	0	0	0	1	0	2	.176	.125	Edgar Martinez	.444	18	8	2	0	2	5	4	1	.545	.889
Terry Steinbach	.167	12	2	0	0	0	0	0	2	.167	.167	Brady Anderson	.429	14	6	0	1	1	3	1	1	.529	.786

Marc Pisciotta — Cubs

Age 27 – Pitches Right

	ERA	W	L	Sv	G	GS	IP	BB	SO	Avg	H	2B	3B	HR	RBI	OBP	SLG	GF	IR	IRS	Hld	SvOp	SB	CS	GB	FB	G/F
1997 Season	3.18	3	1	0	24	0	28.1	16	21	.200	20	5	0	1	13	.314	.280	7	15	5	10	1	2	2	35	30	1.17

1997 Season

	ERA	W	L	Sv	G	GS	IP	H	HR	BB	SO		Avg	AB	H	2B	3B	HR	RBI	BB	SO	OBP	SLG
Home	4.32	3	0	0	14	0	16.2	14	1	8	15	vs. Left	.261	46	12	2	0	1	8	6	10	.346	.370
Away	1.54	0	1	0	10	0	11.2	6	0	8	6	vs. Right	.148	54	8	3	0	0	5	10	11	.288	.204

Jim Pittsley — Royals

Age 24 – Pitches Right

	ERA	W	L	Sv	G	GS	IP	BB	SO	Avg	H	2B	3B	HR	RBI	OBP	SLG	CG	ShO	Sup	QS	#P/S	SB	CS	GB	FB	G/F
1997 Season	5.46	5	8	0	21	21	112.0	54	52	.277	120	14	5	15	66	.361	.436	0	0	5.54	5	87	11	4	159	133	1.20
Career (1995-1997)	5.70	5	8	0	22	22	115.1	55	52	.283	127	15	5	18	71	.364	.459	0	0	5.54	5	86	11	4	166	140	1.19

1997 Season

	ERA	W	L	Sv	G	GS	IP	H	HR	BB	SO		Avg	AB	H	2B	3B	HR	RBI	BB	SO	OBP	SLG
Home	4.82	4	5	0	13	13	74.2	72	10	33	34	vs. Left	.298	205	61	7	3	8	30	35	25	.403	.478
Away	6.75	1	3	0	8	8	37.1	48	5	21	18	vs. Right	.259	228	59	7	2	7	36	19	27	.319	.399
Starter	5.46	5	8	0	21	21	112.0	120	15	54	52	Scoring Posn	.267	116	31	6	3	3	47	11	10	.321	.448
Reliever	0.00	0	0	0	0	0	0.0	0	0	0	0	Close & Late	.111	9	1	0	0	1	2	1	0	.200	.444
0-3 Days Rest (Start)	0.00	0	0	0	0	0	0.0	0	0	0	0	None on/out	.270	100	27	1	1	2	2	16	14	.381	.360
4 Days Rest	4.54	2	2	0	7	7	37.2	43	3	13	19	First Pitch	.443	61	27	3	0	5	13	1	0	.452	.738
5+ Days Rest	5.93	3	6	0	14	14	74.1	77	12	41	33	Ahead in Count	.231	173	40	2	3	2	15	0	41	.251	.312
Pre-All Star	5.58	2	6	0	12	12	69.1	76	11	30	32	Behind in Count	.270	126	34	7	1	7	28	33	0	.420	.508
Post-All Star	5.27	3	2	0	9	9	42.2	44	4	24	20	Two Strikes	.201	174	35	3	2	3	17	20	52	.291	.293

Erik Plantenberg — Phillies

Age 29 – Pitches Left (groundball pitcher)

	ERA	W	L	Sv	G	GS	IP	BB	SO	Avg	H	2B	3B	HR	RBI	OBP	SLG	GF	IR	IRS	Hld	SvOp	SB	CS	GB	FB	G/F
1997 Season	4.91	0	0	0	35	0	25.2	12	12	.255	25	10	0	1	18	.339	.388	9	18	9	3	0	1	0	48	24	2.00
Career (1993-1997)	4.46	0	0	1	61	0	42.1	31	16	.250	40	12	0	1	24	.379	.344	15	42	15	10	1	1	1	87	33	2.64

1997 Season

	ERA	W	L	Sv	G	GS	IP	H	HR	BB	SO		Avg	AB	H	2B	3B	HR	RBI	BB	SO	OBP	SLG
Home	3.68	0	0	0	19	0	14.2	11	0	5	8	vs. Left	.356	45	16	4	0	1	11	3	5	.408	.511
Away	6.55	0	0	0	16	0	11.0	14	1	7	4	vs. Right	.170	53	9	6	0	0	7	9	7	.286	.283
Starter	0.00	0	0	0	0	0	0.0	0	0	0	0	Scoring Posn	.444	27	12	4	0	1	18	3	3	.500	.704
Reliever	4.91	0	0	0	35	0	25.2	25	1	12	12	Close & Late	.300	20	6	1	0	0	2	3	4	.391	.350
0 Days rest (Relief)	3.18	0	0	0	7	0	5.2	3	0	4	2	None on/out	.043	23	1	1	0	0	0	3	2	.154	.087
1 or 2 Days rest	5.40	0	0	0	24	0	18.1	19	1	7	9	First Pitch	.133	15	2	1	0	0	4	0	0	.133	.200
3+ Days rest	5.40	0	0	0	4	0	1.2	3	0	1	1	Ahead in Count	.121	33	4	2	0	0	0	0	11	.147	.182
Pre-All Star	4.91	0	0	0	35	0	25.2	25	1	12	12	Behind in Count	.435	23	10	4	0	1	8	7	0	.548	.739
Post-All Star	0.00	0	0	0	0	0	0.0	0	0	0	0	Two Strikes	.128	39	5	2	0	0	1	5	12	.227	.179

Phil Plantier — Cardinals

Age 29 – Bats Left (flyball hitter)

	Avg	G	AB	R	H	2B	3B	HR	RBI	BB	SO	HBP	GDP	SB	CS	OBP	SLG	IBB	SH	SF	#Pit	#P/PA	GB	FB	G/F
1997 Season	.248	52	121	13	30	8	0	5	18	13	30	3	5	0	3	.331	.438	1	0	2	578	4.16	34	36	0.94
Last Five Years	.233	435	1371	186	320	63	2	73	224	166	349	19	24	10	12	.322	.442	17	2	13	6476	4.12	323	469	0.69

1997 Season

	Avg	AB	H	2B	3B	HR	RBI	BB	SO	OBP	SLG		Avg	AB	H	2B	3B	HR	RBI	BB	SO	OBP	SLG
vs. Left	.154	13	2	0	0	1	1	1	3	.267	.385	Scoring Posn	.273	33	9	3	0	0	13	4	8	.350	.364
vs. Right	.259	108	28	8	0	4	17	12	27	.339	.444	Close & Late	.389	18	7	3	0	1	4	4	4	.522	.722
Home	.246	57	14	3	0	2	10	9	14	.357	.404	None on/out	.208	24	5	1	0	2	2	3	6	.321	.500
Away	.250	64	16	5	0	3	8	4	16	.304	.469	Batting #5	.091	22	2	0	0	1	3	5	7	.300	.227
First Pitch	.333	6	2	0	0	1	1	0	0	.429	.333	Batting #6	.375	24	9	1	0	2	6	3	5	.444	.667
Ahead in Count	.381	21	8	2	0	2	6	5	0	.481	.762	Other	.253	75	19	7	0	2	9	5	18	.305	.427
Behind in Count	.197	66	13	6	0	3	9	0	23	.221	.424	Pre-All Star	.125	8	1	0	0	0	0	2	3	.300	.125
Two Strikes	.171	70	12	4	0	2	9	7	30	.253	.314	Post-All Star	.257	113	29	8	0	5	18	11	27	.333	.460

Last Five Years

	Avg	AB	H	2B	3B	HR	RBI	BB	SO	OBP	SLG		Avg	AB	H	2B	3B	HR	RBI	BB	SO	OBP	SLG
vs. Left	.192	292	56	3	0	17	39	33	86	.284	.377	First Pitch	.241	83	20	4	0	4	19	10	0	.333	.434
vs. Right	.245	1079	264	60	2	56	185	133	263	.332	.460	Ahead in Count	.336	330	111	17	1	37	90	79	0	.464	.730
Groundball	.256	402	103	19	1	24	62	43	107	.332	.488	Behind in Count	.181	656	119	29	1	18	72	0	275	.194	.311
Flyball	.214	201	43	10	0	14	33	23	58	.312	.473	Two Strikes	.165	729	120	28	1	20	72	76	349	.248	.288
Home	.224	662	148	29	2	29	99	81	169	.315	.405	Batting #4	.253	435	110	24	0	32	82	66	103	.360	.529
Away	.243	709	172	34	0	44	125	85	180	.328	.477	Batting #5	.222	473	105	23	1	17	69	46	126	.296	.383
Day	.276	475	131	26	1	28	105	52	117	.348	.512	Other	.227	463	105	16	1	24	73	54	120	.310	.421
Night	.211	896	189	37	1	45	119	114	232	.309	.405	March/April	.205	195	40	10	0	13	25	26	53	.297	.456
Grass	.224	1099	246	48	2	52	173	133	267	.312	.413	May	.262	252	66	16	0	13	49	26	65	.347	.480
Turf	.272	272	74	15	0	21	51	33	82	.360	.559	June	.226	252	57	9	1	13	37	26	61	.306	.425
Pre-All Star	.230	770	177	38	1	41	115	85	197	.314	.442	July	.238	265	63	13	0	10	33	23	70	.296	.400
Post-All Star	.238	601	143	25	1	32	109	81	152	.331	.443	August	.236	229	54	8	1	15	45	37	49	.349	.476
Scoring Posn	.239	393	94	23	1	19	155	61	101	.340	.448	Sept/Oct	.225	178	40	7	0	9	35	28	51	.335	.416
Close & Late	.198	243	48	5	0	14	33	30	72	.291	.391	vs. AL	.220	250	55	10	1	8	33	29	61	.310	.364
None on/out	.220	314	69	11	0	14	14	34	76	.304	.389	vs. NL	.236	1121	265	53	1	65	191	137	288	.325	.459

Batter vs. Pitcher (career)

Hits Best Against	Avg	AB	H	2B	3B	HR	RBI	BB	SO	OBP	SLG	Hits Worst Against	Avg	AB	H	2B	3B	HR	RBI	BB	SO	OBP	SLG
Curt Schilling	.545	11	6	3	0	2	5	0	1	.545	1.364	John Smoltz	.000	14	0	0	0	0	0	0	5	.000	.000
Doug Drabek	.462	13	6	3	0	2	6	2	3	.563	1.154	Greg Maddux	.053	19	1	0	0	0	0	0	6	.053	.053
Rene Arocha	.455	11	5	1	0	2	5	0	2	.455	1.091	Kevin Ritz	.067	15	1	0	0	0	0	0	1	.067	.067
Pete Smith	.333	12	4	0	0	2	6	1	3	.385	.833	Dwight Gooden	.083	12	1	0	0	0	0	0	2	.083	.083
Tim Belcher	.333	9	3	2	0	1	3	1	1	.455	.889	Ben McDonald	.083	12	1	0	0	0	1	2	3	.214	.083

Dan Plesac — Blue Jays

Age 36 – Pitches Left

	ERA	W	L	Sv	G	GS	IP	BB	SO	Avg	H	2B	3B	HR	RBI	OBP	SLG	GF	IR	IRS	Hld	SvOp	SB	CS	GB	FB	G/F
1997 Season	3.58	2	4	1	73	0	50.1	19	61	.244	47	5	1	8	28	.310	.404	18	52	14	27	5	5	1	50	52	0.96
Last Five Years	4.13	16	17	16	315	0	298.1	104	294	.261	302	44	6	34	164	.321	.403	90	201	62	75	32	22	5	358	316	1.13

1997 Season

	ERA	W	L	Sv	G	GS	IP	H	HR	BB	SO		Avg	AB	H	2B	3B	HR	RBI	BB	SO	OBP	SLG
Home	5.14	2	3	0	31	0	21.0	21	4	8	23	vs. Left	.189	90	17	2	0	4	14	7	34	.247	.344
Away	2.45	0	1	1	42	0	29.1	26	4	11	38	vs. Right	.291	103	30	3	1	4	14	12	27	.362	.456
Day	1.86	1	2	0	27	0	19.1	17	1	8	26	Inning 1-6	.500	2	1	0	0	0	1	1	1	.667	.500
Night	4.65	1	2	1	46	0	31.0	30	7	11	35	Inning 7+	.241	191	46	5	1	8	28	18	60	.305	.403
Grass	2.33	0	1	1	38	0	27.0	24	4	10	35	None on	.255	94	24	2	1	4	4	9	27	.320	.426
Turf	5.01	2	3	0	35	0	23.1	23	4	9	26	Runners on	.232	99	23	3	0	4	24	10	34	.300	.384
March/April	5.79	0	2	1	13	0	9.1	13	2	2	11	Scoring Posn	.232	56	13	2	0	2	19	8	19	.323	.375
May	6.23	0	0	0	8	0	4.1	5	2	3	5	Close & Late	.289	128	37	3	1	6	22	14	38	.359	.469
June	2.89	0	1	0	10	0	9.1	9	0	2	11	None on/out	.300	40	12	1	1	0	0	5	13	.378	.375
July	2.16	0	0	0	12	0	8.1	6	1	3	11	vs. 1st Batr (relief)	.227	66	15	3	0	2	12	7	21	.301	.364
August	2.00	0	0	0	14	0	9.0	8	1	5	9	1st Inning Pitched	.250	176	44	5	1	7	27	18	54	.318	.409
Sept/Oct	3.60	2	1	0	16	0	10.0	6	2	4	14	First 15 Pitches	.258	155	40	5	1	7	24	16	45	.326	.439
Starter	0.00	0	0	0	0	0	0.0	0	0	0	0	Pitch 16-30	.194	36	7	0	0	1	4	3	14	.256	.278

1997 Season

	ERA	W	L	Sv	G	GS	IP	H	HR	BB	SO
Reliever	3.58	2	4	1	73	0	50.1	47	8	19	61
0 Days rest (Relief)	3.55	0	0	1	21	0	12.2	11	2	4	19
1 or 2 Days rest	4.74	2	3	0	36	0	24.2	27	4	11	27
3+ Days rest	1.38	0	1	0	16	0	13.0	9	2	4	15
vs. AL	3.86	2	4	1	67	0	44.1	45	8	18	56
vs. NL	1.50	0	0	0	6	0	6.0	2	0	1	5
Pre-All Star	4.44	0	3	1	34	0	24.1	28	4	8	28
Post-All Star	2.77	2	1	0	39	0	26.0	19	4	11	33

	Avg	AB	H	2B	3B	HR	RBI	BB	SO	OBP	SLG
Pitch 31-45	.000	2	0	0	0	0	0	0	2	.000	.000
Pitch 46+	.000	0	0	0	0	0	0	0	0	.000	.000
First Pitch	.385	26	10	2	0	2	5	3	0	.448	.692
Ahead in Count	.168	107	18	2	1	2	9	0	50	.168	.262
Behind in Count	.433	30	13	1	0	2	8	8	0	.538	.667
Two Strikes	.118	110	13	1	1	2	7	8	61	.178	.200
Pre-All Star	.283	99	28	4	1	4	17	8	28	.336	.465
Post-All Star	.202	94	19	1	0	4	11	11	33	.283	.340

Last Five Years

	ERA	W	L	Sv	G	GS	IP	H	HR	BB	SO
Home	4.45	7	9	9	148	0	145.2	150	17	57	148
Away	3.83	9	8	7	167	0	152.2	152	17	47	146
Day	3.34	6	5	5	135	0	132.0	124	13	42	141
Night	4.76	10	12	11	180	0	166.1	178	21	62	153
Grass	4.44	7	7	3	161	0	152.0	158	20	55	151
Turf	3.81	9	10	13	154	0	146.1	144	14	49	143
March/April	5.36	1	4	1	46	0	47.0	51	10	15	47
May	2.89	2	1	3	53	0	53.0	44	4	23	49
June	4.03	4	1	2	54	0	60.1	61	5	16	52
July	4.37	1	4	6	61	0	59.2	69	9	15	69
August	4.14	3	5	1	51	0	41.1	49	4	20	32
Sept/Oct	4.14	5	2	3	50	0	37.0	28	2	15	45
Starter	0.00	0	0	0	0	0	0.0	0	0	0	0
Reliever	4.13	16	17	16	315	0	298.1	302	34	104	294
0 Days rest (Relief)	4.25	3	3	4	83	0	65.2	71	7	22	75
1 or 2 Days rest	3.83	11	11	9	161	0	162.0	157	16	52	151
3+ Days rest	4.71	2	3	3	71	0	70.2	74	11	30	68
vs. AL	3.86	2	4	1	67	0	44.1	45	8	18	56
vs. NL	4.18	14	13	15	248	0	254.0	257	26	86	238
Pre-All Star	4.22	8	6	8	171	0	179.0	181	23	57	171
Post-All Star	4.00	8	11	8	144	0	119.1	121	11	47	123

	Avg	AB	H	2B	3B	HR	RBI	BB	SO	OBP	SLG
vs. Left	.222	409	91	15	5	10	61	31	141	.278	.357
vs. Right	.283	746	211	29	4	24	103	73	153	.344	.429
Inning 1-6	.230	139	32	5	2	2	14	9	36	.275	.338
Inning 7+	.266	1016	270	39	7	32	150	95	258	.327	.412
None on	.249	610	152	28	4	15	15	46	162	.303	.382
Runners on	.275	545	150	16	5	19	149	58	132	.340	.428
Scoring Posn	.270	315	85	12	4	9	125	42	85	.347	.419
Close & Late	.292	538	157	19	5	16	95	58	137	.358	.435
None on/out	.264	261	69	15	2	5	16	66	307		
vs. 1st Batr (relief)	.256	285	73	18	3	7	44	25	77	.312	.414
1st Inning Pitched	.259	880	228	36	6	26	141	86	220	.323	.402
First 15 Pitches	.261	781	204	34	4	22	107	74	185	.323	.399
Pitch 16-30	.257	315	81	9	3	11	47	27	92	.316	.410
Pitch 31-45	.304	56	17	1	2	1	10	2	17	.322	.446
Pitch 46+	.000	3	0	0	0	0	0	1	0	.250	.000
First Pitch	.323	161	52	7	1	3	27	20	0	.396	.435
Ahead in Count	.201	618	124	19	5	12	65	0	251	.202	.306
Behind in Count	.396	187	74	12	1	11	41	52	0	.519	.647
Two Strikes	.181	618	112	17	5	13	65	32	294	.221	.288
Pre-All Star	.262	690	181	27	5	23	99	57	171	.317	.416
Post-All Star	.260	465	121	17	4	11	65	47	123	.327	.385

Pitcher vs. Batter (career)

Pitches Best Vs.	Avg	AB	H	2B	3B	HR	RBI	BB	SO	OBP	SLG
Todd Hundley	.000	11	0	0	0	0	0	1	7	.083	.000
Pete Incaviglia	.045	22	1	0	0	0	2	1	5	.087	.045
Pat Borders	.077	13	1	0	0	0	0	2	1	.200	.077
Travis Fryman	.091	11	1	0	0	0	0	1	1	.231	.091
Ruben Sierra	.130	23	3	0	0	0	2	1	1	.167	.130

Pitches Worst Vs.	Avg	AB	H	2B	3B	HR	RBI	BB	SO	OBP	SLG
Julio Franco	.500	12	6	0	0	1	1	2	1	.571	.750
Steve Finley	.462	13	6	1	1	0	3	0	0	.462	.692
Eric Young	.375	8	3	1	0	1	1	3	0	.545	.875
Barry Bonds	.333	15	5	0	1	1	4	2	1	.412	.667
Ray Lankford	.333	12	4	2	1	1	6	0	7	.333	.917

Eric Plunk — Indians
Age 34 – Pitches Right

	ERA	W	L	Sv	G	GS	IP	BB	SO	Avg	H	2B	3B	HR	RBI	OBP	SLG	GF	IR	IRS	Hld	SvOp	SB	CS	GB	FB	G/F
1997 Season	4.66	4	5	0	56	0	65.2	36	66	.245	62	16	2	12	40	.339	.466	23	46	14	10	2	8	2	60	81	0.74
Last Five Years	2.99	24	16	22	279	0	349.1	164	372	.223	288	58	8	31	144	.313	.352	115	219	53	59	35	44	10	356	353	1.01

1997 Season

	ERA	W	L	Sv	G	GS	IP	H	HR	BB	SO
Home	4.08	2	0	0	24	0	28.2	25	3	16	35
Away	5.11	2	5	0	32	0	37.0	37	9	20	31
Day	4.85	2	4	0	23	0	26.0	25	5	15	25
Night	4.54	2	1	0	33	0	39.2	37	7	21	41
Grass	4.64	3	5	0	46	0	54.1	50	9	29	57
Turf	4.76	1	0	0	10	0	11.1	12	3	7	9
March/April	4.80	0	2	0	13	0	15.0	14	3	7	15
May	5.56	1	0	0	9	0	11.1	9	4	6	13
June	9.39	1	0	0	6	0	7.2	12	2	7	5
July	4.22	1	0	0	10	0	10.2	15	1	6	10
August	3.09	1	2	0	10	0	11.2	9	1	6	12
Sept/Oct	1.93	0	1	0	10	0	9.1	3	1	2	11
Starter	0.00	0	0	0	0	0	0.0	0	0	0	0
Reliever	4.66	4	5	0	56	0	65.2	62	12	36	66
0 Days rest (Relief)	1.17	0	1	0	8	0	7.2	4	1	2	5
1 or 2 Days rest	5.45	3	3	0	28	0	33.0	32	9	19	35
3+ Days rest	4.68	1	1	0	20	0	25.0	26	2	15	26
vs. AL	4.98	3	5	0	52	0	59.2	56	12	34	62
vs. NL	1.50	1	0	0	4	0	6.0	6	0	2	4
Pre-All Star	5.54	3	2	0	30	0	37.1	38	9	22	33
Post-All Star	3.49	1	3	0	26	0	28.1	24	3	14	33

	Avg	AB	H	2B	3B	HR	RBI	BB	SO	OBP	SLG
vs. Left	.277	94	26	3	2	5	12	16	21	.382	.511
vs. Right	.226	159	36	13	0	7	28	20	45	.313	.440
Inning 1-6	.175	40	7	2	0	0	5	5	8	.267	.225
Inning 7+	.258	213	55	14	2	12	35	31	58	.352	.512
None on	.287	122	35	8	1	8		15	33	.370	.566
Runners on	.206	131	27	8	1	4	32	21	33	.312	.374
Scoring Posn	.185	92	17	7	1	2	28	18	24	.313	.348
Close & Late	.262	61	16	4	0	4	9	11	11	.365	.525
None on/out	.267	60	16	2	0	5	5	3	16	.313	.550
vs. 1st Batr (relief)	.271	48	13	1	0	5	8	6	9	.364	.604
1st Inning Pitched	.240	183	44	8	1	11	35	22	45	.322	.475
First 15 Pitches	.278	151	42	9	1	12	33	22	29	.371	.589
Pitch 16-30	.208	77	16	5	1	0	6	10	27	.295	.299
Pitch 31-45	.150	20	3	2	0	0	1	4	8	.292	.250
Pitch 46+	.200	5	1	0	0	0	1	0		.200	.200
First Pitch	.206	34	7	3	0	1	4	5	0	.308	.382
Ahead in Count	.185	119	22	3	1	5	20	0	55	.189	.353
Behind in Count	.319	47	15	5	0	4	10	14	0	.475	.681
Two Strikes	.169	130	22	4	0	5	15	17	66	.267	.315
Pre-All Star	.259	147	38	13	1	9	26	22	33	.357	.544
Post-All Star	.226	106	24	3	1	3	14	14	33	.314	.358

Last Five Years

	ERA	W	L	Sv	G	GS	IP	H	HR	BB	SO
Home	3.10	17	3	10	130	0	156.2	123	11	65	160
Away	2.90	7	13	12	149	0	192.2	165	20	99	212
Day	2.85	8	11	6	105	0	142.0	115	10	64	162
Night	3.08	16	5	16	174	0	207.1	173	21	100	210
Grass	3.11	21	13	17	234	0	292.2	245	25	136	304
Turf	2.38	3	3	5	45	0	56.2	43	6	28	68

	Avg	AB	H	2B	3B	HR	RBI	BB	SO	OBP	SLG
vs. Left	.253	569	144	27	6	12	58	82	141	.351	.385
vs. Right	.199	722	144	31	2	19	86	82	231	.313	.327
Inning 1-6	.185	108	20	3	0	0	13	16	24	.299	.213
Inning 7+	.227	1183	268	55	8	31	131	148	348	.314	.365
None on	.232	664	154	32	5	21	21	73	191	.312	.390
Runners on	.214	627	134	26	3	10	123	91	181	.314	.313

Last Five Years

	ERA	W	L	Sv	G	GS	IP	H	HR	BB	SO		Avg	AB	H	2B	3B	HR	RBI	BB	SO	OBP	SLG
March/April	4.55	4	5	0	44	0	57.1	59	6	31	64	Scoring Posn	.200	420	84	19	3	6	114	68	117	.310	.302
May	2.14	5	2	4	52	0	63.0	41	7	36	68	Close & Late	.239	589	141	26	5	18	74	77	171	.329	.392
June	2.96	8	0	6	47	0	67.0	53	5	30	68	None on/out	.226	297	67	15	1	9	9	22	72	.286	.374
July	2.44	4	2	5	49	0	62.2	49	6	25	61	vs. 1st Batr (relief)	.230	244	56	12	0	8	30	28	56	.319	.377
August	4.17	2	6	4	51	0	58.1	56	6	29	70	1st Inning Pitched	.222	866	192	34	4	28	118	105	247	.309	.367
Sept/Oct	1.32	1	1	3	36	0	41.0	30	1	13	41	First 15 Pitches	.243	725	176	33	2	26	97	86	189	.324	.401
Starter	0.00	0	0	0	0	0	0.0	0	0	0	0	Pitch 16-30	.182	395	72	15	5	5	32	60	126	.296	.284
Reliever	2.99	24	16	22	279	0	349.1	288	31	164	372	Pitch 31-45	.219	137	30	6	0	0	10	13	50	.286	.263
0 Days rest (Relief)	1.94	4	2	7	48	0	51.0	39	2	24	56	Pitch 46+	.294	34	10	4	1	0	5	5	7	.385	.471
1 or 2 Days rest	3.12	14	9	10	145	0	182.0	145	18	91	193	First Pitch	.301	153	46	13	0	4	20	15	0	.368	.464
3+ Days rest	3.25	6	5	5	86	0	116.1	104	11	49	123	Ahead in Count	.158	688	109	17	5	10	61	0	323	.165	.241
vs. AL	3.01	23	16	22	275	0	343.1	282	31	162	368	Behind in Count	.300	217	65	17	0	9	35	74	0	.476	.502
vs. NL	1.50	1	0	0	4	0	6.0	6	0	2	4	Two Strikes	.158	732	116	19	5	13	61	75	372	.241	.251
Pre-All Star	3.10	20	8	12	157	0	206.0	167	20	107	213	Pre-All Star	.221	756	167	38	4	20	82	107	213	.321	.361
Post-All Star	2.83	4	8	10	122	0	143.1	121	11	57	159	Post-All Star	.226	535	121	20	4	11	62	57	159	.301	.340

Pitcher vs. Batter (career)

Pitches Best Vs.	Avg	AB	H	2B	3B	HR	RBI	BB	SO	OBP	SLG	Pitches Worst Vs.	Avg	AB	H	2B	3B	HR	RBI	BB	SO	OBP	SLG
Frank Thomas	.000	16	0	0	0	0	1	2	3	.111	.000	Wally Joyner	.625	16	10	2	0	3	8	3	1	.684	1.313
Jack Howell	.000	12	0	0	0	0	0	2	9	.143	.000	Harold Baines	.583	12	7	0	0	0	2	4	2	.688	.583
Chris Hoiles	.000	7	0	0	0	0	1	3	2	.273	.000	Wade Boggs	.545	11	6	2	1	0	1	7	0	.722	.909
Greg Vaughn	.053	19	1	1	0	0	0	2	6	.143	.105	Paul Molitor	.464	28	13	1	1	2	7	6	5	.559	.786
Mike Stanley	.063	16	1	0	0	0	0	2	2	.167	.063	Edgar Martinez	.333	9	3	0	0	2	4	4	5	.538	1.000

Kevin Polcovich — Pirates
Age 28 – Bats Right

	Avg	G	AB	R	H	2B	3B	HR	RBI	BB	SO	HBP	GDP	SB	CS	OBP	SLG	IBB	SH	SF	#Pit	#P/PA	GB	FB	G/F
1997 Season	.273	84	245	37	67	16	1	4	21	21	45	9	11	2	2	.350	.396	4	2	2	953	3.42	87	61	1.43

1997 Season

	Avg	AB	H	2B	3B	HR	RBI	BB	SO	OBP	SLG		Avg	AB	H	2B	3B	HR	RBI	BB	SO	OBP	SLG
vs. Left	.286	56	16	3	0	2	7	7	9	.379	.446	Scoring Posn	.210	62	13	4	0	1	17	9	8	.329	.323
vs. Right	.270	189	51	13	1	2	14	14	36	.341	.381	Close & Late	.200	35	7	2	0	1	3	2	7	.263	.343
Home	.259	116	30	10	0	0	9	9	22	.333	.345	None on/out	.275	69	19	1	1	2	2	6	14	.367	.406
Away	.287	129	37	6	1	4	12	12	23	.365	.442	Batting #8	.279	226	63	15	1	3	19	20	43	.355	.394
First Pitch	.455	33	15	3	0	1	2	0		.514	.545	Batting #9	.214	14	3	1	0	1	2	0	1	.214	.500
Ahead in Count	.327	49	16	5	1	2	9	11	0	.444	.592	Other	.200	5	1	0	0	0	1	1		.429	.200
Behind in Count	.181	116	21	4	0	1	5	0	41	.215	.241	Pre-All Star	.290	100	29	6	0	1	7	11	15	.385	.380
Two Strikes	.154	104	16	3	0	1	6	8	45	.248	.212	Post-All Star	.262	145	38	10	1	3	14	10	30	.325	.407

Jim Poole — Giants
Age 32 – Pitches Left

	ERA	W	L	Sv	G	GS	IP	BB	SO	Avg	H	2B	3B	HR	RBI	OBP	SLG	GF	IR	IRS	Hld	SvOp	SB	CS	GB	FB	G/F
1997 Season	7.11	3	1	0	63	0	49.1	25	26	.353	72	17	0	6	55	.429	.522	11	53	24	9	0	3	4	71	73	0.97
Last Five Years	4.20	15	6	2	265	0	220.2	101	152	.263	219	48	3	24	141	.343	.414	54	250	65	49	9	13	11	287	265	1.08

1997 Season

	ERA	W	L	Sv	G	GS	IP	H	HR	BB	SO		Avg	AB	H	2B	3B	HR	RBI	BB	SO	OBP	SLG
Home	7.04	1	0	0	32	0	23.0	34	1	17	13	vs. Left	.337	83	28	8	0	3	27	10	15	.412	.542
Away	7.18	2	1	0	31	0	26.1	39	5	8	13	vs. Right	.363	124	45	9	0	3	28	15	11	.440	.508
Day	9.39	1	1	0	27	0	23.0	42	2	11	10	Inning 1-6	.400	55	22	5	0	2	17	4	7	.441	.600
Night	5.13	2	0	0	36	0	26.1	31	4	14	16	Inning 7+	.336	152	51	12	0	4	38	21	19	.425	.493
Grass	7.80	2	1	0	53	0	42.2	67	5	23	25	None on/out	.319	91	29	3	0	3	3	10	9	.392	.451
Turf	2.70	1	0	0	10	0	6.2	6	1	2	1	Runners on	.379	116	44	14	0	3	52	15	17	.456	.578
March/April	2.84	1	0	0	11	0	6.1	6	1	6	3	Scoring Posn	.400	75	30	10	0	2	47	10	11	.472	.613
May	7.82	1	0	0	15	0	12.2	21	1	6	8	Close & Late	.289	38	11	4	0	1	8	9	5	.426	.474
June	4.91	1	1	0	13	0	11.0	14	2	6	2	None on/out	.310	42	13	1	0	1	1	2	3	.341	.405
July	6.00	0	0	0	11	0	9.0	14	1	3	8	vs. 1st Batr (relief)	.315	54	17	3	0	3	15	6	9	.383	.537
August	7.50	0	0	0	9	0	6.0	8	1	0	3	1st Inning Pitched	.350	180	63	16	0	5	53	20	24	.420	.522
Sept/Oct	18.69	0	0	0	4	0	4.1	10	0	4	2	First 15 Pitches	.322	149	48	10	0	5	36	19	21	.401	.490
Starter	0.00	0	0	0	0	0	0.0	0	0	0	0	Pitch 16-30	.400	45	18	4	0	1	16	4	5	.460	.556
Reliever	7.11	3	1	0	63	0	49.1	73	6	25	26	Pitch 31-45	.444	9	4	2	0	0	2	2	0	.583	.667
0 Days rest (Relief)	10.91	2	1	0	18	0	15.2	29	3	9	5	Pitch 46+	.750	4	3	1	0	0	1	0	0	.750	1.000
1 or 2 Days rest	3.72	1	0	0	26	0	19.1	25	1	10	10	First Pitch	.382	34	13	2	0	2	7	4	0	.462	.618
3+ Days rest	7.53	0	0	0	19	0	14.1	19	2	6	11	Ahead in Count	.239	88	21	4	0	0	13	0	23	.250	.284
vs. AL	10.13	0	0	0	5	0	2.2	5	0	1	1	Behind in Count	.471	51	24	8	0	0	19	11	0	.565	.627
vs. NL	6.94	3	1	0	58	0	46.2	68	6	24	25	Two Strikes	.244	90	22	4	0	2	16	10	26	.327	.356
Pre-All Star	5.34	3	1	0	41	0	32.0	41	4	18	14	Pre-All Star	.331	124	41	6	0	4	24	18	14	.418	.476
Post-All Star	10.38	0	0	0	22	0	17.1	32	2	7	12	Post-All Star	.386	83	32	11	0	2	31	7	12	.446	.590

Last Five Years

	ERA	W	L	Sv	G	GS	IP	H	HR	BB	SO		Avg	AB	H	2B	3B	HR	RBI	BB	SO	OBP	SLG
Home	3.64	7	2	0	140	0	118.2	108	5	57	90	vs. Left	.256	363	93	25	2	6	58	35	76	.323	.386
Away	4.85	8	4	2	125	0	102.0	111	19	44	62	vs. Right	.268	471	126	23	1	18	83	66	76	.358	.435
Day	4.54	5	2	1	97	0	81.1	75	5	41	55	Inning 1-6	.313	166	52	12	1	5	37	17	29	.376	.488
Night	4.00	10	4	1	168	0	139.1	144	19	60	97	Inning 7+	.250	668	167	36	2	19	104	84	123	.336	.395
Grass	4.21	13	5	1	230	0	194.2	195	20	88	139	None on	.264	406	107	17	2	15	15	35	73	.325	.426
Turf	4.15	2	1	1	35	0	26.0	24	4	13	13	Runners on	.262	428	112	31	1	9	126	66	79	.360	.402

375

Last Five Years

	ERA	W	L	Sv	G	GS	IP	H	HR	BB	SO		Avg	AB	H	2B	3B	HR	RBI	BB	SO	OBP	SLG
March/April	3.64	3	1	0	38	0	29.2	25	5	12	21	Scoring Posn	.252	266	67	19	0	6	114	51	53	.367	.391
May	3.52	3	1	0	55	0	46.0	49	3	20	39	Close & Late	.197	264	52	12	2	7	38	34	57	.289	.337
June	5.62	3	2	0	50	0	41.2	50	7	22	22	None on/out	.278	176	49	9	0	4	4	15	28	.335	.398
July	3.89	1	1	1	45	0	41.2	46	4	21	33	vs. 1st Batr (relief)	.252	230	58	13	0	6	36	26	49	.326	.387
August	2.43	3	0	0	44	0	29.2	22	3	10	24	1st Inning Pitched	.262	650	170	40	3	18	128	76	121	.340	.415
Sept/Oct	5.91	2	1	1	33	0	32.0	27	2	16	13	First 15 Pitches	.253	588	149	34	2	15	96	71	109	.335	.395
Starter	0.00	0	0	0	0	0	0.0	0	0	0	0	Pitch 16-30	.284	183	52	8	1	7	36	21	36	.359	.454
Reliever	4.20	15	6	2	265	0	220.2	219	24	101	152	Pitch 31-45	.245	53	13	5	0	1	7	7	6	.339	.396
0 Days rest (Relief)	5.15	7	2	0	67	0	57.2	61	4	28	35	Pitch 46+	.500	10	5	1	0	1	2	2	1	.583	.900
1 or 2 Days rest	3.54	6	1	1	111	0	86.1	87	7	45	54	First Pitch	.316	114	36	9	0	6	22	15	0	.402	.553
3+ Days rest	4.23	2	3	1	87	0	76.2	71	13	28	63	Ahead in Count	.190	363	69	13	2	3	45	0	127	.191	.262
vs. AL	3.59	10	4	2	172	0	150.1	136	16	64	108	Behind in Count	.349	192	67	17	1	8	41	54	0	.494	.573
vs. NL	5.50	5	2	0	93	0	70.1	83	8	37	44	Two Strikes	.168	364	61	13	1	4	46	32	152	.235	.242
Pre-All Star	3.96	10	4	0	158	0	134.0	136	15	62	93	Pre-All Star	.269	506	136	28	2	15	78	62	93	.347	.421
Post-All Star	4.57	5	2	2	107	0	86.2	83	9	39	59	Post-All Star	.253	328	83	20	1	9	63	39	59	.338	.402

Pitcher vs. Batter (career)

Pitches Best Vs.	Avg	AB	H	2B	3B	HR	RBI	BB	SO	OBP	SLG	Pitches Worst Vs.	Avg	AB	H	2B	3B	HR	RBI	BB	SO	OBP	SLG
Rafael Palmeiro	.000	11	0	0	0	0	1	1	1	.083	.000	Lance Johnson	.571	14	8	1	2	0	6	0	0	.571	.929
Wade Boggs	.077	13	1	1	0	0	0	4	5	.294	.154	Robin Ventura	.545	11	6	3	0	1	5	0	0	.500	1.091
B.J. Surhoff	.154	13	2	0	0	0	3	1	4	.214	.154	John Olerud	.400	10	4	3	0	1	5	0	2	.500	.700
Paul O'Neill	.182	11	2	0	0	0	1	2	4	.308	.182												

Mark Portugal — Phillies
Age 35 – Pitches Right

	ERA	W	L	Sv	G	GS	IP	BB	SO	Avg	H	2B	3B	HR	RBI	OBP	SLG	CG	ShO	Sup	QS	#P/S	SB	CS	GB	FB	G/F
1997 Season	4.61	0	2	0	3	3	13.2	5	2	.321	17	8	2	0	8	.373	.547	0	0	1.98	0	1	70	1	1	21	18	1.17
Last Five Years	3.63	47	33	0	115	114	696.2	225	409	.256	677	114	15	64	279	.316	.383	4	2	5.31	61	90	53	16	1005	751	1.34

1997 Season

	ERA	W	L	Sv	G	GS	IP	H	HR	BB	SO		Avg	AB	H	2B	3B	HR	RBI	BB	SO	OBP	SLG
Home	4.22	0	1	0	2	2	10.2	13	0	2	2	vs. Left	.364	22	8	3	2	0	3	1	2	.391	.682
Away	6.00	0	1	0	1	1	3.0	4	0	3	0	vs. Right	.290	31	9	5	0	0	5	4	0	.361	.452

Last Five Years

	ERA	W	L	Sv	G	GS	IP	H	HR	BB	SO		Avg	AB	H	2B	3B	HR	RBI	BB	SO	OBP	SLG
Home	3.22	24	18	0	58	58	371.2	356	38	107	229	vs. Left	.245	1270	311	43	8	27	120	124	205	.312	.355
Away	4.10	23	15	0	57	56	325.0	321	26	118	180	vs. Right	.266	1377	366	71	7	37	159	101	204	.320	.408
Day	2.86	23	10	0	43	42	283.1	241	21	85	172	Inning 1-6	.254	2329	592	98	13	52	249	200	361	.315	.374
Night	4.16	24	23	0	72	72	413.1	436	43	140	237	Inning 7+	.267	318	85	16	2	12	30	25	48	.322	.443
Grass	4.09	16	17	0	54	53	317.0	303	38	119	195	None on	.254	1540	391	73	7	32	32	140	242	.320	.373
Turf	3.25	31	16	0	61	61	379.2	374	26	106	214	Runners on	.258	1107	286	41	8	32	247	85	167	.311	.397
March/April	4.60	4	8	0	18	18	109.2	122	10	28	74	Scoring Posn	.263	594	156	26	4	16	203	62	99	.330	.401
May	3.24	7	4	0	22	22	136.0	110	13	61	81	Close & Late	.237	173	41	5	0	6	15	14	31	.293	.370
June	3.56	8	5	0	20	20	129.0	122	10	40	81	None on/out	.272	684	186	33	1	15	15	61	111	.334	.389
July	4.13	12	9	0	23	23	139.1	165	17	43	80	vs. 1st Batr (relief)	1.000	1	1	0	0	0	0	0	0	1.000	1.000
August	3.75	8	5	0	18	18	98.1	96	11	31	49	1st Inning Pitched	.259	436	113	19	6	9	59	38	67	.317	.392
Sept/Oct	2.13	8	1	0	14	13	84.1	62	3	22	44	First 75 Pitches	.251	2052	515	86	13	46	207	168	314	.309	.373
Starter	3.61	47	33	0	114	114	695.2	674	64	225	409	Pitch 76-90	.277	343	95	18	0	14	48	29	51	.341	.452
Reliever	18.00	0	0	0	1	0	1.0	3	0	0	0	Pitch 91-105	.275	193	53	7	2	4	19	20	29	.343	.394
0-3 Days Rest (Start)	1.29	4	0	0	4	4	28.0	17	2	6	10	Pitch 106+	.237	59	14	3	0	0	5	8	15	.324	.288
4 Days Rest	4.06	27	24	0	67	67	409.2	407	39	139	255	First Pitch	.315	429	135	26	3	22	67	7	0	.329	.543
5+ Days Rest	3.14	16	9	0	43	43	258.0	250	23	80	144	Ahead in Count	.217	1166	253	36	8	15	95	0	355	.220	.300
vs. AL	0.00	0	0	0	0	0	0.0	0	0	0	0	Behind in Count	.297	589	175	36	1	17	68	132	0	.427	.448
vs. NL	3.63	47	33	0	115	114	696.2	677	64	225	409	Two Strikes	.191	1129	216	28	9	14	81	86	409	.250	.269
Pre-All Star	3.83	24	20	0	68	68	418.0	402	40	152	265	Pre-All Star	.256	1572	402	70	10	40	175	152	265	.324	.389
Post-All Star	3.33	23	13	0	47	46	278.2	275	24	73	144	Post-All Star	.256	1075	275	44	5	24	104	73	144	.304	.373

Pitcher vs. Batter (career)

Pitches Best Vs.	Avg	AB	H	2B	3B	HR	RBI	BB	SO	OBP	SLG	Pitches Worst Vs.	Avg	AB	H	2B	3B	HR	RBI	BB	SO	OBP	SLG
Tom Pagnozzi	.059	17	1	0	0	0	1	2	1	.150	.059	Jeff Bagwell	.647	17	11	5	0	3	4	1	1	.727	.941
Matt Williams	.067	45	3	0	0	0	1	2	13	.106	.067	Dante Bichette	.500	20	10	0	1	4	8	1	1	.524	1.200
Kevin Elster	.067	15	1	0	0	0	1	0	1	.063	.067	Brian Johnson	.500	10	5	2	0	1	4	0	0	.455	1.000
Vinny Castilla	.077	13	1	0	0	0	0	0	3	.077	.077	Ken Caminiti	.438	16	7	3	0	2	5	1	5	.471	1.000
John Vander Wal	.083	12	1	0	0	0	0	0	0	.083	.083	Darryl Strawberry	.421	19	8	1	0	3	6	3	7	.500	.947

Jorge Posada — Yankees
Age 26 – Bats Both

	Avg	G	AB	R	H	2B	3B	HR	RBI	BB	SO	HBP	GDP	SB	CS	OBP	SLG	IBB	SH	SF	#Pit	#P/PA	GB	FB	G/F
1997 Season	.250	60	188	29	47	12	0	6	25	30	33	3	2	1	2	.359	.410	2	1	2	857	3.83	67	60	1.12
Career (1995-1997)	.238	69	202	30	48	12	0	6	25	31	39	3	3	1	2	.345	.386	2	1	2	916	3.83	73	61	1.20

1997 Season

	Avg	AB	H	2B	3B	HR	RBI	BB	SO	OBP	SLG		Avg	AB	H	2B	3B	HR	RBI	BB	SO	OBP	SLG
vs. Left	.310	42	13	4	0	1	5	0	5	.310	.476	Scoring Posn	.288	59	17	2	0	3	19	7	11	.353	.475
vs. Right	.233	146	34	8	0	5	20	30	28	.370	.390	Close & Late	.250	28	7	3	0	0	2	5	5	.353	.357
Home	.282	78	22	7	0	2	9	9	12	.364	.449	None on/out	.262	42	11	3	0	2		5	4	.367	.476
Away	.227	110	25	5	0	4	16	21	21	.356	.382	Batting #8	.311	106	33	10	0	6	19	17	18	.405	.575
First Pitch	.385	26	10	0	0	1	3	1	0	.407	.500	Batting #9	.169	77	13	2	0	0	4	10	14	.281	.195

1997 Season

	Avg	AB	H	2B	3B	HR	RBI	BB	SO	OBP	SLG		Avg	AB	H	2B	3B	HR	RBI	BB	SO	OBP	SLG
Ahead in Count	.358	53	19	7	0	3	14	15	0	.500	.660	Other	.200	5	1	0	0	0	2	3	1	.500	.500
Behind in Count	.180	61	11	3	0	1	5	0	22	.203	.279	Pre-All Star	.245	94	23	4	0	1	7	10	17	.327	.319
Two Strikes	.147	75	11	4	0	2	6	14	33	.286	.280	Post-All Star	.255	94	24	8	0	5	18	20	16	.388	.500

Scott Pose — Yankees
Age 31 – Bats Left

	Avg	G	AB	R	H	2B	3B	HR	RBI	BB	SO	HBP	GDP	SB	CS	OBP	SLG	IBB	SH	SF	#Pit	#P/PA	GB	FB	G/F
1997 Season	.218	54	87	19	19	2	1	0	5	9	11	0	1	3	1	.292	.264	0	0	0	382	3.98	42	15	2.80
Career (1993-1997)	.211	69	128	19	27	4	1	0	8	11	15	0	1	3	3	.273	.258	0	1	0	533	3.83	67	19	3.53

1997 Season

	Avg	AB	H	2B	3B	HR	RBI	BB	SO	OBP	SLG		Avg	AB	H	2B	3B	HR	RBI	BB	SO	OBP	SLG
vs. Left	.333	15	5	0	0	0	1	0	0	.333	.333	Scoring Posn	.211	19	4	1	1	0	5	3	2	.318	.368
vs. Right	.194	72	14	2	1	0	4	9	11	.284	.250	Close & Late	.250	12	3	0	0	0	1	1	1	.308	.200

Dante Powell — Giants
Age 24 – Bats Right

	Avg	G	AB	R	H	2B	3B	HR	RBI	BB	SO	HBP	GDP	SB	CS	OBP	SLG	IBB	SH	SF	#Pit	#P/PA	GB	FB	G/F
1997 Season	.308	27	39	8	12	1	0	1	3	4	11	0	0	1	1	.372	.410	0	1	0	175	3.98	8	7	1.14

1997 Season

	Avg	AB	H	2B	3B	HR	RBI	BB	SO	OBP	SLG		Avg	AB	H	2B	3B	HR	RBI	BB	SO	OBP	SLG
vs. Left	.381	21	8	1	0	1	1	1	6	.409	.571	Scoring Posn	.333	9	3	0	0	0	2	3	3	.500	.333
vs. Right	.222	18	4	0	0	0	2	3	5	.333	.222	Close & Late	.286	7	2	0	0	0	0	3	3	.500	.286

Jay Powell — Marlins
Age 26 – Pitches Right (groundball pitcher)

	ERA	W	L	Sv	G	GS	IP	BB	SO	Avg	H	2B	3B	HR	RBI	OBP	SLG	GF	IR	IRS	Hld	SvOp	SB	CS	GB	FB	G/F
1997 Season	3.28	7	2	2	74	0	79.2	30	65	.242	71	11	1	3	32	.317	.317	40	77	22	8	24	4	8	3	123	58	2.12
Career (1995-1997)	3.73	11	5	4	150	0	159.1	72	121	.248	149	25	5	8	77	.336	.342	40	77	22	36	9	17	4	253	130	1.95

1997 Season

	ERA	W	L	Sv	G	GS	IP	H	HR	BB	SO		Avg	AB	H	2B	3B	HR	RBI	BB	SO	OBP	SLG
Home	4.67	5	2	1	40	0	44.1	48	2	16	42	vs. Left	.293	92	27	5	0	0	7	10	24	.371	.348
Away	1.53	2	0	1	34	0	35.1	23	1	14	23	vs. Right	.219	201	44	6	1	3	25	20	41	.292	.303
Day	4.20	2	0	0	17	0	15.0	17	1	4	13	Inning 1-6	.000	3	0	0	0	0	0	0	0	.000	.000
Night	3.06	5	2	2	57	0	64.2	54	2	26	52	Inning 7+	.245	290	71	11	1	3	32	30	65	.320	.321
Grass	4.02	7	2	1	61	0	65.0	60	3	27	56	None on	.275	142	39	6	1	2	2	15	39	.348	.373
Turf	0.00	0	0	0	13	0	14.2	11	0	3	9	Runners on	.212	151	32	5	0	1	30	15	26	.289	.265
March/April	2.25	0	0	0	10	0	12.0	13	0	3	6	Scoring Posn	.211	90	19	4	0	1	30	11	17	.292	.289
May	0.90	1	1	1	16	0	20.0	11	0	7	20	Close & Late	.238	160	38	7	1	2	19	20	38	.330	.331
June	3.86	0	0	0	10	0	11.2	14	0	4	12	None on/out	.281	64	18	3	1	0	0	7	20	.361	.359
July	15.63	0	1	0	10	0	6.1	12	2	5	6	vs. 1st Batr (relief)	.308	65	20	3	1	0	4	9	16	.392	.385
August	1.69	3	0	1	15	0	16.0	8	1	5	13	1st Inning Pitched	.265	238	63	8	1	3	32	24	49	.335	.345
Sept/Oct	3.29	3	0	0	13	0	13.2	13	0		8	First 15 Pitches	.283	205	58	5	1	3	23	23	41	.357	.361
Starter	0.00	0	0	0	0	0	0.0	0	0	0	0	Pitch 16-30	.148	81	12	5	0	0	9	5	22	.207	.210
Reliever	3.28	7	2	2	74	0	79.2	71	3	30	65	Pitch 31-45	.143	7	1	1	0	0	0	2	2	.333	.286
0 Days rest (Relief)	0.47	2	0	1	16	0	19.0	9	0	8	15	Pitch 46+	.000	0	0	0	0	0	0	0	0	.000	.000
1 or 2 Days rest	3.88	4	1	1	44	0	46.1	46	1	16	37	First Pitch	.283	46	13	3	0	0		3	0	.320	.348
3+ Days rest	5.02	1	1	0	14	0	14.1	16	2	6	13	Ahead in Count	.134	134	18	2	0	0	6	0	56	.151	.149
vs. AL	2.70	1	0	0	8	0	6.2	5	0	2	6	Behind in Count	.448	58	26	5	1	1	11	12	0	.543	.621
vs. NL	3.33	6	2	2	66	0	73.0	66	3	28	59	Two Strikes	.120	133	16	3	0	0	6	15	65	.225	.143
Pre-All Star	2.03	1	1	1	38	0	44.1	38	0	14	38	Pre-All Star	.232	164	38	4	1	0	11	14	38	.298	.268
Post-All Star	4.84	6	1	1	36	0	35.1	33	3	16	27	Post-All Star	.256	129	33	7	0	3	21	16	27	.340	.380

Career (1995-1997)

	ERA	W	L	Sv	G	GS	IP	H	HR	BB	SO		Avg	AB	H	2B	3B	HR	RBI	BB	SO	OBP	SLG
Home	3.81	8	2	3	78	0	82.2	82	3	37	64	vs. Left	.263	217	57	8	3	3	25	29	48	.364	.369
Away	3.64	3	3	1	72	0	76.2	67	5	35	57	vs. Right	.240	383	92	14	2	5	52	43	73	.320	.326
Day	3.58	2	1	0	37	0	37.2	35	1	16	32	Inning 1-6	.313	48	15	3	0	0	8	5	8	.377	.375
Night	3.77	9	4	4	113	0	121.2	114	5	56	89	Inning 7+	.243	552	134	19	5	8	69	67	113	.333	.339
Grass	3.49	11	3	3	121	0	131.1	117	6	58	100	None on	.240	292	70	12	2	2	2	36	66	.329	.315
Turf	4.82	0	2	1	29	0	28.0	32	2	14	21	Runners on	.256	308	79	10	3	6	75	36	55	.343	.367
March/April	1.62	1	0	0	15	0	16.2	15	0	4	11	Scoring Posn	.228	193	44	7	0	3	65	27	38	.325	.311
May	1.93	1	1	2	24	0	28.0	19	1	13	23	Close & Late	.241	291	70	13	4	4	32	40	58	.339	.354
June	4.13	1	0	0	22	0	24.0	23	0	13	18	None on/out	.263	133	35	8	1	0	0	12	31	.333	.338
July	8.34	0	1	0	25	0	22.2	31	3	15	21	vs. 1st Batr (relief)	.291	134	39	8	1	1	12	14	30	.360	.388
August	2.83	4	1	1	31	0	35.0	30	3	10	30	1st Inning Pitched	.260	477	124	16	4	8	73	56	94	.344	.361
Sept/Oct	3.82	4	2	1	33	0	33.0	31	1	17	18	First 15 Pitches	.263	403	106	14	3	6	51	46	77	.346	.357
Starter	0.00	0	0	0	0	0	0.0	0	0	0	0	Pitch 16-30	.227	181	41	7	2	2	26	22	40	.317	.320
Reliever	3.73	11	5	4	150	0	159.1	149	8	72	121	Pitch 31-45	.125	16	2	1	0	0	0	4	4	.300	.188
0 Days rest (Relief)	1.63	4	0	2	35	0	38.2	25	2	21	30	Pitch 46+	.000	0	0	0	0	0	0	0	0	.000	.000
1 or 2 Days rest	4.83	6	4	1	85	0	87.2	88	4	39	70	First Pitch	.281	96	27	6	1	2	22	4	0	.324	.427
3+ Days rest	3.27	1	1	1	30	0	33.0	36	2	12	21	Ahead in Count	.164	268	44	5	1	0	14	0	104	.178	.190
vs. AL	2.70	1	0	0	8	0	6.2	5	0	2	6	Behind in Count	.376	125	47	9	1	2	21	33	0	.509	.512
vs. NL	3.77	10	5	4	142	0	152.2	144	8	70	115	Two Strikes	.162	271	44	7	2	0	14	35	121	.270	.203
Pre-All Star	2.63	3	1	2	66	0	72.0	61	1	33	55	Pre-All Star	.224	272	61	6	1	1	27	33	55	.316	.265
Post-All Star	4.64	8	4	2	84	0	87.1	88	7	39	66	Post-All Star	.268	328	88	16	4	7	50	39	66	.353	.405

Arquimedez Pozo — Red Sox
Age 24 – Bats Right

	Avg	G	AB	R	H	2B	3B	HR	RBI	BB	SO	HBP	GDP	SB	CS	OBP	SLG	IBB	SH	SF	#Pit	#P/PA	GB	FB	G/F
1997 Season	.267	4	15	0	4	1	0	0	3	0	5	0	0	0	0	.250	.333	0	1	1	71	4.18	7	3	2.33
Career (1995-1997)	.189	26	74	4	14	4	1	1	14	5	15	1	1	1	1	.215	.311	0	2	2	310	3.88	26	23	1.13

1997 Season

	Avg	AB	H	2B	3B	HR	RBI	BB	SO	OBP	SLG		Avg	AB	H	2B	3B	HR	RBI	BB	SO	OBP	SLG
vs. Left	.000	0	0	0	0	0	0	0	0	.000	.000	Scoring Posn	.250	4	1	0	0	0	3	0	1	.200	.250
vs. Right	.267	15	4	1	0	0	3	0	5	.250	.333	Close & Late	.333	3	1	1	0	0	0	0	1	.333	.667

Todd Pratt — Mets
Age 31 – Bats Right

	Avg	G	AB	R	H	2B	3B	HR	RBI	BB	SO	HBP	GDP	SB	CS	OBP	SLG	IBB	SH	SF	#Pit	#P/PA	GB	FB	G/F
1997 Season	.283	39	106	12	30	6	0	2	19	13	32	2	1	0	1	.372	.396	0	0	0	518	4.28	26	28	0.93
Last Five Years	.234	125	355	33	83	20	1	9	45	36	101	3	7	0	2	.308	.372	1	1	2	1667	4.20	110	93	1.18

1997 Season

	Avg	AB	H	2B	3B	HR	RBI	BB	SO	OBP	SLG		Avg	AB	H	2B	3B	HR	RBI	BB	SO	OBP	SLG
vs. Left	.447	38	17	5	0	2	12	7	8	.553	.737	Scoring Posn	.343	35	12	1	0	0	15	6	10	.439	.371
vs. Right	.191	68	13	1	0	0	7	6	24	.257	.206	Close & Late	.111	18	2	0	0	0	0	2	6	.200	.111

Curtis Pride — Red Sox
Age 29 – Bats Left

	Avg	G	AB	R	H	2B	3B	HR	RBI	BB	SO	HBP	GDP	SB	CS	OBP	SLG	IBB	SH	SF	#Pit	#P/PA	GB	FB	G/F
1997 Season	.213	81	164	22	35	4	4	3	20	24	46	1	4	6	4	.316	.341	1	2	1	786	4.09	64	25	2.56
Career (1993-1997)	.258	234	503	87	130	23	10	14	58	60	128	1	8	21	12	.338	.427	2	6	1	2302	4.03	199	95	2.09

1997 Season

	Avg	AB	H	2B	3B	HR	RBI	BB	SO	OBP	SLG		Avg	AB	H	2B	3B	HR	RBI	BB	SO	OBP	SLG
vs. Left	.462	13	6	0	0	0	6	0	3	.500	.462	Scoring Posn	.256	43	11	0	2	1	18	6	5	.340	.419
vs. Right	.192	151	29	4	4	3	14	24	43	.301	.331	Close & Late	.200	35	7	0	3	0	4	5	9	.310	.371
Home	.248	101	25	2	3	3	18	16	31	.350	.416	None on/out	.190	42	8	1	0	1	1	4	15	.261	.286
Away	.159	63	10	2	1	0	2	8	15	.260	.222	Batting #6	.286	21	6	1	0	1	3	6	7	.444	.476
First Pitch	.294	17	5	0	0	1	4	1	0	.333	.471	Batting #7	.211	76	16	2	1	2	12	9	18	.302	.342
Ahead in Count	.276	29	8	0	1	2	7	13	0	.488	.552	Other	.194	67	13	1	3	0	5	9	21	.286	.299
Behind in Count	.132	76	10	3	1	0	5	0	36	.143	.197	Pre-All Star	.233	133	31	3	4	2	18	19	37	.331	.361
Two Strikes	.151	93	14	2	2	0	9	10	46	.233	.215	Post-All Star	.129	31	4	1	0	1	2	5	9	.250	.258

Career (1993-1997)

	Avg	AB	H	2B	3B	HR	RBI	BB	SO	OBP	SLG		Avg	AB	H	2B	3B	HR	RBI	BB	SO	OBP	SLG
vs. Left	.367	30	11	0	0	0	9	0	7	.387	.367	First Pitch	.431	58	25	2	1	2	14	2	0	.450	.603
vs. Right	.252	473	119	23	10	14	49	60	121	.335	.431	Ahead in Count	.372	94	35	6	2	11	23	31	0	.524	.830
Groundball	.212	146	31	4	1	5	14	13	33	.281	.356	Behind in Count	.152	237	36	9	3	0	7	0	104	.155	.215
Flyball	.236	89	21	3	1	0	9	14	30	.340	.292	Two Strikes	.167	270	45	6	5	0	15	27	128	.242	.226
Home	.275	280	77	15	7	8	41	34	72	.354	.464	Batting #1	.300	207	62	15	4	6	22	23	46	.370	.498
Away	.238	223	53	8	3	6	17	26	56	.319	.381	Batting #7	.212	85	18	3	1	2	12	9	22	.295	.341
Day	.235	196	46	6	1	4	25	27	51	.326	.337	Other	.237	211	50	5	5	6	24	28	60	.325	.393
Night	.274	307	84	17	9	10	33	33	77	.346	.485	March/April	.200	55	11	1	1	0	5	8	13	.313	.255
Grass	.275	418	115	20	8	14	52	53	100	.357	.462	May	.296	81	24	3	2	3	9	7	17	.352	.494
Turf	.176	85	15	3	2	0	6	7	28	.239	.259	June	.252	115	29	6	4	1	15	11	32	.315	.400
Pre-All Star	.256	281	72	11	8	5	32	32	67	.333	.406	July	.182	88	16	2	1	2	6	15	26	.301	.295
Post-All Star	.261	222	58	12	2	9	26	28	61	.344	.455	August	.283	99	28	8	1	2	9	8	24	.336	.444
Scoring Posn	.263	118	31	5	3	3	42	12	33	.328	.432	Sept/Oct	.338	65	22	1		6	14	11	16	.434	.692
Close & Late	.221	95	21	2	4	2	13	13	26	.313	.389	vs. AL	.271	414	112	21	8	12	48	49	104	.348	.447
None on/out	.241	166	40	9		4	4	17	37	.311	.392	vs. NL	.202	89	18	2	2	2	10	11	24	.290	.337

Batter vs. Pitcher (career)

Hits Best Against	Avg	AB	H	2B	3B	HR	RBI	BB	SO	OBP	SLG	Hits Worst Against	Avg	AB	H	2B	3B	HR	RBI	BB	SO	OBP	SLG
James Baldwin	.500	8	4	1	1	1	3	4	2	.667	1.250	Charles Nagy	.111	27	3	0	0	1	3	0	11	.111	.222
Mike Mussina	.333	9	3	0	0	0	2	2	3	.455	.333	Orel Hershiser	.182	11	2	0	0	0	0	0	2	.182	.182

Ariel Prieto — Athletics
Age 28 – Pitches Right (groundball pitcher)

	ERA	W	L	Sv	G	GS	IP	BB	SO	Avg	H	2B	3B	HR	RBI	OBP	SLG	CG	ShO	Sup	QS	#P/S	SB	CS	GB	FB	G/F
1997 Season	5.04	6	8	0	22	22	125.0	70	90	.306	155	27	9	16	72	.393	.490	0	0	5.33	9	101	11	5	187	122	1.53
Career (1995-1997)	4.67	14	21	0	57	52	308.2	156	202	.285	342	59	13	29	158	.373	.429	3	0	4.72	24	99	27	12	484	294	1.65

1997 Season

	ERA	W	L	Sv	G	GS	IP	H	HR	BB	SO		Avg	AB	H	2B	3B	HR	RBI	BB	SO	OBP	SLG
Home	3.61	5	2	0	10	10	57.1	69	5	32	47	vs. Left	.309	259	80	12	4	8	34	40	47	.405	.479
Away	6.25	1	6	0	12	12	67.2	86	11	38	43	vs. Right	.304	247	75	15	5	8	38	30	43	.381	.502
Day	5.93	2	2	0	6	6	30.1	43	2	22	27	Inning 1-6	.298	476	142	26	8	15	66	67	84	.388	.481
Night	4.75	4	6	0	16	16	94.2	112	14	48	63	Inning 7+	.433	30	13	1	1	1	6	3	6	.471	.633
Grass	5.11	6	8	0	19	19	107.1	133	13	62	73	None on	.311	257	80	11	4	12	12	38	51	.402	.525
Turf	4.58	0	0	0	3	3	17.2	22	3	8	17	Runners on	.301	249	75	16	5	4	60	32	39	.384	.454
March/April	3.55	2	1	0	6	6	33.0	41	6	20	20	Scoring Posn	.275	142	39	12	2	2	52	22	21	.374	.430
May	5.55	2	2	0	6	6	35.2	43	4	14	26	Close & Late	.400	15	6	1	1	1	2	2	4	.471	.800
June	3.62	2	2	0	5	5	32.1	33	4	18	27	None on/out	.306	124	38	4	3	6	6	19	28	.399	.532
July	10.38	0	1	0	3	3	13.0	25	4	13	12	vs. 1st Batr (relief)	.000	0	0	0	0	0	0	0	0	.000	.000
August	5.73	0	2	0	2	2	11.0	13	2	5	5	1st Inning Pitched	.322	87	28	7	2	2	18	22	14	.459	.517
Sept/Oct	0.00	0	0	0	0	0	0.0	0	0	0	0	First 75 Pitches	.293	358	105	18	6	11	52	52	71	.388	.469

1997 Season

	ERA	W	L	Sv	G	GS	IP	H	HR	BB	SO		Avg	AB	H	2B	3B	HR	RBI	BB	SO	OBP	SLG
Starter	5.04	6	8	0	22	22	125.0	155	16	70	90	Pitch 76-90	.288	73	21	3	2	3	8	8	7	.358	.507
Reliever	0.00	0	0	0	0	0	0.0	0	0	0	0	Pitch 91-105	.420	50	21	5	0	1	5	7	7	.491	.580
0-3 Days Rest (Start)	1.80	0	0	0	1	1	5.0	7	0	1	5	Pitch 106+	.320	25	8	1	1	1	7	3	5	.367	.560
4 Days Rest	4.77	4	3	0	12	12	71.2	85	7	39	61	First Pitch	.365	74	27	6	2	2	14	1	0	.382	.581
5+ Days Rest	5.77	2	5	0	9	9	48.1	63	9	30	24	Ahead in Count	.237	215	51	13	4	4	21	0	72	.241	.391
vs. AL	4.99	5	8	0	20	20	113.2	137	15	60	74	Behind in Count	.411	124	51	4	3	8	27	40	0	.550	.685
vs. NL	5.56	1	0	0	2	2	11.1	18	1	10	16	Two Strikes	.211	218	46	12	2	4	21	29	90	.306	.339
Pre-All Star	4.73	6	5	0	19	19	110.1	136	14	62	82	Pre-All Star	.306	444	136	22	8	14	60	62	82	.393	.486
Post-All Star	7.36	0	3	0	3	3	14.2	19	2	8	8	Post-All Star	.306	62	19	5	1	2	12	8	8	.394	.516

Career (1995-1997)

	ERA	W	L	Sv	G	GS	IP	H	HR	BB	SO		Avg	AB	H	2B	3B	HR	RBI	BB	SO	OBP	SLG
Home	4.26	11	8	0	30	30	148.0	159	14	75	111	vs. Left	.274	650	178	27	7	15	73	102	119	.375	.406
Away	5.04	3	13	0	31	27	160.2	183	16	82	91	vs. Right	.299	548	164	32	6	14	85	54	83	.370	.456
Day	5.08	6	8	0	22	21	111.2	125	6	56	82	Inning 1-6	.285	1079	308	54	12	25	146	142	181	.372	.427
Night	4.43	8	13	0	35	31	197.0	217	23	100	120	Inning 7+	.286	119	34	5	1	4	12	14	21	.377	.445
Grass	4.30	13	18	0	47	43	257.1	277	22	134	167	None on	.283	643	182	27	6	19	19	80	115	.368	.432
Turf	6.49	1	3	0	10	9	51.1	65	7	22	35	Runners on	.288	555	160	32	7	10	139	76	87	.377	.425
March/April	5.23	3	3	0	12	12	62.0	79	11	38	36	Scoring Posn	.263	320	84	19	4	6	120	54	47	.370	.403
May	5.29	3	3	0	9	9	47.2	57	4	20	34	Close & Late	.268	56	15	4	1	2	6	3	9	.328	.482
June	3.62	2	2	0	5	5	32.1	33	4	18	27	None on/out	.289	304	88	12	3	10	10	35	53	.368	.447
July	5.90	1	6	0	10	9	50.1	55	3	24	33	vs. 1st Batr (relief)	.667	3	2	0	0	0	0	1	0	.800	.667
August	3.87	3	6	0	12	12	79.0	79	6	41	47	1st Inning Pitched	.244	205	50	12	4	3	29	39	38	.369	.385
Sept/Oct	3.86	2	1	0	9	5	37.1	39	1	15	25	First 75 Pitches	.272	845	230	41	9	17	109	119	149	.367	.402
Starter	4.77	14	21	0	52	52	301.2	340	29	153	199	Pitch 76-90	.367	177	65	11	3	7	27	14	19	.418	.582
Reliever	0.00	0	0	0	5	0	7.0	2	0	3	3	Pitch 91-105	.274	117	32	5	0	4	15	15	20	.361	.419
0-3 Days Rest (Start)	3.46	0	1	0	3	3	13.0	15	0	5	11	Pitch 106+	.254	59	15	2	1	1	7	8	14	.352	.373
4 Days Rest	4.19	11	9	0	30	30	191.0	206	13	97	133	First Pitch	.352	179	63	12	4	3	27	2	0	.376	.514
5+ Days Rest	6.08	3	11	0	19	19	97.2	119	16	51	55	Ahead in Count	.224	473	106	23	4	7	51	0	151	.229	.334
vs. AL	4.63	13	21	0	55	50	297.1	324	28	146	186	Behind in Count	.375	296	111	13	3	14	51	93	0	.524	.581
vs. NL	5.56	1	0	0	2	2	11.1	18	1	10	16	Two Strikes	.191	507	97	19	2	8	52	61	202	.279	.284
Pre-All Star	5.14	8	9	0	30	29	159.1	195	20	88	112	Pre-All Star	.308	634	195	31	9	20	92	88	112	.394	.479
Post-All Star	4.16	6	12	0	27	23	149.1	147	9	68	90	Post-All Star	.261	564	147	28	4	9	66	68	90	.348	.372

Pitcher vs. Batter (career)

Pitches Best Vs.	Avg	AB	H	2B	3B	HR	RBI	BB	SO	OBP	SLG	Pitches Worst Vs.	Avg	AB	H	2B	3B	HR	RBI	BB	SO	OBP	SLG
Tony Phillips	.111	18	2	0	0	0	1	2	8	.200	.111	Harold Baines	.600	10	6	1	0	0	2	2	2	.667	.700
Ozzie Guillen	.111	9	1	0	0	0	1	1	1	.182	.111	Marty Cordova	.455	11	5	2	0	0	2	0	0	.538	.636
Alex Gonzalez	.118	17	2	1	0	1	4	0	6	.111	.353	Chuck Knoblauch	.417	12	5	1	0	1	2	5	1	.611	.750
Scott Stahoviak	.154	13	2	1	0	0	0	1	4	.214	.231	Garret Anderson	.400	10	4	0	1	1	3	1	0	.455	.900
Omar Vizquel	.188	16	3	0	0	0	0	2	1	.278	.188	Carlos Delgado	.375	16	6	0	0	3	6	1	4	.444	.938

Tom Prince — Dodgers

Age 33 – Bats Right (flyball hitter)

	Avg	G	AB	R	H	2B	3B	HR	RBI	BB	SO	HBP	GDP	SB	CS	OBP	SLG	IBB	SH	SF	#Pit	#P/PA	GB	FB	G/F
1997 Season	.220	47	100	17	22	5	0	3	14	5	15	3	2	0	0	.275	.360	0	4	1	414	3.66	28	41	0.68
Last Five Years	.221	174	389	42	86	27	1	7	54	29	81	12	7	1	1	.291	.350	4	9	6	1616	3.63	106	145	0.73

1997 Season

	Avg	AB	H	2B	3B	HR	RBI	BB	SO	OBP	SLG		Avg	AB	H	2B	3B	HR	RBI	BB	SO	OBP	SLG
vs. Left	.152	33	5	3	0	1	5	3	3	.237	.333	Scoring Posn	.258	31	8	1	0	1	12	0	6	.294	.387
vs. Right	.254	67	17	2	0	2	9	2	12	.296	.373	Close & Late	.176	17	3	0	0	0	4	1	3	.211	.176

Last Five Years

	Avg	AB	H	2B	3B	HR	RBI	BB	SO	OBP	SLG		Avg	AB	H	2B	3B	HR	RBI	BB	SO	OBP	SLG
vs. Left	.203	133	27	13	0	1	11	13	21	.285	.323	First Pitch	.302	53	16	5	0	2	10	1	0	.345	.509
vs. Right	.230	256	59	14	1	6	43	16	60	.295	.363	Ahead in Count	.367	79	29	8	1	4	21	12	0	.442	.646
Groundball	.196	92	18	7	0	1	7	8	19	.304	.200	Behind in Count	.149	175	26	9	0	0	10	0	70	.171	.200
Flyball	.296	54	16	4	0	3	14	3	16	.311	.537	Two Strikes	.144	181	26	8	0	0	12	16	81	.227	.188
Home	.187	139	26	8	0	4	24	9	29	.242	.331	Batting #7	.155	97	15	5	0	3	11	5	21	.231	.299
Away	.240	250	60	19	1	3	30	20	52	.318	.360	Batting #8	.235	234	55	16	1	4	34	22	51	.314	.363
Day	.219	137	30	9	0	1	14	5	28	.273	.307	Other	.276	58	16	6	0	0	9	2	9	.297	.379
Night	.222	252	56	18	1	6	40	24	53	.301	.373	March/April	.275	40	11	2	0	0	7	4	6	.348	.325
Grass	.230	213	49	13	1	5	30	15	41	.297	.371	May	.208	77	16	5	1	2	14	10	16	.315	.377
Turf	.210	176	37	14	0	2	24	14	40	.284	.324	June	.162	74	12	7	0	1	7	2	20	.190	.243
Pre-All Star	.217	217	47	13	1	3	32	18	48	.285	.327	July	.261	69	18	8	0	2	10	7	13	.350	.464
Post-All Star	.227	172	39	14	0	4	22	11	33	.300	.378	August	.176	68	12	1	0	1	9	3	16	.233	.235
Scoring Posn	.314	105	33	8	1	3	48	9	18	.381	.495	Sept/Oct	.279	61	17	8	0	1	7	3	10	.333	.459
Close & Late	.222	72	16	4	0	0	10	6	22	.296	.278	vs. AL	.292	24	7	0	0	1	3	1	3	.320	.417
None on/out	.138	94	13	6	0	2	2	8	14	.214	.266	vs. NL	.216	365	79	27	1	6	51	28	78	.290	.345

Batter vs. Pitcher (career)

Hits Best Against	Avg	AB	H	2B	3B	HR	RBI	BB	SO	OBP	SLG	Hits Worst Against	Avg	AB	H	2B	3B	HR	RBI	BB	SO	OBP	SLG
												Allen Watson	.000	9	0	0	0	0	0	1	3	.182	.000
												John Smoltz	.167	12	2	2	0	0	0	1	3	.231	.333

Tim Pugh — Tigers
Age 31 – Pitches Right (groundball pitcher)

	ERA	W	L	Sv	G	GS	IP	BB	SO	Avg	H	2B	3B	HR	RBI	OBP	SLG	CG	ShO	Sup	QS	#P/S	SB	CS	GB	FB	G/F
1997 Season	5.00	1	1	0	2	2	9.0	5	4	.188	6	3	0	0	5	.297	.281	0	0	9.00	1	67	0	0	14	9	1.56
Last Five Years	5.26	21	26	0	100	51	371.1	145	196	.293	432	58	11	49	216	.358	.446	4	1	5.62	21	84	38	11	600	399	1.50

1997 Season

	ERA	W	L	Sv	G	GS	IP	H	HR	BB	SO		Avg	AB	H	2B	3B	HR	RBI	BB	SO	OBP	SLG
Home	36.00	0	1	0	1	1	1.0	3	0	3	0	vs. Left	.167	18	3	1	0	0	3	3	0	.286	.222
Away	1.13	1	0	0	1	1	8.0	3	0	2	4	vs. Right	.214	14	3	2	0	0	2	2	4	.313	.357

Last Five Years

	ERA	W	L	Sv	G	GS	IP	H	HR	BB	SO		Avg	AB	H	2B	3B	HR	RBI	BB	SO	OBP	SLG
Home	4.92	9	9	0	48	24	184.2	203	25	75	95	vs. Left	.293	685	201	24	9	24	103	80	75	.366	.460
Away	5.59	11	17	0	52	27	186.2	229	24	70	101	vs. Right	.292	791	231	34	2	25	113	65	121	.351	.435
Day	5.87	5	11	0	32	17	119.2	136	22	41	67	Inning 1-6	.299	1186	355	51	10	39	184	115	152	.364	.458
Night	4.97	16	15	0	68	34	251.2	296	27	104	129	Inning 7+	.266	290	77	7	1	10	32	30	44	.335	.400
Grass	5.86	6	14	0	44	20	139.2	173	25	55	86	None on	.273	841	230	39	5	27	69	112	135	.335	.428
Turf	4.89	15	12	0	56	31	231.2	259	24	90	110	Runners on	.318	635	202	19	6	22	189	76	84	.388	.471
March/April	4.22	5	1	0	20	7	70.1	68	6	30	35	Scoring Posn	.324	361	117	16	5	12	167	53	52	.399	.496
May	6.11	5	8	0	24	15	91.1	115	11	47	40	Close & Late	.305	82	25	1	0	1	8	9	16	.374	.354
June	6.12	2	6	0	21	6	64.2	88	12	17	36	None on/out	.254	370	94	17	4	10	10	25	47	.310	.403
July	4.46	4	4	0	14	11	70.2	82	11	18	39	vs. 1st Batr (relief)	.400	45	18	5	0	3	10	3	5	.449	.711
August	7.55	2	3	0	8	6	31.0	42	6	14	19	1st Inning Pitched	.325	385	125	20	4	9	80	48	50	.400	.468
Sept/Oct	3.53	3	4	0	13	6	43.1	37	3	19	27	First 75 Pitches	.285	1288	367	53	9	42	185	125	172	.351	.438
Starter	5.20	19	22	0	51	51	275.0	326	33	105	140	Pitch 76-90	.342	111	38	3	2	5	18	11	18	.398	.541
Reliever	5.42	2	4	0	49	0	96.1	106	16	40	56	Pitch 91-105	.365	63	23	2	0	1	11	7	6	.429	.444
0-3 Days Rest (Start)	0.50	2	0	0	3	3	18.0	7	0	3	8	Pitch 106+	.286	14	4	0	0	1	2	2	0	.375	.500
4 Days Rest	6.15	9	13	0	26	26	137.2	193	18	52	73	First Pitch	.321	271	87	10	2	14	50	3	0	.339	.528
5+ Days Rest	4.83	8	9	0	22	22	119.1	126	15	50	59	Ahead in Count	.223	605	135	11	4	13	62	0	171	.227	.319
vs. AL	5.36	1	2	0	21	3	45.1	48	9	17	31	Behind in Count	.368	342	126	22	3	13	62	86	0	.490	.564
vs. NL	5.25	20	24	0	79	48	326.0	384	40	128	165	Two Strikes	.206	557	115	15	2	7	43	56	196	.283	.278
Pre-All Star	5.28	15	15	0	70	32	255.2	299	34	102	124	Pre-All Star	.294	1017	299	49	7	34	153	102	124	.362	.456
Post-All Star	5.21	6	11	0	30	19	115.2	133	6	43	72	Post-All Star	.290	459	133	9	4	15	63	43	72	.350	.425

Pitcher vs. Batter (career)

Pitches Best Vs.	Avg	AB	H	2B	3B	HR	RBI	BB	SO	OBP	SLG	Pitches Worst Vs.	Avg	AB	H	2B	3B	HR	RBI	BB	SO	OBP	SLG
Darrin Fletcher	.000	10	0	0	0	0	0	1	0	.167	.000	Vinny Castilla	.583	12	7	1	0	2	5	0	0	.583	1.167
David Segui	.100	10	1	0	0	0	0	1	0	.182	.100	Mike Piazza	.545	11	6	0	0	1	3	0	0	.643	.818
Tony Fernandez	.143	14	2	1	0	0	0	1	0	.200	.214	Fred McGriff	.538	13	7	0	1	2	5	4	1	.647	1.154
Ken Caminiti	.143	14	2	1	0	0	2	1	0	.200	.214	Brett Butler	.522	23	12	2	1	1	5	1	2	.542	.826
Craig Biggio	.158	19	3	0	0	0	3	2	3	.238	.158	Sammy Sosa	.462	13	6	0	0	2	6	0	1	.462	.923

Harvey Pulliam — Rockies
Age 30 – Bats Right

	Avg	G	AB	R	H	2B	3B	HR	RBI	BB	SO	HBP	GDP	SB	CS	OBP	SLG	IBB	SH	SF	#Pit	#P/PA	GB	FB	G/F
1997 Season	.284	59	67	15	19	3	0	3	9	5	15	0	2	0	1	.333	.463	0	0	0	288	4.00	25	17	1.47
Last Five Years	.262	101	149	25	39	9	0	5	18	9	37	1	6	0	1	.308	.423	0	0	0	613	3.86	52	35	1.49

1997 Season

	Avg	AB	H	2B	3B	HR	RBI	BB	SO	OBP	SLG		Avg	AB	H	2B	3B	HR	RBI	BB	SO	OBP	SLG
vs. Left	.306	36	11	2	0	3	5	2	9	.342	.611	Scoring Posn	.263	19	5	1	0	0	5	1	4	.300	.316
vs. Right	.258	31	8	1	0	0	4	3	6	.324	.290	Close & Late	.250	16	4	0	0	1	2	2	5	.333	.438

Paul Quantrill — Blue Jays
Age 29 – Pitches Right (groundball pitcher)

	ERA	W	L	Sv	G	GS	IP	BB	SO	Avg	H	2B	3B	HR	RBI	OBP	SLG	GF	IR	IRS	Hld	SvOp	SB	CS	GB	FB	G/F
1997 Season	1.94	6	7	5	77	0	88.0	17	56	.297	103	15	1	5	30	.329	.389	29	55	16	16	10	5	6	162	64	2.53
Last Five Years	4.28	31	48	7	232	64	592.2	171	339	.282	702	133	18	72	305	.346	.461	54	123	39	23	18	44	20	933	602	1.55

1997 Season

	ERA	W	L	Sv	G	GS	IP	H	HR	BB	SO		Avg	AB	H	2B	3B	HR	RBI	BB	SO	OBP	SLG
Home	1.80	5	2	2	36	0	45.0	55	1	7	33	vs. Left	.315	130	41	3	0	3	12	11	18	.366	.408
Away	2.09	1	5	3	41	0	43.0	48	4	10	23	vs. Right	.286	217	62	12	1	2	18	6	38	.305	.378
Day	2.25	4	2	1	29	0	36.0	42	3	6	28	Inning 1-6	.214	56	12	5	0	1	5	6	14	.297	.357
Night	1.73	2	5	4	48	0	52.0	61	2	11	28	Inning 7+	.313	291	91	10	1	4	25	11	42	.336	.395
Grass	2.41	1	5	2	35	0	37.1	42	4	9	21	None on	.393	173	68	12	1	2	2	7	24	.417	.509
Turf	1.60	5	2	3	42	0	50.2	61	1	8	35	Runners on	.201	174	35	3	0	3	28	10	32	.245	.270
March/April	1.98	3	2	0	10	0	13.2	15	1	2	9	Scoring Posn	.176	108	19	2	0	3	28	7	21	.227	.278
May	2.13	1	0	1	9	0	12.2	14	1	1	9	Close & Late	.325	191	62	7	0	4	17	8	27	.352	.424
June	1.32	0	0	3	13	0	13.2	13	0	2	6	None on/out	.280	75	21	3	1	1	3	3	10	.308	.387
July	3.38	0	1	0	14	0	16.0	24	1	7	11	vs. 1st Batr (relief)	.290	69	20	3	0	1	11	5	9	.329	.377
August	1.37	2	2	1	16	0	19.2	22	2	4	14	1st Inning Pitched	.286	245	70	10	0	4	27	12	38	.318	.376
Sept/Oct	1.46	0	2	0	15	0	12.1	15	0	1	7	First 15 Pitches	.324	216	70	12	1	1	19	10	23	.352	.403
Starter	0.00	0	0	0	0	0	0.0	0	0	0	0	Pitch 16-30	.245	98	24	2	0	3	8	3	25	.267	.357
Reliever	1.94	6	7	5	77	0	88.0	103	5	17	56	Pitch 31-45	.190	21	4	0	0	0	3	0	5	.292	.190
0 Days rest (Relief)	1.41	5	1	5	26	0	32.0	34	2	6	22	Pitch 46+	.417	12	5	1	0	1	3	1	0	.462	.750
1 or 2 Days rest	1.63	4	4	0	38	0	38.2	48	1	5	20	First Pitch	.500	46	23	5	0	3	8	1	0	.520	.609
3+ Days rest	3.63	2	2	0	13	0	17.1	21	2	6	14	Ahead in Count	.205	161	33	4	0	1	8	0	48	.204	.248
vs. AL	2.09	6	6	4	69	0	81.2	95	5	14	55	Behind in Count	.333	72	24	1	1	1	5	8	0	.395	.417
vs. NL	0.00	0	1	1	8	0	6.1	8	0	3	1	Two Strikes	.196	163	32	4	0	3	8	6	56	.229	.276
Pre-All Star	1.64	4	2	4	36	0	44.0	47	2	6	27	Pre-All Star	.281	167	47	5	0	2	12	6	27	.307	.347

1997 Season

	ERA	W	L	Sv	G	GS	IP	H	HR	BB	SO		Avg	AB	H	2B	3B	HR	RBI	BB	SO	OBP	SLG
Post-All Star	2.25	2	5	1	41	0	44.0	56	3	11	29	Post-All Star	.311	180	56	10	1	3	18	11	29	.349	.428

Last Five Years

	ERA	W	L	Sv	G	GS	IP	H	HR	BB	SO		Avg	AB	H	2B	3B	HR	RBI	BB	SO	OBP	SLG
Home	4.29	16	23	4	117	33	312.2	376	39	104	182	vs. Left	.316	1067	337	71	10	43	147	99	157	.373	.522
Away	4.28	15	25	3	115	31	280.0	326	33	67	157	vs. Right	.283	1292	365	62	8	29	158	72	182	.323	.410
Day	4.49	10	18	2	80	23	204.1	246	30	59	123	Inning 1-6	.293	1580	463	91	12	55	217	105	219	.337	.470
Night	4.17	21	30	5	152	41	388.1	456	42	112	216	Inning 7+	.307	779	239	42	6	17	88	66	120	.365	.442
Grass	3.95	13	26	3	114	28	280.1	310	33	78	162	None on	.312	1330	415	91	11	41	41	69	194	.350	.489
Turf	4.58	18	22	4	118	36	312.1	392	39	93	177	Runners on	.279	1029	287	42	7	31	264	102	145	.342	.424
March/April	4.08	6	5	0	30	6	70.2	81	13	22	44	Scoring Posn	.264	624	165	28	6	20	237	78	98	.342	.425
May	3.83	7	7	1	40	13	110.1	121	13	22	68	Close & Late	.340	397	135	23	3	13	52	35	58	.397	.511
June	4.39	8	8	4	44	17	133.1	162	17	32	76	None on/out	.291	584	170	41	4	14	25	85	325	.447
July	4.36	4	8	1	42	9	97.0	126	13	29	60	vs. 1st Batr (relief)	.295	149	44	10	0	2	21	12	20	.347	.403
August	4.20	2	10	1	38	7	94.1	106	7	40	48	1st Inning Pitched	.284	804	228	36	3	15	107	60	124	.334	.392
Sept/Oct	4.86	4	10	0	38	12	87.0	106	9	26	43	First 15 Pitches	.308	697	215	41	4	11	70	39	96	.347	.426
Starter	5.03	14	30	0	64	64	359.1	439	54	96	203	Pitch 16-30	.293	502	147	26	1	18	72	51	76	.357	.456
Reliever	3.12	15	18	7	168	0	233.1	263	18	75	136	Pitch 31-45	.281	310	87	10	5	7	33	23	48	.335	.413
0 Days rest (Relief)	2.60	2	1	5	35	0	45.0	51	4	8	31	Pitch 46+	.298	850	253	56	8	36	130	58	119	.343	.509
1 or 2 Days rest	3.06	10	12	1	82	0	106.0	114	9	39	48	First Pitch	.368	372	137	28	1	13	52	24	0	.403	.554
3+ Days rest	3.50	3	5	1	51	0	82.1	98	5	28	57	Ahead in Count	.221	1041	230	50	8	18	93	0	292	.226	.336
vs. AL	4.03	18	33	5	173	34	377.0	443	49	114	222	Behind in Count	.363	490	178	27	4	25	90	66	0	.437	.588
vs. NL	4.72	13	15	2	59	30	215.2	259	23	57	117	Two Strikes	.219	1061	232	42	9	21	97	81	339	.278	.335
Pre-All Star	4.10	22	24	5	126	42	355.2	407	49	89	213	Pre-All Star	.289	1408	407	79	9	49	182	89	213	.334	.462
Post-All Star	4.56	9	24	2	106	22	237.0	295	23	82	126	Post-All Star	.310	951	295	54	9	23	123	82	126	.365	.458

Pitcher vs. Batter (career)

Pitches Best Vs.	Avg	AB	H	2B	3B	HR	RBI	BB	SO	OBP	SLG	Pitches Worst Vs.	Avg	AB	H	2B	3B	HR	RBI	BB	SO	OBP	SLG
Ruben Sierra	.000	15	0	0	0	0	0	1	4	.063	.000	Wil Cordero	.714	14	10	1	0	0	4	0	1	.714	.786
Dean Palmer	.083	12	1	0	0	0	0	1	1	.154	.083	Reggie Jefferson	.667	12	8	3	0	0	3	2	2	.714	.917
Kevin Seitzer	.091	11	1	0	0	0	0	1	1	.167	.091	Orlando Merced	.615	13	8	2	1	1	3	1	1	.643	1.154
Jay Bell	.125	16	2	0	0	0	0	1	2	.176	.125	Paul Sorrento	.500	12	6	2	0	2	3	1	0	.500	1.167
Sandy Alomar Jr	.143	14	2	0	0	0	0	1	0	.200	.143	Rafael Palmeiro	.429	7	3	1	0	1	6	3	0	.500	1.000

Brian Raabe — Rockies
Age 30 – Bats Right

	Avg	G	AB	R	H	2B	3B	HR	RBI	BB	SO	HBP	GDP	SB	CS	OBP	SLG	IBB	SH	SF	#Pit	#P/PA	GB	FB	G/F
1997 Season	.167	4	6	0	1	0	0	0	0	1	3	0	0	0	0	.286	.167	0	1	0	27	3.38	3	0	0.00
Career (1995-1997)	.207	17	29	4	6	0	0	0	2	2	4	0	0	0	0	.250	.207	0	1	1	106	3.21	9	11	0.82

1997 Season

	Avg	AB	H	2B	3B	HR	RBI	BB	SO	OBP	SLG		Avg	AB	H	2B	3B	HR	RBI	BB	SO	OBP	SLG
vs. Left	1.000	1	1	0	0	0	0	0	0	1.000	1.000	Scoring Posn	.000	1	0	0	0	0	0	0	1	.000	.000
vs. Right	.000	5	0	0	0	0	0	1	3	.167	.000	Close & Late	1.000	1	1	0	0	0	0	0	0	1.000	1.000

Scott Radinsky — Dodgers
Age 30 – Pitches Left

	ERA	W	L	Sv	G	GS	IP	BB	SO	Avg	H	2B	3B	HR	RBI	OBP	SLG	GF	IR	IRS	Hld	SvOp	SB	CS	GB	FB	G/F
1997 Season	2.89	5	1	3	75	0	62.1	21	44	.236	54	11	1	4	29	.298	.345	14	56	11	26	5	2	1	87	61	1.43
Last Five Years	3.60	20	5	9	252	0	207.1	74	150	.265	213	37	4	16	111	.325	.381	67	184	50	53	17	7	4	269	229	1.17

1997 Season

	ERA	W	L	Sv	G	GS	IP	H	HR	BB	SO		Avg	AB	H	2B	3B	HR	RBI	BB	SO	OBP	SLG
Home	0.65	2	0	1	36	0	27.2	18	1	6	17	vs. Left	.221	86	19	6	1	2	16	7	18	.281	.384
Away	4.67	3	1	2	39	0	34.2	36	3	15	27	vs. Right	.245	143	35	5	0	2	13	14	26	.308	.322
Day	1.80	1	1	2	20	0	20.0	16	2	9	19	Inning 1-6	.375	8	3	1	0	0	1	0	1	.375	.500
Night	3.40	4	0	1	55	0	42.1	38	2	12	25	Inning 7+	.231	221	51	10	1	4	28	21	43	.296	.339
Grass	2.92	4	0	3	63	0	52.1	42	3	18	32	None on	.276	116	32	8	1	3	3	8	23	.340	.440
Turf	2.70	1	1	0	12	0	10.0	12	1	3	12	Runners on	.195	113	22	3	0	1	26	13	21	.275	.248
March/April	3.65	0	0	0	14	0	12.1	12	0	3	7	Scoring Posn	.246	65	16	3	0	1	26	9	10	.329	.338
May	2.70	2	0	0	12	0	10.0	6	1	5	4	Close & Late	.189	106	20	3	0	3	12	16	24	.286	.302
June	2.70	0	1	0	12	0	10.0	9	1	5	6	None on/out	.308	52	16	5	1	0	0	2	8	.333	.442
July	1.59	2	0	1	13	0	11.1	6	1	2	8	vs. 1st Batr (relief)	.232	69	16	4	1	0	7	4	11	.267	.319
August	2.61	0	0	1	14	0	10.1	13	1	2	13	1st Inning Pitched	.242	207	50	10	1	4	26	13	41	.284	.357
Sept/Oct	4.32	1	0	1	10	0	8.1	8	0	4	6	First 15 Pitches	.253	182	46	10	1	4	24	11	33	.293	.385
Starter	0.00	0	0	0	0	0	0.0	0	0	0	0	Pitch 16-30	.122	41	5	0	0	0	2	8	11	.265	.122
Reliever	2.89	5	1	3	75	0	62.1	54	4	21	44	Pitch 31-45	.500	6	3	1	0	0	3	2	0	.625	.667
0 Days rest (Relief)	0.57	2	0	1	19	0	15.2	10	0	2	11	Pitch 46+	.000	0	0	0	0	0	0	0	0	.000	.000
1 or 2 Days rest	4.31	2	1	1	40	0	31.1	28	4	16	18	First Pitch	.289	38	11	3	0	2	11	4	0	.356	.526
3+ Days rest	2.35	1	0	1	16	0	15.1	16	0	3	15	Ahead in Count	.238	101	24	6	0	1	6	0	30	.238	.327
vs. AL	9.53	1	0	0	9	0	5.2	8	1	4	3	Behind in Count	.208	48	10	1	1	0	7	5	0	.278	.271
vs. NL	2.22	4	1	3	66	0	56.2	46	3	17	41	Two Strikes	.223	103	23	4	0	2	8	11	44	.296	.320
Pre-All Star	3.03	3	1	0	42	0	35.2	29	2	13	18	Pre-All Star	.227	128	29	8	1	2	19	13	18	.292	.352
Post-All Star	2.70	2	0	3	33	0	26.2	25	2	8	26	Post-All Star	.248	101	25	3	0	2	10	8	26	.306	.337

Last Five Years

	ERA	W	L	Sv	G	GS	IP	H	HR	BB	SO		Avg	AB	H	2B	3B	HR	RBI	BB	SO	OBP	SLG
Home	3.50	10	4	4	127	0	105.1	108	9	34	74	vs. Left	.253	296	75	17	2	4	40	19	72	.298	.365
Away	3.71	10	1	5	125	0	102.0	105	7	40	76	vs. Right	.272	507	138	20	2	12	71	55	78	.340	.391

Last Five Years

	ERA	W	L	Sv	G	GS	IP	H	HR	BB	SO
Day	2.39	10	2	5	71	0	67.2	64	7	25	54
Night	4.19	10	3	4	181	0	139.2	149	9	49	96
Grass	3.66	18	4	7	211	0	177.0	182	15	63	126
Turf	3.26	2	1	2	41	0	30.1	31	1	11	24
March/April	2.70	0	0	1	31	0	30.0	25	0	8	19
May	5.35	6	1	1	41	0	33.2	42	6	16	19
June	3.52	0	1	1	51	0	38.1	42	2	19	28
July	3.03	6	1	3	40	0	35.2	26	5	6	24
August	3.86	2	2	2	46	0	35.0	44	2	12	35
Sept/Oct	3.12	6	0	1	43	0	34.2	34	1	13	25
Starter	0.00	0	0	0	0	0	0.0	0	0	0	0
Reliever	3.60	20	5	9	252	0	207.1	213	16	74	150
0 Days rest (Relief)	3.32	5	1	2	63	0	43.1	44	2	13	31
1 or 2 Days rest	3.76	10	4	4	118	0	95.2	103	7	40	65
3+ Days rest	3.56	5	0	3	71	0	68.1	66	7	21	54
vs. AL	5.03	11	3	5	128	0	98.1	115	11	40	61
vs. NL	2.31	9	2	4	124	0	109.0	98	5	34	89
Pre-All Star	3.95	7	3	3	135	0	114.0	121	10	45	70
Post-All Star	3.18	13	2	6	117	0	93.1	92	6	29	80

	Avg	AB	H	2B	3B	HR	RBI	BB	SO	OBP	SLG
Inning 1-6	.278	54	15	6	1	2	18	5	7	.323	.537
Inning 7+	.264	749	198	31	3	14	93	69	143	.325	.370
None on	.289	398	115	19	3	9	9	28	75	.336	.420
Runners on	.242	405	98	18	1	7	102	46	75	.315	.343
Scoring Posn	.263	251	66	12	1	6	98	30	50	.333	.390
Close & Late	.249	346	86	10	2	7	41	38	68	.330	.350
None on/out	.279	172	48	8	1	2	2	12	27	.326	.372
vs. 1st Batr (relief)	.258	229	59	11	1	4	26	19	49	.311	.367
1st Inning Pitched	.265	688	182	32	3	13	103	59	134	.320	.376
First 15 Pitches	.272	606	165	32	3	12	81	55	107	.331	.394
Pitch 16-30	.247	174	43	3	1	3	25	16	36	.306	.328
Pitch 31-45	.227	22	5	2	0	1	5	3	6	.320	.455
Pitch 46+	.000	1	0	0	0	0	0	0	1	.000	.000
First Pitch	.276	98	27	7	0	3	20	15	0	.370	.439
Ahead in Count	.226	372	84	13	1	4	31	0	120	.224	.298
Behind in Count	.360	178	64	11	2	6	36	25	0	.436	.545
Two Strikes	.201	363	73	8	1	4	35	33	150	.264	.262
Post-All Star	.255	361	92	13	2	6	41	29	80	.311	.352

Pitcher vs. Batter (career)

Pitches Best Vs.	Avg	AB	H	2B	3B	HR	RBI	BB	SO	OBP	SLG
Ken Griffey Jr	.063	16	1	0	0	0	0	0	7	.118	.125
John Olerud	.118	17	2	1	0	0	2	2	3	.211	.176
Brian McRae	.167	12	2	0	0	0	0	1	2	.231	.167
Jim Eisenreich	.182	11	2	0	0	0	1	1	2	.250	.182
Greg Vaughn	.200	10	2	0	0	0	0	1	3	.273	.200

Pitches Worst Vs.	Avg	AB	H	2B	3B	HR	RBI	BB	SO	OBP	SLG
Chili Davis	.556	9	5	2	0	1	8	3	3	.615	1.111
Steve Finley	.455	11	5	2	0	0	1	0	1	.455	.636
Tony Phillips	.385	13	5	0	0	1	3	1	0	.429	.615
Ruben Sierra	.375	8	3	0	0	0	1	5	0	.615	.375

Brad Radke — Twins

Age 25 – Pitches Right (flyball pitcher)

	ERA	W	L	Sv	G	GS	IP	BB	SO	Avg	H	2B	3B	HR	RBI	OBP	SLG	CG	ShO	Sup	QS	#P/S	SB	CS	GB	FB	G/F
1997 Season	3.87	20	10	0	35	35	239.2	48	174	.257	238	52	4	28	104	.293	.412	4	1	6.12	20	101	10	7	334	275	1.21
Career (1995-1997)	4.48	42	40	0	99	98	652.2	152	397	.262	664	155	13	100	322	.304	.451	9	2	5.36	48	100	23	16	805	914	0.88

1997 Season

	ERA	W	L	Sv	G	GS	IP	H	HR	BB	SO
Home	4.00	11	5	0	20	20	135.0	143	14	28	101
Away	3.70	9	5	0	15	15	104.2	95	14	20	73
Day	3.07	7	1	0	11	11	76.1	70	6	13	62
Night	4.24	13	9	0	24	24	163.1	168	22	35	112
Grass	4.11	7	5	0	13	13	87.2	84	13	19	60
Turf	3.73	13	5	0	22	22	152.0	154	15	29	114
March/April	5.24	1	1	0	6	6	34.1	43	4	11	27
May	4.65	3	3	0	6	6	40.2	46	4	5	30
June	3.05	5	1	0	6	6	44.1	46	5	9	30
July	1.57	6	0	0	6	6	46.0	32	2	10	30
August	4.35	3	2	0	6	6	41.1	36	4	7	31
Sept/Oct	5.18	2	3	0	5	5	33.0	35	9	6	26
Starter	3.87	20	10	0	35	35	239.2	238	28	48	174
Reliever	0.00	0	0	0	0	0	0.0	0	0	0	0
0-3 Days Rest (Start)	0.00	0	0	0	0	0	0.0	0	0	0	0
4 Days Rest	3.62	16	8	0	27	27	189.0	180	22	39	135
5+ Days Rest	4.80	4	2	0	8	8	50.2	58	6	9	39
vs. AL	3.91	17	10	0	32	32	218.2	216	26	46	159
vs. NL	3.43	3	0	0	3	3	21.0	22	2	2	15
Pre-All Star	4.13	10	5	0	19	19	126.1	139	13	27	90
Post-All Star	3.57	10	5	0	16	16	113.1	99	15	21	84

	Avg	AB	H	2B	3B	HR	RBI	BB	SO	OBP	SLG
vs. Left	.291	471	137	28	1	15	52	30	76	.333	.450
vs. Right	.221	456	101	24	3	13	52	18	98	.251	.373
Inning 1-6	.264	766	202	41	3	26	89	39	138	.298	.427
Inning 7+	.224	161	36	11	1	2	15	9	36	.269	.342
None on	.229	598	137	27	3	17	17	34	117	.272	.370
Runners on	.307	329	101	25	1	11	87	14	57	.331	.489
Scoring Posn	.314	169	53	18	1	5	72	10	34	.339	.521
Close & Late	.180	61	11	3	1	0	5	1	13	.206	.262
None on/out	.198	247	49	11	2	6	6	12	47	.236	.332
vs. 1st Batr (relief)	.000	0	0	0	0	0	0	0	0	.000	.000
1st Inning Pitched	.211	128	27	8	0	4	13	10	27	.271	.367
First 75 Pitches	.246	674	166	34	3	23	68	34	126	.283	.408
Pitch 76-90	.345	116	40	8	0	2	16	7	18	.373	.466
Pitch 91-105	.233	90	21	5	1	2	14	2	19	.255	.378
Pitch 106+	.234	47	11	5	0	1	6	5	11	.308	.404
First Pitch	.361	144	52	12	2	7	24	1	0	.358	.618
Ahead in Count	.189	444	84	17	0	7	34	0	149	.191	.275
Behind in Count	.333	159	53	12	2	7	26	23	0	.418	.566
Two Strikes	.172	424	73	15	0	7	27	24	174	.219	.257
Pre-All Star	.280	496	139	34	2	13	61	27	90	.315	.435
Post-All Star	.230	431	99	18	2	15	43	21	84	.267	.385

Career (1995-1997)

	ERA	W	L	Sv	G	GS	IP	H	HR	BB	SO
Home	4.06	23	20	0	54	53	363.2	364	54	82	235
Away	5.01	19	20	0	45	45	289.0	300	46	70	162
Day	3.99	13	10	0	29	29	194.0	187	24	46	139
Night	4.69	29	30	0	70	69	458.2	477	76	106	258
Grass	5.20	15	18	0	37	37	235.1	252	35	57	122
Turf	4.08	27	22	0	62	61	417.1	412	65	95	275
March/April	4.82	4	4	0	13	12	74.2	85	9	21	56
May	5.26	6	8	0	17	17	106.0	116	15	27	69
June	4.40	6	10	0	18	18	122.2	131	20	24	63
July	3.90	12	5	0	18	18	120.0	102	16	29	74
August	3.84	8	6	0	18	18	126.2	110	16	27	71
Sept/Oct	5.00	6	7	0	15	15	102.2	102	24	24	64
Starter	4.46	42	40	0	98	98	649.2	659	100	152	397
Reliever	9.00	0	0	0	1	0	3.0	5	0	0	0
0-3 Days Rest (Start)	7.84	0	2	0	2	2	10.1	19	3	3	4
4 Days Rest	4.35	32	30	0	74	74	500.2	494	74	117	309
5+ Days Rest	4.61	10	8	0	22	22	138.2	146	23	32	84
vs. AL	4.52	39	40	0	96	95	631.2	642	98	150	382

	Avg	AB	H	2B	3B	HR	RBI	BB	SO	OBP	SLG
vs. Left	.271	1389	377	87	8	53	164	88	188	.315	.460
vs. Right	.250	1148	287	68	5	47	158	64	209	.289	.441
Inning 1-6	.262	2160	565	134	10	88	285	130	334	.303	.455
Inning 7+	.263	377	99	21	3	12	37	22	63	.307	.430
None on	.244	1612	394	93	8	61	61	96	256	.289	.426
Runners on	.292	925	270	62	5	39	261	56	141	.328	.496
Scoring Posn	.288	486	140	37	3	20	208	35	85	.325	.500
Close & Late	.241	166	40	8	1	6	17	8	25	.278	.410
None on/out	.237	679	161	37	7	24	24	38	101	.279	.418
vs. 1st Batr (relief)	.000	1	0	0	0	0	0	0	0	.000	.000
1st Inning Pitched	.252	381	96	24	1	16	47	26	72	.302	.446
First 75 Pitches	.252	1824	460	115	8	65	202	100	292	.291	.431
Pitch 76-90	.320	328	105	18	3	17	65	30	42	.376	.549
Pitch 91-105	.265	260	69	14	2	12	40	11	39	.297	.473
Pitch 106+	.240	125	30	8	0	6	15	11	24	.307	.448
First Pitch	.319	379	121	31	3	17	58	1	0	.319	.551
Ahead in Count	.202	1184	239	53	2	29	103	0	344	.205	.323
Behind in Count	.337	493	166	42	4	30	102	80	0	.428	.621

Career (1995-1997)

	ERA	W	L	Sv	G	GS	IP	H	HR	BB	SO		Avg	AB	H	2B	3B	HR	RBI	BB	SO	OBP	SLG
vs. NL	3.43	3	0	0	3	3	21.0	22	2	2	15	Two Strikes	.189	1135	215	45	4	32	89	71	397	.239	.321
Pre-All Star	4.84	20	22	0	52	51	327.1	360	50	78	202	Pre-All Star	.278	1293	360	80	7	50	175	78	202	.319	.467
Post-All Star	4.12	22	18	0	47	47	325.1	304	50	74	195	Post-All Star	.244	1244	304	75	6	50	147	74	195	.288	.435

Pitcher vs. Batter (career)

Pitches Best Vs.	Avg	AB	H	2B	3B	HR	RBI	BB	SO	OBP	SLG	Pitches Worst Vs.	Avg	AB	H	2B	3B	HR	RBI	BB	SO	OBP	SLG
Brent Gates	.053	19	1	0	1	0	1	2	2	.143	.158	B.J. Surhoff	.556	9	5	1	0	1	1	2	2	.636	1.000
Juan Gonzalez	.059	17	1	0	1	0	2	0	2	.059	.176	Jeromy Burnitz	.500	16	8	2	0	2	4	0	2	.500	1.000
Mickey Tettleton	.091	11	1	0	0	0	0	1	2	.167	.091	Ivan Rodriguez	.500	14	7	1	0	2	3	3	3	.588	1.000
Scott Brosius	.111	18	2	1	0	0	1	0	4	.111	.167	Jay Buhner	.476	21	10	2	1	4	6	1	1	.500	1.238
Johnny Damon	.133	15	2	0	0	0	0	0	2	.133	.133	Jay Buhner	.417	12	5	0	0	3	5	1	4	.462	1.167

Brady Raggio — Cardinals
Age 25 – Pitches Right (groundball pitcher)

	ERA	W	L	Sv	G	GS	IP	BB	SO	Avg	H	2B	3B	HR	RBI	OBP	SLG	GF	IR	IRS	Hld	SvOp	SB	CS	GB	FB	G/F
1997 Season	6.89	1	2	0	15	4	31.1	16	21	.336	44	7	0	1	24	.407	.412	5	3	1	0	0	4	3	56	25	2.24

1997 Season

	ERA	W	L	Sv	G	GS	IP	H	HR	BB	SO		Avg	AB	H	2B	3B	HR	RBI	BB	SO	OBP	SLG
Home	4.50	0	1	0	5	2	12.0	14	0	9	10	vs. Left	.456	57	26	4	0	0	14	7	4	.508	.526
Away	8.38	1	1	0	10	2	19.1	30	1	7	11	vs. Right	.243	74	18	3	0	1	10	9	17	.329	.324

Tim Raines — Yankees
Age 38 – Bats Both

	Avg	G	AB	R	H	2B	3B	HR	RBI	BB	SO	HBP	GDP	SB	CS	OBP	SLG	IBB	SH	SF	#Pit	#P/PA	GB	FB	G/F
1997 Season	.321	74	271	56	87	20	2	4	38	41	34	0	4	8	5	.403	.454	0	0	6	1258	3.96	102	71	1.44
Last Five Years	.291	482	1773	337	516	86	15	51	244	270	193	8	35	65	15	.384	.443	11	9	18	8064	3.88	671	528	1.27

1997 Season

	Avg	AB	H	2B	3B	HR	RBI	BB	SO	OBP	SLG		Avg	AB	H	2B	3B	HR	RBI	BB	SO	OBP	SLG
vs. Left	.339	59	20	3	0	1	4	8	5	.412	.441	First Pitch	.353	34	12	3	0	0	3	0	0	.353	.441
vs. Right	.316	212	67	17	2	3	34	33	29	.400	.458	Ahead in Count	.389	72	28	7	2	2	17	25	0	.535	.625
Groundball	.277	65	18	5	1	1	13	8	10	.347	.431	Behind in Count	.217	92	20	5	0	1	9	0	25	.215	.304
Flyball	.351	37	13	1	0	1	3	9	2	.478	.459	Two Strikes	.246	114	28	4	0	1	12	16	34	.328	.307
Home	.349	149	52	12	2	3	22	20	17	.416	.517	Batting #1	.336	214	72	16	2	4	26	33	26	.417	.486
Away	.287	122	35	8	0	1	16	21	17	.386	.377	Batting #2	.280	50	14	4	0	0	12	6	5	.351	.360
Day	.314	121	38	9	1	1	18	20	15	.406	.430	Other	.143	7	1	0	0	0	0	2	3	.333	.143
Night	.327	150	49	11	1	3	20	21	19	.400	.473	March/April	.245	49	12	3	0	1	6	10	8	.367	.367
Grass	.332	250	83	19	2	4	37	38	29	.413	.472	May	.333	99	33	7	1	0	11	14	15	.409	.424
Turf	.190	21	4	1	0	0	1	3	5	.280	.238	June	.333	3	1	0	0	0	0	2	0	.600	.333
Pre-All Star	.305	151	46	10	1	1	17	26	23	.400	.404	July	.000	0	0	0	0	0	0	0	0	.000	.000
Post-All Star	.342	120	41	10	1	3	21	15	11	.406	.517	August	.283	46	13	4	0	0	10	6	4	.358	.370
Scoring Posn	.306	62	19	6	1	0	32	15	9	.410	.435	Sept/Oct	.378	74	28	6	1	3	11	9	7	.435	.608
Close & Late	.257	35	9	1	0	0	5	9	5	.400	.286	vs. AL	.327	266	87	20	2	4	38	40	32	.407	.462
None on/out	.374	99	37	7	1	1	6	12	9	.410	.495	vs. NL	.000	5	0	0	0	0	0	1	2	.167	.000

1997 By Position

Position	Avg	AB	H	2B	3B	HR	RBI	BB	SO	OBP	SLG	G	GS	Innings	PO	A	E	DP	Fld Pct	Rng Fctr	In Zone	Zone Outs	Zone Rtg	MLB Zone
As DH	.364	55	20	8	0	2	14	8	4	.431	.618	13	13	---	---	---	---	---	---	---	---	---	---	---
As lf	.318	211	67	12	2	2	24	31	28	.398	.422	57	51	452.0	78	1	1	0	.988	1.57	102	77	.755	.805

Last Five Years

	Avg	AB	H	2B	3B	HR	RBI	BB	SO	OBP	SLG		Avg	AB	H	2B	3B	HR	RBI	BB	SO	OBP	SLG
vs. Left	.287	446	128	21	0	8	51	75	42	.391	.388	First Pitch	.308	240	74	14	1	9	40	6	0	.325	.488
vs. Right	.292	1327	388	65	15	43	193	195	151	.381	.461	Ahead in Count	.350	557	195	38	7	24	95	141	0	.477	.573
Groundball	.287	456	131	21	3	10	67	59	54	.371	.412	Behind in Count	.215	586	126	19	3	6	56	0	152	.223	.288
Flyball	.313	352	110	12	3	14	48	60	41	.413	.483	Two Strikes	.245	681	167	23	2	12	75	122	193	.360	.338
Home	.300	864	259	36	9	28	112	136	79	.394	.459	Batting #1	.300	1013	304	48	8	35	124	166	109	.397	.467
Away	.283	909	257	50	6	23	132	134	114	.377	.427	Batting #2	.270	626	169	32	6	13	97	79	69	.352	.403
Day	.297	546	162	29	5	14	70	83	62	.387	.445	Other	.321	134	43	6	1	3	23	25	15	.423	.448
Night	.289	1227	354	57	10	37	174	187	131	.382	.442	March/April	.279	190	53	9	0	10	29	32	23	.385	.484
Grass	.299	1523	456	75	13	44	208	238	151	.393	.452	May	.295	356	105	16	4	9	47	53	38	.383	.438
Turf	.240	250	60	11	2	7	36	32	42	.325	.384	June	.287	268	77	12	2	7	25	46	27	.392	.425
Pre-All Star	.289	930	269	45	8	27	122	142	99	.383	.442	July	.277	307	85	13	5	7	46	35	24	.355	.420
Post-All Star	.293	843	247	41	7	24	122	128	94	.384	.444	August	.301	306	92	18	1	7	53	46	35	.388	.435
Scoring Posn	.304	414	126	26	3	8	186	97	51	.424	.440	Sept/Oct	.301	346	104	18	3	11	44	58	46	.398	.465
Close & Late	.284	275	78	11	0	7	39	49	25	.386	.400	vs. AL	.292	1768	516	86	15	51	244	269	191	.384	.444
None on/out	.310	555	172	25	8	19	19	61	57	.383	.486	vs. NL	.000	5	0	0	0	0	0	1	2	.167	.000

Batter vs. Pitcher (since 1984)

Hits Best Against	Avg	AB	H	2B	3B	HR	RBI	BB	SO	OBP	SLG	Hits Worst Against	Avg	AB	H	2B	3B	HR	RBI	BB	SO	OBP	SLG
Ken Hill	.550	20	11	3	1	0	5	7	2	.667	.800	Felipe Lira	.000	9	0	0	0	0	0	4	2	.308	.000
Andy Benes	.500	16	8	1	1	2	4	1	3	.529	1.063	Jose Mesa	.077	13	1	0	0	0	0	0	0	.077	.077
Mark Leiter	.467	15	7	0	0	3	4	4	2	.579	1.067	Bobby Ayala	.100	10	1	0	0	0	1	1	5	.182	.100
Carlos Reyes	.462	13	6	1	0	2	3	2	0	.533	1.000	Scott Kamieniecki	.125	16	2	0	0	0	0	2	2	.222	.125
Jim Converse	.400	10	4	0	1	0	3	2	3	.500	.900	Mike Morgan	.167	12	2	0	0	0	0	0	0	.167	.167

Manny Ramirez — Indians
Age 26 – Bats Right (flyball hitter)

	Avg	G	AB	R	H	2B	3B	HR	RBI	BB	SO	HBP	GDP	SB	CS	OBP	SLG	IBB	SH	SF	#Pit	#P/PA	GB	FB	G/F
1997 Season	.328	150	561	99	184	40	0	26	88	79	115	7	19	2	3	.415	.538	5	0	4	2617	4.02	193	148	1.30
Career (1993-1997)	.304	552	1938	334	590	134	4	109	372	283	411	15	59	20	16	.393	.546	23	2	22	9236	4.09	584	582	1.00

1997 Season

	Avg	AB	H	2B	3B	HR	RBI	BB	SO	OBP	SLG		Avg	AB	H	2B	3B	HR	RBI	BB	SO	OBP	SLG
vs. Left	.350	137	48	13	0	6	26	19	24	.433	.577	First Pitch	.389	54	21	7	0	5	14	4	0	.441	.796
vs. Right	.321	424	136	27	0	20	62	60	91	.409	.526	Ahead in Count	.441	136	60	11	0	11	26	33	0	.544	.765
Groundball	.288	104	30	8	0	6	21	13	22	.377	.538	Behind in Count	.275	258	71	14	0	7	31	0	91	.291	.411
Flyball	.416	77	32	7	0	4	16	13	16	.500	.662	Two Strikes	.247	275	68	17	0	8	30	42	115	.351	.396
Home	.333	279	93	19	0	14	47	40	61	.420	.552	Batting #3	.325	194	63	11	0	11	32	33	47	.424	.552
Away	.323	282	91	21	0	12	41	39	54	.410	.525	Batting #6	.320	181	58	11	0	8	30	25	32	.405	.514
Day	.368	190	70	14	0	10	40	27	42	.448	.600	Other	.339	186	63	18	0	7	26	21	36	.414	.548
Night	.307	371	114	26	0	16	48	52	73	.398	.507	March/April	.304	92	28	8	0	5	17	11	14	.381	.554
Grass	.343	470	161	34	0	21	74	69	97	.431	.549	May	.369	65	24	2	0	3	14	9	16	.447	.538
Turf	.253	91	23	6	0	5	14	10	18	.327	.484	June	.341	85	29	8	0	2	12	14	16	.440	.506
Pre-All Star	.342	263	90	19	0	13	49	35	49	.422	.563	July	.324	105	34	10	0	3	9	10	20	.393	.505
Post-All Star	.315	298	94	21	0	13	39	44	66	.408	.517	August	.301	103	31	3	0	9	20	28	27	.447	.592
Scoring Posn	.237	152	36	8	0	5	62	29	29	.358	.388	Sept/Oct	.342	111	38	9	0	4	16	7	22	.388	.532
Close & Late	.355	62	22	4	0	4	8	16	16	.487	.613	vs. AL	.327	511	167	37	0	22	82	71	103	.413	.528
None on/out	.360	136	49	8	0	7	7	11	26	.416	.574	vs. NL	.340	50	17	3	0	4	6	8	12	.431	.640

1997 By Position

Position	Avg	AB	H	2B	3B	HR	RBI	BB	SO	OBP	SLG	G	GS	Innings	PO	A	E	DP	Fld Pct	Rng Fctr	In Zone	Zone Outs	Zone Rtg	MLB Zone
As rf	.319	545	174	37	0	25	85	77	114	.408	.525	146	146	1253.2	258	10	7	2	.975	1.92	292	246	.842	.813

Career (1993-1997)

	Avg	AB	H	2B	3B	HR	RBI	BB	SO	OBP	SLG		Avg	AB	H	2B	3B	HR	RBI	BB	SO	OBP	SLG
vs. Left	.347	554	192	50	0	29	106	86	95	.435	.594	First Pitch	.330	179	59	13	0	16	47	15	0	.379	.670
vs. Right	.288	1384	398	84	4	80	266	197	316	.377	.527	Ahead in Count	.419	487	204	47	1	45	132	141	0	.543	.797
Groundball	.295	370	109	28	1	21	65	48	83	.377	.546	Behind in Count	.243	875	213	49	2	28	121	0	329	.252	.400
Flyball	.284	349	99	23	0	24	79	56	82	.381	.556	Two Strikes	.218	970	211	49	2	32	127	127	411	.311	.371
Home	.294	948	279	64	4	54	190	146	211	.389	.541	Batting #6	.313	656	205	44	0	40	128	93	138	.400	.563
Away	.314	990	311	70	0	55	182	137	200	.398	.552	Batting #7	.280	514	144	28	2	30	105	83	108	.377	.518
Day	.325	650	211	47	2	37	129	87	158	.403	.574	Other	.314	768	241	62	2	39	139	107	165	.398	.552
Night	.294	1288	379	87	2	72	243	196	253	.389	.533	March/April	.306	252	77	21	1	17	59	33	48	.384	.599
Grass	.306	1679	514	119	4	91	320	249	361	.396	.544	May	.301	319	96	18	0	22	69	44	68	.383	.564
Turf	.293	259	76	15	0	18	52	34	50	.374	.560	June	.287	342	98	21	2	18	58	67	85	.401	.518
Pre-All Star	.301	1003	302	69	3	64	211	157	219	.394	.567	July	.322	345	111	32	1	18	66	49	71	.409	.577
Post-All Star	.308	935	288	65	1	45	161	126	192	.393	.524	August	.329	340	112	22	0	20	70	64	76	.431	.571
Scoring Posn	.288	528	152	31	0	26	263	98	110	.391	.494	Sept/Oct	.282	340	96	20	0	14	50	26	63	.343	.465
Close & Late	.273	249	68	13	1	15	43	61	64	.417	.514	vs. AL	.303	1888	573	131	4	105	366	275	399	.392	.544
None on/out	.297	458	136	25	3	28	28	49	101	.367	.548	vs. NL	.340	50	17	3	0	4	6	8	12	.431	.640

Batter vs. Pitcher (career)

Hits Best Against	Avg	AB	H	2B	3B	HR	RBI	BB	SO	OBP	SLG	Hits Worst Against	Avg	AB	H	2B	3B	HR	RBI	BB	SO	OBP	SLG
Rick Krivda	.778	9	7	2	0	0	1	3	0	.833	1.000	Roger Pavlik	.000	13	0	0	0	0	1	2	3	.133	.000
Willie Adams	.667	9	6	1	1	1	2	2	2	.727	1.333	Juan Guzman	.111	9	1	0	0	0	0	2	1	.273	.111
Andy Pettitte	.500	18	9	2	0	2	7	0	1	.500	.944	Kevin Appier	.118	17	2	1	0	0	1	1	9	.211	.176
Al Leiter	.500	14	7	1	0	1	3	0	2	.533	.786	Tim Wakefield	.133	15	2	1	0	0	0	1	6	.188	.200
Rich Robertson	.462	13	6	4	0	1	5	1	1	.500	1.000	Bob Tewksbury	.154	13	2	1	0	0	1	0	3	.154	.231

Edgar Ramos — Astros
Age 23 – Pitches Right

	ERA	W	L	Sv	G	GS	IP	BB	SO	Avg	H	2B	3B	HR	RBI	OBP	SLG	CG	ShO	Sup	QS	#P/S	SB	CS	GB	FB	G/F
1997 Season	5.14	0	2	0	4	2	14.0	6	4	.288	15	4	2	3	7	.373	.615	0	0	2.57	0	74	2	1	19	17	1.12

1997 Season

	ERA	W	L	Sv	G	GS	IP	H	HR	BB	SO		Avg	AB	H	2B	3B	HR	RBI	BB	SO	OBP	SLG
Home	0.00	0	0	0	0	0	0.0	0	0	0	0	vs. Left	.391	23	9	1	1	2	5	4	2	.481	.783
Away	5.14	0	2	0	4	2	14.0	15	3	6	4	vs. Right	.207	29	6	3	1	1	2	2	2	.281	.483

Ken Ramos — Astros
Age 31 – Bats Left

	Avg	G	AB	R	H	2B	3B	HR	RBI	BB	SO	HBP	GDP	SB	CS	OBP	SLG	IBB	SH	SF	#Pit	#P/PA	GB	FB	G/F
1997 Season	.000	14	12	0	0	0	0	0	1	2	0	0	1	0	0	.133	.000	0	0	1	63	4.20	6	7	0.86

1997 Season

	Avg	AB	H	2B	3B	HR	RBI	BB	SO	OBP	SLG		Avg	AB	H	2B	3B	HR	RBI	BB	SO	OBP	SLG
vs. Left	.000	2	0	0	0	0	0	1	0	.333	.000	Scoring Posn	.000	3	0	0	0	0	1	0	0	.000	.000
vs. Right	.000	10	0	0	0	0	1	1	0	.083	.000	Close & Late	.000	2	0	0	0	0	0	1	0	.333	.000

Joe Randa — Pirates
Age 28 – Bats Right

	Avg	G	AB	R	H	2B	3B	HR	RBI	BB	SO	HBP	GDP	SB	CS	OBP	SLG	IBB	SH	SF	#Pit	#P/PA	GB	FB	G/F
1997 Season	.302	126	443	58	134	27	9	7	60	41	64	6	10	4	2	.366	.451	1	4	5	1790	3.59	175	124	1.41
Career (1995-1997)	.292	270	850	100	248	53	10	14	112	73	128	7	22	17	7	.349	.427	5	6	9	3350	3.54	340	216	1.57

1997 Season

	Avg	AB	H	2B	3B	HR	RBI	BB	SO	OBP	SLG
vs. Left	.232	99	23	6	0	2	10	10	11	.303	.354
vs. Right	.323	344	111	21	9	5	50	31	53	.383	.480
Groundball	.319	69	22	6	3	1	15	5	12	.360	.426
Flyball	.305	82	25	4	1	1	12	3	16	.330	.415
Home	.304	227	69	17	8	5	37	25	35	.375	.515
Away	.301	216	65	10	1	2	23	16	29	.356	.384
Day	.287	136	39	12	2	1	21	7	21	.327	.426
Night	.309	307	95	15	7	6	39	34	43	.382	.463
Grass	.295	146	43	8	0	1	12	12	22	.358	.370
Turf	.306	297	91	19	9	6	48	29	42	.369	.492
Pre-All Star	.297	249	74	16	7	5	34	22	36	.359	.478
Post-All Star	.309	194	60	11	2	2	26	19	28	.374	.418
Scoring Posn	.317	120	38	8	3	1	50	17	16	.392	.458
Close & Late	.320	75	24	4	1	1	10	9	14	.391	.440
None on/out	.302	106	32	9	0	0		5	15	.351	.387

	Avg	AB	H	2B	3B	HR	RBI	BB	SO	OBP	SLG
First Pitch	.429	56	24	4	0	0	8	1	0	.433	.500
Ahead in Count	.365	126	46	11	3	1	22	29	0	.484	.524
Behind in Count	.220	186	41	11	2	6	21	0	58	.240	.398
Two Strikes	.209	182	38	7	3	5	20	11	64	.269	.363
Batting #5	.335	260	87	15	7	4	45	26	33	.400	.492
Batting #8	.265	113	30	8	1	2	11	11	19	.333	.407
Other	.243	70	17	4	1	1	4	4	12	.284	.371
March/April	.228	79	18	6	0	1	6	6	13	.279	.342
May	.348	92	32	7	3	2	10	11	12	.423	.554
June	.308	78	24	3	4	2	16	5	11	.360	.526
July	.222	18	4	1	0	0	0	0	4	.222	.278
August	.287	101	29	5	1	1	10	11	15	.368	.386
Sept/Oct	.360	75	27	5	1	1	16	8	9	.414	.493
vs. AL	.297	37	11	1	1	1	5	1	3	.300	.459
vs. NL	.303	406	123	26	8	6	55	40	61	.371	.451

1997 By Position

Position	Avg	AB	H	2B	3B	HR	RBI	BB	SO	OBP	SLG	G	GS	Innings	PO	A	E	DP	Fld Pct	Rng Fctr	In Zone	Outs	Zone Rtg	MLB Zone
As 2b	.282	39	11	3	0	1	5	4	4	.349	.436	13	9	84.0	25	41	0	6	1.000	7.07	47	43	.915	.902
As 3b	.303	403	122	24	9	6	55	37	60	.366	.452	120	111	970.1	66	249	21	24	.938	2.92	353	280	.793	.801

Career (1995-1997)

	Avg	AB	H	2B	3B	HR	RBI	BB	SO	OBP	SLG
vs. Left	.281	288	81	23	0	4	35	25	37	.337	.403
vs. Right	.297	562	167	30	10	10	77	48	91	.356	.440
Groundball	.302	149	45	10	4	2	26	12	25	.348	.463
Flyball	.293	140	41	7	1	1	19	9	27	.336	.379
Home	.307	430	132	33	9	8	72	45	59	.373	.481
Away	.276	420	116	20	1	6	40	28	69	.324	.371
Day	.285	253	72	17	3	5	36	15	47	.326	.435
Night	.295	597	176	36	7	9	76	58	81	.359	.424
Grass	.290	511	148	32	1	6	62	40	77	.343	.403
Turf	.295	339	100	21	9	6	50	33	51	.359	.463
Pre-All Star	.282	454	128	26	8	8	57	45	67	.348	.427
Post-All Star	.303	396	120	27	2	6	55	28	61	.351	.427
Scoring Posn	.321	218	70	15	3	2	91	32	27	.398	.445
Close & Late	.277	137	38	9	1	1	14	19	29	.365	.380
None on/out	.289	201	58	13	0	2	2	10	26	.323	.383

	Avg	AB	H	2B	3B	HR	RBI	BB	SO	OBP	SLG
First Pitch	.392	120	47	10	0	3	23	3	0	.402	.550
Ahead in Count	.384	219	84	21	3	2	34	49	0	.494	.534
Behind in Count	.208	375	78	19	2	8	38	0	115	.219	.333
Two Strikes	.192	349	67	12	3	6	33	20	128	.243	.295
Batting #5	.327	266	87	15	7	4	45	26	35	.392	.481
Batting #8	.286	217	62	12	1	5	28	17	35	.340	.419
Other	.270	367	99	26	2	5	39	30	58	.323	.392
March/April	.246	138	34	7	1	1	14	13	23	.307	.333
May	.308	130	40	9	3	4	12	13	18	.375	.515
June	.312	157	49	9	4	2	29	13	22	.368	.459
July	.243	107	26	8	0	2	11	8	16	.299	.374
August	.289	159	46	10	1	2	18	15	23	.356	.403
Sept/Oct	.333	159	53	10	1	3	28	11	26	.374	.465
vs. AL	.282	444	125	27	2	8	57	33	67	.329	.405
vs. NL	.303	406	123	26	8	6	55	40	61	.371	.451

Batter vs. Pitcher (career)

Hits Best Against	Avg	AB	H	2B	3B	HR	RBI	BB	SO	OBP	SLG
Jamie Moyer	.333	12	4	2	0	0	2	0	1	.333	.500
Wilson Alvarez	.333	12	4	1	0	1	2	0	2	.333	.667
Jamey Wright	.333	9	3	1	1	0	2	2	1	.455	.667

Hits Worst Against	Avg	AB	H	2B	3B	HR	RBI	BB	SO	OBP	SLG
Terry Mulholland	.182	11	2	2	0	0	2	0	2	.182	.364

Pat Rapp — Giants
Age 30 – Pitches Right (groundball pitcher)

	ERA	W	L	Sv	G	GS	IP	BB	SO	Avg	H	2B	3B	HR	RBI	OBP	SLG	CG	ShO	Sup	QS	#P/S	SB	CS	GB	FB	G/F
1997 Season	4.83	5	8	0	27	25	141.2	72	92	.288	158	29	3	16	73	.372	.440	1	1	4.83	8	93	9	7	230	143	1.61
Last Five Years	4.26	38	45	0	125	121	698.2	347	412	.278	733	130	19	58	320	.364	.407	7	4	4.84	58	95	37	51	1071	693	1.55

1997 Season

	ERA	W	L	Sv	G	GS	IP	H	HR	BB	SO
Home	4.92	1	3	0	13	12	64.0	64	9	33	48
Away	4.75	4	5	0	14	13	77.2	94	7	39	44
Day	4.66	1	2	0	8	7	38.2	45	4	23	27
Night	4.89	4	6	0	19	18	103.0	113	12	49	65
Grass	5.53	3	6	0	23	21	114.0	132	13	63	79
Turf	1.95	2	2	0	4	4	27.2	26	3	9	13
March/April	5.20	2	1	0	5	5	27.2	33	2	13	11
May	3.38	1	1	0	6	6	37.1	30	5	13	26
June	4.82	1	3	0	5	5	28.0	35	3	14	20
July	5.23	0	1	0	4	4	20.2	30	1	15	15
August	7.90	1	2	0	3	3	13.2	16	3	8	5
Sept/Oct	4.40	0	0	0	4	2	14.1	14	2	9	15
Starter	4.80	5	8	0	25	25	135.0	152	15	67	82
Reliever	5.40	0	0	0	2	0	6.2	6	1	5	10
0-3 Days Rest (Start)	3.52	0	0	0	2	2	7.2	7	2	4	5
4 Days Rest	4.42	3	6	0	14	14	75.1	85	8	37	51
5+ Days Rest	5.54	2	2	0	9	9	52.0	59	6	26	26
vs. AL	5.68	0	1	0	2	2	6.1	10	0	11	4
vs. NL	4.79	5	7	0	25	23	135.1	148	16	61	88
Pre-All Star	4.38	4	6	0	18	18	102.2	114	10	49	60

	Avg	AB	H	2B	3B	HR	RBI	BB	SO	OBP	SLG
vs. Left	.292	260	76	12	0	7	29	34	40	.372	.419
vs. Right	.285	288	82	17	3	9	44	38	52	.373	.458
Inning 1-6	.286	507	145	26	3	14	69	68	87	.372	.432
Inning 7+	.317	41	13	3	0	2	4	4	5	.378	.537
None on	.310	303	94	16	2	13	13	32	49	.380	.505
Runners on	.261	245	64	13	1	3	60	40	43	.364	.359
Scoring Posn	.231	147	34	7	1	2	54	27	30	.346	.333
Close & Late	.450	20	9	2	0	2	4	3	2	.522	.850
None on/out	.321	140	45	6	0	5	5	17	20	.395	.471
vs. 1st Batr (relief)	.500	2	1	1	0	0	1	0	1	.500	1.000
1st Inning Pitched	.339	109	37	11	0	5	23	13	21	.411	.578
First 75 Pitches	.285	417	119	22	2	12	53	53	69	.367	.434
Pitch 76-90	.233	60	14	2	1	2	9	11	10	.347	.400
Pitch 91-105	.404	52	21	4	0	2	10	4	8	.456	.596
Pitch 106+	.211	19	4	1	0	0	1	4	5	.348	.263
First Pitch	.333	78	26	3	0	7	16	2	0	.346	.641
Ahead in Count	.228	215	49	9	0	5	20	0	72	.233	.340
Behind in Count	.331	148	49	11	2	4	27	43	0	.479	.514
Two Strikes	.224	246	55	10	1	1	22	27	92	.303	.285
Pre-All Star	.286	398	114	18	2	10	49	49	60	.365	.417

1997 Season

Post-All Star	ERA	W	L	Sv	G	GS	IP	H	HR	BB	SO		Post-All Star	Avg	AB	H	2B	3B	HR	RBI	BB	SO	OBP	SLG
Post-All Star	6.00	1	2	0	9	7	39.0	44	6	23	32		Post-All Star	.293	150	44	11	1	6	24	23	32	.391	.500

Last Five Years

	ERA	W	L	Sv	G	GS	IP	H	HR	BB	SO			Avg	AB	H	2B	3B	HR	RBI	BB	SO	OBP	SLG
Home	4.23	21	20	0	62	60	349.1	362	31	159	218		vs. Left	.286	1276	365	61	10	25	142	192	153	.378	.408
Away	4.30	17	25	0	63	61	349.1	371	27	188	194		vs. Right	.270	1363	368	69	9	33	178	155	259	.351	.406
Day	4.40	5	14	0	30	28	151.1	169	13	78	99		Inning 1-6	.279	2410	673	111	18	48	299	316	381	.365	.400
Night	4.23	33	31	0	95	93	547.1	564	45	269	313		Inning 7+	.262	229	60	19	1	10	21	31	31	.352	.485
Grass	4.52	31	36	0	102	98	564.0	598	50	276	342		None on	.290	1426	413	76	11	38	38	169	211	.369	.438
Turf	3.21	7	9	0	23	23	134.2	135	8	71	70		Runners on	.264	1213	320	54	8	20	282	178	201	.359	.371
March/April	4.29	4	6	0	15	15	86.0	94	6	34	34		Scoring Posn	.247	695	172	29	2	10	236	116	122	.352	.338
May	4.20	6	6	0	23	22	128.2	132	13	60	77		Close & Late	.320	97	31	14	1	6	14	18	10	.426	.670
June	4.19	5	11	0	22	21	122.1	126	9	68	74		None on/out	.303	659	200	33	7	16	16	85	90	.387	.448
July	4.21	5	10	0	23	23	130.1	141	9	65	96		vs. 1st Batr (relief)	.500	4	2	1	0	0	1	0	1	.500	.750
August	5.85	9	8	0	22	22	110.1	136	17	70	58		1st Inning Pitched	.296	479	142	25	5	12	87	87	82	.408	.445
Sept/Oct	2.95	9	4	0	20	18	119.0	104	4	50	73		First 75 Pitches	.285	1947	554	87	14	38	238	259	318	.371	.402
Starter	4.26	38	44	0	121	121	689.1	725	57	341	400		Pitch 76-90	.215	331	71	18	3	9	33	49	39	.319	.369
Reliever	4.82	0	1	0	4	0	9.1	8	1	6	12		Pitch 91-105	.286	252	72	15	2	7	29	22	41	.350	.444
0-3 Days Rest (Start)	3.52	0	0	0	2	2	7.2	8	1	4	5		Pitch 106+	.330	109	36	10	0	4	20	17	14	.417	.532
4 Days Rest	4.62	23	30	0	74	74	413.1	450	36	222	246		First Pitch	.340	379	129	19	4	10	56	11	0	.359	.491
5+ Days Rest	3.72	15	14	0	45	45	268.1	267	20	115	149		Ahead in Count	.212	1081	229	40	6	20	96	0	337	.218	.315
vs. AL	5.68	0	1	0	2	2	6.1	10	0	11	4		Behind in Count	.320	653	209	44	6	17	91	199		.478	.484
vs. NL	4.25	38	44	0	123	119	692.1	723	58	336	408		Two Strikes	.221	1160	256	46	7	17	115	137	412	.309	.316
Pre-All Star	4.34	16	28	0	68	66	377.2	401	30	192	211		Pre-All Star	.282	1421	401	71	10	30	170	192	211	.371	.410
Post-All Star	4.18	22	17	0	57	55	321.0	332	28	155	201		Post-All Star	.273	1218	332	59	9	28	150	155	201	.357	.405

Pitcher vs. Batter (career)

Pitches Best Vs.	Avg	AB	H	2B	3B	HR	RBI	BB	SO	OBP	SLG	Pitches Worst Vs.	Avg	AB	H	2B	3B	HR	RBI	BB	SO	OBP	SLG
Glenallen Hill	.000	11	0	0	0	0	0	1	0	.083	.000	Charlie O'Brien	.545	11	6	0	0	1	1	2	1	.643	.818
Brett Butler	.000	10	0	0	0	0	0	3	2	.231	.000	Barry Bonds	.500	14	7	0	1	2	8	6	0	.619	1.071
Marquis Grissom	.071	28	2	0	0	0	0	2	5	.133	.071	Jeff Bagwell	.455	11	5	0	0	2	6	3	2	.533	1.000
Chipper Jones	.071	14	1	0	0	0	1	1	2	.133	.071	Ellis Burks	.440	25	11	1	0	4	9	2	4	.481	.960
Jeff Branson	.118	17	2	0	0	0	0	1	1	.118	.118	Jeff Kent	.400	25	10	1	0	0	3	3	4	.464	.920

Jeff Reboulet — Orioles
Age 34 – Bats Right (groundball hitter)

	Avg	G	AB	R	H	2B	3B	HR	RBI	BB	SO	HBP	GDP	SB	CS	OBP	SLG	IBB	SH	SF	#Pit	#P/PA	GB	FB	G/F
1997 Season	.237	99	228	26	54	9	0	4	27	23	44	1	3	3	0	.307	.329	0	11	2	1113	4.20	92	58	1.59
Last Five Years	.253	476	1107	146	280	48	1	12	111	128	172	6	13	13	9	.332	.331	1	24	5	5254	4.14	436	303	1.44

1997 Season

	Avg	AB	H	2B	3B	HR	RBI	BB	SO	OBP	SLG		Avg	AB	H	2B	3B	HR	RBI	BB	SO	OBP	SLG
vs. Left	.198	101	20	4	0	3	10	9	15	.270	.327	Scoring Posn	.224	58	13	2	0	0	21	6	10	.299	.259
vs. Right	.268	127	34	5	0	1	17	14	29	.336	.331	Close & Late	.243	37	9	2	0	1	8	3	9	.317	.378
Home	.221	104	23	4	0	2	11	11	21	.293	.317	None on/out	.262	42	11	1	0	2	2	6	9	.354	.429
Away	.250	124	31	5	0	2	16	12	23	.319	.339	Batting #2	.245	139	34	6	0	3	16	14	29	.316	.353
First Pitch	.438	16	7	1	0	1	0	0	0	.438	.500	Batting #9	.250	48	12	2	0	0	8	6	10	.327	.292
Ahead in Count	.219	32	7	1	0	1	4	12	0	.422	.344	Other	.195	41	8	1	0	1	3	3	5	.250	.293
Behind in Count	.218	124	27	3	0	2	14	0	36	.224	.290	Pre-All Star	.200	90	18	2	0	2	16	11	14	.291	.289
Two Strikes	.199	136	27	4	0	2	15	11	44	.228	.228	Post-All Star	.261	138	36	7	0	2	11	12	30	.318	.355

Last Five Years

	Avg	AB	H	2B	3B	HR	RBI	BB	SO	OBP	SLG		Avg	AB	H	2B	3B	HR	RBI	BB	SO	OBP	SLG
vs. Left	.257	432	111	19	0	9	42	49	54	.336	.363	First Pitch	.386	83	32	5	0	1	4	1	0	.400	.482
vs. Right	.250	675	169	29	1	3	69	79	118	.330	.310	Ahead in Count	.292	212	62	13	0	4	31	84	0	.488	.410
Groundball	.275	236	65	8	0	0	29	31	35	.359	.309	Behind in Count	.204	555	113	12	1	2	43	0	143	.208	.240
Flyball	.216	171	37	2	0	2	14	18	34	.297	.263	Two Strikes	.218	605	132	22	0	3	53	43	172	.273	.269
Home	.250	533	133	21	0	5	47	58	86	.325	.317	Batting #2	.261	463	121	21	1	9	44	51	74	.336	.369
Away	.256	574	147	27	1	7	64	70	86	.339	.343	Batting #9	.260	315	82	17	0	2	33	36	46	.337	.333
Day	.241	423	102	18	0	6	53	52	72	.326	.326	Other	.234	329	77	10	0	1	34	41	52	.323	.274
Night	.260	684	178	30	1	6	58	76	100	.336	.333	March/April	.206	160	33	6	0	4	21	24	19	.310	.319
Grass	.254	567	144	27	0	6	69	70	88	.339	.349	May	.204	181	37	4	0	2	16	15	30	.265	.260
Turf	.252	540	136	21	1	3	45	58	84	.326	.311	June	.276	181	50	9	0	1	19	23	28	.367	.343
Pre-All Star	.232	586	136	24	0	8	64	71	88	.319	.314	July	.297	172	51	15	1	1	21	17	25	.366	.413
Post-All Star	.276	521	144	24	1	4	47	57	84	.348	.348	August	.256	238	61	7	0	3	24	16	41	.327	.324
Scoring Posn	.269	271	73	17	0	3	99	43	43	.368	.365	Sept/Oct	.274	175	48	7	0	1	13	23	29	.359	.331
Close & Late	.282	156	44	6	0	2	25	15	27	.351	.359	vs. AL	.253	1082	274	47	1	12	107	125	163	.332	.332
None on/out	.289	228	66	10	0	6	6	27	37	.365	.280	vs. NL	.240	25	6	1	0	0	4	3	9	.345	.280

Batter vs. Pitcher (career)

Hits Best Against	Avg	AB	H	2B	3B	HR	RBI	BB	SO	OBP	SLG	Hits Worst Against	Avg	AB	H	2B	3B	HR	RBI	BB	SO	OBP	SLG
Ricky Bones	.471	17	8	1	0	2	5	2	2	.526	.882	Kevin Appier	.000	10	0	0	0	0	1	1	3	.091	.000
Angel Miranda	.364	11	4	1	0	1	4	2	0	.462	.727	Juan Guzman	.111	18	2	0	1	0	3	3	5	.238	.222
Wilson Alvarez	.353	17	6	2	0	0	1	3	2	.450	.471	David Wells	.154	13	2	0	0	0	1	1	4	.214	.154
Randy Johnson	.314	35	11	2	0	1	4	6	9	.415	.457	Jaime Navarro	.182	11	2	2	0	0	1	1	4	.182	.364
Tom Gordon	.313	16	5	1	0	0	2	4	2	.450	.375	Jack McDowell	.214	14	3	0	0	0	1	3	1	.353	.214

Jeff Reed — Rockies

	Avg	G	AB	R	H	2B	3B	HR	RBI	BB	SO	HBP	GDP	SB	CS	OBP	SLG	IBB	SH	SF	#Pit	#P/PA	GB	FB	G/F
1997 Season	.297	90	256	43	76	10	0	17	47	35	55	2	8	2	1	.386	.535	1	5	0	1183	3.97	85	72	1.18
Last Five Years	.270	388	932	110	252	38	1	32	112	125	180	4	24	4	4	.358	.416	20	12	4	4182	3.88	346	259	1.34

1997 Season

	Avg	AB	H	2B	3B	HR	RBI	BB	SO	OBP	SLG		Avg	AB	H	2B	3B	HR	RBI	BB	SO	OBP	SLG
vs. Left	.172	29	5	1	0	0	0	0	11	.172	.207	Scoring Posn	.297	64	19	1	0	5	30	10	15	.392	.547
vs. Right	.313	227	71	9	0	17	47	35	44	.409	.577	Close & Late	.333	39	13	3	0	3	8	7	10	.435	.641
Home	.333	132	44	9	0	9	31	24	31	.436	.606	None on/out	.236	55	13	1	0	3	3	8	10	.333	.418
Away	.258	124	32	1	0	8	16	11	24	.328	.460	Batting #6	.226	31	7	1	0	3	4	8	4	.400	.548
First Pitch	.222	27	6	1	0	2	0	0	0	.250	.259	Batting #7	.320	194	62	9	0	12	37	20	41	.386	.552
Ahead in Count	.412	68	28	3	0	9	27	19	0	.545	.853	Other	.226	31	7	0	0	2	6	7	10	.368	.419
Behind in Count	.212	99	21	3	0	3	8	0	43	.212	.333	Pre-All Star	.312	125	39	3	0	7	23	13	27	.377	.504
Two Strikes	.181	116	21	3	0	7	16	55		.280	.284	Post-All Star	.282	131	37	7	0	10	24	22	28	.394	.565

Last Five Years

	Avg	AB	H	2B	3B	HR	RBI	BB	SO	OBP	SLG		Avg	AB	H	2B	3B	HR	RBI	BB	SO	OBP	SLG
vs. Left	.211	90	19	1	0	4	6	8	24	.283	.356	First Pitch	.319	116	37	5	0	1	5	11	0	.392	.388
vs. Right	.277	842	233	37	1	28	106	117	156	.365	.423	Ahead in Count	.354	240	85	12	0	17	56	76	0	.508	.617
Groundball	.289	273	79	9	0	8	34	31	44	.365	.410	Behind in Count	.201	374	75	9	1	8	28	0	144	.200	.294
Flyball	.285	158	45	9	0	6	24	18	34	.354	.456	Two Strikes	.193	429	83	14	1	7	29	38	180	.259	.280
Home	.298	497	148	26	0	21	73	71	90	.384	.477	Batting #7	.303	531	161	26	1	21	68	61	105	.376	.475
Away	.239	435	104	12	1	11	39	54	90	.327	.347	Batting #8	.243	210	51	7	0	5	26	33	31	.346	.348
Day	.248	431	107	18	0	14	52	61	79	.341	.387	Other	.209	191	40	5	0	6	18	31	44	.323	.330
Night	.289	501	145	20	1	18	60	64	101	.372	.441	March/April	.246	130	32	4	0	5	19	22	27	.353	.392
Grass	.281	768	216	33	1	30	99	107	144	.369	.444	May	.291	189	55	5	0	8	25	18	32	.349	.444
Turf	.220	164	36	5	0	2	13	18	36	.306	.287	June	.250	168	42	6	0	7	17	23	36	.344	.411
Pre-All Star	.262	531	139	15	0	20	66	67	108	.344	.403	July	.266	169	45	7	1	2	13	25	35	.364	.355
Post-All Star	.282	401	113	23	1	12	46	58	72	.376	.434	August	.307	150	46	8	0	5	20	16	26	.379	.460
Scoring Posn	.250	224	56	4	0	8	80	56	54	.394	.375	Sept/Oct	.254	126	32	8	0	5	18	21	24	.361	.437
Close & Late	.243	177	43	8	1	5	17	24	32	.333	.384	vs. AL	.391	23	9	1	0	2	5	3	6	.462	.696
None on/out	.269	234	63	11	0	7	7	19	33	.324	.406	vs. NL	.267	909	243	37	1	30	107	122	174	.355	.409

Batter vs. Pitcher (career)

Hits Best Against	Avg	AB	H	2B	3B	HR	RBI	BB	SO	OBP	SLG	Hits Worst Against	Avg	AB	H	2B	3B	HR	RBI	BB	SO	OBP	SLG
Andy Benes	.472	36	17	2	0	2	10	8	5	.543	.694	Bobby Jones	.091	11	1	1	0	0	0	2	1	.231	.182
Jim Bullinger	.462	13	6	1	0	0	3	0	0	.500	.538	David Cone	.095	21	2	0	0	0	2	3	7	.208	.095
Alan Benes	.429	14	6	0	0	0	1	1	2	.467	.429	Andy Ashby	.125	16	2	1	0	0	0	2	2	.222	.188
Pat Rapp	.364	11	4	0	0	0	1	3	2	.500	.364	Mike Bielecki	.158	19	3	1	0	0	0	3	4	.261	.158
Danny Darwin	.333	18	6	4	1	0	3	2	1	.400	.667	Mike Morgan	.167	24	4	0	0	0	1	0	2	.167	.167

Jody Reed — Tigers

	Avg	G	AB	R	H	2B	3B	HR	RBI	BB	SO	HBP	GDP	SB	CS	OBP	SLG	IBB	SH	SF	#Pit	#P/PA	GB	FB	G/F
1997 Season	.196	52	112	6	22	2	0	0	8	10	15	3	2	3	2	.278	.214	0	3	1	468	3.63	33	36	0.92
Last Five Years	.257	569	1896	205	488	83	3	10	165	223	180	14	49	17	18	.337	.320	20	32	16	8020	3.68	771	533	1.45

1997 Season

	Avg	AB	H	2B	3B	HR	RBI	BB	SO	OBP	SLG		Avg	AB	H	2B	3B	HR	RBI	BB	SO	OBP	SLG
vs. Left	.233	30	7	0	0	0	2	4	1	.333	.233	Scoring Posn	.292	24	7	0	0	0	8	3	4	.400	.292
vs. Right	.183	82	15	2	0	0	6	6	14	.256	.207	Close & Late	.200	30	6	1	0	0	2	2	5	.265	.233
Home	.246	57	14	2	0	0	6	8	8	.353	.281	None on/out	.136	22	3	0	0	0	0	1	2	.174	.136
Away	.145	55	8	0	0	0	2	2	7	.190	.145	Batting #2	.205	44	9	1	0	0	2	6	5	.327	.227
First Pitch	.200	15	3	0	0	0	0	0	0	.200	.200	Batting #9	.222	36	8	1	0	0	3	2	2	.282	.250
Ahead in Count	.200	25	5	1	0	0	2	7	0	.394	.240	Other	.156	32	5	0	0	0	3	2	8	.200	.156
Behind in Count	.170	53	9	0	0	0	5	0	14	.182	.170	Pre-All Star	.198	96	19	2	0	0	6	10	14	.291	.219
Two Strikes	.200	50	10	1	0	0	4	1	5	.259	.220	Post-All Star	.188	16	3	0	0	0	2	0	1	.188	.188

Last Five Years

	Avg	AB	H	2B	3B	HR	RBI	BB	SO	OBP	SLG		Avg	AB	H	2B	3B	HR	RBI	BB	SO	OBP	SLG
vs. Left	.265	480	127	23	1	0	28	77	33	.369	.317	First Pitch	.257	183	47	10	1	2	10	12	0	.301	.355
vs. Right	.255	1416	361	60	2	10	137	146	147	.326	.321	Ahead in Count	.306	516	158	35	1	7	60	126	0	.440	.419
Groundball	.264	500	132	25	2	2	46	57	41	.343	.334	Behind in Count	.224	821	184	25	1	0	60	0	154	.229	.257
Flyball	.235	315	74	11	0	3	30	32	32	.307	.298	Two Strikes	.209	752	157	20	0	1	63	85	180	.290	.239
Home	.263	923	243	40	0	6	85	120	76	.349	.326	Batting #2	.260	569	148	27	2	4	43	59	43	.335	.336
Away	.252	973	245	43	3	4	80	103	104	.326	.314	Batting #8	.261	654	171	25	1	3	53	77	82	.341	.317
Day	.246	594	146	28	1	5	61	80	57	.337	.322	Other	.251	673	169	31	0	3	69	87	55	.336	.311
Night	.263	1302	342	55	2	5	104	143	123	.337	.320	March/April	.265	291	77	12	0	0	30	38	22	.357	.306
Grass	.269	1534	412	68	1	9	135	182	152	.347	.334	May	.244	361	88	15	2	1	34	46	30	.327	.305
Turf	.210	362	76	15	2	0	30	41	28	.295	.262	June	.265	339	90	12	0	4	24	42	36	.346	.336
Pre-All Star	.257	1084	279	44	2	5	95	140	99	.345	.315	July	.246	329	81	15	0	1	35	52	35	.353	.301
Post-All Star	.257	812	209	39	1	5	70	83	81	.327	.326	August	.251	303	76	16	1	0	20	17	31	.291	.310
Scoring Posn	.280	453	127	20	0	2	150	105	54	.409	.338	Sept/Oct	.278	273	76	13	0	4	22	28	26	.348	.370
Close & Late	.255	333	85	14	0	1	24	37	36	.332	.306	vs. AL	.259	502	130	24	0	2	45	67	47	.349	.319
None on/out	.263	494	130	24	1	0	35	40	35	.315	.321	vs. NL	.257	1394	358	59	3	8	120	156	133	.333	.321

Batter vs. Pitcher (career)

Hits Best Against	Avg	AB	H	2B	3B	HR	RBI	BB	SO	OBP	SLG	Hits Worst Against	Avg	AB	H	2B	3B	HR	RBI	BB	SO	OBP	SLG
Willie Blair	.571	14	8	1	0	2	5	0	2	.571	1.071	Pedro Martinez	.077	13	1	1	0	0	0	1	3	.143	.154
Rich DeLucia	.533	15	8	4	0	0	3	2	1	.588	.800	Tommy Greene	.091	11	1	0	0	0	0	0	1	.091	.091
Chris Hammond	.500	12	6	2	0	0	2	2	0	.600	.667	Donovan Osborne	.111	18	2	0	0	0	0	1	0	.158	.111

Hits Best Against	Avg	AB	H	2B	3B	HR	RBI	BB	SO	OBP	SLG	Hits Worst Against	Avg	AB	H	2B	3B	HR	RBI	BB	SO	OBP	SLG
Mark Guthrie	.500	10	5	1	0	0	0	4	3	.643	.600	Shane Reynolds	.118	17	2	0	0	0	1	1	1	.167	.118
Juan Guzman	.462	13	6	1	0	1	3	2	1	.533	.769	Dave Burba	.125	16	2	0	0	0	1	0	2	.125	.125

Rick Reed — Mets
Age 32 – Pitches Right (groundball pitcher)

	ERA	W	L	Sv	G	GS	IP	BB	SO	Avg	H	2B	3B	HR	RBI	OBP	SLG	CG	ShO	Sup	QS	#P/S	SB	CS	GB	FB	G/F
1997 Season	2.89	13	9	0	33	31	208.1	31	113	.239	186	33	5	19	68	.272	.368	2	0	3.97	22	.88	3	6	330	197	1.68
Last Five Years	3.39	15	10	0	44	37	249.2	43	140	.247	233	43	5	28	96	.285	.392	2	0	4.18	23	.86	3	9	389	252	1.54

1997 Season

	ERA	W	L	Sv	G	GS	IP	H	HR	BB	SO		Avg	AB	H	2B	3B	HR	RBI	BB	SO	OBP	SLG
Home	3.05	8	5	0	15	15	100.1	89	7	15	65	vs. Left	.231	385	89	18	2	9	30	24	65	.277	.358
Away	2.75	5	4	0	18	16	108.0	97	12	16	48	vs. Right	.247	393	97	15	3	10	38	7	48	.267	.377
Day	2.39	6	3	0	15	14	90.1	81	8	13	53	Inning 1-6	.242	666	161	26	5	18	62	27	97	.275	.377
Night	3.28	7	6	0	18	17	118.0	105	11	18	60	Inning 7+	.223	112	25	7	0	1	6	4	16	.250	.313
Grass	2.52	12	6	0	26	24	167.2	137	15	29	92	None on	.227	502	114	20	3	13	13	19	83	.260	.357
Turf	4.43	1	3	0	7	7	40.2	49	4	2	21	Runners on	.261	276	72	13	2	6	55	12	30	.294	.388
March/April	1.03	2	1	0	5	4	35.0	22	2	5	22	Scoring Posn	.231	156	36	7	1	2	43	9	19	.272	.327
May	2.41	1	1	0	6	5	33.2	33	2	3	17	Close & Late	.217	83	18	4	0	1	3	4	15	.253	.301
June	5.25	2	2	0	6	6	36.0	43	6	8	19	None on/out	.204	211	43	7	1	4	4	3	34	.219	.303
July	2.27	4	0	0	5	5	35.2	31	3	7	16	vs. 1st Batr (relief)	.000	2	0	0	0	0	0	0	1	.000	.000
August	4.09	2	4	0	6	6	33.0	31	3	5	14	1st Inning Pitched	.220	123	27	3	0	3	11	4	25	.260	.337
Sept/Oct	2.31	2	1	0	5	5	35.0	26	3	3	25	First 75 Pitches	.244	635	155	24	5	17	59	22	94	.273	.378
Starter	2.98	13	9	0	31	31	202.2	183	19	31	106	Pitch 76-90	.202	89	18	6	0	2	5	6	11	.260	.337
Reliever	0.00	0	0	0	2	0	5.2	3	0	0	7	Pitch 91-105	.222	36	8	2	0	1	3	5	2	.282	.278
0-3 Days Rest (Start)	0.00	0	0	0	1	1	8.0	5	0	1	1	Pitch 106+	.278	18	5	1	0	0	3	0	3	.278	.333
4 Days Rest	3.00	9	5	0	15	15	102.0	88	10	14	60	First Pitch	.265	151	40	6	0	4	12	3	0	.287	.384
5+ Days Rest	3.21	4	4	0	15	15	92.2	90	9	16	45	Ahead in Count	.198	348	69	14	3	4	21	0	98	.202	.290
vs. AL	3.79	1	1	0	3	3	19.0	15	5	4	6	Behind in Count	.289	142	41	8	1	5	17	15	0	.354	.465
vs. NL	2.80	12	8	0	30	28	189.1	171	14	27	107	Two Strikes	.209	330	69	14	4	5	19	13	113	.241	.321
Pre-All Star	2.93	6	4	0	18	16	110.2	106	11	16	64	Pre-All Star	.252	420	106	23	2	11	38	16	64	.286	.395
Post-All Star	2.86	7	5	0	15	15	97.2	80	8	15	49	Post-All Star	.223	358	80	10	3	8	30	15	49	.255	.335

Steve Reed — Rockies
Age 32 – Pitches Right

	ERA	W	L	Sv	G	GS	IP	BB	SO	Avg	H	2B	3B	HR	RBI	OBP	SLG	GF	IR	IRS	Hld	SvOp	SB	CS	GB	FB	G/F
1997 Season	4.04	4	6	6	63	0	62.1	27	43	.219	49	7	0	10	33	.315	.384	23	34	11	10	13	5	2	68	79	0.86
Last Five Years	3.68	25	18	15	329	0	369.2	123	275	.245	335	52	9	51	197	.313	.408	70	217	69	66	41	23	18	456	423	1.08

1997 Season

	ERA	W	L	Sv	G	GS	IP	H	HR	BB	SO		Avg	AB	H	2B	3B	HR	RBI	BB	SO	OBP	SLG
Home	3.45	1	3	4	32	0	31.1	24	7	10	22	vs. Left	.210	100	21	2	0	5	10	13	15	.319	.380
Away	4.65	3	3	2	31	0	31.0	25	3	17	21	vs. Right	.226	124	28	5	0	5	23	14	28	.312	.387
Day	2.87	2	2	4	32	0	31.1	21	4	15	24	Inning 1-6	.077	13	1	0	0	0	0	0	2	.077	.077
Night	5.23	2	4	2	31	0	31.0	28	6	12	19	Inning 7+	.227	211	48	7	0	10	33	27	41	.328	.403
Grass	3.30	1	3	6	49	0	46.1	37	8	16	32	None on	.220	127	28	2	0	7	7	13	24	.308	.402
Turf	6.19	3	3	0	14	0	16.0	12	2	11	11	Runners on	.216	97	21	5	0	3	26	14	19	.325	.361
March/April	2.45	0	0	0	10	0	11.0	9	1	6	9	Scoring Posn	.200	60	12	4	0	0	20	8	12	.310	.267
May	7.59	0	2	6	13	0	10.2	13	3	7	7	Close & Late	.277	112	31	6	0	8	26	15	17	.379	.545
June	4.50	1	1	0	12	0	12.0	7	3	5	8	None on/out	.185	54	10	0	0	4	4	6	9	.279	.407
July	3.97	1	1	0	11	0	11.1	12	2	6	6	vs. 1st Batr (relief)	.263	57	15	0	0	4	4	5	9	.333	.474
August	3.12	2	1	0	10	0	8.2	4	0	2	7	1st Inning Pitched	.230	200	46	7	0	10	33	24	39	.326	.415
Sept/Oct	2.08	0	1	0	7	0	8.2	4	1	1	6	First 15 Pitches	.223	166	37	5	0	8	25	19	29	.319	.398
Starter	0.00	0	0	0	0	0	0.0	0	0	0	0	Pitch 16-30	.226	53	12	2	0	2	8	7	14	.317	.377
Reliever	4.04	4	6	6	63	0	62.1	49	10	27	43	Pitch 31-45	.000	5	0	0	0	0	0	1	0	.167	.000
0 Days rest (Relief)	6.08	2	1	1	13	0	13.1	15	3	4	9	Pitch 46+	.000	0	0	0	0	0	0	0	0	.000	.000
1 or 2 Days rest	2.34	2	2	5	36	0	34.2	24	4	16	26	First Pitch	.222	36	8	1	0	3	6	1	0	.275	.500
3+ Days rest	6.28	0	3	0	14	0	14.1	10	3	7	8	Ahead in Count	.218	110	24	3	0	3	18	0	37	.225	.327
vs. AL	7.71	0	1	0	5	0	4.2	6	2	1	2	Behind in Count	.235	34	8	3	0	1	3	16	0	.480	.412
vs. NL	3.75	4	5	6	58	0	57.2	43	8	26	41	Two Strikes	.190	100	19	2	0	3	12	10	43	.270	.284
Pre-All Star	5.00	1	3	6	38	0	36.0	33	8	19	25	Pre-All Star	.243	136	33	4	0	8	23	19	25	.344	.449
Post-All Star	2.73	3	3	0	25	0	26.1	16	2	8	18	Post-All Star	.182	88	16	3	0	2	10	8	18	.270	.284

Last Five Years

	ERA	W	L	Sv	G	GS	IP	H	HR	BB	SO		Avg	AB	H	2B	3B	HR	RBI	BB	SO	OBP	SLG
Home	4.45	15	10	8	175	0	198.0	197	35	68	142	vs. Left	.286	521	149	23	3	23	76	62	84	.370	.474
Away	2.78	10	8	7	154	0	171.2	138	16	55	133	vs. Right	.220	847	186	29	6	28	121	61	191	.277	.367
Day	4.16	12	6	9	138	0	151.1	140	25	49	120	Inning 1-6	.245	298	73	11	1	9	47	25	67	.307	.379
Night	3.34	13	10	6	191	0	218.1	195	26	74	155	Inning 7+	.245	1070	262	41	8	42	150	98	208	.315	.416
Grass	3.70	18	13	14	262	0	294.1	272	42	95	217	None on	.241	785	189	25	6	31	31	59	162	.302	.406
Turf	3.58	7	5	1	67	0	75.1	63	9	28	58	Runners on	.250	583	146	27	3	20	166	64	113	.328	.410
March/April	4.99	3	2	0	46	0	48.2	56	10	17	31	Scoring Posn	.273	352	96	18	2	10	141	46	68	.354	.420
May	4.47	1	5	8	54	0	56.1	54	10	22	50	Close & Late	.224	548	123	25	3	22	89	52	107	.301	.401
June	3.27	4	2	2	61	0	74.1	62	11	22	56	None on/out	.242	330	80	12	3	16	16	24	65	.298	.442
July	3.59	5	4	2	65	0	67.2	70	8	25	45	vs. 1st Batr (relief)	.248	303	75	12	3	16	56	21	60	.296	.465
August	3.29	6	3	3	54	0	63.0	57	7	20	48	1st Inning Pitched	.244	1043	255	42	7	42	167	91	212	.310	.419
Sept/Oct	2.87	6	2	0	49	0	59.2	36	5	17	45	First 15 Pitches	.234	913	214	34	6	39	135	75	176	.298	.413
Starter	0.00	0	0	0	0	0	0.0	0	0	0	0	Pitch 16-30	.266	387	103	16	3	9	48	41	85	.345	.393

	ERA	W	L	Sv	G	GS	IP	H	HR	BB	SO		Avg	AB	H	2B	3B	HR	RBI	BB	SO	OBP	SLG
Reliever	3.68	25	18	15	329	0	369.2	335	51	123	275	Pitch 31-45	.290	62	18	2	0	3	14	7	14	.371	.468
0 Days rest (Relief)	4.19	10	7	5	90	0	105.1	112	22	27	72	Pitch 46+	.000	6	0	0	0	0	0	0	0	.000	.000
1 or 2 Days rest	3.00	13	7	9	183	0	204.1	157	21	77	160	First Pitch	.297	192	57	10	2	9	38	10	0	.338	.510
3+ Days rest	5.10	2	4	1	56	0	60.0	66	8	19	43	Ahead in Count	.190	653	124	16	3	14	64	0	231	.200	.288
vs. AL	7.71	0	1	0	5	0	4.2	6	2	1	2	Behind in Count	.321	243	78	12	2	16	60	0	.455	.584
vs. NL	3.62	25	17	15	324	0	365.0	329	49	122	273	Two Strikes	.177	640	113	13	1	14	65	52	275	.244	.266
Pre-All Star	3.91	11	9	11	180	0	200.1	189	32	68	155	Pre-All Star	.250	755	189	27	5	32	111	68	155	.320	.426
Post-All Star	3.40	14	9	4	149	0	169.1	146	19	55	120	Post-All Star	.238	613	146	25	4	19	86	55	120	.305	.385

Pitcher vs. Batter (career)

Pitches Best Vs.	Avg	AB	H	2B	3B	HR	RBI	BB	SO	OBP	SLG	Pitches Worst Vs.	Avg	AB	H	2B	3B	HR	RBI	BB	SO	OBP	SLG
Benito Santiago	.000	16	0	0	0	0	1	1	4	.056	.000	Mike Piazza	.583	12	7	1	0	4	9	1	1	.667	1.667
Gary Sheffield	.000	11	0	0	0	0	2	1	5	.077	.000	Jeff Conine	.500	14	7	2	0	1	2	1	2	.533	.857
Barry Larkin	.000	10	0	0	0	0	0	2	2	.167	.000	Marquis Grissom	.500	10	5	1	1	0	0	2	1	.583	.800
Royce Clayton	.083	12	1	0	0	0	1	1	3	.143	.083	Ron Gant	.364	11	4	1	0	1	3	3	1	.500	.727
Jay Bell	.111	9	1	0	0	0	2	0	1	.091	.111	Eric Karros	.333	15	5	1	0	2	4	3	5	.444	.800

Pokey Reese — Reds
Age 25 – Bats Right

	Avg	G	AB	R	H	2B	3B	HR	RBI	BB	SO	HBP	GDP	SB	CS	OBP	SLG	IBB	SH	SF	#Pit	#P/PA	GB	FB	G/F
1997 Season	.219	128	397	48	87	15	0	4	26	31	82	5	1	25	7	.284	.287	2	4	0	1786	4.09	136	124	1.10

1997 Season

	Avg	AB	H	2B	3B	HR	RBI	BB	SO	OBP	SLG		Avg	AB	H	2B	3B	HR	RBI	BB	SO	OBP	SLG
vs. Left	.172	87	15	3	0	1	6	10	25	.273	.241	First Pitch	.500	30	15	2	0	1	4	1	0	.545	.667
vs. Right	.232	310	72	12	0	3	20	21	57	.287	.300	Ahead in Count	.257	74	19	2	0	2	7	22	0	.427	.365
Groundball	.220	59	13	3	0	1	6	5	7	.292	.322	Behind in Count	.163	196	32	8	0	4	0	68	.176	.204
Flyball	.250	48	12	1	0	1	4	5	9	.321	.333	Two Strikes	.134	209	28	5	0	1	9	8	82	.170	.172
Home	.270	178	48	8	0	3	19	18	32	.350	.365	Batting #1	.216	148	32	8	0	1	7	12	24	.280	.291
Away	.178	219	39	7	0	1	7	13	50	.227	.224	Batting #8	.242	124	30	3	0	2	9	9	25	.314	.315
Day	.239	155	37	11	0	1	16	7	38	.276	.329	Other	.200	125	25	4	0	1	10	10	33	.259	.256
Night	.207	242	50	4	0	3	10	24	44	.289	.260	March/April	.167	18	3	1	0	1	4	0	7	.211	.389
Grass	.179	151	27	5	0	1	6	10	30	.235	.232	May	.250	36	9	0	0	0	2	4	6	.325	.250
Turf	.244	246	60	10	0	3	20	21	52	.314	.321	June	.254	63	16	2	0	1	5	5	18	.319	.333
Pre-All Star	.237	139	33	4	0	2	12	9	38	.298	.309	July	.218	87	19	1	0	0	4	6	18	.284	.230
Post-All Star	.209	258	54	11	0	2	14	22	44	.277	.275	August	.253	99	25	7	0	0	7	6	16	.295	.323
Scoring Posn	.170	94	16	2	0	1	20	10	21	.257	.223	Sept/Oct	.160	94	15	4	0	2	4	10	17	.248	.266
Close & Late	.234	64	15	2	0	1	4	4	18	.300	.313	vs. AL	.265	49	13	3	0	1	5	2	11	.308	.388
None on/out	.234	111	26	5	0	0	0	9	24	.298	.279	vs. NL	.213	348	74	12	0	3	21	29	71	.281	.273

1997 By Position

Position	Avg	AB	H	2B	3B	HR	RBI	BB	SO	OBP	SLG	G	GS	Innings	PO	A	E	DP	Fld Pct	Rng Fctr	In Zone	Zone Outs	Zone Rtg	MLB Zone
As ss	.218	367	80	14	0	4	24	27	77	.281	.289	110	92	853.1	170	262	15	56	.966	4.56	288	285	.990	.937

Bryan Rekar — Rockies
Age 26 – Pitches Right

	ERA	W	L	Sv	G	GS	IP	BB	SO	Avg	H	2B	3B	HR	RBI	OBP	SLG	CG	ShO	Sup	QS	#P/S	SB	CS	GB	FB	G/F
1997 Season	5.79	1	0	0	2	2	9.1	6	4	.282	11	3	0	3	6	.378	.590	0	0	7.71	0	84	0	0	13	19	0.68
Career (1995-1997)	6.54	7	10	0	31	27	152.2	56	89	.307	193	40	9	25	109	.368	.519	1	0	4.89	10	93	3	4	219	212	1.03

1997 Season

	ERA	W	L	Sv	G	GS	IP	H	HR	BB	SO		Avg	AB	H	2B	3B	HR	RBI	BB	SO	OBP	SLG
Home	6.75	0	0	0	1	1	4.0	6	2	2	1	vs. Left	.333	21	7	2	0	2	3	4	0	.440	.714
Away	5.06	1	0	0	1	1	5.1	5	1	4	3	vs. Right	.222	18	4	1	0	1	3	2	4	.300	.444

Desi Relaford — Phillies
Age 24 – Bats Both

	Avg	G	AB	R	H	2B	3B	HR	RBI	BB	SO	HBP	GDP	SB	CS	OBP	SLG	IBB	SH	SF	#Pit	#P/PA	GB	FB	G/F
1997 Season	.184	15	38	3	7	1	2	0	6	5	6	0	0	3	0	.279	.316	0	1	0	155	3.52	14	12	1.17
Career (1996-1997)	.179	30	78	5	14	3	2	0	7	8	15	0	1	4	0	.256	.269	0	2	0	294	3.34	26	22	1.18

1997 Season

	Avg	AB	H	2B	3B	HR	RBI	BB	SO	OBP	SLG		Avg	AB	H	2B	3B	HR	RBI	BB	SO	OBP	SLG
vs. Left	.267	15	4	0	1	0	3	0	3	.267	.400	Scoring Posn	.250	12	3	1	0	0	6	2	3	.357	.333
vs. Right	.130	23	3	1	1	0	3	5	3	.286	.261	Close & Late	.400	5	2	0	1	0	0	1	1	.500	.800

Mike Remlinger — Reds
Age 32 – Pitches Left

	ERA	W	L	Sv	G	GS	IP	BB	SO	Avg	H	2B	3B	HR	RBI	OBP	SLG	GF	IR	IRS	Hld	SvOp	SB	CS	GB	FB	G/F
1997 Season	4.14	8	8	2	69	12	124.0	60	145	.223	100	31	0	11	50	.322	.366	10	50	8	14	2	11	7	130	104	1.25
Last Five Years	4.53	9	15	2	105	25	212.2	119	204	.239	188	53	0	25	102	.345	.403	16	72	13	16	3	19	10	252	198	1.27

1997 Season

	ERA	W	L	Sv	G	GS	IP	H	HR	BB	SO		Avg	AB	H	2B	3B	HR	RBI	BB	SO	OBP	SLG
Home	3.95	3	3	1	42	6	68.1	54	8	30	83	vs. Left	.241	112	27	4	0	5	16	12	25	.338	.411
Away	4.37	5	5	1	27	6	55.2	46	3	30	62	vs. Right	.217	336	73	27	0	6	34	48	120	.316	.351
Day	5.31	3	6	0	28	6	57.2	47	7	27	65	Inning 1-6	.244	266	65	23	0	7	36	35	86	.337	.410
Night	3.12	5	2	2	41	6	66.1	53	4	33	80	Inning 7+	.192	182	35	8	0	4	14	25	59	.300	.302

1997 Season

	ERA	W	L	Sv	G	GS	IP	H	HR	BB	SO		Avg	AB	H	2B	3B	HR	RBI	BB	SO	OBP	SLG
Grass	5.57	2	3	1	17	4	32.1	32	3	20	36	None on	.214	257	55	16	0	7	7	35	84	.318	.358
Turf	3.63	6	5	1	52	8	91.2	68	8	40	109	Runners on	.236	191	45	15	0	4	43	25	61	.327	.377
March/April	1.80	0	1	0	11	0	10.0	5	0	7	14	Scoring Posn	.241	112	27	10	0	2	36	20	36	.355	.384
May	3.86	0	2	2	16	0	14.0	9	2	7	15	Close & Late	.154	91	14	4	0	2	4	15	35	.291	.264
June	2.55	3	0	0	16	1	17.2	9	1	11	23	None on/out	.204	113	23	9	0	3	3	16	36	.313	.363
July	3.75	0	1	0	11	0	12.0	11	1	5	16	vs. 1st Batr (relief)	.160	50	8	3	0	0	6	5	19	.263	.220
August	5.85	3	2	0	8	5	32.1	33	4	18	37	1st Inning Pitched	.213	183	39	15	0	4	23	29	64	.335	.361
Sept/Oct	4.26	2	2	0	7	6	38.0	33	3	12	40	First 15 Pitches	.201	149	30	8	0	4	16	20	49	.316	.336
Starter	4.30	6	4	0	12	12	73.1	65	7	30	81	Pitch 16-30	.216	88	19	8	0	2	9	15	30	.327	.375
Reliever	3.91	2	4	2	57	0	50.2	35	4	30	64	Pitch 31-45	.154	52	8	1	0	1	3	8	23	.279	.231
0 Days rest (Relief)	2.70	2	3	1	21	0	20.0	8	2	10	27	Pitch 46+	.270	159	43	14	0	4	22	17	43	.339	.434
1 or 2 Days rest	4.56	0	0	1	27	0	23.2	20	2	13	30	First Pitch	.286	42	12	3	0	1	5	6	0	.373	.429
3+ Days rest	5.14	0	1	0	9	0	7.0	7	0	7	7	Ahead in Count	.200	245	49	15	0	4	21	0	120	.205	.310
vs. AL	3.00	1	1	0	4	2	12.0	6	1	6	16	Behind in Count	.257	70	18	5	0	4	14	27	0	.469	.500
vs. NL	4.26	7	7	2	65	10	112.0	94	10	54	129	Two Strikes	.180	266	48	18	0	4	23	37	145	.257	.293
Pre-All Star	3.00	3	4	2	44	1	42.0	25	3	25	52	Pre-All Star	.174	144	25	10	0	3	12	25	52	.308	.306
Post-All Star	4.72	5	4	0	25	11	82.0	75	8	35	93	Post-All Star	.247	304	75	21	0	8	38	35	93	.329	.395

Edgar Renteria — Marlins   Age 22 – Bats Right

	Avg	G	AB	R	H	2B	3B	HR	RBI	BB	SO	HBP	GDP	SB	CS	OBP	SLG	IBB	SH	SF	#Pit	#P/PA	GB	FB	G/F
1997 Season	.277	154	617	90	171	21	3	4	52	45	108	4	17	32	15	.327	.340	1	19	6	2485	3.60	267	129	2.07
Career (1996-1997)	.290	260	1048	158	304	39	6	9	83	78	176	6	29	48	17	.340	.365	1	21	9	4115	3.54	448	231	1.94

1997 Season

	Avg	AB	H	2B	3B	HR	RBI	BB	SO	OBP	SLG		Avg	AB	H	2B	3B	HR	RBI	BB	SO	OBP	SLG
vs. Left	.259	108	28	4	0	0	3	13	18	.336	.296	First Pitch	.337	95	32	7	1	1	8	1	0	.347	.463
vs. Right	.281	509	143	17	3	4	49	32	90	.325	.350	Ahead in Count	.320	122	39	2	0	2	10	22	0	.429	.385
Groundball	.311	103	32	5	0	0	5	4	15	.333	.359	Behind in Count	.206	282	58	8	1	0	23	0	90	.206	.241
Flyball	.222	81	18	3	1	0	5	2	20	.241	.284	Two Strikes	.208	284	59	6	1	1	23	22	108	.265	.246
Home	.265	306	81	10	1	3	29	26	45	.324	.333	Batting #2	.281	595	167	20	3	4	51	45	101	.332	.345
Away	.289	311	90	11	2	1	23	19	63	.330	.347	Batting #3	.059	17	1	0	0	0	0	0	5	.059	.059
Day	.270	189	51	6	0	0	12	13	37	.319	.302	Other	.600	5	3	1	0	0	1	0	2	.600	.800
Night	.280	428	120	15	3	4	40	32	71	.331	.357	March/April	.214	98	21	3	0	1	8	8	18	.271	.276
Grass	.276	507	140	14	3	4	44	40	78	.331	.339	May	.293	116	34	6	1	0	13	7	17	.331	.362
Turf	.282	110	31	7	0	0	8	5	30	.310	.345	June	.255	94	24	3	1	0	4	10	19	.327	.309
Pre-All Star	.264	333	88	12	2	1	27	26	56	.316	.321	July	.320	103	33	5	1	2	10	4	22	.360	.447
Post-All Star	.292	284	83	9	1	3	25	19	52	.341	.363	August	.306	108	33	3	0	0	12	13	19	.371	.333
Scoring Posn	.294	136	40	6	1	0	46	11	23	.333	.353	Sept/Oct	.265	98	26	1	0	1	5	3	13	.294	.306
Close & Late	.247	93	23	3	0	1	12	12	15	.333	.312	vs. AL	.367	60	22	3	1	0	7	5	6	.415	.450
None on/out	.289	121	35	8	1	4	4	11	15	.353	.471	vs. NL	.268	557	149	18	2	4	45	40	102	.318	.329

1997 By Position

Position	Avg	AB	H	2B	3B	HR	RBI	BB	SO	OBP	SLG	G	GS	Innings	PO	A	E	DP	Fld Pct	Rng Fctr	In Zone	Zone Outs	Zone Rtg	MLB Zone
As ss	.278	616	171	21	3	4	52	45	107	.328	.341	153	149	1328.2	243	415	17	95	.975	4.46	450	437	.971	.937

Career (1996-1997)

	Avg	AB	H	2B	3B	HR	RBI	BB	SO	OBP	SLG		Avg	AB	H	2B	3B	HR	RBI	BB	SO	OBP	SLG
vs. Left	.253	198	50	10	1	2	12	21	38	.320	.343	First Pitch	.327	171	56	10	3	3	21	1	0	.339	.474
vs. Right	.299	850	254	29	5	7	71	57	138	.345	.369	Ahead in Count	.357	213	76	10	1	4	19	40	0	.459	.469
Groundball	.328	186	61	9	1	0	9	11	24	.364	.387	Behind in Count	.221	484	107	13	1	1	30	0	149	.220	.258
Flyball	.276	181	50	9	1	0	11	7	36	.302	.302	Two Strikes	.204	461	94	9	1	2	29	37	176	.262	.241
Home	.281	494	139	18	4	5	46	48	69	.348	.364	Batting #2	.294	1016	299	38	6	9	82	78	168	.345	.370
Away	.298	554	165	21	2	4	37	30	107	.333	.365	Batting #3	.059	17	1	0	0	0	0	0	5	.059	.059
Day	.283	311	88	13	1	1	20	21	62	.331	.341	Other	.267	15	4	1	0	0	1	0	3	.267	.333
Night	.293	737	216	26	5	8	63	57	114	.344	.374	March/April	.214	98	21	3	0	1	8	8	18	.271	.276
Grass	.286	842	241	27	6	7	68	70	132	.343	.357	May	.289	159	46	10	2	0	13	12	24	.337	.377
Turf	.306	206	63	12	0	2	15	8	44	.329	.393	June	.244	180	44	7	1	1	11	14	30	.296	.311
Pre-All Star	.260	462	120	20	3	2	34	35	74	.309	.329	July	.330	182	60	10	3	3	19	10	36	.376	.467
Post-All Star	.314	586	184	19	3	7	49	43	102	.364	.392	August	.323	223	72	4	0	1	20	26	39	.389	.354
Scoring Posn	.294	221	65	12	1	0	69	22	34	.345	.357	Sept/Oct	.296	206	61	5	0	3	12	8	29	.327	.364
Close & Late	.282	156	44	5	1	2	19	21	29	.365	.365	vs. AL	.367	60	22	3	1	0	7	5	6	.415	.450
None on/out	.298	205	61	11	2	7	7	18	24	.357	.473	vs. NL	.285	988	282	36	5	9	76	73	170	.336	.359

Batter vs. Pitcher (career)

Hits Best Against	Avg	AB	H	2B	3B	HR	RBI	BB	SO	OBP	SLG	Hits Worst Against	Avg	AB	H	2B	3B	HR	RBI	BB	SO	OBP	SLG
Kevin Ritz	.636	11	7	0	0	0	1	0	1	.636	.636	Andy Benes	.071	14	1	0	0	0	0	0	7	.071	.071
Pedro Astacio	.455	11	5	1	0	0	2	0	1	.455	.545	Mike Morgan	.091	11	1	0	0	0	1	2	4	.214	.091
Hideo Nomo	.368	19	7	0	1	0	2	0	5	.368	.474	Danny Darwin	.167	12	2	0	0	0	1	0	1	.167	.250
Donovan Osborne	.364	11	4	1	1	0	0	1	3	.417	.636	Todd Stottlemyre	.167	12	2	0	0	0	1	0	2	.167	.167
Mark Leiter	.357	14	5	2	0	0	2	0	1	.357	.500	Jeff Juden	.214	14	3	0	0	0	0	0	2	.214	.214

Al Reyes — Brewers
Age 27 – Pitches Right (flyball pitcher)

	ERA	W	L	Sv	G	GS	IP	BB	SO	Avg	H	2B	3B	HR	RBI	OBP	SLG	GF	IR	IRS	Hld	SvOp	SB	CS	GB	FB	G/F
1997 Season	5.46	1	2	1	19	0	29.2	9	28	.274	32	6	1	4	20	.341	.444	7	12	2	1	1	1	0	36	39	0.92
Career (1995-1997)	4.19	3	3	2	51	0	68.2	29	59	.230	59	9	3	8	39	.321	.383	22	33	11	5	2	5	0	73	85	0.86

1997 Season

	ERA	W	L	Sv	G	GS	IP	H	HR	BB	SO		Avg	AB	H	2B	3B	HR	RBI	BB	SO	OBP	SLG
Home	6.27	1	2	0	10	0	18.2	25	2	6	16	vs. Left	.333	45	15	1	1	3	11	3	10	.388	.600
Away	4.09	0	0	1	9	0	11.0	7	2	3	12	vs. Right	.236	72	17	5	0	1	9	6	18	.313	.347

Carlos Reyes — Athletics
Age 29 – Pitches Right

	ERA	W	L	Sv	G	GS	IP	BB	SO	Avg	H	2B	3B	HR	RBI	OBP	SLG	GF	IR	IRS	Hld	SvOp	SB	CS	GB	FB	G/F
1997 Season	5.82	3	4	0	37	6	77.1	25	43	.316	101	16	1	13	46	.367	.494	9	21	4	1	1	6	0	118	103	1.15
Career (1994-1997)	4.93	14	23	1	150	26	346.2	158	226	.278	377	69	6	52	203	.355	.452	50	100	39	6	3	29	14	494	389	1.27

1997 Season

	ERA	W	L	Sv	G	GS	IP	H	HR	BB	SO		Avg	AB	H	2B	3B	HR	RBI	BB	SO	OBP	SLG
Home	5.17	1	2	0	20	3	47.0	57	9	16	20	vs. Left	.327	153	50	7	0	6	20	9	16	.370	.490
Away	6.82	2	2	0	17	3	30.1	44	4	9	23	vs. Right	.305	167	51	9	1	7	26	16	27	.364	.497
Starter	8.34	0	4	0	6	6	22.2	34	3	13	9	Scoring Posn	.239	88	21	5	0	5	34	11	12	.324	.466
Reliever	4.77	3	0	0	31	0	54.2	67	10	12	34	Close & Late	.200	25	5	1	0	0	1	0	4	.231	.240
0 Days rest (Relief)	7.04	0	0	0	5	0	7.2	11	3	2	5	None on/out	.430	79	34	3	0	4		4	9	.464	.620
1 or 2 Days rest	4.68	1	0	0	14	0	25.0	37	4	5	9	First Pitch	.404	57	23	1	0	3	12	1	0	.414	.579
3+ Days rest	4.09	2	0	0	12	0	22.0	19	3	5	8	Ahead in Count	.273	121	33	4	1	3	7	0	35	.285	.397
Pre-All Star	3.66	3	0	0	21	0	39.1	40	7	9	26	Behind in Count	.319	69	22	4	0	3	11	15	0	.435	.507
Post-All Star	8.05	0	4	0	16	6	38.0	61	6	16	17	Two Strikes	.281	135	38	7	1	5	13	9	43	.331	.459

Career (1994-1997)

	ERA	W	L	Sv	G	GS	IP	H	HR	BB	SO		Avg	AB	H	2B	3B	HR	RBI	BB	SO	OBP	SLG
Home	4.38	4	7	0	74	13	183.0	174	27	79	120	vs. Left	.286	695	199	38	4	19	87	80	104	.362	.435
Away	5.55	10	16	1	76	13	163.2	203	25	79	106	vs. Right	.268	663	178	31	2	33	116	78	122	.347	.471
Day	3.76	3	7	0	62	10	148.1	141	21	59	100	Inning 1-6	.286	853	244	44	5	35	148	115	135	.372	.472
Night	5.81	11	16	1	88	16	198.1	236	31	99	126	Inning 7+	.263	505	133	25	1	17	55	43	91	.324	.418
Grass	5.21	12	20	1	131	24	304.0	342	50	138	196	None on	.285	729	208	39	2	26	26	71	115	.354	.451
Turf	2.95	2	3	0	19	2	42.2	35	2	20	30	Runners on	.269	629	169	30	4	26	177	87	111	.355	.453
March/April	5.20	3	4	0	16	6	55.1	58	14	21	38	Scoring Posn	.267	359	96	18	2	19	158	63	58	.370	.487
May	5.92	0	7	0	25	5	76.0	84	12	38	43	Close & Late	.269	182	49	9	1	4	17	21	32	.350	.396
June	2.08	4	1	1	36	4	69.1	58	7	36	54	None on	.294	327	96	16	0	11	11	27	44	.355	.443
July	6.55	2	4	0	29	7	56.1	73	8	20	42	vs. 1st Batr (relief)	.297	111	33	6	2	8	29	9	18	.347	.604
August	5.56	3	5	0	24	4	55.0	62	7	25	33	1st Inning Pitched	.254	515	131	28	3	22	91	54	87	.327	.449
Sept/Oct	4.41	2	2	0	20	0	34.2	42	4	18	16	First 15 Pitches	.277	437	121	21	4	19	69	41	65	.341	.474
Starter	5.74	3	14	0	26	26	122.1	138	16	63	73	Pitch 16-30	.284	359	102	21	2	14	55	42	59	.363	.471
Reliever	4.49	11	9	1	124	0	224.1	239	36	95	153	Pitch 31-45	.264	231	61	7	0	4	28	30	47	.348	.346
0 Days rest (Relief)	4.94	2	2	0	16	0	23.2	22	6	9	18	Pitch 46+	.281	331	93	20	0	15	51	45	55	.367	.477
1 or 2 Days rest	4.95	4	4	1	54	0	91.0	109	16	35	70	First Pitch	.309	191	59	9	1	8	32	8	0	.335	.492
3+ Days rest	4.02	5	3	0	54	0	109.2	108	14	51	65	Ahead in Count	.211	536	113	18	3	13	51	0	170	.219	.328
vs. AL	4.93	13	23	1	146	26	337.2	368	49	156	222	Behind in Count	.366	333	122	24	2	21	77	89	0	.499	.640
vs. NL	5.00	1	0	0	4	0	9.0	9	3	2	4	Two Strikes	.193	579	112	26	2	16	59	61	226	.275	.328
Pre-All Star	4.62	7	13	1	89	16	220.1	227	36	100	154	Pre-All Star	.267	849	227	50	4	36	123	100	154	.345	.458
Post-All Star	5.49	7	10	0	61	10	126.1	150	16	58	72	Post-All Star	.295	509	150	19	4	16	80	58	72	.370	.442

Pitcher vs. Batter (career)

Pitches Best Vs.	Avg	AB	H	2B	3B	HR	RBI	BB	SO	OBP	SLG	Pitches Worst Vs.	Avg	AB	H	2B	3B	HR	RBI	BB	SO	OBP	SLG
Sandy Alomar Jr	.000	10	0	0	0	0	0	1	3	.091	.000	Rusty Greer	.643	14	9	3	0	1	5	0	0	.643	1.071
Paul Sorrento	.083	12	1	0	0	0	0	1	4	.154	.083	Paul O'Neill	.600	10	6	0	0	1	5	3	1	.692	.900
Dave Hollins	.100	10	1	0	0	0	0	1	3	.250	.100	Tim Raines	.462	13	6	1	0	2	3	2	0	.533	1.000
Pat Meares	.111	9	1	0	0	0	1	0	0	.273	.111	Roberto Alomar	.375	8	3	3	0	0	1	4	0	.583	.750
Will Clark	.200	10	2	0	0	0	2	1	1	.250	.200	Juan Gonzalez	.333	12	4	0	0	2	6	1	2	.357	.833

Dennis Reyes — Dodgers
Age 21 – Pitches Left

	ERA	W	L	Sv	G	GS	IP	BB	SO	Avg	H	2B	3B	HR	RBI	OBP	SLG	GF	IR	IRS	Hld	SvOp	SB	CS	GB	FB	G/F
1997 Season	3.83	2	3	0	14	5	47.0	18	36	.280	51	8	1	4	19	.347	.401	0	2	0	0	0	7	0	63	47	1.34

1997 Season

	ERA	W	L	Sv	G	GS	IP	H	HR	BB	SO		Avg	AB	H	2B	3B	HR	RBI	BB	SO	OBP	SLG
Home	2.84	1	1	0	7	2	19.0	18	1	8	16	vs. Left	.302	43	13	2	0	2	6	8	12	.423	.488
Away	4.50	1	2	0	7	3	28.0	33	3	10	20	vs. Right	.273	139	38	6	1	2	13	10	24	.320	.374

Shane Reynolds — Astros
Age 30 – Pitches Right (groundball pitcher)

	ERA	W	L	Sv	G	GS	IP	BB	SO	Avg	H	2B	3B	HR	RBI	OBP	SLG	CG	ShO	Sup	QS	#P/S	SB	CS	GB	FB	G/F
1997 Season	4.23	9	10	0	30	30	181.0	47	152	.267	189	39	3	19	83	.313	.410	2	0	4.62	15	93	5	6	288	155	1.86
Last Five Years	3.60	43	36	0	133	110	744.1	155	651	.260	751	131	20	64	288	.300	.385	10	4	4.76	64	95	38	24	1216	587	2.07

1997 Season

	ERA	W	L	Sv	G	GS	IP	H	HR	BB	SO		Avg	AB	H	2B	3B	HR	RBI	BB	SO	OBP	SLG
Home	3.40	6	3	0	15	15	98.0	93	9	13	95	vs. Left	.262	370	97	13	2	8	48	35	78	.326	.373
Away	5.20	3	7	0	15	15	83.0	96	10	34	57	vs. Right	.271	339	92	26	1	11	35	12	74	.297	.451
Day	4.10	0	3	0	7	7	41.2	45	4	15	27	Inning 1-6	.261	618	161	33	3	14	68	42	132	.308	.392

1997 Season

	ERA	W	L	Sv	G	GS	IP	H	HR	BB	SO		Avg	AB	H	2B	3B	HR	RBI	BB	SO	OBP	SLG
Night	4.26	9	7	0	23	23	139.1	144	15	32	125	Inning 7+	.308	91	28	6	0	5	15	5	20	.347	.538
Grass	5.33	1	5	0	10	10	52.1	64	6	23	36	None on	.258	419	108	19	2	12	12	23	94	.300	.399
Turf	3.78	8	5	0	20	20	128.2	125	13	24	116	Runners on	.279	290	81	20	1	7	71	24	58	.331	.428
March/April	2.91	3	2	0	6	6	46.1	35	7	9	39	Scoring Posn	.285	151	43	11	0	1	55	16	33	.343	.377
May	4.95	1	3	0	7	7	40.0	49	3	15	32	Close & Late	.340	53	18	3	0	2	8	1	8	.357	.509
June	4.50	0	1	0	2	2	8.0	9	1	3	3	None on/out	.247	182	45	11	0	4	4	10	42	.286	.374
July	5.32	2	0	0	4	4	22.0	19	0	5	19	vs. 1st Batr (relief)	.000	0	0	0	0	0	0	0	0	.000	.000
August	5.68	0	3	0	6	6	31.2	42	3	10	27	1st Inning Pitched	.239	117	28	5	0	4	15	9	24	.291	.385
Sept/Oct	3.00	3	1	0	5	5	33.0	35	5	5	32	First 75 Pitches	.268	533	143	32	3	14	56	33	113	.311	.418
Starter	4.23	9	10	0	30	30	181.0	189	19	47	152	Pitch 76-90	.293	92	27	4	0	0	11	8	20	.353	.337
Reliever	0.00	0	0	0	0	0	0.0	0	0	0	0	Pitch 91-105	.236	55	13	3	0	4	13	4	10	.295	.509
0-3 Days Rest (Start)	1.29	0	0	0	1	1	7.0	7	1	1	6	Pitch 106+	.207	29	6	0	0	1	3	2	9	.250	.310
4 Days Rest	4.28	6	9	0	23	23	136.2	143	13	37	111	First Pitch	.436	110	48	9	0	5	22	0	0	.430	.655
5+ Days Rest	4.58	3	1	0	6	6	37.1	39	5	9	35	Ahead in Count	.181	331	60	11	1	5	28	0	135	.184	.266
vs. AL	4.26	0	1	0	1	1	6.1	9	0	2	3	Behind in Count	.357	129	46	12	1	6	22	26	0	.465	.605
vs. NL	4.23	9	9	0	29	29	174.2	180	19	45	149	Two Strikes	.178	338	60	10	1	5	26	21	152	.228	.257
Pre-All Star	3.91	4	6	0	15	15	94.1	93	11	27	74	Pre-All Star	.255	364	93	18	0	11	40	27	74	.309	.396
Post-All Star	4.57	5	4	0	15	15	86.2	96	8	20	78	Post-All Star	.278	345	96	21	3	8	43	20	78	.317	.426

Last Five Years

	ERA	W	L	Sv	G	GS	IP	H	HR	BB	SO		Avg	AB	H	2B	3B	HR	RBI	BB	SO	OBP	SLG
Home	3.14	23	13	0	60	53	369.2	343	26	59	357	vs. Left	.254	1395	354	56	7	25	130	89	327	.301	.358
Away	4.06	20	23	0	73	57	374.2	408	38	96	294	vs. Right	.265	1499	397	75	13	39	158	66	324	.300	.410
Day	3.96	5	10	0	33	25	170.2	180	17	46	145	Inning 1-6	.255	2440	622	103	17	52	234	136	552	.297	.375
Night	3.50	38	26	0	100	85	573.2	571	47	109	506	Inning 7+	.284	454	129	28	3	12	54	19	99	.318	.438
Grass	4.50	10	18	0	44	37	230.0	253	30	57	186	None on	.262	1700	445	71	11	43	43	81	365	.298	.392
Turf	3.20	33	18	0	89	73	514.1	498	34	98	465	Runners on	.256	1194	306	60	9	21	245	74	286	.303	.374
March/April	3.72	8	4	0	21	13	104.0	99	10	25	88	Scoring Posn	.250	660	165	36	6	8	207	52	164	.305	.359
May	3.79	7	9	0	26	23	142.2	149	10	32	142	Close & Late	.274	237	65	10	2	3	22	8	49	.303	.371
June	3.37	7	6	0	19	19	117.2	128	10	28	93	None on/out	.287	756	217	42	4	20	20	34	142	.319	.433
July	2.94	10	3	0	26	17	134.2	117	8	22	115	vs. 1st Batr (relief)	.217	23	5	0	1	0	1	0	3	.217	.304
August	3.48	7	8	0	21	20	134.1	134	11	20	108	1st Inning Pitched	.249	502	125	23	3	8	50	26	105	.290	.355
Sept/Oct	4.46	4	6	0	20	18	111.0	124	15	28	105	First 75 Pitches	.254	2211	562	99	18	48	204	116	498	.294	.380
Starter	3.61	40	35	0	110	110	701.0	708	62	145	611	Pitch 76-90	.305	367	112	18	2	7	40	20	88	.342	.422
Reliever	3.53	3	1	0	23	0	43.1	43	2	10	40	Pitch 91-105	.246	224	55	8	0	8	34	14	43	.303	.388
0-3 Days Rest (Start)	2.92	1	3	0	8	8	49.1	45	3	11	55	Pitch 106+	.239	92	22	6	0	1	10	5	22	.276	.337
4 Days Rest	4.12	23	22	0	67	67	417.2	446	41	99	355	First Pitch	.363	457	166	27	4	18	64	11	0	.378	.558
5+ Days Rest	2.85	16	10	0	35	35	234.0	217	18	35	201	Ahead in Count	.199	1468	292	56	6	19	109	0	587	.206	.284
vs. AL	4.26	0	1	0	1	1	6.1	9	0	2	3	Behind in Count	.331	516	171	27	5	17	65	74	0	.415	.502
vs. NL	3.60	43	35	0	132	109	738.0	742	64	153	648	Two Strikes	.177	1424	252	39	7	17	98	70	651	.220	.250
Pre-All Star	3.48	25	19	0	74	58	395.1	403	31	89	350	Pre-All Star	.262	1537	403	67	10	31	147	89	350	.306	.379
Post-All Star	3.74	18	17	0	59	52	349.0	348	33	66	301	Post-All Star	.256	1357	348	64	10	33	141	66	301	.294	.391

Pitcher vs. Batter (career)

Pitches Best Vs.	Avg	AB	H	2B	3B	HR	RBI	BB	SO	OBP	SLG	Pitches Worst Vs.	Avg	AB	H	2B	3B	HR	RBI	BB	SO	OBP	SLG
Don Slaught	.091	11	1	0	0	0	0	0	1	.091	.091	Bip Roberts	.571	14	8	2	1	0	4	2	2	.647	.857
Dave Clark	.091	11	1	0	0	0	0	0	5	.091	.091	Ellis Burks	.538	13	7	1	0	1	2	1	1	.571	.846
Deion Sanders	.091	11	1	0	0	0	0	0	2	.091	.091	T. Hollandsworth	.500	12	6	2	0	2	5	1	3	.538	1.167
Delino DeShields	.125	24	3	0	0	0	0	0	6	.125	.125	Greg Gagne	.444	9	4	1	0	1	1	3	2	.583	.889
Rey Sanchez	.133	15	2	0	0	0	2	0	5	.133	.133	Glenallen Hill	.400	15	6	0	2	2	4	0	5	.375	1.067

Armando Reynoso — Mets
Age 32 – Pitches Right

	ERA	W	L	Sv	G	GS	IP	BB	SO	Avg	H	2B	3B	HR	RBI	OBP	SLG	CG	ShO	Sup	QS	#P/S	SB	CS	GB	FB	G/F
1997 Season	4.53	6	3	0	16	16	91.1	29	47	.275	95	20	6	7	42	.338	.429	1	1	5.32	9	85	2	2	134	93	1.44
Last Five Years	4.63	36	34	0	105	103	594.1	199	317	.287	666	129	27	73	309	.350	.460	6	1	5.41	46	92	32	16	854	727	1.17

1997 Season

	ERA	W	L	Sv	G	GS	IP	H	HR	BB	SO		Avg	AB	H	2B	3B	HR	RBI	BB	SO	OBP	SLG
Home	4.75	3	2	0	9	9	53.0	52	4	21	27	vs. Left	.267	150	40	6	4	2	13	18	22	.347	.400
Away	4.23	3	1	0	7	7	38.1	43	3	8	20	vs. Right	.282	195	55	14	2	5	29	11	25	.330	.451
Starter	4.53	6	3	0	16	16	91.1	95	7	29	47	Scoring Posn	.244	78	19	8	0	1	31	12	11	.360	.385
Reliever	0.00	0	0	0	0	0	0.0	0	0	0	0	Close & Late	.190	21	4	2	1	1	3	2	5	.308	.524
0-3 Days Rest (Start)	0.00	0	0	0	0	0	0.0	0	0	0	0	None on/out	.261	88	23	4	3	0	6	6	13	.309	.375
4 Days Rest	4.75	3	2	0	6	6	36.0	36	2	12	18	First Pitch	.295	44	13	2	1	1	5	2	0	.354	.455
5+ Days Rest	4.39	3	1	0	10	10	55.1	59	5	17	29	Ahead in Count	.188	133	25	4	1	2	11	0	43	.191	.278
Pre-All Star	3.84	6	2	0	14	14	82.0	81	7	23	42	Behind in Count	.344	93	32	7	2	3	12	19	0	.460	.559
Post-All Star	10.61	0	1	0	2	2	9.1	14	0	6	5	Two Strikes	.206	136	28	6	2	1	10	8	47	.253	.301

Last Five Years

	ERA	W	L	Sv	G	GS	IP	H	HR	BB	SO		Avg	AB	H	2B	3B	HR	RBI	BB	SO	OBP	SLG
Home	4.78	20	13	0	52	50	297.2	345	42	100	148	vs. Left	.289	1074	310	65	15	30	144	96	140	.354	.461
Away	4.49	16	21	0	53	53	296.2	321	31	99	169	vs. Right	.286	1246	356	64	12	43	165	103	177	.346	.460
Day	4.71	14	7	0	37	36	204.1	229	16	74	107	Inning 1-6	.288	2118	610	119	24	67	289	182	291	.350	.462
Night	4.59	22	27	0	68	67	390.0	437	57	125	210	Inning 7+	.277	202	56	10	3	6	20	17	26	.347	.446
Grass	4.93	28	25	0	81	79	451.1	521	60	151	236	None on	.281	1353	380	71	18	47	47	94	188	.334	.464
Turf	3.71	8	9	0	24	24	143.0	145	13	48	81	Runners on	.296	967	286	58	9	26	262	105	129	.370	.455
March/April	4.52	4	4	0	14	14	81.2	89	6	21	29	Scoring Posn	.264	576	152	36	6	11	216	83	82	.359	.405
May	3.58	9	6	0	22	22	145.2	142	18	46	93	Close & Late	.217	92	20	6	1	3	12	9	14	.305	.402

Last Five Years

	ERA	W	L	Sv	G	GS	IP	H	HR	BB	SO		Avg	AB	H	2B	3B	HR	RBI	BB	SO	OBP	SLG
June	3.56	6	4	0	17	16	98.2	93	11	32	57	None on/out	.287	596	171	36	12	21	21	35	87	.332	.493
July	6.16	5	10	0	20	20	103.2	127	18	38	50	vs. L (relief)	.500	2	1	0	0	0	0	0	0	.500	.500
August	5.04	7	7	0	16	16	89.1	117	13	35	48	1st Inning Pitched	.322	426	137	29	3	16	67	28	45	.374	.516
Sept/Oct	5.62	5	3	0	16	15	75.1	98	7	27	40	First 75 Pitches	.286	1830	523	101	19	58	231	141	244	.344	.457
Starter	4.62	36	34	0	103	103	592.1	662	73	199	317	Pitch 76-90	.296	247	73	16	4	6	37	32	36	.376	.466
Reliever	9.00	0	0	0	2	0	2.0	4	0	0	0	Pitch 91-105	.291	165	48	7	3	7	33	19	20	.364	.497
0-3 Days Rest (Start)	3.60	1	0	0	1	1	5.0	5	0	1	1	Pitch 106+	.282	78	22	5	1	2	8	7	17	.364	.449
4 Days Rest	4.50	21	20	0	56	56	336.0	375	40	105	168	First Pitch	.369	347	128	17	7	12	62	6	0	.383	.562
5+ Days Rest	4.80	14	14	0	46	46	251.1	282	33	93	148	Ahead in Count	.222	907	201	32	6	19	88	0	263	.239	.333
vs. AL	21.60	0	1	0	1	1	1.2	5	0	2	2	Behind in Count	.325	594	193	52	10	24	88	112	0	.431	.567
vs. NL	4.59	36	33	0	104	102	592.1	661	73	197	315	Two Strikes	.208	945	197	31	7	23	96	81	317	.282	.329
Pre-All Star	4.02	22	16	0	60	59	360.1	369	42	109	193	Pre-All Star	.268	1378	369	72	16	42	160	109	193	.329	.435
Post-All Star	5.58	14	18	0	45	44	234.0	297	31	90	124	Post-All Star	.315	942	297	57	11	31	149	90	124	.380	.498

Pitcher vs. Batter (career)

Pitches Best Vs.	Avg	AB	H	2B	3B	HR	RBI	BB	SO	OBP	SLG	Pitches Worst Vs.	Avg	AB	H	2B	3B	HR	RBI	BB	SO	OBP	SLG
Rico Brogna	.000	13	0	0	0	0	0	0	1	.000	.000	Barry Bonds	.667	15	10	3	1	2	9	8	1	.783	1.400
Kevin Stocker	.000	11	0	0	0	0	0	1	3	.214	.000	Chipper Jones	.545	11	6	1	1	2	4	2	0	.615	1.364
Mark Grudzielanek	.000	10	0	0	0	0	0	0	1	.167	.000	Mickey Morandini	.545	11	6	2	2	0	0	1	2	.583	1.091
Ryne Sandberg	.000	9	0	0	0	0	2	1	2	.083	.000	Mariano Duncan	.538	13	7	0	1	2	5	1	0	.571	1.154
Mike Benjamin	.091	11	1	0	0	0	0	0	1	.091	.091	Reggie Sanders	.500	16	8	0	1	4	7	1	1	.529	1.375

Arthur Rhodes — Orioles

Age 28 – Pitches Left (flyball pitcher)

	ERA	W	L	Sv	G	GS	IP	BB	SO	Avg	H	2B	3B	HR	RBI	OBP	SLG	GF	IR	IRS	Hld	SvOp	SB	CS	GB	FB	G/F
1997 Season	3.02	10	3	1	53	0	95.1	26	102	.218	75	16	1	9	33	.278	.349	6	38	11	9	2	14	4	101	101	1.00
Last Five Years	5.07	29	20	2	127	38	362.0	176	337	.245	333	64	10	52	192	.332	.421	14	75	23	11	4	34	15	392	433	0.91

1997 Season

	ERA	W	L	Sv	G	GS	IP	H	HR	BB	SO		Avg	AB	H	2B	3B	HR	RBI	BB	SO	OBP	SLG
Home	3.81	6	1	0	28	0	49.2	44	7	13	47	vs. Left	.220	118	26	4	0	3	13	6	34	.275	.331
Away	2.17	4	2	1	25	0	45.2	31	2	13	55	vs. Right	.217	226	49	12	1	6	20	20	68	.279	.358
Day	4.44	4	2	0	17	0	24.1	24	4	5	25	Inning 1-6	.209	134	28	8	1	5	18	11	35	.268	.396
Night	2.54	6	1	1	36	0	71.0	51	5	21	77	Inning 7+	.224	210	47	8	0	4	15	15	67	.284	.319
Grass	2.97	10	3	1	48	0	91.0	70	9	22	96	None on	.235	204	48	11	0	6	6	16	63	.300	.377
Turf	4.15	0	0	0	5	0	4.1	5	0	4	6	Runners on	.193	140	27	5	1	3	27	10	39	.245	.307
March/April	3.07	2	1	0	8	0	14.2	12	1	5	17	Scoring Posn	.203	79	16	3	1	1	23	9	25	.272	.304
May	5.91	0	1	0	6	0	10.2	13	5	1	8	Close & Late	.220	118	26	6	0	0	6	7	42	.276	.271
June	0.00	2	0	1	9	0	19.0	6	0	2	26	None on/out	.211	90	19	4	0	4	4	5	29	.260	.389
July	3.48	3	0	0	10	0	20.2	21	2	7	22	vs. 1st Batr (relief)	.184	49	9	4	0	1	7	2	18	.212	.327
August	3.57	3	1	0	11	0	17.2	11	1	6	16	1st Inning Pitched	.187	166	31	10	1	1	19	15	50	.249	.277
Sept/Oct	3.55	0	0	0	9	0	12.2	12	0	5	13	First 15 Pitches	.177	141	25	8	1	4	14	14	40	.226	.255
Starter	0.00	0	0	0	0	0	0.0	0	0	0	0	Pitch 16-30	.292	120	35	7	1	6	12	14	37	.384	.517
Reliever	3.02	10	3	1	53	0	95.1	75	9	26	102	Pitch 31-45	.157	70	11	0	0	2	5	1	24	.169	.243
0 Days rest (Relief)	3.86	0	0	0	2	0	2.1	1	0	1	1	Pitch 46+	.308	13	4	1	0	0	2	1	1	.357	.385
1 or 2 Days rest	4.11	7	2	1	32	0	57.0	46	6	17	58	First Pitch	.222	45	10	3	0	0	5	3	0	.280	.289
3+ Days rest	1.25	3	1	0	19	0	36.0	28	3	8	43	Ahead in Count	.186	188	35	8	0	5	8	0	90	.190	.309
vs. AL	3.16	7	3	1	48	0	85.1	72	8	24	89	Behind in Count	.261	46	12	4	1	1	7	11	0	.417	.457
vs. NL	1.80	3	0	0	5	0	10.0	3	1	2	13	Two Strikes	.158	203	32	6	0	6	16	12	102	.206	.276
Pre-All Star	2.45	6	2	1	26	0	51.1	36	7	11	57	Pre-All Star	.198	182	36	6	1	7	18	11	57	.245	.357
Post-All Star	3.68	4	1	0	27	0	44.0	39	2	15	45	Post-All Star	.241	162	39	10	0	2	15	15	45	.313	.340

Last Five Years

	ERA	W	L	Sv	G	GS	IP	H	HR	BB	SO		Avg	AB	H	2B	3B	HR	RBI	BB	SO	OBP	SLG
Home	5.78	14	11	1	64	17	176.0	169	31	85	168	vs. Left	.225	316	71	11	1	13	44	31	70	.298	.389
Away	4.40	15	9	1	63	21	186.0	164	21	91	169	vs. Right	.251	1044	262	53	9	39	148	145	267	.342	.431
Day	5.97	11	9	0	46	17	126.2	124	21	68	139	Inning 1-6	.267	944	252	53	8	39	157	135	220	.358	.464
Night	4.59	18	11	2	81	21	235.1	209	31	108	198	Inning 7+	.195	416	81	11	2	13	35	41	117	.271	.325
Grass	4.97	26	17	2	111	30	313.1	281	46	151	292	None on	.237	771	183	36	6	26	26	100	183	.327	.401
Turf	5.73	3	3	0	16	8	48.2	52	6	25	45	Runners on	.255	589	150	28	4	26	166	76	154	.338	.448
March/April	6.28	8	5	1	24	11	77.1	77	13	39	84	Scoring Posn	.235	332	78	15	4	10	131	54	94	.334	.395
May	8.87	2	6	0	20	8	47.2	63	13	30	51	Close & Late	.190	216	41	6	1	5	17	22	68	.271	.296
June	2.61	7	0	1	22	4	62.0	41	5	23	65	None on/out	.248	339	84	15	3	12	12	42	81	.332	.416
July	4.01	3	3	0	20	2	49.1	42	7	17	53	vs. 1st Batr (relief)	.179	78	14	5	0	2	15	7	33	.241	.321
August	3.92	7	3	0	25	7	80.1	65	8	43	58	1st Inning Pitched	.222	418	93	19	4	10	61	53	123	.305	.359
Sept/Oct	5.56	2	3	0	16	6	45.1	45	6	24	26	First 15 Pitches	.215	321	69	14	2	7	37	34	84	.285	.336
Starter	6.48	11	14	0	38	38	191.2	202	31	112	153	Pitch 16-30	.257	311	80	18	2	15	37	44	101	.355	.473
Reliever	3.49	18	6	2	89	0	170.1	131	21	64	184	Pitch 31-45	.249	245	61	10	1	9	39	29	58	.332	.408
0 Days rest (Relief)	5.40	0	1	0	3	0	3.1	2	1	1	2	Pitch 46+	.255	483	123	22	5	21	79	69	94	.348	.451
1 or 2 Days rest	3.69	12	3	1	48	0	90.1	67	12	35	92	First Pitch	.304	148	45	8	2	6	27	9	0	.344	.507
3+ Days rest	3.17	6	2	1	38	0	76.2	62	8	28	90	Ahead in Count	.189	641	121	21	2	14	51	0	279	.193	.293
vs. AL	5.16	26	20	2	122	38	352.0	330	51	174	324	Behind in Count	.292	277	81	14	4	15	57	83	0	.455	.534
vs. NL	1.80	3	0	0	5	0	10.0	3	1	2	13	Two Strikes	.178	714	127	21	2	18	76	84	337	.266	.289
Pre-All Star	5.64	19	12	2	72	25	204.1	198	32	98	219	Pre-All Star	.255	777	198	38	6	32	119	98	219	.338	.443
Post-All Star	4.34	10	8	0	55	13	157.2	135	20	78	118	Post-All Star	.232	583	135	26	4	20	73	78	118	.324	.393

Pitcher vs. Batter (career)

Pitches Best Vs.	Avg	AB	H	2B	3B	HR	RBI	BB	SO	OBP	SLG	Pitches Worst Vs.	Avg	AB	H	2B	3B	HR	RBI	BB	SO	OBP	SLG
Omar Vizquel	.056	18	1	0	0	0	0	1	1	.105	.056	Jose Canseco	.625	8	5	0	0	3	6	4	1	.750	1.750

Pitcher vs. Batter (career)

Pitches Best Vs.	Avg	AB	H	2B	3B	HR	RBI	BB	SO	OBP	SLG	Pitches Worst Vs.	Avg	AB	H	2B	3B	HR	RBI	BB	SO	OBP	SLG
Juan Gonzalez	.105	19	2	1	0	0	2	0	8	.095	.158	Gerald Williams	.467	15	7	3	0	1	5	0	2	.467	.867
Mo Vaughn	.167	18	3	0	0	0	2	0	9	.167	.167	Tim Salmon	.455	11	5	0	0	1	6	2	2	.667	.727
Rich Amaral	.182	11	2	0	0	0	1	0	3	.182	.182	Danny Tartabull	.444	9	4	1	0	1	3	3	1	.583	.889
Travis Fryman	.200	15	3	0	0	0	3	1	4	.250	.200	Albert Belle	.400	15	6	3	0	2	7	5	2	.550	1.000

Brad Rigby — Athletics
Age 25 – Pitches Right

	ERA	W	L	Sv	G	GS	IP	BB	SO	Avg	H	2B	3B	HR	RBI	OBP	SLG	CG	ShO	Sup	QS	#P/S	SB	CS	GB	FB	G/F
1997 Season	4.87	1	7	0	14	14	77.2	22	34	302	92	15	1	14	39	.344	.495	0	0	3.71	6	84	2	1	132	88	1.50

1997 Season

	ERA	W	L	Sv	G	GS	IP	H	HR	BB	SO		Avg	AB	H	2B	3B	HR	RBI	BB	SO	OBP	SLG
Home	4.13	1	4	0	9	9	52.1	57	8	17	25	vs. Left	.342	155	53	9	0	7	19	7	13	.365	.535
Away	6.39	0	3	0	5	5	25.1	35	6	5	9	vs. Right	.260	150	39	6	1	7	20	15	21	.323	.453
Starter	4.87	1	7	0	14	14	77.2	92	14	22	34	Scoring Posn	.239	71	17	2	1	1	23	10	8	.311	.338
Reliever	0.00	0	0	0	0	0	0.0	0	0	0	0	Close & Late	.250	12	3	0	0	1	1	1	0	.308	.500
0-3 Days Rest (Start)	2.12	0	0	0	3	3	17.0	10	2	8	8	None on/out	.357	84	30	6	0	7	7	2	6	.379	.679
4 Days Rest	4.43	1	2	0	4	4	20.1	30	2	4	8	Ahead in Count	.258	124	32	3	0	6	14	0	27	.262	.427
5+ Days Rest	6.25	0	5	0	7	7	40.1	52	10	10	18	Behind in Count	.305	82	25	4	0	2	7	16	0	.414	.427
Pre-All Star	5.25	0	2	0	2	2	12.0	16	4	2	4	Two Strikes	.266	124	33	5	0	7	18	5	34	.295	.476
Post-All Star	4.80	1	5	0	12	12	65.2	76	10	20	30												

Adam Riggs — Dodgers
Age 25 – Bats Right

	Avg	G	AB	R	H	2B	3B	HR	RBI	BB	SO	HBP	GDP	SB	CS	OBP	SLG	IBB	SH	SF	#Pit	#P/PA	GB	FB	G/F
1997 Season	.200	9	20	3	4	1	0	0	1	4	3	0	0	1	0	.333	.250	1	0	0	96	4.00	6	7	0.86

1997 Season

	Avg	AB	H	2B	3B	HR	RBI	BB	SO	OBP	SLG		Avg	AB	H	2B	3B	HR	RBI	BB	SO	OBP	SLG
vs. Left	.273	11	3	0	0	0	1	3	2	.429	.273	Scoring Posn	.333	3	1	0	0	0	1	1	1	.500	.333
vs. Right	.111	9	1	1	0	0	0	1	1	.200	.222	Close & Late	1.000	1	1	0	0	0	0	0	0	1.000	1.000

Ricardo Rincon — Pirates
Age 28 – Pitches Left (flyball pitcher)

	ERA	W	L	Sv	G	GS	IP	BB	SO	Avg	H	2B	3B	HR	RBI	OBP	SLG	GF	IR	IRS	Hld	SvOp	SB	CS	GB	FB	G/F
1997 Season	3.45	4	8	4	62	0	60.0	24	71	230	51	9	0	5	22	.309	.338	23	35	9	18	6	3	4	55	62	0.89

1997 Season

	ERA	W	L	Sv	G	GS	IP	H	HR	BB	SO		Avg	AB	H	2B	3B	HR	RBI	BB	SO	OBP	SLG
Home	2.51	4	3	2	33	0	32.1	26	3	12	43	vs. Left	.235	81	19	6	0	2	10	6	28	.287	.383
Away	4.55	0	5	2	29	0	27.2	25	2	12	28	vs. Right	.227	141	32	3	0	3	12	18	43	.321	.312
Day	3.79	1	4	1	17	0	19.0	21	1	6	28	Inning 1-6	.333	3	1	0	0	3	1	0	.500	.667
Night	3.29	3	4	3	45	0	41.0	30	4	18	43	Inning 7+	.228	219	50	8	0	5	19	23	71	.306	.333
Grass	3.86	0	4	1	21	0	21.0	16	1	9	22	None on	.244	127	31	4	0	3	3	9	38	.294	.346
Turf	3.23	4	4	3	41	0	39.0	35	4	15	49	Runners on	.211	95	20	5	0	2	19	15	33	.327	.326
March/April	2.45	2	2	0	9	0	11.0	7	0	5	18	Scoring Posn	.196	56	11	2	0	0	14	12	21	.343	.232
May	1.98	0	0	4	11	0	13.2	9	0	2	14	Close & Late	.245	139	34	5	0	2	13	19	45	.342	.324
June	12.60	0	2	0	8	0	5.0	10	3	3	9	None on/out	.232	56	13	2	0	1	1	4	16	.283	.321
July	2.89	2	0	0	10	0	9.1	9	1	4	13	vs. 1st Batr (relief)	.190	58	11	4	0	2	7	4	21	.242	.362
August	4.15	0	3	0	13	0	13.0	11	1	8	10	1st Inning Pitched	.226	190	43	7	0	5	21	21	59	.308	.342
Sept/Oct	1.13	0	1	0	11	0	8.0	5	0	2	7	First 15 Pitches	.239	163	39	6	0	5	18	19	45	.326	.368
Starter	0.00	0	0	0	0	0	0.0	0	0	0	0	Pitch 16-30	.200	55	11	3	0	0	3	5	24	.262	.255
Reliever	3.45	4	8	4	62	0	60.0	51	5	24	71	Pitch 31-45	.250	4	1	0	0	0	1	0	2	.250	.250
0 Days rest (Relief)	0.73	0	0	0	12	0	12.1	6	0	6	12	Pitch 46+	.000	0	0	0	0	0	0	0	0	.000	.000
1 or 2 Days rest	4.40	3	7	2	34	0	30.2	30	3	12	35	First Pitch	.273	22	6	0	0	1	6	0	.429	.273
3+ Days rest	3.71	1	1	2	16	0	17.0	13	2	6	24	Ahead in Count	.143	112	16	2	0	2	6	0	63	.158	.214
vs. AL	8.31	0	0	0	5	0	4.1	5	2	1	4	Behind in Count	.391	46	18	6	0	1	6	11	0	.509	.587
vs. NL	3.07	4	8	4	57	0	55.2	46	3	23	67	Two Strikes	.120	117	14	1	0	1	7	7	71	.169	.154
Pre-All Star	4.06	2	4	4	29	0	31.0	28	3	11	43	Pre-All Star	.248	113	28	5	0	3	13	11	43	.312	.372
Post-All Star	2.79	2	4	0	33	0	29.0	23	2	13	28	Post-All Star	.211	109	23	4	0	2	9	13	28	.306	.303

Danny Rios — Yankees
Age 25 – Pitches Right

	ERA	W	L	Sv	G	GS	IP	BB	SO	Avg	H	2B	3B	HR	RBI	OBP	SLG	GF	IR	IRS	Hld	SvOp	SB	CS	GB	FB	G/F
1997 Season	19.29	0	0	0	2	0	2.1	2	1	563	9	0	0	3	7	.632	1.125	0	3	3	0	0	0	0	6	1	6.00

1997 Season

	ERA	W	L	Sv	G	GS	IP	H	HR	BB	SO		Avg	AB	H	2B	3B	HR	RBI	BB	SO	OBP	SLG
Home	27.00	0	0	0	1	0	0.2	5	0	0	0	vs. Left	.571	7	4	0	0	2	3	2	0	.667	1.429
Away	16.20	0	0	0	1	0	1.2	4	3	2	1	vs. Right	.556	9	5	0	0	1	4	0	1	.600	.889

Billy Ripken — Rangers

Age 33 – Bats Right (groundball hitter)

	Avg	G	AB	R	H	2B	3B	HR	RBI	BB	SO	HBP	GDP	SB	CS	OBP	SLG	IBB	SH	SF	#Pit	#P/PA	GB	FB	G/F
1997 Season	.276	71	203	18	56	9	1	3	24	9	32	0	7	0	1	.300	.374	0	1	5	771	3.54	85	48	1.77
Last Five Years	.254	218	568	62	144	26	1	7	56	32	83	5	19	2	3	.296	.340	0	8	7	2245	3.62	245	141	1.74

1997 Season

	Avg	AB	H	2B	3B	HR	RBI	BB	SO	OBP	SLG		Avg	AB	H	2B	3B	HR	RBI	BB	SO	OBP	SLG
vs. Left	.299	87	26	6	1	0	9	1	12	.303	.391	Scoring Posn	.271	48	13	1	1	0	20	4	9	.298	.333
vs. Right	.259	116	30	3	0	3	15	8	20	.297	.362	Close & Late	.333	24	8	2	0	0	4	0	2	.320	.417
Home	.344	96	33	6	1	1	13	2	16	.350	.458	None on/out	.350	60	21	1	0	2	2	2	9	.371	.467
Away	.215	107	23	3	0	2	11	7	16	.256	.299	Batting #8	.278	115	32	3	1	1	11	4	19	.295	.348
First Pitch	.429	28	12	1	0	2	3	0	0	.429	.679	Batting #9	.281	64	18	4	0	2	12	4	11	.319	.438
Ahead in Count	.304	56	17	4	1	1	7	3	0	.328	.464	Other	.250	24	6	2	0	0	1	1	2	.269	.333
Behind in Count	.230	87	20	2	0	0	12	0	32	.222	.253	Pre-All Star	.306	121	37	4	1	2	20	5	17	.321	.405
Two Strikes	.190	79	15	2	0	0	7	6	32	.247	.215	Post-All Star	.232	82	19	5	0	1	4	4	15	.267	.329

Last Five Years

	Avg	AB	H	2B	3B	HR	RBI	BB	SO	OBP	SLG		Avg	AB	H	2B	3B	HR	RBI	BB	SO	OBP	SLG
vs. Left	.279	233	65	13	1	1	18	7	31	.315	.356	First Pitch	.366	82	30	7	0	3	10	0	0	.381	.561
vs. Right	.236	335	79	13	0	6	38	25	52	.293	.328	Ahead in Count	.282	124	35	7	1	2	17	20	0	.374	.403
Groundball	.240	121	29	1	0	1	11	9	23	.293	.273	Behind in Count	.211	256	54	8	0	1	23	0	78	.215	.254
Flyball	.318	88	28	3	0	2	9	2	10	.337	.420	Two Strikes	.187	252	47	6	0	1	16	12	83	.226	.222
Home	.298	282	84	13	1	3	34	15	42	.334	.383	Batting #8	.291	206	60	9	1	2	18	10	32	.326	.374
Away	.210	286	60	13	0	4	22	17	41	.258	.297	Batting #9	.231	238	55	13	0	4	28	18	36	.290	.336
Day	.203	172	35	4	0	1	10	7	24	.246	.244	Other	.234	124	29	4	0	1	10	4	15	.256	.290
Night	.275	396	109	22	1	6	46	25	59	.317	.381	March/April	.232	95	22	4	0	0	8	6	15	.291	.274
Grass	.257	518	133	24	1	6	50	28	76	.299	.342	May	.280	157	44	9	1	3	19	8	17	.308	.408
Turf	.220	50	11	2	0	1	6	4	7	.268	.320	June	.274	146	40	5	0	1	18	8	22	.318	.329
Pre-All Star	.262	408	107	18	1	4	45	22	55	.303	.341	July	.179	56	10	0	0	1	3	3	12	.220	.232
Post-All Star	.231	160	37	8	0	3	11	10	28	.276	.338	August	.171	35	6	2	0	0	2	3	7	.237	.229
Scoring Posn	.255	153	39	3	1	0	48	9	24	.297	.288	Sept/Oct	.278	79	22	6	0	2	8	4	10	.313	.430
Close & Late	.300	70	21	5	0	0	9	4	8	.342	.371	vs. AL	.255	545	139	25	1	7	53	32	81	.299	.343
None on/out	.338	136	46	12	0	3	3	8	16	.375	.493	vs. NL	.217	23	5	1	0	0	3	0	2	.217	.261

Batter vs. Pitcher (career)

Hits Best Against	Avg	AB	H	2B	3B	HR	RBI	BB	SO	OBP	SLG	Hits Worst Against	Avg	AB	H	2B	3B	HR	RBI	BB	SO	OBP	SLG
Kenny Rogers	.429	14	6	0	0	0	1	0	0	.429	.429	Charles Nagy	.000	14	0	0	0	0	1	1	4	.067	.000
David Wells	.421	19	8	3	0	1	1	3	0	.500	.737	Andy Pettitte	.000	11	0	0	0	0	0	0	1	.000	.000
Wilson Alvarez	.364	11	4	2	0	0	2	1	1	.417	.545	Scott Erickson	.000	9	0	0	0	0	0	1	3	.182	.000
Greg Swindell	.359	39	14	4	0	0	3	1	6	.375	.462	Mark Gubicza	.059	17	1	0	0	0	0	4	3	.238	.059
Jimmy Key	.333	33	11	1	1	0	0	1	1	.353	.424	Jack McDowell	.077	13	1	0	0	0	0	0	0	.077	.077

Cal Ripken — Orioles

Age 37 – Bats Right

	Avg	G	AB	R	H	2B	3B	HR	RBI	BB	SO	HBP	GDP	SB	CS	OBP	SLG	IBB	SH	SF	#Pit	#P/PA	GB	FB	G/F
1997 Season	.270	162	615	79	166	30	0	17	84	56	73	5	19	1	0	.331	.402	3	0	10	2435	3.55	288	157	1.83
Last Five Years	.274	743	2890	402	793	148	9	97	439	264	309	21	96	4	7	.336	.433	34	1	32	11507	3.59	1217	882	1.38

1997 Season

	Avg	AB	H	2B	3B	HR	RBI	BB	SO	OBP	SLG		Avg	AB	H	2B	3B	HR	RBI	BB	SO	OBP	SLG
vs. Left	.260	181	47	9	0	5	22	19	19	.335	.392	First Pitch	.304	92	28	5	0	1	8	2	0	.313	.391
vs. Right	.274	434	119	21	0	12	62	37	54	.329	.406	Ahead in Count	.280	168	47	9	0	11	33	24	0	.372	.530
Groundball	.231	156	36	6	0	2	19	22	19	.324	.308	Behind in Count	.233	227	53	9	0	4	26	0	63	.241	.326
Flyball	.243	74	18	4	0	1	7	6	7	.296	.338	Two Strikes	.200	225	45	5	0	1	21	30	73	.290	.236
Home	.272	290	79	13	0	10	44	27	36	.337	.421	Batting #5	.287	314	90	16	0	10	49	24	41	.339	.433
Away	.268	325	87	17	0	7	40	29	37	.325	.385	Batting #6	.259	147	38	6	0	3	17	18	23	.333	.361
Day	.304	194	59	11	0	8	33	27	23	.391	.485	Other	.247	154	38	8	0	4	18	14	9	.312	.377
Night	.254	421	107	19	0	9	51	29	50	.300	.363	March/April	.316	95	30	5	0	5	20	5	8	.350	.526
Grass	.274	547	150	25	0	17	78	46	65	.331	.413	May	.250	104	26	5	0	2	20	13	14	.328	.413
Turf	.235	68	16	5	0	0	6	10	8	.333	.309	June	.300	110	33	5	0	2	12	7	9	.342	.400
Pre-All Star	.296	341	101	19	0	11	57	26	33	.344	.449	July	.241	112	27	6	0	1	10	4	10	.274	.321
Post-All Star	.237	274	65	11	0	6	27	30	40	.315	.343	August	.357	98	35	5	0	3	10	11	12	.417	.500
Scoring Posn	.275	153	42	10	0	5	68	26	15	.363	.438	Sept/Oct	.156	96	15	4	0	2	7	16	20	.277	.260
Close & Late	.298	104	31	1	0	5	13	6	15	.336	.452	vs. AL	.259	555	144	28	0	14	73	49	66	.319	.386
None on/out	.253	158	40	10	0	4	4	5	20	.280	.392	vs. NL	.367	60	22	2	0	3	11	7	7	.441	.550

1997 By Position

Position	Avg	AB	H	2B	3B	HR	RBI	BB	SO	OBP	SLG	G	GS	Innings	PO	A	E	DP	Fld Pct	Rng Fctr	In Zone	Zone Outs	Zone Rtg	MLB Zone
As 3b	.268	612	164	30	0	17	83	56	73	.329	.400	162	162	1401.0	98	312	22	25	.949	2.63	444	356	.802	.801

Last Five Years

	Avg	AB	H	2B	3B	HR	RBI	BB	SO	OBP	SLG		Avg	AB	H	2B	3B	HR	RBI	BB	SO	OBP	SLG
vs. Left	.288	813	234	41	0	28	118	82	73	.353	.442	First Pitch	.292	390	114	26	2	10	45	26	0	.338	.446
vs. Right	.269	2077	559	107	9	69	321	182	236	.330	.429	Ahead in Count	.284	825	234	47	1	42	147	116	0	.376	.496
Groundball	.254	650	165	31	0	13	85	73	82	.330	.362	Behind in Count	.253	1123	284	49	3	29	161	0	263	.258	.379
Flyball	.249	502	125	24	3	22	95	33	45	.297	.440	Two Strikes	.231	1065	246	40	4	21	133	112	309	.306	.335
Home	.271	1386	375	62	3	49	228	140	160	.340	.426	Batting #4	.288	800	230	38	4	25	125	73	67	.348	.439
Away	.278	1504	418	86	6	48	211	124	149	.333	.439	Batting #5	.275	1028	283	59	1	30	161	86	127	.330	.422
Day	.276	852	235	45	2	34	148	102	96	.355	.453	Other	.264	1062	280	51	4	42	153	105	115	.333	.438
Night	.274	2038	558	103	7	63	291	162	213	.328	.424	March/April	.299	395	118	26	4	10	68	31	44	.350	.461
Grass	.273	2517	686	125	7	85	385	227	275	.334	.429	May	.241	507	122	22	1	17	77	56	56	.318	.389

Last Five Years

	Avg	AB	H	2B	3B	HR	RBI	BB	SO	OBP	SLG		Avg	AB	H	2B	3B	HR	RBI	BB	SO	OBP	SLG
Turf	.287	373	107	23	2	12	54	37	34	.351	.456	June	.304	553	168	31	1	25	94	44	53	.356	.499
Pre-All Star	.280	1629	456	86	6	59	267	149	166	.341	.449	July	.267	521	139	18	1	17	73	46	56	.329	.403
Post-All Star	.267	1261	337	62	3	38	172	115	143	.330	.412	August	.290	483	140	26	1	15	72	46	45	.334	.441
Scoring Posn	.296	737	218	39	3	29	334	118	73	.383	.475	Sept/Oct	.246	431	106	25	1	13	55	41	55	.314	.399
Close & Late	.259	424	110	21	0	14	62	46	59	.331	.408	vs. AL	.272	2830	771	146	9	94	428	257	302	.334	.430
None on/out	.246	690	170	34	3	29	29	44	73	.296	.430	vs. NL	.367	60	22	2	0	3	11	7	7	.441	.550

Batter vs. Pitcher (since 1984)

Hits Best Against	Avg	AB	H	2B	3B	HR	RBI	BB	SO	OBP	SLG	Hits Worst Against	Avg	AB	H	2B	3B	HR	RBI	BB	SO	OBP	SLG
Tony Castillo	.545	11	6	1	0	1	2	0	1	.545	.909	Orel Hershiser	.000	16	0	0	0	0	2	4	2	.182	.000
Scott Aldred	.450	20	9	1	1	2	5	1	1	.476	.900	Doug Drabek	.000	14	0	0	0	0	0	0	0	.000	.000
Don Wengert	.429	14	6	2	0	1	2	1	1	.467	.786	Roberto Hernandez	.000	10	0	0	0	0	0	1	1	.091	.000
Chris Haney	.400	15	6	0	0	3	7	1	1	.412	1.000	Ed Vosberg	.083	12	1	0	0	0	0	0	4	.083	.083
Mike Jackson	.333	18	6	1	0	3	10	1	4	.368	.889	Mike Morgan	.091	22	2	0	0	0	0	0	4	.091	.091

Bill Risley — Blue Jays
Age 31 – Pitches Right (flyball pitcher)

	ERA	W	L	Sv	G	GS	IP	BB	SO	Avg	H	2B	3B	HR	RBI	OBP	SLG	GF	IR	IRS	Hld	SvOp	SB	CS	GB	FB	G/F
1997 Season	8.31	0	1	0	3	0	4.1	2	2	.188	3	0	0	2	4	.278	.563	1	1	0	0	1	0	0	3	8	0.38
Last Five Years	3.62	11	9	1	112	0	161.2	66	159	.213	124	25	6	24	90	.292	.400	25	81	31	22	12	12	2	130	222	0.59

1997 Season

	ERA	W	L	Sv	G	GS	IP	H	HR	BB	SO		Avg	AB	H	2B	3B	HR	RBI	BB	SO	OBP	SLG
Home	13.50	0	0	0	1	0	1.1	1	1	2	2	vs. Left	.143	7	1	0	0	1	2	0	0	.143	.571
Away	6.00	0	1	0	2	0	3.0	2	1	0	0	vs. Right	.222	9	2	0	0	1	2	2	2	.364	.556

Last Five Years

	ERA	W	L	Sv	G	GS	IP	H	HR	BB	SO		Avg	AB	H	2B	3B	HR	RBI	BB	SO	OBP	SLG
Home	3.91	7	3	1	55	0	69.0	64	10	31	78	vs. Left	.209	287	60	13	4	8	37	36	64	.294	.366
Away	3.40	4	6	0	57	0	92.2	60	14	35	81	vs. Right	.217	295	64	12	2	16	53	30	95	.290	.434
Day	4.26	3	2	0	38	0	61.1	51	12	28	54	Inning 1-6	.218	119	26	4	1	5	23	17	31	.317	.395
Night	3.23	8	7	1	74	0	100.1	73	12	38	105	Inning 7+	.212	463	98	21	5	19	67	49	128	.286	.402
Grass	3.22	2	4	0	44	0	72.2	49	11	27	64	None on	.187	331	62	16	4	10	10	32	93	.261	.350
Turf	3.94	9	5	1	68	0	89.0	75	13	39	95	Runners on	.247	251	62	9	2	14	80	34	66	.331	.466
March/April	5.14	1	0	0	9	0	14.0	13	3	11	12	Scoring Posn	.247	158	39	8	2	10	72	25	43	.340	.513
May	2.43	2	2	1	26	0	37.0	24	2	10	44	Close & Late	.208	236	49	10	3	9	42	27	65	.287	.390
June	4.20	4	3	0	24	0	30.0	24	5	14	38	None on/out	.207	135	28	6	3	6	6	16	40	.296	.430
July	2.73	1	2	0	19	0	29.2	19	6	14	27	vs. 1st Batr (relief)	.245	94	23	1	3	6	15	16	28	.360	.511
August	3.73	3	0	0	17	0	31.1	25	4	8	25	1st Inning Pitched	.230	369	85	16	6	15	72	45	104	.313	.428
Sept/Oct	5.03	0	2	0	17	0	19.2	19	4	9	13	First 15 Pitches	.228	290	66	12	6	9	45	37	82	.315	.403
Starter	0.00	0	0	0	0	0	0.0	0	0	0	0	Pitch 16-30	.204	201	41	8	0	11	36	21	56	.278	.408
Reliever	3.62	11	9	1	112	0	161.2	124	24	66	159	Pitch 31-45	.189	74	14	5	0	4	9	7	17	.256	.419
0 Days rest (Relief)	5.21	0	1	0	16	0	19.0	18	4	6	21	Pitch 46+	.176	17	3	0	0	0	0	1	2	.222	.176
1 or 2 Days rest	4.52	3	5	1	46	0	61.2	54	10	34	64	First Pitch	.257	70	18	1	2	5	16	5	0	.303	.543
3+ Days rest	2.56	2	3	0	50	0	81.0	52	10	26	74	Ahead in Count	.165	267	44	10	2	9	23	0	127	.165	.318
vs. AL	3.57	11	9	1	110	0	158.2	122	23	64	157	Behind in Count	.322	121	39	6	2	9	35	20	0	.415	.628
vs. NL	6.00	0	0	0	2	0	3.0	2	1	2	2	Two Strikes	.156	308	48	12	0	8	27	41	159	.254	.273
Pre-All Star	3.55	7	6	1	65	0	91.1	71	13	38	105	Pre-All Star	.214	332	71	16	5	13	52	38	105	.293	.410
Post-All Star	3.71	4	3	0	47	0	70.1	53	11	28	54	Post-All Star	.212	250	53	9	1	11	38	28	54	.291	.388

Pitcher vs. Batter (career)

Pitches Best Vs.	Avg	AB	H	2B	3B	HR	RBI	BB	SO	OBP	SLG	Pitches Worst Vs.	Avg	AB	H	2B	3B	HR	RBI	BB	SO	OBP	SLG
												Tim Raines	.333	9	3	0	0	0	0	2	1	.455	.333

Todd Ritchie — Twins
Age 26 – Pitches Right (flyball pitcher)

	ERA	W	L	Sv	G	GS	IP	BB	SO	Avg	H	2B	3B	HR	RBI	OBP	SLG	GF	IR	IRS	Hld	SvOp	SB	CS	GB	FB	G/F
1997 Season	4.58	2	3	0	42	0	74.2	28	44	.290	87	12	2	11	41	.353	.453	19	24	7	3	2	4	3	93	114	0.82

1997 Season

	ERA	W	L	Sv	G	GS	IP	H	HR	BB	SO		Avg	AB	H	2B	3B	HR	RBI	BB	SO	OBP	SLG
Home	3.91	1	0	0	23	0	46.0	51	7	9	28	vs. Left	.218	110	24	4	0	8	18	12	22	.301	.473
Away	5.65	1	3	0	19	0	28.2	36	4	19	16	vs. Right	.332	190	63	8	2	3	23	16	22	.385	.442
Starter	0.00	0	0	0	0	0	0.0	0	0	0	0	Scoring Posn	.239	88	21	2	1	2	29	9	15	.320	.352
Reliever	4.58	2	3	0	42	0	74.2	87	11	28	44	Close & Late	.333	12	4	0	0	1	1	1		.385	.333
0 Days rest (Relief)	0.00	0	0	0	3	0	4.1	4	0	0	3	None on/out	.299	67	20	1	0	1	1	7	9	.365	.358
1 or 2 Days rest	4.25	1	0	0	20	0	29.2	30	6	10	17	First Pitch	.255	55	14	3	0	3	11	0	0	.255	.473
3+ Days rest	5.31	1	2	0	19	0	40.2	53	5	18	24	Ahead in Count	.233	116	27	2	1	1	13	0	36	.231	.293
Pre-All Star	5.08	2	3	0	21	0	33.2	39	5	20	21	Behind in Count	.377	77	29	3	0	5	11	18	0	.495	.610
Post-All Star	4.17	0	0	0	21	0	41.0	48	6	8	23	Two Strikes	.270	126	34	5	0	1	12	10	44	.321	.333

Kevin Ritz — Rockies
Age 33 – Pitches Right (groundball pitcher)

	ERA	W	L	Sv	G	GS	IP	BB	SO	Avg	H	2B	3B	HR	RBI	OBP	SLG	CG	ShO	Sup	QS	#P/S	SB	CS	GB	FB	G/F
1997 Season	5.87	6	8	0	18	18	107.1	46	56	.330	142	29	4	16	64	.392	.528	1	0	6.20	6	96	19	8	168	116	1.45
Last Five Years	5.11	39	36	2	99	96	567.1	251	334	.287	637	129	15	61	309	.364	.442	3	0	6.09	38	97	70	28	943	535	1.76

1997 Season

	ERA	W	L	Sv	G	GS	IP	H	HR	BB	SO
Home	7.50	2	4	0	8	8	48.0	72	8	20	27
Away	4.55	4	4	0	10	10	59.1	70	8	26	29
Starter	5.87	6	8	0	18	18	107.1	142	16	46	56
Reliever	0.00	0	0	0	0	0	0.0	0	0	0	0
0-3 Days Rest (Start)	0.00	0	0	0	0	0	0.0	0	0	0	0
4 Days Rest	5.82	5	4	0	12	12	72.2	91	10	33	40
5+ Days Rest	5.97	1	4	0	6	6	34.2	51	6	13	16
Pre-All Star	5.87	6	8	0	18	18	107.1	142	16	46	56
Post-All Star	0.00	0	0	0	0	0	0.0	0	0	0	0

	Avg	AB	H	2B	3B	HR	RBI	BB	SO	OBP	SLG
vs. Left	.359	237	85	15	3	11	41	29	31	.425	.586
vs. Right	.295	193	57	14	1	5	23	17	25	.350	.456
Scoring Posn	.333	117	39	8	3	7	52	18	25	.407	.632
Close & Late	.500	2	1	0	0	0	1	1	0	.667	.500
None on/out	.351	111	39	8	0	5	5	10	6	.405	.559
First Pitch	.292	65	19	3	1	2	4	1	0	.299	.462
Ahead in Count	.315	146	46	13	1	3	16	0	48	.315	.479
Behind in Count	.350	140	49	12	1	6	29	28	0	.448	.579
Two Strikes	.289	142	41	7	2	5	19	17	56	.369	.472

Last Five Years

	ERA	W	L	Sv	G	GS	IP	H	HR	BB	SO
Home	5.88	17	13	2	47	44	263.1	322	36	113	167
Away	4.44	22	23	0	52	52	304.0	315	25	138	167
Day	5.61	15	11	1	41	39	232.2	280	27	101	126
Night	4.76	24	25	1	58	57	334.2	357	34	150	208
Grass	5.23	32	29	2	80	77	461.1	523	54	195	275
Turf	4.58	7	7	0	19	19	106.0	114	7	56	59
March/April	6.50	5	6	0	13	13	70.2	94	11	43	45
May	4.47	8	3	0	19	19	110.2	113	10	44	67
June	4.24	9	9	0	23	23	140.0	145	13	61	75
July	5.67	8	7	0	17	17	101.2	119	14	39	58
August	6.40	3	9	0	15	14	77.1	98	10	45	49
Sept/Oct	4.16	6	2	2	12	10	67.0	68	3	19	40
Starter	5.17	39	36	0	96	96	558.2	632	61	250	329
Reliever	1.04	0	0	2	3	0	8.2	5	0	1	5
0-3 Days Rest (Start)	2.00	1	1	0	3	3	18.0	14	2	3	14
4 Days Rest	5.35	28	25	0	67	67	394.0	447	41	169	220
5+ Days Rest	5.09	10	10	0	26	26	146.2	171	18	78	95
vs. AL	8.68	0	2	0	2	2	9.1	14	2	4	6
vs. NL	5.05	39	34	2	97	94	558.0	623	59	247	328
Pre-All Star	4.72	25	20	0	60	60	355.0	380	37	162	206
Post-All Star	5.76	14	16	2	39	36	212.1	257	24	89	128

	Avg	AB	H	2B	3B	HR	RBI	BB	SO	OBP	SLG
vs. Left	.305	1012	309	69	6	27	144	142	153	.393	.465
vs. Right	.272	1204	328	60	9	34	165	109	181	.338	.422
Inning 1-6	.284	2013	571	114	14	52	277	231	309	.360	.432
Inning 7+	.325	203	66	15	1	9	32	20	25	.396	.542
None on	.284	1217	346	59	7	28		119	163	.353	.413
Runners on	.291	999	291	70	8	33	281	132	171	.376	.476
Scoring Posn	.291	601	175	33	6	24	251	101	112	.390	.486
Close & Late	.294	51	15	2	0	3	13	10	6	.410	.510
None on/out	.292	552	161	29	3	14		54	62	.359	.431
vs. 1st Batr (relief)	.667	3	2	0	0	0	1	0	1	.667	.667
1st Inning Pitched	.337	413	139	23	7	12	77	40	64	.393	.513
First 75 Pitches	.281	1653	465	88	10	40	209	180	235	.355	.419
Pitch 76-90	.302	285	86	22	1	9	51	42	61	.391	.481
Pitch 91-105	.311	183	57	11	1	7	28	22	28	.388	.497
Pitch 106+	.305	95	29	8	3	5	21	7	10	.371	.611
First Pitch	.379	351	133	24	4	18	64	7	0	.393	.624
Ahead in Count	.221	865	191	46	2	11	71	0	269	.232	.317
Behind in Count	.351	555	195	44	7	20	112	148	0	.482	.564
Two Strikes	.205	901	185	40	2	13	76	96	334	.291	.297
Pre-All Star	.280	1359	380	71	10	37	169	162	206	.358	.428
Post-All Star	.300	857	257	58	5	24	140	89	128	.373	.463

Pitcher vs. Batter (career)

Pitches Best Vs.	Avg	AB	H	2B	3B	HR	RBI	BB	SO	OBP	SLG
Phil Plantier	.067	15	1	0	0	0	0	0	0	.067	.067
Charlie Hayes	.077	13	1	0	0	0	0	0	2	.077	.077
Edgardo Alfonzo	.100	20	2	0	0	0	1	2	1	.182	.100
Carlos Garcia	.100	10	1	0	0	0		1	2	.182	.100
Orlando Miller	.118	17	2	0	0	0	1	0	3	.118	.118

Pitches Worst Vs.	Avg	AB	H	2B	3B	HR	RBI	BB	SO	OBP	SLG
Butch Huskey	.600	15	9	2	0	1	4	1	0	.625	.933
Steve Finley	.579	19	11	2	1	3	7	4	1	.652	1.263
Mark Grace	.500	24	12	5	0	3	12	4	1	.552	1.083
David Segui	.500	10	5	0	2	3	1	1		.545	1.100
Ryan Klesko	.417	12	5	2	0	2	5	1	3	.462	1.083

Luis Rivera — Astros
Age 34 – Bats Right

	Avg	G	AB	R	H	2B	3B	HR	RBI	BB	SO	HBP	GDP	SB	CS	OBP	SLG	IBB	SH	SF	#Pit	#P/PA	GB	FB	G/F
1997 Season	.231	7	13	2	3	1	0	0	3	1	6	0	0	0	0	.286	.385	0	1	0	62	4.13	0	3	0.00
Last Five Years	.226	101	186	26	42	10	3	4	15	16	56	3	3	1	3	.296	.376	0	3	1	806	3.86	43	59	0.73

1997 Season

	Avg	AB	H	2B	3B	HR	RBI	BB	SO	OBP	SLG
vs. Left	.333	6	2	0	0	0	0	0	3	.333	.333
vs. Right	.143	7	1	0	1	0	3	1	3	.250	.429

	Avg	AB	H	2B	3B	HR	RBI	BB	SO	OBP	SLG
Scoring Posn	.200	5	1	0	1	0	3	0	3	.200	.600
Close & Late	.667	3	2	0	0	0	0	0	0	.667	.667

Mariano Rivera — Yankees
Age 28 – Pitches Right (flyball pitcher)

	ERA	W	L	Sv	G	GS	IP	BB	SO	Avg	H	2B	3B	HR	RBI	OBP	SLG	GF	IR	IRS	Hld	SvOp	SB	CS	GB	FB	G/F
1997 Season	1.88	6	4	43	66	0	71.2	20	68	.237	65	9	2	5	19	.285	.339	56	17	4	0	52	3	0	86	74	1.16
Career (1995-1997)	2.96	19	10	48	146	10	246.1	84	249	.225	209	33	3	17	86	.291	.323	72	44	12	27	61	11	3	252	267	0.94

1997 Season

	ERA	W	L	Sv	G	GS	IP	H	HR	BB	SO
Home	2.25	4	3	23	38	0	40.0	36	4	8	40
Away	1.42	2	1	20	28	0	31.2	29	1	12	28
Day	1.32	3	0	14	24	0	27.1	29	2	9	27
Night	2.23	3	4	29	42	0	44.1	36	3	11	41
Grass	1.99	5	4	38	59	0	63.1	57	4	15	59
Turf	1.08	1	0	5	7	0	8.1	8	1	5	9
March/April	2.93	0	1	8	12	0	15.1	18	2	1	10
May	0.90	1	0	7	9	0	10.0	11	0	5	13
June	1.80	1	1	11	14	0	15.0	12	1	4	12
July	1.17	1	1	5	8	0	7.2	5	1	2	12
August	1.84	1	1	9	14	0	14.2	11	1	6	12
Sept/Oct	2.00	2	0	3	9	0	9.0	8	0	2	9
Starter	0.00	0	0	0	0	0	0.0	0	0	0	0

	Avg	AB	H	2B	3B	HR	RBI	BB	SO	OBP	SLG
vs. Left	.242	153	37	4	0	1	4	9	33	.282	.288
vs. Right	.231	121	28	5	2	4	15	11	35	.289	.405
Inning 1-6	.000	0	0	0	0	0	0	0	0	.000	.000
Inning 7+	.237	274	65	9	2	5	19	20	68	.285	.339
None on	.267	150	40	4	1	5	5	6	32	.295	.407
Runners on	.202	124	25	5	1	0	14	14	36	.275	.258
Scoring Posn	.151	73	11	4	0	0	13	10	25	.241	.205
Close & Late	.243	214	52	8	2	5	19	15	51	.288	.369
None on/out	.269	67	18	0	0	3	3	0	15	.269	.402
vs. 1st Batr (relief)	.203	64	13	0	0	3	4	2	15	.227	.344
1st Inning Pitched	.237	245	58	8	2	5	18	17	61	.282	.347
First 15 Pitches	.285	186	53	8	2	5	17	14	39	.330	.430
Pitch 16-30	.118	76	9	1	0	0	2	3	27	.150	.132

1997 Season

	ERA	W	L	Sv	G	GS	IP	H	HR	BB	SO		Avg	AB	H	2B	3B	HR	RBI	BB	SO	OBP	SLG
Reliever	1.88	6	4	43	66	0	71.2	65	5	20	68	Pitch 31-45	.300	10	3	0	0	0	0	3	1	.462	.300
0 Days rest (Relief)	2.33	0	1	14	20	0	19.1	21	0	4	21	Pitch 46+	.000	2	0	0	0	0	0	0	0	.000	.000
1 or 2 Days rest	2.54	3	2	17	25	0	28.1	33	3	8	21	First Pitch	.269	26	7	1	0	1	2	4	0	.367	.423
3+ Days rest	0.75	3	1	12	21	0	24.0	11	0	8	26	Ahead in Count	.193	161	31	4	1	1	7	0	62	.191	.248
vs. AL	1.88	6	2	40	61	0	67.0	60	5	19	63	Behind in Count	.409	44	18	3	1	3	4	8	0	.500	.727
vs. NL	1.93	0	2	3	5	0	4.2	5	0	1	5	Two Strikes	.155	155	24	2	1	1	9	7	68	.188	.200
Pre-All Star	1.96	2	2	27	36	0	41.1	42	3	10	38	Pre-All Star	.261	161	42	6	1	3	12	10	38	.301	.366
Post-All Star	1.78	4	2	16	30	0	30.1	23	2	10	30	Post-All Star	.204	113	23	3	1	2	7	10	30	.264	.301

Career (1995-1997)

	ERA	W	L	Sv	G	GS	IP	H	HR	BB	SO		Avg	AB	H	2B	3B	HR	RBI	BB	SO	OBP	SLG
Home	3.33	13	7	27	76	5	121.2	105	11	41	124	vs. Left	.232	509	118	14	0	8	41	49	111	.301	.306
Away	2.60	6	3	21	70	5	124.2	104	6	43	125	vs. Right	.218	418	91	19	3	9	45	35	138	.278	.342
Day	2.13	9	0	17	54	6	101.1	90	4	38	99	Inning 1-6	.265	275	73	14	1	9	40	31	66	.342	.422
Night	3.54	10	10	31	92	4	145.0	119	13	46	150	Inning 7+	.209	652	136	19	2	8	46	53	183	.268	.281
Grass	3.19	18	10	43	131	10	220.1	190	15	74	217	None on	.224	532	119	17	1	9	9	40	124	.280	.310
Turf	1.04	1	0	5	15	0	26.0	19	2	10	32	Runners on	.228	395	90	16	2	8	77	44	125	.304	.339
March/April	1.95	2	1	8	22	0	37.0	28	2	11	34	Scoring Posn	.188	218	41	11	0	5	68	32	71	.290	.307
May	2.14	3	1	9	20	2	33.2	32	1	14	33	Close & Late	.212	467	99	17	2	7	41	39	134	.271	.302
June	4.99	1	3	11	24	2	39.2	45	5	11	40	None on/out	.220	232	51	2	0	6	6	11	57	.258	.306
July	1.43	4	1	5	23	4	50.1	34	3	16	54	vs. 1st Batr (relief)	.156	128	20	1	0	3	5	7	43	.206	.234
August	3.55	2	2	12	28	1	45.2	40	3	20	46	1st Inning Pitched	.196	515	101	16	2	7	44	47	155	.263	.276
Sept/Oct	3.83	7	2	3	29	1	40.0	30	3	12	42	First 15 Pitches	.221	402	89	12	2	7	32	34	103	.282	.313
Starter	5.94	3	3	0	10	10	50.0	64	8	20	38	Pitch 16-30	.165	242	40	9	0	1	15	24	80	.240	.215
Reliever	2.20	16	7	48	136	0	196.1	145	9	64	211	Pitch 31-45	.226	115	26	3	0	2	8	14	29	.311	.304
0 Days rest (Relief)	4.34	0	3	16	29	0	29.0	34	0	7	36	Pitch 46+	.321	168	54	9	1	7	31	12	37	.372	.512
1 or 2 Days rest	1.91	7	3	19	61	0	89.1	69	6	27	87	First Pitch	.266	94	25	5	0	5	16	7	0	.314	.479
3+ Days rest	1.73	9	1	13	46	0	78.0	42	3	30	88	Ahead in Count	.168	541	91	13	2	2	30	0	224	.174	.211
vs. AL	2.98	19	8	45	141	10	241.2	204	17	83	244	Behind in Count	.381	134	51	10	1	5	17	34	0	.506	.582
vs. NL	1.93	0	2	3	5	0	4.2	5	0	1	5	Two Strikes	.149	564	84	10	2	5	40	42	249	.208	.200
Pre-All Star	2.83	7	5	29	73	6	130.1	117	9	41	130	Pre-All Star	.236	495	117	16	2	9	49	41	130	.296	.331
Post-All Star	3.10	12	5	19	73	4	116.0	88	8	43	119	Post-All Star	.213	432	92	17	1	8	37	43	119	.285	.313

Pitcher vs. Batter (career)

Pitches Best Vs.	Avg	AB	H	2B	3B	HR	RBI	BB	SO	OBP	SLG	Pitches Worst Vs.	Avg	AB	H	2B	3B	HR	RBI	BB	SO	OBP	SLG
Ray Durham	.000	12	0	0	0	0	0	0	1	.000	.000	Ken Griffey Jr	.429	7	3	0	0	1	1	4	1	.636	.857
Terry Steinbach	.077	13	1	0	0	0	0	0	4	.077	.077	Tom Goodwin	.364	11	4	0	0	0	0	0	0	.364	.364
Harold Baines	.182	11	2	0	0	0	0	0	2	.182	.182	Geronimo Berroa	.308	13	4	0	0	1	4	1	3	.357	.538
Brent Gates	.182	11	2	0	0	0	2	0	0	.182	.182												
Ozzie Guillen	.200	10	2	0	0	0	0	1	0	.273	.200												

Ruben Rivera — Padres
Age 24 – Bats Right

	Avg	G	AB	R	H	2B	3B	HR	RBI	BB	SO	HBP	GDP	SB	CS	OBP	SLG	IBB	SH	SF	#Pit	#P/PA	GB	FB	G/F
1997 Season	.250	17	20	2	5	1	0	0	1	2	9	0	0	2	1	.318	.300	0	0	0	104	4.73	5	4	1.25
Career (1995-1997)	.275	68	109	19	30	7	1	2	17	15	36	2	1	8	3	.367	.413	0	1	2	564	4.37	24	29	0.83

1997 Season

	Avg	AB	H	2B	3B	HR	RBI	BB	SO	OBP	SLG		Avg	AB	H	2B	3B	HR	RBI	BB	SO	OBP	SLG
vs. Left	.250	12	3	1	0	0	1	0	6	.250	.333	Scoring Posn	.500	4	2	0	0	0	1	1	1	.600	.500
vs. Right	.250	8	2	0	0	0	0	2	3	.400	.250	Close & Late	.250	8	2	0	0	0	0	0	6	.250	.250

Joe Roa — Giants
Age 26 – Pitches Right (groundball pitcher)

	ERA	W	L	Sv	G	GS	IP	BB	SO	Avg	H	2B	3B	HR	RBI	OBP	SLG	GF	IR	IRS	Hld	SvOp	SB	CS	GB	FB	G/F
1997 Season	5.21	2	5	0	28	3	65.2	20	34	.333	86	10	1	8	41	.380	.473	4	23	6	2	0	5	3	112	70	1.60
Career (1995-1997)	5.40	2	6	0	30	4	73.1	25	34	.340	99	14	1	9	48	.391	.488	4	24	7	2	0	5	3	125	79	1.58

1997 Season

	ERA	W	L	Sv	G	GS	IP	H	HR	BB	SO		Avg	AB	H	2B	3B	HR	RBI	BB	SO	OBP	SLG
Home	5.73	1	4	0	15	2	33.0	42	3	9	13	vs. Left	.309	123	38	6	1	5	23	11	15	.360	.496
Away	4.68	1	1	0	13	1	32.2	44	5	11	21	vs. Right	.356	135	48	4	0	3	18	9	19	.399	.452
Starter	6.28	1	2	0	3	3	14.1	25	1	2	6	Scoring Posn	.338	68	23	2	0	4	35	8	10	.388	.544
Reliever	4.91	1	3	0	25	0	51.1	61	7	18	28	Close & Late	.270	37	10	0	1	0	3	6	2	.372	.324
0 Days rest (Relief)	15.43	0	0	0	3	0	4.2	8	2	1	4	None on/out	.318	66	21	1	0	3	5	13	.375	.470
1 or 2 Days rest	4.19	0	2	0	10	0	19.1	26	1	8	8	First Pitch	.463	41	19	0	0	1	5	5	0	.511	.537
3+ Days rest	3.62	1	1	0	12	0	27.1	27	4	9	16	Ahead in Count	.281	128	36	2	1	1	18	0	26	.290	.336
Pre-All Star	5.01	2	4	0	25	2	55.2	71	6	14	28	Behind in Count	.422	45	19	5	0	4	12	9	0	.509	.800
Post-All Star	6.30	0	1	0	3	1	10.0	15	0	6	6	Two Strikes	.287	115	33	3	1	2	16	6	34	.325	.383

Bip Roberts — Indians
Age 34 – Bats Both (groundball hitter)

	Avg	G	AB	R	H	2B	3B	HR	RBI	BB	SO	HBP	GDP	SB	CS	OBP	SLG	IBB	SH	SF	#Pit	#P/PA	GB	FB	G/F
1997 Season	.302	120	431	63	130	20	2	4	44	28	67	3	7	18	3	.345	.385	2	1	5	1800	3.85	193	72	2.68
Last Five Years	.292	471	1761	240	515	83	9	9	170	147	244	13	25	97	27	.348	.365	13	4	16	7066	3.64	790	335	2.36

1997 Season

	Avg	AB	H	2B	3B	HR	RBI	BB	SO	OBP	SLG		Avg	AB	H	2B	3B	HR	RBI	BB	SO	OBP	SLG
vs. Left	.324	145	47	5	0	2	15	4	18	.340	.400	First Pitch	.328	61	20	5	0	0	8	2	0	.343	.410

1997 Season

	Avg	AB	H	2B	3B	HR	RBI	BB	SO	OBP	SLG		Avg	AB	H	2B	3B	HR	RBI	BB	SO	OBP	SLG
vs. Right	.290	286	83	15	2	2	29	24	49	.347	.378	Ahead in Count	.389	72	28	5	1	1	10	14	0	.488	.528
Groundball	.317	63	20	2	1	0	9	3	6			Behind in Count	.235	204	48	8	1	1	17	0	55	.242	.299
Flyball	.279	61	17	4	0	1	4	4	16	.318	.393	Two Strikes	.248	218	54	7	0	1	18	12	67	.292	.294
Home	.309	188	58	9	2	1	16	16	28	.367	.394	Batting #1	.309	291	90	14	2	3	26	17	44	.348	.402
Away	.296	243	72	11	0	3	28	12	39	.327	.379	Batting #3	.290	107	31	5	0	1	11	5	17	.321	.364
Day	.299	137	41	12	0	0	14	7	20	.329	.387	Other	.273	33	9	1	0	0	7	6	7	.381	.303
Night	.303	294	89	8	2	4	30	21	47	.352	.384	March/April	.395	86	34	6	0	1	10	3	8	.416	.500
Grass	.299	345	103	17	2	3	39	21	54	.340	.386	May	.276	76	21	4	0	0	9	6	12	.321	.329
Turf	.314	86	27	3	0	1	5	7	13	.362	.384	June	.235	34	8	1	0	0	4	1	5	.257	.265
Pre-All Star	.321	196	63	11	0	1	23	10	25	.351	.393	July	.338	77	26	5	0	0	4	6	11	.393	.403
Post-All Star	.285	235	67	9	2	3	21	18	42	.340	.379	August	.247	73	18	1	2	0	9	5	17	.291	.315
Scoring Posn	.290	100	29	4	1	0	34	9	18	.333	.350	Sept/Oct	.271	85	23	3	0	3	8	7	14	.333	.412
Close & Late	.333	69	23	5	0	0	4	8	16	.405	.406	vs. AL	.305	419	128	19	2	4	44	27	62	.348	.389
None on/out	.279	154	43	4	0	2	2	12	30	.339	.344	vs. NL	.167	12	2	1	0	0	0	1	5	.231	.250

1997 By Position

Position	Avg	AB	H	2B	3B	HR	RBI	BB	SO	OBP	SLG	G	GS	Innings	PO	A	E	DP	Fld Pct	Rng Fctr	In Zone	Zone Outs	Zone Rtg	MLB Zone
As Pinch Hitter	.250	8	2	0	0	0	2	3	1	.500	.250	12	0	---	---	---	---	---	---	---	---	---	---	---
As 2b	.265	49	13	2	0	3	6	1	8	.302	.490	13	13	93.1	24	31	4	9	.932	5.30	37	33	.892	.902
As 3b	.385	39	15	3	0	0	5	2	5	.405	.462	10	9	69.2	3	12	0	1	1.000	1.94	18	16	.889	.801
As lf	.298	326	97	15	2	1	31	21	51	.337	.365	92	79	682.2	155	5	3	1	.982	2.11	188	152	.809	.805

Last Five Years

	Avg	AB	H	2B	3B	HR	RBI	BB	SO	OBP	SLG		Avg	AB	H	2B	3B	HR	RBI	BB	SO	OBP	SLG
vs. Left	.277	546	151	22	2	4	44	38	69	.324	.346	First Pitch	.367	313	115	22	2	2	49	10	0	.384	.470
vs. Right	.300	1215	364	61	7	5	126	109	175	.359	.374	Ahead in Count	.342	345	118	24	2	3	35	82	0	.466	.449
Groundball	.298	463	138	23	4	1	54	42	53	.357	.371	Behind in Count	.241	765	184	28	3	1	50	0	203	.249	.289
Flyball	.273	256	70	18	1	4	27	19	44	.324	.398	Two Strikes	.219	773	169	21	2	1	50	55	244	.278	.255
Home	.290	853	247	43	6	4	88	66	120	.345	.368	Batting #1	.294	1373	403	64	9	8	119	111	189	.348	.371
Away	.295	908	268	40	3	5	82	81	124	.352	.362	Batting #3	.292	192	56	10	0	1	25	10	34	.330	.359
Day	.289	532	154	28	0	3	51	36	72	.333	.359	Other	.286	196	56	9	0	0	26	26	21	.368	.332
Night	.294	1229	361	55	9	6	119	111	172	.355	.368	March/April	.288	340	98	18	1	2	35	31	39	.348	.365
Grass	.303	1300	394	64	7	8	135	87	177	.348	.382	May	.301	448	135	17	3	2	52	53	59	.377	.366
Turf	.262	461	121	19	2	1	35	60	67	.350	.319	June	.310	361	112	24	2	0	30	21	42	.347	.388
Pre-All Star	.300	1187	356	63	6	4	119	106	145	.358	.373	July	.298	255	76	13	1	0	20	21	42	.354	.357
Post-All Star	.277	574	159	20	3	5	51	41	99	.329	.348	August	.275	171	47	4	2	2	16	10	29	.315	.357
Scoring Posn	.309	418	129	19	4	3	156	44	57	.366	.395	Sept/Oct	.253	186	47	7	0	3	17	11	33	.302	.339
Close & Late	.294	286	84	13	0	1	31	39	48	.383	.350	vs. AL	.296	758	224	40	4	4	96	52	100	.340	.375
None on/out	.291	660	192	32	4	3	3	57	100	.351	.365	vs. NL	.290	1003	291	43	5	5	74	95	144	.355	.358

Batter vs. Pitcher (career)

Hits Best Against	Avg	AB	H	2B	3B	HR	RBI	BB	SO	OBP	SLG	Hits Worst Against	Avg	AB	H	2B	3B	HR	RBI	BB	SO	OBP	SLG
Danny Darwin	.583	12	7	4	0	0	0	1	2	.615	.917	Rick Honeycutt	.000	11	0	0	0	0	0	1	2	.083	.000
Shane Reynolds	.571	14	8	2	1	0	4	2	2	.647	.857	Tim Belcher	.067	15	1	0	0	0	0	2	2	.176	.067
Allen Watson	.556	9	5	0	1	0	4	2	0	.636	.778	Tim Wakefield	.077	13	1	0	0	0	1	3	6	.250	.077
Greg Maddux	.471	34	16	4	0	0	3	7	4	.561	.588	Jimmy Key	.125	24	3	0	0	1	2	4		.192	.125
Pedro Martinez	.438	16	7	1	0	1	2	3	1	.526	.875	James Baldwin	.143	14	2	1	0	0	2	0	1	.143	.214

Mike Robertson — Phillies
Age 27 – Bats Left

	Avg	G	AB	R	H	2B	3B	HR	RBI	BB	SO	HBP	GDP	SB	CS	OBP	SLG	IBB	SH	SF	#Pit	#P/PA	GB	FB	G/F
1997 Season	.211	22	38	3	8	2	1	0	4	0	6	3	0	1	0	.268	.316	0	0	0	144	3.51	12	15	0.80
Career (1996-1997)	.200	28	45	3	9	3	1	0	4	0	7	3	0	1	0	.250	.311	0	0	0	169	3.52	16	16	1.00

1997 Season

	Avg	AB	H	2B	3B	HR	RBI	BB	SO	OBP	SLG		Avg	AB	H	2B	3B	HR	RBI	BB	SO	OBP	SLG
vs. Left	.000	2	0	0	0	0	0	0	1	.333	.000	Scoring Posn	.667	6	4	1	1	0	4	0	0	.667	1.167
vs. Right	.222	36	8	2	1	0	4	0	5	.263	.333	Close & Late	.300	10	3	1	0	0	0	0	1	.364	.400

Rich Robertson — Twins
Age 29 – Pitches Left

	ERA	W	L	Sv	G	GS	IP	BB	SO	Avg	H	2B	3B	HR	RBI	OBP	SLG	CG	ShO	Sup	QS	#P/S	SB	CS	GB	FB	G/F
1997 Season	5.69	8	12	0	31	26	147.0	70	69	.292	169	38	2	19	85	.370	.463	0	0	4.78	8	89	14	6	238	179	1.33
Career (1993-1997)	5.25	17	30	0	109	61	409.2	231	234	.282	449	85	9	47	222	.375	.435	6	3	4.13	23	94	36	18	647	456	1.42

1997 Season

	ERA	W	L	Sv	G	GS	IP	H	HR	BB	SO		Avg	AB	H	2B	3B	HR	RBI	BB	SO	OBP	SLG
Home	6.42	5	7	0	15	15	82.2	98	11	44	44	vs. Left	.336	116	39	8	1	2	20	17	21	.426	.474
Away	4.76	3	5	0	16	11	64.1	71	8	26	25	vs. Right	.281	463	130	30	1	17	65	53	48	.355	.460
Day	5.97	1	2	0	7	6	34.2	44	3	12	13	Inning 1-6	.293	540	158	34	2	19	80	64	65	.370	.469
Night	5.61	7	10	0	24	20	112.1	125	16	58	56	Inning 7+	.282	39	11	4	0	0	5	6	4	.370	.385
Grass	5.83	2	5	0	13	8	46.1	53	7	19	16	None on	.287	317	91	19	2	12	12	38	40	.370	.473
Turf	5.63	6	7	0	18	18	100.2	116	12	51	53	Runners on	.298	262	78	19	0	7	73	32	29	.368	.450
March/April	7.20	2	1	0	4	4	20.0	24	6	10	7	Scoring Posn	.308	143	44	13	0	6	66	22	16	.389	.524
May	5.11	3	2	0	6	6	37.0	37	3	18	19	Close & Late	.333	18	6	3	0	0	3	4	1	.455	.500
June	4.94	2	2	0	5	5	27.1	32	4	12	15	None on/out	.275	153	42	4	1		8	14	22	.335	.471
July	4.50	0	3	0	5	5	28.0	33	3	14	6	vs. 1st Batr (relief)	.200	5	1	0	0	0	0	0	1	.200	.200
August	6.04	1	3	0	6	4	25.1	31	1	10	18	1st Inning Pitched	.298	121	36	12	1	4	17	14	14	.365	.524

1997 Season

	ERA	W	L	Sv	G	GS	IP	H	HR	BB	SO		Avg	AB	H	2B	3B	HR	RBI	BB	SO	OBP	SLG
Sept/Oct	9.64	0	1	0	5	2	9.1	12	2	6	4	First 75 Pitches	.301	472	142	32	2	15	69	53	62	.372	.472
Starter	5.90	8	12	0	26	26	137.1	159	19	69	64	Pitch 76-90	.239	67	16	3	0	3	11	10	5	.342	.418
Reliever	2.79	0	0	0	5	0	9.2	10	0	1	5	Pitch 91-105	.278	36	10	2	0	1	4	5	2	.366	.417
0-3 Days Rest (Start)	3.00	0	0	0	1	1	6.0	6	0	3	3	Pitch 106+	.250	4	1	1	0	0	1	2	0	.500	.500
4 Days Rest	6.68	3	8	0	13	13	68.2	86	9	34	27	First Pitch	.375	88	33	8	1	1	9	2	0	.387	.523
5+ Days Rest	5.31	5	4	0	12	12	62.2	67	10	32	34	Ahead in Count	.194	191	37	6	0	2	13	0	53	.200	.257
vs. AL	5.90	7	11	0	28	23	132.2	153	17	64	59	Behind in Count	.373	185	69	17	0	12	44	39	0	.485	.659
vs. NL	3.77	1	1	0	3	3	14.1	16	2	6	10	Two Strikes	.192	213	41	9	0	4	22	29	69	.291	.291
Pre-All Star	5.36	7	6	0	16	16	90.2	98	14	44	41	Post-All Star	.305	233	71	19	1	14	47	44	41	.374	.459
Post-All Star	6.23	1	6	0	15	10	56.1	71	5	26	28												

Career (1993-1997)

	ERA	W	L	Sv	G	GS	IP	H	HR	BB	SO		Avg	AB	H	2B	3B	HR	RBI	BB	SO	OBP	SLG
Home	5.62	9	19	0	58	36	227.1	253	23	140	142	vs. Left	.274	347	95	16	3	5	47	59	59	.387	.380
Away	4.79	8	11	0	51	25	182.1	196	24	91	92	vs. Right	.284	1247	354	69	6	42	175	172	175	.371	.450
Day	4.51	2	6	0	26	16	107.2	113	10	56	68	Inning 1-6	.284	1343	382	74	7	41	197	195	189	.378	.442
Night	5.51	15	24	0	83	45	302.0	336	37	175	166	Inning 7+	.267	251	67	11	2	6	25	36	45	.359	.398
Grass	5.45	6	11	0	38	20	135.1	148	21	70	62	None on	.281	840	236	38	5	27	27	114	128	.372	.435
Turf	5.15	11	24	0	71	41	274.1	301	26	161	172	Runners on	.282	754	213	47	4	20	195	117	106	.377	.435
March/April	6.45	2	5	0	12	10	53.0	65	10	31	24	Scoring Posn	.276	421	116	27	4	14	172	77	67	.381	.458
May	4.96	4	5	0	23	13	90.2	99	9	42	65	Close & Late	.333	66	22	3	1	3	11	11	5	.429	.545
June	4.32	4	3	0	18	10	66.2	69	8	36	41	None on/out	.286	399	114	14	3	15	15	52	58	.369	.449
July	5.56	1	4	0	19	10	69.2	85	9	43	29	vs. 1st Batr (relief)	.237	38	9	2	1	0	2	8	5	.362	.342
August	5.11	3	7	0	16	9	61.2	65	5	38	43	1st Inning Pitched	.303	379	115	23	5	9	55	64	50	.401	.462
Sept/Oct	5.43	3	6	0	21	9	68.0	66	6	41	32	First 75 Pitches	.297	1271	377	69	7	37	182	177	193	.381	.449
Starter	5.33	16	28	0	61	61	339.1	361	41	187	193	Pitch 76-90	.208	154	32	6	0	3	20	33	19	.352	.305
Reliever	4.86	1	2	0	48	0	70.1	88	6	44	41	Pitch 91-105	.248	113	28	6	1	7	15	18	13	.356	.504
0-3 Days Rest (Start)	5.79	0	0	0	2	2	9.1	11	0	4	6	Pitch 106+	.214	56	12	4	1	0	5	9	9	.333	.321
4 Days Rest	5.97	7	19	0	36	36	193.0	216	25	119	106	First Pitch	.335	233	78	16	2	6	31	9	0	.359	.498
5+ Days Rest	4.40	9	9	0	23	23	137.0	134	16	64	81	Ahead in Count	.211	582	123	15	1	9	45	0	183	.220	.287
vs. AL	5.22	16	28	0	89	58	370.2	398	43	211	211	Behind in Count	.348	471	164	37	4	22	97	123	0	.483	.584
vs. NL	5.54	1	2	0	20	3	39.0	51	4	20	23	Two Strikes	.188	627	118	17	1	8	45	99	234	.304	.257
Pre-All Star	5.13	10	15	0	57	35	222.2	247	29	119	134	Pre-All Star	.287	861	247	44	5	29	117	119	134	.376	.451
Post-All Star	5.39	7	15	0	52	26	187.0	202	18	112	100	Post-All Star	.276	733	202	41	4	18	105	112	100	.373	.416

Pitcher vs. Batter (career)

Pitches Best Vs.	Avg	AB	H	2B	3B	HR	RBI	BB	SO	OBP	SLG	Pitches Worst Vs.	Avg	AB	H	2B	3B	HR	RBI	BB	SO	OBP	SLG
Lyle Mouton	.000	13	0	0	0	0	3	1	2	.063	.000	Albert Belle	.875	8	7	1	0	1	4	3	0	.917	1.375
Ray Durham	.067	15	1	0	0	0	1	3	2	.222	.067	Chad Curtis	.700	10	7	1	0	2	7	1	1	.667	1.400
J.T. Snow	.083	12	1	0	0	0	0	1	2	.083	.083	Mark McGwire	.600	10	6	1	0	3	7	3	1	.692	1.600
Garret Anderson	.118	17	2	1	0	0	1	0	2	.118	.176	Frank Thomas	.455	11	5	0	0	2	5	1	0	.500	1.000
Gary DiSarcina	.125	16	2	0	0	0	0	2	1	.176	.125	Geronimo Berroa	.429	14	6	3	0	3	8	1	1	.438	1.071

Ken Robinson — Blue Jays
Age 28 – Pitches Right (flyball pitcher)

	ERA	W	L	Sv	G	GS	IP	BB	SO	Avg	H	2B	3B	HR	RBI	OBP	SLG	GF	IR	IRS	Hld	SvOp	SB	CS	GB	FB	G/F
1997 Season	2.70	0	0	0	3	0	3.1	1	4	.100	1	0	0	1	1	.182	.400	2	2	0	1	0	0	0	3	0	0.00
Career (1995-1997)	3.91	2	2	0	29	0	48.1	26	40	.199	35	4	3	8	27	.304	.392	13	18	5	1	1	2	0	44	68	0.65

1997 Season

	ERA	W	L	Sv	G	GS	IP	H	HR	BB	SO		Avg	AB	H	2B	3B	HR	RBI	BB	SO	OBP	SLG
Home	0.00	0	0	0	1	0	0.1	0	0	0	0	vs. Left	.000	4	0	0	0	0	0	1	2	.200	.000
Away	3.00	0	0	0	2	0	3.0	1	1	1	4	vs. Right	.167	6	1	0	0	1	1	0	2	.167	.667

Alex Rodriguez — Mariners
Age 22 – Bats Right (groundball hitter)

	Avg	G	AB	R	H	2B	3B	HR	RBI	BB	SO	HBP	GDP	SB	CS	OBP	SLG	IBB	SH	SF	#Pit	#P/PA	GB	FB	G/F
1997 Season	.300	141	587	100	176	40	3	23	84	41	99	5	14	29	6	.350	.496	1	4	1	2484	3.89	235	164	1.43
Career (1994-1997)	.314	352	1384	260	435	100	6	64	228	109	265	9	29	51	12	.366	.534	2	12	9	6096	4.00	524	381	1.38

1997 Season

	Avg	AB	H	2B	3B	HR	RBI	BB	SO	OBP	SLG		Avg	AB	H	2B	3B	HR	RBI	BB	SO	OBP	SLG
vs. Left	.299	157	47	11	2	8	25	9	32	.337	.548	First Pitch	.304	56	17	3	1	2	9	1	0	.339	.500
vs. Right	.300	430	129	29	1	15	59	32	67	.355	.477	Ahead in Count	.403	129	52	13	0	7	24	23	0	.493	.667
Groundball	.333	123	41	12	1	1	14	13	18	.401	.472	Behind in Count	.257	280	72	16	0	8	31	0	88	.261	.400
Flyball	.281	89	25	7	1	3	13	4	20	.319	.427	Two Strikes	.236	288	68	17	0	11	35	17	99	.282	.410
Home	.311	289	90	23	2	16	51	17	55	.351	.571	Batting #2	.298	450	134	32	2	16	62	31	69	.349	.484
Away	.289	298	86	17	1	7	33	24	44	.350	.423	Batting #5	.310	129	40	8	1	5	19	9	29	.355	.504
Day	.306	193	59	10	1	8	28	15	32	.359	.492	Other	.250	8	2	0	0	2	3	1	1	.333	1.000
Night	.297	394	117	30	2	15	56	26	67	.346	.497	March/April	.333	120	40	10	0	4	19	7	15	.380	.517
Grass	.279	269	75	17	1	5	27	23	40	.345	.405	May	.286	112	32	7	1	3	10	10	21	.347	.446
Turf	.318	318	101	23	2	18	57	18	59	.355	.572	June	.358	53	19	6	1	4	10	2	4	.382	.736
Pre-All Star	.312	311	97	24	2	12	42	20	47	.360	.518	July	.294	109	32	7	0	4	15	9	18	.353	.468
Post-All Star	.286	276	79	16	1	11	42	21	52	.339	.471	August	.268	123	33	6	0	7	21	7	27	.313	.488
Scoring Posn	.301	143	43	10	0	6	59	11	24	.361	.497	Sept/Oct	.286	70	20	4	1	1	9	6	14	.342	.414
Close & Late	.333	72	24	4	0	3	8	7	13	.407	.514	vs. AL	.303	548	166	39	3	21	79	38	95	.353	.500
None on/out	.371	116	43	9	1	4	4	5	18	.397	.569	vs. NL	.256	39	10	1	0	2	5	3	4	.310	.436

1997 By Position

Position	Avg	AB	H	2B	3B	HR	RBI	BB	SO	OBP	SLG	G	GS	Innings	PO	A	E	DP	Fld Pct	Rng Fctr	In Zone	Zone Outs	Zone Rtg	MLB Zone
As ss	.299	582	174	40	3	23	82	41	98	.350	.497	140	140	1233.2	210	394	24	85	.962	4.41	456	432	.947	.937

Career (1994-1997)

	Avg	AB	H	2B	3B	HR	RBI	BB	SO	OBP	SLG		Avg	AB	H	2B	3B	HR	RBI	BB	SO	OBP	SLG
vs. Left	.314	370	116	29	4	19	68	36	70	.373	.568	First Pitch	.348	135	47	11	1	8	29	2	0	.371	.622
vs. Right	.315	1014	319	71	2	45	160	73	195	.364	.522	Ahead in Count	.429	294	126	34	1	18	66	59	0	.523	.735
Groundball	.348	325	113	31	1	8	45	31	55	.409	.523	Behind in Count	.253	643	163	28	1	23	81	0	224	.256	.407
Flyball	.279	201	56	8	1	10	30	11	49	.319	.478	Two Strikes	.246	703	173	36	2	30	93	48	265	.296	.431
Home	.332	657	218	51	5	35	116	54	129	.383	.584	Batting #2	.336	982	330	77	4	49	170	85	159	.391	.572
Away	.298	727	217	49	1	29	112	55	136	.351	.488	Batting #9	.246	211	52	12	0	6	30	11	57	.283	.389
Day	.311	434	135	33	1	18	76	36	96	.363	.516	Other	.277	191	53	11	2	9	28	13	49	.324	.497
Night	.316	950	300	67	5	46	152	73	169	.367	.542	March/April	.320	178	57	19	0	7	34	12	24	.370	.545
Grass	.295	638	188	42	1	24	93	48	122	.348	.476	May	.333	234	78	18	1	10	41	14	47	.369	.547
Turf	.331	746	247	58	5	40	135	61	143	.381	.583	June	.307	202	62	13	1	11	30	17	41	.362	.545
Pre-All Star	.314	685	215	55	2	31	116	45	129	.359	.536	July	.308	312	96	22	1	14	45	26	63	.365	.519
Post-All Star	.315	699	220	45	4	33	112	64	136	.372	.532	August	.331	278	92	18	1	18	53	21	59	.377	.597
Scoring Posn	.310	342	106	23	0	17	156	29	70	.362	.526	Sept/Oct	.278	180	50	10	2	4	25	19	31	.347	.422
Close & Late	.310	197	61	12	0	10	30	19	41	.374	.523	vs. AL	.316	1345	425	99	6	62	223	106	261	.368	.537
None on/out	.329	280	92	25	1	9	9	17	55	.371	.521	vs. NL	.256	39	10	1	0	2	5	3	4	.310	.436

Batter vs. Pitcher (career)

Hits Best Against	Avg	AB	H	2B	3B	HR	RBI	BB	SO	OBP	SLG	Hits Worst Against	Avg	AB	H	2B	3B	HR	RBI	BB	SO	OBP	SLG
Dwight Gooden	.600	10	6	2	0	1	3	0	0	.692	1.100	Andy Pettitte	.143	14	2	0	0	1	2	0	3	.143	.357
Shawn Boskie	.533	15	8	3	0	2	6	0	3	.533	1.133	Cal Eldred	.143	14	2	0	0	1	1	1	3	.200	.143
Kenny Rogers	.500	12	6	1	0	2	5	0	2	.500	1.083	John Burkett	.182	11	2	1	0	0	0	0	2	.182	.273
Scott Erickson	.444	18	8	3	0	2	6	2	1	.500	.944	Don Wengert	.182	11	2	2	0	0	0	0	0	.182	.364
John Wasdin	.417	12	5	1	0	2	3	0	2	.417	1.000	Kevin Appier	.231	13	3	0	0	0	0	0	4	.231	.231

Felix Rodriguez — Reds
Age 25 – Pitches Right (flyball pitcher)

	ERA	W	L	Sv	G	GS	IP	BB	SO	Avg	H	2B	3B	HR	RBI	OBP	SLG	GF	IR	IRS	Hld	SvOp	SB	CS	GB	FB	G/F
1997 Season	4.30	0	0	0	26	1	46.0	28	34	.271	48	9	1	2	28	.387	.367	13	13	7	0	0	7	4	60	54	1.11
Career (1995-1997)	3.97	1	1	0	37	1	56.2	33	39	.272	59	12	1	4	37	.381	.392	18	22	13	0	1	7	4	69	70	0.99

1997 Season

	ERA	W	L	Sv	G	GS	IP	H	HR	BB	SO		Avg	AB	H	2B	3B	HR	RBI	BB	SO	OBP	SLG
Home	4.88	0	0	0	15	0	24.0	27	1	16	21	vs. Left	.268	82	22	4	0	2	13	12	16	.358	.390
Away	3.68	0	0	0	11	1	22.0	21	1	12	13	vs. Right	.274	95	26	5	1	0	15	16	18	.410	.347
Starter	3.86	0	0	0	1	1	4.2	5	0	2	0	Scoring Posn	.306	62	19	3	1	2	28	11	14	.429	.484
Reliever	4.35	0	0	0	25	0	41.1	43	2	26	34	Close & Late	.000	0	0	0	0	0	0	0	0	.000	.000
0 Days rest (Relief)	9.00	0	0	0	2	0	4.0	4	1	3	4	None on/out	.243	37	9	0	0	0	0	3	5	.317	.324
1 or 2 Days rest	0.96	0	0	0	7	0	9.1	8	0	5	7	First Pitch	.280	25	7	3	0	1	5	1	0	.357	.520
3+ Days rest	4.82	0	0	0	16	0	28.0	31	1	18	23	Ahead in Count	.246	65	16	2	0	0	8	0	22	.279	.277
Pre-All Star	4.50	0	0	0	5	0	8.0	12	0	5	8	Behind in Count	.239	46	11	2	0	1	10	12	0	.407	.348
Post-All Star	4.26	0	0	0	21	1	38.0	36	2	23	26	Two Strikes	.182	77	14	1	0	0	8	15	34	.319	.195

Frank Rodriguez — Twins
Age 25 – Pitches Right

	ERA	W	L	Sv	G	GS	IP	BB	SO	Avg	H	2B	3B	HR	RBI	OBP	SLG	GF	IR	IRS	Hld	SvOp	SB	CS	GB	FB	G/F
1997 Season	4.62	3	6	0	43	15	142.1	60	65	.271	147	29	3	12	74	.346	.401	5	28	10	4	2	5	4	223	160	1.39
Career (1995-1997)	5.17	21	28	2	106	66	454.2	195	234	.273	479	98	8	50	250	.348	.423	10	36	10	5	4	16	12	722	506	1.43

1997 Season

	ERA	W	L	Sv	G	GS	IP	H	HR	BB	SO		Avg	AB	H	2B	3B	HR	RBI	BB	SO	OBP	SLG
Home	2.97	1	2	0	20	4	69.2	61	5	18	33	vs. Left	.283	233	66	10	2	7	29	38	28	.386	.433
Away	6.19	2	4	0	23	11	72.2	86	7	42	32	vs. Right	.261	310	81	19	1	5	45	22	37	.315	.377
Day	6.75	0	3	0	10	5	29.1	36	4	19	11	Inning 1-6	.258	400	103	21	2	7	58	45	46	.336	.373
Night	4.06	3	3	0	33	10	113.0	111	8	41	54	Inning 7+	.308	143	44	8	1	5	16	15	19	.377	.483
Grass	6.29	1	4	0	19	10	63.0	70	5	39	28	None on	.254	295	75	15	2	7	7	32	32	.333	.390
Turf	3.29	2	2	0	24	5	79.1	77	7	21	37	Runners on	.290	248	72	14	1	5	67	28	33	.362	.415
March/April	7.54	1	2	0	5	5	22.2	26	5	14	10	Scoring Posn	.328	137	45	9	0	3	62	21	18	.413	.460
May	4.13	0	1	0	6	4	28.1	31	2	13	10	Close & Late	.309	55	17	5	0	1	8	10	6	.424	.455
June	2.79	0	0	0	10	0	19.1	17	0	6	8	None on/out	.288	132	38	5	1	4	4	16	12	.369	.432
July	5.82	1	1	0	9	1	21.2	24	2	13	5	vs. 1st Batr (relief)	.250	20	5	1	0	1	7	7	2	.464	.450
August	4.11	0	1	0	7	3	30.2	29	3	9	19	1st Inning Pitched	.286	147	42	11	0	3	32	21	14	.376	.422
Sept/Oct	3.20	1	1	0	6	2	19.2	20	0	5	15	First 15 Pitches	.273	139	38	10	0	5	21	15	11	.350	.453
Starter	6.10	2	6	0	15	15	76.2	88	9	39	36	Pitch 16-30	.186	118	22	7	0	0	8	15	18	.284	.246
Reliever	2.88	1	0	0	28	0	65.2	59	3	21	29	Pitch 31-45	.270	89	24	4	0	2	17	11	9	.350	.382
0 Days rest (Relief)	0.00	0	0	0	2	0	6.0	5	0	3	2	Pitch 46+	.320	197	63	8	3	5	28	19	27	.381	.467
1 or 2 Days rest	4.65	1	0	0	17	0	31.0	36	2	12	18	First Pitch	.316	76	24	7	2	1	16	0	0	.350	.500
3+ Days rest	1.57	0	0	0	9	0	28.2	18	1	6	8	Ahead in Count	.233	219	51	7	1	4	23	0	56	.241	.329
vs. AL	4.75	3	4	0	38	13	125.0	128	11	51	58	Behind in Count	.286	147	42	9	0	4	19	38	0	.432	.429
vs. NL	3.63	0	2	0	5	2	17.1	19	1	9	7	Two Strikes	.209	196	41	8	1	4	23	18	65	.281	.321
Pre-All Star	4.56	1	3	0	23	9	75.0	75	7	39	28	Pre-All Star	.268	280	75	19	1	7	36	39	28	.359	.411
Post-All Star	4.68	2	3	0	20	6	67.1	72	5	21	37	Post-All Star	.274	263	72	10	3	5	38	21	37	.332	.392

Career (1995-1997)

	ERA	W	L	Sv	G	GS	IP	H	HR	BB	SO		Avg	AB	H	2B	3B	HR	RBI	BB	SO	OBP	SLG
Home	4.07	10	11	0	50	31	239.0	225	20	95	129	vs. Left	.275	893	246	46	6	22	115	123	100	.361	.414
Away	6.38	11	17	2	56	35	215.2	254	30	100	105	vs. Right	.270	863	233	52	2	28	135	72	134	.334	.432
Day	5.98	6	12	1	37	24	146.0	160	18	74	67	Inning 1-6	.273	1448	395	83	7	40	218	162	190	.348	.423
Night	4.78	15	16	1	69	42	308.2	319	32	121	167	Inning 7+	.273	308	84	15	1	10	32	33	44	.346	.425
Grass	6.73	9	17	0	51	32	194.0	230	26	95	101	None on	.256	950	243	52	5	32	32	117	132	.342	.422
Turf	4.01	12	11	2	55	34	260.2	249	24	100	133	Runners on	.293	806	236	46	3	18	218	78	102	.355	.424
March/April	7.49	3	5	0	13	12	57.2	68	8	32	25	Scoring Posn	.308	442	136	30	1	14	204	53	59	.375	.475
May	5.37	1	5	0	14	11	67.0	75	7	29	32	Close & Late	.273	139	38	11	0	4	20	22	19	.370	.439
June	3.53	5	1	0	19	6	66.1	65	7	21	38	None on/out	.272	430	117	19	1	15	15	55	46	.360	.426
July	6.03	5	5	0	21	11	74.2	82	7	40	27	vs. 1st Batr (relief)	.219	32	7	1	0	2	8	7	3	.375	.438
August	3.83	4	4	2	21	12	98.2	93	10	33	58	1st Inning Pitched	.304	398	121	25	0	16	83	49	50	.380	.487
Sept/Oct	5.48	3	8	0	18	14	90.1	96	11	40	54	First 15 Pitches	.297	317	94	20	0	13	42	29	30	.360	.483
Starter	5.62	19	27	0	66	66	365.1	403	43	166	190	Pitch 16-30	.216	320	69	17	0	5	43	40	56	.307	.316
Reliever	3.32	2	1	2	40	0	89.1	76	7	29	44	Pitch 31-45	.252	274	69	13	1	6	39	29	35	.327	.372
0 Days rest (Relief)	1.35	0	0	1	4	0	13.1	8	1	5	7	Pitch 46+	.292	845	247	48	7	26	126	97	113	.365	.458
1 or 2 Days rest	4.98	2	0	1	23	0	43.1	49	4	16	27	First Pitch	.320	241	77	19	3	8	47	6	0	.337	.523
3+ Days rest	1.93	0	1	0	13	0	32.2	19	2	8	10	Ahead in Count	.231	720	166	32	3	12	72	0	204	.238	.333
vs. AL	5.23	21	26	2	101	64	437.1	460	49	186	227	Behind in Count	.290	466	135	28	1	16	75	125	0	.438	.457
vs. NL	3.63	0	2	0	5	2	17.1	19	1	9	7	Two Strikes	.220	677	149	29	4	17		64	234	.289	.350
Pre-All Star	5.47	9	13	0	52	31	205.2	223	22	96	101	Pre-All Star	.282	791	223	53	3	22	108	96	101	.361	.440
Post-All Star	4.92	12	15	2	54	35	249.0	256	28	99	133	Post-All Star	.265	965	256	45	5	28	142	99	133	.336	.409

Pitcher vs. Batter (career)

Pitches Best Vs.	Avg	AB	H	2B	3B	HR	RBI	BB	SO	OBP	SLG	Pitches Worst Vs.	Avg	AB	H	2B	3B	HR	RBI	BB	SO	OBP	SLG
John Olerud	.000	8	0	0	0	0	1	3	0	.273	.000	Johnny Damon	.625	8	5	0	2	1	6	3	0	.727	1.500
Shawn Green	.083	12	1	0	0	0	1	0	5	.077	.083	Cecil Fielder	.529	17	9	2	0	4	8	1	3	.526	1.353
Jorge Fabregas	.083	12	1	0	0	0	0	0	2	.154	.083	Frank Thomas	.500	12	6	2	0	2	5	2	3	.571	1.167
Ruben Sierra	.091	11	1	0	0	0	0	3	2	.286	.091	J.T. Snow	.500	10	5	2	0	1	1	1	0	.545	1.000
Ken Griffey Jr	.133	15	2	0	0	0	0	2	0	.235	.133	Tino Martinez	.474	19	9	3	0	2	6	0	2	.474	.947

Henry Rodriguez — Expos
Age 30 – Bats Left (flyball hitter)

	Avg	G	AB	R	H	2B	3B	HR	RBI	BB	SO	HBP	GDP	SB	CS	OBP	SLG	IBB	SH	SF	#Pit	#P/PA	GB	FB	G/F
1997 Season	.244	132	476	55	116	28	3	26	83	42	149	2	6	3	3	.306	.479	5	0	3	1980	3.79	112	147	0.76
Last Five Years	.256	502	1628	202	417	98	7	80	273	118	434	7	32	6	5	.307	.472	18	1	13	6671	3.78	443	509	0.87

1997 Season

	Avg	AB	H	2B	3B	HR	RBI	BB	SO	OBP	SLG		Avg	AB	H	2B	3B	HR	RBI	BB	SO	OBP	SLG
vs. Left	.218	133	29	6	0	5	14	15	42	.305	.376	First Pitch	.348	66	23	3	0	6	11	4	0	.386	.667
vs. Right	.254	343	87	22	3	21	69	27	107	.306	.519	Ahead in Count	.349	83	29	8	0	9	23	18	0	.465	.663
Groundball	.263	114	30	9	0	7	17	7	38	.317	.526	Behind in Count	.162	234	38	10	1	10	29	0	129	.165	.342
Flyball	.226	62	14	5	1	3	12	4	21	.273	.484	Two Strikes	.142	253	36	12	1	9	34	20	149	.204	.304
Home	.266	248	66	20	3	14	46	22	71	.328	.540	Batting #4	.204	93	19	6	3	3	9	8	30	.267	.430
Away	.219	228	50	8	0	12	37	20	78	.281	.412	Batting #5	.278	241	67	13	0	14	45	20	74	.331	.506
Day	.276	145	40	10	0	7	21	9	46	.321	.490	Other	.211	142	30	9	0	9	29	14	45	.289	.465
Night	.230	331	76	18	3	19	62	33	103	.300	.474	March/April	.333	96	32	11	1	6	18	3	27	.350	.656
Grass	.264	140	37	7	0	9	25	14	48	.329	.507	May	.323	96	31	8	0	3	16	10	24	.380	.500
Turf	.235	336	79	21	3	17	58	28	101	.296	.462	June	.188	101	19	2	1	7	17	12	36	.274	.436
Pre-All Star	.271	303	82	21	2	16	51	26	92	.325	.512	July	.160	81	13	2	0	6	17	4	32	.200	.407
Post-All Star	.197	173	34	7	1	10	32	16	57	.272	.422	August	.176	34	6	1	0	2	6	3	11	.263	.382
Scoring Posn	.297	111	33	5	1	10	60	16	37	.377	.631	Sept/Oct	.221	68	15	4	1	2	9	10	19	.329	.397
Close & Late	.171	82	14	3	0	3	8	9	28	.261	.317	vs. AL	.194	36	7	0	0	5	7	8	12	.341	.611
None on/out	.192	120	23	8	1	4	4	9	31	.254	.375	vs. NL	.248	440	109	28	3	21	76	34	137	.303	.468

1997 By Position

Position	Avg	AB	H	2B	3B	HR	RBI	BB	SO	OBP	SLG	G	GS	Innings	PO	A	E	DP	Fld Pct	Rng Fctr	In Zone	Outs	Zone Rtg	MLB Zone
As lf	.245	461	113	27	3	25	77	42	144	.309	.479	126	124	1010.2	197	4	3	2	.985	1.79	232	191	.823	.805

Last Five Years

	Avg	AB	H	2B	3B	HR	RBI	BB	SO	OBP	SLG		Avg	AB	H	2B	3B	HR	RBI	BB	SO	OBP	SLG
vs. Left	.220	295	65	15	1	14	45	23	93	.283	.420	First Pitch	.365	244	89	18	0	18	51	11	0	.393	.660
vs. Right	.264	1333	352	83	6	66	228	95	341	.312	.484	Ahead in Count	.324	296	96	26	1	23	82	54	0	.424	.652
Groundball	.233	416	97	23	3	16	55	26	122	.286	.418	Behind in Count	.189	779	147	32	4	25	87	0	360	.192	.336
Flyball	.263	240	63	16	1	12	36	13	59	.303	.488	Two Strikes	.179	837	150	33	3	26	89	53	434	.230	.319
Home	.263	830	218	53	4	45	152	64	223	.316	.499	Batting #3	.266	403	107	25	1	30	81	33	114	.323	.556
Away	.249	798	199	45	3	35	121	54	211	.297	.445	Batting #5	.279	641	179	40	2	25	103	38	164	.319	.465
Day	.292	487	142	36	1	21	75	29	138	.330	.499	Other	.224	584	131	33	4	25	89	47	156	.283	.423
Night	.241	1141	275	62	6	59	198	89	296	.297	.461	March/April	.313	262	82	23	1	18	56	15	70	.348	.615
Grass	.267	793	212	40	2	37	123	54	190	.314	.463	May	.302	387	117	24	2	18	72	36	79	.356	.514
Turf	.246	835	205	58	5	43	150	64	244	.300	.481	June	.237	283	67	14	2	13	44	19	84	.289	.438
Pre-All Star	.276	1007	278	64	5	51	181	73	258	.324	.501	July	.204	280	57	14	1	13	45	14	81	.241	.400
Post-All Star	.224	621	139	34	2	29	92	45	176	.280	.425	August	.210	195	41	8	0	10	30	12	64	.262	.405
Scoring Posn	.288	431	124	25	4	27	194	47	124	.350	.552	Sept/Oct	.240	221	53	15	1	8	26	22	56	.315	.425
Close & Late	.235	277	65	12	1	12	37	28	85	.309	.415	vs. AL	.194	36	7	0	0	5	7	8	12	.341	.611
None on/out	.235	340	80	26	1	14	14	27	80	.295	.441	vs. NL	.258	1592	410	98	7	75	266	110	422	.306	.469

Batter vs. Pitcher (career)

Hits Best Against	Avg	AB	H	2B	3B	HR	RBI	BB	SO	OBP	SLG	Hits Worst Against	Avg	AB	H	2B	3B	HR	RBI	BB	SO	OBP	SLG
Mark Leiter	.476	21	10	3	1	3	9	1	4	.500	1.143	Bobby Jones	.045	22	1	0	0	0	0	1	5	.087	.045
Osvald Fernandez	.417	12	5	1	0	3	7	1	5	.462	1.250	Mike Williams	.071	14	1	1	0	0	0	2	2	.071	.143
Donovan Osborne	.417	12	5	2	0	1	3	0	3	.417	.833	Rod Beck	.077	13	1	0	0	0	0	0	3	.077	.077
Bret Saberhagen	.400	15	6	1	0	2	7	0	2	.375	.867	Pedro Astacio	.083	12	1	1	0	0	1	0	3	.083	.167
Doug Brocail	.400	10	4	1	0	2	4	0	2	.364	1.100	Jeff Brantley	.091	11	1	0	0	0	0	0	5	.091	.091

Ivan Rodriguez — Rangers

Age 26 – Bats Right (groundball hitter)

	Avg	G	AB	R	H	2B	3B	HR	RBI	BB	SO	HBP	GDP	SB	CS	OBP	SLG	IBB	SH	SF	#Pit	#P/PA	GB	FB	G/F
1997 Season	.313	150	597	98	187	34	4	20	77	38	89	8	18	7	3	.360	.484	7	1	4	2198	3.39	255	140	1.82
Last Five Years	.298	669	2564	382	765	160	14	77	353	152	304	27	70	26	15	.341	.462	24	6	25	9252	3.34	1066	673	1.58

1997 Season

	Avg	AB	H	2B	3B	HR	RBI	BB	SO	OBP	SLG		Avg	AB	H	2B	3B	HR	RBI	BB	SO	OBP	SLG
vs. Left	.321	162	52	10	1	5	25	9	25	.360	.488	First Pitch	.339	109	37	5	1	7	20	6	0	.373	.596
vs. Right	.310	435	135	24	3	15	52	29	64	.360	.483	Ahead in Count	.390	118	46	8	2	6	19	13	0	.450	.644
Groundball	.237	139	33	4	3	3	14	10	25	.285	.374	Behind in Count	.243	280	68	16	1	3	24	0	75	.260	.339
Flyball	.313	96	30	8	0	2	10	8	13	.383	.458	Two Strikes	.227	247	56	13	0	4	22	19	89	.298	.328
Home	.347	311	108	17	3	12	47	12	37	.376	.537	Batting #2	.333	517	172	33	4	19	70	29	65	.372	.522
Away	.276	286	79	17	1	8	30	26	52	.344	.427	Batting #6	.143	49	7	0	0	1	2	4	16	.250	.204
Day	.297	118	35	10	1	3	15	9	21	.354	.475	Other	.258	31	8	1	0	0	5	5	8	.351	.290
Night	.317	479	152	24	3	17	62	29	68	.362	.486	March/April	.323	96	31	6	1	2	15	3	10	.350	.469
Grass	.320	537	172	29	3	18	66	32	76	.366	.486	May	.383	107	41	8	1	3	10	7	13	.422	.561
Turf	.250	60	15	5	1	2	11	6	13	.313	.467	June	.330	115	38	10	1	5	14	6	15	.361	.565
Pre-All Star	.340	341	116	26	3	11	40	17	39	.375	.531	July	.281	89	25	5	1	1	8	5	13	.343	.393
Post-All Star	.277	256	71	8	1	9	37	21	50	.342	.422	August	.243	103	25	2	0	3	11	10	29	.322	.350
Scoring Posn	.320	128	41	9	0	2	54	17	21	.405	.438	Sept/Oct	.310	87	27	3	0	6	19	7	9	.358	.552
Close & Late	.362	94	34	2	1	1	24	10	21	.421	.436	vs. AL	.309	538	166	30	4	18	68	31	82	.353	.480
None on/out	.348	115	40	1	6	6	2	13		.364	.583	vs. NL	.356	59	21	4	0	2	9	7	7	.418	.525

1997 By Position

Position	Avg	AB	H	2B	3B	HR	RBI	BB	SO	OBP	SLG	G	GS	Innings	PO	A	E	DP	Fld Pct	Rng Fctr	In Zone	Zone Outs	Zone Rtg	MLB Zone
As c	.312	574	179	34	4	20	73	35	83	.357	.490	143	139	1201.0	822	74	7	11	.992	---	---	---	---	---

Last Five Years

	Avg	AB	H	2B	3B	HR	RBI	BB	SO	OBP	SLG		Avg	AB	H	2B	3B	HR	RBI	BB	SO	OBP	SLG
vs. Left	.305	676	206	42	2	25	104	54	79	.354	.484	First Pitch	.330	430	142	25	3	23	86	17	0	.357	.563
vs. Right	.296	1888	559	118	12	52	249	98	225	.336	.454	Ahead in Count	.364	536	195	40	7	22	86	64	0	.433	.588
Groundball	.280	561	157	29	4	12	59	30	68	.318	.427	Behind in Count	.246	1209	297	70	1	21	128	0	270	.253	.357
Flyball	.259	483	125	34	1	15	63	32	60	.310	.427	Two Strikes	.226	1009	228	49	0	15	100	71	304	.284	.319
Home	.308	1287	396	78	10	41	191	75	144	.349	.479	Batting #2	.311	1282	399	81	7	44	172	74	129	.351	.488
Away	.289	1277	369	82	4	36	162	77	160	.333	.444	Batting #6	.268	523	140	32	0	15	68	22	73	.299	.415
Day	.321	535	172	35	2	16	68	33	60	.365	.484	Other	.298	759	226	47	7	18	113	56	102	.352	.449
Night	.292	2029	593	125	12	61	285	119	244	.335	.456	March/April	.310	352	109	28	2	7	59	28	43	.365	.460
Grass	.300	2255	676	138	13	69	314	131	262	.342	.464	May	.307	469	144	30	6	11	54	30	58	.352	.467
Turf	.288	309	89	22	1	8	39	21	42	.333	.443	June	.320	441	141	31	3	18	70	22	53	.352	.526
Pre-All Star	.313	1421	445	98	12	43	200	86	168	.356	.490	July	.317	473	150	28	2	19	62	28	47	.362	.505
Post-All Star	.280	1143	320	62	2	34	153	66	136	.322	.427	August	.281	445	125	29	0	13	59	27	56	.328	.434
Scoring Posn	.283	644	182	44	1	10	251	67	82	.350	.401	Sept/Oct	.250	384	96	14	1	9	49	17	47	.281	.362
Close & Late	.307	371	114	17	3	5	63	33	60	.371	.410	vs. AL	.297	2505	744	156	14	75	344	145	297	.339	.460
None on/out	.319	505	161	33	3	26	26	21	50	.350	.550	vs. NL	.356	59	21	4	0	2	9	7	7	.418	.525

Batter vs. Pitcher (career)

Hits Best Against	Avg	AB	H	2B	3B	HR	RBI	BB	SO	OBP	SLG	Hits Worst Against	Avg	AB	H	2B	3B	HR	RBI	BB	SO	OBP	SLG
Rick Aguilera	.500	14	7	1	0	2	5	1	0	.533	1.000	Pat Mahomes	.000	11	0	0	0	0	1	0	0	.000	.000
Jamie Moyer	.481	27	13	5	0	2	6	1	0	.500	.889	Brian Williams	.000	10	0	0	0	0	2	1	0	.091	.000
Brad Radke	.476	21	10	2	1	4	6	1	1	.500	1.238	Shawn Boskie	.091	11	1	1	0	0	0	0	2	.091	.182
Brian Anderson	.455	11	5	2	0	0	0	2	1	.538	.636	David Cone	.133	30	4	2	0	0	1	0	3	.133	.200
Carlos Reyes	.429	14	6	4	0	0	3	0	1	.429	.714	Kevin Tapani	.143	14	2	0	0	0	0	0	0	.143	.143

Nerio Rodriguez — Orioles

Age 25 – Pitches Right (flyball pitcher)

	ERA	W	L	Sv	G	GS	IP	BB	SO	Avg	H	2B	3B	HR	RBI	OBP	SLG	GF	IR	IRS	Hld	SvOp	SB	CS	GB	FB	G/F
1997 Season	4.91	2	1	0	6	2	22.0	8	11	.250	21	7	1	2	15	.309	.429	1	1	0	0	1	0	0	28	32	0.88
Career (1996-1997)	4.66	2	2	0	14	3	38.2	15	23	.257	39	10	1	4	25	.322	.414	3	10	3	0	1	2	0	49	60	0.82

1997 Season

	ERA	W	L	Sv	G	GS	IP	H	HR	BB	SO		Avg	AB	H	2B	3B	HR	RBI	BB	SO	OBP	SLG
Home	4.15	1	1	0	3	1	13.0	13	0	4	9	vs. Left	.286	42	12	3	0	2	8	5	6	.347	.500
Away	6.00	1	0	0	3	1	9.0	8	2	4	2	vs. Right	.214	42	9	4	1	0	7	3	5	.271	.357

403

Rich Rodriguez — Giants
Age 35 – Pitches Left

	ERA	W	L	Sv	G	GS	IP	BB	SO	Avg	H	2B	3B	HR	RBI	OBP	SLG	GF	IR	IRS	Hld	SvOp	SB	CS	GB	FB	G/F
1997 Season	3.17	4	3	1	71	0	65.1	21	32	.264	65	9	3	7	35	.325	.411	15	64	19	14	5	0	4	106	65	1.63
Last Five Years	3.63	9	12	4	198	0	203.1	80	118	.259	200	33	6	23	105	.332	.407	51	145	41	39	15	8	8	284	224	1.27

1997 Season

	ERA	W	L	Sv	G	GS	IP	H	HR	BB	SO		Avg	AB	H	2B	3B	HR	RBI	BB	SO	OBP	SLG
Home	2.73	3	2	0	36	0	33.0	32	3	13	12	vs. Left	.314	102	32	4	3	3	14	9	13	.375	.500
Away	3.62	1	1	1	35	0	32.1	33	4	8	20	vs. Right	.229	144	33	5	0	4	21	12	19	.288	.347
Day	3.19	1	2	0	39	0	36.2	36	4	12	21	Inning 1-6	.229	35	8	1	1	0	7	8	7	.372	.314
Night	3.14	3	1	1	32	0	28.2	29	3	9	11	Inning 7+	.270	211	57	8	2	7	28	13	25	.316	.427
Grass	3.29	4	3	0	59	0	54.2	53	7	16	21	None on	.252	131	33	7	1	5	5	9	20	.305	.435
Turf	2.53	0	0	1	12	0	10.2	12	0	5	11	Runners on	.278	115	32	2	2	2	30	12	12	.346	.383
March/April	1.54	2	1	0	12	0	11.2	10	0	3	8	Scoring Posn	.293	75	22	2	1	1	28	10	7	.376	.413
May	0.53	1	0	1	17	0	17.0	10	0	7	7	Close & Late	.223	103	23	3	2	2	10	9	12	.286	.350
June	4.35	1	1	0	13	0	10.1	15	3	5	3	None on/out	.222	54	12	2	1	1	1	5	5	.250	.352
July	8.71	0	0	0	11	0	10.1	13	4	3	4	vs. 1st Batr (relief)	.284	67	19	1	3	1	10	3	9	.324	.433
August	2.00	1	0	0	9	0	9.0	11	0	2	8	1st Inning Pitched	.269	208	56	7	3	6	33	17	25	.327	.418
Sept/Oct	3.86	0	0	0	9	0	7.0	6	0	1	2	First Pitch	.281	196	55	8	3	7	30	12	25	.325	.459
Starter	0.00	0	0	0	0	0	0.0	0	0	0	0	Pitch 16-30	.188	48	9	1	0	0	5	9	6	.316	.208
Reliever	3.17	4	3	1	71	0	65.1	65	7	21	32	Pitch 31-45	.500	2	1	0	0	0	0	0	1	.500	.500
0 Days rest (Relief)	3.09	2	0	1	25	0	23.1	28	4	6	9	Pitch 46+	.000	0	0	0	0	0	0	0	0	.000	.000
1 or 2 Days rest	3.56	2	1	0	33	0	30.1	26	2	12	15	First Pitch	.314	35	11	3	1	0	6	4	0	.385	.457
3+ Days rest	2.31	0	2	0	13	0	11.2	11	1	3	8	Ahead in Count	.198	111	22	2	2	2	11	0	28	.198	.306
vs. AL	3.18	1	1	0	6	0	5.2	7	1	1	1	Behind in Count	.451	51	23	2	0	3	10	11	0	.548	.667
vs. NL	3.17	3	2	1	65	0	59.2	58	6	20	31	Two Strikes	.172	99	17	1	2	1	11	6	32	.219	.253
Pre-All Star	1.76	3	3	1	44	0	41.0	35	3	16	19	Pre-All Star	.236	148	35	3	2	3	18	16	19	.315	.345
Post-All Star	5.55	1	0	0	27	0	24.1	30	4	5	13	Post-All Star	.306	98	30	6	1	4	17	5	13	.340	.510

Last Five Years

	ERA	W	L	Sv	G	GS	IP	H	HR	BB	SO		Avg	AB	H	2B	3B	HR	RBI	BB	SO	OBP	SLG
Home	3.88	6	5	2	99	0	99.2	104	11	47	56	vs. Left	.263	262	69	8	4	7	31	28	36	.339	.405
Away	3.39	3	7	2	99	0	103.2	96	12	33	62	vs. Right	.257	509	131	25	2	16	74	52	82	.328	.409
Day	3.05	2	3	1	76	0	73.2	68	7	26	48	Inning 1-6	.239	109	26	4	1	2	21	18	19	.352	.349
Night	3.96	7	9	3	122	0	129.2	132	16	54	70	Inning 7+	.263	662	174	29	5	21	84	62	99	.328	.417
Grass	3.23	7	4	2	125	0	125.1	122	16	44	60	None on	.243	415	101	18	4	11	11	34	68	.304	.386
Turf	4.27	2	8	2	73	0	78.0	78	7	36	58	Runners on	.278	356	99	15	2	12	94	46	50	.363	.433
March/April	3.28	4	2	2	36	0	35.2	31	1	15	24	Scoring Posn	.279	226	63	8	2	6	77	38	31	.386	.412
May	2.55	1	5	1	45	0	42.1	37	3	13	30	Close & Late	.257	304	78	9	2	10	40	33	46	.331	.398
June	2.19	2	1	0	36	0	37.0	44	4	14	19	None on/out	.247	182	45	6	3	5	5	10	30	.290	.396
July	7.75	2	1	0	33	0	33.2	41	10	12	15	vs. 1st Batr (relief)	.250	185	50	4	5	6	25	11	33	.315	.443
August	2.78	2	1	0	27	0	32.1	26	3	19	19	1st Inning Pitched	.270	581	157	23	6	18	87	61	88	.343	.423
Sept/Oct	3.63	0	1	1	21	0	22.1	21	2	7	11	First 15 Pitches	.273	556	152	24	6	19	79	43	79	.328	.441
Starter	0.00	0	0	0	0	0	0.0	0	0	0	0	Pitch 16-30	.200	175	35	6	0	4	17	32	32	.329	.303
Reliever	3.63	9	12	4	198	0	203.1	200	23	80	118	Pitch 31-45	.303	33	10	3	0	0	9	3	6	.361	.394
0 Days rest (Relief)	3.53	5	2	2	57	0	51.0	52	9	17	21	Pitch 46+	.429	7	3	0	0	0	0	2	1	.556	.429
1 or 2 Days rest	3.52	4	2	2	97	0	99.2	95	8	44	64	First Pitch	.321	106	34	7	2	4	15	15	0	.410	.538
3+ Days rest	3.93	0	4	0	44	0	52.2	53	6	19	33	Ahead in Count	.191	346	66	10	3	7	34	0	106	.193	.293
vs. AL	3.18	1	1	0	6	0	5.2	7	1	1	1	Behind in Count	.350	180	63	9	1	9	36	36	0	.456	.561
vs. NL	3.64	8	11	4	192	0	197.2	193	22	79	117	Two Strikes	.193	331	64	12	3	5	33	29	118	.260	.293
Pre-All Star	3.24	7	10	3	126	0	125.0	126	12	47	76	Pre-All Star	.266	473	126	17	4	12	62	47	76	.337	.395
Post-All Star	4.25	2	2	1	72	0	78.1	74	11	33	42	Post-All Star	.248	298	74	14	2	11	43	33	42	.324	.426

Pitcher vs. Batter (career)

Pitches Best Vs.	Avg	AB	H	2B	3B	HR	RBI	BB	SO	OBP	SLG	Pitches Worst Vs.	Avg	AB	H	2B	3B	HR	RBI	BB	SO	OBP	SLG
Steve Finley	.063	16	1	0	0	1	1	2	3	.167		Marquis Grissom	.462	13	6	0	0	1	3	0	1	.500	.692
Dave Martinez	.100	10	1	0	0	0	0	1	5	.182	.100	Craig Biggio	.429	14	6	3	0	0	2	6	0	.600	.643
Jay Bell	.125	16	2	1	0	0	0	1	5	.176	.188	Brett Butler	.421	19	8	0	0	0	0	3	0	.500	.421
Darren Daulton	.167	12	2	0	0	1	1	2		.231	.167	Jeff Blauser	.400	15	6	3	0	0	1	2	0	.471	.600
Will Clark	.167	12	2	0	0	3	1	2		.231	.167	Bobby Bonilla	.308	13	4	2	0	1	4	3		.357	.692

Kenny Rogers — Yankees
Age 33 – Pitches Left

	ERA	W	L	Sv	G	GS	IP	BB	SO	Avg	H	2B	3B	HR	RBI	OBP	SLG	CG	ShO	Sup	QS	#P/S	SB	CS	GB	FB	G/F
1997 Season	5.65	6	7	0	31	22	145.0	62	78	.280	161	26	3	18	86	.354	.429	1	0	5.52	4	92	3	6	246	146	1.68
Last Five Years	4.36	62	40	0	151	140	907.2	344	570	.280	911	72	16	102	416	.329	.405	17	4	5.45	71	102	20	34	1353	964	1.40

1997 Season

	ERA	W	L	Sv	G	GS	IP	H	HR	BB	SO		Avg	AB	H	2B	3B	HR	RBI	BB	SO	OBP	SLG
Home	5.57	3	4	0	15	10	72.2	79	8	36	47	vs. Left	.238	101	24	3	0	3	11	13	17	.339	.356
Away	5.72	3	3	0	16	12	72.1	82	10	26	31	vs. Right	.288	475	137	23	3	15	75	49	61	.358	.444
Day	5.95	2	2	0	11	7	42.1	46	5	19	29	Inning 1-6	.284	489	139	22	2	17	83	54	61	.361	.442
Night	5.52	4	5	0	20	15	102.2	115	13	43	49	Inning 7+	.253	87	22	4	1	1	3	8	17	.316	.356
Grass	5.41	6	5	0	28	19	131.1	141	17	59	75	None on	.248	335	83	16	1	7	7	33	50	.319	.364
Turf	7.90	0	2	0	3	3	13.2	20	1	3	3	Runners on	.324	241	78	10	2	11	79	29	28	.401	.519
March/April	5.81	2	1	0	5	5	31.0	29	4	14	19	Scoring Posn	.354	127	45	7	1	6	66	18	11	.434	.567
May	5.20	1	2	0	5	5	27.2	28	2	10	15	Close & Late	.208	24	5	1	0	2	3	5	3	.367	.250
June	6.67	1	1	0	7	4	28.1	37	3	18	15	None on/out	.245	147	36	4	0	1	1	11	25	.306	.293
July	1.00	0	0	0	3	0	9.0	6	1	2	5	vs. 1st Batr (relief)	.000	9	0	0	0	0	0	0	2	.000	.000
August	5.74	1	1	0	5	3	15.2	21	1	11	12	1st Inning Pitched	.270	122	33	3	1	4	17	9	19	.318	.410

1997 Season

	ERA	W	L	Sv	G	GS	IP	H	HR	BB	SO		Avg	AB	H	2B	3B	HR	RBI	BB	SO	OBP	SLG
Sept/Oct	6.21	1	2	0	6	5	33.1	40	7	7	12	First 75 Pitches	.269	464	125	20	2	15	66	47	63	.344	.418
Starter	6.27	6	6	0	22	22	120.2	138	17	49	60	Pitch 76-90	.317	63	20	4	0	1	9	9	9	.403	.429
Reliever	2.59	0	1	0	9	0	24.1	23	1	13	18	Pitch 91-105	.326	43	14	2	1	1	10	4	4	.375	.488
0-3 Days Rest (Start)	9.00	1	0	0	2	2	9.0	10	1	8	7	Pitch 106+	.333	6	2	0	0	1	1	2	2	.500	.833
4 Days Rest	6.33	3	1	0	11	11	58.1	71	8	25	31	First Pitch	.370	73	27	6	0	1	10	1	0	.395	.493
5+ Days Rest	5.74	2	5	0	9	9	53.1	57	8	16	22	Ahead in Count	.199	231	46	8	1	5	20	0	64	.214	.307
vs. AL	5.70	6	6	0	28	20	131.0	146	17	54	73	Behind in Count	.351	154	54	8	2	9	34	29	0	.449	.604
vs. NL	5.14	0	1	0	3	2	14.0	15	1	8	5	Two Strikes	.178	241	43	10	1	6	22	32	78	.282	.303
Pre-All Star	5.90	4	4	0	17	14	87.0	94	9	42	49	Pre-All Star	.273	344	94	15	2	9	53	42	49	.356	.407
Post-All Star	5.28	2	3	0	14	8	58.0	67	9	20	29	Post-All Star	.289	232	67	11	1	9	33	20	29	.352	.461

Last Five Years

	ERA	W	L	Sv	G	GS	IP	H	HR	BB	SO		Avg	AB	H	2B	3B	HR	RBI	BB	SO	OBP	SLG
Home	4.20	36	19	0	79	73	487.0	487	46	188	311	vs. Left	.223	506	113	16	4	16	57	53	112	.305	.366
Away	4.56	26	21	0	72	67	420.2	424	56	156	259	vs. Right	.266	2995	798	154	12	86	359	291	458	.333	.412
Day	5.00	20	13	0	45	41	252.0	264	35	94	135	Inning 1-6	.260	2963	771	139	15	90	379	303	472	.332	.408
Night	4.12	42	27	0	106	99	655.2	647	67	250	435	Inning 7+	.260	538	140	31	1	12	37	41	98	.310	.388
Grass	4.49	57	34	0	135	124	806.1	811	93	315	508	None on	.244	2109	515	101	8	59	59	182	355	.307	.384
Turf	3.38	5	6	0	16	16	101.1	100	9	29	62	Runners on	.284	1392	396	69	8	43	357	162	215	.360	.438
March/April	4.50	7	5	0	19	17	106.0	95	12	47	69	Scoring Posn	.282	758	214	41	3	22	297	103	123	.365	.431
May	4.17	13	8	0	28	28	172.2	173	12	68	109	Close & Late	.258	229	59	12	0	4	14	23	37	.324	.362
June	4.99	12	7	0	31	28	182.1	204	20	76	113	None on/out	.252	922	232	45	2	30	30	76	150	.313	.402
July	3.87	7	6	0	25	22	151.1	142	20	59	118	vs. 1st Batr (relief)	.000	11	0	0	0	0	0	0	3	.000	.000
August	5.10	13	8	0	26	24	150.0	158	20	55	92	1st Inning Pitched	.282	589	166	25	2	19	83	67	99	.356	.428
Sept/Oct	3.47	10	6	0	22	21	145.1	139	18	39	69	First 75 Pitches	.257	2516	646	120	11	75	298	248	393	.327	.403
Starter	4.42	62	39	0	140	140	881.2	888	101	331	550	Pitch 76-90	.275	415	114	21	2	13	54	44	76	.342	.429
Reliever	2.42	0	1	0	11	0	26.0	23	1	13	20	Pitch 91-105	.267	344	92	15	3	12	49	30	53	.328	.433
0-3 Days Rest (Start)	4.46	6	2	0	12	12	78.2	69	10	29	50	Pitch 106+	.261	226	59	14	0	2	15	22	48	.324	.350
4 Days Rest	4.38	38	21	0	86	86	548.1	554	64	205	342	First Pitch	.340	500	170	31	1	17	69	6	0	.351	.508
5+ Days Rest	4.49	18	16	0	42	42	254.2	265	27	97	158	Ahead in Count	.180	1415	254	48	4	22	100	0	469	.187	.266
vs. AL	4.35	62	39	0	148	138	893.2	896	101	336	565	Behind in Count	.340	911	310	55	8	49	173	188	0	.450	.580
vs. NL	5.14	0	1	0	3	2	14.0	15	1	8	5	Two Strikes	.178	1476	263	59	5	21	110	150	570	.259	.268
Pre-All Star	4.58	34	22	0	86	81	511.1	523	53	213	332	Pre-All Star	.264	1979	523	104	12	53	244	213	332	.339	.409
Post-All Star	4.09	28	18	0	65	59	396.1	388	49	131	238	Post-All Star	.255	1522	388	66	4	49	172	131	238	.316	.400

Pitcher vs. Batter (career)

Pitches Best Vs.	Avg	AB	H	2B	3B	HR	RBI	BB	SO	OBP	SLG	Pitches Worst Vs.	Avg	AB	H	2B	3B	HR	RBI	BB	SO	OBP	SLG
Gary Thurman	.000	9	0	0	0	0	1	2	3	.167	.000	Luis Rivera	.500	12	6	3	1	0	3	0	2	.500	.917
Ray Durham	.045	22	1	0	0	0	0	1	9	.087	.045	Alex Rodriguez	.500	12	6	1	0	2	5	0	2	.500	1.083
Ozzie Guillen	.067	15	1	0	0	0	2	0	0	.067	.067	Bernie Williams	.462	13	6	2	0	1	6	3	1	.563	.846
Ron Coomer	.083	12	1	0	0	0	0	0	2	.083	.083	Dave Hollins	.455	11	5	0	0	2	3	4	1	.600	1.000
Gary DiSarcina	.086	35	3	1	0	0	2	0	1	.086	.114	Jack Voigt	.364	11	4	0	0	3	4	0	0	.417	1.182

Dan Rohrmeier — Mariners
Age 33 – Bats Right

	Avg	G	AB	R	H	2B	3B	HR	RBI	BB	SO	HBP	GDP	SB	CS	OBP	SLG	IBB	SH	SF	#Pit	#P/PA	GB	FB	G/F
1997 Season	.333	7	9	4	3	0	0	0	2	2	4	0	0	0	0	.455	.333	0	0	0	47	4.27	3	1	3.00

1997 Season

	Avg	AB	H	2B	3B	HR	RBI	BB	SO		Avg	AB	H	2B	3B	HR	RBI	BB	SO	OBP	SLG
vs. Left	.500	4	2	0	0	0	1	2	2	.667	.500	Scoring Posn	.667	3	2	0	0	0	2	1	1	.750	.667
vs. Right	.200	5	1	0	0	0	1	0	2	.200	.200	Close & Late	.333	3	1	0	0	0	1	0	2	.333	.333

Mel Rojas — Mets
Age 31 – Pitches Right

	ERA	W	L	Sv	G	GS	IP	BB	SO	Avg	H	2B	3B	HR	RBI	OBP	SLG	GF	IR	IRS	Hld	SvOp	SB	CS	GB	FB	G/F
1997 Season	4.64	0	6	15	77	0	85.1	36	93	.241	78	13	2	15	54	.329	.433	50	24	11	7	22	8	2	95	83	1.14
Last Five Years	3.63	16	24	107	334	0	406.1	144	378	.233	354	65	8	39	212	.307	.363	214	154	57	44	138	44	4	522	394	1.32

1997 Season

	ERA	W	L	Sv	G	GS	IP	H	HR	BB	SO		Avg	AB	H	2B	3B	HR	RBI	BB	SO	OBP	SLG
Home	4.01	0	5	10	44	0	51.2	49	8	20	62	vs. Left	.258	159	41	8	0	8	28	19	45	.339	.459
Away	5.61	0	1	5	33	0	33.2	29	7	16	31	vs. Right	.226	164	37	5	2	7	26	17	48	.319	.409
Day	3.53	0	2	8	36	0	35.2	25	6	11	34	Inning 1-6	.000	3	0	0	0	0	0	1	1	.400	.000
Night	5.44	0	4	7	41	0	49.2	53	9	25	59	Inning 7+	.244	320	78	13	2	15	54	35	92	.328	.438
Grass	4.68	0	6	13	68	0	75.0	73	12	31	83	None on	.225	178	40	6	2	7	7	20	55	.317	.399
Turf	4.35	0	0	2	9	0	10.1	5	3	5	10	Runners on	.262	145	38	7	0	8	47	16	38	.343	.476
March/April	5.40	0	1	2	9	0	8.1	8	1	3	7	Scoring Posn	.289	90	26	6	0	6	43	10	24	.359	.556
May	4.24	0	1	3	16	0	17.0	14	4	11	17	Close & Late	.253	190	48	6	2	9	35	23	55	.335	.447
June	5.40	0	0	1	11	0	11.2	13	3	6	14	None on/out	.250	72	18	4	2	4	4	10	22	.357	.528
July	3.78	0	2	7	14	0	16.2	16	2	7	16	vs. 1st Batr (relief)	.262	65	17	5	0	4	11	10	16	.364	.523
August	4.74	0	1	0	16	0	19.0	15	3	7	20	1st Inning Pitched	.229	258	59	9	0	11	40	32	79	.328	.391
Sept/Oct	4.97	0	1	2	11	0	12.2	12	2	2	19	First 15 Pitches	.258	209	54	10	1	9	29	23	60	.349	.445
Starter	0.00	0	0	0	0	0	0.0	0	0	0	0	Pitch 16-30	.214	98	21	2	1	5	21	11	27	.294	.408
Reliever	4.64	0	6	15	77	0	85.1	78	15	36	93	Pitch 31-45	.188	16	3	1	0	1	4	2	6	.278	.438
0 Days rest (Relief)	4.13	0	2	4	20	0	24.0	17	4	12	25	Pitch 46+	.000	0	0	0	0	0	0	0	0	.000	.000
1 or 2 Days rest	4.78	0	2	10	46	0	49.0	47	11	19	59	First Pitch	.378	45	17	0	1	5	10	1	0	.391	.756
3+ Days rest	5.11	0	2	1	11	0	12.1	14	0	5	9	Ahead in Count	.181	182	33	7	0	5	21	0	77	.198	.302

1997 Season

	ERA	W	L	Sv	G	GS	IP	H	HR	BB	SO		Avg	AB	H	2B	3B	HR	RBI	BB	SO	OBP	SLG
vs. AL	0.00	0	0	2	8	0	8.1	4	0	1	11	Behind in Count	.362	47	17	3	0	4	14	21	0	.571	.681
vs. NL	5.14	0	6	13	69	0	77.0	74	15	35	82	Two Strikes	.155	181	28	6	1	3	22	14	93	.222	.249
Pre-All Star	4.46	0	2	9	39	0	40.1	36	8	22	42	Pre-All Star	.240	150	36	5	0	8	24	22	42	.356	.433
Post-All Star	4.80	0	4	6	38	0	45.0	42	7	14	51	Post-All Star	.243	173	42	8	2	7	30	14	51	.304	.434

Last Five Years

	ERA	W	L	Sv	G	GS	IP	H	HR	BB	SO		Avg	AB	H	2B	3B	HR	RBI	BB	SO	OBP	SLG
Home	3.83	11	12	52	166	0	206.2	177	23	72	194	vs. Left	.236	772	182	32	6	22	110	87	197	.314	.378
Away	3.43	5	12	55	168	0	199.2	177	16	72	184	vs. Right	.230	747	172	33	2	17	102	57	181	.300	.348
Day	4.11	6	10	36	138	0	138.0	121	14	49	117	Inning 1-6	.214	28	6	4	0	0	12	6	7	.359	.357
Night	3.39	10	14	71	217	0	268.1	233	25	95	261	Inning 7+	.233	1491	348	61	8	39	200	138	371	.306	.364
Grass	3.84	3	11	49	154	0	178.1	164	19	62	185	None on	.231	796	184	30	5	23		76	202	.309	.368
Turf	3.47	13	13	58	180	0	228.0	190	20	82	193	Runners on	.235	723	170	35	3	16	189	68	176	.304	.358
March/April	3.96	4	3	17	45	0	52.1	49	4	20	47	Scoring Posn	.253	431	109	25	2	12	173	51	105	.332	.404
May	3.48	3	7	22	70	0	88.0	69	9	40	78	Close & Late	.226	933	211	34	4	24	124	94	241	.302	.348
June	4.63	5	5	8	56	0	72.0	70	10	24	59	None on/out	.259	340	88	14	4	11	11	39	78	.344	.421
July	3.79	1	5	27	61	0	73.2	77	6	23	77	vs. 1st Batr (relief)	.250	292	73	15	2	9	32	29	71	.326	.408
August	2.76	2	2	15	55	0	71.2	46	5	23	65	1st Inning Pitched	.231	1120	259	47	4	24	162	109	279	.308	.345
Sept/Oct	3.14	1	2	18	47	0	48.2	43	5	14	52	First 15 Pitches	.238	956	228	42	4	22	114	85	226	.309	.360
Starter	0.00	0	0	0	0	0	0.0	0	0	0	0	Pitch 16-30	.219	470	103	20	4	12	77	53	117	.306	.355
Reliever	3.63	16	24	107	334	0	406.1	354	39	144	378	Pitch 31-45	.250	92	23	3	0	5	21	6	35	.296	.446
0 Days rest (Relief)	3.79	2	6	39	81	0	92.2	81	11	38	90	Pitch 46+	.000	1	0	0	0	0	0	0	0	.000	.000
1 or 2 Days rest	3.69	11	14	55	189	0	231.2	204	22	81	222	First Pitch	.265	219	58	11	1	8	38	9	0	.307	.434
3+ Days rest	3.29	3	4	13	64	0	82.0	69	6	25	66	Ahead in Count	.187	819	153	31	2	13	83	0	334	.196	.277
vs. AL	0.00	0	0	2	8	0	8.1	4	0	1	11	Behind in Count	.339	251	85	12	4	11	50	69	0	.483	.550
vs. NL	3.71	16	24	105	326	0	398.0	350	39	143	367	Two Strikes	.165	808	133	29	1	11	80	65	378	.232	.244
Pre-All Star	4.01	13	16	56	188	0	233.1	206	25	91	209	Pre-All Star	.238	866	206	38	5	25	126	91	209	.320	.380
Post-All Star	3.12	3	8	51	146	0	173.0	148	14	53	169	Post-All Star	.227	653	148	27	3	14	86	53	169	.289	.342

Pitcher vs. Batter (career)

Pitches Best Vs.	Avg	AB	H	2B	3B	HR	RBI	BB	SO	OBP	SLG	Pitches Worst Vs.	Avg	AB	H	2B	3B	HR	RBI	BB	SO	OBP	SLG
Joe Orsulak	.000	10	0	0	0	0	0	0	2	.091	.000	Andres Galarraga	.750	12	9	3	0	1	5	0	2	.750	1.250
Tom Pagnozzi	.071	14	1	0	0	0	0	0	3	.071	.071	Hal Morris	.588	17	10	2	0	1	3	0	1	.556	.882
Reggie Sanders	.077	13	1	0	0	0	1	4		.143	.077	Gary Sheffield	.385	13	5	4	0	1	3	4	1	.556	.692
Mike Piazza	.077	13	1	0	0	0	1	1	7	.143	.077	Todd Zeile	.368	19	7	1	0	2	11	3	2	.440	.737
Luis Gonzalez	.083	12	1	0	0	0	0	2		.083	.083	Jeff Bagwell	.357	14	5	1	0	1	5	4		.524	.643

Scott Rolen — Phillies
Age 23 – Bats Right

	Avg	G	AB	R	H	2B	3B	HR	RBI	BB	SO	HBP	GDP	SB	CS	OBP	SLG	IBB	SH	SF	#Pit	#P/PA	GB	FB	G/F
1997 Season	.283	156	561	93	159	35	3	21	92	76	138	13	6	16	6	.377	.469	4	0	7	2594	3.95	178	156	1.14
Career (1996-1997)	.278	193	691	103	192	42	3	25	110	89	165	14	10	16	8	.367	.456	4	0	9	3118	3.88	227	186	1.22

1997 Season

	Avg	AB	H	2B	3B	HR	RBI	BB	SO	OBP	SLG		Avg	AB	H	2B	3B	HR	RBI	BB	SO	OBP	SLG
vs. Left	.282	131	37	11	0	3	24	21	33	.378	.435	First Pitch	.403	67	27	10	1	1	14	3	0	.427	.627
vs. Right	.284	430	122	24	3	18	68	55	105	.377	.479	Ahead in Count	.350	120	42	9	1	8	22	39	0	.524	.642
Groundball	.342	76	26	2	1	4	16	13	13	.446	.553	Behind in Count	.210	248	52	8	0	8	37	0	109	.217	.339
Flyball	.258	89	23	5	1	4	15	19	28	.387	.472	Two Strikes	.189	286	54	10	1	6	38	34	138	.280	.294
Home	.279	265	74	20	1	11	46	42	57	.382	.487	Batting #3	.303	185	56	12	2	5	27	20	48	.379	.470
Away	.287	296	85	15	2	10	46	34	81	.364	.453	Batting #4	.274	288	79	20	1	15	55	46	72	.380	.507
Day	.257	175	45	7	0	6	23	20	46	.337	.400	Other	.273	88	24	3	0	1	10	10	18	.366	.341
Night	.295	386	114	28	3	15	69	56	92	.395	.500	March/April	.282	85	24	3	0	1	10	9	18	.371	.353
Grass	.287	216	62	9	1	10	36	28	57	.372	.477	May	.309	110	34	6	2	5	18	10	22	.374	.536
Turf	.281	345	97	26	2	11	56	48	81	.381	.464	June	.216	88	19	8	1	2	15	14	23	.327	.398
Pre-All Star	.284	306	87	20	3	10	48	36	67	.368	.467	July	.363	91	33	9	0	5	19	22	19	.478	.626
Post-All Star	.282	255	72	15	0	11	44	40	71	.388	.471	August	.284	81	23	5	0	4	16	8	20	.372	.494
Scoring Posn	.321	159	51	11	2	5	65	27	33	.413	.509	Sept/Oct	.245	106	26	4	0	4	14	13	36	.339	.396
Close & Late	.278	72	20	5	1	2	12	7	19	.341	.458	vs. AL	.339	56	19	2	1	3	8	6	18	.406	.571
None on/out	.256	133	34	4	1	2	2	14	34	.331	.346	vs. NL	.277	505	140	33	2	18	84	70	120	.374	.457

1997 By Position

Position	Avg	AB	H	2B	3B	HR	RBI	BB	SO	OBP	SLG	G	GS	Innings	PO	A	E	DP	Fld Pct	Rng Fctr	In Zone	Zone Outs	Zone Rtg	MLB Zone
As 3b	.283	561	159	35	3	21	92	76	138	.377	.469	155	155	1337.0	144	290	24	30	.948	2.92	406	342	.842	.801

Mandy Romero — Padres
Age 30 – Bats Both

	Avg	G	AB	R	H	2B	3B	HR	RBI	BB	SO	HBP	GDP	SB	CS	OBP	SLG	IBB	SH	SF	#Pit	#P/PA	GB	FB	G/F
1997 Season	.208	21	48	7	10	0	0	2	4	2	18	0	1	1	0	.240	.333	0	0	0	182	3.64	10	11	0.91

1997 Season

	Avg	AB	H	2B	3B	HR	RBI	BB	SO	OBP	SLG		Avg	AB	H	2B	3B	HR	RBI	BB	SO	OBP	SLG
vs. Left	.200	5	1	0	0	0	0	1	2	.333	.200	Scoring Posn	.300	10	3	0	0	0	2	1	4	.364	.300
vs. Right	.209	43	9	0	0	2	4	1	16	.227	.349	Close & Late	.143	7	1	0	0	0	0	0	4	.143	.143

Jose Rosado — Royals

Age 23 – Pitches Left (flyball pitcher)

	ERA	W	L	Sv	G	GS	IP	BB	SO	Avg	H	2B	3B	HR	RBI	OBP	SLG	CG	ShO	Sup	QS	#P/S	SB	CS	GB	FB	G/F
1997 Season	4.69	9	12	0	33	33	203.1	73	129	.264	208	34	4	26	92	.326	.417	2	0	4.56	15	99	10	3	255	268	0.95
Career (1996-1997)	4.18	17	18	0	49	49	310.0	99	193	.259	309	56	7	33	126	.316	.401	4	1	4.56	25	99	16	8	382	392	0.97

1997 Season

	ERA	W	L	Sv	G	GS	IP	H	HR	BB	SO		Avg	AB	H	2B	3B	HR	RBI	BB	SO	OBP	SLG
Home	4.33	5	6	0	14	14	95.2	94	12	30	49	vs. Left	.248	145	36	6	2	7	17	18	33	.325	.462
Away	5.02	4	6	0	19	19	107.2	114	14	43	80	vs. Right	.268	642	172	28	2	19	75	55	96	.326	.407
Day	4.72	3	4	0	10	10	55.1	57	6	23	39	Inning 1-6	.267	692	185	32	4	21	81	63	116	.327	.416
Night	4.68	6	8	0	23	23	148.0	151	20	50	90	Inning 7+	.242	95	23	2	0	5	11	10	13	.314	.421
Grass	5.06	8	10	0	28	28	172.2	179	24	64	105	None on	.260	473	123	18	3	23	23	39	82	.322	.457
Turf	2.64	1	2	0	5	5	30.2	29	2	9	24	Runners on	.271	314	85	16	1	3	69	34	47	.331	.357
March/April	2.59	1	0	0	5	5	31.1	30	4	10	18	Scoring Posn	.241	162	39	8	1	0	60	19	25	.302	.302
May	3.83	2	3	0	6	6	42.1	32	3	17	30	Close & Late	.220	59	13	1	0	2	6	8	8	.313	.339
June	3.27	4	1	0	6	6	44.0	37	5	9	22	None on/out	.244	205	50	5	1	11	11	21	36	.320	.439
July	5.23	0	3	0	5	5	31.0	31	4	12	24	vs. 1st Batr (relief)	.000	0	0	0	0	0	0	0	0	.000	.000
August	7.03	2	3	0	6	6	32.0	44	8	10	18	1st Inning Pitched	.248	129	32	5	0	2	17	18	24	.338	.333
Sept/Oct	7.94	0	2	0	5	5	22.2	34	2	15	17	First 75 Pitches	.262	581	152	23	3	20	66	53	97	.324	.415
Starter	4.69	9	12	0	33	33	203.1	208	26	73	129	Pitch 76-90	.316	98	31	5	1	4	17	11	15	.378	.510
Reliever	0.00	0	0	0	0	0	0.0	0	0	0	0	Pitch 91-105	.227	75	17	5	0	0	5	5	13	.272	.293
0-3 Days Rest (Start)	0.00	0	0	0	0	0	0.0	0	0	0	0	Pitch 106+	.242	33	8	1	0	2	4	4	4	.324	.455
4 Days Rest	4.56	7	9	0	21	21	130.1	130	14	49	86	First Pitch	.330	109	36	6	0	4	17	2	0	.345	.495
5+ Days Rest	4.93	2	3	0	12	12	73.0	78	12	24	43	Ahead in Count	.213	394	84	13	1	5	34	0	106	.215	.289
vs. AL	4.92	8	11	0	31	31	188.1	195	25	70	120	Behind in Count	.360	161	58	11	3	12	27	38	0	.480	.689
vs. NL	1.80	1	1	0	2	2	15.0	13	1	3	9	Two Strikes	.177	361	64	7	1	4	25	33	129	.249	.235
Pre-All Star	3.39	7	4	0	18	18	124.2	109	13	37	73	Pre-All Star	.234	466	109	22	3	13	41	37	73	.287	.378
Post-All Star	6.75	2	8	0	15	15	78.2	99	13	36	56	Post-All Star	.308	321	99	12	1	13	51	36	56	.380	.474

Mel Rosario — Orioles

Age 25 – Bats Both

	Avg	G	AB	R	H	2B	3B	HR	RBI	BB	SO	HBP	GDP	SB	CS	OBP	SLG	IBB	SH	SF	#Pit	#P/PA	GB	FB	G/F
1997 Season	.000	4	3	0	0	0	0	0	0	1	0	0	0	0	0	.000	.000	0	0	0	8	2.67	1	1	1.00

1997 Season

	Avg	AB	H	2B	3B	HR	RBI	BB	SO	OBP	SLG		Avg	AB	H	2B	3B	HR	RBI	BB	SO	OBP	SLG
vs. Left	.000	0	0	0	0	0	0	0	0	.000	.000	Scoring Posn	.000	1	0	0	0	0	0	0	1	.000	.000
vs. Right	.000	3	0	0	0	0	0	0	1	.000	.000	Close & Late	.000	1	0	0	0	0	0	0	0	.000	.000

Brian Rose — Red Sox

Age 22 – Pitches Right

	ERA	W	L	Sv	G	GS	IP	BB	SO	Avg	H	2B	3B	HR	RBI	OBP	SLG	CG	ShO	Sup	QS	#P/S	SB	CS	GB	FB	G/F
1997 Season	12.00	0	0	0	1	1	3.0	2	3	.357	5	1	0	0	4	.438	.429	0	0	9.00	0	73	1	0	6	1	6.00

1997 Season

	ERA	W	L	Sv	G	GS	IP	H	HR	BB	SO		Avg	AB	H	2B	3B	HR	RBI	BB	SO	OBP	SLG
Home	12.00	0	0	0	1	1	3.0	5	0	2	3	vs. Left	.222	9	2	0	0	0	2	2	3	.364	.222
Away	0.00	0	0	0	0	0	0.0	0	0	0	0	vs. Right	.600	5	3	1	0	0	2	0	0	.600	.800

Pete Rose Jr. — Reds

Age 28 – Bats Left

	Avg	G	AB	R	H	2B	3B	HR	RBI	BB	SO	HBP	GDP	SB	CS	OBP	SLG	IBB	SH	SF	#Pit	#P/PA	GB	FB	G/F
1997 Season	.143	11	14	2	2	0	0	0	0	2	9	0	0	0	0	.250	.143	0	0	0	74	4.63	2	1	2.00

1997 Season

	Avg	AB	H	2B	3B	HR	RBI	BB	SO	OBP	SLG		Avg	AB	H	2B	3B	HR	RBI	BB	SO	OBP	SLG
vs. Left	.000	4	0	0	0	0	0	0	3	.000	.000	Scoring Posn	.000	2	0	0	0	0	0	1	2	.333	.000
vs. Right	.200	10	2	0	0	0	0	2	6	.333	.200	Close & Late	.000	1	0	0	0	0	0	1	1	.500	.000

Matt Ruebel — Pirates

Age 28 – Pitches Left

	ERA	W	L	Sv	G	GS	IP	BB	SO	Avg	H	2B	3B	HR	RBI	OBP	SLG	GF	IR	IRS	Hld	SvOp	SB	CS	GB	FB	G/F
1997 Season	6.32	3	2	0	44	0	62.2	27	50	.302	77	15	3	8	52	.373	.478	9	36	12	8	1	7	1	96	74	1.30
Career (1996-1997)	5.49	4	3	1	70	7	121.1	52	72	.290	141	33	5	15	81	.366	.471	12	50	16	12	2	11	4	196	149	1.32

1997 Season

	ERA	W	L	Sv	G	GS	IP	H	HR	BB	SO		Avg	AB	H	2B	3B	HR	RBI	BB	SO	OBP	SLG
Home	6.11	1	0	0	22	0	35.1	46	4	14	29	vs. Left	.277	83	23	4	0	2	21	10	11	.351	.398
Away	6.59	2	2	0	22	0	27.1	31	4	13	21	vs. Right	.314	172	54	11	3	6	31	17	39	.385	.517
Starter	0.00	0	0	0	0	0	0.0	0	0	0	0	Scoring Posn	.322	87	28	6	0	3	44	12	20	.390	.494
Reliever	6.32	3	2	0	44	0	62.2	77	8	27	50	Close & Late	.291	55	16	4	1	2	13	5	10	.371	.509
0 Days rest (Relief)	6.75	0	1	0	5	0	8.0	12	1	5	7	None on/out	.241	54	13	2	1	2	2	4	8	.293	.426
1 or 2 Days rest	7.02	0	1	0	20	0	33.1	45	6	12	28	First Pitch	.273	33	9	2	0	0	4	1	0	.333	.333
3+ Days rest	5.06	3	0	0	19	0	21.1	20	1	10	15	Ahead in Count	.244	119	29	5	0	0	44	0	44	.244	.387
Pre-All Star	8.69	2	2	0	25	0	29.0	40	4	16	27	Behind in Count	.383	60	23	3	2	4	13	15	0	.507	.700
Post-All Star	4.28	1	0	0	19	0	33.2	37	4	11	23	Two Strikes	.228	123	28	8	1	4	26	11	50	.294	.407

Kirk Rueter — Giants
Age 27 – Pitches Left

	ERA	W	L	Sv	G	GS	IP	BB	SO	Avg	H	2B	3B	HR	RBI	OBP	SLG	CG	ShO	Sup	QS	#P/S	SB	CS	GB	FB	G/F
1997 Season	3.45	13	6	0	32	32	190.2	51	115	.264	194	39	3	17	67	.311	.395	0	0	5.62	21	96	4	7	294	193	1.52
Career (1993-1997)	3.72	39	20	0	95	94	518.0	128	270	.268	532	101	4	48	201	.313	.396	2	1	6.20	44	86	15	26	755	603	1.25

1997 Season

	ERA	W	L	Sv	G	GS	IP	H	HR	BB	SO		Avg	AB	H	2B	3B	HR	RBI	BB	SO	OBP	SLG
Home	3.00	7	4	0	17	17	102.0	101	7	33	67	vs. Left	.281	139	39	5	1	4	18	9	19	.322	.417
Away	3.96	6	2	0	15	15	88.2	93	10	18	48	vs. Right	.261	595	155	34	2	13	49	42	96	.308	.390
Day	3.08	4	3	0	13	13	79.0	77	4	21	49	Inning 1-6	.267	670	179	36	3	15	62	47	107	.314	.397
Night	3.71	9	3	0	19	19	111.2	117	13	30	66	Inning 7+	.234	64	15	3	0	2	5	4	8	.279	.375
Grass	3.26	12	5	0	27	27	162.2	162	14	46	104	None on	.279	426	119	24	2	12	12	25	68	.319	.430
Turf	4.50	1	1	0	5	5	28.0	32	3	5	11	Runners on	.244	308	75	15	1	5	55	26	47	.299	.347
March/April	2.73	1	0	0	5	5	29.2	23	2	8	17	Scoring Posn	.215	149	32	7	0	3	48	19	23	.297	.322
May	3.72	1	1	0	5	5	29.0	28	1	8	22	Close & Late	.194	31	6	0	0	1	2	1	4	.219	.290
June	3.97	3	1	0	6	6	34.0	40	5	13	18	None on/out	.321	196	63	11	1	7	7	12	28	.361	.495
July	4.93	2	3	0	6	6	34.2	42	4	7	23	vs. 1st Batr (relief)	.000	0	0	0	0	0	0	0	0	.000	.000
August	3.16	2	1	0	5	5	31.1	32	2	3	13	1st Inning Pitched	.278	126	35	8	0	4	19	10	17	.331	.437
Sept/Oct	1.97	4	0	0	5	5	32.0	29	3	12	22	First 75 Pitches	.267	551	147	31	2	12	49	36	87	.311	.396
Starter	3.45	13	6	0	32	32	190.2	194	17	51	115	Pitch 76-90	.269	93	25	5	1	2	9	7	13	.317	.409
Reliever	0.00	0	0	0	0	0	0.0	0	0	0	0	Pitch 91-105	.284	67	19	3	0	3	9	5	7	.329	.463
0-3 Days Rest (Start)	0.00	0	0	0	0	0	0.0	0	0	0	0	Pitch 106+	.130	23	3	0	0	0	0	3	8	.231	.130
4 Days Rest	3.22	10	4	0	20	20	120.1	124	9	32	77	Ahead in Count	.203	305	62	13	0	4	17	0	97	.204	.285
5+ Days Rest	3.84	3	2	0	12	12	70.1	70	8	19	38	Behind in Count	.356	180	64	12	2	11	30	28	0	.438	.628
vs. AL	4.67	2	1	0	3	3	17.1	24	3	2	17	Two Strikes	.193	326	63	15	0	2	16	18	115	.235	.258
vs. NL	3.32	11	5	0	29	29	173.1	170	14	49	98												
Pre-All Star	3.80	5	3	0	17	17	97.0	100	9	29	61	Pre-All Star	.266	376	100	20	2	9	44	29	61	.316	.402
Post-All Star	3.07	8	3	0	15	15	93.2	94	8	22	54	Post-All Star	.263	358	94	19	1	8	23	22	54	.305	.388

Career (1993-1997)

	ERA	W	L	Sv	G	GS	IP	H	HR	BB	SO		Avg	AB	H	2B	3B	HR	RBI	BB	SO	OBP	SLG
Home	3.89	19	13	0	50	50	270.2	291	24	78	147	vs. Left	.263	357	94	10	1	7	41	23	47	.310	.356
Away	3.53	20	7	0	45	44	247.1	241	24	50	123	vs. Right	.270	1625	438	91	3	41	160	105	223	.313	.405
Day	4.17	10	11	0	37	36	196.1	208	21	48	114	Inning 1-6	.272	1836	500	94	4	43	192	117	252	.316	.398
Night	3.44	29	9	0	58	58	321.2	324	27	80	156	Inning 7+	.219	146	32	7	0	5	9	11	18	.274	.370
Grass	3.45	19	11	0	47	47	273.2	270	23	69	161	None on	.270	1198	323	58	2	30	30	67	162	.310	.396
Turf	4.02	20	9	0	48	47	244.1	262	25	59	109	Runners on	.267	784	209	43	2	18	171	61	108	.317	.395
March/April	4.48	5	2	0	16	16	80.1	83	8	21	43	Scoring Posn	.275	393	108	20	0	12	149	43	56	.341	.417
May	4.70	1	4	0	13	13	61.1	71	4	16	38	Close & Late	.182	88	16	4	0	2	4	6	10	.234	.295
June	4.23	7	3	0	15	15	78.2	87	12	23	38	None on/out	.280	532	149	26	1	15	15	27	65	.316	.417
July	4.36	6	6	0	18	18	97.0	109	11	26	49	vs. 1st Batr (relief)	.000	1	0	0	0	0	0	0	0	.000	.000
August	3.04	8	2	0	15	14	91.2	88	5	17	42	1st Inning Pitched	.302	368	111	19	0	10	50	34	48	.363	.435
Sept/Oct	2.23	12	3	0	18	18	109.0	94	8	25	60	First 75 Pitches	.271	1616	438	85	3	37	159	103	215	.315	.396
Starter	3.72	39	20	0	94	94	515.2	531	48	127	269	Pitch 76-90	.284	222	63	11	1	7	28	15	29	.328	.437
Reliever	3.86	0	0	0	1	0	2.1	1	0	1	1	Pitch 91-105	.243	107	26	4	0	4	14	6	14	.281	.393
0-3 Days Rest (Start)	0.00	0	0	0	0	0	0.0	0	0	0	0	Pitch 106+	.135	37	5	1	0	0	0	4	12	.220	.162
4 Days Rest	3.93	21	10	0	46	46	256.1	280	23	61	140	First Pitch	.300	263	79	13	0	6	35	7	0	.315	.418
5+ Days Rest	3.51	18	10	0	48	48	259.1	251	25	66	129	Ahead in Count	.196	871	171	33	1	15	58	0	231	.197	.288
vs. AL	4.67	2	1	0	3	3	17.1	24	3	2	17	Behind in Count	.362	445	161	33	2	18	64	66	0	.443	.566
vs. NL	3.69	37	19	0	92	91	500.2	508	45	126	253	Two Strikes	.201	884	178	36	1	13	58	55	270	.249	.288
Pre-All Star	4.52	15	13	0	50	50	254.2	276	29	69	139	Pre-All Star	.279	990	276	52	3	29	124	69	139	.325	.425
Post-All Star	2.94	24	7	0	45	44	263.1	256	19	59	131	Post-All Star	.258	992	256	49	1	19	77	59	131	.301	.367

Pitcher vs. Batter (career)

Pitches Best Vs.	Avg	AB	H	2B	3B	HR	RBI	BB	SO	OBP	SLG	Pitches Worst Vs.	Avg	AB	H	2B	3B	HR	RBI	BB	SO	OBP	SLG
Ricky Gutierrez	.000	14	0	0	0	0	0	0	3	.000	.000	Ryan Klesko	.500	12	6	0	0	2	5	1	2	.538	1.000
Brian McRae	.000	11	0	0	0	0	0	0	1	.000	.000	Mariano Duncan	.500	10	5	3	0	0	1	1	1	.545	.800
Barry Larkin	.091	11	1	0	0	0	1	1	1	.154	.091	David Segui	.444	9	4	1	0	1	2	3	0	.583	.889
Royce Clayton	.100	20	2	0	0	0	1	1	1	.143	.100	Sammy Sosa	.429	14	6	2	1	1	2	0	4	.429	.929
Delino DeShields	.143	14	2	0	0	0	0	1	1	.143	.143	Gregg Jefferies	.400	15	6	2	0	2	2	1	0	.438	.933

Scott Ruffcorn — Phillies
Age 28 – Pitches Right

	ERA	W	L	Sv	G	GS	IP	BB	SO	Avg	H	2B	3B	HR	RBI	OBP	SLG	GF	IR	IRS	Hld	SvOp	SB	CS	GB	FB	G/F
1997 Season	7.71	0	3	0	18	4	39.2	36	33	.275	42	14	3	4	33	.423	.484	3	2	1	0	0	6	1	45	47	0.96
Career (1993-1997)	8.57	0	8	0	30	9	70.1	70	46	.310	86	20	4	8	65	.455	.498	5	3	1	0	0	19	3	91	79	1.15

1997 Season

	ERA	W	L	Sv	G	GS	IP	H	HR	BB	SO		Avg	AB	H	2B	3B	HR	RBI	BB	SO	OBP	SLG
Home	7.50	0	2	0	4	2	12.0	13	1	12	8	vs. Left	.262	65	17	3	2	0	8	18	16	.437	.369
Away	7.81	0	1	0	14	2	27.2	29	3	24	25	vs. Right	.284	88	25	11	1	4	25	18	17	.412	.568

Bruce Ruffin — Rockies
Age 34 – Pitches Left (groundball pitcher)

	ERA	W	L	Sv	G	GS	IP	BB	SO	Avg	H	2B	3B	HR	RBI	OBP	SLG	GF	IR	IRS	Hld	SvOp	SB	CS	GB	FB	G/F
1997 Season	5.32	0	2	7	23	0	22.0	18	31	.220	18	5	0	3	16	.360	.390	15	13	7	2	9	3	0	29	14	2.07
Last Five Years	3.84	17	18	60	246	12	321.0	165	319	.246	299	49	3	25	154	.335	.353	137	110	33	22	74	27	12	514	217	2.37

1997 Season

	ERA	W	L	Sv	G	GS	IP	H	HR	BB	SO		Avg	AB	H	2B	3B	HR	RBI	BB	SO	OBP	SLG
Home	3.38	0	0	2	10	0	10.2	12	0	6	19	vs. Left	.296	27	8	1	0	1	9	5	11	.406	.444

1997 Season

	ERA	W	L	Sv	G	GS	IP	H	HR	BB	SO		Avg	AB	H	2B	3B	HR	RBI	BB	SO	OBP	SLG
Away	7.15	0	2	5	13	0	11.1	6	3	12	12	vs. Right	.182	55	10	4	0	2	7	13	20	.338	.364

Last Five Years

	ERA	W	L	Sv	G	GS	IP	H	HR	BB	SO		Avg	AB	H	2B	3B	HR	RBI	BB	SO	OBP	SLG
Home	3.98	11	6	24	121	8	169.2	171	9	88	171	vs. Left	.258	291	75	10	0	6	37	55	70	.372	.354
Away	3.69	6	12	36	125	4	151.1	128	16	77	148	vs. Right	.242	924	224	39	3	19	117	110	249	.322	.353
Day	3.33	12	8	24	106	5	137.2	133	11	67	145	Inning 1-6	.286	385	110	19	3	8	51	50	93	.365	.413
Night	4.22	5	10	36	140	7	183.1	166	14	98	174	Inning 7+	.228	830	189	30	0	17	103	115	226	.320	.325
Grass	4.19	12	15	44	192	10	249.0	248	19	133	245	None on	.237	615	146	24	2	11	81	173	326	.337	
Turf	2.63	5	3	16	54	2	72.0	51	6	32	74	Runners on	.255	600	153	25	1	14	143	84	146	.343	.370
March/April	4.10	3	1	8	45	4	59.1	56	4	39	58	Scoring Posn	.227	352	80	10	0	8	126	61	95	.336	.324
May	3.99	1	5	17	46	2	58.2	54	4	29	52	Close & Late	.225	449	101	14	0	10	70	66	137	.323	.323
June	6.09	5	5	13	41	6	57.2	76	5	27	65	None on/out	.261	272	71	12	2	2	31	76	.337	.342
July	3.88	2	3	9	35	0	51.0	47	6	26	51	vs. 1st Batr (relief)	.219	201	44	8	0	3	13	30	66	.320	.303
August	2.70	3	4	2	36	0	43.1	26	5	16	39	1st Inning Pitched	.226	800	181	26	0	19	107	116	224	.323	.330
Sept/Oct	1.76	3	0	11	43	0	51.0	40	1	28	54	First 15 Pitches	.234	640	150	27	0	14	72	84	167	.323	.323
Starter	6.08	3	4	0	12	12	53.1	73	4	31	46	Pitch 16-30	.232	323	75	6	2	7	45	50	96	.332	.328
Reliever	3.40	14	14	60	234	0	267.2	226	21	134	273	Pitch 31-45	.355	107	38	10	0	1	21	14	26	.424	.477
0 Days rest (Relief)	4.75	1	6	20	67	0	60.2	64	5	37	62	Pitch 46+	.248	145	36	6	1	3	16	17	30	.323	.366
1 or 2 Days rest	2.99	8	6	29	119	0	153.2	120	14	76	157	First Pitch	.348	161	56	7	0	6	37	12	0	.389	.503
3+ Days rest	3.04	5	2	11	48	0	53.1	42	2	21	54	Ahead in Count	.167	615	103	18	3	7	44	0	270	.169	.241
vs. AL	10.80	0	0	0	2	0	1.2	3	0	1	3	Behind in Count	.349	212	74	11	0	2	37	104	0	.556	.429
vs. NL	3.80	17	18	60	244	12	319.1	296	25	164	316	Two Strikes	.133	624	83	19	3	8	36	49	319	.196	.212
Pre-All Star	4.55	9	13	42	143	12	192.0	194	15	107	192	Pre-All Star	.262	741	194	38	2	15	104	107	192	.354	.379
Post-All Star	2.79	8	5	18	103	0	129.0	105	10	58	127	Post-All Star	.222	474	105	11	1	10	50	58	127	.304	.312

Pitcher vs. Batter (career)

Pitches Best Vs.	Avg	AB	H	2B	3B	HR	RBI	BB	SO	OBP	SLG	Pitches Worst Vs.	Avg	AB	H	2B	3B	HR	RBI	BB	SO	OBP	SLG
Jody Reed	.000	7	0	0	0	0	0	4	1	.364	.000	Joe Girardi	.500	12	6	2	0	1	4	1	2	.538	.917
Ray Lankford	.100	20	2	0	0	0	0	4	5	.250	.100	Roberto Kelly	.500	8	4	1	0	0	4	3	3	.636	.625
Carlos Garcia	.100	10	1	1	0	0	0	1	3	.182	.200	Ron Gant	.476	21	10	4	1	1	8	3	2	.542	.905
Steve Finley	.133	15	2	1	0	0	0	5	.133	.200	Eric Davis	.417	24	10	5	0	1	5	5	6	.500	.750
Royce Clayton	.182	11	2	0	0	1		0	.182	.182	Matt Williams	.318	22	7	0	0	3	3	2	.400	.727

Glendon Rusch — Royals

Age 23 – Pitches Left

	ERA	W	L	Sv	G	GS	IP	BB	SO	Avg	H	2B	3B	HR	RBI	OBP	SLG	CG	ShO	Sup	QS	#P/S	SB	CS	GB	FB	G/F
1997 Season	5.50	6	9	0	30	27	170.1	52	116	.301	206	39	3	28	98	.353	.490	1	0	4.28	11	98	6	0	224	197	1.14

1997 Season

	ERA	W	L	Sv	G	GS	IP	H	HR	BB	SO		Avg	AB	H	2B	3B	HR	RBI	BB	SO	OBP	SLG
Home	6.10	0	6	0	14	13	76.2	100	14	28	52	vs. Left	.354	161	57	7	1	9	25	8	26	.386	.578
Away	5.00	6	3	0	16	14	93.2	106	14	24	64	vs. Right	.285	523	149	32	2	19	73	44	90	.344	.463
Day	4.40	2	3	0	8	7	47.0	51	6	16	26	Inning 1-6	.301	605	182	37	3	25	93	49	101	.356	.496
Night	5.91	4	6	0	22	20	123.1	155	22	36	90	Inning 7+	.304	79	24	2	0	3	5	3	15	.329	.443
Grass	5.78	4	8	0	24	23	138.2	173	24	45	94	None on	.279	401	112	18	1	18	18	28	63	.331	.464
Turf	4.26	2	1	0	6	4	31.2	33	4	7	22	Runners on	.332	283	94	21	2	10	80	24	53	.384	.531
March/April	5.00	2	1	0	5	4	27.0	33	3	6	18	Scoring Posn	.343	143	49	13	2	4	66	17	27	.406	.545
May	4.71	1	1	0	6	6	36.1	44	5	15	30	Close & Late	.316	38	12	0	0	2	4	3	6	.366	.474
June	9.64	0	2	0	3	2	14.0	24	2	4	10	None on/out	.268	179	48	7	0	10	10	9	28	.307	.475
July	6.97	0	3	0	6	5	31.0	40	5	8	15	vs. 1st Batr (relief)	.667	3	2	1	0	1	1	0	0	.667	2.000
August	4.31	2	2	0	6	6	39.2	36	9	11	28	1st Inning Pitched	.383	128	49	15	2	2	31	10	16	.415	.578
Sept/Oct	4.84	1	0	0	4	4	22.1	29	4	8	15	First 75 Pitches	.304	497	151	34	3	20	74	40	82	.359	.505
Starter	5.39	6	9	0	27	27	165.1	196	27	52	111	Pitch 76-90	.255	102	26	3	0	5	15	7	22	.306	.431
Reliever	9.00	0	0	0	3	0	5.0	10	1	0	5	Pitch 91-105	.351	74	26	2	0	2	6	5	10	.392	.459
0-3 Days Rest (Start)	1.08	0	0	0	1	1	8.1	5	1	0	3	Pitch 106+	.273	11	3	0	0	1	3	0	2	.273	.545
4 Days Rest	6.01	3	6	0	16	16	97.1	121	18	35	70	First Pitch	.380	100	38	3	0	6	19	0	0	.369	.590
5+ Days Rest	4.98	3	3	0	10	10	59.2	70	8	17	38	Ahead in Count	.227	308	70	12	3	7	29	0	102	.241	.354
vs. AL	5.53	6	8	0	27	25	154.2	187	26	50	107	Behind in Count	.386	140	54	13	0	10	27	23	0	.470	.693
vs. NL	5.17	0	1	0	3	2	15.2	19	2	2	9	Two Strikes	.215	303	65	16	1	8	34	29	116	.287	.353
Pre-All Star	5.94	3	5	0	15	13	83.1	111	11	26	59	Pre-All Star	.326	341	111	25	1	11	51	26	59	.367	.501
Post-All Star	5.07	3	4	0	15	14	87.0	95	17	26	57	Post-All Star	.277	343	95	14	2	17	47	26	57	.340	.478

Ken Ryan — Phillies

Age 29 – Pitches Right (groundball pitcher)

	ERA	W	L	Sv	G	GS	IP	BB	SO	Avg	H	2B	3B	HR	RBI	OBP	SLG	GF	IR	IRS	Hld	SvOp	SB	CS	GB	FB	G/F
1997 Season	9.58	1	0	0	22	0	20.2	13	10	.344	31	4	2	5	25	.430	.600	10	3	2	2	0	0	0	35	31	1.13
Last Five Years	3.63	13	14	29	201	0	240.1	128	195	.250	225	42	5	16	114	.347	.362	108	83	26	25	43	20	7	334	196	1.70

1997 Season

	ERA	W	L	Sv	G	GS	IP	H	HR	BB	SO		Avg	AB	H	2B	3B	HR	RBI	BB	SO	OBP	SLG
Home	5.91	1	0	0	12	0	10.2	13	4	7	6	vs. Left	.279	43	12	1	1	2	9	5	6	.354	.488
Away	13.50	0	0	0	10	0	10.0	18	1	6	4	vs. Right	.404	47	19	3	1	3	16	8	4	.492	.702

Last Five Years

	ERA	W	L	Sv	G	GS	IP	H	HR	BB	SO		Avg	AB	H	2B	3B	HR	RBI	BB	SO	OBP	SLG
Home	4.56	7	9	16	105	0	128.1	125	11	66	104	vs. Left	.248	403	100	21	1	3	52	78	88	.369	.328
Away	2.57	6	5	13	96	0	112.0	100	5	62	91	vs. Right	.252	496	125	21	4	13	62	50	107	.327	.389
Day	2.93	2	2	11	62	0	76.2	57	1	42	73	Inning 1-6	.225	40	9	2	0	1	4	5	7	.311	.350

Last Five Years

	ERA	W	L	Sv	G	GS	IP	H	HR	BB	SO		Avg	AB	H	2B	3B	HR	RBI	BB	SO	OBP	SLG
Night	3.96	11	12	18	139	0	163.2	168	15	86	122	Inning 7+	.251	859	216	40	5	15	110	123	188	.348	.362
Grass	4.08	9	10	21	129	0	145.2	149	8	75	123	None on	.250	464	116	17	3	11	11	64	103	.341	.371
Turf	2.95	4	4	8	72	0	94.2	76	8	53	72	Runners on	.251	435	109	25	2	5	103	64	92	.353	.352
March/April	0.99	0	0	3	22	0	27.1	16	1	9	22	Scoring Posn	.251	255	64	15	1	2	92	53	58	.382	.341
May	4.70	4	2	7	54	0	61.1	64	8	36	51	Close & Late	.248	479	119	21	2	9	61	76	103	.353	.357
June	4.08	2	5	6	39	0	46.1	44	3	35	45	None on/out	.249	213	53	9	0	7	7	22	45	.319	.390
July	4.79	4	4	6	32	0	35.2	44	2	12	28	vs. 1st Batr (relief)	.211	180	38	3	0	4	14	20	30	.294	.294
August	2.25	0	1	4	24	0	32.0	28	1	15	23	1st Inning Pitched	.249	668	166	27	5	14	87	95	131	.345	.367
Sept/Oct	3.35	3	2	3	30	0	37.2	29	1	21	28	First 15 Pitches	.247	535	132	20	4	11	56	75	102	.342	.361
Starter	0.00	0	0	0	1	0	0.0	0	0	0	0	Pitch 16-30	.250	288	72	18	1	3	39	48	72	.362	.351
Reliever	3.63	13	14	29	201	0	240.1	225	16	128	195	Pitch 31-45	.288	73	21	4	0	2	19	5	19	.333	.425
0 Days rest (Relief)	2.66	1	4	7	38	0	40.2	42	1	19	26	Pitch 46+	.000	3	0	0	0	0	0	0	2	.000	.000
1 or 2 Days rest	4.40	6	8	16	107	0	129.0	127	10	72	108	First Pitch	.294	102	30	6	1	0	14	19	0	.411	.373
3+ Days rest	2.80	4	2	6	56	0	70.2	56	5	37	61	Ahead in Count	.199	418	83	20	0	7	39	0	170	.206	.297
vs. AL	3.49	9	9	21	118	0	131.2	123	7	71	115	Behind in Count	.342	193	66	10	5	36	61	0	0	.502	.492
vs. NL	3.81	4	5	8	83	0	108.2	102	9	57	80	Two Strikes	.185	475	88	20	1	9	43	48	195	.264	.288
Pre-All Star	4.02	7	9	18	128	0	150.0	144	13	84	130	Pre-All Star	.253	569	144	27	3	13	70	84	130	.352	.380
Post-All Star	2.99	6	5	11	73	0	90.1	81	3	44	65	Post-All Star	.245	330	81	15	2	3	44	44	65	.339	.330

Bret Saberhagen — Red Sox

Age 34 – Pitches Right

	ERA	W	L	Sv	G	GS	IP	BB	SO	Avg	H	2B	3B	HR	RBI	OBP	SLG	CG	ShO	Sup	QS	#P/S	SB	CS	GB	FB	G/F
1997 Season	6.58	0	1	0	6	6	26.0	10	14	.288	30	12	0	5	19	.353	.548	0	0	7.96	0	78	4	0	26	45	0.58
Last Five Years	3.54	28	18	0	74	74	495.2	73	350	.261	495	100	15	50	191	.292	.408	11	1	5.23	43	98	25	12	669	558	1.20

1997 Season

	ERA	W	L	Sv	G	GS	IP	H	HR	BB	SO		Avg	AB	H	2B	3B	HR	RBI	BB	SO	OBP	SLG
Home	2.70	0	0	0	2	2	10.0	9	0	1	5	vs. Left	.328	61	20	8	0	4	16	9	8	.397	.656
Away	9.00	0	1	0	4	4	16.0	21	5	9	9	vs. Right	.233	43	10	4	0	1	3	1	6	.283	.395

Last Five Years

	ERA	W	L	Sv	G	GS	IP	H	HR	BB	SO		Avg	AB	H	2B	3B	HR	RBI	BB	SO	OBP	SLG
Home	3.52	11	8	0	33	33	214.2	205	17	33	161	vs. Left	.248	963	239	55	11	25	101	48	191	.283	.406
Away	3.56	17	10	0	41	41	281.0	290	33	40	189	vs. Right	.274	935	256	45	4	25	90	25	159	.303	.411
Day	3.79	8	8	0	22	22	147.1	153	18	26	104	Inning 1-6	.263	1546	406	81	14	43	155	62	287	.296	.417
Night	3.44	20	10	0	52	52	348.1	342	32	47	246	Inning 7+	.253	352	89	19	1	7	36	11	63	.278	.372
Grass	3.64	21	13	0	55	55	363.0	368	39	54	262	None on	.257	1192	306	59	12	31	31	39	228	.288	.404
Turf	3.26	7	5	0	19	19	132.2	127	11	19	88	Runners on	.268	706	189	41	3	19	160	34	122	.300	.415
March/April	4.42	5	4	0	11	11	79.1	88	12	12	44	Scoring Posn	.282	358	101	26	0	12	136	27	59	.327	.453
May	2.66	4	4	0	14	14	101.1	92	4	16	72	Close & Late	.277	191	53	13	1	1	23	6	36	.305	.372
June	3.12	8	5	0	18	18	127.0	124	14	10	103	None on/out	.266	508	135	25	4	12	12	13	93	.290	.402
July	2.61	6	3	0	13	13	96.2	85	7	9	74	vs. 1st Batr (relief)	.000	0	0	0	0	0	0	0	0	.000	.000
August	4.34	4	2	0	10	10	58.0	60	5	15	37	1st Inning Pitched	.273	286	78	21	2	6	38	14	57	.314	.423
Sept/Oct	7.02	1	0	0	8	8	33.1	46	8	11	20	First 75 Pitches	.260	1379	358	75	12	38	136	53	259	.292	.414
Starter	3.54	28	18	0	74	74	495.2	495	50	73	350	Pitch 76-90	.259	220	57	13	2	5	17	10	34	.291	.405
Reliever	0.00	0	0	0	0	0	0.0	0	0	0	0	Pitch 91-105	.234	171	40	6	0	5	21	6	33	.267	.357
0-3 Days Rest (Start)	1.50	1	0	0	1	1	6.0	5	0	0	3	Pitch 106+	.313	128	40	6	1	2	17	4	24	.336	.422
4 Days Rest	3.33	16	10	0	42	42	286.1	287	28	43	203	First Pitch	.330	270	89	21	3	8	39	6	0	.353	.519
5+ Days Rest	3.90	11	8	0	31	31	203.1	203	22	30	144	Ahead in Count	.211	1003	212	35	5	15	68	0	308	.220	.301
vs. AL	5.73	0	1	0	5	5	22.0	23	3	9	12	Behind in Count	.344	326	112	21	2	21	51	25	0	.386	.613
vs. NL	3.44	28	17	0	69	69	473.2	472	47	64	338	Two Strikes	.189	935	177	36	6	11	58	42	350	.231	.276
Pre-All Star	3.21	20	15	0	48	48	345.0	332	34	41	246	Pre-All Star	.255	1300	332	61	9	34	124	41	246	.282	.395
Post-All Star	4.30	8	3	0	26	26	150.2	163	16	32	104	Post-All Star	.273	598	163	39	6	16	67	32	104	.315	.438

Pitcher vs. Batter (career)

Pitches Best Vs.	Avg	AB	H	2B	3B	HR	RBI	BB	SO	OBP	SLG	Pitches Worst Vs.	Avg	AB	H	2B	3B	HR	RBI	BB	SO	OBP	SLG
Craig Biggio	.071	14	1	0	0	0	0	0	5	.071	.071	Jim Eisenreich	.667	12	8	0	1	0	2	0	2	.667	.833
Mike Devereaux	.077	13	1	0	0	0	1	0	3	.077	.077	Matt Williams	.533	15	8	2	0	3	6	0	1	.533	1.267
Barry Larkin	.100	10	1	0	0	0	1	3	.182	.100	Alvaro Espinoza	.529	17	9	2	1	0	1	0	0	.529	.765
Luis Rivera	.100	10	1	0	0	0	0	1	2	.182	.100	Barry Bonds	.400	20	8	3	0	3	5	1	2	.429	1.000
Royce Clayton	.133	15	2	0	0	0	0	0	2	.133	.133	Henry Rodriguez	.400	15	6	1	0	2	2	0	2	.375	.867

A.J. Sager — Tigers

Age 33 – Pitches Right (groundball pitcher)

	ERA	W	L	Sv	G	GS	IP	BB	SO	Avg	H	2B	3B	HR	RBI	OBP	SLG	GF	IR	IRS	Hld	SvOp	SB	CS	GB	FB	G/F
1997 Season	4.18	3	4	3	38	1	84.0	24	53	.258	81	11	4	10	47	.307	.414	8	41	12	10	4	4	2	125	85	1.47
Career (1994-1997)	5.05	8	13	3	92	13	224.1	76	141	.289	253	44	9	25	136	.345	.438	15	78	26	11	5	15	10	394	191	2.06

1997 Season

	ERA	W	L	Sv	G	GS	IP	H	HR	BB	SO		Avg	AB	H	2B	3B	HR	RBI	BB	SO	OBP	SLG
Home	2.54	1	2	2	20	1	49.2	37	3	9	31	vs. Left	.260	150	39	4	2	5	18	12	31	.311	.413
Away	6.55	2	2	1	18	0	34.1	44	7	15	22	vs. Right	.256	164	42	7	2	5	29	12	22	.304	.415
Starter	1.80	0	1	0	1	1	5.0	4	1	1	2	Scoring Posn	.240	75	18	4	1	2	34	11	13	.315	.400
Reliever	4.33	3	3	3	37	0	79.0	77	9	23	51	Close & Late	.181	94	17	4	0	2	13	9	14	.243	.287
0 Days rest (Relief)	4.00	0	1	1	5	0	9.0	7	1	2	7	None on/out	.211	76	16	2	2	1	1	3	14	.250	.329
1 or 2 Days rest	5.31	2	2	0	11	0	20.1	17	3	9	17	First Pitch	.270	37	10	1	1	2	8	5	0	.333	.514
3+ Days rest	3.99	1	0	2	21	0	49.2	53	5	12	27	Ahead in Count	.236	144	34	6	1	3	14	0	41	.238	.354
Pre-All Star	3.02	2	2	3	23	1	44.2	39	2	10	26	Behind in Count	.294	68	20	3	0	2	16	10	0	.380	.426

	ERA	W	L	Sv	G	GS	IP	H	HR	BB	SO			Avg	AB	H	2B	3B	HR	RBI	BB	SO	OBP	SLG

1997 Season

	ERA	W	L	Sv	G	GS	IP	H	HR	BB	SO			Avg	AB	H	2B	3B	HR	RBI	BB	SO	OBP	SLG
Post-All Star	5.49	1	2	0	15	0	39.1	42	8	14	27	Two Strikes		.214	145	31	2	2	2	9	9	53	.261	.297

Marc Sagmoen — Rangers
Age 27 – Bats Left

	Avg	G	AB	R	H	2B	3B	HR	RBI	BB	SO	HBP	GDP	SB	CS	OBP	SLG	IBB	SH	SF	#Pit	#P/PA	GB	FB	G/F
1997 Season	.140	21	43	2	6	2	0	1	4	2	13	0	1	0	0	.174	.256	0	0	1	151	3.28	17	11	1.55

1997 Season

	Avg	AB	H	2B	3B	HR	RBI	BB	SO	OBP	SLG			Avg	AB	H	2B	3B	HR	RBI	BB	SO	OBP	SLG
vs. Left	.000	3	0	0	0	0	0	0	2	.000	.000	Scoring Posn		.200	10	2	0	0	0	3	1	1	.250	.200
vs. Right	.150	40	6	2	0	1	4	2	11	.186	.275	Close & Late		.143	7	1	0	0	1	0	1	3	.125	.286

Tim Salmon — Angels
Age 29 – Bats Right (flyball hitter)

	Avg	G	AB	R	H	2B	3B	HR	RBI	BB	SO	HBP	GDP	SB	CS	OBP	SLG	IBB	SH	SF	#Pit	#P/PA	GB	FB	G/F
1997 Season	.296	157	582	95	172	28	1	33	129	95	142	7	7	9	12	.394	.517	5	0	11	2787	4.01	158	187	0.84
Last Five Years	.297	698	2588	456	768	142	11	151	497	415	615	27	33	24	28	.396	.535	21	0	29	12317	4.03	694	820	0.85

1997 Season

	Avg	AB	H	2B	3B	HR	RBI	BB	SO	OBP	SLG			Avg	AB	H	2B	3B	HR	RBI	BB	SO	OBP	SLG
vs. Left	.288	139	40	6	0	9	25	32	34	.423	.525	First Pitch		.457	94	43	7	0	8	34	5	0	.480	.787
vs. Right	.298	443	132	22	1	24	104	63	108	.385	.515	Ahead in Count		.407	108	44	6	0	11	41	34	0	.534	.769
Groundball	.349	106	37	4	1	9	27	9	29	.405	.660	Behind in Count		.208	259	54	10	1	11	40	0	111	.222	.382
Flyball	.261	88	23	6	0	4	20	20	22	.387	.466	Two Strikes		.203	291	59	9	0	7	37	56	142	.333	.306
Home	.283	297	84	12	0	17	62	45	70	.384	.495	Batting #4		.281	317	89	16	1	21	63	55	82	.389	.536
Away	.309	285	88	16	1	16	67	50	72	.405	.540	Batting #5		.326	224	73	12	0	12	62	34	52	.411	.540
Day	.299	167	50	11	1	6	34	18	38	.358	.485	Other		.244	41	10	0	0	0	4	6	8	.340	.244
Night	.294	415	122	17	0	27	95	77	104	.408	.530	March/April		.244	90	22	4	0	3	16	12	29	.337	.389
Grass	.298	524	156	25	1	30	116	79	130	.391	.521	May		.265	98	26	3	0	3	17	15	25	.363	.388
Turf	.276	58	16	3	0	3	13	16	12	.421	.483	June		.319	94	30	9	0	6	20	22	23	.438	.606
Pre-All Star	.282	305	86	19	0	15	60	51	82	.385	.492	July		.390	100	39	6	0	7	32	17	24	.483	.660
Post-All Star	.310	277	86	9	1	18	69	44	60	.405	.545	August		.260	104	27	2	1	7	24	14	28	.355	.500
Scoring Posn	.348	178	62	11	0	10	99	39	44	.450	.579	Sept/Oct		.292	96	28	4	0	7	20	15	13	.381	.552
Close & Late	.245	102	25	6	1	4	26	16	36	.347	.441	vs. AL		.294	521	153	21	1	32	123	85	128	.391	.522
None on/out	.303	152	46	9	0	8	8	22	27	.401	.520	vs. NL		.311	61	19	7	0	1	6	10	14	.419	.475

1997 By Position

Position	Avg	AB	H	2B	3B	HR	RBI	BB	SO	OBP	SLG	G	GS	Innings	PO	A	E	DP	Fld Pct	Rng Fctr	In Zone	Zone Outs	Zone Rtg	MLB Zone
As rf	.298	568	169	27	1	32	128	91	140	.394	.518	153	153	1372.2	352	15	11	6	.971	2.41	396	336	.848	.813

Last Five Years

	Avg	AB	H	2B	3B	HR	RBI	BB	SO	OBP	SLG			Avg	AB	H	2B	3B	HR	RBI	BB	SO	OBP	SLG
vs. Left	.279	649	181	29	3	42	120	145	148	.414	.527	First Pitch		.416	281	117	21	2	22	80	17	0	.451	.740
vs. Right	.303	1939	587	113	8	109	377	270	467	.389	.538	Ahead in Count		.397	600	238	51	2	61	179	186	0	.534	.793
Groundball	.326	527	172	29	1	27	104	65	111	.405	.539	Behind in Count		.226	1113	251	43	3	45	165	0	479	.235	.391
Flyball	.266	500	133	31	2	32	95	101	133	.386	.528	Two Strikes		.195	1238	241	40	2	37	143	212	615	.316	.320
Home	.285	1302	371	64	3	85	252	200	310	.383	.535	Batting #3		.293	1371	402	84	7	76	250	205	337	.387	.531
Away	.309	1286	397	78	6	66	245	215	305	.408	.536	Batting #4		.300	706	212	34	3	44	138	121	159	.405	.544
Day	.281	725	204	39	2	28	124	104	163	.371	.457	Other		.301	511	154	24	1	31	109	89	119	.404	.534
Night	.303	1863	564	103	9	123	373	311	452	.405	.566	March/April		.256	352	90	20	0	16	58	55	91	.355	.449
Grass	.301	2273	685	123	9	135	442	348	533	.396	.542	May		.289	506	146	24	1	25	94	86	132	.391	.488
Turf	.263	315	83	19	2	16	55	67	82	.393	.489	June		.297	488	145	31	2	36	94	92	110	.412	.590
Pre-All Star	.288	1494	430	84	3	88	281	257	364	.394	.525	July		.324	438	142	27	0	28	106	72	95	.423	.578
Post-All Star	.309	1094	338	58	8	63	216	158	251	.398	.549	August		.288	465	134	17	5	32	78	59	120	.373	.553
Scoring Posn	.305	696	212	49	2	39	344	163	160	.430	.549	Sept/Oct		.327	339	111	23	3	14	67	51	67	.414	.537
Close & Late	.298	392	117	20	2	19	78	63	120	.401	.505	vs. AL		.296	2527	749	135	11	150	491	405	601	.395	.537
None on/out	.318	570	181	28	2	43	43	70	117	.396	.600	vs. NL		.311	61	19	7	0	1	6	10	14	.419	.475

Batter vs. Pitcher (career)

Hits Best Against	Avg	AB	H	2B	3B	HR	RBI	BB	SO	OBP	SLG	Hits Worst Against	Avg	AB	H	2B	3B	HR	RBI	BB	SO	OBP	SLG
Scott Kamieniecki	.647	17	11	2	0	2	8	2	5	.667	1.118	Woody Williams	.000	9	0	0	0	0	0	4	0	.308	.000
Scott Karl	.615	13	8	1	0	1	5	2	3	.667	.923	Orel Hershiser	.083	12	1	0	0	0	1	1	4	.154	.083
Ken Hill	.600	15	9	0	0	1	2	2	2	.647	.800	Roger Clemens	.139	36	5	0	0	1	2	1	13	.184	.222
Bobby Witt	.500	22	11	0	0	3	8	3	4	.560	.909	Jack McDowell	.152	33	5	1	0	0	0	3	11	.243	.182
Scott Aldred	.462	13	6	1	0	2	4	2	1	.500	1.000	Alan Mills	.200	10	2	0	0	0	1	1	2	.250	.200

Juan Samuel — Blue Jays
Age 37 – Bats Right (groundball hitter)

	Avg	G	AB	R	H	2B	3B	HR	RBI	BB	SO	HBP	GDP	SB	CS	OBP	SLG	IBB	SH	SF	#Pit	#P/PA	GB	FB	G/F
1997 Season	.284	45	95	13	27	5	4	3	15	10	28	2	2	5	3	.364	.516	0	1	0	418	3.87	18	33	0.55
Last Five Years	.261	367	885	141	231	42	17	32	127	87	221	13	13	34	17	.334	.455	4	2	5	3892	3.92	273	235	1.16

1997 Season

	Avg	AB	H	2B	3B	HR	RBI	BB	SO	OBP	SLG			Avg	AB	H	2B	3B	HR	RBI	BB	SO	OBP	SLG
vs. Left	.284	67	19	3	2	1	9	6	18	.342	.433	Scoring Posn		.303	33	10	2	3	0	12	4	6	.395	.545
vs. Right	.286	28	8	2	2	2	6	4	10	.412	.714	Close & Late		.231	13	3	0	1	0	4	3	4	.375	.385

Last Five Years

	Avg	AB	H	2B	3B	HR	RBI	BB	SO	OBP	SLG		Avg	AB	H	2B	3B	HR	RBI	BB	SO	OBP	SLG
vs. Left	.271	473	128	15	11	18	70	50	128	.343	.463	First Pitch	.370	92	34	9	3	3	19	2	0	.402	.630
vs. Right	.250	412	103	27	6	14	57	37	93	.324	.447	Ahead in Count	.370	189	70	13	5	15	50	46	0	.494	.730
Groundball	.254	205	52	5	5	4	25	22	49	.341	.385	Behind in Count	.188	441	83	8	7	8	35	0	192	.199	.293
Flyball	.229	144	33	9	1	7	17	15	34	.306	.451	Two Strikes	.163	467	76	10	4	9	32	39	221	.232	.259
Home	.289	391	113	18	13	17	58	47	96	.370	.532	Batting #3	.263	160	42	7	1	8	27	14	55	.331	.469
Away	.239	494	118	24	4	15	69	40	125	.305	.395	Batting #6	.279	147	41	5	3	5	21	11	33	.327	.456
Day	.250	300	75	11	9	10	45	26	72	.315	.447	Other	.256	578	148	30	13	19	79	62	133	.337	.452
Night	.267	585	156	31	8	22	82	61	149	.344	.460	March/April	.261	92	24	3	0	4	9	11	30	.340	.424
Grass	.273	528	144	27	6	21	83	45	128	.337	.466	May	.200	115	23	3	4	2	9	7	34	.246	.348
Turf	.244	357	87	15	11	11	44	42	93	.330	.440	June	.299	164	49	11	4	10	39	18	33	.368	.598
Pre-All Star	.274	420	115	20	10	18	60	39	104	.340	.498	July	.286	185	53	10	4	6	30	14	43	.354	.481
Post-All Star	.249	465	116	22	7	14	61	48	117	.330	.417	August	.277	155	43	10	1	4	18	21	34	.364	.432
Scoring Posn	.318	214	68	14	7	6	90	35	50	.421	.533	Sept/Oct	.224	174	39	5	4	6	22	16	47	.308	.402
Close & Late	.241	166	40	8	1	2	18	15	47	.308	.337	vs. AL	.274	624	171	32	13	28	101	64	168	.350	.502
None on/out	.206	214	44	4	5	5	5	15	59	.267	.341	vs. NL	.230	261	60	10	4	4	26	23	53	.298	.345

Batter vs. Pitcher (since 1984)

Hits Best Against	Avg	AB	H	2B	3B	HR	RBI	BB	SO	OBP	SLG	Hits Worst Against	Avg	AB	H	2B	3B	HR	RBI	BB	SO	OBP	SLG
Mike Bielecki	.500	20	10	2	0	2	8	2	2	.500	.900	Jimmy Key	.077	13	1	0	0	0	1	0	3	.077	.077
Stan Belinda	.429	7	3	2	0	0	4	4	0	.636	.714	Bob Tewksbury	.083	12	1	0	0	0	0	1	2	.154	.083
Todd Worrell	.368	19	7	3	1	1	7	0	3	.368	.789	Kent Mercker	.100	10	1	0	0	0	1	2	3	.231	.100
Rheal Cormier	.364	11	4	2	0	1	3	1	1	.462	.818	Steve Avery	.129	31	4	1	0	0	2	0	6	.129	.161
Chris Haney	.364	11	4	0	0	1	3	1	1	.417	.636	Danny Darwin	.133	15	2	0	0	0	1	1	3	.176	.133

Rey Sanchez — Yankees

Age 30 – Bats Right (groundball hitter)

	Avg	G	AB	R	H	2B	3B	HR	RBI	BB	SO	HBP	GDP	SB	CS	OBP	SLG	IBB	SH	SF	#Pit	#P/PA	GB	FB	G/F
1997 Season	.274	135	343	35	94	21	0	2	27	16	47	1	8	4	6	.307	.353	2	9	1	1267	3.42	144	69	2.09
Last Five Years	.268	545	1695	181	454	76	5	6	118	87	188	15	40	20	17	.308	.329	21	38	8	5860	3.18	702	406	1.73

1997 Season

	Avg	AB	H	2B	3B	HR	RBI	BB	SO	OBP	SLG		Avg	AB	H	2B	3B	HR	RBI	BB	SO	OBP	SLG
vs. Left	.308	65	20	5	0	1	10	3	9	.333	.431	First Pitch	.279	61	17	3	0	1	5	1	0	.297	.377
vs. Right	.266	278	74	16	0	1	17	13	38	.301	.335	Ahead in Count	.289	76	22	8	0	0	7	10	0	.372	.395
Groundball	.182	66	12	1	0	0	3	2	6	.206	.197	Behind in Count	.225	142	32	6	0	1	9	0	44	.225	.289
Flyball	.296	54	16	3	0	1	2	2	14	.321	.407	Two Strikes	.216	139	30	2	0	1	9	5	47	.243	.252
Home	.285	137	39	7	0	1	8	4	24	.305	.358	Batting #8	.268	164	44	8	0	1	7	10	25	.310	.335
Away	.267	206	55	14	0	1	19	12	23	.309	.350	Batting #9	.302	139	42	11	0	1	16	3	18	.319	.403
Day	.295	166	49	10	0	1	13	10	25	.335	.373	Other	.200	40	8	2	0	0	4	3	4	.256	.250
Night	.254	177	45	11	0	1	14	6	22	.281	.333	March/April	.273	33	9	2	0	0	3	3	2	.333	.333
Grass	.282	284	80	17	0	2	26	12	40	.312	.363	May	.228	57	13	3	0	0	3	3	9	.267	.281
Turf	.237	59	14	4	0	0	1	4	7	.286	.305	June	.295	61	18	2	0	1	5	3	9	.328	.377
Pre-All Star	.268	153	41	7	0	1	11	10	21	.313	.333	July	.200	40	8	2	0	0	1	1	4	.220	.250
Post-All Star	.279	190	53	14	0	1	16	6	26	.303	.368	August	.359	64	23	5	0	1	8	4	8	.397	.484
Scoring Posn	.276	87	24	6	0	1	26	9	15	.340	.379	Sept/Oct	.261	88	23	7	0	0	7	2	15	.283	.341
Close & Late	.260	50	13	2	0	0	3	2	9	.288	.300	vs. AL	.329	140	46	11	0	1	16	5	20	.354	.429
None on/out	.220	82	18	6	0	0	0	2	14	.293	.293	vs. NL	.236	203	48	10	0	1	11	11	27	.276	.300

1997 By Position

Position	Avg	AB	H	2B	3B	HR	RBI	BB	SO	OBP	SLG	G	GS	Innings	PO	A	E	DP	Fld Pct	Rng Fctr	In Zone	Outs	Zone Rtg	MLB Zone
As Pinch Hitter	.000	11	0	0	0	0	0	0	2	.000	.000	12	0	---	---	---	---	---	---	---	---	---	---	---
As 2b	.302	222	67	18	0	2	21	10	31	.333	.410	69	64	536.2	114	173	5	37	.983	4.81	201	183	.910	.902
As ss	.245	110	27	3	0	0	6	6	14	.284	.273	69	25	302.2	52	94	5	13	.967	4.34	107	96	.897	.937

Last Five Years

	Avg	AB	H	2B	3B	HR	RBI	BB	SO	OBP	SLG		Avg	AB	H	2B	3B	HR	RBI	BB	SO	OBP	SLG
vs. Left	.270	419	113	16	1	2	32	15	35	.302	.327	First Pitch	.279	359	100	17	1	2	32	16	0	.306	.348
vs. Right	.267	1276	341	60	4	4	86	72	153	.310	.330	Ahead in Count	.315	391	123	20	0	1	34	39	0	.373	.373
Groundball	.237	490	116	14	1	1	29	20	59	.274	.276	Behind in Count	.225	661	149	28	3	1	31	0	169	.238	.281
Flyball	.267	251	67	10	1	2	21	10	36	.310	.339	Two Strikes	.207	579	120	20	4	1	28	33	188	.261	.261
Home	.262	778	204	33	1	2	52	35	94	.299	.315	Batting #2	.260	530	138	22	1	2	36	11	48	.277	.317
Away	.273	917	250	43	4	4	66	52	94	.316	.341	Batting #8	.262	756	198	33	4	3	48	57	96	.319	.328
Day	.269	933	251	42	1	3	69	53	100	.313	.326	Other	.289	409	118	21	0	1	34	19	44	.326	.347
Night	.266	762	203	34	4	3	49	34	88	.302	.333	March/April	.250	268	67	10	1	1	18	13	22	.291	.306
Grass	.273	1313	358	60	3	5	91	68	146	.312	.334	May	.267	315	84	13	1	0	19	19	36	.315	.314
Turf	.251	382	96	16	2	1	27	19	42	.293	.312	June	.314	350	110	16	2	1	21	18	34	.348	.380
Pre-All Star	.280	1003	281	41	4	4	68	54	99	.322	.341	July	.255	274	70	14	0	2	23	15	30	.300	.328
Post-All Star	.250	692	173	35	1	2	50	33	89	.288	.312	August	.270	256	69	12	1	2	24	12	31	.310	.348
Scoring Posn	.259	359	93	19	2	2	107	39	53	.338	.340	Sept/Oct	.233	232	54	11	0	0	13	10	35	.265	.280
Close & Late	.303	277	84	8	0	2	20	11	38	.336	.354	vs. AL	.329	140	46	11	0	1	16	5	20	.354	.429
None on/out	.248	427	106	19	1	0	0	16	39	.279	.297	vs. NL	.262	1555	408	65	5	5	102	82	168	.304	.320

Batter vs. Pitcher (career)

Hits Best Against	Avg	AB	H	2B	3B	HR	RBI	BB	SO	OBP	SLG	Hits Worst Against	Avg	AB	H	2B	3B	HR	RBI	BB	SO	OBP	SLG
Armando Reynoso	.556	9	5	0	0	0	0	2	0	.636	.556	Rheal Cormier	.000	10	0	0	0	0	0	1	0	.091	.000
Mark Clark	.444	9	4	2	0	0	2	0	0	.545	.667	Tom Glavine	.045	22	1	0	0	0	0	0	0	.045	.045
Mark Portugal	.429	14	6	2	0	0	0	0	1	.429	.571	Greg Maddux	.071	14	1	0	0	0	0	0	1	.071	.071
John Smiley	.429	14	6	2	0	0	2	0	1	.429	.571	Greg Swindell	.083	12	1	0	0	0	0	0	0	.083	.083

412

Batter vs. Pitcher (career)

Hits Best Against	Avg	AB	H	2B	3B	HR	RBI	BB	SO	OBP	SLG	Hits Worst Against	Avg	AB	H	2B	3B	HR	RBI	BB	SO	OBP	SLG
Pat Rapp	.400	10	4	1	0	0	2	1	2	.455	.500	Bobby Jones	.091	11	1	0	0	0	1	0	0	.091	.091

Ryne Sandberg — Cubs
Age 38 – Bats Right

	Avg	G	AB	R	H	2B	3B	HR	RBI	BB	SO	HBP	GDP	SB	CS	OBP	SLG	IBB	SH	SF	#Pit	#P/PA	GB	FB	G/F
1997 Season	.264	135	447	54	118	26	0	12	64	28	94	2	5	7	4	.308	.403	3	0	3	1813	3.78	154	124	1.24
Last Five Years	.266	459	1680	242	447	83	9	51	225	142	312	12	33	30	17	.325	.417	8	3	14	7258	3.92	634	456	1.39

1997 Season

	Avg	AB	H	2B	3B	HR	RBI	BB	SO	OBP	SLG		Avg	AB	H	2B	3B	HR	RBI	BB	SO	OBP	SLG
vs. Left	.293	116	34	8	0	5	24	12	23	.354	.491	First Pitch	.250	12	3	0	0	0	1	2	0	.400	.250
vs. Right	.254	331	84	18	0	7	40	16	71	.291	.372	Ahead in Count	.373	102	38	10	0	4	15	21	0	.472	.588
Groundball	.263	95	25	4	0	0	8	6	21	.314	.305	Behind in Count	.193	243	47	9	0	5	31	0	84	.193	.292
Flyball	.296	54	16	4	0	1	12	4	10	.339	.426	Two Strikes	.218	225	49	10	0	7	32	5	94	.235	.356
Home	.272	246	67	13	0	9	40	15	50	.316	.435	Batting #5	.245	98	24	5	0	2	14	8	16	.302	.357
Away	.254	201	51	13	0	3	24	13	44	.299	.363	Batting #6	.265	162	43	10	0	3	24	11	32	.313	.383
Day	.250	264	66	15	0	10	43	16	57	.295	.420	Other	.273	187	51	11	0	7	26	9	46	.308	.444
Night	.284	183	52	11	0	2	21	12	37	.328	.377	March/April	.209	67	14	3	0	2	8	6	19	.284	.343
Grass	.247	364	90	17	0	10	51	21	76	.290	.376	May	.200	70	14	4	0	1	8	4	15	.253	.300
Turf	.337	83	28	9	0	2	13	7	18	.389	.518	June	.300	100	30	6	0	0	14	7	20	.343	.360
Pre-All Star	.260	258	67	18	0	5	37	19	56	.313	.388	July	.253	75	19	5	0	2	8	2	10	.269	.400
Post-All Star	.270	189	51	8	0	7	27	9	38	.302	.423	August	.351	74	26	4	0	5	15	7	16	.402	.608
Scoring Posn	.330	112	37	8	0	0	45	13	20	.395	.402	Sept/Oct	.246	61	15	4	0	2	11	2	14	.270	.410
Close & Late	.250	84	21	2	0	1	8	6	24	.300	.310	vs. AL	.313	48	15	5	0	0	9	3	9	.346	.417
None on/out	.274	117	32	8	0	4	4	5	15	.303	.444	vs. NL	.258	399	103	21	0	12	55	25	85	.304	.401

1997 By Position

Position	Avg	AB	H	2B	3B	HR	RBI	BB	SO	OBP	SLG	G	GS	Innings	PO	A	E	DP	Fld Pct	Rng Fctr	In Zone	Zone Outs	Zone Rtg	MLB Zone
As Pinch Hitter	.200	10	2	0	0	0	2	0	5	.200	.200	10	0	---	---	---	---	---	---	---	---	---	---	---
As 2b	.265	434	115	26	0	12	62	28	88	.310	.408	126	115	991.1	204	296	8	59	.984	4.54	319	306	.959	.902

Last Five Years

	Avg	AB	H	2B	3B	HR	RBI	BB	SO	OBP	SLG		Avg	AB	H	2B	3B	HR	RBI	BB	SO	OBP	SLG
vs. Left	.280	407	114	22	1	20	64	47	65	.354	.486	First Pitch	.333	39	13	3	0	0	4	7	0	.481	.410
vs. Right	.262	1273	333	61	8	31	161	95	247	.316	.395	Ahead in Count	.351	382	134	27	4	23	66	87	0	.468	.623
Groundball	.268	477	128	20	4	7	44	48	81	.339	.371	Behind in Count	.222	892	198	31	2	11	92	0	276	.222	.298
Flyball	.257	276	71	17	1	5	36	12	55	.289	.380	Two Strikes	.214	821	176	29	3	17	94	48	312	.257	.319
Home	.266	887	236	39	3	29	129	79	153	.329	.415	Batting #2	.266	706	188	39	6	27	89	64	123	.332	.453
Away	.266	793	211	44	6	22	96	63	159	.321	.420	Batting #6	.259	309	80	19	1	8	48	22	63	.311	.405
Day	.251	975	245	43	5	32	139	86	184	.313	.404	Other	.269	665	179	25	2	16	88	56	126	.324	.385
Night	.287	705	202	40	4	19	86	56	128	.342	.435	March/April	.229	236	54	11	3	9	31	30	56	.321	.415
Grass	.259	1312	340	56	4	40	173	113	228	.320	.399	May	.241	357	86	14	3	11	43	35	72	.310	.389
Turf	.291	368	107	27	5	11	52	29	84	.344	.481	June	.275	320	88	16	2	6	46	18	55	.315	.394
Pre-All Star	.259	1009	261	51	9	29	138	88	193	.320	.413	July	.258	283	73	20	1	7	32	16	41	.298	.410
Post-All Star	.277	671	186	32	0	22	87	54	119	.334	.423	August	.313	288	90	13	0	12	44	26	51	.371	.483
Scoring Posn	.303	396	120	23	5	8	161	53	74	.378	.447	Sept/Oct	.286	196	56	9	0	6	29	17	37	.346	.423
Close & Late	.242	281	68	10	0	5	31	30	70	.318	.331	vs. AL	.313	48	15	5	0	0	9	3	9	.346	.417
None on/out	.244	353	86	19	0	10	10	24	61	.292	.382	vs. NL	.265	1632	432	78	9	51	216	139	303	.325	.417

Batter vs. Pitcher (since 1984)

Hits Best Against	Avg	AB	H	2B	3B	HR	RBI	BB	SO	OBP	SLG	Hits Worst Against	Avg	AB	H	2B	3B	HR	RBI	BB	SO	OBP	SLG
Donovan Osborne	.538	13	7	2	0	2	6	4	2	.647	1.154	Ismael Valdes	.000	13	0	0	0	0	0	1	5	.071	.000
Omar Olivares	.478	23	11	1	0	2	3	4	1	.556	.783	Tim Scott	.000	11	0	0	0	0	0	1	3	.083	.000
Tom Candiotti	.417	12	5	3	0	1	3	1	1	.462	.917	Armando Reynoso	.000	9	0	0	0	0	2	1	2	.083	.000
Allen Watson	.417	12	5	1	0	4	7	1	2	.462	1.500	Rod Beck	.091	11	1	0	0	0	0	2	4	.083	.091
Mark Clark	.400	15	6	0	1	2	3	3	2	.474	.933	Matt Morris	.091	11	1	0	0	0	1	0	2	.167	.091

Deion Sanders — Reds
Age 30 – Bats Left

	Avg	G	AB	R	H	2B	3B	HR	RBI	BB	SO	HBP	GDP	SB	CS	OBP	SLG	IBB	SH	SF	#Pit	#P/PA	GB	FB	G/F
1997 Season	.273	115	465	53	127	13	7	5	23	34	67	6	4	56	13	.329	.363	2	2	2	1778	3.49	173	127	1.36
Last Five Years	.275	387	1455	201	400	59	25	21	107	109	232	16	13	137	45	.331	.393	6	8	8	5634	3.53	539	371	1.45

1997 Season

	Avg	AB	H	2B	3B	HR	RBI	BB	SO	OBP	SLG		Avg	AB	H	2B	3B	HR	RBI	BB	SO	OBP	SLG
vs. Left	.302	126	38	2	1	1	8	6	22	.348	.357	First Pitch	.299	77	23	4	3	1	5	2	0	.309	.468
vs. Right	.263	339	89	11	6	4	15	28	45	.323	.366	Ahead in Count	.352	88	31	5	1	1	6	23	0	.496	.466
Groundball	.281	96	27	3	1	2	7	6	13	.333	.396	Behind in Count	.227	216	49	3	1	2	7	0	59	.241	.278
Flyball	.319	69	22	2	3	0	3	6	7	.377	.435	Two Strikes	.214	206	44	3	2	2	9	9	67	.250	.277
Home	.275	236	65	8	3	0	10	14	35	.325	.335	Batting #1	.272	460	125	13	7	5	23	33	66	.327	.363
Away	.271	229	62	5	4	5	13	20	32	.333	.393	Batting #9	.000	3	0	0	0	0	0	0	1	.000	.000
Day	.256	164	42	5	4	1	9	13	23	.317	.354	Other	1.000	2	2	0	0	0	0	1	0	1.000	1.000
Night	.282	301	85	8	3	4	14	21	44	.336	.369	March/April	.383	107	41	3	4	1	8	7	7	.426	.514
Grass	.251	167	42	4	3	3	11	14	25	.308	.365	May	.252	119	30	7	2	1	6	9	18	.308	.370
Turf	.285	298	85	9	4	2	12	20	42	.342	.362	June	.244	86	21	1	0	1	3	12	12	.301	.291
Pre-All Star	.298	336	100	11	7	4	19	25	41	.351	.408	July	.207	87	18	1	1	1	3	9	16	.296	.276
Post-All Star	.209	129	27	2	0	1	4	9	26	.275	.248	August	.286	56	16	1	0	1	3	2	13	.328	.357
Scoring Posn	.205	88	18	1	0	0	18	10	17	.287	.216	Sept/Oct	.100	10	1	0	0	0	1	0	1	.100	.100

1997 Season

	Avg	AB	H	2B	3B	HR	RBI	BB	SO	OBP	SLG		Avg	AB	H	2B	3B	HR	RBI	BB	SO	OBP	SLG
Close & Late	.235	68	16	2	0	0	3	9	13	.325	.265	vs. AL	.262	42	11	0	0	0	4	3	5	.311	.262
None on/out	.299	201	60	6	4	1	1	10	24	.341	.383	vs. NL	.274	423	116	13	7	5	19	31	62	.331	.374

1997 By Position

Position	Avg	AB	H	2B	3B	HR	RBI	BB	SO	OBP	SLG	G	GS	Innings	PO	A	E	DP	Fld Pct	Rng Fctr	In Zone	Zone Outs	Zone Rtg	MLB Zone
As lf	.207	140	29	2	1	1	5	14	21	.288	.257	37	34	303.1	66	1	1	0	.985	1.99	75	64	.853	.805
As cf	.299	321	96	11	6	4	18	20	45	.346	.408	77	77	654.2	168	2	3	1	.983	2.34	194	156	.804	.815

Last Five Years

	Avg	AB	H	2B	3B	HR	RBI	BB	SO	OBP	SLG		Avg	AB	H	2B	3B	HR	RBI	BB	SO	OBP	SLG
vs. Left	.244	353	86	10	5	2	23	25	72	.301	.317	First Pitch	.312	250	78	13	5	6	30	6	0	.332	.476
vs. Right	.285	1102	314	49	20	19	84	84	160	.340	.417	Ahead in Count	.378	315	119	22	6	7	35	55	0	.471	.552
Groundball	.291	395	115	18	5	6	34	28	56	.342	.408	Behind in Count	.205	643	132	16	10	5	28	0	193	.215	.285
Flyball	.271	203	55	4	5	4	15	17	41	.330	.399	Two Strikes	.194	619	120	14	10	5	31	48	232	.255	.273
Home	.291	721	210	39	13	6	46	52	110	.342	.406	Batting #1	.272	1380	376	53	25	20	98	102	222	.326	.391
Away	.259	734	190	20	12	15	61	57	122	.319	.380	Batting #2	.250	36	9	2	0	0	4	3	6	.364	.306
Day	.278	464	129	20	9	9	35	44	75	.350	.418	Other	.385	39	15	4	0	1	5	4	4	.442	.564
Night	.273	991	271	39	16	12	72	65	157	.321	.381	March/April	.336	256	86	14	4	5	28	20	24	.389	.480
Grass	.274	840	230	36	13	14	68	63	137	.327	.398	May	.256	336	86	16	5	3	21	22	55	.306	.360
Turf	.276	615	170	23	12	7	39	46	95	.330	.387	June	.244	270	66	11	3	1	13	19	44	.296	.319
Pre-All Star	.282	927	261	43	17	10	68	67	137	.335	.397	July	.241	253	61	6	6	3	20	21	46	.306	.348
Post-All Star	.263	528	139	16	8	11	39	42	95	.324	.386	August	.295	241	71	8	6	8	21	19	48	.355	.477
Scoring Posn	.270	274	74	10	6	1	84	30	40	.340	.361	Sept/Oct	.303	99	30	4	1	1	4	8	15	.361	.394
Close & Late	.271	225	61	14	3	0	13	23	34	.339	.360	vs. AL	.262	42	11	0	0	0	4	3	5	.311	.262
None on/out	.278	615	171	22	13	8	8	42	91	.331	.395	vs. NL	.275	1413	389	59	25	21	103	106	227	.331	.397

Batter vs. Pitcher (career)

Hits Best Against	Avg	AB	H	2B	3B	HR	RBI	BB	SO	OBP	SLG	Hits Worst Against	Avg	AB	H	2B	3B	HR	RBI	BB	SO	OBP	SLG
David Cone	.600	10	6	0	0	1	1	1	1	.636	.900	Alan Benes	.000	11	0	0	0	0	0	1	1	.083	.000
John Burkett	.467	30	14	2	3	0	6	1	3	.500	.733	Rick Reed	.056	18	1	0	0	1	3	0	2	.056	.222
Pat Rapp	.429	14	6	0	1	1	1	3	0	.556	.786	Todd Stottlemyre	.083	12	1	0	0	1	0	1	1	.154	.083
Tim Belcher	.385	26	10	2	2	1	1	2	4	.448	.731	Shane Reynolds	.091	11	1	0	0	0	0	0	2	.091	.091
Curt Schilling	.333	24	8	0	2	1	6	5	4	.448	.625	Doug Drabek	.115	26	3	1	0	0	1	5		.148	.154

Reggie Sanders — Reds   Age 30 – Bats Right

	Avg	G	AB	R	H	2B	3B	HR	RBI	BB	SO	HBP	GDP	SB	CS	OBP	SLG	IBB	SH	SF	#Pit	#P/PA	GB	FB	G/F
1997 Season	.253	86	312	52	79	19	2	19	56	42	93	3	9	13	7	.347	.510	3	1	0	1383	3.86	82	105	0.78
Last Five Years	.273	545	1979	348	540	108	21	98	333	247	533	20	38	121	46	.356	.497	19	5	18	8885	3.92	603	559	1.08

1997 Season

	Avg	AB	H	2B	3B	HR	RBI	BB	SO	OBP	SLG		Avg	AB	H	2B	3B	HR	RBI	BB	SO	OBP	SLG
vs. Left	.309	68	21	7	0	4	10	12	15	.420	.588	First Pitch	.378	45	17	7	0	2	14	3	0	.417	.667
vs. Right	.238	244	58	12	2	15	46	30	78	.326	.488	Ahead in Count	.359	64	23	2	0	8	13	20	0	.512	.766
Groundball	.304	69	21	5	1	4	11	11	17	.400	.580	Behind in Count	.176	153	27	7	1	5	17	0	78	.192	.333
Flyball	.333	33	11	1	0	3	7	2	12	.389	.636	Two Strikes	.120	167	20	7	1	5	15	19	93	.222	.263
Home	.263	152	40	9	2	11	30	20	38	.349	.566	Batting #5	.288	118	34	6	1	6	24	20	29	.391	.508
Away	.244	160	39	10	0	8	26	22	55	.346	.456	Batting #6	.234	77	18	5	0	5	12	8	23	.314	.494
Day	.250	104	26	6	1	7	15	8	30	.304	.529	Other	.231	117	27	8	1	8	20	14	41	.323	.521
Night	.255	208	53	13	1	12	41	34	63	.367	.500	March/April	.246	57	14	3	1	3	11	5	15	.328	.491
Grass	.202	119	24	5	0	7	20	19	41	.321	.404	May	.212	52	11	3	0	3	9	7	19	.305	.442
Turf	.285	193	55	14	2	12	36	23	52	.364	.565	June	.000	0	0	0	0	0	0	0	0	.000	.000
Pre-All Star	.229	109	25	6	1	6	20	12	34	.317	.468	July	.200	30	6	1	0	3	4	5	13	.314	.533
Post-All Star	.266	203	54	13	1	13	36	30	59	.363	.532	August	.279	104	29	6	1	10	23	11	29	.353	.462
Scoring Posn	.275	80	22	6	2	6	39	16	16	.408	.625	Sept/Oct	.275	69	19	6	0	9	14	17		.398	.362
Close & Late	.302	43	13	3	0	5	11	5	13	.388	.721	vs. AL	.353	17	6	3	0	0	4	3	7	.450	.529
None on/out	.287	87	25	5	0	7	7	7	29	.340	.586	vs. NL	.247	295	73	16	2	19	52	39	86	.341	.508

1997 By Position

Position	Avg	AB	H	2B	3B	HR	RBI	BB	SO	OBP	SLG	G	GS	Innings	PO	A	E	DP	Fld Pct	Rng Fctr	In Zone	Zone Outs	Zone Rtg	MLB Zone
As rf	.251	311	78	19	2	19	56	42	93	.346	.510	85	84	753.0	184	4	5	1	.974	2.25	206	176	.854	.813

Last Five Years

	Avg	AB	H	2B	3B	HR	RBI	BB	SO	OBP	SLG		Avg	AB	H	2B	3B	HR	RBI	BB	SO	OBP	SLG
vs. Left	.319	454	145	28	6	26	82	64	92	.401	.579	First Pitch	.379	248	94	22	6	13	61	15	0	.415	.673
vs. Right	.259	1525	395	80	15	72	251	183	441	.343	.473	Ahead in Count	.407	428	174	32	7	44	116	125	0	.540	.822
Groundball	.304	608	185	37	9	26	100	81	146	.388	.523	Behind in Count	.196	905	177	38	7	20	86	0	423	.205	.319
Flyball	.264	292	77	18	3	16	50	25	106	.322	.510	Two Strikes	.163	1017	166	36	5	21	91	107	533	.248	.270
Home	.278	967	269	55	13	45	169	128	250	.365	.502	Batting #4	.272	633	172	42	5	39	117	89	174	.366	.539
Away	.268	1012	271	53	8	53	164	119	283	.348	.493	Batting #5	.296	564	167	29	9	25	100	64	143	.370	.512
Day	.263	586	154	39	4	26	101	68	155	.338	.476	Other	.257	782	201	37	7	34	116	94	216	.338	.453
Night	.277	1393	386	69	17	72	232	179	378	.364	.506	March/April	.261	276	72	15	6	11	44	29	73	.341	.478
Grass	.257	637	164	35	5	32	95	82	182	.346	.479	May	.286	350	100	17	4	19	57	56	99	.385	.520
Turf	.280	1342	376	73	16	66	238	165	351	.362	.506	June	.283	343	97	19	3	20	70	25	83	.335	.531
Pre-All Star	.280	1107	310	60	13	55	192	123	287	.355	.507	July	.264	402	106	23	2	18	60	50	107	.348	.465
Post-All Star	.264	872	230	48	8	43	141	124	246	.358	.485	August	.274	365	100	22	3	24	72	55	104	.369	.548
Scoring Posn	.277	573	159	31	9	25	237	120	151	.400	.494	Sept/Oct	.267	243	65	12	3	6	30	32	67	.356	.416
Close & Late	.247	300	74	15	3	13	45	37	95	.336	.447	vs. AL	.353	17	6	3	0	0	4	3	7	.450	.529

Last Five Years

	Avg	AB	H	2B	3B	HR	RBI	BB	SO	OBP	SLG		Avg	AB	H	2B	3B	HR	RBI	BB	SO	OBP	SLG
None on/out	.293	461	135	25	5	27	27	40	122	.353	.544	vs. NL	.272	1962	534	105	21	98	329	244	526	.356	.497

Batter vs. Pitcher (career)

Hits Best Against	Avg	AB	H	2B	3B	HR	RBI	BB	SO	OBP	SLG	Hits Worst Against	Avg	AB	H	2B	3B	HR	RBI	BB	SO	OBP	SLG
Brian Williams	.667	12	8	2	0	2	5	2	2	.714	1.333	Kevin Gross	.050	20	1	0	0	0	0	2	6	.136	.050
Armando Reynoso	.500	16	8	0	1	4	7	1	1	.529	1.375	Mel Rojas	.077	13	1	0	0	0	0	1	4	.143	.077
Butch Henry	.455	11	5	1	0	3	4	1	1	.500	1.364	Todd Jones	.077	13	1	0	0	0	1	1	6	.143	.077
Roger Bailey	.444	9	4	1	0	2	4	2	1	.583	1.222	Mark Wohlers	.083	12	1	0	0	0	0	1	7	.154	.083
Chris Hammond	.438	16	7	1	3	1	6	2	1	.500	1.063	John Burkett	.087	23	2	1	0	0	4	2	2	.148	.130

Scott Sanders — Tigers　　　　　　　Age 29 – Pitches Right

	ERA	W	L	Sv	G	GS	IP	BB	SO	Avg	H	2B	3B	HR	RBI	OBP	SLG	GF	IR	IRS	Hld	SvOp	SB	CS	GB	FB	G/F
1997 Season	5.86	6	14	2	47	20	139.2	62	120	.278	152	38	3	30	100	.350	.523	15	22	12	4	4	13	5	151	183	0.83
Career (1993-1997)	4.54	27	35	3	142	80	537.0	212	511	.247	505	102	9	68	263	.318	.405	23	40	16	9	5	43	25	647	549	1.18

1997 Season

	ERA	W	L	Sv	G	GS	IP	H	BB	SO
Home	5.65	3	9	1	25	11	79.2	83	18	33
Away	6.15	3	5	1	22	9	60.0	69	12	29
Day	5.33	5	5	1	13	9	54.0	51	10	19
Night	6.20	1	9	1	34	11	85.2	101	20	43
Grass	5.66	2	9	1	24	13	82.2	92	17	28
Turf	6.16	4	5	1	23	7	57.0	60	13	34
March/April	8.88	0	4	0	9	4	25.1	30	8	13
May	6.05	1	1	0	7	2	19.1	22	4	16
June	3.14	1	1	2	11	0	14.1	12	3	7
July	5.48	1	2	0	9	3	21.1	27	5	4
August	6.59	1	4	0	6	6	28.2	36	5	16
Sept/Oct	4.11	2	2	0	5	5	30.2	25	5	6
Starter	6.45	4	13	0	20	20	104.2	117	24	43
Reliever	4.11	2	1	2	27	0	35.0	35	6	19
0 Days rest (Relief)	6.75	0	0	0	2	0	1.1	1	1	2
1 or 2 Days rest	4.50	2	1	1	17	0	24.0	25	3	11
3+ Days rest	2.79	0	1	0	8	0	9.2	9	2	6
vs. AL	6.17	6	13	1	42	19	128.1	138	30	56
vs. NL	2.38	0	1	0	5	1	11.1	14	0	6
Pre-All Star	6.68	2	6	2	30	6	62.0	68	16	37
Post-All Star	5.21	4	8	0	17	14	77.2	84	14	25

	Avg	AB	H	2B	3B	HR	RBI	BB	SO	OBP	SLG
vs. Left	.286	266	76	22	2	15	44	43	57	.383	.553
vs. Right	.270	281	76	16	1	15	56	19	63	.316	.495
Inning 1-6	.280	411	115	29	3	25	75	45	81	.349	.547
Inning 7+	.272	136	37	9	0	5	25	17	39	.352	.449
None on	.247	320	79	19	1	17	17	35	78	.325	.472
Runners on	.322	227	73	19	2	13	83	27	42	.383	.595
Scoring Posn	.275	142	39	9	2	7	69	23	29	.362	.514
Close & Late	.410	39	16	1	0	3	11	3	11	.444	.667
None on/out	.243	140	34	9	0	8	8	10	35	.298	.479
vs. 1st Batr (relief)	.273	22	6	3	0	0	4	2	10	.370	.409
1st Inning Pitched	.244	160	39	12	1	6	29	22	42	.337	.444
First 15 Pitches	.267	116	31	10	1	4	21	13	27	.348	.474
Pitch 16-30	.252	107	27	8	0	5	15	11	30	.322	.467
Pitch 31-45	.346	81	28	7	0	2	11	9	12	.411	.506
Pitch 46+	.272	243	66	13	2	19	53	29	51	.343	.576
Ahead in Count	.203	271	55	13	1	7	26	0	109	.210	.336
Behind in Count	.392	102	40	8	1	12	34	24	0	.489	.843
Two Strikes	.197	290	57	16	0	9	33		120	.283	.345
Pre-All Star	.276	246	68	18	1	16	56	37	56	.369	.553
Post-All Star	.279	301	84	20	2	14	44	25	64	.333	.498

Career (1993-1997)

	ERA	W	L	Sv	G	GS	IP	H	HR	BB	SO
Home	4.66	16	19	1	76	43	288.0	275	42	113	279
Away	4.41	11	16	2	66	37	249.0	230	26	99	232
Day	4.39	13	9	1	44	27	170.0	156	19	73	163
Night	4.61	14	26	2	98	53	367.0	349	49	139	348
Grass	4.75	17	26	2	97	58	377.1	369	48	140	358
Turf	4.06	10	9	1	45	22	159.2	136	20	72	153
March/April	5.57	2	6	1	24	9	63.0	59	11	27	57
May	5.36	5	4	0	25	11	82.1	75	15	44	72
June	3.91	4	6	2	33	11	96.2	85	12	42	105
July	5.31	4	8	0	24	17	98.1	107	12	27	110
August	3.52	8	5	0	18	16	99.2	83	8	39	88
Sept/Oct	4.08	4	6	0	18	16	97.0	96	10	33	79
Starter	4.74	24	32	0	80	80	454.0	432	57	175	418
Reliever	3.47	3	3	3	62	0	83.0	73	11	37	93
0 Days rest (Relief)	3.86	0	0	0	3	0	2.1	3	1	2	2
1 or 2 Days rest	3.73	3	3	1	36	0	50.2	47	5	25	55
3+ Days rest	3.00	0	0	2	23	0	30.0	23	5	10	36
vs. AL	6.17	6	13	1	42	19	128.1	138	30	56	108
vs. NL	4.03	21	22	2	100	61	408.2	367	38	156	403
Pre-All Star	4.84	11	19	3	91	36	277.1	248	41	124	278
Post-All Star	4.23	16	16	0	51	44	259.2	257	27	88	233

	Avg	AB	H	2B	3B	HR	RBI	BB	SO	OBP	SLG
vs. Left	.278	945	263	60	6	32	128	140	193	.370	.456
vs. Right	.219	1103	242	42	3	36	135	72	318	.270	.361
Inning 1-6	.250	1651	412	82	8	58	224	166	397	.318	.414
Inning 7+	.234	397	93	20	1	10	39	46	114	.317	.365
None on	.219	1233	270	53	4	38	38	126	323	.297	.361
Runners on	.288	815	235	49	5	30	225	86	188	.349	.471
Scoring Posn	.281	456	128	25	4	16	188	61	113	.352	.458
Close & Late	.285	130	37	3	0	3	16	16	35	.362	.377
None on/out	.223	539	120	25	2	19	19	41	133	.284	.382
vs. 1st Batr (relief)	.288	52	15	5	0	1	7	6	18	.371	.442
1st Inning Pitched	.226	495	112	27	1	13	65	61	126	.313	.364
First 15 Pitches	.233	378	88	21	2	9	44	40	83	.309	.370
Pitch 16-30	.229	367	84	21	0	14	37	36	105	.299	.401
Pitch 31-45	.270	307	83	15	2	7	34	36	68	.346	.401
Pitch 46+	.251	996	250	45	5	38	148	100	255	.319	.421
First Pitch	.324	253	82	17	2	13	45	13	0	.352	.561
Ahead in Count	.172	1001	172	38	2	14	72	0	449	.180	.256
Behind in Count	.358	422	151	27	4	30	99	99	0	.470	.654
Two Strikes	.156	1031	161	33	2	12	67	99	511	.236	.227
Pre-All Star	.237	1048	248	52	5	41	145	124	278	.320	.413
Post-All Star	.257	1000	257	50	4	27	118	88	233	.315	.396

Pitcher vs. Batter (career)

Pitches Best Vs.	Avg	AB	H	2B	3B	HR	RBI	BB	SO	OBP	SLG	Pitches Worst Vs.	Avg	AB	H	2B	3B	HR	RBI	BB	SO	OBP	SLG
Luis Gonzalez	.000	11	0	0	0	0	0	1	3	.083	.000	Gregg Jefferies	.500	14	7	2	0	1	3	0	2	.500	.857
Mike Lansing	.071	14	1	0	0	0	0	3	3	.133	.071	Barry Bonds	.400	15	6	1	0	3	5	4	1	.438	1.067
Jeff Kent	.077	13	1	0	0	0	0	0	5	.077	.077	Larry Walker	.400	10	4	1	0	2	4	1	2	.455	1.100
Bobby Bonilla	.100	10	1	0	0	0	1	2	1	.250	.100	Rich Becker	.375	8	3	1	0	1	2	3	2	.545	.875
Eddie Taubensee	.125	16	2	0	0	0	1	2	3	.222	.125	Bernard Gilkey	.333	9	3	0	0	2	5	1	2	.364	1.000

Julio Santana — Rangers
Age 25 – Pitches Right

	ERA	W	L	Sv	G	GS	IP	BB	SO	Avg	H	2B	3B	HR	RBI	OBP	SLG	GF	IR	IRS	Hld	SvOp	SB	CS	GB	FB	G/F
1997 Season	6.75	4	6	0	30	14	104.0	49	64	.323	141	23	4	16	72	.392	.503	3	15	2	1	1	3	1	151	126	1.20

1997 Season

	ERA	W	L	Sv	G	GS	IP	H	HR	BB	SO
Home	6.30	3	2	0	14	7	50.0	60	7	29	27
Away	7.17	1	4	0	16	7	54.0	81	9	20	37
Starter	7.36	3	5	0	14	14	69.2	103	10	33	44
Reliever	5.50	1	1	0	16	0	34.1	38	6	16	20
0 Days rest (Relief)	0.00	0	0	0	1	0	1.1	2	0	0	1
1 or 2 Days rest	8.10	0	1	0	5	0	6.2	12	2	3	5
3+ Days rest	5.13	1	0	0	10	0	26.1	24	4	13	14
Pre-All Star	6.51	3	4	0	18	10	74.2	92	13	40	43
Post-All Star	7.36	1	2	0	12	4	29.1	49	3	9	21

	Avg	AB	H	2B	3B	HR	RBI	BB	SO	OBP	SLG
vs. Left	.324	216	70	13	2	5	24	24	31	.400	.472
vs. Right	.321	221	71	10	2	11	48	25	33	.384	.534
Scoring Posn	.302	129	39	7	2	7	61	16	22	.371	.550
Close & Late	.318	22	7	1	0	1	3	4	2	.423	.500
None on/out	.304	102	31	3	1	1	1	11	13	.372	.382
First Pitch	.431	72	31	6	0	4	16	2	0	.442	.681
Ahead in Count	.318	179	57	12	1	7	35	0	43	.322	.514
Behind in Count	.314	102	32	3	2	4	15	31	0	.470	.500
Two Strikes	.267	180	48	8	2	6	26	16	64	.330	.433

F.P. Santangelo — Expos
Age 30 – Bats Both

	Avg	G	AB	R	H	2B	3B	HR	RBI	BB	SO	HBP	GDP	SB	CS	OBP	SLG	IBB	SH	SF	#Pit	#P/PA	GB	FB	G/F
1997 Season	.249	130	350	56	87	19	5	5	31	50	73	25	1	8	5	.379	.374	1	12	3	1660	3.77	121	99	1.22
Career (1995-1997)	.268	317	841	121	225	44	11	13	96	111	143	38	7	14	8	.375	.392	5	22	8	3686	3.61	308	241	1.28

1997 Season

	Avg	AB	H	2B	3B	HR	RBI	BB	SO	OBP	SLG
vs. Left	.250	80	20	2	0	2	6	8	19	.365	.350
vs. Right	.248	270	67	17	5	3	25	42	54	.383	.381
Groundball	.202	94	19	5	1	0	6	14	19	.342	.277
Flyball	.209	43	9	2	0	0		8	10	.382	.256
Home	.275	167	46	10	1	5	19	22	36	.397	.437
Away	.224	183	41	9	4	0	12	28	37	.362	.317
Day	.252	111	28	6	2	0	9	16	27	.382	.342
Night	.247	239	59	13	3	5	22	34	46	.377	.389
Grass	.223	121	27	6	2	0	8	19	22	.345	.306
Turf	.262	229	60	13	3	5	23	31	51	.396	.410
Pre-All Star	.307	205	63	15	2	4	21	35	41	.436	.459
Post-All Star	.166	145	24	4	3	1	10	15	32	.292	.255
Scoring Posn	.156	77	12	6	0	1	23	16	13	.327	.273
Close & Late	.238	63	15	1	1	0	3	5	13	.360	.286
None on/out	.292	113	33	8	0	2		12	22	.398	.416

	Avg	AB	H	2B	3B	HR	RBI	BB	SO	OBP	SLG
First Pitch	.333	48	16	3	2	1	8	1	0	.411	.542
Ahead in Count	.304	79	24	9	0	1	11	27	0	.481	.456
Behind in Count	.197	152	30	4	3	2	7	0	60	.256	.303
Two Strikes	.202	168	34	6	3	3	10	22	73	.337	.327
Batting #1	.307	153	47	11	3	3	16	22	35	.427	.477
Batting #7	.216	74	16	2	0	2	8	12	15	.370	.324
Other	.195	123	24	6	2	0	7	16	23	.325	.276
March/April	.283	60	17	4	2	1	8	16	13	.457	.467
May	.220	41	9	1	0	0	4	6	7	.393	.244
June	.372	94	35	10	0	3	9	12	18	.459	.574
July	.153	72	11	3	1	1	6	8	17	.315	.264
August	.200	70	14	0	2	0	3	7	17	.273	.264
Sept/Oct	.077	13	1	1	0	0	1	1	1	.250	.154
vs. AL	.235	51	12	4	0	0	2	7	10	.350	.314
vs. NL	.251	299	75	15	5	5	29	43	63	.383	.385

1997 By Position

Position	Avg	AB	H	2B	3B	HR	RBI	BB	SO	OBP	SLG	G	GS	Innings	PO	A	E	DP	Fld Pct	Rng Fctr	In Zone	Zone Outs	Zone Rtg	MLB Zone
As Pinch Hitter	.111	9	1	0	0	0	1	1	1	.250	.111	15	0	---										
As 3b	.289	97	28	3	0	1	3	11	23	.378	.351	32	25	231.0	17	45	3	0	.954	2.42	64	47	.734	.801
As lf	.190	63	12	1	3	0	3	6	16	.338	.302	40	15	168.1	46	1	0	1	1.000	2.51	56	45	.804	.805
As cf	.381	42	16	5	0	3	8	3	4	.447	.714	13	11	104.0	29	0	0	0	1.000	2.51	36	27	.750	.815
As rf	.221	131	29	10	2	1	16	29	25	.399	.351	51	41	354.1	79	3	0	1	1.000	2.08	91	77	.846	.813

Career (1995-1997)

	Avg	AB	H	2B	3B	HR	RBI	BB	SO	OBP	SLG
vs. Left	.278	187	52	8	1	3	22	24	33	.388	.380
vs. Right	.265	654	173	36	10	10	74	87	110	.371	.396
Groundball	.262	202	53	12	3	1	26	28	37	.375	.366
Flyball	.187	134	25	4	0	2	6	13	21	.284	.261
Home	.305	416	127	29	6	11	62	61	69	.416	.483
Away	.231	425	98	15	5	2	34	50	74	.333	.304
Day	.258	252	65	14	4	2	30	32	47	.362	.369
Night	.272	589	160	30	7	11	66	79	96	.380	.402
Grass	.233	296	69	9	3	2	30	31	49	.318	.304
Turf	.286	545	156	35	8	11	66	80	94	.404	.440
Pre-All Star	.289	401	116	26	5	7	53	64	75	.408	.431
Post-All Star	.248	440	109	18	6	6	43	47	68	.343	.357
Scoring Posn	.255	196	50	13	3	3	78	30	29	.371	.398
Close & Late	.226	146	33	2	1	2	19	17	28	.335	.295
None on/out	.275	255	70	15	2	5	5	30	41	.379	.408

	Avg	AB	H	2B	3B	HR	RBI	BB	SO	OBP	SLG
First Pitch	.360	125	45	9	4	1	19	5	0	.411	.520
Ahead in Count	.354	195	69	16	4	5	33	62	0	.508	.554
Behind in Count	.197	356	70	13	3	2	20	0	116	.239	.267
Two Strikes	.188	351	66	16	3	5	27	44	143	.308	.293
Batting #1	.276	239	66	12	3	6	25	29	49	.382	.427
Batting #7	.243	251	61	12	3	5	27	31	40	.346	.375
Other	.279	351	98	20	5	2	44	51	54	.390	.382
March/April	.304	92	28	6	2	2	15	19	18	.440	.478
May	.228	114	26	7	2	0	14	14	19	.345	.325
June	.329	170	56	12	1	5	22	23	31	.429	.500
July	.169	124	21	5	1	2	11	20	24	.333	.274
August	.291	220	64	12	5	3	22	24	34	.366	.432
Sept/Oct	.248	121	30	2	0	1	12	11	17	.333	.288
vs. AL	.235	51	12	4	0	0	2	7	10	.350	.314
vs. NL	.270	790	213	40	11	13	94	104	133	.376	.397

Batter vs. Pitcher (career)

Hits Best Against	Avg	AB	H	2B	3B	HR	RBI	BB	SO	OBP	SLG
Kevin Brown	.455	11	5	0	0	0	0	1	3	.500	.455
Bobby Jones	.417	12	5	1	0	1	4	1	3	.500	.750
Pedro Astacio	.400	15	6	1	2	0	5	1	3	.438	.733
Darryl Kile	.333	15	5	1	0	0	0	4	2	.474	.400
Mark Gardner	.333	9	3	0	0	2	3	2	0	.455	1.000

Hits Worst Against	Avg	AB	H	2B	3B	HR	RBI	BB	SO	OBP	SLG
Curt Schilling	.083	12	1	0	0	0	0	1	3	.154	.083
Terry Mulholland	.100	10	1	0	0	1	4	0	1	.091	.400
Mike Morgan	.100	10	1	0	0	0	1	1	1	.182	.100
Jason Isringhausen	.111	9	1	0	0	0	0	1	0	.250	.111
Shane Reynolds	.167	12	2	0	0	0	0	2	4	.333	.167

Benito Santiago — Blue Jays

	Avg	G	AB	R	H	2B	3B	HR	RBI	BB	SO	HBP	GDP	SB	CS	OBP	SLG	IBB	SH	SF	#Pit	#P/PA	GB	FB	G/F
1997 Season	.243	97	341	31	83	10	0	13	42	17	80	2	10	1	0	.279	.387	1	1	5	1300	3.55	112	98	1.14
Last Five Years	.257	554	1894	226	486	84	10	78	262	152	377	13	45	16	11	.314	.435	12	3	17	7382	3.55	605	590	1.03

1997 Season

	Avg	AB	H	2B	3B	HR	RBI	BB	SO	OBP	SLG		Avg	AB	H	2B	3B	HR	RBI	BB	SO	OBP	SLG
vs. Left	.301	93	28	0	0	6	16	5	21	.333	.495	First Pitch	.371	62	23	4	0	3	7	1	0	.369	.581
vs. Right	.222	248	55	10	0	7	26	12	59	.259		Ahead in Count	.393	56	22	1	0	5	15	7	0	.469	.679
Groundball	.180	50	9	1	0	3	7	4	9	.232	.380	Behind in Count	.182	165	30	2	0	4	15	0	63	.185	.267
Flyball	.261	46	12	0	0	3	8	1	17	.300	.457	Two Strikes	.146	158	23	2	0	3	16	9	80	.189	.215
Home	.261	184	48	6	0	7	27	7	39	.284	.408	Batting #6	.253	91	23	2	0	3	8	4	30	.278	.374
Away	.223	157	35	4	0	6	15	10	41	.275	.363	Batting #7	.225	182	41	5	0	6	24	11	38	.267	.352
Day	.265	102	27	1	0	4	13	6	21	.303	.392	Other	.279	68	19	3	0	4	10	2	12	.315	.500
Night	.234	239	56	9	0	9	29	11	59	.270	.385	March/April	.161	31	5	1	0	1	4	2	9	.212	.290
Grass	.226	115	26	2	0	3	8	10	28	.297	.322	May	.205	78	16	1	0	2	11	3	23	.235	.295
Turf	.252	226	57	8	0	10	34	7	52	.270	.420	June	.200	65	13	3	0	0	2	3	14	.232	.246
Pre-All Star	.197	183	36	5	0	3	17	8	46	.229	.273	July	.286	42	12	0	0	3	5	3	7	.326	.500
Post-All Star	.297	158	47	5	0	10	25	9	34	.335	.519	August	.286	63	18	3	0	4	9	3	8	.318	.524
Scoring Posn	.205	88	18	2	0	5	32	10	28	.272	.398	Sept/Oct	.306	62	19	2	0	3	11	3	19	.343	.484
Close & Late	.173	52	9	0	0	4	7	4	15	.224	.404	vs. AL	.252	302	76	8	0	13	41	16	70	.285	.407
None on/out	.211	76	16	2	0	2	2	2	16	.241	.316	vs. NL	.179	39	7	2	0	0	1	1	10	.238	.231

1997 By Position

Position	Avg	AB	H	2B	3B	HR	RBI	BB	SO	OBP	SLG	G	GS	Innings	PO	A	E	DP	Fld Pct	Rng Fctr	In Zone	Zone Outs	Zone Rtg	MLB Zone
As c	.243	337	82	10	0	13	42	17	77	.280	.383	95	93	819.1	620	39	2	10	.997	—	—	—	—	

Last Five Years

	Avg	AB	H	2B	3B	HR	RBI	BB	SO	OBP	SLG		Avg	AB	H	2B	3B	HR	RBI	BB	SO	OBP	SLG
vs. Left	.316	450	142	23	3	22	74	47	69	.379	.527	First Pitch	.313	377	118	21	5	20	58	7	0	.331	.554
vs. Right	.238	1444	344	61	7	56	188	105	308	.293	.407	Ahead in Count	.389	350	136	30	1	22	79	65	0	.481	.669
Groundball	.248	520	129	21	2	24	66	45	87	.310	.435	Behind in Count	.179	840	150	18	3	20	74	0	315	.182	.279
Flyball	.261	326	85	14	5	17	47	26	79	.321	.491	Two Strikes	.156	840	131	25	1	18	72	80	377	.231	.252
Home	.267	970	259	49	5	32	126	76	194	.322	.427	Batting #6	.262	866	227	41	5	38	126	53	178	.305	.453
Away	.246	924	227	35	5	46	136	76	183	.305	.444	Batting #7	.252	441	111	23	3	14	54	31	77	.305	.413
Day	.295	448	132	21	3	18	72	53	86	.365	.475	Other	.252	587	148	20	2	26	82	68	122	.331	.426
Night	.245	1446	354	63	7	60	190	99	291	.297	.423	March/April	.245	277	68	17	1	12	43	25	55	.309	.444
Grass	.247	989	244	39	7	38	136	83	194	.307	.416	May	.232	345	80	12	2	9	42	30	70	.294	.357
Turf	.267	905	242	45	3	40	126	69	183	.321	.456	June	.256	309	79	11	5	8	32	24	63	.315	.401
Pre-All Star	.243	1040	253	45	8	32	128	88	207	.304	.394	July	.267	356	95	17	0	18	56	19	73	.302	.466
Post-All Star	.273	854	233	39	2	46	134	64	170	.325	.485	August	.259	367	95	18	1	17	47	21	62	.296	.452
Scoring Posn	.260	489	127	22	3	28	194	68	106	.342	.489	Sept/Oct	.288	240	69	9	1	14	42	33	54	.384	.508
Close & Late	.190	321	61	11	1	11	37	22	81	.244	.333	vs. AL	.252	302	76	8	0	13	41	16	70	.285	.407
None on/out	.268	437	117	18	6	18	18	24	79	.310	.460	vs. NL	.258	1592	410	76	10	65	221	136	307	.319	.440

Batter vs. Pitcher (career)

Hits Best Against	Avg	AB	H	2B	3B	HR	RBI	BB	SO	OBP	SLG	Hits Worst Against	Avg	AB	H	2B	3B	HR	RBI	BB	SO	OBP	SLG
Denny Neagle	.421	19	8	1	0	3	4	2	3	.476	.947	Steve Reed	.000	16	0	0	0	0	1	1	4	.056	.000
Rheal Cormier	.417	12	5	0	1	3	7	1	2	.462	1.333	Doug Drabek	.032	31	1	0	1	0	3	2	5	.118	.097
Andy Benes	.400	15	6	2	0	2	4	2	0	.471	.933	Dave Burba	.056	18	1	0	0	0	0	4	5	.227	.056
Steve Trachsel	.350	20	7	1	1	2	3	3	7	.435	.800	Norm Charlton	.100	20	2	0	0	0	1	2	5	.182	.100
Jaime Navarro	.333	15	5	2	0	2	4	1	5	.375	.867	Hideo Nomo	.100	10	1	0	0	0	0	1	1	.182	.100

Jose Santiago — Royals

	ERA	W	L	Sv	G	GS	IP	BB	SO	Avg	H	2B	3B	HR	RBI	OBP	SLG	GF	IR	IRS	Hld	SvOp	SB	CS	GB	FB	G/F
1997 Season	1.93	0	0	0	4	0	4.2	2	1	.333	7	1	0	0	2	.417	.381	3	2	2	0	0	0	0	8	7	1.14

1997 Season

	ERA	W	L	Sv	G	GS	IP	H	HR	BB	SO		Avg	AB	H	2B	3B	HR	RBI	BB	SO	OBP	SLG
Home	2.45	0	0	0	3	0	3.2	6	0	2	1	vs. Left	.250	8	2	1	0	0	2	0	0	.250	.375
Away	0.00	0	0	0	1	0	1.0	1	0	1	0	vs. Right	.385	13	5	0	0	0	1	2	1	.500	.385

Tony Saunders — Marlins

	ERA	W	L	Sv	G	GS	IP	BB	SO	Avg	H	2B	3B	HR	RBI	OBP	SLG	CG	ShO	Sup	QS	#P/S	SB	CS	GB	FB	G/F
1997 Season	4.61	4	6	0	22	21	111.1	64	102	.244	99	17	2	12	56	.347	.385	0	0	5.34	12	92	7	9	138	122	1.13

1997 Season

	ERA	W	L	Sv	G	GS	IP	H	HR	BB	SO		Avg	AB	H	2B	3B	HR	RBI	BB	SO	OBP	SLG
Home	4.26	3	4	0	12	12	61.1	51	7	48	52	vs. Left	.176	85	15	3	0	2	7	9	31	.263	.282
Away	5.04	1	2	0	10	9	50.0	48	5	16	50	vs. Right	.263	320	84	14	2	10	49	55	71	.368	.413
Starter	4.65	4	6	0	21	21	110.1	99	12	63	100	Scoring Posn	.235	102	24	3	1	3	40	13	20	.311	.373
Reliever	0.00	0	0	0	1	0	1.0	0	0	0	1	Close & Late	.409	22	9	2	1	0	5	2	3	.458	.591
0-3 Days Rest (Start)	10.50	0	0	0	1	1	6.0	8	2	2	8	None on/out	.265	102	27	6	0	3	3	19	26	.380	.412
4 Days Rest	2.92	3	2	0	11	11	61.2	52	3	34	44	First Pitch	.410	39	16	3	1	1	13	1	0	.415	.615
5+ Days Rest	6.33	1	4	0	9	9	42.2	39	7	27	44	Ahead in Count	.154	169	26	3	1	2	9	0	74	.153	.219
Pre-All Star	4.38	2	1	0	7	7	39.0	36	3	12	35	Behind in Count	.323	99	32	8	0	7	24	37	0	.504	.616
Post-All Star	4.73	2	5	0	15	14	72.1	63	9	52	67	Two Strikes	.137	204	28	2	1	2	10	26	102	.234	.186

Steve Scarsone — Cardinals
Age 32 – Bats Right (flyball hitter)

	Avg	G	AB	R	H	2B	3B	HR	RBI	BB	SO	HBP	GDP	SB	CS	OBP	SLG	IBB	SH	SF	#Pit	#P/PA	GB	FB	G/F
1997 Season	.100	5	10	0	1	0	0	0	0	2	5	0	0	1	0	.250	.100				50	4.17	1	2	0.50
Last Five Years	.245	286	732	98	179	39	4	20	80	59	230	8	9	6	8	.306	.391	1	18	5	3093	3.76	179	227	0.79

1997 Season

	Avg	AB	H	2B	3B	HR	RBI	BB	SO	OBP	SLG			Avg	AB	H	2B	3B	HR	RBI	BB	SO	OBP	SLG
vs. Left	.000	2	0	0	0	0	0	0	2	.000	.000	Scoring Posn		.000	2	0	0	0	0	0	2	1	.500	.000
vs. Right	.125	8	1	0	0	0	0	2	3	.300	.125	Close & Late		.000	2	0	0	0	0	0	1	2	.333	.000

Last Five Years

	Avg	AB	H	2B	3B	HR	RBI	BB	SO	OBP	SLG			Avg	AB	H	2B	3B	HR	RBI	BB	SO	OBP	SLG
vs. Left	.299	231	69	17	1	5	22	21	63	.355	.446	First Pitch		.345	113	39	6	2	6	21	0	0	.353	.593
vs. Right	.220	501	110	22	3	15	58	38	167	.283	.365	Ahead in Count		.303	99	30	10	1	5	12	27	0	.457	.576
Groundball	.276	214	59	13	0	8	23	12	54	.314	.449	Behind in Count		.190	401	76	16	1	6	33	0	203	.199	.279
Flyball	.191	131	25	7	1	3	15	13	65	.274	.328	Two Strikes		.158	405	64	13	1	3	23	32	230	.217	.217
Home	.241	373	90	19	3	12	47	31	117	.307	.405	Batting #2		.280	264	74	18	1	10	32	19	77	.334	.470
Away	.248	359	89	20	1	8	33	28	113	.305	.376	Batting #7		.247	227	56	12	1	7	28	13	71	.295	.401
Day	.224	406	91	20	1	12	47	35	131	.290	.367	Other		.203	241	49	9	2	3	20	27	82	.286	.295
Night	.270	326	88	19	3	8	33	24	99	.326	.420	March/April		.231	78	18	5	0	2	7	10	24	.326	.372
Grass	.234	531	124	25	3	15	60	40	169	.296	.377	May		.289	76	22	7	0	4	10	9	25	.365	.539
Turf	.274	201	55	14	1	5	20	17	61	.333	.428	June		.266	154	41	6	2	6	16	6	42	.299	.448
Pre-All Star	.270	385	104	24	2	13	45	30	113	.325	.444	July		.263	217	57	17	2	3	26	16	71	.312	.401
Post-All Star	.216	347	75	15	2	7	35	29	117	.285	.331	August		.176	102	18	3	0	3	14	10	33	.259	.294
Scoring Posn	.215	186	40	15	0	5	57	18	67	.284	.376	Sept/Oct		.219	105	23	1	0	2	9	8	35	.293	.286
Close & Late	.227	119	27	6	0	5	16	10	45	.298	.403	vs. AL		.000	0	0	0	0	0	0	0	0	.000	.000
None on/out	.239	180	43	11	1	4	11	11	47	.294	.378	vs. NL		.245	732	179	39	4	20	80	59	230	.306	.391

Batter vs. Pitcher (career)

Hits Best Against	Avg	AB	H	2B	3B	HR	RBI	BB	SO	OBP	SLG	Hits Worst Against	Avg	AB	H	2B	3B	HR	RBI	BB	SO	OBP	SLG
Danny Jackson	.600	10	6	1	0	0	3	2	1	.667	.700	Ramon Martinez	.000	12	0	0	0	0	0	0	5	.000	.000
F. Valenzuela	.455	11	5	2	0	0	1	0	2	.455	.636	Doug Drabek	.071	14	1	0	0	0	2	0	5	.071	.071
												Pete Schourek	.091	11	1	0	0	0	1	1	4	.167	.091
												Denny Neagle	.200	15	3	0	0	0	1	1	6	.294	.200

Curt Schilling — Phillies
Age 31 – Pitches Right

	ERA	W	L	Sv	G	GS	IP	BB	SO	Avg	H	2B	3B	HR	RBI	OBP	SLG	CG	ShO	Sup	QS	#P/S	SB	CS	GB	FB	G/F
1997 Season	2.97	17	11	0	35	35	254.1	58	319	.224	208	49	7	25	92	.271	.372	7	2	4.14	26	118	9	9	267	201	1.33
Last Five Years	3.52	51	41	0	125	125	871.1	219	859	.237	774	157	17	86	336	.287	.375	24	6	4.26	83	110	40	29	1009	831	1.21

1997 Season

	ERA	W	L	Sv	G	GS	IP	H	HR	BB	SO			Avg	AB	H	2B	3B	HR	RBI	BB	SO	OBP	SLG
Home	2.80	7	6	0	20	20	144.2	111	10	32	186	vs. Left		.232	456	106	21	6	16	51	34	151	.287	.410
Away	3.20	10	5	0	15	15	109.2	97	15	26	133	vs. Right		.215	474	102	28	1	9	41	24	168	.254	.335
Day	3.29	7	5	0	13	13	95.2	78	12	17	123	Inning 1-6		.218	734	160	37	4	20	72	45	264	.265	.361
Night	2.78	10	6	0	22	22	158.2	130	13	41	196	Inning 7+		.245	196	48	12	3	5	20	13	55	.294	.413
Grass	3.72	4	4	0	8	8	55.2	50	11	15	73	None on		.212	612	130	29	4	16	16	32	220	.254	.351
Turf	2.76	13	7	0	27	27	198.2	158	14	43	246	Runners on		.245	318	78	20	3	9	76	26	99	.301	.412
March/April	3.80	3	2	0	6	6	42.2	41	6	11	40	Scoring Posn		.209	187	39	11	3	2	59	14	70	.257	.332
May	2.11	4	2	0	6	6	42.2	32	3	10	53	Close & Late		.233	129	30	8	2	2	14	12	35	.296	.372
June	4.54	2	3	0	6	6	39.2	37	6	15	58	None on/out		.229	249	57	12	4	5	15	15	86	.275	.369
July	2.68	2	3	0	6	6	47.0	36	5	8	61	vs. 1st Batr (relief)		.000	0	0	0	0	0	0	0	0	.000	.000
August	1.45	2	0	0	5	5	37.1	25	1	9	55	1st Inning Pitched		.210	119	25	3	1	6	10	2	47	.280	.403
Sept/Oct	3.20	4	1	0	6	6	45.0	37	4	6	55	First 75 Pitches		.218	570	124	24	4	11	46	29	206	.257	.332
Starter	2.97	17	11	0	35	35	254.1	208	25	58	319	Pitch 76-90		.189	122	23	8	1	4	15	8	39	.235	.369
Reliever	0.00	0	0	0	0	0	0.0	0	0	0	0	Pitch 91-105		.274	106	29	8	1	4	11	9	35	.336	.481
0-3 Days Rest (Start)	0.00	0	0	0	0	0	0.0	0	0	0	0	Pitch 106+		.242	132	32	9	1	6	20	12	39	.306	.462
4 Days Rest	3.10	14	10	0	30	30	218.0	186	24	43	268	First Pitch		.333	105	35	12	1	2	12	0	0	.355	.524
5+ Days Rest	2.23	3	1	0	5	5	36.1	22	1	15	51	Ahead in Count		.162	543	88	17	5	10	39	0	267	.162	.267
vs. AL	3.00	1	1	0	3	3	21.0	20	0	4	31	Behind in Count		.333	108	36	13	0	6	20	25	0	.463	.620
vs. NL	2.97	16	10	0	32	32	233.1	188	25	54	288	Two Strikes		.159	580	92	18	3	12	42	31	319	.201	.262
Pre-All Star	3.59	9	8	0	19	19	133.0	119	15	37	159	Pre-All Star		.242	492	119	23	4	15	61	37	159	.296	.396
Post-All Star	2.30	8	3	0	16	16	121.1	89	10	21	160	Post-All Star		.203	438	89	26	3	10	31	21	160	.242	.345

Last Five Years

	ERA	W	L	Sv	G	GS	IP	H	HR	BB	SO			Avg	AB	H	2B	3B	HR	RBI	BB	SO	OBP	SLG
Home	3.35	22	23	0	60	60	427.0	369	33	108	457	vs. Left		.239	1580	378	73	13	47	179	122	422	.294	.391
Away	3.69	29	18	0	65	65	444.1	405	53	111	402	vs. Right		.235	1683	396	84	4	39	157	97	437	.280	.359
Day	4.17	16	16	0	44	44	295.1	295	39	66	283	Inning 1-6		.233	2661	621	127	12	68	276	180	721	.284	.367
Night	3.19	35	25	0	81	81	576.0	479	47	153	576	Inning 7+		.254	602	153	30	5	18	60	39	138	.300	.410
Grass	3.51	16	11	0	39	39	271.2	240	41	62	253	None on		.222	2081	461	96	8	56	56	119	558	.267	.356
Turf	3.53	35	30	0	86	86	599.2	534	45	157	606	Runners on		.265	1182	313	61	9	30	280	100	301	.321	.408
March/April	3.60	7	7	0	18	18	125.0	117	13	32	96	Scoring Posn		.250	655	164	35	8	12	230	68	202	.315	.383
May	2.97	11	5	0	25	25	176.0	146	20	45	171	Close & Late		.255	341	87	16	3	11	44	29	74	.312	.416
June	4.38	6	11	0	23	23	150.0	134	21	42	147	None on/out		.232	862	200	45	6	20	20	49	221	.277	.368
July	4.16	8	9	0	23	23	151.1	144	16	52	151	vs. 1st Batr (relief)		.000	0	0	0	0	0	0	0	0	.000	.000
August	2.96	7	5	0	19	19	139.2	121	6	30	157	1st Inning Pitched		.230	460	106	25	3	13	52	45	123	.303	.383
Sept/Oct	3.06	12	4	0	17	17	129.1	112	10	18	137	First 75 Pitches		.233	2141	499	102	11	49	207	135	573	.281	.360
Starter	3.52	51	41	0	125	125	871.1	774	86	219	859	Pitch 76-90		.230	427	98	15	3	12	42	27	106	.276	.363
Reliever	0.00	0	0	0	0	0	0.0	0	0	0	0	Pitch 91-105		.261	371	97	23	1	14	46	23	91	.305	.442

Last Five Years

	ERA	W	L	Sv	G	GS	IP	H	HR	BB	SO		Avg	AB	H	2B	3B	HR	RBI	BB	SO	OBP	SLG
0-3 Days Rest (Start)	0.00	0	0	0	0	0	0.0	0	0	0	0	Pitch 106+	.247	324	80	17	2	11	41	34	89	.318	.414
4 Days Rest	3.64	35	35	0	93	93	648.0	607	64	153	636	First Pitch	.319	433	138	31	3	12	49	14	0	.346	.487
5+ Days Rest	3.18	16	6	0	32	32	223.1	167	22	66	223	Ahead in Count	.175	1718	301	55	9	31	130	0	730	.178	.272
vs. AL	3.00	1	1	0	3	3	21.0	20	0	4	31	Behind in Count	.350	505	177	50	4	27	92	88	0	.446	.626
vs. NL	3.54	50	40	0	122	122	850.1	754	86	215	828	Two Strikes	.171	1781	305	48	7	32	133	117	859	.223	.260
Pre-All Star	3.98	24	29	0	73	73	486.2	457	57	140	448	Pre-All Star	.248	1844	457	90	7	57	216	140	448	.303	.397
Post-All Star	2.95	27	12	0	52	52	384.2	317	29	79	411	Post-All Star	.223	1419	317	67	10	29	120	79	411	.266	.346

Pitcher vs. Batter (career)

Pitches Best Vs.	Avg	AB	H	2B	3B	HR	RBI	BB	SO	OBP	SLG	Pitches Worst Vs.	Avg	AB	H	2B	3B	HR	RBI	BB	SO	OBP	SLG
Ryan Klesko	.000	13	0	0	0	0	0	2	7	.133	.000	Phil Plantier	.545	11	6	3	0	2	5	0	1	.545	1.364
Darrin Fletcher	.031	32	1	0	0	0	4	1	6	.059	.031	Lance Johnson	.500	12	6	0	1	1	3	0	1	.462	.917
Derek Bell	.048	21	1	0	0	0	1	2	4	.125	.048	Mark Lemke	.484	31	15	1	0	2	5	3	4	.529	.710
Greg Gagne	.056	18	1	1	0	0	2	0	12	.056	.111	Tony Fernandez	.429	14	6	2	1	0	2	2	3	.500	.714
Brad Ausmus	.091	11	1	0	0	0	0	0	3	.091	.091	David Justice	.360	25	9	2	0	3	11	6	5	.484	.800

Jason Schmidt — Pirates
Age 25 – Pitches Right

	ERA	W	L	Sv	G	GS	IP	BB	SO	Avg	H	2B	3B	HR	RBI	OBP	SLG	CG	ShO	Sup	QS	#P/S	SB	CS	GB	FB	G/F
1997 Season	4.60	10	9	0	32	32	187.2	76	136	.265	193	42	8	16	93	.341	.411	2	0	4.89	16	96	8	8	271	187	1.45
Career (1995-1997)	5.04	17	17	0	60	51	309.0	147	229	.274	328	64	10	28	168	.355	.414	3	0	5.21	23	98	20	9	433	323	1.34

1997 Season

	ERA	W	L	Sv	G	GS	IP	H	HR	BB	SO		Avg	AB	H	2B	3B	HR	RBI	BB	SO	OBP	SLG
Home	5.20	7	6	0	17	17	98.2	101	8	40	70	vs. Left	.274	361	99	18	7	11	41	52	79	.364	.454
Away	3.94	3	3	0	15	15	89.0	92	8	36	66	vs. Right	.257	366	94	24	1	5	52	24	57	.318	.369
Day	4.27	1	2	0	9	9	52.2	52	3	29	33	Inning 1-6	.271	645	175	40	7	15	87	69	115	.348	.425
Night	4.73	9	7	0	23	23	135.0	141	13	47	103	Inning 7+	.220	82	18	2	1	1	6	7	21	.281	.305
Grass	2.72	2	0	0	9	9	56.1	53	6	25	36	None on	.263	411	108	24	3	10	10	39	79	.334	.409
Turf	5.41	8	9	0	23	23	131.1	140	10	51	100	Runners on	.269	316	85	18	5	6	83	37	57	.350	.415
March/April	5.03	1	1	0	4	4	19.2	21	0	17	10	Scoring Posn	.287	171	49	10	3	1	65	25	31	.378	.398
May	5.74	0	2	0	6	6	31.1	37	2	11	24	Close & Late	.186	43	8	1	0	1	3	5	8	.271	.279
June	3.10	2	1	0	5	5	29.0	25	3	6	26	None on/out	.259	185	48	9	0	5	5	17	34	.322	.389
July	2.63	3	2	0	6	6	41.0	34	3	17	31	vs. 1st Batr (relief)	.000	0	0	0	0	0	0	0	0	.000	.000
August	6.23	2	1	0	6	6	39.0	45	5	16	26	1st Inning Pitched	.259	116	30	4	1	2	17	13	30	.336	.362
Sept/Oct	5.20	2	2	0	5	5	27.2	31	3	9	19	First 75 Pitches	.263	525	138	29	5	11	59	52	91	.336	.400
Starter	4.60	10	9	0	32	32	187.2	193	16	76	136	Pitch 76-90	.317	101	32	9	2	4	20	8	18	.369	.564
Reliever	0.00	0	0	0	0	0	0.0	0	0	0	0	Pitch 91-105	.193	57	11	2	1	1	6	14	13	.352	.316
0-3 Days Rest (Start)	0.00	0	0	0	0	0	0.0	0	0	0	0	Pitch 106+	.273	44	12	2	0	0	8	2	14	.319	.318
4 Days Rest	5.30	5	6	0	18	18	103.2	109	13	41	74	First Pitch	.322	118	38	11	1	4	18	1	0	.333	.534
5+ Days Rest	3.75	5	3	0	14	14	84.0	84	3	35	62	Ahead in Count	.193	331	64	10	1	4	18	0	110	.208	.266
vs. AL	2.74	2	0	0	3	3	23.0	18	1	3	23	Behind in Count	.295	146	43	10	2	6	29	37	0	.435	.514
vs. NL	4.86	8	9	0	29	29	164.2	175	15	73	113	Two Strikes	.202	332	67	12	2	4	24	38	136	.294	.286
Pre-All Star	4.25	4	4	0	16	16	89.0	88	5	35	70	Pre-All Star	.257	342	88	21	4	5	41	35	70	.336	.386
Post-All Star	4.93	6	5	0	16	16	98.2	105	11	41	66	Post-All Star	.273	385	105	21	4	11	52	41	66	.346	.434

Pete Schourek — Reds
Age 29 – Pitches Left

	ERA	W	L	Sv	G	GS	IP	BB	SO	Avg	H	2B	3B	HR	RBI	OBP	SLG	CG	ShO	Sup	QS	#P/S	SB	CS	GB	FB	G/F
1997 Season	5.42	5	8	0	18	17	84.2	38	59	.241	78	18	2	18	50	.327	.475	0	0	4.89	3	82	10	0	82	123	0.67
Last Five Years	4.66	39	34	0	122	86	552.0	181	414	.269	573	118	13	66	279	.330	.430	2	0	5.17	37	93	38	24	675	628	1.07

1997 Season

	ERA	W	L	Sv	G	GS	IP	H	HR	BB	SO		Avg	AB	H	2B	3B	HR	RBI	BB	SO	OBP	SLG
Home	5.93	3	4	0	10	9	44.0	42	11	20	32	vs. Left	.273	66	18	2	1	3	10	5	14	.342	.470
Away	4.87	2	4	0	8	8	40.2	36	7	18	27	vs. Right	.233	258	60	16	1	15	40	33	45	.323	.477
Starter	5.34	5	8	0	17	17	84.1	76	18	38	58	Scoring Posn	.294	68	20	6	0	2	27	8	7	.364	.471
Reliever	27.00	0	0	0	1	0	0.1	2	0	0	1	Close & Late	.000	2	0	0	0	0	0	0	0	.000	.000
0-3 Days Rest (Start)	0.00	0	0	0	0	0	0.0	0	0	0	0	None on/out	.207	92	19	4	0	7	7	4	21	.247	.478
4 Days Rest	6.14	1	4	0	6	6	29.1	37	7	15	14	First Pitch	.325	40	13	2	0	3	5	0	0	.372	.600
5+ Days Rest	4.91	4	4	0	11	11	55.0	45	11	23	44	Ahead in Count	.166	145	24	6	2	3	13	0	52	.170	.297
Pre-All Star	5.14	5	5	0	12	12	61.1	51	14	28	46	Behind in Count	.315	73	23	7	0	8	19	24	0	.485	.740
Post-All Star	6.17	0	3	0	6	5	23.1	27	4	10	13	Two Strikes	.187	155	29	8	2	3	13	14	59	.254	.323

Last Five Years

	ERA	W	L	Sv	G	GS	IP	H	HR	BB	SO		Avg	AB	H	2B	3B	HR	RBI	BB	SO	OBP	SLG
Home	4.24	25	17	0	60	42	282.1	275	33	79	216	vs. Left	.314	408	128	21	3	14	60	32	73	.365	.483
Away	5.11	14	17	0	62	44	269.2	298	33	102	198	vs. Right	.259	1720	445	97	10	52	219	149	341	.322	.417
Day	4.62	16	9	0	41	29	195.0	186	28	69	145	Inning 1-6	.271	1826	494	103	13	55	240	161	365	.333	.432
Night	4.69	23	25	0	81	57	357.0	387	38	112	269	Inning 7+	.262	302	79	15	0	11	39	20	49	.308	.421
Grass	5.59	9	20	0	55	36	223.2	260	30	87	156	None on	.242	1287	311	57	7	37	37	91	270	.298	.383
Turf	4.03	30	14	0	67	50	328.1	313	36	94	258	Runners on	.312	841	262	61	6	29	242	90	144	.376	.502
March/April	6.62	6	6	0	17	13	70.2	97	6	33	54	Scoring Posn	.303	462	140	35	3	10	192	59	81	.377	.457
May	4.42	10	10	0	29	22	148.2	139	22	54	108	Close & Late	.287	136	39	9	0	5	22	9	19	.329	.463
June	5.04	4	8	0	19	15	85.2	95	16	21	65	None on/out	.263	560	146	27	4	19	19	34	109	.309	.425
July	4.54	8	5	0	21	17	105.0	107	10	34	82	vs. 1st Batr (relief)	.241	29	7	1	0	1	4	4	6	.314	.379
August	4.41	5	2	0	18	8	65.1	62	8	17	54	1st Inning Pitched	.285	452	129	27	1	15	67	48	86	.355	.449
Sept/Oct	3.29	6	3	0	18	11	76.2	73	4	22	51	First 75 Pitches	.267	1673	446	94	9	48	213	152	339	.331	.420

419

Last Five Years

	ERA	W	L	Sv	G	GS	IP	H	HR	SO		Avg	AB	H	2B	3B	HR	RBI	BB	SO	OBP	SLG
Starter	4.45	36	33	0	86	86	499.2	505	59	374	Pitch 76-90	.305	243	74	13	1	11	40	17	38	.356	.502
Reliever	6.71	3	1	0	36	0	52.1	68	7	22	Pitch 91-105	.212	156	33	5	3	4	14	8	31	.251	.359
0-3 Days Rest (Start)	4.63	2	1	0	4	4	23.1	29	3	11	Pitch 106+	.357	56	20	6	0	3	12	4	6	.410	.625
4 Days Rest	4.00	20	14	0	41	41	249.2	238	25	70	First Pitch	.324	281	91	18	2	11	47	10	0	.361	.520
5+ Days Rest	4.92	14	18	0	41	41	226.2	238	31	78	Ahead in Count	.198	1012	200	42	7	13	84	0	360	.204	.292
vs. AL	4.50	0	1	0	1	1	6.0	3	2	6	Behind in Count	.389	455	177	40	4	32	96	87	0	.484	.705
vs. NL	4.66	39	33	0	121	85	546.0	570	64	179	Two Strikes	.198	1031	204	44	4	11	83	84	414	.263	.280
Pre-All Star	5.05	23	25	0	73	56	342.0	377	46	117	Pre-All Star	.279	1351	377	74	7	46	187	117	258	.341	.446
Post-All Star	4.03	16	9	0	49	30	210.0	196	20	64	Post-All Star	.252	777	196	44	6	20	92	64	156	.311	.402

Pitcher vs. Batter (career)

Pitches Best Vs.	Avg	AB	H	2B	3B	HR	RBI	BB	SO	OBP	SLG	Pitches Worst Vs.	Avg	AB	H	2B	3B	HR	RBI	BB	SO	OBP	SLG
Ricky Gutierrez	.000	12	0	0	0	0	0	2	3	.143	.000	Rondell White	.625	16	10	2	1	1	4	1	1	.647	1.063
Alex Arias	.000	11	0	0	0	0	0	1	0	.154	.000	Joe Oliver	.545	11	6	3	0	1	4	0	2	.545	1.091
Lenny Webster	.000	9	0	0	0	0	0	3	2	.250	.000	Ken Caminiti	.467	15	7	0	0	2	6	2	1	.529	.867
Jose Vizcaino	.067	15	1	0	0	0	0	1	0	.067	.067	Vinny Castilla	.462	13	6	2	0	1	3	0	1	.462	.846
Orlando Merced	.083	12	1	1	0	0	1	0	1	.083	.167	Tom Pagnozzi	.438	16	7	3	0	2	6	0	1	.471	1.000

Tim Scott — Mariners
Age 31 – Pitches Right

	ERA	W	L	Sv	G	GS	IP	BB	SO	Avg	H	2B	3B	HR	RBI	OBP	SLG	GF	IR	IRS	Hld	SvOp	SB	CS	GB	FB	G/F
1997 Season	8.14	1	1	0	17	0	21.0	7	16	.337	30	4	3	2	19	.400	.517	2	5	2	1	1	2	1	36	16	2.25
Last Five Years	3.96	20	12	5	240	0	275.1	112	222	.255	267	47	12	20	137	.335	.380	59	157	46	40	16	63	9	314	313	1.00

1997 Season

	ERA	W	L	Sv	G	GS	IP	H	HR	BB	SO		Avg	AB	H	2B	3B	HR	RBI	BB	SO	OBP	SLG
Home	2.76	0	0	0	11	0	16.1	16	1	3	12	vs. Left	.341	44	15	2	1	0	7	5	9	.412	.432
Away	27.00	1	1	0	6	0	4.2	14	1	4	4	vs. Right	.333	45	15	2	2	2	12	2	7	.388	.600

Last Five Years

	ERA	W	L	Sv	G	GS	IP	H	HR	BB	SO		Avg	AB	H	2B	3B	HR	RBI	BB	SO	OBP	SLG
Home	2.97	10	5	5	117	0	145.2	130	9	51	112	vs. Left	.217	479	104	16	3	9	57	65	109	.316	.319
Away	5.07	10	7	0	123	0	129.2	137	11	61	110	vs. Right	.287	568	163	31	9	11	80	47	113	.352	.431
Day	4.05	9	6	0	75	0	86.2	79	9	29	75	Inning 1-6	.290	169	49	8	1	4	37	22	41	.376	.420
Night	3.91	11	6	5	165	0	188.2	188	11	83	147	Inning 7+	.248	878	218	39	11	16	100	90	181	.327	.372
Grass	4.56	9	5	0	100	0	118.1	130	12	48	87	None on	.254	528	134	25	5	10	10	48	112	.331	.377
Turf	3.50	11	7	5	140	0	157.0	137	8	64	135	Runners on	.256	519	133	22	7	10	127	64	110	.339	.383
March/April	3.16	5	2	0	40	0	51.1	36	4	19	41	Scoring Posn	.257	342	88	11	3	6	111	53	75	.359	.360
May	4.26	1	2	2	56	0	67.2	67	4	24	53	Close & Late	.256	406	104	17	7	7	45	47	92	.348	.384
June	2.93	2	2	1	36	0	40.0	37	2	20	36	None on/out	.230	226	52	11	2	2	21	45	38	.318	.340
July	4.23	4	3	1	43	0	44.2	58	1	22	32	vs. 1st Batr (relief)	.239	209	50	10	1	3	24	22	50	.331	.340
August	3.02	4	0	0	39	0	47.2	44	4	15	39	1st Inning Pitched	.265	769	204	36	10	14	119	85	162	.345	.393
Sept/Oct	7.88	4	1	1	26	0	24.0	25	5	12	21	First 15 Pitches	.266	638	170	29	7	10	77	66	124	.345	.381
Starter	0.00	0	0	0	0	0	0.0	0	0	0	0	Pitch 16-30	.252	329	83	16	4	9	52	38	77	.337	.407
Reliever	3.96	20	12	5	240	0	275.1	267	20	112	222	Pitch 31-45	.169	65	11	2	1	0	7	6	18	.239	.231
0 Days rest (Relief)	5.24	4	4	1	43	0	44.2	46	3	21	30	Pitch 46+	.200	15	3	0	0	1	0	2	3	.294	.400
1 or 2 Days rest	3.63	11	5	4	127	0	143.2	141	13	60	116	First Pitch	.313	147	46	9	1	4	22	5	0	.346	.469
3+ Days rest	3.83	5	3	0	70	0	87.0	80	4	31	76	Ahead in Count	.203	546	111	16	4	4	48	0	192	.214	.269
vs. AL	16.20	0	0	0	2	0	1.2	5	0	1	2	Behind in Count	.300	180	54	9	7	6	34	54	0	.460	.528
vs. NL	3.88	20	12	5	238	0	273.2	262	20	111	220	Two Strikes	.184	539	99	19	2	7	52	53	222	.267	.265
Pre-All Star	3.98	9	8	3	147	0	172.0	164	11	69	137	Pre-All Star	.250	657	164	30	9	11	88	69	137	.331	.373
Post-All Star	3.92	11	4	2	93	0	103.1	103	9	43	85	Post-All Star	.264	390	103	17	3	9	49	43	85	.342	.392

Pitcher vs. Batter (career)

Pitches Best Vs.	Avg	AB	H	2B	3B	HR	RBI	BB	SO	OBP	SLG	Pitches Worst Vs.	Avg	AB	H	2B	3B	HR	RBI	BB	SO	OBP	SLG
Ryne Sandberg	.000	11	0	0	0	0	0	1	1	.083	.000	Jeff Bagwell	.875	8	7	2	0	1	5	1	0	.818	1.500
Mike Piazza	.091	11	1	1	0	0	1	0	4	.091	.182	Tom Pagnozzi	.500	12	6	3	0	0	1	0	2	.500	.750
Orlando Merced	.100	10	1	0	0	0	0	2	5	.250	.100	Craig Biggio	.462	13	6	0	0	1	6	0	3	.500	.692
Ken Caminiti	.200	10	2	1	0	0	0	1	1	.273	.300	Jeff King	.400	10	4	1	0	1	4	2	0	.500	.800
Charlie Hayes	.214	14	3	0	1	0	1	0	1	.214	.357	Reggie Sanders	.333	12	4	3	0	1	3	1	5	.385	.833

Kevin Sefcik — Phillies
Age 27 – Bats Right

	Avg	G	AB	R	H	2B	3B	HR	RBI	BB	SO	HBP	GDP	SB	CS	OBP	SLG	IBB	SH	SF	#Pit	#P/PA	GB	FB	G/F
1997 Season	.269	61	119	11	32	3	0	2	6	4	9	1	4	1	2	.298	.345	0	7	0	438	3.34	40	47	0.85
Career (1995-1997)	.272	110	239	22	65	8	3	2	15	13	27	3	8	4	2	.315	.356	3	8	2	950	3.58	94	74	1.27

1997 Season

	Avg	AB	H	2B	3B	HR	RBI	BB	SO	OBP	SLG		Avg	AB	H	2B	3B	HR	RBI	BB	SO	OBP	SLG
vs. Left	.245	49	12	1	0	2	5	2	5	.275	.388	Scoring Posn	.056	18	1	0	0	1	4	2	3	.150	.222
vs. Right	.286	70	20	2	0	0	1	2	4	.315	.314	Close & Late	.294	17	5	0	0	0	0	1	2	.333	.294
Home	.294	68	20	2	0	2	6	1	4	.314	.412	None on/out	.281	32	9	1	0	0	0	1	1	.324	.313
Away	.235	51	12	1	0	0	0	3	3	.278	.255	Batting #2	.257	70	18	2	0	2	5	0	5	.268	.371
First Pitch	.154	26	4	2	0	0	0	0	0	.154	.231	Batting #9	.238	21	5	1	0	0	0	2	3	.304	.286
Ahead in Count	.314	35	11	0	0	1	4	0	.385	.314	Other	.321	28	9	0	0	0	1	1	0	.367	.321
Behind in Count	.326	43	14	1	0	2	5	0	.326	.488	Pre-All Star	.234	47	11	1	0	1	4	2	3	.265	.319
Two Strikes	.273	44	12	1	0	2	5	0	9	.273	.409	Post-All Star	.292	72	21	2	0	1	2	2	6	.320	.361

David Segui — Expos

	Avg	G	AB	R	H	2B	3B	HR	RBI	BB	SO	HBP	GDP	SB	CS	OBP	SLG	IBB	SH	SF	#Pit	#P/PA	GB	FB	G/F
1997 Season	.307	125	459	75	141	22	3	21	68	57	66	1	9	1	0	.380	.505	12	0	6	1846	3.53	186	121	1.54
Last Five Years	.286	608	2117	312	605	121	9	64	297	248	263	5	51	9	12	.359	.442	31	12	21	8539	3.55	822	620	1.33

1997 Season

	Avg	AB	H	2B	3B	HR	RBI	BB	SO	OBP	SLG		Avg	AB	H	2B	3B	HR	RBI	BB	SO	OBP	SLG
vs. Left	.295	122	36	6	0	5	9	21	18	.396	.467	First Pitch	.466	73	34	5	1	5	18	10	0	.518	.767
vs. Right	.312	337	105	16	3	16	59	36	48	.375	.519	Ahead in Count	.307	127	39	5	0	7	22	34	0	.445	.512
Groundball	.284	102	29	8	0	4	12	11	12	.348	.480	Behind in Count	.264	178	47	10	0	8	18	0	53	.267	.455
Flyball	.250	60	15	1	2	3	9	5	8	.303	.483	Two Strikes	.209	172	36	5	2	6	14	13	66	.265	.366
Home	.345	206	71	12	0	10	39	32	24	.424	.549	Batting #4	.304	438	133	20	3	19	63	53	64	.376	.493
Away	.277	253	70	10	3	11	29	25	42	.343	.470	Batting #5	.381	21	8	2	0	2	5	4	2	.480	.762
Day	.344	157	54	10	1	6	20	24	20	.424	.535	Other	.000	0	0	0	0	0	0	0	0	.000	.000
Night	.288	302	87	12	2	15	48	33	46	.357	.490	March/April	.352	91	32	8	1	4	15	10	14	.412	.593
Grass	.276	181	50	6	1	8	20	19	30	.347	.453	May	.315	73	23	4	0	2	11	15	15	.422	.452
Turf	.327	278	91	16	2	13	48	38	36	.402	.540	June	.286	35	10	2	1	0	3	5	4	.390	.400
Pre-All Star	.321	218	70	16	2	7	33	34	38	.409	.509	July	.256	82	21	2	0	4	15	8	12	.315	.427
Post-All Star	.295	241	71	6	1	14	35	23	28	.353	.502	August	.292	106	31	2	0	5	15	15	10	.377	.453
Scoring Posn	.259	116	30	4	1	4	45	32	17	.406	.414	Sept/Oct	.333	72	24	4	1	6	9	4	11	.368	.667
Close & Late	.234	77	18	1	0	2	6	10	17	.318	.325	vs. AL	.333	33	11	3	1	2	6	5	6	.421	.667
None on/out	.313	147	46	10	1	6	6	8	21	.348	.517	vs. NL	.305	426	130	19	2	19	62	52	60	.377	.493

1997 By Position

Position	Avg	AB	H	2B	3B	HR	RBI	BB	SO	OBP	SLG	G	GS	Innings	PO	A	E	DP	Fld Pct	Rng Fctr	In Zone	Zone Outs	Zone Rtg	MLB Zone
As 1b	.307	459	141	22	3	21	68	57	66	.380	.505	125	125	1071.2	1036	87	6	104	.995	—	202	168	.832	.874

Last Five Years

	Avg	AB	H	2B	3B	HR	RBI	BB	SO	OBP	SLG		Avg	AB	H	2B	3B	HR	RBI	BB	SO	OBP	SLG
vs. Left	.284	588	167	31	1	21	79	70	86	.361	.447	First Pitch	.341	352	120	22	2	16	58	25	0	.380	.551
vs. Right	.286	1529	438	90	8	43	218	178	177	.358	.440	Ahead in Count	.300	520	156	27	1	16	87	134	0	.437	.448
Groundball	.289	505	146	33	2	10	70	47	55	.346	.422	Behind in Count	.245	897	220	40	3	23	85	0	224	.247	.373
Flyball	.261	353	92	21	4	12	38	36	61	.327	.445	Two Strikes	.223	822	183	36	4	21	90	89	263	.300	.353
Home	.296	1050	311	70	3	33	160	129	115	.370	.463	Batting #4	.295	569	168	28	4	21	84	67	86	.366	.469
Away	.276	1067	294	51	6	31	137	119	148	.347	.422	Batting #7	.274	292	80	15	1	7	34	40	34	.356	.404
Day	.303	654	198	43	2	16	93	79	85	.376	.448	Other	.284	1256	357	78	4	36	179	141	143	.356	.439
Night	.278	1463	407	78	7	48	204	169	178	.351	.440	March/April	.322	301	97	19	1	10	58	39	48	.398	.492
Grass	.282	1149	324	62	3	36	162	142	144	.359	.435	May	.278	363	101	21	1	12	47	56	47	.369	.441
Turf	.290	968	281	59	6	28	135	106	119	.359	.450	June	.306	353	108	30	3	6	42	32	41	.363	.459
Pre-All Star	.302	1119	338	77	5	30	162	138	146	.376	.460	July	.263	361	95	18	2	9	45	25	36	.308	.399
Post-All Star	.268	998	267	44	4	34	135	110	117	.340	.422	August	.279	387	108	12	1	10	42	54	49	.369	.393
Scoring Posn	.285	533	152	30	2	12	218	94	69	.383	.417	Sept/Oct	.273	352	96	21	1	17	63	42	42	.348	.483
Close & Late	.232	353	82	12	0	9	36	42	56	.313	.343	vs. AL	.277	483	134	30	1	12	66	63	59	.356	.418
None on/out	.293	501	147	31	1	18	18	47	56	.354	.467	vs. NL	.288	1634	471	91	8	52	231	185	204	.360	.449

Batter vs. Pitcher (career)

Hits Best Against	Avg	AB	H	2B	3B	HR	RBI	BB	SO	OBP	SLG	Hits Worst Against	Avg	AB	H	2B	3B	HR	RBI	BB	SO	OBP	SLG
Jose Bautista	.600	10	6	2	0	2	6	2	0	.667	1.400	Bobby Jones	.000	15	0	0	0	0	0	1	5	.063	.000
Greg McMichael	.545	11	6	1	0	1	3	0	2	.545	.909	Pedro Martinez	.000	10	0	0	0	0	0	1	5	.091	.000
Kevin Ritz	.500	10	5	0	0	2	3	1	1	.545	1.100	Curt Schilling	.071	14	1	0	0	0	0	1	5	.133	.071
Kirk Rueter	.444	9	4	1	0	1	2	3	0	.583	.889	Kevin Tapani	.091	11	1	0	0	0	1	0	1	.091	.182
Ismael Valdes	.417	12	5	2	0	1	5	1	0	.462	.833	Tim Pugh	.100	10	1	0	0	0	0	0	0	.182	.100

Kevin Seitzer — Indians

	Avg	G	AB	R	H	2B	3B	HR	RBI	BB	SO	HBP	GDP	SB	CS	OBP	SLG	IBB	SH	SF	#Pit	#P/PA	GB	FB	G/F
1997 Season	.268	64	198	27	53	14	0	2	24	18	25	0	6	0	0	.326	.369	0	2	2	923	4.20	82	48	1.71
Last Five Years	.303	550	1989	257	602	122	10	36	277	243	247	15	52	17	9	.380	.428	11	19	18	8995	3.94	785	535	1.47

1997 Season

	Avg	AB	H	2B	3B	HR	RBI	BB	SO	OBP	SLG		Avg	AB	H	2B	3B	HR	RBI	BB	SO	OBP	SLG
vs. Left	.268	97	26	6	0	2	10	12	10	.345	.392	Scoring Posn	.255	55	14	5	0	1	23	10	6	.358	.400
vs. Right	.267	101	27	8	0	0	14	6	15	.306	.347	Close & Late	.150	20	3	0	0	1	4	1	4	.174	.300
Home	.282	103	29	8	0	1	13	13	17	.362	.388	None on/out	.282	39	11	3	0	1	1	2	4	.317	.436
Away	.253	95	24	6	0	1	11	5	8	.284	.347	Batting #2	.274	113	31	10	0	1	12	9	12	.325	.389
First Pitch	.250	8	2	1	0	0	2	0	0	.250	.375	Batting #3	.244	41	10	2	0	0	5	5	7	.326	.293
Ahead in Count	.350	60	21	4	0	0	9	9	0	.435	.417	Other	.273	44	12	2	0	1	7	4	6	.327	.386
Behind in Count	.176	85	15	5	0	2	6	0	21	.176	.306	Pre-All Star	.259	108	28	7	0	2	18	11	13	.322	.380
Two Strikes	.194	93	18	6	0	2	9	9	25	.262	.323	Post-All Star	.278	90	25	7	0	0	6	7	12	.330	.356

Last Five Years

	Avg	AB	H	2B	3B	HR	RBI	BB	SO	OBP	SLG		Avg	AB	H	2B	3B	HR	RBI	BB	SO	OBP	SLG
vs. Left	.295	613	181	38	2	10	81	87	69	.380	.413	First Pitch	.320	175	56	11	2	4	33	9	0	.351	.474
vs. Right	.306	1376	421	84	8	26	196	156	178	.379	.435	Ahead in Count	.380	529	201	44	4	17	103	135	0	.505	.575
Groundball	.301	469	141	24	4	6	56	43	52	.365	.407	Behind in Count	.240	896	215	43	2	7	82	0	212	.247	.316
Flyball	.310	365	113	27	0	5	51	43	42	.381	.425	Two Strikes	.224	896	201	43	1	8	86	98	247	.304	.301
Home	.288	979	282	53	4	17	123	138	115	.379	.402	Batting #2	.311	762	237	55	3	14	105	68	84	.371	.468
Away	.317	1010	320	69	6	19	154	105	132	.380	.453	Batting #3	.301	698	210	37	2	12	99	121	95	.405	.411
Day	.315	711	224	52	3	15	111	100	90	.396	.460	Other	.293	529	155	30	5	10	73	54	68	.356	.425
Night	.296	1278	378	70	7	21	166	143	157	.371	.411	March/April	.291	254	74	15	1	12	45	32	32	.371	.500
Grass	.305	1701	518	106	9	30	244	213	205	.383	.430	May	.311	354	110	23	3	3	46	44	38	.390	.418

Last Five Years

	Avg	AB	H	2B	3B	HR	RBI	BB	SO	OBP	SLG		Avg	AB	H	2B	3B	HR	RBI	BB	SO	OBP	SLG
Turf	.292	288	84	16	1	6	33	30	42	.359	.417	June	.332	358	119	24	3	6	55	44	52	.401	.466
Pre-All Star	.312	1107	345	71	7	23	164	131	145	.384	.451	July	.257	366	94	19	0	3	42	45	49	.337	.333
Post-All Star	.291	882	257	51	3	13	113	112	102	.374	.400	August	.304	358	109	19	2	7	50	49	42	.393	.427
Scoring Posn	.323	498	161	32	3	12	235	96	60	.422	.472	Sept/Oct	.321	299	96	22	1	5	39	29	34	.385	.452
Close & Late	.292	284	83	16	0	7	42	31	46	.362	.423	vs. AL	.302	1959	591	118	10	35	273	240	243	.379	.426
None on/out	.253	391	99	27	0	9	9	42	47	.327	.391	vs. NL	.367	30	11	4	0	1	4	3	4	.424	.600

Batter vs. Pitcher (career)

Hits Best Against	Avg	AB	H	2B	3B	HR	RBI	BB	SO	OBP	SLG	Hits Worst Against	Avg	AB	H	2B	3B	HR	RBI	BB	SO	OBP	SLG
Tim Wakefield	.667	9	6	0	0	0	1	2	0	.727	.667	Omar Olivares	.000	11	0	0	0	0	0	2	1	.154	.000
Kevin Ritz	.500	10	5	2	0	0	2	2	1	.538	.700	Doug Jones	.077	13	1	0	0	0	1	0	1	.077	.077
Pat Mahomes	.455	11	5	1	0	1	4	2	1	.538	.818	Paul Quantrill	.091	11	1	0	0	0	0	1	0	.167	.091
Wilson Alvarez	.444	27	12	3	0	1	8	5	2	.531	.667	Scott Erickson	.125	32	4	1	0	0	1	3	3	.222	.156
Chris Haney	.440	25	11	5	0	0	6	4	3	.517	.640	Dennis Cook	.154	13	2	0	0	0	0	1	2	.214	.154

Aaron Sele — Red Sox   Age 28 – Pitches Right (groundball pitcher)

	ERA	W	L	Sv	G	GS	IP	BB	SO	Avg	H	2B	3B	HR	RBI	OBP	SLG	CG	ShO	Sup	QS	#P/S	SB	CS	GB	FB	G/F
1997 Season	5.38	13	12	0	33	33	177.1	80	122	.279	196	41	6	25	98	.361	.461	1	0	6.39	17	92	19	7	257	179	1.44
Career (1993-1997)	4.41	38	33	0	108	108	622.0	269	478	.273	660	126	12	60	308	.352	.409	4	0	5.63	54	100	45	23	884	564	1.57

1997 Season

	ERA	W	L	Sv	G	GS	IP	H	HR	BB	SO		Avg	AB	H	2B	3B	HR	RBI	BB	SO	OBP	SLG
Home	4.49	8	6	0	17	17	102.1	104	12	38	73	vs. Left	.325	378	123	26	4	15	48	49	62	.403	.534
Away	6.60	5	6	0	16	16	75.0	92	13	42	49	vs. Right	.225	325	73	15	2	10	50	31	60	.313	.375
Day	6.75	2	4	0	10	10	44.0	62	10	21	25	Inning 1-6	.275	650	179	39	4	22	92	74	118	.358	.449
Night	4.93	11	8	0	23	23	133.1	134	15	59	97	Inning 7+	.321	53	17	2	2	3	6	6	4	.400	.604
Grass	5.10	10	10	0	27	27	150.0	166	20	63	109	None on	.283	374	106	23	3	16	16	43	66	.372	.489
Turf	6.91	3	2	0	6	6	27.1	30	5	17	13	Runners on	.274	329	90	18	3	9	82	37	56	.349	.429
March/April	4.10	3	1	0	5	5	26.1	27	4	18	17	Scoring Posn	.235	187	44	10	2	3	66	26	36	.321	.358
May	6.67	3	2	0	6	6	29.2	36	4	16	19	Close & Late	.360	25	9	1	1	3	4	5	2	.484	.840
June	5.66	3	3	0	6	6	35.0	43	4	14	23	None on/out	.259	174	45	8	1	9	9	21	33	.355	.471
July	4.91	1	1	0	5	5	33.0	34	5	5	27	vs. 1st Batr (relief)	.000	0	0	0	0	0	0	0	0	.000	.000
August	8.54	2	4	0	6	6	26.1	33	6	15	16	1st Inning Pitched	.316	136	43	10	2	4	23	17	22	.396	.507
Sept/Oct	2.33	1	1	0	5	5	27.0	23	2	12	20	First 75 Pitches	.292	528	154	36	4	18	81	58	97	.370	.477
Starter	5.38	13	12	0	33	33	177.1	196	25	80	122	Pitch 76-90	.202	89	18	2	1	3	8	9	16	.280	.348
Reliever	0.00	0	0	0	0	0	0.0	0	0	0	0	Pitch 91-105	.259	58	15	1	1	3	7	4	5	.338	.466
0-3 Days Rest (Start)	0.00	0	0	0	0	0	0.0	0	0	0	0	Pitch 106+	.321	28	9	2	0	1	2	9	4	.486	.500
4 Days Rest	5.43	8	7	0	20	20	112.2	126	15	43	71	First Pitch	.391	110	43	11	0	9	27	2	0	.397	.736
5+ Days Rest	5.29	5	5	0	13	13	64.2	70	10	37	51	Ahead in Count	.200	300	60	10	1	5	21	0	101	.219	.290
vs. AL	5.55	12	10	0	30	30	159.0	182	23	72	108	Behind in Count	.392	153	60	16	3	8	33	39	0	.523	.693
vs. NL	3.93	1	2	0	3	3	18.1	14	2	8	14	Two Strikes	.171	298	51	9	2	1	19	39	122	.277	.225
Pre-All Star	5.13	10	6	0	18	18	100.0	113	12	48	65	Pre-All Star	.285	397	113	22	2	12	55	48	65	.370	.441
Post-All Star	5.70	3	6	0	15	15	77.1	83	13	32	57	Post-All Star	.271	306	83	19	4	13	43	32	57	.350	.487

Career (1993-1997)

	ERA	W	L	Sv	G	GS	IP	H	HR	BB	SO		Avg	AB	H	2B	3B	HR	RBI	BB	SO	OBP	SLG
Home	4.38	21	19	0	53	53	324.2	332	29	134	260	vs. Left	.300	1265	380	80	9	36	164	166	225	.384	.463
Away	4.45	17	14	0	55	55	297.1	328	31	135	218	vs. Right	.242	1157	280	46	3	24	144	103	253	.316	.349
Day	4.66	15	11	0	38	38	208.2	236	20	92	155	Inning 1-6	.268	2211	593	114	9	52	287	244	441	.348	.398
Night	4.29	23	22	0	70	70	413.1	424	40	177	323	Inning 7+	.318	211	67	12	3	8	21	25	37	.394	.517
Grass	4.50	32	30	0	93	93	542.1	579	52	230	426	None on	.273	1294	353	67	6	41	41	151	255	.359	.429
Turf	3.84	6	3	0	15	15	79.2	81	8	39	52	Runners on	.272	1128	307	59	6	19	267	118	223	.344	.386
March/April	3.89	8	6	0	16	16	90.1	86	9	50	68	Scoring Posn	.263	605	159	29	5	8	228	82	127	.347	.367
May	4.87	8	7	0	22	22	118.1	131	10	60	81	Close & Late	.287	101	29	5	1	4	8	14	18	.387	.475
June	5.32	5	6	0	18	18	108.1	128	8	43	86	None on/out	.237	599	142	22	2	19	19	65	116	.326	.376
July	3.89	8	4	0	20	20	127.1	125	19	37	92	vs. 1st Batr (relief)	.000	0	0	0	0	0	0	0	0	.000	.000
August	5.21	5	8	0	16	16	86.1	99	8	41	70	1st Inning Pitched	.273	421	115	26	2	8	60	42	83	.344	.401
Sept/Oct	3.25	4	3	0	16	16	91.1	91	6	38	81	First 75 Pitches	.268	1703	456	90	6	37	214	185	340	.347	.393
Starter	4.41	38	33	0	108	108	622.0	660	60	269	478	Pitch 76-90	.265	313	83	18	4	10	39	34	62	.341	.444
Reliever	0.00	0	0	0	0	0	0.0	0	0	0	0	Pitch 91-105	.273	256	70	11	2	8	36	27	48	.353	.426
0-3 Days Rest (Start)	3.18	0	0	0	1	1	5.2	4	0	1	5	Pitch 106+	.340	150	51	7	0	5	19	23	28	.432	.487
4 Days Rest	4.05	22	16	0	57	57	340.0	362	28	137	241	First Pitch	.354	305	108	25	1	13	55	5	0	.365	.570
5+ Days Rest	4.89	16	17	0	50	50	276.1	294	32	131	232	Ahead in Count	.207	1068	221	38	2	12	93	0	394	.222	.280
vs. AL	4.43	37	31	0	105	105	603.2	646	58	261	464	Behind in Count	.363	551	200	42	5	24	102	142	0	.491	.588
vs. NL	3.93	1	2	0	3	3	18.1	14	2	8	14	Two Strikes	.194	1142	222	40	5	11	98	122	478	.281	.267
Pre-All Star	4.32	25	16	0	62	62	362.2	371	29	163	269	Pre-All Star	.266	1396	371	66	6	29	168	163	269	.349	.384
Post-All Star	4.55	13	17	0	46	46	259.1	289	31	106	209	Post-All Star	.282	1026	289	60	6	31	140	106	209	.356	.442

Pitcher vs. Batter (career)

Pitches Best Vs.	Avg	AB	H	2B	3B	HR	RBI	BB	SO	OBP	SLG	Pitches Worst Vs.	Avg	AB	H	2B	3B	HR	RBI	BB	SO	OBP	SLG
Mark McLemore	.000	12	0	0	0	0	0	1	3	.077	.000	Shawn Green	.667	12	8	2	0	1	4	2	0	.667	1.083
J.T. Snow	.000	10	0	0	0	0	0	2	4	.167	.000	Garret Anderson	.600	10	6	4	0	1	6	1	0	.636	1.300
Jorge Posada	.000	8	0	0	0	0	0	3	6	.333	.000	Johnny Damon	.545	11	6	3	0	1	4	1	0	.545	1.091
Joey Cora	.083	12	1	0	0	0	0	2	0	.214	.083	Edgar Martinez	.500	8	4	1	0	1	5	3	1	.583	1.000
Chad Curtis	.154	13	2	0	0	0	0	1	3	.214	.154	Tony Clark	.444	9	4	1	0	2	4	3	3	.583	1.222

Dan Serafini — Twins

	ERA	W	L	Sv	G	GS	IP	BB	SO	Avg	H	2B	3B	HR	RBI	OBP	SLG	CG	ShO	Sup	QS	#P/S	SB	CS	GB	FB	G/F
1997 Season	3.42	2	1	0	6	4	26.1	11	15	.273	27	6	1	1	8	.345	.384	1	0	8.20	2	89	2	2	30	36	0.83
Career (1996-1997)	4.40	2	2	0	7	5	30.2	13	16	.288	34	8	1	2	13	.361	.424	1	0	7.63	2	87	2	2	35	47	0.74

1997 Season

	ERA	W	L	Sv	G	GS	IP	H	HR	BB	SO		Avg	AB	H	2B	3B	HR	RBI	BB	SO	OBP	SLG
Home	5.84	1	1	0	3	2	12.1	12	1	5	7	vs. Left	.250	20	5	2	0	0	1	4	6	.375	.350
Away	1.29	1	0	0	3	2	14.0	15	0	6	8	vs. Right	.278	79	22	4	1	1	7	7	9	.337	.392

Scott Servais — Cubs

	Avg	G	AB	R	H	2B	3B	HR	RBI	BB	SO	HBP	GDP	SB	CS	OBP	SLG	IBB	SH	SF	#Pit	#P/PA	GB	FB	G/F
1997 Season	.260	122	385	36	100	21	0	6	45	24	56	6	7	0	1	.311	.361	7	7	3	1409	3.32	148	113	1.31
Last Five Years	.250	494	1603	167	400	89	1	50	228	118	272	32	46	2	5	.310	.400	18	22	19	6191	3.45	598	472	1.27

1997 Season

	Avg	AB	H	2B	3B	HR	RBI	BB	SO	OBP	SLG		Avg	AB	H	2B	3B	HR	RBI	BB	SO	OBP	SLG
vs. Left	.283	92	26	6	0	3	16	6	10	.327	.446	First Pitch	.206	68	14	7	0	1	4	6	0	.289	.353
vs. Right	.253	293	74	15	0	3	29	18	46	.306	.334	Ahead in Count	.385	91	35	5	0	3	17	6	0	.414	.538
Groundball	.351	74	26	5	0	3	13	6	11	.407	.541	Behind in Count	.158	158	25	5	0	1	15	0	46	.178	.209
Flyball	.218	55	12	2	0	0	3	3	10	.267	.255	Two Strikes	.140	143	20	3	0	2	12	56	.210	.203
Home	.262	191	50	12	0	4	23	9	25	.299	.387	Batting #7	.267	146	39	9	0	1	15	7	19	.314	.349
Away	.258	194	50	9	0	2	22	15	31	.322	.335	Batting #8	.249	185	46	7	0	3	19	14	24	.307	.335
Day	.278	209	58	12	0	5	28	10	28	.317	.407	Other	.278	54	15	5	0	2	11	3	13	.316	.481
Night	.239	176	42	9	0	1	17	14	28	.304	.307	March/April	.246	65	16	2	0	1	8	4	8	.306	.323
Grass	.261	318	83	17	0	5	37	15	42	.303	.362	May	.229	70	16	4	0	3	11	8	13	.329	.414
Turf	.254	67	17	4	0	1	8	9	14	.346	.358	June	.293	75	22	3	0	1	8	5	12	.338	.373
Pre-All Star	.270	222	60	10	0	5	29	19	35	.337	.383	July	.219	73	16	4	0	0	8	2	10	.247	.274
Post-All Star	.245	163	40	11	0	1	16	5	21	.272	.331	August	.298	57	17	4	0	4	1	6	.310	.368
Scoring Posn	.256	90	23	6	0	2	37	13	16	.346	.389	Sept/Oct	.289	45	13	4	0	1	6	4	7	.347	.444
Close & Late	.225	71	16	3	0	1	7	4	15	.276	.310	vs. AL	.350	40	14	2	0	0	7	2	7	.381	.400
None on/out	.228	101	23	4	0	1		5	13	.264	.297	vs. NL	.249	345	86	19	0	6	38	22	49	.303	.357

1997 By Position

Position	Avg	AB	H	2B	3B	HR	RBI	BB	SO	OBP	SLG	G	GS	Innings	PO	A	E	DP	Fld Pct	Rng Fctr	In Zone	Zone Outs	Zone Rtg	MLB Zone
As c	.257	378	97	19	0	6	42	23	55	.307	.354	118	110	965.2	735	72	8	11	.990	---	---	---	---	---

Last Five Years

	Avg	AB	H	2B	3B	HR	RBI	BB	SO	OBP	SLG		Avg	AB	H	2B	3B	HR	RBI	BB	SO	OBP	SLG
vs. Left	.281	467	131	39	0	17	88	47	69	.347	.473	First Pitch	.299	294	88	21	0	10	45	12	0	.332	.473
vs. Right	.237	1136	269	50	1	33	140	71	203	.295	.370	Ahead in Count	.338	361	122	23	0	15	67	53	0	.417	.526
Groundball	.255	404	103	20	0	14	69	37	75	.327	.408	Behind in Count	.168	678	114	25	1	15	79	0	231	.189	.274
Flyball	.279	262	73	22	0	12	38	15	51	.322	.500	Two Strikes	.151	661	100	23	1	18	70	53	272	.224	.271
Home	.243	818	199	46	0	26	118	55	139	.299	.395	Batting #7	.238	945	225	49	1	26	124	68	166	.300	.375
Away	.256	785	201	43	1	24	110	63	133	.322	.405	Batting #8	.268	347	93	21	0	14	50	27	53	.326	.450
Day	.270	721	195	41	0	23	106	52	110	.329	.423	Other	.264	311	82	19	0	10	54	23	53	.325	.421
Night	.232	882	205	48	1	27	122	66	162	.295	.381	March/April	.252	230	58	11	0	9	39	21	31	.322	.417
Grass	.271	996	270	51	0	32	140	75	161	.332	.421	May	.216	291	63	17	1	11	40	16	57	.270	.395
Turf	.214	607	130	38	0	18	88	43	111	.274	.366	June	.265	325	86	17	0	8	41	25	53	.329	.391
Pre-All Star	.251	953	239	52	1	32	136	74	165	.315	.408	July	.253	292	74	17	0	6	38	16	49	.312	.373
Post-All Star	.248	650	161	37	0	18	92	44	107	.304	.388	August	.252	266	67	16	0	12	35	21	48	.308	.447
Scoring Posn	.249	413	103	25	1	8	164	44	85	.323	.373	Sept/Oct	.261	199	52	11	0	4	35	19	34	.326	.377
Close & Late	.271	269	73	13	0	9	37	19	48	.327	.420	vs. AL	.350	40	14	2	0	0	7	2	7	.381	.400
None on/out	.237	371	88	13	0	8	8	19	61	.289	.337	vs. NL	.247	1563	386	87	1	50	221	116	265	.309	.400

Batter vs. Pitcher (career)

Hits Best Against	Avg	AB	H	2B	3B	HR	RBI	BB	SO	OBP	SLG	Hits Worst Against	Avg	AB	H	2B	3B	HR	RBI	BB	SO	OBP	SLG
Armando Reynoso	.583	12	7	1	0	0	4	1	1	.615	.667	Kevin Gross	.000	11	0	0	0	0	0	0	1	.000	.000
Ismael Valdes	.500	12	6	1	0	0	1	2	.538	.583	Bobby Jones	.056	18	1	0	0	0	0	1	1	.150	.056
Chris Hammond	.429	21	9	2	0	1	4	3	7	.500	.667	Chan Ho Park	.063	16	1	0	0	0	1	1	4	.167	.063
Steve Cooke	.412	17	7	2	0	1	3	2	2	.474	.706	Ramon Martinez	.083	12	1	0	0	0	1	0	4	.083	.083
Kevin Ritz	.333	12	4	1	0	2	9	0	2	.333	.917	Mark Petkovsek	.100	10	1	0	0	0	0	1	2	.182	.100

Scott Service — Royals

	ERA	W	L	Sv	G	GS	IP	BB	SO	Avg	H	2B	3B	HR	RBI	OBP	SLG	GF	IR	IRS	Hld	SvOp	SB	CS	GB	FB	G/F
1997 Season	6.45	0	3	0	16	0	22.1	6	22	.326	28	7	0	2	15	.366	.477	3	8	2	3	1	0	0	30	19	1.58
Last Five Years	4.42	7	8	2	113	1	154.2	63	146	.259	149	33	6	21	87	.338	.447	23	68	23	16	3	6	7	172	169	1.02

1997 Season

	ERA	W	L	Sv	G	GS	IP	H	HR	BB	SO		Avg	AB	H	2B	3B	HR	RBI	BB	SO	OBP	SLG
Home	6.43	0	1	0	5	0	7.0	7	1	2	11	vs. Left	.371	35	13	4	0	1	8	3	10	.421	.571
Away	6.46	0	2	0	11	0	15.1	21	1	4	11	vs. Right	.294	51	15	3	0	1	7	3	12	.327	.412

Last Five Years

	ERA	W	L	Sv	G	GS	IP	H	HR	BB	SO		Avg	AB	H	2B	3B	HR	RBI	BB	SO	OBP	SLG
Home	4.23	1	2	2	48	0	66.0	68	11	25	65	vs. Left	.270	211	57	12	5	6	35	42	41	.392	.460
Away	4.57	6	6	0	65	1	88.2	81	10	38	81	vs. Right	.253	364	92	21	1	15	52	21	105	.303	.440
Day	4.80	2	6	1	50	0	69.1	63	9	36	69	Inning 1-6	.269	208	56	13	2	7	38	17	54	.338	.452
Night	4.11	5	2	1	63	1	85.1	86	12	27	77	Inning 7+	.253	367	93	20	4	14	49	46	92	.339	.444

423

	ERA	W	L	Sv	G	GS	IP	H	HR	BB	SO		Avg	AB	H	2B	3B	HR	RBI	BB	SO	OBP	SLG
Grass	5.12	2	5	0	59	0	77.1	72	12	35	73	None on	.252	329	83	20	6	13	13	26	81	.322	.468
Turf	3.72	5	3	2	54	1	77.1	77	9	28	73	Runners on	.268	246	66	13	0	8	74	37	65	.358	.419
March/April	11.81	0	0	0	4	0	5.1	11	1	1	3	Scoring Posn	.265	155	41	8	0	3	63	28	44	.365	.374
May	0.00	0	0	0	0	0	0.0	0	0	0	0	Close & Late	.283	145	41	10	2	7	28	23	33	.381	.524
June	0.00	0	0	0	0	0	0.0	0	0	0	0	None on/out	.245	139	34	7	3	7	7	11	31	.318	.489
July	3.61	2	3	0	27	1	42.1	43	6	13	31	vs. 1st Batr (relief)	.247	97	24	5	2	5	17	10	20	.318	.495
August	4.80	3	0	0	40	0	54.1	47	9	24	57	1st Inning Pitched	.244	349	85	17	4	13	62	45	84	.333	.427
Sept/Oct	3.93	2	5	2	42	0	52.2	48	5	25	55	First 15 Pitches	.250	304	76	15	4	10	46	39	68	.340	.424
Starter	5.40	0	0	0	1	1	5.0	8	0	0	2	Pitch 16-30	.259	197	51	11	2	8	25	16	58	.323	.457
Reliever	4.39	7	8	2	112	0	149.2	141	21	63	144	Pitch 31-45	.293	58	17	6	0	2	13	7	19	.379	.500
0 Days rest (Relief)	4.22	0	2	0	23	0	32.0	31	3	18	30	Pitch 46+	.313	16	5	1	0	1	3	1	1	.353	.563
1 or 2 Days rest	5.75	3	4	1	56	0	72.0	73	13	27	79	First Pitch	.356	87	31	4	0	6	23	9	0	.406	.609
3+ Days rest	2.36	4	1	1	33	0	45.2	37	5	18	35	Ahead in Count	.165	278	46	7	2	5	28	0	129	.185	.259
vs. AL	6.57	0	3	0	9	0	12.1	14	1	5	13	Behind in Count	.375	120	45	18	2	3	18	24	0	.479	.633
vs. NL	4.24	7	5	2	104	1	142.1	135	20	58	133	Two Strikes	.154	286	44	6	3	5	32	30	146	.248	.248
Pre-All Star	7.02	1	0	0	11	0	16.2	21	3	3	12	Pre-All Star	.323	65	21	5	2	3	13	3	12	.352	.600
Post-All Star	4.11	6	8	2	102	1	138.0	128	18	60	134	Post-All Star	.251	510	128	28	4	18	74	60	134	.337	.427

Richie Sexson — Indians

Age 23 – Bats Right

	Avg	G	AB	R	H	2B	3B	HR	RBI	BB	SO	HBP	GDP	SB	CS	OBP	SLG	IBB	SH	SF	#Pit	#P/PA	GB	FB	G/F
1997 Season	.273	5	11	1	3	0	0	0	0	0	2	0	0	2	0	.273	.273	0	0	0	34	3.09	8	1	8.00

1997 Season

	Avg	AB	H	2B	3B	HR	RBI	BB	SO	OBP	SLG		Avg	AB	H	2B	3B	HR	RBI	BB	SO	OBP	SLG
vs. Left	.300	10	3	0	0	0	0	0	2	.300	.300	Scoring Posn	.000	1	0	0	0	0	0	0	1	.000	.000
vs. Right	.000	1	0	0	0	0	0	0	0	.000	.000	Close & Late	.333	3	1	0	0	0	0	0	2	.333	.333

Jeff Shaw — Reds

Age 31 – Pitches Right

	ERA	W	L	Sv	G	GS	IP	BB	SO	Avg	H	2B	3B	HR	RBI	OBP	SLG	GF	IR	IRS	Hld	SvOp	SB	CS	GB	FB	G/F
1997 Season	2.38	4	2	42	78	0	94.2	12	74	.227	79	15	1	7	29	.253	.336	62	25	7	5	49	4	1	120	92	1.30
Last Five Years	3.44	20	23	50	316	8	434.1	115	291	.249	406	91	5	41	187	.302	.386	132	171	46	47	68	25	11	631	428	1.47

1997 Season

	ERA	W	L	Sv	G	GS	IP	H	HR	BB	SO		Avg	AB	H	2B	3B	HR	RBI	BB	SO	OBP	SLG
Home	1.90	2	1	24	43	0	52.0	38	3	4	41	vs. Left	.242	178	43	11	0	2	18	6	32	.270	.337
Away	2.95	2	1	18	35	0	42.2	41	4	8	33	vs. Right	.212	170	36	4	1	5	11	6	42	.235	.335
Day	3.48	2	2	8	26	0	33.2	28	1	4	24	Inning 1-6	.000	2	0	0	0	0	0	0	1	.000	.000
Night	1.77	2	0	34	52	0	61.0	51	6	8	50	Inning 7+	.228	346	79	15	1	7	29	12	73	.254	.338
Grass	3.00	1	1	9	21	0	27.0	26	3	5	21	None on	.202	213	43	8	1	7	6	48	.227	.347
Turf	2.13	3	1	33	57	0	67.2	53	4	7	53	Runners on	.267	135	36	7	0	0	22	6	26	.292	.319
March/April	1.23	0	0	3	13	0	14.2	11	1	3	14	Scoring Posn	.229	83	19	5	0	0	22	4	15	.256	.289
May	0.43	1	0	4	13	0	21.0	12	1	2	21	Close & Late	.205	239	49	9	1	4	18	8	51	.228	.301
June	2.89	1	0	9	16	0	18.2	22	2	1	7	None on/out	.227	88	20	4	0	3	3	1	23	.244	.375
July	3.60	1	0	5	8	0	10.0	6	2	2	10	vs. 1st Batr (relief)	.284	74	21	7	0	3	7	2	15	.308	.500
August	5.87	1	2	7	13	0	15.1	16	1	3	12	1st Inning Pitched	.248	278	69	14	1	6	27	11	53	.276	.371
Sept/Oct	1.20	0	0	14	15	0	15.0	12	0	1	10	First 15 Pitches	.251	251	63	12	1	6	18	8	47	.275	.378
Starter	0.00	0	0	0	0	0	0.0	0	0	0	0	Pitch 16-30	.169	83	14	2	0	1	11	4	21	.205	.229
Reliever	2.38	4	2	42	78	0	94.2	79	7	12	74	Pitch 31-45	.154	13	2	1	0	0	0	0	5	.154	.231
0 Days rest (Relief)	2.73	0	2	21	32	0	33.0	23	2	6	24	Pitch 46+	.000	1	0	0	0	0	0	0	1	.000	.000
1 or 2 Days rest	2.51	0	0	13	28	0	32.1	37	2	5	19	First Pitch	.288	52	15	4	0	2	8	2	0	.309	.481
3+ Days rest	1.84	4	0	8	18	0	29.1	19	3	1	31	Ahead in Count	.182	198	36	5	1	2	13	0	66	.184	.247
vs. AL	3.38	0	0	4	7	0	8.0	9	1	1	5	Behind in Count	.350	40	14	3	0	0	5	4	0	.409	.425
vs. NL	2.28	4	2	38	71	0	86.2	70	6	11	69	Two Strikes	.153	177	27	4	0	2	7	6	74	.179	.209
Pre-All Star	1.44	2	0	18	44	0	56.1	45	4	6	44	Pre-All Star	.223	202	45	8	0	4	13	6	44	.246	.322
Post-All Star	3.76	2	2	24	34	0	38.1	34	3	6	30	Post-All Star	.233	146	34	7	1	3	16	6	30	.261	.356

	ERA	W	L	Sv	G	GS	IP	H	HR	BB	SO		Avg	AB	H	2B	3B	HR	RBI	BB	SO	OBP	SLG
Home	3.22	11	10	29	157	6	223.1	206	19	59	142	vs. Left	.260	734	191	40	0	17	82	68	115	.323	.384
Away	3.67	9	13	21	159	2	211.0	206	22	56	149	vs. Right	.239	899	215	51	5	24	105	47	176	.284	.387
Day	3.54	8	8	10	96	2	127.0	118	15	34	80	Inning 1-6	.240	433	104	24	1	8	53	39	74	.303	.356
Night	3.40	12	15	40	220	6	307.1	288	26	81	211	Inning 7+	.252	1200	302	67	4	33	134	80	217	.302	.397
Grass	3.73	5	8	11	107	2	154.1	152	15	37	112	None on	.242	926	224	49	4	34	34	44	168	.286	.414
Turf	3.28	15	15	39	209	6	280.0	254	26	78	179	Runners on	.257	707	182	42	1	7	153	71	123	.322	.349
March/April	2.35	3	3	3	44	0	57.1	47	7	14	47	Scoring Posn	.220	449	99	27	1	3	139	57	94	.301	.305
May	3.18	3	7	5	56	4	87.2	74	7	26	65	Close & Late	.234	595	139	30	2	15	65	52	113	.299	.366
June	4.26	4	3	12	58	4	88.2	103	10	21	47	None on/out	.236	399	94	19	2	12	12	14	75	.274	.383
July	4.28	3	5	6	55	0	73.2	66	9	23	61	vs. 1st Batr (relief)	.230	283	65	13	1	8	26	15	50	.276	.367
August	3.51	3	4	9	55	0	74.1	68	4	21	43	1st Inning Pitched	.259	1065	276	54	5	25	139	77	189	.310	.390
Sept/Oct	2.39	4	1	15	48	0	52.2	48	4	10	28	First 15 Pitches	.256	996	255	50	4	26	105	62	165	.302	.393
Starter	3.96	1	4	0	8	8	36.1	38	3	15	14	Pitch 16-30	.236	450	106	30	1	12	66	34	100	.293	.387
Reliever	3.39	19	19	50	308	0	398.0	368	38	100	277	Pitch 31-45	.273	121	33	9	0	1	11	12	9	.350	.372
0 Days rest (Relief)	3.08	3	9	23	84	0	99.1	74	10	27	59	Pitch 46+	.182	66	12	2	0	2	5	7	7	.270	.303
1 or 2 Days rest	3.67	10	7	17	152	0	191.1	200	15	54	135	First Pitch	.316	288	91	24	2	10	40	17	0	.349	.517
3+ Days rest	3.19	6	3	10	72	0	107.1	94	13	19	83	Ahead in Count	.199	764	152	32	1	11	68	0	253	.208	.287
vs. AL	5.09	0	0	4	16	0	17.2	21	3	2	11	Behind in Count	.279	294	82	20	1	9	43	52	0	.389	.446

Last Five Years

	ERA	W	L	Sv	G	GS	IP	H	HR	BB	SO		Avg	AB	H	2B	3B	HR	RBI	BB	SO	OBP	SLG
vs. NL	3.37	20	23	46	300	8	416.2	385	38	113	280	Two Strikes	.174	691	120	23	0	10	54	46	291	.232	.250
Pre-All Star	3.32	10	14	22	178	8	268.2	253	26	67	190	Pre-All Star	.249	1018	253	57	3	26	116	67	190	.298	.387
Post-All Star	3.64	10	9	28	138	0	165.2	153	15	48	101	Post-All Star	.249	615	153	34	2	15	71	48	101	.308	.384

Pitcher vs. Batter (career)

Pitches Best Vs.	Avg	AB	H	2B	3B	HR	RBI	BB	SO	OBP	SLG	Pitches Worst Vs.	Avg	AB	H	2B	3B	HR	RBI	BB	SO	OBP	SLG
Ruben Sierra	.000	10	0	0	0	0	0	1	1	.091	.000	Bobby Bonilla	.500	12	6	0	0	2	3	0	2	.500	1.000
Royce Clayton	.056	18	1	0	0	0	0	0	2	.105	.056	Ron Gant	.500	10	5	0	0	2	3	3	2	.615	1.100
Bernard Gilkey	.154	13	2	0	0	0	1	0	3	.154	.154	Kevin Stocker	.444	9	4	1	0	0	1	1	1	.455	.556
Derrick May	.182	11	2	0	0	0	1	1	0	.231	.182	Barry Bonds	.429	14	6	2	0	1	4	5	1	.579	.786
Walt Weiss	.200	15	3	0	0	0	0	0	2	.200	.200	Glenallen Hill	.308	13	4	0	0	1	2	2	2	.400	.615

Danny Sheaffer — Cardinals
Age 36 – Bats Right (groundball hitter)

	Avg	G	AB	R	H	2B	3B	HR	RBI	BB	SO	HBP	GDP	SB	CS	OBP	SLG	IBB	SH	SF	#Pit	#P/PA	GB	FB	G/F
1997 Season	.250	76	132	10	33	5	0	0	11	8	17	1	10	1	0	.296	.288	0	4	1	473	3.24	49	40	1.23
Last Five Years	.243	357	864	81	210	37	5	12	105	58	106	5	42	6	8	.292	.339	2	10	8	3169	3.35	380	241	1.58

1997 Season

	Avg	AB	H	2B	3B	HR	RBI	BB	SO	OBP	SLG		Avg	AB	H	2B	3B	HR	RBI	BB	SO	OBP	SLG
vs. Left	.222	63	14	3	0	0	4	4	9	.279	.270	Scoring Posn	.333	33	11	2	0	0	11	2	3	.378	.394
vs. Right	.275	69	19	2	0	0	7	4	8	.311	.304	Close & Late	.407	27	11	2	0	0	5	1	4	.429	.481
Home	.291	55	16	2	0	0	6	3	9	.339	.327	None on/out	.320	25	8	1	0	0	0	2	7	.370	.360
Away	.221	77	17	3	0	0	5	5	8	.265	.260	Batting #6	.310	42	13	3	0	0	5	1	7	.341	.381
First Pitch	.382	34	13	2	0	0	2	0	0	.382	.441	Batting #9	.259	27	7	0	0	0	2	2	2	.310	.259
Ahead in Count	.273	22	6	1	0	0	5	0	0	.407	.318	Other	.206	63	13	2	0	0	4	5	8	.261	.238
Behind in Count	.167	60	10	2	0	0	6	0	16	.180	.200	Pre-All Star	.284	74	21	3	0	0	4	5	10	.338	.324
Two Strikes	.149	47	7	1	0	0	4	3	17	.216	.170	Post-All Star	.207	58	12	2	0	0	7	3	7	.242	.241

Last Five Years

	Avg	AB	H	2B	3B	HR	RBI	BB	SO	OBP	SLG		Avg	AB	H	2B	3B	HR	RBI	BB	SO	OBP	SLG
vs. Left	.248	266	66	12	2	3	38	24	33	.312	.342	First Pitch	.333	186	62	10	1	2	27	2	0	.342	.430
vs. Right	.241	598	144	25	3	9	67	34	73	.283	.338	Ahead in Count	.293	174	51	11	2	2	29	38	0	.413	.414
Groundball	.234	218	51	8	2	2	20	12	27	.280	.317	Behind in Count	.172	361	62	13	1	3	28	0	92	.176	.238
Flyball	.254	134	34	8	1	2	16	8	19	.294	.373	Two Strikes	.169	337	57	12	0	5	24	18	106	.216	.249
Home	.257	420	108	26	3	5	60	32	52	.314	.369	Batting #7	.233	404	94	18	2	8	62	25	49	.281	.347
Away	.230	444	102	11	2	7	45	26	54	.271	.311	Batting #8	.258	178	46	7	1	3	13	12	20	.302	.360
Day	.207	333	69	10	4	4	34	19	34	.255	.297	Other	.248	282	70	12	2	1	30	21	37	.301	.316
Night	.266	531	141	27	1	8	71	39	72	.315	.365	March/April	.264	91	24	5	0	1	12	7	7	.323	.352
Grass	.242	595	144	25	3	8	79	36	69	.289	.334	May	.264	140	37	5	1	1	14	8	15	.304	.336
Turf	.245	269	66	12	2	4	26	22	37	.299	.349	June	.229	170	39	8	0	4	21	7	22	.267	.347
Pre-All Star	.261	452	118	19	2	8	53	26	47	.304	.365	July	.246	191	47	6	1	4	24	16	26	.300	.351
Post-All Star	.223	412	92	18	3	4	52	32	59	.279	.311	August	.247	166	41	11	1	2	25	15	21	.308	.361
Scoring Posn	.263	228	60	8	2	3	89	30	28	.351	.355	Sept/Oct	.208	106	22	2	2	0	9	5	15	.248	.264
Close & Late	.292	144	42	6	1	3	23	11	21	.342	.410	vs. AL	.250	8	2	0	0	0	1	1	0	.333	.250
None on/out	.298	181	54	9	2	5	5	8	21	.328	.453	vs. NL	.243	856	208	37	5	12	104	57	106	.292	.340

Batter vs. Pitcher (career)

Hits Best Against	Avg	AB	H	2B	3B	HR	RBI	BB	SO	OBP	SLG	Hits Worst Against	Avg	AB	H	2B	3B	HR	RBI	BB	SO	OBP	SLG
Denny Neagle	.500	14	7	2	0	0	5	2	2	.563	.643	Mike Hampton	.083	12	1	0	0	0	0	0	3	.083	.083
John Smiley	.429	14	6	1	0	0	2	0	0	.429	.500	Tom Candiotti	.100	10	1	0	0	0	1	1	0	.182	.100
Paul Wagner	.385	13	5	0	1	0	2	1	1	.429	.538	Bobby Jones	.167	12	2	0	0	1	5	0	0	.231	.417
												Carlos Perez	.182	11	2	1	0	0	0	0	1	.182	.273
												Kirk Rueter	.231	13	3	0	0	1	1	0	1	.231	.462

Andy Sheets — Mariners
Age 26 – Bats Right

	Avg	G	AB	R	H	2B	3B	HR	RBI	BB	SO	HBP	GDP	SB	CS	OBP	SLG	IBB	SH	SF	#Pit	#P/PA	GB	FB	G/F
1997 Season	.247	32	89	18	22	3	0	4	9	7	34	0	1	2	0	.299	.416	0	5	1	378	3.71	28	16	1.75
Career (1996-1997)	.216	79	199	36	43	11	0	4	18	17	75	1	3	4	0	.279	.332	0	7	2	832	3.68	60	42	1.43

1997 Season

	Avg	AB	H	2B	3B	HR	RBI	BB	SO	OBP	SLG		Avg	AB	H	2B	3B	HR	RBI	BB	SO	OBP	SLG
vs. Left	.313	16	5	0	0	0	3	4	6	.429	.313	Scoring Posn	.174	23	4	0	0	0	4	1	9	.200	.174
vs. Right	.233	73	17	3	0	4	6	3	28	.263	.438	Close & Late	.000	5	0	0	0	0	0	1	2	.167	.000

Gary Sheffield — Marlins
Age 29 – Bats Right (flyball hitter)

	Avg	G	AB	R	H	2B	3B	HR	RBI	BB	SO	HBP	GDP	SB	CS	OBP	SLG	IBB	SH	SF	#Pit	#P/PA	GB	FB	G/F
1997 Season	.250	135	444	86	111	22	1	21	71	121	79	15	7	11	7	.424	.446	11	0	2	2281	3.92	158	146	1.08
Last Five Years	.290	586	1992	378	577	99	8	126	388	416	304	44	47	75	31	.419	.537	55	0	22	9352	3.78	654	692	0.95

1997 Season

	Avg	AB	H	2B	3B	HR	RBI	BB	SO	OBP	SLG		Avg	AB	H	2B	3B	HR	RBI	BB	SO	OBP	SLG
vs. Left	.343	67	23	4	0	5	13	27	10	.536	.627	First Pitch	.315	54	17	3	0	4	12	8	0	.448	.593
vs. Right	.233	377	88	18	1	16	58	94	69	.402	.414	Ahead in Count	.299	97	29	7	0	5	19	58	0	.570	.526
Groundball	.182	66	12	6	0	2	11	25	13	.407	.364	Behind in Count	.200	195	39	7	1	8	24	0	59	.222	.369
Flyball	.263	57	15	0	0	4	7	19	13	.447	.474	Two Strikes	.225	204	46	11	1	9	29	55	79	.398	.422
Home	.276	214	59	11	0	13	33	65	33	.460	.509	Batting #3	.248	258	64	11	0	13	37	72	48	.420	.442

1997 Season

	Avg	AB	H	2B	3B	HR	RBI	BB	SO	OBP	SLG		Avg	AB	H	2B	3B	HR	RBI	BB	SO	OBP	SLG
Away	.226	230	52	11	1	8	38	56	46	.390	.387	Batting #4	.245	184	45	11	1	8	31	49	31	.426	.446
Day	.207	140	29	6	1	7	23	43	28	.416	.414	Other	1.000	2	2	0	0	0	3	0	0	1.000	1.000
Night	.270	304	82	16	0	14	48	78	51	.429	.461	March/April	.227	75	17	4	0	4	11	29	14	.459	.440
Grass	.267	371	99	20	1	19	56	93	63	.429	.480	May	.222	54	12	3	0	1	5	15	4	.417	.333
Turf	.164	73	12	2	0	2	15	28	16	.406	.274	June	.244	82	20	6	0	3	16	27	19	.451	.427
Pre-All Star	.242	236	57	14	1	9	37	71	39	.436	.424	July	.279	68	19	2	1	4	12	8	13	.372	.515
Post-All Star	.260	208	54	8	0	12	34	50	40	.411	.471	August	.213	94	20	3	0	4	13	28	17	.403	.372
Scoring Posn	.254	114	29	6	0	5	47	42	20	.466	.439	Sept/Oct	.324	71	23	4	0	5	14	14	12	.430	.592
Close & Late	.265	68	18	2	0	2	10	19	18	.451	.382	vs. AL	.260	50	13	3	0	3	9	18	7	.456	.500
None on/out	.191	94	18	3	0	5	5	19	17	.333	.383	vs. NL	.249	394	98	19	1	18	62	103	72	.420	.439

1997 By Position

Position	Avg	AB	H	2B	3B	HR	RBI	BB	SO	OBP	SLG	G	GS	Innings	PO	A	E	DP	Fld Pct	Rng Fctr	In Zone	Outs	Zone Rtg	MLB Zone
As rf	.245	440	108	22	1	20	66	118	79	.419	.436	132	132	1115.1	230	14	5	1	.980	1.97	284	222	.782	.813

Last Five Years

	Avg	AB	H	2B	3B	HR	RBI	BB	SO	OBP	SLG		Avg	AB	H	2B	3B	HR	RBI	BB	SO	OBP	SLG
vs. Left	.300	466	140	17	0	29	87	100	52	.428	.524	First Pitch	.380	279	106	19	2	23	59	34	0	.465	.710
vs. Right	.286	1526	437	82	8	97	301	316	252	.417	.541	Ahead in Count	.352	415	146	29	2	36	113	222	0	.581	.692
Groundball	.273	501	137	22	5	32	98	88	71	.392	.529	Behind in Count	.224	879	197	28	3	37	117	0	232	.238	.389
Flyball	.292	318	93	18	0	21	71	65	51	.416	.547	Two Strikes	.218	880	192	36	2	30	113	160	304	.343	.366
Home	.303	957	290	53	3	61	193	222	134	.444	.556	Batting #3	.291	1343	391	66	4	92	266	284	212	.420	.552
Away	.277	1035	287	46	5	65	195	194	170	.396	.520	Batting #4	.283	639	181	33	4	33	116	128	91	.414	.502
Day	.281	545	153	24	4	33	109	109	89	.409	.521	Other	.500	10	5	0	0	1	6	4	1	.643	.800
Night	.293	1447	424	75	4	93	279	307	215	.423	.543	March/April	.279	351	98	17	2	31	68	75	54	.413	.604
Grass	.301	1580	476	85	8	100	314	335	242	.431	.555	May	.275	363	100	18	1	16	59	87	57	.424	.463
Turf	.245	412	101	14	0	26	74	81	62	.372	.468	June	.295	363	107	19	1	16	60	65	47	.410	.485
Pre-All Star	.285	1195	341	59	5	71	208	244	171	.414	.521	July	.300	343	103	21	2	20	68	49	50	.396	.548
Post-All Star	.296	797	236	40	3	55	180	172	133	.427	.561	August	.273	322	88	15	0	22	73	65	45	.401	.525
Scoring Posn	.295	488	144	27	3	37	250	169	70	.470	.590	Sept/Oct	.324	250	81	9	2	21	60	75	51	.482	.628
Close & Late	.282	305	86	11	3	14	62	82	60	.441	.475	vs. AL	.260	50	13	3	0	3	9	18	7	.456	.500
None on/out	.300	397	119	18	1	21	21	58	50	.398	.509	vs. NL	.290	1942	564	96	8	123	379	398	297	.418	.538

Batter vs. Pitcher (career)

Hits Best Against	Avg	AB	H	2B	3B	HR	RBI	BB	SO	OBP	SLG	Hits Worst Against	Avg	AB	H	2B	3B	HR	RBI	BB	SO	OBP	SLG
Salomon Torres	.625	8	5	2	0	2	4	5	0	.769	1.625	Steve Reed	.000	11	0	0	0	0	2	1	5	.077	.000
Hideo Nomo	.571	14	8	0	0	3	5	2	2	.625	1.214	Mark Wohlers	.063	16	1	1	0	0	0	1	4	.118	.125
Steve Trachsel	.556	18	10	3	0	3	5	6	2	.680	1.222	Bob Tewksbury	.071	14	1	0	0	0	1	2	2	.176	.071
Osvald Fernandez	.444	9	4	0	0	2	3	4	1	.615	1.111	Matt Morris	.100	10	1	0	0	0	1	0	3	.182	.100
John Burkett	.417	12	5	1	0	3	6	1	0	.462	1.250	Tim Belcher	.133	15	2	0	0	0	2	0	2	.167	.133

Scott Sheldon — Athletics
Age 29 – Bats Right

	Avg	G	AB	R	H	2B	3B	HR	RBI	BB	SO	HBP	GDP	SB	CS	OBP	SLG	IBB	SH	SF	#Pit	#P/PA	GB	FB	G/F
1997 Season	.250	13	24	2	6	0	0	1	2	1	6	1	0	0	0	.308	.375	0	1	0	99	3.67	6	8	0.75

1997 Season

	Avg	AB	H	2B	3B	HR	RBI	BB	SO	OBP	SLG		Avg	AB	H	2B	3B	HR	RBI	BB	SO	OBP	SLG
vs. Left	.333	6	2	0	0	0	0	0	1	.333	.333	Scoring Posn	.375	8	3	0	0	0	0	0	2	.444	.375
vs. Right	.222	18	4	0	0	1	2	1	5	.300	.389	Close & Late	.000	1	0	0	0	0	0	0	0	.000	.000

Craig Shipley — Padres
Age 35 – Bats Right

	Avg	G	AB	R	H	2B	3B	HR	RBI	BB	SO	HBP	GDP	SB	CS	OBP	SLG	IBB	SH	SF	#Pit	#P/PA	GB	FB	G/F
1997 Season	.273	63	139	22	38	9	0	5	19	7	20	1		1	1	.306	.446	0	1	1	503	3.40	49	45	1.09
Last Five Years	.281	374	933	115	262	45	5	17	102	36	122	10	20	32	11	.312	.394	5	8	8	3115	3.13	352	274	1.28

1997 Season

	Avg	AB	H	2B	3B	HR	RBI	BB	SO	OBP	SLG		Avg	AB	H	2B	3B	HR	RBI	BB	SO	OBP	SLG
vs. Left	.255	47	12	1	0	3	6	2	7		.468	Scoring Posn	.286	42	12	4	0	1	14	1	8	.295	.452
vs. Right	.283	92	26	8	0	2	13	5	13	.316	.435	Close & Late	.229	35	8	2	0	1	2	1	6	.250	.371
Home	.321	53	17	2	0	3	11	4	5	.368	.528	None on/out	.263	38	10	1	0	2	2	1	6	.300	.447
Away	.244	86	21	7	0	2	8	3	15	.267	.395	Batting #1	.154	26	4	1	0	0	2	2	6	.214	.192
First Pitch	.346	26	9	2	0	1	3	0	0	.333	.538	Batting #7	.310	29	9	4	0	0	6	3	4	.364	.448
Ahead in Count	.333	27	9	2	0	1	4	2	0	.379	.519	Other	.298	84	25	4	0	5	13	2	10	.314	.524
Behind in Count	.230	61	14	3	0	2	7	0	14	.230	.377	Pre-All Star	.333	33	11	4	0	2	4	0	4	.333	.636
Two Strikes	.220	59	13	4	0	3	11	5	20	.281	.441	Post-All Star	.255	106	27	5	0	3	15	7	16	.298	.387

Last Five Years

	Avg	AB	H	2B	3B	HR	RBI	BB	SO	OBP	SLG		Avg	AB	H	2B	3B	HR	RBI	BB	SO	OBP	SLG
vs. Left	.288	379	109	17	2	5	34	16	38	.309	.383	First Pitch	.260	200	52	11	0	1	10	5	0	.289	.330
vs. Right	.276	554	153	28	3	12	68	20	84	.309	.403	Ahead in Count	.355	183	65	11	2	6	25	17	0	.409	.536
Groundball	.252	266	67	12	1	3	23	11	38	.282	.338	Behind in Count	.250	404	101	13	3	9	50	0	109	.255	.364
Flyball	.305	131	40	8	0	2	11	1	17	.308	.412	Two Strikes	.193	336	65	11	2	7	41	14	122	.228	.301
Home	.266	443	118	18	4	8	49	21	53	.299	.379	Batting #2	.301	216	65	10	3	6	32	9	20	.333	.458
Away	.294	490	144	27	1	9	53	15	69	.324	.408	Batting #6	.299	184	55	8	1	6	23	2	30	.318	.451
Day	.286	325	93	18	1	8	38	17	43	.329	.422	Other	.266	533	142	27	1	5	47	25	72	.301	.349
Night	.278	608	169	27	4	9	64	19	79	.303	.380	March/April	.287	136	39	12	0	2	12	4	19	.308	.419
Grass	.289	585	169	27	5	12	76	25	71	.319	.414	May	.333	108	36	7	1	5	22	3	7	.351	.556

Last Five Years

	Avg	AB	H	2B	3B	HR	RBI	BB	SO	OBP	SLG		Avg	AB	H	2B	3B	HR	RBI	BB	SO	OBP	SLG
Turf	.267	348	93	18	0	5	26	11	51	.301	.362	June	.275	153	42	4	2	0	12	9	19	.319	.327
Pre-All Star	.298	453	135	28	4	8	50	18	54	.328	.430	July	.312	170	53	12	2	3	25	9	22	.350	.459
Post-All Star	.265	480	127	17	1	9	52	18	68	.297	.360	August	.235	234	55	8	0	4	20	6	36	.262	.321
Scoring Posn	.274	223	61	14	1	4	84	14	35	.317	.399	Sept/Oct	.280	132	37	2	0	3	11	5	19	.314	.364
Close & Late	.302	199	60	11	2	3	18	8	34	.336	.422	vs. AL	1.000	1	1	0	0	0	0	0	0	1.000	1.000
None on/out	.279	251	70	14	1	4	4	8	30	.301	.390	vs. NL	.280	932	261	45	5	17	102	36	122	.311	.394

Batter vs. Pitcher (career)

Hits Best Against	Avg	AB	H	2B	3B	HR	RBI	BB	SO	OBP	SLG	Hits Worst Against	Avg	AB	H	2B	3B	HR	RBI	BB	SO	OBP	SLG
Greg Swindell	.545	11	6	3	0	0	1	1	1	.538	.818	Steve Avery	.077	13	1	0	0	0	0	1	3	.143	.077
Tom Glavine	.471	17	8	0	0	0	1	0	2	.471	.471	Tom Candiotti	.083	12	1	0	0	0	1	0	5	.083	.083
Orel Hershiser	.364	11	4	0	0	0	1	0	0	.417	.364	Pat Rapp	.091	11	1	0	0	0	0	1	1	.167	.091
Kevin Gross	.364	11	4	0	0	0	2	0	3	.364	.364	Allen Watson	.100	10	1	0	0	0	0	1	1	.250	.100
Ken Hill	.364	11	4	1	0	3	0	2	.364	.455		Tim Belcher	.182	11	2	0	0	0	2	0	1	.182	.182

Paul Shuey — Indians

Age 27 – Pitches Right

	ERA	W	L	Sv	G	GS	IP	BB	SO	Avg	H	2B	3B	HR	RBI	OBP	SLG	GF	IR	IRS	Hld	SvOp	SB	CS	GB	FB	G/F
1997 Season	6.20	4	2	2	40	0	45.0	28	46	.294	52	7	1	5	28	.389	.429	16	18	6	4	3	6	0	56	50	1.12
Career (1994-1997)	4.78	9	7	11	103	0	116.2	71	111	.262	116	21	1	12	60	.362	.395	48	41	14	12	15	14	5	151	111	1.36

1997 Season

	ERA	W	L	Sv	G	GS	IP	H	BB	SO		Avg	AB	H	2B	3B	HR	RBI	BB	SO	OBP	SLG
Home	6.18	3	1	0	21	0	27.2	35	1	17	24	vs. Left	.235	68	16	1	0	1	7	14	16	.369	.294
Away	6.23	1	1	2	19	0	17.1	17	4	11	22	vs. Right	.330	109	36	6	1	4	21	14	30	.403	.514
Starter	0.00	0	0	0	0	0	0.0	0	0	0	0	Scoring Posn	.333	42	14	1	0	1	21	15	10	.492	.429
Reliever	6.20	4	2	2	40	0	45.0	52	5	28	46	Close & Late	.265	34	9	0	0	1	6	10	11	.444	.353
0 Days rest (Relief)	4.15	1	0	1	10	0	8.2	7	1	6	8	None on/out	.311	45	14	4	1	0	0	3	15	.354	.444
1 or 2 Days rest	8.05	2	2	0	16	0	19.0	27	4	9	24	First Pitch	.368	19	7	0	0	0	3	1	0	.400	.368
3+ Days rest	5.19	1	0	1	14	0	17.1	18	0	13	14	Ahead in Count	.182	77	14	2	1	0	5	0	39	.182	.234
Pre-All Star	5.16	2	1	2	23	0	22.2	28	3	13	19	Behind in Count	.373	51	19	4	0	2	7	12	0	.492	.569
Post-All Star	7.25	2	1	0	17	0	22.1	24	2	15	27	Two Strikes	.181	83	15	1	1	2	10	15	46	.303	.289

Career (1994-1997)

	ERA	W	L	Sv	G	GS	IP	H	BB	SO		Avg	AB	H	2B	3B	HR	RBI	BB	SO	OBP	SLG
Home	4.45	7	3	5	53	0	64.2	71	5	35	63	vs. Left	.245	196	48	9	0	2	21	41	48	.373	.321
Away	5.19	2	4	6	50	0	52.0	45	7	36	48	vs. Right	.275	247	68	12	1	10	39	30	63	.351	.453
Day	3.92	4	2	3	37	0	43.2	39	5	24	49	Inning 1-6	.333	51	17	3	0	3	17	11	11	.444	.569
Night	5.30	5	5	8	66	0	73.0	77	7	47	62	Inning 7+	.253	392	99	18	1	9	43	60	100	.350	.372
Grass	4.37	9	6	9	92	0	107.0	106	7	63	98	None on	.276	239	66	10	1	6	6	25	60	.347	.402
Turf	9.31	0	1	2	11	0	9.2	10	5	8	13	Runners on	.245	204	50	11	0	6	54	46	51	.376	.387
March/April	12.15	0	3	2	13	0	13.1	23	5	17	14	Scoring Posn	.265	113	30	5	0	3	46	31	29	.409	.389
May	1.46	1	0	2	13	0	12.1	7	0	7	12	Close & Late	.261	157	41	7	0	5	21	29	36	.376	.401
June	4.45	3	1	4	27	0	28.1	28	2	15	25	None on/out	.250	104	26	5	1	1	1	10	31	.316	.346
July	1.32	1	1	3	13	0	13.2	11	1	8	9	vs. 1st Batr (relief)	.227	88	20	4	0	1	7	12	28	.317	.307
August	4.85	2	0	0	18	0	29.2	27	3	11	38	1st Inning Pitched	.242	327	79	16	0	7	45	60	85	.357	.355
Sept/Oct	4.66	2	2	0	19	0	19.1	20	1	13	13	First 15 Pitches	.255	255	65	13	0	4	27	35	65	.345	.353
Starter	0.00	0	0	0	0	0	0.0	0	0	0	0	Pitch 16-30	.243	136	33	6	1	6	21	28	32	.367	.434
Reliever	4.78	9	7	11	103	0	116.2	116	12	71	111	Pitch 31-45	.326	43	14	1	0	2	10	6	12	.408	.488
0 Days rest (Relief)	4.12	3	1	4	21	0	19.2	15	1	17	18	Pitch 46+	.444	9	4	1	0	0	2	2	2	.500	.556
1 or 2 Days rest	5.16	3	4	3	45	0	52.1	57	8	25	48	First Pitch	.360	50	18	3	0	0	6	5	0	.418	.420
3+ Days rest	4.63	3	2	4	37	0	44.2	44	3	29	45	Ahead in Count	.183	191	35	9	1	2	13	0	89	.182	.272
vs. AL	4.51	9	7	11	98	0	111.2	107	12	67	108	Behind in Count	.368	106	39	7	0	5	22	33	0	.514	.575
vs. NL	10.80	0	0	0	5	0	5.0	9	0	4	3	Two Strikes	.175	228	40	8	1	6	22	22	33	.278	.298
Pre-All Star	5.43	4	5	9	57	0	58.0	62	8	40	52	Pre-All Star	.276	225	62	12	0	8	35	40	52	.383	.436
Post-All Star	4.14	5	2	2	46	0	58.2	54	4	31	59	Post-All Star	.248	218	54	9	1	4	25	31	59	.339	.353

Terry Shumpert — Padres

Age 31 – Bats Right (flyball hitter)

	Avg	G	AB	R	H	2B	3B	HR	RBI	BB	SO	HBP	GDP	SB	CS	OBP	SLG	IBB	SH	SF	#Pit	#P/PA	GB	FB	G/F
1997 Season	.273	13	33	4	9	3	0	1	6	3	4	0	1	0	0	.324	.455	0	0	1	137	3.70	17	12	1.42
Last Five Years	.237	133	304	43	72	13	2	11	39	24	69	1	1	22	5	.292	.401	0	5	3	1308	3.88	90	95	0.95

1997 Season

	Avg	AB	H	2B	3B	HR	RBI	BB	SO	OBP	SLG		Avg	AB	H	2B	3B	HR	RBI	BB	SO	OBP	SLG
vs. Left	.600	5	3	1	0	1	3	3	1	.667	1.400	Scoring Posn	.100	10	1	0	0	0	3	1	2	.167	.100
vs. Right	.214	28	6	2	0	0	3	0	3	.214	.286	Close & Late	.333	3	1	0	0	0	0	0	0	.333	.333

Ruben Sierra — Blue Jays

Age 32 – Bats Both

	Avg	G	AB	R	H	2B	3B	HR	RBI	BB	SO	HBP	GDP	SB	CS	OBP	SLG	IBB	SH	SF	#Pit	#P/PA	GB	FB	G/F
1997 Season	.232	39	138	10	32	5	3	3	12	9	34	0	1	0	0	.277	.377	2	0	1	542	3.66	48	41	1.17
Last Five Years	.250	575	2191	292	547	107	11	79	363	190	354	0	50	42	18	.305	.417	38	0	39	8709	3.60	808	718	1.13

1997 Season

	Avg	AB	H	2B	3B	HR	RBI	BB	SO	OBP	SLG		Avg	AB	H	2B	3B	HR	RBI	BB	SO	OBP	SLG
vs. Left	.184	38	7	0	0	1	3	1	11	.205	.263	Scoring Posn	.171	35	6	1	1	9	5	8	.268	.343	
vs. Right	.250	100	25	5	3	2	9	8	23	.303	.420	Close & Late	.158	19	3	0	0	0	0	2	6	.238	.158
Home	.239	71	17	3	2	3	8	5	15	.289	.465	None on/out	.304	23	7	0	0	1	0	8	.304	.435	

1997 Season

	Avg	AB	H	2B	3B	HR	RBI	BB	SO	OBP	SLG		Avg	AB	H	2B	3B	HR	RBI	BB	SO	OBP	SLG
Away	.224	67	15	2	1	0	4	4	19	.264	.284	Batting #4	.209	43	9	1	0	2	5	2	7	.244	.372
First Pitch	.308	13	4	0	1	1	1	2	0	.400	.692	Batting #6	.266	64	17	3	3	1	6	4	18	.304	.453
Ahead in Count	.300	40	12	1	2	1	7	4	0	.356	.500	Other	.194	31	6	1	0	0	1	3	9	.265	.226
Behind in Count	.175	63	11	3	0	1	3	0	32	.175	.270	Pre-All Star	.232	138	32	5	3	3	12	9	34	.277	.377
Two Strikes	.129	62	8	3	0	0	1	3	34	.169	.177	Post-All Star	.000	0	0	0	0	0	0	0	0	.000	.000

Last Five Years

	Avg	AB	H	2B	3B	HR	RBI	BB	SO	OBP	SLG		Avg	AB	H	2B	3B	HR	RBI	BB	SO	OBP	SLG
vs. Left	.278	712	198	42	1	26	127	65	104	.332	.449	First Pitch	.307	254	78	14	2	14	54	25	0	.361	.543
vs. Right	.236	1479	349	65	10	53	236	125	250	.291	.401	Ahead in Count	.314	566	178	38	6	26	139	101	0	.410	.541
Groundball	.257	494	127	27	7	11	74	33	61	.300	.407	Behind in Count	.205	917	188	34	2	24	108	0	296	.202	.325
Flyball	.257	444	114	18	0	23	81	38	82	.310	.453	Two Strikes	.175	912	160	25	3	18	80	64	354	.228	.269
Home	.243	1065	259	47	7	35	175	98	180	.302	.399	Batting #3	.239	763	182	34	5	30	129	61	118	.290	.414
Away	.256	1126	288	60	4	44	188	92	174	.307	.433	Batting #4	.255	922	235	51	1	32	165	83	132	.311	.416
Day	.253	857	217	47	7	21	115	81	115	.313	.398	Other	.257	506	130	22	5	17	69	46	104	.314	.421
Night	.247	1334	330	60	4	58	248	109	213	.299	.429	March/April	.253	360	91	24	1	18	55	25	60	.297	.475
Grass	.248	1825	453	88	8	64	303	155	293	.302	.410	May	.246	448	110	19	3	14	76	38	62	.298	.395
Turf	.257	366	94	19	3	15	60	35	61	.318	.448	June	.261	429	112	19	2	20	79	39	81	.320	.455
Pre-All Star	.254	1365	347	67	3	55	227	108	220	.305	.434	July	.280	321	90	13	1	12	53	26	45	.326	.439
Post-All Star	.242	826	200	40	4	24	136	82	134	.305	.387	August	.231	381	88	20	2	8	55	37	64	.296	.357
Scoring Posn	.271	613	166	30	2	29	287	84	106	.340	.468	Sept/Oct	.222	252	56	12	2	7	45	25	42	.286	.369
Close & Late	.237	321	76	11	1	12	57	43	66	.321	.389	vs. AL	.250	2100	525	102	10	77	356	184	332	.305	.418
None on/out	.257	487	125	32	3	12	12	29	67	.298	.409	vs. NL	.242	91	22	5	1	2	7	6	22	.289	.385

Batter vs. Pitcher (career)

Hits Best Against	Avg	AB	H	2B	3B	HR	RBI	BB	SO	OBP	SLG	Hits Worst Against	Avg	AB	H	2B	3B	HR	RBI	BB	SO	OBP	SLG
Bill Swift	.444	27	12	2	1	2	8	0	3	.444	.815	Paul Quantrill	.000	15	0	0	0	0	0	1	4	.063	.000
Roberto Hernandez	.417	12	5	1	0	2	7	2	1	.500	1.000	Gregg Olson	.000	12	0	0	0	0	0	1	0	.077	.000
Jose Bautista	.400	10	4	2	0	0	2	0	1	.455	.600	Jeff Shaw	.000	10	0	0	0	0	0	1	1	.091	.000
Scott Bailes	.350	20	7	3	0	2	3	2	2	.409	.800	Ben McDonald	.033	30	1	0	0	0	0	1	1	.065	.033
Dennis Cook	.333	12	4	1	0	3	4	2	.500	.667	David Cone	.045	22	1	0	0	0	0	5	.045	.091	

Jose Silva — Pirates
Age 24 – Pitches Right

	ERA	W	L	Sv	G	GS	IP	BB	SO	Avg	H	2B	3B	HR	RBI	OBP	SLG	GF	IR	IRS	Hld	SvOp	SB	CS	GB	FB	G/F
1997 Season	5.94	2	1	0	11	4	36.1	16	30	.347	52	12	1	4	25	.406	.520	0	4	2	0		3	1	51	39	1.31
Career (1996-1997)	6.34	2	1	0	13	4	38.1	16	30	.354	54	13	1	5	28	.409	.540	0	4	2	0		3	1	58	42	1.38

1997 Season

	ERA	W	L	Sv	G	GS	IP	H	HR	BB	SO		Avg	AB	H	2B	3B	HR	RBI	BB	SO	OBP	SLG
Home	4.64	1	0	0	6	2	21.1	28	1	11	16	vs. Left	.390	59	23	7	1	4	13	8	12	.449	.746
Away	7.80	1	1	0	5	2	15.0	24	3	5	14	vs. Right	.319	91	29	5	0	0	12	8	18	.376	.374

Dave Silvestri — Rangers
Age 30 – Bats Right (flyball hitter)

	Avg	G	AB	R	H	2B	3B	HR	RBI	BB	SO	HBP	GDP	SB	CS	OBP	SLG	IBB	SH	SF	#Pit	#P/PA	GB	FB	G/F
1997 Season	.000	2	4	0	0	0	0	0	0	0	1	0	0	0	0	.000	.000	0	0	0	14	3.50	3	0	0.00
Last Five Years	.208	163	298	39	62	11	1	6	34	56	90	1	9	4	2	.331	.312	6	4	4	1448	3.99	95	66	1.44

1997 Season

	Avg	AB	H	2B	3B	HR	RBI	BB	SO	OBP	SLG		Avg	AB	H	2B	3B	HR	RBI	BB	SO	OBP	SLG
vs. Left	.000	1	0	0	0	0	0	0	0	.000	.000	Scoring Posn	.000	1	0	0	0	0	0	0	0	.000	.000
vs. Right	.000	3	0	0	0	0	0	1	.000	.000	Close & Late	.000	0	0	0	0	0	0	0	0	.000	.000	

Last Five Years

	Avg	AB	H	2B	3B	HR	RBI	BB	SO	OBP	SLG		Avg	AB	H	2B	3B	HR	RBI	BB	SO	OBP	SLG
vs. Left	.212	85	18	2	0	3	16	15	23	.320	.341	First Pitch	.324	34	11	4	0	3	10	4	0	.395	.706
vs. Right	.207	213	44	9	1	3	18	41	67	.336	.300	Ahead in Count	.234	64	15	2	0	1	4	20	0	.412	.313
Groundball	.288	59	17	2	0	1	12	12	18	.397	.373	Behind in Count	.170	141	24	4	1	1	11	0	74	.174	.234
Flyball	.224	58	13	3	0	2	5	10	24	.343	.379	Two Strikes	.139	151	21	2	1	1	11	32	90	.293	.185
Home	.222	153	34	8	0	1	15	41	41	.383	.294	Batting #8	.204	142	29	4	0	2	13	29	34	.337	.275
Away	.193	145	28	3	1	5	19	15	49	.270	.331	Batting #9	.149	67	10	2	1	0	7	9	27	.250	.209
Day	.088	80	7	1	0	1	3	19	29	.263	.138	Other	.258	89	23	5	0	4	14	18	29	.378	.449
Night	.252	218	55	10	1	5	31	37	61	.358	.376	March/April	.171	41	7	1	0	0	5	6	14	.277	.195
Grass	.194	134	26	3	0	5	16	19	41	.297	.328	May	.255	55	14	0	0	1	9	11	10	.377	.309
Turf	.220	164	36	8	1	1	18	37	49	.358	.299	June	.164	55	9	1	0	1	6	13	18	.319	.236
Pre-All Star	.199	171	34	3	0	3	21	36	47	.336	.269	July	.189	37	7	2	1	1	3	10	13	.362	.378
Post-All Star	.220	127	28	8	1	3	13	20	43	.324	.370	August	.192	78	15	5	0	2	10	11	25	.289	.333
Scoring Posn	.238	84	20	4	0	1	26	29	26	.424	.321	Sept/Oct	.313	32	10	2	0	1	1	5	10	.405	.469
Close & Late	.192	52	10	0	0	1	3	10	20	.323	.250	vs. AL	.156	64	10	1	1	3	10	13	22	.300	.344
None on/out	.147	75	11	1	0	2	2	10	24	.267	vs. NL	.222	234	52	10	0	3	24	43	68	.341	.303	

Batter vs. Pitcher (career)

Hits Best Against	Avg	AB	H	2B	3B	HR	RBI	BB	SO	OBP	SLG	Hits Worst Against	Avg	AB	H	2B	3B	HR	RBI	BB	SO	OBP	SLG
												Randy Johnson	.100	10	1	0	0	1	2	1	7	.167	.400

Bill Simas — White Sox
Age 26 – Pitches Right

	ERA	W	L	Sv	G	GS	IP	BB	SO	Avg	H	2B	3B	HR	RBI	OBP	SLG	GF	IR	IRS	Hld	SvOp	SB	CS	GB	FB	G/F
1997 Season	4.14	3	1	1	40	0	41.1	24	38	.279	46	6	1	6	27	.375	.436	11	30	11	3	2	4	1	54	46	1.17
Career (1995-1997)	4.22	6	10	3	118	0	128.0	73	119	.270	136	27	4	12	75	.368	.412	31	85	28	21	10	6	3	152	141	1.08

1997 Season

	ERA	W	L	Sv	G	GS	IP	H	HR	BB	SO		Avg	AB	H	2B	3B	HR	RBI	BB	SO	OBP	SLG
Home	4.64	1	0	0	19	0	21.1	24	1	18	19	vs. Left	.296	54	16	1	1	3	12	9	15	.397	.519
Away	3.60	2	1	1	21	0	20.0	22	5	6	19	vs. Right	.270	111	30	5	0	3	15	15	23	.364	.396
Starter	0.00	0	0	0	0	0	0.0	0	0	0	0	Scoring Posn	.228	57	13	4	1	0	18	12	13	.366	.333
Reliever	4.14	3	1	1	40	0	41.1	46	6	24	38	Close & Late	.222	45	10	2	0	1	5	10	11	.375	.333
0 Days rest (Relief)	0.00	1	0	0	7	0	5.2	7	0	5	6	None on/out	.303	33	10	0	0	2	2	2	9	.343	.485
1 or 2 Days rest	4.91	2	1	1	19	0	22.0	25	6	9	17	First Pitch	.500	20	10	0	0	1	5	1	0	.524	.650
3+ Days rest	4.61	0	0	0	14	0	13.2	14	0	10	15	Ahead in Count	.216	88	19	4	0	3	12	0	32	.231	.364
Pre-All Star	4.54	3	0	1	33	0	33.2	36	5	19	32	Behind in Count	.190	21	4	1	1	4	12			.485	.476
Post-All Star	2.35	0	1	0	7	0	7.2	10	1	5	6	Two Strikes	.217	92	20	3	0	1	12	11	38	.305	.283

Career (1995-1997)

	ERA	W	L	Sv	G	GS	IP	H	HR	BB	SO		Avg	AB	H	2B	3B	HR	RBI	BB	SO	OBP	SLG
Home	4.61	3	3	0	57	0	68.1	70	5	45	62	vs. Left	.267	187	50	9	3	4	24	32	33	.381	.412
Away	3.77	3	7	3	61	0	59.2	66	7	28	57	vs. Right	.272	316	86	18	1	8	51	41	86	.359	.411
Day	4.86	1	8	2	43	0	46.1	41	3	33	44	Inning 1-6	.271	59	16	3	0	3	9	2	14	.317	.475
Night	3.86	5	2	1	75	0	81.2	95	9	40	75	Inning 7+	.270	444	120	24	4	9	66	71	105	.374	.403
Grass	4.45	5	7	3	100	0	109.1	119	10	65	101	None on	.274	230	63	7	2	6	6	31	51	.363	.400
Turf	2.89	1	3	0	18	0	18.2	17	2	8	18	Runners on	.267	273	73	20	2	6	69	42	68	.372	.421
March/April	4.43	0	3	0	21	0	22.1	16	1	18	21	Scoring Posn	.252	159	40	12	1	2	57	32	42	.384	.377
May	1.71	2	0	2	24	0	26.1	23	3	12	23	Close & Late	.278	216	60	15	1	3	31	36	53	.385	.398
June	6.08	1	1	0	23	0	26.2	32	4	12	31	None on/out	.225	102	23	2	0	2	2	10	23	.301	.304
July	6.00	0	4	0	16	0	15.0	22	2	10	10	vs. 1st Batr (relief)	.297	101	30	5	0	1	10	14	28	.398	.376
August	4.71	2	1	0	18	0	21.0	27	1	14	20	1st Inning Pitched	.268	362	97	18	4	8	59	52	82	.366	.406
Sept/Oct	2.70	1	1	1	16	0	16.2	16	1	7	14	First 15 Pitches	.278	295	82	16	4	6	44	35	64	.359	.420
Starter	0.00	0	0	0	0	0	0.0	0	0	0	0	Pitch 16-30	.274	164	45	7	0	5	25	28	41	.387	.409
Reliever	4.22	6	10	3	118	0	128.0	136	12	73	119	Pitch 31-45	.175	40	7	3	0	1	3	9	14	.327	.325
0 Days rest (Relief)	4.37	2	3	0	22	0	22.2	30	1	15	18	Pitch 46+	.500	4	2	1	0	0	3	1	0	.600	.750
1 or 2 Days rest	4.68	4	3	2	57	0	59.2	65	10	28	49	First Pitch	.410	61	25	1	0	3	11	8	0	.493	.574
3+ Days rest	3.55	0	4	1	39	0	45.2	41	1	30	52	Ahead in Count	.203	256	52	12	1	4	27	0	101	.212	.305
vs. AL	4.19	6	10	3	116	0	126.2	135	12	72	116	Behind in Count	.333	81	27	9	2	4	21	30	0	.509	.642
vs. NL	6.75	0	0	0	2	0	1.1	1	0	1	3	Two Strikes	.201	273	55	12	1	2	25	34	119	.294	.275
Pre-All Star	4.29	3	4	2	72	0	77.2	77	8	45	76	Pre-All Star	.252	305	77	17	2	8	49	45	76	.355	.400
Post-All Star	4.11	3	6	1	46	0	50.1	59	4	28	43	Post-All Star	.298	198	59	10	2	4	26	28	43	.387	.429

Mike Simms — Rangers
Age 31 – Bats Right

	Avg	G	AB	R	H	2B	3B	HR	RBI	BB	SO	HBP	GDP	SB	CS	OBP	SLG	IBB	SH	SF	#Pit	#P/PA	GB	FB	G/F
1997 Season	.252	59	111	13	28	8	0	5	22	8	27	0	3	0	1	.298	.459	1	0	2	441	3.64	33	36	0.92
Last Five Years	.231	164	312	34	72	15	1	15	54	25	76	4	7	3	3	.294	.429	1	0	3	1259	3.66	92	110	0.84

1997 Season

	Avg	AB	H	2B	3B	HR	RBI	BB	SO	OBP	SLG		Avg	AB	H	2B	3B	HR	RBI	BB	SO	OBP	SLG
vs. Left	.235	81	19	5	0	3	13	6	21	.284	.407	Scoring Posn	.344	32	11	2	0	1	16	3	5	.378	.500
vs. Right	.300	30	9	3	0	2	9	2	6	.333	.600	Close & Late	.389	18	7	2	0	2	9	2	5	.450	.833

Randall Simon — Braves
Age 23 – Bats Left

	Avg	G	AB	R	H	2B	3B	HR	RBI	BB	SO	HBP	GDP	SB	CS	OBP	SLG	IBB	SH	SF	#Pit	#P/PA	GB	FB	G/F
1997 Season	.429	13	14	2	6	1	0	0	1	1	2	0	1	0	0	.467	.500	0	0	0	40	2.67	7	2	3.50

1997 Season

	Avg	AB	H	2B	3B	HR	RBI	BB	SO	OBP	SLG		Avg	AB	H	2B	3B	HR	RBI	BB	SO	OBP	SLG
vs. Left	.000	1	0	0	0	0	0	0	0	.000	.000	Scoring Posn	.500	2	1	0	0	0	1	0	0	.500	.500
vs. Right	.462	13	6	1	0	0	1	1	2	.500	.538	Close & Late	.250	4	1	0	0	0	0	0	0	.250	.250

Mike Sirotka — White Sox
Age 27 – Pitches Left

	ERA	W	L	Sv	G	GS	IP	BB	SO	Avg	H	2B	3B	HR	RBI	OBP	SLG	CG	ShO	Sup	QS	#P/S	SB	CS	GB	FB	G/F
1997 Season	2.25	3	0	0	7	4	32.0	5	24	.290	36	6	0	4	9	.323	.435	0	0	5.34	2	96	1	4	37	41	0.90
Career (1995-1997)	4.37	5	4	0	28	14	92.2	34	54	.300	109	21	4	9	50	.357	.455	0	0	4.37	4	85	3	7	124	106	1.17

1997 Season

	ERA	W	L	Sv	G	GS	IP	H	HR	BB	SO		Avg	AB	H	2B	3B	HR	RBI	BB	SO	OBP	SLG
Home	2.75	3	0	0	5	3	19.2	25	3	2	15	vs. Left	.269	26	7	1	0	0	2	1	3	.321	.308
Away	1.46	0	0	0	2	1	12.1	11	1	3	9	vs. Right	.296	98	29	5	0	4	7	4	21	.324	.469

Don Slaught — Padres

Age 39 – Bats Right

	Avg	G	AB	R	H	2B	3B	HR	RBI	BB	SO	HBP	GDP	SB	CS	OBP	SLG	IBB	SH	SF	#Pit	#P/PA	GB	FB	G/F
1997 Season	.000	20	20	2	0	0	0	0	0	5	4	0	1	0	0	.200	.000	0	1	0	84	3.23	8	8	1.00
Last Five Years	.294	323	992	95	292	42	2	18	125	92	121	12	40	1	0	.359	.395	6	8	7	3825	3.44	413	231	1.79

1997 Season

	Avg	AB	H	2B	3B	HR	RBI	BB	SO	OBP	SLG		Avg	AB	H	2B	3B	HR	RBI	BB	SO	OBP	SLG
vs. Left	.000	5	0	0	0	0	0	2	1	.286	.000	Scoring Posn	.000	5	0	0	0	0	0	2	0	.286	.000
vs. Right	.000	15	0	0	0	0	0	3	3	.167	.000	Close & Late	.000	3	0	0	0	0	0	1	1	.250	.000

Last Five Years

	Avg	AB	H	2B	3B	HR	RBI	BB	SO	OBP	SLG		Avg	AB	H	2B	3B	HR	RBI	BB	SO	OBP	SLG
vs. Left	.339	313	106	17	2	5	33	29	27	.399	.454	First Pitch	.368	201	74	14	2	6	36	6	0	.389	.547
vs. Right	.274	679	186	25	0	13	92	63	94	.340	.368	Ahead in Count	.360	239	86	13	0	3	39	49	0	.471	.452
Groundball	.309	282	87	7	0	5	38	32	31	.379	.387	Behind in Count	.227	384	87	11	0	5	24	0	106	.238	.294
Flyball	.285	179	51	9	1	5	23	14	24	.342	.430	Two Strikes	.216	365	79	12	0	8	35	37	121	.293	.315
Home	.286	503	144	22	2	5	61	46	62	.350	.368	Batting #7	.311	412	128	12	1	6	43	35	56	.372	.388
Away	.303	489	148	20	0	13	64	46	59	.368	.423	Batting #8	.295	244	72	12	0	5	30	24	25	.364	.406
Day	.205	229	47	12	0	5	25	23	33	.286	.323	Other	.274	336	92	18	1	7	52	33	40	.340	.396
Night	.321	763	245	30	2	13	100	69	88	.381	.417	March/April	.336	143	48	5	1	3	24	23	20	.438	.448
Grass	.288	437	126	17	0	11	63	35	53	.344	.403	May	.244	193	47	6	0	2	18	18	21	.308	.306
Turf	.299	555	166	25	2	7	62	57	68	.370	.389	June	.304	237	72	10	0	7	35	17	26	.355	.435
Pre-All Star	.300	659	198	26	2	15	93	67	80	.369	.414	July	.328	204	67	10	1	3	25	16	28	.385	.431
Post-All Star	.282	333	94	16	0	3	32	25	41	.340	.357	August	.260	100	26	8	0	1	10	9	17	.324	.370
Scoring Posn	.307	267	82	9	0	3	96	35	32	.383	.375	Sept/Oct	.278	115	32	3	0	2	13	9	9	.331	.357
Close & Late	.316	187	59	6	0	3	29	19	21	.379	.396	vs. AL	.313	243	76	10	0	6	36	15	22	.355	.428
None on/out	.298	228	68	9	1	5	5	17	31	.355	.412	vs. NL	.288	749	216	32	2	12	89	77	99	.360	.385

Batter vs. Pitcher (since 1984)

Hits Best Against	Avg	AB	H	2B	3B	HR	RBI	BB	SO	OBP	SLG	Hits Worst Against	Avg	AB	H	2B	3B	HR	RBI	BB	SO	OBP	SLG
Mike Morgan	.533	15	8	1	0	2	4	3	0	.632	1.000	Pedro Martinez	.000	10	0	0	0	0	0	2	3	.167	.000
John Smiley	.533	15	8	1	1	1	5	1	2	.529	.933	Greg Maddux	.091	11	1	0	0	0	0	0	3	.091	.091
Jack McDowell	.455	11	5	2	0	1	1	1	0	.500	.909	Jose Bautista	.091	11	1	0	0	0	1	0	3	.091	.091
Dennis Martinez	.429	21	9	2	1	1	4	1	0	.478	.762	Shane Reynolds	.091	11	1	0	0	0	0	0	1	.091	.091
Pete Harnisch	.368	19	7	2	0	2	9	2	1	.478	.789	Tom Candiotti	.118	17	2	0	1	0	1	0	3	.118	.235

Heathcliff Slocumb — Mariners

Age 32 – Pitches Right (groundball pitcher)

	ERA	W	L	Sv	G	GS	IP	BB	SO	Avg	H	2B	3B	HR	RBI	OBP	SLG	GF	IR	IRS	Hld	SvOp	SB	CS	GB	FB	G/F
1997 Season	5.16	0	9	27	76	0	75.0	49	64	.286	84	17	1	6	49	.393	.412	61	27	12	3	33	11	1	107	66	1.62
Last Five Years	3.56	19	22	90	294	0	334.0	187	295	.266	326	46	2	13	172	.352	.325	200	127	53	29	117	38	7	490	279	1.76

1997 Season

	ERA	W	L	Sv	G	GS	IP	H	HR	BB	SO		Avg	AB	H	2B	3B	HR	RBI	BB	SO	OBP	SLG
Home	5.26	0	4	12	39	0	39.1	38	4	23	35	vs. Left	.266	143	38	7	1	2	20	25	26	.382	.371
Away	5.05	0	5	15	37	0	35.2	46	2	26	29	vs. Right	.305	151	46	10	0	4	29	24	38	.402	.450
Day	6.26	0	2	6	24	0	23.0	27	3	19	27	Inning 1-6	.286	7	2	0	0	0	1	2	2	.444	.286
Night	4.67	0	7	21	52	0	52.0	57	3	30	37	Inning 7+	.286	287	82	17	1	6	48	47	62	.391	.415
Grass	5.37	0	6	16	53	0	52.0	59	4	36	43	None on	.342	120	41	9	0	3	3	23	24	.451	.492
Turf	4.70	0	3	11	23	0	23.0	25	2	13	21	Runners on	.247	174	43	8	1	3	46	26	40	.351	.356
March/April	3.27	0	0	3	11	0	11.0	15	1	11	7	Scoring Posn	.225	111	25	4	0	1	41	21	31	.358	.288
May	10.45	0	2	3	12	0	10.1	16	1	9	6	Close & Late	.259	170	44	12	0	3	29	33	39	.388	.382
June	6.00	0	1	5	14	0	15.0	18	2	9	15	None on/out	.328	64	21	4	0	1	7	14	14	.403	.438
July	3.48	0	2	6	12	0	10.1	9	0	5	8	vs. 1st Batr (relief)	.338	65	22	3	0	1	7	8	12	.419	.431
August	5.63	0	3	4	14	0	16.0	20	2	8	16	1st Inning Pitched	.285	260	74	13	1	4	42	47	56	.399	.388
Sept/Oct	2.19	0	1	6	13	0	12.1	6	0	7	12	First 15 Pitches	.300	190	57	10	1	3	21	30	38	.399	.411
Starter	0.00	0	0	0	0	0	0.0	0	0	0	0	Pitch 16-30	.272	92	25	6	0	3	24	16	22	.387	.435
Reliever	5.16	0	9	27	76	0	75.0	84	6	49	64	Pitch 31-45	.200	10	2	1	0	0	4	3	3	.385	.300
0 Days rest (Relief)	6.38	0	3	13	23	0	18.1	22	1	16	18	Pitch 46+	.000	2	0	0	0	0	0	0	1	.000	.000
1 or 2 Days rest	4.87	0	5	11	40	0	44.1	48	4	20	37	First Pitch	.238	21	5	0	0	0	5	2	0	.292	.238
3+ Days rest	4.38	0	1	3	13	0	12.1	14	1	13	9	Ahead in Count	.230	152	35	9	0	1	16	0	57	.250	.309
vs. AL	5.25	0	9	27	72	0	72.0	80	5	47	59	Behind in Count	.379	58	22	3	0	3	16	26	0	.571	.586
vs. NL	3.00	0	0	0	4	0	3.0	4	1	2	5	Two Strikes	.223	157	35	8	0	2	17	21	64	.326	.312
Pre-All Star	6.57	0	4	11	38	0	37.0	50	4	30	29	Pre-All Star	.333	150	50	11	0	4	34	30	29	.446	.487
Post-All Star	3.79	0	5	16	38	0	38.0	34	2	19	35	Post-All Star	.236	144	34	6	1	2	15	19	35	.333	.333

Last Five Years

	ERA	W	L	Sv	G	GS	IP	H	HR	BB	SO		Avg	AB	H	2B	3B	HR	RBI	BB	SO	OBP	SLG
Home	3.94	8	8	40	149	0	164.1	151	6	91	153	vs. Left	.256	590	151	12	1	4	65	101	121	.367	.300
Away	3.18	11	14	50	145	0	169.2	175	7	96	142	vs. Right	.255	685	175	34	1	9	107	86	174	.339	.347
Day	4.44	6	9	23	96	0	107.1	113	7	64	97	Inning 1-6	.228	79	18	2	0	2	18	10	19	.304	.329
Night	3.14	13	13	67	198	0	226.2	213	6	123	198	Inning 7+	.258	1196	308	44	2	11	154	177	276	.356	.325
Grass	3.70	10	14	53	182	0	201.2	193	10	122	172	None on	.256	598	153	21	0	5	5	73	125	.339	.316
Turf	3.33	9	8	37	112	0	132.1	133	3	65	123	Runners on	.256	677	173	25	2	8	167	114	170	.364	.334
March/April	2.31	3	1	8	37	0	46.2	44	2	19	34	Scoring Posn	.251	426	107	12	1	6	158	77	115	.363	.326
May	4.32	4	4	18	64	0	66.2	59	3	43	55	Close & Late	.256	774	198	28	1	8	114	129	181	.366	.326
June	3.18	3	5	15	64	0	76.1	73	3	49	65	None on/out	.270	282	76	9	0	3	3	30	50	.344	.333
July	4.47	3	3	15	47	0	54.1	60	1	20	50	vs. 1st Batr (relief)	.258	252	65	7	0	3	28	37	54	.353	.321
August	5.08	2	7	17	42	0	44.1	58	2	22	47	1st Inning Pitched	.240	1005	241	33	1	11	137	164	244	.349	.307
Sept/Oct	1.77	4	2	17	40	0	45.2	32	1	34	44	First 15 Pitches	.252	761	192	27	1	9	85	112	167	.349	.326
Starter	0.00	0	0	0	0	0	0.0	0	0	0	0	Pitch 16-30	.255	412	105	18	0	4	65	65	106	.360	.328

430

Last Five Years

	ERA	W	L	Sv	G	GS	IP	H	HR	BB	SO		Avg	AB	H	2B	3B	HR	RBI	BB	SO	OBP	SLG
Reliever	3.56	19	22	90	294	0	334.0	326	13	187	295	Pitch 31-45	.284	95	27	1	1	0	19	10	21	.346	.316
0 Days rest (Relief)	3.68	3	5	44	84	0	80.2	81	2	52	77	Pitch 46+	.286	7	2	0	0	0	3	0	1	.286	.286
1 or 2 Days rest	3.86	12	13	32	149	0	184.0	188	10	97	167	First Pitch	.319	141	45	1	0	1	26	15	0	.393	.348
3+ Days rest	2.60	4	4	14	61	0	69.1	57	1	38	51	Ahead in Count	.191	633	121	17	0	3	47	0	235	.199	.232
vs. AL	4.09	8	15	58	167	0	182.2	176	10	118	165	Behind in Count	.359	237	85	17	0	5	53	91	0	.494	.494
vs. NL	2.91	11	7	32	127	0	151.1	150	3	69	130	Two Strikes	.185	674	125	15	0	5	57	80	295	.276	.230
Pre-All Star	3.72	11	11	42	177	0	205.2	199	9	119	170	Pre-All Star	.254	783	199	31	1	9	121	119	170	.351	.331
Post-All Star	3.30	8	11	48	117	0	128.1	127	4	68	125	Post-All Star	.258	492	127	15	1	4	51	68	125	.354	.317

Pitcher vs. Batter (career)

Pitches Best Vs.	Avg	AB	H	2B	3B	HR	RBI	BB	SO	OBP	SLG	Pitches Worst Vs.	Avg	AB	H	2B	3B	HR	RBI	BB	SO	OBP	SLG
Orlando Merced	.143	14	2	0	0	0	0	1	7	.200	.143	Brady Anderson	.571	7	4	1	0	1	1	4	0	.727	1.143
Jay Bell	.188	16	3	3	0	0	3	2	7	.316	.375	Todd Zeile	.444	9	4	2	0	0	2	2	1	.545	.667
Cal Ripken	.200	10	2	0	0	0	1	2	1	.333	.200												
Bobby Bonilla	.214	14	3	0	0	0	1	4	2	.267	.214												
Rafael Palmeiro	.222	9	2	0	0	0	3	1	3	.273	.222												

Aaron Small — Athletics

Age 26 – Pitches Right (groundball pitcher)

	ERA	W	L	Sv	G	GS	IP	BB	SO	Avg	H	2B	3B	HR	RBI	OBP	SLG	GF	IR	IRS	Hld	SvOp	SB	CS	GB	FB	G/F
1997 Season	4.28	9	5	4	71	0	96.2	40	57	.294	109	19	3	6	50	.362	.410	22	52	15	8	6	10	3	166	90	1.84
Career (1994-1997)	5.05	11	8	4	91	3	133.2	70	79	.300	158	28	3	11	79	.381	.427	28	61	19	8	6	13	4	223	137	1.63

1997 Season

	ERA	W	L	Sv	G	GS	IP	H	HR	BB	SO		Avg	AB	H	2B	3B	HR	RBI	BB	SO	OBP	SLG
Home	4.36	5	1	2	37	0	53.2	54	5	19	28	vs. Left	.327	168	55	9	3	2	27	18	25	.386	.452
Away	4.19	4	4	2	34	0	43.0	55	1	21	29	vs. Right	.266	203	54	10	0	4	23	22	32	.342	.374
Day	4.17	8	2	1	32	0	45.1	42	2	21	22	Inning 1-6	.341	41	14	1	1	0	8	2	6	.378	.415
Night	4.38	1	3	3	39	0	51.1	67	4	19	35	Inning 7+	.288	330	95	18	2	6	42	38	51	.360	.409
Grass	4.22	8	5	4	64	0	89.2	100	6	35	49	None on	.307	179	55	11	0	3	3	22	27	.383	.419
Turf	5.14	1	0	0	7	0	7.0	9	0	5	8	Runners on	.281	192	54	8	3	3	47	18	30	.342	.401
March/April	3.32	3	0	1	9	0	19.0	19	1	9	15	Scoring Posn	.287	115	33	6	2	1	41	15	21	.367	.400
May	6.32	1	1	1	14	0	15.2	23	0	9	9	Close & Late	.261	142	37	7	1	2	18	22	20	.355	.366
June	6.08	1	3	1	10	0	13.1	18	0	7	5	None on/out	.313	83	26	7	0	3	3	10	16	.387	.506
July	2.65	2	1	0	14	0	17.0	13	2	6	7	vs. 1st Batr (relief)	.313	64	20	4	0	2	8	3	13	.329	.469
August	3.45	0	0	0	13	0	15.2	17	0	6	9	1st Inning Pitched	.293	229	67	11	2	2	32	21	46	.353	.384
Sept/Oct	4.50	2	0	1	11	0	16.0	19	3	3	12	First 15 Pitches	.307	218	67	9	0	2	20	19	33	.360	.376
Starter	0.00	0	0	0	0	0	0.0	0	0	0	0	Pitch 16-30	.257	113	29	7	3	3	22	14	22	.346	.451
Reliever	4.28	9	5	4	71	0	96.2	109	6	40	57	Pitch 31-45	.303	33	10	2	0	0	5	3	2	.351	.364
0 Days rest (Relief)	5.75	2	2	1	17	0	20.1	29	0	10	15	Pitch 46+	.429	7	3	1	0	1	3	4	0	.636	1.000
1 or 2 Days rest	4.03	3	2	1	39	0	51.1	55	3	23	31	First Pitch	.308	52	16	1	0	0	3	6	0	.377	.327
3+ Days rest	3.60	4	1	2	15	0	25.0	25	3	7	11	Ahead in Count	.286	185	53	11	2	1	26	0	49	.289	.384
vs. AL	4.85	8	4	2	63	0	81.2	101	6	37	49	Behind in Count	.289	76	22	3	0	0	6	21	0	.443	.329
vs. NL	1.20	1	1	2	8	0	15.0	8	0	3	8	Two Strikes	.265	162	43	12	2	2	26	13	57	.322	.401
Pre-All Star	5.13	6	4	3	36	0	52.2	63	2	27	31	Pre-All Star	.301	209	63	10	2	2	27	27	31	.382	.397
Post-All Star	3.27	3	1	1	35	0	44.0	46	4	13	26	Post-All Star	.284	162	46	9	1	4	23	13	26	.335	.426

John Smiley — Indians

Age 33 – Pitches Left

	ERA	W	L	Sv	G	GS	IP	BB	SO	Avg	H	2B	3B	HR	RBI	OBP	SLG	CG	ShO	Sup	QS	#P/S	SB	CS	GB	FB	G/F
1997 Season	5.31	11	14	0	26	26	154.1	41	120	.298	184	33	1	26	89	.347	.481	0	0	4.72	13	92	15	7	220	168	1.31
Last Five Years	4.22	50	52	0	131	129	812.2	202	587	.273	850	167	17	90	376	.320	.425	6	3	4.84	73	92	69	31	1109	878	1.26

1997 Season

	ERA	W	L	Sv	G	GS	IP	H	HR	BB	SO		Avg	AB	H	2B	3B	HR	RBI	BB	SO	OBP	SLG
Home	7.57	4	6	0	10	10	54.2	70	13	13	39	vs. Left	.383	107	41	7	0	5	12	7	28	.426	.589
Away	4.06	7	8	0	16	16	99.2	114	13	28	81	vs. Right	.280	511	143	26	1	21	77	34	92	.331	.458
Day	6.65	2	7	0	9	9	46.0	64	8	23	33	Inning 1-6	.305	568	173	33	1	24	82	35	109	.351	.493
Night	4.74	9	7	0	17	17	108.1	120	18	18	87	Inning 7+	.220	50	11	0	0	2	7	6	11	.304	.340
Grass	5.04	3	8	0	12	12	69.2	88	13	24	57	None on	.293	345	101	15	1	15	15	28	69	.353	.472
Turf	5.53	8	6	0	14	14	84.2	96	13	17	63	Runners on	.304	273	83	18	0	11	74	13	51	.340	.491
March/April	8.19	1	5	0	6	6	29.2	42	5	18	19	Scoring Posn	.306	144	44	6	0	5	57	9	27	.350	.451
May	2.83	4	1	0	5	5	35.0	34	4	5	31	Close & Late	.130	23	3	0	0	1	3	3	4	.231	.261
June	8.84	0	4	0	4	4	18.1	30	3	7	15	None on/out	.297	155	46	7	0	9	9	17	30	.370	.516
July	3.18	4	0	0	5	5	34.0	33	5	1	29	vs. 1st Batr (relief)	.000	0	0	0	0	0	0	0	0	.000	.000
August	5.54	2	4	0	6	6	37.1	45	9	10	26	1st Inning Pitched	.273	99	27	1	0	2	13	3	20	.298	.343
Sept/Oct	0.00	0	0	0	0	0	0.0	0	0	0	0	First 75 Pitches	.310	487	151	26	1	22	74	29	92	.355	.503
Starter	5.31	11	14	0	26	26	154.1	184	26	41	120	Pitch 76-90	.239	71	17	5	0	2	5	5	15	.299	.394
Reliever	0.00	0	0	0	0	0	0.0	0	0	0	0	Pitch 91-105	.216	51	11	2	0	1	6	5	11	.286	.314
0-3 Days Rest (Start)	0.00	0	0	0	0	0	0.0	0	0	0	0	Pitch 106+	.556	9	5	0	0	1	4	2	2	.636	.889
4 Days Rest	5.18	6	6	0	12	12	73.0	85	11	23	58	First Pitch	.431	102	44	8	1	6	17	3	0	.453	.706
5+ Days Rest	5.42	5	8	0	14	14	81.1	99	15	18	62	Ahead in Count	.235	302	71	12	0	6	29	0	101	.247	.334
vs. AL	5.50	2	4	0	6	6	37.2	46	8	11	29	Behind in Count	.345	116	40	8	0	9	29	19	0	.434	.447
vs. NL	5.25	9	10	0	20	20	116.2	138	18	30	91	Two Strikes	.186	280	52	10	0	5	26	19	120	.245	.296
Pre-All Star	5.97	6	10	0	16	16	89.0	113	13	30	71	Pre-All Star	.310	364	113	23	0	13	58	30	71	.368	.481
Post-All Star	4.41	5	4	0	10	10	65.1	71	13	11	49	Post-All Star	.280	254	71	10	1	13	31	11	49	.316	.480

Last Five Years

	ERA	W	L	Sv	G	GS	IP	H	HR	BB	SO		Avg	AB	H	2B	3B	HR	RBI	BB	SO	OBP	SLG
Home	4.54	23	26	0	60	60	368.1	382	44	108	258	vs. Left	.282	496	140	31	4	17	60	48	96	.347	.464
Away	3.95	27	26	0	71	69	444.1	468	46	94	329	vs. Right	.272	2613	710	136	13	73	316	154	491	.315	.418
Day	4.24	10	17	0	38	36	220.2	245	26	60	160	Inning 1-6	.277	2754	764	152	17	81	345	182	521	.325	.433
Night	4.21	40	35	0	93	93	592.0	605	64	142	427	Inning 7+	.242	355	86	15	0	9	31	20	66	.284	.361
Grass	3.83	15	18	0	46	45	284.1	294	34	60	214	None on	.264	1854	490	88	6	54	54	112	393	.311	.406
Turf	4.43	35	34	0	85	84	528.1	556	56	142	373	Runners on	.287	1255	360	79	11	36	322	90	194	.334	.453
March/April	5.52	4	13	0	23	23	130.1	150	15	58	95	Scoring Posn	.297	703	209	43	4	24	274	63	104	.352	.472
May	3.71	14	10	0	28	28	179.2	177	18	36	119	Close & Late	.219	183	40	6	0	6	17	13	32	.269	.350
June	4.44	12	11	0	26	26	160.0	183	17	36	111	None on/out	.284	827	235	43	2	32	32	47	156	.325	.457
July	3.74	13	4	0	25	24	156.1	165	16	24	116	vs. 1st Batr (relief)	1.000	1	1	1	0	0	0	1	0	1.000	2.000
August	4.27	5	7	0	17	17	109.2	103	19	31	79	1st Inning Pitched	.282	514	145	25	2	14	70	34	93	.329	.420
Sept/Oct	3.64	2	7	0	12	11	76.2	72	5	17	67	First 75 Pitches	.280	2407	673	132	14	69	301	160	446	.328	.432
Starter	4.20	50	52	0	129	129	811.1	848	90	200	586	Pitch 76-90	.268	414	111	24	3	15	44	24	85	.309	.449
Reliever	13.50	0	0	0	2	0	1.1	2	0	2	1	Pitch 91-105	.227	233	53	8	0	5	23	15	44	.273	.326
0-3 Days Rest (Start)	4.82	0	1	0	2	2	9.1	16	0	2	9	Pitch 106+	.236	55	13	3	0	1	8	3	12	.288	.345
4 Days Rest	3.96	35	28	0	79	79	515.1	522	52	118	380	First Pitch	.356	534	190	28	6	29	97	11	0	.371	.594
5+ Days Rest	4.62	15	23	0	48	48	286.2	310	38	80	197	Ahead in Count	.223	1544	345	73	8	21	132	0	513	.230	.322
vs. AL	5.50	2	4	0	6	6	37.2	46	8	11	29	Behind in Count	.341	537	183	35	3	26	99	101	0	.441	.562
vs. NL	4.16	48	48	0	125	123	775.0	804	82	191	558	Two Strikes	.190	1419	269	56	6	19	111	90	587	.242	.277
Pre-All Star	4.45	35	35	0	85	84	515.2	563	54	136	359	Pre-All Star	.282	1994	563	102	9	54	250	136	359	.331	.424
Post-All Star	3.82	15	17	0	46	45	297.0	287	36	66	228	Post-All Star	.257	1115	287	65	8	36	126	66	228	.302	.427

Pitcher vs. Batter (career)

Pitches Best Vs.	Avg	AB	H	2B	3B	HR	RBI	BB	SO	OBP	SLG	Pitches Worst Vs.	Avg	AB	H	2B	3B	HR	RBI	BB	SO	OBP	SLG
Javy Lopez	.000	18	0	0	0	0	0	0	0	.000	.000	Kenny Lofton	.545	11	6	1	0	1	1	0	0	.545	.909
Joey Cora	.000	11	0	0	0	0	0	2	1	.214	.000	Don Slaught	.533	15	8	1	1	1	5	1	2	.529	.933
Rickey Henderson	.063	16	1	0	0	0	0	2	2	.167	.063	Mark McGwire	.500	10	5	2	0	2	3	3	2	.615	1.300
Dean Palmer	.091	11	1	0	0	0	0	0	3	.091	.091	Barry Bonds	.412	17	7	0	0	3	6	7	2	.583	.941
Orlando Miller	.091	11	1	0	0	0	0	0	3	.091	.091	Matt Williams	.395	38	15	3	0	7	15	3	7	.439	1.026

Lee Smith — Expos
Age 40 – Pitches Right

	ERA	W	L	Sv	G	GS	IP	BB	SO	Avg	H	2B	3B	HR	RBI	OBP	SLG	GF	IR	IRS	Hld	SvOp	SB	CS	GB	FB	G/F
1997 Season	5.82	0	1	5	25	0	21.2	8	15	.308	28	4	1	2	14	.370	.440	14	3	2	2	6	8	1	39	21	1.86
Last Five Years	3.84	6	18	123	235	0	222.2	84	201	.252	214	35	4	26	147	.319	.404	184	66	18	10	147	38	11	263	255	1.03

1997 Season

	ERA	W	L	Sv	G	GS	IP	H	HR	BB	SO		Avg	AB	H	2B	3B	HR	RBI	BB	SO	OBP	SLG
Home	10.03	0	1	5	15	0	11.2	19	1	7	7	vs. Left	.255	47	12	2	0	1	4	7	10	.352	.362
Away	0.90	0	0	0	10	0	10.0	9	1	1	8	vs. Right	.364	44	16	2	1	1	10	1	5	.391	.523
Starter	0.00	0	0	0	0	0	0.0	0	0	0	0	Scoring Posn	.455	22	10	1	0	1	12	3	5	.538	.636
Reliever	5.82	0	1	5	25	0	21.2	28	2	8	15	Close & Late	.342	38	13	1	0	2	10	5	7	.432	.526
0 Days rest (Relief)	5.40	0	0	1	2	0	1.2	2	0	3	2	None on/out	.227	22	5	0	0	1	1	1	3	.261	.364
1 or 2 Days rest	4.91	0	0	2	10	0	7.1	9	1	2	6	First Pitch	.286	14	4	2	0	1	4	0	.286	.643
3+ Days rest	6.39	0	1	2	13	0	12.2	17	1	3	7	Ahead in Count	.281	32	9	2	1	0	4	0	10	.281	.406
Pre-All Star	5.82	0	1	5	25	0	21.2	28	2	8	15	Behind in Count	.579	19	11	0	0	1	4	5	0	.680	.737
Post-All Star	0.00	0	0	0	0	0	0.0	0	0	0	0	Two Strikes	.211	38	8	0	0	1	3	15	.268	.211

Last Five Years

	ERA	W	L	Sv	G	GS	IP	H	HR	BB	SO		Avg	AB	H	2B	3B	HR	RBI	BB	SO	OBP	SLG
Home	3.97	2	8	62	116	0	111.0	109	12	35	93	vs. Left	.243	441	107	16	4	13	50	49	105	.315	.385
Away	3.71	4	10	61	119	0	111.2	105	14	49	108	vs. Right	.263	407	107	19	4	13	56	35	96	.342	.425
Day	4.25	2	7	37	76	0	65.2	61	9	31	60	Inning 1-6	.182	11	2	1	0	0	2	2	4	.308	.273
Night	3.67	4	11	86	159	0	157.0	153	17	53	141	Inning 7+	.253	837	212	34	8	26	104	82	197	.319	.406
Grass	3.48	2	12	79	137	0	126.2	125	13	49	120	None on	.275	459	126	23	4	15	15	39	88	.333	.440
Turf	4.31	4	6	44	98	0	96.0	89	13	35	81	Runners on	.226	389	88	12	4	11	91	45	113	.303	.362
March/April	1.45	0	1	26	40	0	37.1	25	0	9	32	Scoring Posn	.226	243	56	7	1	8	80	33	79	.313	.362
May	3.98	3	1	24	45	0	40.2	38	9	17	38	Close & Late	.265	555	147	17	5	23	86	53	133	.329	.438
June	3.94	1	4	32	50	0	48.0	50	4	15	39	None on/out	.262	202	53	10	1	7	7	17	43	.320	.426
July	7.71	1	6	17	37	0	37.1	40	7	16	41	vs. 1st Batr (relief)	.255	212	54	11	0	6	13	20	49	.321	.392
August	2.78	5	1	15	37	0	35.2	36	4	15	31	1st Inning Pitched	.252	806	203	34	8	24	102	83	194	.320	.403
Sept/Oct	2.66	0	1	9	26	0	23.2	19	2	12	20	First 15 Pitches	.263	628	165	28	6	18	69	63	133	.328	.412
Starter	0.00	0	0	0	0	0	0.0	0	0	0	0	Pitch 16-30	.232	211	49	7	2	8	37	20	66	.300	.398
Reliever	3.84	6	18	123	235	0	222.2	214	26	84	201	Pitch 31-45	.000	9	0	0	0	0	0	1	2	.100	.000
0 Days rest (Relief)	3.10	1	2	39	58	0	52.1	51	6	11	44	Pitch 46+	.000	0	0	0	0	0	0	0	0	.000	.000
1 or 2 Days rest	3.12	2	6	45	86	0	83.2	73	8	35	80	First Pitch	.411	107	44	7	3	4	19	8	0	.452	.645
3+ Days rest	4.98	3	10	39	91	0	86.2	90	12	38	77	Ahead in Count	.208	437	91	18	3	11	50	0	166	.209	.339
vs. AL	3.04	1	9	73	114	0	109.2	90	10	44	103	Behind in Count	.344	128	44	3	1	4	15	40	0	.506	.477
vs. NL	4.62	5	9	50	121	0	113.0	124	16	40	98	Two Strikes	.178	460	82	16	3	13	50	33	201	.234	.311
Pre-All Star	3.72	4	9	86	147	0	138.0	132	17	47	122	Pre-All Star	.249	531	132	21	5	17	66	47	122	.309	.403
Post-All Star	4.04	2	9	37	88	0	84.2	82	9	37	79	Post-All Star	.259	317	82	14	3	9	40	37	79	.333	.407

Pitcher vs. Batter (since 1984)

Pitches Best Vs.	Avg	AB	H	2B	3B	HR	RBI	BB	SO	OBP	SLG	Pitches Worst Vs.	Avg	AB	H	2B	3B	HR	RBI	BB	SO	OBP	SLG
Jay Bell	.000	11	0	0	0	0	0	1	5	.083	.000	Mariano Duncan	.500	16	8	0	2	1	7	0	1	.500	.938
Andres Galarraga	.091	11	1	0	0	0	0	2	5	.231	.091	Mark Grace	.400	10	4	1	0	0	3	2	0	.500	.500
Rickey Henderson	.091	11	1	0	0	0	0	3	5	.286	.091	Ryne Sandberg	.385	13	5	0	0	1	3	0	3	.385	.615
Eric Karros	.100	10	1	1	0	0	1	2	2	.250	.200	Barry Bonds	.364	11	4	1	0	2	4	1	4	.417	1.000
Cal Ripken	.222	9	2	0	0	0	2	0	2	.182	.222	Bobby Bonilla	.308	13	4	0	0	0	3	0	2	.308	.769

Mark Smith — Pirates
Age 28 – Bats Right

	Avg	G	AB	R	H	2B	3B	HR	RBI	BB	SO	HBP	GDP	SB	CS	OBP	SLG	IBB	SH	SF	#Pit	#P/PA	GB	FB	G/F
1997 Season	.285	71	193	29	55	13	1	9	35	28	36	0	3	3	1	.374	.503	1	0	1	860	3.87	65	62	1.05
Career (1994-1997)	.259	138	382	49	99	20	1	16	62	43	80	4	7	6	3	.339	.442	3	2	2	1633	3.77	120	135	0.89

1997 Season

	Avg	AB	H	2B	3B	HR	RBI	BB	SO	OBP	SLG		Avg	AB	H	2B	3B	HR	RBI	BB	SO	OBP	SLG
vs. Left	.212	66	14	1	1	5	10	9	9	.307	.485	Scoring Posn	.368	57	21	5	0	5	30	10	11	.456	.719
vs. Right	.323	127	41	12	0	4	25	19	27	.408	.512	Close & Late	.295	44	13	0	1	4	10	7	11	.392	.614
Home	.288	73	21	3	0	6	16	12	12	.388	.575	None on/out	.282	39	11	3	1	3	3	6	8	.378	.641
Away	.283	120	34	10	1	3	19	16	24	.365	.458	Batting #3	.254	63	16	5	0	2	14	10	12	.351	.429
First Pitch	.393	28	11	2	1	2	8	1	0	.400	.750	Batting #6	.325	40	13	2	0	3	7	6	11	.413	.600
Ahead in Count	.354	48	17	7	0	3	10	17	0	.523	.688	Other	.289	90	26	6	1	4	14	12	13	.373	.511
Behind in Count	.162	74	12	0	0	2	9	0	33	.162	.243	Pre-All Star	.302	53	16	7	0	2	11	1	10	.309	.547
Two Strikes	.160	81	13	1	0	2	9	10	36	.253	.247	Post-All Star	.279	140	39	6	1	7	24	27	26	.395	.486

Pete Smith — Padres
Age 32 – Pitches Right

	ERA	W	L	Sv	G	GS	IP	BB	SO	Avg	H	2B	3B	HR	RBI	OBP	SLG	GF	IR	IRS	Hld	SvOp	SB	CS	GB	FB	G/F
1997 Season	4.81	7	6	1	37	15	118.0	52	68	.267	120	14	1	16	60	.343	.410	7	18	7	2	1	13	4	189	118	1.60
Last Five Years	5.09	16	26	1	89	52	364.1	137	197	.278	387	63	8	64	195	.341	.472	12	26	10	3	1	25	19	538	396	1.36

1997 Season

	ERA	W	L	Sv	G	GS	IP	H	HR	BB	SO		Avg	AB	H	2B	3B	HR	RBI	BB	SO	OBP	SLG
Home	5.16	2	3	0	21	7	61.0	64	7	22	41	vs. Left	.269	223	60	4	1	6	29	30	30	.354	.377
Away	4.42	5	3	1	16	8	57.0	56	9	30	27	vs. Right	.265	226	60	10	0	10	31	22	38	.332	.442
Starter	3.96	6	5	0	15	15	84.0	86	9	36	48	Scoring Posn	.315	111	35	7	0	4	44	16	12	.395	.486
Reliever	6.88	1	1	1	22	0	34.0	34	7	16	20	Close & Late	.325	40	13	3	0	0	7	5	7	.404	.400
0 Days rest (Relief)	1.69	0	0	0	5	0	5.1	3	0	5	4	None on/out	.230	113	26	3	1	3	3	12	23	.310	.354
1 or 2 Days rest	6.97	1	0	1	12	0	20.2	19	4	8	10	First Pitch	.300	70	21	3	0	2	12	2	0	.311	.429
3+ Days rest	10.13	0	1	0	5	0	8.0	12	3	3	6	Ahead in Count	.207	193	40	4	0	6	16	0	57	.211	.321
Pre-All Star	5.70	2	1	1	20	1	36.1	30	7	17	22	Behind in Count	.374	107	40	5	0	6	20	23	0	.485	.589
Post-All Star	4.41	5	5	0	17	14	81.2	90	9	35	46	Two Strikes	.203	187	38	5	1	5	20	27	68	.307	.321

Last Five Years

	ERA	W	L	Sv	G	GS	IP	H	HR	BB	SO		Avg	AB	H	2B	3B	HR	RBI	BB	SO	OBP	SLG
Home	5.03	8	16	0	50	27	195.0	207	31	74	108	vs. Left	.289	691	200	22	5	27	89	82	80	.362	.453
Away	5.16	8	10	1	39	25	169.1	180	33	63	89	vs. Right	.266	702	187	41	3	37	106	55	117	.320	.491
Day	6.45	5	7	0	26	16	103.1	116	26	45	56	Inning 1-6	.279	1163	324	56	8	55	165	111	166	.340	.482
Night	4.55	11	19	1	63	36	261.0	271	38	92	141	Inning 7+	.274	230	63	7	0	9	30	26	31	.349	.422
Grass	4.83	13	19	0	65	41	283.1	297	43	102	156	None on	.281	832	234	40	7	39	89	80	130	.346	.487
Turf	6.00	3	7	1	24	11	81.0	90	21	35	41	Runners on	.273	561	153	23	1	25	156	57	67	.334	.451
March/April	3.78	3	5	0	12	9	66.2	65	8	23	37	Scoring Posn	.280	321	90	14	0	12	123	39	47	.346	.436
May	5.60	3	5	1	23	11	88.1	89	21	28	36	Close & Late	.277	101	28	4	0	3	12	10	12	.345	.406
June	6.00	3	7	0	24	11	81.0	84	14	39	50	None on/out	.287	366	105	20	4	18	18	25	53	.338	.511
July	5.86	3	3	0	15	9	55.1	75	13	19	31	vs. 1st Batr (relief)	.258	31	8	2	0	3	6	5	4	.351	.613
August	3.46	1	5	0	7	7	41.2	38	5	14	23	1st Inning Pitched	.279	330	92	9	3	20	59	35	46	.346	.506
Sept/Oct	4.88	3	1	0	8	5	31.1	34	3	14	20	First 15 Pitches	.274	266	73	9	2	16	40	23	35	.330	.504
Starter	5.08	13	24	0	52	52	302.2	330	51	114	160	Pitch 16-30	.275	269	74	10	2	11	35	24	38	.336	.450
Reliever	5.11	3	2	1	37	0	61.2	57	13	23	37	Pitch 31-45	.269	238	64	16	3	5	26	16	43	.314	.424
0 Days rest (Relief)	4.26	0	0	0	6	0	6.1	5	2	5	4	Pitch 46+	.284	620	176	28	1	32	94	74	81	.359	.487
1 or 2 Days rest	5.08	2	0	1	15	0	28.1	27	4	9	14	First Pitch	.318	220	70	15	0	11	44	9	0	.339	.536
3+ Days rest	5.33	1	2	0	16	0	27.0	27	7	9	19	Ahead in Count	.213	602	128	18	5	20	58	0	174	.214	.359
vs. AL	5.93	0	2	0	5	1	13.2	13	2	7	5	Behind in Count	.375	336	126	21	1	21	55	65	0	.475	.631
vs. NL	5.06	16	24	1	84	51	350.2	374	62	130	192	Two Strikes	.218	592	129	20	4	26	72	63	197	.293	.397
Pre-All Star	5.29	10	18	1	65	34	258.2	265	49	98	138	Pre-All Star	.270	983	265	49	6	49	143	98	138	.334	.481
Post-All Star	4.60	6	8	0	24	18	105.2	122	15	39	59	Post-All Star	.298	410	122	14	2	15	52	39	59	.359	.451

Pitcher vs. Batter (career)

Pitches Best Vs.	Avg	AB	H	2B	3B	HR	RBI	BB	SO	OBP	SLG	Pitches Worst Vs.	Avg	AB	H	2B	3B	HR	RBI	BB	SO	OBP	SLG
Sean Berry	.000	10	0	0	0	0	0	1	1	.091	.000	Joe Oliver	.636	11	7	0	0	1	6	0	0	.636	.909
Damon Berryhill	.077	13	1	1	0	0	1	1	3	.143	.154	Bobby Bonilla	.440	25	11	3	0	4	11	5	6	.516	1.040
Hal Morris	.083	12	1	1	0	0	2	0	1	.083	.167	Jeff Conine	.438	16	7	1	1	1	4	3	2	.526	.813
Kevin Elster	.091	11	1	1	0	0	0	0	7	.091	.182	Will Clark	.414	29	12	0	0	4	7	5	4	.500	.828
Jose Offerman	.125	16	2	0	0	0	0	0	0	.125	.125	Darryl Strawberry	.357	14	5	0	0	3	4	5	3	.526	1.000

John Smoltz — Braves
Age 31 – Pitches Right

	ERA	W	L	Sv	G	GS	IP	BB	SO	Avg	H	2B	3B	HR	RBI	OBP	SLG	CG	ShO	Sup	QS	#P/S	SB	CS	GB	FB	G/F
1997 Season	3.02	15	12	0	35	35	256.0	63	241	.242	234	42	4	21	88	.288	.359	7	2	4.85	25	106	14	11	325	247	1.32
Last Five Years	3.31	72	48	0	155	155	1080.2	338	1031	.231	927	183	17	93	403	.292	.355	19	6	5.06	97	105	46	36	1264	1055	1.20

1997 Season

	ERA	W	L	Sv	G	GS	IP	H	HR	BB	SO		Avg	AB	H	2B	3B	HR	RBI	BB	SO	OBP	SLG
Home	3.32	6	7	0	19	19	138.1	135	11	40	131	vs. Left	.246	524	129	19	3	10	47	41	98	.301	.351
Away	2.68	9	5	0	16	16	117.2	99	10	23	110	vs. Right	.238	442	105	23	1	11	41	22	143	.273	.369
Day	4.32	3	5	0	11	11	75.0	82	7	17	77	Inning 1-6	.226	757	171	32	3	14	63	51	198	.275	.332
Night	2.49	12	7	0	24	24	181.0	152	14	46	164	Inning 7+	.301	209	63	10	1	7	25	12	43	.339	.459
Grass	3.23	9	10	0	27	27	195.0	193	17	49	186	None on	.238	609	145	29	3	13	13	30	152	.274	.360
Turf	2.36	6	2	0	8	8	61.0	41	4	14	55	Runners on	.249	357	89	13	1	8	75	33	89	.312	.359
March/April	2.74	2	3	0	6	6	42.2	46	2	12	34	Scoring Posn	.225	213	48	8	1	5	68	23	58	.300	.343

433

1997 Season

	ERA	W	L	Sv	G	GS	IP	H	HR	BB	SO
May	2.86	4	1	0	6	6	44.0	38	3	5	33
June	3.48	1	3	0	6	6	44.0	43	7	13	36
July	4.07	2	2	0	6	6	42.0	42	3	16	42
August	1.48	4	1	0	6	6	48.2	34	2	11	59
Sept/Oct	3.89	2	2	0	5	5	34.2	31	4	6	37
Starter	3.02	15	12	0	35	35	256.0	234	21	63	241
Reliever	0.00	0	0	0	0	0	0.0	0	0	0	0
0-3 Days Rest (Start)	3.86	1	2	0	3	3	21.0	17	2	7	20
4 Days Rest	3.09	10	8	0	22	22	160.0	149	12	43	148
5+ Days Rest	2.64	4	2	0	10	10	75.0	68	7	13	73
vs. AL	5.92	1	2	0	4	4	24.1	27	4	5	28
vs. NL	2.72	14	10	0	31	31	231.2	207	17	58	213
Pre-All Star	2.92	8	7	0	19	19	135.2	131	12	30	106
Post-All Star	3.14	7	5	0	16	16	120.1	103	9	33	135

	Avg	AB	H	2B	3B	HR	RBI	BB	SO	OBP	SLG
Close & Late	.313	144	45	6	0	6	22	7	29	.344	.479
vs. 1st Batr (relief)	.000	0	0	0	0	0	0	0	0	.000	.000
1st Inning Pitched	.240	129	31	6	0	0	8	10	37	.295	.287
First 75 Pitches	.230	651	150	28	2	9	50	40	170	.275	.321
Pitch 76-90	.264	125	33	6	1	4	16	11	33	.321	.424
Pitch 91-105	.277	112	31	6	1	4	9	9	21	.331	.455
Pitch 106+	.256	78	20	2	0	4	13	3	17	.284	.436
First Pitch	.364	162	59	13	0	6	26	6	0	.387	.556
Ahead in Count	.176	535	94	18	1	6	26	0	218	.177	.247
Behind in Count	.346	127	44	8	1	5	18	26	0	.455	.543
Two Strikes	.157	498	78	13	2	7	35	31	241	.205	.233
Pre-All Star	.254	515	131	17	3	12	45	30	106	.296	.369
Post-All Star	.228	451	103	25	1	9	43	33	135	.280	.348

Last Five Years

	ERA	W	L	Sv	G	GS	IP	H	HR	BB	SO
Home	3.63	31	26	0	80	80	552.2	496	54	186	524
Away	2.97	41	22	0	75	75	528.0	431	39	152	507
Day	3.30	21	17	0	49	49	341.0	286	32	101	349
Night	3.31	51	31	0	106	106	739.2	641	61	237	682
Grass	3.43	52	39	0	121	121	843.0	737	82	267	811
Turf	2.88	20	9	0	34	34	237.2	190	11	71	220
March/April	2.74	12	8	0	22	22	161.0	131	11	49	155
May	3.15	14	9	0	29	29	194.1	162	15	63	166
June	3.43	15	11	0	29	29	207.0	174	25	65	200
July	3.92	8	9	0	27	27	181.1	171	11	69	180
August	2.94	13	5	0	24	24	174.1	145	17	43	167
Sept/Oct	3.60	10	6	0	24	24	162.2	144	14	49	163
Starter	3.31	72	48	0	155	155	1080.2	927	93	338	1031
Reliever	0.00	0	0	0	0	0	0.0	0	0	0	0
0-3 Days Rest (Start)	5.26	3	3	0	8	8	51.1	54	8	15	48
4 Days Rest	3.09	50	29	0	101	101	719.0	606	57	215	679
5+ Days Rest	3.48	19	16	0	46	46	310.1	267	28	108	304
vs. AL	5.92	1	2	0	4	4	24.1	27	4	5	28
vs. NL	3.25	71	46	0	151	151	1056.1	900	89	333	1003
Pre-All Star	3.11	43	31	0	87	87	608.1	507	53	191	566
Post-All Star	3.56	29	17	0	68	68	472.1	420	40	147	465

	Avg	AB	H	2B	3B	HR	RBI	BB	SO	OBP	SLG
vs. Left	.250	1961	490	95	12	38	199	208	392	.324	.369
vs. Right	.213	2049	437	88	5	55	204	130	639	.260	.342
Inning 1-6	.221	3281	724	144	12	72	313	277	886	.283	.338
Inning 7+	.278	729	203	39	5	21	90	61	145	.333	.432
None on	.222	2474	550	119	9	47	47	173	648	.276	.335
Runners on	.245	1536	377	64	8	46	356	165	383	.318	.387
Scoring Posn	.231	871	201	40	5	23	297	126	243	.325	.367
Close & Late	.292	466	136	22	4	14	62	39	95	.346	.446
None on/out	.235	1062	250	50	4	25	25	75	239	.287	.361
vs. 1st Batr (relief)	.000	0	0	0	0	0	0	0	0	.000	.000
1st Inning Pitched	.243	585	142	24	1	16	65	66	155	.320	.369
First 75 Pitches	.221	2727	602	118	8	58	244	229	725	.283	.334
Pitch 76-90	.244	524	128	27	2	14	59	40	139	.299	.384
Pitch 91-105	.255	432	110	23	3	11	46	34	101	.308	.398
Pitch 106+	.266	327	87	15	4	10	54	35	66	.335	.428
First Pitch	.331	605	200	41	0	21	91	25	0	.360	.502
Ahead in Count	.164	2050	336	66	9	24	124	0	904	.167	.240
Behind in Count	.322	683	220	49	6	30	111	152	0	.442	.543
Two Strikes	.150	2049	308	59	8	24	121	161	1031	.214	.222
Pre-All Star	.226	2246	507	84	9	53	219	191	566	.288	.342
Post-All Star	.238	1764	420	99	8	40	184	147	465	.298	.371

Pitcher vs. Batter (career)

Pitches Best Vs.	Avg	AB	H	2B	3B	HR	RBI	BB	SO	OBP	SLG
Jermain Allensworth	.000	15	0	0	0	0	1	0	3	.000	.000
Phil Plantier	.000	14	0	0	0	0	0	0	5	.000	.000
Roberto Kelly	.000	13	0	0	0	0	0	1	2	.071	.000
Sammy Sosa	.032	31	1	0	1	0	0	2	17	.091	.097
Willie Greene	.105	19	2	0	0	0	1	0	5	.105	.105

Pitches Worst Vs.	Avg	AB	H	2B	3B	HR	RBI	BB	SO	OBP	SLG
Quilvio Veras	.529	17	9	3	2	0	1	3	3	.600	.941
Al Martin	.513	39	20	5	1	1	7	6	5	.578	.769
Eric Davis	.438	32	14	2	0	5	8	5	5	.514	.969
Ellis Burks	.400	15	6	2	0	2	7	1	5	.438	.933
Billy Ashley	.375	8	3	1	0	1	1	3	3	.545	.875

Chris Snopek — White Sox

Age 27 – Bats Right

	Avg	G	AB	R	H	2B	3B	HR	RBI	BB	SO	HBP	GDP	SB	CS	OBP	SLG	IBB	SH	SF	#Pit	#P/PA	GB	FB	G/F
1997 Season	.218	86	298	27	65	15	0	5	35	18	51	1	4	3	2	.263	.319	0	4	2	1092	3.38	95	102	0.93
Career (1995-1997)	.243	154	470	57	114	25	1	12	60	33	79	2	11	4	3	.293	.377	0	5	3	1768	3.45	154	159	0.97

1997 Season

	Avg	AB	H	2B	3B	HR	RBI	BB	SO	OBP	SLG
vs. Left	.217	115	25	7	0	2	11	2	17	.237	.330
vs. Right	.219	183	40	8	0	3	24	16	34	.279	.311
Groundball	.212	52	11	3	0	0	7	6	10	.288	.269
Flyball	.186	59	11	3	0	1	6	2	12	.226	.288
Home	.220	127	28	7	0	3	18	8	23	.265	.346
Away	.216	171	37	8	0	2	17	10	28	.262	.298
Day	.280	107	30	8	0	3	20	8	14	.330	.439
Night	.183	191	35	7	0	2	15	10	37	.225	.251
Grass	.223	233	52	9	0	5	28	16	37	.272	.326
Turf	.200	65	13	6	0	0	7	2	14	.232	.292
Pre-All Star	.225	236	53	12	0	5	33	15	42	.272	.330
Post-All Star	.194	62	12	3	0	0	2	3	9	.231	.242
Scoring Posn	.238	84	20	4	0	0	28	8	15	.298	.286
Close & Late	.174	46	8	3	0	0	4	5	10	.255	.239
None on/out	.200	65	13	1	0		3	3	8	.267	.483

	Avg	AB	H	2B	3B	HR	RBI	BB	SO	OBP	SLG
First Pitch	.170	53	9	2	0	1	8	0	0	.182	.264
Ahead in Count	.305	59	18	3	0	2	12	12	0	.423	.458
Behind in Count	.193	140	27	6	0	2	7	0	44	.193	.279
Two Strikes	.159	126	20	7	0	0	11	6	51	.197	.214
Batting #6	.196	112	22	5	0	3	15	11	25	.266	.321
Batting #8	.182	88	16	3	0	1	6	3	8	.217	.250
Other	.276	98	27	7	0	1	14	4	18	.301	.378
March/April	.213	75	16	3	0	3	12	10	17	.302	.373
May	.246	57	14	2	0	0	8	4	9	.295	.281
June	.216	88	19	6	0	2	11	1	9	.231	.352
July	.246	65	16	4	0	0	4	2	10	.269	.308
August	.000	13	0	0	0	0	0	1	6	.071	.000
Sept/Oct	.000	0	0	0	0	0	0	0	0	.000	.000
vs. AL	.212	269	57	12	0	4	32	18	46	.263	.301
vs. NL	.276	29	8	3	0	1	3	0	5	.267	.483

1997 By Position

Position	Avg	AB	H	2B	3B	HR	RBI	BB	SO	OBP	SLG	G	GS	Innings	PO	A	E	DP	Fld Pct	Rng Fctr	In Zone	Zone Outs	Zone Rtg	MLB Zone
As 3b	.213	286	61	13	0	5	34	17	49	.258	.311	82	78	692.0	56	117	16	11	.915	2.25	182	138	.758	.801

J.T. Snow — Giants

Age 30 – Bats Both (flyball hitter)

	Avg	G	AB	R	H	2B	3B	HR	RBI	BB	SO	HBP	GDP	SB	CS	OBP	SLG	IBB	SH	SF	#Pit	#P/PA	GB	FB	G/F
1997 Season	.281	157	531	81	149	36	1	28	104	96	124	1	8	6	4	.387	.510	13	2	7	2550	4.00	157	177	0.89
Last Five Years	.264	645	2292	312	604	100	5	93	360	278	447	14	55	12	12	.344	.433	28	18	19	10169	3.88	667	756	0.88

1997 Season

	Avg	AB	H	2B	3B	HR	RBI	BB	SO	OBP	SLG		Avg	AB	H	2B	3B	HR	RBI	BB	SO	OBP	SLG
vs. Left	.188	133	25	6	0	1	16	23	39	.304	.256	First Pitch	.326	43	14	5	0	4	10	8	0	.423	.721
vs. Right	.312	398	124	30	1	27	88	73	85	.415	.595	Ahead in Count	.371	151	56	14	1	9	40	42	0	.505	.656
Groundball	.333	114	38	10	0	6	19	16	17	.412	.579	Behind in Count	.175	229	40	6	0	8	32	0	103	.172	.306
Flyball	.267	60	16	2	0	0	10	14	20	.400	.300	Two Strikes	.175	252	44	9	0	8	32	46	124	.300	.306
Home	.272	257	70	19	0	14	50	52	65	.391	.510	Batting #5	.294	214	63	10	1	15	48	50	54	.424	.561
Away	.288	274	79	17	1	14	54	44	59	.384	.511	Batting #6	.294	201	59	15	0	10	35	30	36	.380	.517
Day	.295	241	71	17	1	12	51	42	56	.397	.523	Other	.233	116	27	11	0	3	21	16	34	.326	.405
Night	.269	290	78	19	0	16	53	54	68	.379	.500	March/April	.235	81	19	4	0	0	7	15	17	.351	.284
Grass	.290	434	126	30	1	24	83	79	97	.397	.530	May	.333	93	31	10	0	1	14	17	24	.432	.473
Turf	.237	97	23	6	0	4	21	17	27	.345	.423	June	.326	92	30	9	0	8	20	18	20	.441	.685
Pre-All Star	.299	288	86	24	0	13	47	51	66	.402	.517	July	.333	90	30	5	0	7	19	13	21	.406	.622
Post-All Star	.259	243	63	12	1	15	57	45	58	.370	.502	August	.232	95	22	2	0	8	28	14	27	.330	.505
Scoring Posn	.278	144	40	13	0	7	75	40	46	.419	.514	Sept/Oct	.213	80	17	6	1	4	16	19	15	.356	.463
Close & Late	.220	82	18	3	1	1	9	22	26	.385	.317	vs. AL	.379	58	22	6	0	9	20	10	9	.471	.948
None on/out	.305	151	46	5	0	10	10	19	28	.386	.536	vs. NL	.268	473	127	30	1	19	84	86	115	.377	.457

1997 By Position

Position	Avg	AB	H	2B	3B	HR	RBI	BB	SO	OBP	SLG	G	GS	Innings	PO	A	E	DP	Fld Pct	Rng Fctr	In Zone	Zone Outs	MLB Rtg	MLB Zone
As 1b	.282	529	149	36	1	28	104	94	123	.387	.512	156	151	1333.1	1308	106	7	135	.995	---	252	212	.841	.874

Last Five Years

	Avg	AB	H	2B	3B	HR	RBI	BB	SO	OBP	SLG		Avg	AB	H	2B	3B	HR	RBI	BB	SO	OBP	SLG
vs. Left	.220	651	143	20	3	13	79	74	146	.301	.320	First Pitch	.304	240	73	15	1	11	33	23	0	.372	.513
vs. Right	.281	1641	461	80	2	80	281	204	301	.361	.478	Ahead in Count	.345	595	205	38	1	35	133	124	0	.454	.588
Groundball	.319	477	152	29	1	17	72	49	83	.380	.491	Behind in Count	.197	969	191	26	2	25	115	0	368	.202	.305
Flyball	.243	411	100	15	1	15	67	49	85	.328	.394	Two Strikes	.171	1045	179	27	2	30	123	131	447	.266	.287
Home	.278	1156	321	45	2	53	201	146	233	.358	.458	Batting #5	.270	892	241	34	2	35	147	127	186	.363	.430
Away	.249	1136	283	55	3	40	159	132	214	.330	.408	Batting #6	.267	641	171	25	2	31	93	78	104	.346	.457
Day	.262	733	192	35	3	32	118	86	159	.341	.449	Other	.253	759	192	41	1	27	120	73	157	.320	.416
Night	.264	1559	412	65	2	61	242	192	288	.346	.426	March/April	.272	250	68	9	2	6	32	30	50	.352	.396
Grass	.267	1985	530	81	5	88	321	236	380	.346	.446	May	.255	385	98	16	0	16	62	55	70	.349	.421
Turf	.241	307	74	19	0	5	39	42	67	.335	.352	June	.274	470	129	22	2	18	72	53	90	.351	.445
Pre-All Star	.268	1251	335	54	4	49	191	157	244	.352	.435	July	.291	446	130	19	0	20	81	49	89	.364	.469
Post-All Star	.258	1041	269	46	1	44	169	121	203	.335	.431	August	.225	369	83	13	0	18	63	53	83	.322	.407
Scoring Posn	.267	603	161	31	2	30	274	111	138	.375	.474	Sept/Oct	.258	372	96	21	1	15	50	38	65	.324	.441
Close & Late	.243	337	82	10	2	7	40	58	86	.355	.347	vs. AL	.262	1819	477	70	4	74	276	192	332	.335	.427
None on/out	.277	538	149	18	1	25	25	46	98	.337	.454	vs. NL	.268	473	127	30	1	19	84	86	115	.377	.457

Batter vs. Pitcher (career)

Hits Best Against	Avg	AB	H	2B	3B	HR	RBI	BB	SO	OBP	SLG	Hits Worst Against	Avg	AB	H	2B	3B	HR	RBI	BB	SO	OBP	SLG
Jamie Moyer	.556	18	10	2	0	1	2	1	1	.579	.833	Aaron Sele	.000	10	0	0	0	0	0	2	4	.167	.000
Frank Rodriguez	.500	10	5	2	0	1	1	1	0	.545	1.000	David Wells	.056	18	1	1	0	0	1	1	4	.105	.111
Bobby Witt	.462	13	6	1	0	1	1	2	2	.533	.769	Jimmy Key	.071	14	1	0	0	0	0	1	5	.133	.071
Scott Kamieniecki	.400	10	4	2	0	0	2	0	2	.500	.600	Rich Robertson	.083	12	1	0	0	0	0	0	2	.083	.083
Alex Fernandez	.318	22	7	3	0	2	3	3	5	.400	.727	Wilson Alvarez	.087	23	2	0	0	0	0	1	6	.125	.087

Clint Sodowsky — Pirates

Age 25 – Pitches Right (groundball pitcher)

	ERA	W	L	Sv	G	GS	IP	BB	SO	Avg	H	2B	3B	HR	RBI	OBP	SLG	GF	IR	IRS	Hld	SvOp	SB	CS	GB	FB	G/F
1997 Season	3.63	2	2	0	45	0	52.0	34	51	.249	49	9	0	6	23	.362	.386	8	23	8	5	2	4	2	99	28	3.54
Career (1995-1997)	5.96	5	7	0	58	13	99.2	72	74	.284	113	16	0	15	64	.398	.437	8	23	8	5	2	5	3	193	73	2.64

1997 Season

	ERA	W	L	Sv	G	GS	IP	H	HR	BB	SO		Avg	AB	H	2B	3B	HR	RBI	BB	SO	OBP	SLG
Home	3.90	1	0	0	24	0	27.2	26	5	20	30	vs. Left	.263	80	21	5	0	2	7	13	16	.358	.400
Away	3.33	1	2	0	21	0	24.1	23	1	14	21	vs. Right	.239	117	28	4	0	4	16	21	35	.364	.376
Starter	0.00	0	0	0	0	0	0.0	0	0	0	0	Scoring Posn	.179	67	12	2	0	0	17	17	20	.337	.209
Reliever	3.63	2	2	0	45	0	52.0	49	6	34	51	Close & Late	.229	35	8	3	0	2	4	4	7	.325	.486
0 Days rest (Relief)	6.30	0	2	0	11	0	10.0	15	2	9	8	None on/out	.327	49	16	1	0	5	5	3	7	.377	.653
1 or 2 Days rest	2.42	1	0	0	19	0	22.1	15	3	16	23	First Pitch	.333	24	8	4	0	1	5	4	0	.467	.625
3+ Days rest	3.66	1	0	0	15	0	19.2	19	1	9	20	Ahead in Count	.155	84	13	3	0	1	7	0	38	.155	.226
Pre-All Star	3.80	0	1	0	20	0	23.2	26	3	8	24	Behind in Count	.391	46	18	0	0	3	6	19	0	.561	.587
Post-All Star	3.49	2	1	0	25	0	28.1	23	3	26	27	Two Strikes	.171	105	18	1	0	2	11	11	51	.250	.267

Luis Sojo — Yankees

Age 32 – Bats Right

	Avg	G	AB	R	H	2B	3B	HR	RBI	BB	SO	HBP	GDP	SB	CS	OBP	SLG	IBB	SH	SF	#Pit	#P/PA	GB	FB	G/F
1997 Season	.307	77	215	27	66	6	1	2	25	16	14	1	5	3	1	.355	.372	0	5	2	864	3.62	96	60	1.60
Last Five Years	.267	356	1101	137	294	45	6	16	113	62	77	1	6	29	11	.307	.362	0	24	6	4310	3.60	461	343	1.34

1997 Season

	Avg	AB	H	2B	3B	HR	RBI	BB	SO	OBP	SLG		Avg	AB	H	2B	3B	HR	RBI	BB	SO	OBP	SLG
vs. Left	.227	66	15	1	0	1	5	6	4	.288	.288	Scoring Posn	.323	62	20	2	1	0	21	6	2	.371	.387

1997 Season

	Avg	AB	H	2B	3B	HR	RBI	BB	SO	OBP	SLG		Avg	AB	H	2B	3B	HR	RBI	BB	SO	OBP	SLG
vs. Right	.342	149	51	5	1	1	20	10	10	.385	.409	Close & Late	.118	34	4	1	0	0	2	3	4	.189	.147
Home	.321	106	34	3	1	2	17	8	7	.371	.425	None on/out	.306	49	15	1	0	0	0	2	3	.346	.327
Away	.294	109	32	3	0	0	8	8	7	.339	.321	Batting #2	.321	137	44	6	1	1	14	9	8	.363	.401
First Pitch	.357	28	10	2	0	1	3	0	0	.345	.536	Batting #9	.273	44	12	0	0	0	5	4	3	.327	.273
Ahead in Count	.176	51	9	1	1	0	5	10	0	.306	.235	Other	.294	34	10	0	0	1	6	3	3	.359	.382
Behind in Count	.347	101	35	3	0	0	12	0	14	.353	.376	Pre-All Star	.305	118	36	2	0	1	16	9	8	.349	.347
Two Strikes	.329	85	28	3	0	0	9	6	14	.380	.365	Post-All Star	.309	97	30	4	1	1	9	7	6	.362	.402

Last Five Years

	Avg	AB	H	2B	3B	HR	RBI	BB	SO	OBP	SLG		Avg	AB	H	2B	3B	HR	RBI	BB	SO	OBP	SLG
vs. Left	.270	345	93	21	0	9	44	28	20	.325	.409	First Pitch	.287	136	39	6	0	5	19	0	0	.285	.441
vs. Right	.266	756	201	24	6	7	69	34	57	.299	.341	Ahead in Count	.341	249	85	14	3	6	36	43	0	.435	.494
Groundball	.291	258	75	13	1	4	22	14	17	.330	.395	Behind in Count	.226	504	114	16	1	3	37	0	66	.231	.280
Flyball	.277	195	54	11	1	3	28	8	13	.311	.390	Two Strikes	.229	442	101	13	1	4	34	19	77	.266	.290
Home	.243	543	132	22	2	11	73	36	49	.292	.352	Batting #2	.314	414	130	24	2	7	52	26	26	.357	.432
Away	.290	558	162	23	4	5	40	26	28	.323	.373	Batting #9	.257	257	66	7	2	3	24	17	18	.305	.335
Day	.276	319	88	15	3	2	28	11	23	.302	.361	Other	.228	430	98	14	2	6	37	19	33	.261	.312
Night	.263	782	206	30	3	14	85	51	54	.310	.363	March/April	.253	91	23	6	0	0	11	6	3	.296	.319
Grass	.293	583	171	25	5	7	52	34	32	.333	.389	May	.269	238	64	7	2	4	21	7	23	.294	.366
Turf	.237	518	123	20	1	9	61	28	45	.278	.332	June	.243	255	62	8	0	5	27	18	20	.292	.333
Pre-All Star	.255	648	165	22	3	9	63	33	48	.293	.340	July	.263	209	55	10	3	2	20	8	13	.294	.368
Post-All Star	.285	453	129	23	3	7	50	29	29	.329	.395	August	.281	196	55	7	1	2	15	13	12	.329	.357
Scoring Posn	.269	264	71	13	4	3	92	15	19	.309	.383	Sept/Oct	.313	115	36	7	0	3	19	10	6	.366	.455
Close & Late	.219	155	34	9	2	1	21	12	16	.278	.323	vs. AL	.268	1078	289	44	6	16	111	61	76	.309	.365
None on/out	.240	258	62	11	1	4	4	13	13	.279	.337	vs. NL	.217	23	5	1	0	0	2	1	1	.250	.261

Batter vs. Pitcher (career)

Hits Best Against	Avg	AB	H	2B	3B	HR	RBI	BB	SO	OBP	SLG	Hits Worst Against	Avg	AB	H	2B	3B	HR	RBI	BB	SO	OBP	SLG
Mark Gubicza	.545	22	12	1	0	1	8	1	0	.565	.727	David Cone	.000	11	0	0	0	0	1	1	2	.083	.000
Mike Mussina	.455	11	5	2	1	0	1	0	0	.455	.818	Wilson Alvarez	.080	25	2	1	0	0	3	3	0	.179	.120
Darren Oliver	.421	19	8	1	0	2	6	1	2	.450	.789	Tom Gordon	.083	12	1	0	0	0	0	0	3	.083	.083
Buddy Groom	.400	10	4	1	0	1	2	1	1	.455	.800	Jose Mesa	.091	11	1	0	0	0	0	0	3	.091	.091
Ricky Bones	.375	16	6	0	0	2	3	0	0	.412	.750	Chuck Finley	.125	16	2	0	0	0	0	3	2	.263	.125

Paul Sorrento — Mariners   Age 32 – Bats Left

	Avg	G	AB	R	H	2B	3B	HR	RBI	BB	SO	HBP	GDP	SB	CS	OBP	SLG	IBB	SH	SF	#Pit	#P/PA	GB	FB	G/F
1997 Season	.269	146	457	68	123	19	0	31	80	51	112	3	13	0	2	.345	.514	9	0	2	1923	3.75	135	130	1.04
Last Five Years	.267	636	2036	303	544	105	2	111	379	251	475	12	50	4	7	.348	.484	42	3	18	8977	3.87	629	601	1.05

1997 Season

	Avg	AB	H	2B	3B	HR	RBI	BB	SO	OBP	SLG		Avg	AB	H	2B	3B	HR	RBI	BB	SO	OBP	SLG
vs. Left	.205	39	8	0	0	4	6	4	14	.279	.513	First Pitch	.417	60	25	3	0	3	11	7	0	.493	.617
vs. Right	.275	418	115	19	0	27	74	47	98	.351	.514	Ahead in Count	.333	117	39	6	0	12	34	19	0	.426	.692
Groundball	.307	114	35	9	0	5	21	13	23	.388	.518	Behind in Count	.199	186	37	5	0	10	18	0	91	.199	.387
Flyball	.247	77	19	2	0	4	8	9	21	.326	.429	Two Strikes	.171	210	36	4	0	13	24	24	112	.255	.376
Home	.299	221	66	10	0	18	38	29	55	.380	.588	Batting #6	.280	318	89	16	0	21	61	26	72	.339	.528
Away	.242	236	57	9	0	13	42	22	57	.312	.445	Batting #7	.162	68	11	1	0	2	4	11	23	.278	.265
Day	.252	163	41	7	0	12	27	15	40	.319	.515	Other	.324	71	23	2	0	8	15	14	17	.430	.690
Night	.279	294	82	12	0	19	53	36	72	.360	.514	March/April	.284	81	23	5	0	2	14	2	22	.301	.420
Grass	.230	200	46	9	0	12	36	20	51	.300	.455	May	.278	79	22	2	0	5	9	10	14	.360	.494
Turf	.300	257	77	10	0	19	44	31	61	.379	.560	June	.291	79	23	3	0	8	17	10	14	.391	.633
Pre-All Star	.281	253	71	10	0	17	42	23	52	.348	.522	July	.246	69	17	4	0	5	10	6	19	.303	.522
Post-All Star	.255	204	52	9	0	14	38	28	60	.341	.505	August	.250	76	19	4	0	6	19	11	18	.341	.539
Scoring Posn	.198	121	24	6	0	4	43	28	32	.344	.347	Sept/Oct	.260	73	19	1	0	5	11	12	25	.365	.479
Close & Late	.149	74	11	4	0	1	7	11	22	.259	.243	vs. AL	.268	411	110	17	0	26	68	41	103	.337	.499
None on/out	.324	108	35	4	0	10	10	4	22	.360	.639	vs. NL	.283	46	13	2	0	5	12	10	9	.411	.652

1997 By Position

Position	Avg	AB	H	2B	3B	HR	RBI	BB	SO	OBP	SLG	G	GS	Innings	PO	A	E	DP	Fld Pct	Rng Fctr	In Zone	Zone Outs	MLB Rtg	Zone
As Pinch Hitter	.304	23	7	1	0	2	6	2	10	.360	.609	25	0	—	—	—	—	—	—	—	—	—	—	—
As 1b	.269	432	116	18	0	29	74	49	101	.346	.512	139	119	1057.2	929	85	4	91	.996	—	176	150	.852	.874

Last Five Years

	Avg	AB	H	2B	3B	HR	RBI	BB	SO	OBP	SLG		Avg	AB	H	2B	3B	HR	RBI	BB	SO	OBP	SLG
vs. Left	.218	303	66	12	1	13	60	27	90	.290	.393	First Pitch	.402	251	101	23	0	21	67	32	0	.471	.745
vs. Right	.276	1733	478	93	1	98	319	224	385	.358	.500	Ahead in Count	.352	537	189	40	1	37	131	115	0	.463	.637
Groundball	.281	477	134	27	0	19	79	53	103	.358	.457	Behind in Count	.184	846	156	23	1	34	111	0	375	.189	.335
Flyball	.241	357	86	16	1	20	64	48	80	.333	.459	Two Strikes	.165	975	161	28	1	42	129	102	475	.245	.325
Home	.289	986	285	56	1	59	188	139	227	.378	.527	Batting #5	.273	571	156	39	0	28	97	75	140	.355	.489
Away	.247	1050	259	49	1	52	191	112	248	.320	.444	Batting #6	.279	865	241	41	2	47	158	91	187	.349	.494
Day	.260	674	175	35	0	39	118	89	177	.346	.488	Other	.245	600	147	25	0	36	124	85	148	.341	.467
Night	.271	1362	369	70	1	72	261	162	298	.349	.482	March/April	.263	315	83	16	0	18	69	27	76	.321	.486
Grass	.257	1340	345	65	1	67	248	163	314	.337	.457	May	.305	341	104	18	0	27	60	44	66	.382	.595
Turf	.286	696	199	40	1	44	131	88	161	.369	.536	June	.269	383	103	22	0	16	67	57	90	.368	.452
Pre-All Star	.279	1155	322	61	0	66	223	138	258	.353	.503	July	.242	380	92	17	0	19	72	37	105	.308	.437
Post-All Star	.252	881	222	44	2	45	156	113	217	.338	.460	August	.261	356	93	22	0	20	73	47	75	.350	.492
Scoring Posn	.268	560	150	34	0	25	255	108	143	.379	.463	Sept/Oct	.264	261	69	10	2	11	38	39	63	.361	.444

	Avg	AB	H	2B	3B	HR	RBI	BB	SO	OBP	SLG		Avg	AB	H	2B	3B	HR	RBI	BB	SO	OBP	SLG
Close & Late	.259	321	83	19	0	13	51	35	86	.331	.439	vs. AL	.267	1990	531	103	2	106	367	241	466	.347	.480
None on/out	.297	437	130	23	0	26	26	34	88	.354	.529	vs. NL	.283	46	13	2	0	5	12	10	9	.411	.652

Batter vs. Pitcher (career)

Hits Best Against	Avg	AB	H	2B	3B	HR	RBI	BB	SO	OBP	SLG	Hits Worst Against	Avg	AB	H	2B	3B	HR	RBI	BB	SO	OBP	SLG
Orel Hershiser	.583	12	7	2	0	0	1	2	2	.643	.750	David Cone	.080	25	2	0	0	0	0	3	6	.179	.080
Bobby Witt	.536	28	15	1	0	2	4	8	5	.649	.786	Carlos Reyes	.083	12	1	0	0	0	0	1	4	.154	.083
Paul Quantrill	.500	12	6	2	0	2	3	1	0	.500	1.167	Mike Trombley	.091	11	1	1	0	0	2	1	3	.154	.182
Dave Telgheder	.400	10	4	2	0	2	3	3	2	.538	1.200	Mike Fetters	.100	10	1	0	0	0	1	2	3	.250	.100
Don Wengert	.400	10	4	1	0	1	6	3	3	.538	.800	Roberto Hernandez	.125	16	2	0	0	0	2	0	5	.125	.125

Sammy Sosa — Cubs   Age 29 – Bats Right

	Avg	G	AB	R	H	2B	3B	HR	RBI	BB	SO	HBP	GDP	SB	CS	OBP	SLG	IBB	SH	SF	#Pit	#P/PA	GB	FB	G/F
1997 Season	.251	162	642	90	161	31	4	36	119	45	174	2	16	22	12	.300	.480	9	0	5	2650	3.82	213	167	1.28
Last Five Years	.268	694	2728	414	732	111	20	170	501	200	669	18	58	132	48	.321	.511	33	1	16	11226	3.79	817	806	1.01

1997 Season

	Avg	AB	H	2B	3B	HR	RBI	BB	SO	OBP	SLG		Avg	AB	H	2B	3B	HR	RBI	BB	SO	OBP	SLG
vs. Left	.270	141	38	7	0	12	34	15	33	.340	.574	First Pitch	.298	84	25	5	1	6	22	5	0	.333	.595
vs. Right	.246	501	123	24	4	24	85	30	141	.288	.453	Ahead in Count	.393	122	48	6	1	14	39	12	0	.441	.803
Groundball	.289	135	39	12	1	5	20	9	26	.333	.504	Behind in Count	.182	303	55	14	1	8	30	0	141	.183	.314
Flyball	.241	87	21	2	0	5	14	6	27	.284	.437	Two Strikes	.159	333	53	11	0	9	34	27	174	.222	.273
Home	.269	312	84	10	2	25	85	31	77	.335	.554	Batting #3	.207	87	18	2	0	4	16	5	29	.266	.368
Away	.233	330	77	21	2	11	34	14	97	.264	.409	Batting #4	.258	554	143	29	4	32	103	40	144	.306	.498
Day	.268	355	95	18	3	23	81	28	96	.322	.530	Other	.000	1	0	0	0	0	0	0	1	.000	.000
Night	.230	287	66	13	1	13	38	17	78	.271	.418	March/April	.216	97	21	5	0	3	13	9	19	.283	.361
Grass	.263	517	136	25	4	31	103	42	133	.318	.507	May	.333	111	37	8	2	10	28	9	32	.380	.712
Turf	.200	125	25	6	0	5	16	3	41	.219	.368	June	.219	114	25	7	0	3	15	4	33	.242	.360
Pre-All Star	.255	349	89	22	2	17	62	22	93	.297	.476	July	.232	112	26	5	0	5	21	9	32	.301	.411
Post-All Star	.246	293	72	9	2	19	57	23	81	.303	.485	August	.228	114	26	4	2	9	25	6	34	.262	.535
Scoring Posn	.246	183	45	10	2	9	78	18	56	.306	.470	Sept/Oct	.277	94	26	2	0	6	17	8	24	.333	.489
Close & Late	.240	96	23	5	0	7	20	10	22	.308	.510	vs. AL	.373	59	22	7	0	3	12	6	17	.424	.644
None on/out	.229	144	33	10	0	10	10	7	29	.265	.507	vs. NL	.238	583	139	24	4	33	107	39	157	.287	.463

1997 By Position

Position	Avg	AB	H	2B	3B	HR	RBI	BB	SO	OBP	SLG	G	GS	Innings	PO	A	E	DP	Fld Pct	Rng Fctr	In Zone	Zone Outs	Zone Rtg	MLB Zone
As rf	.251	641	161	31	4	36	119	45	173	.300	.480	161	161	1416.2	324	16	8	1	.977	2.16	364	310	.852	.813

Last Five Years

	Avg	AB	H	2B	3B	HR	RBI	BB	SO	OBP	SLG		Avg	AB	H	2B	3B	HR	RBI	BB	SO	OBP	SLG
vs. Left	.278	665	185	29	5	48	130	70	151	.346	.553	First Pitch	.335	394	132	19	5	26	87	27	0	.378	.607
vs. Right	.265	2063	547	82	15	122	371	130	518	.312	.497	Ahead in Count	.392	487	191	33	5	56	158	56	0	.449	.825
Groundball	.293	758	222	36	5	48	140	58	161	.349	.544	Behind in Count	.196	1316	258	37	6	52	155	0	552	.201	.352
Flyball	.252	425	107	15	2	23	65	28	132	.298	.459	Two Strikes	.181	1368	247	36	4	47	144	116	669	.248	.316
Home	.275	1380	380	48	12	104	298	113	312	.331	.554	Batting #4	.271	1555	421	66	10	106	317	128	390	.327	.531
Away	.261	1348	352	63	8	66	203	87	357	.310	.467	Batting #5	.252	437	110	17	5	19	55	28	96	.304	.444
Day	.270	1522	411	56	15	109	301	129	369	.329	.541	Other	.273	736	201	28	5	45	129	44	183	.316	.508
Night	.266	1206	321	55	5	61	200	71	300	.310	.472	March/April	.233	391	91	13	4	17	55	27	96	.286	.417
Grass	.281	2150	605	93	17	151	436	170	517	.336	.551	May	.297	518	154	25	6	44	109	35	136	.345	.624
Turf	.220	578	127	18	3	19	65	30	152	.261	.360	June	.269	528	142	22	3	27	90	30	124	.307	.475
Pre-All Star	.267	1612	430	67	14	95	280	106	394	.314	.502	July	.282	542	153	25	1	31	97	42	113	.338	.504
Post-All Star	.271	1116	302	44	6	75	221	94	275	.331	.522	August	.260	446	116	16	4	35	94	35	120	.316	.549
Scoring Posn	.267	768	205	28	7	46	316	83	205	.336	.501	Sept/Oct	.251	303	76	10	2	16	56	31	80	.323	.455
Close & Late	.246	447	110	16	2	23	76	35	117	.299	.445	vs. AL	.373	59	22	7	0	3	12	6	17	.424	.644
None on/out	.266	625	166	29	2	41	41	35	152	.307	.515	vs. NL	.266	2669	710	104	20	167	489	194	652	.318	.508

Batter vs. Pitcher (career)

Hits Best Against	Avg	AB	H	2B	3B	HR	RBI	BB	SO	OBP	SLG	Hits Worst Against	Avg	AB	H	2B	3B	HR	RBI	BB	SO	OBP	SLG
Orel Hershiser	.529	17	9	1	0	3	6	2	2	.579	1.118	Mike Hampton	.000	23	0	0	0	0	0	1	7	.042	.000
Ken Hill	.500	12	6	1	0	2	2	3	1	.600	1.083	John Smoltz	.032	31	1	0	1	0	0	2	17	.091	.097
Mark Petkovsek	.455	11	5	1	0	3	8	1	0	.500	1.364	Ismael Valdes	.103	29	3	0	0	0	1	1	14	.133	.103
Rheal Cormier	.417	12	5	1	0	4	8	1	1	.462	1.500	Steve Cooke	.111	18	2	0	0	0	2	1	4	.158	.111
Robb Nen	.364	11	4	0	1	3	5	0	3	.364	1.364	Darryl Kile	.129	31	4	0	0	0	0	0	13	.129	.129

Tim Spehr — Braves   Age 31 – Bats Right

	Avg	G	AB	R	H	2B	3B	HR	RBI	BB	SO	HBP	GDP	SB	CS	OBP	SLG	IBB	SH	SF	#Pit	#P/PA	GB	FB	G/F
1997 Season	.184	25	49	5	9	1	0	2	6	2	16	1	0	1	0	.231	.327	0	0	0	204	3.92	11	12	0.92
Last Five Years	.203	234	251	35	51	16	1	6	27	21	69	3	1	6	0	.271	.347	1	8	2	1157	4.06	80	61	1.31

1997 Season

	Avg	AB	H	2B	3B	HR	RBI	BB	SO	OBP	SLG		Avg	AB	H	2B	3B	HR	RBI	BB	SO	OBP	SLG
vs. Left	.188	16	3	1	0	1	1	1	5	.235	.438	Scoring Posn	.222	9	2	0	0	1	5	1	5	.300	.556
vs. Right	.182	33	6	0	0	1	5	1	11	.229	.273	Close & Late	.143	7	1	0	0	0	0	1	3	.250	.143

Bill Spiers — Astros
Age 32 – Bats Left (groundball hitter)

	Avg	G	AB	R	H	2B	3B	HR	RBI	BB	SO	HBP	GDP	SB	CS	OBP	SLG	IBB	SH	SF	#Pit	#P/PA	GB	FB	G/F
1997 Season	.320	132	291	51	93	27	4	4	48	61	42	1	4	10	5	.438	.481	6	1	1	1352	3.81	111	80	1.39
Last Five Years	.263	503	1135	153	298	57	11	12	138	141	184	8	21	33	15	.346	.364	14	15	8	4842	3.70	456	285	1.60

1997 Season

	Avg	AB	H	2B	3B	HR	RBI	BB	SO	OBP	SLG		Avg	AB	H	2B	3B	HR	RBI	BB	SO	OBP	SLG
vs. Left	.317	41	13	4	1	0	7	9	7	.451	.463	First Pitch	.353	34	12	3	1	0	7	3	0	.405	.500
vs. Right	.320	250	80	23	3	4	41	52	35	.436	.484	Ahead in Count	.291	55	16	7	0	1	10	48	0	.615	.473
Groundball	.297	64	19	3	1	0	4	8	8	.375		Behind in Count	.268	127	34	8	1	2	18	0	36	.268	.394
Flyball	.265	34	9	8	0	0	8	8	6	.395	.500	Two Strikes	.310	129	40	11	3	2	16	10	42	.360	.488
Home	.310	142	44	14	2	0	20	24	14	.410	.437	Batting #2	.400	70	28	6	0	0	7	14	11	.500	.486
Away	.329	149	49	13	2	4	28	37	28	.463	.523	Batting #6	.259	85	22	3	2	0	11	19	14	.390	.341
Day	.325	83	27	7	1	1	19	21	9	.467	.470	Other	.316	136	43	18	2	4	30	28	17	.436	.566
Night	.317	208	66	20	3	3	29	40	33	.426	.486	March/April	.295	44	13	3	0	1	8	13	8	.456	.432
Grass	.348	112	39	10	2	3	19	28	23	.479	.554	May	.396	48	19	7	0	0	3	6	5	.455	.542
Turf	.302	179	54	17	2	1	29	33	19	.411	.436	June	.229	48	11	2	1	0	6	16	9	.431	.313
Pre-All Star	.307	150	46	12	1	1	18	39	22	.450	.420	July	.292	48	14	4	1	1	7	5	5	.358	.479
Post-All Star	.333	141	47	15	3	3	30	22	20	.423	.546	August	.409	44	18	6	1	0	10	9	9	.509	.591
Scoring Posn	.449	78	35	9	1	3	46	19	10	.551	.705	Sept/Oct	.305	59	18	5	1	2	14	12	6	.423	.525
Close & Late	.347	72	25	11	2	1	16	14	18	.453	.597	vs. AL	.176	34	6	0	0	0	1	5	3	.282	.176
None on/out	.250	72	18	7	1	0	0	12	8	.357	.375	vs. NL	.339	257	87	27	4	4	47	56	39	.457	.521

1997 By Position

Position	Avg	AB	H	2B	3B	HR	RBI	BB	SO	OBP	SLG	G	GS	Innings	PO	A	E	DP	Fld Pct	Rng Fctr	In Zone	Zone Outs	Zone Rtg	MLB Zone
As Pinch Hitter	.455	33	15	6	0	1	11	7	4	.550	.727	40	0	---										
As 3b	.271	188	51	11	3	3	28	36	27	.387	.410	84	48	497.0	44	129	12	11	.935	3.13	181	144	.796	.801
As ss	.347	49	17	5	0	0	7	8	10	.448	.449	28	13	122.1	26	58	6	12	.933	6.18	66	66	1.000	.937

Last Five Years

	Avg	AB	H	2B	3B	HR	RBI	BB	SO	OBP	SLG		Avg	AB	H	2B	3B	HR	RBI	BB	SO	OBP	SLG
vs. Left	.195	164	32	7	2	0	14	21	32	.305	.262	First Pitch	.293	147	43	7	1	3	20	10	0	.348	.415
vs. Right	.274	971	266	50	9	12	124	120	152	.353	.381	Ahead in Count	.259	232	60	13	3	3	35	97	0	.471	.379
Groundball	.241	237	57	9	3	1	18	26	38	.321	.316	Behind in Count	.225	493	111	21	3	3	50	0	156	.231	.298
Flyball	.212	212	45	15	1	3	28	28	37	.299	.335	Two Strikes	.231	494	114	23	4	4	45	34	184	.285	.318
Home	.294	547	161	31	5	5	79	67	82	.372	.397	Batting #2	.268	370	99	14	3	0	33	41	56	.346	.322
Away	.233	588	137	26	6	7	59	74	102	.322	.333	Batting #9	.265	200	53	14	2	5	21	16	32	.317	.430
Day	.273	352	96	16	4	3	42	52	57	.370	.366	Other	.258	565	146	29	6	7	84	84	96	.356	.368
Night	.258	783	202	41	7	9	96	89	127	.335	.363	March/April	.260	177	46	9	1	1	21	27	29	.359	.339
Grass	.267	682	182	28	6	7	83	86	117	.351	.356	May	.259	224	58	12	1	0	16	21	40	.329	.321
Turf	.256	453	116	29	5	5	55	55	67	.338	.375	June	.239	218	52	8	3	3	25	31	33	.333	.344
Pre-All Star	.257	674	173	32	6	4	72	86	114	.343	.340	July	.253	194	49	9	3	3	25	14	34	.307	.376
Post-All Star	.271	461	125	25	5	8	66	55	70	.351	.399	August	.320	175	56	12	1	3	23	25	29	.403	.451
Scoring Posn	.306	307	94	16	2	3	122	41	47	.381	.401	Sept/Oct	.252	147	37	7	2	2	28	22	19	.357	.367
Close & Late	.259	251	65	16	3	6	39	29	51	.337	.418	vs. AL	.240	588	141	18	5	2	54	53	96	.306	.298
None on/out	.237	279	66	9	2	6	6	26	49	.306	.348	vs. NL	.287	547	157	39	6	10	84	88	88	.386	.435

Batter vs. Pitcher (career)

Hits Best Against	Avg	AB	H	2B	3B	HR	RBI	BB	SO	OBP	SLG	Hits Worst Against	Avg	AB	H	2B	3B	HR	RBI	BB	SO	OBP	SLG
Kevin Appier	.500	14	7	1	0	0	4	2	1	.563	.571	Greg Cadaret	.000	11	0	0	0	0	0	0	5	.000	.000
Scott Kamieniecki	.462	13	6	0	1	0	0	0	0	.500	.615	Tom Candiotti	.095	21	2	0	0	0	3	1	5	.130	.095
Scott Erickson	.444	9	4	0	0	1	3	0		.583	.444	Erik Hanson	.100	20	2	0	0	0	0	0		.100	.100
Mark Leiter	.389	18	7	2	0	1	3	6	2	.520	.667	Hipolito Pichardo	.100	10	1	0	0	0	0	2	1	.250	.100
Francisco Cordova	.333	12	4	0	0	2	2	0		.333	.833	Kevin Tapani	.136	22	3	1	0	0	4	0	8	.136	.182

Scott Spiezio — Athletics
Age 25 – Bats Both

	Avg	G	AB	R	H	2B	3B	HR	RBI	BB	SO	HBP	GDP	SB	CS	OBP	SLG	IBB	SH	SF	#Pit	#P/PA	GB	FB	G/F
1997 Season	.243	147	538	58	131	28	4	14	65	44	75	1	12	9	3	.300	.388	2	3	4	2130	3.61	155	203	0.76
Career (1996-1997)	.247	156	567	64	140	30	4	16	73	46	79	1	12	9	4	.305	.399	3	5	4	2257	3.61	164	215	0.76

1997 Season

	Avg	AB	H	2B	3B	HR	RBI	BB	SO	OBP	SLG		Avg	AB	H	2B	3B	HR	RBI	BB	SO	OBP	SLG
vs. Left	.235	149	35	5	1	7	24	17	21	.311	.423	First Pitch	.313	80	25	7	1	2	14	2	0	.325	.500
vs. Right	.247	389	96	23	3	7	41	27	54	.295	.375	Ahead in Count	.233	120	28	5	2	5	18	24	0	.356	.433
Groundball	.286	112	32	8	1	3	11	12	15	.349	.455	Behind in Count	.192	224	43	7	1	4	17	0	61	.196	.286
Flyball	.234	94	22	6	2	2	12	7	16	.294	.404	Two Strikes	.196	224	44	10	1	6	22	18	75	.259	.330
Home	.243	280	68	16	4	6	39	23	36	.300	.393	Batting #6	.229	258	59	12	2	6	27	24	38	.295	.360
Away	.244	258	63	12	0	8	26	21	39	.300	.384	Batting #7	.240	154	37	7	1	3	17	7	20	.270	.357
Day	.274	237	65	13	2	7	29	23	30	.337	.435	Other	.278	126	35	9	1	5	21	13	17	.345	.484
Night	.219	301	66	15	2	7	36	21	45	.270	.352	March/April	.284	102	29	10	0	3	14	9	17	.342	.471
Grass	.251	490	123	27	4	11	60	39	66	.305	.390	May	.259	108	28	5	1	4	14	9	16	.319	.435
Turf	.167	48	8	1	0	3	5	5	9	.245	.375	June	.119	42	5	0	0	0	3	3	7	.170	.119
Pre-All Star	.237	270	64	15	1	8	34	24	44	.298	.389	July	.232	95	22	2	1	2	9	6	13	.275	.337
Post-All Star	.250	268	67	13	3	6	31	20	31	.302	.388	August	.175	97	17	4	0	1	9	5	14	.216	.247
Scoring Posn	.232	125	29	7	4	3	47	15	21	.306	.424	Sept/Oct	.319	94	30	7	2	4	16	12	8	.394	.564
Close & Late	.233	86	20	6	0	2	7	8	13	.295	.372	vs. AL	.246	500	123	27	3	13	58	41	71	.302	.390
None on/out	.228	114	26	3	0	3	3	9	17	.285	.333	vs. NL	.211	38	8	1	1	1	7	3	4	.268	.368

Position	Avg	AB	H	2B	3B	HR	RBI	BB	SO	OBP	SLG	G	GS	Innings	PO	A	E	DP	Fld Pct	Rng Fctr	In Zone	Outs	Zone Rtg	MLB Zone
As 2b	.244	536	131	28	4	14	65	43	75	.300	.390	146	140	1256.0	281	414	7	94	.990	4.98	461	424	.920	.902

Paul Spoljaric — Mariners
Age 27 – Pitches Left (flyball pitcher)

	ERA	W	L	Sv	G	GS	IP	BB	SO	Avg	H	2B	3B	HR	RBI	OBP	SLG	GF	IR	IRS	Hld	SvOp	SB	CS	GB	FB	G/F
1997 Season	3.69	0	3	3	57	0	70.2	36	70	.236	61	16	2	4	32	.333	.359	10	46	12	10	5	5	3	78	61	1.28
Career (1994-1997)	4.22	2	6	4	87	1	111.0	64	110	.234	96	22	2	13	58	.342	.392	22	60	17	15	6	8	4	114	116	0.98

1997 Season

	ERA	W	L	Sv	G	GS	IP	H	HR	BB	SO		Avg	AB	H	2B	3B	HR	RBI	BB	SO	OBP	SLG
Home	4.62	0	0	0	29	0	37.0	34	2	17	40	vs. Left	.244	123	30	6	1	3	20	13	31	.316	.382
Away	2.67	0	3	3	28	0	33.2	27	2	19	30	vs. Right	.228	136	31	10	1	1	12	23	39	.348	.338
Day	3.00	0	0	0	21	0	27.0	19	1	17	37	Inning 1-6	.227	88	20	4	0	1	10	10	22	.314	.307
Night	4.12	0	3	3	36	0	43.2	42	3	19	33	Inning 7+	.240	171	41	12	2	3	22	26	48	.343	.386
Grass	2.35	0	2	3	24	0	30.2	24	2	17	27	None on	.224	134	30	6	0	2	2	14	36	.302	.313
Turf	4.72	0	1	0	33	0	40.0	37	2	19	43	Runners on	.248	125	31	10	2	2	30	22	34	.364	.408
March/April	2.57	0	2	1	6	0	7.0	3	1	3	4	Scoring Posn	.203	74	15	6	1	0	24	14	18	.337	.311
May	2.35	0	0	0	7	0	15.1	11	1	2	8	Close & Late	.225	71	16	4	0	3	13	15	15	.368	.408
June	5.17	0	1	1	12	0	15.2	13	1	11	21	None on/out	.234	64	15	3	0	1	1	2	17	.269	.328
July	1.80	0	0	0	12	0	10.0	10	0	6	10	vs. 1st Batr (relief)	.296	54	16	4	0	1	7	3	13	.333	.426
August	5.68	0	0	0	9	0	12.2	11	1	8	18	1st Inning Pitched	.211	161	34	9	1	1	15	19	49	.299	.298
Sept/Oct	3.60	0	0	0	11	0	10.0	13	0	7	9	First 15 Pitches	.229	140	32	9	1	1	13	17	38	.319	.329
Starter	0.00	0	0	0	0	0	0.0	0	0	0	0	Pitch 16-30	.198	81	16	4	0	3	7	14	24	.313	.358
Reliever	3.69	0	3	3	57	0	70.2	61	4	36	70	Pitch 31-45	.429	21	9	3	0	0	9	5	1	.556	.571
0 Days rest (Relief)	2.77	0	1	0	12	0	13.0	10	0	8	14	Pitch 46+	.235	17	4	0	1	0	3	0	7	.235	.353
1 or 2 Days rest	5.60	0	2	3	27	0	35.1	33	3	20	39	First Pitch	.321	28	9	4	0	0	3	6	0	.441	.464
3+ Days rest	1.21	0	0	0	18	0	22.1	18	1	8	17	Ahead in Count	.150	133	20	5	0	2	7	0	61	.157	.233
vs. AL	3.29	0	2	3	51	0	63.0	54	4	32	65	Behind in Count	.269	52	14	3	1	2	12	15	0	.437	.481
vs. NL	7.04	0	1	0	6	0	7.2	7	0	4	5	Two Strikes	.175	137	24	8	1	2	14	15	70	.257	.292
Pre-All Star	3.35	0	3	2	28	0	40.1	29	3	16	36	Pre-All Star	.206	141	29	8	1	3	16	16	36	.288	.340
Post-All Star	4.15	0	0	1	29	0	30.1	32	1	20	34	Post-All Star	.271	118	32	8	1	1	16	20	34	.386	.381

Jerry Spradlin — Phillies
Age 31 – Pitches Right

	ERA	W	L	Sv	G	GS	IP	BB	SO	Avg	H	2B	3B	HR	RBI	OBP	SLG	GF	IR	IRS	Hld	SvOp	SB	CS	GB	FB	G/F
1997 Season	4.74	4	8	1	76	0	81.2	27	67	.274	86	16	2	9	46	.331	.424	23	40	13	18	5	7	4	109	81	1.35
Career (1993-1997)	4.60	6	9	3	120	0	139.0	38	95	.270	142	24	7	15	81	.316	.428	42	66	23	18	8	13	6	198	150	1.32

1997 Season

	ERA	W	L	Sv	G	GS	IP	H	HR	BB	SO		Avg	AB	H	2B	3B	HR	RBI	BB	SO	OBP	SLG
Home	3.57	3	2	0	42	0	45.1	45	5	9	41	vs. Left	.270	126	34	6	1	4	15	12	30	.329	.429
Away	6.19	1	6	1	34	0	36.1	41	4	18	26	vs. Right	.277	188	52	10	1	5	31	15	37	.333	.420
Day	5.40	1	1	1	21	0	23.1	23	2	10	17	Inning 1-6	.250	12	3	0	0	1	3	1	0	.308	.500
Night	4.47	3	7	0	55	0	58.1	63	7	17	50	Inning 7+	.275	302	83	16	2	8	43	26	67	.332	.421
Grass	6.93	0	3	1	24	0	24.2	28	4	10	21	None on	.275	160	44	9	1	3	3	16	41	.341	.400
Turf	3.79	4	5	0	52	0	57.0	58	5	17	46	Runners on	.273	154	42	7	1	6	43	11	26	.321	.448
March/April	2.92	0	1	0	12	0	12.1	6	0	2	8	Scoring Posn	.234	94	22	3	1	2	33	7	21	.282	.351
May	4.22	1	0	0	11	0	10.2	12	1	3	11	Close & Late	.274	164	45	9	1	5	23	14	40	.331	.433
June	3.94	0	2	0	15	0	16.0	14	1	7	15	None on/out	.132	68	9	0	0	0	0	7	21	.213	.147
July	10.20	0	3	0	14	0	15.0	24	3	7	14	vs. 1st Batr (relief)	.191	68	13	1	0	2	8	7	16	.267	.294
August	2.25	1	0	0	13	0	16.0	13	0	7	7	1st Inning Pitched	.264	258	68	13	1	9	39	21	57	.319	.426
Sept/Oct	4.63	2	2	1	11	0	11.2	17	4	1	12	First 15 Pitches	.271	214	58	11	0	7	29	14	42	.313	.421
Starter	0.00	0	0	0	0	0	0.0	0	0	0	0	Pitch 16-30	.292	89	26	4	2	2	14	9	22	.364	.449
Reliever	4.74	4	8	1	76	0	81.2	86	9	27	67	Pitch 31-45	.100	10	1	0	0	0	0	4	3	.357	.100
0 Days rest (Relief)	5.06	1	3	0	29	0	32.0	38	3	9	24	Pitch 46+	1.000	1	1	0	0	0	3	0	0	1.000	2.000
1 or 2 Days rest	5.17	2	3	0	31	0	31.1	33	6	10	23	First Pitch	.243	37	9	1	0	1	6	1	0	.263	.351
3+ Days rest	3.44	1	2	1	16	0	18.1	15	0	8	20	Ahead in Count	.244	156	38	6	2	3	21	0	54	.247	.365
vs. AL	7.36	1	1	0	7	0	7.1	5	1	5	5	Behind in Count	.350	60	21	6	0	3	10	18	0	.500	.600
vs. NL	4.48	3	7	1	69	0	74.1	81	8	22	62	Two Strikes	.194	160	31	5	2	3	19	8	67	.231	.306
Pre-All Star	5.02	1	4	0	41	0	43.0	39	3	15	36	Pre-All Star	.244	160	39	8	2	3	23	15	36	.311	.375
Post-All Star	4.42	3	4	1	35	0	38.2	47	6	12	31	Post-All Star	.305	154	47	8	0	6	23	12	31	.353	.474

Ed Sprague — Blue Jays
Age 30 – Bats Right

	Avg	G	AB	R	H	2B	3B	HR	RBI	BB	SO	HBP	GDP	SB	CS	OBP	SLG	IBB	SH	SF	#Pit	#P/PA	GB	FB	G/F
1997 Season	.228	138	504	63	115	29	4	14	48	51	102	6	10	0	1	.306	.385	0	0	1	2103	3.74	130	180	0.72
Last Five Years	.244	700	2567	316	627	141	10	91	340	224	524	54	69	2	1	.315	.413	8	5	25	10895	3.79	758	861	0.88

1997 Season

	Avg	AB	H	2B	3B	HR	RBI	BB	SO	OBP	SLG		Avg	AB	H	2B	3B	HR	RBI	BB	SO	OBP	SLG
vs. Left	.250	148	37	10	2	7	19	16	31	.327	.486	First Pitch	.291	79	23	6	0	4	8	0	0	.309	.519
vs. Right	.219	356	78	19	2	7	29	35	71	.297	.343	Ahead in Count	.306	108	33	10	1	7	16	26	0	.444	.611
Groundball	.188	85	16	3	2	2	10	7	14	.258	.341	Behind in Count	.181	221	40	6	3	3	17	0	77	.188	.276
Flyball	.254	67	17	4	1	2	4	2	14	.275	.433	Two Strikes	.162	235	38	7	2	3	16	25	102	.248	.247
Home	.217	254	55	13	3	5	19	21	52	.287	.350	Batting #4	.244	119	29	5	3	5	13	10	25	.313	.462
Away	.240	250	60	16	1	9	29	30	50	.325	.420	Batting #5	.221	280	62	22	1	5	25	26	64	.296	.361
Day	.193	187	36	10	2	4	16	23	44	.288	.332	Other	.229	105	24	2	0	4	10	15	13	.325	.362

439

1997 Season

	Avg	AB	H	2B	3B	HR	RBI	BB	SO	OBP	SLG
Night	.249	317	79	19	2	10	32	28	58	.317	.416
Grass	.245	208	51	11	1	9	23	28	45	.336	.438
Turf	.216	296	64	18	3	5	25	23	57	.284	.348
Pre-All Star	.235	306	72	25	3	10	33	30	65	.311	.435
Post-All Star	.217	198	43	4	1	4	15	21	37	.299	.308
Scoring Posn	.174	115	20	5	1	2	32	12	24	.267	.287
Close & Late	.218	78	17	3	1	1	4	10	23	.322	.321
None on/out	.331	121	40	13	2	6		11	22	.391	.620

	Avg	AB	H	2B	3B	HR	RBI	BB	SO	OBP	SLG
March/April	.286	91	26	13	0	5	17	7	18	.343	.593
May	.268	97	26	6	1	5	9	12	21	.360	.505
June	.198	96	19	6	2	0	7	9	20	.271	.302
July	.155	103	16	2	0	0	1	6	26	.216	.175
August	.255	110	28	2	1	4	14	15	15	.344	.400
Sept/Oct	.000	7	0	0	0	0	0	0	2	.222	.000
vs. AL	.238	454	108	26	3	14	44	47	90	.317	.401
vs. NL	.140	50	7	3	1	0	4	4	12	.204	.240

1997 By Position

Position	Avg	AB	H	2B	3B	HR	RBI	BB	SO	OBP	SLG	G	GS	Innings	PO	A	E	DP	Fld Pct	Rng Fctr	In Zone	Zone Outs	Zone Rtg	MLB Zone
As 3b	.228	474	108	29	4	13	45	48	96	.305	.388	129	129	1120.1	106	201	18	19	.945	2.47	299	229	.766	.801

Last Five Years

	Avg	AB	H	2B	3B	HR	RBI	BB	SO	OBP	SLG
vs. Left	.264	702	185	41	2	31	96	71	111	.332	.460
vs. Right	.237	1865	442	100	8	60	244	153	413	.309	.396
Groundball	.281	545	153	32	3	15	79	34	105	.336	.433
Flyball	.233	424	99	24	1	15	58	31	87	.296	.401
Home	.246	1279	314	70	4	48	167	108	275	.317	.419
Away	.243	1288	313	71	6	43	173	116	249	.313	.408
Day	.246	886	218	42	3	37	127	83	180	.319	.426
Night	.243	1681	409	99	7	54	213	141	344	.313	.407
Grass	.250	1067	267	55	5	37	146	102	191	.323	.415
Turf	.240	1500	360	86	5	54	194	122	333	.310	.412
Pre-All Star	.252	1467	369	88	6	62	201	126	318	.321	.446
Post-All Star	.235	1100	258	53	4	29	139	98	206	.308	.369
Scoring Posn	.214	681	146	31	4	20	242	77	155	.302	.360
Close & Late	.232	379	88	11	3	12	42	37	106	.317	.372
None on/out	.273	629	172	40	3	34	34	41	125	.324	.509

	Avg	AB	H	2B	3B	HR	RBI	BB	SO	OBP	SLG
First Pitch	.354	373	132	41	1	21	60	6	0	.381	.638
Ahead in Count	.299	571	171	36	4	32	111	97	0	.407	.545
Behind in Count	.185	1131	209	35	4	22	99	0	414	.197	.281
Two Strikes	.172	1200	206	38	4	26	115	121	524	.255	.275
Batting #5	.234	1000	234	62	3	42	131	103	235	.315	.428
Batting #6	.246	609	150	30	3	21	77	60	136	.330	.409
Other	.254	958	243	49	4	28	132	61	173	.306	.401
March/April	.283	382	108	27	1	20	71	28	82	.339	.516
May	.258	473	122	26	1	20	56	49	108	.340	.444
June	.241	464	112	28	3	15	54	37	99	.310	.412
July	.210	491	103	24	1	16	59	40	100	.282	.360
August	.248	463	115	20	4	13	65	43	70	.320	.393
Sept/Oct	.228	294	67	16	0	7	35	27	65	.300	.354
vs. AL	.246	2517	620	138	9	91	336	220	512	.317	.417
vs. NL	.140	50	7	3	1	0	4	4	12	.204	.240

Batter vs. Pitcher (career)

Hits Best Against	Avg	AB	H	2B	3B	HR	RBI	BB	SO	OBP	SLG
Sterling Hitchcock	.500	14	7	0	0	1	5	0	1	.500	.714
Orel Hershiser	.421	19	8	1	0	2	4	1	3	.450	.789
Kenny Rogers	.407	27	11	3	0	2	5	4	2	.484	.741
Chris Haney	.368	19	7	4	0	1	2	1	1	.429	.737
Jack McDowell	.313	16	5	3	0	1	3	4	5	.476	.688

Hits Worst Against	Avg	AB	H	2B	3B	HR	RBI	BB	SO	OBP	SLG
Bob Wolcott	.000	11	0	0	0	0	1	0	4	.000	.000
Tim Belcher	.050	20	1	0	0	1	1	0	6	.095	.200
F. Valenzuela	.083	12	1	0	0	0	0		1	.083	.083
Randy Johnson	.118	34	4	1	0	0	1	3	15	.189	.147
Cal Eldred	.130	23	3	0	0	0	0	0	4	.130	.130

Dennis Springer — Angels

Age 33 – Pitches Right (flyball pitcher)

	ERA	W	L	Sv	G	GS	IP	BB	SO	Avg	H	2B	3B	HR	RBI	OBP	SLG	CG	ShO	Sup	QS	#P/S	SB	CS	GB	FB	G/F
1997 Season	5.18	9	9	0	32	28	194.2	73	75	.267	199	50	4	32	112	.335	.473	3	1	5.59	11	100	19	11	223	310	0.72
Career (1995-1997)	5.26	14	18	0	56	47	311.2	125	154	.261	311	66	4	59	170	.336	.472	5	2	5.60	17	99	34	20	373	461	0.81

1997 Season

	ERA	W	L	Sv	G	GS	IP	H	HR	BB	SO
Home	5.23	4	4	0	16	12	93.0	89	18	30	39
Away	5.13	5	5	0	16	16	101.2	110	14	43	36
Day	3.91	4	1	0	8	8	53.0	46	5	22	19
Night	5.65	5	8	0	24	20	141.2	153	27	51	56
Grass	5.37	7	9	0	28	24	166.0	176	30	57	62
Turf	4.08	2	0	0	4	4	28.2	23	2	16	13
March/April	7.82	0	0	0	4	1	12.2	19	0	9	9
May	4.35	3	1	0	5	4	31.0	31	5	12	15
June	5.68	1	1	0	6	6	38.0	39	8	15	17
July	6.60	2	2	0	5	5	30.0	33	6	14	12
August	3.83	2	3	0	7	7	49.1	44	6	10	11
Sept/Oct	5.08	1	2	0	5	5	33.2	33	7	13	11
Starter	5.14	9	8	0	28	28	182.0	184	32	66	64
Reliever	5.68	1	0	0	4	0	12.2	15	0	7	11
0-3 Days Rest (Start)	3.73	2	2	0	6	6	41.0	38	6	8	18
4 Days Rest	6.72	4	2	0	11	11	69.2	71	16	30	21
5+ Days Rest	4.42	2	5	0	11	11	71.1	75	10	28	25
vs. AL	4.96	9	8	0	29	25	179.2	180	26	70	71
vs. NL	7.80	0	1	0	3	3	15.0	19	6	3	4
Pre-All Star	5.82	4	3	0	16	12	86.2	96	15	39	43
Post-All Star	4.67	5	6	0	16	16	108.0	103	17	34	32

	Avg	AB	H	2B	3B	HR	RBI	BB	SO	OBP	SLG
vs. Left	.262	381	100	29	3	16	60	36	35	.323	.480
vs. Right	.271	365	99	21	1	16	52	37	40	.347	.466
Inning 1-6	.267	630	168	42	4	25	99	64	62	.337	.465
Inning 7+	.267	116	31	8	0	7	13	9	13	.323	.517
None on	.257	456	117	32	2	18	18	39	46	.322	.454
Runners on	.283	290	82	18	2	14	94	34	29	.354	.503
Scoring Posn	.263	197	49	11	2	7	79	27	23	.350	.464
Close & Late	.271	59	16	5	0	3	7	5	8	.338	.508
None on/out	.268	194	52	16	0	7	7	18	17	.333	.459
vs. 1st Batr (relief)	.333	3	1	0	0	0	0	1	1	.500	.333
1st Inning Pitched	.267	120	32	8	1	3	26	18	22	.354	.425
First 75 Pitches	.272	540	147	40	4	20	83	53	58	.339	.472
Pitch 76-90	.327	98	32	6	0	8	23	12	8	.411	.633
Pitch 91-105	.213	61	13	2	0	2	4	4	5	.258	.344
Pitch 106+	.149	47	7	2	0	2	4	4	4	.216	.319
First Pitch	.254	118	30	8	0	6	20	0	0	.276	.475
Ahead in Count	.220	291	64	20	2	4	23	0	63	.224	.344
Behind in Count	.392	189	74	17	2	18	49	42	0	.502	.788
Two Strikes	.184	272	50	14	0	4	23	31	75	.266	.279
Pre-All Star	.281	342	96	24	2	15	58	39	43	.358	.494
Post-All Star	.255	404	103	26	2	17	54	34	32	.315	.455

Russ Springer — Astros

Age 29 – Pitches Right (flyball pitcher)

	ERA	W	L	Sv	G	GS	IP	BB	SO	Avg	H	2B	3B	HR	RBI	OBP	SLG	GF	IR	IRS	Hld	SvOp	SB	CS	GB	FB	G/F
1997 Season	4.23	3	3	3	54	0	55.1	27	74	.232	48	16	0	4	29	.329	.367	13	37	12	9	7	8	0	45	61	0.74
Last Five Years	5.30	10	23	6	170	27	336.0	146	297	.273	362	82	3	52	207	.350	.458	40	94	28	16	15	38	6	303	488	0.62

1997 Season

	ERA	W	L	Sv	G	GS	IP	H	HR	BB	SO
Home	5.79	1	1	1	26	0	23.1	30	3	8	31

	Avg	AB	H	2B	3B	HR	RBI	BB	SO	OBP	SLG
vs. Left	.229	96	22	6	0	2	12	13	30	.345	.354

1997 Season

	ERA	W	L	Sv	G	GS	IP	H	HR	BB	SO		Avg	AB	H	2B	3B	HR	RBI	BB	SO	OBP	SLG
Away	3.09	2	2	2	28	0	32.0	19	1	19	43	vs. Right	.234	111	26	10	0	2	17	14	44	.315	.378
Day	1.15	1	1	1	15	0	15.2	11	0	7	20	Inning 1-6	.235	17	4	1	0	0	5	3	6	.364	.294
Night	5.45	2	2	2	39	0	39.2	37	4	20	54	Inning 7+	.232	190	44	15	0	4	24	24	68	.326	.374
Grass	3.63	1	1	2	20	0	22.1	15	1	16	31	None on	.211	95	20	5	0	2	2	14	39	.330	.326
Turf	4.64	2	2	1	34	0	33.0	33	3	11	43	Runners on	.250	112	28	11	0	2	27	13	35	.328	.402
March/April	1.54	1	0	0	9	0	11.2	7	0	6	18	Scoring Posn	.231	65	15	7	0	1	24	10	19	.333	.385
May	2.70	0	2	0	13	0	13.1	10	2	3	20	Close & Late	.228	114	26	7	0	3	19	15	36	.326	.368
June	18.90	0	0	0	6	0	3.1	10	0	4	3	None on/out	.195	41	8	1	0	0		7	18	.327	.220
July	6.75	0	1	1	7	0	6.2	5	1	6	10	vs. 1st Batr (relief)	.186	43	8	1	0	0	6	8	21	.333	.209
August	2.92	1	0	1	10	0	12.1	12	1	2	13	1st Inning Pitched	.241	166	40	13	0	3	26	22	58	.333	.373
Sept/Oct	4.50	1	0	1	9	0	8.0	4	0	6	10	First 15 Pitches	.257	113	29	9	0	2	20	16	43	.353	.389
Starter	0.00	0	0	0	0	0	0.0	0	0	0	0	Pitch 16-30	.211	71	15	5	0	1	7	7	22	.300	.324
Reliever	4.23	3	3	3	54	0	55.1	48	4	27	74	Pitch 31-45	.222	18	4	2	0	1	2	3	5	.333	.500
0 Days rest (Relief)	3.24	1	1	1	9	0	8.1	5	1	1	11	Pitch 46+	.000	5	0	0	0	0	0	0	1	.167	.000
1 or 2 Days rest	4.18	2	1	1	29	0	28.0	25	3	16	38	First Pitch	.250	12	3	1	0	0	4	1	0	.333	.333
3+ Days rest	4.74	0	1	1	16	0	19.0	18	0	10	25	Ahead in Count	.208	125	26	8	0	0	8	0	59	.227	.272
vs. AL	162.00	0	0	0	2	0	0.1	5	0	2	0	Behind in Count	.360	25	9	4	0	0	5	6	0	.469	.520
vs. NL	3.27	3	3	3	52	0	55.0	43	4	25	74	Two Strikes	.185	146	27	9	0	2	12	20	74	.296	.288
Pre-All Star	4.13	1	2	0	28	0	28.1	27	2	13	41	Pre-All Star	.245	110	27	10	0	2	14	13	41	.328	.391
Post-All Star	4.33	2	1	3	26	0	27.0	21	2	14	33	Post-All Star	.216	97	21	6	0	2	15	14	33	.330	.340

Last Five Years

	ERA	W	L	Sv	G	GS	IP	H	HR	BB	SO		Avg	AB	H	2B	3B	HR	RBI	BB	SO	OBP	SLG
Home	5.02	7	8	3	88	14	175.2	191	28	73	152	vs. Left	.282	599	169	38	1	23	77	75	117	.370	.464
Away	5.61	3	15	3	82	13	160.1	171	24	73	145	vs. Right	.266	725	193	44	2	29	130	71	180	.333	.452
Day	5.75	2	9	1	47	7	83.0	84	15	41	80	Inning 1-6	.295	775	229	50	3	29	135	82	141	.365	.480
Night	5.16	8	14	5	123	20	253.0	278	37	105	217	Inning 7+	.242	549	133	32	0	23	72	64	156	.330	.426
Grass	6.17	4	15	5	86	21	201.1	237	38	93	151	None on	.255	693	177	36	2	15	15	77	162	.338	.378
Turf	4.01	6	8	1	84	6	134.2	125	14	53	146	Runners on	.293	631	185	46	1	37	192	69	135	.363	.545
March/April	2.86	2	2	0	21	0	28.1	26	2	12	37	Scoring Posn	.280	368	103	27	0	22	154	51	78	.363	.533
May	6.00	0	5	0	28	1	36.0	40	7	14	43	Close & Late	.273	242	66	14	0	13	46	36	62	.379	.492
June	7.10	2	7	1	34	8	77.1	104	18	29	65	None on/out	.271	303	82	18	1	5	5	41	69	.363	.386
July	5.95	3	7	2	32	15	101.1	110	16	59	67	vs. 1st Batr (relief)	.215	121	26	5	0	3	15	17	43	.322	.331
August	3.43	2	2	2	29	3	57.2	56	4	16	47	1st Inning Pitched	.252	584	147	33	2	23	99	61	163	.327	.433
Sept/Oct	3.82	1	0	1	26	0	35.1	26	5	16	38	First 15 Pitches	.284	444	126	31	2	19	77	45	112	.353	.491
Starter	7.34	5	14	0	27	27	137.1	188	25	64	77	Pitch 16-30	.234	354	83	20	0	14	47	34	98	.311	.410
Reliever	3.90	5	9	6	143	0	198.2	174	27	82	220	Pitch 31-45	.262	164	43	10	0	7	22	26	37	.366	.451
0 Days rest (Relief)	5.65	1	1	1	15	0	14.1	12	4	1	17	Pitch 46+	.304	362	110	21	1	12	61	41	50	.376	.467
1 or 2 Days rest	3.64	2	6	4	82	0	118.2	100	16	55	126	First Pitch	.347	147	51	13	1	8	29	10	0	.390	.612
3+ Days rest	3.97	2	1	1	46	0	65.2	62	7	26	77	Ahead in Count	.221	652	144	35	1	11	69	0	250	.233	.328
vs. AL	6.68	4	10	3	53	20	157.2	191	31	73	97	Behind in Count	.343	271	93	24	0	18	60	64	0	.406	.631
vs. NL	4.09	6	13	3	117	7	178.1	171	21	73	200	Two Strikes	.206	714	147	33	2	13	69	72	297	.284	.312
Pre-All Star	5.65	6	14	1	93	14	180.0	210	32	75	170	Pre-All Star	.289	726	210	48	2	32	118	75	170	.359	.493
Post-All Star	4.90	4	9	5	77	13	156.0	152	20	73	127	Post-All Star	.254	598	152	34	1	20	89	71	127	.339	.415

Pitcher vs. Batter (career)

Pitches Best Vs.	Avg	AB	H	2B	3B	HR	RBI	BB	SO	OBP	SLG
Devon White	.167	12	2	0	1	0	0	1	3	.231	.333

Pitches Worst Vs.	Avg	AB	H	2B	3B	HR	RBI	BB	SO	OBP	SLG
Chuck Knoblauch	.417	12	5	1	0	0	2	2	3	.500	.500
Lance Johnson	.417	12	5	1	0	1	1	0	0	.417	.750
Rickey Henderson	.333	6	2	0	0	0	0	5	1	.636	.333

Scott Stahoviak — Twins
Age 28 – Bats Left (flyball hitter)

	Avg	G	AB	R	H	2B	3B	HR	RBI	BB	SO	HBP	GDP	SB	CS	OBP	SLG	IBB	SH	SF	#Pit	#P/PA	GB	FB	G/F
1997 Season	.229	91	275	33	63	17	0	10	33	24	73	6	7	5	2	.301	.400	1	0	4	1204	3.90	89	83	1.07
Career (1993-1997)	.259	335	1000	134	259	70	3	26	118	116	270	9	21	13	8	.339	.413	9	1	8	4520	3.99	318	263	1.21

1997 Season

	Avg	AB	H	2B	3B	HR	RBI	BB	SO	OBP	SLG		Avg	AB	H	2B	3B	HR	RBI	BB	SO	OBP	SLG
vs. Left	.286	14	4	1	0	0	2	2	3	.375	.357	First Pitch	.366	41	15	6	0	3	6	1	0	.372	.732
vs. Right	.226	261	59	16	0	10	31	22	70	.297	.402	Ahead in Count	.322	59	19	2	0	4	11	18	0	.475	.559
Groundball	.123	57	7	4	0	1	2	7	16	.242	.246	Behind in Count	.110	118	13	1	0	2	6	0	54	.139	.169
Flyball	.268	41	11	1	0	3	7	2	14	.348	.512	Two Strikes	.160	144	23	8	0	3	15	5	73	.209	.278
Home	.241	141	34	11	0	4	18	14	39	.316	.404	Batting #5	.236	55	13	5	0	2	8	9	18	.366	.436
Away	.216	134	29	6	0	6	15	10	34	.285	.396	Batting #6	.236	89	21	3	0	4	14	7	25	.289	.404
Day	.234	77	18	8	0	5	11	5	15	.306	.532	Other	.221	131	29	9	0	4	11	8	30	.277	.382
Night	.227	198	45	9	0	5	22	19	58	.299	.348	March/April	1.000	1	1	0	0	0	0	0	0	1.000	1.000
Grass	.220	118	26	6	0	5	12	10	28	.299	.398	May	.188	32	6	3	0	2	4	4	11	.297	.469
Turf	.236	157	37	11	0	5	21	14	45	.303	.401	June	.339	59	20	3	0	2	11	5	13	.379	.492
Pre-All Star	.274	106	29	6	0	6	17	11	25	.342	.500	July	.222	72	16	6	0	3	5	5	15	.273	.431
Post-All Star	.201	169	34	11	0	4	16	13	48	.275	.337	August	.154	65	10	2	0	5	5	2	24	.277	.277
Scoring Posn	.220	59	13	3	0	2	22	6	20	.315	.373	Sept/Oct	.217	46	10	3	0	1	8	5	12	.309	.348
Close & Late	.162	37	6	2	0	0	1	6	6	.279	.216	vs. AL	.223	242	54	16	0	9	29	22	66	.300	.401
None on/out	.253	75	19	5	0	2	3	3	11	.300	.400	vs. NL	.273	33	9	1	0	1	4	2	7	.306	.394

1997 By Position

Position	Avg	AB	H	2B	3B	HR	RBI	BB	SO	OBP	SLG	G	GS	Innings	PO	A	E	DP	Fld Pct	Rng Fctr	In Zone	Zone Outs	Zone Rtg	MLB Zone
As Pinch Hitter	.375	16	6	3	0	1	3	0	4	.375	.750	16	0	---	---	---	---	---	---	---	---	---	---	---

1997 By Position

Position	Avg	AB	H	2B	3B	HR	RBI	BB	SO	OBP	SLG	G	GS	Innings	PO	A	E	DP	Fld Pct	Rng Fctr	In Zone	Outs	Zone Rtg	MLB Zone
As 1b	.225	244	55	14	0	9	29	24	65	.306	.393	81	71	629.0	606	58	7	68	.990	—	131	118	.901	.874

Career (1993-1997)

	Avg	AB	H	2B	3B	HR	RBI	BB	SO	OBP	SLG		Avg	AB	H	2B	3B	HR	RBI	BB	SO	OBP	SLG
vs. Left	.237	59	14	3	0	1	5	10	21	.357	.339	First Pitch	.287	157	45	15	1	6	20	7	0	.315	.510
vs. Right	.260	941	245	67	3	25	113	106	249	.338	.418	Ahead in Count	.362	174	63	14	1	8	32	75	0	.553	.592
Groundball	.240	250	60	20	0	4	27	35	68	.338	.368	Behind in Count	.198	475	94	23	0	9	48	0	207	.206	.303
Flyball	.228	167	38	9	0	5	20	17	55	.309	.371	Two Strikes	.197	544	107	34	0	11	59	34	270	.250	.320
Home	.273	516	141	35	2	13	60	59	134	.349	.424	Batting #5	.240	200	48	14	0	5	20	33	54	.353	.385
Away	.244	484	118	35	1	13	58	57	136	.328	.401	Batting #6	.256	242	62	12	0	8	30	26	66	.327	.405
Day	.234	286	67	26	1	7	32	32	73	.318	.406	Other	.267	558	149	44	3	13	68	57	150	.339	.427
Night	.269	714	192	44	2	19	86	84	197	.347	.416	March/April	.333	48	16	4	0	4	11	6	22	.418	.667
Grass	.251	414	104	34	1	12	53	46	114	.332	.425	May	.245	147	36	9	1	2	14	17	33	.327	.361
Turf	.265	586	155	36	2	14	65	70	156	.344	.404	June	.314	204	64	14	1	7	28	30	46	.399	.495
Pre-All Star	.280	457	128	30	2	16	60	59	111	.363	.453	July	.252	218	55	17	0	5	23	27	54	.333	.399
Post-All Star	.241	543	131	40	1	11	58	57	159	.318	.379	August	.247	223	55	16	0	4	24	25	66	.328	.372
Scoring Posn	.251	267	67	16	2	8	95	40	81	.350	.416	Sept/Oct	.206	160	33	10	1	4	18	11	49	.267	.356
Close & Late	.226	133	30	9	0	2	9	21	37	.331	.338	vs. AL	.259	967	250	69	3	25	114	114	263	.340	.414
None on/out	.311	238	74	28	1	5	5	22	45	.374	.500	vs. NL	.273	33	9	1	0	1	4	2	7	.306	.394

Batter vs. Pitcher (career)

Hits Best Against	Avg	AB	H	2B	3B	HR	RBI	BB	SO	OBP	SLG	Hits Worst Against	Avg	AB	H	2B	3B	HR	RBI	BB	SO	OBP	SLG
Ricky Bones	.533	15	8	4	0	2	3	0	1	.533	1.200	Ken Hill	.067	15	1	0	0	0	0	1	3	.125	.067
Bobby Witt	.474	19	9	1	0	1	5	2	2	.524	.684	Tom Gordon	.100	10	1	0	0	0	0	3	2	.286	.100
Jimmy Haynes	.455	11	5	2	0	0	2	1	4	.500	.636	Pat Hentgen	.150	20	3	1	0	0	0	1	5	.190	.200
Aaron Sele	.417	12	5	1	0	1	2	2	4	.533	.750	Ariel Prieto	.154	13	2	1	0	0	0	1	4	.214	.231
Chad Ogea	.400	15	6	1	0	1	4	3	3	.500	.667	Roger Pavlik	.158	19	3	0	0	0	3	2	5	.238	.158

Matt Stairs — Athletics
Age 30 – Bats Left

	Avg	G	AB	R	H	2B	3B	HR	RBI	BB	SO	HBP	GDP	SB	CS	OBP	SLG	IBB	SH	SF	#Pit	#P/PA	GB	FB	G/F
1997 Season	.298	133	352	62	105	19	0	27	73	50	60	3	6	3	2	.386	.582	1	1	4	1617	3.94	106	131	0.81
Last Five Years	.289	239	585	92	169	32	2	38	115	73	98	3	2	4	4	.369	.545	3	2	6	2601	3.88	182	207	0.88

1997 Season

	Avg	AB	H	2B	3B	HR	RBI	BB	SO	OBP	SLG		Avg	AB	H	2B	3B	HR	RBI	BB	SO	OBP	SLG
vs. Left	.259	85	22	2	0	8	20	12	20	.347	.565	First Pitch	.304	46	14	4	0	2	4	1	0	.347	.522
vs. Right	.311	267	83	17	0	19	53	38	40	.399	.588	Ahead in Count	.386	83	32	6	0	10	21	31	0	.543	.819
Groundball	.300	80	24	4	0	7	23	9	10	.370	.613	Behind in Count	.272	151	41	7	0	6	27	0	50	.273	.437
Flyball	.192	52	10	1	0	3	9	13	8	.364	.385	Two Strikes	.219	169	37	7	0	7	27	18	60	.296	.385
Home	.305	197	60	9	0	20	46	30	33	.393	.655	Batting #3	.354	96	34	6	0	10	31	20	14	.454	.729
Away	.290	155	45	10	0	7	27	20	27	.378	.490	Batting #4	.224	143	32	8	0	7	18	14	23	.297	.427
Day	.243	148	36	9	0	10	28	21	30	.341	.473	Other	.345	113	39	5	0	10	24	16	23	.432	.655
Night	.338	204	69	15	0	17	45	29	30	.419	.662	March/April	.308	26	8	1	0	3	6	4	3	.419	.692
Grass	.297	310	92	17	0	25	66	47	54	.390	.594	May	.316	38	12	1	0	3	7	8	7	.435	.579
Turf	.310	42	13	2	0	2	7	3	6	.356	.500	June	.458	59	27	8	0	6	22	5	8	.493	.898
Pre-All Star	.356	135	48	10	0	12	35	19	20	.437	.696	July	.300	50	15	1	0	5	12	13	10	.431	.620
Post-All Star	.263	217	57	9	0	15	38	31	40	.355	.512	August	.270	100	27	6	0	8	20	11	13	.348	.570
Scoring Posn	.273	99	27	5	0	7	44	12	19	.345	.535	Sept/Oct	.203	79	16	2	0	2	6	9	19	.284	.304
Close & Late	.278	72	20	1	0	6	16	9	18	.373	.542	vs. AL	.292	298	87	15	0	22	59	47	52	.389	.564
None on/out	.284	67	19	6	0	5	5	11	13	.385	.597	vs. NL	.333	54	18	4	0	5	14	3	8	.368	.685

1997 By Position

Position	Avg	AB	H	2B	3B	HR	RBI	BB	SO	OBP	SLG	G	GS	Innings	PO	A	E	DP	Fld Pct	Rng Fctr	In Zone	Outs	Zone Rtg	MLB Zone
As DH	.250	56	14	2	0	2	13	8	13	.333	.393	17	13	—	—	—	—	—	—	—	—	—	—	—
As Pinch Hitter	.353	34	12	0	0	1	5	5	6	.463	.441	42	0	—	—	—	—	—	—	—	—	—	—	—
As lf	.198	86	17	4	0	1	3	11	18	.286	.279	28	23	197.2	38	2	2	0	.952	1.82	43	36	.837	.805
As rf	.358	173	62	13	0	22	51	25	22	.440	.815	63	44	418.0	85	4	1	0	.989	1.92	98	79	.806	.813

Robby Stanifer — Marlins
Age 26 – Pitches Right

	ERA	W	L	Sv	G	GS	IP	BB	SO	Avg	H	2B	3B	HR	RBI	OBP	SLG	GF	IR	IRS	Hld	SvOp	SB	CS	GB	FB	G/F
1997 Season	4.60	1	2	1	36	0	45.0	16	28	.261	43	6	1	9	28	.337	.473	10	16	7	4	2	4	2	53	53	1.00

1997 Season

	ERA	W	L	Sv	G	GS	IP	H	HR	BB	SO		Avg	AB	H	2B	3B	HR	RBI	BB	SO	OBP	SLG
Home	5.49	1	0	0	17	0	19.2	22	4	7	16	vs. Left	.327	49	16	3	0	3	11	5	4	.389	.571
Away	3.91	0	2	1	19	0	25.1	21	5	9	12	vs. Right	.233	116	27	3	1	6	17	11	24	.315	.431
Starter	0.00	0	0	0	0	0	0.0	0	0	0	0	Scoring Posn	.256	43	11	2	1	1	18	3	3	.304	.419
Reliever	4.60	1	2	1	36	0	45.0	43	9	16	28	Close & Late	.118	34	4	1	0	1	3	7	6	.268	.235
0 Days rest (Relief)	12.00	0	1	0	6	0	6.0	8	4	4	4	None on/out	.179	39	7	0	0	3	3	5	9	.304	.410
1 or 2 Days rest	4.12	1	1	0	15	0	19.2	23	3	7	13	First Pitch	.278	18	5	0	0	2	5	0	0	.278	.611
3+ Days rest	2.79	0	0	1	15	0	19.1	12	2	5	11	Ahead in Count	.176	68	12	3	0	2	6	0	22	.200	.309
Pre-All Star	3.42	1	0	1	19	0	26.1	23	4	11	13	Behind in Count	.396	48	19	3	1	5	14	7	0	.473	.813
Post-All Star	6.27	0	2	0	17	0	18.2	20	5	5	15	Two Strikes	.127	71	9	3	0	4	9	9	28	.244	.211

Andy Stankiewicz — Expos

	Avg	G	AB	R	H	2B	3B	HR	RBI	BB	SO	HBP	GDP	SB	CS	OBP	SLG	IBB	SH	SF	#Pit	#P/PA	GB	FB	G/F
1997 Season	.224	76	107	11	24	9	0	1	5	4	22	0	1	1	1	.250	.336	0	7	1	410	3.45	37	29	1.28
Last Five Years	.221	236	299	44	66	18	1	2	26	35	66	4	5	7	4	.309	.308	3	11	2	1313	3.74	96	82	1.17

1997 Season

	Avg	AB	H	2B	3B	HR	RBI	BB	SO	OBP	SLG		Avg	AB	H	2B	3B	HR	RBI	BB	SO	OBP	SLG
vs. Left	.171	35	6	2	0	1	3	2	6	.216	.314	Scoring Posn	.095	21	2	2	0	0	4	1	5	.130	.190
vs. Right	.250	72	18	7	0	0	2	2	16	.267	.347	Close & Late	.077	26	2	1	0	1	2	2	4	.143	.231

Mike Stanley — Yankees

	Avg	G	AB	R	H	2B	3B	HR	RBI	BB	SO	HBP	GDP	SB	CS	OBP	SLG	IBB	SH	SF	#Pit	#P/PA	GB	FB	G/F
1997 Season	.297	125	347	61	103	26	0	29	79	54	72	6	13	0	1	.393	.507	4	0	8	1613	3.89	97	102	0.95
Last Five Years	.287	576	1856	321	533	111	3	101	358	276	381	23	55	4	3	.381	.513	14	0	27	8626	3.95	514	657	0.78

1997 Season

	Avg	AB	H	2B	3B	HR	RBI	BB	SO	OBP	SLG		Avg	AB	H	2B	3B	HR	RBI	BB	SO	OBP	SLG
vs. Left	.306	144	44	13	0	6	26	28	34	.424	.521	First Pitch	.388	49	19	5	0	3	10	3	0	.446	.673
vs. Right	.291	203	59	12	0	10	39	26	38	.370	.498	Ahead in Count	.500	68	34	12	0	5	23	21	0	.596	.897
Groundball	.271	70	19	3	0	2	12	10	16	.357	.400	Behind in Count	.169	148	25	2	0	3	15	0	54	.171	.243
Flyball	.273	55	15	1	0	6	15	7	8	.359	.618	Two Strikes	.188	165	31	5	0	4	22	30	72	.308	.291
Home	.295	183	54	13	0	6	25	22	39	.379	.464	Batting #4	.222	117	26	6	0	6	24	19	28	.336	.427
Away	.299	164	49	12	0	10	40	32	33	.408	.555	Batting #5	.372	145	54	12	0	9	33	24	26	.462	.641
Day	.248	101	25	6	0	4	23	16	25	.344	.426	Other	.271	85	23	7	0	1	8	11	18	.354	.388
Night	.317	246	78	19	0	12	42	38	47	.414	.541	March/April	.254	59	15	1	0	2	7	7	12	.333	.373
Grass	.304	306	93	23	0	13	56	49	62	.401	.507	May	.313	32	10	3	0	2	16	9	5	.467	.594
Turf	.244	41	10	2	0	3	9	5	10	.326	.512	June	.365	74	27	8	0	4	13	11	14	.437	.635
Pre-All Star	.319	188	60	13	0	9	40	29	35	.410	.532	July	.280	75	21	4	0	4	14	7	13	.365	.493
Post-All Star	.270	159	43	12	0	7	25	25	37	.372	.478	August	.261	46	12	4	0	1	5	11	14	.397	.413
Scoring Posn	.350	100	35	7	0	7	51	19	18	.430	.630	Sept/Oct	.295	61	18	5	0	3	10	9	14	.380	.525
Close & Late	.211	57	12	0	0	1	10	9	10	.314	.263	vs. AL	.291	320	93	21	0	14	62	45	66	.378	.488
None on/out	.313	80	25	3	0	4	4	10	18	.396	.500	vs. NL	.370	27	10	4	0	2	3	9	6	.541	.741

1997 By Position

Position	Avg	AB	H	2B	3B	HR	RBI	BB	SO	OBP	SLG	G	GS	Innings	PO	A	E	DP	Fld Pct	Rng Fctr	In Zone	Zone Outs	Zone Rtg	MLB Zone
As DH	.264	182	48	11	0	7	28	27	46	.367	.440	69	43	—	—	—	—	—	—	—	—	—	—	—
As Pinch Hitter	.357	28	10	3	0	2	9	4	5	.412	.679	34	0	—	—	—	—	—	—	—	—	—	—	—
As c	.297	37	11	2	0	1	6	4	6	.357	.432	15	9	77.0	53	3	1	0	.982	—	—	—	—	—
As 1b	.352	122	43	11	0	8	30	21	19	.442	.639	43	34	304.2	302	22	1	34	.997	—	51	45	.882	.874

Last Five Years

	Avg	AB	H	2B	3B	HR	RBI	BB	SO	OBP	SLG		Avg	AB	H	2B	3B	HR	RBI	BB	SO	OBP	SLG
vs. Left	.302	669	202	38	0	47	141	119	136	.400	.570	First Pitch	.353	238	84	19	0	10	38	10	0	.388	.559
vs. Right	.279	1187	331	73	3	54	217	157	245	.364	.482	Ahead in Count	.419	444	186	43	1	46	170	125	0	.537	.831
Groundball	.289	418	121	28	0	20	87	48	106	.368	.500	Behind in Count	.195	779	152	29	0	19	76	0	301	.205	.306
Flyball	.277	358	99	15	1	23	75	47	65	.364	.517	Two Strikes	.182	876	159	29	2	25	91	141	381	.298	.305
Home	.302	912	275	54	0	54	193	146	175	.400	.538	Batting #5	.311	643	200	39	1	36	132	100	120	.407	.543
Away	.273	944	258	57	3	47	165	130	206	.363	.489	Batting #7	.283	477	135	31	1	26	98	71	96	.378	.516
Day	.289	581	168	36	0	28	115	95	130	.390	.496	Other	.269	736	198	41	1	39	128	105	165	.361	.486
Night	.286	1275	365	75	3	73	243	181	248	.377	.522	March/April	.253	241	61	9	0	7	30	38	41	.359	.378
Grass	.290	1594	463	94	1	87	309	241	320	.386	.514	May	.292	305	89	22	1	14	61	47	69	.391	.508
Turf	.267	262	70	17	2	14	49	35	61	.353	.508	June	.295	366	108	23	0	23	77	56	78	.384	.546
Pre-All Star	.287	1039	298	66	2	48	189	152	213	.379	.493	July	.326	405	132	26	2	31	98	53	72	.412	.630
Post-All Star	.288	817	235	45	1	53	169	124	168	.384	.540	August	.264	330	87	16	0	18	58	45	70	.352	.476
Scoring Posn	.308	493	152	37	1	27	256	102	108	.415	.552	Sept/Oct	.268	209	56	15	0	8	34	37	51	.374	.455
Close & Late	.310	268	83	13	0	6	43	45	48	.400	.425	vs. AL	.286	1829	523	107	3	99	355	267	375	.379	.510
None on/out	.275	461	127	19	1	26	26	44	96	.344	.490	vs. NL	.370	27	10	4	0	2	3	9	6	.541	.741

Batter vs. Pitcher (career)

Hits Best Against	Avg	AB	H	2B	3B	HR	RBI	BB	SO	OBP	SLG	Hits Worst Against	Avg	AB	H	2B	3B	HR	RBI	BB	SO	OBP	SLG
Woody Williams	.571	14	8	1	0	3	5	2	0	.625	1.286	Eric Plunk	.063	16	1	0	0	0	0	2	2	.167	.063
Brian Anderson	.500	12	6	1	0	2	3	1	1	.538	1.083	Mike Timlin	.100	10	1	0	0	0	0	2	3	.250	.100
Scott Aldred	.455	11	5	0	0	3	5	0	2	.500	1.273	Jeff Fassero	.111	9	1	0	0	0	1	1	4	.182	.111
Tony Castillo	.455	11	5	0	0	2	3	1	4	.462	1.000	Kevin Tapani	.154	13	2	1	0	0	2	0	2	.154	.231
Charles Nagy	.435	23	10	1	0	3	9	4	2	.519	.870	Kevin Appier	.188	16	3	0	0	0	0	0	5	.188	.188

Mike Stanton — Yankees

	ERA	W	L	Sv	G	GS	IP	BB	SO	Avg	H	2B	3B	HR	RBI	OBP	SLG	GF	IR	IRS	Hld	SvOp	SB	CS	GB	FB	G/F
1997 Season	2.57	6	1	3	64	0	66.2	34	70	.205	50	5	0	3	21	.310	.262	15	49	13	26	5	1	1	81	59	1.37
Last Five Years	3.65	19	13	35	305	0	283.1	130	231	.252	268	42	2	26	151	.336	.369	121	200	64	71	51	14	13	339	299	1.13

1997 Season

	ERA	W	L	Sv	G	GS	IP	H	HR	BB	SO		Avg	AB	H	2B	3B	HR	RBI	BB	SO	OBP	SLG
Home	1.91	3	0	0	30	0	28.1	21	2	15	28	vs. Left	.159	88	14	0	0	0	5	9	20	.253	.159
Away	3.05	3	1	3	34	0	38.1	29	1	19	42	vs. Right	.231	156	36	5	0	3	16	25	50	.341	.321
Day	2.63	0	0	1	23	0	24.0	17	1	19	22	Inning 1-6	.167	12	2	0	0	0	2	1	3	.286	.167
Night	2.53	3	1	2	41	0	42.2	33	2	15	48	Inning 7+	.207	232	48	5	0	3	19	33	67	.311	.267
Grass	2.54	6	0	2	57	0	60.1	43	3	31	63	None on	.189	127	24	4	0	2	2	15	36	.275	.268

1997 Season

	ERA	W	L	Sv	G	GS	IP	H	HR	BB	SO		Avg	AB	H	2B	3B	HR	RBI	BB	SO	OBP	SLG
Turf	2.84	0	1	1	7	0	6.1	7	0	3	7	Runners on	.222	117	26	1	0	1	19	19	34	.345	.256
March/April	2.70	0	0	0	13	0	6.2	4	0	5	4	Scoring Posn	.229	70	16	1	0	1	19	15	22	.379	.286
May	2.25	0	0	0	8	0	8.0	5	0	5	4	Close & Late	.224	156	35	3	0	1	14	21	49	.324	.263
June	3.68	5	0	0	12	0	14.2	12	1	5	16	None on/out	.161	56	9	1	0	1	1	5	16	.230	.232
July	0.00	0	0	1	7	0	7.1	1	0	5	10	vs. 1st Batr (relief)	.138	58	8	0	0	1	5	4	17	.219	.190
August	3.21	1	0	1	13	0	14.0	16	1	9	20	1st Inning Pitched	.186	177	33	1	0	3	15	21	54	.284	.243
Sept/Oct	2.25	0	1	1	11	0	16.0	12	1	5	16	First 15 Pitches	.169	154	26	1	0	2	11	15	42	.251	.214
Starter	0.00	0	0	0	0	0	0.0	0	0	0	0	Pitch 16-30	.297	64	19	3	0	1	9	11	22	.408	.391
Reliever	2.57	6	1	3	64	0	66.2	50	3	34	70	Pitch 31-45	.211	19	4	1	0	0	1	5	4	.375	.263
0 Days rest (Relief)	0.69	3	0	0	12	0	13.0	11	0	6	12	Pitch 46+	.143	7	1	0	0	0	0	3	2	.400	.143
1 or 2 Days rest	4.03	2	1	2	32	0	29.0	26	3	19	29	First Pitch	.136	22	3	0	0	0	0	1	0	.174	.136
3+ Days rest	1.82	1	0	1	20	0	24.2	13	0	9	29	Ahead in Count	.157	134	21	3	0	1	12	0	63	.169	.201
vs. AL	2.67	3	0	3	58	0	60.2	44	3	29	62	Behind in Count	.216	37	8	1	0	0	4	21	0	.508	.243
vs. NL	1.50	3	1	0	6	0	6.0	6	0	5	8	Two Strikes	.199	146	29	2	0	2	14	12	70	.269	.253
Pre-All Star	3.03	5	0	0	34	0	29.2	21	1	15	25	Pre-All Star	.193	109	21	1	0	1	10	15	25	.296	.229
Post-All Star	2.19	1	1	3	30	0	37.0	29	2	19	45	Post-All Star	.215	135	29	4	0	2	11	19	45	.321	.289

Last Five Years

	ERA	W	L	Sv	G	GS	IP	H	HR	BB	SO		Avg	AB	H	2B	3B	HR	RBI	BB	SO	OBP	SLG
Home	2.98	14	6	16	152	0	142.0	135	13	71	113	vs. Left	.214	369	79	9	1	3	45	38	88	.292	.268
Away	4.33	5	7	19	153	0	141.1	133	13	59	118	vs. Right	.272	694	189	33	1	23	106	92	143	.359	.422
Day	4.28	6	4	10	89	0	80.0	72	8	47	67	Inning 1-6	.268	41	11	0	0	1	11	5	6	.388	.341
Night	3.41	13	9	25	216	0	203.1	196	18	83	164	Inning 7+	.251	1022	257	42	2	25	140	125	225	.334	.370
Grass	3.40	19	10	25	248	0	235.2	223	20	110	194	None on	.236	537	127	22	0	16	16	62	106	.318	.367
Turf	4.91	0	3	10	57	0	47.2	45	6	20	37	Runners on	.268	526	141	20	2	10	135	68	125	.354	.371
March/April	4.43	3	2	8	55	0	40.2	35	4	23	28	Scoring Posn	.278	320	89	16	1	6	125	47	74	.371	.391
May	3.00	2	2	11	56	0	54.0	48	3	22	45	Close & Late	.259	553	143	20	0	15	81	67	138	.339	.376
June	4.08	11	2	5	54	0	57.1	61	8	27	50	None on/out	.226	235	53	12	0	4	4	23	49	.295	.328
July	3.02	1	2	9	49	0	41.2	40	2	21	33	vs. 1st Batr (relief)	.226	270	61	11	1	5	35	27	62	.304	.330
August	4.97	2	2	1	53	0	50.2	53	7	27	46	1st Inning Pitched	.247	878	217	34	2	22	136	102	189	.328	.366
Sept/Oct	2.08	0	3	1	38	0	39.0	31	2	10	29	First 15 Pitches	.233	739	172	27	1	19	97	80	153	.310	.349
Starter	0.00	0	0	0	0	0	0.0	0	0	0	0	Pitch 16-30	.313	259	81	11	1	7	49	38	61	.403	.444
Reliever	3.65	19	13	35	305	0	283.1	268	26	130	231	Pitch 31-45	.265	49	13	4	0	0	5	8	13	.368	.347
0 Days rest (Relief)	3.07	8	3	10	89	0	85.0	68	4	25	80	Pitch 46+	.125	16	2	0	0	0	0	4	4	.300	.125
1 or 2 Days rest	4.32	8	6	15	132	0	114.2	123	14	72	87	First Pitch	.275	120	33	7	0	3	22	14	0	.346	.408
3+ Days rest	3.33	3	4	10	84	0	83.2	77	8	33	64	Ahead in Count	.194	532	103	17	1	5	48	0	201	.197	.258
vs. AL	3.20	8	4	4	161	0	160.1	139	17	64	132	Behind in Count	.327	199	65	9	1	8	41	67	0	.498	.503
vs. NL	4.24	11	9	31	144	0	123.0	129	9	66	99	Two Strikes	.197	558	110	19	1	8	55	49	231	.265	.278
Pre-All Star	3.62	17	7	26	178	0	164.0	153	15	75	135	Pre-All Star	.250	611	153	24	2	15	92	75	135	.333	.370
Post-All Star	3.70	2	6	9	127	0	119.1	115	11	55	96	Post-All Star	.254	452	115	18	0	11	59	55	96	.340	.367

Pitcher vs. Batter (career)

Pitches Best Vs.	Avg	AB	H	2B	3B	HR	RBI	BB	SO	OBP	SLG	Pitches Worst Vs.	Avg	AB	H	2B	3B	HR	RBI	BB	SO	OBP	SLG
Darryl Strawberry	.000	11	0	0	0	0	0	2	4	.154	.000	Ray Lankford	.455	11	5	0	0	1	3	1	4	.500	.727
Delino DeShields	.000	10	0	0	0	0	0	2	3	.167	.000	Gregg Jefferies	.444	9	4	1	0	1	2	0	.545	.556
Eddie Murray	.067	15	1	0	0	0	0	0	1	.067	.067	Darren Daulton	.385	13	5	2	0	1	1	3	3	.500	.769
Brett Butler	.091	11	1	0	0	0	1	3	1	.286	.091	Dave Martinez	.364	11	4	0	0	1	3	0	3	.364	.636
Craig Biggio	.143	14	2	0	0	0	1	1	3	.200	.143	Dave Hollins	.357	14	5	3	0	1	1	2	2	.438	.786

Terry Steinbach — Twins
Age 36 – Bats Right

	Avg	G	AB	R	H	2B	3B	HR	RBI	BB	SO	HBP	GDP	SB	CS	OBP	SLG	IBB	SH	SF	#Pit	#P/PA	GB	FB	G/F
1997 Season	.248	122	447	60	111	27	1	12	54	35	106	1	14	6	1	.302	.394	2	0	4	1792	3.66	166	114	1.46
Last Five Years	.273	588	2125	280	580	118	6	83	319	160	422	13	68	12	9	.325	.451	16	2	17	8110	3.49	766	592	1.29

1997 Season

	Avg	AB	H	2B	3B	HR	RBI	BB	SO	OBP	SLG		Avg	AB	H	2B	3B	HR	RBI	BB	SO	OBP	SLG
vs. Left	.308	117	36	7	0	4	18	13	25	.374	.470	First Pitch	.306	72	22	8	1	1	8	2	0	.324	.486
vs. Right	.227	330	75	20	1	8	36	22	81	.275	.367	Ahead in Count	.292	106	31	5	0	6	19	14	0	.380	.509
Groundball	.268	112	30	4	0	4	17	5	26	.297	.411	Behind in Count	.182	192	35	5	0	3	14	0	90	.179	.255
Flyball	.221	77	17	8	1	0	6	6	16	.277	.351	Two Strikes	.164	201	33	5	0	2	14	19	106	.235	.219
Home	.281	224	63	16	0	6	32	22	56	.345	.433	Batting #4	.253	233	59	15	1	7	27	15	53	.296	.416
Away	.215	223	48	11	1	6	22	13	47	.256	.354	Batting #5	.213	94	20	3	0	2	14	12	23	.308	.309
Day	.230	100	23	7	0	5	12	10	22	.297	.450	Other	.267	120	32	9	0	3	13	8	30	.308	.417
Night	.254	347	88	20	1	7	42	25	84	.303	.378	March/April	.240	75	18	4	0	1	9	8	14	.314	.333
Grass	.236	182	43	10	1	6	19	13	37	.284	.401	May	.303	76	23	5	0	2	10	10	19	.384	.447
Turf	.257	265	68	17	0	6	35	22	69	.314	.389	June	.253	75	19	3	0	5	14	4	19	.288	.493
Pre-All Star	.273	242	66	14	1	8	38	23	55	.335	.438	July	.282	85	24	5	1	2	6	2	15	.299	.435
Post-All Star	.220	205	45	13	0	4	16	12	51	.261	.341	August	.233	73	17	6	0	2	7	7	20	.296	.397
Scoring Posn	.205	127	26	10	0	2	40	15	38	.281	.331	Sept/Oct	.159	63	10	4	0	0	3	4	19	.209	.222
Close & Late	.197	61	12	1	1	1	6	8	17	.286	.295	vs. AL	.258	407	105	24	1	10	49	32	95	.311	.396
None on/out	.248	117	29	10	0	3	3	10	24	.307	.410	vs. NL	.150	40	6	3	0	2	5	3	11	.209	.375

1997 By Position

Position	Avg	AB	H	2B	3B	HR	RBI	BB	SO	OBP	SLG	G	GS	Innings	PO	A	E	DP	Fld Pct	Rng Fctr	In Zone	Zone Outs	Zone Rtg	MLB Zone
As c	.255	436	111	27	1	12	53	35	101	.309	.404	116	112	990.0	654	52	5	4	.993	---	---	---	---	---

444

Last Five Years

	Avg	AB	H	2B	3B	HR	RBI	BB	SO	OBP	SLG		Avg	AB	H	2B	3B	HR	RBI	BB	SO	OBP	SLG
vs. Left	.309	608	188	32	2	31	95	61	115	.372	.521	First Pitch	.340	391	133	28	3	20	74	16	0	.363	.581
vs. Right	.258	1517	392	86	4	52	224	99	307	.306	.423	Ahead in Count	.337	481	162	34	1	32	92	64	0	.417	.611
Groundball	.263	505	133	24	2	16	71	26	100	.301	.414	Behind in Count	.195	906	177	29	2	22	107	0	370	.201	.305
Flyball	.271	417	113	31	3	14	57	29	74	.320	.460	Two Strikes	.187	894	167	29	1	21	103	80	422	.257	.292
Home	.289	1023	296	61	4	41	168	78	222	.341	.477	Batting #5	.266	744	198	37	4	21	98	71	142	.335	.411
Away	.258	1102	284	57	2	42	151	82	200	.310	.427	Batting #6	.263	771	203	40	1	35	124	54	153	.311	.454
Day	.262	766	201	40	2	37	134	60	152	.320	.465	Other	.293	610	179	41	1	27	97	35	127	.330	.497
Night	.279	1359	379	78	4	46	185	100	270	.328	.444	March/April	.278	313	87	21	1	14	52	31	51	.346	.486
Grass	.275	1613	444	85	6	70	249	119	312	.327	.466	May	.275	437	120	33	0	13	62	35	77	.332	.439
Turf	.266	512	136	33	0	13	70	41	110	.321	.406	June	.272	426	116	19	1	18	64	35	96	.325	.448
Pre-All Star	.279	1315	367	79	3	53	204	110	251	.337	.465	July	.304	434	132	17	1	20	66	21	85	.337	.486
Post-All Star	.263	810	213	39	3	30	115	50	171	.307	.430	August	.238	294	70	18	3	11	52	21	62	.293	.432
Scoring Posn	.268	545	146	30	2	28	241	62	117	.337	.484	Sept/Oct	.249	221	55	10	0	7	23	17	51	.304	.389
Close & Late	.238	341	81	11	3	12	55	30	71	.299	.393	vs. AL	.275	2085	574	115	6	81	314	157	411	.327	.453
None on/out	.269	528	142	33	1	21	21	28	94	.307	.455	vs. NL	.150	40	6	3	0	2	5	3	11	.209	.375

Batter vs. Pitcher (career)

Hits Best Against	Avg	AB	H	2B	3B	HR	RBI	BB	SO	OBP	SLG	Hits Worst Against	Avg	AB	H	2B	3B	HR	RBI	BB	SO	OBP	SLG
Mark Guthrie	.545	11	6	0	0	3	13	1	1	.583	1.364	James Baldwin	.000	11	0	0	0	0	0	1	4	.083	.000
Al Leiter	.500	10	5	3	0	1	2	2	3	.583	.800	Mariano Rivera	.077	13	1	0	0	0	0	0	4	.077	.077
Jamie Moyer	.421	19	8	2	0	2	5	2	2	.476	.842	Kevin Gross	.100	10	1	0	0	0	1	1	3	.182	.100
Sterling Hitchcock	.400	10	4	0	0	2	4	1	3	.417	1.000	Alan Mills	.100	10	1	0	0	0	1	1	2	.182	.100
Kevin Tapani	.355	31	11	4	0	4	7	3	4	.412	.871	Mark Clark	.154	13	2	0	0	0	1	0	3	.143	.154

Garrett Stephenson — Phillies
Age 26 – Pitches Right (flyball pitcher)

	ERA	W	L	Sv	G	GS	IP	BB	SO	Avg	H	2B	3B	HR	RBI	OBP	SLG	CG	ShO	Sup	QS	#P/S	SB	CS	GB	FB	G/F
1997 Season	3.15	8	6	0	20	18	117.0	38	81	.244	104	30	3	11	42	.307	.406	2	0	4.15	12	98	2	5	141	146	0.97
Career (1996-1997)	3.65	8	7	0	23	18	123.1	41	84	.257	117	33	3	12	50	.320	.421	2	0	4.23	12	98	3	8	153	155	0.99

1997 Season

	ERA	W	L	Sv	G	GS	IP	H	HR	BB	SO		Avg	AB	H	2B	3B	HR	RBI	BB	SO	OBP	SLG
Home	2.78	6	3	0	12	10	68.0	61	6	21	50	vs. Left	.242	178	43	11	3	6	17	18	33	.315	.438
Away	3.67	2	3	0	8	8	49.0	43	5	17	31	vs. Right	.246	248	61	19	0	5	25	20	48	.302	.383
Starter	3.22	8	6	0	18	18	114.2	103	11	36	81	Scoring Posn	.214	84	18	4	0	4	33	7	17	.260	.405
Reliever	0.00	0	0	0	2	0	2.1	1	0	2	0	Close & Late	.240	25	6	2	0	2	3	2	3	.296	.320
0-3 Days Rest (Start)	1.50	0	0	0	1	1	6.0	4	0	2	7	None on/out	.273	121	33	5	2	6	6	5	28	.307	.496
4 Days Rest	3.52	5	4	0	10	10	64.0	66	6	23	44	First Pitch	.206	68	14	6	0	1	11	0	0	.200	.338
5+ Days Rest	3.02	3	2	0	7	7	44.2	33	5	11	30	Ahead in Count	.250	192	48	12	1	2	12	0	63	.253	.354
Pre-All Star	4.02	2	4	0	9	8	47.0	42	8	18	37	Behind in Count	.259	81	21	4	0	5	11	21	0	.408	.494
Post-All Star	2.57	6	2	0	11	10	70.0	62	3	20	44	Two Strikes	.197	203	40	9	1	4	17	13	81	.260	.310

Dave Stevens — Cubs
Age 28 – Pitches Right (flyball pitcher)

	ERA	W	L	Sv	G	GS	IP	BB	SO	Avg	H	2B	3B	HR	RBI	OBP	SLG	GF	IR	IRS	Hld	SvOp	SB	CS	GB	FB	G/F
1997 Season	9.19	1	5	0	16	6	32.1	26	29	.370	54	15	2	8	31	.466	.664	0	5	3	0	0	10	2	30	51	0.59
Career (1994-1997)	6.00	14	14	21	145	6	201.0	106	129	.298	241	50	8	40	152	.378	.528	78	84	30	6	28	23	9	203	312	0.65

1997 Season

	ERA	W	L	Sv	G	GS	IP	H	HR	BB	SO		Avg	AB	H	2B	3B	HR	RBI	BB	SO	OBP	SLG
Home	11.25	0	3	0	9	3	16.0	31	4	13	15	vs. Left	.356	73	26	7	1	4	12	11	20	.435	.644
Away	7.16	1	2	0	7	3	16.1	23	4	13	14	vs. Right	.384	73	28	8	1	4	19	15	9	.494	.685

Career (1994-1997)

	ERA	W	L	Sv	G	GS	IP	H	HR	BB	SO		Avg	AB	H	2B	3B	HR	RBI	BB	SO	OBP	SLG
Home	7.90	8	8	10	78	3	106.0	142	26	59	70	vs. Left	.316	386	122	27	4	13	67	55	60	.396	.508
Away	3.88	6	6	11	67	3	95.0	99	14	47	59	vs. Right	.282	422	119	23	4	27	85	51	69	.361	.547
Day	5.88	3	6	10	49	4	72.0	90	14	40	46	Inning 1-6	.337	252	85	24	5	10	49	35	39	.416	.591
Night	6.07	11	8	11	96	2	129.0	151	26	66	83	Inning 7+	.281	556	156	26	3	30	103	71	90	.361	.500
Grass	4.12	6	7	7	63	3	91.2	102	12	46	64	None on	.315	397	125	22	1	23	23	50	52	.391	.549
Turf	7.57	8	7	14	82	3	109.1	139	28	60	65	Runners on	.282	411	116	28	7	17	129	56	77	.365	.509
March/April	5.56	1	0	5	11	0	11.1	16	2	6	5	Scoring Posn	.277	271	75	17	5	10	111	36	52	.355	.487
May	5.75	2	0	4	24	0	36.0	39	7	15	24	Close & Late	.278	252	70	14	2	10	49	35	43	.363	.468
June	7.34	3	4	1	24	2	38.0	53	11	17	30	None on/out	.359	184	66	16	0	14	14	22	18	.427	.674
July	6.24	2	3	5	33	4	49.0	52	13	36	28	vs. 1st Batr (relief)	.322	118	38	10	1	7	26	19	17	.410	.602
August	6.68	2	5	4	25	0	31.0	44	5	21	18	1st Inning Pitched	.294	483	142	29	5	23	98	68	82	.379	.518
Sept/Oct	4.04	4	2	2	28	0	35.2	37	2	11	24	First 15 Pitches	.301	372	112	25	4	20	69	51	54	.381	.551
Starter	9.00	1	3	0	6	6	23.0	41	8	17	16	Pitch 16-30	.285	270	77	12	2	12	52	30	47	.359	.478
Reliever	5.61	13	11	21	139	0	178.0	200	32	89	113	Pitch 31-45	.250	92	23	4	1	2	11	11	16	.330	.380
0 Days rest (Relief)	6.12	0	4	8	23	0	25.0	27	3	14	19	Pitch 46+	.392	74	29	9	1	6	20	14	12	.489	.784
1 or 2 Days rest	6.51	7	5	10	63	0	74.2	95	17	40	50	First Pitch	.360	114	41	10	1	8	28	3	0	.376	.675
3+ Days rest	4.60	6	2	3	53	0	78.1	78	12	35	44	Ahead in Count	.254	347	88	13	4	11	48	0	104	.254	.409
vs. AL	5.74	14	14	21	138	6	196.0	234	40	98	118	Behind in Count	.360	189	68	23	2	17	49	53	0	.496	.772
vs. NL	16.20	0	0	0	7	0	5.0	7	0	8	11	Two Strikes	.248	363	90	12	4	10	51	50	159	.338	.386
Pre-All Star	6.29	7	4	12	71	3	101.2	126	23	49	69	Pre-All Star	.307	411	126	23	6	23	84	49	69	.380	.560
Post-All Star	5.71	7	10	9	74	3	99.1	115	17	57	60	Post-All Star	.290	397	115	27	2	17	68	57	60	.376	.496

445

Pitcher vs. Batter (career)

Pitches Best Vs.	Avg	AB	H	2B	3B	HR	RBI	BB	SO	OBP	SLG	Pitches Worst Vs.	Avg	AB	H	2B	3B	HR	RBI	BB	SO	OBP	SLG
Ray Durham	.182	11	2	0	0	1	2	1	3	.250	.455	Frank Thomas	.500	12	6	1	0	0	4	1	1	.538	.583
												Albert Belle	.462	13	6	2	0	1	3	0	0	.462	.846
												Kevin Seitzer	.400	10	4	0	0	0	1	1	0	.455	.400
												Omar Vizquel	.364	11	4	0	0	0	3	1	2	.417	.364

Lee Stevens — Rangers
Age 30 – Bats Left

	Avg	G	AB	R	H	2B	3B	HR	RBI	BB	SO	HBP	GDP	SB	CS	OBP	SLG	IBB	SH	SF	#Pit	#P/PA	GB	FB	G/F
1997 Season	.300	137	426	58	128	24	2	21	74	23	83	1	18	1	3	.336	.514	2	1	3	1501	3.31	168	111	1.51
Last Five Years	.290	164	504	64	146	26	5	24	86	29	105	2	20	1	3	.328	.504	2	1	4	1816	3.36	191	138	1.38

1997 Season

	Avg	AB	H	2B	3B	HR	RBI	BB	SO	OBP	SLG		Avg	AB	H	2B	3B	HR	RBI	BB	SO	OBP	SLG
vs. Left	.284	67	19	4	0	4	12	4	19	.333	.522	First Pitch	.380	92	35	10	0	3	13	2	0	.394	.587
vs. Right	.304	359	109	20	2	17	62	19	64	.336	.513	Ahead in Count	.390	77	30	3	2	7	20	9	0	.453	.753
Groundball	.277	101	28	8	0	3	18	6	23	.315	.446	Behind in Count	.207	203	42	7	0	10	31	0	77	.208	.389
Flyball	.338	74	25	4	1	5	14	8	14	.402	.622	Two Strikes	.188	191	36	5	0	8	25	12	83	.239	.340
Home	.321	218	70	12	1	12	40	8	47	.345	.550	Batting #5	.327	162	53	8	0	9	31	9	23	.366	.543
Away	.279	208	58	12	1	9	34	15	36	.326	.476	Batting #7	.271	133	36	9	1	5	18	9	28	.315	.466
Day	.356	90	32	8	1	5	18	9	19	.406	.633	Other	.298	131	39	7	1	7	25	5	32	.319	.527
Night	.286	336	96	16	1	16	56	14	64	.315	.482	March/April	.278	72	20	2	0	5	18	8	18	.341	.514
Grass	.305	390	119	22	2	20	67	19	74	.338	.526	May	.318	66	21	7	1	2	11	4	13	.352	.545
Turf	.250	36	9	2	0	1	7	4	9	.310	.389	June	.216	37	8	1	0	2	5	2	4	.256	.405
Pre-All Star	.295	193	57	11	2	10	38	14	37	.338	.528	July	.299	67	20	2	1	2	8	3	14	.329	.448
Post-All Star	.305	233	71	13	0	11	36	9	46	.333	.502	August	.299	87	26	4	0	4	10	4	19	.330	.483
Scoring Posn	.318	110	35	7	1	6	53	9	19	.361	.564	Sept/Oct	.340	97	33	8	0	6	22	2	15	.360	.608
Close & Late	.316	57	18	6	0	3	12	5	13	.365	.579	vs. AL	.292	391	114	21	2	19	69	20	77	.325	.501
None on/out	.312	93	29	8	0	5	5	5	19	.347	.559	vs. NL	.400	35	14	3	0	2	5	3	6	.447	.657

1997 By Position

Position	Avg	AB	H	2B	3B	HR	RBI	BB	SO	OBP	SLG	G	GS	Innings	PO	A	E	DP	Fld Pct	Rng Fctr	In Zone	Outs	Zone Rtg	MLB Zone
As DH	.276	127	35	7	1	5	18	4	25	.293	.465	38	33	—	—	—	—	—	—	—	—	—	—	—
As Pinch Hitter	.304	23	7	2	0	1	6	3	5	.385	.522	27	0	—	—	—	—	—	—	—	—	—	—	—
As 1b	.329	213	70	10	0	14	43	12	41	.367	.573	62	54	478.0	455	33	3	45	.994	—	113	94	.832	.874
As rf	.279	61	17	4	0	2	7	4	12	.323	.443	19	18	138.0	27	0	0	0	1.000	1.76	29	27	.931	.813

Andy Stewart — Royals
Age 27 – Bats Right

	Avg	G	AB	R	H	2B	3B	HR	RBI	BB	SO	HBP	GDP	SB	CS	OBP	SLG	IBB	SH	SF	#Pit	#P/PA	GB	FB	G/F
1997 Season	.250	5	8	1	2	1	0	0	0	0	0	0	0	1	0	.250	.375	0	0	0	26	3.25	5	2	2.50

1997 Season

	Avg	AB	H	2B	3B	HR	RBI	BB	SO	OBP	SLG		Avg	AB	H	2B	3B	HR	RBI	BB	SO	OBP	SLG
vs. Left	.333	6	2	1	0	0	0	0	0	.333	.500	Scoring Posn	.000	0	0	0	0	0	0	0	0	.000	.000
vs. Right	.000	2	0	0	0	0	0	0	0	.000	.000	Close & Late	.000	3	0	0	0	0	0	0	0	.000	.000

Shannon Stewart — Blue Jays
Age 24 – Bats Right

	Avg	G	AB	R	H	2B	3B	HR	RBI	BB	SO	HBP	GDP	SB	CS	OBP	SLG	IBB	SH	SF	#Pit	#P/PA	GB	FB	G/F
1997 Season	.286	44	168	25	48	13	7	0	22	19	24	4	3	10	3	.368	.446	1	0	2	722	3.74	67	42	1.60
Career (1995-1997)	.265	63	223	29	59	14	7	0	25	25	33	5	4	13	3	.349	.390	1	0	2	967	3.79	89	56	1.59

1997 Season

	Avg	AB	H	2B	3B	HR	RBI	BB	SO	OBP	SLG		Avg	AB	H	2B	3B	HR	RBI	BB	SO	OBP	SLG
vs. Left	.343	35	12	3	2	0	3	7	8	.452	.543	Scoring Posn	.350	40	14	7	0	0	20	4	4	.391	.525
vs. Right	.271	133	36	10	5	0	19	12	16	.344	.421	Close & Late	.321	28	9	2	0	0	5	4	4	.429	.393
Home	.269	78	21	5	2	0	10	10	12	.352	.385	None on/out	.266	64	17	3	2	0	0	7	14	.356	.375
Away	.300	90	27	8	5	0	12	9	12	.381	.500	Batting #1	.291	165	48	13	7	0	22	18	24	.370	.455
First Pitch	.529	17	9	5	1	0	6	1	0	.600	.941	Batting #4	.000	2	0	0	0	0	0	0	0	.000	.000
Ahead in Count	.333	33	11	3	1	0	7	8	0	.442	.485	Other	.000	1	0	0	0	0	0	1	0	.500	.000
Behind in Count	.223	94	21	3	3	0	7	0	23	.223	.319	Pre-All Star	.000	1	0	0	0	0	0	1	0	.500	.000
Two Strikes	.238	84	20	3	3	0	4	10	24	.326	.345	Post-All Star	.287	167	48	13	7	0	22	18	24	.366	.449

Kelly Stinnett — Brewers
Age 28 – Bats Right

	Avg	G	AB	R	H	2B	3B	HR	RBI	BB	SO	HBP	GDP	SB	CS	OBP	SLG	IBB	SH	SF	#Pit	#P/PA	GB	FB	G/F
1997 Season	.250	30	36	2	9	4	0	0	3	3	9	0	0	0	0	.308	.361	0	0	0	146	3.74	6	15	0.40
Career (1994-1997)	.225	168	408	46	92	18	3	6	35	45	113	4	6	5	4	.320	.328	4	0	1	1799	3.86	128	108	1.19

1997 Season

	Avg	AB	H	2B	3B	HR	RBI	BB	SO	OBP	SLG		Avg	AB	H	2B	3B	HR	RBI	BB	SO	OBP	SLG
vs. Left	.304	23	7	2	0	0	1	2	4	.360	.391	Scoring Posn	.200	10	2	1	0	0	3	1	4	.273	.300
vs. Right	.154	13	2	2	0	0	2	1	5	.214	.308	Close & Late	.167	6	1	0	0	0	1	1	2	.286	.167

Career (1994-1997)

	Avg	AB	H	2B	3B	HR	RBI	BB	SO	OBP	SLG		Avg	AB	H	2B	3B	HR	RBI	BB	SO	OBP	SLG
vs. Left	.228	197	45	7	1	5	20	21	42	.308	.350	First Pitch	.313	67	21	3	1	2	9	2	0	.370	.478
vs. Right	.223	211	47	11	2	1	15	24	71	.331	.308	Ahead in Count	.378	74	28	7	2	3	14	22	0	.520	.649

446

Career (1994-1997)

	Avg	AB	H	2B	3B	HR	RBI	BB	SO	OBP	SLG		Avg	AB	H	2B	3B	HR	RBI	BB	SO	OBP	SLG
Groundball	.278	79	22	4	0	1	9	15	20	.412	.367	Behind in Count	.163	209	34	7	0	1	10	0	98	.218	.211
Flyball	.188	69	13	0	0	1	3	6	24	.260	.232	Two Strikes	.128	218	28	6	0	0	9	21	113	.218	.156
Home	.216	190	41	6	1	1	9	24	55	.315	.274	Batting #2	.267	75	20	4	2	1	8	6	12	.341	.413
Away	.234	218	51	12	2	5	26	21	58	.324	.376	Batting #8	.201	164	33	4	1	2	13	24	53	.321	.274
Day	.220	127	28	4	0	1	10	11	39	.313	.276	Other	.231	169	39	10	0	3	14	15	48	.309	.343
Night	.228	281	64	14	3	5	25	34	74	.323	.352	March/April	.273	33	9	1	0	0	4	4	5	.368	.303
Grass	.233	305	71	12	3	3	23	37	88	.332	.321	May	.235	68	16	2	0	3	5	4	15	.307	.397
Turf	.204	103	21	6	0	3	12	8	25	.281	.350	June	.303	66	20	4	2	0	7	6	18	.373	.424
Pre-All Star	.272	184	50	8	2	4	18	18	42	.354	.402	July	.270	63	17	3	1	1	6	8	15	.370	.397
Post-All Star	.188	224	42	10	1	2	17	27	71	.292	.268	August	.148	115	17	4	0	1	8	14	39	.263	.209
Scoring Posn	.217	92	20	6	2	1	28	20	30	.365	.359	Sept/Oct	.206	63	13	4	0	1	5	9	21	.306	.317
Close & Late	.178	73	13	3	1	0	10	6	24	.268	.247	vs. AL	.172	58	10	4	0	0	3	5	19	.250	.241
None on/out	.221	95	21	1	0	2	2	8	25	.308	.295	vs. NL	.234	350	82	14	3	6	32	40	94	.331	.343

Kevin Stocker — Phillies

Age 28 – Bats Both

	Avg	G	AB	R	H	2B	3B	HR	RBI	BB	SO	HBP	GDP	SB	CS	OBP	SLG	IBB	SH	SF	#Pit	#P/PA	GB	FB	G/F
1997 Season	.266	149	504	51	134	23	5	4	40	51	91	2	13	11	6	.335	.355	7	2	1	2039	3.64	181	132	1.37
Career (1993-1997)	.262	545	1840	223	482	82	19	14	172	211	339	34	37	30	13	.347	.350	44	23	13	7798	3.68	662	453	1.46

1997 Season

	Avg	AB	H	2B	3B	HR	RBI	BB	SO	OBP	SLG		Avg	AB	H	2B	3B	HR	RBI	BB	SO	OBP	SLG
vs. Left	.297	111	33	5	2	1	11	12	13	.376	.405	First Pitch	.374	91	34	9	1	1	14	3	0	.389	.527
vs. Right	.257	393	101	18	3	3	29	39	78	.323	.341	Ahead in Count	.321	106	34	4	1	3	13	31	0	.478	.462
Groundball	.286	84	24	5	2	2	13	11	17	.368	.464	Behind in Count	.196	219	43	5	1	0	6	0	81	.196	.228
Flyball	.226	84	19	4	1	0	5	4	17	.261	.298	Two Strikes	.184	217	40	6	1	0	8	17	91	.247	.221
Home	.305	233	71	14	4	2	21	34	36	.396	.425	Batting #2	.270	37	10	2	0	0	3	2	9	.308	.324
Away	.232	271	63	9	1	2	19	17	55	.298	.295	Batting #8	.275	436	120	21	5	4	37	48	73	.349	.374
Day	.327	162	53	10	0	1	12	12	25	.371	.407	Other	.129	31	4	0	0	0	0	1	9	.156	.129
Night	.237	342	81	13	5	3	28	39	66	.319	.330	March/April	.277	83	23	6	0	0		9	17	.348	.349
Grass	.236	199	47	7	0	2	15	11	47	.276	.302	May	.212	99	21	6	1	0		7	13	.264	.293
Turf	.285	305	87	16	5	2	25	40	44	.371	.390	June	.244	78	19	1	2	0	3	8	20	.322	.308
Pre-All Star	.250	280	70	14	3	1	18	27	52	.318	.332	July	.341	85	29	4	1	3	10	12	16	.423	.518
Post-All Star	.286	224	64	9	2	3	22	24	39	.356	.384	August	.258	93	24	4	0	0	6	10	12	.337	.301
Scoring Posn	.246	118	29	7	1	2	37	23	21	.371	.373	Sept/Oct	.273	66	18	2	1	1	9	5	13	.319	.379
Close & Late	.280	75	21	3	1	0	6	10	13	.365	.347	vs. AL	.256	43	11	2	1		5	2	10	.304	.442
None on/out	.353	102	36	9	2	1	1	7	11	.400	.510	vs. NL	.267	461	123	22	3	3	35	49	81	.338	.347

1997 By Position

Position	Avg	AB	H	2B	3B	HR	RBI	BB	SO	OBP	SLG	G	GS	Innings	PO	A	E	DP	Fld Pct	Rng Fctr	In Zone	Zone Outs	Zone Rtg	MLB Zone
As ss	.267	502	134	23	5	4	40	51	91	.336	.357	147	146	1262.1	191	375	11	75	.981	4.04	422	389	.922	.937

Career (1993-1997)

	Avg	AB	H	2B	3B	HR	RBI	BB	SO	OBP	SLG		Avg	AB	H	2B	3B	HR	RBI	BB	SO	OBP	SLG
vs. Left	.288	438	126	24	3	2	36	46	67	.361	.370	First Pitch	.341	302	103	19	4	2	42	34	0	.408	.450
vs. Right	.254	1402	356	58	16	12	136	165	272	.342	.344	Ahead in Count	.330	385	127	14	6	5	44	102	0	.474	.436
Groundball	.242	454	110	18	4	6	51	61	84	.343	.339	Behind in Count	.182	807	147	24	4	1	45	0	304	.199	.226
Flyball	.243	300	73	15	4	0	32	29	70	.313	.320	Two Strikes	.182	828	151	30	3	5	52	75	339	.259	.244
Home	.269	905	243	48	11	6	89	117	155	.360	.366	Batting #2	.310	142	44	12	3	2	14	9	30	.359	.479
Away	.256	935	239	34	8	8	83	94	184	.333	.335	Batting #8	.262	1618	424	69	16	12	156	194	293	.350	.347
Day	.293	552	162	28	6	6	46	59	87	.365	.393	Other	.175	80	14	1	0	0	2	8	16	.256	.188
Night	.248	1288	320	54	13	9	126	152	252	.339	.332	March/April	.252	226	57	8	1	3	28	36	45	.374	.336
Grass	.258	625	161	21	4	8	60	62	136	.332	.342	May	.198	247	49	9	2	0	19	22	47	.266	.251
Turf	.264	1215	321	61	15	6	112	149	203	.354	.354	June	.235	243	57	9	2	0	17	35	50	.335	.288
Pre-All Star	.237	841	199	29	6	5	74	107	166	.331	.303	July	.300	380	114	13	4	6	41	48	68	.384	.403
Post-All Star	.283	999	283	53	13	9	98	104	173	.360	.389	August	.262	413	108	22	5	4	38	40	64	.340	.368
Scoring Posn	.226	455	103	16	7	4	153	99	82	.370	.319	Sept/Oct	.293	331	97	21	5	1	29	30	65	.359	.396
Close & Late	.289	322	93	18	4	1	31	41	65	.378	.379	vs. AL	.256	43	11	2	1		5	2	10	.304	.442
None on/out	.310	429	133	28	3	3	43	75	383	.420	.348	vs. NL	.262	1797	471	81	17	13	167	209	329	.347	.348

Batter vs. Pitcher (career)

Hits Best Against	Avg	AB	H	2B	3B	HR	RBI	BB	SO	OBP	SLG	Hits Worst Against	Avg	AB	H	2B	3B	HR	RBI	BB	SO	OBP	SLG
Pete Harnisch	.583	12	7	1	0	0	6	0	0	.538	.667	Kevin Brown	.000	12	0	0	0	0	0	1	4	.143	.000
Doug Brocail	.500	10	5	2	0	0	1	0	1	.545	.700	Armando Reynoso	.000	11	0	0	0	0	0	1	3	.214	.000
Denny Neagle	.462	13	6	1	0	0	5	3	4	.563	.538	Todd Worrell	.000	10	0	0	0	0	0	1	4	.091	.000
Steve Cooke	.429	14	6	1	0	1	1	2	0	.500	.714	Andy Benes	.042	24	1	0	0	0	0	1	6	.080	.042
Andy Ashby	.333	15	5	1	0	1	4	6	1	.545	.600	Greg Maddux	.087	23	2	0	0	0	0		5	.125	.087

Todd Stottlemyre — Cardinals

Age 33 – Pitches Right

	ERA	W	L	Sv	G	GS	IP	BB	SO	Avg	H	2B	3B	HR	RBI	OBP	SLG	CG	ShO	Sup	QS	#P/S	SB	CS	GB	FB	G/F
1997 Season	3.88	12	9	0	28	28	181.0	65	160	.231	155	30	3	16	81	.308	.356	0	0	4.52	17	102	18	7	226	175	1.29
Last Five Years	4.26	58	46	1	149	139	931.1	355	762	.260	927	179	21	102	438	.330	.408	11	4	5.25	73	105	109	44	1171	1013	1.16

1997 Season

	ERA	W	L	Sv	G	GS	IP	H	HR	BB	SO		Avg	AB	H	2B	3B	HR	RBI	BB	SO	OBP	SLG
Home	4.89	4	5	0	11	11	70.0	64	9	28	67	vs. Left	.267	359	96	18	2	11	51	46	67	.354	.421
Away	3.24	8	4	0	17	17	111.0	91	7	37	93	vs. Right	.189	312	59	12	1	5	30	19	93	.253	.282

1997 Season

	ERA	W	L	Sv	G	GS	IP	H	HR	BB	SO		Avg	AB	H	2B	3B	HR	RBI	BB	SO	OBP	SLG
Day	3.64	5	4	0	12	12	84.0	59	7	32	74	Inning 1-6	.220	583	128	27	2	12	70	55	142	.298	.334
Night	4.08	7	5	0	16	16	97.0	96	9	33	86	Inning 7+	.307	88	27	3	1	4	11	10	18	.374	.500
Grass	4.39	7	8	0	20	20	131.1	116	13	49	122	None on	.226	403	91	16	1	7	7	31	98	.291	.323
Turf	2.54	5	1	0	8	8	49.2	39	3	16	38	Runners on	.239	268	64	14	2	9	74	34	62	.332	.407
March/April	4.06	1	0	0	6	6	37.2	35	1	13	23	Scoring Posn	.319	135	43	9	2	6	64	24	29	.419	.548
May	3.83	4	2	0	6	6	42.1	32	7	11	46	Close & Late	.333	51	17	1	1	1	5	6	8	.404	.451
June	4.97	2	2	0	5	5	29.0	27	2	11	21	None on/out	.219	178	39	10	0	5	5	14	42	.276	.360
July	2.97	4	2	0	6	6	39.1	30	5	15	44	vs. 1st Batr (relief)	.000	0	0	0	0	0	0	0	0	.000	.000
August	3.86	2	2	0	5	5	32.2	31	1	15	26	1st Inning Pitched	.301	113	34	10	0	4	26	11	23	.382	.496
Sept/Oct	0.00	0	0	0	0	0	0.0	0	0	0	0	First 75 Pitches	.218	478	104	21	1	11	56	45	115	.297	.335
Starter	3.88	12	9	0	28	28	181.0	155	16	65	160	Pitch 76-90	.271	96	26	6	0	0	9	6	24	.317	.333
Reliever	0.00	0	0	0	0	0	0.0	0	0	0	0	Pitch 91-105	.239	67	16	1	1	4	10	7	15	.320	.463
0-3 Days Rest (Start)	0.00	0	0	0	0	0	0.0	0	0	0	0	Pitch 106+	.300	30	9	2	1	1	6	7	6	.421	.533
4 Days Rest	3.66	7	8	0	18	18	118.0	95	10	44	113	First Pitch	.323	93	30	6	0	0	6	3	0	.364	.387
5+ Days Rest	4.29	5	1	0	10	10	63.0	60	6	21	47	Ahead in Count	.167	293	49	6	1	7	28	0	133	.187	.266
vs. AL	2.40	1	1	0	2	2	15.0	8	0	3	18	Behind in Count	.318	151	48	11	0	5	23	33	0	.434	.490
vs. NL	4.01	11	8	0	26	26	166.0	147	16	62	142	Two Strikes	.136	317	43	8	1	5	26	29	160	.217	.215
Pre-All Star	3.95	7	6	0	19	19	123.0	103	11	39	108	Pre-All Star	.227	454	103	18	3	11	54	39	108	.296	.352
Post-All Star	3.72	5	3	0	9	9	58.0	52	5	26	52	Post-All Star	.240	217	52	12	0	5	27	26	52	.333	.364

Last Five Years

	ERA	W	L	Sv	G	GS	IP	H	HR	BB	SO		Avg	AB	H	2B	3B	HR	RBI	BB	SO	OBP	SLG
Home	4.11	26	25	1	74	69	477.0	443	48	185	414	vs. Left	.276	1863	515	104	10	54	223	228	371	.356	.430
Away	4.42	32	21	0	75	70	454.1	484	47	170	348	vs. Right	.243	1698	412	75	11	48	215	127	391	.301	.385
Day	3.78	24	16	0	53	50	348.0	316	31	137	284	Inning 1-6	.262	3001	785	150	18	88	376	301	635	.332	.412
Night	4.55	34	30	1	96	89	583.1	611	71	218	478	Inning 7+	.254	560	142	29	3	14	62	54	127	.320	.391
Grass	4.39	37	31	0	99	93	619.2	622	66	251	535	None on	.263	2077	547	110	16	55	55	168	450	.324	.411
Turf	4.01	21	15	1	50	46	311.2	305	36	104	227	Runners on	.256	1484	380	69	5	47	383	187	312	.338	.404
March/April	4.76	7	5	1	26	19	130.1	132	11	51	78	Scoring Posn	.266	868	231	44	4	31	336	137	186	.358	.433
May	4.00	12	8	0	27	27	175.1	172	24	73	177	Close & Late	.275	287	79	18	1	5	35	33	57	.348	.397
June	3.64	10	9	0	25	23	163.0	140	19	56	145	None on/out	.269	931	250	50	10	30	30	65	199	.319	.440
July	4.08	9	9	0	27	27	181.0	185	21	61	144	vs. 1st Batr (relief)	.200	10	2	0	0	0	1	0	1	.200	.200
August	5.06	14	9	0	26	26	163.2	187	19	73	109	1st Inning Pitched	.257	572	147	28	5	28	99	70	142	.344	.470
Sept/Oct	4.12	8	6	0	18	17	118.0	111	8	41	109	First 75 Pitches	.258	2437	628	118	16	68	297	237	533	.326	.403
Starter	4.31	56	46	0	139	139	912.0	915	102	349	746	Pitch 76-90	.273	473	129	28	2	11	56	41	90	.332	.410
Reliever	1.86	2	0	2	10	0	19.1	12	0	6	16	Pitch 91-105	.279	384	107	19	2	12	48	44	75	.355	.432
0-3 Days Rest (Start)	3.86	0	1	0	2	2	11.2	14	2	7	7	Pitch 106+	.236	267	63	14	1	11	37	33	64	.323	.419
4 Days Rest	4.16	34	30	0	86	86	572.2	579	66	208	467	First Pitch	.352	511	180	28	3	22	86	19	0	.377	.548
5+ Days Rest	4.59	22	15	0	51	51	327.2	322	34	134	272	Ahead in Count	.197	1523	300	47	6	26	137	0	612	.206	.287
vs. AL	4.50	33	27	1	89	80	542.0	589	56	200	426	Behind in Count	.340	792	269	63	3	35	127	172	0	.454	.559
vs. NL	3.93	25	19	0	60	59	389.1	338	46	155	336	Two Strikes	.164	1601	263	43	6	23	120	163	762	.246	.242
Pre-All Star	4.04	32	27	1	87	78	533.0	502	60	198	454	Pre-All Star	.248	2021	502	104	12	60	245	198	454	.319	.401
Post-All Star	4.56	26	19	0	62	61	398.1	425	42	157	308	Post-All Star	.276	1540	425	75	9	42	193	157	308	.344	.418

Pitcher vs. Batter (career)

Pitches Best Vs.	Avg	AB	H	2B	3B	HR	RBI	BB	SO	OBP	SLG	Pitches Worst Vs.	Avg	AB	H	2B	3B	HR	RBI	BB	SO	OBP	SLG
Joe Carter	.000	14	0	0	0	0	0	0	4	.000	.000	Chipper Jones	.500	14	7	1	0	3	7	4	1	.611	1.214
Bobby Bonilla	.000	10	0	0	0	0	0	1	1	.091	.000	Jeff Bagwell	.429	14	6	0	0	2	2	7	2	.667	.857
Dante Bichette	.071	14	1	0	0	0	0	1	4	.071	.071	John Valentin	.423	26	11	1	1	3	6	2	2	.464	.885
Gary DiSarcina	.083	24	2	0	0	0	1	0	0	.083	.083	Marquis Grissom	.364	11	4	0	0	3	3	1	2	.417	1.182
Eric Karros	.083	12	1	0	0	0	1	1	4	.143	.083	Jose Canseco	.306	36	11	0	0	8	15	4	12	.390	.972

Doug Strange — Expos

Age 34 – Bats Both

	Avg	G	AB	R	H	2B	3B	HR	RBI	BB	SO	HBP	GDP	SB	CS	OBP	SLG	IBB	SH	SF	#Pit	#P/PA	GB	FB	G/F
1997 Season	.257	118	327	40	84	16	2	12	47	36	76	2	4	0	2	.332	.428	9	5	2	1217	3.27	112	90	1.24
Last Five Years	.248	498	1375	162	341	73	6	29	177	118	239	11	28	8	12	.310	.373	12	18	10	5146	3.36	513	388	1.32

1997 Season

	Avg	AB	H	2B	3B	HR	RBI	BB	SO	OBP	SLG		Avg	AB	H	2B	3B	HR	RBI	BB	SO	OBP	SLG
vs. Left	.250	112	28	4	0	0	8	8	21	.300	.286	First Pitch	.329	73	24	5	0	1	7	6	0	.395	.438
vs. Right	.260	215	56	12	2	12	39	28	55	.348	.502	Ahead in Count	.383	60	23	3	0	7	19	15	0	.500	.783
Groundball	.246	65	16	4	0	6	17	10	19	.351	.585	Behind in Count	.137	146	20	5	1	1	9	0	72	.136	.205
Flyball	.163	43	7	1	0	1	2	4	15	.234	.256	Two Strikes	.114	140	16	2	1	1	7	14	76	.194	.164
Home	.268	190	51	10	2	6	26	20	43	.341	.437	Batting #7	.264	110	29	5	1	6	24	7	21	.311	.491
Away	.241	137	33	6	0	6	21	16	33	.321	.416	Batting #8	.239	155	37	9	0	5	16	23	36	.341	.394
Day	.221	104	23	5	0	4	14	8	24	.281	.385	Other	.290	62	18	2	1	1	7	6	19	.348	.403
Night	.274	223	61	11	2	8	33	28	52	.356	.448	March/April	.333	27	9	3	0	1	4	3	4	.419	.556
Grass	.263	95	25	3	0	6	16	9	26	.321	.484	May	.350	80	28	5	0	3	19	6	19	.391	.525
Turf	.254	232	59	13	2	6	31	27	50	.337	.405	June	.200	40	8	1	0	0	0	1	14	.220	.225
Pre-All Star	.296	162	48	9	0	4	23	11	42	.343	.426	July	.182	66	12	4	1	1	7	9	14	.286	.318
Post-All Star	.218	165	36	7	2	8	24	25	34	.323	.430	August	.216	74	16	2	0	5	9	9	17	.301	.446
Scoring Posn	.305	82	25	4	2	3	33	18	19	.427	.512	Sept/Oct	.275	40	11	1	1	2	8	8	8	.396	.500
Close & Late	.242	66	16	2	2	3	12	6	17	.311	.470	vs. AL	.269	26	7	1	0	1	3	3	7	.345	.423
None on/out	.242	95	23	4	0	2	2	6	24	.287	.347	vs. NL	.256	301	77	15	2	11	46	33	69	.331	.429

1997 By Position

Position	Avg	AB	H	2B	3B	HR	RBI	BB	SO	OBP	SLG	G	GS	Innings	PO	A	E	DP	Fld Pct	Rng Fctr	In Zone	Zone Outs	Zone Rtg	MLB Zone
As 3b	.249	313	78	16	1	12	44	34	73	.325	.422	105	88	803.1	62	171	13	13	.947	2.61	243	196	.807	.801

Last Five Years

	Avg	AB	H	2B	3B	HR	RBI	BB	SO	OBP	SLG		Avg	AB	H	2B	3B	HR	RBI	BB	SO	OBP	SLG
vs. Left	.222	275	61	13	0	0	23	17	46	.264	.269	First Pitch	.315	289	91	19	1	7	44	9	0	.342	.460
vs. Right	.255	1100	280	60	6	29	154	101	193	.322	.399	Ahead in Count	.331	284	94	22	1	14	67	54	0	.435	.563
Groundball	.244	295	72	18	0	9	42	32	56	.325	.397	Behind in Count	.172	583	100	21	2	2	37	0	215	.179	.225
Flyball	.269	245	66	13	2	5	42	14	42	.315	.400	Two Strikes	.130	546	71	13	2	2	27	54	239	.212	.172
Home	.265	697	185	39	3	16	97	64	120	.333	.399	Batting #7	.233	437	102	23	1	9	57	31	69	.289	.352
Away	.230	678	156	34	3	13	80	54	119	.287	.347	Batting #8	.260	442	115	24	2	9	52	54	78	.339	.385
Day	.193	384	74	15	1	8	44	28	74	.249	.299	Other	.250	496	124	26	3	11	68	33	92	.303	.381
Night	.269	991	267	58	5	21	133	90	165	.334	.402	March/April	.263	156	41	7	1	7	28	9	29	.306	.455
Grass	.253	862	218	50	3	18	112	72	143	.313	.381	May	.273	282	77	18	1	4	38	19	47	.327	.387
Turf	.240	513	123	23	3	11	65	46	96	.306	.361	June	.252	258	65	12	1	3	26	19	45	.307	.341
Pre-All Star	.257	756	194	40	3	14	95	55	136	.312	.373	July	.215	256	55	13	1	2	31	28	39	.297	.297
Post-All Star	.237	619	147	33	3	15	82	63	103	.309	.373	August	.213	267	57	12	1	9	30	23	54	.274	.367
Scoring Posn	.260	369	96	24	3	9	142	50	70	.345	.415	Sept/Oct	.295	156	46	11	1	4	24	20	25	.375	.455
Close & Late	.273	278	76	11	5	7	45	24	56	.333	.424	vs. AL	.246	1074	264	58	4	18	131	85	170	.304	.358
None on/out	.267	330	88	16	0	6	6	20	57	.314	.370	vs. NL	.256	301	77	15	2	11	46	33	69	.331	.429

Batter vs. Pitcher (career)

Hits Best Against	Avg	AB	H	2B	3B	HR	RBI	BB	SO	OBP	SLG	Hits Worst Against	Avg	AB	H	2B	3B	HR	RBI	BB	SO	OBP	SLG
Mark Clark	.500	12	6	0	0	1	3	2	0	.571	.750	Alex Fernandez	.050	20	1	0	0	0	0	0	2	.050	.050
Pat Hentgen	.467	15	7	0	0	0	5	1	1	.500	.467	David Cone	.154	13	2	1	0	0	1	1	1	.214	.231
Ben McDonald	.357	14	5	3	0	0	1	0	1	.357	.571	Kevin Tapani	.167	12	2	0	0	1	0	5	.167	.167
Todd Stottlemyre	.333	12	4	0	0	0	1	5	1	.529	.333	Jack McDowell	.176	17	3	1	0	2	1	2	.222	.235
Mike Mussina	.333	12	4	1	0	1	1	0	3	.333	.667	Al Leiter	.182	11	2	1	0	1	0	1	.182	.273

Darryl Strawberry — Yankees
Age 36 – Bats Left (flyball hitter)

	Avg	G	AB	R	H	2B	3B	HR	RBI	BB	SO	HBP	GDP	SB	CS	OBP	SLG	IBB	SH	SF	#Pit	#P/PA	GB	FB	G/F
1997 Season	.103	11	29	1	3	1	0	0	2	3	9	0	2	0	0	.188	.138	0	0	0	139	4.34	9	8	1.13
Last Five Years	.227	167	510	76	116	23	2	23	80	79	127	5	7	7	8	.333	.416	11	0	7	2381	3.96	154	161	0.96

1997 Season

	Avg	AB	H	2B	3B	HR	RBI	BB	SO	OBP	SLG		Avg	AB	H	2B	3B	HR	RBI	BB	SO	OBP	SLG
vs. Left	.000	7	0	0	0	0	0	1	5	.125	.000	Scoring Posn	.100	10	1	1	0	0	2	2	3	.250	.200
vs. Right	.136	22	3	1	0	0	2	2	4	.208	.182	Close & Late	.200	5	1	0	0	0	0	2	0	.429	.200

Last Five Years

	Avg	AB	H	2B	3B	HR	RBI	BB	SO	OBP	SLG		Avg	AB	H	2B	3B	HR	RBI	BB	SO	OBP	SLG
vs. Left	.180	122	22	4	0	5	13	23	37	.308	.336	First Pitch	.321	53	17	1	1	4	13	9	0	.415	.604
vs. Right	.242	388	94	19	2	18	67	56	90	.341	.441	Ahead in Count	.300	120	36	9	0	6	24	36	0	.456	.525
Groundball	.193	166	32	7	0	4	21	17	44	.273	.294	Behind in Count	.148	223	33	7	0	5	23	0	97	.162	.247
Flyball	.202	89	18	3	1	3	19	11	23	.294	.360	Two Strikes	.140	257	36	11	0	10	27	34	127	.251	.300
Home	.260	227	59	11	0	16	44	32	54	.350	.520	Batting #4	.190	105	20	5	0	5	18	22	21	.338	.381
Away	.201	283	57	12	2	7	36	47	73	.319	.332	Batting #5	.255	157	40	8	1	7	26	23	43	.350	.452
Day	.220	191	42	11	0	7	27	33	54	.335	.387	Other	.226	248	56	10	1	11	36	34	63	.319	.407
Night	.232	319	74	12	2	16	53	46	73	.332	.433	March/April	.125	80	10	2	0	3	8	16	10	.273	.263
Grass	.220	431	95	18	1	20	64	73	104	.333	.406	May	.083	12	1	0	0	1	2	0	3	.083	.333
Turf	.266	79	21	5	1	3	16	6	23	.330	.468	June	.136	22	3	0	0	1	2	2	8	.240	.273
Pre-All Star	.116	129	15	2	0	5	12	20	24	.242	.248	July	.263	133	35	7	0	7	28	25	34	.379	.474
Post-All Star	.265	381	101	21	2	18	68	59	103	.364	.472	August	.265	189	50	9	2	8	27	25	49	.353	.460
Scoring Posn	.238	126	30	6	0	7	56	36	32	.394	.452	Sept/Oct	.230	74	17	5	0	3	13	11	23	.326	.419
Close & Late	.181	72	13	3	0	1	5	18	18	.352	.264	vs. AL	.254	315	80	18	1	14	51	44	84	.348	.451
None on/out	.246	114	28	5	0	4	4	14	27	.333	.395	vs. NL	.185	195	36	5	1	9	29	35	43	.309	.359

Batter vs. Pitcher (since 1984)

Hits Best Against	Avg	AB	H	2B	3B	HR	RBI	BB	SO	OBP	SLG	Hits Worst Against	Avg	AB	H	2B	3B	HR	RBI	BB	SO	OBP	SLG
Mark Portugal	.421	19	8	1	0	3	6	3	7	.500	.947	Mitch Williams	.000	12	0	0	0	0	0	2	7	.143	.000
Tim Wakefield	.385	13	5	0	0	2	6	0	1	.385	.846	Mike Stanton	.000	11	0	0	0	0	0	2	4	.154	.000
Tommy Greene	.375	8	3	0	0	1	2	3	1	.545	.750	Danny Jackson	.056	18	1	0	0	0	1	4	6	.227	.056
Pete Smith	.357	14	5	0	0	3	4	5	3	.526	1.000	Ramon Martinez	.067	15	1	0	0	0	1	0	4	.067	.067
Dennis Cook	.333	9	3	0	0	0	3	4	0	.538	.667	Steve Avery	.118	17	2	0	0	0	0	1	3	.167	.118

Everett Stull — Expos
Age 26 – Pitches Right

	ERA	W	L	Sv	G	GS	IP	BB	SO	Avg	H	2B	3B	HR	RBI	OBP	SLG	GF	IR	IRS	Hld	SvOp	SB	CS	GB	FB	G/F
1997 Season	16.20	0	1	0	3	0	3.1	4	2	.438	7	3	0	1	7	.550	.813	1	0	0	0	0	1	0	3	8	0.38

1997 Season

	ERA	W	L	Sv	G	GS	IP	H	HR	BB	SO		Avg	AB	H	2B	3B	HR	RBI	BB	SO	OBP	SLG
Home	0.00	0	0	0	0	0	0.0	0	0	0	0	vs. Left	.500	8	4	2	0	0	2	2	1	.600	.750
Away	16.20	0	1	0	3	0	3.1	7	1	4	2	vs. Right	.375	8	3	1	0	1	5	2	1	.500	.875

Tanyon Sturtze — Rangers

Age 27 – Pitches Right (flyball pitcher)

	ERA	W	L	Sv	G	GS	IP	BB	SO	Avg	H	2B	3B	HR	RBI	OBP	SLG	CG	ShO	Sup	QS	#P/S	SB	CS	GB	FB	G/F
1997 Season	8.27	1	1	0	9	5	32.2	18	18	.338	45	8	2	6	27	.406	.564	0	0	5.51	0	87	0	1	38	50	0.76
Career (1995-1997)	8.47	2	1	0	17	5	45.2	24	25	.337	63	11	2	10	40	.405	.578	0	0	4.93	0	87	0	1	52	67	0.78

1997 Season

	ERA	W	L	Sv	G	GS	IP	H	HR	BB	SO		Avg	AB	H	2B	3B	HR	RBI	BB	SO	OBP	SLG
Home	10.69	0	1	0	6	2	16.0	27	3	11	8	vs. Left	.328	64	21	3	0	2	15	13	11	.430	.469
Away	5.94	1	0	0	3	3	16.2	18	3	7	10	vs. Right	.348	69	24	5	2	4	12	5	7	.382	.652

Chris Stynes — Reds

Age 25 – Bats Right

	Avg	G	AB	R	H	2B	3B	HR	RBI	BB	SO	HBP	GDP	SB	CS	OBP	SLG	IBB	SH	SF	#Pit	#P/PA	GB	FB	G/F
1997 Season	.348	49	198	31	69	7	1	6	28	11	13	4	5	11	2	.394	.485	1	2	0	691	3.21	96	52	1.85
Career (1995-1997)	.314	107	325	46	102	14	1	6	36	17	21	4	8	16	4	.355	.418	1	3	0	1120	3.21	162	85	1.91

1997 Season

	Avg	AB	H	2B	3B	HR	RBI	BB	SO	OBP	SLG		Avg	AB	H	2B	3B	HR	RBI	BB	SO	OBP	SLG
vs. Left	.195	41	8	0	0	1	6	3	4	.250	.268	Scoring Posn	.388	49	19	1	0	2	22	5	4	.444	.531
vs. Right	.389	157	61	7	1	5	22	8	9	.432	.541	Close & Late	.286	28	8	1	0	1	7	1	2	.310	.429
Home	.347	75	26	2	1	2	9	5	5	.388	.480	None on/out	.192	26	5	0	0	0	0	3		.192	.192
Away	.350	123	43	5	0	4	19	6	8	.398	.488	Batting #2	.636	11	7	0	0	1	1	0	1	.636	.909
First Pitch	.367	30	11	0	0	1	4	1	0	.406	.467	Batting #3	.332	187	62	7	1	5	27	11	12	.381	.460
Ahead in Count	.364	55	20	0	2	6	5	0		.426	.509	Other	.000	0	0	0	0	0	0	0	0	.000	.000
Behind in Count	.291	79	23	4	0	2	11	0	13	.309	.418	Pre-All Star	.000	0	0	0	0	0	0	0	0	.000	.000
Two Strikes	.323	62	20	3	0	3	11	5	13	.391	.516	Post-All Star	.348	198	69	7	1	6	28	11	13	.394	.485

Scott Sullivan — Reds

Age 27 – Pitches Right

	ERA	W	L	Sv	G	GS	IP	BB	SO	Avg	H	2B	3B	HR	RBI	OBP	SLG	GF	IR	IRS	Hld	SvOp	SB	CS	GB	FB	G/F
1997 Season	3.24	5	3	1	59	0	97.1	30	96	.220	79	16	2	12	45	.291	.376	15	39	16	13	2	10	0	104	106	0.98
Career (1995-1997)	3.22	5	3	1	69	0	109.0	37	101	.224	90	16	2	12	47	.301	.364	20	42	16	13	2	10	0	121	117	1.03

1997 Season

	ERA	W	L	Sv	G	GS	IP	H	HR	BB	SO		Avg	AB	H	2B	3B	HR	RBI	BB	SO	OBP	SLG
Home	3.51	3	0	1	32	0	51.1	44	5	17	54	vs. Left	.243	152	37	8	0	7	20	17	27	.324	.434
Away	2.93	2	3	0	27	0	46.0	35	7	13	42	vs. Right	.203	207	42	8	2	5	25	13	69	.265	.333
Day	5.18	1	2	1	20	0	33.0	35	6	10	40	Inning 1-6	.256	117	30	2	0	6	21	9	35	.315	.427
Night	2.24	4	1	0	39	0	64.1	44	6	20	56	Inning 7+	.202	242	49	14	2	6	24	21	61	.279	.351
Grass	3.31	2	2	0	20	0	32.2	24	7	6	32	None on	.201	219	44	11	1	9	9	17	58	.265	.384
Turf	3.20	3	1	1	39	0	64.2	55	5	24	64	Runners on	.250	140	35	5	1	3	36	13	38	.329	.364
March/April	13.50	0	0	0	1	0	0.2	2	0	1	0	Scoring Posn	.245	98	24	3	0	2	31	11	31	.336	.337
May	3.46	0	1	0	7	0	13.0	11	0	7	15	Close & Late	.206	102	21	5	0	2	11	8	19	.274	.314
June	2.63	1	1	0	14	0	24.0	21	2	7	21	None on/out	.170	88	15	4	1	4	4	6	26	.223	.375
July	1.77	0	1	1	13	0	20.1	12	3	5	19	vs. 1st Batr (relief)	.196	56	11	1	1	1	6	3	16	.237	.304
August	4.15	0	0	0	14	0	21.2	21	5	7	26	1st Inning Pitched	.203	192	39	6	1	5	24	15	60	.279	.323
Sept/Oct	4.08	4	0	0	10	0	17.2	12	2	3	15	First 15 Pitches	.213	164	35	3	2	4	18	10	47	.274	.329
Starter	0.00	0	0	0	0	0	0.0	0	0	0	0	Pitch 16-30	.244	131	32	10	0	5	19	17	35	.342	.435
Reliever	3.24	5	3	1	59	0	97.1	79	12	30	96	Pitch 31-45	.180	50	9	2	0	2	5	1	11	.192	.340
0 Days rest (Relief)	2.43	2	1	0	17	0	29.2	19	3	9	32	Pitch 46+	.214	14	3	1	0	1	3	2	3	.313	.500
1 or 2 Days rest	3.70	2	2	1	30	0	48.2	45	5	15	41	First Pitch	.205	39	8	0	0	1	3	8	0	.340	.282
3+ Days rest	3.32	1	0	0	12	0	19.0	15	4	6	23	Ahead in Count	.184	207	38	10	0	8	23	0	86	.206	.348
vs. AL	2.13	0	0	1	9	0	12.2	11	1	2	16	Behind in Count	.397	58	23	6	2	2	14	10	0	.478	.672
vs. NL	3.40	5	3	0	50	0	84.2	68	11	28	80	Two Strikes	.156	192	30	7	0	6	16	12	96	.217	.286
Pre-All Star	2.89	1	2	1	25	0	43.2	37	2	16	40	Pre-All Star	.234	158	37	7	1	2	17	16	40	.311	.329
Post-All Star	3.52	4	1	0	34	0	53.2	42	10	14	56	Post-All Star	.209	201	42	9	1	10	28	14	56	.274	.413

Jeff Suppan — Red Sox

Age 23 – Pitches Right

	ERA	W	L	Sv	G	GS	IP	BB	SO	Avg	H	2B	3B	HR	RBI	OBP	SLG	CG	ShO	Sup	QS	#P/S	SB	CS	GB	FB	G/F
1997 Season	5.69	7	3	0	23	22	112.1	36	67	.305	140	28	0	12	62	.358	.444	0	0	5.69	9	83	25	3	162	140	1.16
Career (1995-1997)	5.99	9	6	0	39	29	157.2	54	99	.309	198	42	2	19	95	.363	.470	0	0	5.31	10	85	33	4	218	190	1.15

1997 Season

	ERA	W	L	Sv	G	GS	IP	H	HR	BB	SO		Avg	AB	H	2B	3B	HR	RBI	BB	SO	OBP	SLG
Home	4.87	4	2	0	11	11	57.1	60	4	23	34	vs. Left	.280	232	65	15	0	8	40	21	32	.337	.448
Away	6.55	3	1	0	12	11	55.0	80	8	13	33	vs. Right	.330	227	75	13	0	4	22	15	35	.379	.441
Starter	5.50	7	3	0	22	22	111.1	137	12	36	67	Scoring Posn	.303	119	36	6	0	5	51	11	18	.356	.479
Reliever	27.00	0	0	0	1	0	1.0	3	0	0	0	Close & Late	.240	25	6	0	0	0	0	0	3	.240	.240
0-3 Days Rest (Start)	0.00	0	0	0	0	0	0.0	0	0	0	0	None on/out	.289	114	33	10	0	3	3	9	15	.347	.456
4 Days Rest	4.32	5	1	0	14	14	77.0	85	8	27	39	First Pitch	.294	68	20	4	0	2	11	1	0	.304	.441
5+ Days Rest	8.13	2	2	0	8	8	34.1	52	4	9	28	Ahead in Count	.275	211	58	12	0	3	18	0	58	.284	.374
Pre-All Star	5.65	2	0	0	9	9	43.0	56	7	17	21	Behind in Count	.394	94	37	8	0	4	24	18	0	.478	.606
Post-All Star	5.71	5	3	0	14	13	69.1	84	5	19	46	Two Strikes	.244	209	51	10	0	4	21	17	67	.309	.359

450

B.J. Surhoff — Orioles

Age 33 – Bats Left (groundball hitter)

	Avg	G	AB	R	H	2B	3B	HR	RBI	BB	SO	HBP	GDP	SB	CS	OBP	SLG	IBB	SH	SF	#Pit	#P/PA	GB	FB	G/F
1997 Season	.284	147	528	80	150	30	4	18	88	49	60	5	7	1	1	.345	.458	14	3	10	2145	3.61	183	195	0.94
Last Five Years	.289	595	2166	312	626	132	18	64	344	185	243	14	32	20	15	.346	.455	31	13	22	8467	3.53	796	719	1.11

1997 Season

	Avg	AB	H	2B	3B	HR	RBI	BB	SO	OBP	SLG		Avg	AB	H	2B	3B	HR	RBI	BB	SO	OBP	SLG
vs. Left	.288	160	46	9	0	3	28	10	21	.335	.400	First Pitch	.320	50	16	1	0	4	12	11	0	.453	.580
vs. Right	.283	368	104	21	4	15	60	39	39	.348	.484	Ahead in Count	.364	121	44	11	1	7	34	24	0	.459	.645
Groundball	.321	137	44	5	2	4	26	14	15	.381	.474	Behind in Count	.254	260	66	15	2	7	32	0	49	.257	.408
Flyball	.273	66	18	5	0	2	11	4	5	.306	.439	Two Strikes	.192	239	46	13	1	3	19	13	60	.234	.293
Home	.269	238	64	8	3	10	34	25	38	.345	.454	Batting #5	.338	151	51	13	2	6	28	12	16	.373	.570
Away	.297	290	86	22	1	8	54	24	22	.345	.462	Batting #6	.276	199	55	9	1	7	32	21	18	.353	.437
Day	.296	159	47	6	3	8	39	19	19	.361	.522	Other	.247	178	44	8	1	5	28	16	26	.312	.388
Night	.279	369	103	24	1	10	49	30	41	.337	.431	March/April	.310	58	18	4	1	1	6	8	7	.388	.466
Grass	.264	462	122	28	4	15	72	42	55	.326	.439	May	.366	101	37	6	2	5	27	7	16	.413	.614
Turf	.424	66	28	2	0	3	16	7	5	.473	.591	June	.231	91	21	4	0	5	17	16	9	.339	.440
Pre-All Star	.298	272	81	15	3	11	54	35	33	.379	.496	July	.253	87	22	4	0	3	12	5	4	.309	.402
Post-All Star	.270	256	69	15	1	7	34	14	27	.306	.418	August	.287	101	29	8	1	2	14	8	10	.339	.446
Scoring Posn	.300	130	39	10	1	4	66	21	17	.380	.485	Sept/Oct	.256	90	23	4	0	2	12	5	14	.286	.367
Close & Late	.265	83	22	1	0	0	11	13	10	.354	.277	vs. AL	.297	478	142	29	4	16	83	41	52	.352	.475
None on/out	.291	117	34	4	0	4	4	11	11	.362	.427	vs. NL	.160	50	8	1	0	2	5	8	8	.279	.300

1997 By Position

Position	Avg	AB	H	2B	3B	HR	RBI	BB	SO	OBP	SLG	G	GS	Innings	PO	A	E	DP	Fld Pct	Rng Fctr	In Zone	Zone Outs	Zone Rtg	MLB Zone
As lf	.285	480	137	26	3	16	84	44	54	.345	.452	133	128	1135.0	246	11	2	3	.992	2.04	277	231	.834	.805

Last Five Years

	Avg	AB	H	2B	3B	HR	RBI	BB	SO	OBP	SLG		Avg	AB	H	2B	3B	HR	RBI	BB	SO	OBP	SLG
vs. Left	.301	670	202	48	2	14	113	49	63	.354	.442	First Pitch	.332	256	85	14	6	7	52	24	0	.387	.516
vs. Right	.283	1496	424	84	16	50	231	136	180	.342	.461	Ahead in Count	.333	559	186	40	5	28	121	93	0	.425	.572
Groundball	.288	552	159	25	9	14	93	43	60	.339	.442	Behind in Count	.249	933	232	50	5	20	116	0	198	.254	.377
Flyball	.258	353	91	20	2	10	47	28	34	.312	.411	Two Strikes	.227	866	197	44	4	15	92	67	243	.286	.339
Home	.292	1042	304	58	13	35	179	98	125	.353	.473	Batting #3	.272	595	162	35	3	16	88	57	51	.333	.422
Away	.286	1124	322	74	5	29	165	87	118	.339	.439	Batting #6	.288	729	210	41	6	23	115	57	86	.343	.455
Day	.297	674	200	41	10	20	119	61	73	.352	.476	Other	.302	842	254	56	9	25	141	71	106	.357	.479
Night	.286	1492	426	91	8	44	225	124	170	.343	.446	March/April	.271	229	62	15	1	7	33	23	32	.335	.437
Grass	.284	1905	541	115	18	57	301	167	218	.343	.453	May	.290	307	89	16	4	10	56	32	35	.358	.466
Turf	.326	261	85	17	0	7	43	18	25	.369	.471	June	.271	439	119	27	4	11	69	44	50	.338	.426
Pre-All Star	.288	1106	318	67	10	34	190	107	131	.352	.458	July	.325	400	130	26	6	15	73	23	42	.366	.533
Post-All Star	.291	1060	308	65	8	30	154	78	112	.339	.452	August	.300	427	128	24	2	14	64	35	40	.356	.464
Scoring Posn	.330	540	178	43	6	16	279	69	63	.395	.520	Sept/Oct	.269	364	98	24	1	7	49	28	44	.318	.398
Close & Late	.249	345	86	9	1	8	52	41	42	.327	.351	vs. AL	.292	2116	618	131	18	62	339	177	235	.347	.459
None on/out	.289	499	144	27	5	17	17	35	60	.341	.465	vs. NL	.160	50	8	1	0	2	5	8	8	.279	.300

Batter vs. Pitcher (career)

Hits Best Against	Avg	AB	H	2B	3B	HR	RBI	BB	SO	OBP	SLG	Hits Worst Against	Avg	AB	H	2B	3B	HR	RBI	BB	SO	OBP	SLG
Scott Aldred	.545	11	6	0	0	1	4	2	0	.615	.818	Jason Jacome	.077	13	1	0	0	0	0	0	1	.077	.077
Chris Haney	.500	16	8	3	0	1	4	0	0	.500	.875	Kevin Gross	.083	12	1	0	0	0	1	1	1	.154	.083
Brad Radke	.500	16	8	2	0	2	4	0	2	.500	1.000	Jason Bere	.083	12	1	0	0	0	0	0	5	.154	.083
Orel Hershiser	.500	12	6	0	1	0	3	2	1	.571	.667	Scott Karl	.083	12	1	0	0	0	0	0	0	.154	.083
Frank Rodriguez	.400	15	6	0	0	2	6	1	0	.438	.800	Scott Bailes	.154	13	2	0	0	0	3	0	0	.154	.154

Larry Sutton — Royals

Age 28 – Bats Left

	Avg	G	AB	R	H	2B	3B	HR	RBI	BB	SO	HBP	GDP	SB	CS	OBP	SLG	IBB	SH	SF	#Pit	#P/PA	GB	FB	G/F
1997 Season	.290	27	69	9	20	2	0	2	8	8	12	0	0	0	0	.338	.406	0	1	0	289	3.85	12	32	0.38

1997 Season

	Avg	AB	H	2B	3B	HR	RBI	BB	SO	OBP	SLG		Avg	AB	H	2B	3B	HR	RBI	BB	SO	OBP	SLG
vs. Left	.000	4	0	0	0	0	0	1	1	.200	.000	Scoring Posn	.429	14	6	0	0	2	8	3	4	.529	.857
vs. Right	.308	65	20	2	0	2	8	4	11	.348	.431	Close & Late	.412	17	7	0	0	1	3	3	4	.500	.588

Dale Sveum — Pirates

Age 34 – Bats Both (flyball hitter)

	Avg	G	AB	R	H	2B	3B	HR	RBI	BB	SO	HBP	GDP	SB	CS	OBP	SLG	IBB	SH	SF	#Pit	#P/PA	GB	FB	G/F
1997 Season	.261	126	306	30	80	20	1	12	47	27	81	0	8	0	3	.319	.451	2	4	2	1263	3.73	95	91	1.04
Last Five Years	.249	178	446	54	111	27	2	16	60	51	118	0	11	0	3	.325	.426	3	5	2	1933	3.84	131	139	0.94

1997 Season

	Avg	AB	H	2B	3B	HR	RBI	BB	SO	OBP	SLG		Avg	AB	H	2B	3B	HR	RBI	BB	SO	OBP	SLG
vs. Left	.196	51	10	1	0	2	9	7	15	.288	.333	First Pitch	.367	49	18	4	1	1	6	2	0	.392	.551
vs. Right	.275	255	70	19	1	10	38	20	66	.326	.475	Ahead in Count	.396	53	21	7	0	4	14	10	0	.492	.755
Groundball	.294	51	15	4	0	2	12	5	21	.357	.490	Behind in Count	.198	131	26	4	0	4	13	0	64	.197	.321
Flyball	.206	63	13	4	0	2	6	5	21	.265	.365	Two Strikes	.148	142	21	4	0	3	13	15	81	.226	.239
Home	.208	149	31	7	1	5	19	11	36	.261	.369	Batting #5	.274	135	37	6	0	7	22	10	29	.320	.442
Away	.312	157	49	13	0	7	28	16	45	.374	.529	Batting #9	.233	43	10	6	0	1	6	5	20	.313	.442
Day	.284	134	38	6	1	6	22	12	34	.342	.478	Other	.258	128	33	8	1	4	19	12	32	.321	.430
Night	.244	172	42	14	0	6	25	15	47	.302	.430	March/April	.250	32	8	5	0	0	2	3	7	.314	.406
Grass	.284	102	29	6	0	5	19	13	30	.362	.490	May	.147	34	5	1	0	1	5	4	12	.237	.265

451

1997 Season

	Avg	AB	H	2B	3B	HR	RBI	BB	SO	OBP	SLG		Avg	AB	H	2B	3B	HR	RBI	BB	SO	OBP	SLG
Turf	.250	204	51	14	1	7	28	14	51	.297	.431	June	.412	51	21	4	0	4	12	3	11	.444	.725
Pre-All Star	.304	138	42	12	0	6	22	14	37	.366	.522	July	.271	85	23	4	0	3	12	8	20	.326	.424
Post-All Star	.226	168	38	8	1	6	25	13	44	.280	.393	August	.227	75	17	4	1	3	12	7	24	.293	.427
Scoring Posn	.204	93	19	5	0	4	33	10	22	.276	.387	Sept/Oct	.207	29	6	2	0	1	4	2	7	.258	.379
Close & Late	.286	70	20	4	0	2	8	9	22	.367	.429	vs. AL	.212	33	7	0	0	3	4	3	6	.270	.485
None on/out	.263	76	20	5	0	4	4	5	26	.309	.487	vs. NL	.267	273	73	20	1	9	43	24	75	.326	.447

1997 By Position

Position	Avg	AB	H	2B	3B	HR	RBI	BB	SO	OBP	SLG	G	GS	Innings	PO	A	E	DP	Fld Pct	Rng Fctr	In Zone	Zone Outs	Zone Rtg	MLB Zone
As Pinch Hitter	.220	41	9	5	0	1	7	6	17	.319	.415	---	---	---	---	---	---	---	---	---	---	---	---	---
As 1b	.143	49	7	1	1	1	6	4	15	.208	.265	21	10	107.2	105	5	0	10	1.000	---	11	12	1.091	.874
As 3b	.270	148	40	6	0	7	22	12	34	.321	.453	47	39	332.2	17	78	6	4	.941	2.57	110	86	.782	.801
As ss	.328	61	20	5	0	3	11	5	15	.379	.557	28	13	146.1	29	54	1	14	.988	5.10	67	55	.821	.937

Dave Swartzbaugh — Cubs   Age 30 – Pitches Right (flyball pitcher)

	ERA	W	L	Sv	G	GS	IP	BB	SO	Avg	H	2B	3B	HR	RBI	OBP	SLG	CG	ShO	Sup	QS	#P/S	SB	CS	GB	FB	G/F
1997 Season	9.00	0	1	0	2	2	8.0	7	4	.364	12	5	1	1	7	.476	.667	0	0	4.50	0	72	2	0	7	15	0.47
Career (1995-1997)	5.72	0	3	0	15	7	39.1	24	22	.285	43	14	1	4	24	.384	.470	0	0	2.75	2	80	8	2	45	52	0.87

1997 Season

	ERA	W	L	Sv	G	GS	IP	H	HR	BB	SO		Avg	AB	H	2B	3B	HR	RBI	BB	SO	OBP	SLG
Home	0.00	0	0	0	0	0	0.0	0	0	0	0	vs. Left	.368	19	7	3	1	1	5	2	2	.435	.789
Away	9.00	0	1	0	2	2	8.0	12	1	7	4	vs. Right	.357	14	5	2	0	0	2	5	2	.526	.500

Mark Sweeney — Padres   Age 28 – Bats Left

	Avg	G	AB	R	H	2B	3B	HR	RBI	BB	SO	HBP	GDP	SB	CS	OBP	SLG	IBB	SH	SF	#Pit	#P/PA	GB	FB	G/F
1997 Season	.280	115	164	16	46	7	0	2	23	20	32	1	3	2	3	.358	.360	1	1	2	688	3.66	57	46	1.24
Career (1995-1997)	.273	250	411	53	112	18	0	7	58	63	76	2	10	6	4	.369	.367	3	7	4	1867	3.83	152	111	1.37

1997 Season

	Avg	AB	H	2B	3B	HR	RBI	BB	SO	OBP	SLG		Avg	AB	H	2B	3B	HR	RBI	BB	SO	OBP	SLG
vs. Left	.286	7	2	0	0	0	1	0	1	.286	.286	Scoring Posn	.327	55	18	2	0	0	19	10	16	.418	.364
vs. Right	.280	157	44	7	0	2	22	20	31	.361	.363	Close & Late	.417	36	15	0	0	1	8	7	7	.500	.500
Home	.257	74	19	3	0	2	12	9	16	.333	.378	None on/out	.225	40	9	0	0	0	0	2	10	.279	.225
Away	.300	90	27	4	0	0	11	11	16	.379	.344	Batting #5	.280	25	7	2	0	0	4	3	6	.357	.360
First Pitch	.370	27	10	2	0	1	6	1	0	.400	.556	Batting #9	.291	55	16	1	0	0	4	6	14	.355	.418
Ahead in Count	.472	36	17	5	0	0	6	14	0	.620	.611	Other	.274	84	23	4	0	0	10	11	12	.361	.321
Behind in Count	.149	74	11	0	0	0	7	0	28	.149	.149	Pre-All Star	.238	80	19	4	0	0	6	11	19	.330	.288
Two Strikes	.133	75	10	0	0	1	6	5	32	.188	.173	Post-All Star	.321	84	27	3	0	2	17	9	13	.387	.429

Mike Sweeney — Royals   Age 24 – Bats Right

	Avg	G	AB	R	H	2B	3B	HR	RBI	BB	SO	HBP	GDP	SB	CS	OBP	SLG	IBB	SH	SF	#Pit	#P/PA	GB	FB	G/F
1997 Season	.242	84	240	30	58	8	0	7	31	17	33	6	8	3	2	.306	.363	0	1	2	970	3.65	89	71	1.25
Career (1995-1997)	.257	138	409	54	105	18	0	11	55	35	54	10	15	4	4	.327	.381	0	0	5	1645	3.58	147	133	1.11

1997 Season

	Avg	AB	H	2B	3B	HR	RBI	BB	SO	OBP	SLG		Avg	AB	H	2B	3B	HR	RBI	BB	SO	OBP	SLG
vs. Left	.189	74	14	2	0	1	8	4	12	.228	.257	Scoring Posn	.224	58	13	1	0	3	25	5	7	.309	.397
vs. Right	.265	166	44	6	0	6	23	13	21	.339	.410	Close & Late	.239	46	11	3	0	3	8	2	13	.314	.500
Home	.241	116	28	4	0	5	17	8	13	.313	.405	None on/out	.333	48	16	2	0	2	2	3	4	.396	.500
Away	.242	124	30	4	0	2	14	9	20	.299	.323	Batting #7	.275	80	22	3	0	4	19	7	9	.363	.463
First Pitch	.313	32	10	3	0	1	4	0	0	.353	.500	Batting #8	.218	87	19	4	0	1	7	5	13	.258	.299
Ahead in Count	.377	53	20	2	0	2	12	5	0	.424	.528	Other	.233	73	17	1	0	2	5	5	11	.296	.329
Behind in Count	.171	117	20	3	0	3	7	0	28	.197	.274	Pre-All Star	.243	70	17	2	0	4	12	6	12	.329	.443
Two Strikes	.141	99	14	3	0	2	10	12	33	.252	.232	Post-All Star	.241	170	41	6	0	3	19	11	21	.296	.329

Bill Swift — Orioles   Age 36 – Pitches Right (groundball pitcher)

	ERA	W	L	Sv	G	GS	IP	BB	SO	Avg	H	2B	3B	HR	RBI	OBP	SLG	CG	ShO	Sup	QS	#P/S	SB	CS	GB	FB	G/F
1997 Season	6.34	4	6	0	14	13	65.1	26	29	.318	85	21	4	11	52	.378	.551	0	0	8.27	3	77	4	0	132	61	2.16
Last Five Years	3.88	43	25	2	91	86	531.1	160	321	.263	534	88	11	52	234	.318	.394	1	1	6.22	44	87	28	20	1038	364	2.85

1997 Season

	ERA	W	L	Sv	G	GS	IP	H	HR	BB	SO		Avg	AB	H	2B	3B	HR	RBI	BB	SO	OBP	SLG
Home	6.25	3	2	0	7	6	31.2	43	5	12	15	vs. Left	.324	136	44	11	2	9	33	18	15	.405	.632
Away	6.42	1	4	0	7	7	33.2	42	6	14	14	vs. Right	.313	131	41	10	2	2	19	8	14	.348	.466
Starter	6.16	4	6	0	13	13	64.1	83	11	25	29	Scoring Posn	.320	75	24	8	1	4	38	8	9	.375	.613
Reliever	18.00	0	0	0	1	0	1.0	2	0	1	0	Close & Late	.000	5	0	0	0	0	0	0	0	.000	.000
0-3 Days Rest (Start)	0.00	0	0	0	0	0	0.0	0	0	0	0	None on/out	.369	65	24	4	1	2	2	7	4	.438	.554
4 Days Rest	6.08	3	3	0	7	7	37.0	47	6	18	17	First Pitch	.391	46	18	4	1	4	15		0	.388	.783
5+ Days Rest	6.26	1	3	0	6	6	27.1	36	5	7	12	Ahead in Count	.255	106	27	6	1	3	11	0	24	.262	.415
Pre-All Star	4.75	4	1	0	7	7	36.0	40	5	12	14	Behind in Count	.359	64	23	8	1	2	13	0		.456	.609
Post-All Star	8.28	0	5	0	7	6	29.1	45	6	14	15	Two Strikes	.184	98	18	4	1	0	6	13	29	.286	.245

452

Last Five Years

	ERA	W	L	Sv	G	GS	IP	H	HR	BB	SO		Avg	AB	H	2B	3B	HR	RBI	BB	SO	OBP	SLG
Home	3.44	24	10	1	46	43	275.0	265	27	83	168	vs. Left	.285	1086	309	53	7	33	144	111	126	.353	.437
Away	4.35	19	15	1	45	43	256.1	269	25	77	153	vs. Right	.238	945	225	35	4	19	90	49	195	.277	.344
Day	3.72	26	12	0	46	44	276.0	270	30	81	171	Inning 1-6	.264	1799	475	77	11	48	216	152	289	.324	.399
Night	4.05	17	13	2	45	42	255.1	264	22	79	150	Inning 7+	.254	232	59	11	0	4	18	8	32	.277	.353
Grass	3.55	36	18	2	70	66	423.2	405	43	131	259	None on	.250	1196	299	39	5	31	92	91	191	.307	.369
Turf	5.18	7	7	0	21	20	107.2	129	9	29	62	Runners on	.281	835	235	49	6	21	203	68	130	.334	.430
March/April	3.06	7	4	0	15	15	94.0	79	9	22	53	Scoring Posn	.291	444	129	27	5	11	173	48	72	.355	.448
May	5.31	10	3	0	18	18	103.1	121	13	44	61	Close & Late	.216	134	29	5	0	2	9	5	18	.245	.299
June	2.67	8	5	0	14	14	91.0	75	4	29	59	None on/out	.251	521	131	15	1	10	10	41	73	.313	.342
July	4.23	8	5	0	16	16	95.2	107	10	23	67	vs. 1st Batr (relief)	.400	5	2	0	0	0	0	0	0	.400	.400
August	5.73	3	5	0	12	11	66.0	76	13	17	38	1st Inning Pitched	.253	332	84	12	1	12	43	40	47	.336	.404
Sept/Oct	2.43	7	3	2	16	12	81.1	76	3	25	43	First 75 Pitches	.256	1657	424	74	6	42	178	137	267	.315	.384
Starter	3.89	43	25	0	86	86	525.1	527	52	158	319	Pitch 76-90	.292	243	71	9	3	6	41	17	37	.335	.428
Reliever	3.00	0	0	2	5	0	6.0	7	0	2	2	Pitch 91-105	.327	110	36	5	1	3	13	5	11	.362	.473
0-3 Days Rest (Start)	1.20	2	0	0	2	2	15.0	5	0	5	6	Pitch 106+	.143	21	3	0	1	1	2	1	6	.182	.381
4 Days Rest	3.58	24	11	0	49	49	309.0	302	33	98	200	First Pitch	.350	343	120	19	2	13	62	10	0	.364	.510
5+ Days Rest	4.56	13	14	0	35	35	201.1	220	19	55	113	Ahead in Count	.205	862	177	30	3	14	64	0	282	.213	.296
vs. AL	0.00	0	0	0	0	0	0.0	0	0	0	0	Behind in Count	.301	498	150	31	3	13	70	96	0	.411	.454
vs. NL	3.88	43	25	2	91	86	531.1	534	52	160	321	Two Strikes	.179	787	141	21	5	12	59	54	321	.238	.264
Pre-All Star	3.67	27	13	0	50	50	308.2	294	27	99	192	Pre-All Star	.254	1157	294	46	6	27	125	99	192	.314	.374
Post-All Star	4.16	16	12	2	41	36	222.2	240	25	61	129	Post-All Star	.275	874	240	42	5	25	109	61	129	.324	.420

Pitcher vs. Batter (career)

Pitches Best Vs.	Avg	AB	H	2B	3B	HR	RBI	BB	SO	OBP	SLG	Pitches Worst Vs.	Avg	AB	H	2B	3B	HR	RBI	BB	SO	OBP	SLG
Luis Alicea	.000	12	0	0	0	0	0	0	4	.000	.000	Ruben Sierra	.444	27	12	2	1	2	8	0	3	.444	.815
Joe Oliver	.063	16	1	0	0	0	0	0	3	.063	.063	Gregg Jefferies	.417	12	5	0	0	2	7	2	0	.500	.917
Chuck Carr	.063	16	1	0	0	0	0	0	3	.063	.063	Dante Bichette	.417	12	5	2	0	2	3	1	2	.462	1.083
Mariano Duncan	.091	22	2	0	0	0	1	0	7	.091	.091	Fred McGriff	.387	31	12	3	0	3	8	4	1	.457	.774
Orlando Merced	.125	16	2	1	0	0	1	0	1	.125	.188	Darren Daulton	.375	24	9	3	1	2	8	4	2	.464	.833

Greg Swindell — Twins
Age 33 – Pitches Left

	ERA	W	L	Sv	G	GS	IP	BB	SO	Avg	H	2B	3B	HR	RBI	OBP	SLG	GF	IR	IRS	Hld	SvOp	SB	CS	GB	FB	G/F
1997 Season	3.58	7	4	1	65	1	115.2	25	75	.238	102	26	4	12	56	.282	.402	12	60	19	12	7	6	6	138	140	0.99
Last Five Years	4.41	38	39	1	174	87	659.0	149	405	.285	738	165	16	90	338	.323	.465	19	74	26	13	11	52	45	878	787	1.12

1997 Season

	ERA	W	L	Sv	G	GS	IP	H	HR	BB	SO		Avg	AB	H	2B	3B	HR	RBI	BB	SO	OBP	SLG
Home	3.79	3	2	1	34	1	57.0	53	6	11	32	vs. Left	.205	151	31	7	2	1	17	3	27	.224	.298
Away	3.38	4	2	0	31	0	58.2	49	6	14	43	vs. Right	.256	277	71	19	2	11	39	22	48	.311	.458
Day	2.89	4	0	0	24	0	43.2	41	1	10	24	Inning 1-6	.272	162	44	11	3	4	25	10	26	.316	.451
Night	4.00	3	4	1	41	1	72.0	61	11	15	51	Inning 7+	.218	266	58	15	1	8	31	15	49	.261	.372
Grass	3.18	4	2	0	26	0	51.0	44	4	12	34	None on	.224	245	55	13	1	8	12	13	41	.264	.384
Turf	3.90	3	2	1	39	1	64.2	58	8	13	41	Runners on	.257	183	47	13	3	4	48	13	32	.305	.426
March/April	4.41	1	1	0	8	0	16.1	20	0	4	7	Scoring Posn	.292	106	31	9	2	2	42	9	16	.345	.472
May	5.21	1	1	0	11	1	19.0	17	3	8	7	Close & Late	.225	138	31	8	1	4	18	8	26	.267	.384
June	2.33	2	0	0	10	0	19.1	12	1	5	13	None on/out	.224	107	24	6	0	2	2	3	20	.245	.336
July	2.45	2	0	0	14	0	22.0	13	1	1	18	vs. 1st Batr (relief)	.311	61	19	5	1	0	16	1	10	.317	.426
August	4.26	1	1	0	11	0	19.0	19	4	2	16	1st Inning Pitched	.229	205	47	15	3	2	32	14	33	.281	.361
Sept/Oct	3.15	0	1	1	11	0	20.0	21	3	5	14	First 15 Pitches	.238	206	49	15	3	3	29	11	29	.279	.383
Starter	12.27	0	1	0	1	1	3.2	6	2	1	3	Pitch 16-30	.239	134	32	7	0	6	18	10	32	.292	.425
Reliever	3.29	7	3	1	64	0	112.0	96	10	24	72	Pitch 31-45	.226	62	14	3	0	2	13	4	5	.262	.371
0 Days rest (Relief)	2.84	1	1	0	11	0	19.0	17	2	3	14	Pitch 46+	.269	26	7	1	1	1	4	1	5	.296	.500
1 or 2 Days rest	3.70	4	2	1	37	0	58.1	51	7	13	33	First Pitch	.296	71	21	4	2	3	8	3	0	.324	.535
3+ Days rest	2.86	2	0	0	16	0	34.2	28	1	8	25	Ahead in Count	.210	200	42	8	1	6	20	0	65	.212	.350
vs. AL	3.83	7	4	1	59	1	105.2	95	12	24	68	Behind in Count	.291	79	23	9	0	2	14	9	0	.364	.481
vs. NL	0.90	0	0	0	6	0	10.0	7	0	1	7	Two Strikes	.186	194	36	6	2	5	24	13	75	.237	.314
Pre-All Star	3.97	4	2	0	32	1	59.0	51	4	17	30	Pre-All Star	.232	220	51	12	2	4	29	17	30	.289	.359
Post-All Star	3.18	3	2	1	33	0	56.2	51	8	8	45	Post-All Star	.245	208	51	14	2	8	27	8	45	.274	.447

Last Five Years

	ERA	W	L	Sv	G	GS	IP	H	HR	BB	SO		Avg	AB	H	2B	3B	HR	RBI	BB	SO	OBP	SLG
Home	4.11	17	21	1	87	42	335.1	372	47	65	207	vs. Left	.276	1125	151	38	5	9	50	26	98	.309	.412
Away	4.73	21	18	0	87	45	323.2	366	43	84	198	vs. Right	.288	2041	587	127	11	81	288	123	307	.327	.480
Day	4.75	16	12	0	59	29	214.0	246	32	50	133	Inning 1-6	.288	1999	576	118	14	68	262	122	307	.328	.463
Night	4.25	22	27	1	115	58	445.0	492	58	99	272	Inning 7+	.275	590	162	47	2	22	76	27	98	.306	.473
Grass	4.55	18	9	0	67	27	233.1	250	33	58	152	None on	.284	1525	433	96	7	51	51	75	243	.320	.456
Turf	4.33	20	30	1	107	60	425.2	488	57	91	253	Runners on	.287	1064	305	69	9	39	287	74	162	.328	.478
March/April	3.29	8	3	0	23	15	112.0	105	7	25	66	Scoring Posn	.280	596	167	38	3	22	240	53	95	.329	.465
May	6.06	7	9	0	33	19	127.2	161	25	36	62	Close & Late	.269	279	75	19	2	9	36	16	52	.308	.448
June	4.04	6	10	0	30	17	127.0	140	14	29	76	None on/out	.270	662	179	49	4	20	20	35	108	.310	.447
July	5.03	6	4	0	32	14	105.2	115	17	22	70	vs. 1st Batr (relief)	.298	84	25	7	1	1	19	1	14	.302	.440
August	4.08	7	9	0	31	13	106.0	119	17	14	71	1st Inning Pitched	.285	635	181	42	8	26	106	38	94	.325	.499
Sept/Oct	3.57	4	4	1	25	9	80.2	98	10	23	60	First 15 Pitches	.293	573	168	42	6	20	80	26	78	.324	.492
Starter	4.62	28	34	0	87	87	506.1	598	71	114	302	Pitch 16-30	.264	518	137	26	4	23	71	33	94	.311	.463
Reliever	3.71	10	5	1	87	0	152.2	140	19	35	103	Pitch 31-45	.288	410	118	25	2	15	43	27	67	.331	.468
0 Days rest (Relief)	2.84	1	1	0	11	0	19.0	17	2	3	14	Pitch 46+	.290	1088	315	72	4	32	144	63	166	.325	.451
1 or 2 Days rest	4.41	7	3	1	49	0	79.2	77	13	20	51	First Pitch	.317	445	141	37	4	15	64	8	0	.326	.519

453

Last Five Years

	ERA	W	L	Sv	G	GS	IP	H	HR	BB	SO		Avg	AB	H	2B	3B	HR	RBI	BB	SO	OBP	SLG
3+ Days rest	3.00	2	1	0	27	0	54.0	46	4	12	38	Ahead in Count	.233	1222	285	56	7	27	115	0	348	.235	.357
vs. AL	4.42	8	5	1	72	3	134.1	126	20	32	89	Behind in Count	.361	471	170	40	1	35	102	65	0	.432	.673
vs. NL	4.41	30	34	0	102	84	524.2	612	70	117	316	Two Strikes	.209	1140	238	45	6	26	102	76	405	.260	.327
Pre-All Star	4.54	23	23	0	95	56	402.0	444	52	99	227	Pre-All Star	.282	1573	444	96	9	52	205	99	227	.325	.454
Post-All Star	4.20	15	16	1	79	31	257.0	294	38	50	178	Post-All Star	.289	1016	294	69	7	38	133	50	178	.320	.483

Pitcher vs. Batter (career)

Pitches Best Vs.	Avg	AB	H	2B	3B	HR	RBI	BB	SO	OBP	SLG	Pitches Worst Vs.	Avg	AB	H	2B	3B	HR	RBI	BB	SO	OBP	SLG
Ron Karkovice	.071	14	1	0	0	0	0	1	7	.133	.071	Bret Boone	.615	13	8	3	0	2	7	1	0	.600	1.308
Rey Sanchez	.083	12	1	0	0	0	0	0	0	.083	.083	Charlie Hayes	.563	16	9	4	0	2	3	0	1	.563	1.188
Jeff Branson	.083	12	1	0	0	0	0	0	4	.083	.083	Marquis Grissom	.500	22	11	2	1	5	9	1	3	.522	1.364
Joe Orsulak	.091	11	1	0	0	0	0	0	1	.091	.091	Kevin Mitchell	.500	12	6	1	0	2	3	0	0	.500	1.083
Mike Macfarlane	.130	23	3	0	0	0	0	0	6	.130	.130	Mark Parent	.364	11	4	2	0	2	4	2	1	.462	1.091

Jeff Tabaka — Reds   Age 34 – Pitches Left (flyball pitcher)

	ERA	W	L	Sv	G	GS	IP	BB	SO	Avg	H	2B	3B	HR	RBI	OBP	SLG	GF	IR	IRS	Hld	SvOp	SB	CS	GB	FB	G/F
1997 Season	4.50	0	0	0	3	0	2.0	1	1	.143	1	0	0	1	1	.400	.571	1	1	0	0	0	0	0	1	3	0.33
Career (1994-1997)	4.88	4	3	2	94	0	94.0	59	76	.248	88	15	4	9	51	.362	.389	22	68	16	6	3	6	4	96	110	0.87

1997 Season

	ERA	W	L	Sv	G	GS	IP	H	HR	BB	SO		Avg	AB	H	2B	3B	HR	RBI	BB	SO	OBP	SLG
Home	0.00	0	0	0	1	0	0.1	0	0	.1	0	vs. Left	.000	1	0	0	0	0	0	1	1	.667	.000
Away	5.40	0	0	0	2	0	1.2	1	1	1	1	vs. Right	.167	6	1	0	0	1	1	0	0	.286	.667

Career (1994-1997)

	ERA	W	L	Sv	G	GS	IP	H	HR	BB	SO		Avg	AB	H	2B	3B	HR	RBI	BB	SO	OBP	SLG
Home	3.72	1	1	1	42	0	48.1	37	2	29	34	vs. Left	.301	133	40	10	1	1	26	31	17	.440	.414
Away	6.11	3	2	1	52	0	45.2	51	7	30	42	vs. Right	.216	222	48	5	3	8	25	28	59	.311	.374
Day	5.22	1	1	0	27	0	29.1	29	3	18	31	Inning 1-6	.253	91	23	5	2	1	12	10	26	.330	.385
Night	4.73	3	2	1	67	0	64.2	59	6	41	45	Inning 7+	.246	264	65	10	2	8	39	49	50	.372	.390
Grass	5.12	3	0	1	48	0	45.2	43	6	29	37	None on	.246	187	46	9	0	5	5	24	48	.338	.390
Turf	4.66	1	3	1	46	0	48.1	45	3	30	39	Runners on	.250	168	42	6	4	4	46	35	28	.386	.405
March/April	7.78	0	1	1	17	0	19.2	25	4	14	15	Scoring Posn	.226	106	24	3	2	2	40	24	20	.371	.349
May	6.05	0	1	1	17	0	19.1	21	3	12	20	Close & Late	.300	80	24	3	0	2	11	16	16	.429	.413
June	7.56	2	1	0	15	0	8.1	9	0	5	6	None on/out	.282	85	24	3	0	1	1	10	22	.358	.353
July	2.61	1	0	0	17	0	20.2	18	0	12	17	vs. 1st Batr (relief)	.265	83	22	4	0	1	12	11	15	.351	.349
August	1.76	0	0	0	16	0	15.1	7	2	7	11	1st Inning Pitched	.253	257	65	11	4	6	41	43	55	.369	.397
Sept/Oct	4.22	1	0	0	12	0	10.2	8	0	9	7	First 15 Pitches	.266	218	58	10	2	5	28	30	38	.363	.399
Starter	0.00	0	0	0	0	0	0.0	0	0	0	0	Pitch 16-30	.182	88	16	3	1	3	13	23	24	.360	.341
Reliever	4.88	4	3	2	94	0	94.0	88	9	59	76	Pitch 31-45	.289	45	13	2	1	1	9	3	8	.333	.444
0 Days rest (Relief)	7.53	1	0	1	19	0	14.1	23	2	10	12	Pitch 46+	.250	4	1	0	0	0	1	3	1	.571	.250
1 or 2 Days rest	4.69	3	3	0	42	0	40.1	37	3	25	32	First Pitch	.227	44	10	1	0	1	3	1	0	.244	.318
3+ Days rest	4.12	0	0	1	33	0	39.1	28	4	24	32	Ahead in Count	.171	158	27	4	1	4	11	0	67	.186	.285
vs. AL	0.00	0	0	0	0	0	0.0	0	0	0	0	Behind in Count	.274	73	20	3	1	2	15	29	0	.480	.425
vs. NL	4.88	4	3	2	94	0	94.0	88	9	59	76	Two Strikes	.184	179	33	6	2	4	24	29	76	.303	.307
Pre-All Star	6.46	2	3	2	54	0	54.1	59	7	35	45	Pre-All Star	.272	217	59	9	3	7	41	35	45	.380	.438
Post-All Star	2.72	2	0	0	40	0	39.2	29	2	24	31	Post-All Star	.210	138	29	4	1	2	10	24	31	.333	.312

Pitcher vs. Batter (career)

Pitches Best Vs.	Avg	AB	H	2B	3B	HR	RBI	BB	SO	OBP	SLG	Pitches Worst Vs.	Avg	AB	H	2B	3B	HR	RBI	BB	SO	OBP	SLG
												Hal Morris	.364	11	4	1	0	0	4	0	2	.364	.455

Kevin Tapani — Cubs   Age 34 – Pitches Right

	ERA	W	L	Sv	G	GS	IP	BB	SO	Avg	H	2B	3B	HR	RBI	OBP	SLG	CG	ShO	Sup	QS	#P/S	SB	CS	GB	FB	G/F
1997 Season	3.39	9	3	0	13	13	85.0	23	55	.242	77	19	1	7	30	.296	.374	1		1	5.29	9	97	3	3	115	86	1.34
Last Five Years	4.52	55	48	0	140	137	882.2	243	577	.277	964	221	19	104	424	.326	.441	12		4	5.10	71	101	92	35	1264	958	1.32

1997 Season

	ERA	W	L	Sv	G	GS	IP	H	HR	BB	SO		Avg	AB	H	2B	3B	HR	RBI	BB	SO	OBP	SLG
Home	1.65	6	0	0	7	7	49.0	40	3	11	34	vs. Left	.230	174	40	9	1	4	21	9	33	.270	.362
Away	5.75	3	3	0	6	6	36.0	37	4	12	21	vs. Right	.257	144	37	10	0	3	9	14	22	.325	.389
Starter	3.39	9	3	0	13	13	85.0	77	7	23	55	Scoring Posn	.258	66	17	2	0	3	21	10	9	.354	.424
Reliever	0.00	0	0	0	0	0	0.0	0	0	0	0	Close & Late	.261	23	6	2	0	1	2	1	4	.292	.478
0-3 Days Rest (Start)	0.00	0	0	0	0	0	0.0	0	0	0	0	None on/out	.244	86	21	7	0	1	3	12	12	.278	.360
4 Days Rest	3.13	6	1	0	7	7	46.0	45	2	12	29	First Pitch	.233	60	14	2	0	1	7	1	0	.246	.317
5+ Days Rest	3.69	3	2	0	6	6	39.0	32	5	11	26	Ahead in Count	.145	131	19	4	0	5	11	0	47	.150	.290
Pre-All Star	0.00	0	0	0	0	0	0.0	0	0	0	0	Behind in Count	.356	59	21	5	0	0	4	8	0	.435	.441
Post-All Star	3.39	9	3	0	13	13	85.0	77	7	23	55	Two Strikes	.135	141	19	3	0	4	14	14	55	.217	.241

Last Five Years

	ERA	W	L	Sv	G	GS	IP	H	HR	BB	SO		Avg	AB	H	2B	3B	HR	RBI	BB	SO	OBP	SLG
Home	4.02	31	21	0	68	66	456.2	467	46	116	290	vs. Left	.273	1887	516	127	14	58	251	130	342	.320	.448
Away	5.05	24	27	0	72	71	426.0	497	58	127	287	vs. Right	.281	1595	448	94	5	46	173	113	235	.333	.433
Day	3.96	20	13	0	49	48	313.1	325	33	83	216	Inning 1-6	.273	2958	807	180	15	87	372	204	504	.322	.432
Night	4.82	35	35	0	91	89	569.1	639	71	160	361	Inning 7+	.300	524	157	41	4	17	52	39	73	.347	.490
Grass	4.92	33	25	0	81	78	484.1	552	65	155	322	None on	.271	2064	560	131	9	60	60	124	351	.317	.431
Turf	4.02	22	23	0	59	59	398.1	412	39	88	255	Runners on	.285	1418	404	90	10	44	364	119	226	.338	.456
March/April	6.53	3	6	0	16	16	91.0	114	11	32	50	Scoring Posn	.274	849	233	49	4	24	303	91	145	.341	.426

	ERA	W	L	Sv	G	GS	IP	H	HR	BB	SO		Avg	AB	H	2B	3B	HR	RBI	BB	SO	OBP	SLG
May	3.74	12	9	0	25	25	166.0	180	16	40	114	Close & Late	.275	258	71	21	1	8	29	25	37	.339	.457
June	3.85	8	12	0	23	23	161.1	177	15	43	110	None on/out	.278	904	251	63	3	26	26	41	146	.315	.449
July	5.55	7	8	0	26	25	155.2	178	23	45	107	vs. 1st Batr (relief)	.000	3	0	0	0	0	0	0	0	.000	.000
August	4.81	12	8	0	26	26	162.2	178	24	46	94	1st Inning Pitched	.288	563	162	39	2	14	76	44	98	.344	.439
Sept/Oct	3.45	13	5	0	24	22	146.0	137	15	37	102	First 75 Pitches	.274	2433	667	151	12	73	290	167	405	.323	.436
Starter	4.53	55	48	0	137	137	877.2	960	103	242	573	Pitch 76-90	.289	461	133	26	4	11	64	26	69	.326	.434
Reliever	1.80	0	0	0	3	0	5.0	4	1	1	4	Pitch 91-105	.288	375	108	28	1	14	47	29	72	.338	.480
0-3 Days Rest (Start)	4.34	3	3	0	9	9	58.0	63	6	9	43	Pitch 106+	.263	213	56	16	2	6	23	21	31	.328	.441
4 Days Rest	4.51	39	35	0	94	94	611.0	668	73	182	390	First Pitch	.348	563	196	51	5	23	98	5	0	.353	.579
5+ Days Rest	4.66	13	10	0	34	34	208.2	229	24	51	140	Ahead in Count	.211	1543	325	70	5	33	139	0	488	.216	.327
vs. AL	4.62	43	43	0	115	114	746.1	822	90	207	484	Behind in Count	.330	684	226	48	4	29	102	114	0	.424	.539
vs. NL	3.96	12	5	0	25	23	136.1	142	14	36	93	Two Strikes	.198	1543	305	67	6	28	125	124	577	.261	.303
Pre-All Star	4.61	24	30	0	72	71	458.2	520	48	129	303	Pre-All Star	.286	1816	520	125	12	48	224	129	303	.336	.448
Post-All Star	4.42	31	18	0	68	66	424.0	444	56	114	274	Post-All Star	.267	1666	444	96	7	56	200	114	274	.314	.433

Pitches Best Vs.	Avg	AB	H	2B	3B	HR	RBI	BB	SO	OBP	SLG	Pitches Worst Vs.	Avg	AB	H	2B	3B	HR	RBI	BB	SO	OBP	SLG
Glenallen Hill	.000	12	0	0	0	0	1	0	2	.000	.000	Joey Cora	.486	35	17	7	0	1	5	0	2	.486	.771
Luis Rivera	.000	11	0	0	0	0	0	0	3	.000	.000	Fred McGriff	.444	9	4	1	0	1	4	3	1	.583	.889
Jon Nunnally	.000	11	0	0	0	0	0	1	5	.083	.000	Paul Sorrento	.400	35	14	6	0	3	9	2	7	.421	.829
Jeff Huson	.042	24	1	1	0	0	1	0	3	.042	.083	Reggie Jefferson	.400	10	4	1	0	1	1	3	.455	.800
Jeffrey Hammonds	.083	12	1	0	0	0	0	0	2	.083	.083	Terry Steinbach	.355	31	11	4	0	4	7	3	4	.412	.871

Tony Tarasco — Orioles

Age 27 – Bats Left

	Avg	G	AB	R	H	2B	3B	HR	RBI	BB	SO	HBP	GDP	SB	CS	OBP	SLG	IBB	SH	SF	#Pit	#P/PA	GB	FB	G/F
1997 Season	.205	100	166	26	34	8	1	7	26	25	33	1	3	2	2	.313	.392	1	1	0	766	3.97	51	63	0.81
Career (1993-1997)	.242	368	855	126	207	37	5	27	96	92	148	4	12	36	9	.317	.392	14	5	5	3588	3.73	291	276	1.05

1997 Season

	Avg	AB	H	2B	3B	HR	RBI	BB	SO	OBP	SLG		Avg	AB	H	2B	3B	HR	RBI	BB	SO	OBP	SLG
vs. Left	.160	25	4	0	0	1	1	1	8	.192	.280	Scoring Posn	.279	43	12	1	0	1	16	10	8	.426	.372
vs. Right	.213	141	30	8	1	6	25	24	25	.331	.411	Close & Late	.172	29	5	3	0	1	6	6	10	.314	.379
Home	.216	74	16	5	0	4	15	9	13	.301	.446	None on/out	.125	40	5	1	0	2	2	4	8	.205	.300
Away	.196	92	18	3	1	3	11	16	20	.321	.348	Batting #7	.210	81	17	3	0	4	13	12	16	.312	.395
First Pitch	.267	30	8	2	0	2	9	1	0	.290	.533	Batting #8	.267	30	8	2	1	2	7	7	2	.405	.600
Ahead in Count	.262	42	11	4	0	3	9	8	0	.380	.571	Other	.164	55	9	3	0	1	6	6	15	.258	.273
Behind in Count	.117	60	7	2	1	0	3	0	27	.131	.183	Pre-All Star	.229	118	27	4	1	6	19	21	21	.345	.432
Two Strikes	.158	76	12	1	0	2	11	16	33	.344	.250	Post-All Star	.146	48	7	4	0	1	7	4	12	.226	.292

Career (1993-1997)

	Avg	AB	H	2B	3B	HR	RBI	BB	SO	OBP	SLG		Avg	AB	H	2B	3B	HR	RBI	BB	SO	OBP	SLG
vs. Left	.245	151	37	5	1	3	15	7	30	.278	.351	First Pitch	.313	144	45	7	0	4	17	11	0	.369	.444
vs. Right	.241	704	170	32	4	24	81	85	118	.325	.401	Ahead in Count	.280	211	59	14	2	14	45	38	0	.388	.564
Groundball	.232	276	64	13	1	5	23	29	43	.311	.341	Behind in Count	.178	338	60	10	3	4	18	0	116	.181	.260
Flyball	.277	119	33	4	0	8	20	17	25	.368	.513	Two Strikes	.185	378	70	10	2	6	24	43	148	.269	.270
Home	.257	435	112	22	1	14	50	40	76	.320	.409	Batting #1	.255	192	49	9	2	7	19	19	31	.322	.432
Away	.226	420	95	15	4	13	46	52	72	.314	.374	Batting #7	.236	212	50	7	2	9	28	25	41	.316	.415
Day	.252	286	72	12	1	8	32	30	49	.322	.385	Other	.239	451	108	21	1	11	49	48	76	.315	.364
Night	.237	569	135	25	4	19	64	62	99	.315	.395	March/April	.271	133	36	4	0	4	10	6	17	.307	.391
Grass	.254	496	126	22	4	18	67	56	78	.330	.423	May	.256	203	52	11	1	8	27	23	41	.332	.438
Turf	.226	359	81	15	1	9	29	36	70	.298	.348	June	.262	183	48	9	1	6	24	23	32	.343	.421
Pre-All Star	.257	571	147	24	4	20	67	61	95	.330	.419	July	.250	148	37	6	2	4	19	20	24	.341	.399
Post-All Star	.211	284	60	13	1	7	29	31	53	.292	.338	August	.144	97	14	3	0	1	5	7	24	.202	.206
Scoring Posn	.258	198	51	8	1	5	62	35	29	.367	.384	Sept/Oct	.220	91	20	4	1	4	11	13	10	.321	.418
Close & Late	.224	152	34	8	0	2	17	16	31	.294	.316	vs. AL	.223	233	52	10	1	7	33	29	45	.309	.365
None on/out	.264	235	62	13	2	6	30	29	38	.297	.413	vs. NL	.249	622	155	27	4	20	63	63	103	.320	.402

Hits Best Against	Avg	AB	H	2B	3B	HR	RBI	BB	SO	OBP	SLG	Hits Worst Against	Avg	AB	H	2B	3B	HR	RBI	BB	SO	OBP	SLG
Dave Weathers	.600	10	6	2	0	0	1	1	1	.636	.800	Joey Hamilton	.077	13	1	0	0	0	1	1	0	.200	.077
Jaime Navarro	.364	11	4	1	0	2	4	2	1	.462	1.000	Ismael Valdes	.143	14	2	0	0	1	1	0	2	.143	.357
												Mark Leiter	.222	9	2	0	0	1	1	2	1	.364	.556
												Ramon Martinez	.222	9	2	0	0	0	1	4	2	.462	.556

Danny Tartabull — Phillies

Age 35 – Bats Right

	Avg	G	AB	R	H	2B	3B	HR	RBI	BB	SO	HBP	GDP	SB	CS	OBP	SLG	IBB	SH	SF	#Pit	#P/PA	GB	FB	G/F
1997 Season	.000	3	7	2	0	0	0	0	0	4	4	0	0	0	0	.364	.000	0	0	0	54	4.91	0	3	0.00
Last Five Years	.249	460	1671	249	416	96	6	85	305	269	481	4	38	2	5	.351	.466	17	0	17	7761	3.96	512	437	1.17

1997 Season

	Avg	AB	H	2B	3B	HR	RBI	BB	SO	OBP	SLG		Avg	AB	H	2B	3B	HR	RBI	BB	SO	OBP	SLG
vs. Left	.000	3	0	0	0	0	0	1	2	.250	.000	Scoring Posn	.000	2	0	0	0	0	0	2	1	.500	.000
vs. Right	.000	4	0	0	0	0	0	3	2	.429	.000	Close & Late	.000	2	0	0	0	0	0	0	2	.000	.000

	Avg	AB	H	2B	3B	HR	RBI	BB	SO	OBP	SLG		Avg	AB	H	2B	3B	HR	RBI	BB	SO	OBP	SLG
vs. Left	.258	531	137	34	2	26	92	127	142	.400	.476	First Pitch	.358	218	78	19	0	16	54	13	0	.392	.665
vs. Right	.245	1140	279	62	4	59	213	142	339	.326	.461	Ahead in Count	.356	340	121	26	2	25	93	131	0	.530	.665

455

Last Five Years

	Avg	AB	H	2B	3B	HR	RBI	BB	SO	OBP	SLG		Avg	AB	H	2B	3B	HR	RBI	BB	SO	OBP	SLG
Groundball	.296	379	112	22	0	18	79	56	90	.385	.496	Behind in Count	.158	754	119	40	4	22	83	0	379	.158	.309
Flyball	.241	344	83	20	0	27	67	57	112	.347	.535	Two Strikes	.135	829	112	28	2	22	82	125	481	.247	.253
Home	.239	766	183	44	1	35	138	105	217	.328	.436	Batting #4	.240	1065	256	60	2	50	183	185	314	.352	.441
Away	.257	905	233	52	5	50	167	164	264	.370	.492	Batting #6	.279	341	95	26	2	20	69	44	84	.357	.543
Day	.235	578	136	33	3	30	121	90	172	.333	.458	Day	.245	265	65	10	2	15	53	40	83	.341	.468
Night	.256	1093	280	63	3	55	184	179	300	.361	.470	March/April	.238	265	63	17	1	11	45	50	78	.357	.434
Grass	.245	1449	355	81	5	74	258	214	420	.340	.461	May	.213	328	70	21	0	12	48	50	96	.313	.387
Turf	.275	222	61	15	1	11	47	55	61	.417	.500	June	.253	281	71	19	2	15	50	43	79	.348	.495
Pre-All Star	.239	1005	240	64	4	46	165	158	291	.339	.448	July	.287	328	94	13	1	22	68	49	82	.377	.534
Post-All Star	.264	666	176	32	2	39	140	111	190	.369	.494	August	.228	202	46	16	0	12	46	38	60	.353	.485
Scoring Posn	.252	468	118	29	2	19	212	102	144	.375	.444	Sept/Oct	.270	267	72	10	2	13	48	39	86	.363	.468
Close & Late	.230	248	57	15	0	9	39	43	75	.347	.399	vs. AL	.250	1664	416	96	6	85	305	265	477	.351	.468
None on/out	.245	412	101	24	1	26	26	44	117	.319	.498	vs. NL	.000	7	0	0	0	0	0	4	4	.364	.000

Batter vs. Pitcher (career)

Hits Best Against	Avg	AB	H	2B	3B	HR	RBI	BB	SO	OBP	SLG	Hits Worst Against	Avg	AB	H	2B	3B	HR	RBI	BB	SO	OBP	SLG
Mike Morgan	.727	11	8	0	0	1	4	1	0	.750	1.000	Kevin Appier	.000	18	0	0	0	0	0	1	11	.053	.000
Scott Bailes	.500	18	9	1	0	3	7	2	0	.550	1.056	David Cone	.000	15	0	0	0	0	0	2	4	.118	.000
Arthur Rhodes	.444	9	4	1	0	1	3	3	1	.583	.889	Sterling Hitchcock	.000	10	0	0	0	0	0	3	6	.231	.000
Mike Mussina	.429	14	6	0	0	3	4	1	4	.467	1.071	Alan Mills	.100	10	1	0	0	0	2	1	6	.167	.100
Wilson Alvarez	.375	16	6	0	0	3	8	5	3	.524	.938	Brian Anderson	.154	13	2	0	0	0	0	0	4	.154	.154

Fernando Tatis — Rangers
Age 23 – Bats Right

	Avg	G	AB	R	H	2B	3B	HR	RBI	BB	SO	HBP	GDP	SB	CS	OBP	SLG	IBB	SH	SF	#Pit	#P/PA	GB	FB	G/F
1997 Season	.256	60	223	29	57	9	0	8	29	14	42	0	6	3	0	.297	.404	0	2	2	903	3.75	76	69	1.10

1997 Season

	Avg	AB	H	2B	3B	HR	RBI	BB	SO	OBP	SLG		Avg	AB	H	2B	3B	HR	RBI	BB	SO	OBP	SLG
vs. Left	.230	61	14	1	0	1	5	4	11	.277	.295	Scoring Posn	.258	66	17	4	0	1	22	6	17	.311	.364
vs. Right	.265	162	43	8	0	7	24	10	31	.305	.444	Close & Late	.129	31	4	0	0	1	3	3	8	.206	.226
Home	.242	95	23	2	0	6	12	7	17	.288	.453	None on/out	.245	49	12	1	0		4	4	6	.302	.510
Away	.266	128	34	7	0	2	17	7	25	.304	.367	Batting #7	.293	75	22	1	0	3	12	10	14	.376	.427
First Pitch	.333	33	11	3	0	3	6	0	0	.333	.697	Batting #8	.261	69	18	7	0	2	11	2	10	.278	.449
Ahead in Count	.452	31	14	3	0	1	7	8	0	.550		Other	.215	79	17	1	0	3	6	2	18	.232	.342
Behind in Count	.190	116	22	2	0	1	8	0	36	.190	.233	Pre-All Star	.000	0	0	0	0	0	0	0	0	.000	.000
Two Strikes	.167	120	20	1	0	2	9	6	42	.206	.225	Post-All Star	.256	223	57	9	0	8	29	14	42	.297	.404

Ramon Tatis — Cubs
Age 25 – Pitches Left (groundball pitcher)

	ERA	W	L	Sv	G	GS	IP	BB	SO	Avg	H	2B	3B	HR	RBI	OBP	SLG	GF	IR	IRS	Hld	SvOp	SB	CS	GB	FB	G/F
1997 Season	5.34	1	1	0	56	0	55.2	29	33	.308	66	9	1	13	39	.394	.542	12	49	15	8	1	2	0	95	48	1.98

1997 Season

	ERA	W	L	Sv	G	GS	IP	H	HR	BB	SO		Avg	AB	H	2B	3B	HR	RBI	BB	SO	OBP	SLG
Home	9.00	1	1	0	32	0	25.0	36	9	18	16	vs. Left	.288	80	23	3	1	2	9	11	10	.380	.425
Away	2.35	0	0	0	24	0	30.2	30	4	11	17	vs. Right	.321	134	43	6	0	11	30	18	23	.401	.612
Day	5.09	0	0	0	34	0	35.1	35	7	22	24	Inning 1-6	.287	87	25	4	0	5	15	8	16	.361	.506
Night	5.75	1	1	0	22	0	20.1	31	6	7	9	Inning 7+	.323	127	41	5	1	8	24	21	17	.414	.567
Grass	6.49	1	1	0	47	0	43.0	59	12	23	25	None on	.317	104	33	5	1	7	7	12	15	.393	.587
Turf	1.42	0	0	0	9	0	12.2	7	1	6	8	Runners on	.300	110	33	4	0	6	32	17	18	.394	.500
March/April	4.32	0	0	0	7	0	8.1	6	1	3	1	Scoring Posn	.296	71	21	1	0	4	28	11	13	.391	.479
May	4.22	0	0	0	6	0	10.2	12	1	6	11	Close & Late	.273	33	9	1	1	3	7	7	6	.381	.455
June	3.86	0	0	0	10	0	14.0	11	1	4	7	None on/out	.289	45	13	3	0	1		6	5	.373	.422
July	4.66	0	1	0	12	0	9.2	12	2	4	5	vs. 1st Batr (relief)	.295	44	13	2	0	2	11	10	3	.429	.477
August	6.97	1	0	0	14	0	10.1	20	4	6	5	1st Inning Pitched	.308	143	44	5	0	10	31	22	22	.408	.552
Sept/Oct	16.88	0	0	0	7	0	2.2	5	1	3	2	First 15 Pitches	.308	133	41	6	0	8	27	23	20	.411	.534
Starter	0.00	0	0	0	0	0	0.0	0	0	0	0	Pitch 16-30	.328	58	19	3	1	4	7	6	6	.409	.621
Reliever	5.34	1	1	0	56	0	55.2	66	13	29	33	Pitch 31-45	.300	20	6	0	0	1	5	0	6	.273	.450
0 Days rest (Relief)	3.65	0	1	0	16	0	12.1	12	1	7	6	Pitch 46+	.000	3	0	0	0	0	0	0	0	.000	.000
1 or 2 Days rest	7.36	1	0	0	20	0	22.0	34	9	7	16	First Pitch	.375	40	15	1	0	3	8	6	0	.468	.625
3+ Days rest	4.22	0	0	0	20	0	21.1	20	3	15	11	Ahead in Count	.222	90	20	3	0	3	10	0	27	.215	.356
vs. AL	9.00	0	0	0	4	0	4.0	5	3	1	2	Behind in Count	.388	49	19	3	0	4	12	15	0	.538	.694
vs. NL	5.05	1	1	0	52	0	51.2	61	10	28	31	Two Strikes	.225	89	20	3	1	2	10	8	33	.290	.348
Pre-All Star	4.05	0	0	0	24	0	33.1	29	6	17	21	Pre-All Star	.244	119	29	5	0	6	15	17	21	.341	.437
Post-All Star	7.25	1	1	0	32	0	22.1	37	7	12	12	Post-All Star	.389	95	37	4	1	7	24	12	12	.459	.674

Eddie Taubensee — Reds
Age 29 – Bats Left

	Avg	G	AB	R	H	2B	3B	HR	RBI	BB	SO	HBP	GDP	SB	CS	OBP	SLG	IBB	SH	SF	#Pit	#P/PA	GB	FB	G/F
1997 Season	.268	108	254	26	68	18	0	10	34	22	66	1	2	0	1	.323	.457	2	1	5	1068	3.77	68	79	0.86
Last Five Years	.275	456	1274	159	350	71	5	48	189	106	257	3	18	8	7	.328	.451	16	5	15	5060	3.61	439	375	1.17

1997 Season

	Avg	AB	H	2B	3B	HR	RBI	BB	SO	OBP	SLG		Avg	AB	H	2B	3B	HR	RBI	BB	SO	OBP	SLG
vs. Left	.161	31	5	1	0	1	2	0	12	.188	.290	Scoring Posn	.250	60	15	3	0	1	22	8	15	.324	.350
vs. Right	.283	223	63	17	0	9	32	22	54	.340	.480	Close & Late	.238	42	10	3	0	2	7	7	12	.340	.452
Home	.283	127	36	9	0	7	21	11	35	.340	.520	None on/out	.279	61	17	4	0	1	1	3	16	.313	.393

1997 Season

	Avg	AB	H	2B	3B	HR	RBI	BB	SO	OBP	SLG		Avg	AB	H	2B	3B	HR	RBI	BB	SO	OBP	SLG
Away	.252	127	32	9	0	3	13	11	31	.305	.394	Batting #5	.235	68	16	6	0	2	9	3	19	.264	.412
First Pitch	.273	33	9	1	0	1	2	1	0	.286	.394	Batting #6	.239	46	11	2	0	2	3	4	15	.294	.413
Ahead in Count	.389	54	21	7	0	5	14	10	0	.470	.796	Other	.293	140	41	10	0	6	22	15	32	.358	.493
Behind in Count	.195	118	23	5	0	0	7	0	52	.192	.237	Pre-All Star	.253	158	40	14	0	6	18	14	38	.310	.456
Two Strikes	.187	123	23	6	0	2	12	11	66	.257	.285	Post-All Star	.292	96	28	4	0	4	16	8	28	.343	.458

Last Five Years

	Avg	AB	H	2B	3B	HR	RBI	BB	SO	OBP	SLG		Avg	AB	H	2B	3B	HR	RBI	BB	SO	OBP	SLG
vs. Left	.238	172	41	7	0	7	30	10	42	.286	.401	First Pitch	.296	186	55	15	1	10	32	10	0	.333	.548
vs. Right	.280	1102	309	64	5	41	159	96	215	.335	.459	Ahead in Count	.384	281	108	19	2	17	60	52	0	.472	.648
Groundball	.271	387	105	15	3	13	40	29	71	.319	.426	Behind in Count	.205	565	116	21	1	12	56	0	210	.205	.310
Flyball	.319	185	59	14	1	10	35	15	33	.364	.568	Two Strikes	.181	565	102	21	2	11	55	43	257	.239	.283
Home	.270	600	162	38	2	23	93	55	122	.331	.455	Batting #6	.292	240	70	12	2	12	32	22	54	.351	.508
Away	.279	674	188	33	3	25	96	51	135	.348	.448	Batting #8	.283	403	114	17	3	15	57	41	67	.346	.452
Day	.281	430	121	20	2	21	61	45	88	.346	.484	Other	.263	631	166	42	0	21	100	43	136	.308	.429
Night	.271	844	229	51	3	27	128	61	169	.319	.435	March/April	.273	205	56	14	1	7	31	21	32	.336	.454
Grass	.273	439	120	20	0	17	56	28	81	.314	.435	May	.228	237	54	10	1	6	23	24	54	.302	.354
Turf	.275	835	230	51	5	31	133	78	176	.336	.460	June	.298	225	67	16	3	10	40	16	49	.342	.529
Pre-All Star	.263	733	193	42	5	28	108	64	151	.321	.449	July	.276	199	55	9	0	10	28	13	41	.316	.472
Post-All Star	.290	541	157	29	0	20	81	42	106	.338	.455	August	.296	223	66	14	0	9	32	15	45	.338	.480
Scoring Posn	.268	347	93	16	2	11	132	51	72	.353	.421	Sept/Oct	.281	185	52	8	0	6	35	17	36	.340	.422
Close & Late	.246	224	55	13	0	7	32	25	47	.321	.397	vs. AL	.333	24	8	2	0	2	5	1	3	.385	.667
None on/out	.296	294	87	12	1	10	10	16	44	.332	.446	vs. NL	.274	1250	342	69	5	46	184	105	254	.327	.447

Batter vs. Pitcher (career)

Hits Best Against	Avg	AB	H	2B	3B	HR	RBI	BB	SO	OBP	SLG	Hits Worst Against	Avg	AB	H	2B	3B	HR	RBI	BB	SO	OBP	SLG
Kevin Foster	.545	11	6	3	0	1	3	0	1	.545	1.091	Ramon Martinez	.071	14	1	1	0	0	0	0	3	.133	.143
Shane Reynolds	.526	19	10	1	2	0	1	1	4	.550	.789	Steve Trachsel	.077	13	1	0	0	0	0	0	3	.077	.077
Kevin Ritz	.444	9	4	0	0	1	2	2	3	.545	.778	Pedro Astacio	.103	29	3	0	0	0	1	0	5	.100	.103
Bobby Jones	.412	17	7	3	0	1	4	0	4	.412	.765	Mike Morgan	.105	19	2	0	0	0	2	0	5	.100	.105
Mark Leiter	.400	10	4	0	1	2	3	1	2	.417	1.200	Scott Sanders	.125	16	2	0	0	0	1	2	3	.222	.125

Jesus Tavarez — Red Sox
Age 27 – Bats Both

	Avg	G	AB	R	H	2B	3B	HR	RBI	BB	SO	HBP	GDP	SB	CS	OBP	SLG	IBB	SH	SF	#Pit	#P/PA	GB	FB	G/F
1997 Season	.174	42	69	12	12	3	1	0	9	4	9	0	2	0	0	.216	.246	0	0	1	245	3.31	31	19	1.63
Career (1994-1997)	.240	220	412	61	99	12	3	3	32	28	59	1	5	13	7	.289	.299	1	7	2	1539	3.42	193	90	2.14

1997 Season

	Avg	AB	H	2B	3B	HR	RBI	BB	SO	OBP	SLG		Avg	AB	H	2B	3B	HR	RBI	BB	SO	OBP	SLG
vs. Left	.211	38	8	2	0	0	3	2	4	.244	.263	Scoring Posn	.182	22	4	2	1	0	9	1	4	.208	.364
vs. Right	.129	31	4	1	1	0	6	2	5	.182	.226	Close & Late	.250	8	2	0	0	0	0	1	2	.333	.250

Career (1994-1997)

	Avg	AB	H	2B	3B	HR	RBI	BB	SO	OBP	SLG		Avg	AB	H	2B	3B	HR	RBI	BB	SO	OBP	SLG
vs. Left	.216	116	25	4	0	0	7	7	11	.256	.250	First Pitch	.230	74	17	1	0	0	6	1	0	.250	.243
vs. Right	.250	296	74	8	3	2	21	21	48	.302	.318	Ahead in Count	.310	100	31	5	1	0	8	6	0	.346	.380
Groundball	.213	94	20	0	1	1	8	8	11	.275	.266	Behind in Count	.192	172	33	4	1	0	13	0	50	.191	.227
Flyball	.274	62	17	4	0	0	6	3	10	.308	.339	Two Strikes	.199	151	30	5	0	2	12	21	59	.297	.272
Home	.294	187	55	8	2	1	20	12	25	.338	.374	Batting #8	.260	131	34	4	2	0	8	11	15	.317	.321
Away	.196	225	44	4	1	1	12	16	34	.248	.236	Batting #9	.174	92	16	4	0	0	3	9	13	.245	.217
Day	.253	99	25	2	0	1	4	4	9	.282	.303	Other	.259	189	49	4	1	2	21	8	31	.291	.323
Night	.236	313	74	10	3	1	28	24	50	.291	.297	March/April	.094	32	3	1	0	0	0	2	8	.147	.125
Grass	.242	297	72	9	3	2	27	22	44	.295	.313	May	.200	30	6	1	0	0	1	1	6	.226	.233
Turf	.235	115	27	3	0	0	5	6	15	.273	.261	June	.212	85	18	1	0	0	7	4	10	.244	.224
Pre-All Star	.187	155	29	4	0	0	10	8	25	.226	.213	July	.233	30	7	2	0	0	5	3	2	.303	.300
Post-All Star	.272	257	70	8	3	2	22	20	34	.326	.350	August	.243	136	33	3	3	1	12	10	21	.299	.331
Scoring Posn	.357	98	35	3	1	1	31	9	14	.409	.439	Sept/Oct	.323	99	32	4	0	1	7	8	12	.370	.394
Close & Late	.250	80	20	4	0	0	5	5	16	.294	.300	vs. AL	.172	58	10	2	1	0	7	4	7	.222	.241
None on/out	.219	114	25	4	1	0	7	7	21	.264	.272	vs. NL	.251	354	89	10	2	2	25	24	52	.300	.308

Julian Tavarez — Giants
Age 25 – Pitches Right (groundball pitcher)

	ERA	W	L	Sv	G	GS	IP	BB	SO	Avg	H	2B	3B	HR	RBI	OBP	SLG	GF	IR	IRS	Hld	SvOp	SB	CS	GB	FB	G/F
1997 Season	3.87	6	4	0	89	0	88.1	34	38	.277	91	16	2	6	56	.344	.392	13	80	32	26	3	5	0	190	67	2.84
Career (1993-1997)	4.31	22	16	0	206	12	292.2	91	171	.286	327	62	6	30	176	.340	.430	41	147	51	58	7	13	7	508	268	1.90

1997 Season

	ERA	W	L	Sv	G	GS	IP	H	HR	BB	SO		Avg	AB	H	2B	3B	HR	RBI	BB	SO	OBP	SLG
Home	4.95	3	1	0	43	0	40.0	47	4	15	19	vs. Left	.258	124	32	7	1	0	18	17	12	.338	.331
Away	2.98	3	3	0	46	0	48.1	44	2	19	19	vs. Right	.288	205	59	9	1	6	38	17	26	.348	.429
Day	4.64	4	2	0	40	0	33.0	39	3	16	17	Inning 1-6	.333	63	21	3	1	2	27	5	3	.380	.508
Night	3.42	2	2	0	49	0	55.1	52	3	18	21	Inning 7+	.263	266	70	13	1	4	29	29	35	.336	.365
Grass	4.58	5	3	0	75	0	70.2	75	6	29	30	None on	.309	165	51	7	1	3	3	12	21	.363	.418
Turf	1.02	1	1	0	14	0	17.2	16	0	5	8	Runners on	.244	164	40	9	1	3	53	22	17	.327	.366
March/April	4.50	0	0	0	13	0	12.0	14	0	4	5	Scoring Posn	.257	101	26	6	1	2	51	15	10	.341	.396
May	9.45	1	2	0	16	0	13.1	20	3	11	5	Close & Late	.279	147	41	7	0	2	18	19	19	.361	.367
June	0.00	0	0	0	18	0	19.1	11	0	4	5	None on/out	.324	74	24	3	1		2	2	14	.351	.473
July	3.07	2	1	0	14	0	14.2	14	1	3	8	vs. 1st Batr (relief)	.375	80	30	5	1	3	22	5	10	.393	.575

1997 Season

	ERA	W	L	Sv	G	GS	IP	H	HR	BB	SO		Avg	AB	H	2B	3B	HR	RBI	BB	SO	OBP	SLG
August	4.32	2	1	0	15	0	16.2	21	1	8	5	1st Inning Pitched	.273	267	73	14	2	5	52	28	30	.337	.397
Sept/Oct	3.65	1	0	0	13	0	12.1	11	1	4	9	First 15 Pitches	.269	242	65	13	2	4	41	21	27	.322	.388
Starter	0.00	0	0	0	0	0	0.0	0	0	0	0	Pitch 16-30	.294	68	20	2	0	1	12	12	9	.412	.368
Reliever	3.87	6	4	0	89	0	88.1	91	6	34	38	Pitch 31-45	.316	19	6	1	0	1	3	1	2	.350	.526
0 Days rest (Relief)	2.87	2	1	0	30	0	31.1	24	1	9	11	Pitch 46+	.000	0	0	0	0	0	0	0	0	.000	.000
1 or 2 Days rest	3.94	4	2	0	50	0	48.0	55	4	20	21	First Pitch	.189	53	10	2	0	0	5	5	0	.274	.226
3+ Days rest	7.00	0	1	0	9	0	9.0	12	1	5	6	Ahead in Count	.220	118	26	3	2	1	20	0	32	.231	.305
vs. AL	4.32	0	0	0	9	0	8.1	14	0	3	2	Behind in Count	.379	95	36	8	0	3	21	20	0	.475	.558
vs. NL	3.83	6	4	0	80	0	80.0	77	6	31	36	Two Strikes	.183	126	23	3	0	3	19	9	38	.243	.278
Pre-All Star	3.97	2	2	0	49	0	45.1	47	3	19	17	Pre-All Star	.276	170	47	11	1	3	28	19	17	.350	.406
Post-All Star	3.77	4	2	0	40	0	43.0	44	3	15	21	Post-All Star	.277	159	44	5	1	3	28	15	21	.337	.377

Career (1993-1997)

	ERA	W	L	Sv	G	GS	IP	H	HR	BB	SO		Avg	AB	H	2B	3B	HR	RBI	BB	SO	OBP	SLG
Home	3.93	12	5	0	100	5	142.0	158	16	34	90	vs. Left	.312	507	158	34	5	12	75	50	61	.372	.469
Away	4.66	10	11	0	106	7	150.2	169	14	57	81	vs. Right	.266	635	169	28	1	18	101	41	110	.314	.398
Day	3.98	10	3	0	78	6	95.0	97	8	36	53	Inning 1-6	.359	348	125	26	4	15	95	29	27	.407	.586
Night	4.46	12	13	0	128	10	197.2	230	22	55	118	Inning 7+	.254	794	202	36	2	15	81	62	144	.310	.361
Grass	4.45	20	13	0	172	9	240.2	266	26	75	141	None on	.294	598	176	32	3	15	15	39	92	.346	.433
Turf	3.63	2	3	0	34	3	52.0	61	4	16	30	Runners on	.278	544	151	30	3	15	161	52	79	.334	.426
March/April	3.06	1	1	0	26	0	32.1	27	1	10	20	Scoring Posn	.277	318	88	19	3	8	145	38	45	.342	.431
May	6.13	4	4	0	38	1	39.2	55	6	16	26	Close & Late	.243	407	99	14	0	10	41	37	78	.307	.351
June	2.29	3	3	0	38	1	59.0	53	3	13	33	None on/out	.277	271	75	13	1	10	10	11	44	.317	.443
July	4.88	4	2	0	28	3	48.0	60	5	13	22	vs. 1st Batr (relief)	.324	176	57	9	1	8	30	11	32	.356	.523
August	4.57	8	6	0	43	4	67.0	81	10	23	40	1st Inning Pitched	.272	680	185	32	5	16	119	56	106	.324	.404
Sept/Oct	5.21	2	0	0	33	3	46.2	51	5	16	30	First 15 Pitches	.270	596	161	28	3	14	83	42	91	.316	.398
Starter	8.83	3	5	0	12	12	52.0	90	12	17	30	Pitch 16-30	.275	298	82	19	2	6	50	33	50	.351	.413
Reliever	3.33	19	11	0	194	0	240.2	237	18	74	148	Pitch 31-45	.286	133	38	7	1	6	21	9	19	.338	.489
0 Days rest (Relief)	2.75	5	2	0	46	0	55.2	45	4	15	28	Pitch 46+	.400	115	46	8	0	4	22	7	11	.435	.574
1 or 2 Days rest	3.69	12	7	0	103	0	129.1	136	12	43	79	First Pitch	.278	176	49	8	0	5	22	11	0	.325	.409
3+ Days rest	3.07	2	2	0	45	0	55.2	56	2	16	41	Ahead in Count	.225	466	105	18	4	6	58	0	145	.234	.309
vs. AL	4.49	16	12	0	126	12	212.2	250	24	60	135	Behind in Count	.372	290	108	24	1	12	59	51	0	.461	.586
vs. NL	3.83	6	4	0	80	0	80.0	77	6	31	36	Two Strikes	.206	475	98	17	1	7	56	29	171	.259	.291
Pre-All Star	3.63	10	8	0	108	3	144.0	151	11	42	84	Pre-All Star	.274	551	151	32	3	11	73	42	84	.327	.403
Post-All Star	4.96	12	8	0	98	9	148.2	176	19	49	87	Post-All Star	.298	591	176	30	3	19	103	49	87	.352	.455

Pitcher vs. Batter (career)

Pitches Best Vs.	Avg	AB	H	2B	3B	HR	RBI	BB	SO	OBP	SLG	Pitches Worst Vs.	Avg	AB	H	2B	3B	HR	RBI	BB	SO	OBP	SLG
												Mo Vaughn	.583	12	7	0	0	0	2	2	1	.643	.583
												Joe Carter	.400	10	4	0	0	1	3	1	1	.455	.700

Billy Taylor — Athletics

Age 36 – Pitches Right (groundball pitcher)

	ERA	W	L	Sv	G	GS	IP	BB	SO	Avg	H	2B	3B	HR	RBI	OBP	SLG	GF	IR	IRS	Hld	SvOp	SB	CS	GB	FB	G/F
1997 Season	3.82	6	4	23	72	0	73.0	36	66	.254	70	17	2	3	39	.348	.362	45	48	15	7	30	10	3	117	57	2.05
Career (1994-1997)	3.91	10	10	41	168	0	179.2	79	181	.237	160	33	3	9	93	.325	.349	86	122	32	13	52	21	3	243	154	1.58

1997 Season

	ERA	W	L	Sv	G	GS	IP	H	HR	BB	SO		Avg	AB	H	2B	3B	HR	RBI	BB	SO	OBP	SLG
Home	4.50	1	0	12	40	0	40.0	35	2	16	36	vs. Left	.323	130	42	11	2	2	22	18	25	.407	.485
Away	3.00	2	4	11	32	0	33.0	35	1	23	30	vs. Right	.192	146	28	6	0	1	17	18	41	.296	.253
Day	5.14	1	0	8	30	0	28.0	29	1	12	21	Inning 1-6	.000	2	0	0	0	0	0	0	0	.000	.000
Night	3.00	2	4	15	42	0	45.0	41	2	24	45	Inning 7+	.255	274	70	17	2	3	39	36	66	.350	.365
Grass	3.78	3	2	19	63	0	64.1	59	3	31	56	None on	.200	130	26	8	2	1	1	11	30	.283	.315
Turf	4.15	0	2	4	9	0	8.2	11	0	5	10	Runners on	.301	146	44	9	0	2	38	25	36	.402	.404
March/April	7.50	1	1	5	12	0	12.0	17	1	10	6	Scoring Posn	.269	104	28	1	0	1	36	19	23	.381	.385
May	4.50	1	2	4	11	0	12.0	12	2	9	12	Close & Late	.222	189	42	12	1	2	28	30	47	.335	.328
June	5.40	0	1	6	13	0	10.0	7	0	6	13	None on/out	.241	54	13	4	2	1	1	5	11	.317	.444
July	0.73	0	0	4	10	0	12.1	5	0	3	10	vs. 1st Batr (relief)	.212	66	14	4	1	1	6	5	17	.278	.348
August	3.86	1	0	2	12	0	14.0	11	0	5	16	1st Inning Pitched	.251	231	58	14	2	3	34	25	53	.335	.368
Sept/Oct	1.42	0	0	2	14	0	12.2	18	0	3	9	First 15 Pitches	.241	191	46	10	2	1	19	20	38	.326	.330
Starter	0.00	0	0	0	0	0	0.0	0	0	0	0	Pitch 16-30	.257	74	19	6	0	2	16	12	26	.360	.419
Reliever	3.82	3	4	23	72	0	73.0	70	3	36	66	Pitch 31-45	.455	11	5	1	0	0	4	4	2	.600	.545
0 Days rest (Relief)	5.40	1	1	6	12	0	10.0	13	0	5	8	Pitch 46+	.000	0	0	0	0	0	0	0	0	.000	.000
1 or 2 Days rest	2.72	2	2	16	48	0	49.2	40	1	25	43	First Pitch	.407	27	11	3	1	0	5	8	0	.543	.593
3+ Days rest	6.75	0	1	1	12	0	13.1	17	2	6	15	Ahead in Count	.224	147	33	7	1	0	15	0	53	.243	.286
vs. AL	3.93	3	4	21	66	0	66.1	65	3	34	58	Behind in Count	.273	44	12	1	0	2	9	16	0	.475	.432
vs. NL	2.70	0	0	2	6	0	6.2	5	0	2	8	Two Strikes	.193	140	27	7	0	1	16	12	66	.274	.264
Pre-All Star	5.40	2	4	16	38	0	36.2	36	3	25	32	Pre-All Star	.255	141	36	9	2	3	21	25	32	.380	.411
Post-All Star	2.23	1	0	7	34	0	36.1	34	0	11	34	Post-All Star	.252	135	34	8	0	0	18	11	34	.311	.311

Career (1994-1997)

	ERA	W	L	Sv	G	GS	IP	H	HR	BB	SO		Avg	AB	H	2B	3B	HR	RBI	BB	SO	OBP	SLG
Home	4.81	6	4	19	87	0	95.1	86	7	40	91	vs. Left	.287	282	81	17	3	6	43	42	46	.384	.433
Away	2.88	4	6	22	81	0	84.1	74	5	39	90	vs. Right	.202	392	79	16	0	6	50	37	135	.280	.288
Day	3.61	5	3	16	66	0	72.1	64	4	27	78	Inning 1-6	.217	46	10	1	0	3	10	5	11	.302	.435
Night	4.11	5	7	25	102	0	107.1	96	8	52	103	Inning 7+	.239	628	150	32	3	9	83	74	170	.326	.342
Grass	3.94	10	8	33	148	0	160.0	137	12	71	162	None on	.205	342	70	17	2	3	3	30	103	.282	.292
Turf	3.66	0	2	8	20	0	19.2	23	0	8	19	Runners on	.271	332	90	16	1	9	90	49	78	.366	.407

Career (1994-1997)

	ERA	W	L	Sv	G	GS	IP	H	HR	BB	SO		Avg	AB	H	2B	3B	HR	RBI	BB	SO	OBP	SLG
March/April	4.24	1	1	8	23	0	23.1	24	2	13	17	Scoring Posn	.252	226	57	15	1	6	84	35	48	.354	.407
May	3.92	2	6	5	38	0	41.1	42	4	18	47	Close & Late	.223	367	82	17	2	5	52	57	100	.334	.322
June	5.40	2	1	9	34	0	33.1	30	2	16	37	None on/out	.238	147	35	8	2	2	2	13	45	.309	.361
July	2.33	3	1	10	35	0	38.2	21	3	15	38	vs. 1st Batr (relief)	.209	153	32	7	1	3	19	12	50	.275	.327
August	5.75	1	1	4	17	0	20.1	18	1	7	23	1st Inning Pitched	.219	512	112	23	3	9	72	50	136	.298	.328
Sept/Oct	2.38	1	0	5	21	0	22.2	25	0	10	19	First 15 Pitches	.216	435	94	18	3	6	48	41	108	.295	.313
Starter	0.00	0	0	0	0	0	0.0	0	0	0	0	Pitch 16-30	.254	201	51	13	0	6	36	30	62	.352	.408
Reliever	3.91	10	10	41	168	0	179.2	160	12	79	181	Pitch 31-45	.395	38	15	2	0	0	9	8	11	.500	.447
0 Days rest (Relief)	2.37	2	2	13	34	0	30.1	23	0	10	32	Pitch 46+	.000	0	0	0	0	0	0	0	0	.000	.000
1 or 2 Days rest	3.63	7	5	23	99	0	111.2	98	8	55	106	First Pitch	.377	61	23	6	1	3	16	14	0	.500	.656
3+ Days rest	5.97	1	3	5	35	0	37.2	39	4	14	43	Ahead in Count	.199	362	72	17	1	1	37	0	150	.216	.260
vs. AL	3.95	10	10	39	162	0	173.0	155	12	77	173	Behind in Count	.297	111	33	4	0	5	22	39	0	.480	.468
vs. NL	2.70	0	0	2	6	0	6.2	5	0	2	8	Two Strikes	.170	364	62	16	0	2	32	25	181	.236	.231
Pre-All Star	4.05	7	8	24	106	0	111.0	102	9	51	112	Pre-All Star	.242	422	102	23	3	9	58	51	112	.335	.374
Post-All Star	3.67	3	2	17	62	0	68.2	58	3	28	69	Post-All Star	.230	252	58	10	0	3	35	28	69	.307	.306

Pitcher vs. Batter (career)

Pitches Best Vs.	Avg	AB	H	2B	3B	HR	RBI	BB	SO	OBP	SLG	Pitches Worst Vs.	Avg	AB	H	2B	3B	HR	RBI	BB	SO	OBP	SLG
Juan Gonzalez	.091	11	1	0	0	0	1	0	4	.091	.091												
Edgar Martinez	.111	9	1	0	0	0	1	2	1	.273	.111												

Miguel Tejada — Athletics
Age 22 – Bats Right

	Avg	G	AB	R	H	2B	3B	HR	RBI	BB	SO	HBP	GDP	SB	CS	OBP	SLG	IBB	SH	SF	#Pit	#P/PA	GB	FB	G/F
1997 Season	.202	26	99	10	20	3	2	2	10	2	22	3	3	2	0	.240	.333	0	0	0	375	3.61	32	32	1.00

1997 Season

	Avg	AB	H	2B	3B	HR	RBI	BB	SO	OBP	SLG		Avg	AB	H	2B	3B	HR	RBI	BB	SO	OBP	SLG
vs. Left	.250	28	7	1	0	1	2	0	2	.276	.393	Scoring Posn	.318	22	7	2	1	1	9	0	2	.348	.636
vs. Right	.183	71	13	2	2	1	8	2	20	.227	.310	Close & Late	.200	15	3	0	0	1	2	0	3	.200	.400

Amaury Telemaco — Cubs
Age 24 – Pitches Right (flyball pitcher)

	ERA	W	L	Sv	G	GS	IP	BB	SO	Avg	H	2B	3B	HR	RBI	OBP	SLG	CG	ShO	Sup	QS	#P/S	SB	CS	GB	FB	G/F
1997 Season	6.16	0	3	0	10	5	38.0	11	29	.303	47	16	1	4	26	.347	.497	0	0	2.13	2	88	4	1	52	42	1.24
Career (1996-1997)	5.65	5	10	0	35	22	135.1	42	93	.287	155	38	2	24	86	.340	.498	0	0	4.72	9	84	13	4	165	169	0.98

1997 Season

	ERA	W	L	Sv	G	GS	IP	H	HR	BB	SO		Avg	AB	H	2B	3B	HR	RBI	BB	SO	OBP	SLG
Home	6.65	0	2	0	6	3	21.2	26	3	8	17	vs. Left	.303	76	23	9	0	1	9	6	12	.354	.461
Away	5.51	0	1	0	4	2	16.1	21	1	3	12	vs. Right	.304	79	24	7	1	3	17	5	17	.341	.532

Anthony Telford — Expos
Age 32 – Pitches Right (groundball pitcher)

	ERA	W	L	Sv	G	GS	IP	BB	SO	Avg	H	2B	3B	HR	RBI	OBP	SLG	GF	IR	IRS	Hld	SvOp	SB	CS	GB	FB	G/F
1997 Season	3.24	4	6	1	65	0	89.0	33	61	.236	77	6	3	11	39	.315	.374	17	53	10	11	5	8	3	137	78	1.76
Last Five Years	3.74	4	6	1	68	0	96.1	34	67	.246	84	7	3	14	47	.321	.399	19	55	10	11	5	9	3	147	91	1.62

1997 Season

	ERA	W	L	Sv	G	GS	IP	H	HR	BB	SO		Avg	AB	H	2B	3B	HR	RBI	BB	SO	OBP	SLG
Home	2.90	2	2	1	34	0	49.2	40	8	17	32	vs. Left	.232	138	32	4	1	5	15	17	19	.314	.384
Away	3.66	2	4	0	31	0	39.1	37	3	16	29	vs. Right	.239	188	45	2	2	6	24	16	42	.316	.367
Day	3.48	2	2	0	19	0	31.0	24	4	12	24	Inning 1-6	.239	113	27	4	0	3	17	14	20	.333	.354
Night	3.10	2	4	1	46	0	58.0	53	7	21	37	Inning 7+	.235	213	50	2	3	8	22	19	41	.305	.385
Grass	3.30	2	1	0	23	0	30.0	25	2	12	23	None on	.239	176	42	2	2	10	10	8	35	.280	.443
Turf	3.20	2	5	1	42	0	59.0	52	9	21	38	Runners on	.233	150	35	4	1	1	29	25	26	.352	.293
March/April	4.80	0	0	0	7	0	15.0	14	3	10	7	Scoring Posn	.258	93	24	3	0	0	26	16	16	.375	.290
May	0.57	1	0	0	14	0	15.2	9	1	6	7	Close & Late	.262	130	34	2	2	7	18	15	29	.345	.469
June	2.31	1	1	0	10	0	11.2	5	2	5	7	None on/out	.295	78	23	2		5	5	4	15	.337	.564
July	3.78	0	2	0	11	0	16.2	18	0	5	9	vs. 1st Batr (relief)	.214	56	12	1	0	2	5	6	12	.323	.339
August	1.10	2	1	0	12	0	16.1	12	1	5	20	1st Inning Pitched	.219	192	42	4	2	3	23	22	38	.311	.307
Sept/Oct	7.24	0	2	1	11	0	13.2	19	4	2	11	First 15 Pitches	.231	173	40	4	2	3	20	16	29	.314	.329
Starter	0.00	0	0	0	0	0	0.0	0	0	0	0	Pitch 16-30	.208	106	22	0	1	5	11	13	25	.292	.368
Reliever	3.24	4	6	1	65	0	89.0	77	11	33	61	Pitch 31-45	.316	38	12	1	0	3	5	3	5	.366	.579
0 Days rest (Relief)	3.52	0	2	0	18	0	30.2	28	4	8	20	Pitch 46+	.333	9	3	1	0	0	3	1	2	.400	.444
1 or 2 Days rest	3.86	2	4	0	30	0	32.2	31	6	14	24	First Pitch	.327	49	16	1	1	3	10	3	0	.400	.571
3+ Days rest	2.10	2	0	1	17	0	25.2	18	1	11	17	Ahead in Count	.171	158	27	3	1	2	13	0	52	.170	.241
vs. AL	10.13	1	1	0	5	0	2.2	3	0	5	1	Behind in Count	.232	56	13	1	1	3	7	16	0	.403	.446
vs. NL	3.02	3	5	1	60	0	86.1	74	11	28	60	Two Strikes	.157	153	24	2	1	3	13	14	61	.232	.242
Pre-All Star	2.49	2	2	0	33	0	47.0	34	6	22	23	Pre-All Star	.202	168	34	2	1	6	21	22	23	.306	.333
Post-All Star	4.07	2	4	1	32	0	42.0	43	5	11	38	Post-All Star	.272	158	43	4	2	5	18	11	38	.326	.418

Dave Telgheder — Athletics
Age 31 – Pitches Right

	ERA	W	L	Sv	G	GS	IP	BB	SO	Avg	H	2B	3B	HR	RBI	OBP	SLG	CG	ShO	Sup	QS	#P/S	SB	CS	GB	FB	G/F
1997 Season	6.06	4	6	0	20	19	101.0	35	55	.324	134	32	3	15	59	.373	.524	0	0	6.33	5	89	9	4	160	123	1.30
Career (1993-1997)	5.34	15	18	0	73	44	291.2	97	153	.301	353	81	12	43	156	.355	.501	1	1	5.31	17	89	21	9	424	359	1.18

1997 Season

	ERA	W	L	Sv	G	GS	IP	H	HR	BB	SO		Avg	AB	H	2B	3B	HR	RBI	BB	SO	OBP	SLG
Home	5.94	2	2	0	8	7	36.1	52	4	8	17	vs. Left	.340	209	71	18	3	9	29	24	26	.403	.584
Away	6.12	2	4	0	12	12	64.2	82	11	27	38	vs. Right	.307	205	63	14	0	6	30	11	29	.341	.463
Starter	6.24	4	6	0	19	19	98.0	133	15	33	53	Scoring Posn	.295	112	33	8	0	1	40	13	10	.353	.393
Reliever	0.00	0	0	0	1	0	3.0	1	0	2	2	Close & Late	.188	16	3	0	1	1	2	3	2	.316	.500
0-3 Days Rest (Start)	0.00	0	0	0	1	1	7.2	6	0	2	1	None on/out	.294	102	30	13	1	2	2	7	13	.345	.500
4 Days Rest	8.05	2	4	0	11	11	50.1	74	6	23	24	First Pitch	.370	54	20	4	0	2	9	0	0	.370	.556
5+ Days Rest	5.18	2	2	0	7	7	40.0	53	9	8	28	Ahead in Count	.274	179	49	11	1	6	21	0	48	.279	.447
Pre-All Star	6.02	2	4	0	15	14	80.2	106	11	26	45	Behind in Count	.362	94	34	10	1	3	16	18	0	.452	.585
Post-All Star	6.20	2	2	0	5	5	20.1	28	4	9	10	Two Strikes	.286	189	54	14	1	6	20	17	55	.348	.466

Career (1993-1997)

	ERA	W	L	Sv	G	GS	IP	H	HR	BB	SO		Avg	AB	H	2B	3B	HR	RBI	BB	SO	OBP	SLG
Home	5.37	9	9	0	32	21	132.1	159	17	40	64	vs. Left	.317	603	191	46	9	21	78	52	79	.369	.527
Away	5.31	6	9	0	41	23	159.1	194	26	57	89	vs. Right	.285	569	162	35	3	22	78	45	74	.339	.473
Day	5.70	4	5	0	26	15	96.1	122	13	39	44	Inning 1-6	.308	949	292	68	8	37	130	82	126	.363	.513
Night	5.16	11	13	0	47	29	195.1	231	30	58	109	Inning 7+	.274	223	61	13	4	6	26	15	27	.321	.448
Grass	5.36	13	15	0	57	37	242.0	292	34	80	123	None on	.307	659	202	48	9	30	30	57	90	.364	.543
Turf	5.26	2	3	0	16	7	49.2	61	9	17	30	Runners on	.294	513	151	33	3	13	126	40	63	.344	.446
March/April	4.91	0	2	0	12	5	44.0	53	7	19	19	Scoring Posn	.279	294	82	24	1	6	105	34	31	.347	.429
May	7.71	1	2	0	6	6	30.1	40	4	12	16	Close & Late	.250	76	19	7	1	1	5	6	8	.305	.408
June	5.17	3	1	0	9	4	31.1	35	5	7	20	None on/out	.288	292	84	29	2	10	10	24	37	.344	.503
July	5.11	1	4	0	9	7	44.0	62	7	10	19	vs. 1st Batr (relief)	.120	25	3	1	1	0	2	4	3	.241	.240
August	5.62	2	4	0	18	7	57.2	70	6	15	34	1st Inning Pitched	.278	277	77	17	2	9	45	26	39	.337	.451
Sept/Oct	4.70	8	5	0	19	15	84.1	93	14	34	45	First 75 Pitches	.311	958	298	62	10	39	134	78	128	.364	.519
Starter	5.38	14	17	0	44	44	241.0	301	36	82	127	Pitch 76-90	.264	121	32	14	1	1	16	13	13	.331	.421
Reliever	5.15	1	1	0	29	0	50.2	52	7	15	26	Pitch 91-105	.200	65	13	1	0	2	3	4	9	.246	.308
0-3 Days Rest (Start)	1.95	2	1	0	4	4	27.2	26	1	7	10	Pitch 106+	.357	28	10	4	1	1	3	2	3	.400	.679
4 Days Rest	6.73	7	11	0	26	26	128.1	178	18	53	57	First Pitch	.335	179	60	17	0	9	34	7	0	.363	.601
5+ Days Rest	4.45	5	5	0	14	14	85.0	97	17	22	60	Ahead in Count	.270	519	140	28	6	16	53	0	137	.276	.439
vs. AL	5.49	7	13	0	34	31	169.0	213	25	60	87	Behind in Count	.316	263	83	20	2	11	42	46	0	.412	.532
vs. NL	5.14	8	5	0	39	13	122.2	140	18	37	66	Two Strikes	.256	488	125	30	4	15	51	44	153	.320	.426
Pre-All Star	6.04	5	6	0	29	17	117.2	148	18	41	58	Pre-All Star	.311	476	148	31	5	18	68	41	58	.366	.511
Post-All Star	4.86	10	12	0	44	27	174.0	205	25	56	95	Post-All Star	.295	696	205	50	7	25	88	56	95	.347	.494

Pitcher vs. Batter (career)

Pitches Best Vs.	Avg	AB	H	2B	3B	HR	RBI	BB	SO	OBP	SLG	Pitches Worst Vs.	Avg	AB	H	2B	3B	HR	RBI	BB	SO	OBP	SLG
Jay Buhner	.182	11	2	0	0	1	4	2	1	.308	.455	Edgar Martinez	.556	9	5	2	0	1	3	2	0	.636	1.111
Jim Thome	.222	9	2	1	0	0	3	2	3	.364	.333	Bernie Williams	.500	10	5	2	1	1	1	1	0	.545	1.200
												Derek Jeter	.455	11	5	0	0	1	1	1	1	.500	.727
												Paul Sorrento	.400	10	4	2	0	2	3	3	2	.538	1.200
												Joey Cora	.364	11	4	1	1	0	1	1	0	.462	.636

Mickey Tettleton — Rangers
Age 37 – Bats Both (flyball hitter)

	Avg	G	AB	R	H	2B	3B	HR	RBI	BB	SO	HBP	GDP	SB	CS	OBP	SLG	IBB	SH	SF	#Pit	#P/PA	GB	FB	G/F
1997 Season	.091	17	44	5	4	1	0	3	4	3	12	1	1	0	0	.167	.318	1	0		190	3.96	13	17	0.76
Last Five Years	.241	553	1825	295	439	89	8	108	326	411	496	16	29	5	9	.381	.476	36	2	21	9847	4.33	475	587	0.81

1997 Season

	Avg	AB	H	2B	3B	HR	RBI	BB	SO	OBP	SLG		Avg	AB	H	2B	3B	HR	RBI	BB	SO	OBP	SLG
vs. Left	.067	15	1	0	0	1	1	0	4	.067	.267	Scoring Posn	.000	7	0	0	0	0	1	3	2	.300	.000
vs. Right	.103	29	3	1	0	2	3	3	8	.212	.345	Close & Late	.125	8	1	1	0	0	0	0	4	.125	.250

Last Five Years

	Avg	AB	H	2B	3B	HR	RBI	BB	SO	OBP	SLG		Avg	AB	H	2B	3B	HR	RBI	BB	SO	OBP	SLG
vs. Left	.236	516	122	33	2	25	81	113	141	.370	.453	First Pitch	.432	88	38	7	0	8	36	19	0	.523	.784
vs. Right	.242	1309	317	56	6	83	245	298	355	.385	.484	Ahead in Count	.325	502	163	34	3	55	150	211	0	.517	.733
Groundball	.254	401	102	18	2	28	71	86	109	.386	.519	Behind in Count	.162	728	118	32	1	19	63	0	369	.176	.287
Flyball	.234	385	90	16	2	24	69	88	97	.377	.473	Two Strikes	.148	940	139	31	3	27	93	181	496	.292	.273
Home	.248	920	228	47	3	63	179	218	245	.391	.511	Batting #5	.218	650	142	35	3	38	100	142	192	.358	.457
Away	.233	905	211	42	5	45	147	193	251	.370	.440	Batting #6	.256	659	169	32	5	44	137	160	176	.404	.520
Day	.225	551	124	22	1	32	96	122	151	.371	.443	Other	.248	516	128	22	0	26	89	109	128	.380	.442
Night	.247	1274	315	67	7	76	230	289	345	.385	.490	March/April	.225	262	59	15	0	18	53	69	76	.389	.489
Grass	.243	1579	384	76	7	99	287	359	427	.385	.488	May	.270	352	95	16	3	19	63	71	89	.392	.494
Turf	.224	246	55	13	1	9	39	52	69	.357	.394	June	.224	361	81	15	0	25	62	66	89	.346	.474
Pre-All Star	.243	1108	269	53	5	70	202	234	294	.377	.489	July	.217	327	71	15	2	18	50	76	109	.370	.440
Post-All Star	.237	717	170	36	3	38	124	177	202	.387	.455	August	.235	277	65	13	1	13	53	69	86	.383	.430
Scoring Posn	.255	462	118	16	3	27	219	158	128	.433	.478	Sept/Oct	.276	246	68	15	2	15	45	60	64	.419	.537
Close & Late	.303	244	74	10	1	16	53	49	66	.422	.549	vs. AL	.241	1821	439	89	8	108	326	410	496	.381	.477
None on/out	.266	515	137	28	3	39	39	79	128	.368	.559	vs. NL	.000	4	0	0	0	0	0	1	0	.200	.000

Batter vs. Pitcher (career)

Hits Best Against	Avg	AB	H	2B	3B	HR	RBI	BB	SO	OBP	SLG	Hits Worst Against	Avg	AB	H	2B	3B	HR	RBI	BB	SO	OBP	SLG
Angel Miranda	.571	14	8	1	0	3	5	0	3	.571	1.286	Jason Bere	.000	14	0	0	0	0	0	6	9	.300	.000
Pat Mahomes	.500	6	3	1	0	2	3	5	2	.727	1.667	Tony Castillo	.000	10	0	0	0	0	1	2	2	.154	.000

460

Batter vs. Pitcher (career)

Hits Best Against	Avg	AB	H	2B	3B	HR	RBI	BB	SO	OBP	SLG	Hits Worst Against	Avg	AB	H	2B	3B	HR	RBI	BB	SO	OBP	SLG
Mark Clark	.444	9	4	1	0	1	3	2	2	.545	.889	Albie Lopez	.000	8	0	0	0	0	0	2	3	.273	.000
Bob Wickman	.375	16	6	0	0	3	7	5	4	.524	.938	Felipe Lira	.091	11	1	0	0	1	0	5	.083	.091
James Baldwin	.333	9	3	1	0	2	3	2	2	.455	1.111	Brad Radke	.091	11	1	0	0	0	1	2	.167	.091

Bob Tewksbury — Twins
Age 37 – Pitches Right (groundball pitcher)

	ERA	W	L	Sv	G	GS	IP	BB	SO	Avg	H	2B	3B	HR	RBI	OBP	SLG	CG	ShO	Sup	QS	#P/S	SB	CS	GB	FB	G/F
1997 Season	4.22	8	13	0	26	26	168.2	31	92	.297	200	46	4	12	75	.325	.430	5	2	4.22	15	95	6	2	279	187	1.49
Last Five Years	4.40	55	50	0	139	136	874.1	136	447	.297	1041	211	21	71	412	.324	.431	16	4	5.30	74	90	66	22	1526	867	1.76

1997 Season

	ERA	W	L	Sv	G	GS	IP	H	BB	SO		Avg	AB	H	2B	3B	HR	RBI	BB	SO	OBP	SLG
Home	4.44	3	7	0	11	11	77.0	96	7	45	vs. Left	.308	351	108	25	2	6	41	22	38	.345	.442
Away	4.03	5	6	0	15	15	91.2	104	5	47	vs. Right	.285	323	92	21	2	6	34	9	54	.304	.418
Day	4.23	2	2	0	6	6	38.1	38	1	22	Inning 1-6	.301	575	173	41	4	12	68	28	82	.331	.449
Night	4.21	6	11	0	20	20	130.1	162	11	70	Inning 7+	.273	99	27	5	0	0	7	3	10	.291	.323
Grass	4.62	4	5	0	11	11	64.1	79	5	35	None on	.297	381	113	28	3	7	7	13	52	.320	.441
Turf	3.97	4	8	0	15	15	104.1	121	7	57	Runners on	.297	293	87	18	1	5	68	18	40	.332	.416
March/April	3.77	1	4	0	6	6	43.0	47	3	10	Scoring Posn	.322	171	55	10	0	4	64	13	21	.359	.450
May	3.15	1	1	0	3	3	20.0	24	2	11	Close & Late	.327	49	16	3	0	0	4	2	4	.353	.388
June	3.27	2	2	0	5	5	33.0	37	1	15	None on/out	.292	171	50	13	2	2	6	27	.316	.427
July	6.35	0	1	0	3	3	17.0	27	1	8	vs. 1st Batr (relief)	.000	0	0	0	0	0	0	0	0	.000	.000
August	4.05	1	2	0	3	3	20.0	19	0	10	1st Inning Pitched	.279	104	29	6	0	1	11	6	12	.324	.365
Sept/Oct	5.30	3	3	0	6	6	35.2	46	5	5	First 75 Pitches	.312	509	159	39	3	11	63	21	67	.338	.466
Starter	4.22	8	13	0	26	26	168.2	200	12	92	Pitch 76-90	.241	83	20	4	0	1	5	13	.281	.325
Reliever	0.00	0	0	0	0	0	0.0	0	0	0	Pitch 91-105	.236	55	13	2	1	0	4	5	9	.295	.309
0-3 Days Rest (Start)	1.13	0	1	0	1	1	8.0	4	0	2	Pitch 106+	.296	27	8	1	0	0	3	.296	.333
4 Days Rest	3.04	8	4	0	16	16	109.2	113	6	21	First Pitch	.327	101	33	7	0	2	14	1	0	.327	.455
5+ Days Rest	7.24	0	8	0	9	9	51.0	83	6	27	Ahead in Count	.234	320	75	23	2	1	19	0	82	.236	.328
vs. AL	4.16	8	12	0	23	23	153.2	176	12	84	Behind in Count	.393	135	53	10	1	5	23	18	0	.458	.593
vs. NL	4.80	0	1	0	3	3	15.0	24	0	8	Two Strikes	.223	283	63	16	2	3	18	12	92	.256	.325
Pre-All Star	3.35	4	7	0	15	15	102.0	116	6	58	Pre-All Star	.288	403	116	22	1	6	34	21	58	.321	.392
Post-All Star	5.54	4	6	0	11	11	66.2	84	6	34	Post-All Star	.310	271	84	24	3	6	41	10	34	.332	.487

Last Five Years

	ERA	W	L	Sv	G	GS	IP	H	HR	BB	SO		Avg	AB	H	2B	3B	HR	RBI	BB	SO	OBP	SLG
Home	4.06	26	25	0	65	62	434.0	496	38	51	236	vs. Left	.297	1758	523	107	13	29	208	81	203	.326	.423
Away	4.72	29	25	0	74	74	440.1	545	33	85	211	vs. Right	.297	1742	518	104	8	42	204	55	244	.321	.439
Day	3.98	15	13	0	35	34	228.1	254	15	30	136	Inning 1-6	.301	3016	909	189	20	61	371	124	386	.329	.438
Night	4.54	40	37	0	104	102	646.0	787	56	106	311	Inning 7+	.273	484	132	22	1	10	41	12	61	.291	.384
Grass	4.51	27	23	0	71	68	431.1	512	36	77	235	None on	.288	2039	588	116	9	42	42	56	244	.310	.416
Turf	4.29	28	27	0	68	68	443.0	529	35	59	212	Runners on	.310	1461	453	95	12	29	370	80	203	.342	.451
March/April	3.99	10	8	0	22	22	149.0	168	16	27	87	Scoring Posn	.306	831	254	53	10	19	335	60	141	.345	.462
May	3.96	13	6	0	26	26	179.2	204	12	23	80	Close & Late	.278	245	68	12	0	2	17	8	32	.305	.351
June	4.74	10	14	0	26	26	163.1	205	12	26	86	None on/out	.304	907	276	55	6	16	16	21	107	.322	.431
July	4.52	8	7	0	26	26	163.1	192	10	25	87	vs. 1st Batr (relief)	.000	3	0	0	0	0	0	0	0	.000	.000
August	3.94	8	6	0	18	17	114.1	129	6	19	51	1st Inning Pitched	.285	547	156	30	3	8	66	29	64	.324	.395
Sept/Oct	5.50	6	9	0	21	19	104.2	143	13	16	56	First 75 Pitches	.301	2767	834	172	19	57	350	109	341	.327	.439
Starter	4.37	55	50	0	136	136	869.0	1034	71	136	445	Pitch 76-90	.292	431	126	25	1	9	49	20	58	.325	.418
Reliever	8.44	0	0	0	3	0	5.1	7	0	0	2	Pitch 91-105	.283	212	60	10	1	4	25	7	31	.308	.396
0-3 Days Rest (Start)	3.65	5	4	0	12	12	74.0	78	4	12	35	Pitch 106+	.233	90	21	4	0	1	8	0	17	.233	.311
4 Days Rest	3.96	31	27	0	76	76	512.0	589	38	84	274	First Pitch	.363	609	221	44	0	15	98	9	0	.367	.509
5+ Days Rest	5.31	19	19	0	48	48	283.0	367	29	40	136	Ahead in Count	.242	1609	390	90	10	17	115	0	405	.247	.342
vs. AL	4.35	16	19	0	44	44	283.1	345	20	45	137	Behind in Count	.357	728	260	49	7	25	122	72	0	.412	.547
vs. NL	4.42	39	31	0	95	92	591.0	696	51	91	310	Two Strikes	.219	1374	301	63	10	14	94	55	447	.251	.310
Pre-All Star	3.96	37	29	0	83	83	557.0	640	40	81	285	Pre-All Star	.289	2215	640	135	9	40	232	81	285	.314	.412
Post-All Star	5.16	18	21	0	56	53	317.1	401	31	55	162	Post-All Star	.312	1285	401	76	12	31	180	55	162	.341	.462

Pitcher vs. Batter (career)

Pitches Best Vs.	Avg	AB	H	2B	3B	HR	RBI	BB	SO	OBP	SLG	Pitches Worst Vs.	Avg	AB	H	2B	3B	HR	RBI	BB	SO	OBP	SLG
Joe Girardi	.056	18	1	0	0	0	0	0	1	.150	.056	Albert Belle	.583	12	7	3	0	0	1	0	0	.583	.833
Gary Sheffield	.071	14	1	0	0	0	1	2	2	.176	.071	Ozzie Guillen	.571	14	8	2	0	0	3	0	1	.533	.714
Juan Samuel	.083	12	1	0	0	0	0	1	2	.154	.083	Ken Griffey Jr	.545	11	6	3	0	2	6	0	2	.545	1.364
Omar Vizquel	.091	11	1	0	0	0	1	1	1	.167	.091	Tim Salmon	.500	12	6	1	0	1	3	0	1	.500	.833
Javy Lopez	.125	16	2	0	0	0	1	2	.125	.125	Paul Molitor	.500	10	5	2	0	0	1	0	.545	.700

Frank Thomas — White Sox
Age 30 – Bats Right (flyball hitter)

	Avg	G	AB	R	H	2B	3B	HR	RBI	BB	SO	HBP	GDP	SB	CS	OBP	SLG	IBB	SH	SF	#Pit	#P/PA	GB	FB	G/F
1997 Season	.347	146	530	110	184	35	0	35	125	109	69	3	15	1	1	.456	.611	9	0	7	2562	3.95	175	193	0.91
Last Five Years	.334	698	2498	534	835	158	1	194	599	575	328	18	79	11	9	.455	.631	99	0	47	12215	3.89	800	863	0.93

1997 Season

	Avg	AB	H	2B	3B	HR	RBI	BB	SO	OBP	SLG		Avg	AB	H	2B	3B	HR	RBI	BB	SO	OBP	SLG
vs. Left	.358	106	38	10	0	12	31	16	11	.435	.792	First Pitch	.339	59	20	5	0	5	15	5	0	.391	.678
vs. Right	.344	424	146	25	0	23	94	93	58	.461	.566	Ahead in Count	.424	158	67	14	0	12	45	69	0	.589	.741
Groundball	.308	117	36	3	0	9	26	21	13	.408	.564	Behind in Count	.259	193	50	10	0	8	28	0	51	.264	.435

461

1997 Season

	Avg	AB	H	2B	3B	HR	RBI	BB	SO	OBP	SLG		Avg	AB	H	2B	3B	HR	RBI	BB	SO	OBP	SLG
Flyball	.293	99	29	8	0	5	19	12	18	.366	.525	Two Strikes	.252	230	58	8	0	12	35	35	69	.350	.443
Home	.319	251	80	12	0	16	53	53	30	.434	.558	Total	.347	530	184	35	0	35	125	109	69	.456	.611
Away	.373	279	104	23	0	19	72	56	39	.476	.659	Batting #3	.347	530	184	35	0	35	125	109	69	.456	.611
Day	.366	175	64	13	0	10	39	32	20	.469	.611	Other	.000	0	0	0	0	0	0	0	0	.000	.000
Night	.338	355	120	22	0	25	86	77	49	.450	.611	March/April	.319	91	29	5	0	2	15	23	11	.452	.440
Grass	.359	460	165	30	0	31	114	98	56	.469	.626	May	.430	86	37	6	0	9	29	27	13	.556	.814
Turf	.271	70	19	5	0	4	11	11	13	.366	.514	June	.390	59	23	5	0	5	16	9	8	.464	.729
Pre-All Star	.368	261	96	19	0	17	63	59	37	.479	.636	July	.321	106	34	8	0	9	31	11	12	.381	.651
Post-All Star	.327	269	88	16	0	18	62	50	32	.433	.587	August	.327	101	33	6	0	5	15	18	17	.430	.535
Scoring Posn	.417	139	58	16	0	10	87	39	14	.524	.748	Sept/Oct	.322	87	28	5	0	5	19	21	8	.459	.552
Close & Late	.333	78	26	4	0	4	20	25	13	.486	.538	vs. AL	.347	496	172	31	0	35	120	108	64	.461	.621
None on/out	.280	100	28	4	0	3	3	16	17	.379	.410	vs. NL	.353	34	12	4	0	0	5	1	5	.378	.471

1997 By Position

Position	Avg	AB	H	2B	3B	HR	RBI	BB	SO	OBP	SLG	G	GS	Innings	PO	A	E	DP	Fld Pct	Rng Fctr	In Zone	Zone Outs	Zone Rtg	MLB Zone
As DH	.314	175	55	10	0	8	30	37	20	.435	.509	49	49	—	—	—	—	—	—	—	—	—	—	—
As 1b	.363	355	129	25	0	27	95	72	49	.467	.662	97	97	822.2	739	48	11	70	.986	—	168	139	.827	.874

Last Five Years

	Avg	AB	H	2B	3B	HR	RBI	BB	SO	OBP	SLG		Avg	AB	H	2B	3B	HR	RBI	BB	SO	OBP	SLG
vs. Left	.366	606	222	42	1	67	164	66	144	.484	.771	First Pitch	.397	315	125	28	0	35	110	76	0	.505	.819
vs. Right	.324	1892	613	116	0	127	435	427	262	.445	.587	Ahead in Count	.394	759	299	61	1	73	200	291	0	.557	.765
Groundball	.336	607	204	31	0	43	135	152	90	.464	.600	Behind in Count	.258	852	220	40	0	44	150	0	244	.261	.460
Flyball	.304	529	161	32	0	40	104	98	72	.411	.592	Two Strikes	.251	1013	254	44	0	50	176	208	328	.377	.442
Home	.329	1207	397	69	1	95	270	276	137	.452	.624	Batting #3	.340	2335	795	153	1	185	563	531	297	.459	.645
Away	.339	1291	438	89	0	99	329	299	191	.458	.638	Batting #4	.247	158	39	5	0	9	35	44	30	.403	.449
Day	.348	739	257	60	1	51	174	167	102	.469	.639	Other	.200	5	1	0	0	0	1	0	1	.200	.200
Night	.329	1759	578	98	0	143	425	408	226	.449	.628	March/April	.323	372	120	26	0	24	89	81	54	.439	.586
Grass	.338	2167	733	137	1	171	530	507	268	.460	.639	May	.352	446	157	35	0	38	119	131	68	.495	.686
Turf	.308	331	102	21	0	23	69	68	60	.424	.580	June	.350	463	162	24	1	39	102	98	60	.461	.659
Pre-All Star	.346	1435	496	98	1	113	347	341	198	.468	.652	July	.350	420	147	32	0	37	116	98	48	.465	.690
Post-All Star	.319	1063	339	60	0	81	252	234	130	.438	.604	August	.323	437	141	25	0	29	95	94	54	.441	.579
Scoring Posn	.341	672	229	55	1	43	387	228	98	.485	.618	Sept/Oct	.300	360	108	16	0	27	78	73	44	.416	.569
Close & Late	.292	367	107	17	0	23	79	107	63	.451	.526	vs. AL	.334	2464	823	154	1	194	594	574	323	.456	.634
None on/out	.329	471	155	23	0	33	33	77	59	.423	.588	vs. NL	.353	34	12	4	0	0	5	1	5	.378	.471

Batter vs. Pitcher (career)

Hits Best Against	Avg	AB	H	2B	3B	HR	RBI	BB	SO	OBP	SLG	Hits Worst Against	Avg	AB	H	2B	3B	HR	RBI	BB	SO	OBP	SLG
Buddy Groom	.667	6	4	0	0	1	3	9	0	.867	1.167	Eric Plunk	.000	16	0	0	0	0	1	2	3	.111	.000
Scott Karl	.583	12	7	1	0	4	8	4	1	.688	1.667	Danny Darwin	.000	15	0	0	0	0	0	4	1	.211	.000
Sterling Hitchcock	.571	14	8	3	0	2	4	2	1	.625	1.214	Mike Timlin	.000	12	0	0	0	0	0	5	5	.333	.000
Willie Adams	.571	7	4	0	0	1	3	5	1	.750	1.000	Dennis Eckersley	.077	13	1	0	0	0	0	0	4	.077	.077
Frank Rodriguez	.500	12	6	2	0	2	5	2	3	.571	1.167	Mark Clark	.100	10	1	1	0	0	0	1	1	.182	.200

Larry Thomas — White Sox

Age 28 – Pitches Left (flyball pitcher)

	ERA	W	L	Sv	G	GS	IP	BB	SO	Avg	H	2B	3B	HR	RBI	OBP	SLG	GF	IR	IRS	Hld	SvOp	SB	CS	GB	FB	G/F
1997 Season	8.10	0	0	0	5	0	3.1	2	0	.250	3	1	0	1	3	.357	.583	0	6				0	0	5	6	0.83
Career (1995-1997)	3.02	2	3	0	79	0	47.2	22	32	.247	43	8	1	3	20	.342	.356	16	70	14	9	2	4	1	56	59	0.95

1997 Season

	ERA	W	L	Sv	G	GS	IP	H	HR	BB	SO		Avg	AB	H	2B	3B	HR	RBI	BB	SO	OBP	SLG
Home	0.00	0	0	0	1	0	1.1	1	0	0	0	vs. Left	.222	9	2	1	0	1	3	1	0	.300	.667
Away	13.50	0	0	0	4	0	2.0	1	1	2	0	vs. Right	.333	3	1	0	0	0	0	0	0	.500	.333

Career (1995-1997)

	ERA	W	L	Sv	G	GS	IP	H	HR	BB	SO		Avg	AB	H	2B	3B	HR	RBI	BB	SO	OBP	SLG
Home	2.00	2	2	0	41	0	27.0	25	2	10	19	vs. Left	.255	94	24	4	0	2	15	9	19	.327	.362
Away	4.35	0	1	0	38	0	20.2	18	1	12	13	vs. Right	.238	80	19	4	1	1	5	13	13	.358	.350
Day	4.02	1	2	0	26	0	15.2	17	2	7	10	Inning 1-6	.294	17	5	1	0	0	1	4	5	.429	.353
Night	2.53	1	1	0	53	0	32.0	26	1	15	22	Inning 7+	.242	157	38	7	1	3	19	18	27	.331	.357
Grass	3.22	2	3	0	71	0	44.2	41	3	20	31	None on	.234	77	18	2	1	0	0	8	13	.314	.286
Turf	0.00	0	0	0	8	0	3.0	2	0	2	1	Runners on	.258	97	25	6	0	3	20	14	19	.363	.412
March/April	2.89	1	1	0	12	0	9.1	8	0	4	7	Scoring Posn	.275	51	14	4	0	1	14	14	14	.448	.412
May	6.75	1	2	0	18	0	8.0	8	1	5	1	Close & Late	.303	76	23	4	0	2	13	9	17	.391	.434
June	1.50	0	0	0	13	0	6.0	9	1	3	3	None on/out	.250	36	9	1	0	0	0	2	6	.289	.278
July	3.60	0	0	0	10	0	5.0	7	0	1	3	vs. 1st Batr (relief)	.324	71	23	4	0	1	9	5	12	.377	.423
August	3.60	0	0	0	16	0	10.0	6	1	4	5	1st Inning Pitched	.269	156	42	8	1	2	18	19	28	.360	.372
Sept/Oct	0.00	0	0	0	10	0	9.1	5	0	5	13	First 15 Pitches	.272	151	41	8	1	2	18	18	26	.360	.377
Starter	0.00	0	0	0	0	0	0.0	0	0	0	0	Pitch 16-30	.087	23	2	0	0	1	2	4	6	.222	.217
Reliever	3.02	2	3	0	79	0	47.2	43	3	22	32	Pitch 31-45	.000	0	0	0	0	0	0	0	0	.000	.000
0 Days rest (Relief)	5.84	2	0	0	27	0	12.1	12	1	10	8	Pitch 46+	.000	0	0	0	0	0	0	0	0	.000	.000
1 or 2 Days rest	2.55	2	1	0	28	0	17.2	15	1	7	11	First Pitch	.211	19	4	1	0	0	1	3	0	.318	.263
3+ Days rest	1.53	0	0	0	24	0	17.2	16	1	5	13	Ahead in Count	.135	74	10	0	0	2	0	30		.147	.162
vs. AL	3.02	2	3	0	79	0	47.2	43	3	22	32	Behind in Count	.380	50	19	5	0	2	13	13	0	.516	.600
vs. NL	0.00	0	0	0	0	0	0.0	0	0	0	0	Two Strikes	.149	74	11	2	0	0	4	6	32	.213	.176
Pre-All Star	3.96	2	3	0	46	0	25.0	28	2	12	14	Pre-All Star	.292	96	28	6	0	2	12	12	14	.382	.417
Post-All Star	1.99	0	0	0	33	0	22.2	15	1	10	18	Post-All Star	.192	78	15	2	1	1	8	10	18	.292	.282

Jim Thome — Indians
Age 27 – Bats Left (groundball hitter)

	Avg	G	AB	R	H	2B	3B	HR	RBI	BB	SO	HBP	GDP	SB	CS	OBP	SLG	IBB	SH	SF	#Pit	#P/PA	GB	FB	G/F
1997 Season	.286	147	496	104	142	25	0	40	102	120	146	3	9	1	1	.423	.579	9	0	8	2799	4.46	137	135	1.01
Last Five Years	.295	580	1928	404	568	113	9	130	365	415	520	18	44	12	10	.421	.565	26	1	19	10312	4.33	610	477	1.28

1997 Season

	Avg	AB	H	2B	3B	HR	RBI	BB	SO	OBP	SLG		Avg	AB	H	2B	3B	HR	RBI	BB	SO	OBP	SLG
vs. Left	.275	131	36	6	0	4	22	18	40	.355	.412	First Pitch	.421	38	16	1	0	7	15	3	0	.452	1.000
vs. Right	.290	365	106	19	0	36	80	102	106	.445	.638	Ahead in Count	.527	112	59	10	0	16	39	61	0	.682	1.045
Groundball	.250	100	25	5	0	7	13	18	30	.361	.510	Behind in Count	.165	206	34	9	0	8	25	0	100	.176	.325
Flyball	.294	68	20	3	0	6	17	20	19	.455	.603	Two Strikes	.163	282	46	12	0	9	30	56	146	.305	.301
Home	.286	238	68	12	0	17	50	64	70	.429	.550	Batting #3	.283	307	87	18	0	27	70	87	91	.438	.606
Away	.287	258	74	13	0	23	52	56	76	.416	.605	Batting #4	.289	152	44	6	0	12	30	30	48	.405	.566
Day	.212	179	38	6	0	10	37	43	62	.363	.413	Other	.297	37	11	1	0	1	2	3	7	.350	.405
Night	.328	317	104	19	0	30	65	77	84	.456	.672	March/April	.338	80	27	6	0	5	17	28	21	.505	.600
Grass	.285	424	121	21	0	35	87	109	129	.426	.583	May	.253	83	21	1	0	5	15	16	25	.390	.446
Turf	.292	72	21	4	0	5	15	11	17	.400	.556	June	.289	83	24	5	0	12	26	16	27	.404	.783
Pre-All Star	.298	258	77	13	0	24	62	67	76	.441	.628	July	.279	68	19	6	0	5	12	24	19	.458	.588
Post-All Star	.273	238	65	12	0	16	40	53	70	.402	.525	August	.290	100	29	3	0	9	23	20	31	.407	.590
Scoring Posn	.288	132	38	11	0	7	63	44	44	.449	.530	Sept/Oct	.268	82	22	4	0	4	9	13	23	.368	.463
Close & Late	.259	54	14	2	0	4	13	20	15	.447	.519	vs. AL	.289	453	131	21	0	39	94	110	131	.425	.594
None on/out	.280	100	28	6	0	10	10	16	27	.385	.640	vs. NL	.256	43	11	4	0	1	8	10	15	.400	.419

1997 By Position

Position	Avg	AB	H	2B	3B	HR	RBI	BB	SO	OBP	SLG	G	GS	Innings	PO	A	E	DP	Fld Pct	Rng Fctr	In Zone	Zone Outs	Zone Rtg	MLB Zone
As 1b	.290	490	142	25	0	40	102	120	144	.427	.586	145	140	1224.2	1234	95	10	124	.993	—	268	230	858	874

Last Five Years

	Avg	AB	H	2B	3B	HR	RBI	BB	SO	OBP	SLG		Avg	AB	H	2B	3B	HR	RBI	BB	SO	OBP	SLG
vs. Left	.252	527	133	27	2	18	85	80	154	.353	.414	First Pitch	.419	172	72	15	2	20	50	15	0	.472	.878
vs. Right	.310	1401	435	86	7	112	280	335	366	.444	.622	Ahead in Count	.434	463	201	43	3	52	144	215	0	.609	.877
Groundball	.276	392	108	26	1	26	63	74	106	.391	.546	Behind in Count	.207	384	79	29	2	29	92	0	386	.215	.352
Flyball	.271	351	95	17	2	28	65	73	98	.396	.570	Two Strikes	.199	1039	207	41	3	39	117	185	520	.321	.357
Home	.290	940	273	59	4	63	188	213	243	.422	.563	Batting #3	.298	625	186	29	1	58	157	149	182	.430	.626
Away	.299	988	295	54	5	67	177	202	277	.419	.567	Batting #6	.296	405	120	25	1	26	70	94	108	.434	.556
Day	.263	646	170	35	2	42	141	137	167	.393	.519	Other	.292	898	262	59	7	46	138	172	230	.407	.527
Night	.310	1282	398	78	7	88	224	278	353	.435	.588	March/April	.293	225	66	13	2	12	40	63	58	.450	.529
Grass	.293	1651	484	98	8	117	325	368	444	.423	.575	May	.285	326	93	20	1	22	51	55	93	.388	.555
Turf	.303	277	84	15	1	13	40	47	76	.409	.505	June	.305	325	99	21	2	29	79	72	90	.438	.554
Pre-All Star	.298	963	287	59	4	70	188	207	264	.425	.588	July	.289	336	97	18	2	23	58	67	85	.403	.554
Post-All Star	.291	965	281	54	4	60	177	208	256	.416	.542	August	.332	358	119	24	0	25	74	93	91	.471	.609
Scoring Posn	.274	521	143	35	2	29	236	134	148	.413	.516	Sept/Oct	.263	358	94	17	3	19	63	65	103	.376	.486
Close & Late	.291	289	84	17	1	19	61	59	84	.410	.554	vs. AL	.295	1885	557	109	9	129	357	405	505	.421	.568
None on/out	.318	465	148	27	3	39	39	65	119	.406	.632	vs. NL	.256	43	11	4	0	1	8	10	15	.400	.419

Batter vs. Pitcher (career)

Hits Best Against	Avg	AB	H	2B	3B	HR	RBI	BB	SO	OBP	SLG	Hits Worst Against	Avg	AB	H	2B	3B	HR	RBI	BB	SO	OBP	SLG
Felipe Lira	.455	11	5	1	0	1	1	4	2	.625	.818	Jesse Orosco	.000	12	0	0	0	0	0	6	6	.333	.000
Buddy Groom	.444	9	4	0	0	2	3	2	2	.545	1.111	James Baldwin	.071	14	1	0	0	0	0	1	3	.133	.071
John Wasdin	.400	10	4	1	0	3	5	4	2	.571	1.400	David Wells	.143	14	2	0	0	0	1	3	.200	.143
Jose Rosado	.400	10	4	0	0	2	5	2	2	.462	1.000	Kevin Gross	.182	11	2	1	0	0	0	4	.182	.273
Bobby Witt	.389	18	7	0	2	3	12	3	6	.455	1.111	Juan Guzman	.200	25	5	0	0	0	0	2	8	.259	.200

Justin Thompson — Tigers
Age 25 – Pitches Left (groundball pitcher)

	ERA	W	L	Sv	G	GS	IP	BB	SO	Avg	H	2B	3B	HR	RBI	OBP	SLG	CG	ShO	Sup	QS	#P/S	SB	CS	GB	FB	G/F
1997 Season	3.02	15	11	0	32	32	223.1	66	151	.233	188	32	3	20	76	.289	.354	4	0	5.00	25	104	20	11	327	210	1.56
Career (1996-1997)	3.35	16	17	0	43	43	282.1	97	195	.241	250	44	3	27	107	.305	.367	4	0	4.72	28	101	27	16	418	269	1.55

1997 Season

	ERA	W	L	Sv	G	GS	IP	H	HR	BB	SO		Avg	AB	H	2B	3B	HR	RBI	BB	SO	OBP	SLG
Home	2.88	11	5	0	19	19	131.1	108	14	42	82	vs. Left	.184	125	23	2	0	4	11	14	37	.266	.296
Away	3.23	4	6	0	13	13	92.0	80	6	24	69	vs. Right	.242	682	165	30	3	16	65	52	114	.294	.364
Day	3.45	7	5	0	12	12	86.0	73	11	24	67	Inning 1-6	.228	671	153	23	2	15	60	55	124	.285	.335
Night	2.75	8	6	0	20	20	137.1	115	9	42	84	Inning 7+	.257	136	35	9	1	5	16	11	27	.309	.449
Grass	2.90	14	7	0	25	25	173.2	143	16	54	110	None on	.227	515	117	22	3	13	13	42	100	.285	.357
Turf	3.44	1	4	0	7	7	49.2	45	4	12	41	Runners on	.243	292	71	10	0	7	63	24	51	.296	.349
March/April	4.50	2	2	0	6	6	38.0	38	3	18	20	Scoring Posn	.264	148	39	7	0	1	50	18	25	.328	.331
May	1.85	3	1	0	5	5	39.0	23	2	9	29	Close & Late	.226	84	19	5	0	5	12	7	19	.283	.464
June	2.03	3	3	0	6	6	44.1	33	4	17	38	None on/out	.225	218	49	7	2	6	6	17	40	.281	.358
July	4.50	1	2	0	4	4	24.0	22	6	3	14	vs. 1st Batr (relief)	.000	0	0	0	0	0	0	0	0	.000	.000
August	2.28	3	2	0	6	6	43.1	41	2	8	26	1st Inning Pitched	.209	110	23	4	1	2	9	9	21	.279	.318
Sept/Oct	3.89	3	1	0	5	5	34.2	31	3	11	24	First 75 Pitches	.227	565	128	20	2	8	44	44	103	.282	.312
Starter	3.02	15	11	0	32	32	223.1	188	20	66	151	Pitch 76-90	.265	113	30	7	1	6	13	12	25	.331	.504
Reliever	0.00	0	0	0	0	0	0.0	0	0	0	0	Pitch 91-105	.226	84	19	4	0	4	14	7	16	.280	.417
0-3 Days Rest (Start)	0.00	0	0	0	0	0	0.0	0	0	0	0	Pitch 106+	.244	45	11	1	0	2	5	3	7	.292	.400
4 Days Rest	3.12	10	8	0	20	20	147.1	122	15	36	95	First Pitch	.300	110	33	1	1	3	11	1	0	.310	.409
5+ Days Rest	2.84	5	3	0	12	12	76.0	66	5	30	56	Ahead in Count	.158	400	63	7	1	7	28	0	126	.158	.233
vs. AL	3.27	13	10	0	29	29	200.2	173	20	58	133	Behind in Count	.333	180	60	17	0	7	25	151	0	.204	.544
vs. NL	0.79	2	1	0	3	3	22.2	15	0	8	18	Two Strikes	.153	391	60	10	1	8	25	52	230	.204	.230

463

1997 Season

	ERA	W	L	Sv	G	GS	IP	H	HR	BB	SO		Avg	AB	H	2B	3B	HR	RBI	BB	SO	OBP	SLG
Pre-All Star	2.95	8	6	0	18	18	128.1	102	12	45	91	Pre-All Star	.225	454	102	23	2	12	40	45	91	.293	.363
Post-All Star	3.13	7	5	0	14	14	95.0	86	8	21	60	Post-All Star	.244	353	86	9	1	8	36	21	60	.284	.343

Mark Thompson — Rockies   Age 27 – Pitches Right

	ERA	W	L	Sv	G	GS	IP	BB	SO	Avg	H	2B	3B	HR	RBI	OBP	SLG	CG	ShO	Sup	QS	#P/S	SB	CS	GB	FB	G/F
1997 Season	7.89	3	3	0	6	6	29.2	13	9	.323	40	8	2	8	26	.399	.613	0	0	8.80	1	85	4	0	46	53	0.87
Career (1994-1997)	5.97	15	18	0	63	41	259.1	117	143	.307	318	74	9	42	172	.384	.517	3	1	6.39	18	95	29	12	393	339	1.16

1997 Season

	ERA	W	L	Sv	G	GS	IP	H	HR	BB	SO		Avg	AB	H	2B	3B	HR	RBI	BB	SO	OBP	SLG
Home	8.44	1	2	0	3	3	16.0	21	6	5	2	vs. Left	.344	61	21	4	1	4	18	6	5	.397	.639
Away	7.24	2	1	0	3	3	13.2	19	2	8	7	vs. Right	.302	63	19	4	1	4	8	7	4	.400	.587

Career (1994-1997)

	ERA	W	L	Sv	G	GS	IP	H	HR	BB	SO		Avg	AB	H	2B	3B	HR	RBI	BB	SO	OBP	SLG
Home	6.99	7	8	0	34	19	128.2	175	26	57	67	vs. Left	.316	475	150	32	4	19	78	62	57	.397	.520
Away	4.96	8	10	0	29	22	130.2	143	16	60	76	vs. Right	.299	561	168	42	5	23	94	55	86	.374	.515
Day	5.88	7	8	0	26	19	113.1	143	22	48	63	Inning 1-6	.302	881	266	56	7	41	151	100	124	.381	.521
Night	6.04	8	10	0	37	22	146.0	175	20	69	80	Inning 7+	.335	155	52	18	2	1	21	17	19	.405	.497
Grass	6.41	12	16	0	56	35	222.0	289	39	107	126	None on	.322	549	177	39	6	24	54	66	.390	.546
Turf	3.38	3	2	0	7	6	37.1	29	3	10	17	Runners on	.290	487	141	35	3	18	148	63	77	.378	.485
March/April	4.81	5	2	0	11	7	43.0	45	8	22	18	Scoring Posn	.304	303	92	18	3	12	129	39	48	.384	.502
May	7.74	2	5	0	12	8	50.0	70	8	23	24	Close & Late	.342	38	13	5	0	0	5	8	6	.468	.474
June	7.65	1	3	0	10	8	42.1	59	7	17	27	None on/out	.283	254	72	16	6	9	9	25	30	.357	.500
July	4.54	2	2	0	13	5	37.2	49	4	17	21	vs. 1st Batr	.389	18	7	0	1	2	5	2	1	.455	.833
August	4.41	3	4	0	8	8	51.0	55	8	16	30	1st Inning Pitched	.312	234	73	16	4	7	53	34	34	.406	.504
Sept/Oct	6.62	2	2	0	9	5	35.1	40	7	22	23	First 75 Pitches	.308	802	247	57	6	34	143	93	111	.388	.521
Starter	6.00	14	17	0	41	41	228.0	272	40	99	123	Pitch 76-90	.356	118	42	10	1	3	15	11	16	.409	.534
Reliever	5.74	1	1	0	22	0	31.1	46	2	18	20	Pitch 91-105	.284	74	21	5	2	5	11	4	9	.338	.608
0-3 Days Rest (Start)	5.25	1	0	0	2	2	12.0	11	2	5	6	Pitch 106+	.190	42	8	2	0	0	3	9	7	.333	.238
4 Days Rest	7.47	6	13	0	23	23	121.2	168	28	59	69	First Pitch	.417	163	68	20	1	10	44	2	0	.435	.736
5+ Days Rest	4.20	7	4	0	16	16	94.1	93	10	35	48	Ahead in Count	.243	415	101	22	3	13	53	0	114	.261	.405
vs. AL	0.00	0	0	0	0	0	0.0	0	0	0	0	Behind in Count	.371	275	102	23	2	12	44	69	0	.501	.600
vs. NL	5.97	15	18	0	63	41	259.1	318	42	117	143	Two Strikes	.219	407	89	13	5	16	60	46	143	.308	.393
Pre-All Star	6.56	8	10	0	34	24	141.1	179	23	62	74	Pre-All Star	.312	573	179	43	5	23	99	62	74	.389	.525
Post-All Star	5.26	7	8	0	29	17	118.0	139	19	55	69	Post-All Star	.300	463	139	31	4	19	73	55	69	.379	.508

Pitcher vs. Batter (career)

Pitches Best Vs.	Avg	AB	H	2B	3B	HR	RBI	BB	SO	OBP	SLG	Pitches Worst Vs.	Avg	AB	H	2B	3B	HR	RBI	BB	SO	OBP	SLG
Sammy Sosa	.154	13	2	1	0	1	1	0	4	.214	.462	Todd Hundley	.556	9	5	0	0	1	4	2	0	.636	.889
Bret Boone	.154	13	2	0	1	0	2	0	2	.214	.385	Ray Lankford	.444	9	4	1	0	1	6	2	1	.500	.889
Brian McRae	.200	10	2	0	0	1	2	3	3	.357	.500	Barry Larkin	.429	14	6	1	0	2	4	1	1	.467	.929
Hal Morris	.231	13	3	0	0	0	1	2	1	.333	.231	Gary Sheffield	.400	5	2	1	0	0	1	6	1	.727	.600
												Raul Mondesi	.357	14	5	1	0	3	6	0	2	.357	1.071

John Thomson — Rockies   Age 24 – Pitches Right (groundball pitcher)

	ERA	W	L	Sv	G	GS	IP	BB	SO	Avg	H	2B	3B	HR	RBI	OBP	SLG	CG	ShO	Sup	QS	#P/S	SB	CS	GB	FB	G/F
1997 Season	4.71	7	9	0	27	27	166.1	51	106	.296	193	36	4	15	85	.351	.433	2	1	4.92	15	92	15	8	262	155	1.69

1997 Season

	ERA	W	L	Sv	G	GS	IP	H	HR	BB	SO		Avg	AB	H	2B	3B	HR	RBI	BB	SO	OBP	SLG
Home	5.90	4	3	0	13	13	71.2	98	10	22	48	vs. Left	.316	354	112	15	3	9	49	35	46	.379	.452
Away	3.80	3	6	0	14	14	94.2	95	5	29	58	vs. Right	.273	297	81	21	1	6	36	16	60	.317	.411
Day	4.96	5	4	0	12	12	74.1	82	8	28	54	Inning 1-6	.298	581	173	30	3	14	77	40	98	.347	.432
Night	4.50	2	5	0	15	15	92.0	111	7	23	52	Inning 7+	.286	70	20	6	1	1	8	11	8	.383	.443
Grass	4.58	7	7	0	23	23	141.1	165	13	43	86	None on	.309	350	108	17	1	7	7	32	66	.371	.423
Turf	5.40	0	2	0	4	4	25.0	28	2	8	20	Runners on	.282	301	85	19	3	8	78	19	40	.326	.445
March/April	0.00	0	0	0	0	0	0.0	0	0	0	0	Scoring Posn	.309	149	46	12	2	3	62	12	20	.358	.477
May	5.56	0	4	0	4	4	22.2	27	1	10	19	Close & Late	.286	35	10	4	1	1	5	2	5	.375	.543
June	5.61	2	1	0	6	6	33.2	43	3	10	23	None on/out	.314	159	50	7	0	4	4	17	28	.381	.434
July	2.97	1	1	0	5	5	33.1	31	1	7	23	vs. 1st Batr (relief)	.000	0	0	0	0	0	0	0	0	.000	.000
August	4.54	3	2	0	6	6	39.2	42	2	15	18	1st Inning Pitched	.295	105	31	6	1	3	19	12	15	.367	.457
Sept/Oct	5.11	1	1	0	6	6	37.0	50	8	9	23	First 75 Pitches	.289	508	147	27	3	13	67	35	83	.338	.431
Starter	4.71	7	9	0	27	27	166.1	193	15	51	106	Pitch 76-90	.342	79	27	5	1	1	9	9	14	.418	.468
Reliever	0.00	0	0	0	0	0	0.0	0	0	0	0	Pitch 91-105	.340	47	16	3	0	0	7	6	6	.392	.404
0-3 Days Rest (Start)	5.40	1	0	0	1	1	6.2	9	2	2	4	Pitch 106+	.176	17	3	1	0	1	2	3	3	.300	.412
4 Days Rest	5.09	5	6	0	17	17	109.2	122	12	33	67	First Pitch	.317	104	33	7	0	3	17	0	0	.327	.471
5+ Days Rest	3.78	1	3	0	9	9	50.0	62	1	16	35	Ahead in Count	.236	313	74	10	2	5	27	0	91	.237	.329
vs. AL	7.80	1	1	0	3	3	15.0	24	0	6	9	Behind in Count	.372	121	45	9	0	5	29	34	0	.510	.570
vs. NL	4.40	6	8	0	24	24	151.1	169	15	45	97	Two Strikes	.199	276	55	7	4	4	17	17	106	.247	.268
Pre-All Star	6.02	2	6	0	11	11	61.1	77	4	23	45	Pre-All Star	.316	244	77	14	1	4	41	23	45	.379	.430
Post-All Star	3.94	5	3	0	16	16	105.0	116	11	28	61	Post-All Star	.285	407	116	22	3	11	44	28	61	.333	.435

Gary Thurman — Mets
Age 33 – Bats Right (groundball hitter)

	Avg	G	AB	R	H	2B	3B	HR	RBI	BB	SO	HBP	GDP	SB	CS	OBP	SLG	IBB	SH	SF	#Pit	#P/PA	GB	FB	G/F
1997 Season	.167	11	6	0	1	0	0	0	0	0	0	0	1	0	1	.167	.167	0	0	0	14	2.33	3	3	1.00
Last Five Years	.233	99	120	25	28	4	2	0	16	12	33	0	3	12	3	.299	.300	0	1	2	508	3.76	37	28	1.32

1997 Season

	Avg	AB	H	2B	3B	HR	RBI	BB	SO	OBP	SLG		Avg	AB	H	2B	3B	HR	RBI	BB	SO	OBP	SLG
vs. Left	.000	3	0	0	0	0	0	0	0	.000	.000	Scoring Posn	.000	1	0	0	0	0	0	0	0	.000	.000
vs. Right	.333	3	1	0	0	0	0	0	0	.333	.333	Close & Late	.000	2	0	0	0	0	0	0	0	.000	.000

Mike Thurman — Expos
Age 24 – Pitches Right

	ERA	W	L	Sv	G	GS	IP	BB	SO	Avg	H	2B	3B	HR	RBI	OBP	SLG	GF	IR	IRS	Hld	SvOp	SB	CS	GB	FB	G/F
1997 Season	5.40	1	0	0	5	2	11.2	4	8	.186	8	3	0	3	9	.271	.465	1	2	2	0	0	1	0	15	17	0.88

1997 Season

	ERA	W	L	Sv	G	GS	IP	H	HR	BB	SO		Avg	AB	H	2B	3B	HR	RBI	BB	SO	OBP	SLG
Home	3.60	1	0	0	3	2	10.0	6	2	4	6	vs. Left	.267	15	4	2	0	2	4	3	0	.421	.800
Away	16.20	0	0	0	2	0	1.2	2	1	0	2	vs. Right	.143	28	4	1	0	1	5	1	8	.172	.286

Mike Timlin — Mariners
Age 32 – Pitches Right (groundball pitcher)

	ERA	W	L	Sv	G	GS	IP	BB	SO	Avg	H	2B	3B	HR	RBI	OBP	SLG	GF	IR	IRS	Hld	SvOp	SB	CS	GB	FB	G/F
1997 Season	3.22	6	4	10	64	0	72.2	20	45	.257	69	6	1	8	32	.309	.375	31	30	8	9	18	3	2	136	55	2.47
Last Five Years	3.74	15	16	49	242	0	267.0	102	220	.255	258	33	4	25	130	.327	.370	149	118	40	29	73	18	3	446	186	2.40

1997 Season

	ERA	W	L	Sv	G	GS	IP	H	HR	BB	SO		Avg	AB	H	2B	3B	HR	RBI	BB	SO	OBP	SLG
Home	3.00	4	1	4	33	0	39.0	37	4	12	22	vs. Left	.263	118	31	5	1	3	15	12	19	.331	.398
Away	3.48	2	3	6	31	0	33.2	32	4	8	23	vs. Right	.252	151	38	1	0	5	17	8	26	.292	.358
Day	3.77	4	0	3	24	0	28.2	28	3	9	18	Inning 1-6	.167	18	3	0	0	1	3	0	5	.167	.333
Night	2.86	2	4	7	40	0	44.0	41	5	11	27	Inning 7+	.263	251	66	6	1	7	29	20	40	.319	.378
Grass	3.86	2	3	4	27	0	30.1	30	4	8	22	None on	.248	153	38	5	0	5	5	7	27	.281	.379
Turf	2.76	4	1	6	37	0	42.1	39	4	12	23	Runners on	.267	116	31	1	1	3	27	13	18	.344	.371
March/April	3.60	0	0	2	9	0	10.0	11	3	3	12	Scoring Posn	.258	66	17	1	0	2	24	11	8	.367	.364
May	1.98	1	0	3	10	0	13.2	12	1	4	11	Close & Late	.294	163	48	4	1	4	22	15	26	.358	.405
June	2.61	0	0	4	10	0	10.1	10	1	1	4	None on/out	.279	61	17	3	0	2	2	9	3	.313	.426
July	3.46	2	2	0	9	0	13.0	8	1	7	9	vs. 1st Batr (relief)	.262	61	16	2	0	3	6	2	9	.286	.443
August	4.96	1	1	1	13	0	16.1	16	2	3	7	1st Inning Pitched	.255	204	52	5	0	6	25	13	36	.301	.368
Sept/Oct	1.93	2	1	0	13	0	9.1	12	0	2	2	First 15 Pitches	.245	192	47	5	0	6	21	7	33	.274	.365
Starter	0.00	0	0	0	0	0	0.0	0	0	0	0	Pitch 16-30	.328	67	22	1	1	2	10	9	8	.408	.463
Reliever	3.22	6	4	10	64	0	72.2	69	8	20	45	Pitch 31-45	.000	9	0	0	0	0	1	4	3	.308	.000
0 Days rest (Relief)	1.50	1	0	5	15	0	12.0	9	0	0	6	Pitch 46+	.000	1	0	0	0	0	0	0	1	.000	.000
1 or 2 Days rest	2.90	3	2	4	32	0	40.1	35	3	10	24	First Pitch	.300	50	15	1	1	3	8	5	0	.375	.540
3+ Days rest	4.87	2	2	1	17	0	20.1	25	5	10	15	Ahead in Count	.236	127	30	3	0	4	13	0	37	.234	.354
vs. AL	3.08	4	2	9	58	0	64.1	60	7	17	40	Behind in Count	.286	42	12	1	0	1	7	8	0	.400	.381
vs. NL	4.32	2	2	1	6	0	8.1	9	1	3	5	Two Strikes	.202	109	22	3	0	3	14	7	45	.248	.312
Pre-All Star	2.41	2	2	9	30	0	37.1	34	5	10	29	Pre-All Star	.250	136	34	3	0	5	15	10	29	.304	.382
Post-All Star	4.08	4	4	1	34	0	35.1	35	3	10	16	Post-All Star	.263	133	35	3	1	3	17	10	16	.315	.368

Last Five Years

	ERA	W	L	Sv	G	GS	IP	H	HR	BB	SO		Avg	AB	H	2B	3B	HR	RBI	BB	SO	OBP	SLG
Home	3.06	10	5	18	125	0	141.1	131	12	53	123	vs. Left	.275	501	138	27	3	10	63	53	95	.343	.401
Away	4.51	5	11	31	117	0	125.2	127	13	49	97	vs. Right	.236	509	120	6	1	15	67	49	125	.310	.340
Day	3.19	7	4	17	90	0	98.2	90	7	41	87	Inning 1-6	.183	60	11	2	0	2	9	6	17	.258	.317
Night	4.06	8	12	32	152	0	168.1	168	18	61	133	Inning 7+	.260	950	247	31	4	23	121	96	203	.331	.374
Grass	4.76	5	10	25	103	0	109.2	113	12	45	86	None on	.234	543	127	16	0	15	15	44	127	.291	.346
Turf	3.03	10	6	24	139	0	157.1	145	13	57	134	Runners on	.281	467	131	17	4	10	115	58	93	.365	.398
March/April	4.85	0	1	7	39	0	39.0	45	7	13	43	Scoring Posn	.264	273	72	9	2	5	99	42	51	.364	.366
May	4.28	3	1	11	53	0	61.0	64	4	26	57	Close & Late	.283	498	141	21	4	12	80	50	96	.353	.414
June	3.92	2	1	10	38	0	41.1	38	4	15	29	None on/out	.243	235	57	5	0	7	7	19	53	.299	.353
July	4.50	5	6	5	32	0	40.0	33	7	20	39	vs. 1st Batr (relief)	.234	214	50	6	0	7	22	22	46	.317	.360
August	3.57	3	2	5	36	0	40.1	38	2	11	17	1st Inning Pitched	.256	790	202	26	2	21	107	74	179	.322	.373
Sept/Oct	1.39	2	5	11	44	0	45.1	40	1	17	35	First 15 Pitches	.266	708	188	27	2	20	91	54	145	.322	.394
Starter	0.00	0	0	0	0	0	0.0	0	0	0	0	Pitch 16-30	.229	240	55	4	1	5	29	36	57	.330	.317
Reliever	3.74	15	16	49	242	0	267.0	258	25	102	220	Pitch 31-45	.255	55	14	2	1	0	8	11	16	.379	.327
0 Days rest (Relief)	5.52	4	3	14	45	0	44.0	47	5	17	35	Pitch 46+	.143	7	1	0	0	0		1	2	.250	.143
1 or 2 Days rest	3.64	6	8	20	113	0	133.2	122	10	46	107	First Pitch	.367	158	58	11	1	7	25	14	0	.422	.582
3+ Days rest	3.02	5	5	15	84	0	89.1	89	10	39	78	Ahead in Count	.189	503	95	10	1	10	43	0	196	.197	.272
vs. AL	3.72	13	14	48	236	0	258.2	249	24	99	215	Behind in Count	.303	188	57	7	2	5	35	59	0	.468	.441
vs. NL	4.32	2	2	1	6	0	8.1	9	1	3	5	Two Strikes	.166	445	74	8	1	9	44	28	220	.221	.249
Pre-All Star	4.10	6	3	29	137	0	153.2	155	16	58	142	Pre-All Star	.262	592	155	16	3	16	76	58	142	.330	.380
Post-All Star	3.26	9	13	20	105	0	113.1	103	9	44	78	Post-All Star	.246	418	103	17	1	9	54	44	78	.321	.356

Pitcher vs. Batter (career)

Pitches Best Vs.	Avg	AB	H	2B	3B	HR	RBI	BB	SO	OBP	SLG	Pitches Worst Vs.	Avg	AB	H	2B	3B	HR	RBI	BB	SO	OBP	SLG
Frank Thomas	.000	12	0	0	0	0	0	5	5	.333	.000	Albert Belle	.462	13	6	0	0	2	3	2	0	.533	.923
Mike Stanley	.100	10	1	0	0	0	0	2	3	.250	.100	Mike Gallego	.444	9	4	0	0	0	3	2	1	.545	.444
Ivan Rodriguez	.167	12	2	0	0	0	1	0	5	.167	.167	Juan Gonzalez	.357	14	5	0	0	1	2	1	5	.400	.571
Carlos Baerga	.167	12	2	0	0	0	2	1	3	.214	.167	Tony Phillips	.333	9	3	1	0	0	5	6	4	.600	.444
Brady Anderson	.167	12	2	0	0	0		1	4	.231	.167	Danny Tartabull	.333	9	3	2	0	0	1		2	.364	.556

Ozzie Timmons — Reds

	Avg	G	AB	R	H	2B	3B	HR	RBI	BB	SO	HBP	GDP	SB	CS	OBP	SLG	IBB	SH	SF	#Pit	#P/PA	GB	FB	G/F
1997 Season	.333	6	9	1	3	1	0	0	0	0	1	0	0	0	0	.333	.444	0	0	0	31	3.44	3	3	1.00
Career (1995-1997)	238	148	320	49	76	15	1	15	44	28	63	1	9	4	0	.300	.431	2	1	1	1374	3.91	96	112	0.86

1997 Season

	Avg	AB	H	2B	3B	HR	RBI	BB	SO	OBP	SLG		Avg	AB	H	2B	3B	HR	RBI	BB	SO	OBP	SLG
vs. Left	.500	2	1	0	0	0	0	0	1	.500	.500	Scoring Posn	.000	2	0	0	0	0	0	0	0	.000	.000
vs. Right	.286	7	2	1	0	0	0	0	0	.286	.429	Close & Late	.000	1	0	0	0	0	0	0	1	.000	.000

Career (1995-1997)

	Avg	AB	H	2B	3B	HR	RBI	BB	SO	OBP	SLG		Avg	AB	H	2B	3B	HR	RBI	BB	SO	OBP	SLG
vs. Left	.271	170	46	9	1	6	22	16	25	.333	.441	First Pitch	.212	33	7	2	0	2	10	2	0	.257	.455
vs. Right	.200	150	30	6	0	9	22	12	38	.262	.420	Ahead in Count	.304	69	21	4	0	3	13	16	0	.442	.493
Groundball	.265	83	22	6	1	3	16	6	19	.311	.470	Behind in Count	.195	154	30	5	0	7	15	0	54	.195	.364
Flyball	.143	42	6	0	0	1	2	2	16	.182	.214	Two Strikes	.172	157	27	4	1	5	13	10	63	.222	.306
Home	.219	169	37	2	1	11	21	15	39	.286	.438	Batting #6	.263	80	21	4	0	5	12	6	15	.314	.500
Away	.258	151	39	13	0	4	23	13	24	.315	.424	Batting #7	.250	60	15	4	1	2	7	2	10	.274	.450
Day	.213	174	37	6	0	9	18	18	37	.286	.402	Other	.222	180	40	7	0	8	25	20	38	.302	.394
Night	.267	146	39	9	1	6	26	10	26	.316	.466	March/April	.184	38	7	1	0	1	3	6	10	.295	.289
Grass	.242	240	58	8	1	12	30	18	52	.297	.433	May	.204	49	10	1	0	1	3	3	9	.250	.286
Turf	.225	80	18	7	0	3	14	10	11	.308	.425	June	.254	67	17	4	0	3	10	4	17	.292	.448
Pre-All Star	.221	163	36	7	1	5	18	14	37	.281	.368	July	.138	29	4	2	1	0	2	4	5	.242	.276
Post-All Star	.255	157	40	8	0	10	26	14	26	.320	.497	August	.346	52	18	6	0	3	11	3	8	.382	.635
Scoring Posn	.253	75	19	5	0	1	24	8	17	.321	.360	Sept/Oct	.235	85	20	1	0	7	15	8	14	.309	.494
Close & Late	.110	73	8	2	0	2	8	4	23	.156	.219	vs. AL	.000	0	0	0	0	0	0	0	0	.000	.000
None on/out	.282	71	20	4	0	5	5	13	13	.329	.549	vs. NL	.238	320	76	15	1	15	44	28	63	.300	.431

Batter vs. Pitcher (career)

Hits Best Against	Avg	AB	H	2B	3B	HR	RBI	BB	SO	OBP	SLG	Hits Worst Against	Avg	AB	H	2B	3B	HR	RBI	BB	SO	OBP	SLG
Mike Hampton	.364	11	4	1	0	1	3	1	2	.417	.727												
Tom Glavine	.357	14	5	2	0	0	1	1	4	.400	.500												
Denny Neagle	.333	12	4	0	0	0	0	0	2	.333	.333												
Steve Avery	.308	13	4	1	0	0	1	0	0	.308	.385												

Lee Tinsley — Mariners

	Avg	G	AB	R	H	2B	3B	HR	RBI	BB	SO	HBP	GDP	SB	CS	OBP	SLG	IBB	SH	SF	#Pit	#P/PA	GB	FB	G/F
1997 Season	.197	49	122	12	24	6	2	0	6	11	34	0	4	2	0	.263	.279	0	0	0	513	3.86	45	27	1.67
Career (1993-1997)	241	361	870	131	210	34	4	13	79	88	231	21	41	20	.313	.334	2	14	3	3736	3.82	338	155	2.18

1997 Season

	Avg	AB	H	2B	3B	HR	RBI	BB	SO	OBP	SLG		Avg	AB	H	2B	3B	HR	RBI	BB	SO	OBP	SLG
vs. Left	.308	13	4	2	0	0	1	1	5	.357	.462	Scoring Posn	.200	40	8	1	1	0	6	3	13	.256	.275
vs. Right	.183	109	20	4	2	0	5	10	29	.252	.257	Close & Late	.190	21	4	1	0	0	2	3	4	.292	.238
Home	.192	73	14	4	1	0	2	7	21	.263	.274	None on/out	.242	33	8	3	0	0	0	1	7	.265	.333
Away	.204	49	10	2	1	0	4	4	13	.264	.286	Batting #1	.182	11	2	0	0	0	1	1	3	.250	.182
First Pitch	.308	13	4	1	1	0	3	0	0	.308	.538	Batting #9	.184	87	16	5	1	0	3	9	25	.260	.264
Ahead in Count	.333	27	9	2	0	0	1	9	0	.500	.407	Other	.250	24	6	1	1	0	2	1	6	.280	.375
Behind in Count	.073	55	4	1	0	0	0	0	27	.073	.091	Pre-All Star	.208	77	16	4	1	0	4	6	19	.265	.286
Two Strikes	.100	60	6	2	0	0	2	2	34	.129	.133	Post-All Star	.178	45	8	2	1	0	2	5	15	.260	.267

Career (1993-1997)

	Avg	AB	H	2B	3B	HR	RBI	BB	SO	OBP	SLG		Avg	AB	H	2B	3B	HR	RBI	BB	SO	OBP	SLG
vs. Left	.218	225	49	8	0	3	17	22	66	.291	.293	First Pitch	.325	83	27	2	1	2	15	2	0	.345	.446
vs. Right	.250	645	161	26	4	10	62	66	165	.321	.349	Ahead in Count	.335	167	56	9	1	2	17	49	0	.484	.437
Groundball	.229	218	50	7	0	0	18	21	59	.300	.261	Behind in Count	.182	439	80	10	1	6	32	0	204	.188	.251
Flyball	.243	148	36	6	1	5	11	18	42	.329	.399	Two Strikes	.169	439	74	13	1	3	25	37	231	.238	.223
Home	.253	442	112	22	2	6	48	44	109	.321	.353	Batting #1	.239	326	78	11	1	5	34	42	75	.327	.325
Away	.229	428	98	12	2	7	31	44	122	.305	.315	Batting #9	.245	364	89	17	2	6	34	28	106	.301	.352
Day	.266	267	71	13	1	5	29	20	65	.316	.378	Other	.239	180	43	6	1	2	11	18	50	.312	.317
Night	.231	603	139	21	3	8	50	68	166	.312	.315	March/April	.209	139	29	5	1	1	13	16	41	.290	.281
Grass	.257	678	174	28	2	13	68	65	169	.324	.361	May	.257	109	28	5	0	1	9	13	33	.341	.330
Turf	.188	192	36	6	2	0	11	23	62	.273	.240	June	.264	193	51	4	2	4	21	17	45	.324	.368
Pre-All Star	.242	520	126	16	3	7	49	53	140	.315	.325	July	.238	223	53	6	0	4	17	16	59	.295	.318
Post-All Star	.240	350	84	18	1	6	30	35	91	.309	.349	August	.270	159	43	13	1	3	18	22	40	.361	.421
Scoring Posn	.231	225	52	6	2	3	66	31	67	.326	.316	Sept/Oct	.128	47	6	1	0	0	1	3	13	.180	.149
Close & Late	.267	131	35	6	0	1	14	19	36	.360	.336	vs. AL	.248	818	203	34	4	13	77	84	209	.320	.347
None on/out	.264	273	72	17	0	5	5	20	66	.314	.381	vs. NL	.135	52	7	0	0	0	2	4	22	.196	.135

Batter vs. Pitcher (career)

Hits Best Against	Avg	AB	H	2B	3B	HR	RBI	BB	SO	OBP	SLG	Hits Worst Against	Avg	AB	H	2B	3B	HR	RBI	BB	SO	OBP	SLG
Felipe Lira	.417	12	5	1	0	0	0	0	0	.417	.500	Jimmy Key	.071	14	1	0	0	0	0	0	5	.133	.071
Al Leiter	.333	15	5	2	0	1	0	3		.333	.467	Kenny Rogers	.143	14	2	0	0	1	1	0	5	.143	.357

Andy Tomberlin — Mets
Age 31 – Bats Left

	Avg	G	AB	R	H	2B	3B	HR	RBI	BB	SO	HBP	GDP	SB	CS	OBP	SLG	IBB	SH	SF	#Pit	#P/PA	GB	FB	G/F
1997 Season	.286	6	7	0	2	0	0	0	0	1	3	0	0	0	0	.375	.286	0	0	0	25	3.13	1	2	0.50
Career (1993-1997)	.237	159	236	32	56	4	2	9	26	23	78	2	2	5	1	.310	.386	0	2	0	995	3.78	67	53	1.26

1997 Season

	Avg	AB	H	2B	3B	HR	RBI	BB	SO	OBP	SLG		Avg	AB	H	2B	3B	HR	RBI	BB	SO	OBP	SLG
vs. Left	.000	0	0	0	0	0	0	0	0	.000	.000	Scoring Posn	.000	1	0	0	0	0	0	0	1	.000	.000
vs. Right	.286	7	2	0	0	0	0	1	3	.375	.286	Close & Late	.667	3	2	0	0	0	0	0	1	.667	.667

Brett Tomko — Reds
Age 25 – Pitches Right (flyball pitcher)

	ERA	W	L	Sv	G	GS	IP	BB	SO	Avg	H	2B	3B	HR	RBI	OBP	SLG	CG	ShO	Sup	QS	#P/S	SB	CS	GB	FB	G/F
1997 Season	3.43	11	7	0	22	19	126.0	47	95	.234	106	25	1	14	47	.306	.386	0	0	4.79	14	97	4	7	124	164	0.76

1997 Season

	ERA	W	L	Sv	G	GS	IP	H	HR	BB	SO		Avg	AB	H	2B	3B	HR	RBI	BB	SO	OBP	SLG
Home	3.68	7	4	0	13	11	73.1	60	9	25	66	vs. Left	.190	221	42	14	1	9	23	34	43	.300	.385
Away	3.08	4	3	0	9	8	52.2	46	5	22	29	vs. Right	.276	232	64	11	0	5	24	13	52	.312	.388
Day	4.47	3	4	0	9	7	48.1	44	6	20	35	Inning 1-6	.225	396	89	22	1	11	38	41	85	.296	.369
Night	2.78	8	3	0	13	12	77.2	62	8	27	60	Inning 7+	.298	57	17	3	0	3	9	6	10	.375	.509
Grass	3.15	2	3	0	7	6	40.0	36	3	17	23	None on	.238	282	67	20	1	9	9	31	68	.320	.411
Turf	3.56	9	4	0	15	13	86.0	70	11	30	72	Runners on	.228	171	39	5	0	5	38	16	27	.284	.345
March/April	0.00	0	0	0	0	0	0.0	0	0	0	0	Scoring Posn	.213	89	19	3	0	1	30	12	15	.282	.281
May	3.00	0	1	0	1	1	6.0	5	1	2	3	Close & Late	.323	31	10	2	0	1	6	2	5	.364	.484
June	2.03	4	0	0	5	5	31.0	20	1	15	23	None on/out	.238	122	29	11	1	4	4	12	29	.311	.443
July	7.50	1	2	0	5	2	18.0	20	6	4	13	vs. 1st Batr (relief)	.000	3	0	0	0	0	0	0	2	.000	.000
August	2.43	4	2	0	6	6	37.0	28	3	12	26	1st Inning Pitched	.141	71	10	3	0	2	4	9	18	.238	.268
Sept/Oct	3.71	2	2	0	5	5	34.0	33	3	14	30	First 75 Pitches	.227	343	78	18	1	13	37	30	79	.290	.399
Starter	3.15	11	6	0	19	19	117.0	98	11	44	88	Pitch 76-90	.259	58	15	3	0	1	5	6	8	.323	.362
Reliever	7.00	0	1	0	3	0	9.0	8	3	3	7	Pitch 91-105	.278	36	10	4	0	0	2	6	7	.386	.389
0-3 Days Rest (Start)	0.00	0	0	0	0	0	0.0	0	0	0	0	Pitch 106+	.188	16	3	0	0	0	3	5	1	.381	.188
4 Days Rest	2.59	7	2	0	10	10	66.0	49	3	28	51	First Pitch	.275	69	19	3	1	2	12	2	0	.307	.435
5+ Days Rest	3.88	4	4	0	9	9	51.0	49	8	16	37	Ahead in Count	.169	219	37	9	0	5	14	0	85	.174	.279
vs. AL	2.84	4	0	0	4	4	25.1	18	2	10	21	Behind in Count	.364	88	32	10	0	6	15	22	0	.482	.682
vs. NL	3.58	7	7	0	18	15	100.2	88	12	37	74	Two Strikes	.156	224	35	9	0	4	11	23	95	.239	.250
Pre-All Star	2.51	5	1	0	7	7	43.0	29	3	18	31	Pre-All Star	.195	149	29	8	0	3	11	18	31	.287	.309
Post-All Star	3.90	6	6	0	15	12	83.0	77	11	29	64	Post-All Star	.253	304	77	17	1	11	36	29	64	.316	.424

Salomon Torres — Expos
Age 26 – Pitches Right

	ERA	W	L	Sv	G	GS	IP	BB	SO	Avg	H	2B	3B	HR	RBI	OBP	SLG	GF	IR	IRS	Hld	SvOp	SB	CS	GB	FB	G/F
1997 Season	9.82	0	0	0	14	0	25.2	15	11	.305	32	8	0	2	22	.403	.438	4	8	4	0	0	3	0	46	23	2.00
Career (1993-1997)	5.71	11	25	0	68	43	283.2	148	159	.279	308	65	3	38	171	.369	.447	11	19	10	0	0	24	12	448	305	1.47

1997 Season

	ERA	W	L	Sv	G	GS	IP	H	HR	BB	SO		Avg	AB	H	2B	3B	HR	RBI	BB	SO	OBP	SLG
Home	11.25	0	0	0	9	0	16.0	24	1	10	7	vs. Left	.340	47	16	3	0	1	12	12	5	.467	.468
Away	7.45	0	0	0	5	0	9.2	8	1	5	4	vs. Right	.276	58	16	5	0	1	10	3	6	.344	.414

Career (1993-1997)

	ERA	W	L	Sv	G	GS	IP	H	HR	BB	SO		Avg	AB	H	2B	3B	HR	RBI	BB	SO	OBP	SLG
Home	6.26	5	15	0	34	23	146.2	164	21	85	90	vs. Left	.301	582	175	33	3	18	86	94	70	.394	.460
Away	5.12	6	10	0	34	20	137.0	144	17	63	69	vs. Right	.255	522	133	32	0	20	85	54	89	.340	.431
Day	5.39	6	12	0	28	21	123.2	128	20	74	70	Inning 1-6	.278	928	258	54	3	36	149	129	138	.371	.459
Night	5.96	5	13	0	40	22	160.0	180	18	74	89	Inning 7+	.284	176	50	11	0	2	22	19	21	.357	.381
Grass	5.89	7	17	0	39	29	168.0	184	27	98	88	None on	.264	607	160	30	1	19	19	75	84	.353	.410
Turf	5.45	4	8	0	29	14	115.2	124	11	50	71	Runners on	.298	497	148	35	2	19	152	73	75	.388	.491
March/April	7.64	0	3	0	9	4	33.0	34	6	17	15	Scoring Posn	.285	277	79	20	0	9	121	45	45	.378	.455
May	4.61	2	1	0	15	6	54.2	58	7	21	36	Close & Late	.348	46	16	5	0	1	11	5	5	.412	.522
June	6.34	2	10	0	18	12	76.2	91	12	46	42	None on/out	.294	279	82	17	1	13	13	30	43	.373	.502
July	7.20	1	3	0	8	5	30.0	39	4	15	13	vs. 1st Batr (relief)	.474	19	9	2	0	1	4	2		.583	.737
August	6.46	1	0	0	4	2	15.1	19	2	7	12	1st Inning Pitched	.326	264	86	20	0	11	50	49	36	.438	.527
Sept/Oct	4.26	5	8	0	14	14	74.0	67	7	42	41	First 15 Pitches	.357	185	66	16	0	9	26	30	23	.457	.589
Starter	5.35	11	24	0	43	43	235.2	245	35	122	134	Pitch 16-30	.277	206	57	11	1	7	33	24	26	.355	.442
Reliever	7.50	0	1	0	25	0	48.0	63	3	26	25	Pitch 31-45	.251	183	46	9	1	1	17	30	38	.353	.328
0 Days rest (Relief)	0.00	0	0	0	1	0	2.0	1	0	0	1	Pitch 46+	.262	530	139	29	1	21	95	64	72	.349	.440
1 or 2 Days rest	5.79	0	0	0	4	0	9.1	14	0	4	6	First Pitch	.321	196	63	4	2	10	43	9	0	.355	.515
3+ Days rest	8.35	0	1	0	20	0	36.2	48	3	22	18	Ahead in Count	.214	429	92	17	1	11	45	0	137	.227	.336
vs. AL	6.01	6	11	0	28	20	124.1	138	17	68	81	Behind in Count	.339	271	92	26	0	11	48	79	0	.492	.557
vs. NL	5.48	5	14	0	40	23	159.1	170	21	80	78	Two Strikes	.209	449	94	22	0	9	48	60	159	.305	.318
Pre-All Star	6.49	5	14	0	45	24	172.0	200	26	90	95	Pre-All Star	.296	676	200	41	3	26	114	90	95	.383	.481
Post-All Star	4.51	6	11	0	23	19	111.2	108	12	58	64	Post-All Star	.252	428	108	24	0	12	57	58	64	.347	.393

Pitcher vs. Batter (career)

Pitches Best Vs.	Avg	AB	H	2B	3B	HR	RBI	BB	SO	OBP	SLG	Pitches Worst Vs.	Avg	AB	H	2B	3B	HR	RBI	BB	SO	OBP	SLG
Gregg Jefferies	.100	10	1	1	0	0	1	1	0	.182	.200	Gary Sheffield	.625	8	5	2	0	2	4	5	0	.769	1.625
Sammy Sosa	.182	11	2	1	0	0	0	4		.182	.273	Jeff Conine	.500	12	6	2	0	2	7	0	3	.500	1.167
Chuck Carr	.182	11	2	0	0	0	0	1	1	.250	.182	Bernard Gilkey	.500	10	5	1	0	1	2	2	2	.583	.900
Todd Zeile	.200	10	2	1	0	0	0	1	1	.273	.300	Mark Grace	.400	10	4	1	0	0	3	1	0	.455	.500

Steve Trachsel — Cubs

Age 27 – Pitches Right (groundball pitcher)

	ERA	W	L	Sv	G	GS	IP	BB	SO	Avg	H	2B	3B	HR	RBI	OBP	SLG	CG	ShO	Sup	QS	#P/S	SB	CS	GB	FB	G/F
1997 Season	4.51	8	12	0	34	34	201.1	69	160	.287	225	45	4	32	101	.344	.476	0	0	4.29	16	98	27	12	288	.192	1.50
Career (1993-1997)	3.98	37	43	0	120	119	732.2	264	531	.260	729	129	21	110	317	.325	.439	6	2	4.47	72	99	71	34	1057	.703	1.50

1997 Season

	ERA	W	L	Sv	G	GS	IP	H	HR	BB	SO		Avg	AB	H	2B	3B	HR	RBI	BB	SO	OBP	SLG
Home	4.15	7	4	0	19	19	121.1	123	17	43	102	vs. Left	.260	377	98	19	3	12	42	32	85	.316	.422
Away	5.06	1	8	0	15	15	80.0	102	15	26	58	vs. Right	.311	408	127	26	1	20	59	37	75	.368	.527
Day	4.87	6	6	0	20	20	118.1	141	19	44	99	Inning 1-6	.279	710	198	39	3	28	90	62	142	.337	.461
Night	4.01	2	6	0	14	14	83.0	84	13	25	61	Inning 7+	.360	75	27	6	1	4	11	7	18	.410	.627
Grass	4.59	7	10	0	28	28	168.2	182	26	65	134	None on	.296	467	138	27	4	22	22	32	98	.345	.512
Turf	4.13	1	2	0	6	6	32.2	43	6	4	26	Runners on	.274	318	87	18	0	10	79	37	62	.342	.425
March/April	7.04	1	3	0	6	6	30.2	38	7	16	26	Scoring Posn	.298	171	51	7	0	9	74	26	35	.376	.497
May	3.19	2	1	0	6	6	36.2	38	4	14	22	Close & Late	.340	53	18	5	0	3	7	5	13	.390	.604
June	4.42	1	2	0	6	6	36.2	46	4	8	36	None on/out	.299	211	63	18	3	11	11	13	48	.345	.569
July	5.22	1	3	0	5	5	29.1	31	6	9	25	vs. 1st Batr (relief)	.000	0	0	0	0	0	0	0	0	.000	.000
August	3.86	1	1	0	5	5	30.1	30	6	11	23	1st Inning Pitched	.289	135	39	10	1	8	19	9	33	.331	.556
Sept/Oct	3.82	2	2	0	6	6	37.2	42	5	11	28	First 75 Pitches	.280	589	165	31	2	23	66	41	117	.327	.457
Starter	4.51	8	12	0	34	34	201.1	225	32	69	160	Pitch 76-90	.282	103	29	6	1	4	14	16	22	.378	.476
Reliever	0.00	0	0	0	0	0	0.0	0	0	0	0	Pitch 91-105	.342	76	26	6	1	4	15	11	19	.420	.605
0-3 Days Rest (Start)	1.29	0	0	0	1	1	7.0	3	0	1	5	Pitch 106+	.294	17	5	2	0	1	6	1	2	.333	.588
4 Days Rest	3.96	4	5	0	21	21	129.2	137	19	49	99	First Pitch	.410	105	43	13	1	7	21	3	0	.422	.752
5+ Days Rest	5.98	4	7	0	12	12	64.2	85	13	19	56	Ahead in Count	.193	353	68	14	2	10	30	0	129	.198	.329
vs. AL	7.27	1	0	0	3	3	17.1	24	2	10	18	Behind in Count	.413	167	69	9	0	12	31	40	0	.521	.683
vs. NL	4.26	7	12	0	31	31	184.0	201	30	59	142	Two Strikes	.196	383	75	17	1	10	32	25	160	.248	.324
Pre-All Star	4.76	4	6	0	19	19	109.2	128	16	38	86	Pre-All Star	.297	431	128	31	3	16	57	38	86	.354	.494
Post-All Star	4.22	4	6	0	15	15	91.2	97	16	31	74	Post-All Star	.274	354	97	14	1	16	44	31	74	.332	.455

Career (1993-1997)

	ERA	W	L	Sv	G	GS	IP	H	HR	BB	SO		Avg	AB	H	2B	3B	HR	RBI	BB	SO	OBP	SLG
Home	3.93	19	25	0	65	64	401.0	403	66	145	292	vs. Left	.241	1244	300	46	11	45	132	122	251	.307	.404
Away	4.04	18	18	0	55	55	331.2	326	44	119	239	vs. Right	.275	1561	429	83	10	65	185	142	280	.338	.466
Day	3.74	21	26	0	73	72	454.1	443	64	165	326	Inning 1-6	.258	2479	639	110	18	97	287	232	468	.323	.434
Night	4.37	16	17	0	47	47	278.1	286	46	99	205	Inning 7+	.276	326	90	19	3	13	30	32	63	.338	.472
Grass	4.18	28	39	0	97	96	590.0	598	92	222	420	None on	.276	1672	461	78	13	83	83	137	295	.334	.487
Turf	3.15	9	4	0	23	23	142.2	131	18	42	111	Runners on	.237	1133	268	51	8	27	234	127	236	.312	.367
March/April	4.71	4	7	0	15	15	86.0	88	19	37	72	Scoring Posn	.214	627	134	20	2	16	195	92	148	.311	.329
May	3.25	8	5	0	23	23	144.0	137	17	44	91	Close & Late	.289	197	57	14	2	8	19	21	40	.356	.503
June	3.36	7	9	0	23	23	150.0	142	16	51	121	None on/out	.283	749	212	41	9	37	37	51	139	.330	.510
July	4.73	7	8	0	20	20	116.0	127	21	43	86	vs. 1st Batr (relief)	.000	1	0	0	0	0	0	0	0	.000	.000
August	3.58	6	5	0	18	18	115.2	101	15	50	70	1st Inning Pitched	.252	440	111	21	2	15	42	48	90	.325	.411
Sept/Oct	4.76	5	9	0	21	20	121.0	134	22	39	91	First 75 Pitches	.258	2050	529	89	15	79	233	181	379	.320	.432
Starter	3.98	37	43	0	119	119	731.0	727	109	263	530	Pitch 76-90	.283	361	102	21	3	14	40	40	77	.353	.474
Reliever	5.40	0	0	0	1	0	1.2	2	1	1	1	Pitch 91-105	.268	284	76	12	1	15	32	24	49	.324	.475
0-3 Days Rest (Start)	4.50	0	1	0	2	2	12.0	10	0	5	9	Pitch 106+	.200	110	22	7	2	2	6	19	26	.315	.355
4 Days Rest	4.11	18	25	0	71	71	444.1	447	71	152	302	First Pitch	.327	422	138	28	3	20	58	12	0	.346	.550
5+ Days Rest	3.74	19	17	0	46	46	274.2	270	38	106	201	Ahead in Count	.195	1280	250	40	10	26	104	0	424	.202	.303
vs. AL	7.27	1	0	0	3	3	17.1	24	2	10	18	Behind in Count	.353	558	197	33	4	39	87	138	0	.477	.636
vs. NL	3.90	36	43	0	117	116	715.1	705	108	254	513	Two Strikes	.190	1340	255	45	7	35	113	113	531	.257	.313
Pre-All Star	3.60	21	23	0	67	67	420.1	402	57	140	308	Pre-All Star	.253	1591	402	74	10	57	162	140	308	.315	.419
Post-All Star	4.50	16	20	0	53	52	312.1	327	53	124	223	Post-All Star	.269	1214	327	55	11	53	155	124	223	.338	.464

Pitcher vs. Batter (career)

Pitches Best Vs.	Avg	AB	H	2B	3B	HR	RBI	BB	SO	OBP	SLG	Pitches Worst Vs.	Avg	AB	H	2B	3B	HR	RBI	BB	SO	OBP	SLG
Orlando Merced	.000	15	0	0	0	0	0	0	2	.000	.000	Carlos Garcia	.563	16	9	0	1	1	4	0	0	.563	.875
Matt Williams	.000	12	0	0	0	0	1	4	1	.235	.000	Gary Sheffield	.556	18	10	3	0	3	5	6	2	.680	1.222
Eddie Taubensee	.077	13	1	0	0	0	0	0	3	.077	.077	Ricky Otero	.538	13	7	0	1	1	2	0	1	.500	.923
Dmitri Young	.083	12	1	1	0	0	0	0	3	.083	.167	Todd Hundley	.462	13	6	0	0	3	4	0	2	.462	1.154
Todd Hollandsworth	.091	11	1	0	0	0	0	1	1	.167	.091	Tom Pagnozzi	.438	16	7	4	1	1	3	2	3	.500	1.000

Bubba Trammell — Tigers

Age 26 – Bats Right

	Avg	G	AB	R	H	2B	3B	HR	RBI	BB	SO	HBP	GDP	SB	CS	OBP	SLG	IBB	SH	SF	#Pit	#P/PA	GB	FB	G/F
1997 Season	.228	44	123	14	28	5	0	4	13	15	35	0	2	3	1	.307	.366	0	0	2	561	4.01	35	39	0.90

1997 Season

	Avg	AB	H	2B	3B	HR	RBI	BB	SO	OBP	SLG		Avg	AB	H	2B	3B	HR	RBI	BB	SO	OBP	SLG
vs. Left	.261	46	12	3	0	3	7	5	15	.327	.522	Scoring Posn	.192	26	5	1	0	2	11	1	6	.207	.462
vs. Right	.208	77	16	2	0	1	6	10	20	.295	.273	Close & Late	.200	15	3	0	0	0	1	2	3	.294	.200
Home	.188	64	12	1	0	2	5	6	23	.257	.297	None on/out	.185	27	5	2	0	1	1	6	4	.333	.370
Away	.271	59	16	4	0	2	8	9	12	.357	.441	Batting #6	.206	34	7	2	0	1	3	1	9	.216	.353
First Pitch	.294	17	5	2	0	0	1	0	0	.294	.412	Batting #7	.183	71	13	2	0	1	6	9	23	.275	.254
Ahead in Count	.417	24	10	2	0	1	4	8	0	.563	.625	Other	.444	18	8	1	0	2	4	5	3	.565	.833
Behind in Count	.133	60	8	1	0	0	3	0	28	.129	.150	Pre-All Star	.239	67	16	1	0	4	9	14	16	.370	.433
Two Strikes	.130	69	9	1	0	2	6	7	35	.208	.217	Post-All Star	.214	56	12	4	0	0	4	1	19	.220	.286

Ricky Trlicek — Mets

Age 29 – Pitches Right (groundball pitcher)

	ERA	W	L	Sv	G	GS	IP	BB	SO	Avg	H	2B	3B	HR	RBI	OBP	SLG	GF	IR	IRS	Hld	SvOp	SB	CS	GB	FB	G/F
1997 Season	5.57	3	4	0	27	0	32.1	23	14	.293	36	6	0	4	21	.405	.439	12	16	4	1	1	3	1	56	30	1.87
Last Five Years	5.15	5	8	1	85	1	124.0	63	65	.273	130	23	3	12	80	.362	.410	34	70	22	2	3	10	2	239	84	2.85

1997 Season

	ERA	W	L	Sv	G	GS	IP	H	HR	BB	SO		Avg	AB	H	2B	3B	HR	RBI	BB	SO	OBP	SLG
Home	5.27	0	1	0	11	0	13.2	14	3	5	6	vs. Left	.327	52	17	3	0	2	14	10	1	.435	.500
Away	5.79	3	3	0	16	0	18.2	22	1	18	8	vs. Right	.268	71	19	3	0	2	7	13	13	.384	.394
Starter	0.00	0	0	0	0	0	0.0	0	0	0	0	Scoring Posn	.244	41	10	1	0	0	15	11	4	.396	.268
Reliever	5.57	3	4	0	27	0	32.1	36	4	23	14	Close & Late	.273	44	12	2	0	1	5	13	6	.448	.386
0 Days rest (Relief)	1.93	1	2	0	6	0	9.1	7	0	9	7	None on/out	.357	28	10	3	0	1	4	3	.455	.571
1 or 2 Days rest	8.04	2	2	0	14	0	15.2	24	3	10	4	First Pitch	.296	27	8	3	0	1	4	3	0	.367	.519
3+ Days rest	4.91	0	0	0	7	0	7.1	5	1	4	3	Ahead in Count	.289	38	11	1	0	1	8	0	10	.289	.395
Pre-All Star	5.57	3	4	0	27	0	32.1	36	4	23	14	Behind in Count	.282	39	11	2	0	2	7	10	0	.420	.487
Post-All Star	0.00	0	0	0	0	0	0.0	0	0	0	0	Two Strikes	.359	39	14	1	0	1	7	9	14	.490	.462

Mike Trombley — Twins

Age 31 – Pitches Right (flyball pitcher)

	ERA	W	L	Sv	G	GS	IP	BB	SO	Avg	H	2B	3B	HR	RBI	OBP	SLG	GF	IR	IRS	Hld	SvOp	SB	CS	GB	FB	G/F
1997 Season	4.37	2	3	1	67	0	82.1	31	74	.248	77	11	1	7	39	.317	.357	21	51	17	11	1	6	1	101	88	1.15
Last Five Years	4.81	19	18	9	198	28	411.1	157	316	.269	432	97	14	52	245	.336	.443	56	149	59	24	16	31	12	511	513	1.00

1997 Season

	ERA	W	L	Sv	G	GS	IP	H	HR	BB	SO		Avg	AB	H	2B	3B	HR	RBI	BB	SO	OBP	SLG
Home	4.78	0	1	1	34	0	43.1	43	7	14	42	vs. Left	.211	109	23	4	0	2	13	13	19	.298	.303
Away	3.92	2	2	0	33	0	39.0	34	0	17	32	vs. Right	.267	202	54	7	1	5	26	18	55	.327	.386
Day	8.59	1	1	0	22	0	22.0	30	4	16	19	Inning 1-6	.274	84	23	5	0	1	14	9	22	.337	.369
Night	2.83	1	2	1	45	0	60.1	47	3	15	55	Inning 7+	.238	227	54	6	1	6	25	22	52	.310	.352
Grass	3.71	2	1	0	27	0	34.0	32	0	12	28	None on	.241	162	39	6	0	3	12	40	.301	.333
Turf	4.84	0	2	1	40	0	48.1	45	7	19	46	Runners on	.255	149	38	5	1	4	36	19	34	.333	.383
March/April	3.60	0	0	0	9	0	15.0	14	1	5	12	Scoring Posn	.286	91	26	2	0	2	31	14	26	.370	.374
May	4.67	1	0	0	12	0	17.1	15	3	6	16	Close & Late	.167	84	14	1	1	0	7	11	24	.263	.202
June	5.02	0	1	0	13	0	14.1	10	0	8	14	None on/out	.217	69	15	2	0	1	3	16	.270	.290
July	6.08	0	0	0	11	0	13.1	14	2	3	11	vs. 1st Batr (relief)	.350	60	21	2	1	2	12	6	14	.403	.517
August	1.26	0	1	1	12	0	14.1	12	1	6	12	1st Inning Pitched	.279	208	58	8	1	6	36	25	47	.354	.413
Sept/Oct	6.75	1	1	0	10	0	8.0	12	0	3	9	First 15 Pitches	.259	185	48	6	1	4	25	21	41	.335	.368
Starter	0.00	0	0	0	0	0	0.0	0	0	0	0	Pitch 16-30	.208	96	20	4	0	2	11	10	25	.287	.313
Reliever	4.37	2	3	1	67	0	82.1	77	7	31	74	Pitch 31-45	.300	30	9	1	0	1	3	0	8	.300	.433
0 Days rest (Relief)	5.93	1	1	1	14	0	13.2	14	3	8	9	Pitch 46+	.000	0	0	0	0	0	0	0	0	.000	.000
1 or 2 Days rest	3.55	1	1	0	37	0	50.2	40	3	15	48	First Pitch	.250	36	9	1	0	1	4	3	0	.308	.361
3+ Days rest	5.50	0	1	0	16	0	18.0	23	1	8	17	Ahead in Count	.195	159	31	5	1	2	13	0	71	.199	.277
vs. AL	4.75	1	3	1	57	0	72.0	72	7	25	68	Behind in Count	.400	65	26	3	0	3	18	9	0	.468	.585
vs. NL	1.74	1	0	0	10	0	10.1	5	0	6	6	Two Strikes	.177	158	28	4	1	1	14	19	74	.270	.272
Pre-All Star	4.14	1	1	0	37	0	50.0	43	4	19	43	Pre-All Star	.232	185	43	8	1	4	18	19	43	.304	.351
Post-All Star	4.73	1	2	1	30	0	32.1	34	3	12	31	Post-All Star	.270	126	34	3	0	3	21	12	31	.336	.365

Last Five Years

	ERA	W	L	Sv	G	GS	IP	H	HR	BB	SO		Avg	AB	H	2B	3B	HR	RBI	BB	SO	OBP	SLG
Home	4.97	8	9	6	101	12	212.0	214	34	64	173	vs. Left	.288	737	212	50	8	25	114	95	121	.370	.479
Away	4.65	11	9	3	97	16	199.1	218	18	93	143	vs. Right	.253	871	220	47	6	27	131	62	195	.307	.413
Day	5.07	6	4	2	56	6	103.0	106	13	45	77	Inning 1-6	.284	884	251	67	9	33	154	98	161	.356	.492
Night	4.73	13	14	7	142	22	308.1	326	39	112	239	Inning 7+	.250	724	181	30	5	19	91	59	155	.312	.384
Grass	4.24	9	6	3	79	13	165.2	176	14	77	127	None on	.263	848	223	58	8	30	30	66	165	.324	.456
Turf	5.20	10	12	6	119	15	245.2	256	38	80	189	Runners on	.275	760	209	39	6	22	215	91	151	.350	.429
March/April	4.72	3	0	0	25	1	53.1	57	8	20	40	Scoring Posn	.267	475	127	26	4	10	184	70	106	.352	.402
May	7.15	2	2	1	26	2	39.0	39	8	19	36	Close & Late	.221	280	62	8	3	5	39	24	73	.284	.325
June	4.17	4	5	1	35	3	69.0	60	7	22	53	None on/out	.278	371	103	23	4	11	11	27	66	.335	.450
July	4.95	2	4	2	37	4	80.0	97	7	30	50	vs. 1st Batr (relief)	.287	150	43	7	2	5	27	16	40	.359	.460
August	4.15	3	3	2	41	8	89.0	88	15	28	74	1st Inning Pitched	.303	684	207	37	4	26	146	81	144	.375	.482
Sept/Oct	4.89	5	4	3	34	10	81.0	98	7	38	63	First 15 Pitches	.301	562	169	30	3	18	101	60	121	.369	.461
Starter	5.78	7	13	0	28	28	146.1	170	22	64	99	Pitch 16-30	.238	428	102	22	2	15	65	49	77	.318	.404
Reliever	4.28	12	5	9	170	0	265.0	256	30	93	217	Pitch 31-45	.230	239	55	15	4	8	28	17	53	.287	.427
0 Days rest (Relief)	5.52	4	1	1	30	0	31.0	33	5	15	20	Pitch 46+	.280	379	106	30	5	11	51	31	65	.339	.472
1 or 2 Days rest	3.62	5	2	5	91	0	141.2	123	18	45	123	First Pitch	.344	195	67	13	0	8	27	12	0	.392	.533
3+ Days rest	4.87	3	2	3	49	0	92.1	100	7	33	74	Ahead in Count	.216	778	168	41	8	13	78	0	282	.225	.339
vs. AL	4.89	18	18	9	188	28	401.0	427	52	151	310	Behind in Count	.361	371	134	31	3	25	109	79	0	.469	.663
vs. NL	1.74	1	0	0	10	0	10.1	5	0	6	6	Two Strikes	.188	750	141	32	9	14	68	66	316	.261	.311
Pre-All Star	4.66	10	7	2	96	7	183.1	177	24	69	142	Pre-All Star	.252	701	177	37	8	24	109	69	142	.324	.431
Post-All Star	4.93	9	11	7	102	21	228.0	255	28	88	174	Post-All Star	.281	907	255	60	6	28	136	88	174	.346	.453

Pitcher vs. Batter (career)

Pitches Best Vs.	Avg	AB	H	2B	3B	HR	RBI	BB	SO	OBP	SLG	Pitches Worst Vs.	Avg	AB	H	2B	3B	HR	RBI	BB	SO	OBP	SLG
Ruben Sierra	.091	11	1	0	0	0	4	0	1	.091	.182	Brady Anderson	.545	11	6	2	1	1	1	2	2	.615	1.182
Paul Sorrento	.091	11	1	1	0	0	2	1	3	.154	.182	John Jaha	.538	13	7	2	0	3	9	1	2	.571	1.385
Danny Tartabull	.100	10	1	1	0	0	0	1	2	.182	.200	Mo Vaughn	.500	8	4	1	0	1	3	0	0	.636	1.000
Ivan Rodriguez	.133	15	2	1	0	0	0	0	6	.133	.200	Albert Belle	.368	19	7	3	1	2	4	0	6	.368	.947
Rich Amaral	.182	11	2	1	0	0	0	0	2	.182	.182	Geronimo Berroa	.357	14	5	2	0	2	6	0	3	.357	.929

469

Michael Tucker — Braves
Age 27 – Bats Left

	Avg	G	AB	R	H	2B	3B	HR	RBI	BB	SO	HBP	GDP	SB	CS	OBP	SLG	IBB	SH	SF	#Pit	#P/PA	GB	FB	G/F
1997 Season	.283	138	499	80	141	25	7	14	56	44	116	6	7	12	7	.347	.445	0	4	1	2126	3.84	150	130	1.15
Career (1995-1997)	.271	308	1015	158	275	53	11	30	126	102	236	14	16	24	14	.344	.433	3	9	5	4503	3.93	297	281	1.06

1997 Season

	Avg	AB	H	2B	3B	HR	RBI	BB	SO	OBP	SLG		Avg	AB	H	2B	3B	HR	RBI	BB	SO	OBP	SLG
vs. Left	.283	113	32	5	0	0	12	8	27	.352	.327	First Pitch	.351	77	27	2	1	3	6	0	0	.367	.519
vs. Right	.282	386	109	20	7	14	44	36	89	.346	.479	Ahead in Count	.412	97	40	9	0	5	15	19	0	.504	.660
Groundball	.274	95	26	4	3	0	6	5	28	.317	.379	Behind in Count	.204	240	49	7	3	5	28	0	101	.211	.321
Flyball	.313	64	20	3	1	3	5	9	11	.397	.531	Two Strikes	.179	246	44	6	3	3	24	25	116	.257	.264
Home	.280	239	67	10	4	5	22	21	55	.342	.418	Batting #2	.283	406	115	20	7	11	48	34	90	.348	.448
Away	.285	260	74	15	3	9	34	23	61	.352	.469	Batting #7	.263	19	5	1	0	1	3	3		.348	.474
Day	.222	158	35	5	2	5	16	14	40	.301	.373	Other	.284	74	21	4	0	2	5	7	23	.346	.419
Night	.311	341	106	20	5	9	40	30	76	.369	.478	March/April	.418	79	33	0	2	2	20	4	8	.446	.544
Grass	.283	400	113	20	7	9	43	33	96	.345	.435	May	.260	104	27	10	2	2	8	13	28	.347	.452
Turf	.283	99	28	5	0	5	13	11	20	.355	.485	June	.257	105	27	6	1	4	13	7	23	.333	.448
Pre-All Star	.304	313	95	16	5	8	42	27	66	.370	.463	July	.228	101	23	5	1	2	5	11	28	.304	.356
Post-All Star	.247	186	46	9	2	6	14	17	50	.309	.414	August	.208	53	11	2	1	1	3	8	15	.311	.340
Scoring Posn	.258	128	33	3	2	3	37	9	28	.304	.383	Sept/Oct	.351	57	20	2	0	3	7	1	14	.356	.544
Close & Late	.200	75	15	4	1	1	7	8	20	.294	.320	vs. AL	.277	47	13	1	0	0	1	4	9	.346	.298
None on/out	.250	100	25			8	1	3	15	27	.348	.440	vs. NL	.283	452	128	24	7	14	55	40	107	.347	.460

1997 By Position

Position	Avg	AB	H	2B	3B	HR	RBI	BB	SO	OBP	SLG	G	GS	Innings	PO	A	E	DP	Fld Pct	Rng Fctr	In Zone	Zone Outs	Zone Rtg	MLB Zone
As Pinch Hitter	.000	9	0	0	0	0	0	2	3	.182	.000	12	0	—	—	—	—	—	—	—	—	—	—	—
As lf	.284	102	29	6	1	2	15	5	24	.336	.422	53	21	242.1	56	2	1	2	.983	2.15	61	49	.803	.805
As rf	.289	388	112	19	6	12	41	37	89	.354	.461	102	100	828.0	181	4	4	0	.979	2.01	207	169	.816	.813

Career (1995-1997)

	Avg	AB	H	2B	3B	HR	RBI	BB	SO	OBP	SLG		Avg	AB	H	2B	3B	HR	RBI	BB	SO	OBP	SLG
vs. Left	.260	204	53	7	1	5	25	14	43	.326	.377	First Pitch	.365	137	50	6	1	5	13	0	0	.383	.533
vs. Right	.274	811	222	46	10	25	101	88	193	.349	.448	Ahead in Count	.398	211	84	18	1	13	48	57	0	.518	.678
Groundball	.296	243	72	13	4	4	25	17	64	.350	.432	Behind in Count	.184	477	88	17	4	8	43	0	206	.196	.287
Flyball	.268	153	41	7	3	5	21	22	35	.362	.451	Two Strikes	.166	512	85	16	6	5	41	45	236	.243	.250
Home	.266	493	131	27	7	8	49	51	111	.340	.398	Batting #2	.284	409	116	20	7	11	48	36	90	.350	.447
Away	.276	522	144	26	4	22	77	51	125	.348	.467	Batting #5	.257	171	44	14	2	6	20	18	39	.332	.468
Day	.230	296	68	11	5	8	35	30	70	.314	.382	Other	.264	435	115	19	2	13	58	48	107	.343	.407
Night	.288	719	207	42	6	22	91	72	166	.357	.455	March/April	.333	171	57	5	3	5	36	13	29	.385	.485
Grass	.276	848	234	47	11	20	103	80	197	.346	.428	May	.209	254	53	16	2	5	23	30	60	.293	.346
Turf	.246	167	41	6	0	10	23	22	39	.337	.461	June	.265	132	35	8	2	4	16	9	29	.349	.447
Pre-All Star	.264	606	160	30	7	16	79	58	128	.338	.416	July	.237	173	41	7	2	4	13	17	44	.307	.370
Post-All Star	.281	409	115	23	4	14	47	44	108	.354	.460	August	.315	181	57	11	2	8	26	29	40	.415	.530
Scoring Posn	.264	250	66	10	3	6	91	26	51	.335	.400	Sept/Oct	.308	104	32	6	0	4	12	4	34	.330	.481
Close & Late	.221	145	32	8	1	5	16	18	54	.319	.393	vs. AL	.261	563	147	29	4	16	71	62	129	.342	.412
None on/out	.237	232	55	15	2	11	11	27	56	.322	.461	vs. NL	.283	452	128	24	7	14	55	40	107	.347	.460

Batter vs. Pitcher (career)

Hits Best Against	Avg	AB	H	2B	3B	HR	RBI	BB	SO	OBP	SLG	Hits Worst Against	Avg	AB	H	2B	3B	HR	RBI	BB	SO	OBP	SLG
Pat Hentgen	.400	10	4	1	0	1	4	4	3	.571	.800	Darryl Kile	.111	9	1	0	0	0	0	2	2	.273	.111
Mark Clark	.385	13	5	2	0	2	3	0	0	.385	1.000	Orel Hershiser	.182	11	2	1	0	0	0	1	4	.250	.273
Ricky Bones	.357	14	5	1	0	0	3	0	0	.400	.429	Alex Fernandez	.200	10	2	0	0	0	0	2	5	.333	.200
Roger Clemens	.308	13	4	1	0	0	1	1	5	.357	.385	Dwight Gooden	.222	9	2	0	0	0	0	2	2	.364	.222

Chris Turner — Angels
Age 29 – Bats Right

	Avg	G	AB	R	H	2B	3B	HR	RBI	BB	SO	HBP	GDP	SB	CS	OBP	SLG	IBB	SH	SF	#Pit	#P/PA	GB	FB	G/F
1997 Season	.261	13	23	4	6	1	1	1	2	5	8	0	0	0	0	.393	.522	0	1	0	124	4.28	4	6	0.67
Career (1993-1997)	.250	105	260	37	65	13	2	3	29	25	56	2	3	4	1	.316	.350	0	2	4	1168	3.99	80	79	1.01

1997 Season

	Avg	AB	H	2B	3B	HR	RBI	BB	SO	OBP	SLG		Avg	AB	H	2B	3B	HR	RBI	BB	SO	OBP	SLG
vs. Left	.400	10	4	1	1	0	1	2	4	.500	.700	Scoring Posn	.167	6	1	1	0	0	1	1	2	.286	.333
vs. Right	.154	13	2	0	0	1	1	3	4	.313	.385	Close & Late	.400	5	2	1	0	0	1	2	1	.571	.600

Tim Unroe — Brewers
Age 27 – Bats Right

	Avg	G	AB	R	H	2B	3B	HR	RBI	BB	SO	HBP	GDP	SB	CS	OBP	SLG	IBB	SH	SF	#Pit	#P/PA	GB	FB	G/F
1997 Season	.250	32	16	3	4	1	0	2	5	2	9	0	0	0	2	0	.333	.688	0	0	0	95	5.28	1	4	0.25
Career (1995-1997)	.222	48	36	8	8	1	0	2	5	6	14	0	0	0	2	1	.333	.417	0	0	0	204	4.86	7	9	0.78

1997 Season

	Avg	AB	H	2B	3B	HR	RBI	BB	SO	OBP	SLG		Avg	AB	H	2B	3B	HR	RBI	BB	SO	OBP	SLG
vs. Left	.182	11	2	0	0	1	4	2	7	.308	.455	Scoring Posn	.333	3	1	0	0	1	4	0	1	.333	1.333
vs. Right	.400	5	2	1	0	1	1	0	2	.400	1.200	Close & Late	.200	5	1	0	0	1	1		3	.333	.800

Ugueth Urbina — Expos

Age 24 – Pitches Right

	ERA	W	L	Sv	G	GS	IP	BB	SO	Avg	H	2B	3B	HR	RBI	OBP	SLG	GF	IR	IRS	Hld	SvOp	SB	CS	GB	FB	G/F
1997 Season	3.78	5	8	27	63	0	64.1	29	84	.215	52	8	2	9	33	.301	.376	50	36	9	1	32	8	0	55	73	0.75
Career (1995-1997)	4.02	17	15	27	103	21	201.2	87	207	.214	4	33	99	.312	.416	52	41	11	7	33	32	5	229	223	1.03

1997 Season

	ERA	W	L	Sv	G	GS	IP	H	HR	BB	SO		Avg	AB	H	2B	3B	HR	RBI	BB	SO	OBP	SLG
Home	3.38	5	4	12	30	0	32.0	23	3	14	42	vs. Left	.282	103	29	7	2	4	17	16	23	.378	.505
Away	4.18	1	4	15	33	0	32.1	29	6	15	42	vs. Right	.165	139	23	1	0	5	16	13	61	.242	.281
Day	2.88	2	2	7	24	0	25.0	17	4	9	33	Inning 1-6	.000	0	0	0	0	0	0	0	0	.000	.000
Night	4.35	3	6	20	39	0	39.1	35	5	20	51	Inning 7+	.215	242	52	8	2	9	33	29	84	.301	.376
Grass	4.57	0	3	9	22	0	21.2	21	3	12	26	None on	.230	122	28	5	1	5	5	10	40	.288	.410
Turf	3.38	5	5	18	41	0	42.2	31	6	17	58	Runners on	.200	120	24	3	1	4	28	19	44	.314	.342
March/April	1.46	1	1	2	11	0	12.1	5	2	4	15	Scoring Posn	.253	75	19	2	1	4	28	14	27	.378	.467
May	6.00	1	3	6	14	0	12.0	11	1	9	16	Close & Late	.213	183	39	7	1	6	27	27	62	.318	.361
June	5.79	0	1	6	8	0	9.1	13	2	5	10	None on/out	.286	56	16	3	0	3	3	5	14	.344	.500
July	5.40	1	2	4	10	0	10.0	10	2	3	17	vs. 1st Batr (relief)	.339	56	19	4	0	3	8	7	14	.413	.571
August	1.64	0	1	5	12	0	11.0	6	1	4	12	1st Inning Pitched	.211	204	43	6	1	7	29	25	63	.300	.353
Sept/Oct	2.79	2	0	4	8	0	9.2	7	1	4	14	First 15 Pitches	.206	170	35	5	1	5	20	17	52	.282	.335
Starter	0.00	0	0	0	0	0	0.0	0	0	0	0	Pitch 16-30	.250	64	16	3	1	3	12	12	27	.368	.469
Reliever	3.78	5	8	27	63	0	64.1	52	9	29	84	Pitch 31-45	.125	8	1	0	0	1	1	0	5	.125	.125
0 Days rest (Relief)	3.07	1	1	9	15	0	14.2	7	2	6	15	Pitch 46+	.000	0	0	0	0	0	0	0	0	.000	.000
1 or 2 Days rest	4.91	1	5	12	26	0	25.2	25	2	13	38	First Pitch	.400	20	8	0	1	2	6	2	0	.455	.800
3+ Days rest	3.00	3	2	6	22	0	24.0	20	5	10	31	Ahead in Count	.167	132	22	3	0	3	5	0	71	.173	.258
vs. AL	1.13	1	0	5	7	0	8.0	4	0	2	14	Behind in Count	.318	44	14	4	1	3	13	11	0	.455	.659
vs. NL	4.15	4	8	22	56	0	56.1	48	9	27	70	Two Strikes	.129	140	18	3	0	2	8	16	84	.223	.193
Pre-All Star	4.93	2	6	15	36	0	34.2	32	5	19	43	Pre-All Star	.242	132	32	6	2	5	21	19	43	.342	.432
Post-All Star	2.43	3	2	12	27	0	29.2	20	4	10	41	Post-All Star	.182	110	20	2	0	4	12	10	41	.250	.309

Ismael Valdes — Dodgers

Age 24 – Pitches Right

	ERA	W	L	Sv	G	GS	IP	BB	SO	Avg	H	2B	3B	HR	RBI	OBP	SLG	CG	ShO	Sup	QS	#P/S	SB	CS	GB	FB	G/F
1997 Season	2.65	10	11	0	30	30	196.2	47	140	.234	171	35	4	16	65	.282	.358	0	0	3.25	20	99	16	6	241	214	1.13
Career (1994-1997)	3.03	41	30	1	117	91	647.2	162	491	.237	579	110	11	55	225	.285	.358	6	2	4.22	64	100	53	14	869	644	1.35

1997 Season

	ERA	W	L	Sv	G	GS	IP	H	HR	BB	SO		Avg	AB	H	2B	3B	HR	RBI	BB	SO	OBP	SLG
Home	2.07	5	5	0	15	15	104.1	82	4	22	75	vs. Left	.262	367	96	19	1	8	36	25	54	.310	.384
Away	3.31	5	6	0	15	15	92.1	89	12	25	65	vs. Right	.206	364	75	16	3	8	29	22	86	.253	.332
Day	2.22	4	2	0	8	8	52.2	33	5	16	35	Inning 1-6	.237	634	150	32	2	15	61	43	125	.286	.364
Night	2.81	6	9	0	22	22	144.0	138	11	31	105	Inning 7+	.216	97	21	3	2	1	4	4	15	.255	.320
Grass	2.55	8	9	0	26	26	169.1	152	12	36	120	None on	.240	470	113	23	4	12	12	23	82	.277	.383
Turf	3.29	2	2	0	4	4	27.1	19	4	11	20	Runners on	.222	261	58	12	0	4	53	24	58	.290	.314
March/April	3.14	1	3	0	5	5	28.2	31	2	6	15	Scoring Posn	.244	164	40	9	0	1	45	19	48	.321	.317
May	2.43	2	3	0	6	6	40.2	35	1	9	35	Close & Late	.237	76	18	3	2	1	4	4	13	.275	.368
June	3.82	1	3	0	6	6	37.2	34	6	15	25	None on/out	.260	204	53	12	2	7	7	6	28	.281	.441
July	1.64	2	0	0	2	2	11.0	10	0	1	8	vs. 1st Batr (relief)	.000	0	0	0	0	0	0	0	0	.000	.000
August	1.84	3	1	0	6	6	44.0	31	3	5	31	1st Inning Pitched	.226	106	24	4	1	0	9	9	17	.282	.283
Sept/Oct	2.60	1	1	0	5	5	34.2	30	4	12	26	First 75 Pitches	.235	537	126	28	1	12	46	30	106	.275	.358
Starter	2.65	10	11	0	30	30	196.2	171	16	47	140	Pitch 76-90	.284	95	27	5	1	3	14	9	17	.349	.453
Reliever	0.00	0	0	0	0	0	0.0	0	0	0	0	Pitch 91-105	.157	70	11	1	1	0	3	4	13	.213	.200
0-3 Days Rest (Start)	0.00	0	0	0	0	0	0.0	0	0	0	0	Pitch 106+	.241	29	7	1	1	1	2	4	4	.333	.448
4 Days Rest	2.70	6	5	0	17	17	113.1	90	11	28	72	First Pitch	.280	100	28	9	2	3	15	0	0	.280	.500
5+ Days Rest	2.59	4	6	0	13	13	83.1	81	5	19	68	Ahead in Count	.197	370	73	10	1	3	21	0	116	.198	.254
vs. AL	3.67	0	2	0	4	4	27.0	21	6	11	19	Behind in Count	.341	132	45	11	1	7	17	22	0	.436	.598
vs. NL	2.49	10	9	0	26	26	169.2	150	10	36	121	Two Strikes	.169	373	63	11	1	4	22	25	140	.220	.236
Pre-All Star	2.97	5	9	0	18	18	112.0	102	9	30	78	Pre-All Star	.243	419	102	24	2	9	41	30	78	.292	.375
Post-All Star	2.23	5	2	0	12	12	84.2	69	7	17	62	Post-All Star	.221	312	69	11	2	7	24	17	62	.268	.337

Career (1994-1997)

	ERA	W	L	Sv	G	GS	IP	H	HR	BB	SO		Avg	AB	H	2B	3B	HR	RBI	BB	SO	OBP	SLG
Home	2.42	20	13	0	58	44	334.1	261	21	79	261	vs. Left	.245	1157	284	54	4	30	110	85	186	.298	.377
Away	3.68	21	17	1	59	47	313.1	318	34	83	230	vs. Right	.229	1287	295	56	7	25	115	77	305	.272	.342
Day	2.73	11	8	1	33	26	191.1	144	14	51	152	Inning 1-6	.240	1958	470	97	7	43	190	136	385	.289	.363
Night	3.16	30	22	0	84	65	456.1	435	41	111	339	Inning 7+	.224	486	109	13	4	12	35	26	106	.266	.342
Grass	2.74	34	22	1	97	75	541.1	468	45	134	415	None on	.240	1523	365	71	7	32	32	79	283	.279	.359
Turf	4.49	7	8	0	20	16	106.1	111	10	28	76	Runners on	.232	921	214	39	4	23	193	83	208	.294	.358
March/April	2.82	3	4	0	13	12	76.2	74	7	15	53	Scoring Posn	.229	542	124	24	3	12	162	63	143	.304	.351
May	2.92	5	7	1	19	14	101.2	89	5	26	87	Close & Late	.233	313	73	4	7	1	19	20	75	.278	.351
June	3.30	9	6	0	23	18	131.0	114	15	42	91	None on/out	.237	646	153	30	3	11	11	32	109	.276	.344
July	2.68	9	3	0	23	13	94.0	86	6	21	77	vs. 1st Batr (relief)	.208	24	5	1	0	0	0	2	8	.269	.250
August	3.34	9	6	0	23	18	132.0	128	10	28	101	1st Inning Pitched	.219	420	92	20	4	8	41	44	83	.293	.343
Sept/Oct	2.88	6	4	0	16	16	112.1	88	12	30	82	First 75 Pitches	.240	1790	429	85	8	37	162	118	357	.286	.358
Starter	3.04	38	29	0	91	91	610.2	552	53	149	456	Pitch 76-90	.273	300	82	17	1	10	38	23	62	.325	.437
Reliever	2.92	3	1	1	26	0	37.0	27	2	13	35	Pitch 91-105	.200	225	45	4	1	5	18	11	42	.239	.293
0-3 Days Rest (Start)	4.50	0	1	0	3	3	12.0	9	2	7	11	Pitch 106+	.178	129	23	4	1	3	7	10	30	.243	.295
4 Days Rest	2.89	24	15	0	51	51	349.1	299	28	85	269	First Pitch	.298	383	114	24	3	11	51	12	0	.317	.462
5+ Days Rest	3.18	14	13	0	37	37	249.1	244	23	57	176	Ahead in Count	.188	1173	220	35	5	14	73	0	406	.188	.262
vs. AL	3.67	0	2	0	4	4	27.0	21	6	11	19	Behind in Count	.315	463	146	27	1	24	67	67	0	.402	.533
vs. NL	3.00	41	28	1	113	87	620.2	558	49	151	472	Two Strikes	.163	1169	190	33	4	15	74	83	491	.219	.236

Career (1994-1997)

	ERA	W	L	Sv	G	GS	IP	H	HR	BB	SO		Avg	AB	H	2B	3B	HR	RBI	BB	SO	OBP	SLG
Pre-All Star	3.21	20	19	1	64	48	339.1	306	32	89	252	Pre-All Star	.239	1281	306	59	3	32	121	89	252	.289	.365
Post-All Star	2.83	21	11	0	53	43	308.1	273	23	73	239	Post-All Star	.235	1163	273	51	8	23	104	73	239	.280	.352

Pitcher vs. Batter (career)

Pitches Best Vs.	Avg	AB	H	2B	3B	HR	RBI	BB	SO	OBP	SLG	Pitches Worst Vs.	Avg	AB	H	2B	3B	HR	RBI	BB	SO	OBP	SLG
Neifi Perez	.000	13	0	0	0	0	0	2	0	.000	.000	Jim Eisenreich	.524	21	11	0	0	1	6	2	0	.565	.667
Ryne Sandberg	.000	13	0	0	0	0	0	1	5	.071	.000	Tony Gwynn	.480	25	12	5	0	1	3	1	1	.500	.800
Brad Ausmus	.000	10	0	0	0	0	0	1	2	.091	.000	David Segui	.417	12	5	2	0	1	5	1	0	.462	.833
Jay Bell	.077	13	1	0	0	0	0	0	6	.077	.077	Ken Caminiti	.400	20	8	0	0	4	8	2	5	.455	1.000
Mark Parent	.091	11	1	0	0	0	0	0	4	.091	.091	Gary Sheffield	.400	10	4	0	1	2	2	2	0	.500	1.200

Marc Valdes — Expos
Age 26 – Pitches Right (groundball pitcher)

	ERA	W	L	Sv	G	GS	IP	BB	SO	Avg	H	2B	3B	HR	RBI	OBP	SLG	GF	IR	IRS	Hld	SvOp	SB	CS	#P	FB	FB/G
1997 Season	3.13	4	4	2	48	7	95.0	39	54	.240	84	17	3	2	37	.326	.323	9	33	10	1	2	6	2	166	68	2.44
Career (1995-1997)	4.18	5	7	2	62	18	150.2	71	69	.279	164	31	4	8	72	.362	.387	9	35	10	1	3	15	2	273	138	1.98

1997 Season

	ERA	W	L	Sv	G	GS	IP	H	HR	BB	SO		Avg	AB	H	2B	3B	HR	RBI	BB	SO	OBP	SLG
Home	3.76	2	3	1	21	3	38.1	35	2	12	17	vs. Left	.250	136	34	8	0	1	13	21	19	.352	.331
Away	2.70	2	1	1	27	4	56.2	49	0	27	37	vs. Right	.234	214	50	9	3	1	24	18	35	.309	.318
Starter	3.86	0	3	0	7	7	35.0	32	1	16	21	Scoring Posn	.165	109	18	6	2	0	34	16	17	.278	.257
Reliever	2.70	4	1	2	41	0	60.0	52	1	23	33	Close & Late	.279	43	12	2	1	0	7	11	9	.404	.372
0 Days rest (Relief)	1.35	0	0	1	4	0	6.2	6	0	1	4	None on/out	.286	84	24	5	0	0	0	5	12	.333	.345
1 or 2 Days rest	3.31	4	1	1	26	0	35.1	34	1	17	16	First Pitch	.255	55	14	5	0	0	2	4	0	.311	.345
3+ Days rest	2.00	0	0	0	11	0	18.0	12	0	5	13	Ahead in Count	.171	140	24	1	2	1	13	0	48	.199	.250
Pre-All Star	3.79	3	2	1	25	2	38.0	31	1	20	22	Behind in Count	.270	89	24	6	1	0	17	22	0	.409	.360
Post-All Star	2.68	1	2	1	23	5	57.0	53	1	19	32	Two Strikes	.190	147	28	5	1	1	12	13	54	.274	.272

Mario Valdez — White Sox
Age 23 – Bats Left

	Avg	G	AB	R	H	2B	3B	HR	RBI	BB	SO	HBP	GDP	SB	CS	OBP	SLG	IBB	SH	SF	#Pit	#P/PA	GB	FB	G/F
1997 Season	.243	54	115	11	28	7	0	1	13	17	39	3	3	1	0	.350	.330	0	0	2	566	4.13	31	30	1.03

1997 Season

	Avg	AB	H	2B	3B	HR	RBI	BB	SO	OBP	SLG		Avg	AB	H	2B	3B	HR	RBI	BB	SO	OBP	SLG
vs. Left	.188	16	3	1	0	0	0	2	6	.316	.250	Scoring Posn	.200	35	7	1	0	0	12	8	15	.362	.229
vs. Right	.253	99	25	6	0	1	13	15	33	.356	.343	Close & Late	.200	15	3	0	0	0	1	0	6	.200	.200
Home	.268	56	15	6	0	0	7	13	18	.408	.375	None on/out	.324	34	11	4	0	1	0	0	8	.343	.529
Away	.220	59	13	1	0	1	6	4	21	.288	.288	Batting #7	.179	28	5	4	0	0	1	5	10	.324	.321
First Pitch	.545	11	6	1	0	1	4	0	0	.545	.909	Batting #8	.280	75	21	3	0	1	11	10	23	.371	.360
Ahead in Count	.263	19	5	1	0	0	6	7	0	.464	.316	Other	.167	12	2	0	0	0	1	2	6	.286	.167
Behind in Count	.190	58	11	3	0	0	3	0	30	.200	.241	Pre-All Star	.313	16	5	1	0	0	3	2	7	.368	.375
Two Strikes	.156	64	10	2	0	0	3	10	39	.276	.188	Post-All Star	.232	99	23	6	0	1	10	15	32	.347	.323

Javier Valentin — Twins
Age 22 – Bats Both

	Avg	G	AB	R	H	2B	3B	HR	RBI	BB	SO	HBP	GDP	SB	CS	OBP	SLG	IBB	SH	SF	#Pit	#P/PA	GB	FB	G/F
1997 Season	.286	4	7	1	2	0	0	0	0	0	3	0	0	0	0	.286	.286	0	0	0	27	3.86	1	1	1.00

1997 Season

	Avg	AB	H	2B	3B	HR	RBI	BB	SO	OBP	SLG		Avg	AB	H	2B	3B	HR	RBI	BB	SO	OBP	SLG
vs. Left	.500	2	1	0	0	0	0	0	1	.500	.500	Scoring Posn	.000	2	0	0	0	0	0	0	1	.000	.000
vs. Right	.200	5	1	0	0	0	0	0	2	.200	.200	Close & Late	.000	0	0	0	0	0	0	0	0	.000	.000

John Valentin — Red Sox
Age 31 – Bats Right (flyball hitter)

	Avg	G	AB	R	H	2B	3B	HR	RBI	BB	SO	HBP	GDP	SB	CS	OBP	SLG	IBB	SH	SF	#Pit	#P/PA	GB	FB	G/F
1997 Season	.306	143	575	95	176	47	5	18	77	58	66	5	21	7	4	.372	.499	5	1	5	2349	3.65	219	186	1.18
Last Five Years	.298	637	2391	390	712	179	15	78	353	293	307	27	55	42	24	.377	.483	10	28	26	10686	3.86	783	834	0.94

1997 Season

	Avg	AB	H	2B	3B	HR	RBI	BB	SO	OBP	SLG		Avg	AB	H	2B	3B	HR	RBI	BB	SO	OBP	SLG
vs. Left	.221	154	34	12	1	5	12	24	22	.322	.409	First Pitch	.341	88	30	10	3	4	12	3	0	.370	.659
vs. Right	.337	421	142	35	4	13	65	34	44	.391	.532	Ahead in Count	.407	145	59	17	1	5	25	33	0	.514	.641
Groundball	.355	107	38	7	2	5	17	11	10	.415	.598	Behind in Count	.221	235	52	8	1	6	22	0	55	.221	.340
Flyball	.298	84	25	9	1	1	13	6	10	.348	.464	Two Strikes	.235	238	56	12	0	6	23	22	66	.303	.361
Home	.328	287	94	25	2	11	47	36	33	.402	.544	Batting #2	.291	354	103	28	2	14	43	35	46	.359	.455
Away	.285	288	82	22	3	7	30	22	33	.340	.455	Batting #7	.313	64	20	5	0	0	11	9	4	.395	.391
Day	.245	159	39	7	0	9	19	22	19	.339	.459	Other	.338	157	53	14	3	4	23	14	16	.390	.541
Night	.329	416	137	40	5	9	58	36	47	.385	.514	March/April	.160	94	15	3	0	2	5	9	15	.245	.255
Grass	.320	507	162	41	4	17	69	53	57	.387	.517	May	.324	74	24	8	1	0	9	5	6	.370	.459
Turf	.206	68	14	6	1	1	8	5	9	.257	.368	June	.373	110	41	9	1	4	23	13	10	.432	.582
Pre-All Star	.286	304	87	22	3	6	39	29	35	.350	.438	July	.342	117	40	12	1	6	16	14	15	.417	.615
Post-All Star	.328	271	89	25	2	12	38	29	31	.396	.568	August	.370	108	40	10	2	3	19	8	9	.410	.583
Scoring Posn	.312	141	44	14	1	3	55	27	18	.414	.489	Sept/Oct	.222	72	16	5	0	3	5	9	11	.317	.417
Close & Late	.374	99	37	9	1	0	12	11	13	.441	.485	vs. AL	.302	530	160	42	5	16	69	47	59	.361	.491
None on/out	.330	115	38	8	1	6	6	9	12	.384	.574	vs. NL	.356	45	16	5	0	2	8	11	7	.482	.600

1997 By Position

Position	Avg	AB	H	2B	3B	HR	RBI	BB	SO	OBP	SLG	G	GS	Innings	PO	A	E	DP	Fld Pct	Rng Fctr	In Zone	Zone Outs	Zone Rtg	MLB Zone
As 2b	.294	313	92	25	3	7	42	30	35	.357	.460	79	79	707.1	181	259	11	68	.976	5.60	287	247	.861	.902
As 3b	.322	261	84	22	2	11	35	28	31	.390	.548	64	63	552.2	59	122	11	15	.943	2.95	178	146	.820	.801

Last Five Years

	Avg	AB	H	2B	3B	HR	RBI	BB	SO	OBP	SLG		Avg	AB	H	2B	3B	HR	RBI	BB	SO	OBP	SLG
vs. Left	.301	612	184	48	7	18	79	102	82	.402	.490	First Pitch	.375	291	109	27	5	11	41	6	0	.396	.615
vs. Right	.297	1779	528	131	8	60	274	191	225	.368	.481	Ahead in Count	.366	648	237	70	5	33	132	163	0	.487	.642
Groundball	.334	488	163	41	4	13	78	55	54	.402	.514	Behind in Count	.226	934	211	42	4	17	70	0	246	.238	.334
Flyball	.277	452	125	30	4	10	66	48	63	.346	.427	Two Strikes	.226	1016	230	47	3	18	111	124	307	.317	.332
Home	.319	1196	381	103	6	44	193	175	162	.408	.525	Batting #2	.293	1367	401	93	7	54	195	180	176	.380	.490
Away	.277	1195	331	76	9	34	160	118	145	.345	.441	Batting #8	.308	299	92	28	0	6	44	29	47	.369	.462
Day	.281	740	208	49	4	21	103	101	100	.371	.443	Other	.302	725	219	58	8	18	114	84	84	.375	.479
Night	.305	1651	504	130	11	57	250	192	207	.380	.501	March/April	.226	318	72	18	2	7	30	37	40	.312	.362
Grass	.305	2073	633	159	11	66	302	254	264	.385	.488	May	.305	377	115	27	3	11	56	49	60	.389	.480
Turf	.248	318	79	20	4	12	51	39	43	.328	.450	June	.300	497	149	34	4	19	76	58	62	.373	.499
Pre-All Star	.287	1343	386	96	10	41	185	162	180	.365	.465	July	.316	462	146	41	2	15	66	69	60	.405	.511
Post-All Star	.311	1048	326	83	5	37	168	131	127	.392	.506	August	.326	405	132	31	3	14	75	38	48	.386	.521
Scoring Posn	.307	612	188	51	3	16	262	106	87	.403	.479	Sept/Oct	.295	332	98	28	1	12	50	42	37	.380	.494
Close & Late	.327	364	119	33	1	13	56	42	52	.400	.530	vs. AL	.297	2346	696	174	15	76	345	282	300	.375	.481
None on/out	.307	479	147	33	2	21	21	49	55	.379	.516	vs. NL	.356	45	16	5	0	2	8	11	7	.482	.600

Batter vs. Pitcher (career)

Hits Best Against	Avg	AB	H	2B	3B	HR	RBI	BB	SO	OBP	SLG	Hits Worst Against	Avg	AB	H	2B	3B	HR	RBI	BB	SO	OBP	SLG
Buddy Groom	.647	17	11	1	0	1	6	0	0	.647	.882	Andy Pettitte	.067	15	1	1	0	0	1	1	2	.125	.133
Angel Miranda	.500	12	6	1	1	0	1	3	0	.625	.750	Jack McDowell	.083	24	2	0	0	1	3	2	7	.154	.208
Jason Bere	.444	9	4	1	0	1	3	2	2	.545	.889	Jeff Nelson	.091	11	1	0	0	0	1	1	2	.167	.091
Bob Wickman	.429	14	6	3	0	2	6	1	1	.438	1.071	Woody Williams	.118	17	2	1	0	0	2	1	1	.167	.176
Todd Stottlemyre	.423	26	11	1	1	3	6	2	2	.464	.885	Jason Dickson	.143	14	2	1	0	0	0	0	4	.143	.214

Jose Valentin — Brewers

Age 28 – Bats Both (flyball hitter)

	Avg	G	AB	R	H	2B	3B	HR	RBI	BB	SO	HBP	GDP	SB	CS	OBP	SLG	IBB	SH	SF	#Pit	#P/PA	GB	FB	G/F
1997 Season	.253	136	494	58	125	23	1	17	58	39	109	4	5	19	8	.310	.407	4	4	5	2035	3.73	115	183	0.63
Last Five Years	.246	518	1722	267	423	99	13	64	255	187	428	7	11	65	23	.320	.430	15	23	15	7610	3.89	403	593	0.68

1997 Season

	Avg	AB	H	2B	3B	HR	RBI	BB	SO	OBP	SLG		Avg	AB	H	2B	3B	HR	RBI	BB	SO	OBP	SLG
vs. Left	.259	158	41	3	0	2	9	7	35	.299	.316	First Pitch	.309	68	21	2	0	1	6	3	0	.333	.382
vs. Right	.250	336	84	20	1	15	49	32	74	.315	.449	Ahead in Count	.280	107	30	8	0	7	20	18	0	.381	.551
Groundball	.288	80	23	4	0	7	12	2	18	.305	.600	Behind in Count	.224	219	49	8	1	7	21	0	91	.233	.365
Flyball	.172	99	17	4	0	2	7	13	23	.274	.273	Two Strikes	.178	230	41	8	0	6	18	18	109	.241	.291
Home	.208	231	48	12	1	4	26	28	52	.298	.320	Batting #2	.260	196	51	13	0	8	20	14	42	.313	.449
Away	.293	263	77	11	0	13	32	11	57	.321	.483	Batting #6	.235	115	27	3	1	5	16	12	31	.307	.409
Day	.210	176	37	9	0	2	17	14	34	.268	.295	Other	.257	183	47	7	0	4	22	13	36	.308	.361
Night	.277	318	88	14	1	15	41	25	75	.333	.469	March/April	.100	20	2	0	0	0	1	2	6	.182	.100
Grass	.259	424	110	21	1	14	54	35	93	.318	.413	May	.319	72	23	5	1	2	14	9	13	.393	.500
Turf	.214	70	15	2	0	3	4	4	16	.257	.371	June	.271	96	26	1	0	4	13	4	25	.300	.406
Pre-All Star	.269	208	56	9	1	6	32	17	45	.323	.409	July	.250	100	25	6	0	3	9	9	15	.321	.400
Post-All Star	.241	286	69	14	0	11	26	22	64	.300	.406	August	.288	118	34	9	0	5	14	9	26	.338	.492
Scoring Posn	.258	124	32	7	1	4	40	13	34	.322	.427	Sept/Oct	.170	88	15	2	0	3	7	6	24	.223	.295
Close & Late	.200	80	16	2	0	1	5	6	26	.264	.263	vs. AL	.259	440	114	21	1	15	52	38	99	.320	.414
None on/out	.284	109	31	3	0	6	6	8	20	.350	.477	vs. NL	.204	54	11	2	0	2	6	1	10	.218	.352

1997 By Position

Position	Avg	AB	H	2B	3B	HR	RBI	BB	SO	OBP	SLG	G	GS	Innings	PO	A	E	DP	Fld Pct	Rng Fctr	In Zone	Zone Outs	Zone Rtg	MLB Zone
As ss	.252	488	123	23	1	17	58	39	109	.310	.408	134	132	1150.1	208	384	20	88	.967	4.63	435	406	.933	.937

Last Five Years

	Avg	AB	H	2B	3B	HR	RBI	BB	SO	OBP	SLG		Avg	AB	H	2B	3B	HR	RBI	BB	SO	OBP	SLG
vs. Left	.217	433	94	10	3	4	35	41	122	.288	.282	First Pitch	.318	233	74	15	2	5	40	12	0	.348	.464
vs. Right	.255	1289	329	89	10	60	220	146	306	.330	.479	Ahead in Count	.319	367	117	33	4	22	85	81	0	.436	.610
Groundball	.258	391	101	28	1	19	63	26	77	.304	.481	Behind in Count	.188	794	149	33	5	26	80	0	355	.192	.340
Flyball	.242	331	80	25	1	7	42	48	90	.339	.387	Two Strikes	.169	848	143	37	5	28	89	93	428	.253	.323
Home	.237	852	202	51	10	26	135	101	191	.320	.412	Batting #6	.248	278	69	14	2	17	50	27	74	.315	.496
Away	.254	870	221	48	3	38	120	86	237	.320	.447	Batting #9	.241	638	154	42	5	23	99	71	167	.318	.431
Day	.230	595	137	33	6	19	91	67	145	.306	.402	Other	.248	806	200	43	6	24	106	89	187	.323	.406
Night	.254	1127	286	66	7	45	164	120	283	.326	.445	March/April	.255	137	35	7	3	3	22	18	31	.342	.416
Grass	.245	1501	368	86	13	53	223	168	365	.321	.426	May	.235	319	75	21	2	9	52	33	75	.305	.398
Turf	.249	221	55	13	0	11	32	19	63	.307	.457	June	.285	362	103	19	5	15	59	19	92	.319	.489
Pre-All Star	.261	917	239	57	10	31	148	90	226	.325	.446	July	.227	362	82	22	0	15	48	51	95	.325	.412
Post-All Star	.229	805	184	42	3	33	107	97	202	.313	.411	August	.268	328	88	23	1	16	47	32	76	.333	.491
Scoring Posn	.263	476	125	32	7	19	194	61	119	.339	.479	Sept/Oct	.187	214	40	7	2	6	27	34	59	.299	.322
Close & Late	.195	256	50	12	2	6	28	38	86	.300	.328	vs. AL	.247	1668	412	97	13	62	249	186	418	.322	.432
None on/out	.245	379	93	23	1	20	20	35	93	.314	.422	vs. NL	.204	54	11	2	0	2	6	1	10	.218	.352

Batter vs. Pitcher (career)

Hits Best Against	Avg	AB	H	2B	3B	HR	RBI	BB	SO	OBP	SLG	Hits Worst Against	Avg	AB	H	2B	3B	HR	RBI	BB	SO	OBP	SLG
Danny Darwin	.545	11	6	1	1	2	4	1	2	.583	1.364	Randy Johnson	.000	13	0	0	0	0	0	2	6	.133	.000

Batter vs. Pitcher (career)

Hits Best Against	Avg	AB	H	2B	3B	HR	RBI	BB	SO	OBP	SLG	Hits Worst Against	Avg	AB	H	2B	3B	HR	RBI	BB	SO	OBP	SLG
Ken Hill	.500	18	9	4	0	1	3	3	4	.571	.889	Bobby Witt	.059	17	1	0	0	1	1	1	5	.111	.235
Tim Belcher	.412	17	7	3	0	0	3	3	3	.500	.588	Sterling Hitchcock	.077	13	1	0	0	0	0	0	6	.077	.077
Orel Hershiser	.381	21	8	1	0	5	7	0	3	.381	1.143	Ben McDonald	.100	10	1	0	0	0	0	0	2	.308	.100
Alex Fernandez	.357	14	5	0	1	1	2	1	5	.400	.714	David Wells	.125	16	2	0	0	0	1	1	5	.176	.125

Fernando Valenzuela — Cardinals
Age 37 – Pitches Left

	ERA	W	L	Sv	G	GS	IP	BB	SO	Avg	H	2B	3B	HR	RBI	OBP	SLG	CG	ShO	Sup	QS	#P/S	SB	CS	GB	FB	G/F
1997 Season	4.96	2	12	0	18	18	89.0	46	61	.295	106	18	1	12	50	.381	.451	1	0	3.74	4	90	8	7	138	90	1.53
Last Five Years	4.40	32	35	0	120	102	574.2	233	310	.274	605	135	8	71	272	.343	.438	6	2	5.17	41	93	41	35	812	689	1.18

1997 Season

	ERA	W	L	Sv	G	GS	IP	H	HR	BB	SO		Avg	AB	H	2B	3B	HR	RBI	BB	SO	OBP	SLG
Home	4.11	1	6	0	9	9	50.1	58	9	19	27	vs. Left	.313	67	21	4	0	2	9	8	13	.410	.463
Away	6.05	1	6	0	9	9	38.2	48	3	27	34	vs. Right	.291	292	85	14	1	10	41	38	48	.374	.449
Starter	4.96	2	12	0	18	18	89.0	106	12	46	61	Scoring Posn	.267	105	28	3	0	2	37	10	25	.336	.352
Reliever	0.00	0	0	0	0	0	0.0	0	0	0	0	Close & Late	.500	4	2	0	0	1	2	0	0	.500	1.250
0-3 Days Rest (Start)	0.00	0	0	0	0	0	0.0	0	0	0	0	None on/out	.281	89	25	4	0	4	4	7	17	.340	.461
4 Days Rest	5.33	1	5	0	10	10	50.2	63	6	26	38	First Pitch	.372	43	16	2	0	2	5	0	0	.400	.558
5+ Days Rest	4.46	1	7	0	8	8	38.1	43	6	20	23	Ahead in Count	.209	139	29	0	0	2	13	0	47	.224	.295
Pre-All Star	4.80	2	11	0	17	17	86.1	104	12	40	60	Behind in Count	.379	87	33	6	0	5	18	28	0	.530	.621
Post-All Star	10.13	0	1	0	1	1	2.2	2	0	6	1	Two Strikes	.196	158	31	6	1	1	11	18	61	.277	.259

Last Five Years

	ERA	W	L	Sv	G	GS	IP	H	HR	BB	SO		Avg	AB	H	2B	3B	HR	RBI	BB	SO	OBP	SLG
Home	4.04	19	16	0	61	56	316.1	336	39	113	166	vs. Left	.283	375	106	24	1	9	41	42	66	.358	.424
Away	4.84	13	19	0	59	46	258.1	269	32	120	144	vs. Right	.272	1836	499	111	7	62	231	191	244	.340	.441
Day	5.01	10	14	0	38	31	167.0	187	21	69	89	Inning 1-6	.276	1996	550	119	8	64	248	209	282	.345	.439
Night	4.15	22	21	0	82	71	407.2	418	50	164	221	Inning 7+	.256	215	55	16	0	7	24	24	28	.328	.428
Grass	4.49	25	29	0	90	77	428.2	458	53	173	231	None on	.267	1290	344	92	2	42	42	122	191	.332	.439
Turf	4.13	7	6	0	30	25	146.0	147	18	60	79	Runners on	.283	921	261	43	6	29	230	111	119	.358	.438
March/April	3.47	1	6	0	15	12	62.1	65	8	24	40	Scoring Posn	.257	556	143	26	3	13	188	67	84	.332	.385
May	4.79	6	11	0	24	21	118.1	133	16	48	73	Close & Late	.308	65	20	4	0	2	10	12	6	.410	.462
June	4.38	4	7	0	22	19	111.0	120	14	39	55	None on/out	.284	592	168	52	1	24	24	43	78	.333	.497
July	3.59	7	7	0	24	18	115.1	103	10	41	41	vs. 1st Batr (relief)	.313	16	5	3	0	1	4	1	3	.353	.688
August	5.64	6	2	0	18	15	81.1	90	13	42	51	1st Inning Pitched	.288	458	132	30	3	14	66	34	63	.335	.459
Sept/Oct	4.48	8	2	0	17	17	86.1	94	10	39	50	First 75 Pitches	.277	1679	465	106	7	49	210	177	241	.345	.436
Starter	4.39	30	35	0	102	102	555.1	589	67	225	298	Pitch 76-90	.259	270	70	12	0	15	34	28	36	.336	.470
Reliever	4.66	2	0	0	19	0	19.1	16	4	8	12	Pitch 91-105	.283	180	51	9	1	5	21	23	23	.363	.428
0-3 Days Rest (Start)	7.71	0	1	0	3	3	11.2	14	1	7	3	Pitch 106+	.232	82	19	8	0	2	7	5	10	.273	.402
4 Days Rest	4.47	18	20	0	58	58	318.0	337	39	127	184	First Pitch	.339	289	98	21	1	7	35	4	0	.349	.491
5+ Days Rest	4.11	12	14	0	41	41	225.2	238	27	91	111	Ahead in Count	.220	858	189	44	1	17	76	0	226	.224	.333
vs. AL	4.95	8	11	0	33	32	183.2	184	19	82	81	Behind in Count	.343	519	178	35	4	26	94	118	0	.463	.576
vs. NL	4.14	24	24	0	87	70	391.0	421	52	151	229	Two Strikes	.202	993	201	50	2	18	75	111	310	.283	.311
Pre-All Star	4.25	13	29	0	70	60	341.0	359	43	109	188	Pre-All Star	.272	1318	359	79	5	43	165	129	188	.338	.438
Post-All Star	4.62	19	6	0	50	42	233.2	246	28	104	122	Post-All Star	.275	893	246	56	3	28	107	104	122	.350	.439

Pitcher vs. Batter (since 1984)

Pitches Best Vs.	Avg	AB	H	2B	3B	HR	RBI	BB	SO	OBP	SLG	Pitches Worst Vs.	Avg	AB	H	2B	3B	HR	RBI	BB	SO	OBP	SLG
Edgardo Alfonzo	.000	10	0	0	0	0	2	3	.167	.000		Mark Parent	.583	12	7	1	0	2	4	0	1	.583	1.167
Al Martin	.000	8	0	0	0	0	3	0	.273	.000		Eric Karros	.571	14	8	0	0	2	5	0	1	.571	1.000
Ed Sprague	.083	12	1	0	0	0	0	1	.083	.083		Sean Berry	.467	15	7	1	0	2	4	1	1	.500	.933
Rafael Belliard	.100	20	2	0	0	0	2	0	1	.100	.100	James Mouton	.462	13	6	0	0	2	2	0	.500	.923
Eric Young	.100	10	1	0	0	0	0	1	.182	.100		Tony Eusebio	.400	10	4	1	0	2	5	2	1	.500	1.100

John Vander Wal — Rockies
Age 32 – Bats Left

	Avg	G	AB	R	H	2B	3B	HR	RBI	BB	SO	HBP	GDP	SB	CS	OBP	SLG	IBB	SH	SF	#Pit	#P/PA	GB	FB	G/F
1997 Season	.174	76	92	7	16	2	0	1	11	10	33	0	2	1	1	.255	.228	0	0	0	400	3.92	34	18	1.89
Last Five Years	.248	482	669	88	166	26	8	21	108	88	155	2	13	12	8	.335	.405	9	0	5	2898	3.79	245	170	1.44

1997 Season

	Avg	AB	H	2B	3B	HR	RBI	BB	SO	OBP	SLG		Avg	AB	H	2B	3B	HR	RBI	BB	SO	OBP	SLG
vs. Left	.000	7	0	0	0	0	0	1	2	.125	.000	Scoring Posn	.250	28	7	1	0	1	11	2	9	.300	.393
vs. Right	.188	85	16	2	0	1	11	9	31	.266	.247	Close & Late	.156	32	5	1	0	1	7	4	17	.250	.281

Last Five Years

	Avg	AB	H	2B	3B	HR	RBI	BB	SO	OBP	SLG		Avg	AB	H	2B	3B	HR	RBI	BB	SO	OBP	SLG
vs. Left	.186	43	8	2	0	0	4	6	9	.286	.233	First Pitch	.381	97	37	7	3	6	32	8	0	.417	.701
vs. Right	.252	626	158	24	8	21	104	82	146	.338	.417	Ahead in Count	.360	150	54	5	2	9	36	36	0	.484	.600
Groundball	.269	193	52	8	2	9	32	25	34	.355	.472	Behind in Count	.141	284	40	6	3	3	25	0	121	.146	.215
Flyball	.200	95	19	3	0	2	9	16	28	.315	.295	Two Strikes	.132	318	42	5	2	2	27	44	155	.240	.179
Home	.285	288	82	16	2	9	59	42	56	.375	.448	Batting #5	.181	116	21	2	0	5	17	14	21	.267	.328
Away	.220	381	84	10	6	12	49	46	99	.304	.373	Batting #9	.282	206	58	14	2	7	34	29	54	.369	.471
Day	.261	268	70	10	3	7	49	32	59	.340	.399	Other	.251	347	87	10	6	9	57	45	80	.338	.392
Night	.239	401	96	16	5	14	59	56	96	.332	.409	March/April	.265	102	27	3	3	1	16	10	20	.336	.382
Grass	.259	448	116	20	6	15	78	58	111	.343	.431	May	.270	122	33	5	1	6	23	14	33	.343	.475
Turf	.226	221	50	6	2	6	30	30	44	.319	.353	June	.280	143	40	7	1	6	29	19	32	.362	.469
Pre-All Star	.261	402	105	15	5	14	73	51	94	.345	.428	July	.185	119	22	1	0	4	21	20	36	.303	.294

Last Five Years

	Avg	AB	H	2B	3B	HR	RBI	BB	SO	OBP	SLG		Avg	AB	H	2B	3B	HR	RBI	BB	SO	OBP	SLG
Post-All Star	.228	267	61	11	3	7	35	37	61	.320	.371	August	.224	107	24	2	1	1	9	15	22	.317	.290
Scoring Posn	.311	190	59	8	6	8	88	32	39	.401	.542	Sept/Oct	.263	76	20	8	2	3	10	10	12	.349	.539
Close & Late	.221	172	38	3	2	4	24	22	58	.306	.331	vs. AL	.083	12	1	0	0	0	0	2	5	.214	.083
None on/out	.262	126	33	6	1	1	1	8	25	.316	.349	vs. NL	.251	657	165	26	8	21	108	86	150	.337	.411

Batter vs. Pitcher (career)

Hits Best Against	Avg	AB	H	2B	3B	HR	RBI	BB	SO	OBP	SLG	Hits Worst Against	Avg	AB	H	2B	3B	HR	RBI	BB	SO	OBP	SLG
John Smoltz	.438	16	7	0	0	1	7	4	3	.550	.625	Darryl Kile	.000	12	0	0	0	0	0	3	3	.200	.000
Todd Worrell	.400	10	4	0	0	1	2	1	4	.455	.700	Mark Portugal	.083	12	1	0	0	0	0	0	2	.083	.083
Pete Harnisch	.375	8	3	1	0	0	2	3	1	.545	.500	Kevin Gross	.143	14	2	0	0	0	1	0	4	.143	.143
Doug Drabek	.360	25	9	4	1	0	1	2	0	.429	.583	Frank Castillo	.167	18	3	0	0	0	0	0	7	.167	.167
Bill Swift	.333	12	4	0	0	1	1	2	0	.429	.583	Rod Beck	.182	11	2	0	0	0	0	0	3	.182	.182

William VanLandingham — Giants
Age 27 – Pitches Right

	ERA	W	L	Sv	G	GS	IP	BB	SO	Avg	H	2B	3B	HR	RBI	OBP	SLG	CG	ShO	Sup	QS	#P/S	SB	CS	GB	FB	G/F
1997 Season	4.96	4	7	0	18	17	89.0	59	52	.257	470	95	11	46	229	.345	.396	0	0	3.74	7	89	19	3	115	127	0.91
Career (1994-1997)	4.54	27	26	0	84	81	477.1	220	300	.257	470	95	11	46	229	.337	.396	1	0	4.86	37	94	71	24	628	601	1.04

1997 Season

	ERA	W	L	Sv	G	GS	IP	H	HR	BB	SO		Avg	AB	H	2B	3B	HR	RBI	BB	SO	OBP	SLG
Home	4.01	1	5	0	9	9	51.2	39	7	28	27	vs. Left	.272	162	44	7	2	5	25	31	19	.377	.432
Away	6.27	3	2	0	9	8	37.1	41	4	31	25	vs. Right	.206	175	36	6	2	6	20	28	33	.314	.366
Starter	5.13	4	7	0	17	17	86.0	78	11	58	48	Scoring Posn	.232	82	19	3	2	1	30	20	16	.358	.354
Reliever	0.00	0	0	0	1	0	3.0	2	0	1	4	Close & Late	.091	11	1	0	0	1	2	1	2	.167	.364
0-3 Days Rest (Start)	0.00	0	0	0	0	0	0.0	0	0	0	0	None on/out	.205	83	17	4	0	5	5	18	18	.347	.434
4 Days Rest	4.87	3	3	0	8	8	40.2	29	5	30	17	First Pitch	.333	54	18	2	2	0	1	2	0	.357	.444
5+ Days Rest	5.36	1	4	0	9	9	45.1	49	6	28	31	Ahead in Count	.186	129	24	7	0	4	14	0	44	.183	.333
Pre-All Star	5.11	4	6	0	16	16	81.0	71	10	55	44	Behind in Count	.267	90	24	2	1	5	20	37	0	.462	.478
Post-All Star	3.38	0	1	0	2	1	8.0	9	1	4	8	Two Strikes	.181	144	26	7	1	3	16	20	52	.279	.306

Career (1994-1997)

	ERA	W	L	Sv	G	GS	IP	H	HR	BB	SO		Avg	AB	H	2B	3B	HR	RBI	BB	SO	OBP	SLG
Home	4.21	14	14	0	43	43	267.0	252	27	108	175	vs. Left	.280	828	232	43	5	18	102	88	87	.349	.409
Away	4.96	13	12	0	41	38	210.1	218	19	112	125	vs. Right	.237	1004	238	52	6	28	127	132	213	.328	.384
Day	4.11	15	10	0	44	43	265.0	248	20	116	175	Inning 1-6	.254	1655	421	88	10	42	216	197	267	.335	.396
Night	5.09	12	16	0	40	38	212.1	222	26	104	125	Inning 7+	.277	177	49	7	1	4	13	23	33	.363	.395
Grass	4.39	22	21	0	66	63	377.1	366	38	166	249	None on/out	.238	1071	255	57	3	26	26	113	193	.314	.370
Turf	5.13	5	5	0	18	18	100.0	104	8	54	51	Runners on	.283	761	215	38	8	20	203	107	107	.368	.432
March/April	5.64	2	6	0	10	10	59.0	58	4	29	32	Scoring Posn	.273	439	120	23	5	11	175	81	69	.381	.424
May	5.30	4	4	0	14	13	69.2	68	10	41	39	Close & Late	.259	108	28	2	1	2	8	11	19	.328	.352
June	4.54	5	7	0	21	21	113.0	114	16	57	79	None on/out	.232	474	110	24	1	12	12	48	86	.305	.363
July	4.20	7	4	0	19	17	111.1	104	9	42	86	vs. 1st Batr (relief)	.000	2	0	0	0	0	0	1	1	.333	.000
August	4.32	7	4	0	13	13	81.1	84	6	30	45	1st Inning Pitched	.267	318	85	21	0	11	49	49	50	.363	.437
Sept/Oct	3.14	2	1	0	7	7	43.0	42	1	21	19	First 75 Pitches	.254	1390	353	70	8	39	179	164	222	.334	.400
Starter	4.61	27	26	0	81	81	468.2	466	46	215	292	Pitch 76-90	.277	253	70	12	2	6	29	22	41	.336	.411
Reliever	1.04	0	0	0	3	0	8.2	4	0	5	8	Pitch 91-105	.238	143	34	9	1	1	15	24	24	.345	.336
0-3 Days Rest (Start)	3.00	2	2	0	4	4	27.0	28	2	11	19	Pitch 106+	.283	46	13	4	0	0	6	10	13	.414	.370
4 Days Rest	5.06	13	13	0	42	42	242.0	249	24	110	144	First Pitch	.335	281	94	15	3	8	44	11	0	.361	.495
5+ Days Rest	4.28	12	11	0	35	35	199.2	189	20	94	129	Ahead in Count	.189	831	157	36	3	15	65	0	268	.192	.294
vs. AL	9.82	1	1	0	2	2	7.1	6	1	11	5	Behind in Count	.318	418	133	25	2	18	81	133	0	.476	.517
vs. NL	4.46	26	25	0	82	79	470.0	464	45	209	295	Two Strikes	.183	797	146	33	2	13	70	76	300	.257	.279
Pre-All Star	5.07	13	18	0	51	50	275.1	282	33	140	181	Pre-All Star	.263	1072	282	52	9	33	151	140	181	.349	.421
Post-All Star	3.83	14	8	0	33	31	202.0	188	13	80	119	Post-All Star	.247	760	188	43	2	13	78	80	119	.321	.361

Pitcher vs. Batter (career)

Pitches Best Vs.	Avg	AB	H	2B	3B	HR	RBI	BB	SO	OBP	SLG	Pitches Worst Vs.	Avg	AB	H	2B	3B	HR	RBI	BB	SO	OBP	SLG
Charlie Hayes	.000	15	0	0	0	0	0	2	4	.118	.000	Thomas Howard	.800	10	8	1	0	0	3	0	0	.727	.900
Eric Young	.100	10	1	0	0	0	0	0	0	.250	.100	Jose Vizcaino	.600	10	6	1	0	0	1	0	0	.636	.700
Brian L. Hunter	.143	14	2	0	0	0	2	0	4	.133	.143	Ken Caminiti	.538	13	7	2	0	1	7	1	3	.600	.923
Terry Pendleton	.167	18	3	1	0	0	3	0	2	.167	.222	Ray Lankford	.455	11	5	1	0	2	6	2	1	.538	1.091
Gregg Jefferies	.176	17	3	0	0	0	1	1	2	.222	.176	Joe Oliver	.333	9	3	2	1	0	3	3	1	.500	.778

Jason Varitek — Red Sox
Age 26 – Bats Both

	Avg	G	AB	R	H	2B	3B	HR	RBI	BB	SO	HBP	GDP	SB	CS	OBP	SLG	IBB	SH	SF	#Pit	#P/PA	GB	FB	G/F
1997 Season	1.000	1	1	0	1	0	0	0	0	0	0	0	0	0	0	1.000	1.000	0	0	0	2	2.00	1	0	0.00

1997 Season

	Avg	AB	H	2B	3B	HR	RBI	BB	SO	OBP	SLG		Avg	AB	H	2B	3B	HR	RBI	BB	SO	OBP	SLG
vs. Left	.000	0	0	0	0	0	0	0	0	.000	.000	Scoring Posn	.000	0	0	0	0	0	0	0	0	.000	.000
vs. Right	1.000	1	1	0	0	0	0	0	0	1.000	1.000	Close & Late	.000	0	0	0	0	0	0	0	0	.000	.000

Greg Vaughn — Padres
Age 32 – Bats Right (flyball hitter)

	Avg	G	AB	R	H	2B	3B	HR	RBI	BB	SO	HBP	GDP	SB	CS	OBP	SLG	IBB	SH	SF	#Pit	#P/PA	GB	FB	G/F
1997 Season	.216	120	361	60	78	10	0	18	57	56	110	2	7	7	4	.322	.393	1	0	3	1739	4.12	99	107	0.93
Last Five Years	.247	622	2208	381	546	100	5	125	385	333	540	14	36	45	23	.347	.467	30	0	17	9891	3.85	608	750	0.81

1997 Season

	Avg	AB	H	2B	3B	HR	RBI	BB	SO	OBP	SLG		Avg	AB	H	2B	3B	HR	RBI	BB	SO	OBP	SLG
vs. Left	.237	76	18	1	0	8	20	18	21	.385	.566	First Pitch	.288	52	15	2	0	1	6	0	0	.288	.385
vs. Right	.211	285	60	9	0	10	37	38	89	.304	.347	Ahead in Count	.357	70	25	6	0	8	25	18	0	.494	.786
Groundball	.155	71	11	2	0	2	8	10	26	.259	.268	Behind in Count	.178	163	29	2	0	6	15	0	77	.182	.301
Flyball	.236	55	13	0	0	3	7	9	16	.344	.400	Batting #5	.178	152	27	3	0	8	22	21	49	.254	.213
Home	.202	163	33	4	0	11	29	21	49	.294	.429	Batting #6	.227	163	37	5	0	6	24	25	46	.330	.368
Away	.227	198	45	6	0	7	28	35	61	.345	.364	Other	.304	46	14	2	0	4	11	10	15	.429	.609
Day	.181	116	21	5	0	5	21	22	36	.307	.353	March/April	.181	83	15	1	0	5	6	11	17	.277	.373
Night	.233	245	57	5	0	13	36	34	74	.330	.412	May	.268	56	15	2	0	2	10	3	23	.323	.411
Grass	.215	284	61	9	0	16	48	41	86	.314	.415	June	.212	52	11	0	0	2	6	9	16	.328	.327
Turf	.221	77	17	1	0	2	9	15	24	.351	.312	July	.294	34	10	3	0	2	7	5	9	.385	.559
Pre-All Star	.224	196	44	4	0	10	24	25	56	.317	.398	August	.147	75	11	2	0	3	11	17	27	.298	.293
Post-All Star	.206	165	34	6	0	8	33	31	54	.328	.388	Sept/Oct	.262	61	16	2	0	4	17	11	18	.375	.492
Scoring Posn	.213	108	23	5	0	3	38	18	35	.318	.343	vs. AL	.273	33	9	1	0	3	7	6	10	.385	.576
Close & Late	.254	67	17	2	0	3	9	13	25	.370	.418	vs. NL	.210	328	69	9	0	15	50	50	100	.316	.375
None on/out	.247	81	20	3	0	5	13	13	25	.351	.469												

1997 By Position

Position	Avg	AB	H	2B	3B	HR	RBI	BB	SO	OBP	SLG	G	GS	Innings	PO	A	E	DP	Fld Pct	Rng Fctr	In Zone	Zone Outs	Zone Rtg	MLB Zone
As Pinch Hitter	.217	23	5	0	0	2	3	5	9	.357	.478	28	0	---										
As lf	.213	324	69	10	0	14	49	48	96	.316	.373	94	88	758.1	153	7	1	0	.994	1.90	182	144	.791	.805

Last Five Years

	Avg	AB	H	2B	3B	HR	RBI	BB	SO	OBP	SLG		Avg	AB	H	2B	3B	HR	RBI	BB	SO	OBP	SLG
vs. Left	.265	563	149	25	2	37	100	117	109	.391	.513	First Pitch	.311	351	109	22	0	17	74	20	0	.354	.519
vs. Right	.241	1645	397	75	3	88	285	216	431	.331	.451	Ahead in Count	.354	520	184	30	4	50	140	142	0	.488	.715
Groundball	.219	494	108	21	0	22	73	79	118	.329	.395	Behind in Count	.178	894	159	26	1	29	93	0	395	.181	.306
Flyball	.272	416	113	15	2	29	84	65	102	.370	.526	Two Strikes	.142	1018	145	27	0	30	100	170	540	.264	.257
Home	.265	1044	277	52	4	62	197	162	257	.363	.501	Batting #4	.247	1148	284	53	4	57	182	189	274	.356	.449
Away	.231	1164	269	48	1	63	188	171	283	.333	.436	Batting #5	.242	504	122	21	0	38	110	81	129	.346	.514
Day	.237	742	176	40	2	33	118	125	185	.347	.430	Other	.252	556	140	26	0	30	93	63	137	.330	.460
Night	.252	1466	370	60	3	92	267	208	355	.347	.486	March/April	.248	274	68	9	1	18	45	47	59	.357	.485
Grass	.245	1854	454	85	5	105	326	268	440	.341	.466	May	.257	447	115	17	0	26	85	62	122	.351	.470
Turf	.260	354	92	15	0	20	59	65	100	.380	.472	June	.261	444	116	27	1	31	97	65	107	.356	.536
Pre-All Star	.261	1311	342	65	2	79	248	190	327	.356	.494	July	.263	441	116	28	2	18	71	43	102	.331	.458
Post-All Star	.227	897	204	35	3	46	137	143	213	.334	.427	August	.209	374	78	14	1	20	52	76	96	.344	.412
Scoring Posn	.243	642	156	32	1	26	255	133	151	.366	.417	Sept/Oct	.232	228	53	5	0	12	35	40	54	.347	.412
Close & Late	.203	340	69	13	0	10	36	55	108	.314	.329	vs. AL	.258	1739	448	88	4	100	313	259	409	.355	.485
None on/out	.271	502	136	30	3	32	32	59	112	.351	.534	vs. NL	.209	469	98	12	1	25	72	74	131	.320	.399

Batter vs. Pitcher (career)

Hits Best Against	Avg	AB	H	2B	3B	HR	RBI	BB	SO	OBP	SLG	Hits Worst Against	Avg	AB	H	2B	3B	HR	RBI	BB	SO	OBP	SLG
Doug Jones	.500	14	7	4	0	1	3	0	2	.500	1.000	Jon Lieber	.000	12	0	0	0	0	0	0	3	.000	.000
Andy Pettitte	.500	10	5	1	0	1	5	3	0	.615	.900	Dave Burba	.000	9	0	0	0	0	0	2	2	.182	.000
Paul Quantrill	.417	12	5	1	0	2	3	1	0	.462	1.000	Eric Plunk	.053	19	1	1	0	0	0	2	6	.143	.105
Scott Erickson	.394	33	13	4	0	4	12	2	7	.429	.879	Roger Clemens	.069	29	2	0	0	0	0	4	16	.182	.069
Jason Bere	.385	13	5	0	1	1	6	0	2	.385	.769	Mark Guthrie	.071	14	1	0	0	0	0	0	4	.133	.071

Mo Vaughn — Red Sox
Age 30 – Bats Left

	Avg	G	AB	R	H	2B	3B	HR	RBI	BB	SO	HBP	GDP	SB	CS	OBP	SLG	IBB	SH	SF	#Pit	#P/PA	GB	FB	G/F
1997 Season	.315	141	527	91	166	24	0	35	96	86	154	12	9	2	2	.420	.560	17	0	3	2466	3.93	161	115	1.40
Last Five Years	.310	705	2645	458	820	140	6	173	548	385	700	58	62	23	13	.406	.564	96	0	24	11795	3.79	772	628	1.23

1997 Season

	Avg	AB	H	2B	3B	HR	RBI	BB	SO	OBP	SLG		Avg	AB	H	2B	3B	HR	RBI	BB	SO	OBP	SLG
vs. Left	.337	196	66	8	0	15	33	30	61	.440	.607	First Pitch	.397	68	27	4	0	6	10	14	0	.517	.721
vs. Right	.302	331	100	16	0	20	63	56	93	.409	.532	Ahead in Count	.473	112	53	3	0	12	32	38	0	.607	.821
Groundball	.347	95	33	3	0	4	15	17	28	.466	.505	Behind in Count	.213	230	49	11	0	7	27	0	117	.231	.352
Flyball	.262	84	22	3	0	3	7	9	25	.330	.405	Two Strikes	.173	277	48	10	0	7	30	34	154	.269	.285
Home	.338	260	88	12	0	20	55	48	80	.453	.615	Batting #3	.311	441	137	19	0	28	84	75	131	.422	.544
Away	.292	267	78	12	0	15	41	38	74	.387	.506	Batting #4	.341	85	29	5	0	7	12	11	23	.417	.647
Day	.292	171	50	10	0	10	28	29	52	.404	.526	Other	.000	1	0	0	0	0	0	0	0	.000	.000
Night	.326	356	116	14	0	25	68	57	102	.428	.576	March/April	.286	91	26	3	0	6	17	21	23	.431	.516
Grass	.324	463	150	17	0	34	89	78	126	.431	.581	May	.337	95	32	6	0	8	14	11	22	.407	.653
Turf	.250	64	16	7	0	1	7	8	28	.342	.406	June	.415	53	22	1	0	6	14	11	15	.516	.774
Pre-All Star	.335	239	80	10	0	20	45	43	60	.443	.628	July	.300	80	24	2	0	4	14	22	27	.467	.475
Post-All Star	.299	288	86	14	0	15	51	43	94	.403	.503	August	.322	118	38	8	0	9	41		38	.380	.542
Scoring Posn	.301	146	44	5	0	10	62	35	48	.439	.541	Sept/Oct	.267	90	24	4	0	5	14	12	26	.368	.478
Close & Late	.276	76	21	3	0	6	17	21	25	.439	.553	vs. AL	.317	496	157	23	0	31	90	83	148	.424	.550
None on/out	.358	106	38	3	0	7	7	12	30	.447	.585	vs. NL	.290	31	9	1	0	4	6	3	6	.353	.710

1997 By Position

Position	Avg	AB	H	2B	3B	HR	RBI	BB	SO	OBP	SLG	G	GS	Innings	PO	A	E	DP	Fld Pct	Rng Fctr	In Zone	Outs	Zone Rtg	MLB Zone
As 1b	.321	492	158	23	0	35	91	82	142	.428	.581	131	131	1137.0	1089	73	14	116	.988	—	232	175	.754	.874

Last Five Years

	Avg	AB	H	2B	3B	HR	RBI	BB	SO	OBP	SLG		Avg	AB	H	2B	3B	HR	RBI	BB	SO	OBP	SLG
vs. Left	.298	860	256	40	1	54	179	99	255	.388	.535	First Pitch	.412	357	147	20	2	37	102	81	0	.533	.790
vs. Right	.316	1785	564	100	5	119	369	286	445	.414	.578	Ahead in Count	.420	591	248	43	0	49	149	179	0	.552	.741
Groundball	.300	503	151	27	0	29	99	72	129	.396	.527	Behind in Count	.216	1206	260	49	2	47	183	0	570	.232	.376
Flyball	.296	517	153	25	0	32	83	67	139	.386	.530	Two Strikes	.198	1325	263	50	2	49	186	124	700	.275	.350
Home	.334	1336	446	85	2	90	289	212	361	.432	.603	Batting #3	.310	1653	513	76	4	111	353	242	443	.407	.563
Away	.286	1309	374	55	4	83	259	173	339	.378	.524	Batting #4	.316	633	200	37	1	43	128	90	179	.409	.581
Day	.317	862	273	46	1	52	179	121	254	.410	.553	Other	.298	359	107	27	1	19	67	53	78	.396	.538
Night	.307	1783	547	94	5	121	369	264	446	.404	.569	March/April	.330	364	120	21	1	24	84	62	88	.429	.591
Grass	.311	2306	718	108	4	155	479	344	594	.409	.563	May	.328	506	166	23	2	42	104	71	128	.418	.630
Turf	.301	339	102	32	2	18	69	41	106	.386	.566	June	.301	448	135	22	1	26	79	71	122	.407	.529
Pre-All Star	.318	1429	455	70	5	104	302	217	368	.414	.593	July	.309	431	133	17	2	31	109	68	118	.411	.573
Post-All Star	.300	1216	365	70	1	69	246	168	332	.396	.530	August	.288	479	138	32	0	24	85	67	132	.383	.505
Scoring Posn	.328	711	233	42	2	51	380	177	195	.462	.608	Sept/Oct	.307	417	128	25	0	26	87	46	112	.391	.554
Close & Late	.271	373	101	13	1	21	66	67	97	.387	.480	vs. AL	.310	2614	811	139	6	169	542	382	694	.406	.562
None on/out	.302	589	178	30	2	36	36	46	153	.362	.543	vs. NL	.290	31	9	1	0	4	6	3	6	.353	.710

Batter vs. Pitcher (career)

Hits Best Against	Avg	AB	H	2B	3B	HR	RBI	BB	SO	OBP	SLG	Hits Worst Against	Avg	AB	H	2B	3B	HR	RBI	BB	SO	OBP	SLG
Ken Hill	.563	16	9	3	0	1	3	1	1	.611	.938	Hipolito Pichardo	.000	11	0	0	0	0	0	1	3	.083	.000
Shawn Boskie	.556	18	10	4	0	3	10	1	2	.591	1.278	Norm Charlton	.000	8	0	0	0	0	0	2	5	.273	.000
Bob Wickman	.500	10	5	3	0	1	3	3	2	.643	1.100	Roberto Hernandez	.071	14	1	0	0	1	1	0	8	.071	.286
Mike Trombley	.500	8	4	1	0	1	1	3	0	.636	1.000	Bobby Ayala	.077	13	1	0	0	0	0	1	6	.143	.077
Jamie Moyer	.444	9	4	0	0	2	3	1	2	.583	1.111	Arthur Rhodes	.167	18	3	0	0	0	2	0	9	.167	.167

Jorge Velandia — Padres
Age 23 – Bats Right

	Avg	G	AB	R	H	2B	3B	HR	RBI	BB	SO	HBP	GDP	SB	CS	OBP	SLG	IBB	SH	SF	#Pit	#P/PA	GB	FB	G/F
1997 Season	.103	14	29	0	3	2	0	0	0	1	7	0	0	0	0	.133	.172	0	0	0	105	3.50	8	7	1.14

1997 Season

	Avg	AB	H	2B	3B	HR	RBI	BB	SO	OBP	SLG		Avg	AB	H	2B	3B	HR	RBI	BB	SO	OBP	SLG
vs. Left	.000	1	0	0	0	0	0	0	0	.000	.000	Scoring Posn	.000	7	0	0	0	0	0	1	3	.125	.000
vs. Right	.107	28	3	2	0	0	0	1	7	.138	.179	Close & Late	.000	3	0	0	0	0	0	0	1	.000	.000

Robin Ventura — White Sox
Age 30 – Bats Left

	Avg	G	AB	R	H	2B	3B	HR	RBI	BB	SO	HBP	GDP	SB	CS	OBP	SLG	IBB	SH	SF	#Pit	#P/PA	GB	FB	G/F
1997 Season	.262	54	183	27	48	10	1	6	26	34	21	0	3	0	0	.373	.426	5	0	3	885	4.02	68	62	1.10
Last Five Years	.279	613	2216	344	619	105	5	106	396	353	351	8	49	9	13	.375	.475	57	4	33	10416	3.98	708	717	0.99

1997 Season

	Avg	AB	H	2B	3B	HR	RBI	BB	SO	OBP	SLG		Avg	AB	H	2B	3B	HR	RBI	BB	SO	OBP	SLG
vs. Left	.256	39	10	1	0	0	7	8	4	.375	.282	Scoring Posn	.295	44	13	2	1	0	18	15	6	.452	.386
vs. Right	.264	144	38	9	1	6	19	26	17	.372	.465	Close & Late	.320	25	8	2	1	1	8	4	4	.414	.600
Home	.290	93	27	5	1	2	14	18	6	.398	.430	None on/out	.310	42	13	6	0	3	3	8	3	.420	.667
Away	.233	90	21	5	0	4	12	16	15	.346	.422	Batting #5	.273	139	38	9	1	5	24	27	17	.385	.460
First Pitch	.448	29	13	3	0	0	6	4	0	.515	.552	Batting #6	.100	20	2	0	0	0	5	3	.280	.100
Ahead in Count	.262	42	11	1	1	3	8	18	0	.475	.548	Other	.333	24	8	1	0	1	2	2	1	.385	.500
Behind in Count	.209	67	14	1	0	1	6	0	15	.206	.269	Pre-All Star	.000	0	0	0	0	0	0	0	0	.000	.000
Two Strikes	.205	88	18	4	0	3	11	12	21	.297	.352	Post-All Star	.262	183	48	10	1	6	26	34	21	.373	.426

Last Five Years

	Avg	AB	H	2B	3B	HR	RBI	BB	SO	OBP	SLG		Avg	AB	H	2B	3B	HR	RBI	BB	SO	OBP	SLG
vs. Left	.266	654	174	29	3	28	133	78	142	.340	.448	First Pitch	.434	244	106	18	0	14	61	46	0	.524	.680
vs. Right	.285	1562	445	76	2	78	263	275	209	.390	.486	Ahead in Count	.326	610	199	36	1	40	143	192	0	.481	.585
Groundball	.241	540	130	23	1	13	76	84	101	.339	.359	Behind in Count	.201	890	179	22	4	26	103	0	287	.203	.322
Flyball	.293	447	131	23	3	30	118	84	69	.403	.559	Two Strikes	.206	1029	212	36	3	37	137	114	351	.283	.355
Home	.288	1036	298	46	1	43	182	172	151	.385	.458	Batting #4	.270	508	137	27	0	22	94	79	84	.368	.453
Away	.272	1180	321	59	4	63	214	181	200	.367	.489	Batting #5	.282	1364	384	58	5	70	255	231	219	.381	.485
Day	.265	660	175	28	1	32	105	99	110	.358	.456	Other	.285	344	98	20	0	14	47	43	48	.364	.465
Night	.285	1556	444	77	4	74	291	254	241	.383	.483	March/April	.266	282	75	13	0	13	38	45	50	.365	.450
Grass	.277	1918	532	85	4	89	347	308	302	.374	.465	May	.299	344	103	16	1	22	84	69	66	.411	.544
Turf	.292	298	87	20	1	17	49	45	49	.385	.537	June	.258	395	102	15	0	21	68	57	71	.348	.456
Pre-All Star	.273	1159	316	50	2	63	218	183	207	.368	.482	July	.281	416	117	23	2	16	67	56	56	.365	.462
Post-All Star	.287	1057	303	55	3	43	178	170	144	.384	.466	August	.296	405	120	18	1	20	73	70	59	.398	.494
Scoring Posn	.278	665	185	36	2	27	294	164	104	.408	.460	Sept/Oct	.273	374	102	20	1	14	66	56	49	.365	.444
Close & Late	.269	364	98	17	3	9	53	49	63	.352	.407	vs. AL	.279	2196	612	105	4	106	392	350	351	.375	.475
None on/out	.272	514	140	30	3	30	30	60	85	.351	.510	vs. NL	.350	20	7	1	0	4	3	0	.417	.450

Batter vs. Pitcher (career)

Hits Best Against	Avg	AB	H	2B	3B	HR	RBI	BB	SO	OBP	SLG	Hits Worst Against	Avg	AB	H	2B	3B	HR	RBI	BB	SO	OBP	SLG
Tim Belcher	.545	22	12	2	0	1	9	2	0	.583	.773	Buddy Groom	.077	13	1	0	0	0	1	0	4	.071	.077
Jim Poole	.545	11	6	3	0	1	5	0	0	.500	1.091	Orel Hershiser	.083	12	1	0	0	0	0	1	1	.214	.083
Jesse Orosco	.500	12	6	1	1	2	4	3	3	.600	1.250	Bob Wickman	.100	10	1	0	0	0	0	2	0	.250	.100
Tony Fossas	.500	8	4	0	0	1	2	4	2	.667	.875	Hipolito Pichardo	.136	22	3	0	0	0	0	2	2	.208	.136

Batter vs. Pitcher (career)

Hits Best Against	Avg	AB	H	2B	3B	HR	RBI	BB	SO	OBP	SLG	Hits Worst Against	Avg	AB	H	2B	3B	HR	RBI	BB	SO	OBP	SLG
Omar Olivares	.462	13	6	2	0	1	5	2	0	.500	.846	Brad Radke	.143	14	2	0	0	0	0	1	1	.200	.143

Dario Veras — Padres
Age 25 – Pitches Right

	ERA	W	L	Sv	G	GS	IP	BB	SO	Avg	H	2B	3B	HR	RBI	OBP	SLG	GF	IR	IRS	Hld	SvOp	SB	CS	GB	FB	G/F
1997 Season	5.11	2	1	0	23	0	24.2	12	21	.280	28	7	0	5	20	.368	.500	7	15	8	2	1	2	3	33	25	1.32
Career (1996-1997)	3.86	5	2	0	46	0	53.2	22	44	.255	52	11	0	8	33	.335	.426	13	30	14	3	1	6	3	71	53	1.34

1997 Season

	ERA	W	L	Sv	G	GS	IP	H	HR	BB	SO		Avg	AB	H	2B	3B	HR	RBI	BB	SO	OBP	SLG
Home	3.38	1	1	0	12	0	16.0	17	2	7	11	vs. Left	.237	38	9	5	0	1	10	9	7	.383	.447
Away	8.31	1	0	0	11	0	8.2	11	3	5	10	vs. Right	.306	62	19	2	0	4	10	3	14	.358	.532

Quilvio Veras — Padres
Age 27 – Bats Both

	Avg	G	AB	R	H	2B	3B	HR	RBI	BB	SO	HBP	GDP	SB	CS	OBP	SLG	IBB	SH	SF	#Pit	#P/PA	GB	FB	G/F
1997 Season	.265	145	539	74	143	23	1	3	45	72	84	7	9	33	12	.357	.328	0	9	4	2527	4.00	235	110	2.14
Career (1995-1997)	.261	342	1232	200	322	51	9	12	91	203	194	18	19	97	41	.372	.347	1	17	7	6039	4.09	516	279	1.85

1997 Season

	Avg	AB	H	2B	3B	HR	RBI	BB	SO	OBP	SLG		Avg	AB	H	2B	3B	HR	RBI	BB	SO	OBP	SLG
vs. Left	.194	124	24	5	0	0	5	17	14	.296	.234	First Pitch	.295	61	18	3	1	0	5	0	0	.313	.377
vs. Right	.287	415	119	18	1	3	40	55	70	.375	.357	Ahead in Count	.354	113	40	10	0	0	15	33	0	.493	.442
Groundball	.283	106	30	8	0	0	6	14	11	.382	.358	Behind in Count	.229	249	57	5	0	1	13	0	72	.243	.261
Flyball	.216	88	19	3	1	1	5	9	20	.290	.307	Two Strikes	.203	261	53	5	0	3	16	39	84	.308	.257
Home	.276	261	72	12	1	3	18	35	38	.365	.364	Batting #1	.221	226	50	8	0	2	19	35	42	.335	.283
Away	.255	278	71	11	0	0	27	37	46	.350	.295	Batting #2	.293	242	71	12	0	1	20	33	34	.384	.355
Day	.250	180	45	9	0	2	17	22	30	.333	.333	Other	.310	71	22	3	1	0	6	4	8	.338	.380
Night	.273	359	98	14	1	1	28	50	54	.368	.326	March/April	.220	91	20	4	0	2	11	13	13	.324	.330
Grass	.273	444	121	21	1	3	41	52	63	.351	.345	May	.185	65	12	4	0	0	5	6	13	.270	.246
Turf	.232	95	22	2	0	0	4	20	21	.381	.253	June	.333	93	31	4	1	0	8	8	8	.379	.398
Pre-All Star	.269	271	73	14	1	3	26	33	36	.352	.362	July	.385	104	40	5	0	1	13	16	17	.463	.462
Post-All Star	.261	268	70	9	0	0	19	39	48	.362	.295	August	.214	103	22	5	0	0	5	15	18	.331	.262
Scoring Posn	.267	116	31	5	0	0	39	23	20	.382	.310	Sept/Oct	.217	83	18	1	0	0	3	14	15	.337	.229
Close & Late	.281	89	25	7	0	0	13	11	12	.360	.360	vs. AL	.353	68	24	4	0	0	6	6	6	.408	.412
None on/out	.215	144	31	3	1	1	21	7	21	.323	.326	vs. NL	.253	471	119	19	1	3	39	66	78	.350	.316

1997 By Position

Position	Avg	AB	H	2B	3B	HR	RBI	BB	SO	OBP	SLG	G	GS	Innings	PO	A	E	DP	Fld Pct	Rng Fctr	In Zone	Zone Outs	Zone Rtg	MLB Zone
As 2b	.266	534	142	22	1	3	45	72	82	.358	.328	142	134	1192.1	277	407	11	68	.984	5.16	461	420	.911	.902

Career (1995-1997)

	Avg	AB	H	2B	3B	HR	RBI	BB	SO	OBP	SLG		Avg	AB	H	2B	3B	HR	RBI	BB	SO	OBP	SLG
vs. Left	.235	298	70	9	2	4	18	44	39	.345	.355	First Pitch	.254	134	34	7	1	3	16	1	0	.277	.388
vs. Right	.270	934	252	42	7	8	73	159	155	.380	.355	Ahead in Count	.358	299	107	23	5	3	33	89	0	.503	.498
Groundball	.236	276	65	13	0	1	15	36	37	.332	.293	Behind in Count	.210	534	112	9	1	3	21	0	165	.226	.247
Flyball	.219	178	39	5	2	3	10	32	34	.341	.320	Two Strikes	.186	597	111	12	1	6	27	113	194	.318	.240
Home	.261	582	152	24	4	6	41	98	90	.375	.347	Batting #1	.254	866	220	32	7	10	64	151	143	.373	.342
Away	.262	650	170	27	5	6	50	105	104	.369	.346	Batting #2	.283	279	79	15	1	2	21	45	39	.387	.366
Day	.224	326	73	19	1	4	25	44	60	.318	.325	Other	.264	87	23	4	1	0	6	7	12	.313	.333
Night	.275	906	249	32	8	8	66	159	134	.390	.354	March/April	.227	185	42	8	0	4	17	32	29	.347	.335
Grass	.262	971	254	43	6	8	70	147	146	.365	.343	May	.225	187	42	7	0	2	16	29	32	.342	.294
Turf	.261	261	68	8	3	4	21	56	48	.397	.360	June	.271	210	57	10	2	2	12	29	23	.360	.367
Pre-All Star	.253	660	167	31	2	9	48	102	93	.359	.347	July	.299	278	83	11	1	1	19	47	46	.405	.356
Post-All Star	.271	572	155	20	7	3	43	101	101	.386	.346	August	.258	213	55	10	3	2	16	35	35	.370	.362
Scoring Posn	.232	246	57	6	1	3	74	53	47	.372	.301	Sept/Oct	.270	159	43	5	3	1	11	31	29	.396	.358
Close & Late	.274	186	51	9	4	0	20	34	25	.386	.364	vs. AL	.353	68	24	4	0	0	6	6	6	.408	.412
None on/out	.264	432	114	19	5	5	84	84	68	.392	.366	vs. NL	.256	1164	298	47	9	12	85	197	188	.370	.343

Batter vs. Pitcher (career)

Hits Best Against	Avg	AB	H	2B	3B	HR	RBI	BB	SO	OBP	SLG	Hits Worst Against	Avg	AB	H	2B	3B	HR	RBI	BB	SO	OBP	SLG
John Smoltz	.529	17	9	3	2	0	1	3	3	.600	.941	Jon Lieber	.118	17	2	0	0	0	0	2	3	.211	.118
Steve Trachsel	.500	10	5	2	0	0	1	1	1	.583	.700	Bobby Jones	.133	15	2	0	0	0	2	3	1	.278	.133
Donne Wall	.500	10	5	1	0	0	0	1	1	.545	.600	Greg Maddux	.154	13	2	0	0	0	0	1	3	.214	.154
Michael Mimbs	.462	13	6	1	0	0	2	6	2	.650	.538	Jeff Fassero	.154	13	2	1	0	0	0	1	1	.214	.231
Pedro Astacio	.375	16	6	0	0	1	1	4	1	.500	.563	Esteban Loaiza	.182	11	2	0	0	0	0	1		.250	.182

Dave Veres — Expos
Age 31 – Pitches Right

	ERA	W	L	Sv	G	GS	IP	BB	SO	Avg	H	2B	3B	HR	RBI	OBP	SLG	GF	IR	IRS	Hld	SvOp	SB	CS	GB	FB	G/F
1997 Season	3.48	2	3	1	53	0	62.0	27	47	.278	68	15	4	5	30	.353	.433	11	33	15	10	4	2	4	85	74	1.15
Career (1994-1997)	3.07	16	10	7	225	0	284.0	96	250	.260	281	50	8	24	120	.324	.388	55	145	52	47	14	22	9	381	301	1.27

1997 Season

	ERA	W	L	Sv	G	GS	IP	H	HR	BB	SO		Avg	AB	H	2B	3B	HR	RBI	BB	SO	OBP	SLG
Home	4.10	1	2	0	25	0	26.1	31	3	15	24	vs. Left	.292	106	31	9	2	2	12	21	21	.409	.472
Away	3.03	1	1	1	28	0	35.2	37	2	12	23	vs. Right	.266	139	37	6	2	3	18	6	26	.304	.403
Day	3.38	0	0	1	15	0	16.0	16	2	8	13	Inning 1-6	.375	32	12	3	1	1	3	3	3	.429	.625
Night	3.52	2	3	0	38	0	46.0	52	3	19	34	Inning 7+	.263	213	56	12	3	4	27	24	44	.342	.404

1997 Season

	ERA	W	L	Sv	G	GS	IP	H	HR	BB	SO
Grass	2.35	1	1	0	19	0	23.0	23	1	10	13
Turf	4.15	1	2	1	34	0	39.0	45	4	17	34
March/April	2.84	0	0	1	13	0	19.0	14	2	6	12
May	5.73	1	1	0	12	0	11.0	11	2	7	9
June	0.87	1	1	0	9	0	10.1	10	0	4	8
July	3.65	0	1	0	10	0	12.1	15	1	3	12
August	1.50	0	0	0	5	0	6.0	8	0	4	5
Sept/Oct	10.80	0	0	0	4	0	3.1	10	0	3	1
Starter	0.00	0	0	0	0	0	0.0	0	0	0	0
Reliever	3.48	2	3	1	53	0	62.0	68	5	27	47
0 Days rest (Relief)	3.14	1	2	1	13	0	14.1	11	1	7	11
1 or 2 Days rest	3.96	1	0	0	20	0	25.0	29	2	5	18
3+ Days rest	3.18	0	1	0	20	0	22.2	28	2	15	18
vs. AL	2.70	0	0	0	3	0	3.1	6	0	0	2
vs. NL	3.53	2	3	1	50	0	58.2	62	5	27	45
Pre-All Star	3.14	2	2	1	36	0	43.0	41	4	17	31
Post-All Star	4.26	0	1	0	17	0	19.0	27	1	10	16

	Avg	AB	H	2B	3B	HR	RBI	BB	SO	OBP	SLG
None on	.333	129	43	10	3	3	3	10	18	.386	.527
Runners on	.216	116	25	5	1	2	27	17	29	.319	.328
Scoring Posn	.203	74	15	4	1	1	25	12	19	.318	.324
Close & Late	.252	115	29	7	1	1	17	13	26	.336	.357
None on/out	.328	64	21	5	2	2	2	2	11	.348	.563
vs. 1st Batr (relief)	.388	49	19	4	2	2	10	2	8	.415	.673
1st Inning Pitched	.258	163	42	10	2	3	24	19	32	.337	.399
First 15 Pitches	.289	142	41	9	2	3	23	12	26	.350	.444
Pitch 16-30	.288	80	23	6	1	0	3	13	16	.387	.388
Pitch 31-45	.150	20	3	0	1	2	4	0	5	.150	.550
Pitch 46+	.333	3	1	0	0	0	0	2	0	.600	.333
First Pitch	.250	28	7	3	0	1	4	2	0	.323	.464
Ahead in Count	.191	110	21	5	2	0	8	0	39	.196	.273
Behind in Count	.407	59	24	4	1	2	14	17	0	.539	.610
Two Strikes	.205	117	24	6	3	1	9	8	47	.260	.333
Pre-All Star	.247	166	41	8	2	4	20	17	31	.319	.392
Post-All Star	.342	79	27	7	2	1	10	10	16	.422	.519

Career (1994-1997)

	ERA	W	L	Sv	G	GS	IP	H	HR	BB	SO
Home	3.31	10	2	3	108	0	130.2	126	11	48	109
Away	2.88	6	8	4	117	0	153.1	155	13	48	141
Day	4.24	3	1	2	66	0	74.1	81	7	41	65
Night	2.66	13	9	5	159	0	209.2	200	17	55	185
Grass	2.82	2	6	2	72	0	95.2	97	9	35	96
Turf	3.20	14	4	5	153	0	188.1	184	15	61	154
March/April	4.12	2	0	2	29	0	39.1	40	7	15	36
May	3.10	6	6	1	48	0	58.0	53	5	18	55
June	3.24	4	2	2	38	0	50.0	53	5	17	38
July	2.21	0	1	1	46	0	57.0	47	3	17	50
August	2.60	1	1	1	34	0	45.0	48	4	15	38
Sept/Oct	3.63	3	0	0	30	0	34.2	40	0	14	33
Starter	0.00	0	0	0	0	0	0.0	0	0	0	0
Reliever	3.07	16	10	7	225	0	284.0	281	24	96	250
0 Days rest (Relief)	2.18	5	4	3	49	0	62.0	46	3	17	61
1 or 2 Days rest	3.44	8	3	3	119	0	154.1	161	13	50	135
3+ Days rest	3.06	3	3	1	57	0	67.2	74	8	29	54
vs. AL	2.70	0	0	0	3	0	3.1	6	0	0	2
vs. NL	3.08	16	10	7	222	0	280.2	275	24	96	248
Pre-All Star	3.27	12	8	5	128	0	165.1	161	17	55	141
Post-All Star	2.81	4	2	2	97	0	118.2	120	7	41	109

	Avg	AB	H	2B	3B	HR	RBI	BB	SO	OBP	SLG
vs. Left	.275	432	119	26	4	10	39	65	85	.369	.424
vs. Right	.250	648	162	24	4	14	81	31	165	.292	.364
Inning 1-6	.281	203	57	9	3	2	21	12	43	.319	.384
Inning 7+	.255	877	224	41	5	22	99	84	207	.325	.389
None on	.279	592	165	28	6	19	19	39	126	.329	.443
Runners on	.238	488	116	22	2	5	101	57	124	.319	.322
Scoring Posn	.211	317	67	14	2	3	95	41	86	.303	.297
Close & Late	.257	444	114	16	2	9	51	42	107	.327	.363
None on/out	.283	265	75	17	4	8	8	13	58	.321	.468
vs. 1st Batr (relief)	.294	201	59	14	3	5	30	14	41	.348	.468
1st Inning Pitched	.244	705	172	36	3	14	97	74	158	.319	.363
First 15 Pitches	.269	598	161	37	4	12	86	55	121	.333	.405
Pitch 16-30	.247	372	92	13	3	7	24	33	97	.315	.355
Pitch 31-45	.235	98	23	0	1	3	8	6	31	.276	.347
Pitch 46+	.417	12	5	0	0	2	2	2	1	.533	.917
First Pitch	.302	149	45	11	1	3	13	11	0	.358	.450
Ahead in Count	.201	498	100	16	3	6	47	0	193	.208	.281
Behind in Count	.378	209	79	15	2	10	39	38	0	.476	.612
Two Strikes	.166	530	88	16	4	5	44	47	250	.236	.240
Pre-All Star	.256	629	161	28	5	17	55	55	141	.321	.397
Post-All Star	.266	451	120	22	3	7	49	41	109	.329	.375

Pitcher vs. Batter (career)

Pitches Best Vs.	Avg	AB	H	2B	3B	HR	RBI	BB	SO	OBP	SLG
Glenallen Hill	.000	11	0	0	0	0	1	0	5	.000	.000
Eric Young	.077	13	1	0	0	0	0	0	3	.077	.077
Sammy Sosa	.111	9	1	0	0	0	2	1	2	.182	.111
Royce Clayton	.182	11	2	1	0	0	0	0	3	.182	.273

Pitches Worst Vs.	Avg	AB	H	2B	3B	HR	RBI	BB	SO	OBP	SLG
Vinny Castilla	.545	11	6	0	0	1	4	1	3	.538	.818

Randy Veres — Royals

Age 32 – Pitches Right (groundball pitcher)

	ERA	W	L	Sv	G	GS	IP	BB	SO	Avg	H	2B	3B	HR	RBI	OBP	SLG	GF	IR	IRS	Hld	SvOp	SB	CS	GB	FB	G/F
1997 Season	3.31	4	0	1	24	0	35.1	7	28	.273	36	4	0	4	23	.313	.394	7	28	13	4	3	3	0	44	39	1.13
Last Five Years	4.94	9	9	2	106	0	124.0	54	92	.276	132	14	1	19	103	.350	.429	34	105	46	18	9	12	2	195	127	1.54

1997 Season

	ERA	W	L	Sv	G	GS	IP	H	HR	BB	SO
Home	3.45	2	0	0	11	0	15.2	15	1	2	9
Away	3.20	2	0	1	13	0	19.2	21	3	5	19

	Avg	AB	H	2B	3B	HR	RBI	BB	SO	OBP	SLG
vs. Left	.273	55	15	1	0	1	7	4	10	.323	.345
vs. Right	.273	77	21	3	0	3	16	3	18	.306	.429

Last Five Years

	ERA	W	L	Sv	G	GS	IP	H	HR	BB	SO
Home	4.64	5	3	0	50	0	54.1	55	12	16	43
Away	5.17	4	6	2	56	0	69.2	77	7	38	49
Day	5.45	1	2	2	28	0	34.2	37	7	13	23
Night	4.74	8	7	0	78	0	89.1	95	12	41	69
Grass	4.50	8	6	1	83	0	94.0	95	15	39	68
Turf	6.30	1	3	1	23	0	30.0	37	4	15	24
March/April	6.37	1	3	1	22	0	29.2	32	5	17	24
May	4.85	4	3	0	32	0	39.0	38	3	20	36
June	2.35	1	1	2	18	0	23.0	22	4	4	14
July	4.63	1	2	0	14	0	11.2	13	5	2	7
August	7.82	1	2	0	13	0	12.2	20	1	6	7
Sept/Oct	3.38	1	0	0	7	0	8.0	7	1	5	4
Starter	0.00	0	0	0	0	0	0.0	0	0	0	0
Reliever	4.94	9	9	2	106	0	124.0	132	19	54	92
0 Days rest (Relief)	6.12	1	2	0	27	0	25.0	29	6	7	18
1 or 2 Days rest	4.48	4	6	2	52	0	66.1	65	10	32	56
3+ Days rest	4.96	4	1	0	27	0	32.2	38	3	15	18

	Avg	AB	H	2B	3B	HR	RBI	BB	SO	OBP	SLG
vs. Left	.297	195	58	5	1	11	43	31	36	.399	.503
vs. Right	.261	283	74	9	0	8	60	23	56	.313	.378
Inning 1-6	.254	114	29	5	0	5	32	14	23	.353	.430
Inning 7+	.283	364	103	9	1	14	71	40	69	.348	.429
None on	.247	247	61	9	1	13	13	19	51	.303	.449
Runners on	.307	231	71	5	0	6	90	35	41	.393	.407
Scoring Posn	.335	167	56	5	0	5	88	28	33	.418	.455
Close & Late	.298	161	48	4	0	9	39	16	30	.349	.491
None on/out	.250	100	25	4	1	3	3	8	17	.306	.400
vs. 1st Batr (relief)	.367	90	33	2	0	6	34	5	17	.394	.589
1st Inning Pitched	.284	328	93	8	1	14	87	39	69	.358	.442
First 15 Pitches	.281	285	80	7	1	12	69	31	52	.349	.439
Pitch 16-30	.255	145	37	5	0	5	27	17	30	.339	.393
Pitch 31-45	.308	39	12	2	0	2	4	5	10	.378	.513
Pitch 46+	.333	9	3	0	0	0	3	1	0	.400	.333
First Pitch	.341	85	29	1	0	5	23	0	0	.423	.529
Ahead in Count	.168	208	35	4	1	3	20	0	85	.170	.240

Last Five Years

	ERA	W	L	Sv	G	GS	IP	H	HR	BB	SO		Avg	AB	H	2B	3B	HR	RBI	BB	SO	OBP	SLG
vs. AL	5.80	4	4	1	48	0	63.2	72	10	30	55	Behind in Count	.438	105	46	8	0	8	41	24	0	.522	.743
vs. NL	4.03	5	5	1	58	0	60.1	60	9	24	37	Two Strikes	.163	203	33	3	1	3	24	22	92	.242	.232
Pre-All Star	4.85	6	6	2	76	0	94.2	96	15	41	79	Pre-All Star	.268	358	96	12	1	15	77	41	79	.343	.433
Post-All Star	5.22	3	0	0	30	0	29.1	36	4	13	13	Post-All Star	.300	120	36	2	0	4	26	13	13	.370	.417

Jose Vidro — Expos
Age 23 – Bats Both

	Avg	G	AB	R	H	2B	3B	HR	RBI	BB	SO	HBP	GDP	SB	CS	OBP	SLG	IBB	SH	SF	#Pit	#P/PA	GB	FB	G/F
1997 Season	.249	67	169	19	42	12	1	2	17	11	20	2	1	0	1	0	.297	.367	0	0	3	680	3.68	82	42	1.95

1997 Season

	Avg	AB	H	2B	3B	HR	RBI	BB	SO	OBP	SLG		Avg	AB	H	2B	3B	HR	RBI	BB	SO	OBP	SLG
vs. Left	.213	47	10	3	0	0	3	5	6	.302	.277	Scoring Posn	.265	34	9	3	0	1	16	3	3	.300	.441
vs. Right	.262	122	32	9	1	2	14	6	14	.295	.402	Close & Late	.366	41	15	4	0	2	11	4	6	.435	.610
Home	.226	62	14	6	1	0	7	5	8	.300	.355	None on/out	.294	34	10	4	0	0	0	3	5	.368	.412
Away	.262	107	28	6	0	2	10	6	12	.296	.374	Batting #3	.211	57	12	4	0	2	6	2	7	.237	.386
First Pitch	.292	24	7	3	0	0	2	0	0	.280	.417	Batting #6	.105	19	2	0	0	0	1	3	3	.250	.105
Ahead in Count	.263	38	10	1	0	0	3	10	0	.408	.289	Other	.301	93	28	8	1	0	11	6	10	.343	.409
Behind in Count	.247	81	20	7	1	2	8	0	14	.265	.432	Pre-All Star	.130	23	3	2	0	0	1	1	3	.160	.217
Two Strikes	.220	82	18	5	1	2	8	1	20	.247	.378	Post-All Star	.267	146	39	10	1	2	16	10	17	.319	.390

Ron Villone — Brewers
Age 28 – Pitches Left (flyball pitcher)

	ERA	W	L	Sv	G	GS	IP	BB	SO	Avg	H	2B	3B	HR	RBI	OBP	SLG	GF	IR	IRS	Hld	SvOp	SB	CS	GB	FB	G/F
1997 Season	3.42	1	0	0	50	0	52.2	36	40	.271	54	3	0	4	26	.386	.347	15	37	8	8	2	0	2	57	53	1.08
Career (1995-1997)	4.09	4	4	3	132	0	140.2	95	141	.247	129	9	1	21	89	.368	.389	49	104	42	23	10	5	7	135	151	0.89

1997 Season

	ERA	W	L	Sv	G	GS	IP	H	HR	BB	SO		Avg	AB	H	2B	3B	HR	RBI	BB	SO	OBP	SLG
Home	3.52	0	0	0	19	0	23.0	23	3	17	15	vs. Left	.353	68	24	0	0	2	13	14	12	.470	.441
Away	3.34	1	0	0	31	0	29.2	31	1	19	25	vs. Right	.229	131	30	3	0	2	13	22	28	.340	.298
Day	2.70	0	0	0	21	0	23.1	25	0	17	16	Inning 1-6	.171	41	7	0	0	1	4	5	7	.277	.244
Night	3.99	1	0	0	29	0	29.1	29	4	19	24	Inning 7+	.297	158	47	3	0	3	22	31	33	.413	.373
Grass	3.27	0	0	0	42	0	44.0	43	4	34	31	None on	.233	90	21	1	0	2	2	16	17	.355	.311
Turf	4.15	1	0	0	8	0	8.2	11	0	2	9	Runners on	.303	109	33	2	0	2	24	20	23	.411	.376
March/April	6.14	0	0	0	8	0	7.1	9	2	6	4	Scoring Posn	.300	60	18	0	0	2	24	11	8	.408	.400
May	1.13	0	0	0	7	0	8.0	4	0	7	3	Close & Late	.283	46	13	0	0	1	7	13	8	.441	.348
June	7.20	0	0	0	8	0	5.0	7	2	5	4	None on/out	.273	44	12	0	0	2	2	10	7	.407	.409
July	7.45	0	0	0	14	0	9.2	19	0	7	8	vs. 1st Batr (relief)	.282	39	11	0	0	0	4	10	7	.429	.282
August	0.79	0	0	0	7	0	11.1	11	0	5	12	1st Inning Pitched	.292	144	42	2	0	4	25	25	26	.400	.389
Sept/Oct	0.79	1	0	0	6	0	11.1	4	0	6	9	First 15 Pitches	.300	110	33	2	0	2	12	18	18	.403	.373
Starter	0.00	0	0	0	0	0	0.0	0	0	0	0	Pitch 16-30	.280	50	14	1	0	2	10	8	11	.379	.420
Reliever	3.42	1	0	0	50	0	52.2	54	4	36	40	Pitch 31-45	.167	24	4	0	0	0	3	4	8	.286	.167
0 Days rest (Relief)	4.76	0	0	0	13	0	11.1	11	3	8	12	Pitch 46+	.200	15	3	0	0	0	1	6	3	.429	.200
1 or 2 Days rest	4.76	0	0	0	19	0	17.0	24	0	15	9	First Pitch	.143	21	3	0	0	0	2	2	0	.217	.143
3+ Days rest	1.85	1	0	0	18	0	24.1	19	1	13	19	Ahead in Count	.198	101	20	0	0	0	7	0	31	.206	.198
vs. AL	3.26	0	0	0	46	0	47.0	47	4	31	35	Behind in Count	.462	39	18	2	0	2	9	18	0	.632	.667
vs. NL	4.76	1	0	0	4	0	5.2	7	0	5	5	Two Strikes	.191	110	21	0	0	1	9	16	40	.299	.218
Pre-All Star	5.87	0	0	0	26	0	23.0	28	4	20	13	Pre-All Star	.326	86	28	2	0	4	17	20	13	.453	.488
Post-All Star	1.52	1	0	0	24	0	29.2	26	0	16	27	Post-All Star	.230	113	26	1	0	0	9	16	27	.331	.239

Career (1995-1997)

	ERA	W	L	Sv	G	GS	IP	H	HR	BB	SO		Avg	AB	H	2B	3B	HR	RBI	BB	SO	OBP	SLG
Home	3.63	1	2	2	61	0	69.1	62	10	40	65	vs. Left	.292	168	49	2	0	5	34	43	42	.442	.393
Away	4.54	3	2	1	71	0	71.1	67	11	55	76	vs. Right	.226	354	80	7	1	16	55	52	99	.330	.387
Day	2.96	0	2	1	49	0	51.2	44	4	38	44	Inning 1-6	.178	73	13	0	0	3	15	18	19	.355	.301
Night	4.75	4	2	2	83	0	89.0	85	17	57	97	Inning 7+	.258	449	116	9	1	18	74	77	122	.371	.403
Grass	3.25	2	2	3	111	0	119.0	102	16	79	114	None on	.222	257	57	6	1	9	9	43	70	.340	.358
Turf	8.72	2	2	0	21	0	21.2	27	5	16	27	Runners on	.272	265	72	3	0	12	80	52	71	.395	.419
March/April	5.79	0	0	0	10	0	9.1	10	3	6	6	Scoring Posn	.294	160	47	1	0	9	74	34	38	.423	.469
May	3.55	0	1	0	14	0	12.2	11	1	16	10	Close & Late	.280	164	46	4	0	8	33	28	39	.390	.451
June	4.85	0	1	0	30	0	29.2	27	6	25	32	None on/out	.237	114	27	2	1	5	5	24	28	.370	.404
July	7.88	1	1	0	23	0	16.0	22	2	8	16	vs. 1st Batr (relief)	.290	100	29	0	1	5	24	27	25	.454	.460
August	3.09	1	1	2	29	0	35.0	25	6	21	37	1st Inning Pitched	.250	380	95	5	1	17	78	68	103	.371	.403
Sept/Oct	2.61	2	0	1	26	0	38.0	28	3	19	40	First 15 Pitches	.269	297	80	5	1	14	59	51	71	.385	.434
Starter	0.00	0	0	0	0	0	0.0	0	0	0	0	Pitch 16-30	.225	151	34	2	0	6	21	28	48	.348	.358
Reliever	4.09	4	4	3	132	0	140.2	129	21	95	141	Pitch 31-45	.208	53	11	2	0	1	7	8	14	.311	.302
0 Days rest (Relief)	5.09	0	1	0	26	0	23.0	19	6	16	25	Pitch 46+	.190	21	4	0	0	0	2	8	8	.414	.190
1 or 2 Days rest	3.80	1	1	2	64	0	64.0	65	9	42	67	First Pitch	.258	62	16	3	0	2	13	2	0	.303	.403
3+ Days rest	4.02	3	2	1	42	0	53.2	45	6	37	49	Ahead in Count	.166	265	44	1	0	3	25	0	118	.180	.204
vs. AL	4.25	0	2	2	88	0	91.0	81	14	72	80	Behind in Count	.442	104	46	4	1	11	34	51	0	.626	.817
vs. NL	3.81	4	2	1	44	0	49.2	48	7	23	61	Two Strikes	.154	292	45	1	0	4	29	42	141	.266	.199
Pre-All Star	5.17	0	2	0	59	0	55.2	58	10	49	52	Pre-All Star	.279	208	58	3	0	10	37	49	52	.419	.438
Post-All Star	3.39	4	2	3	73	0	85.0	71	11	46	89	Post-All Star	.226	314	71	6	1	10	52	46	89	.333	.357

Fernando Vina — Brewers

	Avg	G	AB	R	H	2B	3B	HR	RBI	BB	SO	HBP	GDP	SB	CS	OBP	SLG	IBB	SH	SF	#Pit	#P/PA	GB	FB	G/F
1997 Season	.275	79	324	37	89	12	2	4	28	12	23	7	4	8	7	.312	.361	1	2	3	1086	3.12	122	101	1.21
Career (1993-1997)	.270	435	1335	202	361	46	19	14	111	88	100	44	29	39	18	.334	.365	4	15	9	4970	3.33	494	404	1.22

1997 Season

	Avg	AB	H	2B	3B	HR	RBI	BB	SO	OBP	SLG		Avg	AB	H	2B	3B	HR	RBI	BB	SO	OBP	SLG
vs. Left	.253	91	23	2	2	0	8	1	8	.277	.319	First Pitch	.387	62	24	4	0	2	13	1	0	.412	.548
vs. Right	.283	233	66	10	0	4	20	11	15	.325	.378	Ahead in Count	.260	73	19	1	1	1	7	8	0	.329	.342
Groundball	.267	60	16	2	0	0	2	2	7	.290	.300	Behind in Count	.237	135	32	6	0	1	4	0	21	.259	.304
Flyball	.351	57	20	4	0	1	6	5	2	.431	.474	Two Strikes	.228	101	23	6	0	1	5	3	23	.264	.317
Home	.302	172	52	5	2	1	15	6	11	.337	.372	Batting #1	.273	322	88	12	2	4	28	12	23	.311	.360
Away	.243	152	37	7	0	3	13	6	12	.284	.349	Batting #5	.000	1	0	0	0	0	0	0	0	.000	.000
Day	.262	122	32	4	1	0	6	3	7	.280	.311	Other	1.000	1	1	0	0	0	0	0	0	1.000	1.000
Night	.282	202	57	8	1	4	22	9	16	.330	.391	March/April	.321	56	18	5	1	1	10	1	1	.339	.500
Grass	.296	270	80	9	2	4	28	11	18	.332	.389	May	.000	0	0	0	0	0	0	0	0	.000	.000
Turf	.167	54	9	3	0	0	0	1	5	.211	.222	June	.000	0	0	0	0	0	0	0	0	.000	.000
Pre-All Star	.321	56	18	5	1	1	10	1	1	.339	.500	July	.218	55	12	3	0	0	2	2	9	.259	.273
Post-All Star	.265	268	71	7	1	3	18	11	22	.307	.332	August	.319	119	38	2	0	2	12	6	5	.366	.387
Scoring Posn	.306	62	19	1	1	1	25	5	4	.352	.403	Sept/Oct	.223	94	21	2	1	1	4	3	8	.255	.298
Close & Late	.203	59	12	0	1	0	5	2	3	.230	.237	vs. AL	.280	300	84	12	2	4	28	10	23	.316	.373
None on/out	.232	125	29	6	1	1	2	8	.256	.320		vs. NL	.208	24	5	0	0	0	0	2	0	.269	.208

1997 By Position

Position	Avg	AB	H	2B	3B	HR	RBI	BB	SO	OBP	SLG	G	GS	Innings	PO	A	E	DP	Fld Pct	Rng Fctr	In Zone	Zone Outs	Zone Rtg	MLB Zone
As 2b	.278	316	88	12	2	4	28	12	21	.317	.367	78	75	657.1	149	227	7	53	.982	5.15	246	219	.890	.902

Career (1993-1997)

	Avg	AB	H	2B	3B	HR	RBI	BB	SO	OBP	SLG		Avg	AB	H	2B	3B	HR	RBI	BB	SO	OBP	SLG
vs. Left	.248	262	65	7	4	0	23	21	29	.318	.305	First Pitch	.296	233	69	7	4	3	29	3	0	.335	.399
vs. Right	.276	1073	296	39	15	14	88	67	71	.338	.379	Ahead in Count	.287	317	91	17	7	4	33	55	0	.395	.423
Groundball	.280	343	96	7	3	2	24	20	23	.339	.335	Behind in Count	.225	529	119	14	3	5	27	0	88	.254	.291
Flyball	.311	244	76	14	4	2	25	17	19	.372	.426	Two Strikes	.239	469	112	17	5	6	38	29	100	.301	.335
Home	.280	693	194	23	12	5	68	46	53	.342	.369	Batting #1	.261	804	210	27	13	10	69	55	63	.325	.364
Away	.260	642	167	23	7	9	43	42	47	.326	.360	Batting #2	.271	247	67	8	5	1	16	10	17	.318	.356
Day	.254	473	120	17	7	1	29	32	41	.318	.326	Other	.296	284	84	11	1	3	26	23	20	.373	.373
Night	.280	862	241	29	12	13	82	56	59	.343	.386	March/April	.313	163	51	10	4	2	22	11	9	.365	.460
Grass	.274	1120	307	35	15	12	103	70	82	.335	.364	May	.276	185	51	8	2	2	14	19	16	.360	.373
Turf	.251	215	54	11	4	2	8	18	18	.331	.367	June	.278	209	58	6	2	3	15	17	11	.364	.368
Pre-All Star	.285	618	176	26	9	7	55	48	42	.356	.390	July	.249	261	65	10	5	1	23	15	26	.313	.337
Post-All Star	.258	717	185	20	10	7	56	40	58	.314	.343	August	.258	264	68	5	1	2	14	16	16	.317	.307
Scoring Posn	.277	285	79	6	6	4	96	28	26	.354	.382	Sept/Oct	.269	253	68	7	5	4	23	10	22	.307	.383
Close & Late	.245	220	54	4	2	0	15	20	16	.336	.382	vs. AL	.274	1187	325	40	19	14	105	74	89	.331	.375
None on/out	.261	449	117	22	4	3	3	19	27	.317	.370	vs. NL	.243	148	36	6	0	0	6	14	11	.356	.284

Batter vs. Pitcher (career)

Hits Best Against	Avg	AB	H	2B	3B	HR	RBI	BB	SO	OBP	SLG	Hits Worst Against	Avg	AB	H	2B	3B	HR	RBI	BB	SO	OBP	SLG
David Cone	.625	16	10	2	0	0	3	1	1	.667	.750	Jamie Moyer	.182	11	2	0	0	0	0	2	2	.357	.182
Brian Williams	.444	9	4	0	0	0	1	2	2	.545	.444	Roger Clemens	.200	20	4	0	0	0	0	4	5	.360	.200
Brian Moehler	.385	13	5	2	0	0	1	1	0	.429	.538	Frank Rodriguez	.231	13	3	0	0	0	1	0	1	.214	.231
Don Wengert	.364	11	4	0	0	1	2	0	0	.417	.636	Roger Pavlik	.231	13	3	0	0	0	0	1	2	.286	.231
Andy Pettitte	.364	11	4	1	0	1	0	0	0	.364	.636	Alex Fernandez	.238	21	5	1	0	0	0	2	2	.238	.286

Joe Vitiello — Royals

	Avg	G	AB	R	H	2B	3B	HR	RBI	BB	SO	HBP	GDP	SB	CS	OBP	SLG	IBB	SH	SF	#Pit	#P/PA	GB	FB	G/F
1997 Season	.238	51	130	11	31	6	0	5	18	14	37	2	2	0	0	.322	.400	1	0	0	558	3.82	45	26	1.73
Career (1995-1997)	.244	189	517	53	126	25	1	20	79	60	131	9	18	2	0	.331	.412	3	0	3	2365	4.02	183	109	1.68

1997 Season

	Avg	AB	H	2B	3B	HR	RBI	BB	SO	OBP	SLG		Avg	AB	H	2B	3B	HR	RBI	BB	SO	OBP	SLG
vs. Left	.236	72	17	3	0	3	11	7	22	.313	.403	Scoring Posn	.250	40	10	2	0	1	13	6	14	.348	.375
vs. Right	.241	58	14	3	0	2	7	7	15	.333	.397	Close & Late	.214	14	3	0	0	0	1	2	4	.313	.214
Home	.234	77	18	4	0	4	8	7	18	.314	.442	None on/out	.235	17	4	1	0	0	0	5	3	.409	.294
Away	.245	53	13	2	0	1	10	7	19	.333	.340	Batting #5	.237	38	9	2	0	0	6	8	11	.383	.289
First Pitch	.316	19	6	1	0	1	3	0	0	.316	.526	Batting #6	.233	43	10	3	0	2	6	3	14	.302	.449
Ahead in Count	.333	30	10	1	0	3	8	7	0	.459	.667	Other	.245	49	12	1	0	3	6	3	12	.302	.449
Behind in Count	.197	61	12	3	0	2	0	0	30	.210	.246	Pre-All Star	.225	102	23	5	0	2	14	13	29	.325	.333
Two Strikes	.108	65	7	3	0	1	7	37	.194	.154		Post-All Star	.286	28	8	1	0	3	4	1	8	.310	.643

Career (1995-1997)

	Avg	AB	H	2B	3B	HR	RBI	BB	SO	OBP	SLG		Avg	AB	H	2B	3B	HR	RBI	BB	SO	OBP	SLG
vs. Left	.257	253	65	13	0	13	48	33	67	.352	.462	First Pitch	.339	59	20	4	0	4	14	2	0	.369	.610
vs. Right	.231	264	61	12	1	7	31	27	64	.311	.364	Ahead in Count	.336	113	38	6	0	7	21	23	0	.449	.575
Groundball	.272	125	34	7	0	3	13	12	27	.341	.400	Behind in Count	.195	251	49	10	1	7	28	0	114	.210	.327
Flyball	.232	69	16	3	0	2	10	12	19	.361	.362	Two Strikes	.148	270	40	11	1	6	28	35	131	.255	.263
Home	.253	289	73	16	0	10	39	34	68	.340	.412	Batting #4	.204	181	37	7	1	8	25	26	54	.310	.387
Away	.232	228	53	9	1	10	40	26	63	.319	.412	Batting #6	.244	127	31	9	0	3	22	15	31	.326	.386
Day	.281	146	41	8	1	8	28	21	39	.385	.514	Other	.278	209	58	9	0	9	32	19	46	.353	.450
Night	.229	371	85	17	0	12	51	39	92	.308	.372	March/April	.284	102	29	10	0	1	17	26	33	.431	.412
Grass	.241	452	109	24	0	18	65	49	114	.324	.414	May	.219	96	21	4	0	4	12	13	29	.318	.385

Career (1995-1997)

	Avg	AB	H	2B	3B	HR	RBI	BB	SO	OBP	SLG		Avg	AB	H	2B	3B	HR	RBI	BB	SO	OBP	SLG
Turf	.262	65	17	1	1	2	14	11	17	.377	.400	June	.198	106	21	4	1	3	15	6	26	.256	.340
Pre-All Star	.226	319	72	18	1	9	46	48	94	.333	.373	July	.162	37	6	0	0	3	6	3	12	.225	.405
Post-All Star	.273	198	54	7	0	11	33	12	37	.327	.475	August	.313	96	30	6	0	4	15	8	16	.383	.500
Scoring Posn	.227	141	32	6	0	5	55	27	33	.356	.376	Sept/Oct	.238	80	19	1	0	5	14	4	15	.282	.438
Close & Late	.250	64	16	2	0	1	8	12	14	.377	.328	vs. AL	.245	515	126	25	1	20	79	60	130	.332	.414
None on/out	.248	121	30	7	0	4	4	11	26	.316	.405	vs. NL	.000	2	0	0	0	0	0	0	1	.000	.000

Batter vs. Pitcher (career)

Hits Best Against	Avg	AB	H	2B	3B	HR	RBI	BB	SO	OBP	SLG	Hits Worst Against	Avg	AB	H	2B	3B	HR	RBI	BB	SO	OBP	SLG
Jimmy Key	.400	10	4	2	0	1	4	0	5	.364	.900	Randy Johnson	.182	11	2	0	0	1	3	4	6	.400	.455
												Jamie Moyer	.200	10	2	2	0	2	1	2	.333	.400

Jose Vizcaino — Giants
Age 30 – Bats Both (groundball hitter)

	Avg	G	AB	R	H	2B	3B	HR	RBI	BB	SO	HBP	GDP	SB	CS	OBP	SLG	IBB	SH	SF	#Pit	#P/PA	GB	FB	G/F
1997 Season	.266	151	568	77	151	19	7	5	50	48	87	0	13	8	8	.323	.350	1	13	1	2237	3.55	259	113	2.29
Last Five Years	.279	684	2580	334	721	89	27	16	238	197	378	9	49	44	38	.330	.353	10	49	22	10044	3.52	1130	538	2.10

1997 Season

	Avg	AB	H	2B	3B	HR	RBI	BB	SO	OBP	SLG		Avg	AB	H	2B	3B	HR	RBI	BB	SO	OBP	SLG
vs. Left	.240	125	30	6	0	0	12	16	26	.324	.288	First Pitch	.390	100	39	4	1	2	15	1	0	.396	.510
vs. Right	.273	443	121	13	7	5	38	32	61	.322	.368	Ahead in Count	.346	107	37	6	0	0	10	30	0	.486	.402
Groundball	.246	126	31	3	2	1	9	6	23	.280	.325	Behind in Count	.184	255	47	5	4	2	14	0	81	.184	.259
Flyball	.212	66	14	2	0	1	5	7	8	.288	.288	Two Strikes	.175	251	44	6	2	2	16	17	87	.228	.239
Home	.237	279	66	8	4	1	21	29	45	.307	.305	Batting #2	.256	445	114	12	4	3	35	40	71	.317	.321
Away	.294	289	85	11	3	4	29	19	42	.338	.394	Batting #7	.316	98	31	7	3	2	14	5	13	.350	.510
Day	.266	252	67	10	6	4	26	19	51	.316	.401	Other	.240	25	6	0	0	0	1	3	3	.321	.240
Night	.266	316	84	9	1	1	24	29	36	.328	.310	March/April	.224	85	19	1	0	1	3	9	13	.298	.271
Grass	.253	474	120	14	7	3	40	38	69	.308	.331	May	.290	93	27	4	2	0	10	14	12	.380	.376
Turf	.330	94	31	5	0	2	10	10	18	.394	.447	June	.257	105	27	2	0	1	10	11	14	.328	.305
Pre-All Star	.261	303	79	9	2	2	23	34	42	.334	.323	July	.282	103	29	4	1	0	8	3	17	.302	.340
Post-All Star	.272	265	72	10	5	3	27	14	45	.308	.381	August	.279	104	29	3	2	3	13	7	20	.324	.433
Scoring Posn	.318	132	42	6	0	1	41	9	16	.359	.386	Sept/Oct	.256	78	20	5	2	0	6	4	11	.293	.372
Close & Late	.368	95	35	5	0	1	12	7	12	.412	.453	vs. AL	.273	55	15	2	0	1	5	3	10	.310	.364
None on/out	.280	100	28	4	1	2	10	15	15	.345	.400	vs. NL	.265	513	136	17	7	4	45	45	77	.324	.349

1997 By Position

Position	Avg	AB	H	2B	3B	HR	RBI	BB	SO	OBP	SLG		G	GS	Innings	PO	A	E	DP	Fld Pct	Rng Fctr	In Zone	Zone Outs	Zone Rtg	MLB Zone
As ss	.268	557	149	19	7	5	50	48	87	.323	.354		147	140	1221.0	204	444	16	96	.976	4.78	474	443	.935	.937

Last Five Years

	Avg	AB	H	2B	3B	HR	RBI	BB	SO	OBP	SLG		Avg	AB	H	2B	3B	HR	RBI	BB	SO	OBP	SLG
vs. Left	.292	643	188	20	0	0	51	51	100	.343	.323	First Pitch	.358	480	172	21	5	4	59	6	0	.366	.448
vs. Right	.275	1937	533	69	27	16	187	146	278	.326	.363	Ahead in Count	.325	495	161	21	5	3	52	119	0	.454	.406
Groundball	.267	735	196	23	3	2	50	45	97	.309	.314	Behind in Count	.234	1146	268	29	13	5	86	0	335	.235	.295
Flyball	.302	387	117	15	4	5	36	29	59	.352	.401	Two Strikes	.220	1125	247	33	8	6	88	72	378	.267	.279
Home	.277	1275	353	31	13	6	114	106	179	.332	.336	Batting #1	.253	474	120	13	3	3	38	43	68	.314	.312
Away	.282	1305	368	58	14	10	124	91	199	.328	.371	Batting #2	.279	1514	422	46	19	9	126	112	219	.328	.352
Day	.287	1025	294	34	14	8	88	78	160	.335	.371	Other	.302	592	179	30	5	4	74	42	91	.347	.390
Night	.275	1555	427	55	13	8	150	119	218	.327	.342	March/April	.294	343	101	9	4	5	33	33	56	.354	.388
Grass	.278	2037	567	65	24	11	180	150	300	.328	.350	May	.298	480	143	14	6	1	37	48	66	.367	.358
Turf	.284	543	154	24	3	5	58	47	78	.339	.366	June	.266	488	130	14	5	2	42	28	66	.305	.328
Pre-All Star	.283	1461	413	46	16	8	126	116	211	.335	.352	July	.266	470	125	24	3	1	50	36	72	.316	.336
Post-All Star	.275	1119	308	43	11	8	112	81	167	.323	.355	August	.262	435	114	14	5	5	45	28	74	.306	.352
Scoring Posn	.300	590	177	22	1	6	208	56	83	.352	.371	Sept/Oct	.297	364	108	14	4	2	31	24	44	.338	.374
Close & Late	.297	434	129	17	1	2	62	34	76	.350	.355	vs. AL	.282	234	66	7	2	1	18	10	34	.310	.342
None on/out	.273	609	166	21	8	4	4	47	85	.335	.353	vs. NL	.279	2346	655	82	25	15	220	187	344	.332	.355

Batter vs. Pitcher (career)

Hits Best Against	Avg	AB	H	2B	3B	HR	RBI	BB	SO	OBP	SLG	Hits Worst Against	Avg	AB	H	2B	3B	HR	RBI	BB	SO	OBP	SLG
Alan Benes	.692	13	9	1	2	0	2	0	3	.692	1.077	Pete Schourek	.067	15	1	0	0	0	0	0	0	.067	.067
VanLandingham	.600	10	6	1	0	0	0	1	0	.636	.700	Shane Reynolds	.091	22	2	1	0	0	2	2	1	.167	.136
Tim Belcher	.563	16	9	1	1	0	4	1	2	.611	.750	Omar Olivares	.105	19	2	0	0	0	0	1	1	.150	.105
Robb Nen	.545	11	6	3	1	0	1	0	2	.545	1.000	Greg Maddux	.120	25	3	0	0	0	1	1	6	.148	.120
Mark Petkovsek	.500	12	6	2	0	0	0	0	0	.500	.667	Bobby Witt	.182	11	2	0	0	0	0	0	0	.182	.182

Omar Vizquel — Indians
Age 31 – Bats Both (groundball hitter)

	Avg	G	AB	R	H	2B	3B	HR	RBI	BB	SO	HBP	GDP	SB	CS	OBP	SLG	IBB	SH	SF	#Pit	#P/PA	GB	FB	G/F
1997 Season	.280	153	565	89	158	23	6	5	49	57	58	2	16	43	12	.347	.368	1	16	2	2487	3.87	211	154	1.37
Last Five Years	.274	667	2495	381	684	111	10	23	233	245	253	11	41	132	50	.338	.354	3	62	26	10716	3.77	972	699	1.39

1997 Season

	Avg	AB	H	2B	3B	HR	RBI	BB	SO	OBP	SLG		Avg	AB	H	2B	3B	HR	RBI	BB	SO	OBP	SLG
vs. Left	.265	151	40	7	0	2	14	9	13	.306	.351	First Pitch	.182	44	8	0	0	0	3	0	0	.200	.182
vs. Right	.285	414	118	16	6	3	35	48	45	.361	.374	Ahead in Count	.310	116	36	4	2	2	18	34	0	.467	.431
Groundball	.224	98	22	3	1	0	9	16	.300	.276	Behind in Count	.251	283	71	12	3	1	17	0	53	.252	.325
Flyball	.275	80	22	7	1	0	4	7	13	.333	.388	Two Strikes	.244	270	66	11	2	3	14	23	58	.305	.333
Home	.300	290	87	14	4	3	26	25	34	.354	.407	Batting #2	.250	200	50	5	1	1	14	18	21	.312	.300

1997 Season

	Avg	AB	H	2B	3B	HR	RBI	BB	SO	OBP	SLG		Avg	AB	H	2B	3B	HR	RBI	BB	SO	OBP	SLG
Away	.258	275	71	9	2	2	23	32	24	.339	.327	Batting #9	.303	234	71	13	2	2	18	21	23	.366	.402
Day	.295	193	57	11	2	1	19	19	23	.362	.389	Other	.282	131	37	5	3	2	17	18	14	.364	.412
Night	.272	372	101	12	4	4	30	38	35	.339	.358	March/April	.289	97	28	2	3	0	9	11	11	.361	.371
Grass	.289	484	140	21	6	4	45	44	47	.349	.382	May	.214	84	18	4	0	1	4	11	9	.305	.298
Turf	.222	81	18	2	0	1	4	13	11	.333	.284	June	.287	94	27	5	2	1	14	7	9	.340	.415
Pre-All Star	.279	290	81	11	5	2	27	30	30	.348	.372	July	.301	83	25	3	1	0	3	6	9	.348	.361
Post-All Star	.280	275	77	12	1	3	22	27	28	.345	.364	August	.299	117	35	6	0	0	5	9	13	.354	.350
Scoring Posn	.224	143	32	6	1	1	42	12	17	.289	.301	Sept/Oct	.278	90	25	3	0	3	14	13	7	.365	.411
Close & Late	.382	68	26	4	2	0	10	5	5	.425	.500	vs. AL	.288	507	146	22	5	3	37	51	49	.355	.369
None on/out	.316	152	48	10	1	1		19	16	.392	.414	vs. NL	.207	58	12	1	1	2	12	6	9	.277	.362

1997 By Position

Position	Avg	AB	H	2B	3B	HR	RBI	BB	SO	OBP	SLG	G	GS	Innings	PO	A	E	DP	Fld Pct	Rng Fctr	In Zone	Zone Outs	Zone Rtg	MLB Zone
As ss	.281	563	158	23	6	5	49	57	58	.348	.369	152	149	1307.1	245	428	10	102	.985	4.63	474	465	.981	.937

Last Five Years

	Avg	AB	H	2B	3B	HR	RBI	BB	SO	OBP	SLG		Avg	AB	H	2B	3B	HR	RBI	BB	SO	OBP	SLG
vs. Left	.248	734	182	42	0	9	75	62	73	.308	.342	First Pitch	.337	252	85	5	0	2	24	2	0	.344	.381
vs. Right	.285	1761	502	69	10	14	158	183	180	.351	.359	Ahead in Count	.298	524	156	27	2	6	69	146	0	.447	.391
Groundball	.281	469	132	18	3	3	48	49	47	.353	.352	Behind in Count	.240	1218	292	52	5	9	92	0	229	.243	.313
Flyball	.296	456	135	29	1	5	47	38	51	.345	.397	Two Strikes	.213	1120	238	50	4	12	79	97	253	.296	.296
Home	.285	1237	353	62	5	9	127	120	116	.347	.365	Batting #2	.273	1219	333	54	3	11	125	123	119	.337	.349
Away	.263	1258	331	49	5	14	106	125	137	.330	.343	Batting #9	.278	800	222	41	3	8	76	69	74	.338	.366
Day	.276	768	212	42	3	3	76	80	78	.343	.350	Other	.271	476	129	16	4	4	32	53	60	.344	.347
Night	.273	1727	472	69	7	20	157	165	175	.336	.356	March/April	.260	334	87	16	3	4	31	39	34	.337	.362
Grass	.272	1905	519	85	8	14	188	181	191	.334	.348	May	.255	392	100	13	0	5	29	40	40	.323	.327
Turf	.280	590	165	26	2	9	45	64	62	.351	.376	June	.322	478	154	20	3	3	59	46	44	.382	.395
Pre-All Star	.286	1366	391	56	6	13	131	137	138	.351	.365	July	.279	488	136	26	1	4	37	34	53	.324	.361
Post-All Star	.260	1129	293	55	4	10	102	108	115	.324	.342	August	.258	462	119	18	2	2	31	44	55	.322	.318
Scoring Posn	.267	640	171	27	3	6	208	56	67	.318	.347	Sept/Oct	.258	341	88	18	1	5	46	42	27	.339	.361
Close & Late	.298	369	110	17	3	2	42	38	31	.365	.377	vs. AL	.276	2437	672	110	9	21	221	239	244	.340	.354
None on/out	.279	596	166	29	1	9	9	70	64	.356	.376	vs. NL	.207	58	12	1	1	2	12	6	9	.277	.362

Batter vs. Pitcher (career)

Hits Best Against	Avg	AB	H	2B	3B	HR	RBI	BB	SO	OBP	SLG	Hits Worst Against	Avg	AB	H	2B	3B	HR	RBI	BB	SO	OBP	SLG
Kevin Gross	.750	12	9	2	0	0	3	0	0	.750	.917	David Wells	.036	28	1	0	0	0	0	1	5	.069	.036
Aaron Sele	.583	12	7	1	0	1	6	0	1	.583	.917	Arthur Rhodes	.056	18	1	0	0	0	0	1	1	.105	.056
Jaime Navarro	.486	35	17	2	1	0	3	3	1	.526	.600	Bob Tewksbury	.091	11	1	0	0	0	0	1	1	.167	.091
Mike Trombley	.462	13	6	1	1	0	3	1	1	.533	.692	Eddie Guardado	.182	11	2	0	0	0	2	0	0	.182	.182
Pat Hentgen	.400	25	10	1		2	3	2	2	.444	.800	Mark Gubicza	.200	15	3	0	0	0	1	0	2	.200	.200

Jack Voigt — Brewers

Age 32 – Bats Right (flyball hitter)

	Avg	G	AB	R	H	2B	3B	HR	RBI	BB	SO	HBP	GDP	SB	CS	OBP	SLG	IBB	SH	SF	#Pit	#P/PA	GB	FB	G/F
1997 Season	.245	72	151	20	37	9	2	8	22	19	36	1	5	1	2	.331	.490	2	2	1	687	3.95	47	48	0.98
Last Five Years	.248	236	516	77	128	28	3	19	73	72	110	2	10	2	2	.340	.424	3	3	4	2279	3.82	158	178	0.89

1997 Season

	Avg	AB	H	2B	3B	HR	RBI	BB	SO	OBP	SLG		Avg	AB	H	2B	3B	HR	RBI	BB	SO	OBP	SLG
vs. Left	.311	90	28	8	2	6	15	11	21	.386	.644	Scoring Posn	.294	34	10	3	1	1	14	5	7	.375	.529
vs. Right	.148	61	9	1	0	2	7	8	15	.254	.262	Close & Late	.053	19	1	0	0	1	2	6	7	.296	.211
Home	.268	82	22	6	1	5	12	12	17	.362	.549	None on/out	.306	36	11	3	0	4	4	3	9	.359	.722
Away	.217	69	15	3	1	3	10	7	19	.295	.420	Batting #5	.293	41	12	4	2	1	6	3	9	.341	.561
First Pitch	.450	20	9	4	0	2	6	2	0	.500	.950	Batting #6	.148	27	4	1	0	2	4	2	5	.207	.407
Ahead in Count	.500	36	18	5	1	4	10	4	0	.550	1.028	Other	.253	83	21	4	0	5	12	14	22	.364	.482
Behind in Count	.078	64	5	0	1	1	4	0	28	.077	.156	Pre-All Star	.229	35	8	3	0	2	7	3	5	.300	.486
Two Strikes	.092	76	7	0	1	2	4	13	36	.225	.197	Post-All Star	.250	116	29	6	2	6	15	16	31	.341	.491

Last Five Years

	Avg	AB	H	2B	3B	HR	RBI	BB	SO	OBP	SLG		Avg	AB	H	2B	3B	HR	RBI	BB	SO	OBP	SLG
vs. Left	.293	273	80	16	2	16	49	30	54	.363	.553	First Pitch	.390	77	30	7	1	3	17	2	0	.407	.623
vs. Right	.198	243	48	9	1	3	24	42	56	.316	.280	Ahead in Count	.386	132	51	12	1	13	29	32	0	.506	.788
Groundball	.233	90	21	3	1	1	9	13	17	.330	.322	Behind in Count	.163	208	34	7	1	2	18	0	91	.161	.236
Flyball	.256	86	22	7	0	4	11	9	7	.329	.477	Two Strikes	.137	227	31	7	1	3	19	38	110	.259	.216
Home	.251	287	72	16	1	13	42	41	61	.343	.449	Batting #8	.276	105	29	8	1	5	13	13	16	.350	.514
Away	.245	229	56	12	2	6	31	31	49	.336	.393	Batting #9	.246	138	34	5	0	3	19	12	22	.340	.348
Day	.219	146	32	6	1	2	16	22	29	.320	.315	Other	.238	273	65	15	2	11	41	39	62	.337	.429
Night	.259	370	96	22	2	17	57	50	81	.348	.468	March/April	.185	27	5	0	0	1	6	3	5	.290	.296
Grass	.243	452	110	21	3	19	66	63	93	.336	.429	May	.250	104	26	1	0	3	12	9	22	.304	.394
Turf	.281	64	18	7	0	0	7	9	17	.368	.391	June	.245	98	24	7	2	2	17	14	14	.336	.378
Pre-All Star	.234	261	61	10	0	8	41	32	46	.318	.364	July	.234	107	25	7	2	6	18	15	26	.331	.505
Post-All Star	.263	255	67	18	3	11	32	40	64	.363	.486	August	.287	87	25	7	1	4	9	16	21	.398	.529
Scoring Posn	.270	137	37	7	1	4	55	19	30	.354	.423	Sept/Oct	.247	93	23	6	0	3	11	15	22	.352	.409
Close & Late	.169	77	13	2	0	3		14	20	.301	.312	vs. AL	.249	511	127	27	3	19	72	71	108	.340	.425
None on/out	.306	111	34	8	1	9	9	18	27	.403	.640	vs. NL	.200	5	1	1	0	0	1	1	2	.375	.400

Batter vs. Pitcher (career)

Hits Best Against	Avg	AB	H	2B	3B	HR	RBI	BB	SO	OBP	SLG	Hits Worst Against	Avg	AB	H	2B	3B	HR	RBI	BB	SO	OBP	SLG
Randy Johnson	.417	12	5	1	0	1	2	1	4	.462	.750	Mark Langston	.000	12	0	0	0	0	0	0	3	.000	.000

Ed Vosberg — Marlins

Age 36 – Pitches Left (groundball pitcher)

	ERA	W	L	Sv	G	GS	IP	BB	SO	Avg	H	2B	3B	HR	RBI	OBP	SLG	GF	IR	IRS	Hld	SvOp	SB	CS	GB	FB	G/F
1997 Season	4.42	2	3	1	59	0	53.0	21	37	.285	59	11	2	3	33	.359	.401	22	45	13	8	3	0	0	77	66	1.17
Last Five Years	3.68	8	11	13	171	0	146.2	63	117	.282	158	23	3	12	86	.355	.398	65	153	47	26	21	3	5	223	142	1.57

1997 Season

	ERA	W	L	Sv	G	GS	IP	H	HR	BB	SO		Avg	AB	H	2B	3B	HR	RBI	BB	SO	OBP	SLG
Home	4.33	2	2	0	31	0	27.0	27	2	9	20	vs. Left	.230	74	17	3	0	2	12	8	22	.322	.351
Away	4.50	0	1	1	28	0	26.0	32	1	12	17	vs. Right	.316	133	42	8	2	1	21	13	15	.380	.429
Day	2.70	0	0	0	12	0	10.0	11	0	6	7	Inning 1-6	.278	36	10	3	1	1	6	4	7	.366	.500
Night	4.81	2	3	1	47	0	43.0	48	3	15	30	Inning 7+	.287	171	49	8	1	2	27	17	30	.357	.380
Grass	4.81	2	3	0	50	0	43.0	51	3	16	31	None on	.303	99	30	5	1	2	2	3	23	.337	.434
Turf	2.70	0	0	1	9	0	10.0	8	0	5	6	Runners on	.269	108	29	6	1	1	31	18	14	.376	.370
March/April	10.29	0	1	0	6	0	7.0	11	1	3	3	Scoring Posn	.264	72	19	2	1	1	29	13	14	.360	.361
May	1.35	1	0	0	10	0	6.2	8	0	3	5	Close & Late	.412	51	21	4	1	1	15	9	7	.500	.588
June	5.40	0	1	0	11	0	8.1	6	1	4	8	None on/out	.360	50	18	3	1	1	1	0	10	.373	.520
July	1.42	0	0	0	11	0	12.2	11	0	3	6	vs. 1st Batr (relief)	.389	54	21	4	1	0	8	4	7	.441	.500
August	3.46	0	0	0	12	0	13.0	15	1	4	12	1st Inning Pitched	.317	164	52	10	2	2	29	19	27	.395	.439
Sept/Oct	8.44	1	1	1	9	0	5.1	8	0	4	3	First 15 Pitches	.326	141	46	9	2	2	25	16	19	.405	.461
Starter	0.00	0	0	0	0	0	0.0	0	0	0	0	Pitch 16-30	.176	51	9	1	0	0	1	5	13	.259	.255
Reliever	4.42	2	3	1	59	0	53.0	59	3	21	37	Pitch 31-45	.308	13	4	1	0	0	2	0	5	.286	.385
0 Days rest (Relief)	3.63	0	1	0	14	0	17.1	17	2	4	12	Pitch 46+	.000	2	0	0	0	0	0	0	0	.000	.000
1 or 2 Days rest	5.21	0	2	1	24	0	19.0	23	0	9	18	First Pitch	.324	37	12	0	1	1	13	5	0	.395	.541
3+ Days rest	4.32	2	0	0	21	0	16.2	19	1	8	7	Ahead in Count	.241	83	20	1	0	1	5	0	30	.259	.277
vs. AL	4.72	2	2	0	41	0	40.0	45	3	16	30	Behind in Count	.293	41	12	3	0	0	6	9	0	.423	.366
vs. NL	3.46	0	1	1	18	0	13.0	14	0	5	7	Two Strikes	.207	87	18	1	1	1	5	7	37	.271	.276
Pre-All Star	5.32	1	2	0	29	0	23.2	26	2	10	16	Pre-All Star	.283	92	26	6	1	2	18	10	16	.362	.435
Post-All Star	3.68	1	1	1	30	0	29.1	33	1	11	21	Post-All Star	.287	115	33	5	1	1	15	11	21	.356	.374

Last Five Years

	ERA	W	L	Sv	G	GS	IP	H	HR	BB	SO		Avg	AB	H	2B	3B	HR	RBI	BB	SO	OBP	SLG
Home	2.51	5	7	7	85	0	82.1	76	6	24	59	vs. Left	.253	221	56	8	1	7	35	26	51	.335	.394
Away	5.18	3	4	6	86	0	64.1	82	6	39	58	vs. Right	.300	340	102	15	2	5	51	37	66	.368	.400
Day	1.60	1	0	6	42	0	39.1	31	1	19	34	Inning 1-6	.269	78	21	4	1	3	14	10	21	.360	.462
Night	4.44	7	11	7	129	0	107.1	127	11	44	83	Inning 7+	.284	483	137	19	2	9	72	53	96	.354	.387
Grass	3.54	8	10	12	147	0	129.2	136	12	54	105	None on	.292	267	78	12	2	7	7	13	61	.330	.431
Turf	4.76	0	1	1	24	0	17.0	22	0	9	12	Runners on	.272	294	80	11	1	5	79	50	56	.375	.367
March/April	4.43	0	1	5	18	0	22.1	23	2	9	12	Scoring Posn	.294	194	57	6	1	5	77	36	42	.391	.412
May	4.02	2	1	1	24	0	15.2	21	1	8	16	Close & Late	.330	212	70	10	2	3	40	35	39	.424	.439
June	3.48	1	2	0	25	0	20.2	24	2	10	21	None on/out	.331	121	40	5	2	1	1	5	23	.362	.430
July	2.56	3	1	2	44	0	38.2	31	2	15	32	vs. 1st Batr (relief)	.307	150	46	6	2	3	29	16	22	.373	.433
August	2.83	1	1	3	32	0	28.2	35	4	11	21	1st Inning Pitched	.299	432	129	21	3	8	76	56	84	.379	.417
Sept/Oct	6.10	1	5	2	28	0	20.2	24	1	10	15	First 15 Pitches	.306	389	119	20	3	9	66	49	70	.386	.442
Starter	0.00	0	0	0	0	0	0.0	0	0	0	0	Pitch 16-30	.211	128	27	1	0	3	18	13	35	.283	.289
Reliever	3.68	8	11	13	171	0	146.2	158	12	63	117	Pitch 31-45	.297	37	11	2	0	2	1	1	12	.308	.351
0 Days rest (Relief)	5.61	0	5	2	36	0	33.2	42	7	8	29	Pitch 46+	.143	7	1	0	0	0	0	0	0	.143	.143
1 or 2 Days rest	3.71	3	4	5	67	0	53.1	64	2	28	44	First Pitch	.289	76	22	6	1	2	18	9	0	.360	.474
3+ Days rest	2.56	5	2	6	68	0	59.2	52	3	27	44	Ahead in Count	.237	241	57	3	0	3	19	0	97	.242	.286
vs. AL	3.70	8	10	12	153	0	133.2	144	12	58	110	Behind in Count	.363	124	45	7	1	4	27	28	0	.474	.532
vs. NL	3.46	0	1	1	18	0	13.0	14	0	5	7	Two Strikes	.213	254	54	5	1	4	26	26	117	.286	.287
Pre-All Star	3.89	4	4	7	80	0	69.1	75	7	29	60	Pre-All Star	.275	273	75	11	1	7	44	29	60	.346	.399
Post-All Star	3.49	4	7	6	91	0	77.1	83	5	34	57	Post-All Star	.288	288	83	12	2	5	42	34	57	.363	.396

Terrell Wade — Braves

Age 25 – Pitches Left (flyball pitcher)

	ERA	W	L	Sv	G	GS	IP	BB	SO	Avg	H	2B	3B	HR	RBI	OBP	SLG	CG	ShO	Sup	QS	#P/S	SB	CS	GB	FB	G/F
1997 Season	5.36	2	3	0	12	9	42.0	16	35	.349	60	10	0	6	24	.400	.512	0	0	5.14	3	77	13	5	54	48	1.13
Career (1995-1997)	3.89	7	4	1	59	17	115.2	67	117	.275	120	27	1	16	49	.370	.451	0	0	5.21	4	80	29	9	121	127	0.95

1997 Season

	ERA	W	L	Sv	G	GS	IP	H	HR	BB	SO		Avg	AB	H	2B	3B	HR	RBI	BB	SO	OBP	SLG
Home	3.82	2	2	0	8	6	30.2	42	3	11	27	vs. Left	.489	45	22	2	0	3	1	8	.489	.533
Away	9.53	0	1	0	4	3	11.1	18	3	5	8	vs. Right	.299	127	38	8	0	6	21	15	27	.372	.504

Billy Wagner — Astros

	ERA	W	L	Sv	G	GS	IP	BB	SO	Avg	H	2B	3B	HR	RBI	OBP	SLG	GF	IR	IRS	Hld	SvOp	SB	CS	GB	FB	G/F
1997 Season	2.85	7	8	23	62	0	66.1	30	106	.204	49	8	0	5	31	.299	.300	49	34	13	1	29	2	2	55	43	1.28
Career (1995-1997)	2.66	9	10	32	100	0	118.1	60	173	.187	77	13	0	14	49	.298	.299	69	55	17	4	42	7	3	96	92	1.04

1997 Season

	ERA	W	L	Sv	G	GS	IP	H	HR	BB	SO		Avg	AB	H	2B	3B	HR	RBI	BB	SO	OBP	SLG
Home	3.41	4	4	10	30	0	31.2	25	3	16	53	vs. Left	.237	38	9	2	0	0	3	5	18	.326	.289
Away	2.34	3	4	13	32	0	34.2	24	2	14	53	vs. Right	.198	202	40	6	0	5	28	25	88	.294	.302
Day	4.82	3	5	7	21	0	18.2	15	2	8	33	Inning 1-6	.000	0	0	0	0	0	0	0	0	.000	.000
Night	2.08	4	3	16	41	0	47.2	34	3	22	73	Inning 7+	.204	240	49	8	0	5	31	30	106	.299	.300
Grass	2.63	3	4	8	23	0	27.1	21	1	11	41	None on	.168	119	20	5	0	3	3	14	65	.261	.286
Turf	3.00	4	4	15	39	0	39.0	28	4	19	65	Runners on	.240	121	29	3	0	2	28	16	41	.336	.314
March/April	0.60	2	1	5	11	0	15.0	7	1	4	26	Scoring Posn	.254	71	18	2	0	1	25	13	20	.372	.324
May	3.00	1	1	4	10	0	12.0	9	1	3	23	Close & Late	.226	177	40	5	0	4	26	23	73	.320	.322
June	2.89	2	1	5	10	0	9.1	10	0	3	13	None on/out	.096	52	5	1	0	1	1	5	31	.175	.173
July	0.69	3	0	5	10	0	13.0	7	0	6	19	vs. 1st Batr (relief)	.148	54	8	1	0	1	6	8	27	.258	.222
August	9.72	0	3	0	9	0	8.1	14	3	6	11	1st Inning Pitched	.168	190	32	4	0	3	25	23	86	.264	.237
Sept/Oct	3.12	0	2	4	12	0	8.2	2	0	8	14	First 15 Pitches	.184	141	26	4	0	2	16	15	61	.266	.255
Starter	0.00	0	0	0	0	0	0.0	0	0	0	0	Pitch 16-30	.241	83	20	4	0	3	14	12	36	.351	.398
Reliever	2.85	7	8	23	62	0	66.1	49	5	30	106	Pitch 31-45	.214	14	3	0	0	0	1	3	8	.353	.214
0 Days rest (Relief)	2.25	2	1	5	12	0	12.0	8	0	5	13	Pitch 46+	.000	2	0	0	0	0	0	0	0	.000	.000
1 or 2 Days rest	2.87	3	5	10	31	0	37.2	28	4	18	64	First Pitch	.478	23	11	1	0	2	6	1	0	.520	.783
3+ Days rest	3.24	2	2	8	19	0	16.2	13	1	7	29	Ahead in Count	.146	151	22	2	0	3	13	0	83	.151	.219
vs. AL	0.00	1	0	0	3	0	2.0	0	0	1	3	Behind in Count	.318	22	7	1	0	0	5	10	0	.529	.364
vs. NL	2.94	6	8	23	59	0	64.1	49	5	29	103	Two Strikes	.135	170	23	3	0	2	18	19	106	.226	.188
Pre-All Star	1.83	5	3	15	34	0	39.1	27	2	11	67	Pre-All Star	.191	141	27	6	0	2	13	11	67	.260	.277
Post-All Star	4.33	2	5	8	28	0	27.0	22	3	19	39	Post-All Star	.222	99	22	2	0	3	18	19	39	.350	.333

Paul Wagner — Brewers

	ERA	W	L	Sv	G	GS	IP	BB	SO	Avg	H	2B	3B	HR	RBI	OBP	SLG	GF	IR	IRS	Hld	SvOp	SB	CS	GB	FB	G/F
1997 Season	4.50	1	0	0	16	0	18.0	13	9	.290	20	1	0	4	9	.398	.478	3	8	1	0	1	4	0	29	21	1.38
Last Five Years	4.69	25	40	3	138	74	525.2	216	410	.276	559	96	10	54	271	.349	.413	17	46	22	7	7	74	23	784	514	1.53

1997 Season

	ERA	W	L	Sv	G	GS	IP	H	HR	BB	SO		Avg	AB	H	2B	3B	HR	RBI	BB	SO	OBP	SLG
Home	5.40	1	0	0	6	0	8.1	8	2	5	2	vs. Left	.321	28	9	1	0	1	3	4	6	.406	.464
Away	3.72	0	0	0	10	0	9.2	12	2	8	7	vs. Right	.268	41	11	0	0	3	6	9	3	.392	.488

Last Five Years

	ERA	W	L	Sv	G	GS	IP	H	HR	BB	SO		Avg	AB	H	2B	3B	HR	RBI	BB	SO	OBP	SLG
Home	4.60	17	22	1	68	37	272.0	286	25	96	220	vs. Left	.291	949	276	42	5	19	127	111	161	.366	.406
Away	4.79	8	18	2	70	37	253.2	273	29	120	190	vs. Right	.263	1077	283	54	5	35	144	105	249	.334	.420
Day	4.16	10	13	0	46	27	192.2	196	24	74	160	Inning 1-6	.272	1646	448	86	10	46	234	178	337	.347	.420
Night	5.00	15	27	3	92	47	333.0	363	30	142	250	Inning 7+	.292	380	111	10	0	8	37	38	73	.356	.382
Grass	4.28	6	8	2	46	23	164.0	170	18	70	123	None on	.282	1102	311	56	5	32	32	111	213	.352	.429
Turf	4.88	19	32	1	92	51	361.2	389	36	146	287	Runners on	.268	924	248	40	5	22	239	105	197	.345	.394
March/April	3.92	4	5	2	24	10	80.1	80	6	25	86	Scoring Posn	.278	562	156	26	5	17	220	81	123	.364	.432
May	5.07	5	11	0	28	18	119.0	130	13	55	89	Close & Late	.328	177	58	6	0	5	27	12	33	.366	.446
June	4.77	4	8	0	20	16	94.1	98	8	41	65	None on/out	.304	507	154	31	4	16	16	49	76	.369	.475
July	5.63	3	9	0	29	12	88.0	98	11	41	53	vs. 1st Batr (relief)	.396	53	21	2	0	2	12	9	6	.476	.547
August	4.70	3	2	1	24	7	69.0	76	6	32	63	1st Inning Pitched	.278	504	140	19	2	11	92	72	100	.368	.389
Sept/Oct	3.72	6	5	0	13	11	75.0	76	10	22	54	First 15 Pitches	.312	397	124	16	3	10	66	53	71	.392	.443
Starter	4.76	19	35	0	74	74	433.0	454	45	176	331	Pitch 16-30	.250	388	97	19	0	11	48	36	84	.319	.384
Reliever	4.37	6	5	3	64	0	92.2	105	9	40	79	Pitch 31-45	.242	306	74	12	2	8	31	34	70	.325	.373
0 Days rest (Relief)	4.50	0	0	1	10	0	12.0	16	1	3	8	Pitch 46+	.282	935	264	49	5	26	126	93	185	.350	.426
1 or 2 Days rest	4.91	4	4	2	42	0	62.1	72	6	31	56	First Pitch	.350	326	114	13	2	13	57	12	0	.376	.521
3+ Days rest	2.45	2	1	0	12	0	18.1	17	2	6	15	Ahead in Count	.194	847	164	23	3	15	85	0	369	.197	.281
vs. AL	9.00	1	0	0	2	0	2.0	3	1	0	0	Behind in Count	.337	498	168	37	4	14	90	113	0	.459	.512
vs. NL	4.67	24	40	3	136	74	523.2	556	53	216	410	Two Strikes	.181	878	159	24	3	15	78	91	410	.261	.267
Pre-All Star	4.88	14	29	2	80	48	321.0	347	32	135	260	Pre-All Star	.281	1235	347	66	8	32	169	135	260	.353	.425
Post-All Star	4.40	11	11	1	58	26	204.2	212	22	81	150	Post-All Star	.268	791	212	30	2	22	102	81	150	.342	.394

Pitcher vs. Batter (career)

Pitches Best Vs.	Avg	AB	H	2B	3B	HR	RBI	BB	SO	OBP	SLG	Pitches Worst Vs.	Avg	AB	H	2B	3B	HR	RBI	BB	SO	OBP	SLG
Walt Weiss	.000	17	0	0	0	0	1	7	3	.292	.000	Jeff Bagwell	.545	11	6	1	0	1	2	3	3	.667	.909
Joe Girardi	.000	11	0	0	0	0	0	0	4	.000	.000	Barry Larkin	.524	21	11	3	1	1	4	4	0	.600	.905
Charlie Hayes	.067	15	1	0	0	0	4	1	2	.176	.067	Tony Gwynn	.438	16	7	2	0	2	6	2	1	.500	.938
Todd Hundley	.125	16	2	0	0	0	1	0	3	.125	.125	Raul Mondesi	.364	11	4	0	0	2	4	0	4	.364	.909
Benito Santiago	.125	16	2	1	0	0	1	1		.176	.188	Mike Piazza	.353	17	6	0	0	3	7	1	3	.389	.882

David Wainhouse — Pirates

	ERA	W	L	Sv	G	GS	IP	BB	SO	Avg	H	2B	3B	HR	RBI	OBP	SLG	GF	IR	IRS	Hld	SvOp	SB	CS	GB	FB	G/F
1997 Season	8.04	0	1	0	25	0	28.0	17	21	.301	34	8	0	2	27	.403	.425	6	25	8	1	0	1	1	47	27	1.74
Last Five Years	7.83	1	1	0	45	0	54.0	32	39	.293	63	13	0	6	51	.390	.437	12	38	14	2	0	9	1	81	59	1.37

1997 Season

	ERA	W	L	Sv	G	GS	IP	H	HR	BB	SO		Avg	AB	H	2B	3B	HR	RBI	BB	SO	OBP	SLG
Home	5.54	0	0	0	12	0	13.0	13	1	9	10	vs. Left	.306	36	11	4	0	0	11	8	8	.435	.417

1997 Season

	ERA	W	L	Sv	G	GS	IP	H	HR	BB	SO		Avg	AB	H	2B	3B	HR	RBI	BB	SO	OBP	SLG
Away	10.20	0	1	0	13	0	15.0	21	1	8	11	vs. Right	.299	77	23	4	0	2	16	9	13	.386	.429
Starter	0.00	0	0	0	0	0	0.0	0	0	0	0	Scoring Posn	.333	54	18	8	0	0	25	5	11	.383	.481
Reliever	8.04	0	0	1	25	0	28.0	34	2	17	21	Close & Late	.385	13	5	1	0	1	4	2	1	.500	.692
0 Days rest (Relief)	7.36	0	1	0	4	0	3.2				6	None on/out	.421	19	8	0	0	1	1	5	1	.560	.579
1 or 2 Days rest	6.28	0	0	0	14	0	14.1	18	2	10	10	First Pitch	.526	19	10	2	0	1	8	0	0	.560	.789
3+ Days rest	10.80	0	0	0	7	0	10.0	14	0	6	5	Ahead in Count	.156	45	7	1	0	0	0	0	18	.174	.178
Pre-All Star	8.04	0	1	0	25	0	28.0	34	2	17	21	Behind in Count	.433	30	13	4	0	0	12	15	0	.617	.567
Post-All Star	0.00	0	0	0	0	0	0.0	0	0	0	0	Two Strikes	.200	40	8	1	0	0	1	5	21	.256	.300

Tim Wakefield — Red Sox
Age 31 – Pitches Right (flyball pitcher)

	ERA	W	L	Sv	G	GS	IP	BB	SO	Avg	H	2B	3B	HR	RBI	OBP	SLG	CG	ShO	Sup	QS	#P/S	SB	CS	GB	FB	G/F
1997 Season	4.25	12	15	0	35	29	201.1	87	151	.256	193	43	6	24	88	.343	.425	3	0	4.47	15	104	25	18	214	262	0.82
Last Five Years	4.40	48	47	0	118	108	736.2	320	469	.262	739	147	16	98	361	.344	.430	19	5	4.81	56	106	76	32	855	996	0.86

1997 Season

	ERA	W	L	Sv	G	GS	IP	H	HR	BB	SO		Avg	AB	H	2B	3B	HR	RBI	BB	SO	OBP	SLG
Home	4.18	4	8	0	16	14	97.0	100	13	36	67	vs. Left	.269	368	99	23	5	9	38	43	68	.347	.432
Away	4.31	8	7	0	19	15	104.1	93	11	51	84	vs. Right	.244	385	94	20	1	15	50	44	83	.339	.418
Day	4.08	4	6	0	13	10	79.1	72	13	35	61	Inning 1-6	.265	608	161	38	5	17	74	67	124	.348	.428
Night	4.35	8	9	0	22	19	122.0	121	11	52	90	Inning 7+	.221	145	32	5	1	7	14	20	27	.324	.414
Grass	4.25	10	15	0	31	27	184.1	181	24	77	135	None on	.257	436	112	24	6	13	13	52	79	.352	.429
Turf	4.24	2	0	0	4	2	17.0	12	0	10	16	Runners on	.256	317	81	19	0	11	75	35	72	.331	.420
March/April	4.24	1	1	0	3	3	17.0	14	1	4	4	Scoring Posn	.242	182	44	9	0	5	62	22	45	.322	.374
May	5.76	0	3	0	5	5	29.2	30	3	19	26	Close & Late	.233	73	17	3	1	4	10	13	26	.356	.466
June	5.73	2	4	0	6	6	33.0	40	5	22	29	None on/out	.229	192	44	8	3	4	10	22	38	.330	.365
July	2.06	2	4	0	7	4	43.2	30	4	12	36	vs. 1st Batr (relief)	.200	5	1	0	0	0	1	0	1	.167	.200
August	5.43	4	3	0	9	7	44.2	54	9	14	34	1st Inning Pitched	.250	124	31	6	1	2	15	15	38	.333	.363
Sept/Oct	2.16	3	0	0	5	4	33.1	25	2	16	22	First 75 Pitches	.263	536	141	31	5	18	68	61	114	.345	.440
Starter	4.32	12	13	0	29	29	185.1	183	23	79	135	Pitch 76-90	.281	89	25	5	1	3	9	6	15	.354	.461
Reliever	3.38	0	2	0	6	0	16.0	10	1	8	16	Pitch 91-105	.210	62	13	4	0	2	9	9	8	.319	.371
0-3 Days Rest (Start)	4.82	4	2	0	6	6	37.1	41	5	10	26	Pitch 106+	.212	66	14	3	0	1	2	11	14	.338	.303
4 Days Rest	4.54	4	6	0	12	12	77.1	84	13	36	63	First Pitch	.351	97	34	4	2	9	17	2	0	.390	.711
5+ Days Rest	3.82	4	5	0	11	11	70.2	58	5	33	46	Ahead in Count	.221	389	86	21	1	6	33	0	117	.232	.326
vs. AL	3.91	12	12	0	31	26	184.1	164	21	77	141	Behind in Count	.278	133	37	10	3	4	20	44	0	.453	.489
vs. NL	7.94	0	3	0	4	3	17.0	29	3	10	10	Two Strikes	.194	372	72	22	1	5	29	41	151	.284	.298
Pre-All Star	4.95	3	9	0	16	14	87.1	86	9	47	70	Pre-All Star	.261	330	86	19	3	9	41	47	70	.364	.418
Post-All Star	3.71	9	6	0	19	15	114.0	107	15	40	81	Post-All Star	.253	423	107	24	3	15	47	40	81	.326	.430

Last Five Years

	ERA	W	L	Sv	G	GS	IP	H	HR	BB	SO		Avg	AB	H	2B	3B	HR	RBI	BB	SO	OBP	SLG
Home	4.01	23	21	0	57	53	372.1	378	48	150	234	vs. Left	.268	1413	379	82	11	41	172	182	216	.353	.429
Away	4.79	25	26	0	61	55	364.1	361	50	170	235	vs. Right	.256	1406	360	65	5	57	189	138	253	.334	.431
Day	3.00	13	12	0	32	28	215.2	179	30	87	140	Inning 1-6	.264	2316	612	130	14	78	317	265	402	.343	.434
Night	4.98	35	35	0	86	80	521.0	560	68	233	329	Inning 7+	.252	503	127	17	2	20	44	65	67	.346	.414
Grass	4.27	39	39	0	91	87	592.0	604	87	235	379	None on	.258	1595	411	78	12	57	57	186	259	.345	.429
Turf	4.91	9	8	0	27	21	144.2	135	11	85	90	Runners on	.268	1224	328	69	4	41	304	134	210	.342	.431
March/April	4.89	6	6	0	13	13	84.2	82	9	54	45	Scoring Posn	.248	703	174	33	3	24	258	85	138	.327	.405
May	5.09	3	8	0	18	18	111.1	125	14	58	73	Close & Late	.234	274	64	9	2	11	26	34	34	.326	.401
June	5.26	8	10	0	24	20	125.0	149	17	52	80	None on/out	.242	707	171	32	5	22	22	80	113	.332	.395
July	3.28	11	7	0	20	17	131.2	122	14	42	96	vs. 1st Batr (relief)	.111	9	1	0	0	0	1	0	3	.100	.111
August	4.88	10	7	0	21	19	131.0	130	29	47	89	1st Inning Pitched	.257	447	115	18	3	18	73	53	108	.338	.432
Sept/Oct	3.47	10	9	0	22	21	153.0	131	15	67	86	First 75 Pitches	.264	1923	508	104	13	64	244	208	337	.343	.432
Starter	4.42	47	45	0	108	108	714.2	723	97	311	449	Pitch 76-90	.273	344	94	19	1	17	54	33	54	.345	.483
Reliever	3.68	1	2	0	10	0	22.0	16	1	9	20	Pitch 91-105	.254	287	73	13	1	10	42	32	40	.332	.411
0-3 Days Rest (Start)	4.78	6	6	0	13	13	86.2	93	15	25	49	Pitch 106+	.242	265	64	11	1	7	21	47	38	.364	.370
4 Days Rest	3.87	29	22	0	60	60	414.0	397	62	171	256	First Pitch	.311	386	120	19	3	23	70	3	0	.335	.554
5+ Days Rest	5.34	12	17	0	35	35	214.0	233	20	115	144	Ahead in Count	.221	1359	301	62	2	36	139	0	373	.226	.350
vs. AL	4.03	42	33	0	90	85	591.1	565	81	235	400	Behind in Count	.303	575	174	44	7	26	94	175	0	.465	.539
vs. NL	5.88	6	14	0	28	23	145.1	174	17	85	69	Two Strikes	.198	1268	251	53	4	28	123	142	469	.284	.312
Pre-All Star	4.95	19	27	0	62	56	361.2	392	46	182	228	Pre-All Star	.278	1409	392	76	10	46	198	182	228	.366	.444
Post-All Star	3.86	29	20	0	56	52	375.0	347	52	138	241	Post-All Star	.246	1410	347	71	6	52	163	138	241	.322	.416

Pitcher vs. Batter (career)

Pitches Best Vs.	Avg	AB	H	2B	3B	HR	RBI	BB	SO	OBP	SLG	Pitches Worst Vs.	Avg	AB	H	2B	3B	HR	RBI	BB	SO	OBP	SLG
Joe Girardi	.000	10	0	0	0	0	0	1	1	.167	.000	Kevin Seitzer	.667	9	6	0	0	0	0	2	0	.727	.667
Gary DiSarcina	.063	16	1	0	0	0	0	0	0	.063	.063	Dave Nilsson	.640	25	16	5	0	1	4	7	1	.719	.960
Tomas Perez	.100	10	1	0	0	0	0	1	1	.182	.100	Dean Palmer	.500	12	6	1	0	1	1	2	2	.571	.833
Jay Buhner	.105	19	2	0	0	0	2	1	8	.150	.105	Paul O'Neill	.333	9	3	1	0	2	5	3	1	.429	1.111
Willie McGee	.133	15	2	0	0	0	1	0	4	.133	.133	Jose Canseco	.333	9	3	1	0	2	6	0	2	.364	1.111

Matt Walbeck — Tigers

Age 28 – Bats Both

	Avg	G	AB	R	H	2B	3B	HR	RBI	BB	SO	HBP	GDP	SB	CS	OBP	SLG	IBB	SH	SF	#Pit	#P/PA	GB	FB	G/F
1997 Season	.277	47	137	18	38	3	0	3	10	12	19	0	4	3	3	.331	.365	0	0	2	562	3.72	51	36	1.42
Career (1993-1997)	.235	333	1113	116	262	45	1	12	119	64	167	3	28	10	6	.277	.310	3	3	7	4075	3.42	446	327	1.36

1997 Season

	Avg	AB	H	2B	3B	HR	RBI	BB	SO	OBP	SLG		Avg	AB	H	2B	3B	HR	RBI	BB	SO	OBP	SLG
vs. Left	.229	48	11	2	0	0	1	3	5	.275	.271	Scoring Posn	.261	23	6	1	0	1	8	3	3	.321	.435
vs. Right	.303	89	27	1	0	3	9	9	14	.360	.416	Close & Late	.231	26	6	0	0	1	1	4	5	.333	.346
Home	.279	61	17	2	0	1	6	6	8	.338	.361	None on/out	.359	39	14	2	0	1	1	3	5	.405	.487
Away	.276	76	21	1	0	2	4	6	11	.325	.368	Batting #8	.280	125	35	3	0	3	10	11	18	.333	.376
First Pitch	.304	23	7	0	0	2	3	0	0	.304	.565	Batting #9	.286	7	2	0	0	0	1	0	1	.375	.286
Ahead in Count	.296	27	8	1	0	0	3	7	0	.429	.333	Other	.200	5	1	0	0	0	0	0	1	.200	.200
Behind in Count	.267	60	16	0	0	1	2	0	19	.267	.317	Pre-All Star	.276	29	8	2	0	1	5	5	3	.361	.448
Two Strikes	.281	64	18	1	0	1	4	5	19	.344	.344	Post-All Star	.278	108	30	1	0	2	5	7	16	.322	.343

Career (1993-1997)

	Avg	AB	H	2B	3B	HR	RBI	BB	SO	OBP	SLG		Avg	AB	H	2B	3B	HR	RBI	BB	SO	OBP	SLG
vs. Left	.272	309	84	15	1	2	38	16	28	.306	.346	First Pitch	.306	229	70	13	0	4	25	1	0	.310	.415
vs. Right	.221	804	178	30	0	10	81	48	139	.266	.296	Ahead in Count	.269	249	67	10	0	0	30	35	0	.355	.309
Groundball	.241	294	71	14	0	1	36	25	56	.299	.299	Behind in Count	.191	451	86	12	1	5	34	0	150	.193	.255
Flyball	.248	214	53	9	0	6	34	8	26	.275	.374	Two Strikes	.172	436	75	12	1	7	40	28	167	.221	.252
Home	.242	538	130	26	1	4	55	34	80	.288	.316	Batting #7	.229	192	44	7	0	1	20	10	34	.271	.281
Away	.230	575	132	19	0	8	64	30	87	.267	.304	Batting #8	.245	695	170	29	1	9	78	40	96	.284	.328
Day	.212	307	65	15	0	4	37	18	50	.253	.300	Other	.212	226	48	9	0	2	21	14	37	.260	.279
Night	.244	806	197	30	1	8	82	46	117	.286	.314	March/April	.226	137	31	5	0	2	20	7	16	.270	.307
Grass	.241	543	131	18	0	6	63	33	77	.284	.308	May	.266	143	38	8	0	3	23	10	23	.310	.385
Turf	.230	570	131	27	1	6	56	31	90	.271	.312	June	.182	181	33	7	0	0	12	7	26	.212	.221
Pre-All Star	.221	524	116	24	0	6	62	31	79	.265	.302	July	.234	239	56	9	0	5	23	13	43	.272	.335
Post-All Star	.248	589	146	21	1	6	57	33	88	.288	.317	August	.260	215	56	9	1	2	21	15	31	.312	.340
Scoring Posn	.272	290	79	20	0	5	109	18	46	.310	.393	Sept/Oct	.242	198	48	7	0	0	20	12	28	.286	.278
Close & Late	.232	194	45	6	0	4	24	10	38	.271	.325	vs. AL	.237	1076	255	43	1	11	113	63	160	.279	.309
None on/out	.244	295	72	13	0	3	3	14	36	.281	.319	vs. NL	.189	37	7	2	0	1	6	1	7	.211	.324

Batter vs. Pitcher (career)

Hits Best Against	Avg	AB	H	2B	3B	HR	RBI	BB	SO	OBP	SLG	Hits Worst Against	Avg	AB	H	2B	3B	HR	RBI	BB	SO	OBP	SLG
Ken Hill	.636	11	7	0	0	0	2	3	0	.733	.636	Alex Fernandez	.091	11	1	0	0	0	0	2	0	.231	.091
Chuck Finley	.412	17	7	0	0	0	2	3	0	.474	.412	Mark Gubicza	.100	10	1	0	0	0	1	0	.182	.100
Jason Bere	.400	10	4	1	0	2	1	4	.455	.500	Roger Clemens	.111	9	1	0	0	1	2	4	.250	.111
Wilson Alvarez	.357	14	5	1	0	0	1	1	3	.400	.429	Tom Gordon	.118	17	2	0	0	0	0	5	.118	.118
Juan Guzman	.353	17	6	0	0	0	3	1	2	.389	.353	Dennis Martinez	.158	19	3	0	0	0	1	0	.158	.158

Jamie Walker — Royals

Age 26 – Pitches Left

	ERA	W	L	Sv	G	GS	IP	BB	SO	Avg	H	2B	3B	HR	RBI	OBP	SLG	GF	IR	IRS	Hld	SvOp	SB	CS	GB	FB	G/F
1997 Season	5.44	3	3	0	50	0	43.0	20	24	.271	46	6	2	6	33	.354	.435	15	46	17	3	1	4	1	59	51	1.16

1997 Season

	ERA	W	L	Sv	G	GS	IP	H	HR	BB	SO		Avg	AB	H	2B	3B	HR	RBI	BB	SO	OBP	SLG
Home	5.92	3	1	0	24	0	24.1	29	3	8	16	vs. Left	.275	69	19	3	1	2	16	8	14	.358	.435
Away	4.82	0	2	0	26	0	18.2	17	3	12	8	vs. Right	.267	101	27	3	1	4	17	12	10	.351	.436
Day	0.98	2	1	0	16	0	18.1	10	1	8	4	Inning 1-6	.292	48	14	2	0	2	11	3	5	.340	.458
Night	8.76	1	2	0	34	0	24.2	36	5	12	20	Inning 7+	.262	122	32	4	2	4	22	17	19	.359	.426
Grass	4.65	3	3	0	43	0	40.2	43	5	17	21	None on	.238	84	20	1	1	1	1	10	14	.333	.310
Turf	19.29	0	0	0	7	0	2.1	3	1	3	3	Runners on	.302	86	26	5	1	5	32	10	10	.374	.558
March/April	7.94	1	1	0	9	0	5.2	3	0	3	3	Scoring Posn	.333	48	16	3	0	2	24	7	7	.414	.521
May	9.00	2	1	0	12	0	6.0	8	2	5	3	Close & Late	.333	27	9	1	0	1	7	6	3	.472	.481
June	3.86	0	0	0	3	0	2.1	2	0	1	2	None on/out	.256	39	10	0	1	0	0	3	5	.310	.308
July	3.09	0	0	0	10	0	11.2	14	2	4	3	vs. 1st Batr (relief)	.341	44	15	2	1	2	14	4	9	.400	.568
August	3.18	0	1	0	9	0	11.1	9	0	2	5	1st Inning Pitched	.250	120	30	4	1	4	28	16	16	.348	.400
Sept/Oct	9.00	0	0	0	7	0	6.0	10	2	5	6	First 15 Pitches	.259	108	28	3	1	4	28	16	14	.364	.417
Starter	0.00	0	0	0	0	0	0.0	0	0	0	0	Pitch 16-30	.262	42	11	2	1	0	2	4	7	.326	.357
Reliever	5.44	3	3	0	50	0	43.0	46	6	20	24	Pitch 31-45	.313	16	5	0	0	2	0	3	.313	.500
0 Days rest (Relief)	5.25	1	0	0	10	0	12.0	14	2	4	3	Pitch 46+	.500	4	2	1	0	1	0	0	.500	1.500
1 or 2 Days rest	6.92	0	1	0	17	0	13.0	16	3	8	10	First Pitch	.364	22	8	0	1	2	8	3	0	.423	.727
3+ Days rest	4.50	2	2	0	23	0	18.0	16	1	8	11	Ahead in Count	.145	69	10	2	0	1	8	0	21	.155	.217
vs. AL	5.77	3	3	0	46	0	39.0	44	5	19	22	Behind in Count	.245	49	12	1	3	12	10	0	.383	.449
vs. NL	2.25	0	0	0	4	0	4.0	2	1	1	2	Two Strikes	.209	67	14	2	0	7	7	24	.299	.239
Pre-All Star	6.35	3	2	0	26	0	17.0	15	2	10	10	Pre-All Star	.234	64	15	1	1	2	13	10	10	.355	.375
Post-All Star	4.85	0	1	0	24	0	26.0	31	4	10	14	Post-All Star	.292	106	31	5	1	4	20	10	14	.353	.472

Larry Walker — Rockies

Age 31 – Bats Left (groundball hitter)

	Avg	G	AB	R	H	2B	3B	HR	RBI	BB	SO	HBP	GDP	SB	CS	OBP	SLG	IBB	SH	SF	#Pit	#P/PA	GB	FB	G/F
1997 Season	.366	153	568	143	208	46	4	49	130	78	90	14	15	33	8	.452	.720	14	0	4	2224	3.35	216	150	1.44
Last Five Years	.311	608	2219	458	691	163	20	144	461	274	370	47	50	111	25	.395	.598	54	0	24	8649	3.37	840	628	1.34

1997 Season

	Avg	AB	H	2B	3B	HR	RBI	BB	SO	OBP	SLG		Avg	AB	H	2B	3B	HR	RBI	BB	SO	OBP	SLG
vs. Left	.299	144	43	14	0	6	23	17	25	.400	.521	First Pitch	.443	122	54	11	3	10	33	11	0	.500	.828
vs. Right	.389	424	165	32	4	43	107	61	65	.470	.788	Ahead in Count	.433	134	58	11	1	15	35	39	0	.563	.866

1997 Season

	Avg	AB	H	2B	3B	HR	RBI	BB	SO	OBP	SLG
Groundball	.426	115	49	11	1	10	34	13	17	.489	.800
Flyball	.404	94	38	8	2	8	17	14	12	.486	.787
Home	.384	302	116	30	4	20	68	36	34	.460	.709
Away	.346	266	92	16	0	29	62	42	56	.443	.733
Day	.414	261	108	29	3	25	73	37	42	.495	.835
Night	.326	307	100	17	1	24	57	41	48	.415	.622
Grass	.371	469	174	38	4	38	106	65	67	.457	.757
Turf	.343	99	34	8	0	11	24	13	23	.425	.758
Pre-All Star	.398	309	123	25	3	25	68	49	50	.496	.741
Post-All Star	.328	259	85	21	1	24	62	29	40	.397	.695
Scoring Posn	.364	140	51	10	0	5	68	34	21	.495	.543
Close & Late	.352	71	25	5	1	7	17	14	12	.459	.746
None on/out	.381	97	37	8	1	11	11	4	20	.417	.825

	Avg	AB	H	2B	3B	HR	RBI	BB	SO	OBP	SLG
Behind in Count	.263	217	57	15	0	13	40	0	71	.281	.512
Two Strikes	.242	215	52	12	0	9	29	28	90	.343	.423
Batting #3	.371	536	199	44	3	47	125	73	83	.455	.728
Batting #4	.290	31	9	2	1	2	5	3	7	.371	.613
Other	.000	1	0	0	0	0	0	0	2	.667	.000
March/April	.456	90	41	6	1	11	29	14	16	.538	.911
May	.365	104	38	11	2	4	18	19	14	.472	.625
June	.408	98	40	8	0	10	21	15	17	.427	.762
July	.305	95	29	6	0	5	20	9	12	.361	.526
August	.362	105	38	10	1	10	21	11	17	.427	.762
Sept/Oct	.289	76	22	5	0	9	21	10	14	.375	.711
vs. AL	.373	59	22	5	0	7	14	4	5	.431	.814
vs. NL	.365	509	186	41	4	42	116	74	85	.454	.709

1997 By Position

Position	Avg	AB	H	2B	3B	HR	RBI	BB	SO	OBP	SLG	G	GS	Innings	PO	A	E	DP	Fld Pct	Rng Fctr	In Zone	Zone Outs	Zone Rtg	MLB Zone
As rf	.373	547	204	45	4	47	127	76	85	.457	.728	150	143	1235.1	230	12	2	5	.992	1.76	303	220	.726	.813

Last Five Years

	Avg	AB	H	2B	3B	HR	RBI	BB	SO	OBP	SLG
vs. Left	.289	660	191	45	6	29	125	69	118	.376	.508
vs. Right	.321	1559	500	118	14	115	336	205	252	.403	.636
Groundball	.324	561	182	46	6	30	120	49	84	.383	.588
Flyball	.339	348	118	25	6	23	74	50	61	.428	.644
Home	.351	1105	388	104	14	76	262	125	167	.425	.677
Away	.272	1114	303	59	6	68	199	149	203	.365	.519
Day	.318	781	248	58	7	57	168	96	137	.404	.629
Night	.308	1438	443	105	13	87	293	178	233	.390	.581
Grass	.328	1368	449	95	16	96	296	160	214	.407	.632
Turf	.284	851	242	68	4	48	165	114	156	.376	.543
Pre-All Star	.321	1294	416	96	11	87	267	160	221	.406	.614
Post-All Star	.297	925	275	67	9	57	194	114	149	.379	.574
Scoring Posn	.296	624	185	44	9	22	284	124	116	.413	.502
Close & Late	.278	309	86	18	4	16	54	55	48	.390	.518
None on/out	.311	518	161	40	5	36	36	40	89	.367	.616

	Avg	AB	H	2B	3B	HR	RBI	BB	SO	OBP	SLG
First Pitch	.383	517	198	43	9	32	130	39	0	.436	.687
Ahead in Count	.400	453	181	44	3	46	114	144	0	.543	.815
Behind in Count	.223	873	195	47	7	37	138	0	309	.241	.420
Two Strikes	.204	867	177	41	5	33	117	91	370	.289	.377
Batting #3	.344	770	265	63	4	60	164	93	131	.425	.670
Batting #4	.298	1413	421	100	16	82	292	176	233	.381	.565
Other	.139	36	5	0	0	2	5	6	8	.289	.306
March/April	.329	340	112	27	2	25	78	39	59	.413	.641
May	.308	465	143	40	7	24	85	57	77	.390	.578
June	.344	363	125	27	1	29	77	51	68	.435	.664
July	.302	384	116	22	2	18	76	43	60	.372	.510
August	.296	389	115	33	3	26	85	46	67	.369	.596
Sept/Oct	.288	278	80	14	5	22	60	38	39	.369	.612
vs. AL	.373	59	22	5	0	7	14	4	5	.431	.814
vs. NL	.310	2160	669	158	20	137	447	270	365	.394	.592

Batter vs. Pitcher (career)

Hits Best Against	Avg	AB	H	2B	3B	HR	RBI	BB	SO	OBP	SLG
Chris Hammond	.600	15	9	0	0	2	3	1	2	.647	1.000
Kevin Foster	.500	18	9	0	0	4	9	3	4	.545	1.167
Greg McMichael	.500	12	6	0	1	2	3	1	0	.538	1.167
Tom Candiotti	.444	18	8	0	0	4	7	3	0	.500	1.111
Scott Sanders	.400	10	4	1	0	2	4	1	2	.455	1.100

Hits Worst Against	Avg	AB	H	2B	3B	HR	RBI	BB	SO	OBP	SLG
Bob Patterson	.000	9	0	0	0	0	1	1	3	.091	.000
Allen Watson	.077	13	1	0	0	0	2	2	0	.200	.077
Mike Bielecki	.083	12	1	0	0	0	0	1	3	.154	.083
Mike Maddux	.100	10	1	0	0	0	0	2	0	.091	.100
Paul Assenmacher	.111	18	2	0	0	0	2	2	5	.200	.111

Todd Walker — Twins

Age 25 – Bats Left

	Avg	G	AB	R	H	2B	3B	HR	RBI	BB	SO	HBP	GDP	SB	CS	OBP	SLG	IBB	SH	SF	#Pit	#P/PA	GB	FB	G/F
1997 Season	.237	52	156	15	37	7	1	3	16	11	30	1	5	7	0	.288	.353	1	1	2	657	3.84	62	46	1.30
Career (1996-1997)	.244	77	238	23	58	13	1	3	22	15	43	1	9	9	0	.286	.345	1	1	5	954	3.67	94	69	1.36

1997 Season

	Avg	AB	H	2B	3B	HR	RBI	BB	SO	OBP	SLG
vs. Left	.357	14	5	1	0	0	3	1	3	.375	.429
vs. Right	.225	142	32	6	1	3	13	10	27	.279	.345
Home	.209	67	14	4	0	1	6	4	16	.257	.313
Away	.258	89	23	3	1	2	10	7	14	.313	.382
First Pitch	.474	19	9	3	0	1	6	1	0	.500	.789
Ahead in Count	.355	31	11	3	0	1	7	4	0	.432	.548
Behind in Count	.143	84	12	1	0	0	2	0	28	.141	.155
Two Strikes	.165	79	13	1	0	0	2	6	30	.221	.177

	Avg	AB	H	2B	3B	HR	RBI	BB	SO	OBP	SLG
Scoring Posn	.213	47	10	4	0	1	13	3	10	.250	.362
Close & Late	.348	23	8	2	0	0	1	1	5	.375	.435
None on/out	.250	40	10	0	0	1	1	2	7	.286	.325
Batting #7	.229	48	11	2	0	1	6	2	8	.275	.333
Batting #8	.326	43	14	4	0	2	6	4	9	.375	.558
Other	.185	65	12	1	1	0	4	5	13	.239	.231
Pre-All Star	.194	108	21	5	0	1	6	10	26	.264	.269
Post-All Star	.333	48	16	2	1	2	10	1	4	.347	.542

Donne Wall — Reds

Age 30 – Pitches Right

	ERA	W	L	Sv	G	GS	IP	BB	SO	Avg	H	2B	3B	HR	RBI	OBP	SLG	CG	ShO	Sup	QS	#P/S	SB	CS	GB	FB	G/F
1997 Season	6.26	2	5	0	8	8	41.2	16	25	.317	53	8	2	8	28	.384	.533	0	0	3.46	3	88	3	5	67	41	1.63
Career (1995-1997)	5.00	14	14	0	40	36	216.0	55	140	.290	256	54	6	30	117	.342	.477	2	1	4.58	16	89	13	14	325	240	1.35

1997 Season

	ERA	W	L	Sv	G	GS	IP	H	HR	BB	SO
Home	3.63	2	2	0	4	4	22.1	26	2	6	16
Away	9.31	0	3	0	4	4	19.1	27	6	10	9

	Avg	AB	H	2B	3B	HR	RBI	BB	SO	OBP	SLG
vs. Left	.311	61	19	3	0	4	7	4	6	.354	.557
vs. Right	.321	106	34	5	2	4	21	12	19	.400	.519

Career (1995-1997)

	ERA	W	L	Sv	G	GS	IP	H	HR	BB	SO
Home	3.79	7	6	0	19	18	114.0	112	11	26	91
Away	6.35	7	8	0	21	18	102.0	144	19	29	49
Day	6.23	3	4	0	11	9	47.2	62	6	16	25
Night	4.65	11	10	0	29	27	168.1	194	24	39	115
Grass	7.20	6	7	0	16	15	80.0	116	18	25	40

	Avg	AB	H	2B	3B	HR	RBI	BB	SO	OBP	SLG
vs. Left	.266	357	95	21	4	13	40	22	54	.309	.457
vs. Right	.318	507	161	33	2	17	77	33	86	.364	.491
Inning 1-6	.294	761	224	48	5	26	102	51	122	.342	.473
Inning 7+	.311	103	32	6	1	4	15	4	18	.336	.505
None on	.292	503	147	35	2	16	16	25	80	.331	.465

Career (1995-1997)

	ERA	W	L	Sv	G	GS	IP	H	HR	BB	SO		Avg	AB	H	2B	3B	HR	RBI	BB	SO	OBP	SLG
Turf	3.71	8	7	0	24	21	136.0	140	12	30	100	Runners on	.302	361	109	19	4	14	101	30	60	.356	.493
March/April	1.35	1	0	0	1	1	6.2	5	0	0	4	Scoring Posn	.279	222	62	11	2	7	82	22	40	.340	.441
May	6.39	1	2	0	6	6	31.0	38	5	8	13	Close & Late	.283	60	17	1	1	1	9	2	13	.306	.383
June	3.97	6	3	0	10	10	65.2	73	9	19	43	None on/out	.302	222	67	18	1	8	8	9	39	.338	.500
July	5.73	0	3	0	6	6	33.0	46	5	12	24	vs. 1st Batr (relief)	1.000	3	3	1	0	0	0	1	0	1.000	1.333
August	2.76	3	1	0	6	4	32.2	28	2	5	24	1st Inning Pitched	.270	148	40	7	1	5	18	11	29	.325	.432
Sept/Oct	7.09	3	5	0	11	9	47.0	66	9	11	32	First 75 Pitches	.287	689	198	43	5	21	84	42	115	.332	.456
Starter	4.98	14	14	0	36	36	209.2	244	29	54	137	Pitch 76-90	.327	101	33	7	0	5	17	7	12	.373	.545
Reliever	5.68	0	0	0	4	0	6.1	12	1	1	3	Pitch 91-105	.375	56	21	3	1	3	13	5	9	.426	.625
0-3 Days Rest (Start)	6.35	0	1	0	2	2	11.1	9	1	4	9	Pitch 106+	.222	18	4	1	0	1	3	1	4	.263	.444
4 Days Rest	4.83	6	6	0	17	17	98.2	113	14	28	54	First Pitch	.324	145	47	7	0	6	20	2	0	.331	.497
5+ Days Rest	4.97	8	7	0	17	17	99.2	122	14	22	74	Ahead in Count	.234	402	94	15	2	8	41	0	122	.244	.341
vs. AL	5.91	0	2	0	2	2	10.2	15	1	6	3	Behind in Count	.424	177	75	20	3	12	39	29	0	.500	.774
vs. NL	4.95	14	12	0	38	34	205.1	241	29	49	137	Two Strikes	.220	381	84	13	2	9	36	24	140	.276	.336
Pre-All Star	4.69	8	6	0	19	19	111.1	128	16	32	67	Pre-All Star	.292	438	128	28	3	16	58	32	67	.345	.479
Post-All Star	5.33	6	8	0	21	17	104.2	128	14	23	73	Post-All Star	.300	426	128	26	3	14	59	23	73	.338	.474

Pitcher vs. Batter (career)

Pitches Best Vs.	Avg	AB	H	2B	3B	HR	RBI	BB	SO	OBP	SLG	Pitches Worst Vs.	Avg	AB	H	2B	3B	HR	RBI	BB	SO	OBP	SLG
Vinny Castilla	.000	11	0	0	0	0	1	1	1	.077	.000	Dante Bichette	.625	16	10	5	0	1	6	0	0	.625	1.125
Walt Weiss	.071	14	1	0	0	0	0	1	3	.133	.071	Andres Galarraga	.500	16	8	3	0	1	5	1	2	.529	.875
Brian McRae	.167	12	2	1	0	0	0	0	0	.167	.167	Quilvio Veras	.500	10	5	1	0	0	0	1	1	.545	.600
Jermain Allensworth	.200	10	2	0	0	0	1	0	3	.273	.200	Mark Grace	.400	10	4	1	0	1	2	0	2	.364	.800
Al Martin	.235	17	4	0	0	2	3	0	1	.235	.588	Jeff King	.333	12	4	0	0	1	5	1	2	.357	.583

Jeff Wallace — Pirates
Age 22 – Pitches Left

	ERA	W	L	Sv	G	GS	IP	BB	SO	Avg	H	2B	3B	HR	RBI	OBP	SLG	GF	IR	IRS	Hld	SvOp	SB	CS	GB	FB	G/F
1997 Season	0.75	0	0	0	11	0	12.0	8	14	.200	8	2	0	0	3	.327	.250	1	3	1	3	1	1	1	12	11	1.09

1997 Season

	ERA	W	L	Sv	G	GS	IP	H	HR	BB	SO		Avg	AB	H	2B	3B	HR	RBI	BB	SO	OBP	SLG
Home	1.08	0	0	0	8	0	8.1	6	0	7	10	vs. Left	.118	17	2	1	0	0	1	1	9	.167	.176
Away	0.00	0	0	0	3	0	3.2	2	0	1	4	vs. Right	.261	23	6	1	0	3	7	5	.419	.304

Jerome Walton — Orioles
Age 32 – Bats Right (groundball hitter)

	Avg	G	AB	R	H	2B	3B	HR	RBI	BB	SO	HBP	GDP	SB	CS	OBP	SLG	IBB	SH	SF	#Pit	P/PA	GB	FB	G/F
1997 Season	.294	26	68	8	20	1	0	3	9	4	10	0	3	0	0	.333	.441	0	2	0	251	3.39	29	17	1.71
Last Five Years	.300	216	347	61	104	22	1	13	44	31	59	4	6	12	10	.360	.481	0	7	4	1454	3.70	121	89	1.36

1997 Season

	Avg	AB	H	2B	3B	HR	RBI	BB	SO	OBP	SLG		Avg	AB	H	2B	3B	HR	RBI	BB	SO	OBP	SLG
vs. Left	.250	40	10	1	0	2	6	2	6	.286	.425	Scoring Posn	.308	26	8	0	0	2	8	0	6	.308	.538
vs. Right	.357	28	10	0	0	1	3	2	4	.400	.464	Close & Late	.200	10	2	0	0	0	0	0	3	.200	.200

Turner Ward — Pirates
Age 33 – Bats Both

	Avg	G	AB	R	H	2B	3B	HR	RBI	BB	SO	HBP	GDP	SB	CS	OBP	SLG	IBB	SH	SF	#Pit	P/PA	GB	FB	G/F
1997 Season	.353	71	167	33	59	16	7	33	18	17	2	1	4	1	.420	.587	2	3	1	729	3.80	69	43	1.60
Last Five Years	.247	332	897	134	222	40	7	26	132	120	149	7	22	22	7	.337	.395	9	8	12	3991	3.82	326	267	1.22

1997 Season

	Avg	AB	H	2B	3B	HR	RBI	BB	SO	OBP	SLG		Avg	AB	H	2B	3B	HR	RBI	BB	SO	OBP	SLG
vs. Left	.375	24	9	3	1	1	7	5	2	.483	.708	Scoring Posn	.404	47	19	6	0	1	24	6	3	.463	.596
vs. Right	.350	143	50	13	0	6	26	13	15	.409	.566	Close & Late	.395	38	15	4	0	2	9	3	5	.439	.658
Home	.422	83	35	9	1	5	19	10	8	.495	.735	None on/out	.282	39	11	3	0	2	2	4	7	.349	.513
Away	.286	84	24	7	0	2	14	8	9	.344	.440	Batting #2	.381	105	40	9	1	4	19	10	10	.431	.600
First Pitch	.423	26	11	3	1	0	5	2	0	.464	.615	Batting #9	.296	27	8	2	0	2	7	1	1	.321	.593
Ahead in Count	.429	35	15	3	0	2	13	12	0	.563	.686	Other	.314	35	11	5	0	1	7	7	6	.455	.543
Behind in Count	.320	75	24	7	0	4	10	0	12	.338	.368	Pre-All Star	.429	14	6	1	0	1	2	0	1	.429	.714
Two Strikes	.224	76	17	5	0	2	4	17		.280	.368	Post-All Star	.346	153	53	15	1	6	31	18	16	.420	.575

Last Five Years

	Avg	AB	H	2B	3B	HR	RBI	BB	SO	OBP	SLG		Avg	AB	H	2B	3B	HR	RBI	BB	SO	OBP	SLG
vs. Left	.225	204	46	11	3	4	28	23	35	.303	.368	First Pitch	.299	144	43	8	2	3	22	6	0	.327	.444
vs. Right	.254	693	176	29	4	22	104	97	114	.347	.403	Ahead in Count	.271	192	52	9	0	6	31	76	0	.473	.411
Groundball	.226	199	45	7	1	5	22	16	32	.285	.347	Behind in Count	.208	389	81	13	3	12	42	0	121	.217	.350
Flyball	.210	176	37	5	1	6	24	22	36	.300	.352	Two Strikes	.195	416	81	17	2	12	53	38	149	.266	.332
Home	.271	410	111	22	6	15	70	54	69	.358	.463	Batting #2	.316	234	74	13	1	11	40	20	32	.366	.521
Away	.228	487	111	18	1	11	62	66	80	.319	.337	Batting #3	.257	214	55	12	2	4	29	32	32	.357	.388
Day	.251	347	87	15	5	15	52	43	52	.329	.452	Other	.207	449	93	15	4	11	63	68	85	.313	.332
Night	.245	550	135	25	2	11	80	77	97	.342	.358	March/April	.239	159	38	7	2	8	33	37	27	.381	.459
Grass	.247	599	148	22	4	15	89	87	105	.342	.372	May	.258	233	60	8	2	4	24	21	36	.317	.361
Turf	.248	298	74	18	3	11	43	33	44	.326	.440	June	.231	108	25	2	1	4	19	17	24	.346	.380
Pre-All Star	.240	578	139	21	6	17	83	77	103	.331	.386	July	.233	210	49	8	1	3	19	25	39	.314	.324
Post-All Star	.260	319	83	19	1	9	49	43	46	.348	.411	August	.247	89	22	9	0	3	17	11	14	.330	.449
Scoring Posn	.260	246	64	16	3	4	97	42	41	.353	.398	Sept/Oct	.286	98	28	6	1	4	20	9	5	.351	.490
Close & Late	.290	162	47	9	1	7	25	22	26	.376	.488	vs. AL	.226	743	168	26	6	19	102	103	133	.322	.354

Last Five Years

	Avg	AB	H	2B	3B	HR	RBI	BB	SO	OBP	SLG			Avg	AB	H	2B	3B	HR	RBI	BB	SO	OBP	SLG
None on/out	210	195	41	5	1	5	5	18	35	277	323	vs. NL		351	154	54	14	1	7	30	17	16	.413	.591

Batter vs. Pitcher (career)

Hits Best Against	Avg	AB	H	2B	3B	HR	RBI	BB	SO	OBP	SLG	Hits Worst Against	Avg	AB	H	2B	3B	HR	RBI	BB	SO	OBP	SLG
Mark Clark	.364	11	4	0	0	1	1	0	0	.364	.636	David Cone	.077	13	1	0	0	0	0	2	2	.200	.077
												Tim Belcher	.111	9	1	0	0	0	0	3	1	.333	.111
												Mark Gubicza	.130	23	3	1	0	0	1	0	2	.130	.174
												Ben McDonald	.154	13	2	0	0	0	0	2	3	.143	.154
												Hipolito Pichardo	.182	11	2	0	0	0	0	3	1	.154	.182

John Wasdin — Red Sox
Age 25 – Pitches Right (flyball pitcher)

	ERA	W	L	Sv	G	GS	IP	BB	SO	Avg	H	2B	3B	HR	RBI	OBP	SLG	GF	IR	IRS	Hld	SvOp	SB	CS	GB	FB	G/F
1997 Season	4.40	4	6	0	53	7	124.2	38	84	.251	121	29	2	18	71	.306	.432	10	28	12	11	2	18	2	121	182	0.66
Career (1995-1997)	5.17	13	14	0	83	30	273.1	91	165	.264	280	63	4	46	169	.324	.462	15	34	14	11	3	36	5	288	399	0.72

1997 Season

	ERA	W	L	Sv	G	GS	IP	H	HR	BB	SO		Avg	AB	H	2B	3B	HR	RBI	BB	SO	OBP	SLG
Home	5.04	2	4	0	25	4	60.2	74	9	18	46	vs. Left	.272	235	64	15	1	10	43	26	33	.341	.472
Away	3.80	2	2	0	28	3	64.0	47	9	20	38	vs. Right	.231	247	57	14	1	8	28	12	51	.271	.393
Day	4.88	2	1	0	19	4	48.0	43	9	16	33	Inning 1-6	.235	302	71	19	0	11	45	24	50	.292	.407
Night	4.11	2	5	0	34	3	76.2	78	9	22	51	Inning 7+	.278	180	50	10	2	7	26	14	34	.328	.472
Grass	4.71	2	6	0	46	6	105.0	109	14	33	69	None on	.223	291	65	16	1	8	8	22	51	.280	.368
Turf	2.75	2	0	0	7	1	19.2	12	0	5	15	Runners on	.293	191	56	13	1	10	63	16	33	.343	.529
March/April	4.65	0	0	0	5	5	31.0	25	5	11	26	Scoring Posn	.274	124	34	10	1	6	55	14	22	.336	.516
May	6.95	0	3	0	9	2	22.0	23	4	10	14	Close & Late	.292	89	26	6	1	4	15	6	20	.330	.517
June	4.05	3	0	0	12	0	20.0	26	2	7	10	None on/out	.233	120	28	6	1	3	3	7	18	.276	.375
July	3.65	0	2	0	8	0	12.1	13	3	4	6	vs. 1st Batr (relief)	.310	42	13	1	1	1	9	4	6	.370	.452
August	4.00	1	0	0	10	0	27.0	20	4	4	20	1st Inning Pitched	.250	192	48	9	2	5	34	12	36	.292	.396
Sept/Oct	1.46	0	1	0	9	0	12.1	14	0	3	8	First 15 Pitches	.259	162	42	9	1	5	27	9	24	.295	.420
Starter	5.63	0	1	0	7	7	40.0	39	6	17	30	Pitch 16-30	.234	137	32	5	1	5	15	11	25	.291	.394
Reliever	3.83	4	5	0	46	0	84.2	82	12	21	54	Pitch 31-45	.178	73	13	3	0	5	9	4	14	.221	.425
0 Days rest (Relief)	15.43	0	1	0	4	0	2.1	7	1	0	2	Pitch 46+	.309	110	34	12	0	3	20	14	21	.389	.500
1 or 2 Days rest	3.76	2	2	0	27	0	52.2	56	6	12	33	First Pitch	.214	56	12	4	0	2	8	2	0	.237	.393
3+ Days rest	3.03	2	2	0	15	0	29.2	19	5	9	19	Ahead in Count	.229	249	57	8	2	7	35	0	73	.232	.361
vs. AL	4.25	3	6	0	47	7	114.1	108	16	36	80	Behind in Count	.298	94	28	10	0	4	16	19	0	.414	.532
vs. NL	6.10	1	0	0	6	0	10.1	13	2	2	4	Two Strikes	.218	248	54	9	1	8	32	17	84	.270	.359
Pre-All Star	4.93	3	3	0	28	7	76.2	75	11	28	51	Pre-All Star	.257	292	75	23	2	11	44	28	51	.319	.462
Post-All Star	3.56	1	3	0	25	0	48.0	46	7	10	33	Post-All Star	.242	190	46	6	0	7	27	10	33	.284	.384

Pat Watkins — Reds
Age 25 – Bats Right

	Avg	G	AB	R	H	2B	3B	HR	RBI	BB	SO	HBP	GDP	SB	CS	OBP	SLG	IBB	SH	SF	#Pit	P/PA	GB	FB	G/F
1997 Season	.207	17	29	2	6	2	0	0	0	5	0	1	0	1	0	.207	.276	0	1	0	103	3.43	10	5	2.00

1997 Season

	Avg	AB	H	2B	3B	HR	RBI	BB	SO	OBP	SLG		Avg	AB	H	2B	3B	HR	RBI	BB	SO	OBP	SLG
vs. Left	.167	12	2	0	0	0	0	0	2	.167	.167	Scoring Posn	.000	7	0	0	0	0	0	0	3	.000	.000
vs. Right	.235	17	4	2	0	0	0	3		.235	.353	Close & Late	.200	5	1	1	0	0	0	0	0	.200	.400

Allen Watson — Angels
Age 27 – Pitches Left

	ERA	W	L	Sv	G	GS	IP	BB	SO	Avg	H	2B	3B	HR	RBI	OBP	SLG	CG	ShO	Sup	QS	#P/S	SB	CS	GB	FB	G/F
1997 Season	4.93	12	12	0	35	34	199.0	73	141	.279	220	39	4	37	115	.344	.480	0	0	5.38	18	98	17	11	265	254	1.04
Career (1993-1997)	4.91	39	45	0	123	119	700.2	264	441	.279	755	154	19	108	374	.347	.469	2	0	5.07	54	92	68	42	957	856	1.12

1997 Season

	ERA	W	L	Sv	G	GS	IP	H	HR	BB	SO		Avg	AB	H	2B	3B	HR	RBI	BB	SO	OBP	SLG
Home	5.85	5	7	0	20	19	104.2	130	23	38	83	vs. Left	.254	142	36	6	1	4	19	13	30	.325	.394
Away	3.91	7	5	0	15	15	94.1	90	14	35	58	vs. Right	.285	646	184	33	3	33	96	60	111	.348	.498
Day	3.65	5	2	0	11	11	69.0	69	12	24	44	Inning 1-6	.273	718	196	34	4	32	103	63	134	.336	.465
Night	5.61	7	10	0	24	23	130.0	151	24	49	97	Inning 7+	.343	70	24	5	0	5	12	10	7	.425	.629
Grass	5.28	10	10	0	31	30	172.0	200	36	65	125	None on	.260	462	120	19	4	18	18	41	77	.327	.435
Turf	2.67	2	2	0	4	4	27.0	20	1	8	16	Runners on	.307	326	100	20	0	19	97	32	64	.368	.543
March/April	7.50	0	2	0	5	5	24.0	33	5	4	20	Scoring Posn	.294	170	50	12	0	7	73	23	32	.373	.488
May	4.34	3	1	0	7	6	37.1	43	5	14	11	Close & Late	.240	25	6	1	0	2	3	2	2	.321	.400
June	4.45	4	1	0	5	5	28.1	28	5	12	27	None on/out	.253	198	50	9	3	4	4	20	31	.324	.389
July	3.99	1	2	0	6	6	38.1	29	7	22	29	vs. 1st Batr (relief)	1.000	1	1	1	0	0	2	0	0	1.000	2.000
August	4.70	3	2	0	6	6	38.1	44	7	12	28	1st Inning Pitched	.333	141	47	12	1	3	27	13	21	.385	.496
Sept/Oct	5.51	1	4	0	6	6	32.2	43	8	7	26	First 75 Pitches	.276	587	162	30	4	22	82	47	106	.332	.453
Starter	4.79	12	12	0	34	34	199.0	216	36	73	141	Pitch 76-90	.318	110	35	6	0	12	27	10	21	.380	.700
Reliever	—	0	0	0	1	0	0.0	4	1	0	0	Pitch 91-105	.235	68	16	1	0	2	4	10	10	.346	.338
0-3 Days Rest (Start)	3.06	0	2	0	5	5	35.1	28	6	14	19	Pitch 106+	.304	23	7	2	0	1	2	6	4	.448	.522
4 Days Rest	5.67	8	7	0	19	19	106.1	128	20	41	72	First Pitch	.347	98	34	4	1	4	19	0	0	.343	.531
5+ Days Rest	4.24	4	3	0	10	10	57.1	60	10	18	50	Ahead in Count	.227	370	84	17	1	12	35	0	115	.237	.376
vs. AL	4.69	12	9	0	32	31	184.1	200	33	63	128	Behind in Count	.353	173	61	9	0	10	40	41	0	.468	.578
vs. NL	7.98	0	3	0	3	3	14.2	20	4	10	13	Two Strikes	.219	384	84	15	1	15	39	32	141	.283	.380
Pre-All Star	5.23	7	5	0	18	17	94.2	108	15	36	61	Pre-All Star	.288	375	108	24	1	15	56	36	61	.351	.477

490

1997 Season

	ERA	W	L	Sv	G	GS	IP	H	HR	BB	SO		Avg	AB	H	2B	3B	HR	RBI	BB	SO	OBP	SLG
Post-All Star	4.66	5	7	0	17	17	104.1	112	22	37	80	Post-All Star	271	413	112	15	3	22	59	37	80	.338	.482

Career (1993-1997)

	ERA	W	L	Sv	G	GS	IP	H	HR	BB	SO		Avg	AB	H	2B	3B	HR	RBI	BB	SO	OBP	SLG
Home	4.93	20	20	0	62	61	349.0	366	52	149	232	vs. Left	.226	456	103	15	4	14	57	49	74	.309	.368
Away	4.89	19	25	0	61	58	351.2	389	56	115	209	vs. Right	.289	2253	652	139	15	94	317	215	367	.354	.490
Day	4.79	13	15	0	45	45	264.2	288	41	99	175	Inning 1-6	.277	2467	683	134	19	99	343	238	414	.345	.467
Night	4.97	26	30	0	78	74	436.0	467	67	165	266	Inning 7+	.298	242	72	20	0	9	31	26	27	.363	.492
Grass	5.16	20	28	0	73	69	415.0	465	77	150	281	None on	.267	1568	418	83	10	60	60	168	250	.344	.447
Turf	4.54	19	17	0	50	50	285.2	290	31	114	160	Runners on	.295	1141	337	71	9	48	314	96	191	.351	.500
March/April	6.01	4	6	0	17	17	97.1	116	19	27	71	Scoring Posn	.292	633	185	43	5	24	252	62	117	.354	.490
May	5.00	7	6	0	20	18	108.0	119	17	40	46	Close & Late	.276	127	35	10	0	4	17	14	12	.342	.449
June	3.81	8	5	0	17	17	101.2	100	15	42	80	None on/out	.273	692	189	41	7	25	25	82	111	.352	.461
July	5.14	8	7	0	22	22	124.1	123	18	62	76	vs. 1st Batr (relief)	.500	4	2	1	0	0	3	0	0	.500	.750
August	4.01	9	7	0	23	22	141.1	145	18	50	91	1st Inning Pitched	.280	465	130	32	5	13	74	55	78	.357	.454
Sept/Oct	5.63	3	14	0	24	23	128.0	152	21	43	77	First 75 Pitches	.274	2107	577	117	19	74	269	190	351	.338	.453
Starter	4.96	39	44	0	119	119	687.1	741	107	262	435	Pitch 76-90	.309	343	106	25	0	23	72	41	47	.386	.583
Reliever	2.03	0	1	0	4	0	13.1	14	1	2	6	Pitch 91-105	.258	186	48	8	0	5	18	23	30	.346	.382
0-3 Days Rest (Start)	3.12	0	2	0	6	6	43.1	37	6	15	23	Pitch 106+	.329	73	24	4	0	6	15	10	13	.417	.630
4 Days Rest	5.40	22	27	0	67	67	384.2	432	68	150	245	First Pitch	.365	425	155	32	5	17	66	3	0	.373	.584
5+ Days Rest	4.62	17	15	0	46	46	259.1	272	33	97	167	Ahead in Count	.212	1191	253	52	7	27	113	0	373	.223	.336
vs. AL	4.69	12	9	0	32	31	184.1	200	33	63	128	Behind in Count	.333	600	200	39	2	37	120	144	0	.458	.590
vs. NL	4.99	27	36	0	91	88	516.1	555	75	201	313	Two Strikes	.205	1194	245	52	8	31	119	117	441	.284	.340
Pre-All Star	4.89	22	19	0	60	58	338.2	365	53	128	211	Pre-All Star	.279	1307	365	81	7	53	179	128	211	.346	.474
Post-All Star	4.92	17	26	0	63	61	362.0	390	55	136	230	Post-All Star	.278	1402	390	73	12	55	195	136	230	.347	.465

Pitcher vs. Batter (career)

Pitches Best Vs.	Avg	AB	H	2B	3B	HR	RBI	BB	SO	OBP	SLG	Pitches Worst Vs.	Avg	AB	H	2B	3B	HR	RBI	BB	SO	OBP	SLG
Mike Simms	.000	12	0	0	0	0	0	0	2	.000	.000	Ellis Burks	.700	10	7	1	0	0	1	2	1	.750	.800
Tom Prince	.000	9	0	0	0	0	0	1	3	.182	.000	Chipper Jones	.500	12	6	1	0	2	6	0	2	.500	1.083
Tony Gwynn	.067	15	1	0	0	0	1	0	6	.067	.067	Ryne Sandberg	.417	12	5	1	0	4	7	1	2	.462	1.500
Roberto Kelly	.077	13	1	0	0	0	1	0	6	.077	.077	Mike Piazza	.400	10	4	1	0	2	4	1	3	.417	1.100
Larry Walker	.077	13	1	0	0	0	2	2	0	.200	.077	Matt Williams	.357	14	5	1	0	3	7	1	4	.471	1.071

Age 28 – Pitches Right (groundball pitcher)

Dave Weathers — Indians

	ERA	W	L	Sv	G	GS	IP	BB	SO	Avg	H	2B	3B	HR	RBI	OBP	SLG	GF	IR	IRS	Hld	SvOp	SB	CS	GB	FB	G/F
1997 Season	8.42	1	3	0	19	1	25.2	15	18	.355	38	4	3	3	24	.435	.533	5	17	4	0	—	2	1	38	27	1.41
Last Five Years	5.68	17	27	0	127	58	385.1	181	237	.307	473	77	13	35	239	.384	.442	16	53	20	4	1	30	13	644	368	1.75

1997 Season

	ERA	W	L	Sv	G	GS	IP	H	HR	BB	SO		Avg	AB	H	2B	3B	HR	RBI	BB	SO	OBP	SLG
Home	9.28	1	1	0	9	0	10.2	22	1	8	7	vs. Left	.354	48	17	2	2	2	11	4	9	.404	.604
Away	7.80	0	2	0	10	1	15.0	16	2	8	10	vs. Right	.356	59	21	2	1	1	13	11	9	.458	.475

Last Five Years

	ERA	W	L	Sv	G	GS	IP	H	HR	BB	SO		Avg	AB	H	2B	3B	HR	RBI	BB	SO	OBP	SLG
Home	6.13	10	12	0	60	27	183.2	240	12	103	101	vs. Left	.329	756	249	44	10	14	114	97	95	.409	.470
Away	5.27	7	15	0	67	31	201.2	233	23	78	136	vs. Right	.285	785	224	33	3	21	125	84	142	.359	.415
Day	5.87	4	6	0	38	13	99.2	118	12	48	67	Inning 1-6	.306	1295	396	65	10	30	200	147	190	.379	.441
Night	5.61	13	21	0	89	45	285.2	355	23	133	170	Inning 7+	.313	246	77	12	3	5	39	34	47	.406	.447
Grass	6.24	13	24	0	101	44	293.0	377	30	152	178	None on	.294	810	238	42	7	17	17	81	132	.360	.426
Turf	3.90	4	3	0	26	14	92.1	96	5	29	59	Runners on	.321	731	235	35	6	18	222	100	105	.408	.460
March/April	3.24	4	2	0	27	5	58.1	63	6	26	33	Scoring Posn	.307	424	130	22	3	7	190	75	66	.415	.422
May	5.00	4	4	0	17	12	77.1	88	4	39	44	Close & Late	.367	79	29	3	1	2	15	12	17	.468	.506
June	4.38	3	5	0	15	14	74.0	85	5	29	33	None on/out	.335	385	129	22	3	11	11	30	39	.388	.494
July	8.26	2	7	0	33	10	77.1	111	9	39	58	vs. 1st Batr (relief)	.310	58	18	3	0	0	11	0	6	.406	.362
August	8.45	2	5	0	13	10	43.2	65	9	22	29	1st Inning Pitched	.313	447	140	19	4	8	82	57	76	.397	.427
Sept/Oct	5.10	2	4	0	22	7	54.2	61	2	26	40	First 15 Pitches	.315	356	112	16	4	6	45	38	51	.391	.426
Starter	5.56	15	23	0	58	58	299.2	371	28	133	171	Pitch 16-30	.298	319	95	15	1	8	60	44	59	.354	.343
Reliever	6.09	2	4	0	69	0	85.2	102	7	48	66	Pitch 31-45	.262	248	65	11	3	1	29	34	36	.354	.343
0 Days rest (Relief)	3.24	0	0	0	15	0	16.2	21	2	4	9	Pitch 46+	.325	618	201	35	5	20	105	65	91	.393	.498
1 or 2 Days rest	4.65	1	2	0	25	0	31.0	30	2	24	27	First Pitch	.366	235	86	16	3	8	51	12	0	.405	.562
3+ Days rest	8.53	1	2	0	29	0	38.0	51	3	20	30	Ahead in Count	.237	637	151	23	8	5	66	0	194	.248	.322
vs. AL	8.79	1	5	0	30	5	43.0	61	4	29	31	Behind in Count	.348	382	133	19	1	16	75	90	0	.472	.529
vs. NL	5.28	16	22	0	97	53	342.1	412	31	152	206	Two Strikes	.230	656	151	28	6	8	64	79	237	.319	.328
Pre-All Star	4.55	12	12	0	65	35	231.1	263	18	104	124	Pre-All Star	.291	903	263	39	9	18	117	104	124	.369	.414
Post-All Star	7.36	5	15	0	62	23	154.0	210	17	77	113	Post-All Star	.329	638	210	38	4	17	122	77	113	.404	.481

Pitcher vs. Batter (career)

Pitches Best Vs.	Avg	AB	H	2B	3B	HR	RBI	BB	SO	OBP	SLG	Pitches Worst Vs.	Avg	AB	H	2B	3B	HR	RBI	BB	SO	OBP	SLG
Kevin Stocker	.071	14	1	0	0	0	1	1	2	.188	.071	Dave Clark	.667	15	10	2	0	1	4	0	0	.667	1.000
Charlie Hayes	.077	13	1	1	0	0	0	0	3	.250	.154	Jeff Kent	.600	15	9	3	1	0	8	3	2	.684	.933
Jeff Bagwell	.083	12	1	0	0	0	0	0	3	.083	.083	Tony Tarasco	.600	10	6	2	0	0	1	1	1	.636	.800
Jay Bell	.091	11	1	0	0	0	1	2	3	.231	.091	Barry Bonds	.545	11	6	1	0	1	5	3	1	.643	.909
Al Martin	.167	18	3	0	0	0	1	2	2	.250	.167	Bobby Bonilla	.400	10	4	1	0	1	1	5	1	.538	1.000

Lenny Webster — Orioles

Age 33 – Bats Right (groundball hitter)

	Avg	G	AB	R	H	2B	3B	HR	RBI	BB	SO	HBP	GDP	SB	CS	OBP	SLG	IBB	SH	SF	#Pit	#P/PA	FB	G/F
1997 Season	.255	98	259	29	66	8	1	7	37	22	46	2	10	0	1	.317	.375	0	3	1	1056	3.68	112	57	1.96
Last Five Years	.248	331	832	92	206	39	1	19	99	90	126	10	32	1	1	.328	.365	4	6	2	3473	3.69	371	190	1.95

1997 Season

	Avg	AB	H	2B	3B	HR	RBI	BB	SO	OBP	SLG		Avg	AB	H	2B	3B	HR	RBI	BB	SO	OBP	SLG
vs. Left	.259	81	21	5	0	3	12	9	15	.330	.432	Scoring Posn	.265	68	18	2	1	2	28	3	10	.301	.412
vs. Right	.253	178	45	3	1	4	25	13	31	.311	.348	Close & Late	.225	40	9	2	0	1	5	3	6	.279	.350
Home	.216	134	29	2	0	3	16	9	24	.274	.299	None on/out	.254	67	17	1	0	0	4	12	.306	.269
Away	.296	125	37	6	1	4	21	13	22	.362	.456	Batting #7	.216	37	8	2	0	1	6	6	8	.326	.351
First Pitch	.256	43	11	3	0	1	9	0	0	.250	.395	Batting #8	.251	219	55	6	0	5	27	15	38	.304	.347
Ahead in Count	.409	66	27	2	1	6	17	9	0	.487	.742	Other	1.000	3	3	0	1	1	4	1	0	1.000	2.667
Behind in Count	.105	105	11	1	0	0	6	0	40	.113	.114	Pre-All Star	.256	125	32	3	0	3	18	11	21	.314	.352
Two Strikes	.118	110	13	1	0	4	13	46	.218	.127		Post-All Star	.254	134	34	5	1	4	19	11	25	.320	.396

Last Five Years

	Avg	AB	H	2B	3B	HR	RBI	BB	SO	OBP	SLG		Avg	AB	H	2B	3B	HR	RBI	BB	SO	OBP	SLG
vs. Left	.265	294	78	23	0	7	37	42	39	.364	.415	First Pitch	.262	126	33	9	0	4	26	3	0	.291	.429
vs. Right	.238	538	128	16	1	12	62	48	87	.307	.338	Ahead in Count	.336	229	77	13	1	13	42	42	0	.447	.572
Groundball	.282	202	57	13	0	6	28	20	32	.354	.436	Behind in Count	.152	335	51	4	0	0	18	0	111	.160	.164
Flyball	.279	111	31	7	0	4	17	15	15	.375	.450	Two Strikes	.162	346	56	9	0	1	21	45	126	.262	.197
Home	.234	436	102	20	0	8	44	35	60	.302	.335	Batting #7	.235	281	66	15	0	4	31	32	40	.317	.331
Away	.263	396	104	19	1	11	55	55	66	.355	.399	Batting #8	.261	364	95	13	0	7	41	34	54	.326	.354
Day	.234	320	75	14	1	8	41	39	49	.320	.359	Other	.241	187	45	11	1	8	27	24	32	.346	.439
Night	.256	512	131	25	0	11	58	51	77	.332	.369	March/April	.205	73	15	5	0	1	7	11	7	.326	.315
Grass	.239	402	96	13	1	13	55	44	69	.319	.373	May	.257	148	38	6	0	2	17	14	27	.327	.338
Turf	.256	430	110	26	0	6	44	46	57	.336	.358	June	.267	150	40	7	0	2	22	14	24	.331	.353
Pre-All Star	.243	423	103	18	0	8	54	43	64	.321	.343	July	.191	157	30	4	0	4	14	12	18	.257	.293
Post-All Star	.252	409	103	21	1	11	45	47	62	.335	.389	August	.266	139	37	8	0	4	22	17	21	.358	.410
Scoring Posn	.232	233	54	7	1	4	78	26	44	.322	.322	Sept/Oct	.279	146	46	9	1	6	17	22	29	.364	.455
Close & Late	.234	141	33	5	0	3	16	18	26	.321	.333	vs. AL	.218	335	73	10	0	5	35	31	49	.285	.293
None on/out	.250	192	48	8	0	1		15	22	.304	.307	vs. NL	.268	497	133	29	1	14	64	59	77	.355	.414

Batter vs. Pitcher (career)

Hits Best Against	Avg	AB	H	2B	3B	HR	RBI	BB	SO	OBP	SLG	Hits Worst Against	Avg	AB	H	2B	3B	HR	RBI	BB	SO	OBP	SLG
Chuck Finley	.417	12	5	1	0	0	1	0	3	.417	.500	Robert Person	.000	11	0	0	0	0	0	0	2	.000	.000
Denny Neagle	.385	13	5	0	0	1	1	2	2	.467	.615	Charles Nagy	.000	10	0	0	0	0	0	2	3	.167	.000
Kenny Rogers	.364	11	4	0	0	1	1	1	4	.417	.364	Pete Schourek	.000	9	0	0	0	0	0	3	2	.250	.000
												Roger Clemens	.100	10	1	0	0	0	0	1	1	.182	.100
												Tom Glavine	.200	20	4	1	0	0	1	1	4	.273	.250

John Wehner — Marlins

Age 31 – Bats Right (groundball hitter)

	Avg	G	AB	R	H	2B	3B	HR	RBI	BB	SO	HBP	GDP	SB	CS	OBP	SLG	IBB	SH	SF	#Pit	#P/PA	GB	FB	G/F
1997 Season	.278	44	36	8	10	2	0	0	2	2	5	1	2	1	2	.333	.333	0	1	0	137	3.43	19	4	4.75
Last Five Years	.265	213	321	44	85	12	4	2	23	26	55	1	7	5	6	.320	.346	3	9	2	1229	3.42	146	70	2.09

1997 Season

	Avg	AB	H	2B	3B	HR	RBI	BB	SO	OBP	SLG		Avg	AB	H	2B	3B	HR	RBI	BB	SO	OBP	SLG
vs. Left	.000	9	0	0	0	0	1	2	1	.182	.000	Scoring Posn	.000	11	0	0	0	0	1	0	1	.000	.000
vs. Right	.370	27	10	2	0	0	1	0	4	.393	.444	Close & Late	.375	8	3	1	0	0	0	1	.375	.500

Walt Weiss — Rockies

Age 34 – Bats Both (groundball hitter)

	Avg	G	AB	R	H	2B	3B	HR	RBI	BB	SO	HBP	GDP	SB	CS	OBP	SLG	IBB	SH	SF	#Pit	#P/PA	GB	FB	G/F
1997 Season	.270	121	393	52	106	23	5	4	38	66	56	2	7	5	2	.377	.384	3	7	1	1832	3.91	179	98	1.83
Last Five Years	.266	681	2260	314	602	85	16	15	182	379	322	16	34	49	17	.373	.338	29	36	15	10173	3.76	993	506	1.96

1997 Season

	Avg	AB	H	2B	3B	HR	RBI	BB	SO	OBP	SLG		Avg	AB	H	2B	3B	HR	RBI	BB	SO	OBP	SLG
vs. Left	.192	99	19	3	1	0	6	17	16	.310	.273	First Pitch	.340	53	18	3	0	0	4	2	0	.364	.396
vs. Right	.296	294	87	20	4	3	32	49	40	.399	.422	Ahead in Count	.344	90	31	8	1	3	18	31	0	.512	.556
Groundball	.244	82	20	2	1	1	9	15	14	.361	.329	Behind in Count	.193	145	28	8	0	0	6	0	40	.199	.248
Flyball	.193	57	11	3	0	0	3	10	8	.323	.246	Two Strikes	.185	173	32	9	2	1	8	31	56	.309	.277
Home	.301	206	62	13	4	2	23	38	25	.411	.432	Batting #1	.272	114	31	9	0	2	10	28	15	.417	.404
Away	.235	187	44	10	1	2	15	28	31	.338	.332	Batting #8	.247	251	62	11	3	2	25	34	36	.339	.339
Day	.264	197	52	14	2	2	24	26	29	.348	.386	Other	.464	28	13	3	2	0	3	4	5	.531	.714
Night	.276	196	54	9	3	2	14	40	27	.403	.383	March/April	.269	67	18	5	1	0	9	7	8	.347	.373
Grass	.277	339	94	21	5	4	33	55	48	.379	.404	May	.256	86	22	4	1	2	8	14	10	.360	.395
Turf	.222	54	12	2	0	0	5	11	8	.364	.259	June	.266	79	21	2	0	0	5	14	12	.376	.291
Pre-All Star	.254	244	62	11	3	2	22	35	35	.350	.348	July	.321	28	9	2	2	0	2	1	10	.345	.536
Post-All Star	.295	149	44	12	2	2	16	31	21	.418	.443	August	.267	60	16	6	1	0	8	10	7	.375	.400
Scoring Posn	.300	80	24	5	1	0	29	14	7	.400	.388	Sept/Oct	.274	73	20	4	0	2	6	20	9	.430	.411
Close & Late	.250	56	14	2	0	0	6	11	3	.373	.286	vs. AL	.340	47	16	5	0	1	6	10	9	.458	.511
None on/out	.231	121	28	4	1	2	2	24	22	.359	.331	vs. NL	.260	346	90	18	5	3	32	56	48	.365	.367

1997 By Position

Position	Avg	AB	H	2B	3B	HR	RBI	BB	SO	OBP	SLG	G	GS	Innings	PO	A	E	DP	Fld Pct	Rng Fctr	In Zone	Zone Outs	Zone Rtg	MLB Zone
As ss	.265	389	103	22	4	4	38	65	56	.372	.373	119	112	971.2	192	372	10	89	.983	5.22	401	377	940	.937

Last Five Years

	Avg	AB	H	2B	3B	HR	RBI	BB	SO	OBP	SLG		Avg	AB	H	2B	3B	HR	RBI	BB	SO	OBP	SLG
vs. Left	.258	578	149	20	2	2	37	100	82	.367	.310	First Pitch	.338	325	110	15	2	3	43	19	0	.372	.425
vs. Right	.269	1682	453	65	14	13	145	279	240	.376	.348	Ahead in Count	.302	530	160	21	4	5	54	185	0	.480	.385
Groundball	.275	629	173	20	4	2	42	104	90	.381	.329	Behind in Count	.214	936	200	32	4	4	54	0	273	.223	.269
Flyball	.252	369	93	16	0	1	24	54	71	.347	.304	Two Strikes	.194	952	185	26	4	1	43	173	322	.323	.233
Home	.287	1142	328	40	10	8	112	206	158	.396	.361	Batting #1	.269	616	166	24	5	4	47	110	80	.383	.344
Away	.245	1118	274	45	6	7	70	173	164	.350	.315	Batting #8	.266	1266	337	46	8	6	106	216	181	.376	.329
Day	.248	814	202	40	6	8	76	131	119	.353	.342	Other	.262	378	99	15	3	5	29	53	61	.349	.357
Night	.277	1446	400	45	10	7	106	248	203	.385	.336	March/April	.276	344	95	8	4	2	36	50	51	.370	.340
Grass	.274	1818	499	69	13	13	152	308	258	.380	.348	May	.297	451	134	19	6	2	32	74	55	.400	.379
Turf	.233	442	103	16	3	2	30	71	64	.345	.296	June	.254	457	116	14	0	2	31	67	66	.348	.298
Pre-All Star	.270	1377	372	46	11	6	109	211	195	.369	.333	July	.245	388	95	16	2	2	34	59	66	.345	.312
Post-All Star	.260	883	230	39	5	9	73	168	127	.380	.347	August	.259	332	86	16	3	3	30	59	46	.377	.352
Scoring Posn	.238	496	118	20	3	1	154	107	78	.368	.296	Sept/Oct	.264	288	76	12	1	4	19	70	38	.407	.354
Close & Late	.266	354	94	10	1	1	31	73	51	.391	.308	vs. AL	.340	47	16	5	0	1	6	10	8	.458	.511
None on/out	.253	655	166	17	5	5	116	116		.368	.318	vs. NL	.265	2213	586	80	16	14	176	369	314	.372	.334

Batter vs. Pitcher (career)

Hits Best Against	Avg	AB	H	2B	3B	HR	RBI	BB	SO	OBP	SLG	Hits Worst Against	Avg	AB	H	2B	3B	HR	RBI	BB	SO	OBP	SLG
Todd Worrell	.556	9	5	1	0	0	5	0	2	.455	.667	Sid Fernandez	.000	9	0	0	0	0	0	2	4	.182	.000
Kirk Rueter	.545	11	6	2	0	0	1	2	0	.615	.727	Jack McDowell	.048	21	1	0	0	0	1	0	4	.048	.048
Esteban Loaiza	.462	13	6	3	0	1	4	2	1	.533	.923	Donne Wall	.071	14	1	0	0	0	0	1	3	.133	.071
Kevin Foster	.444	9	4	2	0	1	3	4	2	.615	1.000	David Wells	.077	13	1	0	0	0	2	1	1	.143	.077
Mark Wohlers	.429	7	3	1	0	0	1	5	2	.667	.571	Rheal Cormier	.091	11	1	0	0	0	0	1	2	.167	.091

Bob Wells — Mariners

Age 31 – Pitches Right (flyball pitcher)

	ERA	W	L	Sv	G	GS	IP	BB	SO	Avg	H	2B	3B	HR	RBI	OBP	SLG	GF	IR	IRS	Hld	SvOp	SB	CS	GB	FB	G/F
1997 Season	5.75	2	0	2	46	1	67.1	18	51	.314	88	21	0	11	49	.360	.507	19	21	8	5	4	3	6	75	102	0.74
Career (1994-1997)	5.43	20	10	2	119	21	283.2	107	189	.286	325	81	6	47	174	.351	.491	30	77	27	6	5	14	11	297	450	0.66

1997 Season

	ERA	W	L	Sv	G	GS	IP	H	HR	BB	SO		Avg	AB	H	2B	3B	HR	RBI	BB	SO	OBP	SLG
Home	4.68	1	0	1	21	1	32.2	42	4	12	25	vs. Left	.301	113	34	2	0	3	15	11	21	.370	.398
Away	6.75	1	0	1	25	0	34.2	46	7	6	26	vs. Right	.323	167	54	19	0	8	34	7	30	.352	.581
Starter	9.00	0	0	0	1	1	3.0	4	0	3	3	Scoring Posn	.354	79	28	7	0	2	33	4	11	.376	.519
Reliever	5.60	2	0	2	45	0	64.1	84	11	15	48	Close & Late	.240	50	12	5	0	2	7	2	9	.269	.460
0 Days rest (Relief)	9.00	0	0	0	4	0	2.0	4	0	0	3	None on/out	.318	66	21	0	0	2	2	3	11	.357	.500
1 or 2 Days rest	6.11	1	0	2	21	0	28.0	42	6	4	23	First Pitch	.333	33	11	1	0	2	5	1	0	.371	.545
3+ Days rest	4.98	1	0	0	20	0	34.1	38	5	11	22	Ahead in Count	.273	139	38	6	0	3	20	0	40	.277	.381
Pre-All Star	7.59	2	0	0	25	1	32.0	46	7	14	25	Behind in Count	.460	50	23	9	0	4	10	4	0	.509	.880
Post-All Star	4.08	0	0	2	21	0	35.1	42	4	4	26	Two Strikes	.236	144	34	7	0	2	21	13	51	.300	.326

Career (1994-1997)

	ERA	W	L	Sv	G	GS	IP	H	HR	BB	SO		Avg	AB	H	2B	3B	HR	RBI	BB	SO	OBP	SLG
Home	5.28	7	5	1	56	10	133.0	151	19	52	89	vs. Left	.299	521	156	33	3	21	75	58	73	.374	.495
Away	5.56	13	5	1	63	11	150.2	174	28	55	100	vs. Right	.274	617	169	48	3	26	99	49	116	.331	.488
Day	5.17	7	3	2	43	8	102.2	115	15	37	62	Inning 1-6	.289	752	217	53	6	31	120	66	117	.350	.499
Night	5.57	13	7	0	76	13	181.0	210	32	70	127	Inning 7+	.280	386	108	28	0	16	54	41	72	.351	.477
Grass	6.10	9	5	1	54	9	121.0	147	26	46	79	None on	.282	621	175	46	3	21	56	120		.347	.467
Turf	4.92	11	5	1	65	12	162.2	178	21	61	110	Runners on	.290	517	150	35	3	26	153	51	69	.355	.520
March/April	4.35	2	1	0	15	2	31.0	29	4	15	24	Scoring Posn	.291	282	82	20	2	11	114	35	37	.364	.493
May	5.49	6	3	0	29	3	57.1	62	7	24	48	Close & Late	.316	95	30	9	0	4	15	8	15	.369	.537
June	5.11	6	0	0	19	5	49.1	57	9	19	28	None on/out	.286	276	79	22	1	9	9	22	42	.343	.471
July	4.21	3	2	2	21	6	72.2	73	14	21	54	vs. 1st Batr (relief)	.384	86	33	10	0	3	20	11	9	.449	.605
August	7.04	2	3	0	23	4	55.0	77	11	20	23	1st Inning Pitched	.294	432	127	34	1	14	82	49	70	.374	.475
Sept/Oct	7.85	1	1	0	12	1	18.1	27	2	8	12	First 15 Pitches	.320	300	96	22	1	11	51	33	40	.398	.510
Starter	7.04	7	8	0	21	21	99.2	126	21	33	62	Pitch 16-30	.262	279	73	19	1	12	48	36	60	.351	.466
Reliever	4.55	13	2	2	98	0	184.0	199	26	74	127	Pitch 31-45	.257	202	52	12	1	6	22	12	35	.302	.416
0 Days rest (Relief)	7.71	2	0	0	6	0	7.0	9	0	1	7	Pitch 46+	.291	357	104	28	3	18	53	26	54	.336	.538
1 or 2 Days rest	4.61	4	1	2	38	0	56.2	65	8	17	43	First Pitch	.336	146	49	11	1	9	32	8	0	.373	.610
3+ Days rest	4.34	7	1	0	54	0	120.1	125	18	56	77	Ahead in Count	.230	508	117	29	1	11	53	0	152	.242	.356
vs. AL	5.35	18	10	2	107	21	269.1	305	42	102	179	Behind in Count	.352	227	80	24	3	17	48	48	0	.466	.709
vs. NL	6.91	2	0	0	12	0	14.1	20	5	5	10	Two Strikes	.217	557	121	27	0	12	60	51	189	.289	.330
Pre-All Star	5.22	14	5	0	69	12	160.1	175	26	67	117	Pre-All Star	.274	638	175	43	3	26	102	67	117	.348	.473
Post-All Star	5.69	6	5	2	50	9	123.1	150	21	40	72	Post-All Star	.300	500	150	38	3	21	72	40	72	.354	.514

Pitcher vs. Batter (career)

Pitches Best Vs.	Avg	AB	H	2B	3B	HR	RBI	BB	SO	OBP	SLG	Pitches Worst Vs.	Avg	AB	H	2B	3B	HR	RBI	BB	SO	OBP	SLG
Chuck Knoblauch	.091	11	1	0	0	1	2	0	3	.167	.364	Cecil Fielder	.571	7	4	1	0	2	8	4	1	.727	1.571
Mo Vaughn	.125	8	1	0	0	0	2	2	2	.364	.125	Greg Myers	.455	11	5	1	0	2	4	1	1	.500	1.091
Marty Cordova	.182	11	2	1	0	0	2	1	2	.250	.273	John Valentin	.417	12	5	2	0	0	0	3	0	.533	.583
Chili Davis	.200	10	2	0	0	0	1	2	0	.333	.200	Frank Thomas	.400	10	4	1	0	2	4	1	1	.455	1.100
Tony Phillips	.200	10	2	0	0	0	1	2	2	.333	.200	Mike Matheny	.364	11	4	1	1	1	2	0	4	.364	.909

David Wells — Yankees
Age 35 – Pitches Left

	ERA	W	L	Sv	G	GS	IP	BB	SO	Avg	H	2B	3B	HR	RBI	OBP	SLG	CG	ShO	Sup	QS	#P/S	SB	CS	GB	FB	G/F
1997 Season	4.21	16	10	0	32	32	218.0	45	156	.278	239	53	5	24	100	.317	.434	5	2	5.12	17	102	19	8	287	243	1.18
Last Five Years	4.19	59	48	0	143	141	943.2	215	629	.267	976	199	20	118	424	.310	.429	19	3	5.18	81	101	80	34	1251	1096	1.14

1997 Season

	ERA	W	L	Sv	G	GS	IP	H	HR	BB	SO		Avg	AB	H	2B	3B	HR	RBI	BB	SO	OBP	SLG
Home	3.88	8	5	0	17	17	116.0	136	13	22	89	vs. Left	.327	159	52	9	2	3	22	3	23	.344	.465
Away	4.59	8	5	0	15	15	102.0	103	11	23	67	vs. Right	.266	702	187	44	3	21	78	42	133	.311	.427
Day	4.31	4	4	0	10	10	64.2	70	10	14	53	Inning 1-6	.281	701	197	44	4	20	85	38	131	.323	.441
Night	4.17	12	6	0	22	22	153.1	169	14	31	103	Inning 7+	.263	160	42	9	1	4	15	7	25	.290	.406
Grass	4.37	13	9	0	28	28	187.1	214	21	38	131	None on	.284	483	137	26	5	10	10	28	83	.327	.420
Turf	3.23	3	1	0	4	4	30.2	25	3	7	25	Runners on	.270	378	102	27	0	14	90	17	73	.304	.452
March/April	3.66	2	1	0	6	6	39.1	48	5	10	27	Scoring Posn	.239	209	50	9	0	8	74	15	46	.293	.397
May	4.21	3	2	0	5	5	36.1	34	4	5	20	Close & Late	.286	77	22	5	1	2	9	4	10	.317	.455
June	4.20	3	1	0	5	5	30.0	31	3	5	20	None on/out	.288	215	62	11	2	3	16	36	.341	.400
July	2.75	3	1	0	5	5	36.0	29	3	9	32	vs. 1st Batr (relief)	.000	0	0	0	0	0	0	0	0	.000	.000
August	5.95	3	3	0	6	6	42.1	49	8	10	35	1st Inning Pitched	.263	118	31	8	0	10	10	29	.331	.331
Sept/Oct	4.24	2	2	0	5	5	34.0	48	1	6	22	First 75 Pitches	.275	596	164	38	3	17	69	33	112	.319	.435
Starter	4.21	16	10	0	32	32	218.0	239	24	45	156	Pitch 76-90	.333	126	42	11	2	5	20	3	16	.348	.571
Reliever	0.00	0	0	0	0	0	0.0	0	0	0	0	Pitch 91-105	.200	85	17	1	0	1	4	6	20	.253	.247
0-3 Days Rest (Start)	0.00	0	0	0	0	0	0.0	0	0	0	0	Pitch 106+	.296	54	16	3	0	1	7	3	8	.328	.407
4 Days Rest	3.86	12	6	0	20	20	137.2	139	14	27	101	First Pitch	.413	138	57	16	1	4	20	0	0	.418	.630
5+ Days Rest	4.82	4	4	0	12	12	80.1	100	10	18	55	Ahead in Count	.198	424	84	15	1	10	44	0	141	.205	.309
vs. AL	4.23	15	9	0	30	30	202.0	224	21	44	143	Behind in Count	.379	161	61	13	2	6	21	28	0	.471	.596
vs. NL	3.94	1	1	0	2	2	16.0	15	3	1	13	Two Strikes	.168	394	66	12	1	7	32	17	156	.206	.256
Pre-All Star	3.82	9	4	0	17	17	113.0	118	12	23	73	Pre-All Star	.269	438	118	24	1	12	47	23	73	.310	.411
Post-All Star	4.63	7	6	0	15	15	105.0	121	12	22	83	Post-All Star	.286	423	121	29	4	12	53	22	83	.324	.459

Last Five Years

	ERA	W	L	Sv	G	GS	IP	H	HR	BB	SO		Avg	AB	H	2B	3B	HR	RBI	BB	SO	OBP	SLG
Home	3.32	38	18	0	75	74	526.2	512	54	101	365	vs. Left	.260	680	177	28	7	15	76	26	116	.292	.388
Away	5.29	21	30	0	68	67	417.0	464	64	114	264	vs. Right	.268	2976	799	171	13	103	348	189	513	.314	.439
Day	4.76	16	17	0	44	43	276.0	292	44	56	191	Inning 1-6	.265	3045	807	166	16	98	369	186	548	.310	.427
Night	3.95	43	31	0	99	98	667.2	684	74	159	438	Inning 7+	.277	611	169	33	4	20	55	29	81	.310	.442
Grass	4.29	48	39	0	118	116	780.0	817	100	174	503	None on	.269	2219	598	110	16	64	64	99	383	.306	.420
Turf	3.68	11	9	0	25	25	163.2	159	18	41	126	Runners on	.263	1437	378	89	4	54	360	116	246	.316	.443
March/April	3.53	9	6	0	20	20	130.0	133	16	27	78	Scoring Posn	.257	783	201	47	1	28	290	91	146	.329	.427
May	4.01	8	8	0	22	22	150.1	143	19	32	94	Close & Late	.293	317	93	24	3	9	33	17	39	.327	.473
June	4.59	12	8	0	28	28	188.1	195	26	52	122	None on/out	.294	971	285	53	8	33	33	44	172	.328	.467
July	3.78	13	9	0	27	27	188.1	184	20	39	130	vs. 1st Batr (relief)	.500	2	1	0	0	1	1	0	0	.500	2.000
August	4.22	11	7	0	23	21	145.0	152	19	31	100	1st Inning Pitched	.252	532	134	29	3	11	58	40	111	.307	.380
Sept/Oct	4.96	6	10	0	23	23	141.2	169	18	34	100	First 75 Pitches	.262	2580	677	138	13	84	293	159	466	.308	.424
Starter	4.18	59	48	0	141	141	940.1	971	117	215	626	Pitch 76-90	.295	485	143	35	4	17	68	21	72	.327	.489
Reliever	5.40	0	0	0	2	0	3.1	5	1	0	3	Pitch 91-105	.265	347	92	16	1	10	39	17	56	.300	.403
0-3 Days Rest (Start)	3.66	7	3	0	13	13	78.2	91	10	22	47	Pitch 106+	.262	244	64	10	2	7	24	18	35	.312	.406
4 Days Rest	4.17	39	28	0	89	89	603.2	595	75	142	418	First Pitch	.330	546	180	41	5	18	68	19	0	.352	.516
5+ Days Rest	4.36	13	17	0	39	39	258.0	285	32	51	161	Ahead in Count	.205	1720	353	66	4	38	149	0	548	.212	.315
vs. AL	4.24	52	42	0	130	128	855.0	887	109	198	566	Behind in Count	.356	742	264	57	8	42	128	108	0	.437	.624
vs. NL	3.65	7	6	0	13	13	88.2	89	9	17	63	Two Strikes	.185	1678	310	62	3	36	130	86	629	.230	.290
Pre-All Star	4.16	33	24	0	78	78	524.0	530	68	121	328	Pre-All Star	.263	2019	530	106	7	68	233	121	328	.307	.423
Post-All Star	4.22	26	24	0	65	63	419.2	446	50	94	301	Post-All Star	.272	1637	446	93	13	50	191	94	301	.314	.437

Pitcher vs. Batter (career)

Pitches Best Vs.	Avg	AB	H	2B	3B	HR	RBI	BB	SO	OBP	SLG	Pitches Worst Vs.	Avg	AB	H	2B	3B	HR	RBI	BB	SO	OBP	SLG
Jeff King	.000	10	0	0	0	0	0	2	2	.167	.000	Ron Coomer	.615	13	8	0	0	1	2	0	0	.615	.846
Omar Vizquel	.036	28	1	0	0	0	1	1	5	.069	.036	Ray Durham	.500	20	10	3	0	1	3	1	0	.500	.800
Rusty Greer	.071	14	1	0	0	0	1	0	1	.067	.071	Rex Hudler	.400	15	6	1	0	2	4	1	1	.438	.867
Paul O'Neill	.071	14	1	0	0	0	0	0	1	.071	.071	Cecil Fielder	.381	21	8	0	0	4	10	5	4	.500	.952
Dave Nilsson	.077	13	1	0	0	0	0	0	1	.077	.077	Frank Thomas	.372	43	16	4	1	5	10	11	7	.500	.860

Turk Wendell — Mets
Age 31 – Pitches Right

	ERA	W	L	Sv	G	GS	IP	BB	SO	Avg	H	2B	3B	HR	RBI	OBP	SLG	GF	IR	IRS	Hld	SvOp	SB	CS	GB	FB	G/F
1997 Season	4.36	3	5	5	65	0	76.1	53	64	.240	68	21	3	7	38	.361	.410	21	22	6	2	7	5	3	86	85	1.01
Career (1993-1997)	4.45	11	14	23	191	6	253.0	139	213	.253	243	50	4	29	134	.349	.404	89	95	29	11	28	13	9	343	248	1.38

1997 Season

	ERA	W	L	Sv	G	GS	IP	BB	SO		Avg	AB	H	2B	3B	HR	RBI	BB	SO	OBP	SLG
Home	4.50	3	3	4	33	0	40.0	35	6	28	34	vs. Left	.316	114	36	10	3	4	20	22	16	.431	.561
Away	4.21	0	2	1	32	0	36.1	33	1	25	30	vs. Right	.189	169	32	11	0	3	18	31	48	.314	.308
Day	3.82	1	4	4	31	0	37.2	32	3	26	34	Inning 1-6	.222	45	10	4	0	1	7	7	12	.327	.378
Night	4.89	2	1	1	34	0	38.2	36	4	27	30	Inning 7+	.244	238	58	17	3	6	31	46	52	.367	.416
Grass	4.11	3	4	5	54	0	61.1	52	6	46	54	None on	.250	148	37	11	1	3	3	24	37	.358	.399
Turf	5.40	0	1	0	11	0	15.0	16	1	7	10	Runners on	.230	135	31	10	2	4	35	29	27	.363	.422
March/April	4.80	0	2	1	12	0	15.0	13	1	10	19	Scoring Posn	.284	74	21	8	2	3	32	22	15	.440	.568
May	6.10	2	1	0	10	0	10.1	11	1	5	5	Close & Late	.237	97	23	6	2	2	19	20	24	.370	.402
June	2.08	0	0	3	12	0	17.1	10	1	10	15	None on/out	.273	66	18	5	1	2	2	16	17	.415	.470
July	3.86	1	2	0	15	0	14.0	13	1	13	12	vs. 1st Batr (relief)	.191	47	9	3	1	1	4	17	16	.400	.362
August	3.95	0	0	0	12	0	13.2	13	1	14	8	1st Inning Pitched	.216	185	40	15	3	4	28	40	51	.357	.395

494

1997 Season

	ERA	W	L	Sv	G	GS	IP	H	HR	BB	SO		Avg	AB	H	2B	3B	HR	RBI	BB	SO	OBP	SLG
Sept/Oct	9.00	0	0	1	4	0	6.0	8	2	1	5	First 15 Pitches	.235	153	36	10	2	4	19	35	36	.382	.405
Starter	0.00	0	0	0	0	0	0.0	0	0	0	0	Pitch 16-30	.255	98	25	9	1	2	14	16	22	.353	.429
Reliever	4.36	3	5	5	65	0	76.1	68	7	53	64	Pitch 31-45	.185	27	5	2	0	0	3	2	6	.241	.259
0 Days rest (Relief)	6.00	1	0	2	18	0	15.0	16	1	15	13	Pitch 46+	.400	5	2	0	0	1	2	0	0	.400	1.000
1 or 2 Days rest	3.65	1	1	0	28	0	37.0	28	1	26	33	First Pitch	.250	36	9	2	0	2	8	5	0	.372	.472
3+ Days rest	4.44	1	4	3	19	0	24.1	24	5	12	18	Ahead in Count	.182	159	29	7	1	2	11	0	57	.180	.277
vs. AL	2.89	0	0	3	6	0	9.1	5	2	5	9	Behind in Count	.356	45	16	7	1	2	9	31	0	.610	.689
vs. NL	4.57	3	5	2	59	0	67.0	63	5	48	55	Two Strikes	.182	154	28	8	1	1	12	17	64	.260	.266
Pre-All Star	4.63	2	3	4	37	0	44.2	38	3	28	40	Pre-All Star	.229	166	38	16	1	3	23	28	40	.338	.392
Post-All Star	3.98	1	2	1	28	0	31.2	30	4	25	24	Post-All Star	.256	117	30	5	2	4	15	25	24	.392	.436

Career (1993-1997)

	ERA	W	L	Sv	G	GS	IP	H	HR	BB	SO		Avg	AB	H	2B	3B	HR	RBI	BB	SO	OBP	SLG
Home	4.06	8	7	12	101	1	133.0	114	15	75	121	vs. Left	.299	401	120	23	3	11	56	62	63	.394	.454
Away	4.88	3	7	11	90	5	120.0	129	14	64	92	vs. Right	.220	559	123	27	1	18	78	77	150	.317	.369
Day	3.82	7	10	17	110	2	141.1	125	13	79	128	Inning 1-6	.297	303	90	20	0	9	60	38	66	.374	.452
Night	5.24	4	4	6	81	4	111.2	118	16	60	85	Inning 7+	.233	657	153	30	4	20	74	101	147	.338	.382
Grass	4.05	10	11	19	155	3	206.2	186	23	108	183	None on	.249	511	127	28	2	11	11	59	118	.330	.376
Turf	6.22	1	3	4	36	3	46.1	57	6	31	30	Runners on	.258	449	116	22	2	18	123	80	95	.370	.437
March/April	4.29	2	3	3	25	1	35.2	33	3	19	45	Scoring Posn	.288	267	77	14	2	11	106	58	55	.409	.479
May	6.16	4	2	1	24	1	30.2	30	3	27	21	Close & Late	.219	310	68	15	2	8	40	55	72	.341	.358
June	4.41	1	3	7	41	3	63.1	63	7	28	45	None on/out	.246	224	55	10	1	6	6	27	50	.332	.379
July	4.04	2	3	3	30	0	35.2	39	5	21	26	vs. 1st Batr (relief)	.212	156	33	6	1	5	21	23	38	.314	.359
August	4.36	0	1	5	39	0	43.1	40	6	25	38	1st Inning Pitched	.224	584	131	25	4	17	87	95	143	.334	.368
Sept/Oct	3.86	2	4	4	32	1	44.1	38	5	19	38	First 15 Pitches	.233	477	111	19	3	14	60	74	105	.339	.373
Starter	7.24	1	3	0	6	6	27.1	37	2	10	19	Pitch 16-30	.264	284	75	16	1	11	42	45	68	.364	.444
Reliever	4.11	10	11	23	185	0	225.2	206	27	129	194	Pitch 31-45	.272	114	31	11	0	1	17	11	23	.336	.395
0 Days rest (Relief)	5.11	2	4	8	47	0	49.1	53	7	30	48	Pitch 46+	.306	85	26	4	0	3	15	9	17	.372	.459
1 or 2 Days rest	3.31	4	2	9	82	0	100.2	81	8	59	93	First Pitch	.330	103	34	7	0	5	26	14	0	.417	.544
3+ Days rest	4.52	4	5	6	56	0	75.2	72	12	40	53	Ahead in Count	.186	505	94	20	2	10	39	0	183	.191	.293
vs. AL	2.89	0	0	3	6	0	9.1	5	2	5	9	Behind in Count	.370	181	67	12	1	10	42	72	0	.545	.613
vs. NL	4.51	11	14	20	185	6	243.2	238	27	134	204	Two Strikes	.177	498	88	23	1	6	39	53	213	.257	.263
Pre-All Star	4.87	8	8	11	96	5	135.0	135	13	79	113	Pre-All Star	.260	519	135	33	1	13	77	79	113	.358	.403
Post-All Star	3.97	3	6	12	95	1	118.0	108	16	60	100	Post-All Star	.245	441	108	17	3	16	57	60	100	.339	.406

Pitcher vs. Batter (career)

Pitches Best Vs.	Avg	AB	H	2B	3B	HR	RBI	BB	SO	OBP	SLG	Pitches Worst Vs.	Avg	AB	H	2B	3B	HR	RBI	BB	SO	OBP	SLG
Archi Cianfrocco	.000	11	0	0	0	0	0	0	4	.000	.000	Gregg Jefferies	.455	11	5	0	1	0	1	2	0	.538	.636
Bernard Gilkey	.000	8	0	0	0	0	0	3	4	.273	.000	Raul Mondesi	.455	11	5	1	0	0	2	0	3	.417	.545
Ron Gant	.111	9	1	0	0	0	0	2	2	.273	.111												
Dante Bichette	.182	11	2	0	0	0	1	0	1	.182	.182												
Walt Weiss	.200	10	2	0	0	0	1	1	1	.273	.200												

Don Wengert — Athletics

Age 28 – Pitches Right

	ERA	W	L	Sv	G	GS	IP	BB	SO	Avg	H	2B	3B	HR	RBI	OBP	SLG	GF	IR	IRS	Hld	SvOp	SB	CS	GB	FB	G/F
1997 Season	6.04	5	11	2	49	12	134.0	41	68	.321	177	41	1	21	93	.372	.514	16	36	14	0	3	5	5	221	147	1.50
Career (1995-1997)	5.57	13	23	2	104	37	325.0	113	159	.309	407	86	8	43	202	.367	.508	28	62	24	3	3	14	9	489	385	1.27

1997 Season

	ERA	W	L	Sv	G	GS	IP	H	HR	BB	SO		Avg	AB	H	2B	3B	HR	RBI	BB	SO	OBP	SLG
Home	6.65	3	7	0	26	6	66.1	98	11	17	30	vs. Left	.326	270	88	23	0	9	40	23	27	.383	.511
Away	5.45	2	4	2	23	6	67.2	79	10	24	38	vs. Right	.317	281	89	18	1	12	53	18	41	.362	.516
Day	6.37	2	3	0	27	6	65.0	88	10	19	29	Inning 1-6	.306	366	112	30	0	17	70	29	47	.364	.527
Night	5.74	3	8	2	22	6	69.0	89	11	22	39	Inning 7+	.351	185	65	11	1	4	23	12	21	.389	.486
Grass	5.97	4	10	2	46	10	120.2	163	19	35	58	None on	.302	295	89	24	0	10	10	11	37	.335	.485
Turf	6.75	1	1	0	3	2	13.1	14	2	6	10	Runners on	.344	256	88	17	1	11	83	30	31	.411	.547
March/April	4.00	1	2	1	9	0	18.0	19	2	8	10	Scoring Posn	.288	170	49	7	1	8	73	23	21	.363	.482
May	5.40	1	1	0	10	1	25.0	38	3	5	14	Close & Late	.481	52	25	4	0	1	10	8	3	.550	.615
June	7.55	1	4	0	6	6	31.0	36	9	12	14	None on/out	.328	134	44	15	0	4	4	3	17	.343	.530
July	4.82	2	2	0	10	2	28.0	34	3	7	17	vs. 1st Batr (relief)	.417	36	15	2	0	3	12	2	1	.447	.722
August	8.14	0	1	0	7	3	21.0	31	2	8	8	1st Inning Pitched	.298	181	54	11	0	5	35	11	21	.345	.442
Sept/Oct	5.73	0	1	1	7	0	11.0	19	2	1	5	First 15 Pitches	.262	145	38	8	0	4	23	9	16	.310	.400
Starter	7.13	2	6	0	12	12	59.1	72	13	18	29	Pitch 16-30	.381	126	48	9	0	7	22	12	14	.443	.468
Reliever	5.18	3	5	2	37	0	74.2	105	8	23	39	Pitch 31-45	.345	119	41	12	0	1	15	8	16	.377	.471
0 Days rest (Relief)	5.40	0	0	0	3	0	8.1	13	0	4	8	Pitch 46+	.311	161	50	12	1	9	33	12	22	.368	.565
1 or 2 Days rest	4.61	2	2	2	22	0	41.0	50	5	12	20	First Pitch	.398	83	33	5	1	2	14	3	0	.424	.554
3+ Days rest	5.34	2	3	0	13	1	30.1	49	4	9	14	Ahead in Count	.221	208	46	12	0	5	27	0	54	.230	.351
vs. AL	5.53	5	9	2	45	10	123.2	159	18	35	64	Behind in Count	.423	130	55	12	0	7	22	22	0	.510	.677
vs. NL	12.19	0	2	0	4	2	10.1	18	3	6	4	Two Strikes	.234	218	51	15	0	8	26	16	68	.291	.413
Pre-All Star	6.15	3	8	1	26	8	79.0	99	15	27	42	Pre-All Star	.307	322	99	28	1	15	59	27	42	.366	.540
Post-All Star	5.89	2	3	1	23	4	55.0	78	6	14	26	Post-All Star	.341	229	78	13	0	6	34	14	26	.382	.476

Career (1995-1997)

	ERA	W	L	Sv	G	GS	IP	H	HR	BB	SO		Avg	AB	H	2B	3B	HR	RBI	BB	SO	OBP	SLG
Home	5.71	7	11	0	52	19	168.2	217	32	48	81	vs. Left	.315	667	210	44	4	29	103	67	64	.380	.523
Away	5.41	6	12	2	52	18	156.1	190	21	65	78	vs. Right	.304	649	197	42	4	24	99	46	95	.354	.492
Day	5.97	7	8	0	49	17	143.1	187	24	42	59	Inning 1-6	.303	965	292	65	4	42	158	78	120	.359	.509
Night	5.25	6	15	2	55	20	181.2	220	29	71	100	Inning 7+	.328	351	115	21	4	11	44	35	39	.391	.504

Career (1995-1997)

	ERA	W	L	Sv	G	GS	IP	H	HR	BB	SO		Avg	AB	H	2B	3B	HR	RBI	BB	SO	OBP	SLG
Grass	5.44	11	20	2	95	32	292.2	367	48	97	137	None on	.303	720	218	50	5	32	32	47	85	.353	.519
Turf	6.68	2	3	0	9	5	32.1	40	5	16	22	Runners on	.317	596	189	36	3	21	170	66	74	.383	.493
March/April	4.14	1	4	1	19	0	37.0	36	4	17	17	Scoring Posn	.270	363	98	15	2	11	141	49	46	.349	.413
May	1.67	2	2	0	19	6	61.0	72	10	16	35	Close & Late	.379	103	39	7	1	1	14	16	8	.462	.495
June	6.90	2	8	0	11	11	60.0	78	13	20	32	None on/out	.318	330	105	23	1	17	17	18	31	.357	.548
July	4.62	4	3	0	22	7	74.0	83	14	22	39	vs. 1st Batr (relief)	.365	63	23	2	1	3	16	4	5	.403	.571
August	5.83	3	0	0	16	8	54.0	75	5	19	18	1st Inning Pitched	.291	375	109	20	1	9	60	31	41	.352	.421
Sept/Oct	7.85	0	3	1	17	5	39.0	63	7	19	18	First 15 Pitches	.290	317	92	18	2	8	43	22	30	.343	.435
Starter	6.09	9	16	0	37	37	199.2	248	39	67	96	Pitch 16-30	.314	271	85	17	1	13	42	31	35	.389	.528
Reliever	4.74	4	7	2	67	0	125.1	159	14	46	63	Pitch 31-45	.291	234	68	15	0	3	24	17	34	.337	.393
0 Days rest (Relief)	4.91	0	0	0	4	0	11.0	14	0	4	13	Pitch 46+	.328	494	162	36	5	29	93	43	60	.384	.597
1 or 2 Days rest	4.52	2	2	2	36	0	65.2	79	8	24	31	First Pitch	.392	204	80	14	1	10	40	10	0	.425	.618
3+ Days rest	4.70	3	5	0	28	1	53.2	73	7	20	22	Ahead in Count	.241	514	124	27	5	18	64	0	122	.251	.418
vs. AL	5.35	13	21	2	100	35	314.2	389	50	107	155	Behind in Count	.385	299	115	23	2	15	52	56	0	.478	.625
vs. NL	12.19	0	2	0	4	2	10.1	18	3	6	4	Two Strikes	.227	534	121	30	4	19	62	47	159	.295	.404
Pre-All Star	5.45	7	15	1	53	20	176.2	208	32	60	96	Pre-All Star	.292	712	208	52	4	32	112	60	96	.351	.511
Post-All Star	5.70	6	8	1	51	17	148.1	199	21	53	63	Post-All Star	.329	604	199	34	4	21	90	53	63	.386	.503

Pitcher vs. Batter (career)

Pitches Best Vs.	Avg	AB	H	2B	3B	HR	RBI	BB	SO	OBP	SLG	Pitches Worst Vs.	Avg	AB	H	2B	3B	HR	RBI	BB	SO	OBP	SLG
Jay Buhner	.083	12	1	0	0	0	0	3	4	.267	.083	Edgar Martinez	.600	10	6	1	0	1	3	4	0	.733	1.000
Rusty Greer	.167	12	2	0	0	0	3	1	1	.333	.167	Juan Gonzalez	.556	9	5	0	0	4	9	2	0	.583	1.889
Alex Rodriguez	.182	11	2	2	0	0	0	0	1	.182	.364	Roberto Alomar	.500	14	7	0	0	2	6	0	0	.500	.929
Marty Cordova	.182	11	2	1	0	0	0	0	4	.182	.273	Mo Vaughn	.462	13	6	1	0	2	4	0	3	.462	1.000
Cecil Fielder	.200	10	2	1	0	0	1	1	2	.273	.300	Paul Sorrento	.400	10	4	1	0	1	6	3	3	.538	.800

John Wetteland — Rangers

Age 31 – Pitches Right (flyball pitcher)

	ERA	W	L	Sv	G	GS	IP	BB	SO	Avg	H	2B	3B	HR	RBI	OBP	SLG	GF	IR	IRS	Hld	SvOp	SB	CS	GB	FB	G/F
1997 Season	1.94	7	2	31	61	0	65.0	21	63	.182	43	11	0	5	22	.248	.292	58	19	5	0	37	1	1	68	75	0.91
Last Five Years	2.31	23	19	173	305	0	339.0	105	379	.196	241	47	9	28	130	.260	.317	273	119	33	0	205	35	6	289	401	0.72

1997 Season

	ERA	W	L	Sv	G	GS	IP	H	HR	BB	SO		Avg	AB	H	2B	3B	HR	RBI	BB	SO	OBP	SLG
Home	1.05	5	0	15	33	0	34.1	19	1	14	35	vs. Left	.167	126	21	4	0	1	10	15	29	.254	.222
Away	2.93	2	2	16	28	0	30.2	24	4	7	28	vs. Right	.200	110	22	7	0	4	12	6	34	.241	.373
Day	2.50	1	1	10	18	0	18.0	12	2	7	15	Inning 1-6	.000	0	0	0	0	0	0	0	0	.000	.000
Night	1.72	6	1	21	43	0	47.0	31	3	14	48	Inning 7+	.182	236	43	11	0	5	22	21	63	.248	.292
Grass	2.03	7	2	28	58	0	62.0	42	5	21	60	None on	.162	142	23	7	0	2	2	11	41	.222	.254
Turf	0.00	0	0	3	3	0	3.0	1	0	0	3	Runners on	.213	94	20	4	0	3	20	10	22	.286	.351
March/April	0.90	1	0	6	10	0	10.0	6	0	4	5	Scoring Posn	.261	46	12	3	0	1	16	9	14	.375	.391
May	1.74	1	0	6	9	0	10.1	8	0	4	10	Close & Late	.216	162	35	9	0	5	21	14	43	.277	.364
June	4.97	2	1	5	12	0	12.2	14	3	4	16	None on/out	.105	57	6	1	0	0	0	4	15	.164	.123
July	1.69	1	1	5	10	0	10.2	6	0	2	9	vs. 1st Batr (relief)	.107	56	6	1	0	0	3	4	18	.164	.125
August	0.64	2	0	5	12	0	14.0	6	2	2	12	1st Inning Pitched	.192	213	41	11	0	5	22	21	56	.264	.315
Sept/Oct	1.23	0	0	4	8	0	7.1	3	0	4	11	First 15 Pitches	.178	169	30	6	0	5	15	13	40	.235	.302
Starter	0.00	0	0	0	0	0	0.0	0	0	0	0	Pitch 16-30	.200	65	13	5	0	0	7	8	22	.288	.277
Reliever	1.94	7	2	31	61	0	65.0	43	5	21	63	Pitch 31-45	.000	2	0	0	0	0	0	0	1	.000	.000
0 Days rest (Relief)	3.78	1	2	13	18	0	16.2	19	3	6	18	Pitch 46+	.000	0	0	0	0	0	0	0	0	.000	.000
1 or 2 Days rest	1.35	5	0	6	21	0	26.2	12	1	5	25	First Pitch	.233	30	7	1	0	0	1	3	0	.303	.267
3+ Days rest	1.25	1	0	12	22	0	21.2	12	1	10	20	Ahead in Count	.161	112	18	6	0	3	12	0	50	.159	.295
vs. AL	1.09	6	1	27	53	0	58.0	33	2	16	53	Behind in Count	.217	46	10	3	0	1	4	8	0	.333	.348
vs. NL	9.00	1	1	4	8	0	7.0	10	3	5	10	Two Strikes	.142	120	17	4	0	4	14	10	63	.208	.292
Pre-All Star	2.57	4	1	18	33	0	35.0	28	3	12	32	Pre-All Star	.215	130	28	8	0	3	16	12	32	.280	.346
Post-All Star	1.20	3	1	13	28	0	30.0	15	2	9	31	Post-All Star	.142	106	15	3	0	2	6	9	31	.209	.226

Last Five Years

	ERA	W	L	Sv	G	GS	IP	H	HR	BB	SO		Avg	AB	H	2B	3B	HR	RBI	BB	SO	OBP	SLG
Home	2.42	16	8	80	154	0	167.1	117	13	54	174	vs. Left	.204	692	141	22	5	18	83	68	204	.277	.328
Away	2.20	7	11	93	151	0	171.2	124	15	51	205	vs. Right	.186	537	100	25	4	10	47	37	175	.238	.304
Day	2.72	7	7	57	101	0	109.1	84	11	30	125	Inning 1-6	.000	0	0	0	0	0	0	0	0	.000	.000
Night	2.12	16	12	116	204	0	229.2	157	17	75	254	Inning 7+	.196	1229	241	47	9	28	130	105	379	.260	.317
Grass	2.20	10	11	112	199	0	212.2	150	19	61	234	None on	.187	700	131	25	5	16	16	53	213	.246	.306
Turf	2.49	13	8	61	106	0	126.1	91	9	44	145	Runners on	.208	529	110	22	4	12	114	52	166	.278	.333
March/April	2.57	2	1	14	31	0	35.0	29	3	12	26	Scoring Posn	.208	332	69	14	2	5	95	38	114	.285	.307
May	2.63	5	4	28	55	0	68.1	48	6	27	74	Close & Late	.203	917	186	37	7	24	115	89	281	.274	.337
June	2.69	3	3	39	62	0	67.0	54	8	22	80	None on/out	.176	284	50	10	4	4	4	22	88	.235	.282
July	1.85	6	4	38	64	0	68.0	47	3	13	75	vs. 1st Batr (relief)	.183	279	51	10	3	5	21	21	84	.241	.294
August	3.34	5	6	25	49	0	56.2	48	7	20	59	1st Inning Pitched	.205	1036	212	43	8	25	119	84	321	.265	.334
Sept/Oct	0.41	2	1	29	44	0	44.0	15	1	11	65	First 15 Pitches	.205	797	163	33	7	22	78	63	228	.265	.346
Starter	0.00	0	0	0	0	0	0.0	0	0	0	0	Pitch 16-30	.190	384	73	14	2	5	47	33	133	.254	.276
Reliever	2.31	23	19	173	305	0	339.0	241	28	105	379	Pitch 31-45	.114	44	5	0	0	1	4	8	17	.245	.182
0 Days rest (Relief)	2.20	4	5	64	88	0	90.0	76	7	28	90	Pitch 46+	.000	4	0	0	0	0	1	1	1	.200	.000
1 or 2 Days rest	2.37	15	9	78	145	0	171.0	109	13	52	197	First Pitch	.283	145	41	9	3	5	25	11	0	.333	.490
3+ Days rest	2.31	4	5	31	72	0	78.0	56	8	25	92	Ahead in Count	.157	674	106	16	3	14	58	0	321	.161	.252
vs. AL	2.31	9	9	101	175	0	183.0	127	17	51	188	Behind in Count	.285	179	51	11	1	5	28	35	0	.394	.441
vs. NL	2.31	14	10	72	130	0	156.0	114	11	54	191	Two Strikes	.148	737	109	21	4	16	62	59	379	.213	.354
Pre-All Star	2.50	11	9	93	168	0	190.2	145	18	62	207	Pre-All Star	.208	698	145	34	7	18	80	62	207	.271	.354

Last Five Years

	ERA	W	L	Sv	G	GS	IP	H	HR	BB	SO		Avg	AB	H	2B	3B	HR	RBI	BB	SO	OBP	SLG
Post-All Star	2.06	12	10	80	137	0	148.1	96	10	43	172	Post-All Star	181	531	96	13	2	10	50	43	172	.246	.269

Pitcher vs. Batter (career)

Pitches Best Vs.	Avg	AB	H	2B	3B	HR	RBI	BB	SO	OBP	SLG	Pitches Worst Vs.	Avg	AB	H	2B	3B	HR	RBI	BB	SO	OBP	SLG
Jeff King	.050	20	1	0	0	0	1	1	8	.091	.050	Ken Caminiti	.455	11	5	1	0	1	2	0	4	.455	.818
Barry Larkin	.077	13	1	1	0	0	3	0	0	.071	.154	Benito Santiago	.438	16	7	1	0	0	1	4	1	.471	.500
Ryne Sandberg	.100	10	1	0	0	0	1	3	1	.308	.100	Craig Biggio	.417	12	5	0	0	2	6	3	4	.533	.917
Fred McGriff	.182	11	2	0	0	0	0	0	3	.182	.182	Kevin Mitchell	.400	10	4	0	0	1	3	2	.538	.400
Bip Roberts	.208	24	5	0	0	0	4	1	4	.240	.208	Kevin Elster	.333	9	3	0	0	1	4	2	4	.417	.667

Matt Whisenant — Royals
Age 27 – Pitches Left (groundball pitcher)

	ERA	W	L	Sv	G	GS	IP	BB	SO	Avg	H	2B	3B	HR	RBI	OBP	SLG	GF	IR	IRS	Hld	SvOp	SB	CS	GB	FB	G/F
1997 Season	4.57	1	0	0	28	0	21.2	18	20	.229	19	2	0	0	11	.385	.253	5	23	7	5	0	0	0	35	15	2.33

1997 Season

	ERA	W	L	Sv	G	GS	IP	H	HR	BB	SO		Avg	AB	H	2B	3B	HR	RBI	BB	SO	OBP	SLG
Home	5.56	0	0	0	13	0	11.1	12	0	9	12	vs. Left	.282	39	11	1	0	0	7	9	9	.451	.308
Away	3.48	1	0	0	15	0	10.1	7	0	9	8	vs. Right	.182	44	8	1	0	0	4	9	11	.321	.205
Starter	0.00	0	0	0	0	0	0.0	0	0	0	0	Scoring Posn	.258	31	8	1	0	0	11	8	9	.439	.290
Reliever	4.57	1	0	0	28	0	21.2	19	0	18	20	Close & Late	.182	22	4	0	0	0	3	4	8	.308	.182
0 Days rest (Relief)	0.00	0	0	0	4	0	1.2	3	0	1	2	None on/out	.133	15	2	1	0	0	0	5	4	.381	.200
1 or 2 Days rest	4.26	1	0	0	17	0	12.2	10	0	11	10	First Pitch	.333	12	4	1	0	0	1	0	0	.333	.417
3+ Days rest	6.14	0	0	0	7	0	7.1	6	0	6	8	Ahead in Count	.206	34	7	0	0	0	4	0	17	.229	.206
Pre-All Star	0.00	0	0	0	1	0	1.0	1	0	1	1	Behind in Count	.261	23	6	1	0	0	4	6	0	.433	.304
Post-All Star	4.79	1	0	0	27	0	20.2	18	0	17	19	Two Strikes	.139	36	5	0	0	0	5	12	20	.380	.139

Devon White — Marlins
Age 35 – Bats Both (groundball hitter)

	Avg	G	AB	R	H	2B	3B	HR	RBI	BB	SO	HBP	GDP	SB	CS	OBP	SLG	IBB	SH	SF	#Pit	#P/PA	GB	FB	G/F
1997 Season	.245	74	265	37	65	13	1	6	34	32	65	7	3	13	5	.338	.370	2	0	4	1243	4.04	100	62	1.61
Last Five Years	.271	567	2245	358	609	139	24	61	272	177	468	32	23	91	20	.331	.436	13	12	21	9613	3.87	786	569	1.38

1997 Season

	Avg	AB	H	2B	3B	HR	RBI	BB	SO	OBP	SLG		Avg	AB	H	2B	3B	HR	RBI	BB	SO	OBP	SLG
vs. Left	.188	48	9	1	0	1	8	6	8	.286	.271	First Pitch	.464	28	13	3	0	1	9	2	0	.515	.679
vs. Right	.258	217	56	12	1	5	26	26	57	.349	.392	Ahead in Count	.414	58	24	3	0	4	16	13	0	.514	.672
Groundball	.214	28	6	2	0	0	4	3	8	.313	.286	Behind in Count	.143	126	18	6	0	0	3	0	53	.168	.190
Flyball	.209	43	9	0	0	2	3	3	9	.271	.349	Two Strikes	.118	144	17	4	0	0	6	17	65	.229	.146
Home	.250	152	38	8	0	4	21	16	33	.335	.382	Batting #1	.237	190	45	5	1	6	29	18	53	.313	.368
Away	.239	113	27	5	1	2	13	16	32	.341	.354	Batting #6	.261	46	12	0	0	0	5	13	9	.433	.391
Day	.228	92	21	7	0	4	20	12	20	.318	.435	Other	.276	29	8	2	0	0	0	1	3	.323	.345
Night	.254	173	44	6	1	2	14	20	45	.348	.335	March/April	.245	49	12	6	0	0	5	13	11	.413	.367
Grass	.244	225	55	11	1	6	28	24	57	.327	.382	May	.333	6	2	2	0	0	0	0	2	.429	.667
Turf	.250	40	10	2	0	0	6	8	8	.392	.300	June	.333	15	5	0	0	0	0	1	0	.375	.333
Pre-All Star	.271	70	19	8	0	5	14	13	40	.407	.386	July	.059	17	1	0	0	0	1	0	4	.111	.059
Post-All Star	.236	195	46	5	1	6	29	18	52	.311	.364	August	.253	99	25	4	1	1	12	11	30	.336	.343
Scoring Posn	.308	52	16	2	0	2	30	11	10	.412	.462	Sept/Oct	.253	79	20	1	0	5	16	7	18	.310	.456
Close & Late	.213	47	10	2	0	0	4	7	15	.351	.255	vs. AL	.368	19	7	1	0	1	7	4	6	.480	.579
None on/out	.263	95	25	5	1	3	3	7	24	.346	.432	vs. NL	.236	246	58	12	1	5	27	28	59	.325	.354

1997 By Position

Position	Avg	AB	H	2B	3B	HR	RBI	BB	SO	OBP	SLG	G	GS	Innings	PO	A	E	DP	Fld Pct	Rng Fctr	In Zone	Zone Outs	Zone Rtg	MLB Zone
As cf	.249	261	65	13	1	6	34	32	63	.342	.375	72	67	586.2	150	4	2	1	.987	2.36	175	147	.840	.815

Last Five Years

	Avg	AB	H	2B	3B	HR	RBI	BB	SO	OBP	SLG		Avg	AB	H	2B	3B	HR	RBI	BB	SO	OBP	SLG
vs. Left	.274	576	158	42	4	15	85	38	107	.329	.439	First Pitch	.365	277	101	17	2	12	44	8	0	.397	.570
vs. Right	.270	1669	451	97	20	46	187	139	361	.331	.435	Ahead in Count	.347	453	157	50	4	22	84	101	0	.462	.620
Groundball	.271	436	118	26	3	10	56	29	107	.324	.413	Behind in Count	.209	1078	225	45	10	20	93	0	398	.219	.325
Flyball	.258	427	110	18	8	10	43	25	81	.304	.407	Two Strikes	.198	1150	228	47	12	15	91	68	468	.248	.293
Home	.275	1144	315	75	16	28	131	86	243	.332	.442	Batting #1	.269	1660	447	96	18	49	189	118	351	.325	.437
Away	.267	1101	294	64	8	33	141	91	225	.329	.430	Batting #2	.280	254	71	19	5	2	23	27	52	.350	.417
Day	.281	720	202	42	8	30	101	63	154	.342	.486	Other	.275	331	91	24	1	10	60	32	65	.340	.444
Night	.267	1525	407	97	16	31	171	114	314	.325	.412	March/April	.292	274	80	20	4	7	34	34	51	.380	.471
Grass	.252	1257	317	68	12	33	149	100	258	.310	.396	May	.300	460	138	33	8	11	49	27	97	.344	.478
Turf	.296	988	292	71	17	28	123	77	210	.356	.487	June	.254	402	102	22	3	14	44	25	70	.303	.438
Pre-All Star	.286	1260	360	88	18	37	141	80	229	.343	.472	July	.251	459	115	29	3	10	50	37	107	.314	.392
Post-All Star	.253	985	249	51	6	24	131	80	229	.314	.390	August	.284	250	71	11	4	10	45	24	56	.345	.456
Scoring Posn	.318	453	144	32	3	15	213	58	94	.390	.501	Sept/Oct	.276	1447	400	90	17	39	161	111	310	.334	.443
Close & Late	.266	331	88	19	4	11	56	35	75	.347	.447	vs. AL	.262	798	209	49	7	22	111	66	158	.325	.424
None on/out	.274	820	225	46	10	34	34	43	155	.323	.479	vs. NL											

Batter vs. Pitcher (career)

Hits Best Against	Avg	AB	H	2B	3B	HR	RBI	BB	SO	OBP	SLG	Hits Worst Against	Avg	AB	H	2B	3B	HR	RBI	BB	SO	OBP	SLG
Scott Kamieniecki	.500	16	8	0	1	2	5	1	3	.529	1.000	Cal Eldred	.000	18	0	0	0	0	1	2	4	.095	.000
Arthur Rhodes	.429	21	9	2	1	0	6	0	6	.409	.667	Pete Harnisch	.000	13	0	0	0	0	0	0	3	.071	.000
Steve Trachsel	.417	12	5	1	1	0	0	3	2	.533	.667	Terry Mulholland	.000	10	0	0	0	0	0	2	2	.167	.000
Mark Gardner	.385	13	5	1	0	2	2	0	4	.385	.923	Dennis Martinez	.071	14	1	0	0	0	0	1	3	.133	.071

497

Batter vs. Pitcher (career)

Hits Best Against	Avg	AB	H	2B	3B	HR	RBI	BB	SO	OBP	SLG	Hits Worst Against	Avg	AB	H	2B	3B	HR	RBI	BB	SO	OBP	SLG
Ricky Bones	.382	34	13	3	1	2	2	2	5	.417	.706	Bret Saberhagen	.114	35	4	2	0	0	0	0	9	.114	.171

Gabe White — Reds
Age 26 – Pitches Left (flyball pitcher)

	ERA	W	L	Sv	G	GS	IP	BB	SO	Avg	H	2B	3B	HR	RBI	OBP	SLG	CG	SHO	3up	QC	#P/E	SB	CS	GB	FB	G/F
1997 Season	4.39	2	2	1	12	6	41.0	8	25	.253	39	12	0	6	20	.291	.448	0	0	4.83	2	89	3	0	43	63	0.68
Career (1994-1997)	5.58	4	5	2	38	12	90.1	28	67	.257	89	26	2	17	55	.313	.491	0	0	4.08	4	80	11	2	82	146	0.56

1997 Season

	ERA	W	L	Sv	G	GS	IP	H	HR	BB	SO		Avg	AB	H	2B	3B	HR	RBI	BB	SO	OBP	SLG
Home	3.86	1	1	0	6	3	21.0	19	4	4	15	vs. Left	.500	18	9	4	0	0	5	1	1	.526	.722
Away	4.95	1	1	1	6	3	20.0	20	2	4	10	vs. Right	.221	136	30	8	0	6	15	7	24	.260	.412

Rondell White — Expos
Age 26 – Bats Right (groundball hitter)

	Avg	G	AB	R	H	2B	3B	HR	RBI	BB	SO	HBP	GDP	SB	CS	OBP	SLG	IBB	SH	SF	#Pit	#P/PA	GB	FB	G/F
1997 Season	.270	151	592	84	160	29	5	28	82	31	111	10	18	16	8	.316	.478	3	1	4	2163	3.39	252	133	1.89
Career (1993-1997)	.283	432	1570	231	444	94	15	51	208	110	285	21	43	57	22	.336	.459	4	3	10	6150	3.59	688	335	2.05

1997 Season

	Avg	AB	H	2B	3B	HR	RBI	BB	SO	OBP	SLG		Avg	AB	H	2B	3B	HR	RBI	BB	SO	OBP	SLG
vs. Left	.255	137	35	5	2	10	25	8	24	.304	.540	First Pitch	.381	97	37	3	0	7	12	3	0	.400	.629
vs. Right	.275	455	125	24	3	18	57	23	87	.319	.459	Ahead in Count	.402	122	49	13	0	8	22	12	0	.456	.705
Groundball	.246	130	32	6	0	3	10	5	27	.300	.362	Behind in Count	.175	257	45	9	2	9	26	0	90	.199	.331
Flyball	.420	69	29	8	0	10	28	5	11	.453	.971	Two Strikes	.159	251	40	8	2	6	24	16	111	.228	.279
Home	.290	269	78	16	4	9	36	17	52	.340	.480	Batting #3	.296	324	96	15	4	15	47	14	59	.339	.506
Away	.254	323	82	13	1	19	46	14	59	.294	.477	Batting #6	.218	110	24	6	0	2	8	7	23	.271	.327
Day	.323	198	64	10	1	12	28	13	42	.367	.566	Other	.253	158	40	8	1	11	27	10	29	.298	.525
Night	.244	394	96	19	4	16	54	18	69	.289	.434	March/April	.276	98	27	4	1	4	12	6	20	.321	.459
Grass	.274	226	62	10	0	13	33	10	47	.320	.491	May	.328	116	38	7	1	5	17	4	18	.368	.534
Turf	.268	366	98	19	5	15	49	21	64	.313	.470	June	.162	74	12	4	0	0	5	4	17	.229	.216
Pre-All Star	.265	313	83	15	2	12	38	14	58	.310	.441	July	.301	93	28	5	1	8	18	2	11	.323	.634
Post-All Star	.276	279	77	14	3	16	44	17	53	.322	.520	August	.270	111	30	5	1	5	18	11	23	.341	.468
Scoring Posn	.207	140	29	8	2	3	44	13	31	.294	.357	Sept/Oct	.250	100	25	4	1	6	12	4	22	.279	.490
Close & Late	.282	103	29	7	0	7	19	4	23	.315	.553	vs. AL	.231	52	12	1	0	2	7	1	10	.250	.365
None on/out	.281	135	38	8	1	5	5	4	26	.307	.467	vs. NL	.274	540	148	28	5	26	75	30	101	.322	.489

1997 By Position

Position	Avg	AB	H	2B	3B	HR	RBI	BB	SO	OBP	SLG	G	GS	Innings	PO	A	E	DP	Fld Pct	Rng Fctr	In Zone	Zone Outs	Zone Rtg	MLB Zone
As cf	.270	592	160	29	5	28	82	31	111	.316	.478	151	151	1339.0	375	6	3	3	.992	2.56	448	363	810	.815

Career (1993-1997)

	Avg	AB	H	2B	3B	HR	RBI	BB	SO	OBP	SLG		Avg	AB	H	2B	3B	HR	RBI	BB	SO	OBP	SLG
vs. Left	.323	418	135	35	5	14	64	28	61	.372	.531	First Pitch	.351	239	84	17	3	7	25	4	0	.367	.536
vs. Right	.268	1152	309	59	10	37	144	82	224	.323	.433	Ahead in Count	.363	317	115	21	3	17	55	56	0	.458	.609
Groundball	.246	386	95	21	5	5	38	24	80	.303	.365	Behind in Count	.219	713	156	37	4	16	75	0	232	.231	.349
Flyball	.294	231	68	14	0	17	51	26	37	.367	.576	Two Strikes	.199	709	141	36	3	14	75	50	285	.260	.317
Home	.297	721	214	42	8	19	97	65	133	.362	.456	Batting #1	.301	299	90	18	5	9	30	31	60	.367	.485
Away	.271	849	230	52	7	32	111	45	152	.313	.462	Batting #3	.288	549	158	25	6	20	85	27	102	.332	.464
Day	.302	494	149	32	4	21	71	41	102	.355	.510	Other	.271	722	196	51	4	22	93	52	123	.326	.445
Night	.274	1076	295	62	11	30	137	69	183	.327	.427	March/April	.286	227	65	8	4	8	35	13	43	.326	.463
Grass	.278	564	157	34	3	22	68	30	107	.322	.466	May	.325	169	55	12	1	9	30	16	31	.394	.568
Turf	.285	1006	287	60	12	29	140	80	178	.344	.455	June	.238	160	38	11	1	2	15	9	28	.303	.356
Pre-All Star	.272	621	169	33	6	22	87	38	112	.324	.451	July	.267	296	79	20	2	13	44	22	50	.328	.480
Post-All Star	.290	949	275	61	9	29	121	72	173	.344	.465	August	.289	346	100	21	5	9	38	24	64	.339	.457
Scoring Posn	.247	405	100	22	3	8	146	47	79	.333	.375	Sept/Oct	.288	372	107	22	2	10	46	26	69	.333	.438
Close & Late	.250	248	62	13	5	10	38	20	49	.307	.464	vs. AL	.231	52	12	1	0	2	7	1	10	.250	.365
None on/out	.307	417	128	30	3	12	12	26	70	.351	.480	vs. NL	.285	1518	432	93	15	49	201	109	275	.339	.462

Batter vs. Pitcher (career)

Hits Best Against	Avg	AB	H	2B	3B	HR	RBI	BB	SO	OBP	SLG	Hits Worst Against	Avg	AB	H	2B	3B	HR	RBI	BB	SO	OBP	SLG
Pete Schourek	.625	16	10	2	1	1	4	1	1	.647	1.063	Mark Clark	.000	10	0	0	0	0	0	0	3	.091	.000
John Smiley	.471	17	8	4	0	1	0	3		.471	.706	Mike Morgan	.071	14	1	1	0	0	0	1	1	.133	.143
Greg Swindell	.429	14	6	1	0	1	2	1		.467	.714	Ismael Valdes	.125	16	2	1	0	0	0	0	2	.125	.188
F. Valenzuela	.364	11	4	0	1	1	3	1	1	.417	.818	Mark Portugal	.167	12	2	0	0	0	1	0	2	.154	.167
Armando Reynoso	.308	13	4	1	0	2	4	2		.400	.923	Terry Mulholland	.182	11	2	0	0	0	0	0	2	.182	.182

Mark Whiten — Yankees
Age 31 – Bats Both (groundball hitter)

	Avg	G	AB	R	H	2B	3B	HR	RBI	BB	SO	HBP	GDP	SB	CS	OBP	SLG	IBB	SH	SF	#Pit	#P/PA	GB	FB	G/F
1997 Season	.265	69	215	34	57	11	0	5	24	30	47	2	6	4	2	.360	.386	5	1	0	953	3.84	94	39	2.41
Last Five Years	.262	541	1843	299	482	75	8	78	294	245	445	9	46	54	24	.346	.438	30	1	8	7849	3.74	762	385	1.98

1997 Season

	Avg	AB	H	2B	3B	HR	RBI	BB	SO	OBP	SLG		Avg	AB	H	2B	3B	HR	RBI	BB	SO	OBP	SLG
vs. Left	.259	81	21	3	0	3	10	11	21	.362	.407	Scoring Posn	.293	58	17	2	0	2	19	13	17	.423	.431
vs. Right	.269	134	36	8	0	2	14	19	26	.359	.373	Close & Late	.191	47	9	1	0	1	7	10	10	.333	.277
Home	.212	99	21	5	0	4	10	13	22	.310	.384	None on/out	.174	46	8	1	0	0	0	12	9	.356	.196
Away	.310	116	36	6	0	1	14	17	25	.403	.388	Batting #6	.184	49	9	2	0	2	5	8	15	.310	.347

1997 Season

	Avg	AB	H	2B	3B	HR	RBI	BB	SO	OBP	SLG		Avg	AB	H	2B	3B	HR	RBI	BB	SO	OBP	SLG
First Pitch	.424	33	14	0	0	1	7	3	0	.486	.515	Batting #7	.261	111	29	6	0	2	14	17	23	.359	.369
Ahead in Count	.236	55	13	4	0	1	5	8	0	.333	.364	Other	.345	55	19	3	0	1	5	5	9	.410	.455
Behind in Count	.278	90	25	7	0	2	7	0	40	.286	.422	Pre-All Star	.258	182	47	10	0	5	23	28	41	.360	.396
Two Strikes	.184	103	19	3	0	3	7	19	47	.317	.301	Post-All Star	.303	33	10	1	0	0	1	2	6	.361	.333

Last Five Years

	Avg	AB	H	2B	3B	HR	RBI	BB	SO	OBP	SLG		Avg	AB	H	2B	3B	HR	RBI	BB	SO	OBP	SLG
vs. Left	.244	544	133	15	1	27	79	59	116	.324	.425	First Pitch	.355	310	110	9	1	17	66	21	0	.397	.555
vs. Right	.269	1299	349	60	7	51	215	175	329	.356	.443	Ahead in Count	.360	461	166	26	4	37	112	110	0	.480	.675
Groundball	.259	557	144	21	0	16	92	64	139	.335	.382	Behind in Count	.179	720	129	24	0	13	58	0	335	.187	.267
Flyball	.238	290	69	13	4	14	38	42	66	.338	.455	Two Strikes	.159	837	133	26	2	18	73	103	445	.256	.259
Home	.251	853	214	34	1	36	139	112	212	.342	.420	Batting #5	.263	586	154	22	4	21	85	67	121	.337	.422
Away	.271	990	268	41	7	42	155	122	233	.350	.454	Batting #6	.259	501	130	16	3	24	90	59	109	.341	.447
Day	.259	559	145	23	2	21	80	85	127	.352	.420	Other	.262	756	198	37	1	33	119	108	215	.356	.444
Night	.262	1284	337	52	6	57	214	149	318	.341	.445	March/April	.248	274	68	8	1	11	29	51	77	.368	.405
Grass	.244	876	214	41	5	28	113	117	212	.334	.398	May	.266	327	87	20	0	9	42	28	73	.326	.410
Turf	.277	967	268	34	3	50	181	117	233	.357	.474	June	.225	342	77	11	1	10	50	40	80	.309	.351
Pre-All Star	.252	1010	255	40	4	33	135	127	252	.338	.398	July	.268	272	73	11	3	12	48	35	64	.348	.463
Post-All Star	.273	833	227	35	4	45	159	107	193	.356	.486	August	.299	314	94	12	2	17	57	44	64	.386	.513
Scoring Posn	.276	529	146	21	1	26	221	94	138	.382	.467	Sept/Oct	.264	314	83	13	1	19	68	36	87	.344	.494
Close & Late	.235	332	78	10	1	15	55	54	88	.342	.407	vs. AL	.268	437	117	21	0	18	67	52	101	.350	.439
None on/out	.253	438	111	19	2	14	14	43	103	.324	.402	vs. NL	.260	1406	365	54	8	60	227	182	344	.345	.437

Batter vs. Pitcher (career)

Hits Best Against	Avg	AB	H	2B	3B	HR	RBI	BB	SO	OBP	SLG	Hits Worst Against	Avg	AB	H	2B	3B	HR	RBI	BB	SO	OBP	SLG
Darryl Kile	.526	19	10	1	1	1	4	2	1	.571	.842	Chris Hammond	.077	13	1	0	0	0	2	0	6	.077	.077
Willie Blair	.455	11	5	1	0	1	2	1	3	.500	.818	Pete Schourek	.077	13	1	0	0	0	1	2	5	.200	.077
Rich Robertson	.444	9	4	0	0	1	2	2	2	.545	.778	Mark Portugal	.143	14	2	0	0	0	0	2	5	.250	.143
Chuck Finley	.429	21	9	3	1	1	4	2	6	.478	.810	Andy Ashby	.143	14	2	0	0	0	0	2	3	.250	.143
Greg Swindell	.385	13	5	0	0	2	4	1	2	.429	.846	Juan Guzman	.182	11	2	0	0	0	3	0	3	.182	.182

Matt Whiteside — Rangers

Age 30 – Pitches Right

	ERA	W	L	Sv	G	GS	IP	BB	SO	Avg	H	2B	3B	HR	RBI	OBP	SLG	GF	IR	IRS	Hld	SvOp	SB	CS	GB	FB	G/F
1997 Season	5.08	4	1	0	42	1	72.2	26	44	.296	85	18	1	4	49	.355	.408	8	38	16	2	4	0	6	116	74	1.57
Last Five Years	4.87	13	9	5	203	1	292.0	107	181	.284	322	44	5	30	170	.345	.411	59	187	55	31	16	7	14	444	313	1.42

1997 Season

	ERA	W	L	Sv	G	GS	IP	H	HR	BB	SO		Avg	AB	H	2B	3B	HR	RBI	BB	SO	OBP	SLG
Home	4.89	2	1	0	21	1	42.1	46	2	12	26	vs. Left	.341	129	44	10	0	3	28	10	14	.389	.488
Away	5.34	2	0	0	21	0	30.1	39	2	14	18	vs. Right	.259	158	41	8	1	1	21	16	30	.328	.342
Starter	11.25	0	0	0	1	1	4.0	6	0	0	1	Scoring Posn	.303	89	27	6	1	1	41	12	14	.380	.427
Reliever	4.72	4	1	0	41	0	68.2	79	4	26	43	Close & Late	.305	59	18	2	0	0	7	8	4	.382	.339
0 Days rest (Relief)	7.84	0	0	0	7	0	10.1	21	1	3	6	None on/out	.185	65	12	0	0	1	1	3	11	.221	.231
1 or 2 Days rest	3.30	1	0	0	16	0	30.0	25	1	7	18	First Pitch	.333	48	16	2	0	1	15	3	0	.370	.438
3+ Days rest	5.08	1	1	0	18	0	28.1	33	2	16	19	Ahead in Count	.227	119	27	3	1	0	11	0	38	.227	.269
Pre-All Star	6.23	1	1	0	18	0	26.0	33	3	7	16	Behind in Count	.333	75	25	10	0	2	17	8	0	.395	.547
Post-All Star	4.44	3	0	0	24	0	46.2	52	1	19	28	Two Strikes	.223	103	23	2	0	0	6	15	44	.319	.243

Last Five Years

	ERA	W	L	Sv	G	GS	IP	H	HR	BB	SO		Avg	AB	H	2B	3B	HR	RBI	BB	SO	OBP	SLG
Home	4.10	8	4	2	103	1	164.2	162	16	46	99	vs. Left	.303	435	132	23	2	8	61	38	57	.361	.421
Away	5.87	5	5	3	100	0	127.1	160	14	61	82	vs. Right	.271	700	190	21	3	22	109	69	124	.335	.404
Day	6.28	2	3	2	43	0	61.2	87	7	29	36	Inning 1-6	.294	320	94	18	3	8	63	28	50	.352	.444
Night	4.49	11	6	3	160	1	230.1	235	23	78	145	Inning 7+	.280	815	228	26	2	22	107	79	131	.342	.398
Grass	4.60	11	7	5	173	1	256.1	270	27	93	160	None on	.269	581	156	20	3	16	16	48	90	.326	.396
Turf	6.81	2	2	0	30	0	35.2	52	3	14	21	Runners on	.300	554	166	24	2	14	154	59	91	.363	.426
March/April	5.14	1	1	0	20	0	28.0	27	2	9	17	Scoring Posn	.261	333	87	13	2	4	128	50	65	.353	.348
May	4.13	1	0	0	40	0	52.1	59	2	19	34	Close & Late	.278	363	101	8	2	8	46	31	68	.336	.377
June	4.89	4	2	0	41	0	57.0	61	11	17	39	None on/out	.258	256	66	7	3	9	9	23	36	.319	.414
July	4.55	2	3	3	43	1	59.1	69	6	25	36	vs. 1st Batr (relief)	.250	176	44	4	2	3	27	21	32	.325	.347
August	5.57	3	2	1	25	0	42.0	47	3	21	28	1st Inning Pitched	.263	665	175	26	4	14	107	67	111	.330	.377
Sept/Oct	5.23	2	1	1	34	0	53.1	59	6	16	27	First 15 Pitches	.273	609	166	22	4	14	90	58	86	.336	.391
Starter	11.25	0	0	0	1	1	4.0	6	0	0	1	Pitch 16-30	.296	311	92	15	0	8	51	33	69	.361	.421
Reliever	4.78	13	9	5	202	0	288.0	316	30	107	180	Pitch 31-45	.288	118	34	3	1	2	9	12	18	.351	.381
0 Days rest (Relief)	5.19	4	1	1	36	0	50.1	64	8	16	25	Pitch 46+	.309	97	30	4	0	6	20	4	8	.343	.536
1 or 2 Days rest	4.13	2	5	4	97	0	143.2	141	15	44	94	First Pitch	.372	183	68	6	1	8	39	13	0	.411	.546
3+ Days rest	5.55	7	3	0	69	0	94.0	111	7	47	61	Ahead in Count	.241	506	122	15	1	10	56	0	148	.242	.334
vs. AL	4.95	11	9	5	199	1	285.1	316	30	106	180	Behind in Count	.321	252	81	15	2	8	51	41	0	.416	.492
vs. NL	1.35	2	0	0	4	0	6.2	6	0	1	1	Two Strikes	.219	479	105	14	0	11	49	53	181	.297	.317
Pre-All Star	4.56	7	5	2	118	0	156.0	166	18	51	100	Pre-All Star	.276	602	166	28	2	18	86	51	100	.332	.419
Post-All Star	5.23	6	4	3	85	1	136.0	156	12	56	81	Post-All Star	.293	533	156	16	3	12	84	56	81	.359	.402

Pitcher vs. Batter (career)

Pitches Best Vs.	Avg	AB	H	2B	3B	HR	RBI	BB	SO	OBP	SLG	Pitches Worst Vs.	Avg	AB	H	2B	3B	HR	RBI	BB	SO	OBP	SLG
Rickey Henderson	.111	9	1	0	0	0	0	2	2	.273	.111	Tino Martinez	.462	13	6	1	0	0	5	1	1	.500	.538
Mark McGwire	.154	13	2	0	0	0	0	2	4	.267	.154	Edgar Martinez	.417	12	5	1	0	1	2	4	0	.563	.750
Jay Buhner	.188	16	3	0	0	1	5	2	4	.278	.188	Travis Fryman	.412	17	7	1	0	2	6	0	4	.389	.824
Terry Steinbach	.214	14	3	0	0	3	0	4	.214	.214	Bernie Williams	.400	10	4	0	0	0	1	1	2	.500	.400

499

Pitcher vs. Batter (career)

Pitches Best Vs.	Avg	AB	H	2B	3B	HR	RBI	BB	SO	OBP	SLG	Pitches Worst Vs.	Avg	AB	H	2B	3B	HR	RBI	BB	SO	OBP	SLG
Chuck Knoblauch	.214	14	3	1	0	0	0	0	0	.214	.286	Tim Salmon	.364	11	4	0	0	1	3	3	2	.500	.636

Bob Wickman — Brewers   Age 29 – Pitches Right (groundball pitcher)

	ERA	W	L	Sv	G	GS	IP	BB	SO	Avg	H	2B	3B	HR	RBI	OBP	SLG	GF	IR	IRS	Hld	SvOp	SB	CS	GB	FB	G/F
1997 Season	2.73	7	6	1	74	0	95.2	41	78	.252	89	15	0	8	38	.333	.000	20	48	15	28	5	15	4	159	60	2.65
Last Five Years	3.89	35	19	12	301	20	481.1	214	330	.263	482	86	6	40	253	.344	.382	80	232	81	72	37	58	16	864	351	2.46

1997 Season

	ERA	W	L	Sv	G	GS	IP	H	HR	BB	SO		Avg	AB	H	2B	3B	HR	RBI	BB	SO	OBP	SLG
Home	3.69	5	2	0	40	0	46.1	42	5	19	38	vs. Left	.260	146	38	7	0	1	19	24	29	.364	.329
Away	1.82	2	4	1	34	0	49.1	47	3	22	40	vs. Right	.246	207	51	8	0	7	19	17	49	.310	.386
Day	1.99	3	3	1	30	0	40.2	27	5	15	36	Inning 1-6	.182	22	4	2	0	1	6	4	8	.296	.409
Night	3.27	4	3	0	44	0	55.0	62	3	26	42	Inning 7+	.257	331	85	13	0	7	32	37	70	.336	.360
Grass	3.16	7	6	1	65	0	82.2	80	8	36	64	None on	.290	176	51	8	0	5	5	16	34	.356	.420
Turf	0.00	0	0	0	9	0	13.0	9	0	5	14	Runners on	.215	177	38	7	0	3	33	25	44	.312	.305
March/April	3.38	2	1	0	10	0	13.1	11	2	4	11	Scoring Posn	.164	110	18	5	0	2	29	23	30	.309	.264
May	4.08	0	1	1	12	0	17.2	23	2	8	15	Close & Late	.263	240	63	11	0	3	24	29	47	.343	.346
June	2.61	3	1	0	9	0	10.1	9	2	4	9	None on/out	.272	81	22	3	0	3	3	4	11	.306	.420
July	1.02	1	0	0	17	0	17.2	11	0	8	11	vs. 1st Batr (relief)	.214	70	15	4	0	2	9	3	13	.243	.357
August	3.66	0	3	0	14	0	19.2	21	0	8	13	1st Inning Pitched	.232	241	56	12	0	7	32	27	56	.314	.369
Sept/Oct	1.59	1	0	0	12	0	17.0	14	2	9	19	First 15 Pitches	.233	202	47	7	0	6	20	20	42	.307	.356
Starter	0.00	0	0	0	0	0	0.0	0	0	0	0	Pitch 16-30	.291	117	34	7	0	1	13	16	29	.381	.376
Reliever	2.73	7	6	1	74	0	95.2	89	8	41	78	Pitch 31-45	.250	28	7	1	0	0	2	4	5	.344	.286
0 Days rest (Relief)	1.17	2	2	0	21	0	23.0	15	1	11	19	Pitch 46+	.167	6	1	0	0	1	3	1	2	.250	.667
1 or 2 Days rest	3.27	2	3	0	37	0	52.1	55	3	20	49	First Pitch	.283	46	13	2	0	1	5	0	0	.353	.391
3+ Days rest	3.10	3	1	1	16	0	20.1	19	4	10	10	Ahead in Count	.180	150	27	5	0	2	10	0	58	.194	.253
vs. AL	2.95	6	6	1	68	0	88.1	84	8	40	72	Behind in Count	.390	82	32	4	0	4	13	18	0	.500	.585
vs. NL	0.00	1	0	0	6	0	7.1	5	0	1	6	Two Strikes	.153	157	24	5	0	1	10	18	78	.250	.204
Pre-All Star	3.09	5	3	1	35	0	46.2	46	6	17	38	Pre-All Star	.261	176	46	3	0	6	22	17	38	.328	.381
Post-All Star	2.39	2	3	0	39	0	49.0	43	2	24	40	Post-All Star	.243	177	43	12	0	2	16	24	40	.338	.345

Last Five Years

	ERA	W	L	Sv	G	GS	IP	H	HR	BB	SO		Avg	AB	H	2B	3B	HR	RBI	BB	SO	OBP	SLG
Home	3.66	22	4	3	152	8	238.2	223	19	100	164	vs. Left	.282	791	223	42	2	16	108	110	118	.373	.401
Away	4.12	13	15	9	149	12	242.2	259	21	114	166	vs. Right	.248	1043	259	44	4	24	145	104	212	.321	.367
Day	3.50	16	8	4	123	8	205.2	190	15	92	143	Inning 1-6	.269	659	177	35	3	18	111	85	103	.355	.413
Night	4.18	19	11	8	178	12	275.2	292	25	122	187	Inning 7+	.260	1175	305	51	3	22	142	129	227	.337	.364
Grass	3.79	33	16	10	265	17	422.2	421	37	185	292	None on	.271	933	253	40	2	22	96	96	169	.344	.389
Turf	4.60	2	3	2	36	3	58.2	61	3	29	38	Runners on	.254	901	229	46	4	18	231	118	161	.343	.374
March/April	4.62	5	2	0	37	3	60.1	69	5	31	33	Scoring Posn	.245	550	135	33	4	11	212	95	108	.357	.380
May	3.69	9	2	3	50	7	101.0	108	11	41	75	Close & Late	.260	670	174	28	3	11	89	74	126	.337	.360
June	3.46	7	6	3	55	5	91.0	86	7	36	53	None on/out	.276	428	118	20	1	15	15	28	69	.322	.432
July	3.74	5	3	1	62	3	86.2	76	7	45	67	vs. 1st Batr (relief)	.223	256	57	11	0	7	43	19	65	.280	.348
August	4.18	3	6	4	56	1	88.1	92	3	40	60	1st Inning Pitched	.235	944	222	43	4	18	142	111	201	.319	.346
Sept/Oct	3.97	6	0	1	41	1	47.2	51	7	21	42	First 15 Pitches	.243	839	204	37	3	18	114	87	162	.319	.359
Starter	4.91	8	5	0	20	20	113.2	136	14	57	51	Pitch 16-30	.267	528	141	27	1	9	59	64	108	.352	.373
Reliever	3.57	27	14	12	281	0	367.2	346	26	157	279	Pitch 31-45	.250	196	49	6	2	5	34	26	28	.341	.378
0 Days rest (Relief)	2.71	7	5	2	74	0	76.1	62	2	34	61	Pitch 46+	.325	271	88	16	0	8	46	37	32	.404	.472
1 or 2 Days rest	3.83	12	7	6	140	0	204.1	200	13	89	160	First Pitch	.318	274	87	15	0	5	40	18	0	.358	.427
3+ Days rest	3.72	8	2	4	67	0	87.0	84	11	34	58	Ahead in Count	.208	742	154	32	0	15	84	0	258	.220	.311
vs. AL	3.95	34	19	12	295	20	474.0	477	40	213	324	Behind in Count	.335	451	151	23	3	9	80	99	0	.456	.459
vs. NL	0.00	1	0	0	6	0	7.1	5	0	1	6	Two Strikes	.195	763	149	32	2	14	88	97	330	.290	.298
Pre-All Star	3.84	22	12	6	158	17	291.0	290	27	125	185	Pre-All Star	.260	1116	290	45	3	27	150	125	185	.338	.378
Post-All Star	3.97	13	7	6	143	3	190.1	192	13	89	145	Post-All Star	.267	718	192	41	3	13	103	89	145	.353	.387

Pitcher vs. Batter (career)

Pitches Best Vs.	Avg	AB	H	2B	3B	HR	RBI	BB	SO	OBP	SLG	Pitches Worst Vs.	Avg	AB	H	2B	3B	HR	RBI	BB	SO	OBP	SLG
Pat Borders	.000	12	0	0	0	0	1	0	1	.000	.000	John Olerud	.556	9	5	2	1	0	0	2	0	.636	1.000
Cal Ripken	.077	26	2	0	0	0	3	1	4	.111	.077	Scott Cooper	.545	11	6	2	0	1	4	0	3	.545	1.000
Shane Mack	.083	12	1	0	0	0	0	2	4	.214	.083	Chris Hoiles	.500	12	6	0	0	2	3	3	1	.588	1.000
Brady Anderson	.083	12	1	0	0	0	0	2	2	.214	.083	Mo Vaughn	.500	10	5	3	0	1	3	3	2	.643	1.100
Sandy Alomar Jr	.091	11	1	0	0	0	1	1	3	.167	.091	John Valentin	.429	14	6	3	0	2	6	1	1	.438	1.071

Chris Widger — Expos   Age 27 – Bats Right

	Avg	G	AB	R	H	2B	3B	HR	RBI	BB	SO	HBP	GDP	SB	CS	OBP	SLG	IBB	SH	SF	#Pit	#P/PA	GB	FB	G/F
1997 Season	.234	91	278	30	65	20	3	7	37	22	59	1	7	2	0	.290	.403	1	2	2	1166	3.82	86	89	0.97
Career (1995-1997)	.228	122	334	33	76	20	3	8	39	25	75	2	7	2	0	.283	.377	1	2	3	1390	3.80	101	106	0.95

1997 Season

	Avg	AB	H	2B	3B	HR	RBI	BB	SO	OBP	SLG		Avg	AB	H	2B	3B	HR	RBI	BB	SO	OBP	SLG
vs. Left	.277	101	28	8	2	4	19	10	19	.342	.515	First Pitch	.286	28	8	3	1	1	4	0	0	.276	.571
vs. Right	.209	177	37	12	1	3	18	12	40	.260	.339	Ahead in Count	.340	50	17	8	0	3	15	10	0	.459	.680
Groundball	.231	78	18	4	1	2	8	1	19	.250	.385	Behind in Count	.171	140	24	7	1	1	13	0	52	.171	.257
Flyball	.161	31	5	2	0	1	4	2	11	.212	.323	Two Strikes	.169	136	23	5	1	2	11	12	59	.236	.265
Home	.225	142	32	12	2	4	20	9	32	.270	.423	Batting #7	.208	48	10	1	0	2	8	4	7	.264	.354
Away	.243	136	33	8	1	3	17	13	27	.311	.382	Batting #8	.236	178	42	16	2	3	24	17	34	.305	.399

1997 Season

	Avg	AB	H	2B	3B	HR	RBI	BB	SO	OBP	SLG		Avg	AB	H	2B	3B	HR	RBI	BB	SO	OBP	SLG
Day	.248	101	25	6	2	2	12	9	16	.306	.406	Other	.250	52	13	3	1	2	5	1	18	.264	.462
Night	.226	177	40	14	1	5	25	13	43	.281	.401	March/April	.237	38	9	3	0	2	6	1	6	.250	.474
Grass	.221	95	21	5	1	2	14	11	20	.306	.358	May	.283	46	13	4	1	1	11	2	5	.306	.478
Turf	.240	183	44	15	2	5	23	11	39	.282	.426	June	.291	55	16	4	2	1	7	5	16	.350	.491
Pre-All Star	.270	152	41	12	3	4	24	8	30	.302	.467	July	.228	57	13	2	0	2	7	2	12	.267	.368
Post-All Star	.190	126	24	8	0	3	13	14	29	.277	.325	August	.130	46	6	2	0	1	5	5	9	.216	.239
Scoring Posn	.333	72	24	8	0	2	28	7	16	.390	.528	Sept/Oct	.222	36	8	5	0	0	1	7	11	.349	.361
Close & Late	.261	46	12	1	1	1	7	8	11	.364	.391	vs. AL	.276	29	8	1	1	0	1	2	7	.323	.379
None on/out	.203	64	13	4	0	3	3	3	12	.239	.406	vs. NL	.229	249	57	19	2	7	36	20	52	.287	.406

1997 By Position

Position	Avg	AB	H	2B	3B	HR	RBI	BB	SO	OBP	SLG	G	GS	Innings	PO	A	E	DP	Fld Pct	Rng Fctr	In Zone	Zone Outs	Zone Rtg	MLB Zone
As c	.239	272	65	20	3	7	37	22	57	.296	.412	85	78	694.1	516	40	11	2	.981	---	---	---	---	---

Marc Wilkins — Pirates
Age 27 – Pitches Right (groundball pitcher)

	ERA	W	L	Sv	G	GS	IP	BB	SO	Avg	H	2B	3B	HR	RBI	OBP	SLG	GF	IR	IRS	Hld	SvOp	SB	CS	GB	FB	G/F
1997 Season	3.69	9	5	2	70	0	75.2	33	47	.242	65	11	2	7	27	.333	.375	21	31	5	15	4	6	5	112	70	1.60
Career (1996-1997)	3.76	13	8	3	117	2	150.2	69	109	.254	140	25	3	13	64	.345	.381	32	47	15	19	9	18	10	224	128	1.75

1997 Season

	ERA	W	L	Sv	G	GS	IP	H	HR	BB	SO		Avg	AB	H	2B	3B	HR	RBI	BB	SO	OBP	SLG
Home	4.05	5	0	1	35	0	40.0	35	3	12	22	vs. Left	.246	114	28	6	0	2	11	18	25	.353	.351
Away	3.28	4	1	1	35	0	35.2	30	4	21	25	vs. Right	.239	155	37	5	2	5	16	15	22	.318	.394
Day	3.93	3	4	2	31	0	34.1	32	5	13	21	Inning 1-6	.211	38	8	1	0	1	5	6	10	.318	.316
Night	3.48	6	1	0	39	0	41.1	33	2	20	26	Inning 7+	.247	231	57	10	2	6	22	27	37	.336	.385
Grass	3.38	2	4	1	22	0	21.1	20	2	18	15	None on	.259	158	41	7	1	5	5	15	23	.331	.411
Turf	3.81	7	1	1	48	0	54.1	45	5	15	32	Runners on	.216	111	24	4	1	2	22	18	24	.336	.324
March/April	6.00	1	0	0	11	0	12.0	11	0	11	10	Scoring Posn	.226	62	14	4	1	2	22	14	12	.368	.419
May	4.40	3	0	0	11	0	14.1	14	3	5	10	Close & Late	.202	109	22	6	0	2	10	12	18	.287	.312
June	4.63	1	1	0	12	0	11.2	13	2	1	6	None on/out	.243	70	17	2	0	1	1	2	10	.274	.314
July	1.50	1	1	1	12	0	12.0	7	1	8	7	vs. 1st Batr (relief)	.175	63	11	1	0	0	3	5	10	.246	.190
August	3.52	2	2	1	13	0	15.1	14	1	5	10	1st Inning Pitched	.239	205	49	9	2	6	24	26	32	.336	.390
Sept/Oct	1.74	1	1	0	11	0	10.1	6	0	3	4	First 15 Pitches	.247	186	46	9	2	4	18	18	26	.327	.382
Starter	0.00	0	0	0	0	0	0.0	0	0	0	0	Pitch 16-30	.209	67	14	2	0	2	7	10	18	.312	.328
Reliever	3.69	9	5	2	70	0	75.2	65	7	33	47	Pitch 31-45	.250	12	3	0	0	1	1	4	1	.438	.500
0 Days rest (Relief)	3.86	3	2	2	18	0	18.2	17	2	3	10	Pitch 46+	.500	4	2	0	0	0	1	1	0	.600	.500
1 or 2 Days rest	3.40	5	2	0	39	0	42.1	36	3	15	25	First Pitch	.242	33	8	3	1	0	7	2	0	.306	.394
3+ Days rest	4.30	1	1	0	13	0	14.2	12	2	15	12	Ahead in Count	.157	115	18	4	0	2	3	0	41	.164	.243
vs. AL	3.86	0	1	0	5	0	4.2	4	1	4	1	Behind in Count	.368	68	25	3	0	3	12	17	0	.494	.544
vs. NL	3.68	9	4	2	65	0	71.0	61	6	29	46	Two Strikes	.164	116	19	2	0	3	6	14	47	.254	.259
Pre-All Star	4.69	6	1	1	37	0	40.1	38	5	19	28	Pre-All Star	.257	148	38	5	1	5	20	19	28	.341	.405
Post-All Star	2.55	3	4	1	33	0	35.1	27	2	14	19	Post-All Star	.223	121	27	6	1	2	7	14	19	.324	.339

Rick Wilkins — Mariners
Age 31 – Bats Left (flyball hitter)

	Avg	G	AB	R	H	2B	3B	HR	RBI	BB	SO	HBP	GDP	SB	CS	OBP	SLG	IBB	SH	SF	#Pit	#P/PA	GB	FB	G/F
1997 Season	.198	71	202	20	40	6	0	7	27	18	67	0	0	0	0	.259	.332	0	0	4	836	3.73	52	57	0.91
Last Five Years	.246	508	1574	225	387	75	5	65	217	221	434	7	22	6	7	.338	.424	33	1	19	7191	3.95	433	440	0.98

1997 Season

	Avg	AB	H	2B	3B	HR	RBI	BB	SO	OBP	SLG		Avg	AB	H	2B	3B	HR	RBI	BB	SO	OBP	SLG
vs. Left	.103	39	4	0	0	0	1	4	17	.186	.103	Scoring Posn	.159	63	10	3	0	0	18	11	29	.269	.206
vs. Right	.221	163	36	6	0	7	26	14	50	.276	.387	Close & Late	.219	32	7	1	0	2	8	5	13	.308	.438
Home	.155	103	16	3	0	2	14	9	40	.216	.243	None on/out	.137	51	7	0	0	1	1	2	13	.170	.196
Away	.242	99	24	3	0	5	13	9	27	.306	.424	Batting #7	.182	44	8	2	0	0	5	4	12	.245	.227
First Pitch	.156	32	5	1	0	0	3	0	0	.152	.188	Batting #8	.195	128	25	2	0	5	14	10	42	.250	.328
Ahead in Count	.429	35	15	3	0	2	8	10	0	.543	.686	Other	.233	30	7	2	0	2	8	4	13	.314	.500
Behind in Count	.147	102	15	2	0	3	9	0	59	.147	.255	Pre-All Star	.190	163	31	5	0	4	21	13	58	.246	.294
Two Strikes	.137	102	14	1	0	2	9	8	67	.198	.206	Post-All Star	.231	39	9	1	0	3	6	5	9	.311	.487

Last Five Years

	Avg	AB	H	2B	3B	HR	RBI	BB	SO	OBP	SLG		Avg	AB	H	2B	3B	HR	RBI	BB	SO	OBP	SLG
vs. Left	.169	260	44	8	0	8	27	34	103	.270	.292	First Pitch	.253	198	50	9	1	5	32	22	0	.329	.384
vs. Right	.261	1314	343	67	5	57	190	187	331	.351	.450	Ahead in Count	.388	366	142	30	1	28	82	89	0	.499	.705
Groundball	.228	470	107	23	1	15	50	62	123	.319	.377	Behind in Count	.166	705	117	24	3	19	65	0	362	.171	.289
Flyball	.248	246	61	10	0	14	38	46	79	.363	.459	Two Strikes	.152	808	123	24	2	20	64	110	434	.257	.261
Home	.214	774	166	34	1	25	88	91	235	.297	.358	Batting #6	.273	501	137	33	4	21	79	66	128	.359	.481
Away	.276	800	221	41	4	40	129	130	199	.376	.488	Batting #8	.249	349	87	12	0	18	44	43	111	.331	.438
Day	.223	730	163	35	0	23	74	101	200	.319	.366	Other	.225	724	163	30	1	26	94	112	195	.327	.373
Night	.265	844	224	40	5	42	143	120	234	.354	.474	March/April	.216	250	54	12	0	8	29	40	63	.322	.360
Grass	.244	1092	266	49	2	48	155	147	306	.334	.424	May	.230	361	83	15	0	12	32	51	119	.325	.371
Turf	.251	482	121	26	3	17	62	74	128	.347	.423	June	.240	341	82	15	4	14	43	48	97	.336	.431
Pre-All Star	.232	1027	238	47	4	37	115	150	305	.330	.393	July	.231	238	55	11	1	10	35	32	65	.324	.412
Post-All Star	.272	547	149	28	1	28	102	71	129	.353	.481	August	.287	181	52	11	0	11	37	21	47	.354	.530
Scoring Posn	.227	423	96	21	1	12	148	103	134	.369	.366	Sept/Oct	.300	203	61	11	0	10	41	29	43	.384	.502
Close & Late	.213	258	55	8	0	10	41	45	86	.327	.360	vs. AL	.250	20	5	1	0	1	4	1	6	.273	.450

Last Five Years

	Avg	AB	H	2B	3B	HR	RBI	BB	SO	OBP	SLG		Avg	AB	H	2B	3B	HR	RBI	BB	SO	OBP	SLG
None on/out	.215	405	87	19	2	11	11	34	106	.279	.353	vs. NL	.246	1554	382	74	5	64	213	220	428	.339	.423

Batter vs. Pitcher (career)

Hits Best Against	Avg	AB	H	2B	3B	HR	RBI	BB	SO	OBP	SLG	Hits Worst Against	Avg	AB	H	2B	3B	HR	RBI	BB	SO	OBP	SLG
Rene Arocha	.600	10	6	0	0	1	1	2	2	.667	.900	Curt Leskanic	.000	11	0	0	0	0	0	0	7	.000	.000
Ken Hill	.452	31	14	4	0	2	5	2	5	.486	.774	Trevor Hoffman	.000	8	0	0	0	0	0	3	5	.273	.000
Kevin Gross	.400	20	8	3	0	2	4	2	5	.455	.850	Greg Maddux	.071	14	1	1	0	0	1	2	4	.176	.143
Tommy Greene	.375	8	3	0	0	1	1	3	2	.545	.750	Todd Stottlemyre	.100	10	1	0	0	0	0	2	4	.250	.100
Willie Blair	.357	14	5	0	0	2	4	3	4	.471	.786	Scott Sanders	.133	15	2	1	0	0	0	1	2	.188	.200

Bernie Williams — Yankees
Age 29 – Bats Both (groundball hitter)

	Avg	G	AB	R	H	2B	3B	HR	RBI	BB	SO	HBP	GDP	SB	CS	OBP	SLG	IBB	SH	SF	#Pit	#P/PA	GB	FB	G/F
1997 Season	.328	129	509	107	167	35	6	21	100	73	80	1	10	15	8	.408	.544	7	0	8	2204	3.73	218	116	1.88
Last Five Years	.299	663	2598	455	778	150	27	92	409	344	410	13	65	65	36	.381	.484	22	5	23	11231	3.77	1061	655	1.62

1997 Season

	Avg	AB	H	2B	3B	HR	RBI	BB	SO	OBP	SLG		Avg	AB	H	2B	3B	HR	RBI	BB	SO	OBP	SLG
vs. Left	.326	141	46	11	0	9	32	31	22	.443	.596	First Pitch	.324	74	24	5	0	4	11	6	0	.370	.554
vs. Right	.329	368	121	24	6	12	68	42	58	.393	.524	Ahead in Count	.460	137	63	13	3	10	44	33	0	.557	.818
Groundball	.283	99	28	8	0	2	9	19	24	.395	.424	Behind in Count	.246	203	50	15	2	4	28	0	66	.243	.399
Flyball	.241	79	19	5	3	3	13	11	11	.333	.494	Two Strikes	.235	213	50	11	2	4	28	34	80	.336	.362
Home	.300	240	72	16	3	13	43	26	39	.366	.554	Batting #3	.333	436	145	28	4	18	81	68	62	.419	.539
Away	.353	269	95	19	3	8	57	47	41	.443	.535	Batting #4	.308	65	20	5	2	3	18	4	15	.338	.585
Day	.333	201	67	13	2	11	34	18	30	.387	.582	Other	.250	8	2	2	0	0	1	1	3	.333	.500
Night	.325	308	100	22	4	10	66	55	50	.420	.519	March/April	.345	110	38	9	1	2	19	21	11	.444	.500
Grass	.345	429	148	29	6	19	92	61	69	.420	.573	May	.297	101	30	6	0	6	18	19	19	.405	.535
Turf	.238	80	19	6	0	2	8	12	11	.344	.388	June	.294	51	15	4	0	2	13	10	10	.410	.490
Pre-All Star	.306	278	85	19	1	10	51	51	45	.410	.489	July	.167	30	5	0	0	3	3	6	.235	.167	
Post-All Star	.355	231	82	16	5	11	49	22	35	.405	.610	August	.395	119	47	10	1	8	23	12	15	.448	.697
Scoring Posn	.335	161	54	7	2	6	79	24	28	.407	.516	Sept/Oct	.327	98	32	6	4	3	24	8	19	.370	.561
Close & Late	.250	80	20	3	3	2	13	14	14	.362	.438	vs. AL	.330	473	156	32	6	20	96	69	75	.410	.550
None on/out	.283	99	28	5	1	4	4	11	17	.355	.475	vs. NL	.306	36	11	3	0	1	4	4	5	.375	.472

1997 By Position

Position	Avg	AB	H	2B	3B	HR	RBI	BB	SO	OBP	SLG	G	GS	Innings	PO	A	E	DP	Fld Pct	Rng Fctr	In Zone	Zone Outs	Zone Rtg	MLB Zone
As cf	.329	508	167	35	6	21	100	73	79	.408	.545	128	127	1122.2	269	2	2	1	.993	2.17	332	264	.795	.815

Last Five Years

	Avg	AB	H	2B	3B	HR	RBI	BB	SO	OBP	SLG		Avg	AB	H	2B	3B	HR	RBI	BB	SO	OBP	SLG
vs. Left	.337	845	285	56	4	51	162	120	126	.417	.594	First Pitch	.372	363	135	30	4	13	81	13	0	.393	.584
vs. Right	.281	1753	493	94	23	41	247	224	284	.364	.431	Ahead in Count	.383	720	276	50	10	41	143	182	0	.502	.651
Groundball	.294	582	171	33	5	8	73	77	93	.379	.409	Behind in Count	.221	1027	227	41	8	23	113	0	329	.227	.344
Flyball	.275	484	133	27	6	20	60	70	68	.366	.479	Two Strikes	.213	1071	228	40	11	22	112	148	410	.310	.332
Home	.299	1219	365	72	11	41	181	164	166	.382	.477	Batting #1	.273	575	157	35	8	17	77	54	98	.338	.450
Away	.299	1379	413	78	16	51	228	180	244	.381	.490	Batting #6	.295	509	150	30	2	13	63	64	75	.373	.438
Day	.289	960	277	54	8	38	130	125	152	.371	.480	Other	.311	1514	471	85	17	62	269	226	237	.399	.513
Night	.306	1638	501	96	19	54	279	219	258	.387	.487	March/April	.270	370	100	21	2	13	61	62	49	.373	.443
Grass	.306	2213	678	129	22	83	370	298	343	.387	.497	May	.268	384	103	19	3	14	60	61	70	.368	.443
Turf	.260	385	100	21	5	9	39	46	67	.345	.410	June	.311	456	142	31	5	24	92	57	73	.388	.559
Pre-All Star	.278	1373	382	73	12	55	229	196	220	.368	.469	July	.283	453	128	15	2	13	57	60	68	.366	.411
Post-All Star	.323	1225	396	77	15	37	180	148	190	.397	.501	August	.341	522	178	38	6	16	71	49	79	.397	.529
Scoring Posn	.307	716	220	29	10	24	315	109	103	.389	.476	Sept/Oct	.308	413	127	26	9	12	68	55	73	.391	.501
Close & Late	.278	371	103	14	4	9	61	47	73	.359	.410	vs. AL	.299	2562	767	147	27	91	405	340	405	.381	.484
None on/out	.281	588	165	34	5	29	29	66	85	.358	.503	vs. NL	.306	36	11	3	0	1	4	4	5	.375	.472

Batter vs. Pitcher (career)

Hits Best Against	Avg	AB	H	2B	3B	HR	RBI	BB	SO	OBP	SLG	Hits Worst Against	Avg	AB	H	2B	3B	HR	RBI	BB	SO	OBP	SLG
Jamie Moyer	.514	37	19	6	0	5	10	2	3	.538	1.081	Scott Karl	.059	17	1	0	0	0	0	1	4	.111	.059
Dave Telgheder	.500	10	5	2	1	1	1	1	0	.545	1.200	Rick Aguilera	.100	10	1	0	0	0	0	0	3	.182	.100
Jose Rosado	.500	10	5	0	0	2	3	0	1	.455	1.100	Mike Oquist	.100	10	1	0	0	0	1	1	2	.182	.100
Kenny Rogers	.462	13	6	2	0	1	6	3	1	.563	.846	Ricky Bones	.133	30	4	2	0	0	2	4	3	.235	.200
Eddie Guardado	.429	14	6	2	0	2	5	2	2	.500	1.000	Al Leiter	.167	12	2	0	0	0	0	2	3	.231	.167

Brian Williams — Orioles
Age 29 – Pitches Right

	ERA	W	L	Sv	G	GS	IP	BB	SO	Avg	H	2B	3B	HR	RBI	OBP	SLG	GF	IR	IRS	Hld	SvOp	SB	CS	GB	FB	G/F
1997 Season	3.00	0	0	0	13	0	24.0	18	14	.220	20	6	1	0	13	.345	.308	8	14	8		0	1	0	0	34	29	1.17
Last Five Years	5.75	16	29	5	159	41	377.1	220	266	.291	432	80	10	40	256	.387	.439	46	69	28	10	13	19	11	572	391	1.46

1997 Season

	ERA	W	L	Sv	G	GS	IP	H	HR	BB	SO		Avg	AB	H	2B	3B	HR	RBI	BB	SO	OBP	SLG
Home	2.61	0	0	0	5	0	10.1	7	0	8	5	vs. Left	.273	44	12	2	1	0	7	10	7	.400	.364
Away	3.29	0	0	0	8	0	13.2	13	0	10	9	vs. Right	.170	47	8	4	0	0	6	8	7	.291	.255

Last Five Years

	ERA	W	L	Sv	G	GS	IP	H	HR	BB	SO		Avg	AB	H	2B	3B	HR	RBI	BB	SO	OBP	SLG
Home	5.15	7	10	4	76	19	192.1	197	21	106	146	vs. Left	.331	704	233	46	4	21	125	110	123	.425	.497
Away	6.37	9	19	1	83	22	185.0	235	19	114	120	vs. Right	.255	781	199	34	6	19	131	110	143	.352	.387

Last Five Years

	ERA	W	L	Sv	G	GS	IP	H	HR	BB	SO		Avg	AB	H	2B	3B	HR	RBI	BB	SO	OBP	SLG
Day	5.23	8	13	1	60	17	155.0	160	16	93	107	Inning 1-6	.300	946	284	57	6	25	158	124	163	.385	.452
Night	6.11	8	16	4	99	24	222.1	272	24	127	159	Inning 7+	.275	539	148	23	4	15	98	96	103	.389	.416
Grass	6.18	7	20	3	102	24	230.0	253	24	158	167	None on	.275	737	203	34	6	16	16	108	139	.376	.403
Turf	5.07	9	9	2	57	17	147.1	179	16	62	99	Runners on	.306	748	229	46	4	24	240	112	127	.397	.475
March/April	6.00	1	3	2	22	2	39.0	45	4	30	26	Scoring Posn	.315	447	141	26	3	12	206	79	87	.413	.468
May	4.83	1	6	1	37	7	76.1	88	7	41	54	Close & Late	.293	205	60	3	1	9	40	35	37	.411	.449
June	5.14	5	7	2	31	10	91.0	99	9	49	64	None on/out	.296	338	100	16	3	9	9	49	67	.394	.441
July	6.44	7	8	0	28	14	86.2	103	12	45	69	vs. 1st Batr (relief)	.250	104	26	5	0	0	10	12	19	.331	.298
August	9.73	1	3	0	11	7	37.0	52	5	24	14	1st Inning Pitched	.285	564	161	24	5	16	116	96	111	.391	.431
Sept/Oct	3.80	1	2	0	30	1	47.1	45	3	31	39	First 15 Pitches	.283	435	123	19	4	11	59	64	77	.376	.421
Starter	6.26	13	17	0	41	41	214.1	263	28	122	139	Pitch 16-30	.322	323	104	14	1	9	72	56	69	.427	.455
Reliever	5.08	3	12	5	118	0	163.0	169	12	98	127	Pitch 31-45	.277	224	62	17	2	5	39	34	39	.380	.438
0 Days rest (Relief)	5.74	0	1	0	12	0	15.2	24	0	11	11	Pitch 46+	.284	503	143	30	3	15	86	66	81	.372	.445
1 or 2 Days rest	5.72	1	8	4	52	0	67.2	68	8	38	55	First Pitch	.376	221	83	20	2	7	62	7	0	.397	.579
3+ Days rest	4.41	2	3	1	54	0	79.2	77	4	49	61	Ahead in Count	.199	607	121	23	3	7	60	0	214	.215	.282
vs. AL	6.00	3	10	2	52	17	144.0	161	21	101	85	Behind in Count	.350	357	125	21	2	18	82	143	0	.533	.571
vs. NL	5.59	13	19	3	107	24	233.1	271	19	119	181	Two Strikes	.199	642	128	24	4	9	66	70	266	.287	.291
Pre-All Star	5.12	10	19	5	100	23	237.1	270	21	130	163	Pre-All Star	.292	925	270	47	5	21	141	130	163	.382	.422
Post-All Star	6.81	6	10	0	59	18	140.0	162	19	90	103	Post-All Star	.289	560	162	33	5	19	115	90	103	.394	.468

Pitcher vs. Batter (career)

Pitches Best Vs.	Avg	AB	H	2B	3B	HR	RBI	BB	SO	OBP	SLG	Pitches Worst Vs.	Avg	AB	H	2B	3B	HR	RBI	BB	SO	OBP	SLG
Ivan Rodriguez	.000	10	0	0	0	0	2	1	0	.091	.000	Reggie Sanders	.667	12	8	2	0	2	5	2	2	.714	1.333
Marquis Grissom	.111	9	1	0	0	0	1	4	2	.357	.111	Mark Grace	.583	12	7	2	0	0	4	6	0	.722	.750
Derrick May	.167	12	2	1	0	0	2	1	4	.231	.250	Gregg Jefferies	.571	14	8	1	1	1	4	3	1	.647	1.000
Sammy Sosa	.182	11	2	0	0	0	3	2	3	.286	.182	Terry Pendleton	.571	14	8	1	0	1	7	0	3	.571	.857
Darren Daulton	.182	11	2	0	0	0	1	4	3	.400	.182	Todd Zeile	.500	16	8	1	1	3	7	0	2	.500	1.250

Eddie Williams — Pirates
Age 33 – Bats Right

	Avg	G	AB	R	H	2B	3B	HR	RBI	BB	SO	HBP	GDP	SB	CS	OBP	SLG	IBB	SH	SF	#Pit	#P/PA	GB	FB	G/F
1997 Season	.240	38	96	12	23	5	0	3	12	11	25	2	2	1	0	.327	.385	2	1	1	432	3.89	34	24	1.42
Last Five Years	.257	261	782	101	201	32	2	32	127	67	148	11	40	1	3	.323	.426	3	3	5	3340	3.84	301	208	1.45

1997 Season

	Avg	AB	H	2B	3B	HR	RBI	BB	SO	OBP	SLG		Avg	AB	H	2B	3B	HR	RBI	BB	SO	OBP	SLG
vs. Left	.233	30	7	0	0	2	4	3	3	.303	.433	Scoring Posn	.233	30	7	1	0	0	9	7	5	.368	.267
vs. Right	.242	66	16	5	0	1	8	8	22	.338	.364	Close & Late	.190	21	4	1	0	0	3	4	6	.320	.238

Last Five Years

	Avg	AB	H	2B	3B	HR	RBI	BB	SO	OBP	SLG		Avg	AB	H	2B	3B	HR	RBI	BB	SO	OBP	SLG
vs. Left	.269	283	76	10	0	13	42	24	47	.324	.442	First Pitch	.341	85	29	4	0	5	15	2	0	.371	.565
vs. Right	.251	499	125	22	2	19	85	43	101	.322	.417	Ahead in Count	.331	172	57	8	0	15	43	33	0	.438	.640
Groundball	.297	185	55	6	1	4	29	22	38	.381	.405	Behind in Count	.191	362	69	12	2	8	40	0	123	.203	.301
Flyball	.244	119	29	5	0	4	14	7	16	.289	.387	Two Strikes	.164	372	61	11	2	8	42	32	148	.238	.269
Home	.258	345	89	17	1	13	55	33	75	.333	.426	Batting #4	.278	263	73	15	2	8	37	20	51	.336	.441
Away	.256	437	112	15	1	19	72	34	73	.314	.426	Batting #5	.279	269	75	12	0	11	49	26	51	.343	.446
Day	.300	263	79	9	1	17	57	25	32	.369	.536	Other	.212	250	53	5	0	13	41	21	46	.287	.388
Night	.235	519	122	23	1	15	70	42	116	.298	.370	March/April	.242	91	22	4	1	3	15	11	25	.330	.407
Grass	.255	577	147	21	2	25	92	42	110	.313	.428	May	.237	156	37	5	0	5	21	10	23	.292	.365
Turf	.263	205	54	11	0	7	35	25	38	.349	.420	June	.322	118	38	6	0	6	25	11	15	.386	.525
Pre-All Star	.261	429	112	16	1	18	78	37	77	.328	.429	July	.275	200	55	8	0	11	41	17	32	.339	.480
Post-All Star	.252	353	89	16	1	14	49	30	71	.315	.422	August	.242	153	37	7	1	6	19	11	39	.295	.418
Scoring Posn	.277	242	67	11	2	8	95	27	38	.350	.438	Sept/Oct	.188	64	12	2	0	1	6	7	14	.278	.266
Close & Late	.219	137	30	4	1	4	18	12	25	.280	.350	vs. AL	.208	226	47	5	0	6	28	19	51	.277	.310
None on/out	.232	198	46	9	0	7	7	16	45	.305	.300	vs. NL	.277	556	154	27	2	26	99	48	97	.341	.473

Batter vs. Pitcher (career)

Hits Best Against	Avg	AB	H	2B	3B	HR	RBI	BB	SO	OBP	SLG	Hits Worst Against	Avg	AB	H	2B	3B	HR	RBI	BB	SO	OBP	SLG
Greg Swindell	.385	13	5	0	0	1	3	0	1	.357	.615	Jimmy Key	.071	14	1	1	0	0	0	0	3	.071	.143
Tom Candiotti	.364	11	4	3	0	0	2	0	0	.364	.636	Jeff Fassero	.154	13	2	0	0	0	2	0	4	.154	.154
Pedro Martinez	.308	13	4	1	0	0	1	1	3	.357	.385	Frank Castillo	.167	12	2	0	0	0	0	0	1	.231	.167

George Williams — Athletics
Age 29 – Bats Both

	Avg	G	AB	R	H	2B	3B	HR	RBI	BB	SO	HBP	GDP	SB	CS	OBP	SLG	IBB	SH	SF	#Pit	#P/PA	GB	FB	G/F
1997 Season	.289	76	201	30	58	9	1	3	22	35	46	2	2	0	1	.397	.388	0	2	1	993	4.12	61	61	1.00
Career (1995-1997)	.245	161	412	60	101	19	2	9	46	74	99	7	6	0	1	.366	.367	3	4	4	2020	4.03	113	138	0.82

1997 Season

	Avg	AB	H	2B	3B	HR	RBI	BB	SO	OBP	SLG		Avg	AB	H	2B	3B	HR	RBI	BB	SO	OBP	SLG
vs. Left	.324	68	22	3	0	2	5	7	11	.387	.456	Scoring Posn	.264	53	14	1	0	0	19	4	17	.322	.283
vs. Right	.271	133	36	6	1	1	17	28	35	.402	.353	Close & Late	.289	38	11	3	0	0	8	5	6	.372	.368
Home	.343	99	34	5	0	2	12	18	22	.454	.455	None on/out	.292	48	14	3	1	0	14	7		.452	.396
Away	.235	102	24	4	1	1	10	17	24	.342	.324	Batting #7	.293	82	24	4	0	0	8	15	20	.398	.341
First Pitch	.448	29	13	2	0	1	6	0	0	.467	.621	Batting #8	.358	53	19	4	1	2	4	7	9	.433	.585
Ahead in Count	.444	45	20	4	0	2	7	15	0	.574	.667	Other	.227	66	15	1	0	1	10	13	17	.370	.288
Behind in Count	.129	85	11	1	0	0	3	0	38	.140	.141	Pre-All Star	.256	160	41	8	1	1	15	32	39	.381	.338
Two Strikes	.154	104	16	3	1	0	5	20	46	.296	.202	Post-All Star	.415	41	17	1	0	2	7	3	7	.467	.585

Gerald Williams — Brewers

Age 31 – Bats Right

	Avg	G	AB	R	H	2B	3B	HR	RBI	BB	SO	HBP	GDP	SB	CS	OBP	SLG	IBB	SH	SF	#Pit	#P/PA	GB	FB	G/F
1997 Season	.253	155	566	73	143	32	2	10	41	19	90	6	9	23	9	.282	.369	1	5	5	2122	3.53	208	169	1.23
Last Five Years	.249	479	1226	179	305	79	11	25	122	65	212	14	29	40	23	.291	.392	5	8	15	4887	3.68	440	364	1.21

1997 Season

	Avg	AB	H	2B	3B	HR	RBI	BB	SO	OBP	SLG		Avg	AB	H	2B	3B	HR	RBI	BB	SO	OBP	SLG
vs. Left	.274	157	43	11	0	6	15	7	24	.303	.459	First Pitch	.309	94	29	7	0	1	7	1	0	.330	.415
vs. Right	.244	409	100	21	2	4	26	12	66	.274	.006	Ahead in Count	.350	100	35	10	0	3	12	10	0	.404	.540
Groundball	.294	85	25	7	0	1	6	3	20	.326	.412	Behind in Count	.209	287	60	10	2	3	15	0	84	.213	.289
Flyball	.241	112	27	4	1	2	10	3	14	.265	.348	Two Strikes	.180	266	48	9	1	3	8	8	90	.211	.256
Home	.262	267	70	14	1	3	19	12	39	.299	.356	Batting #7	.305	174	53	12	0	4	14	6	26	.328	.443
Away	.244	299	73	18	1	7	22	7	51	.266	.381	Batting #8	.245	159	39	11	2	0	8	7	32	.287	.340
Day	.250	216	54	12	1	3	14	8	43	.281	.356	Other	.219	233	51	9	0	6	19	6	32	.244	.335
Night	.254	350	89	20	1	7	27	11	47	.283	.377	March/April	.309	68	21	5	1	1	6	6	14	.382	.456
Grass	.252	485	122	25	2	8	34	17	74	.282	.361	May	.268	112	30	4	0	4	11	5	14	.299	.411
Turf	.259	81	21	7	0	2	7	2	16	.279	.420	June	.245	106	26	4	0	2	11	4	14	.274	.340
Pre-All Star	.266	308	82	13	1	7	30	15	45	.304	.383	July	.252	107	27	4	0	3	6	1	18	.257	.393
Post-All Star	.236	258	61	19	1	3	11	4	45	.255	.353	August	.210	105	22	7	1	0	5	2	18	.239	.295
Scoring Posn	.205	127	26	5	1	1	28	7	25	.248	.283	Sept/Oct	.250	68	17	6	0	0	2	1	12	.264	.338
Close & Late	.220	100	22	6	1	2	10	2	13	.224	.360	vs. AL	.248	517	128	30	2	9	34	16	83	.277	.366
None on/out	.235	170	40	6	0	2	2	6	28	.266	.306	vs. NL	.306	49	15	2	0	1	7	3	7	.327	.408

1997 By Position

Position	Avg	AB	H	2B	3B	HR	RBI	BB	SO	OBP	SLG		G	GS	Innings	PO	A	E	DP	Fld Pct	Rng Fctr	In Zone	Zone Outs	Zone Rtg	MLB Zone
As lf	.287	115	33	6	0	2	11	2	15	.308	.391		39	35	245.1	53	3	0	0	1.000	2.13	60	53	.883	.805
As cf	.244	450	110	26	2	8	30	17	75	.276	.364		129	124	1071.2	301	8	3	4	.990	2.60	358	286	.799	.815

Last Five Years

	Avg	AB	H	2B	3B	HR	RBI	BB	SO	OBP	SLG		Avg	AB	H	2B	3B	HR	RBI	BB	SO	OBP	SLG
vs. Left	.270	508	137	40	4	17	61	41	86	.324	.465	First Pitch	.335	194	65	17	2	5	26	5	0	.361	.521
vs. Right	.234	718	168	39	7	8	61	24	126	.267	.341	Ahead in Count	.326	218	71	22	3	8	28	29	0	.403	.564
Groundball	.301	216	65	18	2	3	20	9	40	.333	.444	Behind in Count	.211	616	130	28	5	6	46	0	190	.216	.302
Flyball	.272	224	61	14	6	6	30	18	28	.329	.469	Two Strikes	.184	593	109	28	1	8	38	31	212	.229	.275
Home	.256	590	151	35	6	12	67	35	93	.298	.397	Batting #7	.283	367	104	29	1	7	35	26	56	.334	.425
Away	.242	636	154	44	5	13	55	30	119	.284	.388	Batting #8	.252	420	106	27	7	8	46	16	81	.287	.407
Day	.254	481	122	31	6	9	51	21	94	.287	.399	Other	.216	439	95	23	3	10	41	23	75	.257	.351
Night	.246	745	183	48	5	16	71	44	118	.291	.388	March/April	.325	120	39	11	3	3	18	9	26	.386	.542
Grass	.245	1080	265	66	9	21	103	56	188	.285	.381	May	.280	268	75	12	4	10	34	17	36	.328	.466
Turf	.274	146	40	13	2	4	19	9	24	.331	.473	June	.263	228	60	15	1	5	30	10	38	.296	.404
Pre-All Star	.280	675	189	41	8	19	87	40	113	.326	.449	July	.244	213	52	12	2	6	18	12	42	.281	.404
Post-All Star	.211	551	116	38	3	6	35	25	99	.248	.323	August	.167	215	36	18	1	0	14	10	36	.209	.260
Scoring Posn	.213	320	68	16	4	3	88	23	56	.268	.316	Sept/Oct	.236	182	43	11	0	1	8	7	34	.273	.313
Close & Late	.250	184	46	11	2	2	15	8	37	.273	.364	vs. AL	.246	1177	290	77	11	24	115	62	205	.289	.392
None on/out	.256	305	78	22	2	6	6	16	54	.299	.400	vs. NL	.306	49	15	2	0	1	7	3	7	.327	.408

Batter vs. Pitcher (career)

Hits Best Against	Avg	AB	H	2B	3B	HR	RBI	BB	SO	OBP	SLG	Hits Worst Against	Avg	AB	H	2B	3B	HR	RBI	BB	SO	OBP	SLG
Arthur Rhodes	.467	15	7	3	0	1	5	0	2	.467	.867	Jose Rosado	.000	9	0	0	0	0	1	1	2	.091	.000
Charles Nagy	.462	13	6	1	0	0	3	0	3	.462	.692	Kenny Rogers	.083	12	1	0	0	0	0	1	1	.154	.083
Scott Karl	.364	11	4	1	0	0	2	3	.462	.455	James Baldwin	.100	10	1	0	0	0	1	1	3	.182	.100
Paul Quantrill	.364	11	4	3	0	0	0	1	.364	.636	Jamie Moyer	.154	26	4	1	0	0	1	1	6	.185	.192
Rich Robertson	.313	16	5	1	0	0	3	0	1	.313	.500	Kevin Appier	.154	13	2	1	0	0	0	0	4	.154	.231

Matt Williams — Indians

Age 32 – Bats Right (flyball hitter)

	Avg	G	AB	R	H	2B	3B	HR	RBI	BB	SO	HBP	GDP	SB	CS	OBP	SLG	IBB	SH	SF	#Pit	#P/PA	GB	FB	G/F
1997 Season	.263	151	596	86	157	32	3	32	105	34	108	4	14	12	4	.307	.488	4	0	2	2173	3.42	172	209	0.82
Last Five Years	.287	589	2307	387	663	114	12	158	461	163	424	18	54	17	9	.336	.553	32	0	23	8705	3.47	717	792	0.91

1997 Season

	Avg	AB	H	2B	3B	HR	RBI	BB	SO	OBP	SLG		Avg	AB	H	2B	3B	HR	RBI	BB	SO	OBP	SLG
vs. Left	.281	139	39	10	1	13	31	9	22	.327	.647	First Pitch	.308	107	33	10	0	4	18	4	0	.333	.514
vs. Right	.258	457	118	22	2	19	74	25	86	.300	.300	Ahead in Count	.368	114	42	10	0	7	26	15	0	.438	.640
Groundball	.241	108	26	2	1	6	13	9	13	.299	.444	Behind in Count	.193	274	53	7	3	13	42	0	91	.201	.383
Flyball	.244	86	21	1	1	4	9	4	17	.286	.419	Two Strikes	.175	263	46	6	3	12	41	15	108	.224	.357
Home	.265	272	72	15	1	18	50	20	50	.313	.404	Batting #4	.238	290	69	19	0	15	47	19	60	.289	.459
Away	.262	324	85	17	2	25	67	14	58	.301	.559	Batting #6	.307	264	81	11	3	16	55	14	35	.344	.553
Day	.315	203	64	10	1	12	38	9	36	.347	.552	Other	.167	42	7	2	0	1	3	1	13	.186	.286
Night	.237	393	93	22	2	20	67	25	72	.286	.454	March/April	.290	107	31	11	0	7	25	10	15	.356	.589
Grass	.263	506	133	28	3	26	90	32	87	.309	.484	May	.227	88	20	3	0	6	11	5	29	.277	.466
Turf	.267	90	24	4	0	6	15	2	21	.290	.511	June	.181	94	17	2	0	6	18	4	18	.214	.394
Pre-All Star	.243	309	75	16	0	20	64	20	64	.292	.489	July	.250	100	25	1	1	4	14	6	16	.287	.400
Post-All Star	.286	287	82	16	3	12	54	14	44	.322	.488	August	.325	114	37	10	0	5	25	2	17	.342	.544
Scoring Posn	.282	177	50	12	0	7	72	17	36	.342	.469	Sept/Oct	.290	93	27	5	2	4	17	7	13	.347	.516
Close & Late	.304	79	24	2	1	5	20	6	18	.360	.544	vs. AL	.266	531	141	29	3	30	96	33	94	.312	.501
None on/out	.297	148	44	7	1	13	13	7	21	.333	.622	vs. NL	.246	65	16	3	0	2	9	1	14	.258	.385

1997 By Position

Position	Avg	AB	H	2B	3B	HR	RBI	BB	SO	OBP	SLG	G	GS	Innings	PO	A	E	DP	Fld Pct	Rng Fctr	In Zone	Zone Outs	Zone Rtg	MLB Zone
As 3b	.264	595	157	32	3	32	105	34	107	.307	.489	151	148	1284.2	88	299	12	21	.970	2.71	405	337	.832	.801

Last Five Years

	Avg	AB	H	2B	3B	HR	RBI	BB	SO	OBP	SLG		Avg	AB	H	2B	3B	HR	RBI	BB	SO	OBP	SLG
vs. Left	.301	572	172	32	3	59	137	55	88	.362	.677	First Pitch	.325	425	138	30	0	35	92	25	0	.362	.642
vs. Right	.283	1735	491	82	9	99	324	108	336	.327	.512	Ahead in Count	.359	460	165	26	3	46	123	76	0	.445	.728
Groundball	.292	630	184	23	3	40	111	45	107	.341	.529	Behind in Count	.226	1019	230	37	9	48	162	0	355	.231	.421
Flyball	.305	338	103	18	2	25	62	20	65	.346	.592	Two Strikes	.196	979	192	35	8	42	148	61	424	.248	.377
Home	.288	1099	316	56	5	68	213	95	214	.346	.533	Batting #4	.290	1803	522	96	9	128	370	135	335	.340	.566
Away	.287	1208	347	58	7	90	248	68	210	.327	.570	Batting #6	.307	264	81	11	3	16	55	14	35	.344	.553
Day	.299	1057	316	51	3	80	221	87	192	.353	.580	Other	.250	240	60	7	0	14	36	14	54	.300	.454
Night	.278	1250	347	63	9	78	240	76	232	.321	.530	March/April	.312	404	126	29	1	30	85	42	64	.378	.611
Grass	.288	1853	533	89	10	118	360	144	337	.341	.538	May	.285	527	150	21	4	42	116	37	122	.333	.579
Turf	.286	454	130	25	2	40	101	19	87	.316	.615	June	.240	384	92	12	1	27	70	24	75	.288	.487
Pre-All Star	.281	1389	390	62	6	104	290	108	277	.335	.559	July	.295	366	108	12	1	23	75	23	65	.339	.522
Post-All Star	.297	918	273	52	6	54	171	55	147	.338	.544	August	.289	304	88	22	1	13	46	11	54	.319	.497
Scoring Posn	.295	674	199	36	3	41	304	81	136	.362	.540	Sept/Oct	.307	322	99	18	4	23	69	26	44	.357	.602
Close & Late	.277	336	93	10	4	18	63	28	69	.334	.491	vs. AL	.266	531	141	29	3	30	96	33	94	.312	.501
None on/out	.309	580	179	32	4	50	50	30	87	.346	.636	vs. NL	.294	1776	522	85	9	128	365	130	330	.343	.568

Batter vs. Pitcher (career)

Hits Best Against	Avg	AB	H	2B	3B	HR	RBI	BB	SO	OBP	SLG	Hits Worst Against	Avg	AB	H	2B	3B	HR	RBI	BB	SO	OBP	SLG
Bret Saberhagen	.533	15	8	2	0	3	6	0	1	.533	1.267	Steve Trachsel	.000	12	0	0	0	0	1	4	1	.235	.000
Xavier Hernandez	.438	16	7	3	0	2	9	0	2	.438	1.000	Mark Portugal	.067	45	3	0	0	0	0	2	13	.106	.067
Frank Castillo	.429	28	12	3	0	4	11	1	5	.448	.964	Cal Eldred	.100	10	1	0	0	0	1	2	0	.250	.100
John Smiley	.395	38	15	3	0	7	15	3	7	.439	1.026	Pat Rapp	.125	16	2	1	0	0	2	1	5	.182	.143
Allen Watson	.357	14	5	1	0	3	7	1	4	.471	1.071	Danny Darwin	.143	21	3	0	0	0	0	0	6	.182	.143

Mike Williams — Royals

Age 29 – Pitches Right

	ERA	W	L	Sv	G	GS	IP	BB	SO	Avg	H	2B	3B	HR	RBI	OBP	SLG	GF	IR	IRS	Hld	SvOp	SB	CS	GB	FB	G/F
1997 Season	6.43	0	2	1	10	0	14.0	8	10	.333	20	3	0	1	13	.414	.433	4	4	1	1	0	0	0	18	19	0.95
Last Five Years	4.89	12	26	1	104	49	370.0	146	232	.278	397	77	12	48	203	.346	.449	16	48	21	2	1	37	16	518	404	1.28

1997 Season

	ERA	W	L	Sv	G	GS	IP	H	HR	BB	SO		Avg	AB	H	2B	3B	HR	RBI	BB	SO	OBP	SLG
Home	6.48	0	1	1	5	0	8.1	13	0	6	5	vs. Left	.269	26	7	1	0	1	3	3	6	.345	.423
Away	6.35	0	1	0	5	0	5.2	7	1	2	5	vs. Right	.382	34	13	2	0	0	10	5	4	.463	.441

Last Five Years

	ERA	W	L	Sv	G	GS	IP	H	HR	BB	SO		Avg	AB	H	2B	3B	HR	RBI	BB	SO	OBP	SLG
Home	4.78	8	9	1	53	24	196.0	207	23	74	117	vs. Left	.259	638	165	40	5	23	83	84	83	.344	.445
Away	5.02	4	17	0	51	25	174.0	190	25	72	115	vs. Right	.293	792	232	37	7	25	120	62	149	.348	.452
Day	4.95	3	12	1	33	15	111.0	125	14	37	80	Inning 1-6	.276	1205	333	71	8	43	170	115	193	.342	.456
Night	4.86	9	14	0	71	34	259.0	272	34	109	152	Inning 7+	.284	225	64	6	4	5	33	31	39	.368	.413
Grass	5.34	3	10	1	36	16	119.2	143	18	53	72	None on	.284	810	230	44	5	30	30	64	132	.341	.462
Turf	4.67	9	16	0	68	33	250.1	254	30	93	160	Runners on	.269	620	167	33	7	18	173	82	100	.352	.432
March/April	5.76	0	2	0	7	5	29.2	38	4	14	17	Scoring Posn	.281	374	105	19	3	14	153	55	70	.367	.460
May	5.99	2	4	0	21	8	70.2	91	12	30	54	Close & Late	.295	122	36	4	1	4	22	17	37	.400	.443
June	4.79	1	7	1	22	11	77.0	84	9	25	41	None on/out	.267	359	96	17	2	10	10	22	60	.315	.409
July	3.78	3	4	0	20	7	64.1	60	6	25	42	vs. 1st Batr (relief)	.154	52	8	1	0	0	6	2	11	.200	.173
August	6.02	3	3	0	18	5	49.1	56	10	23	25	1st Inning Pitched	.278	378	105	21	5	14	78	44	59	.356	.471
Sept/Oct	3.87	3	6	0	16	13	79.0	68	7	29	53	First 15 Pitches	.262	305	80	16	3	6	40	28	45	.327	.393
Starter	4.83	10	21	0	49	49	274.0	297	37	103	165	Pitch 16-30	.289	287	83	13	4	16	58	35	50	.370	.530
Reliever	5.06	2	5	1	55	0	96.0	100	11	43	67	Pitch 31-45	.298	255	76	21	3	8	32	14	44	.335	.498
0 Days rest (Relief)	4.26	1	0	0	9	0	19.0	21	1	9	16	Pitch 46+	.271	583	158	27	2	18	73	69	93	.349	.417
1 or 2 Days rest	5.50	1	0	0	10	0	18.0	18	3	11	12	First Pitch	.320	228	73	16	1	11	36	11	0	.358	.544
3+ Days rest	5.19	0	5	1	36	0	59.0	61	7	23	39	Ahead in Count	.230	631	145	23	6	12	64	0	197	.237	.342
vs. AL	6.97	0	1	1	7	0	10.1	13	0	6	9	Behind in Count	.311	315	98	26	2	14	55	80	0	.446	.540
vs. NL	4.83	12	25	0	97	49	359.2	384	48	140	223	Two Strikes	.210	614	129	20	8	13	64	55	232	.277	.332
Pre-All Star	5.00	6	14	1	59	26	208.2	240	27	75	130	Pre-All Star	.292	821	240	50	7	27	119	75	130	.353	.469
Post-All Star	4.74	6	12	0	45	23	161.1	157	21	71	102	Post-All Star	.258	609	157	27	5	21	84	71	102	.337	.422

Pitcher vs. Batter (career)

Pitches Best Vs.	Avg	AB	H	2B	3B	HR	RBI	BB	SO	OBP	SLG	Pitches Worst Vs.	Avg	AB	H	2B	3B	HR	RBI	BB	SO	OBP	SLG
Henry Rodriguez	.071	14	1	1	0	0	0	0	2	.071	.143	Terry Pendleton	.500	12	6	4	0	0	3	1	0	.538	.833
Darrin Fletcher	.100	10	1	1	0	0	0	1	0	.182	.200	Ray Lankford	.462	13	6	2	0	2	3	1	4	.500	1.077
Steve Finley	.133	15	2	1	0	0	2	0	1	.133	.200	Mike Piazza	.417	12	5	1	1	1	4	3	1	.533	.917
Thomas Howard	.154	13	2	1	0	0	0	0	0	.154	.231	Fred McGriff	.417	12	5	1	0	2	4	1	0	.462	1.000
Kurt Abbott	.182	11	2	1	0	0	1	0	2	.167	.273	Sammy Sosa	.400	10	4	0	0	2	6	1	0	.417	1.000

Mitch Williams — Royals
Age 33 – Pitches Left

	ERA	W	L	Sv	G	GS	IP	BB	SO	Avg	H	2B	3B	HR	RBI	OBP	SLG	GF	IR	IRS	Hld	SvOp	SB	CS	GB	FB	G/F
1997 Season	10.80	0	1	0	7	0	6.2	7	10	.367	11	3	0	2	10	.474	.667	4	3	3			0	1	11	3	3.67
Last Five Years	5.07	5	14	49	117	0	99.1	96	100	.267	101	14	0	10	64	.417	.384	82	37	21	7	58	16	1	110	101	1.09

1997 Season

	ERA	W	L	Sv	G	GS	IP	H	HR	BB	SO		Avg	AB	H	2B	3B	HR	RBI	BB	SO	OBP	SLG
Home	12.00	0	0	0	3	0	3.0	7	0	1	3	vs. Left	.364	11	4	0	0	1	4	1	2	.385	.636
Away	9.82	0	1	0	4	0	3.2	4	2	6	7	vs. Right	.368	19	7	3	0	1	6	0	0	.620	.684

Last Five Years

	ERA	W	L	Sv	G	GS	IP	H	HR	BB	SO		Avg	AB	H	2B	3B	HR	RBI	BB	SO	OBP	SLG
Home	5.72	2	7	22	56	0	50.1	54	4	43	49	vs. Left	.266	94	25	0	0	3	17	16	23	.388	.362
Away	4.41	3	7	27	61	0	49.0	47	6	53	51	vs. Right	.268	284	76	14	0	7	47	80	77	.427	.391
Day	6.61	2	6	13	33	0	31.1	40	4	29	30	Inning 1-6	.381	21	8	2	0	2	11	10	7	.581	.762
Night	4.37	3	8	36	84	0	68.0	61	6	67	70	Inning 7+	.261	357	93	12	0	8	53	86	93	.406	.361
Grass	5.26	3	4	16	47	0	39.1	43	5	40	37	None on	.247	166	41	5	0	3	3	44	43	.408	.331
Turf	4.95	2	10	33	70	0	60.0	58	5	56	63	Runners on	.283	212	60	9	0	7	61	52	57	.425	.425
March/April	6.08	1	3	13	28	0	26.2	31	2	24	27	Scoring Posn	.268	138	37	6	0	5	57	32	34	.401	.420
May	7.67	2	6	7	38	0	27.0	30	6	30	28	Close & Late	.277	220	61	5	0	5	40	55	58	.423	.368
June	1.69	0	1	9	15	0	10.2	10	1	10	11	None on/out	.250	80	20	2	0	2	2	20	23	.406	.350
July	2.08	1	0	5	13	0	13.0	7	0	9	7	vs. 1st Batr (relief)	.244	90	22	3	0	4	10	25	24	.419	.378
August	4.35	1	1	8	10	0	10.1	12	0	11	13	1st Inning Pitched	.263	358	94	13	0	10	61	93	96	.418	.383
Sept/Oct	3.86	0	3	7	13	0	11.2	11	1	12	14	First 15 Pitches	.283	254	72	9	0	8	37	67	60	.440	.413
Starter	0.00	0	0	0	0	0	0.0	0	0	0	0	Pitch 16-30	.239	117	28	5	0	2	23	27	38	.377	.333
Reliever	5.07	5	14	49	117	0	99.1	101	10	96	100	Pitch 31-45	.143	7	1	0	0	0	4	2	2	.273	.143
0 Days rest (Relief)	4.02	3	5	14	37	0	31.1	28	3	29	28	Pitch 46+	.000	0	0	0	0	0	0	0	0	.000	.000
1 or 2 Days rest	5.40	0	6	21	43	0	35.0	34	3	40	39	First Pitch	.296	27	8	2	0	0	3	0	0	.355	.370
3+ Days rest	5.73	2	3	14	37	0	33.0	39	4	27	33	Ahead in Count	.216	204	44	7	0	4	21	0	75	.217	.309
vs. AL	8.31	1	3	0	27	0	17.1	24	3	28	19	Behind in Count	.424	66	28	3	0	3	23	64	0	.701	.606
vs. NL	4.39	4	11	49	90	0	82.0	77	7	68	81	Two Strikes	.190	205	39	7	0	6	22	29	100	.288	.312
Pre-All Star	5.89	4	10	29	87	0	70.1	76	9	68	71	Pre-All Star	.279	272	76	9	0	9	54	66	71	.425	.412
Post-All Star	3.10	1	4	20	30	0	29.0	25	1	28	29	Post-All Star	.236	106	25	5	0	1	10	28	29	.397	.311

Pitcher vs. Batter (career)

Pitches Best Vs.	Avg	AB	H	2B	3B	HR	RBI	BB	SO	OBP	SLG	Pitches Worst Vs.	Avg	AB	H	2B	3B	HR	RBI	BB	SO	OBP	SLG
Darryl Strawberry	.000	12	0	0	0	0	0	2	7	.143	.000	Gregg Jefferies	.556	9	5	0	0	0	2	1	0	.636	.556
Marquis Grissom	.063	16	1	1	0	0	1	3	1	.211	.125	Ray Lankford	.500	10	5	1	1	0	2	4	3	.643	.800
Mark Grace	.067	15	1	0	0	0	0	3	0	.067	.067	Delino DeShields	.429	7	3	1	0	0	2	0	1	.615	.571
Tony Gwynn	.083	12	1	1	0	0	1	1	1	.154	.167	Ken Caminiti	.417	12	5	0	0	0	3	3	4	.533	.667
Rex Hudler	.091	11	1	0	0	0	0	0	3	.091	.091	Jay Bell	.316	19	6	1	1	1	2	4	6	.435	.632

Shad Williams — Angels
Age 27 – Pitches Right (flyball pitcher)

	ERA	W	L	Sv	G	GS	IP	BB	SO	Avg	H	2B	3B	HR	RBI	OBP	SLG	GF	IR	IRS	Hld	SvOp	SB	CS	GB	FB	G/F
1997 Season	0.00	0	0	0	1	0	1.0	1	0	.250	1	0	0	0	0	.400	.250	1	0	0			0	0	2	2	1.00
Career (1996-1997)	8.59	0	2	0	14	2	29.1	22	26	.339	43	11	0	7	36	.441	.591	4	13	9	0	0	5	1	28	38	0.74

1997 Season

	ERA	W	L	Sv	G	GS	IP	H	HR	BB	SO		Avg	AB	H	2B	3B	HR	RBI	BB	SO	OBP	SLG
Home	0.00	0	0	0	0	0	0.0	0	0	0	0	vs. Left	.000	2	0	0	0	0	0	1	0	.333	.000
Away	0.00	0	0	0	1	0	1.0	1	0	1	0	vs. Right	.500	2	1	0	0	0	0	0	0	.500	.500

Woody Williams — Blue Jays
Age 31 – Pitches Right (flyball pitcher)

	ERA	W	L	Sv	G	GS	IP	BB	SO	Avg	H	2B	3B	HR	RBI	OBP	SLG	CG	ShO	Sup	QS	#P/S	SB	CS	GB	FB	G/F
1997 Season	4.35	9	14	0	31	31	194.2	66	124	.269	201	44	5	31	89	.329	.465	0	0	3.19	18	103	8	9	197	286	0.69
Career (1993-1997)	4.21	18	25	0	134	44	403.2	170	288	.255	393	84	6	52	174	.331	.419	1	0	3.81	22	98	23	11	397	570	0.70

1997 Season

	ERA	W	L	Sv	G	GS	IP	H	HR	BB	SO		Avg	AB	H	2B	3B	HR	RBI	BB	SO	OBP	SLG
Home	4.14	5	8	0	17	17	111.0	114	12	30	75	vs. Left	.271	395	107	17	3	15	42	46	67	.349	.443
Away	4.63	4	6	0	14	14	83.2	87	19	36	49	vs. Right	.266	353	94	27	2	16	47	20	57	.305	.490
Day	5.28	1	9	0	12	12	76.2	78	17	32	51	Inning 1-6	.263	666	175	39	4	27	80	63	115	.327	.455
Night	3.74	8	5	0	19	19	118.0	123	14	34	73	Inning 7+	.317	82	26	5	1	4	9	3	9	.341	.549
Grass	4.23	3	4	0	10	10	61.2	61	11	25	37	None on	.270	452	122	29	2	25	25	34	79	.324	.509
Turf	4.40	6	10	0	21	21	133.0	140	20	41	87	Runners on	.267	296	79	15	3	6	64	32	45	.336	.399
March/April	3.04	0	1	0	4	4	26.2	20	3	6	16	Scoring Posn	.253	166	42	6	3	3	55	27	32	.347	.380
May	4.97	1	4	0	6	6	38.0	34	3	15	26	Close & Late	.304	46	14	3	1	2	7	1	3	.319	.543
June	5.52	2	2	0	5	5	29.1	33	9	12	14	None on/out	.280	200	56	15	0	12	12	12	35	.327	.535
July	3.34	3	2	0	5	5	32.1	31	5	6	18	vs. 1st Batr (relief)	.000	0	0	0	0	0	0	0	0	.000	.000
August	5.65	1	4	0	6	6	36.2	50	6	14	24	1st Inning Pitched	.271	118	32	5	2	4	20	14	20	.346	.449
Sept/Oct	3.13	2	1	0	5	5	31.2	33	5	13	26	First 75 Pitches	.262	520	136	28	3	19	60	45	92	.322	.437
Starter	4.35	9	14	0	31	31	194.2	201	31	66	124	Pitch 76-90	.308	104	32	8	1	6	14	10	14	.362	.577
Reliever	0.00	0	0	0	0	0	0.0	0	0	0	0	Pitch 91-105	.282	85	24	5	0	6	13	9	12	.358	.553
0-3 Days Rest (Start)	0.00	0	0	0	0	0	0.0	0	0	0	0	Pitch 106+	.231	39	9	3	1	0	2	2	6	.268	.359
4 Days Rest	4.14	7	10	0	21	21	137.0	142	21	44	88	First Pitch	.344	93	32	7	0	6	12	1	0	.351	.613
5+ Days Rest	4.84	2	4	0	10	10	57.2	59	10	22	36	Ahead in Count	.237	355	84	21	4	11	36	0	97	.244	.411
vs. AL	4.46	8	13	0	28	28	175.2	190	31	54	115	Behind in Count	.316	152	48	12	0	5	36	0	0	.442	.533
vs. NL	3.32	1	1	0	3	3	19.0	11	0	12	9	Two Strikes	.205	361	74	17	4	8	25	29	124	.270	.341
Pre-All Star	4.59	3	8	0	16	16	100.0	95	15	34	60	Pre-All Star	.247	385	95	22	1	15	48	34	60	.312	.426

1997 Season

	ERA	W	L	Sv	G	GS	IP	H	HR	BB	SO		Avg	AB	H	2B	3B	HR	RBI	BB	SO	OBP	SLG
Post-All Star	4.09	6	6	0	15	15	94.2	106	16	32	64	Post-All Star	.292	363	106	22	4	16	41	32	64	.347	.507

Career (1993-1997)

	ERA	W	L	Sv	G	GS	IP	H	HR	BB	SO		Avg	AB	H	2B	3B	HR	RBI	BB	SO	OBP	SLG
Home	4.23	11	13	0	69	24	223.2	220	26	88	162	vs. Left	.255	807	206	37	3	23	78	110	160	.347	.394
Away	4.20	7	12	0	65	20	180.0	173	26	82	126	vs. Right	.255	732	187	47	3	29	96	60	128	.314	.447
Day	4.85	3	10	0	45	16	137.1	135	24	62	100	Inning 1-6	.258	1036	267	55	4	37	122	113	182	.332	.426
Night	3.89	15	15	0	89	28	266.1	258	28	108	188	Inning 7+	.250	503	126	29	2	15	52	57	106	.331	.406
Grass	3.76	6	7	0	53	15	146.0	134	16	65	103	None on	.259	874	226	49	3	36	36	84	167	.326	.445
Turf	4.47	12	18	0	81	29	257.2	259	36	105	185	Runners on	.251	665	167	35	3	16	138	86	121	.338	.385
March/April	3.35	0	1	0	14	4	37.2	29	3	15	30	Scoring Posn	.250	368	92	19	3	10	122	63	84	.356	.399
May	5.13	1	6	0	34	6	80.2	83	8	40	58	Close & Late	.227	203	46	7	1	7	23	28	39	.322	.374
June	4.42	6	4	0	29	5	73.1	71	12	36	52	None on/out	.277	394	109	26	0	20	20	33	72	.339	.495
July	3.09	4	3	0	21	8	67.0	56	8	20	42	vs. 1st Batr (relief)	.213	75	16	5	0	3	14	13	19	.337	.400
August	5.30	3	7	0	24	11	74.2	92	11	32	49	1st Inning Pitched	.246	452	111	23	3	11	65	69	105	.350	.383
Sept/Oct	3.33	4	4	0	12	10	70.1	62	10	27	57	First 75 Pitches	.255	1232	314	65	4	38	141	142	241	.334	.407
Starter	4.34	14	19	0	44	44	265.1	270	41	90	173	Pitch 76-90	.277	141	39	10	1	7	16	15	22	.342	.511
Reliever	3.97	4	6	0	90	0	138.1	123	11	80	115	Pitch 91-105	.270	111	30	5	0	7	15	10	17	.336	.505
0-3 Days Rest (Start)	0.00	0	0	0	0	0	0.0	0	0	0	0	Pitch 106+	.182	55	10	4	1	0	2	3	8	.224	.291
4 Days Rest	3.77	11	12	0	28	28	181.2	179	27	55	121	First Pitch	.299	197	59	10	0	8	23	7	0	.333	.472
5+ Days Rest	5.59	3	7	0	16	16	83.2	91	14	35	52	Ahead in Count	.226	733	166	38	5	17	73	0	239	.233	.362
vs. AL	4.26	17	24	0	131	41	384.2	382	52	158	279	Behind in Count	.315	317	100	25	0	17	53	85	0	.456	.555
vs. NL	3.32	1	1	0	3	3	19.0	11	0	12	9	Two Strikes	.206	751	155	32	5	14	60	78	288	.285	.318
Pre-All Star	4.34	8	13	0	85	18	220.0	205	25	99	159	Pre-All Star	.244	841	205	46	1	25	99	99	159	.326	.390
Post-All Star	4.07	10	12	0	49	26	183.2	188	27	71	129	Post-All Star	.269	698	188	38	5	27	75	71	129	.338	.454

Pitcher vs. Batter (career)

Pitches Best Vs.	Avg	AB	H	2B	3B	HR	RBI	BB	SO	OBP	SLG	Pitches Worst Vs.	Avg	AB	H	2B	3B	HR	RBI	BB	SO	OBP	SLG
Tim Salmon	.000	9	0	0	0	0	0	4	0	.308	.000	Mike Stanley	.571	14	8	1	0	3	5	2	0	.625	1.286
Cecil Fielder	.095	21	2	1	0	0	0	0	7	.095	.143	Joey Cora	.545	11	6	2	0	1	1	0	0	.545	1.000
John Valentin	.118	17	2	1	0	0	2	1	1	.167	.176	Chuck Knoblauch	.545	11	6	2	0	1	2	0	1	.545	1.000
Jeff Frye	.167	12	2	0	0	0	0	1	1	.167	.167	Frank Thomas	.500	12	6	1	0	3	0	0	0	.500	.917
Jim Edmonds	.182	11	2	0	0	0	1	0	0	.182	.182	Derek Jeter	.357	14	5	1	0	2	2	0	4	.357	.857

Antone Williamson — Brewers   Age 24 – Bats Left

	Avg	G	AB	R	H	2B	3B	HR	RBI	BB	SO	HBP	GDP	SB	CS	OBP	SLG	IBB	SH	SF	#Pit	#P/PA	GB	FB	G/F
1997 Season	.204	24	54	2	11	3	0	0	6	4	8	0	2	0	1	.254	.259	0	1	1	220	3.67	24	19	1.26

1997 Season

	Avg	AB	H	2B	3B	HR	RBI	BB	SO	OBP	SLG		Avg	AB	H	2B	3B	HR	RBI	BB	SO	OBP	SLG
vs. Left	.000	2	0	0	0	0	0	1	1	.333	.000	Scoring Posn	.231	13	3	1	0	0	6	0	2	.214	.308
vs. Right	.212	52	11	3	0	0	6	3	7	.250	.269	Close & Late	.333	9	3	2	0	0	2	1	1	.400	.556

Dan Wilson — Mariners   Age 29 – Bats Right

	Avg	G	AB	R	H	2B	3B	HR	RBI	BB	SO	HBP	GDP	SB	CS	OBP	SLG	IBB	SH	SF	#Pit	#P/PA	GB	FB	G/F
1997 Season	.270	146	508	66	137	31	1	15	74	39	72	5	12	7	2	.326	.423	1	8	3	2119	3.76	174	174	1.00
Last Five Years	.265	530	1756	187	466	94	6	45	243	123	296	11	53	11	7	.315	.403	8	32	12	7045	3.64	603	545	1.11

1997 Season

	Avg	AB	H	2B	3B	HR	RBI	BB	SO	OBP	SLG		Avg	AB	H	2B	3B	HR	RBI	BB	SO	OBP	SLG
vs. Left	.357	129	46	11	0	9	28	11	12	.404	.651	First Pitch	.262	42	11	4	0	1	10	1	0	.283	.429
vs. Right	.240	379	91	20	1	6	46	28	60	.300	.346	Ahead in Count	.282	131	37	7	0	2	13	21	0	.386	.382
Groundball	.219	105	23	4	0	2	12	5	12	.259	.314	Behind in Count	.241	232	56	13	1	9	34	0	58	.247	.422
Flyball	.289	83	24	8	0	4	14	9	13	.359	.530	Two Strikes	.263	224	59	14	0	11	32	17	72	.317	.473
Home	.265	253	67	17	1	9	45	24	42	.336	.447	Batting #6	.253	75	19	4	0	3	8	4	15	.288	.427
Away	.275	255	70	14	0	6	29	15	30	.316	.400	Batting #7	.279	319	89	23	0	9	51	25	47	.335	.436
Day	.322	149	48	10	1	8	26	12	21	.377	.564	Other	.254	114	29	4	1	3	15	10	10	.325	.386
Night	.248	359	89	21	0	7	48	27	51	.305	.365	March/April	.349	86	30	8	1	0	11	10	14	.418	.465
Grass	.260	219	57	11	0	6	25	11	28	.295	.393	May	.247	93	23	5	0	3	11	6	16	.293	.398
Turf	.277	289	80	20	1	9	49	28	44	.349	.446	June	.214	84	18	5	0	3	13	2	13	.239	.393
Pre-All Star	.273	286	78	20	1	6	38	20	44	.323	.413	July	.302	86	26	5	0	2	16	11	11	.384	.430
Post-All Star	.266	222	59	11	0	9	36	19	28	.331	.437	August	.224	85	19	5	0	4	14	3	13	.258	.424
Scoring Posn	.347	121	42	6	1	5	63	11	23	.401	.537	Sept/Oct	.284	74	21	2	0	3	9	7	5	.354	.432
Close & Late	.321	81	26	8	0	4	13	2	8	.349	.568	vs. AL	.281	455	128	30	1	14	67	36	65	.337	.444
None on/out	.201	134	27	5	0	4	4	13	18	.272	.328	vs. NL	.170	53	9	1	0	1	7	3	7	.237	.245

1997 By Position

Position	Avg	AB	H	2B	3B	HR	RBI	BB	SO	OBP	SLG	G	GS	Innings	PO	A	E	DP	Fld Pct	Rng Fctr	In Zone	Zone Outs	Zone Rtg	MLB Zone
As c	.268	503	135	31	0	15	72	39	72	.325	.419	144	136	1202.0	1050	72	6	14	.995	---	---	---	---	---

Last Five Years

	Avg	AB	H	2B	3B	HR	RBI	BB	SO	OBP	SLG		Avg	AB	H	2B	3B	HR	RBI	BB	SO	OBP	SLG
vs. Left	.272	448	122	24	1	18	77	34	60	.322	.451	First Pitch	.342	202	69	19	2	6	53	4	0	.352	.545
vs. Right	.263	1308	344	70	5	27	166	89	236	.313	.386	Ahead in Count	.296	419	124	16	2	14	60	67	0	.394	.444
Groundball	.248	443	110	23	1	8	62	10	16	.299	.359	Behind in Count	.210	822	173	42	2	18	85	0	258	.216	.332
Flyball	.282	309	87	21	0	11	44	24	58	.337	.456	Two Strikes	.198	756	150	39	1	17	72	52	296	.253	.320
Home	.260	861	224	55	4	22	126	72	152	.320	.410	Batting #7	.295	484	143	31	0	13	81	40	66	.353	.440

507

Last Five Years

	Avg	AB	H	2B	3B	HR	RBI	BB	SO	OBP	SLG		Avg	AB	H	2B	3B	HR	RBI	BB	SO	OBP	SLG
Away	.270	895	242	39	2	23	117	51	144	.311	.396	Batting #8	.249	760	189	32	3	15	83	52	134	.299	.358
Day	.292	472	138	30	3	21	79	38	86	.347	.502	Other	.262	512	134	31	3	17	79	31	96	.303	.434
Night	.255	1284	328	64	3	24	164	85	210	.304	.366	March/April	.282	234	66	15	2	7	35	22	45	.345	.453
Grass	.266	745	198	33	2	20	93	40	122	.305	.396	May	.269	338	91	17	1	5	41	26	53	.324	.370
Turf	.265	1011	268	61	4	25	150	83	174	.323	.408	June	.252	326	82	20	1	9	44	17	56	.290	.402
Pre-All Star	.270	998	269	58	4	20	132	70	166	.320	.405	July	.287	321	92	19	1	7	41	28	48	.348	.417
Post-All Star	.260	758	197	36	2	22	111	53	130	.310	.400	August	.232	285	66	11	0	6	37	14	54	.269	.333
Scoring Posn	.312	465	145	30	1	11	200	42	77	.366	.452	Sept/Oct	.274	252	69	12	1	11	41	16	40	.316	.460
Close & Late	.302	265	80	22	0	9	47	17	47	.348	.487	vs. AL	.270	1627	440	90	6	44	228	111	273	.319	.414
None on/out	.249	450	112	20	2	12	12	35	82	.305	.382	vs. NL	.202	129	26	4	0	1	15	12	23	.276	.256

Batter vs. Pitcher (career)

Hits Best Against	Avg	AB	H	2B	3B	HR	RBI	BB	SO	OBP	SLG	Hits Worst Against	Avg	AB	H	2B	3B	HR	RBI	BB	SO	OBP	SLG
Cal Eldred	.471	17	8	4	0	0	8	1	2	.500	.706	John Wasdin	.000	12	0	0	0	0	0	0	2	.000	.000
Mike Mussina	.375	24	9	2	0	2	4	1	3	.400	.708	Tom Gordon	.077	13	1	0	0	0	1	2	4	.200	.077
David Wells	.368	19	7	1	0	2	4	0	3	.368	.737	Ben McDonald	.100	10	1	1	0	0	0	1	4	.182	.200
Brad Radke	.333	15	5	1	0	1	3	2	1	.412	.600	Orel Hershiser	.125	16	2	2	0	0	1	0	2	.125	.250
Felipe Lira	.308	13	4	0	0	2	2	1	5	.357	.769	Jack McDowell	.182	11	2	0	0	0	0	0	2	.182	.182

Enrique Wilson — Indians
Age 22 – Bats Both

	Avg	G	AB	R	H	2B	3B	HR	RBI	BB	SO	HBP	GDP	SB	CS	OBP	SLG	IBB	SH	SF	#Pit	#P/PA	GB	FB	G/F
1997 Season	.333	5	15	2	5	0	0	0	1	0	2	0	0	0	0	.333	.333	0	0	0	48	3.20	7	4	1.75

1997 Season

	Avg	AB	H	2B	3B	HR	RBI	BB	SO	OBP	SLG		Avg	AB	H	2B	3B	HR	RBI	BB	SO	OBP	SLG
vs. Left	.500	6	3	0	0	0	0	0	1	.500	.500	Scoring Posn	1.000	2	2	0	0	0	1	0	0	1.000	1.000
vs. Right	.222	9	2	0	0	0	1	0	1	.222	.222	Close & Late	.500	2	1	0	0	0	1	0	0	.500	.500

Scott Winchester — Reds
Age 25 – Pitches Right

	ERA	W	L	Sv	G	GS	IP	BB	SO	Avg	H	2B	3B	HR	RBI	OBP	SLG	GF	IR	IRS	Hld	SvOp	SB	CS	GB	FB	G/F
1997 Season	6.00	0	0	0	5	0	6.0	2	3	.360	9	1	1	1	5	.429	.600	4	0	0	0	0	0	0	13	5	2.60

1997 Season

	ERA	W	L	Sv	G	GS	IP	H	HR	BB	SO		Avg	AB	H	2B	3B	HR	RBI	BB	SO	OBP	SLG
Home	6.00	0	0	0	3	0	3.0	3	0	2	3	vs. Left	.400	5	2	0	1	0	0	0	0	.500	.800
Away	6.00	0	0	0	2	0	3.0	6	1	0	0	vs. Right	.350	20	7	1	0	1	5	2	3	.409	.550

Darrin Winston — Phillies
Age 31 – Pitches Left (flyball pitcher)

	ERA	W	L	Sv	G	GS	IP	BB	SO	Avg	H	2B	3B	HR	RBI	OBP	SLG	GF	IR	IRS	Hld	SvOp	SB	CS	GB	FB	G/F
1997 Season	5.25	2	0	0	7	1	12.0	3	8	.178	8	3	0	4	8	.260	.511	1	4	0	1	0	0	0	16	18	0.89

1997 Season

	ERA	W	L	Sv	G	GS	IP	H	HR	BB	SO		Avg	AB	H	2B	3B	HR	RBI	BB	SO	OBP	SLG
Home	0.00	1	0	0	5	1	9.1	1	0	1	6	vs. Left	.111	9	1	0	0	1	1	0	1	.200	.444
Away	23.63	1	0	0	2	0	2.2	7	4	2	2	vs. Right	.194	36	7	3	0	3	7	3	7	.275	.528

Jay Witasick — Athletics
Age 25 – Pitches Right

	ERA	W	L	Sv	G	GS	IP	BB	SO	Avg	H	2B	3B	HR	RBI	OBP	SLG	GF	IR	IRS	Hld	SvOp	SB	CS	GB	FB	G/F
1997 Season	5.73	0	0	0	8	0	11.0	6	8	.304	14	2	0	2	9	.385	.478	1	4	2	1	0	0	0	18	18	1.00
Career (1996-1997)	6.00	1	1	0	20	0	24.0	11	20	.274	26	2	1	7	19	.346	.537	7	11	3	1	1	1	0	35	33	1.06

1997 Season

	ERA	W	L	Sv	G	GS	IP	H	HR	BB	SO		Avg	AB	H	2B	3B	HR	RBI	BB	SO	OBP	SLG
Home	9.45	0	0	0	6	0	6.2	12	2	1	5	vs. Left	.333	18	6	1	0	1	4	3	3	.429	.556
Away	0.00	0	0	0	2	0	4.1	2	0	5	3	vs. Right	.286	28	8	1	0	1	5	3	5	.355	.429

Bobby Witt — Rangers
Age 34 – Pitches Right

	ERA	W	L	Sv	G	GS	IP	BB	SO	Avg	H	2B	3B	HR	RBI	OBP	SLG	CG	ShO	Sup	QS	#P/S	SB	CS	GB	FB	G/F
1997 Season	4.82	12	12	0	34	32	209.0	74	121	.294	245	45	6	33	113	.350	.481	3	0	5.21	16	101	14	9	255	254	1.08
Last Five Years	4.71	55	58	0	155	150	936.1	399	661	.284	1042	189	29	111	472	.354	.442	17	4	5.08	70	102	67	47	1247	1038	1.20

1997 Season

	ERA	W	L	Sv	G	GS	IP	H	HR	BB	SO		Avg	AB	H	2B	3B	HR	RBI	BB	SO	OBP	SLG
Home	5.05	5	7	0	19	18	117.2	146	21	44	62	vs. Left	.334	410	137	24	4	20	64	43	50	.398	.559
Away	4.53	7	5	0	15	14	91.1	99	12	30	59	vs. Right	.255	423	108	21	2	13	49	31	71	.303	.407
Day	7.21	2	3	0	8	8	43.2	65	9	15	30	Inning 1-6	.291	714	208	41	6	27	101	68	104	.352	.479
Night	4.19	10	9	0	26	24	165.1	180	25	59	91	Inning 7+	.311	119	37	4	0	6	12	6	17	.339	.496
Grass	4.79	11	11	0	31	29	193.1	223	30	69	106	None on	.297	491	146	25	2	19	19	38	62	.350	.473
Turf	5.17	1	1	0	3	3	15.2	22	3	5	15	Runners on	.289	342	99	20	4	14	94	36	59	.351	.494
March/April	2.30	5	0	0	6	4	31.1	37	5	5	19	Scoring Posn	.245	192	47	9	3	8	78	22	41	.312	.448
May	4.57	2	2	0	6	6	41.1	42	5	14	22	Close & Late	.273	66	18	2	0	2	6	4	12	.310	.394
June	4.19	2	2	0	6	6	38.2	42	4	14	17	None on/out	.266	214	57	9	2	8	8	18	28	.326	.439
July	4.18	1	2	0	5	5	32.1	34	6	11	25	vs. 1st Batr (relief)	.500	2	1	0	0	0	0	0	0	.500	.500
August	6.46	1	3	0	6	6	39.0	54	8	17	20	1st Inning Pitched	.292	130	38	6	2	6	23	17	20	.372	.508

508

1997 Season

	ERA	W	L	Sv	G	GS	IP	H	HR	BB	SO
Sept/Oct	7.52	1	3	0	5	5	26.1	36	5	13	18
Starter	4.90	11	12	0	32	32	205.2	240	33	73	120
Reliever	0.00	1	0	0	2	0	3.1	5	0	1	1
0-3 Days Rest (Start)	11.25	0	0	0	1	1	4.0	7	0	2	2
4 Days Rest	4.70	8	11	0	23	23	155.0	177	23	57	90
5+ Days Rest	5.01	4	1	0	8	8	46.2	56	10	14	28
vs. AL	5.15	10	12	0	30	28	181.2	220	31	66	105
vs. NL	2.63	2	0	0	4	4	27.1	25	2	8	16
Pre-All Star	3.62	10	4	0	19	17	119.1	124	15	36	61
Post-All Star	6.42	2	8	0	15	15	89.2	121	18	38	60

	Avg	AB	H	2B	3B	HR	RBI	BB	SO	OBP	SLG
First 75 Pitches	.295	570	168	30	6	20	79	58	84	.359	.474
Pitch 76-90	.325	114	37	9	0	6	17	9	18	.371	.561
Pitch 91-105	.281	96	27	5	0	4	11	5	11	.314	.458
Pitch 106+	.245	53	13	1	0	3	6	2	8	.273	.434
First Pitch	.377	130	49	11	1	4	17	3	0	.387	.569
Ahead in Count	.275	360	99	17	1	16	40	0	99	.277	.461
Behind in Count	.301	193	58	10	2	9	37	39	0	.413	.513
Two Strikes	.231	351	81	17	1	11	34	32	121	.297	.379
Pre-All Star	.268	463	124	24	3	15	50	36	61	.321	.430
Post-All Star	.327	370	121	21	3	18	63	38	60	.386	.546

Last Five Years

	ERA	W	L	Sv	G	GS	IP	H	HR	BB	SO
Home	4.41	32	24	0	79	77	509.2	548	58	212	365
Away	5.06	23	34	0	76	73	426.2	494	53	187	296
Day	5.19	18	20	0	48	47	289.2	324	33	127	214
Night	4.50	37	38	0	107	103	646.2	718	78	272	447
Grass	4.69	48	49	0	135	130	821.2	899	97	359	557
Turf	4.87	7	9	0	20	20	114.2	143	14	40	104
March/April	4.54	10	4	0	21	19	119.0	123	19	57	79
May	5.32	11	13	0	30	30	179.1	206	23	83	122
June	3.97	9	11	0	29	29	181.1	175	18	78	127
July	4.80	7	11	0	28	26	165.0	196	21	52	141
August	4.68	8	9	0	24	24	154.0	185	13	80	79
Sept/Oct	4.97	10	10	0	23	22	137.2	157	17	49	113
Starter	4.74	53	58	0	150	150	920.0	1023	111	396	441
Reliever	2.76	2	0	0	5	0	16.1	19	0	3	12
0-3 Days Rest (Start)	10.94	1	5	0	7	7	26.1	52	5	13	15
4 Days Rest	4.40	36	36	0	96	96	617.1	653	70	250	441
5+ Days Rest	4.92	16	17	0	47	47	276.1	318	28	133	193
vs. AL	4.89	51	51	0	132	127	798.1	913	101	344	550
vs. NL	3.65	4	7	0	23	23	138.0	129	10	55	111
Pre-All Star	4.54	33	32	0	88	86	537.1	563	68	235	371
Post-All Star	4.94	22	26	0	67	64	399.0	479	43	164	290

	Avg	AB	H	2B	3B	HR	RBI	BB	SO	OBP	SLG
vs. Left	.304	1918	583	112	20	61	255	224	312	.377	.479
vs. Right	.262	1749	459	77	9	50	217	175	349	.329	.403
Inning 1-6	.284	3146	893	157	29	96	433	367	569	.358	.444
Inning 7+	.286	521	149	32	0	15	39	32	92	.327	.434
None on	.280	2090	585	105	14	57	57	212	355	.348	.425
Runners on	.290	1577	457	84	15	54	415	187	306	.361	.465
Scoring Posn	.260	881	229	40	10	32	346	115	210	.335	.437
Close & Late	.265	245	65	15	0	5	16	18	45	.317	.388
None on/out	.283	942	267	54	5	24	24	88	148	.347	.428
vs. 1st Batr (relief)	.400	5	2	1	0	0	0	0	1	.400	.600
1st Inning Pitched	.287	581	167	32	6	16	93	101	115	.389	.446
First 75 Pitches	.285	2516	717	128	24	74	351	294	448	.358	.444
Pitch 76-90	.290	462	134	22	1	14	50	42	87	.352	.433
Pitch 91-105	.246	382	94	19	2	11	37	36	62	.313	.393
Pitch 106+	.316	307	97	20	2	12	34	27	64	.372	.511
First Pitch	.339	548	186	40	5	11	69	14	0	.355	.491
Ahead in Count	.239	1671	400	72	11	44	171	0	537	.242	.375
Behind in Count	.352	753	265	42	6	35	139	205	0	.486	.563
Two Strikes	.212	1682	356	63	12	43	156	179	661	.289	.340
Pre-All Star	.271	2075	563	96	18	68	261	235	371	.346	.433
Post-All Star	.301	1592	479	93	11	43	211	164	290	.365	.454

Pitcher vs. Batter (career)

Pitches Best Vs.	Avg	AB	H	2B	3B	HR	RBI	BB	SO	OBP	SLG
Mike Devereaux	.053	19	1	0	0	0	1	1	3	.095	.053
Joe Girardi	.091	11	1	1	0	0	0	1	3	.091	.182
Dave Hollins	.100	10	1	0	0	0	0	1	1	.182	.100
Warren Newson	.100	10	1	0	0	0	0	1	4	.182	.100
Troy O'Leary	.154	13	2	0	0	0	0	0	3	.154	.154

Pitches Worst Vs.	Avg	AB	H	2B	3B	HR	RBI	BB	SO	OBP	SLG
Johnny Damon	.571	14	8	1	1	1	4	1	0	.600	1.000
Tim Salmon	.500	22	11	0	0	3	8	3	4	.560	.909
Geronimo Berroa	.500	10	5	1	0	2	2	3	1	.615	1.200
Dean Palmer	.417	12	5	1	0	3	6	2	3	.500	1.250
Jim Thome	.389	18	7	0	2	3	12	3	6	.455	1.111

Mark Wohlers — Braves

Age 28 – Pitches Right (groundball pitcher)

	ERA	W	L	Sv	G	GS	IP	BB	SO	Avg	H	2B	3B	HR	RBI	OBP	SLG	GF	IR	IRS	Hld	SvOp	SB	CS	GB	FB	G/F
1997 Season	3.50	5	7	33	71	0	69.1	38	92	.224	57	8	1	4	27	.321	.311	55	15	4	1	40	13	0	74	55	1.35
Last Five Years	3.42	27	18	98	310	0	310.1	138	385	.231	267	39	8	17	140	.312	.323	196	143	44	22	115	40	3	379	225	1.68

1997 Season

	ERA	W	L	Sv	G	GS	IP	H	HR	BB	SO
Home	4.76	4	4	15	37	0	34.0	30	3	18	42
Away	2.29	1	3	18	34	0	35.1	27	1	20	50
Day	4.63	0	3	11	23	0	23.1	22	2	16	28
Night	2.93	5	4	22	48	0	46.0	35	2	22	64
Grass	4.02	5	6	24	59	0	56.0	45	4	31	75
Turf	1.35	0	1	9	12	0	13.1	12	0	7	17
March/April	3.48	1	0	6	11	0	10.1	5	1	10	14
May	0.00	1	0	5	12	0	11.2	6	0	4	18
June	3.75	0	3	6	12	0	12.0	9	1	7	14
July	2.25	0	1	8	12	0	12.0	11	1	4	14
August	4.20	2	1	7	16	0	15.0	17	1	9	21
Sept/Oct	8.64	1	2	1	8	0	8.1	9	0	4	11
Starter	0.00	0	0	0	0	0	0.0	0	0	0	0
Reliever	3.50	5	7	33	71	0	69.1	57	4	38	92
0 Days rest (Relief)	5.51	1	2	13	18	0	16.1	17	2	10	26
1 or 2 Days rest	3.25	2	4	16	38	0	36.0	26	1	19	39
3+ Days rest	2.12	2	1	4	15	0	17.0	14	1	9	27
vs. AL	3.38	0	1	2	5	0	5.1	3	1	5	6
vs. NL	3.52	5	6	31	66	0	64.0	54	3	33	86
Pre-All Star	2.17	2	3	20	38	0	37.1	22	2	24	50
Post-All Star	5.06	3	4	13	33	0	32.0	35	2	14	42

	Avg	AB	H	2B	3B	HR	RBI	BB	SO	OBP	SLG
vs. Left	.225	142	32	4	1	2	15	25	53	.337	.310
vs. Right	.223	112	25	4	0	2	12	13	39	.299	.313
Inning 1-6	.000	0	0	0	0	0	0	0	0	.000	.000
Inning 7+	.224	254	57	8	1	4	27	38	92	.321	.311
None on	.211	142	30	5	1	1	1	22	55	.317	.282
Runners on	.241	112	27	3	0	3	26	16	37	.326	.348
Scoring Posn	.203	74	15	2	0	1	21	12	26	.305	.270
Close & Late	.235	200	47	8	1	3	24	34	71	.340	.330
None on/out	.190	63	12	3	1	0	0	9	19	.292	.270
vs. 1st Batr (relief)	.226	62	14	3	1	1	5	9	19	.324	.355
1st Inning Pitched	.222	239	53	6	1	4	25	36	85	.336	.305
First 15 Pitches	.234	197	46	5	1	4	17	25	70	.317	.330
Pitch 16-30	.185	54	10	2	0	0	9	13	21	.333	.222
Pitch 31-45	.333	3	1	1	0	0	1	0	1	.333	.667
Pitch 46+	.000	0	0	0	0	0	0	0	0	.000	.000
First Pitch	.341	44	15	1	1	0	7	0	0	.326	.409
Ahead in Count	.102	127	13	1	0	0	5	0	80	.110	.110
Behind in Count	.396	48	19	5	0	3	9	21	0	.571	.688
Two Strikes	.107	131	14	1	0	1	9	17	92	.208	.137
Pre-All Star	.172	128	22	4	0	2	11	24	50	.301	.250
Post-All Star	.278	126	35	4	2	2	16	14	42	.343	.373

Last Five Years

	ERA	W	L	Sv	G	GS	IP	H	HR	BB	SO
Home	4.02	20	14	50	166	0	170.1	148	12	70	193
Away	2.70	7	4	48	144	0	140.0	119	5	68	192
Day	3.67	6	6	25	95	0	88.1	82	7	48	120
Night	3.32	21	12	73	215	0	222.0	185	10	90	265

	Avg	AB	H	2B	3B	HR	RBI	BB	SO	OBP	SLG
vs. Left	.234	547	128	17	6	8	56	84	194	.334	.331
vs. Right	.229	608	139	22	2	9	84	54	191	.316	.316
Inning 1-6	.121	33	4	1	0	0	6	2	13	.167	.152
Inning 7+	.234	1122	263	38	8	17	134	136	372	.316	.328

Last Five Years

	ERA	W	L	Sv	G	GS	IP	H	HR	BB	SO		Avg	AB	H	2B	3B	HR	RBI	BB	SO	OBP	SLG
Grass	3.54	25	17	75	249	0	252.0	208	15	110	307	None on	.217	621	135	19	6	9	9	64	217	.292	.311
Turf	2.93	2	1	23	61	0	58.1	59	2	28	78	Runners on	.247	534	132	20	2	8	131	74	168	.335	.337
March/April	3.05	4	0	12	39	0	38.1	27	4	31	45	Scoring Posn	.230	361	83	12	2	3	118	64	121	.339	.299
May	3.32	3	2	8	46	0	43.1	38	2	21	71	Close & Late	.232	729	169	25	4	10	84	92	240	.317	.318
June	2.87	3	4	19	59	0	62.2	45	4	25	73	None on/out	.178	264	47	6	4	3		23	88	.244	.265
July	2.29	9	4	22	60	0	63.0	48	1	19	70	vs. 1st Batr (relief)	.206	277	57	7	3	4	26	27	88	.277	.296
August	3.45	4	4	26	61	0	57.1	58	3	24	66	1st Inning Pitched	.230	1018	234	33	7	13	123	110	046	.207	.314
Sept/Oct	6.11	4	4	11	45	0	45.2	51	3	18	60	First 15 Pitches	.241	849	205	27	7	15	90	88	273	.312	.343
Starter	0.00	0	0	0	0	0	0.0	0	0	0	0	Pitch 16-30	.212	273	58	10	1	2	45	47	103	.322	.278
Reliever	3.42	27	18	98	310	0	310.1	267	17	138	385	Pitch 31-45	.121	33	4	2	0	0	5	3	9	.231	.182
0 Days rest (Relief)	3.14	7	4	40	89	0	86.0	84	6	39	107	Pitch 46+	.000	0	0	0	0	0	0	0	0	.000	.000
1 or 2 Days rest	3.65	15	12	45	159	0	157.2	128	8	72	187	First Pitch	.372	164	61	6	3	5	27	15	0	.418	.537
3+ Days rest	3.24	5	2	13	62	0	66.2	55	3	27	91	Ahead in Count	.138	614	85	14	3	3	50	0	343	.139	.186
vs. AL	3.38	0	1	2	5	0	5.1	3	1	5	6	Behind in Count	.366	202	74	13	1	7	40	59	0	.506	.545
vs. NL	3.42	27	17	96	305	0	305.0	264	16	133	379	Two Strikes	.125	630	79	11	1	4	51	62	385	.204	.165
Pre-All Star	2.99	13	7	45	163	0	162.2	127	10	82	207	Pre-All Star	.215	592	127	20	3	10	73	82	207	.309	.309
Post-All Star	3.90	14	11	53	147	0	147.2	140	7	56	178	Post-All Star	.249	563	140	19	5	7	67	56	178	.315	.337

Pitcher vs. Batter (career)

Pitches Best Vs.	Avg	AB	H	2B	3B	HR	RBI	BB	SO	OBP	SLG	Pitches Worst Vs.	Avg	AB	H	2B	3B	HR	RBI	BB	SO	OBP	SLG
Barry Bonds	.000	7	0	0	0	0	0	4	2	.364	.000	Dante Bichette	.429	14	6	1	0	0	4	1	4	.467	.500
Gary Sheffield	.063	16	1	1	0	0	0	1	4	.118	.125	Walt Weiss	.429	7	3	1	0	0	1	5	2	.667	.571
Reggie Sanders	.083	12	1	0	0	0	0	1	7	.154	.083	Andres Galarraga	.385	13	5	1	0	1	3	1	4	.429	.692
Jeff Conine	.182	11	2	0	0	0	0	1	4	.250	.182	Vinny Castilla	.357	14	5	0	0	2	4	0	3	.357	.786
Hal Morris	.231	13	3	0	0	0	0	0	5	.231	.231	Jay Bell	.333	9	3	2	0	0	3	3	2	.500	.556

Steve Wojciechowski — Athletics

Age 27 – Pitches Left

	ERA	W	L	Sv	G	GS	IP	BB	SO	Avg	H	2B	3B	HR	RBI	OBP	SLG	CG	ShO	Sup	QS	#P/S	SB	CS	GB	FB	G/F
1997 Season	7.84	0	2	0	3	2	10.1	1	5	.386	17	1	0	2	7	.400	.545	0	0	2.61	0	79	2	2	21	8	2.63
Career (1995-1997)	5.65	7	10	0	33	24	138.2	57	48	.298	165	30	6	19	76	.364	.477	0	0	5.52	6	86	20	8	202	184	1.10

1997 Season

	ERA	W	L	Sv	G	GS	IP	H	HR	BB	SO		Avg	AB	H	2B	3B	HR	RBI	BB	SO	OBP	SLG
Home	7.84	0	2	0	2	2	10.1	17	2	1	5	vs. Left	.000	3	0	0	0	0	0	0	1	.000	.000
Away	0.00	0	0	0	1	0	0.0	0	0	0	0	vs. Right	.415	41	17	1	0	2	7	1	4	.429	.585

Bob Wolcott — Mariners

Age 24 – Pitches Right (flyball pitcher)

	ERA	W	L	Sv	G	GS	IP	BB	SO	Avg	H	2B	3B	HR	RBI	OBP	SLG	CG	ShO	Sup	QS	#P/S	SB	CS	GB	FB	G/F
1997 Season	6.03	5	6	0	19	18	100.0	29	58	.314	129	33	3	22	66	.365	.569	0	0	6.57	6	87	3	3	125	140	0.89
Career (1995-1997)	5.66	15	18	0	56	52	286.0	97	155	.303	351	87	10	54	172	.362	.535	1	0	6.39	16	85	3	6	373	406	0.92

1997 Season

	ERA	W	L	Sv	G	GS	IP	H	HR	BB	SO		Avg	AB	H	2B	3B	HR	RBI	BB	SO	OBP	SLG
Home	5.08	3	2	0	10	9	56.2	68	12	16	34	vs. Left	.328	201	66	14	3	14	39	21	21	.390	.637
Away	7.27	2	4	0	9	9	43.1	61	10	13	24	vs. Right	.300	210	63	19	0	8	27	8	37	.339	.505
Starter	6.11	5	6	0	18	18	98.2	128	22	29	57	Scoring Posn	.298	104	31	4	0	7	45	8	16	.353	.538
Reliever	0.00	0	0	0	1	0	1.1	1	0	0	1	Close & Late	.500	2	1	0	0	0	0	1	0	.667	.500
0-3 Days Rest (Start)	0.00	0	0	0	0	0	0.0	0	0	0	0	None on/out	.267	101	27	8	1	3	8		11	.333	.455
4 Days Rest	5.02	3	1	0	6	6	37.2	42	8	11	19	First Pitch	.393	61	24	8	0	3	12	2	0	.422	.672
5+ Days Rest	6.79	2	5	0	12	12	61.0	86	14	18	38	Ahead in Count	.276	192	53	11	2	8	30	0	49	.289	.479
Pre-All Star	5.53	4	4	0	13	12	70.0	87	13	23	38	Behind in Count	.380	79	30	7	1	5	13	15	0	.474	.684
Post-All Star	7.20	1	2	0	6	6	30.0	42	9	6	20	Two Strikes	.244	180	44	10	1	7	22	12	58	.303	.428

Career (1995-1997)

	ERA	W	L	Sv	G	GS	IP	H	HR	BB	SO		Avg	AB	H	2B	3B	HR	RBI	BB	SO	OBP	SLG
Home	5.53	6	10	0	29	27	148.0	180	30	53	84	vs. Left	.342	602	206	52	8	32	97	62	61	.404	.615
Away	5.80	9	8	0	27	25	138.0	171	24	44	71	vs. Right	.261	556	145	35	2	22	75	35	94	.315	.450
Day	5.68	5	4	0	18	17	90.1	104	14	34	61	Inning 1-6	.305	1076	328	83	10	48	164	93	147	.365	.534
Night	5.66	10	14	0	38	35	195.2	247	40	63	94	Inning 7+	.280	82	23	4	0	6	8	4	8	.322	.549
Grass	6.26	7	8	0	23	21	115.0	147	24	39	59	None on	.319	646	206	52	6	30	30	54	91	.377	.567
Turf	5.26	8	10	0	33	31	171.0	204	30	58	96	Runners on	.283	512	145	35	4	24	142	43	64	.343	.508
March/April	6.24	3	4	0	10	10	53.1	11	11	21	28	Scoring Posn	.265	268	71	14	2	14	110	26	33	.332	.489
May	5.77	2	4	0	9	8	43.2	60	5	23	16	Close & Late	.297	37	11	2	0	1	2	2	4	.333	.432
June	6.04	4	3	0	11	11	56.2	76	11	18	26	None on/out	.316	301	95	19	1	15	15	21	42	.372	.535
July	3.17	2	1	0	8	8	54.0	50	13	11	32	vs. 1st Batr (relief)	.500	4	2	0	0	2	0	0	0	.500	1.000
August	8.44	3	5	0	9	9	37.1	67	8	12	31	1st Inning Pitched	.284	218	62	12	1	12	36	23	30	.359	.560
Sept/Oct	5.05	1	1	0	9	6	41.0	39	6	12	22	First 75 Pitches	.299	946	283	68	8	39	131	79	135	.358	.512
Starter	5.62	15	18	0	52	52	275.1	341	51	94	151	Pitch 76-90	.278	133	37	13	1	8	26	9	16	.333	.571
Reliever	6.75	0	0	0	4	0	10.2	10	3	3	4	Pitch 91-105	.373	67	25	5	1	5	12	8	3	.442	.701
0-3 Days Rest (Start)	1.80	1	0	0	1	1	5.0	6	0	4	1	Pitch 106+	.500	12	6	1	0	2	3	0	0	.538	1.083
4 Days Rest	4.93	9	8	0	26	26	142.1	168	24	44	74	First Pitch	.439	164	72	19	2	8	35	7	0	.463	.726
5+ Days Rest	6.54	5	10	0	25	25	128.0	167	27	46	76	Ahead in Count	.229	516	118	24	3	17	60	0	136	.240	.386
vs. AL	5.45	15	17	0	53	49	271.0	328	49	93	147	Behind in Count	.340	268	91	22	2	18	47	46	0	.436	.638
vs. NL	9.60	0	1	0	3	3	15.0	23	5	4	8	Two Strikes	.222	472	105	23	4	14	43	44	155	.296	.377
Pre-All Star	5.86	9	11	0	31	30	161.1	201	28	64	77	Pre-All Star	.306	656	201	57	7	28	102	64	77	.372	.543
Post-All Star	5.41	6	7	0	25	22	124.2	150	26	33	78	Post-All Star	.299	502	150	30	3	26	70	33	78	.348	.526

Pitcher vs. Batter (career)

Pitches Best Vs.	Avg	AB	H	2B	3B	HR	RBI	BB	SO	OBP	SLG	Pitches Worst Vs.	Avg	AB	H	2B	3B	HR	RBI	BB	SO	OBP	SLG
Chuck Knoblauch	.000	14	0	0	0	0	0	0	2	.000	.000	Matt Stairs	.667	12	8	2	0	2	2	0	1	.667	1.333
Ed Sprague	.000	11	0	0	0	1	0	0	4	.000	.000	Tim Naehring	.500	12	6	1	0	1	3	3	1	.625	.833
Scott Brosius	.083	12	1	0	0	0	0	1	4	.154	.083	Bob Hamelin	.429	14	6	3	0	1	5	2	0	.500	.857
Jason Giambi	.143	14	2	1	0	0	0	0	2	.143	.214	Joe Carter	.364	11	4	1	0	2	5	0	0	.417	1.000
Greg Myers	.167	12	2	0	0	0	2	1	2	.231	.167	Tony Clark	.333	12	4	0	0	2	2	1	1	.385	.833

Tony Womack — Pirates
Age 28 – Bats Left

	Avg	G	AB	R	H	2B	3B	HR	RBI	BB	SO	HBP	GDP	SB	CS	OBP	SLG	IBB	SH	SF	#Pit	#P/PA	GB	FB	G/F
1997 Season	.278	155	641	85	178	26	9	6	50	43	109	3	6	60	7	.326	.374	2	2	0	2613	3.79	248	139	1.78
Career (1993-1997)	.274	192	707	105	194	29	10	6	58	54	116	4	6	64	7	.329	.369	2	6	0	2915	3.78	275	158	1.74

1997 Season

	Avg	AB	H	2B	3B	HR	RBI	BB	SO	OBP	SLG		Avg	AB	H	2B	3B	HR	RBI	BB	SO	OBP	SLG
vs. Left	.310	129	40	4	1	0	14	9	34	.360	.357	First Pitch	.377	77	29	3	1	2	11	1	0	.385	.519
vs. Right	.270	512	138	22	8	6	36	34	75	.318	.379	Ahead in Count	.365	104	38	9	2	0	8	21	0	.476	.490
Groundball	.286	105	30	4	2	1	9	7	16	.330	.318	Behind in Count	.225	355	80	7	0	3	21	0	102	.229	.270
Flyball	.290	124	36	6	1	2	7	3	25	.318	.403	Two Strikes	.223	332	74	8	3	2	22	21	109	.271	.283
Home	.277	314	87	10	5	5	26	23	47	.330	.389	Batting #1	.277	636	176	25	9	6	50	43	109	.326	.373
Away	.278	327	91	16	4	1	24	20	62	.322	.361	Batting #3	.000	1	0	0	0	0	0	0	0	.000	.000
Day	.332	226	75	10	5	3	22	19	41	.384	.460	Other	.500	4	2	1	0	0	0	0	0	.500	.750
Night	.248	415	103	16	4	3	28	24	68	.294	.328	March/April	.210	100	21	3	3	1	5	7	17	.269	.330
Grass	.290	231	67	13	2	1	17	13	46	.328	.377	May	.291	103	30	1	2	1	10	10	24	.354	.369
Turf	.271	410	111	13	7	5	33	30	63	.325	.373	June	.289	114	33	1	1	1	9	2	19	.302	.342
Pre-All Star	.272	342	93	6	7	3	29	22	62	.318	.357	July	.311	122	38	6	3	1	14	8	14	.359	.434
Post-All Star	.284	299	85	20	2	3	21	21	47	.335	.395	August	.279	111	31	8	0	2	6	5	18	.310	.405
Scoring Posn	.295	139	41	4	2	1	44	12	25	.364	.374	Sept/Oct	.275	91	25	7	0	0	6	11	17	.359	.352
Close & Late	.223	94	21	4	1	0	11	6	18	.277	.287	vs. AL	.267	60	16	4	1	1	4	4	6	.313	.417
None on/out	.253	273	69	9	6	4	4	18	50	.299	.374	vs. NL	.279	581	162	22	8	5	46	39	103	.327	.370

1997 By Position

Position	Avg	AB	H	2B	3B	HR	RBI	BB	SO	OBP	SLG	G	GS	Innings	PO	A	E	DP	Fld Pct	Rng Fctr	In Zone	Zone Outs	Zone Rtg	MLB Zone
As 2b	.277	638	177	26	9	6	50	43	109	.326	.375	152	148	1292.2	335	429	20	83	.974	5.32	485	413	.852	.902

Steve Woodard — Brewers
Age 23 – Pitches Right (flyball pitcher)

	ERA	W	L	Sv	G	GS	IP	BB	SO	Avg	H	2B	3B	HR	RBI	OBP	SLG	CG	ShO	Sup	QS	#P/S	SB	CS	GB	FB	G/F
1997 Season	5.15	3	3	0	7	7	36.2	6	32	.269	39	13	1	5	23	.307	.476	0	0	2.70	3	87	3	1	38	49	0.78

1997 Season

	ERA	W	L	Sv	G	GS	IP	H	HR	BB	SO		Avg	AB	H	2B	3B	HR	RBI	BB	SO	OBP	SLG
Home	7.15	2	3	0	5	5	22.2	30	3	4	26	vs. Left	.293	82	24	8	1	3	13	2	19	.310	.524
Away	1.93	1	0	0	2	2	14.0	9	2	2	6	vs. Right	.238	63	15	5	0	2	10	4	13	.304	.413

Tim Worrell — Padres
Age 30 – Pitches Right

	ERA	W	L	Sv	G	GS	IP	BB	SO	Avg	H	2B	3B	HR	RBI	OBP	SLG	GF	IR	IRS	Hld	SvOp	SB	CS	GB	FB	G/F
1997 Season	5.16	4	8	3	60	10	106.1	50	81	.280	116	20	4	14	67	.363	.449	14	28	11	16	7	16	6	144	121	1.19
Career (1993-1997)	4.30	16	23	4	143	40	356.0	143	259	.258	354	66	10	36	185	.332	.400	27	61	21	27	9	36	22	464	406	1.14

1997 Season

	ERA	W	L	Sv	G	GS	IP	H	HR	BB	SO		Avg	AB	H	2B	3B	HR	RBI	BB	SO	OBP	SLG
Home	4.76	4	7	0	30	7	64.1	62	10	22	50	vs. Left	.303	195	59	10	3	5	28	26	26	.383	.462
Away	5.79	0	1	3	30	3	42.0	54	4	28	31	vs. Right	.260	219	57	10	1	9	39	24	55	.340	.438
Day	8.18	1	1	0	21	2	22.0	33	4	12	18	Inning 1-6	.277	195	54	8	2	7	33	21	30	.351	.446
Night	4.38	3	7	3	39	8	84.1	83	10	38	63	Inning 7+	.283	219	62	12	2	7	34	29	51	.373	.452
Grass	5.53	4	8	2	52	9	94.1	104	14	44	71	None on	.264	216	57	11	3	9	24	45	36	.383	.429
Turf	2.25	0	0	1	8	1	12.0	12	0	6	10	Runners on	.298	198	59	9	1	5	58	26	36	.383	.429
March/April	5.19	1	3	0	5	4	26.0	22	4	14	12	Scoring Posn	.265	132	35	6	1	2	50	20	25	.360	.371
May	6.00	1	3	1	7	6	30.0	40	3	11	25	Close & Late	.276	123	34	6	2	2	19	19	28	.378	.407
June	4.41	1	0	1	14	0	16.1	17	2	9	7	None on/out	.240	96	23	3	2	4	4	10	22	.324	.438
July	0.82	0	1	1	12	0	11.0	6	0	5	13	vs. 1st Batr (relief)	.318	44	14	2	1	1	4	2	7	.375	.477
August	2.45	0	0	0	12	0	14.2	17	2	4	14	1st Inning Pitched	.280	200	56	12	2	6	38	25	42	.363	.450
Sept/Oct	14.04	1	1	0	10	0	8.1	14	3	7	10	First 15 Pitches	.274	164	45	10	1	5	23	15	31	.346	.439
Starter	5.23	2	5	0	10	10	51.2	55	7	22	33	Pitch 16-30	.310	100	31	8	2	5	23	13	22	.385	.580
Reliever	5.10	2	3	3	50	0	54.2	61	7	28	48	Pitch 31-45	.306	49	15	0	0	0	7	10	9	.424	.306
0 Days rest (Relief)	9.82	0	2	1	14	0	11.0	16	2	10	7	Pitch 46+	.248	101	25	2	1	4	14	12	19	.336	.406
1 or 2 Days rest	2.19	1	0	0	21	0	24.2	22	2	8	21	First Pitch	.365	63	23	4	0	3	16	0	0	.394	.571
3+ Days rest	6.16	1	1	2	15	0	19.0	22	3	10	20	Ahead in Count	.182	203	37	4	3	4	18	0	73	.188	.291
vs. AL	6.23	0	0	1	9	0	8.2	10	1	9	7	Behind in Count	.451	82	37	8	0	6	26	18	0	.538	.768
vs. NL	5.07	4	8	2	51	10	97.2	106	13	41	74	Two Strikes	.137	182	25	4	3	3	13	32	81	.271	.242
Pre-All Star	5.30	3	6	2	30	10	74.2	81	9	36	45	Pre-All Star	.278	291	81	12	2	9	49	36	45	.364	.426
Post-All Star	4.83	1	2	1	30	0	31.2	35	5	14	36	Post-All Star	.285	123	35	8	2	5	18	14	36	.359	.504

Career (1993-1997)

	ERA	W	L	Sv	G	GS	IP	H	HR	BB	SO		Avg	AB	H	2B	3B	HR	RBI	BB	SO	OBP	SLG
Home	4.47	11	17	0	75	27	217.2	211	27	72	162	vs. Left	.279	645	180	33	8	11	75	82	91	.360	.406
Away	4.03	5	6	4	68	13	138.1	143	9	71	97	vs. Right	.240	725	174	33	2	25	110	61	168	.306	.394

Career (1993-1997)

	ERA	W	L	Sv	G	GS	IP	H	HR	BB	SO		Avg	AB	H	2B	3B	HR	RBI	BB	SO	OBP	SLG
Day	3.61	5	3	1	49	9	102.1	104	8	36	80	Inning 1-6	.270	879	237	42	7	24	129	90	146	.339	.415
Night	4.58	11	20	3	94	31	253.2	250	28	107	179	Inning 7+	.238	491	117	24	3	12	56	53	113	.319	.373
Grass	4.31	16	20	3	119	34	304.2	300	33	115	222	None on	.237	768	182	36	4	24	24	71	147	.307	.388
Turf	4.21	0	3	1	24	6	51.1	54	3	28	37	Runners on	.286	602	172	30	6	12	161	72	112	.363	.415
March/April	3.67	3	4	0	13	7	54.0	37	4	26	34	Scoring Posn	.262	381	100	18	4	7	143	53	78	.348	.386
May	4.12	3	3	1	15	6	43.2	45	3	15	39	Close & Late	.218	248	54	10	3	5	28	31	54	.316	.343
June	4.66	2	4	1	24	5	56.0	56	8	18	33	None on/out	.246	338	83	15	2	10	10	24	51	.305	.391
July	3.88	2	4	2	29	7	60.1	56	5	29	44	vs. 1st Batr (relief)	.250	92	23	4	1	1	8	7	18	.317	.348
August	4.13	1	4	0	27	10	76.1	91	7	25	47	1st Inning Pitched	.244	476	116	20	5	9	74	51	114	.322	.363
Sept/Oct	5.21	5	4	0	35	5	65.2	69	9	30	62	First 15 Pitches	.233	395	92	16	4	7	43	34	86	.304	.347
Starter	4.97	7	19	0	40	40	217.1	240	24	83	131	Pitch 16-30	.244	308	75	21	3	7	48	38	66	.325	.399
Reliever	3.25	9	4	4	103	0	138.2	114	12	60	128	Pitch 31-45	.296	199	59	8	0	4	28	22	33	.368	.397
0 Days rest (Relief)	6.00	1	2	1	19	0	18.0	17	2	12	13	Pitch 46+	.274	468	128	21	3	18	66	49	74	.345	.447
1 or 2 Days rest	2.88	3	1	0	47	0	59.1	47	5	23	54	First Pitch	.306	196	60	11	1	8	36	4	0	.333	.495
3+ Days rest	2.79	5	1	3	37	0	61.1	50	5	25	61	Ahead in Count	.198	627	124	19	5	9	47	0	221	.203	.287
vs. AL	6.23	0	0	1	9	0	8.2	10	1	9	7	Behind in Count	.333	288	96	20	1	12	61	67	0	.458	.535
vs. NL	4.25	16	23	3	134	40	347.1	344	35	134	252	Two Strikes	.176	630	111	16	6	9	47	72	259	.266	.263
Pre-All Star	4.60	9	14	2	60	22	174.0	173	20	70	118	Pre-All Star	.258	670	173	28	5	20	100	70	118	.332	.404
Post-All Star	4.01	7	9	2	83	18	182.0	181	16	73	141	Post-All Star	.259	700	181	38	5	16	85	73	141	.331	.396

Pitcher vs. Batter (career)

Pitches Best Vs.	Avg	AB	H	2B	3B	HR	RBI	BB	SO	OBP	SLG	Pitches Worst Vs.	Avg	AB	H	2B	3B	HR	RBI	BB	SO	OBP	SLG
Ryan Klesko	.091	11	1	1	0	0	0	2	3	.231	.182	Mike Piazza	.615	13	8	1	0	3	6	2	0	.667	1.385
Barry Larkin	.100	10	1	1	0	0	0	0	0	.182	.200	Andres Galarraga	.500	10	5	1	0	1	3	0	3	.545	.900
Jeff Blauser	.154	13	2	0	0	0	3	0	3	.133	.154	Mark Grace	.500	10	5	0	0	1	3	1	0	.545	.800
Ryne Sandberg	.154	13	2	1	0	0	2	0	2	.154	.231	Hal Morris	.417	12	5	1	0	1	5	2	1	.500	.750
Mark Lemke	.182	11	2	1	0	0	0	1	0	.250	.182	Eric Karros	.313	16	5	1	0	3	6	0	3	.313	.938

Todd Worrell — Dodgers

Age 38 – Pitches Right (flyball pitcher)

	ERA	W	L	Sv	G	GS	IP	BB	SO	Avg	H	2B	3B	HR	RBI	OBP	SLG	GF	IR	IRS	Hld	SvOp	SB	CS	GB	FB	G/F
1997 Season	5.28	2	6	35	65	0	59.2	23	61	.250	60	10	1	12	35	.316	.450	55	11	5	0	44	7	0	62	80	0.78
Last Five Years	3.93	17	19	127	269	0	268.0	80	263	.254	254	43	2	31	146	.307	.390	224	88	37	6	160	40	1	288	320	0.90

1997 Season

	ERA	W	L	Sv	G	GS	IP	H	HR	BB	SO		Avg	AB	H	2B	3B	HR	RBI	BB	SO	OBP	SLG
Home	5.52	0	3	19	32	0	29.1	29	4	11	30	vs. Left	.225	138	31	3	1	7	20	12	33	.287	.413
Away	5.04	2	3	16	33	0	30.1	31	8	12	31	vs. Right	.284	102	29	7	0	5	15	11	28	.354	.500
Day	3.66	0	1	9	19	0	19.2	16	3	6	15	Inning 1-6	.000	0	0	0	0	0	0	0	0	.000	.000
Night	6.07	2	5	26	46	0	40.0	44	9	17	46	Inning 7+	.250	240	60	10	1	12	35	23	61	.316	.450
Grass	5.33	1	5	30	55	0	50.2	51	8	20	52	None on	.244	135	33	6	0	9	9	13	39	.311	.489
Turf	5.00	1	1	5	10	0	9.0	9	4	3	9	Runners on	.257	105	27	4	1	3	26	10	22	.322	.400
March/April	6.17	0	1	7	13	0	11.2	11	0	4	14	Scoring Posn	.310	58	18	4	1	1	22	8	19	.394	.466
May	0.93	0	0	7	10	0	9.2	6	1	4	7	Close & Late	.232	155	36	3	0	9	24	14	37	.296	.426
June	11.05	1	0	2	8	0	7.1	12	3	5	11	None on/out	.214	56	12	3	0	3	3	6	20	.290	.429
July	2.92	0	1	11	14	0	12.1	15	3	2	10	vs. 1st Batr (relief)	.207	58	12	3	0	2	4	7	20	.292	.362
August	7.15	1	3	6	12	0	11.1	9	5	3	14	1st Inning Pitched	.250	232	58	10	1	12	34	22	60	.315	.457
Sept/Oct	4.91	0	1	2	8	0	7.1	7	1	5	5	First 15 Pitches	.251	175	44	6	1	11	21	13	47	.303	.486
Starter	0.00	0	0	0	0	0	0.0	0	0	0	0	Pitch 16-30	.237	59	14	3	0	1	12	10	13	.348	.389
Reliever	5.28	2	6	35	65	0	59.2	60	12	23	61	Pitch 31-45	.333	6	2	1	0	0	2	0	1	.333	.500
0 Days rest (Relief)	3.68	0	1	14	18	0	14.2	14	3	4	13	Pitch 46+	.000	0	0	0	0	0	0	0	0	.000	.000
1 or 2 Days rest	4.39	2	3	16	27	0	26.2	23	7	8	29	First Pitch	.281	32	9	0	0	2	6	1	0	.303	.469
3+ Days rest	7.85	0	2	5	20	0	18.1	19	2	11	19	Ahead in Count	.206	136	28	5	1	6	16	0	53	.206	.390
vs. AL	6.75	0	2	4	6	0	5.1	7	0	2	5	Behind in Count	.364	33	12	3	0	2	6	5	0	.447	.636
vs. NL	5.13	2	4	31	59	0	54.1	53	12	21	56	Two Strikes	.196	143	28	6	1	4	15	17	61	.281	.336
Pre-All Star	5.01	1	1	20	35	0	32.1	32	3	13	35	Pre-All Star	.250	128	32	8	1	3	18	16	35	.319	.398
Post-All Star	5.60	1	5	15	30	0	27.1	28	9	10	26	Post-All Star	.250	112	28	2	0	9	19	10	26	.311	.509

Last Five Years

	ERA	W	L	Sv	G	GS	IP	H	HR	BB	SO		Avg	AB	H	2B	3B	HR	RBI	BB	SO	OBP	SLG
Home	3.76	10	8	62	134	0	138.2	123	12	37	139	vs. Left	.235	544	128	19	2	18	78	44	142	.291	.377
Away	4.11	7	11	65	135	0	129.1	140	19	43	124	vs. Right	.276	490	135	24	0	13	68	36	121	.325	.404
Day	3.66	2	5	38	83	0	83.2	74	7	27	86	Inning 1-6	.000	0	0	0	0	0	0	0	0	.000	.000
Night	4.05	15	14	89	186	0	184.1	189	24	53	177	Inning 7+	.254	1034	263	43	2	31	146	80	263	.307	.390
Grass	3.85	13	14	99	215	0	217.1	213	20	63	216	None on	.242	571	138	25	0	19	19	37	153	.290	.385
Turf	4.26	4	5	28	54	0	50.2	50	11	17	47	Runners on	.270	463	125	18	2	12	127	43	110	.327	.395
March/April	2.39	2	2	17	38	0	37.2	29	0	9	48	Scoring Posn	.285	281	80	15	2	3	107	33	68	.347	.384
May	3.10	2	4	19	42	0	40.2	39	7	12	33	Close & Late	.243	723	176	23	0	20	112	59	182	.300	.358
June	4.17	4	3	21	44	0	41.0	34	4	10	42	None on/out	.214	238	51	11	0	8	8	13	59	.255	.361
July	5.54	3	3	24	47	0	50.1	62	10	15	47	vs. 1st Batr (relief)	.224	250	56	11	0	6	22	13	64	.258	.340
August	4.55	6	5	26	57	0	55.1	59	7	20	55	1st Inning Pitched	.253	932	236	39	2	26	133	69	237	.304	.383
Sept/Oct	3.14	0	2	20	41	0	43.0	40	3	14	38	First 15 Pitches	.253	748	189	30	2	22	84	49	187	.299	.386
Starter	0.00	0	0	0	0	0	0.0	0	0	0	0	Pitch 16-30	.265	257	68	12	0	8	56	28	70	.334	.405
Reliever	3.93	17	19	127	269	0	268.0	263	31	80	263	Pitch 31-45	.207	29	6	1	0	1	6	3	6	.273	.345
0 Days rest (Relief)	3.60	5	4	49	77	0	70.0	78	7	16	69	Pitch 46+	.000	0	0	0	0	0	0	0	0	.000	.000
1 or 2 Days rest	4.05	10	10	50	113	0	117.2	115	15	40	117	First Pitch	.324	148	48	9	0	4	25	6	0	.346	.466
3+ Days rest	4.03	2	5	28	79	0	80.1	70	9	24	49	Ahead in Count	.195	555	108	17	1	11	57	0	227	.198	.288
vs. AL	6.75	0	2	4	6	0	5.1	7	0	2	5	Behind in Count	.344	157	54	11	0	10	37	25	0	.422	.605

Last Five Years

	ERA	W	L	Sv	G	GS	IP	H	HR	BB	SO		Avg	AB	H	2B	3B	HR	RBI	BB	SO	OBP	SLG
vs. NL	3.87	17	17	123	263	0	262.2	256	31	78	258	Two Strikes	.185	572	106	17	1	8	52	49	263	.250	.260
Pre-All Star	3.16	10	10	63	135	0	133.2	111	13	34	136	Pre-All Star	.222	499	111	20	1	13	62	34	136	.274	.345
Post-All Star	4.69	7	9	64	134	0	134.1	152	18	46	127	Post-All Star	.284	535	152	23	1	18	84	46	127	.338	.432

Pitcher vs. Batter (career)

Pitches Best Vs.	Avg	AB	H	2B	3B	HR	RBI	BB	SO	OBP	SLG	Pitches Worst Vs.	Avg	AB	H	2B	3B	HR	RBI	BB	SO	OBP	SLG
Ron Gant	.000	14	0	0	0	0	0	2	5	.125	.000	Will Clark	.500	10	5	2	0	1	3	3	2	.615	1.000
Todd Hundley	.000	10	0	0	0	0	0	0	5	.091	.000	Marquis Grissom	.444	9	4	0	0	1	1	2	2	.545	.778
Kevin Stocker	.000	10	0	0	0	0	0	1	4	.091	.000	John Vander Wal	.400	10	4	0	0	1	2	1	4	.455	.700
Terry Pendleton	.100	10	1	0	0	0	2	1	3	.182	.100	Barry Bonds	.385	13	5	0	0	1	2	4	3	.529	.615
Shawon Dunston	.211	19	4	0	0	0	2	0	5	.211	.211	Juan Samuel	.368	19	7	3	1	1	7	0	3	.368	.789

Jamey Wright — Rockies
Age 23 – Pitches Right (groundball pitcher)

	ERA	W	L	Sv	G	GS	IP	BB	SO	Avg	H	2B	3B	HR	RBI	OBP	SLG	CG	ShO	Sup	QS	#P/S	SB	CS	GB	FB	G/F
1997 Season	6.25	8	12	0	26	26	149.2	71	59	.327	198	43	6	19	99	.406	.512	1	0	5.65	10	93	10	10	292	152	1.92
Career (1996-1997)	5.75	12	16	0	42	41	241.0	112	104	.317	303	69	10	27	151	.397	.494	1	0	5.41	19	94	17	15	464	229	2.03

1997 Season

	ERA	W	L	Sv	G	GS	IP	H	HR	BB	SO		Avg	AB	H	2B	3B	HR	RBI	BB	SO	OBP	SLG
Home	7.67	5	7	0	15	15	88.0	125	12	37	35	vs. Left	.394	254	100	25	1	8	52	28	21	.453	.594
Away	4.23	3	5	0	11	11	61.2	73	7	34	24	vs. Right	.279	351	98	18	5	11	47	43	38	.372	.453
Day	6.61	4	4	0	11	11	62.2	89	6	33	22	Inning 1-6	.324	540	175	36	6	16	86	67	53	.406	.502
Night	6.00	4	8	0	15	15	87.0	109	13	38	37	Inning 7+	.354	65	23	7	0	3	13	4	6	.403	.600
Grass	6.57	7	9	0	19	19	112.1	155	13	46	43	None on	.336	333	112	23	4	14	14	28	27	.393	.556
Turf	5.30	1	3	0	7	7	37.1	43	6	25	16	Runners on	.316	272	86	20	2	5	85	43	32	.420	.460
March/April	7.52	3	1	0	5	5	26.1	45	5	10	12	Scoring Posn	.305	167	51	11	1	3	75	32	16	.422	.437
May	9.20	1	1	0	3	3	14.2	17	2	16	9	Close & Late	.355	31	11	1	0	1	6	2	4	.412	.484
June	9.60	0	2	0	3	3	15.0	18	1	9	9	None on/out	.327	153	50	6	1	9	9	10	9	.380	.556
July	4.68	1	3	0	5	5	32.2	38	3	14	9	vs. 1st Batr (relief)	.000	0	0	0	0	0	0	0	0	.000	.000
August	5.60	1	3	0	6	6	35.1	45	4	15	11	1st Inning Pitched	.387	106	41	6	2	5	24	13	10	.459	.623
Sept/Oct	4.21	2	2	0	4	4	25.2	35	4	7	9	First 75 Pitches	.333	472	157	31	4	15	74	51	45	.405	.511
Starter	6.25	8	12	0	26	26	149.2	198	19	71	59	Pitch 76-90	.299	77	23	7	1	1	13	10	7	.400	.455
Reliever	0.00	0	0	0	0	0	0.0	0	0	0	0	Pitch 91-105	.317	41	13	4	1	3	8	9	5	.431	.683
0-3 Days Rest (Start)	0.00	0	0	0	0	0	0.0	0	0	0	0	Pitch 106+	.333	15	5	1	0	0	4	1	2	.389	.400
4 Days Rest	5.23	5	5	0	14	14	86.0	98	9	42	35	First Pitch	.309	110	34	9	1	7	22	3	0	.353	.600
5+ Days Rest	7.63	3	7	0	12	12	63.2	100	10	29	24	Ahead in Count	.332	211	70	12	1	5	33	0	51	.343	.469
vs. AL	7.27	0	1	0	3	3	17.1	19	2	10	7	Behind in Count	.320	172	55	12	3	5	31	44	0	.461	.512
vs. NL	6.12	8	11	0	23	23	132.1	179	17	61	52	Two Strikes	.321	209	67	16	0	4	27	24	59	.397	.455
Pre-All Star	8.17	4	5	0	12	12	61.2	88	9	37	31	Pre-All Star	.337	261	88	21	3	9	51	37	31	.424	.544
Post-All Star	4.91	4	7	0	14	14	88.0	110	10	34	28	Post-All Star	.320	344	110	22	3	10	48	34	28	.391	.488

Jaret Wright — Indians
Age 22 – Pitches Right

	ERA	W	L	Sv	G	GS	IP	BB	SO	Avg	H	2B	3B	HR	RBI	OBP	SLG	CG	ShO	Sup	QS	#P/S	SB	CS	GB	FB	G/F
1997 Season	4.38	8	3	0	16	16	90.1	35	63	.238	81	20	2	9	38	.314	.387	0	0	6.38	9	94	15	1	123	97	1.27

1997 Season

	ERA	W	L	Sv	G	GS	IP	H	HR	BB	SO		Avg	AB	H	2B	3B	HR	RBI	BB	SO	OBP	SLG
Home	5.20	3	2	0	7	7	36.1	38	4	16	29	vs. Left	.280	175	49	11	2	4	22	14	26	.335	.434
Away	3.83	5	1	0	9	9	54.0	43	5	19	34	vs. Right	.193	166	32	9	0	5	16	21	37	.293	.337
Starter	4.38	8	3	0	16	16	90.1	81	9	35	63	Scoring Posn	.273	88	24	7	0	3	32	10	20	.340	.455
Reliever	0.00	0	0	0	0	0	0.0	0	0	0	0	Close & Late	.500	2	1	0	0	0	0	0	0	.500	.500
0-3 Days Rest (Start)	0.00	0	0	0	0	0	0.0	0	0	0	0	None on/out	.258	89	23	7	0	3	3	7	15	.313	.438
4 Days Rest	3.49	6	2	0	9	9	56.2	49	3	23	40	First Pitch	.283	46	13	4	1	1	10	0	0	.306	.478
5+ Days Rest	5.88	2	1	0	7	7	33.2	32	6	12	23	Ahead in Count	.141	149	21	5	0	2	9	0	51	.215	.215
Pre-All Star	5.59	1	0	0	2	2	9.2	8	3	5	6	Behind in Count	.282	71	20	5	0	5	11	16	0	.409	.563
Post-All Star	4.24	7	3	0	14	14	80.2	73	6	30	57	Two Strikes	.172	163	28	6	1	1	9	19	63	.267	.239

Esteban Yan — Orioles
Age 24 – Pitches Right (flyball pitcher)

	ERA	W	L	Sv	G	GS	IP	BB	SO	Avg	H	2B	3B	HR	RBI	OBP	SLG	CG	ShO	Sup	QS	#P/S	SB	CS	GB	FB	G/F
1997 Season	15.83	0	1	0	3	2	9.2	7	4	.417	20	2	1	3	16	.500	.688	0	0	3.72	0	97	2	0	14	22	0.64
Career (1996-1997)	10.89	0	1	0	7	2	19.0	10	11	.379	33	3	1	6	22	.450	.644	0	0	6.16	0	97	2	0	21	41	0.51

1997 Season

	ERA	W	L	Sv	G	GS	IP	H	HR	BB	SO		Avg	AB	H	2B	3B	HR	RBI	BB	SO	OBP	SLG
Home	15.19	0	0	0	2	1	5.1	9	2	4	3	vs. Left	.364	22	8	0	0	2	7	4	2	.462	.636
Away	16.62	0	1	0	1	1	4.1	11	1	3	1	vs. Right	.462	26	12	2	1	1	9	3	2	.531	.731

Dmitri Young — Cardinals
Age 24 – Bats Both

	Avg	G	AB	R	H	2B	3B	HR	RBI	BB	SO	HBP	GDP	SB	CS	OBP	SLG	IBB	SH	SF	#Pit	#P/PA	GB	FB	G/F
1997 Season	.258	110	333	38	86	14	3	5	34	38	63	2	8	6	5	.335	.363	3	1	3	1391	3.69	148	74	2.00
Career (1996-1997)	.257	126	362	41	93	14	3	5	36	42	68	3	9	6	6	.337	.354	3	1	3	1510	3.67	156	84	1.86

1997 Season

	Avg	AB	H	2B	3B	HR	RBI	BB	SO	OBP	SLG		Avg	AB	H	2B	3B	HR	RBI	BB	SO	OBP	SLG
vs. Left	.265	83	22	3	0	1	9	7	17	.330	.337	First Pitch	.346	52	18	1	1	2	8	3	0	.375	.519

1997 Season

	Avg	AB	H	2B	3B	HR	RBI	BB	SO	OBP	SLG		Avg	AB	H	2B	3B	HR	RBI	BB	SO	OBP	SLG
vs. Right	.256	250	64	11	3	4	25	31	46	.337	.372	Ahead in Count	.231	65	15	1	0	0	5	20	0	.414	.246
Groundball	.203	69	14	5	0	1	8	9	13	.288	.319	Behind in Count	.227	154	35	12	0	1	8	0	46	.232	.325
Flyball	.260	50	13	1	1	0	5	3	13	.315	.320	Two Strikes	.183	153	28	7	2	1	11	15	63	.259	.275
Home	.240	175	42	9	0	2	15	24	31	.330	.326	Batting #5	.283	60	17	2	0	1	7	3	8	.313	.367
Away	.278	158	44	5	0	2	19	14	32	.341	.405	Batting #6	.354	96	34	4	0	2	15	14	17	.436	.458
Day	.217	129	28	3	1	1		11	30	.282	.279	Other	.199	177	35	8	3	2	12	21	38	.287	.311
Night	.284	204	58	11	2	4	25	27	33	.368	.417	March/April	.273	66	18	4	2	1	7	7	12	.000	.129
Grass	.241	266	64	11	2	3	23	31	51	.319	.331	May	.243	37	9	1	0	1	7	7	7	.378	.351
Turf	.328	67	22	3	1	2	11	7	12	.400	.493	June	.322	87	28	5	1	1	15	3	16	.352	.437
Pre-All Star	.288	208	60	10	3	3	25	20	36	.353	.409	July	.174	69	12	2	0	0	5	5	15	.224	.203
Post-All Star	.208	125	26	4	0	2	9	18	27	.306	.288	August	.231	13	3	0	0	0	0	7	2	.500	.231
Scoring Posn	.256	82	21	2	1	0	28	11	15	.347	.305	Sept/Oct	.262	61	16	2	0	2	6	9	11	.357	.393
Close & Late	.203	64	13	1	0	0	5	9	17	.297	.219	vs. AL	.286	28	8	0	0	0	2	6		.333	.286
None on/out	.308	65	20	3	1	2	2	6	10	.366	.477	vs. NL	.256	305	78	14	3	5	32	36	57	.335	.370

1997 By Position

Position	Avg	AB	H	2B	3B	HR	RBI	BB	SO	OBP	SLG	G	GS	Innings	PO	A	E	DP	Fld Pct	Rng Fctr	In Zone	Outs	Zone Rtg	MLB Zone
As Pinch Hitter	.143	14	2	0	0	0	3	4	7	.316	.143	19	0	---										
As 1b	.266	256	68	12	3	3	26	25	46	.333	.371	74	68	590.2	603	45	10	50	.985	---	114	108	.947	.874
As rf	.281	32	9	0	0	2	3	6	4	.395	.469	10	10	84.0	23	2	2	0	.926	2.68	24	20	.833	.813

Eric Young — Dodgers

Age 31 – Bats Right (groundball hitter)

	Avg	G	AB	R	H	2B	3B	HR	RBI	BB	SO	HBP	GDP	SB	CS	OBP	SLG	IBB	SH	SF	#Pit	#P/PA	GB	FB	G/F
1997 Season	.280	155	622	106	174	33	8	8	61	71	54	9	18	45	14	.359	.397	1	10	6	2500	3.48	277	182	1.52
Last Five Years	.294	650	2274	406	668	106	30	32	243	268	172	41	43	193	71	.376	.409	9	24	18	9561	3.64	992	667	1.49

1997 Season

	Avg	AB	H	2B	3B	HR	RBI	BB	SO	OBP	SLG		Avg	AB	H	2B	3B	HR	RBI	BB	SO	OBP	SLG
vs. Left	.280	157	44	11	1	3	15	16	11	.358	.420	First Pitch	.235	81	19	2	0	0	7	0	0	.226	.259
vs. Right	.280	465	130	21	7	5	46	55	43	.359	.389	Ahead in Count	.338	154	52	9	1	4	20	53	0	.505	.487
Groundball	.319	119	38	8	2	1	20	16	11	.415	.445	Behind in Count	.234	265	62	14	6	0	20	0	47	.250	.332
Flyball	.240	75	18	4	2	2	5	13	7	.348	.427	Two Strikes	.231	225	52	13	4	2	25	18	54	.301	.351
Home	.292	277	81	15	3	2	32	41	19	.391	.390	Batting #1	.278	565	157	32	8	7	56	67	51	.358	.400
Away	.270	345	93	18	5	6	29	30	35	.331	.403	Batting #2	.260	50	13	0	0	1	3	3	3	.327	.320
Day	.296	274	81	15	4	3	33	42	18	.391	.412	Other	.571	7	4	1	0	0	2	1	0	.625	.714
Night	.267	348	93	18	4	5	28	29	36	.332	.385	March/April	.346	104	36	8	2	0	7	12	7	.415	.462
Grass	.275	480	132	25	6	5	50	59	37	.359	.385	May	.287	108	31	7	1	2	10	16	6	.379	.426
Turf	.296	142	42	8	2	3	11	12	17	.359	.444	June	.270	111	30	4	2	0	11	12	5	.346	.396
Pre-All Star	.293	338	99	20	6	4	28	44	20	.378	.423	July	.242	99	24	6	1	2	11	14	13	.345	.384
Post-All Star	.264	284	75	13	2	4	33	27	34	.335	.366	August	.288	104	30	8	1	1	11	8	12	.348	.413
Scoring Posn	.270	126	34	9	1	0	48	18	10	.359	.357	Sept/Oct	.240	96	23	0	1	1	11	9	11	.315	.292
Close & Late	.303	76	23	7	0	1	10	12	11	.396	.434	vs. AL	.250	60	15	3	1	1	6	7	4	.361	.383
None on/out	.280	250	70	15	5	5	5	31	20	.362	.440	vs. NL	.283	562	159	30	7	7	55	64	50	.358	.399

1997 By Position

Position	Avg	AB	H	2B	3B	HR	RBI	BB	SO	OBP	SLG	G	GS	Innings	PO	A	E	DP	Fld Pct	Rng Fctr	In Zone	Outs	Zone Rtg	MLB Zone
As 2b	.279	621	173	33	8	8	61	71	54	.358	.396	154	151	1327.1	319	493	18	111	.978	5.51	555	521	.939	.902

Last Five Years

	Avg	AB	H	2B	3B	HR	RBI	BB	SO	OBP	SLG		Avg	AB	H	2B	3B	HR	RBI	BB	SO	OBP	SLG
vs. Left	.301	615	185	39	4	11	65	68	47	.380	.444	First Pitch	.302	281	85	13	2	2	38	7	0	.323	.384
vs. Right	.291	1659	483	67	22	21	178	200	125	.374	.396	Ahead in Count	.327	593	194	27	6	18	85	195	0	.492	.484
Groundball	.267	570	152	23	4	8	69	64	49	.363	.363	Behind in Count	.252	943	238	47	13	4	72	0	143	.273	.343
Flyball	.310	332	103	11	6	8	33	50	30	.405	.452	Two Strikes	.247	892	220	43	14	9	83	66	172	.314	.357
Home	.335	1128	378	48	21	23	167	158	66	.422	.476	Batting #1	.294	1996	586	96	28	25	210	228	147	.374	.407
Away	.253	1146	290	58	9	9	76	110	106	.327	.343	Batting #2	.232	138	32	6	0	4	9	15	11	.325	.362
Day	.316	851	269	44	13	17	97	111	63	.404	.458	Other	.357	140	50	4	2	3	24	25	14	.449	.479
Night	.280	1423	399	62	17	15	147	157	109	.358	.379	March/April	.310	261	81	15	4	5	28	34	18	.393	.456
Grass	.302	1800	543	84	25	29	211	225	125	.386	.424	May	.253	379	96	18	5	5	33	47	26	.342	.367
Turf	.264	474	125	22	5	3	32	43	47	.334	.350	June	.311	392	122	17	3	4	49	55	25	.403	.401
Pre-All Star	.291	1178	343	58	14	17	123	153	79	.379	.407	July	.302	473	143	21	6	7	52	52	41	.382	.416
Post-All Star	.297	1096	325	48	16	15	120	115	93	.372	.411	August	.277	411	114	22	7	5	46	42	37	.353	.401
Scoring Posn	.295	501	148	24	8	2	201	69	31	.386	.387	Sept/Oct	.313	358	112	13	5	6	46	38	25	.387	.427
Close & Late	.319	298	95	14	5	1	36	48	25	.417	.409	vs. AL	.250	60	15	3	1	1	6	7	4	.361	.383
None on/out	.285	895	255	39	14	19	19	107	79	.376	.423	vs. NL	.295	2214	653	103	29	31	237	261	168	.376	.410

Batter vs. Pitcher (career)

Hits Best Against	Avg	AB	H	2B	3B	HR	RBI	BB	SO	OBP	SLG	Hits Worst Against	Avg	AB	H	2B	3B	HR	RBI	BB	SO	OBP	SLG
Kevin Brown	.600	10	6	1	1	0	1	1	0	.636	.900	Alex Fernandez	.000	10	0	0	0	0	0	1	0	.091	.000
Mike Hampton	.563	16	9	2	0	0	4	1	1	.611	.688	Dave Veres	.077	13	1	0	0	0	0	0	3	.077	.077
Carlos Perez	.556	9	5	0	0	1	1	1	0	.636	.889	F. Valenzuela	.100	10	1	0	0	0	0	1	0	.182	.100
John Burkett	.485	33	16	2	3	0	3	1	0	.514	.727	Tommy Greene	.100	10	1	0	0	0	0	1	0	.182	.100
Dan Plesac	.375	8	3	1	0	1	1	3	0	.545	.875	Darren Oliver	.111	9	1	0	0	0	1	0	0	.182	.111

Ernie Young — Athletics

	Avg	G	AB	R	H	2B	3B	HR	RBI	BB	SO	HBP	GDP	SB	CS	OBP	SLG	IBB	SH	SF	#Pit	#P/PA	GB	FB	G/F
1997 Season	.223	71	175	22	39	7	0	5	15	19	57	2	6	1	3	.303	.349	0	2	2	767	3.84	63	32	1.97
Career (1994-1997)	.227	249	717	105	163	30	4	26	87	80	195	9	21	8	8	.310	.389	1	5	6	3182	3.89	227	192	1.18

1997 Season

	Avg	AB	H	2B	3B	HR	RBI	BB	SO	OBP	SLG		Avg	AB	H	2B	3B	HR	RBI	BB	SO	OBP	SLG
vs. Left	.180	61	11	2	0	0	4	8	23	.268	.213	Scoring Posn	.140	43	6	1	0	1	6	6	19	.235	.233
vs. Right	.246	114	28	5	0	5	11	11	34	.323	.421	Close & Late	.143	28	4	2	0	0	1	3	15	.226	.214
Home	.223	94	21	6	0	3	9	11	29	.306	.383	None on/out	.160	50	8	2	0	2	2	3	17	.208	.320
Away	.222	81	18	1	0	2	6	8	28	.300	.309	Batting #8	.260	77	20	3	0	2	5	5	26	.318	.377
First Pitch	.406	32	13	2	0	2	6	0	0	.412	.656	Batting #9	.261	46	12	4	0	2	8	5	15	.327	.478
Ahead in Count	.280	25	7	2	0	1	3	7	0	.424	.480	Other	.135	52	7	0	0	1	2	9	16	.262	.192
Behind in Count	.088	80	7	1	0	0	0	0	42	.099	.100	Pre-All Star	.130	46	6	0	0	1	1	8	13	.259	.196
Two Strikes	.138	94	13	3	0	3	12	57	.243	.170		Post-All Star	.256	129	33	7	0	4	14	11	44	.319	.403

Career (1994-1997)

	Avg	AB	H	2B	3B	HR	RBI	BB	SO	OBP	SLG		Avg	AB	H	2B	3B	HR	RBI	BB	SO	OBP	SLG
vs. Left	.231	216	50	8	1	7	22	26	59	.317	.375	First Pitch	.364	110	40	8	0	7	20	1	0	.374	.627
vs. Right	.226	501	113	22	3	19	65	54	136	.307	.395	Ahead in Count	.297	128	38	7	0	7	19	36	0	.446	.516
Groundball	.198	172	34	6	0	5	13	16	40	.270	.320	Behind in Count	.144	319	46	7	3	4	17	0	148	.157	.223
Flyball	.248	109	27	6	1	2	18	12	36	.320	.376	Two Strikes	.141	368	52	9	3	5	27	43	195	.236	.223
Home	.234	384	90	17	2	15	43	38	104	.306	.406	Batting #1	.236	191	45	8	2	7	30	22	55	.318	.408
Away	.219	333	73	13	2	11	44	42	91	.315	.369	Batting #8	.235	311	73	13	2	12	37	38	85	.327	.405
Day	.236	314	74	12	3	9	40	32	84	.313	.379	Other	.209	215	45	9	0	7	20	20	55	.278	.349
Night	.221	403	89	18	1	17	47	48	111	.309	.397	March/April	.215	107	23	4	1	1	9	16	30	.317	.299
Grass	.232	641	149	27	4	24	76	71	174	.314	.399	May	.168	113	19	3	0	6	20	9	27	.236	.354
Turf	.184	76	14	3	0	2	11	9	21	.276	.303	June	.269	108	29	5	2	6	16	11	29	.339	.519
Pre-All Star	.215	358	77	12	3	14	46	42	92	.300	.383	July	.209	129	27	5	0	5	13	17	39	.306	.364
Post-All Star	.240	359	86	18	1	12	41	38	103	.320	.396	August	.233	163	38	10	0	4	14	18	43	.317	.368
Scoring Posn	.206	180	37	6	1	4	53	26	57	.300	.317	Sept/Oct	.278	97	27	3	1	4	15	9	27	.349	.454
Close & Late	.163	104	17	6	0	5	13	13	42	.254	.365	vs. AL	.227	704	160	30	4	26	87	79	190	.311	.392
None on/out	.225	204	46	12	2	6	21	57	.307	.392		vs. NL	.231	13	3	0	0	0	0	1	5	.286	.231

Batter vs. Pitcher (career)

Hits Best Against	Avg	AB	H	2B	3B	HR	RBI	BB	SO	OBP	SLG	Hits Worst Against	Avg	AB	H	2B	3B	HR	RBI	BB	SO	OBP	SLG
												Wilson Alvarez	.100	10	1	0	0	0	0	1	5	.250	.100
												Charles Nagy	.118	17	2	0	0	1	1	0	2	.118	.294
												Pat Hentgen	.133	15	2	1	0	0	0	0	3	.133	.200
												Kenny Rogers	.154	13	2	1	0	1	0	0	3	.214	.231
												Juan Guzman	.182	11	2	1	0	1	1	0	3	.231	.273

Kevin Young — Pirates

	Avg	G	AB	R	H	2B	3B	HR	RBI	BB	SO	HBP	GDP	SB	CS	OBP	SLG	IBB	SH	SF	#Pit	#P/PA	GB	FB	G/F
1997 Season	.300	97	333	59	100	18	3	18	74	16	89	4	6	11	2	.332	.535	1	1	8	1320	3.65	95	94	1.01
Last Five Years	.251	408	1217	145	305	64	8	39	177	79	290	16	25	17	12	.300	.412	6	9	21	5051	3.76	343	382	0.90

1997 Season

	Avg	AB	H	2B	3B	HR	RBI	BB	SO	OBP	SLG		Avg	AB	H	2B	3B	HR	RBI	BB	SO	OBP	SLG
vs. Left	.360	86	31	6	0	5	19	4	22	.376	.605	First Pitch	.383	47	18	4	0	4	12	1	0	.412	.723
vs. Right	.279	247	69	12	3	13	55	12	67	.317	.510	Ahead in Count	.403	67	27	3	1	4	24	9	0	.450	.657
Groundball	.419	43	18	3	0	3	11	3	9	.447	.698	Behind in Count	.219	155	34	8	2	3	17	0	71	.226	.355
Flyball	.250	52	13	3	1	5	17	4	21	.310	.635	Two Strikes	.157	166	26	6	0	5	23	6	89	.190	.283
Home	.277	173	48	9	2	11	41	7	47	.311	.543	Batting #3	.333	9	3	1	0	1	3	0	3	.333	.778
Away	.325	160	52	9	1	7	33	9	42	.357	.525	Batting #4	.302	298	90	15	2	15	62	15	81	.335	.517
Day	.299	117	35	9	0	6	34	8	32	.346	.530	Other	.269	26	7	2	1	2	9	1	5	.296	.654
Night	.301	216	65	9	3	12	40	8	57	.325	.537	March/April	.318	22	7	0	0	1	6	0	7	.304	.455
Grass	.314	105	33	4	0	4	15	8	31	.360	.467	May	.297	64	19	7	3	3	17	2	15	.324	.641
Turf	.294	228	67	14	3	14	59	8	58	.320	.566	June	.305	95	29	6	0	4	16	4	25	.350	.495
Pre-All Star	.306	206	63	14	3	10	43	8	54	.339	.549	July	.337	104	35	4	0	7	26	9	29	.379	.577
Post-All Star	.291	127	37	4	0	8	31	8	35	.321	.512	August	.286	7	2	0	0	1	3	0	1	.250	.714
Scoring Posn	.299	107	32	9	0	5	54	4	26	.308	.523	Sept/Oct	.195	41	8	1	0	2	6	1	12	.209	.366
Close & Late	.333	60	20	7	1	4	20	3	17	.369	.683	vs. AL	.300	30	9	2	0	1	6	0	7	.323	.467
None on/out	.322	87	28	5	0	6	6	8	23	.379	.586	vs. NL	.300	303	91	16	3	17	68	16	82	.333	.541

1997 By Position

Position	Avg	AB	H	2B	3B	HR	RBI	BB	SO	OBP	SLG	G	GS	Innings	PO	A	E	DP	Fld Pct	Rng Fctr	In Zone	Zone Outs	Zone Rtg	MLB Zone
As 1b	.328	259	85	15	1	16	59	12	69	.352	.579	77	64	576.0	618	56	2	48	.997	---	149	141	.946	.874
As 3b	.133	30	4	0	1	0	3	2	11	.188	.200	12	5	61.0	7	16	3	2	.885	3.39	24	20	.833	.801
As lf	.250	36	9	2	1	2	10	2	7	.325	.528	10	10	79.0	17	0	0	0	1.000	1.94	19	16	.842	.805

Last Five Years

	Avg	AB	H	2B	3B	HR	RBI	BB	SO	OBP	SLG		Avg	AB	H	2B	3B	HR	RBI	BB	SO	OBP	SLG
vs. Left	.257	440	113	25	0	18	61	35	97	.311	.436	First Pitch	.375	168	63	14	1	6	27	6	0	.412	.577
vs. Right	.247	777	192	39	8	21	116	44	193	.294	.399	Ahead in Count	.301	246	74	12	3	11	53	33	0	.374	.508
Groundball	.259	301	78	16	1	6	35	17	65	.307	.379	Behind in Count	.196	578	113	27	3	12	63	0	244	.213	.315
Flyball	.229	192	44	8	3	8	36	10	53	.271	.427	Two Strikes	.163	606	99	25	1	10	59	40	290	.221	.271
Home	.247	627	155	38	3	27	106	48	145	.305	.447	Batting #4	.296	314	93	17	2	15	63	17	86	.332	.506
Away	.254	590	150	26	5	12	71	31	145	.294	.376	Batting #8	.227	299	68	20	3	6	31	25	77	.289	.375
Day	.244	361	88	19	2	8	51	20	95	.286	.374	Other	.238	604	144	27	3	18	83	37	127	.289	.382

515

Last Five Years

	Avg	AB	H	2B	3B	HR	RBI	BB	SO	OBP	SLG		Avg	AB	H	2B	3B	HR	RBI	BB	SO	OBP	SLG
Night	.254	856	217	45	6	31	126	59	195	.306	.429	March/April	.241	133	32	3	1	3	22	10	38	.297	.346
Grass	.249	437	109	17	4	10	49	29	107	.301	.375	May	.243	169	41	12	4	6	28	12	30	.307	.467
Turf	.251	780	196	47	4	29	128	50	183	.300	.433	June	.264	277	73	15	2	7	35	15	66	.312	.408
Pre-All Star	.249	675	168	30	7	20	99	40	161	.299	.407	July	.251	275	69	12	0	10	47	25	74	.311	.404
Post-All Star	.253	542	137	31	1	19	79	39	129	.301	.419	August	.282	170	48	12	0	7	31	8	33	.317	.476
Scoring Posn	.227	331	75	17	1	11	134	36	186	.292	.384	Sept/Oct	.218	193	42	10	1	6	24	9	49	.246	.373
Close & Late	.258	225	58	19	2	6	45	16	56	.308	.440	vs. AL	.253	162	41	8	0	9	29	11	39	.305	.469
None on/out	.266	305	81	15	0	13	13	18	65	.311	.443	vs. NL	.250	1055	264	56	8	30	148	68	251	.299	.404

Batter vs. Pitcher (career)

Hits Best Against	Avg	AB	H	2B	3B	HR	RBI	BB	SO	OBP	SLG	Hits Worst Against	Avg	AB	H	2B	3B	HR	RBI	BB	SO	OBP	SLG
Pete Schourek	.438	16	7	1	0	1	3	0	2	.438	.688	Kevin Gross	.083	12	1	0	0	0	1	0	6	.143	.083
Danny Jackson	.364	11	4	0	0	0	1	0	1	.417	.364	Mark Portugal	.083	12	1	0	0	1	2	2	.214	.083
Armando Reynoso	.364	11	4	2	0	0	1	0	1	.364	.545	Donovan Osborne	.091	11	1	0	0	0	0	0	7	.091	.091
Orel Hershiser	.333	15	5	1	0	0	0	1	3	.375	.400	Jeff Fassero	.133	15	2	0	0	0	0	6	.133	.133
												Darryl Kile	.188	16	3	0	0	0	2	1	6	.222	.188

Gregg Zaun — Marlins
Age 27 – Bats Both

	Avg	G	AB	R	H	2B	3B	HR	RBI	BB	SO	HBP	GDP	SB	CS	OBP	SLG	IBB	SH	SF	#Pit	#P/PA	GB	FB	G/F
1997 Season	.301	58	143	21	43	10	2	2	20	26	18	2	3	1	0	.415	.441	4	1	0	614	3.57	42	54	0.78
Career (1995-1997)	.269	158	386	59	104	24	3	7	49	56	52	4	10	3	1	.366	.402	7	4	2	1655	3.66	127	143	0.89

1997 Season

	Avg	AB	H	2B	3B	HR	RBI	BB	SO	OBP	SLG		Avg	AB	H	2B	3B	HR	RBI	BB	SO	OBP	SLG
vs. Left	.286	14	4	1	0	0	2	5	3	.500	.357	Scoring Posn	.286	42	12	3	0	0	16	16	7	.492	.357
vs. Right	.302	129	39	9	2	2	18	21	15	.404	.450	Close & Late	.263	38	10	3	0	2	7	8	6	.391	.500
Home	.311	61	19	4	2	0	11	10	6	.425	.443	None on/out	.290	31	9	3	0	1	2	1	.333	.484
Away	.293	82	24	6	0	2	9	16	12	.408	.439	Batting #7	.311	45	14	2	1	0	4	5	6	.380	.400
First Pitch	.385	26	10	0	0	1	6	3	0	.467	.500	Batting #8	.301	73	22	6	0	1	14	16	8	.440	.425
Ahead in Count	.361	36	13	5	0	1	5	13	0	.540	.583	Other	.280	25	7	2	1	1	2	5	4	.400	.560
Behind in Count	.250	56	14	3	1	0	3	0	17	.250	.339	Pre-All Star	.310	84	26	7	0	2	16	15	8	.420	.464
Two Strikes	.179	56	10	1	1	0	6	10	18	.303	.232	Post-All Star	.288	59	17	3	2	0	4	11	10	.408	.407

Todd Zeile — Dodgers
Age 32 – Bats Right

	Avg	G	AB	R	H	2B	3B	HR	RBI	BB	SO	HBP	GDP	SB	CS	OBP	SLG	IBB	SH	SF	#Pit	#P/PA	GB	FB	G/F
1997 Season	.268	160	575	89	154	17	0	31	90	85	112	6	18	8	7	.365	.459	7	0	6	2757	4.10	207	169	1.22
Last Five Years	.265	706	2604	361	690	132	2	106	419	323	424	14	75	16	15	.346	.439	20	4	28	12015	4.04	939	827	1.14

1997 Season

	Avg	AB	H	2B	3B	HR	RBI	BB	SO	OBP	SLG		Avg	AB	H	2B	3B	HR	RBI	BB	SO	OBP	SLG
vs. Left	.257	140	36	6	0	5	18	23	20	.361	.407	First Pitch	.279	43	12	2	0	2	3	4	0	.340	.465
vs. Right	.271	435	118	11	0	26	72	62	92	.366	.476	Ahead in Count	.457	129	59	4	0	13	35	48	0	.602	.791
Groundball	.281	89	25	4	0	5	14	16	20	.402	.494	Behind in Count	.184	272	50	10	0	7	32	0	87	.194	.298
Flyball	.176	74	13	1	0	3	8	8	19	.262	.311	Two Strikes	.166	289	48	9	0	6	28	33	112	.256	.260
Home	.271	284	77	7	0	17	46	37	44	.357	.475	Batting #5	.235	85	20	0	0	3	9	10	18	.320	.341
Away	.265	291	77	10	0	14	44	48	68	.372	.443	Batting #6	.286	360	103	13	0	22	63	65	75	.397	.506
Day	.267	165	44	6	0	11	27	27	34	.374	.503	Other	.238	130	31	4	0	6	18	10	19	.296	.408
Night	.268	410	110	11	0	20	63	58	78	.361	.441	March/April	.175	80	14	2	0	2	10	11	16	.290	.275
Grass	.268	473	127	14	0	26	74	65	87	.360	.463	May	.280	100	28	4	0	7	16	14	19	.365	.530
Turf	.265	102	27	3	0	5	16	20	25	.384	.441	June	.214	112	24	1	0	7	13	12	21	.288	.411
Pre-All Star	.229	314	72	8	0	16	41	41	64	.320	.408	July	.236	89	21	2	0	5	14	20	19	.375	.427
Post-All Star	.314	261	82	9	0	15	49	44	48	.415	.521	August	.324	108	35	4	0	3	18	17	16	.417	.444
Scoring Posn	.228	158	36	5	0	5	56	36	30	.363	.354	Sept/Oct	.372	86	32	4	0	7	19	11	21	.450	.663
Close & Late	.283	106	30	1	0	7	12	19	19	.402	.491	vs. AL	.220	59	13	1	0	3	8	11	13	.343	.390
None on/out	.324	136	44	6	0	11	14	14	28	.399	.610	vs. NL	.273	516	141	16	0	28	82	74	99	.367	.467

1997 By Position

Position	Avg	AB	H	2B	3B	HR	RBI	BB	SO	OBP	SLG	G	GS	Innings	PO	A	E	DP	Fld Pct	Rng Fctr	In Zone	Zone Outs	Zone Rtg	MLB Zone
As 3b	.268	574	154	17	0	31	90	85	111	.365	.460	160	159	1431.1	105	247	26	27	.931	2.21	360	285	792	801

Last Five Years

	Avg	AB	H	2B	3B	HR	RBI	BB	SO	OBP	SLG		Avg	AB	H	2B	3B	HR	RBI	BB	SO	OBP	SLG
vs. Left	.257	604	155	36	1	25	96	85	70	.346	.444	First Pitch	.326	187	61	16	0	6	28	13	0	.368	.508
vs. Right	.268	2000	535	96	1	81	323	238	354	.346	.438	Ahead in Count	.320	607	194	30	0	44	139	179	0	.470	.586
Groundball	.258	678	175	34	0	21	105	84	113	.341	.401	Behind in Count	.220	1197	263	58	1	27	146	0	344	.224	.338
Flyball	.244	422	103	19	1	18	70	56	81	.331	.422	Two Strikes	.200	1238	247	52	1	24	136	131	424	.278	.301
Home	.277	1223	339	57	1	52	200	139	174	.350	.453	Batting #4	.276	1137	314	61	1	48	206	156	181	.361	.458
Away	.254	1381	351	75	1	54	219	184	250	.342	.427	Batting #6	.282	579	163	27	0	26	94	91	103	.381	.463
Day	.271	798	216	41	2	33	129	107	131	.356	.451	Other	.240	888	213	44	1	32	119	76	140	.302	.400
Night	.262	1806	474	91	0	73	290	216	293	.341	.434	March/April	.243	334	81	17	0	12	47	46	51	.335	.401
Grass	.261	1314	343	63	0	61	217	171	230	.348	.448	May	.259	478	124	22	0	21	77	59	82	.341	.437
Turf	.269	1290	347	69	2	45	202	152	194	.344	.430	June	.243	511	124	27	0	14	57	46	68	.304	.378
Pre-All Star	.256	1479	378	74	2	51	205	168	235	.331	.412	July	.290	489	142	27	2	28	105	64	86	.367	.526
Post-All Star	.277	1125	312	58	0	55	214	155	189	.365	.476	August	.279	469	131	20	0	14	71	65	84	.371	.412
Scoring Posn	.263	737	194	41	0	27	301	146	126	.377	.429	Sept/Oct	.272	323	88	19	0	17	62	43	53	.359	.489
Close & Late	.242	425	103	18	0	13	51	55	79	.331	.376	vs. AL	.233	176	41	9	0	8	27	26	29	.332	.420

Last Five Years

	Avg	AB	H	2B	3B	HR	RBI	BB	SO	OBP	SLG		Avg	AB	H	2B	3B	HR	RBI	BB	SO	OBP	SLG
None on/out	272	659	179	39	0	30	30	51	110	328	467	vs. NL	267	2428	649	123	2		98	392	297	395	347	441

Batter vs. Pitcher (career)

Hits Best Against	Avg	AB	H	2B	3B	HR	RBI	BB	SO	OBP	SLG	Hits Worst Against	Avg	AB	H	2B	3B	HR	RBI	BB	SO	OBP	SLG
Brian Williams	.500	16	8	1	1	3	7	0	2	.500	1.250	Danny Darwin	.000	11	0	0	0	0	1	0	2	.000	.000
Heathcliff Slocumb	.444	9	4	2	0	0	2	2	1	.545	.667	Bryan Rekar	.000	11	0	0	0	0	0	0	2	.000	.000
Tim Wakefield	.417	12	5	1	0	1	3	2	2	.500	.750	Chuck McElroy	.071	14	1	0	0	0	0	2	1	.188	.071
Andy Ashby	.389	18	7	2	0	1	5	6	1	.560	.667	Richie Lewis	.100	10	1	0	0	0	0	1	4	.182	.100
Mel Rojas	.368	19	7	1	0	2	11	3	2	.440	.737	Bobby Jones	.118	17	2	0	0	0	0	1	7	.167	.118

Team/League Profiles

Here are our statistical splits for all 28 big league teams, the American and National Leagues, and all of Major League Baseball. Included are home/road and lefty/righty breakdowns, how leadoff men fared, hitting in the clutch and starter vs. reliever comparisons.

So go ahead, turn the page and check out just how much Coors Field inflates offense. The Rockies scored 167 more runs and hit 68 points higher at home, though they did bash just nine more homers than they did on the road.

Major League Baseball

	Avg	G	AB	R	H	2B	3B	HR	RBI	BB	SO	HBP	GDP	SB	CS	OBP	SLG	IBB	SH	SF	#Pit	#P/PA	GB	FB	G/F
1997	.267	2266	155438	21604	41471	8004	883	4640	20468	15666	29937	1449	3436	3308	1564	.337	.419	1169	1577	1383	650935	3.71	56062	42668	1.31

1997 Batting

	Avg	AB	H	2B	3B	HR	RBI	BB	SO	OBP	SLG
vs.Left	.266	40760	10040	2059	190	1202	5346	4145	7823	.336	.414
vs.Right	.267	114672	30631	5945	693	3438	15122	11521	22114	.007	.421
Groundball	.268	30039	8065	1549	180	793	3923	3015	5670	.338	.411
Flyball	.257	23017	5919	1210	141	759	2902	2213	4894	.325	.421
Home	.272	75873	20646	3975	462	2299	10357	8087	14260	.345	.428
Away	.262	79565	20825	4029	421	2341	10111	7579	15677	.329	.411
Day	.270	54327	14654	2891	292	1620	7293	5662	10618	.341	.423
Night	.265	101111	26817	5113	591	3020	13175	10004	19319	.334	.417
Grass	.269	111281	29939	5512	589	3400	14795	11418	20864	.339	.421
Turf	.261	44157	11532	2492	294	1240	5673	4248	9073	.330	.415
Pre-All Star	.268	81941	21955	4326	456	2383	10804	8525	15390	.340	.419
Post-All Star	.266	73497	19516	3678	427	2257	9664	7141	14547	.334	.419
Scoring Posn	.267	39521	10538	2101	261	1058	15266	5686	8037	.355	.413
Close&Late	.261	24695	6453	1145	144	672	3368	2966	5405	.343	.401
None on/out	.268	38702	10359	1964	228	1229	1229	3267	7058	.329	.425

	Avg	AB	H	2B	3B	HR	RBI	BB	SO	OBP	SLG
First Pitch	.333	21916	7302	1445	154	812	3556	857	0	.363	.524
Ahead in Cnt	.346	33409	11546	2345	245	1621	6417	8014	0	.470	.576
Behind in Cnt	.204	70538	14410	2656	295	1265	6283	0	25068	.211	.304
Two Strikes	.187	71633	13367	2522	287	1308	6349	6778	29937	.201	.285
Leadoff	.274	18995	5198	931	198	295	1724	1982	3010	.347	.390
Batting #2	.277	18611	5153	1000	120	418	2045	1778	3140	.343	.411
Batting #3	.293	17736	5191	1041	92	803	3061	2328	3176	.376	.498
March/April	.265	23731	6285	1229	125	655	3124	2662	4362	.342	.410
May	.266	26415	7027	1361	145	765	3458	2720	5007	.338	.415
June	.272	26102	7107	1439	154	781	3461	2592	4952	.341	.429
July	.266	25819	6864	1314	146	795	3366	2513	5072	.334	.420
August	.267	28010	7491	1401	163	870	3730	2686	5407	.334	.422
Sept/Oct	.264	25361	6697	1260	150	774	3329	2493	5137	.333	.417
vs.AL	.272	78307	21281	4124	404	2468	10576	7859	14440	.341	.429
vs.NL	.262	77131	20190	3880	479	2172	9892	7807	15497	.333	.409

	ERA	W	L	Sv	Opp	G	IP	BB	SO	Avg	AB	H	2B	3B	HR	RBI	OBP	SLG	CG	ShO	Sup	QS	#P/S	SB	CS	GB	FB	G/F
1997	4.38	2266	2266	1139	1706	4532	40454.0	15666	29937	.267	41471	8004	883	4640	20468	.337	.419	266	211	4.81	2240	96	3308	1564	56062	42668	1.31

1997 Pitching

	ERA	W	L	Sv	G	GS	IP	H	HR	BB	SO
Home	4.18	1213	1053	537	7981	2266	20789.1	20825	2341	7579	15677
Away	4.60	1053	1213	602	7879	2266	19664.2	20646	2299	8087	14260
Day	4.51	791	791	389	5666	1582	14106.1	14654	1620	5662	10618
Night	4.31	1475	1475	750	10194	2950	26347.2	26817	3020	10004	19319
Grass	4.43	1618	1618	812	11449	3236	28913.1	29939	3400	11418	20864
Turf	4.26	648	648	327	4411	1296	11540.2	11532	1240	4248	9073
March/April	4.35	347	347	178	2477	694	6194.0	6285	655	2662	4362
May	4.31	387	387	197	2624	774	6890.0	7027	765	2720	5007
June	4.45	381	381	195	2597	762	6767.1	7107	781	2592	4952
July	4.39	377	377	198	2577	754	6728.1	6864	795	2513	5072
August	4.45	406	406	198	2809	812	7258.1	7491	870	2686	5407
Sept/Oct	4.34	368	368	173	2776	736	6616.0	6697	774	2493	5137
Starters	4.46	1583	1587	0	4532	4532	27168.0	28056	3198	9867	19171
Relievers	4.23	683	679	1139	11328	0	13286.0	13417	1442	5799	10766
0-3 Dys Rest(SP)	4.45	60	59	0	200	200	1119.2	1161	129	382	720
4 Days Rest	4.34	948	905	0	2542	2541	15597.0	15905	1824	5510	11132
5+ Days Rest	4.63	573	623	0	1789	1789	10440.2	10979	1244	3969	7312
vs.AL	4.57	1142	1122	570	7813	2264	20207.2	21171	2477	7962	14617
vs.NL	4.19	1124	1144	569	8047	2268	20246.1	20300	2163	7704	15320
Pre-All Star	4.38	1199	1199	616	8258	2398	21333.1	21955	2383	8525	15390
Post-All Star	4.39	1067	1067	523	7602	2134	19120.2	19516	2257	7141	14547

	Avg	AB	H	2B	3B	HR	RBI	BB	SO	OBP	SLG
vs.Left	.274	64873	17795	3416	452	1952	8644	7377	11770	.350	.431
vs.Right	.261	90565	23676	4588	431	2688	11824	8289	18167	.327	.411
Inning 1-6	.269	104487	28078	5579	592	3185	14006	10206	19311	.337	.425
Inning 7+	.263	50951	13393	2425	291	1455	6462	5460	10626	.330	.408
None on	.263	87379	22943	4410	484	2698	2698	7821	16993	.328	.417
Runners on	.272	68059	18528	3594	399	1942	17770	7845	12944	.348	.422
Scoring Posn	.267	39521	10538	2101	261	1058	15266	5686	8037	.355	.413
Close & Late	.261	24695	6453	1145	144	672	3368	2966	5405	.343	.401
None on/out	.268	38702	10359	1964	228	1229	1229	3267	7058	.329	.425
vs. 1st Batr (relief)	.262	9991	2622	466	55	298	1444	1034	2226	.334	.410
1st Inning Pitched	.267	53054	14180	2605	295	1531	8466	6210	11195	.346	.414
First 75 Pits (SP)	.269	16006	4308	852	98	459	2024	1412	2839	.331	.421
Pitch 76-90	.280	13566	3804	767	93	486	1877	1328	2386	.347	.458
Pitch 91-105	.259	9157	2376	463	52	283	1117	911	1636	.330	.414
Pitch 106+	.254	4670	1187	228	40	141	568	500	965	.329	.411
First Pitch	.333	21916	7302	1445	154	812	3556	857	0	.363	.524
Ahead in Count	.204	70538	14416	2656	295	1265	6283	0	25068	.211	.304
Behind in Count	.346	33412	11546	2345	245	1621	6417	8014	0	.470	.576
Two Strikes	.187	71634	13367	2522	287	1308	6349	6778	29937	.261	.285
Pre-All Star	.268	81941	21955	4326	456	2383	10804	8525	15390	.340	.419
Post-All Star	.266	73497	19516	3678	427	2257	9664	7141	14547	.334	.419

Games Finished: 4266   Inherited Runners: 7145   Inherited Runners Scored: 2298   Holds: 1562

American League

1997	Avg	G	AB	R	H	2B	3B	HR	RBI	BB	SO	HBP	GDP	SB	CS	OBP	SLG	IBB	SH	SF	#Pit	#P/PA	GB	FB	G/F
1997	.271	1239	78235	11164	21171	4097	398	2477	10592	7962	14617	676	1787	1491	723	.340	.428	540	547	740	330429	3.75	27621	22251	1.24

1997 Batting

	Avg	AB	H	2B	3B	HR	RBI	BB	SO	OBP	SLG
vs.Left	.271	22040	5976	1124	96	681	2934	2164	4147	.338	.424
vs.Right	.270	56195	15195	2973	302	1796	7658	5798	10470	.341	.416
Groundball	.269	15745	4234	795	85	450	2093	1192	1570	.331	
Flyball	.263	12226	3216	677	70	405	1570				
Home	.275	38191	10493	2026	212	1230	5325	4123	7032	.348	.436
Away	.267	40044	10678	2071	186	1247	5267	3839	7585	.333	.421
Day	.269	26000	7005	1381	127	798	3490	2830	5005	.343	.424
Night	.271	52235	14166	2716	271	1679	7102	5132	9612	.339	.430
Grass	.272	60980	16611	3125	303	1946	8309	6310	11079	.343	.429
Turf	.264	17255	4560	972	95	531	2283	1652	3538	.332	.424
Pre-All Star	.273	40897	11158	2165	193	1305	5678	4387	7477	.345	.431
Post-All Star	.268	37338	10013	1932	205	1172	4914	3575	7140	.335	.420
Scoring Posn	.270	19847	5367	1108	117	581	7893	2860	3966	.357	.426
Close & Late	.265	12090	3207	552	62	345	1676	1470	2621	.346	.407
None on/out	.272	19418	5287	991	106	650	650	1605	3440	.332	.435

	Avg	AB	H	2B	3B	HR	RBI	BB	SO	OBP	SLG
First Pitch	.339	10598	3593	717	70	424	1770	406	0	.367	.540
Ahead in Count	.346	16986	5870	1170	122	872	3340	3993	0	.467	.583
Behind in Count	.211	35462	7468	1391	137	665	3258	0	12108	.217	.314
Two Strikes	.194	36218	7014	1343	127	707	3317	3559	14617	.269	.296
Leadoff	.276	9537	2634	479	100	163	913	1010	1511	.349	.399
Batting #2	.273	9309	2541	523	58	215	1089	945	1552	.343	.411
Batting #3	.294	8942	2633	501	31	413	1562	1158	1723	.375	.496
March/April	.275	12088	3323	648	52	386	1712	1431	2158	.342	.433
May	.269	13121	3534	657	61	406	1810	1410	2382	.342	.422
June	.275	12857	3538	718	65	410	1752	1263	2401	.342	.437
July	.267	13028	3479	664	68	415	1705	1251	2470	.334	.424
August	.270	14238	3845	739	81	477	1948	1334	2672	.335	.434
Sept/Oct	.268	12903	3452	671	71	383	1665	1273	2534	.335	.420
vs.AL	.272	70992	19287	3718	364	2248	9640	7202	13142	.341	.429
vs.NL	.260	7243	1884	379	34	229	952	760	1475	.333	.417

1997	ERA	W	L	Sv	Opp	G	IP	BB	SO	Avg	H	2B	3B	HR	RBI	OBP	SLG	CG	ShO	Sup	QS	#P/S	SB	CS
1997	4.56	1122	1142	568	860	2478	20198.1	7859	14440	.272	21281	4124	404	2468	10576	.341	.429	123	98	4.97	1028	97	1537	741	27778	22242	1.25

1997 Pitching

	ERA	W	L	Sv	G	GS	IP	H	HR	BB	SO
Home	4.42	585	547	258	3911	1132	10374.0	10797	1242	3812	7456
Away	4.71	537	595	310	3914	1132	9824.1	10484	1226	4047	6984
Day	4.55	375	375	186	2679	750	6721.2	7073	792	2786	4920
Night	4.57	747	767	382	5146	1514	13476.2	14208	1676	5073	9520
Grass	4.60	875	887	444	6165	1762	15745.0	16694	1948	6215	11015
Turf	4.44	247	255	124	1660	502	4453.1	4587	520	1644	3425
March/April	4.76	174	174	86	1247	348	3119.1	3323	386	1431	2158
May	4.61	191	191	93	1237	382	3385.2	3534	406	1410	2382
June	4.38	190	182	105	1247	372	3314.1	3504	395	1176	2325
July	4.42	187	193	92	1275	380	3382.1	3493	404	1231	2442
August	4.73	200	210	105	1415	410	3665.1	3922	482	1339	2640
Sept/Oct	4.47	180	192	87	1404	372	3331.1	3505	395	1272	2493
Starters	4.75	770	812	0	2264	2264	13469.0	14426	1724	4935	9103
Relievers	4.19	352	330	568	5561	0	6729.1	6855	744	2924	5337
0-3 Dys Rest (SP)	4.52	37	34	0	120	120	679.2	703	83	223	393
4 Days Rest	4.62	472	477	0	1275	1274	7779.1	8248	1008	2740	5359
5+DaysRest	5.00	260	301	0	869	869	5005.0	5468	632	1970	3348
vs.AL	4.60	1025	1025	514	7086	2050	18303.1	19287	2248	7202	13142
vs.NL	4.23	97	117	54	739	214	1895.0	1994	220	657	1298
Pre-All Star	4.58	594	592	301	4004	1186	10551.1	11138	1279	4280	7373
Post-All Star	4.54	528	550	267	3821	1078	9647.0	10143	1189	3579	7067

	Avg	AB	H	2B	3B	HR	RBI	BB	SO	OBP	SLG
vs.Left	.278	32588	9068	1756	200	1088	4497	3683	5746	.353	.445
vs.Right	.267	45719	12213	2368	204	1380	6079	4176	8694	.331	.418
Inning 1-6	.275	52804	14508	2929	268	1726	7351	5122	9220	.341	.438
Inning 7+	.266	25503	6773	1195	136	742	3225	2737	5220	.339	.410
None on	.267	43677	11681	2287	222	1415	1415	3929	8053	.333	.427
Runners on	.277	34630	9600	1837	182	1053	9161	3930	6387	.350	.432
Scoring Posn	.271	19967	5415	1093	119	587	7897	2812	3936	.356	.427
Close & Late	.266	11989	3191	552	65	339	1654	1459	2611	.347	.408
None on/out	.272	19400	5276	997	107	640	640	1611	3394	.332	.433
vs. 1st Batr (relief)	.267	4923	1315	222	20	148	767	482	1082	.334	.411
1st Inning Pitched	.266	26012	6924	1285	125	765	4166	3060	5434	.345	.413
First 75 Pits (SP)	.274	8026	2202	432	52	235	1049	716	1293	.337	.429
Pitch 76-90	.289	6889	1991	404	46	273	1005	640	1161	.351	.480
Pitch 91-105	.268	4887	1312	249	24	158	621	435	816	.331	.426
Pitch 106+	.256	2469	633	111	19	74	278	280	492	.335	.407
First Pitch	.340	10717	3644	712	77	424	1814	409	0	.367	.540
Ahead in Count	.211	35403	7476	1395	138	664	3246	0	11977	.218	.315
Behind in Count	.346	17049	5904	1186	123	869	3965	0		.467	.583
Two Strikes	.195	36045	7030	1362	122	702	3286	3478	14440	.270	.298
Pre-All Star	.272	40879	11138	2169	195	1279	5578	4280	7373	.343	.429
Post-All Star	.271	37428	10143	1955	209	1189	4998	3579	7067	.337	.430

Games Finished: 2141   Inherited Runners: 3893   Inherited Runners Scored: 1215   Holds: 792

521

National League

	Avg	G	AB	R	H	2B	3B	HR	RBI	BB	SO	HBP	GDP	SB	CS	OBP	SLG	IBB	SH	SF	#Pit	#P/PA	GB	FB	G/F
1997	.263	1241	77203	10440	20300	3907	485	2163	9876	7704	15320	773	1649	1817	841	.333	.410	629	1030	643	320506	3.67	28441	20417	1.39

1997 Batting

	Avg	AB	H	2B	3B	HR	RBI	BB	SO	OBP	SLG
vs.Left	.200	10728	1994	935	94	521	2412	1981	3676	.334	.403
vs.Right	.264	58477	15436	2972	391	1642	7464	5723	11644	.333	.412
Groundball	.268	14294	3831	754	95	343	1830	1356	2741	.335	.406
Flyball	.250	10791	2703	533	71	354	1332	1021	2488	.319	.411
Home	.269	37682	10153	1949	250	1069	5032	3964	7228	.343	.420
Away	.257	39521	10147	1958	235	1094	4844	3740	8092	.325	.401
Day	.270	28327	7649	1510	165	822	3803	2832	5613	.340	.422
Night	.259	48876	12651	2397	320	1341	6073	4872	9707	.330	.403
Grass	.265	50301	13328	2387	286	1454	6486	5108	9785	.335	.411
Turf	.259	26902	6972	1520	199	709	3390	2596	5535	.330	.410
Pre-All Star	.263	41044	10797	2161	263	1078	5126	4138	7913	.334	.407
Post-All Star	.263	36159	9503	1746	222	1085	4750	3566	7407	.333	.413
Scoring Posn	.263	19674	5171	993	144	477	2826	2826	4071	.353	.401
Close & Late	.258	12605	3246	593	82	327	1692	1496	2784	.340	.395
None on/out	.263	19284	5072	973	122	579	579	1662	3618	.326	.416

	Avg	AB	H	2B	3B	HR	RBI	BB	SO	OBP	SLG
First Pitch	.328	11318	3709	728	84	388	1786	451	0	.359	.510
Ahead in Count	.346	16423	5676	1175	123	749	3077	4021	0	.472	.599
Behind in Count	.198	35073	6948	1265	158	600	3025	0	12960	.206	.295
Two Strikes	.179	35415	6353	1179	160	601	3032	3219	15320	.252	.273
Leadoff	.271	9458	2564	452	98	132	811	972	1499	.345	.381
Batting #2	.281	9302	2612	477	62	203	956	833	1588	.343	.411
Batting #3	.291	8794	2558	540	61	390	1499	1170	1453	.377	.499
March/April	.254	11643	2962	581	73	269	1412	1231	2204	.329	.386
May	.263	13294	3483	704	84	359	1648	1310	2625	.333	.409
June	.269	13245	3569	721	89	371	1709	1329	2551	.340	.421
July	.265	12791	3385	650	78	380	1661	1262	2602	.334	.417
August	.265	13772	3646	662	82	393	1782	1352	2735	.333	.410
Sept/Oct	.260	12458	3245	589	79	391	1664	1220	2603	.331	.415
vs.AL	.273	7315	1994	406	40	220	936	657	1298	.337	.429
vs.NL	.262	69888	18306	3501	445	1943	8940	7047	14022	.333	.410

	ERA	W	L	Sv	Opp	G	IP	BB	SO	Avg	H	2B	3B	HR	RBI	OBP	SLG	CG	ShO	Sup	QS	#P/S	SB	CS	GB	FB	G/F
1997	4.20	1144	1124	571	846	2482	20255.2	7807	15497	.262	20190	3880	479	2172	9892	.333	.409	143	113	4.64	1212	95	1771	823	28284	20426	1.38

1997 Pitching

	ERA	W	L	Sv	Opp	G	GS	IP	H	HR	BB	SO
Home	3.93	628	506	279		4070	1134	10415.1	10028	1099	3767	8221
Away	4.48	516	618	292		3965	1134	9840.1	10162	1073	4040	7276
Day	4.47	416	416	203		2987	832	7384.2	7581	828	2876	5698
Night	4.05	728	708	368		5048	1436	12871.0	12609	1344	4931	9799
Grass	4.23	743	731	368		5284	1474	13168.1	13245	1452	5203	9849
Turf	4.15	401	393	203		2751	794	7087.1	6945	720	2604	5648
March/April	3.93	173	173	92		1230	346	3074.2	2962	269	1231	2204
May	4.02	196	196	104		1387	392	3504.1	3493	359	1310	2625
June	4.51	191	199	92		1350	390	3453.0	3603	386	1416	2627
July	4.36	190	184	106		1302	374	3346.0	3371	391	1282	2630
August	4.15	206	196	91		1394	402	3593.0	3569	388	1347	2671
Sept/Oct	4.20	188	176	86		1372	364	3284.2	3192	379	1221	2644
Starters	4.16	813	775	0		2268	2268	13699.0	13630	1474	4932	10068
Relievers	4.28	331	349	571		5767	0	6556.2	6560	698	2875	5429
0-3 Dys Rest(SP)	4.36			0		80	80	440.0	458	46	159	327
4 Days Rest	4.06	476	428	0		1267	1267	7817.2	7657	816	2770	5773
5+Days Rest	4.30	313	322	0		920	920	5435.2	5511	612	1999	3964
vs.AL	4.32	117	97	56		727	214	1904.1	1884	229	760	1475
vs.NL	4.19	1027	1027	515		7308	2054	18351.1	18306	1943	7047	14022
Pre-All Star	4.18	605	607	315		4254	1212	10782.0	10817	1104	4245	8017
Post-All Star	4.23	539	517	256		3781	1056	9473.2	9373	1068	3562	7480

	Avg	AB	H	2B	3B	HR	RBI	BB	SO	OBP	SLG
vs.Left	.270	32285	8727	1660	252	864	4147	3694	6024	.347	.418
vs.Right	.256	44846	11463	2220	227	1308	5745	4113	9473	.323	.403
Inning 1-6	.263	51683	13570	2650	324	1459	6655	5084	10091	.332	.411
Inning 7+	.260	25448	6620	1230	155	713	3237	2723	5406	.335	.405
None on	.258	43702	11262	2123	262	1283	1283	3892	8940	.323	.406
Runners on	.267	33429	8928	1757	217	889	8609	3915	6557	.345	.412
Scoring Posn	.262	19554	5123	1008	142	471	7369	2874	4101	.353	.400
Close & Late	.257	12706	3262	593	79	333	1714	1507	2794	.339	.394
None on/out	.263	19302	5083	967	121	589		1656	3664	.326	.418
vs.1st Batr(relief)	.258	5068	1307	244	35	150	677	552	1144	.335	.409
1st Inning Pitched	.268	27042	7256	1320	170	766	4300	3150	5761	.348	.415
First 75 Pits (SP)	.264	7980	2106	420	46	224	975	696	1546	.326	.412
Pitch 76-90	.272	6677	1813	363	47	213	872	688	1225	.343	.436
Pitch 91-105	.249	4270	1064	214	28	125	496	476	820	.328	.400
Pitch 106+	.252	2201	554	117	21	67	290	220	473	.324	.415
First Pitch	.327	11199	3658	733	77	388	1742	448	0	.358	.510
Ahead in Count	.198	35135	6940	1261	157	601	3037	0	13091	.205	.294
Behind in Count	.345	16363	5642	1159	122	752	3093	4049	0	.473	.568
Two Strikes	.178	35589	6337	1160	165	606	3063	3300	15497	.252	.271
Pre-All Star	.263	41062	10817	2157	261	1104	5226	4245	8017	.336	.409
Post-All Star	.260	36069	9373	1723	218	1068	4666	3562	7480	.330	.409

Games Finished: 2125   Inherited Runners: 3252   Inherited Runners Scored: 1083   Holds: 770

Anaheim Angels

	Avg	G	AB	R	H	2B	3B	HR	RBI	BB	SO	HBP	GDP	SB	CS	OBP	SLG	IBB	SH	SF	#Pit	#P/PA	GB	FB	G/F
1997	.272	162	5628	829	1531	279	25	161	775	617	953	45	128	126	72	.346	.416	37	40	57	23620	3.70	2048	1602	1.28

1997 Batting

	Avg	AB	H	2B	3B	HR	RBI	BB	SO	OBP	SLG
vs. Left	.277	1627	451	73	3	45	221	179	281	.349	.409
vs. Right	.270	4001	1080	206	22	116	554	438	672	.353	.441
Groundball	.283	1009	286	46	7	33	140	104	193	.346	.403
Flyball	.256	880	225	53	4	23	117	107	133	.339	.403
Home	.277	2813	779	145	9	87	418	324	469	.354	.428
Away	.267	2815	752	134	16	74	357	293	484	.337	.405
Day	.259	1604	416	88	6	31	178	168	273	.329	.380
Night	.277	4024	1115	191	19	130	597	449	680	.352	.431
Grass	.273	5044	1378	256	23	144	707	546	861	.346	.419
Turf	.262	584	153	23	2	17	68	71	92	.344	.396
Pre-All Star	.279	3021	844	153	12	79	409	310	468	.349	.416
Post-All Star	.264	2607	687	126	13	82	366	307	485	.342	.416
Scoring Posn	.278	1484	413	81	9	40	603	218	269	.364	.426
Close & Late	.276	934	258	52	6	20	131	120	189	.360	.409
None on/out	.266	1376	366	69	12	44	44	132	228	.336	.430

	Avg	AB	H	2B	3B	HR	RBI	BB	SO	OBP	SLG
First Pitch	.345	830	286	53	6	26	141	28	0	.367	.517
Ahead in Count	.337	1167	393	73	6	52	213	298	0	.467	.543
Behind in Count	.218	2575	561	94	10	50	243	0	808	.226	.320
Two Strikes	.203	2527	512	89	7	54	268	291	953	.226	.307
Leadoff	.243	659	160	31	3	11	73	104	108	.346	.349
Batting #2	.281	655	184	40	7	15	74	87	107	.371	.432
Batting #3	.293	659	193	39	2	23	106	70	141	.363	.463
March/April	.283	867	245	37	2	19	116	77	130	.341	.396
May	.285	980	279	52	3	30	146	102	147	.354	.436
June	.276	970	268	54	7	20	121	111	150	.353	.408
July	.284	970	275	47	6	36	158	114	183	.361	.456
August	.243	964	234	57	5	27	129	106	177	.321	.396
Sept/Oct	.262	877	230	32	2	29	105	107	166	.342	.403
vs. AL	.273	5062	1383	248	22	147	714	550	850	.345	.418
vs. NL	.261	566	148	31	3	14	61	67	103	.346	.401

	ERA	W	L	Sv	Opp	G	IP	BB	SO	H	2B	3B	HR	RBI	OBP	SLG	CG	ShO	Sup	QS	#P/S	SB	CS	GB	FB	G/F
1997	4.52	84	78	39	66	162	1454.2	605	1050	269	1506	287	26	202	758	.343	.437	9	5	5.13	76	99	101	64	1842	1707	1.08

1997 Pitching

	ERA	W	L	Sv	G	GS	IP	H	HR	BB	SO
Home	4.48	46	36	18	300	82	760.0	787	123	294	566
Away	4.56	38	42	21	262	80	694.2	719	79	311	484
Day	3.97	23	23	13	160	46	415.0	416	46	182	314
Night	4.74	61	55	26	402	116	1039.2	1090	156	423	736
Grass	4.54	78	67	36	511	145	1308.1	1364	189	544	935
Turf	4.31	6	11	3	51	17	146.1	142	13	61	115
March/April	5.09	12	12	2	90	24	222.2	248	31	95	166
May	4.52	16	12	9	92	28	245.0	252	29	100	155
June	4.52	13	15	7	97	28	248.2	267	39	108	197
July	4.21	19	9	8	90	28	248.0	241	35	121	194
August	4.28	14	15	9	99	29	258.2	269	36	88	146
Sept/Oct	4.55	10	15	4	94	25	231.2	229	32	93	192
Starters	5.01	53	51	0	162	162	965.1	1055	154	377	618
Relievers	3.55	31	27	39	400	0	489.1	451	48	228	432
0-3 Days Rest (SP)	4.42	9	8	0	27	27	169.0	171	28	46	105
4 Days Rest	5.44	26	26	0	75	75	443.0	497	82	167	237
5+ Days Rest	4.74	18	17	0	60	60	353.1	387	44	164	237
vs. AL	4.45	80	66	36	502	146	1310.0	1340	175	550	949
vs. NL	5.16	4	12	3	60	16	144.2	166	27	55	101
Pre-All Star	4.61	44	42	19	266	86	770.1	820	104	327	558
Post-All Star	4.41	40	36	20	266	76	684.1	686	98	278	492

	Avg	AB	H	2B	3B	HR	RBI	BB	SO	OBP	SLG
vs. Left	.260	2048	533	115	7	71	260	255	372	.343	.427
vs. Right	.274	3556	973	172	19	131	498	350	678	.342	.443
Inning 1-6	.281	3779	1061	203	16	147	552	390	631	.349	.460
Inning 7+	.244	1825	445	84	10	55	206	215	419	.329	.391
None on	.263	3181	837	163	18	125	125	309	594	.334	.444
Runners on	.276	2423	669	124	8	77	633	296	456	.353	.429
Scoring Posn	.264	1397	369	69	5	37	533	222	276	.358	.400
Close & Late	.247	968	239	40	3	31	127	120	232	.335	.390
None on/out	.268	1399	375	76	9	47	47	124	253	.331	.436
vs. 1st Batr (relief)	.232	353	82	15	0	12	55	32	88	.295	.377
1st Inning Pitched	.259	1821	471	96	9	53	281	232	445	.345	.409
First 75 Pits (SP)	.280	567	159	34	2	16	84	60	92	.353	.432
Pitch 76-90	.303	512	155	26	2	32	91	51	80	.367	.549
Pitch 91-105	.242	372	90	11	0	13	34	34	54	.307	.376
Pitch 106+	.198	177	35	6	1	3	10	28	37	.314	.294
Ahead in Count	.313	712	223	48	2	27	115	30	0	.343	.500
Behind in Count	.218	2500	545	99	9	51	225	0	852	.226	.326
Two Strikes	.200	2645	528	97	9	62	241	252	1050	.275	.313
Pre-All Star	.275	2977	820	150	13	104	408	327	558	.350	.439
Post-All Star	.261	2627	686	137	13	98	350	278	492	.334	.435

Games Finished: 153   Inherited Runners: 290   Inherited Runners Scored: 77   Holds: 55

Baltimore Orioles

	Avg	G	AB	R	H	2B	3B	HR	RBI	BB	SO	HBP	GDP	SB	CS	OBP	SLG	IBB	SH	SF	#Pit	#P/PA	GB	FB	G/F
1997	.268	162	5584	812	1498	264	22	196	780	586	952	65	120	63	26	.341	.429	44	46	59	23580	3.72	1963	1762	1.11

1997 Batting

	Avg	AB	H	2B	3B	HR	RBI	BB	SO	OBP	SLG
vs. Left	.258	1800	465	80	6	61	237	175	315	.329	.411
vs. Right	.273	3784	1033	184	16	135	543	411	637	.347	.437
Groundball	.283	1383	392	64	7	36	208	183	221	.370	.418
Flyball	.265	642	170	35	2	30	90	70	92	.341	.466
Home	.265	2691	712	108	5	107	374	271	470	.337	.428
Away	.272	2893	786	156	17	89	406	315	482	.346	.430
Day	.279	1841	513	83	9	86	288	243	321	.366	.474
Night	.263	3743	985	181	13	110	492	343	631	.329	.407
Grass	.267	4960	1324	233	18	181	699	518	836	.341	.431
Turf	.279	624	174	31	4	15	81	68	116	.348	.413
Pre-All Star	.272	2939	800	127	13	103	430	322	504	.333	.428
Post-All Star	.264	2645	698	137	9	93	350	264	448	.333	.428
Scoring Posn	.264	1360	359	72	6	36	552	208	234	.360	.405
Close & Late	.258	855	221	32	1	27	122	112	184	.347	.393
None on/out	.261	1396	364	63	5	54	54	111	240	.321	.429

	Avg	AB	H	2B	3B	HR	RBI	BB	SO	OBP	SLG
First Pitch	.344	786	270	44	2	39	130	35	0	.374	.553
Ahead in Count	.338	1298	439	76	6	71	240	276	0	.455	.570
Behind in Count	.208	2414	501	97	9	50	232	0	784	.216	.317
Two Strikes	.182	2484	452	88	7	48	231	274	952	.267	.281
Leadoff	.297	664	197	42	9	21	83	90	104	.394	.482
Batting #2	.297	663	197	35	4	16	81	66	100	.360	.434
Batting #3	.254	665	169	27	2	31	103	64	139	.320	.441
March/April	.295	808	238	34	3	29	124	84	116	.363	.452
May	.269	944	254	40	4	37	153	114	177	.353	.438
June	.251	938	235	40	2	24	104	92	173	.321	.374
July	.267	950	254	46	6	37	139	86	139	.332	.445
August	.258	943	243	46	4	34	130	98	158	.332	.423
Sept/Oct	.274	1001	274	58	3	35	130	112	189	.349	.443
vs. AL	.269	5057	1362	251	20	176	713	524	849	.341	.431
vs. NL	.258	527	136	13	2	20	67	62	103	.342	.404

Baltimore Orioles

	ERA	W	L	Sv	Opp	G	IP	BB	SO	Avg	H	2B	3B	HR	RBI	OBP	SLG	CG	ShO	Sup	QS	#P/S	SB	CS	GB	FB	G/F
1997	3.91	98	64	59	69	162	1461.0	563	1139	.253	1404	267	29	164	650	.323	.401	8	10	5.00	89	98	149	50	1995	1574	1.27

1997 Pitching

	ERA	W	L	Sv	G	GS	IP	H	HR	BB	SO		Avg	AB	H	2B	3B	HR	RBI	BB	SO	OBP	SLG
Home	3.98	46	35	27	281	81	741.0	717	89	276	575	vs. Left	.249	2252	560	115	14	73	280	264	422	.328	.409
Away	3.84	52	29	32	281	81	720.0	687	75	287	564	vs. Right	.257	3299	844	152	15	91	370	299	717	.320	.395
Day	4.15	33	20	19	185	53	479.0	481	61	183	389	Inning 1-6	.264	3728	984	193	20	116	474	349	700	.320	.420
Night	3.79	65	44	40	377	109	982.0	923	103	380	750	Inning 7+	.232	1812	420	74	9	48	176	214	439	.313	.362
Grass	4.07	85	60	50	503	145	1307.0	1274	147	517	1013	None on	.262	3201	838	161	19	83	83	279	662	.324	.402
Turf	2.57	13	4	9	59	17	154.0	130	17	46	126	Runners on	.242	2339	566	106	10	81	567	284	477	.322	.400
March/April	3.86	16	7	13	76	23	209.2	184	21	90	168	Scoring Posn	.229	1335	306	60	6	46	479	200	285	.324	.387
May	3.20	20	8	13	90	28	250.0	219	28	92	169	Close & Late	.221	895	198	32	6	20	85	119	255	.313	.337
June	3.35	15	12	9	93	27	244.1	224	23	86	199	None on/out	.267	1411	377	69	8	38	103	270	318	.408	
July	3.90	16	11	7	97	27	247.0	265	35	91	202	vs. 1st Batr (relief)	.216	348	75	13	3	8	44	43	100	.339	
August	3.90	18	10	11	97	28	254.0	230	31	95	224	1st Inning Pitched	.238	1834	437	84	9	52	276	255	422	.330	.379
Sept/Oct	5.20	13	16	6	109	29	256.0	282	26	109	177	First 75 Pits (SP)	.286	574	164	29	6	16	63	54	97	.349	.441
Starters	4.19	65	40	0	162	162	983.1	996	115	335	701	Pitch 76-90	.268	507	136	31	2	20	69	39	95	.323	.456
Relievers	3.33	33	24	59	400	0	477.2	408	49	228	438	Pitch 91-105	.254	401	102	18	2	10	38	27	64	.306	.384
0-3 Days Rest (SP)	4.17	4	1	0	6	6	36.2	33	2	11	13	Pitch 106+	.294	136	40	6	1	3	12	17	27	.368	.419
4 Days Rest	3.63	40	21	0	97	97	612.1	612	65	196	440	First Pitch	.343	706	242	38	11	33	119	24	0	.363	.568
5+ Days Rest	5.22	21	18	0	59	59	334.1	351	48	128	248	Ahead in Count	.190	2561	487	94	8	44	183	0	936	.193	.285
vs. AL	3.87	90	57	54	502	147	1320.0	1263	144	507	1033	Behind in Count	.315	1135	357	69	6	50	196	279	0	.450	.518
vs. NL	4.28	8	7	5	60	15	141.0	141	20	56	106	Two Strikes	.183	2684	492	97	7	53	217	260	1139	.257	.284
Pre-All Star	3.63	55	30	37	282	85	764.0	693	85	300	588	Pre-All Star	.242	2864	693	127	13	85	315	300	588	.314	.384
Post-All Star	4.22	43	34	22	280	77	697.0	711	79	263	551	Post-All Star	.266	2676	711	140	16	79	335	263	551	.333	.419

Games Finished: 154   Inherited Runners: 277   Inherited Runners Scored: 72   Holds: 68

Boston Red Sox

1997 Record: 78 – 84

	Avg	G	AB	R	H	2B	3B	HR	RBI	BB	SO	HBP	GDP	SB	CS	OBP	SLG	IBB	SH	SF	#Pit	#P/PA	GB	FB	G/F
1997	.291	162	5781	851	1684	373	32	185	810	514	1044	59	152	68	48	.352	.463	54	21	55	23643	3.68	2165	1492	1.45

1997 Batting

	Avg	AB	H	2B	3B	HR	RBI	BB	SO	OBP	SLG		Avg	AB	H	2B	3B	HR	RBI	BB	SO	OBP	SLG
vs. Left	.266	1720	457	116	7	51	210	177	365	.340	.430	First Pitch	.354	805	285	67	7	25	102	43	0	.397	.548
vs. Right	.302	4061	1227	257	25	134	600	337	679	.358	.477	Ahead in Count	.366	1335	489	125	7	71	278	260	0	.466	.630
Groundball	.294	1041	306	65	6	28	149	103	179	.362	.449	Behind in Count	.225	2523	567	106	11	48	241	0	868	.231	.333
Flyball	.287	936	269	61	4	27	125	66	170	.337	.448	Two Strikes	.203	2585	526	106	6	44	248	211	1044	.266	.300
Home	.301	2840	854	197	15	90	408	274	512	.365	.476	Leadoff	.306	732	224	48	12	31	108	38	97	.342	.531
Away	.282	2941	830	176	17	95	402	240	532	.339	.451	Batting #2	.270	693	187	48	2	19	78	61	114	.332	.427
Day	.276	1769	489	112	4	46	236	160	325	.337	.422	Batting #3	.312	638	199	29	1	34	108	91	178	.406	.520
Night	.298	4012	1195	261	28	139	574	354	719	.359	.481	March/April	.296	898	266	56	2	38	139	104	170	.372	.490
Grass	.293	5056	1483	323	29	157	702	458	902	.355	.462	May	.274	900	247	50	5	29	114	79	169	.336	.438
Turf	.277	725	201	50	3	28	108	56	142	.332	.470	June	.300	1056	317	67	4	36	159	92	167	.357	.473
Pre-All Star	.291	3069	893	187	13	106	443	293	541	.355	.464	July	.312	1021	319	74	9	28	143	107	180	.384	.485
Post-All Star	.292	2712	791	186	19	79	367	221	503	.349	.462	August	.298	1056	315	71	10	30	162	73	190	.344	.470
Scoring Posn	.284	1501	426	104	11	49	609	225	304	.372	.466	Sept/Oct	.259	850	220	55	2	24	93	59	146	.311	.413
Close & Late	.274	942	258	58	7	18	135	110	205	.353	.408	vs. AL	.294	5285	1556	338	31	170	746	456	946	.354	.467
None on/out	.315	1437	452	80	9	55	55	81	237	.358	.498	vs. NL	.258	496	128	35	1	15	64	58	98	.337	.423

	ERA	W	L	Sv	Opp	G	IP	BB	SO	Avg	H	2B	3B	HR	RBI	OBP	SLG	CG	ShO	Sup	QS	#P/S	SB	CS	GB	FB	G/F
1997	4.85	78	84	40	65	162	1451.2	611	987	.277	1569	330	30	149	809	.351	.424	7	4	5.28	69	92	171	53	2036	1578	1.29

1997 Pitching

	ERA	W	L	Sv	G	GS	IP	H	HR	BB	SO		Avg	AB	H	2B	3B	HR	RBI	BB	SO	OBP	SLG
Home	4.46	39	42	12	283	81	749.0	800	62	294	522	vs. Left	.288	2451	707	162	20	64	352	308	425	.369	.449
Away	5.26	39	42	28	296	81	702.2	769	87	317	465	vs. Right	.268	3219	862	168	10	85	457	303	562	.337	.405
Day	5.29	22	28	11	181	50	445.1	511	60	201	291	Inning 1-6	.278	3793	1054	222	20	106	551	394	649	.350	.431
Night	4.65	56	56	29	398	112	1006.1	1058	89	410	696	Inning 7+	.274	1877	515	108	10	43	258	217	338	.354	.411
Grass	4.73	68	74	31	502	142	1278.1	1383	125	517	867	None on	.270	3004	811	176	17	78	78	313	543	.346	.418
Turf	5.71	10	10	9	77	20	173.1	186	24	94	120	Runners on	.284	2666	758	154	13	71	731	298	444	.356	.432
March/April	4.52	13	12	7	96	25	225.0	233	27	118	131	Scoring Posn	.283	1564	442	89	11	38	648	228	274	.370	.426
May	5.61	9	17	3	90	26	227.2	261	19	113	155	Close & Late	.275	865	238	54	6	26	133	123	152	.369	.442
June	5.49	14	15	9	107	29	265.2	318	29	115	181	None on/out	.275	1370	377	84	9	37	37	129	238	.344	.431
July	3.92	15	13	7	83	28	254.2	253	21	81	180	vs. 1st Batr (relief)	.288	372	107	29	3	6	58	32	72	.354	.430
August	5.68	16	13	7	107	29	260.0	294	40	99	185	1st Inning Pitched	.281	2013	565	117	11	44	353	241	375	.360	.415
Sept/Oct	3.70	11	14	7	96	25	218.2	210	13	85	155	First 75 Pits (SP)	.281	545	153	32	3	16	78	55	92	.351	.439
Starters	4.95	50	53	0	162	162	909.1	980	102	365	619	Pitch 76-90	.280	428	120	21	4	9	54	42	70	.351	.411
Relievers	4.68	28	31	40	417	0	542.1	589	47	246	368	Pitch 91-105	.241	257	62	13	1	9	35	26	58	.321	.405
0-3 Days Rest (SP)	4.01	2	2	0	10	10	60.2	59	5	16	42	Pitch 106+	.245	151	37	10	0	3	7	27	28	.365	.371
4 Days Rest	5.02	24	28	0	85	85	487.1	544	57	190	314	First Pitch	.338	794	268	54	3	34	153	37	0	.369	.547
5+ Days Rest	5.01	20	23	0	67	67	361.1	377	40	159	263	Ahead in Count	.218	2624	571	117	7	45	258	0	832	.227	.319
vs. AL	4.88	72	75	36	525	147	1318.0	1428	129	560	899	Behind in Count	.352	1186	417	95	13	36	238	302	0	.480	.545
vs. NL	4.58	6	9	4	54	15	133.2	141	20	51	88	Two Strikes	.203	2612	529	117	8	42	249	270	987	.285	.302
Pre-All Star	5.11	38	48	20	307	86	769.2	865	77	358	500	Pre-All Star	.284	3041	865	189	13	77	461	358	500	.363	.431
Post-All Star	4.55	40	36	20	272	76	682.0	704	72	253	487	Post-All Star	.268	2629	704	141	17	72	348	253	487	.337	.417

Games Finished: 155   Inherited Runners: 281   Inherited Runners Scored: 103   Holds: 51

Chicago White Sox

1997 Record: 80 – 81

1997	Avg	G	AB	R	H	2B	3B	HR	RBI	BB	SO	HBP	GDP	SB	CS	OBP	SLG	IBB	SH	SF	#Pit	#P/PA	GB	FB	G/F
	.273	161	5491	779	1498	260	28	158	740	569	901	33	133	106	52	.341	.417	40	47	60	22665	3.66	2040	1580	1.29

1997 Batting

	Avg	AB	H	2B	3B	HR	RBI	BB	SO	OBP	SLG		Avg	AB	H	2B	3B	HR	RBI	BB	SO	OBP	SLG
vs. Left	.268	1400	375	56	4	43	176	128	227	.329	.406	First Pitch	.315	825	260	37	7	27	137	26	0	.336	.475
vs. Right	.275	4091	1123	204	24	115	564	441	674	.345	.420	Ahead in Count	.335	1312	439	74	10	61	247	313	0	.460	.546
Groundball	.264	1138	300	52	8	30	150	119	191	.333	.402	Behind in Count	.216	2332	503	89	4	35	188	0	742	.220	.302
Flyball	.263	995	262	57	7	38	132	85	190	.324	.449	Two Strikes	.202	2403	486	86	7	40	212	230	901	.274	.294
Home	.272	2655	723	132	17	73	376	290	413	.343	.417	Leadoff	.275	673	185	32	2	11	42	71	113	.346	.377
Away	.273	2836	775	128	11	85	364	279	488	.339	.416	Batting #2	.286	658	188	24	4	15	65	66	109	.350	.403
Day	.281	1736	488	87	13	47	243	204	281	.357	.427	Batting #3	.329	602	198	35	0	36	129	115	88	.435	.566
Night	.269	3755	1010	173	15	111	497	365	620	.334	.412	March/April	.254	855	217	33	5	20	99	121	152	.346	.374
Grass	.276	4689	1296	216	24	136	648	504	735	.346	.420	May	.301	895	269	45	4	28	148	107	139	.374	.454
Turf	.252	802	202	44	4	22	92	65	166	.312	.399	June	.277	964	267	46	4	36	137	81	167	.334	.445
Pre-All Star	.276	2911	802	137	13	86	407	317	499	.347	.420	July	.272	917	249	45	2	25	120	72	144	.323	.407
Post-All Star	.270	2580	696	123	15	72	333	252	402	.335	.413	August	.262	1010	265	51	6	26	127	106	163	.334	.402
Scoring Posn	.281	1383	388	75	8	36	570	212	236	.367	.424	Sept/Oct	.272	850	231	40	7	23	109	82	136	.338	.416
Close & Late	.274	803	220	29	4	18	119	117	156	.364	.387	vs. AL	.275	5006	1377	238	27	143	686	534	803	.345	.419
None on/out	.252	1372	346	57	10	40	40	104	220	.307	.396	vs. NL	.249	485	121	22	1	15	54	35	98	.304	.392

	ERA	W	L	Sv	Opp	G	IP	BB	SO	Avg	2B	3B	HR	RBI	OBP	SLG	CG	ShO	Sup	QS	#P/S	SB	CS	GB	FB	G/F
1997	4.73	80	81	52	70	161	1422.1	575	961	271	1505	305	28	175	790	.340	.430	6	7	4.93	76	99	119	52	1835	1784	1.03

1997 Pitching

	ERA	W	L	Sv	G	GS	IP	H	HR	BB	SO		Avg	AB	H	2B	3B	HR	RBI	BB	SO	OBP	SLG
Home	4.32	45	36	27	275	81	734.0	745	78	270	518	vs. Left	.278	2293	638	129	12	82	344	274	377	.354	.452
Away	5.18	35	45	25	275	80	688.1	760	97	305	443	vs. Right	.265	3267	867	176	16	93	446	301	584	.329	.414
Day	4.66	27	23	20	196	50	453.2	503	40	196	322	Inning 1-6	.264	3743	990	209	16	113	522	370	637	.331	.419
Night	4.77	53	58	32	354	111	968.2	1002	135	379	639	Inning 7+	.283	1817	515	96	12	62	268	205	324	.357	.452
Grass	4.75	70	68	44	479	138	1224.2	1293	147	497	831	None on	.272	3025	822	174	17	95	95	276	504	.337	.435
Turf	4.60	10	13	8	71	23	197.2	212	28	78	130	Runners on	.269	2535	683	131	11	80	695	299	457	.342	.424
March/April	4.49	8	17	3	81	25	222.1	224	24	103	163	Scoring Posn	.276	1464	404	80	4	44	593	202	289	.355	.426
May	4.64	15	11	8	92	26	231.0	234	23	107	162	Close & Late	.282	829	234	36	5	25	124	102	163	.360	.428
June	4.24	17	11	10	96	28	250.1	272	23	91	149	None on/out	.280	1356	380	62	6	48	48	117	211	.344	.441
July	4.61	13	14	9	89	27	236.0	248	30	75	148	vs. 1st Batr (relief)	.296	341	101	23	0	9	53	38	62	.365	.443
August	4.93	15	15	13	99	30	262.2	270	39	120	192	1st Inning Pitched	.278	1825	507	95	8	55	298	212	358	.352	.429
Sept/Oct	5.52	12	13	9	93	25	220.0	257	36	79	147	First 75 Pits (SP)	.232	586	136	28	4	10	69	48	86	.288	.345
Starters	4.97	57	64	0	161	161	965.1	1028	121	370	628	Pitch 76-90	.322	500	161	32	3	27	90	49	74	.386	.560
Relievers	4.23	23	17	52	389	0	457.0	477	54	205	333	Pitch 91-105	.253	360	91	20	1	13	53	31	58	.309	.422
0-3 Days Rest (SP)	4.63	1	1	0	4	4	23.1	31	3	6	12	Pitch 106+	.292	226	66	13	2	9	36	26	39	.362	.487
4 Days Rest	4.45	27	32	0	76	76	465.2	475	56	184	300	First Pitch	.317	735	233	56	4	29	137	35	0	.347	.522
5+ Days Rest	5.50	29	31	0	81	81	476.1	522	62	180	316	Ahead in Count	.222	2568	571	113	15	44	249	0	801	.227	.329
vs. AL	4.84	72	74	46	503	146	1293.1	1374	163	537	884	Behind in Count	.341	1183	403	84	5	69	242	268	0	.460	.595
vs. NL	3.63	8	7	6	47	15	129.0	131	12	38	77	Two Strikes	.197	2572	507	91	12	40	243	272	961	.276	.288
Pre-All Star	4.42	43	42	22	287	85	755.2	786	73	308	505	Pre-All Star	.266	2950	786	164	17	73	403	308	505	.335	.408
Post-All Star	5.09	37	39	30	263	76	666.2	719	102	267	456	Post-All Star	.275	2610	719	141	11	102	387	267	456	.345	.455

Games Finished: 155   Inherited Runners: 277   Inherited Runners Scored: 86   Holds: 62

Cleveland Indians

1997 Record: 86 – 75

1997	Avg	G	AB	R	H	2B	3B	HR	RBI	BB	SO	HBP	GDP	SB	CS	OBP	SLG	IBB	SH	SF	#Pit	#P/PA	GB	FB	G/F
	.286	161	5556	868	1589	301	22	220	810	617	955	37	152	118	59	.358	.467	39	45	49	23972	3.80	1953	1554	1.26

1997 Batting

	Avg	AB	H	2B	3B	HR	RBI	BB	SO	OBP	SLG		Avg	AB	H	2B	3B	HR	RBI	BB	SO	OBP	SLG
vs. Left	.296	1477	437	86	5	59	218	149	239	.360	.481	First Pitch	.355	696	247	51	6	38	130	25	0	.379	.609
vs. Right	.282	4079	1152	215	17	161	592	468	716	.358	.462	Ahead in Count	.362	1292	468	85	6	74	259	300	0	.480	.609
Groundball	.265	1042	276	58	4	37	133	107	174	.336	.435	Behind in Count	.220	2463	542	104	8	61	248	0	778	.225	.343
Flyball	.302	776	234	47	4	28	117	87	145	.374	.481	Two Strikes	.198	2511	497	90	8	64	242	292	955	.285	.317
Home	.287	2702	776	148	11	96	395	324	475	.363	.457	Leadoff	.263	678	178	32	8	18	82	67	98	.329	.413
Away	.285	2854	813	153	11	124	415	293	480	.354	.477	Batting #2	.268	683	183	33	2	9	66	52	97	.319	.403
Day	.298	1852	552	97	4	68	301	225	340	.375	.465	Batting #3	.292	590	172	32	0	38	112	132	154	.420	.539
Night	.280	3704	1037	204	18	152	509	392	615	.350	.468	March/April	.305	898	274	57	5	49	159	138	140	.399	.543
Grass	.287	4747	1362	258	19	189	699	537	813	.360	.469	May	.265	861	228	38	0	31	113	103	154	.343	.447
Turf	.281	809	227	43	3	31	111	80	142	.349	.456	June	.281	833	234	50	2	28	122	81	155	.345	.447
Pre-All Star	.289	2769	799	153	8	115	425	335	470	.365	.474	July	.275	894	246	47	7	26	109	101	154	.350	.431
Post-All Star	.283	2787	790	148	14	105	385	282	485	.351	.460	August	.297	1048	311	53	5	50	163	112	186	.366	.500
Scoring Posn	.278	1460	406	85	3	48	590	221	267	.367	.439	Sept/Oct	.290	1022	296	56	3	36	144	82	166	.344	.456
Close & Late	.309	718	222	40	3	33	130	87	135	.380	.511	vs. AL	.286	5038	1442	272	20	204	736	567	853	.359	.470
None on/out	.309	1375	425	65	8	71	71	132	211	.373	.523	vs. NL	.284	518	147	29	2	16	74	50	102	.350	.440

Cleveland Indians

1997	ERA	W	L	Sv	Opp	G	IP	BB	SO	Avg	H	2B	3B	HR	RBI	OBP	SLG	CG	ShO	Sup	QS	#P/S	SB	CS	GB	FB	G/F
1997	4.73	86	75	39	54	161	1425.2	575	1036	.276	1528	276	28	181	768	.347	.434	4	3	5.48	70	96	126	55	2060	1427	1.44

1997 Pitching

	ERA	W	L	Sv	G	GS	IP	H	HR	BB	SO		Avg	AB	H	2B	3B	HR	RBI	BB	SO	OBP	SLG
Home	4.59	44	37	18	294	81	736.0	778	89	275	535	vs. Left	.293	2491	730	131	15	84	369	286	432	.367	.459
Away	4.88	42	38	21	296	80	689.2	750	92	300	497	vs. Right	.262	3044	798	145	13	97	399	289	604	.330	.414
Day	5.12	29	24	10	194	53	464.0	499	59	207	349	Inning 1-6	.281	3735	1049	195	16	118	541	382	620	.350	.436
Night	4.54	57	51	29	396	108	961.2	1029	122	368	687	Inning 7+	.266	1800	479	81	12	63	227	193	416	.341	.429
Grass	4.70	73	65	32	509	138	1228.2	1307	156	507	889	None on	.279	3067	856	161	16	111	111	276	552	.344	.451
Turf	4.93	13	10	7	81	23	197.0	221	25	68	147	Runners on	.272	2468	672	115	12	70	657	299	484	.350	.414
March/April	6.28	12	13	7	98	25	222.0	287	40	108	164	Scoring Posn	.269	1455	391	76	9	37	572	222	308	.360	.410
May	3.52	15	11	6	85	26	227.2	216	31	100	173	Close & Late	.256	714	183	27	3	29	94	87	177	.339	.424
June	4.88	13	11	3	94	24	216.0	248	28	80	140	None on/out	.274	1369	375	72	7	48	48	112	238	.334	.442
July	4.59	14	13	6	95	27	241.0	246	21	87	175	vs. 1st Batr (relief)	.275	382	105	10	1	16	56	38	81	.343	.432
August	4.66	16	14	8	106	30	264.1	269	39	90	202	1st Inning Pitched	.264	1923	508	82	9	64	288	221	440	.342	.416
Sept/Oct	4.52	16	13	9	112	29	254.2	262	22	110	182	First 75 Pits (SP)	.284	588	167	23	4	27	96	53	86	.346	.474
Starters	4.90	60	53	0	161	161	955.0	1034	121	364	607	Pitch 76-90	.295	491	145	24	4	20	74	39	73	.352	.483
Relievers	4.38	26	22	39	429	0	470.2	494	60	211	429	Pitch 91-105	.272	313	85	18	1	10	49	33	59	.346	.431
0-3 Days Rest (SP)	3.49	3	1	0	7	7	38.2	35	2	7	21	Pitch 106+	.278	158	44	7	1	3	16	14	31	.345	.405
4 Days Rest	4.62	40	34	0	87	87	543.1	562	69	192	355	First Pitch	.348	775	270	48	6	21	131	38	0	.382	.507
5+ Days Rest	5.45	17	18	0	67	67	373.0	437	50	165	231	Ahead in Count	.205	2471	506	88	8	39	211	0	862	.212	.294
vs. AL	4.79	77	69	35	532	146	1293.2	1387	171	530	948	Behind in Count	.362	1198	434	79	10	77	246	281	0	.481	.638
vs. NL	4.09	9	6	4	58	15	132.0	141	10	45	88	Two Strikes	.192	2538	487	91	6	44	220	256	1036	.270	.284
Pre-All Star	4.91	44	36	18	295	80	709.2	798	102	302	501	Pre-All Star	.287	2785	798	139	10	102	408	302	501	.359	.454
Post-All Star	4.55	42	39	21	295	81	716.0	730	79	273	535	Post-All Star	.265	2750	730	137	18	79	360	273	535	.334	.415

Games Finished: 157   Inherited Runners: 294   Inherited Runners Scored: 81   Holds: 71

Detroit Tigers

1997 Record: 79 – 83

1997	Avg	G	AB	R	H	2B	3B	HR	RBI	BB	SO	HBP	GDP	SB	CS	OBP	SLG	IBB	SH	SF	#Pit	#P/PA	GB	FB	G/F
1997	.258	162	5481	784	1415	268	32	176	743	578	1164	49	121	161	72	.332	.415	37	34	47	23663	3.82	1950	1428	1.37

1997 Batting

	Avg	AB	H	2B	3B	HR	RBI	BB	SO	OBP	SLG		Avg	AB	H	2B	3B	HR	RBI	BB	SO	OBP	SLG
vs. Left	.263	1469	387	75	12	49	214	153	313	.336	.431	First Pitch	.365	654	239	46	6	38	131	25	0	.388	.628
vs. Right	.256	4012	1028	193	20	127	529	425	851	.330	.409	Ahead in Count	.335	1127	378	87	11	60	228	291	0	.469	.592
Groundball	.255	1093	279	55	3	25	132	133	226	.338	.380	Behind in Count	.195	2596	505	87	8	34	230	0	958	.202	.273
Flyball	.252	970	244	46	7	33	124	102	231	.321	.415	Two Strikes	.185	2702	500	81	10	49	250	262	1164	.261	.277
Home	.255	2644	674	119	19	98	385	338	580	.342	.425	Leadoff	.266	677	180	28	8	4	4	67	127	.331	.349
Away	.261	2837	741	149	13	78	358	240	584	.322	.405	Batting #2	.276	624	172	37	8	25	90	85	106	.371	.481
Day	.259	2113	548	103	11	71	303	245	436	.340	.419	Batting #3	.270	644	174	34	3	27	119	60	130	.332	.458
Night	.257	3368	867	165	21	105	440	333	728	.327	.412	March/April	.260	919	239	42	4	31	131	98	190	.334	.416
Grass	.262	4814	1261	233	26	164	687	539	1012	.339	.423	May	.252	820	207	36	6	25	118	102	158	.340	.402
Turf	.231	667	154	35	6	12	56	39	152	.273	.355	June	.265	877	232	53	8	32	131	98	186	.340	.453
Pre-All Star	.262	2842	746	142	19	105	427	331	585	.342	.437	July	.256	893	229	43	4	36	120	109	211	.341	.434
Post-All Star	.254	2639	669	126	13	71	316	247	579	.320	.392	August	.262	1027	269	49	6	28	124	83	196	.319	.403
Scoring Posn	.273	1351	369	69	8	52	562	200	392	.362	.452	Sept/Oct	.253	945	239	45	4	24	119	88	223	.319	.385
Close & Late	.252	829	209	31	5	21	102	94	205	.331	.378	vs. AL	.259	4989	1290	244	27	158	672	529	1044	.333	.413
None on/out	.248	1385	343	57	10	37	37	115	291	.309	.383	vs. NL	.254	492	125	24	5	18	71	49	120	.320	.433

1997	ERA	W	L	Sv	Opp	G	IP	BB	SO	Avg	H	2B	3B	HR	RBI	OBP	SLG	CG	ShO	Sup	QS	#P/S	SB	CS	GB	FB	G/F
1997	4.56	79	83	42	64	162	1445.2	552	982	.266	1476	276	34	178	753	.334	.424	13	8	4.88	75	96	130	48	2020	1540	1.31

1997 Pitching

	ERA	W	L	Sv	G	GS	IP	H	HR	BB	SO		Avg	AB	H	2B	3B	HR	RBI	BB	SO	OBP	SLG
Home	4.14	42	39	19	283	81	740.0	716	91	270	505	vs. Left	.273	2465	674	136	17	82	342	260	428	.345	.442
Away	5.00	37	44	23	296	81	705.2	760	87	282	477	vs. Right	.260	3087	802	140	17	96	411	292	554	.325	.409
Day	4.69	32	31	17	224	63	564.1	567	75	233	367	Inning 1-6	.273	3747	1022	205	24	120	505	362	606	.339	.436
Night	4.47	47	52	25	355	99	881.1	909	103	319	615	Inning 7+	.252	1805	454	71	10	58	248	190	376	.322	.398
Grass	4.52	73	69	38	506	142	1274.2	1297	158	488	838	None on	.254	3179	808	149	16	107	107	289	590	.320	.412
Turf	4.84	6	14	4	73	20	171.0	179	20	64	144	Runners on	.282	2373	668	127	18	71	646	263	392	.351	.440
March/April	5.29	11	16	5	117	27	239.2	263	22	139	130	Scoring Posn	.283	1338	379	87	11	32	544	204	231	.370	.436
May	3.17	14	11	6	76	25	221.1	176	22	81	165	Close & Late	.255	839	214	30	5	29	132	97	189	.328	.406
June	4.58	11	15	6	88	26	230.0	234	34	78	154	None on/out	.266	1402	373	65	10	57	57	109	243	.323	.449
July	5.52	13	14	10	101	27	239.2	282	31	86	154	vs. 1st Batr (relief)	.271	365	99	12	4	15	66	41	87	.344	.449
August	4.43	14	16	7	100	30	266.0	288	38	84	192	1st Inning Pitched	.257	1863	478	90	14	55	316	224	377	.337	.408
Sept/Oct	4.27	16	11	8	105	27	249.0	233	31	84	187	First 75 Pits (SP)	.263	555	146	30	5	13	69	47	98	.323	.405
Starters	4.46	58	63	0	162	162	958.0	988	112	336	602	Pitch 76-90	.292	473	138	24	3	25	71	53	83	.364	.514
Relievers	4.74	21	20	42	417	0	487.2	488	66	216	380	Pitch 91-105	.241	348	84	15	1	11	44	24	46	.290	.385
0-3 Days Rest (SP)	4.03	1	1	0	4	4	22.1	24	3	5	16	Pitch 106+	.201	159	32	5	0	3	12	9	30	.285	.289
4 Days Rest	4.46	36	32	0	86	86	532.2	548	65	172	326	First Pitch	.335	743	249	41	7	33	119	25	0	.363	.542
5+ Days Rest	4.49	21	30	0	72	72	403.0	416	44	159	260	Ahead in Count	.197	2487	490	87	13	49	217	0	808	.201	.302
vs. AL	4.68	71	76	38	529	147	1314.2	1348	169	517	894	Behind in Count	.346	1244	431	100	10	59	269	297	0	.468	.585
vs. NL	3.30	8	7	4	50	15	131.0	128	9	35	88	Two Strikes	.187	2556	478	83	12	54	227	230	982	.256	.292
Pre-All Star	4.51	41	44	21	302	86	754.0	750	86	323	483	Pre-All Star	.262	2866	750	150	15	86	389	323	483	.339	.415
Post-All Star	4.61	38	39	21	277	77	691.2	726	92	229	499	Post-All Star	.270	2686	726	126	19	92	364	229	499	.328	.434

Games Finished: 149   Inherited Runners: 306   Inherited Runners Scored: 110   Holds: 65

Kansas City Royals

1997	Avg	G	AB	R	H	2B	3B	HR	RBI	BB	SO	HBP	GDP	SB	CS	OBP	SLG	IBB	SH	SF	#Pit	#P/PA	GB	FB	G/F
1997	264	161	5599	747	1478	256	35	158	711	561	1061	42	106	130	66	333	407	34	51	42	23643	3.76	1951	1563	1.25

1997 Batting

	Avg	AB	H	2B	3B	HR	RBI	BB	SO	OBP	SLG		Avg	AB	H	2B	3B	HR	RBI	BB	SO	OBP	SLG
vs. Left	.272	1707	465	82	7	51	211	140	324	.328	.418	First Pitch	.342	745	255	48	5	26	119	24	0	.368	.525
vs. Right	.260	3892	1013	174	28	107	500	421	737	.336	.402	Ahead in Count	.331	1107	366	69	8	62	239	283	0	.464	.575
Groundball	.288	938	270	33	6	28	129	90	165	.354	.425	Behind in Count	.208	2612	542	91	17	37	219	0	882	.213	.298
Flyball	.241	916	221	41	4	25	99	91	192	.313	.377	Two Strikes	.189	2627	497	85	11	34	210	254	1061	.263	.269
Home	.272	2764	751	121	20	88	369	294	471	.345	.425	Leadoff	.297	703	209	39	9	3	61	57	110	.351	.391
Away	.256	2835	727	135	15	70	342	267	590	.322	.389	Batting #2	.256	661	169	29	4	8	60	68	125	.327	.348
Day	.263	1806	475	89	12	54	231	186	376	.333	.415	Batting #3	.292	640	187	29	3	24	96	76	105	.367	.459
Night	.264	3793	1003	167	23	104	480	375	685	.333	.403	March/April	.270	781	211	40	5	22	106	85	147	.342	.419
Grass	.265	4807	1272	210	30	137	604	478	904	.333	.406	May	.256	956	245	41	5	20	108	108	162	.337	.372
Turf	.260	792	206	46	5	21	107	83	157	.334	.410	June	.277	904	250	41	7	29	129	79	168	.336	.434
Pre-All Star	.266	2808	747	129	17	73	362	283	506	.335	.402	July	.254	944	240	43	5	19	108	88	157	.322	.371
Post-All Star	.262	2791	731	127	18	85	349	278	555	.331	.412	August	.266	1018	271	44	8	43	144	81	214	.323	.423
Scoring Posn	.266	1372	365	71	15	38	534	191	256	.352	.423	Sept/Oct	.262	996	261	47	5	25	116	120	213	.342	.395
Close & Late	.261	1011	264	39	7	24	117	104	215	.334	.385	vs. AL	.263	5091	1340	223	34	140	637	497	954	.331	.403
None on/out	.254	1382	351	67	6	29	29	119	240	.316	.374	vs. NL	.272	508	138	33	1	18	74	64	107	.358	.447

1997	ERA	W	L	Sv	Opp	G	IP	BB	SO	Avg	H	2B	3B	HR	RBI	OBP	SLG	CG	ShO	Sup	QS	#P/S	SB	CS	FB	G/F
1997	4.70	67	94	29	50	161	1443.0	531	961	274	1530	260	28	186	773	340	430	11	5	4.66	73	99	72	42	1974	1586 1.24

1997 Pitching

	ERA	W	L	Sv	G	GS	IP	H	HR	BB	SO		Avg	AB	H	2B	3B	HR	RBI	BB	SO	OBP	SLG
Home	4.80	33	47	8	265	80	743.0	794	94	245	457	vs. Left	.281	2203	620	100	15	89	321	235	388	.353	.462
Away	4.59	34	47	21	289	81	700.0	736	92	286	504	vs. Right	.269	3380	910	160	12	97	452	296	573	.331	.410
Day	4.59	21	31	8	187	52	464.1	500	60	182	338	Inning 1-6	.276	3757	1036	199	17	121	527	347	645	.340	.434
Night	4.75	46	63	21	367	109	978.2	1030	126	349	623	Inning 7+	.271	1826	494	61	10	65	246	184	316	.340	.422
Grass	4.83	55	83	22	470	138	1247.0	1344	166	455	818	None on	.264	3181	840	139	14	116	116	253	535	.324	.426
Turf	3.86	12	11	7	84	23	196.0	186	20	76	143	Runners on	.287	2402	690	121	13	70	657	278	426	.359	.436
March/April	4.18	11	12	4	75	23	206.2	211	23	74	139	Scoring Posn	.287	1354	388	71	12	35	569	186	257	.365	.434
May	4.77	12	16	4	86	28	253.0	256	36	123	186	Close & Late	.270	895	242	27	4	35	134	112	186	.353	.427
June	4.25	13	13	6	80	26	230.2	249	26	59	135	None on/out	.267	1384	370	61	5	51	51	112	220	.328	.429
July	5.35	8	19	2	92	27	237.0	251	37	86	155	vs. 1st Batr (relief)	.278	353	98	12	1	14	71	22	73	.331	.436
August	5.07	11	18	6	107	29	259.0	284	36	77	164	1st Inning Pitched	.267	1833	490	84	6	56	314	196	351	.341	.411
Sept/Oct	4.45	12	16	7	114	28	256.2	279	28	112	182	First 75 Pits (SP)	.264	568	150	25	1	12	61	46	85	.326	.375
Starters	4.81	47	61	0	161	161	1002.0	1082	131	344	645	Pitch 76-90	.311	553	172	32	6	23	87	50	101	.369	.515
Relievers	4.43	20	33	29	393	0	441.0	448	55	187	316	Pitch 91-105	.272	383	104	22	0	7	37	30	57	.323	.384
0-3 Days Rest (SP)	3.20	2	1	0	4	4	25.1	29	2	3	17	Pitch 106+	.275	182	50	6	0	10	35	18	31	.338	.473
4 Days Rest	4.78	26	38	0	94	94	591.2	642	79	199	400	First Pitch	.330	807	266	32	2	38	139	30	0	.357	.515
5+ Days Rest	4.98	19	22	0	63	63	385.0	411	50	142	228	Ahead in Count	.213	2572	549	97	14	43	229	0	812	.222	.312
vs. AL	4.74	61	85	27	502	146	1314.0	1390	172	492	883	Behind in Count	.340	1232	419	80	9	71	248	266	0	.456	.593
vs. NL	4.26	6	9	2	52	15	129.0	140	14	39	78	Two Strikes	.202	2506	505	90	7	48	235	234	961	.275	.300
Pre-All Star	4.55	36	46	14	256	82	730.1	774	93	269	481	Pre-All Star	.274	2825	774	136	14	93	381	269	481	.338	.431
Post-All Star	4.85	31	48	15	298	79	712.2	756	93	262	480	Post-All Star	.274	2758	756	124	13	93	392	262	480	.342	.430

Games Finished: 150   Inherited Runners: 270   Inherited Runners Scored: 101   Holds: 39

Milwaukee Brewers

1997	Avg	G	AB	R	H	2B	3B	HR	RBI	BB	SO	HBP	GDP	SB	CS	OBP	SLG	IBB	SH	SF	#Pit	#P/PA	GB	FB	G/F
1997	260	161	5444	681	1415	294	27	135	643	494	967	58	123	103	55	325	398	31	48	52	22810	3.74	1890	1619	1.17

1997 Batting

	Avg	AB	H	2B	3B	HR	RBI	BB	SO	OBP	SLG		Avg	AB	H	2B	3B	HR	RBI	BB	SO	OBP	SLG
vs. Left	.260	1689	439	84	10	39	184	130	315	.319	.391	First Pitch	.318	664	211	46	4	19	108	25	0	.352	.485
vs. Right	.260	3755	976	210	17	96	459	364	652	.328	.402	Ahead in Count	.330	1139	376	84	8	49	188	274	0	.457	.547
Groundball	.269	927	249	50	4	33	118	67	170	.322	.438	Behind in Count	.211	2601	549	102	13	41	218	0	829	.218	.308
Flyball	.232	1003	233	49	2	20	97	109	201	.312	.345	Two Strikes	.198	2555	507	105	10	48	220	195	967	.261	.304
Home	.269	2643	711	146	18	56	331	274	459	.341	.401	Leadoff	.269	695	187	30	4	11	61	38	82	.315	.371
Away	.251	2801	704	148	9	79	312	220	508	.310	.395	Batting #2	.274	632	173	45	5	20	83	79	104	.363	.456
Day	.263	2029	534	111	7	37	219	204	377	.334	.379	Batting #3	.285	635	181	43	1	14	80	66	87	.355	.422
Night	.258	3415	881	183	20	98	424	290	590	.320	.409	March/April	.270	774	209	45	5	18	100	88	143	.348	.411
Grass	.268	4680	1254	248	26	116	570	439	817	.334	.406	May	.266	900	239	55	4	23	126	94	144	.339	.412
Turf	.211	764	161	46	1	19	73	55	150	.271	.348	June	.268	907	243	44	7	22	107	67	183	.321	.405
Pre-All Star	.265	2767	732	155	17	66	352	269	500	.333	.404	July	.245	938	230	49	4	32	97	60	169	.295	.408
Post-All Star	.255	2677	683	139	10	69	291	225	467	.318	.392	August	.265	1049	278	56	5	26	129	88	163	.326	.402
Scoring Posn	.267	1343	358	83	10	28	488	157	248	.337	.406	Sept/Oct	.247	876	216	45	2	14	84	97	165	.325	.350
Close & Late	.244	949	232	41	6	21	101	103	173	.320	.367	vs. AL	.262	4971	1303	267	26	126	598	454	875	.327	.402
None on/out	.256	1362	348	76	5	37	37	107	239	.316	.400	vs. NL	.237	473	112	27	1	9	45	40	92	.305	.355

Milwaukee Brewers

1997	ERA	W	L	Sv	Opp	G	IP	BB	SO	Avg	H	2B	3B	HR	RBI	OBP	SLG	CG	ShO	Sup	QS	#P/S	SB	CS	GB	FB	G/F
	4.22	78	83	44	59	161	1427.1	542	1016	.261	1419	274	24	177	697	.333	.418	6	8	4.29	70	96	106	52	1927	1553	1.24

1997 Pitching

	ERA	W	L	Sv	G	GS	IP	H	HR	BB	SO		Avg	AB	H	2B	3B	HR	RBI	BB	SO	OBP	SLG
Home	3.93	47	33	23	267	80	733.0	727	92	266	535	vs. Left	.267	2355	628	125	14	76	299	269	421	.346	.428
Away	4.52	31	50	21	261	81	694.1	692	85	276	481	vs. Right	.257	3002	701	150	10	101	398	273	595	.322	.410
Day	4.22	27	33	17	200	60	528.2	518	64	202	387	Inning 1-6	.263	3716	976	202	18	133	521	377	649	.336	.434
Night	4.22	51	50	27	328	101	898.2	901	113	340	629	Inning 7+	.257	1721	443	73	6	44	176	165	367	.326	.383
Grass	4.11	70	68	38	458	138	1234.0	1227	156	468	873	None on	.258	3124	807	156	16	103	103	273	571	.323	.417
Turf	4.93	8	15	6	70	23	193.1	192	21	74	143	Runners on	.265	2313	612	119	8	74	594	269	445	.345	.419
March/April	4.64	12	11	5	75	23	200.0	207	25	117	137	Scoring Posn	.256	1326	340	68	5	42	508	187	280	.348	.410
May	4.51	13	14	8	82	27	233.1	247	30	94	175	Close & Late	.253	936	237	45	5	18	92	98	207	.326	.370
June	4.40	12	15	7	80	27	235.1	237	29	79	160	None on/out	.278	1383	385	81	8	53	53	113	226	.337	.463
July	3.62	16	12	10	98	28	251.1	225	23	78	169	vs. 1st Batr (relief)	.246	329	81	17	0	10	45	29	75	.308	.389
August	4.27	15	15	7	102	30	274.0	281	29	93	199	1st Inning Pitched	.253	1812	458	84	5	56	277	228	409	.340	.397
Sept/Oct	3.97	10	16	7	91	26	233.1	222	41	81	176	First 75 Pits (SP)	.287	593	170	34	7	16	73	64	88	.362	.449
Starters	4.47	57	62	0	161	161	950.0	946	124	346	617	Pitch 76-90	.279	488	136	24	4	19	67	41	78	.336	.461
Relievers	3.71	21	21	44	367	0	477.1	473	53	196	399	Pitch 91-105	.247	312	77	13	3	14	48	33	50	.321	.442
0-3 Days Rest (SP)	2.86	4	0	0	8	8	44.0	30	4	20	32	Pitch 106+	.190	100	19	3	0	3	6	10	20	.270	.310
4 Days Rest	4.68	40	47	0	112	112	663.0	692	98	235	442	First Pitch	.316	687	217	47	3	29	106	16	0	.343	.520
5+ Days Rest	4.19	13	15	0	41	41	243.0	224	22	91	143	Ahead in Count	.200	2436	487	79	7	47	213	0	826	.210	.296
vs. AL	4.30	70	76	39	482	146	1298.1	1298	170	499	927	Behind in Count	.330	1208	399	88	8	64	216	283	0	.456	.575
vs. NL	3.35	8	7	5	46	15	129.0	121	7	43	89	Two Strikes	.184	2547	469	82	8	48	220	243	1016	.261	.279
Pre-All Star	4.66	39	44	21	261	83	720.2	755	92	302	502	Pre-All Star	.272	2772	755	137	15	92	389	302	502	.347	.432
Post-All Star	3.77	39	39	23	267	78	706.2	664	85	240	514	Post-All Star	.249	2665	664	138	9	85	308	240	514	.318	.403

Games Finished: 155   Inherited Runners: 226   Inherited Runners Scored: 71   Holds: 57

Minnesota Twins

1997 Record: 68 – 94

1997	Avg	G	AB	R	H	2B	3B	HR	RBI	BB	SO	HBP	GDP	SB	CS	OBP	SLG	IBB	SH	SF	#Pit	#P/PA	GB	FB	G/F
	.270	162	5634	772	1522	305	40	132	730	495	1121	60	116	151	52	.333	.409	32	20	56	23230	3.71	2025	1603	1.26

1997 Batting

	Avg	AB	H	2B	3B	HR	RBI	BB	SO	OBP	SLG		Avg	AB	H	2B	3B	HR	RBI	BB	SO	OBP	SLG
vs. Left	.286	1283	367	72	5	28	187	119	230	.350	.415	First Pitch	.338	801	271	58	6	23	135	27	0	.362	.512
vs. Right	.265	4351	1155	233	35	104	543	376	891	.327	.407	Ahead in Count	.349	1208	422	83	13	45	237	234	0	.453	.551
Groundball	.264	1272	336	72	12	30	167	116	257	.331	.410	Behind in Count	.205	2556	524	96	14	36	217	0	929	.216	.296
Flyball	.268	868	233	50	5	18	93	65	177	.325	.400	Two Strikes	.191	2573	492	99	13	33	220	234	1121	.266	.278
Home	.274	2777	761	160	17	59	374	250	564	.339	.408	Leadoff	.291	657	191	26	11	10	62	85	94	.383	.409
Away	.266	2857	761	145	23	73	356	245	557	.327	.410	Batting #2	.258	655	169	39	4	14	89	78	140	.337	.394
Day	.276	1699	469	110	9	38	232	160	334	.341	.418	Batting #3	.302	668	202	45	6	11	101	52	88	.348	.437
Night	.268	3935	1053	195	31	94	498	335	787	.329	.405	March/April	.269	877	236	55	4	19	118	110	167	.354	.406
Grass	.267	2389	637	124	19	60	295	207	455	.327	.401	May	.273	986	269	51	8	19	129	98	196	.341	.399
Turf	.273	3245	885	181	21	72	435	288	666	.336	.408	June	.292	883	258	53	6	24	125	70	161	.346	.447
Pre-All Star	.276	2958	817	171	20	69	394	288	566	.343	.418	July	.265	947	251	50	6	22	114	53	171	.309	.400
Post-All Star	.263	2676	705	134	20	63	336	207	555	.321	.399	August	.257	969	249	50	8	23	113	73	230	.314	.396
Scoring Posn	.275	1474	405	91	13	36	575	180	342	.349	.427	Sept/Oct	.266	972	259	46	8	25	131	91	196	.332	.417
Close & Late	.267	763	204	29	6	16	91	79	163	.338	.384	vs. AL	.270	5113	1379	277	35	117	656	461	1012	.334	.406
None on/out	.268	1372	368	66	8	26	26	100	241	.324	.385	vs. NL	.274	521	143	28	5	14	30	34	109	.322	.434

	ERA	W	L	Sv	Opp	G	IP	BB	SO	Avg	H	2B	3B	HR	RBI	OBP	SLG	CG	ShO	Sup	QS	#P/S	SB	CS	GB	FB	G/F
1997	5.00	68	94	30	49	162	1434.0	495	908	.283	1596	338	33	187	815	.342	.454	10	4	4.85	61	90	85	46	1997	1751	1.14

1997 Pitching

	ERA	W	L	Sv	G	GS	IP	H	HR	BB	SO		Avg	AB	H	2B	3B	HR	RBI	BB	SO	OBP	SLG
Home	4.94	35	46	15	280	81	741.0	820	92	224	482	vs. Left	.290	2257	654	135	15	79	325	214	361	.352	.468
Away	5.05	33	48	15	272	81	693.0	776	95	271	426	vs. Right	.278	3384	942	203	18	108	490	281	547	.335	.445
Day	5.53	19	29	8	179	48	424.2	495	50	170	261	Inning 1-6	.292	3859	1127	251	25	132	577	344	555	.351	.473
Night	4.77	49	65	22	373	114	1009.1	1101	137	325	647	Inning 7+	.263	1782	469	87	8	55	238	151	353	.322	.414
Grass	5.24	27	41	13	228	68	577.1	658	85	228	354	None on	.274	3126	858	176	16	104	104	262	503	.334	.441
Turf	4.83	41	53	17	324	94	856.2	938	102	267	554	Runners on	.293	2515	738	162	17	83	711	233	405	.351	.470
March/April	5.80	11	15	5	98	26	229.2	265	30	96	142	Scoring Posn	.305	1441	440	99	10	51	616	159	237	.367	.494
May	5.19	12	16	7	101	28	251.2	269	38	93	154	Close & Late	.249	683	170	35	5	16	95	61	155	.311	.385
June	4.55	12	13	4	80	25	219.1	248	26	67	138	None on/out	.268	1390	373	69	7	46	46	111	237	.326	.427
July	4.43	13	14	5	89	27	243.2	255	27	98	152	vs. 1st Batr (relief)	.295	342	101	14	3	7	58	39	69	.366	.415
August	4.97	8	20	4	87	28	244.1	272	27	69	156	1st Inning Pitched	.267	1833	490	104	10	57	288	190	339	.337	.428
Sept/Oct	5.03	12	16	5	97	28	245.1	287	39	72	166	First 75 Pits (SP)	.295	576	170	34	5	19	86	47	75	.346	.470
Starters	5.42	50	76	0	162	162	906.0	1070	128	318	515	Pitch 76-90	.309	444	137	29	1	11	62	41	61	.364	.453
Relievers	4.26	18	18	30	390	0	528.0	526	59	177	393	Pitch 91-105	.305	262	80	15	6	11	49	26	39	.368	.534
0-3 Days Rest (SP)	4.19	2	6	0	10	10	53.2	52	4	22	19	Pitch 106+	.248	101	25	9	0	2	11	7	18	.296	.396
4 Days Rest	5.26	35	49	0	98	98	563.0	667	80	177	328	First Pitch	.345	840	290	71	9	34	149	19	0	.361	.573
5+ Days Rest	5.97	13	21	0	54	54	289.1	351	44	119	168	Ahead in Count	.220	2475	544	105	9	41	229	0	780	.223	.319
vs. AL	5.15	61	86	27	502	147	1303.1	1456	175	451	835	Behind in Count	.362	1267	459	96	9	69	272	266	0	.471	.616
vs. NL	3.44	7	8	3	50	15	130.2	140	12	44	73	Two Strikes	.209	2441	510	99	9	49	244	210	908	.273	.317
Pre-All Star	5.04	37	48	17	299	85	752.0	831	98	285	460	Pre-All Star	.283	2937	831	181	12	98	420	285	460	.347	.453
Post-All Star	4.95	31	46	13	253	77	682.0	765	89	210	448	Post-All Star	.283	2704	765	157	21	89	395	210	448	.335	.455

Games Finished: 152   Inherited Runners: 285   Inherited Runners Scored: 91   Holds: 52

New York Yankees
1997 Record: 96 – 66

1997	Avg	G	AB	R	H	2B	3B	HR	RBI	BB	SO	HBP	GDP	SB	CS	OBP	SLG	IBB	SH	SF	#Pit	#P/PA	GB	FB	G/F
	.287	162	5710	891	1636	325	23	161	846	676	954	37	138	99	58	.362	.436	51	34	70	24590	3.77	2217	1463	1.52

1997 Batting

	Avg	AB	H	2B	3B	HR	RBI	BB	SO	OBP	SLG		Avg	AB	H	2B	3B	HR	RBI	BB	SO	OBP	SLG
vs. Left	.284	1670	474	90	3	50	255	205	279	.361	.431	First Pitch	.339	822	279	64	1	24	125	36	0	.368	.507
vs. Right	.288	4040	1162	235	20	111	591	471	675	.362	.438	Ahead in Count	.362	1272	461	98	11	55	267	331	0	.489	.586
Groundball	.276	1194	329	59	2	27	163	145	237	.354	.396	Behind in Count	.230	2461	565	105	10	47	272	0	756	.233	.338
Flyball	.279	893	249	48	6	31	118	86	146	.341	.450	Two Strikes	.208	2578	537	99	8	53	282	309	954	.294	.315
Home	.285	2704	770	147	13	75	377	309	431	.358	.432	Leadoff	.317	694	220	39	9	11	81	84	118	.392	.447
Away	.288	3006	866	178	10	86	469	367	523	.365	.440	Batting #2	.271	679	184	40	3	8	78	83	93	.349	.374
Day	.283	2140	605	130	8	70	312	236	369	.354	.449	Batting #3	.343	647	222	41	4	28	129	103	96	.430	.549
Night	.289	3570	1031	195	15	91	534	440	585	.366	.428	March/April	.293	967	283	61	4	23	149	138	143	.380	.435
Grass	.289	4985	1439	280	23	143	747	603	794	.365	.440	May	.265	959	254	43	2	34	133	112	174	.343	.420
Turf	.272	725	197	45	0	18	99	73	160	.340	.408	June	.285	883	252	50	4	25	134	130	154	.376	.436
Pre-All Star	.276	2998	828	163	10	83	428	396	519	.360	.420	July	.282	873	246	46	2	21	117	87	136	.349	.411
Post-All Star	.298	2712	808	162	13	78	418	280	435	.363	.464	August	.307	1047	321	67	3	31	161	105	166	.371	.465
Scoring Posn	.298	1590	474	88	8	50	686	262	292	.385	.458	Sept/Oct	.285	981	280	58	8	27	152	104	181	.351	.443
Close & Late	.264	872	230	37	6	26	128	123	168	.357	.409	vs. AL	.292	5219	1526	301	22	157	809	621	847	.367	.449
None on/out	.291	1380	402	83	5	32	32	123	215	.353	.428	vs. NL	.224	491	110	24	1	4	37	55	107	.303	.301

1997	ERA	W	L	Sv	Opp	G	IP	BB	SO	Avg	H	2B	3B	HR	RBI	OBP	SLG	CG	ShO	Sup	QS	#P/S	SB	CS	GB	FB	G/F
	3.84	96	66	51	76	162	1467.2	532	1165	.260	1463	270	27	144	650	.327	.394	11	10	5.46	84	99	111	47	2080	1368	1.52

1997 Pitching

	ERA	W	L	Sv	G	GS	IP	H	HR	BB	SO		Avg	AB	H	2B	3B	HR	RBI	BB	SO	OBP	SLG
Home	3.69	47	33	25	257	80	735.0	722	71	248	597	vs. Left	.264	1971	520	86	10	55	210	198	393	.334	.401
Away	3.99	49	33	26	273	82	732.2	741	73	284	568	vs. Right	.258	3655	943	184	17	89	440	334	772	.323	.391
Day	3.70	37	23	19	203	60	552.0	542	54	206	470	Inning 1-6	.260	3721	966	175	15	104	441	330	737	.324	.399
Night	3.92	59	43	32	327	102	915.2	921	90	326	695	Inning 7+	.261	1905	497	95	12	40	209	202	428	.333	.386
Grass	3.86	85	57	44	467	142	1291.0	1284	127	468	1008	None on	.253	3159	800	151	18	79	79	272	646	.317	.387
Turf	3.67	11	9	7	63	20	176.2	179	17	64	157	Runners on	.269	2467	663	119	9	65	571	260	519	.340	.403
March/April	4.04	14	13	9	102	27	245.1	253	25	111	188	Scoring Posn	.263	1409	370	72	4	40	504	197	333	.353	.405
May	3.71	15	12	8	81	27	245.0	255	23	76	196	Close & Late	.270	954	258	53	8	17	122	116	234	.351	.396
June	3.92	17	8	11	84	25	231.2	226	20	81	184	None on/out	.247	1392	344	53	6	31	31	116	276	.309	.361
July	3.08	15	11	7	72	26	231.0	201	23	75	185	vs. 1st Batr (relief)	.199	321	64	9	0	12	40	36	84	.282	.340
August	4.34	18	11	12	96	29	261.1	277	34	101	221	1st Inning Pitched	.249	1765	440	77	8	43	216	179	412	.321	.375
Sept/Oct	3.87	17	11	4	95	28	253.1	251	19	88	191	First 75 Pits (SP)	.252	583	147	32	1	21	68	50	104	.313	.419
Starters	4.12	72	42	0	162	162	1017.1	1051	103	341	775	Pitch 76-90	.298	524	156	33	4	16	69	39	99	.347	.468
Relievers	3.20	24	24	51	368	0	450.1	412	41	191	390	Pitch 91-105	.285	400	114	19	4	5	46	32	86	.344	.390
0-3 Days Rest (SP)	7.17	1	1	0	8	8	42.2	59	8	19	27	Pitch 106+	.276	210	58	6	3	5	26	24	42	.352	.405
4 Days Rest	3.75	47	22	0	93	93	592.1	574	54	203	485	First Pitch	.356	739	263	55	2	22	96	31	0	.387	.525
5+ Days Rest	4.35	24	19	0	61	61	382.1	418	41	119	263	Ahead in Count	.192	2672	513	84	8	45	225	0	970	.199	.280
vs. AL	3.89	91	56	48	481	147	1331.2	1337	134	484	1051	Behind in Count	.336	1165	391	79	11	50	197	264	0	.457	.551
vs. NL	3.31	5	10	3	49	15	136.0	126	10	48	114	Two Strikes	.180	2694	485	93	9	43	218	234	1165	.249	.266
Pre-All Star	3.73	48	37	29	282	85	774.0	775	71	284	612	Pre-All Star	.262	2963	775	139	10	71	338	284	612	.329	.387
Post-All Star	3.96	48	29	22	248	77	693.2	688	73	248	553	Post-All Star	.258	2663	688	131	17	73	312	248	553	.325	.403

Games Finished: 151   Inherited Runners: 245   Inherited Runners Scored: 62   Holds: 62

Oakland Athletics
1997 Record: 65 – 97

1997	Avg	G	AB	R	H	2B	3B	HR	RBI	BB	SO	HBP	GDP	SB	CS	OBP	SLG	IBB	SH	SF	#Pit	#P/PA	GB	FB	G/F
	.260	162	5589	764	1451	274	23	197	714	642	1181	49	133	71	36	.339	.423	23	49	40	24925	3.91	1781	1673	1.06

1997 Batting

	Avg	AB	H	2B	3B	HR	RBI	BB	SO	OBP	SLG		Avg	AB	H	2B	3B	HR	RBI	BB	SO	OBP	SLG
vs. Left	.260	1509	392	63	5	48	187	183	334	.341	.404	First Pitch	.333	682	227	52	7	32	116	18	0	.355	.570
vs. Right	.260	4080	1059	211	18	149	527	459	847	.338	.430	Ahead in Count	.332	1164	387	77	6	64	222	313	0	.471	.574
Groundball	.265	1227	325	62	6	37	145	150	250	.348	.416	Behind in Count	.206	2560	528	88	6	59	217	0	960	.213	.314
Flyball	.246	853	210	42	4	35	106	90	186	.325	.428	Two Strikes	.191	2761	526	93	9	55	223	311	1181	.276	.290
Home	.269	2773	747	140	11	107	365	332	546	.352	.444	Leadoff	.235	673	158	28	6	10	35	95	178	.334	.339
Away	.250	2816	704	134	12	90	349	310	635	.326	.402	Batting #2	.263	666	175	37	2	12	85	78	108	.341	.378
Day	.259	2358	610	106	10	86	296	289	487	.343	.422	Batting #3	.296	641	190	34	2	34	129	94	147	.386	.515
Night	.260	3231	841	168	13	111	418	353	694	.336	.423	March/April	.261	914	239	42	3	37	115	120	164	.352	.435
Grass	.259	4993	1291	239	22	176	641	594	1041	.341	.421	May	.247	1028	254	48	2	34	132	125	219	.328	.397
Turf	.268	596	160	35	1	21	73	48	140	.320	.436	June	.270	906	245	53	1	36	123	99	221	.346	.450
Pre-All Star	.259	3045	790	148	9	118	406	375	644	.343	.430	July	.243	888	216	35	5	35	111	115	219	.333	.412
Post-All Star	.260	2544	661	126	14	79	308	267	537	.334	.414	August	.257	945	243	44	5	33	109	95	182	.330	.419
Scoring Posn	.239	1356	324	73	6	39	488	201	325	.334	.388	Sept/Oct	.280	908	254	52	7	22	124	88	176	.345	.425
Close & Late	.271	873	237	37	0	34	125	118	211	.360	.431	vs. AL	.259	5043	1306	250	18	177	630	574	1070	.338	.421
None on/out	.263	1390	365	62	9	57	57	147	304	.336	.443	vs. NL	.266	546	145	24	5	20	84	68	111	.349	.438

Oakland Athletics

1997	ERA	W	L	Sv	Opp	G	IP	BB	SO	Avg	H	2B	3B	HR	RBI	OBP	SLG	CG	ShO	Sup	QS	#P/S	SB	CS	GB	FB	G/F
	5.48	65	97	38	61	162	1445.1	642	953	301	1734	346	38	197	897	372	476	2	1	4.76	50	91	131	48	2170	1627	1.33

1997 Pitching

	ERA	W	L	Sv	G	GS	IP	H	HR	BB	SO		Avg	AB	H	2B	3B	HR	RBI	BB	SO	OBP	SLG
Home	5.57	35	46	18	344	81	750.0	907	96	324	473	vs. Left	.310	2704	837	177	24	98	430	309	416	.381	.501
Away	5.38	30	51	20	299	81	695.1	827	101	318	480	vs. Right	.283	9006	897	169	14	99	467	333	537	.365	.454
Day	5.46	30	38	13	288	68	617.0	735	77	280	382	Inning 1-6	.304	3900	1186	249	26	139	624	412	621	.372	.400
Night	5.50	35	59	25	355	94	828.1	999	120	362	571	Inning 7+	.293	1870	548	97	12	58	273	230	332	.373	.451
Grass	5.52	58	87	33	583	145	1300.1	1573	180	577	829	None on	.298	3029	904	192	19	114	114	293	504	.365	.487
Turf	5.15	7	10	5	60	17	145.0	161	17	65	124	Runners on	.303	2741	830	154	19	83	783	349	449	.379	.464
March/April	5.18	13	13	7	96	26	236.1	289	31	116	160	Scoring Posn	.276	1656	457	90	11	46	672	256	281	.365	.427
May	6.59	9	21	6	103	30	263.2	346	41	121	159	Close & Late	.284	757	215	39	5	19	133	125	134	.390	.424
June	4.94	12	15	10	100	27	233.1	257	33	96	156	None on/out	.309	1389	429	101	13	55	122	223	.370	.519
July	5.32	8	19	5	110	27	235.1	270	28	99	152	vs. 1st Batr (relief)	.287	428	123	17	1	12	69	38	91	.342	.416
August	5.26	11	16	4	118	27	246.1	287	28	108	145	1st Inning Pitched	.293	2118	620	106	12	71	395	267	390	.373	.455
Sept/Oct	5.47	12	13	6	116	25	230.1	285	36	102	181	First 75 Pits (SP)	.315	562	177	42	6	19	102	49	80	.373	.512
Starters	5.95	29	73	0	162	162	858.2	1056	127	366	545	Pitch 76-90	.327	447	146	26	5	21	76	41	58	.385	.548
Relievers	4.80	36	24	38	481	0	586.2	678	70	276	408	Pitch 91-105	.294	245	72	18	1	8	33	31	49	.377	.473
0-3 Days Rest (SP)	5.16	1	9	0	17	17	82.0	98	9	33	38	Pitch 106+	.298	104	31	6	2	5	15	13	21	.380	.538
4 Days Rest	6.35	17	35	0	83	82	434.0	536	64	191	311	First Pitch	.362	810	293	56	10	29	146	39	0	.392	.563
5+ Days Rest	5.68	10	29	0	62	62	337.2	415	53	140	193	Ahead in Count	.244	2474	604	124	14	58	287	0	788	.251	.376
vs. AL	5.49	58	88	32	582	146	1304.2	1564	179	584	845	Behind in Count	.359	1368	491	93	7	57	264	340	0	.484	.562
vs. NL	5.37	7	9	6	61	16	140.2	170	18	58	108	Two Strikes	.232	2533	587	139	11	69	289	263	953	.308	.377
Pre-All Star	5.66	37	52	25	320	89	784.1	958	114	354	517	Pre-All Star	.304	3154	958	202	27	114	508	354	517	.376	.493
Post-All Star	5.27	28	45	13	323	73	661.0	776	83	288	436	Post-All Star	.297	2616	776	144	11	83	389	288	436	.367	.455

Games Finished: 160   Inherited Runners: 386   Inherited Runners Scored: 121   Holds: 49

Seattle Mariners

1997 Record: 90 – 72

1997	Avg	G	AB	R	H	2B	3B	HR	RBI	BB	SO	HBP	GDP	SB	CS	OBP	SLG	IBB	SH	SF	#Pit	#P/PA	GB	FB	G/F
	.280	162	5614	925	1574	312	21	264	890	626	1110	49	145	89	40	.355	.485	53	46	49	24229	3.79	1864	1728	1.08

1997 Batting

	Avg	AB	H	2B	3B	HR	RBI	BB	SO	OBP	SLG		Avg	AB	H	2B	3B	HR	RBI	BB	SO	OBP	SLG
vs. Left	.293	1442	423	78	6	70	249	159	284	.365	.501	First Pitch	.353	711	251	43	4	36	132	39	0	.393	.577
vs. Right	.276	4172	1151	234	15	194	641	467	826	.351	.479	Ahead in Count	.372	1297	483	94	6	96	292	331	0	.498	.676
Groundball	.275	1214	334	68	6	47	174	141	218	.354	.457	Behind in Count	.213	2527	537	107	5	85	300	0	913	.271	.360
Flyball	.274	868	238	49	6	46	142	88	180	.342	.503	Two Strikes	.198	2624	520	112	5	95	301	253	1100	.271	.353
Home	.284	2738	778	176	11	131	448	387	568	.365	.500	Leadoff	.294	693	204	41	4	12	66	57	75	.349	.417
Away	.277	2876	796	136	10	133	442	289	542	.345	.470	Batting #2	.281	690	194	48	3	26	93	51	114	.335	.472
Day	.269	1782	479	93	11	88	267	203	377	.346	.481	Batting #3	.299	639	191	34	3	59	152	82	130	.379	.638
Night	.286	3832	1095	219	10	176	623	423	733	.359	.486	March/April	.292	938	274	61	4	33	151	109	176	.369	.471
Grass	.270	2467	665	121	7	106	364	252	469	.340	.453	May	.287	962	276	50	2	42	151	103	167	.359	.474
Turf	.289	3147	909	191	14	158	526	374	641	.367	.509	June	.280	912	255	64	2	50	148	97	181	.353	.519
Pre-All Star	.286	3020	865	182	8	139	487	339	559	.362	.490	July	.289	921	266	54	5	36	149	96	182	.355	.476
Post-All Star	.273	2594	709	130	13	125	403	287	551	.347	.478	August	.261	1011	264	49	5	55	151	118	217	.342	.483
Scoring Posn	.276	1407	389	85	4	54	600	214	306	.367	.458	Sept/Oct	.275	870	239	34	3	48	140	103	187	.352	.466
Close & Late	.254	785	199	41	2	30	113	106	187	.346	.425	vs. AL	.281	5069	1426	280	20	231	792	548	1001	.354	.481
None on/out	.294	1386	407	81	5	67	135	242	361	.504	vs. NL	.272	545	148	32	1	33	98	78	109	.363	.516

1997	ERA	W	L	Sv	Opp	G	IP	BB	SO	Avg	H	2B	3B	HR	RBI	OBP	SLG	CG	ShO	Sup	QS	#P/S	SB	CS	FB	G/F
	4.78	90	72	38	65	162	1447.2	598	1207	267	1500	313	21	192	782	342	433	9	8	5.75	83	100	99	66	1945	1605	1.21

1997 Pitching

	ERA	W	L	Sv	G	GS	IP	H	HR	BB	SO		Avg	AB	H	2B	3B	HR	RBI	BB	SO	OBP	SLG
Home	4.80	45	36	18	279	81	738.0	746	102	312	657	vs. Left	.295	1926	568	100	12	84	314	260	350	.383	.490
Away	4.76	45	36	20	275	81	709.2	754	90	286	550	vs. Right	.252	3694	932	213	9	108	468	338	857	.320	.403
Day	4.17	30	21	15	176	51	464.1	447	50	218	382	Inning 1-6	.263	3764	989	211	12	135	508	362	781	.333	.433
Night	5.07	60	51	23	378	111	983.1	1053	142	380	825	Inning 7+	.275	1856	511	102	9	57	274	236	426	.361	.432
Grass	4.68	38	32	18	235	70	613.2	655	81	240	475	None on	.259	3106	806	162	12	100	100	314	678	.334	.416
Turf	4.86	52	40	20	319	92	834.0	845	111	358	732	Runners on	.276	2514	694	151	9	92	682	284	529	.353	.453
March/April	5.44	16	11	7	90	27	241.2	257	39	116	171	Scoring Posn	.263	1457	383	92	6	52	580	199	318	.351	.441
May	6.17	11	16	3	90	27	239.1	277	35	119	187	Close & Late	.282	849	239	49	3	23	144	109	204	.366	.428
June	3.68	20	7	10	80	27	240.0	220	27	83	204	None on/out	.260	1375	358	72	7	41	41	129	270	.330	.412
July	5.19	13	13	5	81	26	230.2	255	37	94	219	vs. 1st Batr (relief)	.304	342	104	22	3	11	55	37	60	.382	.482
August	4.43	15	15	6	98	30	268.1	264	29	96	244	1st Inning Pitched	.264	1871	494	98	9	54	314	239	409	.353	.431
Sept/Oct	3.80	15	10	7	105	25	227.2	227	25	90	182	First 75 Pits (SP)	.257	569	146	30	2	22	70	47	111	.318	.432
Starters	4.47	66	46	0	162	162	985.2	985	132	362	808	Pitch 76-90	.227	476	108	33	2	18	63	54	103	.308	.418
Relievers	5.44	24	26	38	392	0	462.0	515	60	236	399	Pitch 91-105	.293	369	108	23	1	13	47	43	75	.331	.409
0-3 Days Rest (SP)	3.96	1	3	0	7	7	38.2	38	7	16	23	Pitch 106+	.243	247	60	7	2	10	35	32	75	.331	.409
4 Days Rest	4.13	48	24	0	90	90	580.1	563	77	204	487	First Pitch	.343	706	242	53	5	32	129	28	0	.373	.568
5+ Days Rest	5.08	17	19	0	65	65	366.2	384	48	142	298	Ahead in Count	.203	2600	528	101	6	53	233	0	993	.212	.308
vs. AL	4.63	83	63	35	498	146	1308.1	1340	161	542	1098	Behind in Count	.370	1215	449	92	7	76	254	283	0	.488	.644
vs. NL	6.20	7	9	3	56	16	139.1	160	31	56	109	Two Strikes	.175	2695	471	96	6	54	251	286	1207	.259	.275
Pre-All Star	5.15	49	38	20	291	87	771.1	808	115	342	607	Pre-All Star	.271	2987	808	174	10	115	444	342	607	.350	.451
Post-All Star	4.36	41	34	18	263	75	676.1	692	77	256	600	Post-All Star	.263	2633	692	139	11	77	338	256	600	.334	.412

Games Finished: 153   Inherited Runners: 269   Inherited Runners Scored: 92   Holds: 56

530

Texas Rangers

	Avg	G	AB	R	H	2B	3B	HR	RBI	BB	SO	HBP	GDP	SB	CS	OBP	SLG	IBB	SH	SF	#Pit	#P/PA	GB	FB	G/F
1997	.274	162	5651	807	1547	311	27	187	773	500	1116	34	118	72	37	.334	.438	39	28	52	23181	3.70	1964	1555	1.26

1997 Batting

	Avg	AB	H	2B	3B	HR	RBI	BB	SO	OBP	SLG		Avg	AB	H	2B	3B	HR	RBI	BB	SO	OBP	SLG
vs. Left	.274	1593	437	84	5	49	198	135	318	.332	.426	First Pitch	.342	798	273	55	3	37	136	31	0	.366	.558
vs. Right	.274	4058	1110	227	22	138	575	365	798	.334	.442	Ahead in Count	.357	1170	418	80	12	58	231	249	0	.465	.595
Groundball	.250	1310	328	65	7	34	156	109	268	.307	.389	Behind in Count	.208	2648	551	126	8	49	248	0	958	.214	.317
Flyball	.280	881	247	54	7	30	130	79	186	.340	.460	Two Strikes	.190	2667	507	112	9	54	234	220	1116	.256	.300
Home	.288	2786	803	155	20	95	393	247	521	.347	.461	Leadoff	.248	682	169	36	6	8	54	78	112	.327	.353
Away	.260	2865	744	156	7	92	380	253	595	.320	.415	Batting #2	.308	695	214	41	4	21	87	39	109	.347	.469
Day	.269	1283	345	77	7	41	179	118	278	.332	.436	Batting #3	.322	639	206	45	3	28	92	84	96	.402	.534
Night	.275	4368	1202	234	20	146	594	382	838	.334	.438	March/April	.249	791	197	39	1	24	107	86	156	.325	.392
Grass	.275	5047	1388	269	24	171	687	449	961	.335	.439	May	.281	978	275	60	8	33	139	96	195	.343	.460
Turf	.263	604	159	42	3	16	86	51	155	.323	.422	June	.285	963	274	59	5	29	117	76	164	.338	.447
Pre-All Star	.276	2941	813	173	15	95	403	279	550	.339	.442	July	.276	954	263	54	5	33	128	84	213	.337	.447
Post-All Star	.271	2710	734	138	12	92	370	221	566	.327	.432	August	.269	1091	293	48	4	33	160	96	234	.330	.411
Scoring Posn	.270	1421	384	72	6	39	568	189	309	.350	.412	Sept/Oct	.280	874	245	51	4	35	122	62	154	.327	.468
Close & Late	.289	841	243	53	6	29	139	86	206	.354	.470	vs. AL	.270	5076	1368	278	23	171	672	445	1029	.329	.434
None on/out	.290	1408	409	87	7	65	65	107	249	.344	.501	vs. NL	.311	575	179	33	4	16	101	55	87	.370	.466

	ERA	W	L	Sv	Opp	G	IP	BB	SO	Avg	H	2B	3B	HR	RBI	OBP	SLG	CG	ShO	Sup	QS	#P/S	SB	CS	GB	FB	G/F
1997	4.69	77	85	33	57	162	1429.2	541	925	.283	1598	304	34	169	784	.347	.439	8	9	5.08	66	96	60	54	2019	1613	1.25

1997 Pitching

	ERA	W	L	Sv	G	GS	IP	H	HR	BB	SO		Avg	AB	H	2B	3B	HR	RBI	BB	SO	OBP	SLG
Home	4.82	39	42	16	273	81	734.0	826	91	284	458	vs. Left	.287	2483	712	126	12	75	342	282	404	.361	.438
Away	4.55	38	43	17	271	81	695.2	772	78	257	467	vs. Right	.280	3159	886	178	22	94	442	259	521	.335	.440
Day	4.40	21	16	10	126	37	321.0	360	39	118	237	Inning 1-6	.292	3866	1127	222	26	126	563	368	606	.354	.460
Night	4.77	56	69	23	418	125	1108.2	1238	130	423	688	Inning 7+	.265	1776	471	82	8	43	221	173	319	.330	.393
Grass	4.70	68	77	29	490	145	1284.1	1436	155	490	805	None on	.277	3119	863	168	15	100	100	263	509	.337	.436
Turf	4.58	9	8	4	54	17	145.1	162	14	51	120	Runners on	.291	2523	735	136	19	69	684	278	416	.358	.442
March/April	3.80	14	10	7	75	24	208.2	206	22	77	145	Scoring Posn	.279	1464	409	76	11	47	607	189	272	.353	.443
May	4.54	15	13	7	91	28	246.0	275	27	107	143	Close & Late	.291	793	231	43	4	19	120	95	147	.366	.427
June	4.71	10	17	5	93	27	239.0	277	26	80	159	None on/out	.275	1386	381	63	9	41	41	109	220	.331	.422
July	4.68	11	16	5	90	27	238.2	257	26	81	145	vs. 1st Batr (relief)	.261	345	90	16	1	6	54	28	74	.311	.365
August	5.54	14	14	5	109	31	278.0	335	47	111	172	1st Inning Pitched	.280	1843	516	100	11	54	323	205	338	.352	.434
Sept/Oct	4.64	13	12	4	86	25	219.1	248	21	85	161	First 75 Pits (SP)	.297	590	175	34	5	12	78	53	83	.358	.492
Starters	5.11	49	66	0	162	162	959.0	1132	130	355	586	Pitch 76-90	.292	510	149	34	3	17	69	51	82	.356	.471
Relievers	3.84	28	19	33	382	0	470.2	466	39	186	339	Pitch 91-105	.299	394	118	18	2	17	44	31	56	.348	.485
0-3 Days Rest (SP)	5.75	2	0	0	7	7	40.2	39	4	18	25	Pitch 106+	.238	193	46	9	3	7	20	18	24	.307	.425
4 Days Rest	4.90	29	50	0	99	99	591.0	700	78	220	337	First Pitch	.370	880	326	62	8	32	171	31	0	.390	.568
5+ Days Rest	5.39	18	16	0	56	56	327.1	393	48	117	224	Ahead in Count	.233	2396	559	107	12	56	274	0	774	.238	.358
vs. AL	4.74	67	79	29	491	146	1285.2	1437	151	500	840	Behind in Count	.331	1294	428	77	10	57	221	281	0	.446	.538
vs. NL	4.25	10	6	4	53	16	144.0	161	18	41	85	Two Strikes	.207	2377	491	94	9	49	237	229	925	.278	.316
Pre-All Star	4.35	43	42	20	278	85	746.2	801	83	280	480	Pre-All Star	.275	2916	801	158	14	83	386	280	480	.340	.424
Post-All Star	5.06	34	43	13	266	77	683.0	797	86	261	445	Post-All Star	.292	2726	797	146	20	86	398	261	445	.354	.455

Games Finished: 154   Inherited Runners: 304   Inherited Runners Scored: 96   Holds: 42

Toronto Blue Jays

	Avg	G	AB	R	H	2B	3B	HR	RBI	BB	SO	HBP	GDP	SB	CS	OBP	SLG	IBB	SH	SF	#Pit	#P/PA	GB	FB	G/F
1997	.244	162	5473	654	1333	275	41	147	627	487	1138	59	102	134	50	.310	.389	26	38	52	22678	3.71	1810	1629	1.11

1997 Batting

	Avg	AB	H	2B	3B	HR	RBI	BB	SO	OBP	SLG		Avg	AB	H	2B	3B	HR	RBI	BB	SO	OBP	SLG
vs. Left	.246	1654	407	85	18	38	187	132	323	.305	.388	First Pitch	.307	779	239	53	6	34	128	24	0	.332	.521
vs. Right	.242	3819	926	190	23	109	440	355	815	.311	.390	Ahead in Count	.320	1098	351	65	12	54	199	240	0	.440	.548
Groundball	.234	957	224	46	7	25	129	92	180	.306	.375	Behind in Count	.190	2594	493	99	14	33	185	0	943	.197	.277
Flyball	.243	745	181	45	8	21	80	67	177	.314	.409	Two Strikes	.174	2621	455	98	17	36	176	223	1138	.243	.265
Home	.246	2661	654	132	26	68	312	259	553	.302	.387	Leadoff	.262	657	172	27	9	2	60	79	95	.341	.339
Away	.241	2812	679	143	15	79	315	228	585	.302	.387	Batting #2	.232	655	152	27	6	7	60	52	126	.293	.324
Day	.242	1988	482	95	16	35	205	189	431	.312	.359	Batting #3	.235	635	149	34	1	26	106	69	144	.306	.414
Night	.244	3485	851	180	25	112	422	298	707	.308	.407	March/April	.243	801	195	46	5	24	98	73	164	.313	.403
Grass	.244	2302	561	115	13	66	259	186	479	.304	.391	May	.250	952	238	48	8	21	100	67	181	.301	.383
Turf	.243	3171	772	160	28	81	368	301	659	.314	.388	June	.242	861	208	44	6	19	95	90	171	.315	.373
Pre-All Star	.243	2809	682	145	19	68	305	250	566	.308	.381	July	.212	918	195	31	2	29	92	79	212	.280	.345
Post-All Star	.244	2664	651	130	22	79	322	237	572	.311	.399	August	.273	1060	289	54	7	38	146	100	196	.337	.444
Scoring Posn	.228	1345	307	59	10	36	468	182	286	.317	.367	Sept/Oct	.236	881	208	52	13	16	96	78	214	.305	.379
Close & Late	.230	915	210	33	3	28	123	111	224	.314	.364	vs. AL	.247	4973	1229	251	39	131	579	442	1009	.313	.392
None on/out	.244	1397	341	78	7	36	36	92	283	.297	.387	vs. NL	.208	500	104	24	2	16	48	45	129	.278	.360

Toronto Blue Jays

1997	ERA	W	L	Sv	Opp	G	IP	BB	SO	Avg	H	2B	3B	HR	RBI	OBP	SLG	CG	ShO	Sup	QS	#P/S	SB	CS	GB	FB	G/F
1997	3.92	76	86	34	55	162	1442.2	497	1150	263	1453	277	25	167	650	326	413	19	16	4.08	86	104	77	64	1878	1529	1.23

1997 Pitching

	ERA	W	L	Sv	G	GS	IP	H	HR	BB	SO		Avg	AB	H	2B	3B	HR	RBI	BB	SO	OBP	SLG
Ilomo	3.41	42	39	14	230	81	740.0	712	72	230	572	vs. Left	.255	2689	687	119	13	76	309	269	557	.325	.394
Away	4.46	34	47	20	268	81	702.2	711	95	267	578	vs. Right	.270	2838	766	158	12	91	341	228	593	.327	.430
Day	3.70	24	35	6	180	59	528.1	499	57	208	431	Inning 1-6	.255	3690	941	192	17	116	445	335	783	.319	.410
Night	4.05	52	51	28	318	103	914.1	954	110	289	719	Inning 7+	.280	1831	512	84	8	51	205	162	367	.340	.418
Grass	4.47	27	39	16	224	66	575.2	599	76	219	480	None on	.262	3176	831	159	9	100	100	257	662	.320	.412
Turf	3.55	49	47	18	274	96	867.0	854	91	278	670	Runners on	.265	2351	622	118	16	67	550	240	488	.333	.414
March/April	3.73	11	12	5	76	23	209.2	196	26	71	154	Scoring Posn	.258	1307	337	64	14	40	472	161	295	.337	.420
May	4.23	15	13	5	78	28	251.0	251	24	84	203	Close & Late	.290	1012	293	42	3	32	119	95	197	.353	.432
June	3.72	11	15	8	75	26	230.0	227	32	73	169	None on/out	.272	1394	379	69	3	47	47	105	269	.327	.427
July	3.55	13	15	6	88	28	248.1	244	30	79	212	vs. 1st Batr (relief)	.281	302	85	13	0	10	43	29	66	.343	.424
August	4.53	15	15	6	90	30	268.1	302	29	108	198	1st Inning Pitched	.271	1658	450	68	4	51	227	171	369	.340	.410
Sept/Oct	3.63	11	16	4	91	27	235.1	233	26	82	214	First 75 Pits (SP)	.249	570	142	25	1	16	52	43	116	.304	.381
Starters	3.99	57	62	0	162	162	1054.0	1023	124	356	837	Pitch 76-90	.246	536	132	35	3	15	63	50	104	.314	.407
Relievers	3.73	19	24	34	336	0	388.2	430	43	141	313	Pitch 91-105	.265	471	125	26	1	17	64	34	83	.320	.433
0-3 Days Rest (SP)	22.50	0	0	0	1	1	2.0	5	2	1	3	Pitch 106+	.277	325	90	16	4	8	37	27	69	.339	.425
4 Days Rest	3.99	37	39	0	100	100	679.2	636	84	210	558	First Pitch	.335	783	262	49	4	31	104	26	0	.360	.526
5+ Days Rest	3.89	20	23	0	61	61	372.1	382	38	145	276	Ahead in Count	.203	2567	522	100	8	49	213	0	943	.209	.306
vs. AL	3.94	72	75	32	455	147	1307.2	1325	155	449	1056	Behind in Count	.343	1111	381	68	9	53	201	232	0	.453	.563
vs. NL	3.67	4	11	2	43	15	135.0	128	12	48	94	Two Strikes	.186	2645	491	93	9	47	195	239	1150	.257	.281
Pre-All Star	3.80	40	43	18	248	83	748.2	724	86	246	579	Post-All Star	.272	2685	729	154	13	81	322	251	571	.336	.429
Post-All Star	4.05	36	43	16	250	79	694.0	729	81	251	571												

Games Finished: 143   Inherited Runners: 183   Inherited Runners Scored: 52   Holds: 63

Atlanta Braves

1997 Record: 101 – 61

1997	Avg	G	AB	R	H	2B	3B	HR	RBI	BB	SO	HBP	GDP	SB	CS	OBP	SLG	IBB	SH	SF	#Pit	#P/PA	GB	FB	G/F
1997	270	162	5528	791	1490	268	37	174	755	597	1160	52	143	108	58	343	426	45	83	52	23061	3.65	2061	1360	1.52

1997 Batting

	Avg	AB	H	2B	3B	HR	RBI	BB	SO	OBP	SLG		Avg	AB	H	2B	3B	HR	RBI	BB	SO	OBP	SLG
vs. Left	.268	1518	407	73	10	39	194	171	319	.345	.406	First Pitch	.327	927	303	55	7	41	163	33	0	.354	.534
vs. Right	.270	4010	1083	195	27	135	561	426	841	.343	.433	Ahead in Count	.355	1165	413	75	10	61	239	307	0	.484	.593
Groundball	.253	1018	258	51	9	30	120	97	228	.324	.410	Behind in Count	.197	2418	476	79	10	39	202	0	973	.205	.286
Flyball	.262	676	177	25	3	24	100	69	155	.332	.414	Two Strikes	.185	2547	470	90	13	36	198	256	1160	.263	.272
Home	.273	2700	737	118	21	76	366	310	563	.350	.417	Leadoff	.312	676	211	30	7	12	72	87	126	.394	.430
Away	.266	2828	753	150	16	98	389	287	597	.337	.435	Batting #2	.272	668	182	30	10	21	80	68	149	.346	.442
Day	.260	1622	421	85	12	58	209	157	348	.329	.434	Batting #3	.303	646	196	43	5	20	118	78	101	.375	.478
Night	.274	3906	1069	183	25	116	546	440	812	.349	.422	March/April	.317	865	274	43	7	24	135	84	139	.377	.466
Grass	.269	4443	1197	204	34	128	593	483	940	.343	.417	May	.253	922	233	45	6	24	114	106	195	.330	.393
Turf	.270	1085	293	64	3	46	162	114	220	.344	.462	June	.281	974	274	54	6	38	148	115	203	.362	.466
Pre-All Star	.283	2971	842	154	20	92	429	324	583	.356	.442	July	.265	955	253	59	6	34	135	99	199	.336	.446
Post-All Star	.253	2557	648	114	17	82	326	273	577	.329	.408	August	.244	925	226	32	9	26	119	106	221	.327	.383
Scoring Posn	.257	1411	362	59	9	37	548	200	311	.343	.390	Sept/Oct	.259	887	230	35	3	28	104	87	203	.329	.400
Close & Late	.245	878	215	34	6	24	98	113	218	.337	.379	vs. AL	.269	536	144	26	3	19	69	46	113	.333	.435
None on/out	.285	1381	393	77	7	58	58	146	273	.355	.476	vs. NL	.270	4992	1346	242	34	155	686	551	1047	.345	.425

1997	ERA	W	L	Sv	Opp	G	IP	BB	SO	Avg	H	2B	3B	HR	RBI	OBP	SLG	CG	ShO	Sup	QS	#P/S	SB	CS	GB	FB	G/F
1997	3.18	101	61	37	53	162	1465.2	450	1196	242	1319	242	31	145	545	301	354	21	17	4.86	114	99	124	54	1954	1391	1.40

1997 Pitching

	ERA	W	L	Sv	G	GS	IP	H	HR	BB	SO		Avg	AB	H	2B	3B	HR	RBI	BB	SO	OBP	SLG
Home	3.20	50	31	15	282	81	749.0	664	55	240	615	vs. Left	.247	2125	524	95	7	40	208	213	444	.315	.354
Away	3.16	51	30	22	254	81	716.2	655	56	210	581	vs. Right	.238	3336	795	142	15	71	337	237	752	.291	.354
Day	3.55	27	21	12	162	48	426.1	385	35	126	363	Inning 1-6	.240	3597	865	155	17	70	351	262	754	.293	.351
Night	3.03	74	40	25	374	114	1039.1	934	76	324	833	Inning 7+	.244	1864	454	82	5	41	194	188	442	.314	.359
Grass	3.28	78	53	27	444	131	1191.0	1075	91	375	971	None on	.239	3263	780	142	14	56	56	231	720	.292	.343
Turf	2.75	23	8	10	92	31	274.2	244	20	75	225	Runners on	.245	2198	539	95	8	55	489	219	476	.312	.371
March/April	2.56	19	6	7	82	25	221.1	192	7	66	162	Scoring Posn	.228	1245	284	45	7	27	406	164	294	.313	.341
May	3.14	17	11	6	90	28	252.0	246	20	66	200	Close & Late	.245	1030	252	45	3	23	127	132	253	.331	.361
June	3.80	16	12	6	83	28	251.0	248	24	81	182	None on/out	.247	1407	348	60	9	25	95	95	299	.298	.356
July	3.47	17	11	8	89	28	251.2	220	21	84	202	vs. 1st Batr (relief)	.258	326	84	16	2	14	43	43	87	.344	.448
August	2.78	16	11	7	95	27	252.1	219	20	86	228	1st Inning Pitched	.245	1774	435	70	7	34	217	190	430	.320	.350
Sept/Oct	3.26	16	10	3	91	26	237.1	194	19	67	222	First 75 Pits (SP)	.240	600	144	33	4	9	63	41	130	.293	.353
Starters	3.05	75	37	0	162	162	1096.2	990	78	270	843	Pitch 76-90	.269	502	135	25	1	13	59	49	100	.335	.400
Relievers	3.56	26	24	37	374	0	369.0	329	33	180	353	Pitch 91-105	.259	371	96	17	3	8	35	27	66	.308	.385
0-3 Days Rest (SP)	2.94	3	4	0	11	11	70.1	64	5	18	57	Pitch 106+	.234	252	59	12	0	9	30	14	47	.275	.389
4 Days Rest	2.86	52	19	0	99	99	685.1	599	46	158	524	First Pitch	.315	829	261	46	4	24	98	36	0	.343	.467
5+ Days Rest	3.46	20	14	0	52	52	341.0	327	27	94	262	Ahead in Count	.182	2716	494	91	11	25	151	0	1062	.188	.251
vs. AL	2.99	8	7	2	42	15	138.2	120	13	33	115	Behind in Count	.323	967	312	61	4	41	165	229	0	.446	.521
vs. NL	3.20	93	54	35	494	147	1327.0	1199	98	417	1081	Two Strikes	.164	2656	435	76	10	28	185	184	1196	.222	.232
Pre-All Star	3.11	57	30	22	278	87	777.1	727	54	228	578	Pre-All Star	.249	2914	727	128	14	54	288	228	578	.305	.359
Post-All Star	3.26	44	31	15	258	75	688.1	592	57	222	618	Post-All Star	.232	2547	592	109	8	57	257	222	618	.296	.349

Games Finished: 141   Inherited Runners: 147   Inherited Runners Scored: 44   Holds: 43

Chicago Cubs

1997	Avg	G	AB	R	H	2B	3B	HR	RBI	BB	SO	HBP	GDP	SB	CS	OBP	SLG	IBB	SH	SF	#Pit	#P/PA	GB	FB	G/F
1997	.263	162	5489	687	1444	269	39	127	642	451	1003	34	119	116	60	.321	.396	40	83	38	22048	3.62	2038	1373	1.48

1997 Batting

	Avg	AB	H	2B	3B	HR	RBI	BB	SO	OBP	SLG		Avg	AB	H	2B	3B	HR	RBI	BB	SO	OBP	SLG
vs. Left	.263	1286	338	57	7	37	157	103	209	.320	.404	First Pitch	.287	799	229	40	5	19	105	28	0	.316	.421
vs. Right	.263	4203	1106	212	32	90	485	348	794	.321	.393	Ahead in Count	.342	1177	403	79	13	46	199	229	0	.446	.549
Groundball	.267	1103	295	60	9	18	126	93	326	.326	.387	Behind in Count	.202	2489	504	87	16	32	205	0	860	.208	.289
Flyball	.241	781	188	33	7	22	83	53	172	.289	.385	Two Strikes	.188	2450	460	77	8	33	190	193	1003	.249	.266
Home	.281	2716	763	127	19	79	374	245	488	.342	.429	Leadoff	.275	691	190	35	9	11	45	45	81	.321	.399
Away	.246	2773	681	142	20	48	268	206	515	.300	.363	Batting #2	.274	654	179	33	6	10	51	57	93	.334	.388
Day	.277	3068	851	147	25	90	417	266	556	.337	.430	Batting #3	.284	623	177	27	5	17	84	84	80	.370	.425
Night	.245	2421	593	122	14	37	225	185	447	.300	.353	March/April	.228	829	189	42	4	15	87	81	137	.302	.343
Grass	.267	4472	1193	197	33	108	533	372	797	.325	.398	May	.267	960	256	52	10	26	116	82	191	.326	.423
Turf	.247	1017	251	72	6	19	109	79	206	.302	.385	June	.267	936	250	48	3	17	105	85	168	.329	.379
Pre-All Star	.259	2931	760	160	18	64	346	264	529	.323	.392	July	.264	960	253	56	4	17	110	78	178	.320	.383
Post-All Star	.267	2558	684	109	21	63	296	187	474	.319	.400	August	.270	977	264	25	9	31	115	63	185	.315	.409
Scoring Posn	.265	1319	350	70	8	22	476	177	261	.347	.381	Sept/Oct	.281	827	232	46	9	21	109	62	144	.332	.434
Close & Late	.263	862	227	35	8	17	97	76	171	.323	.382	vs. AL	.327	513	168	27	5	12	79	43	81	.380	.470
None on/out	.253	1386	350	70	10	35	35	90	207	.302	.393	vs. NL	.256	4976	1276	242	34	115	563	408	922	.315	.388

1997	ERA	W	L	Sv	Opp	G	IP	BB	SO	Avg	2B	3B	HR	RBI	OBP	SLG	CG	ShO	Sup	QS	#P/S	SB	CS	FB	G/F
1997	4.44	68	94	37	55	162	1429.0	590	1072	.266	1451	303	32	185	728	.339	.435	6	4	4.33	83	94	146	59	1857	1539	1.21

1997 Pitching

	ERA	W	L	Sv	G	GS	IP	H	HR	BB	SO		Avg	AB	H	2B	3B	HR	RBI	BB	SO	OBP	SLG
Home	4.14	42	39	19	81	740.0	719	106	298	583		vs. Left	.262	2384	625	131	23	63	284	273	451	.338	.416	
Away	4.77	26	55	18	294	81	689.0	732	79	292	489	vs. Right	.269	3072	826	172	9	122	444	317	621	.340	.450
Day	4.38	44	47	21	342	91	803.2	813	112	329	636	Inning 1-6	.259	3677	952	202	23	110	468	381	699	.331	.416
Night	4.52	24	47	16	261	71	625.1	638	73	261	436	Inning 7+	.280	1779	499	101	9	75	260	209	373	.357	.474
Grass	4.52	56	76	27	1172.0	1195	159	482	890	None on	.267	3080	821	169	17	110	110	295	609	.334	.440		
Turf	4.06	12	18	10	105	30	257.0	256	26	108	182	Runners on	.265	2376	630	134	15	75	618	295	463	.345	.429
March/April	4.84	6	19	4	94	25	214.0	234	28	93	153	Scoring Posn	.263	1405	370	77	11	43	527	214	300	.355	.426
May	3.56	15	13	9	102	28	253.0	242	28	90	183	Close & Late	.283	884	250	49	5	33	144	111	203	.361	.462
June	4.52	11	17	6	101	28	243.0	245	28	104	193	None on/out	.269	1366	367	83	8	47	47	125	256	.334	.444
July	4.61	11	17	8	112	28	253.2	261	41	101	194	vs. 1st Batr (relief)	.230	379	87	18	0	13	57	51	79	.322	.380
August	4.76	12	16	5	109	28	249.1	266	36	117	178	1st Inning Pitched	.266	1940	516	87	8	69	322	246	423	.349	.426
Sept/Oct	4.42	13	12	5	85	25	216.0	203	24	85	171	First 75 Pits (SP)	.247	600	148	32	3	16	63	43	104	.299	.390
Starters	4.43	56	61	0	162	162	958.2	974	122	367	668	Pitch 76-90	.288	473	136	38	3	27	75	66	88	.378	.552
Relievers	4.46	12	33	37	441	0	470.1	477	63	223	404	Pitch 91-105	.274	314	86	17	3	13	39	29	70	.335	.471
0-3 Days Rest (SP)	6.75	0	3	0	5	5	24.0	31	3	9	14	Pitch 106+	.272	81	22	7	0	3	16	9	17	.341	.469
4 Days Rest	4.17	38	28	0	95	95	569.1	565	68	218	385	First Pitch	.324	791	256	50	4	42	133	34	0	.352	.556
5+ Days Rest	4.68	18	30	0	62	62	365.1	378	51	140	269	Ahead in Count	.202	2495	503	104	10	63	237	0	922	.205	.327
vs. AL	4.40	9	6	4	51	15	131.0	137	13	52	96	Behind in Count	.352	1163	409	88	6	58	224	316	0	.490	.587
vs. NL	4.44	59	88	33	552	147	1298.0	1314	172	538	976	Two Strikes	.181	2524	456	101	11	49	232	238	1072	.254	.288
Pre-All Star	4.22	37	50	23	318	87	763.0	776	90	309	565	Pre-All Star	.267	2905	776	184	14	90	374	309	565	.340	.433
Post-All Star	4.69	31	44	14	285	75	666.0	675	95	281	507	Post-All Star	.265	2551	675	119	18	95	354	281	507	.338	.437

Games Finished: 156   Inherited Runners: 291   Inherited Runners Scored: 88   Holds: 63

Cincinnati Reds

1997	Avg	G	AB	R	H	2B	3B	HR	RBI	BB	SO	HBP	GDP	SB	CS	OBP	SLG	IBB	SH	SF	#Pit	#P/PA	GB	FB	G/F
1997	.253	162	5484	651	1386	269	27	142	612	518	1113	45	105	190	67	.321	.389	35	75	30	22853	3.71	2045	1461	1.40

1997 Batting

	Avg	AB	H	2B	3B	HR	RBI	BB	SO	OBP	SLG		Avg	AB	H	2B	3B	HR	RBI	BB	SO	OBP	SLG
vs. Left	.252	1239	312	62	4	28	145	137	270	.332	.376	First Pitch	.325	769	250	41	7	26	121	26	0	.351	.498
vs. Right	.253	4245	1074	207	23	114	467	381	843	.317	.393	Ahead in Count	.321	1182	380	79	6	51	181	280	0	.452	.528
Groundball	.240	960	230	41	4	20	95	96	187	.313	.353	Behind in Count	.191	2512	481	92	9	39	181	0	959	.197	.282
Flyball	.231	732	169	33	5	22	73	60	159	.290	.380	Two Strikes	.171	2581	441	88	9	43	204	211	1113	.237	.262
Home	.264	2675	706	141	11	73	324	273	505	.335	.407	Leadoff	.250	689	172	23	8	8	37	52	104	.308	.341
Away	.242	2809	680	128	16	69	288	245	608	.306	.373	Batting #2	.270	664	179	34	4	14	62	62	128	.332	.396
Day	.251	2071	519	113	13	52	239	187	439	.317	.393	Batting #3	.271	634	172	40	2	16	71	73	79	.351	.416
Night	.254	3413	867	156	14	90	373	331	674	.323	.387	March/April	.243	849	206	40	2	16	83	87	144	.319	.370
Grass	.234	1879	439	74	9	48	183	166	401	.298	.359	May	.257	992	255	49	6	20	102	102	191	.328	.379
Turf	.263	3605	947	195	18	94	429	352	712	.332	.405	June	.257	880	226	51	1	19	93	69	157	.331	.382
Pre-All Star	.252	2917	736	147	17	61	307	275	542	.320	.377	July	.237	831	197	32	2	25	90	78	204	.307	.371
Post-All Star	.253	2567	650	122	10	81	305	243	571	.322	.403	August	.268	996	267	47	6	37	128	76	224	.324	.439
Scoring Posn	.226	1384	313	61	8	35	463	208	317	.327	.358	Sept/Oct	.251	936	235	48	3	25	116	106	193	.330	.389
Close & Late	.231	845	195	38	4	23	94	92	202	.309	.367	vs. AL	.272	497	135	32	1	13	66	42	82	.335	.419
None on/out	.244	1383	338	60	9	30	30	101	277	.299	.366	vs. NL	.251	4987	1251	237	26	129	546	476	1031	.319	.386

Cincinnati Reds

1997	ERA	W	L	Sv	Opp	G	IP	BB	SO	Avg	H	2B	3B	HR	RBI	OBP	SLG	CG	ShO	Sup	QS	#P/S	SB	CS	GB	FB	G/F
	4.41	76	86	49	63	162	1449.0	558	1159	256	1408	311	30	173	725	.330	.417	5	8	4.04	74	89	139	48	1826	1627	1.12

1997 Pitching

	ERA	W	L	Sv	G	GS	IP	H	HR	BB	SO		Avg	AB	H	2B	3B	HR	RBI	BB	SO	OBP	SLG
Home	4.40	40	41	27	309	81	740.0	699	91	283	617	vs. Left	.269	2038	549	125	12	62	274	217	380	.347	.434
Away	4.42	36	45	22	270	81	709.0	709	82	275	542	vs. Right	.247	3471	859	186	18	111	451	341	779	.320	.407
Day	5.29	21	39	12	224	60	534.1	559	72	235	427	Inning 1-0	.266	3726	991	219	20	128	517	384	741	.339	.439
Night	3.90	55	47	37	361	102	914.2	849	101	323	732	Inning 7+	.234	1783	417	92	10	45	200	174	418	.311	.372
Grass	4.87	21	34	13	193	55	476.1	505	59	194	358	None on	.239	3183	761	172	15	105	105	301	690	.311	.402
Turf	4.18	55	52	36	392	107	972.2	903	114	364	801	Runners on	.278	2326	647	139	15	68	620	257	469	.356	.439
March/April	6.36	7	18	4	105	25	216.2	258	28	121	182	Scoring Posn	.268	1390	373	76	6	38	526	194	306	.361	.414
May	3.22	13	16	7	105	29	268.1	232	30	84	224	Close & Late	.215	820	176	43	2	14	87	77	198	.290	.323
June	4.25	14	12	9	103	26	235.0	239	23	101	186	None on/out	.239	1395	333	82	7	53	53	115	287	.301	.422
July	4.19	11	14	6	76	25	219.1	192	36	69	171	vs. 1st Batr (relief)	.239	380	91	23	2	11	54	28	103	.304	.397
August	4.82	14	15	8	100	29	255.2	236	33	100	208	1st Inning Pitched	.249	1983	494	117	9	53	278	198	456	.328	.397
Sept/Oct	3.93	17	11	15	96	28	254.0	251	23	83	188	First 75 Pits (SP)	.267	576	154	30	3	21	90	54	111	.334	.439
Starters	4.67	60	66	0	162	162	914.1	911	115	347	657	Pitch 76-90	.273	411	112	25	2	14	48	49	68	.353	.445
Relievers	3.97	16	20	49	423	0	534.2	497	58	211	502	Pitch 91-105	.246	224	55	14	2	6	26	26	44	.324	.406
0-3 Days Rest (SP)	5.73	3	3	0	7	7	37.2	40	4	16	39	Pitch 106+	.283	60	17	4	0	4	19	13	6	.408	.550
4 Days Rest	4.21	32	25	0	75	75	446.2	417	48	163	307	First Pitch	.328	784	257	51	6	31	130	47	0	.375	.527
5+ Days Rest	5.04	25	38	0	80	80	430.0	454	63	168	311	Ahead in Count	.201	2636	530	113	11	52	241	0	983	.212	.311
vs. AL	4.02	9	6	5	50	15	132.0	118	15	46	116	Behind in Count	.333	1104	368	91	6	61	225	268	0	.462	.592
vs. NL	4.45	67	80	44	535	147	1317.0	1290	158	512	1043	Two Strikes	.174	2591	451	106	8	48	217	242	1159	.250	.277
Pre-All Star	4.40	38	48	23	328	86	772.1	763	86	321	624	Pre-All Star	.259	2946	763	165	15	86	382	321	624	.338	.413
Post-All Star	4.42	38	38	26	257	76	676.2	645	87	237	535	Post-All Star	.252	2563	645	146	15	87	343	237	535	.321	.422

Games Finished: 157   Inherited Runners: 246   Inherited Runners Scored: 89   Holds: 74

Colorado Rockies

1997 Record: 83 – 79

1997	Avg	G	AB	R	H	2B	3B	HR	RBI	BB	SO	HBP	GDP	SB	CS	OBP	SLG	IBB	SH	SF	#Pit	P/PA	GB	FB	G/F
	.288	162	5603	923	1611	269	40	239	869	562	1060	63	140	137	65	.357	.478	35	73	35	23080	3.64	2108	1515	1.39

1997 Batting

	Avg	AB	H	2B	3B	HR	RBI	BB	SO	OBP	SLG		Avg	AB	H	2B	3B	HR	RBI	BB	SO	OBP	SLG
vs. Left	.271	1332	361	64	7	51	185	126	243	.340	.444	First Pitch	.345	841	290	43	9	46	185	23	0	.369	.581
vs. Right	.293	4271	1250	205	33	188	684	436	817	.362	.488	Ahead in Count	.391	1208	472	78	10	85	275	305	0	.512	.683
Groundball	.314	1134	356	56	9	47	206	118	179	.382	.504	Behind in Count	.213	2497	531	97	11	59	249	0	894	.220	.331
Flyball	.288	909	262	45	9	55	145	94	188	.358	.539	Two Strikes	.188	2532	477	90	11	54	241	231	1060	.260	.297
Home	.321	2841	912	155	23	124	516	288	449	.386	.523	Leadoff	.275	654	180	42	6	8	63	92	67	.368	.394
Away	.253	2762	699	114	17	115	353	274	611	.327	.432	Batting #2	.300	660	198	23	3	34	93	81	111	.377	.498
Day	.302	2683	811	149	15	123	451	296	510	.376	.507	Batting #3	.347	639	222	46	4	49	136	81	108	.430	.662
Night	.274	2920	800	120	25	116	418	266	550	.340	.451	March/April	.316	841	266	41	5	38	159	93	153	.391	.512
Grass	.291	4559	1328	221	35	196	729	464	819	.361	.484	May	.266	987	263	44	6	39	143	112	173	.345	.442
Turf	.271	1044	283	48	5	43	140	98	241	.339	.450	June	.297	1018	302	48	9	44	166	102	183	.366	.491
Pre-All Star	.283	3030	857	138	22	123	472	318	558	.357	.465	July	.267	931	249	45	7	30	111	85	199	.334	.427
Post-All Star	.293	2573	754	131	18	116	397	244	502	.358	.493	August	.299	993	297	58	7	48	149	90	191	.361	.517
Scoring Posn	.295	1419	418	74	6	42	591	187	263	.376	.444	Sept/Oct	.281	833	234	33	6	40	141	80	161	.347	.479
Close & Late	.275	778	214	38	6	31	121	82	165	.346	.459	vs. AL	.295	572	169	34	3	24	88	46	108	.352	.491
None on/out	.276	1371	378	61	12	55	136	241	345	.345	.458	vs. NL	.287	5031	1442	235	37	215	781	516	952	.358	.476

1997	ERA	W	L	Sv	Opp	G	IP	BB	SO	Avg	H	2B	3B	HR	RBI	OBP	SLG	CG	ShO	Sup	QS	#P/S	SB	CS	GB	FB	G/F
	5.25	83	79	38	60	162	1432.2	566	870	300	1697	342	41	196	870	.367	.479	9	5	5.80	62	92	130	54	2360	1492	1.58

1997 Pitching

	ERA	W	L	Sv	G	GS	IP	H	HR	BB	SO		Avg	AB	H	2B	3B	HR	RBI	BB	SO	OBP	SLG
Home	5.67	47	34	19	305	81	738.0	932	121	263	451	vs. Left	.318	2663	847	179	22	93	442	291	380	.385	.507
Away	4.81	36	45	19	284	81	694.2	765	75	303	419	vs. Right	.284	2994	850	163	19	103	428	275	490	.352	.454
Day	5.17	42	35	20	283	77	680.1	808	80	267	429	Inning 1-6	.306	3867	1183	237	32	140	600	358	557	.369	.492
Night	5.32	41	44	18	306	85	752.1	889	116	299	441	Inning 7+	.287	1790	514	105	9	56	270	208	313	.364	.450
Grass	5.26	72	60	32	486	132	1175.1	1422	161	450	706	None on	.302	3054	922	175	19	113	113	277	458	.364	.483
Turf	5.21	11	19	6	103	30	257.1	275	35	116	164	Runners on	.298	2603	775	167	22	83	757	289	412	.371	.474
March/April	4.61	17	7	8	81	24	213.0	248	31	71	121	Scoring Posn	.284	1545	439	94	13	48	646	213	272	.371	.455
May	5.60	12	17	9	111	29	255.1	297	29	123	136	Close & Late	.284	767	218	44	6	21	130	100	140	.374	.439
June	5.65	14	15	2	111	29	255.0	310	34	117	158	None on/out	.304	1384	421	78	6	56	56	118	184	.361	.491
July	5.88	8	19	2	95	27	238.2	302	34	83	148	vs. 1st Batr (relief)	.310	384	119	25	2	13	48	36	71	.370	.487
August	4.94	17	12	9	101	29	253.0	297	29	98	153	1st Inning Pitched	.310	2067	641	114	17	76	270	243	359	.385	.492
Sept/Oct	4.67	15	9	8	90	24	217.2	243	39	74	154	First 75 Pits (SP)	.305	580	177	47	3	21	92	55	90	.367	.505
Starters	5.48	54	59	0	162	162	954.1	1177	143	363	526	Pitch 76-90	.327	499	163	35	6	15	78	48	80	.391	.511
Relievers	4.80	29	20	38	427	0	478.1	520	53	203	344	Pitch 91-105	.298	258	77	19	2	8	35	35	39	.391	.481
0-3 Days Rest (SP)	9.28	1	1	0	2	2	10.2	19	4	5	9	Pitch 106+	.313	99	31	6	2	7	20	10	12	.383	.626
4 Days Rest	5.52	31	32	0	90	90	541.0	651	73	223	297	First Pitch	.342	897	307	64	8	41	171	15	0	.362	.569
5+ Days Rest	5.32	22	26	0	70	70	402.2	507	66	135	220	Ahead in Count	.245	2313	567	108	10	55	275	0	739	.251	.372
vs. AL	5.43	9	7	2	59	16	141.0	167	14	57	94	Behind in Count	.356	1420	506	110	10	66	268	331	0	.478	.587
vs. NL	5.23	74	72	36	530	146	1291.2	1530	182	509	776	Two Strikes	.209	2217	463	83	8	53	248	220	870	.284	.325
Pre-All Star	5.36	43	45	19	324	88	772.1	916	100	329	445	Pre-All Star	.299	3064	916	194	18	100	476	329	445	.370	.472
Post-All Star	5.12	40	34	19	265	74	660.1	781	96	237	425	Post-All Star	.301	2593	781	148	23	96	394	237	425	.365	.487

Games Finished: 153   Inherited Runners: 239   Inherited Runners Scored: 86   Holds: 71

Florida Marlins

1997	Avg	G	AB	R	H	2B	3B	HR	RBI	BB	SO	HBP	GDP	SB	CS	OBP	SLG	IBB	SH	SF	#Pit	#P/PA	GB	FB	G/F
1997	259	162	5439	740	1410	272	28	136	703	686	1074	61	133	115	58	.346	.395	55	71	42	23625	3.75	2008	1502	1.34

1997 Batting

	Avg	AB	H	2B	3B	HR	RBI	BB	SO	OBP	SLG		Avg	AB	H	2B	3B	HR	RBI	BB	SO	OBP	SLG
vs. Left	.276	1014	280	56	4	33	149	139	195	.367	.437	First Pitch	.319	789	252	55	4	24	128	43	0	.362	.490
vs. Right	.255	4425	1130	216	24	103	554	547	879	.342	.385	Ahead in Count	.334	1239	414	79	9	46	224	321	0	.471	.524
Groundball	.251	868	218	47	5	16	98	108	147	.336	.372	Behind in Count	.195	2349	458	88	12	43	216	0	871	.203	.298
Flyball	.227	697	158	20	8	18	82	94	169	.321	.356	Two Strikes	.178	2488	443	82	9	45	231	322	1074	.277	.273
Home	.263	2616	689	121	17	63	343	369	511	.359	.395	Leadoff	.243	690	168	27	2	7	56	61	148	.312	.319
Away	.255	2823	721	151	11	73	360	317	563	.334	.394	Batting #2	.284	665	189	26	3	6	58	54	119	.340	.359
Day	.243	1701	413	78	5	42	197	221	312	.334	.369	Batting #3	.256	606	155	29	3	23	81	102	110	.368	.427
Night	.267	3738	997	194	23	94	506	465	762	.352	.406	March/April	.252	806	203	36	4	21	102	127	152	.359	.385
Grass	.260	4377	1139	210	25	111	557	560	854	.348	.396	May	.278	949	264	61	5	17	116	105	174	.357	.407
Turf	.255	1062	271	62	3	25	146	126	220	.339	.390	June	.243	906	220	46	6	16	106	120	187	.334	.360
Pre-All Star	.258	2876	743	155	16	56	345	368	551	.347	.382	July	.264	886	234	46	6	26	105	87	192	.336	.418
Post-All Star	.260	2563	667	117	12	80	358	318	523	.345	.409	August	.267	984	263	47	3	25	145	141	200	.360	.397
Scoring Posn	.259	1441	373	64	11	37	543	265	301	.370	.396	Sept/Oct	.249	908	226	36	4	31	129	106	169	.330	.400
Close & Late	.248	942	234	44	3	24	131	138	206	.349	.378	vs. AL	.260	506	129	29	2	10	72	66	93	.341	.379
None on/out	.265	1343	356	63	4	40	40	137	242	.339	.407	vs. NL	.260	4933	1281	243	26	126	631	620	981	.347	.396

1997	ERA	W	L	Sv	Opp	G	IP	BB	SO	Avg	H	2B	3B	HR	RBI	OBP	SLG	CG	ShO	Sup	QS	#P/S	SB	CS	GB	FB	G/F
1997	3.83	92	70	39	59	162	1446.2	639	1188	250	1353	232	49	131	638	.334	.384	12	10	4.60	95	101	95	70	1913	1494	1.28

1997 Pitching

	ERA	W	L	Sv	G	GS	IP	H	HR	BB	SO		Avg	AB	H	2B	3B	HR	RBI	BB	SO	OBP	SLG
Home	3.55	52	29	17	298	81	742.1	653	65	340	614	vs. Left	.256	2059	527	89	25	41	210	258	439	.342	.383
Away	4.11	40	41	22	268	81	704.1	700	66	299	574	vs. Right	.247	3345	826	143	24	90	428	381	749	.329	.385
Day	4.05	24	28	12	170	52	453.2	447	37	180	367	Inning 1-6	.249	3603	896	157	32	82	409	435	783	.333	.378
Night	3.73	68	42	27	396	110	993.0	906	94	459	821	Inning 7+	.254	1801	457	75	17	49	229	204	405	.335	.396
Grass	3.84	75	57	29	467	132	1182.1	1100	103	535	960	None on	.249	3017	751	132	31	85	85	330	695	.329	.398
Turf	3.75	17	13	10	99	30	264.1	253	28	104	228	Runners on	.252	2387	602	100	18	46	553	309	493	.340	.367
March/April	3.75	15	10	7	79	25	220.2	189	12	89	154	Scoring Posn	.238	1388	330	52	13	24	484	211	303	.336	.346
May	3.10	16	11	8	92	27	247.0	227	23	85	217	Close & Late	.247	923	228	35	11	28	127	114	219	.335	.420
June	3.94	17	11	10	92	28	244.1	225	18	116	204	None on/out	.252	1344	339	64	15	44	44	156	293	.335	.420
July	4.09	13	13	4	89	26	233.0	220	26	112	202	vs. 1st Batr (relief)	.246	341	84	14	7	7	30	55	85	.356	.390
August	3.44	19	10	6	103	29	261.1	237	22	103	227	1st Inning Pitched	.264	1921	507	87	18	46	285	256	429	.354	.400
Sept/Oct	4.68	12	15	4	111	27	240.1	255	30	114	184	First 75 Pits (SP)	.250	569	142	22	5	11	54	65	110	.329	.364
Starters	3.76	64	49	0	162	162	988.1	905	88	423	801	Pitch 76-90	.252	489	123	17	10	16	69	54	98	.330	.425
Relievers	3.97	28	21	39	404	0	458.1	448	43	216	387	Pitch 91-105	.228	369	84	16	3	12	43	43	79	.320	.385
0-3 Days Rest (SP)	7.36	1	0	0	2	2	11.0	13	2	9	13	Pitch 106+	.221	244	54	8	4	6	24	23	56	.288	.361
4 Days Rest	3.47	35	30	0	91	91	567.1	520	40	229	451	First Pitch	.325	684	222	32	4	24	102	34	0	.362	.488
5+ Days Rest	4.06	28	19	0	69	69	410.0	372	46	185	337	Ahead in Count	.194	2471	479	85	19	39	220	0	967	.203	.291
vs. AL	3.55	12	3	3	62	15	137.0	115	8	81	118	Behind in Count	.325	1158	376	76	14	42	181	317	0	.470	.523
vs. NL	3.86	80	67	36	504	147	1309.2	1238	123	558	1070	Two Strikes	.173	2629	455	88	22	39	243	288	1188	.258	.268
Pre-All Star	3.65	50	36	26	284	86	765.0	703	59	323	604	Pre-All Star	.247	2843	703	130	33	59	321	323	603	.339	.378
Post-All Star	4.03	42	34	13	282	76	681.2	650	72	316	584	Post-All Star	.254	2561	650	102	16	72	317	316	584	.330	.390

Games Finished: 150   Inherited Runners: 184   Inherited Runners Scored: 58   Holds: 60

Houston Astros

1997	Avg	G	AB	R	H	2B	3B	HR	RBI	BB	SO	HBP	GDP	SB	CS	OBP	SLG	IBB	SH	SF	#Pit	#P/PA	GB	FB	G/F
1997	259	162	5502	777	1427	314	40	133	720	633	1085	100	104	171	74	.344	.403	63	74	53	23482	3.69	2049	1515	1.35

1997 Batting

	Avg	AB	H	2B	3B	HR	RBI	BB	SO	OBP	SLG		Avg	AB	H	2B	3B	HR	RBI	BB	SO	OBP	SLG
vs. Left	.252	1297	327	69	9	25	155	157	245	.337	.377	First Pitch	.338	807	273	70	7	24	126	46	0	.388	.532
vs. Right	.262	4205	1100	245	31	108	565	476	840	.345	.412	Ahead in Count	.312	1146	357	85	12	43	206	344	0	.470	.519
Groundball	.263	822	216	39	11	15	116	94	177	.342	.398	Behind in Count	.211	2503	527	104	12	41	238	0	906	.225	.311
Flyball	.256	750	192	57	2	24	109	93	145	.345	.433	Two Strikes	.188	2566	482	96	12	37	227	242	1085	.267	.278
Home	.257	2653	682	152	23	59	345	294	520	.341	.398	Leadoff	.307	648	199	41	8	22	82	87	109	.412	.497
Away	.261	2849	745	162	17	74	375	339	565	.346	.408	Batting #2	.294	673	198	42	6	17	90	61	105	.361	.450
Day	.252	1681	424	102	7	37	218	198	330	.342	.387	Batting #3	.289	588	170	43	3	44	138	130	126	.426	.597
Night	.262	3821	1003	212	33	96	502	435	755	.344	.411	March/April	.249	887	221	47	5	17	105	94	181	.329	.371
Grass	.260	2058	535	103	14	49	260	248	406	.345	.395	May	.256	954	244	65	5	23	111	102	183	.334	.407
Turf	.259	3444	892	211	26	84	460	385	679	.343	.409	June	.258	934	241	47	4	19	111	123	177	.347	.378
Pre-All Star	.253	2964	751	168	17	64	350	340	571	.335	.386	July	.260	885	230	43	10	25	134	92	180	.337	.416
Post-All Star	.266	2538	676	146	23	69	370	293	514	.353	.424	August	.259	959	248	55	6	26	126	126	185	.352	.410
Scoring Posn	.260	1499	389	85	14	26	551	209	302	.366	.387	Sept/Oct	.275	883	243	57	10	23	133	96	179	.362	.441
Close & Late	.234	1002	234	48	6	23	118	141	242	.337	.362	vs. AL	.245	478	117	20	4	8	43	47	79	.321	.354
None on/out	.252	1370	345	82	9	38	38	121	269	.322	.408	vs. NL	.261	5024	1310	294	36	125	677	586	1006	.346	.408

Houston Astros

1997	ERA	W	L	Sv	Opp	G	IP	BB	SO	Avg	H	2B	3B	HR	RBI	OBP	SLG	CG	ShO	Sup	QS	#P/S	SB	CS	GB	FB	G/F
1997	3.66	84	78	37	59	162	1459.0	511	1138	252	1379	255	23	134	631	319	380	16	12	4.79	97	98	92	57	2144	1333	1.61

1997 Pitching

	ERA	W	L	Sv	G	GS	IP	H	HR	BB	SO		Avg	AB	H	2B	3B	HR	RBI	BB	SO	OBP	SLG
Home	3.29	46	35	15	248	81	747.0	667	56	221	659	vs. Left	.258	2217	571	102	10	57	260	248	421	.333	.390
Away	4.06	38	43	22	200	81	712.0	712	78	290	479	vs. Right	.247	3266	808	153	13	77	371	263	717	.309	.373
Day	3.39	27	23	13	162	50	443.2	393	34	173	355	Inning 1-6	.253	3040	823	167	15	89	406	317	692	.317	.381
Night	3.78	57	55	24	354	112	1015.1	986	100	338	783	Inning 7+	.248	1840	456	88	8	45	225	194	446	.324	.378
Grass	4.15	26	32	17	196	58	512.0	517	56	214	340	None on	.247	3117	771	137	12	80	80	267	647	.312	.376
Turf	3.40	58	46	20	320	104	947.0	862	78	297	798	Runners on	.257	2366	608	118	11	54	551	244	491	.328	.385
March/April	3.17	15	11	10	77	26	235.2	203	19	73	184	Scoring Posn	.255	1315	335	64	4	27	469	179	293	.340	.371
May	4.29	11	17	4	100	28	251.2	265	24	102	197	Close & Late	.269	1031	277	43	5	28	146	113	230	.347	.402
June	4.40	14	14	7	90	28	247.2	261	28	93	183	None on/out	.260	1375	358	65	5	32	32	123	261	.326	.385
July	2.95	19	7	8	73	26	240.2	205	10	60	186	vs. 1st Batr (relief)	.228	303	69	10	1	6	54	36	93	.313	.327
August	3.85	11	17	3	90	28	252.1	249	33	87	187	1st Inning Pitched	.249	1712	427	74	6	43	270	203	433	.332	.375
Sept/Oct	3.23	14	12	5	86	26	231.0	196	20	96	201	First 75 Pits (SP)	.247	611	151	27	5	17	67	54	111	.310	.391
Starters	3.61	62	50	0	162	162	1043.0	1003	99	344	722	Pitch 76-90	.252	516	130	23	1	11	55	43	96	.310	.364
Relievers	3.81	22	28	37	354	0	416.0	376	35	167	416	Pitch 91-105	.237	333	79	18	1	11	34	35	55	.316	.396
0-3 Days Rest (SP)	3.83	3	1	0	7	7	40.0	43	2	14	30	Pitch 106+	.246	203	50	10	2	3	17	18	44	.313	.360
4 Days Rest	3.55	40	33	0	98	98	646.2	616	57	213	443	First Pitch	.331	836	277	57	6	25	112	9	0	.344	.504
5+ Days Rest	3.69	19	16	0	57	57	356.1	344	40	117	249	Ahead in Count	.189	2528	479	77	8	42	215	0	957	.199	.276
vs. AL	4.57	4	11	0	40	15	130.0	138	14	48	81	Behind in Count	.330	1112	367	79	5	45	192	280	0	.461	.531
vs. NL	3.58	80	67	37	147	147	1329.0	1241	120	463	1057	Two Strikes	.176	2596	456	72	8	40	212	222	1138	.247	.256
Pre-All Star	3.97	43	45	22	285	88	789.0	783	76	283	613	Post-All Star	.260	3009	783	144	14	76	365	283	613	.327	.393
Post-All Star	3.30	41	33	15	231	74	670.0	596	58	228	525	Pre-All Star	.241	2474	596	111	9	58	266	228	525	.309	.363

Games Finished: 146   Inherited Runners: 226   Inherited Runners Scored: 86   Holds: 32

Los Angeles Dodgers

1997 Record: 88 – 74

1997	Avg	G	AB	R	H	2B	3B	HR	RBI	BB	SO	HBP	GDP	SB	CS	OBP	SLG	IBB	SH	SF	#Pit	#P/PA	GB	FB	G/F
1997	268	162	5544	742	1488	242	33	174	706	498	1079	33	108	131	64	330	418	46	105	36	22582	3.63	2061	1402	1.47

1997 Batting

	Avg	AB	H	2B	3B	HR	RBI	BB	SO	OBP	SLG		Avg	AB	H	2B	3B	HR	RBI	BB	SO	OBP	SLG
vs. Left	.265	1463	388	78	5	45	179	133	274	.327	.418	First Pitch	.314	792	249	40	5	27	112	33	0	.346	.480
vs. Right	.270	4081	1100	164	28	129	527	365	805	.332	.418	Ahead in Count	.363	1124	408	65	6	66	238	271	0	.485	.608
Groundball	.269	886	238	46	8	19	110	78	175	.303	.403	Behind in Count	.206	2577	531	89	15	46	218	0	929	.211	.306
Flyball	.238	664	158	24	5	18	68	57	152	.299	.370	Two Strikes	.188	2558	480	86	12	43	199	194	1079	.247	.281
Home	.265	2667	708	114	14	85	332	248	492	.330	.414	Leadoff	.276	680	188	25	10	3	52	59	99	.336	.356
Away	.271	2877	780	128	19	89	374	250	587	.331	.422	Batting #2	.276	675	186	23	6	18	71	42	109	.318	.407
Day	.280	1613	452	76	13	51	228	161	341	.348	.438	Batting #3	.330	646	213	35	2	46	136	63	100	.391	.604
Night	.264	3931	1036	166	20	123	478	337	738	.323	.410	March/April	.254	814	207	28	6	18	83	85	135	.327	.370
Grass	.269	4533	1221	194	23	151	575	399	855	.330	.422	May	.243	934	227	49	6	27	97	70	185	.296	.395
Turf	.264	1011	267	48	10	23	131	99	224	.331	.400	June	.271	980	266	46	6	37	137	96	177	.337	.444
Pre-All Star	.262	2940	769	137	19	87	351	267	533	.324	.410	July	.296	922	273	45	5	38	145	73	180	.350	.479
Post-All Star	.276	2604	719	105	14	87	355	231	546	.337	.427	August	.270	1023	276	37	3	25	124	105	218	.339	.385
Scoring Posn	.265	1404	372	63	14	38	516	177	294	.342	.411	Sept/Oct	.274	871	239	37	7	29	120	69	184	.332	.433
Close & Late	.239	938	224	33	5	29	117	109	208	.318	.377	vs. AL	.284	560	159	27	3	22	83	43	97	.338	.461
None on/out	.288	1404	405	58	8	46	46	111	265	.344	.439	vs. NL	.267	4984	1329	215	30	152	623	455	982	.330	.413

1997	ERA	W	L	Sv	Opp	G	IP	BB	SO	Avg	H	2B	3B	HR	RBI	OBP	SLG	CG	ShO	Sup	QS	#P/S	SB	CS	GB	FB	G/F
1997	3.62	88	74	45	65	162	1459.1	546	1232	241	1325	257	32	163	612	313	389	6	6	4.58	96	100	118	58	1821	1518	1.20

1997 Pitching

	ERA	W	L	Sv	G	GS	IP	H	HR	BB	SO		Avg	AB	H	2B	3B	HR	RBI	BB	SO	OBP	SLG
Home	3.00	47	34	24	280	81	746.0	613	76	246	616	vs. Left	.256	2606	666	120	16	78	298	295	510	.333	.404
Away	4.26	41	40	21	294	81	713.1	712	87	300	616	vs. Right	.228	2887	659	137	16	85	314	251	722	.295	.375
Day	3.78	27	20	12	163	47	419.1	393	56	154	347	Inning 1-6	.240	3637	874	175	22	109	404	369	842	.315	.390
Night	3.56	61	54	33	411	115	1040.0	932	107	392	885	Inning 7+	.243	1856	451	82	10	54	204	177	390	.311	.385
Grass	3.54	72	61	38	478	133	1207.2	1079	134	449	989	None on	.245	3217	787	153	16	107	107	283	717	.310	.402
Turf	4.01	16	13	7	96	29	251.2	246	29	97	243	Runners on	.236	2276	538	104	16	56	505	263	515	.318	.370
March/April	3.24	13	11	8	99	24	222.1	182	16	88	176	Scoring Posn	.229	1326	304	68	11	23	421	202	335	.331	.349
May	2.89	13	15	7	92	28	249.1	217	19	87	211	Close & Late	.232	957	222	33	4	31	119	106	207	.308	.372
June	4.38	13	16	4	99	29	256.2	241	35	112	230	None on/out	.252	1407	355	82	9	43	43	106	282	.308	.415
July	2.87	20	7	12	91	27	241.2	232	24	85	182	vs. 1st Batr (relief)	.217	360	78	17	3	6	35	43	92	.301	.331
August	3.27	19	11	10	94	30	269.2	237	32	73	180	First 75 Pits (SP)	.255	1914	489	93	15	55	264	200	411	.329	.406
Sept/Oct	5.20	10	14	2	99	24	219.2	216	37	101	180	Pitch 76-90	.229	547	125	22	1	13	46	53	147	.300	.344
Starters	3.73	63	52	0	162	162	1014.1	928	115	373	863	Pitch 91-105	.298	524	156	33	4	20	74	57	112	.374	.490
Relievers	3.38	25	22	45	412	0	445.0	397	48	173	369	Pitch 106+	.180	356	64	13	2	8	36	40	79	.272	.295
0-3 Days Rest (SP)	1.95	2	0	0	5	5	32.1	25	2	11	19	First Pitch	.308	769	237	50	4	31	121	24	0	.337	.505
4 Days Rest	3.88	37	30	0	91	91	578.0	513	70	208	488	Ahead in Count	.162	2480	401	66	9	34	165	0	1020	.167	.237
5+ Days Rest	3.65	24	22	0	66	66	404.0	390	43	154	356	Behind in Count	.349	1213	423	87	14	58	190	267	0	.465	.587
vs. AL	4.31	9	7	5	58	16	142.0	137	23	65	122	Two Strikes	.148	2610	386	71	9	43	178	253	1232	.227	.231
vs. NL	3.55	79	67	40	516	146	1317.1	1188	140	481	1110	Pre-All Star	.236	2911	688	151	13	77	313	308	654	.312	.377
Pre-All Star	3.43	45	42	23	312	87	782.1	688	77	308	654	Post-All Star	.247	2582	637	106	19	86	299	238	578	.315	.402
Post-All Star	3.84	43	32	22	262	75	677.0	637	86	238	578												

Games Finished: 156   Inherited Runners: 217   Inherited Runners Scored: 49   Holds: 75

Montreal Expos

	Avg	G	AB	R	H	2B	3B	HR	RBI	BB	SO	HBP	GDP	SB	CS	OBP	SLG	IBB	SH	SF	#Pit	P/PA	GB	FB	G/F
1997	.258	162	5526	691	1423	339	34	172	659	420	1084	73	96	75	46	.316	.425	40	72	40	21545	3.51	2030	1485	1.37

1997 Batting

	Avg	AB	H	2B	3B	HR	RBI	BB	SO	OBP	SLG		Avg	AB	H	2B	3B	HR	RBI	BB	SO	OBP	SLG
vs. Left	.244	1441	352	73	7	47	169	122	275	.309	.402	First Pitch	.339	874	296	69	8	32	110	30	0	.368	.546
vs. Right	.262	4085	1071	266	27	125	490	298	809	.319	.432	Ahead in Count	.344	1141	392	105	2	58	200	222	0	.448	.592
Groundball	.259	1237	321	86	6	38	137	84	260	.317	.431	Behind in Count	.187	2559	479	108	14	53	205	0	936	.199	.302
Flyball	.262	660	173	43	4	31	96	52	140	.321	.480	Two Strikes	.161	2445	393	90	16	43	182	167	1084	.223	.263
Home	.267	2703	723	187	19	81	339	221	527	.330	.441	Leadoff	.274	675	185	45	4	5	53	42	103	.331	.375
Away	.248	2823	700	152	15	91	320	199	557	.303	.409	Batting #2	.279	663	185	53	4	20	73	52	104	.336	.462
Day	.280	1819	510	116	10	65	224	139	347	.336	.462	Batting #3	.270	664	179	42	6	26	93	32	117	.317	.468
Night	.246	3707	913	223	24	107	435	281	737	.306	.406	March/April	.279	821	229	63	6	30	114	63	155	.331	.480
Grass	.262	1980	518	102	6	70	232	147	383	.317	.425	May	.290	953	276	56	3	29	134	79	179	.353	.446
Turf	.255	3546	905	237	28	102	427	273	701	.316	.424	June	.255	928	237	62	6	25	99	72	193	.317	.416
Pre-All Star	.273	2911	794	194	16	90	368	231	566	.332	.443	July	.237	903	214	52	7	27	105	66	172	.298	.400
Post-All Star	.241	2615	629	145	18	82	291	189	518	.299	.404	August	.250	999	250	50	5	31	110	77	181	.309	.403
Scoring Posn	.244	1295	316	76	10	39	463	161	269	.320	.435	Sept/Oct	.235	922	217	56	7	30	97	63	204	.289	.409
Close & Late	.247	937	231	47	5	27	115	86	200	.320	.394	vs. AL	.249	503	125	30	2	20	58	42	99	.313	.435
None on/out	.262	1418	372	95	8	33	33	73	260	.307	.410	vs. NL	.258	5023	1298	309	32	152	601	378	985	.317	.423

	ERA	W	L	Sv	Opp	G	IP	BB	SO	Avg	H	2B	3B	HR	RBI	OBP	SLG	CG	ShO	Sup	QS	P/S	#P	SB	CS	GB	FB	G/F
1997	4.14	78	84	37	55	162	1447.0	557	1138	.251	1365	253	38	149	699	.325	.393	27	14	4.30	82	90	192	42	1966	1454	1.35

1997 Pitching

	ERA	W	L	Sv	G	GS	IP	H	HR	BB	SO		Avg	AB	H	2B	3B	HR	RBI	BB	SO	OBP	SLG
Home	3.99	45	36	19	269	81	742.0	696	69	272	590	vs. Left	.252	2290	577	106	13	55	289	295	439	.339	.382
Away	4.29	33	48	18	283	81	705.0	669	80	285	548	vs. Right	.250	3158	788	147	25	94	410	262	699	.314	.401
Day	4.46	26	26	11	180	52	464.0	410	56	184	365	Inning 1-6	.249	3644	909	178	23	94	471	381	749	.326	.388
Night	3.98	52	58	26	372	110	983.0	955	93	373	773	Inning 7+	.253	1804	456	75	15	55	228	176	389	.323	.402
Grass	4.00	23	33	11	197	56	488.1	457	54	196	367	None on	.249	3130	779	141	20	89	89	252	661	.311	.392
Turf	4.21	55	51	26	355	106	958.2	908	95	361	771	Runners on	.253	2318	586	112	18	60	610	305	477	.342	.394
March/April	4.94	12	12	6	89	24	209.2	206	21	97	141	Scoring Posn	.254	1387	352	63	12	33	529	227	292	.357	.388
May	4.04	16	12	9	105	28	247.0	225	26	105	190	Close & Late	.250	957	239	38	7	29	133	111	220	.331	.395
June	2.99	17	11	7	73	28	250.0	205	19	89	196	None on/out	.267	1380	369	62	11	42	42	111	269	.327	.420
July	4.86	10	16	5	87	26	237.0	247	31	74	197	vs. 1st Batr (relief)	.320	341	109	16	4	13	57	40	67	.395	.504
August	4.48	12	17	5	99	29	255.0	251	28	103	220	1st Inning Pitched	.261	1802	470	83	15	46	302	243	371	.351	.400
Sept/Oct	3.66	11	16	5	99	27	248.1	231	24	89	194	First 75 Pits (SP)	.245	534	131	22	4	18	69	51	120	.321	.403
Starters	3.93	57	57	0	162	162	965.2	876	97	346	773	Pitch 76-90	.245	433	106	18	3	12	47	34	79	.304	.383
Relievers	4.54	21	27	37	390	0	481.1	489	52	211	365	Pitch 91-105	.212	278	59	11	1	8	34	25	54	.277	.345
0-3 Days Rest (SP)	7.47	1	1	0	4	4	15.2	15	1	9	8	Pitch 106+	.230	187	43	8	1	6	16	12	48	.282	.380
4 Days Rest	3.72	31	35	0	89	89	553.1	489	60	202	471	First Pitch	.319	797	254	56	7	32	110	40	0	.362	.527
5+ Days Rest	4.08	25	21	0	69	69	396.2	372	36	136	293	Ahead in Count	.171	2539	433	73	12	37	199	0	995	.179	.252
vs. AL	2.29	12	3	5	40	15	137.2	97	11	36	116	Behind in Count	.366	1119	410	87	11	47	251	294	0	.494	.590
vs. NL	4.33	66	81	32	512	147	1309.1	1268	138	521	1022	Two Strikes	.161	2498	402	68	14	41	203	223	1138	.235	.249
Pre-All Star	4.05	47	39	23	286	86	764.1	697	73	314	579	Pre-All Star	.243	2866	697	141	24	73	359	314	579	.323	.386
Post-All Star	4.23	31	45	14	266	76	682.2	668	76	243	559	Post-All Star	.259	2582	668	112	14	76	340	243	559	.327	.401

Games Finished: 135   Inherited Runners: 251   Inherited Runners Scored: 80   Holds: 30

New York Mets

	Avg	G	AB	R	H	2B	3B	HR	RBI	BB	SO	HBP	GDP	SB	CS	OBP	SLG	IBB	SH	SF	#Pit	P/PA	GB	FB	G/F
1997	.262	162	5524	777	1448	274	28	153	741	550	1029	57	122	97	74	.332	.405	45	58	59	22890	3.66	2058	1487	1.38

1997 Batting

	Avg	AB	H	2B	3B	HR	RBI	BB	SO	OBP	SLG		Avg	AB	H	2B	3B	HR	RBI	BB	SO	OBP	SLG
vs. Left	.265	1510	400	77	5	40	217	166	265	.343	.402	First Pitch	.322	720	232	39	2	24	119	25	0	.351	.482
vs. Right	.261	4014	1048	197	23	113	524	384	764	.328	.406	Ahead in Count	.351	1273	447	110	6	60	249	312	0	.476	.588
Groundball	.291	1090	317	50	4	20	161	117	192	.361	.399	Behind in Count	.200	2472	494	78	12	36	213	0	857	.207	.285
Flyball	.251	748	188	37	2	29	91	58	175	.305	.422	Two Strikes	.173	2442	422	69	12	47	228	212	1029	.244	.269
Home	.274	2688	737	146	15	74	382	281	473	.345	.422	Leadoff	.265	676	179	32	9	10	56	69	113	.340	.383
Away	.251	2836	711	128	13	79	359	269	556	.319	.389	Batting #2	.293	663	194	33	2	11	74	62	102	.355	.398
Day	.270	2158	583	104	5	67	321	216	386	.339	.416	Batting #3	.295	614	181	36	2	28	125	100	80	.396	.497
Night	.257	3366	865	170	23	86	420	334	643	.327	.398	March/April	.244	902	220	45	2	17	114	92	165	.316	.355
Grass	.265	4599	1219	233	20	125	621	461	823	.335	.406	May	.279	909	254	48	7	28	132	95	150	.348	.440
Turf	.248	925	229	41	8	28	120	89	206	.319	.400	June	.273	889	243	47	6	29	112	86	175	.342	.438
Pre-All Star	.268	2926	784	152	16	79	389	297	516	.337	.412	July	.264	902	238	42	5	25	122	96	162	.337	.405
Post-All Star	.256	2598	664	122	12	74	352	253	513	.326	.397	August	.275	998	274	56	4	22	136	90	157	.337	.409
Scoring Posn	.291	1381	402	80	9	33	561	184	263	.369	.434	Sept/Oct	.237	924	219	36	2	32	125	91	220	.312	.384
Close & Late	.265	961	255	40	4	31	161	133	185	.356	.412	vs. AL	.275	520	143	36	0	13	62	45	90	.340	.419
None on/out	.260	1374	357	65	8	44	44	132	246	.331	.415	vs. NL	.261	5004	1305	238	28	140	679	505	939	.331	.403

New York Mets

1997	ERA	W	L	Sv	Opp	G	IP	BB	SO	Avg	H	2B	3B	HR	RBI	OBP	SLG	CG	ShO	Sup	QS	#P/S	SB	CS	GB	FB	G/F
	3.95	88	74	49	78	162	1459.1	504	982	262	1452	282	35	160	669	326	411	7	8	4.79	96	92	106	44	2143	1387	1.55

1997 Pitching

	ERA	W	L	Sv	G	GS	IP	H	HR	BB	SO		Avg	AB	H	2B	3B	HR	RBI	BB	SO	OBP	SLG
Home	3.55	50	31	25	258	81	747.0	703	71	250	542	vs. Left	.273	2416	659	123	21	69	300	248	420	.341	.427
Away	4.36	38	43	24	280	81	712.1	749	85	254	440	vs. Right	.253	3135	793	159	14	91	369	256	562	.314	.400
Day	3.99	38	26	20	208	64	570.0	576	62	196	357	Inning 1-6	.263	3704	973	186	26	102	449	319	601	.321	.410
Night	3.92	50	48	29	330	98	889.1	876	98	308	625	Inning 7+	.259	1847	479	96	9	58	220	185	351	.330	.415
Grass	3.95	75	60	42	446	135	1226.2	1199	138	442	835	None on	.258	3206	828	142	23	93	93	257	580	.318	.404
Turf	3.91	13	14	7	92	27	232.2	253	22	62	147	Runners on	.266	2345	624	140	12	67	576	247	420	.336	.422
March/April	3.34	12	14	8	88	26	242.2	216	22	90	153	Scoring Posn	.260	1351	351	77	7	34	479	183	256	.345	.403
May	3.21	18	9	9	83	27	238.1	227	25	76	153	Close & Late	.260	992	258	55	6	28	123	111	193	.336	.412
June	4.76	15	12	7	90	27	238.1	282	31	74	158	None on/out	.248	1399	347	58	13	38	38	102	243	.305	.390
July	4.54	15	11	12	90	26	230.0	234	27	80	139	vs. 1st Batr (relief)	.289	329	95	20	1	12	44	36	69	.363	.465
August	4.38	13	16	6	100	29	263.0	275	32	94	164	1st Inning Pitched	.269	1876	504	97	7	60	272	192	377	.339	.424
Sept/Oct	3.46	15	12	7	87	27	247.0	218	23	90	215	First 75 Pits (SP)	.288	611	176	30	5	14	71	54	83	.348	.422
Starters	3.90	61	48	0	162	162	993.2	990	106	317	621	Pitch 76-90	.248	468	116	33	3	12	56	47	72	.322	.408
Relievers	4.04	27	26	49	376	0	465.2	462	54	187	361	Pitch 91-105	.244	279	68	13	2	10	27	31	42	.321	.412
0-3 Days Rest (SP)	2.59	1	2	0	5	5	31.1	30	2	6	15	Pitch 106+	.264	106	28	8	0	1	10	10	16	.342	.368
4 Days Rest	3.69	31	23	0	78	78	478.0	458	46	156	307	First Pitch	.298	890	265	57	7	28	119	30	0	.329	.472
5+ Days Rest	4.20	29	23	0	79	79	484.1	502	58	155	299	Ahead in Count	.201	2452	493	94	9	40	200	0	835	.206	.296
vs. AL	4.58	7	8	6	51	15	133.2	130	29	54	98	Behind in Count	.345	1187	410	82	12	59	208	257	0	.460	.584
vs. NL	3.88	81	66	43	487	147	1325.2	1322	131	446	884	Two Strikes	.192	2411	464	80	14	40	186	216	982	.261	.287
Pre-All Star	3.88	48	38	26	284	86	774.1	788	88	355	502	Pre-All Star	.267	2955	788	151	17	88	345	255	502	.327	.419
Post-All Star	4.02	40	36	23	254	76	685.0	664	72	249	480	Post-All Star	.256	2596	664	131	18	72	324	249	480	.324	.403

Games Finished: 155   Inherited Runners: 169   Inherited Runners Scored: 64   Holds: 43

Philadelphia Phillies

1997 Record: 68 – 94

1997	Avg	G	AB	R	H	2B	3B	HR	RBI	BB	SO	HBP	GDP	SB	CS	OBP	SLG	IBB	SH	SF	#Pit	#P/PA	GB	FB	G/F
	.255	162	5443	668	1390	290	35	116	622	519	1032	40	105	92	56	322	385	32	74	50	22677	3.70	1934	1515	1.28

1997 Batting

	Avg	AB	H	2B	3B	HR	RBI	BB	SO	OBP	SLG		Avg	AB	H	2B	3B	HR	RBI	BB	SO	OBP	SLG
vs. Left	.260	1336	348	69	7	30	185	142	253	.332	.390	First Pitch	.341	757	258	65	6	18	119	21	0	.359	.514
vs. Right	.254	4107	1042	221	28	86	437	377	779	.319	.384	Ahead in Count	.334	1180	394	86	11	44	197	292	0	.466	.537
Groundball	.265	871	231	49	9	19	109	87	171	.332	.408	Behind in Count	.190	2511	476	85	9	36	199	0	884	.194	.274
Flyball	.240	867	208	56	4	21	92	85	202	.309	.386	Two Strikes	.177	2491	440	80	11	37	191	205	1032	.242	.262
Home	.265	2687	713	153	19	61	328	287	497	.339	.405	Leadoff	.263	676	178	35	9	8	54	68	80	.331	.377
Away	.246	2756	677	137	16	55	294	232	535	.305	.367	Batting #2	.292	643	188	45	2	3	50	61	99	.357	.383
Day	.261	1719	449	83	7	31	177	155	319	.323	.372	Batting #3	.259	626	162	36	6	16	80	76	104	.342	.412
Night	.253	3724	941	207	28	85	445	364	713	.321	.392	March/April	.233	808	188	41	2	12	82	80	160	.305	.333
Grass	.246	2009	495	93	9	40	210	174	389	.307	.361	May	.249	958	239	54	5	23	90	76	157	.306	.388
Turf	.261	3434	895	197	26	76	412	345	643	.331	.400	June	.244	874	213	54	10	13	87	91	172	.315	.373
Pre-All Star	.246	2847	700	164	17	58	285	268	521	.312	.377	July	.272	875	238	47	7	25	116	112	158	.355	.427
Post-All Star	.266	2596	690	126	18	58	337	251	511	.333	.395	August	.274	942	258	46	0	20	130	72	172	.329	.398
Scoring Posn	.256	1386	355	74	8	29	484	175	275	.333	.384	Sept/Oct	.258	986	254	48	11	23	117	88	213	.321	.399
Close & Late	.266	758	202	39	7	18	99	78	146	.334	.408	vs. AL	.244	505	123	24	4	9	44	39	95	.299	.360
None on/out	.268	1360	364	80	12	28	28	113	212	.327	.406	vs. NL	.257	4938	1267	266	31	107	578	480	937	.324	.388

1997	ERA	W	L	Sv	Opp	G	IP	BB	SO	Avg	H	2B	3B	HR	RBI	OBP	SLG	CG	ShO	Sup	QS	#P/S	SB	CS	GB	FB	G/F
	4.85	68	94	35	50	162	1420.1	616	1209	265	1441	341	43	171	807	342	437	13	7	4.26	80	99	107	57	1791	1548	1.16

1997 Pitching

	ERA	W	L	Sv	G	GS	IP	H	HR	BB	SO		Avg	AB	H	2B	3B	HR	RBI	BB	SO	OBP	SLG
Home	4.26	38	43	17	289	81	743.0	714	81	271	638	vs. Left	.273	2288	624	135	30	66	335	297	473	.358	.444
Away	5.49	30	51	18	282	81	677.1	727	90	345	571	vs. Right	.259	3155	817	206	13	105	472	319	736	.331	.432
Day	5.20	20	31	12	182	51	445.0	471	50	187	401	Inning 1-6	.264	3698	978	241	27	125	555	407	833	.340	.446
Night	4.69	48	63	23	389	111	975.1	970	121	429	808	Inning 7+	.265	1745	463	100	16	46	252	209	376	.346	.420
Grass	5.73	20	39	13	208	59	490.0	531	72	266	422	None on	.255	3097	789	184	27	96	96	286	720	.324	.425
Turf	4.38	48	55	22	363	103	930.1	910	99	350	787	Runners on	.278	2346	652	157	16	75	711	330	489	.365	.454
March/April	4.42	8	16	5	88	24	212.0	205	18	102	153	Scoring Posn	.276	1446	399	97	14	39	610	234	324	.370	.443
May	5.67	11	18	7	105	29	251.0	258	38	122	192	Close & Late	.257	775	199	40	5	17	105	105	188	.347	.387
June	5.92	4	22	2	103	26	225.0	262	29	117	189	None on/out	.252	1339	337	67	13	47	47	131	288	.326	.426
July	5.91	10	16	5	94	26	225.1	248	38	108	212	vs. 1st Batr (relief)	.217	359	78	20	2	10	42	45	68	.310	.368
August	3.25	17	10	7	84	27	244.0	219	14	96	220	1st Inning Pitched	.269	1964	529	111	13	62	342	269	424	.359	.434
Sept/Oct	4.07	18	12	9	97	30	263.0	249	34	71	243	First 75 Pits (SP)	.311	515	160	40	3	21	83	38	107	.366	.522
Starters	4.63	51	71	0	162	162	971.2	966	119	367	835	Pitch 76-90	.217	461	100	21	5	18	60	53	100	.298	.401
Relievers	5.32	17	23	35	409	0	448.2	475	52	249	374	Pitch 91-105	.279	333	93	25	1	10	43	36	78	.347	.450
0-3 Days Rest (SP)	2.53	3	1	0	5	5	32.0	17	4	8	19	Pitch 106+	.238	239	57	17	3	11	39	25	60	.310	.473
4 Days Rest	4.66	28	41	0	95	95	581.1	592	79	195	524	First Pitch	.306	729	223	70	6	15	131	28	0	.337	.480
5+ Days Rest	4.77	21	23	0	62	62	358.1	357	36	164	292	Ahead in Count	.202	2524	509	106	19	56	235	0	1002	.208	.325
vs. AL	4.83	5	10	2	50	15	128.2	141	12	61	110	Behind in Count	.346	1117	387	67	6	56	250	339	0	.497	.594
vs. NL	4.85	63	84	33	521	147	1291.2	1300	159	555	1099	Two Strikes	.184	2689	495	101	18	66	256	248	1209	.254	.309
Pre-All Star	5.51	24	61	15	321	85	740.0	793	94	366	572	Pre-All Star	.277	2859	793	208	22	94	480	366	572	.362	.464
Post-All Star	4.13	44	33	20	250	77	680.1	648	77	250	637	Post-All Star	.251	2584	648	133	21	77	327	250	637	.319	.408

Games Finished: 149   Inherited Runners: 204   Inherited Runners Scored: 72   Holds: 38

Pittsburgh Pirates

	Avg	G	AB	R	H	2B	3B	HR	RBI	BB	SO	HBP	GDP	SB	CS	OBP	SLG	IBB	SH	SF	#Pit	#P/PA	GB	FB	G/F
1997	262	162	5503	725	1440	291	52	129	686	481	1161	92	106	160	50	329	404	27	77	47	22756	3.67	2068	1391	1.49

1997 Batting

	Avg	AB	H	2B	3B	HR	RBI	BB	SO	OBP	SLG		Avg	AB	H	2B	3B	HR	RBI	BB	SO	OBP	SLG
vs. Left	.272	1186	322	50	9	34	156	124	246	.344	.415	First Pitch	.354	756	268	58	9	20	114	18	0	.377	.534
vs. Right	.259	4317	1118	241	43	95	530	357	915	.325	.401	Ahead in Count	.356	1066	379	78	13	39	217	254	0	.478	.563
Groundball	.266	856	228	48	6	16	112	66	177	.322	.393	Behind in Count	.196	2658	520	101	12	42	207	0	998	.210	.290
Flyball	.251	1045	262	53	10	27	114	64	274	.306	.398	Two Strikes	.174	2603	453	82	17	40	216	209	1161	.245	.265
Home	.263	2659	698	139	33	68	345	245	552	.333	.416	Leadoff	.275	697	192	29	10	8	60	53	118	.332	.380
Away	.261	2844	742	152	19	61	341	236	609	.325	.392	Batting #2	.261	647	169	35	4	9	69	61	114	.333	.369
Day	.271	1881	510	114	18	43	269	166	429	.338	.419	Batting #3	.272	629	171	36	8	18	84	75	123	.356	.440
Night	.257	3622	930	177	34	86	417	315	732	.324	.396	March/April	.238	843	201	48	6	13	83	81	197	.311	.356
Grass	.260	1886	490	97	6	40	225	164	399	.324	.381	May	.249	931	232	42	15	25	118	102	209	.334	.407
Turf	.263	3617	950	194	46	89	461	317	762	.331	.416	June	.266	916	244	46	12	19	118	60	180	.323	.405
Pre-All Star	.253	2890	731	145	36	63	346	263	628	.324	.393	July	.269	969	261	52	7	23	118	77	212	.327	.409
Post-All Star	.271	2613	709	146	16	66	340	218	533	.334	.415	August	.272	983	267	58	6	25	128	79	188	.331	.419
Scoring Posn	.254	1514	384	75	13	34	538	175	307	.334	.388	Sept/Oct	.253	861	235	45	6	24	121	82	175	.345	.423
Close & Late	.282	893	252	54	8	18	132	91	203	.357	.421	vs. AL	.253	491	124	23	5	11	47	26	70	.301	.387
None on/out	.264	1351	356	68	15	38	38	121	292	.333	.420	vs. NL	.263	5012	1316	268	47	118	639	455	1091	.331	.405

	ERA	W	L	Sv	Opp	G	IP	BB	SO	Avg	H	2B	3B	HR	RBI	OBP	SLG	CG	ShO	Sup	QS	#P/S	SB	CS	GB	FB	G/F
1997	4.28	79	83	41	59	162	1436.0	560	1080	.271	1503	296	35	143	707	.343	.415	6	8	4.54	90	90	109	66	2253	1267	1.78

1997 Pitching

	ERA	W	L	Sv	G	GS	IP	H	HR	BB	SO		Avg	AB	H	2B	3B	HR	RBI	BB	SO	OBP	SLG
Home	4.26	43	38	19	306	81	735.0	763	77	269	572	vs. Left	.288	2374	683	129	22	66	294	264	427	.361	.444
Away	4.30	36	45	22	307	81	701.0	740	66	291	508	vs. Right	.259	3165	820	167	13	77	413	296	653	.328	.393
Day	4.80	26	28	14	217	54	479.2	562	58	195	368	Inning 1-6	.275	3757	1035	213	23	97	501	351	700	.341	.422
Night	4.02	53	55	27	396	108	956.1	941	85	365	712	Inning 7+	.263	1782	468	83	12	46	206	209	380	.345	.400
Grass	4.04	26	28	17	201	54	468.1	487	45	207	340	None on	.279	3049	850	163	19	95	95	253	570	.340	.438
Turf	4.40	53	55	24	412	108	967.2	1016	98	353	740	Runners on	.262	2490	653	133	16	48	612	307	510	.345	.386
March/April	4.28	12	13	6	96	25	222.2	230	18	102	149	Scoring Posn	.269	1444	389	80	9	28	537	223	305	.363	.395
May	4.06	14	14	8	95	28	248.0	255	23	78	182	Close & Late	.257	864	222	45	4	21	106	93	189	.334	.391
June	4.81	11	16	3	98	27	236.0	253	24	85	175	None on/out	.289	1387	401	66	6	44	44	98	243	.340	.441
July	3.95	16	12	10	105	28	250.2	263	19	103	213	vs. 1st Batr (relief)	.257	401	103	15	1	18	62	42	88	.333	.434
August	4.76	15	14	9	113	29	255.0	289	31	121	188	1st Inning Pitched	.275	2048	564	93	15	64	328	255	448	.359	.429
Sept/Oct	3.78	11	14	5	106	25	223.2	213	28	71	173	First 75 Pits (SP)	.251	549	138	28	1	15	55	43	99	.310	.388
Starters	4.25	53	57	0	162	162	943.0	1001	88	317	659	Pitch 76-90	.311	472	147	32	5	16	73	44	72	.370	.502
Relievers	4.34	26	26	41	451	0	493.0	502	55	243	421	Pitch 91-105	.241	245	59	13	3	2	27	40	47	.351	.343
0-3 Days Rest (SP)	0.00	0	0	0	0	0	0.0	0	0	0	0	Pitch 106+	.297	118	35	7	0	2	17	7	25	.346	.407
4 Days Rest	4.79	31	32	0	88	88	490.0	546	54	174	344	First Pitch	.338	864	292	61	5	26	152	47	0	.377	.510
5+ Days Rest	3.66	22	25	0	74	74	453.0	455	34	143	315	Ahead in Count	.200	2468	494	96	11	42	184	0	898	.209	.299
vs. AL	4.59	7	8	5	48	15	131.1	137	15	39	105	Behind in Count	.354	1186	420	79	8	51	231	294	0	.480	.563
vs. NL	4.25	72	75	36	564	147	1304.2	1366	128	521	975	Two Strikes	.183	2449	447	86	12	41	196	218	1080	.254	.278
Pre-All Star	4.25	43	43	21	309	86	761.2	790	66	283	550	Pre-All Star	.271	2912	790	165	18	66	369	283	550	.340	.408
Post-All Star	4.31	36	40	20	304	76	674.1	713	77	277	530	Post-All Star	.271	2627	713	131	17	77	338	277	530	.345	.422

Games Finished: 156   Inherited Runners: 247   Inherited Runners Scored: 87   Holds: 65

St. Louis Cardinals

	Avg	G	AB	R	H	2B	3B	HR	RBI	BB	SO	HBP	GDP	SB	CS	OBP	SLG	IBB	SH	SF	#Pit	#P/PA	GB	FB	G/F
1997	255	162	5524	689	1409	269	39	144	654	543	1191	42	128	164	60	324	396	54	58	44	22748	3.66	2049	1377	1.49

1997 Batting

	Avg	AB	H	2B	3B	HR	RBI	BB	SO	OBP	SLG		Avg	AB	H	2B	3B	HR	RBI	BB	SO	OBP	SLG
vs. Left	.247	1345	332	73	8	35	164	128	317	.315	.391	First Pitch	.328	895	294	63	5	24	115	40	0	.358	.491
vs. Right	.258	4179	1077	196	31	109	490	415	874	.327	.398	Ahead in Count	.339	1107	375	73	12	50	188	262	0	.465	.562
Groundball	.257	1127	290	52	5	23	118	101	237	.320	.374	Behind in Count	.190	2545	484	96	12	39	214	0	992	.196	.283
Flyball	.247	781	193	45	6	20	88	64	190	.310	.397	Two Strikes	.170	2599	442	77	14	44	231	240	1191	.243	.261
Home	.261	2682	701	144	13	68	327	288	538	.334	.401	Leadoff	.275	683	188	34	11	10	69	59	109	.332	.401
Away	.249	2842	708	125	26	76	327	255	653	.315	.392	Batting #2	.255	687	175	35	6	13	56	42	145	.298	.380
Day	.271	1920	520	91	12	48	246	190	411	.337	.406	Batting #3	.280	601	168	34	3	39	109	106	161	.387	.541
Night	.247	3604	889	178	27	96	408	353	780	.317	.391	March/April	.229	830	190	39	9	14	79	81	173	.303	.348
Grass	.259	4485	1162	223	31	119	543	451	933	.324	.402	May	.266	915	243	51	5	26	117	83	200	.327	.417
Turf	.238	1039	247	46	8	25	111	92	258	.302	.370	June	.285	963	274	54	10	24	133	97	204	.352	.436
Pre-All Star	.262	2921	766	154	24	67	346	288	611	.331	.400	July	.250	908	227	40	3	24	93	92	189	.319	.380
Post-All Star	.247	2603	643	115	15	77	308	255	580	.316	.392	August	.245	972	238	45	9	20	103	90	208	.313	.371
Scoring Posn	.258	1353	349	72	13	34	501	209	308	.356	.406	Sept/Oct	.253	936	237	40	3	36	129	100	217	.327	.418
Close & Late	.241	1053	254	49	8	25	130	112	256	.317	.374	vs. AL	.259	498	129	27	5	11	51	51	93	.332	.400
None on/out	.252	1399	353	62	11	39	39	109	274	.310	.396	vs. NL	.255	5026	1280	242	34	133	603	492	1098	.323	.396

St. Louis Cardinals

1997	ERA	W	L	Sv	Opp	G	IP	BB	SO	Avg	H	2B	3B	HR	RBI	OBP	SLG	CG	ShO	Sup	QS	#P/S	SB	CS	GB	FB	G/F
1997	3.88	73	89	39	58	162	1455.2	536	1130	259	1422	232	32	124	669	329	380	5	3	4.26	95	99	134	66	2021	1385	1.46

1997 Pitching

	ERA	W	L	Sv	G	GS	IP	H	HR	BB	SO		Avg	AB	H	2B	3B	HR	RBI	BB	SO	OBP	SLG
Home	3.34	41	40	21	288	81	747.0	687	59	258	595	vs. Left	.265	2421	642	108	18	53	311	276	471	.342	.390
Away	4.44	32	49	18	273	81	708.2	735	65	278	535	vs. Right	.254	3072	780	124	14	71	358	260	659	.318	.373
Day	4.46	26	30	13	186	56	504.1	498	54	175	405	Inning 1-6	.250	3621	906	154	21	80	447	352	762	.320	.371
Night	3.57	47	59	26	375	106	951.1	924	70	361	725	Inning 7+	.276	1872	516	78	11	44	222	184	368	.345	.400
Grass	3.78	62	70	32	457	132	1195.1	1146	101	429	942	None on	.249	3081	767	128	13	71		276	654	.317	.368
Turf	4.32	11	19	7	104	30	260.1	276	23	107	188	Runners on	.272	2412	655	104	19	53	598	260	476	.342	.396
March/April	3.33	11	14	5	81	25	219.0	210	11	83	172	Scoring Posn	.271	1381	374	63	13	25	512	200	282	.356	.390
May	3.51	13	14	6	84	27	238.2	228	20	74	194	Close & Late	.279	967	270	38	6	22	123	121	190	.364	.399
June	3.36	15	13	7	89	28	251.2	243	20	88	226	None on/out	.259	1369	355	69	4	31	31	120	270	.325	.383
July	3.86	12	15	9	92	27	244.2	224	26	105	216	vs. 1st Batr (relief)	.242	359	87	12	3	7	28	27	65	.302	.351
August	4.28	12	17	7	101	29	256.2	247	22	100	172	1st Inning Pitched	.269	1878	505	80	11	38	258	183	381	.337	.384
Sept/Oct	4.85	10	16	5	114	26	245.0	270	25	86	150	First 75 Pits (SP)	.279	563	157	26	2	14	77	50	116	.336	.407
Starters	3.92	50	58	0	162	162	1001.0	946	80	371	802	Pitch 76-90	.252	484	122	26	1	7	54	42	110	.317	.353
Relievers	3.78	23	31	39	399	0	454.2	476	44	165	328	Pitch 91-105	.236	347	82	12	3	10	37	37	76	.318	.375
0-3 Days Rest (SP)	4.97	1	1	0	6	6	29.0	34	1	11	26	Pitch 106+	.265	200	53	9	5	2	30	29	46	.359	.390
4 Days Rest	3.78	29	36	0	99	99	624.1	568	50	229	505	First Pitch	.336	742	249	36	7	23	109	29	0	.364	.496
5+ Days Rest	4.09	20	21	0	57	57	347.2	344	29	131	271	Ahead in Count	.203	2502	509	72	9	34	207	0	943	.213	.280
vs. AL	4.01	8	7	6	51	15	132.1	131	16	38	110	Behind in Count	.337	1158	390	75	6	41	208	270	0	.459	.518
vs. NL	3.86	65	82	33	510	147	1323.1	1291	108	498	1020	Two Strikes	.173	2573	444	66	7	27	187	236	1130	.248	.366
Pre-All Star	3.42	41	45	19	274	86	765.1	730	57	265	647	Pre-All Star	.253	2881	730	121	16	57	312	265	647	.321	.366
Post-All Star	4.38	32	44	20	287	76	690.1	692	67	271	483	Post-All Star	.265	2612	692	111	16	67	357	271	483	.337	.397

Games Finished: 157   Inherited Runners: 205   Inherited Runners Scored: 53   Holds: 48

San Diego Padres

1997 Record: 76 – 86

1997	Avg	G	AB	R	H	2B	3B	HR	RBI	BB	SO	HBP	GDP	SB	CS	OBP	SLG	IBB	SH	SF	#Pit	#P/PA	GB	FB	G/F
1997	.271	162	5609	795	1519	275	16	152	761	604	1129	35	129	140	60	.342	.407	40	63	58	23852	3.74	1993	1426	1.40

1997 Batting

	Avg	AB	H	2B	3B	HR	RBI	BB	SO	OBP	SLG		Avg	AB	H	2B	3B	HR	RBI	BB	SO	OBP	SLG
vs. Left	.263	1294	340	62	4	44	190	158	260	.345	.419	First Pitch	.335	787	264	49	3	28	139	29	0	.362	.512
vs. Right	.273	4315	1179	213	12	108	571	446	869	.341	.403	Ahead in Count	.349	1222	427	92	3	47	230	289	0	.469	.545
Groundball	.283	1158	328	70	3	28	146	115	217	.348	.421	Behind in Count	.205	2530	519	73	4	46	243	0	944	.210	.292
Flyball	.258	883	228	36	1	27	104	88	202	.326	.393	Two Strikes	.188	2571	483	87	8	42	243	285	1129	.270	.277
Home	.262	2742	718	130	6	75	350	277	558	.330	.396	Leadoff	.250	653	163	28	0	13	58	111	135	.363	.352
Away	.279	2867	801	145	10	77	411	327	571	.354	.418	Batting #2	.311	676	210	37	1	20	72	65	98	.372	.457
Day	.280	1912	536	114	8	46	276	196	363	.347	.434	Batting #3	.324	669	217	51	5	18	138	56	48	.373	.496
Night	.266	3697	983	161	8	106	485	408	766	.340	.400	March/April	.235	787	185	29	2	18	93	89	150	.314	.346
Grass	.271	4524	1228	222	12	125	615	484	883	.342	.409	May	.277	982	272	50	1	31	140	82	216	.336	.425
Turf	.268	1085	291	53	4	27	146	120	246	.343	.399	June	.292	1065	311	63	4	28	159	113	178	.360	.438
Pre-All Star	.272	3034	825	155	7	85	423	309	588	.341	.412	July	.285	922	263	49	4	25	146	124	196	.369	.428
Post-All Star	.270	2575	694	120	9	67	338	295	541	.344	.401	August	.254	1017	258	53	5	24	116	111	215	.325	.386
Scoring Posn	.290	1446	420	75	11	37	589	211	303	.371	.434	Sept/Oct	.275	836	230	31	0	26	107	85	174	.344	.406
Close & Late	.287	885	254	45	6	13	127	123	192	.372	.395	vs. AL	.299	579	173	38	2	20	97	62	96	.370	.475
None on/out	.264	1374	363	62	2	44	44	143	287	.336	.408	vs. NL	.268	5030	1346	237	14	132	664	542	1033	.339	.399

1997	ERA	W	L	Sv	Opp	G	IP	BB	SO	Avg	H	2B	3B	HR	RBI	OBP	SLG	CG	ShO	Sup	QS	#P/S	SB	CS	GB	FB	G/F
1997	4.98	76	86	43	63	162	1450.0	596	1059	280	1581	291	16	172	845	352	435	5	2	4.93	67	91	171	75	2164	1395	1.55

1997 Pitching

	ERA	W	L	Sv	G	GS	IP	H	HR	BB	SO		Avg	AB	H	2B	3B	HR	RBI	BB	SO	OBP	SLG
Home	4.48	39	42	17	300	81	749.0	774	96	263	564	vs. Left	.281	2349	660	120	19	67	345	282	415	.360	.434
Away	5.52	37	44	26	288	81	701.0	807	76	333	495	vs. Right	.279	3306	921	171	17	105	500	314	644	.346	.436
Day	4.98	27	29	14	200	56	495.1	563	53	202	376	Inning 1-6	.286	3796	1086	197	21	121	562	372	665	.353	.445
Night	4.99	49	57	29	388	106	954.2	1018	119	394	683	Inning 7+	.266	1859	495	94	15	51	283	224	414	.350	.415
Grass	4.88	63	68	34	473	131	1185.0	1286	145	468	866	None on	.271	3107	843	160	18	96	96	288	616	.338	.427
Turf	5.43	13	18	9	115	31	265.0	295	27	128	193	Runners on	.290	2548	738	131	16	76	749	308	443	.368	.446
March/April	3.59	9	15	3	76	24	210.2	203	23	89	155	Scoring Posn	.285	1567	446	86	12	40	654	223	276	.373	.431
May	5.47	13	15	7	99	28	250.0	290	28	104	187	Close & Late	.258	822	212	45	10	16	123	115	187	.354	.395
June	6.00	14	15	10	105	29	265.1	319	36	130	185	None on/out	.277	1369	379	79	9	41	41	131	250	.347	.438
July	4.80	16	11	11	106	27	241.2	263	27	103	179	vs. 1st Batr (relief)	.251	370	93	19	2	11	52	40	101	.337	.403
August	4.44	13	17	7	96	30	265.1	279	29	73	184	1st Inning Pitched	.281	2021	567	106	16	59	388	250	435	.364	.436
Sept/Oct	5.39	11	13	5	106	24	217.0	227	29	97	169	First 75 Pits (SP)	.276	555	153	29	6	19	81	55	86	.342	.452
Starters	4.98	47	62	0	162	162	933.2	1042	117	348	613	Pitch 76-90	.293	484	142	19	1	17	66	44	71	.355	.442
Relievers	4.99	29	24	43	426	0	516.1	539	55	248	446	Pitch 91-105	.292	264	77	11	1	8	34	31	44	.368	.432
0-3 Days Rest (SP)	4.54	3	6	0	14	14	71.1	74	9	36	54	Pitch 106+	.307	88	27	6	0	5	15	3	21	.330	.545
4 Days Rest	4.64	30	37	0	94	94	570.1	629	70	194	365	First Pitch	.358	815	292	59	6	22	148	25	0	.385	.526
5+ Days Rest	5.76	14	19	0	54	54	292.0	339	38	118	194	Ahead in Count	.207	2516	520	89	10	41	244	0	895	.214	.299
vs. AL	5.63	8	8	5	61	16	144.0	158	24	80	92	Behind in Count	.363	1243	451	78	6	63	256	290	0	.483	.591
vs. NL	4.91	68	78	38	527	146	1306.0	1423	148	516	967	Two Strikes	.185	2532	468	80	12	47	264	281	1059	.271	.282
Pre-All Star	5.19	38	49	21	304	87	779.0	877	97	353	563	Pre-All Star	.288	3045	877	156	22	97	468	353	563	.366	.449
Post-All Star	4.75	38	37	22	284	75	671.0	704	75	243	496	Post-All Star	.270	2610	704	135	14	75	377	243	496	.335	.418

Games Finished: 157   Inherited Runners: 293   Inherited Runners Scored: 110   Holds: 43

1997	Avg	G	AB	R	H	2B	3B	HR	RBI	BB	SO	HBP	GDP	SB	CS	OBP	SLG	IBB	SH	SF	#Pit	#P/PA	GB	FB	G/F
1997	.258	162	5485	784	1415	266	37	172	746	642	1120	46	111	121	49	.337	.414	72	64	59	23307	3.70	1939	1608	1.21

1997 Batting

	Avg	AB	H	2B	3B	HR	RBI	BB	SO	OBP	SLG		Avg	AB	H	2B	3B	HR	RBI	BB	SO	OBP	SLG
vs. Left	.244	1465	357	72	8	33	167	175	305	.325	.371	First Pitch	.312	805	251	41	7	35	130	56	0	.358	.511
vs. Right	.263	4020	1058	194	29	139	579	467	815	.342	.430	Ahead in Count	.348	1193	415	91	10	53	234	333	0	.489	.574
Groundball	.262	1164	305	59	7	34	154	102	205	.325	.412	Behind in Count	.191	2453	468	88	10	49	235	0	957	.195	.295
Flyball	.246	598	147	26	5	16	87	90	157	.346	.386	Two Strikes	.184	2542	467	85	8	57	251	252	1120	.260	.291
Home	.251	2653	666	122	17	83	361	338	555	.338	.404	Leadoff	.255	670	171	26	5	7	54	87	107	.342	.340
Away	.264	2832	749	144	20	89	385	304	565	.337	.424	Batting #2	.271	664	180	28	5	7	57	65	112	.337	.360
Day	.262	2479	650	138	15	69	331	284	522	.341	.413	Batting #3	.287	609	175	42	7	30	106	114	116	.399	.527
Night	.254	3006	765	128	22	103	415	358	598	.335	.415	March/April	.240	761	183	37	6	16	93	94	163	.324	.368
Grass	.259	4497	1164	214	29	144	610	535	903	.340	.415	May	.248	948	235	38	4	21	118	114	222	.335	.363
Turf	.254	988	251	52	8	28	136	107	217	.328	.408	June	.273	982	268	55	6	43	135	100	197	.342	.473
Pre-All Star	.256	2886	739	138	18	89	369	326	616	.334	.409	July	.271	942	255	42	5	36	131	103	181	.344	.441
Post-All Star	.260	2599	676	128	19	83	377	316	504	.341	.420	August	.259	1004	260	53	8	33	153	126	190	.341	.426
Scoring Posn	.259	1422	368	65	10	34	549	248	297	.365	.390	Sept/Oct	.252	848	214	41	8	23	116	105	167	.335	.401
Close & Late	.292	873	255	49	6	24	152	122	190	.379	.444	vs. AL	.280	557	156	33	1	28	77	59	102	.348	.494
None on/out	.250	1370	342	70	7	51	51	129	273	.317	.423	vs. NL	.255	4928	1259	233	36	144	669	583	1018	.336	.405

1997	ERA	W	L	Sv	Opp	G	IP	BB	SO	Avg	H	2B	3B	HR	RBI	OBP	SLG	CG	ShO	Sup	QS	#P/S	SB	CS	GB	FB	G/F
1997	4.39	90	72	45	69	162	1446.0	578	1044	.270	1494	248	31	160	747	.340	.412	5	9	4.85	81	96	108	73	2071	1596	1.30

1997 Pitching

	ERA	W	L	Sv	G	GS	IP	H	HR	BB	SO		Avg	AB	H	2B	3B	HR	RBI	BB	SO	OBP	SLG
Home	3.96	48	33	25	329	81	750.0	744	76	293	565	vs. Left	.279	2055	573	98	14	54	297	237	354	.353	.419
Away	4.86	42	39	20	314	81	696.0	750	84	285	479	vs. Right	.264	3484	921	150	17	106	450	341	690	.332	.408
Day	4.57	41	33	17	308	74	665.0	703	69	273	502	Inning 1-6	.269	3713	999	169	22	112	511	396	703	.340	.417
Night	4.24	49	39	28	335	88	781.0	791	91	305	542	Inning 7+	.271	1826	495	79	9	48	236	182	341	.340	.403
Grass	4.37	74	60	36	540	134	1198.0	1246	134	496	863	None on	.262	3101	813	125	18	87	87	296	603	.330	.398
Turf	4.50	16	12	9	103	28	248.0	248	26	82	181	Runners on	.279	2438	681	123	13	73	660	282	441	.352	.430
March/April	2.90	17	7	11	95	24	214.1	186	15	67	149	Scoring Posn	.276	1364	377	66	10	42	569	207	263	.365	.432
May	4.49	14	14	8	118	28	254.2	284	26	114	159	Close & Late	.261	917	239	40	5	22	121	98	177	.332	.387
June	4.46	16	13	10	113	29	254.0	270	37	109	162	None on/out	.271	1381	374	52	6	46	46	125	243	.336	.417
July	5.18	12	15	6	103	27	238.0	260	31	95	189	vs. 1st Batr (relief)	.298	436	130	19	5	9	71	30	76	.342	.427
August	4.67	16	13	4	109	29	260.1	268	27	96	185	1st Inning Pitched	.284	2142	608	108	13	61	373	222	384	.351	.432
Sept/Oct	4.49	15	10	6	105	25	224.2	226	24	97	200	First 75 Pits (SP)	.263	570	150	32	1	15	64	40	132	.312	.402
Starters	4.25	60	48	0	162	162	920.2	921	107	379	685	Pitch 76-90	.271	461	125	18	2	15	56	58	79	.352	.416
Relievers	4.64	30	24	45	481	0	525.1	573	53	199	359	Pitch 91-105	.284	299	85	15	1	11	45	41	57	.370	.452
0-3 Days Rest (SP)	5.45	1	2	0	7	7	34.2	53	7	8	23	Pitch 106+	.214	140	30	4	2	1	11	26	37	.349	.293
4 Days Rest	4.39	31	27	0	85	85	486.0	494	55	208	362	First Pitch	.345	772	266	44	3	24	106	50	0	.385	.503
5+ Days Rest	3.99	27	19	0	69	69	394.1	370	45	159	296	Ahead in Count	.212	2495	529	87	9	41	264	0	873	.218	.303
vs. AL	5.28	10	6	6	64	16	145.0	158	22	66	102	Behind in Count	.340	1216	413	69	12	64	244	297	0	.464	.574
vs. NL	4.30	80	66	39	579	146	1301.0	1336	138	512	942	Two Strikes	.197	2614	515	82	12	44	256	231	1044	.266	.288
Pre-All Star	4.06	51	36	32	347	87	776.0	786	87	308	521	Pre-All Star	.266	2952	786	119	21	87	374	308	521	.336	.409
Post-All Star	4.78	39	36	13	296	75	670.0	708	73	270	523	Post-All Star	.274	2587	708	129	10	73	373	270	523	.345	.416

Games Finished: 157   Inherited Runners: 333   Inherited Runners Scored: 117   Holds: 85

Leader Boards

On the pages that follow, we provide top 10 lists in a variety of statistical categories, for both 1997 and the last five years as a whole. We'll tell you who the top hitter was with runners in scoring position last year (Tony Gwynn, .459), and which pitcher was the toughest in the same situation (Randy Johnson, .154). And much, much more.

As you might expect, "Batting #9" includes only American League players.

1997 Batting Leaders

Overall
(Minimum 502 PA)

Player, Team	AB	H	AVG
T Gwynn, SD	**592**	**220**	**.372**
L Walker, Col	568	208	.366
M Piazza, LA	556	201	.362
F Thomas, ChA	530	184	.347
K Lofton, Atl	493	164	.333
E Martinez, Sea	542	179	.330
D Justice, Cle	495	163	.329
B Williams, NYA	509	167	.328
M Ramirez, Cle	561	184	.328
W Joyner, SD	455	149	.327

LHP
(Minimum 150 PA)

Player, Team	AB	H	AVG
E Alfonzo, NYN	**135**	**51**	**.378**
G Berroa, Bal	148	53	.358
T Gwynn, SD	163	58	.356
M Ramirez, Cle	137	48	.350
B Huskey, NYN	139	47	.338
M Vaughn, Bos	196	66	.337
M Grace, ChN	143	48	.336
K Lofton, Atl	152	51	.336
C Davis, KC	147	48	.327
B Williams, NYA	141	46	.326

RHP
(Minimum 200 PA)

Player, Team	AB	H	AVG
L Walker, Col	**424**	**165**	**.389**
T Gwynn, SD	429	162	.378
R Alomar, Bal	299	109	.365
M Piazza, LA	432	156	.361
R Jefferson, Bos	383	135	.352
P O'Neill, NYA	364	126	.346
E Martinez, Sea	411	142	.345
F Thomas, ChA	424	146	.344
W Joyner, SD	375	128	.341
J Valentin, Bos	421	142	.337

Home
(Minimum 175 PA)

Player, Team	AB	H	AVG
L Walker, Col	**302**	**116**	**.384**
R Alomar, Bal	211	80	.379
T Gwynn, SD	296	112	.378
R Greer, Tex	300	111	.370
D Bichette, Col	301	109	.362
M Grace, ChN	276	98	.355
M Piazza, LA	279	99	.355
D Justice, Cle	238	84	.353
W Clark, Tex	202	71	.351
I Rodriguez, Tex	311	108	.347

Away
(Minimum 175 PA)

Player, Team	AB	H	AVG
F Thomas, ChA	**279**	**104**	**.373**
M Piazza, LA	277	102	.368
T Gwynn, SD	296	108	.365
B Williams, NYA	269	95	.353
S Alomar Jr, Cle	230	81	.352
H Baines, Bal	221	77	.348
L Walker, Col	266	92	.346
K Lofton, Atl	235	81	.345
E Martinez, Sea	274	93	.339
P O'Neill, NYA	290	98	.338

Groundball Pitchers
(Minimum 125 PA)

Player, Team	AB	H	AVG
L Walker, Col	**115**	**49**	**.426**
T Gwynn, SD	119	45	.378
A Galarraga, Col	119	44	.370
T Martinez, NYA	123	43	.350
N Garciaparra, Bos	118	40	.339
J Snow, SF	114	38	.333
A Rodriguez, Sea	123	41	.333
M Bordick, Bal	129	42	.326
J Olerud, NYN	112	36	.321
B Surhoff, Bal	137	44	.321

Grass
(Minimum 150 PA)

Player, Team	AB	H	AVG
L Walker, Col	**469**	**174**	**.371**
T Gwynn, SD	484	177	.366
F Thomas, ChA	460	165	.359
M Piazza, LA	465	164	.353
B Williams, NYA	429	148	.345
P Meares, Min	166	57	.343
M Ramirez, Cle	470	161	.343
R Alomar, Bal	351	120	.342
W Joyner, SD	365	124	.340
M Grace, ChN	452	153	.338

Turf
(Minimum 150 PA)

Player, Team	AB	H	AVG
E Martinez, Sea	**305**	**101**	**.331**
B Larkin, Cin	149	49	.329
D Segui, Mon	278	91	.327
H Morris, Cin	219	71	.324
R Coomer, Min	297	96	.323
J Kendall, Pit	321	102	.318
A Rodriguez, Sea	318	101	.318
K Griffey Jr, Sea	336	104	.310
C Knoblauch, Min	358	110	.307
P Molitor, Min	319	98	.307

Flyball Pitchers
(Minimum 100 PA)

Player, Team	AB	H	AVG
T Gwynn, SD	**96**	**41**	**.427**
L Walker, Col	94	38	.404
J Cora, Sea	99	38	.384
D Jeter, NYA	102	38	.373
M Morandini, Phi	94	34	.362
E Martinez, Sea	82	29	.354
P O'Neill, NYA	99	35	.354
C Knoblauch, Min	99	34	.343
J Bagwell, Hou	77	26	.338
A Belle, ChA	113	38	.336

Day
(Minimum 150 PA)

Player, Team	AB	H	AVG
L Walker, Col	**261**	**108**	**.414**
M Piazza, LA	159	60	.377
M Ramirez, Cle	190	70	.368
F Thomas, ChA	175	64	.366
T Gwynn, SD	192	70	.365
D DeShields, StL	171	62	.363
R Greer, Tex	133	48	.361
D Justice, Cle	166	59	.355
R Alomar, Bal	125	44	.352
W Joyner, SD	166	58	.349

Night
(Minimum 200 PA)

Player, Team	AB	H	AVG
T Gwynn, SD	**400**	**150**	**.375**
M Piazza, LA	397	141	.355
K Lofton, Atl	357	123	.345
E Martinez, Sea	379	130	.343
J Frye, Bos	277	94	.339
M Stairs, Oak	204	69	.338
F Thomas, ChA	355	120	.338
R Mondesi, LA	451	150	.333
W Clark, Tex	320	106	.331
C Biggio, Hou	431	142	.329

Scoring Position
(Minimum 100 PA)

Player, Team	AB	H	AVG
T Gwynn, SD	**146**	**67**	**.459**
P O'Neill, NYA	159	68	.428
E Alfonzo, NYN	115	48	.417
F Thomas, ChA	139	58	.417
J Olerud, NYN	130	50	.385
R Coomer, Min	135	50	.370
L Walker, Col	140	51	.364
J Cirillo, Mil	149	54	.362
M Piazza, LA	147	53	.361
C Biggio, Hou	123	44	.358

1997 Batting Leaders

April
(Minimum 100 PA)

Player, Team	AB	H	AVG
L Walker, Col	**90**	**41**	**.456**
K Lofton, Atl	114	45	.395
D Justice, Cle	83	32	.386
D Sanders, Cin	107	41	.383
B Anderson, Bal	79	30	.380
T Gwynn, SD	98	36	.367
M Alou, Fla	86	31	.360
B Butler, LA	89	32	.360
V Castilla, Col	89	32	.360
J Olerud, NYN	101	36	.356

May
(Minimum 100 PA)

Player, Team	AB	H	AVG
J Cora, Sea	**107**	**48**	**.449**
T Gwynn, SD	103	46	.447
F Thomas, ChA	86	37	.430
W Clark, Tex	99	39	.394
I Rodriguez, Tex	107	41	.383
B Bonilla, Fla	102	39	.382
B Larkin, Cin	84	32	.381
D Justice, Cle	84	32	.381
E Martinez, Sea	101	38	.376
C Baerga, NYN	95	35	.368

June
(Minimum 100 PA)

Player, Team	AB	H	AVG
M Piazza, LA	**109**	**47**	**.431**
M Loretta, Mil	95	40	.421
L Walker, Col	98	40	.408
W Joyner, SD	102	40	.392
R Greer, Tex	104	40	.385
J Valentin, Bos	110	41	.373
F Santangelo, Mon	94	35	.372
R Henderson, Ana	92	34	.370
S Javier, SF	90	33	.367
T Gwynn, SD	105	38	.362

July
(Minimum 100 PA)

Player, Team	AB	H	AVG
R Jefferson, Bos	**96**	**39**	**.406**
T Salmon, Ana	100	39	.390
T Gwynn, SD	106	41	.387
Q Veras, SD	104	40	.385
W Clark, Tex	96	35	.365
S Rolen, Phi	91	33	.363
B Bonds, SF	94	34	.362
M Grace, ChN	93	33	.355
C Biggio, Hou	96	34	.354
P O'Neill, NYA	99	35	.354

August
(Minimum 100 PA)

Player, Team	AB	H	AVG
B Williams, NYA	**119**	**47**	**.395**
D Justice, Cle	104	40	.385
K Caminiti, SD	109	41	.376
N Garciaparra, Bos	121	45	.372
J Valentin, Bos	108	40	.370
K Lofton, Atl	113	41	.363
L Walker, Col	105	38	.362
V Castilla, Col	111	40	.360
C Ripken, Bal	98	35	.357
C Counsell, Fla	84	30	.357

September-October
(Minimum 100 PA)

Player, Team	AB	H	AVG
M Piazza, LA	**96**	**39**	**.406**
E Burks, Col	91	35	.385
T Zeile, LA	86	32	.372
J Nunnally, Cin	92	34	.370
J Giambi, Oak	93	34	.366
D DeShields, StL	93	33	.355
M Ramirez, Cle	111	38	.342
L Stevens, Tex	97	33	.340
J Gonzalez, Tex	95	32	.337
G Anderson, Ana	101	34	.337

1st Pitch
(Minimum 100 PA)

Player, Team	AB	H	AVG
T Salmon, Ana	**94**	**43**	**.457**
J Lopez, Atl	90	41	.456
L Walker, Col	122	54	.443
T Gwynn, SD	97	41	.423
J Vizcaino, SF	100	39	.390
N Garciaparra, Bos	135	52	.385
R White, Mon	97	37	.381
M Alou, Fla	100	38	.380
B Anderson, Bal	103	39	.379
J Carter, Tor	93	35	.376

Ahead in Count
(Minimum 150 PA)

Player, Team	AB	H	AVG
J Thome, Cle	**112**	**59**	**.527**
V Castilla, Col	124	60	.484
M Vaughn, Bos	112	53	.473
B Williams, NYA	137	63	.460
M Piazza, LA	122	56	.459
T Zeile, LA	129	59	.457
E Martinez, Sea	161	73	.453
M Ramirez, Cle	136	60	.441
M McGwire, StL	114	50	.439
L Walker, Col	134	58	.433

Behind in Count
(Minimum 150 PA)

Player, Team	AB	H	AVG
T Gwynn, SD	**220**	**78**	**.355**
M Piazza, LA	246	76	.309
R Greer, Tex	225	68	.302
D Glanville, ChN	227	66	.291
N Garciaparra, Bos	289	84	.291
P O'Neill, NYA	235	68	.289
R Kelly, Sea	180	52	.289
E Alfonzo, NYN	243	70	.288
R Alomar, Bal	192	54	.281
C Biggio, Hou	303	85	.281

Two Strikes
(Minimum 150 PA)

Player, Team	AB	H	AVG
T Gwynn, SD	**176**	**63**	**.358**
M Piazza, LA	238	74	.311
R Greer, Tex	263	74	.281
M Loretta, Mil	231	64	.277
D Glanville, ChN	188	52	.277
P O'Neill, NYA	256	70	.273
R Alomar, Bal	182	49	.269
D Magadan, Oak	153	41	.268
K Lofton, Atl	243	65	.267
E Alfonzo, NYN	225	60	.267

Full Count
(Minimum 40 PA)

Player, Team	AB	H	AVG
B Spiers, Hou	**33**	**16**	**.485**
P Molitor, Min	27	13	.481
M Loretta, Mil	57	24	.421
M Lewis, SF	30	12	.400
M Lieberthal, Phi	39	15	.385
M Piazza, LA	47	18	.383
W Clark, Tex	40	15	.375
R Alomar, Bal	40	15	.375
T Gwynn, SD	33	12	.364
T Womack, Pit	44	16	.364

Close & Late
(Minimum 75 PA)

Player, Team	AB	H	AVG
T Gwynn, SD	**86**	**34**	**.395**
O Vizquel, Cle	68	26	.382
J Blauser, Atl	89	34	.382
D Erstad, Ana	84	32	.381
T Martinez, NYA	90	34	.378
J Valentin, Bos	99	37	.374
J Kendall, Pit	75	28	.373
J Vizcaino, SF	95	35	.368
I Rodriguez, Tex	94	34	.362
E Alfonzo, NYN	94	34	.362

1997 Batting Leaders

Batting #1
(Minimum 175 PA)

Player, Team	AB	H	AVG
T Raines, NYA	**214**	**72**	**.336**
K Lofton, Atl	492	163	.331
D Jeter, NYA	427	137	.321
D Glanville, ChN	248	78	.315
C Biggio, Hou	614	191	.311
B Roberts, Cle	291	90	.309
J Offerman, KC	350	108	.309
F Santangelo, Mon	153	47	.307
N Garciaparra, Bos	683	209	.306
L Johnson, ChN	396	121	.306

Batting #2
(Minimum 175 PA)

Player, Team	AB	H	AVG
I Rodriguez, Tex	**517**	**172**	**.333**
R Alomar, Bal	337	112	.332
E Alfonzo, NYN	406	134	.330
B Higginson, Det	253	80	.316
E Burks, Col	331	102	.308
R Kelly, Sea	179	55	.307
M Morandini, Phi	510	155	.304
D Erstad, Ana	303	91	.300
A Rodriguez, Sea	450	134	.298
S Finley, SD	195	58	.297

Batting #3
(Minimum 175 PA)

Player, Team	AB	H	AVG
L Walker, Col	**536**	**199**	**.371**
P O'Neill, NYA	190	70	.368
M Piazza, LA	468	169	.361
T Gwynn, SD	465	167	.359
F Thomas, ChA	530	184	.347
B Williams, NYA	436	145	.333
C Stynes, Cin	187	62	.332
M Ramirez, Cle	194	63	.325
R Greer, Tex	598	192	.321
R Lankford, StL	258	82	.318

Batting #4
(Minimum 150 PA)

Player, Team	AB	H	AVG
R Jefferson, Bos	**344**	**119**	**.346**
M Ramirez, Cle	159	55	.346
E Martinez, Sea	531	178	.335
A Galarraga, Col	539	168	.312
D Segui, Mon	438	133	.304
K Young, Pit	298	90	.302
J Edmonds, Ana	150	45	.300
D Daulton, Fla	144	43	.299
T Martinez, NYA	463	138	.298
J Gonzalez, Tex	529	157	.297

Batting #5
(Minimum 150 PA)

Player, Team	AB	H	AVG
M Stanley, NYA	**145**	**54**	**.372**
G Berroa, Bal	186	63	.339
B Surhoff, Bal	151	51	.338
D Justice, Cle	478	160	.335
J Randa, Pit	260	87	.335
W Joyner, SD	255	85	.333
R Mondesi, LA	425	141	.332
W Clark, Tex	335	111	.331
L Stevens, Tex	162	53	.327
T Salmon, Ana	224	73	.326

Batting #6
(Minimum 150 PA)

Player, Team	AB	H	AVG
B Bonilla, Fla	**215**	**71**	**.330**
S Dunston, Pit	146	48	.329
P O'Neill, NYA	169	55	.325
M Alou, Fla	177	57	.322
M Ramirez, Cle	181	58	.320
T O'Leary, Bos	287	90	.314
G Anderson, Ana	319	99	.310
J Kendall, Pit	337	104	.309
M Williams, Cle	264	81	.307
C Baerga, NYN	251	77	.307

Batting #7
(Minimum 100 PA)

Player, Team	AB	H	AVG
D Cedeno, Tex	**89**	**35**	**.393**
C Curtis, NYA	139	51	.367
J Reed, Col	194	62	.320
J Vizcaino, SF	98	31	.316
S Alomar Jr, Cle	157	49	.312
J Franco, Mil	118	36	.305
G Williams, Mil	174	53	.305
R Sandberg, ChN	102	31	.304
M Loretta, Mil	102	31	.304
D Martinez, ChA	109	33	.303

Batting #8
(Minimum 100 PA)

Player, Team	AB	H	AVG
J Blauser, Atl	**157**	**57**	**.363**
J Frye, Bos	118	40	.339
R Becker, Min	124	41	.331
S Alomar Jr, Cle	103	34	.330
W Guerrero, LA	96	31	.323
P Meares, Min	118	38	.322
J Posada, NYA	106	33	.311
M Alexander, ChN	135	42	.311
T Fernandez, Cle	100	31	.310
N Perez, Col	142	43	.303

Batting #9
(Minimum 100 PA)

Player, Team	AB	H	AVG
J Damon, KC	**94**	**34**	**.362**
R Sanchez, NYA	113	38	.336
J Frye, Bos	115	38	.330
D Hocking, Min	131	40	.305
O Vizquel, Cle	234	71	.303
D Bragg, Bos	167	48	.287
J Levis, Mil	144	41	.285
C Garcia, Tor	158	42	.266
A Gonzalez, Tor	181	48	.265
P Meares, Min	280	73	.261

None On/None Out
(Minimum 100 PA)

Player, Team	AB	H	AVG
L Walker, Col	**97**	**37**	**.381**
J Kendall, Pit	106	40	.377
E Martinez, Sea	125	47	.376
T Raines, NYA	99	37	.374
R Mondesi, LA	156	58	.372
A Rodriguez, Sea	116	43	.371
R Lankford, StL	100	37	.370
T Gwynn, SD	103	38	.369
G Anderson, Ana	113	41	.363
M Ramirez, Cle	136	49	.360

Pre-All Star
(Minimum 175 PA)

Player, Team	AB	H	AVG
L Walker, Col	**309**	**123**	**.398**
T Gwynn, SD	330	130	.394
S Alomar Jr, Cle	240	90	.375
F Thomas, ChA	261	96	.368
M Piazza, LA	300	107	.357
J Blauser, Atl	283	98	.346
K Lofton, Atl	288	99	.344
M Ramirez, Cle	263	90	.342
E Martinez, Sea	310	106	.342
R Jefferson, Bos	229	78	.341

Post-All Star
(Minimum 175 PA)

Player, Team	AB	H	AVG
M Piazza, LA	**256**	**94**	**.367**
B Williams, NYA	231	82	.355
C Stynes, Cin	198	69	.348
T Ward, Pit	153	53	.346
T Gwynn, SD	262	90	.344
E Burks, Col	179	61	.341
B Mayne, Oak	169	57	.337
P O'Neill, NYA	265	89	.336
J Frye, Bos	269	90	.335
K Caminiti, SD	251	83	.331

5-Year Batting Leaders

Overall
(Minimum 1800 PA)

Player	AB	H	AVG
T Gwynn	2486	916	.368
M Piazza	2489	838	.337
F Thomas	2498	835	.334
K Lofton	2664	868	.326
E Martinez	2013	649	.322
M Grace	2651	851	.321
R Alomar	2498	797	.319
P Molitor	2813	897	.319
P O'Neill	2425	769	.317
J Eisenreich	1660	525	.316

LHP
(Minimum 525 PA)

Player	AB	H	AVG
F Thomas	606	222	.366
T Gwynn	818	289	.353
M Piazza	542	191	.352
M Ramirez	554	192	.347
P Molitor	653	225	.345
B Williams	845	285	.337
J Bagwell	598	199	.333
E Burks	535	178	.333
V Castilla	523	173	.331
E Martinez	491	162	.330

RHP
(Minimum 700 PA)

Player	AB	H	AVG
T Gwynn	1668	627	.376
P O'Neill	1629	562	.345
R Alomar	1783	610	.342
K Lofton	1767	593	.336
M Piazza	1947	647	.332
R Jefferson	1245	409	.329
J Eisenreich	1405	456	.325
F Thomas	1892	613	.324
M Grace	1854	599	.323
H Morris	1567	505	.322

Home
(Minimum 625 PA)

Player	AB	H	AVG
T Gwynn	1242	471	.379
D Bichette	1440	528	.367
L Walker	1105	388	.351
A Galarraga	1361	476	.350
M Grace	1368	468	.342
V Castilla	1146	391	.341
E Burks	980	334	.341
P Molitor	1421	483	.340
E Martinez	934	314	.336
W Boggs	1135	381	.336

Away
(Minimum 625 PA)

Player	AB	H	AVG
T Gwynn	1244	445	.358
M Piazza	1253	447	.357
F Thomas	1291	438	.339
K Lofton	1334	428	.321
L Johnson	1366	436	.319
K Seitzer	1010	320	.317
M Ramirez	990	311	.314
J Bagwell	1286	403	.313
H Baines	1085	339	.312
R Kelly	1009	315	.312

Groundball Pitchers
(Minimum 450 PA)

Player	AB	H	AVG
T Gwynn	660	229	.347
W Joyner	447	154	.345
G Jefferies	611	207	.339
F Thomas	607	204	.336
A Galarraga	723	242	.335
J Valentin	488	163	.334
J Conine	677	223	.329
T Salmon	527	172	.326
B Butler	524	171	.326
J Eisenreich	466	152	.326

Grass
(Minimum 525 PA)

Player	AB	H	AVG
T Gwynn	1915	719	.375
F Thomas	2167	733	.338
R Alomar	1520	506	.333
M Grace	2098	692	.330
K Lofton	2299	757	.329
L Walker	1368	449	.328
M Piazza	1992	650	.326
D Bichette	2237	729	.326
A Galarraga	2138	688	.322
P O'Neill	2091	671	.321

Turf
(Minimum 525 PA)

Player	AB	H	AVG
M Piazza	497	188	.378
T Gwynn	571	197	.345
E Martinez	1108	373	.337
J Eisenreich	938	312	.333
P Molitor	1663	551	.331
A Rodriguez	746	247	.331
K Mitchell	551	180	.327
H Morris	1358	440	.324
J Kendall	599	191	.319
C Knoblauch	1671	530	.317

Flyball Pitchers
(Minimum 450 PA)

Player	AB	H	AVG
D Bichette	466	171	.367
R Alomar	410	140	.341
P O'Neill	469	156	.333
W Clark	412	135	.328
J Cora	476	155	.326
P Molitor	488	157	.322
M Grace	398	128	.322
K Lofton	490	155	.316
C Knoblauch	488	154	.316
B Bonds	356	109	.306

Day
(Minimum 525 PA)

Player	AB	H	AVG
T Gwynn	789	300	.380
M Piazza	656	238	.363
F Thomas	739	257	.348
M Grace	1478	497	.336
T Naehring	495	166	.335
P Molitor	896	292	.326
M Ramirez	650	211	.325
P O'Neill	879	284	.323
I Rodriguez	535	172	.322
K Lofton	845	271	.321

Night
(Minimum 700 PA)

Player	AB	H	AVG
T Gwynn	1697	616	.363
E Martinez	1424	471	.331
F Thomas	1759	578	.329
K Lofton	1819	597	.328
M Piazza	1833	600	.327
R Alomar	1727	559	.324
D Slaught	763	245	.321
S Mack	667	213	.319
A Rodriguez	950	300	.316
R Greer	1422	449	.316

Scoring Position
(Minimum 350 PA)

Player	AB	H	AVG
T Gwynn	558	216	.387
P Molitor	795	279	.351
M Piazza	667	234	.351
F Thomas	672	229	.341
P O'Neill	683	231	.338
A Galarraga	782	262	.335
K Lofton	533	176	.330
B Surhoff	540	178	.330
C Knoblauch	574	189	.329
M Vaughn	711	233	.328

547

5-Year Batting Leaders

March/April
(Minimum 250 PA)

Player	AB	H	AVG
P O'Neill	311	116	.373
T Gwynn	360	134	.372
K Lofton	397	137	.345
J Olerud	373	128	.343
E Burks	324	108	.333
P Molitor	355	118	.332
R Alomar	366	121	.331
M Vaughn	364	120	.330
M Alou	358	118	.330
M Piazza	355	117	.330

May
(Minimum 400 PA)

Player	AB	H	AVG
M Piazza	404	150	.371
T Gwynn	509	180	.354
F Thomas	446	157	.352
E Martinez	427	143	.335
K Lofton	532	177	.333
P O'Neill	407	135	.332
A Belle	507	168	.331
B Bonilla	481	159	.331
M Grace	494	163	.330
M Vaughn	506	166	.328

June
(Minimum 400 PA)

Player	AB	H	AVG
F Thomas	463	162	.350
T Gwynn	467	163	.349
A Galarraga	525	182	.347
M Piazza	480	166	.346
L Walker	363	125	.344
D Bichette	569	192	.337
E Martinez	406	136	.335
R Alomar	496	165	.333
K Seitzer	358	119	.332
M Grissom	542	180	.332

July
(Minimum 400 PA)

Player	AB	H	AVG
T Gwynn	425	164	.386
F Thomas	420	147	.350
W Joyner	418	141	.337
C Biggio	520	172	.331
B Bonds	469	155	.330
P Molitor	527	173	.328
M Stanley	405	132	.326
C Knoblauch	507	165	.325
B Surhoff	400	130	.325
T Salmon	438	142	.324

August
(Minimum 325 PA)

Player	AB	H	AVG
T Gwynn	412	158	.384
R Greer	352	123	.349
B Williams	522	178	.341
M Piazza	430	145	.337
J Thome	358	119	.332
K Lofton	501	166	.331
P Molitor	511	169	.331
J Olerud	403	133	.330
M Ramirez	340	112	.329
J Bagwell	338	111	.328

September-October
(Minimum 325 PA)

Player	AB	H	AVG
T Gwynn	313	117	.374
L Johnson	395	139	.352
H Baines	304	103	.339
G Jefferies	295	99	.336
K Caminiti	368	123	.334
R Alomar	321	106	.330
O Nixon	391	129	.330
H Morris	291	96	.330
T Salmon	339	111	.327
M Piazza	385	126	.327

1st Pitch
(Minimum 425 PA)

Player	AB	H	AVG
A Galarraga	406	172	.424
M Vaughn	357	147	.412
T Gwynn	399	160	.401
D Bichette	502	201	.400
D Bell	430	171	.398
P O'Neill	383	149	.389
H Baines	395	153	.387
L Walker	517	198	.383
M Alou	449	168	.374
E Murray	401	146	.364

Ahead in Count
(Minimum 525 PA)

Player	AB	H	AVG
A Galarraga	618	280	.453
J Thome	463	201	.434
E Martinez	555	235	.423
J Bagwell	590	249	.422
M Vaughn	591	248	.420
M Stanley	444	186	.419
M Ramirez	487	204	.419
K Lofton	763	314	.412
E Burks	521	213	.409
R Sanders	425	173	.407

Behind in Count
(Minimum 525 PA)

Player	AB	H	AVG
T Gwynn	936	305	.326
C Knoblauch	1266	361	.285
J Eisenreich	663	186	.281
M Piazza	1148	318	.277
J Frye	686	190	.277
G Jefferies	893	247	.277
W Boggs	962	266	.277
R Alomar	1117	307	.275
M Grace	905	248	.274
L Johnson	870	233	.268

Two Strikes
(Minimum 525 PA)

Player	AB	H	AVG
T Gwynn	735	248	.337
G Jefferies	779	216	.277
J Eisenreich	647	176	.272
C Knoblauch	1220	327	.268
W Boggs	1067	284	.266
R Alomar	1148	304	.265
B Larkin	942	245	.260
L Johnson	752	195	.259
M Grace	857	220	.257
G Anderson	705	177	.251

Full Count
(Minimum 125 PA)

Player	AB	H	AVG
T Gwynn	131	55	.420
D Magadan	195	68	.349
B Spiers	116	38	.328
J Eisenreich	132	43	.326
P Molitor	201	65	.323
T Raines	212	67	.316
D May	105	33	.314
M Grace	198	62	.313
F Viña	93	29	.312
G Hill	152	47	.309

Close & Late
(Minimum 250 PA)

Player	AB	H	AVG
T Gwynn	416	170	.409
M Grace	410	141	.344
E Martinez	268	92	.343
P O'Neill	316	107	.339
S Alomar Jr	266	89	.335
J Valentin	364	119	.327
P Meares	238	76	.319
W Joyner	351	112	.319
E Young	298	95	.319
W McGee	290	92	.317

5-Year Batting Leaders

Batting #1
(Minimum 625 PA)

Player	AB	H	AVG
K Lofton	2658	866	.326
D Jeter	601	194	.323
L Johnson	1647	524	.318
C Knoblauch	2397	750	.313
W Boggs	766	239	.312
N Garciaparra	689	209	.303
B Butler	1796	540	.301
T Raines	1013	304	.300
C Biggio	1477	442	.299
J Offerman	778	231	.297

Batting #2
(Minimum 625 PA)

Player	AB	H	AVG
A Rodriguez	982	330	.336
E Burks	752	241	.320
W Boggs	1152	369	.320
R Alomar	1341	425	.317
I Rodriguez	1282	399	.311
K Seitzer	762	237	.311
J Frye	612	189	.309
J Edmonds	764	235	.308
E Alfonzo	760	232	.305
J Cirillo	555	169	.305

Batting #3
(Minimum 625 PA)

Player	AB	H	AVG
T Gwynn	1723	630	.366
L Walker	770	265	.344
R Alomar	616	212	.344
F Thomas	2335	795	.340
M Piazza	1800	607	.337
P Molitor	2298	741	.322
W Joyner	651	209	.321
D Bichette	1576	505	.320
R Greer	962	308	.320
M Grace	2205	699	.317

Batting #4
(Minimum 525 PA)

Player	AB	H	AVG
R Jefferson	505	176	.349
K Mitchell	739	246	.333
E Martinez	1184	387	.327
A Galarraga	1855	601	.324
B Jordan	534	169	.316
M Vaughn	633	200	.316
O Merced	554	175	.316
A Belle	2769	849	.307
H Baines	914	279	.305
D Nilsson	605	183	.302

Batting #5
(Minimum 525 PA)

Player	AB	H	AVG
J Eisenreich	497	169	.340
B Bonds	546	180	.330
P O'Neill	761	250	.329
J Olerud	1260	407	.323
W Clark	507	162	.320
D Bichette	770	246	.319
G Berroa	637	199	.312
M Stanley	643	200	.311
H Baines	712	216	.303
T Salmon	502	152	.303

Batting #6
(Minimum 525 PA)

Player	AB	H	AVG
J Eisenreich	514	170	.331
G Anderson	915	286	.313
M Ramirez	656	205	.313
V Castilla	1369	424	.310
D Jackson	487	146	.300
J Mabry	575	172	.299
B Williams	509	150	.295
E Burks	462	136	.294
J Kent	643	189	.294
B Surhoff	729	210	.288

Batting #7
(Minimum 350 PA)

Player	AB	H	AVG
T Eusebio	383	119	.311
D Slaught	412	128	.311
R Greer	369	114	.309
J Reed	531	161	.303
J Lopez	702	212	.302
D Wilson	484	143	.295
L Johnson	779	230	.295
T O'Leary	410	120	.293
C Hoiles	521	150	.288
S Alomar Jr	424	121	.285

Batting #8
(Minimum 350 PA)

Player	AB	H	AVG
J Kendall	445	135	.303
R Velarde	319	96	.301
P Meares	354	104	.294
T Fernandez	326	95	.291
J Blauser	298	86	.289
M McLemore	572	165	.288
R Gutierrez	381	109	.286
E Taubensee	403	114	.283
P Sorrento	308	87	.282
S Brosius	397	112	.282

Batting #9
(Minimum 350 PA)

Player	AB	H	AVG
S Alomar	471	147	.312
O Vizquel	800	222	.278
L Alicea	341	93	.273
G DiSarcina	1755	474	.270
O Guillen	2136	568	.266
J Reboulet	315	82	.260
M Bordick	1252	321	.256
P Kelly	990	253	.256
P Meares	1239	314	.253
L Tinsley	350	88	.251

None On/None Out
(Minimum 350 PA)

Player	AB	H	AVG
T Gwynn	474	181	.382
M Piazza	482	167	.346
D Jeter	403	139	.345
W Clark	485	167	.344
R Alomar	576	197	.342
E Martinez	465	158	.340
G Anderson	342	115	.336
B Larkin	434	145	.334
S Dunston	398	131	.329
F Thomas	471	155	.329

Pre-All Star
(Minimum 650 PA)

Player	AB	H	AVG
T Gwynn	1475	536	.363
F Thomas	1435	496	.346
M Piazza	1388	478	.344
P O'Neill	1337	450	.337
K Lofton	1568	525	.335
E Martinez	1154	383	.332
L Walker	1294	416	.321
M Grace	1435	459	.320
R Alomar	1479	473	.320
M Vaughn	1429	455	.318

Post-All Star
(Minimum 650 PA)

Player	AB	H	AVG
T Gwynn	1011	380	.376
P Molitor	1275	420	.329
W Boggs	963	317	.329
L Johnson	1199	393	.328
M Piazza	1101	360	.327
D Jeter	605	196	.324
B Williams	1225	396	.323
M Grace	1216	392	.322
G Jefferies	1057	338	.320
F Thomas	1063	339	.319

1997 Pitching Leaders

Overall
(Minimum 162 IP)

Pitcher, Team	IP	ER	ERA
P Martinez, Mon	**241.1**	**51**	**1.90**
R Clemens, Tor	264.0	60	2.05
G Maddux, Atl	232.2	57	2.20
R Johnson, Sea	213.0	54	2.28
D Kile, Hou	255.2	73	2.57
I Valdes, LA	196.2	58	2.65
K Brown, Fla	237.1	71	2.69
D Cone, NYA	195.0	61	2.82
A Pettitte, NYA	240.1	77	2.88
R Reed, NYN	208.1	67	2.89

Home
(Minimum 75 IP)

Pitcher, Team	IP	ER	ERA
R Clemens, Tor	**147.2**	**25**	**1.52**
R Johnson, Sea	114.0	24	1.89
P Martinez, Mon	140.1	31	1.99
I Valdes, LA	104.1	24	2.07
T Glavine, Atl	97.1	23	2.13
G Maddux, Atl	132.0	32	2.18
A Leiter, Fla	75.0	19	2.28
S Estes, SF	104.1	27	2.33
K Brown, Fla	125.1	35	2.51
D Mlicki, NYN	89.0	25	2.53

Away
(Minimum 75 IP)

Pitcher, Team	IP	ER	ERA
P Martinez, Mon	**101.0**	**20**	**1.78**
G Maddux, Atl	100.2	25	2.24
D Cone, NYA	105.0	29	2.49
D Kile, Hou	123.2	35	2.55
J Smoltz, Atl	117.2	35	2.68
R Clemens, Tor	116.1	35	2.71
R Johnson, Sea	99.0	30	2.73
R Reed, NYN	108.0	33	2.75
D Neagle, Atl	112.2	36	2.88
K Brown, Fla	112.0	36	2.89

April
(Minimum 25 IP)

Pitcher, Team	IP	ER	ERA
R Reed, NYN	**35.0**	**4**	**1.03**
G Maddux, Atl	32.0	4	1.13
T Glavine, Atl	44.0	8	1.64
R Clemens, Tor	36.2	7	1.72
E Loaiza, Pit	34.1	7	1.83
K Brown, Fla	41.1	9	1.96
F Cordova, Pit	32.0	7	1.97
A Ashby, SD	38.1	9	2.11
R Bailey, Col	33.0	8	2.18
S Estes, SF	27.2	7	2.28

May
(Minimum 25 IP)

Pitcher, Team	IP	ER	ERA
B Jones, NYN	**39.0**	**5**	**1.15**
D Kile, Hou	45.0	6	1.20
G Stephenson, Phi	27.0	4	1.33
P Hentgen, Tor	48.0	8	1.50
F Cordova, Pit	36.0	6	1.50
D Cone, NYA	43.2	8	1.65
P Martinez, Mon	46.0	9	1.76
J Thompson, Det	39.0	8	1.85
G Maddux, Atl	42.2	9	1.90
T Mulholland, SF	41.2	9	1.94

June
(Minimum 25 IP)

Pitcher, Team	IP	ER	ERA
W Alvarez, SF	**43.1**	**4**	**0.83**
R Johnson, Sea	49.0	5	0.92
R Clemens, Tor	38.1	7	1.64
P Martinez, Mon	50.2	10	1.78
C Perez, Mon	46.0	10	1.96
K Mercker, Cin	41.1	9	1.96
Al Benes, StL	44.1	10	2.03
J Thompson, Det	44.1	10	2.03
B Tomko, Cin	31.0	7	2.03
T Glavine, Atl	47.1	11	2.09

July
(Minimum 25 IP)

Pitcher, Team	IP	ER	ERA
R Clemens, Tor	**50.1**	**5**	**0.89**
L Hernandez, Fla	26.0	4	1.38
T Saunders, Fla	31.1	5	1.44
B Radke, Min	46.0	8	1.57
D Kile, Hou	51.0	9	1.59
G Maddux, Atl	38.0	7	1.66
C Park, LA	41.1	9	1.96
J Key, Bal	40.2	9	1.99
T Wakefield, Bos	43.2	10	2.06
M Morris, StL	41.1	10	2.18

August
(Minimum 25 IP)

Pitcher, Team	IP	ER	ERA
P Martinez, Mon	**49.1**	**6**	**1.09**
K Brown, Fla	45.0	7	1.40
C Schilling, Phi	37.1	6	1.45
J Smoltz, Atl	48.2	8	1.48
D Neagle, Atl	43.2	8	1.65
I Valdes, LA	44.0	9	1.84
R Johnson, Sea	29.0	6	1.86
R Helling, Tex	28.2	6	1.88
D Hermanson, Mon	30.1	7	2.08
S Erickson, Bal	47.0	11	2.11

September-October
(Minimum 25 IP)

Pitcher, Team	IP	ER	ERA
C Perez, Mon	**30.1**	**4**	**1.19**
D Mlicki, NYN	31.2	5	1.42
K Hill, Ana	37.2	6	1.43
B Henry, Bos	30.1	5	1.48
G Maddux, Atl	36.0	6	1.50
K Tapani, ChN	38.1	7	1.64
G Stephenson, Phi	30.1	6	1.78
C Carpenter, Tor	33.2	7	1.87
M Valdes, Mon	28.1	6	1.91
R Garcia, Hou	32.1	7	1.95

Grass
(Minimum 75 IP)

Pitcher, Team	IP	ER	ERA
G Maddux, Atl	**204.2**	**43**	**1.89**
R Clemens, Tor	102.1	25	2.20
D Kile, Hou	90.0	24	2.40
A Benes, StL	138.1	38	2.47
R Reed, NYN	167.2	47	2.52
I Valdes, LA	169.1	48	2.55
G McMichael, NYN	76.0	23	2.72
R Johnson, Sea	91.0	29	2.87
K Brown, Fla	202.1	65	2.89
J Thompson, Det	173.2	56	2.90

Turf
(Minimum 75 IP)

Pitcher, Team	IP	ER	ERA
R Johnson, Sea	**122.0**	**25**	**1.84**
R Clemens, Tor	161.2	35	1.95
P Martinez, Mon	184.2	42	2.05
G Stephenson, Phi	84.0	23	2.46
D Kile, Hou	165.2	49	2.66
C Schilling, Phi	198.2	61	2.76
P Hentgen, Tor	152.0	50	2.96
M Hampton, Hou	142.2	48	3.03
F Rodriguez, Min	79.1	29	3.29
J Fassero, Sea	125.0	47	3.38

1st Batter
(Minimum 50 BFP)

Pitcher, Team	AB	H	AVG
D Bochtler, SD	**39**	**1**	**.026**
J Orosco, Bal	57	4	.070
T Percival, Ana	47	5	.106
J Wetteland, Tex	56	6	.107
M Stanton, NYA	58	8	.138
J Nelson, NYA	63	9	.143
T Hoffman, SD	68	10	.147
B Wagner, Hou	54	8	.148
R Myers, Bal	52	8	.154
M Remlinger, Cin	50	8	.160

1997 Pitching Leaders

Overall
(Minimum 625 BFP)

Pitcher, Team	AB	H	AVG
P Martinez, Mon	860	158	.184
R Johnson, Sea	758	147	.194
C Park, LA	700	149	.213
R Clemens, Tor	957	204	.213
D Cone, NYA	710	155	.218
Al Benes, StL	585	128	.219
S Estes, SF	726	162	.223
C Schilling, Phi	930	208	.224
D Kile, Hou	924	208	.225
T Gordon, Bos	686	155	.226

LHB
(Minimum 125 BFP)

Pitcher, Team	AB	H	AVG
J Wetteland, Tex	126	21	.167
P Martinez, Mon	469	86	.183
J Thompson, Det	125	23	.184
T Hoffman, SD	157	29	.185
B Tomko, Cin	221	42	.190
R Hernandez, SF	160	31	.194
C Perez, Mon	139	27	.194
A Benitez, Bal	103	21	.204
R Clemens, Tor	498	102	.205
G Swindell, Min	151	31	.205

RHB
(Minimum 225 BFP)

Pitcher, Team	AB	H	AVG
P Martinez, Mon	391	72	.184
R Johnson, Sea	681	127	.186
C Park, LA	337	63	.187
T Stottlemyre, StL	312	59	.189
A Fernandez, Fla	428	82	.192
B Wagner, Hou	202	40	.198
S Belinda, Cin	207	42	.203
S Sullivan, Cin	207	42	.203
Al Benes, StL	293	60	.205
I Valdes, LA	364	75	.206

None On/None Out
(Minimum 150 BFP)

Pitcher, Team	AB	H	AVG
R Johnson, Sea	194	30	.155
B Jones, NYN	190	36	.189
Al Benes, StL	152	29	.191
D Neagle, Atl	234	46	.197
B Radke, Min	247	49	.198
J Gonzalez, ChN	140	28	.200
P Martinez, Mon	231	47	.203
R Reed, NYN	211	43	.204
R Clemens, Tor	249	51	.205
D Burba, Cin	162	34	.210

None On
(Minimum 250 BFP)

Pitcher, Team	AB	H	AVG
P Martinez, Mon	549	100	.182
R Johnson, Sea	477	96	.201
Al Benes, StL	344	72	.209
R Clemens, Tor	587	123	.210
S Estes, SF	432	91	.211
C Park, LA	434	92	.212
C Schilling, Phi	612	130	.212
D Neagle, Atl	569	121	.213
M Remlinger, Cin	257	55	.214
An Benes, StL	377	81	.215

Runners On
(Minimum 250 BFP)

Pitcher, Team	AB	H	AVG
R Johnson, Sea	281	51	.181
P Martinez, Mon	311	58	.186
R Martinez, LA	226	43	.190
D Kile, Hou	388	78	.201
T Glavine, Atl	323	66	.204
C Park, LA	266	57	.214
D Cone, NYA	293	63	.215
R Clemens, Tor	370	81	.219
G Maddux, Atl	306	67	.219
I Valdes, LA	261	58	.222

1st Pitch
(Minimum 100 BFP)

Pitcher, Team	AB	H	AVG
M Clark, ChN	126	23	.183
D Neagle, Atl	122	31	.254
D Springer, Ana	118	30	.254
M Morris, StL	114	29	.254
K Appier, KC	112	29	.259
R Reed, NYN	151	40	.265
J Dickson, Ana	117	31	.265
B Jones, NYN	101	27	.267
I Valdes, LA	100	28	.280
P Hentgen, Tor	177	50	.282

Two Strikes
(Minimum 150 BFP)

Pitcher, Team	AB	H	AVG
P Martinez, Mon	501	46	.092
R Johnson, Sea	451	43	.095
H Nomo, LA	371	39	.105
J Powell, Fla	133	16	.120
C Park, LA	339	41	.121
R Clemens, Tor	512	63	.123
U Urbina, Mon	140	18	.129
P Astacio, Col	326	42	.129
An Benes, StL	348	45	.129
A Benitez, Bal	161	21	.130

Scoring Position
(Minimum 125 BFP)

Pitcher, Team	AB	H	AVG
R Johnson, Sea	143	22	.154
B Wickman, Mil	110	18	.164
M Valdes, Mon	109	18	.165
D Kile, Hou	210	36	.171
S Belinda, Cin	112	20	.179
J Key, Bal	156	28	.179
G McMichael, NYN	100	18	.180
R Clemens, Tor	194	35	.180
T Glavine, Atl	164	30	.183
K Mercker, Cin	118	22	.186

Ahead in Count
(Minimum 150 BFP)

Pitcher, Team	AB	H	AVG
P Martinez, Mon	492	55	.112
P Astacio, Col	318	38	.119
R Johnson, Sea	406	49	.121
R Martinez, LA	220	28	.127
J Juden, Cle	282	39	.138
H Nomo, LA	353	49	.139
T Gordon, Bos	337	47	.139
C Park, LA	314	44	.140
S Estes, SF	320	45	.141
J Wright, Cle	149	21	.141

Behind in Count
(Minimum 150 BFP)

Pitcher, Team	AB	H	AVG
K Mercker, Cin	121	30	.248
K Appier, KC	169	44	.260
J Pittsley, KC	126	34	.270
J Gonzalez, ChN	129	35	.271
T Glavine, Atl	205	56	.273
D Kile, Hou	218	60	.275
T Wakefield, Bos	133	37	.278
D Cone, NYA	118	33	.280
J Key, Bal	184	52	.283
A Fernandez, Fla	137	39	.285

Close & Late
(Minimum 50 BFP)

Pitcher, Team	AB	H	AVG
K Brown, Fla	66	9	.136
S Estes, SF	49	7	.143
M Remlinger, Cin	91	14	.154
M Trombley, Min	84	14	.167
M Pisciotta, ChN	60	10	.167
A Benitez, Bal	161	27	.168
P Astacio, Col	59	10	.169
B Clontz, Atl	47	8	.170
P Assenmacher, Cle	82	14	.171
B Radke, Min	61	11	.180

5-Year Pitching Leaders

Overall
(Minimum 575 IP)

Pitcher	IP	ER	ERA
G Maddux	**1156.1**	**274**	**2.13**
R Johnson	916.0	291	2.86
P Martinez	904.1	302	3.01
I Valdes	647.2	218	3.03
D Cone	922.0	325	3.17
T Glavine	1078.2	383	3.20
K Brown	1045.2	373	3.21
J Smoltz	1080.2	397	3.31
R Clemens	1009.0	372	3.32
H Nomo	627.0	233	3.34

Home
(Minimum 250 IP)

Pitcher	IP	ER	ERA
G Maddux	**589.1**	**143**	**2.18**
I Valdes	334.1	90	2.42
R Johnson	497.0	144	2.61
H Nomo	343.0	104	2.73
K Brown	579.0	176	2.74
P Martinez	451.0	140	2.79
A Pettitte	339.0	107	2.84
A Leiter	403.1	134	2.99
T Glavine	512.2	171	3.00
D Osborne	290.2	101	3.13

Away
(Minimum 250 IP)

Pitcher	IP	ER	ERA
G Maddux	**567.0**	**131**	**2.08**
D Cone	481.1	158	2.95
J Smoltz	528.0	174	2.97
R Johnson	419.0	147	3.16
P Martinez	453.1	162	3.22
J Fassero	470.2	169	3.23
K Appier	522.0	193	3.33
J Key	419.1	156	3.35
R Clemens	499.2	186	3.35
T Glavine	566.0	212	3.37

March/April
(Minimum 80 IP)

Pitcher	IP	ER	ERA
G Maddux	**174.2**	**37**	**1.91**
R Clemens	154.1	46	2.68
P Martinez	103.1	31	2.70
T Glavine	148.1	45	2.73
J Smoltz	161.0	49	2.74
A Fernandez	150.2	49	2.93
B Swift	94.0	32	3.06
A Ashby	140.1	48	3.08
K Hill	158.0	55	3.13
W Alvarez	132.0	46	3.14

May
(Minimum 100 IP)

Pitcher	IP	ER	ERA
D Cone	**195.2**	**47**	**2.16**
B Jones	166.1	43	2.33
P Martinez	175.2	47	2.41
G Maddux	214.0	59	2.48
B Saberhagen	101.1	30	2.66
C Finley	213.0	65	2.75
K Hill	174.0	56	2.90
I Valdes	101.2	33	2.92
C Schilling	176.0	58	2.97
K Brown	198.2	66	2.99

June
(Minimum 100 IP)

Pitcher	IP	ER	ERA
R Johnson	**183.2**	**47**	**2.30**
K Appier	182.1	54	2.67
G Maddux	206.0	62	2.71
T Candiotti	160.1	50	2.81
H Nomo	130.0	42	2.91
An Benes	196.1	65	2.98
S Cooke	110.0	37	3.03
P Martinez	178.0	61	3.08
A Leiter	144.1	50	3.12
B Saberhagen	127.0	44	3.12

July
(Minimum 100 IP)

Pitcher	IP	ER	ERA
G Maddux	**220.2**	**50**	**2.04**
H Nomo	102.1	29	2.55
T Candiotti	178.0	51	2.58
D Cone	167.2	53	2.84
S Reynolds	134.2	44	2.94
J Fassero	172.0	57	2.98
B McDonald	157.2	53	3.03
P Harnisch	146.1	50	3.08
D Martinez	126.1	44	3.13
J Key	166.0	58	3.14

August
(Minimum 90 IP)

Pitcher	IP	ER	ERA
G Maddux	**201.2**	**41**	**1.83**
M Mussina	166.2	45	2.43
P Martinez	160.2	46	2.58
R Johnson	142.1	41	2.59
R Martinez	145.0	45	2.79
J Smoltz	174.1	57	2.94
A Fernandez	188.2	62	2.96
C Schilling	139.2	46	2.96
K Rueter	91.2	31	3.04
K Brown	181.0	62	3.08

September-October
(Minimum 75 IP)

Pitcher	IP	ER	ERA
G Maddux	**139.1**	**25**	**1.61**
R Johnson	121.2	24	1.78
K Brown	166.1	39	2.11
M Portugal	84.1	20	2.13
K Rueter	109.0	27	2.23
B Swift	81.1	22	2.43
P Harnisch	84.1	24	2.56
P Astacio	131.2	39	2.67
B McDonald	100.0	30	2.70
A Pettitte	115.0	35	2.74

Grass
(Minimum 250 IP)

Pitcher	IP	ER	ERA
G Maddux	**882.2**	**213**	**2.17**
R Hernandez	300.1	89	2.67
I Valdes	541.1	165	2.74
G McMichael	333.2	105	2.83
T Hoffman	286.1	95	2.99
R Beck	261.0	88	3.03
C Park	259.2	89	3.08
E Plunk	292.2	101	3.11
D Cone	562.2	197	3.15
K Brown	915.2	322	3.16

Turf
(Minimum 250 IP)

Pitcher	IP	ER	ERA
G Maddux	**273.2**	**61**	**2.01**
R Clemens	260.1	75	2.59
R Johnson	564.1	166	2.65
K Appier	286.2	90	2.83
P Martinez	578.0	185	2.88
T Glavine	251.1	85	3.04
S Reynolds	514.1	183	3.20
D Cone	359.1	128	3.21
M Portugal	379.2	137	3.25
J Shaw	280.0	102	3.28

1st Batter
(Minimum 150 BFP)

Pitcher	AB	H	AVG
D Bochtler	**124**	**15**	**.121**
T Percival	160	21	.131
R Bottalico	172	30	.174
J Orosco	258	47	.182
J Wetteland	279	51	.183
T Hoffman	289	57	.197
Y Perez	161	32	.199
T Fossas	278	56	.201
T Borland	132	27	.205
M Wohlers	277	57	.206

5-Year Pitching Leaders

Overall
(Minimum 2200 BFP)

Pitcher	AB	H	AVG
R Johnson	**3303**	**671**	**.203**
P Martinez	3271	696	.213
H Nomo	2303	497	.216
D Cone	3361	735	.219
G Maddux	4241	950	.224
R Clemens	3739	860	.230
J Smoltz	4010	927	.231
K Appier	3840	890	.232
A Leiter	2815	666	.237
I Valdes	2444	579	.237

LHB
(Minimum 425 BFP)

Pitcher	AB	H	AVG
T Hoffman	**653**	**127**	**.194**
J Wetteland	692	141	.204
B Patterson	402	82	.204
T Fossas	382	78	.204
G Maddux	2066	445	.215
T Scott	479	104	.217
R Hernandez	658	143	.217
J Fassero	597	130	.218
M Langston	408	90	.221
B Florie	369	82	.222

RHB
(Minimum 800 BFP)

Pitcher	AB	H	AVG
E Plunk	**722**	**144**	**.199**
P Martinez	1531	307	.201
J Nelson	775	157	.203
R Johnson	2980	607	.204
K Appier	1791	365	.204
H Nomo	1217	253	.208
D Cone	1506	317	.210
J Smoltz	2049	437	.213
J Juden	700	150	.214
Al Benes	738	159	.215

None On/None Out
(Minimum 525 BFP)

Pitcher	AB	H	AVG
R Johnson	**863**	**169**	**.196**
S Sanders	539	120	.223
P Martinez	862	192	.223
D Cone	897	200	.223
H Nomo	608	137	.225
R Clemens	966	220	.228
C Schilling	862	200	.232
K Brown	1040	243	.234
A Leiter	692	162	.234
J Smoltz	1062	250	.235

None On
(Minimum 900 BFP)

Pitcher	AB	H	AVG
R Johnson	**2058**	**422**	**.205**
P Martinez	2033	423	.208
H Nomo	1420	299	.211
S Sanders	1233	270	.219
D Cone	2049	449	.219
C Schilling	2081	461	.222
J Smoltz	2474	550	.222
R Clemens	2223	501	.225
S Fernandez	939	212	.226
G Maddux	2712	616	.227

Runners On
(Minimum 900 BFP)

Pitcher	AB	H	AVG
R Johnson	**1245**	**249**	**.200**
D Cone	1312	286	.218
G Maddux	1529	334	.218
P Martinez	1238	273	.221
H Nomo	883	198	.224
I Valdes	921	214	.232
K Appier	1563	364	.233
P Astacio	1302	306	.235
W Alvarez	1598	376	.235
S Trachsel	1133	268	.237

1st Pitch
(Minimum 425 BFP)

Pitcher	AB	H	AVG
G Maddux	**770**	**203**	**.264**
A Fernandez	556	148	.266
D Martinez	420	117	.279
M Clark	479	135	.282
K Appier	447	126	.282
P Harnisch	402	115	.286
R Martinez	466	135	.290
R Bones	535	156	.292
M Mussina	571	168	.294
K Hill	595	177	.297

Two Strikes
(Minimum 525 BFP)

Pitcher	AB	H	AVG
H Nomo	**1132**	**116**	**.102**
C Park	573	68	.119
R Johnson	2005	242	.121
M Wohlers	630	79	.125
M Jackson	618	78	.126
B Ruffin	624	83	.133
J Orosco	478	64	.134
G Maddux	1807	243	.134
P Martinez	1785	242	.136
X Hernandez	597	84	.141

Scoring Position
(Minimum 425 BFP)

Pitcher	AB	H	AVG
T Hoffman	**362**	**67**	**.185**
R Johnson	707	138	.195
E Plunk	420	84	.200
D Cone	754	152	.202
G Maddux	866	177	.204
T Jones	376	78	.207
H Nomo	536	112	.209
G McMichael	415	87	.210
P Martinez	668	141	.211
S Trachsel	627	134	.214

Ahead in Count
(Minimum 525 BFP)

Pitcher	AB	H	AVG
H Nomo	**1065**	**128**	**.120**
R Johnson	1854	255	.138
M Wohlers	614	85	.138
X Hernandez	571	85	.149
P Martinez	1693	258	.152
J Juden	583	89	.153
T Hoffman	774	119	.154
J Wetteland	674	106	.157
R Clemens	1774	279	.157
M Jackson	584	92	.158

Behind in Count
(Minimum 525 BFP)

Pitcher	AB	H	AVG
D Cone	**652**	**186**	**.285**
F Rodriguez	466	135	.290
M Portugal	589	175	.297
T Glavine	972	289	.297
W Alvarez	725	218	.301
B Swift	498	150	.301
T Wakefield	575	174	.303
J Hamilton	534	163	.305
J Moyer	648	198	.306
B McDonald	799	246	.308

Close & Late
(Minimum 150 BFP)

Pitcher	AB	H	AVG
T Percival	**477**	**80**	**.168**
D Gooden	148	26	.176
H Nomo	157	28	.178
J Orosco	469	87	.185
A Benitez	253	47	.186
A Rhodes	216	41	.190
P Martinez	141	27	.191
M Jackson	626	123	.196
J Poole	264	52	.197
P Martinez	491	97	.198

Glossary

There are quite a few abbreviations in the book with which most of you are probably familiar. But for the sake of completeness, here is a rundown of all the abbreviations, plus descriptions of many of the categories for the stat splits and some of the formulas used.

For Hitters:

Avg=batting average, G=games played, AB=at-bats, R=runs scored, H=hits, 2B=doubles, 3B=triples, HR=home runs, RBI=runs batted in, BB=walks, SO=strikeouts, HBP=times hit by pitch, GDP=times grounded into double play, SB=stolen bases, CS=caught stealing, OBP=on-base percentage, SLG=slugging percentage, IBB=intentional walks received, SH=sacrifice hits, SF=sacrifice flies, #Pit=number of pitches offered to the hitter, #P/PA=average number of pitches per plate appearance, GB=number of fair ground balls hit (hits, outs and errors), FB=number of fly balls hit (excludes line drives), G/F=ratio of grounders to fly balls.

For Fielders:

G=number of games the player appeared at that position, GS=number of starts the player made, Innings=number of innings played at that position, PO=putouts, A=assists, E=errors, DP=double plays turned, Fld. Pct=fielding percentage, Rng. Fctr=Range Factor, In Zone=balls hit in the player's area, Outs=number of outs resulting from a ball hit to a player, Zone Rtg=Zone Rating (see below), MLB Zone=major league average zone rating for that position.

For Pitchers:

ERA=earned run average, W=wins, L=losses, Sv=saves, G=games pitched, GS=games started, IP=innings pitched, BB=walks issued, SO=strikeouts, Avg.=opposition batting average against the pitcher, H=hits allowed, 2B=doubles allowed, 3B=triples allowed, HR=homers allowed, RBI=RBI allowed, OBP=on-base percentage against the pitcher, SLG=slugging percentage against the pitcher, CG=complete games, ShO=shutouts, Sup=run support per nine innings, GF=games finished, IR=inherited runners, IRS=inherited runners who scored, QS=quality starts, Hld=holds, SvOp=save opportunities, SB=stolen bases against the pitcher, CS=times runners were caught stealing while the pitcher was on the mound, GB=groundballs hit against the pitcher (hits, outs and errors), FB=fly balls hit against the pitcher (excludes line drives), G/F=ratio of grounders to flies.

Formulas and Definitions

OBP = (H + BB + HBP) / (AB + BB + HBP + SF); SLG = Total Bases / At Bats; Fld.Pct. = (PO + A) / (PO + A + E); Rng.Fctr. = (PO + A) * 9 / defensive innings played, or the average number of plays a fielder makes over a nine-inning game. Zone Rating = The Zone Rating measures all the balls hit in the area where a fielder can reasonably be expected to record an out, then counts the percentage of outs actually made. Thus, a zone rating of .965, like the one Deivi Cruz had at shortstop last year, means that he got 445 outs on the 461 balls hit into his general area last year, or 96.5%. GF = games in which the pitcher was the last reliever in the game. Hold = A pitcher gets a hold when he enters the game in a save situation, records at least one out, and leaves the game having never relinquished the lead. A player cannot finish the game and get a hold, nor can he get credit for a hold and a save in the same game.

Player Breakdowns

There are three styles of player breakdowns in this book. The first is for all the *Regulars*, the second is for Subs and the final type is for the "cup-of-coffee" players. We defined Regulars as being any batters with 325 or more plate appearances last season or pitchers with either 162+ innings or 60+ appearances. *Subs* are hitters with between 126 and 324 plate appearances or pitchers who threw between 60 and 161.2 innings last year or appeared in between 25 and 59 games. The final type of player includes everyone else who appeared in a game in 1997. What this means is that the Regulars have stat splits in every category, the Subs have splits in most categories and the fringe players have just a couple of listings.

The multi-year section (career or five-year) is shown for any hitter whose career exceeds his 1997 playing time by 325+ appearances or for any pitcher whose career exceeds his 1997 playing time by 162 innings or 60 games.

Starting pitchers have slightly different formats than relief pitchers. In the top section, starters have stats for CG, ShO, Sup, QS and #P/S. For relievers, defined as pitchers with more games relieved than started, we show GF, IR, IRS, Hld and SvOp. In the stat breakdowns, starters have statistics based on longer rest between starts and higher pitch levels per outing.

Breakdown Categories

Most of the categories are fairly straightforward, but below is some information that could make a few of them a little less ambiguous.

The "1997 Season" label refers to his total stats for last year, even if he got traded midway through the season. So Mark McGwire's line is for both the Athletics and the Cardinals. The next line is either the hitter's or pitcher's performance since the start of the 1993 season, or his career if he debuted since 1993.

AGE indicates how old the player will be on July 1, 1998, or midway through next season.

GROUNDBALL and FLYBALL are a hitter's stats against pitchers that induce mostly grounders or flies, respectively. So Travis Fryman's "Groundball" line is his performance against pitchers like Orel Hershiser, who throw mostly grounders. If a player's Groundball/Flyball ratio is less than 1.00, then he is a Flyball hitter. If the ratio is greater then 1.50, then he is a Groundball hitter. Anything else is classified as neutral. The same cutoffs are used for pitchers in classifying them as flyball/groundball pitchers. Also, anybody with less then 50 plate appearances is automatically called neutral.

DAY/NIGHT designations differ between the leagues. Officially, night games in the National League are those that start after 5:00 p.m., while night games in the AL are those that begin after 6:00 p.m. So a game starting at 5:30 in Yankee Stadium is a day game while one in Shea Stadium at the same time is a night contest. We avoid this silliness by calling all games starting after 5:00 p.m. night games. GRASS is grass and TURF is artificial turf.

FIRST PITCH refers to the first pitch of a given at-bat, and any walks listed here are intentional walks. For hitters, AHEAD IN COUNT includes 1-0, 2-0, 3-0, 2-1, and 3-1. BEHIND IN COUNT includes 0-1, 0-2, 1-2, and 2-2. For pitchers, it's the opposite.

SCORING POSITION is having at least one runner at either second or third base. CLOSE AND LATE occurs when a) the game is in the seventh inning or later and b) the batting team is either leading by one run, tied, or has the potential tying run on base, at bat or on deck. NONE ON/OUT is when there are no outs and the bases are empty (generally leadoff situations).

INNING 1-6 and INNING 7+ refer to the actual innings in which a pitcher worked. NONE ON/RUNNERS ON is the status of the baserunners.

VS. 1ST BATR (RELIEF) is what happened to the first batter a reliever faced. FIRST INNING PITCHED is the result of the pitcher's work until he recorded three outs.

Vs. AL/NL is the numbers a player produced facing AL teams and NL teams.

The NUMBER OF PITCHES section shows the results of balls put into play while his pitch count was in that range.

All of the above is the same for the multi-year data as well.

In the PITCHER/BATTER MATCH-UPS, the following conditions must be met before a player is added to the list: a) There must be greater than 10 plate appearances between the batter and the pitcher; and b) Batters must have a .300 average against a pitcher to be considered as a "Hits Best Against" candidate, and pitchers must limit hitters to under .250 to be listed under "Pitches Best Vs." Thus, not all hitters will have five pitchers that qualify, and not all pitchers will have five batters that qualify.

—*Tony Nistler*

About STATS, Inc.

STATS, Inc. is the nation's leading independent sports information and statistical analysis company, providing detailed sports services for a wide array of commercial clients.

As one of the fastest-growing sports companies—in 1994, we ranked 144th on the "Inc. 500" list of fastest-growing privately held firms—STATS provides the most up-to-the-minute sports information to professional teams, print and broadcast media, software developers and interactive service providers around the country. Some of our major clients are ESPN, the Associated Press, Fox Sports, Electronic Arts, MSNBC, SONY and Topps. Much of the information we provide is available to the public via STATS On-Line. With a computer and a modem, you can follow action in the four major professional sports, as well as NCAA football and basketball. . . as it happens!

STATS Publishing, a division of STATS, Inc., produces 12 annual books, including the *Major League Handbook*, *The Scouting Notebook*, the *Pro Football Handbook*, the *Pro Basketball Handbook* and the *Hockey Handbook* as well as the *STATS Fantasy Insider* magazine. These publications deliver STATS' expertise to fans, scouts, general managers and media around the country.

In addition, STATS offers the most innovative—and fun—fantasy sports games and support products around, from *Bill James Fantasy Baseball* and *Bill James Classic Baseball* to *STATS Fantasy Football* and *STATS Fantasy Hoops*. Check out the latest STATS and Bill James fantasy game, *Stock Market Baseball* and our immensely popular Fantasy Portfolios.

Information technology has grown by leaps and bounds in the last decade, and STATS will continue to be at the forefront as a supplier of the most up-to-date, in-depth sports information available. For those of you on the information superhighway, you can always catch STATS in our area on America Online or at our Internet site.

For more information on our products, or on joining our reporter network, contact us on:

America On-Line — (Keyword: STATS)

Internet — www.stats.com

Toll Free in the USA at 1-800-63-STATS (1-800-637-8287)

Outside the USA at 1-847-676-3383

Or write to:

STATS, Inc.
8131 Monticello Ave.
Skokie, IL 60076-3300

MORE OF STATS' STARTING LINEUP...

STATS Scouting Notebook: 1998

- Extensive scouting reports on over 700 major league players
- Evaluations of nearly 200 minor league prospects
- Expert analysis from nationally-known writers
- Manager profiles section evaluates skipper style and strategy

"A phenomenal resource!" Jayson Stark, Baseball America

- **Item #SN98, $19.95, Available 1/1/98**

STATS Minor League Scouting Notebook 1998

- Evaluation of each organization's top prospects
- Essays, stat lines and grades for more than 400 prospects
- Author John Sickels' exclusive list of baseball's top 50 prospects
- Each prospect rated with a grade from A to C-minus

"John Sickels knows the minor leagues like no one else." John Benson, Baseball Weekly

- **Item #MH98, $19.95, Available 1/15/98**

STATS analyzes baseball like nobody else!

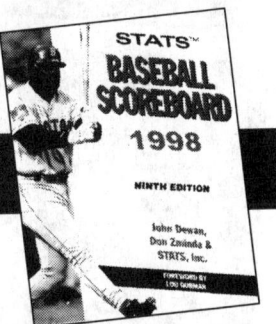

STATS Diamond Chronicles 1998

- Essays, debates and discussions from the 1997 season and offseason
- In-depth, often heated dialogue between well-known baseball analysts
- Learn what experts think of trades, managerial styles, realignment, etc.
- Featuring commentary by Bill James, Don Zminda, Steve Moyer and John Dewan
- **Item #CH98, $19.95, Available 2/15/98**

STATS Baseball Scoreboard 1998

- Oh Yeah? Prove It! STATS' experts answer all the tough questions about baseball today
- Easy-to-understand charts and graphs answer the questions fans always ask
- In-depth coverage for each major league team
- Equal measures informative and entertaining
- **Item #SB98, $19.95, Available 3/1/98**

Order from STATS INC. Today!

Use Order Form in This Book, or Call 1-800-63-STATS or 847-676-3383 or visit www.stats.com

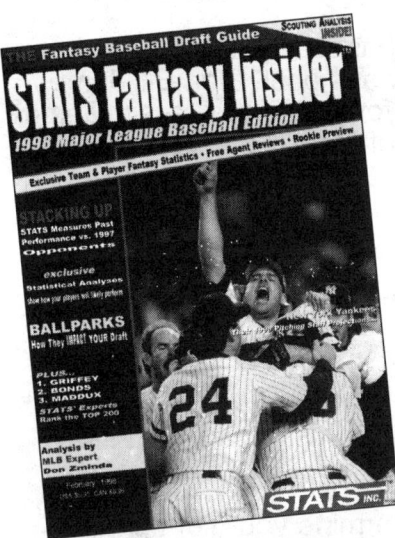

Get Into STATS Fantasy Hoops!

Soar into the 1997-98 season with STATS Fantasy Hoops! SFH puts YOU in charge. Don't just sit back and watch Grant Hill, Shawn Kemp and Michael Jordan — get in the game and coach your team to the top!

How to Play SFH:
1. Sign up to coach a team
2. You'll receive a full set of rules and a draft form with SFH point values for all eligible players - anyone who played in the NBA in 1996-97, plus all 1997 NBA draft picks
3. Complete the draft form and return it to STATS
4. You will take part in the draft with nine other owners, and we will send you league rosters
5. You make unlimited weekly transactions including trades, free agent signings, activations, and benchings
6. Six of the 10 teams in your league advance to postseason play, with two teams ultimately advancing to the Finals

SFH point values are based on actual NBA results, mirroring the real thing. Weekly reports will tell you everything you need to know to lead your team to the SFH Championship!

PLAY STATS Fantasy Football!

STATS Fantasy Football puts YOU in charge! You draft, trade, cut, bench, activate players and even sign free agents each week. SFF pits you head-to-head against 11 other owners.

STATS' scoring system applies realistic values, tested against actual NFL results. Each week, you'll receive a superb in-depth report telling you all about both team and league performances.

How to Play SFF:
1. Sign up today!
2. STATS sends you a draft form listing all eligible NFL players
3. Fill out the draft form and return it to STATS, and you will take part in the draft along with 11 other team owners
4. Go head-to-head against the other owners in your league. You'll make week-by-week roster moves and transactions through STATS' Fantasy Football experts, via phone, fax, or on-line!

STATS Fantasy Football on the Web? Check it out! www.stats.com

Order from STATS INC. Today!

Use Order Form in This Book, or Call 1-800-63-STATS or 847-676-3383 or visit www.stats.com

STATS, Inc. Order Form

Name_____

Address_____

City_____ State_____ Zip_____

Phone_____Fax_____ E-mail Address_____

Method of Payment (U.S. Funds Only):
☐ Check ☐ Money Order ☐ Visa ☐ MasterCard

Credit Card Information:

Cardholder Name_____

Credit Card Number_____ Exp. Date_____

Signature_____

PUBLICATIONS (STATS books now include FREE first class shipping; magazines — add $2)

Qty.	Product Name	Item #	Price	Total
	STATS All-Time Major League Handbook	ATHA	$54.95	
	STATS All-Time Baseball Sourcebook	ATSA	$54.95	
	STATS All-Time Major League COMBO (BOTH books!)	ATCA	$99.95	
	STATS Major League Handbook 1998	HB98	$19.95	
	STATS Major League Handbook 1998 (Comb-bound)	HC98	$21.95	
	STATS Projections Update 1998 (MAGAZINE)	PJUP	$9.95	
	The Scouting Notebook: 1998	SN98	$19.95	
	The Scouting Notebook: 1998 (Comb-bound)	SC98	$21.95	
	STATS Minor League Scouting Notebook 1998	MN98	$19.95	
	STATS Minor League Handbook 1998	MH98	$19.95	
	STATS Minor League Handbook 1998 (Comb-bound)	MC98	$21.95	
	STATS Player Profiles 1998	PP98	$19.95	
	STATS Player Profiles 1998 (Comb-bound)	PC98	$21.95	
	STATS 1998 BVSP Match-Ups!	BP98	$19.95	
	STATS Baseball Scoreboard 1998	SB98	$19.95	
	STATS Diamond Chronicles 1998	CH98	$19.95	
	Pro Football Revealed: The 100 Yard War (1997 Edition)	PF97	$18.95	
	STATS Pro Football Handbook 1997	FH97	$19.95	
	STATS Basketball Handbook 1997-98	BH98	$19.95	
	STATS Hockey Handbook 1997-98	HH98	$19.95	
	STATS Fantasy Insider: 1998 Major League Baseball Edition (MAGAZINE)	IB98	$5.95	
	STATS Fantasy Insider: 1998 Pro Football Edition (MAGAZINE)	IF98	$5.95	
Prior Editions	**(Please circle appropriate year)**			
	STATS Major League Handbook '90 '91 '92 '93 '94 '95 '96 '97		$9.95	
	The Scouting Report/Notebook '94 '95 '96 '97		$9.95	
	STATS Player Profiles '93 '94 '95 '96 '97		$9.95	
	STATS Minor League Handbook '92 '93 '94 '95 '96 '97		$9.95	
	STATS BVSP Match-Ups! '94 '95 '96 '97		$5.95	
	STATS Baseball Scoreboard '92 '93 '94 '95 '96 '97		$9.95	
	STATS Basketball Scoreboard/Handbook '93-'94 '94-'95 '95-'96 '96-'97		$9.95	
	Pro Football Revealed: The 100 Yard War '94 '95 '96		$9.95	
	STATS Pro Football Handbook '95 '96		$9.95	
	STATS Minor League Scouting Notebook '95 '96 '97		$9.95	
	STATS Hockey Handbook '96-'97		$9.95	

FANTASY GAMES

Qty.	Product Name	Item Number	Price	Total
	Bill James Classic Baseball	BJCB	$129.00	
	STATS Fantasy Hoops	SFH	$79.00	
	STATS Fantasy Football	SFF	$69.00	
	Bill James Fantasy Baseball	BJFB	$89.00	

1st Fantasy Team Name (ex. Colt 45's):_____

  What Fantasy Game is this team for?_____

2nd Fantasy Team Name (ex. Colt 45's):_____

  What Fantasy Game is this team for?_____

NOTE: $1.00/player is charged for all roster moves and transactions.

For Bill James Fantasy Baseball:

Would you like to play in a league drafted by Bill James? ❏ Yes ❏ No

MULTIMEDIA PRODUCTS (Prices include shipping & handling charges)

Qty.	Product Name	Item Number	Price	Total
	Bill James Encyclopedia CD-Rom	BJCD	$49.95	

TOTALS

	Price	Total
Product Total (excl. Fantasy Games)		
Canada—all orders—add:	$2.50/book	
Magazines—shipping—add:	$2.00/each	
Order 2 or more books—subtract:	$1.00/book	
(**NOT** to be combined with other specials)		
Subtotal		
Fantasy Games Total		
IL residents add 8.5% sales tax		
GRAND TOTAL		

For Faster Service, Please Call 800-63-STATS or 847-676-3383
Visit STATS on the World Wide Web at www.stats.com
Fax Your Order to 847-676-0821
STATS, Inc • 8131 Monticello Avenue • Skokie, Illinois 60076-3300

NOTE: *Orders for shipments outside of the USA or Canada are Credit Card only. Actual shipping charges will be added to the product cost.*

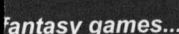